THE GOOD SCHO
SPECIAL EDUCATIONAL NEEDS

A critical and independent guide, which takes no money or advertising from schools or SEN service providers

First Edition

Edited by Sandra Hutchinson

With free online access to a comprehensive, continually updated database of special schools and of SEN provision in special and mainstream schools

www.goodschoolsguide.co.uk/?SEN

LUCAS
PUBLICATIONS

First Edition published 2006

by Lucas Publications Ltd

Bowland House, West Street, Alresford SO24 9AT

ISBN 09532 659 94

A CIP catalogue record for this book is available from the British Library.

Publishing Project Management by Pencil-Sharp Editors

Designed and typeset by Optima Information Design

Print management by Susan Sutterby

Printed and bound in Great Britain by Polestar Wheatons Ltd

Writers:

Simon Arbuthnott
Lindsey Aspinall
John Richard Badham
Ellen Baylis
Godfrey Bishop
Susannah Camps Harris
Elizabeth Coatman
Charles Cowling
Sarah Crabb
Sarah Drummond
Arabella Dymoke
Sue Fieldman
Sara Freakley
Lisa Freedman
Pippa Goedkoop
Elizabeth Grahamslaw
Paul Grahamslaw
Debra Hamblin
Susan Hamlyn
Bernadette Henniker
Sylvia Howe
Sandra Hutchinson
Ali Hutchison
Sophie Irwin
Christine Jefferson
Caroline Karwowska
Emma Lee-Potter
Priscilla McCall
Victoria McKee
Elizabeth Moody-Stuart
Patrea More Nisbett
Beth Noakes
Suzie Oweiss
Stephanie Page
Jill Parsons
Harriet Plyler
Anne Prendergast
Catriona Prest
Angela Pullin
Rosemary Taylor
Carolyn Thomas
Anthony Verity
Janette Wallis
Sue Wood

Research:

Annie Finn
Shari Lord
Janet Griffiths

Assistant:

Olivia Hamlyn

Cover design: Matthew Knight

Editorial review: Susan Hamlyn

Organisational help: Anthea Palmer

Acknowledgements

And with particular thanks to all the charities which have given us their support, especially:

ADDISS

AFF (Army Families Federation)

Barnardo's

Dyspraxia Foundation

National Autistic Society

RADAR

RNIB Royal National Institute For The Blind

Skill

The Rett Syndrome Association

We should also like to thank the countless friends, pupils, parents, staff (not to mention moles because they would rather we didn't) who have contributed enormously valuable information and to whom we are deeply indebted.

Contents

The Good Schools Guide Advisory Service

The **Good Schools Guide Advisory Service**® is a consultancy run by The Good Schools Guide® to advise parents, on a one-to-one basis, on choosing the best schools for their children.

The Good Schools Guide is in a unique position to do this because its advisors have visited hundreds of schools over the past twenty years, and have gathered an enormous reservoir of information and experience. *The Good Schools Guide – Special Educational Needs* is only a glimpse of this. We would be happy to put our knowledge and our wide network of personal contacts to work for you.

The advisory service is provided by our most experienced editors, most of whom are parents like you, although some have been professionally involved with education. We offer access to advice on that basis.

Not even the best school is perfect. Good schools differ enormously in what they offer and in the kind of child they suit best. Our service can help you with:

- Finding schools which are likely to suit your child
- Inside information on what a particular school is really like
- Suggesting good schools that you may not know about
- Checking out specific schools for you
- Information on strong specialist departments and unusual features
- Suggestions on how to improve your chances of getting your child accepted by a school.

Tell us what you need, and we will tell you if we are able to help. All information is treated in the strictest confidence. We act as agent for our advisers, and, if we can help, the next step is for us to put you in touch directly with an appropriate adviser who will agree directly with you about a consultation in person or by e-mail, fax or telephone. If we cannot refer you to an appropriate adviser, we may be able to suggest someone else who can meet your needs.

Our standard fee is £250. The adviser may suggest a higher or lower fee, which is between you and the adviser to agree in particular cases.

The Good Schools Guide on the Web

www.goodschoolsguide.co.uk

Half price for owners of this book

There's a lot more to *The Good Schools Guide – Special Educational Needs* than we were able fit in this book!

We have a dedicated special needs section on our website carrying even more advice, information and help.

You will find a small but fast increasing number of short reviews that are only on the web, not in the printed guide.

For English schools there is the A level data: results analysed at the level of subject and grade, so that you can see exactly how popular each subject is and how well pupils do. You can use our search program to look for schools which are particularly good at individual subjects, or at least have enough pupils doing them for you to be sure that they are really on offer.

Again for English schools, there's the five-year history of performance table data, which you can use to track how a school has been improving (or not), and how it rates in comparison with other schools (we provide performance tables based on a total of 10 different measures).

(We are doing our best, too, to provide data on Scottish, Welsh and Northern Irish schools: having made some progress in our negotiations, with luck it will find its way onto a website during 2006.)

We also include there a summary of where pupils go after GCSE, and (as we are able to obtain data under the Freedom of Information Act) doubtless we will be adding other fascinating analyses over the course of the year.

All of these are in addition to the facilities that have always been there for our online subscribers: searches based on geography and on school characteristics; searches of The Good Schools Guide text and of our links pages; links to school websites and to Ofsted and other inspection reports; links to hundreds of other websites that contain information that we think will be useful to parents who are looking for schools.

You will also find that the Good Schools Guide online is updated regularly as rewrites and new schools are added, and as we make thousands of minor alterations throughout the year.

All this is yours for a year if you subscribe to the Good Schools Guide online. And, because you have already paid to purchase this book, we will only charge you half price (for as long as this first edition is in print). Go to www.goodschoolsguide.co.uk, click on 'buy the guide' and, book in hand, answer a question to prove your ownership. When, later in the year, we introduce an updated version of our Good Schools Guide online shop, you will also be asked for a reference code. Use 'Chesnut'.

Introduction

I have, or I think I may have, a child with a special educational need.

At the risk of sounding like a group therapy session, if you identify with this statement, or are wondering if there is something the matter with your child, this may well be the book you've been looking for.

Like many parents, I thought there was something different about my child but wasn't sure what – I had all the pieces for the jigsaw but not the box, so it was hard to work out exactly what I was looking for. Nevertheless I was determined to do what I thought was best for my child and to get the help and support he deserved. I managed to work my way through the system for what, on the SEN scale, is a relatively minor but nevertheless important need; but it wasn't easy.

The world of SEN can be a minefield: there's information out there but finding out what you need to know can be difficult – hence this guide. We'd never pretend that buying this book will solve your problems, but we hope it will guide you to the sources of help, support and advice that can ease what is often, at best, a difficult and very stressful process. We hope it will help you identify what may be wrong, what you can do, who you can consult, to provide food for thought, provoke debate and demonstrate there is some cracking provision out there: super ideas; innovative approaches ... Ask yourself, if one school can do it, why can't others?

There are marked differences between this guide and our long-established sister publication, *The Good Schools Guide*. Column inches devoted to school reviews are fewer; indeed, the schools in this guide are illustrations of schools that do at least a good job for children with SEN rather than a comprehensive directory of all schools with terrific provision. However, information on all schools is available, if not in this publication then through our comprehensive website, www.goodschoolsguide.co.uk/?SEN.

In a new departure, instead of saying solely what *we* think a school provides for SEN, we've asked all schools to tell us what *they* think they provide, via a detailed questionnaire. Where schools have responded, the information is available to you online. We haven't verified the comments as such but we hope the phone will be hot, the post bag heavy and cyberspace jammed as you pick up the blower, put pen to paper or tap the keyboards, spilling the beans, telling the truth ...

Unusually, but perhaps not unexpectedly, some schools have played down their provision. Radley College told us: 'We would rather not appear in any guide of schools offering SEN provision so will not be completing a questionnaire.' A shame really, because a parent of a child with SEN who attends the school said they're doing a fantastic job for him. Don't they value the child and the work they are doing with him? Are they ashamed to be doing a good job for a child who has fulfilled the entrance criteria, made the grade, yet happens to have a learning difference?

Alas, Radley isn't alone. We've written some very complimentary things about SEN provision at some schools, yet they've asked, nay demanded, that we remove the comments. Would they have acted in a similar fashion if we'd said how terrific their provision for the gifted and talented kids is? We don't recall schools asking us not to mention the number of scholars, the newly refurbished dorms, state-of-the-art ICT packages ...

The truth seems to be that they are frightened of what parents might think if they found out the school was good at dealing with SEN. With some reason: as our website survey has shown, half of the hundreds who replied to the survey think that having SEN children in a school harms other children's education, mostly because they feel that SEN children get all the attention. Hiding your light under a bushel is one solution, we suppose – but we much prefer to see the torch held proudly aloft by the likes of Winchester College, or the ever-glorious St John's College School, Cambridge whose head writes:

> Each child is special; each child has needs; each child has special needs.'

This is a message that has come through at high volume in the very many special schools we've visited. We know that more than a few were surprised to get our call; they shouldn't have been. There is so much expertise and diversity in special schools, an uncanny knack of being able to think outside the box, see things differently, offer a real chance to the youngsters in their care. We fully understand the calls for inclusion, for children to have the opportunity to be educated in mainstream schools, but the special schools we've visited have proved time and again that inclusion isn't just, if at all, about a mainstream experience, it is about being included on terms that best fit the needs of the individual. When we visited TreeHouse, a school originally established by a group of parents to meet the needs of children with autism, the head said:

> People think children [with autism] benefit from inclusion in mainstream because they're getting the chance to communicate and socialise with other typically developing children, but this isn't necessarily the case ... children do benefit from visits; they offer a chance to generalise their skills.

And added:

> I'd love to unpick what is meant by a peer group for the children: one of our pupils was in a mainstream setting, but he wasn't in a peer group, wasn't actually accessing the curriculum, and staff didn't have the training or opportunity to undo his learning or the stages and steps his learning needed.

We had heard good things about TreeHouse, and following on from this introduction one of its founding parents, the author Nick Hornby, writes about the difference it has made to his son's life.

Special schools and units attached to mainstream schools are two alternatives to being educated in a mainstream setting. Many parents battle for a statement that names such schools or units. Would they really do this if mainstream schools offered the quality of education and provision they feel their child deserves?

We suspect (hope?) that there'll be more than an eyebrow or two raised at the inclusion in this first edition of some of the schools we've chosen as illustrations of good schools for SEN. The criterion for inclusion was reasonably straightforward: are they doing a good job for a child with special needs? We didn't stipulate IQ or need.

We've kept the reviews in the familiar *Good Schools Guide* style. For the most part we've visited the schools, spent time uncovering the foibles and fancies of each one, chatting to the head, staff, parents and children. Sometimes our task has been difficult. A handful of schools haven't allowed us to visit so we've sent a spy along, then interviewed a parent or ten, asked questions in and out of the locality, submitted our findings to the school and printed them! We've upset the odd school – because we tell the truth. If the accommodation is shabby, why lie? You'll notice the instant you visit. On the other hand, if our reporting is accurate, you'll know what to expect, won't be put off by the shabby surroundings and might just concentrate on the excellent education and care they can give your child!

The *Good Schools Guide* has never just been about the schools but about the package that is the education of the child. With SEN, that can be a pretty big parcel. There's so much SEN information and expertise out there, but few places where the information is brought together and nowhere where schools have been visited and written up *independently* with the parents of children with SEN in mind. (We'd like to stress the 'independently', because there are some guides or recommendation lists out there you just pay to get yourself on.) Hence this, *The Good Schools Guide for Special Educational Needs*, with a simple aim, not of re-inventing the wheel but of providing the hub and attaching the spokes.

We know there are hundreds more very good schools out there that we haven't yet visited. We rely very much on parents, users of schools and moles to tell us about them, to unearth them on our behalf.

A final introductory comment: throughout the production of this book I've often thought 'if only' – if only I'd made notes during the speech and language therapy sessions (which incidentally I – and my child – used to love), during the occupational therapy sessions – a real eye-opener, not a basket in sight – and during the assessments with the many professionals, including the orthoptist. Shamefully I must admit I have even misplaced the records – I think I sent them to the school but I should have known better and made at least one copy. If I could offer one piece of advice to any parent who suspects that their child is different, it would be to write everything down. Keep a record: dates, times, personnel, issues, observations and outcomes. Record anything, everything, not just formal meetings but things you notice about your child: behaviour, difficulties, what they were doing at the time etc. So, with my parent hat on, that would be a 'do as I say, not as I do!' Get your notebook (or voice recorder) out and scribble away.

To provide an all-round picture, we needed the thoughts and opinions of those with in-depth knowledge of SEN. We wanted to tap into that knowledge and share it with you, so we did. We've been fortunate that so many experts have joined us in this project, to provide reliable and authoritative information: experienced therapists, specialist educators, eminent lawyers – and parents and young people themselves, because there is nothing like going through the mill yourself for gathering expertise. Several charities have worked with us to help uncover schools for this first edition. We are grateful for their support. We've donated £1 to them for every usable comment received. We will continue to do so: the second edition needs you.

Sandra Hutchinson
Editor

Nick Hornby and TreeHouse

Nick Hornby is the best-selling author of Fever Pitch, High Fidelity, About A Boy *and, most recently,* A Long Way Down. *Nick has a son, Danny, with autism. Here he shares some of his thoughts on autism, on bureaucracy, and tells why he and a group of like-minded parents founded their own school to help children like Danny.*

All the research suggests that early intervention is key. On the one hand getting a diagnosis was a huge shock, devastating. Danny's birth was difficult, and there were early signs; but however prepared you think you are, hearing those words is still a huge shock. You don't know what to do or even how to react.

Initially we were told Danny had some kind of global developmental delay, and that the most difficult time would be when he was 5 or 6 and behind other kids. That was far harder to take than when we got the official diagnosis of autism. We were prepared by then. In a way we were fortunate: Danny was diagnosed with autism when he was 2, which is really young. The majority aren't diagnosed until they're 6 or 7. This means many parents have years of anxiety, stress and heartache before they have a label for their child's developmental and behavioural problems.

Autism is a broad term – that's why people talk about the autistic spectrum. Some children can be educated in mainstream schools and go on to be very successful; others don't even know who their family members are. Danny is at the more severe end of the spectrum. Autism is a particularly devastating disorder: an autistic child's development is erratic, unpredictable and shrouded in uncertainty. It is a lifelong condition and the future for any child, upon diagnosis, can seem very bleak indeed. Even the basics, such as toilet training, and the forming of emotional bonds were things, we were told, he might never achieve.

Danny is a lovely, happy, sunny, playful little boy. It wasn't always like that: just before he was 2 he went into a tail-spin – regressing, losing words and skills he had previously had, grinding his teeth and shutting out the rest of the world. He seemed desperately alone and unhappy, and we felt we were losing him. Some of the phrases and words he had then he's never re-acquired.

Parenting a child with autism is demanding enough without the stresses of having to fight every step of the way for everything. Yet however hard or difficult it is for you, you can guarantee that someone else is having a tougher time. I know of people who've been involved in five separate tribunals, involving just about every aspect of their child's life.

Having a child with autism is physically demanding and mentally exhausting, and on top of that there are all the bureaucratic nightmares. You have to find somewhere to educate your child. There are currently around 76,000 autistic children fighting for 3,000 specialist school places, yet experts tell us it is only specialist education that can make any difference.

TreeHouse is unique. Its children receive an education unlike anything else offered in the UK, which is why those of us involved are so passionate about their work. What is being provided for the 90,000 children with autism in the UK is hopelessly inadequate, which is why we want to share the pioneering work of TreeHouse. We want schools like TreeHouse to sprout up all over the country, and we want to help many more teachers get the training that they need to engage, motivate and teach essential skills, in order that all children with autism can achieve their potential and live as independent a life as possible.

Danny has nearly lost TreeHouse several times, even though there was no educational provision for him elsewhere (which is why desperate parents set it up in the first place). Its future is now secure and the school will soon have a permanent home, but it's been a long, hard battle. Danny has been at TreeHouse for five years now.

His progress is remarkable – he listens, he copies, he plays, he has fun, he has a special friend. This is something of a miracle given what the textbooks say about autism. He is affectionate and gentle. Danny's communication skills have developed dramatically.

TreeHouse is incredibly proud of its achievements to date, none of which would have been possible without the support of our many friends who give their precious time, money and energy to help us achieve our vision that 'all children with autism will be empowered through whole life learning'. If you are considering joining us I encourage you to contact TreeHouse to discuss the many ways that you can help our cause; your support will be deeply appreciated.

The TreeHouse Trust is a London-based charity, established in 1997 to provide an educational centre of excellence for children with autism. It was set up by a group of parents (including Nick) whose children had recently been diagnosed with autism.

Part of this piece is reproduced with kind permission from Nick's website at http://www.penguin.co.uk/static/cs/uk/0/minisites/nickhornby/treehouse/index.html

Speaking with the Angel *is a collection of new short stories edited by Nick Hornby and written by Roddy Doyle, Helen Fielding, Robert Harris, Irvine Welsh, Zadie Smith and others. It is published by Penguin and for every copy sold £1 goes to TreeHouse.*

TreeHouse has been reviewed for this book. To find out what we thought, see Part 2.

About this guide

This book isn't just about schools. How could it be? Special needs is a complex area; there are so many factors to consider even before requirements for schooling can be discussed. For most, having a diagnosis is a relief; for many, getting the diagnosis is the tricky bit. Even with a diagnosis you may have to battle to get help, recognition and support for your child. We're not just talking the dyslexic or dyspraxic either; children with severe hearing impairments, autism and an array of more complex needs end up at tribunals with stressed parents fighting the system every step of the way.

We originally intended simply to include more information and more schools for children with special needs in our sister publication, *The Good Schools Guide*. But it soon became apparent that there was so much we needed to tell you it needed a book of its own! So just what have we come up with? A one-stop shop to set you on the road to understanding not only your child's special needs, but the system, support and, alas, the obstacles and hurdles too.

So, what are the areas in which this book can help?

Identifying different kinds of special needs

Even defining a special educational need (SEN) is not cut and dried, so we start off with that, and a positive action plan for schools and parents. Then there's an overview of key conditions, in which we not only describe their characteristics but outline their educational implications and provide information on where to find additional help and advice. (Please don't take lists of characteristics to mean your child has an SEN – how many medical students thought they were riddled with cancer because they happened to have some of the symptoms outlined in the oncology module?) We hope the section will be a useful reference for anyone who thinks their child has a special need or who has been told their child has. However, we cannot stress enough the importance of getting expert professional opinion.

Who's who

We wanted to clear the myths about SENCos SaLTS, OTs, PT, EPs – all have invaluable roles to play in helping children with SEN but just who are they? What do they do and how can they help your child?

The SEN debate

Mainstream or special, independent or state? Everyone seems to have an opinion. Some groups make sure their voices are heard loud and clear, and why not? We feature the opinions of parents, young people with SEN, teachers, charities, the government ... those who know us well will not be surprised that we haven't shirked from debate, we've encouraged it! Whatever your views, we think Chapter 4 makes for an interesting and thought-provoking read.

Choosing a school

Choosing a school is not only about the cut of the cloth, it's about getting the perfect fit, everything from the first tack to the last stitch. Of course, there's a difference between buying a suit off the peg and having one tailor made. Some schools cater extremely well for the very bright, mildly dyslexic child but would be hopeless for other SEN. Having good dyslexia provision alone doesn't necessarily make it the right school for your child with dyslexia, just as having a wheelchair-accessible school doesn't make it a haven for the wheelchair bound. You need to examine a school from all perspectives to ensure the fit is a good one.

We have visited all the schools in this guide that have a full write-up. Most of these have been done with the full co-operation of the schools but a couple didn't want us to write about them – so we visited and wrote about them anyway.

The schools in this guide are illustrations of schools that do well by children with special needs – a cross-section rather than a definitive list. At one extreme, some of the schools in this guide are only really suitable for, say, the bright child with dyslexic-type difficulties. The reviews for these schools concentrate on what the school offers across the board, with only minor reference to SEN. At the other extreme, some schools are very specialised, suitable perhaps for children with severe communication difficulties. When writing about these schools, we maintain our style and review headings, but concentrate much more on the entry criteria and any specialist or 'different' provision offered to meet the child's SEN, while not in any way detracting from the importance of the very many other aspects of the school and school life.

We have a fair few local day schools. Not much point reading about them, you might think, unless you happen to live on their doorstep? Not quite, because these reviews give an insight into what makes a good school: what it is they offer, their outlook, facilities and com- passion, all things that may provide useful pointers, to help you decide what you are looking for, for your child. We already know of parents who, before they spoke to us, were told certain provision can't be made or doesn't exist anywhere, until they spoke to us. Sometimes provision really doesn't exist. There are a number of schools in this guide that were founded by parents, teachers or other professionals exactly because nothing suitable was on offer.

Naturally we've provided a guide to choosing a school: questions to ask, things to look for – but often the real guide is instinct: 'what feels right'. Visit a selection of schools, visit shortlisted schools more than once. If you're anything like me you'll shortlist with your head but select with your heart.

Don't choose a school just because it says it offers provision for dyslexia or whatever; choose a school because it suits your child. If a school doesn't advertise that it caters for SEN but you like it and think it suits your child – ask. You'd be surprised how many schools that do well by children with SEN don't advertise the fact ('we don't want to be seen as a special school').

We also devoted a lot of time and energy to getting schools to tell us what they do for children with SEN. We had some interesting and helpful responses and wanted to share these with you, so we've included a number of these (and there are more online). We have to stress these are school statements not ours, so if you know differently, do tell.

Help in the classroom

School Action Plus, IEPs, the statementing process – we hope Chapter 6 will help you work out what's going on and also what help and concessions your child may be entitled to. And we didn't just examine SEN, we asked those who offer exams for SEN to tell you what's on offer, from ASDAN to A levels via the National Curriculum and P levels.

The law

Misinterpret a phrase in the regulations and it might be a case of go directly to jail do not pass go – parents have a legal obligation to make sure their children receive a suitable education. With this in mind we approached David Ruebain, a highly regarded (some would say the country's top) SEN solicitor and other legal eagles to lead us along the right path. We highlight some of the key points of education law (with a special feature on Scotland's new Education Act), spell out the rights and responsibilities embedded in the statementing process and include a first-hand experience of what it's like to have to go through the trauma of a tribunal. Peter Woodroffe, familiar to users of the Good Schools Guide Advisory Service, gives advice on taking the legal route when things go wrong.

Where to turn for help and advice

However much you know, there's always something else to learn – special needs shouldn't be a DIY job. So we include information on support organisations, where school-leavers can turn to for help, and lots of useful sources of support and advice, including those of the very many contributors to the guide. There's even a glossary to help you decode the TLAs of SEN and a whole lot more besides; if you think differentiation is something to get to grips with in a maths lesson, check the glossary – times they are a changing. And because there's always more to uncover we want to enlist your help too…

How you can help

We know there are plenty of very good, even excellent, schools that should be in future editions of this guide but we need you to help us sort the gems from the paste. We rely on your help to uncover the best; the ones that do well by children with special needs. If you have experience of a school that does well by children with SEN (or indeed want to share your experience of any school) then do tell us. Either online at www.goodschoolsguide.co.uk or by contacting us at:

The Good Schools Guide
3 Craven Mews, London SW11 5PW

Tel: 020 7801 0191
Fax: 0870 052 4067
E-mail: editor@goodschoolsguide.co.uk

We'll even pay £1 to charity for a usable comment.

PART 1

ABOUT SEN

Chapter 1

Entering the world of special needs

Identifying special needs

Does my child have a special need or are the difficulties they seem to have 'normal'? You don't have to have a formal diagnosis to request help for your child. If you suspect your child has a 'learning difference' or difficulty, or you're just worried, seek advice. Here we explain what constitutes a special educational need (SEN) and outline help and support available for your child even if they haven't yet started school.

Children with special educational needs are defined as those who have learning difficulties or disabilities that make it harder for them to learn than most children of the same age. These can be social, emotional, intellectual, behavioural, physical or sensory or a mixture of some or all.

Not all children with special needs are readily identified. Some develop coping strategies to mask their difficulties; others may have for example a hearing loss that has not been identified or may be considered naughty, a fidget, a daydreamer – symptoms of everyday childhood but also ones that can conceal underlying special needs. Parents know their children well – so don't feel, just because nobody else has said anything, that 'it's just you'.

It's thought that approximately 20 per cent of children have special needs at some point during their school life. Many think the figure is higher; indeed it seems to be getting harder to find a family not touched in some way by special needs. Why? Better recognition, detection and diagnosis of SEN on the one hand, coupled with medical advances and better neo-natal survival rates on the other. What's more it seems it's not just children who are being diagnosed with SEN, we know anecdotally of a number of parents who, on getting a diagnosis for their child, realise they have a previously undetected difficulty themselves.

For some children having an SEN is a transitory phase; it may be that following suitable intervention the child will be 'cured'. At the other extreme some will have special educational needs throughout school and possibly into adult life. The type, nature and severity of SEN varies but approximately 2 per cent of children have needs that require a statement (or in Scotland a record of need or co-ordinated support plan).

The government aims to ensure that the majority of children with special needs attend and have their needs met in ordinary mainstream schools: inclusion is the order of the day. However, for a minority of children (but not all those with statements), special schools or other provision will be better placed to cater for their needs.

What problems might a child with special needs have?

Almost anything (see Chapter 2 for information on some of the conditions associated with SEN). The degree and extent of SEN also vary considerably between and within conditions. Difficulties may occur with:

- all school work
- specific areas of school work such as reading, writing, numeracy, understanding or processing information
- self-expression or expressing and understanding what others are saying
- listening or paying attention
- establishing relationships, making friends or relating to adults
- behaving appropriately in or out of school
- personal organisation
- motor skills: may be impaired or slower-processing
- sensory or physical needs
- a combination of any of the above.

Action to take if you think your child has a special need

Firstly bear in mind that children progress at different rates and have different ways in which they learn best. If this doesn't reassure you then trust your instincts and seek a second (or third) opinion.

- Talk to your child's teacher, or headteacher. Make sure you are prepared before you go in – write down all the points you want to make, better still keep a diary or record of incidents and experiences that support your case, remember you know your child best.

- Find out if the school also thinks your child may have difficulties or special needs, whether your child is making the progress expected for their age and if there is anything you can do to help at home. If the school shares your concerns they will decide on the appropriate type and level of support or intervention. If the school doesn't share your concerns and you are still not happy with the explanations given, pursue the matter, seeking independent advice or information if necessary.

- You may find it useful to make an appointment to speak to the school's special educational needs co-ordinator (SENCo).

- Hopefully working together with your child's teachers will help to sort out many worries and problems, but be prepared to be the person keeping on top of matters – schools focus on all children but it's your child that matters to you. The closer you work with your child's teachers, the more successful any help for your child should be. If you disagree with something said or done, ask for an explanation but try not to be defensive or aggressive: antagonising teachers won't help, but don't let them railroad you either – they don't always know best.

- Parents are often the first ones to identify a difficulty, so they can rightly request help for their child. Seek the help and support of professionals. Your GP (or health visitor for pre-school children) will be a useful starting point.

- Use the Useful contacts section in this book to get in touch with people and organisations who can help. There's a lot of experience out there to be tapped into.

How a school can help

There is statutory guidance (see Chapter 9) on inclusive schooling for all maintained (state) schools for children with SEN in England, including city academies and maintained nursery schools. This doesn't apply to schools in other parts of the United Kingdom or those in the independent sector, who can please themselves. However, fears of future litigation mean independent schools are beginning to take special needs very seriously and many will follow the guidelines or similar.

With or without the guidance, many schools are getting much better at detecting and managing special needs, but some are still slow to recognise and assess problems. As a rule:

- Good teachers will choose the best way to help a child learn from a range of activities and will differentiate the curriculum (teacher-speak for adapt lessons) to take account of individual learning need.

- Teachers should carefully organise lessons, the classroom, social groupings, books, materials and the way they teach to ensure a child can make the most of any given learning opportunity – if this isn't happening for your child ask why. (Where it is happening let GSG know – we are keen to share with our readers all good ideas and practice.)

- Every school should have a policy that explains how they provide education for children with SEN. Do ask a school for a copy of the policy and for an explanation of how the policy is implemented. (If it's full of jargon ask for the information in plain-speak.)

- Where a school believes a child's difficulties require extra measures they will follow the guidance given in the SEN Code of Practice on how to provide help for children with SEN. Basically this uses a graduated approach to help those children identified as having SEN. If a child's needs are clearly greater than the norm, stages can be skipped and the process speeded up. Remember, the current Code of Practice expects a lot from schools, and some may have genuine difficulties in successfully meeting those expectations, so do keep on top of issues and concerns. You can order a free copy of the SEN Code of Practice from the DfES (details in Part 4) if you think you may have to do battle or if you need to know what should or could be happening.

- If a school thinks your child requires it, they may recommend that your child is placed on School Action or School Action Plus – more on this form of extra or different help in Chapter 6. The school must tell parents when they first start giving extra or different help for a child because of their SEN; it's your right to be involved.

- Some schools use Individual Education Plans (IEPs) to write down actions or help for a child (see Chapter 6 for a detailed explanation). These contain targets for your child to work towards.

- If you haven't yet decided on which school your child should attend, see Chapter 5 on choosing a school for children with SEN.

What you can do if you're dissatisfied with the provision currently being made for your child

If you are not happy with your child's progress, whatever the reason, there are several things you can do, but most importantly keep in sight the fact that your child will get one shot at education and deserves at all times to get appropriate help and support. So if you think you have a genuine gripe but are being fobbed off, pursue the issues.

If your child is already being given additional or different provision but you think they need more support, then discuss with the child's class teacher, SENCo or headteacher whether to ask the local education authority (LEA) to make a statutory assessment of your child to see if they need a statement. An assessment will only be necessary if the school can't provide all the help a child needs (sometimes just asking for an assessment is enough to keep the school on its toes with regard to provision made for a child).

At a meeting with a member of the school staff about the school's handling of your child's educational needs, do write everything down – make notes before, during and after the meeting. It often helps to take a friend or relative with you, if only for much-needed moral support. If you feel you want someone experienced in such matters, representatives of local parent partnership services, local voluntary organisations or parents' groups may also be able to help.

If you have concerns that you feel are not being properly addressed you can speak to the governor with responsibility for SEN or the chair of the governing body, or ask for a copy of the school's complaints procedure and follow the procedure outlined. If necessary speak to the LEA – they should have a special needs adviser or similar.

Finding schools that provide for particular educational or medical needs

Seek advice from your LEA about the range of school provision available locally, including special school provision. Charities also have lists of schools they recommend for certain conditions.

Further information about particular schools – including independent and non-maintained special schools – can be obtained from the schools themselves. Additionally the local parent partnership service will be able to offer factual and impartial information and advice: ask the LEA for the service's phone number.

It's also invaluable to talk with other parents who have had similar experiences and to use guides such as this one for an independent insight into schools based on the experiences of other parents. Most importantly, though, you need to visit schools to see if they really will meet your child's needs before making any decisions (see Chapter 5).

Preschool children and special needs

You do not have to wait until a child starts school to get help and support.

You may have concerns about your child's sensory development (sight, hearing, speech and language); physical, social, emotional development or behaviour; or the way in which they play, learn and interact with others and their environment.

It's recognised that early intervention can make a big difference so if you think your child needs extra support to develop and learn, speak to your health visitor, family GP or preschool. They will either allay your fears that it is quite normal for little Lawrie not to be able to recite War and Peace by the age of 2 (whatever other mothers at nursery say), or, if professionals share your concerns, they may want to look more closely at your child's needs and may involve staff based at one of the child development centres.

In addition, you may be able to get extra help through the Portage Service, a preschool home visiting educational service for children with additional support needs.

A young child identified as having SEN may be put on Early Years Action or Early Years Action Plus to enable them to learn and develop. When preschool and other support services can't provide all the help needed they may request a statutory assessment of the child's needs, which can lead to a statement of special educational needs (see Chapter 6 for more about what this entails). Parents too can request a statutory assessment. The decision on whether to carry out an assessment rests with the LEA.

At whatever age, or whatever the nature of the difficulty or worry, if you think your child has special educational needs, then seek help, advice and support from all quarters. Your child isn't alone and you shouldn't be either.

Chapter 2

Conditions

For a few parents, especially where the child has a genetic disorder or sensory impairment, diagnosis of a handicap or difficulty will be made at birth or during early infancy. Other difficulties may not be apparent (or even exist) until the child is older, perhaps even a teenager. In a few cases diagnosis isn't made until well into adult life and perhaps only then because a family member is identified as having a particular difficulty. Yet even those undetected until adult life often feel a sense of relief when they finally realise why they struggled or experienced problems and finally have a name to pin to these.

Over the years there has been a great deal of controversy about the effect of labelling a child as dyslexic or blind or whatever. Clearly labelling can have a very negative impact if the child is seen only for their disability and not appreciated for their strengths. That said, many parents are extremely relieved to uncover the problem:

I was so glad when my child was diagnosed as dyspraxic. The school had told me there wasn't anything to worry about but I knew my child was experiencing greater difficulties than he should. He couldn't jump or hop; his handwriting was illegible; he struggled with laces, bumped into things. At least now I felt he'd get the help he needed instead of people thinking he was just clumsy and stupid.

So many parents worry and want a label to hang on to but then find that, unlike chickenpox or a broken leg, there isn't a neat cure or even in many cases a neat list of symptoms. Few children with special educational needs have just one difficulty: a child may have other difficulties – what's commonly referred to as co-morbidity. It's not unusual for a child to have dyslexia and dyspraxia, to have emotional and social difficulties as well as learning difficulties etc. However, often a child will have one condition that requires greater attention, so for an autistic child with Down's syndrome, autism is likely to be the dominant condition.

Complexities, co-morbidity, multiple disorders – describe them as you will, special needs are seldom textbook cases. A term used for some of these is neuro-diversity. Neuro-diverse people are those who, to a greater or lesser degree, experience the world differently from most people. Many of the greatest thinkers and creators of our time were neuro-diverse: Einstein, Samuel Coleridge Taylor, Winston Churchill and Jamie Oliver to name just a few! They all had a difficult time at school because their way of thinking was different and did not fit in with the norm.

The causes of neuro-diversity are not known. It is possibly linked to premature or delayed birth and has a higher prevalence in boys. It is considered to be a developmental delay or immaturity in part of the brain, a predisposition that may be inherited. Neuro-diversity does not affect intelligence, but it can affect performance.

What to look out for

This varies. Just as an example, a child with dyspraxia, may

- be clumsy
- have difficulty with tasks such as tying laces, catching balls (may be last to be picked for team games)
- be slow with activities like getting dressed
- experience problems with speed and presentation of handwriting (slow, untidy, messy), frequently find tasks such as copying from the board a real challenge.
- have poor balance or proprioception (sense of body position in space, may invade the space of others too)
- be hypersensitive to some stimuli
- get lost easily in new surroundings
- have difficulty with left and right

- be unaware of environment
- have asymmetric tonic neck reflex (ATNR) which can cause a lack of integration to both sides of the body, with resultant difficulty working across the midline.

Children who exhibit these traits are not necessarily dyspraxic – a child may be disruptive in class because of hypersensitivity to some stimuli, or be finding it difficult to screen out information coming through their sensory systems, or be trying to avoid the unpleasant visual sensations that occur when they try to read. Symptoms or similar behaviour may have different causes.

This chapter describes over 20 different conditions. Some are well known; some you may never have heard of before. Just like delving into a medical dictionary, it's very easy to read something and think: 'Aha, that's it, that explains the problem!' But don't use this chapter to make an instant diagnosis. Diagnosis is not easy, and as children grow, different problems may come to the fore – in dyspraxia, for example, as children get older, some of the physical difficulties lessen but organisational difficulties become more noticeable.

Of course there are many conditions other than these that can affect a child's ability to learn, ranging from severe physical handicap to psychological disturbance. Circumstances, such as being the victim of bullying or having to act as a carer for a parent, can also profoundly affect a child's educational needs. Some of the organisations whose work is described in Chapter 8 are especially helpful in this regard.

However, we hope that the information in this chapter will shed light on the types of difficulty that can arise with different conditions and what you may expect (remember, every child is different and Harry may not know that he's supposed to be dyspraxic because he's got Asperger's), and that it will help you understand – and explain to others – what's going on inside your child. But please, if you suspect your child has a problem seek out expert help and advice: health visitors, the school or your GP are good starting points.

The autistic spectrum

Autism is a lifelong developmental disability that affects the way a person communicates and relates to people around them. Some people with the condition have accompanying learning disabilities, while others have average or above-average intelligence.

Autism is characterised by impairments in three areas: social interaction, communication, and imagination (shown in difficulties in the development of play, flexibility of thought, or restricted or repetitive interests). This 'triad of impairments' is found in varying degrees and forms, so the concept of the autistic spectrum has been developed, and the term autistic spectrum disorder (ASD) covers a wide range of abilities and disabilities, including childhood autism at the less able end of the spectrum, to Asperger's syndrome at the more able end. Autistic spectrum disorders are not rare; it is estimated that about 1 in 110 people have an ASD.

How ASD affects people

Children with the more narrowly defined condition of childhood autism develop language later than typically developing children, and some may remain non-verbal. In contrast, children who have Asperger's syndrome develop language at the same time as other children, but their language use is often unusual. They may use rather formal words and phrases, which make them seem old-fashioned and different from their peers, or they may speak in a stilted or monotonous way.

The difficulties in social interaction pose very particular problems. Children with an ASD find it difficult to read social cues and non-verbal signals about what other people are feeling. For instance, a person with an ASD may not be able to spot when a companion is upset, angry or bored. They come across as lacking in empathy for other people's feelings, which could be interpreted by someone not aware of their disability as wilful self-centredness. Children with autism may show no interest in what other people are doing and avoid joining in games with their siblings, peers or parents. Their parents often describe them as being engrossed in a world of their own. Children with Asperger's syndrome, on the other hand, often show a desire to be sociable, but their attempts to make friends may be thwarted by their lack of comprehension of the social nuances of negotiating friendships.

People with an ASD often say they like 'sameness'. They dislike things that upset their routines, because routine gives them a sense of security. Children with autism often repetitively perform the same actions and show no signs of developing imaginative play. Others may become fascinated by a particular topic, for example dinosaurs, and become extremely knowledgeable about it, but be uninterested in branching out to other related subjects. The close focus they give to their chosen interests may help in certain disciplines, for example in some aspects of maths and science. Impairment of imagination does not mean that people with an ASD are necessarily uncreative; some are very creative. It is more that flexibility of thought, the ability to foresee the consequences of their actions and to put themselves in another person's place and understand their point of view are all likely to be areas of difficulty for them.

Diagnosis

Autistic spectrum disorders can usually be diagnosed from about two years. Children with Asperger's syndrome usually learn to speak at the same age as typically developing children, so their disability may not be picked up quite so early. Diagnosticians most commonly interview the parent about the child's development and observe the child in a number of situations to arrive at a diagnosis. If you think your child may have an ASD you should go to your GP and request a referral to a consultant or diagnostic team with an understanding of the condition.

Some disorders on the spectrum have their own specific labels.

Pervasive developmental disorder (PDD) is the name given to a group of neurological disorders characterised by severe and pervasive impairment or delay in several areas of development, including social interaction, communication skills, and/or the presence of stereotyped behaviour and activities that may be frequently copied and pursued rigidly and repetitively.

You may also come across the term PDD (NOS): 'similarly pervasive development disorder not otherwise specified'. This may be used to describe individuals who, although they do not meet the full criteria for autism, nevertheless display autistic symptoms. Late-onset autism would be considered a PDD (NOS).

Often associated with the autistic spectrum disorders, semantic pragmatic disorder (SPD) is usually identified between 18 months and 2 years. Typically a child has good hearing but few if any real words, and has problems with comprehension (but responds well to speech therapy). By school age the child appears 'different' – sometimes appearing to follow very little conversation, while at other times giving a detailed explanation of an event. Later on in school they are often good at maths, science and information and communications technology (ICT) but have great difficulty in writing a coherent sentence or playing with other children. They may have difficulty sharing and with taking turns. They can appear aggressive, selfish, bossy, over-confident, shy or withdrawn. In school, they may be misdiagnosed as children with behavioural problems.

Current thinking is that children with SPD have many more problems than just speaking and understanding words; the underlying difficulty may be in the way they process information. Children with SPD find it more difficult to extract the central meaning or the saliency of an event. They tend to focus on detail instead: they may, for example, find the duck hidden in the picture but fail to grasp the situation or story in the picture, or may point out the spot on your face before saying hello.

Early support for parent and child

The National Autistic Society (NAS) has developed two parent-training programmes for parents whose child has just been diagnosed: EarlyBird (for under 5s) and EarlyBird Plus (for infant school age). These programmes are designed to help the parents understand the condition and provide strategies to help with their child's communication, interaction, play skills and behaviour. They are provided by licensed practitioners, in different local authorities, throughout the UK. Other local authorities may use similar programmes for parent support and training such as Portage and Hanen. The NAS also has a programme called *help!*, consisting of six sessions on different aspects of caring for a child or adult with an ASD; this is offered to parents/carers where the diagnosis has been received in the last 18 months.

Approaches for improving skills

Some children with autism can show very difficult behaviour. It is not always immediately obvious why it is happening, and it can be difficult to control the situation without knowing more about what lies behind it and what strategies to use. Behaviour is a form of communication; it sends messages to other people and gets results. With limited verbal communication, a child with autism may not be able to express their feelings of anxiety, discomfort, or frustration except in an outburst of unwanted behaviour. They may have learnt from experience that such behaviour generally achieves their desired objective. So it becomes important to analyse what had been going on before the outburst that might have upset the child, and then teach some other way of communicating what they want.

Parents and teachers are trained to use various approaches to help develop children's language and communication skills.

Children with autism tend to be visual learners and find it easier to understand the world about them through visual aids. The Picture Exchange Communication System (PECS) is a commonly used approach in which the adult will use pictures as symbols to teach the names of different objects. Gradually, children are taught to exchange a picture for the object they want, to construct simple sentences using the pictures, and to indicate choices between various objects. Visual supports are helpful to children with an ASD even if they are verbal. At school the teacher may use a visual timetable showing times and simple drawings of the activities, so that the pupil knows exactly what they will be doing when. Many schools use sophisticated computer software packages to write out stories, descriptions and instructions in both words and symbols simultaneously.

Most schools that educate children with autism have adopted the TEACCH approach (Treatment and Education of Autistic and related Communication-handicapped Children). It is based on the principle that children with autism learn better in a structured educational environment, and that each child should have a unique programme based on regular assessment of their abilities. The educational approach is also grounded in theories of cognition and behaviour. Understanding the causes of unwanted behaviour is important in the process of trying to reduce it. The strengths of the individual children with ASD are recognised and built on, taking into account their visual learning styles and their love of pattern, rules and order. The physical environment in which the child is learning is organised in a structured way to help them learn what activities take place in particular areas and to avoid sensory distractions. They are given clear instructions for every stage of an activity, usually presented in a visual way. The TEACCH approach is one in which you can work with the professionals to continue the techniques at home.

Children with autism who can read may be taught how to cope with different situations using the technique of Social Stories™. These stories are written for the individual child, explaining in words and pictures, step by step, what will happen in any situation they are likely to feel anxious about or how they should cope with situations they find difficult. For instance, a story might explain what to do when they go on a bus journey or hear the fire alarm.

A number of children with ASD respond well to drama and role-play activities. Sometimes social skills such as greetings, turn-taking in conversation and watching for cues in social skills groups are taught in sessions which may be run by speech and language therapists or teachers.

What kind of school is best?

Children with autistic spectrum disorders differ from each other considerably in the kind of schooling that best suits them. It is not even true to say that a child with autism will need a special school, while a child with Asperger's syndrome will get along fine in a mainstream school. Some do and some don't.

There are children with autism who are well supported in mainstream schools if the staff are well trained, the staff/pupil ratio is high and the classroom environment can be adapted sufficiently for their needs. Conversely, there are some children with Asperger's syndrome, at the more able end of the spectrum, who are very unhappy in mainstream schools, because they feel misunderstood and isolated, and they find the noise and busyness oppressive. Bullying of pupils who are different from the majority is sadly not uncommon.

It is a good idea to visit as many types of school as you can to get a broad view of what's available. Some key features you should look out for include:

- approachable teaching staff and a named person, perhaps the SENCo, who can guide staff on the needs of children with ASD
- good communication between staff and parents, and between staff and pupils
- good planning for the child's day and any changes that may occur

■ staff able to communicate clearly to the pupils using visual as well as verbal means.

Social skills are hard to learn if the child has no friends. In mainstream schools the teachers may have set up a Circle of Friends or buddy system to help a child with an ASD in the social world of the classroom and playground. Fellow pupils are trained to understand their classmate's difficulties and give them friendship and support.

And here are some questions to ask:

■ Do the teachers have a flexible outlook on teaching strategies, which may need to be adapted to suit the individual child?

■ Is there a clear whole-school policy on bullying?

■ What training have the staff had in the needs of children with autism?

■ To whom do pupils with ASD go if they have any anxieties or problems?

We are grateful to the NAS for their extensive help with the information above.

Further information and help

See also Part 4: Useful contacts.

National Autistic Society (NAS)

Web: www.nas.org.uk. E-mail: nas@nas.org.uk.
Tel: 020 7833 2299. Fax: 020 7833 9666.
Helpline (10am-4pm Mon-Fri): 0845 070 4004
or 0845 070 4003 (minicom).
Address (head office): 393 City Road, London EC1V 1NG

The NAS was set up by parents in 1962. It now runs six schools and 17 adult day and residential services, and advises other schools through outreach work. The NAS helps thousands of people with autism, their parents and carers through its national services such as the Autism Helpline, parent support groups at NAS branches, the Advocacy for Education service, befriending schemes, social groups, seminars and programmes of parent training. The NAS training department delivers tailored training courses for professionals in education and other fields. The NAS also has a publications department, which produces and sells a wide variety of literature for parents, teachers and carers.

The NAS website is a rich repository of information about autism for people with an autistic spectrum disorder, parents and professionals. Information sheets about the topics and approaches mentioned above can be found at www.autism.org.uk/infosheets.

The Public Autism Resource and Information System, PARIS, an online directory of autism services, can be found at www.info.autism.org.uk.

NAS schools

Broomhayes School.
Web: www.autism.org.uk/broomhayes.
E-mail: Broomhayes@nas.org.uk.
Tel: 01237 473830. Fax: 01237 421097.
Address: Kingsley House, Alverdiscott Road, Bideford, North Devon EX39 4PL

Daldorch House School.
Web: www.autism.org.uk/daldorch.
E-mail: Daldorch@nas.org.uk.
Tel: 01290 551666. Fax: 01290 553399.
Address: Sorn Road, Catrine, East Ayrshire, KA5 6NA

The Helen Allison School.
Web: www.autism.org.uk/helenallison.
E-mail: Helen.Allison@nas.org.uk.
Tel: 01474 814878. Fax: 01474 812033.
Address: Longfield Road, Meopham, Kent DA13 0EW

Radlett Lodge School.
Web: www.autism.org.uk/radlett.
E-mail: Radlett.Lodge@nas.org.uk.
Tel: 01923 854922. Fax: 01923 859922.
Address: Harper Lane, Radlett, Hertfordshire WD7 9HW

The Robert Ogden School.
Web: www.autism.org.uk/robertogden.
E-mail: Robert.Ogden@nas.org.uk.
Tel: 01709 874443. Fax: 01709 870701.
Address: Clayton Lane, Thurnscoe, Rotherham, South Yorkshire S63 0BE

The Sybil Elgar School.
Web: www.autism.org.uk/sybilelgar.
E-mail: SybilElgarSchool@nas.org.uk.
Tel: 020 8813 9168. Fax: 020 8571 7332.
Address: Havelock Road, Southall, Middlesex UB2 4NR

Behavioural disorders

Educating children with behavioural difficulties in mainstream schools provokes much debate between the pro- and anti-inclusion lobbies. Such pupils may frequently lack concentration finding it difficult to remain on task, fiddle or fidget, call out in class, disrupt those around them, meddle or interfere with the property of others, behave inappropriately for their age, demonstrate aggressive or unacceptable behaviour, and display social difficulties – perhaps cry easily or recoil from social situations and find it difficult to make friends and sustain relationships.

Attention deficit (hyperactivity) disorder: ADD/ADHD

Attention deficit disorder (ADD) is one of the most challenging and controversial areas of special education facing teachers in UK schools today. Parents of ADD children live in chaos; they have to supervise and cope with unrealistic limits (often with little or no support), leading to stress and frustration in the family.

ADD is a neurological condition, probably genetic in origin, where the sufferer has a limited ability to sustain attention, and has reduced control over words or actions as a result of impulsiveness and lack of appropriate forethought. When there is also hyperactivity (ADHD), sufferers find it hard to control the amount of physical activity appropriate to a situation and their behaviour may be highly disruptive.

No one has precise data on the cause of ADD/ADHD and much still needs to be studied, but recent research seems to suggest that it is due to an inherited imbalance of neurotransmitters. There are many examples of adults who were never diagnosed (or who were misdiagnosed) as children, who are later diagnosed by an ADD/ADHD-aware professional. Often the evidence was always there, but little or no appropriate action taken.

The most recent explanation for those more obvious hyperactive/impulsive types is 'response inhibition', which seems to suggest that individuals live essentially in a constant state of being on high alert and are unable to shut out any sensory, visual or auditory stimuli coming their way and therefore unable to concentrate enough to make use of incoming information.

ADD/ADHD is an extremely distressing condition affecting up to 8 per cent of school-age children. An early diagnosis and treatment can save a child the pain of inappropriate social skills and deflated confidence, and is crucial to a child's chances of achieving a good quality of life. Referral to a specialist in the field of ADD/ADHD is important to ensure the correct diagnosis and care. ADD/ADHD is a complex disorder that varies greatly in type and severity between individuals and requires a multi-professional approach. Traditionally, ADD/ADHD has been poorly understood and not very well catered for, but enhanced knowledge and understanding of the condition particularly within education has led to recent improvements.

Typical signs

ADD sufferers are inattentive, may have problems in concentrating and focusing, and may have difficulties with verbal and emotional impulsiveness. Schoolwork is often erratic and unpredictable. Parents and teachers assume the child is lazy; their school reports may say 'Needs to concentrate and pay attention'. Often clingy, quiet and over-shy, they are easily led yet find instructions difficult to understand. They tend to be daydreamers. Both ADD and ADHD sufferers are prone to become victims of bullying.

It is generally agreed that ADD/ADHD does not have a significant effect on intellectual ability. ADD/ADHD sufferers are usually of normal to high intelligence, highly creative and intuitive, with enhanced physical ability. However, the difficulty with concentration means they frequently do not fulfil their true potential. This underachievement, and persistent criticism because of behaviour, can lead to low self-esteem and depression. Sufferers may lack motivation and organisational skills, are often the class clown and may play truant. Sleep disorders often accompany ADD/ADHD and if the condition is not treated before puberty other problems may emerge.

The weight of the law

Some schools seem to find it difficult to accept the condition and any appropriate treatment, despite being unwilling victims of the consequences of ignoring it. It has been stated in Parliament, and clearly proven in the courts, that ADD/ADHD is one of a number of conditions which give rise to special educational needs.

If you suspect your child has ADD/ADHD consult your GP who will be able to rule out any physical causes for your child's behaviour (hearing loss, thyroid problems etc) and refer you to appropriate professionals who will be able to assist with a diagnosis and appropriate help. If schooling is an issue, the LEA should have a list of suitable mainstream and specialist provision.

The impact ...

Conservative estimates as described by Paul Cooper, Professor of Education at Leicester University, place the number of school-age children with ADD/ADHD within the UK at this time at approximately 500,000, though fewer than 50,000 students have a diagnosis at present. In reality, however, in every class of 30 children it is likely that there will be between one and two students with ADD/ADHD. Because of the potential impact of these children on the class dynamics in terms of teacher time and social interaction, it could well be argued that ADD/ADHD either directly or indirectly will affect every student within every classroom in the UK.

Managing ADD/ADHD

Fintan J O'Regan, international expert in ADD/ADHD, behaviour management and SEN

The *American Diagnostic and Statistical Manual of Mental Disorders* (DM1V) recognises three subgroups, which it describes as Hyperactive Impulsive Type, Predominately Impulsive Type and Combined Type. However, in practice we are usually looking at two specific patterns of behaviour: those children who cannot sit still, are highly impulsive and appear driven by a motor and those who appear to be mentally somewhere else other than in your presence most of the time ... the space cadets.

These typical examples might help to clarify the variability further.

Daniel

It's 8.25 and Daniel's brother and elder sister are waiting for him so they can go to school together. But 4-year-old Daniel decides he does not want to wear his coat. He is crying and says he doesn't want to go to school today. Pleading is ignored, as are threats. He will not put his coat on. The clock is ticking ... soon they will all be late for school. This has been a pattern of the last few days – Daniel difficult and disruptive, his mother tense with frustration. Options are limited. Sending him to his room is not a possibility at this time, and Daniel probably even knows this. In the end the coat is forced on him and he's dragged screaming down the street, howling all the way to school with his bemused and embarrassed brother and sister and a highly agitated and embarrassed mother. The next morning the same thing happens ... and the next ... Then Daniel's mother tries the sticker chart formula. For every morning that no complaints occur Daniel gets a sticker; ten stickers he gets a present – and to make it fair the whole family goes out for dinner. Daniel likes the concept. He wears his coat, he gets his sticker, he is able to self-regulate.

Ivan

Ivan was having a typical day: he just couldn't keep still. He kept on fiddling with a pen which, once taken away by the teacher, was replaced by an elastic band. When it was flicked across the room and struck Sadie across the face she stood up yelling in the middle of the class. The teacher Mr Flynn had had enough of this and of year 8c in general. 'Out!' he said to Ivan. 'Off to the LSU. Go and see Ms Parker.' Ivan didn't mind as he quite liked Ms Parker and preferred the sanctuary of the learning support unit. But as he left the classroom he passed Mark and whispered something to him. Now Mark flew out of his seat and ran after Ivan out of the classroom. The two of them began pummelling each other in the corridor. Before Mr Flynn could move, five other students had rushed out of the classroom to watch the action. Mr Flynn pulled the two boys apart, with Ivan laughing and Mark spluttering, still furious: 'He cussed my mother, Sir!'

Simon

Instead of being at homework club after school 13-year-old Simon was spotted outside on the street on his skateboard. The teacher asked him to come inside and join the others. Simon appeared flustered and disorientated and was finding it hard to settle at his desk. Also his skateboard kept getting in his way. Simon, though badly disorganised, was usually a most passive and generally compliant student. After watching him struggle to get started the teacher said that he would remove his skateboard until later. It came as a tremendous shock to the teacher when Simon's response was to jump out of his seat in a furious temper, yelling 'If you do that you'll be sorry!' The room became a deadly hush. After his outburst Simon now sat slumped, spent in his chair. When the teacher approached him Simon put his hands over his ears and started sobbing, saying 'I'm such a bad kid.'

It is obviously difficult to assess the time and costs to support children with ADD/ADHD, but one thing is clear: learning difficulties accompanied by behavioural issues take up a great deal of both. As in most businesses today, the most expensive resource in schools is personnel. Learning and behaviour difficulties engage vast amounts of personnel time in terms of specialist teaching (often one- to-one provision), additional learning support staffing and a range of time-consuming meetings, conferences, phone calls, paper administration and communication with external agencies. I recently spent most of a particular Tuesday on one issue, for which seven other adults, including the senior LEA educational psychologist, a social worker, the child's headteacher, the classroom teacher, two learning support teachers, the careers adviser and the parent also needed to be involved. This is not a unique scenario: on a day-to-day basis throughout the UK vast resources are absorbed in planning, managing and teaching children with ADD/ADHD.

Within mainstream schools children with ADD/ADHD will require varying amounts of support dependent in part on the nature of their difficulties, the type of school they attend and, to a very large extent, the training of the special needs teacher and the SEN skills/knowledge/attitude of the majority of the regular teaching staff.

Although many teachers, support staff and administrators are aware of the term ADD/ADHD, few see it as medical disorder rather than a behavioural issue. This to some extent is understandable: teachers at the 'coal face' will have to address the core symptoms of inattention, impulsivity, hyperactivity and often other behavioural/socialisation difficulties. As a group they are often quite defensive about behavioural issues with specific students, which, unlike learning difficulties, can often make individual teachers feel uncomfortable about how their management of particular students is perceived

… and some management strategies

Educational support such as special help from a trained teacher outside the child's class plus extra help within the class can enable a child to remain in mainstream school. Sometimes needs may be best met via a statement of SEN (see Chapter 6). One-to-one interaction generally results in improvements in concentration and behaviour (for a short duration).

'Management of ADD/ADHD = SF3R' translates as the core principles for successful management of children with ADD/ADHD: Structure and Flexibility supported by the 3Rs of Respect, Relationships and Role Models. The overriding message is a structured learning environment, with differentiated work to address the children's learning weaknesses and adaptations to fit their learning style.

Within this term one of the letter Rs is often mistaken for Ritalin. Of course medication can have a major role to play in ADD/ADHD management. ADD/ADHD is a medical diagnosis and it therefore may require a medical strategy or option to complement (complement being the key word) the other principles of SF3R.

Overall, a school needs an SEN department that has an understanding of ADD/ADHD. In addition to this a calm, encouraging and consistent approach, with a well-structured routine, clear rules and standards of work in school and for homework are beneficial for a child with ADD/ADHD.

Strategies for a child with ADD/ADHD must be individualised and involve both the whole-school approach and strategies for the specific child. Persistent difficulties, despite the implementation of reasonable strategies, suggest the need for a medical review. It must be remembered that the concurrent use of medication must not be seen as a threat or criticism of teaching strategies, but as a necessary adjunct. In reality, the most effective teaching of a child with ADD/ADHD arises from taking an open-minded view to using another option or adaptive approach to the teaching and management.

Finally there are two extremely important principles to understand when managing a child with ADD/ADHD. The first of these is that it is not the child's fault, nor is it your fault. Working together with the school on behalf of the child is the most effective way of achieving success. And this will involve what I label the three Cs: Clarity, Co-operation and Communication. Secondly, support from other parents is vital.

How to spot the ideal teacher for a child with ADD/ADHD

- Thoroughly knowledgeable about ADD/ADHD and accepts the legitimacy of the disorder.

- Tough as nails about rules but always calm and positive.

- Ingenious about modifying teaching strategies and materials in order to match the child's learning style.
- Tailors academic material to suit the child's abilities and skills.
- Creates assignments that require as much activity on the child's part as possible.
- Mixes high- and low-interest tasks in tune with the child's learning style.
- Deals with homework in a pragmatic way.
- Knows when to back off when the child's level of frustration begins to peak.
- Knows when to back off when the parent's level of frustration begins to peak.
- Speaks clearly in brief, understandable sentences.
- Looks the child straight in the eye when communicating.
- Runs an absolutely predictable and organised classroom.
- Controls the classroom without being controlling.
- Provides immediate and consistent feedback regarding behaviour.
- Develops a private signal system with the child to gently notify them when they are off task or acting inappropriately.
- Maintains close proximity without being intrusive.
- Ignores minor disruptions; knows how to choose battles.
- Has no problem acting as an auxiliary organiser.
- Maintains an interest in the child as a person even after a trying day.
- Willing to call and meet with parents.
- Has a sense of humour you wouldn't believe.

Helping your child at home

- Acknowledge and accept your child's weaknesses and strengths, and design activities around their strengths to help their confidence levels.
- Try to work out the times in the day when they work most productively, and ensure that a task begins and ends with an activity that they enjoy.
- Bolster and maintain your child's self-esteem, to help the 'whole child' develop.
- School and the home must maintain close contact to ensure that your child receives consistent messages.
- Don't personalise situations: it is the behaviour that you do not approve of, not the child.
- Never discipline in anger: everyone says things in the heat of the moment that they later regret – you will say things you don't mean and, more importantly, sometimes you can't back up.

Finally, have fun with your children. Look at specific situations not as problems but as opportunities for developing your relationship, as the father and son do in this little story.

> For Mr Bailey and Freddy, his 10-year-old son with ADHD, the big issue was that both of them were highly charged individuals who would not back down in the course of an argument. Each wanted the final word. When Freddy got the final word, this would send his father into a frenzy – he felt the last word was his by right as head of the family. It was suggested to Mr Bailey that perhaps he could pay Freddy 50p so that he, the father, could have the last word. Two weeks later the father called to say thank you. Things at home were calmer and he and Freddy were getting along fine. He said the sight of Freddy biting his lip in order to get the 50p was worth every penny and he would have paid £5 for the outcome ... I told him not to tell Freddy ...
>
> F O'Regan, *How to Teach and Manage Children with ADHD* (LDA Learning, 2002)

Fintan J O'Regan works as a behavioural/SEN adviser for Surrey LEA, tutor at Leicester University and external expert at Worcester University. He is a consultant/trainer for the Metropolitan Police and the Youth Justice Board and an international trainer in the field of ADD/ADHD, behaviour management and SEN. He has written a number of published articles on the subject of behaviour management and ADD/ADHD and is the co-author of the Times Educational Supplement *award-winning book* Educating Children with ADHD *(Routledge/Falmer, 2000). Fintan is the current board member of the ADHD Global Network and Education Director of ADDISS Charitable Trust.*

Behavioural emotional and social difficulties (BESD)

Behavioural emotional and social difficulties (BESD) describes a wide range of conditions including: withdrawn, depressive or suicidal attitudes; an obsessive preoccupation with eating habits; school phobia; substance misuse; disruptive, antisocial and unco-operative behaviour; and frustration, anger and threat of or actual violence. All affect a child's own learning and can impact significantly on the education of peers. BESD is associated with problems that have, or are assumed to have, their roots in 'nurture' rather than 'nature'.

Specialist approaches are often required for children with emotional and behavioural difficulties (EBD) or social, emotional and behavioural difficulties (SEBD). For some children medication or psychiatric intervention may be needed and attendance at a BESD school will be the most appropriate way for the child to receive the specialist help and attention required.

There is no easy answer to appropriate classroom strategies for a child with BESD because of the wide range of conditions that can underpin the label; however, the following may help:

- small, carefully thought-out group settings or one-to-one working
- use of learning mentors (or key workers or equivalent)
- careful monitoring and targeting
- structured routine
- individual education plans (IEPs)
- SMART (specific, measurable, achievable, realistic and time-related) targets
- clear guidelines
- involving and working closely with parents and the child
- differentiated work tailored to learning need
- rewarding and reinforcing positive behaviour
- enhanced personal social and health education programmes
- programmes for managing and controlling behaviour
- anger-management programmes
- counselling and peer support.

One special school we visited found the use of circle time at the end of the day to discuss the day, problems and their resolutions, to be effective and positive. Another mainstream school told us that early intervention and the introduction of nurture groups appears to have lessened problems with behaviour and had a positive impact on all pupils, not just those in the nurture group.

Oppositional defiant disorder (ODD)

Oppositional defiant disorder is used to describe long-lasting, aggressive and defiant behaviour that is extreme and outside the normal range. It is characterised by a persistent disobedience and opposition to authority figures (such as parents, teachers or other adults). Such behaviour is usually less severe than conduct disorders but equally persistent. The basic rights of others are still respected and age-appropriate societal rules and behaviour are not violated. ODD is characterised by aggressive, negative, hostile and defiant behaviour, which may be strongest in the home. Children with ODD will blame others rather than themselves and may seem angry and resentful, especially towards adults. Outwardly a child may appear irritable, with frequent temper outbursts, frustration and intolerance. Self-esteem is usually low though it's likely the child will project an image of toughness. Additional symptoms of anxiety and depression are common.

Conduct disorders

Conduct disorders embrace behaviour that violates the social rules and rights of others and are typically present in the home, school and wider community. Children and adolescents with conduct disorders tend to be physically aggressive. They may fight, bully, be cruel to people and animals, destroy other people's property (possibly including arson) or steal. Stealing ranges from 'borrowing' others' possessions to shoplifting, forgery, car theft and burglary. Children with this disorder often lie, are truants, cheat at schoolwork and display callous behaviour. They may use or abuse tobacco, alcohol and other drugs at an unusually early age and be sexually precocious. Such behaviour must have persisted for six months or more for a conduct disorder diagnosis.

Schools employ a variety of strategies when working with youngsters with conduct disorders, including behaviour management, social skills (often through enhanced personal, social and health education (PSHE) input), strategies to improve self-esteem and self-control, and close liaison and involvement with parents or carers.

Obsessive compulsive disorder (OCD)

This is a condition where the sufferer experiences recurrent thoughts or images which they recognise as senseless but which nevertheless disturb them. Obsessions are often accompanied by excessively repetitive acts (compulsions or rituals such as continually washing hands), carried out in order to reduce the anxiety resulting from an obsession. Sufferers try to avoid situations or activities that remind them of their obsession. A sufferer may worry about acting on unwanted or senseless urges or impulses, such as harming someone they are close to, or worry obsessively about terrible things happening to them, or repeatedly experience unpleasant thoughts or images. Symptoms may manifest as physical difficulties, fast heartbeat, trembling or panic attacks. OCD usually appears in adolescence or early childhood. Medication and counselling may be of help to some sufferers.

Tourette's syndrome and other tic disorders

Tics are movements or sounds that are repeated over and over again – anything from eye blinking to obscene words. They are involuntary: sufferers describe tics as compelling – if they don't do them they don't 'feel right'. The problem may be transient and cause no ill effect, or be chronic and/or multiple. There are no diagnostic tests, and it is common for the tics to disappear as soon as the doctor is consulted and return again straight afterwards.

The technical bit

Tourette's syndrome (TS) occurs before a child is 18 and is characterised by many varied, frequently changing motor tics (eye blinking/rolling; head jerking; facial grimacing/contortions; body jerking; hitting self/others; shoulder shrugging; lip smacking; arm flapping/flailing; or vocal tics (grunting, sniffing, yelling, barking, making 'tsk' or 'pft' noises, puffing expirations, spitting). TS is a neurological disorder, and so cannot be controlled by the sufferer without their having more severe tics.

There are three types of vocal tics: repeating own words (pallilalia), repeating the words of others (echolalia), and uttering obscenities (coprolalia). For TS to be diagnosed the frequency of tics must be many times a day, nearly every day, for more than one year, with no period of remission during that year lasting longer than two months. TS can be inherited, and is often associated with OCD and ADD/ADHD (see Chapter 2, Behavioural disorders).

The practical bit: a parent's-eye view

It is possible for a person with TS to suppress their tics for a limited period of time but eventually the tics have to come out. In class a TS sufferer may suppress a grunting tic but in effect this creates a backlog of tics. Bullying is always an issue for Tourette's sufferers, though we've yet to find a school willing to admit it happens in their school! One mother describes the tactics she and her son have evolved:

> My son signals he needs to leave the room to release a flurry of tics by asking the teacher if he can get a drink of water. Depending on the nature of the tics, it may be necessary to lie down to release them; remaining upright can cause discomfort. The only private place for him is the school toilets – hardly ideal!
>
> Thankfully my son's tics are only shoulder shrugging, eye rolling, head nodding, and grunting. Stress and tiredness can make the tics worse. Tics often continue until he falls asleep. We have sought the school's co-operation in bringing him in later if he's had a bad night. When tics are very severe, we keep him at home. Listening to audio cassettes can help relieve stress and fatigue.

The knock-on effect

There are physical problems associated with tics: a tic in the arm a sufferer writes with will adversely affect handwriting; eye rolling or head nodding tics can make reading difficult. When tics are severe, it may not be possible to drink out of a normal cup. (A car cup saves being soaked!) Even when speaking, tics can be very frustrating, as vocal tics such as grunting continue, making it difficult to get a sentence out. Understandably, word processors/computers are useful tools for a TS sufferer.

TS sufferers may also have an OCD. They may be concerned with symmetry, or cleanliness, or repeatedly have to perform a physical action such as squeezing fingers and thumb together. Or they may focus obsessively on right/wrong issues or repeatedly ask the same question. The movie *Matchstick Men* – with Nicholas Cage, in which he had to switch a light on and off a certain number of times, was a pretty good example of mild Tourette's and OCD!

The medication used to treat TS was originally designed for other conditions. Some are anti-psychotics; others lower blood pressure. One mother says:

> We tried both. Everyone is different but my son became volatile, depressed, very overweight, and moved about as if sedated so we stopped the medication and sought the help of a food intolerance expert. This has been more successful, reducing the frequency and severity of tics by as much 80 per cent. Now my son avoids sugar, cannot use mint toothpaste, doesn't take any cow's dairy products (he has goat's milk products) and is better if food is free from yeast, colourings, added salt and preservatives.

On the plus side kids with TS are generally hardworking and conscientious. If they are high functioning they actually don't require much more attention than other children. A regular SEN meeting, perhaps just a chat once a week or so, may be all that is needed to check all is well.

Compiled with reference to Tictionary *by Betty Ottinger (Karnac Books, 2003).*

Further information and help

See also Part 4: Useful contacts.

National Attention Deficit Disorder Information and Support Service (ADDISS)
Web: www.addiss.co.uk. E-mail: info@addiss.co.uk.
Tel: 020 8906 9068. Fax: 020 8959 0727.
Address: 10 Station Road, Mill Hill, London NW7 2JU

ADDISS is the UK national advocacy group for parents and professionals concerned with ADD/ADHD. ADDISS is a registered charity, run by unpaid staff that provides information, training and support for parents, sufferers and professionals in the fields of ADD/ADHD and related learning and behavioural difficulties. ADDISS holds a three-day national conference each year, bringing together professionals and people living with ADD/ADHD, and convenes many practical workshops and training events on ADD/ADHD around the UK.

OCD Action. Formerly Obsessive Action: the national organisation for obsessive compulsive disorder (OCD), body dysmorphic disorder (BDD), compulsive skin picking (CSP) and trichotillomania – a very helpful site.
Web: www.ocdaction.org.uk.
E-mail: info@ocdaction.org.uk.
Help and information line: 0845 390 OCDA (6232).
Office: 0870 360 OCDA (6232). Fax: 020 7288 0828.
Address: 22-24 Highbury Grove, Suite 107,
London N5 2EA

Tourette Syndrome Association.
Web: www.tsa.org.uk. E-mail: enquiries@tsa.org.uk.
Tel: 01892 669151. Helpline: 0845 458 1252.
Admin: 01383 629600.
Address: Tourette Syndrome (UK) Association,
PO Box 26149, Dunfermline KY12 9WT

Genetic and related disorders

Down's syndrome

Down's syndrome is the most frequently recognised genetic cause of intellectual disability and occurs in all races and economic groups. It is a chromosomal disorder caused by an error in cell division that results in the presence of an additional chromosome in pair 21 or 'trisomy 21'. It isn't known what causes this extra chromosome, which can come from either the mother or the father, but there is a definite link with advanced maternal age, the incidence of Down's syndrome rising from 1 in 2,000 in babies born to mothers under 20, to 1 in 20 for women over 45 – although most babies with Down's syndrome are born to women under the age of 35, as younger women have higher fertility rates.

It is estimated that there are around 60,000 people with Down's syndrome living in the UK, and about 600 babies with the condition born in the UK each year. There are slightly more boys born with Down's syndrome than girls, but this difference is small. The number of Down's babies who die in infancy is significantly higher than the general population, but less than 20 per cent, and a child surviving the first five years has the same chance of reaching age 40 as the general population. After age 40 there is a definite increase in mortality, though many adults survive in good health into their sixties.

Diagnosis

A new-born baby with Down's syndrome often has physical features recognisable in the delivery room. These may include a flat facial profile, an upward slant to the eyes, a short neck, abnormally shaped ears, white spots on the iris of the eye (called Brushfield spots), and a single, deep transverse crease on the palm of the hand. However, a child with Down's syndrome may not possess all of these features, some of which may be found in people who don't have Down's. To confirm the diagnosis, the doctor will request a blood test called a chromosomal karyotype. This involves 'growing' the cells from the baby's blood for about two weeks, followed by a microscopic visualisation of the chromosomes to determine if extra material from chromosome 21 is present.

Difficulties Down's syndrome children experience

Bob Black, Education Information Officer for the Down's Syndrome Association

Children will have some degree of developmental delay – they are often slow to turn over, sit, stand and respond. This may be related to the child's poor muscle tone. Development of speech and language abilities may take longer than expected and may not occur as fully as parents would like. Several other well-known medical conditions, including hearing loss, congenital heart disease, and vision disorders are more prevalent among those with Down's syndrome. However, children with Down's syndrome do develop communication skills and learn effectively.

The abilities of children with Down's syndrome vary enormously, but most tend to be within the mild to moderate learning disability range. Speech is often indistinct, owing to the typical mouth formation; and there is developmental delay in language, which may be improved by specialist speech and language therapy. Children are prone to middle-ear problems and conductive hearing loss. Learning difficulties are also compounded by disorders of vision.

The main problems to expect are that a child with Down's will take longer than most to process information, and require more practice when learning skills. Some learning may never be completely mastered. Teaching methods should include visual as well as linguistic clues to help learning.

Going to school

Choosing a school for a child with Down's syndrome can appear challenging but ultimately is fairly simple. A good school that takes a range of children from its local area, a school that values diversity and understands children is equally a good school for a child with Down's syndrome.

Parents have the right to ask for a special school if they particularly want one or if their child has significant additional or complex needs, but at 'rising 5' over 80 per cent of Down's children go to a local mainstream school with additional support. Parents will generally choose the school that is local to them, which their other children go to, or the one that the child's preschool peers are likely to be attending. Both state and private schools can easily include a child with Down's syndrome, and many will network with other schools in their area to share information and strategies.

In many cases yours may be the first child with Down's syndrome that the school will have included, and some adjustments will need to be made to understand and accommodate a child who may have more significant learning difficulties than they have previously encountered. Schools that are welcoming and committed to inclusion will accept these challenges for what they are, and will look at the needs of your child as a child first. All good schools celebrate the individual successes of those that are slow learners as well as the high achievers.

A good school will listen to parents' concerns and seek outside information from expert sources on the learning and other needs of children with Down's syndrome. It will look at your child's inclusion as a matter of right and will be committed to them for the whole time they are in the school and not as some part-time social experiment. A good school will seek to offer access to a broad and balanced curriculum and will be creative at finding ways to include your child in the whole range of school life.

The benefits to the school are profound. Many report that looking at the needs of this group of children has enhanced the learning experience of the whole school and helped to find a range of strategies for dealing with other special needs, and the impact of inclusion has had many other advantages. Many who are not even directly in contact with the child will feel better informed and less intimidated. PHSE and disability awareness become part of everyday practice rather than a separate simply academic activity, and schools report improvement of understanding, achievement and provision across the ability range.

Parents are often concerned that a vulnerable child will be bullied or picked on, but experience suggests that the reverse is often the case; children who have been perceived to be prone to this kind of behaviour have responded by offering support and protection to the less able child, bringing out positive behaviour and increasing self-esteem and self-worth in many who struggled to find any.

With sensible differentiation, assessment and tools such as the P scales for measuring and celebrating individual achievement, children with Down's syndrome are successfully included throughout their infant and primary education. By the time children transfer to secondary school only 27 per cent currently continue in mainstream, but this figure increases every year and with planning and forethought increasing numbers of children are staying in the mainstream as schools learn to make the necessary adjustments. Until secondary schools have caught up with their primary colleagues in supporting and celebrating inclusive practice, many children will continue to need good special school placements through to transition into further education.

Fragile X

Fragile X is the second most commonly occurring inherited condition after Down's syndrome. It gets its name from the discovery of a link between mental handicap and an abnormal 'fragile' site on the X chromosome. Fragile X occurs in approximately 1 in 4,000 males and 1 in 8,000 females, and its severity is more marked in boys than girls, with intellectual disability varying from mild to severe.

Adults with fragile X syndrome often show strengths in domestic daily living skills, relative to their communication and socialisation abilities. Nevertheless, many need a degree of supported living.

Diagnosis

Diagnosis is by blood test using DNA analysis. Prenatal diagnosis is also possible either by chronic villus or foetal blood sampling. However prenatal diagnosis cannot always distinguish affected from unaffected carrier females.

There is a 50-50 chance of a female carrier passing on the fragile X chromosome to her children. Of these, boys are almost certain to be affected whilst girls have a 1 in 3 chance of being affected. Men can also be unaffected carriers of the fragile X chromosome, passing it to their daughters but not to their sons.

Although it was discovered in the 1970s the gene associated with fragile X wasn't identified until 1991 so many individuals with the condition may remain undiagnosed. In many families a diagnosis is not made until after the birth of a second or third affected child. Carriers of the syndrome can be offered genetic counselling if appropriate. In the case of children, once a diagnosis is made specialist help in the areas of education, speech and language development can be put in place along with any special care and understanding, appropriate medical, psychological and social help that can be given

Problems associated with fragile X

Not all children will have all these problems but even those with intelligence in the average or above-average range may exhibit many of these features.

Learning difficulties

Approximately 80 per cent of boys and a quarter of girls with fragile X have learning difficulties varying from subtle educational delays to severe mental handicap. Overall, strengths are verbal abilities such as vocabulary, aspects of simultaneous information processing and some visual perceptual tasks. But there may be difficulty with organising thoughts and planning ahead, processing new information, especially where abstract reasoning, sequential processing, visual-spatial abilities, short-term memory and numeracy are involved. With puberty and adolescence the rate of intellectual development appears to decline.

Speech and language problems

Language difficulties range from a complete absence of speech through to mild communication problems. The rate of talking may be fast and fluctuating, with swings in pitch and even garbled and disorganised speech with corrections or frequent shifts of conversation from topic to topic. Speech may be delayed, distorted or lack fluency. Articulation problems are also common. You may find children repeat their own and other people's speech as a way of maintaining participation in conversation while trying to process what is being said.

Challenging behaviour

Boys with fragile X tend to be overactive and impulsive with marked concentration problems, attention deficit, restlessness, fidgeting and distractibility. Irritability, tantrums and aggressive outbursts are aggravated by environmental over-stimulation, confusing situations or heightened anxiety. Girls are usually less affected than boys but have similar attention difficulties and are often extremely shy and socially withdrawn. However, emotional difficulties are common even in girls with a normal IQ.

Clumsiness

Fine motor co-ordination problems are common but not usually apparent until later. Over-sensitiveness to sensory stimuli means that people with fragile X are easily overwhelmed by sights, sounds, smells, tastes and textures – poor eye contact and gaze avoidance may be attempts to avoid excessive stimulation.

Autistic-like features

Although only a minority have 'typical autism', many display autistic characteristics such as poor eye contact, repetitive behaviour or speech, resistance to change, strong preoccupations or fascinations, social anxiety, abnormal shyness and an insistence on routine. However, unlike those who are autistic, fragile X sufferers tend to be affectionate and have an interest in relating socially even though they may be shy and anxious in social situations.

Physical features

Features ascribed to fragile X syndrome include a relatively large head, a long face with prominent ears, largish jaw and double-jointedness. However as these are less marked in young children a fragile X diagnosis is often missed or delayed. Epilepsy is developed by up to 30 per cent of people with fragile X syndrome.

Medical help

A combination of medical, psychological, educational and social interventions tailored to your child's needs can help substantially. In some cases medication may be helpful, especially for those with attention deficit or who suffer seizures. Over-activity in fragile X syndrome tends to decrease with age, but attention difficulties, restlessness and impulsiveness can remain problematic for many adolescents and adults.

Rett syndrome

Rett syndrome is a complex neurological disorder that affects mainly girls. A large proportion of people with Rett syndrome have a mutation on the MECP2 gene on the X chromosome.

Initial development appears normal but after the first 12 months head growth slows, followed by social withdrawal and a deterioration in speech and mobility. Whilst there is variability in the severity of the disorder, most people with Rett syndrome are profoundly and multiply disabled with high dependency needs throughout life. Rett syndrome is probably the most common genetic cause of profound intellectual and physical disability in girls, occurring in more than 1 in 10,000 female births.

Typical signs of Rett syndrome

- Appearing to make normal progress, but with a period of stagnation in development from about the end of the first year until regression occurs.
- A regression period when skills in speech and hand movement are reduced; this usually occurs between 9 and 30 months.
- Development of repetitive hand movements such as wringing, patting, clapping, tapping or mouthing.
- A stiff or clumsy posture or gait, or an unsteady, wide-based gait.
- A slowing of head growth between 2 months and 4 years.

Other features include:

- breathing irregularities including hyperventilation, breath holding and air swallowing
- EEG abnormalities
- epilepsy

- with age, muscles become increasingly rigid, and there may be joint deformities and muscle wasting
- development of scoliosis (curvature of the spine)
- growth retardation.

Information reproduced by kind permission of the Rett Syndrome Association UK, a national organisation providing information, advice and support to parents, carers, siblings and professionals. Their work includes proactive support for families, liaison with a wide range of professionals to support good practice in care and management of Rett syndrome, a wide range of accessible written and video information and research. They produce a quarterly magazine, Rett News, *have support groups across the UK, a regional parent contact network, and an annual family weekend and family day. They also fund research and work in partnership internationally. We found them to be a friendly and approachable organisation offering information and guidance, including useful and practical advice on the statementing process, how to write a statement, questions to ask, organisations to approach etc.*

Rare chromosome disorders

Prader-Willi and Angelman syndromes are rare genetic conditions both caused by irregularities in chromosome 15. They aren't diseases but are neurological disorders which can cause severe learning difficulties.

Children with Angelman syndrome (AS) used to be termed 'puppet children' because of their characteristic happy demeanour, small head, sometimes inappropriate laughter and stiff jerky movements. They also have a tendency to extreme thinness. Other characteristics include sleep problems, lack of speech (greater receptive than expressive language), and developmental delay. To date only about 350 cases have been diagnosed in the UK. Some children with AS have been wrongly diagnosed as having an autistic spectrum disorder or cerebral palsy.

Prader-Willi syndrome (PWS) is often characterised by an insatiable appetite for food and tendency to gain weight very rapidly, often leading to serious obesity and associated medical problems. Characteristics include: poor muscle tone, co-ordination and balance; emotional and social difficulties; immature physical development, immature development of sexual organs (few reach full sexual maturity); and possibly learning difficulties. As with Down's syndrome, many people with PWS also exhibit characteristic facial and other physical features. These include small hands and feet, almond-shaped eyes, a narrow forehead and a down-turned mouth with a triangular-shaped upper lip.

There is no cure for PWS, although some aspects can be treated. The Prader-Willi Syndrome Association UK recommends that help of a dietitian, paediatrician, physiotherapist, educational psychologist and (if necessary) speech therapist should be sought as soon as a diagnosis is made.

Williams syndrome is a rare, non-hereditary chromosome disorder which occurs at random and affects intellectual development. There may be associated physical problems ranging from slight muscle weakness to heart defects. Each sufferer has a unique set of physical, emotional and mental strengths and weaknesses, which need to be monitored and understood by those caring for the sufferer.

As with Down's, sufferers have a facial similarity. They are characterised by 'elfin' features – a wide mouth, turned-up nose with flattened bridge, slightly puffy cheeks and widely spaced irregular teeth. Some may have a squint. Initial signs of Williams syndrome include low birth weight, slow weight gain, below average growth, missing developmental milestones, slow feeding, restlessness, hyperactivity and possible excess vomiting. A raised calcium level is found in some babies. Older children may demonstrate uninhibited, inappropriate behaviour, and feel compelled to talk to adults but unable to relate to their peers. May have obsessional interests, a short attention span, exaggerated emotions, emotional immaturity, poor motor skills and learning difficulties but with a high verbal ability. Heart problems are common as all sufferers have a narrowing of the aorta. Most notable of all is a hypersensitivity to noise, becoming distressed by balloons bursting, fireworks exploding or other such loud noises.

Careful consideration should be given to finding an appropriate educational setting for the Williams sufferer. Learning difficulties may make mainstream education problematic but a child may lack the stimuli of verbal communication and social interaction if placed in a special school.

Further information and help

See also Part 4: Useful contacts.

Down's syndrome

Down's Syndrome Association (DSA).
Web: www.dsa-uk.com.
E-mail: info@downs-syndrome.org.uk.
Tel: 0845 230 0372. Fax: 0845 230 0373.
Address: Langdon Down Centre, 2a Langdon Park, Teddington TW11 9PS

Case studies and examples of children's work at all Key Stages are shown in the association's award winning Education Support Pack for Schools. Simple factsheets and guides to specific topics are available from the DSA's website and publications guide. The DSA has released its support pack online as a free PDF download. It includes chapters on strategies for inclusion, the development of literacy, numeracy and language skills, successful transition and the effective use of computers. It can be downloaded at www.dsa-uk.com.

As well as several regional offices throughout England there are offices in:

Northern Ireland:
Tel: 028 9070 4606. Fax: 028 9070 4075.
Address: Graham House, Knockbracken Healthcare Park, Saintfield Road, Belfast BT8 8BH

Wales:
E-mail: dsa.wales@lineone.net.
Tel: 029 2052 2511. Fax: 029 2052 2511.
Address: Suite 1, 206 Whitechurch Road, Heath, Cardiff CF4 3NB

Down's Syndrome Scotland is the a Scottish cousin of the DSA.
Web: www.dsscotland.org.uk.
E-mail: info@dsscotland.org.uk.
Tel: 0131 313 4225. Fax: 0131 313 4285.
Address: 158/160 Balgreen Road, Edinburgh EH11 3AU

The Downs Syndrome Educational Trust offers an advisory and consultancy service – website not that useful in itself unless you want to subscribe for access to the Trust's online library and archive.
Web: www.downsed.org.
E-mail: enquiries@downsed.org.
Tel: 023 9285 5330. Fax: 023 9285 5320.
Address: The Sarah Duffen Centre, Belmont Street, Southsea, Hampshire PO5 1NA

Mencap is a campaigning charity covering Down's and other brain-damage disorders.
Web: www.mencap.org.uk.
E-mail: information@mencap.org.uk.
Tel: 020 7454 0454. Fax: 020 7696 5540.
Address: 123 Golden Lane, London EC1Y 0RT

National Downs Syndrome Association (USA). Produces a Down's syndrome education support pack for schools.
Web: www.ndss.org. E-mail: info@ndss.org.
Tel: (9am-5pm East Coast USA time):
00 1 212 460 9330. Freephone: 00 1 800 221 4602.
Fax: 00 1 212 979 2873.
Address: National Down Syndrome Society, 666 Broadway, New York, NY 10012, USA

Other genetic conditions

ASSERT. A UK-based support group run by volunteers who have direct contact with people with Angelman syndrome, and the best Angelman syndrome website that we have found.
Web: www.angelmanuk.org.
Address: PO Box 13694, Musselburgh, East Lothian EH21 6XZ

Fragile X Society. The society offers support, information and advice to affected families and professionals.
Web: www.fragilex.org.uk.
E-mail: info@fragilex.org.uk. Tel: 01371 875100.
Address: Rood End House, 6 Stortford Road, Great Dunmow, Essex CM6 1DA

Prader-Willi Syndrome Association UK (PWSA). The only organisation in the UK and the Republic of Ireland to address the needs of people with Prader-Willi. Much information in the 'A-Z of Prader-Willi'. Web links to many international organisations and personal PWSA (UK) PWSA (Prader-Willi Syndrome Association UK).
Web: www.pwsa.co.uk.
E-mail: admin@pwsa-uk.demon.co.uk.
Tel (9.30am-3.30pm Mon-Fri): 01332 365676 (office hours: 9.30am-3.30pm Mon-Fri.). Answerphone at other times. Fax: 01332 360401.
Address: PWSA (UK), 125a London Road, Derby DE1 2QQ

Rett Syndrome Association UK. A national charity offering information, advice, practical help, friendship and sup-

port to people with Rett syndrome, their families and carers.
Web: www.rettsyndrome.org.uk.
E-mail: info@rettsyndrome.org.uk.
Tel (national): 0870 770 3266 (local) 020 8361 5161.
Fax (national): 0870 770 3265 (local): 020 8368 6123.
Address: 113 Friern Barnet Road, London N11 3EU

Unique – The Rare Chromosome Disorder Support Group.
Tel: 01883 330766.
Address: PO Box 2189, Caterham, Surrey CR3 5GN

Williams Syndrome Foundation UK: Plenty of information, diagnosis, treatment etc, including a profile of special educational needs. Check the 'Guidelines' section for advice for parents, teachers, families and professionals who come into contact with Williams syndrome sufferers.
Web: www.williams-syndrome.org.uk.
E-mail: John.nelson-wsfoundation@btinternet.com.
Tel: 01732 365152. Fax: 01732 360178.
Address: 161 High Street, Tonbridge, Kent TN9 1BX

Specific learning difficulties

'Specific learning difficulties' is an umbrella term to cover a number of problems: dyslexia (reading and writing), dyscalculia (maths), dyspraxia (co-ordination), dysgraphia (writing). Children may have difficulties in just one of these areas – a purely dyscalculic child will stumble only with numbers and may excel in non-mathematical subjects – but it is not uncommon for a dyslexic pupil to have difficulties in some areas of maths, most likely in number, or to have some co-ordination difficulties. Difficulties with numeracy are often accompanied by the language difficulties of dyslexia.

Some children with specific learning difficulties may exhibit behavioural difficulties, though frequently these diminish when the child receives appropriate help and support with the subsequent growth in confidence and self-esteem.

Dyslexia

Steve Chinn, Former Principal of Mark College, Somerset

The first recorded case of dyslexia was in Scotland over 100 years ago. It wasn't called dyslexia then and some people still get agitated over what it could or should be called now. So you may still see 'specific learning difficulties' used instead of or even in conjunction with 'dyslexia'. Whatever the issues some academics and some educational administrators have with 'dyslexia', most people now have some ideas about what dyslexia is about. It is primarily about difficulties with reading, spelling and writing. There are other issues, but more on those later.

Dyslexia is a fairly common difficulty. Researchers say around 10 per cent of people have a problem that affects their work and life and that for 4 per cent these problems are very significant. Whatever the statistics suggest, I know if people ask me what I do for a living and I say 'I work with dyslexics' I frequently am told, 'Oh my son/brother/husband/auntie/neighbour is dyslexic and I think I may be, too.' Another indicator of the prevalence of dyslexia is that provision for dyslexic students in higher education exceeds provision for all the other disabilities put together.

Dyslexia is a common difficulty, but that does not make it less of a problem. Despite its being so well recognised, there are still those who deny its existence or, more subtly, underestimate or ignore the significance of the problem for a particular individual.

Indicators of dyslexia

- Incidence of dyslexia in the family.

- Problems with speech and language, including mispronouncing or jumbling words, poor use of syntax, difficulties with rhymes, inaccurate and inconsistent use of words, word-naming problems.

- Problems with sequencing, and poor organisational skills including difficulty dressing.

- Visual difficulties: standard eye tests may reveal perfect vision but there may be underlying problems with tracking, ordering or sorting.

- There may be auditory difficulties. The child may hear but not be able to distinguish sounds. Hearing test results may be normal but the child may have problems remembering a string of instructions, learning nursery or other rhymes, learning tables, the alphabet, days of the week or months of the year, or have poor rhythm. Counting, especially counting backwards, may be problematic. Fine motor skill problems may be apparent – perhaps holding a pencil awkwardly, having difficulty with scissors or cutlery, problems tying shoe laces.

■ Gross motor skill difficulties may be apparent: the child may be slow to hop, skip or jump, appear clumsy and bump into things, have difficulty distinguishing right from left.

In isolation or indeed in young children these indicators of dyslexia should not give cause for concern. It is when several indicators are present that dyslexia (or another specific learning difficulty) may be present. Those who suspect that their child may have a learning difficulty should arrange for screening.

In *No Easy Answers: The Learning Disabled Child at Home and at School* (Bantam, 1995), Sally Smith wrote 'Who is this child?'

It is the child who usually:

■ Fails at school despite adequate intelligence.

■ At school age writes 41 for 14, reads 'on' for 'no', writes b for d and can't remember the sequence of letters that make up a word.

■ Hears a clock ticking, the sound of pencils scratching on paper, but doesn't hear what the teacher says.

■ Forgets the names of people, places, his own phone number, date of birth, but remembers the ads on TV.

■ Loses homework, misplaces a book, doesn't know what day it is.

■ Has a messy room, a shirttail hanging out, shoelaces undone, attracts dirt like a magnet.

■ Doesn't look where he is going, bumps into doors, doesn't look at the person who is talking to him.

■ Has trouble lining up, doesn't stop talking, fiddles with anything and everything.

■ Calls breakfast 'lunch', says 'Good morning' in the afternoon, has little sense of time.

■ Has a limited concentration span, especially with anything written.

■ Is reluctant to try new things, to accept even minor changes in routine.

■ Says 'I don't care' or 'I won't' when he means 'I can't', and would rather be labelled bad than stupid.

■ Or it is maybe the quiet child who has withdrawn from involvement in any classroom activity.

■ Or the child who has a headache or tummy ache on the same day each week, the day of the lesson he dreads.

A child with dyslexia? Remember that it is very difficult for any individual to realise why they are different. They may recognise that what they can and cannot do is different, for example spelling accurately or remembering times-table facts, but they are unlikely to know why.

Screening

It is wise, from many perspectives, to screen pupils for the possibility of dyslexia or dyscalculia. There are several ways in which teachers can do this, so if you have worries, ask if this can be done. NFER-Nelson publish, on CD-ROM, screening tests for both of these specific learning difficulties. Lucid Research also publish a computer-based screening test for dyslexia.

Facing the school day

Dyslexia is mainly associated with reading and writing, but it affects more than just English lessons. For example, the writing and sequencing demands of history can be a problem and the multi-tasking of many sports can create a problem if the coaching style is not empathetic. Dyslexics can also run into difficulties in maths if not taught appropriately – many dyslexics find learning times-table facts very difficult, which can be a great source of frustration for child, parent and teacher.

The impact of dyslexia depends on the tasks you are asked to do and on the circumstances that surround you. Dyslexics can flourish in the cosy, reassuring atmosphere of a good primary school, but many things about the structure of secondary schools make them inherently difficult for dyslexics. For example, pupils now meet many teachers instead of just the class teacher, and they are expected to be more independent in their learning, to read more and write more, to adjust to more new demands from each new lesson, to be organised. Dyslexic children will struggle with all of these to a greater or lesser degree.

What pupils say

In 2000, I organised a day conference for dyslexic pupils from a neighbouring comprehensive school. At the end of the day, the pupils got together in groups and listed what they found helpful and what they found unhelpful in schools.

Things that hinder:

- Teachers who go too fast and expect too much. Being expected to produce the same amount of work (as non-dyslexic pupils) in the same time.
- Teachers who do not stick to the point.
- Teachers who know I am dyslexic but don't help me enough. Being patronised.
- Too much copying off the board and/or dictating notes. Rubbing work off the board too soon.
- Having test results read out loud. People who make fun of me or who are sarcastic.
- Being told off when I ask a friend for help.
- Not being allowed to use my laptop in lessons.
- Confusing 'dyslexic' with stupidity. Lack of understanding/empathy for dyslexia (from teachers and other students).
- Being made to read aloud in class.

Things that help:

- Help being given discretely to individuals.
- Being given more time.
- Handouts with summaries of work.
- Marking work in dark colours ... tidily.
- Working in smaller groups.
- Trained teachers. An awareness of dyslexic difficulties. Teachers who care.
- Grades that show individual improvement.
- Marking that is clear and helpful.
- Catch-up exercises.
- Work judged for content, not spelling.

These issues should be addressed in any school's policy for special educational needs. Ask to see the policy and ask for examples as to how it is implemented in the school.

(The above lists are reproduced from Thomson and Chinn in *Dyslexia: Theory and Good Practice,* Whurr, 2001.)

Dyslexia friendly schools

The British Dyslexia Association (BDA) has lobbied for the formation of 'dyslexia friendly schools', a term coined by Neil Mackay. Local authorities will know which of their schools have this status. There is still some way to go on setting and monitoring a common standard, but this is a really important step. Find out more at the BDA website.

The Council for the Registration of Schools Teaching Dyslexic Pupils (CReSTeD) has a list of schools who have agreed to have their provision for dyslexic pupils examined by the council and who have met set criteria, which are listed on their website. CReSTeD's Handbook also gives a list of useful questions to ask when you visit a school.

Quick cures

Over the years I have worked in the dyslexia field I have met many 'cures' for dyslexia. Sometimes they make a difference for some people, sometimes that difference is dramatic, but not always and not with all people. For example, it was thought by some that a deficiency in zinc was the problem. Some difficulties can be identified and treated; for example, glue ear (otitis media), common in children with dyslexia, can affect the acquisition of auditory discrimination skills, which in turn affects the development of phonics in reading. Other aids, such as coloured lenses (it is important to screen for this), are likely to be effective in only 20 per cent of cases (see 'Orthoptist' in Chapter 3). Fish oils, kinaesthetic exercises, computer games and reading books held upside down whilst draping a coloured scarf over the left shoulder have all been tried with variable and often doubtful results.

I fear that a 'cure' from such interventions alone is unlikely. Vulnerable parents may have their hopes raised, so enter those doors carefully and at your own risk.

A bright future

For those who persevere, and many dyslexics persevere at levels non-dyslexics will never attain, the results can be impressive. Ex-pupils of my school have done some great things. For example, one is a partner in a tree surgery, one presented his Masters degree research into dyslexia at the last BDA international conference, one has worked as a master plasterer, one teaches special needs children in the Bronx, New York, one is a Sergeant in the Army, one runs a catering equipment business, one is an engineer at Lotus. The range of destinations is impressive and not always predictable.

Well-known dyslexics include Tom Cruise, Lord Rogers, Sir Jackie Stewart, Susan Hampshire, Linda LaPlante, Cher, Sir Richard Branson and Sir Steve Redgrave. The great Olympian rower was guest speaker at the British Dyslexia Association's international conference at which he received a standing ovation. Afterwards the committee presented him with a special hardbound copy of the conference book. He thanked the committee, smiled wryly and said 'I guess this won't be the fifth book I have ever read!'

Dyscalculia – a learning difficulty in maths skills or something else?

The first references to dyscalculia are over 30 years old, yet this specific learning difficulty is only just becoming recognised in mainstream education, perhaps as a result of the continuing bad press for GCSE maths?

Just what is dyscalculia? Many people have a 'difficulty' with maths – hated it at school, couldn't see the point – and, like all skills, it is a matter of use it or lose it. Few adults practise the maths of fractions or algebra after leaving school; indeed, in 1995 a study on behalf of the Basic Skills Agency of 1,714 adults aged 35 years found that just under a quarter had such low numeracy skills that completing everyday tasks successfully would be difficult. However, dyscalculia is more than just a difficulty in learning maths skills, in the same way that dyslexia is more than just a difficulty in learning language skills. Very little is known about the prevalence of dyscalculia, its causes or treatment. There isn't a single reason why many people fail to master maths, and academic consensus suggests that only 3 to 6 per cent of pupils are dyscalculic.

The DfES booklet (2001) on supporting pupils with dyslexia and dyscalculia in the National Numeracy Strategy defines dyscalculia as

> a condition that affects the ability to acquire mathematical skills. Dyscalculic learners may have difficulty understanding simple number concepts, lack an intuitive grasp of numbers, and have problems learning number facts and procedures. Even if they produce a correct answer or use a correct method, they may do so mechanically and without confidence.

So, dyscalculia could be described as a difficulty in the brain with the whole concept of numbers and how they relate to one another. At its extreme, acalculia, it means an inability even to count.

Does it matter?

Early maths is mostly numbers. Later topics such as measure, algebra, data handling and spatial topics appear on the scene, but up to GCSE the major component remains number, especially for the less able in maths. So a weakness in number skills will be the most significant handicap to learning 'school' maths.

Maths can be concrete, but fairly quickly moves to the abstract and symbolic (perhaps too quickly?). Many children experience difficulty because they rely on memory – trying to learn rules and answers by rote rather than investigating and understanding how the numbers are working in relation to each other. Even more fundamentally, maths is a 'building' subject, and new information will never make sense unless all the foundation blocks are firmly fixed. Perhaps in part because some teachers, particularly in primary schools, are not sufficiently skilled to develop this aspect of maths and mathematical thought, foundation blocks often get missed. Gaps in knowledge affect ability in maths in a basic way quite different from, say, history or geography, and if pupils who are slow processors do not grasp every principle before moving on, the whole subject quickly becomes ridden with anxiety and negative attitudes.

But an inability with numbers is also a handicap in real life. Everyday maths rarely includes algebra, fractions (other than 1/4 and 1/2), co-ordinates or indeed much of what is taught in secondary schools, but it does include a lot of money, measurement, some time and the occasional percentage. Paying for a family meal in a restaurant, for instance, requires estimation skills, possibly accurate addition skills, subtraction skills if using cash, and percentage skills for the tip. Not being able to tell if you have been short-changed, or work out how long a train journey is or whether your bank balance is enough to pay the bills puts you at a constant disadvantage.

The demands maths makes on pupils are varied, sequential and developmental, so gaps in learning can be very damaging and cumulative – poor or weak foundations and the whole shakes, even collapses. Basic skills could include good short-term and working memory, vital for mental arithmetic, particularly for those maths thinkers who are very sequential in their thinking processes. And, of course, there is also a need for long-term, mathematical memory.

Spotting problems early on

An early indicator of difficulty in maths is the persistent use of counting in ones rather than developing a recall of basic facts and relationships between numbers. The first number test on the Butterworth Dyscalculia Screener is for subitising – that is, looking for a sense of what numbers are worth by testing the ability to look at a random cluster of dots and know how many there are without counting.

A later test examines how quickly and accurately children find the answers to basic addition sums such as 4 + 7. If children still count, they are likely to be slow and inaccurate. At a very basic level of skill development they will count all of the 4 + 7, rather than start at 4 (or better still at 7). Relying entirely on counting for addition and subtraction is a severe handicap in terms of speed and accuracy, the more so when trying to use it for bigger numbers and tasks such as multiplication and division.

Often a child's page is covered in endless tally marks, and frequently these are just lined up, with no attempt at grouping. If you show them patterns of dots or groups, say tally groups of 5, they still prefer to see lines of individual markers.

Moving on from one-by-one counting to grouped tallies is just the beginning. Skill in numeracy requires the ability to recognise and use relationships in all numbers, such as seeing 9 as one less than 10; 6 + 5 as 5 + 5 + 1; counting on in twos, tens, fives, especially if the pattern isn't the basic one of 10, 20, 30 ... but 13, 23, 33, 43 ...; to see the relationship between the four operations (+ x – and ÷); to see patterns and relationships in numbers and be able to manipulate them.

Early indicators of dyscalculia include some or all of:

- a difficulty in recognising 'How many' when looking at a small group of objects
- an over-reliance on counting to arrive at number facts and answers
- a persistent difficulty in recalling basic facts (addition facts when younger, multiplication facts when older)
- a problem recognising the symbols of maths (in giving them the right name and in knowing what they mean)
- difficulties with the vocabulary and the language of maths
- working at a slow speed
- inaccuracies
- a distinctly lower level of achievement than in other subjects and in comparison with their peers
- an avoidance of maths and lack of confidence with maths tasks
- anxieties around anything mathematical
- poor awareness of money values
- poor mental arithmetic skills and/or poor written arithmetic skills
- persistence of the difficulties despite lots of help.

Things to do to help:

- Never make the problem an 'issue'.
- Don't say 'Never mind, I could never do maths, either.'
- Practise in low-stress ways ... and a little at any one time.
- Use practical examples (which may well often be based around money).
- Make learning multi-sensory.
- Make your expectations realistic.
- Have lots of small targets rather than a few big targets.
- Look for improvement, not perfection.
- Don't stick with one target, move around a little, but keep revisiting previous work.
- Negotiate with the school to get a better empathy for your child.

- Link facts and learning, so the child has an anchor fact(s) to return to.

Remember: being dyscalculic does not necessarily condemn a child to failure in maths. Ex-pupils of mine have been flagged up as dyscalculic, but have gone on to get A and A* in GCSE maths. Some, however, haven't! The outcome will depend a lot on empathetic and appropriate teaching and, of course, the pupil, the severity and perseverance with the dyscalculic problems.

Steve Chinn has many years of teaching experience with specific learning difficulties. He has written a number of books on the subject and his The Trouble with Maths *(Routledge/Falmer, 2004) won the 2004 TES/NASEN Teaching and Learning Book Award.*

Dyspraxia/developmental co-ordination difficulty

Dr Amanda Kirby, doctor, lecturer and author in the field of dyspraxia

Dyspraxia has often in the past been referred to as 'clumsy child syndrome', but in practice it is more complex than that. It is a developmental difficulty that can overlap with other conditions such as dyslexia and attention deficit hyperactivity disorder (ADHD) and social and communication difficulties including Asperger's syndrome. Many children actually have a combination of co-ordination difficulties and other learning difficulties as well. Each child is unique – there is no classic child with dyspraxia.

Dyspraxia or DCD?

The umbrella term DCD (developmental co-ordination difficulty) is often preferred by medical experts and is in common usage in some other countries (bear this in mind if you are searching the web) and dyspraxia specifically means a motor-planning difficulty. Motor planning? Consider it as thinking about how to make a jam sandwich and the plan you need in order to do so; if you don't have a plan, you may know what the finished thing may look like but you don't know the steps to get there. Only a few children have this difficulty. However, dyspraxia is more generally used in the UK to describe the broader range of co-ordination difficulties.

Indications of dyspraxia

Most children who are given the diagnosis of dyspraxia have other reasons for their co-ordination difficulties. Your child may be a bit floppy (low toned) for example and find it hard to stay sitting up straight at the table or desk and tend to slouch when they eat (this usually provokes an argument in many families, being told to 'sit up' – it may be hard for the child to stay sitting up and concentrate on eating at the same time). On the other hand, a child may be bendy or very flexible and so not so good at controlling the range of movements some of their joints can make. This also often runs in families and has also been called joint hypermobility syndrome. Some children find completing more than one task at a time difficult to do, especially at speed.

Early signs of co-ordination difficulties may include late to sit and walk, and not crawling. Some babies with dyspraxia reach all their milestones but still have some difficulties.

As dyspraxic children get older they may be more likely to fall or trip up, or bump into things. They may be messy eaters, find it hard to use a knife and fork together or spill drinks and be slower at dressing than brothers and sisters. Older children may be very disorganised and leave possessions and clothes all over the place.

They may have greater difficulty in learning skills such as throwing and catching a ball, hopping and jumping, or riding a bike. Some children may also have a delay in language development or may have rather 'sloppy' sounding speech.

Once at school, writing becomes one of the major difficulties and is the one that tends to stay with the child more than other difficulties. A child with dyspraxia may have overlap with other conditions; they may find concentrating and staying on task difficult to do and be fidgety, wanting to move around and fiddle with things around them. However, they are often of average or above-average intelligence, and the inability to do what they can clearly see how to do can be very frustrating for them. Often they are articulate and can voice their ideas but have difficulty transferring them to paper.

Diagnosis

Dyspraxia affects about 6 per cent of the population, with three times as many boys as girls.

The commonest test used to aid diagnosis is the Movement ABC Battery. This is a series of tests usually undertaken by an occupational therapist as well as other tests looking at vision and hearing skills. Symptoms of DCD/Dyspraxia are usually grouped into those affecting small movements (eg dressing, eating, scissors, writing), big movements (running, jumping, skipping), balance and co-ordination (riding a bicycle, standing on one leg, walking along a wall, climbing on playground equipment), and being in a moving environment (such as playing football with others). Some children will be more affected by big movements whereas other children may only have difficulties with smaller, finer movements. However, your child may have difficulties with all forms of co-ordination to varying degrees.

A paediatrician will also usually want to rule out any other causes for motor difficulties. Teachers sometimes watch the child in class and use a checklist to see where the difficulties lie and may refer to an educational psychologist for further testing as well.

If you are worried about your child's progress, first talk to the teacher in school and ask them if they agree with your concerns. They may have a referral system in the school for further help. Some schools run 'motor programmes' to help. Go and see your GP – some will know more than others, but they can refer you to an occupational therapist, paediatrician or physiotherapist – whichever is more appropriate.

It is always important to remember your child's strengths as well as their difficulties – having an assessment can highlight all the bits your child cannot do and can be very stressful for the family.

How does dyspraxia affect your life?

On first glance, children with dyspraxia may not seem different from other children around them, until they are asked, perhaps, to do a co-ordination task at speed. Passing the ball in football might, literally, trip them up. Anxiety, concentration and understanding the rules may also be a problem, but controlling the ball and running may be too much and the child may land in a heap on the pitch, and end up being the target of others' laughter.

Making friends and keeping friends can also be hard. Coping with others' reactions can be as hard for you as a parent as for your child. A thick skin and a quick answer are worth adopting early on. Differences can lead to the child being noticed by other children and being bullied or left out of games and sometimes more alone in the playground.

Some typical problems in school include:

- difficulties following long instructions, and in planning and organising work and themselves
- difficulty copying text from book or whiteboard
- variable ability – better some days than others and may get tired more easily
- low self-esteem and frustration, which will sometimes result in disruptive behaviour
- difficulty in ball sports
- difficulty writing at speed or drawing neatly
- slower getting changed for games lessons.

Other people often find it hard to get their heads round what dyspraxia means in practical terms. 'Hidden disabilities uncovered!' (see Chapter 4) is an amusing and graphic description of what it's like to be a 12-year-old dyspraxic.

Dyspraxia varies with the age, and your child's co-ordination may improve. Looking back, the things you worried about so much, like catching a ball, may drift into insignificance as your child becomes an adult and can choose never to play football again but enjoy swimming instead.

A lot of the co-ordination difficulties your child experiences may also be dependent on what is expected of them. Times of transition from primary to secondary and when leaving school can be the hardest, as change can make children with dyspraxia (as well as their parents!) feel 'wobbly'. When the need for writing fast and legibly, or of organising possessions and themselves, presents problems, this is when good communication with school may be of the greatest help, so that sloppy work or losing things 'again and again' is not seen as something done on purpose.

What parents can do to help children with dyspraxia/DCD

Dyspraxia can't be cured and there are no quick fixes, much as everyone would love their child not to have difficulties. However, with appropriate help and understanding your child can improve a great deal, function well and reach their potential.

Early identification of where the difficulties lie can minimise some of the problems, so enlist support from school and treatment by either occupational therapists or physiotherapists.

Practising skills with your child at home can make a big difference. Encourage activities to enhance co-ordination – you don't need to be an expert: playing ball in the garden, going swimming, teaching your child to ride a bike can all be of great help. Often physically showing a child, perhaps moving their limbs, rather than simply demonstrating a task, will also help. Talk through activities with your child and ask them how they think they could do something better or differently, such as putting on a piece of clothing or kicking the ball in a goal.

Help them learn necessary social skills by encouraging them to make friends and to take part in activities outside the home.

Dyspraxia is not just an educational problem even though this is where it may manifest first. Some adults find tasks like learning to drive or getting a hot meal on the table for the family hard to do. Gaining good organisational skills can be started early by using to-do lists and establishing a clear routine and labelling clothes and drawers. If belongings are forever being mislaid you may find yourself forever buying pens, pencils and protractors late on a Sunday evening. (Three pencil cases is one way of resolving this – one for the bag, one for the desk and one for home as well as name tapes on everything!)

Clumsiness and lack of co-ordination can make meal times with young children a nightmare. Using specialised cutlery, a bowl with a lip and a cup with a lid can all help. Also, make sure your child has feet on the floor and table at waist height, so that sitting up is not a strain.

A little smart thinking about what's actually required in specific tasks can make all the difference. Something simple such as shoes with easy-close fastenings rather than laces means being the first dressed after PE rather than the last every time.

What schools can do to help children with dyspraxia

A great deal can be achieved even with few obvious resources if there is a 'can do' attitude and a sensible, supportive approach.

■ Reduce the number of tasks and allow additional time for their completion.

■ Provide extra supervision and encouragement if required, especially in practical subjects where there are health and safety implications and results may be poor – getting children to work in teams can be a help.

■ Give single instructions rather than a string, which may result in a muddle, and reinforce verbal instructions by repetition.

■ Never assume the child cannot achieve – just give them a bit longer to learn the task and break it down into more manageable parts.

■ Talk through with the child what is expected of them so he can see what the plan of action is and check they have understood – ask them to tell you what you have said rather than accept a nod for yes.

■ Place the child where they can easily see the teacher, and where there are as few distractions as possible.

■ Seat the child at a desk of optimum height and size, without the necessity for moving to see the teacher. A sloping desk or angle board may help.

■ Teach the child strategies to help remember and assist themselves, by use of lists and diaries or use a to-do list so the child can tick off as they go.

■ Ensure the child is well prepared for any changes to routine which can be both problematic and distressing – plan for changes rather than waiting for the problems. Extra visits to a new school, a map of the school and the names and pictures of the teachers may make starting a new school less stressful.

Helping parents

■ It may be a long road so don't try to do everything at once.

■ Ask your child what is troubling them and what does they want to do better. Concentrate on that for starters.

- Don't tell them off if they spill something over themselves or others – they are not doing it on purpose.
- See your child for the kind and sensitive child they are, and see that the world around is making it harder and they are a different child not a difficult child.
- Take a break from therapy and try to incorporate helping your child into everyday family life – if you like swimming together do that rather than exercises without any meaning to the child.
- Be patient!
- Don't worry about the small stuff, think about what skills your child will require for adult life. Getting from A to B on time will matter more than doing a 64-piece jigsaw or cutting out a circle perfectly.
- Have fun. Remember your child has difficulties – they are not a difficult child.

Finally, I am a parent of an adult with DCD. He is now in university making his own way in the world and is a tall, good-looking man who is kind hearted and sensitive. His brother and sister have supported him through his growing years. The journey may be long but I would not have changed my son for anything for the man he has become – dyspraxia and all.

Dr Amanda Kirby is a doctor running a centre for children and adults with specific learning difficulties. She is also a parent of three children 23,19 and 17 years of age. She has lectured to over 15,000 professionals and parents nationally and internationally over the past years and has written books in the field of dyspraxia and related subjects. She is a medical adviser to the Dyspraxia Foundation and also a patron of the New Zealand Dyspraxia Association.

Developmental verbal dyspraxia

Another type of dyspraxia is developmental verbal dyspraxia (DVD). This is a speech condition resulting from an immaturity of the speech-production area of the brain. The child has difficulty making consistent speech sounds or producing words because the speech area does not send out consistent messages to the tongue, lips and larynx.

Indications of DVD are:

- Delayed expressive language skills but normal or above average receptive language skills.
- Inconsistent speech sounds in the first few years, ie pronouncing the same word differently each time.
- Words learnt may be forgotten.
- Very slow development of speech in the first few years.
- Sounds may be acquired in an unusual order, ie more complex sounds may be learned before simpler ones.

There may be long plateau stages in the early stages of speech development where little or no progress is made.

It is best to avoid putting pressure on children with DVD as this may inhibit them and reduce confidence still further. Usually they would like to communicate but are unable to do so effectively. Expressive language skills may be helped by use of poems such as nursery rhymes and songs.

Further information and help

See also Part 4: Useful contacts.

British Dyslexia Association (BDA). A helpful and well put-together site; the BDA has associations for assessing and teaching dotted around the country. Good links.
Web: www.bda-dyslexia.org.uk.
Tel: 0118 935 1927. Fax: 0118 935 1927.
Address: 98 London Road, Reading RG1 5AU

CReSTeD (Council for the Registration of Schools Teaching Dyslexic Pupils). For independent schools (and some state schools).
Web: www.crested.org.uk.
E-mail: crested@crested.org.uk.
Tel/Fax: 01242 604852.
Address: Greygarth, Littleworth, Winchcombe, Cheltenham, Gloucestershire GL54 5BT

Dyspraxia Foundation. Explains the condition and its symptoms well; has a network of local groups. Includes a section about dyspraxia in secondary schools.
Web: www.dyspraxiafoundation.org.uk.
E-mail: dyspraxia@dyspraxiafoundation.org.uk.
Tel: (10am-1pm Mon-Fri.) 01462 454986.

Fax: 01462 455052.
Address: 8 West Alley, Hitchin, Hertfordshire SG5 1EG

Dyscovery Centre. Founded by Dr Amanda Kirby, a Welsh GP who left practice to set it up when her second son was diagnosed with dyspraxia. It offers a full range of assessment and treatment for kids and adults who may have a difficulty on the Autism spectrum. Amanda Kirby speaks at conferences on SEN all over the world and has written a number of books.
Web: www.dyscovery.co.uk.
E-mail: dyscovery.centre@btinternet.com.
Tel: 029 2062 8222. Fax: 029 2062 8333.
Address: 4a Church Road, Whitchurch, Cardiff F14 2DZ

Non-specific learning difficulties

When children have learning difficulties that are more generalised and don't relate to a specific neural problem or immaturity, they can be described as MLD, SLD or PMLD (see below), depending on their degree of difficulty.

According to the DfES, for a child to be classified as MLD, SLD or PMLD they must be on School Action Plus or have a statement. In addition, MLD, SLD or PMLD must be the child's primary or secondary need – the numbers of children with generalised learning difficulties may well be masked because, for example, a child may have autism and MLD, but have the overriding diagnosis of autism.

Some special schools exist specifically for children with learning difficulties although in recent years there has been a move to educate a growing number of children with MLD in mainstream schools.

Moderate learning difficulty (MLD)

Children described as having doderate learning difficulties experience great difficulty following the curriculum, despite receiving suitable help and intervention. Their attainments are significantly below expected levels in most areas of the curriculum, ie below level 2 of the National Curriculum at the start of senior school. Generally they will have difficulty understanding basic concepts and acquiring basic skills in reading, writing and numeracy and there may be a resultant lack of confidence to use and develop the skills they do have.

For many children with MLD there will be additional needs to address: speech and language delay; poor co-ordination; difficulty concentrating; emotional and behavioural difficulties; sensory impairment or a lack of social skills. Children with MLD may appear immature and find it difficult to mix with their regular peer group, many are vulnerable and may experience bullying as a result. Often they are needy with an over-reliance on adult help and support.

The majority of children with MLD are educated in mainstream schools, with provision made for additional help and support appropriate to their needs. Schools have the flexibility to decide how best to meet the pupils' needs: in the classroom; in small group settings; in the learning support unit. Children with MLD may be assisted not just by trained teachers but also by learning support assistants (LSAs), who work under the direction of the classroom teacher and special educational needs co-ordinator (SENCo) or equivalent. Other sections explain in more detail the role of these professionals. Many schools issue individual education plans (IEPs) detailing a child's needs and targets. Targets set should be closely monitored and regularly reviewed, with work for some or all of the time specifically designed to address the needs of the individual.

Many children with MLD cope in mainstream nursery and primary schools but often, by secondary school age, the gaps between children with MLD and other learners have widened to such an extent that the child may find the demands of secondary education too stressful: different teachers; a wide range of subjects; the need to move around the school; to be organised; to change for PE. At this stage intellectual gaps tend to widen too.

Choice of school for a child with MLD will vary according to individual needs and demands, the extent of additional needs, your and your child's wishes, and the LEA policy. Although the vast majority remain in mainstream education, this doesn't mean those who attend special schools are 'excluded'. The Good Schools Guide has visited several schools for children with MLD. One such school, The Park School in Woking, is highly praised by parents. It operates along mainstream lines with children following the National Curriculum and working in smaller groups not dissimilar in size from the lower sets often found in mainstream education. They mix with their peers and with children from other years, have specialist teachers and move around the school independently. They feel included because they can participate in all elements of school life – not just the academic, artistic and sporting, but socially and emotionally too. Many spend part of their time working in mainstream schools, while some of the least able attend other special schools for some of the time if it's felt beneficial.

Severe learning difficulty (SLD)

Children with severe learning difficulties have acute global development delay, such that intellectual or cognitive impairment, coupled with possible sensory, physical, emotional and social difficulties, will make it difficult for the child to follow the curriculum without substantial help and support. These difficulties may be further compounded by poor co-ordination, and they may use symbols, or signing such as Makaton, to help with communication.

A child with SLD will require substantial help in gaining independence or self-help and social skills. It is likely that most areas of academic achievement will be affected, not just basic skills. Their attainments are likely to remain below level 1 of the National Curriculum (in the upper P scale range, P4-P8) for much of their school careers. Accurate statistics are not available for the number of children with SLD educated in mainstream or special schools, in part because the presence of other impairments (autism, communication difficulties etc) often supersedes a diagnosis of SLD.

Children with SLD are likely to find it difficult to understand, learn and remember new skills. As a result they will have problems with both learning skills and applying them to new situations. Additional problems with a number of social tasks, such as communication, self-care and awareness of health and safety, may mean they require supported living.

Profound and multiple learning difficulty (PMLD)

Approximately 7 per cent of children in special schools are diagnosed as having PMLD. Children with profound and multiple learning difficulties have complex learning needs. In addition to very severe learning difficulties, they have other significant problems, such as physical disabilities, sensory impairment or possibly a severe medical condition. They will require a high level of adult support for both learning needs and personal care. They are likely to need sensory stimulation and a curriculum broken down into very small steps. Some pupils communicate by gesture, eye pointing or symbols, others by very simple language. Their attainments are likely to remain below level 1 of the National Curriculum in the P1-P4 range.

Further information and help

These non-specific learning difficulties are very broad based and can have a multiplicity of causes/effects. See Part 4: Useful contacts for sources of information and help.

Sensory problems

Visual impairment

Elizabeth Clery, expert in the teaching and provision of services for visually impaired children

Having a child with visual impairment (VI) is relatively rare. There are around 24,000 children in the UK between birth and 16 who are blind or partially sighted, some of whom may be registered. For about half these children, visual impairment is their only problem, but some 20 per cent have some additional need or needs and 30 per cent have profound or complex needs with associated learning difficulties. Many children with a visual impairment have a statement of special educational need (see Chapter 6).

The number of schools that exist specifically for children with visual impairment has fallen significantly in recent years, and those that remain are educating pupils with increasingly complex needs. However, most children with complex needs that include a visual impairment attend generic special schools maintained by local authorities, rather than schools specialising in sight problems. Around 4 per cent of the total number of children with visual impairment use Braille as their primary learning medium.

Over half of blind or partially sighted children (59 per cent, to be precise) are educated in mainstream schools. They may attend their local school with specialist support from a local authority service or go to a mainstream school that is specifically designated for blind and partially sighted pupils. In these, specialist support forms part of the permanent school staffing. It is common for teaching assistants to provide much of the support to children with visual impairment.

Help schools can give

Wherever pupils with a visual impairment are educated it is essential to provide the range of educational and social opportunities that enable them to participate on an equal basis with their fully sighted peers. But children don't all have the same requirements. They may require different levels of support for different reasons and the level and type of support may vary over time; for some this will be minimal, for others it may be substantial.

Much depends on the effectiveness of the individual school and class teacher. When considering what is best for your own child, you'll naturally look for a school that is inclusive, positive and welcoming to all children, especially those with diverse or special needs, and which welcomes parental support and input and is keen to work as a team. Here are some more specific things to ask about or to look out for:

■ Teachers and those who will be working with your child should receive (or have had) additional training and support necessary to help them in their work with VI. The best schools will ensure training is ongoing, not just a half-day session tagged on to an INSET day.

■ It's important that the teacher is organised and plans to make sure that your child can follow the curriculum fully and isn't disadvantaged. A good teacher will use a range of strategies and approaches, including adapting materials in advance so that your child receives or can use them at the same time as others in the class.

■ A good teacher will ensure that all those working with your child – classroom assistants, therapists and any additional adults – co-ordinate as a team, ensuring the best possible provision and support for your child.

■ Make sure that additional support and the ways in which it is to be supplied are clearly defined and shared with all concerned, including yourself and, at an appropriate level, your child. A good school will listen to your child and take account of their wishes.

■ Make sure responsibility for your child's learning rests with the teacher and not with support assistants.

■ Independence should be encouraged and mechanisms in place to ensure that your child doesn't become overly dependent on one particular adult helper, and that no barriers build up to stop your child interacting with other children.

Approaches and strategies in the classroom may include:

■ backing up visual information with verbal instructions or descriptions (eg reading out loud what is being written on the board)

■ providing the pupil with their own copy of information

■ using all pupils' names and giving more verbal feedback to compensate for difficulty in seeing body language

■ taking careful account of seating and grouping – this may apply particularly when a pupil is using additional technology to ensure they are not separate from their peers

■ ensuring that resources are well organised so that the pupil will have independent access.

Elizabeth Clery has a son and daughter, both of whom are visually impaired. She trained as a teacher for children with visual impairment in 1989 and worked for 11 years in a London authority, establishing and running VI services for children. During this time she set up provision for many children in their local schools, including five pupils who were Braillists, all of whom went to local schools. She has worked closely with many teaching assistants and set up training for them across the authority. For the past five years she has worked for the Royal National Institute for the Blind (RNIB) and with local authorities in developing their provision for blind and partially sighted pupils as well as co-ordinating training for teaching assistants in the London area. She is the author of 'Planned Support' in Visibility no 31*, an RNIB publication.*

Vision and reading problems

Dr Nadia Northway, lecturer and researcher at Glasgow Caledonian University

Sometimes, problems with reading or focusing have nothing to do with actual visual impairment, but with control over how the eyes move or how what they see is interpreted by the brain.

Difficulty with the control of the eyes often results in unpleasant visual symptoms which commonly include:

- blurring
- movement
- shimmering
- flickering
- fading
- distortion of print
- merging of print and background
- double vision
- patterns in print
- colours in print
- difficulty copying
- losing the place when reading
- reversing letters
- difficulty organising and spacing print
- headaches
- sore eyes

Symptoms may be worse under certain lighting conditions, in particular fluorescent lighting, and if print is small and densely packed. Sufferers may also feel that the page is too bright to look at. The symptoms may be constant or intermittent and may be caused by several visual difficulties.

Visual problems do not in themselves cause dyslexia or dyspraxia but they are a considerable additional barrier to learning to read and write, and research has shown that people experiencing reading problems, such as dyslexics, often experience these unpleasant symptoms. The more visual symptoms a person has the more likely they are to have problems with reading. Equally, of course, visual problems can afflict children and adults who do not have dyslexia or dyspraxia.

Symptoms can be indicative of a number of problems, such as poor ocular dominance, unstable fixation or a weakness in focusing ability. An orthoptist (see Chapter 3) will check for and treat problems. Undetected, they can lead to children lagging behind or missing out on learning at crucial times.

Below are some of the key areas of difficulty for dyslexic readers.

Binocular vision difficulties

Binocular vision involves the control and co-ordination of both eyes. Although each eye sees two separate images these images are blended in our brain into one single picture. There are many aspects of binocular vision which are crucial to comfortable and accurate reading.

Our eyes are rarely completely straight. In most people the eyes drift slightly and this is controlled without our even noticing. If the eyes drift too much this can cause headaches and discomfort, especially when reading. Three essential components of eye control, if faulty, affect our ability to read for prolonged periods. These are

- convergence (pulling the eyes in)
- accommodation (fine focusing of vision to stop things looking blurred)
- fusion (a brain function which compensated for drifting of the eyes and keeps the eyes aligned).

It is known that these aspects of vision are weak in many people who find reading difficult. Difficulty with accommodation and convergence will result in problems seeing print clearly and maintaining single clear vision. If there is insufficient fusion the eyes will tire and visual symptoms will result which will make reading difficult. Some people have problems with focusing and co-ordinating the eyes, resulting in fatigue when doing close work.

The good news is that binocular vision problems are easily remedied for most people with some simple exercises and in some cases glasses

Meares-Irlen syndrome (MIS)/visual stress/ scotopic sensitivity

This is caused by pattern sensitivity. Children (and adults) with MIS may complain of many of the visual symptoms in the list above. They may appear to have sore eyes and will get tired easily when reading. In extreme cases they may avoid reading altogether.

It has been shown that patterns or stripes like the one below can create uncomfortable visual distortions which can cause headaches.

NB: Please do not look at this pattern if you suffer from migraine or epilepsy.

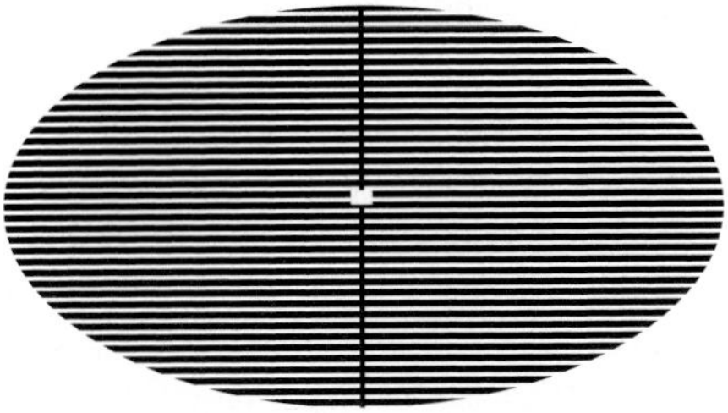

Print can also take on the appearance or illusion of stripy patterns, creating uncomfortable visual symptoms and distortions when reading. These distortions are common (they are an exaggeration of a normal phenomenon) and are not exclusively experienced by people with dyslexia, but can affect up to 50 per cent of dyslexic readers. MIS sufferers find their problems are worse with small print, shiny paper and some font types.

This condition can be treated with tinted overlays and precision-coloured lenses. Each person has an individual colour preference, and the right colour (ascertained by a specially trained orthoptist) will typically reduce the symptoms and discomfort, increase reading speed, reduce headaches and so possibly improve attention and concentration.

Eye movements

Good eye movements are essential to reading. There is a lot of evidence that eye movements may be abnormally controlled or co-ordinated in people experiencing reading difficulty. Abnormal control of eye movements is particularly common in children with other co-ordination problems such as dyspraxia or developmental co-ordination disorder.

Saccadic (jumping) eye movements are used in reading to change focus from one word to another. If these little leaps are poorly controlled then the reader may lose their place or miss words out. This may also cause problems when copying, and the student may not be able to copy accurately especially if they have problems directing their gaze accurately. Common indications of this include

- excessive use of head movements when changing gaze
- difficulty changing focus from one target to another (called an initiation problem)
- poor control of reflexive eye movements, making the person easy to distract
- inaccurate eye movements.

Gaining better control of saccades can make reading more accurate and faster.

Tracking ability

Tracking is used when reading to search for information and follow a line of writing. The ability to do this improves with age and practice. If it is underdeveloped a child will have problems keeping their place when reading and copying. This can be improved with exercises and by using a ruler or window to keep the place. Copying can be improved by placing the material to be copied on the desk directly above, rather than to the side of the paper the child is writing on.

Dr Nadia Northway has always had an interest in dyslexia and has a degree in educational studies. She has completed a PhD on visual function in dyslexia. She is an adviser to the British and Irish Orthoptic Society on dyslexia. She has her own company which sees patients and develops material for use by other practitioners in the field of dyslexia. Her clinic within the university, which specialises in assessing vision in people with reading and writing difficulties, sees patients from all over the UK. It has grown considerably since it started as a research project in 1997. Dr Northway and her team of orthoptists see around 800 patients a year – children and adults with dyslexia, dyspraxia, autism, brain injury, migraine, cerebral palsy and other medical conditions.

Hearing impairment

Children with a hearing impairment range from those with a mild hearing loss to those who are profoundly deaf. For educational purposes, pupils are regarded as having a hearing impairment if they require hearing aids, adaptations to their environment and/or particular teaching strategies in order to follow the curriculum. Deafness alone is not defined as a special educational need, although, as with any SEN, there may be an associated disability or learning difficulty, for which you can get a statement of SEN.

Children may pass the hearing screen tests in school, and be subsequently labelled lazy or disruptive because mild hearing loss has gone undetected. Warning signs include:

- limited attention span
- daydreaming
- slowness of responses
- breathing through the mouth
- irritability

Four categories of hearing impairment are generally used: mild, moderate, severe and profound. Some pupils with a significant loss communicate through sign language (British Sign Language (BSL) is in widespread use) instead of, or as well as, speech. Children with mild or intermittent losses will not receive specialist educational support (even if they attend outpatient clinics) and neither will their families and schools.

There are two main types of hearing loss: conductive and sensori-neural.

Conductive deafness

This occurs when there is some abnormality in the outer or middle ear. Transmission and amplification of sound vibrations are affected as they are conveyed to the inner ear. Generally, conductive deafness involves mild hearing loss, and is temporary.

Any blockage of the outer ear – glue, wax or a cyst – will cause a degree of deafness. The most common cause is otitis media, or glue ear, associated with an infection of the upper respiratory tract that leads to inflammation of the middle-ear cavity. If this becomes chronic a thick fluid develops in the middle ear. Glue ear is treated with antibiotics, and/or surgery to ventilate the middle ear by inserting a grommet in the drum.

About 20 per cent of primary age children suffer from conductive hearing loss caused by middle-ear problems; this reduces to 2 per cent by secondary age.

The consequences on development of undetected hearing impairment may be long lasting. Children who do not hear clearly or whose hearing varies may:

- be late to start talking
- have immature language and difficulties with speech sounds
- fail to develop good listening skills, making learning in school very difficult
- have poor memory and language-processing skills, resulting in more basic vocabularies, reading and spelling problems, sentence structure and comprehension, with lower attainments in reading and maths.

Pupils with a conductive hearing loss have a higher tendency to behaviour problems, poor motivation and attention, shyness and withdrawal. The most vulnerable are those whose conductive deafness started in early infancy and persisted undiagnosed for long periods.

Sensori-neural deafness

Sometimes called nerve deafness, this type of hearing impairment is usually more serious than conductive deafness, and medicine or surgery can do little or nothing to remedy it. The causes of sensori-neural deafness can be hereditary, or associated with diseases such as meningitis or rubella, or induced by trauma. It is relatively rare (4 per 10,000) but is permanent, and may worsen over time.

Sensori-neural deafness is rooted in the inner ear or neural pathways, and usually means that the cochlea is not processing the sound effectively. Sounds will appear quieter and may also be distorted. There may be variations in perception of sounds at different times, and difference in sensitivity to sound at different frequencies. It can be extremely difficult for people with moderate sensori-neural hearing loss to acquire normal speech and language.

Although this type of deafness is incurable, many children benefit from powerful hearing aids or (for older children) cochlear implants. Some pupils may prefer to be placed in a school with a unit attached and specialist teachers, or in a specialist schools for the deaf. These offer a range of services such as speech and language therapy, or specialist equipment such as group hearing aids.

There is a great divide between those who believe that deaf children can be taught to speak using auditory-oral approaches (assisted by hearing aids, cochlear implants, radio aids etc) and be integrated into mainstream society, and those who believe they should be taught through sign language. What suits your child best may depend on the degree of hearing loss and the extent of the delay in language acquisition.

What makes a difference in the classroom

- Pupils with hearing loss should be placed near to the teacher.
- Background noise should be kept to a minimum.
- Use of small group teaching or individual tuition is helpful.
- Where possible, quiet areas for teaching should be used.
- Time spent having to listen to the teacher should be limited.
- The teacher's face should always be clearly visible.
- To maximise communication, visual aids should be used where possible.
- Key words should be written on the blackboard, and be provided in notes for reference.
- An acoustically treated environment should be created.
- Other pupils can help by repeating instructions.

Central auditory processing disorder (CAPD)

Some children do not have a hearing loss but cannot make sense of what they hear. The sounds, words and sentences take much longer than expected to take shape into meaningful patterns so, when other babies are looking and listening and learning from what they see and hear, these children are surrounded by meaningless noises that can be frustrating and sometimes frightening. This is sometimes called a processing disorder because the child's brain is not working out the meaning of sounds properly – the ear and the brain are not co-ordinating fully.

The causes of CAPD are varied and can include head trauma, lead poisoning, possibly chronic ear infections, as well as other unknown reasons. Because there are many different possibilities – even combinations of causes – each child has to be assessed on an individual basis.

Some children benefit from very specific treatment to re-educate the part of the brain that changes noise into sound patterns that make sense.

Characteristics

There five main problem areas for children with CAPD, which can affect home and school activities.

- Auditory figure-ground problems: This is when the child cannot pay attention when there is noise in the background. Noisy, low-structured classrooms could be very frustrating to this child.
- Auditory memory problems: This is when the child has difficulty remembering information such as directions, lists or study materials. It can exist on an immediate basis ('I can't remember it now') and/or on a deferred basis ('I can't remember it when I need it for later').
- Auditory discrimination problems: This is when the child has difficulty hearing the difference between sounds or words that are similar (coat/boat or ch/sh). This problem can affect following directions, reading, spelling and writing skills, among others.
- Auditory attention problems: This is when the child cannot maintain focus for listening long enough to complete a task or requirement (eg listening to a lecture in school). Health, motivation and attitude may also affect attention, but among other factors a child with CAPD cannot (*not* will not) maintain attention.
- Auditory cohesion problems. This relates to higher-level listening tasks: finding it difficult to draw inferences from conversations, understanding riddles or comprehending verbal maths problems which require heightened auditory processing and language levels. Auditory cohesion develops best when all the other skills listed above) are intact.

How to recognise CAPD

- Is your child easily distracted or unusually bothered by loud or sudden noises?
- Are noisy environments upsetting?
- Does behaviour and performance improve in quieter settings?
- Does your child have difficulty following directions, whether simple or complicated?

■ Does your child have reading, spelling, writing or other speech/language difficulties?

■ Is abstract information difficult to interpret?

■ Are verbal maths problems difficult?

■ Is your child disorganised and forgetful?

■ Are conversations hard for your child to follow?

Many of these may also appear in other conditions such as attention deficit hyperactivity disorder (ADHD; see above), or with learning difficulties and even depression. For this reason CAPD is often misdiagnosed. CAPD is also sometimes confused with semantic pragmatic disorder (see above), but SPD has very different roots. Symptoms of CAPD can range from mild to severe, and can take many different forms. Trained professionals, such as speech and language therapists and audiologists who specialise in CAPD, can determine if your child has a central auditory processing disorder.

What the school can do to help

■ One of the most important things that both parents and teachers should do is to realise that CAPD is real. Symptoms and behaviour are not within the child's control.

■ A speech and language therapist can help with drawing up a statement, and/or an individual education plan.

■ School personnel should keep in regular contact with the parents regarding your child's progress.

■ The teacher should accept and help with whatever aids may assist in class, such as an assignment pad or a tape recorder.

■ Sitting towards the front of the classroom facing away from the windows will help concentration and minimise distraction.

What parents can do to help

■ Reduce background noise.

■ Have your child look at you when you are speaking, and use simple, expressive sentences.

■ Speaking at a slightly slower rate and at a mildly increased volume may also help.

■ Difficulty with following directions is possibly the single most common complaint. Ask your child to repeat the directions back to you aloud and to keep repeating them aloud (or to themselves) until the directions are completed. Make certain your child understands the directions and is not just repeating your words. For directions that are to be completed at a later time, writing notes, wearing a watch and maintaining a predictable routine in the household also help.

■ General organisation and scheduling appear beneficial to many children with CAPD. Provide your child with a quiet study place. Regular tasks and responsibilities help to build self-esteem.

Help your child to understand that they can be actively involved in giving themselves the best chances, such as moving to a quieter place when listening is necessary and applying the strategies taught in speech and language therapy. A positive, realistic attitude and healthy self-esteem in a child with CAPD can work wonders.

Multi-sensory impairment (MSI)

Children with multi-sensory impairment have both visual and hearing difficulties and are sometimes referred to as deafblind. Although they may have some residual sight and/or hearing, the combination can result in high anxiety and multi-sensory deprivation. Pupils with multi-sensory impairment have much greater difficulties in following the curriculum and participating in school life than those with a single sensory impairment. Many also have additional disabilities and their complex needs can make it difficult to assess intellectual ability. Incidental learning is limited and children may experience difficulties in perception, communication and acquisition of information. Pupils need teaching approaches that make good use of their residual hearing and vision, together with their other senses. They may require alternative means of communication.

Further information and help

See also Part 4: Useful contacts.

National Blind Children's Society (NBCS).
Web: www.nbcs.org.uk.
E-mail: enquiries@nbcs.org.uk. Tel: 01278 764764.
Address: Bradbury House, Market Street, Highbridge, Somerset TA9 3BW

RNIB (Royal National Institute for the Blind). A good chunk on education under 'Services'.

Web: www.rnib.org.uk. E-mail: helpline@rnib.org.uk.
Tel (helpline): 0845 766 9999. Fax: 020 7388 2034.
Address: 105 Judd Street, London WC1H 9NE

Hearing impairment

British Deaf Association. Exists to ensure that deaf people using sign language have the same rights and entitlement as any other citizens.
Web: www.britishdeafassociation.org.uk.
BDA London: E-mail: tonyp@signcommunity.org.uk.
Tel: 020 7588 3520. Textphone: 020 7588 3529.
Fax: 020 7588 3527. Videophone IP: 81.138.165.105.
Address: Tony Pilkington, 69 Wilson Street,
London EC2A 2BB

National Deaf Children's Society. Provides lists of deaf-friendly schools and detailed advice on what to look for.
Web: www.ndcs.org.uk. E-mail: ndcs@ndcs.org.uk.
Tel: 0207 490 8656. Fax: 020 7251 5020.
Address: 15 Dufferin Street, London EC1Y 8UR

RNID (Royal National Institute for Deaf People).
Information on education is disappointingly sparse and hard to find.
Web: www.rnid.org.uk. E-mail: information@rnid.org.uk.
Tel: 020 7296 8000. Textphone: 020 7296 8001.
Fax: 020 7296 819919.
Address: 23 Featherstone Street, London EC1Y 8SL

CAPD

APDUK. A new site for those affected by CAPD.
Web: www.apduk.org. Tel (1pm-6pm): 01656 766651 (6pm-10pm): 01442 214555.
Address: Mark Mitchell, Hon Secretary APDUK,
c/o Dacorum CVS, 48 High Street, Hemel Hempstead,
Hertfordshire HP1 3AF

Dolfrog. The site's layout and design is an example of how visual spatial learners or (C)APDs think and work, in comparison to non-APDs (who may find it a bit disorientating). Web: www.dolfrog.com.
The same author has a site on 'Invisible disabilities in the UK: www.geocities.com/dolfrog

Speech and language difficulties

It is estimated that communication disorders (including speech, language, and hearing disorders) affect between 5 and 10 per cent of children in the UK. This estimate does not include children who have speech/language problems secondary to other conditions such as hearing impairment or language disorders related to other disabilities such as autism, or cerebral palsy.

When a child is noticeably behind their peers in acquiring speech and/or language skills, communication is considered delayed. Sometimes a child will have greater receptive (understanding) than expressive (speaking) language skills, but this is not always the case. The causes of speech and language disorders may range from hearing loss, neurological disorders or brain damage to drug abuse, physical impairments such as cleft palate, or psychological trauma. Often, however, the cause is unknown.

Speech disorders involve difficulties producing speech sounds or problems with voice quality. They might be characterised by an interruption in the flow or rhythm of speech, such as stuttering (which is called dysfluency). Speech disorders include problems with articulation (the way sounds are formed), or phonological disorders, or difficulties with the pitch, volume or quality of the voice. There may be a combination of several problems. Experiencing difficulty with some speech sounds may be a symptom of a delay, or of a hearing impairment. It can be difficult to understand what someone with a speech disorder is trying to say.

Language disorder is an impairment in the ability to understand and/or use words in context, both verbally and non-verbally. Characteristics of language disorders include improper use of words and their meanings, problems with sentence structure, inappropriate grammatical patterns, reduced vocabulary and inability to express ideas, or follow directions. One or a combination of these may occur in children who are affected by language-learning disabilities (such as dyslexia) or developmental language delay. Children may hear or see a word but not be able to understand its meaning. Often, being unable to communicate frustrates them.

What parents can do

Because of the way the brain develops, it is easier to acquire language and communication skills before the age of 5. When children have muscular disorders, hearing problems or developmental delays, their acquisition of speech, language and related skills is often affected. Because all communication disorders carry the potential to isolate individuals from their social and educational surroundings, appropriate timely intervention is essential.

While many speech and language patterns can be called 'baby talk' and are part of a young child's normal development, they can become problems if they are not outgrown as expected. In this way an initial delay in speech and language or an initial speech pattern can become a disorder, which can cause difficulties in learning.

If you have concerns, you may refer your child to a speech and language specialist without a referral from the GP or educational psychologist.

Educational implications

Learning is done mainly through language, so it is critical that children develop a language for learning, through intensive and specialised help. Some children may require specialist assistance from a resourced school such as a language unit with speech therapy. Others may need a special school environment with a curriculum geared to children with severe communication difficulties. Some may require alternative means of communication, such as sign language, symbols, or voice boxes.

Technology can help children whose physical conditions make communication difficult. The use of electronic communication systems allows those with no speech and people with severe physical disabilities to express themselves.

Speech and language therapy

Children may be referred for speech and language therapy for a variety of reasons, including:

- mild, moderate or severe learning difficulties
- physical disability
- language delay
- language deprivation
- specific language impairment
- specific difficulties in producing sounds
- hearing impairment
- cleft palate
- stammering/dysfluency
- autism/social interaction difficulties
- dyslexia.

Parents, GPs, health visitors, school or early years staff can make a referral to a therapist. Speech and language therapists assist children who have communication disorders in various ways. They work to assess, diagnose and develop a programme of care to maximise the communication potential of those referred to them; they may consult the child's teacher about the most effective ways to facilitate the child's communication in the class setting; and they work closely with the family to develop goals and techniques for effective therapy in class and at home.

At the first session you will be asked for information about your child and the therapist will carry out a screening assessment of all aspects of your child's communication skills. The results will be discussed with you, and the proposed therapy explained, including when it will be offered and the timescale.

Therapy varies but usually involves individual sessions with the parent and child. You will be expected to be involved in helping your child to practise and learn new skills so it is important to be clear about the aims and the results of each phase of therapy. Sometimes a child will be placed on review – formal therapy sessions will be discontinued during this time; however, you should be told the reason for the review and what your child should be doing during the review period.

In some cases, perhaps where a child has a learning difficulty or where a severe and specific speech and language problem makes following the curriculum difficult, their education may be adversely affected. If this is the case for your child ask the therapist who else needs to be involved, the expected procedures, timescales and what you can do to help.

Although the NHS provides speech and language therapy, it is often considered as an educational provision and may be provided or funded by the local education authority. There are many specialist areas within speech and language therapy, so if you feel your child's needs aren't being met by the therapist assigned ask to be referred to the specialist therapist for your child's problem. If there is no specialist available or you want a second opinion, ask the therapist or GP to arrange this or contact one of the organisations listed below for help.

Elective mutism

The term elective (or selective) mutism describes the behaviour of children who are able to speak but remain silent with certain people or in certain settings. It is most commonly noticed when a child joins a school. It is a form of social phobia, and should be treated as such; it has no connection with pervasive developmental disorders such as autism.

The diagnostic criteria for elective mutism are:

■ Consistent failure to speak in specific social situations (in which there is an expectation for speaking, eg at school), despite speaking in other situations.

■ The mutism interferes with educational or occupational achievement or with social communication.

■ The duration of the disturbance is at least one month (not limited to the first month of school).

■ The failure to speak is not due to a lack of knowledge of, or comfort with, the spoken language required in the social situation.

■ The disturbance is not accounted for by a communication disorder (eg stuttering) and does not occur exclusively during the course of a pervasive developmental disorder, schizophrenia, or other psychotic disorder.

Children with elective mutism are often misunderstood. They may be punished for their inability to speak and communicate. Many are still being misdiagnosed with autism, oppositional defiant disorder, or learning disabilities. Children with elective mutism should not be forced to speak, as this leads to worsening of anxiety and mutism. Electively mute children are not manipulative, nor are they developmentally delayed; they are simply too anxious to speak.

There are very few children with elective mutism; more of these are girls than boys. There may be a variety of causes. When it persists for a long time teachers and parents may experience high levels of frustration and even anger. It does not help to force a child to speak. Children tend not to simply grow out of it, so when the condition persists a planned approach is usually helpful. Approaches and interventions, which require patience, time and imagination, tend to work best when they occur in the places where the child does not speak. However, the involvement of the parents is critical.

What the school can do to help

■ It is essential that all adults who come into contact with the child are aware of the difficulty. They must not force the child to speak, but should praise any speech or sound which the child does produce, and possibly use rewards.

■ Emphasis should be placed on activities that do not involve spoken language, such as writing, silent reading, drawing etc.

■ The child should be allowed other means of communicating, for example via the computer.

■ A child with elective mutism normally benefits from being in a mainstream class, and from working and playing with other children, so it is helpful to put the child in small groups for classroom tasks.

The educational psychologist may be involved in planning an intervention programme for the child. Parents and others, with whom the child does speak, should be involved, but the targeted activities should be carried out at school. As more speech emerges, other people may be involved, but very gradually. This disability is usually overcome, but the best chance the child has is when the school works closely with parents and outside support services.

Further information and help

Afasic. A parent-led organisation founded to help children with speech and language problems, and their families.
Web: www.afasic.org.uk. E-mail: info@afasic.org.uk.
Tel (admin): 020 7490 9410. Fax: 020 7251 2834.
Address: 2nd floor, 50-52 Great Sutton Street,
London EC1V 0DJ

ASLTIP (Association of Speech and Language Therapists in Independent Practice). All ASLTIP therapists are Registered Members of RCSLT and registered with the Health Professions Council.
Web: www.helpwithtalking.com.
E-mail: asltip@awdry.demon.co.uk.
Tel (answerphone): 0870 241 3357. Fax: 01494 488590.
Address: WSS Coleheath Bottom, Speen,
Princes Risborough, Buckinghamshire HP27 0SZ

I CAN (Invalid Children's Aid Nationwide).
Web: www.ican.org.uk.

Tel: 0845 225 4071. Fax: 0845 225 4072.
Address: 4 Dyers Building, London. EC1N 2QP

Royal College of Speech and Language Therapists (RCSLT).
Web: www.rcslt.org. E-mail: postmaster@rcslt.org.
Tel: 020 7378 1200. Fax: 020 7403 7254.
Address: 2 White Hart Yard, London SE1 1NX

Talking Point. Website for information about speech, language and communication difficulties in children. Talking Point is run by I CAN, working with the RCSLT and Afasic.
Web: www.talkingpoint.org.uk

Medical conditions

There are a number of medical conditions affecting children that may give rise to a child needing additional help and support in school, though not all will result in a child having special educational needs. The following information, produced in conjunction with Contact a Family, a UK-wide charity which specialises in providing medical information on hundreds of conditions affecting children, is not intended as a comprehensive list but covers some of the more commonly occurring medical conditions.

The Contact a Family Directory of Specific Conditions and Rare Disorders can be seen in full at www.cafamily.org.uk/dirworks.html.

Contact a Family is always delighted to give information to teachers about any disability – teachers can phone free on 0808 808 3555 or e-mail info@cafamily.org.uk.

Spina bifida and hydrocephalus

Spina bifida occurs very early in pregnancy and means split spine. The neural tube, which should develop to form the spinal cord, brain and spine, is split and one or more vertebrae fail to form properly. A gap appears, the bones do not close round the spinal cord and the nerves may bulge out on the unborn baby's back and become damaged.

There are three main types of spina bifida. With spina bifida occulta, a dimple or hair at the site of the defect, on the skin of the back, is the only sign of malformation. This condition is usually very mild and without symptoms although occasionally there may be continence problems and difficulties with mobility.

In spina bifida cystica a sac or cyst is visible on the back covered by a thin layer of skin. There are two forms: a meningocele and a myelomeningocele. In a meningocele the sac contains tissues which cover the spinal cord and cerebro-spinal fluid. The nerves are not normally badly damaged and there is little or no malfunction. This is the least common form of spina bifida. Myelomeningocele is the more common form and more severe because the sac includes nerves and part of the spinal cord as well as tissue and cerebral-spinal fluid. Some degree of paralysis and loss of sensation occurs below the site of the defect. The extent of the disability is dependent upon the extent of nerve damage.

Cranium bifida is a failure of development of the bones of the skull. In this form the sac is called an encephalocele. In some cases part of the brain is also enclosed in the sac while in others it contains only tissue and cerebro-spinal fluid. Spina bifida has some genetic predisposition. For an affected person the risk of an affected child is 1 in 25.

Hydrocephalus

About 80 per cent of people with spina bifida have hydrocephalus. The term hydrocephalus is from the Greek meaning 'water in the head'. The 'water' is cerebrospinal fluid (CSF), a clear liquid which is produced continually in the four ventricles inside the brain. Passing from one ventricle to the next through narrow pathways, it circulates around the surface of the brain – a little also goes down the spinal cord – and is absorbed back into the bloodstream. The absorption takes place through specialised veins inside the skull which have a sieve-like surface. Though much slower than the circulation of the blood, the CSF is constantly being produced, circulated and reabsorbed.

Hydrocephalus can result when either (rarely) too much CSF is produced, or more commonly when it is prevented from circulating or being reabsorbed. As a result, the CSF is produced but cannot get out; this causes raised pressure inside the brain, the ventricles swell and the brain tissue is stretched and squashed. The skull bones in babies and young children are not fixed together as they are in later life, and the pressure causes the head to increase in size. However, it is important to realise that hydrocephalus can also arise in older children and in adults, when the skull bones are fixed and the head cannot increase in size.

Helping the child with spina bifida/hydrocephalus in school

Strategies and help for children will vary according to individual need and should be pertinent to the child. However, some general implications include:

■ Safety: if a child is hit on the head or abdomen and doesn't recover quickly, damage to the shunt should be considered and help sought.

■ Children may be easily distracted, have difficulty staying on task or have poor short-term memory. Say the child's name so that they are aware the instruction is meant for them, gain eye contact and repeat instructions as necessary.

■ Break down tasks and limit the number of instructions given. Visual clues and timetables may help, as will routine and good organisation, both personal and at school.

■ Progress may be inconsistent so be prepared to reinforce, and practise tasks. Children may find it difficult to apply skills learned so these will probably need to be reinforced in a variety of situations.

■ Difficulties with dexterity or co-ordination may be the result of poor visual perception or a lack of fine motor skills. Some children have balance difficulties. They may need extra time and space to get around. Motor skills can be improved with the use of activities designed to improve co-ordination, develop grip, manipulation, strength and dexterity. The physio or occupational therapist may work closely with the child to develop and encourage co-ordination. Special equipment isn't necessarily needed: multi-link cubes, plasticine, playdough all can play a part.

Children with spina bifida are not necessarily all wheelchair users. Those with some paralysis below the damaged area of the spine may be able to walk but have bowel and bladder control problems. Although some preschool establishments are reluctant to take children still in nappies, they must be careful not to discriminate when incontinence is the result of a disability. All schools now have to take note of the Disability Discrimination Act. Parents, too, need that extra support.

Some children may exhibit behavioural difficulties. As with all children, clear boundaries and a safe, caring environment with routine and structure will help. Forewarn and prepare children, especially young children, of anticipated changes to routine, even exciting ones such as a school trip, a special visitor, or a new activity.

Some children don't like noise or over-excitement; others may have difficulty relating to their peers, preferring adult company. Adults can help support a child by building up a good relationship and helping them move towards independence, becoming less reliant on adult assistance and support as confidence and esteem develop.

Epilepsy

Epilepsy is the tendency to have recurrent seizures originating in the brain as a result of excessive or disordered discharge of brain cells. Seizures are divided into two categories:

■ Generalised seizure: both hemispheres of the brain are involved and the sufferer loses consciousness. The seizures include major convulsions with jerking of all limbs and unconsciousness (tonic clonic); seizures when the body goes stiff (tonic) or floppy (atonic); jerks of the limbs (myoclonic jerks) and momentary lapses of consciousness (absences).

■ Partial (or focal) seizure: the disturbance of brain activity starts in, or involves, a specific part of the brain. The nature of such seizures depends upon the area of the brain involved. Partial seizures may be simple or complex. Consciousness is not lost in a simple partial seizure, but is impaired in a complex partial seizure.

Causes of epilepsy are variable.

Idiopathic epilepsy often starts in childhood or adolescence and is largely due to genetic causes. People with idiopathic epilepsy may inherit a low seizure threshold. This would mean that given certain conditions (individual to each person) they might have a greater susceptibility to having a seizure.

Symptomatic epilepsy may be due to brain damage or anomaly from any cause, for example infection, tumours, brain damage or specific syndromes such as Sturge-Weber syndrome, tuberous sclerosis or some metabolic disorders. The pattern of events will depend upon the underlying cause (sporadic in the case of Sturge-Weber syndrome, for instance)

In cryptogenic epilepsy no known cause may be found for the epilepsy, which can begin at any time in the individual's life.

Coping at school

Some children with severe epilepsy may need to attend a special school, of which a limited number exist. However, most children with epilepsy attend mainstream schools and do not require any additional provision, aside from special consideration or understanding.

Epilepsy does not have any bearing on intelligence, although epilepsy may be an additional aspect of learning or physical difficulties. Where seizures are frequent or severe, daily activities and routines may be compromised. It is important not to underestimate the impact on a sufferer's self-esteem of the attitudes of family and friends. If a child suffers ongoing (subclinical) seizures without any outward signs, or is on medication, their behaviour or learning may be affected.

Cerebral palsy

Cerebral palsy, a non-progressive disorder, describes a group of chronic conditions characterised by an inability to fully control motor function, particularly muscle control and co-ordination.

Causes can be multiple and complex. Recent studies suggest that cerebral palsy is mostly due to factors affecting the brain before birth. Known possible causes can include infection, difficult or premature birth, cerebral bleeds, infection or accident in early years and abnormal brain development. In a few cases, cerebral palsy may be caused by a genetic link, but this is quite rare. Parents who may be concerned should ask their GP for referral to a genetic counsellor.

Cerebral palsy is frequently categorised into three main types although many people will have a combination of these types:

- spasticity (stiff and tight muscles)
- athetoid or dyskinetic (involuntary movements, change of tone in muscles from floppy to tense)
- ataxic (unsteady, unco-ordinated shaky movements and irregular speech).

You will also hear terms that indicate the parts of the body affected: hemiplegia (one half of body), diplegia (legs more affected than arms) and quadriplegia (all four limbs equally affected).

As cerebral palsy is such a wide-ranging condition, its effects vary with each individual. In some people, cerebral palsy is barely noticeable; others will be more severely affected. Symptoms depend on the parts of the brain affected but can include:

- involuntary movement
- difficulties with mobility
- abnormal sensation and perception
- sensory impairment of any or all of sight, hearing or speech
- seizures
- poor listening skills
- problems with attention and memory.

The root of the problem is in the brain rather than the affected limbs, and as yet no cure exists to repair the damaged brain cells. Physiotherapy and speech therapy can be used to help with difficulties and prevent deformities developing or the condition worsening. Implications for learning depend on the area of the brain affected and severity of the condition.

Cerebral palsy at school

As a result of muscle weakness and spasticity, a child with cerebral palsy will often appear clumsy when walking, talking, using their hands or carrying out everyday tasks and activities such as using scissors, jumping, painting, with resultant health and safety implications. Pupils with cerebral palsy may tire faster than their peers as motor impairment means they may have to try much harder and use more energy performing tasks.

Some children may have learning difficulties, behavioural problems, epilepsy or sensory impairment (especially communication). It is common for children with cerebral palsy to have difficulty with fine or gross motor skills and visual perception, and to have significant dietary requirements. Early support and therapeutic intervention can undoubtedly help (a fact emphasised by *Removing Barriers to Achievement*, the government's strategy for SEN).

The severity of cerebral palsy together with any additional learning needs will determine the help and support an individual child requires. Many can follow the full mainstream curriculum with some sufferers requiring only the minimum of intervention or consideration. Sufferers with mild symptoms may not receive help from specialists but teachers should be made aware of the difficulties they may encounter, especially in PE, practical subjects and with writing. Chapter 4 has an inspiring account – 'In search of normality' – of one bright young man's experiences at different schools.

Those with severe and complex needs may find a special school with specialist equipment and resources beneficial. Time spent on therapy will vary according to the needs of the individual. Additional help and intervention may include some or all of: educational psychology, physiotherapy, occupational therapy, assistance with speech and language including augmentative and alternative communication (AAC) or conductive education (see below), for varying amounts of time and in differing degrees.

Conductive education

One adult with cerebral palsy told how clinicians said he would never walk, yet, following conductive education he and others in his class achieved this milestone by their sixth birthdays.

Conductive education, based on the work of the Peto Institute in Hungary, is a holistic system that incorporates therapies, learning and exercise; it is an intensive regime and requires a massive commitment from all those involved with the child, especially parents, but those who follow the programmes do acclaim the benefits.

One of the first programmes in the UK was developed at Ingfield Manor School in West Sussex. Now operating within the school as The Dame Vera Lynn School for Parents, the centre can be used by anyone with SEN arising from cerebral palsy and physical and associated difficulties. Officially it's for children from 1 to 5 years, though some as young as 9 months attend. Families used to come from far afield but the opening of additional centres throughout the UK has reduced the catchment area. The programmes cover many aspects, including the basics, such as falling, head control, sitting and standing. (Babies are born with reflex responses to stimuli, prior to the brain developing vital neural pathways. Children with cerebral palsy who retain these reflexes beyond infancy need to be taught to override them.)

Further information and help

See also Part 4: Useful contacts.

Spina bifida and hydrocephalus

Association for Spina Bifida and Hydrocephalus (ASBAH). A reasonable amount of information.
Web: www.asbah.org. E-mail: info@asbah.org.
Tel: 01733 555988. Fax: 01733 555985.
Address: 42 Park Road, Peterborough PE1 2UQ

ASBAH is a charity established in 1966. It offers advice and information to individuals with hydrocephalus and/or spina bifida and their families. It has a network of area advisers covering most parts of the country, backed up by a team of specialist advisers in medical aspects of the conditions and education matters. It works with around 50 local associations in England, Wales and Northern Ireland. ASBAH publishes LINK Journal quarterly and has a wide range of information available, details on request. The association has over 8,000 families and individuals on its database. Information for teachers is available on its website at www.asbah.org/Information/Education.html.

Epilepsy

Epilepsy Action. Web: www.epilepsy.org.uk.
E-mail: helpline@epilepsy.org.uk.
Tel (admin/membership): 0113 210 8800.
Helpline (9am-4.30pm Mon-Thurs, 9am-4pm Fri): 0808 800 5050. Fax (admin/membership): 0113 242 8804. Helpline: 0808 800 5555.
Address: New Anstey House, Gate Way Drive, Yeadon, Leeds LS19 7XY

Epilepsy Action is a national registered charity founded in 1950. It offers a nationwide network of branches. It publishes a quarterly newsletter and has a wide range of information available, details on request. Epilepsy Action has nearly 20,000 members. There is useful information for teachers at www.epilepsy.org.uk/info/teachers.html

National Society for Epilepsy (NSE)
Web: www.epilepsynse.org.uk. Tel: 01494 601300.
Helpline (10am-4pm Mon-Fri): 01494 601400.
Fax: 01494 871927.

Address: Chesham Lane, Chalfont St Peter, Buckinghamshire SL9 0RJ

This charity, established in 1892, provides medical services through outpatient clinics and in-patient assessment; short breaks and residential care services for adults with epilepsy. It has a comprehensive research programme into epilepsy, offers a membership scheme, epilepsy training services and information services. The latter include leaflets, books and videos, a helpline that gives information and listening support, and a network of epilepsy information services in hospital settings around the country. There is useful information for teachers at www.epilepsynse.org.uk/pages/info/leaflets/educatio.cfm.

Cerebral palsy

Scope. Web: www.scope.org.uk.
E-mail: cphelpline@scope.org.uk. Tel: 020 7619 7100.
Freephone helpline (9am-9pm Mon-Fri, 2pm-6pm Sat-Sun): 0808 800 3333.
Address: 6 Market Road, London N7 9PW

Scope is a registered charity that aims to help all disabled people achieve equality. Scope's work is focused on four main areas: early years, employment, education and daily living. In addition to a range of national and local services, Scope has over 250 affiliated local groups. In-depth information and advice is provided on all aspects of cerebral palsy and disability issues as well as information about and referral to Scope services as appropriate. A team of trained counsellors provides clients with emotional support and initial counselling. Scope publishes *Disability Now* monthly. Useful information for teachers can be found at www.scope.org.uk/information/factsheets/.

Chapter 3
SEN personnel

> My child was diagnosed with physical difficulties and I was told he'd need to see either a physiotherapist or an occupational therapist (OT). When we got the referral it was to the OT. Initially I was disappointed, I thought OT was to physio what a nurse is to a doctor but I couldn't have been more wrong. Intensive and on-going occupational therapy was absolutely the right thing, I just wish I'd known more beforehand.

There is a wide variety of health and educational professionals specialising in SEN who can advise, assess and treat your child, to help give them the best possible chances to realise their potential. But who does what?

In an ideal world, a multi-disciplinary team made up of an occupational therapist, physiotherapist, educational psychologist, speech and language therapist and paediatrician would be available to help each child who needed it. Each discipline can add an important part to the jigsaw that is assessment and treatment. Unfortunately, lack of funding for staff, or staff shortages (a national problem), means this situation is rarely found, with difficulties arising even for those who have provision identified on their statement.

Mostly, practitioners assess and treat a range of needs and there may be a degree of overlap or interdependence between therapies and treatments – an occupational therapist's role is a crucial one in independence training of all neuro-diverse conditions; physiotherapists provide exercise regimes to improve a child balance, proprioception and co-ordination over a wide range of conditions. Speech and language therapists are especially helpful with feeding difficulties; where language is delayed; or where there are communication problems in autistic spectrum disorders or dyspraxia. Osteopathy can be very helpful for children who have lower-back problems and have never crawled, while cranio-sacral therapy may be helpful for autism or for children who had difficult or caesarean births.

Exercise has its place too; t'ai chi is an excellent exercise and mediation regime that promotes gentle balanced movement on each side of the body. Karate helps promote good co-ordination skills organisation and movement – particularly beneficial to children with dyspraxia as well as promoting a positive outlook for asthma sufferers and helping those with behavioural or confidence problems. Pilates is helpful in developing co-ordination and muscle strength, especially core muscles. Homeopathy may be helpful for sleep or behaviour problems. Chinese medicine and acupuncture can be helpful for sleep and energy problems (too much energy or tiredness). A nutritional therapist will advise not only on a healthy diet but also on the effects of specific factors; for example, research into the benefits of essential fatty acids hit the media spotlight in early 2005 following the perceived success of the Durham schools trial, and vitamin B6 and magnesium have been helpful to some children with attention deficit hyperactivity disorders (ADHD).

As with all therapies, some trial and error may be needed before you find the therapy to suit your child. However, these therapies treat the whole person with gentle non-addictive methods and support natural development and maturation. Finally do remember there are cowboys out there, so please, only work with qualified practitioners.

Who to turn to first?

If you have concerns, speak to your health visitor or your child's school, or seek a referral from your GP to your local child development centre or paediatric service. Early diagnosis from a paediatrician, occupational therapist, speech and language therapist or educational psychologist is important; the sooner the correct support is put in place, the better. Unfortunately, long waiting lists and limited therapy time are not uncommon. If this is the case it may be worth considering contacting a private therapist who can work with your child and the school over a longer period.

Educational psychologist

Dr Enid Alston, South Thames College of Further Education

It is not easy to forget the day when a teacher throws a grubby and rather tired folder of exercise books in front of you and says scornfully 'This is Jennifer.' My reaction, perhaps wrongly, was to feel mortified. I should have defended my daughter against such an unfair attack, but nevertheless I had the reaction that I was perhaps not the parent that I thought I was, that my child was not meeting other people's expectations and this reflected on me. While I wanted to leap to the defence of my child, the evidence in that little pile was quite clear: the work looked more like that of a drunken spider with a leg missing crawling across the page than a child of 9 years old.

Of course nobody at that time suggested that we should contact an educational psychologist or have Jennifer assessed for differences in learning. The funny child who could speak intelligently and amusingly on endless different subjects and be a source of facts and information as well as mimic and act, was not the same as the mute, frustrated one sitting in lessons trying to meet with an approval that never came. She was found wanting because of the presentation and the written content that so under-represented what she really was.

Sadly, although one hopes that a reaction such as this would now be the exception rather than the norm, from my work with older students and adults I have found that many have still not received the understanding and support that they need in school to make the most of their potential. Students of 16+ are still coming out of school saying that they did not receive an assessment or any support with learning in their school years. The moral of this story is that if a school does suggest that they will refer your child to an educational psychologist or for a statement of SEN, you are in fact fortunate. It may not seem so at the time, but this is a comfort. It tells you the school is already knowledgeable about special needs and the needs of the learner and is concerned for the welfare of your child and for others in the class.

I have found that parents need as much information as they can get about both the kind of difficulties that could be affecting their child's learning and also the process their child will experience when they are assessed for learning difficulties. They are then in a position to ensure that their child gets the best assessment, resulting in the best available help for their particular needs.

The assessment process

To a parent, the process of obtaining an assessment or a statement of SEN can seem like one for bottling yoghurt. The object is packed, the cap is fitted and the label popped on all very neatly and the product comes out at the end looking beautiful on paper but not really relating to your child. It doesn't empower parents or give them confidence or reassurance about how to help their child and how to ensure that they make the most of their years in school, which, in the end, is all that any parent wants.

So what will be the process that your child will encounter? First of all you should already be aware that your child would have had an individual education plan (IEP) for some time (see Chapter 6). This will have been discussed with you at parents evenings and individually in meetings with the class teacher or school special needs co-ordinator (SENCo). You will also know that your child has been placed on what is called 'School Action' or 'School Action Plus' with a Wave 2 (small group) or Wave 3 (individual) intervention.

It is when you get to School Action Plus that, as the term suggests, assessment by an educational or other psychologist is a probability. This process may not be quick because the school has to make the application and funding has to be put in place for the assessment. In the meantime, try to find out as much background as you can about the differences in your child's behavioural and learning style that have been mentioned by the teachers. Some sources of information are listed below.

The purpose of the assessment is to find out how the school can best help your child. To understand this a close look must be taken at how your child learns, their profile of strengths and weaknesses and the difficulties that they have in a number of different areas – behaviour, speaking, concentration, organisation, cohesion of movement and memory being just some of them.

The first step will be to arrange a consultation meeting that involves those who know the child best: parents or carers, teachers, the SENCo and the psychologist. The educational psychologist (EP) may also observe your child in class to make observations on social interactions and behaviour that leads to completion of tasks and learning.

If a further assessment is needed a consultation will be arranged. This will entail your child completing a number of tasks, which include reading, spelling, writing and maths tasks as well as verbal reasoning and reasoning with shapes, figures and pictures. The whole process will take about two to three hours and your child should be helped to understand what the assessment is for and what it will involve. Leaflets can often be supplied by the EP to help with this explanation. EPs are well trained to put the children at ease and relate to them during these sessions, and most children find the session a positive experience with an element of challenge or fun involved somewhere in the procedure.

The assessment will result either in a verbal report, or a written one, or both. The written report will contain a great deal of technical jargon as well as the nitty-gritty, ie the recommendations for the future education of your child and an overview of your child's strengths and weaknesses. A report that does not contain some reference to strengths or learning strengths is missing the plot because these are the crucial areas through which your child will need to learn in the future and other professionals need to be guided to look for them. Recommendations or referrals may also be made to other professionals such as a speech and language therapist, occupational therapist, optometrist or a paediatrician, as well as sources of help such as the child and family consultation services. Don't be unduly alarmed if this happens – the more information available the better the help that can be obtained.

This assessment and the report will also play a key role in both the preparation of a statement of SEN and the possibility of obtaining access arrangements for examinations. It is therefore an important document, and once it is obtained you should ensure you have a copy and keep it in a safe place. A copy should also be made available to new centres of education if your child moves school or goes to college.

Starting the ball rolling

What do you do if no one suggests that your child is having difficulties in learning that are interfering with their progress?

Sandy is the child of highly educated professional parents who were working in India when he was conceived. Several months into his pregnancy his mother got dysentery, which affected her on and off until after he was born. Sandy suffered from frequent ear infections and at one point it was noticed that he could not hear what was being said around him. He had grommets fitted when he was 3 years old, which solved this problem. He scraped by in school and remained unobtrusive, but his parents were a bit worried that he didn't seem to be doing as well in school as his brothers. His teachers reassured them that he was about average and there was no need to worry, and they thought for a long time 'it's just Sandy'. Eventually when he was doing A levels a friend persuaded them that he should be assessed and he was found to be dyslexic and with a specific language impairment which had affected his learning to a significant degree. By this time it had also affected his motivation and his self-esteem.

If you are worried about your child but the teachers don't seem concerned or maintain that he will catch up given time, or is just average, follow up on your hunch. Remember miracles do happen; some children will catch up given time, but not very often, so err on the safe side and insist your child is assessed by a trained professional sooner rather than later. Time matters!

The key thing to remember is that the sooner your child's difficulties are isolated, identified and dealt with, the less their education will suffer, the more successfully they will learn and the less their self-esteem and self-confidence will be affected. It is difficult to overestimate the importance of self-esteem in the classroom, and the more this can be protected the better for your child.

If you suspect a difficulty with learning, concentration, behaviour or any other source of problem and the school is not responding to your concerns, you are at liberty to seek a psychologist's assessment yourself or get a second opinion. The professional bodies listed below can supply names of accredited psychologists who can carry out an assessment and give appropriate advice. Sometimes parents need to know a lot more than the professionals, so always remember this is your child and you do know them best!

Dr Enid Alston, AMBDA, DipSpLD, CPsychol, Star Learning Consultancy, is currently an Advanced Practitioner and Lecturer in Specific Learning Difficulties at South Thames College of Further Education.

Further information and help

See also Part 4: Useful contacts.

British Psychological Society. 34,000 psychologists are members but this is a disappointingly inward-looking site with little of use to parents – except for the 'Find a psychologist' service that lists inter alia a few hundred members who offer educational psychology services.
Web: www.bps.org.uk. E-mail: enquiry@bps.org.uk.
Tel: 0116 254 9568. Fax: 0116 247 0787.
Address: St Andrews House, 48 Princess Road East, Leicester LE1 7DR

Educational-Psychologist.co.uk. 'Find a psychologist' section, listing nine educational psychologists (ie very few); you can e-mail or telephone for advice. 'SEN information' section with advice on how to spot various conditions and what to do in various situations.
Web: www.educational-psychologist.co.uk.
E-mail: tim@edpsych.screaming.net; edpsych@hotmail.com

Every Child Matters. A site giving details of the educational psychology service. It includes a brief description of what an educational psychologist does, plus contact details for various services.
Web: www.everychildmatters.gov.uk/ete/psychology

PATOSS (Professional Association of Teachers of Students with Specific Learning Difficulties). Information on specific learning difficulties. Lists of specialists in assessment and tutoring.
Web: www.patoss-dyslexia.org.
E-mail: patoss@evesham.ac.uk.
Tel: 01386 712650. Fax: 01386 712716.
Address: PO Box 10, Evesham, Worcestershire WR11 1ZW

Dyslexia counsellor

Dr Rosemary Scott, specialist dyslexia counsellor and psychologist

At its best, counselling has helped alleviate misery and confusion in pretty much every social group imaginable, with one exception: dyslexics. There are up to six million child and adult dyslexics in this country, but remarkably few take advantage of counselling. This is a great pity, because many dyslexics would benefit enormously from counselling.

On the surface, dyslexics are unhappy for the same reasons as everyone else. Work, relationships, appearance, education and worries about their future can make them thoroughly miserable, sometimes (but surprisingly rarely) to the point of severe clinical depression. Where dyslexic unhappiness can differ from non-dyslexic unhappiness, however, is in its origins. It is often the dyslexia itself – with its powerful but indirect effects (not just the literacy problems) – that creates very singular forms of unhappiness in the dyslexic. If asked which dyslexics would benefit from counselling, I would say all those who are unhappy and who want to make changes in their life. It really is as simple as that.

Is dyslexic unhappiness just about not being able to read, write and spell?

No. This is a hopelessly inadequate and simplistic explanation. Problems with reading, writing and spelling are like a splinter in your foot. If the splinter is removed quickly, then there is some local pain but no long-term harm. But if the splinter is ignored, the effects can be unpredictable. If you are lucky, the body builds a protective carapace of toughened skin around the splinter, and you learn to live with it. If you are not so lucky, the splinter can lead to infection that not only poisons the whole body, but also disables you for life.

In the same way, dyslexic problems are minor if remediated early by sympathetic, specialist teaching, but if not, the wider, long-term effects can be unpredictable. Some dyslexics go on to cope perfectly well, and are simply toughened, rather than disabled, by their experiences. For others, dyslexia can lead to a wretched, reduced existence and lifelong unhappiness. Some dyslexic children have squandered their entire childhood living with the daily terror that their parents might stop loving them if they don't start to succeed. For others, school bullying can lead to ingrained victim behaviour that will contaminate a lifetime of relationships. Dyslexia can also cause unpredictable emotional fallout, emerging as sudden volcanic fury, bewildered isolation, feverish extroversion and numbing shyness. It can even distort family life, where a dyslexic child is circled by a frantic mother, an angry, critical father and jealous siblings, the whole mess leading to the dyslexic child being as isolated at home as they are at school.

Dyslexic children also become dyslexic parents who can struggle so hard to make things different for their own dyslexic child that they end up causing even more harm through overprotection. And there is many a dyslexic father who lies to his children about why he won't read them a bedtime story, and many a marriage where the dyslexic partner is blamed for having the 'bad gene' that 'infected' their children with dyslexia.

Dyslexia is also about the endless gnat-bites of daily hassles. These range from the frustration of not understanding recipes, equipment instructions, road signs and washing instructions, to the more serious side-effects of clumsiness, disorganisation, untidiness, forgetting and losing things, getting lost and being endlessly late so that vital appointments and even long-studied-for exams are missed.

How counselling helps

A counsellor cannot magic away the brutal facts of a dyslexic child's school life, or the waste of a dyslexic adult's abilities. On the other hand, just 'coming to terms with these problems' is not very helpful in the long run. After all, dyslexia will never leave the dyslexic. It is integral to their genes and their brain structure. It is there forever. Problems associated with dyslexia will not go away, so they must be faced, negotiated, re-framed, dismissed, laughed at, built around but not, I believe, just passively 'come to terms with'.

As a first step to this more proactive approach, a good counsellor will acknowledge the problems but also challenge the view that these problems are insuperable. This is especially important to a dyslexic child, and their parents, who need so much to see a way through; a transformation from 'dyslexic' to 'only dyslexic'.

Does child counselling differ from adult counselling?

To some extent. Feelings, for example, will be the main focus in most counselling. But the route to a feeling, and the thoughts and decisions that lead from it, can differ. While counselling of adults – including teenagers and students – will focus on adult relationships, work, further education and the thornier areas of substance addiction, with children the focus will be on the immediate problems of peers, teachers and bullying at school, family problems (dyslexic children can disrupt the family dynamic in spectacular ways), or simply learning social skills – such as more socially useful body language and speech patterns. (Although this is primarily aimed at child dyslexics, it is worth noting that 80 per cent of dyslexics are over 16 years old, and many older newly diagnosed dyslexics can benefit hugely from counselling – I remember an 83-year-old woman who was delighted to discover her dyslexia because now she would die 'dyslexic' and not 'stupid' or 'subnormal' as she had been labelled all her life.)

Counselling techniques

Technique is really is a matter of personal preference but, in my experience, approaches that concentrate on the thinking patterns behind a dyslexic's problems are very well suited to the dyslexic way of thinking.

Broadly, a counsellor working in this way will focus on what is going wrong in the dyslexic's life, understand how the problems might have arisen (particularly from early experiences which, for a dyslexic, will certainly include school), how and why they are still problems and, finally, how to make changes. The search for a way of doing things differently, of using more positive, creative strategies and 'Why not?' solutions is usually very appealing to the dyslexic way of thinking. For a change, they are using their dyslexic strengths, and they are using those strengths to help themselves.

This type of counselling works by making things clear. Not better, necessarily – at least not in the short run. But clear. And when things are clear, when dyslexics understand how they have become unhappy, when they see how the experiences they have had and the decisions they have made in their life have got them where they are – then they are equipped to make a choice about what to do next. With their counsellor by their side to support them, dyslexics can then choose to do things differently, and make dramatic changes in their lives.

A successful counselling relationship is also, in itself, beneficial to dyslexics. A good counselling relationship should be empathic, accepting, respectful, congruent, real and warm. But, for most dyslexics, the simple experience of having such a good relationship is valuable in its own right. Many dyslexics – child or adult – have few experiences of being properly listened to; of having their feelings acknowledged and their distressing history heard by someone who will not dismiss its sheer awfulness (as many parents can do). Dyslexic children may have had relatively few experiences of decent communication. They are not accustomed to being addressed courteously or listened to with genuine curiosity. So, a counselling relationship can also provide a new model of how they might expect to be treated by others.

Some counsellors do 'open-ended counselling' which takes a journey through the dyslexic's life, wherever they want to go, and lasts as long as they want it to. This may take months or years. More solution-focused (or cognitive-behavioural) therapies can be much shorter – just one to six sessions can be effective in some cases. You can negotiate what you want. Sessions can be one to one or you can find a therapy group.

How do I find a counsellor?

First of all, do remember word of mouth. Ask around. Children may also have access to a school counsellor, and universities have some of the best counselling support systems for dyslexic students, including specialist mentors and tutors. Doctors' surgeries may have a counsellor attached.

If you or your child wants private counselling, then you can try going through your private medical insurance, or, alternatively, contact the British Association for Counselling and Psychotherapy (BACP) who will give you a list of registered/accredited counsellors, along with their areas of expertise and contact details. These counsellors carry the BACP counselling kitemark, which means that they have the correct training and practise in a safe and ethical way.

Whoever you choose, trust your instincts. Arrange just one test session with a counsellor, and then do some thinking. Were they warm, likeable and trustworthy? Did you feel safe and accepted? Did your child enjoy the session and want to go back again? Remember that it is your time and your money. You are the customer, and you are in control.

Dr Rosemary Scott has worked with dyslexic children and adults for 20 years. She is co-proprietor, with Dr Michael Thomson, of East Court School for Dyslexic Children, a specialist school approved by the DfES for the education and care of dyslexic and dyspraxic children. Her Dyslexia and Counselling *was published by Whurr in 2004.*

Further information and help

See also Part 4: Useful contacts.

British Association for Counselling and Psychotherapy (BACP). Web: www.bacp.co.uk.
E-mail: bacp@bacp.co.uk. Tel: 0870 443 5252.
Address: BACP House, 35-37 Albert Street, Rugby, Warwickshire CV21 2SG

Dr Scott can be contacted at East Court School on 01843 592077, or e-mail: rscott@eastcourtschool.co.uk.

Occupational therapist

Parents are sometimes flummoxed about what an occupational therapist does. 'Occupational' doesn't explain itself as readily as 'speech and language' or 'physio', and it may conjure up images of basket-weaving or learning to type!

What does a paediatric occupational therapist do to help?

Frances Beaumont, occupational therapist and dyspraxia specialist

Occupational therapy can help a wide range of children, whether they have physical disabilities, behavioural problems or neural differences.

An occupational therapist will begin by assessing your child holistically – that is, they will look not just at the problems but the whole child and their environment. They assess the sensory skills, motor (muscle) control and understanding skills of your child. This will include some standardised tests, but don't worry, these are often more like games and usually very enjoyable!

The standardised test results are important if a statement of SEN is required, and they are also useful for the SENCo or additional needs co-ordinator (AENCo) at school. They should disseminate any relevant information to all the teachers who work with your child, but don't assume they automatically leap into action and put into place all or even anything that is recommended!

A diagnosis is often a relief and enables children to understand their strengths and difficulties in a new light, but treatment may be required to help them cope with life in and out of school. Treatment is usually recommended to help improve one or more of the following: sensory integration, balancing skills, fine motor skills (like handwriting), gross motor skills (like kicking a ball) hand-eye co-ordination, organisational skills. This is where occupational therapy comes in.

Occupational therapy in practice

Treatment can be fun, and might include exercises, games, learning strategies and self-care. It will be geared to the age of your child and their particular problem areas, and might involve:

- games such as 3D noughts and crosses and maze games to give practice with fine hand control
- throwing hoop games to improve hand-eye co-ordination and balance
- practising lace tying, buttons and zips on large toy versions
- games of strategy involving memory and sequencing
- looking at the seating and desk your child uses to see if it gives the correct support and writing angle.

Computer games – often the bane of many a parent's life – also have considerable value in the world of occupational therapy as a treatment tool.

An occupational therapist will also help older children to improve their organisational skills, devising strategies with your child to help conquer the confusing muddle in which neuro-diverse children so often find themselves without knowing why.

Achieving skills that once seemed impossible not only makes life easier and brighter on a practical level, it is a huge boost to self-esteem and sense of independence, which are all part of an occupational therapist's aims.

It is recognised that different teaching approaches are needed according to the way children experience the world. In some cases this may require additional training, and an occupational therapist can help in planning and classroom management.

Frances Beaumont, DipCOT, SROT, Cert Ed of Occupational Therapy Services, is an independent practitioner with over 30 years' experience of occupational therapy. She is also a trained teacher. She specialises in assessing children (from the age of 11), students, and adults with dyspraxia.

Compiled with thanks for comments from Wendy Clarke, Head Occupational Therapist, Mary Sheridan Centre, Canterbury, Kent CT1 3AT, and Jill Christmas, Independent Paediatric Occupational Therapist, Christmas Childrens' Clinic, Manor Road, Rusthall, Tunbridge Wells TN4 8UE.

Further information and help

OT Services. An independent occupational therapy website offering help and advice with dyspraxia assessments, stress management, medico-legal reports, disability advice, and design in the home, garden and workplace.
Web: www.otservices.co.uk.
E-mail: info@otservices.co.uk.
Tel/Fax: 01795 531998. Mobile: 07903 559888.
Address: OT Services, PO Box 198, Faversham, Kent ME13 7YQ

Occupational Therapists in Independent Practice (OTIP). A specialist section of the College of Occupational Therapists. The online Directory lists members of OTIP providing a wide range of services throughout the country. Web: www.otip.co.uk. Tel: 0800 389 4873

Orthoptist

Dr Nadia Northway, lecturer and researcher at Glasgow Caledonian University

You have probably heard of opticians and optometrists. Their primary role is in the prescription and dispensing of glasses. Orthoptists do a completely different job; they are specially trained in how the eyes work as a pair, how the eyes are controlled and how we use vision.

A large proportion of orthoptic work is concerned with squints and the visual development of young children. Orthoptists have a detailed knowledge of the eye and the muscles systems which control the eyes. They commonly see patients of all ages who are experiencing difficulty with control of their vision, such as blurring and flickering, seeing patterns or double vision. (See the section 'Vision and reading problems' in Chapter 2 for more on the difficulties that can be experienced and their causes.)

How to find an orthoptist

There are about 1,000 orthoptists registered in the UK. Most are based in hospitals but they also carry out their work in the community.

I would strongly advise anyone experiencing reading problems or eye problems that are not due to any sort of visual impairment to see an orthoptist. You will need to get a GP referral to your local orthoptic department. You may see an optometrist (optician) and an ophthalmologist (eye doctor) in addition to the orthoptist. They are all part of the eye-care team and have specialised roles.

How an orthoptist can help

An orthoptist will test for a variety of possible causes for vision problems. Difficulties with binocular vision are common with dyslexics and some other conditions, and so they will measure how well the eyes are held straight, how well and quickly they adjust their focusing and the eyes' fusion. Fusion is the 'glue' which allows the two eyes to work in unison for prolonged periods. Measuring this and comparing it to normal ranges shows the amount of drifting of the eyes.

One treatment that you may already associate with orthoptics is a temporary eye patch. This occlusion therapy (as it is more formally known) was traditionally followed when a test called the Dunlop test showed unstable fixation (the inability of the eye to look steadily at something) or lack of eye dominance. The Dunlop test has been shown to be unreliable and orthoptists now use alternative methods such as symptom and history documentation (although some orthoptists still use the Dunlop to aid diagnosis). Although the Dunlop test itself is less popular, recent research has shown that occlusion can improve reading function and is the treatment of choice to improve ocular dominance and fixation.

An orthoptist will also check eye movements and tracking ability (ie following a line of writing). The developmental eye movement test compares a person's ability to read vertical numbers with horizontal numbers and also gives an indication of automaticity (the ability to see and say out loud).

Some problems an orthoptist deals with are to do with automatic muscle control and co-ordination, while others relate to how our brain reacts to what it sees. MIS (Meares-Irlen syndrome; see the section 'Vision and reading problems' in Chapter 2) is caused by a heightened sensitivity to pattern. This can be treated firstly by using coloured overlays, and subsequently by using precision coloured lenses. The colour required for an overlay may be different from that in lenses and a special assessment is needed to find the correct colour for spectacles (see Cerium under 'Further information and help' below). Most orthoptists working in the NHS can assess patients for MIS using overlays. Some have access to a colorimeter but others will know of an optometrist or orthoptist in your area who can provide tinted lenses if they are required. An increase in reading speed or tracking is used to determine that the correct colour has been selected and that this is a useful form of treatment for you.

Orthoptists and dyslexia

Some orthoptists have more specialised knowledge of dyslexia than others, but the British and Irish Orthoptic Society has a specialist interest group with a list of members interested in and working in the field of specific learning difficulties including dyslexia and dyspraxia. Your local orthoptist should be able to seek out a colleague in their area who can help dyslexic readers.

Dr Nadia Northway has always had an interest in dyslexia and has a degree in educational studies. She has completed a PhD on visual function in dyslexia. She is an adviser to the British and Irish Orthoptic Society on dyslexia. She has her own company which sees patients and develops material for use by other practitioners in the field of dyslexia. Her clinic within the university, which specialises in assessing vision in people with reading and writing difficulties, sees patients from all over the UK. It has grown considerably since it started as a research project in 1997. Dr Northway and her team of orthoptists see around 800 patients a year – children and adults with dyslexia, dyspraxia, autism, brain injury, migraine, cerebral palsy and other medical conditions.

Further information and help

See also Part 4: Useful contacts.

British and Irish Orthoptic Society
Web: www.orthoptics.org.uk.
E-mail: bos@orthoptics.org.uk.
Tel: 020 7387 7992. Fax: 020 7387 2584.

Address: Tavistock House North, Tavistock Square, London WC1H 9HX

The society is aiming to publish a Code of Conduct this year. Optometrists and orthoptists with an interest in dyslexia can sign up to the code if they meet the criteria. Practitioners who sign up to the code will only carry out treatments which have a scientific basis and will keep themselves up to date in the field of reading difficulty and dyslexia. This should give anyone seeking advice peace of mind that the person they are seeing is knowledgeable and complying with professional guidelines.

Cerium Visual Technologies. Provides a list of people with the specialist MIS equipment in the UK.
Web: www.ceriumvistech.com.
E-mail: CeriumUK@ceriumvistech.co.uk.
Tel: 01580 765211. Fax: 01580 765573.
Address: Cerium Group Headquarters,
Cerium Technology Park, Tenterden, Kent TN30 7DE

Rainbow Readers. Dr Northway's very useful website.
Web: www.rainbowreaders.co.uk.
E-mail: admin@rainbowreaders.co.uk.
Tel: 07776 191628

Physiotherapy – the motor way to learning

Sally Wright, specialist in neurological and neuro-developmental disorders

Most people are aware that physiotherapy helps children to improve their muscle tone, core stability, balance, posture and co-ordination. Fine – but how can physiotherapy help children with special educational needs become successful learners?

Perhaps the clearest way of explaining is to look at physiotherapists' developmental framework of reference, which we use to work out where to start and what gaps need to be filled in children's learning.

Imagine a tiered pyramid. The top tier is academic learning, but it is supported by several underlying 'themes' of vital developmental tiers.

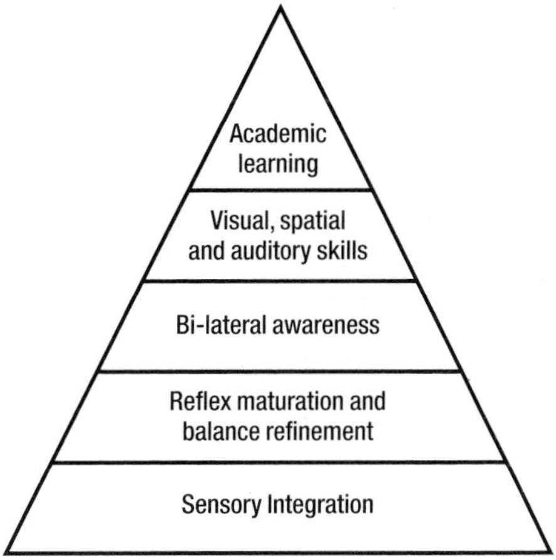

The bottom tier

Sensory integration is a complex neural process. It starts in the womb and is the process by which we process sensations, not just from our five senses, but also muscles (proprioception) and balance receptors (vestibular). All this information is registered, filtered and integrated in the brain to result in movements becoming more and more refined and appropriate. It is a normal process, ongoing throughout life, but is particularly active in children up to the age of 7 years.

Second tier

Reflex maturation, refinement of balance, posture, postural organisation and motor planning. This develops as a result of the child's active interaction with their physical environment and through active problem solving. For example a child has to 'work out' how to climb up onto the sofa and it is through this working out that new neural connections are made and reinforced. Of course some children with special educational needs can't work out how to do this by themselves and they may need to be taken through the movements first – this is something we may do as part of physiotherapy treatment

Third tier

Awareness of the two sides of the body involves developing a preferred hand, learning to co-ordinate the two sides of the body together in actions and learning to co-ordinate the eyes and hands – in other words more sophisticated refinement of motor skills.

Fourth tier

To interpret information we see and hear we need to develop our visual, spatial and auditory perceptual skills. Children start to be able to make abstract judgements about things, such as recognising a cube just by seeing it because earlier they have handled the cube and looked at it form various different angles.

Putting it all together

In reality these tiers are not separate but rather a jigsaw that gradually fits together as the baby learns to overcome gravity, walk, negotiate its environment and handle tools and toys successfully. Physiotherapists work mostly in the first, second and third tiers of this developmental pyramid.

Sensory integration is both a theory and a treatment approach and is used by both paediatric physiotherapists and paediatric occupational therapists. We believe sensory integration is the fundamental foundation from which all learning arises.

Integrating sensations are basic prerequisites for successful academic learning, because it means that children can

- sit still
- shift attention appropriately
- make sense of what they see and hear
- develop a preferred hand
- develop fine and gross motor sills to a good enough degree, for example, to control a pencil.

Children need to be posturally and emotionally secure so that they can attend to instructions and concentrate on what they have to do. They should also have acquired some basic organisational skills. Children who haven't mastered these fundamentals find themselves at a disadvantage in the classroom.

Why do children have these problems?

Some have a recognised genetic disorder, some have suspected genetic disorder but as yet unrecognised, while others have suffered some form of brain damage or brain abnormality. This can be genetic, or due to complications during pregnancy, birth or after the birth. Poor feeding can be an indicator of future difficulties, as can excessive crying, irritability or poor sleep patterns.

The good news is that there is always something positive that can be done to help your child, and a physiotherapist with the right area of specialisation can contribute to that.

How does physiotherapy work for children with SEN?

Most children with SEN and associated physiotherapy needs will have some problem with the way the network of 'wires' in their brain connects up. Ideally, this network becomes increasingly more efficient as the child problem-solves its way through developmental challenges. But if a child's brain is not as successful at reinforcing the most successful neural pathways, messages will travel along extended routes, increasing the time for processing, or information may not reach the required destination or may go to the wrong destination. Problems with this sort of development include developmental co-ordination disorder and dyspraxia (see Chapter 2). These children have more difficulty adapting their behaviour appropriately and thus may have difficulties with academic learning.

Fortunately the brain has the capacity to re-route connections, and physiotherapy (like occupational therapy) can help this in various ways.

We can work to strengthen muscles that have never been worked properly.

Isabel, for example, had low muscle tone. This meant she never tipped her pelvis back as she reached for her feet. This had affected the alignment of her pelvis and meant her abdominal muscles were overly long and weaker than average. The right exercises helped improve her muscular strength and alignment. Jake also had low muscle tone, and as a baby had spent more time sitting than moving in and out of the hands-and-knees position. Because of this his trunk muscles were shorter than average and he seldom twisted his body sideways. This made it difficult for him to carry out co-ordinated actions between the two sides of the body.

Physiotherapists can work to improve balance and postural control by improving a child's core stability and equilibrium responses. Sometimes we have to passively take children through motor patterns before they can learn to do by themselves and later automatically as the pathways in the brain forge new and more effective connections .

General Information about physiotherapists

All NHS hospitals have a paediatric physiotherapy department, which can be accessed via referral through GPs or medical consultants. Private physiotherapists can be accessed directly by parents but most will notify the child's GP or consultant as best practice.

Most children with SEN will need to locate a physiotherapist with neuro-developmental experience. Physio-therapists with this specialised expertise work with many children who have cerebral palsy, developmental delay, prematurity, Down's syndrome and similar conditions. We are trained to assess muscle tone, muscle strength, muscle balance, posture, balance, co-ordination and neuro-development. We work to develop the background posture, alignment and balance the children need to carry out all motor skills. By guiding children's muscular and neural development along the right path we aim to prevent later problems as well as helping to put right difficulties that have already arisen. We'll work on components of skills and then integrate these into skills training. One important benefit of building up children's physical confidence is that they gain self-esteem too.

More specialised paediatric neuro-developmental physiotherapists work with children who have dyspraxia, developmental co-ordination disorder (DCD), dyslexia, Asperger's syndrome and related conditions. These physiotherapists are likely to be trained in sensory integration and may extend their work into the top two tiers of the pyramid. At this level of specialisation there is a degree of overlap with paediatric occupational therapists.

Finding a physiotherapist

When finding the right physiotherapist for your child, begin with the following questions:

Are you a chartered physiotherapist?

Chartered physiotherapists will have MCSP (Member of the Chartered Society of Physiotherapy) and SRP (State Registered Physiotherapist) after their name. This means they will have completed a recognised undergraduate training and will be properly insured to carry out physiotherapy work.

What experience have you had working with children with (describe your particular child's difficulties)?

All children with special educational needs will need a physiotherapist with paediatric experience but not all need highly specialised paediatric physiotherapists. It depends on the complexity of the case.

What tools/frameworks of reference do you use in your work?

All paediatric physiotherapists will use a developmental framework of reference but some may also have training in sensory integration.

Of course you need a physiotherapist with the relevant paediatric and neuro-developmental expertise but, as with any form of therapy, you need to feel that they have a highly positive attitude and a personality with which both you and your child feel confident and secure. The relationship your child develops with a therapist is very important, especially if there are also emotional difficulties.

For your part, physiotherapy will probably mean not just fitting in sessions with a therapist but working through or encouraging your child with a programme of exercises between visits. Much of the benefits of physiotherapy come from repeated practice!

What does a physiotherapist do?

An initial assessment involves:

- Establishing concerns.
- Finding out background medical, developmental and family history.
- Detailed evaluation of muscles and joints including strength, length, alignment; core stability; posture in sitting and standing; neuro-development including anti-gravity ability and co-ordination; balance responses and gross motor skills. Specialist physiotherapists like myself would also evaluate sensory integration, writing, fine motor skills and visual perceptual skills.
- Interpretation of findings taking early medical and developmental history into consideration.
- Feedback to parents.
- Advice about how we can help.
- Decision with parent about plan of action.

Treatment depends on what each child may need, and might involve advice and a programme to follow at home, or weekly treatment plus home programme, or perhaps an intensive course of treatment. Children can be seen individually or in small groups and may be seen in clinics, at home or in school. The length of time children will need to attend for physiotherapy depends on the age of the child, need, and practical considerations such as whom else the child is seeing. The average length of time I would work with a 6-year-old who has developmental co-ordination disorder in my practice would be two to three terms.

Treatment is goal directed and our aim is to improve skills needed for more successful learning. Typical goals might be:

- to re-train writing so their hand doesn't hurt
- to improve posture so their back doesn't hurt
- to improve ball skills
- to help them use cutlery more easily
- to improve their strength and stamina so they are not so tired by the end of the day
- to improve their sitting posture by working to improve core stability
- to improve their visual tracking by working on balance and bilateral co-ordination.

Many parents talk about a 'halo' effect from treatment and notice that is not just the goals of treatment that improve but self-esteem and confidence, thinking skills and concentration. Going back to our tiered pyramid, this makes sense as consolidating those abilities in the lower tiers makes a stronger foundation for the higher tiers.

Most children really enjoy their treatment, even though it is hard work. Therapists are very good at adapting the activities to make them fun and always aim to develop the child's self-esteem and self-confidence. For some children it is the highlight of their week and they literally run in to the treatment room desperate to start. It is an opportunity for them to improve in a safe, empathetic environment where they can trust enough to risk success.

The best result for us is to hear a child cry excitedly: 'I did it!!!'

Sally Wright, MCSP, SRP, works with a group of paediatric occupational therapists and paediatric physiotherapists. The practice is based in London W8 and NW10 and specialises in helping children with neurological and neuro-developmental disorders. Tel: 020 8208 1361 for further information.

Further information and help

Chartered Society of Physiotherapists.
Web: www.csp.org.uk. Tel: 020 7306 6666.
Address: 14 Bedford Row, London WC1R 4ED

Speech and language therapist

Katherine Tweedie, specialist in specific language impairment

Communication is central to the learning process – it is the main tool for teaching, learning and building relationships. So a child who is experiencing any sort of difficulty in this area, perhaps having trouble in making themselves understood, embarrassment over a speech impediment, or difficulty understanding the meaning of what people are saying to them, is likely to find not only lessons but social interaction a struggle.

Speech and language therapists (SaLTs) work with children with a range of communication difficulties, ideally working in partnership with parents and teachers to maximise the child's communication and learning skills.

Who can benefit from seeing an SaLT?

An estimated one in ten children experience a communication difficulty. The type of difficulty can be very different, for example:

- Difficulty with speech sounds. It might be hard to work out what a child is trying to say if they have problems with specific sounds – for example, a 4-year-old who says 'tat' instead of 'cat'.
- Problems with spoken language. Some children use less vocabulary than their peers or their utterances are jumbled and immature. They may also have problems understanding spoken language.
- Social communication difficulties. For some children the problem lies with the pragmatic aspects of communication, for example using and interpreting facial

expression and eye contact. They may tend to take things too literally.

■ Stammering: children who get 'stuck' when talking. They might repeat part of a word or a whole word or struggle to start off a sentence.

While some children have a specific communication difficulty in just one area and generally good development otherwise, therapists also see children whose speech and language difficulties are part of additional learning, physical or medical difficulties.

Because of their specialist knowledge of speech and oral anatomy, therapists also work with babies and children who have difficulty in eating, drinking or swallowing. A child who is inclined to choke easily on lumpy food, for example, may be referred to an SaLT, whose role will be to assess and provide advice. This may involve liaison with other professionals such as a dietician.

What will happen on my child's first session?

The therapist will want to gather as much information as possible about your child's skills and difficulties. They need to know about their general development and hearing skills as well as, for instance, when your child said their first words. It helps the therapist to know about your child's strengths as well as the things they find hard – what sort of toys and games they enjoy, what they quickly tire of. Sessions can then be geared to the most effective way of reaching and helping your child in a way that they enjoy and respond to.

The therapist may ask to talk to other professionals involved with your child, such as teaching staff. This is important as it helps them gain a better understanding of your child and how they communicate in different situations.

Throughout the session the therapist will be assessing your child's communication skills. With a young child this may be through play and observation, while older children may complete a more formal assessment. Some tests provide standardised scores, which help the therapist decide whether a child's skills are appropriate for their age. You and the therapist will then discuss together whether your child will benefit from therapy and what form this should take.

How will the therapist work with my child?

SaLTs work with children in a variety of ways. This may mean one-to-one sessions or group sessions. Parents sometimes worry that a group will amount to 'watered down' therapy. In fact, group sessions can be very effective, provided the group meets your child's specific needs.

As well as working directly with a child, therapists work indirectly. This might take the form of home or school activities and advice to parents and teachers – therapists also provide formal training and workshops for parents and professionals. It makes sense for all the key adults in your child's life to know how best to support your child's skills.

Some schools have regular visits from therapists, or even resident therapists. Work with your child in the classroom can be of considerable benefit, because it is desirable to establish good communication everywhere.

Case studies

The names and specific personal details of these children are fictional, but they closely reflect the experiences of children who are frequently seen by SaLTs.

Sarah

Sarah first saw an SaLT shortly after her fourth birthday. Her parents were able to understand her, but knew that unfamiliar listeners often found it hard to work out what she was saying. One of the specific difficulties she had was in pronouncing the /f/ sound. Sarah's parents and the therapist decided that it would be a good idea to refer Sarah for a second hearing check. The therapist also showed Sarah's parents how to help her make an /f/ sound, while playing a game.

Sarah began going to the speech and language clinic for a weekly session with five other children. They played games that helped them listen and use particular speech sounds. Sarah's mum watched and joined in with some of the sessions so that she knew how to help Sarah practise the activities at home.

With Sarah soon to start school, her parents were worried that her teachers would not be able to understand her, and whether learning to read would be difficult. They talked this through with the therapist, and it was agreed that information and advice would be sent to her new teachers. Sarah attended a review appointment shortly after starting school; she was now using the /f/ sound, which made her easier to understand, and with the understanding teachers had of her difficulties she had also settled into school well, to her parents' relief.

Peter

Peter moved to a new school when he was 13 years old; he had just received a diagnosis of Asperger's syndrome. The SaLT who worked in his new school came to see Peter a few weeks after he started. They talked about the things he was interested in, what he liked and didn't like about school, and who his friends were. Peter's whole class had a session once a week with the therapist and their teacher, each week practising a different social communication skill. One week, for example, they practised 'making a compromise'. They talked about why this was important, and role-played situations in which the children had to agree a compromise. Peter found that specifically thinking and practising difficult social situations helped him get on with his peers.

Ben

Ben's parents first took him to see an SaLT when he was 2 years old. They were worried because he had not yet started using any words. The therapist suggested encouraging his first spoken words by using signs. To start with his parents decided to use ten signs, which related to things Ben often wanted to talk about. They continued to learn more signs together, and gradually they found that Ben started to use the signs as well. Later, when he was able, Ben said the word and dropped the sign.

Before Ben started school it was agreed that a teaching assistant (TA) would be able to support him in his first year. Ben's parents and his TA attended a course on signing and using visual symbols, run by the SaLT, and Ben's therapist came to visit him at school in his first term. The therapist, his TA and teacher planned how to adapt the teaching environment for Ben, as a result of which Ben enjoyed his first year in school and his teachers were confident that he was participating and learning.

Katherine Tweedie works for Bexhill and Rother NHS Primary Care Trust, working in community clinics in Bexhill and Hastings and in a language unit attached to a mainstream school.

Further information

See also Part 4: Useful contacts.

ASLTIP (Association of Speech and Language Therapists in Independent Practice). All ASLTIP therapists are Registered Members of RCSLT and registered with the Health Professions Council.
Web: www.helpwithtalking.com.
E-mail: asltip@awdry.demon.co.uk.
Tel (answerphone): 0870 241 3357.
Fax: 01494 488590.
Address: WSS Coleheath Bottom, Speen,
Princes Risborough, Buckinghamshire HP27 0SZ

Royal College of Speech and Language Therapists (RCSLT).
Web: www.rcslt.org. E-mail: postmaster@rcslt.org.
Tel: 020 7378 1200. Fax: 020 7403 7254.
Address: 2 White Hart Yard, London SE1 1NX

Music therapist

Dr Ann Woodward, music therapist

Music therapy helps children communicate, interact and express their feelings. It makes use of the innate musicality that all humans have: babies respond to music even before they are born, and respond to and join in with the musical elements of speech (such as tone of voice, turn taking and so on) long before they understand or use words. Music can be fun, engaging and playful, and the ability to respond to and engage with music can remain despite disability. Music allows children to develop their non-verbal communication, or to put into music feelings that would be hard to express in words.

What are the aims of music therapy?

The aims of music therapy vary according to a child's individual needs, but might include:

- developing communication and interaction (verbal and non-verbal)
- encouraging the use of the voice
- self-expression
- developing awareness of self and others
- increasing self-confidence

- developing skills such as listening, turn taking and sharing
- developing co-ordination and motor control
- providing emotional support.

Music therapy does not aim to teach musical skills. Rather, it uses music as a way to open up communication and to facilitate positive change.

What happens in a music therapy session?

Music therapy may be on an individual or group basis, depending on the needs of a child. Typically, a child will have music therapy once a week, and sessions last between about 20 minutes and an hour, depending on their age and needs. Although different therapists work in slightly different ways (and vary their approach to meet the needs of each child), central to any approach is the development of a relationship between the child and therapist.

Music making is the main tool for developing this relationship, and usually both the child and the therapist make music together. Often, this music will be improvised. This means that it is spontaneously created, with the therapist responding to the sounds and movements that the child makes. The music therapist may also use musical activities to focus on particular aims, such as turn taking, listening or awareness of others.

Sometimes, and particularly with very young children, parents may be invited to attend their child's sessions. This can nurture the parent-child relationship and help positive change to transfer into other settings.

Who can benefit from music therapy?

Children of any age and ability can benefit from music therapy. Usually the therapist will start by doing a music therapy assessment to find out if the child is likely to respond, and to identify the areas in which it might be helpful. Children do not need any musical ability or training to benefit. Here are a few examples of children who have benefited from music therapy (all names and identifying information have been changed to protect confidentiality).

Alisha is a 16-year-old girl with Rett syndrome. She was not able to talk, and had little control of her hands or feet. Alisha's music therapy aimed to give her ways of interacting and communicating, and motivating her to use her hands and feet. Alisha sometimes made very quiet vocal sounds, and the therapist responded to these by singing an answer. Alisha quickly realised that the therapist was responding to her. She was very engaged by this and began to use her voice more, in short turn-taking exchanges.

When sitting in her wheelchair, Alisha was able to move her feet a little, so the therapist positioned some wind chimes near them so that even a small movement would produce a sound. The therapist responded in a dramatic way on the piano to any sounds or movements that Alisha made. Alisha was delighted to be able to have this effect, and this motivated her to try to move her feet more.

Jamie has Down's syndrome. At 4 he was very shy and usually played by himself. He and his mother attended a music therapy group for five children and their parents which took place each week at Jamie's school. The group's aims included developing interaction, awareness, communication and self-confidence. One activity was a game where everyone had to stop and start playing together, following the 'leader'. At first Jamie did not want to lead the group, but after a few weeks his confidence grew and he was able to have a go. He quickly realised that he could direct the group's stops and starts, and he really enjoyed doing this in a playful way. This game helped him develop his awareness of other children and his ability to interact with them in a way that he felt comfortable with. Jamie's mum also valued the group as it gave her a chance to develop her relationship with her son, and to meet other parents of children with special needs.

Martin is a bright 13-year-old with Asperger's syndrome. Acutely aware that he was different from his peers, he was struggling to understand and come to terms with his diagnosis. Martin was often very angry, and felt that he did not fit in. Through improvising with the music therapist, Martin was able to express and share some of his feelings in a constructive way. The sessions provided a setting where Martin knew he could safely express difficult feelings, and that he would be heard and accepted by another person. Having put his feelings into the music, Martin was then able to begin to talk about how he felt. Gradually, over the course of a year, Martin's confidence developed. He began to come to terms with his diagnosis, and to feel hopeful about the future.

Where to find a musical therapist

Many special schools and some mainstream schools employ a music therapist, so your child might be offered music therapy in school. Some assessment units or child development centres have a music therapist on their team, so you might also come across a music therapist in this context. Some music therapists work in private practice. Before you take your child to a private music therapist, check that they are registered with the Health Professions Council (see 'Further information and help' below). If they are not registered with the HPC, they are not a qualified music therapist.

Dr Ann Woodward qualified as a music therapist in 1996. Since then she has worked as a music therapist in mainstream and special schools with children of all ages and abilities. For six years Ann was an Executive Committee member of the Association of Professional Music Therapists, and she worked with the Health Professions Council to develop the music therapy profession's standards of proficiency. She has a particular interest in autism, and has worked for the charity Resources for Autism since 2000. In January 2005 she became its Director of Resources for Autism, but she still continues with some hands-on work as a music therapist.

Further information and help

Association of Professional Music Therapists (APMT). The professional body for music therapists in the UK. The APMT can help you find a music therapist near to you.
Web: www.apmt.org. E-mail: APMToffice@aol.com.
Tel/Fax: 020 8440 4153.
Address: 61 Church Hill Road, East Barnet, Hertfordshire EN4 8SY

British Society for Music Therapy (BSMT). A charity promoting the use and development of music therapy. It is a source of information about music therapy.
Web: www.bsmt.org. E-mail: info@bsmt.org.
Tel: 020 8441 6226.
Address: 61 Church Hill Road, East Barnet, Hertfordshire EN4 8SY

Health Professions Council. Website includes an online register of qualified music therapists.
Web: www.hpc-uk.org. Tel: 020 7582 0866

The SENCo

Most schools have one yet until relatively recently few of us had even heard of them – so just what is a SENCo?

A SENCo or special educational needs co-ordinator is the person who will advise you of how the school can/will meet your child's additional requirements. If you have a child with special needs, whether the merest niggle of an speech problem or more grave and inhibiting difficulties, consider any visit to a school incomplete without a chat to the head (find out what they really feel about SEN, rather than what they have to say in order to stay within the confines of the law) and a meeting with the SENCo. If your child's needs amount to more than a minor concern the SENCo may well be the person you spend copious amounts of time phoning, chasing, talking to ... Any SENCo worth their salt will at the very least have an empathetic ear and a man-sized box of tissues.

So what does a SENCo actually do?

In a nutshell most try hard to ensure a child with SEN has their needs met as fully as possible. As with all, there are the good, the bad and the ugly, but fortunately (in our experience) the vast majority of SENCos fall into the first category. However, the reality of budgetary and other constraints can make life hard for both you and them.

Once your child is placed in a school they may be assigned help from someone other than the SENCo. However, the SENCo will still be involved and should have a good understanding of a child's needs and requirements. The SENCo takes responsibility for what should be the effective operation and implementation of the school's SEN policy. This is done by identifying, assessing, planning for, monitoring, managing and supporting SEN.

In English state schools a SENCo will ensure all staff follow the Code of Practice. They will ensure that regular observations of children with SEN take place and are acted on. This may involve the development of support programmes to meet needs and break down barriers to learning. For some children an individual education plan (IEP) or individual learning programme (ILP) will be deemed appropriate. These should be monitored and reviewed regularly. Records of all children with SEN should be kept up to date with relevant background information added. A child does not need to have a statement or record of need to be supported by the SENCo but in English state schools it is likely a child in need of SEN support will be placed on School Action or School Action Plus (see Chapter 6).

Competent SENCos consult and liaise with staff, parents and carers, external agencies and appropriate professionals and voluntary bodies to ensure support is coordinated and targeted appropriately. They manage learning support staff, and advise and support other practitioners (therapists etc). Usually they will provide professional guidance to staff who support children with SEN and often they contribute to appropriate in-service training.

Most importantly, the really good SENCos listen to others, especially parents!

One SENCo's story

Maureen Whitehead, Malsis Prep School, North Yorkshire

When my daughter was 8 years old she had the luck to encounter a new teacher, with a new type of training, who immediately pointed out that my daughter was dyslexic. Feeling remorseful over the three years of unbelievable friction during homework sessions and wracked by memories of children who had passed through my care (as a primary school teacher) who could possibly have been aided by the type of teaching advocated by the Dyslexia Institute, I was fired up with determination to do my best in this sphere of education. I set out to further improve my, obviously at that point, inadequate teaching skills by studying for the British Dyslexia Association Diploma and my daughter and I became best friends.

In the early days the SENCo could be spotted fairly easily in the staff room. This was the teacher in the corner, on their knees, in an attitude of fervent prayer. The role was often foisted on an unsuspecting member of staff whose only qualifications for the post were a kind heart and willing nature. They battled against staff of the 'old school' whose type of teaching did not lend itself to differentiation, meaning that the whole class had to fit into the lesson plan whether it was suitable for them or not.

Fortunately things have changed dramatically. Independent schools are required to take note of legislation, which previously they could ignore. Excellent guidelines are now in place for the adoption of a whole-school special needs policy and it would be remarkable to find an independent school that does not attend carefully to the drawing up and execution of such a document; even a highly academic school cannot be exempt from a special needs policy, which is there to benefit all child-ren – the gifted and talented, students with Asperger's syndrome and the highly intelligent 'hidden' dyslexics all will need this security if they are to make the most of their potential and leave school as well-balanced individuals.

Training is now readily available for the role of SENCo and this training is usually best undertaken by a learning support teacher who has gained experience of teaching children with special needs and is confident enough to take on the staff. Less of a battleground atmosphere exists nowadays thanks to far better awareness, but staff will often require the same comfort and guidance as the children on the Special Needs Register. Having one child with attention deficit hyperactivity disorder within the class can mean minute-by-minute monitoring on the part of the teacher who has already differentiated the lesson to suit other children with special needs. A kind heart and willing nature continue to be good assets, but are complemented by training to give support wherever it is needed: to the children, the staff and the parents.

Ensuring your child will receive the full care necessary to proceed down the academic road requires diligent homework and detailed, searching questions during interview. My daughter's senior schoolteachers were blissfully unaware that she was dyslexic until the first parent/staff meeting during her third term. This lack of communication between head and staff was regrettable. There were indeed extenuating circumstances but this did not appease an irate mother who had to listen to the staff's uninformed opinions on her daughter's abilities!

Maureen Whitehead is Head of Learning Support and the SENCo of Malsis Prep School (a Good Schools Guide *school), a school praised for its excellent SEN provision in its recent Independent Schools Inspectorate report.*

Two-way street

A conscientious SENCo will do their best to ensure that all staff are informed and updated about children on the SEN register and that all have an understanding of how best to help the child. A SENCo will help individual staff draw up IEPs if appropriate (see Chapter 6), ensure they are regularly reviewed, and keep everyone – you and your child as well as teachers – informed and involved. The SENCo will also work closely with support staff and outside agencies, therapists and other professionals to ensure a child's needs are met.

SENCos rely on parents' help and support too: if you are aware that your child has any kind of difficulty, inform the staff at the earliest opportunity (preferably before the child starts at the school) and hand over all relevant documentation. This will give staff time to put plans in place to ensure a smooth integration into the new school environment. If you think there may be something holding your child back, express those concerns. Pretesting can highlight hindrances to learning that can usually be addressed. This openness will be much appreciated, especially by the SENCo.

Teaching assistants and learning support assistants

Traditionally, a teaching assistant (TA) assists the teacher, and a learning support assistant (LSA) provides support, sometimes quite specialised, to an individual child or group. However, the roles and titles have become blurred and are interchangeable. The DfES uses the term teaching assistant and has introduced higher level teaching assistants (HLTAs); these are qualified personnel who may take on added responsibilities. In Scotland the term auxiliary may be used for supporting children with special educational needs. Other terms used include curriculum assistant and classroom assistant.

Whatever their job title, assistants are taking on increasingly important roles within the classroom. Most work towards nationally recognised qualifications. They are not a replacement for a trained teacher who should maintain overall responsibility for the teaching and learning of all children in their care. A teaching/learning support assistant works alongside them on agreed targets and, given adequate training and support, may help with the acquisition of new skills. As well as offering in-class support an LSA or TA may be involved with assessment and record keeping, lesson planning and preparation and the modification of teaching and learning materials to meet specific needs.

Teaching/learning support assistants can support pupils of all ages, but their input depends on a number of factors. These include the age of the pupil, the nature of the difficulty and the context in which they are being educated. Their role is far-reaching and varied. Often they will assist a child with organisation, helping them to become more self-reliant over time. Typically they will help a child achieve behavioural objectives in and out of lessons.

A bridge not a barrier

In most cases the aim of extra support is to give a child access to the mainstream curriculum (though possibly not the whole programme of study). Work shouldn't be too different from that undertaken by the rest of the class but may be adapted to take account of learning need. The assistant acts as a bridge, helping with what they need to do to get from where they are currently to where they want to be. An assistant may ensure different learning styles are adopted, perhaps kinaesthetic, visual, practical, or act as a scribe or amanuensis to help the child achieve the learning objectives.

An assistant shouldn't be a barrier to the child working with other children, and all good ones are aware that the more success the child achieves, the less reliant they will be on their support.

It's easy for a child to cling to their support, but while a good assistant will offer social and emotional support, they will at the same time encourage a child to develop friendship groups and rely less on the help and support of others in doing so. Helping a child develop independence in all aspects of life is a key part of the role, and this includes allowing a child to make mistakes and to look for ways to solve problems rather than just being told the right answers or solutions. Rather than taking over when a child is struggling to achieve something, they will offer the tools to help the child to succeed.

The success of TA/LSA support is dependent on close liaison between the teaching staff and the whole school's determination that the pupil be a fully included member from the outset. What must be avoided is the situation where an assistant is 'glued' to the side of a pupil, in the mistaken belief that this is the only way of giving adequate support. Nothing could be further from the truth, as this leads only to dependency, reduced interaction between the teacher and the pupil and their peers, and lowered self-esteem. Effective support will enable the pupil to develop the skills necessary to become an independent learner, competent, confident and valued within the school and the wider community.

A teaching assistant in action

Kathryn Lees, a TA who supports pupils with visual impairment

Good support for the pupil with visual impairment does not remain the same throughout their school career; it constantly evolves to meet the demands of the curriculum and to take into account the developing skills and independence of the pupil.

In nursery, a TA may help to foster the child's natural curiosity, by encouraging them to explore the environment safely, developing language and reasoning. They may help the pupil with practical tasks such as learning to put on, button and unbutton their coat and change into their PE kit.

Once a child moves into the Foundation Stage the role will be to assist in developing the new skills, which are required to access the curriculum. Depending on the type of visual impairment and what adaptations are necessary, I will produce reading books and class material in large print or Braille. Planning with the class teacher and, possibly, a specialist teacher for pupils with visual impairment will have identified how to prepare these in the most appropriate way, and I allocate time to produce them to a high standard. Once they are available the pupil can take part in the class activities along with the other members of the class. Good support at this stage may mean working with the child on the additional curriculum, ie Braille, reinforcing new skills that have previously been taught by the class or specialist teacher.

In the next few years in primary school a touch-typing programme might be introduced, using a screen-reading program such as Jaws or Supernova. I may help the pupil to practise these skills, which can prove invaluable in the years to come, both in terms of speed and presentation of work. The teacher will give me the class's work well in advance so that I can prepare it in a suitable format and return it before the relevant lesson. This ensures that pupils with visual impairment receive their work at the same time as their peers. This introduces more formality and structure into the system and reduces the need for in-class support. Developing this independence now will smooth the transition to high school.

At high school the emphasis will be on the preparation of the vast range of curriculum materials. Again, I will prepare these in advance after close consultation with the teacher. Materials might include tactile maps, diagrams, graphs and charts. I may also be involved in pre-teaching, revision and study skills sessions if these have been identified as a priority, and may act as a scribe or a reader in examinations (with the permission of the examinations board). I may also help the pupil to access the Internet and, at A level, act as a research assistant!

Kathryn Lees is a teaching assistant working for Harrow Sensory and Communication Team (VI), in north London. Her post is centrally funded so she can work in different schools and is deployed where her particular skills are most needed. Kathryn is a Braillist, as are all the centrally funded TAs in this authority, and she uses technology to produce many of the materials needed for pupils. Kathryn is a major source of support to new TAs, especially during their induction period. She has provided assistance to pupils with a wide range of visual impairment across the age range, and over the years has supported, among many others, a Braillist in a sixth form, a pupil who used both Braille and large print in a secondary school, and a pupil with some additional needs in a primary school. She can be seen and heard on a DVD produced by the DfES as part of the induction pack for TAs.

SEN governor

If you want someone to talk to about what is going on in a school or about how to get the best out of a school, without upsetting relationships between you and the staff, that person may be one of the governors. It very much depends upon the individual school – we know some schools where the board of governors is as friendly and as interested in parents' troubles as a nest of vipers, and others where the governors are unknown or invisible. But in most schools, particularly state schools, they play an active and visible role.

In most schools an individual governor will have been given responsibility for SEN; consider talking to him or her. Or perhaps the time has come when you want to make a contribution to the school, and this is a role which you would like to fill. So what does such a governor do, and what are they likely to be able to do? One school governor describes this special role within the board of governors:

> Being the governor with special responsibilities in the area of pupils with special needs is not that different from being a governor per se. You are involved in all the stuff that all governors do, but the area that you 'specialise' in is not a curriculum subject but spreads

across the range. Typically, the SEN governor will liaise with the school's special educational needs co-ordinator (SENCo) or equivalent, and aim to meet them formally once a term. From this meeting comes a report which is presented at the next full governors' meeting.

There is a policy that covers all such 'formal' governors' visits to the school. It simply says that the objectives of the meeting are decided before the meeting and that any written report/notes has to be checked with the member of staff concerned before being presented. So what subjects are covered at these meetings? There is a statutory need for the SENCo, SEN governor and headteacher to produce an annual review of the SEN and how they are provided for, including the number of children involved, the budgeting and what the current educational thinking and policies are. This can be quite time consuming. Recently, for example, the SEN governor on our board has helped the SENCo produce the self-evaluation form required under the new Ofsted rules. She is also there to help the SENCo in any way possible.

SEN governors are not inspectors but a source of support and a critical friend to the school and will probably have a special interest in checking how children with special needs are involved and integrated into school life. As with all the other areas/subjects, it's worth remembering that, while SEN governors may have a personal, even a passionate, interest in this 'special' subject, they won't have (or are extremely unlikely to have!) expert knowledge of the subject or teaching methods, so probably don't know better than staff how to handle a certain area! However, they have a duty to ensure that parents of children with SEN are kept informed and consulted about their child's progress and that all parents are kept informed about SEN – via the prospectus, policies, newsletters, meetings of the parent-teacher association, and the governors' annual report to parents.

At their best, then, the SEN governor will have a clear understanding of what is going on in the school, and will be prepared to talk to you openly about what might be done to help, and to keep the conversation confidential. Don't expect any governor to instruct you on how to take up arms against the school, though; they are generally too much involved and too committed for that.

Chapter 4
The provision debate

Which school? Special, mainstream or something else?

If we're to believe the headlines, that special schools are closing in their droves, there seems little point debating the merits of special versus mainstream schools. By the time we go to press all the special schools will be shut and converted to affordable housing – or will they? A recent debate in the House of Lords, which called for a moratorium on special school closures, met with the response that the rate of closure of special schools has slowed (not stopped though), together with assurances that special schools are here to stay and will have an important role to play in providing expertise and sharing good practice.

So what is actually happening? It's true that many special schools have closed since the Warnock Report, *Special Educational Needs*, was published in 1978. There has been a good deal of reorganisation, reassigning and amalgamation of provision too. However, a report by Ofsted published in 2004, *Special Educational Needs and Disability: Towards Inclusive Schools*, found that since 1999, the proportion of pupils placed in special schools remains more or less static. Moreover, since 2001 there has been a 10 per cent increase in the number of pupils placed in independent special schools and between 2001 and 2003 a 25 per cent increase in the numbers placed in pupil referral units (PRUs). Furthermore some children don't attend schools, either because suitable provision isn't available, or because home education is seen as the best way forward.

The government has made a firm commitment to increasing and enhancing inclusion opportunities. In its white paper on SEN provision, *Removing Barriers to Achievement: The Government's Strategy for SEN* (2004), it suggests that children with severe and complex needs will continue to require special provision but expects the proportion of children educated in special schools to fall, as mainstream schools develop the skills and capacity to meet a wider range of needs. However, it acknowledges that not all pupils get a fair deal at school and thus seeks to encourage schools and education providers to recognise and overcome barriers to learning and to embrace and promote inclusion.

Where you live may make a difference to perceptions. Local education authorities (LEAs) are free to provide as they think fit so SEN provision can be something of a postcode lottery. Some LEAs offer far more places in special schools than others. Lack of special school places doesn't necessarily mean a lack of provision. Some LEAs are much further down the road and much better at inclusion than others.

So just how did the whole notion of inclusion and hence the special versus mainstream debate begin?

A little bit of history

It can be traced back to the Warnock report of 1978. The report coined the phrase 'special educational needs' (incidentally, in Scotland, SEN is being replaced by additional support needs or ASN) and revolutionised the way we view children with special needs.

The report called for a greater number of children with SEN to have their needs met in a mainstream setting, suggesting that 20 per cent of children have SEN but only 2 per cent require access to specialist provision. It didn't, as is widely misreported, call for all children to be educated in mainstream schools or for wholesale closure of special schools. That Lady Warnock is now pushing to ensure special school provision remains for those who need it, is not so much a U-turn as some journalists imply, but a switch in emphasis. When the Warnock report was published there was a need to stress that many children with SEN could, with the right support, be educated in a mainstream setting. Today the emphasis is on maintaining that view, but stressing that for some children a special school will be the most inclusive environment. Having a statement of SEN (see Chapter 6) doesn't mean a child's needs cannot or should not be met in mainstream education, and many children with statements flourish in the ordinary classroom as long as the support they need is provided effectively. Special needs are many and varied; having an SEN doesn't mean a child lacks intelligence, and indeed many mainstream schools readily comment that a number of their children appear on both the SEN and the gifted and talented registers.

Why choose a special school?

Like their mainstream counterparts, special schools must apply the National Curriculum and its assessment procedures, and have broadly the same duties and responsibilities to children in their care, as mainstream schools. The perceived advantages are that class sizes tend to be much smaller, even exceeding one-to-one help in some cases; work is usually geared to the individual rather than to a group; children have a peer group with similar needs and therefore don't appear different; and staff generally have an excellent understanding of the needs of the children and how to address those needs. It's worth noting that many of the SEN experts we've spoken to admit their first forays into the world of SEN weren't planned; they didn't all acquire the expertise then look to share it, and for a good number it was a needs-must situation. Similarly, many specialist schools we've visited recruit good staff then train them.

Undoubtedly special school places cost more; funding tends to be determined by the complexity of learning needs that the school has to address and linked to a set number of places, so an average placement in an independent special school is likely to be twice as expensive as that in a maintained school (in mainstream schools, funding is allocated mainly according to pupil numbers, though there are additions for special factors, such as SEN). A statement of educational need is invariably required to secure a place, often a lengthy and stressful process. (Once a special school is named in a statement, the school is under a duty to admit the child.)

Critics say special schools don't push the children as much academically, have lower expectations, and that mixing with other children with the same needs doesn't create a model or even comprehensive peer group.

So is inclusion the answer?

An increasing number of mainstream schools see themselves as inclusive, though not all have the experience, skills and resources to make effective provision. The Disability Discrimination Act 2001 calls for schools to make reasonable adjustments to prevent pupils with disabilities from being at a disadvantage and to plan to improve their access to the curriculum.

Denying a child a place in a mainstream school may be discriminatory, but not all mainstream schools have the capacity to cope. Some staff aren't confident about admitting and supporting pupils with more complex needs, especially those with social and behavioural difficulties. Overriding concerns about the behaviour of some children and the detrimental effect it has on other children in a class resonate loud and clear – see the sample responses to our survey below. Headteachers struggle to marry the rights of the individual child with that of the whole school or class.

While many schools are happy to take children with special needs, there is a perception that this responsibility should be shared by all schools. Building up a reputation for SEN isn't always helpful; the school can become a magnet for those with SEN and this can adversely affect the balance of the pupil population, even jeopardising the number of positive role models for those with SEN. There are benefits in terms of planning provision and developing staff expertise from having a 'critical mass' of children with particular needs attending a school, but there is also a risk that individual schools may be swamped.

By attending a mainstream school it's suggested that children are on an even footing, not marked out as different. Yet children with special needs are often perceived as different and reports of bullying are not unheard of. Academic expectations may be higher but pastoral support is not always so great (detractors may argue that too much of a crutch is unhelpful). Class sizes tend to be bigger – 30 in Key Stages 1 and 4, 32 in Key Stages 2 and 3 are common.

Specialist help is not always available, as many teachers have received little if any training in SEN; indeed the National Autistic Society (NAS) in its report *Autism in Schools* (2002) found that only 20 per cent of teachers who teach children with autism have had any training at all, and there may be a number of children with many and varied SEN in the same classroom. Even a dedicated learning support assistant (LSA) may not be qualified. Having an LSA can mark a child out as different and alienate them from their peers. Learning support must be organised, allowing sufficient opportunity for a child to develop their skills and independence with access to the teacher, not just the LSA.

In some schools pupils are withdrawn from class, to work in a learning resource base or equivalent. This may provide security and specialist help for the child, but is teaching pupils apart from their peers, in a learning support unit or with an LSA, inclusion?

What's best is what's best for your child

Ultimately what seems to matter to parents of children with SEN is getting the best deal for their child, with the most appropriate provision, and having a choice available. The choice isn't necessarily static. Some parents may choose a special school early on, to get the added input, the early intervention that will help their child cope in a mainstream school later.

Others find that primary school is ideally suited for their child with SEN but secondary provision isn't. At secondary level, demands can seem overwhelming to any child, let alone one with SEN: the additional organisational skills required; moving from class to class; seeing five or six different teachers a day, none of whom may know you well; boisterous older children whose actions may be harmless but to a tiny 11-year-old seem fearsome; the size of the place; new subjects to grapple with. Many schools are working to address these issues by special classes with fewer teachers for some children, the use of learning mentors, inclusive policies etc.

As provision changes, boundaries blur. It's no longer a straight choice between special and mainstream education.

Specialist or resourced provision, a sort of halfway house, is an increasingly popular option. Such units are usually attached to a mainstream school and tend to specialise in a particular SEN, perhaps in autism, or hearing impaired provision. Specialised facilities and specialists are attached to the unit, not just teachers but therapists and others whose expertise is needed. Children will be based in the resource unit but may spend time in the mainstream classroom, and/or children from the mainstream may spend time in the unit. A couple of thousand children are dual registered, spending part of their time in a special school and part in a mainstream.

It isn't only resourced provision that works in this way; many special schools actively encourage their children to spend as much time as possible in a mainstream environment. Visits have to be carefully planned to suit the needs of the child and indeed the other members of the class the child will be integrated into. Admittedly some inclusion into mainstream simply pays lip service and the benefits to the child are neither tangible nor overt. At the other end of the spectrum some children have benefited hugely from spending time in both special and mainstream schools. We've even visited schools where children in special schools are included for part of their time in other more specialised settings. What is evident is that forays into either setting need to be carefully planned with motivations identified.

The one message that comes through loud and clear is: in the world of SEN there's no such thing as one size fits all. Flexibility and catering to the needs of the individual are paramount. The personal experiences described later on in this chapter show how true this is.

Collecting views

A week seldom goes by without a major press feature or TV programme airing the many, often controversial, issues surrounding SEN. As this book is a guide written by parents for parents, we too courted your views. Not every family will have a child with special needs but it's becoming far more difficult to find a family that isn't touched by special needs in some way, perhaps via a relative, friend or neighbour.

As ever, we wanted to know your views and much of what follows in this chapter is devoted to the voices of parents, schools, individuals and groups with an interest in special needs. These don't necessarily concur with our thoughts but we are genuinely interested in sharing opinion – remember, we aim not to give balanced opinion but to give a balance of opinion.

Views from schools ...

We faxed and e-mailed all schools in the country asking them to fill in our SEN questionnaire, designed to outline what they can, or do, offer for children with SEN. Some of the responses we include in this guide; others, including those that missed the publication deadline, can be found online at www.goodschoolsguide.co.uk. An overview of what schools said is included in this chapter; additionally, individual responses are included in the school reviews, not just for the schools we visited but for a good number of others too.

Just what did the questionnaire responses tell us? That a good many schools show a great willingness to work with children with special needs, while a few appear reluctant, or at least reluctant to let on.

Radley College's response was: 'we would rather not appear in any guide of schools offering SEN provision so will not be completing a questionnaire'. This somewhat confused us; many schools in the main *Good Schools Guide* offer SEN provision, so we're not sure if they want out of that guide (and we suspect just about every other guide on the market therefore), or if it was a request not to be included in guides such as this one, which focus on SEN provision. Shortly after we received the Radley response, a parent told the GSG how good the SEN provision was at Radley ...

There was little ambiguity surrounding the response from Sexey's school, which wrote: 'Thank you for your e-mail requesting details for inclusion in the *Good Schools Guide*; however Sexey's school has repeatedly asked to be deleted from the schools included in this guide and would be grateful for this to be actioned.' Well, Sexey's, there's no room at the inn for you in this guide (unless someone tells us you have very good SEN provision) but for anyone who's interested, the GSG review of the school appears both online and in the recently published 11th edition of the guide and the 10th edition and ... So they don't want anything to do with us but we want to keep telling you about Sexey's because it may well be of interest to parents. Not only is Sexey's a Church of England school whose 'Christian values underpin the school's ethos' but it's one of only 32 state schools with boarding, so tuition is free and naturally, like all state schools, they are expected to adhere to the SEN Code of Practice and to be inclusive.

Some responses were short and to the point. Exeter Junior School wrote 'No special provision' and ticked all the 'currently no provision for' boxes. We wonder: do they have some provision that they automatically include for children with special needs but don't view as special or out of the ordinary in any way, or do they simply have no provision at all for SEN? They do have staff that will administer medicines though, so if poorly Pete requires a panacea, someone will dish out the required dose.

Some schools were much clearer in their response. Ipswich High School wrote: 'We do not cater for special educational needs and have not completed the questionnaire for this reason.' Others feel they aren't really geared up for special needs. Francis Holland Junior School wrote: 'as a school we really do not cater particularly for Special Needs Children – indeed one might struggle here. We have the occasional mild dyslexic but that is all but they do not get "special" treatment. I hope that is helpful.' Yes it is helpful and honest, thank you. It gives a clear steer to parents, exactly what we asked for. Indeed in the GSG review of the school we wrote: 'Head looked blank at the mention of special needs, but parents say there is super support in the classrooms for anyone lagging behind.'

Some schools, perhaps those struggling to maintain numbers or a balanced pupil population, said they didn't want to broadcast their provision, feeling it would skew the population if they received any more children with SEN. A handful of others said they'd only complete the gifted and talented bits. There didn't seem to be any pattern to this. Some 'top' independent schools sallied forth, singing the greatness of their departments; others want to keep their light firmly hidden under their bushel.

Positive responses came in all sorts of shapes and forms, Lady Eleanor Holles is one of many schools which told us about their existing provision and added: 'Special educational needs are always dealt with on an individual basis and enquiries about the level of provision that can be offered are welcome.' James Allen's Prep School wrote: 'JAPS was praised in its 2002 ISI Inspection Report for the "excellence" of its provision for Special Needs ...' and we read: 'Notting Hill Prep School has a well established Learning Support Centre that strives to be a centre of excellence.' Wonderful news.

Not all the schools with accolades are in this guide. Some, such as St John's Catholic School for the Deaf, a school not only with 'Beacon' status but more importantly one you've told us does a terrific job, isn't in because we couldn't agree a mutually convenient time to review the school prior to publication. However, we hope to review it in the coming year, and if it's as good as our spies tell us the write-up will appear on the web as soon as we have it. There are a good many other schools that have told us very positive things about their work but we don't know enough about them to review so if you do, please tell. One such is William Henry Smith School in Brighouse, which wrote:

> We are a renowned and highly effective non-maintained residential special school catering for boys with severe social, emotional and behavioural difficulties. A caring, stable and stimulating environment combined with a high ratio of skilled and dedicated staff enables each young person at the school to have the opportunity to develop their full academic and social potential.

Medina High School in Newport, Isle of Wight, wrote at length and included information on how they do things differently: 'We also utilise a bungalow which has been turned into a learning centre for children who find High School difficult to access ... Each year we try to offer our "special" students a residential trip to an outdoor activities centre.'

There are a good many others who've told us they are doing something very special for children with special needs and we've included their responses in this guide. We need your help to find the best, so please tell us about schools you know well that are doing a good job for children with special needs, even if it is a school that hasn't yet responded to our SEN questionnaire. Finding a good school for children with SEN isn't easy but we hope those of you who have, will share your knowledge to help those who need to.

See About this guide, following the introduction, for details of how to contact us. We'll donate £1 to charity for every usable comment we receive.

... and from the Great British Public

Special needs is a widely debated topic with views ranging from those who are sceptical that special needs exist at all to those who say all children have special needs. So we asked the general public: 'Is a school that does well for children with special educational needs (and has lots of them) likely to be good for other children too?' Here's what we found.

The divisions between the yes and no camps were almost 50-50, but of greater interest than the raw statistics were the perceptions and comments included with responses. In a nutshell the yes camp said:

> Such a school will be expert at knowing children as individuals and making the most of their potential ... It shows a school is prepared to rise to a challenge and see potential.

With the overriding concern of the no faction:

> Having SEN kids around disrupts my child's education.

Gone are the days of spiriting away children who are different, hiding them in the attic, denying their existence (and however medieval that may seem, it continued to happen in Britain until the latter part of the 20th century). Inclusion is with us, and can be extremely successful and absolutely the right call for very many children with SEN. Today, in England and Wales, every child with a special need can ask to be educated in a mainstream school and the LEA has to agree to this unless after careful consideration it thinks it is unsuitable for the child, beyond its resources, or will have an adverse effect on other children. It isn't specific so there will be variability not just between authorities but within them too – one authority may think a child's needs can be met suitably, within its resources and without 'prejudice' to others; another may disagree. With such variability it's perhaps not surprising that unsuitability, availability of resources and the impact on other children are concerns raised:

> I do not agree though that all special needs children are best placed in mainstream schools. Some children need such a high level of supervision that mainstream schooling isn't a feasible option.

On the other hand:

> It is good for children to be aware of children who have problems. However, it can sometimes be difficult for a child with severe problems to fit in, causing problems for teachers, children and parents alike.

There was plenty of support for the idea that a school that is good for SEN is good for all, but a strong theme of 'SEN kids get all the attention so mine does not'. There were a few misunderstandings too. Some thought having a special need equates to low ability; this isn't necessarily true – Einstein, Edison, Branson are all high-profile dyslexics with more than their fair share of the old grey matter. Others think that being labelled as SEN means children must be physically different (again, not always true, and importantly having a physical disability does not necessarily equate to having special educational needs). Caveats centred round support, funding, behaviour, class size and training issues.

> It is important to recognise that each child learns differently, each child has needs that are special – this may sound a dreadful cliché, but it's true.

Many felt the biggest plus of having children with special needs is associated with seeing children as individuals:

> All children are individuals; a school with lots of SEN pupils has to recognise this, which is good.

> As long as the school also does well for the other children then it's good for children to learn to live with people from all walks of life. If they can deal with children with all kinds of learning problems, imagine what they can do for kids who have no trouble learning.

> If staff work closely with those who have special needs, surely it follows that they will recognise the needs of other individuals and respond to them. If they can care for a special child, an able child should be no problem.

> Many schools are very inclusive and find having children with special needs adds a positive dimension to school life.

Some go one step further, believing:

> Every child has a special need. It is the educator's job to identify that need in order that all children reach their full potential. Some needs might not be as obvious as others but the very nature of children is complex and diverse. They cannot all be the same, pressed into an unrealistic mould of who they should be. This does untold damage to our young people, far more than an acceptance of self and others for who they are and freedom to become all they should be.

To further support this argument we were told:

> I went to a school that has always done well for special needs, yet me and my friends all left with good examination results too.

> [I am] a student from a school with a large special needs department which I think is very important and has much to offer. It allows acceptance and understanding by pupils, of others who may appear different, as well as helping to incorporate children with special educational need into as normal an education as possible. This often results in an acceleration of their learning potential. I also believe that a school that can get a child with special needs to, for example, read by the age of 15, shows far greater teaching ability than one that does not take special needs children but boasts that all their pupils pass their exams. Not hard if you only take clever pupils!

However, not all agree:

> The attention needs to be fully on the capable students.

And

> If the teachers are concentrating on the children with special needs they will not help the other children. It would require more teachers as well because they may be at a different levels.

> The SEN children hold back the clever children.

Others tell us that too many children with special needs in a class has a detrimental effect:

> There are 5 children with special needs in my daughter's class. Lots of parents feel their child's education has been held back because there is not enough help for the children.

With state school class sizes around the 30-pupil mark, six children with SEN should be expected if 20 per cent of children have an SEN.

> In a state school where the class sizes are large, there is not enough time and energy for the teachers to spend on the other [non SEN] children.

Sometimes it's not just about the numbers of children with SEN in the class but the nature of the SEN or even where the SEN child is placed in a class:

> Due to the seating plan, my daughter had to sit next to someone with special needs in all her lessons. I had to move her schools because she couldn't concentrate.

> There's too much time spent on them [SEN children] at the expense of other children and some of their behaviour rub off on others!!

> My daughter's class has quite a lot of children with special educational needs and behaviour problems. The constant disruption has greatly affected my daughter's education.

Disruptive behaviour, both low level and serious outbursts are a key factor among those who believe that children with SEN should not be in the mainstream classroom. However, it must be stressed that not all 'naughty' children have special needs and not all special needs children are naughty. Interestingly, one of the most recent government reports, the Steer Report into learning behaviour, states: 'We acknowledge that while our time and remit did not allow for significant consideration of pupil attendance or Special Educational Needs (SEN), these are extremely important issues with great relevance to pupil behaviour' *(Learning Behaviour The Report of the Practitioners Group on School Behaviour and Discipline*, DfES 2005). So clearly SEN is not the only cause of poor behaviour. Behaviour of children in and out of the classroom is a major, and growing, concern with a belief in some quarters that pupils have too much power and teachers too little. More than a few have experienced the detrimental effects of children with SEN whose behaviour has had a negative impact. Whereas pupils with behavioural issues are seen to have a largely negative impact on the classroom, it appears those with specific learning needs bring something more positive:

> Dyslexic children are creative and improve many aspects for other children, like quite original art, developed sense of fun, practical minds.

And have a positive impact on the quality of teaching:

> Staff who are skilled at developing individual learning strategies for pupils will be good at it across the board and are more likely to be able to accommodate individual learning ... They are used to catering for individuals and ensuring each child is working at their potential.

> It would appear that the school has developed strategies or curriculum that caters for many learning styles and in so doing is able to assist them in reaching their full potential.

> If a school is really committed to children, then whatever their ability or needs, that will place all children in good stead ...

There's no such thing as a free lunch. Placing SEN children in mainstream education should not be viewed as a cheap option. The need to ensure that support, funding and training are in place was highlighted:

> If adequately staffed, and not just by teaching staff, children who attend such schools are more accepting and understanding of other people's needs. They mature into well balanced individuals and positive citizens.

> Having children with SEN teaches acceptance and respect for others. It's just hard for teachers who lack experience in SEN. They may be able to pitch work for the children in the year group but not meet individual needs.

> I am a teacher in a mainstream school. We have quite a few SEN children. There are advantages for the other children as they become aware of the difficulties children with SEN face, and see them as part of the community and their lives. They make friends with each other and are involved with life in the school and the wider community. All children have special needs and teachers are able to deal with them if they remember the children are just children who learn at different speeds and in different ways. As a teacher it is difficult. Problems include lack of support from county, insufficient funding to support SEN children and lack of guidance provided or time given to attend courses or visit other schools to learn techniques such as using Makaton, or developing visual timetables etc. For most mainstream teachers such techniques are new but they are things we need to know to support the children. Most teachers end up doing this in their own time and at their own expense.

> If the money is there, if they are well supported with lots of teaching assistants and as long as all efforts are not placed solely with SEN students. It's important all students have this wealth of help!!

Undoubtedly, supporting children with SEN can be costly:

> [Children with SEN] Take up too much funding and teachers' time and get all the attention.

If that seems harsh, perhaps this tilts the perspective?

> Special needs children take up too much time and the other children suffer.
>
> The children without special needs do not get the attention that they need as the children with special needs need extra care.

Because it's not just children with SEN who need attention but all children:

> I am a student and like it when I get my individual needs met. With lots of special needs students I, and lots of other students, are missing out on getting the best quality education.
>
> Sometimes, children who are above average are overlooked because they are not struggling, yet aren't given any incentive to try harder.
>
> Very bright children are not classed as 'special educational needs' and in my experience, they are left very much to 'get on with it' because they can. They do not benefit.
>
> The school would not meet the needs of children without disabilities.

And it seems it's not just the ordinary child who might suffer:

> Children without special needs wouldn't be suited to the way staff teach.
>
> Children learn at different rates. It would be unfair to expect a child with learning difficulties to keep up with faster learners.

And not just with learning:

> The disabled children are more likely to be bullied.

A sad fact but many children we spoke to in special schools, not just the disabled but others with special needs, said bullying in their mainstream schools made their lives intolerable. In this context perhaps the following response isn't so unexpected:

> All special needs people are freaks keep dem away.

We're just thankful far more of you said:

> This gives the opportunity to give them all the experience to learn all about each other, in all aspects of life.'

And

> I value the 'care about everyone' style; good for all.
>
> It tells me the school is committed to bring out the best in all children and not just concentrate on the brightest ones.

SEN is no respecter of social class, affecting children from all walks of life and every corner of society. Undoubtedly deprivation and poverty exacerbate difficulties. Some initiatives such as the excellence in cities schemes aim to redress the balance for children in areas of deprivation but are not targeted specifically at children with SEN. One respondent reports:

> I came to think that our 'popular' state school would not be right for us. One-fifth of the children had SEN. I noticed the statistics after reading the school behaviour policy, which indicated inclusion on the SEN register as one measure to deal with unacceptable behaviour. The Ofsted report remarked that most children were well below average when they came to school but improved due to good teaching. Apparently most of them came from a council estate nearby ... I decided that it would not be fair to put a bright child in the company of 20 or more 'well below average' kids at least four of whom are also hyper. Whatever the standard of teaching it was very unclear what incentive teachers would have to stretch a relatively less 'disadvantaged' bright child.

So, a school with good teaching, popular with parents, a school looking to address issues of poor behaviour rather than pretend they don't exist, but that isn't enough? We don't know if being near to a council estate put the writer off or if they asked the school what they do with bright non-SEN children. Many have a gifted and talented register for the able with specialist activities and master classes, so do ask and of course check out what really happens in practice.

As with all schools, some do a better job than others. Our views become tarnished or gilded by our experiences and those of people around us. Many schools eschew the benefits of having children with special needs, though we wonder if opinion depends on the type and severity of the special need as well as the number of children with special needs. Educating any child has costs, financial as well as social and emotional. The one thing all respondents have in common is the acknowledgement that special needs exist. SEN is an issue. With views clearly split, the desire for choice in education is, it seems, greater than ever. Although not all of you agree with the comment 'We are in one and it is really good for all children.' If this applies to you, whatever the type of school, do tell the Good Schools Guide; we even donate money to charity for usable comments about good schools so scribe away.

Insider information

Naturally it was important to include the views of those who are directly affected by SEN, both parents and young people. So here is a small but representative sample of these, including opinions from those who have experienced both the mainstream and special sectors.

Life in – and after – a pupil referral unit

Here a young adult who had behavioural problems at his mainstream school describes how his transfer to a pupil referral unit transformed his behaviour and attitude and enabled him to gain qualifications and a job that would otherwise have been out of his reach.

Right from the start of year 8 at mainstream school I started misbehaving and losing my temper very easily. I still don't really know why I did. From the start of year 9, my school told me that if I did not go on an anger-management course I would probably not last at the school, as I would be expelled if it carried on. Deep down I wanted to sort my problems out so I agreed to attend an anger-management course. Twelve weeks later and it was over. I thought that this was the end of me misbehaving. It was, for about a year, then I started again. This time, my school had enough of me and they wanted me out.

My headteacher did not want to expel me so instead he applied for me to go to Millbrook Pupil Referral Unit (PRU). I went for an interview, then, as I had been accepted, I met the headteacher and also the teacher who would be teaching me during the next year. They were great and treated me like an adult, unlike my last school. I told myself that it would be different here (in a good way) and I would probably change for the best.

When September came I couldn't wait to start afresh. In my first week we were told what was planned: two and a half days in class; one day work experience and one day at college. I thought: wow, I am going to really like this.

There were six pupils in a class and our teacher plus a teacher's help. They were the best teachers anybody could have. I think they understood how we felt as they both had teenage sons. We all got on like a family. It was so different to my mainstream school because the teachers there didn't care if you did bad in your exams or anything like that. Because our new teachers treated us like adults, I think we started to behave like them. We had no reason to misbehave now. They rewarded good behaviour all week with a Friday afternoon at the local snooker hall or bowling alley. Not once did anybody miss this, it showed we could behave all week, every week.

If we had any problems even if it was problems at home then you could talk to one of the teachers – they listened, understood and helped in any way. At mainstream I would never ever have talked to one of the teachers if I had a problem as I would have felt embarrassed but at Millbrook it was like they were family and you could open up to them. They were there any time for you – whenever you needed them they were there. I started working to my ability again. I was pleased. My favourite subject was maths, I was good but wanted to improve even more. My teacher, who also loved maths, showed me how to improve and taught me new stuff, stuff I didn't already know. I started to enjoy school more and loved going there every day. I don't think that I ever had a day off because I enjoyed it so much.

So from going from hating school and hating doing my work I went to loving it. I think it helped others, as there was no one to show off to, which I think is the main reason why kids misbehave. It's like me, we were showing off in front of the lasses, trying to impress them, but in my new group it was five lads, there was no one to show off to. Everyone just got on with the work and they behaved like adults. I think a good PRU must treat all pupils the same, and reward good behaviour with treats such as days out which our class did. My fave was the motorbike scheme in Hull. We went every end of term, for the day. Every teenage lad loves motor bikes so I think that was a good way of rewarding us.

Parents often think the worst when they hear about a PRU but it's just a school where your children will learn to behave properly and to start to work to their ability, which is something all parents want for their children and it helps prevent you from getting expelled for good, which won't help you in the future when you want a good job or to be on a good course at college.

At Millbrook they didn't sit GCSEs so we worked towards key skills. When I first started I was aiming at key skills level 1 but come the end of the year I had gained key skills level 2 in maths, IT and communications. These were the only subjects we did. I also got an OCR in science (silver award). My teacher knew for sure that if he could get me entered for science and maths GCSE at my old school then I would pass them too. I was allowed to enter them even though I had not done any coursework because I'd been at Millbrook. When my results came through, I passed them, I got a D in maths and an E in science. I was so happy, I would never have achieved this if I had not gone to Millbrook PRU. I owe them everything.

My teacher at Millbrook even taught me how to play the guitar, something which I'd always wanted to do. Even though every pupil there had some kind of behaviour problem I can't really remember one occasion where anybody kicked off. It was as if nobody had a problem and I believe that if they had gone back to mainstream school they would be different for sure and would end up in trouble. Our class was the leavers' group and we knew that by the end of the year our school life would be over and we would be in the big open world. I think we all changed for the best.

From leaving the PRU I went on a course at my local college. As I found a job I dropped out of college but it didn't turn out right and I found myself on a YTS scheme, learning car valeting. I got an NVQ in that. Then I got a job back with my previous employer but at a different company, doing groundworks. I have slowly worked my way up the wage ladder from earning £80 a week to earning £500 a week. Which is a big difference.

If I had not gone to Millbrook then I was going to end up getting expelled with no qualifications and no belief in myself and my abilities, If I hadn't grown up when I did then who knows where I would be now. If all schools treated kids like adults then there wouldn't be a problem half the time. Thank you Millbrook PRU, you have made me who I am today.

In search of normality

Howard Sanders was born with cerebral palsy. Now an undergraduate at Wolverhampton University, he describes his experiences of both mainstream and special schools and his desire to experience normality.

I was born in early February 1984 ten weeks prematurely, which resulted in me developing cerebral palsy. (Premature, low birth-weight babies can suffer head trauma, leading to damage to the part of the brain that controls motor function.) In my case, this only affected my ability to walk. The early years were difficult. Cerebral palsy affects every part of your life, creating problems parents may find difficult to deal with. It is a 'brick wall' feeling – you can push and push, but the wall will only give so much, then it cannot be moved any more. People deal with things differently; my parent's response was very focused, almost obsessively committed to obtaining the best possible support for me, in all ways.

First stop was the Peto Institute in Birmingham, to undergo conductive education. This regime, a strict programme of learning and exercises, is designed to improve mobility and achieve greater personal independence. In my case it was designed solely to improve my mobility and flexibility. Contrary to conventional medical expectation, I was walking by the age of 6.

After this success, I went to The Dower House, a local independent junior school. For two years it proved an excellent school but gradually I began to slip behind my peers, particularly in basic literacy and numeracy. My parents decided to send me to a more specialised school that could help me academically: Birchfield School in Albrighton. Unfortunately they weren't equipped or able to accommodate my physical needs. I became isolated, and within a week we parted company! From there I went to Grange House, an independent school in Herefordshire. This was great.

Thanks to the support of a teacher called Mrs Taylor, affectionately known as Mrs T, my literacy skills developed in leaps and bounds. Unfortunately the school began to experience difficulties; I left in the spring of 1994. I am not too sure whether the school still exists; I hope it does as it did a great deal for me.

Last stop was Bredon School near Tewkesbury. Without doubt, a turning point in my life. The school was quirky, a little odd, full of characters; you had to be strong willed and stand up for yourself, but it was absolutely superb in what it did for me. It improved my basic skills, developed my independence and made me a more rounded individual. They didn't always get it right – in swimming classes I was automatically placed in the training pool with kindergarten children. I remained in the training pool for the whole academic year. Actually, I had a lot of swimming ability, but they didn't assess my abilities in the same way as the other children – they made assumptions without actually finding out, thought that because I used sticks, I didn't have a voice. They tended to ask others about me, and use their opinions as facts. However, in other areas I was given support to develop, though often this only arose because I stood up for myself, became strong in how I dealt with things.

There is great debate about where a child should be educated. I have been to both special and mainstream schools. I believe, regardless of disability, a school should explore you as well as you exploring it. For a disabled person, the crux is support and the whole point of support is to provide a sense of normality. But what is normality? Is it black, white, rich or poor? A house in the Cotswolds, or a caravan on someone else's land? Without support, I think you are constantly teetering on the edge of craziness with an almost obsessive desire for normality, even though you are not sure what that is. If the school has a well thought out learning support system, which gives support to the child, the teachers and the parents, then I favour a mainstream education. I found the expectations much higher in mainstream; I developed faster, and more completely as a person. I believe there is a danger that by categorising disabled children they are not allowed to stretch and increase their abilities – lack of achievement is therefore a self-fulfilling prophecy. Disability is not about easy, straightforward answers – there is no right or wrong, there is only more right, and more wrong. I think the only person who can define what is normal is the individual. My views have changed from those of a child with no concept of difference, through teenage depression, made more acute by a sense of my own difference, to where I am now: successfully completing a degree course at Wolverhampton University, something I have only reached through support, and developing and accepting my own perception of normality. For me it's been a lonely journey, one I had to explore for myself. My parents supported me in the journey, but as my mother used to say to me, 'I can't do it for you.'

Nurture groups

Many teachers, as well as parents, will not have come across nurture groups, but they are gaining popularity as their beneficial effects are observed. One school governor describes her introduction to one and how it has helped her school.

When our headteacher first mentioned the idea of adding a nurture group to our primary school, he was met – at least amongst the governors – with blank looks. However, his persuasive description of how it would fit in with the school's ethos of inclusion, combined with the fact that, for a rural school, we have a high proportion (about a third) of pupils with special needs, made it worth having a closer look. And the more we looked at nurture groups the more we liked them. Then, as funding became available (at the time) and a classroom fell vacant as a result of falling rolls, we began the venture.

Nurture groups are a form of early intervention for children who look as if they might have difficulties in their education because of social and emotional problems. As early as possible in their schooling, a Boxall test is run on the children identified as those who may benefit for a stint in the group. This test, in the form of structured observation of children in the classroom, has been developed by teachers and classroom staff to support the work of nurture groups by highlighting behavioural problems and assessing children's skills or difficulties at building relationships.

With parental consent, a child who is suitable can join the nurture group. Ours is called Penguins, to reflect the strong emphasis on nurturing and caring for others. Children will spend up to four terms in the class. They register, share playtime and lunch, and end the day with their original class, but the rest of the time up to nine of them are in their own dedicated classroom with a teacher and full-time teaching assistant (TA). As well as schooling, care and consideration for others are important emphases in the Penguins' day. A unique feature of the classroom, for example, is the kitchen. The idea of eating together and sometimes cooking for each other is central to the concept of nurturing. The class has a daily snack time – toast and a drink – to which outsiders are invited; I always enjoy my visits.

Other important features are that the classroom is as peaceful as possible and that there is a sense of routine and continuity. To this end the teacher and TA are superhumanly calm and consistent – and this rubs off on the children. If for any reason one or other of them is not in school, there is only one supply teacher who comes in – if she is not available then the children will spend time in their original class. They have a daily timetable which is discussed at the beginning of the day and is prominently displayed on a whiteboard.

It must be stressed that it is not simply disruptive children who benefit – children who are extremely subdued also profit enormously. One little boy who entered Penguins when he was in year 2, about two years ago, was painfully shy – my first memory of him is hiding behind a group of his classmates when they were presenting their work at assembly. He spent a year in Penguins and this year he sang an unexpected solo (the partner in his duet failed to show) in his class's Christmas performance.

Over the three years we have been running the group we have learnt a lot. We have found that the earlier a child is identified (preferably in reception class), the better the effect of the procedure. When we started we had a mixture of Key Stage 1 and Key Stage 2 children and it wasn't as effective as it is now that most are Foundation and Key Stage 1 children. We were warned that at the beginning it would take at least a term for the group to reach an even keel, as all the children would be new together and therefore could egg each other on. Sure enough, as some go out and new ones come in every term, the new ones pick up the existing children's (hopefully) good habits.

The nurture group has also had a knock-on effect on the rest of the school, partly because the children who spend time in Penguins tend to re-integrate back into their classes successfully at the end of their stint and (if that was their bent) are not disruptive. The existence of the group has enabled what was already a nurturing atmosphere to develop even more widely throughout the school.

Two contrasting viewpoints

At this stage you may be thinking, as many people do, that some educational needs can be met in mainstream schools whereas others require special schools. But debate rages over the best educational route even for children with very similar conditions.

Deafness is something about which many people have strong opinions, and parents and other deaf people can be passionate in their arguments. This is Charlie's father:

> My child is severely deaf, not profoundly deaf. He has a very chatty older sister and Mum – a language rich family – and his temperament and nature is outgoing and socially confident. He has no additional problems, though some deaf children do. That I am prepared when necessary – and there have been occasions – to stand up to authority and to question professionals is also (mostly!) in his favour.

But attitudes and approaches vary. The divide is enormous, for instance, between parents who choose a cochlear implant for their child and those who treat their child's deafness as natural and teach them sign language as their first language. Then there are the needs of a deaf child of deaf parents, of a deaf child for whom English is not a first language, children for whom deafness is only one of several problems ... and so it goes on.

Often problems really begin when negotiating secondary schools – this is where many of the really serious difficulties start, when a child has to move around different classes and teachers and can easily get overwhelmed. It is at this stage that many parents consider specialist schools for academically bright deaf children. Here, two parents of deaf children tell about their own experiences and different approaches to the mainstream/special debate.

Ian's story

Ian got meningitis when he was 8 months old and was diagnosed profoundly deaf in both ears early on – there is difficulty detecting deafness and degree of deafness in babies. He wore hearing aids from then on. We were lucky as we had a home help and were able, in the preschool years, to spend time trying to get him to make sounds and words. This is probably the most crucial time as the decision to sign or speak is made during this period. Ian went for cochlear implant assessment when he was 8 but we decided not to proceed – we are now going through the assessment again!

We put Ian into a normal state primary school where he received additional help. Getting this help needs a statement of SEN from the local authority who effectively makes the funds available to the school. It is crucial that the right ingredients are cited – help at school (we had full-time help to begin with which has tailed down as Ian wanted independence and has found ways to cope), speech therapy (crucial), peripatetic visits, support from other bodies. If these ingredients are not there they need to be lobbied for with vigour. We certainly had to lobby. We also moved during this period, which provided interesting insights into the levels of help different local authorities were willing to provide.

Ian was clearly bright and passed his entrance exams into a boys' grammar school. We had to overcome resistance from the headmaster who didn't want someone with disabilities affecting the school performance! After that 'battle', which we won, he has been very supportive, as has the school. Ian has also fully participated in sport, which is important in growing self-confidence and making friends.

We wanted to avoid any school with a hearing unit, including deaf grammar schools, as we felt standards and expectations may be lower. Nonetheless, it is vital to have someone who understands about the radio aid or the hearing aid, can check it and is capable of either getting it to work or replacing it. We did this at home, relying on peripatetic help and support from the local hospital. This is of course complemented by support from hearing tests which monitor things on a regular basis, and regular visits to an ear, nose and throat specialist.

We feel it's important to meet others with deaf children with similar aspirations, to establish what help/support should be provided during school time. Ian is now 17 studying for A levels with the expectation of going to university.

Lucy's story

I am the mother of a 14-year-old child who was totally deafened at the age of 18 months by meningitis (she had a cochlear implant at the age of 3). I have witnessed many parents, myself included, desperately trying to work through the stages of bereavement (denial, bargaining, anger, depression, acceptance) as they gradually come to terms with the fact that their son or daughter has a permanent disability, which is never going to go away.

The problem for parents of a disabled child is that there is an additional agenda, which may prevent them from doing what is best for their child and may instead result in their doing what is most comfortable for them, based on their state of psychological adjustment to their child's disability.

Some parents seem to latch onto 'normality' as a target, convincing themselves that interventions (such as the cochlear implant) are going to make their child 'normal' again. This then means living a normal life, going to a normal school and doing everything to avoid the label of 'disability' raising its ugly head.

For these parents, mainstream education is the goal, because they can then say that their child is going to a normal school. This makes them comfortable about their child's disability. 'They're doing alright because, look, they're going to the local secondary school with all their friends. So that means they are normal and their deafness is not a problem.'

In some cases, this may simply be an expression of the denial or bargaining (using rationalisations to make you feel better), which is an integral part of the psychological state of bereavement. Normal bereavement processes generally take a year to reach resolution. However, having a disabled child results in abnormal bereavement, because the source of the grief is (literally) ever present and cannot be forgotten, so emotions continue to be raised years after the event. I still find myself unexpectedly in tears when I am asked to talk about my daughter's illness and our early struggles to cope with its consequences, even though it all happened more than ten years ago.

So the issue is: does getting your deaf child into a local mainstream secondary school indicate success in the management of their deafness? It depends. There are undoubtedly some deaf children who get the support they need in mainstream and function extremely well, reaching their full potential and coming out with excellent qualifications to set them up for life.

However, there are others who suffer in a mainstream class. Imagine the effect of noisy classrooms; large class sizes; poor class discipline (leading to disruptive behaviour); teachers who, having no training in the needs of hearing impaired students, may inadvertently make learning difficult (eg failing to face the deaf pupil; talking too quickly or quietly); lack of subtitling on video presentations; lack of written support (eg text on a smartboard behind the teacher) so that the lesson is being transmitted simultaneously in writing as well as orally. A hearing-impaired child may be unable to contribute to class discussions because they fail to hear their fellow students, feel socially isolated (because they are just too hard to talk to) and refuse to use a radio aid or have support staff present in the classroom (because it makes them different from their peers and is 'seriously uncool'). All that is a hell of a high price to pay for the title of 'normal'.

I would be dishonest, however, if I did not also identify the very real concerns of sending a child to a specialist school for the deaf. These schools are generally residential, which means boarding unless you are lucky enough to live locally or are prepared to move house. They could also be viewed as deaf ghettos, where your child will be surrounded exclusively by hundreds of deaf pupils (some of whom may have additional physical or behavioural issues) and where schoolwork is pursued in isolation from the normal world outside. Is this secluded community the best place for your child to prepare for the hearing world?

It can be. What these schools enable is easy access to learning, without the exhaustion and frustration of the fight to be understood or to understand. Everything is geared up to enable your child to overcome the technical difficulties of their deafness. Class sizes are much smaller than mainstream, classroom environments may well be fitted with every technological gizmo known (and there is an awful lot available now with the introduction of smartboard technology into the classroom and lots more to come). These aids enable written support for every word spoken. There are also other systems allowing pupils access to each other's speech, so that interactive class discussions are the norm. The teachers are not only subject specialists, but also trained teachers for the deaf. They know how to facilitate learning in deaf children and are far less likely to make errors in their teaching style that act as a barrier to effective communication in the classroom.

If your child has poor speech quality, the likelihood is that they will be much better understood by the teachers in a specialist school. In this way barriers to learning are removed and your child can then have the 'normal' child's experience of school, which is listening to the teacher and understanding the words that they say, and being understood in their turn. This then liberates them to concentrate solely on understanding the subject material itself. This is exactly what a normal child's experience of school should be.

So perhaps the definition of 'normal' education is not sending a deaf child to a mainstream school, where they have limited access to what is going on in the classroom, but instead sending them to a specialist school where they can experience learning in a normal way by concentrating solely on understanding the subject material.

Difficulties with hearing aids (or any other gadget to improve hearing) are also not an issue at a specialist school for the deaf. Everybody is in the same boat. They are all dependent on some kind of electronics. It is not hidden, it is simply forgotten about. There are also no barriers to communication. If speech is too difficult, the kids revert to sign language. Even oral kids will soon be signing away with the best of them. Communication without barriers, without effort, without prejudice.

This use of sign language may horrify parents who have embraced the oral approach. However, there is no evidence to suggest that sign language is in any way damaging to oral learning, if it is used in a social context. Instead, it could be said to enrich the deaf child's life, providing a more relaxing method of communicating outside class. After all, your child is deaf. Nothing is going to change that. Current technology can only provide advanced forms of hearing assistance. We cannot currently undo or reverse the physiological damage that causes sensori-neural deafness (although this remains a possibility in the future). In the meantime, pretending that the natural state of your child is anything other than deaf is to be in a state of denial, and that's not good either for you or for your child.

Yes, undoubtedly, allowing your child to go to a specialist school for the deaf does emphasise the fact that they are disabled. Is that a problem? It shouldn't be. Your child's confidence about their own deafness is dependent on their being completely comfortable in both their partially hearing state (with aids) and their stone-deaf or hearing-impaired state (without aids). Going to a specialist school should certainly help them to come to terms with their disability. The 'Why me?' is a lot easier to handle if they can see hundreds of others with similar difficulties.

A special school for the deaf may be an isolated community, but it often represents an oasis where a deaf child can drink their fill from the pool of knowledge with ease. Having reached their potential they are then ready to enter the outside world, equipped with the qualifications they need to do well and the confidence concerning their deafness, which should significantly reduce the barriers to their success. The ghetto issue is also fairly easily resolved: by weekly boarding and/or encouraging active socialising with hearing peers in the holidays.

You want your child to experience a normal education? Think about a special school.

Hidden disabilities uncovered!

It isn't necessarily the type of school you attend, it's about others understanding and accepting that people are different even if they look the same on the outside. Here one youngster with dyspraxia describes (with a bit of help from his mum) some of the obstacles and how it's possible to hurdle over some, dodge round others or simply put up with (or even avoid) the rest!

Would you tell a blind man to see? or someone who is deaf to hear?

Actually you might, but I hope you'd help the blind man to see, perhaps by providing a guide dog to lead the way, a stick to feel objects, Braille to make the written word come alive. Or perhaps you'd spend time describing what you see in your world so you could share your sighted experiences.

Most of us have some experience of not being able to hear properly – when we have a bad cold or have too much water in our ears from swimming, or when mum asks you to tidy your room then gets cross because you simply didn't hear. Not much fun, is it? Of course a deaf person hears but in a different way – they listen to music by feeling vibrations, they hear what people are saying by lip reading or using sign language, they use equipment or aids to help them. Being deaf doesn't prevent them from sharing our world or making huge contributions to it.

Usually if someone is blind or deaf we soon spot this, but sometimes disabilities aren't so easy to see or hear. Dyspraxia and dyslexia are two of these. So welcome to my world, the world of the dyspraxic, possibly with a bit of dyslexia thrown in for good measure.

I want you to imagine that you are on the sports field – perhaps you're the best catcher in cricket, the top try scorer in rugby or the super slogger in rounders. If you're right handed hold out your arm, picture I'm going to fit a very heavy lead sleeve on it. If you're left handed it's going to go on your left arm. It goes all the way from top to bottom just past your knuckles. Now try making that catch – tricky? Oh, and for good measure, stick out your opposite leg. I'm going to put that in armour too, all the way from hip to foot, large enough so you can bend your knee inside the armour but – you've probably guessed it – the armour itself doesn't bend. Now try running to make that catch, score the try or get the rounder. Not so easy, is it?

Of course, I'm sure you'll be determined to overcome these minor obstacles, but you might have to spend quite a bit of time learning how to cope with these new additions. Keep the armour on for the full duration of the game or practice session and you'll probably find it's a lot more tiring than usual. Exhausted? I hope not because it's now time to go in, get dressed and move swiftly to your next lesson. Leave the armour on and see how you cope getting into the clothes you've just taken off. OK, OK, take the armour off, then, but don't expect me to give you any extra time. Now run along or you'll be late.

Bonjour Madame Jaune, Guten tag mein kinder. Confused? Don't be, it's French but with a twist of course. Today's French dictation is going to be in German. Let me explain. Madame Jaune says what we have to write down in German but we don't write it in German, we write it in French. So if she says Guten Tag we write Bonjour! Easy peasy. I thought you'd agree, so let's just make it a little bit trickier. Instead of writing with the hand you normally use, you have to put your crayon – yes crayon, not pencil or pen – in the opposite hand. If you're clever enough to be ambidextrous use your mouth or toes to hold the crayon. Don't worry if you don't understand German – there's a special machine at the side of your desk. Press the buttons and it will translate the German to French, but try not to use it too much because – I'm sure you've guessed it – there'll be no extra time. Oh, and make the writing legible – in fact nothing less than copperplate will do, otherwise you'll be back at break with your armour on copying the work out until it looks pristine.

French over, it's time for the final lesson before lunch: literature. At last a chance for a bit of a rest, a nice relaxing read, chance to put your feet up, unwind. Well yes ... and no.

Today's reading book had a bit of an accident at the printers. It looks fine on the outside but turn the page – all the words are there, they're just jumbled about a bit.

CHAPTER ONE

Everyone looked six foot wide no in horror. Mr Roberts, was about to turn into a rather rotund explosive, human six-foot tall cannon ball tunnel. His angry roar moustache rushed twitched, from his lumbering eyes opened wider than his lips. The Mesrey tunnel you've done what my lad?

OK, so I exaggerate a bit, but words do get jumbled, especially the easy ones like 'was' and 'saw', and it's not easy for me to track, I often end up on the wrong line if I'm not careful. Usually I manage to work out that what I should be reading, is:

Everyone looked on in horror. Mr Roberts, a rather rotund rugby teacher, six foot tall and six foot wide, was about to turn into one explosive human cannon ball. His moustache twitched, his eyes opened wider than the Mersey tunnel. An angry roar rushed from his lumbering lips. 'You've done what, my lad?'

Though sometimes I think my versions are more fun!

Still, can you imagine how dizzy you'd feel after reading a few pages of that – bet you wouldn't race through books nearly so quickly and I think you might have to read it a few times before the words make any sense. At least I hope you can see why I need extra time in exams.

Everyone has their failings but I can tell you that dyspraxia isn't one of mine. I know bits let me down – for example, every single report mentions my handwriting and how bad it is. My occupational therapist got me into touch typing when I was quite young – she said it would help, and it does. Not all her suggestions were great. She wanted me to have a sloping desk but I had other ideas about that, I didn't want to be different from the other kids in my class and thankfully school never got round to getting me one. When I go to senior school next year I'm going to be allowed to type everything; I'm really looking forward to that. I like ICT, and using the computer means I won't have to worry about presentation. I'll be able to spell check too as I must admit spellings are a bit of a disaster area for me.

I don't look any different from anyone else, more handsome possibly, but you know what I mean! I can do most things other people can do, but often have to try a lot harder. Getting dressed can be troublesome – nothing seems to quite fit. Catching a ball doesn't come naturally. I have to try and try, then try a bit more and a bit more still but, boy, do I feel like a champion when I succeed and a grandmaster when I succeed every time.

My brain works just fine but my body doesn't always do what it's meant to. Don't make me write things out time and again – my brain is so fired up it will explode if I don't get all the information out. Give me a word processor instead. Understand when I take a bit longer to read what's written or to write down what you're telling me. I'm not stupid. In fact, dyslexics and dyspraxics are in great company – Churchill, yes Sir

Winston Churchill no less, was dyspraxic, and General Eisenhower was dyslexic – but together they helped defeat one of the biggest tyrants the world has ever seen. Adolf Hitler of course. Think Olympic champions and you might just think Sir Steve Redgrave: five gold medals and you've guessed it – dyslexic. Richard Branson? yes you've guessed it ...

So I'm not complaining. To be honest, I don't really know any different. I do know, though, that dyspraxia helps shape me, makes me determined to try harder, to understand why I have to go the extra mile so often. Yes, I think I can safely say dyspraxia helps determine my success.

From purgatory to pride: a parent's experience of ADHD

Celia Mannings is a part-time GP and photojournalist, and mother of Matthew, 8, who has attention deficit hyperactivity disorder (ADHD), and Christopher, 7. She writes for a parenting magazine, Right Start, *about childhood medical problems, and is currently working on a photographic book about patients in general practice. Here she shares her experiences as a mother of a child with ADHD.*

No one teaches you how to be a parent, let alone of a child like ours. Our son has ADHD. Looking back, it hasn't been an easy road, but he's now enjoying life to the full, as a bright and sensitive 8-year-old in a mainstream school – some of our strategies must have paid off ... At one time, we didn't think this was ever going to happen; he couldn't keep or even make friends, threw violent tantrums, bit and hit other children, was defiant with adults and usually did the opposite of what he was told at every opportunity.

Now I look at Matthew, and my eyes well up with pride. He has overcome huge personal obstacles with great courage for a little boy. It's clear he still has ADHD, and he's been taking medication for four years, but he's developing into a caring, thoughtful young man with enormous energy and a drive to achieve more every day. Family life is what I imagine to be near-normal for us now!

It hasn't always been like this. Matt was a difficult baby, not sleeping, crying, always restless, but the problems began in earnest as he turned 1, and his little brother arrived. All hell broke loose. We didn't understand, and it was put down to 'sibling rivalry'; I muddled on, not knowing that other little boys didn't behave like mine. One friend's toddler lost a nail because Matthew bit him so hard. We'd go to toddler groups and each time a child cried it'd either be Matthew himself or a child he'd pushed off the slide or whose toy he'd stolen. I'd get angry and upset and leave in despair, never to return for embarrassment. Life became pretty lonely, especially as I was an 'Army wife', newly posted to London. Nobody wanted to befriend the hopeless mother with the uncontrollable and destructive child.

Things didn't improve when we sought help. Family therapy told us to 'take away his favourite toy'. One friend said to me 'Why don't you give him the thrashing of his life so he doesn't do it again?' Everybody had suggestions, assuming I was doing nothing. Even at home we disagreed; my husband and I have come close to divorce on several occasions. I began taking anti-depressants, and periodically still do. Life was about getting through one day and on to the next, in a fog of exhaustion and depression.

The turning point was being given a diagnosis. Overnight, I was allowed to stop thinking of Matthew as a naughty child, but rather as one who is special, needing a completely different approach. I no longer had to try to make him conform, but could begin to love him for the way he is. Things at last began to make sense, and I can remember the overwhelming sense of relief and oddly, happiness, to be told there was something wrong with my child. Knowing the reason, there was something tangible to work on, and at last I began to develop the relationship I'd always longed for with my little boy.

The next invaluable step was starting medication. There are many opinions about Ritalin, but our experience has been only of good. About half an hour after his morning dose, it's as though Matthew's true character starts to emerge; he isn't doped up, or a 'zombie' as has been suggested about Ritalin. On the contrary, he's no quieter than usual, but is able to interact with his friends without flying out of control, concentrate at school, relax, enjoy his games and hobbies and take a full part in family life. Stimulant medication like Ritalin provides a 'window of opportunity' to learn, and the more he learns, the less he needs the medication. I'm a GP, so am perhaps more comfortable with the idea of medication than some parents may be, but I think it would be sad for others to miss out through misinformation that's often written about stimulants in the press.

In praise of school angels

Choosing a school is always very individual. I spoke to the headteacher, and gauged the school's attitude to 'difficult' children first. I also made sure they had programmes in place for special needs children. We'd learnt that Matthew responds so much better to calmness and praise rather than punishment. I was terrified he would be made to stand in the corner or outside the class, for talking or fidgeting, and that he'd then hate school for ever more. I was also terrified that he wouldn't be able to make friends, or would make them, then push them too far and lose them again. I never really thought about him achieving at school, only that I longed for him to fit in and be happy.

I have always been very impressed with how the school have responded to Matthew. I find it works for parents and school to be firm, but not to overdiscipline (especially important for the very young child), to state rules and help him conform but also to support, show the way, encourage. Matt gets angry when he feels he hasn't been able to express what has happened. There's usually a reason why he's done something, even if it was trivial and his response wasn't appropriate. We, and the school, have learnt to talk to him, and to listen, not to single him out – ADHD children are usually low on self-esteem in any case. Matt is incredibly oversensitive, and something going wrong that a 'normal' child might shrug off easily, stays with Matthew for far longer; he will fret for days if he thinks he's been misunderstood.

Matthew began his medication just before he started school. At first, when he had a lunchtime tablet at school, the school secretary gave it to him without fail for a year before he went on to a long-acting preparation. She was under no obligation to do so, but she's just that kind of helpful lady. This, together with being blessed with two wonderful teachers, really began to turn things around.

I've heard many ways to help ADHD children at school, such as allowing them to move to another chair in the classroom without having to ask, to help the 'fidgety' feeling. One boy was allowed to do star jumps in the toilets to get rid of excess energy in private, without drawing attention to himself. Matthew hasn't done these, but has had a hugely positive experience of school, with one lovely teacher for two years in a row. I read once in an ADDISS newsletter, in response to the question 'What single thing has helped your ADHD child the most?', an answer that brought tears to my eyes. A family had simply written the name of their child's school teacher. I could say this has been true for Matthew too, in the form of Mrs Hannah Chivers. She understood his personality perfectly, and managed to bring out his strengths and give him confidence. She told me she'd enjoyed seeing the change in him as he progressed; in short, she was nothing short of an angel. Not only is he now achieving expected grades, he's ahead in subjects he enjoys.

Undoubtedly, schools can do a great deal to help a child with ADHD; I think Matthew's future has been turned around by Colerne Primary School. They liaise with parents; don't make you feel you're being a nuisance or, worse still, at fault for the child's problems. I ask them for strategies they have found which help and use them. They tell me when he's doing well; there's nothing better than praise (especially if previously all comments have been bad).

If Matt upsets one of his friends, I explain to them that he does want to be their friend, but he has an illness that makes it hard for him to always be good. Usually, they say 'Oh, fine', cheer up and run off to play with him again.

Facing the future

Things still aren't always easy. It's only a few months since Matthew last threatened me with the carving knife, and it's frightening to see how he can fly off the handle and physically attack his brother in a disagreement. It sounds surreal, but the nature of ADHD is impulsivity and lack of control, and it's an ongoing learning process. Thankfully, we've come a long way down the road already, and are progressing every day.

I'm worried again, now it's just three years before he moves schools. We'd like to choose private education, and being an Army family need to look into grants. I think Matt might be easily led because he is desperate to fit in, and I need to be confident about the environment he'll experience. I just want him to be happy more than anything else – if this is the case, I think he'll flourish and do well academically.

Heading for Inclusion

Nigel Utton is Chair of Heading for Inclusion, a group of headteachers and senior school leaders dedicated to the ideals of a fully inclusive mainstream education system. Together they share and develop best practice and act as a pressure group on government to speed up and contribute to the inclusion agenda.

As parents of children with special needs many of you will be experts on what it is like to be excluded. Experiences ranging from the serious tones of professionals when your child's disabilities first became apparent, to the 'nice' way that the local school said 'I don't think we will be able to cope with John/Joanna's difficulties here – had you thought of the local special school?'

As headteacher of a mainstream primary school I believe I play a powerful role in cutting through the alienation many of our young people feel. Our school system is the key place in our society where people of all races, phy ical need, intellectual ability, backgrounds, religions, sexual orientation and skin colours can be together. Inclusion is not just about a few children with learning, physical or behavioural difficulties being 'placed' in mainstream schools. It is about human beings learning to move on from the mistakes of the past and to learn to live well with each other. It is about creating a society where all people can find their own unique place and work to the benefit of all. If this work is not started at school, then what hope do we have as a society? The Heading for Inclusion group has a long-term vision of *all* children having their learning needs met in their local school.

Schools that do not include children well are not good schools

I am deeply saddened when I hear stories of children who have poor experiences of inclusion. Maria, who has physical disabilities, told not to give out invitations to her birthday party because the headteacher did not think it appropriate; Karen kept apart from the other children in case the look of her body might scare them; Peter, whose parents were told the school was full – only to hear that another child (without impairment) was given a place in the same class the next day. These tragic stories often come from schools with 'good reputations'. No parent who has heard such stories would want their child to go to such a school. And yet, what would have happened if the civil rights movement in America had given up its call for desegregation because some schools were not doing it well?

There is no formula for inclusion

I have often heard teachers say 'I treat all the children in my class the same.' Be wary of those teachers. It is neither desirable nor possible to treat all children the same.

When Alice joined our school at the age of 4 with Down's syndrome we spent time listening to her, listening to her mum, listening to her brothers, talking to the class and the school – preparing us all for a time when she would be joining us. All the school staff and all the children in her class learnt Makaton, as this was Alice's primary means of communication, and we engaged an assistant to help include her in the activities of the class. When John joined our school, also aged 4, also with Down's syndrome, he had good speech and his parents did not want him to learn Makaton – so we did different things to ensure his full inclusion. Both children are successfully moving through the school, making friends, becoming a part of their local communities.

When Ali, an Egyptian Muslim with very little English, joined my class, I saw it as my job to make sure I adapted everything to make it accessible to him and to let him know he was welcome in our class. He was given buddies, he was given a display board in the classroom so he could show the children about the country he had come from, he learnt English, he made friends – he stopped the behaviour problems he had developed in the infant school the term before.

In one sense we treated these children very differently, in that we did different things to ensure their inclusion and full participation; in another way they were treated the same – their particular needs were identified and met to the best of our ability.

Possibilities without limits

When I was teacher in charge of resourced provision for children with EBD I was able to prove that it is possible to include children with severe behavioural difficulties into a mainstream setting. I am not arguing that it is easy, but it is certainly desirable. Mark had moved to us in year 3 from a special school. His behaviour was sometimes violent and unpredictable. At first the other children were wary of him. I invited six members of his class to join a circle of friends for him. We discussed his behaviour, good and bad, once a week or if there was a particular problem to sort out or issue to celebrate. The other children gained great skills in listening and empathising – I also encouraged them to practise being assertive with Mark – letting him know in no uncertain terms that hurting others was simply not acceptable!

The class grew to be unafraid of Mark, to accept that sometimes he did lose control of himself, and that they had a right to expect and demand better of him. As they learned to appreciate his courage and ability to stand up for himself – and others – they elected him their school council representative every year because they knew he would challenge authority and ensure that things went well for the children. We did not need to have lessons in social responsibility or citizenship – we lived it!

At present, inclusion is a learning process. The main problem is that those of us who lead schools have only experienced a non-inclusive education system. That clouds our thinking and tends to make us work along tried, tested and unsuccessful lines. Many schools cannot see how children with special needs can be included. And indeed, without significant changes in attitude, in many cases they cannot!

Heading for Inclusion: what we are learning

In Heading for Inclusion we do not believe there are different types of children – some of whom can be included and some of whom it is too difficult to include. Our experience is that if we get things right for children with extremes of need it improves things for many more children. To be included some children require very concentrated physical or behavioural support – this may mean that several adults are needed in a classroom to allow a particular child to be included successfully. Some children require low-stimulus environments, light rooms, ball pools, intensive physiotherapy. All of these can be provided in an inclusive school, and our experience shows that many 'mainstream' children also benefit from such environments!

Heading for Inclusion believes that the current model of 'mainstream' and 'special' education is not a long-term solution. We want to help create an inclusive society where all people are valued regardless of their achievements or their abilities. We plan for a future where schools are adaptable places which change and grow depending on the needs of the young people learning there, where needs are constantly re-evaluated and changes are made to accommodate them; where all stakeholders (particularly the young people themselves) are listened to.

Those of us who are dedicated to inclusion find ourselves working differently. Our basic assumption is that all children can be included. Our job as school leaders is to work out how best that can be done. The process is very clear: we need to continually ask questions; look for solutions; seek advice; support each other – but, most importantly, keep *thinking*.

From 2006 Heading for Inclusion will hold an annual conference to broaden our membership and spread our accumulated experience and knowledge. Great things are already happening in many schools and these ideas need to be shared and developed – schools are already changing for the better!

Nigel Utton has worked as a primary school teacher in a wide variety of schools since 1990. He has been a firm supporter of inclusion since the age of 10, when his mainstream school was flooded and the children were shipped into the local 'special school'. He asked himself then: why are we kept separate? When in charge of a provision for children with emotional and behavioural difficulties (EBD) in Hampshire he helped to show that even children with statements for EBD can be successfully included into mainstream school. He is currently headteacher of St Lawrence Church of England Primary School in Alton, which is working towards being an inclusive school.

The special learning – and teaching – needs of further education

Dr Enid Alston and Malcolm Starrs of Star Learning Consultancy have done some preliminary research at London's South Thames College of Further Education which suggests that many children are still going through the school system with learning problems unidentified.

All students carry into further education (FE) the baggage picked up during their years in the school education system. Generally, the average university student will have had reasonable learning experiences and gained a number of high-grade A levels, but many students go to FE colleges as disaffected or disillusioned learners whose passage through school has been troubled or difficult. The baggage that comes with some of these students can be weighty and uncomfortable, and correspondingly the student's self-confidence and esteem, particularly regarding learning, can be disastrously poor.

The government sees FE as a way to increase the base level of skills available to employers (hence the ALS, additional learner support). Legislative changes are driving the momentum for increases in the teaching of literacy and numeracy and providing access courses to both employment and degree-level studies, so that even those with difficulties can be found a place in the workforce. At the other end of the spectrum FE colleges aim to provide a wider selection of routes into higher education.

To meet these aims, colleges must address the needs of the large section of their students who require specialist support. To do this effectively they must be proactive rather than reactive, recognising needs before students arrive, so that resources are in place.

Two years ago we set up a mini research project within the dyslexia support department of South Thames College. We intended to revamp the procedure for assessing students and wanted to pinpoint the range of difficulties students were experiencing so that we had a clearly identified base from which to progress. Identifying problem areas would also enable students to understand better the reasons for particular areas or ways of learning. Part of this involved recording the history of assessment and support of those who came to the college – we were particularly interested in those who'd received no help of this kind during their school years and the resultant problems they brought with them to further education.

What the figures showed

Although the material obtained has come only from those students who were assessed for specific learning difficulties within the learning support department and more specifically for dyslexia during the two years that it has run to date (2003-5), we think the findings are significant and alarming but not altogether unexpected. Since students have come looking for help to the learning support department either voluntarily or by referral; this strongly suggests that they have always had some difficulties with learning. Obviously some of the students participating in our survey had been identified as having difficulties while at school and had received some levels of support, but the figures obtained suggest that the levels of both identification and support in schools are woefully inadequate for the needs we encountered.

The figures obtained during the project are based on self-report and therefore have to be interpreted with caution – with ages ranging up to 61, and a mean age of 27.5, it is possible that memories of schooldays may be inaccurate. However, where possible we checked details, and the results speak for themselves.

For our project we involved 79 students – 28 men and 51 women, reflecting the predominance of women in the college as a whole (and mirroring the increase in uptake of FE courses by women nationwide).

We found that, overall, only 24 per cent of the students positively identified in college with a specific learning difficulty(SpLD) or dyslexia had ever received an assessment during their school career. Even then, a number were done privately at the instigation of parents rather than the school.

When the data was analysed by gender, the difference was equally startling: 87 per cent of the women (56 per cent of the men) said they'd never been assessed. This is a large discrepancy when you consider it is now understood there is no gender difference in the occurrence of dyslexia.

We realised that age was likely to influence these figures. Until 20 years ago or less, an assessment for SpLD/dyslexia was relatively rare and thought by many to be a 'cop out'. So we divided the groups into 10-year age cohorts and re-examined the figures. We were unsurprised to find that in the 35-65 age range only one woman (less than 5 per cent of the total sample) had been assessed and identified as dyslexic. However, and of much greater concern, was that of the 44 participants in the youngest age range (16-25 years) fewer than half said that they had been assessed for their obvious difficulties with learning and underachievement.

Considering the level of knowledge and awareness that is now available, including the Dyslexia Friendly Schools initiative promoted by the British Dyslexia Association, this suggests much less awareness regarding specific learning difficulties in schools than might be expected, or hoped for.

We also questioned the students on the level of support that they had received in school. Here are some of the findings (which, we recognise, may be more open to memory error than the fact of an assessment).

- 61 per cent said they hadn't received any support for learning during their school years.

- 73 per cent of the women, as opposed to 37 per cent of the men, said they didn't receive support whilst at school. In fact only four women reported receiving support at both primary and secondary school (once again reflecting the unbalanced gender distribution we found regarding assessments at school).

- Only 8 per cent of the 51 women in our project had received continuous support in school, and only 14 per cent of them reported receiving any support at all during their school years. The equivalent figures for men were 30 per cent and 63 per cent.

- 65 per cent of the youngest age group (16-25 years) reported receiving no support during their school years, while in the older age groups the incidence of learning support was, predictably, even lower.

The implications of these findings

At a recent session on reading remediation it was reported that three out of every five schoolchildren are not able to read text commensurate with their age. It has also been demonstrated that the illiteracy rate increases in correlation with levels of social inequality and deprivation, with as many as 80 per cent of prison inmates estimated to be illiterate or to have severe difficulty with functional literacy.

The means of teaching used by dyslexia specialists, such as the MEMSC model (multi-sensory, errorless, metacognitive, sequential and cumulative) used in South Thames College, are proven to be the most powerful methods of producing readers and therefore productive, literate members of the community. So, we have the means, and we should be concentrating, not on debating how the students we teach should be categorised, but on how to train those who teach them. No longer is it sufficient to think that only primary school teachers need to be aware of the rudiments of teaching language and literacy; it is becoming increasingly evident that this needs to be a tool for teachers at all levels.

Even allowing for the possibility of memory lapses on the part of some of the participants after extended periods, the figures produced by our small survey are disturbing to say the least, and should be informing decisions at policy level. In FE we often receive the halt, the lame and the weary of the learning world and it is our job as tutors to provide new focus and motivation for students' valid but sometimes haphazard aspirations. This requires further research to validate and expand on what our project is uncovering. And therein lies a further problem.

While it is taken for granted that research is an integral if not the major function of universities it is not considered the norm in colleges of further education, which feel they are the poor relation in the world of tertiary education. Departments wishing to undertake research such as is being done at South Thames College have no, or very limited, access to funding within FE college budgets, while source after source outside have no provision that makes their funding open to FE. Until a department has funding to do some research it cannot take time out from teaching to plan the research or source further funding. Until this changes these highly charged issues within further education will not be adequately addressed. Yet surely, need is high?

Removing barriers to achievement

A plethora of documentation exists to support children with special needs in schools. These are weighty documents and not the sort of thing to sit down and read with one eye on the TV. The documents are aimed at schools and those involved with the education and well-being of children but are not written with parents as the readers in mind (though they do make mention of the importance of parents). We include an overview here, for those who have an interest in what informs school policy and practice. If you want something light-hearted and entertaining read the *Beano* – this is only for insomniacs and a few others. You have been warned!

A key document (see the SEN timetable in Part 4) is the 2004 white paper *Removing Barriers to Achievement*. This outlines the government's vision for giving children with SEN and disabilities the opportunity to succeed. It moves the definition of inclusion away from simply placing a child with SEN in a mainstream setting, seeking instead to reduce the barriers to learning and participation that children experience. It works from the premises that:

> All children have the right to a good education and the opportunity to fulfil their potential. All teachers should expect to teach children with special educational needs (SEN) and all schools should play their part in educating children from their local community, whatever their background or ability.

But it recognises:

> Too many children wait for too long to have their needs met; children who should be able to be taught in mainstream settings are sometimes turned away and many staff feel ill equipped to meet the wide range of pupil needs in today's classrooms; many special schools feel uncertain of their future role; families face unacceptable variations in the level of support available from their school, local authority or local health services.

Below is our interpretation of this document and the points we feel are key.

The document proposes working towards a unified system where children can more easily move between mainstream and special schools or be dual registered. It acknowledges that special schools will remain the best place to educate some children with severe and complex needs but proposes children with less significant needs, including moderate learning difficulties (MLD) and some behavioural, emotional and social difficulties (BESD) should, as staff expertise and capacity within mainstream schools develops, have their needs met in mainstream schools. It envisages special schools sharing their expertise and experience to support greater inclusion.

Four areas are identified as key to delivering more inclusive education. These are:

- early intervention
- removing barriers to learning
- raising expectations and achievement
- delivering improvements in partnership (the way organisations and agencies work together and with parents and the child).

It recognises that severe and complex needs, requiring support from more than one specialist agency, will continue to need the protection a statement provides, but hopes that by removing these obstacles there will be less reliance on statements.

Early years intervention

> Give me a child until he is seven, and I will give you the man.

At the Good Schools Guide we know of nurture groups where early intervention is making a real difference to the lives not just of the children on the programme, but of others who reap rewards from the knock-on benefits. Early intervention can help children catch up with their peers, not just academically but socially, emotionally and behaviourally, as necessary. Additionally those who require support on a continuing basis get help early, reducing the risk of long-term under-achievement and disaffection.

The merits of early intervention are supported by findings (from the Effective Provision of Pre-school Education (EPPE) project and the associated Early Years Transitions and SEN (EYTSEN) project) that 'pre-school can be an effective intervention for reducing SEN, especially for the most disadvantaged and vulnerable children'.

An integrated approach to early education and childcare is recommended, and there's recognition that information for parents needs to improve (hear, hear!) Advice, support, staff training and evidence gathering are key and it's felt that unnecessary bureaucracy can be reduced, for example by streamlining annual reviews and individual education plans (IEPs), and using information and communications technology (ICT) for record keeping.

It's acknowledged that childcare, a problem for many parents, is trickier still where children have SEN or disabilities, so the white paper recommends improving information on the availability of suitable childcare locally (not the same as improving childcare locally); professional toolkits; and funding.

As more children are identified with special needs earlier, demand for specialist advice and support has outstripped supply in some areas. It's suggested that early years special educational needs co-ordinators (SENCos) and area SENCos can help identify children's needs. We're told: 'There is already a wealth of expertise in schools and local authorities, which early years settings should be able to tap into ... sharing learning and expertise, problem solving, and planning to support a smooth transition to primary school.'

There's a training pack complete with video for SENCos to help identify young children with SEN. So that's all right then – to think we thought training might be a costly and time-consuming exercise!

Will this be enough? There's recognition that prevention is better than cure, but we still wonder how much is a sticking-plaster approach. Do staff in early years settings receive appropriate training to deal with the variety of needs presented, to identify a child with SEN, to know when to seek specialist advice? Research by the Audit Commission found that 68 per cent of SEN resources are focused on pupils with statements. So, you've guessed it, a recommendation is that the number of statements should be reduced, rather than funding increased. Which is fine if suitable provision is available but not so great if it's simply a cost-cutting exercise.

Funding of special school places comes under the spotlight too, with calls for greater accountability, better use of residential placements; agreements by providers to keep fee increases within a given framework etc. Little wonder the special schools we visit all tell of the battles parents have with local education authorities to secure a place.

The role of local authorities in allocating resources, promoting early intervention and effective practice in schools and providing schools with access to specialist SEN support services is seen as crucial. It's acknowledged that effectiveness varies: 'Some authorities delegate resources for children with statements, enabling schools to take action more promptly and giving them greater flexibility over how they use their funding ... This in turn has tended to reduce demand for statements.'

Needless to say, all LEAs are being encouraged in this direction. The advantages of this approach are outlined as:

- addressing needs as they arise rather than waiting for failure to be reinforced
- allowing resources to be managed on a whole-school basis rather than piecemeal
- equitable distribution of resources between schools (does this mean all schools get the same per capita funding or that funding will vary according to the number of children identified as having SEN? Some educational settings tell us they don't have any children with SEN – will they need any funding?)
- greater clarity about the respective responsibilities of schools and the LEA and less bureaucracy as fewer children need statements (is that 'need', or 'will be able to get'?).

It's widely recognised that the statementing process is expensive, time consuming, bureaucratic and stressful, yet parents still fight to get a statement. Why? Reducing bureaucracy is one thing, eliminating it without a suitable alternative is another. It's acknowledged that the number of statements issued won't fall overnight: 'Reducing reliance on statements is a long-term (ie 4-5 year) change process, requiring a cultural shift, extensive capacity-building at school level, a realignment of advice and support services, strengthened accountability arrangements, and additional support for parents, particularly those most affected by the changes.'

Worryingly, the document is now a couple of years into publication so the long term draws ever nigh.

Removing barriers to learning

There is recognition that inclusion isn't just about the type of school a child attends; it's about being able to take part in school life, being included, having a peer group, getting the right kind of help and support to achieve and fulfil potential, being able to successfully access the curriculum.

For inclusion to work properly and be effective, schools need expertise among staff together with the resources to deal with increasingly complex needs. Furthermore, there are concerns, especially where children have demanding behavioural, emotional or social difficulties, of the impact on other children. Some SEN require specialist services. How will these be provided and will provision be cost effective? This also raises the question of what, if any, is the future role of special schools within an inclusive education system. The white paper says the government wants to see:

■ Special schools educating children with the most severe and complex needs, and sharing their specialist skills and knowledge to support inclusion in mainstream schools

■ Schools with the confidence to innovate and the skills and specialist support to meet the needs of all pupils successfully

■ Schools working together to support the inclusion of all children from their local community, backed up by good quality specialist advice from local authority and health services, working in multi-disciplinary teams.

■ Parents with confidence that, in choosing a local mainstream school, their child will receive a good education and be a valued member of the school community.

To support these aims the government says it will:

■ Bring together education, health, social care and the voluntary sector, with the focus on those children whose needs place growing demands on schools (autistic spectrum disorder, behavioural, emotional and social difficulties, speech, language and communication difficulties, and moderate learning difficulties etc)

■ Provide practical tools and materials for schools and local authorities to improve access for disabled pupils

■ Work to ensure leadership programmes promote inclusive practice

■ Clarify the future of special schools, focusing on high standards, working with mainstream schools

■ Improve the quality of education for children with more severe behavioural, emotional and social difficulties

■ Pump prime regional centres of expertise, building on the work of leading special schools and local authority support services

■ Help reduce reliance on high-cost placements in residential special schools

■ Set minimum standards for SEN advisory and support services, for self-evaluation, and for use by Ofsted, to achieve greater consistency in quality, availability and cost effectiveness.

Do check how this is working in your child's school (or proposed school). Find out how far down the line the school is in meeting these proposed aims. We suspect there will be wide variations, not just between LEAs but across providers within an LEA.

Raising expectations and achievement

The third aim is described as providing 'a personalised education that brings out the best in every child, that builds on their strengths, enables them to develop a love of learning, and helps them to grow into confident and independent citizens, valued for the contribution they make'.

To meet this aim schools need to respond effectively to the wide range of pupil needs; ensure appropriate help is in place that will enable children with SEN to achieve to the full; provide suitable curriculum and examination options for children with SEN; and ensure quality advice is available on options beyond school.

To do this, the document proposes:

■ Helping schools vary pace and approach to learning to meet individual needs

■ Delivering practical teaching and learning resources to raise achievement

■ Developing strategies and teaching approaches

■ Delivering quality teacher training and continuous professional development in core skills and knowledge of SEN

■ Assessing the scope for developing specialist qualifications

■ Collecting data on, promoting and extending the use of P Scales to measure progress made by those working below level 1 of the National Curriculum

■ Changing performance tables so schools get credit for the achievements of all pupils, including those with SEN

■ Publishing practical tools for involving young people with SEN and disabilities in decisions about their learning

■ Working across government to improve the quality of transition planning, setting national standards for health and social care

■ Working to expand educational and training opportunities and develop new opportunities for transition to work.

Naturally what's really important is ensuring that the proposals actually enable schools and providers to meet and fulfil the aim in an effective way.

Delivering improvements in partnership

Too often parents continue to face a postcode lottery in the support available from their school, local authority and health services, resulting in a fight to secure entitlement. Furthermore, confusion too often arises about who should provide what, leading to disputes and delays, often further hindered by shortfalls in some local authorities' provision.

The report says the government wants to see:

■ More consistency between local authorities particularly in their use of statements, funding to schools and special school provision

■ Schools regularly reviewing the effectiveness of their SEN provision, with local authorities, providing support and challenge where concerns are raised

■ Parents with greater confidence that their child's SEN will be met in school – whether or not they have a statement

■ Greater integration of education, health and social care.

And will:

■ Promote more consistent practice ... provide support and challenge on key SEN issues, including the use of statements, management of SEN resources, identifying and sharing good practice and tackling underperformance

■ Make SEN Regional Partnerships directly accountable to the DfES for their work on the implementation of this strategy

■ Ensure that schools make inclusion an integral part of self-evaluation

■ Share best practice and improve comparative data on SEN performance.

So, SEN provision varies widely. Some children still face real barriers to learning and some parents lack confidence in a school's ability to meet their child's needs. Progress has been made but much remains to be done. The white paper concludes:

> we will know we have made a difference when: children with SEN have their needs met as soon as they become apparent, without the need for a period of failure; children with SEN feel valued members of their school community and the barriers that divide mainstream and special schools have disappeared and all schools work in partnership with other services and the voluntary sector to meet the needs of local children.

We, at the Good Schools Guide, very much look forward to that day.

Part 2

THE SCHOOLS

Chapter 5

Choosing a school

Few things cause so much angst for parents as finding the right school for their child. Once offspring have been through the system most parents wise up to what's really on offer, how good a school actually is, what they really want for their child. But unless you've got a crystal ball the best advice we can give is: do your homework; check out inspection reports; seek the opinions of neighbours, friends, fellow parents, specialist advisors; visit schools; and use unbiased guides such as this one.

Begin by thinking of the end point. What would you realistically expect your son or daughter to be doing in 20 years' time? Education must be challenging, and bring out a child's full potential if possible, going beyond what that potential is currently perceived to be. Look for schools that are excellent in areas where your child can shine despite their disability; achievement in one specific area often gives a child confidence to succeed in others.

Crucially, your child may have special educational needs but they have other things too – hobbies, interests, strengths, a personality ... For the child who finds classroom tasks a burden, search for an all-round school which has the ability and desire to turn out an all-round child who will reach their potential.

Practical advice

Before you decide

Be honest with yourself. Neither emphasise your child's problems nor diminish them. Be honest with the school too. The more a school knows about your child, the greater their ability to decide if they can cope/help.

Get as good a professional assessment as possible. Use an appropriate support group, which will be able to recommend professionals who can give you a frank description of your child's needs. For a child with a physical/genetic problem you will have lots of useful expert information from the clinicians who have worked with them. For the child with behavioural difficulties, autistic spectrum disorder difficulties, learning difficulties, specific or global, get as much up-to-date advice as you can. Generally, a school will require a report from an educational psychologist (EP or edpsych for short) at some point for all but the mildest of cases. You can pay for a private EP report, though the local education authority may decide you must use the EPs they recommend (there's more on how EPs can help in Chapter 3).

Parent support groups are often brilliant, with more information than your so-called experts. The web is a good hunting ground, too, and don't be afraid of looking up sites in other countries – Australian and American ones are often packed with information. If you're bemused by all the categories and terminology relating to different types of school, take a look at the ready-reference in Part 4.

Health warning

State schools by law have to be inclusive, so in theory they should cater for anything and everything. It's extremely important to visit and to ask lots of probing questions to make sure they really can get it right for your child. The flip side is that many independent schools do very well by children with SEN but don't advertise the fact as they don't want to be viewed as a special needs school.

Prior to a visit

At this stage you're trying to find out if the school is worth visiting. Find out about:

■ Attitudes to special needs and the types of special needs the school can cater for. Consult guides such as this one – we're beginning to gather information on attitudes to SEN from a broad cross-section of schools.

■ The SEN policy and/or inclusion policy or similar. Ask for a copy; this may be in teacher-speak but will be a useful benchmark from which you can formulate questions on the visit and it shows you're on the ball. Remember to ask how the policy would work for your child and check when you visit if the school really is doing what it says it is.

■ Fees. If it's a fee-paying school ask about additional charges made for SEN provision. A few mainstream schools include provision in the fees but many don't, and SEN or learning support can work out a very costly extra. Remember, even special schools may charge extra for some therapies so always check how inclusive the fees really are.

■ Ask what procedures are in place for home-school contact.

■ Ask for copies of recent newsletters. Do they celebrate pupil achievement? Which pupils, what kind of achievements? Are they informative, bossy or just a glossy marketing tool?

■ Try to get the views of parents with children already at the school, especially those whose children may have similar difficulties.

■ Check out what the school's inspection report says about SEN provision – see 'Reading the reports' below.

■ Outline the needs of your child and (if the school doesn't offer) ask for the visit to include time with the special educational needs co-ordinator (SENCo), learning support department or teacher in charge of special needs. Ensure your visit will include departments where your child has interests/talents as well as those where difficulties are expected to occur.

■ Ask for advice from the school on entry requirements and how these may be adapted to accommodate your child's SEN.

On a visit

SENs and their associated problems are as wide-ranging and individual as the child. The list below is geared to looking at mainstream schooling for a child who needs a moderate level of support. It isn't definitive but should provide useful prompts for a visit – select the questions that are most important to you prior to the visit, make a list and ask away.

If you decide to visit a school allow at least half a day, longer if your child will be boarding or has more complex needs. Be prepared to visit a school on more than one occasion. Ask for names and addresses of other parents.

The head

If the head isn't enthusiastic about helping SEN children then staff may not be as supportive or understanding as they should be. Be sure that your child will never be asked 'Is this the best you can do?'

■ What is the head's attitude to special needs?

■ Do they have high expectations of children with SEN?

■ Do they celebrate their successes? (on a weekly basis, for anything and everything, in front of the whole school at assembly)

■ Ask about end-of-year prize giving – what are prizes awarded for?

■ How does the head ensure children with SEN really are included?

■ For some SENs the level of pastoral care may be as important as specialist understanding of a particular disability – question the head about the academic/pastoral balance.

Academic matters: teaching, learning and the curriculum

■ Is the school's special needs support an integral part of the school, with a two-way flow of information between specialist teachers and subject teachers? As a rule of thumb, schools where SEN support is an add-on, with help found when needed and specialist teachers having little contact with the school, are really only suitable for mild cases. Ask a teacher or two where they turn to for advice, how often and how good it has been.

■ Ask if your child will be excluded or disabled from certain activities or parts of the curriculum because of their SEN. How flexible are they prepared to be about this? What do pupils miss in order to receive extra help? Do you mind?

■ How is the balance of the curriculum adjusted to take account of individual need? Extra English or maths instead of an additional GCSE?

■ Are teaching methods appropriate for SEN children – are support materials provided? How long are lessons? Are they in relatively short sections or are there long periods of dictation/copying off the board? Is this a school where lessons are typically half an hour's chat and then 'Now make notes of what I have said'?

■ Ask about the use of videos, information and commun- ications technology (ICT), tape recorders, Braille computers, practical equipment etc.

■ What teaching styles are used? If it's all chalk and talk it'll be fine for monkeys but not much use to anyone else. Find out if children are allowed/expected to think, discover, question. If so, how is this encouraged?

■ How are tasks adapted for those children who may, for example, have difficulty concentrating or writing for long periods? Are there individualised learning programmes and is work suitably adapted to take account of pupil need?

■ Try to find out how individual departments adapt teaching and learning for children with SEN. Are they as clued up as they should be to your child's needs? If not, will specialist provision be made available for your child and what guarantees can the school give that it will meet your child's needs?

■ Ask what lengths the school would go to, to accommodate a child with SEN? For example, are all areas of the school accessible to a wheelchair user? If not, would they consider capital projects such as building a ground floor lab to accommodate a child in a wheelchair? – we know some who have so don't be afraid to ask. By law all schools have to be inclusive and have disabled access, so make a serious fuss.

■ What learning support and classroom assistance would be made available to your child and how often? Does this meet with your expectations and your child's requirements?

■ Ask what specialist facilities, equipment and resources the school uses for SEN. There are concessions permitted to SEN pupils taking public exams. Is the school alert to these, such as providing a laptop or an amanuensis? (Push for the legitimate use of these via an EP report.) Is a full degree of training available for your child in how to make best use of any aids provided?

■ Ask how many pupils in the school have special needs like your child's and how many teachers offer specialist support. A sizeable peer group will ensure that support is there in depth, and that your child's difficulties are not underestimated, misunderstood or looked down on by staff or pupils. What about class sizes?

■ Are SEN pupils withdrawn from class for specialist tuition, or does the school double-teach, with a classroom assistant for those with problems? Deaf children often have a mentor at all times and the teacher in charge will often have a specially linked microphone. Ditto children with dyslexia, where a teaching assistant will offer help to the struggling pupil and also to the very bright who may be easily bored and lose interest.

The pastoral system: behaviour and support mechanisms

■ Find out how the school's sanction/reward system flexes to take account of problems, difficulties and specific needs of children. Is positive behaviour praised? How? What behaviour management programmes are in operation? Is there a planned programme to help build self-esteem? – if so, what?

■ Are all staff briefed on potential triggers for outbursts by individual children? What contingency plans are in place should confrontation arise in class?

■ Will the school control and administer medication if need be?

■ Home-school liaison and contact. How often are reports sent home? Does the school communicate on a regular basis with parents? How? Do they hold information meetings or run courses for parents? Do they have a parent support group, social group or other activities?

■ Are there any quiet or time-out areas where children who may become stressed or anxious can spend part of the day? Are there distraction-free work areas? Are they used? How? When?

■ Is there any peer support, mentoring or buddying, where an older child assists a younger, perhaps because of shared problems or difficulties?

■ Is a key-worker system or equivalent used? If so how is the key worker used in supporting the child? (A good key worker will have a positive relationship with the child, monitor progress, pull together multi-agency support, pass on relevant information to staff and mediate between teacher and pupil where relationships are strained.) Try to find out how pupils perceive their key worker.

■ What is the school's policy on bullying? (Beware the school that says they don't have any bullying!) How are children taught to respond to or deal with bullying and teasing?

Atmosphere

■ Speak to children. Ask them what they think about learning support, children with disabilities etc. This can be very telling of how accepted children with SEN are.

■ What is the atmosphere like in classrooms? Do teachers and learning staff appear to be working well together? Are children relaxed, happy and learning?

■ Talk to some pupils with the same diagnosis as your child. Are they bubbling with pride and confidence?

Specialist provision

■ When you speak with the SENCO or equivalent ask which SEN they feel the school caters particularly well for. Ask if there is a dedicated inclusion team or similar?

■ Ask if the school tests all children on entry. If not, who? When? How often? What conditions are screened for? What do they do once they have the screening results? There are lots of ways of screening and if a school is really switched on to SEN they will be testing and proactive with the findings.

■ What facilities does the library have to support children with SEN?

■ Are there any extra-curricular activities linked to SEN, such as signing classes for non-hearing-impaired children?

■ What staff training has recently taken place? What changes have recently taken place in teaching and learning for children with SEN? There has been an awful lot put out by the government and DfES on SEN in the last few years so there should be plenty of changes and developments afoot.

■ Ask if any of the teaching staff hold specific qualifications in the teaching of your child's SEN.

■ What, if any, in-class support is there?

■ Ask if children will be given individual education plans (IEPs) or set targets. If so, how are targets decided upon? By whom? Are pupils involved in the process? What involvement do parents have with this process? Do children know what their targets are and do they understand them? Are targets linked to work set? Do targets take account of personal goals? How are they monitored? How regularly are they reviewed? If IEPs are used ask to see a sample: is it useful?

■ If relevant, ask how often specialists such as the educational psychologist or speech therapist visit. How are requirements met? – in class, via small groups, individually, or a mixture of these?

■ What ICT provision is available, how frequently is it used and by whom? Who pays for any specialist provision such as individual laptops for individual need?

■ Are there any outreach teams or similar working with or from the school? For what? Outreach teams should provide and cascade expertise.

Additional guidelines if you're seeking a high level of support or specialist facilities

When it comes to choosing a specialist school beware of those schools that offer all things to all people. Remember that headteachers of specialist schools, like their mainstream counterparts, need to fill places in order to balance the books. Be wary of those schools who say they will take special measures for a child who is obviously going to be treated differently from the other children in the school. Examine carefully how they will carry out these measures.

If a child has a substantial learning difficulty, exam results may not be particularly useful to measure the success of a school (though they will give an indication of how well it is possible to do in that school). Try to find another baseline from which to work. See if you can discover what the typical child has in terms of both emotional and educational status on arriving at the school, and see if you can determine what value has been added to that child when they leave.

What success does the school have in getting their students into further education, or employment, and how successful are they in keeping a relationship with their ex-students to see if they are successful in their chosen field of work?

Look for signs of confidence in the older children, and see what help they are given with 'life skills', either formally through programmes in the curriculum, or informally in the way the pastoral side of the school is run. Ask for contacts with existing parents of children like yours, and phone three or four across the age range.

And again, what is the head's attitude, and what are the kids like? There is simply no excuse for any school to have low expectations and dulled kids.

Reading the reports

Ofsted and others

There's no longer any great secrecy surrounding school inspections. For some years now, reports have been published and available to view on the web. Log on to Ofsted, ISI (for independent schools), HMIE (for Scottish schools), DENI (in Northern Ireland) or Estyn (for Wales) (see 'Further information and help' below). But as with most reports there's a code to decipher and a few questions to ask. Inspection reports tell us lots if you know how to read the reports and understand what happens (or rather happened until very recently) when the notice of inspection drops through the letterbox.

Teachers suddenly discover the switch for the interactive whiteboard; lessons have a zing (must be the three months' planning). Work from last term isn't only marked, it's graded, with targets written in, ticked off and achieved all in one go (wow!). The graffiti disappears overnight. Perhaps more worryingly, there have been reported cases of some pupils being asked to stay away from school (which schools hotly deny), of being taken away on trips during the inspection, or, more commonly,of difficult classes being taught by senior management until the inspectors disappear.

Now there's a new Ofsted system in place. Instead of months of notice, followed by blood, sweat, tears, tantrums, exhaustion, depression (and that's just the head); there's a mere two minutes (well, as little as two days) before the inspectors scrutinise every last policy document, using only the finest-toothed nit-comb ever wielded by even the starchiest of school nurses. It's now a short sharp shock! Followed by a couple of days under the magnifying glass before the painful process is gone; quicker than a molar extraction and certainly too quick for the long-term sick to be dragged from beds or malingerers sent to theirs.

So what happens? They look at the data to hand: the Performance AND Assessment Report (PANDA – something that eats, shoots and leaves?), school improvement plan (SIP) and the self-evaluation form (SEF), trickier than the latest England team selection. Say all the teaching is fantastic and everything hunky-dory? Seeing is believing! Say all hopeless, they'll definitely carry out an observation. Something in the middle? Does this mean wishy-washy and in need of a kick? Things have to be kept up to date: no more last-minute marking of books. Setting targets and monitoring them is now part of the daily grind; writing lesson plans no longer something waved goodbye to at the end of teaching practice – there's even an expectation they'll be delivered to support assistants before, not after, lessons! Observations are shorter – as little as five minutes (because teaching was so impressive ... or boring?) and feedback faster.

The new reports are slimmer (so you can print them out without using an entire ink cartridge). Each section is headed and graded. Grade 1: outstanding (and we've seen several of these), grade 4: inadequate, with good and satisfactory in between. Where a section isn't grade 1, helpful comments will be made about what the school should do to improve. They grade overall effectiveness, achievements and standards, including how well learners with disabilities or learning difficulties progress, personal development and well-being of pupils including behaviour and healthy lifestyles (so the cola and chocolate machines are a no-no then, drat), and how well learners develop workplace skills (no, not how to have a sneaky fag break).

As you'd expect, the quality of provision is reported on. This isn't so much about how pretty the corridors are (though undoubtedly these will make an impression), it's how effective teaching and learning is, in meeting the full range of learners' needs (teaching to the middle no longer an option). A key part of the leadership and management section refers to how effectively management raises achievement and supports learners (but not really about how they support staff in doing so); governors can expect to be grilled (and they don't even get paid for the privilege of doing their job!) plus a comment on what pupils and parents think of the school (although the parent and student questionnaires have gone).

After the inspection, not only do the schools receive the report, with an opportunity to reply to it, but a delightful letter is sent to the children of the school. The one to secondary age is quite formal, though in pupil-friendly language, beginning: 'Dear pupils and students'. Primary ones we've seen have pretty graphics in colour and start 'Dear children'. Both thank the children for letting the inspection team visit (as if they had a choice). Ticks (primary) or bullet points (secondary) indicate what the inspectors liked best about the school, and an arrow (not a cross) or further bullet points mark out what they've asked the head to think about, so the school can improve (retirement?). Both end with a 'thank you for all your help'.

If you are looking through older inspection reports, or non-Ofsted ones (some of the others are well below Ofsted standard), the key bits are usually under headings along the lines of 'what the school does well and what the school could do better'. This provides a useful summary. If the school still looks interesting, some reports have grading, comparing the school with all schools, similar schools etc.

Beware, inspection reports can date very quickly – that can be a plus or a minus. In smaller schools, a change of head can alter the whole dynamics of the school. In large schools a previously outstanding report for Spanish may well be down to one member of staff.

Individual subject reports have disappeared from the new reports ... and don't be fooled into thinking specialist status means the school really is the best in the area for a subject – only one school can have the status. If another school nabbed maths and science first, schools may be left with limited options to grab the extra cash that goes with the status.

Read reports with care, and use your imagination – inspectors have seen too many schools and tend to think everyone knows what's meant by, for example, 'low-level disruption'. Does this mean 'Nothing much' then? No! It actually means the most annoying kind. Where lessons are constantly spoiled and marred by an individual or handful who know how to play the system, throw bits of paper while the teacher writes on the board, make silly noises, call out inappropriately. The sort that's much worse for other pupils than the occasional spectacular blow-out followed by a quick expulsion.

So read the reports: they're intended for the parents of the school and are a valuable part of the picture. But you will be lucky if the report is recent enough to be decisive. Ask those who know the school well to give the inside story, and consult guides such as this one. And always take a critical look yourself, before you entrust your child to a school.

The Commission for Social Care Inspection (CSCI)

Just when Flashman-era horrors have faded to a distant memory, the CSCI, the lead inspectorate for social care in England, has been given responsibility to inspect 'welfare arrangements' at state and independent boarding schools and to check they meet national minimum standards. For users of mainstream schools the CSCI's reports are not often a vital read, but for residential special schools they plug a vital hole. Not that standards in special schools are worse – the CSCI's reports are mostly full of praise – but it's much harder for a parent to judge what's going on after hours when your child has communication difficulties.

CSCI inspectors usually visit schools in teams of four, spending three days questioning staff and talking to small groups of boarders in private to ascertain whether their welfare is being 'adequately safeguarded and promoted'. They then write a detailed report, which is sent to the school head to sign and confirm as 'fair and accurate'.

Each school is judged on 52 standards. These cover a wide range of issues, including bullying, relationships between staff and boarders, racial and sexual discrimination, intrusions into privacy, accommodation, food, and access to information about events in the world outside.

So far, inspectors have concluded that most boarding schools look after children well. But they have found areas of concern in some schools. A handful have been criticised for the quality of accommodation and furnishings on offer to boarders, while others have been taken to task over the quality of food served up or for allowing raunchy posters on bedroom walls.

Eton, for instance, received high praise for providing 'a positive boarding experience for its pupils'. But inspectors also drew attention to the fact that rules on posters in boys' rooms varied considerably among the 25 boarding houses. 'In one house domestic staff reported that they were uncomfortable with some of the posters on display in the boys' rooms', they said. 'It is advised that school-wide guidance on posters be developed and implemented.'

At other schools boarders complained that they found it difficult to sleep at night and didn't have enough privacy and space. Some pupils at Clifton College said their dorms were noisy when they were trying to get to sleep. And although girls, parents and staff were 'very complimentary' about the boarding provision at Cheltenham Ladies' College, a few complained about the morning waking-up procedure. 'The pupils felt that they were woken up rather harshly, with loud greetings and bright lights, and on occasions staff knocked on doors whilst simultaneously opening the door', said the inspectors. Oh, the poor darlings.

But despite these quibbles, boarding schools are perceived as doing a good job. In 2004, Dr Roger Morgan, the Children's Rights Director for England – based within the CSCI – questioned 2,000 boarders and their parents and found they were generally positive about boarding schools. 'They are seen as offering a positive social life, with plenty of friends and activities – often across cultures – and with strong benefits of learning social skills and independence', reported Dr Morgan. 'The public caricature of boarding is very negative, with people imagining lots of bullying, poor care and extreme homesickness. These are not major issues for today's boarders or their parents.'

Indeed not. Parents' memories may stray back to the days when they were lads and lasses at boarding school; some of their schools would have had to have been transformed into the penal institutions that they resembled to accommodate those who had been convicted of crimes that, these days, would keep the *Daily Mail* fulminating for a week.

Bear in mind, though, that there is a long tradition in many schools of not talking to anybody about what's really going on. If, when you go around a school, the pupils are open and talk to you easily about how the little miseries of school life are dealt with, then they probably talked to the CSCI too.

Interview time

With thanks to Maureen Whitehead, SENCo of Malsis School, for additional information.

Once you've found the perfect school for your offspring how do you ensure they make the cut?

Processes vary from school to school. Some independent and selective schools interview and assess candidates up to 18 months prior to entry (and expect parents to shell out a hefty deposit too); others will assess children at any time provided a place is available. Some groups of schools, the Girls' Day School Trust (GDST), for example, have co-ordinated admission arrangements.

Some schools interview all their prospective pupils and even their parents as well. Others interview only scholarship candidates. Most interview those who have passed a minimum standard in the examinations. We know of some schools that expect the child to prepare a four-page CV, undergo a couple of interviews and have written confirmation of likely performance at common entrance, all many months prior to common entrance. Interviews may be with the headteacher or with other senior teachers. There may well be further tests done at the interview. For example, if Jessica did well in her English paper but less well in her maths, she may be taken off by the maths department and given some maths exercises to do. This should not be a cause for alarm but it is as well to be prepared for the possibility.

While, obviously, it is a good idea to be able to talk about a book you have read recently and know well enough to discuss, you cannot prepare for interviews. In fact, it is unwise to try to prepare. Children who have been drilled beforehand usually sit tongue-tied trying to remember what was practised at home, what she said in the practice, what Daddy told her to say. Interviewers will look for spontaneity, friendliness, and a willingness to think, to join in and to listen. This is especially important if Jessica is interviewed in a group with maybe two or three other candidates. If she is seen on her own, again, the interviewer will look for a relaxed, open approach, not a prepared speech.

When a child has known special needs, interview and assessment are the norm. This is to make sure school and child are a good match, and to consider any further adjustments needed to existing provision, if the school is to successfully meet the child's needs.

If there is a selection procedure for entry that involves a test or exam and your child qualifies for extra time or concessions in exams, let the school know in advance so they can make the necessary arrangements. The Joint Council for Qualifications (JCQ) updates the Regulations and Guidance for Candidates with Particular Requirements annually, so do make sure you refer to the most recent version (see the section 'Extra exam support' in Chapter 6).

Most schools will ask for relevant documentation – specialist reports such as those prepared by an educational psychologist or a statement of SEN – to be forwarded prior to interview or assessment (in some cases even prior to inviting you to look round). If not sent beforehand, inform the staff at the first interview of your child's special needs or any general concerns you have. This will give them time to put plans in place to ensure a smooth integration into the new school environment. This openness will be much appreciated, especially by the SENCo.

Assessments will usually be carried out by the special needs or learning support department or equivalent, and are designed to ensure they get the best out of the child. This may involve the child spending a day or two in school being assessed formally and informally. In some cases professionals, such as speech and language therapists, who would be working with the child, will be involved with the assessment process. Pre-testing can highlight hindrances to learning that can usually be addressed.

Interviews and assessments should be a two-way process, enabling both parties to ensure there will be a good fit. In a boarding school the matrons are also worth interviewing. They can be invaluable in helping with any exercises that need to be undertaken in a quiet and comfortable atmosphere, and you may find that they are also part of the support team. It has been said that the best person to interview is a child on the SEN Register. Ask them if their needs are being catered for, what they think of the support department and, best of all, do they know what their targets are!

And finally ...

Know your rights. Don't be bullied into a decision you might later regret. Many parents of children with special needs have to go to tribunal to fight for the school or provision they feel is right for their child. Don't be put off if you fall at the first hurdle. LEAs are notoriously mean: it is cheaper to educate within mainstream. Go to the Secretary of State if need be, and remember your final arbiter is the House of Lords. Finally, when you find the ideal school do tell us.

Further information and help

See also Part 4: Useful contacts.

CSCI (Commission for Social Care Inspection).
Web: www.csci.org.uk.
E-mail: enquiries@csci.gsi.gov.uk.
Tel (head office): 020 7979 2000
(helpline): 0845 015 0120. Fax: 020 7979 2111.
Address: 33 Greycoat Street, London SW1P 2QF

DENI (Department of Education Northern Ireland). Website has a clear link to SEN information from the main page.
Web: www.deni.gov.uk. E-mail: mail@deni.gov.uk.
Tel: 028 9127 9279. Fax: 028 9127 9100.
Address: Rathgael House, Balloo Road, Bangor, Northern Ireland BT19 7PR

Estyn. Office of HM Chief Inspector of Education and Training in Wales.
Web: www.estyn.gov.uk.
E-mail: enquiries@estyn.gsi.gov.uk (general enquiries) or publications@estyn.gsi.gov.uk.
Tel: 029 2044 6446. Fax: 029 2044 6448.
Address: Anchor Court, Keen Road, Cardiff CF24 5JW

HMIE. HM Inspectorate of Education in Scotland.
Web: www.hmie.gov.uk.
E-mail: enquiries@hmie.gov.uk. Tel: 01506 600200.

ISI (Independent Schools Inspectorate).
Web: www.isinspect.org.uk.
E-mail: info@isinspect.org.uk.
Tel: 020 7600 0100. Fax: 020 7776 8849.
Address: CAP House, 9-12 Long Lane, London EC1A 9HA

Ofsted. See website under 'Publications by topic' to view Ofsted's Guidelines for inspection, review, analysis and good practice etc regarding special schools, or for a complete list, 'A-Z of Ofsted publications'.
Web: www.ofsted.gov.uk.
E-mail: freepublications@ofsted.gov.uk.
Tel: 0700 263 7833.
Address: Ofsted, Alexandra House, 33 Kingsway, London WC2B 6SE

THE SCHOOLS

Good Schools Guide reviews

This section covers schools that we have visited, so we can describe them in detail. The write-ups follow the pattern set in our long-established sister publication The Good Schools Guide, with additional material on special needs.

The extent of the additional SEN information we've added reflects the complexity of special needs catered for. Where a school provides for the more severe end of special needs we've concentrated our reviews on the specialist support given, while retaining the character, personality and nuances of the school. Where a school does well by children with milder SEN our reviews concentrate less on the additional SEN provision and more on everything else, to help you decide which best fits your child's likes, interests and character. For example, lots of schools cater for the mildly dyslexic child so we concentrate on what else the school offers. Fewer schools cater for the severely autistic child, so the review will indicate how the school deals with autism, specialist programmes on offer, support for parents and siblings etc.

To this we have added 'What the school told us about their SEN provision', based on each school's answers to a detailed questionnaire. You can view these questionnaires, and search the information contained in them, online at www.goodschoolsguide.co.uk/?SEN. We haven't verified this information, but include it as a useful addition to our own researches. A few schools didn't want to tell us anything so we've made our own observations and would welcome yours.

Under 'What the school told us ...' are two sections: 'Summary' and 'Detail'. Under 'Summary', we encouraged schools to describe their SEN provision as a whole. We find the way that different schools have done this quite illuminating.

The second section, 'Detail', lists a school's SEN provision. Our questionnaire listed a wide range of conditions, frequently subdivided into 'mild', 'moderate' and 'severe'. The meanings of these terms varies with the condition (see Chapter 2), but 'mild' generally indicates a condition that can be accommodated with some extra learning support, individual tuition or a specific adaptation of learning tools, while experience with a 'severe' level of a condition indicates full-support specialist provision (such as teachers trained in sign language to cope with profound deafness).

We asked schools to indicate for each condition how experienced they were at dealing with it: whether they had had experience of children with this condition, whether they currently provided for such children in the school or whether they regarded themselves as a centre of excellence. To see the full range of answers, and to search our schools database using them, log on to www.goodschoolsguide.co.uk/?SEN. In this book we have listed the answers in abbreviated form:

Autistic spectrum disorders

ASP	Asperger's syndrome
AUT	autism
SPD	semantic pragmatic disorder
AUT(other)	other autistic: any autistic spectrum disorder that the school does not wish to put into one of the above categories

Behavioural difficulties

ADD	attention deficit disorder
ADHD	attention deficit hyperactivity disorders
CD	conduct disorders: behaviour that violates social rules and the rights of others
EBD	emotional and behavioural difficulties
OCD	obsessive compulsive disorders
ODD	oppositional defiant disorders
TIC	Tourette's syndrome and other tic disorders

Genetic and related disorders

DS	Down's syndrome
FRX	fragile X
GEN	other genetic: indicates a special provision or expertise not listed above. A description should be included in the summary of SEN provision

Learning difficulties

MLD	moderate learning difficulties
PMLD	profound and multiple learning difficulties
SLD	severe learning difficulties

Specific learning difficulties

DYSC	dyscalculia
DYSL	dyslexia
DYSP	dyspraxia
EAL	English as an additional language: facilities for non-native speakers with little or very poor English
SpLD	other specific learning difficulties: covers an increasing number of SENs not otherwise specified, such as dysgraphia, dysphasia etc

Sensory impairment

HI	hearing impairment
MSI	multi-sensory impairment: combination of visual and hearing difficulties possibly with additional disabilities
Sp&LD	speech and language difficulties
VI	visual impairment

Medical and related needs

CP	cerebral palsy
DEL	'delicate' children: a catch-all for conditions which require the school to take particular care with a child, although there are no learning difficulties as such. Haemophilia is an example, as might be leukaemia, cystic fibrosis or allergies
Epi	epilepsy
Eat	eating disorders: anorexia etc
PD	physical difficulties: may be specific or cover a wide range of physical disabilities
Oth	other: indicates specialist provision that does not fall within any of the descriptions above. Should be outlined in the summary

Other types of facility or support

BSU	behaviour support unit
Gifted	special provision for exceptionally gifted children
GWA	good wheelchair access. Access could be good even if the school is in a Victorian building on three floors with no lift, as long as the school is prepared to make major adjustments (eg moving a science lab) to accommodate a wheelchair user
LSU	learning support unit
POS	provides outreach support
ROS	receives outreach support
SLC	specialist language centre

ABBERLEY HALL

Worcester, Worcestershire, WR6 6DD

Tel: 01299 896 275
Fax: 01299 896 875
Email: john.walker@abberleyhall.co.uk
Website: www.abberleyhall.co.uk

• Pupils: 117 boys, 54 girls; 70 per cent board, the rest day. Also pre-prep/nursery with 50 boys, 35 girls • Ages: 7-13, pre-prep 2+ - 7 • Religion: C of E • Fees: Boarders £4,950; day £3,965. Pre-prep and nursery £955-£2,120
• School status: Independent • Opendays: October
• School gender: Mixed • Day/boarding: Takes boarders

SEN provision

Detail:
Now provide for in school:
Mild: DYSL; DYSP;
Moderate: MLD; DYSL; DYSP;
Severe: DYSL;
Experience of:
Mild: ASP; ADD; EBD; HI; VI;
Others: Sp&LD; Epi;

Summary: Abberley Hall has a strong learning support unit which deals with mild to moderate forms of the conditions stated below. Each child needing learning support is assessed by the team prior to registration.

What we say about the school – the full Good Schools Guide review

Head: Since 1996, Mr John Walker BSc (fiftyish) who was educated at Bradfield, and took his degree (in psychology from Surrey) on the wing. He went straight into schoolmastering from school itself, with stints at West Hill Park, Edgeborough and Sunningdale, before going to Pembroke House in Kenya, where he became head of studies (retains strong links – a rugby team was visiting when we were at the school). He also spent four years at Bramcote. His wife, Janie, is 'fully involved with the school, particularly on the pastoral side'; she also supervises the school ponies. A charming and delightful couple, with three grown up children, they love being in the 'people business'. Head comments that the 'golden thing about a small school is small classes – not only can you see the problems but you can always get on top of them'. He teaches maths to scholars and the bottom rung of the CE ladder and monitors work cards – both the good and the bad.

Entrance: Informal interview, no exam as such but children are tested before their interview to give the school some idea of their strengths and weaknesses. All ability in-take, a few means-tested awards on offer 'for nice children who need boarding, who will fit in and for whom the school can do something'. This is not a scholarship award and, often as not, will go to a single parent. Main entry in September but can and will take at any time.

Exit: Historical links with Winchester and still sends a regular supply; also to Shrewsbury, Radley, Cheltenham, a few to Eton, Malvern, Marlborough – all over. Girls to Cheltenham Ladies, Malvern Girls, Haberdashers' Monmouth, Cheltenham College, Malvern College, Tudor Hall, Rugby, Marlborough etc. New Malvern day house popular with locals.

Remarks: This is predominantly an English school (check the number of green wellies in the cloakrooms) so 'no need for EFL', despite the 'odd Spaniard or two who come for a couple of terms' (via the Astec agency in Madrid). Mixture of parents, mostly from Shropshire, Hereford, Warwickshire, Worcs and Derbyshire with a trickle from London; trad families and quite a number of first time buyers and, strangely enough, a growing number of expats and Services personnel. Excellent feedback and regular reports to parents. Super parents' book too, with alphabetical lists of subjects of possible concern eg. 'Teddies: These are a delightful feature of boarding school life and most pupils' beds are awash with them' (they were). School only offers full boarding with all-in and all-out weekends, plus some optional outs, no weekly boarding then. Top two years have their own bedside lights. Fabulous dorms carved out of stable lofts, the old drama studio, bachelor quarters.

The school is housed in a remarkable Grade II listed Victorian country house, complete with fine crumbling stucco and a ceiling to die for in the main drawing room. Outstanding conversion of existing buildings and sympathetic additions make this one of the most pleasing schools this (incredibly fussy) editor has visited in many years. A delight. School was originally founded in 1889 at Blackheath in south London – then called Lindisfarne after the monastery – and moved to Worcestershire in 1917 under the aegis of the remarkable Ashton family who eventually endowed the place when it became a charitable trust. Mostly quite jolly extensions, enlivened by a giant chess board which slightly suffers from courtyard cricket; plus peacocks and a guinea pig club. Fishing lake, 'the ink pot', popular with children. School digging own bore hole during our visit, sadly out of bounds, could have provided hours of pleasure, rather like the somewhat bizarre clock tower, popularly used for abseiling.

Wide range of abilities, so fairly tight academic standards; no prep; lessons and homework are combined and, after the first two years, school runs on a 29½ hour week. Reading encouraged, library has £750 worth of books new each term, pupils read in chapel and once a year they prepare and give a speech. Great for self-confidence. More than 40 per cent have some sort of learning support in super suite of rooms in the old lofts (there may be an extra charge). French from eight, with newspapers, telly programmes and articles as important as text books, regular study trips to France, with their own chalet near Bourg Saint Maurice in the French Alps. Groups of 9 and 10-year-olds spend three weeks there during the term learning 'to speak French but also to discover the mountains and to learn about the French way of life'. Latin on tap for all, with Greek option for the brightest; school has its own Latin course: Disce Latinum. Older children must spend 18 months doing German and Spanish – 'no choice'. Tiny classes, 12 the norm, usually streamed and set where necessary. School has abandoned Key Stage 2 tests in English, maths and science – 'they were a waste of time', head asserts, 'they disrupted teaching' – and embraced modern technology plus all the usual suspects, touch-typing for all at eight and a huge recent investment in machines and networks. School proud of its interactive whiteboards. 'We only bought them where they could be of use'. Class names vary according to form teacher.

No problems with staff either on the academic or the pastoral side, 'they like our way of life'. The entire span of British history is taught over three years. Extremely competent academic briefing booklet. Art, design, music and drama all important with stunning new music dept underneath the octagonal Ashton Hall in the former shooting range. Ambitious woodwork, DT and art rooms open each evening. Own kiln and good pottery. This is a keen sporting school, pupils regularly qualify for regional and local championships. Ricochet court (sort of mini-squash – not a lot of 'em around) plus astroturf, huge sports hall which is used by the local cricket club, climbing wall, super 25 metre indoor swimming pool and a proper manege. This is a terrific child-inspired school, no uniform except for 'formal', lots of visits, with firm discipline, jolly high standards producing self-confident, articulate pupils with a fair number of scholarships and an enviable CE record.

THE ABBEY SCHOOL READING

Kendrick Road, Reading, Berkshire, RG1 5DZ

Tel: 0118 987 2256
Fax: 0118 987 1478
Email: schooloffice@theabbey.co.uk
Website: www.theabbey.co.uk

• Pupils: 685 girls, all day • Ages: 11-18 • Religion: Non-denom • Fees: £2,980 • School status: Independent • Opendays: Early October; sixth form late October • School gender: Girls • Day/boarding: Day pupils

SEN provision

Detail:

Now provide for in school:
Mild: ADD; ADHD; EBD; DYSC; DYSL; DYSP;
Moderate: ADD; ADHD; EBD; MLD; DYSC; DYSL; DYSP;
Severe: DYSC; DYSL; DYSP;

Experience of:
Mild: HI; VI;
Severe: ADD; ADHD; EBD;
Others: CD; OCD; EAL;

Summary: The Abbey School is able to manage almost any specific learning difficulty (SpLD) eg dyslexia, dyspraxia, attention deficit (hyperactivity) disorder (ADD/ADHD), dyscalculia and possibly Asperger's syndrome, although this would always be after girls have already passed the entrance examination. The most common requirement is for pupils with dyslexia.

The SEN programme is managed by a full-time teacher, OCR certificated to give individual teaching to pupils with SpLD (dyslexia) through a 30 minute lesson once a week outside lesson time. Approximately 20 pupils are currently on this programme which usually lasts about two years.

The school also runs a special programme for Gifted and Talented pupils, developing strategies to assist them with their individual learning programmes, as well as assisting pupils where English is not their first language. Study skills are taught through SEN together with the PSHE programme.

What we say about the school - the full Good Schools Guide review

Head: Since 2002, Mrs Barbara Stanley BA PGCE FRGS (mid fifties). Educated at Glenlola Collegiate School, County Down, and universities of Belfast and Leicester. A geographer. Headed up Bedford High and Alexandra College Dublin before coming to the Abbey, where her predecessor left big shoes to fill. Her first year had its scrunchy moments and, through earnest dialectic with some miffed girls, staff and parents, she won affection and admiration. Direct, 'calls a spade a spade'. Humane. Approachable. Listens. Knows all the girls by name and levels with them – they like that. 'An educationist, a thinker, just right for the Abbey in these fast-moving times.' A quietly impressive person who blends strong purpose with open-minded curiosity. Her mission is to urge these exam-clever girls to try their hands at everything. Strong commitment to social responsibility, she is a member back home of the inter-faith Corrymeela Community (www.corrymeela.org), which reconciles riven communities post-Troubles.

Academic Matters: To have a daughter at the Abbey is to elicit the response 'Oh – ah' followed by a reverential nod. This is a premiership school with more about it of Chelsea than West Brom. At A level you're looking at 87 per cent A/B, 99 per cent A/C. Sciences very strong – a benefit of single sex – so we find 29 biologists, 24 chemists and 20 mathematicians compared with 17 Eng literati and 17 psychologists. Close to 20 per cent go on to med/vet degree courses. Art and des tech are straight-A subjects, history (difficult) exceptional. Few if any weak links (psychology could do better). Low numbers in IT ought to be boosted by recent investment. At GCSE it's 99.9 per cent A*-C (pity the one poor girl who got a D). Girls know the moment they get their results if they can step up to the sixth form.

Not an exam factory, 'no!' they emphatically say, though a visitor's first impressions are mostly of statistics glistening on noticeboards and even on classroom doors – everywhere you go you're up against last year's results. Parents – some crossly – assert that there's more, much more, going on than meets the untutored eye. 'Marvellous teachers', 'they respond to parental queries within 24 hours' – and get pretty good reviews from the girls, too. They want to know about problems and, said one mum, 'we wish we'd spoken out earlier'. Teachers' work ethic, the need to pack every day, imposes a focus which, for us as visitors, came over too frequently as blinkers. There were warm, well-mannered exceptions. Girls invariably jolly nice. Trad flavour – not much evidence of rebs or boundary pushers – this is the sort of place where attitude would probably come over as, like, so irrelevant. Tutors urge girls to wander outside the curriculum and follow their own intellectual curiosity – good results are not enough. Progress minutely, scientifically monitored, non-thrivers, 'coasters and sliders' chivvied and egged on by mentors abetted by parents.

Parents praise the way the school bends over backwards to accommodate unconventional A level choices – 'the timetabler is a genius'. They laud savvy university application advice and the way they back you to the hilt however you opt. They also praise teachers' expert understanding of their daughters, the way they set apt expectations. Marvellous drama and art, inspirationally led music, terrific sport, all examinable. Sumptuous LRC. Attractively grown-up routines for sixth formers. Own clothes, own classrooms, damn fine common room constitute a counter-lure to local excellent sixth form colleges.

SEN provision not high profile given the requirement to pass the entry exam and cope with the subsequently sprightly pace of life here notwithstanding an SpLD. Around 50 girls come to the attention of the SENCo, who also runs the gifted and talented programme. Most are mildly dyslexic, some dyspraxic. ADHD is not unknown. Around half of these get just 30 mins a week one-to-one.

Games, Options, The Arts: Sports England's Sportsmark Gold says it all. It means they coax the reluctant kindly and make it fun – parents agree – and they regale the very best and catapult them as high as they can go. Hockey, netball and cricket are tops, but it's all top notch – regular county and UK representation. Rowing growing: one GB oarsgirl and others coming through, but it's DIY – no school boats, girls join one of the several local clubs. Links with borough council brings in the local community. Fine swimming pool. Music very strong – 45+ per cent learn an instrument. Ensembles of all kinds from swing to Stravinsky, thrash metal in your own time, please. Drama is adventurous, art well resourced, well done. Considering they're all off the campus by 4 it's amazing what product they get. Good breadth of extra-curricular activities – plus D of E, Young Enterprise, the usual suspects. Trips and expeds in the hols.

Background and Atmosphere: School began in 1887 as Reading High School then, in 1914, after divorcing the Church Schools Company, took their present name in commemoration of a school which had conked out years before having, for two years, had Jane Austen on its books (she reckons they taught her nothing). Buildings turn-of-the-century, typical school brick, gloomy exterior but bright enough inside with some classy add-ons. Spacious playing fields and no sense of the crampedness you get at so many of these off-street city schools.

Pastoral Care and Discipline: Careful attention to best emotional health – this a particular preoccupation of the head. Teachers are appraised 50 per cent on their teaching skills, 50 per cent on their pastoral value. Compared with schools with similar pressures to succeed, it's amazing what a sunny lot they are. Sixth formers are buddies to younger girls and talk them through stuff as it happens. No matter how hard we peered, no evidence of anorexia or drugs – parents concurred, praised the PSHE and general caring vigilance. A striking feature, this. Community values and 'spiritual awareness' instilled by hymn and prayers each morning. They look beyond, too. Every year group must raise money for charity using their own initiative. Discipline is strict but reasonable. When a girl gets baleful they normally bring her round. Expulsion rare.

Pupils and Parents: Parents are professionals who want a powerhouse. Not all by any means awash with money – 20 to 30 per cent dropout after GCSE a symptom, though the growing excellence of local sixth form colleges encourages a fee holiday. Evident ethnic mix enriched by BBC monitoring station at nearby Caversham. No way snobby, too meritocratic. Not a school for a daffy lass, these are sorted girls all going for it. Pleasant social atmosphere, sense of pace, but we were charmed to see a little catching game happening in a corridor. They come also from Maidenhead (1/2 hr) and Windsor (3/4). Fleets of buses. Busy-bee PTA with own website – www.theabbeypa.org.uk.

Entrance: Own entry exam in maths, English and verbal reasoning. Interview picks up on any other desirable attribute. Around 45 per cent come up from the juniors, joined by girls from more than 60 other schools including sizeable wodges from Eton End, Highfield and St Joseph's. New sixth formers need min seven GCSEs at A*-C plus glowing reference.

Exit: Around 10 per cent to Oxbridge. They like London, Birmingham and Nottingham especially. Proper subjects at proper places – as you'd expect. Good range, preponderantly scientific. Heard-of high-fliers include the late Baroness Brigstocke, Sally Taylor (BBC South Today) and Helen Ganly, artist and social reformer. They lay no claim to Miss Austen but cherish Elizabeth Taylor, 'one of the great neglected voices of English fiction.' We know how she felt.

Money Matters: Fees decidedly competitive. Scholarships at age 11 up to 20 per cent for the best 10 per cent. Reverse these numbers in the sixth form, where 20 per cent get 10 per cent – another inducement to stay. Music awards win free instrumental tuition. Some bursaries for those in financial peril, esp in sixth form.

Remarks: It's an anxious business being and staying this good. League table place matters because parents obsess about it (they deny it, of course, and blame politicians). Defection to free sixth form colls post-GCSE has stimulated both a more young adult-friendly sixth form regime and greater efforts in all areas. This is a school which does the biz examwise, no doubt, but also tries with sincerity and enlightenment of purpose, especially under this humane head, to turn out girls who are in touch with everything they can do well and who will go on to be good citizens.

THE ACADEMY SCHOOL

2 Pilgrims Place, Rosslyn Hill, Hampstead, London, NW3 1NG

Tel: 020 7435 6621

• Pupils: 70 boys and girls, all day • Ages: 6-13

• Fees: £3,950 • School status: Independent

• School gender: Mixed • Day/boarding: Day pupils

What we say about the school - the full Good Schools Guide review

Head: Mr Garth Evans BA (forties), who started the school with Chloe Sandars in 1997. Taught English at Trevor Roberts (qv) for two periods of five years each, as well as private tutoring, and started the Academy School partly at the request of clients. 'They liked the way I taught – their children were inspired and given confidence – and suggested I set up a school along those lines.' Relaxed, informal and completely dedicated; at the end of a phone 24 hours a day, even for pupils who have moved on to secondary school. 'For a whole term I used to ring him up every day,' said a parent. 'He was totally involved.'

Entrance: Most come in at seven or ten years old but applications welcome at any time. Some pupils move on from pre-preps, others transfer from any of the local prep schools, a few from state primaries. Most have failed to thrive in more traditional and inflexible environments. Children spend a morning at the school, taking part in lessons, to see if they will fit into the group socially and educationally.

Exit: Girls usually leave at 11, boys at 13, to selective London day schools ranging from Mill Hill to Westminster, Queen's College to St Paul's Girls.

Remarks: The school was set up to fill the need for a small, nurturing, co-ed environment. 'Children need emotional security and to feel good about themselves. Then work falls into place.' Classes of up to about 14 pupils, but often fewer, meet in small rooms in two adjacent cottages, in the adjoining Unitarian chapel, complete with stained glass windows, and in its hall. The science teacher heats a solution over a portable Bunsen burner to a rapt class in a basement classroom. Another teacher sits on the steps in the sun marking books. 'It feels like going round to your favourite teacher's house for tea, only there happen to be other teachers and children there too,' said a parent.

Classes are not strictly by school year – they often encompass an 18-month age range but similar abilities. Specialist teachers for every subject, including French and Latin. Lessons start at 8am, and continue with a short break till (packed) lunch at 1pm. As far as possible, academia takes up the first part of the day, with art, music and sport in the afternoon. The school is mixed-ability, the teaching rigorous and lively. High praise from parents for the dedication of the staff, which includes several charismatic young men. No scholarship classes, though children do sometimes get scholarships. 'We want to make very little of the differences in ability. You can't improve the intellect but you can praise the endeavour. There's lots of praise here.' Parents value the breadth of learning, 'my 10-year-old has astounded us with his general knowledge.' As 11+ and Common Entrance exams approach, the level and pace of learning increases. 'They really work the kids hard – but the teachers work hard too,' said a parent. 'They'll stay till seven at night and give up their holidays if necessary.' Computers are the weakest link. 'All the children have one in their bedroom, so we don't use them overtly. But it would be desirable to teach them to touch-type if we could find the time.'

Not a school for a special needs, though it can accommodate mild learning difficulties, and behavioural problems provoked by more rigid environments. Children must be able to sit down and learn at an appropriate level. The small class sizes mean they get plenty of individual attention, with some one-to-one help where necessary. 'But our curriculum is flexible. We can help children catch up and improve their performance skills but they must not disrupt the group and they need to function as part of our community.'

Two afternoons a week of sport plus extra PE periods. Swimming and eg badminton at the nearby Royal Free leisure centre; football and hockey on Hampstead Heath when weather permits; PE in the hall next door. The school does on occasion put together a team to play a match but its small pool of players means success is a bonus. 'We were excited to lose by only 5-4 to Westminster Under School, until we found out we had played their 12th or so team.'

Art, however, is strong, with a specialist pottery teacher and – unlikely as it seems in such a small space – a kiln. Co-proprietor Chloe Sandars was trained at the Royal Academy of Music and teaches singing plus another music lesson every week. Children can also learn the violin, clarinet and saxophone, and there is a small orchestra. Rehearsals for the big school musical take over the school for several weeks of every summer term. 'The standard is phenomenal,' said a parent, 'and we're used to the performances put on by the big senior schools.'

Informal environment; everyone is on first name terms, and rules and regulations are minimal. 'Everything is based on mutual respect. Our children get plenty of freedom but they have to meet their responsibilities. It's a far more sophisticated concept than having a list of rules. You put the mirror up in front of them and let them look at themselves. That's far worse than any punishment.

'The main ethos of the school is that we really care for the individual needs of each child. They feel completely safe and secure emotionally.' Parents concur, 'my son, who felt alienated at his previous school, loved it here from the start. It's small, cosy and very nurturing. They steer a steady course between being too strict and too lax, and they get the most out of every child.'

Families are mostly wealthy, from Hampstead and environs. Most have already tried the more conventional prep schools. 'I just had a gut feeling my son wasn't happy at his old school. As soon as I walked in here I knew he would adore it and he did. It gave him the confidence to feel he could succeed.'

ACKWORTH SCHOOL

Ackworth, Pontefract, West Yorkshire, WF7 7LT

Tel: 01977 611 401

Fax: 01977 616 225

Email: admissions@ackworthschool.com

Website: www.ackworthschool.com

• Pupils: 180 boys and 190, girls of whom 100 board

• Ages: 11-18 • Religion: Quaker (but other faiths welcome)

• Fees: Senior: day £3,118; boarding £5,166. Coram House: day £1,890 • School status: Independent

• Opendays: A Saturday in early October • School gender: Mixed

• Day/boarding: Takes boarders

SEN provision

Detail:

Centre of excellence for:

Mild: DYSL; DYSP;

Moderate: ASP; AUT;

Severe: ASP; AUT;

Others: EAL;

Experience of:

Mild: ADD; ADHD; EBD; DS; DYSC; HI; CP;

Moderate: MLD;

Others: Sp&LD; Epi;

Summary: The school has an autism resource which provides education for four students with Asperger's syndrome taught individually and integrated as is appropriate to mainstream classes.

The school has a qualified SEN teacher providing support to students with dyspraxia and dyslexia and working with teachers to support student learning. However the school does not have learning support assistants.

What we say about the school - the full Good Schools Guide review

Head: Since 2004, Mr Peter J Simpson MA (early forties) educated at Dartford Grammar, read history at Oxford and got his MA in education management from Keele. Was deputy head at Kimbolton and head of humanities at The Grange School in Cheshire. Loves singing and has two passions – opera, especially Wagner, and outdoor pursuits. Spent five years running an outdoor pursuits unit, and behind the thick-rimmed spectacles his face lights with enthusiasm as he tells of the range of activities available at Ackworth, everything from caving through mountaineering to cross-country skiing. He thinks the school is a real gem and should celebrate achievements more overtly. Pupils say the head understands, is in tune and in touch, 'it's the small things he does that make a difference,' he's keen to please, completely at ease with them and always has a quip or witticism. All this about a head who expelled a couple of youngsters shortly after his arrival – surprisingly, pupils sympathised with him.

Academic Matters: Not an academic hothouse, majority of pupils study for 9 GCSEs with a creditable 90 per cent A*-C. At A level A/B grades fluctuate between 43 and 63 per cent. Class sizes average 18 in the senior school and 8 in the sixth form. Science and maths are ever popular but it is in the creative subjects where the real strengths lie. Plenty of IT facilities including a new ICT suite, next step is to improve the integration of IT into all areas of teaching. Pupils say that lessons are interesting, lively and fun and that they are encouraged to think for themselves and to question.

The school identifies fifteen per cent of pupils as having special educational needs, mainly dyslexia and dyspraxia, though the school can cater for those with dyscalculia, behavioural difficulties and autism. For more than one in seven pupils English is not their first language, of these more than half receive EAL support. School has a newly opened International Language School – doesn't guarantee admission to sixth form but is a step in the right direction.

Not a school for special needs – but a school that caters outstandingly well for children who have them. Pupils display a broad range of aptitudes, characters and academic ability. Head proudly tells of a recent star autistic pupil who got seven A*s and three As at GCSE – talented teaching and a genuine understanding of the needs of the individual child. Special needs children thrive in part because the Quaker ethos – 'that of God is in each of us' – is reinforced by school's motto – non sibi sed omnibus (not for oneself but for everybody.)

The school houses a fantastic, heart-warming and deservedly highly regarded autism resource where four statemented pupils are educated. Expert and compassionate resource head, develops confidence and self-esteem. Attention is paid to developing social and communication skills at all levels including specialist speech and language therapy, computer conversations and using interests such as snooker to promote conversation. Teaching is painstakingly geared to the individual. Each child has an individually designed curriculum, and with the help of dedicated learning support assistants pupils are integrated into a range of classes. Inclusion is a two-way process: children in the main school welcome the pupils from the resource and clamour to spend break and lunchtimes at the resource's Shed Court Club. Two major drawbacks – what lies ahead after Ackworth for those lucky enough to have spent time here and, with only four places available, it's likely to be 'no room at the inn'.

Games, Options, The Arts: Oodles of clubs and societies; those old enough can learn to drive, others take up jewellery, silversmithing, join Amnesty International, relax with yoga, philosophise, fence, play golf – you name it they offer it (well maybe not CCF, rugby or wargaming but pretty much everything else). Students must participate in at least two activities. All pupils play sport, and the school offers outreach support to local physically disabled through Sports Ability, which is modelled on the Paralympics. Music, music technology and drama very popular with plenty of opportunities to participate. Technology and design including HE and textiles are sought after options – over the years school has boasted several Arkwright scholars. There is a fabulous DT department – school full of desks, chairs, cupboards etc made by them ... who needs IKEA with these chaps around?

Background and Atmosphere: One of the first Quaker schools, founded by John Fothergill in 1779. Set among undulating fields and pastures, the school was a Foundling Hospital until the magnificent site and elegant sandstone Georgian buildings were purchased by a group of eminent Friends to provide a place to educate Quakers 'not in affluence.' Recent sympathetic additions blend into the Georgian splendour with the little changed rural landscape providing a contrast to the nearby earthy industrial heartlands. A magnificent setting, it's no wonder an overwhelming sense of joy pervades. Indeed this is such a friendly, welcoming school you probably need to allow two days for a visit instead of the usual one. We were constantly hijacked, not just by staff (who in some schools sprint faster than Kelly Holmes when they see us beckoning) but also by enthusiastic youngsters with a refreshing openness. They had no idea who we were but nonetheless were keen (and determined) to relate the many joys of being at the school and the fun they have, whether we wanted to know or not! We tried desperately hard to ease out a few negatives but all were either too canny to fall for our wily ways or genuinely too enthused by everything.

Pastoral Care and Discipline: There's a great family feel to this school and, as you might expect, discipline errs on the side of tolerance and understanding but that doesn't mean those who push the boundaries don't get punished. Tutors oversee pastoral care but others are involved. Boarding is an integral part of the school and accommodation is very good, some rooms even have en-suite facilities. Day pupils are always welcome to stay for both tea and supervised prep at no extra cost; the weekend activity programme set up for boarders is open to day pupils too. A full(ish) programme is rounded off on Sunday evenings with a Quaker meeting followed by a special tea and activity perhaps a talk, lecture or musical event.

Pupils and Parents: Mostly from professional and business families living in Ackworth and Pontefract with some travelling from Sheffield and Doncaster. Of the 100 boarders, two thirds live abroad, half of these are Chinese. School takes students who will both benefit from the education provided and are willing to make the most of the opportunities offered.

Entrance: Half the pupils come from Coram House, the rest in equal numbers from local state and prep schools. Entry is based on tests in maths and English together with a non-verbal reasoning test. For sixth form entry a minimum of five GCSEs at grade C or above are required.

Exit: Almost half leave at the end of year 11 mostly for local colleges but are replaced by new entrants, mainly boarders. Majority (97 per cent) of sixth form goes on to university, a couple a year to Oxbridge, some overseas, rest to a range of destinations with Leeds, Nottingham and Newcastle perennially popular.

Money Matters: Over 15 per cent of pupils receive help with fees either through scholarships (academic, art, music), bursaries or staff concessions. Discounts for second and subsequent children.

Remarks: If you want to be miserable or bored, go somewhere else. Rule breakers and those easily fatigued would find this school hard to cope with, but anyone wanting to experience and enjoy life will have a lot of fun.

Aiglon College

1885, Chesières-Villars, Switzerland,

Tel: +41244 966 161
Fax: +41244 966 162
Email: info@aiglon.ch
Website: www.aiglon.ch

• Pupils: 350 boys and girls, almost all board • Ages: 13-18 • Religion: Ecumenical • Fees: SFr 45,800-SFr 64,600 annually for boarding • School status: Independent • School gender: Mixed • Day/boarding: Takes boarders

SEN provision

Detail:
Centre of excellence for:
- Mild: DYSL;
- Moderate: DYSL;
- Severe: DYSL;

Now provide for in school:
- Mild: ASP; ADD; ADHD; EBD; DYSC; DYSP; HI; VI;
- Moderate: ADD; ADHD; MLD; DYSP;
- Others: EAL; Sp&LD;

Summary: We are a small department of four experienced teachers. At Aiglon the following deterines determines that a student needs support: he or she may already have received literacy and/or maths support in a previous school, be found to have weaknesses in school screening tests or have difficulties in one or more subjects reported by teachers and/or houseparents. A course of appropriate action is decided. This may involve further testing by an educational psychologist, counselling, speech therapy, sophrology or sessions of one on one specialist teaching. Aiglon is the only International School in Switzerland that uses the Davis Method as an integral part of a young dyslexic student's training. The Head of Department is a Davis® Dyslexia Correction Facilitator.

What we say about the school - the full Good Schools Guide review

Head: Since 2000, Rev Dr Jonathan Long DPhil MTh (University of South Africa) BA (Natal) MA (plus one or two others that he doesn't use) (forties), who came to Aiglon as chaplain in 1998. Educated at Monkton Combe, Bath, he first taught in South Africa and was previously chaplain and housemaster at The Dragon School, Oxford. While in Oxford, apart from adding to his degree portfolio and breaking athletic records, he was instrumental in helping independent schools develop sound approaches to PSE/PSHE and pastoral care. He is married to Sue, DipEd (primary education), BPhilEd (Hons) (Warwick) who teaches special needs. The Longs have two daughters. A manic triathlete, snowboarder and enthusiast, Dr Long was dead worried before he took up his post at Aiglon, having 'spent the last years looking after little ones, I've forgotten how to deal with the older version'. Obviously not a problem now, this is a supremely happy and self-confident headmaster.

The GSG has long been a fan of the gifted and inspirational Dr Long (or Revlong as he used to be). Dr Long took over as head of Aiglon following a period of some turmoil – the previous headmaster left in the context of an acrimonious divorce. At the same time, media interest in the school was especially high after it was announced that the Duke of York's children were coming to Aiglon. A suspected intruder in a girls' boarding house led to heightened media attention and a great deal of anxiety. Six years later – no royalty but a very expensive new security system.

Already familiar with the running of the school, Dr Long has busied himself over the last five years with restoring confidence. A sensitive and sensible head, he regularly spends time with various student groups thrashing out the problems of the moment. Still a pastor at heart – albeit a slightly unconventional one – Dr Long and his two deputy heads (pastoral and academic) run an 'open-door policy' and are always on hand for advice. 'No problem at all about getting staff' – a recent ad for houseparents elicited almost 200 replies and a shortlist and their spouses were flown out to Aiglon so that both parties 'could take a look'. The days of photographs of Swiss mountains and interviews at the East India Club are long past.

Academic Matters: Follows a British curriculum, adopting the pick 'n' mix attitude to GCSE, IGCSE, AS and A2 levels. Setted according to ability in English, French and maths. A level and GCSE results have risen steadily over the past five years (99 per cent pass at A level and 87 per cent A*-C at GCSE in 2005). Most students have English as a second language and the tiny classes means creditable results at A level and a good university track record. The school is an accredited SATs centre (US qualification) and we were particularly impressed by the school's American university entrance programme. All students must study English and some maths in sixth form, though SATs qualify. A good, but not enormous, range of A level subjects on offer – the sciences, maths, humanities, languages – French, Spanish and German – plus philosophy, psycology, media, business studies economics etc. Cyberspace link-up lessons where tutors in the UK can, via a pan-tilt-zoom camera, have instant access to pupils' work in Switzerland. Critical thinking popular.

Small classes, max 16, fabulous new teaching block and very recent modern languages centre with state-of-the-art computers and networked throughout (Internet screened), history seminar room more like a boardroom than a classroom – cushy chairs, posh tables etc. 'But', says Dr Long, 'this is not a school for the straight academic who requires a lot of time to achieve results'. EFL and well-established dyslexia help available, computers on hand to pull up pupil's assignments in special learning needs dept for extra assistance. There are four dedicated and well-qualified specialist teachers in the SEN department pulling in feedback and info from a variety of sources. Cope well with the range of 'dys-strata'. Mark Readings two or three times a term are noted and go towards the final Transcript, which counts for university entrance in the States.

Games, Options, The Arts: Snazzy new art department with imaginative work and dramatic sculpture at entrance – bets were taken locally how long the thing would stay up – six years now and no sign of a wobble. Drama and music technology up to A2. Music department (along with computers and the like) in JCB building, four grand pianos, plus own recording studio. School puts out a local English radio station.

More team games than before (including rugby) but not a cricket school. Brand new Astroturf football facility on campus. Football popular, plus the minor sports; tennis strong, five courts, which adapt to basketball, scattered throughout the campus – well, it is on a mountainside. Skiing strong, but don't expect to spend all winter on planks, minimum four hours a week isn't bad though. Swimming in the local pool further up the village. PE compulsory, plus Exes (expeditions) which range from guided tours of the European capitals, to four-day ski-touring sleeping in huts, climbing Mont Blanc, community service and the like. Aiglon is part of the Round Square Association.

Background and Atmosphere: First founded in 1947 by John Corlette, who had previously taught at Gordonstoun, the school hiccuped along until 6th January 1949 when it opened with six pupils (including a Siamese princess), a headmaster, four teachers and two staff. Most of the pupils came to Villars for health reasons (think TB). The early years were beset with financial disasters, usually to do with currency fluctuations, but the school survived, went co-ed in 1969, and is the only British international school in Switzerland.

The school buildings – boarding houses/classroom blocks or a mixture of both – we are on a slope here so plenty of opportunity for multi-use, each with its own front door – are scattered around the bottom of Chesières (with one family still resolutely remaining in the middle of the campus). The boarding houses are single sex, with the opposite sex being allowed into the ground floor only. Major re-vamp nearly completed including brand new senior boys' boarding house. Dorms, usually in threes, but occasional singles, ski boots everywhere when we visited. Think a rash of slightly oversize chalets with lots of pine inside and out, juxtaposed with some fabulous modern architecture. No 'grounds' to speak of and no fenced-off areas.

Serious amount of fundraising for 55th anniversary and recently bought the local post office, no apparent current intention to sell stamps though, more likely that the '2,000 square meters of building land' will become part of an as-yet undesigned 'multi-purpose sports facility'. Serious house upgrading under way, school has leased le Cerf hotel as a sixth form girls' house. Ah the misery of life on a mountain.

Food much improved since out-sourced catering introduced; salad bars, and 'students are also served more of their preferred dishes and the different tastes and preferences between the boys' and girls' houses are taken into account'. Surprisingly strict dress code, no visible tattoos or piercing, no tongue studs, boys may not wear earrings but girls can have several. Fifteen minutes' meditation (much appreciated by pupils) scheduled daily before lessons.

Pastoral Care and Discipline: Houseparents, personal tutors, head and his two deputies all on hand to help. Enormous amount of support – with 57 different nationalities sometimes little problems can escalate out of all proportion. Fifty-seven nationalities also means grey areas in what is perceived as 'normal' behaviour in a British school. No smoking allowed on campus, or in any public place, but difficult to enforce a total ban when parents offer their children ciggies at home though help with quitting smoking available. Wine and beer from 17 OK with meals in the village. Regular random drugs testing – at least ten a week, from the third form upwards. Public displays of affection (PDA) discouraged, but the Italians are a warm and affectionate race, so forget the six-inch rule. 'Holding hands, or a friendly goodnight kiss after a school event are acceptable; heavy clinches, sitting on partner's lap, petting, couples being alone together in a closed room' are not. Strongly enforced PSE/PSHE programme. Series of punishments – laps, gating, suspension, expulsion.

Pupils and Parents: Truly international, half term only in the autumn term, long weekends in winter and summer, local students allowed out the odd weekend. Fifty-seven different nationalities, split in dorms as far as possible by language, max six from any one country. Mixture of princes, industrialists and the global A stream.

Entrance: Own series of admissions tests, interview with head and refs from present school for all. Satisfactory GCSE or equivalent for sixth form entrants.

Exit: Post-GCSE for sixth form elsewhere – A levels or IB. Otherwise to universities all over. Modest recent Oxbridge successes and tranches to Bristol, King's and University Colleges, London, LSE, Edinburgh, Durham (and quite a lot to the British 'new' universities – Oxford Brookes, Napier etc) as well as an impressive collection to America, Ivy League as well as Boston, Tufts, John Hopkins, NYU and Georgetown.

Remarks: Strong educationally, strong emotionally, tough physically. Aiglon, for all the glamour and the hype, is not an easy option. Neither for the shy and retiring nor the unstreetwise. Exciting, challenging, purposeful.

ALBYN SCHOOL

17-23 Queen's Road, Aberdeen, AB15 4PB

Tel: 01224 322 408

Fax: 01224 209 173

Email: information@albynschool.co.uk

Website: www.albynschool.co.uk

• Pupils: 420 boys and girls in the whole school (but that includes toddlers doing a half day in the nursery); Junior school: 130 girls with (eventually) 150 boys; senior school: 200 girls • Ages: 3 months to 18 • Religion: Ecumenical • Fees: £2,633. NB termly fees vary with the length of the term • School status: Independent • School gender: Mixed • Day/boarding: Day pupils

SEN provision

Detail:

Now provide for in school:

Mild: ASP; DYSL; DYSP;

Severe: HI;

Summary: No response – but in our view well disposed to SEN children. SEN details added by us.

What we say about the school - the full Good Schools Guide review

Head: Since 2002, Dr John D Halliday BA PhD (fiftyish) who was educated at Abingdon School, did his BA in German and linguistics at Exeter and his PhD in Cambridge where his thesis was on Austrian literature. He just loves teaching and enjoys 'the developing relationship with children'. Married, with three children. Dishy, with a delicious sense of humour. His career path is a varied one, he started by teaching English in Passau uni, became a freelance translator for a couple of years before going to Merchiston as head of German, followed by head of langs and housemaster at Sedbergh thence to Rannoch, where he was head, which must have been a pretty dispiriting experience ('it was tough latterly but the school was inspirational'). Post Rannoch he taught langs at Dollar for a year.

Albyn had had a 'pretty rocky ride over the past five years', and was 'slightly wobbly' when Dr Halliday arrived but with 'an incredibly good core of loyal kids and parents' he has succeeded in turning the place around and attracting new blood. Ten year plan = boys. They start in the junior department (only) from August 2005 and two brave eight-year-olds were spending a day in the place when we visited. Clutching their tennis rackets they seemed undaunted by the monstrous regiment. Twenty-five boys have confirmed places, and 2005 saw 18 new girls arrive in P1 and P2. So numbers are up. New heads of geography, history, chemistry and PE appointed and school pretty much back on track, 'good common room, good supportive atmosphere'.

Academic Matters: No particular specialisms, broad range of subjects and results 'achieved with girls of varying ability', one or two fall below C. School follows Scottish system, with Intermediate II offered in art and design, sciences, business management, English and maths. Classical studies and Latin, not much take up of the latter above Standard Grade, accountancy and finance make a welcome addition to the usual suspects. Information systems to intermediate 2 only; business management (very popular and pleasing results) plus modern studies all offered up to Advanced Higher (school adds that all subjects can be taken at Advanced Higher). Higher biology produced an outstanding 11 candidates out of 16 examinees getting As, chemistry and physics both threw up six A candidates (out of nine and eleven candidates respectively). 100 per cent A-C in maths (with eight at A out of 19 takers); quite a number of takers and fair showing in English, more take up in German than French but better marks in the latter. Good music and creditable performance in art and design. Certain amount of almost individual teaching with only one pupil taking the subject; whilst one expects this with Latin (actually three) and Gaelic (learners), it is surprising to find only one candidate taking higher accountancy, and penny numbers doing business management, classical studies and history, but the results are impressive (if hardly cost effective).French and German throughout but Spanish only in the sixth form. Max class size 23, with low teens for practical subjects (school sez 20, but in practice this is much smaller; most classes are 10/15). Comprehensive computer system, class taught as well as in suites, laptops abound, pupils can bring in their own. All pupils have their own e-mail and can e-mail homework and queries to staff. Impressive online support system in most subjects. European computer driving licence for all, key boarding taught early in the school; no interactive whiteboards (yet). Surprisingly only one learning support teacher, based in the primary department who covers the whole school, Dr Halliday talked of employing another SEN specialist who will probably be equally overworked as school caters for dyslexia, dyspraxia, mild Asperger's as well as having one pupil who is profoundly deaf (she came to the school with special microphone and class assistant funded by the LEA, who 'actually refused to give the girl any support at all once she came to us'). No EFL help available as such, but 'lots of support in the classroom', SEN teacher takes individual groups and double teaches a bit – she is very 'willing'. She would need to be. Scribing, readers and all the rest – extra time available for exams – this is no longer a blanket 20 per cent per pupil per exam, but different pupils may need different concessions in different subject. Case must be made for each. No extra charge for SEN help.

Games, Options, The Arts: Main games field at Milltimber five miles away, pupils are bused (and new games changers in pipeline to cope with the boys). Positive netball and hockey with regional representation, and masses of individual sports: national representation in athletics, swimming, rowing, riding, sailing and ten pin bowling. Stunning art dept, with a number of pupils going on to higher things in the art world. Very jolly with papier maché, acrylic and silk screen work. Hot on costume design and much use made of local museums. Strong art and architectural stream. Fantastic music, 'most girls play a musical instrument' and loads of participation in either choir or instrumental ensembles. Good representation in the National Youth Orchestra plus jazz, ceilidh bands and flute ensembles. Keen drama and dance (Dancercise important), the former still extra-curricular. Couldn't do better. Enthusiastic YE, sweeties were the latest offering and highly competitive D of E with oodles of golds. Strong club culture, quizzes, chess, photography, gardening and Scottish country dancing. Keen on public speaking and debating.

Background and Atmosphere: School was founded in 1867 by Harriet Warrack who started teaching girls at home, advertising locally for pupils. Albyn Place (just down the road) became the school's home in 1881, hence the name, and Albyn School for Girls moved to Queen's Road in 1925 – all of which is pretty confusing as St Margaret's School for Girls is still based in Albyn Place. The son of one of the gardeners at Duff House, Alexander Mackie was an early moving light, writing books on English (he was university examiner) and made the school an Aberdeen institution, with emancipated Albyn girls on Aberdeen uni student council by 1907. The current school is based in four attached Victorian merchants' houses, with fantastic ceilings, two well-used libraries and the predictable garden expansion. An enchanting new-build houses the tinies (cots, high chairs and nappies). Dr H seems pretty nonplussed by this addition ('I never thought I would become a Pampers expert when I was at Cambridge') but it pulls in the punters. Tinies (as opposed to babies) are housed in the old stables, and there is a splendid new-build housing a dramatic science wing; equally impressive music dept above hall and gym in the west end of the school. New dedicated purpose-built primary on the stocks (to be opened in 2007); loos etc as well as classrooms will deplete the play area further. But it is not that cramped and there are dedicated enclosed nursery and preschool play areas. School hopes to increase numbers to 650. The school has a strong family feel, which Dr Halliday is keen to keep, but logistically it is a complicated complex of corridors between the houses. Fire doors everywhere. Rather expensive looking prospectus tied up in a tartan ribbon which will have to have a new cover as it still boasts Albyn School for Girls.

Pastoral Care and Discipline: School divided into four clans, pupils can relate to heads of years and guidance staff when in difficulty. Sense of community – school aims to boost the confidence of the shyest child. Head has a policy of zero tolerance for drink 'n' drugs 'n' rock 'n' roll. So expect to be out for persistent bullying or drugs. Dr H has expelled elsewhere and would have no hesitation. Fags and booze on school premises = detention followed by exclusion followed by out. 'Bullying is usually changing friendship groups' seems about right, but actual bullying is regarded as a no-no.

Pupils and Parents: Mixture of professionals, lot of oil and gas, but farmers and marine engineers in the parent body. All hugely supportive and 'tightly knit' – as are the governors. Fair number of first time buyers, parents can drop off early and pick up late for pupils in the lower school but there is an extra charge. International bias, but lots of home grown ones too; nice strong middle class ethos with girlies neat in check dresses and a good line in frilly white socks which seems to be the craze of the moment. Check head bands too. Kilts mandatory for high days and holidays – even in the summer term – and they have to be proper kilts and not the kilted skirt variety – any tartan.

Entrance: Assessment for tinies up to senior school when formal exam (not many turned away, automatic advancement throughout the school, pupils can and do join at any time – throughout the year assuming space available; a very few years are full). Not many come post Standard Grades.

Exit: About five leave post-Highers, the rest stay; most (95 per cent or so) will end by going to uni, often after a gap year, and almost all to Scottish unis. Aberdeen popular – their business admin is particularly good, though surprisingly not that many opt for it. One recent candidate to Cambridge and the odd maverick to Sheffield, Belfast or film studies in Southern California and marine science at Miami.

Money Matters: Incredibly strict scale of rules for payment but (Aberdeen, remember) parents can get a 2 per cent discount if they pay the whole annual whack within a fortnight of the beginning of the autumn term. Discounts of 5 per cent for second child from preschool nursery up, and fifty per cent rebate for third and subsequent children. School 'will do what it can to help parents in difficult times, as long as they are open and talk to us'.

Remarks: With numbers of potential pupils dropping along with the national birth rate this was a school in decline but new initiatives and a stab at lads have reversed this. Worth thinking about if you have tender flowers of either sex whom you would like to have educated together.

Aldenham School

Elstree, Borehamwood, Hertfordshire, WD6 3AJ

Tel: 01923 858 122
Fax: 01923 854 410
Email: enquiries@aldenham.com
Website: www.aldenham.com

• Pupils: 451 boys, 33 girls (years 7 and 8 and sixth form only); 137 'proper' boarders (45 from overseas) + 30 flexi-boarders, rest either day or weekly boarders • Ages: 11-18
• Religion: C of E foundation with ecumenical overtones
• Fees: Day: pre-prep £2,560; prep £2,831, junior £3,266; senior £4,741. Day boarders: junior £4,098; senior £5,662. Boarding: junior £4,892; senior £6,888.
• School status: Independent • Opendays: June and October
• School gender: Mixed • Day/boarding: Takes boarders

SEN provision

Detail:
Experience of:
Mild: ASP; AUT; ADD; ADHD; DYSC; DYSL; DYSP; SpLD; VI;
Others: SPD; EAL;

Summary: We have an extremely good SEN Department. However, pupils do need to be able to cope in the normal classroom situation; they are not taught separately, but have extra individual tuition as and when necessary with qualified SEN teachers.

What we say about the school - the full Good Schools Guide review

Head: Since 2000, Mr Richard Harman MA PGCE (forties), educated at The King's School, Worcester, and read English at Cambridge. Tried his hand at the marketing side of publishing for a couple of years, then five years at Marlborough (with a sabbatical to do a PGCE) teaching English and drama, and twelve at Eastbourne College where he progressed from head of English via housemaster of girls' boarding to becoming part of the senior management team. Whilst at Marlborough, he met and married his wife, who currently teaches at South Hampstead High School. One daughter at Uppingham.

Urbane, charming, film star looks. Lots of staff changes – giving the place a shake-up – but off to head Uppingham in July 2006. New head is to be Mr James Fowler, currently deputy head of Highgate School.

Academic Matters: Not a fiercely academic place. Classes are small, 20 and lower, with four parallel forms, streamed across the board, and setted for English, maths, languages and science – three subjects taught separately but, below the top set, taken as dual award at GSCE. Six per class post-GCSE. Lots of modular exams. Classics back in the mainstream, plus a myriad of languages (native speakers). Best ever A level results 2004; excellent results in biology, business studies, chemistry, maths and further maths, as well as Japanese.

Excellent dyslexia provision with a head of learning support plus a dedicated peripatetic team – dyspraxia, 'mild Asperger's' and ADHD not a problem. One to one or just general support, computers important here – ie support staff can call up work in progress and give positive assistance. Indeed computers important all over, with network manager sitting in a little office below the art room (and next to the two computer suites) – all boarding houses have access to the school's network.

Games, Options, The Arts: A seriously sporty school. Intensely competitive, inter-house as well as inter-school matches in everything. Enormous sports hall with weights room attached, Aldenham Park with sailing lake, no swimming pool (it's on the ten year wish list), cricket popular, masses of footie fields, tennis courts all over. Fives court hosts trillions of matches, shooting range, hockey popular for both sexes, fencing, badminton, cross-country, judo (and a dedicated judo hall which is also used for aerobics and dance). Climbing walls everywhere, both vertical and horizontal, look terrifying.

D of E, huge selection of clubs and rather grand expeditions all over the world. Excellent art results with some ambitious pieces of art on display within the art studios and around the school. Terrific pair of gates in a combination of MDF and pâpier maché depicting the whole sixth form – looked like the gates to hell. Impressive CDT complex adjacent to art rooms and computer suites, humming with activity, graphics room at the back, plus CAD-CAM. Our guide was justly proud of his fish tank coffee table, hell for hoovering, but an interesting conception, as were many others on show.

Imaginative conversion of the old chapel into music centre, with sympathetic recital hall and recording studio adjacent. Loads of practice rooms below – fairly pedestrian conversion here – very shabby, but computer linked to keyboards and networked round the school. Drama very popular in the somewhat utilitarian hall (new hall also on wish list). Good selection of plays and musicals in the past.

Background and Atmosphere: Stunning. Founded in 1597 by Richard Platt and endowed with 'three Pastures of Ground lying nighe the Churche of St Pancrasse in the County of Mid'x besides London.' Cometh the railway, cometh ornate Victorian gothic. Magnificent parquet floored dining hall, with benches and tables like an Oxbridge college. Impressive Robert Adam-style library, which is connected to a rather dreary careers library opened by Lord Denning. Guides hadn't a clue about the buildings, nor did they appear to have any interest or pride in the school's history or traditions, but knew all about the food (much improved recently). Chapel across the (quite busy) road; magical Burne Jones windows, and fairly hefty war memorial feel. School fell on hard times during the recession of the 1990s and caused waves when they saved their bacon by selling Stanley Spencer's altarpiece of the Crucifixion for around two million.

Games fields surrounded by gigantic red brick houses, three for boarders (the largest co-ed) and three for day. Single rooms post-GCSE. Quantity of rather uninspired sixties/seventies buildings around – school went all out to celebrate its quartercentenary. New state-of-the-art classroom block housing English, media studies and modern languages opened in February 2005. Despite being an Anglican foundation, school pays more than just lip service to other faiths, and Muslims, Hindus and Jews all get time off for their own holy days (though they may have to do Saturday morning school).

Pastoral Care and Discipline: Very much based on the house system, loads of back-up. Those from abroad are taken on visits during exeats, to the Dusseldorf Fair, shopping in Calais etc. Tough on drugs, smoking and the like but head has only expelled one pupil, basically for going OTT. Good anti-bullying and PSE programme; 'the school is so small that we can smell trouble before it happens'.

Pupils and Parents: An interesting combination of boarding and day, with many of the day pupils coming from north London's very ethnically mixed community. Fair number from the Middle East and Asia, pupils happily chatting in Japanese in the art room. High proportion of first time buyers, often with two working parents who like to have their children home at weekends. Flexi-boarding popular. The pupils cover the entire spectrum, from those with a high IQ to those who need extra help across the board, but all are here because they flourish better in a small school environment away from the conveyor belt mentality. Pupils all wear uniforms, with sixth form of both sexes graduating to suits; praes (prefects) get to wear satiny grey ties. Manners immaculate.

Entrance: Tests in January for entry at 11, 13 and 16, plus interview and previous school's report. Waiting lists at 11 and 13. Pupils come either from local preps or primaries and the head is anxious not to be seen to poach, hence the double entry date.

Exit: Some leave after GCSEs, and places fill up with new blood, though a tiny trickle of pupils leave after AS levels. School takes enormous care in getting leavers into the right form of tertiary education, which the pupils will enjoy and last the course. Masses of new universities in the leavers' list, occasionally one to Oxbridge; some gap year. Business and IT type courses popular.

Money Matters: After the blip in the 1990s, the Brewers' Company gave the school its 120 acres, which is nice to have in your pocket when you go to the bank manager. Huge array of scholarships at 13 and 16, as well as bursarial help in financial need, plus Brewers' support as well.

Remarks: On the up. Good new head, fab surroundings; perfect for those needing an unpressurised school.

Alexandra Park School

Bidwell Gardens, London, N11 2AZ

Tel: 020 8826 4880

Fax: 020 8888 2236

Email: admin@alexandrapark.haringey.sch.uk

• Pupils: 1,100 boys and girls, all day • Ages: 11-18

• Religion: Non-denom • School status: State

• School gender: Mixed • Day/boarding: Day pupils

SEN provision

Detail:
Centre of excellence for:
  Mild: ASP; AUT; DS;
  Moderate: ASP; AUT; DS;
  Others: SPD; AUT(other); Sp&LD;
Now provide for in school:
  Mild: ADD; ADHD; EBD; DYSC; DYSL; DYSP; HI; VI;
  Moderate: ADD; ADHD; EBD; MLD; DYSL; DYSP; SpLD; HI;
  Others: EAL; Epi; Eat;

Summary: The school provides support for a large number of children with Statements of Special Educational Need as well as students at school action and school action +. We support students with a wide range of need including ASD, speech, language and communication, Down's syndrome, SpLd and general learning difficulties. Certain members of the department have particular qualifications and experience in speech and language impairment. The departmental team consists of teachers, learning mentors and a large number of teaching assistants. In addition, we have specialist TAs with responsibility for literacy, numeracy and year 7 Transition whose work is co-ordinated by a lead teaching assistant.

Students are assessed on entry to school and using this baseline date may be allocated additional support with literacy and numeracy, on a withdrawal basis. This support is in addition to the in-class support provided by T.A's and Learning Mentors. All Statemented students have a Key teacher and TA who are both responsible for giving support to students and parents, liaising with other teaching staff and meetings with parents.

What we say about the school - the full Good Schools Guide review

Head: Since the school's opening in 1999, Ms Rosslyn Hudson, MA PGCE (fifties). Studied English at Edinburgh University, worked for VSO in Indonesia and the Bahamas, then started her teaching career at Latymer School in Edmonton. Was appointed head of English at Edmonton County School, then spent 10 years as deputy head at William Ellis School. Married with two children. Excellent leader and driving force behind the school's success. Was responsible more-or-less single handed for getting the school off the ground. 'It wouldn't have opened in 1999 if I hadn't been bloody-minded and determined.' Has put together a very strong senior management team and appointed many energetic young teachers (who tend to get short-listed for teaching awards). About half of the original staff is still at the school.

Academic Matters: Very mixed intake, with a large percentage coming in with lower than average attainment. However most do better than predicted: 'High expectations start at the top and permeate the whole school,' said Ofsted.

In the first GCSE results, with 51 per cent of students getting 5+ good grades, the traditional subjects of RE, English, history, geography, maths, science and modern languages showed up particularly well. More practical subjects with large amounts of course-work were less successful. 'We didn't have sufficiently robust systems in place, and we weren't strict enough. But that side has been addressed.' The school confidently predicts sharply improving results in future years. 'Our small really able cohort did brilliantly, with clutches of A*s and As.' Single sciences and classical civilisation are available as twilight classes. Everyone studies French or Spanish in year 7 and can take up the other language too in year 8.

The school has maths and science specialist status, and is using its position in the shadow of Alexandra Palace to follow a telecommunications theme, including topics on the health risks of mobile phones and the history of television. Staff are training in cognitive acceleration in science and maths. Some of the extra funds brought by specialist status are being used to split less able students into small science and maths groups.

Pupils with a practical bent can spend a day a week at the College of North East London studying construction crafts, hairdressing, beauty therapy or health and care. 'Our Key Stage 4 curriculum is phenomenally flexible. Whatever they want to study, we do our best to accommodate them.'The first sixth form cohort will take A levels in summer 2006; popular AS subjects include psychology, philosophy and critical thinking.Excellent SEN support, mostly in class. Three full-time SEN teachers, who all teach whole classes and are also form tutors. 'They are not shut away in little rooms doing one-on-one all the time. I have a vision for SEN. If you have sensible numbers of children you can do powerful work.' There are also some 20 teaching assistants, many highly-qualified. The school has been a honey-pot for parents of children with SEN statements. 'We have children here with very complex needs,' says SENCo Pauline Smith. 'Staff here are so receptive and willing to try different things to meet these needs. Everyone accepts that these children are part of the whole school community.'

Games, Options, The Arts: Large gym and spacious sports hall with a climbing wall, plus a tarmac sports area used for sports including netball, basketball and football, and a fitness suite. Plenty of inter-school matches, and sports and cultural clubs. High-quality art teaching; facilities include a dark room, kiln room and print room. Good drama; whole school musical every year. Music groups include a jazz orchestra, brass ensemble, cello quartet, boys' and girls' choirs and a rock group. Language trips to Spain and France, ski trips, football and netball trips to Europe, Duke of Edinburgh award scheme.

Background and Atmosphere: Opened in 1999 on a five-acre site between Muswell Hill Golf Course and Durnsford Park, which had been through several incarnations including Cecil Rhodes Secondary Modern and a sixth form centre for Fortismere School. Pleasant brick buildings with a rural outlook, including new science labs, performing arts rooms and sixth form centre. Friendly and welcoming but highly structured.

Pastoral Care and Discipline: The school includes its fair share of children with challenging behaviour, which is kept firmly in check. It has a structured behaviour management programme which includes rewards as well as sanctions, and does not tolerate unacceptable behaviour. The head is quite prepared to exclude those who try the patience of the school too far. 'We work very hard on behaviour management. I've got to protect the learning and safeguard the students that want to be here. I have to be ferocious about that.' Each form has the same tutor throughout the school, and staff get to know their pupils well. Teachers talk about feeling well supported: 'There's a real bond between staff to make the school a better place.'

Pupils and Parents: When the school first opened, middle class parents were wary and its first intake included large numbers of children with special needs from a wide area. It has since become extremely popular and massively over-subscribed, with a genuinely comprehensive intake including children from the leafy west part of the borough and those from the grittier east. Mostly friendly, polite pupils who are enthusiastic and proud of their school, with a committed parent body.

Entrance: Those with statements get first preference, then siblings. The catchment area is in practice about three quarters of a mile, with most pupils coming from Rhodes, Bounds Green and Nightingale primary schools.

Exit: About two thirds have, so far, gone through to the sixth form, which is open-access, though some are encouraged to make a fresh start elsewhere. A few have moved on to FE colleges.

Money Matters: The maths and science specialist status has brought extra funds and school now employs a bursar, who is responsible for ferreting out other sources of finance and has an expert knowledge of what funds are available.

Remarks: Increasingly popular and over-subscribed comprehensive that caters well for pupils of all abilities, with dynamic and focused head, and staff who are keen to find areas where all children can excel.

ALLEYN'S JUNIOR SCHOOL

Townley Road, Dulwich, London, SE22 8SU

Tel: 020 8557 1519

Fax: 020 8693 3597

Email: juniorschool@alleyns.org.uk

Website: www.alleyns.org.uk

• Pupils: 230; 115 girls, 115 boys • Fees: Junior £2,930-£3,050 • School status: Independent • Opendays: Autumn • School gender: Mixed • Day/boarding: Day pupils

---

What we say about the school - the full Good Schools Guide review

Head: Since 2003, Mr Mark O'Donnell BA, PGD Des MSc (Arch) EdM PGD ES (mid-forties). Previously deputy head of Thorpe House School, Gerrards Cross. Educated at Stonyhurst and St Ignatius College, New South Wales. Married to Esther with three sons of junior school age, this is a quietly-spoken but intensely committed and dedicated head who has his finger on every detail of his super school, its management, its assets, its achievements and its plans. Clearly assiduous, though almost disconcertingly earnest, Mr O'Donnell is clearly a prize catch for the school and has an excellent working relationship with Mr Diggory (head of the senior school) and the other senior staff. He will put himself out to a, perhaps, unique degree to help a child or family with a problem.

Entrance: Around 160 applicants for 16 places in reception. Days are spent assessing hopeful 4-year-olds; immense care is taken and candidates are given a range of developmental exercises. As the school is reluctant to say a final 'no', children are regularly invited back for re-tries. Lots of helpful feedback to parents. The result is a happy, homogeneous bunch of eagerly collaborative, exploring and creative learners in a safe, comfortable and stimulating environment.

Exit: Almost all to the senior school (automatic right of entry, though they all sit the exam). Some go for scholarships elsewhere.

Remarks: The 'two schools within one school' format really works here, for the benefit of all. A 'safe routes' scheme funded by £250,000 of local authority cash, has made a green path for safe travel around the site from the main school to the junior school end. The school is at the far end of the main site, behind the music block but has the benefit of a huge field for outdoor play. It has a special science garden with a wildlife pond and herb, flower and vegetable plots. Two adjoining semis newly acquired will provide an inviting garden entrance just for the tinies – a lovely and imaginatively thought-up way to enter your school.

The building itself, purpose-built in 1992, is a model of what a junior school should be. School day begins with an enlightened 40 minutes of time for chat, admin and 'warm-up' and then a smooth transition into a 'calm and orderly' day. Spaces are big enough to allow a sense of freedom but not overwhelming – bright, stimulating, but not over-busy, classrooms, a first rate IT room with passionately committed specialist staff (when we visited pupils were peacefully absorbed at individual PCs to the sound of evensong from St Paul's Cathedral), excellent library – 'the hub of the school' – and a good, multi-purpose hall/gym. A sense of purposeful, pleasurable work pervades the whole – super textiles and excellent artwork everywhere, rooms have French names, everyone has two years learning a string instrument and around a third take it further. Lots of other music, individual and collaborative. Lots of drama including a major production annually. Plenty of sport and games to suit everyone. SEN have exceptional resources for a junior school – two super little roomlets for individual help, after careful assessment, and bright, dedicated and expert support. As in the main school, loads of clubs – 35+ for chess, gardening, judo, drama and everything else you could imagine.

There are other super junior schools in the area – ones you'd practically reproduce for – but you'd be hard put to find a happier, more secure environment than this and one run with more dedication, vision and enthusiasm.

ALLEYN'S SCHOOL

Townley Road, Dulwich, London, SE22 8SU

Tel: 020 8557 1500

Fax: 020 8557 1462

Email: registrar@alleyns.org.uk

Website: www.alleyns.org.uk

• Pupils: 570 boys, 588 girls; all day • Ages: 4-18

• Religion: C of E • Fees: senior £3,560.

• School status: Independent • Opendays: Autumn

• School gender: Mixed • Day/boarding: Day pupils

SEN provision

Detail:

Now provide for in school:

Mild: ASP; ADD; ADHD; DYSL; DYSP;

Experience of:

Mild: EBD; DYSC; HI; VI;

Moderate: ASP;

Others: SPD; TIC; GEN; DEL; Epi;

Summary: The school works with parents, staff and external professionals to identify conditions relating to specific learning difficulties. The school has a learing support co-ordinator who will give advice and support to students with specific learning difficulties to help them achieve their potential. Where appropriate external support can also be enlisted.

What we say about the school - the full Good Schools Guide review

Head: Since 2002, Dr Colin Diggory BSc MA EdD CMath FIMA FRSA (fiftyish). Married to Sue, with three adult children. Previously teacher of maths at Manchester Grammar, St Paul's and head of maths at Merchant

Taylors, Northwood, his first headship was at Latymer Upper where he stayed for 11 years. A physically impressive man, Dr Diggory moves and speaks with the alacrity and enthusiasm of a nimble and eager sixth former. Volubly articulate on all matters educational, both local and national, Dr Diggory knows his stuff and has done the homework. His doctoral thesis on leadership in independent schools is now complete, he has masses of experience and knowledge of management strategies, a special interest in the performing arts in schools, is a former A level examiner, a current HM school inspector and active on HMC committees.

If that gives the impression of a head forever away at conferences, the reverse is true. Parents speak of how he appears with his wife to cheer on school teams at weekends and, now in his fourth year at Alleyn's, he clearly knows what's what and has big development plans. Dr Diggory is a modest man but one who is generous with praise of others – staff, pupils and a very supportive board of governors. He is keen both to develop staff opportunities and improve delegation – 'leadership density' – yuk! He exudes a nervous energy and is clearly thrilled to take over this thriving school from his friend and predecessor, the much-loved Colin Niven. 'I've inherited a wonderful school and my priority is to protect and promote it.'

Academic Matters: 'We don't aspire to be a league-table killer,' says head but the results here need not hang their heads. 2005 GCSE students achieved 81 per cent per cent A*/A grades and 12 students got all A*s. At A level, 88 per cent got A/Bs, the average points per student being 339 which is better than AAB. Everyone takes the three separate sciences for the first five years and then can take them as individual GCSEs or as a dual award. Modern languages now being further developed to allow for enthusiasts to take three at GCSE if they so choose, as well as Latin. Greek still holding its own. This level of opportunity is rare.

Head has introduced politics and psychology (two of his own children did psychology degrees), which, together with business studies, photography, theatre studies and RS, get respectable numbers of takers at A level as well as the more trad subjects. English attracts large numbers and does well. History and geography also among the stars. Good IT suite and school recently upgraded resources here and the use of IT throughout curriculum – though not as a religion. SENs are quickly spotted and well-supported. 'We have a brilliant SENCo'. Those who need it get an individual education plan (IEP). 'Ideally everyone should have one,' says head -' that's the way education should go'. Buzz words here are 'choice' and opportunity' and parents speak appreciatively of the opportunities available in all areas of the curriculum. 'There's more to life than academics,' says head. But the academics are doing fine.

Games, Options, The Arts: Opportunities for everything. Games are big here but less sporty types are encouraged to do less competitive and intimidating things like fives, swimming, fitness, fencing, t'ai chi, trampolining. Very strong representation at county level in many sports though recent quirkiness in results – superb cricket and hockey and football now reviving after a noticeable glitch. Good pool – 'if they can't swim when they arrive here we make sure they can by the end of their first year', super huge sports hall, vast range of sports available and teams travel far for fixtures. School buildings spread around good fields; more fields plus an athletics track across the road. This is good provision in a grand suburb with a fair bit of local competition for large open spaces!

Opportunities in other areas – an excellent carousel programme for the first senior school years so that everyone has a shot at food tech – they design, cook and eat their own meals and love it, and CDT in metalwork, woodwork and ceramics etc. All taught in small groups. Results are weird, wonderful, clever and exciting. The art – taught in five studios – is astonishingly good – among the most impressively assured and proficient painting we have seen. Music thrives in converted brewery, loads of ensembles of all sizes and types. Recording studio, CDs, tours, concerts large and small, both on site and in grander venues like St John's Smith Square and the Queen Elizabeth Hall. An biennial concert with the two other foundation schools. Drama does remarkably well in the large and imposing, splendidly-beamed, school hall, a dingy old gym and various smaller spaces. An ambitious programme of development – planned for 2006 – is underway to provide a 300-seat theatre, sixth form centre and conference centre – will considerably enhance the school's facilities in all respects and do much to dispel any sense of being the poor relation in the trio of schools. The National Youth Theatre started here and school keen to exploit the link. 40+ clubs and activities, thriving D of E and CCF – the largest voluntary corps in the country, we're told. Community service is busy locally. Loads of trips to everywhere – educational and adventurous, and a good range of language exchanges. Posters advertising interesting speakers from outside make you want to book a seat.

Background and Atmosphere: In 1619 Edward Alleyn, actor and theatre manager who made most of his money from bear-baiting and who, at the age of 57, married the 19-year-old daughter of John Donne, founded his 'College of God's Gift' in Dulwich. This became Dulwich College (cf) but it had always had a lower school. In 1882, this lower school became a separate educational establishment – the present Alleyn's – continuing to share the College board of governors until recent times. The third school in the Dulwich estate is JAGS (cf) – the James Allen's Girls' School – which dates from the mid-19th century. Don't ask about the missing 'y'. The schools are a unique triumvirate, dominating independent education in this, mostly prosperous, part of South-East London and providing a rich – sometimes difficult – choice for local parents. Alleyn's is the co-ed one, the first independent school in London to go fully co-ed, and that is its particular distinction and selling point.

The main building, with its broad, unpretentious, 4-storey redbrick façade, on quiet Townley Road, faces chic Dulwich village to the south and the more modest terraced streets of East Dulwich to the north. Behind is the main site – around the fields – and the buildings are less impressive, plain and functional. The Derek Fenner library (named after pioneering past head) is terrific, well-run, well-stocked and here, almost uniquely, silent study seemed to mean just that. Sciences taught in a separate block and most subjects have their own teaching areas.

The atmosphere is relaxed, with the feeling of any well-run, mixed comprehensive except that it's, for the most part, in good nick, feels very orderly and well-resourced. Pupils are polite, friendly, articulate. Relations with staff seem open and co-operative. You get the feeling everyone is pleased to be here. Plain and sensible uniform. Good food – vegetarian option and salad bar – served efficiently in huge canteen with separate staff area. Sixth form have their own large common room with snacks available all day and their own servery at lunchtime so they can maintain their separate space. Feels like a university student bar. Hot breakfast available for everyone.

Parents speak warmly of the speed with which most pastoral problems are sorted out, especially in the lower school, of the good communications, excellent SEN support and happy children. The 'fantastic' music and brilliant sports are cited and the caring nature of the staff in general. Some feel that girls go there because of the boys, some feel that girls become cliquey in ways that don't happen in single sex schools but, for the most part, it's happy families all round.

Pastoral Care and Discipline: Junior school starts at 4 and school hopes for a nursery before too long. Lower school is for the 11 to 13-year-olds, middle school for the 13 to 16-year-olds and upper school is the sixth form. Lower school is comfortably separate from main school so that the youngsters have a haven but they are in the main building for about half their classes. Everyone has a tutor and, on entering middle school also joins a house. In year 9, heads of houses take over as tutors and establish close relationships with tutees. There are also academic tutors from year 10. Full-time school chaplain. School encourages pupils to be self-reliant and sort out their own problems but support is there if needed. Lower school staff highly praised for 'having it sussed'. Drugs policy clear but seldom needed – supply would mean 'out' and random testing used on rare occasions if felt necessary. Bullying is 'nipped in the bud' very quickly, we're told and most concur – though a few parental eyebrows raised at occasional less-well-handled instances. Head feels relaxed and orderly atmosphere is fed by the space and fields around the school site – less pressure from a harsh external world mean less within. A sense that, as head says, 'the community values everyone'.

Pupils and Parents: Strictly co-ed and any imbalance due to 11-year-old girls outperforming boys at 11+ is levelled when more boys than girls arrive at 13. Pupils come from a wide range of socio-economic and ethnic backgrounds, inner and outer London boroughs, nearish bits of Kent. Common denominators are brains and attitude and a relish of the all-round nature of what's on offer here. At 11, around 1/3 of new intake come from state primaries and much-admired head of lower school now spends a day a fortnight visiting these schools, telling them about the 30 scholarships and bursaries on offer (current total of 171 scholars and 71 on bursaries) to encourage more applicants. Notable former pupils include actors Julian Glover, Sam West, Jude Law and playwright Ray Cooney; writers CS Forester and VS

Pritchett; surgical scientist Prof Ajay Kakkar and defence systems designer Prof RV Jones; industrialist Sir Ronald Leach and banker Sir Keith Whitson.

Entrance: Entry is now automatic from the junior school. Exams – taken by all in maths, English and reasoning. Interview given equal weight – not just the numerically top candidates are chosen. Priority to siblings and 'those with a prior connection'. Over-subscribed, of course. 125 places on offer at 11; in 2004, 600 applied. 10 places at 13. 20 places post-GCSE.

Exit: Lots of gap years. Otherwise to as wide a range of courses and destinations as anywhere – medicine at Leeds, London, Manchester; architecture at Edinburgh, Oxford Brookes, Nottingham; English at York, Homerton, Sussex; various kinds of engineering or IT courses everywhere. 2004 saw 19 to Oxbridge and the first ever leaver off to Harvard. Given the standard of art here, surprisingly few to art schools – but maybe that's where all the gappers end up.

Money Matters: Benefits both from the Dulwich estates (£1m) and Saddlers' Company (£1/4m) support – both of which fund generously. Scholarships at 11+, 13+ for which all candidates are automatically considered. More schols at 16+ – all worth up to 1/3 of fees. Means-tested bursaries at 11+ and 16+ worth up to 100 per cent of fees. Art, music and sports schols at different stages worth varying percentages. All worth serious investigation.

Remarks: Who would get on well here? – 'someone very self-reliant who has their own opinions, someone happy in a relaxed set-up, someone outgoing,' – so says head and parents concur. Perhaps the most academic, shyer girls will still head for JAGS. For boys the choice depends even more on individual personality. 'We're very holistic in our approach to education,' says Mr Diggory and this word, along with 'relaxed', 'opportunity' 'community' and 'valued' set the tone. Jot them down and now go and see the big brother down the road.

Altarnun Community Primary School

Five Lanes, Altarnun, Launceston, Cornwall, PL15 7RZ

Tel: 01566 86274

Fax: 01566 86274

Email: head@altarnun.cornwall.sch.uk

Website: www.altarnun.cornwall.sch.uk

• Pupils: 70 boys and girls; all day • Ages: 4-11

• Religion: Non-denom • School status: State

• School gender: Mixed • Day/boarding: Day pupils

SEN provision

Detail:

Now provide for in school:

Mild: DYSC; DYSL; DYSP;

Moderate: MLD; DYSC; DYSL; DYSP;

Severe: DYSP;

Others: Sp&LD; DEL; PD;

Experience of:

Mild: ADD; ADHD; EBD;

Moderate: ADD; ADHD; EBD;

Summary: Ofsted 2004 reported that: 'Provision for pupils with special educational needs is good with teaching assistants making a strong contribution. Overall pupils make satisfactory progress, especially those with SEN.'

What we say about the school - the full Good Schools Guide review

Head: Since 1991, Mr Malcolm Vian (early fifties). Educated at Queen College, Taunton and Chester College. Various teaching posts – a Liverpool comp, Biscovey Junior School, primary school in Dudley. Became deputy head of Bosvigo primary in Truro (six years), then head at Blisland. Seen as focused and hard-working. Enjoys reading, football and keep-fit. Juggles heavy teaching commitment with effective management. Married with two children.

Entrance: Criteria: sibling already or previously at school, other family connection, geographical proximity, medical, psychological or social service recommendation. Any mitigating circumstances considered by head in consultation with governors to be important. Pupils are from mixed social backgrounds, majority are one-car owners from local farming community but this is changing to include middle class parents moving away from the London rat-race to idyllic Cornish countryside (now 20 per cent). Caters for ten under-fives part-time. Competition includes the newer schools of Lewannick and Tregadillen.

Exit: Virtually 100 per cent to Launceston College.

Remarks: A happy, extremely family-like, school with strength being teaching quality, assisted by volunteer parents. Teachers (who stay a while) communicate and work well together. Pupils taught in three mixed-age classes, with average size of 22. Attainments at end of each Key Stage in line/above national average with 100 per cent achievement at level 4+ in maths and science at Key Stage 2. English not far behind.

Typically Cornish and under-funded. Sadly lacks canteen – classroom blackboard drawn back to reveal through-hatch to kitchen. However, children seem happy enough to sit with dinner tray at worktable. No main hall on-site – children walk 10 mins to use village hall. Indoor PE constrained due to lack of space but situation compensated by excellent outdoor facilities – activity area and wonderfully large playing field that could give school more building space. Governor recently appointed to achieve such building funds. Hot on netball and football. Swim all year at Launceston Leisure Centre. After-school/lunchtime clubs include chess, gardening, recorder, performing arts, music, netball, football, swimming.

Situated eight miles west of Launceston, Altarnun boasts stunning views of Bodmin Moor (on a clear day) and serves largest catchment area for Cornwall. Founded in 1878, moved from smaller village green premises to existing development in 1935. Three permanent classrooms are stacked in a line next to cramped and inadequate office, administration and storage facilities. One classroom doubles as library/resource, music and staff room. Due to be transformed into £15,000 stimulating hi-tech bridge of Starship Enterprise with more IT. Two additional pre-fab classrooms. Teaching staff are fond of school and pupils. Caters well for children with SEN including physically disabled – 14 per cent of total roll.

School colours are grey/black and red, a watch and stud earrings (only) are acceptable. Parent involvement welcomed and there is a lot. Good communication between home and school which seems to support homework programme with an active PTA.

Parents overall are happy with way their children are helped by the school. Effective discipline system (liked and mostly respected by children); yellow card issued when rule broken, red card if two are broken in same day, resulting in loss of choice play session at week end – computers, drawing, chess, instrument etc.

APPLEFORD SCHOOL

Elston Lane, Shrewton, Nr Salisbury, Wiltshire, SP3 4HL

Tel: 01980 621 020

Fax: 01980 621 366

Email: secretary@appleford.wilts.sch.uk

Website: www.appleford.wilts.sch.uk

• Pupils: 70 boys, 15 girls, most boarding with limited number of day places • Ages: 7-13 • Religion: Inter-denominational • Fees: Day £3,998; boarding £6,058 • School status: Independent • Opendays: November • School gender: Mixed • Day/boarding: Takes boarders

SEN provision

Detail:

Now provide for in school:

Mild: ADD; ADHD; DYSC; DYSL; DYSP;

Moderate: ADD; ADHD; DYSC; DYSL; DYSP;

Severe: DYSC; DYSL; DYSP;

Others: Sp&LD;

Experience of:

Mild: ASP; HI;

Moderate: ASP;

Severe: ADD; ADHD;

Summary: Appleford was founded in 1988 to provide help for dyslexic pupils of average or above-average intelligence. In recent times, the spectrum of difficulties has increased so that our category with the DfES is now an Approved Residential Special School for Dyslexic pupils and those with associated learning differences.

Admissions policy: educational psychologist's report, school reports and Appleford assessment during tester visit.

What we say about the school - the full Good Schools Guide review

Head: Since 2001, Revd Bob Clarke BD (fifties). Married to Kate, a nurse, they have grown-up children. A cheerful, friendly, approachable head who knows and understands all the pupils and their specific needs. With advice from Prof Miles and at the beginning of his teaching career, Bob Clarke set up the specialist unit at St David's College Llandudno. He then studied with Sally Childs and began an impeccable career in SpLD. He was later ordained into the Church and combined both disciplines. Took over from Paul Stanley who moved on to Northease Manor after nine years. Appleford continues to be owned by its founders, Dr Peter Gardner and Gerald Trump.

Entrance: At any age from 7 to 13, from anywhere but must have English as a first language. All new entrants are internally assessed and each child is given their own multi-sensory individual education plan to promote self-confidence, self-esteem and success. A good proportion have monitoring statements but only nine are currently funded by their LEAs.

Exit: At 13 the majority of pupils return to mainstream education at schools such as Clayesmore, Milton Abbey, Shiplake and St David's College. Some pupils who still need whole school provision move on to Mark College, Shapwick and Northease Manor. Appleford hosts a Schools' Day every two years to assist parents in making decisions about future schooling.

Remarks: Situated in an area of outstanding natural beauty, this is a small outstanding specialist school for boys and girls with dyslexia and associated learning difficulties such as dyspraxia and ADHD (CReSTeD Category now SP.) Core subjects are taught before lunch every day when the children are fresh, with other subjects after lunch, but with a whole school specialist approach right across the curriculum. All children learn to touch-type in the newly-equipped IT department but not to the detriment of acquiring good handwriting skills. Conversational French is taught to the older children, a plus for all those struggling dyslexics. Every child participates in the school musical production and more than 60 per cent learn a musical instrument in free time. The art and science blocks are impressive and the sports hall is quite magnificent. A variety of sports including rugby, hockey, cricket, riding, soccer and swimming are offered. Despite its size the school appears to lack nothing much in the way of facilities or amenities.

All teachers are DfES qualified. Half of them hold a specialist diploma and all of them have the opportunity to regularly attend specialist courses or events, which the school is renowned for hosting. Teacher:pupil ratio is approximately 1:8 supported by a team of classroom assistants, an educational psychologist, speech and language and occupational therapists – on site.

The pastoral care is superb with each child being given an individual care plan. Dorms are sweet smelling and cosy and food is first class. Children are kept busy and happy with an extensive list of activities and stimulating weekend programmes. There are no signs of homesickness. Parents comment that anyone lucky enough to place their child at this idyllically situated, specialist, popular school can breath a long sigh of relief.

ARDINGLY COLLEGE

College Road, Ardingly, Haywards Heath, West Sussex, RH17 6SQ

Tel: 01444 893 000

Fax: 01444 893 001

Email: registrar@ardingly.com

Website: www.ardingly.com

• Pupils: 458 • Ages: 13-18 • Religion: C of E • Fees: Day £5,120; boarding £6,840 • School status: Independent • Opendays: Some Saturdays in October, March and May. • School gender: Mixed • Day/boarding: Takes boarders

SEN provision

Detail:

Centre of excellence for:
- Mild: DYSL;
- Others: EAL;

Now provide for in school:
- Mild: DYSC; DYSP;
- Moderate: DYSL;

Experience of:
- Mild: ASP; ADD; ADHD; VI;
- Others: Epi; Eat;

Summary: The learning support department offers individual lessons for pupils who have a mild specific learning difficulty. All pupils however must be able to cope in the classroom without individual learning assistant support.

What we say about the school - the full Good Schools Guide review

Headmaster: Since 1998 Mr John Franklin BA Dip Teaching M Ed Admin, fiftyish. An Australian with loads of teaching (English and geography) and boarding experience in both hemispheres including at Sedbergh and Marlborough. Previous job deputy, then acting, head St Peter's College, Adelaide. Mr Franklin inherited a benign but, perhaps, somewhat neglected institution with a brief to bring it up-to-date and beef up discipline. This he has clearly, rather spectacularly, done and all pay tribute to how much has been achieved. Friendly, communicative, with a sparkly wit lurking behind slight reserve, Mr Franklin talks of his regime as the iron fist in the glove. Certainly, he has made changes in standards of behaviour and discipline expected of pupils and, while some might chafe a bit, few would deny the benefits of the overall tightening up under his occasionally steely eye. Parents have welcomed the changes, colleagues admire what is being achieved. 'A lovely man and an excellent head,' was a fellow head's comment. Immensely and warmly proud of his pupils and their achievements, clearly hard-working and enthusiastic, a head to whose care most parents would confidently entrust their children.

Academic Matters: As part of head's drive to up the academic profile and aspirations, college adopted the International Baccalaureate in 2001 and this is having beneficial effects on both the quality of education offered and results. Head a great advocate -' it's a good, broad preparation for tertiary study ... I like the overarching philosophy...it formalises all the things that a good independent education does anyway, emphasising creativity, academics and community service.' The first IB candidates achieved promisingly, getting an average of 34.5 points (45 is max) – comparing well with other schools. Five students scored the Oxbridge requirement 39 points or over. Now around 50/50 IB/A level students. Good choice of A level subjects – theatre studies, business studies (popular) along with more trad options. Good results especially in languages, art, physics and music; less good in business studies and DT but these often the choices of the less academic. Value added is good here. GCSE subjects include PE and drama plus all the usuals with 90 per cent achieving A-C grades and 36 per cent getting A*/A. Languages do well – so surprising how few take them in the sixth despite school's support – 'we might even encourage good linguists to take three languages in the sixth form', says head and certainly there are trips and links enough to fire enthusiasm.

ICT seen as a tool. Huge new PC suite September 2004. Every teaching room now networked and new access to school's library of 400+ CD Roms. Ceiling-mounted data projectors and more upgrading in progress. SEN well understood. 'We have a brilliant SENCo,' says head. 'If she says they will cope here, they will. She hasn't got it wrong yet.' All new entrants screened and individual support programmes drawn up for all who need one. Newest boys' boarding houses have lifts and, in general, school feels they could 'make it work' for the physically disabled on this large and undulating site. EAL available to few who need it.

Games, Options, The Arts: As far as you can see, pitches and sports fields stretch away into the Sussex landscape. School set in 275 acres, a third of which is let as fields. School has Astroturf pitch used for hockey or tennis, plus hard courts, plus use of reservoir for sailing and rowing five minutes walk from main buildings. More than 80 sports offered during the year and school especially successful in football, girls' hockey, cross-country and shooting. Sports not compulsory here but everyone finds something they like. Sports hall built in 2000 but no weights/fitness rooms. Duke of Edinburgh Award scheme is popular here, as is CCF – a wide and challenging programme of activities. Music – now in attractive one-storey block at school entrance – very strong under charismatic director. A super choir – not, sadly, singing to herald our visit – was practising as we arrived – and bands, groups, ensembles, productions of all kinds flourish. Chapel choir sings in all the best places – St Paul's, Canterbury, St George's, Windsor. Individual lessons to top standards – some taught by London orchestral players and teachers include legendary bass guitarist and tuba maestro Herbie Flowers. Drama also good and adventurous, mostly in 'The Under', a super old three hundred seater theatre or in the smaller 'Friends' Barn'. Art is varied and lively – ceramics, sculpture, textiles among the try-outs.

Background and Atmosphere: A Woodard school ie founded in the mid nineteenth century by Canon Nathaniel Woodard and run on Christian principles, Ardingly moved to present impressive location in 1870. Main school in an imposing, three storey, H-shaped red-brick building high on the Sussex downs and with marvellous views over the landscape in all directions. Grandly solemn vaulted chapel used for weekly senior school services. In the winter, site can be cold and windswept but in the summer is a delight. Not a rich foundation and shackled by buildings' Grade II listings and doubtful privilege of being in an 'area of outstanding natural beauty;' school has major job to maintain and upgrade site and facilities but, under Mr Franklin, major changes have happened and more are planned. Good management, prudent changes, summer lets – all help to provide major investment now transforming school. Library to be greatly extended and upgraded by autumn 2004 and 3-year re-stocking plan in progress. Few spartan portakabins still around – one is to be a cybercafe we were told. While some stairwells, labs and corridors remain bleak, some depts, notably art, still awaiting relocating and updating and some boarding accommodation still to be raised to today's standards, Ardingly is on track and can now compete with the best in the area.

All but year 13 boarders now in village-like, small estate of three-storey houses, moments from main building. Newest houses have ICT rooms, well-equipped games rooms, kitchens, 'brew rooms' and gardens with picnic tables. year 9s are in 'pods' of four all with basins – one between two. year 10s are in doubles and years 11-13 in singles. Beds look alarmingly narrow compared to some of the hefty types walking the campus. Attractive blue and white decor in house we visited. New day house made on top floor of one wing – from former boys' boarding rooms – comfortable, well furnished, spacious and with super views! Houseparents all living in house, many with families. All home-cooked, rather delicious food. Site is spacious, leafy, be-gardened, well maintained and feels relaxed.

Pastoral Care and Discipline: Pastoral care relies on tutorial system. Everyone has weekly meeting with tutor who is pupil's confidante, broker, spokesman and school's link with parents. Thereafter, hierarchy of support/discipline ending at the top. Long-term pupils appreciate Mr Franklin's tightening up. Foreign, principally German, boarders who enter for the sixth, strain at bedtimes and dress code but no major revolts after settling in period. Sixth form has dress code, lower forms have uniform – trouser option for girls. No recent drugs incidents but clear policy – automatic out for class A/B and possible police involvement, second chance over cannabis with testing/counselling/collaboration with parents regimen.

Pupils and Parents: Very much a Sussex school with a third of pupils living within 40 minutes drive, a further third – the English boarders – living within fifty miles and final third being overseas boarders. 'I could fill the school with Germans,' says head – the IB being, now, a prime attraction – but no more than 15 taken per year and those who come are, mostly, keen, highly appreciative of all on offer here and achieve impressively. Further few annually from everywhere else but no other large national contingents. Previously popular with Service families, numbers now in decline while diplomatic and other expat numbers increasing. Generally families are unpretentious, many making sacrifices to give their children 'the best'. Largest number from college's own prep. Former Ardines include racing driver Mike Hawthorn, Ian Hislop, composer Stephen Oliver, actors Terry-Thomas and Alan Howard.

Entrance: Selective via scholarship, CE or other exams depending on point of entry – English, maths, VR tested.

Exit: Around 20 leave after GCSE, mostly to local sixth form colleges. Rest stay and go on to everything from Oxbridge science to Nottingham Trent sport studies to employment to university abroad.

Money Matters: As part of necessary belt-tightening some scholarships funds have been reassigned however much still remains. Large number of academic, music, art, drama, sport and DT awards on offer at various stages – up to 50 per cent tuition remission. Special awards for clergy, Services, Sussex and Old Ardines' children. Worth scrutinising the literature.

Remarks: 'I would like to change the fact that we are the best kept secret in Southern England,' says head. Parents accosted on our way out were in no doubt. 'They praise the individual... they'll look at each child and work with them... they don't try to fit child into a mould... it's a very happy place.' We couldn't help noticing that, wherever we went, we were smiled at and that doesn't happen everywhere.

Ash Field School

Broad Avenue, Leicester, Leicestershire, LE5 4PY

Tel: 01162 737 151

Fax: 01162 739 962

Email: office@ashfield.leicester.sch.uk

Website: www.ashfieldschool.co.uk

• Pupils: 40 girls, 70 boys. Some residential provision.
• Ages: 4-19 • School status: State • School gender: Mixed
• Day/boarding: Takes boarders

SEN provision

Detail:

Centre of excellence for:

Mild: CP;
Moderate: CP;
Severe: CP;
Others: Epi; PD;

Experience of:

Mild: ASP; DS; DYSC; DYSL; HI; VI;
Moderate: HI; VI;
Others: PMLD; MSI; Sp&LD;

Summary: Ash Field School and Microtechnology Centre is a day and residential school for 110 pupils aged 4-19 whose main presenting difficulties are physical but usually compounded by one or more additional needs of a communication, sensory, learning or medical nature. In addition to its day and residential work, the school assesses pupils in mainstream for their curriculum access requirements and recommends, installs, and provides training for, ICT equipment and software. More than 500 pupils are currently supported in mainstream in this way

Ash Field is a Leading Edge school, replacing its Beacon status, and is an SEN trailblazer specialist school. Over recent years Ash Field has provided training in leadership and management, ICT, SEN and moving and handling to more than 100 other educational schools, colleges and universities.

What we say about the school - the full Good Schools Guide review

Head: Since 1998, Mr David Bateson MA BEd Cert Ed (fifty). Read education at Birmingham, gained a first, later studied for a masters in 'special needs in the ordinary school' from the University of East Anglia. Previously head of Dawn House School, Rainworth. A leader in his field: an Ofsted inspector; an external adviser; a consultant and trustee of the East Midlands Leadership Centre and the first head of a special school to chair the Leicester Secondary Heads Association (for two years) – 'a fantastic honour.' Head says: 'We are happy to pass on everything that we have learned and achieved here to anyone else. Our involvement with many other bodies also helps us learn and improve here too.'

Inspirational and enthusiastic. Great sense of humour and infectious laugh. Diverted from possible career in journalism after a day helping out at a playgroup for children with special needs. 'I had such a fantastic day and from that moment decided there was no better thing to do than work with these special young people.' Married to Pauline, a teacher at a special school in Chesterfield, two grown-up boys. Music/song writing is a passion and as a birthday treat is recording his own album of contemporary folk music. Writes the school panto. As a parent said to us: 'the school has a headteacher who is, quite frankly, remarkable. He is a friend and mentor to his pupils and an inspiration to everyone. What he and his staff achieve is unbelievable.'

Academic Matters: State special community school and micro assessment centre for mainstream schools. Bucketloads of accolades: one of just 12 Government 'trail-blazer' special schools; in Ofsted's top 1 per cent of schools; twice named as 'excellent' in HMCI annual report to Parliament ...

Effectively three schools in one – primary, secondary, FE. Pupils 'move up' through the separate stages, giving a sense of progression through the school. Class size averages 9 with a maximum 11. Multi-disciplinary team approach to teaching – school staff, staff from special needs teaching service and medical staff work together. School uses peripatetic teachers to help pupils with particular difficulties. Some children have individual teaching sessions. Excels in helping youngsters with hearing and vision difficulties, drafting in specialist staff when needed and offering British Sign Language and Makaton. Extra support is also available for pupils for whom English is a second language.

All pupils have an individual education plan detailing short-term targets for English, maths and personal development. As far as possible, lessons follow the

National Curriculum and elements of the foundation curriculum for pupils working towards level one. National Literacy Strategy and the National Numeracy Strategy are incorporated into English and maths in primary. Head says: 'My staff get just as excited about a child with enormous difficulties making a small step forward – recognising letters, counting – as they do for SATS, GCSEs and other academic attainment.' 'Everyone can achieve. Those achievements are not important in relation to other people, but are important to them and to what they are capable of.' A parent told us: 'The school has changed my son's life for the best, and that applies to many, many other children as well.'

Allows an extra year for children to take GCSEs. Most post-17 students spend some time in local FE college and in work experience or work shadowing.

Games, Options, The Arts: Residential wing with18 beds in 10 bedrooms is open to all pupils during their time at Ash Field. Provides excellent independence training and plays respite role for parents too. Children build up their use of the wing by, for example, staying late for tea, then overnight, then for up to a week. It offers a chance to continue school work, do homework, and add in extra-curricular activities (IT, sports, outings to the cinema, theatre, parks, Beavers, Cubs, Brownies etc). Head is included in a sleep-in rota. Parents visit to maintain routine. Independence, social skills and pride in personal appearance encouraged. Residential staff run activities for parts of Easter and summer holidays. In main school, youngsters make best use of free time, through clubs and sport. Wheelchair hockey/football popular in secondary and post-17. A youth club for over-11s run by youth workers and residential care staff. Regular residential stays at Stoke Mandeville for their sports competition. Plus trips galore: to Cornwall, Belgium, Holland, France and Germany.

Background and Atmosphere: There's a real sense of fulfilment and pleasure; evidence everywhere of children expressing themselves through work, music and play. Traditional-looking school, uninspiring corridors enlivened by joyous, colourful examples of the youngsters' work. A parent said: 'How lucky we are that Ash Field is around. It has transformed my child's education, upbringing and general love for life.'

Pastoral Care and Discipline: Primary pupils have a class teacher and secondary a group tutor as main pastoral link. Each pupil also has a member of the day support staff to act as educational care officer. In the residential wing, each has an identified member of staff to look after pastoral needs. Close links between home and school.

High standards of behaviour and work are expected (and achieved). While recognising the kind of problems the pupils face, the school encourages respect for each other, staff, visitors, property, buildings and achievement. Good work is rewarded with certificates and, for primary pupils, a visit to the head for praise and a sticker.

In secondary, the pupils are in groups or 'parks' – Abbey, Evington and Humberstone. Slips for good work and behaviour are awarded during the week and totalled on a Friday. Totals displayed in the entrance hall. When pupils achieve 10 slips, they receive a tutor's certificate; five tutor's certificates earn a headteacher's certificate. All receive praise at the annual certificate giving. Emphasis is on rewarding good behaviour but, school will withdraw privilege, give detention or send letters to parents if behaviour merits it. Very rare for pupils to be excluded.

Pupils and Parents: From surrounding area: a good mix. Emphasis is on what pupils can do and the ways in which they are like other pupils in the school. Head sums it up: 'We get a chance to work with some of the most interesting children in the country, youngsters who get a tremendous level of enjoyment from the simplest of things. They are ready and willing to learn – all they want is for you to unlock the doors for them. They are not moaning about their lot, they are just trying to do the best they can – that is so humbling and so inspirational.'

Entrance: Pupils referred from five LEAs – City of Leicester, Leicestershire, Rutland, Northamptonshire and Derbyshire – usually with Statement. Pupils can come to the school at any age. Small number (9) split time with a mainstream school. All pupils have physical disability; 25 per cent of those are of average ability but two thirds have moderate learning difficulties and 8 per cent have severe learning difficulties.

Exit: All leave at 19. In 2005 all leavers went on to colleges of further education. Small number leave earlier to join/rejoin mainstream school.

Remarks: Inspirational, led by a very special head. Ethos of making every moment count. Time here fills a visitor with a sense of what can and should be achieved.

ASHBY FIELDS PRIMARY SCHOOL

Wimborne Place, Ashby Fields, Daventry, Northamptonshire, NN11 0YP

Tel: 01327 310 068

Email: head@ashby.northants-ecl.gov.uk

• Pupils: 410 girls and boys, all day • Ages: 4-11

• School status: State • School gender: Mixed

• Day/boarding: Day pupils

SEN provision

Detail:

Now provide for in school:

Mild: ASP; EBD; DYSL;

Moderate: ASP; ADHD; EBD; MLD; DYSL; HI; VI;

Severe: ADHD; EBD; DYSL; DYSP; CP;

Others: SPD; ODD; TIC; GEN; EAL; Sp&LD; PD;

Summary: Although a mainstream school, we include a large number of children with a diverse range of medical, physical and learning needs. We have recently completed the final phase of building to the school which includes a physiotherapy suite for children to carry out personal movement programmes in a warm and private environment.

What we say about the school - the full Good Schools Guide review

Head: Interregnum.

Entrance: LEA standard with SEN overtones.

Remarks: A fairly new foundation, opened in 1999 in a bland new Daventry housing estate. Buildings imaginatively designed: a series of interlocking cloisters surrounded by attractive and extensive play- and sports-grounds. At first sight the school appears to be part of a large shopping complex and this, together with its closeness to a busy ring road, detract noticeably from the overall ambience. The Ofsted report dates from 2001 – very positive, but deals with what was then a tiny institution. Current results at Key Stage 2 – absolute and value added – place the school in the middle of the Northamptonshire range: school recognises that it could do better.

The SENCo is the well-qualified and delightfully enthusiastic and perceptive Deborah Gunby. With the recent move of the founding headmistress into an advisery role in Leicestershire, she has been promoted to acting deputy head. As clear a statement of the importance of special needs as the school could make. SEN intake average: 20 per cent overall, 2 per cent statemented. Full range of supportive strategies: from withdrawal of a child for an hour a week to a full-time teaching assistant for a child with significant problems. SEN children included in all possible aspects of school life. Pupils encouraged to see disability in all its various aspects as matters of everyday inconsequentiality. Staff are fully involved and committed to the school's SEN policy. Regular meetings take place to discuss individual child's progress, and at every stage too the school welcomes parental involvement. Challenging behavioural and academic problems can be a source of tension between school and parent, but this is handled with growing finesse

Extremely well-equipped to deal with all aspects of SEN. Laptops for use in the computer room or throughout the school – particularly useful for dyslexic or dyspraxic pupils (the largest SEN group). Physiotherapy suite for children with cerebral palsy or similar conditions (not many on the roll at present); impressively inclusive that this suite is in the main school concourse.

Dyspraxic and physically impaired children join in class games lessons where this is 'practical, safe and appropriate', sometimes with one-to-one support (especially for swimming). Physically impaired children might do their personal physiotherapy programmes whilst the rest of the class is at PE, to avoid losing time out of the rest of the curriculum – so to some extent the school cannot avoid differentiation; no sense of this presenting any real problems. The quality of artwork is especially good with colourful displays in and out of the classrooms; a real sense of imaginative and lively self-expression throughout the whole campus, which enhances the atmosphere of energetic enthusiastic endeavour which pervades the whole place. Art of course gives a special opportunity to many children with SEN needs and this seems fully exploited.

Music and drama important, children encouraged to take a full part – limited opportunities for individual musical tuition, but choir and a small orchestra, and competes in local competitions and festivals. Unusually wide range of out-of-school activities. Currently this includes a parachute club for infant aged children – though not quite what one might imagine! Buildings designed to allow total disabled access; specially designed playground equipment allows physically impaired children to take a more active part.

The school's recent foundation has both helped and hindered it in the development of a workable system of pastoral care and discipline. The staff are overwhelmingly young and it might be suggested that there is a lack of experience. However, this criticism, if that is what it is, cuts both ways. The school is remarkably open to new thinking and is incredibly self-critical. Recently it has introduced a house system with a competitive system of house points and demerits; thus happily borrowing from what is best in independent schools. One has the clear impression of cheerful children who are well motivated and well disciplined. The anti-bullying policy is rigorous and strictly enforced. Genuine mutual tolerance and respect. Situations can be challenging and difficult: we witnessed a potentially explosive situation that was handled with great care, expertise, and sensitivity.

The children, as one would expect from this catchment area, are overwhelmingly middle class, though this area of Daventry is an entirely new build estate and as such lacks the social cohesion of more established neighbourhoods. Thus the school plays a very important role in developing a sense of community identity. This may be one reason why there is an especially strong parental involvement in the PTA, but also assisting in the library and in out-of-school clubs. The school has secured a particular reputation for its SEN work from a much wider area, but this does not appear to be deterring local parents: one of the most popular primary schools in the Daventry area.

A new school that has yet to fully prove itself (though encouraging signs of problems being tackled). Much will depend on the choice of a replacement for the dynamic founding headmistress. Has already secured an enviable reputation for its SEN provision, largely because of its enthusiastic and youthful staff.

Ashville College

Green Lane, Harrogate, North Yorkshire, HG2 9JP

Tel: 01423 566 358

Fax: 01423 505 142

Email: ashville@ashville.co.uk

Website: www.ashville.co.uk

• Pupils: 830 boys and girls, 145 board • Ages: 4-18 • Religion: Methodist • Fees: Senior school day £2,766-£2,789; boarding £5,206-£5,286. Junior school day £1,948-£2,348; boarding £4,758-£4,845. Pre-prep £1,590 • School status: Independent • Opendays: October • School gender: Mixed • Day/boarding: Takes boarders

SEN provision

Detail:

Now provide for in school:

Mild: DYSC; DYSL; DYSP; VI;

Moderate: DYSL; VI;

Severe: DYSL; VI;

Others: EAL; DEL; Epi; PD; Eat;

Experience of:

Mild: ASP; ADD;

Summary: The school provides English Support using a classroom as a learning support base. Dyslexic pupils are withdrawn from lessons for one period per week and IEPs plus reports are written as appropriate. The dyslexic pupils receive individual programmes of multi-sensory tuition, directed towards their specific learning requirements. Full liaison with parents and staff is a priority and the pupils' progress is monitored throughout the three schools. All pupils on entering the Junior and Senior Schools are screened for dyslexia as part of their induction programme. The English support teacher works with children, either individually or in small groups throughout the three schools.

What we say about the school - the full Good Schools Guide review

Head: Since 2003 Mr Andrew Fleck MA BSc, early forties, educated at Marlborough College, did an MA in education at Sussex having read geology at Nottingham and studied for a PGCE at University College, North Wales. Previously deputy head of St Bede's School,

Sussex, head of geography at Hurstpierpoint and teacher of geography at Ballakermeen High School. Married to Anne, with twin daughters, both at Ashville pre-prep. Older pupils describe the head as confident, amiable and dynamic, younger ones as strict but nice. Loves watersports (especially sailing) and problem solving, spent four seasons canoeing in the Arctic. Believes balance and creativity are key, adds, 'sustainable success doesn't come from hammering the same nail all the time.'

Academic Matters: Good value added at GCSE, approximately 46 per cent of all passes are graded A/A* with 95 per cent graded C or above. Music GCSE is successfully replaced with AS and all pass. Art, Latin and RE traditionally strong, no let downs though slightly fewer pass German than other subjects. Approximately 50 per cent of A level passes are graded A or B, none fail altogether. Loiters round the lower regions of the independent schools' league tables but isn't highly selective in the first place. Taken as a whole, results wouldn't set the world on fire but most pupils exceed predicted potential and clearly those who are able do very well. In recent GCSE exams the school had three pupils in the top five nationally for German and Latin and were curriculum finalists of the National Maths Olympiad.

Average class size 18 with a maximum of 24. Shortish school day, 4pm finish and no Saturday school but option of after school care at extra cost. Six times Winners of the Institute of Directors Award for Business and Technology between 1995 and 2003 when (perhaps not surprisingly) the award was discontinued. All year 7 pupils (and year 3 in the Junior school) are screened for dyslexia using the Philips and Leonard Screening test with further testing and screening as necessary. No pupil has a statement of special educational need but the school identifies almost 100 pupils, mostly boys, as in need of special provision. Over half of these require extra English as English isn't their first language and approximately one third are dyslexic for whom specialist help is available at no extra cost. All access full curriculum, and are generally educated in the mainstream classroom by the class teacher with support as required. The norm is for pupils to be withdrawn for one period per week when assessments are carried out and help given on an individual basis. Individual Education Programmes (IEPs) are included in school reports. Those with dyslexia thrive thanks to the caring environment and carefully planned programmes of study; indeed in recent years only one child didn't get the benchmark five A-Cs at GCSE and most gain at least a B in English.

Games, Options, The Arts: Well-resourced music suite is home to a selection of choirs and bands. Talented musicians play in the National Children's and National Youth Orchestras but there are playing and performing opportunities for those just starting out too. Plenty of productions, latest offerings, Carmina Burana and Finzi's Imitations of Immorality well received. Sports facilities: two gyms, swimming pool, fabulous climbing wall, squash court, fitness room and ample pitches show importance of sport. All usual suspects on offer plus American influenced disc golf, something for everyone.

Background and Atmosphere: Founded in 1877 by the Methodist Church, the pleasant, uncontroversial site sprawls across an otherwise residential area. The school was evacuated to Windermere during the war as the premises were requisitioned for the war effort and used by Air Ministry. Run as a Christian school in the Methodist tradition. Plenty of well kept facilities, atmospheric Memorial Hall is home to lectures, meetings and some concerts with larger gatherings filling the school hall.

Pastoral Care and Discipline: All year 7 are taken to the Lake District for a bonding weekend early in the autumn term, this receives rave reviews not only from the new pupils but also from sixth formers who work as liaison prefects. Those lucky enough to be assigned to year 7 go on the trip too. Duke of Edinburgh Award Scheme available for pupils from year 10. Trip for older students to Malawi ties in with charity fundraising to support the Open Arms Orphanage which has close links with the school. School viewed as a day school with boarding. Four boarding houses are comfortably furnished with usual facilities: kitchens, common rooms, games areas and computers. A couple of largish dorms remain for younger boarders otherwise mainly one or two-man rooms. Biggest grumble is imbalance of pupil nationality – almost two thirds of boarders are Chinese with some resultant friction in an otherwise happy and relaxed environment. New head keen to redress the balance, possibly with enhancement of weekly boarding. Girls and boys encouraged to socialise, half-termly theme evening provides fun for all boarders. Plenty of activities on offer after school but all optional, pupils think everyone should do at least one or two to get the most out of boarding life. Fines if caught smoking with possibility of exclusion for repeated offences. Drugs: out for intending to or supplying, couple of expulsions in recent times.

Pupils and Parents: Hail from local professional and business families, quite a few first time buyers of independent education. A number of Americans from nearby Menwith Hill military base. For about ten per cent of pupils English is not a first language and overall approximately fourteen per cent come from a variety of minority ethnic backgrounds. Thriving Friends of Ashville run regular well-supported activities. Old boys: Ian Dodds (designer of the Moon Buggy), Commander Ian Grieve (head of anti-terrorism Scotland Yard).

Entrance: Interview, report from previous head and day of tests: academic and practical for year 7. Sixth form entry is via interview and satisfactory reference, minimum five grade Cs with grade Bs in subjects to be studied. Exams, interview and reference are norm for entry at other times. Majority of pupils come from own junior school and nearby preps: Belmont Grosvenor and Brackenfield in Harrogate, Westville in Ilkley and Richmond House and Moorlands in Leeds.

Exit: Just under a fifth leave at the end of year 6 and a third at the end of year 11. Majority of sixth formers go onto higher education, a couple to Oxbridge rest to a wide range of universities.

Money Matters: Means tested academic, music, art and drama scholarships available and worth between 10 and 50 per cent of fees. All scholarships are reviewed at the end of the stage of education ie year 9 for year 7 entry. Concessions available for the children of Methodist ministers and bursaries given to Service families.

Remarks: Plenty of happy pupils in a nurturing environment. High fliers tend to fly off to local competitors but those who stay thrive. Popular with locals and overseas Chinese alike. Worth a look if one school from nursery to university suits your child.

Aysgarth School

Bedale, North Yorkshire, DL8 1TF

Tel: 01677 450 240

Fax: 01677 450 736

Email: enquiries@aysgarthschool.co.uk

Website: www.aysgarthschool.co.uk

• Pupils: 123 boys in the prep school, 80 boys and girls in pre-prep and nursery; 90 per cent plus board in the prep school • Ages: 3-13 • Religion: Christian • Fees: Pre-prep £1,625-£1750 day. Prep £4,015 day, £5,015 boarding • School status: Independent • School gender: Boys • Day/boarding: Takes boarders

SEN provision

Detail:

Now provide for in school:

Mild: DYSC; DYSL; DYSP;

Moderate: DYSC; DYSL;

Experience of:

Mild: ADD; ADHD; EBD;

Moderate: ADD;

Others: EAL; Epi;

Summary: Aysgarth School has a learning support department. This comprises a team of teachers with extra qualifications and experience concerned with a variety of special educational needs. They work in support of the whole teaching staff from the Pre-Prep upwards to provide a comprehensive package of support in line with the Code of Practice in the Identification and Assessment of Special Needs' published by the DES in 1994 and the revised Code of Practice 2001.

Aysgarth School follows a graduated approach to Learning Support. Literacy and numeracy assessments are undertaken by pupils. Those pupils with concerns are offered Dyslexia Screening Tests and more detailed assessments. Discussion between parents, child and teachers takes place. Support is offered with targets placed on an individual education plan. The learning support department also offers support in Handwriting, Reading, Balance and co-ordination through Brain Gym and Study Skills.

What we say about the school - the full Good Schools Guide review

Head: Since 2002, Mr Anthony Goddard (fiftyish); succeeded popular ex-Uppingham housemaster Mr John Hodgkinson (Mr Goddard went from Cambridge to ICI and thence to Accenture – head of chemicals practice). Successful manager and marketing expert; no teaching experience but was an Aysgarth governor for ten years – imaginative appointment and numbers have risen by 20 per cent whilst maintaining the boarding focus. He teaches geography, some games and is very involved on the pastoral side. His wife Caroline ran her own Montessori school and is now a special needs teacher; she is very involved on the pastoral side, especially the settling in of new boys, and teaches Religious Studies. Three children, one at university and two working in London. Energetic and charming Mr Philip Southall (married to Louise, two boys on their way through Aysgarth and one at Uppingham) continues as assistant head; much liked and respected by the boys.

Entrance: By interview and assessment, no exam. 'We try not to turn anyone away.' A few scholarships and some bursary help. Siblings' discount.

Exit: Excellent record to public schools. Eton, Harrow, Shrewsbury, Ampleforth, Radley, Sedbergh, Stowe, Uppingham. Good sprinkling of academic and music scholarships.

Remarks: Beautiful rural setting in fifty acres of parkland; purpose-built 19th century school, including splendid tower from whose roof bagpipes may occasionally be heard. Sports facilities to die for especially cricket field and swimming pool. Traditional demanding curriculum (nearly all do Latin), taught by capable and committed staff; all lessons rated 'good or very good' in recent (2000) ISC inspection. Gaps noted by inspectors in DT and PSHE have been filled, with an impressive new creative arts centre just opened. Music outstanding under charismatic director, both instrumentally and chorally; Victorian chapel, with organ, is a gem. New staff and facilities have given a boost to the art, design and technology activities – creative side in general needed a boost. Very thoughtful SEN provision – clear and helpful leaflet for parents.

Sport has high profile – for all but the less sporty are offered various options. Not unusual for seven cricket sides to be fielded on one day. Golf and clay-pigeon shooting on offer. Great rivalry with Bramcote. Parties go regularly to an outdoor centre in the Hebrides run by the exotically named Torquil Johnson-Ferguson (old boy). Pastoral and boarding care excellent – inspected 2005 and met or exceeded all standards assessed; staff know boys well and boys look after each other (these easy relationships praised in ISI report). Plenty to do at weekends, though boys are not forced into multiple activities. Two exeats and a half term every term. Boarding accommodation has been renewed, top quality matrons and school nurse. Very strong parental support, including on governing body. Clientele mainly solid (upper) middle class from the north (including Scotland) and midlands, though a few NCOs' children from Catterick are starting to appear. Governors very active and close to headmaster. Lively Old Aysgarthian association – useful reporting from recent leavers at senior schools and former pupils keep in touch in adult life; a healthy family atmosphere centred on school.

Many of the boys look as though they are about to take Eton in their stride. There's an almost Edwardian ease about the place and few families seem to live in large towns. Some parents new to the game might be put off by this but they would probably be wrong. Aysgarth is a happy, lively place, full of confident, industrious lads, without a trace of snobbishness. And if you want a boys-only boarding school in the north of England, it's the only one there is.

Balfron High School

Roman Road, Balfron, By Glasgow, G63 0PW

Tel: 01360 440 469

Fax: 01360 440 260

Email: balfronhs@stirling.gov.uk

Website: www.balfronhigh.org

• Pupils: 950 boys and girls, all day • Ages: 11-18

• Religion: Non-denom • School status: State

• School gender: Mixed • Day/boarding: Day pupils

SEN provision

Summary: No comment. Frightened of being exposed as seriously SEN friendly? Perhaps – they are extraordinarily welcoming for such a highly academic school.

What we say about the school - the full Good Schools Guide review

Head: Since 2002, Mrs Val Corry BSc(Eng) ARSM PGCE (fifties) who was educated at Morpeth Girls' Grammar School, followed by Imperial College, London, where she read metallurgy and engineering and started her professional career as a researcher for British Steel. Into teaching via Moray House, she taught first at Grangemouth High and then ran a ceramics business before returning to teaching and leapfrogging up the academic ladder via Linlithgow Academy, Stirling High and Wallace High where she became assistant and then depute head. Very much the new girl, she has been involved with advising the government on staff development for the Advanced Highers programme and is in the midst of doing the SQH (Scottish Qualification for Headship) which encompasses leadership and key management skills, and is now working for her Masters – she is 120 points off, and is about to go back to uni to do her dissertation. She currently teaches one period of physics a week but hopes to increase this.

Academic Matters: Max class size 30. Fiercely academic, strong science school – and marvellous labs, but marvellous everything, see below – 24 students doing Advanced Higher biology, 'and huge numbers' coming through in the years below, biology lab has a greenhouse incorporated into its roof. Labs are an astonishing carpeted 90 metres square. Other sciences not far behind, good solid run of the mill academia, 'nothing esoteric' in the timetable, French and German on offer, Gaelic 'might be possible' as indeed is Russian. Flexible learning not a problem and sixth formers and local adults (evenings) can log on to do distance learning courses, psychology particularly popular. Computers abound, three pupils per machine, and emails for all. Mrs Corry is 'looking at' re-active whiteboards – trouble is they cost around £4,000, and you can buy an awful lot of books with £4,000. Humanities divided and pupils do either history or geography during their first year and the other in the year following. No problems with support for learning, the state can and will supply everything, one-to-one where needed, plus scribes etc; three full-time and two part-time staff plus a child ed psych on hand. This is an inclusive school, capable of dealing with physical handicaps (lifts all over the shop). Terrific library overlooking the atrium, with views out over the games pitches to The Campsies.

Games, Options, The Arts: School incorporates a fabulous leisure complex with pool, sports hall and weights much used by the local community and open from 7am to 10pm 365 days a year. Fantastic fitness then. Excellent swimming (25-metre pool), Astroturf, pitches and athletics track. Masses of games after school, Stirling Council (and the lottery) provide a sports co-ordinator; rugby good – and both national and international players in the school. Art is state of, with every possible medium catered for and finished products creeping on to the walls and a rather natty patio. Computer-linked CDT with every machine imaginable. First and third years do home economics – flash new kitchens with microwaves. Terrific theatre and drama, the theatre available to the community, and masses of music; with local involvement. Work experience for all at 14. Masses of trips and exchanges, for culture as well as skiing etc, Japanese exchange in November, school will underwrite those who can't afford it. Huge amount of charity work and much local involvement.

Background and Atmosphere: This is a split-new school, formally opened in May 2002 by Helen Liddle, Secretary of State for Scotland. Cathy Jamieson, MSP and Minister for Education and Young People, celebrated the partnership between Stirling Council and Jarvis by sticking the first leaf on the 'school tree of learning' which climbs up the corner of the atrium. How on earth later leaves will be added is anyone's guess – the tree is some thirty-odd feet high. The atrium adjoins the dining room, pupils bring their own or use swipe cards (which conceals the free school meals problem). This is a magnet school. State of the art in every dimension, each subject has a pod of rooms off the main core, terrific views, marvellous outside area – it does occasionally shine North of the Highland Line. Fortunately there is some scope for expansion, for, having built houses on the adjacent site where the old school stood (now demolished), the school roll is already dangerously near capacity. The school, built under a PFI/PPP will be run by Jarvis (of Railtrack fame) for the next 25 years, they provide the caterers and do all maintenance, the final design was a combination of staff and local community involvement. Slight big brother feel, all the rooms are networked for sound (as well as inter/intra netted) and at 9.55am and again at 10.05am, loudspeaker announcements about sin on the school bus and extra music lessons boomed over the speakers. Electronic noticeboard advertising weekend jobs at the local pub – £3.70 an hour. School became a community school proper in 2003 but the old boards still reassuringly in place. School uniform for all, trainers out, otherwise just polo shirts, sweatshirts etc; smart blue blazers with green trim loaned annually to sixth formers, who must have them cleaned before they are returned. Houses – Camsie, Endrick and Lomond – really only used for games.

Pastoral Care and Discipline: State system of guidance teachers, good PSHE and anti-bullying strategies in place. 'Balfriending' is a buddy system between first and sixth years which really works. Masses of contact, sixth pick up problems early; bullying incidents are logged, the victim supported and the bully sanctioned – and sanctions range from verbal warnings through 'the imposition of a written exercise' to temporary or even permanent exclusions and ed psychs etc.

Pupils and Parents: Mainly country folk, so friendly and welcoming children, few from ethnic minority backgrounds. Good middle class ethos prevails; a teacher at one of the local private schools (so discounted education) has sent his child here as the facilities are 'so much better'.

Entrance: From local primaries, 30 placing requests at the moment.

Exit: Few leave after Standard Grades, rather more post-Highers. Most to Scottish Unis and trad three or four to Oxbridge.

Remarks: Stunning school, happy staff, good work ethos, some of the best views in Scotland. Worth moving to the Trossachs for.

BARNARDISTON HALL PREPARATORY SCHOOL

Barnardiston Hall, Nr. Haverhill, Suffolk, CB9 7TG

Tel: 01440 786 316

Fax: 01440 786 355

Email: info@barnardiston-hall.co.uk

Website: www.barnardiston.com

• Pupils: 115 girls, 125 boys (50 boys and girls board) • Ages: nursery and pre-prep; 2-7; prep 7-11 • Religion: non-denom • Fees: nursery-pre-prep: £1,100-£2,300; prep: £2,950; boarding: £4,500 • School status: Independent • Opendays: None. Prospective parents visit at any time to tour school and meet children • School gender: Mixed • Day/boarding: Takes boarders

SEN provision

Detail:

Centre of excellence for:

- Mild: ASP; AUT; ADD; ADHD; EBD; DYSC;
- Moderate: AUT; ADD; ADHD; EBD; DYSC;
- Severe: ADD; ADHD; EBD;
- Others: CD;

Experience of:

- Mild: DS; DYSL; DYSP; CP;
- Moderate: DS; MLD; DYSL; DYSP; CP;
- Severe: ASP; AUT; DS; DYSC; DYSL; DYSP; CP;
- Others: AUT(other); FRX; PMLD; SLD; MSI; Sp&LD; Epi; Oth;

Summary: Barnardiston Hall provides a first-class education to chidren with special needs ranging from dyslexia and dyspraxia to autism and Asperger's syndrome with in-class support, small group work or one-to-one tuition in 'The Bridge'. Children with mild EBD are given strategies to help them cope with school life and we have received excellent reports from visiting outside agencies.

Broadlands Hall is a 10-bedded residential children's home which is located some two miles from Barnardiston Hall. Broadlands offers education to children with a full range of learning difficulties and/or EBD. Most children are residential and are referred via local authorities. However, day children can be accepted and private placements can be made. Broadlands Hall offers a supportive, safe and caring environment in which children are encouraged to reach their full potential.

What we say about the school - the full Good Schools Guide review

Headmaster: Since 1990, Colonel Keith Boulter (fifties), married to Gail, who is deeply involved in the school; three grown up children, all working in education. Cambridge theology graduate, hockey blue and keen musician, he joined the Royal Army Educational Corps in 1973 and administered five Gurkha schools in Hong Kong, Nepal and Brunei. Also worked at MOD, briefing four star generals.

On leaving the army in 1990, Colonel Boulter bought Barnardiston when there were 52 children and no boarders. In 1995 a £1m pre-prep department was opened, and in 2004 a £1.5m prep extension, including classrooms, language lab and the Bridge (the SEN department). A straightforward, direct person, he is devoted to education and, although he claims not to be much of an administrator, he has more than put the school on the map and is thoroughly acquainted with every last nut and bolt of the organisation. He is very much hands-on, teaching hockey, maths to pupils from 9-13, training the choir, and leading frequent expeditions to the Derbyshire Dales, Ben Nevis and Snowdon. An ISC inspection report described his leadership as enthusiastic and visionary, others call him charismatic. He believes that a flexible approach is the key to bringing out the best in individual pupils and is keen to challenge and stretch them, both physically and mentally. Camping out in the grounds starts early. When the headmaster retires he would like to hand over the school to his own children, one of whom has already taught there.

Entrance: Children spend a day attending lessons and being observed and tested by subject teachers. The school's educational psychologist is used in the case of children with learning difficulties, to assess their particular needs.

Exit: Pupils tend to go on to independent schools of their first choice broadly in the area (there is always a good smattering of scholarships), or (a few) to local state schools.

Remarks: The school is in a lovely rural setting with about 15 acres (including an exciting adventure playground), where children are given a lot of freedom to roam around, build dens and explore. The main house, which is wood panelled and rambling and contains the office and boarding area, is also the Boulter home and has all the comfy domesticity and attractive clutter of a family house. Children, staff and large dogs mill around everywhere and there is clearly little or no distinction between private and public areas. Prospective parents are left to face up to 30 children crammed into the family sitting room, where the latter give an exuberant, no-holds-barred account of the school, which leaves the parents in no doubt as to the brilliance of the sport, the dubious quality of the macaroni cheese, the low tolerance of bullying and the bubbling confidence and happiness of the pupils.

Academically, the school does very well, with the pre-prep scoring well above the national average in maths and English tests. Children are streamed more or less from the word go, then setted for various subjects later on. French is taught from the nursery and Latin from year 1 of the prep, with 'A' set French pupils taking Latin on to year 6. IT provision is excellent, with a computer to every three children, and there is a fully computerised weather station. Full sets of armour doubtless add a touch of realism to history lessons.

About 50 children in the school, with anything from mild dyslexia, a problem with a specific subject to autism, are looked after by the Bridge. The name is apt, as it is both a long suite of cheerful, well-equipped first floor rooms, and also the department which aims to keep children with problems happily integrated in normal lessons. Up to 12 staff 'man' the Bridge, including five classroom assistants, who give help to small groups of children within the classroom, and specialists (two of whom are fully qualified SEN teachers) who deliver one-to-one help outside lessons. Staff at the Bridge have been trained to run a highly successful programme called 'Sound Foundation', which helps children with reading difficulties to make rapid progress. All subject and class teachers are fully briefed about SEN children and armed with teaching strategies. There are several statemented children (with Asperger's, dyslexia, dyspraxia and autism) whose school fees are paid by the state. Children talk openly about their experience of the Bridge, which they clearly love, and there is absolutely no sense of any stigma, as all children see it as part of normal school life. The atmosphere of the Bridge is warm and lovely, as are people who work there. Colonel Boulter won't accept children he knows he cannot help, but the school quite literally 'turned round' more than one child rejected by every other school. The Bridge is also used for TEFL, to cope with some of the 15 per cent or so temporary or full-time pupils from overseas.

Art, music and drama are strong. The art studio, commanding stunning views of the countryside, produces highly colourful and creative work. Eighty children play instruments and music plays a key role in the annual drama production. Choirs are regularly asked to perform at functions throughout the county.

Sporting competition between houses and with other school is keen and teams do well. A recently erected semi-permanent marquee provides quite a reasonable sports hall until funds can be found for the real thing and, although Astroturf is also on the agenda, children seem to be very happy running about in the mud and rain.

Children wax lyrical about the wealth of extra-curricular activities and expeditions (one will be going soon to the base camp of Mount Everest), and children and their parents raise large sums for charities from Swaziland to Venezuela and Nepal, where a school party visited a school in 2004.

The ISC report referred to the very high standard of pastoral care. Parents who choose this school can feel confident that no child will fall through the net in the warm family atmosphere that prevails. There is a 'I just wanted to tell you' letter box for anyone feeling shy about a particular issue, and the fact that several staff have or have had children at the school speaks volumes in itself. Staff say what a wonderfully happy place it is to work, and parents are similarly enthusiastic. This school comes highly recommended.

BASIL PATERSON TUTORIAL COLLEGE

66 Queen Street, Edinburgh, MIDLOTHIAN, EH2 4NA

Tel: 0131 225 3802

Fax: 0131 226 6701

Email: info@basilpaterson.co.uk

Website: www.basilpaterson.co.uk

• Pupils: 35 boys and girls. EFL College operates separately on same site • Ages: 16-19 (but currently some in their 20s) • Religion: Non-denom • Fees: On application. • School status: Independent • School gender: Mixed • Day/boarding: Takes boarders

SEN provision

Detail:
Experience of:
Mild: DYSC; DYSL; DYSP;

Summary: Our Tutorial College offers student-centred individual tuition as well as tuition for examinations in small classes of up to eight students. Our tutors are familiar with teaching students with a variety of learning difficulties and can work with them on an individual basis. We are experienced in presenting students who require special arrangements (readers, scribes etc.) for examinations. Being a small college we are able to offer a caring, supportive environment for students with particular learning difficulties. Our new premises in Queen Street (from July 2005) has facilities for students who require wheelchair access.

We share our facilities with our English Language School which specialises in teaching English to overseas students.

What we say about the school - the full Good Schools Guide review

Principal: Since 2004, Mr Colin M Smith MA, previously Depute Principal St Margaret's School, Edinburgh. Educated at George Heriot's school followed by St Andrews University, where he read French and German. Having taught extensively in Scotland and been Depute Principal for 9 years, he is now in the process of changing Basil Paterson into a 'Scottish Sixth Form College' with a full-time programme as well as into a centre of flexible tuition (any subject, any level, any time). Twilight, evening and weekend tuition are now on offer. He leads the EFL College as well.

Academic Matters: Edinburgh's oldest and most famous tutorial college, BP was founded in 1929, and grafted onto Dugdale's Secretarial College (now defunct) which started in 1893. Currently owned by the Oxford Intensive School of English (OISE). Huge number of subjects on offer: Scottish Highers, Advanced Highers, Intermediates and Standard Grades plus all three of the English exam boards GCSE and AS/A levels. A team of part-time tutors to cover the various examination subjects (Edinburgh is rich in tutors). Max class size eight, plus many individual lessons where necessary. One well-equipped lab on site. Four lessons tuition per subject for Standard Grade/GCSE per week, five for Highers/AS Levels and six for Advanced Highers/'normal two year' A levels. An accredited exam centre for all four boards. Impressive success rate, 'but it does rather depend on the individual student'. Good careers advice, help with UCAS and clearing. The full-time course includes supervised study, general skills classes as well as the social programme.

Popular Easter revision courses in (almost) everything. In addition, flexible tuition is offered in any subject (twilight/evening and weekend). This is proving very popular with both parents and pupils. A suite of evening classes will soon be offered to the local community and beyond.

Background and Atmosphere: The college is now in superb new premises at 66 Queen Street, formerly home to one of Scotland's most prestigious solicitors' companies. It comprises two light airy Georgian buildings joined together with some original ceilings still visible and boasts state-of-the art computers, a student common room and student study centre, a wireless area for students to use their own laptops, 12 excellent classrooms and an outside cafe area. Classes can flow over into the EFL side during the busy Easter period. Outside café area. New computers with e-mail for all. Good self-study area.

Pastoral Care and Discipline: Students on the whole live with families or in flats in and around Edinburgh, accommodation no problem for those from abroad or further afield. But students are expected to take a certain amount of responsibility for their own studies. The new social programme combines activities for both tutorial and EFL students. Each student and parent/guardian must sign a student support agreement.

Pupils and Parents: Currently 10 per cent from abroad plus first-time candidates, retakes and those hopeful of upping previous marks.

Entrance: An interview with the principal as well as a report from the previous school attended.

Remarks: Up and running and delivering the goods.

BEARSDEN ACADEMY

Morven Road, Bearsden, G61 3SU

Tel: 0141 942 2297

Fax: 0141 942 4681

Email: office@bearsdenacademy.e-dunbarton.sch.uk

Website: www.bearsdenacademy.org

• Pupils: 1,255 boys and girls (55/45), capped at 210 first-year intake (seven classes of 30); all day • Ages: 11-18 • Religion: Non-denom • School status: State • School gender: Mixed • Day/boarding: Day pupils

SEN provision

Detail:

Now provide for in school:

- Mild: AUT; ADHD; DYSL; DYSP; VI;
- Moderate: HI;
- Others: EAL;

Experience of:

- Mild: ADD; EBD; HI;
- Moderate: ASP;

Summary: We have limited facilities for pupils with physical disabilities owing to the nature of the building and the extensive campus.

We do provide good curricular support for pupils with additional support needs such as dyslexia or dyspraxia and we currently have several pupils with communication disorders on the autistic spectrum.

Our four special needs auxiliaries provide strong support for individual pupils according to their particular needs. We have also had excellent success with our bilingual pupils, many of whom gain qualifications in their first language.

What we say about the school - the full Good Schools Guide review

Head: Since 2000, Mr P Michael (Mike) R Doig MA FRSA PGCE (mid fifties), who was educated at The High School of Glasgow (then in the state system), read mod langs at Glasgow University and did his teacher training at Aberdeen. Started his teaching career at Milngavie, followed by head of langs at Cumbernauld High School, was depute head at Kirkintilloch High and assistant head at Hermitage Academy in Helensburgh. Then head for 8+ years at Cumbernauld High. A state school baby then. He still teaches the 'occasional spot of PSE but it would be unfair to have a timetabled slot'.

Married, with two children who went through the school but who are now graduates and, as they say in Scotland, he stays locally. He arrived in the school after an unsettling period, the previous head having retired early through ill-health, and the one before that died in post. Bearsden was a school in a timewarp. However, now, head says, 'the school is in good heart again', with the staff 'united' after some pretty 'dramatic changes'. Head is 'largely autonomous' as far as choosing staff is concerned and is obviously running a successful school – the school that the Bearsden 'youngsters' ('nice neutral term') deserve. Although appearing almost horizontally calm and relaxed, head admits that life can occasionally be 'interesting'. An iron fist in a velvet glove perhaps?

Academic Matters: School takes Standard, Intermediate I, Intermediate 2, Highers and Advanced Highers. (Pupils may also be presented for both Intermediate 2 and 1 instead of the Standard; they have different weighting.) German and French but no Spanish, and three separate sciences; maths and English results had been disappointing (although head claimed 'they were the best in East Dumbarton') but now looking up – school says 'consistently strong'. New IT staff improving results are consistently strong. Youngsters (follow the drift) are setted in their second year for English, maths, French and sciences. Not a vast choice of subjects but totally adequate with the non-academic well represented. Most pupils take eight subjects at standard grade.

Pupils are allocated a guidance teacher during their last year at primary, who acts as tutor throughout their time in secondary. Smashing new library which also includes a careers office and much used sixth form study centre. Six fully equipped computing/business rooms – the library has a well-equipped computer room – fabulous dedicated space (more books needed). Work ethos is important here, ditto homework, and homework diary must be signed by parent or guardian but pupils can complain 'to their Guidance teacher if they feel that they are unable to cope with homework'.

Support for learning throughout, with learning support staff visiting the linked primary schools to ensure a smooth transition. Four support for learning assistants, who work with children both on an individual basis and in class, scribing if need be; no diagnosed ADHD, one or two 'high end' Asperger's – head 'is aware of their needs' – and they are integrated wherever possible. 'Can't cope with wheelchairs' (except in the new library) but no problem with a profoundly deaf child who gets peripatetic support. EAL on hand, over 22 different nationalities in the school, many of whom do not speak English at home.

Games, Options, The Arts: Stunning new games hall and, as a community school, this is much used by locals too. Good spread of games pitches; school does remarkably well at rugby, football, with hockey and athletics well-represented. Outstanding success in basketball, a former national basketball coach is head of the PE squad and the school was runner-up in the Scottish finals. No tennis courts or swimming pool but skiing, snowboarding are popular options, with regular trips abroad – the Alps as well as Aviemore. Superb home economics facility, with pupils learning how to wash and iron, as well as cook and operate electronic sewing machines.

Cultural trips to Paris and Florence and large successful art department, with fabric design as well as pure art. Music fantastic, choirs and orchestras of all description and a very sedate but popular rock band. Drama extra-curricular but a popular club – pantomime and Shakespeare in alternating years. Long standing Young Enterprise. Work experience in fourth year, with loads of private placements. Clubs highly popular, and the board game club specialises in esoteric conundrums which make the mind boggle. The web club is also well attended. Massive charity input from seniors in particular, with five-figure sums raised every year. World Challenge Expeditions to Thailand in 2003 and Mongolia in 2005.

Background and Atmosphere: Perched in the midst of leafy Bearsden and surrounded by seriously grand houses (whose denizens must love all the playing fields) the school was built in 1958 to a 1938 design, and has long outgrown its building. The site is littered with temporary structures and there are plans afoot to re-face and re-build (with a spot of selling of surplus land for little boxes to finance the new-build – derelict land we were assured – actually it looked really quite pretty). The alternative suggestion is a total new-build on the outskirts – we are looking at around eight million quids' worth of real estate. and well-maintained. Grounds tidy and well-maintained with staff parking in droves. Classrooms fairly old-fashioned but perfectly serviceable and in good heart; jolly canteen, though pupils often prefer 'to pop down to the cross for a carry-out'. Prefectorial duties include keeping a weather eye on behaviour around school premises. Pupils all neat and tidy in school uniform which is mandatory, with a very strict dress code – no advertising, track suit tops, denim, baseball caps or trainers outwith PE and particularly no football colours or any item of clothing which could potentially cause friction.

Pastoral Care and Discipline: Exemplary. School has a very positive attitude to bullying – 'Friends against Bullying', senior pupils volunteer to work with the first year group, visit them first thing each day and wear badges indicating that anyone who feels they are being bullied can come to them to discuss the problem. There are also 'supervised' lunchtime clubs that youngsters can come to, as well as study-buddies. Chaplaincy team of five – Church of Scotland, Baptist, all take a year each – Church of Rome refuses to allow Catholic priests to join this ecumenical team which is a bit odd considering one of the local primary schools (St Andrews) is Catholic and 85 per cent of their pupils come on. Room set aside during Ramadan for prayer.

Strong discipline code, range of punishments, from Behaviour Card which must be signed by all staff, with the ultimate sanction being exclusion. Pupils who persist in being disruptive or who are late are sent to the Behaviour Support Base for the rest of the lesson which they have disrupted and often for the next lesson in that subject; they also have detention at lunchtime. Head will exclude but has done so only temporarily so far; 'don't tolerate offences to staff'. 'No significant' drugs problem, 'hand on my heart, we've had nothing in the school as such' – they were patted on the back by drugs supremo Maxi Richards, who has an input in the senior PSHE programme.

Pupils and Parents: 5 per cent on free school meals; a good middle class bunch from Milngavie, Bearsden, Canniesburn as well as Drumchapel, north west Glasgow. 'Somewhat' over-subscribed, school has a fair reputation and is handy for buses and trains. Priority to siblings, followed by East Dumbartonshire location (distance from front door to front door). Large number of ethnic backgrounds, over 100+ youngsters from non-English speaking families – most Asians and Chinese but Africans, middle eastern and east Europeans are well represented. Absolutely no problems with the mix, the school is a 'seriously harmonious group'. Good PTA with parents getting quite deeply involved with the school programme of speakers and interview skills as well as the trad charity role.

Entrance: Automatic from local primaries; then by formula. New arrivals can get immediate entry if space available.

Exit: 10 per cent leave post-Standard to do further education elsewhere or go into employment. Indeed one such came to the door to have his application signed by Mr Doig whilst we were with him – three weeks into the winter term and he'd decided he would be better off elsewhere. A few leave post-Highers with university entrance qualifications but most stay for sixth form, notably those going to uni down south. Majority of leavers go to central Scottish universities – no particular bias – industry, dentistry and medicine popular (12 medics in 2004). Regular two or three to Oxbridge annually. Some to study music, some to art school. Youngsters tend to go straight to uni, not a lot of gap year take up.

Money Matters: State, with help on hand to supplement low-income families to go on school trips. Two forms of financial help available to those who stay at school after the age of 16. Footwear and clothing grant for those whose family or guardian qualify as low-income; and the other, the Scottish Executive Education Maintenance Allowance Scheme (EMA), for any pupils living in the area and going to school in East Dunbartonshire.

Remarks: A positive school, firmly setting its sights on the 21st century, with an expert captain at the helm.

Beatrix Potter Primary School

Magdalen Road, Earlsfield, London, SW18 3ER

Tel: 020 8874 1482

Fax: 020 8871 9416

Email: Info@beatrixpotter.wandsworth.sch.uk

Website: www.beatrixpotterschool.com

• Pupils: 230; all day, 50/50 girls and boys • Ages: 3-11

• Religion: Non-denom • School status: State

• School gender: Mixed • Day/boarding: Day pupils

SEN provision

Detail:

Now provide for in school:

Mild: AUT; ADD; ADHD; EBD; DS; DYSC; DYSL; HI; VI; CP;

Moderate: AUT; ADD; ADHD; EBD; DS; MLD; DYSC; DYSL; HI; VI; CP;

Severe: ADD; ADHD; EBD;

Others: CD; OCD; PMLD; Epi; PD; Eat;

Experience of:

Mild: DYSP; SpLD;

Moderate: DYSP;

Severe: AUT; DS; DYSC; DYSL; DYSP; VI; CP;

Others: SPD; AUT(other); TIC; FRX; GEN; SLD; MSI; Sp&LD; DEL;

Summary: Beatrix Potter is an inclusive school, we have catered for a range of needs over several years with great success. Like any school with a 30's building and no space there are limitations to some SEN children. In the future capital investment may address this. In the years 2000-2006 we had on average 11 children with statements and some 32 children on the SEN register. There are always some tensions catering for SEN children but the impact on all children has been very positive. Clearly changes to the funding of SEN have an impact and will inevitably cause questions to be asked on what can and cannot be done. However in an inclusive society at some point these issues will have to be properly addressed.

What we say about the school - the full Good Schools Guide review

Head: Since 1988, Mr Stephen Neale MA DipEdTec (late forties), educated St Bede's, Guildford. Previously taught at a variety of London primaries, married with one grown-up son. Relaxed, a delightful person to talk to, might appear too easy going but, fear not, he fights hard for his school and knows exactly where he is going. A man with insight in many different areas, well-liked by parents and staff.

Entrance: Always over subscribed, 3+ nursery or 4+ reception, attending the nursery does not guarantee a school place. Very local clientele as priority given to those living closest to the school, sibling policy also only applies to those living in the priority area.

Exit: At 11+, 50/50 to independent/state sector, including Dulwich College, Streatham High, JAGS, Lady Margaret and the Sutton Grammar schools.

Remarks: A popular choice for some years. Took its name from the author (who used to draw on Wandsworth Common) – they have a display area for her works and memorabilia. Purpose-built, 1927, single-level accommodation reminiscent of a village school. Fabulous landscaped garden, imaginative range of play equipment including giant chessboard, pond with great crested newts.

Standard National Curriculum with added value, delivered by mainly long-serving, committed staff. Display boards brimming with colourful artwork and an area dedicated to news from schools abroad where they have links: the next trip is to Louisiana. Good sports programme, works with Sport England. A choir and a talented dance teacher who undertakes anything from salsa to modern ballet. Head committed to everyone being involved, parents help in the school, open session every Thursday when pupils show visitors round the school and tell them what it's like to be a pupil there.

SEN and EFL are catered for in-house by a specialist teacher. The head has housed The Rainbow Autistic School for the past couple of years which has recently found a permanent larger site.

A variety of after-school clubs are on offer but pupils have to find outside tutors for 11+ preparation. 'Busy children are happy children' atmosphere, there is something for everyone. Sadly, Beatrix Potter is only one class entry, the size of the school is part of its success and consistently high standards. Do not be put off by the prospectus, definitely not a glossy.

BEDALES SCHOOL

Church Road, Steep, Petersfield, Hampshire, GU32 2DG

Tel: 01730 300 100

Fax: 01730 300 500

Email: admissions@bedales.org.uk

Website: www.bedales.org.uk

• Pupils: 446 boys and girls. 302 boarders, 144 day. • Ages: 13-18 • Religion: Non-denom • Fees: Boarding £7,845; day £6,040 • School status: Independent • Opendays: Five each year • School gender: Mixed • Day/boarding: Takes boarders

SEN provision

Detail:

Experience of:

Mild: ASP; ADD; ADHD; EBD; DYSC; DYSL; DYSP; HI; VI; CP;

Moderate: DYSL; DYSP; VI; CP;

Severe: DYSL;

Others: EAL; Epi;

Summary: At Bedales, those students with specific learning difficulties receive one-to-one support on a weekly basis with an SEN teacher. Typically, these students will receive one learning support lesson per week, and most of them will go on to achieve high grades at GCSE and A level. All but a few enter higher education where they read a wide range of subjects, notably maths and sciences but also history and English.

What we say about the school - the full Good Schools Guide review

Head: Since 2001, Mr Keith Budge MA (forties). Educated at Rossall, read English at University College, Oxford and PGCE from Oxford. Rugby blue. Previously a housemaster at Marlborough and head 1995 to 2000 of Loretto. Married to Moony. Three children – one at Dunhurst, two at Marlborough.

A complex character. 'High calibre,' said a parent, 'But not a leader, not a visionary which is what Bedales requires.' We have previously called him a disciplinarian and some parents hold on to this view but others differ, saying 'he simply draws a line.' Whatever his gifts, they do not seem to lie in public relations and he can come across as cold/shy/arrogant, depending on one's point of view. Has weathered last year's troubles over the school's structure in the face of loudly voiced revolt from many parents (see below), and has brought to completion a stylish £7.5 million building project that would have been the undoing of many heads. Appears to have finally convinced sceptical parents that he is not set on turning Bedales into another Marlborough and that he is here for the duration. After five years as head, is finally becoming an accepted part of the furniture.

Academic Matters: Good results – notably better than other schools based on non-conventional principles. Students (they are not called pupils here) taught to organise themselves like university students. Average class size 15 with 22 max. Most subjects doing well. Maths, history and modern languages (how refreshing) particularly shine. Science well taught (chemistry classrooms must be best in the country) and head keen to point out that a fifth of Bedalians read science or engineering at university. Art, design and theatre see no more than average results. English, economics and art the most popular A level subjects. Plenty of spiritual discussion and theology and ethics are compulsory subject for all in year 13. Setting in maths and languages.

One sixth of the pupils is classified as having special educational needs of mild to moderate severity and are given help by three qualified special needs teachers – who also increasingly aid children without specific learning problems who need help improving their organisation and study skills. The whole is known as 'learning support' and is eulogised by those it supports and their families.

From September 2006 the school will offer a new curriculum. At the lower end of the school, there will be increased integration with the curriculum of (junior school) Dunhurst. In the GCSE years, Bedales students will take core GCSEs plus one or two others to a maximum of seven plus 'Bedales-accredited courses', which will include some that are parallel to GCSE courses, some which will replace GCSE as a preparation for A level, some which will combine aspects of several subjects and may underpin work in a variety of A levels, and some (such as courses in Outdoor Work) that are independent of any external assessment programme. The courses are intended to be ambitious, wide-ranging, creative and less restricting than the current GCSE straightjacket.

Games, Options, The Arts: Enlightened. All students must participate in games or 'outdoor work', the latter a godsend to youngsters who loathe lugging themselves around a rugby field. Three quarters opt for games. PE once a week for all (except the upper sixth). The school is almost comically sensitive about outsiders, like this guide, not taking Bedales' games seriously. It points out its sporting achievements, particularly in boys' and girls' tennis, hockey (four boys from Under 14 team represented East Hampshire, one-half of Under 17 Girls Hockey County squad from Bedales) and athletics. Bedales has poured money into its sports hall, indoor pool (renovated 2002) and floodlit Astroturf, and even rugby is starting to get a look-in. However, we still beg to suggest that it is a rare parent who chooses Bedales for its prowess at games. Quite the contrary, many choose it for the reverse. Still, we receive the odd moan from parents who want the school to do better at sport – lord knows why.

Outdoor work involves gardening, organic farming, tree-planting and livestock husbandry on school's farm. Also on offer are spinning and weaving (of farm's own wool, later used by textile department), blacksmithing, riding, baking bread in a wood-burning oven. We think the school would do better to crow about these phenomenal and unique opportunities rather than bang on about sport – perhaps Keith Budge agrees, as he told us that he would like to see more emphasis given to outdoor work. Quality art – though a few parents we spoke to called it elitist and say it is aimed at the talented few rather than the inept many. In students' first year they spend a half term experimenting with different artistic genres: painting and drawing, pottery, craft, textiles, technology. School runs own art gallery showing work of outsiders as well as students. Brilliant craft (DT) produces near-professional creations.

Amazingly high standards in music. 60 per cent of students learn at least one musical instrument, 20 per cent learn two or more, and many reach diploma level. Lots of concerts and opportunities to play in front of an audience, including a weekly performance for the poppets at nearby Dunannie pre-prep. Several school choirs encourage the masses and the most talented few. Music technology on its way in. Spectacular theatre, with Japanese-influenced architecture, used by outside companies and the public. Twice-a-week activities programme with options like 'tools for self-reliance', hydrotherapy (along with wide range of sports!). Lots of opportunity for creating your own thing.

Background and Atmosphere: Founded by visionary J H Badley in 1893 as an antidote to the education he received at Arnold's Rugby, with its emphasis on muscular Christianity, classics and rugby. Instead, the school would teach academic subjects alongside arts and crafts, rural skills, outdoor work and tolerance. Girls were admitted in 1898, partly to solve the horrendous bullying problem that had exploded in Badley's atmosphere of free choice.

Over the century since then Bedales has had to make periodic concessions to the mainstream – mostly for economic reasons – expanding in size and catering more for local children. Many mainstream schools have moved in the other direction, incorporating Bedales' 'alternative' approach, but the school remains distinctive and given the events of 2004-5 is likely, though not certain, to stay that way.

In September 2004, the board of governors announced plans to change Bedales' three school formula (pre-prep, prep and 13-18 senior school) to a two school system. In so doing, Dunhurst and Dunannie would have merged into a single 3-11 prep, and the entry age of Bedales would have come down to 11. It is no exaggeration that the storm of fury that this plan unleashed shook the school to its core setting parents against governors, parents against parents, governors against governors. 80 per cent of the Bedales' parents committee voted to keep the 3-tier system and the board of governors ultimately voted to back this by a majority of one, leading to the resignation of the board's chairman. For now, both sides have gone off to lick wounds. The governors have all but vanished under an invisibility cloak and are, parents say, conspicuously silent. 'There is a feeling of the craft being a little rudderless at present,' said a long-term parent 'which for the moment is no bad thing.' Meanwhile the dust has settled and the school has emerged surprisingly fit and well. It still offers parents a genuine alternative and, for all the disharmony, there are few parents who do not appreciate this.

That said, the school is not the school it was five years ago. Discipline has been greatly tightened, the trust that used to govern relationships with pupils has been replaced by eg the breathalyser, staff made much more 'accountable'. And perhaps that is inevitable. Many aspects of the old Bedales way of doing things are hard for conventional locals to accept – and their custom is increasingly important. Staff and students still call each other by their first names (reflecting the reality of the underlying relationship – hard for staff trained elsewhere and parents wanting respect from their children). Still no uniform – though the current Bedales fashion tends to muted colours, well cut and clean, this was not always so. The expression of opinions of all kinds continues, but also in a more muted way; mass student protest (eg over the abolition of 'Martin's Game') is dealt with politely – but without concessions – so the motivation for it fades; the B-Daily has lost its cutting edge – at least as far as opinions on school management are concerned, though it remains a startling read for conventional parents. Rules are increasingly enforced, under (by general standards) quite a fierce policy document.

Stunningly beautiful grounds, with arts and crafts style buildings making the whole look like some sort of Quaker or Pennsylvania Dutch utopian community. An aesthetic wonderland, with care and attention to detail in everything – a fertile setting for scholarship. Eyesore 'temporary' huts (have been up thirty years) now largely replaced by sumptuous new classroom/admin block (2005) within Bedales' arts and crafts tradition. Lovely grade I listed library is a war memorial with names of the dead listed along the walls. Food could be better.

Pastoral Care and Discipline: New head has discipline as a priority. 'It had got very lax,' said a student, referring to sex, drugs, illegal drinking, smoking, 'but now multi-busted people are expelled.' Students aware the school has a mostly-undeserved reputation for loose behaviour and are keen to rebut this. Two boarding houses with mixed-age dormitories, girls in Steephurst and boys in Boys' Flat. Noticeably fewer girly pictures on boys' dorm walls than in other schools. Final year students reside in a co-ed boarding house, with single-sex corridors. Sixth form bar open four times a week. Students expected to look after one another eg students caught accompanying a smoker will be given the same punishment as the smoker. Punishments include 'useful work' eg litter clearing and community service. Some parents have expressed concerns about cases of anorexia in this environment where being thin and beautiful is at a premium.

Pupils and Parents: Students a confident, verbal lot, concerned with one another's unique qualities and letting the individual bloom – order of priorities for them is work, then relationships. Not a lot of self-esteem problems among these kids. Extremely at ease talking to adults. If that's just not your child, be careful of plunging in here, but if you are the sort of parent who believes in reasoning with your child rather than barking out 'because I said so', then this could be the school for you. The students look little different from those at other no-uniform schools except for being a bit better-looking on the whole.

Parents with strong opinions and 'bloody impossible to govern,' according to one dad. For good or ill, Bedales parents 'mind terribly' what goes on here. It's not just the fees and natural concern for one's offspring. There is a depth of feeling here that has no parallel elsewhere. Making the decision to send one's child to Bedales is to take an exhilarating plunge – 'it's a way of life,' said a mum, 'and you have to continually defend yourself against those who question your decision to educate your children here – which increases your loyalty to the place.'

40 children of overseas Brits. 27 foreigners, ten with English as a second, but fluent, language (there is ESL tuition). Parents in media, arts, the British Council, Foreign Office, and professions. Famous OBs include successful musicians, artists and craftsmen (including the son and daughter of Princess Margaret), two ambassadors to Russia, business magnates, academics and actors, notably Daniel Day-Lewis and Minnie Driver.

Entrance: 88 students at 13, 60 per cent from Bedales' junior school, Dunhurst, the rest from preps mainly in London and the south east. 20 join at sixth form. At 13, candidates for entry spend two days at the school shortly before beginning of spring term preceding September entry. Applicants sit standard maths, English and reasoning tests, have a groovy time with art and games, and are 'observed' in their interactions with others. Will they fit in, deal with the freedoms of Bedales, show other talents? Used to be as much a chance for the school to sell itself as it is a way of vetting potential students, but now more of a real test (though league table ambitions are not yet overt). Overseas students may sit the tests abroad and UK applicants may be interviewed at other times of year, though the school discourages this. School is still full, despite last year's tumult. Indeed, Bedales is now taking a few extra day pupils, presumably to help fund its ambitious building programme.

Exit: Up to a quarter leaves after GCSE, often because they have been in the Bedales conglomerate since age 3 and need a change. Most go to sixth form colleges, almost none to other independent schools. Post-A level leavers mainly to degree courses; around 20 per cent to art foundation courses. Most popular destinations over past five years have been Leeds, Bristol, Oxford and Edinburgh (in that order). The net is wide beyond that but, in general, an impressively top-drawer list.

Money Matters: 13+ scholarships available for exceptional ability in almost anything, plus a separate category for music. At 16, scholarships are given for academics, art, design and music and, occasionally, science. From September 2006, a number of awards will be made to drama students at the end of their first year in the sixth form. NB All scholarships, with the exception of music, are means-tested. If you fail the means test, the maximum award is £750.

Remarks: Getting back on track and we look forward to seeing the new curriculum in action. Still good for 'individuals,' articulate nonconformists, and people who admire such qualities. But less distinctive than in the past. Said a parent who weathered Bedales' recent turbulent times, 'it wasn't perfect but if I had to go back and choose a school again, knowing everything I know now, I would choose Bedales all over again.'

Bedford School

De Parys Avenue, Bedford, Bedfordshire, MK40 2TU

Tel: 01234 362 200
Fax: 01234 362283
Email: registrar@bedfordschool.org.uk
Website: www.bedfordschool.org.uk

• Pupils: 1,112 boys (includes prep), senior school – 849 day, 263 boarding • Ages: 7-18 • Religion: C of E
• Fees: Day £8,151-£12,600 pa; weekly boarding £12,861-£19,161 pa; full boarding £13,491-£19,812.
• School status: Independent
• Opendays: Late November and early May.
• School gender: Boys • Day/boarding: Takes boarders

SEN provision

Detail:

Now provide for in school:
Mild: ADD; ADHD; DYSL; DYSP;
Moderate: DYSL;
Others: EAL;

Experience of:
Mild: ASP; EBD; DYSC; HI; VI;
Moderate: ADD; ADHD; EBD;
Others: TIC;

Summary: The Academic Support Department

The SEN and Disability Act 2001 (DfES) promotes inclusive education and emphasises meeting pupils' needs effectively. We seek to identify pupils with specific learning difficulties (SpLDs) and to monitor the progress of these pupils efficiently.

We provide support for pupils with

1 physical disabilities
2 dyslexia
3 dyspraxia
4 dyscalculia

Subject Teachers work together with the Academic Support Department, Heads of Department and Tutors to make sure that the pupils receive the support necessary in order to reach their potential. The Head of Academic Support co-ordintes the provision of education for pupils with special educational needs.

Parental Involvement: Literature is available to parents who wish to learn more about special educational needs. It is important that parents provide special educational needs information before transfer. The school values the role of parents in supporting literacy and numeracy development.

Admissions: Pupils with special educational needs are allowed additional time in entrance examinations. Before transition, the school liaises with feeder schools and parents regarding future pupils' special educational needs.

Screening: On entry to year 9 pupils sit the WRAT (Wide Range Achievement Tests) in literacy. These tests, in conjunction with other assessment results (see the School's Assessment Policy) are used to indicate whether a boy may have a specific learning difficulty. The Academic Support Department will inform parents if there is cause for concern and advise further testing with an educational psychologist. If a specific learning difficulty is subsequently identified, a recommendation for academic support may be made. Support is one-to-one, usually for one period per week. This normally takes place during a Study Period. Tuition fees are charged each term.

Referrals: When parents and/or teachers suspect that a pupil has a profile of AD(H)D, dyslexia, dyspraxia or dyscalculia, the pupil is referred, through the Tutor and House Master to the Academic Support Department. Once an assessment of need has been made, the parent(s), pupil and the school discuss the possibility of academic support.

Internal examinations and tests: Those pupils in year 9 and year 10 who have an educational psychologist's report that recommends additional time in examinations receive 15 minutes extra per exam in some of their end-of-year examinations.

When there are time constraints that prevent additional time being given to pupils with special educational needs in examinations or class tests, the mark scheme will take this into account. We aim to ensure that no pupil is disadvantaged.

External Examinations: The department and the examination officer will be responsible for special arrangements in GCSE and GCE examinations, if granted by a qualified professional such as an educational psychologist. The school will keep parents informed at every stage.

Other Facilities: Pupils who have an educational psychologist's report that recommends the use of a computer are encouraged to use a laptop or PC when it is useful and allowed by the Examination Bodies. For Example, some course work can be word processed, some examinations may be taken using a computer and it is possible for pupils to take notes on a laptop in some subject lessons.

Links with external organisations: The school can provide information about educational psychologists, occupational therapists, chartered psychologists, local and national voluntary organisations, which offer advice on special educational needs, and other professionals in the field.

In-service training for staff: All staff are encouraged to follow courses and attend lectures and workshops related to special educational needs. Specialists from outside the school are invited to speak at various times during the academic year.

What we say about the school - the full Good Schools Guide review

Headmaster: Since 1990, Dr Philip Evans OBE MA FRSC (mid fifties). Fiendishly bright and highly entertaining, this is a man of ideas and an ethical approach, not only to his own, impressive, school but to education in general. Forward and outward looking, Dr Evans runs his, on first sight, conservative school, imaginatively and innovatively, drawing on a powerful combination of idealism, pragmatism and energy. A major player in HMC (chairs universities sub-committee, on academic policy committee etc), he is set to bring to his school the greater prominence it deserves. Clearly passionate about science and the teaching of science (he has a Cambridge first in natural sciences), his enthusiasms reach out to all areas of the curriculum and, to the capacities and the achievements of his pupils of whom he is touchingly proud. A hard-edged Welshman with a mission, whose determination to get the best for and out of his pupils, within a liberal and considerate community, permeates the ethos of the school. A good man to have on your side.

Academic Matters: Results are excellent. Almost 100 per cent get A-C at GCSE, almost 75 per cent get A/B at A level. Maths, sciences and French seem especially strong. Increasingly successful IB Diploma course offered since 2003 as an alternative to traditional A levels, 'provides diversification of opportunity, allowing for both the specialist and the talented student wanting to continue with a broad curriculum', says head. Good range of subjects available for the interested few: astronomy, Greek, German, Japanese, Spanish, Mandarin (school now twinned with one in Shandong province enabling joint projects, exchanges etc.)

On-site observatory and planetarium with astronomer in residence, 'allowing us to be undriven by assessment', justifiably enthuses head. Excellent IT facilities throughout school, including in boarding houses. Classics and English taught in two linked houses, with attractive 'schools' feel. Recently completed new facilities include 'state-of-the-art' library/resource centre (opened 2003) and £3m music school (opened 2005). Boys like 'Skills' syllabus – useful preparation for univ application. Academic Support Dept helps able boys with SEN and EAL (necessary as 150 boys from overseas – 25 different countries, making for excellent culturally diverse and homogenising mix). Good teacher/pupil ratio and impressive staying power of staff – over half have been in post for 10+ years.

On-site innovative and enterprising Bedford School Study Centre, a house for international students in which they spend 1-3 terms, mostly in intensive EFL, in preparation for entry to UK school to which they are best suited. Only two or three a year stay at Bedford but best advice given to help in choice. Integrated into whole school which includes prep, all under excellent leadership.

Games, Options, The Arts: Main sports rugby, hockey, rowing, cricket but 12 others played at team level. Rugby exceptionally strong, tours to S. Africa, Australia, New Zealand, junior internationals in 6 sports. Super fields integral to school site, good pool, sports hall, Astroturfs, rifle range. Also uses outside resources, eg athletics stadium. CCF is strong here, keenly supported by head who sees it as fostering leadership and believes it 'helps people to become rounded members of society, developing skills they didn't know they had.' Popular with boys, especially older ones, who see it as a chance to mix with girls from sister schools. Masses of varied activities on offer including Duke of Edinburgh Award, community service – visiting the local elderly or disadvantaged, as well as on-site theatre skills, pottery, journalism, house maintenance etc. Unusually rich choice which embraces CAS requirements for IB Diploma students. Annual ambitious music festival. Impressive and architecturally significant chapel used for concerts. Well-equipped theatre visited by outside companies. Pupils take productions to Edinburgh Festival. Imaginative DT.

Background and Atmosphere: An attractive site. Large fields, landscaped garden feel here and there and solid, unassuming school buildings. Calamitous fire in 1979 destroyed interior of main school building, now rebuilt, including large, light and unusual school hall. 450 years old in 2002, school enjoys its distinguished and significant history and relishes its promising future. Run by the Harpur Trust (along with Dame Alice Harpur and Bedford High Schools, both for girls) this charitable foundation still takes its status seriously and promotes outreach activities in the local community. Increased links with sister schools appreciated by pupils and enables sharing of some teaching and resources. Otherwise, resolutely but not aggressively single sex. Civilised atmosphere with touches of the antique, a 'Poem for the Day' in the library – Adlestrop on day of last visit. Pupils appreciate liberal and encouraging attitude of staff. 'Whatever type of student you are, you're given a chance to do your best,' said one. A chance most seem to take.

Pastoral Care and Discipline: 6 boarding houses on-site or nearby. The universally claimed 'family atmosphere' really is true of the converted, large Victorian houses with inviting sofas, well-equipped games rooms, computer facilities, decent bedrooms and a sensible regime, lovingly maintained by live-in housemaster and wife. Weekly boarding available (ie until after Saturday morning school). All boys in tutor groups, vertically grouped, all boarding houses twinned with day houses to encourage integration. Anti-bullying workshops. Inspection was enthusiastic about all aspects of pastoral care and boarding provision.

Pupils and Parents: Despite coming from more than 25 countries (including Estonia, Germany, Italy, Nigeria, Russia, Spain and many from the Far East) 90 per cent have English as 1st language and all mix happily irrespective of origins. School best-known in region and day places much sought after in locality. Boys seem relaxed and appreciative of school ethos. Not super-selective, induces loyalty in pupils, parents and OBs. Supportive parents increasingly involved. OBs include H H Munro (Saki), John Fowles, Paddy Ashdown.

Entrance: Most from on-site prep school but also from a range of local preps. School draws from five surrounding counties but 50 per cent of boarders from overseas. Prep school candidates take CE, state sector candidates tested in maths, English, science, French and VR. About 25 taken into sixth form. The IB has proved to be a successful attraction at this level.

Exit: Mostly to good universities, 'serious subjects' and a decent annual crop to Oxbridge. Head ensures best possible advice and guidance.

Money Matters: 18 page booklet details awards and requirements. Many and varied scholarships, bursaries and exhibitions. School generously endowed in specific arts subjects as well as general academic. Worth investigating for both boarding and day pupils.

Remarks: Key phrases in the head's vocabulary - 'creative and innovative' and 'not anodyne' – very much characterise the approach along with 'not pretentious'. School much-respected by those in the know though not one of the big names, perhaps, says head, due to being in an 'unfashionable county'. Something, then, of a well-kept secret, likely, though, to be let out of its bag sooner rather than later as has so much to offer on all serious counts.

Bedgebury School

Goudhurst, Cranbrook, Kent, TN17 2SH

Tel: 01580 878 143

Fax: 01580 879 136

Email: registrar@bedgeburyschool.co.uk

Website: www.bedgeburyschool.co.uk

• Ages: 2-18 • Religion: Church of England Affiliated

• Fees: £6,575 for boarding (full and weekly). £4,115 day

• School status: Independent • Opendays: March and May

• School gender: Girls • Day/boarding: Takes boarders

SEN provision

Detail:

Centre of excellence for:

Mild: DYSL;

Moderate: DYSL;

Severe: DYSL;

Now provide for in school:

Mild: DYSP; SpLD;

Moderate: DYSC; DYSP;

Others: EAL;

Experience of:

Mild: ADD; ADHD; DYSC; HI; VI;
Moderate: HI;
Severe: DYSC; DYSP;
Others: Epi;

Summary: We have a separate learning support unit where pupils come for individual support once or twice a week depending on their level of need. Help is also available in some classes. The majority of pupils who come to the unit are dyslexic, but we also deal with other learning difficulites as outlined below.

What we say about the school - the full Good Schools Guide review

Head: Since 2000, Mrs Hilary Moriarty BA Hons, PGCFE, MA, diploma in educational leadership (late fifties, seems younger.) Married with four children – three grown up, one in sixth form at Worth. Educated Denbigh grammar school, read English. Previously deputy head of Red Maids' school in Bristol. An ISI Inspector. Has a regular monthly column in Home and Country, the national magazine of the WI and regularly contributes to the educational press. Straight talking, energetic and enthusiastic, wants the best for her students. Has a 'how can we do it better?' approach. Well-liked by the girls who say she has a good sense of humour, is approachable, friendly and understands their needs. Highly professional, runs a tight ship, cares passionately about the school.

Academic Matters: Small non-selective, nurturing school. Wouldn't set the world alight academically but good value-added and provides some unusual options and creditable successes – past two years a Bedgebury girl has come within the top five in A level art and design. Most take nine GCSEs – 84 per cent graded C or above with 52 per cent graded A or B at A level. Average class size 12 reducing to 5 or 6 in sixth form. All usual curriculum subjects offered with additions of Btec (Equestrian) – continually assessed, no written exams but equal to three A levels for University entrance; A level equivalent NVQ3 fashion course communications studies; textiles. PE and drama GCSEs and PE and photography at A level are popular choices.The qualified and experienced learning support team cater for a range of mild to moderate special needs including ADD, ADHD, hearing and visual impairments, Asperger's and specific learning difficulties but a girl must be able to cope with demands of the mainstream curriculum. Approximately one third are on the learning support (LS) register – mostly for dyslexia; a high(ish) figure in part because school want to ensure potential is maximised so will offer support rather than risk leaving a girl to flounder. Norm is to withdraw for one or two lessons but support is geared to individual needs so eg child with dyscalculia may be withdrawn from all maths lessons and given individual tuition for a limited period. Senior girls tend to be supported with course work, lower school via specialised programmes. Limited, but valuable, in-class support exists but generally small classes, setting arrangements and differentiated work and prep reduce need for one-to-one assistance. LS register is used to monitor pupils with IEPs and where practical, staff, parents and pupils are involved with target-setting. Small successes celebrated. Gifted and talented belong to the NAGC and as well as the provisions of in-class extension materials, a range of activities is offered including competitions, spellathons, maths challenge and summer schools.

Games, Options, The Arts: Excellent and renowned equestrian facilities (BHS Registered) with stabling for 60 horses – third ride at least once a week benefiting from top class instruction provided in all major equestrian disciplines. Lots of other sports offered including lacrosse and swimming (outdoor heated pool). The very good facilities include a new sports hall with super abseil tower and climbing wall, fitness room and 22-acre lake for water sports and purpose-built arts centre for ceramics, photography, art, design, jewellery and fashion. Drama not as good but refurbishment is on school's to-do list. All girls belong to one of four houses, lots of competitions in sport, drama, art, music, public speaking and photography. Plenty of clubs and activities, participation in Duke of Edinburgh Award scheme encouraged. A quarter of girls learn a musical instrument and regular concerts and recitals offer ample opportunities to perform. Day girls encouraged to join after school activities, choirs, orchestras and societies. Weekly boarders attend all school events so although there isn't any teaching on a Saturday, girls aren't always free to go home at the weekends.

Background and Atmosphere: The school was established in 1920 by the Church Education Corporation. The main building is a delightful nineteenth century version of a French chateau, complete with spectacular rose gardens, terraces and a fountain, set in 200 acres (and oft requested as a film location).

Pastoral Care and Discipline: Dedicated team of supportive teachers, pastoral care a strength. Anorexia, drinking and smoking checked for but not a problem, indeed girls seemed rather surprised that we'd mentioned them at all. Boarding a popular option with many day girls choosing to board in senior years. Junior boarders sleep in small dormitories in the main school, progressing to shared or single rooms as they move up the school. Sixth formers housed in a purpose-built block divided into 6 wings each with a common room, TV and kitchen – all have own study bedroom. Girls are expected to eat lunch and supper in the main school. No Saturday school but plenty happening at weekends including shopping trips to local towns, ice-skating, bowling etc. A few dances and socials are held with local boys' schools; girls would like more. Chapel twice a week and on Sundays, broadly Church of England but other faiths and denominations welcomed.

Pupils and Parents: Mostly professional, from a fairly wide geographical area – a number from London; school operates a weekly bus service to Waterloo. Approximately one quarter from a wide range of overseas destinations including: Spain, Germany, Croatia, Estonia, Ireland, Nigeria, Thailand, Japan, Hong Kong and Mainland China. Famous old girls include: Virginia Leng (Olympic Rider) and Trinny Woodall.

Entrance: Not overly difficult, girls are admitted at any time provided there's a place. Take school's own entrance papers and/or common entrance at 13. Many from own junior school otherwise from a wide range of prep schools. Entrance into sixth form relatively open, school attempts to tailor courses, academic cultural and vocational, to needs of students.

Exit: Twenty five per cent leave after GCSEs mostly to schools where there are boys – Stowe, Uppingham and Eastbourne popular. At 18 a few to the major universities eg Durham and Newcastle but majority go to new universities – art and fashion foundation courses popular.

Money Matters: Sixth form scholarships in Btec National Diploma in business and finance (Equestrian Studies), art and design, fashion, drama, music and sports as well as academic and riding. Academic scholarships and music, art, drama and sport awards available for years 7 and 9 but not all offered annually.

Remarks: A homely school that aims to bring out the best in each girl – values the individual and regards vocational success as at least as important as academic achievement. A girl may arrive feeling she isn't much good at anything but will leave with a strong sense of self-worth. Record number of hits on Friends Reunited supports view that girls make friends for life here. Parent commented, 'Bedgebury produces nice, level-headed girls with no airs and graces.'

BEECHWOOD PARK SCHOOL

Markyate, St Albans, Hertfordshire, AL3 8AW

Tel: 01582 840 333

Fax: 01582 842 372

Email: admissions@beechwoodpark.herts.sch.uk

Website: www.beechwoodpark.herts.sch.uk

• Pupils: 500 boys and girls, flexi-boarding and day

• Ages: 2 1/2 -13 • Religion: Inter-denom

• Fees: Day fees £2,350-£3,214; weekly boarding fees £4,138

• School status: Independent • Opendays: Termly

• School gender: Mixed • Day/boarding: Takes boarders

SEN provision

Detail:

Now provide for in school:

Mild: DYSC; DYSL; DYSP;

Moderate: DYSC; DYSL; DYSP;

Severe: DYSL;

Experience of:

Mild: ASP; ADD; ADHD; EBD; HI;

Moderate: ADD;

Severe: DYSP;

Others: SPD; EAL; Sp&LD;

Summary: The school has some learning support provision run by one full-time and two part-time members of staff. The staff are responsible for assessing and identifying children throughout the school who might not be achieving their potential or who are finding some aspects of the curriculum difficult. In order to help these children the staff offer advice to the teachers on how to make provison for them and in some cases will teach pupils individually or in small groups for between one and four short sessions per week. The staff also provide in-class support, particularly in the Junior Department.

What we say about the school - the full Good Schools Guide review

Head: Since 2002, Mr P C E Atkinson BSc MIBiol PGCE (mid forties). BSc and PGCE from Nottingham (a biologist), introduced IB biology at Sevenoaks School, deputy headmaster at the New Beacon School, Sevenoaks, then eleven years as head of Lochinver House School. Married to Claire, an educational psychologist; two children. Believes in breadth.

Took over from Mr D S (David) Macpherson, who was here for 15 years.

Entrance: Assessment and interview. The head stresses every child must qualify but entrance is non-competitive. Priority is given to siblings then date of registration is used. There are no scholarships but there is a bursary fund for those families who have fallen on hard times. Register early.

Exit: Co-ed choices anywhere in the country but most frequently to Rugby, Haileybury, Oundle, Mill Hill, Uppingham and Berkhamsted. Girls tend towards St Albans High, Abbot's Hill, Haberdashers' Aske's and Queenswood; boys also choose St Albans, Haberdashers, Aldenham and Bedford. Regular academic, music, art scholarships – including one recently to Winchester.

Remarks: Once the home of the Saunders Sebright family, set in 37 acres of countryside on the Hertfordshire/Bedfordshire borders just outside Markyate. The original grade 1 listed building has been carefully maintained with new buildings housing the junior/middle departments, sports hall and performance hall. The stable block has been converted into a music school. There are two well-equipped computer rooms and each pupil has his/her own e-mail address. Impressive,if, perhaps, a bit imposing for a young child, traditional wood-panelled library with modern computer catalogue system. Original parkland designed by Capability Brown and film buffs will recognise the drawing room from The Dirty Dozen.

Montessori nursery for children aged 2 1/2 to 5 years recently acquired. Daily bus and coach services pick up from surrounding towns and villages. Boarding is offered on a flexi-system from one or two days each week to weekly. The average age of teachers is 38. French is taught from reception, maths is set at year 4 and Latin and Greek are offered at year 6. Science is strong; the subject benefits from bright and well-equipped science labs. Pupils are continuously assessed and parents receive termly reports; school exams twice a year. Children are taught in class sizes of 20 with sets generally reducing class sizes. SATS results usually at level 5 for Key Stage 2.

The school takes special needs seriously. All children are screened for learning difficulties and those with special needs (dyslexia, dyspraxia) are given extra help from three SEN teachers. Several boys with dyslexia have gone on to become head of school. The school places equal emphasis on the 'special needs' of the academically gifted and those with outstanding talents. There's a special scholars' group in years 7 and 8 and a 'sparklers group' for academically gifted children lower down the school.

Pupils are taught that bullying is not acceptable via regular talks by the head and a pamphlet which is given to all children. Discipline is enforced via the 'pink card' which lists a pupil's merits and offences and must be signed by his/her parent. Those with rather more offences than others are sent to the head. Star badges are awarded every few weeks for effort rather than attainment. Certificates of merit given every term for special achievement.

Inter-school sporting fixtures on Saturdays. As well as outdoor playing fields, facilities include an indoor sports hall, squash courts, covered and heated swimming pool, tennis courts. Plans are underway for an all-weather pitch. Music, art and drama are strong here. Some 150 children learn a musical instrument. The choir was voted Choir of the Year in 1991 and 1992 and was also a finalist in the National Choir competition in 2000. Several children gain art scholarships and the new theatre stages many drama productions and concerts.

Beechwood comes across as a caring school with a warm, friendly atmosphere. Pupils are polite, happy and confident and achieve high standards.

Beeston Hall School

West Runton, Cromer, Norfolk, NR27 9NQ

Tel: 01263 837 324

Fax: 01263 838 177

Email: office@beestonhall.co.uk

Website: www.beestonhall.co.uk

• Pupils: 165. Co-educational (boys:girls 5:3) 95 boarding and 70 day, 'daily boarders' free at weekends • Ages: 7-13 Religion: Mainly C of E, but provision made for RCs.

• Fees: Boarding £5,025; day £3,755.

• School status: Independent • Opendays: Twice yearly

• School gender: Mixed • Day/boarding: Takes boarders

SEN provision

Detail:

Now provide for in school:

Mild: ASP; DYSC; DYSL; DYSP;

Moderate: MLD; DYSL;

Others: EAL;

Experience of:

Mild: ADD; ADHD; EBD; SpLD;

Moderate: ASP; DYSC; DYSP;

Others: OCD; ODD; MSI; PD; Eat;

Summary: Beeston Hall provides SEN support at various levels, depending upon each child's specific need. At the outset children are supported in very small classes through specialist teaching by Dyslexia trained English staff, ably supported by Classroom Assistants. Many concerns can be immediately addressed without the creation of the stigmna attached when children are sent to the SEN Unit, as is the case at some schools. With positive reinforcemnent and additional individual one-to-one sessions many children thrive in confidence and rapidly come to grips with concerns. Should a child require additional help, there is the opportunity to 'drop' Latin as a subject and attend Extra English or maths sessions instead. These small classes are, again, taken by our Dyslexia trained English staff who ensure continuity. Beyond this, children can then attend for a one-to-one session with the school's special needs specialist, although by this stage the school would most probably have recommended the parents seek additional guidance form an educational psychologist, with whom the school would work in close liason. A maximum of three sessions is allowed for each pupil with the school's Specialist and these sessions are charged to a parent's account.

What we say about the school - the full Good Schools Guide review

Head: Since 1998, Mr Innes MacAskill BEd (late forties). Spent 17 years at Caldicott Prep ultimately as deputy head. Married with three teenage daughters. Clearly a 'hands-on' head, knowing each child well and taking a fatherly interest in their concerns. Keen to keep the size and character of the school as it is, though clearly has both space and resources to expand if he wants to. Pristine yet inviting state of boarding houses testament to his belief that school has to be 'homely and comfortable as this is their home in term time.' A popular head, supported by his wife, Sandy, lively and fun, this is a partnership. Mr MacAskill clearly knows his market well and, through hard work and a twenty-four hours approach, gives parents exactly what they want for their children. A fellow head says he 'has all the best bits of headmastering under his belt and actually likes the children' – not a universal characteristic.

Entrance: Candidates seen in spring prior to entry and assessed via 'reading and reasoning tasks'. Potential boarders invited to 'try it out'. Boarding numbers slightly down but most children opt to board before they leave. Entry not a foregone conclusion.

Exit: Wide spread of good schools, including Eton, Harrow, Oundle, Uppingham. Largest group go to Gresham's – several with academic and/or music scholarships here as well as to other excellent schools. Large number of awards 2002-3. On average, 30 – 40 per cent of leavers get them – in academic, music, art, all rounder and sporting fields – to schools as diverse as Queen Margaret's, Tudor Hall, Radley, Harrow, Oundle, Downe House and Uppingham. CE results good even for children in lower sets – recently all children have got into their first choice schools.

Money Matters: New means-tested bursaries for talented children and school has own in-house charity for parents who 'fall on hard times'.

Remarks: A very different ethos and atmosphere from, for example, Home Counties preps. Few video games, play stations and, even, TVs in evidence here. Children less sophisticated but open, natural, spontaneously friendly. Head stresses the pleasure children take in outdoor play – in the woods, in the extensive fields around school site, on the nearby beach in West Runton. School benefits from its position a couple of miles from north Norfolk coast, surrounded by farmland, National Trust woods and heathland. Most pupils come from trad country families but also now attracting families from very different backgrounds too. Shooting a popular activity here, as are sailing, golf and archery. School recently bought own fleet of toppers. National champions in several sports at this level in recent years, as well as many children gaining county, regional and national recognition.

Main school building a super Regency hall, sensitively adapted and beautifully maintained, extended and transformed. New buildings fit well into the site, being small scale and inviting. Super music school, new library, DT and IT rooms. Newly refitted labs, wonderfully civilised dining hall with conservatory extension looking onto putting green, surrounded by traditional Norfolk flintstone walls. Everywhere is beautifully decorated and kept in very good condition – remarkable given the age of the residents! Children are encouraged to keep their habitat orderly and given various duties and responsibilities – seen as part of their general education. Attractive boarding houses – recent ones like 'real' houses in scale. Rooms for 10s, 8s and 4s, dependent on age; a senior pupil in each room for younger children acts as a kind of 'room parent', for which they are given extra privileges in compensation. Boarding rooms not huge but colourful and snug with home duvets and toys, photos etc. Recent inspection praised pastoral care.

School rich in activities and clearly scarcely time enough in the day to do everything on offer. Superb, richly imaginative, witty and highly skilled artwork of all kinds, taught by teacher 30 years in post who clearly gets the best out of the children – beyond expectations. Pupils' art is everywhere, deservedly, in the school and a good thing too. Also everywhere are sofas – in the library, in the Common Room etc – giving lovely relaxed, civilised feel. Music also good – 80 per cent learn instruments – a huge variety offered, including bagpipes and harp. Ensembles of all kinds flourish, as does solo work. Strong SEN dept supports 15 per cent of children, mostly with mild dyslexia. Most children, against national trend, come from traditional boarding school families though few parents will have experienced comfort and care on this scale. Parents travel considerable distances to support weekend activities, although most do come from Norfolk or surrounding counties.

One of the very few full-boarding prep schools in East Anglia. Its small size creates rare family atmosphere. It does well by its pupils and turns out friendly, eager, purposeful and confident children who have been taught to take a pride in their school and in themselves.

BELMONT HOUSE SCHOOL

Sandringham Avenue, Newton Mearns, Glasgow, G77 5DU

Tel: 0141 639 2922

Fax: 0141 639 9860

Email: headmaster@belmontschool.co.uk

Website: www.belmontschool.co.uk

• Pupils: 260 boys and 60 girls; plus nursery 30 boys and girls; All day • Ages: 3-18 • Religion: Non-denom • Fees: Senior 3-6: £2,408; Transitus-S2: £2,281; J4 – J6: £1,992; J1 – J3: £1,738 • School status: Independent • School gender: Mixed • Day/boarding: Day pupils

SEN provision

Detail:

Now provide for in school:

Mild: ASP; DYSL; DYSP;

Moderate: ASP; DYSL; DYSP;

Summary: Keeping mum. Generaly good provision, though, in our view. SEN details added by us.

What we say about the school - the full Good Schools Guide review

Headmaster: Since 2005, Mr Melvyn D Shanks BSc DipEd MInstP CPhys.

Academic Matters: Tiny classes: results fluctuate. School even managed a surprising 105 per cent one year, the result of chaps joining post Standard Grades. Max class size 19 with core subjects, English and maths in the low teens, and most other subjects only nine or ten in a class. Good strong individual teaching methods, but because the pupil base is so small results are 'only as good as the pupils themselves': eight Standard Grades the norm, with Intermediate II an option in many subjects. Most stay on for Advanced Highers, and can add the odd free standing modules in sixth. No particular bias: strong on the science front and on languages: French from the age of seven, German at 12. Spanish is taught as an exam subject only, pupils can do it post standard. Regular curriculum Latin, but no Greek. Vast array of cups for academic and personal excellence. Good range of computers, throughout school and not just in suites, two trolleys of laptops motor round classes. Learning support 'exists'; broad intake, and siblings etc give the school an even broader base. High functioning children with Asperger's, dyslexia, dyspraxia et al are OK, school not wheel-chair friendly. Pupils withdrawn from class, double taught in class and can use the after-school tutorial system in all subjects if they feel the need.

Games, Options, The Arts: For a small school they do remarkably well at rugby, girls now numerous enough to form a netball team, school has playing fields some half a mile away, but are bussed. Jolly art room, variety of different disciplines, fabric strong and fun fashion on display. Kiln. CAD part of the syllabus. Music important, with spectacular performance of West Side Story in rehearsal for the seventy-fifth celebrations. Good charity concert output. Extracurricular drama. Variety of clubs, D of E well supported. Strong on public speaking and take part in local competitions, debating club formed last year. Keen on tennis and golf, and recently took part in the British Ski Championships. Lots of interhouse athletics. Not really a school that does brilliantly in team games against other schools.

Background and Atmosphere: School founded in the heart of Newton Mearns in 1929, moving to this jolly white stucco building on the Broom estate in 1930. Massive add-ons round the back of Belmont create a positive rabbit warren of hutches really quite gloomy even on the sunny day we visited. But most are quite large and many of the rooms open into each other. New build on the cards, school has an option on the Whitecraigs rugby club land and planning is being applied for. Spectacular on paper, though no provision either for drama, a dedicated assembly hall or a library (in reverse order of importance). We have found that architects and planners of new builds seem to think that assembly halls are unimportant and libraries now superseded by classroom libraries and the Internet; however when schools get t the next round of building it appears that the first thing they add is an assembly hall and the second a library. The final building will have two stories round a quad, with juniors on the ground floor and senior school above. Music dept is to the back of the stage. The school will be wired for interactive technology. Whole project is costed at twelve million quid, some of which will come from selling the current site for development and the rest is, apparently, under control. The only bugbear would appear to be planning permission. The new school building is expected to be up and running by 2008. It could be quite noisy, the site is alongside the M77, just over a mile from their current position.

Pastoral Care and Discipline: Not really a naughty school, standard disciplines apply, no drugs scene (at school) but head 'would come down like a ton of bricks'. Detentions the favoured punishment, and for regular miscreants Saturday detention. Bullying stamped on, graffiti instantly removed, head has expelled once. Pupils have tutors (a promoted position) with each tutor having 12 tutees, possible to change tutors if there is a personality clash. Strong discipline, children line up in the playground in twos at the end of break. Charming. Older pupils open doors and stand aside to let us past. 'God not that important' per se, the school does what 'is necessary' as far as the curriculum is concerned, but it is not a single faith school with a strong Christian ethos: twice-weekly ecumenical assembly. 'We do the lot'.

Pupils and Parents: Good middle class collection: ten per cent from the Glasgow Asian population, most of whom have 'strong traditional family businesses'; core of Jewish pupils, smattering of Chinese etc, broad multicultural community. Pupils come from as far away as Ayr, Kilmarnock, East Kilbride, Paisley as well as nearby Pollockshiels. Busses integrate with other schools, and school looks to extending this service in their new campus which is not as well fed by public transport.

Entrance: No test for nursery, automatic transfer to upper school, separate test for children from age seven upwards based on CAT school reports and interview if necessary.

Exit: Not all stay on for either Highers or Advanced Highers. Some may leave post Standard to follow vocational training, others leave to join the family business. Most go to Scottish universities, Glasgow popular, Edinburgh, St Andrews. Occasional one or two to Oxbridge but none recently.

Money Matters: Not a rich school, but will do their darndest to hang onto pupils to next public exam if parents who fall on hard times are upfront about it.

Remarks: Jolly little school; look forward to seeing if they get planning permission. Definitely worth considering.

Belmont Primary School

Belmont Road, Chiswick, London, W4 5UL

Tel: 020 8994 7677

Fax: 020 8742 7866

Email: belmontprimary@dingwall.demon.co.uk

• Pupils: 470; boys and girls equally; all day • Ages: 3-11
• Religion: non-denom • School status: State
• Opendays: Regular Oct-Feb • School gender: Mixed
• Day/boarding: Day pupils

SEN provision

Detail:

Now provide for in school:

Mild: EBD; DS; DYSC; DYSL; DYSP; HI; VI; CP;
Moderate: DS; DYSC; DYSL;
Severe: DYSL;

Experience of:

Mild: ASP; AUT; ADD; ADHD;
Moderate: ASP; MLD;
Others: EAL; Sp&LD;

Summary: Belmont is able to offer a range of learning support to its pupils who have special educational needs. The special educational needs co-ordinator (SENCo) oversees the provision: each child has an individual education plan, which is reviewed regularly with parents and others involved in the child's education. The SENCo and specialist reading recovery trained teacher provide focused support for individuals and groups, where this is identified as appropriate. In addition, a team of trained classroom assistants work alongside the teaching staff to provide support. This enables children with SEN to be taught in smaller more focused groups, generally within the class setting, and also makes it possible for them to receive individualised support, when particular programmes are indicated. The school makes use of external services who are able to help by providing advice, assessment or support, where this is relevant for an individual. Belmont is well resourced with materials to promote learning. Good communication with parents is fostered so that home and school are able to work in partnership to support a child and meet his or her needs effectively.

What we say about the school - the full Good Schools Guide review

Head: Since 2000, Ms Anne Williams BA Dip Sch Management, fiftyish. Mrs Williams was previously head of Hathaway Primary, a borough down the road in Ealing. Hathaway was a very different place – a tough estate school with a high proportion of children whose first language is not English and a poor level of attendance. However, Belmont in prosperous Chiswick, was no pushover. Ms Williams took on a neglected school with a somewhat disaffected school population and 'got on with it'. Quietly spoken, measured and highly methodical, Ms Williams has transformed her school and parents who have been there for the whole ride pay tribute. 'I thought it was good before,' said one, 'but she has really brought it up. She's terrific'. She manages to teach the lower set in year six – always a good sign in a head. Clearly, she has also known how to mobilise resources of all kinds and the result is an orderly, oversubscribed and popular school.

Entrance: Preference given to those who live within the 'Primary Admissions Area' – that's 'catchment' to you and me. Second come siblings who, in effect, are more-or-less guaranteed a place. Children with SENs and medical/social needs who fit these criteria,come higher on the admission list. A few places each year are offered to those living outside the PAA but very close to the school. After that – don't even try. Very over-subscribed, despite head's telling all-comers from outside the area that, really, there is really no chance. Parents are known to rent property within the area just to qualify and then....... – However, although the area is largely made up of quiet Victorian streets with large Victorian semis in private ownership, it's not all like that and a sizeable proportion of pupils comes from non-home-owning families, those on temporary contracts and those who need EAL support. School's inclusion policies help to level these differences and there no appreciable differences in achievement between those of such diverse backgrounds – much to the school's credit.

Exit: Around half to two thirds to Chiswick Community School. Some to other local state comprehensives such as Twyford C of E or The Green School. The rest to the local independents eg Godolphin and Latymer, Notting Hill and Ealing, Latymer Upper, City of London. Belmont does nothing extra to prepare children for such schools so many do have outside coaching. However, education levels in school are such that in

2003 one child won a top scholarship with no outside help at all.

Remarks: Belmont is housed in a large, 3-storey, London brick building and celebrated its centenary in 2004. Thanks to a very extensive refurbishment programme initiated by Ms Williams with the support of both public money and funds raised by parents, it looks pretty good for its age. It has a decent amount of outside space too and all ages have their own designated play areas with equipment and surfaces appropriate for their needs and capacities. No green anywhere apart from a small nature garden with pond – certainly no playing fields – but there is no feeling of being cramped or choked here as with so many schools in comparable urban situations. The locality is certainly urban – it's on a crossroads with Sainsbury's and Starbucks opposite, lots of residential streets and light industry all around. It's near the tube and on a bus route but, once inside, the environment feels safe, comfortable and peaceful and the outside world is decidedly outside.

The ground floor is home to the nursery, reception and year 1 children and is remarkably spacious. The nursery in particular – 26 children – has three large rooms and a hall. Few chic little independent nurseries provide as much as this. The quality of work, as demonstrated by the classroom displays, is exceptional. In one nursery room we saw 'The Belmont Hospital' with a very expert game of doctors and nurses in progress aided by real X-rays of hands, skulls, chests and ankles suspended over the enthusiastic patient's bed; we saw work on textures, water play, construction toys and individual reading – this with one of the army of parents who help with many aspects of class work. Reception was similar – very orderly classrooms with everyone at a table for 5-6 and working away at a large variety of topics between which they swap during the course of a morning. Parents come and help with cooking – everyone wears a 'Belmont Bites' apron and a deliciously slurpy Strawberry Fool was developing when we visited.

The first floor houses years 2 and 3 and is the 'transition floor'. Again a good hall for PE with £8,000 worth of new equipment paid for by the Parents' Association. A designated music room in which everyone has two class music lessons weekly – singing and 'composition' – and, we are told, few children leave the school unable to read music. We witnessed a year 6 class, all armed with instruments, mostly percussive, and singing away with gusto. 'Music permeates the school,' said Ofsted and, in addition to class music, many learn individually. Annually, year 6 puts on a Shakespeare play – 'Twelfth Night' and 'Macbeth' in recent years – and the 'Dream' was in rehearsal as we visited. Photographs on display suggest a high level of production, again much supported, especially with costumes, make-up etc, by parents, many of whom are, of course, 'in 'the arts'.

Teaching up to the end of year 2 is mixed ability. Setting in maths and English arrives in year 3. There are two sets – the higher being slightly the larger and having, therefore, around 33 children to the lower set's 27-ish. The upper set has just one teacher, no classroom assistant being needed with these children because, of course, they are motivated and keen to learn. We couldn't see much problem with the lower sets either. Years 3-6 are on the top floor and, again, all classrooms are orderly and full of displays you want to stop and look at – both of the children's own work and of materials from outside. Years 3-6 have 40 minutes French weekly. There are libraries – well-stocked (parents again!) for both infants and juniors and two excellent IT suites – 15 PCs for the younger children and 30 for the older ones – intelligently used by specialist staff and, when we visited, a year 3 class was concentratedly working on a maths programme about 'capacity' – well beyond ours! Interactive whiteboards also now in use and Ofsted's one and only quibble about ICT being under-used now decidedly out-of-date. Everyone has 2 hours of physical activity weekly and it was especially pleasurable to see a dance class with budding Billy Elliots clearly not at all embarrassed to be dancing – quite balletically!

Belmont does very well academically. SATs results in all subjects are at least 10 per cent above local and national averages and are far higher by year 6. The achievement and value-added results from those from ethnic minority groups especially remarkable. SENs of all kinds are well-supported here. Hounslow borough has a well-established language service and those with EAL needs are seen individually or in small groups for up to a year until they are up to the general standard. A SENCo gives three full days to individuals, pairs or groups. A 'reading recovery' teacher sees individuals who, by year 1, are falling behind – with 'fantastic' results. School has children with a large range of physical disabilities – lots of asthma but also cerebral palsy, Down's syndrome, Cystic Fibrosis and parents clearly grateful for the care and individual attention their children are sure of here. Head pays tribute to her staff –

'they are very highly committed – they go that extra mile – we work as a team.' When we visited there had been no staff changes for two years.

Outside, in the extensive playground areas, there are lots of bike sheds, a covered stage with costume boxes, all kinds of different trails, apparatus, a super climbing wall painted by parents. Inside is cheerily decorated in a rich yellow and aqua blue and it feels cosy and bright. The rooms are all good sizes, the furniture is in good nick and everywhere are thoughtful, orderly displays in a stimulating, orderly environment. The uniform – seemingly strictly adhered to – is attractive, navy and, again, orderly and neat. We saw not one scruffy child. Three male teachers – always a bonus – six staff have been in school for 10+ years and staff covers the whole age range. Two thirds of children bring their own lunch. The local borough delivers the hot lunches – we saw the menu rather than the real thing – and there is a clear emphasis on starch, though tasty starch, and a sad lack of fresh fruit and veg, though the children are offered a salad bar every day. Everyone eats in the canteen – possibly not the most attractive area in the school – two rooms being given over for lunchbox eaters.

A transformed school. Ms Williams is greatly aided by a posse of 'liberal middle class' parents only too eager to help in all areas of school life including in giving unobtrusive financial support when needed for the disadvantaged pupils who wouldn't otherwise be able to take part in trips etc. She is aided, too, by an excellent governing body entirely made up of new members since her advent, as well as by a good relationship with her local authority. She had, at first, to be tough and there were a number of early exclusions. There had been no exclusions in the two years preceding our visit. There is a proper and well-understood system of sanctions. There is an established homework system with extension work on the school website for those who want to push their offspring further – this school is working on all fronts. 'We got the systems in so pupils could learn,' says this thoroughly professional head. The 2003 Ofsted report concluded, 'the school ensures that all children do as well as they can...the leadership of the headteacher, in partnership with the governing body, is excellent... an imaginative and innovative curriculum promotes high levels of achievement. Partnership with parents is very good. The school provides very good value for money.' Find the 'Primary Admissions Area' and move in.

Beverley Grammar School

Queensgate, Beverley, East Riding of Yorkshire, HU17 8NF

Tel: 01482 881 531

Fax: 01482 881 564

Email: office@bgs.karoo.co.uk

Website: www.BGS.eril.net

• Pupils: 800 boys, all day • Ages: 11-18 • Religion: Non-denom • School status: State • School gender: Boys • Day/boarding: Day pupils

SEN provision

Detail:

Experience of:

Mild: ASP; ADD; ADHD; EBD; DS; DYSC; DYSL; DYSP; HI; VI; CP;

Moderate: ASP; ADD; ADHD; EBD; DS; MLD; DYSC; DYSL; DYSP; HI; VI; CP;

Severe: ASP; DYSC; DYSL; DYSP; CP;

Others: SPD; Sp&LD;

Summary: We have a large and successful learning support department which prides itself on its open, caring and inclusive ethos in which support is available to all. Every student is encouraged to participate fully in the life of the school.

Each student on the SEN register has a named TA who meets with them at least once a week. IEPs are written and reviewed three times a year and all staff are required to indicate SEN provision for each teaching group the take. TAs are based in the department but some work largely in one subject area or specialise in a particular disability.

The department has a well-equipped resource and staff base, two physiotherapy rooms, an interview room and an office. The LS area has an 'open door' policy providing support for homework, a refuge for anxious students and learning aids every break and lunchtime and after school one day a week. The department is always staffed from 8am and a number of students start their school day there. TAs staff clubs for socially vulnerable students and support school visits.

Year 12 students are recruited as part of their Enrichment programme to work as support in classrooms and produce materials. In addition over 25 per cent of year 7 students are supported one-to-one by year 12 students for reading, spelling and maths programmes. The programme works in close partnership with parents who reinforce it at home.

Parents are always welcome in school. A parenting support group is run by the school social worker – a full-time appointment. She also works with vulnerable and challenging students on a one-to-one and small group basis. The department supports the Healthy Schools initiative by providing support for healthy choices groups run by the school nurse.

The SENCo has delivered full staff training on Down's syndrome, Asperger's syndrome, dyslexia and physical disability. TAs have a comprehensive in-school training programme and a staff evaluation programme is in place. The department has a weekly meeting at which student issues are discussed and which teaching and pastoral staff may attend to raise particular issues.

What we say about the school - the full Good Schools Guide review

Head: Since 1998, Mr Gerald Broadbent LRAM (sixty-ish). Studied at Royal Academy of Music and Westcott House Theological College, Cambridge, before becoming Church of England priest. Asked by vicar to become more involved with local youngsters, he took part-time job as a music teacher and loved it so much he gave up the priesthood! Went into full-time teaching because, 'I hugely enjoy working with young people'. Held various posts including head at Archbishop Thurstan School, Hull, before moving to Beverley. Genuinely loves his job and infects his school with fun.

Retiring July 2006.

Academic Matters: A solid performer. 75 per cent plus get five or more A*-C grades at GCSE – on a six-year upward trend. School graded A* at Key Stages 3 and 4, putting it in top 5 per cent of schools nationally. Students can also study for NVQ in engineering and GNVQ in IT. In the joint sixth form, almost half of all grades are either A or B. Sixth form blocks at both boys' grammar and nearby girls' high school so students divide their time between the two. 'I argue that it's a good half-way house between the school where they feel comfortable and what it will be like going to university where everything is new,' says head.

Games, Options, The Arts: Strong on music by state standards – about 120 have individual music lessons. Various choirs, orchestras, bands including a year 7 choir for all new intake. 'If any of the boys are reluctant, we take the view, 'what do you mean you don't sing 'Everybody sings!' And because it's the norm, they all do.' Drama has included an all-boy production of Macbeth. 'We had a boy as Lady Macbeth. It didn't cause a ripple.'

Also strong on sport ('you name it, we do it') and highlights include annual cross-country race. 'The boys love it. I can't work it out, I used to hate it,' confesses head. And extra-curricular is, well, take your pick. 'If a boy wants a club to be started, we find a member of staff to start it.'

Background and Atmosphere: Founded in 700 AD, Beverley Grammar is England's oldest state secondary school. Cherishes its traditions but prides itself on moving with the times. On its present site since 1903 and now mix of the old (museum piece of a hall) and the new (£750,000 sixth form block). Though Grammar by name, it's a comprehensive by nature. There are no entrance tests, no fees, and it takes all-comers from its catchment area.

One of a handful of free-standing voluntary aided schools which means it can bid direct to the DfES for some of its finance. Downside is that the trustees have to find 10 per cent of the cost of major building projects. Recently granted specialist status in engineering bringing investment in technology, maths and science. All prizes at speech day awarded for effort – 'at least as important as achievement,' says head.

Pastoral Care and Discipline: Uses more carrot, less stick approach to learning. 'We believe in working hard, but having a lot of fun doing it so there's a lot of leg pulling goes on in the classrooms. And because we have a relaxed approach to learning, the boys learn because they want to, not because they're being threatened what will happen if they don't,' says head. 'We encourage everyone to show respect for everyone else and that's often about the little things – the way staff talk to pupils, the way teachers hold doors open for the kids as well as the kids for the teachers.'

Parents involved at earliest stage over any slips in discipline. School's own social worker may visit child's home to talk over problems. Only one permanent exclusion in three years and exemplary behaviour around school. Credible reward system of 'green slips' which lead to certificates and ultimate prize of special school tie. And mentoring system with a difference to keep learning on track – as well as teachers, mentors can also be volunteers from the community – industrialists, careers advisers, etc – to drum home the value of learning.

Pupils and Parents: Very supportive parents, encouraged to be involved with school from the off. Parents of new intake invited to sit with their child for half a day of lessons. One mum, fresh from a science lesson, described school as 'absolutely brilliant'. 'There's such an eagerness and keenness here. It's renewed in my son that excitement for learning.'

Entrance: Living in catchment area – Beverley and the surrounding villages of Tickton, Walkington and Bishop Burton – is pretty much a must.

Exit: About 70 per cent go on to sixth form and many more into some other form of further education. Ultimately, most go to university.

Remarks: A grown-up school, mature enough to nurture mutual respect and to know when to let its hair down. A school with a sense of humour. No wonder boys love it.

Birkdale School

Oakholme Road, Sheffield, South Yorkshire, S10 3DH

Tel: 0114 266 8409

Fax: 0114 267 1947

Email: admissions@birkdale.sheffield.sch.uk

Website: www.birkdaleschool.org.uk

• Pupils: 460 boys in the senior school; 132 boys and 49 girls in the sixth form. All day • Ages: 11-18 • Religion: Christian, but all faiths welcome • Fees: Seniors £2,577; juniors £2,128; pre-prep £1,799 • School status: Independent • Opendays: October/November • School gender: Boys • Day/boarding: Day pupils

SEN provision

Detail:

Experience of:

Mild: ADD; ADHD; EBD; DYSC; DYSL; DYSP; HI;
Moderate: DYSL; DYSP;
Severe: DYSL;
Others: OCD; EAL; DEL; Epi; Eat;

Summary: The learning support department at Birkdale Senior School is organised on a one-to-one withdrawal system. Pupils are screened in their first term to identify need so that appropriate support can be offered.

Support is tailored to an individual's needs and is reviewed regularly Although the main focus is on literacy skills, study and revision skills become increasingly important as a pupil moves through school. However, personal skills, such as organisation, are reinforced at all stages, and particular emphasis is placed on developing and maintaining a positive self-image for all pupils.

What we say about the school - the full Good Schools Guide review

Head: Since 1998, Mr Robert J Court MA PGCE (fiftyish) who was educated at St Paul's, and read physics at Clare College, Cambridge. Previously twenty years as master, housemaster and in, 1994, second master at Westminster School. He lives on site with his wife, Andrea, who occasionally acts as receptionist at parents' evenings. He came to the school 'because of its strong Christian ethos'. God very important to the head and to the school.

Charming, incredibly prompt with a deliciously dry sense of humour, he has made a certain number of staff changes here, more difficult perhaps, than elsewhere, because of the high cost of housing (in local terms). Head has a house in the Peak District, and 'can be out walking' within thirty minutes of leaving the school. He has no intention of quitting but of raising academic standards – stabilising what he has.

Academic Matters: The sciences, maths, Eng lit and the humanities appear the most popular and successful A levels. Rather jolly ecology pool and masses of trips for geographers and historians. General studies for all at A level; not a lot of take up in either French or German (five in the former and two in the latter – twice as many pupils did Latin and performed considerably better) despite regular exchanges. However, recent GCSE results in the language dept were a great improvement, Spanish now on the curriculum and thriving. Greek on offer at lunchtime and can be taken to exam level. Dual award science at GCSE. Open-door policy in the common room, pupils can approach staff for help at any time. Dyslexia provision costs extra, mild dyslexics only, one pupil in the school is statemented. Huge library, many computer rooms, all linked, with e-mail addresses for all; strong DT presence, subdivided into electronics, graphics and resistant materials.

Games, Options, The Arts: Rather jolly school mag with quizzes as well as the usual sporting achievements. Rugby important here, with trips to New Zealand and Fiji last year. Footie very popular and school has joined the independent schools' competition. Girls may do team or individual sport. 30-metre sports hall and designer gym with weights room. 125 year lease on a sports field some ten minutes drive away, complete with pavilion – new upgraded pavilion completed 2006.

Fabulous art complex run by husband and wife team, concentrating on perspective when we visited via a rather complicated machine of their own design 'which never fails'. Truly exciting work here. Regular As and A* at A level and GCSE respectively, masses of good 3D stuff and the walls of the art dept were positively papered in lively pics. Nice 3D guitar, and some Modigliani look-alikes. Well-equipped drama studio at Johnson House, with recording capabilities and an impressive wardrobe room. Theatre studies at A level. Much use made of the local countryside with trips to the Peak District, D of E. Whole school supports a school in Nepal, with annual visits both from members and friends of the school.

Background and Atmosphere: School founded at the turn of the twentieth century as a boys' private prep school, went up to 16 in 1988, then 18, and added girls in the sixth form only in 1996. Moved into current site in 1998, nice bit of Sheffield but hideously complicated campus, embracing Oakholme Road, Ashdell Road, Endcliffe Crescent and Fulwood Road. Masses of to-ing and fro-ing between the various Victorian/new-build houses on an incredibly steep site. Good octagonal concert hall, school hall bursting at the seams and it doubles as a dining room and badminton court, as well as stage – extension still planned.

Pupils are encouraged to get involved in a variety of lunchtime activities in the period when they are not eating. Pupil-inspired water fountains throughout the school. Separate sixth form block, the Grayson building, which also includes computers. Super Johnson House with listed (£20,000 to replace, said our guide) marble fireplaces, and RE dept on the top floor with a quote from Micah painted on the wall. 'What does the Lord require of you 'To act justly and to love mercy and to walk humbly with your God'. Pupils not allowed to go down the main staircase (one-way system). Lockers line the broad passages throughout. As we said before, the atmosphere is lively, scruffy and fun with, it must be admitted, some of the dirtiest carpets we have come across – bits of chewing gum as well as scraps of paper and the odd pencil. Steps all over the place and no use for wheelchairs.

Pastoral Care and Discipline: Strong Christian ethos, pastoral care important here. And according to the school's policy statement, 'it is the policy of Birkdale School to promote a Christian lifestyle ... any illegal use of controlled drugs by either staff or pupils will be treated as serious misconduct' – which is the first time we have seen staff mentioned in such context. Dealing in drugs equals out and no questions. If found using on the premises, the matter is 'taken very seriously' and previous conduct is taken into account. Pupil might be allowed to remain under a strict regime of testing. (Hasn't happened yet.) 'Drugs are contrary to all our teaching'. Smoking on site rare in school, would result in detention, increasing in severity if problem persists. Ditto booze. Occasional incidents of bullying are dealt with by (usually) confronting the perpetrator, 'might suspend', 'certainly involve parents'. Head of year groups, plus form tutors for all. Tutors first point of call if a pupil has problems but prefects equally used. Prefects spend a training weekend in the Peak District. School uniform throughout the school, blue, grey and white with dashing striped ties for the boys.

Pupils and Parents: Local lads and lasses, many first-time buyers, huge catchment area, parents operate local buses from as far away as Bawtry, Doncaster, the Peak District and North Derbyshire – over a thirty-mile radius. OBs Michael Palin, a couple of judges, a racing driver and an MP or two.

Entrance: Entrance test for all at 11, including those in the junior school, who don't come up 'if it is not the right school for them'. Perhaps a handful each year. CE at 13, but tiny intake then. Girls (and boys) join sixth form from many local schools, around 30 each year. Five passes at GGSE, with four Bs minimum, and at least B at GCSE in any subject to be studied at A level.

Exit: Excellent careers library and online for sixth form. Leeds the most popular university, plus ex-polys, which often offer more esoteric courses: De Montfort, Leeds Met etc. 9 per cent annually to Oxbridge. Business, medics, engineering, computing and law are popular degree subjects.

Money Matters: Not the rich school it appeared to be, having lost assisted places. Certain number of academic scholarships on offer – which can be topped up in case of need. Will carry a pupil to next stage if in real financial need.

Remarks: School has had a meteoric rise from a boys only prep school to a full blown senior school with girls in the sixth. No current thoughts about girls throughout, though anything is possible. Happily ensconced in Sheffield's education alley; strong and both academically and socially tough.

Bishop Luffa Church of England School, Chichester

Bishop Luffa Close, Chichester, West Sussex, PO19 3LT

Tel: 01243 787 741
Fax: 01243 531 807
Email: webadmin@bishopluffa.org.uk
Website: www.bishopluffa.org.uk

• Pupils: 1,374, 50/50 boys and girls • Ages: 11-18
• Religion: C of E • School status: State • Opendays: October
• School gender: Mixed • Day/boarding: Day pupils

SEN provision

Detail:
Centre of excellence for:
Mild: ASP; ADD; ADHD; EBD; DYSL; DYSP; HI; VI; CP;
Moderate: ASP; ADD; ADHD; EBD; DS; MLD; DYSC; DYSL; DYSP; HI; VI;
Severe: ASP; ADD; ADHD; DYSL; DYSP; HI; VI;
Others: OCD; ODD; TIC; Sp&LD;

Summary: A thirteen strong learning support team (SENCo, three teachers and nine learning support assistants) provide support (in-class and out), guidance and advice for pupils with additional needs and their teachers.

The department's work in the school includes providing opportunities for continuing professional development to extend staff knowledge of particular syndromes and disorders which underpins good classroom management, differentiation and pupils' learning styles. In addition we ensure all staff are aware of the needs of the pupils in our care through the inclusion register, The learning support list, individual education plans and case conferences.

We encourage parents to contact the department and to meet with us. We are in regular and close contact with many outside agencies. We participate fully in the 14-16 Increased Flexibility courses, part of the 14-19 Curriculum, providing opportunities for Key Stage 4 pupils to study at our local college and monitoring their progress there.

Overall, the approachability of all the learning support team members and the full co-operation of the teaching stafff means that pupils with additional needs take a full and active part in school life at Bishop Luffa.

What we say about the school - the full Good Schools Guide review

Headmaster: Since 2000, Mr Nicholas Taunt MA PGCE NPQH (forties) educated at Exeter College, Oxford. Previously head of creative arts at Harwich School and then deputy head of Hedingham School. Married to a social worker, they have three children. Enormously positive about continuing and developing his school's excellent reputation. Mature, pleasant, a head who relates well to both parents and pupils; his interests in literature, drama and music are reflected throughout the school.

Academic Matters: Impressive results for a non-selective school, GCSE 81 per cent A*-C in 2005, A level 99 per cent pass rate; 46 per cent A and B grades in 2005. Able pupils take up to 12 subjects at GCSE. Won the National Achievement Award for Excellence in 2001, 2002 and 2003. Pupils carry off a good share of competition prizes for arts, sports, debating and academics.

Well-resourced school, with capable staff and facilities to match; parents comment particularly on the school's innovative teaching of mathematics. A technology college, so ICT is used to facilitate all types of learning. A Leading Edge school too, and keen on professional development, staff training and thinking and learning skills. Strong English and drama, pupils produce their own poetry magazine and have had their poems published in the TES. Setting in some subjects. Motivated, caring and committed staff, hugely appreciated by parents, more than half have been at the school for 10 years.

SEN organised at both ends of the scale. Full-time learning support teachers, and extra training is provided for teachers to assist pupils with specific difficulties as the need arises. A programme of extension classes is run for the very able, which pupils from other schools attend. Individual needs really appear to be met and potential developed as opposed to just talked about as is sadly so often the case. Numbers with SEN tend to be below average but needs are wide ranging and include pupils with specific learning difficulties as well as some with physical or sensory needs.

Games, Options, The Arts: Sports have quality and breadth. Large playing fields, gym and indoor sports hall. Nine pupils in county or UK under-18 teams. Sailing judo and fencing. Good range of creative arts, modern/jazz dance, ballet, two choirs, orchestra, swing band; children compose their own music for productions. Much of the drama curriculum is linked with the English department – this happens far too rarely elsewhere – lots of productions, some produced at Chichester Theatre. One of few schools selected by the National Theatre for its International Connections programme. Actors and theatre directors amongst past pupils.

Background and Atmosphere: Founded in 1963, in a residential area on the edge of Chichester, by a group of parents who wanted a Christian based education for their children. They have been expanding and adding buildings ever since. Extensive new buildings opened in September 2004. A very busy place, with a warren of corridors, easy to get lost. Pupils appeared well behaved and hard working. School's philosophies are 'Nothing but the best' and 'Everyone matters'.

Pastoral Care and Discipline: House system, pupils are taught to support each other, feel valued and respect differences. Clear set of school rules and emphasis on Christian values. Parents and pupils feel a strong sense of community.

Pupils and Parents: From a diversity of backgrounds, as the school is non-selective. Mainly local and from surrounding villages, a few from as far as Arundel and Midhurst. Past pupils include Jonathan Thompson, Amanda Ursell, Paul Millar, Rupert Wingfield-Hayes and Zoe Rahnmar.

Entrance: At 11 from 75 different Sussex primaries, both state and independent; Central School is a feeder. Majority of places go to practising Christians, then children living closest to the school. Unsurprisingly, always over subscribed.

Exit: A handful leaves at 16 to go to local colleges, most stay for A levels. 90 per cent go to university most years, eight to Oxford and Cambridge in 2004; other popular choices are Imperial, Durham, York, Bristol and Cardiff.

Money Matters: Parents' group raise enough money to help less well-off children pay for school trips, foreign exchanges and in some cases instrumental tuition.

Remarks: A comprehensive that works. Interesting school to visit, offering wide range of opportunities to all its pupils whatever their ability, getting the results too at a personal level as well as academic. Parents comment, 'if all state schools were run and resourced as this one, British children could be really confident of competing and improving our world in the 21st century. I don't know any parent who does not feel blessed by attending such a wonderful school.'

Blossom House School

8 The Drive, Wimbledon, London, SW20 8TG

Tel: 020 8946 7348

Fax: 020 8944 5848

Email: blossomhouse@hotmail.com

Website: www.blossomhouseschool.co.uk

• Pupils: 80 boys, 20 girls; all day • Ages: 3-16 • Religion: Non-denom • Fees: £6,135 -£6,350 • School status: Independent • School gender: Mixed • Day/boarding: Day pupils

SEN provision

Detail:

Experience of:

Mild: ASP; AUT; ADD; ADHD; DYSP;

Moderate: ASP; AUT; ADD; ADHD; DYSL; DYSP;

Severe: ASP; ADD; DYSL; DYSP;

Summary: Our school caters for children with speech, language and communication impairments whose cognitive ability is within the broadly average range.

What we say about the school - the full Good Schools Guide review

Head: Since its founding in 1983, Mrs Joanna (Joey) Burgess (fifties) DipCST MRCSLT Dip RSA SpLD PGCE. Educated at St Paul's Girls School and Oldry Fleming School of Speech and Language Therapy. Married to Patrick, a retired stockbroker, with four grown-up daughters. Wealth of experience gained in part from previous employment as a speech and language therapist, dyslexia therapist and teacher. Has a good business brain coupled with real empathy for parents who've been through the mill – 'if there's a problem she'll help sort it.' Runs her school her own way.

Academic Matters: All follow the National Curriculum, adapted as necessary. An abundance of experienced therapists: occupational, speech, art, music and physio, support the children's educational, emotional and physical needs. Each child has an individual learning programme (ILP) with personal learning styles taken into consideration. Classes are multisensory, with much 'over-teaching'. The provision of visual cues such as timetables of the day and of each lesson helps with communication. All (from 7 and up) learn to touch-type. Classes are small, ten or fewer, with children divided into groups of three or four for literacy, numeracy and speech and language therapy (some have individual sessions). Classrooms are spacious, well-organised and calm but playtimes are as lively and as rowdy as in any school!

As the school grows, senior pupils will work towards GCSEs, vocational qualifications and practical courses in a range of subjects including food technology, ICT, D&T and the arts. Some parental grouses , 'brighter children are not sufficiently stretched and stimulated at top end of the school' and, conversely, 'homework (a project to do by end of term) is too open-ended, children can't cope with this, I feel like it's the parents who end up doing all the work that teachers should be doing.' School points out that an open meeting to settle the perennial homework debate found that many wished for even more! Says others praise 'highly motivated' classes and 'focused teaching' for enabling their children 'to cope so well with all that is required'.

Games, Options, The Arts: Sport and the arts are an important and integral part of the curriculum. A wide range of opportunities encourages pupils to understand the benefits of physical activity. Strengths are football and hockey – all get the chance to participate in team games. Fantastic PE teacher who really motivates the children, runs lots of activities after school, organises matches etc. Two annual drama productions; again, all may be involved. Regular visits by children to art galleries, and sessions in school with artists. Music a strength – lively, run by a professional musician – offers regular informal concerts and performing opportunities. All have group music lessons, some have individual instrumental tuition – a few have even recorded their own CDs. Two music therapists work with pupils to help them acquire a sense of identity, build self-esteem, develop creativity and encourage interaction and communication. Both music and art therapy are available and use a psychotherapeutic approach to help pupils focus on the emotional aspect of their difficulties.

Background and Atmosphere: In a quiet residential road close to Wimbledon Common – no signs. Started life as a junior school but now expanding to take older children (year 9 from Sept 05). Moving to purpose-built school on neighbouring site in due course, swimming pool and sports hall included in new facilities. Current school is smartly decorated and well-maintained with a young(ish) staff, mostly in their twenties and thirties (first names used throughout). Head likes staff to be flexible, prepared to adapt and develop – little room for those who've 'always done it this way.'

Pastoral Care and Discipline: Parents say pastoral care is wonderful and appreciate the good ratio of male staff – 'incidence of autism higher among boys so it's lovely to have so many positive male role models.' School rules are simple and clear. Ethos of positive reinforcement means there are consequences rather than punishments for bad behaviour. Emotional issues are taken very seriously and dealt with sensitively. Some say there's scope for closer dialogue between home and school – 'we don't know what's happening on a daily basis so it's difficult to reinforce at home.' School says 'others praise the open-door policy and feedback meetings; communication between school and home is always encouraged.'

Pupils and Parents: From London and the Home Counties, more middle class than not. Fees are high and it can be very difficult for parents to get LEA funding. 'Those of us prepared to go to a tribunal are more likely to get here but it's not easy and some parents just don't have the stamina or know-how.'

Entrance: School caters mainly for children with speech, language and communication impairments, most also have overlapping conditions such as ASD, dyspraxia, sensory integration difficulties, dyslexia and ADHD. Children with language disorders may have associated difficulties with behaviour but the school is not set up to take children with severe behaviour problems. From 3+ into the nursery; term of their fifth birthday to the junior school; 11+ to the senior school. The odd vacancy at other times. Entry is by detailed assessment – need to ensure child will benefit from the specialist education available and school best placed to meet child's needs. Many go to tribunal.

Exit: Some now stay at 11+ others to specialist schools: More House (Farnham), More House (Oxted), The Moat, St Dominic's Godalming, Sibford, Kingham Hall. A few to (supported) mainstream state schools: Wimbledon College, Ursuline Convent etc.

Money Matters: Around 70 per cent are LEA funded. Hope to offer some bursaries in the future.

Remarks: A very special school for special children; continues to expand. Parents full of praise – 'staff dedication and patience are admirable'.

BLOXHAM SCHOOL

Bloxham, Near Banbury, Oxfordshire, OX15 4PE

Tel: 01295 720 222
Fax: 01295 721 897
Email: registrar@bloxhamschool.com
Website: www.bloxhamschool.com

• Pupils: 260 boys, 145 girls (55 per cent board) • Ages: 11-18 • Religion: C of E • Fees: Senior school: boarders £7,235-£7,380; day boarders £5,595-£5,695. Lower school: weekly boarders £4,695-£4,795; day £3,775-£3,850 • School status: Independent • Opendays: March and September • School gender: Mixed • Day/boarding: Takes boarders

SEN provision

Detail:

Centre of excellence for:

Mild: DYSL;
Moderate: DYSL;

Summary: Bloxham School runs a special three-year course for up to six dyslexic pupils each year from year 9 to the GCSE year. This course, which replaces modern foreign languages on the timetable, was opened in 1985. For entry, pupils should have a WISC or BAS combined score of 120 or more. After-school tuition is also available for dyslexic pupils in years 7 and 8, and for dyslexic pupils in years 9 to 11 who are not on the course. Because the course has for so many years drawn high-achieving pupils to the school, dyslexia has a high standing in the school community. The course is taught by Mr Hugh Alexander (Cantab) AMBDA, and after-school tuition is by Mrs Alison McLellan, MA (Cantab).

What we say about the school - the full Good Schools Guide review

Head: Since 2002, Mr Mark Allbrook (fifties) MA PGCE, who was educated at Tonbridge, and read classics at Trinity Hall; where he gained four cricket blues. Did his PGCE at Cambridge. Previously deputy head of Felsted. Helpful, articulate. Teaches classics six times a week, he reintroduced the subject on his arrival. He and his wife Mary, 'a computer wizard', have no children, are happy to be at Bloxham and much enjoy the local life. An enthusiast, the head has an open door policy, and our meeting was punctuated by knocks on the door from small people. Reckons 'he fell on his feet getting this job'. Has boosted the academic side of the school, appointing a new director of studies, which is having 'a knock-on effect'.

Academic Matters: Results good, given the intake, and last year saw one pupil getting four As at A level. School is aiming for serious academic improvement. Huge spread of languages (though less now than previously, as the number of exotic foreigners decreases – currently 10 per cent of pupils come from abroad: Germans, Russians, Hong Kong Chinese 'a good spread'. French, German, Italian, Spanish and Russian showed commendable results at A level last year, though the take-up in all cases was penny numbers, ditto the GCSE language results which included an A in Chinese. Stunning business studies department, fields more candidates at A level than any other subject, with varying results but a pleasing number of As. School plays the system (as do they all), certain amount of modules each term for A level candidates. All pupils now do the new IBtech qualification which covers the whole spectrum of ICT skills. Laptops (free) for all from 14 at the start of their GCSE years, and much in use in the dyslexia department. School now 'fully wireless networked' and it works all over. No keyboarding taught as such, the head maintains that 'voice recognition' programs will make basic keyboarding skills redundant. And he is, himself, trying out ViaVoice.

Superb remedial facilities for dyslexia under Hugh Alexander (still) though school is anxious not to be known as a school for dyslexics and says it 'only accepts children with an IQ in the high 120s as members of the dyslexia course'. Maximum 20 in school at any one time. Serious dyslexia input, school has now gained CReSTed B status, with scribing and 'translating' for exams (ie a teacher who knows the pupil's work and writing will transcribe his or her answers into 'proper' English). Registered dyslexics gain 15 minutes per hour in official exams.

Games, Options, The Arts: Not the rugby powerhouse it used to be but lots of good variety. Two tennis/hockey Astroturfs, huge modern sports hall all just off campus, with two charming little cricket grounds a couple of hundred metres in the other direction (cricket professional recently appointed) and great indoor swimming pool, much used by locals, in the middle of the main school grounds. Sixth form club room now established above the cricket pavilion, complete with electronic score board. School good at individual sports, huge range of sports on offer from a highly acclaimed polo team via cross-country, show jumping and dressage on the equine front to very serious clay shooting. Both girls and boys participate successfully at the National Championships on a regular basis. 'I challenge a keen sporting pupil not to be fulfilled at Bloxham,' says the proud head.

Music is on the up, recent senior school performance of West Side Story met with huge acclaim. Extension to music school planned, but currently still firmly based in the old converted gym. According to the young, Blox still more or less added to everything: guitar = fret-blox, jazz = swing-blox, you get the picture, latest additions = blox-idol and paper-blox. Art department open at weekends, much improved from our last visit, masses of quite successful uptake at GCSE and more at A than previously. Some exciting ceramics. Brilliant textiles. Drama in The Wesley, the old converted chapel popular and thriving. Young Enterprise, D of E etc. Workshops open at weekends too, staff put a lot of extra hours.

Background and Atmosphere: Founded in 1860 and given to the Woodard Foundation (group of schools originally founded by Canon Woodard to promote muscular Christianity) in 1896. Handsome building of Hornton stone, quarried from below the foundations (very economical) with stunning chapel on first floor. Glorious re-shaping of dining room and kitchen area has released the basement to business studies (and an extra computer room). Extended light and airy dining room has good buffet and veggie options.

School proper is contained in playing-field-filled eighty acre campus with quite a lot of out-houses, pitches and buildings, a lot of walking ('max five minutes' said our guide – he must walk even faster than on our gallop round the grounds). Fabulous DT building on site, The Raymond Tec Centre; the top floor floats above the lower work stations joined with an alarming glass staircase. Lower school opened in May 2000 – this palace for 11 to 13-year-olds is a magnificent transformation of the White Lion pub overlooking the main street and feels just like a ship with decking and portholes, though some of the passages seem a little narrow to accommodate two chattering creatures carrying books. Boys and girls allowed a certain amount of free visiting between houses, girls' houses much posher with girls graduating early from dorms to individual study bedrooms at fifth form while boys progress to shared studies – though many have their own at fifth form. Lots of repaints and reorganisation here, jolly colours abounds and the house captains have their own showers – even their personal jacuzzi. School uniform for all but sixth formers, who have a certain freedom in dress.

A tranche of day pupils and weekly boarding for years 7 and 8, and the odd flexi-boarding but a boarding school at heart. Days are long, from 8.30am – 9pm, but the week now ends on Friday for the lower school, and the rest can usually go home after games from 4pm on Saturday. Boarders 'are expected' to be in for the first weekend of term and the first after half term. Raft of school buses for day-boarders ferry them from 'convenient pick-up points'. The advent of boarding for tinies has pushed the numbers up and they recently moved into the former manor house, Park Close, really grand.

Pastoral Care and Discipline: Strong tutorial system via houses, children stay with same tutor throughout. Each house has five tutors who are often on hand during prep in the evening. God important here ('head prefers 'Christian ethos important') and indeed a goodly showing in RS at GCSE, but no A level provision apparently). Discipline 'not as big a problem here, we're a small school where you feel you might be letting someone down'. Urine testing on demand if drug use suspected, followed by probable rustication for a week and random testing thereafter. No pupil is automatically expelled, though they would be for repeated offences. Booze not a major problem, the villagers complain if they drop fag ends in the (very pretty) village, and the campus is too busy to find a quiet corner. Intra-house, boy/girl visiting in communal areas only, contact fairly controlled. 'But caught in flagrante equals out'.

Pupils and Parents: Lots of first time buyers. Parents with children in the state sector come to the school because they see it as 'an upmarket alternative to the state system' and parents from the independent sector come to the school because they want a smaller, more local school (as opposed to Stowe, St Edward's, Uppingham etc). Still suits the 'gentle and less able', but also numbers of very able who could have got in anywhere. Basically north Oxfordshire (not to be confused with North Oxford) farmers, businessmen, the services, considerable mix. 4x4s all over the car park when we visited. Pupils happy and confident, very polite and ready to help when you're lost. The teenage boys' rooms (relatively) wholesome.

Entrance: Large tranche from state primaries at 11, own test and assessment. At 13 from trad prep schools, Beachborough, Bilton Grange, Swanbourne, Winchester House, New College etc. CE pass mark of 50 per cent, but rest assured this is in no way an academic hothouse. Sixth form entrance by interview, report from previous school, and GCSE results.

Exit: Small leakage after GCSE. Majority go on to higher education. Great variety – from Russell Group to former polys and universities favouring practical hands-on courses, art foundation courses very popular plus, Southampton, Loughborough, Harper Adams (for ag/land management) Bristol (UWE). More or less the same as last time, possibly more reading business studies than before.

Money Matters: Parents in real need still get helped via the 'dreaded blue form means test'. Woodard Foundation can give help in an emergency for children of old Bloxhamists. Huge collection of scholarships for everything from music, sport (not at 11+), DT, art and academic, for all ages, take as many as you want, as often as you want, 11+, 13+ and 16+. Amazing.

Remarks: Interesting developments, and they continue. A thriving school with Christian values, academically more challenging than before. Very strong dyslexia course.

Blundell's School

Blundell's Road, Tiverton, Devon, EX16 4DN

Tel: 01884 252 543

Fax: 01884 243 232

Email: registrars@blundells.org

Website: www.blundells.org

• Pupils: 565; 335 boys, 230 girls (400 board/weekly board, rest day) • Ages: 11-18 • Religion: C of E

• Fees: Junior: day £2,740-£4,585. Senior: day £3,520 (locals) £4,400 (the rest) £6,485 • School status: Independent

• Opendays: Mid September • School gender: Mixed

• Day/boarding: Takes boarders

SEN provision

Detail:

Experience of:

Mild: DYSC; DYSL; DYSP;

Summary: There are about 150 pupils in the school with special needs of one sort or another, so we are very much aware that some children need special help and there is close liaison between the English department and other subject teachers.

Sp.L.D. pupils are tested informally in the learning support department and given help by Mrs A'Lee, a highly experienced learning support teacher, or her assistant Mrs Lane. This support usually takes place once or twice a week, by withdrawal. As it is a specialist individual requirement, there has to be a termly charge. Mrs A'Lee reports regularly on pupils' progress, and currently sees about 80 students.

Work is centred on discovering what the individual's problem is and concentrating on it. Poor spelling is covered by repetitive work on basic rules, indifferent vocabulary by extension and slow reading by improvement of skills. In particular, pupils are given support in subject areas where they are having problems. A great effort is made to spark imaginative writing. Dyslexics are encouraged to devise strategies to overcome difficulties of spelling and organising work. For some this may include the use of special filters or glasses as well as the use of techniques such as mind mapping or visualisation.

Dyslexic diagnostic tests (Aston, Digit Span, etc.) at a simple level are given and referral made, where necessary, for full testing to enable students to claim extra time allowance in public examinations.

There are no standard textbooks, as worksheets are prepared individually. However Hornsby's 'Alpha to Omega', Butterworth's 'Using the Oxford Dictionary' and The Sunday Times Word Power are helpful.

Official testing is usually done by Dr Hornby from St Luke's Exeter. Her certification is accepted by exam boards and tests are usually carried out in the Autumn. About twenty-five pupils are tested each year. In 2002 for the first time, the Boards agreed to accept just one certification for the student's entire secondary career. (In Further Education, such certification often entitles students to IT equipment discounts.)

Dyslexia, Dyspraxia, Attention Deficit syndrome: it is very difficult to pinpoint or label problems as every child is different, but at Blundell's we aim to ensure sympathetic treatment, individual support and a positive approach, focusing on the learning difference with its positives rather than any negative associations connected with a learning disability. It is not unusual for dyslexic pupils, with the full extra time allowance in exams, to gain the highest grades in both GCSE and A level examination.

Above all, our students are taught to think of themselves as Blundellians, not as Dyslexics, developing confidence and expertise in as many areas as possible.

What we say about the school - the full Good Schools Guide review

Headmaster: Since 2004, Mr Ian Davenport BA (mid forties). Educated at Bloxham and Durham where he read politics. After five years in the city, Mr Davenport went to St George's Weybridge and thence to Radley where he was senior tutor, housemaster and head of dept (economics), also coaching rugby, fives and other school teams. Married with two young children.

Academic Matters: Strong results for a broadly comprehensive intake. Top of the tree recently are chemistry, geography and history, with mathematics and the other sciences not far behind. Class sizes between 6 and 22. Three new modern technology suites completed in 2003. Full-time EFL specialist teacher, who is backed up by two part-timers. Requirements of some 60 special needs pupils are not over-looked. 'Some' special provision for dyslexia. Education consultant used in advisory capacity.

Games, Options, The Arts: Some 16 annual school trips available. School planning for an indoor pool. Lively music department largely due to 'brilliant director of music' and possibly some intake from Exeter Cathedral prep. Choir tours central Europe each year. Art is equally impressive with enthusiastic teacher who, after 15 years, is quite at home in idyllic classroom with lush green outlook. Theatre taken seriously – West Side Story, Oklahoma-type productions, participation in Edinburgh Festival, hosting of English Shakespeare Company.

Lunchtime in huge canteen is a highlight – mouth-watering menu suits varying tastes; pupils extremely disciplined – queuing patiently, no pushing, shoving or shouting; returning trays to efficient conveyer-belt collection point. No parental concerns over diet. Good workshops (textiles, silver-smithing, cabinet making, engine repairs). Blundell's maintains traditional link with past through military service – all year 9 pupils join CCF for two compulsory terms. Ten Tors and D of E taken seriously. All mainstream sports offered, like hockey, football and cricket but rugby is particularly strong, alongside county-standard girls' hockey teams.

Background and Atmosphere: Set in 80 acres. Charming setting reminiscent of rural university campus; bisected by public road – a wakening reminder of outside world. Dignified collegiate main blocks, cloister and chapel; over the road the newer music block, huge dining hall, excellently designed Ondaatje Hall housing theatre plus photography, art, pottery – named after its Old Blundellian benefactor, self-effacing financier and explorer Christopher Ondaatje (brother of the Booker Prize winner). Do not be put off by the majestic-looking buildings though, as there's a friendly and supportive community atmosphere inside, where individuals count. Unpressurised environment, 'young adults' expected to make own decisions, consequently little sloppiness. Lots of banter among happy staff who tend to stay. Tiverton is 'proud to have it on the doorstep' although interaction with community is limited due to packed and varied schedules. Ginger brown tweedy jackets for 13 to 16-year-olds, not every parent's cup of tea, sixth form boys and girls now wear navy blazers with 13-16 girls in red jackets and navy skirts.

Special burgundy and black striped jackets awarded to exceptional pupils as full colours – can be for sport, music, drama, academics or service to school. Founded in 1604 through the will of a local clothier Peter Blundell. Well served through long association with Amory family. Became fully co-ed in 1993. School mentioned in Lorna Doone by (Old Blundellian)R D Blackmore.

Pastoral Care and Discipline: Smokers caught on campus ordered to report to member of staff six times a day; boarders also put under curfew. Drunken pupils face temporary exclusion. No room for anyone bringing drugs into Blundell's; pupils also known to dabble off campus could face exclusion, although agreeing to random urine testing may save their bacon. Parents were comfortable with the 'fair' way a one-off incident was handled. Pioneering system of flexi-boarding allows pupils to stay as and when they wish and encourages them to come to board when they feel confident to do so; facilities are being adjusted to accommodate this.

Pupils and Parents: Farming intake has dropped from 20 to 2 per cent. Parents working in the professions (probably also looking at Kings Taunton); increasingly from the West Country, although some far-flung including Londoners with local connections. Fair number of Services children. 10 per cent are foreign nationals, especially German – Munich agency sends high-class pupils. Others from Eastern bloc, Japan, Canada. Strongly loyal and supportive Old Boys, include Christopher Ondaatje, Donald Stokes, Michael Mates MP, Anthony Smith. Pupils are pleasant, un-pushy, unspoilt – not afraid to hold opinions.

Entrance: Not a problem although some selection is being forced by oversubscription. CE at 11 and 13 from traditional prep schools (eg Mount House, St Peter's, St Michael's and King's Hall). Good sprinkling from local state schools. Internal and external candidates at sixth form need five C grades at GCSE.

Exit: Rising number to Oxbridge – 10 in 2001; 90-95 per cent to university. Mr Davenport considers that pupils who enter on a low entrance mark and leave with lowly A levels have achieved. Law and the Services are popular career paths; more recently graphic design. Not much migration towards London. The school has traditional links through Peter Blundell with Sidney Sussex, Cambridge and Balliol, Oxford.

Money Matters: Generous number of scholarships – academic and also for music, art, sport and drama, at different ages – well worth enquiring about. Approximately one-third of entrants hold awards of some sort, up to 50 per cent off basic fees. Foundation awards allow local boys and girls to attend as day pupils.

Remarks: Popular school if you can afford the fees. Don't be put off by any grandeur as it is only in the bricks and mortar. Everything else is really down-to-earth.

BOOTHAM SCHOOL

51 Bootham, York, North Yorkshire, YO30 7BU

Tel: 01904 623 261

Fax: 01904 652 106

Email: office@bootham.york.sch.uk

Website: www.bootham.york.sch.uk

• Pupils: 278 boys, 168 girls and 130 at Ebor, the Junior School • Ages: 11-18 and 3-11 at Ebor, the Junior School • Religion: Quaker (but other faiths welcome) • Fees: Full and weekly boarders (y9 to y13) £5,700-£6,072; junior boarding (y7 and y8) £3,893; part weekly boarding (y9 to y13): £4,316-£4,980; day pupils and day boarders £3,614-£3,850; Ebor:£1,470-£1,800 • School status: Independent • Opendays: Saturdays in October, November, May • School gender: Mixed • Day/boarding: Takes boarders

SEN provision

Detail:

Now provide for in school:

Mild: DYSL; DYSP; HI;

Others: PD;

Experience of:

Mild: ASP;

Summary: We do not feel that we have particular special needs facilities which would mark us out as being better equipped than any other school of our type ie one focused on a traditional academic curriculum aimed at selector university application. Obviously we do feel that the Quaker ethos gives a particular style to the school which is manifest in the way individuals are treated but this is open to all our pupils and not targeted on those with special needs or gifts.

We do not for example have a special needs department, we do not have a dyslexia unit, we do not have particular facilities for physical special needs (indeed the old buildings present us with a real challenge in simply meeting the basic legislative requirements for accessibility!). We will always treat each application sympathetically as any school is bound to do but we feel that there is a real danger for us in fostering expectations, because of our reputation for friendliness, which can not be met.

GSG says: this is taking modesty to extremes. SEN details added by us.

What we say about the school - the full Good Schools Guide review

Head: Since 2004, Jonathan Taylor BA Hons Oxon, English, MEd, Sussex. Previously deputy head at Bedales School in Hampshire (described by his head there as 'my Mr Discipline'), he describes Bootham as his 'ideal headship'. Wife, Nicola. His interests include the arts, gardening and the outdoor life.

Academic Matters: Majority of pupils study for 11 GCSEs with a creditable 56 per cent graded A/A*. Particular strengths are DT, maths, music and art with no significant weaknesses. Usual range of subjects but no textiles, food technology or equivalent courses. 75 per cent of A levels are graded A/B with very few below D. Class sizes are between 10 and 20 for GCSE groups and 6 to 14 for A level. School tries to be as flexible as possible about A level combinations, pupils make guided choices then timetable is, as far as possible, designed around these. School houses a specialist science and geography centre, a music school, art and design studios and an IT centre. Computers are much more plentiful following the inspection report and a wireless network has been installed to facilitate the use of laptops. The super John Bright non-fiction library is well used and frequently updated. Teaching is lively and interactive, the expectation is that children will question, investigate and take responsibility for their learning. A wide range of special needs is catered for, including dyslexia, profound deafness and physical handicaps. The buildings have been partly modified for wheelchair provision but needs must be discussed prior to admission. School will do all it can to help – for example a biology lab was created on the ground floor to enable a pupil with a motor disability to be educated alongside her peers.

Games, Options, The Arts: All play sport including sixth form; tennis and football traditionally very popular. Facilities include a lovely new galleried sports hall – the result of an appeal, two squash courts, tennis courts, swimming pool (has had new roof and flooring but still requires further attention) and extensive playing fields. Competitiveness is not a dominant feature of the Quaker ethos, so teams will give as many players as possible the opportunity to compete, not just the most talented. This makes successes all the more commendable – both team (district basketball champions) and individual, where successes include a junior international fencer, Olympic games swimmer and Olympic cyclist, member of the England junior table-tennis team, county netball, hockey and cricket squad members and Leeds and York academy football players. Fantastic design work has received national critical acclaim and is mentioned in the design council guide as an exemplar for good practice. An impressive motorised go-kart designed and built by a sixth former was tested during the visit. We were offered a trial run but decided to leave that to the expertise of Jeremy Clarkson! Vibrant art department with results to match. Exciting expeditions to places as far flung as Peru, Bolivia, Iceland and Russia with regular exchanges in France and Germany. Over 60 per cent learn a musical instrument. Emphasis is on the individual enjoying music not pushing to achieve, yet several attain grade 8 and beyond as well as regular scholarships to the Guildhall and Royal Colleges. Pupils sing and play in national choirs and orchestras. Music technology rooms have digital recording facilities and variety of software to assist composition. All players afforded the opportunity to perform if they want to. School holds regular buffet concerts in the main hall, home to a permanent staging area with tiered seating and theatre lighting. Full-scale senior productions include a regular joint venture with the Mount School. Oh What A Lovely War, The Comedy of Errors and Guys and Dolls have taken centre stage in recent years. School has own well-used observatory and boasts the oldest school natural history society in the country. Hard to be bored here; plenty to do including regular activities and trips at the weekend for boarders.

Background and Atmosphere: The school was founded in 1823 based on liberal intellectual tolerant ideology. Originally a boys' school, it went co-ed in 1983. From the busy main road (minutes from York city centre) the only visible part of the school is a collection of fine Georgian terraces, so it is surprising to find such a deceptively spacious and tranquil campus to the rear. The school, originally the distinguished town house and grounds of the merchant, Sir Richard Johnstone, has been sympathetically extended over the years to provide mostly bright, modern, purpose-built facilities. Quaker meetings are held daily yet only a small percentage of the children and less than half the staff are Quakers. It is faith rather than a particular faith that is important. Head's joy is that the school is non-hierarchical (something that confused the inspectorate), staff are on first name terms and some pupils address certain staff by Christian names, no sirs or madams here.

Pastoral Care and Discipline: Street cred not important, just a warm and caring school with the intimate feel of a close-knit family. Pupils encouraged to question and to probe. Said one member of staff, 'the only thing you can be sure of is that you might be wrong.' Children are not judged, they are valued. No litany of rules exists; discipline is based on trust and mutual respect yet despite, or because of, high level of care, children are very self-sufficient. Pupils are encouraged to consider the impact of their actions not just on themselves but on others too. Effective punishment system operates whereby individuals are given columns of commonly misspelt words to write out, the number of columns depending on the offence. Columns are recorded collectively alongside credits for good work. Forms which achieve a positive number of credits are rewarded with a half-day off school to pursue an activity of their choice. The collectiveness of punishments and rewards works well and encourages pupils to think about the effects of their actions on the wider community. It also encourages the group to take responsibility for individuals and to help them. Alcohol not allowed on premises, drugs (3 expulsions in last couple of years) and bullying are no-nos, as are CCF and games involving violence, but war gaming based on model making and strategy is perceived as constructive and therefore permitted. Plenty of support, everyone from form teachers through to independent counsellors and the health centre, which may be used as a respite, on hand to help.

Good standard of boarding accommodation for both boys and girls. Houses are well decorated and rooms are generously proportioned; houses have a range of facilities but no computers although pupils are encouraged to bring laptops. Rowntree is the girls house, junior boys are housed in Penn, lower and upper senior boys in Fox with sixth form boys having the luxury of en-suite accommodation and single rooms in Evelyn. Children eat in the school dining hall, very good food, plenty of choice. All pupils belong to one of four houses independent of the boarding houses; these contain a mix of ages, sexes and boarding and day pupils.

Pupils and Parents: Regarded locally as the thinking parents' school, lots of children of dons, lecturers and those from the medical world as well as several first time buyers of independent education. Undoubtedly some well heeled parents but not the sort who flash their cash. Day pupils mainly from York and up to a 25-mile radius. 30 per cent of boys and 20 per cent of girls board. Boarders from UK and worldwide, all are English speaking or near fluent if foreign. Children are a happy, confident, savvy bunch accepted for who they are, individuality is appreciated and celebrated – no wonder they enjoy coming to school. Not a smart school, a sweat-shirt based uniform exists for the younger pupils with the older ones asked to dress in a clean, tidy and modest manner, so great variations on a theme! School supported by the Bootham School Association (BSA) and the Old Scholars' Association. The active BSA holds regular coffee mornings, barbecues, walks, lectures etc for parents and has even introduced Grandparents' day. Notable old boys: AJP Taylor, Brian Rix, Philip Noel Baker (Nobel Peace prize-winner and gold medal Olympic athlete), John Bright (parliamentarian), Stuart Rose (head of Marks & Spencer) and Silvanus Thompson (eminent physicist).

Entrance: Main feeder school is Ebor, the junior school to Bootham. Those entering at 11 and 13 sit school's own exam (and CE for those entering at 13). For sixth form (college) entry a minimum of six good passes at GCSE are required which must include maths and English. The head interviews applicants and a report is sought from the previous school. School is now at capacity so don't leave it too late to apply.

Exit: A few leave post-GCSE mainly to York sixth form college, either to follow vocational courses or to avoid Saturday school. Pupils encouraged to take a gap year prior to university and many do. Five or six per year to Oxbridge, rest mainly to wide-range of good universities. York, Newcastle and Leeds are popular choices.

Money Matters: Not a rich school, most income generated through fees and fundraising. Up to four scholarships for boarders of up to one half of fees. Major scholarships worth up to half fees and minor scholarships worth between twelve and twenty five per cent of fees. One art and one music scholarship worth up to half fees and some sixth form scholarships also available.

Remarks: Does well by all, especially the lost sheep and those considered different, but don't expect to find lots of meek souls. The end result is a bright, considerate, confident and articulate individual. Not many the school wouldn't suit after a time because Bootham is addictive – it gets under your skin – but rugby players, the very competitive and attention seekers may find it a tad too nice.

Box Hill School

Mickleham, Dorking, Surrey, RH5 6EA

Tel: 01372 373382

Fax: 01372 363942

Email: registrar@boxhillschool.org.uk

Website: www.boxhillschool.org.uk

• Pupils: 190 day pupils 160 boarders (rising to 400 by 2008) 63 per cent boy 37 per cent girls • Ages: 11-18 • Fees: Day £3,100 to £3,775; weekly boarding: £5,200 to £5,275; full boarding: £6,150- £6,225; International Study Centre: weekly boarding £5,990, full boarding £6,945 • School status: Independent • School gender: Mixed • Day/boarding: Takes boarders

SEN provision

Detail:

Centre of excellence for:

- Mild: DYSL;
- Moderate: DYSL;
- Others: EAL;

Now provide for in school:

- Mild: ADD; ADHD; DYSC; DYSP; SpLD; CP;
- Moderate: ADD;
- Others: Sp&LD; PD;

Experience of:

- Mild: ASP; EBD; HI;
- Moderate: ADHD; EBD; MLD; DYSP; HI;
- Severe: ADD;
- Others: SPD; OCD; Eat;

Summary: Box Hill has a long tradition of supporting pupils with special needs, particularly those with dyslexia. We offer tuition on site by withdrawing pupils, usually on a one-to-one basis, from lessons on a rotational system. The majority receive one or two forty minute lessons a week. GCSE and A level students often have one, one hour lesson a week outside their academic timetable. At present, there are four specialist teachers who have well-equipped rooms. The constant liaison between the specialist teachers and all members of the teaching and House staff helps form a relaxed and effective working environment in which the pupils can maximise their potential.

What we say about the school - the full Good Schools Guide review

Head: Since 2003 Mr Mark Eagers MA(Cantab) MA (Bath) PGCE (forties). Previously deputy head of Ardingly College, was a senior examiner for IB (history) and is an NCA coach (cricket). Married to Jane who teaches economics, business studies and ESL at the school. They have three children, oldest two at the school. Loves sport especially cricket, enjoys hacking round the golf-course and spending time with the family. Pupils say head goes by his name – Eager by name eager by nature. Personable, chatty, popular, his boundless enthusiasm and energy has lifted the spirit and atmosphere. Had a mandate to kick start the school in what is a highly competitive market.

Spent first year settling in and prioritising then started on the very many (and much needed) planned changes and upgrades. Not just facilities (more later) but a school council, greater communication with parents, captains' dinner, more sport etc. No room for complacency on the academic side, most staff swept along with him, a few voting with their feet, some retiring (staff profile older than in many schools). Staff say: 'he has vision, holds onto what's strong and good and that although changes are good, speed of changes have rattled a few cages, but he knows where school is going and where it needs to be.' Head gets universal thumbs up from pupils who say: 'school is more active, lively, he's younger, plays games with us, knows us all and has children the same age so he's in touch.' Teaches younger years and gets really involved in sport especially soccer matches (coaches the thirds) where he's often heard cheering on the lads and occasionally questioning the referee. Pupils love the fact he's revamping things and making everything more student friendly, younger ones agree adding: 'he's funny and nice; even if you're naughty he makes sure you understand what you've done.'

Academic Matters: Teaching styles vary but pupils say most staff work hard to make lessons interesting and accessible and use TVs, interactive whiteboards or OHPs to help. School introducing laptops for all from year 7 (included with fees). Smallish classes average 16. No Saturday school but prep on Saturdays for boarders. Positive value added with art, English language, French and History scores showing pupils gaining a grade higher than anticipated at GCSE. Lowest (though still positive) value added found in sciences and maths. Fashion very popular, A level theatre studies gaining in popularity, English, maths, history, science and art fine, modern languages come in for pupil criticism though German results are among the best at A level. Handful of U grades at A level but no particular subject – representative of policy of entering all who wish to.

Parents and pupils full of praise for SEN and learning support. Get one-to-one or small group support as necessary. One mildly dyslexic boy with poor organisational skills was thrilled to achieve 2. As in GCSE English, another told us, 'I was quite severely dyslexic when I came here but I'm not so bad now, teachers help you at every stage. You learn to get on with it. My teachers collaborate with the dyslexic teacher – it makes a difference.' Keen not to flood classes with learning difficulties as they don't have room for classroom support. Work on literacy and English plus strategies to help pupils in the classroom and with organisation, though older pupils may be given subject-specific help. Majority come out of activities on rotation but some drop a subject to fit learning support in. Department produce IEPs and meet, liaise and interact regularly with all teachers. Learning support staff say strength is the staff: all teachers are SEN aware and dedicated. Range of SENs catered for: physical difficulties (though not junior girl boarders), dyslexia, dyspraxia, mild Asperger's, cerebral palsy, moderate hearing impairment, OCD and dyscalculia. Mild to moderate only. A quarter of pupils receive ESL tuition, 30 of whom attend the International Study Centre full-time.

Games, Options, The Arts: All usual sports, good range of facilities: gym (doubles as main hall), small outdoor heated swimming pool, super climbing centre adjacent to a fantastic outdoor high ropes set-up, brand new assault/team-working course, a well-used, equipped and supervised multi-gym, dance studio with surround sound, etc etc.

Music and music technology is housed in an ugly brown Portakabin. Plenty of opportunities to perform in concerts, productions, tours (Lake Garda for past three years), cabarets etc. Don't have to be grade 8 and gifted to join in, enthusiasm counts. Practical art, theatre, drama all popular. An hour and half compulsory activity slot is built into the daily timetable with diverse choice of activities ranging from candle making to ice skating. Plenty of outings – ys7-9 go on camping/out-door pursuits orientated expeditions twice a year; a big hit with pupils. Senior years do D of E (10 golds recently) and older children get opportunities to go overseas.

Background and Atmosphere: Founded as a co-ed school in 1959 by Roy McComish, a master at Gordonstoun. Still very much a Round Square school, following Kurt Hahn's principles of allowing children to discover themselves, furthering international co-operation, serving the community and participating in adventurous activities calling for initiative and responsibility. Main school in pleasant village of Mickleham, an important and integral part of the community. Pleasant redbrick building believed to have originally been a wedding present from DH Evans to his daughter. Mix of the old, modern buildings that blend well and incongruous ugly prefabs well past sell by date. Some refurbishment in progress.

Pastoral Care and Discipline: No plans to turn into an academic hothouse, believe education should be enjoyed not endured. Stress importance of finding something child is good at; success in one area enhances confidence, makes child feel better about self, leads to success in other areas. International centre attracts lots of overseas boarders – indeed it accounts for a high proportion of those who board in sixth-form, though some stay with guardians.

Boarding facilities vary considerably. Smart new house just built; other houses vary: mansions, cosy but comfortable; modern blocks in need of an upgrade and the externally hideous Ralph house (another brown prefab). Grim and impersonal living space in the junior girls' house – the girls loathe it. Another grumble is the cramped dinning hall (one of the worst we've seen but school says it's being revamped this summer). We sympathise with pupils who moan about the rush to get three sittings through lunch, not that we can imagine why they'd want to linger: for a school that prides itself on atmosphere the very blue dining room with its cafeteria system, plastic furniture, and poor acoustics is decidedly lacking; think gritty visions of transport cafés not romantic images of Hogwarts. Food ranges from healthy salad bar to stodgy puddings – not that anyone should go hungry, there's a school shop, vending machines stocked with sweets and a cyber café selling a range of snacks which provides a well-used communal area for juniors. Over 18s are allowed a couple of visits a week to the King William pub in the village (landlady checks ID) though we're told: 'anyone coming back hammered will get punished, but the cost of a pint in Surrey tends to limit quantity consumed anyway!' Sensible drinking allowed for older students at formal dinners. Clear guidelines are issued for those caught smoking, drinking or involved with drugs, random testing may be used.

The new tutor group system comes in for universal praise: pupils, parents and staff love it – only disadvantage is that tutor system is house based so you end up with single-sex tutor groups. Good and staged discipline system of coloured cards works well. Head introduced a student council which sixth formers praise but younger ones want improving – say they'd like to be asked for their opinions not just rely on a rep that doesn't always do the job properly.

Pupils and Parents: Lots of first time buyers of independent education. Majority from Surrey or Sussex, a quarter from overseas (24 nationalities). Pupils say it's more sporty, less academic than other schools they looked at and entry assessment procedure is more relaxed. 'I didn't want to be stuck in classroom and knew school really didn't approve of bullying and would do a lot to stop it.'

Children love the fact it's a small, close-knit community, where everyone knows each other. Need a 'have a go' attitude, good for the sporty. Couch potatoes and the vain may struggle as outward bound expeditions are compulsory A couple of girls told us how they hadn't fancied caving (water and the dark) but made to try and found they thoroughly enjoyed it. All agree expeditions are a highlight of the year, a great way to get to know people and make new friends. Pupils struggled to say what they hadn't enjoyed, other than exams. All agree school isn't known for its academic prowess, will never soar up the league tables but it does well with its intake and those capable of getting to Oxbridge do.

Entrance: Selection is by tests in maths and English and by interview, with previous school reports considered. Majority enter in year 7 or year 9 with selection days held in November and February prior to year of entry. Numbers are up and school is meeting challenges to find extra space. A truly comprehensive intake from those who achieve five grade A levels and take up Oxbridge places to those who struggle academically but may have talents in sports, the arts etc. Range of SENs catered for: physical difficulties (though not junior girl boarders), dyslexia, dyspraxia, mild Asperger's, cerebral palsy, moderate hearing impairment, OCD and dyscalculia. Withdraw from lessons up to four times a week for 40 minute sessions. A third receive learning support vast majority for dyslexia but it's not the place for those with severe difficulties who need classroom support though it's fine for mild to moderate who will benefit from intervention. A quarter of pupils receive ESL tuition, 30 of whom attend the International Study Centre full-time.

Exit: Handful leave after GCSEs to local colleges. Majority of sixth form go to a range of universities selecting and recruiting, some to study degrees others HND. Odd one to Oxbridge otherwise range from Imperial to Thames Valley. Handful take a gap year, couple into employment.

Money Matters: Range of scholarships and bursaries offered, mainly means tested and worth up to 50 per cent of fees.

Remarks: We've been in far smarter schools with much better facilities but as a pupils told us, 'you don't need state of the art sports halls to play football, it's the package – the teachers, the atmosphere, the community, everyone is positive and school really helps to develop your talents.'

Bramcote School, North Yorkshire

22-30 Filey Road, Scarborough, North Yorkshire, YO11 2TT

Tel: 01723 373 086

Fax: 01723 364 186

Email: headmaster@bramcoteschool.com

Website: www.bramcoteschool.com

• Pupils: 110 (60 boys and 50 girls), 60 per cent full boarding, with 30 per cent regular boarders and 10 per cent day pupils • Ages: 7-13 • Religion: C of E • Fees: Boarding £3,065 per term (for younger pupils in first year at Bramcote) to £4,565; day £3,275 • School status: Independent • School gender: Mixed • Day/boarding: Takes boarders

SEN provision

Detail:
Now provide for in school:
Mild: ASP; DYSC; DYSL; DYSP; SpLD; HI; VI;
Moderate: ADD; ADHD; MLD; DYSC; DYSL; DYSP; SpLD;
Others: SPD; EAL; Sp&LD; Eat;
Experience of:
Mild: EBD;
Moderate: EBD;
Others: OCD;

Summary: No comment offered – but excellent and wide-ranging provision as the SEN details show.

What we say about the school - the full Good Schools Guide review

Head: Since 2003, Mr Andrew G W Lewin BA PGCE (forties), geography degree from Newcastle, then taught at Dunchurch – Winton Hall, Winchester House and Loretto – before coming to Bramcote as deputy head in 1999. He and wife, Debbie, form the core of the pastoral responsibility and live on site. Two of their own three young children are already pupils at the school. High standards, strong community spirit and a sound Christian understanding continue at Bramcote. Andrew, a keen sportsman, used to run the rugby and the cricket, is an MCC playing member and a single figure handicap golfer. Numbers at the school have been rising since his arrival.

Entrance: By interview, non-selective. Children come from all over UK and abroad, but predominantly from Yorkshire and Humberside. Several Forces families. Tedious travel time slashed for parents collecting children for exeats by escorted buses taking children to rendezvous points north and south, and by escorted train journeys to London.

Exit: Excellent record of Common Entrance success and scholarships. Pupils go regularly to Winchester, Oundle, Radley, Shrewsbury, Eton, Ampleforth, Repton, and St Peter's York. Queen Margaret's York, and Wycombe Abbey are favourites with girls when they leave at 13.

Remarks: Founded on Yorkshire coast in 1893 on Scarborough's South Cliff, 15-minute walk from the beach with sweeping views to the sea. Prides itself on feeling like home, and to the headmaster that means being around for the pupils not just weekdays but weekends. More than half the school stays at weekends and joins Mr Lewin for Sunday lunch. Not much chance of a lie-in for him anyway – he and his family live directly below the boys' dorms! Half staff live in and all are involved in Sunday afternoon activities. Entertainment includes trips to cinema, ten pin bowling, clay pigeon shooting, Flamingo Land theme park and, of course, the beach.

'Boarding for me is the whole package,' says Mr Lewin. 'It's everything – the activities, the fun of being with your friends, the sense of community. The younger pupils have the flexibility to start boarding maybe one or two nights a week and then start introducing more nights. The majority convert to full boarding by the time they are in the senior part of the school. We have children who live in Scarborough who choose to board.' Even day pupils over the age of ten stay until after 7. Parents can visit, particularly on Wednesdays and Saturdays and are 'warmly entertained'. A little too warmly perhaps, 'We often find a father dozing on the sofas in the library in front of an open fire.' Whether parents visit children between exeats or not (almost all do), they know how their offspring are doing. On top of the weekly effort grades that the pupils receive in assembly, parents receive reports every few weeks detailing their child's progress in each subject, with comments from a tutor and the headmaster.

Some long-established and outstanding teaching staff. Bramcote believes achievement comes in many forms, and pupils not destined for a string of A*s should be just as valued as those who are. Just as the school gives extra exam preparation to pupils heading for top academic schools, so it gives additional help to pupils finding learning a struggle. A full-time learning support specialist helps pupils with all kinds of difficulties – dyslexia, ADHD, dyspraxia, Asperger's – at no extra charge. 'The first thing I did when I became headmaster was to move the learning support right to the centre of the school, next to my office,' Mr Lewin said. 'It is an important part of Bramcote. There is no stigma at all here for pupils who need learning support.' An issue close to his heart even before one of his own children was diagnosed with dyslexia. 'I know exactly how it feels being the parent of a dyslexic child,' he said. 'But it's important to remember that whether you find reading and writing easy or not, you can still achieve in the classroom and enjoy music, sport, drama or whatever it might be. I firmly believe that the learning support we offer gives the school a breadth and richness which is very, very healthy.

'Once a boys' prep, girls have been admitted to Bramcote since 1996. Transition managed without an entrenched battle of the sexes. The girls enjoy not only activities laid on for them, such as dance and ballet, but are generally happy to take part in the rough and tumble of traditional boys' sports, such as the evening cricket and soccer leagues, as part of a very busy programme of extra-curricular activities. For its size, it can claim an embarrassment of riches in terms of facilities – whopping playing fields, a heated indoor pool, a big sports hall, a dedicated art and music centre, a large school hall and a small gym.

And when time comes to say goodbye to its pupils, it does it in unforgettable style. A school which drums into its pupils a sense of loyalty, history and tradition rounds off the Bramcote experience with an excellent 'Leavers' Programme' which includes a visit to the Somme.

Bredon School

Pull Court, Bushley, Tewkesbury, Gloucestershire, GL20 6AH

Tel: 01684 293 156

Fax: 01684 298 008

Email: enquiries@bredonschool.org

Website: www.bredonschool.org

• Pupils: 235; 20 per cent girls; 60 per cent board

• Ages: Lower School 7-14, Upper School 14-18

• Religion: C of E • Fees: Boarding £4,555 – £6,465; day £1,825 – £4,215 • School status: Independent

• School gender: Mixed • Day/boarding: Takes boarders

SEN provision

Detail:

Now provide for in school:

Mild: ASP; ADD; ADHD; EBD; DYSC; DYSL; DYSP; HI;

Moderate: ASP; ADD; ADHD; EBD; MLD; DYSC; DYSL;

Severe: DYSL;

Others: SPD; EAL;

Experience of:

Mild: AUT;

Moderate: DYSP;

Others: OCD; TIC; Sp&LD; Epi;

Summary: Individual and individualised SEN teaching and learning is at the heart of the Bredon School philosophy. Students may have a specific learning difficulty such as dyslexia, dyspraxia or dyscalculia, as well as ADHD or ADD and Asperger's syndrome. A specialist in EAL and speech and language is also available. A range of multi-sensory teaching methods are used including the more traditional approaches and methods such as the Davis Learning Strategy. All students are assessed at the start of their individual programme of work and assessed after, against their targets. Targets are set with the student and parents working together with the teacher to achieve a formative document which is reviewed at least twice a year. Real progress is achieved with students both academically and with self-esteem. ICT is also at the heart of our approach, with voice activated software having a tremendous impact upon standards. We also have a fully qualified teacher who assesses all students for their individual special arrangements for the GCSE and other examination courses. The fully qualified SEN staff together with the teaching staff work alongside each other to ensure the curriculum is differentiated to meet individual needs. The school also runs training programmes on a regular basis for its staff on SEN issues and encourages staff to become fully qualified teachers of specific learning difficulties.

What we say about the school - the full Good Schools Guide review

Head: Since 2005, M David Keyte, who's also the proprietor. Parents say he's not an 'out in the front head', contact is more likely to be with one of his very capable leadership team. However we're told he has vision and a knack of developing good junior staff.

Academic Matters: Maximum 15 to a class, but in reality probably 7, often with a teacher and support assistant. School is good at identifying pupil needs and designing programmes to suit. 'They really get to know and understand the individual child, how they learn, what makes them tick, but most importantly my child has grown in confidence and he's happy.' Good facilities, interactive whiteboards, lots of visual and kinaesthetic teaching.

Results wouldn't set the league table world on fire but children often achieve beyond expectation and prediction. This isn't a special school, they take a range of abilities, but some 40 per cent of all children have a recognised learning difference, primarily dyslexia or dyspraxia with others such as Asperger's, ADD and ADHD well catered for. School has a 15 strong learning support team and parents say the head of learning support is bringing the department on in leaps and bounds. She's not afraid to try out new ideas and avenues. What's more this has a knock on effect for those who don't have an SEN: they look at the individual; if taking GCSE maths a year early is right for a child, that's what they'll do.' 'Giving confidence won't cure a child, won't turn an average child into a brilliant scholar, but will help them find themselves and develop learning potential.'

Support is provided in class and at the Access Centre where small group or individual tuition is offered (charged as an extra). Outside support via occupational therapy, speech and language, ed psych etc is used as necessary. Help is also on hand for the 10 per cent or so with EAL requirements. SEN is not viewed as a hindrance. the recent speaker at Founders day, Jon Merricks, a multi-millionaire ex-pupil, said Bredon had been his last hope. Previous schools saw only an angry, lazy child. Bredon uncovered a dyslexic with ADD and gave him vision and confidence. He says he believes dyslexia and ADD are gifts: 'I came to see that while I may not be any good at detail and concentration, I am gifted with vision and being able to see the bigger picture.' Recognised the ADD traits when he met Bill Gates: 'I was just the same, had to sit on my hands to concentrate.'

As well as all the usual curriculum, there's a wide-variety of vocationally orientated courses including GCSEs in catering, art and design, drama, rural and agricultural science, astronomy, dance and PE. A level options are limited but most of the core subjects are offered. Additionally school provides a range of alternative sixth form studies including vocational courses (GNVQ, AVCE, Btec etc) in areas such as business, sport, media, countryside and environment, health and social care, engineering, hospitality and catering and ICT.Has a working farm which children have access to through the curriculum and which provides practical, hands on learning opportunities. Hoping to add a teaching area in the near future. Children help with lambing, muck out the pigs, tend sheep or look after some of the thousands of bedding plants grown in the school greenhouses.

Games, Options, The Arts: All usual sports with a range of others including basketball, trampolining, badminton, tae kwon do. Play regular competitive fixtures. Older students encouraged to work for awards such as sports leader awards, basic education leader award (BELA), British Canoe Union (BCU), D of E or to become qualified lifeguards. Music not a strength, but guitar and woodwind popular with opportunities to perform each term. Range of other activities offered including war hammer, nature studies. Good art, into different mediums: textiles, sculpture, plus woodwork, metal work, plastics. Array of design projects on view: BBQ stands, trailers, go-karts etc.

Background and Atmosphere: Founded in 1962 by Lt-Col Tony Sharp OBE and Hugh Jarrett with just 17 boys, school expanded rapidly under the second headmaster: Brian Llewelyn Thomas. Hit a sticky patch in the late 1990s (school very open about this) but has built up reputation steadily since. At the heart of the 84-acre school campus is Pull Court, a super, Victorian mansion, complete with sweeping staircase and surrounded by park and woodland. Many acres are given over to the school farm but there's plenty left over for the BMX cycle track, adventure play circuit, climbing wall, assault course, zip wire and the open-air swimming pool. Ongoing programme of updating with permission recently granted to develop the listed walled garden. Pupils stand up when adults enter the room, healthy mutual respect. Children recognised for their individuality.

Pastoral Care and Discipline: Parents impressed with pastoral care, see it as a strength of the school. 'My son was very averse to school before his time at Bredon. But Bredon boosted his confidence and self-esteem.' Pastoral care system recently overhauled and largely separated from the academic. Introduced housemistresses and additional nursing staff, children seem more comfortable with this regime. Parents assure us any problems are sorted immediately; say staff listen then act. Bullying not an issue but any that arises immediately stamped on. Mobile phones allowed, child protection issues always taken seriously.

Boarding options are flexible, no Saturday morning school so children can enjoy long weekends at home if they choose. Plenty of activities for those who stay including outings eg to Cotswold wildlife park plus regular shopping trips as well as free time to relax, chill or simply explore and play in the extensive, safe grounds. There is a new, purpose-built sixth form area but much of the boarding accommodation is on the basic side but clean and tidy with lockers etc. Building is old and some areas are tatty. There's a healthy eating initiative, salads always available with choice of warm dishes; that said, we're told the food could be better especially for fussy eaters and apparently the chips are too greasy!

Entrance: Via interview and assessment. All prospective pupils invited to spend a taster day in school. For those with SEN, school will consider both current reports and own assessment to ensure needs can be met by the learning support centre.

Exit: 80 per cent to college or university. Range of courses but typically business studies, agricultural/environmental studies or leisure and tourism.

Remarks: A nurturing school ideal for any child battered and bruised from not ticking the usual boxes. Provides a restorative experience. Parents say: they would recommend to anyone who has a 'sensitive' child with SEN and their other siblings, as they cater well for both.

BRENTWOOD SCHOOL

Ingrave Road, Brentwood, Essex, CM15 8AS

Tel: 01277 243 243

Fax: 01277 243 299

Email: headmaster@brentwood.essex.sch.uk

Website: www.brentwoodschool.co.uk

• Pupils: 697 boys and 425 girls (includes 73 boarders)
• Ages: 11-18 • Religion: C of E • Fees: £3,647 day; £6,318 boarding • School status: Independent • Opendays: October
• School gender: Mixed • Day/boarding: Takes boarders

SEN provision

Detail:

Now provide for in school:

Mild: DYSL; DYSP;

Others: EAL;

Experience of:

Mild: ASP; ADD; EBD; DYSC; HI; CP;

Moderate: DYSL; DYSP;

Severe: DYSL;

Others: OCD; DEL; Epi; Eat;

Summary: The Learning Development Department at Brentwood School aims to support those students who need additional help to access the curriculum fully and become more efficient and effective learners.

The Department provides specialist teaching and resources. Throughout the secondary years, small group tuition, targeted intervention and English as a Foreign Language classes take place.

International students are prepared for IGCSE and IELTS. Students with specific learning difficulties or other special needs are advised and assisted in all aspects of school life. The emphasis of the department is on developing independent learners fully integrated into school life assisted by specialist and subject teachers.

What we say about the school - the full Good Schools Guide review

Headmaster: Since 2004, Mr Ian Davies, formerly head of St Dunstan's College, south London. A graduate of St John's, Oxford, Mr Davies, mid-forties, is a theologian, is married and enjoys skiing, golf, tennis and reading. He is an ISI inspector and helps select naval officers for training at Dartmouth for the Admiralty Interview Board.

Academic Matters: A good spread of subjects and school's size enables it to support strong modern languages dept and seven full-time classicists – one of the biggest such departments in the country. Good choice of A level subjects includes business studies, economics, classical civilisation, D&T product design, drama, ICT, Latin and Greek, PE, psychology and political studies in addition to the usuals. RS is a core subject at GCSE.Results are good. In 2005, 96 per cent GCSE passes A*-C. The sciences, Latin and RS especially strong. At A level, a steeper improvement in recent years and results especially impressive in sciences and minority subjects. SENs supported by two full-time SENCos and 30-plus other staff all of whom have had training. Entrants tested on arrival and individual programmes devised where necessary. 'We want to minimise extraction from lessons ... but we will take them out if necessary.' Children with SENs who inform the school prior to taking entrance tests will be given extra time. 'This is an important part of school life – it's our responsibility.'All subjects taught in their own buildings, floors or wings, many with bang-on modern facilities eg fantastic sports hall (used for major school occasions and weekly whole school assembly), dance studios etc, super new science study centre. Impressive, purpose-built Hardy Amies Design Centre, named after and opened by OB Sir Hardy Amies – the Queen's favourite couturier – houses DT, food tech, and ICT and is an inspiration to exceptional work. Elsewhere, in more antiquated areas, a few tired-looking classrooms and labs lag behind. Last head said, 'we're particularly good at getting the best out of those who are academically average ... we operate fairly small groups ... there is a tradition here of regularly monitoring progress, especially of those who are middle-of -the-road ... we do it very thoroughly indeed.'

Games, Options, The Arts: Outstanding, above all in fencing. Current head of school is the U17 Sabre World Champion. At time of our visit, the 1st, 2nd and 3rd in the national U17s boys fencing squad and the Under 20 National Champion are pupils. In 2002 Commonwealth Games a sixth form girl achieved two gold medals. Coaches include two Commonwealth silver medallists. Superb facilities and school very proud and conscious of its prowess. Equally good at football – school holds best overall playing record in the Boodle and Dunthorne FA Cup in its 12 years. Other top sports include tennis, cross-country, cricket and squash. An excellent pool, acres of pitches, fields and courts provide something for everyone. Games rooms for those who prefer not to get hot or muddy.

School has country's largest voluntary CCF corps. Also popular and still expanding community service unit does good things in the locality. Good spacious facilities for music and drama and a lively, ambitious programme for both. Galleried, adaptable music studio. Orchestra tours annually to Siena. Big Band much in demand for local events. Lots of instrumentalists and a whole, huge room devoted to the Sibelius computer programme. Good art studios in the Hardy Amies Design Centre with focused themed work and, when we visited, lots of exuberant work going up for the annual art exhibition. Unique and glorious asset – an outdoor stage with grassed platform in a gorgeous walled and tree-lined garden.

Background and Atmosphere: An ancient foundation – school started life in 1557 and still has a building dating from not long after that – 'Old Big School' – in which relics are tenderly preserved. School clearly proud of its history and documents displayed on walls. John Donne signed its charter in 1622! Well-endowed and well-husbanded, school maintains its vast site, plus many buildings of varying architectural vintages and merits, with care and flair. Lots of domestic properties on the perimeter owned by school in which staff are housed – adding to the solid community feel of the place. Well-stocked and nurtured gardens fill spaces between blocks and pitches. Chapel built in 1867 is heart of pastoral life and is a bit of a gem. Also Memorial Hall – good wood-panelled building with splendid proscenium arch, organ, gallery and notable ceiling.

Unusual feature of daily life is that boys and girls are taught separately until the sixth form – popular with both sexes and parents and seems to resolve the perennial problem of single sex v co-ed in a sensible and equitable way. Also works academically, 'the gap between our boys' and girls' GCSE results is much smaller than the national one,' said head. Largely a day school, with a minority of indigenous boarders, life at weekends can seem a little limited for those who don't want to work all the time – though school stresses that all school facilities are available throughout weekends and explains that timetabled lessons, formerly on Saturdays, now take place during the week allowing more time for extra-curricular activities during the weekend with a hugely increased programme. Saturday school abandoned 2004. Uniform throughout – and stiffly enforced – though a relaxation of styles in the sixth. Girls are noticeably and distinctively smart in Amies designed mid-calf skirts and box jackets which seem not to have dated since arrival in 1995, though they are hot on warm days ('shirt sleeve order is applied on hot days' says the school). Brentwood is a prosperous area though, according to an insider,' the most boring town in England'. Fast trains into Liverpool Street and two minutes to the M25 help if you need to escape.

Pastoral Care and Discipline: Girls board in super late Victorian Mill Hill house. 2-4 share in first three years, 2 share in years 10-12 and most upper sixth have single rooms. These rooms are the largest we have seen in boarding houses – real nesting places and very unlike the cupboards and cubicles being built elsewhere. Boys in 1960s block on edge of pitch – with similar facilities – though less attractive ambiance. Both houses well-kept and well-maintained, comfortable and with a real family feel. Food, eaten in attractive and civilised dining hall with Head, staff and children all together, is good. We spotted chocolate sponge with chocolate custard for the first time since junior school days and – well, what would you have done? Discipline is tight. Pupils are tidy, the place is orderly and behaviour is unusually good. Praepostors – 'praes' – are prefects and do lots of jobs involving minor discipline etc. Have own room in sixth form centre and some privileges. Clear drugs policy. Works with parents, police and a testing régime after single offence but no mercy if you deal or 'persuade' a friend. Generally friendly relations between staff and students – a relaxed and purposeful feel. Previous head felt by some to be too heavy on the discipline and much interest now in how the atmosphere changes under new regime.

Pupils and Parents: Vast majority from immediate locality. Proximity of Ford's UK HQ means plenty of high-paid execs send their children here but also builders, retailers and everyone else. Not much independent sector competition but lots from Chelmsford's highly selective – free – grammars, though no one can compete with school's site and facilities. Boarders from all over the world. Many first time buyers but also loyal OBs who send their offspring. Pupils are friendly, courteous and unpretentious. Weekly boarding, and flexi is growing in popularity but little room for expansion at present. OBs include Robin Day, Douglas Adams, Peter Stothard, Griff Rhys-Jones, Noel Edmonds, Frank Lampard jnr, Nick Scheele – and Sir Hardy Amies.

Entrance: Significant number from own prep school but also from other good local preps and juniors. Assessment via school's own tests or CE – school looks for 55 per cent across the board but 'if they dip below and they're strong in the core subjects, I can take them on,' said last head. For the sixth, you need minimum of 6 Bs at GCSE with an A grade in subjects to be studied at A level.

Exit: Great range of destinations includes Reading, Loughborough, Birmingham, Kent, Essex, Royal Holloway and King's London. Seven to Oxbridge in 2005. Large numbers study economics/business studies; engineering also popular as are other science-based subjects – courses from robotics to criminology.

Money Matters: Fair range of academic scholarships and bursaries. Head believes in non-means-tested awards to attract academically top-flight students, 'though we do have an increasing number of means-tested bursaries'. Music, drama, sports and art scholarships.

Remarks: A good, orderly school offering a sound start in life. Especially worth considering if you like the separate teaching of girls and boys, if a small school is not a prerequisite or if you aren't likely to make it past the stiff competition of the local grammars. So much going for it, it could hit the heights under promising new incumbent and well worth watching.

BRIGHTON AND HOVE HIGH SCHOOL

Montpelier Road, Brighton, East Sussex, BN1 3AT

Tel: 01273 734 112

Fax: 01273 737 120

Email: enquiries@bhhs.gdst.net

Website: www.gdst.net/bhhs

• Pupils: 420 girls, all day • Ages: 11-18 • Religion: Non-denom • Fees: £2,455 • School status: Independent • Opendays: Late September, October, late February and early May • School gender: Girls • Day/boarding: Day pupils

SEN provision

Detail:

Experience of:

Mild: DYSL; DYSP; HI; VI;
Moderate: DYSL; DYSP;
Others: PD;

Summary: A careful register is kept of special needs and individual support clinics are offered as needed. Teaching staff are advised regularly of developments and special support needed.

In the Senior School there are or have been pupils with registered special needs. Some are dyslexic or dyspraxic, others mildly so. There are or have been pupils with hearing or visual difficulties, others with motor difficulties of various kinds. No current pupils have EFL requirements. In the Junior School pupils are supported within the class.

What we say about the school - the full Good Schools Guide review

Head: Since 2004, Mrs Ann Greatorex (rising 50), married no children. A linguist, with an MA in educational politics from Sussex University. Was head of City of

Portsmouth boys' school and before that was deputy head at Bishop Luffa School Chichester. A wide range of experience and during her four years in Portsmouth she very quickly turned around a failing school. Took over from Miss Ros Woodbridge who had been in post for some considerable time and was loved by all, but new head is energetic, friendly and competent with a good sense of humour.

The school has a traditional and academic reputation and, whilst careful not to diminish this or make sweeping changes too soon, head has plenty of ideas up her sleeve. Believes in single sex education between 11-16 years but is considering the setting-up of Diamond schools (ie co-ed 3-11 and co-ed 16-18) the latter about to be launched in another Trust school in Cardiff. Wants to broaden the range of subjects, see the sixth form grow in size, and would like to cater for girls with a broader range of educational needs particularly the dyslexic and the very gifted.

Academic Matters: Academic results excellent, dedicated staff passionate about their subjects. Bright, stimulating, independently minded, confident girls – a description approved by parents, staff and the local general public. Pupils are very conscientious and pile the pressure on themselves but are encouraged to progress as individuals rather than through competitive peer rivalry. English very popular; particularly hot on poetry and awarded 1st place by the Keats House and the Poetry Society for the school Poetry Landmark of the Year. For book week 2005 they lured the Poet Laureate to work with the girls on war poetry.Also involved with raising funds for the British Library for the specific conservation costs of editions of Pride and Prejudice and Robinson Crusoe. A published authoress is on staff; the book week runs as a cross-curricular activity involving history front page competitions, geography travel brochures and a dress up day – the new head dressed as Cruella de Vil calling the staff her 'puppies'. History is taught well – we popped into one lesson and witnessed a virtuoso performance in how to elicit facts and develop arguments with a captivated audience of year 11 girls. Some parents report that a watchful eye had to be kept on the volume of homework. Many girls leave for sixth form colleges because of the limited range of subjects available here; head is keen to eg extend languages beyond Europe and introduce Mandarin.Careers programme very impressive with close links with the local careers service and employers. Year 9 girls receive individual careers guidance with consultants; all girls have free psychometric testing in year 10 and prepare their own action plan. There is an intensive programme of visiting speakers and workshops. The Minerva network puts girls in touch with past pupils who are successful in the career in which they are showing an interest.

Games, Options, The Arts: Facilities much improved by the addition of modern new light sports hall with disabled access (lifts), two outdoor netball courts and an Astroturf court. Winners of the U12/U13 netball County Championship for the last three years, and recent Athletic Sports Champions. Plenty of clubs appear to be on offer, but the general consensus is that sport is not hugely high profile. Girls remark, 'if you are very keen on sport, you wouldn't choose this school or would have to follow up with activities outside the school' – disputed by school which considers that they fully support good athletes in their chosen sport.

Parents laud the singing. Policy of music for all, plenty of experimenting with instruments and sound. Drama well taught, housed in a brand new studio. The Art and Design block has a bright, industrious fizz about it. Excellent photography, sculptures, textiles/costumes.

Background and Atmosphere: The original building (the Temple) became part of the GDST schools in 1880. Still central to the site with pillars said to represent inverted cannons. The school has vastly changed in the past few years – the GDST has carried out extensive improvements, refurbishment and contemporary glass additions so that the past dowdiness has been transformed into a bright cluster of buildings. Food most acceptable – although many pupils bring packed lunches.

Pastoral Care and Discipline: Strong pastoral support system with form teachers and sixth form tutors and year heads – set up for easy communication and accessibility. Sixth forms and year 10 offer a mentoring service for younger girls – this is made easy by the amount of inter-year, inter-house contact through drama, sport competitions and end of year entertainment. Imaginative PSHE – we have encountered this in other Trust schools – the special events and whole days given over to topical issues all help to raise awareness and assist pupils with self-expression on current affairs. Parents agree that the school exudes a disciplined, contained, respectful industrious environment that suits an ambitious, organised, self-motivated pupil. Some believe that within this there is still room for the individual eccentric, others feel that staff were fazed by combative girls. One past pupil told us 'they often celebrated feisty pupils – but distinctly rebels with a cause and not those without – there was plenty of room for spirited girls but not for those who did not value what the school offers'. Bullying not a problem – the school would take a serious stance and anti-bullying workshops are held.

Pupils and Parents: Principally Brighton with a good percentage coming from surrounding Pulborough, Eastbourne, Worthing, etc. A real social and ethnic mix and, due to competitive fees, a good economic mix. OGs Karen Pickering MBE – Olympic Swimming Gold Medallist, Heidi Cooper who won the 2004 Young Director of the year (IoD), Beth Cordingley from The Bill, several recent University Challenge competitors. One girl from the school won the Minerva Prize this year – national GDST award for all round excellence and jolly good egg!

Entrance: Not as heavily over-subscribed as in the recent past; girls come from a wide range of local maintained and independent schools and also the junior school. GDST entrance assessment for the main school, at junior level there are a range of tests, see children at play and interview them. Entry at sixth form requires five GCSEs at C grade or above with A or B in subjects to be taken at A level.

Exit: Some 20-30 leave at 16+ to enjoy co-ed at the local sixth form college, or because other institutions offer a wider range of subjects; some leave to go to co-ed private education. Those that stay are mainly destined for serious universities studying serious subjects, many into medicine, including medical science and veterinary medicine, sport science, natural sciences, earth systems science, geology, zoology, engineering, etc. 37 per cent have taken science degrees. A handful take a gap year.

Money Matters: A healthy bundle of bursaries. Academic scholarships up to 50 per cent of the fees.

Remarks: A successful and thriving school where girls grow focused and confident in their abilities. New head should bring in more flair and breadth.

BRIGHTON COLLEGE

Eastern Rd, Brighton, East Sussex, BN2 0AL

Tel: 01273 704 200

Fax: 01273 704 204

Email: registrar@brightoncollege.net

Website: www.brightoncollege.net

• Pupils: 720; 450 boys, 270 girls; 575 day, 145 board • Ages: 13-18 • Religion: Non-denom • Fees: Day £4,617; weekly boarding £6,286; full boarding £7,157 • School status: Independent • Opendays: One Saturday per term • School gender: Mixed • Day/boarding: Takes boarders

SEN provision

Detail:

Centre of excellence for:
- Mild: DYSL; DYSP;
- Moderate: DYSL;
- Severe: DYSL;
- Others: EAL;

Experience of:
- Mild: ASP; AUT; ADD; EBD; DYSC; SpLD;
- Moderate: ASP; DYSC; DYSP;

Summary: Brighton College specialises in helping bright dyslexic children to achieve their academic potential whilst, at the same time, providing them with a stimulating environment in which to develop their strengths and talents. The school has its own Dyslexia Centre which supports children from each of the three schools of Brighton College: the Pre-Prep School, the Prep School and the Senior School. Up to the end of year 6, pupils receive a combination of in-class support in English and small group withdrawal for specialist teaching. From year 7 onwards, full members of the Dyslexia Centre receive all their English lessons in the centre in groups no larger than 9. In addition, most (but not all) dyslexic pupils substitute their modern languages time for additional support. For those pupils whose needs require less support, ad hoc provision is available. In the sixth form, an AS/A Level study skills course is available, together with individual support lessons.

Pupils with other special educational needs are the responsibility of the three special needs co-ordinators (SENCos). The school is always happy to discuss individual needs with parents, although it recognises that the level of provision it can currently offer may not be sufficient to support all special educational needs.

The school has a separate department for the support of those pupils whose first language is not English.

What we say about the school - the full Good Schools Guide review

Headmaster: From 2006, Mr Richard Cairns, previously Usher (sole deputy head) of Magdalen College School. Succeeds high profile Dr Anthony Seldon who has taken over at Wellington College.

Academic Matters: Performing very strongly, despite not being particularly selective. Over 77 per cent grades A/B at A level, over 67 per cent A/A* at GCSE ('I could push us radically up the league tables if I got rid of the bottom 10 per cent but I don't think that's the moral thing to do,' said Dr Seldon, the previous, very high profile, head). Twenty-nine subjects offered at A level. Class sizes are capped at 20 up to GCSE; after GCSE, the average class size is eight. No Saturday morning school. Good support for bright dyslexics and dyspraxics limited support for other SEN but will strive to work with any child in the school and to manage their needs. Occasionally advises parents to seek an alternative school.

School has a dyslexia centre with separate admission arrangements. Actively seeks out and welcomes the bright child with dyslexia. Entry based on recent EP report, assessment morning (observed in groups) and interviews by head and excellent head of centre, Mr David Ollosson. Severity of dyslexia isn't an issue, looking for potential. Says, 'if we feel a child will get there we will take them on that basis regardless of CE performance, even if they can barely read and write on entry.' Stresses, 'staff and peers recognise potential of dyslexics, we believe in their abilities, talents and needs, they often do better than their peers, we provide an environment in which they achieve.'

Approximately 160 children are taught in the centre (from all three schools). Work in groups, believes this is best way to offer full support, says group is very important, chuldren become fantastically supportive of one another, offer each other support even though it's not a discrete group within the year (included with peers in main school for all other subjects). One to one teaching offered only in sixth form but anyone can seek help outside of timetable if they have individual concerns.

Younger children are offered a mix of in class support and withdrawal. Senior pupils taught English in centre (max group size 9), offered maths support too if needed. Takes additional time from languages (though pupils can still study languages if desired). Concentrates on remediation with younger ones and study skills with older. Says taking complete control of English makes a huge difference, removes embarrassment and stress. Time to finish tasks not an issue – a good end product motivates students. Giving time results in outstanding imaginative works, brings on their English and increases confidence. Facilities include 'text help read and write' which was deemed fantastic by inspector on recent visit. (Programme reads back work punctuated as written and will read out spellings when spell checking.) Adds, 'take control of English as a whole process and help manage reading, writing and spelling together rather than in isolation. Can work up a particular area but for dyslexics, organisation and managing tasks simultaneously is difficult so we try to integrate skills from the start rather than concentrate on individual components.'

Games, Options, The Arts: Sport is enormously important here, with most pupils taking part in games two afternoons a week. Cricket, rugby, athletics, soccer and netball are popular, and pupils sail at a local reservoir. Wisden cricket school of the year in 2003. Girl cricketers reached the finals of the national girls' cricket competition at Lords at 2000, and one (while 15) played in an Ashes test. Clare Connor, captain of the England Women's Cricket team and former pupil, is Head of PR, teaches English and coaches girls' cricket. Heated swimming pool, two Astroturf hockey pitches.

Music thriving – the school has a choir, orchestra, concert band and various chamber groups – and parents rave about the school's drama productions. Excellent art department. Dance facilities much improved with the opening of a new performing arts centre. Lots of cultural trips and an impressive sixth form lecture programme – speakers range from diplomats to the chaplain of Wormwood Scrubs.

Community service is a vital part of school life – pupils help elderly people and disabled children, raise money for charity; some have even visited a Romanian orphanage. The college has formed strong links with disadvantaged state schools and Dr Seldon was involved in various (much-needed) initiatives to rejuvenate Brighton – 'I want our children to be aware they're in a privileged position. If we just turn out successful stockbrokers or lawyers without a social conscience, I think we've failed,' he said.

Background and Atmosphere: Imposing Victorian buildings designed by Sir George Gilbert Scott. In the winter, the buildings have a rather severe, Hound of the Baskervilles air; altogether more welcoming in summer. A short walk into central Brighton; sea views.

The school has had mixed fortunes since it was founded as a nursery for Christian gentlemen – bankrupt three times and almost closed twice. Dr Seldon was appointed head after its most recent financial crisis, in 1997. Enormous hoo-ha – 15 staff were made redundant – but he succeeded in turning the school around and there are now two-year waiting lists in some age groups. Lots of new teachers.

Massive (£4 million) recent building programme included putting in nine extra classrooms, building the performing arts centre, upgrading the sports hall, improving IT facilities, creation of the Rose Lecture theatre and upgrading the library. Pupils love the Café de Paris, a French-style café where they eat lunch once a week and meet to socialise. Despite the improvements, this is a town school and there is limited room for expansion. The new sports ground is a 15-minute walk away and some classrooms are rather cramped.

Pastoral Care and Discipline: Caring, motivated, youngish staff. 'They're very aware of what's going on and the kids trust them,' comments a parent. A 'family school,' with pupils encouraged to treat each other decently. The school's ethos is that discipline has to come from within – pupils who repeatedly step out of line will be told to leave. Liberal in many ways, but not on drugs (Brighton and Hove have a serious druggy culture, alas). Religion offered but not emphasised – indeed, the prep school chapel was recently turned into a library.

Pupils and Parents: The school's increasingly high profile means that more of its pupils commute from outside the Brighton area. Parents are an intriguing mix of old money and funky arty types – mothers waiting outside the school gates are just as likely to sport combat trousers and navel rings as Prada handbags. Serious commitment to co-education, as evidenced by the number of women in the senior management team. In 1997, 25 per cent of pupils were girls; that number has risen to almost 38 per cent. Pupils are generally cheerful, enthusiastic, friendly and polite and have an easy, relaxed relationship with teachers.

Entrance: At 13, by CE if they attend prep school; if not, after an assessment. Children who achieve 55 (used to be 50) per cent at CE are accepted, especially if they excel at music, sport or another activity. Entrance also at sixth form.

Exit: Almost all to university, with many taking a gap year. Wide range of subjects chosen. Old Brightonians include sculptor David Nash, racing driver Jonathan Palmer, writer Peter Mayle, explorer Sir Vivian Fuchs and actor Sir Michael Hordern (who has a performance space named after him).

Money Matters: Fees reasonable. Some scholarships and bursaries available.

Remarks: Happy, modern, un-snobby, forward-looking school that has staged a remarkable comeback over the past few years – thanks mainly to its inspiring last head. Terrific for bright, energetic, robust pupils who like to keep busy; not ideal for the shy and retiring.

BRIGHTON COLLEGE JUNIOR SCHOOL PRE-PREPARATORY

Sutherland Road, Brighton, East Sussex, BN2 2EQ

Tel: 01273 704 200

Fax: 01273 704 204

Email: registrar@brightoncollege.net

Website: www.brightoncollege.net

• Pupils: 185 boys and girls • Ages: 3-7 • Religion: Non-denom
• Fees: £1,154-£2,419 • School status: Independent
• Opendays: One or two mornings and evenings per term
• School gender: Mixed • Day/boarding: Day pupils

SEN provision

Summary: Brighton College specialises in helping bright dyslexic children to achieve their academic potential whilst, at the same time, providing them with a stimulating environment in which to develop their strengths and talents. The school has its own Dyslexia Centre which supports children from each of the three schools of Brighton College: the Pre-Prep School, the Prep

School and the Senior School. Up to the end of year 6, pupils receive a combination of in-class support in English and small group withdrawal for specialist teaching. From year 7 onwards, full members of the Dyslexia Centre receive all their English lessons in the centre in groups no larger than 9. In addition, most (but not all) dyslexic pupils substitute their modern languages time for additional support. For those pupils whose needs require less support, ad hoc provision is available. In the sixth form, an AS/A Level study skills course is available, together with individual support lessons. Pupils with other special educational needs are the responsibility of the three special needs co-ordinators (SENCos). The school is always happy to discuss individual needs with parents, although it recognises that the level of provision it can currently offer may not be sufficient to support all special educational needs. The school has a separate department for the support of those pupils whose first language is not English. Please see Brighton College for response to questionnaire which covers all three schools.

Brighton College Prep School

Walpole Lodge, Walpole Road, Brighton, East Sussex, BN2 0EU

Tel: 01273 704 210
Fax: 01273 704 286
Email: registrar@brightoncollege.net
Website: www.brightoncollege.net

• Pupils: 295 boys and girls, all day • Ages: 8-12 • Religion: Non-denom • Fees: £2,945-£3,775 • School status: Independent • Opendays: One Saturday per term • School gender: Mixed • Day/boarding: Day pupils

SEN provision

Detail:

Centre of excellence for:
- Mild: DYSL; DYSP;
- Moderate: DYSL;
- Severe: DYSL;
- Others: EAL;

Experience of:
- Mild: ASP; AUT; ADD; EBD; DYSC; SpLD;
- Moderate: ASP; DYSC; DYSP;

Summary: Brighton College specialises in helping bright dyslexic children to achieve their academic potential whilst, at the same time, providing them with a stimulating environment in which to develop their strengths and talents. The school has its own Dyslexia Centre which supports children from each of the three schools of Brighton College: the Pre-Prep School, the Prep School and the Senior School. Up to the end of year 6, pupils receive a combination of in-class support in English and small group withdrawal for specialist teaching. From year 7 onwards, full members of the Dyslexia Centre receive all their English lessons in the centre in groups no larger than 9. In addition, most (but not all) dyslexic pupils substitute their modern languages time for additional support. For those pupils whose needs require less support, ad hoc provision is available. In the sixth form, an AS/A Level study skills course is available, together with individual support lessons.

Pupils with other special educational needs are the responsibility of the three special needs co-ordinators (SENCos). The school is always happy to discuss individual needs with parents, although it recognises that the level of provision it can currently offer may not be sufficient to support all special educational needs.

The school has a separate department for the support of those pupils whose first language is not English. Please see Brighton College for response to questionnaire which covers all three schools.

Bruern Abbey School

Chesterton House, Chesterton, Bicester, Oxfordshire, OX26 1UY

Tel: 01869 242 448
Fax: 01869 243 949
Email: bruernabbey2002@yahoo.com
Website: www.bruernabbey.org

• Pupils: 51 boys, most board • Ages: 7/8-13 • Religion: Inter-denom • Fees: Day £4,395; boarding £5,505 • School status: Independent • School gender: Boys • Day/boarding: Takes boarders

SEN provision

Detail:

Now provide for in school:
- Mild: ASP; AUT; ADD; ADHD; DYSC; DYSL; DYSP; VI;

Moderate: ADD; MLD; DYSC; DYSL; DYSP;
Severe: DYSL;
Others: SPD; PMLD; Sp&LD;
Experience of:
Mild: HI;
Moderate: ASP; HI;
Severe: DYSC;
Others: SLD; EAL;

Summary: Bruern Abbey is in so many ways a traditional preparatory school, with its raison d'etre being to prepare boys for Common Entrance to reputable Public Schools. Yet, all the boys at Bruern experience some kind of specific learning difficulty, or range of difficulties, to a degree that for confidence to be restored and for academic potential to be fufilled, they would benefit from small classes, an intensive focus on literacy and numeracy and a genuinely multi-sensory approach to delivering the curriculum, including the use of a personal laptop.

Children are taught by trained and experienced 'specialists' in special needs education and by subject teachers who have an ongoing, in-service training programme, monitored by the Helen Arkell Dyslexia Centre, that helps them understand the difficulties encountered by the dyslexic or dyspraxic child.

What we say about the school - the full Good Schools Guide review

Headmaster: Since 2002, succeeding founder, Mr Sterling Stover, Mr Philip Fawkes MBA CertEd (early fifties). The wonderful Mr Fawkes was head of Twyford School, Winchester for five years before he and his wife, Jane, arrievd at Bruern. Educated at Embley Park (where he also taught and set up the junior school), and Keele University, where he took his MBA in education – a rare commodity 'and it shows', commented a parent, appreciatively. Prior to Twyford he was head of Lathallan Prep in Scotland, which he took from being a somewhat small and sleepy underfunded establishment to, perhaps, the most dynamic prep school in Scotland, by dint of 'man management' and 'marketing skills', not to mention use of Pavlovian techniques to get parents through the door. Senior coach for the national Cricket Association, former chairman of selectors for the Hampshire Schools' Cricket Association under 19 XI. Dogs Kristy and Bonnie. One daughter, Sophie, studying medicine at Exeter University.

Remarks: Although the school runs from 7-8 to 13, many boys come at nine or ten; ie they have gone to a conventional prep school and their dyslexia or whatever has been picked up and frantic parents have finally found the answer to their prays. Recent increase in staff. Not cheap, the school is nearing capacity, but a capital expenditure programme is underway. Recent developments include repair to the old eighteenth-century 'orangery', which is now back in use as a theatre and chapel, more classroom provision and a new science complex. Tiny classes plus one-to-one teaching. Computers everywhere, laptops for all and early keyboarding skills taught. French for all. Most go on to the school of their choice (and we have met them there) – Stowe, Tonbridge, Wellington, Haileybury, Shiplake, Canford, Milton Abbey and Winchester College were on the 2005 list.

Masses of extra-curricular, plus real games against real schools (albeit it may be The Dragon's umpteenth rugby team, but they do get out and play). Golf, judo, fencing, ornithology, polo, shooting; good art and a fantastic rapport with the kitchen. When we visited, almost half the school (which is basically weekly boarding) had opted to help John 'do an Octoberfest' and were just off to the woods to pick mushrooms. As a matter of principle, the food – which if the excellent lunch we had was anything to go by – is carefully controlled, no tuck, no fizzy drinks. And there are magical parents-invited dinners by candlelight on Tuesdays and Thursdays.

Stars for glory, stripes for disobedience, 'most boys have thirty or forty stars by half term'. This is a perfect boy-orientated school, woods, a stream, masses of dens and really rather a handsome building; some slight (!) disrepair still but rolling programme of refurbishment and the boys love the place. No disgrace in coming here.

Some ecstatic reports from parents, but the school has a very particular style. No longer a stop-over for good staff – they appear to be staying. Recent ISI (May 2005)and National Care Standards Commission Inspections went 'swimmingly'. Report was highly complimentary about special needs provision.

Brymore School

Cannington, Bridgwater, Somerset, TA5 2NB

Tel: 01278 652 369
Fax: 01278 653 244
Email: office@brymore.somerset.sch.uk
Website: www.brymore.somerset.sch.uk

• Pupils: 150 boarders, 40 day; all boys • Ages: 13-17 • Religion: Inter-denom • Fees: Boarding £1,900 • School status: State • Opendays: Last Saturday in June – plus country fair • School gender: Boys • Day/boarding: Takes boarders

SEN provision

Detail:

Now provide for in school:

Mild: ADD; ADHD; EBD; DYSC; DYSL; SpLD; VI;
Moderate: ASP; ADD; DYSC; DYSL; DYSP; SpLD;
Others: Epi;

Experience of:

Mild: DYSP; HI;
Moderate: EBD; VI;
Severe: ADD; DYSC; DYSL;
Others: CD; OCD; TIC; Eat;

Summary: The SEN department at Brymore is staffed by a friendly and experienced team. We aim to support 90 per cent of the timetable in year 9 lower sets. We offer daily reading sessions for small groups and individuals, also daily help is offered to support prep.

What we say about the school - the full Good Schools Guide review

Head: Since 2003, Mr Malcolm Lloyd (early fifties), who was a boarder at Woodbridge, Suffolk before training as a PE teacher at College of St Mark and St John when it was still in Chelsea. Added PGCE in youth and community to his BEd degree and started career as PE teacher cum youth tutor at Tessbourne Community School, Barnstaple before moving to Harrow as youth officer. Spent 15 years as community education co-ordinator in Frome prior to appointment at Brymore. Whilst at Frome had organised joint skiing trips with Brymore so governors were aware that he would suit. Refreshingly honest and straightforward, he is respected by boys who catch his understated enthusiasm. Equally at home in front of a computer, on the rugby pitch or in the milking parlour. Lives on site during term time whilst partner Hilary still teaches in Frome and joins him at weekends. Had hoped to bring golfing handicap below 10 by age fifty. Loves sea and mountains. Enjoys painting and photography. Something of an entrepreneurial maverick who understands how boys tick and fits Brymore to a T.

Academic Matters: The curriculum is dominated by horticulture, agriculture and engineering which occupy a third of the time-table and most of a boy's spare time. Despite this, one third of pupils gain at least five GCSEs grade A-Cs – remarkable when a large proportion of 13-year-olds arrive with a reading age less than chronological age. Recently introduced for year 12, and much applauded by Ofsted, a one-year Btec Intermediate Diploma course in land-based skills and a one year NVQ level 2 course in engineering. Both involve 6+ weeks of work experience.

Special needs dept kept busy with 24 statemented pupils and some 100 others with moderate learning difficulties/dyslexia.

Games, Options, The Arts: In keeping with the school's ethos, there is emphasis on team effort rather than individual winners. A rugby team for each year group have a healthy jostle with Millfield B teams. An impressive 19 athletes at county level (hammer, pole-vaulting, cross-country, road-running gets to Nationals), much made of D of E (bronze and silver). Enthusiastic golf, fishing, mountain biking, and badger watching. A resurgence of Young Farmers Club. Business incentive scheme linked with Barnardo's offers year 12 chance to be involved with a business venture while raising money for charity.

Background and Atmosphere: The Brymore school of Rural Technology was set up in 1952 for the sons of Somerset farmers in a stunning site of 60 acres between the sea and the Quantock Hills. A half-mile tree lined drive divides rape fields to the left, farm buildings to the right. The school and main boarding housed in a 17th cent mansion originally owned by a notorious Civil War figure, John Pym, Oliver Cromwell's right hand man. The original stable yard, complete with clock tower has been converted to metal and wood workshops, two blacksmiths' forges, and foundry to industrial standards. No wonder the ghost of John Pym still roams the ex-stable (noises of restless horse hooves on cobbles at night).

Motto 'Diligentia et Labore'. Classrooms in utilitarian blocks left behind by US Cavalry billeted during the war. In the impeccably kept one-acre walled garden dating from 1753 the school vegetables are tended and every boy can have his own allotment. The pupils are responsible for complete upkeep of entire estate – tree pruning, grass cutting, weeding, planting flower beds all lead to a NVQ. A self-financing farm is at the heart of this unique set-up, lambing a flock of 50 ewes, rearing free-range chickens, beef cattle and pigs (much of which ends up in delicious meals for pupils) and milking cows at 6am on a crisp winter morning are essential parts of the learning. 'Backing a tractor through a gateway and getting 10 out of 10 in a spelling test are of equal value here,' says the head, who takes boys who have not thrived in mainstream schools. The knack of his resourceful staff is to turn boys who have seen themselves as failures into confident, responsible young men who all progress to further education or employment.

Golden jubilee 2002/3, supported by Prince of Wales, involved heli-pad purpose-built for his visit.

Pastoral Care and Discipline: No religious affinity. No written set of school rules. Instead, boys are instilled with common sense, given responsibility at an early age and taught by example. Ofsted was moved to wax lyrical – 'pupils respond like buds opening in the sunshine' and praised the personal development and behaviour of pupils. Serious offences dealt with by counselling, withdrawal of privileges, detention and ultimately exclusion. Years 11 and 12 become prefects to assist staff with operating rewards system. In farm and horticultural dept senior boys have real responsibility.

Pupils and Parents: Mostly white with one or two overseas. Mixed backgrounds: 40 per cent come from Somerset, rest mainly from Wilts, Devon, Dorset, Cornwall, South Wales but some from much further afield. All pupils wear blazers and ties for assembly each day, though black sweatshirt is the norm for daywear. OBs include Neil Parish the Euro MP; Mark Irish, English U21 rugby player; Julian Anderson, world windsurfing champion.

Entrance: Between 60 and 70 admitted at 13, selected on aptitude and commitment. Parents and boys interviewed after applying with questionnaire and short essay.

Exit: 71 per cent to horticultural/agricultural colleges such as Lackam, Sparsholt, Kingston Manward, Dutchy College, Cornwall or closer to home – Cannington College and Bridgewater. 13 per cent into employment. 10 per cent to apprenticeships/work based learning.

Money Matters: Boarding fees moderate. Some pupils funded by educational grants from their own LEAs. Up to 10 bursaries in each year, means tested, for one third of fees.

Remarks: State boarding school with a strong practical bias. Magnificently warm and empathetic staff know how to get the best from their boys. No-frills boarding with excellent teaching in practical domain. The only school of its kind in the country.

Cademuir International School

Crawfordton House, Moniaive, Thornhill, DG3 4HG

Tel: 01848 200 212

Fax: 01848 200 336

Email: cademuir1@aol.com

Website: www.cademuir.com

• Pupils: 60 boys, 20 girls (max 85); all board but one
• Ages: 9-18 • Religion: Non-denom • Fees: £5,600-£7,000
• School status: Independent • School gender: Mixed
• Day/boarding: Takes boarders

SEN provision

Detail:

Centre of excellence for:

Mild: ASP; AUT; ADD; ADHD; DYSL; DYSP;
Moderate: ASP; ADD; ADHD; DYSL; DYSP;

Summary: No comment. Determined to remain a well-kept secret? Seriously good provision. SEN details added by us.

What we say about the school - the full Good Schools Guide review

Head and Founder: Since 1990, Mr Robert Mulvey BA DIL (sixties) who read languages at Edinburgh University (and was busy practising them during our recent visit), followed by Aix Marseille University and previously taught in Paris and at Aberlour. Mr Mulvey, married, with two sons (one is dyslexic and has an honours degree in

English from Stirling University) and a daughter, who is bursar at the school.

Convinced that there was no easy answer for either the dyslexic (and that includes all forms of learning difficulties) nor for the gifted pupil, Mr Mulvey founded the school in the former Dr Barnardo's campus in Peebles to cater for both. This is his baby. And though he will be 65 this year, he has no thoughts of retiring; he is, after all, chairman of the governors (a very respectable bunch) and is still looking for an acceptable successor. Meantime he continues to keep an overall eye (albeit sometimes a slightly remote one) and does much of the marketing. The school is handled on a day-to-day basis by Mr Hornby, Dr Francis and Mrs Hill who run the weekend activities, the academic and the pastoral (in that order). Mr Hornby is acting principal.

Academic Matters: Follows the Scottish system but this is misleading. Classes are tiny – often two or three pupils per lesson – and children do exams when they are ready; moving between classes according to their ability. This is not an age-led establishment. Pupils may take Advanced Higher in maths at 14, and then join 11-year-olds for beginners' Spanish, and an earlier 14-year-old was offered two unconditional places at university. Results excellent, numbers too small to qualify for any statistic! Pupil to staff ratio 4:1 (unheard of in our experience); native speakers for all languages. EFL on offer where needed. Some children take three languages in the Scottish Higher system whilst coming from a fourth country. French, German, Spanish on tap. Sciences no problem, and really good maths, English and the humanities.

Mentors on hand for each age group and learning support throughout. Extra tutorials on hand and no shame to ask the staff for help at anytime (even if often at inappropriate moments). No 'real difficulties' in getting suitable staff, those whom we met were enthusiastic and dedicated; many have training in special learning needs and pupils are assessed on arrival. Statemented and children with records of needs welcomed. Computers all over, though not the most modern that we have seen and the computer class when we visited had eight pupils all working on their own projects in a variety of languages and 'no you can't buy another iPod on eBay' then became a topic of discussion. 'Why not?' 'Was it too expensive?'

Games, Options, The Arts: Tiny school, so games not a serious option, but soccer, lacrosse, tennis, athletics, cricket and squash, though the court needs repair. Swimming pool for summer only, and a gym which needs tlc.

Enthusiastic drama, and music. Art impressive, and almost every discipline, including fashion (but no sewing machines) attacked with gusto. Excellent results, pupils continue their work out of hours.

Background and Atmosphere: When Cademuir bought Crawfordton House, home of the defunct Crawfordton prep school, in 1995, they acquired a magnificent, hugely impractical, 1865 Victorian mansion with 26 acres rolling across Annie Laurie country, a very good hour and a half's drive from either Edinburgh or Glasgow. However cheapo flights to Prestwick less than an hour away have opened up the European market, and whilst Moniaive is not a large or sophisticated town, it is only a couple of hours from many European capitals. Theatre and museum visits locally and to Edinburgh, Glasgow, Carlisle and Dumfries. The house was revamped in 2001 after an edict from the local fire department which resulted in stunning girls' accommodation in the basement and super boys' dorms, though these are scattered around the main building. The refurbished rooms are great but some of the original classrooms need updating, elegant ceilings though. Dining room a bit bleak with vending machines etc, vegetarian options available but no vegan or special diets for those with ADHD. And in all honesty, an injection of dosh is needed to fix up some of the outbuildings.

Cademuir runs a thriving and popular summer school, devoted part-time to learning support and part-time to Scottish history, customs, visits, plays, music and the like.

Pastoral Care and Discipline: Moderate physical handicap is not a problem. School well-equipped to deal with mild Asperger's ('as long as they are not aggressive'), top end of the autism spectrum, ADHD etc. Ritalin regarded as 'normal' and 'some of our pupils jolly well ought to be on it' says Mr Mulvey, and every form of medical assistance is cared for (unlike most schools) – eyes, ears, speech – also dentistry. God three times a term, obligatory for all, unless 'they have a letter'.

No bedroom visiting between the sexes, but no six-inch rule either as many of the pupils come from mainland Europe where holding hands with either sex is the norm. Strict discipline code (but fairly relaxed on dress whatever the prospectus says). Suspected drinkers have their bags searched on return from exeats (and that includes Moniaive); if booze is found it is confiscated. Zero tolerance on drugs. Would like to take a firmer stand on fags, but a bit difficult with the prevailing European culture, where parents will insist on offering the little blighters ciggies. Stunning new navy blue sweatshirts which look frightfully smart.

Pupils and Parents: An amorphous bunch, ranging from the statemented in Britain to the grandest of the grand Europeans and everything else between. The UK, Germany and Luxembourg all send children with special needs, Germany also statements exceptionally gifted children, so you get the lot, though less now from Germany and quite a tranche from France which has no specialised schools for any form of SEN within the private sector. 70 per cent from 'mainland Europe', 30 per cent from the UK. Delightful, charming, interested teenagers.

Entrance: No exam – by recommendation and, if necessary, educational psychologist's report. Prospective pupils come and stay for a week and we 'suss each other out'.

Exit: Over 90 per cent to university; school has strong links with the Scottish universities, particularly St Andrews.

Money Matters: Not a rich school; no scholarships, every available surplus goes into the fabric.

Remarks: This school is a national treasure, possibly Scotland's best kept secret, the answer to many a challenged parent's prayer.

Caedmon School

Airy Hill, Whitby, North Yorkshire, YO21 1QA

Tel: 01947 602 570

Fax: 01947 820 315

Email: admin@caedmon.n-yorks.sch.uk

Website: www.caedmon.n-yorks.sch.uk

• Pupils: 530 boys and girls • Ages: 11-14

• Religion: Non-denom • School status: State

• School gender: Mixed • Day/boarding: Day pupils

SEN provision

Detail:

Experience of:

Mild: ASP; AUT; ADD; ADHD; EBD; DS; DYSC; DYSL; DYSP; SpLD; HI; VI; CP;

Moderate: ASP; ADD; ADHD; EBD; MLD; DYSC; DYSL; DYSP; SpLD; HI; VI;

Severe: HI;

Others: SPD; CD; OCD; ODD; EAL; MSI; Sp&LD; Epi; PD; Eat;

Summary: 1. We aim to identify and remove all barriers to learning for all children

2. To provide for all their needs.

i) Physical. This can range from providing spare PE kit, uniform, equipment, breakfast, wheelchair access where possible etc.

ii) Medical. Storing and administering medicines, to training staff for special conditions.

iii) Sensory Impairment. Adapting equipment, training and advising staff, providing support and staff a place to re-charge batteries.

iv) Emotional Needs. Ranging from informed supportive staff to a quiet place/person to go to. To bring in social skills programme, circle time, and circle of friends group (called zinc in our school).

3. Behaviour. Ranging from consistent loss of school rewards, sanctions system, to T.A. support. The use of the inclusion unit on premises and time to reflect on their reasons and the way forward.

4. Learning. Pupils may be taught in mixed ability (for practical subjects) streamed for academic subjects, or taught in smaller groups or some one-to-one. We offer all manner of extra's-tables club, homework club, spelling groups and SRA corrective reading scheme.

5. Support is also offered and given to parents. Our home and school ties are a strength. If we are all working together we are half way there.

6. We aim to educate the whole child and in addition to all timetabled lessons also offer a comprehensive and extensive list of extra-curriculum activities at dinner times and after school. TAs and teaching staff give willingly of their time.

What we say about the school - the full Good Schools Guide review

Head: Since 2001, Tony Hewitt BEd MA NPQH. Taught in four state secondary schools, most recently Blackfyne School, Consett, as deputy head. Still a principal examiner in history and sets GCSE paper for AQA examining board. Has written five GCSE history textbooks and teachers' guides. Married to Jenn, a special needs teacher. Two children. Enthusiastic, committed, with unstuffy sense of humour.

Academic Matters: With no GCSEs or A levels to steal the limelight, Key Stage 3 results are king. And, boy, does it show. Caedmon's results are in top 5 per cent nationally, rated an A* performance. Almost 90 per cent of pupils reach level 5 or above. Outstanding achievement regularly wins Caedmon the DfES's School Achievement Award – effectively a cash bonus for staff which Caedmon shares amongst everyone from teachers to dinner ladies. Placed in top twenty schools nationally in 2003 for value added. Across ability range, pupils judged to leave Caedmon a full academic year ahead of the progress they were expected to make on intake which means a flying start on GCSEs at their next school.

Caedmon also working on 'demystifying' exams by offering volunteers a chance to take information technology GCSE at 14. Impressive results from pupils – and even some teachers who were brave enough to sit the exam alongside them. School prides itself on doing well by less able pupils, including special needs. Intense monitoring means that any slip in standards is noticed and acted on.

Ofsted in 2005 reported 'no weaknesses' and head got an invitation to St James' Palace 'as head of an outstanding school'.

Games, Options, The Arts: One of only three schools in North Yorkshire to win Sport England's Sportsmark Gold. Huge grounds including its own wood for cross-country. £500,000 new floodlit Astroturf, the first in the town, was completed 2004. New classrooms and changing facilities underway. Some pupils opt for junior sports leadership awards and pass on their skills in primary schools. Others return to coach Caedmon's athletes in their lunch hours after they leave. Wealth of after-school activities, including clog dancing.

Good music and drama, including two productions a year – though expect the unexpected. The sublime – performing a home-grown play on board the replica of Captain Cook's ship, Endeavour – was soon followed by the ridiculous – Caedmon's own Stars In Their Eyes with staff and parents doing their Freddie Mercury and Cher routines. Whitby's Captain Cook links mean that the school trip is as ambitious as they come. Caedmon gave up on its round-the-world tours after September 11th but still manages to bob over to Australia where civic receptions are part of the package.

Background and Atmosphere: Get up early, very early, to see what puts Caedmon in a class of its own. Its open school policy means that pupils are welcome from 7.45am onwards to use the library, computer rooms, do their homework or just socialise. The last pupils drift home around 6.00pm. And still the 1960s building, above Whitby harbour, is as tidy as your grandma's front room on Easter Sunday. So how do they do it? Largely, through a very structured system of rewards and merits and efficient prefects, given a heady level of responsibility which includes running the school council and helping to suss out job candidates. Hard to believe they're still only 14.

And if you thought the days when house points meant anything in state comprehensives were long gone, Caedmon has found a way of making them doubly precious. The more points your house gets, the more balls it's awarded in the school's weekly lottery. And the prize? First place for your house in the school dinner queue. Priceless.

Pastoral Care and Discipline: Part of Caedmon's success is down to knowing its pupils well. And, while most would claim the same, Caedmon is small enough to mean it. Teachers pool knowledge of individual pupils at staff meetings. As much chance of disappearing in this school as of scooping a double rollover. Those who work hard are rewarded, those who don't are under the microscope. The head, who tours school several times a day, also does spot-checks on pupils' books. Bad behaviour means formal warnings and sometimes a phone call home to mum. And the ultimate deterrent? Saturday morning detention in full uniform. 'You see this forlorn figure in white shirt and tie trudging into school? They don't do it again,' says head.

Pupils and Parents: Very supportive parents who appreciate that Caedmon goes that extra mile. Accessibility to head verging on saintly. Gives parents his personal e-mail address and mobile phone number. 'I know if they use that number, they're desperate to speak to me.' Blimey. And a newsletter goes home every Friday. That's more contact than most adults have with their mums.

Entrance: Mainly, but not exclusively, down to catchment area. About 20 per cent come from outside in one of those rare instances where parental choice means you can actually get into a very good school without having to move into the grounds.

Exit: Most go to Whitby Community College, the local 14 to 19 state school. Some come out of private sector for their three years at Caedmon.

Remarks: A peach of a school which combines respect and responsibility and still finds room for some classroom banter. You don't just send your child there, you wish you'd gone yourself.

The Cardinal Vaughan Memorial RC School

89 Addison Road, London, W14 8BZ

Tel: 020 7603 8478
Fax: 020 7602 3124
Email: mail@cvms.co.uk
Website: www.cardinalvaughan.kensington-chelsea.sch.uk

• Pupils: 780 boys, plus 120 girls in sixth form; all day
• Ages: 11-18 • Religion: RC • School status: State
• School gender: Boys • Day/boarding: Day pupils

SEN provision

Detail:

Now provide for in school:

Mild: ADD; ADHD; EBD; DYSL; SpLD; HI;
Moderate: ASP; ADD; ADHD; EBD; MLD; DYSL; DYSP; SpLD; VI;
Severe: ASP; AUT; ADHD; EBD; DYSL; HI;
Others: CD; TIC; GEN; SLD; EAL; Sp&LD; PD;

Experience of:

Mild: ASP;
Severe: ADD; VI;
Others: ODD; Epi;

Summary: Cardinal Vaughan Memorial School has, for many years, provided high quality SEN provision for pupils with a diverse range of special educational needs. The department comprises four experienced, qualified teachers with learning support or SEN commitment and five learning support assistants. Staff are experienced in teaching and supporting a wide range of pupils, including severeley autistic boys and others with Autistic Spectrum Disorders; pupils with Dyslexia and Dyspraxia and those with Hearing or Visual Impairments.

Staff work thorughout the school, supporting pupils in class and, at times, on a withdrawal basis. Pupils with Emotional and Behavioural Difficulties are well supported, with the school able to offer Individual Behaviour Plans and additional pastoral suuport when necessary. Home-School communication is strong and departmental members have excellent relationships with pupils and parents alike. Additionally, the school has strong links with external agencies and pupils can receive regular input from outside professionals.

The school makes excellent provision for Gifted and Talented pupils. Masterclasses, Advanced Skills Courses, university taster courses, Latin and visiting speakers are all on offer to pupils alongside Departmental provision.

All the pupils on the school's SEN register take public examinations and disapplication is rare. A wide range of examination provisions are available to those that require them and often, pupils with special educational needs achieve enviable results with many continuing their studies at Key Stage 5 in the school's Sixth form. The school offers a range of subjects, particularly at Key Stage 5, including vocational courses.

What we say about the school - the full Good Schools Guide review

Head: Since 1997, Mr M A Gormally (Michael) BA FRSA ACP (forties) who was educated in Lancashire, read modern languages at London but teaches Latin 'to the first formers, 'it's my way of getting to know them'. He enjoys teaching Latin enormously, 'a secret garden'. He was previously deputy head and has been with the school for 25 years. He is a practising Catholic, as are three quarters of his staff, and religion is important here. Glorious sense of humour – we wanted to describe him as 'giggly' but he would prefer to be 'jocund'. Obviously enjoying the job, he exudes enthusiasm from every pore. Very much the traditionalist, he is affable and popular with pupils and parents alike. 'A rotund and orotund bon viveur,' said one witty member of staff – orotund = either of booming voice, or bombastic prose, neither of which seems appropriate. (Head spent much of our interview playing word games with the assistant headmaster who showed us round.) Thrilled with the 2002 Ofsted report, which is so good he could have written it himself. Goods, Excellents and Very Goods litter the pages, and the only adverse criticism was the size of the site (though interestingly the report describes the sixth form as containing 272 boys 'of whom 93 are young women').

Academic Matters: School has moved to teaching five one-hour periods a day, rather than the traditional 40 minutes; this has worked well, with pupils having to move round less and, according to staff, getting more done in the week. 'Less disruption'. Max 30 per class, with fewer for practical subjects and only 15 for art. Wow! First-formers are divided into four streams on entry and setted from the second year in maths and English but can move up and down. French for all but only the top two streams do Latin; Greek option 'sua sponte' for GCSE 'Latinists' (30 last year, plus 9 at A level) though this is not timetabled, and is not always available – depends on numbers. Alas, German has fallen by the wayside. All must take Eng lit and lang, maths, RE and DT. Pleasing number of As and A*s across the board, 2004 the best ever year for both GCSE and A level results. Christian theology important. Ablest pupils streamed into separate sciences for GCSE in the second year, with their weaker brethren taking dual award; strong science department, 'school ferociously keen on science' and a group in the second year came first in the Salters' science chemistry competition at Queen Mary's College, London. English, maths, history and economics the popular choices at A level. Small but vigorous classics department.

Design Technology (CAD/CAM and the like) in the new Pellegrini building is popular, with successes across the board at all levels. Not too much hands-on stuff in evidence. Computers abound, though not in every classroom.

Super SEN plus support for learning, part of the Excellence in Cities for Gifted and Talented strand, which encourages the ablest. 20 pupils are statemented, with a further 70 on the school's own special educational needs register – they get support both within the class (mentor system by full qualified staff, as well as by older pupils) and on a one-to-one basis. 'This is a truly comprehensive school in every sense of the word'. Great emphasis put on homework. No major changes in staff, though there is a fair turnover in the younger members who find London living expensive and London weighting 'risible'.

Games, Options, The Arts: Extremely active sports – soccer popular but rugby catching up fast, and cricket gaining enthusiasts. Excellent playing fields next to the holy of holies at Twickenham. Pupils do one whole afternoon of sport a week and play other senior schools; large integrated gym. Pupils are bused to the river for rowing (strong), good fencing too. Swimming at the local Kensington Sports Centre. New art dept in the Pellegrini building, buzzing with terrific paintings and some fab 3D; impressive selection of AS stuff on show, being assessed when we visited.

Orchestra now of a 'quasi' professional standard – 'wonderful' – recently performed the whole of Beethoven's fifth and Dvorák's eighth. Impressive, plus a highly acclaimed big band jazz which has a regular monthly gig in the Bull's Head in Barnes, and travels abroad with great success. They sound pretty good too. Variety of ensembles plus 'the jewel in our crown' – the Schola Cantorum, which travels internationally, recently played in the Vatican, singing vespers in the basilica of St Peter's itself, when the choir was blessed by the Pope. This editor was given one of their recent CDs and jolly nice it sounds too – though not perhaps the high liturgy we were promised (there have to be some perks). Massive choral production at Easter and a range of other choirs. All these marvels come from a music suite in the basement, all singing and dancing, sure enough, but pretty grisly. New music suite due for completion 2005 to give this dept the accommodation it deserves. Drama is 'not taught as a discrete subject'; musicals rather than straight plays, put on by a combination of the English and music depts (fantastic much-praised head of music – a maestro). Guys and Dolls, West Side Story among recent productions. Regular French exchanges and trips all over the place both at home and abroad. Strong sense of community service fostered, pupils raise thousands for charity, with weekly charity collections in every form. Lots of voluntary work done in local primaries and with old people in the area.

Background and Atmosphere: The Victorian redbrick building which houses the senior three years was, apparently, originally built as a music hall, The Addison Hall, and we saw pupils doing their GCSEs in what could easily have been the auditorium. 1914 saw the building in use as a private school, it became a grammar school in 1944, and started taking girls in the sixth form in 1980. The Vaughan, as it is known, is a memorial to the third Archbishop of Westminster, Herbert Vaughan, and there is some rather jolly stained glass in the senior building, and a much neglected collection of mitres outside the tiny chapel – dedicated to self-reflection, the benediction is given here on Friday afternoons at the end of school, every week. Voluntary, it is usually well attended.

The uninspired junior block across Addison Road (one way, humps, guarded crossing) dates from the sixties, functional and flat roofed, with a spanking new addition, the Pellegrini building, called after the previous head who was in the job for 21 years. Pretty boring collection of classrooms. All the classrooms have a crucifix in prime position. The mezzanine addition in the assembly/dining hall is a great improvement acoustically and certainly breaks up the barn. Not over-large library considering the number of pupils. Every nook and cranny crammed in the new building which houses the art room, DT and classrooms. It's jolly and bright, full of stainless steel – opened in 1988 by Cardinal Hume and the floor coverings are already showing bad signs of wear. When they decide to expand upwards, they had better stipulate a different contractor. Black and grey uniform, burgundy and grey for girls (school hot on this – 'no variation of uniform is permitted', nor are unconventional hair styles). Ties for sports teams. The Vaughan is possibly the tidiest school we have visited. Busy caring atmosphere, peaceful and friendly, where many other city schools are jungles.

Pastoral Care and Discipline: The Vaughan is a Catholic school and faith is important here. Junior pupils must attend Mass twice a week ('Mass is NOT optional'). The fifth and sixth forms have Mass once a month and the whole school attends the local Our Lady of Victories church on holy days of obligation. The Angelus is said each day at noon and the rosary recited at lunch between May and October (serious stuff this) and vocational education is part of the GCSE curriculum. Sex education is taught by a combined science and religious education clique – according, you understand, to the Catholic ethos. 40 of the sixth form are prefects with distinctive ties, the 'rest are pressed into service as and when necessary'. ' No real problems' with the perennial drugs 'n' booze 'n' fags, 'virtually zero-tolerance for illegal substances'. But discipline is 'under control'; school would like us to say that 'our discipline and pastoral care arrangements are excellent: see Ofsted report on this' – certainly more than under control, if younger pupils continue the habit of lining up in pairs at the end of break (leafy area, junior school) and filing inside, saluting our guide as they did so.

Pupils and Parents: No strategically placed primaries help here. Pupils come from all over the London area, from Tower Hamlets to Aylesbury, Hackney, Hampstead, south London and Bethnal Green, often travelling for an hour or so each way. Homework centre open until 4.45pm. 'School reflects the average inner London population', ditto the number of free school meals. Everyone from true working class to toffs. Huge amount of parental support with 'more than 300 turning up for the recent Ofsted parents' evening. Lots of moral support too. Head calls the parents 'exceptional, the secret of our success'. Almost 50 per cent from ethnic minorities from 50 different countries, with 22 per cent non-white according to Ofsted. Eng lang help on hand if needed.

Entrance: Primary criterion for admission – 'evidence of baptism or reception into the Roman Catholic Church'. As of 2004, new additional entrance tests – of how RC you are. Fiendlishly difficult and demanding questions and test has been failed by devoutly church-going and serious-minded RC candidates – much distress thereafter. Overall, the RC criteria for entrance now v v demanding and, some might think, pretty exclusive.

Massively over-subscribed – 300 for 120 places. 'All applicants are tested to ensure a balanced intake' – diagnostic rather than selective in maths and English – and designed to ensure that 'coaching is now useless'. The Vaughan does not aim to be an academic hothouse. Two As and four Bs or above for entry to the sixth form. Pupils come at 11 from a variety of primaries, and even some private prep schools, and at 16 from roughly the same spread, 40 girls and a handful of boys.

Exit: About 20 boys or so leave after GCSE, usually to take up some form of vocational education not available at The Vaughan. Otherwise a stunning ten to Oxbridge last year (six boys, four girls); Bristol popular, York and Warwick, as well as the London unis etc plus a selection to art schools. Some take a gap year, 'it is increasingly popular'.

Money Matters: Voluntary aided.

Remarks: A kind, religious state school with dedicated staff and a comprehensive intake which, by national state school standards, has consistently good exam results. 'More than good,' said the head indignantly. 'Our results are outstanding by any standards and bear comparison with those of many grammar and independent schools.'

CARRDUS SCHOOL

Overthorpe Hall, Blacklocks Hill, Banbury, Oxfordshire, OX17 2BS

Tel: 01295 263 733

Fax: 01295 263 733

Email: office@carrdusschool.co.uk

Website: www.carrdusschool.co.uk

• Pupils: 120 girls, 30 boys, all day • Ages: 3-11 (boys 3-8)
• Religion: Non-denom • Fees: £2,180-£2,320
• School status: Independent • Opendays: May
• School gender: Mixed • Day/boarding: Day pupils

SEN provision

Detail:

Now provide for in school:

Mild: DYSL;

Moderate: DYSL;

Experience of:

Mild: ASP; AUT; ADD; ADHD; EBD; DS; DYSP; HI; VI; CP;

Moderate: MLD; DYSP; HI;

Others: CD; EAL; Sp&LD; DEL; Epi;

Summary: SEN to us covers both ends of the spectrum: gifted-and-talented to pupils with quite a level of learning difficulties. Our provision aims to meet needs as fully as possible; which will be some one-to-one work with ALL children in school, and individual or small-group work with a number of them. Three teachers work in this way, one each for English, maths and Science. A further two teachers give general support or extension work. This additional tuition, given at our discretion, is a 'value-added' part of our normal school curriculum, usually much enjoyed by the children concerned.

What we say about the school - the full Good Schools Guide review

Head: Since 1985, Miss Susan Carrdus BA (fifties). Educated at The Carrdus School (her mother Kathleen founded school in 1952) and Banbury Grammar School, followed by Southampton University, where she read English. Previously head of English at nearby Tudor Hall. Has a grown-up daughter and two grandchildren.

Warm, approachable and immensely dedicated. Unusually for a head, she spends a third of her time in the classroom and is responsible for all year 5 and 6 English teaching. 'I love it,' she says. 'I really like and enjoy the company of children.' Very child-centred and doesn't miss a trick, whether greeting pupils by name as they race around the garden at break-times, searching out pencil sharpeners in the stationery cupboard or crouching down to help a nursery child put her shoes on the right way round. Throws herself into all school activities, even painting, decorating and sorting out the garden during the holidays. 'I drive a mean dumper truck,' she laughs. Enjoys walking and learning to play the piano in her spare time (not that there's much of it.)

Entrance: No entrance test. Very broad intake. Majority of pupils come from Banbury and surrounding villages, with parents registering children up to three years in advance. Most common entry points are nursery, reception and year 3 but it's worth trying in between too.

Exit: At 11, girls leave for a plethora of schools, including Tudor Hall, King's High, Headington, Rye St Antony, Oxford High, Cheltenham Ladies' College and Bloxham. Good smattering of scholarships over the years. At seven or eight, boys head for prep schools like Winchester House, Warwick Junior, Cothill and Bilton Grange.

Remarks: School moved to present site in 1970, when Kathleen Carrdus (now in her eighties but still taking a huge interest in school activities) bought Overthorpe Hall for the princely sum of £22,500. Became an educational trust in 1991, with 100 per cent of fee income ploughed back into the school. Main building a rambling 1880s hunting lodge set in 11 acres of grounds. Latest ISI report (2004) says school gives pupils 'a very caring and positive education'. Friendly staff pride themselves on making sure children are happy and secure in 'informal yet stimulating' atmosphere. Place feels straight out of a Mary Wesley novel – lots of fresh air, smiley faces, muddy knees and heaps of praise.

Despite relaxed ambience, pupils work hard and academic record is impressive. Hugely experienced staff (average age 48 and around a quarter have been at school for more than ten years.) Maximum class size

24 but in practice more like 18. No setting, but most able get chance to move faster in 'sparkle sessions.' Head of maths holds walk-in surgery first thing every morning for anyone who needs help, including parents puzzled by modern maths! School has number of pupils with dyslexia, dyspraxia and/or learning difficulties and they get support from two specially trained staff. No extra subjects apart from instrument lessons – school ethos is that everyone does everything. Children learn French from reception and take Latin for last two terms of year 6. Homework for all. Reception children take reading books home; year 3 pupils get prep three times a week, year 5 and 6 pupils every night. Thousands of books, all colour-coded for different reading abilities – head reckons school possesses virtually every children's book published since her mum was a girl in the 1920s. At least one computer in each classroom.

Arts strong, with children encouraged to play instruments, speak confidently in public and take part in concerts. Pupil's work on display everywhere you look. African tribal masks dangling from the main staircase, a collage of moles burrowing underground (using real mud!) and a poll of favourite books in the entrance hall – just for the record, year 6 voted for Private Peaceful and Holes while year 3 reckoned Roald Dahl's BFG was tops. Music terrific, with youngest children all playing percussion instruments and everyone from seven upwards learning the recorder. Many older pupils also learn piano, violin, guitar, saxophone or flute. Daily assembly, as well as weekly hymn practice and bible story. Delightful – and short – list of school rules advises pupils 'no sticks, no stones – only climb as high as your friend's head' and 'it's only fun if everybody is enjoying it.' No school uniform, games kit aside. Dress code is 'not smart, not scruffy,' with parents advised to send children in comfy, machine-washable clothes because there's 'lots of mud and trees.' Pupils, mainly kitted out in mini Boden-type leggings and stripy jumpers (no jeans or bare midriffs) approve wholeheartedly. When we visited only one girl said she'd quite like to wear uniform – as long as it was blue.

Sport is compulsory for all. Children do hockey, netball, athletics, gym, tennis, gymnastics, dance, cycling proficiency and swimming (heated outdoor pool set in pretty walled garden.) Cross-country a particular strength – pupils have won every cup going. Lots of school trips, to Stratford-upon-Avon, Oxford's Ashmolean Museum, Roald Dahl Museum etc. All year 6 girls get annual expedition to Normandy – French-speaking only from the minute the coach leaves school.

Nutritious, wholesome lunches cooked on-site and served by friendly dinner ladies who know children well. At break-time youngsters help themselves to cheese, crispbread, raw vegetables and fruit before racing off to play in the garden in virtually all weathers.

Very strong, sociable PTA, with activities ranging from new parents' breakfasts to annual bonfire party, Christmas fair and spring sale. Parents arriving to collect their children in the afternoons gather in the entrance hall, complete with squashy sofas and, in winter, a roaring fire. Way ahead of its time, school launched annual Carrdus At Work day 15 years ago, giving mums and dads the chance to work alongside their children in class for a day during the spring term.

Children have a whale of a time here, while achieving good results. Devoted pupils and parents stay in touch for years after they leave, ringing for advice about everything from university entrance to career choices. Much to head's amusement, old girls frequently implore her, 'can't you start a secondary school like this?'

Castle Court

Knoll Lane, Corfe Mullen, Wimborne, Dorset, BH21 3RF

Tel: 01202 694 438

Fax: 01202 659 063

Email: hmsec@castlecourt.com

Website: www.castlecourt.com

• Pupils: 350, boys and girls; all day • Ages: 3-13
• Religion: C of E • Fees: £3,700 • School status: Independent
• Opendays: October and May, but ring for visits at other times
• School gender: Mixed • Day/boarding: Day pupils

SEN provision

Detail:

Now provide for in school:
Mild: DYSC; DYSL; DYSP;
Others: Oth;
Experience of:
Mild: ADD; HI; VI;
Moderate: MLD; DYSL; DYSP;
Others: MSI;

Summary: Our hope is that all the children will be able to keep up with the general pace of academic life in the school, and appreciate that for some children to reach their full potential they will need a little extra support – usually for mild to moderate dyslexia or dyspraxia. An attractive purpose-built suite of rooms in a quiet part of the school provides a welcoming environment for those children with special needs. The department is well-equipped, including up-to-date computer software for pupils with mild learning difficulties. Four suitably qualified staff are able to deliver teaching programmes, generally on a one-to-one basis, tailored to meet the needs of the individual child.

In the junior part of the school we also provide assistance in the classroom, either to individuals or to small groups, as the need arises.

We have a full-time, fully qualified nurse in the school as our Matron, to administer any medicine or treatment and to take responsibility for particular needs.

What we say about the school - the full Good Schools Guide review

Head: Since 1989, Richard Nicholl BA (enviably youthful early fifties). Shared his schooldays at Stowe with Richard Branson, then diverged. After Durham and Oxford came teaching at Haileybury where he administered English and religious studies to Dom Joly, coached all species of gamesplayer and housemastered sixth form girls. Bright-eyed, effective, engaging, thoughtful. Unexpectedly humorous. Innerly lit by his Christian faith, which permeates everything that happens here. His wife, Vicky, is equally beloved by parents and children. As admissions secretary, she will be your first point of contact. She also oversees catering and cleaning. Two daughters, one ex-Oxford, one at Durham. Will stay until 2011.

Entrance: For 3-5 year-olds, first come, first in. Thereafter, informal assessment 'to ensure that children will be comfortable with the pace here'. Mild dyslexia only. They flock from all compass points: Weymouth-Shaftesbury-Burley-Swanage. First choice for Poole-Bournemouth conurbanites. Scholarships from 7+ for those likely to repeat the performance at a senior school. Automatic discounts for brothers and sisters.

Exit: Canford. If not, one of a scattering of premiership independents. Impressive numbers of awards. Around a quarter leave at 12 for the excellent local grammars, or the equally good comps. Golden alumni include Tony Blackburn, pop singer Amy Studt and rugby sevens hero Ben Gollings.

Remarks: Though held in highest esteem, this school is beguilingly unpretentious. Parents span old and new Dorset – farmers to flashy over-achievers/ entrepreneurs. Expect no quirks. Castle Court is the product not of evolution but meticulous planning and it all stems from the top. Everything is tickety-boo, but never too good to be true. Beautifully behaved children walk to assembly in marshalled lines, evenly spaced. They sit in rapt silence – contentedly. They listen to the Word as it relates to contemporary events, as it applies to daily lives, the delivery humorous, interactive, thought-inspiring, backed by PowerPoint. The objective lies not in the act of worship but in what they call out-working: being kind to each other, raising money for charity. That's why parents like it – there's no sense whatever of evangelical mind-stealing. Zealous atheists may wince, though.

In the classroom the pace is rapid, for this is a blue-chip school. Slower children will puff a bit but they are supported and almost all subjects are setted. The brightest are not worked to death, yet mop up scholarships by the barrowload. Every lesson we invaded was calm and, yes, orderly, but with masses going on. It's that sort of school. They want the children to work well together, and they do. So do the teachers. Marvellously focused. Careful as can be. Results are no happy accident because each child is so painstakingly tracked – every building block is put in place before the next block is added. One mum says, 'pupils miss nothing academically, socially or extra-curricularly. A child can enter at 3 and leave at 13 and you can be absolutely confident that there is no chink in what they have learned or experienced.' Those with emergent SENs are pit-stopped and fine-tuned, mostly one-to-one, expertly, and equipped with 'special skills'. The void left by those off to grammar school is instantly filled for those who remain with extra attention from really impressive form teachers.

Does such an environment favour passive conformity? No. At break-time we saw reassuringly semi-feral high spirits in the rough-and-tumble covered playground and the surrounding woods. This really is a school for all sorts where problems are earnestly remedied, never shuffled off. Sport is played with exuberance and winning is prized. Everyone has a go in a team at some level. Pastoral care is attentive and personal. Music is strong, 75 per cent learn an instrument, and there are performance opportunities of all shapes and genres. Art is superb and has wide appeal, including a thriving after-lunch drop-in club where children do their own thing. Children are urged to try their hands at everything, so the IT suite has outward bound posters above the monitors. Juniors have a go at riding and sailing. From year 5 children can stay till 6pm for 'tea and prep' and activities – a good range. Camping weekends for year 3 and up, some at the wonderful Kingcombe environmental centre.

Classrooms and facilities generally sound but not snazzy. Knoll House, the homely Regency mansion, lies at the heart of a roomy 30 acres. Lovely gardens, azalea-smitten in early summer, where we watched weenies playing Grandma's Footsteps before lunch, an Edwardian vision. All-weather pitch. Constantly uplifted IT. Classrooms comely if unremarkable. Building and upgrading under way subject to planning regs.

This is a kind, gentle school which inspires in parents admiration and affection in equal measure. It is as good as they get.

CATERHAM SCHOOL

Harestone Valley Road, Caterham, Surrey, CR3 6YA

Tel: 01883 343 028
Fax: 01883 347 795
Email: enquiries@caterhamschool.co.uk
Website: www.caterhamschool.co.uk

• Pupils: 746 boys and girls, roughly 3:2 • Ages: 11-18 • Religion: Christian • Fees: Prep £1,141-£2,939; senior day £3,495 – £3,660; boarding £6,477 – £6,827 • School status: Independent • Opendays: September and November • School gender: Mixed • Day/boarding: Takes boarders

SEN provision

Detail:

Now provide for in school:

Mild: ASP; AUT; ADD; ADHD; EBD; DYSC; DYSL; DYSP; VI;

Others: EAL; PD;

Experience of:

Mild: HI;

Moderate: ASP; ADD; MLD; HI;

Others: CD; OCD; TIC; Sp&LD; Epi; Eat;

Summary: Caterham School is a high achieving, academic school from which most pupils go on to the universities of their first choice.

Pupils with mild specific learning difficulties are catered for individually by qualified specialist staff. The SEN provision we provide depends on a pupil's Specific Learning difficulty having been formally diagnosed; it ranges from one-to-one support to group support within the classroom. All subject staff are kept informed and up-to-date with effective learning and teaching strategies and are skilled at coping with pupils with specific learning difficulties.

What we say about the school - the full Good Schools Guide review

Headmaster: Since 1995, Mr Rob Davey MA, Palmes Academiques (mid-fifties). Reminding this aged editor a mite of the young James Stewart, Mr Davey has a grave manner, a soft, engaging southern Irish voice, a tendency to talk at immense length when having begun his answer, 'I'll tell you exactly what it means...' and a smile which appears unexpectedly, betraying the fact that, despite his seriousness about his school, he finds it all tremendously exciting and fun. A modern linguist who has spent nine years driving this school to the considerable heights it has now attained, Mr Davey has a masterplan in mind which, in addition to yet more new-build on this large and leafy site, includes a much needed intention to up the profile of modern languages in his school which currently achieves very highly on the scientific and technical sides. Enthusiastic about 'independent learning' and cites many examples of what this means in practice. Previously deputy head of Wells Cathedral school, this gentle giant is a committed internationalist who was made an officer of the prestigious Palmes Academiques (an order set up by Napoleon Bonaparte for those who have made a notable contribution to culture and education) for his work on cultural exchanges. He is an elder in the United Reform Church, to which this school is affiliated, and is clear about the Christian nature and ethos of the school. 'We're not ashamed of being Christian and we're basically a very British school but we look at other viewpoints.' His school, its general approach and the substantial numbers of pupils from all over the world are testament to this open and truly internationalist attitude – a bit of a treasure in an, otherwise, very much Surrey-based community. Mr Davey was an Oxford Rugby Blue, is a member of the HMC Drugs Guidelines Working Group, is married and is clearly a popular and respected head.

Academic Matters: Caterham can now hold its head high in any company, especially in maths, the sciences and IT. 2004 results included 86 per cent A*-B grades at GCSE (a full 10 per cent improvement on 2000) and, at A level, 100 per cent A-C grades (in 1999 it was 78 per cent). Ninety per cent of leavers secured their first choice university place. Something is going right here. A good set of subject options (international students can take their own languages) includes business studies, economics, government and politics, textiles, psychology, photography and theatre studies, in addition to the usual staples. Modern languages, though encouraged by many foreign trips of all kinds, need beefing up to encourage more takers and this is now in hand. Excellent language lab will help. Greek survives here – hooray. Years 7 and 8 take a course in citizenship and all sixth formers take general studies. A good combination of the trad and the trendy but all in a sensible, purposeful manner. SENs are efficiently diagnosed and well-supported here though those with physical disabilities would find parts of this valley/hills site difficult to negotiate. Parents pay tribute to the caring and dedicated staff who 'really enthuse the pupils' but don't have unrealistic expectations of them.

Games, Options, The Arts: All onsite playing fields, pitches, all-weather surfaces abound. Superb sports hall, plus pool, giant fitness room with 25+ exotic-looking machines, plus plus plus opened in 1996 by Sebastian Coe and open to 'members' ie school families, former pupils etc. Superbly maintained Home Field for athletics etc. Boarding football enthusiasts are coached by a trainer from Crystal Palace FC and school achieves highly in sports which include swimming, rugby, hockey, lacrosse, netball, cricket and cross-country. Riding too. CCF, Young Enterprise and D of E all popular.

Lots of drama though no designated studio; recent productions range from Bugsy Malone to The Comedy of Errors. Drama is an A level option. Workmanlike, well stocked workshops for DT and IT. Art is well catered for, though not in top-notch accommodation, and popular, especially with girls. Printmaking, graphic design, pottery and photography among many options. Nice inter-disciplinary enterprises like a recent, beautifully produced, pamphlet of art and writings – a truly imaginative exercise done just for the pleasure of it and wonderfully encouraging for those whose work appears. Flourishing music with many in-school lessons on around 20 different instruments and every kind of band and ensemble – a range of small recitals to major choral concerts in the Humphreys Hall. Arcane and eclectic choice of other extra-curriculars includes Amnesty, bridge, chemistry, Christian Union, debating, various language and minority sports and the splendid Melting Pot – a chance to exchange multi-cultural experience with over 20 countries represented. Visits here, there and everywhere – Bolivia, Botswana, mosques and temples, skiing and Spain.

Background and Atmosphere: In 1995 two schools merged. Boys' school, Caterham, founded in 1811, merged with nearby girls' school Eothen, founded in 1892. Both Christian foundations. Caterham had been set up to educate the sons of Congregationalist ministers – even thirty years ago around a third of pupils were Welsh and the relationship to the United Reform Church is still close. Christian background informs the ethos and is neither exclusive nor punitive. In fact, this is about as inclusive as a school can get.

School moved to its present, 100 acre site in 1884. One arrives at the school down a quiet lane out of Caterham centre with substantial, well spaced detached houses on one side and the school appears on rising ground to one's left. A three storey, immensely long, red-brick building, it is imposing though built in a plain and solid style – free from the excesses of later in that century. It faces banks of glorious, tree-festooned hills and its own sports grounds. Battalions of white mini-buses wait on hard standing. Further down is the prep and pre-prep, wonderfully secluded, be-treed and traffic-free. Later building has added necessary facilities and some views can seem a little cramped but, in general, there is a sense of space and light.

Inside the main building, there are redbrick and tile corridors which could be prison-like but aren't thanks to sensitive lighting and general decoration – even the somewhat violent yellow of the boys' boarding areas upstairs is well chosen. Boarding for girls and boys recently expensively upgraded. Years 7-9 in good sized rooms for 6, year 10 for 4, year 11 for 2 and year 13 students all have good rooms with en-suite loo and shower – better than most recently built undergraduate rooms. Good kitchens, lots of staff living in and school well-up on parents' need for flexi-boarding and very keen to help. New science block and dining hall now has planning permission. Uniform a sensible black/white/ grey mix though 'smart business suits' for sixth form girls interpreted somewhat surprisingly by some.

Pastoral Care and Discipline: Commitment to excellent pastoral care evidenced by huge and touchingly accessible booklet, strong RSPE curriculum and general air of happy purposefulness everywhere. Clear but flexible structure. House system. Head believes links with parents work to mitigate problems and sees alcohol as a greater menace than drugs – no drugs exclusions for three years at time of visit. Around 70 per cent stay in over weekends – good programme. Many staff live onsite, either in purpose-built houses or in boarding houses. Boarding staff seen as parents rather than staff.

Pupils and Parents: Most boarders from abroad and currently from 38 countries. Largest numbers from Hong Kong, China and eastern Europe. Day pupils from Surrey and a few from Kent or Sussex borders. Good bus services bring from all over. Large proportion of city and professional families, many first-timers – this is easy, prosperous, commuter country. Perennial problems of getting some hard-working foreign students to join extra-curricular activities and to mix generally being keenly tackled but remains an issue. Former pupils include Angus Deayton, Jon Finch, Michael Jecks and cricketers Alastair Brown, James Benning and David Sales.

Entrance: Getting harder for those outside school's own prep, especially as more folk grasp the fact that boys and girls from 3-18 get a pretty unbeatable start in life here. Usual tests at 11 and 13, via interview,and 6 good GCSEs expected at 16.

Exit: A spread of courses with economics most popular in 2003. Range of universities with Birmingham, Nottingham and Southampton most favoured. Three or four to Oxbridge.

Money Matters: Good number of scholarships awarded at 10, 11, 13 and 16. Extra science scholarships at sixth form. Also art and music awards. Bursaries available for children of clergy, OCs, Services and Foreign Service personnel. Special Caterham assisted places for the able but less well-off.

Remarks: Unaccountably neglected by the Guide before this edition, this is a top school. Parents pay tribute to the caring and dedicated staff who 'really enthuse the pupils' but don't have unrealistic expectations of them. Well-appointed in virtually every area and performing outstandingly in maths, science and IT, the school is set to build on the achievements of the last decade. Christian background informs the ethos only in good ways and is neither exclusive nor punitive. In fact, this is about as inclusive as a school can get. The site is leafy, spacious and comfortable. Hard to beat if a co-ed school in the Home Counties with a boarding option is your thing. It is exceptionally well-placed for commuters and those for whom Gatwick/Heathrow are significant – connections couldn't be better. 2004 inspection found no major weaknesses and commented on the 'humane values, the importance of the individual and the sense of community ... the school ... is very successful in preparing its pupils for their future beyond school'.

Centre Academy

92 St John's Hill, Battersea, London, SW11 1SH

Tel: 020 7738 2344

Fax: 020 7738 9862

Email: ukadmin@centreacademy.com

Website: www.centreacademy.com

• Pupils: 54 boys, 16 girls; all day • Ages: 7-19 • Religion: Non-denom • Fees: Lower school £5,875. Middle school £6,090. Senior school £6,350 • School status: Independent • School gender: Mixed • Day/boarding: Day pupils

SEN provision

Detail:

Centre of excellence for:

Mild: ASP; AUT; ADD; ADHD; DYSC; DYSL; DYSP;
Moderate: ADD; ADHD; DYSC; DYSL; DYSP;
Severe: ADD; ADHD; DYSC; DYSL;
Others: EAL; Sp&LD;

Now provide for in school:

Mild: HI;
Moderate: ASP;
Others: ODD; TIC; Epi;

Experience of:

Mild: EBD; SpLD; VI;
Moderate: AUT; MLD; SpLD;

Severe: DYSP;
Others: SPD; CD; OCD; FRX;

Summary: London's Centre Academy, one of the most unique schools in the UK, enables students with various learning difficulties to reclaim their futures. We do so by teaching the skills and coping strategies that students with Dyslexia, ADD, ADHD, Dyspraxia and other learning challenges require in order to succeed.

With exceptionally small classes (usually 6 or 7 students), significant one-to-one instruction and dedicated and experienced faculty members, Centre Academy makes it possible for its students to work to their fullest potential. Following testing and evaluation, we design a programme of instruction tailored to meet the student's individual needs.

Equally unique is the curriculum or rather, the fact that the school offers both the British National Curriculum through GCSE and the traditional American High School Diploma. By offering both systems, we are able to cater to the strengths of the individual student rather than being limited to a 'one size fits all' approach.

English and maths form the core of a student's studies. Other areas involve the Humanities, Science, ICT, Art, Drama, Music, PSHE, Citizenship, and in most instances, Foreign Languages (Spanish and French). Individual counselling, speech and language therapy, and occupational therapy are available. We also offer an after-school Homework club and a range of extgra-curricular activities. GCSE students have a 100 per cent record of acceptance to sixth form and other colleges. Diploma students regularly receive unconditional offers to some of the finest universities in the UK and the US (including Edinburgh, Aberdeen, London, Plymouth, Essex, Hull, to name but a few).With so much emphasis on the individual, Centre Academy must of necessity remain small. The co-educational student body of 70 (ages 7-19) views itself as a community, and the family atmosphere adds to the sense of caring and nurturing.

What we say about the school - the full Good Schools Guide review

Head: Since 2002, Ms Claudine Hakim BA MA (mid thirties), originally from the Lebanon. Previously spent two years as deputy head of Schiller International School, prior to that was director of studies and head of maths at Centre Academy. Returned as head because she has a passion for working with children with learning differences and she felt there was great scope to develop the school in terms of teaching and the curriculum.

Anyone visiting the school could be forgiven for thinking there are three 'heads' in this marriage – school adopts a collegiate approach between the head, the proprietor and the deputy head/director of studies. Parents who pursue a place at the school will initially meet with Dr Duncan Rollo BA MA PhD Post-Doc Fellow (sixties), kindly, personable very much the face of Centre Academy; parents say his 'dedication and positive can-do approach is really making a difference to the calibre of the school.' Parents meet the head during the trial period.

Academic Matters: Small classes and setting enable some group and class teaching as well as individual programmes of study with support from full-time speech and language therapists, four dyslexia specialists and occupational therapist. Pupils follow the National Curriculum and at 14 embark on GCSE or the four-year American High School Diploma (some do both). American system has advantage of being continuously assessed. Usual subjects on offer plus Spanish, no vocational courses as yet. Facilities improving – well-equipped ICT room, small science lab, dedicated art room, some interactive whiteboards, small playground but no dedicated music or PE facilities on site (use local sports centres and nearby municipal playing fields). Children bring packed lunches (lots of pot noodles spotted on our visit), the library is housed in a store cupboard (old school didn't have one) – not ideal – but better than nothing, books are up-to-date and appropriate with provision supplemented by trips to local library. Not at the forefront of teaching and learning but certainly improving (we saw a couple of shaky lessons but recent Ofsted gave a clean bill of health). We found pupils to be confident about their learning with results suggesting some are achieving beyond expectations – not bad when you consider majority are here because they had 'failed' in their previous schools.

Background and Atmosphere: Founded in 1974. Following a period of rapid decline in the late 1990s the school was sold and renamed Centre (rather than American Center) Academy. Current head inherited a school with few resources, very little structure and high staff turnover. LEAs were beginning to question quality of provision at the Academy and enrolment was shaky. Size and urgency of task prompted the head (with the blessing of the proprietor, Mike Murphy, who also owns the Old Rectory in Ipswich), to enlist the help of her former colleague, Dr Rollo. New books were bought, a library created, staff brought in and trained, a uniform introduced, teaching and learning reviewed, procedures tightened and work to transform the Edwardian buildings began (still ongoing, plans afoot for new additions in near future). Latest ventures include introduction of prefects, a school council, a PTA and overhaul of prospectus (old one rife with errors!)

They make a great team – educational nous, vision and experience of Ms Hakim, the marketing, strategy and personnel skills of Dr Rollo and the financial clout of Mike Murphy. Despite all the problems, school never lost its happy, caring, family feel and the three musketeers have successfully preserved this while ensuring the importance of teaching and learning is once again to the fore. Rome wasn't built in a day and likewise work at Centre Academy is far from finished but now task is manageable.

Pastoral Care and Discipline: All children are assigned a mentor as a main point of contact for child and parents, some more proactive than others so provision variable, school counsellor also available. Parents very much part of the school. Careers advice provided by Connexions. Plenty of after school clubs. Children enjoy being here, they like the smallness, intimacy and sense of belonging. As one boy said, 'teachers are like your parents, they make you feel welcome and wanted.'

Pupils and Parents: A mixed bag from all over London, 40 per cent funded by LEAs. Majority is British but a sizeable minority from a myriad of countries with all continents represented. Clientele has changed, used to be lots of expats only here for a couple of years, now vast majority in it for the duration.

Entrance: School traditionally took a broad range of SENs including ADHD. Today emphasis on specific learning difficulties (SpLD) and Asperger's but will take behaviourally eccentric and embrace AD/HD as long as they're not violent or aggressive. Additionally, accommodates children who are 'non-traditional' learners, rather than SEN. Must cope with demands of the National Curriculum.

Admission at any time if a place is available, rolling admissions allows one-to-one or one-to-two input as necessary. Anyone requesting a prospectus will be invited to chat with Dr Rollo. If following the initial chat the school thinks it appropriate, a prospectus will be sent (explains why we were never sent one, though you can download it from the web page). The next step is to forward any relevant documentation such as the EP report to the school. Family then invited to meet Dr Rollo and, if both sides agree, the child spends a trial week in school. Essentially asking, 'is this a good match?' Ability to socialise is at least as important as academic fit. If the trial period doesn't work out the school will try to assist with finding an alternative placement for the child. In some cases they may suggest an intensive period of one-to-one at Lindamood Bell and then a further trial at the school.

Exit: Most to University. New English and US universities a popular options, as are Scottish universities, which offer a foundation year. A few return to mainstream schooling before end of Key Stage 3.

Remarks: On the up again. Just nudges into the guide but we have great expectations.

CHEAM SCHOOL

Headley, Newbury, Berkshire, RG19 8LD

Tel: 01635 268 381

Fax: 01635 269 345

Email: office@cheamschool.co.uk

Website: www.cheamschool.com

• Pupils: 286; 160 boys, 120 girls; half boarding, half day. Plus pre-prep with 110 boys and girls • Ages: 8-13, pre-prep 3-7 • Religion: C of E • Fees: Boarders £5,775; day: £2,445 for Reception - year 2; £4,275 for years 8, 7 and 6 • School status: Independent • School gender: Mixed • Day/boarding: Takes boarders

SEN provision

Detail:

Now provide for in school:

Mild: DYSL;

Moderate: MLD; DYSL;

Others: EAL; Sp&LD;

Experience of:

Mild: ASP; AUT; ADD; ADHD; DYSC; DYSP;

Moderate: AUT;

Summary: Cheam caters for children with certain special needs. There is a thriving learning support department on site which assists children with mild forms of dyslexia and dyspraxia. The staff are very experienced and fully attuned to the needs of the children. Detailed and accurate profiles are kept up-to-date and such information shared with the staff. There is effective communication between the LS Department and the teaching staff thus ensuring that each child's specific needs are met. Children can be screened in house and, if required, tested at school by an educational psychologist.

Bright and gifted children are also well catered for and can fast track through the school into the scholarship streams in the final two years. Pupils are streamed from year 4 upwards. Bright and gifted pupils are prepared for scholarship exams to their public schools in small, 'stand alone' scholarship forms in years 7 and 8.

What we say about the school - the full Good Schools Guide review

Head: Since 1998, Mr Mark R Johnson Bed(Hons) (forties). A West Country product – educated at Buckland House, Devon, and Exeter School; got his degree at the College of St Mark and St John, Plymouth. His last post was as deputy headmaster at Summer Fields, where he was hugely popular. Nickname: Mr J (from his initials – M R J). Bursting with enthusiasm and energy, slightly hail-fellow-well-met, describes himself as 'restless – bubbling with ideas for and about the school we 'whizzed' (regularly) all round the place. Does not (currently) teach, because he reckons it is more important for him to be seeing parents, potential and present. 'He's very parent-friendly,' remarked one, warmly, 'an overgrown prep school boy', said another. Married to Jane, a lovely bouncy lady, a classicist, who does a little Latin and Greek teaching (NB Greek back on course). Two daughters, one now at Teddy's, the other in the school.

Entrance: Informal tests – children spend one day at the school four terms before entry. First come, first served (but at the time of writing over-subscribed, so book early). But figures are meaningless here, as not all year groups are full and there is often place for the odd child 'further up the school'. Can come at half term throughout the year if space available. School holds four in-days for up to ten potential pupils on the list under the watchful eye of the former head of the pre-prep who is accustomed to the vagaries of six-year-olds, a gentle assessment, parents come too and meet the head.

Exit: Boys to Marlborough, Sherborne, Stowe, Eton, Radley, St Edward's Oxford, Winchester 'creeping in' plus Wellington and a number of others; Harrow occasionally. Girls (mostly at 13) to Downe House, Marlborough, Cheltenham Ladies, Sherborne Girls, St Mary's Calne, and Ascot, Heathfield, St Edward's Oxford. Most famous Old Boys: HRH The Duke of Edinburgh, HRH The Prince of Wales, Lord Randolph Churchill, William Pitt the Younger.

Remarks: Back on course as a vibrant and strong prep school after several years in the wilderness. Claims to be the oldest of all the prep schools, traces its history back to 1645. Set in gloriously well-kept grounds with an elegant terraced garden, the main house is partly by Detmar Blow, although the expanded new chapel and Taylor building makes the turn-in to the main school somewhat cramped and surprising, some tree pruning would be a great improvement. Lots of new buildings (classroom block and music school 2002, sports centre and additional ICT suite 2003). Plans for further expansion and improvements in the pipeline (art centre and Astroturf). Six years ago the local pre-prep had to close and 'offered to merge'. Numbers have, therefore, shot up and the school is now choc-a-bloc. Day numbers have also increased and presumably will continue to increase as the local pre-prep children grow into the main school, 'but remember, a lot of them insist on boarding in the last two years.' The boarding/day split in the prep school is about 50/50. Boarding accommodation completely renovated over last two years and Cheam's boarding provision was praised highly following a recent CSCI inspection; splendid new boarders' common room. Large London contingent and a few from overseas (one term, one year, EFL an option). Strong on PSHE, tutors for all. Flexi-ish boarding available but pupils and parents must commit, min two nights. Serious weekend programme for those left behind. New and younger staff have been brought in, adding zest to staid older teachers, and planning permission has been granted for ten staff house units in the grounds which will make getting younger staff easier (prices are high round Newbury).

Setting and streaming in most subjects. Latin considerably beefed up with a Latin reading competition now on the menu. Scholarship forms in the top two years; top stream and 'scholars' take Greek in their final year. Strong on outings and trips to provide hands-on teaching eg workshops at archaeological digs, French classes in Bayeux, environmentalists to the Wyld Court Rainforest, plus all the usual museum visits. All children spend a week in France in their penultimate year for a complete immersion in the language in the build-up to CE and scholarships. Help for the gifted and for the SEN pupils, some may come with a statement of needs, others are spotted in their original assessments, currently 40 pupils have some form of serious help either one-to-one or in small groups. 'Quite a lot' of dual teaching. Two full-time and three part-time assistants, most problems fall within the dys-strata, couple currently with mild Asperger's. 'Always someone to turn to' if problems hit (more or less at any time) and laptops for most in the SEN stream. (learning support knocks in at £17 per individual 40 minute lesson, £10 if shared and for EFL £15 per 30 minute lesson, £8 if shared). The school is otherwise completely-friendly.

Music is on the up (school says 'outstanding') – the school boasts four choirs (40 choristers toured New York Christmas 2005); 90 recently performed Fauré's Requiem, helped by adults; 60 perform regularly in school orchestra; numerous ensemble groups and jazz band. Keen drama for all ages (drama now on the curriculum) and very good art displayed all over the school (art scholars embark on a four day art retreat to Paris in the autumn term). Minimum TV watching, reading period (Digest) after lunch; computer games rationed, digital games forbidden here. Cooking for all, sewing machines for girls – who are allowed to be gentle – that having been said, there is a dedicated lax pitch. Popular Scottish country dancing a regular feature. School day starts at 8.15am with daily chapel and all the children must say good morning and make eye contact with the head on the way out. Saturday morning school. Huge numbers (75) of extra-curricular activities, from copper etching to fly fishing. No winter timetable, throughout the year children work all morning, after lunch do more lessons until 3.30pm, then games, floodlighting, though not over all the hundred or so acres.

Games are big here, with matches and competitions at all levels, so practically everyone is in a team – and, by the way, they beat other schools. Competitive on the house front (divisions). Wide range of sports on offer including rugger, football, cricket, hockey, netball and rounders. Polo (courtesy of Lord Lloyd Webber – 20+ players) and fencing popular, the latter with streams of ribbons and mega cupboards full of cups for each house. Notably good tennis. New sports hall, opened by Martin Johnson, now offers plethora of opportunities for games for pre-prep and prep children. Overseas tours in abundance – girls' hockey to Barcelona, boys' cricket to South Africa. Notice-boards everywhere along passages and meeting places, bulging with (computer generated) information, lists, newspaper cuttings, news etc. 'We know where every pupil is at any time and can pull up his or her profile at will'. The first notice to hit you in the eye as you enter the school asks, 'Are You Happy?' Head's stated aim is to have 'blissfully happy children'. Manners well taken care of and the school operates a fierce anti-bullying policy. Magical head, magical school, all things for all children. Terrific, but much better if they get the loppers out.

Cheltenham College Junior School

Thirlestaine Road, Cheltenham, GL53 7AB

Tel: 01242 522 697

Fax: 01242 265 620

Email: ccjs@cheltcoll.gloucs.sch.uk

Website: www.cheltcoll.gloucs.sch.uk

• Pupils: 450 girls and boys; boarding and day • Ages: 3-13
• Fees: Day: £1,705-£4,160; boarding £4,125-£5,400.
• School status: Independent • Opendays: October and March
• School gender: Mixed • Day/boarding: Takes boarders

SEN provision

Detail:

Now provide for in school:

Mild: ADD; EBD; DYSL; DYSP; HI;

Moderate: HI;

Others: EAL; DEL; PD;

Experience of:

Mild: ASP; AUT; ADHD; DYSC; SpLD; VI; CP;

Others: Epi; Eat;

Summary: The learning support department has been created to ensure that we provide each child the opportunity to fulfil his or her individual potential by creating a secure and sensitive environment for effective learning, in order to assist them to function in our mainstream school. We aim to develop a positive attitude towards learning by providing support where appropriate to develop self-esteem and general self-confidence. To achieve this, the pupils are provided with programmes to develop improved techniques and address areas of difficulties. From entry, our assessment procedure allows us to monitor progress to ensure each child's requirements are catered for. We provide small group teaching, in class support and individual teaching and work very closely with subject staff and class teachers to ensure continuity within the curriculum.

What we say about the school - the full Good Schools Guide review

Head: Since 1992, Mr Nigel Archdale BEd MEd (forties). Educated John Lyon School and Bristol and Edinburgh universities. Previously at Edinburgh Academy junior school. Then four years as head of Royal Wolverhampton Junior School before putting down roots in leafy Cheltenham. Only 10th head in school's history. Three children (daughter at university, sons at Cheltenham College) and ex-teacher wife, now head's right arm. 'I couldn't do this job without her,' he insists. Very sporty, keeps trim with daily swim or run. Energy is hallmark of his headship. 'There are so many exciting things coming to fruition,' he says. 'It's a truly dynamic school.'

Entrance: At 3, 4, 7 and 11. Non-selective below age 11 with entry by assessment and interview. More choosy later on as pupils must be able to pass CE at 13. Lots of local interest. Tiny intake from overseas. Popular with Services. Doors opened to girls in 1993. Discount available for third and subsequent siblings, bursary scheme for Services, and 11+ scholarship up to 50 per cent of fees.

Exit: In 2005, 100 per cent of pupils got into their first choice school. Vast majority move across the road to mixed senior school, Cheltenham College. CE entry pass around 50 per cent, other schools vary. Number of girls leave at 11 for Cheltenham Ladies' College, despite efforts to hang onto them for another two years. A few also to good local grammars. Parents advised on best senior option for their child. Famous OBs (head calls them OJs as in Old Juniors) include General Sir Michael Rose and actor Nigel Davenport.

Remarks: Known simply as The Junior. Set in conservation area, large Edwardian red-brick purpose-built (in 1908) school house with seamless (and some not so seamless) additions over the decades. Newest building for lower school the best yet and overlooking lake. Head's decision to go co-ed caused great ructions but school has never looked back – there were fewer than 240 pupils when he took over, most in years 7 and 8, now there's twice as many.

School day action packed – hardly enough hours in it. Lessons start 8.15am for all but youngest (Kingfishers pre-prep department launched in 1993 in own well-designed extension) and include daily class music. Not at expense of anything else though. Still find time to fit in French from age of 3 alongside staple diet of core subjects. ICT extremely well catered for with annually updated computers, 24-hour Internet connection, and school network. Laptops everywhere. Internal e-mail system keeps staff in touch – replaced old-style staff notice-boards. Academically thrusting for a non-selective school but geared up to the individual. Help available (at no extra charge) for mild dyslexics, dyspraxics and other minor learning difficulties. 'We're not a special school,' says head. 'The emphasis is on mild.' But parent with criticisms elsewhere in the school is unstinting in his praise of the help for SEN. Well-run shuttle system boosts youngsters' intake of core subjects in place of occasional French or Latin. Extra charge for EFL lessons. Well-stocked pleasant library, used to be school gym.

Artwork on show quite unbelievable (it was easy to forget you were in a junior school) so it seemed a shame more was not spread around the school. Main exception is outstanding series of murals along one corridor wall, painted in 2000. Justly proud of working scale model fleet of warships (made by past pupils and maintained by current pupils) which are sailed each year on Junior's own shallow lake. Bags more innovative projects emerging from tech department – great merging of design, woodwork and electronics – as big a hit with girls as boys. Super sports hall and indoor pool (shared with senior school, as are science labs). Lovely cricket pitch, good hockey and rugby tradition, hard courts for tennis. Brand new assembly hall, attached sympathetically to old school, is all their own. Has transformed the big event, put drama back on the map and given school a unique venue for major productions, concerts and gatherings. Only non-purpose building is music school, a lovely wood-panelled setting for individual lessons and small group recitals. Four choirs (chapel choir regularly tours).

Boarding not at full capacity but allows for sleep-overs. Large airy dorms in old building, shared curtained cubicles for older children, all well kept with enough pictures, toys and own duvets to make it homely. Boarders' privileges extend to use of library, computers, art and DT studios at any time of day. Can also use pool for special supervised sessions. Only pupils to be allowed mobile phones though use strictly controlled. Fabulous grounds and lush green setting provide plenty of scope for outside play. Pupils allocated houses for competitive and pastoral reasons. Strict anti-bullying policy rigidly enforced. 'Bullying is a fact of life,' admits head. Will go to great lengths to resolve difficulties but head has been known to ask repeat offenders to leave.

Weekly chapel on Saturday, Sunday service three or four times a term. Chapel 'essential but not in an over-arching way,' says head. Saturday school a bone of contention with some parents; now being made optional for year 3, still compulsory for all above. Topic constantly raises its head at annual parents forum and three-yearly parental survey – so watch this space.

Plenty of moneyed backgrounds, landed gentry and self-made millionaires (there's soon to be an addition to the fact-packed parents' handbook on landing helicopters at school), but there are ordinary folk too. 'We have a very broad parental constituency.' No parent teacher association. Tried it once, didn't work. No fund-raising for extras either. 'Parents are already paying enough through fees,' says head. 'I don't think it's fair to keep on asking them for more.' Extra activities include twice-weekly dry slope skiing in nearby Gloucester, squash, trampolining, and paddle-boating on lake.

Smashing bunch of children seen around school, no one apparently at a loose end, and a certain confidence clearly evident from the youngest Kingfisher up. Head sums up school in one word – enthusiasm. The enthusiasm of pupils, staff and 'most parents'. There's an overwhelming feeling here of purpose and activity. Everything is designed 'to produce a child who can make meaningful sense of this incredibly confusing 21st century,' says head. In other words, kids with street cred as well as an appreciation of their privileged circumstances.

THE CHERWELL SCHOOL

Marston Ferry Road, Oxford, Oxfordshire, OX2 7EE

Tel: 01865 558 719

Fax: 01865 311 165

Email: Headteacher.4116@cherwell.oxon.sch.uk

Website: www.cherwell.oxon.sch.uk

• Pupils: 1,055, boys and girls, all day • Ages: 11-18

• Religion: Non-denom • School status: State

• School gender: Mixed • Day/boarding: Day pupils

SEN provision

Detail:

Experience of:

Mild: ASP; AUT; ADD; ADHD; EBD; DYSC; DYSL; DYSP; HI; VI; CP;

Moderate: ASP; ADD; ADHD; EBD; DS; MLD; DYSC; DYSL; DYSP; HI; VI; CP;

Severe: ASP; ADD; ADHD; EBD; DS; DYSC; DYSL; HI; CP;

Others: CD; ODD; TIC; EAL; Sp&LD; DEL; Epi; PD; Eat;

Summary: Many students at the school have special educational needs – physical, academic, social or emotional and behavioural. There is a learning base and a behaviour base on both sites providing support to students in a variety of ways. In-class support involves a Teaching Assistant being in a class to give help to students who are thus enabled to keep pace with the rest of the class. In a few cases this support is for a particular student, but more generally it is shared between several. Small group withdrawal caters for a small number of students who need extra help with basic literacy, numeracy or social skills. Very occasionally a student is withdrawn for one-to-one work.

Learning support staff also act in an advisory capacity to staff in all curriculum areas, providing resources and strategies for students with special educational needs.

What we say about the school - the full Good Schools Guide review

Head: Since 2003, Mrs K J Judson BA Med FRSA (forties), previously head of Maidstone Grammar School for

Girls. Took over from Mr Martin Roberts, who was head from 1981.

Academic Matters: Arguably best state secondary in Oxford. Head hoped relatively slow rate of improvement at GCSE would be boosted when school became 11-18 in 2003. Cherwell has also applied for specialist science status. Wide and interesting range of subjects at GCSE, including sports studies, child development and information studies. Of the core subjects, above average results in English, strong scores in maths, and exceptional grades in French, history, art, drama, information technology (after a slow start and with the benefit of new IT facilities) and business studies. Most subjects well above national average. German second language on offer, with other languages subject to requirements and backgrounds of pupils. Girls reap many more high grades at GCSE than boys, with a sizeable 20 per cent gap in most subjects between those achieving five A* to C grades. At A level they are much more on a par. Star subjects at A level are art, chemistry, French, geography (clearly popular with able sixth form girls) and maths and further maths, where the boys shine. Some A level courses offered at other sites (including Oxford College of Further Education), including law, graphics and psychology – small number of candidates, excellent grades. Very good AS results despite their hasty introduction – art the real success. Lots of distinctions in advanced GNVQs, offered in business and tourism.

Comprehensive SEN resources, with a full learning support programme and units for hearing-impaired and autistic pupils. 313 pupils currently on the SEN register, 53 IEPs, 25 or so picked up via school action plus. SENCo, who has an RSA diploma in dyslexia, plus administrator plus five teaching assistants, usually one-to-one, but popular small literacy group, withdrawn from class – normally a modern foreign language; all attend mainstream school. It may happen that SEN pupils are directed towards GNVQs or ASDN youth awards rather than GCSEs or A levels, but no harm in that. School is also home to hearing impairment centre for Oxfordshire with a number of outreach staff who work with families. Autistic centre.

Games, Options, The Arts: The setting is everything here. Adequate gym and good all-weather tennis courts and basketball area is supplemented by lots of green space for a big range of sports, including rugby and football, at which both boys and girls represent the county sides. Site also borders Ferry sports centre, which houses pools, larger sports hall and squash courts. Compact but well-resourced library. Drama very popular, with regular theatre visits to London and Stratford, an after-school club and excellent productions. Well-used, separate music block shows music of all kinds taken seriously and to a high standard – around a quarter take individual music lessons and a recent Young Musician of the Year was a Cherwell pianist. Regular concerts from school orchestras, wind band and choirs. Strong art – student sculptures grace the entrance and paintings line the stairwells. Sixth form art students study abroad for a week each year. More than 100 terminals on school computer network and Internet use encouraged. Lively, interesting website includes the headteacher's regular and forthright newsletters. Linked to schools in France and Germany. Trips of all kinds in all subjects 'organised by staff at the drop of a hat'.

Background and Atmosphere: When it opened in 1963, The Cherwell School was a small secondary modern, for ages 11-16, surrounded by allotments and fields near Oxford's upmarket Summertown area. Two 1970s events shattered its peace: first, the building of the inner Oxford ring road; secondly, the shake-up of Oxford's schools. The Cherwell School became an ever-growing comprehensive upper school (ages 13-18), separated from its main feeder middle schools (9-13) by fast-flowing traffic. Its original box-shaped buildings were supplemented by a library and sixth form block and then, when the money ran out in the 1980s, rows of ugly temporary classrooms. When building restarted in 1991, a music and drama block and new permanent classrooms were finally added. The site was also landscaped with help from the parents' association. It really shows, with a modern school that looks tidy and comfortable in its leafy surroundings, if clearly bursting at its seams. Many more changes are afoot as the revamped 11-18 school swallows and extends Frideswide Middle School, across the main road, to house younger Cherwell pupils for the bulk of their lessons.

Pastoral Care and Discipline: Form tutors are first port of call for general matters – pupils retain the same form tutor for three years. School council, made up of elected representatives from years 9-11, discusses and formulates policy affecting the school community and arranges social and charity events. Sixth-formers lead working parties of younger pupils to deal with specific issues. Common sense, 'firm but fair' rules, formal detentions coupled with a positive approach results in, for the most part, decent behaviour and polite young people, though small number of pupils disrupt lessons on occasions. Temporary exclusions used sparingly, usually for bullying or fighting, and permanent exclusions very rare – a couple for violence and drug dealing in the last few years. But the lack of a uniform does leave some particularly scruffy pupils looking as if they have been pulled from a skip.

Pupils and Parents: Pupils are generally all a school could wish for – bright, encouraged at home, used to academic endeavour (this is Oxford, after all), imaginative and ambitious to realise their dreams. Parents are often academics themselves or work in the mass of white-collar, high-brow and highly paid jobs on offer in Oxford. There are, however, pockets of poverty and disaffection in the heart of Oxford and Cherwell has its share of troubled and troublesome children. Famous ex-pupils include Rachel Seiffert (novelist) and Yasmin le Bon (model).

Entrance: Only distance from school matters – unfortunately, this varies from year to year according to numbers applying. Oversubscribed by at least 50 for 220 places for last few years. Distraught parents falling just outside this year's boundary make up ever-increasing number appealing – half a dozen usually succeed. Rise to 270 places per year from 2003 leads head to hope the problem will be solved. Most come from two nearest middle schools and the rest from within a small radius. A few arrive from private prep schools in Oxford.

Exit: Around 80-90 per cent go into sixth form, 60 per cent staying at Cherwell and the remainder usually joining Oxford's FE college. Almost all taking A levels will go on to higher education, while others take vocational qualifications and a small number start work. A few reach Oxbridge, with Cambridge favoured over the grand university round the corner.

Money Matters: Two successive years of financial cuts (1995-6 and 1996-7) in Oxfordshire mean that class sizes are larger, learning support has been cut and there are five fewer staff.

Remarks: A school whose star is very clearly rising, where a great deal is on offer for all abilities – and where one senses that the best is yet to come.

Chethams School of Music

Long Millgate, Manchester, Lancashire, M3 1SB

Tel: 0161 834 9644

Fax: 0161 839 3609

Email: lesleyhaslam@chethams.com

Website: www.chethams.com

• Pupils: 285, mostly boarding (60 day pupils) • Ages: 8-18 • Religion: Non-denom • Fees: Day £5,978, boarding £7,723. Choristers considerably less • School status: Independent • School gender: Mixed • Day/boarding: Takes boarders

SEN provision

Detail:

Now provide for in school:

Mild: ASP; DYSC; DYSL; DYSP; HI;
Moderate: ASP; DYSL; DYSP; HI;
Severe: DYSL;
Others: AUT(other); EAL; Sp&LD;

Experience of:

Mild: ADD; ADHD; EBD;
Moderate: ADD; ADHD; MLD; DYSC;
Severe: ASP; VI;
Others: CD; OCD; ODD; TIC; GEN; PD; Eat;

Summary: Pupils with special educational needs and/or English as a Second language are catered for in the Compensatory Education Department. All of our pupils are musically gifted. At present we have three teachers including the Head of Department (SENCo) and a learning support assistant. A wide age range is covered, 8-18 years old. Lessons take place in the department on an individual basis sometimes combined with in-class support as appropriate. Some pupils have just half an hour per week of additional support whereas others may need as much as three hours. The Department also aims to equip pupils with relevant study skills and specific equipment eg Alphasmart, in order to make the best use of study time. At present we have pupils with SEN ranging from mild dyslexia to high functioning autism. Some of our previous pupils have had Tourette's syndrome, ADHD and Visual Impairment and have managed to procede with music and further their musical careers. We have also catered for a pupil who had

Ehlers Danlos syndrome. Staff are qualified to assess for access arrangements for public examinations.

English as a Second Language is another important part of the department's work. Pupils need to have a working knowledge of English in order to make the most of their time at Chetham's but English support is also available. Pupils enter into the school in different year groups, from Juniors (8 years old) right through to the sixth form. It is important that they have sufficient time to develop their English skills before facing public examinations. There are also opportunities to take specific E2L examinations, eg Cambridge Exams KET, PET First Certificate etc. We also offer IELTS and TOEFL and the International GCSE English as a Second Language. In addition to language support every effort is made to help E2L pupils feel at home with the change in culture whilst affirming their own cultural background.

What we say about the school - the full Good Schools Guide review

Head: Since 1999, Mrs Claire J Moreland MA (mid forties). Read modern languages at Oxford. Previously housemistress and deputy head at Rugby School. Divorced, one son. Interests are music, literature, theatre, travel and walking. Plays classical guitar in private. Viewed by pupils as firm but fair and approachable; they comment that tightening up in discipline since her arrival has been properly explained to them, not just dropped from on high. Her ambitions for the school are that it be 'even better known both locally and nationally' and properly understood as a 'centre of excellence', not of elitism. Developing outreach and partnership programmes to make Chetham's resources, eg expertise and buildings, more widely available. Views not having come up through the music world as 'a bonus' enabling her to bring an independent and impartial perspective to the job. Has all-round support of staff and parents.

Academic Matters: About one third of timetabled time devoted to music. In view of this, and the fact that the school is academically non-selective, exam results are pretty good. Fewer GCSEs and A levels taken than in most schools (generally 7 GCSEs and three or four AS levels) to allow for exceptional music timetabling but the highly motivated attitude of pupils to their music seems to carry over into other subjects. Classes small – average size 15, maximum 22. Ratio of staff to pupils 1:7. Pupils keen to be perceived as highly successful across the board, not just as musicians. School careful to ensure that 'a decent Plan B' is in place, for those pupils who don't make it in a musical career or don't wish to pursue one. 39 pupils currently have some form of SEN, including dyslexia, dyspraxia and a few requiring ESL support. School uses the services of three SEN members of staff.

Musically, the school is highly thought of nationally and internationally. Head keen to emphasise that broad-based western classical tradition also complemented by other facets of musical education, including jazz and electronic music (a state-of-the-art music tech and recording suite available 2006) and use/impact of Internet, as appropriate, 'to equip pupils for the 21st century'. Whiteley Hall (school concert hall) six years old. Numerous competition and other successes.

Games, Options, The Arts: Emphasis on personal fitness. Attention to physical well-being strongly encouraged. Gym open every evening and as much as possible at weekends – also walking trips and sailing activities. No compulsory team sports due to demands of timetabling music lessons, practice sessions, performances etc, though friendly matches, eg between staff and pupils, do take place. Prospective parents fearing that this might mean no competitive spirit in the school would be wrong; energy and adrenaline merely re-routed and very much in evidence in musical teamwork. Strong sense of pride in achievements of the school. Drama popular, including staff productions.

Background and Atmosphere: Site small, 15th-century listed buildings at its core, and located in the heart of Manchester city centre. Became school of music in 1969. Site a mixed blessing; on the one hand, absolutely beautiful, architecturally (something which the aesthetically finely tuned pupils appreciate) but on the other hand, its smallness and the security issues that any such city-centre location would pose, bring their own problems. These should not be over-emphasised, however. Bedrooms are not very big but not too many sharing. Three or four to a room lower down the school, in sixth form 2 people per room. Girls in upper sixth not required to share. Bedroom tidiness evidently not a particularly high priority!

Atmosphere of school is tangibly charged with the excitement and enthusiasm of the pupils and has all the pros and cons of any tight-knit community. School has fairly close relationship with Manchester Cathedral (it educates the choristers) but has multi-ethnic and international intake and looks for common spiritual ground between people and religions rather than following any particular doctrine. The diversity of backgrounds of pupils is viewed as a plus. Pupils take advantage of good links with the musical community in Manchester, attend many concerts in the city.

Pastoral Care and Discipline: Various people to whom pupils can and do turn in difficulties. Relationship with instrument teacher generally very close. House parents, tutors, are available, also house assistants who are often a popular choice of confidant/e (not forgetting the laundry ladies, viewed by some as a bevy of 'mums'). Older pupils look after the younger members of the school and are touchingly fond of their 'little ones'.

Pupil handbook, setting out anti-bullying policy, general information and school rules, is a model document ('busking is strictly against the rules' – hard luck to the more entrepreneurially inclined pupils!). Due to extent of government funding, pupils not permitted to fall by the wayside – school has to justify, and be seen to justify, government support.

Pupils and Parents: Parents from many countries and all walks of life. Some are active in the musical world themselves, others have had no contact with world of music and are astonished to find themselves with a musical prodigy on their hands. Very occasionally a parent has musical ambitions for their child that the child does not share, leading to problems of motivation. Mostly the pupils are immensely motivated and committed, excited at the opportunity to learn at a specialist school. Pupils view 'modesty' and 'having your feet firmly on the ground' as essential prerequisites to happiness at the school. Mutually supportive atmosphere, in which pupils 'live or die' by remembering to read the notice-boards (there is a long corridor of them) and checking school's intranet several times a day – the more absent-minded pupils being suitably organised by the switched-on ones. Famous old boys/girls include Wayne Marshall, Peter Donohoe, Anna Markland, Max Beesley, David Hill.

Entrance: Most applicants hear of school, and are encouraged to apply, through their instrument/music teachers. The only criterion for entry is exceptional musical ability, which is assessed by two auditions. No academic criteria.

Exit: The majority (about two thirds) to music conservatoires and colleges, some to study music at university, others to read other subjects – a good proportion to Oxbridge, bearing out head's view that good musicians tend also to be very bright.

Money Matters: 98 per cent of pupils are at Chetham's with government support via DfES. Successful recent appeal to improve boys' boarding house by 2006.

Remarks: Very special pupils but not remotely 'precious'. Whereas a lot of schools like to pass themselves off as one big, happy family, Chetham's actually feels like one.

CHEW VALLEY SCHOOL

Chew Lane, Chew Magna, Bristol, BS40 8QB

Tel: 01275 332 272

Fax: 01275 333 625

Email: chewvalley_sec@bathnes.gov.uk

Website: www.chewvalleyschool.co.uk

• Pupils: 1,150 boys and girls, all day • Ages: 11-18

• Religion: Non-denom • School status: State

• Opendays: September for y7 entry, November for sixth form. Tours by appointment any time • School gender: Mixed

• Day/boarding: Day pupils

What we say about the school - the full Good Schools Guide review

Head: Since 2003, Mark Mallett, LLB, MA and PGCE, University College, London. He taught in Borneo with VSO, London and Bristol before taking up deputy headship in Hexham, Northumberland. A passionate educationalist and classroom practitioner, he is a teaching head and enthusiastic promoter of extra-curricular activity in sport and the arts.

Academic Matters: Outstanding teaching in science, maths, English, technology and languages; small class sizes in the sixth form. 43 per cent A or B at A level; 75 per cent 5A*-C at GCSE. Highly effective special needs team (rated excellent by Ofsted) deals sensitively with 30 statemented pupils and varying degrees of specific learning difficulty through a modified curriculum. Also brilliant liaison with feeder primary schools on this score. Ofsted report (Jan 2005) confirmed it was a very good school with very good leadership and management, teaching, learning and value for money.

Games, Options, The Arts: Sportsmark, a lottery funded leisure centre and 35 acres of playing fields surrounding the landscaped grounds mean that sport has a high profile. County teams for rugby, badminton, squash, hockey, tennis. Two teams do Ten Tors challenge each year with 35- and 55-mile expeditions on Dartmoor. Sailing offered as sixth form option. Hockey and rugby teams toured Australia in summer 2003.

240 students learn an instrument and frequent concerts include a wide range of music and dance. Recent projects have included an artist in residence, Duncan Morrell, who worked with students on a large whale and dolphin mural. School diary is choc-a-bloc with debating visits, choirs at Bath Festival, drama performances including Twelfth Night at the Bristol Old Vic. Michael Eavis opened the new Music Centre in February 2005.

Background and Atmosphere: Most marvellous location in the midst of a beauty spot/green-belt between the affluent villages of Chew Magna and Chew Stoke, nestled behind the Chew Valley Lake. Unceremonious entrance hall gives you the feeling you had wandered past a back door of a Centre Parcs village. The photo-call of staff (beaming, bright, healthy smiles) could well be those at an up-market health hydro but these are highly skilled teachers and staff who inspire high achievement across the board.

Pastoral Care and Discipline: Much care taken over transplanting tender shoots at age 11. Parents' evenings are civilised, with private appointments – 'no scrums in the hall with everyone listening in,' remarks the head of careers. Sixth formers work with the year 7 students to help them settle into their new surroundings.

Pupils and Parents: So much in demand that 20 per cent of pupils live outside the catchment area. Pupils are a well-ordered bunch. Confident and happy. No signs of tension. They know exactly what they're here for and get on with it.

Old Boys and Girls become sporting stars (4 girls in England students' rugby team), successful musicians, fast-stream civil servants, careers in law, medicine or TV designers.

Entrance: Apply direct to the Director of Education, Bath and North East Somerset Council, Admissions and Transport Section, P O Box 25, Riverside, Keynsham, Bristol BS31 1DN by the 19th October prior to the year of entry. Outside entry into the sixth form needs five grades A*-C GCSEs but a key deciding factor is motivation and behaviour.

Exit: 60 per cent of GCSE students go on into the sixth form, 25 per cent to FE courses, 10 per cent into modern apprenticeship or employment – the rest move out of the area. 90 per cent of sixth formers go on to university (many after a gap year). Steady numbers to veterinary science, sports science, medicine and Oxbridge. In 2005, two students to Oxbridge and a further two to medical school.

Remarks: Hugely popular school in blissful rural setting.

CHRIST COLLEGE, BRECON

Brecon, Powys, LD3 8AF

Tel: 01874 615 440

Fax: 01874 615 475

Email: enquiries@christcollegebrecon.com

Website: www.christcollegebrecon.com

• Pupils: 190 boys, 130 girls. 260 board • Ages: 11-18 Religion: Christian • Fees: Day £3,490-£3,975; boarding £4,650-£5,940 • School status: Independent • School gender: Mixed • Day/boarding: Takes boarders

SEN provision

Detail:

Now provide for in school:

Mild: DYSL;

Moderate: DYSL;

Others: EAL;

Experience of:

Mild: DYSP;

Severe: DYSL;

Others: Eat;

Summary: Highly qualified/experienced SENCo/specialist teacher. Timetabled sessions for learning support on one-to-one group basis. Emphasis on teaching strageties for managing in the classroom. Support for Sixth form as well as younger pupils – which focuses on time management and organisation of self and work.

What we say about the school - the full Good Schools Guide review

Head: Since 1996, Mr Philip Jones MA (fifties), educated at Midsomer Norton Grammar School and read geography at Fitzwilliam College, Cambridge. Taught at Downside and for twenty-four years at Sherborne where he was senior master, housemaster, head of department and a legendary rugby coach. Came relatively late to headmastering but has shown in his time at Brecon that he has a natural talent for the job. Has transformed Brecon into perhaps the leading co-educational boarding school in Wales.

Married to Jane and has two grown up children. When not involved in school (which is not often) he can think of nothing more wonderful than to fish the Tywi, which meanders right past the college. Exudes integrity and is a delightfully unpretentious and honest man who is very clear what he wishes Christ College to become. Steeped in his Welsh heritage (his father was a miner and later the first principal of Midsomer (Mining and later Technical) College) whilst at the same time with a wide and extensive experience of the independent school system. His long service as a very effective and popular housemaster at Sherborne has led him to focus particularly on the quality of pastoral care. Brecon has a particularly strong and vibrant house structure. At least as impressive is the fact that he knows and greets every pupil he meets on his main excursions around the campus. A man who believes in the old-fashioned principle that the first obligation of a head is to walk the job. Understands that happy and fulfilled pupils are those who are stretched in a wide variety of academic disciplines and activities.

Academic Matters: Wide ability range – results are extraordinarily good. 90 plus per cent A* to C at GCSE, 75 per cent A-C at A level. In the sciences, A level pass rates were over 90 per cent. Design and technology is another great strength.

The range of subjects offered in such a small institution amazes one. Enormous choice offered for GCSE and even more at A level. Sixth form teaching groups are often very small with individual progress being very closely monitored – a particular strength. Not a school that has compromised its scholastic ideals in the pursuit of transitory success in league tables. The vast majority of sixth form pupils are undertaking real and demanding subjects even if this depresses the school's league table showing. Strong learning support provided (unusually) as part of the basic fee. The 12 per cent foreign student contingent is offered considerable assistance with English; again as part of the basic fee.

Games, Options, The Arts: Brecon is a boarding school. This means that, even nominally, day pupils will spend at least ten hours a day in school and sometimes as much as fourteen. The school is a hive of activities with the glorious Brecon Beacons being well used as a resource for adventure training and CCF activities. Christ College is perhaps most famous for its prowess on the rugby field. The annual match (perhaps better described as a battle!) between Brecon and Llandovery is a highlight of the Welsh school rugby scene. Yet it is clear that all sports are taken very seriously. Now the College is co-educational this is particularly true of hockey and netball. If proof were needed of the sporting focus of the College the twenty-odd pupils who have represented their country in ten different sports surely speaks volumes.

Art one of the particular strengths and some extraordinary work in photography. The way the pupils' success in this area is acknowledged and even celebrated shows that Brecon has totally shrugged off the bone-headed rugby image it once had. Also shown in the fine dramatic tradition the school has recently developed. Major dramatic productions take place in most terms and are designed to involve as many of the pupils as possible. 'Sweet Charity' and 'Oh What a Lovely War' are recent examples that do precisely this as well as exploiting and developing Brecon's strong choral tradition. Despite this tradition, only 33 per cent of pupils learn a music instrument.

Background and Atmosphere: Founded in 1541 by Henry VIII, together with Eton one of the two independent school royal foundations. Nestles on the edge of the sleepy Welsh market town of Brecon – the views are truly spectacular and whole assemblage is reminiscent of an idealised Dylan Thomas film set. The school campus is nicely compact with boarding houses, chapel, games fields and classrooms all jumbled together in a rather eclectic mixture of architectural styles. In truth one would not celebrate the majority of the post-war developments, yet on the whole the campus is of a human scale that enhances the very modest and unpretentious atmosphere of the institution. The key to Brecon's success is the friendliness and warmth that pervades the relationships here. The head's determination to be accessible to all is a key factor. His office right in the centre of the campus ensures that pupils and staff can simply pop in if need be. Bullying is hardly evident here.

Quite deliberately the head celebrates the old-fashioned values. The College has something of the feel of a 1950s grammar school. Everything and everybody is neat and tidy and a great emphasis is put on respect and courtesy.

Pastoral Care and Discipline: Very strong house system. Head focused on the need to deliver top quality pastoral care. A huge amount of money spent in recent years in upgrading the boarding accommodation. The two girls' boarding houses are now very attractive with charismatic and effective housemothers. Whilst the school expects high standards of behaviour from its pupils (and usually achieves them) discipline is enforced with a light touch. The emphasis is on the quality of personal relationships that seem to be especially good. Escapes some of the more extreme drugs and drink difficulties that plague schools closer to the fleshpots of the south east.

Pupils and Parents: Most of the pupils hail from within 50 miles, pretty evenly divided between those from Wales and from the English marches. There are small numbers from a total of 19 different countries as well as significant and unusually not declining numbers of military and expat families. Not a smart school and has never attempted to be so. Significant numbers come from an agricultural background, although this is very much in the decline. The growth in the number of refugees fleeing London to the good life in Powys suggests that the English proportion will grow.

Entrance: About 60 per cent of the intake at 11, for two years in the delightfully prep school atmosphere of the Junior House, mostly from relatively local Powys and Herefordshire primary schools. A significant and growing intake from prep schools at 13 plus: St John's on the Hill, Llandaff, St Richard's Bredonbury, Abberley Hall, Moor Park and Moffats. Entrance is by a simple mathematics, English and verbal reasoning test and not usually Common Entrance. The growing popularity of the school has made it more selective than it was but it remains relatively relaxed in its selection criteria.

Exit: 97 per cent go on to university, between two and four a year to Oxbridge. A larger than expected number go on to read science degrees, a reflection of the College's particular strength here.

Money Matters: Extraordinarily good value. Lots of very generous scholarships and bursaries for the able and deserving. A rare and very attractive feature is that despite a competitive fee level there are no compulsory extras.

Remarks: No one is going to choose Brecon as an elitist icon, but it's a school that is very much on the up and achieves much more than one would expect given its size and location. Offers at least as much as many more prestigious and expensive alternatives; becoming seriously popular.

Cirencester Deer Park School

Stroud Road, Cirencester, Gloucestershire, GL7 1XB

Tel: 01285 653 447

Fax: 01285 640 669

Email: enquiries@deerparkschool.net

Website: www.deerparkschool.net

• Pupils: 1,112, boys and girls, all day • Ages: 11-16

• Religion: Non-denom • School status: State

• Opendays: Late September • School gender: Mixed

• Day/boarding: Day pupils

SEN provision

Detail:

Now provide for in school:

Mild: ASP; AUT; ADD; ADHD; EBD; DYSC; DYSL; DYSP;

Moderate: ADD; ADHD; EBD; MLD; DYSC; DYSL; DYSP;

Others: CD; EAL; Sp&LD;

Experience of:

Mild: VI; CP;

Moderate: ASP; VI;

Severe: ADD; ADHD; EBD; DYSC; DYSL; DYSP;

Others: OCD; ODD; SLD; Epi; Eat;

Summary: Cirencester Deer Park School provides a range of provision for pupils with special educational needs. We are a high achieving school and our value added work is testament to this. However our intake profile shows that on entry to the school we have a fully comprehensive population covering a range of abilties. The provision for SEN falls broadly into two categories: learning support and inclusion support. These fall under the responsibility of the deputy head: pupil services who is also responsible for the pastoral teams – heads of year, tutors etc.

Learning Support: this area provides support for pupils with specific learning difficulties (dyslexia), general learning difficulties, autistic spectrum disorders, dyspraxia etc. Our provision ranges from in-class support to withdrawal for targeted small groups. We offer alternative curriculum pathways to pupils at Key Stage 4 in order to match their learning needs.

Inclusion Support: this area provides support for pupils with behavioural, emotional and social difficulties and involves intensive work, usually on a one-to-one basis with specialist staff who can offer counselling, behaviour modification, anger management and work on self-awareness.

The two areas are not mutually exclusive and work together often with outside agencies to ensure good provision for all pupils with special and differing needs at Deer Park.

What we say about the school - the full Good Schools Guide review

Head: Since 2003, Mrs Chiquita Henson BA(Hons) NPQH (forties). Read English at Sheffield University followed by PGCE at Bristol; subsequent professional training in leadership and headship. Educated at a comprehensive school herself, Chiquita Henson has been at Deer Park since 1989, becoming head of English when the school still had a sixth form and then deputy head from 1994 to 2003. Knows the patch inside out and has been at forefront of school's recent development as a 'Leading Edge' and 'Training' school. Outwardly reserved but combines steely professionalism with a passion to drive Deer Park forwards. Makes full use of ex-accountant director of support to do the number crunching she finds a chore. 'Incredibly hard-working,' said one parent; 'children find her a bit scary,' said another. A modern, no nonsense head who is good at getting recognition and money for the school. Partner, Tim is a science teacher with children at primary school in Stroud where they live. Still teaches some English. Predecessor was 'a hard act to follow' but general parental agreement that she is good news.

Academic Matters: Has made application to add second specialism to become a college for arts and technology. A truly comprehensive school with results fluctuating from year to year; incredible 80 per cent five GCSEs at grades A*-C achieved in 2003 partly attributable to a significant GNVQ factor. Has averaged 70 per cent plus over past four years; consistently impressive Key Stage 3 levels and improving results in value-added tables with boys and girls doing equally well. Over 20 per cent gain five or more A* and A grades at GCSE. Curriculum structure is divided into modules across a 50 (hour long) lesson fortnight, run by faculties and overseen by mentors – brings the nearest thing to a personal timetable by GCSE level. Interesting links with industry. Mix of traditional and newer courses at GCSE where the 'normal' subject load for pupils is being reduced from 11.5 to 10.5 subjects, giving more time for non-examinable PE (4 hours per fortnight) and global citizenship. Dual award science so quite a challenge for those who go to academic science sixth forms. Can take science as a single subject – plus rural science or child development or a choice from citizenship/RE/ICT. 'Fabulous maths teaching,' said a parent; we saw a class tackling probability with plenty of intelligent participation. Innovative maths and drama scheme for year 7 pupils. 'Faculty in Focus' puts pupils and staff from a given area into the spotlight for a short period – visits to 'Starlab' and 'Maths Magic' have resulted. Parents like homework which they described as 'challenging without being too difficult.'

Well-sited learning support unit adjacent to art area. SENCo carries out audit in year 7; 16 statemented pupils; about 20 per cent of pupils receive help in some form: extraction, spelling and literacy groups; alternative curriculum pathway with support from teaching assistants based in different faculties; value-added results highlight successes, with one pupil in 2005 achieving five GCSEs at grades A*-C from a baseline VRQ of 70. Enrichment activities for gifted and able have included designing a refectory in collaboration with Plymouth University.

Games, Options, The Arts: Vibrant young head of expressive arts having tremendous impact. Orchestra, choir and jazz band with music tours abroad. Major drama production every two years with plenty of shorter works in between. We saw a drama class which was totally absorbed and never noticed us watching. NCFE award in music technology rarely found in 11-16 sector. Good sports hall plus larger Astroturf for football, hockey and lacrosse (!) plus smaller one for netball. Plenty of teams and extra-curricular sports activity. Art is well taught (parents amazed at what their offspring have achieved); adequate accommodation with some impressive pieces on display. Standstill days give each year group a chance to do something outside the curriculum and the annual enrichment week approaches citizenship from a different angle eg 'European Awareness' for year 8 and 'Personal Challenge' for year 9. Hosts South Cotswold Science Fair – a fun event to bring science into everyday experience.

Background and Atmosphere: Celebrates fortieth anniversary as a comprehensive school in 2006. Origins stretch back to middle ages but 1960s legacy evident in featureless external appearance. School shares attractively wooded site on western edge of town with Cirencester College next door and the Royal Agricultural College opposite. Youngish staff with the average age below 40 but over one third have taught here over ten years. Specialist technology status translates into computers everywhere plus digital projectors and interactive whiteboards in every classroom; Powell's Learning Centre a hive of activity and remains open after school. Some aesthetically pleasing internal features such as the drama studio, atrium social area and art exhibition corridor. We liked the simple polo shirt uniform and the positive buzz in lessons and corridors.

Pastoral Care and Discipline: Strong pupil services team divides years into half-year groups with learning co-ordinators for each supported by tutors and mentors. We felt that pupils here have a positive attitude to work and an understanding of a good range of global issues. Pastoral database is bought by other schools. Emphasis on restorative justice. Good attendance levels point to policies working.

Pupils and Parents: Mainly middle class catchment but with some from surprisingly deprived areas in Cirencester. Friendly, polite bunch who get stuck into the challenging work environment. Year 11 pupils seem more mature for age than in average 11-18 school. Some pupils involved in unusual exchanges with Inuit children from Canadian Arctic and with a day school in New Delhi. Most of school's governors are parents. Friends of Deer Park is active in supporting school events and raising funds. Website allows parents access and publishes weekly newsletter.

Entrance: Over-subscribed – comprehensive intake with geography and siblings most important criteria. Majority from Cirencester primaries and outlying villages but quite a few come from Stroud direction where it is seen as an attractive alternative to secondary moderns for some.

Exit: About 90 per cent go into further education with majority going to Cirencester College next door. Significant number go further afield to sixth forms such as Pate's in Cheltenham where Deer Park pupils have done extremely well.

Remarks: 'Can do' philosophy rubs off on everyone – 'everything is an opportunity,' said one teacher. Plenty of human endeavour and creativity behind the high tech world on offer here which 'doesn't take over.' Quite a place, with pupils liking the modern approach and responding well across the board.

Clayesmore Preparatory School

Iwerne Minster, Blandford Forum, Dorset, DT11 8PH

Tel: 01747 811 707

Fax: 01747 811 692

Email: prepadmissions@clayesmore.com

Website: www.clayesmore.com

• Pupils: 265 boys and girls; 65 board. 15 in nursery • Ages: 2-13 • Religion: C of E • Fees: Boarders £4,675-£5,124; day £3,565-£3,805. Pre-prep (including after school care) £1870 • School status: Independent • School gender: Mixed • Day/boarding: Takes boarders

---

SEN provision

Detail:

Centre of excellence for:
- Mild: DYSL; DYSP;
- Moderate: DYSL;

Now provide for in school:
- Mild: DYSC; SpLD;
- Moderate: DYSP;
- Severe: DYSL;
- Others: EAL; Epi;

Experience of:
- Mild: HI; VI;
- Moderate: DYSC;
- Severe: DYSP;

Summary: Clayesmore Preparatory School has an excellent reputation for its provision of support for dyslexic pupils. Our learning support department ensures that pupils have effective and targeted teaching, either individually or in very small groups, to meet their specific needs. Pupils are withdrawn at carefully selected times during the school day to attend their specialist lessons. They may also benefit from the support given by LS Teaching Assistants, who work alongside the teachers in some mainstream lessons. All learning support tutors are fully qualified teachers with additional qualifications in teaching pupils with specific learning difficulties. Mainstream teachers are empathetic with the needs and difficulties of some of the children in the mainstream classes and differentiate accordingly. The school is registered with CReSTeD.

What we say about the school - the full Good Schools Guide review

Head: Mr Martin Cooke (see senior school).

Entrance: Interview with HM, report from previous school, all come for a trial day and are informally assessed, with an ed psych's report if necessary.

Exit: 'More or less an automatic transfer to senior school – about 85 per cent go on' though Mr Cooke 'makes an effort to see parents again and make them welcome'. Some may return to maintained sector (Poole Grammar popular), Canford and Millfield pick up one or two.

Remarks: A separate school which this year celebrates its seventy-fifth birthday; Mr Cooke, head of the senior school, is currently running both with the aid of a deputy and assistant head in each. Charming, with a delightful combo building on a sort of cruciform shape with dormitories and classrooms dotted around (in a rather more organised fashion than it reads), it is first on Mr Cooke's wish list for improvement. Previously based in Charlton Marshall, the school was sold by its founder to Lt Col Ivor Edwards-Stewart who, when he retired in 1974, 'funded a school of a most modern design' on the senior school campus, with a dedicated play area (hopscotch and climbing frames) – it uses senior school facilities, indeed the old squash court, which has a tremendously grand entrance on the school side and forms part of the senior school music department, is divided, with the nether end currently used for tinies' cooking (a bit under used if the truth be told).

Trails of children (some being carried) skipping back from lunch in the big school dining room (terrific lunch), and good use made of the sports pitches, dining room, music school, chapel and leisure centre. Runs popular Arts Week at the end of the summer term. Similar emphasis to the senior school on good pastoral care and the importance of the individual. A very popular school with parents in the area, also has a sprinkling of expat children, some foreigners; fair number of Forces children plus siblings of those in the senior school, plus a number of first time buyers and ex-London refugees. Seventy-five boarders max, flexi-boarding not a problem (£16.65 per night), and no charge if doing sport or choir or sleeping bags on mattresses. Dedicated team of houseparents, plus matrons who are known as 'the sisters'.

All are assessed at five, COPS on the computer, and each child is monitored, and the results held for future referral at all times. A centre of excellence. Pupils have learning support as and when it is required and may spend an hour or two in the unit daily, and then transfer back into the main school for the rest of the day. SENCo, plus fully trained learning support assistants (not teachers) and gappers help in the classroom, plus properly qualified teachers. Gym club and OT group, touch-typing, speech and lang therapy once a week, sloping desks, special pens, all sorts of tricks brought into play. IEP for every child, some need full-time special needs assistant for which parents must pay. Register of gifted and able, staff aim to stretch them. Social and emotional needs are catered for here, as well as individual educational programmes. Three live-in dedicated assistants, plus two part-timers. Though if a child has really severe learning problems, this may not be the school for them.

Trad school curriculum, strong tutorial system: tutors are also responsible for PSHE. Maths, German, Spanish (not French) plus study skills though French and Latin. Strong music, as per the rest of the school, drama and good art. For the challenged child this could be just the place, for the less challenged, or those who need challenging, this school is all singing and dancing. Continuation scholarships to senior school.

Clayesmore School

Iwerne Minster, Blandford Forum, Dorset, DT11 8LL

Tel: 01747 812122

Fax: 01747 813187

Email: hmsec@clayesmore.com

Website: www.clayesmore.com

• Pupils: 234 boys, 136 girls; 220 board, the rest day
• Ages: 13-18 (but Clayesmore Prep School offers 2-13 on the same site) • Religion: C of E • Fees: Boarding £6,915; day £5,060 • School status: Independent • Opendays: Late September/early October, May. Prep school holds its own Open Days and very popular boarding taster weekends.
• School gender: Mixed • Day/boarding: Takes boarders

SEN provision

Detail:

Centre of excellence for:
- Mild: DYSL;
- Moderate: DYSL;
- Severe: DYSL;
- Others: EAL;

Now provide for in school:
- Mild: DYSC; DYSP;
- Others: Epi;

Experience of:
- Mild: VI;
- Moderate: DYSC;
- Others: DEL;

Summary: The learning support centre is an integral part of the school's academic provision. We work sensitively to develop academic abilities, enabling pupils to grow in self-esteem and achieve optimum results in exams. All pupils who receive learning support follow a mainstream academic programme, taking both GCSE and A level examinations in due course. Therefore, individual learning plans are tailored to developed the unique gifts of every girl and boy, enabling them to be proud of their talents and achievements.

What we say about the school - the full Good Schools Guide review

Headmaster: Since 2000, Martin Cooke BEd (Hons) FCollP (forties), an ex-St Paul's chorister and organ scholar who was educated at Monkton Combe and did his BEd in music at Sussex. Describes his hobbies as music in general, playing the organ and information technology. A human dynamo, he originally came to the school in 1994 as head of Clayesmore Prep, a job which he has now resumed and he whizzes between the two (closely interlinked) sites like a dervish. We met and lunched with him (and his pretty wife Eleanor who plays an active part in both schools) in the senior school and found him again in the prep when we hi-jacked his office for a chin-wag. He was previously head of music at Bembridge school and, whilst he no longer teaches, he plays the organ for chapel on occasion and 'interferes' (his word) with the musical output 'occasionally'. He reckons that running a music dept is excellent training for a headship as 'you do a lot of handling people, dealing with the whole 'congo' (as in congregational choir practice).

Vast number of new appointments since his arrival in the senior school – though junior school too during his reign there – eg new deputy, assistant head, director of studies, heads of maths, English, drama and major building programme. (Four staff houses in the village, most commute from Shaftesbury, Blandford et al). Enthusiastic IT pundit, one of his two children is currently 'gapping' and 'earning a fortune' writing websites in the Cooke spare room; his daughter is still in the school.

Trenchantly hands-on, keeps himself well-informed on all pupil issues including bullying. Has focused lots of attention on making the sixth form an exciting environment and spruced up the school's image. Clayesmore is now a member of HMC and Mr Cooke had just come back from his first conference when we met. 'We are now a small school of 400 rather than of 300,' but there is no intention of changing the central ethos of a small, caring school dedicated to bringing out the potential in each individual child. Wish list includes new prep school building and classrooms, improved boarding facilities plus new upper sixth house and an extension to the chapel.

Academic Matters: Year groups of 90, five sets in most subjects except maths for which there may be six. Pupils are setted in French, science and maths. French, Spanish and German are all available to A level, with a goodly number getting As and Bs at A level, splendid number of As in business studies, 30 candidates and 29 passes; history, English, maths, French and art all in the ribbons. Good sprinkling of A*s across the board at GCSE – double science particularly impressive, followed by French, German and English, plus art and PE. ICT provision is very strong. First year in senior school tends to be a 'stabilising year' for children to get up to speed. Tiny class sizes equals more attention from committed staff. Tutors responsible for a small group of pupils and monitor assessments every three weeks. Autumn half-term report for new students. Fantastic new extensive builds all over the shop including the award-winning Jubilee Building housing an entire new science department, two large computer suites and the new learning support centre with small lecture hall. Plus the Spinney Centre, which opened in 2004 with new classrooms for geography, history, business studies and careers, all bristling with the latest computer technology. Impressive.

This is a school on a roll. All the dys-strata catered for and a certain amount of Asperger's, autism and ADHD, new build fine for physical handicaps, rest a bit dodgy. Outstanding learning support for children with moderate to medium learning difficulties from a full and part-time staff of 12 (all fully qualified) in the superb new learning support centre (LSC) atop the new Jubilee building 'and anyone can get there' though, sadly, the senior school SENCo was on a school trip in Rhodes during our visit. All children are assessed, edpsyched if needed, extra help in maths, English and science (but not mod langs). More than 35 per cent of all pupils have some form of support, and a 'tiny number' have serious needs. Progressively more group lessons, max eight in a group, particularly in study skills. 'Need children to laugh and feel successful'. Pupils generally come out of language classes and extra sessions can be timetabled if necessary, plus evenings, but can pop in whenever, early morning sessions, exam and course work, 'try anything'. 'The Dore' exercise programme 'quite beneficial'. Good communication between LSC staff and subject teachers means that each pupil will have the individual attention they need, detailed pupil profiles for each. Help for the most able too. CReSTeD category B – CReSTeD listing essential for 'forces stock' who will be deprived of 'unlimited help indefinitely' if the school is not part of the system. Strong EFL too, with up to six hours a week, either individual or in pairs. Extra charge for both, from £21.50 for individual lessons to £5.43 for lessons shared by up to five.

Games, Options, The Arts: All pupils do sport three times a week. You name it, they play it: swimming, rugby, squash, badminton, hockey, football, netball, athletics, cross-country, rounders, sailing and tennis. Lots of matches and some notable successes against bigger schools. A good sprinkling of county players. School is 'potty on orienteering', and regularly in the ribbons. Locals use the 'leisure complex' on site with pool, gym, squash courts and modern fitness suite, including weights (from 16 and under supervision), and a mirrored salle, but pupils say 'the public are not that much of a hassle'. Presumably a planning requirement. Sports science strong. CCF for pupils in years 10 and 11, and enthusiastic D of E participants – tranches of golds et al (New Chaplain keen on D of E too). Sailing at Ringwood popular. Thriving music school in purpose-built building run by enthusiastic head of music. Vibrant, terrific impromptu piano recital during our visit ('actually my main instrument is the flute'), terrific head of music in a classroom filled with primitive instruments collected from all over the world. And some of them sound amazing. Sophisticated electronic key boards too, recording studio and good participation in national choirs and yoof orchestras. Composition master class in Salisbury, loads of internal concerts, plus masses of travel, pupils can play almost anything, plus woodwind ensemble, brass group, flute choir and string ensemble. Trails of visiting artistes – including Evelyn Glennie who only goes barefoot on stage.

Strong thespian tradition, with a terrific head of drama, whom we met in the (tiny) black theatre, but he is keen that actors should give several performances and not just be a one off. Tremendously strong, with masses of tripettes: Bristol, the Old Vic, London. Pupil technicians (approximately 60 in the school at the moment) as important as actors themselves; fantastic costume dept, with sewing machines and London type input. 'Reading plays' gives access to more pupils, who need not learn the part, but can perform, on stage, in costume, with script in hand. 'Theatre Studies A level and drama work closely together'. Mystery plays for all, including the prep, at Christmas. Outstanding art department housed in lovely old primary school past the pub in the village – pottery, photography, textiles, drawing, painting and ceramics, really bustling and fun, sixth formers have a dedicated wall. Pupils sometimes take their lives in their hands when they cross the A350.

Trips to galleries in London and Paris. Huge range of extra activities four afternoons a week and all staff are expected to run at least one. Pupils can do anything from fencing and yoga to textiles and pottery. There is even a wine tasting club (sixth form only) though, post November 2005, the school bar can only function if it serves food as well as booze, and the wine tasting may well get Blairised or nanny-stated too.

Background and Atmosphere: Idyllic setting; large country house set in sixty two acres of well-maintained grounds with lake, in the pretty village of Iwerne Minster in rural Dorset, five miles north of Blandford Forum, which boasts a post office and butchers (and an awfully large collection of those blue/grey morris minors), plus a school shop which sells skool uniform as well as other essentials for school life. NB sixth form uniform is not provided by skool shop. Some slightly surprising room divisions in the main house, but fireplaces to die for (and glorious computer room on ground floor still showing signs of the most recent roof leak). Well-used social centre, lots of inter-house competitions, sixth form bar twice a week (but see above). Superb grub with salads and vegetarian option. Good cross-cultural influences; staff helped the small group of Chinese pupils cook a celebration meal for Chinese New Year and school meals are occasionally themed around different international celebrations.

Pastoral Care and Discipline: Head keeps a well-practised eye: 'no overt and terrible sin', 'occasional smoking bush' – dissing (as in dismissed which was a new word to the head) about once a year, the odd fag equals letter home and it can get more severe; 'jolly cross' about 'smoking in the building'. A tiered system of punishments ranging from academic 'satis' for prep missed/inappropriate clothing etc to gating and suspension for more serious behaviour problems. Tight eye kept on discipline by the deputy head. Pupils air complaints and suggestions at pupil forum with the head, who is well on top of the situation and not as relaxed as you might think. Has a 'very bad memory' for sin, which means that the next time a pupil sins 'he is down upon him like a ton of bricks' but otherwise the offence is deleted.

'Fantastic collection of house parents' currently, five boarding houses (three boys' and two girls' houses) – all on site except one boys' house in the village. Trad smell of toast, pupils graduate from dorms to study bedrooms. Houses run by married staff often with small children and dogs, with full support staff of matrons and house tutors (choose own in sixth form), 'a good school for the expatriate child who might otherwise have been lost with parents far away'. Campus living in a small school is a double edged sword, on the one hand there is this big family feel with lots of people to turn to, and on the other there can be pervasive claustrophobia and great efforts are made to have buzzy weekends for boarders, including discos, talent contests and popular sixth form parties, houses take turns to organise.

Shopping buses are organised to local towns such as Blandford, Shaftesbury and Sherborne (none of which will set the world alight). The new Southampton shopping mall streaks ahead of the rest, staff go too. Duty staff organise excursions to local places of interest such as Bath (ditto) after Sunday Chapel, which is compulsory twice a year. C of E school chaplain much involved in the whole school. Children of any denomination are welcome.

Pupils and Parents: Number of day children, local buses: Salisbury, Poole, Bournemouth, Dorchester and the A30; can't flexi-board, but can stay over if late night activities, weekly boarding OK (casual boarding – for parents' or pupils' convenience £20, post school function £20). Senior pupils can bring their own cars. 'Always 150 boarders at weekends'. Progressively more London refugees (this is getting to be the norm) Home Counties and a good sprinkling of expat children (Services, diplomatic etc) plus a small number of foreign students, Dubai, Barbados, the Channel Islands. Fair number of first time buyers. No great green wellie influence. Two-night exeats have recently been introduced twice a term.

Entrance: Waiting list of 20 currently. By Common Entrance at 13 (50ish per cent) and interview with the head who looks for potential, and the all-roundedness of prospective boys and girls. Just under half come through from the prep with the rest from a variety of local (and some further afield) prep schools: Forres Sandle Manor, Hordle Walhampton, Highfield, Durlston Court, Port Regis, Dumpton, Sherborne Prep and Castle Court plus local maintained schools. Rash of academic, music and art scholarships, several species of all-rounder awards are made each year. Sixth form entrants need five A/C passes at GCSE. Popular, but space will become a problem as the larger number further down the school progress up – next project is expanded sixth form. Currently year group expands from 90 to 110 (number of Germans plus overseas as well as Brits).

Exit: Some unis, certain number of Oxbridge candidates, some Services, some vocational courses. School turns out vets, medics, all the usual suspects plus strong art, drama and music stream.

Money Matters: Oodles of scholarships: sixth form up to eight, ranging from 75 per cent down, with min four reserved for those not presently in the school, plus for local candidates (means-tested) plus internal, plus music (string players preferred). Trillions too (though not quite so many) of scholarships, exhibitions and bursarial help for academics, music and art for entry into senior school, plus continuity awards from 11 to A level via the prep school (bursarial help available here too) and more closed awards at 13 – means-tested again. Plus closed School Service bursaries for serving members of the armed forces, and a further bursary occasionally for children of past and present members of the Devonshire and Dorset Regiment. Impressive collection.

Remarks: A well-structured school, ideal for a child needing a supportive environment, with a bubbling far-sighted head in charge. Not a snooty school, perfect for the child who needs extra care.

CLIFTON COLLEGE

32 College Road, Clifton, Bristol, BS8 3JH

Tel: 0117 3157 000

Fax: 0117 3157 101

Email: admissions@clifton-college.avon.sch.uk

Website: www.cliftoncollegeuk.com

• Pupils: 660 boys and girls (60 per cent board) • Ages: 13-18 • Religion: C of E but pupils come from many different faith backgrounds • Fees: Boarding £7,305; day £4,835 • School status: Independent • Opendays: Termly • School gender: Mixed • Day/boarding: Takes boarders

SEN provision

Detail:

Now provide for in school:

Mild: DYSL;

Others: EAL;

Experience of:

Mild: ASP; AUT; ADD; DYSC; DYSP;

Moderate: DYSC; DYSL; DYSP;

Severe: ADD;

Others: Eat;

Summary: Clifton College is able to make learning support provision for pupils who have certain difficulties, for example dyslexia, or who have a need for specialist or additional help in some areas of their learning.

What we say about the school - the full Good Schools Guide review

Headmaster: Since 2005, Mr Mark Moore MA (mid forties). Educated at Wolverhampton Grammar School and Downing College Cambridge, where he read English. Taught at Marlborough followed by seven years at Eton, then eleven years as head of English, and latterly director of University Entrance as well, at Radley. Captained Cambridge and a National Champion at Eton Fives; also enjoys squash and soccer (anything with a round ball really). Married to Jo with four children (two boys, two girls). 'Very enthusiastic and energetic, clearly with a love of ideas and learning, and good at celebrating the work and achievements of pupils. A fine sportsman too,' says a (possibly partisan) source.

Academic Matters: In a pilot of 200 schools, Clifton College came out top of the value-added table – on average, a two grade advantage at GCSE. Wide choice of subjects, with non-examined courses and balancing of arts and sciences designed to reap long-term rewards rather than short-term gains. Flexible timetable means that all options and subjects, however diverse, are possible. Excellent range of GSCE options, with strong performance in maths, Eng lit and history. French and Spanish grades consistently high. Sciences mostly examined separately – (they have a lot to live up to – Clifton has produced two Nobel prize-winners in science).

At A level a diverse and comprehensive selection, with lots of As in maths and science. Excellence also in both fine art and history of art. Huge range of languages which may include Polish, Japanese, Hebrew and Mandarin (growing rapidly, currently 80 in the Pre and Upper School). Many As in German. Previous head supported broadening principle of AS levels; results are admirable across the board with a big increase in A grades at A level in 2004 and 2005. Pupils take four AS courses with a fifth, non-examined, course to broaden horizons. Small classes, lots of individual attention. learning support (eg for mild dyslexia) reflected by performance of former strugglers turned Oxbridge candidates.

Games, Options, The Arts: Sport is compulsory throughout the school but the choice is broad and the facilities outstanding, with rackets and fives courts as well as squash and tennis, a sports hall with indoor cricket nets, indoor swimming pool, huge gym full of state-of-the-art equipment and a miniature shooting range. And that's just one side of the Clifton Suspension Bridge – on the other side are new international-standard Astroturf hockey pitches, a new covered pitch allowing year-round tennis and netball, 24 tennis courts, a Real Tennis court, a new fitness centre and pavilion. Oarsmen and oarswomen row on the River Avon. A school used to winning at sport, particularly at cricket and rugby, with England players galore. Girls' games very successful at County and National levels.

Music and drama also a vital part of school life, with its music school stuffed with Steinway grands and rehearsal and practice space, yet embracing modern technology in the shape of synthesisers, a computerised composition suite and a new DJ course. Thriving choirs and all kinds of ensembles, from the full orchestra to a swing band, give regular concerts. Named after old Cliftonian Sir Michael, the Redgrave Theatre hosts up to 40 productions each year. The art department, with two main studios, caters for potters and photographers (with a well-equipped darkroom) as well as fine artists. Wonderful ICT suites, including the library's newly refurbished (to the tune of £1 million) centre of learning, seamlessly integrated into lofty Gothic spaces at the heart of the school.

Long and strong Services connection reflected by 250 in CCF, with girls as enthusiastic as boys. D of E also very popular. School has own property in Wales as base for orienteering or walking weekends. Amazing trips – Ecuador and Himalayas for mountain lovers, Australia and Canada for CCF. Everyone involved in some form of community service.

Background and Atmosphere: Justly famous for the beauty of its campus, overlooking the lovely Close, Clifton College was founded in 1862 by Bristol merchants. It expanded by building or buying the correspondingly tall, Gothic townhouses that surround the main buildings. Backs onto Bristol Zoo in thriving Bristol's jaw-droppingly expensive Clifton. Fully co-ed since 1987. Main entrance through Memorial Arch marks the hundreds of Old Cliftonians, privates and generals among them, who have died in wars – a very poignant daily reminder of which pupils are touchingly conscious. Recently refurbished Percival Library is the jewel in the crown. Houses (literally, in this case) for day and boarding pupils – East Town or West Town, for example, for day, Worcester and School House for boarding. Day houses are well-used for studying, chatting and slumping in breaks. Boarding houses have had major face-lifts – introducing a clever fusion of traditional and modern designs. New houses (one for girls to reflect increased per cent in the school) opened in September 2004. Strong Jewish presence remains, though no longer with their own house and now fully integrated into the life of the school. Nicely laid out dining hall, more popular since advent of new chef with more extensive repertoire than the last, complemented by Grubber, a tuck-cum-uniform shop with an offshoot of little tables. Bustling, busy and cosy feel to the school.

Pastoral Care and Discipline: Comprehensive, compassionate support, with a family feel, via the house system, particularly for the many pupils thousands of miles from home. Forays to the pub or into town usually foiled by houseparents or the Marshal, a former serviceman based on the edge of the site and in charge of security, discipline and general reining in of excess. Clifton's lovely chapel, with its stained-glass window depicting a cricket match, also gives a spiritual focal point. The whole school meets here four days a week, and three or four Sundays a term, with each house choosing a theme for the week and expanding it – recent topics have ranged from immortality to WWF wrestling.

Pupils and Parents: Parents mostly professionals – lots of solicitors and accountants – and many in the Services. Boarders make the most of the flexi-, weekly- and full-boarding options, with a significant number from a wide range of countries abroad. Many day pupils within walking distance, although a few travel from as far as Weston-super-Mare. Famous Old Cliftonians run the gamut – legendary schoolboy cricketer A E J Collins, Victorian poet Sir Henry Newbolt, Sir Michael Redgrave, Earl Haig and John Cleese.

Entrance: Cut-off is 50 per cent at CE and signs of potential. Also internal tests and interviews. Around 70 per cent from own prep (entry to Upper School not a given). Few leave at 16 and popular sixth form is massively over-subscribed.

Exit: Almost all to universities of their first choice and 10 plus to Oxbridge. Many also go on to captain sporting sides and some to Olympic glory.

Money Matters: Variety of scholarships and bursaries. Maximum 25 per cent on merit but supplementary means-tested bursaries up to 100 per cent possible.

Remarks: Traditional school with a modern outlook, offering much to pupils with a range of talents. Lovely to look at, too.

CLIFTON COLLEGE PREPARATORY SCHOOL (THE PRE) + PRE-PREP

The Avenue, Clifton, Bristol, BS8 3HE

Tel: 0117 3157 502
Fax: 0117 3157 504
Email: admissions@clifton-college.avon.sch.uk
Website: www.cliftoncollegeuk.com

• Pupils: 380 girls and boys; one fifth board • Ages: 3-13
• Religion: Pupils come from many different faith backgrounds
• Fees: Boarding max £5,240; day max £3,575
• School status: Independent • Opendays: Termly
• School gender: Mixed • Day/boarding: Takes boarders

SEN provision

Detail:
Now provide for in school:
Mild: DYSC; DYSL; DYSP;
Moderate: DYSC; DYSL; DYSP;
Others: EAL;
Experience of:
Mild: ASP; ADD; ADHD; EBD; HI; VI;
Moderate: ASP; MLD;
Severe: DYSC; DYSL; DYSP;
Others: MSI; Sp&LD; DEL; Epi;

Summary: Children's needs are dealt with very effectively through the Coach House, a facility of six individual teaching rooms which are very well resourced. There are four full-time SEN teachers – all qualified. The department has 'CReSTeD' accreditation and has evoked excellent comments from inspectors.

What we say about the school - the full Good Schools Guide review

Head: Preparatory school: Since 1993, Dr Bob Acheson. Aims to provide a focused, happy environment in which his bright-as-a-button pupils can thrive. Ably assisted by wife, Jill.

Pre-prep: Butcombe, with its own headmistress, Dr Wendy Bowring, operates separately from the prep but is just down the road.

Remarks: Prep school places particular emphasis on ICT and languages, with new science suite kitted out with new computer terminals, tuition in French from day one and German, Spanish and Mandarin as options in years 7 and 8.

Head knows his SEN – even Asperger's – and is thoroughly supportive – though five-and-a-half day week can be overwhelming for some. Rambling club for those who don't enjoy sports.

Most boarders here are from overseas, many from Service families. Succession of artists-in-residence, unusual for prep school. Flexi-boarding, from age 8, very popular and well-used by local parents. Thriving music and choir. Produces easy-going, confident, well-mannered young people and aims at academic success for all.

COBHAM HALL

Cobham, Gravesend, Kent, DA12 3BL

Tel: 01474 823 371
Fax: 01474 825 906
Email: enquiries@cobhamhall.com
Website: www.cobhamhall.com

• Pupils: 200 girls of whom about 55 per cent board
• Ages: 11-18 • Religion: Multi-faith • Fees: £3,800 to £4,900; boarding £5,800 to £7,100 • School status: Independent
• Opendays: May and November • School gender: Girls
• Day/boarding: Takes boarders

SEN provision

Detail:
Centre of excellence for:
Mild: DYSL; DYSP;
Moderate: DYSL;
Others: EAL;
Now provide for in school:
Mild: DYSC;
Experience of:
Mild: ADD; ADHD; EBD; HI; VI; CP;
Others: Epi; PD;

Summary: We have provision for children who need support for dyslexia, dyspraxia and dyscalculia. Students are given an assessment and have timetabled lessons in our centre at the time when other girls are studying Latin.

What we say about the school - the full Good Schools Guide review

Head: Since 2003, Mrs Helen Davy (forties). Read modern history at Oxford followed by postgraduate study at King's College, London. Then worked as a radiographer at the Royal Free Hospital for four years before beginning teaching. Has taught history, history of art and politics at Roedean and The Towers Convent School. Before coming to Cobham she was head of the faculty of cultural studies and acting senior mistress at Roedean. During a career break she ran a small fine wine business and still retains an interest. A warm and enthusiastic person who seems to be very much in touch with the outside world. Married but has no children; her husband works in the City and spends much of his time travelling abroad. He is a biodiversity enthusiast.

Academic Matters: 68 per cent A/B at A level. GCSE 90 per cent A*-C. 3D design, fine art, photography and maths have the best results at A level but increasingly strong in modern foreign languages and sciences; a breadth of courses including critical thinking, theatre studies, IT and business studies. All do Latin for three years and can take it to GCSE. Head says that her aim is to teach children to see the value in themselves and to release it. Encouraged to 'think outside the box or even take the lid off'.

Cobham Hall accepts students with a broad range of abilities and is a truly international school, with 40 per cent coming from abroad. Pupils come from 25 different countries with a growing proportion coming from mainland Europe but there's no dominance from any one country. Strong and impressive EAL presence: about 20 per cent of pupils have EAL requirements. Lessons are timetabled alongside the general curriculum, and students are given extra English tuition either individually or in small groups as well as attending mainstream lessons.

The Susan Hampshire Centre for girls with specific learning difficulties was founded in 1990 and can cater for a fair spectrum of learning problems, providing one-to-one, multisensory support in most subjects. About 15 per cent of pupils have some form of learning assistance under the aegis of the very experienced Mrs Christine Ostler (who has written several books on teaching dyslexics). The centre is recognised by CReSTeD as a dyslexia unit. Pupils need to be of at least good average ability – they are expected to attend mainstream lessons. Specialist help available for dyscalculia. well-equipped computer suites – all wireless networked.

Games, Options, The Arts: Games are compulsory for everyone throughout the school. Stunning games and fitness centre for aerobics, dance, self-defence, etc – locals use it in the evenings and summer schools in the holidays. Good success both with team games and individual sports – netball and volleyball rather than lacrosse and hockey. Rowing on the river Medway is a popular option. A Cobham girl won a bronze medal in British Junior Modern Pentathlon team.

Varied and impressive art, with kiln, mixed media, photography. The fusion of cultures makes for some wonderful artwork. Drama a popular subject and theatre studies is offered as an A level. LAMDA exams on offer too. Tenison Smith Studio Theatre recently opened with state of the art sound and lighting. Drama and music of some sort are compulsory for the first three years and music technology and music are both offered at A level. Fifteen peripatetic teachers, masses of small choirs and bands. Some go to Trinity School of Music or the Guildhall for extra tuition. two girls got distinction at grade 8 violin in 2005. Extracurricular activities for everything from craft to cooking and including riding, gardening and golf – ice skating lessons can be arranged at Gillingham. Duke of Edinburgh also popular.

Background and Atmosphere: Founded in 1962. A member of the Round Square, an organisation of schools (eg Gordonstoun) throughout the world committed to education through service, conservation, adventure and international understanding, and run along the lines of Kurt Hahn's philosophy though the outdoor life perhaps not as prominent as in some other schools in the group. Member schools arrange exchange visits for pupils and teachers, and undertake aid projects in places such as India, Kenya, Venezuela and Eastern Europe. Pupils encouraged to see themselves as genuinely international citizens. Cultural Festival a highlight of spring term. Different nationalities cook their local dishes for a feast which is followed by an entertainment or storytelling – Cobham Hall ethos of students from all over the world working together learning from each other and enjoying the experience.

The elegant Tudor hall, previously the home of the Earls of Darnley, is surrounded by 150 acres of parkland designed by Humphrey Repton with a deer park and golf course. The hall itself is pure magic with magnificent marble fireplaces and a fantastic coach on the first floor. Assemblies are held in the Gilt Hall, a masterpiece of high relief plasterwork covered in gold and superb marble fireplace. English Heritage help with the upkeep of the fabric of the building and the house is open to the public during the holidays.The BBC have recently filmed Dickens' Bleak House here. Worship is available locally for almost all faiths – C of E in the village, Catholic and Sikh in Gravesend, and there's a synagogue nearby too; the chef can provide food early and late during Ramadan.

Modern classrooms are strategically placed away from the main building. Boarders progress from the main building to sixth form houses with their own kitchens – due for refurbishment. Lots of privileges for sixth formers, who wear their own clothes and run the dungeon café in the basement as a commercial venture.

Pastoral Care and Discipline: School run on democratic lines with each girl expected to take responsibility for themselves. The election of the new guardian (head girl) is run like a general election with a manifesto and pupils and staff vote by secret ballot. Guardian and three deputies and four heads of house elected in March and serve for three terms. They meet with the headmistress once a week, and see their role very much as a pastoral one. Links with other head girls to compare leadership styles. Lots of work in keeping open atmosphere and making girls self-assertive. New girls supported by 'big sister' scheme. Genuine sense of family.

Pupils and Parents: Lots of first time buyers, many of whom scrimp and save to send their children here. The main UK catchment area is north Kent, London and the Thames Gateway. Strong overseas contingent. Famous Old Girls include journalist Mary Anne Sieghart, photographer Amelia Troubridge and newsreader Mishal Husain.

Entrance: Not overly difficult. At 11+, 13+ and post GCSE but pupils can usually be accommodated at any time with a letter from the current school and possibly a test. School's newcomers' entrance test day in early January: English, maths and a general paper plus two areas of assessment out of music, drama, art and sport. Plus confidential report from present headteacher plus interview. Scholarships usually awarded as a result of performance in the school's entrance exam. Dyslexic candidates also sit the entrance tests although their results are viewed in the light of the educational psychologist's findings.

Exit: Wide diversity of universities all over the world – lots to art school, some to top universities, one or two to Oxbridge. Several to London University to read medicine. Lots seem to end up in media and the arts.

Money Matters: Cobham Hall Scholarships for the academic, awards for special talents and abilities. Four major sixth form scholarships worth up to 50 per cent of fees plus several subject scholarships. Plus bursarial help, usually only for those with acute temporary financial problems and often only to the next public exam.

Remarks: A gentle school which somehow manages to meet the educational needs of a polyglot community of pupils, provide excellent help for those with specific learning needs, and release potential at all levels of ability. Stunning house and grounds bring creativity to the whole.

COKETHORPE SCHOOL

Witney, Oxon, Oxfordshire, OX29 7PU

Tel: 01993 703 921

Fax: 01993 773 499

Email: admin@cokethorpe.org

Website: www.cokethorpe.org.uk

• Pupils: 605 boys and girls. All day • Ages: 5-18

• Religion: Joint C of E and RC foundation

• Fees: £2,440-£3,940 • School status: Independent

• Opendays: First Saturday in October, Early Lent term, May

• School gender: Mixed • Day/boarding: Day pupils

SEN provision

Detail:

Centre of excellence for:

Mild: DYSL;

Now provide for in school:

Mild: DYSC; DYSP;

Others: EAL;

Experience of:

Mild: HI; VI; CP;

Moderate: MLD; DYSL; HI;
Others: Sp&LD; Epi; Eat;

Summary: The learning support department is a resource which exists to strengthen and support learning across the whole ability range. This encompasses a very wide range of issues. As a consequence, our response must be a flexible one which includes a variety of approaches to the varying needs of our pupils. Our role also requires us to support the staff and to disseminate good practice throughout the school.

Our main teaching and learning objectives can be summarised as follows:

Basic Skills: First and foremost we are here to improve the skills of those students who have difficulties acquiring the basics of literacy and numeracy. There is a need to recognise, however, that there comes a time when other needs predominate and there is a gradual move towards the teaching of basic skills through other, curriculum based tasks.

Study Skills: The recognition and understanding of individual learning styles – the highlighting of strengths and the application of strategies.The improvement of thinking skills.Time management and planning.Revision and exam techniques. Knowledge and use of ICT.

Personal Skills:The encouragement of self-awareness and self-analysis.Organisation. Boosting confidence and self-esteem. Acceptance of constructive criticism. Pro-active problem-solving and the discussion of issues of importance to the individual.

What we say about the school - the full Good Schools Guide review

Headmaster: Since 2002 Mr Damian Ettinger BA MA PGCE, late thirties. Educated St Joseph's College (Beulah Hill), Universities of Manchester and Surrey. Previously head of theology and housemaster, Prior Park College, Bath, 1989-96; head of St Oliver's and head of theology, Downside 1996-2002. Mr Ettinger is married and has four sons and 1 daughter. Brisk, relaxed, confident, this is a young man in a hurry. He has inherited a school which he believes was seriously underperforming and in which under-achievement was almost part of the culture and has set himself in double-quick time to change entirely its character, aims and reputation.

Certainly he's right in that the place has masses going for it in terms of location and site and he has initiated extensive staff changes. His Roman Catholic faith underpins his ethical approach to this job – 'I want to introduce a prayer life into the school' – but this is no preaching softie – 'I want teachers to get angry with the children. How can anyone give 6 out of 10 and say, 'Well done?' This is a tough, modernising head who wants his own high standards reflected in all areas of this, traditionally rather relaxed, school and means, in particular, to move away from the name it had established for being 'a special needs school'. A roller-coaster of a man going, perhaps, too fast for some but he looks pretty unstoppable from where we're standing.

Academic Matters: Results are moving steeply upward – remarkably quickly. Hard to gauge, owing to the widely varying numbers in each year, but in 2002 7 out of 40 A level entries got A/B grades and 17 got D/E/Us; in 2004, 63 out of 101 entries got A/B/C and 38 got D/E/U. Hardly extraordinary, but this school had a high proportion of children with learning difficulties and this represents a considerable improvement and, no doubt, for many, a huge achievement. GCSE grades show a comparable shift. Also notable is that more good candidates are now staying on here post-GCSE and school keen to build on this.

Excellent head of sixth form has introduced range of new A level subjects – psychology, politics, media studies and law; new performing arts space should also help in retention as must centrally located 'bistro' – for sixth and staff – a good idea. £80,000 spent on upgrading ICT and school has startling new block housing two large IT rooms – well-used, if not only for work. We wondered whether some supervision might help here.

Head has beefed up modern langs – all do French, and Spanish is on offer from year 8 (as, now, is Latin). German from year 10. School has a link with school in Lyon and there are some trips abroad – more, perhaps, needed to boost this vital area. At GCSE, geography and business studies are popular. Most take double science but triple also available – taken by decent number. Head has also introduced discrete subject setting – you are setted separately for each core subject not, as before, put in the same set for everything irrespective of your varying aptitudes. He has also moved to a two-week timetable of one-hour lessons – more flexible and better for consistent work.

More controversial is the resolute shift away from learning support. More rigorous assessment at entry and the refusal any longer to take children with more than mild specific learning difficulties – head sees the school as being less able than the nearby special schools to give such children appropriate help – means a decided change in the culture and aspirations of the entire school community. Not that the head doesn't want to help children with SEN but he is convinced that these children, as much as any, need higher aims and need to be helped to achieve far more highly than before – 'when a child is shown excellence in one area it raises his or her expectations across the board ... when they've done something brilliant they need to know it'. As it is, most of children with SEN have some degree of dyslexia or dyspraxia. Some of the older children look mildly shell-shocked – possibly also because of the far stricter discipline than they were used to – but they haven't pulled out and that must be telling.

Games, Options, The Arts: School has 150 acres of parkland and a vast sports hall. Clay pigeon shooting is a passion here – available four times weekly and very popular. Lots of pitches and Astroturf arriving March 2006. Everyone takes part in inter-house cross-country. Head has reintroduced house system, importantly for competitive sports, and believes in excellence – 'we're elitist about our sports'. Rugby, netball and football played. Also on offer are golf, fencing, riding, canoeing, aerobics and judo inter alia. New young head of music set to revitalise dept – at present, fewer than a quarter learn individually and, apart from two class teaching rooms, dept's current housing isn't inviting. Good DT studio but art, too, needs a bit of a boost – nothing specially striking on display here, though graphics, textiles and photography on offer – but head has plans! Old huge maintenance hut now converted to make new performing arts space seating 200+ – a good new asset. Various clubs – chess, sketching, cookery, design, film, BMX biking and very popular 'gadgets and gizmos' – should be something for everyone here. However, a school with this amount of space can offer more and it's hard to imagine that, under the new regime, our next visit here won't be struggling with the range of options.

Background and Atmosphere: A very attractive, solid-looking (though long-standing member of staff called it 'jerry-built') Queen Anne house – 'the Mansion' – greets the visitor. It's set in acres of flattish but undeniably rural parkland with grazing sheep and even has its own Norman church – St Mary the Virgin – a hundred yards or so from the house – used for services and assemblies. Estate has a worthy history and links with the literati of the eighteenth century – Pope, Swift and Gay were visitors here. The mansion now houses the junior school and administration and the entrance hall and some of the rooms are quite splendid. The mansion fronts three courtyards around which, partly in converted farm buildings, teaching takes place, mostly in subject blocks. Some new buildings have been added to complete the quadrangular arrangements – all sensitive and in the appropriate Cotswold stone except for the prosaic and incongruous canteen which is something of an eyesore in this, otherwise immensely attractive, site. Lovely features like a centrally placed little round building – formerly a dovecote – now the school shop and a rather grand arch to one side of the estate.

Site is well-maintained and orderly – very visible maintenance team hard at it. Atmosphere is hard to judge. School still feels something like the boarding school it was until 2003 but also something like a fee-paying, mixed comprehensive which, essentially, it is. Head is moving towards a far more trad public school ethos – new crests on blazers are emblematic in many ways as are reintroduction of real life versions of school emblem – the peacock.

Pastoral Care and Discipline: Again, the Ettinger Effect creating palpable ripples on the discipline front – 'I want pupils to stand up when I come into the room and feel proud of their uniform ... I can't stand children eating and walking ... I can't stand mobile phones'. Has long had local reputation for good pastoral care. Teacher:pupil ratio is unusually high – most classes between 5-15 pupils and never more than 18. Joint RC and C of E foundation underpins ethos. School lunches look appetising and have improved – 'we've tried really hard to give them proper food,' says cook.

Pupils and Parents: From wide catchment area and school runs in 400+ children using 16 buses with many pick-up points – a real plus for working parents. Children come from as far as Oxford, Swindon, Wantage, from Witney and all villages round about. Some complain of the long school day and it is tough if you have an hour's journey each way on top of a school day that ends at 5.00pm. Wide range of families – old school to first-timers – a sizeable proportion. Copies of Homes and Antiques and Cotswold Life on reception room table. Pupils do not look particularly smart – unkempt hair is clearly height of cool here – hard to imagine the reforming Ettinger eye won't be trained on this soon. Parents increasingly involved – head sees this as essential – and school community set to grow in this area. Overall, head wants a 20:60:20 school ie good 'middle order batsmen' with a starry top and a slower bottom and aims 'to get the best out of every child'.

Entrance: Getting tougher and no longer automatic from the school's own junior dept. Maths, English and VR assessed along with applicant's social and sporting skills so other aptitudes taken into account – 'if he's a fantastic fly-half I'd be interested even if he's not academically strong – the question is, what can he offer the school?' says head. Hitherto, 'we've obviously gone with what's come through the door' but that's changed now and increased competition for places seems to justify the change. Between 2-4 applicants now for each place depending on the school stage. At year 5, parents of junior school pupils unlikely to make it into the senior school are helped to look elsewhere – 'we have to learn to say 'no' to parents'. Juniors enter mostly from local nurseries including school's own linked nursery, Westfield House, and primary schools. Seniors from outside come at 11 via Chandlings, The Manor, Ferndale, Our Lady's Convent Junior, St Andrew's Wantage, or, at age 13, from Josca's, The Dragon, New College School, Christ Church Cathedral School and St Hugh's. Criteria for sixth form entry also upped – must have 5+ GCSEs at A*-C including maths, English and a science plus good grades in your A level subjects.

Exit: Some to redbricks eg Manchester, Bristol; most to newer universities eg Nottingham Trent, Oxford Brookes though this trend will probably be reversed. Courses taken cover the range though 2004 saw a lot of embryonic psychologists.

Money Matters: Lots of schols/bursaries of all kinds – academic, art, music, sports, drama, classics, modern langs, and (nice!) all-rounder – now all means-tested. Minor schols for two years from 11. All gauged on exam performance and interview with head. Sixth form schol candidates take two subject papers, a general paper, a reasoning paper and have interviews. Value of schols from 5 to 50 per cent of fees depending on parental means.

Remarks: Ettinger-speak: 'we have to get away from too much patting on the head of children who could have done much better ... we haven't got time, we've got to get on with it. I love this job ... I'm free at the moment, I've got nothing to do ... I'll practise my golf swing.' Interesting to see if he can stay on the ride without too many people – including himself – falling off.

COLET COURT

Lonsdale Road, London, SW13 9JT

Tel: 020 8748 3461

Fax: 020 8746 5357

Email: hmseccc@stpaulsschool.org.uk

Website: www.coletcourt.org.uk

• Pupils: 430 boys, all day • Ages: 7 to 13

• Religion: Colet Court is a Christian foundation, but boys of all faiths are represented at the school • Fees: £3,640

• School status: Independent • Opendays: November

• School gender: Boys • Day/boarding: Day pupils

SEN provision

Detail:

Now provide for in school:

Mild: DYSL; DYSP;

Experience of:

Mild: ADD;

Others: DEL; Epi;

Summary: If a boy passes our entrance exam and is dyslexic or dyspraxic and it is felt useful, we will provide one lesson of one-to-one support each week. In addition, boys who have been recommended by an educational psychologist to use a laptop may do so in lessons and exams.

What we say about the school - the full Good Schools Guide review

Headmaster: Since 1992, Mr Geoffrey Thompson (fifties), who has more qualifications than you ever dreamed of: BA from Newcastle in biology, MEd, CertEd, MIBiol, CBiol, Fellow of the College of Preceptors, Fellow of the Linnaean Society. In other words, the man is formal, professional, experienced. Married to a teacher. Parents say he's sociable but not likely to engage in in-depth conversation. Not surprising, said one, when you consider many parents micro-manage their children's education, beating a path to his door for the slightest triviality. Pupils say, 'we don't see a lot of him but he is kind and patient and he's doing the play; we like that, it's good to see more of him.'

On entering his study your eyes are drawn to the 'sulking boy' and your nose to the fab coffee machine –

a gift from an appreciative parent. Then there's the 'doll' bought from a shop in Helmsley, the coffee, Taylor's of Harrogate and very quickly the conversation turns to the head's passion for Yorkshire. 'I escape there as often as possible. We have school trips too. Many drag their parents back to share the beauty.' So a part-time job with the Yorkshire tourist board? Not quite, not yet. For now he's settled at the school – still a long time to serve if he's to beat the tenure of many previous heads but he clearly enjoys it here and who wouldn't? His current passion is 'Jones' a musical written by a master at St Paul's that he's producing and directing. He hopes it will be the next Joseph. Not so crazy, when you remember that Joseph was originally written by Lloyd Webber for pupils at Colet Court to sing at their Easter end of term concert...

Entrance: At 7, 8, 10 and 11 – these last two ages are now a good route in for beady parents with kids at state primaries. Name down asap. Heavyweight test changed yearly to confound preparation – looking for those who can take the pace.

Exit: Around 98 per cent to St Paul's (when you sign on at Colet you sign up for St Paul's). Handful to boarding schools: Winchester, Eton, occasional to Charterhouse.

Remarks: This isn't a good school – it's an excellent school – says who? Says the ISI inspection report (gushing, there's a void in the 'could do better' section); say the parents (who admit to feeling a slight thrill the first time they enter the school gates); say the results – among the best, if not the best, in the country – 18 scholarships in 2005, one to Winchester, 17 to St Paul's – and say the pupils, read on.

This is a school for bright young things (IQ 120 plus). All will sail through exams, no need to spoon-feed, encourages lateral, imaginative and creative thinking. The entrance exam is designed to weed out the coached from the innately intelligent and seems to do so successfully. So you have to be intelligent? Definitely. Rich? Well it's not cheap but no child who passes the entrance exam will be turned away because of parents' inability to pay the fees. There are generous bursaries up to 100 per cent of fees, plus help with funding extras such as trips and tours abroad. SEN free? No, a generous handful of boys have a learning difficulty and before you choke on your muesli, Einstein was dyslexic. The reality is some 30 plus boys have a difficulty of some sort, mostly mild dyslexia or dyspraxia but ADD, ADHD (Ritalin okay), and Asperger's are found among the numbers. The lovely (phenomenal said one parent) 'dys lady' – 'dyslexia, dyspraxia, dysgraphia, dispirited' is on hand to help out. Boys may receive one-to-one for up to one lesson a week (and never withdrawn from core subjects). There's great communication between staff so problems are quickly spotted, PE will flag up those who present with co-ordination problems; with handwriting, problems are eased by use of laptops and some self-refer. 'Some of our best and brightest have a difficulty. Ironically the baggage can help. They have to develop strategies to cope, they think differently and some get to Oxbridge.'

Wonderful facilities. Yes the buildings are 1960s, not monstrosities by any stretch, though definitely not the ivory towers you'd expect from a school with such long-standing traditions. The 40-acre green site, immaculate, classrooms, airy with frequently changing, stimulating displays, vibrant corridors and naturally everything you'd want to find in a prep school (though some facilities are shared with senior school). There's a full size swimming pool, large sports hall, fencing salle, dojo for aikido, racquets court and tennis courts, plus cricket nets, basketball courts, ICT suites, technology workshops, fully equipped science labs, music school, music hall, large assembly hall, separate dining hall, playground with wood, ropes, swings for littlest boys, a great addition. Class sizes on the biggish side: 18-24 pupils. No setting or streaming in first three years, then setted in maths, Latin and French and a scholarship group is selected by the end of that year. All boys study Latin from year 6 and scholars study Greek (small Greek group for non-scholars).

Hotshot music department. Three choirs, full to bursting, with invigorating schedule of appearances. Three orchestras, chamber ensemble, string quartet. Piles of distinctions on music exams. Over 80 per cent of boys learn one or more musical instruments. Art superb, in bright, spacious art classroom overlooking Thames. Excellent chess team (with national players); super well used library, regular additions. Sports abundant. Compulsory rugby in autumn (except 7-year-olds), soccer in spring, cricket in summer. Games for two hours, two afternoons a week, plus a session of PE. Loads of teams – most boys can represent the school at some level. One of the few independent preps to take boys on overseas soccer tours. Cricket tour to

Barbados, football to Brazil. Saturday morning games or practice, for boys in teams. Golf off-site.

The biggest draw though is the inspirational and fizzy teaching – excellent. 'We do lots of practical things in all kinds of subjects and staff use the interactive whiteboards, show us things from the net or use special packages.' The boys have a genuine thirst for knowledge, a desire to learn, to discover. The beauty is, that here, it's permitted. There's no laddish culture, no fear of being branded a swot – bliss. So what of the boys? Privileged? Yes but privileged to be at the school. But, and this is a big but, the boys are grounded (yes, the odd trace of arrogance from the odd boy but no more than in the poorest comp), they huddle round with trading cards or top trumps at break, or kick a football; shirts hang out as often as they're found in; they teased us and their masters that they were being paid to say great things about the school (perhaps they were!) They have a wicked sense of humour, great sense of fun, not all geniuses, but hard working and polite – it's the parents one worries about. Many see entry to Colet Court as grasping the Holy Grail itself, when in reality it is just the beginning of their worries. They can now look forward to 11 years of making sure their son makes the grade, at least the many parents' activities promote a sense of 'in it together.' There are downsides for the pupils too. From being top dog at previous schools, many will find they're placed in lower sets but the boys are bright enough to realise that being in a low set here is still a great achievement and all are on course for a glowing array of A levels, a few years down the line. 'Sometimes it would be nice to have longer to assimilate a new topic, or idea. Some people grasp things instantaneously. I find that a problem in maths but I know I'm the one getting things straight away in science.' That seems to be the key. Every boy is good and virtually every boy, excellent in something, be it music, sport, science. The pace is frenetic but the boys handle it – no let-up (holidays are known in school jargon as 'remedies').

Everything you'd expect from one of the country's top preps and a whole lot more too. But do not be tempted by the designer label unless your son is the genuine article – bright, keen and robust.

COLFE'S SCHOOL

Horn Park Lane, Lee, London, SE12 8AW

Tel: 020 8852 2283

Fax: 020 8297 1216

Email: head@colfes.com

Website: www.colfes.com

• Pupils: 510 boys and 200 girls, all day • Ages: 11-18
• Religion: C of E • School status: Independent
• School gender: Mixed • Day/boarding: Day pupils

SEN provision

Detail:
Now provide for in school:
Mild: DYSC; DYSL; DYSP;
Moderate: DYSL; DYSP;
Experience of:
Mild: ASP;

Summary: No comment.

What we say about the school - the full Good Schools Guide review

Head: Since 2005, Mr Richard Russell (forties) read slassics at Jesus College Cambridge. Previously deputy warden at Forest School and, before that, director of studies at Sevenoaks.

Academic Matters: Strong academic record, but it's also strong in sport, music and drama. Don't want to simply produce eggheads; it's a school that turns out rounded people. The pupils do get a lot of homework, the school expects results, but at Colfe's they're told the most important lesson of all is how to learn, so they are equipped to cope with university. The school is great at putting pupils forward for exams – it's more interested in encouraging them than worrying about them pulling the results down.

Results pretty consistent. 2002 was a record year with 66 per cent grades A or B at A level and, at GCSE, 93 per cent, with 37 per cent A*/A grades. 2003 grades rather lower at A level but better at GCSE. Performing well, particularly as they draw on a cross-section of academic ability and there are many highly selective schools nearby. Class sizes are small. Nearly a third of the staff have been there for over 10 years, although staff are mainly youngish, around 40 years old. Plenty of children have special learning needs including dyslexia and dyspraxia. Help for this is mainly confined to mild cases, with only one or two having more serious problems.

Games, Options, The Arts: Sport is an important part of the curriculum: rugby training twice per week at eleven for almost all (soccer is also played). Other schools may have a better sporting record but, again, the all inclusive ethos pervades; for example, if you're taken as a reserve to a match you still get a chance to play, unlike some schools. Typically inter-house competitions and inter-school competitions abound, as do sports tours abroad. Sporting personalities, John Gallagher, rugby and Grahame Clinton, cricket, among the committed sports staff. 30 acre site with a modern sports complex and an Astroturf pitch planned in the foreseeable future. Girls' sport was lagging behind – it hadn't really been thought about as the school moved to co-education, but it's now developing in netball, hockey and rounders.

Visual and performing arts centre opened in spring 2003 with facilities for practice and recitals, art and a dark room for photography. Walls adorned with very impressive works – looked like an art gallery in town. Soloists perform, group performances, ballroom dancing – all sorts of activities. 400 pupils in the senior school learn a musical instrument up to post-grade 8.

Various expeditions. Extra-curricular very important – each pupil must attend two (of forty) clubs during the week, either during lunch or after school, ranging from pet care to cookery. Most attend five. You can change clubs each term and they reflect the all round ethos of the school – a club is still learning but it's fun.

Background and Atmosphere: Dates back to 1652; the Leathersellers' Livery Company supports the school, which went independent in 1977. The frontage is an unprepossessing 1960s ILEA building – don't be put off, it's better behind. Tucked away, but there is a real feeling of space once in the grounds, which is quite something when it is so close to London. Generally in good order, bits such as the science block and staff room due for an upgrade. The pre-prep and prep schools are situated in self-contained buildings at the far end of the site, although the younger ones visit the main school for regular assemblies and lunch.

A welcoming school, with a genuinely all-inclusive feel – the sports centre is used by the local community. Broadminded and encouraging, would appeal to parents who believe, 'a happy child is an achieving child' – not a hothouse. A sufficiently small sixth form for the head of sixth to know every pupil. They have not found undue discrimination from universities like Bristol – possibly because Colfe's is a lesser-known independent school.

Pastoral Care and Discipline: 'Firm but fair' is an expression that rolls off the tongue of pupils – they've obviously heard it often. They know bullying, stealing and drugs would not be tolerated (and parents know of no bullying), the school's strategy is tough and well documented but it seems to be accepted that there's a class clown in each year who will be in trouble all the time. Mentors from sixth form help year 7 settle in, not surprisingly, the girls seem more conscientious over this.

Pupils and Parents: Parents are very happy with the school – 'I rave about it to everybody, both my boys love it'. Parents range from ladies with manicured nails to those who've just raced back from a quick trip to Sainsburys after work – though some of the pushier ones push off to Eltham and Dulwich College after pre-prep. Lots of professional parents but not an old boys' network. 18 per cent from ethnic minority families, which reflects the immediate local community, but all pupils speak English. Lots of two-parents-working families, so school opens at 7am for breakfast, the library is supervised until 5pm, and the prep school runs an after school club till 6pm (you don't have to commit to a whole term). Network of school coaches.

Children level-headed and pleasantly not over-indulged. Wearing of home clothes on comic relief day does not turn into a fashion competition, as in some schools. Old Colfeians society is active and maintains the heritage.

Entrance: School is over-subscribed at 11. Colfe's promotes itself as taking a cross-section of pupil abilities (well, it is at least noticeably less selective than some of its neighbours), so the interview (of child and parent) is crucial. Not unknown for the child to pass the interview but the parents to fail – eg not committed enough. Said to be harder for boys to get in than girls – better local provision for girls means less competition for places.

11+ entry by exam in January, reference from present school and interview. Examination consists of maths, English and Verbal Reasoning. Half the pupils come from own prep school, though it's not a foregone conclusion that you'll get into the senior school from there: one or two fail each year, but parents are warned well in advance.

Entry to sixth form by interview, reference and conditional offers on GCSE results.

Exit: Most to good universities, with around four to Oxbridge.

Money Matters: Fees are competitive for a London day school. The Leathersellers' Company helps over 100 children in the school through bursaries (and to a lesser extent scholarships) if the household income is below £30,000. The school also has its own bursary funds.

Remarks: Pleasant, family atmosphere. Takes a broad mix of children yet it still performs well. Not the place for social climbers or swots.

COLLINGHAM

23 Collingham Gardens, London, SW5 0HL

Tel: 020 7244 7414

Fax: 020 7370 7312

Email: london@collingham.co.uk

Website: www.collingham.co.uk

• Pupils: 250 in total: 50 in GCSE dept, 200 over two years in senior dept; roughly 50/50 boys and girls • Ages: 14-19 • School status: Independent • School gender: Mixed • Day/boarding: Day pupils

SEN provision

Detail:

Now provide for in school:

Mild: DYSC; DYSL; DYSP;

Others: EAL; DEL; Epi; Eat;

Experience of:

Mild: ADD; ADHD; EBD; HI; VI;

Others: PD;

Summary: We can give effective learning support to those with mild learning difficulties, such as dyslexia.

What we say about the school - the full Good Schools Guide review

Head: Still under the thriving leadership of Gerald Hattee who has been in the position since 1989. Educated at St Peter's, York and read history at Keble. Teaches history and politics. Very amiable man who clearly has a good rapport with the students, whose welfare is paramount.

James Allder, BA, is in charge of the GCSE department in Queen's Gate Place. A keen skier and snowboarder.

Academic Matters: Offers an impressive range of subjects and in any combination. Popular subjects are English, history, maths and business studies. Photography at AS increasingly popular and some take it on to A2 where it works well with media studies. Sciences are strong with a number of students going on to read medicine. 75 per cent ABCs at A2. Music is taught to A2 but there are no rehearsal rooms.

Students can join a course half way through and the college will pick up the threads, preparing the student for examination. Class sizes are on average five at AS and A2 with a maximum of nine at GCSE. It's a long day starting at 9.30am and finishing at 6pm with lessons taught in two-hour slots, with a short break in the middle. Students can expect six hours tuition per subject a week at A2, with individual lessons if deemed necessary. For November and January re-takes, this goes up to eight hours.

The college runs Easter revision courses for A, AS and GCSEs, fitting in a staggering amount of tuition, enabling a keen student to thoroughly revise three AS/A2s or six GCSEs. Not surprisingly, these are very popular.

Games, Options, The Arts: The college makes use of its location in central London, with gallery and theatre visits. Weekly football match in Wandsworth – voluntary but very popular. Students can keep fit using the facilities at Imperial College where there is a pool, gym, squash and tennis. Sport is compulsory in the GCSE department. Chess is about to take hold of the college and there is also a thriving debating group.

Background and Atmosphere: Founded 30 years ago. Housed in a seven storey building in a leafy residential square, it's in good condition. Space is obviously a limitation but the house has been cunningly divided up, making 27 classrooms, with three well-equipped laboratory, art and dark rooms. You couldn't expect the facilities to be state of the art but they are surprisingly good and combined with teaching excellence, it all adds up to the provision of a sound education. The library, with a bank of computers, overlooks the square, providing a tranquil place to study and is always monitored by a tutor. The coffee room in the basement allows students to meet and sandwiches are made to order. For a tutorial college, there is a strong sense of community that seems to go beyond the boundaries of the classroom. There is an air of inspiration about the place.

Pastoral Care and Discipline: The college prides itself in its pastoral care and is clearly good at it, cleverly bridging the gap between the care that you would expect to find at school and the degree of freedom that the students enjoy here. The support of staff is subtle but highly effective. The overriding mood at Collingham is decidedly upbeat on both the student and staff fronts. The head's door is always open and he is happy to talk. He is keen that students develop and succeed in their own interests outside school hours.

Registers are taken at the beginning of each class and should a student fail to show, this is followed up immediately. Students have personal tutors for their two years, who are adept at picking up on problems and praising the triumphs.

There are no boundaries within the building and so tutors and students are free to go wherever they like. This garners openness. The smokers can usually be found on the pavement opposite the school at break and are not fussed when a member of staff pops out for a word. Mr Hattee prefers to have them in sight rather than round the corner.

Pupils and Parents: You might expect a London tutorial to be full of misfits. This is certainly not the case at Collingham. Many of the students come from the larger public schools: for one reason or another it hasn't worked out. They may have found the set up just too large or the rules too confining. The friendly environment that Collingham provides is often the catalyst needed to fire the imagination and the will to succeed.

It is often the first time that the students themselves have been in part responsible for making a decision in their future education. This means that they are unlikely to fight the system and consequently put more effort into their work.

Students are largely local, travelling in by public transport. Generally there is parental support, with a parent or guardian at the end of a telephone, should the need arise.

Entrance: Students are interviewed and need five GCSE passes to get a place. The student also has to assure the Head that he really wants to come here.

Exit: Students are taken through the UCAS process with a number of presentations and are given guidance with personal statements. The majority go on to the major universities and art schools. A number to Oxbridge.

Remarks: Collingham appeals to children who haven't quite fitted into the public school system. The level of support given to students is exceptional and this is reflected in a growth of confidence and the desire to succeed.

COOMBE HILL INFANT SCHOOL

Coombe Lane West, Kingston upon Thames, Surrey, KT2 7DD

Tel: 020 8942 9481

Fax: 020 8949 7496

Email: chi@rbksch.org

Website: www.coombehilli.kingston.sch.uk

• Pupils: 270 boys and girls • Ages: 4-7 • Religion: Non-denom
• School status: State • School gender: Mixed
• Day/boarding: Day pupils

SEN provision

Detail:

Now provide for in school:

Mild: ASP; AUT; ADD; EBD; DYSC; DYSL; DYSP; VI;
Moderate: EBD; MLD; DYSL;
Others: FRX; PMLD; EAL; Sp&LD;

Summary: We have designated time when our SENCo manages a large team of SEN assistants. At present we have a team of four different assistants who work with individual children and with small groups. One of these assistants is trained in teaching children with dyslexia, another is trained in teaching children with speech and language problems. In addition, we have teacher assistants in every class.

What we say about the school - the full Good Schools Guide review

Head: Since 1991, Mrs Sarah Hobhouse CertEd DipSE in school management (early fifties). Comes from Somerset, educated at Sherborne School in Dorset and Surrey University. Tall, elegant, previously deputy head at St Paul's Chessington. Describes herself as 'user-friendly,' with an open door policy; described by more than one parent as 'fantastic.' Teaches RE and obviously has a great rapport with the children – all clamouring for her attention with 'Mrs Hobhouse look at this' and 'Watch this Mrs Hobhouse.' V. impressive the way she knew every child by name and all wanted to show her something they had done or tell her something about themselves.

Entrance: You need to live almost on the school's posh doorstep to get in. Substantially over-subscribed – more so than any other infant school in the borough: typically 162 applications for 90 places. Priority: to children with sibling attending the school or the associated junior school at the time of admission; pupils with a medical or social need and then those living nearest the school. In practice, about a third of places to siblings. one or two have medical or social needs and the rest tend to live within three-quarters of a mile of the school.

Exit: Majority trot off to the junior school next door. A few to independent schools – Kings College School Wimbledon, Surbiton High School, Wimbledon High School, Putney High School, Rokeby and Shrewsbury House.

Remarks: Top notch school in upmarket area, with winning combination of supportive middle class parents, rich cultural mix and good achievement. Located in one of the most prestigious residential locations in the borough and surrounded by substantial detached houses bristling with security alarms and locked gates to their private roads. A most favourable location for any school, so hugely refreshing that the intake is very ethnically diverse, with 50 per cent of the children having EAL, a third speaking more than one language and some speaking more than two. They get great support – EAL teacher virtually full-time. Many children from European background, together with some Korean and Japanese. School celebrates this rich mix of cultures to the full; highly popular international week and international evenings every year for the whole family – they are invited to wear national dress (even the Brits), have national dancing shows and sample many homemade culinary delights.

Three forms of mixed ability entry – 30 per form. Key Stage 1 results are v. good, but head points out that with so many children having EAL, the higher grades in literacy are harder to achieve for many pupils. SEN – typical of the national average – 21 per cent.

School recently updated to a v. high standard, on a semi-open plan basis with lots of natural light. Amazingly for a state primary school, computerised interactive (and expensive) whiteboards (we have seen many independent prep schools without these), together with a new IT suite. Lovely grounds with far-reaching views. Shares swimming pool with junior school, used by each class twice a week in summer. Buildings adapted for disabled users.

Super school to visit with loads going on and children very absorbed. Great range of after school activities: clubs for gym, drama and music, art and craft, German, French, construction, cooking and a dinosaur club – charge of approx. £3 per session. Lending library for videos, games, reading and maths schemes. Do look at the super website, a lot of it created by the children. Support from the solid middle class parents is tremendous: ' The parents raise a fortune,' says the head, – the school's swimming pool is heated and maintained from proceeds raised by the PTA.

No lunch provided, children have to bring packed lunch from home. Parking problematical, as ever, with busy main road outside. No problems dropping off in the mornings – a quick in and out – not so easy in the afternoon when Head insists parents park in adjacent side roads and walk to collect.

School has everything going for it – great head, vibrancy, enviable buildings, grounds, location and catchment area. Deservedly v. popular, worth moving to be near – or should we say very near – to get a place, assuming of course you have the money to buy in its largely upmarket catchment area.

Coworth-Flexlands School

Valley End, Chobham, Surrey, GU24 8TE

Tel: 01276 855 707

Fax: 01276 856 043

Email: secretary@coworthflexlands.co.uk

Website: www.coworthflexlands.co.uk

• Pupils: 140 girls 15 boys, including nursery, all day
• Ages: 3-11, boys until 7 • Religion: Inter-denom
• Fees: £1,045-£2,450 • School status: Independent
• Opendays: October, November, March • School gender: Mixed
• Day/boarding: Day pupils

SEN provision

Detail:
Now provide for in school:
  Mild: DYSC; DYSL; DYSP;
  Moderate: DYSC; DYSL; DYSP;
  Severe: DYSC;
  Others: DEL; PD;

Summary: Coworth-Flexlands is a Prep School of approximately 150 pupils (nursery to year 6). The school recognises that all pupils have individual needs most of which can be met within the normal environment of the classroom through a differentiated curriculum. The needs of a small number of pupils cannot be met fully without some special support. This additional support is offered as an integral part of the school's provision. The special needs department aims to identify all children who need special consideration to support their physical, social, emotional or intellectual development. Some children are offered extra support within the classroom, others may require individual tuition.

What we say about the school - the full Good Schools Guide review

Head: Since 2004, Mrs Sandy Stephen (late fifties) who was head of Coworth Park (from 2003), and when nearby Flexlands school merged with Coworth Park in September 2004, Mrs S was appointed head of the newly combined school Coworth-Flexlands. A widow with two married daughters, she first came to Coworth Park in 1984 as a parent when her children attended the school; she subsequently joined the teaching staff (moving from a secondary school in London). She has risen up the ranks and was deputy head prior to the headship. Her younger daughter taught piano at the school for two years and the family tradition will continue when her granddaughter starts in 2006. A delightful lady, informally dressed and very grandmotherly – a refreshing change from the business-suited heads of many other preps.

Entrance: Non-selective. Places are offered following a meeting with the head and a tour and introduction to the school (together with the receipt of registration fee) on a first-come-first-served basis. Children join the nursery in the term they become 3. The merged school is not yet full to capacity, so worth trying for vacancies at other times.

Exit: Papplewick, Lambrook Haileybury and Woodcote House popular destinations for the boys when they leave at 7. Girls depart to a whole variety of places including St Georges, Ascot, The Marist and Luckley Oakfield locally, but some move further afield to Guildford High, St Catherine's Bramley and Cheltenham Ladies' College. On average about five or six each year win scholarships.

Remarks: A delightful school which has been going through an unsettled time but, now the merger is complete, they can continue with their vision of developing the 'whole' child – an ethos which has pleased parents, with the good results achieved in a relaxed atmosphere.

Our visit took place a couple of weeks into the opening of the newly merged school on the site of the previous Coworth Park. The school is set in 13 acres of grounds on the edge of Chobham Common and attracts pupils from the local (and very expensive) Surrey/Berkshire area – Chobham, Ascot, Windlesham and Woking. The school is centred on a large old house with later additions – something of a rabbit warren to find your way around but there are big plans for expansion to provide new classrooms, music rooms, staff room and ICT suite in 2006. Until then, the nursery, kindergarten and some others are housed in temporary classrooms. Excellent library – well-stocked with lots of new books: pupils use the library during lesson time and are also encouraged to visit at lunchtimes when they can sit and read quietly on one of the comfy beanbags!

Average class size is smallish: 18 – 20 or less in some years as the year group has been split into two where space allows. Year group sizes vary as a result of the merger. Several young and enthusiastic staff members and 'some who have been there for a very long time' according to one parent. Mrs S is very proud that this non-selective school achieves good SATS results and that many pupils go on to gain places (and also scholarships) at some top senior schools – she is convinced they do well because they do not pressurise the children. Pupils are encouraged to be enthusiastic and creative and to follow a broad-based curriculum. School offers SEN assistance readily to those who require it. They can cater for dyslexia, dyspraxia, hearing impairment and physical disability and also offer a gifted child programme. There are two SEN qualified staff members and the school is happy to discuss individual requirements. Maybe not top of an SEN school list, but the relaxed and happy atmosphere combined with lack of academic pressure could make this a good choice.

Sport is compulsory for all and children are encouraged to take part in a variety of activities including netball, rounders, athletics and swimming once a week in Woking for years 2 – 6. About half the children play an instrument, they have a free choice – piano is very popular as is guitar; others learn cello, clarinet, sax and one is even learning to play the double bass. Music lessons are timetabled mainly before and after school to minimise class disruption, which is a popular move with staff and parents. Pupils take part in the local Chobham music festival and put on a musical production each summer.

Very attractive uniform – blue tartan pinafores or kilts for the girls and the more usual grey shorts or trousers for the boys – the younger ones wear tracksuits in the nursery – very practical commented parents. Lunch is excellent said the staff, and this was confirmed by pupils. All have a hot meal cooked on site, with a choice of salads.

Pupils are encouraged in areas of decision making – two representatives from each year are on the school council and attend weekly meetings chaired by a member of staff. A lively place throughout the day and this continues after school with all the usual extra-curricular activities including clubs for gardening, science and homework (groan!). The school also has its own Rainbow and Brownie packs. Outside space is good – despite the addition of the temporary classrooms – there is a fantastic adventure playground and a separate smaller area for the younger children. Pupils have access to the extensive school grounds and playing fields. Security is tight with key pad entry and plans to enclose the front of the school to increase security.

The six 'golden rules' are displayed all around the place. Lovely family atmosphere and the pupils are friendly and polite. Mrs S is keen to send all her pupils away confident in their own abilities (whatever they may be) and with high self-esteem.

The Craighalbert Centre

1 Craighalbert Way, Cumbernauld, G68 0LS

Tel: 01236 456 100

Fax: 01236 736 889

Email: lillemor@craighalbert.org.uk

Website: www.craighalbert.org.uk

• Pupils: Around 49-50 at any one time • Ages: babies to around 7; plus the odd former pupil who comes back for a week's refresher course a term (five in the school when we visited) • School status: Independent • School gender: Mixed • Day/boarding: Day pupils

SEN provision

Detail:

Centre of excellence for:
- Mild: CP;
- Moderate: CP;
- Severe: CP;
- Others: Epi; PD;

Experience of:
- Mild: DYSP; HI; VI;
- Moderate: DYSP; HI; VI;
- Severe: DYSP;
- Others: MSI; Sp&LD;

Summary: The Craighalbert Centre is the national centre for children with motor impairments and combines the principles of conductive education, as devised at the Peto Institute in Budapest, with national advice on the curriculum in Scotland, to teach the children independence, everyday activities and life skills, within a nursery or school day.

What we say about the school - the full Good Schools Guide review

Head: Since 1991, Dr Lillemor Jernqvist (sixties) who is Swedish and trained in Gothenberg as an educational psychologist; she previously worked with the Spastics Society in London and has always worked in special needs and 'just happened to be around at the right time'. A lovely reassuring person with a tinkling laugh and a halo of blond hair. Her office walls are covered with photographs of blond grandchildren.

Entrance: For pupils with motor impairments, West syndrome, or other 'non-progressive' motor impairment; some may also have epilepsy, visual, aural, speech and language problems though a 'conductive education is a learning process' – 'children should have an ability to learn with understanding. By referral from a local LEA. Determined bullying by parents is often required. Children and their parents (who are a vital part of the conductive education programme) come daily from all over Scotland: the Borders, Galashiels, Perth, Dundee, Angus.

Exit: Pupils officially leave at 7 some to mainstream, some to special schools: Richmond Park, Windsor Park, Greenburn School or Corseford to name but a few.

Remarks: The purpose-built centre set slightly unceremoniously off Cumbernauld's northern ring road and surrounded by a pretty ratty-looking building site ('Scottish wildlife garden' we were told) follows the methods taught by the Budapest-based Peto Institute and opened in 1992, having started life in temporary accommodation some fifteen months earlier. The centre, which is on a sloping site, with ramps, lifts and stairs, has four large remedial rooms (with quite big one-way glassed viewing rooms), a hydrotherapy pool and an extension where children who have been through the centre can come back to check that their progress is up to speed. The large roomy hall is of necessity cluttered with wheelchairs of every conceivable colour and design, plus the odd hard hat, and a number of 'specials', wooden (honestly) double and quadruple chairs with seat belts and adjustable foot rests – usually used for taking children to the loo, we were told. 'Staff try and get them out of nappies.' The loos themselves come in banks of four, with an extra extended shelf at the back so that staff can lend a hand inconspicuously. The open-ended loo block includes showers.

Children may have to be taught to chew, life skills are important. Wherever possible, children are encouraged to walk and to do as much for themselves as they can – the first challenge is to hold their heads straight. Babies and those under two have two one-and-a-half hour sessions a week with their parents who are taught the right way to handle, communicate with, feed (and some may have gastronomy tubes, particularly those who are underweight), dress and 'develop good pattern of movement'. These sessions are free (funded by the Friends of Craighalbert) and often include some time in the hydrotherapy pool (Halliwick swimming method) – blowing water bubbles is important. Local physios use the pool at lunchtime).

Babies from North Lanarkshire are funded by their education service under the new ASL Act. Parents (grandparents, whatever) are integral to conductive education, and many become lifelong friends. Two- to three-year-olds come with their parents four times a week – great importance is made of bonding, communicating and encouraging.

Parental confidence is vital, they are part of the team and we saw really quite badly disabled little ones lying on mats having their limbs massaged and then being shown how to stand, sit, and take tentative steps, 'rhythmical intention'. They are also taught to eat and encouraged to dress themselves. All staff wear blue breeks and white tops with Craighalbert embroidered over the heart, whilst children wear white shirts and shorts and a variety of Velcro-ed splints.

The first thing the children do each day is to change into school clothes (school has its own well-used laundry). Two nursery groups, one for those who have already been in the school and the other for those who are coming in for the first time, follow Scottish guidelines for nursery schools and currently Friday is free and children are encouraged to attend mainstream nursery. Post-five the children are subdivided; conductive education is combined with the Scottish syllabus for that age group (joint IEP), and children are grouped according to ability within the age group. Those who have a mainstream placement go to that school on Fridays but, for some, this may not be suitable and whilst the centre provides Friday school for these pupils, they also advise on what happens next. Very often graduates (well, what else?) go on to mainstream school with a dedicated mentor; there is a rolling programme to take senior pupils back for a couple of weeks (plus parents or mentors) to brush up their motor skills.

The centre has two fully equipped self-catering flats (six twins, one double) upstairs (with perhaps the worst case of bedmaking we have ever seen) which are available to returning students and their families and much used by those who attend conferences either because they want to start their own centres, or to do training modules. An occasional child will come with their parents from the north of England, or the islands or indeed Romania for periods up to three months at a time, when the parents are trained in continuing the treatment themselves. There are no overnight staff. The school itself is highly staffed (over 40 including 21 teaching staff); physios are the most difficult to find. 'Most' are professionally qualified in 'something' and can take Craighalbert modules; each group will have a teacher, nursery nurse, nurse, physio, audiologist, a speech and language therapist and a raft of assistants (the most common complaint is sore knees from all the kneeling they have to do).

Craighalbert modules cover Conductive Education, Cerebral Palsy, Early Education in the Context of Conductive Education and Human Movement from a Conductive Education Perspective. Toys and learning aids are cunningly designed to make the child work for any achievement which is then lavishly praised. Children sit on stools, no quarter from chair backs here. Normal school terms but school also runs a Saturday morning course and a summer school for those with CP who can walk a bit and go to mainstream school, the basic aim is to improve 'abnormal patterns of movement, maintaining and topping up physical skill and mobility'. The Ramblers Group supports and encourages those with less spasticity whose 'disabilities would become minimal if they learned early on how to make the best use of the whole body'. Outstanding; if necessary kill to get your child here.

Cranleigh Preparatory School

Horseshoe Lane, Cranleigh, GU6 8QH

Tel: 01483 542 051

Fax: 01483 277 136

Email: fjmb@cranprep.org

Website: www.cranleighprepschool.org

• Pupils: 165 boys, 105 girls, 200 day, 70 board • Ages: 7-13 • Religion: Non-denom • Fees: Day: £3,160-£3,825; boarding: £4,155-£4,820 • School status: Independent • Opendays: October • School gender: Mixed • Day/boarding: Takes boarders

SEN provision

Detail:

Centre of excellence for:
- Mild: DYSL;
- Moderate: DYSL;

Now provide for in school:
- Mild: DYSC; DYSP;
- Moderate: DYSC; DYSP;
- Severe: DYSL;

Experience of:
- Mild: ADD; ADHD; EBD;
- Moderate: MLD;
- Severe: DYSP;
- Others: EAL; Sp&LD;

Summary: The learning support department at Cranleigh Prep School deals with pupils who have a learning difficulty which in some way hinders their ability to learn fully in the main classroom. The aim of the department is to provide a safe learning environment for pupils to achieve their potential. We provide specialist tuition for pupils with dyslexia, dyspraxia and dyscalculia. Support can be provided for pupils for whom English is a second language. We tailor our teaching to the pupil's specific learning difficulties. Every pupil has an IEP made specifically to suit their needs. A multi-sensory approach to learning is taken with our students.

The department offers specialist teacher assessments to identify pupils who may have a specific need. All teachers in the school are made aware of pupils receiving support and their needs. We can also recommend outside specialists such as educational psychologists, speech and language therapists, occupational therapists and opticians.

All the teachers in the learning support department are qualified special needs teachers. They all hold diplomas in SpLD. We also have a trained Phono-Graphix tutor and Visualising and Verbalising tutor.

What we say about the school - the full Good Schools Guide review

Headmaster: Since 2000, Mr Michael Roulston MBE CertEd BPhil MEd (late forties). Married to Janet, who teaches food technology at the school. Previously headmaster of the British School in Tokyo where he transformed the place. He has worked the same magic here, taking a lacklustre boys-only prep and turning it into a 21st century co-ed prep school of huge merit. Lovely man – approachable, humorous, interested and interesting, also somehow remarkably unassuming. 'I love what I do – there's a feel good factor here,' he says. Certainly his enthusiasm knows no bounds and touches everything and everyone around the school. Says that he has been hugely supported by the governing body and has felt he has been allowed to 'run with it'- and run he has. There aren't enough positive epithets in existence to describe the man as far as parents are concerned: 'incredibly dynamic,' 'wonderful,' 'inspirational,' 'not your average head,' 'a real leader,' 'fabulous'. One parent going so far as to say 'he walks on water.' That we would like to see.

Entrance: The main entry point is at 7+, and then another at 11+: usually about 50/60 applicants for the available places. Pupils are selected on academic merit, and ability to contribute to the life of the school -'we're looking for girls and boys who love school, are fired by it, and can give as much to the school as we can give them,' says Mr R. At 7+ pupils take written and/or oral assessments in English, maths and non-verbal reasoning as well as assignments in art and sport. At 11+ candidates also sit a general knowledge paper and have an interview with a senior member of staff. A report from the head of the pupil's present school is also sought. Prospective pupils spend a day at the school and are observed for their interaction: it's not just about paper results but more about the whole person, and how the Cranleigh ethos will suit them.

Exit: Around 60 per cent over the road to Cranleigh School – the majority sit CE and CASE. Other pupils go on to Charterhouse, Eton, Marlborough, Winchester, Wellington, Cheltenham Ladies, Heathfield Ascot, Lancing, Royal Grammar Guildford, amongst others.

Remarks: A super go-getting, can-do place, but tempered with a tangible warmth and friendliness. Remarkable transformation of buildings, teaching, extra-curricular activities – in fact everything has had the Roulston touch. Academically, it is a challenging atmosphere where children are inspired to learn. Energised approach to education – 'there's no drudgery here – it's a fun atmosphere,' says one parent. 'My children virtually skip in to school – even on a Saturday,' said another. School encourages lateral thinking and asking questions – 'to think outside of the box,' says a parent. Mr R looking at introducing the primary years programme of the IB. Parents feel that the teaching is 'leagues ahead' without huge pressure on the children.

Children start off in mixed ability groups with the majority of time spent with their form teacher, and in the third year are streamed for English and maths. In the upper school every subject is streamed, and there is a scholars' set.

SEN provision v. good. Dedicated learning support department and specialist tuition for pupils with dyslexia, dyspraxia and dyscalculia – which parents pay extra for. The school's SENCo has a team of three part-time tutors and teachers. Pupils are not specifically tested for learning difficulties: 'our own entry tests may reveal weaknesses,' says the head. School asks for any educational psychologist's assessment, so that the SENCo can advise if the school is right for the child. A multi-sensory approach and teaching is tailored to the child's needs – every pupil has an individual educational plan. One parent commented that her dyslexic daughter's confidence 'had soared.' Another parent said that her very academic child was 'stretched and challenged.'

On a musical note, vast range of activities on offer from singing lessons to electronic music. Lots of individual music lessons (27 specialists teaching 400 pupils a week). Dance teacher gets a pat on the back for getting boys up on their feet – street dance is very popular with the boys here. Impressive drama and art facilities – head of art believes everyone capable of doing amazing things, which is obviously filtering through to pupils as standard is extremely good and children's art is everywhere round the school.

Sport is very definitely for all, regardless of talent, the very unsporty may find this aspect tough but as Mr

R says 'Everyone is encouraged to do everything – we'll find what they're good at.' One parent commented on the competitiveness for team places, and resultant disappointments. Whole gamut of usual sports, in addition, options for riding, squash, golf, judo and Eton fives. Extracurricular opportunities abound: pupils are busy, busy, busy all day and beyond – hence encouragement to board so that these can be enjoyed to the full. Boarding is actively on the agenda in the last couple of years of school and the head feels this is important: 'At 12 and 13 the children positively look for opportunities to be independent and boarding gives that opportunity – they can flex their wings in a nurturing environment.' No question that the boarding aspect of the school adds another edge to the prep school atmosphere, but this constant go-getting all day atmosphere is not for everyone: sit down and read a book at home types may feel it is all too much. Saturday school for everyone, every alternate weekend.

Opposite its big sister, Cranleigh, in rolling Surrey countryside. Money has obviously been chucked at the place, but it has been done with intelligence. Integrity of the original buildings has been kept, whilst transforming the interior into a light, bright and breezy welcoming environment. Reception area is full of squashy sofas, giving impression of a swish hotel. Design and technology block impressive – Mr R has been busy knocking down walls (not personally) to create one huge workshop. Inventions are created on computers and then made in the workshop which is gadget heaven – every possible piece of machinery is available there. Dorms are light and bright – again with really attractive furnishings. One has a funky living room called 'the Ikea Room' – apparently according to matron because some brave soul went to Ikea and bought all the furnishings in one go. Matrons seem lovely – 'you can always talk to them'.

Pupils are a remarkably self-possessed and happy bunch. Parents are mostly local, middle class professionals, but the school is currently riding high and is becoming increasingly popular out of the immediate area.

CRANLEIGH SCHOOL

Horseshoe Lane, Cranleigh, Surrey, GU6 8QQ

Tel: 01483 273 666
Fax: 01483 267 398
Email: enquiry@cranleigh.org
Website: www.cranleigh.org

• Pupils: 401 boys, 205 girls; about 70 per cent board
• Ages: 13-18 • Religion: C of E • Fees: Boarding £7,450, day £6,035 • School status: Independent
• Opendays: Usually end of September • School gender: Mixed
• Day/boarding: Takes boarders

SEN provision

Detail:

Now provide for in school:
- Mild: DYSL; DYSP;
- Moderate: DYSL;

Experience of:
- Mild: HI;
- Others: EAL; Eat;

Summary: Learning support is available on an individual basis for any pupil requiring it, including those with mild specific learning dificulties. There is a specially designated centrally located room where pupils have access to a networked computer. Tuition may be given in all aspects of literacy, numeracy, EFL, study skills and personal organisation. Weekly lessons are provided (typically a 35 minute session) depending on individual requirements. Sessions usually take place outside normal lesson times unless a pupil has study periods. These lessons are charged as an extra to parents at the pro rata hourly rate which is set annually by the Governors. Assessment of any pupil with a suspected learning difficulty can be undertaken using standardised tests and dyslexia screening software with referral to an educational psychologist if necessary. Cranleigh has a long standing working relationship with the Helen Arkell Dyslexia Centre, Farnham.

What we say about the school - the full Good Schools Guide review

Headmaster: Since 1997, Mr Guy de W Waller, MA MSc PGCE FRSA (fifties), educated at Hurstpierpoint, and read chemistry at Worcester College and educational psychology at Wolfson College. Cricket and hockey blue. Former headmaster of Lord Wandsworth College. He has obvious enthusiasm, energy and self-confidence. Clearly doesn't feel he has to impress anybody – PR machine was definitely switched off the day we looked round – also a tendency to be rather glib and flippant (he doesn't have much time for this guide!). Describes himself as a 'frustrated housemaster – definitely not a career headmaster.' Feels that co-ed schools 'reflect the world we live in.' Has no doubts that school is doing it right – right balance of boys and girls, right approach to education. Describes the school fondly as 'this crazy place with heart.' Still teaches chemistry and philosophy – believes being in the classroom 'focuses you'. Likes to be kept informed and involved with pupils and he says 'the key is to have a good team in place.' Cuts something of a controversial figure amongst parents – variously described as 'charming, dynamic, running a tight ship' as well as 'distant, arrogant, autocratic, doesn't listen to parents' and all range of comments in between. Some parents feel that he is rather resting on his laurels (head hotly denies this – he has recently researched and completed a major development plan for the school), the school really being the only serious contender for senior co-ed in this part of Surrey, and thus a virtual monopoly. For others, he can do no wrong.

Academic Matters: Although academia is not wholly what Cranleigh is about, academic results have improved greatly of late, not least because of the introduction of girls throughout the school. At GCSE 60 per cent A/A* with particular success in drama and classical civilisation. At A/AS level, individual strengths vary from year to year but drama, economics, business studies, English, history and the sciences are usually up there with good grades. At A level between 75-80 per cent A/B grades. Head says that pupils 'don't have to be superstars,' but one parent commented that the academic side is definitely hotting up and 'B and C students may struggle.' School employs a SENCo who screens all entrants, support offered for those who need it – one-to-one sessions which cost extra.

Games, Options, The Arts: 'Sport is a very important part of just about every Cranleighan's life,' says head. The sheer range of sports available is staggering – there really is something for everyone. Sports facilities are extremely impressive – 100 of the 200 acres of the school land are given over to playing fields. Facilities include the Trevor Abbott sports centre (opened in Jan 2002), an all weather pitch for hockey in winter which converts to 12 tennis courts in summer (all packed with Wimbledon wannabees when we visited), indoor and outdoor swimming pools, cricket and rugby pitches stretching away as far as the eye can see, championship standard squash courts, six Eton fives courts, nine hole golf course, stables with own horses (pupils can bring their own horse(s) if desired), and so on. Key sports include rugby, cricket, hockey, lacrosse, netball, tennis and athletics. Football has nowhere near the same emphasis as rugby – might put off a soccer-mad boy. There are opportunities for all levels of talent – parents with non-sporty but enthusiastic children say that they really enjoy what they do. But certainly don't bother applying if your child absolutely loathes sport.

Art generally praised but one informed parental critic 'wasn't that impressed'. Drama is particularly strong with fantastic theatre facilities (very professional tiered auditorium) and lots of chance to perform throughout the year in a variety of different shows. Musically, the opportunities are vast, with choirs, orchestras, individual instrument tuition, concerts throughout the year. Interestingly though, music has not been hugely popular at either GCSE or A level.

Head does not feel that the description 'after-school activities' is apt for Cranleigh – 'it's not an expression that fits with our ethos as here after-school activities equal going to sleep. You have to be careful not to say 'going to bed' in a co-ed school.' Quite! However, call it what you will, other than sport, the options are wide ranging and children have loads of opportunities to fill their day – 'too many' says head.

Background and Atmosphere: Founded in 1865 for farmers' sons, is going through something of a renaissance and is currently wildly fashionable – 'the school has become very popular since Guy Waller became head,' was how one prospective parent put it. Another described how it was her daughter's 'dream come true' to get in. Set in stunning grounds totalling some 200 acres, the school certainly fulfils every expectation of an English boarding school. Beautiful, impressive façade – breathtaking architecture which continues inside to the chapel, library, quad.

Six houses: four boys, two girls. Boarding houses seem well designed – the newer ones are obviously more swish with bright and airy feel, dorms (generally sleep four) on the whole seem like the typical teenage bedroom – posters on wall, clothes strewn everywhere, but a homely atmosphere. Dining hall atmospheric, pupils help themselves from a choice of food – 'rather like motorway services,' says head.

Boarding is actively encouraged – majority do board – not out of necessity but desire to engage in all the school has to offer. If you are looking for a school where the kids are home at 4.00pm lounging around and chatting to parents, forget it – this is not the school for you. Absolutely key at Cranleigh are the sporting/extra-curricular opportunities and a long school day – whether you are boarding or not. A parent of a day pupil commented 'she loves the social whirl and doesn't want to come straight home.'

Pupils are encouraged to eat, sleep, and breathe Cranleigh. They are busy from dawn till dusk – school day is from 7.30am until potentially 9.00pm at night. 'If they really want to go home after that, they can,' says head. Everyone is expected to participate in the school fully and the head is very pro boarding and quite disparaging of what he calls 'five day' schools. Do expect resistance if your boarding child wishes to change to being a day pupil. Parents have been told it's disruptive to boarders, and affects the school's cash flow.

Everyone has Saturday school virtually every Saturday, and over a third of boarders stay at the weekend – although one boarding pupil said 'we all go home at the weekend' so it depends what a particular peer group does. A number of parents we talked to felt that there should be more weekend exeats. 'My children aren't usually home till 6.30pm on a Saturday, which makes going away for the weekend or seeing friends very difficult' said one parent of day pupils. Boarders need to be back by 7.00pm on a Sunday, so an even shorter weekend for them.

Pastoral Care and Discipline: Christian values underpin school society. Huge crackdown in recent years on sloppy discipline – drugs definitely not tolerated in any way; two boys expelled recently for drugs possession, although 'those expulsions surprised nobody,' says a not-particularly-shocked parent. Personal possession of alcohol and smoking are also big no-nos leading to a variety of sanctions including gating and detentions. Persistent offenders will be suspended. Sex education, not surprisingly, is quite high up the agenda here and romantic attachments between pupils are definitely discouraged. 'Inappropriate' sexual behaviour will lead to suspension or expulsion.

Head says that whole feel of school is 'more like a university' and that pupils will need self-reliance. Pupils' daily pastoral care is managed within each of the six houses and weekly meeting between head and tutors allows specific problems to be discussed. Bullying is tackled via the tutorial/house system where pupils can talk in confidence. Individual housemasters and housemistresses have their own views on mobile phones, going out etc – it's the luck of the draw – 'nonsense!' says the head, 'the only variation is whether the house actually collects phones overnight/during prep.' Surprisingly, considering tough line on transgression, school is not a pageant of well turned out pupils – lots of customised uniform in evidence, stiletto heels, short skirts, and funky hairstyles. Sixth formers wear suits – but for some girls the word suit is no way synonymous with smart and Mr W is trying to tidy them up. All this trendy dishevelment and urban cool seems a bit incongruous in such glorious surroundings.'

Pupils and Parents: Interestingly, for a predominantly boarding school, parents tend to be from quite a small, local radius (certainly no more than 30 miles is the norm) – and it's not unusual for parents to actually live in Cranleigh. Parents are 'a mix of backgrounds' says head – although as the school is hardly cheap presumably most are well-heeled (though Mr W keen to stress that a significant number have bursarial assistance). One parent said that school is 'like a movie set – full of beautiful people' and certainly pupils are particularly cool souls who come across as mature, self-possessed individuals.

Entrance: The entrance list is opened in May, 2½ years before September entry. Candidates and parents interviewed for interests/values/aspirations – conditional offers based on these and prep school reports, pending CE results. School very over-subscribed so they can afford to be choosy about who gets in. Head is looking for pupils who 'enjoy being at school and have the capability to be interested in a wide range of things.' For entrance to the sixth form (about 15-20 come in at this stage), the expectations are fairly modest: three Bs and three Cs at GCSE. Candidates will also be interviewed and reports sought from previous head. Sixth formers in general would be expected to board.

Exit: 15 or 20 a year leave at 16 for 'places offering more diverse AS/A2 courses than us', but the vast majority stay and go on to a wide range of universities – most popular recently include Nottingham, Exeter,

Bristol. Leeds, Oxford Brookes with 8 or 9 a year to Oxbridge.

Money Matters: Fees are by no means cheap, but most parents seem to feel that 'you get what you pay for' with the huge amount on offer. There are scholarships available – academic, music, art and the Eric Abbott for candidates of 'strong academic ability and at least one other area of excellence' – up to a maximum of 25 per cent of fees for the top awards. Other than that you'll need to remortgage.

Remarks: Hugely popular school with loads on offer, improving academia and mega street cred. Ideal for the sporty, energetic, sociable, and independent child.

D'Overbroeck's College

The Swan Building, 111 Banbury Road, Oxford, Oxfordshire, OX2 6JX

Tel: 01865 310 000
Fax: 01865 552 296
Email: mail@doverbroecks.com
Website: www.doverbroecks.com

• Pupils: 210 boys and girls in the sixth form, of whom approx 45 per cent board. About 80 in Leckford • Ages: 16-19; Leckford Place 11-16 • Religion: Non-denom • Fees: Years 9-11 £3,370; sixth form £4,850. Boarding £6,050-£7,265 • School status: Independent • Opendays: February, May and October • School gender: Mixed • Day/boarding: Takes boarders

SEN provision

Detail:
Now provide for in school:
- Mild: ASP; ADD; ADHD; DYSL; VI;
- Moderate: DYSL;
- Others: EAL;

Experience of:
- Mild: EBD; DYSC; DYSP; SpLD; HI;
- Moderate: ADD; ADHD; MLD; DYSC; DYSP; VI;
- Severe: DYSL;
- Others: Epi; PD; Eat;

Summary: We have had considerable experience over the years of teaching students with dyslexia and other mild learning difficulties, and we have a strong track record of success in this area. Our small classes, flexible teaching methods and strong focus on meeting individual needs makes this a positive, confidence-building environment with a clear emphasis on identifying strengths and building on them.

Students quickly realise that we are always ready to understand and address their particular needs and to help them find strategies that work for them – without in any way singling them out or making them feel self-conscious.

What we say about the school - the full Good Schools Guide review

Principal: Since 1996, Mr Sami Cohen BSc (forties). Educated in the Middle East followed by A levels in London, Mr Cohen read chemistry and French at Leeds. He first joined d'Overbroeck's in 1979, became director of studies, left, went to Paris, came back, et voilà ... Teaches languages, though not currently, French, Italian; sympa, thoughtful, quiet sense of humour, knows absolutely everything about everyone,thoroughly competent. Married, with three young children.

Head of Leckford Place School: Since 2005, Mr Mark Olejnik (late forties); has a first in history and ancient history. Joined d'Overbroeck's from Bury Lawn School in Milton Keynes, where he was deputy head.

Academic Matters: d'Overbroeck's Sixth form – huge numbers of subjects on offer (40 at present); serious labs, good library, tiny classes – max ten. 'Rigorously academic', excellent teaching (north Oxford of course), terrific staff specialising in A levels need one say more? Third-year-sixth picks up any retakes from other schools or extra A levels for a career change. Almost any combination possible, three or four A levels the norm. Good university advice and UCAS pick up.

Leckford Place School – for many years d'Overbroeck's had some students joining at 13 – something of an 'alternative' environment. In 2005 they established Leckford Place School 11 to 16-year-olds on a separate site. Target intake per year group of 40-45, max class size is 15. Entry at 11+ and 13+. d'Overbroeck's says 'focus still very much on the individual, small class approach, a school where the individual child is at the centre of everything the school does'. We have yet to visit – or indeed hear much from parents.

Games, Options, The Arts: Sixth form: serious art room, with sculpture, pottery, ceramics, fashion design, print making et al. Good music, games provision improving all the time from previous rather ad hoc basis (now two afternoons a week) – voluntary in the sixth form. Theatre studies dept have an arrangement with a company in Oxford for hands-on experience. Strong debating. Good IT and music technology. Special medic and vet and Oxbridge courses. The facilities are there, it is rather up to the pupil to enjoy.

Leckford Place School: 'PE and sport play important part in the life of the school'.

Background and Atmosphere: Sixth form: two main sites near to each other and close to city centre. All pupils expected to find their own lunch but food available to buy in the student common room/cafe. University environment, informal, relaxed, friendly but focused. No uniform.

Leckford Place School: we shall see.

Easter revision courses (GCSE, AS and A levels). Jazz holiday courses for ages 10-16

Pastoral Care and Discipline: Sixth form: 40 per cent of all sixth formers board, either in the college-owned student accommodation – super bedrooms, ghastly carpet – or with host families organised by and well known to the college. The rest are day. No boarding facilities for juniors. All students have personal tutors. Attendance and work rate very closely monitored. Regular feedback to parents.

Pupils and Parents: Sixth form: Those who want or need an alternative to more trad schools.

Leckford aiming to see parents 'as partners: open door policy.'

Entrance: At 11+ and 13+: own exam, references and interview.

Sixth form entry: references,interview and minimum of five GCSE passes.

Exit: Universities all over. Tops (in order) for 2004 were Bristol, Imperial, Oxford Brookes, University College, Edinburgh, Manchester, Oxford, Royal Holloway, St Andrews, Warwick.

Money Matters: Academic scholarships, science scholarships and art scholarships available. New performing art scholarship.

Remarks: Probably the most exciting school for secondary education in Oxford, and a very strong candidate for the best independent sixth form college in the UK.

The new Leckford Place junior school is, to us, an unknown.

Dame Hannah Rogers School

Woodland Road, Ivybridge, Devon, PL21 9HQ

Tel: 01752 892 461

Fax: 01752 898 101

Email: mail@damehannah.com

Website: www.damehannah.com

• Pupils: 45 girls and boys (all boarders except for 2 day girls)
• Ages: 8-19 • Religion: Non-denom
• School status: Independent • School gender: Mixed
• Day/boarding: Takes boarders

SEN provision

Detail:

Now provide for in school:
- Mild: AUT; DYSP; SpLD; CP;
- Moderate: AUT; MLD; DYSP; CP;
- Severe: DYSP; CP;
- Others: PMLD; SLD; Epi; Eat;

Experience of:
- Mild: DYSC; DYSL; HI; VI;
- Moderate: DYSC; DYSL; HI; VI;
- Severe: AUT; DYSC; DYSL;
- Others: DEL;

Summary: Dame Hannah Rogers School is a non-maintained residential special school and further education department.

Whose needs do we meet? Students with physical difficulties and associated learning difficulties (from moderate to profound). In addition many have sensory impairments usually associated with their disabilities. Many of our students have complex physical or medical problems. We are greatly experienced in working with young people who have communication difficulties. Our current age range is from 8 to 19 years but we hope to extend this to 5 to 19 years.

How do we meet those needs? By providing a multidisciplinary team approach alongside a waking hour curriculum. Students within the school (8-16 years) have access to a broad and balanced inclusive curriculum, which is specifically matched to individual needs. We zfollow the National Curriculum and offer a range of accredited courses at Key Stage 4 and above. The high staff-to-student ratio, which includes 24 hour nursing cover, ensures that all students have access to a high standard of support for all aspects of their school/residential experience. Standards of care are very high and the school has had excellent inspection results from the Commission for Social Care Inspection.

Within our Further Education department (16-19 years) we offer life skills alongside basic educational skills and the students are housed in specially adapted bungalows in order to maximise their independence skills. A range of therapies is provided including physiotherapy, speech and language therapy, hydrotherapy, rebound therapy, riding for the disabled. From October 2005 we will also be offering music therapy. Dame Hannah Rogers School has been included on the Ofsted Roll of Honour having received two outstanding inspection reports. We have an exceptional learning environment.

What we say about the school - the full Good Schools Guide review

Head: Since 2005, Mrs Angela Murray CertEd NPQH (early fifties). Trained as a teacher after working in a bank but 'never wanted to teach in mainstream'. Began career in Bristol teaching pupils with severe learning difficulties, moved to Dame Hannah Rogers in 1979. Promoted from deputy following retirement of predecessor; very empathetic and competent; understands profound and multiple learning difficulties inside out. Enjoyed NPQH training – especially time spent with colleagues from other sectors. Lives locally: husband Ian teaches ICT at FE college, two teenage daughters.

Academic Matters: Pupils have severe physical difficulties and communication disorders, with learning difficulties on a scale from moderate to profound. Emphasis on being a 'total communication environment' – ie where all forms of communication are respected, with all staff learning 'sign along'. Pupils use a range of VOCAs (electronic communication aids with voice output) and low tech communications systems (according to which suits each pupil best). Staff regularly review nine topic areas (eg 'food') through which foundation subjects are delivered; differentiated curriculum with value-added coming largely through life and social skills. Four spacious classrooms with attractive, topic relevant displays where teachers and learning support assistants often outnumber pupils.

Average class size is seven; individual timetables to accommodate different needs; we watched a girl counting with the use of blocks as part of Key Stage 3 maths whilst a boy with some vocal ability was using a touch-screen computer to move and match items in front of him. Variety of externally accredited courses such as Accreditation for Life and Living and National Skills Profile. FE curriculum for post-16s is life skills centred, and offers ASDAN in addition to OCR. The curriculum is adapted according to individual needs in each class. Leisure skills taught include games, sensory work and the arts.

Games, Options, The Arts: Lots of outings for pupils to eg ten-pin bowling and curling. Exchange visits to Germany and France. Involvement in local and national sporting events eg Stoke Mandeville games and Ten Tors (special seven mile wheelchair friendly course); came second nationally in Kielder Challenge, teaming up with students from local community college. Therapeutic riding popular, three sessions a week. New physiotherapy suite includes multi-activity hall, wheelchair maintenance workshop and all singing and dancing interactive hydrotherapy pool with computerised lighting and music. Separate multi-sensory room with range of stimuli including touch sensitive music wall with capacity similar to electronic keyboard. Dynamic head of physiotherapy teaches medics on placement. Speech therapists develop AAC skills of those with little or no speech through a combination of individual work, communication groups and class based sessions. Therapists provide training to school and care staff. LEA funding for some so-called 'additional' items can be hard to come by, but charities (eg Whizzkids for wheelchairs) often plug a gap.

Background and Atmosphere: OK buildings, pleasantly landscaped; sensory garden and a memorial garden. School mantra is 'from potential to achievement – a quality provision where individuals matter' and what we saw was just that. Dame Hannah's portrait hangs in the entrance looking down altruistically at new arrivals and we felt she would approve of what the school has become. DHR offers highest standards of care and training to severely challenged young people; all the staff we met showed dedication, energy and professionalism. Trustees combine lots of useful expertise and give it freely, as do many friends and other volunteers; two local charity shops help oil the wheels, and a trust director orchestrates vital financial support. DHR is used for placements for 1st and 3rd year medical students from Peninsular Medical School.

Justifies its national reputation. Upgrading its facilities; staff are trained to top levels. We liked the way that everything seemed to flow effortlessly with therapies being as natural a part of the day as eating or relaxing. Parents clamouring for year-round respite care here: it is giving what they and their children most want.

Pastoral Care and Discipline: Whole team approach; multi-disciplinary meetings and in-house training help to pull in everyone; class teachers write IEPs with therapists twice yearly and have regular meetings with care staff. School now registering as a children's home to allow some respite care for 50 weeks of year in response to increased parental demand. Experienced care team, care staff work separate waking and night shifts and give huge amounts of personal care; six nurses with specialist knowledge and experience (eg of epilepsy, tracheostomies and gastrostomies) provide 24 hour medical support from health centre in residential wing. Most bedrooms being converted to singles with swish toilet facilities shared between two; privacy and dignity important in view of some medical conditions. Hoists in upgraded bedrooms as well as in classrooms. All areas scrupulously clean with cheery decor and space for personal posters, photos from home etc. Staff not daunted by challenges faced by pupils; everything is done (eg chat books; family and friends albums) to encourage communication. Senior students are accommodated in one of five bungalows which struck us as being 'homes away from home'.

Pupils and Parents: Pupils come from a wide area. Lots of phone traffic between staff and parents, plus website with news of events, e-mail and webcam. Old Students' organisation run by 50-year-old former student; newsletter twice a year and occasional reunions.

Entrance: Pre-application visit recommended. Two-day assessment involves meeting staff and students, teaching and care staff as well as therapists, educational psychologist and consulting paediatrician. Families can use parents' flat overnight during the assessment visit.

Exit: Some go on to tertiary specialist colleges.

Money Matters: Fees are normally met by local authorities and are set on a scale starting at £51,000 according to the level of need and provision.

Remarks: Students gain greatly in self-esteem, and will have vastly improved life and educational skills with which to face the outside world.

Dane Court Grammar School

Broadstairs Road, Broadstairs, Kent, CT10 2RT

Tel: 01843 864 941

Fax: 01843 608 811

Email: admin@danecourt.kent.sch.uk

Website: www.danecourt.kent.sch.uk

• Pupils: 1,150 boys and girls, all day • Ages: 11-18

• Religion: Non-denom • School status: State

• School gender: Mixed • Day/boarding: Day pupils

SEN provision

Detail:

Now provide for in school:

Mild: ASP; AUT; ADD; ADHD; EBD; DYSC; DYSL; DYSP; SpLD; HI; VI; CP;

Moderate: ASP; ADD; ADHD; EBD; MLD; DYSL; DYSP; SpLD; HI; VI;

Severe: VI;

Others: SPD; EAL; PD;

Summary: We are a designated unit for students with visual impairments. We have a team of 7 learning support assistants, five of whom are Braille trained.

We offer study skills lessons to a small number of students in years 8 and 9, particularly those with dyslexia.We also have a lunchtime group targeting pupils with social communication difficulties. Two of our LSAs have done autism and Asperger's courses. At present we have seven pupils with statements and about 25 at school action plus.Support is given in class to pupils from years 7 to 11. A few pupils also have one-to-one support a few times a week.

What we say about the school - the full Good Schools Guide review

Head: Since 2004, Mr Paul Luxmoore (mid forties). Read history at University College London and trained to be a teacher at the Institute of Education, London. Taught at Chelmsford High School and says this has had a very strong influence on him. Came here from being acting head at Bourne Grammar School. Dapper. A personable and articulate man with lots of energy and commitment, a welcome arrival.

Believes in state education and has always taught in it. This is his first substantial headship, and he is already making his presence felt. Has introduced a house system, which has gone down well, and is working on involving the sixth form more in the life of the school. Realistic about the school, but clear in his aim to take it up a level: believes, for instance, that all in the sixth form should aim to go to university (not the norm in this economically stretched part of Britain). Wants the school to do better by exceptionally able students.

Academic Matters: Superb results, both actual and value-added, by the uninspiring standards of the Thanet area, and not at all bad by national standards: in the top 25 per cent. Almost all get the requisite five A*-C grades at GCSE; 46 per cent A/B grades at A level: 'an indication of the very hard work done by both staff and students', says Mr Luxmoore.

The school is a specialist language college, though you would be hard put to guess this from the A level results – it shows more in a determination to develop an international approach to the curriculum and in students' attitudes. Spanish has been introduced in year 7, and the school is looking at the IB. Students teach French at local primary schools.

Students enthusiastic about media studies and English. Physics popular – always a surprise – and strong indications of good teaching elsewhere too. Boys keep up with the girls – another welcome anomaly. Facilities reasonable, much new spending on ICT.

Splendid SEN provision. For the past few years, Dane Court has been a designated grammar school for visually impaired (VI) students. A handful scattered throughout the school; one student is profoundly deaf, one is completely blind. A significant number of students have dyslexia, dyspraxia or Asperger's. Staff training for SEN is a high priority: three are qualified in Braille, and this is soon to be four. Each department has its SEN co-ordinator to ensure continuity of provision, and staff work closely with families. SEN children are featured in an album, ensuring all staff are aware of their needs. Other students are accepting of SEN pupils, and rather proud of them being there and being involved in the life of the school. Genuinely inclusive.

Games, Options, The Arts: A strong PE department, with successful teams at all levels: some students competing at county level. Successful climbing team. Art very good, with vivid and skilful displays around the school. Music strong, with a large number of orchestras and bands.

Background and Atmosphere: Shabby. Years of neglect and tight budgets. Faint but pervasive smell of school dinners. When head arrived he was dismayed by the premises, but soon found that, compared to other local schools, facilities are good. School, though, feels full of pupils who like being there and are busy, and head sees lots of possibilities for improvement. He has plans for eg revamping the learning resource centre, having a primary school built on the site, also a sports hall. The spirit of the school shines through. Forward looking, enthusiastic, aiming at widening the often narrow parameters of pupils' and parents aspirations.

Pastoral Care and Discipline: Sixth form 'buddies' (also a club run at lunchtimes where years 7-11 can meet others, play games and talk to the staff) and 'form friends'; senior students very much involved in helping younger ones. Much appreciated. Sixth form generally given responsibility: the sixth form centre belongs entirely to them – they have a telly, do their own decoration. Sixth form newspaper and Year Book. Firm policy on drugs – the few incidents rapidly dealt with; apparently not much of a problem with alcohol. Bullying not tolerated: 'I can't stand it,' says the head, and he sees to it that any infringements are dealt with appropriately, and the right message gets across.

Pupils and Parents: Varied socio-economic background, with much deprivation. School spirit gets through to parents as well as kids: many parents involved in eg language evening classes, PTA activities and fundraising. Free Spanish evening classes for parents and pupils attracted 240 people, so another tutor has been recruited. The highly presentable sixth formers who showed us round were chosen at random and told us 'we don't know anyone who doesn't want to be here.'

Entrance: From local primary schools by the Kent Test – the county's version of the 11-plus. Sixth form entry not tough – five A* to C grades with B grades in the subjects studied at A level.

Exit: To university or other FE if the head has anything to do with it, and not just to the local branch of Christ Church University down the road either. Although that's perfectly good, he is keen to encourage wider horizons.

Remarks: A good school in less than easy circumstances, showing the way on inclusion and aspiration.

DANES HILL SCHOOL

Oxshott, Leatherhead, Surrey, KT22 0JG

Tel: 01372 842 509

Fax: 01372 844 452

Email: registrar@daneshillschool.co.uk

Website: www.daneshillschool.co.uk

• Pupils: 470 boys, 385 girls, all day • Ages: 2 1/2-13 (nursery, pre-prep school (known as Bevendean), middle and upper school) • Religion: Christian non-denom • Fees: reception and yr 1 £2393, yr 2 to yr 8 £3375 • School status: Independent • School gender: Mixed • Day/boarding: Day pupils

SEN provision

Detail:

Centre of excellence for:

Mild: DYSL;

Moderate: DYSL;

Others: EAL;

Now provide for in school:

Mild: ASP; ADD; SpLD;

Experience of:

Mild: AUT; ADHD; EBD; DYSC; DYSP; HI; VI; CP;

Moderate: ASP; ADD; DYSC; DYSP; SpLD; VI;

Severe: DYSL;

Others: SPD; Sp&LD; PD; Eat;

Summary: Danes Hill School is committed to providing equal access for all pupils to a broad and balanced curriculum to which they are entitled. The school makes provision for pupils with special educational needs whether they have specific learning difficulties or are exceptionally able or 'gifted'. The director of learning support co-ordinates provision from the nursery to year 8. Children are withdrawn for individual lessons and groupwork is also provided. Weekend Workshops are offered for some exceptionally able pupils. All learning support staff have specialist qualifications. The school has a comprehensive assessment and monitoring system to ensure that each pupil has the opportunity to develop their true potential.

What we say about the school - the full Good Schools Guide review

Headmaster: Since 1989, Mr Robin Parfitt MA MSc (late fifties). Two headships prior to Danes Hill, Mr Parfitt has grown and developed the school considerably since he has been at the helm. Married to Angela (director of studies). A very confident, business-like man who is seen by parents as a strong leader. Wants to be at the cutting edge of change and he believes the school is 'very different from smaller local preps.' Demands respect. Lots of very efficient support staff around him.

Entrance: Waiting lists are not generally an issue, but they do exist for some year groups (although they do not operate more than two years ahead) so get names down early. Entry points at nursery (2 1/2-3 years), transition (3-4 years) reception (4-5 years) and year 3 (7-8 years) when they are tested in English, maths and reading.

In such a large school, worth ringing at odd times to see what is available. From September 2007, the school will take fewer new children into transition making spaces available for entry into reception. Some scholarships and bursaries on offer. Extremely approachable registrar, Mrs Shattock, described by one parent as 'fantastic'.

Exit: Boys and girls theoretically both leave at 13 (although about 25 per cent of girls exit at 11). Pupils go on to City of London Freemen's School, Epsom College, Royal Grammar School Guildford, King's Wimbledon and Guildford High School amongst others. Impressive list of school awards particularly academic and sports from a wide range of schools including St John's and Cranleigh.

Remarks: A very large school with traditional values and a strong feeling of discipline and achievement. Academically strong with a broad curriculum and a very good level of general education. Main aim is to prepare children for CE and public school scholarships with a high success rate in both. Some parents feel not as much importance is put on 11+ and that the focus on girls leaving at 11 is lost.

So what about the school's reputation as an academic hot-house? Yes, academia is extremely important, yet there's a real sense of pride in helping the less able to achieve their best. According to the head, as long as your child shows 'enormous compassion and imagination' then their achievements are valued. On average 22 pupils in each class, but children are placed into small sets from year 3 and scholarship streams from year 6. Class groups are mixed at year 3 and 6, so children get the opportunity to make new friends. Classroom layout is traditional with pupils taught at individual desks facing the teacher from an early age. The head is strongly of the view that this method gets the best from his pupils. There is controlled discipline in the classroom – children stand automatically as you enter – and this is well balanced by 'friendly teachers who help to bring fun to the lessons.' Lots of hands-on experimentation and practical work. Computerised whiteboards in every classroom. Two noticeably impressive computer suites.

Unanimous parental comments that there are no weak teachers. Mr Parfitt says he pays his staff well and expects high standards in return. Languages v strong: all introduced to three languages – more if they study the classics! French in the pre-prep, a 'taster' course in Spanish and German (six months each) in year 3 and then either Spanish or German as their single language in year 4. French is introduced again in year 5. After that, French and Spanish or German are taught on an equal basis. Works well – a high pass rate for language GCSE at age 13. Lots of exchange trips with very intense language study whilst abroad. Latin, and classical Greek- about twenty 10-year-olds studying this option.

Significant learning support unit that works hard to provide additional help. The unit also plucks out the very bright, gifted and talented children and enjoys bringing them on. Some parental feeling that 'there's not such a focus on the average child – who must be self-motivated to succeed.'

Great emphasis on the arts, many arts scholarships to senior schools... Three separate art rooms (3-dimensional, graphic design and general). Some beautiful and very mature 3-D work and an extremely enthusiastic art teacher. Artwork adorns the walls in the most unexpected places and children use visual work in all areas of study. Design technology, drama and music equally strong. Drama teachers write their own plays, so parents don't know what to expect. Isolated comment from a parent that 'it's always the same kids who get the lead roles.' A high percentage of pupils learn a musical instrument (up to grade 8) and many play more than one. Practice takes place at home although orchestra and ensembles, as well as choirs, rehearse in timetabled sessions at school. Performances recently at the Royal Albert Hall, Guildford Cathedral and Southwark Cathedral. Pupils also in the National Children's Orchestra and the National Children's Choir.

Sport flourishes helped by the school's extensive grounds, and sporty children really thrive here. Grand display cabinet full of sporting trophies in the reception. Lots of tournaments. Rosslyn Park 7-a-side semi-finalists and finalists, and national biathlon champions. One parent comments 'There's a huge focus on rugby. It's given so much priority each year that football peters out.' Despite this, there's such a variety of sport on offer that any child should find something to suit.

School site is large and wooded with many areas for the children to play and explore. Lovely naturalistic feel, with beautiful sculptures and building names – The Rookery, The Ark. Tidy and litter free. A real feel of history and tradition about the place – the school has only existed since 1947, but the Victorian buildings and choice of décor in reception areas make it appear more long-standing. New buildings have been sympathetically added to the main house, some temporary classrooms. Bevendean is being rebuilt with a new double storey classroom block due for completion Dec 2006.

Head sees himself as 'a facilitator who allows his senior management and heads of department to get on with the job.' There's a feeling of strict order and control. Children don't mill around, but move along with purpose. A large school. 'Without the size', the head says, 'Danes Hill would not be able to offer such a wide and well resourced curriculum with so many specialist teachers'. On the negative side, parents feel that the management structure stops them from talking directly to the head about day-to-day matters. Parental opinions vary from the disgruntled – 'It's hard to see the head. You are referred to the head of year or head of school' to the more positive 'If you want to see the head he'll make time for you'. But it's often better to deal with the head of year because they know your child better.' (Unanimous thumbs up for the head of the upper school: 'He is excellent. He's very in touch with the children' and 'Lots of help when discussing where your child should go next').

Pastoral care is much praised. Children taught to be responsible for their own actions from an early age. 'The school makes children very independent' says one parent, 'They're very responsible. There's sex education and puberty education!' Good home cooking with plenty of healthy choices.

The large number of international children creates a unique atmosphere (there's even a specialist EAL teacher). The school is the only factor that binds all these disparate people together – may explain why there is such a strong sense of community. Parents are corporate chieftains and the like, and mostly rather wealthy. They put in a large amount of effort and commitment to the school and this is strongly encouraged by the head. A few comments that the parents form cliques. Drop-off and pick-up times are a nightmare – the entrance to the school is on the brow of a steep hill. School runs a bus service from and to the immediate surrounding areas (Walton, Weybridge, Esher, Claygate and Bookham).

Suits bright, confident, sporty children happy to get involved in school life and who would not get lost in the crowd.

Davies Laing and Dick College

100 Marylebone Lane, London, W1U 2QB

Tel: 020 7935 8411

Fax: 020 7935 0755

Email: dld@dld.org

Website: www.dld.org

• Pupils: 400 boys and girls, all day • Ages: 14-19

• Religion: Non-denom • Fees: £4,920

• School status: Independent • School gender: Mixed

• Day/boarding: Day pupils

SEN provision

Detail:

Now provide for in school:

Mild: DYSL;

Moderate: DYSL;

Experience of:

Mild: ADD; ADHD; DYSP;

Moderate: ADD;

Others: EAL;

Summary: DLD has two specialist tutors to help students with moderate dyslexia and other learning difficulties.

What we say about the school - the full Good Schools Guide review

Principal: Since 1996, Ms Elizabeth Rickards MA PGCE (fifties). Read history at St Andrews University. Spent ten years at Duff Miller College, including five years as Vice Principal. Joined DLD in 1993, and was appointed principal three years later. Has also worked at the Young Vic, and is passionate about the importance of creativity in education. Outstanding leader. 'She's very sharp, very quick, really on the ball,' said a parent. 'The kids know that they can't get away with anything.' 'She's fantastically persuasive,' said another, 'but most of what she said has been borne out by our experience.' Known to staff and students as 'Topsy': 'which shows our affection as well as our respect,' said one. Married.

Academic Matters: A small minority of pupils are there to do one- or two-year GCSE courses, the rest one- or two- year A level courses. There are also retake courses of varying length. Maximum class size: 10. Commendable results from a mixed-ability intake. Most GCSE students take eight subjects, from a limited list that includes the basics plus French, Spanish, business studies, ICT, art and drama. Latin, Greek and German are available via individual tuition. Generally over 80 per cent get 5+ A*-C grades.

A level students get a choice of 40 subjects, including Chinese, photography, film studies and law, in more-or-less any combination. Art, business studies and psychology are consistently popular, alongside English and maths; just over half of all grades are generally A or B.

Some students are disaffected when they arrive. 'But it is unusual for them to be anti-education after a few weeks. It's important to fit the right course to the right student. Because of the small class sizes they get lots of individual feedback and huge amounts of encouragement, and most start making progress very quickly.'

The college can cope with special needs such as dyslexia and dyspraxia, though not ADHD, generally picking up several previously undiagnosed cases each year. Most need group support with study and essay-writing skills; individual help is also available at extra cost. 'Our SEN students get more or less the same level of results as the others – due to getting the subjects right, and to plenty of support.'

No quarter is given academically: 'We will not accept scrappy work. We believe in raising standards and in making students believe they can move up to the next level.' Many staff are from Oxbridge, and come from non-teaching backgrounds: the theatre, the City, the BBC. 'They work unbelievably hard,' said an insider. 'They put in a lot of effort for the students.'

Games, Options, The Arts: A surprisingly arty college: A level art is one of the most popular and successful subjects, and several students are refugees from high-powered academic institutions where the creative side is less valued. The main aim of most students is to pass their exams, and extra-curricular activities are not high on the agenda except for those in plays and sports teams. A level students, in particular, often work long days. However, all GCSE students play sport at local centres on Friday afternoons, including football, basketball, tennis, netball and aerobics, and there are sports clubs and matches after school. The DLD youth theatre puts on two performances a year; the house band – organised by the drummer of Van der Graaf Generator, who is also the music technology teacher – plays well-attended gigs; there are film, debating and art clubs.

Year 10 and 12 students take part in Activities Week at the end of June, which could involve putting together a newspaper or a CD, making a film, playing plenty of sport or going on an art trip to Italy.

Background and Atmosphere: Now one of a group owned by Alpha Plus, the college was founded in 1931 to provide tutoring for Oxbridge and Colonial Service entrance exams. After the second world war it began to specialise in A and O level teaching. In 2004 it moved from Notting Hill to light, airy, refurbished premises in Marylebone, with an 80-seater theatre, recording studio, three art studios, science labs and photography studio.

Informal atmosphere, closer to a college than a school, with staff and students on a first name basis. 'They're unfussy about clothes, and about students in clinches on the stairs,' said an insider. 'But academically they're pretty tough. Students don't get away with things.'

Pastoral Care and Discipline: Strong pastoral system. 'Many students have had a shifting lifestyle, and it's a real haven for them,' said an insider. 'There is a lot of respect, because students know we care about them.' An attendance officer checks that students are present at each lesson and contacts parents of absconders. Each student has a weekly meeting with their personal tutor, to talk about progress and future plans. Tough sanctions for misusing drink and drugs; those under suspicion are sent for drugs tests, to general parental approval. 'There are a few troubled and troublesome students,' said a parent, 'but most buckle down eventually.'

'Occasionally there are students we don't manage to turn round,' says the head. 'Then I'll often suggest to parents a gap year in the middle of the sixth form, preferably working in Waitrose. It concentrates their minds on the consequences of failing to work, and the difference in maturity when they come back is often amazing.'

Sanctions include detentions and supervised study, and there is a system of verbal and written warnings based on employment law. Bullying is taken very seriously. A few students are excluded, mostly for consistently failing to turn up, some for drug offences. 'They don't care about superficial things, but on work, drink, drugs and bullying they clamp down very quickly.'

Pupils and Parents: Most students have come from private schools. Some have had enough of boarding; some have been ill; some have found their previous school too rigid or too stressful. Others come from peripatetic diplomatic families. Some lack confidence, and need to learn good working habits. Most thrive in the informal but structured atmosphere.

Entrance: Those going into the sixth form need a minimum of five grade Cs at GCSE; if they haven't passed maths or English they will need to retake these. Everyone is interviewed, and previous schools are asked for references. The college will not consider students who have been disruptive elsewhere.

Exit: A few GCSE students move on elsewhere – perhaps to state sixth form colleges – but most go through to the sixth form. Those aiming at Oxbridge are given an intensive course including lectures, seminars, mock interviews and individual tuition; around half a dozen a year generally get places. Extra help also for potential vets, doctors and dentists. Arts foundation courses are popular; other students move on to a huge range of courses varying from mechanical engineering at Edinburgh to sports and exercise science at Brighton.

Money Matters: Several scholarships available, usually of 20 – 50 per cent of fees, plus bursaries.

Remarks: Good at stimulating the very bright as well as re-motivating the disaffected. Informal atmosphere with strong staff/student relationships underlies a structured regimen where everyone is kept up to scratch.

DEAN CLOSE SCHOOL

Shelburne Road, Cheltenham, Gloucestershire, GL51 6HE

Tel: 01242 258 000
Fax: 01242 258 003
Email: office@deanclose.org.uk
Website: www.deanclose.org.uk

• Pupils: 468 boys and girls: 118 day boys, 92 day girls plus 137 boys and 121 girls boarding • Ages: 13-18 • Religion: C of E (Anglican Foundation) although all denominations welcome • Fees: Day £4,640; boarding £6,585 • School status: Independent • Opendays: September, November, March and May • School gender: Mixed • Day/boarding: Takes boarders

SEN provision

Detail:
Experience of:
Mild: ASP; DYSC; DYSL; DYSP; SpLD; VI; CP;
Moderate: DYSL; DYSP;

Summary: We provide the following support services: literacy support, numeracy support, curriculum support, study skills.

What we say about the school - the full Good Schools Guide review

Head: Since 1998, the Revd Tim Hastie-Smith MA CertTheol (fortyish), who was educated at Cranleigh, followed by Magdalene. He took orders at Wycliffe Hall, Oxford. One of our favourite heads, dashing (lilac shirt, purple-patterned tie, orange and turquoise socks when we visited), personable and fun; he is relishing the challenge and enjoying it hugely. Taught briefly at Felsted between Oxford and Cambridge: St Nicholas Scholar, with three years curacy at St Ebbe's before going to Stowe in 1991 where he was chaplain (and a very popular one too), admissions tutor and head of theology. Married to 'the beautiful Joanne', with three children, the elder two are in the school, plus a 'brilliant new baby'. Hastie-Smith (nicknames Tastie-Hastie, Tastie Bits haven't changed) arrived to find the school in less affluent circumstances than he had been led to believe, and spent the first couple of years performing financial miracles. With two new boarding houses under his belt, a new pre-prep and a £2.5 million refurbishment of one of the boys' boarding houses underway (autumn 2003), he is now set to go for it. New sports hall scheduled for 2004. Lots of new staff employed, certain amount of 'dead wood' replaced, plus some dynamic new appointments: almost every housemaster/mistress and many new heads of departments. All bar one of the senior posts have changed. This is a school in flux. 'Shaking the school out of its time warp', says the head. New director of studies, new management structure (previous head insisted on signing all the cheques himself), loads of delegation. 'Each department should be autonomous'.

Head has spent time introducing pupils to the real world: regular and interesting programme of external speakers – ranging from Jonathan Aitken via Lord Marshall (of BA) to John Julius Norwich and Jilly Cooper. Plus serious entertaining in his own (rather grand) home, when he has up to 70 (mostly local) guests for a visiting speaker and supper, which 'raises the school profile'. Tries to get away from the previous slightly introverted evangelical image and invites both staff and pupils to face important challenges. Enthusiastic on promoting confidence (as do they all) and 'develop as people, YOU matter, you have a unique roll to play; you are significant, you have the ability to do something'.

Keen to raise the academic standard (and has already done so) and is 'flirting with the idea of IB'. Though whether he finds time to read all the books in his study is open to question: this editor will be first in line when he does a rummage sale (and he says he has many more at home).

Academic Matters: 'On the cusp, academically', increasingly more selective, though the average ability of students can vary from year to year. Class size 20, five streams in each year; all pupils must do RE at GCSE, and take it a year early, most also take the three sciences and English early too. Super labs, combining practical areas with 'proper' lecture auditorium. Huge variety of GCSEs: French, German, Spanish. Latin, Russian and Chinese successes.

We originally said that 'pupils are equipped with laptops on arrival, and can connect into the infrared networking facility throughout (only occasional glitches) which should connect them both to printers and to the Internet'. This is apparently no longer true and, while they are essential for some lessons, only 90 per cent now have them, others lease them from the school. Head says 'IT is not an educational panacea, but it is a basic piece of kit which all must be competent and confident at using'. Pupils do super PowerPoint presentations. Excellent dyslexia provision, with a dedicated unit, including dyslexia-sensitive software, programme targeted for each child as necessary; as is EFL; pupils are assessed on arrival, and they are encouraged to take the relevant exams to enable them to enter British or American universities.

Games, Options, The Arts: Little change here: primarily a hockey school with national representation still at all levels, Decanians regularly feature at county and regional levels as well, and regularly reach National finals, their under 14 boys' team won in 2001 and, in 2002, the under 14 girls' team won. Rugby, cricket, tennis, sailing etc all on offer, 25-metre swimming pool not yet up to speed, and sports hall due for a revamp shortly (£1.5 million campaign). Water polo strong. Huge number of clubs, 120+ 'activities' on offer currently, everything from astronomy via clay pigeon shooting, to theatre maintenance and woodwork. The kit car building option means real cars, though perhaps not popular for driving lessons. Polo, yoga and Tai Bo are new entrants into the list. Plus octa hockey 'in which a small piece of wood around eight inches long is used to push a lead puck around on the bottom of the pool'; masks, fins and protective gloves are the only equipment required. Heptathlon as well as pentathlon. D of E as you might expect, CCF from the age of 13, though sixth formers have dropped it for community service: working with asylum seekers and wheelchair basketball popular, as well as teaching in a special needs school. Head is chairman of ISC Community Service Group.

Thriving Young Enterprise. And a host of spectacular trips all over. Currently seven scholars on various expeditions organised by the British Schools Exploration Society 'to undertake expeditions to harsh environments and to carry out adventure-related scientific fieldwork'.

Superlatives fail to describe the brilliant new music wing, attached by overhead bridge to professional theatre, much used by locals. Music vibrant, with a strong choral tradition and various orchestras. Music and drama very strong and timetabled with spectacular productions. Outdoor Tuckwell theatre in the grounds, CDT with CAD, and home economics for both sexes.

Background and Atmosphere: The school was founded in 1886 in memory of Dean Francis Close, Rector of Cheltenham for 30 years, before becoming Dean of Carlisle. 'Voluntary' Christian Union and Bible study still feature in each house; Christian ethics important. School worships together three times a week in the slightly austere chapel (porch with interesting stained glass). Head has replaced the compulsory weekly Sundays service for all (including day pupils) with evensong on Fridays, though all must still attend chapel on two fixed Sundays a term.

Set in 80 acres of manicured grounds, shared with prep school, who also share sports, some drama and music facilities. Original buildings much altered, with fantastic library like an upturned boat with beech galleries and refurbished parquet flooring. Spectacular lofty dining room, with 'God's Word a Guiding Light' inscribed below the rafters. Café-style feeding, vegetarian option. Modern cloisters with unusual sculptures contrast with older classrooms – many now revamped; and boarding houses, now almost all state of the art. Larger dorms have been divided into smaller cabins. Boarding encouraged and flexi-boarding on offer, strong family feel. Single rooms for (almost) all at the top of the school. Brilliant new girls' house.

New uniform 'on the stocks'; suits and trouser suits for older girls, and head was amazed to be approached by female staff on his arrival to be asked whether it was OK for them to wear trouser suits. Wow.

Pastoral Care and Discipline: House system, with houseparents and ancillary tutors. Dedicated houses for day children. Strong anti-bullying policy. Head expelled 'masses' his first year, but now discipline is 'firmly under control'. Out for OTT, but 'hardly anyone lately' – the odd one or two. Automatic expulsion for drugs and sex; warnings, followed by 'junkers' (hard labour/estate work) for booze, fines for fags.

Pupils and Parents: As we predicted, under the new regime, the profile has been gradually creeping up: the green wellie brigade is advancing. Fair number of expats, military parents on the up (20 per cent) – they tend to choose the school and then buy a house in the area. Around 15 per cent of locals board, lots of self-employed people 'the mercantile gang', quite a number of proper foreigners – who must attend chapel.

Entrance: To prep school by own entrance exam (English, maths, verbal reasoning). To senior school by Common Entrance, special arrangements for children from state primaries. More or less automatic from own prep school but school has now a vast number of feeder prep schools on its books and head is governor of an amazing six of them: Aldro, Orwell Park, St Anselm's et al. 30 pupils joined at sixth form level last year: VR plus six GCSEs four Bs, and two Cs, plus 'special exams' in potential A level subjects.

Exit: Almost 50 per cent took a gap year last year (a sign of changing profile – parents can afford it – right); fair number of re-applications, and 'applying this year', no particular bias, three baby doctors, five art foundationers. No particular bias either in university choice (re-applying and applying this year are undoubtedly the favourites in the leavers' list) and only one to Oxbridge (head says they usually apply after A level results). One or two train for holy orders, but business and economics are important.

Money Matters: School now back on a firm financial footing, squillions of scholarships: academic, art, music, sports, and bursarial help where needed – automatic for clergy children, and popular with the Services. Tough on non-payers, but lenient in family crisis or emergency.

Remarks: Non-stuffy new head is performing miracles, and kicking the school out of its time warp; less dauntingly evangelical than before, though Christian ethos still prevails, but, we suspect, the c is getting smaller. No challenge from Cheltenham College going co-ed.

Devonport High School for Boys

Paradise Road, Stoke, Plymouth, Devon, PL1 5QP

Tel: 01752 208 787

Fax: 01752 208 788

Email: headmaster@dhsb.org

Website: www.dhsb.org

• Pupils: 1,150 boys • Ages: 11-18 • Religion: Non-denom • School status: State • Opendays: Early July and mid September • School gender: Boys • Day/boarding: Day pupils

SEN provision

Detail:

Experience of:

Mild: ASP; ADD; DS;

Moderate: ASP;

Summary: The school now employs a number of support staff to work in and outside the classroom so that all the boys who pass the 11-plus test can expect to have their individual needs catered for. For example, the school has successfully supported pupils with physical, sight and hearing disabilites, Asperger's syndrome, ADHD and Tourette's syndrome.

What we say about the school - the full Good Schools Guide review

Headmaster: Since 1993, Dr Nic Pettit (early fifties). Graduated in biochemistry at University of Herts, PGCE at Bristol, PhD in microbiology, University of Kent. Research scientist for five years. Offered biology teaching post at Simon Langton Boys Grammar, Canterbury. Loved it so much changed career to teaching. Head of biology at Dane Court Grammar, Broadstairs; deputy head of Royal Latin School. Firm disciplinarian who believes research background enabled him to work fast and hard but also taught him when to stop. A country lad at heart who enjoys family life. Likes to share a joke. More familiar with boys who share his passions for academic excellence, the great outdoors and orienteering. Married to Pam, Bristol University classicist, now part-time school librarian. One son, David, educated at DHSB (now at Cambridge reading engineering) and younger daughter, Ruth, educated at Devonport High School for Girls (DHSG)(also now at Cambridge, reading classics)

Academic Matters: Excellent results. Average class size 29, reducing in number for practical subjects such as science and technology and for GCSE. Setting from year 9 provides small sets for pupils who need more help. Latin compulsory in years 7 and 8 and an option in year 9. Year 9 mini option system allows additional drama, music, Latin or physical education. In year 10 all boys study ten GCSEs, RE and PE. Four/five AS subjects in year 12 and three/four A levels in year 13 is common, sometimes five or six. 26 A level subjects at DHSB; consortium arrangement with four local schools (DHSG, Notre Dame, St Boniface and Eggbuckland) increases number to 30+ and gives boys opportunity to work alongside girls. 'The teachers are brilliant, they don't push but guide pupils to bring them up to speed,' comment parents. As the new engineering curriculum is developed, partnerships with Plymouth and Loughborough University enhance course provision.

Games, Options, The Arts: Regular county, regional and often national sporting achievements in rugby, football, athletics, basketball, cross-country running, cricket, fencing, judo and water polo. No swimming pool, so civic facilities are used. Hockey off campus. Picturesque Mount Edgcumbe Country Park and Dartmoor used for cross-country and orienteering. Art is on the up with newly appointed head of department working in newly refurbished art rooms. Music in new department base from autumn 2003. Lots of before and after school clubs – scrabble, poetry, French conversation, robot wars/robotics, rock climbing, running. Community drama productions and musicals co-presented with DHSG. D of E and Ten Tors popular. School boasts French centre in Brittany where up to 400 pupils, including year 7, enjoy week's break for £168, practising French, orienteering, canoeing and riding.

Background and Atmosphere: DHSB founded in 1896 by headteacher Alonzo Rider to give able boys opportunities that they otherwise might not have – still true today. Moved to present splendid Grade II* listed building in 1945 alongside Tamar Technical High School. DHSB took over whole site in 1991. The interior is now being extensively refurbished, the school benefiting from engineering sponsorship and LEA capital grants, although DHSB still prioritises spending on teachers. Smart and tidy, talented-looking students. The youngest seem inquisitive and polite, while the older 'young-gentlemen' seem quietly confident, a trait Dr Pettit approves of.

Pastoral Care and Discipline: Since Dr Pettit's arrival, pastoral care team has more than doubled to ten. 'Dr Pettit's very approachable, always there at the end of the telephone,' say parents. 'My child suffered mild name-calling because he wore glasses but as soon as I contacted the school the problem stopped with no lasting side effects.'

Behaviour on-site seems remarkably good, minus the odd scribble on toilet cubicles. It's perhaps less presentable outside school, eg food fights on the buses. Three caught with cannabis in eight years, resulting in fixed term exclusion and police involvement. Dr Pettit is a realist, 'I don't like mistakes but can tolerate one in some circumstances.' Rules state hair must be of 'natural colour and conventional style' although short-cropped dreadlocks have crept in; more lax sixth form style allows ponytails. No jewellery includes earrings.

Pupils and Parents: Mixed bag. Pupils from extremely impoverished backgrounds have achieved success at Oxbridge via DHSB. Pupils from 160 feeder schools desperately want to come here, dragging their non-committal parents along on open day. DHSB takes up to 12 per cent of Plymouth's boys.

Pupils travel from within 750 sq-mile catchment area, even from Truro, Exeter, Okehampton. Parents established contract with local bus company for eight double-deckers to bring children in from neighbouring Plymouth districts to city's three grammar schools. Many old boys in positions of influence, including Sir Austin Pearce, chairman of British Aerospace, many Navy admirals and professors, MP Ann Widdecombe's dad.

Entrance: Written English paper (comprehension and composition), two multiple choice papers on mathematics and verbal reasoning. PTFA organised practice exam held beforehand, then the real exam on two successive Saturdays. If 174 places over-subscribed (happens often) candidates are admitted in the order of their score, with siblings (of those at DHSB, DHSG and Plymouth High School for Girls) having priority in the event of a tie for 174th place (rare). Results are age-standardised. Transfer to DHSB is possible at 12, 13, 14 and 16.

Exit: 80 per cent proceed to sixth form, remainder begin GNVQs, modern apprenticeships, local employment. 90 per cent of sixth form to higher education. Popular university choices include Plymouth (increasingly), Durham, Cardiff, Bristol, Nottingham and Imperial London, not forgetting Oxbridge. Various careers – medicine, dentistry, sports management. Many engineers, mathematicians and scientists a testament to the school's generous sponsorship from the consortium led by the Engineers Employers Federation and BAE Systems.

Remarks: Provider of broad and demanding education. Well-driven and focused head.

THE DOMINIE

55 Warriner Gardens, Battersea, London, SW11 4DX

Tel: 020 7720 8783
Fax: 020 7720 8783
Email: lrdominie@aol.com
Website: www.thedominie.co.uk

• Pupils: 18 boys 12 girls, capacity 32. All day • Ages: 6-13
• Religion: Non-denom • Fees: £4,950 - physiotherapy extra
• School status: Independent • School gender: Mixed
• Day/boarding: Day pupils

SEN provision

Detail:
Now provide for in school:
Mild: ASP; ADD; DYSL; DYSP;
Moderate: DYSL; DYSP;
Severe: DYSL; DYSP;
Others: SPD; Sp&LD;

Summary: The Dominie provides specialist support for dyslexic and dyspraxic children of average or above average ability. This support is delivered in small classes and one-to-one lessons. The National Curriculum is followed and specific remediation programmes are woven throughout.

What we say about the school - the full Good Schools Guide review

Head: Since 1987, Mrs Lesley Robertson, a founder and co-owner of the school. Prior to that she spent three years working with mentally handicapped adolescents in Canberra and a year as a clinician in Pimlico. A diminutive Scot with an eye for success, enthusiasm for learning and talent for teaching, she leads by example spending much of the day in the classroom carefully teasing out the best from her eager brood.

The running of the school is shared equally with her partner, co-owner and school director Miss Anne O'Doherty, previously head of lower school at Thomas's Kensington. Miss O'Doherty's interest in helping dyslexic children grew steadily until in 1988 she gave up mainstream teaching to be a successful therapist (and eventual co-director) at the Dyslexia Teaching Centre, Kensington. She oversees much of the running of the school including entry, assessment, school transfer and special needs provision. Her friendly, reassuring face lights up when she speaks of her passion not only for children but for the parents too.

Entrance: An independent prep school for children with dyslexia or dyspraxia, who are of average, or above average ability. The school can also cater for children with other SEN such as Asperger's or speech and language difficulties but only if they are secondary to dyslexia or dyspraxia. Entry at any time if a place is available. Pupils undergo an intensive two-day assessment. Part of the assessment is class based and part one-to-one. Any formal evidence such as an educational psychologist's reports or LEA referral will be used in conjunction with the assessment. The majority of places at the school are privately funded but a few have LEA funding.

Exit: To a range of schools, mainstream and special. Much care taken in helping parents choose. Recent leavers to St Bede's, Marymount International, More House and The Moat.

Remarks: Bright, modern, purpose-designed premises close to Battersea Park. Compact, well-equipped. Informative and frequently changing displays; exciting artwork and examples of student achievements.

The National Curriculum is followed but carefully adapted and modified with additions ('specials') – a range of remedial lessons from problem-solving to brain gym. Speech and language therapy is an integral part of the curriculum with the therapist providing primary support and promoting involvement in music and drama.

Mornings focus on literacy and numeracy – afternoons on practical and sporting activities. Children are placed in age related forms but are taught according to need and ability. Group sizes vary with a maximum of eight per class, all aided by experienced learning support assistants. Varied teaching styles and strategies. Pupils say learning is enjoyable, successful and fun – 'I couldn't take away [ie subtract] until I came here,' said one child, 'but the teachers worked with me and showed me new ways. I can't believe it's so easy or that I learned so quickly. They really cheer you up.'

An amiable, articulate bunch, they recognise and champion the benefits of school, especially the way everyone cares for each other. The pastoral system isn't a structure, it's a continuum that involves everyone the whole of the time. Formal recognition of pupil achievements in the weekly assembly – merit badges and the lucky dip are firm favourites with pupils.

Home school links are good – an open door policy, and parents are expected to be involved with their child's learning. Homework is an important and integral part of school life and is set in abundance – staff recognise it can be a source of friction and angst so they're on hand to offer support.

The school doesn't have any outdoor facilities of its own but children visit nearby Battersea Park daily and use a local sports centre for swimming, football, PE and gym. All bring a packed lunch – school encourages but doesn't insist on healthy eating. Lunchtimes are social occasions – younger children have a story read or are entertained by staff. Improvements suggested by the children were a drinks area, somewhere to cook, a bigger library (the joy of reading has certainly been discovered here), own playground and use of the ICT facilities at break. They all love the place as it is, though.

Not the place for those demanding stacks of sports. A delightful, heartening oasis for average to bright children hindered by dyslexia or dyspraxia, who require an intimate, industrious and caring environment.

DONALDSON'S COLLEGE

West Coates, Edinburgh, EH12 5JJ

Tel: 0131 337 9911

Fax: 0131 337 1654

Email: admin@donaldsons-coll.edin.sch.uk

Website: www.donaldsons-coll.edin.sch.uk

• Pupils: 70 boys and girls – 15 full-time (as in four nights a week) boarders. 55 day, a floating number of whom are occasional boarders who stay for the socialising • Ages: School divided into Baby Blocks for tinies and siblings: 3 and under; Nursery: 3-5; Primary: 5-11; Secondary 11-19 • School status: Independent • School gender: Mixed • Day/boarding: Day pupils

SEN provision

Summary: No comment. SEN details added by us: we have only included the SENs that pupils must have to be here – a wide range of accompanying SENs are also catered for.

What we say about the school - the full Good Schools Guide review

Head: Since 2005, Mrs Janice MacNeill (fifties though looks ten years younger) who has been in special education since 'God knows when' and has come from setting up the inclusion sector of West Lothian College where she increased the numbers attending the life skills courses from 80 to 550. Before that she was head of Stanmore House School in Lanark. Educated in Irvine, she did her BEd at Craigie College, now part of Strathclyde University, and qualified in special needs at Moray House in 1979. Takes over from the redoubtable Janet Allan (who did so much to improve the academics in the college) and has the jolly prospect of masterminding the move to Linlithgow. Learning BSL – the school is a centre of excellence and BSL the acknowledged method of communication (estimates from signing staff say that it takes three or four years to get good and you know you've got there when you stop moving your lips). Early days yet in her administration, but there is no doubt that this is a challenge she relishes. Determined, charming, knowledgeable.

Academic Matters: School follows – as far as possible – a normal curriculum. That having been said, pupils here are either born profoundly deaf or have severe speech and language problems. Few are just deaf: as far as possible the 'just deaf' children are absorbed into mainstream. Many here have additional needs: social and emotional problems; certain amount of autism; high functioning Asperger's or ADHD. Many have statements of needs. Fair number of cochlear implants and a range of hearing devices, radios and mikes. Consultant educational audiologist on the staff, children are constantly monitored in an office full of high tech gadgets and child-friendly furniture. He spends much time in class: 'everything has to be a game' with little ones. Part of the audiologist's job is to teach the children to hear, and develop the hearing part of the brain by tweaking 'auditory development', and checking whether a temporary blip might not be caused by something as simple as glue ear.

102 staff on site, the largest class is six and the smallest two. BSL used whenever a deaf child is in the room ('so they don't feel left out') and it is decidedly eerie to be part of a group who are totally silent, but communicating like mad (except for one young man determined to emulate Evelyn Glennie – who is not

regarded as proper deaf by the deaf community – only with a hammer on a work bench). Computers for all from nursery up, and in every classroom. Primary pupils are classroom based, graduating to subject rooms as they reach secondary level; this transition often causes problems, particularly with the autistic child. Lots of case discussions, regular reviews 'may have to change targets, change the IEP'. If realistically feasible Donaldson's pupils sit external exams, though they may not take them at the pre-ordained chronological age – three pupils got standard grades whilst in S3 (earlier than the normal). Few failures, which is a testimony to the sympathetic staff; art and design kicked up a B at higher and an A at intermediate 2. Biology, hospitality (very popular as a subject) and science completed the achievements. School is looking at 'how best we can deliver modern languages to the deaf' and are 'reinterpreting' the 5 to 14 curriculum into sign language (the second most popular language in the UK).

Games, Options, The Arts: Too few to form teams, but football perennially popular but was briefly banned during our visit (spot of window damage), fantastic swimming pool and dedicated gym with own staff. Outrageously good art dept with some splendid pieces: the coursework featuring lizard-patterned trainers was particularly fetching and one of last year's leavers was visiting (she is doing a pre-foundation year at Heriot-Watt) to help one of the younger pupils who has cerebral palsy. Trips wherever possible 'but they may take more planning'; D of E, outward bound courses; 'need high staffing' – the priority is to keep the children safe and happy. Music important, and a specialist, and well used hall and theatre. Children are encouraged through role play, specialist drama coach. Vast number of bikes, electric scooters and skate boards. Youngsters are encouraged to be as normal as possible and take part in as many different activities as they can.

Background and Atmosphere: Designed by WH Playfair in 1841 with a £210,000 legacy from Edinburgh publisher Sir James Donaldson who died in 1830 'to build and endow an orphan hospital', which subsequently became Donaldson's school for the deaf. The original hospital, which was designed for 300 children, took ages to build, described as a 'Jacobean Palace' and built on a quadrangle of 79 x 63 metres, is quite magnificent but could hardly be less suitable for the deaf. Good news, then, that the Playfair palace is to be divided into seventy executive apartments, plus seventy more in the grounds, and the school is moving in 2007 to a purpose-built and audiologically friendly new-build on an eight acre brownfield site in Preston Road, Linlithgow, some fifteen miles west of Edinburgh. Building will be painted in primary colours and designed as far as possible to be acoustically friendly which 'will give children the skills to listen'. Antiques, including a pair of chairs used by Queen Victoria when she visited the incomplete palace in 1850, were recently sold to fund the school's website development: bums on seats has ever been the key to a school's finances.

Pastoral Care and Discipline: Wherever possible siblings of deaf children are included in activities, particularly in the younger age groups. The care staff are second to none; masses of them. Individual bedrooms: some of the children can be 'rowdy' at bed time, and 'it is easier if they don't share'. The older boys' house is a sort of half way house, gearing them for independent living. Pupils can and do shop for themselves and cook tea here once a week, they also cook lunch in home economics (and do their own washing). Learning to budget and live a normal day-to-day life is part of education here. Day pupils usually spend a couple of days a week staying over, it's more fun to do things with friends and home life can be lonely for the deaf. Problem-solving and life skills all important. Good collection of table football, billiards, pretty much anything you would expect to find in any boarding school. Care staff help with PSHE; deafness is no bar to normal teenage angst or wickedness; no 'touch wood' drug or alcohol difficulties. Appropriate behaviour is a constant theme.

Pupils and Parents: Children from all over Scotland, plus from the North of England since the closure of the Newcastle unit. Parents often have to battle with their LEAs to come here, and Donaldson's is enormously supportive of them; a fair number of children who come here have deaf parents.

Entrance: Via LEAs.

Exit: As far as possible pupils will be able to take on some form of training, but often English is required at standard grade and for many this is an insurmountable barrier.

Remarks: A national treasure: fantastic for those who need it.

DOUGLAS ACADEMY

Mains Estate, Milngavie, G62 7HL

Tel: 01419 562 281

Fax: 01419 561 533

Email: office@douglas.e-dunbarton.sch.uk

• Pupils: 1,060 boys and girls • Ages: 11-18

• Religion: Non-denom • School status: State

• School gender: Mixed • Day/boarding: Day pupils

SEN provision

Detail:

Centre of excellence for:

Mild: ASP; ADD; ADHD; EBD; DYSC; DYSL; DYSP; SpLD; VI;

Moderate: ASP; ADD; ADHD; EBD; MLD; DYSC; DYSL; DYSP; SpLD; HI; VI;

Severe: ASP; ADD; ADHD; EBD; DYSC; DYSL; DYSP; SpLD;

Others: SPD; CD; OCD; ODD; TIC; SLD; EAL; PD; Oth;

Now provide for in school:

Mild: AUT;

Moderate: AUT;

Severe: AUT;

Others: AUT(other); PMLD; Sp&LD; Eat;

Experience of:

Mild: DS; CP;

Moderate: CP;

Severe: HI; VI; CP;

Others: FRX; GEN; MSI; DEL; Epi;

Summary: Douglas Academy staff as a whole, and support for learning staff in particular, aim to provide an appropriate teaching and learning experience to enable each student to fulfil their potential. Support is offered in terms of suitable pupil tuition, co-operative teaching, resource allocation, consultancy, liaison and staff development. Support is offered for all pupils including needs of both the moreable child as well as pupils with general or specific learning difficulties. Support for Learning provide appropriate staff development on a range of initiatives featuring social communication, developmental co-ordination disorders and English as an Additional Language during the 2005/06 session to raise awareness of best practice.

What we say about the school - the full Good Schools Guide review

Head: Since 1989, Mr Gordon Wilson BSc PGCE (fifties) who came to the school as depute in 1983, rising to acting head, and, with the coming of the School Board, had to announce his own appointment as head. He formally took over in December 1989. Educated at the then Bellahouston Grammar School, he read chemistry at Glasgow University and did his PGCE at Jordanhill. Married, with three grown-up children, two of whom came to the school on 'placing request', he lives 'three and a half minutes' away. He 'misses classroom teaching, but enjoys running the school and manages to fit in hockey on Saturdays', relaxed and proud of his pupils' achievements; no problems in getting staff. Keen that pupils do not necessarily make career decisions at 11 or 12, but take a spectrum of subjects across the board. Care and welfare are equally important as exam results.

Academic Matters: School is on the up academically, with last year's results brill. Three sciences on offer, many take two, outstanding results in the Chemistry Olympiad, ditto Biology Olympiad; junior success in Junior Maths Challenge, and Junior Maths Olympiad. Successes in Physics Challenge and Physics Olympiads. Get the message? French and Italian (replaced German, 'nothing to do with the music school'); Spanish option at sixth form, had more pupils with five Highers than any other state school in Scotland a couple of years ago. 'Fair amount of autonomy' in employing staff', 'but if there are teachers free within the authority, then we have to take them'; otherwise school advertises and can make their own appointments. Regular success across the board at Standard Grades, music specialists take both Standard and Higher music without fuss and, 'effortless'. Specialists take 'specially tailored courses', but see below. Most pupils get a clutch of eight subjects at Standard Grade, some may leave after Highers, and some stay on for the Advanced Higher – school responds to 'the needs of the pupil' and there is a certain amount of mix and match with Intermediate grades.

Staff visit local primaries and meet new pupils the term before they hit big school. Children are setted for maths in October of their first term, and in the second year for everything else. Programme in place for teachers to be trained in how to make use of ICT in the classroom, which software to use and how to make

PowerPoint presentations. Exceptional computing department, school got best results in Advanced Highers in Scotland, and won the STAR trophy (well 'equal top marks'). Computers all over the shop – a certain amount of room revamping to form study areas. School also acquired a couple of dedicated computers via the Tesco voucher scheme – parents had to buy £270,000 worth of shopping to fund them! Two rooms for CDT, plus computer studies, business studies, as well as a computer suite in the library – well stocked, which also contains the careers department. Excellent support for learning, with a strong team which offers both guidance and support in class. When we visit a school we always ask for detailed exam results over the last three years, regretably not available here – an unacceptable attitude to parents, we feel. School responds,'exam results outstanding. Published annually in School Handbook, updated in December'. Douglas Academy, apparently uniquely in Scotland, was hit by a national, targeted strike by Unison, 'owing to the high profile of the school' and the teaching staff ran the school with no janitorial, office or technician staff for over three months. Now that's dedication.

Games, Options, The Arts: The school does outstandingly well – head says 'embarrassingly well' – at rugby, hockey and athletics. 'Strong competitive edge'. This is not a school for layabouts, this is a doing school. 'Lots of land', internal cross-country course, pool – much used by the community, who also do evening and keep-fit classes here. Mass of charity involvement. Spectacular art, and marvellous art complex at the top of the building, with three dimensional as well as pottery etc. Home economics classrooms reduced from an astonishing five to two, but well used. Regular charity fashion shows. Mass of extra-curricular activities ranging from fitness training to paired reading and debating. French exchanges.

School became a Centre of Excellence for Music in 1979 and boasts a first orchestra of 'almost professional standard' plus 'an outstanding chamber orchestra, senior wind band, second orchestra – very full (60+) which often has first year pupils playing, as well as non-music specialists. 'On a par with St Mary's Music School in Edinburgh. Adjectives tend to fail when dealing with Centres of Excellence but take it as read that any superlative would be inadequate. Pupils follow the normal curriculum, but 20 per cent of their time is spent on music. Music specialists come from all over Scotland, Ullapool to Newton Stewart, and their chosen instrument can be in any discipline from fiddle to piano. (There are no quotas for entry, 'around about eight or ten annually', and 'might all play the flute'.) Places at the school are free and open to all (help given with transport), with pupils from further away boarding at Dalrymple House, opposite the Botanic Gardens in Glasgow's west end (they share with pupils from the centre of Excellence for Dance at nearby Knightswood). Two homework tutors. Music lessons carry a nominal charge for non-music specialists (22 per cent), and local concerts are always a sell-out, particularly the annual Christmas concert at St Paul's in Milngavie. Not as many boy choristers but very good girls' choir and serious senior choir, the junior one is merely 'good' but, by any other school's standards, it would be outstanding. Most of the music staff have top jobs in Scotland's orchestras and choirs.

Background and Atmosphere: Fairly boring square sixties building round a grass quadrangle with a mass of interesting add-ons. Magical views of the Campsies to the North. Millennium project involved re-landscaping the campus and revamping most of the fixtures and furnishings. Health and Safety complain that there is too much glass, but it is clean, light and airy. School dress equals white shirt/blouse, school ties, trousers or skirts and NO trainers. School monitors occasionally do a dress-code blitz. Music specialists wear blazers, as do the debating team, who won the 2002 European Parliament UK final in York and travelled to Turin to represent the UK.

Pastoral Care and Discipline: Team of ministers from local churches welcome involvement with the school. 'Drugs not an issue' in the school and good (state) guidance system in place, plus link tutors who have informal relationships with the pupils offering both emotional and social support. Recent HMI Inspection was enthusiastic about the fact that 'almost all enjoyed coming to school and were treated as family'. Clearly defined rules about bullying and loads of staff back-up. 'Good extended team'.

Pupils and Parents: No 'significant number' from ethnic minorities and no problems with religious festivals – 'praying (as in five times a day) never an issue'. Parents 'feel welcome', and good fund-raising and pastoral parents association in place. Homework diary and home study invitations plus the Home Study Pack 'really bumps up exam performance' and gives parents detailed info as to what is going on at school; and the results have improved spectacularly over the last six years.

Entrance: Four associated primary schools; one of which is tiny and rural. Pupils from (the Catholic) St Joseph's may come here, and almost all do, or they may prefer to be bused the 30 minutes or so there and back to the local secondary Catholic school in Kirkintilloch. Excellent child-orientated joining handbook.

Exit: Some leave after Standard Grades, ditto after Highers, most stay on for Advanced Highers. Good percentage to uni, 75 per cent of leavers go to higher education with five or six Highers, local unis popular with a regular trickle to Oxbridge. Some to art school, most music specialists to some form of further music.

Money Matters: Funds available for trips, those on 'free meals' not expected to pay, though the take-up here is less than anticipated and with swipe cards, this is not an issue.

Remarks: Stunning state school for musicians but worth moving house for if you are not in the catchment area. Exam results impressive and getting even more so.

DOVER COLLEGE

Effingham Crescent, Dover, Kent, CT17 9RH

Tel: 01304 205 969
Fax: 01304 242 208
Email: registrar@dovercollege.demon.co.uk
Website: www.dover-college.kent.sch.uk

• Pupils: 356 50:50 boys/girls; 2/3 day pupils to 1/3 boarders – ratio reversed in the sixth form • Ages: 11-18 • Fees: day £2,565-£3,175; weekly boarding £4,420-£4,960; full boarding £4,750-£6,355 • School status: Independent • School gender: Mixed • Day/boarding: Takes boarders

SEN provision

Detail:
Centre of excellence for:
Mild: DYSL; DYSP;
Moderate: DYSL; DYSP;
Now provide for in school:
Mild: HI;
Moderate: HI;
Severe: HI;

Summary: No comment. Shhhh – it's a secret? One worth sharing, in our view. SEN details added by us.

What we say about the school - the full Good Schools Guide review

Headmaster: Since 2004, Mr Stephen Jones MSc MLitt (mid forties), previously social tutor (housemaster) at Radley for eight years, where he taught maths and coached rugby, sailing and fives. Before that he taught at Berkhamsted, Cheltenham and The Dragon. Educated at Hurstpierpoint, Lord Wandsworth College and Durham University where he acquired an MSc in maths and MLitt in philosophy. Married to Katie, a priest, who occasionally conducts services in the school. Three children, one of whom is in the sixth form here. Very enthusiastic about the school, warm and approachable, knows all the children. At first meeting it seems rather surprising that someone of this pedigree and quality should have ended up somewhere so unsmart as Dover, but he appears totally happy here, and committed to the place and its ethos.

Academic Matters: A refuge from the Kent grammar school system and smart, selective independents, with a strong international flavour. 45 per cent A/B at A level – pretty respectable, given the intake, and pupils speak warmly of good teaching, small classes and lots of support. Few get three A grades: but then almost nobody fails, either. Travel and tourism, PE, business studies and drama, ICT, DT, music offered at A level as well as core subjects. Foreign students start off in the International Study Centre and gradually move into more mainstream lessons. Do IGCSE in English, PET English test and International Language Testing System (IELTS) needed for University. Staff draw up individual study plans for English as a second language leading to university accredited qualifications. About 60 children have some form of EAL requirement. Dyslexics, dyspraxics well supported here (CReSTeD category WS), but probably would not suit a child with very severe problems as no LSA or teaching assistants. Some children with hearing impairments, one statemented. Children withdrawn from lessons (but not from maths, science or English) – rotate through the other subjects and then given time to catch up on what has been missed – some extra help available. Would not, for example, take a very artistic child out of art lessons. Computers networked, with special software packages to support literacy and numeracy. Two well-qualified SEN teachers; specialist maths support too. Year 7s screened for reading and spelling; NFER and CAT testing for all. Some problems still emerge later but close eye is kept on all children by subject teachers and through the house system. Difficult to slip through the net here, even if not picked up by previous schools. Exercise programmes and INPP (Institute for Neuro Physiological Psychology) developmental course – a respectable outfit despite the weird sounding name, and we know children who have benefited considerably from their programmes. Saturday school every other Saturday with lessons until lunchtime and sport and activities until 4pm – works well as non-lesson Saturdays used for whole school events – play and music rehearsals and sponsored walks etc so as not to waste lesson time.

Games, Options, The Arts: Not a notably sporty school: it's just too small to make competitive teams, but sport is much enjoyed, and taken seriously, and there are some examples of excellence in individual sports. Boys play football, hockey and cricket/tennis. Girls play hockey, netball and rounders/tennis. Major sport is compulsory up to fifth form. Sixth form have to do some sort of exercise but doesn't have to be team games – fitness classes a popular option particularly for the girls. Can do art instead of team sport. Sailing with Dover Sailing Club. Some notable sportsmen, including: Oleksiy Udovenko, Kent Cross Country League Champion, and Ashley Burton, Captain of England Independent Schools Soccer XI.

Music, drama and art are what the pupils like to put their surplus energies into. Burgeoning music, strong choral tradition. Art good but headmaster keen to develop it further – would like to make an art gallery to exhibit pupils' work and that of local artists. As head says, drama is good but could be better – recent investment in new technical equipment, lights etc. Lots of plays throughout the year – major school and individual house productions. 11 to 13-year-olds do outdoor play in King Stephen's Garden in the summer – wonderful walled garden where King Stephen is apparently buried.

Background and Atmosphere: Founded in 1871 by a group of local businessmen to educate local children and is housed in the grounds of St Martin's Priory, an oasis of green in the middle of Dover with wonderful views of the castle and nestling behind the famous white cliffs. Went co-ed in 1974 – one of the first boys' schools to do this – now 50:50. Although much of the original priory has been destroyed there is still a feeling of history here and the overall impression is uplifting despite the hotchpotch of buildings added as the school has grown over the years, from late Victorian houses through the 1930s and 1950s and uninspiring modern.

Although not part of the Round Square group of schools (Gordonstoun et al) it follows many of Kurt Hahn's principles of service to the community; the new headmaster is keen to strengthen the service element. Children are expected to be involved in some form of service which could be through Duke of Edinburgh scheme or helping with sport and music in local primary schools. Leadership training trips to the Italian Alps and Wales. There is a school council, and the children are encouraged to be concerned with environmental issues. Despite the strong military traditions of the school there is no CCF – a previous headmaster abolished it and knocked down the armoury!

Pastoral Care and Discipline: A broadly Christian school. The headmaster does not believe in multiculturalism but in the celebration of all cultures. Everyone required to attend chapel three times a week, very much a spiritual whole-school event. A comfortable, caring place, high on TLC; headmaster says they try to be proactive through the house systems and low self-esteem and lack of confidence picked up pretty quickly. The children we met seemed thoroughly happy and at ease with themselves.

Usually about 100 children in at weekends and pupils tend to want to 'chill' but shopping trips to Canterbury etc organised, and perhaps a celebration of different cultures eg each member of house might cook their national dish. All children, both day and boarding, belong to a house – Priory and five others – three boys' houses two girls'. Younger children (11-13) start off in the Priory House (mainly day with about 10 boarders) 'wonderful pastoral care and lots of feedback' according to one parent. 'Housemaster really seems to know the children and what they are up to.' Ethos of tolerance throughout the school; people look after each other.

Pupils and Parents: 30 per cent from abroad – over 30 nationalities in the school – lots from mainland Europe – Germany, Russia, Belarus, Ukraine, some from Nigeria. Everyone gets on well with each other, and with the English: all the hoped-for benefits of international diversity are here. The mainland Chinese find integration a little more difficult than everyone else (as always). A number of Forces children: headmaster wants to encourage Forces families from all ranks to send their children here. Some refugees from the state system cannot believe their luck in having an average of 15 per class for GCSE and an average of 5 in the sixth form. Popular with those who have not made it in the Kent Test for entrance to the grammar schools.

Children are well dressed, thoroughly natural, altogether comfortable. Lots of mixing between ages and interests: a delightfully hierarchy-free school. Old Boys include: Sir Frederick Ashton of Royal Ballet fame, film producer Guy East, Simon Cowell of 'Pop Idol' and 'The X Factor' fame and Nick Cowell of 'Big Brother' and 'The Block'.

Entrance: Almost non-selective. Most come in at 11+, 13+ and sixth form but pupils can be admitted at any time if there are spaces. 11+ by entrance exam and interview, 13+ by Common Entrance and at any other time by interview and a report from previous school.

Exit: Some movement after GCSEs – some to local Sixth form colleges (fees) more come. Most on to further education – some to major universities eg Leeds, Edinburgh, London, plus others to newer universities and to performing arts, film and media and fashion courses.

Money Matters: Fees widely regarded as good value, and then there are a number of useful academic, music arts and sports scholarships, means tested to ensure that the most deserving families get the biggest discounts.

Remarks: One of those crucial and hard to find schools which sets out to do well for the ordinary child, and succeeds. A happy, relaxed place. Jeffrey Archer taught here as a young man and apparently proved to be an excellent teacher.

DRIFFIELD SCHOOL

Manorfield Road, East Riding of Yorkshire, Driffield, YO25 5HR

Tel: 01377 253 631

Fax: 01377 256 922

Email: office@driffieldschool.eril.net

Website: www.driffieldschool.net

• Pupils: Almost 2,000 boys and girls • Ages: 11-18

• Religion: Non-denom • School status: State

• School gender: Mixed • Day/boarding: Day pupils

SEN provision

Detail:

Now provide for in school:

Mild: ASP; AUT; ADD; ADHD; EBD; DYSC; DYSL; DYSP; HI; VI; CP;

Moderate: ASP; AUT; ADD; ADHD; EBD; MLD; DYSC; DYSL; DYSP; HI; VI; CP;

Severe: DYSL; DYSP; HI; VI; CP;

Others: EAL; Sp&LD; Epi; PD; Eat;

Summary: Driffield School has always been held in very high regard for our inclusive approach to education. There are many examples of excellent practice of student support across the whole curriculum. However, we are not complacent. We continue to evaluate our practice in line with government strategy to respond to the changing needs of young people. The launch of the new Student Services Team this September has allowed a 'joined up' multi-agency approach to issues that occur in the classroom. We strive to remove all barriers to learning by identifying children's needs early and providing effective support and intervention. Student Services consists of a team of highly qualified, motivated and enthusiastic teachers and teaching assistants with a diverse range of experience. Support is provided for all student needs, ranging from learning, social, communication, emotional, behavioural and physical difficulties, as well as English as an Additional Language.

What we say about the school - the full Good Schools Guide review

Head: Since 2004, Mr Martin Green BEd MA (late forties). BEd from University of Leeds, MA Educational Leadership, University of Hull. Started career as chemistry teacher in Hull area, later deputy head of Winifred Holtby School, Hull, and head of Withernsea High School and Technology College. Married to a teacher wife with two daughters at university.

Academic Matters: Exam results on oxygen-sapping uphill gradient as children benefiting from changes in recent years reach exam age. In 2003, 55 per cent of pupils achieved at least five GCSEs at A*-C; 67 per cent in 2005. A level results currently among the best in the East Riding. How do they do it? By tracking every single child in every subject all the time. Teachers log progress of pupils every four weeks on an electronic registration system. Computer flags up any student who fails to make hoped-for progress and hapless pupil is brought up to speed in whatever way the school decrees, be it extra homework or late study. Child is attached to a mentor – a teacher designated to get them instantly back on track. Parents love it, school loves it, even students accept it's for their greater good. Apparently. And it's not all bad news for pupils. The mentor can negotiate deadline extensions, etc for a student genuinely snowed under.

Debbie Dalton fronts the SEN dept, now called Student Services (ie inclusive); can cope with (almost) any learning difficulty from moderate to severe – the entire dys-strata, ADHD, plus severely (rather than profoundly) deaf – the school operates a soundfield system. 200 children on the register with IEPs for all including 49 with statements. One to one, one to two, small groups, anything from one hour to two/three hours a week, alpha smart (computers) – in and out of school, and all networked. 18 teaching assistants, all highly trained, most remedial help is provided in class, but occasional one-to-one, max one and a half hours a week, but 'can buy in more'. Very accommodating, 'can adapt to different needs'; special co-ordinator for their able, gifted and talented programme too.

Games, Options, The Arts: International recognition for performing arts. Winners many times of international Rock Challenge competition for dance, drama and music. Represented UK in Australia in 2003. Strong on sport, particularly cricket, rugby, hockey. Thriving Duke of Edinburgh scheme. Range of activities outside lessons excellent. Extra-curricular activities given priority because of rural catchment area where, for many children, school is core element of their social life.

Background and Atmosphere: A whopper of a school, among the biggest in the country, set in a vast 40-acre site and with considerably more people than most of the students' home villages in the Yorkshire Wolds. Feels less like a school, more like a campus, not least in sixth form which boasts own Internet café. School only 40 years old but has just spent millions on new design and technology and ICT blocks with specialist performing arts building imminent. Shares use of council swimming pool and sports centre.

Biggest asset? Its own residential studies centre in the North York Moors National Park for everything from geography field trips to intensive study seminars. Pupils encouraged to use school with its 600-plus Internet-linked computers out of hours. Doors open at 7am and library is open until at least 7pm, sometimes later. Children can go home for a meal, then catch special late bus back to school for more study or activities before school bus takes them home again.

Pastoral Care and Discipline: Potential for swamping enormous as intake largely from relatively small rural primaries. Problems prevented by putting students into six houses and having registration forms comprising six students from each year group. New pupils instantly taken under wing of old hands. One of many ways school encourages responsibility. Sixteen-year-old student governor says views of pupils are taken seriously. 'They really listen to us.'

Discipline tight. School prides itself on standing absolutely no nonsense. Will not tolerate pupils disturbing lessons and disrupting education of the majority.

Pupils and Parents: Parents from wide range of backgrounds but many have caught school's ambitious bug and work hard to support it. Pupils' progress reports to parents three times a year and full report annually. Newsletters to many parents sent out via e-mail so no chance to 'lose' that letter about extra homework. Parents' briefing evenings about, for instance, study leave.

Entrance: Seriously over-full and only takes pupils from 130 square mile catchment area.

Exit: Most stay on to sixth form and then to universities including Oxbridge.

Remarks: A beacon state school combining innovation and risk-taking to fire up the ambitions of a whole community. Outstanding.

DURHAM HIGH SCHOOL FOR GIRLS

Farewell Hall, Durham, County Durham, DH1 3TB

Tel: 0191 384 3226
Fax: 0191 386 7381
Email: headmistress@dhsfg.org.uk
Website: www.dhsfg.org.uk

• Pupils: 600 girls, all day • Ages: 3-18 • Religion: C of E, accepts all faiths and none • Fees: seniors £2,550; infants/juniors £1,770-£1,900 • School status: Independent • School gender: Girls • Day/boarding: Day pupils

SEN provision

Detail:
Now provide for in school:
- Mild: DYSC; DYSL; HI;
- Moderate: DYSC; DYSL;
- Severe: DYSL;
- Others: EAL;

Experience of:
- Mild: ASP; EBD; DYSP; SpLD;
- Others: Eat;

Summary: We have in-school screening for specific learning difficulties. We have a designated learning support room with appropriate resources. We have an educational psychologist who works with the school, assessing and following up individual needs. SpLD students are given a weekly lesson with a qualified SpLD teacher and support within the curriculum, if parents request it. For those with literacy and numeracy difficulties, we give help on an individual or small group basis. Other support for hearing difficulties is given usually through the LEA sensory support services working with the school.

What we say about the school - the full Good Schools Guide review

Head: Since 1998, Mrs A Templeman MA DipT (fifties), previously deputy at Haberdashers' Aske's, Elstree. Married with three children; calm, reflective, gentle style; teaches classics. Educated at Watford Grammar School for Girls and at St Hugh's Oxford (Lit Hum). Reader in the Church of England. Wants girls who are 'excited about life and learning', encourages hard work and dedication alongside a social conscience.

Academic Matters: 98 per cent five or more good GCSEs, 94 per cent grades A to C at A level. Stronger than average take-up in maths and science; geography and religious studies also strong. French, German and Latin taught from 11, though not the widest range of languages for keen linguists; a safe but not expansive range of A level options includes politics and sociology. Average class sizes, a number of age groups surprisingly not yet at capacity. Some girls with mild to moderate dyslexia, the occasional one with other special needs; teaching assistance offered at extra charge.

Games, Options, The Arts: Sports not overly obvious around the place (in contrast to Durham School), though a good range of the usual options – hockey, netball and tennis being favourites; represented at county level in hockey, national level in tennis and skiing. World Challenge expeditions to Rajasthan and Madagascar; Duke of Edinburgh awards also popular; community service and charity work encouraged. Music workshops, outdoor activity trips and overseas visits invite the wider world in and encourage the girls out; music, art and drama popular with larger productions held in Durham's Gala Theatre, the girls not afraid to tackle the occasional all-male play with an all-female cast.

Background and Atmosphere: Founded in 1894 by the Church of England, now accepts all faiths and none. Relatively new site with mostly modern buildings and programme of refurb throughout. Attractive open location in good residential area, convenient for city centre. Juniors in attractive new buildings, including delightful Rainbow nursery ('the promise of a good beginning'); all very proud of new senior library and dedicated librarian forging links with a school in New York to share ideas and opinions across the Atlantic. Upgraded ICT and science labs. A translation of the school motto causes some consternation – 'The fear of the Lord is the beginning of wisdom' which, for avoidance of misunderstanding, rarely surfaces these days. Yet there are reminders everywhere that this is a church school, the affirmation of faith and 'spiritual growth' is mentioned throughout. The recent appointment of a lay chaplain proved a great success, inspiring girls with her desire to learn salsa dancing as well as her teaching. Staff are 'wonderful and slightly wacky'; average age 44; a number of 'characters' generating real fondness between staff and pupils.

Pastoral Care and Discipline: House system (though the girls had some difficulty remembering what they were). Form tutor for each class. Staff and girls vote for head girls and deputy. Buddy system; nurturing approach to discipline.

Pupils and Parents: Very diverse social spread, significant number from educational action zones in East Durham, others from business and professional families. 10 pupils on free places; 20 per cent of senior house on bursaries. Intake chiefly from County Durham and Sunderland; fairly narrow cultural spread, reflective of the local community. Supportive Old Girls' association. Girls are bright, vivacious and enthusiastic with that refreshing naivety that they can take on the world – and win. Free (but not too free) thinking, challenging but not groundbreaking, girls are glad to be here and feel 'safe'. No uniform for sixth form and unusually relaxed dress code, rare to see girls in denim in this type of school, girls admit they relax and 'stop thinking about what to wear for school after the first couple of weeks or so', apparently an advantage of a 'boy-free zone'.

Entrance: Assessed 'by observation' for nursery and reception, appropriate testing in subsequent years for junior house. English and maths tests at 11 based on Key Stage 2 SATs with references from junior heads and interview, style of testing reflects intake from local feeder state primary schools. For entry at 16 five GCSE passes A* to C, references and interview with head. Generous number of scholarships and bursaries 'to attract bright, enthusiastic and gifted pupils who can make a real impact on the life of the school'.

Exit: Some leave post-GCSE for the boys of Durham School or local state schools, most stay for sixth form then go on to trad, predominantly northern, universities, plus a good number of Oxbridge candidates. Notable old girls include Wendy Craig (actress), Joanna Burton (opera), Wendy Gibson (BBC journalist), Sarah Blair (sister of PM).

Remarks: A refreshing change, a school that doesn't oversell itself. A combination of all that is new in education with core traditional values.

EASINGWOLD SCHOOL

York Road, Easingwold, York, North Yorkshire, YO61 3EF

Tel: 01347 821 451

Fax: 01347 823 301

Email: admin@easingwold.n-yorks.sch.uk

Website: www.easingwoldschool.com

• Pupils: 1365 boys and girls, all day • Ages: 11-18

• School status: State • School gender: Mixed

• Day/boarding: Day pupils

SEN provision

Detail:

Now provide for in school:

Mild: ASP; AUT; ADD; ADHD; EBD; DYSC; DYSL; DYSP; VI;

Moderate: ASP; AUT; ADD; EBD; MLD; DYSL; VI;

Severe: ASP;

Others: SPD; OCD; EAL; Sp&LD; DEL; Epi; Eat;

Experience of:

Mild: CP;

Moderate: ADHD; DYSC; DYSP;

Severe: DYSL; HI;

Others: AUT(other); PD;

Summary: The school aims to provide entitlement for all pupils to a broad and balanced curriculum appropriate to the needs of the individual child, so that they can make maximum progress and achieve their full potential. The school believes it is important to work in partnership with parents, pupils and all outside agencies to promote the development of all pupils, especially those with special educational needs. The SEN team take particular care to demonstrate there is a caring and supportive community that builds on the interests and strengths of individuals, within an atmosphere that is challenging and also enjoyable. Responsibility for one's actions and a duty to help others make progress are key factors in the success of our provision.

What we say about the school - the full Good Schools Guide review

Head: Since 2001, Mrs Carey Chidwick, BA Hons Diplomée (fifty). Friendly and outgoing. Popular with pupils and staff. Qualified King's College, London.

Previously head at Berwick-upon-Tweed Community High School. Began as a modern languages teacher in Kent. Became head of department and joined Kent education department's teacher training team. Then went to Northumberland as adviser/inspector for modern languages. Qualified as an Ofsted inspector in 1992 and continued to participate in inspections after returning to mainstream schools. Knows most of the children's names and chats to them in the corridors.

Academic Matters: 70-ish per cent five A* to C grades at GCSE. As proud of the less-academic student who achieves D at A level or E at GCSE as those who record straight As. Expectation is high, but not too driven by league tables. This philosophy embraces children with special needs, championed by an achievement manager whose job title says it all. School caters for children with a range of special needs such as Asperger's, autism, hyperactivity, ADD, learning difficulties, and speech, vision and hearing difficulties. Not bound by the SEN register: help is targeted at children who need it, regardless of whether they are on register or not. Aim is to get children off the register, not perpetuate their place. Parent of a special needs student told us: 'The school values every pupil individually and the staff are amazing. We have been absolutely thrilled, and for our son it has been marvellous, he has come on in leaps and bounds.' School works with primary schools to get a picture of the pupils before they come to Easingwold, and an idea of any special needs they may have. Does not prejudge, but those needing extra help will get an individual plan, including specific targets, regularly reviewed. Recently introduced, at year 10, a computerised tracking system monitors individual children's progress and alerts school where they are in danger of under-achieving. A model of inclusive education with reams of enthusiastic parents.

Traditional subjects studied at GCSE, with all pupils taking core subjects – English, maths, science etc – and selecting two options from art, business studies, child development, music etc. In sixth form students take intermediate (GNVQ) courses or AS/A levels. A variety of vocational studies on offer throughout. Life after Easingwold is important. School includes careers education as part of the curriculum. Quality of work placements recognised with national award and work related learning is strong thread in the curriculum. Always looking for ways to do better, using both national and international research to identify best practice. Staff encouraged to develop their own learning while they teach: teaching assistants go on to qualify as teachers, teachers get masters degrees, and so on.

Games, Options, The Arts: Fabulous sporting pedigree. Regularly excels in competitions on a Yorkshire-wide/regional basis in cricket, football, basketball, rugby, netball and hockey. Many other sports are offered and there is a pool and multi-gym. Music (choirs and orchestra that tour home and abroad) and drama (strong tradition with frequent productions and theatre visits) with good facilities. Lots of extracurriculars, and plenty of opportunity for language exchange visits and many other trips, community work, IT access and Duke of Edinburgh Awards.

Background and Atmosphere: Opened as a bilateral school in 1954 but roots can be traced to the foundation of Easingwold Grammar School in 1784. Has outgrown its buildings. Uninspiring corridors hide pleasant and vibrant classrooms, decked in the children's own impressive work, filled with attentive children working, enjoying.

School is proud of its achievements – sporting and academic – and the noticeboards are testament. One pupil told us: 'Easingwold is a very friendly school and very nice, there is always someone there to help when you need it.' Most pupils feel very positive about their school and its sense of community.

Pastoral Care and Discipline: Well structured: form tutors, and house system. Praise and punishments graded, gradual. Mentoring system to pick up children who develop any difficulties – academic, emotional, behavioural – and address them.

Pupils and Parents: 10 miles north of York, on outskirts of market town of Easingwold; pupils also come from York, Thirsk, Helperby and surrounding rural villages. An outward-looking school. Almost all pupils are English and white – but school is aware that this inhibits pupils' learning of cultural diversity and addresses this. Applying for specialist language college status to expand experience of different cultures and offer broader employment prospects to pupils. Strong cultural links with French and German schools with regular exchange visits. Very much part of the community – Friends of Easingwold as much social as educational.

Entrance: Popular. Preference for SEN, then for locals who put school as their first preference, then for locals who put another school first and failed to get in there. Cut-off usually somewhere in this latter group, resulting in panic-stricken appeals that succeed more often than usual (the alternative school may be many miles away).

Exit: About two-thirds go on to school's own sixth form after year 11, with many others going on to further education elsewhere. Post A level, 75 per cent to university and higher education.

Remarks: A happy comprehensive school where it is a pleasure to teach and be taught. Pupils and staff are at ease, know what is expected of them and strive to achieve their best.

EAST COURT SCHOOL

Victoria Parade, Ramsgate, Kent, CT11 8ED

Tel: 01843 592 077

Fax: 01843 592 418

Email: dyslexia@eastcourtschool.co.uk

Website: www.eastcourtschool.co.uk

• Pupils: 79 (65 boys. 14 girls. 53 boarders) Capacity 90
• Ages: 7 to 14 • Fees: Day £4,550; weekly boarding £5,650; full boarding £6,250. Inclusive of speech/language therapy, motor development etc • School status: Independent
• School gender: Mixed • Day/boarding: Takes boarders

SEN provision

Detail:

Centre of excellence for:
- Mild: DYSL; DYSP;
- Moderate: DYSL;
- Severe: DYSL;

Now provide for in school:
- Mild: DYSC; SpLD;
- Moderate: DYSC; DYSP; SpLD;
- Severe: DYSC; DYSP; SpLD;

Experience of:
- Mild: ASP; ADD; ADHD; HI; VI;
- Others: SPD; OCD; EAL; Sp&LD;

Summary: We cater for children with dyslexia/specific learning difficulties and some may have dyspraxic problems as well as some phonological processing difficulties. In general, the school accepts children of at least average ability, with no primary behavioural difficulties. Our aim is to return children to mainstream education at 13 years of age, with reading, writing and spelling up and running.

The purpose of SEN provision at East Court is to teach pupils to read, write and spell. East Court is a specialist school for dyslexic children. It is approved by the DfES under Section 347(1) of the 1996 Education Act for Dyslexia and Dyspraxia. The school offers specialist literacy and numeracy programmes and has support from a speech and language therapist for phonological difficulties as well as specialist dyslexia support. The school also has a motor development programme run by a specialist teacher. East Court is widely known as a centre of excellence in dyslexia. In addition to the school we run a psychological and educational assessment service. Many staff publish work on dyslexia teaching or research. We regularly run conferences for teachers and educational psychologists. East Court specialises in specific learning difficulties and is unable to provide for children who have general learning difficulties, autistic spectrum disorders, behaviour problems or severe ADHD.

What we say about the school - the full Good Schools Guide review

Principal: Since 1983 Dr Michael Thomson BSc MSc PhD AFBPsS FIARLD C Psychol Chartered Psychologist (fifties). Internationally renowned dyslexia specialist has written many books and papers including the dyslexia teaching handbook and is an ex-academic. Teaches and tutors at the school but hasn't followed traditional teaching route – worked as an academic prior to co-founding school. Continues to write and edit books on dyslexia (sometimes with staff input) and is currently updating 'Word Quest', a children's adventure game for spelling which is connected to books he's written. Says have to look after parents and loves being with the children. Believes it's important to work hard, have fun (pranks and jokes) and to encourage self-belief. Regarded affectionately by the children who say: 'he's old on the outside, young on the inside with the world's worst jokes!'

Academic Matters: All follow National Curriculum – with additions of calligraphy and typing, daily brain gym but no modern languages (will help with provision if a child has a need – perhaps for common entrance or similar). Lots of flexibility, view success as important: 'if a child is good at something we'll accommodate it.' Do not sit SATs – feel inappropriate and unreliable for children with dyslexia. Evaluate children's performance over the year using baseline measures for reading, writing and spelling. Masses of tests and profiles help pinpoint areas of difficulty. Published papers tell of successes they have with children. Prep is integrated into the school day though oldest get additional homework. Want to get children back to mainstream so looking for a level of self-discipline. Don't have year groups: children join one of seven levels, these reflect age and most importantly, reading, writing and spelling attainments – 'if a child begins to overachieve we'll re-group, don't want boredom to set in.'

Use an eclectic mix of resources including multi-sensory structured phonics course and high-interest low-reading-age books. Encourage paired reading between older and younger children, both benefit. Curriculum is very structured and organised: 'we have to be because the children aren't.' Stacks of IT taught as a discrete subject and integrated into curriculum, laptops encouraged. Experimenting with use of interactive white-board: 'expensive so we want to make sure they're used to enhance teaching and learning before we get more.' Classes average 6 for core-curriculum, 12 for rest. Subjects taught by specialists in dedicated facilities, classrooms small but well-equipped. We saw mainly teacher led lessons or one-to-one tutorials; mostly using differentiated materials. Pupils say best lessons are those such as science where they get to do lots of practical work. Full-time teaching staff are supported by two LSAs; psychologists, a speech and language therapist who works mainly on phonological skills and motor development for dyspraxic difficulties; and counsellor (for parents and children). Staff stay so profile older than in many schools though head keen to introduce young blood with new teaching and learning ideas.

Games, Options, The Arts: Have own small gym, astroturf and guaranteed use of nearby sports field. Play football, rugby, netball, lacrosse, cricket and rounders against local prep schools. Extra-curricular activities include: squash, swimming, ten-pin bowling, cycling, golf, art, woodwork, karate, play station and pool. Lots of trips: to London, theatre, skiing, sailing etc. Dedicated art room with kiln and woodwork area. Music and drama limited – small ensemble, individual instrumental tuition available and all participate in annual production – ten minutes per class! Enter local music and drama festival for mime, theatre and poetry, two first places this year. Pupils complain taught drama lesson is like another English lesson (school keen to address this).

Background and Atmosphere: School looks onto stunning sea views (France on a clear day) and sits comfortably in the smart residential area. Housed in a Grade 2 listed, Victorian mansion (former home of the Wills family). Founded in 1983 by four proprietors, now only two: Dr Thomson and Dr Rosemary Scott (academic and author) who's also the bursar, care manager and counsellor – a formidable team – two strong personalities, work extremely well together; say they can turn on a sixpence as they don't have governors. Both run professional training and inset courses. Grounds are well kept and fun, there's a mini cave, fountain, astroturf, roller blading ramps and rockery with model trains, windmills etc (made by children, semblance of a model village). Not a large school but space thoughtfully used – ongoing programme of development and refurbishment has a touch of the Forth Bridge about it. Recent purchase of adjacent Orchard House provides improved teaching accommodation for youngest and boarding for girls.

Pastoral Care and Discipline: Majority board. Girls' dorms are well kept, homely and noticeably smarter than the boys' which have a lived-in feel with some in need of redecoration (on the cards), though alas even the Changing Rooms team couldn't tamper with the listed avocado bathroom suite! Children get to personalise, theme and name their dorms. Proud of healthy, wholesome, quality food – realised a long time ago importance of a good diet – pupils encouraged to bring recipes from home for catering staff to trial. School say: 'it's a small school with a terrific bush telegraph so we don't miss much.' Deal swiftly with any bullying or suspicious incidents; indeed pupils we interviewed couldn't actually think of any incidences of bullying. Fallings out between pupils dealt with practically – must say three things they like about the other person (now there's an idea to try!)

Care staff act as parents: talk to, communicate with and organise the children. Credit system of ticks, and stars important and result in tangible rewards both collectively and individually, supported by card system, green for good, yellow for caution and red resulting in parental involvement. Couple of exclusions in past few years – won't let individuals spoil things for group: 'children are vulnerable, must do what's in their collective best interests.' Make it clear they don't cater for children whose core problems relate to behavioural difficulties.

Pupils and Parents: Mostly from SE England but smattering from the north plus expats from Chile and

Taiwan. Majority have English as a first language, odd one bilingual. Have an open door policy for parents and encourage involvement, try to dispel parental guilt and recognise many may have dyslexia. Several ex-pupils have obtained very good degrees, some from Oxbridge, and one old boy is a member of the England U21 rugby squad.

Entrance: From 7 though majority enter at 9 or 10 for a three or four year input, but good readers may only need a one or two year boost. Younger arrivals often leave at 11. Take a broad range of learning difficulties but children must have dyslexia and/or dyspraxia. Once parents express an interest school will ask for copy of the EP report. Will offer interview if think they can offer the right educational diet (parents can look round first if they prefer). Child will be looked after by fellow pupils and invited to join lessons, have lunch, share jokes, talk and do puzzles and games; try to ensure experience is stress free. Get feedback from staff, talk to parents then either offer a place or explain why school isn't appropriate. Looking for ordinary children who have dyslexic difficulties: not a place for slow learners, those with ADHD or behaviour problems.

Exit: Aim to get children back into mainstream, majority to independent schools: Stowe, Brighton College, Kent College, Bethany, St Bede's, St Lawrence College, Oakham, Bloxham, St David's College, Grenville College.

Money Matters: Majority privately funded, handful by LEA usually after going to tribunal.

Remarks: Encourages each child to become an individual true to self. A 'can-do' school for average to bright dyslexics keen to get the required boost to return to and thrive in mainstream.

EDGE GROVE PREPARATORY SCHOOL

Aldenham, Aldenham Village, Hertfordshire, WD25 8NL

Tel: 01923 855 724

Fax: 01923 859 920

Email: admissions@edgegrove.indschools.co.uk

Website: www.edgegrove.co.uk

• Pupils: 243 boys and 109 girls; 60 board, the rest day • Ages: 3-13 • Religion: C of E • Fees: Pre-prep £1,220-£2,225. Prep: day £3,040- £3,650; boarding £4,065-£4,975. Casual boarding £29 per night • School status: Independent Opendays: Oct/Feb/June • School gender: Mixed • Day/boarding: Takes boarders

SEN provision

Detail:

Now provide for in school:

Mild: DYSC; DYSL;

Summary: No comment offered – and very modest in the SEN details section too.

What we say about the school - the full Good Schools Guide review

Headmaster: Since 2002, Mr Michael Wilson BSc (early forties). Setting about turning this beautiful school into a top-flight co-ed prep. He and his highly capable wife, Carolyn, a SEN specialist, make a dedicated team, clearly fired by the potential of the site, the buildings, grounds and the position – in the country but just outside London. Not driven by lists or leagues but by the possibility of offering the best to each child.

Three boys – one still at the school, two now moved on to Haileybury. Mr Wilson, brought up in Kenya and with experience of schools there, in Thailand as well as over here, wants to create, as he says, an African school in England, by which he means a place of excellence across the board, a total curriculum with academics at its heart and a twenty four hour culture of creative involvement and enjoyment. Judging by the absorbed and relaxed faces we saw, this is already happening.

Entrance: Interviews for children from 3+ along with parents, plus assessment over a day's visit via games and lessons and general observation. Later via tests in English, maths, reasoning, plus interviews. School not aiming to cream off the brightest, 'I want the range,' says head and looks as much for character, personality and the capacity to make the most of what school offers as for academic potential. While not a school with an SEN specialism, school does well by such children and is unashamedly mixed ability. Now very over-subscribed at bottom end.

Exit: Not a place where children will be hot-housed to leave at 7 for some more glitzy establishment. You're in for the whole ride here. A proportion of girls leave at 11 for St Albans Girls School, Haberdashers, Abbots Hill, Queenswood, St Margaret's, Watford Girls' Grammar, The Mount and other good local schools. Boys stay until 13 with a few leaving at 11. Day pupils go on to St Albans, Merchant Taylor's, Mill Hill, Aldenham, Haberdashers', Watford Boys' Grammar or Queen Elizabeth's, Barnet and boarders make for Harrow, Haileybury, Eton, Sherborne, Uppingham, Oundle, Canford and Rugby among many others. 2005 saw scholarships being awarded to 22 of the 42 leavers, including a King's Scholarship to Eton. The pupils were heading for 19 schools and head works assiduously – visiting schools and chatting with heads – to make links with senior schools everywhere. A head who will take great care in placing your child.

Remarks: Just inside the M25, minutes from junction 5 on the M1, you're on a country estate with a delicious 1751 house at its centre, walled gardens (one with heated pool), plentiful playing fields, flower beds, lake, woods, neighbourly cows. There are twenty-five acres here – only fifteen miles from the centre of London – and it's a bit of a miracle. You arrive down a short drive through fields, just past the pretty village of Aldenham. A quiet, tree-studded, safe-feeling school. Formerly the home of JP Morgan, the house is a gem, magical trails of wisteria hanging over the main entrance porch. Three boys were happily and co-operatively playing croquet on the inviting lawn when we arrived. Wonderful entrance hall – all wood panels, stucco ceiling, glass dome and civilised furnishings – 'you put up your own pictures and nobody breaks anything,' says head – houses admin offices. Onsite pre-prep is Hart House – one storey modern block – bright and cheery with spacious, well-organised rooms and good facilities.

Edge Grove became a school in 1935. Boys only until 1997, it is now co-ed and takes children from 3-thus has recently expanded rapidly. Still 3:1 boys:girls. Mixed ability classes for 7 to 9-year-olds but streamed thereafter – though in a flexible structure. Saturday morning school gradually receding – no longer compulsory for 7 to 10-year-olds – and now consists of activities for 7-10's and mix of activities and lessons for the older ones. Day goes on until 5.00pm. Day pupils may opt to stay until 5.45pm if they wish to complete their prep at school – useful for two working parents. New head immediately set about huge updating and upgrading programme – curriculum, buildings, resources, grounds. 'I was brought up in East Africa where you have to move quickly or someone runs over you!'

Curriculum now runs on a streamlined 'whole school' system. Much done but far more still to be done as part of ambitious ten-year plan. Catchment area suggests no lack of available funds – some of country's richest send their offspring here. So, while some lessons still in upmarket Portakabin, changes already in train mean that much of school's teaching accommodation will be new-build or seamless extension in five years time. SENs well identified and then exceptionally well catered for under Mrs Ryder and Mrs Wilson's eye. Carefully structured and graded individual programmes plus in-class support. In 2004/5, 43 pupils having varying levels of support. Extra maths and English given instead of Latin where appropriate. Charges for one-to-one and some small group work additional to fees. Aiming to 'support the less able and stretch the most able', school also has an ABCo – ie teacher extending the range of the brightest. Policy of employing both SENCo and ABCo widely in the school to meet needs everywhere. Head takes particular pleasure in 2005 drama, music, sport and all-rounder scholarships won by pupils in every stream – 'that's what I'm after'. Overall, impressive 63 scholarships to senior schools won in 2000-2005, including – why not say it again? – a King's Scholarship to Eton – third in four years. EAL link with Mill Hill school supports few who need it.

Boarding expanding rapidly. Accommodation, though glamorous in wood-panelled, beautiful rooms, is overcrowded by modern standards and, though well furnished with sofas and books, is not homely. Necessary changes imminent and plans have been submitted. New extensions and rearrangements will mean fewer boarders in lovely, main house, rooms with views and space. Carpet everywhere. Super, reassuring housemistress in relaxed, though secure-feeling, environment. Boarders increasingly from Services families, many based at Northwood but also from everywhere overseas – Hong Kong, Korea, Cyprus etc. Weekly boarding increasingly popular and available. Walkabout phone available so that parents can be carried to children. Good pastoral care throughout in this happy, relaxed and civilised community.

Rapid improvements in teaching accommodation. Average class size 16. Greek taught to scholars. ICT was updated in 2005 and now consists of two fixed labs with wireless technology throughout the school to support a mobile laptop trolley with 20 units. Art among the best anywhere with extraordinarily sophisticated, careful yet free and creative work in many media – most notably in ceramics. (The Indian slippers in painted clay are alone worth a visit!) Drawing to a staggeringly high standard. Visits to galleries, an annual resident artist – all helps but this is seriously good stuff. Good, bright classrooms, good displays for the most part. A gorgeous library in main house – may become a common room which would be a sensible change. Music very strong – 90 per cent learn an instrument – loads of bands, ensembles. Twenty-five plus sports, excellent sports hall – school does well in competitions and sends representatives to local and national sides. Head is an ex-Davis cup coach. Cubs, scouts, beavers etc etc etc.

Edington and Shapwick School

Shapwick Manor, Shapwick, Bridgwater, Somerset, TA7 9NJ

Tel: 01458 210384
Fax: 01458 210 111
Email: shapwick@edingtonshapwick.co.uk
Website: www.edingtonshapwick.co.uk

• Pupils: 180: 40 in junior school, 112in senior school, 13 in sixth form. 30 per cent girls. 75 per cent board • Ages: 8-18 • Religion: Non-denom • Fees: £3,900-£5,935 • School status: Independent • School gender: Mixed • Day/boarding: Takes boarders

SEN provision

Detail:
Centre of excellence for:
- Mild: DYSC; DYSL; DYSP;
- Moderate: DYSC; DYSL; DYSP;
- Severe: DYSC; DYSL;
- Others: Sp&LD;

Summary: Specialist Independent Dyslexia School, approved by the DfES and CReSTeD Category 'SP'.

What we say about the school - the full Good Schools Guide review

Director of Studies: Since 1983, Mr David Walker BSc (fifties). From Keele University. Captain of club rugby and veteran of five marathons including the awesome Cornwall Marathon. Wife Annette teaches at the school – 'they've all suffered before they get here. We run as a normal school with the extra bits woven in, but nobody minds if they don't know what the date is'. Gave short shrift to one of our correspondents who wanted to know why her child had been refused entry (so that she could better judge from 5,000 miles away which school to try next): could not remember and was not inclined to find out.

Head (Pastoral): since 1981, Mr John Whittock Cert Ed (forties), married to Sandra with four children from 2 to 20, has been here since the school's inception. 'When the senior school began with just 24 pupils it was an exciting opportunity to provide dyslexic children with an education that was then very hard to come by. The strength of this school is that when pupils come here they stop feeling isolated'. Rugby captain and member of Somerset County RFU as well as leading adventure expeditions of all types.

Academic Matters: GCSE results consistently good. Resistant materials technology, graphic products, drama, science, art, photography do exceedingly well with 80 per cent of grades above B. Maths taken 18 months early – 70 per cent achieve grade C or above.

CReSTeD Category A (the highest level of provision) for the last nine years. Accreditation from RCSLT for language therapy work – the only school in the country to have it. Dragon Dictate and Keystone software, networked computers, most have laptops provided by their LEAs.

Until three years ago, post-16 students simply stayed on for re-takes or moved to sixth form colleges local to their homes. Without the continued special support in busy institutions even those who had done brilliantly at GCSE floundered or panicked and fled – crash and burn in SEN-speak. Now a co-operative scheme between Bridgwater College and Shapwick has created a dyslexia-friendly sixth form, which enables pupils to have all the advantages of the wide choices offered for A level and GNVQ by a large college without losing the multi-sensory teaching and speech and language therapy back at their familiar base. Learning to get the correct bus and find their way round Bridgwater prepare them for life in the world outside Shapwick.

Centre of excellence for language and occupational therapy.

Games, Options, The Arts: Sport compulsory for all until sixth form. County-level players in badminton, athletics and rugby. Teams play state and private schools. D of E generates much enthusiasm and bronze awards. Annual ski trip to France combines junior and senior schools; improves co-ordination, listening, confidence, high-level organisation while they learn to bum-board, snow board and ski. Art trips to Egypt, years 7, 8, 9/10 to Normandy.

Summer Arts festival – local artists do workshops on tapestry, painting, willow-weaving; pottery made by the pupils on the theme of 'The Scream'. Drum, guitar and keyboard taught to a handful. Choir at junior school.

Background and Atmosphere: Magic atmosphere. Motto: *Gradu diverso via una* – The same road by different steps. Shapwick Manor, owned by Lord Vestey, is the hub of the school. Fine early stable block, listed rotund dovecote, lesser architectural delights such as a few Portakabins cleverly hidden so as not to offend the eye. All seven boarding houses are run as cosy family units with a pair of house parents attached to each. Furthest away is The Lakes, a boys' house in Meare (the next village), while Little Lawn, Church Farm and Greystones are closer to the Manor.

The country's first and largest specialist school for dyslexics and the only independent school of its kind to board from 8 to 18, Shapwick has the endearing element of being so self-contained as to appear uninterested in its outward packaging. The prospectus may be mistaken for one that launched the school in 1974, and newsletters still resemble a parish magazine from the 1930s, but wade past the minuscule print and it's full of action.

Pastoral Care and Discipline: The staff here are everything – they bring a new meaning to the word dedication. Many have family members and some children who have suffered with dyslexia or dyspraxia, so their compassion and zeal does not stop when the bell goes. 12 parents' meetings a year. Strong parental involvement contributes to its success. Discipline is firm but fair. Definite exclusion for cannabis.

Pupils and Parents: All severely dyslexic/dyspraxic from both state and independent sector from Wales, North Yorkshire, Channel Islands, Germany, India, Nigeria, Jordan. 75 per cent are statemented. 'Often parents only realise that they themselves are dyslexic after they sort it out for their kids', says Cynthia, the speech therapist who has become to the children an angel incarnate. The office is awash with letters of gratitude from delighted parents of pupils past and present who have come from years of the wrong schooling, being made to feel inadequate or bullied because of their impediment and, after a very short time, have gained self-esteem and begun to flourish.

Entrance: No emotional or behavioural problems catered for. Entry at any age by psychologist's report and interview. Minimum 85-90 IQ. Mark College has sent their post-16 students here.

Exit: For some a 2-3 year course results in a return to the mainstream at 11 or 13. Post-16, 100 per cent stay on to take A levels or Btec leading to university courses. Plymouth University has now devised a programme for dyslexics to obtain entry without A levels.

Money Matters: Small number of limited bursaries and scholarships. Sibling discount applies.

Remarks: Parents full of praise. 'Staff are miracle workers', says one.

THE ELMS SCHOOL

Colwall, Malvern, Worcestershire, WR13 6EF

Tel: 01684 540 344

Fax: 01684 541 174

Email: office@elmsschool.co.uk

Website: www.elmsschool.co.uk

• Pupils: 70 boys, 60 girls; 80 per cent board; plus 70 children in pre-prep • Ages: 3-13 • Religion: C of E • Fees: Boarding £5,695; day £4,945; pre-prep £1,850-£3,150 • School status: Independent • School gender: Mixed • Day/boarding: Takes boarders

SEN provision

Detail:

Experience of:

Mild: ASP; ADD; ADHD; DYSC; DYSL;

Moderate: MLD;

Others: EAL; Epi;

Summary: The school intentionally includes a wide ability range including SEN and gifted children who receive support either individually or within the usual teaching environment according to individual requirements.

What we say about the school - the full Good Schools Guide review

Head: Since 1985 Clive Ashby BA Cert Ed (fifties), single (unusual in prep schools these days). Educated in a number of schools both in England and Spain; most notably Belmont Abbey in Hereford: now defunct.

Degree in science from Nottingham. Interesting background, firstly in commerce, then St Richard's in Bromyard in Herefordshire and finally Sunningdale, where he was hugely influenced by the Dawson twins. Truly gargantuan appetite for work. He not only teaches, mainly maths, but is also his own bursar and even finds time to maintain the beautifully kept school garden. Has an almost obsessive love for all things rural. The school attended the countryside march en masse and the banners are still displayed over the school entrance. This is a man who provokes the most partisan reactions. His energy, focus and determination to succeed do not always make him popular with some of his independent school colleagues but he is highly regarded and even loved by many of his staff, parents and pupils. One especially notes the real affection many parents feel for him. The school has its own working farm and he breeds a string of thoroughbred racehorses. Lucky to have a wonderfully warm enthusiastic and extraordinarily accessible head of boarding in Sarah Wilson, who fulfils many of the traditional functions of headmaster's wife.

Took over a moribund school of 48 children in 1985 and has transformed it into one of the most successful preparatory schools in the Welsh Marches, currently with numbers in excess of 200. He has what are now regarded as rather old fashioned views on education. Hates the pressurised tick box concept of so much modern educational ideology. He is concerned with the breadth of education and the need for every pupil to succeed at something – a philosophy that goes down jolly well in rural Herefordshire! Has a very clear understanding of his potential market and a considerable flair for attracting the 'right' parents – very largely the richer smarter rural set; owners of agricultural estates are not untypical. The school is entirely in his image and its success is an extraordinary testament to the fact that it is still possible for unusual eccentric heads to thrive in the post-modern landscape of modern education.

Entrance: Over-subscribed, but not excessively so. Entrance into pre-prep as early as 3, regular intake at 7 and 8. A few children from local state schools but the majority from very traditional independent school families. Most children from Herefordshire, Gloucestershire, Monmouthshire and Powys but a significant number from other parts of the country – notably London.

Exit: A few girls still leave at 11, but increasingly rare says head. The largest number goes to Malvern College, Shrewsbury School or Malvern Girls' College but, over the last five years, pupils have exited to 23 different schools including Cheltenham College, Eton, Winchester, Marlborough, Monmouth, Uppingham, Rugby, Cheltenham Ladies' College and Tudor Hall. The majority of girls still seem to go on to single sex schools. Respectable scholarship list, seven in 2004; about 25 per cent of leavers get some kind of award but one needs to bear in mind that a number of awards over the last few years have been for art, drama, sport etc reflecting the head's aim to provide a breadth of education. This is not an academic hothouse!

Remarks: The oldest prep school in England, founded by Humphry Walwyn in 1614. In the middle of the attractive village of Colwall just outside Malvern. Not immediately impressive, the main school buildings abut the main road, yet to walk through the gates is a revelation. The school backs on to 150 acres of pristine gardens, beautifully maintained games fields and a small working farm complete with pigs, cows and horses. Perhaps unique amongst prep schools in having rural studies as part of the curriculum. The animals are not just here for show, one is assured – 'we eventually eat the pigs, chickens and cows' (not the horses!) The farm is a wonderful asset for all the children but especially for the less sporty and the academically challenged, who can get a real sense of achievement in helping in the farm. Riding and shooting are important parts of the school activity programme with children having achieved success at national equestrian events – and school is said to provide, in one way or another, half the Ledbury hunt. Winners of the prep school National shooting competition in 13 out of the last 18 years!

Remarkable number of new buildings including a vast sports hall, indoor swimming pool and brand new changing facilities. There are plans to build a new girls' boarding house and further classroom to start in the next twelve months. There cannot be many small schools with equivalent facilities. Remarkably, so successful has the financial management of the school been, that all this has been achieved without an overdraft. A factor in this is no doubt the somewhat high fees with little distinction made between the charges for boarding or day. The Elms charges the highest termly fee of any prep school in the area but, perhaps, this just adds to its exclusive appeal.

The least impressive part of the school is the children's dormitories (although one is assured that this will be addressed in the new development programme). Every child in the prep school (not pre-prep) has a designated bed; there are rest periods after lunch every day. This means that day children can board when they want, provided it is not more than four nights a week when they must convert to full boarder and stay over the weekend. However, this policy has meant that the dormitories are overcrowded and not very homely.

Academically sound with many long-serving staff (very low staff turnover). Inspection imminent. Traditional curriculum which includes a strong classics department. Follows a traditional prep school policy of moving children through classes as the need appears – this the head describes as the ladder system – which can mean that the brighter sparks might spend the last two years in the top class. However, it is quite clear that the head is very sensitive to parental concerns and there is a certain flexibility in the system. His determination to maintain this structure cocks a snook at current educational theory – it will be interesting to see what the inspectors make of this. Groups are very small and no class is larger than thirteen, the smallest just nine. It seems to work well and both parents and children seem happy with it.

Delightful well-mannered, cared-for children. Head places great emphasis on developing polite, confident children and in this he is very largely successful. Very few foreign pupils, fewer than half a dozen. Very conventional school uniform, boys wear corduroy shorts until they leave at 13. Wonderful cosy family atmosphere, not only the farm animals but lots of friendly dogs wander around the school, children are even encouraged to bring in their own (smaller) animals. Difficult to imagine much problem with homesickness here! The small size of the school means that each child is known as an individual and it is clear that the head knows and understands his charges extremely well. There is a wide range of activities which are well chronicled in very full termly newsletters (NB the school does not have an annual magazine). It is nice to see so many children involved in a wide sporting programme with the emphasis on participation rather than producing a sporting elite. Very strong art and drama but the head is refreshingly honest in admitting music is not especially strong although nearly 60 per cent of pupils learn at least one instrument

An ancient foundation but the resurrected present Elms School is very much in the image of the current head. In many ways an idiosyncratic and very unusual school, offering a traditional prep school experience increasingly rarely found. Not everyone will care for it but those who do have nothing but good to say of it.

ELSTREE SCHOOL

Woolhampton, Reading, Berkshire, RG7 5TD

Tel: 01189 713 302

Fax: 01189 714 280

Email: secretary@elstreeschool.org.uk

Website: www.elstreeschool.org.uk

• Pupils: 185 boys plus 65 boys and girls in pre-prep (Home Farm). 80 full boarders, 20 regular flexi-boarders, rest day • Ages: 7-13, pre-prep 3-7 • Religion: C of E • Fees: Pre-prep £2,332; prep: day £4,030; boarding £5,460 • School status: Independent • Opendays: December, March, May and October • School gender: Boys • Day/boarding: Takes boarders

SEN provision

Detail:

Experience of:

Mild: ASP; DYSC; DYSL; DYSP; SpLD; HI; VI;

Moderate: MLD; DYSL;

Others: EAL; Sp&LD; Epi;

Summary: Elstree has an outstanding reputation for supporting boys with special educational needs, as has been recognised in recent ISI inspections. There is a team of committed and well-qualified staff, under the leadership of Mrs Vicky Bateman, who care and look after boys with a variety of needs. The department is very well integrated and the boys' success at Common Entrance and Scholarship examinations is impressive.

What we say about the school - the full Good Schools Guide review

Headmaster: Since 1995, Mr Syd Hill MA (mid fifties). Read geography and education at Cambridge; previously housemaster at Malvern College. Typical headmaster in appearance – tall, ruddy, sporty, slightly shy but knows all boys and is extremely quick to praise. Runs a tight ship with strict rules. Has successfully shaken off Elstree's 'snooty' image. No plans to bow under parental pressure to go co-ed. Firmly believes in single-sex schooling at this age. 'We much prefer to set ourselves up as a first-class boys' school,' he says. Encourages boarding from early age but very flexible. Wife Jane very lively, supportive, with good people skills. 'She's everything a headmaster's wife should be.' A son now following in father's footsteps at Mount House (qv), two daughters at university.

Entrance: Non-selective. 50 per cent move up from Home Farm, rest from far and wide (large proportion from London and Home Counties, around 10 overseas). No test, but prospective pupil assessment. Report from previous head also important 'just to make sure we're the right school' and identify any learning difficulties.

Exit: Clear favourites over last eight years (in descending order) are Bradfield, Eton and Radley closely followed by Marlborough, Harrow and Wellington. Other popular choices include Stowe and Charterhouse. 'We know by age 10 which school a boy would be suited to and we advise parents accordingly,' says head.

Remarks: Prides itself on a traditional character. Established in 1848. At the outbreak of war, staff and 70 boys upped sticks from Elstree, Herts and never went back. Glorious Georgian country house and 150-acre estate set in heart of leafy Berkshire, formerly home to a Polish family (Gurowski). Intricate carvings and floor-to-ceiling wood-panelled walls form welcoming main entrance. Freshly painted dorms in rooms above. Bright, very cheerful and homely with lots of home photos pinned up. 'It's like after the match at Twickenham in here there's so much noise and chatter,' quips the head. Housemaster looks after boarders' welfare while younger boys cared for by housemistress. 'Our pastoral care is second to none,' claims head, and this was clearly identified in recent ISI inspection. There are also resident matrons and a qualified nurse. Parents invited to visit as often as possible. No mobiles permitted. Letters home written weekly. Academic studies obviously important but not be all and end all. Plenty of help for dyslexics/learning difficulties. 'I feel the atmosphere of the school is enhanced by different abilities and strengths,' he says. 'We offer an all-round education; developing self-esteem is crucial.'

Few boys fail to get into next school of their choice. Lessons six days a week (for day boys too). Brand new ICT room of networked terminals, plus bank of laptops for use in other classrooms, skills taught to all (starting with top year from Home Farm) and used in all subjects. Streamed classes from age 9 – average size 15. Setting in mathematics. Boys were attentive and responsive in lessons we saw. Not shy to speak up. Big, functional classrooms in new-ish block. Wide subject range (as curriculum demands), focus on Common Entrance – scholarship hopefuls creamed off early and taught in separate class. Hugely successful. Regularly produce six scholars a year, including awards in art, music and sport – 2002 a bumper year with 15 awards including 6 music scholarships. Awards in 2003 included King's Scholarship to Eton. Class music tuition as well as individual lessons. Violin and piano particularly strong. Two to three even learn bagpipes. Orchestra and bands in abundance. Senior choir performs often at concerts, not just in church every Sunday.

Religion a fundamental part of school life. Scriptures studied closely, boys encouraged to read Bible for themselves and morning prayers held daily. 'I think it's our job to plant the seed,' explains head. 'It also has a major influence on the boys' behaviour.' Certainly what we witnessed was impeccable – excellent table manners, courtesy and respect for others. 'There's absolutely no bullying here,' stressed one boy now in his final year. When pressed, he admitted there's a certain amount of teasing but no worse. 'All boys know precisely what is right and wrong,' says head. Remarkable.

Four school houses (North, South, East and West) for purely competitive reasons. Stars earned by boys go towards house cup. Games played daily (usual rugby, football, hockey, tennis, athletics) to good competitive level but seen more as good experience. 'Every boy has played for the school, that's what's important to us and to him,' head says. Brand spanking new sports hall opened in 2000 by Elstree old boy Field Marshal Lord Bramall (other famous OBs include Sebastian Faulks, an active school governor) – a great improvement on old school hall. 'One of the best gyms I've seen,' commented visiting fencing tutor. New all-weather tennis courts. Superb new library just opened last year in main house. New junior classroom block opened in Summer 2005 as part of ongoing development programme. Good facilities for art and DT – boys happy to show off their work. Large teaching staff – good mix of experience and more youthful enthusiasm. Type of boy, also mixed. Head asserts 'it's a school for all sorts. I'm very keen that parents should not choose Elstree for the wrong reasons just because it has the right social status'. There are not many families here for whom independent education and boarding is a first.' Might this be changing?

Home Farm School (pre-prep): Head since 1999, Mrs Sue Evans CertEd (early fifties), previously taught at Crosfields. Widowed, two daughters – one in fashion industry, the other in gap year. Runs happy, friendly mixed pre-prep in lovely converted 18th century farmhouse and barn a short walk from Elstree. First opened in 1993 with just eight children – now flourishing. Small class sizes. All rooms and corridors exhibit children's work. 'Every child has something up,' says head. 'And it's all their own work – I don't believe in putting teachers' work up on the walls.' Non-selective. Parents register son/daughter before assessment day. Computers in every room. Music taught to all from nursery up with special extra sessions for mothers and toddlers – useful focal point for new parents. Automatic transition to Elstree, no additional test taken, but screened for learning difficulties at 5. Lots of learning through play as well as focus on literacy and numeracy. Really cosy, homely atmosphere. After school club is asset for working parents. Popular with families moving out from London as well as from more immediate locality but it's well worth a car journey.

Epsom College

College Road, Epsom, Surrey, KT17 4JQ

Tel: 01372 821 234

Fax: 01372 821 237

Email: admissions@epsomcollege.org.uk

Website: www.epsomcollege.org.uk

• Pupils: 720; 498 boys of whom 263 board, including 151 weekly boarders. 222 girls: 127 board, including 81 weekly boarders • Ages: 13-18 • Religion: C of E • Fees: Day £5,266; day boarding £5,607; weekly boarding £7,159; full boarding £7,463 • School status: Independent • Opendays: May and September/October • School gender: Mixed • Day/boarding: Takes boarders

SEN provision

Detail:

Experience of:

Mild: ASP; AUT; ADD; DS;

Moderate: ASP; ADD;

Severe: ADD;

Summary: Learning support at Epsom College

The philosophy of the learning support department (LSD) is that all pupils can improve and achieve, given the appropriate support for their special educational needs (SEN). At Epsom we have very well-qualified and experienced staff who are able to work with a wide range of SEN.

Our aim is to support individuals with a specific teaching programme, according to their needs, eg a structured literacy and/or spelling programme for pupils with a specific learning difficulty (SpLD). We will help them to develop and use strategies and techniques to support their learning.

We also teach pupils how to improve or develop organisational skills, exam and revision techniques, study skills, time management and handwriting. We consider the development of confidence and self-esteem vital to our pupils' success – the one-to-one support can prove to be an important role here. We are aiming for pupils to become independent, both in learning and thinking, and to use their relevant strategies and techniques automatically.

Testing or assessments may take place following referrals from staff, parents or the pupils themselves. Assessments in respect of special arrangements for external exams can be made and the report and recommendations submitted. Occasionally it may be necessary to suggest a referral to an educational psychologist.

Our usual one-to-one programme consists of 30 lessons, over three terms, of 45 mins each. These are always arranged in consultation with the pupil and are held outside of the academic timetable and extra-curricular activities. The sixth form pupils have their lessons during a study period and these are 35 mins. Other programmes of support are offered according to need and vary from 6 to 12 weeks. There is a charge made to parents towards the cost of these extra lessons which is added to the school bill at the end of each term.

We liaise with Housemasters and Housemistresses, Tutors and individual teaching staff. It is important that all staff are aware of a pupil's needs and how to support them in class. The LSD produces and maintains a Special Needs Register which identifies each pupil. Staff can then refer to each individual's specific needs/difficulties and recommendations for teaching/support. We are able to assess and monitor progress and then report to all concerned. We are always available to offer support to both staff and parents.

What we say about the school - the full Good Schools Guide review

Head: Since 2000, Mr Stephen R Borthwick (early fifties), previously head of Aldenham. Educated at a Surrey grammar school, then physics at the University of Wales, Bangor. Previously head of physics at Marlborough and then deputy head at Bishop's Stortford. Enjoys golf, walking, portrait photography and music. Personable and business-like. Married to Glynis, a modern linguist (they met at university), who teaches English as an Alternative Language at the school. Parents' main point of contact seems to be with house masters/mistresses rather than the head.

Academic Matters: Not a premier league academic powerhouse but very strong overall performance. At GCSE consistently good A/A* performance in languages (French, German, Spanish), art, maths, geography, history and the separate sciences. Overall GCSE pass rate of 100 per cent grades A-C. A level results also impressive with 80 per cent achieving A or B.

In the lower school there is a broad curriculum. Choice between German and Spanish. Generally, pupils take 10 GCSEs; the most able at maths can sit a year earlier. Sixth formers take four A/S levels, some continuing with four subjects for A2s but most taking 3. Recent introductions proving popular for A/S level include classical civilisation, theology, philosophy, business studies, politics and government and theatre studies. The newly introduced critical thinking has also proved a popular choice for candidates. One parent with a son keen on serious computer programming settled on Epsom after a long and frustrating search.

Each subject has its own teaching block, except for economics, business studies, history and geography which are housed in the new Mackinder building. Each block has a dedicated library, seminar room and departmental office. Impressive modern main library converted from the old gym in 1996, with link to the careers department. Qualified librarian always on duty and it also functions as a community area, with broad selection of daily newspapers and current cinema guides.

Average class size 18 in the lower school; 10 in sixth form. Pupils with SEN admitted provided that they can cope with academic mainstream (full-time teacher and assistant solely for this), but extra charge. Support for dyslexic pupils is 'impressive', according to one satisfied parent. Saturday morning lessons for all with games or activities in the afternoon, after which weekly boarders can depart until Sunday evening.

Games, Options, The Arts: Sport compulsory for all – more than 25 sports available. PE is offered at A level and the sports centre has a dedicated form room for this. The centre also houses two large sports halls (one with cricket nets), a fencing salle with two pistes, a multigym, climbing wall and everything else you would expect. School very, very good at target rifle shooting, with a 25m indoor range – popular with both boys and girls and the master in charge of shooting (an historian) has been adjutant to the British cadet rifle team. Epsom has been Public Schools' Champion nine times during the last 14 years.

Better spectator provision for the swimming pool almost complete at time of writing. Hockey very popular with both sexes (master in charge was member of British Olympic team); rugby is main boys' field sport (winners of The Daily Mail U15 Rugby Cup). Soccer also on offer, although budding David Beckhams should note that soccer is not often played competitively below sixth form. Good squash courts, some with spectator galleries, and golf available on the neighbouring private Epsom Downs course.

School surrounded by extensive playing fields. Splendid CCF assault course (used by the Army as well) and which has featured in ITV's 'The Bill'. CCF compulsory for first two years – it's not popular with everyone – thereafter optional. Duke of Edinburgh Award scheme also operated at all three of its levels. School exceptionally strong on art (see famous OB artists), with most pupils having their own studio space for their work – no tedious packing away after each lesson. One parent said, 'my son was especially talented at pottery and he was given the greatest encouragement.' Music also very good (over 350 lessons per week) and sensibly scheduled so that no pupil misses an academic lesson – other schools take note! Modern music block has own recording studio. Vocal groups very popular with both sexes, including the Downs Singers (secular as well as holy music) and the chapel choir. Old squash courts destined to become a centre for performing arts, relieving the somewhat small school hall (also being developed) from housing these activities as well as exams and assemblies.

Background and Atmosphere: School founded in 1855 along with The Royal Medical Foundation for the sons of doctors and occupies 80 acres on Epsom Downs – an oasis in the heart of the built-up Surrey commuter belt. All accommodation, facilities and sports are within the grounds or adjacent (except for sailing in the summer at Ripley). Used to have small, idiosyncratic museum housing, probably unique, collection of medical instruments and items of biological interest – still on view and of great interest to some parents and, we hope, to the fortunate pupils.

Buildings of mellow red brick, including the chapel and the modern structures blend in well, creating a collegiate atmosphere – although some would argue the site is not over-endowed with character and atmosphere. A recently developed 'social centre' very popular with both sexes and all age groups – open at specified times during day and 'good for hanging out,' says one sixth former. Boarding houses cosy, each with small library, music and IT rooms. Meals are compulsory for all (peace of mind for mothers with potentially anorexic daughters). Girl boarders share no more than four to a room, with a single room in the upper sixth. Boys boarding share between four and six in first year, then between two from second year, with own room in upper sixth.

School now fully co-ed and has benefited enormously from this, says head, becoming a 'more civilised and congenial community.' Numbers expanding, mainly to cope with demand from girls, which has necessitated an additional house, increasing houses from 11 to 12. Around 30 day boarders (20 boys, 11 girls), who stay at school to do their prep.

Large numbers of brothers and sisters in the school which, head says, brings a better sense of partnership with the families. Courteous, middle class pupils, with noticeably easy relations between boys and girls. All wear uniform, with wider choice available to sixth formers including trousers for girls. Generally smart but some girls a bit dishevelled and with surprisingly short skirts.

Pastoral Care and Discipline: We have had a few reports of bullying in the past (head accepts that this may have been the case) but it is now definitely history. Recent parental survey on key issues resulted in 97 per cent voting that pastoral care was either satisfactory or very satisfactory. There is a published anti-bullying policy and the issue is addressed in PSE lessons and in-house talks. House support for pupils is strong with a house tutor for each year group in each house, providing supervision for academic and pastoral matters as well as house matters. More than 50 per cent of the staff have been here over 10 years, indicating a stable and contented bunch. School counsellor available. Zero-tolerance on drugs with head finding it 'difficult to envisage any circumstances in which a pupil found in possession or dealing could remain.' Recent social services report on boarding very positive.

Chapel compulsory on Wednesdays and on Saturday, together with a weekly congregational hymn practice, alternative arrangements eg supervised study for non-C of E students. Chapel on Sunday morning is voluntary, followed by optional sports and visits eg to Tate Modern. One pupil says, 'very few boarders want a seventh day of being organised, they want flexibility.' Boarders allowed into Epsom but control exercised depending on age, numbers and time.

Pupils and Parents: Predominantly from Surrey and fringes, even among the boarders. Pupils come from a wide range of local prep schools but no formal links with any particular one. Ample daily school transport laid on from west London and several Surrey towns, with minibuses between school and local rail stations – means many parents can avoid the dreaded school run.

Parents mainly professionals and company directors, with 14 per cent expats and non-UK. ' The school is not a pretentious one,' says one mother. Has a long tradition of overseas students and the sixth form entry especially reflects this, with pupils continuing to come from the same schools in SE Asia and Hong Kong, many of them the children of former pupils.

Well-known Old Epsomians include artists John Piper and Graham Sutherland and, for no obvious reason, a strong line in TV reporters, including Jeremy Vine, Nicholas Witchell, Mark Mardell and Jonathan Maitland (also the author of 'How to Make Your Million From the Internet' and, subsequently, the same with 'And What to Do If You Don't' added to the title), together with lots of medical luminaries and some politicians.

Entrance: Via CE at 13 (pass mark for entrance 55 – 60 per cent). An 11-plus exam can be sat before CE based on tests in English, maths, IQ and an interview – useful for borderline candidates. Non-CE takers can sit special tests at 13. At sixth form, there is an intake of about 50 – including 30 girls. Sixth form entry is subject to entrance exams, interviews and actual performance achieved at GCSE.

Exit: Vast majority to university (most popular are Southampton, Edinburgh, Nottingham and Cambridge or gap year). Subject-wise, of 155 about 10-15 go on to study medicine and 10-20 engineering or economics, with business, English, law and geography next in popularity. School has reputation for producing more medics than any other and used to be the number one choice for doctors' sons – intake broader now.

Money Matters: The usual awards for art, music and sport, together with academic, all-rounder but also design technology and theatre studies awards and all available at both 13 and 16. Closed scholarships for children of doctors who have fallen on hard times. More than 40 awards made each year – their value is up to 20-25 per cent of full fees but can be topped up by bursaries.

Remarks: Solid co-educational school with healthy proportion of boarders both weekly and full-time. Good academic achievement, very good on-site facilities and increasingly popular with girls who generally integrate well.

ETON COLLEGE

Eton, Windsor, Berkshire, SL4 6DW

Tel: 01753 671 249

Fax: 01753 671 248

Email: admissions@etoncollege.org.uk

Website: www.etoncollege.com

• Pupils: 1,298 boys (all boarding) • Ages: 13-18 • Religion: C of E (other faiths 'excused' chapel, but many attend anyway) • Fees: £7,896 • School status: Independent • Opendays: Tours and briefings on 60 afternoons a year • School gender: Boys • Day/boarding: Takes boarders

SEN provision

Summary: Special educational needs are met through individual and small-group tuition rather than in classes. Please consult the tutor for admissions about our special needs provision and the allowances made in the selection process.

GSG writes: sounds pretty bleak and unwelcoming, but we have heard some lovely stories of how well they have supported SEN. Becoming a seriously SEN-friendly school, perhaps in honour of the current Old Etonian prime ministerial hopeful, but not yet ready to bruit it abroad.

What we say about the school - the full Good Schools Guide review

Headmaster: Since 2002, Mr Anthony (Tony) Little ARM MA PGCE (forties) who was educated at Eton, read English at Corpus Christi (where he was a choral exhibitioner) and did his PGCE at Homerton. Previously head of Oakham, having taught English at Tonbridge and Brentwood, and was head of Chigwell ('a steep learning curve') before Oakham. Keen on music, the theatre, film and rowing (nostalgically the latter). A lovely man; he speaks immaculate English, in paragraphs, with 'whoms'.

Some radical moves – the head man (as all Eton heads are known) has instituted a parent/teacher evening in E and F block, before long leave in the first half (Eton speak: read before half term in the first term); this is a dramatic turnaround and no longer will parents be able to complain that they 'don't know what the darlings are up to'.

Certain amount of jealousy from other headmasters – 'he hasn't even been head of a first division school and now he is head of the heap' – but he appears comfortable in his (holey) shoes and is good at working the public and the parents, 'super directed, makes a terrific impression'. 'Keen on raising the public perception of the school.' 'Not a stuffed shirt and always open to new ideas.'

This is a head who reckons that, 'there must be a regular appraisal of teachers and housemasters'. Health and Safety are also much involved, and there has been a pro-active appointment. The head's wife, Jenny, is very involved in school activities ('too involved' said one beak (ie teacher); 'not at all hands-off' said the head man; she regularly acts as school guide. And no, she has not done her colours test. The Littles have a grown up daughter.

The lower man (as the previous deputy head was known) is now a two-man position, with 'computer freak', the erstwhile head of maths, Rev. John Puddifoot ('jumped up director of studies,' said one colleague) running the curriculum side, with Dr Bob Stevenson looking after the trad pastoral role of lower master.

Academic Matters: First class all round, though not necessarily first class in all the league tables. Outstandingly good teaching, Eton can pick and choose (and cash has quite a lot to do with it – heads of departments elsewhere join the also-rans for extra pay). Prospective staff have a series of interviews, spending time in the department, taking a class (head man is 'keen that everyone should be in a class with boys') and culminating with lunch (knives and forks test). Boys setted by ability from the first year and all take some (it varies) GCSEs early, plus a full complement the following year. Boys can reduce the number of GCSEs they take and embark on an early start on AS level courses; quite a few do. More time for real education, fewer exam hoops to be jumped through. Plenty of va et vient among sets, boys are constantly changing beaks and peer groups.

Tutors allotted for junior boys, who may then request their specialist tutor post-GCSE. Highly structured, lots of sticks and carrots. Monthly order cards and show-ups – the former now apparently delivered by e-mail. Certain amount of irritation from older beaks about 'having to fill in the class register by computer'. Fab langs, one of the most successful departments in the country in terms of results – packs in talk and chalk. Japanese, Chinese, Arabic are options (NB if Eton offers a subject it really happens – unlike many other schools which often have an element of window dressing). Proper language exchanges throughout the school (like two weeks in Japan, a whole term in Germany – usually on an exchange basis). Indeed exchanges in every discipline – France, Spain, Russia ... Plus Casa Guidi in Florence.

Vast choice of A levels, results outstanding; maths a popular subject, with ancillary economics; geography and history strong. English results are phenomenal. Twice yearly internal exams ('trials' – the top boys' results are read out). Boys are treated much as university students and need considerable stamina and self-discipline to cope with the work load, no quarter is given for those who fall by the wayside. (School comments that 'this is utterly untrue, and every effort is made by housemasters, tutors and teachers to help boys through difficult periods').

School reports sent to parents have a curious formula: beaks report to tutors, who in turn report to housemasters, who in turn write to parents, enclosing relevant reports as well as their personal assessment of the situation.

School took us to task for saying that 'this is absolutely not the school for a dyslexic' and though school has good links with the Dyslexia Association, and has had for many years, pupils and beaks alike say that 'it is not really the best place for pupils who are seriously challenged'. 'Too much working on your own,' said one former (mildly dyslexic) Etonian of our acquaintance. But that having been said, there is a strong learning support system in place and the school takes in 'a significant number of dyslexic and indeed dyspraxic boys corresponding to the proportion in the general population ... and does so consciously at the point of selection where their potential is recognised, and it then provides them with extensive support'. Dyslexia unit in place, with one-to-one, and group therapy on tap, school can also cope with boys with Asperger's and ADHD, on the 'mild to moderate' spectrum in all cases.

Most of Little's previous headships have leant in the direction of co-education and/or the IB. When we asked him about the possibilities of such radical change his reaction was to say that, 'I first learnt that we were going down the IB route on the radio when I was filling the car with petrol in Norfolk'. He doesn't reckon it is 'good for enthusiasts, nor for scientists', but is 'much better for girls'. 'The best part of the IB is the extended essay or Theory of Knowledge – complete with footnotes – but now that all lower sixth do divinity' (which he teaches) 'this acts as an embryonic ToK, and we find nuggets of outstanding excellence, exposing as many boys as possible.' On the question of girls: we got an enigmatic 'who knows?' (the boys wondered about their uniform).

Games, Options, The Arts: Excellent all round – every conceivable extra-curricular activity is on offer to amazing standards in some cases. IT now in the vanguard, with the local expert maintaining that he had rarely come across such infrastructure. (Head man complains about 'the tyranny of the e-mail culture'). Each room in every house now with infra-red and net connections; all boys have mobiles and discount-available laptops. Brill music, generally acknowledged to be one of the best departments in the country; and attracts the brightest and best in music scholarships. Regular and very polished concerts; wonderful chapel choir.

Superb and inspirational art department, oodles of dosh spent here in the last few years – marvellous open aspect over playing fields to the northwest. Remarkable and challenging work; masses of prizes and skols here too. The art department that all other schools envy. Drama important. Skule plays as well as house plays; both housemaster and boy-inspired, plus more trad stuff.

Main games are soccer, rugby, fives, hockey, cricket – very good; plus Eton's own Wall Game and the Field Game; good fencing, swimming (squad recently trained to swim the Channel), water polo, sailing etc, also judo, polo, beagling. Over forty teams in action most Saturdays but, though still successful, the school does not appear to be winning the way it once did. And sport is no longer worshipped the way it once was. Housemasters not pushing hard enough say some. Head encourages boys to continue with sports through exam terms – brownie points for this.

Huge number of outings, visits and field trips etc, and good provision for amusing pupils post-exams. CCF very popular – pace Harry Windsor, and full-time officer seconded. Excellent and popular post-school camp offers fantastic range of experiences – helicoptering, parachuting, speedboat driving licence (popular this and essential for hiring boats in the hols). Vast number of clubs and societies, with top notch speakers, often run by boys themselves, and almost all of which boast a variety of club sox – by which Etonians can be easily identified – they usually wear a non-matching pair (warning here, the school bill may well be augmented by several hundred quid's worth of extra 'essential' club kit – sox and scarves only).

Background and Atmosphere: Founded in 1440 by Henry VI (sister college of King's College, Cambridge, which was founded a year later), and 70 King's Scholars still live in the original buildings (most elegant dining hall and really ancient classroom still with original benches and graffiti). Buildings of mellow old red brick, grounds run down to the Thames. Magnificent chapel built by Henry VI and a second chapel for Lower Boys; war memorials all over the shop, deep nostalgia. School has appointed an Imam, RC chaplain on staff too.

Twenty-four boarding houses, including separate one for King's Scholars; single study bedsits for all, from day one. Huge variety in spec, housemasters employ different strategies as to which boy chooses first. Décor differs – one mother described one as 'like a working brothel'; another has carpet up the walls. Boarding houses scattered down the High Street and beyond; houses are known not by name but by the initials of the housemaster in charge – housemasters in the job for 13 years, so of course the name of the house changes... irritating for Eton buffs who like to pretend they know the place. Boys no longer wear bum freezers but tail coats for all, with stiff (paper) collars except for office bearers, who wear proper wing collars and white ties. Brilliant for posture, as boys stuff pockets in their tails with all sorts of essential school kit, pulling even the most round-shouldered creature straight. (Must be the cheapest school uniform out, with good second-hand trade both boy-inspired and via the school tailors in the High Street). Head describes the uniform as 'anally retentive'. Fancy waistcoats worn by members of the Eton Society ('Pop'), most memorable one was entirely made of condoms. However pupils no longer wear tails across the bridge to Windsor, or even now (much) in the High Street, and much changing and half-changing throughout the day.

Atmosphere very much alive, not easy, and every day is structured and active. Everyone – boys, beaks (often flying round Eton on their bikes – in white tie, with their black gowns flying and trousers tucked into their socks). All beaks must wear gowns and these come into their own during their three line whip coffee break – Chambers – when one beak will attract the attention of another by tugging at his gown... this can become addictive, with long lines of tugging beaks forming. 'Like a line of elephants,' says the head man.

Eton has its own trad but ever evolving school language: halves (terms) long leave (half term) etc, currently the buzz is to add 'age': as in 'pubage', 'birdage', 'tabage' (tobacco), lebage (as in plebs) etc. In general the school is a solipsistic attitude to life. Excellent school mags (The Chronicle, The Junior Chronicle) which are sold on high days and holidays for commission (usually by younger boys). An unwritten law discourages boys from speaking to the press, which may be the reason why beaks often hear the latest gossip via their houses and not from their peers – this can lead to not so funny situations, when a quick e-mail to all housemasters concerned could calm the matter down. All boys now allowed mobile phones, though talking on them outwith the house is frowned upon, if not action is usually taken.

New poet in residence: the normally yellow PVC clad (in night clubs) Patience Agbabi. Chosen by the head for her 'raw vitality' and she has lines from her poems tattooed on her body. Keen on lesbianism and sado-masochism – or so says the Evening Standard.

Pastoral Care and Discipline: Broad-minded and liberal in principle, though quite capable of firing a pupil at a moment's notice for drugs offences, often to the consternation of parents. Drugs and booze and fags a perennial problem. If there is a suspicion that a pupil may be dabbling with drugs, then a 'more flexible' view is taken, to 'motivate' the pupil. Parents are informed and boy is subjected to lectures and random drugs testing. The idea, according to the head man is to 'turn around the drug culture'; this is not necessarily how it is perceived by housemasters and dames who may be involved. 'Not so much boozing' now, but 'smoking is still fairly prevalent'. Expect dismissal for repeat performances. Drunken boys are usually sobered up in house – with much love and care from housemaster and dame – other boys equally supportive. The alternative is an overnight stay in the local (extremely expensive) private hospital with stomach pumps et al. Immediate rustication thereafter, and not a lot of sympathy either. The most normal punishment is 'to go on the bill' – this involves a quick trip to the head man with a preposter (aka sixth former) within and without the head man's office. The former acts as watchman, and the latter as marshal. The only time a preposter is not used is in the case of bullying when the head man deals with suspected culprits on his own.

The most popular form of punishment – and here the range is from missing chapel to going AWOL – is early rising. Some pupils are never 'off the bill' and some are never on it. School takes exception to our comments that 'boys are allowed out on any Sunday', and indeed true that younger boys have to have some sort of permission in place, usually given by e-mail or fax, and on a fairly laissez-faire basis. But the King's Road in London heaves with Etonians of all shapes and sizes on any given Sunday, with boys in C having one extra weekend off in each half, B blockers two such indulgences. For those left at school though, there are masses of extra-curricular activities, choral, dramatic, what have you. The art and music schools are open, as well as the swimming pool, plus organised cross-country runs (strong house competition here) rowing, cricket, football, whatever. This is a school well provided with opportunities as well as the staff to run them, and house noticeboards bulge with info on rehearsals, debates, groups, matches (both inter-house, and friendlies), clubs and activities.

Pupils and Parents: Still the trad school it always was, with numbers of Old Etonian families in the ascendant again. The Fourth of June (aka school speech day) is still as buzzy as ever, with minibuses decanting lovelies from local girls' schools to join the baying throng of picnickers but (fortunately for the school), the mass of royal watchers have gone, and the hype has subsided. A huge mix of families, from scholarship boys in the remote Welsh valleys via a percentage of first time buyers to foreign princelings and the deeply grand.

Numerous notable Old Etonians: Hubert Parry, 19 Prime Ministers, Captain Oates, the poets Gray and Shelley, Keynes, Fielding. Surprisingly few real stars among the living; politicians (William Waldegrave, Nicholas Soames, Douglas Hurd, Boris Johnson) a clutch of journalists (Charles Moore, Nicholas Coleridge, Craig Brown) also Martin Taylor, Humphrey Lyttleton, Nicholas Charles Tyrwhitt Wheeler, Matthew Pinsent and Michael Chance; plus gaol birds: Jonathan Aitken and Darius Guppy amongst others. Successful old boys tend not to describe themselves as Old Etonians; preferring to describe themselves as 'having been at school'; as in 'there is no truth in the rumour that Jeffrey Archer was at school'.

Entrance: 700 candidates for 256 places; currently from 91 different prep schools. 'A record' says the tutor for admissions. New (as in not the trad put down at birth and forget about it regime) entry procedures appear to be working well. The head man has taken the new exam himself – 'I did pass, but did rather better in the oral part'. Boys do a combination of an interview and a multiple choice computer driven exercise and results are marked by five independent assessors who then spend two days discussing their findings. Prep school reports are important, and family background is taken into account when reaching the 'global mark'. It is important that a boy 'will thrive in a boarding environment', and be able to cope 'working under his own steam'.

Successful candidates then make their choice from a possible four houses – as each housemaster has a potential 13 year tenure, then the odds on actually getting the particular housemaster you opt for is higher than if you chose him when little Johnnie is two or three months old. So that's a bonus. Housemasters find the extra strain of these late interviews a bit of a bind, and sometimes reflect nostalgically on the days of the general list. School has taken to visiting prep schools, we think for the first time ever, to reassure them that Eton is still the place for their darlings. Prep schools to whom we have spoken report that yes, after the first year's blip, when school seemed to 'be choosing clever creatures without much oomph', procedure does seem to be working well, and the chaps who get in would mostly have been the chaps who got in under the old procedure. They did, however, express concern that Eton should be 'pleased with the results' when boys chosen by the new procedure have not yet gone right through the school.

Entries for King's Scholarships (14 per annum) accepted until the beginning of May for exam in May at 12/13+ (these scholarships may be up to 100 per cent, with school paying for uniform, and occasionally travelling expenses). Scholars still chosen by the examiners sitting as an electoral college, looking for imagination and enterprise as much as competence – hopeless Latin forgiven if maths superb, or vice versa. Past papers freely available from the school.

Up to four continuation scholarships (aka junior scholarships) for younger boys from state schools at 10, at which point Eton pays for three years' prep school education in trad Eton 'feeds' for successful candidates. Eight scholarships for state school pupils at sixth form – for the whole two years.

Exit: Average of 70+ boys to Oxbridge, though not all who might be Oxbridge material apply. 'Anyway, who would we meet there?' is a regular comment from potential Oxbridge scholars. Successful in organ scholarships to Oxbridge. Most go on to university, to Bristol, Exeter and Edinburgh in droves, plus over 70 different institutions in the UK, 10-15 annually abroad. The army is popular in some quarters (*pace* Prince Harry), and one or two fall through every net. Tranches of gap year. Thereafter the City, estate agencies, auction houses, journalism, family estates, politics.

Money Matters: Pots and pots of money and assets; it is said that Eton is funded not by fees but by rental income; popular sideline from films (The Madness of King George etc). Eton can afford to, and does, have everything of the best, and pays its staff very well indeed. Good value. Large number of bursaries etc for parents on hard times plus eight music scholarships year, plus countless exhibitions. The posh thing is to win a King's Scholarship and turn it down in favour of someone who needs it financially. The original Key Stage then has the (less important than ever) kudos of E marked against his name in the school house list, ditto for regularly coming tops in trials. Regular subsidised summer schools – rowing a popular option for prep school wannabes. Masses of public activity; the rowing lake is used nationally for training international rowers, and the new athletics hall and track are much in demand by locals. Eton is one of the few schools confident in its charitable status and, if it goes, they assume that parents will be able to pay the VAT on fees which is what the government is after.

Remarks: Still the number one boys' public school. The teaching and facilities are second to none. School was cross about our saying that it was 'a hard place to be for a boy who is neither one of the lads nor a gifted sportsman'; a quick survey of recent starry leavers thought, 'it must have been ghastly' for those whom they regarded as nonentities or nerds; the nonentities disagreed, saying 'that they had great fun', and 'wouldn't have been anywhere else for the world'.

FAIRLEY HOUSE SCHOOL

30 Causton Street, London, SW1P 4AU

Tel: 020 7976 5456

Fax: 020 7976 5905

Email: af@fairleyhouse.org.uk

Website: www.fairleyhouse.westminster.sch.uk

• Pupils: 130 boys and girls, all day • Ages: 5-13 • Religion: Inter-denom • Fees: £7,300 • School status: Independent • Opendays: Autumn term for parents and visiting professionals. Parents invited to tour the school throughout the year if they telephone for an appointment • School gender: Mixed • Day/boarding: Day pupils

SEN provision

Detail:

Now provide for in school:

Mild: ADD; DYSC; DYSL; DYSP; SpLD;

Moderate: ADD; DYSC; DYSL; DYSP; SpLD;

Severe: DYSC; DYSL; DYSP; SpLD;
Others: Sp&LD;
Experience of:
Mild: VI; CP;
Others: SPD; EAL; Epi;

Summary: Fairley House School has a whole school approach to specific learning difficulties for children from 5 to 13. Speech and language therapy and occupational therapy are fully integrated with children's education. All teachers hold a qualification in specific learning difficulties. The school's aim is to enhance children's literacy and numeracy skills and to teach them to compensate for their specific learning difficulties so that they can return to mainstream schooling after two to three years. We aim to raise children's self-esteem and confidence through nurturing children's talents and giving them a level playing field by offering them a peer group of other children with specific learning difficulties.

What we say about the school - the full Good Schools Guide review

Principal: Principal since 1997, Ms Jacqueline Patricia Murray BA MEd DipPsychol MSc RSA Dip SpLD (fifties). Educated at Rickmansworth Grammar and Sussex University (American studies), then studied in the US and the UK for teaching and special needs qualifications. Qualified as an educational psychologist at UCL in 2000. Worked as a teacher in the US and UK and ran the Watford Dyslexia Unit and trained teachers to teach dyslexic pupils at London University. Calm, measured, softly spoken, genuinely proud to be a key part of the school and keen to disseminate knowledge. Would love to see training courses run at Fairley House – 'we've been at it a long time and have built up a lot of expertise that we should be sharing.'

Academic Matters: Approximately 20 per cent of pupils in the junior department are statemented with majority paid for by their LEAs – many parents go to tribunal to secure a place, head will support if they have a good case – passionate that needy children have equal opportunities. Believes fervently in the right for a child to learn to read.

Parents very involved with school, standing room only at plays and performances. School is possibly unique in that it actively seeks to keep children for as short a time as possible. The aim is re-integration and inclusion in mainstream as soon as appropriate. Teaches the primary National Curriculum with emphasis on literacy including language extension (LEX) and numeracy. All study proper science, humanities, art, design technology, drama and games. No languages, but masses of multi-sensory activities. Good library; reading, study and social skills important. Feels like a normal primary school, evidence of all usual curriculum topics, from Vikings to Victorians, covering every conceivable display area. Art a strength, supported by arts week with artists in residence and trips to nearby Tate gallery. School say normality is important if the children are to be confident and included when they return to mainstream settings. Small amount of homework set most evenings.

Children are taught in classes of up to 12 but most are sub-divided. A lot of thought goes into groupings, they're not purely based on ability: 'we had a group of sports mad boys who weren't so keen on reading so their literacy group was led by the sports master – hey presto – motivation.' Other groups may be designed for identified input from the team of occupational therapists, speech and language therapists, the EP/principal or one of the specialist teachers. Support here isn't velcroed on, it's integral, effective and continual. Occupational therapists will work with children in PE and help children in the classroom acquire the necessary visual perceptual skills for reading and spelling as well as with gross and fine motor co-ordination, posture, handwriting etc. Speech and language therapists help link language development to the acquisition of skills in literacy which is re-assessed annually against baseline – very powerful, can show up to two years' progress. On-site assessments of sight and hearing by orthoptist and audiologist (and all leavers re-assessed by EP). Specialist facilities include adjustable desks to improve posture; coloured lenses, and use of coloured transparencies. Large computer room all networked, as are the photocopying machines. Laptops provided by the school for all who can touch-type (school teaches this using in-house programme).

Senior department caters for and teaches Key Stage 3 of the National Curriculum with German for all. Building not ideal for secondary curriculum but space is carefully planned and well used. There are four key teaching areas: English room, maths/science base, Art/DT area plus a larger room used for assembly, fencing, drama and music plus a library section. All rooms have a computer linked to the school's wireless network plus other gadgets including smartboard, e-beam, scanner and digital camera used by staff and pupils.

Exciting problem-solving activities link years 7 to 9; plenty of project based tasks and cross-curricular work eg maths class cooking when we visited. Clear marking policy ensures pupils know what's expected from work. Variety of teaching and learning strategies used – eg spellings supported by scanning exercises, word-search and dictation with kinaesthetic exercises acting as a memory trigger so knickers successfully used to teach 'kn' words. Lesson objectives are displayed, sometimes with key words and usually with a plenary session.

Pupils have a broad spectrum of specific learning difficulties ranging from problems with written language to those with motor planning, motor skills and co-ordination. Common factor is a marked discrepancy between potential and performance. School acts as a learning bridge useful for those who respond well to intense intervention for a short period, need help in becoming independent learners or seem too young for boarding school. Each pupil has a written individual education plan (IEP) review and meeting at the end of each term with pupil attending at least part of the meeting. Targets are suggested and comments amalgamated into the IEP for the forthcoming term. The special provision team reviews the pupils' needs termly and allocates provision. Speech and language therapy (SaLT), occupational therapy (OT) and special provision are available on a one-to-one or small group basis. Pupils are withdrawn from some lessons; aim to develop the pupils' skills, reducing extra provision as soon as appropriate, and moving to in-class support. Group sizes vary but 12 usually maximum, important that pupils can cope in larger classes. All grouped by ability for reading, literacy and maths. All are tested using standardised tests in literacy and maths. New pupils have a hearing and orthoptic screening. Use wireless laptops throughout the day and all learn to touch-type.

Games, Options, The Arts: Limited outdoor space at the junior department, so use Battersea Park for hockey, football and cricket, Latchmere leisure centre for netball and indoor games and the Queen Mother's Sports Centre for swimming. The school's large hall is used for PE, assembly, music and lunch (great emphasis on healthy eating – no E-numbers). Good selection of after school clubs, say 'it's important to give children what they need' so plenty of trips and visits too. House system and ample rewards encourage youngsters in all aspects of school life.

Senior department doesn't have own sports facilities either, other than a small hall used for fencing and Kung Fu but uses nearby Archbishops Park for football, basketball, rounders, cricket and tennis, gym next door for indoor PE and local swimming pool also used. Lovely artwork especially pottery (own kiln) and textiles. No instrumental lessons but all get a weekly group music lesson.

Background and Atmosphere: A CReSTeD category A school, founded 25 years ago by Daphne Hamilton Fairley, a speech and language therapist. Junior department at Lambeth Road (5 to 9-year-olds) and a senior department at Causton Street (9 to 13-year-olds). Junior started first, senior department opened in 2001 in a Grade 2 former Victorian school with its own separate head. Whole school now under one rule again.

This is a school that others look up to. Not cheap but offers value for money. Pupils from London and beyond, spend on average two to three years at the school – whatever is beneficial. Children come as young as six but the school profile broadens at nine and ten.

Lots of chatty children, many whose feeling of failure and floundering elsewhere has turned to pride and success here. Indeed school justifiably claims that no child has ever left Fairley without the ability not only to read but to do so with purpose and understanding. Children move on from here with heads held high and most achieve at least that nationally expected at the end of Key Stage 2, some do much better.

A caring and industrious environment where children develop a 'can do' attitude.

Pastoral Care and Discipline: A system of merits, demerits and detentions is supported by weekly assembly that celebrates achievement and termly prize giving. Letter sent home to anyone receiving ten demerits or five certificates of merit in a week. Use behaviour modification programmes if necessary to help combat any bullying or similar. Contact with parents is maintained through homework diary, the IEP and IEP reviews, reports, parent meetings and newsletters. Homework is often colour-coded to aid organisation with zero tolerance on un-attempted homework unless a written explanation from the parent is received.

All bring packed lunches, microwaves available, strict policy – ask parents to provide a balance of food types without preservatives, flavourings or colourings. Chilled water provided, fizzy drinks, sweets and chocolate are banned, not even allowed in pupil's bag for the journey home. Demerits and detention for offenders!

Selection of after school activities, clubs and homework sessions for those staying till 4.30pm. School Council has a small budget to spend each term with money used to buy fish for the pond, water cooler and make a donation to a favourite charity.

Pupils and Parents: From all over London and as far as St Albans. A genuine social mix from the titled to those on benefits.

Entrance: Entry, over two days, is by a serious and detailed assessment. It costs £650 but for that you'll get reports from an educational psychologist, a speech therapist, an occupational therapist – and most likely a place. Apply anytime; always have spaces for September.

Caters mainly for dyslexia/dyspraxia (but ADD, ADHD, Asperger's accepted if primary difficulty an SpLD), also take non-conventional learners who may have difficulties in mainstream. Latter tend to stay two years until problems fixed. Junior department takes children they think they can help. Basically need to have tried and not succeeded elsewhere – shouldn't be first port of call hence only take from 6. Find older children have more drive: 'they know what it's like to fail and it isn't a good feeling so they're more receptive to help.'

Prior to a visit existing reports should be forwarded to the school to ensure there will be some kind of fit as school isn't suitable for those with global learning difficulties. Each pupil will spend a day or two in school and will complete a screening assessment before a place is offered. Charged £650 for a full assessment, £350 for report from OT and SaLT. Looking for average or above IQ, both verbal and performance and a spark. Just under half have LEA statements and funding. Children must be able to cope with routine and structure.

Exit: Encourage children to leave as soon as they are ready. School very supportive of next move – appreciate it can be a real worry. Help parents make a guided choice via a general talk then as many individual appointments as necessary to ensure they get it right. Look at child's abilities, strengths, weaknesses, interests and the level of support needed. Children are prepared for entrance exams and interviews to next school – some receive several offers. Destinations for leavers from the junior department include Fairley House senior department, London day schools, or to boarding schools eg Millfield, Stanbridge Earls, Frewen, Sibford, Windlesham, St Christopher's, Bedgebury. From the senior department, Royal Russell, St Bede's, Portland Place, Stowe, Bradfield College, Bedgebury, The Moat are popular options.

Remarks: Children like warmth, support and smallness and say best bits are making good friends and not being bullied. Rebuilds shattered egos, develops confidence, equips majority for mainstream education and importantly it gives parents their child back.

Farleigh School

Red Rice, Andover, Hampshire, SP11 7PW

Tel: 01264 710 766

Fax: 01264 710 070

Email: office@farleighschool.co.uk

Website: www.farleighschool.com

• Pupils: 233 boys and 160 girls; 115 boarders (two-thirds boys, one-third girls), more weekly than full, 278 day pupils • Ages: 3-13 • Religion: RC • Fees: Boarding £5,325; day £4,075; flexible boarding £27.50 per night; pre-prep £2,240 • School status: Independent • Opendays: October • School gender: Mixed • Day/boarding: Takes boarders

SEN provision

Detail:

Centre of excellence for:
  Mild: DYSL; DYSP;
  Moderate: DYSL;
Now provide for in school:
  Mild: DYSC;
  Moderate: DYSP;
Experience of:
  Mild: ASP; AUT; ADD; ADHD; EBD; HI;
  Others: Sp&LD;

Summary: Due to the very nature of learning, all pupils require support at some time in their school life, whether it is educational, social or emotional. Support for our young learners includes literacy, numeracy, study skills, gross and fine motor skills, access to word processing and support with organisation. In school, the learning support team works with the staff, both individually and through INSET, so that they too feel informed and supported in working with all aspects of special educational needs.

Our provision of support for learning includes the use of educational psychologists, speech therapists, occupational therapists and child therapists who work in the areas of social and emotional development. An exciting new area for us is working to meet the needs of our able and gifted pupils.

The ISI inspection report of 2003 remarked 'The teaching within the learning support centre is excellent. It is highly skilled, well organised and appropriate to the needs of the pupils and is a major factor in the progress made by pupils.'

What we say about the school - the full Good Schools Guide review

Head: Since 2004, Father Simon Everson, a central figure in the school and still its resident chaplain. Father Simon Everson (rather unusually for an RC priest) resides on site with his wife and two children. The explanation is that he was formerly an Anglican vicar in an inner London parish, who subsequently converted to Catholicism. Fr Simon was ordained in Westminster Cathedral by the Archbishop of Westminster, accompanied by a party of 600 from the school, including parents. He teaches RE and PSHE, which includes sex education within the context of a loving relationship within marriage. Highly regarded by pupils and parents, both RC and otherwise. Took over suddenly as head following the abrupt departure of Mr John Alcott.

Entrance: To kindergarten at 3 and into the pre-prep at 5, both on non-selective basis. Assessment (not too rigorous) at 7 if coming from outside, plus reference from existing school. Oversubscribed in most years so priority given to RCs, boarders, siblings and children of former pupils. Presently 50 per cent RCs, who come from all over the country. Others come from London and local preps and primaries, mostly within a 25-mile radius. Boarding numbers holding steady.

Exit: To wide selection of prestigious schools, including, for the boys, Ampleforth, Eton, Downside, Sherborne, Radley, Harrow, Marlborough, Winchester and, for the girls, St Mary's Shaftesbury, St Mary's Ascot, Downe House, Marlborough, Godolphin and St Swithun's. About 10 per cent leave at 11, some to take up places at sought-after state grammars in nearby Salisbury (boys to Bishop Wordsworth and girls to South Wilts) and also girls to take up places at senior boarding schools. About 10 scholarships won per year.

Remarks: Appealing school with friendly, family atmosphere (lots of children of former pupils and many brothers and sisters) and good academic achievement. Formerly a boys' Catholic prep, now co-ed boarding with strong day element. Based in a lovely Georgian house in the Test Valley, full of light and surrounded by 60 acres of parkland with impressive cedar trees and woodland. Lovely, recently constructed kindergarten and pre-prep department and the former gym now houses a well-equipped theatre with tiered seating. A new art and design block was opened in April 2004 and an indoor heated swimming pool, located alongside the new sports hall, was opened in April 2005. The old outdoor swimming pool is still used by hardier boarders in the summer months.

A new junior boarding house for boys and girls aged 7 to 10. One boarding house for senior boys and one for senior girls, in dormitories, some parts of which have been sub-divided, nothing fancy but homely. Flexible boarding available with many day pupils requesting to board two to three nights per week, as a stepping stone to weekly boarding. Food 'really nice', according to the children, with popular fish and chips every Friday and themed suppers twice a term.

Academically very sound, with children proceeding to very well-respected senior schools. Excellence Board affixed to wall outside head's room to display outstanding work. Children setted according to ability in a gradual process over years 4 and 5. Average class size 16. Latin begins in year 6. Strong learning support with four fully qualified staff. Experience of most areas of learning difficulties, which include dyslexia, dyspraxia and mild social/communication difficulties. 68 pupils on the learning support register. Of those, approximately 20 pupils identified as gifted and able, and are catered for. A mature, stable, staff base, up-to-date with current thinking.

Mass is held every Thursday and Sunday morning and parents and locals are welcome in the lovely chapel. Grace said at all meal times. Fr Simon wants children at the school to have a strong awareness of their faith, but he stresses that all faiths are welcomed.

A feature of the school is its five GAs – the gap year students recruited on to the staff each year from the UK, Australia and South Africa. They act as older cousins to the children, supervising breaks, taking on boarding duties, running clubs and societies. These popular people live on site, together with 23 other resident staff.

Parents generally regard the school as sporty. 'Nearly every' child who wants to play for the school has the opportunity to do so, providing matches can be arranged with enough teams. Lots of emphasis on outdoor activities, not just sport. Making dens in the school woods, cycling, roller blades and scooters are very popular with the children and not something found at your average London prep. For the non-sporty children, there is a chance to excel at activities like public speaking, ICT, art and reading competitions. Mobile phones banned, as are electronic games.

Not many pupils from abroad, but school has traditional links with Spanish children from Madrid and Seville and there are usually a couple of pupils from there and about 10 overseas Brits. No local transport laid on, except for escorted train collections together with deliveries to Waterloo and airports for boarders. Parents mainly professional and managerial (lots with boarding experience themselves) – a very well-heeled, upmarket, bunch. Strong contingent of London parents and some Services families. A growing number are so taken by the Hampshire lifestyle, with its spaciousness and picturesque thatched villages that they sell up and move to the area, commuting to London on the 70-minute train journey from Andover to Waterloo. Good social life for local parents as well as the London ones – the Friends of Farleigh is a purely social association, which organises bonfire nights, fish and chip race evenings, Family Fun Day and so on. When we visited, a charity tennis tournament for parents was in full swing and well supported. Happy mums here, which make for a happy school. Notable Old Boys include the actor Rupert Everett (star of the 2002 film of 'The Importance of Being Earnest'), the journalist Craig Brown, Lords Stafford (pro-chancellor of Keele University), Hesketh (of Formula 1 racing fame) and Grantley, and Hugh Vyvyan, member of the England rugby squad.

FELSTED SCHOOL

Felsted, Great Dunmow, Essex, CM6 3LL

Tel: 01371 822 600

Fax: 01371 822 607

Email: info@felsted.org

Website: www.felsted.org

• Pupils: 450 boys and girls (around 40 per cent girls, 150 day and 290 boarders) • Ages: 13-18 • Religion: C of E • Fees: Boarders £6,847; day £5,124. (Prep day £1,179-£2,945) • School status: Independent • Opendays: October and May • School gender: Mixed • Day/boarding: Takes boarders

SEN provision

Detail:

Now provide for in school:

Mild: ADD; ADHD; EBD; DYSC; DYSL; DYSP; HI; VI;

Moderate: MLD;

Others: EAL; Sp&LD; DEL; Epi; PD;

Experience of:

Mild: ASP; AUT;

Others: ODD; GEN;

Summary: The ambition of the learning support department is to support and to develop pupils' learning so that they can achieve their full potential within the curriculum. This will be achieved mainly through one-to-one and small group work with some assistance in individual lessons. Pupils' difficulties will vary and so the level and nature of support given will reflect this. Pupils who are dyslexic or have a specific learning difficulty will follow specially devised courses in order to meet their particular needs. Pupils are screened for learning difficulties and a register is kept up-to-date to ensure that teaching staff are aware of the needs of the pupils they are teaching. Individual education plans are produced to assist pupils. When appropriate, assessment occurs so that pupils can qualify for extra time in public exams if deemed necessary. It is hoped that pupils will increasingly take responsibility for their learning and make use of the support this department offers as and when they require it.

What we say about the school - the full Good Schools Guide review

Head: Since 1993, Mr Stephen Roberts MA (mid forties). Educated at Mill Hill and University College, Oxford. Degree in physics. Formerly head of department and housemaster at Oundle. Spent an unfulfilling year as a credit analyst before switching to teaching. Friendly, chatty and approachable. Enjoys golf and reading when he has time. Married to Joanna, an occupational psychologist. Two teenage sons.

Academic Matters: Setting according to ability in core subjects from the beginning of year 9. French is a core subject, with a choice of Spanish or German as a second language; Latin to A level, Greek to GCSE. IT is integrated into all subjects, not taught separately. The International Baccalaureate is to be offered from September 2006 in addition to A levels; lower sixth pupils all attend a selection of four five-week courses to 'broaden their intellectual horizons and to complement their mainstream studies'. Exam results are impressive at GCSE, with around 95 per cent achieving C or above. A level results are good, particularly considering that the GCSE grade requirements for sixth formers are lower than those of many competing schools, and are improving year by year. Currently about 50 on the SEN register, the majority of them dyslexic. About 30 have extra time in exams. 'We provide extra support for those children who need it but the school isn't right for the severely dyslexic,' says the head. Full-time EAL support. Children with EAL take extra English instead of French in year 9. After that, language study is dependent on progress.

Games, Options, The Arts: Rugby, hockey, cricket and tennis for the boys; hockey, netball, tennis and rounders for the girls. Winners of Twenty/20 Cricket Schools Championship for two years running. Boys' and girls' hockey is strong. Plenty of other sports on offer as extra-curricular activities, including soccer, golf, squash and shooting. D of E and Combined Cadet Force. Many pupils involved in community service. Around 50 music scholars and many more taking music lessons. Regular overseas music tours and a recent tour of the USA with a theatre production. A 30-strong social committee ensures that there is no shortage of entertainment for boarders, particularly at the weekends.

Background and Atmosphere: Set in the rural Essex village of Felsted. Founded in 1564 by Richard, Lord Riche, Lord Chancellor of England, a villain who developed a social conscience after playing a part in the decapitation of Thomas More. A building dating from this time is still in use for music but the main building dates from 1860. Some grade I and II listed buildings. New additions, the latest being an extra boarding house for girls, are architecturally pleasing and fit well with the existing buildings. Extensive and well-kept grounds and an extremely pleasant environment. Girls came to the sixth form in 1971 but not to the rest of the school until 1993. Numbers grew fairly rapidly and Felsted feels like a proper co-ed school now.

Pastoral Care and Discipline: Strong house system with plenty of inter-house competitions. Parents choose their children's houses several years in advance. Eight boarding houses – five for boys and three for girls – with small dormitories and single rooms for everyone in their last year, if not before. Home-from-home atmosphere in the boarding houses, with house staff performing tasks beyond the call of duty – ie picking boarders' clothes up off the floor and putting them away. Many of the day pupils board several days a week, often because they want to take full advantage of the extra-curricular activities but 'a child won't feel second- rate as a day pupil,' says the head. Home boarding option (school day starts at 8.30am and ends at 9pm) also available. Pupils attend chapel three mornings a weeks, plus boarders attend on two out of three Sundays. Three grades of detention, with the most serious – and most effective deterrent – being the Saturday night detention.

Pupils and Parents: Pupils come from Essex (daily buses run from a number of Essex towns), Suffolk, Cambridgeshire, north London and Hertfordshire. A fair number from abroad, with around 50 speaking English as an additional language. The sixth form is particularly popular with Germans. Notable old pupils include theatre director Max Stafford-Clark, England cricketers Derek Pringle, John Stephenson and Nick Knight and architect Prof Sir Colin Wilson.

Entrance: CE for pupils from schools that prepare for the exam. The pass rate is 50 per cent, although around four or five pupils are taken on each year who don't quite make it. 'It would be absurd to put up a solid black line,' says the head. 'And usually those who don't make 50 per cent go on to achieve good A levels.' Entrance from schools that do not prepare for CE is by interview, VRQ test and confidential reference. Lots come in from Felsted Prep School – of a prep year group of 60, 50-55 will move on to the senior school. Holmwood House in Colchester also provides a significant number of pupils. Entrance to the sixth form is with five GCSEs at grade C or above.

Exit: All but a few go on to university. Five plus to Oxbridge per year.

Money Matters: An unspecified percentage of fee income goes towards bursaries and a variety of academic, music and art scholarships worth up to 50 per cent of the fees at 13 and 16. Scholarships also at 11 and some means-tested awards. Had around 80 assisted places (at last count). School does not have heavy endowments.

Remarks: Plenty to attract parents to this school whether they are looking for a day or boarding place for their offspring.

Feltonfleet School

Byfleet Road, Cobham, Surrey, KT11 1DR

Tel: 01932 862 264
Fax: 01932 860 280
Email: office@feltonfleet.co.uk
Website: www.feltonfleet.co.uk

• Pupils: 335 girls and boys. 40 weekly boarders, rest day. Nursery and pre-prep (Calvi House) 70 boys and girls • Ages: 7-13, pre-prep 3-7 • Religion: mainly C of E • Fees: nursery £1,296 (mornings only); pre-prep £2,424; main school £3,553; weekly boarding £4,964 • School status: Independent • Opendays: Saturday in October and February; during school day in May • School gender: Mixed • Day/boarding: Takes boarders

---

SEN provision

Detail:
Experience of:

Mild: ADD; ADHD; DYSC; DYSL; DYSP;
Moderate: DYSC; DYSL; DYSP;
Severe: DYSL;
Others: EAL; Sp&LD;

Summary: At Feltonfleet, we endeavour to provide for the individual learner. We have a full-time Head of SEN who works closely with the teaching staff, providing teachers with advice on planning and teaching through INSET and working to ensure that pupils with a specific learning difficulty (such as dyslexia) or with other educational needs are given the best opportunities to achieve their potential throughout the curriculum. The Head of SEN also supports sets in academic subjects as an additional teacher, thus keeping to small groups with ratios of on average 1 to 6. In addition to this, there is a full-time one-to-one specialist teacher based at Feltonfleet who teaches children with SpLD or other literacy difficulties. She incorporates multisensory teaching methods focusing on specific targets in her lessons during the school day. The Head of SEN ensures that all teachers are aware of the targets taught in these lessons and that they are used, where appropriate, in their own teaching objectives. A specialist teacher for children with English as an Additional Language is also part of the team and works on specific targets with them. Again, the Head of SEN ensures that these pupils are given every opportunity to develop their English across the curriculum by advising teachers and ensuring that teachers are aware of their targets.

What we say about the school - the full Good Schools Guide review

Head: Since 2000, Mr Philip Ward BEd (mid-forties, but looks younger). Educated at Reigate Grammar School and Exeter University. Spent 17 years at Uppingham (he is a huge fan) working his way up the ranks to senior housemaster. Married to Sue, who plays an active wife-of-the-headmaster role, as well as running junior department and having overall pastoral responsibility for girls. Two children – both of whom were pupils of Feltonfleet and now at Cranleigh. Clearly passionate about his school; a charismatic, family man who enjoys a chat. Full of energy, he says he wants 'fizzy-buzzy staff'- fresh faces and fresh approaches. Very approachable, 'cares greatly that this is a place where children feel at ease.'

Entrance: Waiting list for entry into pre-prep on a first-come-first-served basis – get names down early. Most join at age 7 into year 3; 18 from the pre-prep and about 30 from many feeder schools including Milbourne Lodge Junior, Wimbledon College Prep, Grantchester House, Emberhurst, Glenesk, the Hurlingham and Putney Park. Tested in English and maths but it's a 'gentle approach' to pupil evaluation. Head says they're looking for long-term commitment and potential, known as 'headmaster's eye test.' Entry possible higher up as odd gaps appear – always worth a try.

Exit: Mainly at 13 after Common Entrance. A few leave at 11. Leavers go all over the place: local schools Reeds Cobham, St George's Weybridge, St John's Leatherhead, Cranleigh and Epsom College get a chunk, but popularity goes in peaks and troughs. Increasingly to co-ed schools and weekly boarding is popular. Number of scholarships increasing – more to all round schools than to real academic hothouses.

Remarks: Family feel, love-of-life atmosphere, an incredibly energetic and sporty school. Suits active kids who like to be busy – as one parent says 'not for the child who needs stillness and down-time as pupils are always on the go.' Has come a long way in recent years and feels like it's still evolving.

Buildings centred on a large Edwardian house, hidden from view behind woodland and high fences. Centenary Building houses 'super-duper' new library and spacious classrooms for geography, history, French and Latin, networked wireless laptops and interactive whiteboards. Lots of space outside, well maintained and tidy, but the school is next to the A3 which gives a constant background hum to the otherwise peaceful surroundings.

Academic standards are high, but a broad range of children are accepted and it is not a school for parents who want hot-housing. Staff believe happy kids flourish – every class has a newly introduced 'circle time' to help build their self-esteem. Teachers are young and friendly, although the ever youthful Mr Ward says 'the average age of staff is 40 – we have several wise and energetic ones too.' Progressive style of teaching – mixture of few desks facing forward and desks in circles. School reckons that a variety of different teaching styles gives children more chances of success.

Average 16 children per class from year 3 upwards; setting in English and maths begins in year 3. From year 5, teaching is by subject specialists, with setting in French (starts in the nursery and very well taught) and science. Scholarship streams in year 7. School fully supports 11+, though one isolated parental comment that 'they do as much as they can to prepare for 11+, but are limited by majority continuing to CE.' Languages are strong. Spanish from year 6 introduced in 2004. Year 8 scholars do some Italian and Greek. Science, ICT and DT are together in a newly refurbished building.

Pupils with moderate learning disabilities welcome – about 38 children have support. School has full-time SENCo and team of peripatetic learning support staff. Also a Gifted and Talented co-ordinator.

Music has seen a revival under a new director. Own computer room where pupils experiment with melodies. Lots of positive changes, and loads of new music clubs including pop bands. 180 children learn a musical instrument and there's an annual Party in the Park every May. Drama also strong despite being taught in the old gym, and takes productions to The Edinburgh Festival. Art is on the way up.

Sport is an incredibly important part of a Feltonfleet child's life. There's a well-used covered swimming pool, a large leisure centre with two squash courts, a small astroturf pitch and loads of space for rugby, hockey, cricket etc. Matches every Wednesday in school hours. Girls have a super games mistress who also takes on role of 'big sister'. Lots of overseas tours and national tournaments. Girls strong in netball and hockey, boys in rugby. Squash scholarship to Millfield awarded in 2005. Head very involved with sport – he referees, runs golf and senior girls' tennis.

Massive choice of clubs: pupils encouraged to be busy. One parent felt too much is expected of their child – 'I get the impression they spend a lot of time dashing about.' Long school day with flexible finish times. Weekly boarding is part of the ethos – 25 boys and 15 girls. Boys and girls get along very well and mix at 'activity time'. Dorms are cosy and homely. New boarding master has built boarding up to a very high standard and there's a good feeling of closeness. Flexi-boarding also available for occasional use.

Pupils are a happy, active and lively bunch but boys outnumber girls by almost 3:1 – the effect of local competition. Some see this as an advantage – 'girls get lots of opportunities to play in teams because there are fewer to choose from.' – others do not. Head hopes that plans to extend the pre-prep will mean more girls moving up the school. Uniform guidelines are adhered to but a certain amount of individuality glimmers through.

Pupils get lots of praise and encouragement from staff, especially from the head who opens his doors to a queue of children every morning to show him good work for 'headmaster's initials.' Thumbs up from the parents for the school's pastoral care – 'it's a caring, nurturing and supportive environment.' Mix of parents, lots of first time buyers and professionals. Growing number from SW London. The school is perceived as full of moneyed souls – the usual convoy of suburban 4x4s does little to allay the perception. Plenty of parking for drop-off and pick-up but allow time in the morning to battle with the rush-hour congestion. School bus runs from Wimbledon and Cobham with more routes planned.

Filey School

Muston Road, Filey, North Yorkshire, YO14 0HG

Tel: 01723 512 354
Fax: 01723 512 165
Email: admin@filey.n-yorks.sch.uk
Website: www.filey.n-yorks.sch.uk

• Pupils: 780 boys and girls • Ages: 11-16
• Religion: Non-denom • School status: State
• School gender: Mixed • Day/boarding: Day pupils

SEN provision

Detail:
Now provide for in school:
Mild: AUT; ADD; ADHD; EBD; DYSC; DYSL; DYSP; HI; VI; CP;
Moderate: ADD; ADHD; EBD; MLD; DYSL; VI;
Severe: EBD; DYSL;
Others: CD; ODD; TIC; Sp&LD; Epi; PD; Eat;
Experience of:
Mild: ASP;
Moderate: DYSC; CP;
Others: OCD; EAL;

Summary: The school aims to create successful learning by providing curriculum access, giving equality of opportunity and developing the interests, abilities and aptitudes of all students, whether they have specific learning difficulties or they are gifted and talented. The SEN department consists of a well-established team of teachers and teaching assistants. Methods of support include in-class support, withdrawal, group activities at lunchtimes and one-to-one pastoral care. The school has introduced a teaching group dedicated to the vulnerable students in years 7 and 8. These groups are taught for the majority of their lessons in a home room by the same teacher and receive a high level of TA support and additional help with literacy, numeracy and social skills. Enrichment activities are available for gifted and talened students. We are fast developing alternative curriculum opportunities for Key Stage 4 students who wish to enhance their skills in a vocational capacity.

What we say about the school - the full Good Schools Guide review

Head: Since 2003, Mrs Lorraine Gill BA (Hull) (late forties). Twenty-five years a teacher, latterly as deputy head at Kelvin Hall School, Hull. Married, used to foster children. Extremely focused, mightily determined. Previously specialised in boosting under-performing schools. 'Here, I want to take a good school and turn it into an outstanding school. I'm going to complete my career here so it has to be right. It's my mission.' So, no pressure there, then.

Academic Matters: Awesome improvement in exam results. 2002 saw school's best ever GCSE results with 66.4 per cent of students achieving five or more A*-C grades, a 27 per cent increase over three years. Winner of Government's School Achievement Awards bonus scheme for three consecutive years, and dubbed 'Ofsted-on-Sea' by one national paper. Not bad for a true comprehensive – the only one serving the Filey area – with often a below-average ability intake despite excellent feeder schools. Special educational needs numbers often 20 per cent plus, partly because children with disrupted schooling move in and out of resort; does well by special needs students and just as well by the gifted. Gifted and talented co-ordinator nurtures students with special skills – academic, musical, sporting, whatever.

Under-achievement is spotted and dealt with, whichever side of the fence it falls. 'We have a rigorous programme of performance management,' says head. 'Myself and my deputies observe all our teachers, and samples of books and homework planners are seen on a regular basis.' Teachers are keen to start videoing their own lessons to see how they can improve. They are committed to becoming excellent. 'We touch and change people's lives and to me that's a sacred trust. I can't do with teachers who come in to this profession for bad reasons. They have to be on a mission. The students have to come first.' Now you know why she got the job.

Games, Options, The Arts: Good sporting achievement but thank the staff, not the facilities. It's not just the school that lacks a sports centre, it's the town. Head and community now working together on bid for sports centre funding. School also has the only community swimming pool, 30 years old and still open to the public. New music suite but as yet no adequate drama space. Usual hobby clubs. Accessible community education with facilities open 50 weeks of the year.

Background and Atmosphere: Built in the sixties, school's growing reputation and thriving population have seen numbers virtually double in 14 years. One minute you're in a science lab straight out of your childhood with roller blackboards and woodwork by Noah, the next you're in a state-of-the art IT suite. Schizophrenic, or what? The solution? Specialist technology college status, hopefully by October 2004, bringing a much-needed £1m investment. 'That doesn't mean technology at the expense of the rest of the curriculum,' assures Mrs Gill. 'We want to use the best of technology to enhance, say, drama and music. We want a 21st century school.'

Meanwhile, head stamps her mark on the school in ways all those little ways teenagers love. The word 'pupil' is out, 'student' is in – and that's how they're treated. Youngsters who once sat on the floor in assemblies now sit on chairs, the canteen – though still hopelessly too small – has been given the Ikea look, toilets are graffiti-free and Mrs Gill checks personally that the new soap dispensers are always full. She's fanatical about litter – and she's no time for teenage slouches. 'Come on, tuck your shirts in,' she says with a hint of good humour to some 16-year-old boys in the library. And they do. They don't even seem to mind. This is a school buzzing with good pupil/teacher rapport. No wonder they learn.

Pastoral Care and Discipline: School rules mercifully brief and standards of behaviour high. Isolated study, possibly with head, as ultimate deterrent for bad behaviour. Parents informed if pupils misbehave. 'Disturbances in lessons cannot go unchallenged,' Mrs Gill says. Well, hurrah to that.

We spring a visit on one class where the pupils are heads down working when we go in, polite when I address them, complimentary about the school. 'Some of our most challenging pupils are in that class,' Mrs Gill says later. You could have fooled us.

Pupils and Parents: Parents, desperate to secure children's future in an area hard-hit by fishing and farming decline, treasure school as a focal point in community. Good school/home links. 'Nothing is too much trouble,' says one parent. Head sets aside regular sessions when her door is open to any pupil for any reason. 'Well, they are my kids.'

Entrance: Same old story. Unless you live in catchment area, appealing for a place in this chock-full school is your only hope.

Exit: Two thirds go to sixth form or further education colleges in nearby Scarborough, most ultimately to university. Modern apprenticeships take much of the remainder.

Remarks: If it's gloss you're looking for, this is neither the school nor the town for you. What you see is what you get – good behaviour, good teaching, good results.

FINTON HOUSE SCHOOL

171 Trinity Road, London, SW17 7HL

Tel: 020 8682 0921

Fax: 020 8767 5017

Email: admissions@fintonhouse.org.uk

Website: www.fintonhouse.org.uk

• Pupils: 125 boys, 185 girls; all day • Ages: 4-11 • Religion: Non-denom • Fees: £2,900-£3,225 • School status: Independent • Opendays: First Wednesday in February • School gender: Mixed • Day/boarding: Day pupils

---

SEN provision

Detail:

Now provide for in school:

Mild: ASP; AUT; DS; DYSC; DYSL; DYSP; SpLD; HI; VI; CP;

Moderate: ASP; AUT; DS; MLD; DYSC; DYSL; DYSP; SpLD; HI; VI;

Severe: HI;

Others: SPD; GEN; Sp&LD;

Experience of:

Mild: ADD; EBD;

Moderate: ADD; ADHD; EBD; CP;

Others: CD; OCD; Epi;

Summary: At Finton House there is a Head of Special Needs who is responsible for co-ordinating and running the special needs department and representing the department at both Management and Governors meetings. There are two SENCos, one is responsible for the co-ordination and delivery of support to children on special needs places, who have a special needs assistant (LSA) assigned to them. The other SENCo is responsible for the co-ordination and management of learning support to children with specific learning difficulties.

Finton House has the provision to support a variety of children with special needs ie hearing or visual impairment, autistic spectrum – including Asperger's, speech and language difficulties, hemiplegia, Down's syndrome, dyspraxia, dyscalculia and dyslexia etc. There are currently one full-time and five part-time learning support teachers. Learning support is provided both one-to-one and free of charge in group sessions for mathematics, spelling, writing and reading comprehension. One learning support teacher provides support for both foundation stage and Key Stage 1 children, as part of our Early Years Intervention Programme. There is no charge for this support to parents. As well as learning support teachers, and assistants for specific children, there are currently two part-time therapists on the staff, an occupational therapist and speech and language therapist. There are both group and one-to-one speech and language sessions provided for specific children. Group speech and language sessions are free for Reception children.

Finton House provides a range of free clubs before and after school to support the specific needs of children eg touch-typing, Brain Gym, Early Birds, handwriting, maths and SRA (reading comprehension). There are also excellent links with Wandsworth Local Education Authority SEN division. They supply peripatetic teachers to meet the needs of specific children.

What we say about the school - the full Good Schools Guide review

Headmaster: Since 2005, Mr Adrian Floyd. Mr Floyd came from Newton Prep, where he was head of upper school. Previously had taught at Tower House, East Sheen, as head of English. Prior to working in London, taught at Summer Fields, Oxford.

Entrance: Much sought after. Non-selective first-come-first-served – put names down early. Places appear in later years, always worth checking – children very welcoming to newcomers. At least three special needs places per year for children with significant but not severe needs. LEA funding may be available for statemented children – very over-subscribed – following Ed Psych assessment places are offered to children with the greatest need that can be met by the school's resources. Siblings have priority. Comprehensive academic ability ranges from gifted and talented to SEN with some children appearing on both registers.

Exit: Some move to 'the country' before 11. A handful of boys leave at 8 for boys' prep schools: King's Wimbledon, Westminster Under, Northcote Lodge, Eaton House, Dulwich Prep, or go on to board at Summer Fields, Windlesham, Ludgrove etc. At 11, guided choice to wide variety of day and boarding schools: Putney High, Wimbledon High, JAGS, Alleyn's, Francis Holland, St Mary's, Ascot, Woldingham, Benenden, Dulwich, Wycombe Abbey etc.

Remarks: Caring, welcoming, environment with parent-friendly atmosphere. Children are local to smart Wandsworth. Smallish school accommodated in two handsome and well-proportioned Victorian houses sensitively adapted for school use. Light rooms – gym (doubles as dining hall), specialist science, art, ICT and DT rooms, purpose-built music block (plenty of extra-curricular music and opportunities to perform), good library, lots of stairs (would be difficult for children with physical disabilities). New, purpose-built reception block opened in autumn 2005. Decent sized playground packed with equipment including Wendy houses, friendship bench, climbing frame and much used barrels – great for rolling on and in. Plenty of sporting opportunities and regular successes in local competitions – inclusive policy means every child has the opportunity to represent the school in matches. All usual curriculum subjects offered including French from reception and Latin as a club.

School fizzes with enthusiastic youngsters – comfortable with adults, look you in the eye and clearly love school – 'it's fun and we do loads of sport' (fixtures from year 1). Respect for teachers (all called by first names prefixed with Miss or Mr) and sensitivity to each other are virtues to the fore. Interactive whiteboards, used by pupils and staff, add a new dimension to already sparky teaching and learning. Even assemblies were deemed great fun – 'especially the trust one where a teacher pretended to be late then ate cat food – which was actually mars bar and jelly.' School walls burst with fantastic displays of work by all pupils reflecting the very inclusive nature of the school. Plenty of theme days (India, Romans, Vikings ...) lots of project based work and trips throughout but especially for year 6 once exam pressure removed – 'it's important to educate in the broadest sense not just to pass exams,' insists the head.

This is not a special needs school but the school's team including speech and language, occupational therapists and special needs assistants (a staggering fourteen full-time and eight part-time) means that children with learning difficulties can be helped on site on a one-to-one basis (many schools claim this, few actually deliver). Some help is free but one-to-one specialist support outside the classroom incurs a cost – 'kept to absolute minimum, we don't want to make a profit out of SEN.' The head of special needs is assisted by two SENCos; one for the 10 per cent of children who arrive with more complex needs, the other for children with specific learning difficulties who may require monitoring or intervention. Cater for wide-ranging SEN: profoundly deaf (must have some form of communication), Down's, Asperger's, speech and language disorders, specific learning difficulties etc. An early intervention programme has been established to identify mainstream pupils who require additional support. Keen to stress all gain from having SEN children in the school and happily co-exist in a non-patronising environment where differences don't matter. Lots of clubs and activities: some such as brain gym target SEN, super siblings the brothers and sisters of children with SEN, others such as chess, football, dance, rugby for all. School stresses even the most able, outgoing and ebullient child needs nurturing and care.

Emphasis on inclusion, individuality and results without pressure is its forte.

Forres Sandle Manor School

Sandle Manor, Fordingbridge, Hampshire, SP6 1NS

Tel: 01425 653 181

Fax: 01425 655 676

Email: office@forressandlemanor.hants.sch.uk

Website: www.forressandlemanor.com

• Pupils: 290 boys and girls, 100 board • Ages: 3-13 • Religion: Broadly C of E • Fees: £5,280 boarding and £3,880 day • School status: Independent • School gender: Mixed • Day/boarding: Takes boarders

SEN provision

Detail:

Centre of excellence for:
- Mild: DYSL;
- Moderate: DYSL;

Now provide for in school:
- Mild: DYSC; DYSP;
- Moderate: DYSC; DYSP;

Experience of:
- Mild: ADD; ADHD; EBD;
- Moderate: ADD;
- Severe: DYSL; DYSP;
- Others: EAL;

Summary: The Learning Centre at Forres Sandle Manor provides support for up to forty children with identified specific learning difficulties with literacy or with mathematics. The level of difficulty ranges from mild to severe. Teaching is one-to-one or in small groups depending on the need of the child. Children coming to the centre must be able to cope with the intellectual demands of a mainstream prep school although a great deal of support is put in place. In addition, we have a fully qualified specialist teacher who supports children within the class. These may be children whose problems are very mild and they only require a 'boost' or they may be children within the centre who require support within the class in order to access the curriculum. We liaise closely with Senior Schools so that the child's transition is a smooth one and we aim to ensure that the appropriate support will be in place. All children participate in Common Entrance examinations although, occasionally, these are modified in agreement with the Senior School. We believe that when children are happy and achieve, their learning differences should not be a barrier to their success.

What we say about the school - the full Good Schools Guide review

Head: Since 1988, Mr Dick Moore (late forties). Headed Forres from 1988-93, then oversaw the fusion with Sandle Manor, now FSM in quickspeak. Educated at Cranleigh, where he returned after sociology at Durham to be housemaster and director of rugby. There's nothing recycled about him, though – here's where he learned how it could be done better. Anything but hidebound – 'nothing is set in stone', he says. Change, here, is always afoot, not the sea-change sort, more the fine-tuning variety, but enough, perhaps, to unsettle some parents. Married to Sheena, astrophysicist, hers is the still, small voice to his earthquake, wind and fire. She superintends the children's well-being in everything from food to boarding. An impressive partnership of complementary attributes. Four sons, 20 to 12.

Entrance: Most at age 3 or 8. Boarders at 8 only 'if the headmaster is satisfied that the child wishes to board'. Non-selective and they get the full rainbow. The superb learning centre for those with SENs is a draw. Day children bypass perfectly good schools in a 25-mile radius – Winchester, Poole, Salisbury. A good crowd from the New Forest, Avon valley and environs of Cranborne. Boarders a 50-50 mix of expats, mostly Services and locals. Around 50 per cent of parents first time buyers. Geography is against ethnic mix but there's always a wodge of migratory Norwegians (a quirky historic link) and a handful of Spaniards. Start when you like, if there's room. Lists of day children wishing to convert to boarding run to 2011 and rising. No schols or bursaries, but 10 per cent off for Services' children.

Exit: Canford's a staple. Then comes the full gamut of locals – the Sherbornes, Bryanston, Marlborough, Blundells, Millfield, Wells. For the less conventionally academic, Milton Abbey, Clayesmore, Grenville. Impressive numbers of schols in everything. 80 per cent stay to 13. At 11, 20 per cent to single-sex girls, grammars or comp. Eminent outcomes: Michael Foot (Forres), Alec Guinness (Sandle Manor).

Remarks: It feels good and it looks good – the Jacobean manor, the bosky grounds, the engorged rhododendrons – but reality matches it. The educational idea is simple enough – children thrive when they feel good about themselves. This is the exclusive focus and all achievements are reckoned a by-product. No SATs. Parents don't call for regular benchmarking 'because they trust the school'. Expectations must be high because academic results are boast-worthy and rising. Annual Headmaster's Prize to each year group for the child who has worked the hardest.

The school does not apply a play-safe policy to staff appointments, preferring passion, character and kindness. Teachers must be 'up for it'. Plenty of that. Rob Harvey, avant-garde music teacher, has the children playing fruit – even bicycles. Lots of new young faces and a reassuring leavening of wise ones.

The flagship learning centre for children with information processing difficulties – average to above-average IQs only – has no whiff of casualty about it. The brightest are tweaked there, too, and none are hived off: it is integral to mainstream learning, and the techniques in use have pervaded all classrooms. Teaching methods accord with up-to-the-minute thinking. Impressively led. The children rate attendance enviable.

Boarding is well done and a matter of some vanity. Over half the 7-13s do it. The secret lies in the supervision – there are always from 7 to 10 adults on duty and 10 sleep in the main building. Rooms are amusingly painted in colours children delight in. Plenty to do, Wednesday fun evenings the biggest hit. Always around 50 in at weekends, and rising. Genuinely humane. Parents say the children look after each other. Sports facilities are adequate. All-weather pitch coming soon. Heated outdoor pool.

For all the equal emphasis on everything, music is transcendent under the inspirational Dave Andrews. Here, democracy of opportunity defers to a little light elitism and the less able are less indulged. They do the lot, from hip-hop to holiness. We heard the jazz band (breath-stopping) and delighted in the number of girls playing sassy brass. More than three quarters learn an instrument and they perform, perform, perform. Ensembles of everything and choirs too. Demand the CD with your prospectus pack.

FSM is an un-snobby, unselfconscious school apparently too busy to bother with narcissistic PR or bigging itself up, which it could frankly do more of. Manners work on a democracy of respect basis, with the staff reciprocally holding doors open for children. Discipline is intelligent – errant year 8 children may be despatched to devise their own punishment. Discipline extends to parents, too. Strict rules of courtesy and self-restraint govern their conduct at sports events. The excellent parents' handbook both informs and requires – with no shred of bossiness or hauteur. The children themselves are delightfully at ease with everyone – we recall three slightly smudged girls out sketching – but live, reassuringly, in a child's world. Parents tell us they always feel welcome and listened to. Those whose children had problems say they were dealt with quickly and expertly.

This is a school where, clearly, most of the children and staff have a lot of fun most of the time but the philosophy of fun is underpinned by strong seriousness and rigour. Parents who prefer FSM do so over schools they reckon 'too precious' – the sort where toil is tightly focused. The prospectus and website give you the flavour of the place and act as an effective filter. Take it from there.

FORTISMERE SCHOOL

South Wing, Tetherdown, Muswell Hill, London, N10 1NE

Tel: 020 8365 4400
Fax: 020 8444 7822
Email: anixon@fortismere.haringey.sch.uk
Website: www.fortismere.haringey.sch.uk

• Pupils: 1,651 boys and girls; all day • Ages: 11-19
• Religion: Non-denom • School status: State
• School gender: Mixed • Day/boarding: Day pupils

SEN provision

Detail:
Centre of excellence for:
Mild: HI;
Moderate: DYSL; HI;
Severe: HI;

Summary: No comment. Light firmly under bushel – but quite a bright light, in the opinion of the GSG. SEN details added by us.

What we say about the school - the full Good Schools Guide review

Head: Since 2005, Mr David Jones has been acting head while consultants seek a new head 'for up to £100k'.

Academic Matters: This is a comprehensive, but has more than its fair share of bright children (it is, after all, at the top of middle class, liberal, intellectual Muswell Hill). It also has a number at the lower end of the academic spectrum but relatively few middle-of-the-roaders. Not overtly pushy, it does well by its intake, with a respectable 80 per cent or so of pupils getting five A-Cs at GCSE. Art, English, mathematics, science and history are particularly strong and popular at GCSE and A level; Spanish is improving; ditto IT, due largely to a reorganisation and re-staffing of both departments, plus a considerable investment in the learning resources centre so everyone has easy access to computers. There are 50 interactive whiteboards in the school.

French, German and Spanish are all taught to A level; each pupil is allocated to a language group in year 7. ('Of course nearly everyone wants to learn French, so people do tend to feel disgruntled if they're given German or Spanish,' commented a parent. 'And they deliberately don't let you learn a language if you've already got experience of it.') Two thirds now take up a second language in year 9; an accelerated learning programme is available only to particularly able linguists. 27 A level options, including business studies, drama, economics, media studies, philosophy, performing arts, physical education, psychology and photography, plus some GNVQs.

Although this is a technology college (and has smart labs and DT rooms to show for the extra funds), there is no particular technological emphasis. 'It is my pride and joy that they all get a fully rounded education up to GCSE.' But the school does run a Neighbourhood Engineers scheme, which sees older pupils working on projects with companies like Arup. 'We've made engineering really fashionable – it's no longer seen as a blue collar activity. It now has the cachet it has in countries like Germany and Switzerland.' Pupils have also worked with Interbrand, whose founder is now on the governing body, and whose aim is to put the design world in touch with the education world.

Money from the government's Excellence in Cities programme – 'the best bit of government policy there is – it recognises the extra challenges of inner cities and gives them extra money to cope' – funds two learning mentors, who mostly do outreach work with families and counsel children on a one-to-one basis. Part of the project is to encourage youngsters from non-academic backgrounds to stay on to the sixth form and go to university. The money also funds curriculum extension work and extra-curricular activities as part of the government's gifted and talented programme. These are available to everyone, though high-achievers are particularly encouraged to take part. 'Extras can benefit everyone. You need to make sure you're not selling anyone short.'

This is an inclusive school and the teaching is as mixed ability as it can manage, though maths is setted from year 8 and modern languages from year 9. 'Our intake is skewed towards the top end and these bright, motivated pupils help to pull up the tail end – they encourage the less motivated to do their best. You have to take each child as you find them, get to know them inside out, set appropriate targets and go for it in a big way.' Some parents are less than totally convinced about mixed ability teaching – 'my son has expressed frustration about the influence of disruptive pupils in a couple of science subjects. But he did two science papers early and got As in both of them, so the teaching is obviously good.'

Effective special needs department – 'we've cornered the north London market in dyslexia'. On site, and part of the rebuilding programme, is the secondary department of the Blanche Nevile School for deaf and hearing-impaired children. These pupils are integrated into the main school for anything from 5 to 95 per cent of the time.

Games, Options, The Arts: Enviably for a London school, Fortismere has a 20-acre site which includes three football pitches, cricket pitch and outdoor swimming pool, as well as a sports hall and gym, a dance studio and seven tennis courts. Football, tennis and athletics particularly strong. It runs endless clubs and teams, down to C teams, 'so even if you're not that good you can still join in,' said a pupil approvingly. There's a full Saturday mornings sports programme. Fortismere was awarded the Sports Mark in 2003. Art, as mentioned before, is extremely strong, with excellent results. 'It's stunning,' said a parent. 'The children take it very seriously and work very hard.' Drama, dance and music are all taken seriously; there are three choirs, a string quartet, steel band, jazz band and orchestra. 'The jazz is wonderful,' said a parent. Music students have visited Prague and Beijing. On the head's wish list is a new performing arts building.

Background and Atmosphere: Bracing hill-top site amidst leafy Muswell Hill Edwardiana. An amalgamation of a grammar school and a secondary modern in 1967, the school mirrors the history of secondary education in Haringey. It has two wings, joined by a quarter-mile pathway round the playing fields – 'in the depths of winter, in the midst of a hailstorm, it's like being out in the North Sea,' says the head. A rebuilding programme completed 2003/4 funded by the government's private finance initiative scheme. This is providing a library/learning resource centre, four new labs, food technology rooms, the all-weather pitches and new tennis courts. No uniform, relaxed atmosphere.

Pastoral Care and Discipline: Each class keeps its form tutor and head of year for five years (staff turnover permitting), – 'it is nice to have the continuity in such a big school,' said a parent. Bullying is mostly dealt with well, with disruptive behaviour kept in check. Good home-school communication, and accessible teachers. A parent commented, 'there's very little for the children to rebel against – with no uniform, and very basic rules. And it works, partly because the parents of the majority are very proactive at home.'

Pupils and Parents: 'It's a good reflection of what I'd describe as a balanced society,' said a parent. 'It's very multi-cultural, very multi-ethnic, with a good solid base.' Plenty of middle class professional and creative types from the surrounding leafy streets (many of whom moved there with Fortismere in mind), plus a good number from less affluent parts. 'One big advantage of the school is that I know all my son's friends, because they nearly all live nearby. They can walk to school and to each other's houses, which is brilliant for their independence. And they're all very nice kids.'

Entrance: After special needs and siblings, preference goes to those living nearest as the crow flies. In practice, the catchment area is about a mile. Although technology colleges are allowed to select 10 per cent, Fortismere does not do so – 'my governors would never select by aptitude. We believe very strongly in inclusiveness.' All year 11 students get the opportunity to move up to the sixth form and are joined by about 50 new students, from independent as well as state schools. Those wanting to do A levels need a minimum of five A*-C grades at GCSE.

Exit: About 80 per cent go on to higher education, mostly the traditional universities, including three or four a year to Oxbridge.

Money Matters: Technology college status has brought extra funds for improvements, as has refurbishment under the council's private finance initiative scheme. This is a comfortable area with a high proportion of professional families, many of whom are enthusiastic fund-raisers.

Remarks: One of the successful genuine comprehensives that put a premium on the prices of nearby houses. Excellent facilities, an inclusive ethos and highly creditable exam results. 'My kids might have been pushed slightly harder at a selective school,' said a parent. 'But here they get an excellent balance and recognise the broader range of society. It's a lovely school.'

Framlingham College

Framlingham, Woodbridge, Suffolk, IP13 9EY

Tel: 01728 723 789

Fax: 01728 724 546

Email: admissions@framcollege.co.uk

Website: www.framlingham.suffolk.sch.uk

• Pupils: 274 boys, 153 girls; 304 board, 123 day

• Ages: 13-18 • Religion: C of E - Inter-denom

• Fees: Day: £1,740- £3,026 Brandeston Hall and £3,967 Framlingham College per term. Boarding: £4,866 (BH) and £6,172 (FC) • School status: Independent

• Opendays: Late Jan, May and early October

• School gender: Mixed • Day/boarding: Takes boarders

What we say about the school - the full Good Schools Guide review

Head: Since 1994, Mrs Gwen Randall BA, early fifties, husband retired, budding barrister daughter. Read French at Bristol University, was head of modern languages and drama at St Mary's, Calne, then deputy head of Dauntsey's, before setting about, with enormous energy and considerable publicity, transforming and modernising the college. A very lively person, completely open about the downs as well as the ups, much in love with the school and excited about future plans. Describes herself as 'one of the pithier backbenchers at HMC.'

Academic Matters: A well performing school at both GCSE and A level, not amongst the highest fliers, but nowadays more top than bottom heavy. Prides itself on catering well for the whole ability range. Provision for ESL and learning support is excellent, with a separate suite of rooms and a lovely atmosphere. Facilities in general, for such a large, rambling place, are very sensibly thought out, business-like and well-equipped. This is very much due to Mrs Randall's excellent eye for maximisation of space, of which the superb split-level library is a prime example. Class sizes are small, with rooms deliberately designed to hold no more than 22. Maths very strong through to A level; Design & Technology department is stunning and produces quite exceptional work.

Games, Options, The Arts: Sport clearly of major importance (there is a fine new indoor pool) and highly successful but the head makes a point of musical and academic achievement featuring strongly in inter-house competition. Drama is immensely popular -quite a few pupils go on to RADA and the like – with frequent first-rate performances. Lots of concerts too and exciting plans afoot for the updating of the theatre. Endless interesting leisure activities. Radio enthusiasts have their own room bursting with equipment.

Background and Atmosphere: College founded in 1864 with rather austere Victorian main building. Beautiful setting, perched on a hillside with a gorgeous view across the valley to Framlingham castle. Everything beautifully kept, including 50 acres of playing fields. A woman's hand at the helm has helped to give a greater sense of light and cohesion to what was a bit of a hotch-potch. Boarding facilities are pleasant enough and have certainly come a long way since the best boast of a (very) early prospectus that, 'each boy has a separate bed.' The school is enviably tidy and well-organised. Relaxed politeness the order of the day for relationships between staff and pupils and the atmosphere is tangibly unpressured but businesslike. Some very nice touches, like the airy central meeting hall, where pupils can gather and chat, currently being extended into a charming outside piazza.

Pastoral Care and Discipline: A major change has been the abolition of day houses and the absorption of day pupils into boarding houses, where they have desks and can sleep over in boarders' rooms; clearly a good move, as now the tutor system looks after day pupils and boarders with complete even-handedness. Prefects are carefully trained (the top ones do a week's residential leadership course) and given plenty of responsibility. Open discussion of problems such as bullying is encouraged and prevalent. Occasional cannabis experimenters are given a second chance but not one has ever re-offended. Discipline in general is good – a calm atmosphere prevails.

Pupils and Parents: Pupils are drawn largely from middle class East Anglian families, although there is a largish contingent of students from abroad including numbers of German students who come for one year in the sixth form and frequently stay for two. Most integrate seamlessly into the school. The college is highly thought of locally. No problems recruiting on any front.

Entrance: Most applicants and Brandeston Hall pupils accepted but only if the head considers they will cope. Big influx into the sixth form (dependent on GCSE results), where virtually all subject combinations are accepted.

Exit: Most to university, with a fair smattering of Oxbridge

Money Matters: Head says she likes to balance the books and give value for money and has worked small miracles on the site. One coup in 1999, when she changed the 'scruffy' uniform, now remarkably tidy (including the sixth form who all, boys and girls, wear suits), was to give every pupil a free set! Good number of scholarships of all sorts, reductions for siblings.

Remarks: Very pleasant, well-ordered school which bears the stamp of a lively, charismatic head. When she came she saw 'pockets of excellence in a sea of despair.' No sign of despair now.

Freemantles School

Pyrcroft Road, Chertsey, Surrey, KT16 9ER

Tel: 01932 563 460

Fax: 01932 569 679

Email: info@freemantles.surrey.sch.uk

Website: www.freemantles.surrey.sch.uk

• Pupils: 86 pupils: 16 girls 70 boys (94 from September 05) • Ages: 4- 15, will eventually take children from 4-19 following a site move • School status: State • School gender: Mixed • Day/boarding: Day pupils

SEN provision

Detail:

Centre of excellence for:

Mild: AUT;

Moderate: ASP; AUT;

Severe: ASP; AUT; ADD; ADHD;

Others: AUT(other); SLD; Sp&LD;

Summary: Freemantles is a local authority day school for pupils with autistic spectrum disorder. We take children mainly from NW and NE of Surrey.

We are gradually increasing our age range and will be moving to a new site to accommodate pupils from rising 5-19. We will also have a residential facility for 24 children.

We use TEACCH and PECS as well as many other strategies to support the development of our students and have a maximum of eight students in a group with an average ratio of one adult to two students.

What we say about the school - the full Good Schools Guide review

Head: Since 1987 Ms Ruth Buchan BA Dip EBD. Previously taught in primary and secondary mainstream, in special schools and in a child guidance clinic and tutorial class in Surrey and London. Sensitive, professional, compassionate. Believes autism is fascinating and that it's essential to be receptive to new ideas and to try to keep a step ahead. Has huge respect for parents, their motivation and way they're willing to be open and pool their ideas. Study teeming with photos of pupils, samples of their work and heart-warming letters. Parents say it's such a loving, caring school and that head 'knows every child, could work with the diplomatic service, always makes you feel positive, has a fantastic knack of getting to the real problem and a ready supply of tissues.'

Academic Matters: Maximum class size 8. Every class has a qualified teacher, welfare assistant and classroom assistant so majority have one staff member to two pupils with staff rotating between groups. Each classroom has a play area (common room in senior school), workstations and quiet/relaxation area, plus life-skills area in Key Stage 3/4 rooms. Some have wonderful wall displays others deliberately minimalist to avoid over-stimulation. Specialist facilities include a soft-play room, hydrotherapy pool, art, music, occupational and speech therapy rooms, laundry, small library and different well-equipped playgrounds for the Key Stages. Pupils are carefully grouped within each of the Key Stages with changes made if necessary. Pupils follow the National Curriculum with particular emphasis on PSHE, behaviour and communication plus conversational and food based French for older children. All children, including those with good verbal communication, start out using PECs, at home and throughout school even in lunch, with varying degrees of dependency. Good resources – mix of commercial and in-house; needed age appropriate literacy materials for older children and wanted them to have access to National Curriculum so have re-written parts of texts and put in PECS. All have a visual timetable of the day and match colours to work trays to encourage independence. Some pupils work solely one-to-one but aim is always to encourage group participation. If a child isn't going to be able to manage group work a move to another school may be in child's best interests.

Sensory curriculum very important – we saw a super sensory cookery lesson involving smells, sounds, textures, grating, blending, mixing etc. Individual education plans (IEPs), behaviour drills, target setting and reflections are integral to both the pastoral and the academic. Good home school communication vital – each child has a home school book and a visual/sensory scrapbook completed at weekends and in the holidays to show what they've been doing – lots of photos (thank goodness for digital cameras) but also the tactile – sand, hair, jigsaws, carrier bags. Speech therapists available daily, work both in classes and one-to-one with teachers continuing any agreed programmes. Senior school developing – eventually take children up to age 19, have year 10 from Sept, older pupils will follow ASDAN accredited courses plus others as appropriate.

Games, Options, The Arts: Music a strength of the school with some music therapy funded by friends of Freemantles; lots of lovely examples of teacher-led art brighten the corridors, and range of sporting opportunities – swimming at the local pool, sailing, football etc – plus weekly outing, ranging from a shopping trip to culture at the British Museum, ensure pupils get lots of inclusive, mainstream type activities. Residential trips – sailing, skiing, camping with the scouts, staying in the school's caravans – play an important part in social development, give parents a break and help staff to be like parents: 'without that experience we could be quite condemning.' School is about the whole family so opportunities for siblings too including a sibling sailing weekend, fun days etc.

Background and Atmosphere: School founded 32 years ago in a tiny cottage hospital with approximately 20 children. Moved to current site in 1996 now very much at capacity and reaching its sell-by date – hope for new building, planning permission granted, site identified and school designed but now has to go before a public enquiry – school remains optimistic of getting green light. New premises will have residential respite centre for 24 children run in conjunction with social services on a needs basis in term times with opportunity for those outside of the school to use the provision at weekends and in the holidays. Impact on parents and family life never underestimated – 'autism doesn't go away, it affects every aspect of family life – parents often have to give up work, holidays, their social life; we try to ensure they can have some fun too.' School employs two outreach teachers and runs lots of training courses for professionals, parents and support staff (stacks on their website too).

Pastoral Care and Discipline: Cares about what is in the child's best interests. Celebration wall – everything from licking an ice-lolly to success in numeracy skills recognises achievements. Good eye contact and behaviour constantly praised with parents encouraged to support rewards, individual to the pupil, at home. Reflections session held at the end of each day to discuss daily target, how did you feel or what worked well. If target achieved (some learning, some PSHE) then move closer to bull's-eye on target board. Staff phone parents if there are any worries and talk through reasons with the family and child. Have target ladders for longer term goals. Where possible, children are included in mainstream or specialist Learning Difficulties (LD) schools – gives experience of being in a large classroom, of fending for themselves and being sociable.

School happy to help host birthday parties in school or out (ten-pin bowling etc) – reduces the stress for parents and allows children to be on familiar territory. Lunch (lots of different diets) and play seen as important opportunities for the children to let off steam and practise social skills. School supportive of the whole family, hosts parent groups, activities and conferences, works with siblings and runs an Asperger's group after school for children in mainstream who may benefit from additional support.

Pupils and Parents: Majority from the NW and NE of Surrey LEA.

Entrance: All children have statements of SEN for autistic spectrum disorders, some children have associated problems – epilepsy, SLD, ADD etc. Surrey LEA put together two panels (one meets in Nov the other in March) of schools and units that have provision for ASD/SCD pupils. Has a reputation for taking a wide range of ability and working hard for all including the most troubled. Panel considers all appropriate children and places them in the most suitable provision. Consider reception and year 1 at one panel and secondary age and years 2 to 6 at the other. High demand for places, parents of ASD children known to move into the catchment area to try to get a place.

Exit: At 11 to Surrey special schools including The Park, Carwarden House Community School, The Ridgeway, West Hill and The Abbey, some to boarding, though many now stay on to own secondary school. Not many to mainstream, keep tabs on those who do via outreach team which supports mainstream and other special schools. No senior leavers as yet but dialogue engaged in with local colleges to ensure those who eventually leave will be well catered for.

Money Matters: Friends of Freemantles raise money to support and run the school mini-buses, music therapy caravans etc. Otherwise funding through LEA.

Remarks: Parents say school amply fulfils its aim of finding a twinkle in each child and demonstrating it. A lovely, caring school – not only nurtures the child but helps and supports the whole family unit.

FRENSHAM HEIGHTS SCHOOL

Rowledge, Farnham, Surrey, GU10 4EA

Tel: 01252 792561

Fax: 01252 794 335

Email: headmaster@frensham-heights.org.uk

Website: www.frensham-heights.org.uk

• Pupils: 480, roughly 50/50 boys and girls; Boarding from 11 (37 per cent board, 62 per cent in sixth form) • Ages: 11-18, juniors 3-11 • Religion: Non-denom • Fees: First school: £1,480-£2,220. Lower school: £2,220-£3,920; boarding £6,040. Upper school: day: £4,130; boarding £6,250 • School status: Independent • Opendays: Five each year - see website • School gender: Mixed • Day/boarding: Takes boarders

SEN provision

Detail:

Now provide for in school:

Mild: DYSL; DYSP;

Experience of:

Mild: ADD; ADHD; DYSC;

Others: EAL; Sp&LD;

Summary: Frensham Heights provides group lessons from year 1 for those considered to have mild learning difficulties. These lessons not only offer support but enable the teacher to monitor individual progress. From year 7 the school uses a diagnostic test to assess the learning needs of all pupils and this is then influential on how lessons are planned and how those with IEPs are managed. Frensham Heights does not have a Special Needs Unit, our provision is managed by a head of learning support working with a team of peripatetic specialist teachers who provide support on a one-to-one basis but this is charged separately.

What we say about the school - the full Good Schools Guide review

Headmaster: Since 2004, Mr Andrew Fisher BA MA (forties), educated at Geelong Grammar in Australia (where his father was headmaster) followed by the University of New South Wales (history and Eng lit) and a masters in education management at Sheffield. Comes from Wrekin College in Shropshire, where he rose through the ranks to become deputy head. Married to Catherine, with two young children who are not in the school: 'as the son of a head, grandson of a head and nephew of a head I realise that they must have a bit of a life outside school'. Teaches 14-year-olds, 'loves teaching', 'children only get one chance', 'school should be the best experience they ever have', 'students should get the chance to make mistakes'.

Recently appointed deputy head academic whose job it is to 'ensure that all pupils fulfil their potential – not with the eye to any league table but with an eye to them not wasting their own time, other pupils' time or their parents' money.' 'Several got quite a bump when Andrew did as he said he would and did not allow them up into the next year as they had not worked hard enough. It has had a remarkably salutary effect'. Head is, nonetheless, delighted to be fronting this seriously artistic school, but keen on rugby and cricket too, so watch out for a slight change in emphasis.

Personable and fun, some pupils are still slightly wary of Andrew (this is a first name school): those who have regular contact were reassuring: 'he's OK' (highest form of praise). 'You can hear him whistling in the morning', but not apparently later in the day. Suspects that he is probably a people's person rather than a builder.

Predecessor, Peter de Voil, went to head The English College in Prague.

Academic Matters: Average class size 17. Not the best collection of A levels we have ever seen, but that's not really what this school is about. Fair number of As in German, French and Chinese, but Eng lang and lit scoring more Bs and Cs in GCSE, and ditto at A level recently. Science and maths strongest, history OK. Two of: drama, dance, music, art, ceramics, DT required at GCSE, the first by far the most popular. Vast range of different and busy A levels: photography, PE new additions. Setting in maths and science but not other subjects to avoid labelling perennial slow-streamers. 100 plus pupils receive support for mild specific learning difficulties, and virtually all get extra tuition. Parents interested in personal development, not league tables. No classics. No RE after age 14 (pupils thought they might like it). Some good, unconventional teaching, using drama etc to get the message across.

Lower school classrooms are dotted along the ground floor of the converted and much expanded stables, IT in the hay loft (PowerPoint presentations the norm), ditto (but not the same hay loft) busy multi-media library, well-used with audio books, videos and appealing paperbacks and classical music buzzing gently in the background. Ceramics everywhere. Library is open till 6.30pm, points for laptops, teaching sessions on how to run a library and use a catalogue, along with quizzes and games for 13+ make this one of the more imaginative libraries we have visited.

Games, Options, The Arts: Head keen on sport, rugby now in place, and first XI have just beaten Charterhouse 'and are walking about 50 foot tall'. Sport is 'improving'. Enormously. 'Both in the quality of the schools against whom they play (for instance boys' matches v Eton, Winchester and Charterhouse) and in the results they are achieving – several sides are unbeaten'. Games compulsory twice a week, whole class play the same games up to sixth form, when they can choose. All the usual games are played but probably not yet the place to send a prep school rugby champion. Plenty of minority sports – basketball strong, also fitness training. One or two already involved in colt County cricket, all-weather nets in the offing. (Apparently the original cricket ground was laid down by the Charringtons in 1900 so that Daddy could play and Mummy could entertain the Prince of Wales).

The most terrifying high frame ('it looks even higher from the top,' said Andrew) which combines every conceivable superman movement plus some that even stunt men would be amazed at. Woods filled with serious and popular climbing frames: Jacob's ladder impressive. School was the first to be licensed as a centre for outdoor education, and 'the ropes course is partly about personal challenge, but it is actually far more about respecting and supporting others, and taking responsibility for one's own actions, which is why it is a timetabled lesson'. Forges strong staff/pupil links and is much used in summer by business workshops. Forget convention: this is the most imaginative playground we have ever seen. Trad gym looks Neanderthal by comparison. Certain amount of D of E, but not the religion you find in many schools. Expeditions important, huge range, staff 'give up weeks of holiday time to take pupils to The Red Sea and the Sahara'. Trekking, camping, mountain climbing, survival skills, first aid. Lots of weekend trips away for boarders which day pupils can join, most sound rather scary.

Intimidatingly good performing arts, the building itself has won oodles of awards, with several pupils in current TV programmes and films. Award-winning dance in stunning dance studio: shiny black floor, wall of mirrors and no shoes allowed. New slightly surprising music centre (fires are in fashion at Frensham: this time it was a squirrel which apparently ate the wires; horrifying photographs of the detritus left by the blaze). Music centre has a glass roof in the main auditorium which means that it is almost useless sound-wise when it rains, and like an oven when the sun shines. Fortunately the house itself boasts a glorious ballroom which can be co-opted for concerts. Music strong, with loads of opportunities to play and sing, including an annual concert tour abroad. 22 peripatetic music staff, some of them international performers, two orchestras, three choirs, string quartets, masses of concerts and a soirée in June – for some reason they also teach the bagpipes. More ceramics dotted all round the place, with children's art on every wall, everywhere, the main hall, the passages. 'We like having our work on show, it is very encouraging,' said our 11-year-old guide. Not quite big enough art department (extension probably on next wish list), but some superb results. Glorious pupil-designed panther in foyer of the Performing Arts Centre.

Background and Atmosphere: Founded in 1925, this was a school ahead of its time: co-ed school capable of taking children virtually from cradle to university with no uniforms, no bullying, no competition, no house points, no prize-givings. Creative learning, creative thinking important, plus the arts. Think Bloomsbury in the country. Teachers and students all on first-name basis. No uniform, vague dress code, 'we do insist on more formal dress when the occasion demands' but no overt fashion dictates.

Magnificent Edwardian pile, built by a brewery magnate, set in beautiful 150 acre grounds with stupendous views – over fifty miles on a clear day, Frensham ponds just over the hill. Massive outside use of Performing Arts Centre, which was set ablaze by an electrician's halogen light just days before it was due to open. Fair amount of new build lately, and lots of titivating going on. No Saturday school, day pupils may leave at 4.10 on weekdays. Boys' houses across the road, girls live in the main building in not very satisfactory conditions: dorms are perfectly OK, with decent study bedrooms for older girls, but if they want to invited boys into their common room they must 'find a member of staff and ask them to come and sit in the common room too'. The new sixth form centre (due 2006) and consequent re-jigging of accommodation should deal with this problem.

Pastoral Care and Discipline: Very nurturing pupil/teacher relationships with teachers widely available out of school hours. 'If you get a bad mark it's easy to discuss it with your teacher,' said a pupil. 'Mentors counsel younger students: 'nice and easy to talk to'. Strict about getting prep in, discipline is taken seriously. Smoking used to be allowed here, no longer; bar twice a week, school gets cross if boozing overdone. Drugs the same perennial problem: though Andrew will always give everyone a second chance, even to taking on pupils dissed by other schools. Though immediate expulsion if caught indulging on school premises. Pupils with a drug history coming from other schools must agree to a contract, and will be subject to regular – periodic – drugs testing. Three pupils out last term. No chapel or assembly, but morning talks on Wednesdays, varying from the 'enlightened to the mundane'. Annual parent teachers meeting, which doesn't seem quite enough, plus parents' committee 'which meets each term to discuss matters of common interest'. (Fly on the wall stuff that).

Pupils and Parents: Pupils come from state and independent schools in Surrey, East Hampshire, West Sussex and the A3/M3 corridor into South West London. About 7 per cent expat and no more than 10 per cent from overseas. Unusual international dimension, echoing the founders' international conscience, with the head keen on bringing overseas kids into a 'parochial part of Surrey'. Large numbers of those whom we met lived 'within two minutes' of the school, and neighbouring villages are rapidly becoming school annexes. Sir Claus – now Lord – Moser is an Old Boy (he came as a refugee from Nazi Germany). Many from the arts, publishing, film, entertainment, design etc. Also academics, professionals and IT people.

Entrance: Mainly at 3+, 11+, 13+ or 16+. Assessment, interview and school report at age 10 (or below). Entrance exam required for the older children. Considerably 'over-subscribed for our January entrance exam'; 'there will therefore be those who are not offered places. BUT, and it is a big but, the selection will never be just about academics (the reason we have our own entrance exam: the reason we offer all pupils the chance to show us skills/interests they have irrespective of whether these skills are of themselves scholarship standard'. Need six Cs or better at GCSE for sixth form entry. Hate to turn anyone away, 'the worst thing you can say to anyone is – you failed'. Some children come here from schools where they were not happy.

Exit: Some to music conservatories, drama schools and art colleges in the UK and abroad. Most to a wide range of universities, studying everything from marine biology and coastal ecology to Arabic with politics, dance and fashion. The odd one or two to Oxbridge. Some Gap.

Money Matters: Some help for academia, music and other creative and performing arts. Bursarial help reserved for 'funding those pupils of excellence whose parents would not otherwise be able to afford a Frensham Heights' education?. Busy-bee development officer, helping the school to make a bob or two letting out facilities like the outdoor education centre to visiting schools, the Prince's Trust. Also does a brisk trade in weddings. Competitive music festival and summer schools also pull in the loot.

Remarks: Friendly and inspiring school, achieving its aim of providing good alternative education with lots of freedom but no hint of chaos.

FREWEN COLLEGE

Northiam, Rye, East Sussex, TN31 6NL

Tel: 01797 252 494

Fax: 01797 252 567

Email: office@frewencollege.org

Website: www.frewencollege.co.uk

• Pupils: 85 boys and girls; about one third board • Ages: 7-17 • Religion: non-denom • Fees: The Oaks: day £4,300; boarding £6,400. Senior school: £4,600-£5,600; boarding £7,000-£7,750 • School status: Independent • Opendays: Contact school • School gender: Mixed • Day/boarding: Takes boarders

SEN provision

Detail:

Centre of excellence for:

- Mild: DYSL; DYSP;
- Moderate: DYSL; DYSP;
- Severe: DYSL; DYSP;

Now provide for in school:

- Mild: ASP; DYSC;
- Moderate: DYSC;

Summary: The central aim of the school is to help every child realise and achieve their full potential. Most pupils will have encountered difficulties during their previous educational experiences and many will be far more aware of their limitations than their capabilities. At Frewen, each pupil is seen as an individual with unique talents and abilities. By working to emphasise and develop their strengths, we create the confidence to address their limitations in a positive and creative environment.

We offer the full National Curriculum, teaching in small groups (average class size 5.5) through specialist staff, supported by our own full-time speech and language and occupational therapists. All new pupils undergo thorough assessment and educational and therapy programmes are tailored to their individual needs. While placing great emphasis on literacy and numeracy, we have particular strengths in IT, art and design, and music. We have a wide range of excellent facilities, including playing fields, gardens, and access to parkland extending to over 100 acres.

Above all, Frewen College is a community in which respect for the individual is at the core of our philosophy. Each member of the community has an important role to play and is expected to understand their responsibilities and help others whenever possible.

What we say about the school - the full Good Schools Guide review

Principal: Since 2003, Mrs Felicity Youlten BSc PGCE (sixtyish) a biologist. Previously deputy head in the maintained sector in a large comprehensive school in Kent and before that in inner London where she gained much experience in teaching children with special needs. Mrs Youlten is contracted until August 2006 but will stay in post until the right successor is found. Dedicated and committed and having invested heavily of both effort and devotion in the rebirth of Frewen, Mrs Youlten is in no more rush to depart than the school is to lose her. She was appointed shortly after Mr Jeremy Field took over as Business Manager and Bursar and together they have transformed Frewen into the kind of special school that most parents of dyslexics dream of.

Academic Matters: 'Individual education plan' is one of the two guiding principles here. 'Targets' is the other. Every child knows his own plan. The targets of junior pupils in all key areas are kept on little cards in cups, ready to be referred to at any point in the day. Most classes have no more than six children and all are carefully monitored. The school specialises in supporting dyslexics and dyspraxics with the associated speech and language difficulties such children can have, as well as a small number of children with Asperger's. They do not take those whose primary problem is ADHD or MLD, nor those with profound speech and language problems. The nature of the building and its unalterability (planning regs) do not allow for wheelchair users to come as boarders.

The Oaks – the junior school for years 3-6 – in a house opposite the main one, is spacious and incorporates classrooms and a small hall in which a play written for the children and tailored to them as individuals was being rehearsed with everyone contentedly partaking when we visited. There is an IT room, a therapy room for small groups or one-to-one which is used for 'time out' space, especially for Asperger's children for whom class activities can be stressful. There is also a speech and language therapy room, also used for occupational therapy. Here children are helped with social skills and 'good listening' and 'good looking'. Lots of outdoor play – in all weathers – in wellies and overalls. All is overseen by The Oaks' own teacher in charge, Mrs Sally Welch – young, enthusiastic and very clued-up.

But the two schools are decidedly one. At year 7 most move into the main site, but a few each year have so successfully caught up they are able to rejoin mainstream education elsewhere, some passing entrance exams to local independents. School takes national SATs and some reach level 5 in maths and science at Key Stage 2 and level 6 at Key Stage 3. In the main school, the small class sizes persist and all the classes we visited were relaxed, with everyone seemingly absorbed and involved. A sense of each child's individual needs is pervasive. We visited an English class where everyone was writing on a PC and we learned how, in public exams, many will use an amanuensis to read the questions and/or transcribe the pupils' dictated answers – all according to the individual needs. School follows National Curriculum, students take GCSEs and an AS or two – some few stay on for year 12 and can take art, photography and/or design technology – and results are improving. 2004 saw an average of seven subjects taken at GCSE and 19 per cent of pupils with five grades within the A*-C range. Given careful targeting and recently beefed-up staff, these results look set to improve. Pupils in years 10/11 given weekly careers lessons.

Most teachers have SEN qualifications and school supports several others through distance learning courses at the Dyslexia Institute. A full-time speech therapist and a full-time occupational therapist and other specialists eg art therapists are brought in for individuals according to need.

Games, Options, The Arts: There is a good outdoor pool in the exquisite gardens at the back of the house – a rarely privileged setting – no sports hall, though one is wistfully talked of. There is a cricket field, football and rugby pitches, tennis/basketball courts, an all-weather five-a-side football and hockey pitch, a good fitness suite in its own house in the old stables. Alternatives to PE for dyspraxics. A sports hall would be nice but hardly feels essential.

We saw enthusiastic DT classes, MDF chairs in mid-construction and an array of imaginative and colourful gardening boxes. Art is excellent – varied in both inspiration and media – super ceramics decorate window sills. Music is popular – many learn individually, principally keyboard, guitar and drums. There is one band – surely scope for more ensemble work here? – but former pupils have gone on to read music at university.

Background and Atmosphere: The main house, formerly called Brickwall, is quite stunning and a bursar's nightmare. The 1633 black and white Jacobean façade, original leaded lights 'n' all, fronts some quite splendid plasterwork ceilings, C17th painted oriental leather wall-coverings, concealed staircases and who-knows-what behind and a ghost called Martha – the poor darling ran out with her nightie on fire and expired on the onion patch c1752. The house came with numerous family portraits, other paintings and furniture and artefacts, the curatorship and/or sale of which is an abiding feature of the school's management. Fierce English Heritage regulations constrain what can/must be done to alter or preserve and it is easy to forget that this is a school. This is especially true in the glorious Sissinghurst/Knole style gardens which are a knock-out mix of beautifully planted borders and formal yeweries – maintained by gardener with 47 years of service at time of our visit. Converted stables house a number of depts. And there are some 'temporary' classrooms – which never are, of course – plus good, newish teaching block with central atrium housing library and display area.

The school is named after the family who owned the place for 300+ years, having made their money in furs and spices. It became, first, a boys' school, then a billet for Canadian forces in WWII and, finally, the last resident Frewen, Admiral Sir John, turned it into a school in 1972 with four dyslexic boys. Frewen believes it was the first specialist dyslexic school. The atmosphere is relaxed, civilized and measured – helped hugely by the spaciousness and peace of this quiet nook where East Sussex peeps into the Garden of England next door. The Oaks is housed in an old brick building with sensitive add-ons. Gardens with an adventure playground – gardening club is popular. No good-sized towns for miles – a good place for anyone to de-stress. We heard no raised voices on our visit. Boarding being refurbished but looks pretty good as it is. Year 6s are four to a dorm with en-suites – amps and guitars in rooms. Seniors are two to a pretty spacious room or have a room to themselves. Full boarding offered from September 2005. Good wholesome food including salad bar and school works with special diets where necessary. System of three different tablecloths for different types of food – everyone takes something from each to ensure a balanced diet.

Pastoral Care and Discipline: An established pastoral system but, clearly, 'anyone can talk to anyone if they want to'. Deputy head deals with most behavioural problems. System of good and bad order marks, leading to yellow and red cards for misdemeanours. Few problems severe enough to reach the head. Excellent 'incentive scheme' devised to tackle problems of litter and minor vandalism highly successful and popular and school looked very orderly and beautifully kept throughout – despite massive upkeep challenges. Since Mrs Youlten's arrival one permanent exclusion for fighting, none for drugs. A sense of a whole school approach here to general welfare – 'everyone understands the difficulties' said a teacher and pupils work with maintenance and kitchen staff on work experience – terrific for self-esteem.

Pupils and Parents: Most are local though, in effect, that means a few from south London boroughs, from well into Kent and into Sussex. About 50 per cent supported by LEAs so a good, homogenous social mix. Girls a new innovation and full boarding arrives in September 2005. Currently two-thirds are day pupils. Parents mixed in all ways, largely realistic about their children's aspirations, and school works hard to foster links.

Entrance: Infinitely painstaking. All prospective pupils invited for trial days and they may stay for as long as a week, participating in classes with all appropriate teachers who then report back. Specialised assessments also made of individual needs and problems – all goes to create fullest possible picture and school will advise if they feel they are not the best place. EPs and current school's reports also important, of course.

Exit: Most to some sort of further education – usually a practical, vocational or art course at a local college. Some straight into work. Given the educational difficulties of some of these young people, an encouraging record.

Money Matters: No schols but means-tested bursaries may be made available in cases of need. Bursaries for Forces families.

Remarks: Still more to do here in terms of the school's growth and development but the essentials are in place – the main one being a confident, dedicated and enthusiastic staff. With good recent Ofsted, CReSTeD and the Commission for Social Care (CSCI) inspections, Frewen provides a privileged setting for its clear-sighted, gentle and encouraging approach. If the school feels you're 'a Frewen child' and takes you, they'll give you of their best.

FRIENDS' SCHOOL

Mount Pleasant Road, Saffron Walden, Essex, CB11 3EB

Tel: 01799 525 351

Fax: 01799 523 808

Email: admin@friends.org.uk

Website: www.friends.org.uk

• Pupils: 220 boys and girls; 50 boarders • Ages: 11-18 • Religion: Quaker ethos • Fees: Day £2,050-£3,590; boarding £5,790 • School status: Independent • Opendays: Termly • School gender: Mixed • Day/boarding: Takes boarders

SEN provision

Detail:

Now provide for in school:

Mild: DYSC; DYSL; DYSP; HI;

Moderate: DYSL;

Experience of:

Mild: ASP; AUT; ADD; ADHD; VI;

Severe: CP;

Others: DEL; Epi;

Summary: The Study Centre aims to develop strategies to improve an individual's study, organisation and thinking skills. Study Centre staff complement and support the work of teachers in the classroom. Your child may benefit from one-to-one teaching, or support within the classroom from fully qualified learning support assistants; both are designed to ensure equal access to the curriculum.

The Study Centre will monitor your child's progress closely and modify support where appropriate. The cost of support will depend on your child's needs. Additional costs will be kept to a minimum and will be discussed during the application process.

Friends' School is regarded as having particular strength in working with children with dyslexia.

What we say about the school - the full Good Schools Guide review

Head: Since 2001, Mr Andy Waters BEd MA (forties); went to local grammar and then London University, was house tutor of St Christopher's, Letchworth and deputy head at Oswestry in Shropshire. A human dynamo;

meticulous, ambitious, verbal, going hammer and tongs on marketing the assets with new prospectus to mark 300th year. Climbs mountains and does Triathlon for kicks (ex-tutor of Outward Bound Wales) so serious reconstruction of the place is merely his warm-up exercise. Still time to teach history, play guitar and mandolin in a ceilidh band. Says he has a complete intolerance of bullying. Bends over backward to be Robin Hood with deserving cases who can't afford fees – 'my door is always open though my desk is seldom clear.' Wife Hazel works in Cambridge, with son at junior school and daughter in senior school. Sixth formers like his tenacity but still undecided on suitable nickname.

Off to head Grenville College, Devon in July 2006.

Academic Matters: For a school whose policy is to select as wide a range of pupils as will benefit from its curriculum, it does wonders: 83+ per cent five or more GCSE A-C grades, half of them gaining eight or more. Does not worship at altar of league tables – no policy of withdrawing borderline candidates in order to improve GCSE statistics. In year 11 pupils achieved on average 2.6 more A*-C grades than expected from standardised tests in year 9 – due to quality of teaching. French and German taught to all in years 7 and 8.

Member of National Association of Gifted Children – the more able as well as special needs catered for. three dedicated full-time specialists and 6 assistants assist dyslexics, mild Asperger's syndrome, impaired hearing and some statemented pupils.

Cosy sixth form (most tutor groups only 6) attracts those who can't face 'factory farm' sixth form colleges nearby. Bias towards science, maths, exotic languages, history of art and art. Recent additions to A level subjects are film studies, theatre and media studies. 25 per cent A or B grades at A level, about 8 per cent fail – around the national average. Adequate IT facilities but don't hold your breath. Well-meaning careers advice needs more business-like approach from the real world.

Games, Options, The Arts: Despite acres of playing fields, hard tennis courts, a 25 yard indoor pool (one of first in the country) and a sports hall for indoor hockey, badminton, basketball, football and cricket, no county teams as yet. Much enthusiasm though and 90 per cent of girls represent school in hockey teams; 80 per cent of boys in football teams. D of E given full rein. Mr Waters will no doubt improve the motivation to compete.

Young Enterprise Scheme gains an extra qualification. 185 instrumental lessons in purpose-built music school ranges to post grade 8. Zestful drama puts on flamboyant musicals with casts of all ages. LAMDA exams.

Established ESOL takes Chinese, Japanese, Russian students and integrates them into all classes. The Octopus Art Gallery (in fabulous space of disused water tower) provides ample exhibition space for local artists as well as pupils and very vibrant artist in residence.

Background and Atmosphere: Founded in 1702 this well-travelled school began its life in Clerkenwell attached to a workhouse, lifted off to Croydon and, when typhoid threatened, came to its present site 20 minutes away from Cambridge in an imposing gothic Victorian building (land donated by two Friends).

Stunning artwork by ex-students and various artists in residence displayed in the old wood-panelled dining room and all round the school. Otherwise not a penny wasted on vanity. Has the atmosphere of an unpretentious grammar combined with a small country school with tight community ties. With its cosily old-fashioned feel it's a place where individuality is cherished, catered for and celebrated. Head is pumping new blood into the school with heads of departments, so give it a year or two under his energetic reign and this friendly teddy-bear could metamorphose into a savvy 21st century fox.

Pastoral Care and Discipline: Where the Quaker element comes up trumps. School-phobics or those bullied elsewhere come and thrive here. Day scholars encouraged to stay on after school hours to join in activities/prep/tea. Boarders live in comfy, large and airy rooms with cheery resident staff. Quartet of senior scholars are the head boy/girl and deputies.

Pupils and Parents: Only a sprinkle of teachers and pupils from Quaker background these days, though the governing body is still essentially Quaker. Day pupils come from a 30 mile radius, boarders from London, Herts, Suffolk, Essex, Cambridge – teachers, doctors, entrepreneurs and 'estuary up-market East-Enders', commented local taxi driver.

Uniform is due for overhaul. Sixth formers in own clothes. No trendies, alcohol banned, campus is strictly a no smoking zone. Old Scholars: BBC 'Blue Planet' producer Martha Holmes, rock star Tom Robinson, former Speaker of the House of Commons, Lord Newton of Braintree and quite a few of the Rowntree clan.

Entrance: Easy for those who fit the type of pupil the school looks for. Interview and assessment at 11. 40 per cent arrive from junior school. Most outside entries to sixth form are currently via EFL.

Exit: 3-4 to Oxbridge. 70 per cent to universities like Bristol, University College London, Lancaster. 30 per cent leave post-16 for sixth form colleges in London and Cambridge which offer a broader range of subjects.

Money Matters: Despite 70 assisted places lost, school continues to grow strongly (by over a third in three years in senior school). Two scholarships for academic excellence in years 7 and 9 (means tested); bursaries in art, music, sport in years 7 and 9 and for new entrants in year 9. Sixth form: head's discretion to award (max) £2,000 to those who contribute substantially to school life. Quaker bursaries for Quaker families.

Remarks: Head is contracted till retirement so major improvements are expected. Thus very good value until fees catch up with 21st century. Ideal for an unusual child or one who would shrink in the high pressured hot-houses.

THE FROEBELIAN SCHOOL

Clarence Road, Horsforth, Leeds, West Yorkshire, LS18 4LB

Tel: 01132 583 047

Fax: 0113 258 0173

Email: office@froebelian.co.uk

Website: www.froebelian.co.uk

• Pupils: Around 190 boys and girls; all day • Ages: 3-11

• Religion: Christian, non-denom • Fees: £1,040-1,685

• School status: Independent • Opendays: March

• School gender: Mixed • Day/boarding: Day pupils

SEN provision

Detail:

Experience of:

Mild: ASP; ADD; ADHD; DYSC; DYSL; DYSP;

Moderate: ASP; ADD; ADHD; MLD; DYSC; DYSL; DYSP;

Others: EAL;

Summary: We aim to be as inclusive as possible to a wide range of children. Our 'Increasing Access' policy includes a commitment to gradual, realistic changes that will allow us to welcome an increasingly diverse cross-section of pupils.

Currently, our main provision is for children with mild to moderate learning needs. A qualified learning support specialist works with teachers to help them adjust their learning and teaching techniques to meet the needs of all pupils. Those children who benefit, are withdrawn form some lessons for individual support from the learning support co-ordinator.

What we say about the school - the full Good Schools Guide review

Headmaster: Since 1991, Mr John Tranmer MA PGCE (late forties), read history at St John's, Cambridge, PGCE at St Martin's Lancaster. Has had varied career – teaching at Bolton School, HMS Indefatigable (nautical school), Parkside School, Cobham (ran history, RE and games). Two 2-year career breaks, with a building society and at GCHQ. Wife works for a charity and both their children attended the school when younger.

Very articulate, with a firm intellectual grip on what is going on. Easy, unaffected manner, very much at home in a small prep school, sees himself as an enabler, relieving staff of tedious admin tasks (he treats them regularly to cream cakes). A teaching head – one-fifth timetable, mainly history; coaches sport, runs marathons. His office has sweeping views over wooded valley to ruined Kirkstall Abbey.

Entrance: Almost exclusively at 3; first 24 to register are invited to spend two hours in school, where they are informally assessed by staff. One-form entry of 24, perpetual waiting-list of between 20 and 30. Places occasionally available for older children.

Exit: About 80 per cent to Bradford and Leeds independent grammar schools (boys and girls). Harrogate Ladies' College, Ashville and Woodhouse Grove also popular. Occasional entrant to boarding (eg St Peter's, York) or reputable maintained (St Aidan's, Harrogate).

Remarks: Small, intimate, family-atmosphere prep school on a cramped (school says 'compact') site, on the northern fringes of the Leeds-Bradford conurbation. Founded 1913, but no longer any formal connection with the Froebel Institute. A recent extension has provided two large additional classrooms, a multi-purpose studio and a welcome enlargement of the playground.

Serious academic ethos but by no means a sweatshop. Consistently high SATs results. Top-quality, feet-on-ground staff dedicated to helping children enjoy learning. Average class size 24 – but early years always have one or two classroom assistants. Exposure to IT from the start – 4-year-olds manipulate enormous mice, year 5s e-mail and surf the net on their own – and they're taught how to use the conventional library. Much specialist teaching in junior (8-11) department – science, D&T, French, music, IT, games and drama. Teacher/pupil ratio 1:11. All pupils screened for SEN at ages 7 and 8 (eight pupils currently have one-to-one support with a specialist teacher). Plenty of sport on offer, despite limited facilities (school uses nearby fields and pool) with the emphasis on taking part. PE/games co-ordinator, Wendy Staniland, was awarded the 'Sports Teacher of the Year Award, 2003' by the National Council for School Sport. Music and drama very strong – over 90 per cent of juniors learn at least one instrument, school is famous locally for its musicals (Bugsy Malone, Oliver). Also field trips, outings, juniors' week in France.'Pastoral care', says Mr Tranmer, 'exists in the fabric of the place; given that staff and pupils live in each other's pockets, it can function largely through teachers' intuition.' Very clear school code and anti-bullying policy. Parents happy with all this. Pupils wear neat, bright-red sweaters (staff, too, are encouraged to dress smartly), and go about their daily business calmly and cheerfully. Strong emphasis on children allowing each other to be happy in their school lives – and older boys and girls (amazingly) help supervise tinies' lunchtime. All in all, a happy and successful little school, which turns out well-prepared and confident children ready for local high-reputation day schools (where they do well). Mr Tranmer thinks wistfully of moving to a more spacious site but this must be long-term. Not for those who want a stately home in hundreds of acres. Very popular with Leeds-Bradford medical mafia; governors are mostly current and past parents. Excellent value, too.

GATEWAYS SCHOOL

Harewood, Leeds, West Yorkshire, LS17 9LE

Tel: 0113 288 6345

Fax: 0113 288 6148

Email: gateways@gatewayschool.co.uk

Website: www.gatewayschool.co.uk

• Pupils: 535 girls, 25 boys aged 3-7 • Ages: 3-18

• Religion: C of E foundation, but 'all faiths or none' accepted

• Fees: £1,089-£2,655 • School status: Independent

• School gender: Girls • Day/boarding: Day pupils

SEN provision

Detail:

Now provide for in school:

Mild: AUT; DYSL; DYSP;

Moderate: DYSL;

Severe: DYSL; SpLD;

Others: SPD; EAL;

Experience of:

Mild: HI;

Summary: Gateways School welcomes children of all abilities, each with their own strengths, interests and weaknesses. We strive to provide a full and balanced curriculum for all our pupils in a professional and caring environment.

The early identification of individual pupils' special needs allows us to put in place a variety of measures and support programmes aimed at enabling each and every pupil to achieve success.

Diagnostic screening tests and referral by teaching staff, help the learning support co-ordinator to decide if SEN intervention is needed. In consultation with the pupils, parents and teachers, a specific and individual programme of support for each pupil is then negotiated.

This can take the form of: adult support for the pupil in the classroom; small group work on a withdrawal basis; a pupil operating on a reduced timetable; tuition in English for non-English speaking pupils; referrals to outside agencies such as speech therapists and educational psychologists.

Gateways is proud of its success over the years in enabling each and every girl to achieve her full potential in all areas of life, be it academic, vocational or social.

What we say about the school - the full Good Schools Guide review

Head: Since 1997, Mrs Denise Davidson BA MEd (fifties). Read history at Manchester, and has done just about everything since then, including living in a Little Gidding community with her family, teaching history to Borstal boys and car maintenance to motor mechanics, starting a school on Tuvalu (where her husband was attorney general), running a smallholding, being appointed as the first housemistress at Oundle, and picking up an MEd in educational management at Cambridge. Five grown-up children. This all adds up to a range of experience and knowledge of the world unusual at the top of any school. It's said the more conservative elements on the staff were somewhat startled by her arrival. Warm, attractive and welcoming personality; a good listener, much respected by pupils and parents, also clear-sighted about where she wants the school to go and how to guide it there – which includes extensive professional development for her staff (two senior teachers were recently awarded MAs from Leeds, in education and music). Her immediate ambition is to construct a winter garden between the school's attractive main buildings.

Academic Matters: Results getting better all the time (value-added index too), as numbers grow and teaching becomes more focused; former 'rejects' now getting Ds and Es at A2 level, while more As are coming from the brightest – 'identified and pushed' by staff. Girls at opposite ends of the ability range seem to coexist contentedly. English outstanding at both levels, art and IT show very well. 2004 GCSE was a bumper year in numbers and achievement, with strong languages (including Greek and Latin) and dual award science. Interestingly, some girls were entered ahead of or behind their chronological group, thus 'highlighting our policy of treating each pupil as an individual'. Average class size 17, and student:staff ratio 8.7 to 1. Serious SEN provision: currently two statemented pupils (one-to-one attention), while another 17 get extra support.

Games, Options, The Arts: Games flourish under recently-appointed male director of sports. The usual netball, hockey and swimming, plus some football, and an emphasis on general health; fitness suite just opened, with an astroturf area in the pipeline. Wittily titled games news sheet – 'Sporta', school mag is 'Porta', OK you Latinists? – helps to raise profile. Enthusiastic involvement in drama (some with boys of nearby Leeds GS), art and music (director is an expert on music and liturgy). D of E and World Challenge cater for the adventurous.

Background and Atmosphere: Founded in 1941, the school occupies the handsome former dower house of the nearby Harewood estate, midway between Leeds and Harrogate. Plenty of additions since then, much of it good to look at and work in, especially recent science/languages building, sports hall, and performing arts centre. An attractive site, if a touch bleak in winter – but these are (mostly) Yorkshire lasses who can cope with a bit of wind and rain. Mrs Davidson is a strong advocate of single-sex education, for all the familiar reasons but with a gritty extra dimension – self-esteem in adolescence depends to an extent on experience in risk-taking, public speaking and conflict handling. Much is made of providing opportunities for these – and preparing girls for a changing world where teamwork and communication skills count for more than old hierarchies – in the school's admirably terse and guff-free prospectus. Fine if it all works in practice; the intention is certainly there. Equally, you find evidence of thought for others, something a good small school can do very well – from 'wraparound care' for the 3 to 11s (ie before and after school provision, charged as an extra) to involvement in the locality (ask about the Gateways Link). A senior girl observed how satisfactory it was that younger pupils weren't altogether separated on the site, and that prefects could keep a motherly eye on the little ones as they played. Neat, trad uniform: cherry red blazers and black skirts, with sixth formers in acceptable own clothes. Altogether, an impression of quiet, unpushy confidence, and girls ready to converse unaffectedly but respectfully with adults.

Pastoral Care and Discipline: As you might expect, a well-conceived pastoral system in which every teacher is involved, and just about everyone knows everyone else. Very little problem with the common school sins, though Mrs Davidson did suspend two girls for smoking – on safety grounds, since they were standing next to some gas bottles.

Pupils and Parents: This used to be a faintly posh establishment for girls perceived to be nice but dim and who couldn't make it to boarding school or the grammar schools of Leeds and Bradford. No more – Gateways increasingly figures on the local prep school circuit for parents who choose what it offers in preference to other places. Local primary schools are also taking an interest. Girls come from Leeds' more comfortable suburbs and the affluent arc of villages from its NW to NE; also Harrogate, and further afield from Skipton and York. Parents are typically doctors, lawyers and financiers, also transient foreigners (Danes, Australians, French) drawn to Leeds' booming economy. Plenty of large shiny cars and smart mums in the car park at picking-up time. Prominent OG: Henrietta Hill, human rights barrister.

Entrance: Applicants for nursery places spend some time in the school on a 'carousel' of activities; 4-11s assessed. 11+ tested in English, maths and VR, also art, ICT and PE. Selection 'not on academic criteria alone'. Transfer from prep to main school is automatic; parents warned in good time if this is unrealistic. Relocation at any age considered if the school has room; post-16 candidates need a minimum of six GCSEs at A*-C. All 11+ girls have a 30-minute slot with Mrs Davidson, then asked to say what they thought of the process (and each other).

Exit: Vast majority to northern universities and colleges; subjects range from molecular biology to equine science.

Money Matters: Some scholarships at present, but system being revised to offer only bursaries; reductions for siblings.

Remarks: An impressive small school on the way up, with strong visionary leadership and a real concern for the all-round development of the individual, but by no means comfy and girly. Increasingly making its mark, and respected by big-hitter neighbouring schools. It may suffer temporarily from the forthcoming amalgamation of Leeds Boys and Girls, but it has the confidence to continue carving out its own niche. Definitely worth a trip into the Yorkshire countryside.

George Heriot's School

Lauriston Place, Edinburgh, EH3 9EQ

Tel: 01312 297 263

Fax: 01312 296 363

Email: admissions@george-heriots.com

Website: www.george-heriots.com

• Pupils: 900 boys and girls • Ages: 11-18

• Religion: Non-denom • Fees: Senior school: £2,348; Juniors £1,557-£1,909 • School status: Independent

• School gender: Mixed • Day/boarding: Day pupils

SEN provision

Detail:

Now provide for in school:

Mild: ASP; ADD; ADHD; DYSL; DYSP;

Moderate: ADD; DYSL; DYSP;

Others: EAL;

Summary: Not a squeak from this mousie – but there's a good tale to tell of its SEN provision. SEN details added by us.

What we say about the school - the full Good Schools Guide review

Head: Since 1998, Mr Alistair Hector MA (fiftyish), who was educated at Edinburgh Academy, read modern languages at St Andrews and came to Heriot's from Warwick School, where he was deputy head. Before that he taught at King Edward's School. Started his career at Merchiston, after a spell in Germany teaching EFL. Married, one of his children currently attends the school. Pleased to be back in Scotland and quite liked taking over mid-way through the session – 'you don't have to worry about the timetable and you've got a couple of terms to settle in'. He is head of the whole school. No longer has a timetabled class to teach but pops in and does the 'odd bit of supply teaching for PSHE'; rather misses the daily contact – 'pupils are the core of what the school does'.

Academic Matters: Not easy to extract detailed examination results (by subject by grade) – so keep asking. Solid results at all levels. Max class size 26, 'but usually much less'. Classes streamed early, setted for maths at 9; also for English from 11. Steeped in 'Euro-awareness' a sort of Euro-starter course at 8; with either French, German or Spanish at 10. A second lang can be taken at 13. Strong sciences across the board but actually no particular bias. Eight Standard Grades the norm; Latin available to Standard and classical civilisation to Higher level is surprisingly popular. Finely-tuned support for learning but limited in the amount of help they can give, will not take children with a formal statement of needs except in 'exceptional circumstances' but any child with a suspected problem is seen by the Support for Learning department, which then swings into action. Both withdrawn and team teaching on hand, either individual or in small groups. School will bear the cost of extra lessons and may, in certain circs, cover the cost of an outside ed psych; they have their own who is free. Can cope with ADD/ADHD up to a certain degree. Ritalin is not an issue – 'we would consult with parents to see how their children might be best served'. EFL lessons are charged for. Computers all over the shop, loads of new suites.

Games, Options, The Arts: This is a games school. Outstanding rugby and cricket and girls' hockey very powerful; games played down at Goldenacre, along with all the other Edinburgh schools mafia; FPs use the pitches too. Pupils bused across Edinburgh, cross-country running and rowing are favourite alternative sports – the school has a boat house on the canal. Badminton and extra-curricular football are all in the frame, plus fencing and very good swimming, there is a small training pool on the (very cramped) site, but basically they use the baths at Warrender. Drama now timetabled and taken at both Standard and Higher levels. New head of music recently appointed which has done wonders for this department – choirs as well as a variety of chamber and other orchestras. Art streaking ahead, and photography on offer but not to exam level. Sixth year does voluntary service, working in the nursery, helping with lower primary pupils and outside placements eg the outpatients at the Ashley Ainslie.

Background and Atmosphere: George Heriot, jeweller to King James the VI (and I), who had started business life in a booth by St Giles, left the princely sum of £23,625 'for the building of a hospital' (ie a charity school) on a 'site at the foot of Gray's Close', for boys whose fathers had died. Fabulous ogee curved-roofed towers, the place was first inhabited by Cromwell in 1650 and, whilst principally designed by William Wallace, the magical inner-city school can boast almost every important 17th century Scottish architect – finishing with the court favourite, Robert Mylne. The school claims to be the longest-inhabited school in Scotland. Magnificent Pugin chapel revamped by James Gillespie Graham in 1837; pupils still sit on backless benches. A rather snazzy library in the lower half of a hall has been disastrously (school rejects this epithet – not surprisingly) split in two to provide a concert hall above. While all schools are perennially short on space, this is the most blatant piece of architectural sacrilege we have ever come across.

Founders day celebrated with 'buskins' (garlands) round the founder's statue on June Day. The foundation was feudal superior of great tracts of Edinburgh, and has close links with Donaldson's hospital for the deaf (the school's after-school club is held there daily). The hospital became a school in 1886, changed its name and the 180 foundationers were joined by paying pupils but the 180 registration marks are still visible in the quadrangle. Boarding was phased out in 1902 and girls admitted in 1979; the school became 'fully independent' in 1985. FPs are known as Herioters. School has fantastic views of Edinburgh Castle but the site is cramped; they had hoped to be able to buy part of the about-to-be-defunct Edinburgh Royal Infirmary but were thwarted by developers who propose transforming the place into upmarket flats and office blocks. The former, says the head, 'will be handy for more pupils' but they currently need space more than bums on seats. One or two possibilities in the pipeline – a certain amount of in-filling, plus some internal revamping (the head's office smelled of paint during our visit). The school has leased space from Edinburgh College of Art and the wish list includes plans to improve the old gym, expand the music department and create a sixth form centre for starters. Uniform for all, different ties for prefects and sixth. Trips all over the shop in every discipline.

Pastoral Care and Discipline: Code of conduct equals schools rules which parents and pupils have to sign, based on 'personal safety, safety for others and respect for others, property and the environment'. Ladder of sanctions. Good PSHE team who are proactive in reducing tension, both sides must face up to an issue. Persistent misbehaviour and not responding = out; detentions and discussions with parents more normal. Occasional suspensions, no real problems with drugs, booze and fags but head is on the ball – 'can honestly say that there have been no expulsions because of drugs in my time here'. Concern if school work suffers, no random drugs tests. Church of Scotland chaplain; school uses Grey Friars Kirk (of Bobby fame) for services.

Pupils and Parents: Sturdy middle class lot, Edinburgh-average ethic. Thriving parents' association.

Entrance: Test (English, maths, VRQ) at primary and senior level, including from own junior school; predicted grades for pupils joining post-Standard Grades.

Exit: Regularly four or five to Oxbridge; school runs induction weekends down to Oxbridge along with St Mary's Music School to familiarise pupils with the collegiate system, otherwise mostly to Scottish unis, some leave after Standard Grades either to employment or further education elsewhere.

Money Matters: School felt the loss of Assisted Places keenly but is pretty well back up to speed. Foundation still provides 100 per cent bursary for 'children of primary or secondary school age, who are resident in Edinburgh or the Lothians, whose father has died and whose mother might not otherwise afford the cost of private education'. Raft of other bursaries and scholarships, will keep children in place during financial crisis – but rather depends on child for how long.

Remarks: Thunderingly good inner-city school in a spectacular position, doing what it does do well.

GEORGE WATSON'S COLLEGE

Colinton Road, Edinburgh, EH10 5EG

Tel: 0131 446 6000

Fax: 0131 446 6090

Email: admissions@gwc.org.uk

Website: www.gwc.org.uk

• Pupils: 1,100 (boy:girl ratio 55:45) • Ages: 12-18 • Religion: Non-denom • Fees: Junior £1,681-2,026; senior: £2,606 • School status: Independent • Opendays: October • School gender: Mixed • Day/boarding: Day pupils

SEN provision

Detail:

Centre of excellence for:
- Mild: DYSL;
- Moderate: DYSL;
- Severe: DYSL;

Now provide for in school:
- Mild: DYSP;
- Moderate: DYSP;

Experience of:
- Mild: ASP; AUT; ADD; ADHD; DYSC; HI; VI; CP;
- Moderate: DYSC; HI; VI; CP;
- Severe: DYSP; HI;
- Others: SPD; Sp&LD;

Summary: George Watson's has a long tradition of supporting pupils with specific learning difficulties in the mainstream, and our focus is upon optimum inclusion for each pupil. As well as a learning support staff of five full-time staff and a number of support staff, the whole staff is experienced in recognising and providing for pupils who have particular barriers to their learning. Labelling these barriers is less important than understanding the different strands of difficulty that may be affecting a learner – usually several strands rather than the single barrier often implied by a single label; and our support resources are focused upon working with pupils, staff, families and other professionals to understand each pupil's unique strengths and weaknesses, and to find ways around any barriers.

Emphasis is put upon sharing ideas with teaching staff, with using every possible means to minimise barriers in the classroom (support staff, S6 helpers, parent helpers, use of ICT, and personalised teaching and learning tips for each pupil with difficulties). Pupils may reduce their curriculum to find time for a study programme in the LS Centre – this may focus upon their wider curriculum, or the specific skillls they wish to develop, or a mixture of both. The school is well resourced, and there is real commitment to accessibility and inclusion. LS staff are actively involved in research, development and publication in the field of learning difficulties, collaborating with the University of Edinburgh as well as a range of other professionals and agencies nationwide.

What we say about the school - the full Good Schools Guide review

Principal: Since 2001, Mr Gareth Edwards MA (forties). Born in Wales and has a 'keen affinity with the Celts.' Educated at Tudor Grange Grammar, Solihull; read classics at Exeter, Oxford. Taught at King Edward VIth Edgbaston, before becoming head of department at Bolton Boys, followed by vice principal of Newcastle-under-Lyme School. He was previously rector at Morrison's Academy in Crieff. Married, with one daughter.

A slow speaking, deep thinking head, he has all the Welsh charm and a quiet charisma. He is also very giggly, though he was considerably offended by this comment saying that 'a reputable publication such as ours would not pass such personal comments'. Little does he know.

Academic Matters: One of Scotland's most successful schools; follows the Scottish system; excellent results. One of a few schools to teach study skills throughout the school. Careers advice starts from 15 upwards beginning with Morrisby testing so that pupils can make informed choices when deciding on five or six subjects from the choice of 26. Extension modules and additional subjects available for the last year. Foreign language teaching is strong, with great emphasis put on speaking skills. Numerous native speakers within the department and opportunities for exchanges. Superb networked ICT department used for backing up the curriculum.

Dr Weedon, a practitioner at the forefront of dyslexia research and development, is still strongly at the helm of their special needs team. In this buzzing department all manner of support is made available for pupils, and parents speak highly of special needs provision. Dr Weedon seems to have adopted the school credo of 'developing independence of thought'. Lots of children referred for help but most feel confident enough to refer themselves. Frequent 'inset' and personal development training for all staff throughout the school.

Games, Options, The Arts: Renowned for their successes on the rugby field and strong rowing but now most definitely on the map for their success in winning the juvenile World Pipe and Drum Championships. A wealth of music and sports to choose from as well as the chance to appear in spectacular dramatic productions. But with clubs and societies galore, at the last count close to 80, including 20 sports clubs, four orchestras, three bands, musical ensembles and several choirs, they are spoilt for choice. Many school trips too, at home and abroad. The third year 10-day excursion backpacking with their peers and teachers, features high in most students' memories. Amazing art (students sit English board for this).

Background and Atmosphere: Founded by a legacy left by George Watson, the merchant and financier, in 1741. Some 250 years on, the school still adopts his original principles in offering a good academic and moral education, making room for children from less privileged backgrounds along with the more fortunate. Moved to current site in 1932, now a listed building. Splendid and impressively approached on a long sweeping driveway.

Pastoral Care and Discipline: Ethos of respect for others. Excellent system in place to control such a large school, with a year head following pupils all the way through the school. First year pupils keep the same form teacher for the first two years; the next two years follow suit and get to choose a tutor. Sixth formers are actively involved throughout the school. Strong anti-bullying policy, parents immediately informed and consulted if child is involved. Overall, parents report being impressed with the help given in difficult situations. Detentions plentiful but expulsion rare. Regular training for specialist guidance staff who help with listening and advising.

Pupils and Parents: Bright pupils, stretched in every direction. Claim never to be bored. Mainly children of professionals. Very much a local school but some travelling quite a distance. OBs and OGs include Sir David Steele (The Right Hon Lord Steel of Aikwood KBE DL, presiding officer of the Scottish Parliament), Sir Malcolm Rifkind, former foreign secretary, Chris Hoy, Olympic and Commonwealth medal cyclist, Gavin and Scott Hastings, former Scottish rugby internationals, Sheena McDonald and Martha Kearney, broadcasters and journalists.

Entrance: At 12 and upwards where vacancies arise by selection taking maths, English and VR papers along with interview.

Exit: 90 per cent plus stay on after Highers for further studies. 90 per cent plus go on to higher education. 66 per cent to Scottish universities.

Money Matters: A range of up to 11 academic and two music scholarships each year. Also sports bursaries, Enablement Fund and part of Ogden Trust Science Scholarship Scheme. Numerous short-term or long-term bursaries for those in need with assistance for more than 100 pupils. In 1997 the school's own foundation was established to maintain the original Watson purpose and replace the loss of Assisted Places. It also funded the new music school extension and a lift for disabled students.

Remarks: A fine traditional reputation. Well-organised structured school. Despite the size, communication with parents and pupils is very strong. Every pupil treated as an individual.

GEORGE WATSON'S COLLEGE JUNIOR SCHOOL

Colinton Road, Edinburgh, EH10 5EG

Tel: 0131 447 7931

Fax: 0131 452 8594

Email: admissions@gwc.org.uk

Website: www.gwc.org.uk

• Pupils: boys and girls; all day • Ages: 3-12

• Fees: £1,723-£1,940 • School status: Independent

• School gender: Mixed • Day/boarding: Day pupils

SEN provision

Detail:

Now provide for in school:

Mild: DYSL; HI; CP;

Moderate: DYSL; HI; CP;

Severe: DYSL;

Others: EAL;

Experience of:

Mild: ASP; ADD; ADHD; DYSC; DYSP; VI;

Moderate: AUT; DYSP;

Severe: DYSP;

Others: MSI; Sp&LD;

Summary: Learning support is provided throughout the Junior School, responding to and supporting a wide range of children with different kinds of difficulties, through direct support to individuals, small groups, and through in-class support and co-operative teaching.

What we say about the school - the full Good Schools Guide review

Head: Since 1989, Mr Donald McGougan DipCE (forties), educated at Campbeltown Grammar School and then Moray House. Internally appointed and well liked by staff and pupils.

Entrance: From 3 to the nursery. Early entries by interview but after 7 by English, maths and VR assessment.

Exit: No guarantee of advancement from nursery to main primary school but, once in, majority go on to senior school unless family circumstances dictate otherwise.

Remarks: Learning begins through play in nursery. The Watson's claim is that learning should be fun – even at home; homework given from first year and parents encouraged to support. Specialist subject teaching for the older children but French begins at 6 years old with native speakers. Special catch-up classes run for any latecomers. ICT skills taught and used widely to support other subjects. Mixed ability groups with setting only for maths at the top end of the school. Extensive library, and audio books. And quite a rarity for a primary school, a librarian on hand to help make choices. Good dyslexia support throughout. All for inclusive education, anxious to get away from any image of having 'a school with a unit'.

Lots of opportunities for children to exhibit their dramatic or musical talents on stage. Four choirs, two recorder groups, chamber orchestra, ensembles and pipes. Oodles of extra activities and clubs. Out on the field there's hockey for girls and rugby for the boys and back inside swimming for all. No official scholarships but in line with the ethos of the school, financial help given in unforeseen circumstances. Mostly children from professional parents who are pleased to have the 'extended day' for just a little extra, breakfast and after-school clubs. A big school and, at 23+, biggish classes. But manages its size well, taking advantage of its senior school's facilities. Good teaching and good value for money.

GIGGLESWICK SCHOOL

Giggleswick, Settle, North Yorkshire, BD24 0DE

Tel: 01729 893 000

Fax: 01729 893 150

Email: enquiries@giggleswick.org.uk

Website: www.giggleswick.org.uk

• Pupils: 325 boys and girls (215 board, 110 day) • Ages: 13-18 (associated junior schools, Catteral Hall 7-13 and Mill House pre-prep 3-8) • Religion: C of E • Fees: Senior school: boarding £6,990; day £4,700. Catteral Hall, years 7 and 8 boarding £4,910; day £3,835. Catteral Hall years 3-6 boarding £4,140; day £3,400. Mill House pre-prep £1,700

• School status: Independent • Opendays: October - nursery to year 9; February - sixth form

• School gender: Mixed • Day/boarding: Takes boarders

SEN provision

Detail:
Experience of:
Mild: ASP; AUT; ADD; ADHD; EBD; DYSC; DYSL; DYSP; HI; CP;
Moderate: ASP; AUT; MLD; DYSC; DYSL; DYSP; HI;
Severe: DYSL;
Others: EAL; DEL;

Summary: Giggleswick School learning support department offers appropriate help to any pupil with SEN across the entire 3-18 age range. At the Senior School this is normally in the form of additional individual withdrawal lessons based on either literacy, numeracy or curriculum support. Some SEN pupils pursue a reduced curriculum of modern foreign languages, studying only one instead of two languages in year 9 and dropping this at GCSE. Withdrawal lessons are from non-GCSE subjects, but sport and Music are also usually not withdrawn from. Provision can be made for additional support either in the classroom or one-to-one from classroom assistants should this be necessary.

The provision is broadly similar at Catteral Hall, the prep school. In addition to the withdrawal lessons classes also receive some in-class support from a teaching assistant or from two gap year students. At Mill House, the pre-prep school support can be arranged as above. In addition, support may be provided by North Yorkshire LEA for pupils of nursery age.

School currently has three pupils with statements of SEN, some of whom are day pupils and some are boarders. The SENCo works closely with parents and the LEAs concerned to ensure that appropriate provision and progress is made in line with the statements.

What we say about the school - the full Good Schools Guide review

Head: Since 2001, Mr Geoffrey Boult BA (mid forties). Read geography at Durham University. Previously a housemaster at St Edward's, Oxford. Married to Katie, four daughters, two at Giggleswick. A friendly, good-humoured, youthful figure, well liked and respected by pupils, teaches civics and religious studies. Fast developing a love of life in the north; appreciates the straightforwardness of northerners who 'tell it like it is.' A committed Christian and keen sportsman, once a county hockey player now enjoys coaching games and indulging his passion for golf. Staff now used to the new boss, lots of positive feedback, emphasis on academic target setting caused a stir but now accept head wants to balance the academic, blending it with the breadth of opportunity that Giggleswick offers.

Academic Matters: Hard working pupils confident but not arrogant, good solid staff, blend of age and experience. School selective, but not greatly so, good value added. Separate and combined sciences offered, 94 per cent A* to C pass rate at GCSE (100 per cent in single sciences) and new generation of enthusiastic science teachers. Sets for English, French, maths, science with top set French taking GCSE a year early then studying Russian. A good selection of A level courses offered though these 'have been rationalised to ensure viable teaching groups'. Those wanting to pursue vocational courses are directed elsewhere at 16. Most subjects sport a few Ds and Es but none fail altogether, art a particular strength. No massaging of results here, if you study for a subject you sit the exam. 'Failure not necessarily a bad thing,' says the head, 'sometimes it can provide a much needed wake-up call.'

Full-time special educational needs co-ordinator and successful buddy system where older children with experience of a learning difficulty mentor younger ones. EFL provided (two to four lessons a week), one-to-one, in study periods but anyone arriving from abroad must have a basic level of English. Class sizes 22 maximum, 4-12 for A level. Lots of computers, including some in each boarding house; every pupil has e-mail and a computer link in their study bedroom.

Games, Options, The Arts: Keen drama started by Russell Harty, several OGs and some pupils active in the profession, but luvvies and their tantrums not tolerated. Art and design taken seriously – impressively ambitious design work in particular. Strong links with half a dozen large companies and all pupils take IT qualifications. Public speaking encouraged.

Sport keen, traditionally cross-country and rugby, international level coaching over the past few years has led to success in hockey, cricket and athletics. Seven hard and four grass courts, together with the opportunity to train in Portugal, ensure continued popularity of tennis. A third of pupils learn an instrument (some play professionally), glorious chapel choir and lots of bands regularly tour home and abroad. Splendid sixth form centre with bar, alcohol allowed at weekends but consumption strictly monitored. Oozing with outward-bound opportunities including Duke of Edinburgh Award Scheme and CCF (compulsory in year 10) but plenty of other activities: car maintenance, conservation projects and all the usual opportunities. Exchanges with schools in France and Spain, tours, eg of drama and jazz, to the US, sports to Barbados, Australia and Hong Kong and historians to the WW1 battlefields. Sports' trips charged as extras but those identified as curriculum trips included in the fees.

Background and Atmosphere: Set in the western margins of the magnificent Yorkshire dales beneath an imposing limestone escarpment, 60 minutes' drive north of Manchester. Giggleswick was founded in 1512, moved to present site in 1869. Attractive buildings overlook Giggleswick village beneath the fabulously restored chapel complete with landmark copper dome well worth the walk up the steep hill (bring your crampons). Large development plan continues but wonderful new library with IT suite and Internet café now complete (a popular venue for nightly prep). Other recent additions include floodlit all-weather pitch and dining hall (cafeteria system, separate sittings, lots of choice, quality middling rather than Michelin.) Work on the new science centre is underway and once finished a new sports hall will be built on the site of the old. Girls' quarters in better decorative order than boys' where a lick of paint and the odd new carpet wouldn't go amiss. Pupils welcome to decorate their own study bedrooms, most do but some communal areas impersonal. A full boarding school, exeats only one weekend out of three. Happy relaxed but purposeful atmosphere: James Herriot meets Wainwright.

Pastoral Care and Discipline: Six houses (four boys, two girls) mix of boarding and day. Senior house staff tutor year 9 and 10 with pupils choosing their tutors in year 11. Pastoral care is supported by the medical centre, school doctor, professional counsellors and chaplain. Expulsions are rare, a couple a year. Sniffer dogs brought in termly for drugs checks and compulsory drugs testing is used on known and suspected offenders. Anyone caught supplying faces immediate expulsion. Boys and girls are allowed to visit each other's houses but permission must be sought to move away from public areas. Behaviour between sexes 'should not cause embarrassment to anyone.' Staff vigilant for anorexia and similar, system in place to check on pupils suspected of skipping meals including height/weight monitoring and meal attendance cards. Chapel an integral and important part of the school but faith more important than denomination.

Pupils and Parents: 75 per cent board, the rest are local children from a large catchment area, more boys (65 per cent) than girls, mid-range academically. School fully co-ed since 1983. Fifteen per cent foreign, 15 per cent expats and Services and popular with all these. Suits those who are team players, keen on the out doors and enjoy the varieties of life. Not for city types, loners or those who mind getting wet! Parents in business and the professions. OGs: James Agate, Richard Whitely, William Gaunt, Sarah Fox. OG society well established on the Internet.

Entrance: Not a great problem. At 3 (pre-prep, Mill House); at 7 (junior department, Catteral Hall) via own test and reports; at 13 CE or Giggleswick entrance exam for those from state schools and Catteral Hall together with interview and previous school's report. Entrance into sixth form is by a minimum of five GCSEs at A*-C grade with AS level subjects at B grade. Around 25 new sixth form entrants per year. Catteral Hall Prep school, the main feeder for Giggleswick, is situated in the same grounds and has moved away from following what it describes as the rigidity of common entrance to the breadth of National Curriculum. Year 7 and year 8 pupils at Catteral Hall use the senior school facilities for some lessons easing the transition from junior to senior school and allowing for specialist teaching.

Exit: Five plus to Oxbridge, others principally to a wide spread of universities or art foundation courses. 20 per cent do a gap year.

Money Matters: 30ish scholarships a year, including general distinction, art, music, and locals, ranging in value from 10 per cent for an exhibition to 50 per cent for a top scholarship award, bursaries including Services available. School in good shape financially owing to large gifts from OG Norman Sharpe and more recently Graham Watson (late governor).

Remarks: Friendly, character building co-ed boarding school serving the locals and the English community abroad. Extremely strong links with business reflected in curriculum and attitudes through the school. Doing a good job for a broad intake in this relatively isolated area. A useful school for the less academic pupil, those who don't know what to do next or the multi-talented who want to pursue a diverse range of interests.

GLENALMOND COLLEGE

Glenalmond, PH1 3RY

Tel: 01738 842 056
Fax: 01738 842 063
Email: registrar@glenalmondcollege.co.uk
Website: www.glenalmondcollege.co.uk

• Pupils: 385 pupils (235 boys, 150 girls; all board except for 59 day pupils) • Ages: 12-18 • Religion: Episcopalian
• Fees: Day: £3,635-£4,840. Boarding: £5,325-£7,100
• School status: Independent • School gender: Mixed
• Day/boarding: Takes boarders

SEN provision

Detail:
Now provide for in school:
Mild: DYSL; DYSP;
Others: EAL;
Experience of:
Mild: ASP; ADD; ADHD; EBD; DYSC; HI; VI;
Others: DEL; Epi; Eat;

Summary: Significant experience of mild dyslexia. Learning support for dyslexia and dyspraxia, using one-to-one withdrawal from main classes perhaps once or twice a week.

Teaching of English as a Second language for individuals and groups. Intermediate level required for entry (tested in UK or abroad).

What we say about the school - the full Good Schools Guide review

Warden: Since 2003, Mr Gordon Woods MA (Oxon) PGCE (forties) who was educated at Durham where he was head boy, and previously taught at Shrewsbury, where he rose through the ranks to become head of geography and finally second master. He also ran a couple of houses. Keen on rowing, he stroked the winning Oxford lightweight crew in 1976 and 1977. He and his wife, Emma, are much enjoying their Perthshire appointment, couple of partridges hanging in the porch, that sort of thing. Two teenagers, one in the school, and one still at Shrewsbury.

A human geographer, he is 'passionate about geography and the part that the subject can play on the way the other half lives'. 'You must always look outwards.' Currently teaching upper sixth Highers geography – to learn about the pupils as well as the Scottish system. Has retained the practice of breakfast for new pupils that he inherited from his predecessor who was here from 1992 and directed a considerable recovery of the school's fortunes. He and his wife also have lunches for the lower sixth. Articulate and enthusiastic, 'he is a good thing', the pupils reckon, apart from the occasional (and more than that) mutterings about being a little 'petty-minded'. Mr Woods says of his aims, 'Glenalmond needs to be outward-looking and not just outward bound, to retain a strong sense of its own past but to be modern in its approach to pupils and parents. Seeing boys and girls through the teenage years has to be a three way partnership – pupils, parents and the school'. A credo that was seriously put to the test two summers back, when miscreants included the son of one of the governors.

Academic Matters: 71 per cent A and B grades at A level. Some good staff at all levels, but still one or two who reckon that teaching at Glenalmond is 'a way of life'. Pupils complain about 'inadequate teaching aids', and head admits that 'teaching methods are under review'. Several recent retirements and seven new and enthusiastic staff appointed, including a new deputy head (Academic), a new head of geography from UCL and a new head of girls' games. The new chaplain, previously a choral scholar, keen on rugby and cross-country running, is a real plus. New(ish) science and maths block, awkwardly placed on the slope to the north of the main complex and connected at various levels – the trad build-it-by-numbers confection we see so often, with tubular rails and bog standard three level classrooms (well difficult to be imaginative with the sciences but given some of the glorious architecture around ...). Some excellent science results, but school still leans towards the arts. Fibre optics in place, two networks throughout school, apple and PCs, computers in most classrooms and houses, intranetted, nanny Internet all over, and broadband. Software used to detect fraud with pupils down-loading course work from elsewhere (does it work we wonder?).Setting in the third year, core subjects still setted individually, four sets. Exotic new additions to the A level syllabus: music technology, RS, PE at GCSE level; history of art, apparently, with Internet input, which most other schools find difficult if their Internet is properly nannied. Ditto politics AS (language in the House of Lords can be truly blue). Good GCSE results with quantities of As and A*s across the board.School follows mixed bag of A levels and Highers. Always a difficult row to hoe. About ten per cent take Highers over two years: maths, English, geography popular plus economics and theatre studies. Loads of class related trips. Dyslexia support now represented at meetings of heads of departments (goodness gracious) and salaried professional in charge of learning support 'loads of one-to-one lessons'. All screened on entry, and certified with Ed Psych report for extra time in exams. Most of the male chauvinists are now a thing of the past, though girls still complain of one beak.

Games, Options, The Arts: This is still a school which majors in outward bound activities and uses its fantastic site to good advantage – all sorts of activities (and active is the word) – conservation projects, Munro Club, terrific CCF (remember Coll has strong army links), full-bore shooting as well as clays, indoor and outdoor .22 range, Scottish Islands Peaks Race, skiing (own artificial ski slope now out of commission thanks to Health and Safety regs) regular trips to freezing Glenshee – school boasts a number of past and current members of Scottish ski teams), curling a surprising newcomer, own nine hole golf course at Cairnies, sailing. Two gold D of E assessors on the staff, and hugely popular, with trips to Norway and the ruggeder parts of the USA.

Rugby is a religion, but good, rather than sweeping all before it. Boys' hockey coming up fast, girls' hockey and lacrosse strong, the appointment of hockey international as head of girls' games has done wonders. Enough girls now to muster full strength sports teams who keep tennis/netball teams flying the Glenalmond flag. Sports are a key part of life here, and daily participation is compulsory, but the constitutionally disinclined can get by with a spot of umpiring. NB sports regularly interrupted with vile weather. Rich in all-weather spectacularly floodlit pitches and more in the pipeline. Fishing (on the River Almond), sports hall, indoor heated pool. Two Pipe bands – which is hot shot on the charity front.

Design and technology now holding its own. First XV matches timetabled to ensure that players can participate in music and art – which they do with enthusiasm. Head keen that we would be as keen on the new art dept head as he is. He also did not like us calling her 'a jolly dolly', insisting that 'there is an intensity and passion about her art that goes well beyond the jolly dolly image'. We stand corrected. Head of art very keen on fabric and design and appeared proudest of the hat collection pupils had fabricated during the previous session. Hat making seems the strangest choice for what is a pretty butch school, but the art room is filled with zany pics of girls modelling their own creations, with one or two chaps as well. Fifth form CCF (both sexes) now an option, regular camps throughout the term very popular (our girlie guide was not absolutely convinced how much she loved the expeditions, but it is so much fun to look back on). Sixth form can grannie bash or work in special schools instead.

Background and Atmosphere: Known to the pupils as Coll. Founded in 1847 by Prime Minister Gladstone, this is Scotland's oldest, most elegant, school. Spectacular self-contained quadrangle of cloisters, centred round the chapel and set in its own mini 300 acre estate, beautifully tended parkland and surrounded by some of the smartest grouse shooting in Scotland. Several modern additions stuck round the back, including Basil Spence music block. Also the aforementioned science and maths block.

This is a proper boys' boarding school which admitted girls at sixth form in 1990 and went 'all the way' in 1995; admissions now running 50/50. School currently sports five boys' boarding houses and two girls' and, whilst a third girls' house is on the wish list, a new boys' house will be open in 2007 in order to totally revamp the somewhat jealous boys and to convert some of the current boys housing into staff flats (all staff must live on site, part of their contract). Boys and girls mix socially during the day and after prep in school and not in each other's houses, although moves are afoot for each house to have a co-ed common room for limited access. All houses will also have one dedicated common room. Sixth form bar on Saturdays.

Rather set apart from the world and protective – you can't just wander round at will. 'Shopping bus' to Perth twice a week. Fixed exeats on either side of half term, 'parents have free and welcome access to their children at any time and can take them out on Saturdays and Sundays (after chapel). New trenchant school prospectus, which actually acknowledges that parents and guardians can read the spoken word rather than resembling a Scottish Tourist Board guide to Perthshire, is full of muscular pics of kids in action. Boy and girl now joint heads of Coll for the first time ever.

Pastoral Care and Discipline: Following a fairly hectic last few weeks at Glenalmond two summers back, head has been accused of regarding high jinks as serious. Certainly the affair saw some rather boring removals. Head has counteracted with a massively impressive tightly worded code of behaviour which covers everything from cycling without a helmet to public displays of affection between pupils as well as a massive drugs etc document. 'Smoking is a major social gateway to the smoking of illegal drugs, the College may regard persistent tobacco smoking as a reason for asking parents and pupils to agree to future drug testing'. These documents are unique in our experience and we are slightly concerned that sometimes alleged offences may be judged in black and white.

Basically, random drugs testing on suspicion, out if positive; fags equals house gating, Warden's gating and letters home, followed by suspension. Smoking in a building equals suspension even for the first time. Boozing to excess in permitted zones equals Warden's gating, followed by bans and possible suspension, no spirits allowed in the recognized pubs and watering holes. No bringing booze back to school under any circs. Stories of booze trenches, which we have heard ad infinitum over the years from staff and boys alike (well known to staff cos they borrow it and replace like with like), dismissed by the warden as 'nothing other than an unsubstantiated allegation'. No reported bullying, senior mistress both neutral and approachable. Anorexia said to be less of a problem, couple of girls under watchful eye, but nothing serious. 'Not completely clean' admits the head. Local keepers still complain about empties and other detritus on the neighbouring grouse moor.

Pupils and Parents: Scotland's school for toffs. 'Jolly nice parents'. Traditionally Scottish upper middle and middle class, army, Highland families. About twenty per cent locals and ten per cent foreigners from all over, plus three to four per cent expats. School has previously trawled abroad and this year seven Chinese pupils arrived from Shanghai via an agency. All real foreigners must have guardians, either via parents or contacts or school will fix them up with guardianship agencies 'with whom we have worked successfully in the past'. Large number of first time buyers. FPs (known as OGs) a generous bunch and include Sandy Gall, Robbie Coltrane, Miles Kington, Allan Massie, David Sole and Andrew MacDonald (Train Spotting fame), Charlie (Lord) Falconer, erstwhile flatmate of Tony Blair – who was of course at arch-rival school, Fettes.

Entrance: Own entrance exam at 12, most at 13+ via CE, oodles from Ardvreck, Craigclowan, Lathallan (who are about to take pupils up to age 16) St Mary's Melrose and Belhaven, with a clutch from Cargilfield, state primaries or overseas. Some at sixth form; twenty this year, with a number from Germany, six passes at standard grade or GCSE or entrance test and previous school's recommendation. Entrance not a difficult hurdle at the moment.

Exit: 96 per cent + to university of some form of higher education. Half a dozen to Oxbridge.

Money Matters: Discounts for siblings of 25 per cent, a whopping 50 per cent for fourth child. 10 per cent for children whose parents are in the Armed Forces, and Fil Cler Bursaries for offspring of the Clergy. Otherwise a clutch of bursaries (means-tested) plus help if circumstances change. Music, art and academic scholarships too.

Remarks: School popular and highly thought of, saved by the 'belles' after a period of falling numbers, more girl friendly than previously, but still really a boys' school at heart. Not for retiring flowers, rebels or non-joiners in. We gave the school the soubriquet 'the Eton of the North' in our first edition; despite its best endeavours, we still don't think it's fully back on form.

GLYNE GAP SCHOOL

School Place, Hastings Road, Bexhill-on-Sea, East Sussex, TN40 2PU

Tel: 01424 217 720

Fax: 01424 734 962

Email: office@glynegap.e-sussex.sch.uk

Website: www.glynegap.e-sussex.sch.uk

• Pupils: 100 boys and girls • Ages: 2-19 • School status: State • School gender: Mixed • Day/boarding: Day pupils

SEN provision

Summary: No comment. Just a wonderful place. SEN details added by us.

What we say about the school - the full Good Schools Guide review

Head: Since whenever, Mr John Hassell OBE (late forties). His staff love him, and he is deadly serious in his commitment to the school's goals – to encourage its pupils to lead the most independent and self-determining lives of which they are capable. The school is the most important thing in his life, very reluctant to put himself forward – hence the lack of detail above. Wrote to every soap opera actor and producer to ask them to write in a character with learning difficulties – the disabled should be in the public eye, not him. Delegates, staff involved and empowered. He says 'I've got the best job in the world. As well as teaching all the National Curriculum subjects, we give them skills they never had or thought they would have, such as how to cross a road, feed themselves, get on a bus, go shopping in another town. If you are dependent on someone throughout your life your quality of life is restricted.'

Deputy Di Gargett (mid forties) is the one that parents are likely to see most of, a substantial presence in the school, dependable, supportive, endlessly enthusiastic about the head, the staff and the school. 'There is still a huge fear borne out of ignorance. We believe our pupils' differences should be celebrated. That can only be achieved through knowledge and understanding and we're committed to challenging people's prejudices and misconceptions about disabled people.'

Academic Matters: Aims to offer children the same curriculum opportunities, at an appropriate level, as their brothers and sisters in mainstream schools. No public exams, though many take nationally recognised qualifications. Classes are arranged to provide a progression for all pupils passing through the school, with two to three years being the usual time spent in any one class. Special high dependency classes for pupils with very profound and multiple disabilities. All pupils of a similar age are brought together for some activities during the week.

Co-operation with other schools in the town is a key part of Glyne Gap's success. Mr Hassell explained: 'Already some of our pupils attend lessons at Pebsham and St Richard's and we envisage working with other schools and making that much more widespread.' 'Some of our older students do voluntary work at charity shops or nursery schools. We're into flexible attendance; if pupils can attend mainstream lessons they will.'

The new Bexhill College site includes a £1.5 million Glyne Gap annex. 'We will have our own specialist learning facilities for our 16 to 19-year-olds but they are able to use the rest of the college as well.' Immensely impressive to visit – kids you never would have imagined would be operating at this level, included, involved and appreciated. Annexe in Bexhill (a large detached house) used exclusively to provide community-based FE.

72 staff. Lots of applications to work at the school. 'A very spiritual place to be.' Regular training too. Specialist staff (in direct co-operation and consultation with the child's class teacher) come to work with pupils: nurses, social workers, physiotherapists, music therapist, occupational therapists, speech therapists, an aromatherapist, a teacher for the visually impaired and a dance teacher.

Games, Options, The Arts: Many older students take part in the Duke of Edinburgh award scheme or the Youth Award Scheme and go on vocational (work) experience placements. Sport for all: team sports like football, cricket and volleyball as well as individual sports like trampolining, swimming and riding. For older pupils the school runs an out of school hours sports and leisure club. There have been sleepovers in classrooms, a camp on the school field, trips to the theatre...

Some excellent facilities including a pool, trampoline room, adventure playground and large sports field. A large number of staff hold specialist sports and leisure qualifications.

Background and Atmosphere: Does it all for parents – pick up and drop off, breakfast in school, whatever it takes. Good facilities – nursery (integrated with the primary school next door) bright, light. well-equipped with books, specialist toys and physiotherapy aids. Sensory resource centre with a rebound therapy room, vision stimulation room, soft play room and music room. Smells good – always a test of a caring school.

For children who will always need others to help meet their needs, they give a means of making choices and friendships, to provide the widest possible range of experiences, and to maintain and improve their physical abilities. All staff work to raise the children's confidence.

Pastoral Care and Discipline: The health education syllabus runs through the whole school, ensuring that knowledge is gradually built up over a period of years. So for example, at five years old children may be learning about washing hands, while at 19 students may learn about alcohol abuse. As well as this syllabus, individual needs will be met, as they arise, through individual programmes. A full copy of the school sex education policy is available on request.

Glyne Gap School aims...'to teach children the knowledge, skills and confidence that will enable them to lead as full, normal and independent a life as possible'. Behaviour can be a real barrier to achieving this and can handicap a pupil more than their primary disability does. The school employs practical strategies to promote good behaviour particularly to encourage good order and conduct in the life of the school. For some pupils, possibly because of the nature of their disability or other factors, addressing their behaviour may require a more structured intensive approach. For such cases careful individual planning precedes a how, when and what agreement to dealing with the behaviour.

'We do a good job of teaching our own pupils that they can contribute and play an important part in society. This is a group of people we can be proud of in our town.'

Pupils and Parents: Parents seem very pleased with what the school does for their children. They are encouraged to take an active part in, and contribute to, the setting of their children's termly goals and in post school placements. Parents are made welcome in school, without appointment if necessary. Staff make home visits; to help communication: each pupil has a book which passes daily between home and school, with news and achievements being immediately exchanged. A family and personal adviser is funded by the school and Connexions. Free holiday scheme, home learning and sibling workshops. Family days – including grandparents. Annual planning and review meeting for every pupil, with parents and professionals (if involved).

Entrance: The school operates an Open School policy – parents who believe their child may benefit from the education provided at Glyne Gap (because, for instance, their child is falling behind at another school) contact the school directly to meet the headteacher and to visit. Formal referral for all pupils is through the LEA either in the form of an educational psychologist's recommendation for an assessment placement or through a completed East Sussex Statement of Special Educational Needs.

Exit: Occasionally a student leaves for a full-time further education place at a local or residential college. Most move to establishments that are either run or funded by Social Services.

Careers Education in the school is a process of learning whereby pupils are given the opportunities, experiences and responsibilities to equip them for adult life. Its close relationship with personal and social education means it is at the core of the school's work, particularly in the Secondary and Further Education years. The school works very closely with other agencies to investigate possible placements post-19. One boy, when we visited, was working with the school carpenter, who had just bought him a tool as a present.

Remarks: A very positive, happy place that deals sensitively, imaginatively, professionally and caringly for the pupils who are lucky enough to get a place. Deservedly popular and inspirationally led.

GODSTOWE PREP SCHOOL

High Wycombe, Buckinghamshire, HP13 6PR

Tel: 01494 529 273

Fax: 01494 429 009

Email: head@godstowe.org

Website: www.godstowe.org

• Pupils: 100 boarders, 210 day girls. Also pre-prep of 100 boys and girls, all day • Ages: 7-13, pre-prep 3-7 • Religion: C of E • Fees: £1,660-£3,565; boarding £5,240 • School status: Independent • Opendays: Termly on Fridays, check website for dates • School gender: Mixed • Day/boarding: Takes boarders

SEN provision

Detail:

Now provide for in school:

Mild: DYSC; DYSL; DYSP;

Moderate: DYSC; DYSL; DYSP;

Severe: DYSC; DYSL; DYSP;

Others: EAL; Sp&LD;

Summary: Godstowe Preparatory School provides support for children with learning difficulties within school and within the learning support department. Children can receive specialist help in leteracy and numeracy alongside their usual lessons. The department has close links with an independent speech and language therapist who regularly visits the school, and also well-respected educational psychologists.

What we say about the school - the full Good Schools Guide review

Head: Interregnum. In late June 2005 Mrs Frances Henson, head since 1991, departed precipitately over the course of a weekend. This appears to have been the culmination of long-running disagreements as to the future direction of the school. Not brilliantly handled, putting it mildly. We do not, though, detect any underlying malaise that could not be put right by a good new head. Governors remain committed to Godstowe as it always was – girls only through to 13 – but with better provision for those who want to try for state selectives at 11.

Said good new head is to be (from September 2006) Mr David St Clair Gainer BEd (forties), currently head of Belmont near Dorking. Educated at Claires Court, Maidenhead and Belmont Abbey in Herefordshire followed by St Mary's, Strawberry Hill, London, where he studied mathematics and drama. Began career at Llanarth Court Prep School in South Wales then housemaster of junior house at his old school Belmont Abbey, followed by three years at Forest Grange prep in Horsham where he was deputy head, before becoming head of Belmont in 1991. Friendly, jovial and approachable. Believes in being visible around the place. Married to Cathy who teaches geography and is Belmont's SENCo. Responsible for all drama productions, and also reads to all pre-prep pupils every Friday afternoon. Has two teenage children.

Entrance: Not a selective school, and numbers are down anyway. Entry at 7 for the main school. Academic scholarships at 8 and 11.

Exit: Pre-prep boys usually go to traditional boys' boarding at seven. Girls to major senior schools, including Wycombe Abbey, Cheltenham Ladies' College, Downe House, Haileybury, Rugby, Badminton, Benenden etc etc. Most take CE at 13, with scholarships and exhibitions on all fronts. 30 per cent won scholarships to senior schools in 2003. Small trickle to state sector at 11.

Remarks: The first girls' boarding prep in the country, purpose-built 1900 (with later extensions). Magical new music school (with spectacular views across the valley), serious re-vamp of older buildings, particularly the dining room, and other new building. Brilliant use of very hilly ground on outskirts of High Wycombe, assault course and outdoor activity areas. Masses of activities at weekends, plus free clubs and options – 2 hours per day from 4.30pm. Early drop-off plus breakfast (7.30am) and late pick-up plus supper (7.30pm) for 'a few pounds'. Excellent PSHE in place and girls get lifestyle course after CE which includes lectures from representatives of The Body Shop.

Pre-prep has expanded hugely; now has new separate buildings. French from age four. Latin or Spanish at ten. Classes 'subtly' streamed. Maximum class size 18, scholarship stream. IT, art, marvellous textiles and ceramics; fantastic music (long tradition of this) with masses of girl-inspired concerts. Dyslexia help on hand, with one-to-one help where necessary, regular spelling and reading help available. EFL also available, though only about 5 per cent foreigners (not counting expats). Some MoD parents.

A parent said to us, 'excellent pastoral care, really fantastic homely feel to the boarding houses. All the girls are friendly and caring with good manners. I am really pleased with the high academic standard. My daughter has consistently received a very sound education without feeling at all pressured, despite arriving there in year 6. We have just done the rounds of 13+ interviews to very selective senior schools, and were welcomed at all with a big smile and exclamation of 'Ah ... Godstowe' – acceptance letters poured in soon after! Girls well prepared for interviews, confident and cheerful (and smart).' School is very much on form as a boarding school with a large day element – 'the only good one (ie girls' prep) in the area,' say parents.

That, at least, is what applied until things came unglued. We look to the new head to get it back on the rails fast.

GREENHEAD COLLEGE

Greenhead Road, Huddersfield, West Yorkshire, HD1 4ES

Tel: 01484 422 032

Fax: 01484 518 025

Email: college@greenhead.ac.uk

Website: www.greenhead.ac.uk

• Pupils: 1,750 boys and girls; all in the sixth form

• Ages: 16-18 • Religion: Non-denom • School status: State

• School gender: Mixed • Day/boarding: Day pupils

SEN provision

Detail:
Now provide for in school:
Mild: ASP; ADD; EBD; DYSL; DYSP; HI; VI;
Moderate: EBD; MLD; DYSL; DYSP; HI; VI;
Severe: DYSL; VI;
Others: OCD; TIC; EAL; Epi; PD; Eat;
Experience of:
Mild: ADHD; DYSC; CP;
Moderate: DYSC;
Severe: DYSC;
Others: DEL;

Summary: Greenhead College provides AS/A level programmes of study for 16 to 19-year-olds. The college welcomes all students who reach its entry requirements and endeavours to ensure that they have equal access to the opportunities and experiences on offer. Every student has a personal tutor who monitors their progress and well-being. There is also a counselling service and additional help with academic work is available from subject teachers and the college's study centre. Where a student has a specific learning difficulty or disability, the college's learning support co-ordinator works closely with the student, teachers and tutor to ensure that any special requirements are met.

What we say about the school - the full Good Schools Guide review

Principal: Since 2002, Mr Martin Rostron BA PGCE (early fifties) who was educated at Chadderton Grammar School in Oldham and read English at Liverpool. He came to Greenhead in 1991 and was previously vice principal. He has always taught in the maintained sector and has taught all ages from 11-18 but, more recently, at Priestley Sixth Form College in Warrington. He has had a son and daughter at Greenhead; third child (son) hopes to come. Much enjoying his time here, 'life has got to be fun', 'people here work extraordinarily hard', and 'the staff are quite phenomenal'; good intra-staff support, little turnover of staff. Took over from the seriously wonderful Kevin Conway, the foundation of Greenhead's excellence.

Academic Matters: College is one of three in Huddersfield and they have a concordat whereby all will provide the basic AS and A level subjects but each will specialise in a different sphere. Hence Greenhead offers a business studies at AVCE level (much more difficult than NVQ) as well as A and AS levels in law, government and politics, IT, maths ad infinitum and the humanities and sciences. Psychology and RS currently top of the pops and sociology. An astonishing 199 students took psychology last year, with 40 per cent getting A. French, German, Spanish and Italian on offer but no classics or esoteric languages – one might have expected Urdu, given the ethnic mix but that is studied elsewhere. Computers all over the place. Fantastic suite of brand new labs.

Good take-up for RSA qualifications. Average class size 18 for A levels, and 19 at AS. Most students opt for four AS and three or more As; College will 'tolerate' retakes but only if space available in that particular course and candidates 'have a realistic chance of improving their grades' – perhaps half a dozen a year. They will also 'investigate the possibility' of grafting on extra subjects if 'there is sufficient demand' and if there is sufficient space. A level general studies for 'almost all'. No real break between some lessons – the distances can be quite far. College operates an 'open door' policy, staff cluster in subject rooms during their free time and any pupil can walk in to any subject room and ask for help. Magic. We met a larger than normal cross-section of teachers during our visit. Library designated a 'place of silent study', well, quiet rather than silent, but ferociously well-equipped. Supplemented in 2004 by the 'Reading Room', a new large area for 'sociable' study.

Kevin Conway developed the College's own value-added system, now widely followed – picks up students who are falling behind or who deserve particular praise very early and, most particularly and without rancour, helps bring teachers who are performing below par up to scratch.

Games, Options, The Arts: PE and music popular; enormous art rooms in £2 million new building, shared with law and business. Stunning, with inspired work in progress. No large sports hall of their own but has 'use of' one five minutes' walk across the park; major playing fields (cheap to hire, use all the facilities going, and dance studios.) 92 took PE last year, one third grade As. Strongest rugby side in the county, cups all over the place, squash, basketball good; national representative in hockey – popular, and football 'expanding' – four competitive teams. Music 'absolutely stunning at the moment', orchestra, plus jazz, string quartets – positively 'humming'. Impressive music dept with full recording gear, music computers and PCs. Vibrant drama, often with play rehearsals at 7.30am as well as pm and at weekends. Serious enrichment programme, students are offered an amazing 70 different courses, everything from Freudian psychology, to crime in society or yoga. D of E, Young Enterprise, any key skills you want plus hints on how to handle Oxbridge. Every student MUST attend one course but if you don't fancy any of them, then you can start your own. Probably the best work placement programme anywhere.

Background and Atmosphere: Plumb in the middle of Huddersfield and a stone's throw from the centre of town with train and bus stations, Greenhead, set in what is now an enormous car park, bustles with purposeful students. Huge complex with masses of add-ons, very handsome hall, big wide corridors with lockers on either side, and remarkably tidy. College has 'no problems with disabled'; 'we move the teaching room to the ground floor to accommodate wheelchairs' but possessed of four new lifts; most areas are now fully accessible. They have blind students and, of course, support for learning is a given. Prospective students are advised to contact the college's learning support co-ordinator for advice prior to admission so any specialist support or facilities can be put in place (strive to meet all reasonable requests). Good support and back up once in the system. This is, after all, state-funded. Student Union, self-elected prefects, social areas are the hall and canteen; smokers exiled to cancer ward = outdoor area beside canteen, with huge chimney, presumably from the boiler, presiding over all.

Pastoral Care and Discipline: Excellent pastoral system, with tutors taking a personal interest in each student, and all students having a day off each term to discuss their grades with their teachers and being given a rocket if they are not up to scratch. PSHE for all. College will exclude for violent or abusive behaviour, smoking 'not tolerated' but see above (they all light up as they leave the campus anyway). Students with real problems can make an appointment to see a counsellor. No racial tension, though ethnic groups tend to stick together – 'most stick with their school peer groups'. Regular 'whole block' assemblies – unusual in most sixth form colleges.

Pupils and Parents: What you would expect, mainly solid middle class, not a lot of 'twocers' (taking without owner consent). Strong work ethos. Huge catchment area, about two thirds of the students come from partner schools.

Entrance: Apply well before mid-Feb of the year you want to go to, College nearly 40 per cent over-subscribed, fed by 12 local partner schools in the same catchment area, and around 55 other schools nearby on a placement basis. Places allocated on the basis of interview, plus results of mock GCSEs, and school reports. 8 per cent from the independent sector.

Exit: About 90 per cent go directly to higher education, including 30 or so to Oxbridge; very strong medical bias – at one point the college was responsible for 1 per cent of the new medical intake in the country. Musicians may choose the Northern College of Music or the Conservatoire but, equally, may decide to go to uni first and then study music full-time. 5 per cent gap (and then presumably to higher ed) and rest to work.

Money Matters: Students qualify for state hand-out (EMA), to keep them in sixth form education.

Remarks: As we said before, an outstanding sixth form college, with an ordinary load of students in an ordinary town doing extraordinarily well. The brightest do succeed here and all can expect to do markedly better than in the average state (or independent) school. Terrific.

Gresham's Preparatory School

Cromer Road, Holt, Norfolk, NR25 6EY

Tel: 01263 714600

Fax: 01263 714060

Email: prep@greshams.com

Website: www.greshams.com

• Pupils: roughly 60/40 boys and girls; boarding and day

• Ages: 3-13 including pre-prep and nursery

• Fees: Prep school: boarding: £5,025; day £3,855. Pre-prep: from £1,905-£2,115 • School status: Independent

• Opendays: First May Bank Holiday Saturday, plus taster days in September, October and November • School gender: Mixed

• Day/boarding: Takes boarders

SEN provision

Detail:
Now provide for in school:
Mild: ASP; EBD; DYSC; DYSL; DYSP;
Moderate: ADD; EBD; MLD; DYSC; DYSL; DYSP;
Others: SPD; EAL; Sp&LD;
Experience of:
Mild: ADHD; HI;
Moderate: ADHD;
Others: OCD; TIC; DEL; Epi; PD; Eat;

Summary: A well-resourced department with four qualified members of staff, operating from an excellent learning support centre. Pupils who receive learning support vary from those with mild dyslexic and organisational problems to those with more severe problems with reading and writing. We cater for some children with other conditions on a case-by-case basis.

What we say about the school - the full Good Schools Guide review

Head: Since 2003, Mr James Quick BA PGCE (forties), educated at Rendcomb, did his BA and PGCE at Durham, and teaches history as much as possible – 'I do like being in the classroom... you can find out what's really happening'. Previously taught at The Dragon in Oxford, where he was housemaster (and taught this editor's children history) and subsequently at St Edwards. He did a sabbatical at Geelong Grammar in Australia before coming here with his wife, Kim, and their four daughters, all at Gresham's.

Entrance: Either through the pre-prep or via own test.

Exit: Predominantly to the senior school, though one or two may go elsewhere.

Remarks: Jolly little school, autonomous as far as it goes, but within walking distance of Gresham's (minibus for smalls) for all the main facilities like games, swimming pool and theatre, though the prep does have its own integrated games pitches and a fab new play area with wizard wooden climbing frames and a somewhat strange pagoda. Stunning art dept – with pottery and ceramics and their own kiln; terrific pupil pics all over the shop. Terrific music too; many jazz, wind, string and rock bands, plus little theatrical performances; they have taken a 'production to the Edinburgh fringe for the last ten years.

Big jolly library, with computers and more computers all over the school. Terrific selection of board games, chess popular and giant chess in the garden, and spit new wooden climbing frame. Dedicated classrooms, langs from seven, Latin from nine. One full-time and three part-time SEN assistants, again extra charge for this, but will take ADHD (which senior school is chary about) and finds no problems with Ritalin. This is a charming school within a school, dedicated boy and girl houses, cheerful bright (dare one say garish?) colours in the dorms, with a happy mixture of full, weekly and flexi boarders. Head reckons that shortly the full and weekly boarders will become as one. School nominally full, but 'could take the odd one at the odd time'. Worth a try.

GRESHAM'S SCHOOL

Cromer Road, Holt, Norfolk, NR25 6EA

Tel: 01263 714500
Fax: 01263 712 028
Email: bmccombie@greshams.com
Website: www.greshams.com

• Pupils: 450 boys and girls (two thirds board, one third day) • Ages: 13-18 • Religion: C of E • Fees: Senior school: boarding £6,890; day £5,340. Prep school: boarding: £5,025; day £3,855. Pre-prep: from £1,905-£2,115 • School status: Independent • Opendays: First May Bank Holiday Saturday, plus taster days in September, October and November • School gender: Mixed • Day/boarding: Takes boarders

---

SEN provision

Detail:
Now provide for in school:
Mild: DYSC; DYSL; DYSP;
Moderate: DYSC; DYSL; DYSP;
Experience of:
Mild: ASP; SpLD;
Moderate: SpLD;

Summary: Gresham's learning support department deals mainly with pupils who are dyslexic, dyspraxic or dyscalculic. There are currently 124 pupils on the learning support register; 53 are receiving regular individual lessons from a suitably qualified teacher, whilst those who have become independent learners may only need occasional help. All pupils are screened on entry to the school to ensure that anyone that needs help is identified and appropriate help arranged. Pupils that are known to have a specific learning difficulty before they enter the school are tested by the head of learning support before entry. There is some limited in-class support for pupils who will need a scribe for examinations and many pupils use laptops as their normal method of presenting work. In the GCSE years pupils who have individual lessons usually take nine rather than ten GCSEs and the one-to-one sessions are supplemented by small study groups led by a teacher from the department. The results for pupils on the learning support register are good; all pupils achieved GCSE English, English literature and mathematics with at least a grade C in 2005 and we would expect almost all of our pupils to take A levels and then go on to university.

What we say about the school - the full Good Schools Guide review

Head: Since 2002, Mr Antony Clark MA HDE (forties), educated at St Andrew's College, South Africa, followed by Rhodes University; read history (and played cricket) at Downing, Cambridge and started his teaching career at Westerford High School in Cape Town.

After a brief spell in the 'investment business' he was appointed head of St Joseph's Marist College in Cape Town, which is RC and 'non-racial, ahead of Independence'. Challenging stuff. He expanded the school roll by almost 50 per cent during his time there, before becoming head of St Andrew's College in Grahamstown.

Married to (Dr) Brigitte, who lectures in law at the University of East Anglia; three children in the school. Very much a hands-on head, pupils say 'he is everywhere', turns up at (almost) all matches, has a good recall of their names (all were impressed – apparently his wife tests him in the kitchen). According to a previous head boy, 'he appears to be shaking up the whole school with a new regime'. Teaches history – though probably not enough to satisfy the teacher in him. A 'listening head', he is gradually 'making changes to the pattern of education here'. Asked for a wish list, he replied he 'would like to make the school as happy a place as possible' (first time we have had a metaphysical here), 'build an all-embracing sports pavilion' (the school sports ground hosts a mass of ex-Gresham's matches on the astroturf, so it could also be a permanent fundraiser) and 'build a resources centre to house the library etc, etc'). And, yes, when pushed, the sports pavilion beat the resource centre on priority.

Academic Matters: 50 per cent pass rate at Common Entrance is probably the reason for the really quite large number of Ds and Es at A level, though the bright do really well, with a starring number of pupils in the top five per cent in English literature at GCSE, and 25 pupils (out of fifty) getting A in maths at A level (English and French good too). Classics currently popular, Greek is an option. Huge variety of languages: French, German, Japanese, Russian (good take-up here from the German contingent) and Spanish, and proper brand new lang labs.

No class larger than 21, mostly much much smaller. Pupils are setted from 13 in English and a variety of disciplines thereafter. Utilitarian collection of classrooms, the width of corridors depends on the age of the building. Business studies and the sciences all good, pupils usually do two sciences at GCSE. And one bright chap not only got an A in physics last year, but was also published in the States. CLT (chemistry lecture theatre) in newish science block, with the tiniest staircase imaginable up to the chemistry library. Powerpoint presentation under way during our visit in the biology lab but not a sign of an interactive whiteboard anywhere. Masses of flat-screened computers and, in every department, good use of laptops, school internetted and nannied.

Excellent booklet on sixth form choices. Pupils coming into the school from outside, ie not from the prep school, are screened for suspected problem areas during the year before they arrive: spelling, comprehension, writing and reading and dyscalculia. They may also have an IQ test and an ed psych's report. They may then be given extra help in the lamentably tiny SEN department, which strives manfully to cope with both accelerated learning and dyslexia et al. The visitor creeps past three pupils, each on different programmes, to reach the head of department's over-cluttered hq; three other pupils are tucked away in corners, working away with individual teachers, who may also be teaching EFL. The department boasts three full-time learning support teachers and one dedicated EFL in about the same area as half of one normal classroom. Money needs spending here – we are surprised that games facilities should be given priority. Pupils are usually withdrawn from study periods, but support teaching in class is also on offer, and any pupil in the system is offered 'supervised' study time. The school 'can cope' with very mild Asperger's, ADD but not ADHD, and offers scribes, readers, and voice-activated computers, all for £200 extra per pupil per term.

Games, Options, The Arts: Strong games, particularly hockey – fantastic say the pupils – national championships, county players all over the place. Probably over-used astroturfs, masses of pitches, keen external coaches and a sports physio on hand at important matches. Cricket spectacular and head regards himself as assistant coach. Rugby on the up. Much used swimming pool (and open to all comers) with three mornings a week for early swimmers ex school, BASC course an option. (Indeed masses of options). Weights room, gym, rowing machines regularly used by both boys and girls. Regular prizewinners at Bisley, CCF (army and RAF) popular and D of E, imaginative car building also part of CCF, grannie bashing for non-joiners-in.

Aerobics and dance at GCSE, but no proper dance studio, school needs larger, properly mirrored premises. Auden theatre much used by locals and tremendously varied selection of performances, free to school. Mass of dressing rooms, and sophisticated professional lighting and sound systems for those interested in theatre studies who don't want to strut the boards, enthusiastic set designers happily painting when we visited. Spectacular music with vast range of instruments on offer and good collection of orchestra, band and choral activities. Loads of tours in all disciplines.

Strong art, with good showing at A level, but sadly only flat art and photography, the latter particularly impressive. Our pupil advisors were at odds as to whether the art was fab or not – one who had come here on an art scholarship was particularly dismissive. 'Better in my last place,' she said. Life class open to outsiders and the art rooms were filled with naked fat ladies from every conceivable angle. Regular artists in residence but no history of art. Some of the pics around the school are fantabulous; the photography master recently held an almost sell-out (when we visited) exhibition in the foyer of the art block. Pupils' work is displayed there too. Pupils wondered about textiles, with painted fabrics and the like; though there is a tapestry and embroidery option 'it isn't the same'.

Background and Atmosphere: Founded by Sir John Gresham, Lord Mayor of London and 'a wealthy Midlands landowner' in 1555, 'the school was placed in the control of the Worshipful Company of Fishmongers', with which it still has close links. Somewhat haphazard development of a 170 acre site (including 90 acres of woodlands) demonstrates a variety of architectural styles around 'the parade ground'. Lutyens-style classroom blocks mingle with The Big School, a vast Edwardian hall with polished wood floors. Greek theatre in the woods, optimistically used for prize giving, 'but it almost always rains and we have to run for cover'. Charming chapel. Curious combination of Norfolk knapped flint, and 'temporary' twenties thatched huts ('scruff shacks') which are now listed buildings. Fair amount of walking involved, school straddles (the now by-passed but still fairly busy) main road: bridge for all but upper sixth mandatory.

Friendly, happy and relaxed atmosphere between pupils and staff, 'they don't put us under any pressure' said a pupil (why not?). Masses of lectures, concerts and debates, lively internal social life within the school. More or less ad hoc clothes for upper sixth, lots of jolly jerseys and 'no more than one ring per finger,' said our informant – she was sporting at least three on each. Fetching line in female make-up too, no need for this lot to learn about life skills. No bleached hair (house gating). Sixth form divided by those who do, and those who don't, qualify for BOP (bar on premises). Much used tuck shop, Dave's Diner, offers solace to the rest. Both open five nights a week: post-prep hot spots.

Houses important here, with a host of inter house competitions, 'hysterical house music competition' where all indulge in a spot of cross-dressing. Houses undergoing a senior revamp: Farfield now decorated in what the boys call vomit green, but jolly and with real flowers in strategic places. Ditto the jolly girls' houses. Huge light dining hall (CFB – central feeding block or 'trough'), all pupils eat in houses with staff strategically placed, standard buffet fare, with vegetarian option. All eat at the headmaster's table once a year – empty during our visit, he was wandering around with a rather sad ham sandwich and some salad. Milk and water machines all over the shop, we didn't see a fizzy drink dispenser anywhere. Pupils are allowed into Holt (not a den of iniquity) three times a week, and would love to have a cooking option.

Pastoral Care and Discipline: Good pastoral backup with tutor, house parents, school counsellor and popular school chaplain. Escalating scale of punishments for fags: smoking 'within school buildings will normally involve a movement of two points up the scale' (which could mean permanent exclusion). 'Pupils found in the company of smokers can expect to be punished at 50 per cent severity. (Brill: more schools should copy). Over-18s are allowed to visit The Feathers with permission, otherwise there is an equally comprehensive scale of punishment for boozers, head 'reserves the right to impose the punishments in whatever order seems to him appropriate', which could equal expulsion for a first offence. Zero tolerance for drugs. Sixth formers have sessions on stress, strong anti-bullying policy. Laziness and non-participation frowned upon, particularly by pupils. This is a joining-in school. Sixth formers baby new pupils for their first couple of days.

Pupils and Parents: Delightful, open and friendly, not over-sophisticated boys and girls. Interesting mix of boarders, both weekly and full and day pupils where the day pupils often live further away than the weekly boarders. Some flexi-boarding. By and large farmers, solicitors, accountants, etc., about nine per cent real foreigners (Hong Kong Chinese, Russians, Bulgarians and Germans the main players) plus a handful of expats, some of whom live in Holland (oil: good links via Norwich airport to Amsterdam). Most come from East Anglia, Lincolnshire etc, plus refugees from London. Old boys include Sir Stephen Spender, W H Auden, Benjamin Britten, Ben Nicholson, Sir Christopher Cockerell (inventor of the hovercraft) James Dyson, Lord Reith, Prof Alan Hodgkin.

Entrance: CE, pass 50 per cent plus interview, keen on siblings, though will not take siblings if not up to standard. Either up from own preschool, or from Taverham Hall, Beeston, Town Close (Norwich) or many many others, plus the maintained sector. Some arrive at 16.

Exit: Annual trickle to Oxbridge. Otherwise all over the place with the (regular) odd one to Harper Adams, UMIST, London Guildhall plus the perennial Durham, Newcastle, Leeds etc. About 90 per cent go on to higher education with a percentage taking a gap year, practical subjects like engineering, business, economics and accounting feature strongly.

Money Matters: 450th anniversary appeal launched to give increased bursarial help as well as a spot of building; Fishmongers give generous scholarships. Restricted scholarships to those who have lived in Norfolk for five years, pupils from African prep schools and candidates from the maintained sector. Otherwise 12 academic scholarships or bursaries (up to 100 per cent 'upon demonstration of financial need'), plus art, drama, music, sports and all-rounders awards, plus sixth form scholarships either for those doing fantastically well in GCSE within the school (who are not already getting a scholarship) or for those coming in at sixth form – academic, art, music etc. Annual award of £1,500 for mathematical genius. Plus a bursary of £750 for pupils who 'undertake voluntary work through Students Partnership Worldwide'. Though staff told us that 'school will hold pupils whose parents fall upon hard times until the next public exam, 'head is not quite so sure.'

Remarks: All singing, all dancing, unsophisticated public school catering for a not so niche market under the positive direction of a powerful head. As we said before, well worth driving to the top of Norfolk for.

THE GRYPHON SCHOOL

Bristol Road, Sherborne, Dorset, DT9 4EQ

Tel: 01935 813 122

Fax: 01935 816 992

Email: john.jordan@gryphon.dorset.sch.uk

Website: www.gryphon.dorset.sch.uk

• Pupils: 1,327 boys and girls • Ages: 11-18 • Religion: C of E • School status: State • School gender: Mixed • Day/boarding: Day pupils

SEN provision

Detail:

Centre of excellence for:
- Mild: ASP; DYSL;
- Moderate: ASP; DYSL;
- Severe: ASP; DYSL;

Now provide for in school:
- Mild: ADD; ADHD; EBD; DYSC; DYSP;
- Moderate: ADD; ADHD; EBD; MLD; DYSC; DYSP;
- Severe: ADHD; EBD; DYSC; DYSP;
- Others: CD; EAL; DEL; PD; Oth;

Experience of:
- Mild: SpLD; HI;
- Moderate: SpLD;
- Severe: ADD; SpLD;
- Others: Sp&LD;

Summary: The SEN and dyslexia centre is outstanding and draws pupils over the borders from Dorchester, Gillingham, Shaftesbury, Blandford. We serve a total of 230 (23 dyslexic, 53 statemented) with help for mild Asperger's too. Says an LEA official, 'the Gryphon School has created an ethos over the past ten years which is based upon inclusive practice. All teaching and support staff are actively engaged in designing, creating and delivering a curriculum appropriate to meeting the needs of all pupils. The school has developed highly effective tracking and monitoring systems and analyses data in a very systematic way to inform future planning and pupil progress. This ensures that the additional resources provided for pupils with SEN have very positive outcomes.' Says the school, 'we provide special needs right up to A level. A student with Asperger's who had been rejected by mainstream schools in his area and basically written off came here and we got him through six GCSE levels. Our dyslexia base is full simply because of the excellent provision. We never take more than four in each year group. We offer special needs right up to A level so children with severe learning difficulties are not excluded from acquiring good A levels.' The school has 100 per cent access for students in wheelchairs.

What we say about the school - the full Good Schools Guide review

Head: Since 1992, Mr Chris Shepperd BA (fifties), educated Queen's College, Oxford, and Warwick University. Was head of maths at Hinchingbrooke School, Huntingdon under the renowned Peter Downes before arriving for baptism of fire: amalgamation of three schools into one. When not writing mathematical tomes, he sings and is learning to fly. Has been known to take assembly seated in a gryphon-crested wooden throne which may give lead to his nickname – God. Says the Gryphon is rising from the ashes – 'we have finally brought together a divided community'.

Academic Matters: 50 per cent of A level results are A or B, with 315 UCAS point score average for students (equivalent to better than three Bs). Strong on business and economics, arts, ICT, history, languages. Sixth form has breadth and variety, 27 subjects – ancient history, Latin at GCSE, law, history, philosophy and ethics, further mathematics, theatre studies, sports studies and economics with a range of vocational advanced subjects. At GCSE, 70 per cent of students gain five A* to C, 58 per cent gaining five A* to C with maths and English included. New learning resource centre with Internet and a regularly updated set of books – open three afternoons per week after school for additional study. Maths and science setted from year 7, modern languages from year 8. Five IT suites and 350 computers with all departments networked. Gifted and talented programme includes provision within the curriculum and outside of timetable with whole day activities, residential stays and summer schools. SEN provision has a strong reputation, attracting students from some distance away, lots of good inclusive practice, so that SEN students are made to feel an integral part of the school, and are given the support that they need to do their best.Realistic careers advice begins as motivation for work-related curriculum in year 10; a new programme provides one or two day vocational training for students in agriculture, mechanics, health and childcare, catering, electical and plumbing and hair dressing.

Games, Options, The Arts: Thirty per cent plays an instrument in one of two school bands or four ensembles. Tuition for any instrument possible. Three choirs with umpteen lunchtime musical groups get frequent showcases and three main concerts. Recording studio and main music rooms have composing software on 15 computers. Artsmark silver awarded 2001 in recognition of results in drama, music, art, design, media and literature. Art exhibitions raise local critical acclaim for arts, crafts and photography. Recent theatrical productions range from Lorca to Les Miserables to West Side Story with a cast of fifty and an orchestra of thirty.

Leisure centre on site provides fitness suite, squash courts, outdoor pool, dance studio. Attempts to gain Sportsmark to match attained Artsmark seen as ambitious by some who feel school ought to focus on sciences. Rugby and football teams play private schools and links with Sherborne rugby club; athletes get to county level but team sports further down the school don't often get the attention or the manpower to keep them going. Healthy menu of foreign exchange trips/theatre and dance shows and art trips everywhere.

Background and Atmosphere: The result of an amalgamation of three schools in 1992 is a bustling, well-marketed, consumer-orientated institution with snappy newsletters and an eye-popping social calendar. For a purpose-bred school it lacks some essentials (lockers for pupils) but youngsters are cheerful as they hover round large quadrangles and foyers. Pretty it ain't but locals are won over with the new and well maintained buildings. Hot on parent-rapport and student voice but PTA has fizzled out.

Pastoral Care and Discipline: Bursting with political correctness it bends over backwards for children from difficult homes, employs a counsellor to see pupil referrals of any age; provides access so the disabled can reach every part of this vast building; puts emphasis on charity activities.

Pupil guidance centre for youngsters with problems integrating, eg school phobics, can have specialist attention from senior staff in much smaller groups here, and move back into classrooms as confidence grows. Parents moan that well-behaved plodders don't stand as good a chance here as kids 'with problems'. Care taken over tender shoots before re-planting at 11; teachers visit the eight rural primaries to familiarise youngsters with the big move and each is allowed two friends to have in their tutor group. Tutors remain for five years.

Pupils and Parents: Many teachers from independent Sherborne schools – and state schools – choose Gryphon for their own children. Education is the largest employer in Dorset, thus a huge proportion of teachers' children. Nearby Yeovilton airbase instils a drop or two of Malaysian, Dutch or Spanish blood (pilots on 3-year stints) into an otherwise white community – 'we also have top lawyers, dentists, doctors and they want a proper university!' says head. Uniform strictly adhered to, sixth form wears mufti. Ex-Sherborne, first-team rugby player who chose Gryphon for his sixth form, says he likes it because 'it's relaxed and liberated'.

Entrance: Non-selective. At least 220 enter at 11 from 80 square mile catchment, 25 or so from local independent schools. For sixth form five A-Cs but will make exceptions for students with special needs.

Exit: Post-16, 30+ per cent or so leave for further education at agricultural college, vet training school, engineering apprenticeships, Yeovil College and art foundation courses. 'All but 1 or 2 per cent of our pupils have a positive outcome. Just because they don't get an A level it does not mean they are on the scrap heap. Of the 30+ per cent not staying on for our A level, about 28 per cent go into work-based learning or colleges of further education (Strode College, Weymouth Tech etc). The best way forward for them might be to be a motor mechanic and I'm sure you will be very pleased to see them the next time your car breaks down.' Parents of children who have left at 16 confirm that Gryphon did well for them while they were there. Post-A level, four or so to Oxbridge, 91 per cent to first choice or second of universities.

Remarks: A modern school. No longer reserves its academic emphasis for A levels, with very good GCSE results as well. Parents say it does well for a non-selective school in a rural area; good SEN teaching too.

Gumley House RC Convent School, FCJ

St John's Road, Isleworth, Middlesex, TW7 6XF

Tel: 020 8568 8692

Fax: 020 8758 2674

Email: general@gumley.hounslow.sch.uk

Website: www.gumley.hounslow.sch.uk

• Pupils: 1,180 girls; all day • Ages: 11-18 • Religion: RC • School status: State • Opendays: Early July, late September and early October • School gender: Girls • Day/boarding: Day pupils

SEN provision

Detail:

Experience of:

Mild: DS; DYSP;

Others: PD;

Summary: We have wheelchair access to all areas of the curriculum and to 90 per cent of the facilities/sites.

What we say about the school - the full Good Schools Guide review

Headteacher: Since 1988, Sister Brenda (Miss B Wallace BA PhD) (mid fifties). Previously taught French and Italian and loved it. Now a non-teaching head – felt she was not giving enough time to lesson preparation and this was unfair to girls. Read modern languages at Liverpool and a PhD in Italian poetry at London. Diminutive and approachable, whereas her study is large, airy and reassuringly cluttered; 'you'll just have to take us as you find us,' she declared in a soft Lancashire accent. An outstandingly successful inspection by Ofsted in 2001 showed that they liked what they found very much indeed.

Academic Matters: For a non-selective state school very good results. Compares extremely favourably with local and national averages. Comes top in local league tables. 80-ish per cent gain five or more GCSE grades A*-C. A and A/S levels well ahead of local and national averages. On vexed subject of A/S levels, head feels weaker pupils benefit from leaving school with some qualification but regrets loss of free study periods 'so essential for independent learning'.

Very committed to special needs provision. Two fully qualified teachers and fourteen learning support assistants. SENs catered for include physical difficulties, learning difficulties, ASD, dyslexia, Down's syndrome. To make sure that they miss nobody, policy is to screen for literacy at the start of year 7 and to organise support as appropriate eg literacy tuition, in-class support, reading clubs or monitoring as appropriate. Preferred method of support is in the classroom. Where possible, try to avoid withdrawing girls from subject lessons. Classroom support now widely accepted by staff and students alike. No stigma associated with classroom support, in fact the girls often ask for it. Wheelchair access throughout the school seen as part of ethos – 'we encourage concern for the disabled, the marginalised and the needy'. Sixth formers involved in helping younger pupils.

Games, Options, The Arts: Netball, hockey and athletics all very strong. School regularly wins all local tournaments. Eight tennis courts, a new all-weather surface hockey/football pitch set in spacious 10 acres. New dance and fitness studio (very popular), new drama studio. Thriving orchestra and plethora of private instrument lessons on offer.

Background and Atmosphere: Founded in 1841 as a school and convent by the Faithful Companions of Jesus. The Queen Anne house surrounded by lovely grounds creates a peaceful oasis in west London. Strong support from parents, 'we couldn't run it without them'. Superbly equipped library in former chapel (just the place for inspired contemplation), sensational octagonal assembly hall for whole school events. Despite rigorous religious requirements at entry level the atmosphere is cheerful and tolerant with no hint of religious oppression.

Pastoral Care and Discipline: Prides itself on discipline. Truancy very rare. Emphasis on strong school/home links. Distinctive uniform worn with pride. Strong emphasis on religious, spiritual and moral formation of pupils. Very supportive staff.

Pupils and Parents: The catchment area covers a wide area of west London from Southall to Twickenham so a broad mix of intake. Most parents make a voluntary contribution to the school's development fund each month.

Entrance: Non-selective academically at age 11. However (and here's the rub), girls and their parents must be practising Roman Catholics (written proof required from parish priest) and that means attending Mass every Sunday. Other entrance criteria are distance from school and first choice on application form. School is heavily over-subscribed; head has no plans for further expansion – 'we'd rather like to keep our grounds as they are'.

Exit: 60 per cent and rising each year go on to higher education. The remainder either take a gap year (increasingly popular) or go directly into employment.

Money Matters: Voluntary aided so run by head and board of governors. Funded through the local council but parents' contributions (voluntary) keep it running as a Catholic school, provide extra facilities and offset maintenance costs.

Remarks: For a budding Mr Bennet who is also a fully paid-up member of the Catholic Church now would be a good time to visit an estate agent in Isleworth. This is an excellent school in lovely surroundings, which will give all your daughters a good education. Well worth a visit.

THE HALL SCHOOL

23 Crossfield Road, Hampstead, London, NW3 4NU

Tel: 020 7722 1700

Fax: 020 7483 0181

Email: office@hallschool.co.uk

Website: www.hallschool.co.uk

• Pupils: 440 boys; all day • Ages: 4-13 • Religion: Christian foundation, all faiths welcome • Fees: £2,785-£3,390 • School status: Independent • Opendays: Open evenings for those who have registered their sons • School gender: Boys • Day/boarding: Day pupils

SEN provision

Detail:

Now provide for in school:

Mild: DYSC; DYSL; DYSP; SpLD;

Moderate: DYSL; DYSP;

Others: Sp&LD;

Experience of:

Mild: ADHD;

Others: EAL;

Summary: We have a small number of part-time specialist staff to provide learning support to boys with dyspraxia and dyslexia. There is a full-time co-ordinator to oversee this. We also specifically cater for reading and writing problems not on the dyslexia spectrum.

What we say about the school - the full Good Schools Guide review

Head: From 2006, returning to hold the fort during an interregnum, popular previously head, Mr Ramage. His successor left to head the junior school of Geelong Grammar. New head due September 2006, is to be Mr Philip Lough (pronounced Lock) MA PGCE (fifties), head of Windlesham for the past 10 years. A catch.

Married to Mrs Christine Lough MA PGCE (fifty) who is assistant head at Windlesham. Both are linguists; Mr Lough was educated at Sherborne, followed by Trinity College, Oxford and Mrs Lough went to Madras College in St Andrews, followed by Aberdeen University. The Loughs, who have three grown up children, met and married whilst doing their respective PGCEs at Durham. Both of them teach French – he to the scholars at the top end plus RE, and she to the tinies as well as preparing older children for their next step. 'Drugs, drink, relationships (including sex) and how to deal with peer pressure.' 'Learn to say no, consider the consequences'. Thoughtful and fun, glowing reports come in from happy parents of children who find themselves 'watching telly and eating crisps' in the Loughs' flat to overcome a temporary blip of homesickness.

Entrance: Register before your son is a year old (though it's worth trying for gaps at odd moments and the school often takes four or five new boys into year 4). The school registers and takes a £50 deposit from the first 200 applicants. Around 30 boys come into reception at 4 and 20 or so into year 1 at 5 – parents decide whether or not their son would be better off at nursery for another year. Boys are assessed in groups of six or so: 4+ applicants in the January before they join; 5+ applicants in May of the same year (they join the school 16 months later). 'These are not real academic assessments. We're looking for boys who will make the most of our opportunities.' Parents have already met the head and the head of the junior school in the autumn term. 'We need to like them and feel they will support us and they need to like us. It's important that the boys have got help at home when they need it.' Those accepting a place pay a deposit of £1,000, of which £500 is returned at the end of their son's first term, the rest when he leaves the school.

Exit: Westminster and St Paul's are the most popular destinations (there are apparently more boys from The Hall at Westminster than from any other prep school); also City, UCS, Highgate, Eton, Winchester and Harrow. Seven academic, four music and one art and one sports scholarships in 2004.

Remarks: Highly academic prep school which is extremely effective at getting boys into the top senior schools. Work and play both proceed at a brisk pace, and life skills and study skills are part of the curriculum. 'The quality of the teaching is fantastic,' said a parent. 'They do a lot more for the boys than just getting good results from them. They have such a broad education.' High praise for most of the staff. 'It feels as if they are really committed to the boys,' said another parent.

French, science, art, PE, music and ICT are taught by specialists from reception onwards, other subjects by class teachers in the junior school. The middle school, years 4 and 5, is a transition between junior and senior schools, with lessons taught by specialist staff but in the boys' own form-rooms. Setting for maths and English in year 6; in year 7, one form is hived off 'to work at a faster pace with a greater degree of challenge'. Most, but not necessarily all, of this group will become the scholarship form in year 8. This, naturally, upsets some of the parents, who complain about their boys being treated as second-class citizens. 'It is an unnecessary elitism,' said a parent whose son is one of the chosen, 'but they do some fantastic things in that class.' 'The parents do create pressures,' agrees the head, 'but I expect them to support what we are doing. All the boys will achieve good results.' Everyone, particularly the scholarship class, works very hard. 'They have a very strong foundation of learning and they are taught to work hard consistently – which is a wonderful asset to them,' said a parent. 'There are some extraordinarily talented children in the school and I think all the boys benefit from this. It gives them an insight into excellence and the hard work it takes to attain it. And they realise that everyone can shine in their own way with a bit of effort.'

A full-time learning support co-ordinator and part-time specialist staff support boys with moderate dyspraxia and dyslexia. Individual programmes in place for the 40 or so children with additional needs, help extends beyond the basics to eg ICT. 'My son had some difficulties with writing, and they've been brilliant at providing extra support,' said a parent. Boys who cannot take the pace may be asked to move elsewhere ' but generally the parents will have formed a good relationship with the teachers and any decision is usually arrived at on an amicable basis,' says the head. Not surprising then, that school doesn't approve of pupils being coached outside of school unless it's for handwriting issues or similar and only with school's agreement. Strongly believe own staff should be addressing issues (hear hear!).

Building work has resulted in the new middle school, opened in 1998, a refurbished senior school, new DT centre, pottery room and library – all light, bright and airy. The junior school, reception and playground have all been refurbished and were completed in 2004.

'There is the most amazing sense of things going on all the time,' said a parent. 'The kids are fired on all cylinders.' Lots of sport – two afternoons' sport a week for middle and senior boys at the school's sports ground at Finchley, pitches in Mill Hill or the athletics track at Parliament Hill; fencing, squash at Lord's and golf are also offered; the senior school has a large-ish playground and a multi-purpose sports hall which doubles as a setting for concerts, plays and assemblies. 'The sport has been fantastic,' said a parent. 'There's lots of opportunities for everyone, not just the first team.' And indeed the school magazine lists zillions of awards for everything from U9 Most Improved Cricketer to Snooker Doubles Shield.

Excellent drama – it is on the timetable throughout and, alongside impressive school productions, there is informal drama for year 5 upwards. 'For a whole term the children are writing their own skits and rehearsing to perform in each other's,' said a parent. 'They get the chance to try their hand at all sorts of different roles and they have wonderful fun.'

Prolific and high quality art and pottery; strong music – about three-quarters of the boys play one or more instruments and are expected to perform in the numerous concerts from year 1 upwards. 'I was surprised when my son told me his favourite music was a piece by Vaughan Williams,' said a parent. 'Then he explained that they hear music and discuss it in assembly every week.'

Numerous outings – ranging from junior school trips to Whipsnade Zoo, Madame Tussaud's and Mountfitchet Castle and middle school outings to Southwark Cathedral, Verulamium and The Ragged School, to senior school trips to Normandy, Holland and Devon.

Parents find, unexpectedly, that the pastoral side is strong. 'My son used to be very shy and sensitive and they have really nurtured him and brought him out,' said a parent. 'When I've had a problem it's always been easy to sort it out with the teachers.' The school is in the process of introducing a new anti-bullying policy, in consultation with boys and parents. 'We keep revisiting pastoral care because it's important to keep looking at your policies. There will always be someone who slips through the net but we do our best.'

The school unashamedly rewards the brightest and best but boys and parents agree that it is also good at spotting, nurturing and rewarding more hidden talents and effort. 'Everyone's got something they're good at and the school really brings it out,' said a pupil.

Parents are a high-powered lot, mostly wealthy, very demanding, inclined to drive local residents mad by thoughtless double-parking but kept under control by

Mr Pierson. 'They expect a lot of the boys and drive them very hard,' said a parent. 'But my son is always really keen to go to school – which is fantastic.' Another commented, 'my son has said that his sons will go to The Hall – and you can't get a higher recommendation than that.'

HALL SCHOOL WIMBLEDON (THE)

17 The Downs, Wimbledon, London, SW20 8HF

Tel: 020 8879 9200

Fax: 020 8946 0864

Email: enquiries@hallschoolwimbledon.co.uk

Website: www.hallschoolwimbledon.co.uk

• Pupils: 155 boys, 80 girls • Ages: 11-16 • Religion: Non-denom • Fees: £2,957 • School status: Independent • Opendays: Open days twice termly, parents must apply to attend • School gender: Mixed • Day/boarding: Day pupils

SEN provision

Detail:

Centre of excellence for:
- Mild: AUT;
- Moderate: AUT;
- Severe: AUT;

Now provide for in school:
- Mild: DYSC; DYSL; DYSP; SpLD;
- Moderate: MLD; DYSC; DYSL; DYSP; SpLD;
- Others: EAL;

Experience of:
- Mild: ASP; ADD; ADHD; EBD; HI; VI;
- Moderate: ASP; ADD;
- Severe: ASP; DYSC;
- Others: SPD; AUT(other); Sp&LD; PD;

Summary: In the main school, children's learning is supported by three specialist teachers. Most support is carried out within the classroom, any one-to-one will incur an additional charge.

We have a small, dedicated unit for children with autism. We are recruiting children with moderate to low functioning autism from ages 5 to 10. The unit is attached to our junior school so that the pupils can participate in mainstreaming and reverse mainstreaming. We accept both LEA and privately funded pupils.

What we say about the school - the full Good Schools Guide review

Head: Since 1999, Mr Timothy Hobbs MA (forties), educated at Eastbourne College and St Andrews where he read medieval and modern history. Abandoned accountancy training in favour of a teaching post at Hill House International Junior School, which he left six years later (encouraged by parents) to set up in 1990 his own school – the original Hall Junior School (qv). (In 1999 his brother Jonathan joined as principal of the junior school). Unmarried – other than to the school where he spends seven days a week in any of his five offices which range from a gorgeous cream sitting-room complete with three-legged black cat, to a more functional workspace in a converted garage where the children can drop in as they pass by. Erudite, energetic, entrepreneurial, passionate about the school and a stickler for old-fashioned good manners. He has the demeanour of a favourite uncle. Entertainingly opinionated, he writes the most readable newsletters we've seen – wonderfully indiscreet and quite philosophical at times. He prides himself on his prescience – currently has a date in a sealed envelope in his safe, predicting abolition of the Euro. More pertinently, he served his first home-cooked organic school dinner when Jamie Oliver was still a school boy, and wrote The Hall's code on bullying eight years before it became law for all schools to have one. He has recently closed down the school's ICT suite and predicts that computers will no longer be used in classrooms in the UK by 2015. He (and his school) have a certain local reputation for being quirky – but underpinning some of the less conventional practices, he espouses traditional, old-fashioned values. 'It can only come out as the usual collection of clichés, but I absolutely cherish the individual and want to foster their spirit,' he says. 'He puts the needs of the children above all,' agrees one mother. 'And truly celebrates their individuality.' TJH is The Hall School Wimbledon – parents should consider all the pluses and minuses such a close association with the brand can bring. You wouldn't want him falling under a bus the day after your child starts the school or any time during their time there.

Academic Matters: If you love league tables and prize academia above all else, look away now. As a mixed ability school with a largely non-selective entry, exam results are not the be all and end all here. Ethos is that learning must be a pleasure, not a burden. The prospectus says that 'thought is the most important activity taking place at our school.' That said, the school works to the Common Entrance and GCSE syllabuses, while 'noting the spirit and content' of the National Curriculum, all combined in its own 'Works Programme'. Pre-GCSE, the core subjects are English, French, maths and science, alongside the usual history, geography, religious studies art, music and the less common 'gardening'. No SATs. At GCSE, the timetable will be written around that year's cohort and always include German and PE – 'PE is our most popular choice,' says TJH – additionally a broad choice of languages, textiles, and rural science among others. Generally academic matters are not considered more important than any other matters at this school. (That's not to say that the children don't work hard – they do.) But TJH stresses equal emphasis across the school day: 'Maths is as important as lunch, which is as important as poetry and football.' He is anti-league tables – would be more interested in something which gave a better idea of value-added. 'Getting a 'refuser' to take exams is a success' he says. 'A year 10 boy who joined us with not much more than his 2 times table and went on to get a B in his GCSE a year later – those are success stories.' For the record, in 2005 84 per cent gained five GCSE passes at A*-C.

Class sizes average 20. English and maths classes (for which the pupils are set) usually have a second teacher with them. Language classes (also set) have about 15 pupils. At GCSE class sizes are anything from 1 to 20, averaging 10. The school no longer offers ICT as a GCSE option and use of computers in other lessons is selective: 'IT skills are taught to avail real curriculum needs rather than as a general subject – we don't teach how to use a hammer, we teach the skills to make a box,' says TJH in typical TJH fashion. Books are preferred. 'I simply felt that the ICT GCSE syllabus did not deliver,' he adds. However, the school aims to have all the children touch-typing by the end of year 9. GCSE year groups additionally study the ASDAN programme promoting 'key life skills.'

School has its own unique and rather elaborate homework system called 'Flints'. Based on a 'little and often' philosophy, the pupils get bite-size exercises in four or five different subjects every night, and are then tested at school on Friday morning in what is called 'a flint wall'. These results are fed back to parents each week. One mother said she felt the children aiming for Common Entrance were pushed harder than the rest. No weekend homework (the envy of other private school pupils?) except for GCSE coursework in years 10 and 11, though the students invariably have a project on the go.

Special needs are met within the classroom with as little one-to-one as possible. Three learning support teachers are on the staff (parents contribute towards the cost of special needs provision). School currently caters for mild dyslexia and for two amputees from the Iraq war who both have one-to-one help in all classes for writing and translation. The specialist autistic unit based at the junior school (qv) can take secondary age pupils. Around 15 pupils have EAL needs – met by an EAL teacher and classroom support as necessary.

Games, Options, The Arts: Sport is an integral part of school life. Every day begins with the major wake-up call of 30 minutes circuit training from 8.30am – and this goes on all through the year, rain or shine. Similarly a hurricane would have to pass through before outside playtime was dropped, and some parents grumble about slightly damp children trooping back for lessons – school's attitude is that a drop of rain never hurt anybody. Sport is timetabled every day – a good range with the emphasis on racquets and netball (pupils recently returned from a netball tour of New Zealand). There are no elite teams – places are rotated to allow everyone to have a go. Some parents of sports 'stars' would prefer set teams and can resent the wobbly beginnings of newcomers – but the school will not leave someone on a bench all term.

A very active school – makes the most of any opportunity to get out of the classroom for anything from a 45-minute investigation of the school's ponds, to a three-week field trip incorporating literature, history, philosophy and geography. The field-trip programme is enormous and led by TJH, includes expeditions such as walking the 105 mile South Downs Way, climbing in the Brecon Beacons in Wales and camping in Pevensey. 'This is a huge plus point,' says one mother. 'TJH really gets to know the children on these trips and follows up when they are back in school.' Downside according to another is that it makes him hard to track down: 'parents are not his priority- though he's very good when you get him.' The head replies that 'any parent that wants to see me does so – parents can always see a senior tutor who will contact me and may act on my behalf.' Additionally, all the children are taught to climb (head likes the analogy with achievement in life). Musical abilities are strongly encouraged – no orchestra but there is a choir and a regular pantomime and musical production each year ('always a treat' says one parent). Art facilities have recently expanded to fill the space vacated by ICT suite. No after school clubs (school day runs from 8.30 to 5pm) but there are break time clubs in design technology, art and music. There are also inter-house sports competitions in morning break (which is 45 minutes long).

Background and Atmosphere: TJH founded the school in 1990 and began teaching in a church hall in Wimbledon Village with nine pupils, intending to steer them through to Common Entrance. He was teaching, cooking, keeping animals – and it's probably from these early beginnings that the 'wacky' reputation gathered hold. Things took off very quickly as word spread and new pupils joined. The senior school (formerly Hazlehurst's school premises) was purchased in 1998 – an extended Victorian residential property 10 minutes from Wimbledon station. Grounds not huge, but beautiful and well-used. There is a gazebo, a grassy area, five ponds, some landscaping and other interesting nooks and crannies. Some classrooms on the small side – functional rather than fantastic. Walls a bit bare when we visited but it was the beginning of term. Impressive central staircase hung with professional artwork belonging to the head. Lunchtime is a pleasant social occasion. The children get wholesome organic food (no packed lunches allowed, nor any vending machines) and they set and clear tables themselves. A child having a bad day may be distracted by an invitation to come and help prepare the food – all done on site. Lunchtime functions as an 'assembly' – there is no other whole school gathering. 'It's a wholesome school rather than a faith school,' says TJH. Children look ready for action in outward-bound style uniform of polo shirts, sweat shirts and chinos. They are proud of their school. All encouraged to do lots for charity. Overall a happy, stimulating environment, with a relaxed atmosphere.

Pastoral Care and Discipline: A tolerant regime with as little regulation as possible. No punishments as such and certainly no detentions or being kept in at break time ('What message does that give 'That fresh air and exercise are not important,' says TJH). Zero tolerance of bullying – which has a wide-ranging definition including ignoring somebody. This is about the only 'crime' for which there is a punishment. Serial offender would be deemed to have 'spoilt his/her community' (his class) and would be moved to another year group while things were sorted out, otherwise suspension and expulsion follow. 'Some of the children who join us have been bullied elsewhere and we simply will not tolerate it here,' says TJH. Children are encouraged to report any incident, to sit with somebody different in each lesson (no saving places for friends) and indeed not to have a 'best friend' to the exclusion of others.

Every child is given a cake to celebrate their birthday – whole school sings and there's enough to share with their class. Until recently TJH made each cake himself ('great chance to really focus on that child and think about their needs in the coming year,' he says.) Has had less time for this lately but would like to reinstate. 'Tutors always very supportive. It is like a family', said one parent. Average age of teaching staff is 35. Around 20 per cent have been with the school at least 10 years, others put in more fleeting appearances – a hefty contingent are recruited from Australia and New Zealand (their can-do attitude appeals to the school).

Pupils and Parents: A cosmopolitan school including lots of nationalities and social groups. Ideal for parents looking for an international school type atmosphere: 'our children slotted in quickly and happily,' says one well-travelled parent. 'Children with a need will have it catered for here,' says another mother. 'Consequently it attracts children with a 'story' or history of some kind.' TJH worries that people will equate quirky/eccentric with mediocre achievement – 'we have many very bright children and a few 'gifted,' he says. Pupils are not obviously different, and the youngsters who showed us round were pleasingly confident. School is boy heavy – 60/40. Very mixed parent population but notable minorities of actors/playwrights and producers; others from the music world, and football and tennis players. No PTA or sports day (by design) so parents don't get to know each other so easily – particularly if they have not had children in the junior school.

Entrance: By assessment at 11+. All applicants take papers in English and maths, are observed undertaking arts and sports activities and are interviewed. Parents must supply a report from the previous school and disclose any ed psych reports. TJH says purpose of interview is to ensure compatibility with existing children and ensure that all who join 'may benefit from our teaching,' and he aims to make it a good experience for the child even if no place is offered at the end. Special consideration is given to children with particular merit in a non-academic field. Around two thirds of the places go to pupils from the junior school. These children also take the 11+ exams, but are guaranteed a place. Lots of word of mouth recommendations. 60 per cent of pupils live within three miles of school.

Exit: Bit of an exodus at 13 – 'it is about 15 per cent, sometimes fewer' – when the Common Entrance bunch leave. No particular trend, but pupils go to King's Wimbledon, St Paul's, Epsom College and Latymer among others. Off in all directions at 16+, Epsom College a popular sixth form choice. To the question 'Any notable old boys/girls?' comes the reply 'They are all notable!'

Remarks: An unusual place – conventional parents may balk at some of the thinking here – but it's different rather than completely alternative. Mixes the off the wall with the traditional and could be perfect for children who are the 'square pegs' in more traditional establishments.

THE HALL SCHOOL WIMBLEDON JUNIOR SCHOOL

Stroud Crescent, Putney Vale, London, SW15 3QE

Tel: 020 8788 2370

Fax: 020 8788 2121

Email: principal@hsw.co.uk

• Pupils: 340 boys and girls, all day • Ages: 3-11

• Fees: KS1: £2,323. KS2: £2,656 • School status: Independent

• School gender: Mixed • Day/boarding: Day pupils

SEN provision

Detail:

Now provide for in school:

Mild: AUT; DYSC; DYSL;

Moderate: AUT; MLD; DYSC; DYSL;

Severe: AUT;

Others: EAL; Sp&LD;

Experience of:

Mild: ASP; ADD; ADHD; DYSP; SpLD; HI; VI; CP;

Moderate: ASP; ADD; DYSP;

Severe: DYSC; DYSL;

Others: SPD; AUT(other); PD; Eat;

Summary: We have a small, dedicated unit for children with autism. We are recruiting children with moderate to low functioning autism from ages 5 to 10. The unit is attached to our junior school so that the pupils can participate in mainstreaming and reverse mainstreaming. We accept both LEA and privately funded pupils.

In the main schoolchildren's learning is supported by two full-time specialist teachers.

What we say about the school - the full Good Schools Guide review

Head: Since 1990, Mr Timothy J Hobbs MA. Educated at Eastbourne College and St Andrew's, founded The Hall in 1990, after teaching at Hill House and becoming disillusioned with the sausage factory approach to teaching and learning. In 1999 his brother Jonathan M Hobbs MA (Education Management from OU) also educated at Eastbourne College and then at the British School of Osteopathy, joined as principal of the school. Jonathan is responsible for the daily running of the junior school, staffing, trouble-shooting and the minutiae that TJH openly professes to dislike. Not that parents are likely to meet either brother on a visit, admissions are handled by a very capable admissions team but any parent requesting an appointment with head or principal will have their wish granted.

TJH oversees both senior and junior schools, working tirelessly at the sharp end, devoting his energies to preserving the spirit of the schools and looking after the children. Seen by some as a bit of a maverick, not afraid to ruffle feathers for the greater good, there for the children. Thinks outside the box. Fans say he's charming and charismatic, others disagree. TJH is passionate about education in the broadest sense, he wants children to discover themselves, celebrate their individuality yet have due regard and care for others. Says: 'he'd like to feel children leave school not only well educated academically but with practical skills and confidence in all areas in preparation for their future'.

Entrance: Hold a number of open mornings each year. Try to keep a realistic waiting list, must visit school prior to requesting a place. First-come-first-served for reception places. In other years they look to see if a child is compatible with their system. Non-selective but assess all to determine where the child will fit into the school. Parents from wide socio-economic spread, 20 per cent from overseas, several first time buyers.

Exit: Pupils can be prepared for 7-11+ exams and Common Entrance to all major London schools (a minority to boarding). Don't prepare children for scholarships even though some win them. Approximately two thirds to own senior school – automatic entry.

Remarks: Follows the National Curriculum, or rather leads it: all mainstream subjects taught a year ahead of schedule, ensuring children are well-prepared for demands of Common Entrance. Set for maths and English from year 3. Totally committed to hearing every child read daily until they're confident, fluent readers. Strong on history and geography, 150 day/residential field trips and outings annually, with plenty of hands-on learning, both home and abroad. School runs a monitoring and homework system called 'Flints', which: 'enables efficiency and independence in all subjects.' Each child has a folder with weekly Flint sheets to complete. Flints, popular with staff and parents, demonstrates how 'little-and-often produces success.' Extension work is given through a similar system 'Pyrite.'

Classes average 20. Good SEN support, with two full-time staff. Provides a wonderful environment for the mild dyslexic or dyspraxic. Recognises that a bright dyslexic child often makes highly valued verbal contributions and is able to engage in lively, informed debate. Can cater for MLD, mild visual impairment, physical difficulties, and mild Asperger's – but those who need in-class support for behavioural difficulties should look elsewhere. Say everything should work well for children at the school, believe too much teacher intervention can hinder progress. Provision varies according to needs but must be able to manage mainstream and need no more than a couple of half-hour one-to-one sessions per week. Will refuse children who need specialist support that school is not able to provide.

This fast developing school opened in April 1990 in Wimbledon Village, moving to current site (former council school) in 1992. Classrooms are light, well-equipped and set in a terraced site where children have helped plant trees, make ponds and develop a tranquil, stimulating place to learn. There's an Anderson shelter, an American garden to commemorate 9/11, flags portraying the international flavour of the school, a Shepherd's caravan, a partly constructed Cruck house using resources available in medieval times, chickens (rescued from a battery farm) and rabbits but no pigs (locals got tetchy). School, extended with the most delightful log cabins, backs onto Wimbledon Common so plenty of rural science opportunities and terrific views. One bright-eyed youngster told us: 'sometimes we have sleepovers to badger watch.' Swallows and Amazons eat your heart out; an idyll in this playstation orientated world.

Strong and keen sports, games everyday good facilities: tennis court, basketball court, adventure playground, garden, outdoor climbing wall. All children from 7 years old start the day with circuit training: healthy body, healthy mind, attitude (good wholesome food too). All get to be in teams, not just the best. Emphasise sportsmanship, team skills, fun and joining in, rather than always winning. Lots of after school activities (small additional charge). Art and technology well served, we spied giant Jimmy Choo shoes made by pupils, a whole new take on Cinderella! No dedicated music teacher when we visited but school sang tunefully: in the classrooms, we saw a fine example of cross-curricular work – music mixed with PSHE and literacy, during lunch (rousing rendition of happy birthday complete with parent guests and cake provided by TJH) and at the impressive and energetic year 4 'Oliver' dress rehearsal.

Staff committed to pastoral care, good code of morals and behaviour, anti-bullying policy that works. No formal punishments, persistent offenders can be suspended but head feels pupils benefit more from discussion or counselling (some staff don't always adhere to this policy).

A can-do school with a positive and enlightened outlook on education. Produces confident, caring, tolerant, informed youngsters.

Ann Margaret House. Opened in 1998 to cater for children with a diagnosis of severe autism. Founded in response to a plea from a former teacher whose quest to find appropriate provision for her autistic granddaughter proved fruitless. Currently run by senior tutor Jackie England (managed by JMH). Provision exists for four children (three with statements, one private) but plans afoot to extend to six (limited by space). Fees of £50,000 a year are based on inclusive provision so all reasonable needs met immediately without recourse to LEA. No yearly intake – places as and when a space arises. Plan to greatly expand provision when new premises become available.

Unit is housed in own well-equipped, secure building within the grounds of the junior school. All children have a workstation in minimally decorated rooms to avoid over-stimulation. There's a decked play area built in the style of a castle; well-equipped kitchen where pupils help prepare snacks and food purchased as part of a daily trip to Asda (a favourite part of the day according to one pupil); a large classroom for group activities such as role play and a sensory room for the daily kinder kinetics session (a cross between physio and occupational therapy), working on muscle development, balance, co-ordination fine and gross motor skills. A speech and language therapist visits weekly and designs programmes that promote speech 'in context'. Use PECS with all. Each child has visual timetable with photo's or symbols.

Believe having a small unit and being able to work so closely with each individual on communication, social and independent skills, really helps, recognise: 'children with autism don't always follow natural path of development, behaviours can be hard to break, they like their own company.' The children have varying levels of ability, some are learning to read, write and do basic calculations, others concentrate on social and life skills and working with distractions. New concepts taught on an individual basis moving to paired or group work when appropriate. IEPs set out targets that are reviewed regularly in partnership with parents and relevant professionals.

All follow key curriculum elements of language and communication, reading, writing, PSHE and citizenship, maths, science, PE, ICT, humanities and creative and expressive arts. Challenging behaviour impedes learning so address and control with lots of positive reinforcement, praise, and by encouraging 'good learning'. Realise children with autism rely heavily on adult support but recognise need to encourage independent work. If a child can cope with time in mainstream they will look at ways to include. All integrate for weekly PE when small group of children from mainstream come and take part in PE skills at the unit (works well, helps children socialise and follow examples of others). Top year group from junior school visit daily during break times and play with children, say: 'need right role models as autistic children aren't great for each other.' Add 'children in mainstream are fantastic, they love to come over and are tolerant and accepting.' Mainstream children are naturally curious too and ask questions such as: Can they speak? Why can't they? What is autism? Do they live at home, go on holiday etc? Do production with mainstream including sing-along, dance performance etc. Children swim twice a week and trampoline at the senior school. Plenty of trips supplement the curriculum, recent outings to London Aquarium and the science museum using public transport – a skill they need to learn to cope with. Twice yearly, short field trips to the Queen Elizabeth Jubilee activity centre (for SEN), horse riding, climbing, canoeing, caving, all popular.A lovely unit for a handful of children lucky enough to be supported by enlightened, professional, caring staff in a tolerant and inclusive setting.

HAMPSTEAD SCHOOL

Westbere Road, Hampstead, London, NW2 3RT

Tel: 020 7794 8133

Fax: 020 7435 8260

Email: enquiries@hampsteadschool.org.uk

Website: www.hampsteadschool.org.uk

• Pupils: 1,300 pupils; 55 per cent boys and 45 per cent girls
• Ages: 11-19 • Religion: Non-denom • School status: State
• Opendays: September and October • School gender: Mixed
• Day/boarding: Day pupils

SEN provision

Detail:
Now provide for in school:
Mild: ASP; ADD;
Moderate: ASP; ADD;

Summary: SEN is very strong in Hampstead school. The staff strive to include all students regardless of their needs. The school is keeen to stress that it is not specialist in any key area but is always willing to aquire the necessary skills in order to support its students.

What we say about the school - the full Good Schools Guide review

Head: Since 2000, Mr Andy Knowles (forties). Was deputy head here for 10 years and head of the technology department before that. Has also taught technology in Greenwich and EFL in Greece. He is a widower with two primary aged children. Full of energy and enthusiasm. He is 'utterly wedded to the job and cares passionately about the school,' said a parent, 'but he is also very good at looking at the bigger picture'. Very concerned about the children and can understand their problems. Respected by both staff and children.

Academic Matters: Hampstead got a special mention from the Chief Inspector of Schools in 2001 for its outstanding inspection report, which gave it a grade A for its 1999 GCSE results in relation to similar schools. Its results have now risen and 55 per cent of its students now get five A*-Cs at GCSE. It now takes more disabled pupils, including two with cerebral palsy, and 14 each year with statements of special education need. Nearly half the pupils are bilingual, speaking a total of 48 languages, and there is an enormous ability range. 'We have what we call a mixed economy,' says the head, 'and that is one of our real strengths.' Nearly all the lower school teaching is mixed ability, with some setting from year 10 in maths, science and languages. Heads of departments who want to change the system must have good reasons. Setting in maths, science and languages for GCSE is more or less inevitable because of the syllabus differences between the foundation and higher level papers. 'But when we tried setting in DT it made no difference to high-achieving students, while the low attainers did slightly worse. We stress to staff during interviews that mixed-ability teaching takes far more teacher input and preparation – but most of our teachers like Hampstead because of our philosophy.'

Plenty of young, able, enthusiastic teaching staff, many of whom are studying for further qualifications and many of whom move on to be heads of department elsewhere. 'The teachers are so creative,' said a parent. 'They can achieve the most amazing things – like getting the least academic kids to appreciate Romeo and Juliet.' There is extension work available for bright children as part of the curriculum, 'though a lot depends on the child,' said a parent. 'If they're happy to coast along, they're mostly left to get on with it' and some take maths and a humanity GCSE early. The school gets government funds for its Gifted and Talented programme, which provides workshops and master-classes, though these activities rather go against the school's ethos of providing equal opportunities for everyone and are not emphasised. 'And, of course, some parents are very bitter that their children aren't ever chosen,' said a parent. Some complaints that the lack of homework in the first three years does not prepare children for the rigours of GCSE preparation.

Very effective SEN support on and off the site, with help for disruptive pupils which includes a behaviour modification programme. 'We're very successful with students who couldn't cope elsewhere.' The school stresses that while it is not specialist in any key areas of SEN, it is always willing to acquire the necessary skills in order to support its students. All those with a reasonable attendance record who complete the course work – and this does not apply to a significant minority – are entered for exams. 'We give them a chance right up to the last minute. Some of our students achieve enormously by getting a D.'

There is a open recruitment policy into the sixth form, with one-year vocational courses available to the less academic. A level options include electronics, sociology, media studies and government and politics alongside more conventional subjects. There are intermediate GNVQs in leisure and tourism, health and social care, art and design, business and performing arts; the latter three can also be studied to advanced VCE level. The extra funds brought by technology college status have provided excellent ICT resources which are used across the curriculum.

Games, Options, The Arts: No playing fields on site and pupils are bused to Hendon to play games. However, the school does its best and there's a good range of sports clubs and fixtures. There are three gyms on site, including one used mainly for dance, a swimming pool in the basement of the DT building and two tarmac courts called the Front Cage and Back Cage. Students can also go skiing, camping and orienteering.

Perhaps surprisingly for a technology college, there's lots of emphasis on the creative arts, to a very high standard. Art, music and drama are consistently strong at GCSE. The school has links with the National Theatre and, with local theatres and drama schools, puts on ambitious musical productions and co-ordinates the National Playwright Commissioning Group which commissions plays for schools from well-known writers. Pupils are very enthusiastic about drama productions they have been involved in and several students have had their plays performed in various London theatres.

Very high calibre art department with an excellent head – over 90 per cent of art A levels have been grade A for some years. There's plenty of diverse artwork on display including textiles and 3D art, and visits to galleries in London, Barcelona, Paris and Venice. Some of the many choirs, orchestras and smaller music groups – which include steel bands, salsa band and boys' a capella choir – do regular tours abroad. The school won a national award for curriculum extension in 2000. There's a full-time youth worker based at the school, which also employs a community manager to run adult ICT courses. 'We hope to be seen as a focal point for community activities.' The school's Children of the Storm charity supports refugee pupils, of whom there are over 100.

Recently became the first comprehensive to win the cup for Best Delegation to the Model United Nations international debating competition, beating the likes of Eton and other top public schools.

Background and Atmosphere: Situated on the Brent and Camden borders, surrounded by a mixture of local authority housing and genteel West Hampstead suburbia. The school buildings are a mixture of red-brick Edwardiana and 1960s pebble-dash concrete, with paved areas somewhat reminiscent of an underground car park, and a pond full of lilies and yellow irises. A mixture of shabby and refurbished, with plenty of computers, extensive modifications to accommodate a severely disabled pupil, and a new library with state-of-the-art multi-media facilities. An excellent new sixth form facility has just been added which was badly needed; also on the head's wish-list is a sports hall. Relaxed atmosphere; while it has its fair share of difficult pupils, many others are intensely loyal, enthusiastic about the drama, the science projects, the support they have had from teachers. 'It's a very caring school,' said a parent.

Pastoral Care and Discipline: This is a very inclusive school, taking on and coping with children who would struggle elsewhere. 'We can do this because our population is so diverse. We don't have that negative critical mass that can sink other schools.' The discipline is quite strict – 'I can honestly say that my children's education has not been disrupted by the disturbed kids,' said a parent. Excellent pastoral care system. Bullying 'is a fact of life in all schools and you need to be vigilant. We encourage parents to look out for signs. Aggressors are dealt with very severely but most bullies have also been bullied in their lives and we provide anger management and behaviour modification courses.' Parents confirm that any bullying is dealt with very quickly – 'and the head of year rang me when she thought my son might be being bullied – when in fact he wasn't.' There's formal and informal peer support; permanent exclusions 'are very rare but likely to be for extreme acts of aggression.' The school has the usual policies on drugs, with exclusion for dealing and an extensive drug education programme. 'It's about making sure children have the right information and having clear, explicit boundaries.'

Pupils and Parents: Immensely diverse, from Hampstead and West Hampstead intelligentsia to those from nearby local authority housing estates. A great ethnic mix, a high proportion of refugee children, children with disabilities and children with learning difficulties. OG: author Zadie Smith.

Entrance: Those with special educational needs get first preference – the school takes 14 with statements each year – then siblings, then pupils living closest, which, in practice, means less than a mile. Anyone already in the school may go on to the sixth form and about 70 per cent do. Most of the rest go on to FE colleges. Around 15-20 students, mostly from abroad, join the sixth form each year. 'We have an open recruitment policy into the sixth form, because we run vocational courses that can give people an extra year to develop.' Students aiming at A levels need six grade Cs at GCSE, with Bs in the subjects they intend to continue. Advanced vocational courses need four grade Cs; the one-year intermediate vocational course has lower requirements. 'We don't like to turn anyone away.'

Exit: About half go to university, including two or three a year to Oxbridge. Many students get into higher education via the vocational route at Hampstead. School feels that this is a particular strength of its sixth form. Others go to further education colleges, training and employment.

Remarks: Successful, inclusive inner-city comprehensive which has its fair share of disaffected as well as high-flying pupils but also has enthusiastic and creative teachers and 'fantastic' performing and visual arts. A parent commented, 'they do their utmost to give everyone the opportunities and make them all feel valued.'

HAMPTON SCHOOL

Hanworth Road, Hampton, Middlesex, TW12 3HD

Tel: 020 8979 5526
Fax: 020 8941 7368
Email: registrar@hamptonschool.org.uk
Website: www.hamptonschool.org.uk

• Pupils: 1,110 boys; all day • Ages: 11-18
• Religion: Inter-denom • Fees: £3,530
• School status: Independent • Opendays: Open morning late September. Visitors' afternoons throughout the year
• School gender: Boys • Day/boarding: Day pupils

SEN provision

Detail:
Now provide for in school:
Mild: DYSL; DYSP;
Moderate: DYSL; DYSP;

Summary: Please contact Hampton School for details of SEN provision.

GSG says: sounds unhelpful, but they're not. SEN details added by us.

What we say about the school - the full Good Schools Guide review

Head: Since 1997, Mr Barry Martin MA MBA FIMgt FRSA (fiftyish). Educated, and later assistant master, at Kingston Grammar School. Bags of experience in independent schools; formerly director of studies at Mill Hill and principal of Liverpool College. Career in economics for Bank of England before teaching. Maintains interest in world of business; author of business studies textbooks and chief examiner A level business studies. Slightly difficult to read, with a bluff manner, but innovative, humanitarian and admired by the boys – a capable hand on the rudder. Married to Fiona, with teenage son (at the school) and daughter at university.

Academic Matters: Fairly exigent academically, increasing pressure on places is pushing up pass mark for 11+ entry test which is, locally, already considered demanding. Head expresses concern that this is the case, with equal pride in the pupils' intellectual prowess. Levels of homework average-high, tempered by emphasis on extra-curricular involvements. 'We have set our face against being a hothouse pure and simple, the main thing is that boys are busy and happy.'

Results are of high standard; typically 99 per cent pass at GCSE A-C (70 per cent grades A*/A) but, unlike some other schools, no one asked to leave as a result of GCSE results alone. For incumbents and newcomers alike, minimum of GCSE A grade in given subject is preferred for A, A/S level options. 99 per cent pass at A level (70 per cent grades A-B). Languages are strong and well represented in A level choices which, otherwise, show science/maths bias. Year 7 boys choose between French, German and Spanish for modern language slot in timetable, Latin is compulsory until year 8. Maximum class size is 25, lower school tends not to exceed 22. Approximately 70 dyslexic/dyspraxic pupils, offered specialist individual support at extra charge.

Games, Options, The Arts: Sport is of a very high quality. Each boy is allowed to choose the sport he wants to play with no compulsion to play a particular game. Visiting physiotherapist. Leading UK rowing school (by medals and representations) – rowing has been established here for over 50 years – also rugby – spawns several professional players. Football likewise. The sports hall is large enough and has a multigym built in. Four well-equipped IT suites. Modern extension houses English, technology and art with art gallery-cum-corridor adjacent to large light studios with plenty of easels and equipment and reserved space for sixth formers. Recently installed, state-of-the-art, design suite – row upon row of inviting, funky Apple Macs. Design technology workshops are spacious and stuffed with tools and heavy machinery. Wonderful library with open access even in school holidays, large, cheerful, well-stocked, enormous selection of newspapers and periodicals – great libraries are rare and it is good to see a boys' school leading the way. Another comparative rarity is its cellular language laboratory.

Opportunities for performance in national-level debating, drama company that travels to Edinburgh Fringe and takes Shakespeare (back!) to Hampton Court. Plenty of music – choir, orchestra and several pop/rock/jazz and chamber music groups. Individual instrument lessons are school-subsidised and boys routinely win scholarships to music colleges. Most clubs and much sport take place during long lunch breaks. Meals are fitted around extra-curricular activities, but so sufficient is the service (school is well-known on the culinary front) that school lunches are taken up by 80 per cent of pupils, despite being completely optional. Exciting field trips to far-flung destinations plus school travel awards and some worthy links with Africa.

Background and Atmosphere: Spacious suburban location, low on traffic. Central building dates from 1939 and, if not glorious, is at least attractive. Unlisted and, therefore, unimpeded, sympathetic extensions have been added over the years. It all hangs together very well; roomy classrooms, new buildings that link smoothly with the old, added floors and corridors that are distinctly unwarren-like and maintenance which is tip-top. Outdoor space in the form of quads and lawns allow for plenty of steam-letting at break-times. On-site playing fields (27 acres) are, by London standards, downright magnificent. The new sixth form centre feels quite separate, offering status and privacy to the older boys.

Formerly a state grammar school (went independent in 1975) and about half the pupils come from state primary schools, majority from state-educated parents. This said, in atmosphere, school makes a good fist of resembling a traditional public school of long-standing – blazers and flannels, jacketed and tied sixth formers, Old Hamptonians' Association, flourishing cadet corps, burgeoning rowing, shooting and field sports societies; all very Tom Brown's Schooldays.

Not surprisingly, given the head's background, there's a sharp business-minded approach to the running of the school. Member of staff dedicated to PR and fund-raising from alumni and other corporate sponsors. Semi-funded fabulous performing arts centre is the project in progress. Super-slick lunchtime programme of speakers (high-profile Old Boys, left/right politicians and others) keeps boys enthralled and ensures oodles of local press coverage. Upper school divides into two competing entrepreneurial businesses with laurels going annually to the most profitable enterprise. Valentine's Day roses selling well on day of visit! Omni-supportive careers department, responsible for comprehensive handbook, UCAS pamphlet, annual careers convention, high-profile work placement programme and 'mock' interviews. Much emphasis on achievement post-Hampton (after all they may need you to dig deep towards another extension one day!). Ex-pupils' university successes are published back to back with current year's A level results. Illustrious Old Boys include lions of industry, lawyers, politicians and the like.

Pastoral Care and Discipline: Youngish staff with plenty of female role models – one of the deputy heads, head of modern languages, head of maths and head of art – are all women. Proximity to The Lady Eleanor Holles (adjacent premises, some shared facilities, drama and music, same bus service) ensures all-round healthy access to the opposite sex. Informal support pyramid whereby newcomers are paired with a mentor in the upper school. Boys and parents are encouraged to approach form tutors and heads of year with any concerns and pupils rate the 'very friendly nurse' as a good back-up. Ready access to counsellors. Plenty of commendations and merit marks and all-round opportunities to shake the head's hand. On the other side of the coin, detentions, work clinics and suspensions for serious infractions of school rules. Stringent illegal substance policy – expulsion is a serious threat.

Pupils and Parents: Wide west London and Surrey catchment area, bolstered by extensive school bus network. Good mix of boys – not at all pushy and precocious – and an unpretentious parental set 'You can tip up there in your anorak.' All faiths represented and celebrated according to the head.

Entrance: 120 join at 11 (85 per cent from state primaries) and 60 or so at 13 (65 per cent required score in Common Entrance). Majority of 13+ candidates are pre-selected, sitting school's test at 11, success in which reserves a place. Advance place examination available for 10-year-olds, sufficient precocious intellectual ability sees exemption from the scramble for places at 11. Failures at this test are encouraged to re-sit for unprejudiced reconsideration at 11. To join at sixth form, there is an absolute requirement of 6 GCSEs at A or A*.

Exit: Almost all to university, up to 25 to Oxbridge. Oxford, Cambridge and Leeds the three most popular universities in terms of numbers – impressive.

Money Matters: Academic, all-rounder, art, music and choral scholarships are available to candidates demonstrating exceptional promise. A limited number of means-tested bursaries may be offered by the head.

Remarks: High-achieving, well-respected, unpretentious, modern meets traditional independent boys' school. Reasonably large (but not expanding) numbers accommodate a refreshingly wide range of personalities/interests. Possibly not for trembly snowdrops or non-joiners, however. Should your 10-year-old son need convincing of the school's merits, note that Hampton once fielded a team in the BBC's 'Robot Wars'!

Harris Academy

Perth Road, Dundee, DD2 1NL

Tel: 01382 435 700

Fax: 01382 435 701

Email: harris@dundeecity.gov.uk

Website: www.harris-academy.com

• Pupils: 1250 boys and girls, all day • Ages: 11-18
• Religion: Non-denom • School status: State
• School gender: Mixed • Day/boarding: Day pupils

SEN provision

Detail:

Now provide for in school:

Mild: ASP; AUT; ADD; ADHD; EBD; DYSC; DYSL; DYSP; SpLD; HI; VI; CP;

Moderate: ASP; AUT; ADD; ADHD; EBD; MLD; DYSC; DYSL; DYSP; SpLD;

Severe: ADD; ADHD; EBD;

Others: OCD; ODD; TIC; EAL; MSI; Sp&LD; Epi; PD;

Summary: Harris Academy has a Support for Learning department to help all pupils fulfil their potential. In addition there is a Resourced Location which caters for pupils with Autistic Spectrum Disorder. There are pupils in each year group S1 to S6. The provision has been designed specifically to meet the needs of the young people.

In the six years it has been open, the school has managed to rise to the challenge of inclusion for all the young people, and has benefitted greatly as a result.

What we say about the school - the full Good Schools Guide review

Rector: Since 1997, Mr John Thewliss (the name comes from the North of England) BSc PGCE (fifties) who was educated at Broadhurst High in Motherwell, read geography at Glasgow University and did his PGCE at Hamilton College. Previously depute head at Dalziel High in Motherwell and before that depute head at Wallace High. V experienced, a chap who knows the area, married, with two children, his daughter is up and flying and his son is about to take up residence at Dundee University (and as the halls of residence are opposite Harris Academy, he is dreading the bags of washing). Charming, articulate and fun, 'love this job, I cannot believe how lucky I am to have it. 'Everyone thinks I am nuts'. It's not so easy to get good staff, fairly high turnover, and this problem is reflected in the 2004 HMI report 'Overall, the quality of learning and teaching was variable'.

Academic Matters: Well above average: no particular bias, but with around fifty per cent of all pupils leaving after standard grades (most go to Dundee College) it is a little difficult to give an accurate picture. Masses of computers etc, all heavily used with waiting systems in place if need be. Impressive library with yet more machines, class teaching on computers as well as IT. Pupils do keyboarding and basic ICT skills and use the skills in presentations: PowerPoint, sound, film-making, animated flow charts and present to the rest of the class. Max class size (legal limit) 33, but down to 20 for practical subjects. First couple of years all study Eng, maths, science, hist, geog, mod studies, home economics (magic), technology (great etc etc) plus one mod lang: French, German or Spanish. Latin on hand, but no Greek. Streaming after first year when a fast track for English, maths and mod langs comes into force. Teaching disciplines are a combination of individual, small group, whole class teaching and discussion. Strong learning support (but see below).

School attracts a number of ethnic minorities whose parents are billeted to the local uni, hospital or area, 14 currently in the school. Russian, Bengali, Urdu and Cantonese the most frequently spoken at home – native speakers can take these at standard grade. EAL is taught by the special educational needs team, and the HMI thought they were a bit stretched. Pupil support staff co-teach where necessary in class, but 'such support may result in a revised elaborated or alternative curriculum and include individual or small group tuition'. Supported study includes homework clubs, and a teacher is in waiting early on Tuesday mornings or Thursday evenings to help pupils with problems. Good encouragement too, for the more gifted. Terrific use of external facilities.

Eight standard grades for all as far as possible. Langs, humanities and modern studies above average and good showing in the Scottish and UK Maths Challenges; ditto the Dundee Enterprising Maths competition. Wish list includes re-vamped labs on the top floor. Good diversity, inspiring programme of lectures from outside speakers. Serious advice for all pupils on which road to take. Good choice post Standard with the option of intermediates 1 and 2 as well as Highers and Advanced Highers in a raft of subjects, plus tourism and hospitality at standard grades. Regular assessments and good parental feedback.

Autism: School is an important cog in the education of children in the autistic spectrum and, since 2000, takes ten pupils (never less) by request and allocation from the west of Dundee and the city itself (Morgan Academy takes those who live East of Dundee). These pupils are scattered across the age range, and school only accepts the next pupil when space becomes available. 'Lovely laddies' (mainly boys, but that's the nature of autism) all have individual educational programmes which are regularly monitored and amended. Some are totally supported individually and educated in the base (only one currently); others attend mainstream lessons, but may be entirely supported in class, or allowed to attend certain classes for a short period – eg physics: in mainstream for six weeks, and then back to the unit. Most take standard grade maths and all have speech and oral communication. School OK for physical handicaps – 'only one lift, but there are ways of moving round the school'. The base is popular with 'normal kids' who choose to join those in the autistic spectrum at lunchtime – a reverse integration. Many of these pupils will go on to Elmwood College in Fife, where the school has close links.

Games, Options, The Arts: Games fields half a mile away, gyms (still labelled boys and girls) on site – but used by all, ditto swimming pool. Large sports complex off-site. PE timetabled, and impressive line-up of games (extra-curricular) but including the v popular rugby, hockey, football for boys and girls, athletics, basketball (enthusiastic coach) water polo etc. Art, as you might imagine, deeply computer-linked: ceramics, painting, ICT, no CAD as such but the facility to use computer based design. Computer suite in art room, home economics, metalwork area, all computer based and hands on. Other schools please note. Mass of instrumentalists, music strong and popular with ceilidhs and rock concerts (including FPs) – huge charitable input, 'everything and anything'. Choirs, bands, orchestras. Popular theatre club, though not available as an exam subject despite pupils' requests. Outstanding debating, thrashing all comers; vibrant YE and truly popular D of E, with a whacking list of Gold, Silver and Bronze successes. Not the longest list of clubs we have ever seen, but thoroughly active, mass of trips abroad: humanities with proper exchanges popular.

Background and Atmosphere: Founded in 1885 and 'the oldest public school in Dundee', moved to the handsome granite building in 1930, school then added on a hotchpotch of flat-roofed excrescences in the '60s. Thirties classrooms elegant and airy with corridors wide enough for children and their bags to pass: '60s nasties – apart from the inevitable flat roof drip – boast beastly narrow passages, scarred by teenage book bags. Stunning views to the south, with really quite a lot of playground. Tiny dining hall in basement, next to library, students wait their turn in a surprisingly orderly queue at the 'red line'. Work experience at 14; some – less academic – pupils can study vocational subjects; Access courses in communication and maths or apprentice-shops locally.

Free school meals (but the cafeteria is cashless). Help with school uniform (skool provides the basics ex-stock) and trips. Grants available. If pupils stay for fifth year the odds are they will stay on to sixth: five Highers the norm; school qualifies for £40 educational maintenance allowance for those staying on after 16, which is a carrot.

Pastoral Care and Discipline: Sixth formers buddy first formers- 'very protective and good anti-bullying strategy'. Strong PSE reinforced by RME. Pupils are divided into four houses, and the pupil support strategy is handled by house representatives, each house having two guidance and two support-for-learning teachers. Defined sanction system: if pupils disobey one of five clearly defined rules then they 'may be excluded for up to three days' for continuous disobedience and head will meet with the parents. He 'is not prepared for disruptive children or anti-social behaviour' to permeate the school and would much rather produce 'decent sensible sensitive citizens' who are a lot 'more use than an anti-social chemist'. To this end (and this is a first for us) he has installed a splendid reward system: (Pavlov eat your heart out). Each pupil (who has the school code drilled into them during their first week 'so they can't say they don't know what is expected of them') is given a personal plan which must be stamped at the end of each lesson. Pupils earning 250 marks are awarded a certificate, can skip an afternoon's school and see a film of their choice – and get a Mars Bar. 500 stamps qualify for a silver certificate and a free ticket for Megabowl, gold equals a trip to Alton Towers and a certain amount of parent in-put and platinum a three day trip to London. Platinum winners have to have their cards stamped after almost every lesson to qualify. Head just loves these trips. Links with top year of feeder primaries, guidance staff and teacher visit regularly (HMI reckoned the school 'could try harder') and first year pupils all decamp with their teachers to Falkland Youth Centre for bonding and team-building stuff.

Pupils and Parents: A mixed bunch, some here briefly, a caring bunch of kids, charming and well-mannered. (The lure of London perhaps?) Good parental support and school booklet encourages this. Farmers, business people as well as the uni and hospitals.

Entrance: Always full. Pupils come from five main feeders with a couple of dozen placement requests annually. Certain amount of logistical movement. Standard rules about addresses and siblings.

Exit: Either post Standard Grade, or (usually) post sixth form. Some 70 odd per cent to unis, mostly to Scotland but the occasional trickle to Oxbridge. Inspired careers advice.

Remarks: Inspirational. An outstanding head, pity he can't inspire the building with as much enthusiasm as the children.

THE HARRODIAN SCHOOL

Lonsdale Road, London, SW13 9QN

Tel: 020 8748 6117

Fax: 020 8563 7327

Email: admin@harrodian.com

Website: www.harrodian.com

• Pupils: 812 • Ages: 4-18 • Religion: non-denom

• Fees: Pre-prep £2,944; prep £3,306; senior school £3,786; sixth £4,146 • School status: Independent • Opendays: Regular small group tours. Phone for appointment. 11+ open afternoon, October • School gender: Mixed • Day/boarding: Day pupils

---

SEN provision

Detail:

Experience of:

Mild: DYSL; DYSP; HI;

Moderate: DYSL;

Others: EAL;

Summary: The Harrodian School has a dedicated learning support department staffed by teachers qualified to assess and support a wide range of specific learning requirements of pupils of all ages. This support is provided mainly through individual teaching outside the classroom, in close liaison with subject teachers.

What we say about the school - the full Good Schools Guide review

Headmaster (Mr Hooke); Principal (Mr Thomson): Since 1999, Mr James Hooke BSc Hons PGCE, a geographer, mid-forties. Mr Hooke was director of studies and deputy head for four years prior to taking over as head so he has been at the heart of the building of this remarkable school from the start. Quietly spoken and serious, Mr Hooke produces a first impression of an eager sixth former but this quickly gives way to a sense of a man intensely proud of the school he has helped to form and of a very focused, though understated, professionalism and pleasure in the achievement.

Before the Harrodian, Mr Hooke spent three years at St John's School in Buenos Aires and it is perhaps this experience which informs the internationalism he sees as so important and which is reflected in the very mixed backgrounds of his pupils. Mr Hooke is the headmaster, deals with the curriculum and the day-to-day running of this fast-developing school. He is a head who clearly knows his children. The school also has its principal, Mr Peter Thomson. Mr Thomson was headmaster in the early years until his 'retirement' in 1999 but, if he is in any sense retired, it is far from obvious in his intimate involvement with all aspects of school life and his clear delight in what the school has become in so short a time. If Mr Hooke is the head in all the usual senses, Mr Thomson is the benign eminence grise, dealing, perhaps, with the more public face of the school among various other responsibilities he is clearly happy to shoulder. A former head of history and surmaster at St Paul's Boys, yards up the road, this is a highly experienced, more 'old-school', type of master who seems to have taught, during a long career, everyone one meets on the tour, and many of their parents too. An enthusiast, Mr Thomson pays fulsome tribute to the founders of the school in all aspects of their vision and approach.

Academic Matters: 2004 saw the pioneer sixth formers leave for higher education with much success at A level. As the school has grown, it has become academically more selective. Concurrently, fewer parents have seen it just as a prep and taken their children out at Common Entrance. Nonetheless those who do are winning places at good schools elsewhere.

Results are now making the dramatic improvements we predicted some years ago. 2005 GCSE results included 97 per cent with A*-C, and 49 per cent with A*/A grades and eight pupils scored all A*/As. Impressive stuff. Pupil numbers at this level have more than doubled in the last four years and results show steady improvement. Modern languages are essential to the school's being, and all learn French to a more-or-less bi-lingual level, taught wholly by native speakers. Other popular languages include Italian and Spanish; Russian and German are also taught. Japanese, Chinese etc are available by arrangement. It is a rare pleasure to find a school where a command of modern languages is seen as central to civilised life.

The curriculum is a mainstream one with all traditional subjects on offer. Classical Civilisation has been introduced 2004 at GCSE; Latin and Greek survive. Media studies and business studies also popular options. ICT in two good rooms, everyone has a lesson a week and is encouraged to use it in other academic areas. GCSE and A/S options. Senior school and sixth form centre fully networked for laptops etc and science facilities recently updated with new whiteboards. School not rushing into this area. An appealing suite of four rooms nicely tucked away at the top of the main building houses strong SEN department – mostly for one-to-one. 'Support staff work closely with mainstream staff,' says principal, and explains that, with so much sport on offer, school can afford to withdraw pupils from a lesson or so for SEN or, with the less academic children, from Latin. 'We like to think we can cope with mild dyslexia or dyspraxia but we have to be confident they can survive on the academic curriculum,' says head.

Overall, good and promising better academically. Head has aim of upping the overall performance and, increasingly, with the pick of the local clientele, he won't have a problem.

Games, Options, The Arts: You'd be forgiven for imagining that the builders of the old Harrodian Country Club knew that one day it would become a school. Or for being pretty impressed with the vision that has transformed an old squash court into a good modern dance studio, the ballroom – art deco skylight and all – into the school hall and theatre, the kitchen into a library and so on. This school has no sports hall or designated gym – maybe a drawback for some – but it has, half a mile from Hammersmith, 25 acres of pitches, courts, play areas and gardens. Sport is seen as central to the school day. 'We have a very good sports dept', stresses head. 'I'm very proud of what they've achieved. Everyone does sport daily and even the youngest are taught by highly qualified staff – not just a granny in a track suit', says head. All the usual sports on offer as well as lots of dance. Small but heated outdoor pool in super courtyard setting. Art in various art rooms – not over-spacious and pleasantly cluttered with variety of lively work. GCSE class were thoughtfully painting and varnishing bottles when we visited and some textile and fashion work, somewhat haphazardly on display. Good, careful drawing done lower in the school. Music school opened in 2003 provides flexible small recital/theatre studio with fixed raked seating and other facilities including teaching/practice rooms. New 'high energy' head of music set to build on recent 'huge progress'. All usual instruments taught to increasingly high levels. Bands allowed to record CDs on site and make their own photographed cover – very popular, of course. Battle of the Bands competition judged by celeb from music world. Performing of various kinds going on contentedly in pairs or small groups everywhere we went. Extra-curricular options include board games, dance, film, music ensembles and umpteen bands, computer club and 'animation' – many of which happen after school.

Background and Atmosphere: Unusual to say the least. Not a very 1990s idea – buy an old country club on the banks of the urban Thames and turn it into a co-ed school with a bias to modern languages and civilised values. Preserve the faux-neo-classical architectural style, add to it seamlessly with first class new-build and imaginative, charming features eg a pool in a cloister with ambulatory, and embellish it tastefully with any number of inessential but elegant and stylish jeux d'esprit – little fountains and stone vases, olive trees, balustrades, loggias and parterres, York stone courtyards and reception areas, real carpet, real gardens, real three course lunches, yet manage not to be precious or to spoil the pleasant and unpretentious children lucky enough to start life here. Space is used to create large halls and atria, a feeling of space everywhere except in some of the smaller teaching rooms/studios/labs which would be cramped with more than one or two more children. This place began life in the 1920s as the resort of staff from Harrods – clearly Mr H wanted his employees to have a taste of the grand style. After a tri-partite bidding match in 1993, a couple with vision, Sir Alford and Lady Houstoun-Boswall, he the eighth baronet and she an American multi-lingual teacher, headmistress and restorer of historical buildings, bought the site (beating St Paul's Boys and the Lycée to it) and proceeded to create a dream – a co-ed school run according to civilised values in a civilised environment to produce relaxed, happy children. School has expanded up and down – now taking from 4 to 18 though it began with ambitions to be no more than a prep. Existing prep and pre-prep part of the whole school in all respects – all share facilities though designated areas for younger pupils all purpose-built, thoughtful and charming. Mini 3-piece suites abound in social areas – velvety sofas and clubland chairs. Thus the school is the newest of its kind in London and unique in many of its qualities. A visitor chances her luck – there are no signs directing you to reception – or anywhere else. There are no bells or buzzers, children are smart but uniform is not a religion – there is a dress code. Few restrictions, 'children are civilised, cultured, accepting and disciplined without huge numbers of rules', says head. 'If the school had a motto, it would be 'Support The Individual', he thinks and parental noises convey that it does exactly that. Head and parents agree about the strong pastoral support, the 'fantastic' success in integrating new children – whatever their educational background, the general happiness. Staff seem to love working here – 'it's such a joy,' said a prep school teacher, in passing. It's certainly about as civilised an environment as one could find – perhaps not wholly surprising in leafy Barnes – the river on one side and large, detached houses on the other side of the school site – but there are older, less congenial schools taking from similar clientele not a million miles away so something is different here. It's not trendy liberal either – conventional and traditional in many things including the teaching style and the curriculum.

Pastoral Care and Discipline: A carefully structured system which works. High teacher pupil ratio which helps create the excellent relationships the school fosters. Parents are lavish in their praise,'... it's very much for the individual ... so positive about each child ... seems to find the best in everyone ... such good support throughout the exam period ...'. Few discipline problems, though, says head, 'children who push too far at the boundaries wouldn't fit in.' Zero tolerance for drugs and no safe haven here for those who have been expelled elsewhere. 'I have expelled children for drugs and wouldn't hesitate to do so again. We try to deal with such matters with PSHE and advice and try never to get into that situation.'

Pupils and Parents: Very middle class, professional, mostly very local though with very international – mostly European – origins. The cosmopolitan west London area not yet really reflected in the ethnic mix of the intake but this presumably only a matter of time and word getting out.

Entrance: Now has huge waiting lists for pre-prep. Non-selective. Strong sibling policy. Competitive at 8+ and 11+ and for occasionals. 'I will interview lots,' says head, 'and try to find children who are happy and have something to offer. I don't just take the top twenty off the list.' Takes few more at CE. Entry to the sixth now requires 6 A/s at GCSE and As in A level subjects.

Exit: A decreasing few at CE to trad day and boarding schools eg St Paul's Boys, King's Wimbledon, Marlborough, Eton, Bryanston, Haileybury and a bunch to Stowe. A few at 16 to tutorial colleges. Thereafter – it seems likely – to range of further education – good universities and art colleges.

Money Matters: Fees pretty average for location and what is on offer. No scholarships or bursaries.

Remarks: When it opened, school developed a local reputation for being for 'the thick rich' but this has been rapidly dispelled. An unusual, gentle and happy place, with a liberal but purposeful atmosphere, harmonious relationships, an exciting present in which everyone takes pride and a promising future in which everyone takes an interest. Set to gain from local Latymer Upper's becoming co-ed – more clever boys looking for a good school – and from the secret now being out that something rare and special is happening up river.

The Hertfordshire and Essex High School

Warwick Road, Bishop's Stortford, Hertfordshire, CM23 5NJ

Tel: 01279 654 127

Fax: 01279 508 810

Email: admin.hertsandessex@thegrid.org.uk

Website: www.hertsandessex.herts.sch.uk

• Pupils: 1,015, mostly girls; some boys in the sixth form
• Ages: 11-18 • Religion: Non-denom • School status: State
• Opendays: End of September or beginning of October
• School gender: Girls • Day/boarding: Day pupils

SEN provision

Detail:
Now provide for in school:
 Mild: DYSC; DYSL; DYSP; SpLD; HI; VI;
 Moderate: MLD; DYSC; DYSL; DYSP; SpLD; HI; VI;
 Severe: DYSL; DYSP;
 Others: FRX; GEN; EAL; DEL; Epi; Eat;
Experience of:
 Mild: ASP; AUT; ADD; ADHD; EBD;
 Moderate: ADD; ADHD; EBD;
 Severe: VI;
 Others: SPD; Sp&LD; PD;

Summary: Herts and Essex adopt a whole school approach to special educational needs. All staff have a role to play in the development and well-being of pupils. All Faculties have a representative on the Link committee, which discusses and shares concerns and good practices about individual pupils and whole school SEN policies. Time is given in all faculty meetings for the representative to feed back information and discuss proposals or individual pupil's needs. The school and staff have considerable experience in dealing with a variety of educational, physical and behavioural needs. The needs of pupils are met in various ways:

- In-class support, with a learning support assistant or additional within the class who can focus on pupils with difficulties.
- Specialist resources where appropriate.
- Differentiation of tasks in class and homework.
- Small group or individual work, where appropriate, allowing for practice or alternative or expanded explanations.
- Short courses, during the school day, in literacy or numeracy or language.
- Links with other secondary schools in the area who offer short courses for gifted and talented pupils.
- Supported homework club twice a week.
- Paired reading programme for pupils in year 7 and 8.
- Buddy system for year 7.
- Behaviour support programmes.

On entering the school all year 7 pupils are assessed by means of the NFER Cognitive Ability Tests and by various literacy and numeracy assessments. This ensures that pupils who need additional support or access to different resources have their academic needs met. Monitoring and assessment of pupils with additional educational needs continues throughout their school career. Access arrangements for exams are assessed early and wherever possible, exam board permission permitting, special arrangements are made and pupils given time and training in using these arrangements effectively.

What we say about the school - the full Good Schools Guide review

Head: Since 2005, Ms Alison Garner BA (forties). Married, no children. Has spent all of her career in the state sector, for the past 9 years in single-sex girls schools.

Academic Matters: An all-ability comprehensive and very good too. Results at GCSE are exemplary with 90-ish per cent five A* to C grades – in the top five per cent of state schools in England. History notably strong. The school has Science College status. Because of the churn post-GCSE, the sixth form are a rather different cohort; results at both A level and GNVQ (business education and ICT) are above the national average but by no means startling. Sciences a popular choice for girls at A level. At 11, pupils are taught in mixed ability classes of around 32 pupils in each; setting in maths in year 7 and languages from year 8. French in year 7, then German, Latin or Spanish added in year 8. One written report a year, with tracking grades 2-3 times a year, plus annual parents' evenings and regular home-school contact.

Games, Options, The Arts: Sport is strong with individual representatives at all levels. The main sports pitches, five-minutes' walk away, include four hockey pitches and a 400-metre grass athletics' track. On site there are tennis courts, rounders pitches, netball and basketball courts and a football pitch a 25-metre indoor swimming pool, a gym and a dance studio. School competes at district, county and regional levels. Clubs in trampolining, gymnastics, judo, dance, basketball and lifesaving – RLSS Lifesaving Awards at bronze, merit and distinction levels.

Some 10 per cent of girls learn one or more musical instruments – so not a great feature here – but there are flourishing choirs, an orchestra, wind band, swing band and several instrumental groups. A wide variety of extra-curricular clubs, many at lunchtime.

Background and Atmosphere: Opened in 1908 as The Bishop's Stortford Secondary School for Girls; fees were £3 a term and girls were trained for teaching careers. Stopped charging fees in 1944 when it was granted self-governing status and committed to remaining an all-ability school. Grammar-schooly buildings with adequate later additions – not much room to build more. The girls are proud of the uniform because it is associated with Herts and Essex High School even though it – long brown kilt-type skirt, matching blazer and fawn jumper – might just make you think this an old-fashioned school, stuck in the dark ages. Far from it. Plans to re-locate school to a new site with state-of-the-art buildings in Bishop's Stortford, possibly by 2010, planning permission allowing.

Pastoral Care and Discipline: The first point of contact is a pupil's form tutor although there is a 'buddy' system where pupils can talk to a particular sixth former about any worries or concerns. Pupils are encouraged always to act with honesty, equality and fairness and the head expects the girls to show respect and consideration to each other. Links with a school in Uganda. Strong policy on bullying.

Pupils and Parents: Large catchment area. Although the town is affluent there are pockets of deprivation, so there is a range of pupils from diverse backgrounds.

Entrance: About 300 apply for a total of 160 places at 11. Priority is given to those who can offer a compelling medical and/or social reason for admission, followed by siblings. Daughters of someone who works at the school come next. A total of 10 per cent of places (16) is allocated to girls with a proven aptitude in music or sport. Any further places go to children on the basis of distance in relation to primary school attended.

Exit: Up to 35 per cent leave after GCSE to pursue courses elsewhere. Minimum entry at sixth form is five C grades at GCSE. Vast majority goes on to higher education after A levels. Pupils are encouraged to sit Oxbridge if they wish; a handful succeed each year.

Remarks: Traditional values but prepares pupils well for the modern world. Girls are encouraged to do well academically and they seem to do so, whatever their ability.

HIGH SCHOOL OF DUNDEE

Euclid Crescent, Dundee, DD1 1HU

Tel: 01382 202 921

Fax: 01382 229 822

Email: admissions@highschoolofdundee.co.uk

Website: www.highschoolofdundee.co.uk

• Pupils: 730 (roughly 50/50 boys/girls) • Ages: 11-18

• Religion: Non-denom • Fees: £1,740 rising to £2,475

• School status: Independent • Opendays: Early November

• School gender: Mixed • Day/boarding: Day pupils

SEN provision

Detail:

Now provide for in school:

Mild: ASP; DYSC; DYSL; DYSP; HI; VI;

Moderate: MLD; DYSL;

Others: DEL;

Experience of:

Mild: ADD;

Summary: Learning Support – The learning support department works closely with the school management and class teachers to provide additional support for pupils with general or specific learning difficulties, sensory impairment, medical needs, or with English as a second language. The length of support can range from being minimal and short-term to complex and long-term. The staff in the department work with pupils both in the junior and senior school. Learning support staff employ a number of inter-related strategies to support pupils by:

- Working in collaboration with other staff to ensure that the curriculum is challenging yet accessible to all.
- Working in co-operation with colleagues to deliver the curriculum as effectively as possible and helping individual pupils.
- Continuing the monitoring and assessment of pupils with specific learning difficulties/dyslexia.

- Providing varying degrees of curriculum support and assessment arrangements.
- Supporting the development of literacy skills as well as paired reading and before school spelling clubs.
- Providing supported study facilities after school.
- Liaising with parents when a need has been identified.
- Liaising with parents, school staff and external agencies, where appropriate, at the stages of transition: junior/secondary, form 2/3 subject choice, Prelim and SQA exam arrangements, form 5/6 UCAS applications.

What we say about the school - the full Good Schools Guide review

Rector: Since 1997, Mr Michael Duncan (Mike) MA Dip Ed BPhil (fifties) who was previously deputy head of Robert Gordon's in Aberdeen whence he arrived in the late seventies as head of English before becoming assistant and then deputy. Read English at St Andrews, did his teacher training at Dundee College of Education (with a Diploma from Dundee University) he then 'taught for a bit' before winning a research scholarship at St Andrews where he spent a happy two years studying popular fiction in 19th Century Scottish periodicals.

Articulate and very much in control of his school, he is quietly proud of his achievements. Certain amount of structural re-jigging: offices, proper reception area, that sort of thing. The junior school has been pulled together: and a new teaching block has been created for English, plus a sixth form common room and separate study area. Computers all over the place and masses of dosh spent here, but head is keen for them to be working computers and not just dust-gatherers. Fair number of new heads of departments, and exam results reflect this in the main. Rector has introduced strong links with Dundee University where some members of S6 can follow uni modules which, if successfully completed, will allow them to start in the second year here (if that is their uni of choice). This pilot has now been copied by a number of state schools – a super initiative.

The rector believes it is vital for pupils to be 'happy in the school' and keen to encourage more independent learning so that pupils do 'not just parrot out facts': ('Abandon spoon feeding'); and would like to be able to offer a broader syllabus to accommodate the small minority of pupils who needs a more vocational programme. The school is academically selective, but there is a broad church of ability (siblings et al) and the rector is concerned that one or two may slip through the net. He has also just appointed a member of staff to pick up the minority of pupils who don't even join in activities. Charming, affable and well in control, Mr Duncan, who is not married, has a nice sense of the ridiculous, and is – quite definitely – prudent.

Academic Matters: School follows the Scottish system: Standard Grades mixed with Intermediate I and II, plus Highers and Advanced Highers. A good collection of subjects offered, including quite a few esoteric ones: technical studies, computing studies plus health and food technology, hospitality, information and modern studies as well as drama, business management and graphic communications. PE at Higher level only. Philosophy and moral ethics a new addition, home economics popular, with cooking courses for sixth formers to prepare them for uni. Tranches of success in chemistry, physics, biology and history. Top chemistry and top history marks in last year's Highers (wow); good links with Burn House at Edzell where historians go for weekends of outside speakers. 14 labs revamped so far and science strong over all. Impressive. Recent English results disappointing, new head of dept in place, so these should improve; head of English busy building relations with the English department at Dundee uni, creative writing popular last year. Mathematics not all that it could be: too many failures and D grades around. Pretty poor take-up in languages, even though all must take two, starting French at Primary 6. French and Spanish the leading contenders, with German a poor third – but new head of dept on stream, so watch this space. Latin scholars in penny numbers (no official Greek, but 'can be organised'. Classics trip to Italy last year.

Max class size 28ish (though usually 'in the teens or low twenties') and 20 for practical matters. No bias in subjects chosen by gender. Efficient looking computer rooms, locked at lunchtime, but used for classroom teaching as well as for IT, 300 desk tops, the Internet link comes via adjacent Abertay University. Old computers are tweaked by pupils and sold via YE for charity and rows of computers wait for attention in the design department, their red guts hanging out like a butcher's shop. Computer links with art, graphic art and design et al. No laptops yet 'not ruled out for a year and a day'. Library in the undercroft below elegant school hall, used for year assemblies (the whole school gathers in the nearby Caird Hall), has been re-furbished; computers and good tables to work at as well as a plethora (but not a huge plethora) of books, but the school mag says that borrowing has gone up by 50 per cent. Free photocopying for skool stuff. Learning support throughout the school, two dedicated staff about to be joined by another. Support starts in the junior school (exercises for all to help dyspraxic students), keen on early intervention, some ADHD but 'not much below', mild Asperger's and dyslexia OK, some help for the very gifted, head keen to avoid the bored child syndrome. Extra English on hand where necessary.

Games, Options, The Arts: Sports field a mile away with brand new three million quid Mayfield Sports Centre under construction as we write, pupils bussed. Strong on rugby, regularly at the finals of the Scottish cup, number of district and Scottish players. Girls' hockey strong, boys play too, cricket, athletics, tennis, swimming at Dundee uni, netball popular and athletics 'very powerful'. New outdoor instructor has taken over D of E which is thriving. Strong CCF and pipe band. Impressive music, with lots of charity concerts, ensemble groups: 500 pupils do instrumental music, a huge range: symphony orchestras, choirs, regular trips to Europe and masses of participation in local competitions. Separate drama department, plus media studies both curricular and extra-curricular. 'Art is stronger on design' says the rector, 'than on painting'; and a jolly art suite stretches across one wing of the building: jewellery expert has recently joined the art staff, and the extra-curricular jewellery club is incredibly popular. Fearsome debating with school regularly thrashing all others and often in the ribbons in the Oxford, Cambridge, Durham etc. uni/schools debating competitions.

Background and Atmosphere: Claims to be the oldest school in Britain: tracing links back to the thirteenth century 'when the Abbot of Lindores was instructed to build a grammar school in the burgh of Dundee'. Good adaptation of old building plumb in the centre of Dundee and surrounded by secure patrolled playground and janitors all over the place (though they did let me park there for a couple of hours). CCTV cameras everywhere. The junior school, based in the 1880s former girls' school (the Margaret Harris Building) is adjacent. School has acquired all the buildings down Bell Street and the school is rapidly expanding along. School uniform for all (boys may wear highland dress as an alternative – though we didn't see any), with girls wearing rather jolly Dundee High check, pinafores for juniors, skirts for the rest – another of the Rector's changes. Those sixth formers who are following classes at the university are allowed to change into mufti on site. Goonies for posh for all staff, the head wears his for assembly. Thrift shop once a month. School has good strong links with the Dundee worthies: directors elected by the Chamber of Commerce, the Guildry and Nine Trades of Dundee, as well as ex-officio the Lord Dean of Guild and the Parish Minister of Dundee and whilst nominally following the Presbyterian ethic, this is truly a broad church.

Pastoral Care and Discipline: Not many problems with drugs or booze or rock and roll, brief incident three years ago equalled pupils out. Tough and stringent anti-bullying policy, pupil welfare committee meets regularly, with regular reviews and impressive PSE. Two dedicated members of staff deal with 'child protection' – this is a first for us. List of possible misdemeanours includes hacking (another first), gambling or bringing laser pens or camera phones into school. Mobiles OK but mustn't be used during school hours or taken into exams. Sanctions range from a 'mild reprimand' via punishments, detention, letters home, suspension and very very occasionally expulsion – though children under threat of expulsion these days are more likely to be withdrawn by their parents first. Sixth formers befriend juniors both buddying and helping with reading or learning support. Four houses run throughout the school each house providing guidance as well as academic support and individual tutors for all.

Pupils and Parents: Fair number of first time buyers, ditto ethnic minorities, traditionally a mixture of – predominantly – farmers and professionals. A number of incomers from the universities and the life science department (particularly) of nearby Ninewells Hospital. 50 per cent come from outside Dundee, with buses from St Andrews, Perth, Forfar, Blairgowrie, Alyth and Arbroath: one or two pupils from Kirkaldy, school is close to railway station. Drivers can bring their own transport with the usual strictures about driving other pupils in place. Famous former pupils include Sir Lewis Robertson, Lord Cullen (Lord President), Lord Ross (Former Lord Justice Clerk) Andrew Marr of the beeb, the novelist AL Kennedy and former Scottish rugby captain Andy Nicoll.

Entrance: Pupils can and do arrive throughout the school year if space available. Two thirds come up from the junior school, the rest from other primaries. Waiting lists currently at P4, P5 and P7. 'School readiness' test for tinies; entrants for P2 up take standardised tests in maths and English for the junior school, and all pupils take the senior school entrance exam – no automatic transfer. Not many come post Standard Grades.

Exit: Logistic throughout the school, otherwise few post Standard (six or so), some post S5 and Highers, with uni entrance, or stay on for Advanced Highers. 93 per cent of those who do stay on go to uni, with a regular trickle of 4/6 to Oxbridge.

Money Matters: School not that rich, and loads of cash recently poured into the infrastructure. Number of bursaries (only); school will move heaven and earth to help families who have come financially unstuck, but hard on non-payers who won't co-operate. Selection of continuation scholarships available for FPs going on to university, some of which are dedicated to The High School and some of which are directed to inhabitants of Dundee. Trusts can often be persuaded to help an individual but might not be prepared to help the school itself. Foundation set up four years ago, and rafts of FPs are under pressure to give little and often 'which when combined might pay for one pupil for one year'.

Remarks: This is a thunderingly good school in the best of the Scottish tradition with all the right vibes and modern teaching aids in place, though some of the results need tweaking a bit. And, with the projected demand from the junior end, the Rector might abandon prudence.

HIGH SCHOOL OF GLASGOW JUNIOR

27 Ledcameroch Road, Bearsden, Glasgow, G61 4AE

Tel: 0141 942 0158

Fax: 0141 570 0020

Email: rector@hsog.co.uk

Website: www.glasgowhigh.co.uk

• Pupils: 380 boys and girls in the junior school, 55 in the nursery. All day • Ages: 4-10; plus nursery (kindergarten) 3-4 • Religion: Non-denom • Fees: Primary £1,527-£2,151; nursery £813 • School status: Independent • School gender: Mixed • Day/boarding: Day pupils

SEN provision

Detail:
Now provide for in school:
Mild: ADD; ADHD; DYSL; DYSP; SpLD;

Summary: The High School of Glasgow Junior and Senior Schools have members of staff with appropriate training who offer learning support to pupils with certain identified learning difficulties. Most of these are youngsters with mild dyslexia, dysmetria (lack of co-ordination of movement) or dyspraxia. We do not have the wide range of resources available in a school which specialises in assisting youngsters with major learning difficulties, but the rector and the headteacher of the Junior School would be pleased to explain to prospective parents what levels of support the school is able to offer. The school buildings have been adapted to provide access to youngsters with physical disabilities.

SEN questionaire details added by GSG.

What we say about the school - the full Good Schools Guide review

Head: Since 2001, Mrs Karen Waugh BA DipPrimEd (forties) who was educated at Hutcheson's Girls' Grammar, followed by a DipEd at Jordanhill College and took her BA via the Open University. Married, with a flexible husband, her children are in the school. Enthusiastic and fun, as well as very pretty, she brings a wealth of experience to this much sought after school. She was previously head of Mearns Primary (700 pupils), depute head of Carolside Primary (800 pupils) and then acting head; and before that she taught at Carlibar, team-taught at Crookfur and taught at the open plan Torrance Primary. Her current appointment is her first in the independent sector. The rector much in evidence during our visit – he carries out regular monthly assemblies here – and does a 'state visit' on Fridays, 'when Karen and I have a blether'. New staff appointments very much a joint activity. School has moved seamlessly forward under new head.

Entrance: 80/100 applicants at kindergarten level (max 54), though this is now 'capped at 50 to allow for the odd beginner at primary 1'. But get in early. School 100 per cent over-subscribed for entrance thereafter. Parents have coffee and cakes and the children are taken to the kindergarten and assessed individually. Social interaction and 'emotional readiness' rather than crammed academics is the yardstick, so children with a reading age of six will not necessarily come up trumps. Interviews are held annually, if you don't get a place the first time round, you may be kept 'on hold' and may be accepted – so don't give up. Recently there have been 63 applications for two places between primaries 1 and 6. Priorities to siblings, FPs' children and the rest of the field.

Exit: Automatic transfer to senior school and usually all do.

Remarks: The Glasgow prep they all – with good reason – fight to get into. Still holds true. Huge number of pupils shoe-horned with enormous skill into tiniest site imaginable; (rector doesn't like this description: he would prefer 'restricted site'). But think Victorian villa, think stained glass windows, think very steep site, think 380 odd children, think the impossible. Massive new build since our last visit, positively Swiss engineering to construct a magical new basement, fantastic kindergarten (with its own entrance); masses of light, this is imaginative architecture at its most productive. (Step forward Dr Easton, rector and architect manqué.)

Junior school shares senior school facilities, bused to Anniesland for rugby and hockey, swimming at the Allander centre, not a huge amount of playground on site (a couple of converted tennis courts) but each age group has their own. Small gym (ie not a sports hall) and impressive convertible hall/theatre. Excellent and imaginative drama. Superb music, three choirs, orchestra, wind, guitar, chamber, chanter – you name it. Specialist art teacher, the entire complex (building is too simple a word) is covered in child-paintings and models.

One (only) male teacher, dedicated French, drama, music, art and PE teachers, otherwise form teacher throughout. Two parallel classes for each year group, with 'group teaching where appropriate'. Support for learning at both ends of the spectrum with specialised learning support (as in dyslexia, dyspraxia, and those whom the rector would prefer us to call 'slow learners') upstairs in main building. No 'problem' with ADHD or children on Ritalin (none in the school at the moment). Sixth formers at senior school act as buddies when pupils move up to senior school. Class size 27 and down, French from the age of eight, IT from the start – IT Works, spread sheets, word processing, databases. Dedicated computer lab. The works.

Same ethos as senior school, positive relationships and anti-bullying plans. Elected junior school council – who have a serious input and recently quizzed the catering manager about the lunch supplied. Trips for everything everywhere. This is a busy school, own tartan for children. Mainly middle class parents, some from far away, children can be left early and collected late. Buses which link up with senior school runs. Kindergarten super with dedicated area, children on the academic ladder at four – play learning at its best. All wear badges with their name on it – automatic for the first few weeks, but then, 'the children love wearing them'. Charming, convenient, couldn't do better.

Hill House St Mary's

65 Bawtry Road, Doncaster, South Yorkshire, DN4 7AD

Tel: 01302 535 926
Fax: 01302 534 675
Email: info@hillhousestmarys.co.uk
Website: www.hillhousestmarys.co.uk

• Pupils: 225 boys and 235 girls • Ages: 3-16
• Religion: Non-denom • Fees: £1,850-£2,643
• School status: Independent • School gender: Mixed
• Day/boarding: Day pupils

SEN provision

Detail:

Experience of:

Mild: ASP; ADD; ADHD; DYSC; DYSL; DYSP; HI;
Moderate: MLD;
Others: EAL; Epi; PD;

Summary: The school employs a multi-sensory tutor who withdraws children from lessons for additional support. In addition the school's three SENCos will work with children in their normal working environment. Where children do present problems, these are usually of a mildly dyslexic nature. All staff are regularly trained to be aware of particular learning difficulties, from which some of our children may be suffering. The school does not consider itself as a specialist provider for SEN children.

What we say about the school - the full Good Schools Guide review

Head: Mr Jack Cusworth BA CertEd (fifties), who has been head of Hill House since 2000 and joined the school in 1973, teaching maths and PE, and 'gradually worked my way up'; sole deputy head and principal from 1990. Educated at a grammar school in Doncaster, followed by Sheffield College of Education and the Open University, his wife is head of the sixth form at Danum school – the local centre of excellence for 16-19 year-olds ('very, very good,' he says, 'but then I am a bit biased'). As nice a chap as you could hope to meet, open, friendly, frank; the children think he's brill. The governors of Hill House effectively bought out the proprietors of St Mary's and the whole is now run as a charitable trust.

Entrance: From reception upwards, put name down on the list. Mini-testette if joining later. Progressively more pupils staying on to combined senior school, with others joining from the state sector. Pupils come from within a fifteen-mile radius of Doncaster.

Exit: A few leave at 11 or 13 and go to trad public schools with fair number of scholarships – Repton, Worksop and the like. Older pupils at 16 mostly go to further education, with a fair number to trad sixth forms and local techs.

Remarks: The combination of these two independent schools in Doncaster happened over the summer hols 2002. St Mary's previously had pupils till 16, as well as in the prep; Hill House, a much stronger and bigger prep, had an enviable reputation locally. GCSE results include a goodly collection of A*s and As across the board and a very commendable pass rate all over. However, when we arrived, the chaos in the office was such that they appeared to have 'thrown everything away', well, couldn't find it anyway. Pupils can take GCSEs early, otherwise, French, Spanish, business studies, ICT, geography, history, art, CDT, home economics, Eng lang and lit, music and maths. Brightest pupils studying at AS and A2 levels. Very good recent ISI inspection report.

Going upwards in age: nursery perfect, lovely collection of Victorian houses with secure play areas (masses of white fences – infuriating for drivers). Excellent pre-prep and prep mostly housed in converted convent, brimful of up to 11-year-olds when we visited, each wearing their own school uniform and each with their class teacher in charge. Special needs catered for, both withdrawn from class, small groups as well as one-to-one, the school adopts a multisensory approach, dyspraxia, Asperger's, 'will cope if we can'. One of the current pupils, an epileptic, has full-time learning support (parents pay). Dedicated labs, wizard libraries, masses of computers and IT, vast hall with stage which doubles as gym, bags of child-inspired art on all the walls.

Art dept full of sumptuous art, pottery, papier mâché and textiles and masses of art scholarships further up. Altogether humming. Thriving music dept with staff travelling between the two buildings. Impressive dining room, tinies are served, otherwise canteen style, staff preside at the ends of the tables. Halal meals on offer and special kitchen. Late supervision till 6pm, plus activities and juice and bikkies for the prep and nursery. Both convent and the extensions overlook Town Field, much used for games by school and town, and absolutely charming. Indeed the whole Rutland Street complex is absolutely charming, with only one smallish property for sale which would complete the corner (and as the school is planning to sell this inner-city site and move further out, this would be a logical – and financially rewarding – step).

At 11, all youngsters move to the more spacious Bawtry Road site, out past the racecourse; regular shuttle between the two sites. Sadly the detached Victorian villa, with its stables and various purpose-built outhouses in a fairly substantial garden (netball pitch, loads of play area) came with a limited lease, now extended to five. The main house is in good heart and the numerous outbuildings have been appropriately refurbished to a high standard to accommodate an additional rather smart science laboratory, new music area and larger home economics room. Certain amount of other internal tinkering with space, smashing art dept atop the stables, good CDT, enviable oak room, used for assemblies and mini-productions. Dining cafeteria-style with stools, halal food, always salads, fruit and cheese and bikkies. Much use made of local facilities sports-wise. PSHE important – 'occasional problems always possible' but good pastoral systems in place. Each division of the school has its own head, plus tutors (pastoral). The academic and the pastoral operate side by side.

Exciting developments. Watch this space.

HILLS ROAD SIXTH FORM COLLEGE

Hills Road, Cambridge, Cambridgeshire, CB2 2PE

Tel: 01223 247 251
Fax: 01223 416 979
Email: aclarke@hillsroad.ac.uk
Website: www.hillsroad.ac.uk

• Pupils: 1,750 girls and boys • Ages: 16-19 • Religion: Non-denom • School status: State • Opendays: Evenings in November • School gender: Mixed • Day/boarding: Day pupils

SEN provision

Detail:

Now provide for in school:

Mild: ASP; DYSL;

Moderate: ASP; DYSL;

Others: EAL;

Summary:

I loved you since I knew you
I wouldn't talk down to you
I have to tell you just how I feel
I won't share you with another boy
I know my mind is made up
So put away your make up
Told you once I won't tell you again ...

The last line, at least, is directed at us (the whole by Sting at Roxanne, in case you wondered). We lost it. The dog ate it. Sorry. As you can see from our write-up, Hills Road is that rarity, a truly SEN-friendly first class academic institution. SEN details added by us.

What we say about the school - the full Good Schools Guide review

Principal: Since 2002, Dr Rob Wilkinson BA PhD (fifties) to whom we spoke but did not meet. Vast experience of sixth form education and as a college inspector. Came here after eight years as principal of Wyggeston and Queen Elizabeth I College in Leicester. Before that he was vice principal at Hills Road (1989-1994), head of history at John Leggott College, Scunthorpe, and taught at Scarborough Sixth Form College.

Academic Matters: Most years tops the league tables as highest achieving sixth form college. The great majority of its students – 85 per cent – come from maintained schools in Cambridge, south Cambridgeshire and surrounding areas. The remaining 15 per cent come from private schools, some of which haemorrhage 16-year-olds each year to Hills Road. Latest inspection report (2001) awarded Hills Road 11 grade ones – 'outstanding' – for every subject inspected and for the college's leadership and management – a unique achievement nationally. The college has a distinctive, palpable academic buzz; it may have a top class sports centre and be renowned for music but many students choose this college first and foremost for its academic reputation. No snobbishness about A level offerings – the more the merrier, including accounting, archaeology, electronics, film studies, Italian, media studies, music technology, dance, sociology, performance studies (not to be confused with theatre studies – also on offer) to name a few. Despite these more glamorous options, maths remains the most popular A level subject – double many other departments. All students do four subjects in their second year – which can include either A level general studies or AS level critical thinking.

One of the most technologically impressive colleges in the UK. Awash with computers, more than 650, all networked and Internet capable, they are wedged into every spare open space, not just IT rooms (head of IT was brought in from Unilever). Two language labs (many private schools have none), video cameras to loan, media studies studio with three editing suites, darkroom, two satellite systems for receiving foreign language programmes and meteorological information. £5m building programme has provided a new science building, new teaching accommodation for psychology and computing, student guidance centre, student cafe, more music facilities, and new landscaping around the campus.

Excellent study skills centre copes with everything from time management, handwriting and essay writing to ESL, dyslexia and Asperger's syndrome. Centre is available to all students and helps over 20 per cent of the student body and this percentage is growing each year. Laptops used by a few students with special needs. Average class size is 19 with 22 max; lunchtime surgeries in all subjects give students an opportunity for more individual attention.

Games, Options, The Arts: Students must attend at least one 'enrichment' session once a week in a discipline outside their studies. Massive range of options available, including most sports. Fields teams in major sports and many unusual ones and those not already going can be rustled up if interest demands. Girls' swimming team, set up by four students, won the English Schools' Swimming Association's Senior Girls' Freestyle and Medley Relay titles against the likes of Millfield School (2001) – some achievement as the college does not have a pool. Recent national players in cricket, hockey, rowing, rugby and tennis. College's sports and tennis centre includes superb cricket hall, opened in 1997 by Sir Colin Cowdrey, indoor and outdoor tennis courts run in conjunction with the Lawn Tennis Association, sports hall and squash court. Ten acres of sports fields a 5-minute walk away.

Drama, theatre administration and stage management flourish in college's Robinson Theatre, built 30 years ago through the donation of a multi-millionaire Old Boy, but looking as fresh as if it were completed yesterday. High standards in music with incredible range of ensembles and fab facilities, including top class recording studio and new music technology suite. Artists in residence and spacious areas for creating art masterpieces. Lots of clubs, including language groups (for non-linguists), life skills, art, fitness, D of E. 60 students involved in Young Enterprise. Overseas visits and exchanges with 17 destinations in Europe, the USA and Africa, including work placements in Germany for language students, a brilliant idea.

Background and Atmosphere: Has been described in the press as a half-way house to university but could more accurately be called a seven-eighths-way house. After coping here, university is a doddle. Opened in 1903 as a selective boys' grammar (nearby private school, the Perse, complained to the government and tried to get it closed down). In 1974 relaunched as a co-ed sixth form college. In the early 1980s there were 600 students, no adult education (4,500 adults now attend evening and weekend classes) and the college site consisted of the original building plus decrepit temporary huts. Foundation building now swallowed up by tasteful, bright, well-designed blocks. Social area in basement a bit of a squash for all these students but almost everything else rivals some universities for excellence of facilities. Big, bustling, friendly; looking out over the central quad as 1,750 sixth form students move from lesson to lesson, the scene resembles a mammoth beehive, or a film on fast forward with everyone moving at double time. New students may feel anxious at first as they have to become used to academic challenges, a diversity of social and economic backgrounds, co-education, and independent work and study. There is nevertheless strong support and guidance for students from day one. 'Although we treat them as young adults, we don't really expect them to be adults', the principal said. Thanks to felicitous Cambridge location, state school cred and excellent reputation, the college enjoys a stream of celebrated speakers, eg Professor Stephen Hawking, John Major, Lord Dearing, Zandra Rhodes and Sir Martin Rees, the Astronomer Royal.

Pastoral Care and Discipline: Hills Road requires teenagers to have a measure of self-discipline, subtly reinforced by the pastoral system. Students have been consulted on most college rules, are expected to behave like adults, and generally rise to meet expectations. There is no smoking behind the bike sheds because the college provides an area for those who choose – despite the principal's advice! – to smoke. Students can freely come and go from campus – as long as they are there for lessons. As well as working hard, students are quick to point out the fun they have: freshers' disco, two annual balls and ... all this freedom. The tutor is the pastoral care mainstay and students see their tutors regularly in tutor groups of around 20 students. There are also regular individual sessions and careers guidance. Previously some gripes about this system but a review of student guidance has been completed and a specialist tutor team, based in a brand new large student guidance centre, became operational in September 2005. Drugs and drink not problems here, although – as everywhere – opportunities exist.

Pupils and Parents: Students do not choose to come here unless they want to work (there are lots of good local alternatives) so are mostly motivated and mature. Some commute well over an hour each way to be here, bus stop opposite and Cambridge rail station five minutes away. Popular with parents of independent school pupils who move their children to Hills Road from local independents like the Perse and the Leys and even from famous London public schools trusting their kids will have a better chance of getting into Oxbridge from a state school than from an independent. Parents are involved, committed, ambitious for their youngsters. Former students include prominent government officials and Anil Gupta, director of the TV programme, Goodness Gracious Me.

Entrance: All prospective students from the local 'Collegiate Board' area are interviewed – a phenomenal feat given the numbers. For A level courses, students need GCSE grade Bs or better in the subjects they will be pursuing or related subjects. Priority is given to students living within the Collegiate Board area and most students come up from one of the area's 11-16 community or village colleges. Up to 80 places offered to pupils outside the area, mostly within a 30-mile radius of the college, but a few from other parts of England. Each year 200 applicants are turned down, some because they do not meet academic requirements.

Exit: Around 95 per cent to degree courses, over 70 a year to Oxford and Cambridge. 35 per cent take gap years and the college is unusually proactive in helping students arrange these, even providing limited funding. A few students don't stay the course but retention rates are well above sixth form college norms. The college has occasionally asked unmotivated students not to continue.

Money Matters: Previous head was a genius at magicking pots of funding out of thin air. With luck, this happy pattern should continue and the signs are that it will, with over £50,000 already raised from donors and the £5m building project having just been completed.

Remarks: Big, powerful, ambitious, top of the range sixth form college for confident and motivated young adults. Challenging atmosphere but most students positively thrive here.

Holmewood House School

Langton Green, Tunbridge Wells, Kent, TN3 0EB

Tel: 01892 860 000

Fax: 01892 863 970

Email: registrar@holmewood.kent.sch.uk

Website: www.holmewood.kent.sch.uk

• Pupils: 515; 322 boys, 193 girls; 6 weekly boarders, the rest day • Ages: 3-13 • Religion: Inter-denom • Fees: Weekly boarding £5,400; day £2,750-£4,285; nursery £1,250 (half-day) £1,875 (full day) • School status: Independent • Opendays: None. Individual attention on private tours of the school • School gender: Mixed • Day/boarding: Takes boarders

---

SEN provision

Detail:

Now provide for in school:

Mild: ASP; DYSL; DYSP; VI;

Moderate: DYSL;

Others: Sp&LD; Epi;

Experience of:

Mild: AUT; ADD; EBD; DYSC; HI;

Moderate: MLD; DYSP;

Others: SPD; EAL; Eat;

Summary: We have an excellent learning support department with four specialist teachers and three learning support assistants who provide monitoring, evaluation and specific teaching for children throughout the school.

In order to ensure that every child reaches his or her academic potential, the learning support department administers nationally standardised assessment tests to all pupils. This screening process starts in Reception and continues until year 8.

Learning support is all-inclusive in the Pre-Prep unless a specialist tutor or individual learning support assistant is specifically required. In the Prep School, pupils are charged pro rata for learning support and detailed assessments.

We are proud of the achievements of our pupils who have experienced problems in their early years. These children usually succeed in gaining places at Common Entrance to a variety of schools.

What we say about the school - the full Good Schools Guide review

Head: Since 1998, Mr Andrew S R Corbett MA PGCE (mid-fifties). Educated at Marlborough and at Edinburgh where he read history of European art and architecture. PGCE at London University. Came here from King's College School, Cambridge where he was headmaster for 5 years. Prior to that, head of history, director of studies and girls' houseparent at Port Regis and before that head of history and housemaster at The Hall, Hampstead. Very approachable, open and kind – diplomatic but firm with some demanding parents. Wife is a very popular full-time teacher here and they have two daughters who were at Holmewood but who now attend King's, Canterbury. Very keen on golf and takes pupils to inter-school competitions. Took over from Mr David Ives, who was head from 1980.

Entrance: Some at 3 into school's own newly built nursery (with 36 places), some into reception and some into year 3, although children can and do join at any age. All pupils assessed (extra time, laptops etc permitted for those with special needs if recommended by EP). Won't shy away from trying to accommodate pupils with physical or learning difficulties provided they have ability to cope with demands of the curriculum and the school. Majority stay until 13 but some leave at 11 to local grammar schools and girls' secondary schools.

Exit: Many pupils to Tonbridge, also Sevenoaks, Eastbourne, King's Canterbury, Cranbrook, Lancing, St Leonards-Mayfield, Marlborough and various other top independent schools. Very much the exception for pupils not to pass into their first choice school. Many prestigious scholarships won.

Remarks: Top prep school, top fees but with such extensive facilities you would expect this. Exceptionally academic; considering the non-selective procedures, the children achieve some wonderful results which reflect the quality and enthusiasm of the teachers. Also very focused on sport. The school tries to put out as many teams as possible in each age group so that all pupils have the opportunity to represent their school. 1st XV rugby team unbeaten last season. Under 11 IAPS national netball champions. Regular gymnastics success at national level. Stunning indoor 25-metre swimming pool built in 2001 – swimming teams national champions four years in succession; full-time swimming coach. Apart from usual team games, squash, athletics, tennis, golf and shooting too.

Extremely active music department – over 70 per cent of pupils learn an instrument – five choirs, two orchestras, a swing band, pop group and two jazz groups to name a few; over last five years they have had 20 major music scholarships to various schools. Music department also has its own computerised keyboard room where pupils can compose. Art equally impressive with two very dedicated and enthusiastic teachers. In 2003, they won two awards given by Artworks – Young Artists of the Year Awards. The award-winning work by the children was featured in a virtual reality exhibition at Tate Modern. Well-equipped DT workshop producing some impressive work. Drama popular as an afternoon and after-school activity in fully equipped theatre.

Lovely fully computerised library with full-time librarian; library lessons also given. Computers in evidence all round the school – all pupils have their own e-mail address – and there are over 30 interactive whiteboards. Pre-prep and nursery in separate blocks with their own head; very well organised; they have full use of all main school facilities. Separate junior department for years 3 and 4. An accelerated band is introduced in year 3 and further setting is carried out in later years. Excellent special needs department – problems are spotted very early on (all children screened in year 3) and help is given. Boarding offered only on weekly basis; some flexi-boarding by younger pupils. Dorms very light, airy, cosy and tidy.

Its reputation as a highly competitive school doesn't seem to phase the children, who are confident, bubbly, honest and well-mannered.

Hordle Walhampton School

Walhampton, Lymington, Hampshire, SO41 5ZG

Tel: 01590 672 013

Fax: 01590 678 498

Email: office@hordlewalhampton.co.uk

Website: www.hordlewalhampton.co.uk

• Pupils: 330 (more boys than girls), 200 in the main school (inc 50 boarders), 130 in pre-prep • Ages: 7-13; pre-prep 2-7 • Religion: C of E • Fees: Boarding £4,750; day £1,805-£3,610 • School status: Independent • Opendays: Near the start of each term • School gender: Mixed • Day/boarding: Takes boarders

SEN provision

Detail:

Experience of:

Mild: ASP; ADD; ADHD; EBD; DYSC; DYSL; DYSP; SpLD; HI; VI;

Others: CD; FRX; EAL; Sp&LD;

Summary: Hordle Walhampton has a learning support unit with four specialists including one to help with EFL needs. Children are helped, on a one-to-one basis or in small groups where appropriate, with a variety of learning needs including dyslexia. Moderate or severe levels of disorder are beyond the resources of the school.

What we say about the school - the full Good Schools Guide review

Head: Since 1998, Mr Henry Phillips BA (fifties), educated at Harrow, worked as a stockbroker before doing an Open University degree in English. Deputy head at Summer Fields, then head of Hordle House, which subsequently amalgamated with Walhampton (see below). 'He's larger than life,' said a parent. 'He says what he thinks and doesn't tolerate fools,' said another. 'He's got a wicked sense of humour and the children think he's fantastic. Every year he hosts a grandparents' lunch and they all adore him.' His 'wonderful' wife, Jackie, helps out with the boarders, teaches and works hard around the school. Three children.

Entrance: First-come-first-served entry at two into the very popular pre-prep, with preference for siblings. Nearly everyone goes through to the prep at seven; more join at that point. There is a fair amount of to-ing and fro-ing; a few leave the pre-prep for state primaries, some come in from abroad for a term or two to improve their English, others move into or out of the area. Always worth trying for a place; those coming in higher up are assessed. 'We're comfortably full but will always take a good child at the last minute.' That doesn't necessarily mean academically gifted. 'All children have something to offer, whether on the games field or in the concert hall. We're a school for good all-rounders.'

Exit: A few leave at 11, for eg King Edward VI in Southampton, but most stay till 13, moving on to a wide variety of secondaries, particularly co-ed Wessex boarding schools such as Bryanston, Marlborough, Canford, but also Eton, Harrow, Winchester, St Swithuns, Downe House. Very few to selective state schools.

Remarks: Has put behind it the traumas of the merger between Hordle House and Walhampton in 1997. Splendid Queen Anne/Victorian building with panelled, galleried entrance hall and chapel in what was once the music room, with original cornices. Glorious 100 acre grounds on the edge of the New Forest with lakes for ducks and sailing, extensive playing fields, outdoor swimming pool backed by Italianate colonnade and shell grotto, stables (bring your own pony), pet shed, new sports hall and performing arts centre. Non-selective. French from 4, Latin from 9, German club. Years 3 and 4 have two parallel classes; years 5-7 are divided by ability into two classes; about a third of year 8 form a scholarship class. The latest Independent Schools Inspectorate report commented that work set in years 3-5 tended to aim at the middle range; the school has addressed this by setting for maths and English and differentiating work in other subjects. 'We're not an academic hot-house, but children fulfil their potential.' 'They teach the children to their own level but don't cram them,' agreed a parent approvingly. Having said that, in 2005 six children gained entrance to Winchester, three gained academic scholarships, two gained sports scholarships, one gained an all-rounder scholarship (for prowess in art, music and sports) and one a music scholarship – a school record.

Has an excellent SEN department (individual and shared teaching at extra charge, plus extra help in class). Good at spotting problems. Will cater for mild Asperger's, ADD, specific learning difficulties (dyslexia unit is registered with CReSTeD). Children with behavioural or severe learning problems may be turned away. Hot on spotting SpLDs and will arrange EP assessments. Go back to basics if necessary – fill in gaps. Very bright boys get help too, if they need it. Children view one-to-one as a real treat, no stigma. Make great strides not just academically but socially too. Only grumble: parents say sometimes they wish school would tell them a little more be a bit more open – tend to say doing fine, don't worry, but parents do worry.

IT is now particularly strong; art and DT good too; plenty of drama. Music, say parents, is more patchy but about 80 per cent of pupils learn an instrument. There is now a school orchestra, a number choirs and specific music groups (including a steel band) and a couple of rock bands. 'We have a very cool guitar teacher. Activities range from cookery to canasta to camp craft. 'My son learned bee keeping and we now have our own hive,' said a parent. Games features very strongly. Individual sports such as archery cater for those who aren't team players. Some mutterings that girls' sport is perhaps slightly less strong than boys' – 'I have appointed an experienced coach to bolster that area and results this year have been pretty good,' says the head. 'We love sport, and are not afraid of competition.' Planning permission for a new astroturf has just been approved to back this up. School teams win medals for tetrathon and sailing as well as the more usual swimming, tennis, rounders and so on. In 2003, rugby and hockey teams toured South Africa.

Towards the end of the summer term the whole school goes off on expeditions, which include a year 7 leadership skills week at the school's own base on the Isle of Mull. This week, which features highly in children's fond memories of the school, helps staff to choose the head boy and girl, prefects and patrol leaders. The school's four houses are divided into mixed aged patrols, whose leaders look after the younger children. 'My children revere their patrol leaders,' says a year 3 teacher.

Excellent pastoral care; staff and parents emphasise that it is a very happy school. 'Parents are amazed at the staff's depth of knowledge of their children.' It takes a no-blame approach to bullying. 'We're very vigilant and try to knock it on the head as fast as we can. Usually a word here and there sorts it out.' Mentors are allocated to new children and there are flexible behaviour strategies for individuals if necessary. Strongly Christian ethos. Assembly takes place in the chapel every morning and there is a service on Friday evenings. 'It is an important part of communal living.' 'Everyone is encouraged to board in the last two years and a few do so lower down – weekly and flexi-boarding available. The school runs a boarding timetable, with sports and activities every afternoon until 6.15pm (except for year 3, who leave at 3.45). There are also Saturday morning activities and afternoon sports matches, and special outings on Sunday for boarders.

Links with local state primaries, whose pupils come up for multi-activity days. 'We're very keen not to be seen as that snobby school on the hill.' Pupils come from the Channel Islands and the Isle of Wight as well as mainland Hampshire and Dorset. Popular with army and civil service families.

Probably not the school for children whose favourite activity is sitting in the corner with a book. "Robust' conjures up our outlook,' says the head. There is a wide enough range of activities for everyone to shine at something, whether clocking up runs for the 3rd XI, singing in the chapel choir or performing in Bugsy Malone. 'We chose the school because it had so many different activities on offer and we haven't been disappointed,' said a parent. 'My boys have always wanted to go to school every day.'

HORNSBY HOUSE SCHOOL

Hearnville Road, London, SW12 8RS

Tel: 020 8673 7573

Fax: 020 8673 6722

Email: school@hornsby-house.co.uk

Website: www.hornsby-house.co.uk

• Pupils: 320 girls and boys, 50/50; all day • Ages: 4-6 infants, 7-11 juniors • Religion: Non-denom • Fees: £2,800-£3,048 • School status: Independent • School gender: Mixed • Day/boarding: Day pupils

SEN provision

Detail:

Now provide for in school:

Mild: DYSC; DYSL;

Moderate: DYSC; DYSL;

Summary: No comment. Good provision, but shy of being known for it? SEN details added by us.

What we say about the school - the full Good Schools Guide review

Head: Since 1998, Mrs Jenny Strong BEd (fifties). Married with four grown-up children, she was brought up in Scotland and educated at St George's Edinburgh. Formerly the deputy head at Alleyn's Junior School also taught at JAPS. Mrs Strong has an interest in maths and science. Very much a hands-on head with a firm belief in co-education.

Retiring July 2006.

Entrance: Non-selective at 4-6 years. From 7 and for occasional places in the junior school an assessment test and interview with the head. Places are allocated on a first-come-first-served basis, so it is worth putting your child's name down in advance. Sibling priority.

Exit: At 11 years to a range of London day schools including Wimbledon and Streatham and Clapham Girls High Schools, Dulwich College, King's College, Emanuel, Alleyn's, James Allen and The Hall. Handful to boarding schools such as Woldingham, Windlesham House, Wycombe Abbey and Heathfield.

Remarks: Hornsby House was founded in 1988 by Professor Beve Hornsby. The school opened with 20 pupils in a church hall premises, they moved to a permanent site in 1993 and have gone from strength to strength ever since. New buildings were opened in September 2000 and 2003 providing further classrooms, a science room, music rooms, art room, library and a state-of-the-art ICT suite complete with all the new technology a good prep school needs.

Has a good reputation for being a friendly, welcoming school where everyone knows each other as it has not grown too large. The staff are mostly long serving. The pupils are predominantly local, especially in the younger age groups. The school is now housed on a well-modernised Victorian (ex local authority) primary school site; spacious light classrooms, a large gym/assembly hall, two playground areas, a well-stocked library, art room. Displays of the children's work everywhere.

Reception classes in a separate building – a cosy and secure atmosphere for the 4 to 6-year-olds, with their own small hall and playground. Class sizes are between 18-22, all classes are mixed ability, have a teacher and an assistant teacher some of whom are graduates. No meals are provided, all bring packed lunches. Good music, drama and sport – the school produces some very colourful shows each term and also has theatre groups to visit. Three choirs, orchestra and a wide choice of individual instrumental tuition. An enthusiastic new sports master arrived recently, the children use the nearby Trinity Fields. A strong parents' group, 'Friends of Hornsby House', runs social events, fetes etc for school and charity fund-raising.

Children with known specific learning difficulties entering the school will be asked to have a full assessment. There is a full-time SEN co-ordinator and three part-time dyslexia therapists who work with children on maths and English. The school is also able to accommodate some children with physical disabilities. Where necessary, pupils use laptops, and the school has good links with touch-typing tutors. A parent comments, 'having moved my children to Hornsby from another school this was a good decision, it is much more relaxed.'

HORTON LODGE COMMUNITY SPECIAL SCHOOL

Rudyard, Leek, Staffordshire, ST13 8RB

Tel: 01538 306 214

Fax: 01538 306 006

Email: headteacher@hortonlodge.staffs.sch.uk

Website: www.atschool.eduweb.co.uk

• Pupils: 59 boys and girls, all statemented, 20 high dependency • Ages: 2-11 • Religion: non-denominational • School status: State • Opendays: Phone for personal appointment • School gender: Mixed • Day/boarding: Takes boarders

SEN provision

Detail:

Centre of excellence for:
- Mild: CP;
- Moderate: CP;
- Severe: CP;

Now provide for in school:
- Mild: HI; VI;
- Moderate: MLD; HI; VI;
- Severe: HI;
- Others: PMLD; MSI; Sp&LD; Epi;

Experience of:
- Mild: ADD; EBD; DS; DYSC; DYSL; DYSP; SpLD;
- Moderate: EBD; DS; DYSC; DYSL; DYSP; SpLD;
- Severe: DYSC; DYSL; DYSP; SpLD; VI;
- Others: SPD; AUT(other); FRX; GEN; EAL; DEL; PD;

Summary: Horton Lodge Community Special School is a primary school for pupils with Physical Disabilities and associated learning difficulties. The school uses Conductive Education to promote active learning for all the pupils – all teachers in the school are fully qualified Conductor Teachers.

The school is a key learning centre and provides support for many pupils with physical disablities who are in mainstream schools. In addition to this the school supports the transition of pupils from Horton Lodge into their mainstream school if and when appropriate.

What we say about the school - the full Good Schools Guide review

Head: Since 2004, Ruth Zimmerman (mid thirties). Enthusiastic dynamo with high expectations and seriously joined-up thinking, building on tradition of school excelling in its provision for pupils, staff and the community. Four year degree course in Conductive Education at the Peto Institute, Hungary. Wholeheartedly committed to school doing its very best for pupils but also, 'serving as a resource base to help shape how the whole community thinks', as well as supporting parents of SEN children from birth and creating a rewarding place to work.

Entrance: For any child with physical disabilities, many have learning difficulties as well. Staffordshire LEA but out-of-county children negotiate with own LEAs to pay Staffordshire. This can be a struggle and parents question why there aren't schools like this one everywhere.

Exit: Some to mainstream schools, often with increasing days out in mainstream primaries to prepare for transition. Lots to Blackfriars Special School, Newcastle-under-Lyme.

Remarks: Idyllic setting surrounded by woods down to lake, paddocks with ponies and abundant fresh air in 10 acres of rolling Staffordshire Moorlands countryside. Very happy, working atmosphere in former 1850s hunting lodge with plainer, single storey, flat roof extensions and colourful play areas, one covered. Teachers all trained in conductive education with holistic approach where, for example, physio and speech therapists work alongside children during normal school activities. Children are out of wheelchairs most of the time, actively sitting. 'We strive for excellence and enjoyment,' says head, 'our children have to work so hard to achieve things that, unless they're enjoying it, they won't, but we're teaching them to cope with what's going to be a very difficult world for them.'

Each child has a Gold File with individual targets, lots of celebrations of achievements and digital photographs to prove them. Staff/pupil ratio is good, 1:6, with eight conductor teachers and 24 support staff. Described as 'outstanding' by Ofsted, with no significant shortcomings. Class work beautifully presented all over school. Visits from theatre, ballet, story telling groups. Glyndebourne Opera expressed doubts before visit but found the children amazingly creative and motivated in finding ways to do things. Recent visits include London, France and Bendrigg Outdoor Adventure Centre in the Lake District. Interactive whiteboards in every classroom. Lots of equipment, including state-of-the-art sensory room (from fundraising) with star-lit tunnel, sound beam, multi-coloured bubble tube etc that work as reward for pressing buttons.

Swimming pool with designated instructor, lighting effects and music, open to local primary school and adults with disabilities. School has open policy for parents and many join children for swimming, as do physiotherapists. Sailability on lake, RDA riding for all 5 to 7-year-olds, then an after-school option with volunteers. Grounds used for camping trips. 'They love it,' says head, 'and I believe they deserve everything mainstream children enjoy'. Pet donkeys, Ed and Dusty, look on from their fundraised stables.

Kiplings residential unit offers four brightly coloured four-bedded rooms. One full-time boarder from Yorkshire and some 20 children choose to stay on a rolling programme. 'Not for respite care,' says head, 'but to continue exercising skills from morning to night', but, she admits, they do enjoy the sleepover atmosphere. Bathrooms with hoists, bubble and lighting effects and choice of eight evening clubs; brownies, art, gym etc. Hands-free phone for private calls home.

'School for Parents' in two staffed rooms for mums, dads and grandparents of babies from birth with suspected or diagnosed disabilities. Parents find it supportive to meet others in the same situation and say of staff, 'it was wonderful to have somewhere to go where they understand what you're going through and can help you with your baby.'

Upstairs rooms used for training mainstream teachers in conductive education and for continuing professional development of own staff in individual specialist areas. House in grounds let to private day nursery (a social enterprise giving profits back to community projects) used by many of predominantly female staff including head. Staff also enjoy well-equipped new gym, from grant applications. Business manager works 'pro-actively' with budget and extra funds raised by governors, parents, friends and several community groups. Resources manager helps plan extra-curricular activities and their follow-up leaving staff to concentrate on teaching. Fleets of minibus taxis deliver and collect children though some parents prefer to do it themselves, driving up to an hour and a half each way. 'You won't find anyone with a bad word about the school,' they say, 'the only thing wrong is that our children can't stay here forever.'

HOWELL'S SCHOOL, LLANDAFF

Cardiff Road, Llandaff, Cardiff, South Glamorgan, CF5 2YD

Tel: 02920 562 019
Fax: 02920 578 879
Email: headsec@how.gdst.net
Website: www.howells.cardiff.sch.uk

• Pupils: 535 girls, all day – but boys in the sixth form from 2005 • Ages: 11-18 • Religion: Non-denom • Fees: Junior £1,293 to £1,565. Senior £2,159 • School status: Independent • School gender: Girls • Day/boarding: Day pupils

SEN provision

Detail:
Centre of excellence for:
Mild: DYSL; DYSP;
Others: EAL;

Summary: Our aim at Howell's School, Llandaff is to support the educational development of all girls within the capabilities of our resources and expertise, so they can achieve their full potential.

What we say about the school - the full Good Schools Guide review

Principal: Since 1991, Mrs Jane Fitz (forties) was born and educated in Tasmania, then London University (chemistry). Has always taught in GSDT schools, rising through the ranks in London. Husband is a professor at Cardiff University; teenage daughter presently at the school. Diligent, professional, able and committed. Chaired the Welsh Independent Schools Council, now a council member of Cardiff University. Described as 'fascinating' and 'a visionary with the ability to see the whole picture and work through the minutiae of detail to see things through to completion'. Such tenacity has not always endeared her to staff but, when applied to the welfare and aspiration of pupils, has proved very successful. Bubbly and delightful deputy principal, Mrs Sally Davis.

Academic Matters: Academically very strong indeed – a selective entry and a busy, vibrant management team ensures there's no room for slack. 87 per cent A/Bs at A level in 2005 and 64 per cent with A/A* at GCSE. Parents make contented noises at the quality of teachers and general standards. Science does very well – eight labs with a collection of enthusiastic staff – and many girls later taking up medicine. We sat in for part of a biology lesson with very attentive pupils who eagerly informed us that we had missed the 'best and gory bits'. Only dual award at GCSE, to leave room for ICT, DT, drama within the school's limit of eight or nine GCSEs. Keen that all students take at least one creative subject – which they do. Maths sure-footed – 'my less mathematically able daughter felt safe and confident due to the dedication of the teachers'.

The breadth of curriculum is not extensive, but is improving: no social sciences, but government and politics, psychology, critical thinking, theatre studies, drama, business studies and IT recently introduced. The head is keen to point out that many go on to study social sciences at university and choices are pragmatic and made with each pupil's university requirements in mind, and the school will jump through hoops to accommodate an individual's passion. There's a pupil doing Arabic, another Italian, another (as a result of some girls winning a national science competition, visiting Cape Kennedy and Houston, returning to form an astronomy club) astronomy.The school celebrates its Welshness and pupils learn about and play their part in Welsh culture – plenty of exhibitors in the Eisteddfod with one pupil winning the Learners' Recitation. Raises the profile of the languages generally in the school. The emphasis on Welsh language and the uniqueness of Welsh culture is strongly supported by parents but does elbow some other subjects out of the curriculum. Wales as famous for exporting teachers as it is for coal – Welsh lilts can be heard in staffrooms across the land and many of the best have come back here. A congenial, jovial and committed bunch.Ten-ish mild/moderate dyslexic pupils annually – satellite unit gives individual tuition at extra cost. Talented children with specific gifts are also catered for. Clear ethos of the school is that the girls can achieve academically and be productive in society.The sixth form is housed opposite the main school in two large Victorian redbrick houses with gardens that stretch to the Llandaff fields. An exciting time is ahead for Howells as – uniquely within the GDST –

they have become co-ed at sixth form with capacity increased from 120 to 200 (they argue that single sex education works well from 11 to 16 but co-ed is equal or better from 16 to 18).

Games, Options, The Arts: Some fine art and textiles on display. A couple of quality drama productions a year, drama perceived as very important in the curriculum. Sport includes badminton, horse riding, fencing, a dry ski team (currently Welsh champions) apart from the usual netball, hockey, swimming and gymnastics, where national successes are numerous. Lacrosse has been a long tradition at the school although fixtures are limited due to the lengthy trip to rivals Malvern and Haberdashers Monmouth. Dance is popular – but not taken to GCSE level.

50 per cent pupils play an instrument, significant numbers at county level (some at national) – parents really laud this department. Light, fresh, octagonal, concert hall and plenty of practice rooms – soon to be extended. We saw pupils being talked through Dawn (by Benjamin Britten) by one of the celebrated music staff who broke into extravagant, enraptured gestures much to the amusement of the girls – very infectious enthusiasm. All types of bands, five choirs, three large orchestras and many chamber groups.

Duke of Edinburgh increasingly popular – we met a large troop setting off for their gold award. Impressive involvement in community and charity work – working with a local special school, Envision, Fair Trade etc; the canteen stocks only fair trade approved goods. Also links with a school in their sister country, Lesotho; staff have already visited for a week and now the pupils are raising money for a new science laboratory and library. Excellent careers programme – conventions, visiting speakers etc.

Background and Atmosphere: In 1537, Thomas Howell left a substantial sum to the Drapers Company for orphans and from this charitable bequest the school was founded in 1860. Joined the GDST in 1980. A short walk from the centre of Cardiff off a busy main road. On entering the school, all feeling of congestion disappears – the site is much larger than is visible from the road. A grey stone chateau-style building of turrets and spires with extensions bolted on over the years. Grand old cast iron staircase, wood panelling, stain-glassed windows, original fresco in the Grand Hall, etc. Much fustiness dispensed with over the past 10 years – no more straw boaters, even the pink and white striped shirt is soon to change. Good food. An atmosphere of 'hwyl' ie spirit and heartiness, respect but not deference.

Pastoral Care and Discipline: Head is not fazed by feisty pupils – 'I often find they become great contributors to society' and the deputy says their motto is 'don't let small things become big things' and 'work hard with parents to nip problems in the bud'. Very effective pastoral systems. Drugs, alcohol not big issues, but out if caught.

Pupils and Parents: Catchment area from Cardiff to Newport, Bridgend and the Valleys means a diverse group of pupils – a lot of bursaries so the selection is academic and not exclusively social. 15 per cent ethnic minority and 60 per cent from state and own linked junior schools, the rest well-heeled parents from eg the medical and legal professions. A shared desire to achieve – the parents are as ambitious as the pupils. Parents very involved with life of school. OGs include the first woman QC in Wales, Jane Crowley; the first women chair in Egyptology, Professor Rosalie David; and Charlotte Church.

Entrance: Usual GDST entrance criteria at nursery and junior school of observing at play and interview. Years 3 to 6 sit papers in maths, English, non-verbal reasoning. Entrance papers mainly taken at year 7 in maths/English. Scholars are chosen from results and interview. Mainly automatic entry from junior to senior unless a pupil is struggling with the level of work.

Exit: Only a handful escape university. Some to art foundation, a double handful go to Oxbridge, others mainly to top brass universities with the highest numbers reading medicine, dentistry, pharmacy, veterinary sciences, engineering and law. Plenty do business studies, IT or performing arts.

Money Matters: Healthy. Apart from the support of the Minerva Trust common to all GDST schools, there is the added benefit of the Thomas Howell Trust managed by the prosperous Drapers Company. About 20 per cent of the senior school are on some kind of bursary – with a small pot available to those falling on hard times.

Remarks: A school where academic excellence, the arts and Welsh culture are celebrated.

HUISH EPISCOPI SCHOOL

Wincanton Road, Langport, Somerset, TA10 9SS

Tel: 01458 250 501

Fax: 01458 250 262

Email: office@huishepiscopi.somerset.sch.uk

Website: www.huishepiscopi.somerset.sch.uk

• Pupils: 615 boys, 595 girls. All day • Ages: 11-16

• Religion: Non-denom • School status: State

• School gender: Mixed • Day/boarding: Day pupils

SEN provision

Detail:

Now provide for in school:

Mild: ASP; AUT; ADD; ADHD; EBD; DYSL; DYSP; HI; VI; CP;

Moderate: ASP; AUT; ADD; ADHD; EBD; MLD; DYSL; DYSP; HI;

Severe: ADD; ADHD; DYSL;

Others: CD; ODD; Sp&LD;

Experience of:

Mild: DYSC;

Moderate: CP;

Others: SPD; OCD; EAL; Epi; Eat;

Summary: Students with special educational needs are initially identified through close liaison with the primary schools. Students' needs are also identified through the initial screening process of assessment and by teacher referral. The school is also very keen to listen to parents' concerns and work in partnership with parents.

Students identified as having additional needs are fully integrated within the school by use of additional resources, including staffing and facilities, following consultation with staff, parents and the student. All teachers are responsible for meeting the needs of all students with special educational needs (as indicated by the revised Code of Practice). Teachers contribute to the development of learning targets for these students through the setting up, monitoring and review of individual education plans (IEPs) for all students at School Action, School Action Plus and with statements.

The special educational needs co-ordinator (known as SENCo) will also liaise with outside agencies for the benefit of students identified as having special educational needs. A sensitive approach, which instils confidence, motivation, pride and success in all students, is a fundamental philosophy of the learning support department.

What we say about the school - the full Good Schools Guide review

Head: Since 1996, Mr Graham Roff BEd MEd AdDipEdMngt (early fifties). Educated in Stockport then Madeley College before reading geography and education at Keele and adding further qualifications along the way. Has moved around the country and was deputy head at Cheadle Hulme High School for six years before coming to Huish Episcopi. Lives locally and wife Pam teaches infants in Ilminster; both their sons have gone through the school. Takes a keen interest in sport particularly basketball which he used to play. Enjoys hill walking and foreign travel but says he has little time for these. Slightly reserved but shrewd with a pragmatic approach to educational issues. Likes to engage with parents and staff; chats to pupils informally in corridors and says that they are 'comfortable' about seeking his help when needed. Proud of what has already been achieved and would love to see school develop a sixth form.

Academic Matters: Head believes in setting children from the outset. School operates two distinct 'populations' (or bands) in each year group. Two 'top ability' groups identified within each band for English and a number of other subjects but 'tight' setting in maths and science. Choice of second foreign language from year 7 (for all except those with 'extreme' special needs) allows pupils to see whether to continue with one or two languages from year 9. GCSE results have improved consistently over recent years, in top 25 per cent nationally in value-added tables. Noticeable effort being put into making teaching livelier and more flexible. Strong emphasis on ICT with more than 250 computers in the school; specialist science status has provided funding for additional laboratories. Majority take dual award science but similar numbers of gifted and weaker scientists take triple science or GNVQ (due to end in 2006) courses respectively.

Attractive languages area with particularly impressive GCSE results in French. History, English and art also good but in all these subjects it's mostly girls who get the best grades; boys fare better in geography. A large number of pupils are entered for statistics in year 10 (a policy questioned by some parents) and many take short GCSE courses in RE and citizenship. Some pupils follow an optional extra subject after school. Large laboratories accommodate up to 32 pupils in top sets allowing lower ability groups of 16-19. Less flexibility in other core subjects. Links with Bridgwater College have led to highly popular and useful courses in practical skills such as engineering and vehicle maintenance with a few in year 11 getting extended work placements.

All year 7 children are screened on entry using computer based (Cats) testing despite close liaison providing plenty of information beforehand from feeder primary schools. SENCo works with staff to support pupils with SpLD and other special needs largely within normal timetable and the 13 learning support assistants work alongside mainstream teachers. Small numbers of statemented children. Few with Asperger's traits get help with socialisation and use of free time in school.

Games, Options, The Arts: Longstanding reputation especially in boys' football, girls' hockey and cross-country with huge numbers involved. Regularly comes out as county champion in football, cricket and hockey; also individual representation at district and county level. Has produced national champions in athletics and high national placings in cross-country. PE is a popular GCSE option and pupils have benefit of purpose-built leisure centre on site which is shared with the community and includes fitness centre, dance studio and superb squash courts; floodlit multi-use outside courts, heated 25 metre open air pool and extensive playing fields.

Music and drama join forces for many productions with good results considering lack of sixth form. Dance is popular but not a GCSE option yet. Lower school hall doubles up as a drama studio. Well-resourced music area where pupils get hands-on experience in lessons. 120 learning music instruments plus choirs and ensembles with regular concerts. Art is well displayed despite the limitations of the buildings; innovative and enthusiastic department which gets good number of students into specialist art and design courses at local colleges.

Background and Atmosphere: Motto: Conemur (Let us strive) which head feels is as appropriate now as ever. The unassuming, single storey, redbrick buildings at the front of the school date from 1939 with seven subsequent additions behind them. From outside and on entering it still feels like a small, rural school. Enjoys its village location and for many years was a 'lovely secondary modern' able to go comprehensive slowly and steadily. No nine day wonder, it has built up a reputation locally as a school which 'gets the best out of children' who go there.

School opens up inside like a tardis but despite its multiplicity of specialist accommodation the original appeal of the place has not been lost. The assembly hall which doubles up as a dining (snacking is probably nearer the truth) area can only accommodate a year group at a time. We witnessed an unusual year 10 assembly which used overhead projection of a Liverpool FC footballer as a positive rôle model and succeeded in carrying pupils along in a way which had relevance for them. Five lessons per day of one hour duration – four before lunch break (which doesn't start until 1.20pm) – a pattern which brings good trade for mid-morning snacks (breakfast for some). Old style classrooms can be viewed from corridors which are now too narrow during lesson changeovers (fortunately not too frequent). Many groups seen knuckling down to real academic work.

Pièce de résistance is the vanguard pupils' loo – all gleaming hardware and surfing murals – which has provoked local media interest. CCTV 'not infringing pupils' privacy' has stopped vandalism. Languages and science suites particularly impressive with results to match the facilities provided. Study Centre is perhaps the greatest success of all offering multi-media facilities including well stocked library. A real oasis of civilisation where pupils are allowed to bring food into a hugely popular weekly storytime. Workshops with visiting authors for both the gifted and those with low literacy levels.

Pastoral Care and Discipline: Pastoral care in hands of experienced senior staff and year heads who make themselves accessible to parents. Year 7 head is especially active around feeder primary schools to make sure children look forward to joining senior school. Attendance is carefully monitored with dedicated staff member to ensure first day notification of absence. Small but adequate learning support area in the heart of the school and separate student guidance and learning centre introduced recently to tackle the educational and social needs of the disruptive and disaffected few.

Pupils and Parents: From within and outside a 200 square mile catchment area. Slightly undersubscribed at present which is good news for those parents willing to ferry their offspring. Martock parents have clubbed together to run their own coach. Informal parental car sharing gets pupils back home if they stay for sports, rehearsals etc.

Parental views are sought and involvement is maintained through regular newsletters; turn-out at parents' evenings is usually about 90 per cent. We heard no parental gripes about discipline or teaching standards but some criticism of homework policy as being both too little and too much. School tries to strike the right balance but may have to work harder with parents on this one. Parents' strong support for sixth form was revealed in a recent survey. At present students move on to any of five tertiary colleges located in the main towns of Somerset, all some miles away.

A certain amount of scruffiness but staff chip away at keeping pupils' appearance up to the mark. Children we met definitely enjoy the school, thought the teachers were good – 'no evil teachers' said one of them – and were keen to show us the best bits. Interesting array of former pupils include fashion designer Alice Temperley, winner of the Walpole Award for British Excellence as well as Sarah Ball, creator of 'Bob the Builder.'

Entrance: Children come from about thirty villages across mid-Somerset including 17 per cent from outside the catchment area.

Exit: Vast majority proceed to tertiary colleges in Somerset.

Remarks: Friendly, close-knit and not daunting for the younger ones. Not many 11-16 comprehensive schools do as well as this.

HURST LODGE SCHOOL

Bagshot Road, Ascot, Berkshire, SL5 9JU

Tel: 01344 622 154

Fax: 01344 627 049

Email: admissions@hurstlodgesch.co.uk

Website: www.hurstlodge.freeserve.co.uk

• Pupils: 220 girls, 18 boys (aged 3-7 only); 28 boarding (weekly and flexi), 192 day • Ages: 3-18 • Religion: Non-denom

• Fees: Senior day £3500, Junior day £2,920, boarding £5,750

• School status: Independent • Opendays: Autumn

• School gender: Girls • Day/boarding: Takes boarders

SEN provision

Detail:

Experience of:

Mild: ASP; ADD; ADHD; EBD; DYSC; DYSL; DYSP; SpLD; HI; VI; CP;

Moderate: ADD; MLD; DYSC; DYSL; DYSP; SpLD; HI;

Severe: DYSC; DYSL; DYSP;

Others: SPD; OCD; EAL; Sp&LD; Epi; Eat;

Summary: No comment, but (as you can see) wide ranging provision.

What we say about the school - the full Good Schools Guide review

Principal: Since 1999, Miss Victoria Smit (early forties), a Hurst Lodge old girl. Unusually for a head, she doesn't have a teaching background. Spent early part of career in industry and reckons it helps to have worked 'in the real world.' Took over from her mother, Mrs Anthea Smit, who bought the school in 1978 to save it from closure. A dynamic, hands-on, open-minded head with a great sense of humour, Miss Smit is a 'chronic dyslexic' who tells pupils she's never let it stop her doing anything. 'If a child ever says, 'I can't do that – I'm dyslexic,' I tell them that I am too,' she says matter-of-factly. Works very closely with deputy principal and experienced teacher, Siobhan O'Connor – they form impressive senior management team. Miss Smit knows all pupils by name and encourages girls to pop into her study to chat about successes and/or disappointments. Spends spare time studying for OU degree, learning Chinese and going to theatre.

Academic Matters: Definitely not an academic hothouse but school gets very solid results. In 2005, 88 per cent of GCSE grades A*-C and 29 per cent A*/A. Tiny number of A level candidates but all A-C grades last time round. School firmly believes in tailoring approach to girls' needs and abilities – a few take French, maths and RE GCSEs a year early but pupils who aren't ready may well wait an extra year. 'It plays havoc with the league tables but we don't just push people through,' says principal. Long-serving and loyal staff who know pupils well. Small classes – rarely more than 16 to a class. Girls setted for English, maths and science.

About 70 pupils – a third of the school – have specific learning difficulties, including dyslexia, dyspraxia,

Asperger's syndrome, ADD, ADHD and mild deafness. Lots of individual help available, with SEN pupils offered one-to-one classes (up to five sessions a week) in cosy dyslexia and educational support dept. Mrs Judith Parker runs the department with trained staff of six dyslexia and SpLD teachers, who follow multi-sensory approach. Speech therapist comes in twice a week and occupational therapist available too.

Games, Options, The Arts: Sport definitely on the up. Small numbers used to mean that netball, hockey, rounders teams etc regularly got thrashed but this is no longer the case – several teams were undefeated in 2005. School excels at swimming (open-air pool in walled garden) and also holds annual biathlon and cross-country championship for local schools. Currently boasts national synchronised swimming and polo champions among pupils. Performing arts form a key part of school – past pupils have gone on to work at the RSC and the National. All pupils have timetabled dance classes every week up till year 10 and ballet, tap, modern dance, jazz and musical theatre offered as extras too. Three performing arts studios for ballet shows, drama productions, concerts etc. Girls' creativity encouraged as much as possible. This must be one of the only schools in the country to allow two and a half tons of sand to be deposited in its performing arts studio for a drama production. 'Some schools are far too anxious about what people will think,' says deputy principal. 'And the kindergarten loved getting what was left over afterwards!' Around 85 per cent of girls take music lessons, with singing far and away the most popular choice. School has junior and senior choir as well as ensemble groups and a mini recording studio where girls can compose own music. Art and photography very popular at GCSE and A2 and loads of extra activities on offer, from flower arranging and cookery to football and judo.

Background and Atmosphere: Founded as ballet school in London in 1942 by Doris Stainer, sister of Oscar-winning actor Leslie Howard (Gone with the Wind...) – 'a very formidable woman with a cane,' recalls present head, who was one of her pupils. School later moved next door to Agatha Christie in Sunningdale and then to leafy 22-acre site on outskirts of Ascot in 1997. Main school building a rambling Victorian country house. Poignant rolls of honour from First and Second World Wars take pride of place in tiny chapel, now used for choir rehearsals. With 220 girls currently on roll, school is bigger than it's ever been and fizzes with activity from dawn till dusk. Small number of boarders live at far end of house – traditional dorms for younger girls, with older ones getting singles or doubles.

Strong family atmosphere abounds. Despite its posh reputation the school isn't in the least bit snooty. Smart frocks and a marquee for prizegiving are 'as posh as we get,' says principal, who hands out gongs for all sorts – from the kindergarten child with smiliest face to the Spirit of Hurst Lodge award, given to the pupil who embodies 'all the things we think are important, like enthusiasm, politeness and hard work.' Girls tolerate old-fashioned brown uniform with good humour. 'People are always complaining about it but it's very comfy,' says one girl. Sixth form wear suits, though they look more like trendy art students than city-slickers.

Pastoral Care and Discipline: Emphasis placed on good manners, respect for others and integrity. Clear list of school rules – girls getting fresh air at break-times and making sure they eat properly at lunch – but discipline not a problem here. Principal says can count on fingers of one hand the number of times she's ever had to raise her voice! Very helpful welcome book for new girls lists everything they need to know, from what to call the teachers to the stationery they need in their pencil cases. Head girl and prefect system, as well as three competitive houses – one named after Miss Stainer and the others after ballet legends Margot Fonteyn and Ninette De Valois. Weekly school council gives girls chance to have their say. Recent innovations include water fountain and more comfy (and back-friendly) school bags. Girls also run buddy system to look after new pupils and offer friendly ear to anyone who needs it. Head prides herself on regular contact with parents and produces weekly newsletter to update them on forthcoming events. Each form has parent rep who attends a termly school management meeting.

Pupils and Parents: Day pupils from up to 50 miles away, boarders from as far away as Hong Kong (eight EFL students). Friendly, personable girls who are very proud of their school and stand up when teachers or visitors enter the room. Notable old girls include Duchess of York, actresses Juliet Stevenson and Claudie Blakeley and TV presenter Emma Forbes.

Entrance: Entrance exam at 11. Girls entering at other stages spend day at school and have interview with principal. Most girls starting year 7 come from Hurst Lodge's own junior school, others from local primaries and preps. School looks at educational psychologists' reports but always keeps an open mind. 'Reports sometimes bear no relation to the child we see,' says principal. Girls entering sixth form must have a C or more in chosen A level subjects and 'a commitment to work hard.'

Exit: Junior school has handful of boys, who leave at seven for preps like Woodcote House, Hall Grove and Papplewick. A big exodus of girls after GSCEs, mainly to sixth form colleges – 'they want to see boys,' says principal with note of exasperation in her voice. Not the place for girls wanting to do A level chemistry and physics but reasonable choice otherwise. Sixth form leavers head in loads of different directions, to university (LSE, Exeter etc), art college and performing arts careers.

Money Matters: Academic, dance, drama, music and art scholarships on offer, as well as the school's annual Racov award – three terms of basic fees given in memory of eminent neuroscientist Achi Racov.

Remarks: Mainstream school that caters for all. Great for raising self-esteem and getting the best out of pupils in nurturing, friendly, purposeful environment. Splendid performing arts and more academic than sometimes given credit for. Particularly good at helping pupils who have the ability to succeed academically but may need individual help.

IMMANUEL COLLEGE

87-91 Elstree Road, Bushey, Hertfordshire, WD23 4EB

Tel: 020 8950 0604

Fax: 020 8950 8687

Email: enquiries@immanuel.herts.sch.uk

Website: www.immanuel.herts.sch.uk

• Pupils: 273 boys, 287 girls • Ages: 11-18 • Religion: Jewish • Fees: £10,398 pa • School status: Independent • School gender: Mixed • Day/boarding: Day pupils

SEN provision

Detail:

Centre of excellence for:
- Mild: DYSL;
- Moderate: DYSL;

Now provide for in school:
- Mild: ASP; ADD; ADHD; EBD; DYSC; DYSP;
- Moderate: DYSC; DYSP;
- Others: EAL; PD; Eat;

Experience of:
- Mild: HI; CP;
- Moderate: CP;
- Others: SPD; Sp&LD;

Summary: Immanuel College offers teaching and guidance for average to bright children who experience mild to moderate specific learning difficulties. We have a team of five teachers and two teaching assistants who are qualified in different aspects of student support.

Teachers also liaise with staff across the curriculum to ensure that suitable provision is made. We enjoy good parental contact which benefits both them, the staff and students.

We aim to provide a nurturing environment in which all students can achieve their potential.

What we say about the school - the full Good Schools Guide review

Head: Since 2000, Philip Skelker MA (late fifties). Previously headmaster of King David School in Liverpool and Carmel College and a beak (master) at Eton. A very impressive and hugely experienced man. Fatherly without being paternalistic, a motivator, amusing, energetic, knows every child. Mr Skelker has two of his six children at the school, one as a teacher. His commitment to enlarge the school and elevate its academic standing as a whole are paralleled by his enthusiasm for and personal interest in the development of each individual student.

That Immanuel College's reputation has grown immensely over the past year is due in no small measure to his regime, with parents hoping that their children will want to model themselves on a head who himself embodies the school's motto, 'Torah im Derekh Erez', the study of Torah together with secular education. Amongst a devoted and enthusiastic staff he is primus inter pares and makes a point of teaching English to all age groups. 'Although my son really has no great love for the subject, he absolutely loved Mr Skelker's English lessons and was inspired by them,' says a mother.

Academic Matters: Solid teaching in very small classes (girls and boys separated except for ICT and art in the upper years and all subjects in the sixth form) with an impressive teacher/student ratio especially in the sixth form. 'The separation works well, making girls feel more confident in their academic studies and boys more confident about expressing their feelings,' says the head.

Throughout the syllabus there is a very strong emphasis on linking secular subjects with Jewish history, tradition, literature and ethos. 'There is no reason why, for example, matters of kashruth (dietary laws) cannot be linked with the issue of, say, zoology,' says a Jewish Studies teacher, reciting chapter and verse. The modern language department is surprisingly imaginative and solid, with these subjects, again, being linked with Jewish studies. Students speak fondly of their teachers and feel they can always approach them with any questions and do so at all times in the corridors.

While some parents welcome the relaxed atmosphere, in which students of all levels are taught together and streaming is reserved for only a few subjects and only in some age groups, others would like to 'see more drive'. The aim, however, is to boost the confidence of students and nurture their potential, says Skelker who, in the same vein has expanded the A level curriculum to include subjects like psychology and theatre studies. The result seems to be a very happy student body, one that enjoys learning for its own sake rather than simply for the marks. The results are impressive by any comparison, almost all pupils achieving grades A*-C at GCSE. About 20 per cent of pupils score A or A* grades in eight or more subjects. At A level, all but a few achieve A-C.

Support teachers on hand for students with learning difficulties but this area seems to be kept rather 'low key' – students get a very large amount of individual attention in all subjects at all times.

Jewish studies takes up almost one third (taking morning prayers into account) of the school day. The enthusiasm and dynamic teaching of this department's head is reflected by students' immense interest, knowledge and love for the subject. The Jewish studies staff clearly take both their subject and their students very seriously. While being completely versed in Jewish texts, teachers are capable of broadening class discussions to include consideration of other religions and of dealing with sophisticated political issues without being exclusive or unduly partisan. 'Since there is no need to do outreach for our children,' says a teacher, 'we can focus on the actual study of text and issues.' All pupils take Jewish Studies to AS level, very many continue to A level, thus being superbly prepared for Yeshiva (further study of the Jewish holy books) and seminary studies. Indeed study at Yeshiva or seminary is very much the preferred gap year option for Immanuel graduates, though this may also reflect a certain hesitation to venture beyond the tried and true.

Games, Options, The Arts: Thanks to the very large and beautifully equipped grounds, sporting activities could be featuring high on the curriculum but these take third place after the intensive Jewish studies and secular curricula. Late coach service encourages take up of sports after school. The music department is in the process of being built up – a tempting scheme through which students are being offered free instrumental tuition and free use of instruments. 'I was absolutely amazed by the level, creativity, and brilliant results achieved in the arts department and the GCSE projects are worthy of exhibition,' said a parent – we can only agree. School trips aimed at enhancing students' understanding and appreciation of Jewish history start in year 7 with a week's visit to York, a trip to Strasbourg and Israel in the middle years and, finally, in sixth form, a trip to Eastern Europe.

Background and Atmosphere: With its very rural setting, late Victorian main building, surrounded by a medley of nondescript modern buildings and bungalows and long school days, Immanuel College has the atmosphere of a boarding school. A warm community, with wafts of home-made cooking as you walk across the campus.

Pastoral Care and Discipline: While disciplinary rules are in place, these do not seem to be imposed on students but simply reinforce family values. On the whole, students support, promote and talk kindly and respectfully to one another.

Pupils and Parents: Most students hail from solidly middle class, warm and quite protective homes. This makes for quite a homogeneous student body, with children socialising comfortably during and after school. This is 'exactly what we were looking for when my child left a very protective primary school environment and was not really able to cope with a more anonymous large scale inner-city operation,' says a father. The dress and language of the students as well as the cars of the parents are 'rather swish', comments a staff member.

There is definitely a feeling of well-behaved, quite docile and 'fortunate' children, perhaps at the expense of not being exposed to a more diverse or cosmopolitan way of life. You will not see these students roaming around aimlessly in the coffee shops of north London. A leaning towards the conservative/modern orthodox way of life does not preclude pupils/parents from all backgrounds and of all degrees of religiousness being welcomed and respected.

Entrance: Students come from varied academic and Jewish backgrounds but have to be committed to want to pursue both these areas with equal zest, says Mr Skelker. About 40 per cent of the students come from non-Jewish primary schools. Very few students join the college at sixth form level, since the head feels quite strongly that students should continue their sixth form studies in the school in which they started their secondary education.

Exit: Historically, a flood left after GCSE. Under the new head and owing to improvements in the sixth form, this has slowed to a trickle. After A levels most students continue to university, after having taken a year off to study at a yeshiva or Seminary.

Money Matters: Several scholarships are awarded annually and bursaries are offered in cases of proven need. Sixth form scholarships may be awarded for outstanding results at GCSE level.

Remarks: While Immanuel College would not feature in a list of scholastically vigorous secondary schools, it certainly would rate among the most caring. A place where no one will 'slip through the net'.

Impington Village College

New Road, Impington, Cambridge, Cambridgeshire, CB4 9LX

Tel: 01223 200 400

Fax: 01223 200 419

Email: office@impington.cambs.sch.uk

Website: www.impington.cambs.sch.uk

• Pupils: 1,370 boys and girls, all day but provision made for far-travelled pupils to be put up locally • Ages: 11-19 • Religion: Non-denom • School status: State • School gender: Mixed • Day/boarding: Day pupils

SEN provision

Detail:

Centre of excellence for:
- Mild: DS; DYSL; CP;
- Moderate: MLD; DYSL; CP;
- Others: PD;

Experience of:
- Mild: HI;

Summary: The special needs team provides flexible and supportive provision for a wide range of special educational needs at Key Stages 3, 4 and 5. The college is fully accessible for students with physical disabilities. Enhanced resource provision from the Local Education Authority funds specialised facilities and support for students with physical disabilities. The IDEAL course specifically designed for post-16 students with moderate learning difficulties is also available.

What we say about the school - the full Good Schools Guide review

Warden: Since 1997, Jacqueline E Kearns MA FRSA (early fifties). Earned a BA Hons degree in German from Liverpool and MA in German Literature from the Freie Universität, Berlin. First teaching jobs were at inner London schools. Then headed a large comprehensive in Kent and two international schools in Germany before taking the reins here. Totally dedicated and inspirational, she is a popular head and an ideal spiritual guide for the multi-layered Impington enterprise. Speaks in a calming and reflective manner and is warm, humorous and genuine (as far as we know, the only head to have addressed an unfamiliar Good Schools Guide editor phoning to arrange an interview as 'my lovely'). Interests include theatre, concerts and dance. Husband, a former teacher, stays busy at home doing up their 16th century house. Two children – both attend Impington Village College.

Academic Matters: A unique school with a split personality. For ages 11-16, it is a happy, successful comprehensive, with unusually strong arts provision and a healthy international conscience. The sixth form is something else – a bona fide international college, offering both the International Baccalaureate (since 1991) and A levels, and taking pupils from 33 nationalities. Running throughout the school is its excellent languages programme (it is one of the government's specialist schools for languages). All pupils learn French in year 7, then German is added, and in years 10 and 11, Spanish and Japanese and, in the sixth form, Russian becomes available. The school won a European Language Award (2001) for its non-traditional approach in introducing French to local primary schools. Lots of extra challenges available for the most able (eg studying Latin and Greek and sitting some GCSEs early).

Pupils praise the school for its excellent teachers and rewards for achievement. Said one, 'you don't get laughed at for wanting to work hard.' As for exam results, what other schools summarise in half a page here extends through 23 pages of statistics, tables and graphs. We think they are telling us that 70 per cent of pupils normally gain five A*-C GCSEs, a solid result given the mixed intake. And the IB/A level scores must be good – in 2001, Impington Village College ranked first among all British comprehensives in the Financial Times' league table of sixth form examination results. This put it above Cambridge's famously good Hills Road Sixth Form College and many independent schools in the area.

Currently 75 per cent of students follow the International Baccalaureate diploma programme – a huge increase in the last two years; 24 per cent take AS/A2 levels and 1 per cent follow the IDEAL course for students with special needs. Of the A level cohort approximately 30 per cent will be taking the full arts provision, and be members of 'The Performance School'.

Games, Options, The Arts: Pupils encouraged to try everything, with spectacular results. Usual range of sports in the lower school, though even in games, Impington's emphasis on individuality, creativity and social justice can be felt. Pupils speak solemnly of the school's scrupulously fair methods of team selection, and where but Impington would we have found a group of cool 12-year-old footballers chatting enthusiastically about how much they enjoy their dance class? Games not mandatory in sixth form and enthusiasm for team sports, abundant among the younger kids, tends to fizzle out.

Deservedly one of the first schools to achieve the government's Artsmark Gold in September 2001 (a composer, a fine artist and a professional dancer in residence). Performing arts are a particular strength and sixth form candidates without academic qualifications may apply directly to Impington's School of Performance via audition. The college stages a dance performance every term, and there is an annual showcase at a venue in Cambridge. Ballet classes available before school. Music department provides masses of opportunities and good teaching (excellent, says Ofsted), popular and successful at GCSE. Lots of clubs, including active Amnesty International group and SFPAN (sixth formers political awareness network!). IB requirement of 150 hours of community service fits in nicely. Many international exchanges and assorted trips overseas. Enthusiastic and popular D of E. Active student council and pupils say they feel 'listened to.'

Background and Atmosphere: Founded in 1939 as part of Cambridgeshire Education Secretary Henry Morris' village college movement – an attempt to provide rural England with educational and social centres serving all ages. Main building designed by the founder of the Bauhaus, Walter Gropius. True to its roots, the college offers adult evening classes, runs a workplace nursery, provides a base for local youth clubs and maintains a sports centre open 364 days a year from 6am to 10pm. Much emphasis is put on international politics, the environment, human rights and other global issues (the student council has been debating whether to introduce Fair Trade vending machines). Pupils' views are respected and children of all ages are encouraged to speak out and share their beliefs. Some elegant facilities (indoor pool, beautiful library with separate sixth form area, cutting-edge language teaching lab, good science labs, dance and drama studios, editing suite). This equipment, along with the international buzz of the place, amusingly at odds with overall down-at-heel condition of the mostly-standard-government-issue-drab site. Head hopes to build a new sixth from centre, and new building for 600 students, replacing temporary huts, opened in 2005. Would also benefit from a larger canteen and a bigger cleaning budget. Sixth form feels separate from the rest of the school but has a beautiful 'learning centre'. No sixth form uniform.

Pastoral Care and Discipline: Behaviour we witnessed was impressive, including an assembly of several hundred 15-year-olds who sat in rapt silence through a twenty minute exposition by a teacher. Behaviour policy speaks in 1970s psycho-babble (much discussion of 'spiritual development', 'unique human beings' and 'the self' – with miscreants requiring an 'inclusion manager behaviour support plan' – yuk) but it is all meant well, and the overall caring and friendly atmosphere is the first thing to hit any visitor. With all the talk of inclusion and social conscience, the college's zero tolerance drugs policy comes as a (pleasant) shock. Any pupils found to be taking illegal substances (including alcohol) or who are under the influence of illegal substances on site or during the school day will be excluded permanently. Only a hip state comprehensive could get away with such a firm stance at a time when most independent schools speak more of counselling and second chances. 'The children love the policy,' says the head, 'because it is clear. Cambridge is a druggy town and the rule makes it much easier for them to say no.' International pupils and youngsters from outside Cambridgeshire are housed (carefully) with local host families.

Pupils and Parents: Parents of 11-16 year-olds range from Cambridge academics to severely underprivileged. 25 per cent of children are on the special educational needs register (including a small group of children with severe disabilities – wheelchairs possible here). In the international sixth form one third of the pupils come up from Impington and a further third from other schools in the area and throughout the UK (a few from independent schools). The rest hail from 33 countries all over the world, although the majority come from Europe. Sixth formers we met (of several nationalities) were mature, non-competitive and self-motivated. 'We're not spoon-fed', said one boy who came here from an independent school.

Entrance: Oversubscribed, but appeals often succeed, boosting class sizes above the target level of 28 pupils (12 in the sixth form). Intake at 11 mainly from neighbourhood primaries. At sixth form, from a wide area in Cambridgeshire and adjoining counties, plus abroad. The sixth form offers four distinct courses. The selective IB course is aimed at highly motivated students earning mostly B grades or above at GCSE. Somewhat less academic children may be steered towards A levels, though they will still normally need five C-or-better GCSEs. The School of Performance accepts pupils with virtually no academic qualifications and, although these pupils will take one or two A/AS levels, it is essentially vocational training for young people planning a career in dance, theatre or music. There is also a special course providing one-to-one tuition to youngsters with severe learning disabilities.

Exit: Leavers at 16 (about two thirds of the school) go to local colleges (Hills Road, Long Road etc) for A levels and GNVQ. Those who leave at 18 go on to a dazzlingly wide array of destinations. Examples from last year's list of leavers: London School of Contemporary Dance (BA programme), Academy of Arts in Rome (to study sculpture), Trust House Forte (hotel management training), Cambridge University (Anglo-Saxon, Norse and Celtic Studies), national service in Germany, medical studies at the University of Padua (Italy), employment in Uzbekistan. 87 per cent to university. Many gap years, deferred entries.

Money Matters: Pupils from outside the EU (very few) must pay roughly £4,700 annually for tuition. Free for everyone else. Pupils residing with host families pay for room and board.

Remarks: The state school system's best kept secret. A genuinely international sixth form college, on the outskirts of one of the most appealing towns in England, offering the IB and A levels, free of charge to all EU residents. And a brilliant head to boot.

INGFIELD MANOR SCHOOL

Five Oaks, Billinghurst, West Sussex, RH14 9AX

Tel: 01403 782 294

Fax: 01403 785 066

Email: ingfield.manor@scope.org.uk

• Pupils: 30, 10 board • Ages: 3-11

• School status: Independent • School gender: Mixed

• Day/boarding: Takes boarders

SEN provision

Detail:

Centre of excellence for:

Mild: CP;

Moderate: CP;

Severe: CP;

Others: PD;

Experience of:

Mild: VI;

Others: PMLD; SLD; MSI;

What we say about the school - the full Good Schools Guide review

Head: Since 2005, Mr Alistair Bruce MA Bed. Previously head of Chailey Heritage School. Liked by parents who say he's proactive and on the ball. Acutely aware of inclusion debate says: 'We have a fantastic provision here, conductive education gets results, there's so much expertise it would be a shame to throw baby out with the bath water. Many of our children would find mainstream too stressful. We have links with mainstream but we'd like to expand these, share expertise and offer genuine inclusion opportunities.'

Entrance: Cater for children with special needs related to physical difficulties especially cerebral palsy. Take youngsters with enough physical and cognitive ability to make the most of Conductive Education. Not currently equipped to cater for extreme medical problems would have to go elsewhere. All have LEA statement. Currently seeking DfES approval to cover the 3-19 age range. Numbers have fallen slightly but parental requests are increasing. Parents like the school, but getting the funding can be a problem.

Exit: To Treloar, Chailey Heritage, other special or local mainstream schools.

Remarks: A long, winding, bumpy, lane (totally unsuited to wheelchairs) leads to the school's spacious, leafy, grounds. The original, Edwardian manor house, marred by incongruous sixties additions, shows some signs of age but is generally well maintained (odd lick of paint here and there wouldn't go amiss). Primarily single storey with good disabled access, all key facilities are fine and resources excellent. One third are residential (because of distance not need). Bedrooms have cheery posters, lots of toys and provide a home from home. Classrooms are bright and lively, typical of any good primary school. Outside there's a delightful play area with sand pit, train, huts, slide and a garden. However, wheelchairs lining the corridors, slatted desks, communication aids, and variety of seating and standing aids indicate some of the very many additional issues children have to cope with on a daily basis.

Learning is centred on conductive education – a programme pioneered by the Peto Institute in Hungary. Everyone, from the team leader down, works shifts to enable the whole day to be a learning opportunity. Conductors are akin to leaders of an orchestra, combining the different therapies: occupational therapy (OT), physio, speech and language into a veritable composition, the whole being greater than the sum of the parts. Therapists cascade knowledge to team staff, who are active and proactive in developing the curriculum, with therapies integrated and carried out throughout the waking day. A wonderfully caring environment. Staff acknowledge children have a lot of demands placed on them. Stress it's okay for children to get it wrong or say they don't know. Conductive education isn't a soft option, not easy on parents either who are encouraged to continue the approach at home. Parents say daily communication is brilliant: 'they write everything down, tell you about problems from the tinniest bruise. They're diplomatic, if they pick things up, they advise and help but don't patronise. You get everything that's offered in mainstream and so much more besides.'

All follow the National Curriculum (NC), adapted as necessary; some work at P levels some beyond. Children are taught in small groups, often with one-to-one support. NC not originally geared for children with SEN so subdivide by physical and intellectual capabilities. Even subjects like music can be tricky, some have ability to compose with computers, others, unable to use machines, will be 'banging something out.' The first part of every day is spent on exercises in the task series room developing solutions to physical problems. Plinths (basically a slatted table), ladder back chairs and stools are used to develop a child's ability to grasp, fix, change place; balance, hold, stand and walk. Communication can be problematic, tend to have good understanding but can't speak at the same level, so try to bridge gap. Physically able, use Makaton signing but for many, augmentative and alternative communication (AAC) is key. Communication aids and books are likened to a pizza base, essential but meatier once toppings are added. School developed own communication using symbols to help deliver the curriculum. In addition to low-tech symbols they've developed a set of vocabulary for high tech speaking devices, published as Ingfield dynamic, these vocabularies and symbols are viewed as the industry standard.

Parents say it's a great place for children to be and believe conductive education really makes a difference. 'School is so right for my daughter I dread the day she has to leave.' Let's hope provision will be around for others, in years to come.

The Dame Vera Lynn School for Parents

Fantastic, on-site, conductive resource, managed by the school, on behalf of the Dame Vera Lynn Trust (she's an active governor of the school too). Currently used by 60 families a week (traditionally from as far away as Isle of White and Chelmsford though opening of other centres has reduced catchment). Can be used by anyone with SEN arising from CP and physical and associated difficulties. Officially for children from 1 to 5 years, but some as young as 9 months. Stipulate parents must be willing to make a commitment to attend regularly. Attending the centre doesn't mean child will attend the school. Support is offered for all from 5 to 11 years who are in mainstream. There's a swim group for 5 to 7-year-olds, gym skills for 9+ and changing skills for 7 to 9-year-olds. Offer support in schools too and encourage their LSAs to work with them at the centre.

There's a cheery parents room with catering facilities (doubles up as a training room for many of the regular parent training sessions) and well-equipped activity rooms where the conductive programmes are held. The two-and-a-half hour sessions allow youngsters to benefit from conductive education and teach parents how to play with and develop their child's skills. Sessions are generally held in groups but one-to-one is offered if needed. Most welcome the opportunity to meet and mix with other parents. For many it's a lifeline. Often they've had only negative feedback with medical staff stressing what a child can't/won't be able to do. Centre looks at what they can do. Teach parents how to practice tasks in home situation. Recognise success is important. If we can't achieve we give up, so we must find steps where children succeed, feel safe and secure and get on with controlling their lives.' Reflexes don't go from CP children so must teach about falling, getting dressed etc. Can't take basics for granted lots of skills to learn.

'They looked at my child and saw potential. You have to go slowly but it helped me accept the situation, they were my salvation.'

Inscape House

Inscape House, Silkhey Grove, Worsley, Manchester, Lancashire, M28 7FG

Tel: 0161 975 2340

Fax: 0161 975 4751

Email: inscapesalford@togethertrust.org

Website: www.bgws.org.uk/inscape/inscsalford.htm

• Pupils: 55 boys and girls all statemented with ASD • Ages: 4-16 • Religion: non- denominational • School status: Independent • School gender: Mixed • Day/boarding: Day pupils

SEN provision

Summary: No comment. Autism specialist. SEN details added by us.

What we say about the school - the full Good Schools Guide review

Head: Since September 2004, Keith Cox, early forties. Came from a year as deputy head here and has 14 years experience with autism in teaching and as adviser for the National Autistic Society. Unpretentious, down to earth, with huge heart for pupils. Hopes he'll be here for a good long while, 'we've a fantastic staff and there's a lot more we can do. I want us to be a centre of excellence for autism.' Staff say, 'you couldn't ask for a nicer head.'

Academic Matters: Every level from P3 to one or two taking a few GCSEs. Class groups average five with three staff, one teacher and two assistants. Children grouped for compatibility as well as age, so some class groups have little spoken language, others are more chatty. Intense support from speech and language therapists each class receiving some six hours per week, each SaLT having a caseload of 15 pupils. Some day-long one-to-one support, lots of individual work in distraction-free areas screened from rest of class or one-to-one in separate rooms as appropriate. Emphasis on development of communication, social and independence skills, for example during snack time at break which also gives practice making choices.

Every class has access to cooking facilities for life skills. There are new specialist rooms for art, science, technology and speech therapy. School currently has four interactive whiteboards with plans for one in each classroom. Every class has digital camera to record achievements and relationships. Daily diary home with voluntary homework possibilities and in-school photographic record/diary kept to record achievements for pupils and parents. Head describes most significant progress as being in behaviours, and the ability of pupils to live and function in the community. Thanks to two minibuses, each class group spends half day a week out on trips to the library, museums, supermarkets, shopping centres etc. School mission statement includes the objective of promoting understanding and acceptance of pupils by raising awareness of ASD. Residential trips to Children's Adventure Farm in Cheshire and Bendrigg

Lodge in Lake District, 'it's the first time away from home for some, the longest for most'.

Games, Options, The Arts: Structured exercise programmes take place in school gym. Bright soft play room includes ball pool and interactive sound panels. School also runs relaxation exercises and has a multi-sensory room and a sensory garden. Play in four separate secure playgrounds is split into two shifts dividing children into compatible groups both in age and level of functioning. Playing fields beyond are shared with neighbouring mainstream primary school. Plans for a five-a-side football team. Groups swim weekly at local community pool. Trampolining is an option.

Background and Atmosphere: School began life as a mid-twentieth century special school and the ageing original brick and wood single storey buildings now also boast new classrooms and playgrounds. Friendly welcome with obvious affection between staff and pupils. 'We're a family, of staff, pupils and parents,' says head, 'and attempting to make a difference to the lives of children with ASD and their parents is what makes us all get up in the morning'. Big photo boards in entrance show life of school and everyone in it and staff point particularly to shots of children without language relating well to their carers. The attitude of service is exemplified by sufficient staff voluntarily giving up two weeks of the summer break to offer a full-time holiday club, 'five weeks is too long for many of these families to cope'; described by parents as 'a lifesaver'. School cook has a child with autism himself so understands that food can be a huge issue and willingly caters for individuals' special medical dietary needs including cooking food brought from home. Parents really appreciate teachers and therapists providing home visits as requested and willingly acting as advocates for them with social services and over respite issues.

Pastoral Care and Discipline: Good behaviour rewarded with charts. All staff trained in PROACT SCIP behaviour management programme, 'to keep youngsters and staff safe'. All areas of school are secure with high fencing, high door handles on internal doors and ultra secure front door operated only by staff swipe card. The Together Trust also runs a small unit in South Manchester for short-term care of children with ASD who're temporarily unable to attend other schools.

Pupils and Parents: Complete socio-economic mix, mainly white reflecting local demographics, although five children come from families where English isn't first language. School has an open door policy to parents and offers workshops, coffee mornings or afternoons and sleep counselling. Just 8 out of 55 pupils are girls, reflecting autism's male predominance. Very happy parents with by far the majority responding to inspectors in 2004 saying they find contact with school, pupil support and provision of advice and assistance 'outstanding' and praising the availability and dedication of staff.

Entrance: Fifty per cent places offered first to Salford LEA though vacancies don't always match their need. Children taken from 12 LEAs on north of Manchester as appropriate places become available. Inscape sister school in Cheadle similarly serves 12 LEAs south of city.

Exit: Head describes huge problem of lack of post-16 and adult autistic provision. New Together Trust sixth form unit opened Sept 2005 with four pupils in Withington, Manchester with plans to expand to 20 places over two years. Some go at 16 to sector colleges and generic special schools, some to specialist residential centres. A small number of pupils across the school may make very slow and careful transitions to mainstream schools.

Money Matters: The school has developed from a partnership between a North West children's charity The Together Trust (formerly The Boys and Girls Welfare Society), The National Autistic Society and Salford LEA. Inscape House has non-maintained special school status with all fees paid by local authorities who also offer optional transport. Parents generally not asked to contribute financially, even for trips away, or break snacks, but some are very actively involved with fundraising through Inscape Friends or on a separate committee with staff.

Remarks: Not much to look at but never judge a book by the cover; beautiful things are happening inside.

James Allen's Preparatory School (JAPS)

East Dulwich Grove, London, SE22 8TE

Tel: 020 8693 0374
Fax: 020 8693 8031
Email: Japsadmissions@jags.org.uk
Website: www.japs.org.uk

• Pupils: 105 boys and girls in pre-prep, 190 girls in middle school, all day • Ages: 4-7 pre-prep, 7-11 middle school
• Religion: C of E Foundation, but all are welcome
• Fees: £2,766 • School status: Independent
• Opendays: September, October and November
• School gender: Mixed • Day/boarding: Day pupils

SEN provision

Detail:
Centre of excellence for:
Mild: DYSL;
Moderate: DYSL;
Severe: DYSL;
Now provide for in school:
Mild: EBD; DYSC; DYSP; SpLD;
Moderate: MLD; DYSC;
Others: EAL;
Experience of:
Mild: ASP; AUT; ADD; ADHD; HI; VI; CP;
Moderate: ADD; ADHD; EBD; DYSP; SpLD; HI; CP;
Severe: DYSC; DYSP; SpLD;
Others: SPD; CD; OCD; ODD; PMLD; MSI; Epi; PD; Eat;

Summary: JAPS was praised in its 2002 ISI Inspection Report for the 'excellence' of its provision for special needs. JAPS is extremely well resourced in terms of special needs/learning support teaching. The main help provided is for pupils with mild/moderate dyslexia but the school caters for pupils with a range of special educational needs.

In the pre-prep (4-7 year-old boys and girls), there is a qualified SENCo for three days per week plus a further learning support teacher for two-and-a-half days per week. In the Middle School (7-11 year-old girls) there is a SENCo for three days per week plus two further full-time learning support teachers. There are three specialist rooms in the school as a whole dedicated to special needs/learning support.

What we say about the school - the full Good Schools Guide review

Head: Since 1992, Mr Piers Heyworth MA PGCE (early fifties) Marlborough and Christ Church, Oxford, where he read English and founded the Oxford Survival Society (keen on environment). Previously celebrated head of English at JAGS, and appointment here an unusual and inspired choice – there's even more scope for his enthusiasm. Comments that the school takes 'a hundred and ten per cent of my time'. Married in 1998 Sarah Russell, who teaches at neighbouring Alleyn's Junior School. Two young children. As school recently expanded to double the size, most of the staff are his own appointments.

Entrance: From 'a hundred different nurseries', mainly in Dulwich and Clapham. Selective entry test in December and January for September, teachers watch out for 'adventurousness of spirit'. Followed by interviews.

Exit: Girls get sackfuls of scholarships. Boys at 7 go on to Dulwich, Dulwich College Preparatory School, Alleyn's junior school, etc.

Remarks: God's gift to the people of Dulwich. Part of the same foundation as JAGS, etc, and consequently very well funded. As the prep department of JAGS, has now spread its wings, with IAPS membership and co-education up to 7. On two sites – littles in Edwardian mansion down the road, 'middle school' tucked beside JAGS, with large extension opened in 1993 to include large sports hall, and super user-friendly library with own librarian – light and much used. Separate IT room, IT is being 'firmly incorporated in all subjects'. Timetabled computing for all, large sunny science room.

Specialist staff in a wide range of subjects – a tremendous strength. Brilliant 'immersion' French from age 4, with Mm Helène Gilbert, who speaks entirely in French and so far children have not cottoned on to the fact she speaks English as well – lots of fun games, impeccable accents and, by the time these children leave the school they will need special fast stream to keep up the good work. French taught in half classes in the middle school by another French specialist who produces an annual play en français. Chosen by the French Embassy to represent the UK in the Parlement des

Enfants in the Assemblée Nationale in Paris 2004. Eighteen per class in pre-prep, rising to 24 in middle school, though most classes have two members of staff and can be split. Consequently 'we feel no need for setting or streaming'. Year 6 pupils take the National Curriculum Key Stage 2 and come out considerably above other IAPS schools. According to Sunday Times in 2005, JAPS 5th best in the UK.

Brilliant art and music. Drama strong (head keen and experienced). Fifty-five clubs after school and a staggering 420 pupils – from JAPS and 60 other local schools – turn up for 'Saturday school' – brain child of staff member, Miss Beverly Sizer – music, drama, dance from 8.30am till 2.30pm – wonderful way for pupils to work off excess energy and parents to get to Tescos in peace. Share new £4m JAGS' swimming pool – JAPS' pupils always in Bazuka national swimming finals. Active parents' committee organising social events etc. Two part-time qualified specialists provide one-to-one tuition for the small proportion of children – 'often the brightest' – needing it – special rooms set aside for this. Also two full-time and one part-time learning support staff. School absolutely full of fizz, top-class staff, strong all round. Has to be contender for one of the two best London preps south of the Thames.

JAMES GILLESPIE'S HIGH SCHOOL

Lauderdale Street, Edinburgh, EH9 1DD

Tel: 0131 447 1900

Fax: 0131 452 8601

Email: headteacher@jamesgillespies.edin.sch.uk

Website: www.jamesgillespies.edin.sch.uk

• Pupils: 595 boys, 540 girls • Ages: 11-18

• Religion: Non-denom • School status: State

• School gender: Mixed • Day/boarding: Day pupils

SEN provision

Detail:

Centre of excellence for:

Mild: ASP; AUT; EBD; DYSL; HI;
Moderate: ASP; AUT; EBD; MLD; DYSL; HI; VI;
Severe: DYSL; HI; VI;
Others: FRX; PMLD; SLD; EAL;

Now provide for in school:

Mild: DYSC; DYSP; VI;
Moderate: DYSC; DYSP;
Severe: EBD; DYSC; DYSP;
Others: DEL; Epi; PD; Eat;

Experience of:

Mild: ADD; ADHD; DS;
Moderate: ADD; ADHD;
Severe: ASP;
Others: SPD; OCD; ODD;

Summary: All children and young people have entitlement to an educational experience of the highest quality. We are committed to the effective inclusion of all pupils in the life of the school. The special educational needs of any individual pupil can be described as whatever is necessary for that young person to gain access to a broad and balanced curriculum. For most pupils most of the time the source of support will be the classroom teacher.

The learning support department offers assistance in a number of ways:

- Publishing annual advice giving information about the needs of particular pupils together with a strategies pack offering advice on how to deal with various difficulties;
- Direct teaching in subject classes or in a tutorial setting;
- Support by Learning Assistants in class;
- Working co-operatively in classes and in consultation with subject teachers to help make the curriculum accessible for all pupils;
- Organising the Befrienders scheme where sixth year pupils support first years in a variety of classes;
- Working with parents, Guidance, subject and other professionals to assess needs and to set and monitor targets;
- Administering the SQA special exam arrangements for those with specific learning difficulties.

What we say about the school - the full Good Schools Guide review

Head: Since 2005, Alex Wallace, previously assistant headteacher and depute headteacher over the past 12 years.

Academic Matters: Class size 30 (20/25 for practical subjects), setted early for maths in the September of their first year, second year setted for English. Three separate sciences for all from the third year onwards. No classics, but French, German and Urdu, a tiny number also learn Gaelic (there is a feeder school where pupils do all subjects in Gaelic). All languages are taught up to Higher level. School does complicated mix of Standard, Higher, Advanced Highers and A levels for physics, art (in order to form a portfolio) and geography. An interesting diversification for a state school. Good support for learning, dyslexia, dyspraxia, and help with exams, both withdrawn from class and team teaching in class. ADHD is OK, 'most reasonably well-behaved'. 250 of the pupils come from 40 different countries 'the most diverse population in Scotland', EFL available (free) for all who need it. CDT is 50/50 craft and design and all computer-based – 350 computers in the school. Recent BECTa award for best website.

Games, Options, The Arts: PE and swimming on site; huge games hall plus astroturf, much used by local community. Football, rugby, hockey pitches about 1.5 miles away at Kirkbrae, pupils are bused. Games are basically extra-curricular, girls' football and netball are popular. Short lunchbreak, 45 mins, so no lunch clubs, kids either go home or to the local carry-outs, rather jolly dining room. Massive music uptake, with carol service in the Usher Hall last year, this year they are off to The McEwan Hall, over 350 regularly on the stage. Senior orchestra, junior orchestra, lessons free, but music dept needs drastic revamping. Ditto labs, DT, libraries and PE area. Strong, spectacular art, photography, 'the lot', impressive fabric design. Huge dance area, media popular with lights and editing studios, three drama studios. Wizard home economics dept – better than most homes we know. Trips all over the place, in many disciplines, skiing, Paris for art, historians to the trenches, geographers to do glacial research in Norway.

Background and Atmosphere: Founded in 1803 as a result of a legacy from James Gillespie, 'a wealthy Edinburgh manufacturer of snuff and tobacco', who was born in Roslin. The school started with 65 students and one master and led a peripatetic existence. At one point it was the prep school for the Merchant Company's secondary schools. By 1908 the school had a roll of over a thousand, including girls, and offered secondary education under the aegis of The Edinburgh School Board, moving to Bruntsfield House, just off The Meadows, in 1966 and going fully co-ed in 1978. The earliest building on this site dates from 1300, and the current schloss was built in 1605, with later additions and improvements. (Sir George Warrender, whose family was to be awarded the title Bruntsfield, bought the house from the original owners and was intrigued to find that if you hung a sheet from every window you could access from the inside, there were still sheetless windows outside. A secret room was discovered, with blood-stained floor, ashes in the grate and a skeleton under the wainscot. The Green Lady haunts the top storeys to this day.)

The head has a grand office in the main building, with a spectacular ceiling, and an impressive fireplace, almost exactly replicated by the music room not quite next door. Now surrounded by predominantly sixties-type classroom blocks, relieved by swards of green and mature trees with a singular clock in the middle of the campus which, despite thousands spend on renovation, will never work properly as the hands were found to be too long. It remains as a memorial to the follies of the architects of the day, though interestingly, Colin MacWilliam has nothing but praise for the design. The campus is hidden amongst decent Victorian tenements, and more grass and trees than you would expect. Woefully short of space, there was a certain frisson when the local electricity board sold an adjoining sub-station without first offering it to the school, who desperately need room to expand. No uniform 'at the moment'.

Pastoral Care and Discipline: Follows the state guidelines, good PSHE, good anti-bullying strategy in place, 'we get the youngsters to talk it through ... we bring them together and get the bully to accept their behaviour is wrong'. 'No current problems' with fags (though pupils light up as they leave the school gates), booze or drugs, but head will exclude on either a temporary or permanent basis if necessary. Last head only ever made two drugs-related temporary exclusions, but it would be permanent if there were any hint of dealing. Also out permanently for a violent attack, though merely temporary exclusion for 'physical violence'. Homework books which must be signed by parent or guardian.

Pupils and Parents: Free intake, so diverse. Large number of professional families, Marchmont is a popular area for the university, plus 'a significant group of working class, with relatively poor backgrounds'. Huge ethnic mix, with some girls wearing the chador – they may well do PE and swim wearing full leggings and long-sleeved T-shirts (though parents can ask to withdraw their daughters from these lessons, few do). Lifts being installed next year for wheelchair-bound pupil, minor physical handicaps OK. Strong parent/teacher involvement.

Entrance: First year capped at 200 but catchment area usually only offers 140, the extra 60 places are by request (and some come from as far as Musselburgh). Last year there were 150 such placement requests; school is obliged to take children on a first-come-first-served basis.

Exit: Number leaves after Standard Grades, either to further education or work; good proportion to unis, mainly Scots, studying medicine, science, art college, followed by social subject and music in that order. Annual trickle to Oxbridge.

Remarks: Much at stake here as new head succeeds very successful predecessor.

JFS School

The Mall, Kenton, Harrow, HA3 9TE

Tel: 020 8206 3100

Fax: 020 8206 3101

Email: admin@jfs.brent.sch.uk

Website: www.jfs.brent.sch.uk

• Pupils: 900 girls; 980 boys • Ages: 11-18 • Religion: Jewish
• School status: State • School gender: Mixed
• Day/boarding: Day pupils

SEN provision

Detail:

Now provide for in school:

Mild: ASP; AUT; ADD; ADHD; EBD; DYSC; DYSL; DYSP; HI; VI; CP;

Moderate: ASP; AUT; ADD; ADHD; EBD; MLD; DYSC; DYSL; DYSP; HI;

Severe: ADHD; EBD; DYSL; DYSP;

Others: SPD; AUT(other); CD; OCD; ODD; TIC; PMLD; Sp&LD; PD; Oth;

Summary: Genetic and related disorders – Triple X, F.D. medical and related needs – Erhler's Danlos syndrome

What we say about the school - the full Good Schools Guide review

Head: Since 1993, after twenty years of working herself up the ranks, Dame Ruth Robins DBE BA TTHD (early fifties); hails from South Africa. Her life is committed to the school, where she is often the first one in and the last one out. Although slight in appearance she is almost military in presence. Her message on Open Days on discipline and hard work is repeated throughout the years and conveys to students and parents alike a feeling of 'I mean business'. When speaking of her pupils one gets a Jean Brodie impression, which is substantiated by her students. She continues to teach French, as she always has and her reputation as an inspired teacher is known to all students. Although Dame Ruth does not hover over students or over her staff, her presence behind the scenes is felt throughout the school. 'I don't know how she does it but she knows every single student even if they have not been to her office,' marvels one student. It takes in fact a long route indeed until a student actually ends up at Dame Ruth for any disciplinary reason and whatever steps ultimately taken are without question with the student's welfare in mind.

Her teaching staff respects her and tries to live up to her high standards and expectations. They seem to do so most successfully.

Academic Matters: JFS has now thoroughly left behind its reputation as a school for the less bright and is now one of the top comprehensive schools in the country, showing up well in value-added tables. 88 per cent got 5+ A*-C grades at GCSE in 2005; 75 per cent of A level grades were A or B. Strong GNVQ courses – all this is impressive for a genuine mixed-ability intake. Maths, sciences, history and geography are strong depts but students less enthusiastic about the modern langs depts especially French. At GCSE students may choose any two of French, Hebrew and Spanish. A particular strength of the school's policy is to set students in each subject early on, with students being constantly evaluated and new targets set. No student, however, is ever 'labelled' and can easily move down or make their way up. Some excellent teachers take on lower sets.

At awards ceremonies, effort and achievement are rewarded on an equal footing. It is thus 'heart warming to see a student with learning difficulties pick up the academic prize of his year or a child with a handicap receive the certificate for PE,' says a parent. A lot of other 'incentive prizes' encourage students to participate in the community life of JFS – and the wider community – with rewards going to students who, for example, help with fund-raising – a high item on the JFS agenda – or with visiting the elderly or contributing to the religious life of the school.

Across years 7-13, a range of programmes is offered for the gifted and talented, as well as for students in need of one-to-one mentoring. Much thought has clearly been given to special needs at JFS, dyslexia, for example, already becoming almost a 'cachet' – with dyslexic students proudly walking with their laptops through the corridors. Their academic achievements seem to prove that, with the right support, results can be very satisfactory. SEN services range from one-to-one tuition to in-class support.

In addition to the standard Key Stage 3 and Key Stage 4 curriculum is Jewish education (including Jewish studies, Israel studies and modern Hebrew). Jewish education has a strong moral basis and takes into account the concerns of, and dilemmas encountered in, today's world. PSE is part of the Jewish education curriculum. Diploma in Childcare and Education (DCE level 3) is also offered.

Games, Options, The Arts: There is little opportunity for formal sport, with the curriculum being occupied by secular and religious studies. However sports are offered and include dance, gymnastics, trampolining, badminton, volleyball, football, netball, hockey, rounders, cricket and athletics.

There are quite enjoyable drama performances; music (choir, barbershop quartets, instrumental performances etc) is quite outstanding, above all due to the enthusiasm and camaraderie inspired by the department's staff. Every performance is received by fellow pupils like an Oscar performance and self-confidence soars. Unlike her predecessor, Dame Ruth likes music and can be spotted at every school concert (albeit in the wings). Teachers, who themselves are excited about a particular type of instrument or style of music, have readily joined in.

The (selective) year 9 Israel residential scheme, which is a 3-month stay on a Kibbutz in Israel, offers students a unique experience to study and live in Israel whilst keeping pace with the academic progress of their counterparts back at home '... the best thing that has ever happened in my life', enthuses a student. Visits to galleries, museums, theatres etc are 'an integral part of school life', says school – to the surprise of some. Music master classes, a week-long reading festival, a three-week long music festival, poetry and debating competitions, an architecture project, the science Olympiad, D of E and Young Enterprise.

Lots of trips abroad.

Background and Atmosphere: While the origins of JFS go back to 1732 and to the East End, the school moved to Camden after the second World War and, in 2002, to a superb new purpose-built campus in Kenton with 15 science labs, an ecological garden, five technology labs, a 450-seat theatre, a television/media studio, a music suite with recording studio and keyboard laboratory, a large learning resources centre, an ICT suite, an open-air amphitheatre, 2 large sports halls, a dance studio, a multi-gym and acres of playing fields. The school has its own beautiful synagogue.

Pastoral Care and Discipline: Religious staff, professional counsellors and individual tutors are on hand at all times and deal with personal problems swiftly and with sensitivity. On entry, each class is allocated to a tutor who accompanies the students until graduation. This is a very effective system that helps students and parents communicate and sort out personal or academic problems. 'It's an overwhelmingly big school but you would never know it, once your child has settled down,' comments a father. However, information about the school can be hard to extract.

Students come from a very wide range of backgrounds (ten per cent on free dinners), displaying different abilities and talents all of which become recognised and appreciated at JFS very early on. On the reverse side, there is zero tolerance for bullying, roughness and discourteous behaviour. 'There are clear guidelines on the school's ethos on entry. Anybody displaying contravention of this does not get a second warning', says the head. 'School has very high standards of discipline and believes in 'old-fashioned values.'

Pupils and Parents: JFS students are extremely happy and enthusiastic and mix in such a way that transcends economic and social barriers. They are friendly and respectful to visitors and care about one another. Those more able need little encouragement to help those with difficulties, the school's paired reading scheme being a case in point. For the most part, students are very proud of their school and of who they are; they carry themselves with confidence. JFS is a very large school but students quickly find their feet. Senior students ease the integration of the new arrivals and make them feel welcome. It is not, say parents, the comprehensive nightmare so many parents fear exposing their protected children to; indeed, the vast majority of students are bright, cheerful and Jewishly committed with 70 per cent coming from Jewish primary schools.

Entrance: The school seeks to have a fully comprehensive intake. Prospective applicants sit tests which are used to divide them into four ability bands. Interviews (which take place after acceptance) are used to allow teachers to gain a wider insight into the interests of each child. Priority is given to looked after children, siblings, those at a Jewish primary school continuously since the start of year 3, siblings of former students and then distance from the school, proportionate to the numbers from each borough. Oversubscription criteria are listed in the full policy, available from the school. The sixth form has 500 places. Approximately 25 per cent join from other schools, many from the private sector.

Parents should not be surprised at being asked to produce their marriage certificate (United Synagogue or equivalent) on application, nor at being asked at the interview about the stability of their marriage.

Exit: Almost all students go on to university; well over half go to Russell Group institutions. Six to Oxbridge in 2005.

Remarks: A big school, but with a warm and caring family atmosphere; students reach their full potential. Aims to guide students 'towards a fulfilling career and towards becoming tolerant and responsible citizens and committed members of the Jewish community'.

JORDANHILL SCHOOL

45 Chamberlain Road, Glasgow, G13 1SP

Tel: 0141 576 2500

Fax: 0141 950 2587

Email: info@jordanhill.glasgow.sch.uk

Website: www.jordanhill.glasgow.sch.uk

• Pupils: 575 boys and girls, all day • Ages: 11-18

• Religion: Non-denom • School status: State

• School gender: Mixed • Day/boarding: Day pupils

SEN provision

Detail:

Now provide for in school:

Mild: ASP; AUT; ADD; ADHD; EBD; DYSC; DYSL; DYSP; SpLD; HI; VI; CP;

Moderate: ASP; ADHD; EBD; MLD; DYSC; DYSL; DYSP; SpLD; HI; VI;

Severe: DYSC;

Others: SPD; ODD; Sp&LD; DEL; Epi; PD; Eat;

Summary: Jordanhill School operates within the terms of the Education (Additional Support for Learning) (Scotland) Act 2004. Specific conditions apply due to the school's grant-aided status. Relevant policy statements can be accessed through the 'Parents' section of the school website.

What we say about the school - the full Good Schools Guide review

Rector: Since 1997, Dr Paul Thomson BSc PhD Dip Ed (forties), educated at Dollar Academy and took combined honours in maths and physics at Glasgow University where he also did his PhD, and then did his teacher training at Jordanhill College next door. Started his teaching career at Boclair in Bearsden followed by Chryston High School where he was principal teacher of physics, then assistant head at the Vale of Leven and depute head at Hermitage Academy: a speedy career path. Dr Thomson, whose wife is depute head of St Margaret's High School in Airdrie, has two children; he is also exceedingly keen on cooking. That apart, he has a fearsome intellect and spouted facts and figures faster than most heads we have met, adding all the while 'that it is available on the web page' which then turned out to be off-line for a spot of tinkering.

Jordanhill is the only direct grant-aided non-special school in Scotland, runs its own budget and indeed so does each department. A block grant comes from the Scottish Executive Education department to whom the school is answerable. Dr Thomson regards himself quite rightly as a CEO, working 'with the staff' and running the place with a budget of £4,500 per child per annum. One of the youngest heads – state or independent – in Scotland he says he has no intention of moving though he obviously misses teaching, and his entire demeanour changed during our tour round the school; whenever we found a child to be talked to – about anything – gone was the efficiency question-answering model and in its place appeared an interested smiley friend. (He also does all the 'early' UCAS references). But youngsters apart, we suspect he does not tolerate fools with ease. (He thinks he has 'mellowed a little' recently). The school is due for a spot of new build to accommodate the reduced class sizes in primaries 1 and 2 and to replace some 'hutted' classrooms well past their sell-by date. Unlike many heads, Dr Thomson regards this as a pupil-necessity and therefore worth spending time and thought on rather than an end in itself for the glorification of Jordanhill and his own cleverness in getting the necessary funding.

Academic Matters: The school is inclusive, but is still the most successful state school (albeit grant-aided) in Scotland. Four classes of 25 (rather than the trad legal limit of 33) with practical classes of 15 (max 20). Some setting in maths and French. French from primary, German taster at 13, and enormous success with credits all over the shop at intermediate II; Spanish is only open to those who do OK in French and only in S5 and S6. Head doesn't seem to think that Latin happens anymore, but the current website happily talks of minimus and classical civilisation clubs (the latter cunningly disguised as lives and cultures of the Romans), and there is much discussion of classical availability at higher still level. The school plies both standard and intermediate II (and results have become sharper in the last eight years); biology and art and design results strong at both standard and higher grade. English, French and maths results are impressive as is French, physics and chemistry. Masses of external activity in the science department with pupils doing project work with the university of Lyons, taking part in the Royal Society of Chemistry quiz and challenges run by Paisley uni.

Outstanding music results with seventeen candidates getting A. The recent HMI report praises the economics results (eight at A, five at B at higher level). Higher psychology in conjunction with Anniesland College and a good partnership developing. Terrific art. Excellent use of computers: everywhere, in the art rooms as well as the classrooms, three hundred of them, interactive whiteboards all over the place too. Smart new media studies room which doubles for English having interesting star-shaped six seater tables and two overhead projectors with an interactive whiteboard, pupils won a prize with their first film. One of the best equipped schools we have visited. Ever. Clusters of laptops motor round classrooms.

Homework clubs and some homework online. Ditto supported study. Several groups of pupils doing research projects have direct links with staff. PowerPoint demos by all, from P7; P6 are observers and rector then discusses the P7 presentation with them (face lit up like a beacon when he described this). Loads of interaction. Evening support classes for exam years, labs are open at lunchtime and post-school. Good modern library, more computers and even more in the careers department. Special needs well catered for, 'if they can cope then we will take them, unless their needs are such that the school cannot accommodate them', some pupils have a record of needs. Two dedicated staff who work across both primary and secondary schools, plus a host of classroom assistants and auxiliaries, scribing where necessary. Lifts and ramps all over the shop. With one or two exceptions, the staffroom looks incredibly young and vibrant.

Games, Options, The Arts: Fantastic games and oodles of caps: capped pupils wear green ties, though we didn't spot any. Rugby, hockey, football (and school was second in the Glasgow league – a stupendous achievement), volleyball, basketball and athletics. Two gyms and a recently acquired sports hall nearby courtesy of Hutchies who bought the former Laurel Park complex. Stunning if cramped art complex, and excellent art on display all over the place: the staff room and on various corridors. None of it too big, but impressive. Kiln and new silk screen machine in place. Sculpture and good CDT. Drama strong, though not the biggest studio we have seen. Inspiring music, with specialist staff from P6 up. 'The best music department in the country' says Dr Thomson, 300 plus pupils play an instrument, 26 different ensembles, serious orchestras. All swinging, and particularly keen on composing.

Clubs for everything, chess particularly popular and a current pupil is in the international squad. Hot on debating, and citizenship. Home economics a serious contender now, but rather more post standard grades when students also study international cuisine (head's face lit up again). Ambitious outdoor education programme with pupils spending afternoons or weeks away depending on year group: Raasay, Castle Toward, senior pupils have a bi-annual trip to the developing world, part project part tourism (forty in Thailand when we visited). World Challenge in Peru a couple of years ago. Oodles of trips abroad: Euroscola at the European Parliament in Strasbourg, Paris, Spain et al. Massive charity involvement, both fund-raising and community work in the locality. Jolly pupil produced school mag, clearly laid out with brilliant editing: nice one, easy to read, with none of the trendy undershadowing that doting grannies find so irritating (not to mention GSG editors).

Background and Atmosphere: School founded in 1920 as a demo school for Jordanhill College of Education and became direct grant aided in 1987. Handsome classical grade B listed building – plus some temporary accommodation which is about to be replaced on the other side of the (rather sad) games pitch. Rector has stunning panelled offices (think Eltham Palace); super huge classrooms with wide pupil-proof corridors. School surrounded by (some) games pitches but a high fence now divides them from the university. Strong links with local Jordanhill Parish church. Strong links too with Glasgow state schools, joint improvement meetings for staff and pupils whilst the latter have a joint pre-vocational programme plus Your Turn project involving pupils across the city. Pupils from other schools can come to Jordanhill to pick up the odd higher or advanced higher not catered for in their own schools.

Jordanhill pupils are neat in brown uniforms – except for the primary when we visited who were in mufti as were their staff – the head of primary particularly dashing in a black T-shirt. Efficient and fairly unforgiving uniform guide-lines in the prospectus supplement. Sixth year have a dedicated common room and two separate ones for boys and girls in S5, the new build will give them better social areas. JOSS operate an after-school club for tinies in the nearby church hall.

Pastoral Care and Discipline: Four houses, the heads of houses are guidance staff with a combined office and interview rooms. Pupils have tutors who are responsible for PSE and the school policy is to clamp down hard on any form of bullying. Neither Dr Thomson nor his predecessor have ever permanently excluded; and there is a clearly defined code of sanctions, including letters home, litter duty (brill) and detention. Regular links between sixth form and littles, combined reading, and the BFG club. Minister from Jordanhill Parish church takes assemblies, but this is an ecumenical school, with all religions' festivals observed, rector is keener that pupils learn 'to conduct themselves properly in church' and understand other faiths (by eg visiting local synagogues, mosques and temples) than pay lip service to any particular religion.

Pupils and Parents: Jordanhill serves a predominantly owner-occupier area; professionals, who form an enthusiastic parent teachers association, with parent volunteers in primary dept and loads of fundraising. Seven per cent ethnic minority.

Entrance: Inclusive, by address, over-subscribed, waiting lists. Siblings get priority. Some places (never advertised) available post standard grades. First come, first served.

Exit: Some 75 per cent to university. Trickle to Oxbridge, certain number to unis down south, Imperial for engineering, Liverpool, Manchester, the odd musician to the Royal Academy of Music, and tranches to art school, with or without a foundation course. But most stay in the West of Scotland. Dentistry, medicine and vet school all popular.

Remarks: Outstanding, with an inspirational if slightly left of centre rector. Better resourced than many schools in the independent sector: and it's free. A beacon. Glasgow independent sector eat your hearts out.

KILGRASTON SCHOOL

Bridge of Earn, Perthshire, PH2 9BQ

Tel: 01738 812 257

Fax: 01738 813 410

Email: registrar@kilgraston.pkc.sch.uk

Website: www.kilgraston.com

• Pupils: 235 girls; 98 board, the rest day • Ages: 13-18 • Religion: RC but inter-denom as well • Fees: Junior school from £2,020 day to £4,950 for boarding; Senior school from £3,500 day to £5,930 boarding • School status: Independent • Opendays: May and October • School gender: Girls • Day/boarding: Takes boarders

---

SEN provision

Detail:

Centre of excellence for:

Mild: DYSC; DYSL; DYSP;

Moderate: DYSL;

Severe: DYSL;

Others: EAL;

Experience of:

Mild: EBD; SpLD;
Moderate: DYSP; SpLD;
Severe: DYSC; DYSP; SpLD;
Others: TIC; Epi; PD; Eat;

Summary: SEN provision at Kilgraston concentrates on meeting the needs of pupils with specific learning difficulties and includes individual lessons, class support and parent/teacher consultations. The learning support department is situated within the learning resources centre and is open until 6.30pm.

What we say about the school - the full Good Schools Guide review

Principal: Since 2004, Mr Michael Farmer BA PGCE (forties), who was educated in the state system in Leicestershire, did economics at Portsmouth and then became a yacht skipper. He did his PGCE at Bristol and comes from Headington School in Oxford, where he was deputy head and head of sixth form (having moved there from Godolphin with the erstwhile headmistress Mrs Hilary Fender). A Roman Catholic. Mr Farmer heads a school very different to that to which he first applied. Kilgraston absorbed the 8-13 section of the much loved girls-only prep school, Butterstone (which was going broke) at the end of the summer term 2003. The girls from Butterstone have now almost all gone (most went down south) and the junior school is no longer Butterstone Grange at Kilgraston, but Kilgraston Preparatory school.

An open door head, he is looking forward to 'teaching economics next year' but currently still admits to 'wearing big L plates'. His wife Mary Ann 'is deeply supportive' and runs the sixth form creative cuisine course. They have a son at Strathallan and a daughter in the school – 'who never comes home, she really loves the place'.

Academic Matters: Not the sleepy place it used to be, placed in top three at Higher in 2005. School runs primarily on the Scottish system, with Standard grades followed by Highers to university in lower sixth, and A levels. Certain amount of fast track standard grades in French and English. Science on the up, with new head of physics, excellent science labs. English lit not strong. 'Bright and encouraging results from lesser sparks,' claimed the previous head. Pupils can 'top up' Standard grades in sixth form, and often take French, maths and Latin a year early. Tiny classes, 8/20, with tiny maths classes to bring the less academic up to status. No change here. Piloting Scotvec clusters, four modules equals one cluster. Only one or two do secretarial studies/keyboarding skills. Business studies popular. Computers everywhere plus two dedicated computer rooms. Really good IT and laptops for everyone on the way (still). E-mail for all. Mass of personal laptops. Library a mess, needs a new broom, drastic re-organisation and a whole lot of new books. Good remedial unit (CReSTeD B status – Wow), with specialist teachers for dyslexia and dyspraxia – one-to-one teaching and EFL on offer. Language labs popular. Masses of exchanges, French, German and Spanish (both pupils and staff) via Sacred Heart network.

Games, Options, The Arts: Magnificent sports hall faced in sandstone, with niches echoing those in the stable building (well converted into junior school with attached nursery); Historic Scotland at its best. Nine astroturfs with floodlighting (good grief). Wide choice of other sports. Climbing wall. Indoor swimming pool on the wish list. Strong drama, and inspired art -'going from strength to strength'; the art department overlooks the Rotunda and currently boasts an enormous computer-linked loom. Tremendous ceramics and regular masterclasses. D of E, debating, leadership courses. Music centre in the attics, with keyboards and individual study rooms; guitars and stringed instruments everywhere, sound recording studio on wish list too. Writers' group. Cooking and brilliant needlework, the girls make their own ball gowns for the annual ball with Merchiston. Couple of school ponies and several more due to arrive shortly, but school is not yet totally into the equestrian scene: pathetic pic of uncollected, out of control pony and rider in current prospectus (stirrups too short, back not straight, air below the seat, pony's neck not bent, ears back etc). The page is entitled 'Balance, poise and composure in all things'! New director of weekend activities recently appointed, and all sorts of options in the pipeline, whitewater rafting, canyoning, sailing.

Background and Atmosphere: Founded in 1920, and one of 200 networked schools and colleges of the Society of the Sacred Heart. Moved to the handsome red Adamesque sandstone house in 1930, masses of extensions including spectacular Barat wing, light and airy with huge wide passages. We previously said that 'religion was very much in evidence, with saints on tap,' this is no longer the case. Mr Farmer has removed many of the saints from the Central Hall, as it was felt that this would be an excellent place 'to show off some off some of our superb artwork'. And indeed pupils' work does look smashing but school looks a bit bleak. A Lawrence Bowen-Jones makeover is desperately needed. Sixth form common room needs an influx of books. Bedsits from third year, tinies dorms now divided into attractive cabins for each. Huge development following the Butterstone debacle, and masses of revamping going on in the dorms area. School stops at 4.10 on Fridays for day and weekly boarders, but masses of alternative activities for those who stay back – though usual moans about 'not having enough to do', these should now be under arrest with the new appointment. Computers, games hall/courts, art, music and sewing rooms open throughout the weekend. Boyfriends can and do visit at weekends. God still important here, most attend assembly and mass on Sundays. Feast Days still special. Local priest holds regular confession.

Pastoral Care and Discipline: Sacred Heart ethos prevails, staff enormously caring, and staff 'will go the extra mile'. Pastoral conferences every week, independent counsellor on tap. Disciplinary Committee, gatings, suspensions, fatigues round school for smoking. Drinkers are suspended and a not so recent problem was 'nipped in the bud'. Will test areas, not girls, if drugs suspected. The girls here are not the dozy lot they used to be. Counsellor on hand, and bullying handled by BFG (Big Friendly Group). Charming little handbook for new pupils full of helpful advice.

Pupils and Parents: Day children from Fife and Perthshire, though bus no longer collects children from the school's front door – the main gate was damaged too often. Boarders from all over Scotland, and Old Girls' children. Toffs' daughters, including non-Catholics, and Muslims. Academically pushy parents may move their children elsewhere but the school breeds loyalty among those who value 'other things'. Currently 21 from overseas ('the Internet is handy,' says the head).

Entrance: Not that difficult. All sit the school's own exam in February in tandem with scholarship exam. Junior school entrants also do CE. Otherwise 11+ from primary schools, and 12+ from prep schools. Pupils can come whenever, half term if space available. Sixth form entry – 'good Standard grades/GCSEs to follow A level course, pupils come 'from overseas', or from local state schools. Pupils steered to 'appropriate' levels of study. Has been known to 'pick up' the odd casualty' from Glenalmond – 'they (the pupils) weren't tough enough'.

Exit: Toffs still abandon at 11+ or 13+ to go elsewhere. 80/90 per cent annually to universities. Occasional departure for sixth form in boys' schools; some leave after Highers, though not currently.

Money Matters: OK financially, the nuns have left rich pickings. Up to ten academic, art and music scholarships. Also riding, tennis and sporting scholarships. Almost one third receive assistance of some sort. School is 'good at finding Trust funding' for those who have fallen on hard times.

Remarks: The only all-girls boarding school left in Scotland and popular. Small, gentle, not overtly Catholic, with terrific facilities. Useful prep facilities; Scots parents see it as a viable alternative to St Leonards (recently gone not very successfully co-ed).

King Edward's School (Birmingham)

Edgbaston Park Road, Birmingham, West Midlands, B15 2UA

Tel: 0121 472 1672

Fax: 01214 154 327

Email: office@kes.bham.sch.uk

Website: www.kes.bham.sch.uk

• Pupils: 840 boys; all day • Ages: 11-18 • Religion: C of E/ multi-faith • Fees: £2,583 • School status: Independent • Opendays: Early July, October, November • School gender: Boys • Day/boarding: Day pupils

SEN provision

Detail:

Experience of:

Mild: ASP; AUT; ADD; EBD; DYSC; DYSL; DYSP; HI; VI;

Moderate: HI;

Others: SPD; OCD; DEL; Epi;

Summary: By the definition of 'gifted and talented', virtually all pupils at King Edward's School would qualify. Therefore our curriculum provision incorporates teaching strategies to stimulate and stretch the most able as a matter of course. Within the school however, we take special educational needs very seriously and to that end we employ both a SENCo and a part-time support teacher as well.

What we say about the school - the full Good Schools Guide review

Chief Master: From 2006, Mr John Claughton, MA Hons (an Oxford classicist) (fiftyish). Educated at King Edward's, he was previously housemaster at Eton and then headmaster at Solihull School 2001-2005. Married with three young sons. Loves cricket, having gained his blue at Oxford and subsequently played County cricket for Warwickshire. He now serves on the Warwickshire CC Committee.

Succeeds popular, successful and charismatic Mr Roger Dancey who retired in December 2005.

Academic Matters: School gets outstanding results by means of first-rate teaching, a well-organised curriculum and an emphasis on educating the whole person, not merely turning out impressive exam statistics. Roughly 12:1 boys to full-time teachers, no class bigger than 26, sixth form 16. Results among the best in the country, especially so in maths, chemistry and geography. Maths A level in 2005, 42 out of 57 candidates got As, out of 59 chemistry candidates 55 got As or Bs; all 25 boys who took history got either A or B. Maths and geography seem especially strong among so many strengths. French compulsory to GCSE, other languages having to be taken as options.

Almost all passes at GCSE, the overwhelming number of grades in all subjects being A*s or As. Head emphasises the importance of special needs support, 'a bit of a crusade', and its place in enabling all candidates to achieve their potential. The recent full inspection which regarded the school as 'outstanding' in all but a very few respects, did point out the need to upgrade the library. This currently enthusiastically in hand. Middle school curriculum also re-evaluated with a view to making it more flexible in the light of report.

Games, Options, The Arts: Main sports rugby, hockey, basketball, cricket, athletics. Boys can also take archery, badminton, cross-country, Eton fives, fencing, golf, orienteering, sailing, squash, swimming, table tennis, tennis and water polo. Boys participate in many regional teams in various sports, also in U15 and U16 national sides in rugby, water polo, cricket. Extensive playing fields, extraordinary in a school one mile from centre of city. Also huge new astroturf pitch shared with King Edward's VI High School for Girls (qv) which shares the school's huge campus and many activities, facilities and some staff. Extra-curricular options include conservation and environmental studies, leadership, CCF. Arts are famously good. Drama to professional standards under inspirational, unequalled teaching and production values. Music similarly outstanding – school justifiably proud of both. Art also impressive.

Background and Atmosphere: School founded in 1552 by King Edward VI, now flagship of King Edward Foundation group of seven Birmingham schools, including King Edward VI Camp Hill, an excellent grammar and school's main academic local rival. The chief master is head of the Foundation though each school is autonomous. School moved to a famous Charles Barry building in 1838 but in true Birmingham spirit of renewal and regeneration, this was demolished and the school moved to its current impressive 32-acre site in 1936.

Buildings are 1930s red brick and solid-looking, and manage to be both elegant and functional, though the length of the corridors might daunt newcomers! Newer buildings have been sensitively incorporated, including latest addition, an imaginative 'tea pavilion' for the entertainment of parents during matches and so on, known, up to now, as 'Dancey's Diner'. Now to be...? Much recent refurbishment especially flooring and lighting, greatly improves ambience.

The adjacent King Edward VI girls' school, founded 1883, is a real boon to the school, especially in matters dramatic, musical, social. Good friendly working relations between the two schools, assisted by some shared staff. Most pervasive feeling in school is a genuine warmth and unaffected enthusiasm among both staff and pupils and a sense of privilege – of the best kind – and good fortune in being there. The school has a sense of being geared to the realities of working life. A cooked breakfast is served every day and school uniform buying arrangements are geared to a working parent's schedule.

Pastoral Care and Discipline: School publishes an impressive-looking Pastoral Handbook with a carefully constructed Code of Conduct and Policies on sex education, PSE, drugs, bullying etc as well as advice on whom to speak to in the event of 'matters of pastoral concern'. System, however, is not restrictive and boys are encouraged to talk to person who is right for them, rather than to specific tutor or master. School has trained student counsellor. Also very approachable masters, including deputy head. Prefect system. Head would assess individual infringements of rules individually but hypothetical serious issues, eg drug selling, would mean instant expulsion.

Pupils and Parents: Intake reflects greatly diverse local ethnic and social mix. Between 35 – 40 per cent of boys from ethnic minorities, only 35 per cent from the city of Birmingham, many commute from as far as Coventry, Wolverhampton, Lichfield and consider it 'worth it'. 45 per cent from primary schools and 55 per cent from prep schools. Uniform throughout the school but sixth formers don't seem to mind. Liberal attitude to self-expression in hair etc and on 'own clothes' days. A place at this school clearly regarded as a prize by parents and pupils alike.

Entrance: Highly competitive (400 candidates for 125 places) at 11+. Entrance tests in English, maths, verbal reasoning, interview, report from current head. Five or so places available at 13+. Sixth form entry dependent on entrance examination in proposed AS subjects, Headteacher's report and interview. Academic scholarships decided on performance in entrance tests. Music scholarships (up to one-half fees) also offered.

Exit: Vast majority take up places at good universities (24 out of last year's 121 leavers went to Oxbridge, 26 to London colleges, 10 to Birmingham, 9 to Nottingham, 9 to Leeds and so on.) Unsurprisingly for a school which is so strong in maths and science, maths and medicine accounted for 30 leavers; natural sciences, computer sciences, engineering, economics made up a further 22. The traditional bias towards science has changed over recent years; leavers are now fairly evenly divided between science and the humanities. Old Edwardians include Tolkien, Enoch Powell, Nobel medical Laureate Sir John Vane, Kenneth Tynan, Bill Oddie.

Money Matters: School – and pupils – hugely fortunate to have Foundation able to compensate to great extent for loss of Assisted Places. Up to 14 places a year still funded out of school resources including 2 HSBC scholarships. Means-tested remission of up to full fees. Additional help in subsidising educationally useful school trips for those who need it. Altogether generous help for the genuinely worthy. Fees compare very favourably to comparable schools elsewhere.

Remarks: On all counts this is a very impressive school combining academic excellence, a real commitment to wider values of education, genuine exuberance and enthusiasm and turning out unpretentious, independent-minded, well-behaved and confident young men. Worth moving for.

King's Bruton

Plox, Bruton, Somerset, BA10 0ED

Tel: 01749 814 200/ Registrar 01749

Fax: 01749 813 426

Email: office@kingsbruton.com

Website: www.kingsbruton.com

• Pupils: 235 boys, 85 girls; 220 board, 100 day • Ages: 13-18

• Religion: Christian • Fees: Boarding £6,700; day £4,910

• School status: Independent • Opendays: October

• School gender: Mixed • Day/boarding: Takes boarders

SEN provision

Detail:

Now provide for in school:

Mild: ASP; ADD; DYSC; DYSL; DYSP; HI;

Moderate: DYSL;

Others: EAL;

Experience of:

Mild: ADHD; EBD; VI;

Moderate: MLD; HI;

Others: CD; Sp&LD; Eat;

Summary: At King's we endeavour to provide a whole school policy for pupils with special needs. They receive help usually on a one-to-one basis in the Special Learning Unit, and follow a programme specifically suited to their needs. We help with literacy, study skills, and in areas of the curriculum where the pupils are experiencing problems.

What we say about the school - the full Good Schools Guide review

Head: Since 2004, Mr Nigel Lashbrook (forties). Chemist. Read it at Oxford – where he played in the university 2nd cricket XI and captained his college rugby side – then taught it at Manchester Grammar where he also coached top rugby and cricket teams. Moved to Tonbridge in 1992, was a boarding housemaster then deputy head. They reckon he's 'totally different' from predecessor Richard Smyth and, for that reason, an 'inspired choice'. Not that there was anything wrong with the excellent Mr Smyth (now at St Peter's, York), he just defied imitation. He was also pretty defiant of contradiction, while with Mr Lashbrook 'you don't feel as if you've gone 15 rounds after you've raised a problem'. He's softly-softly, carefully consensual, rigidly insistent. He's approachable, affable, humorous, with that restless intelligence and ambition you want to see in a head. He's also clearly loving the job. Parents now say they feel confident that, under him, the school is 'really going to go places'. The change of style has led to no change in ethos – 'old fashioned but with a modern outlook' in the words of a parent – but he wants, particularly, to up the academic standard and raise the profile of drama. In both causes he has made firm first strides. He's also kicked out the caterers and improved the food immeasurably, thereby eliminating a long running gripe. He worries that the school is a 'well-kept secret' – this despite years of earnest marketing and some very good building – and he wonders why. Answer: because the school has always been unexceptionable. Sorry. And yet, and yet, the very qualities that have made it so may, in today's boarding market, make it exceptional. We rather think so.

Academic Matters: Good standard fare served up just as you would expect. No eccentricities and no vocational A level equivalents – a shame, perhaps. Some outstanding facilities – top science centre, IT and technology labs with computer-aided design and metal forges. Admirable IT, fully intranetted campus-wide. Classes really are remarkably small – max 20 to GCSE, max 14 in the sixth form. Expectations are rising, underpinned by statistical pupil monitoring. The head interviews every boy and girl at A level revision time, mulls over what they're up to, puts them on the spot. Smart move. 2005 has yielded a best-ever crop of exam results at all levels and the new school year was launched with Henry V-style oratory, but this is not the sort of place where youth grows pale and spectre thin and dies, good heavens no. There's pressure but, observes a sixth form girl fresh from a single sex school, it's not relentless neither does it nag – it's there, yes, but not so you're acutely aware of it. Parents feel the school does a good job by the brightest (always an Oxbridge handful) and the not so bright. Very bright director of studies. The social atmosphere is remarkably free of academic snobbery. Established special needs department – 1 full-time, 2 part-time – caters for 35 dyslexics and dyspraxics, and is reckoned to do well by them, most fall within the dyslexia stream, literacy and study skills important. One pupil currently has a statement of needs. Some help with study skills, especially the sixth form, one-to-one throughout with pupils withdrawn from ancillary rather than core subjects, 'we nurse them through literacy and study skills plus organisation and curricular support'. School not good for wheelchairs, but would 'never turn anyone away'; can and have coped with mild Asperger's, profoundly deaf (hearing aid and voice magnifier for teacher rather then specialist mentor). All the normal aids, scribing, readers (expensive in public lessons = extra invigilators) the odd 'Irlen lens' but not a proven treatment', extra cost for lessons about £25.

Games, Options, The Arts: Terrific sport – a heritage feature. Stirring feats of valour weekly. There's a Spartan quality about the boys' rugby team (the haircuts, of which more anon, add to the impression), as this small school confronts overweening opponents and habitually overcomes them. Coaching excellent all round. Girls not yet quite so mighty but getting there. Parents, lots of them, pound touchlines intently and with camaraderie, while visiting parents comment on the warm welcome. You don't have to be sporty to be happy here, but it must help. Old boy Haydn Thomas is now Gloucester scrum half, Joe Mbu plays for Wasps. Long, strong cross-country tradition: the Tickner brothers were here. Rugby compulsory in first year only. Superb fitness suite approached by way of an art gallery – good art. Drama in its brilliant little in-the-round theatre is going from strength to strength as the head, having just appointed a full-time manager, has added dance to the menu and is looking to involve the community. They already do the Edinburgh Fringe. This is a notably team-spirited school. Music is strong, ambitious director, ensembles of all sorts, a military band and, jewel in the crown, a very good swing band – ask for the cd. 40 per cent learn an instrument. Strong choral tradition and collaboration with the community to make the very biggest noises. Growing trend to do things with other schools in this school-filled town, including the Steiner school. Activities convention on first day of each term to advertise the array on offer. It's the usual long list but, observed a pupil, 'they all actually happen'. Now, that's rare! A thoughtful touch for parents coming to watch their progeny play away matches – a booklet with detailed maps and directions to 25 other schools in the vicinity.

Background and Atmosphere: When the Bishop of London founded King's in 1519 he intended to turn out 'perfyt latyn men' in a school where prayers were said only in Latin. They've gone vernacular now but the golden stone emanates ancientness of an agreeable, lost-world sort of quality. At times, as you walk about the campus, you feel as if you are in a Cambridge college. The town lies in a part of Somerset where the busy world is hushed, making it increasingly attractive to metro-exiles, downsizers, good-lifers, artsy folk, but it's neither ragged-arse bohemian nor is it Cotswold-twee. It's intelligent. The railway station at nearby Castle Cary is the last frontier of the commuter. There are five schools in this wee town and they rub along in a contentedly unfederated way. Co-ed since 1997. Good prospectus, gorgeous long-lens photos which, unusually, depict the boys and girls much as they appear in real life. Very good website. Splendid school mag which offers lots of insights.

Pastoral Care and Discipline: Boarding is apparently so well done here that we were inspired by incredulity to investigatively expose its underside for, as we know, to visit many a boarding school on a wet Saturday night in November is to spectate adolescents falling into hedges. We found no shred of evidence. As one mum put it, 'other schools turn a blind eye to drink. Not Bruton.' 75 per cent of the students board (no weekly, no flexi), and they do so in safety. Expect to see 65 per cent of them on any weekend. Why the good order? 'It's the measure of control we exert,' says the head. 'And the boys and girls like this place, they don't want to rock the boat.' Parents concur – 'there's a healthy respect for the line – this is a tight-knot community. They look after each other.' There's also a breathalyser to focus minds and, clever touch this, a chill-out period in houses every Saturday from 7 till 8 which tames the fever in the blood. Vigilance is the key, not the sanctions. Pastoral care here has got so much better. Parents talk of some splendid housemasters coming through – 'my son responds to e-mails almost by return'.

Relationships with the community are necessarily good and, because town-gown standoffs sometimes inevitably happen, the school part-pays the salary of the local bobby. Boarders can go home for four weekends a term – you choose. Not all take them all up. Why not? 'Because they are happy in the company of their friends,' reflects the head to whom, in his first year, this seems to have been a happy revelation. It is certainly evident in the tenor of relationships as you walk around and is corroborated by the social care inspectors' report, which uncovered one of the lowest bullying rates in the country. They're an unusually well-turned-out lot, boys' hair collar length mostly, giving them a preppie look, especially the sixth formers in their business suits. Oh, they're all terribly nice, some would say terribly conventional. No sign of attitudinous rebs and rads. Character is indulged and enjoyed, says the head, 'unless it undermines safety.' Day boys and girls join boarding houses and feel hardly different at all.

Pupils and Parents: Those who want trad values. Increasingly popular with sophisticated incomers, ever popular with local families who reckon the big school nearby lah-di-dah. Not a school of choice by any means for the M4 corridor brat pack. All the small pool attractions and, yes, good at nurturing those who need it, but by no means exclusively so. Around 20 expats, 30 Europeans and 35 from China and Japan.

Entrance: The intake is truly comprehensive, so the hurdle is the waiting list. Main feeder schools are Hazlegrove (own prep), Chafyn Grove, Salisbury Cathedral, Port Regis, with a smattering from any of the many prep schools hereabouts. The academic range is wide because parents and children choose the school for its own sake, not for its place in the academic pecking order.

Exit: Almost all to higher education – all manner of courses everywhere. For a school that not many people have heard of, it's produced lots of former pupils that people have: R D Blackmore (Lorna Doone) explorer William Dampier, Air Marshal Sir Peter Squire, The Sunday Telegraph's Mandrake, Adam Helliker, historian and author of 'Fortress Malta', James Holland, and comedian Marcus Brigstocke.

Money Matters: Masses of generous scholarships and awards including sixth form, academic and music.

Remarks: A thoroughly well turned-out school in every respect and – we think it high time someone blew their cover – a pre-eminently eligible candidate for parents looking for boarding.

King's College School (Cambridge)

West Road, Cambridge, Cambridgeshire, CB3 9DN

Tel: 01223 365 814

Fax: 01223 461 388

Email: office@kingscam.demon.co.uk

Website: www.kcs.cambs.sch.uk

• Pupils: 30 boys and 35 girls in the pre-prep; 170 boys and 90 girls in the prep. All day except for 34 boarders (including 16 choristers and 8 probationers) • Ages: 4-13 • Religion: C of E – other faiths welcome • Fees: Boarding (boys only) £5,050; choristers £1,685; day £3,260; pre-prep £2,535 • School status: Independent • School gender: Mixed • Day/boarding: Takes boarders

SEN provision

Detail:

Centre of excellence for:

Mild: ASP; ADD; DYSL; DYSP;

Others: SPD; EAL;

Summary: The learning support centre (formerly the dyslexia centre) has approximately 40 pupils who attend the centre on a daily or weekly basis. Some pupils receive help in groups of two or three but most have individual tuition if it is thought that they can take part in the full curriculum.

Teaching programmes are highly effective in boosting reading, writing, spelling and study skills. Careful attention is given to helping children's self-esteem. The learning support centre works closely with teaching staff, parents and outside specialists to achieve the best possible progress with the children.

What we say about the school - the full Good Schools Guide review

Head: Since 1998, Mr Nicholas Robinson BA (forties). Educated at Worth, read English at Anglia Polytechnic, PGCE in maths at Goldsmith's College. Master and subsequently housemaster for twelve years at Worth, where he gained a well- deserved reputation for raising money and getting things moving. A bachelor, a charming man – keen sportsman (skiing his especial forte), seriously musical (conducts). Very energetic and has a nice sense of humour. Has radically restructured the management of the whole place. He has two deputies and has increased the emphasis on the pastoral side. Popular with staff, boys and parents – quite a rarity.

Entrance: At 4, children are invited to spend an afternoon in the reception class; at 7, via assessments in English, maths and verbal reasoning and, occasionally, at other ages via assessment. A fairly broad intake. Annual choir auditions – lots apply. Pre-prep, opened 1992, and the learning support centre (mild Asperger's, ADD, dyslexia, fine) – both over-subscribed. Children of local farmers, business people and academics.

Exit: Half to The Perse (boys and girls). Also The Leys, King's Ely, Harrow, Eton, King's Canterbury, Uppingham, Oundle, Queenswood, Tonbridge, Rugby, Kimbolton. As you would expect, masses of music scholarships awarded. (NB Girls leave at 11 and 13). Old Boys include Orlando Gibbons, Michael Ramsey, Christopher Tugendhat, John Pardoe, Professor Andrew Wiles (who solved Fermat's Last Theorem).

Remarks: One of the top Cambridge prep schools and the smallest by far of the three – St John's and St Faith's being the others – and the only one to operate a sibling policy. Dates back to the 15th century, though buildings are largely 19th and 20th century, away from the centre of Cambridge. Originally boys only, the school went co-ed 25 years ago, then sprouted a highly popular pre-prep and has inevitably evolved from being a boarding plus day prep to become a day school with not many boarders. All choristers must be full boarders, the rest are weekly boarders. Choristers are all boys. King's choristers are of world renown, well used to being in the public eye (gowns, top hats and stiff collars). In 2003, for instance, they gave 11 concerts on a world tour that included Hong Kong, Tokyo, New York, Chicago and their diary reports that, 'we went through 6 time changes and arrived in New York before we left Tokyo'. Which said, the choristers are extremely well-integrated with the rest of the school – 'sometimes the children don't know who is a chorister', said a parent – and it is not unheard of for a chorister to be an academic scholar as well, or an outstanding cricketer.

Three classes of 15 for 7-year-olds and up. Children taught in small groups within each class. Scholarship class for the top year. Classics getting a boost now ('much needed,' say parents). High standards of teaching in all areas. Staff, half male, half female, include a useful recent injection of young blood, also some of long-standing, for example Mr David Higginbottom, deputy headmaster for decades, now the registrar, and official school listener, a real Mr Chips. DT is excellent, art is imaginative. Spacious new library. School inspectors commented positively on the readability of all the books here, though we did not find children here to be particularly enthusiastic readers. 'They don't have enough time to read,' complained a mother. However, enormously enthusiastic on other fronts.

The school has a very good learning support department run by Mrs Karen Richardson who works alongside four part-timers – all qualified to deal with specific learning difficulties. There are another three part-time teachers who help those who don't have a specific educational need but would benefit from additional support in English. Kings will take children who have been identified as having mild SEN (but can cope intellectually) and recognises that needs can crop up after entry. In these cases in-house assessments are made (prior to a referal to an educational psychologist if necessary) and there are useful contacts with educational psychologists. Support in the lower school is given in the classroom or in the learning support department. In the upper school it happens outside lesson times (first thing in the morning, break, lunch) except in cases where French or Latin has been dropped. Times don't vary 'otherwise the children would get muddled'. Additional charges are made for the thirty minute sessions.

Open door policy. A professionally run department – individual learning programs, learning strategies, liaison with class teachers, comments with the termly reports plus a yearly overview. Once a term there's a themed open evening for parents of children who use the unit – topics include paired reading and home support.

Good keen sport, some on site, some five minutes walk away at the athletics ground; full-time tennis coaching throughout the year (only this and individual instrument lessons at extra cost). Classes end at 4.20pm but children regularly stay on until 6pm. Outstanding music – of course – with 270 children learning an instrument, and many learning two or even three. Thirty-seven chamber groups (a prep school record?) and all manner of orchestras. Head of music is Mr Simon Brown, previously head of the academic side of music at the Purcell School. New music centre (rather, the old one cleverly re-jigged) opened summer 2001 by Sir David Willcocks. Space everywhere carefully used – the headmaster skilfully turned the building programme on its head on arrival. This traditional, liberal prep school is in fine fettle, somewhat bursting at the seams, and bursting with energy, producing friendly, cheerful and happy children.

King's Hall

Pyrland, Kingston Road, Taunton, Somerset, TA2 8AA

Tel: 01823 285 920

Fax: 01823 285 922

Email: kingshall@aol.com

Website: www.kingshalltaunton.co.uk

• Pupils: Prep: 60 boarders, 245 day pupils (50/50 girls and boys). Pre-prep: 120 day pupils • Ages: 3-13 • Religion: C of E • Fees: Day £1,200 nursery; £1,770 year 4; £3,365 year 8. Weekly boarding £3,650-£4,750; full boarding £3,650-£4,750 • School status: Independent • Opendays: Early May (usually the first Friday and Saturday but please phone for confirmation) • School gender: Mixed • Day/boarding: Takes boarders

SEN provision

Detail:

Experience of:

Mild: DYSC; DYSL; HI;

Others: EAL; Sp&LD; Epi; Eat;

Summary: Although not a specialist school, King's Hall makes provision for pupils with mild learning difficulties. The SEN department was praised by ISI Inspection in 2004 as being a strength of the school. It is also recognised by the Services Education Allowances (SENA).

What we say about the school - the full Good Schools Guide review

Headmaster: Since 1999, Mr James Macpherson (fifties).

Entrance: Assessment in English and maths, report from present school and informal interview.

Exit: Two thirds transfer to King's College, Taunton at 13, the remainder to other senior schools both in the west country and further afield.

Money Matters: Generous discounts for Services families. Scholarships available at various ages, notably those awarded at 11 continue through King's College as well (subject to annual review).

Remarks: The junior school for King's College (Taunton). Set in country surrounding National Trust farmland on edge of the Quantocks, the original house (1780s) has had recent additions – a new theatre, sports hall and classroom complex.

Majority of boarders are from Services families. Children streamed from year 4, and set for maths. Pupils with learning difficulties accepted provided they are 'of above average intelligence'. Not a school for 'serious' special needs children according to a member of staff. However, very good inspection report for special needs and 20 per cent of pupils take advantage of some learning support. Needs range from the slight eg 'help settling in' and learning skills, to speech therapy and dyslexia. Eight part-time staff and one full-time SENCo.

The King's School (Chester)

Wrexham Road, Chester, Cheshire, CH4 7QL

Tel: 01244 689 500
Fax: 01244 689 501
Email: info@kingschester.co.uk
Website: www.kingschester.co.uk

• Pupils: 855 boys and girls • Ages: 7-18
• Religion: C of E, cathedral foundation • Fees: Junior £2,010; senior £2,625. Plus lunch • School status: Independent
• Opendays: Second or third Saturday in November
• School gender: Mixed • Day/boarding: Day pupils

SEN provision

Detail:
Now provide for in school:
  Mild: DYSL;
Experience of:
  Mild: ASP; AUT; ADD; ADHD; EBD; DYSP; CP;
  Moderate: DYSL;
  Others: SPD; OCD; EAL; MSI; Epi; Eat;

Summary: The King's School currently has 44 pupils with specific learning difficulties on its SEN register. In the junior school, basic screening takes place in September within each year group. This helps to identify particular learning needs and enables teachers to pick up on students whose progress has stalled or is patchy, and for whom there might be an underlying difficulty. Further diagnostic testing then takes place to provide a broader picture of strengths and weaknesses, and a small number of students may receive some additional support with general literacy on a one-to-one basis. In the senior school, basic screening takes place when pupils enter year 7, and this is repeated at the start of year 8 so that any pupils who have arrived after the main intake can be tested. From the test results, pupils with untypical scores are observed carefully by all their teachers and further diagnostic testing may take place if a specific learning difficulty is suspected. Most pupils with SpLD are expected to follow a full curriculum, with reasonable adjustments being made in the context of classroom teaching. In exceptional circumstances, an adapted timetable will be provided – with learning support replacing the study of a second foreign language. One-to-one support is available every day before the start of school from an SEN specialist. Many of our SEN students are very successful both academically and in a wide range of extra-curricular activities.

What we say about the school - the full Good Schools Guide review

Headmaster: Since 2000, Mr Tim Turvey BSc FIBiol FLS (fifties). Read botany and zoology at University College, Cardiff. Came from The Hulme Grammar School, Oldham, where he spent the 1990s as deputy head and head from 1995 – 'Oldham's huge mix of urban, ethnic minority backgrounds was a big contrast with Chester.' Principal examiner for Nuffield A level biology from 1981 until 2001 and editor and author of various Nuffield biology textbooks. Commutes from Didsbury in Manchester where he lives with his wife (a principal manager at AQA). Keen churchgoer, BBC radio 'Pause for Thought' contributor and takes seriously the school's cathedral foundation and faith implications – 'we, as a community, are founded in faith'. Describes the main changes he has made in five years as being, 'initiating major improvements in and additions to the facilities of the school for the benefit of the pupils and the introduction of full co-education.' Pupils describe him as modern, with a driven approach. Mr Turvey is very enthusiastic about the recent admission of girls, 'we believe that educating bright girls and boys alongside each other is the best preparation for university and careers'. Some parents had mixed feelings though most embraced the changes enthusiastically.

Academic Matters: Strongly and unashamedly academic with consistently outstanding GCSE results – 91 per cent A or B grades, around 70 per cent As, very few Cs and only a handful below that. Outstanding at A level too with 30 students gaining three, four or even five A grades; a few Ds, Es and Us which school puts down to not pressurising pupils to choose subjects in which they are bound to excel and not insisting that pupils who have only mediocre prospects should leave. Active SEN provision with SENCo giving extra support before school. Parents describe school as 'not too pushy.' Head explains that an A at GCSE might indicate an A, B or C at A level and says that where A level grades are not what they should be it reflects the difficulties students face making the transition to A level study. Most pupils choose to take general studies AS level. Most popular, and most successful, subjects are maths and sciences. Pupils do well in Maths Challenge and some reach dizzy heights in the maths and physics Olympiads.

Games, Options, The Arts: Very strong rowing tradition (since 1877) with boathouse on the River Dee in city centre though recent coaching style doesn't appeal to all boys. Teams compete with universities and at Henley regatta etc and one of the recent Olympic eight was a pupil here. Boys proud of football, first XI players have hero status and match reports dominate school newsletter but rugby is also on the up. Heated indoor pool on site, acres of flat playing fields, an outstanding new all-weather pitch for hockey and soccer, six full and four half tennis courts and an annual fitness test for students, D of E, Combined Cadet Force, outdoor pursuits trips for first years and trips abroad aplenty – Italy for classics students, WW2 sites for history, geographers go all over Europe, language-related trips and skiing to Europe and North America.

Enthusiastic drama performances, four or five productions a year, enhanced by presence of sixth form girls. Pupils say art has taken huge leap for the better with new teacher and recent results show significant upward trend. Plenty of music activity, private instrument tuition and opportunities for involvement in cathedral worship. Parents like new brochure with forthcoming arts programme.

Background and Atmosphere: Founded by King Henry VIII in 1541, the school moved out of its city centre cathedral site in 1960. Plenty of air and space around the campus just inside Chester ring road where large car parks and bus bays (school bus services are organised by parents and shared by Queen's girls) lead to dignified central buildings and less elegant later additions. New art and design technology studios opened in summer 2004 and a new music school in spring 2005. The 'head's house' used to be exactly that but is now agreeable space for sixth form economics though, from the outside, is dated. But sixth formers say it has a nice atmosphere and love being set apart – 'we get priority at lunch too.' The sixth form block has common and private study rooms and a careers reference room. The common room has a newly introduced cafeteria service with seating to match – a foretaste of student life. Relaxed atmosphere with head of sixth in his room with door open and corridor full of chatting students during private study period. Super new 'Wickson' library named after previous head, over 10,000 books, 60 journals and daily papers. 'The librarians are helpful but they're strict about noise,' say pupils. Hooray! Circle of twenty computers for accessing info adjoins extensive IT suites. And at the heart of it all a beautifully planted quad with dramatic statues – 'that garden's only for the teachers,' pupils shrug.

Pastoral Care and Discipline: Head says that, despite prevailing youth culture in Chester, the school is drug free, 'although you never know what tomorrow will bring.' Pupils seem genuinely aghast at the question of having anything to do with drugs. Head says he believes alcohol is far more of a danger for today's youngsters, 'in a culture where smoking is very uncool they can still be naïve about drinking.' The school does appear genuinely friendly – parents think that new pupils joining any year are welcomed and present pupils say there's a great social life amongst students, which is encouraged by staff, who sit among the children in dining hall.

Removes in first year have prefect mentors to look up to, otherwise pupils say form tutors sort out problems and parents praise the accessibility of teachers, many of whom make personal numbers and voice mail available. An on-site school nurse is appreciated by parents, pupils and head. Head has strengthened links with cathedral, moving from what he calls a superficial spirituality to one which, 'in an unobtrusive way makes faith lived and talked about.' He has introduced two Christian Unions, weekly staff prayer meetings, a Christian parents' group and a significant input from boys in the cathedral on the first Sunday of each term. Pupils have noticed a change of emphasis in assemblies but say, 'he doesn't ram it down our throats.'

Pupils and Parents: The school reflects its catchment area and is predominantly white and middle class, with a few very wealthy Cheshire families represented. Pupils come from miles around, from far along the North Wales coast to areas south of Manchester. Pupils are self-assured, polite, friendly and unpretentious. Smart uniform with dark green, navy and gold striped blazer and sixth form attire only slightly relaxed. Since going co-ed in 2003, years 7, 8 and 9 have thirty per cent girls; 'very encouraging', says head, 'the girls are loving it and they're contributing hugely'. Still some joint ventures with Queen's, notably CCF.

Entrance: By examination at 11. Academic entrance scholarships reintroduced in September 2005 for pupils entering at 11. Every place has 1.6 applicants – 'we take from the top 25 per cent of ability,' say staff. Most seniors carry on into sixth form needing at least 7 GCSEs at a minimum of grade B and an A in prospective A level subjects, so a few are encouraged to go elsewhere for sixth form.

Exit: Most leavers go on to traditional universities to study a wide variety of subjects including film studies, aerospace engineering, equine and human sports and dairy herd management as well as the more traditional PPE, law, medicine and engineering. Thirteen to Oxbridge in 2005, lots to Nottingham, Manchester, Leeds and London. Notable OBs include comedy actor Hugh Lloyd and former M&S finance director Keith Oates, but, 'alas,' says head, 'no serious benefactors proffering huge endowments!'

Money Matters: Some bursaries available, after means-testing, for pupils of high academic ability.

Remarks: Friendly and unpretentious with great results and lots of opportunities. Head is revamping the infrastructure at the same time as encouraging deeper thinking on matters spiritual, in keeping with the school's cathedral foundation.

King's School, Rochester

Satis House, Boley Hill, Rochester, Kent, ME1 1TE

Tel: 01634 888 555

Fax: 01634 888 505

Email: walker@kings-school-rochester.co.uk

Website: www.kings-school-rochester.co.uk

• Pupils: 310. Boys outnumber girls 2:1 throughout the school • Ages: 13-18 • Religion: C of E • Fees: Day: pre-prep/prep £2,375-£3,460; senior £4,470 plus lunch. Boarding: prep £5,335, senior £7,520 • School status: Independent • Opendays: Second Saturday in October • School gender: Mixed • Day/boarding: Takes boarders

SEN provision

Detail:

Now provide for in school:

Mild: DYSL;

Others: EAL;

Experience of:

Mild: ADD; ADHD; EBD; DYSC; DYSP; HI;

Moderate: DYSL;

Others: SPD;

Summary: King's School is co-educational with selective entry and a wide range of ability. It is the school's avowed aim to satisfy the educational needs of all the children on the roll, regardless of ability. As part of this responsibility, we seek to identify children with special needs and to make suitable provision for them.

What we say about the school - the full Good Schools Guide review

Headmaster: Since 1986, Dr Ian Walker (fiftyish), hyperactive and charming Australian polymath whose PhD on Plato and string of degrees are complemented by his multilingualism, artistic and sporting enthusiasms and complete involvement with every aspect of his extraordinary school. Wife, super, ex-teacher and now a practising solicitor, warmly and closely involved with the school. Two children, both at university.

Head's passionate dedication to the school, its staff and pupils informed by powerful personal morality and exuberance which makes the highest demands – of no one more, it seems, than of himself. Loopy sense of humour as evidenced by his published collection of 'Howlers', available from the school.

Academic Matters: Extraordinary, because this is a school with a truly comprehensive intake. Takes at 4 years old pupils it keeps, with no academic weeding, throughout. Gets results comparable with the academically selective competition with an intake 70 per cent of whom would not make it into grammar school. 60 per cent A*/A/B at GCSE, 53 per cent A/B at A level. Special features: German taken from pre-prep level so pupils leave school bilingual, cross-over between the three schools on site so that younger children are taught by senior school teachers and vice versa, unusual emphasis and level of achievement in divinity, reflecting head's commitment, no rigid three science GCSE insistence though all three sciences on offer, flexible curriculum allowing for Russian, Irish and other languages to be studied and, across the board, very impressive results, getting the best from all pupils. Excellent individual support for children with special needs of all kinds. School not afraid to take on children that other schools would shy away from – and then get the best out of them.

Games, Options, The Arts: High standards in all sports especially rowing, fencing, rugby, hockey. Excellent outdoor facilities, less extensive hard surface areas. Wide range of options including wine tasting, bridge, home economics, CCF. Drama excellent despite lack of proper drama studio or special facilities. Music good and enthusiastically supported and includes various ensembles, classical, jazz and pop. School supplies choristers for cathedral choir. Outstanding art under inspirational teaching.

Background and Atmosphere: School inseparable from cathedral and chapter, to which the school buildings are integral. Ancient foundation, dating from 604, re-established in 1541 by Henry VIII, many classes take place in buildings of astonishing elegance and beauty. Sixth form centre in The College, 17th century gem in which new sixth form common rooms are panelled, painted, superbly furnished and immaculately kept, self-policed in this disciplined, though relaxed, atmosphere. School blends ancient with state-of the-art, having fully networked computer centres, direct satellite linked systems and a pioneering European Initiative. First rate new buildings include Chadlington House, stunning new pre-prep. Some older buildings in need of refurbishment and school well-aware of its responsibility to maintain its inheritance. Seven new buildings or major refurbishments in current head's fourteen year regime.

Pastoral Care and Discipline: Pastoral care via tutor system though pupils also encouraged to go to anyone in case of need and many feel comfortable going direct to the head. Clearly a well-run and happy school. Discipline and considerate conduct is emphasised and high standards of dress and behaviour are expected and achieved. Very warm, open and spontaneously polite pupils.

Pupils and Parents: Most pupils live within 10 miles of the school, Rochester, Chatham, Gillingham, Gravesend, Maidstone, Tonbridge, Sevenoaks. Ethnic and cultural mix comfortable with the unashamedly Christian ethic and atmosphere. Parents are warmly supportive and appreciative, especially of the school's clear commitment to the pastoral welfare of each pupil as well as to his or her academic achievement. Only 48 boarders (with room for more) – many happily from abroad – in delightful, family atmosphere, separate girls and boys boarding houses.

Entrance: Over-subscribed at all stages. Common Entrance or special entrance test for maintained sector candidates. Sixth form entry conditional on five GCSEs at A*-C, preferably B or higher in chosen A level subjects and especially if maths or sciences are to be studied. Most children start at 4 and stay until 18.

Exit: Virtually all to university to study the full range of academic and vocational subjects. A decent number to Oxbridge and more to the University of London colleges. Old Roffensians include the brothers John and Peter Selwyn Gummer (now Lord Chadlington,) the late actors David King and Dinsdale Landen, and many Services and industry chiefs.

Money Matters: Scholarships include cathedral choristerships for boys of 40 per cent tuition fees plus a reduction on music tuition fees, King's Exhibitions (from 11), up to five awarded annually, of 50 per cent of tuition fees; King's scholarships (at 13+), up to five awarded annually, of 50 per cent of tuition fees and five Minor King's scholarships of 25 per cent tuition fees. At least five of these for pupils from the maintained sector. Also one art, five music, an organ, and a sports scholarship on comparable bases. Governors' exhibitions, means-tested awards for able children from less well-off homes. Reductions for clergy, service personnel and siblings after the second child. Bursaries in case of sudden need.

Remarks: 'In theory we shouldn't survive,' says the head of his 'best performing comprehensive intake school in the country'. 100 applicants for 8 places at 11+ despite the formidable competition from 26 local grammar schools. Deserves to be far more widely known and appreciated.

KNIGHTON HOUSE SCHOOL

Durweston, Blandford Forum, Dorset, DT11 0PY

Tel: 01258 452 065

Fax: 01258 450 744

Email: enquiries@knighton-house.co.uk

Website: www.knightonhouse.dorset.sch.uk

• Pupils: 90 girls, of whom 75 board. Pre-prep with 33 children including 20 boys, and around 10 at any given moment in the nursery • Ages: 7-13; pre-prep 4-7; nursery 2+ - 3+ • Religion: C of E • Fees: Pre-prep £1,844. Prep: day £3,644; boarding £4,850 • School status: Independent • School gender: Mixed • Day/boarding: Takes boarders

SEN provision

Detail:

Centre of excellence for:

Mild: DYSL;

Moderate: MLD; DYSL;

Now provide for in school:

Mild: DYSC;

Moderate: DYSC;

Summary: Knighton House is a mainstream academic school. It provides tuition for children with mild to moderate learning difficulties in the areas of numeracy and literacy. The school has a learning support unit and staff are qualified to meet the needs of children with specific learning difficulties.

What we say about the school - the full Good Schools Guide review

Head: Since 2004, Mrs Claire Renton MA DipRE, a classicist. Mrs Renton took over after three years as deputy head at Perrott Hill in Somerset where she tutored the scholars and headed the classics and RS depts. Nominated in 2005 Tatler schools award for the best girls' prep school head. Classics remain her first love and she teaches both Latin and Greek to the senior pupils.

Entrance: Via own pre-prep or at seven or eight, informal interview plus report from previous school. Rather tougher quarantine period for ponies, who may be sent home after a trial period, 'mine was expelled after three weeks for kicking', said one pupil. Any child can come – more or less at any time – providing space is available.

Exit: Usually now at 13, to Sherborne, Bryanston, St Mary's Shaftesbury (popular with Catholics), but girls go anywhere and everywhere: all the top girls' schools feature in the list. Pre-prep boys go on to – mainly – Sandroyd, Clayesmore and the Old Malthouse – tranches of scholarships, though surprisingly, the boards only go back to the 1980s, which is a bit sad if children want to look up their parents or grandparents.

Remarks: Founded in 1950, by Christopher Booker's parents, this delightful, happy, unassuming school, is perched on a windy hilltop beside Bryanston's western gate surrounded by paddocks and games fields. Breezy garden with an orchard full of apples, greengages and plums. Rather boring old-rectory type house – said to be the dower house for Bryanston, but it seems unlikely – with usual carbuncular collection of add-ons. However, a new building containing two classrooms and a preparation room for the science lab has just been opened. This is phase one – more new classrooms are planned. Perched on the edge of Bryanston's west drive, the school makes much use of the Bryanston connection, not only because of the Booker association but the school uses their astroturf hockey pitches and swimming pool, as well as riding through their grounds.

Forget the elitist past, this school is now thoroughly integrated into the locality, with a raft of day girls, as well as pre-prep and nursery. Flexi-boarding available if required though twice the price of Sandroyd's up the road. Buses to Wareham and Shaftesbury area, most pupils come from a 20-mile catchment area. Certain proportion of non-Brits – never more than one or two per form. Good dyslexia provision, plus SEN, excellent, plus EFL as required. French from six, Latin from ten, Greek an option – if good at Latin, plus a whole raft of extras as you might expect.

Tiny classes, max 16/18, with some setting as required in maths; French from the early years and Latin. Regular half-termly assessments. Two libraries:

reference and fiction. State-of-the-art IT, girls all have their own e-mail, Spanish is a club; home economics is part of the curriculum (and posh it is too – with very low sinks, what do they do, the poor dears, when they try and cook at home?), dress-making (at last!) and touch-typing (ditto) the norm.

Difficult to decide which is the more important – the horsy factor or the music. The latter has (again rather boring) dedicated red-brick buildings, with recital room and masses of individual practice rooms. This is a school with a musical heritage (and should probably be a feeder for the Yehudi Menuhin School but that name has, surprisingly, not cropped up); squillions of different bands, and groups and an orchestra that 'sounds like an orchestra', says the head. Certainly, as we arrived, there was a flautist sounding like one but there was also a ride going out, with nary a pelham between them, and only one leading rein.

The much-loved red dungarees were disastrously changed from cotton to rather a nasty polyester – they hang very badly and don't fade. Now revamped 'best uniform' – red knitted jersey, checked blouse with Peter Pan collar and dark grey kilt. Cotton dungarees and grey cloaks are back.

This is a school which has weathered and adapted to the changes of a turned millennium; all the pupils, and girls in particular, are friendly, mutually supportive, many from the country. This is a school where they can stay relatively unsophisticated until they go to public school, though whether this is what the girls themselves want, in this, the 21st century, is anyone's guess. But a jolly useful school nonetheless, well-integrated with the local community.

Knowl Hill School

School Lane, Pirbright, Woking, Surrey, GU24 0JN

Tel: 01483 797 032

Fax: 01483 797 641

Email: info@knowlhill.org.uk

Website: www.knowlhill.org.uk

• Pupils: 45 pupils, 12 girls and 32 boys • Ages: 7-16
• Fees: £4,454 plus: speech therapy £334 per term; occupational therapy £334; Clubs £25/£30 per term. Some compulsory extras: trips, sports, and clubs
• School status: Independent • School gender: Mixed
• Day/boarding: Day pupils

SEN provision

Detail:

Now provide for in school:

Mild: DYSL; DYSP; HI;
Moderate: DYSL; DYSP; HI;
Severe: DYSL;

Experience of:

Mild: ASP; AUT; ADD; ADHD; EBD; DYSC; SpLD; VI;
Moderate: ADD; ADHD; EBD; DYSC; SpLD; VI;
Severe: ADD; DYSC; DYSP; SpLD;
Others: SPD; OCD; ODD; MSI; Sp&LD; Epi; Eat;

Summary: Knowl Hill is a co-educational day school for children between the ages of 7 and 16. It was founded in 1984 to teach children with specific learning difficulties (dyslexia). Pupils have specific learing difficulties (dyslexia) and may also have slight emotional and behavioural difficulties and may require either a modified or mainstream curriculum with support. The National Curriculum is followed in a normal classroom setting, in addition to which each child has individual tuition for specific areas of difficulty if needed.

What we say about the school - the full Good Schools Guide review

Principal: Since 2005, Mr James Dow Grant MA PGCE IE Dip, Dip DS Cert SpLD Cert Prof Std (fifties), spent 11 years at the school, four as deputy head. Pupils say, 'he's very nice, charismatic and clever; knows his stuff and what he's doing but he can be strict.' Hopes to continue to teach CDT and keep school moving forward and progressing.

Succeeds founder Mrs Angela Bareford AGSM Teachers Dip Ed AMBDA (Dys Inst Dip) IE Dip who started school in 1984 when she was unable to get help for her own dyslexic son (now in his 30s).

Academic Matters: Maximum class size eight but smaller groups and one-to-one as required. Good range of compact specialist facilities, science lab, small library, large room for assemblies and lunch (packed lunches only, healthy eating actively encouraged). All follow National Curriculum (modified as appropriate) and take Key Stage tests. No foreign languages though older pupils participate in conversational French. Senior pupils study for GCSEs or literacy and numeracy proficiency tests for those unable to cope with GCSE. Great emphasis placed on the multi-sensory, holistic programme for literacy skills (either Dyslexia Institute's multi-sensory literacy or their units of sound programmes). A similar approach is used in maths for those with dyscalculia. Integration of speech and language and occupational therapy is central to learning programme. The therapists go into and run some lessons – the SaLT runs social skills session and assists with English Speaking Board (ESB) preparation – helping pupils focus on voice production, breathing as well as organisation of language, vocab and memory.

Weekly thinking skills sessions help address any difficulties experienced with perceptual, sequencing and memory skills. Additional therapy, tailored to the needs of each child, is available to small groups or individually (extra charge). LEAs prefer blocks of therapy but school feels strongly (and is prepared to argue the case) that regular integrated support is more beneficial. All learn to touch-type (but active handwriting policy encourages good pencil grip and cursive writing) and school provides each pupil with a laptop computer (wireless networked). ICT playing an increasingly important role in teaching and learning – enhanced by use of interactive whiteboards. All have an IEP, regular reports and bi-annual testing supplemented by statutory annual review for those with statements or annual appraisal run along broadly similar lines for rest with regularly monitored and updated targets for all.

Games, Options, The Arts: Good facilities in new creative arts block for art, pottery, 3D, CDT and drama. Art a strength – 'some pupils have spatial difficulties but we show them tricks and teach techniques.' Drama important and used to give guidance, social training and act out day-to-day problems.' Limited sports on offer within school, principally football and basketball but good use made of local facilities. Compulsory educational trips including annual overseas visit (Italy this year) seen as integral and important to building confidence, encouraging independence, reinforcing sense of community, and developing social skills. A variety of clubs including choir, sports archaeology, IT, art, media studies, prep and electronics keeps pupils gainfully occupied at lunchtimes and after school. No sports fixtures or instrumental tuition at present (school hoping to address latter) but pupils have instrumental enrichment and a listening programme – use specific music to channel ideas and concentration. Good links with community and local army base provides outward-bound opportunities and PSHE support.

Background and Atmosphere: The charming, red-brick, former Victorian schoolhouse occupies a small but well-maintained site in a pleasant village location. Sympathetically extended over the years the compact but modern, pristine facilities adequately support the curriculum. Much thought has gone into all aspects of the school's development – even the playground is carefully divided – a yard for those needing to let off steam or simply enjoy a game of footie, a quiet area complete with fountain for those wanting to de-stress, a work/picnic area and a well-equipped adventure playground.

Pastoral Care and Discipline: 'Some children have spent a considerable amount of time out of school, it's important that we provide an empathic atmosphere and environment so we work hard to develop confidence and foster enthusiasm for school.' That doesn't mean misdemeanours go unchecked; a sliding scale of sanctions and detentions exists and the occasional pupil is excluded if behaviour merits it. A couple of permanent exclusions over past few years. 'We have to consider safety and well-being of all our pupils and balance that with the needs of the individual.' Merits and rewards aplenty, including collective rewards for the best class. Pupils very positive – 'if you need help you get it...it's like a family... Knowl Hill is the best thing that happened to me.' Pupils appreciate smallness of the school – 'you get more friends here because everyone knows each other.' Careers advice via Connexions. Regular counselling available (charged as an extra) or open door drop-in sessions (free). No complaints but pupils say they'd like to have a school council or similar for their views and suggestions.

Pupils and Parents: Children of multi-millionaires to those with minimal incomes but all rub along nicely. From a large catchment area Richmond, Farnham, Southall, Cobham, Weybridge, Gerrards Cross, Godstone. Majority are English but smattering from Germany, Sweden and Norway plus a few Americans referred from the two local American Schools. Most epitomise the severe dyslexic – they are appealing, they like talking, are creative but have significant problems with organising, sequencing etc. A significant minority have had very negative experiences of school life and some so traumatised by past experience that a graduated programme is used to integrate the child into school – 'we might start with the child attending for a couple of days a week or maybe just mornings – whatever it takes.' Parents very positive – 'it's made a tremendous difference, we just wish we'd sought out help sooner.'

Entrance: All pupils have to be dyslexic and may be dyspraxic. Additionally pupils may have hearing impairments, elective mutism, epilepsy, or mild to moderate emotional and behavioural difficulties requiring either a modified or mainstream (plus support) curriculum. Won't take those with severe behaviour problems and all accepted on a half-term's trial basis. Referrals may be made privately, by educational psychologists (EP) or by local education authorities (currently eight different LEAs refer pupils). Expected that prospective pupils will already have an EP report. Initially parents come to look round the school and have an interview with the head. 'Parents are often worried, upset and don't know where to go for help and advice – even if we can't help we can usually point them in the right direction.' If school thinks they can help they'll invite the child for a day visit to see how they integrate in class and in the school with speech and language and occupational therapists monitoring and assessing any specific needs. If appropriate, a place will be offered. Mainstream education often has a devastating impact on these children – 'they're bright and know a lot but they can't get it down on paper, that's where we come in.' School won't go to tribunals with parents – feel it's better to have an independent eye. Pupils come at almost any time though rarely in years 10 and 11. Hope is that after a few years they'll be streamed back into mainstream, either to an independent or state school. Waiting lists in younger years – always worth a try to get older ones in.

Exit: Majority to mainstream education or sixth form college.

Money Matters: Occasional means-tested bursary worth up to 50 per cent of fees.

Remarks: A caring school with a happy community feel; refreshes the parts other schools failed to reach.

THE LADY ELEANOR HOLLES SCHOOL

Hanworth Road, Hampton, Middlesex, TW12 3HF

Tel: 020 8979 1601

Fax: 020 8941 8291

Email: office@lehs.org.uk

Website: www.lehs.org.uk

• Pupils: 880 girls; all day • Ages: 7-18 • Religion: C of E

• Fees: Senior £3,401; junior £2,565

• School status: Independent • Opendays: Contact the Registrar

• School gender: Girls • Day/boarding: Day pupils

SEN provision

Detail:

Now provide for in school:

Mild: DYSL; DYSP;

Experience of:

Mild: SpLD; HI;

Others: DEL; Epi; Eat;

Summary: The school caters particularly well for gifted and talented children for whom our normal school curriculum is designed. Additional provision is made for the exceptionally gifted or talented child. The selective nature of the school entrance test means that all pupils are able to follow the same curriculum, but the school does provide short one-to-one courses of learning support, when needed, for those with specific learning difficulties such as dyslexia and dyspraxia, the cost of which is additional to the normal school fee. Pupils with physical disabilities can be accommodated depending on the severity of their condition: there will be wheelchair access to most parts of the school by September 2006. Special educational needs are always dealt with on an individual basis and enquiries about the level of provision that can be offered are welcome.

What we say about the school - the full Good Schools Guide review

Head: Since 2004, Mrs Gillian Low MA Oxon PGCE Cantab (mid forties), formerly head of Francis Holland NW1. Educated at North London Collegiate School, read English at Oxford, taught at various comprehensive schools, former deputy head of Godolphin and Latymer School. Approachable, down-to-earth. 'She's very warm and caring,' said a FH parent. Another commented that she will deal immediately with any concerns. Three children, all at independent schools.

Academic Matters: Undoubtedly, one of the top academic schools in the country. As one parent says, 'given the high level of intake, exam results ought to be good and they are.' Typical pass rate of 100 per cent A*-C at GCSE, with over 90 per cent of these at A*/A grades. Separate sciences more popular than the double award. Latin is popular. General studies compulsory for A level and average points per candidate including this subject is around 34; excluding this subject it is 26. About 70 per cent of grades are A at A level, with English literature, mathematics, biology and psychology being the most popular subjects. Not many do art and few do music but those who do obtain top grades. A parent says that great efforts are made to accommodate unusual combinations of subjects. In spite of terrific results (and probably because the school is an academic front runner), last head had no truck whatsoever with league tables. Clearly there is some exceptional teaching but one parent said that 'pupils do complain that some of the older teachers bore them rigid.' Not a school for slackers. A parent sums up academic life – 'pupils and staff have high expectations of their academic achievements and though it is not cool to be seen to work hard, a great deal of hard work goes on. Most pupils take this in their stride but it must be hard for the ones at the bottom of the class.'

Games, Options, The Arts: Great rowing school – the Millennium Boat House (opened by Sir Steve Redgrave) was a joint project with neighbouring Hampton School, enabling 80 boats to be stored; balcony with far-reaching views over the Thames at Sunbury, 'it would be the envy of any professional rowing club,' says one appreciative parent. For winter, there is lacrosse (lacrosse teacher plays for England, and three girls have recently played in the England squad) and netball (netball teacher played for England in Commonwealth Games 2002) and in the summer, athletics, tennis and rounders. Usual complaint from parents that sports are played to win and 'once the teams are picked, there is not much chance for the rest to represent the school.' Swimming in on-site heated pool. Fencing optional. Splendid new sports hall and trampolining especially popular. No compulsory PE in sixth form but options broaden to include other activities such as Real Tennis at Hampton Court, aerobics, jazz dancing and use of the climbing wall at Hampton School. Recent sports tours have been to the US and Australia.

Dedicated art block enjoys great natural light and shows high quality work. 'Art is done to a very high standard with some fabulous artwork up on the walls,' confirms an impressed parent. Good music – 350 girls have individual music tuition, a considerable number attaining grade 8, with wide variety of choice available. Instruments can be safely left at school. Lots of ensembles, orchestras and choirs. 'The pupil has to be keen,' says a parent, 'no one tells you to go to the practices.' Annual choral and orchestral concert with the boys at Hampton School. Speech and drama is optional extra and annual drama festival of plays by sixth formers (with participation from throughout the school) held with Hampton. Lots of clubs from Scrabble to Amnesty International. Young Enterprise groups in sixth form and CCF.

Background and Atmosphere: School dates from 1711, when it was established in the Cripplegate Ward of the City of London. Moved to Hackney in 1878 and then to its present site in 1936. It has to be said that the main building is not an aesthetic gem by any stretch of imagination, unless one has a special passion for the functional 1930s early Gaumont style, but art historians may appreciate the touches of art deco here and there. Set in the heart of suburbia in largely terra incognita for public transport – shares large school bus network with Hampton School, which means that those keen on after school activities may have a tricky and time-consuming journey home. 'Advantage is that at the end of the day the girls go home, so you don't see any sign of bored teenagers hanging around the school gates,' says a parent. Not that these girls would fall into the bored teenagers category – they are too busy working and doing after school activities.

Has a huge (for outer London standards) thirty acre site, which includes gardens, playing fields and many, mostly modern, additions to the original building. Of particular note is the splendid sixth form centre, which has its own library and where sixth form lessons are taken in most subjects, using small seminar rooms. Both upper and lower sixth have their own well-equipped and comfortable common rooms. The school's 'Statement of Purpose' reflects one of the earliest documents relating to the school. It aims (among other things) 'to produce young women of grace and integrity,' 'which', sighed the previous head, characteristically, 'can occasionally require nothing short of a miracle.' Very much a grammar school feel to the place, although it has never been a state school. The uniform is distinctly understated, being mostly grey, with flashes of cherry red; many skirts considerably above the knee and lots of chunky shoes in sight. In fact, the pupils are surprisingly a bit on the scruffy side – in some ways rather endearing – a change from all those prissy, not above the knee, hair tied back, bags must be black, girls' private schools. No uniform for sixth form – required to dress 'suitably'. Sixth formers can also bring their cars into school and park in their dedicated car park. Security is tight, all girls have swipe cards to gain access to site and buildings. Many parents appreciate the easy relationship with Hampton boys' school next door, 'it's a great leveller. If any LEH girls show signs of getting up themselves (as teenagers quaintly put it), the Hampton boys soon bring them down to earth,' says one parent.

Pastoral Care and Discipline: One mother says, 'I find the staff very considerate and open, with genuine kindness.' Another says: 'Staff are very highly motivated and get the best out of the girls and many of them are great characters.' The girls stay in the same form groups throughout the school until they enter the lower sixth, with four forms of around 24 girls each with a form tutor and deputy, although the tutors tend to change every other year. 14 tutor groups in the sixth form. The girls are bright and confident and a parent says that any trouble is soon nipped in the bud. The school encourages independence and self-reliance from day 1 – 'could be a bit daunting for new pupils who are having trouble adjusting to life in a big new secondary school,' says one parent. School counsellor available. Sixth formers can leave premises at lunchtime (some have driving lessons then) and invite Hampton boys into their common rooms (arrangement is reciprocal).

Pupils and Parents: Intake is mainly suburban, middle class from professional and middle management families; many first time buyers. Increasing numbers from the London postal districts but otherwise from Guildford, Esher, Richmond, Twickenham, Walton, Windsor and Weybridge. 'Definitely not a snobby school,' says a parent, 'you do not get the impression that parents are likely to show off their money – there aren't really any opportunities to do so.' Famous OGs include actresses Charlotte Attenborough and Saskia Reeves.

Entrance: By interview and examination at 11 in maths, English and a general paper. Over-subscribed and some girls do get dropped at interview stage. Intake is 100, around a third of whom enter from the junior school, via exam, but transfer not automatic. The rest tend to come from a wide selection of private preps including Newland House, Twickenham; Rowan, Claygate; Old Vicarage, Richmond; Bute House, Hammersmith and Queens Junior School, Kew; about 20 per cent from state primaries. £50 application fee and £500 reservation fee (refundable on completion of studies). At 16, entrance is by comprehension and analysis, maths and modern language(s) if appropriate, required standard at GCSE and satisfactory school report. About eight or ten places at sixth form level available to replace those who leave (see Exit). Registration should be by 1 November for entry to sixth form in following autumn term.

Exit: Virtually everyone to university – Oxford, Cambridge, Bristol and Leeds recently the favourites. Those who leave after GCSE tend to go to co-ed independent schools such as Westminster, Marlborough, Wellington or Charterhouse, or to sixth form colleges.

Money Matters: A few entrance bursaries are available for 11, based on the results of the entrance exam. A small number of scholarships for excellence in music or academic subjects. Some sixth form scholarships of up to 25 per cent of fees for the two year course – these are awarded on basis of performance in entrance exam.

Remarks: Top-notch academic, highly sought-after, girls' day school, run adeptly by a redoubtable head. Forget private tutoring for borderline candidates, academic expectations are high and it would not be a lot of fun struggling at the bottom of the lowest sets – choose somewhere else. Probably best suited to the outgoing, self-reliant type; the wilting wallflower and those in need of the gentle touch might find it hard to find their feet (and survive) unless they already have a talent to offer, for example, in music or sport. As one mother says, 'it's a 'go for it' school for a 'go for it' child.'

Latchmere Infant School

Latchmere Road, Kingston upon Thames, Surrey, KT2 5TT

Tel: 020 8546 6507

Fax: 020 8547 0187

Email: lti@rbksch.org

• Pupils: 268 boys and girls, all day • Ages: 3-7
• Religion: Non-denom • School status: State
• School gender: Mixed • Day/boarding: Day pupils

SEN provision

Detail:

Now provide for in school:

Mild: ASP; AUT; ADD; ADHD; EBD; DYSC; DYSL; DYSP; SpLD; HI; CP;

Moderate: ASP; ADD; ADHD; EBD; MLD; DYSC; DYSL; DYSP; SpLD; HI;

Others: CD; GEN; EAL; Sp&LD; DEL;

Summary: A wide range of SEN catered for, including growth hormone deficiency and unusual syndromes such as Prader-Willi. However we do not have the resources for severe cases requiring specialised help. Cater for a wide range of SEN within our resources but no specialist groups, other than withdrawal groups for a range of difficulties. We divide the whole school by ability for English and maths, this allows additional support for those who are struggling and extension material for high fliers. Lots of staff have SEN expertise. Speech and language help available. Fewer than 2 per cent of our children have one-to-one support funded by the LEA.

What we say about the school - the full Good Schools Guide review

Head: Mrs Anne Delaney BEd (Hons) MA no personal details – 'let's concentrate on the school,' she said. Not as touchy feely as some infant school heads, but a highly efficient operator (her professionalism would do credit to a senior school head) with great pride in her school and a welcoming smile on her face. 'She is very approachable,' said one parent.

Entrance: Latchmere and Fern Hill (qv) are the two top-notch, over-subscribed schools in N Kingston. For those who live equidistant between the two schools, it must be an agonising decision which to choose – 'I had to keep ringing both schools to find out how many parents had applied from which roads so that I could decide which one to put down as my first choice,' said one prospective parent. We're talking 'savvy' parents in this area, many could afford independent schooling at a pinch, but instead 'I want my child to be part of the local community.' Worth putting all your energies into getting a child into the nursery.

Exit: To Latchmere Junior – transition between the infant and junior school well organised through visits and a buddy system with year 5 children.

Remarks: A super infant school – the atmosphere of 'welcome' hits you even before you read the word in various different languages around the entrance hall. 'We chose the school because it's so open and friendly,' said one parent who's had three children there. Partnership with the school starts before the child does – 'our initial tour was very detailed so that we felt we were already part of the school,' said one new parent.

Key Stage 1 SATS results have fluctuated over the last few years but recently children have done well – many above the national average. However, head hates the divisive effect of league tables. Assessment procedures are very strong in the school and she believes they know the needs of their pupils.

Children enjoy lessons and are able to work independently and quietly from an early stage. 'High quality teaching is a strength throughout the curriculum,' said one mother. Opportunities for grouping by ability are timetabled into the day, so that all abilities can be dealt with including the very able and those with special needs. Good expertise in SEN. Full-time SENCo and both the head and the SENCo have advanced qualifications in SEN which includes dyslexia. Within the school there is also considerable expertise in dyspraxia, ADHD, and autistic spectrum disorder. Very few children need one-to-one support, but group support is much more widely employed. Approximately 24 children currently receive speech and language support from trained staff. All year 1 and 2 grouped by ability in English and maths, so most able are stretched and those experiencing problems helped in small group settings.

Particular curriculum strengths are art, music and sport. Dedicated art area and super art teaching – stunning artwork for all to see (which often wins awards). Music teacher comes in twice a week and runs a choir for year 2 – regular performances. School shares a covered swimming pool with the juniors.

Social education (to teach children how to be part of a community) starts in the nursery and is given much prominence. Pupils delightfully self-confident. Pastoral care is felt to be strength – 'my child's class teacher will tell me exactly what action has been taken if there is a problem,' remarked one mother.

Nursery in an attractive new building. Play areas packed full of every type of climbing equipment, quiet areas and games. School promotes healthy eating; children have the opportunity of cooking and eating a wide range of dishes to widen their experiences of different food – chips with everything is definitely not on the culinary menu here.

After school club offers childcare and curriculum extension activities exclusively for full-time infants and their siblings who attend the junior school. You get the feeling that the school would suffer financially – and thereby educationally – without the help of the parents. Loads of parents help in the school, while the parents' association concentrates on (hugely successful) fund-raising – a staggering £60,000 was raised to renovate the swimming pool with professional fund-raising help given for free.

LATCHMERE JUNIOR SCHOOL

Latchmere Road, Kingston Upon Thames, Surrey, KT2 5TT

Tel: 020 8546 7181

Fax: 020 8549 9182

Email: LTJ@rbksch.org

Website: www.latchmerej.kingston.sch.uk

• Pupils: 360 boys and girls, all day • Ages: 7-11

• Religion: Non-denom • School status: State

• School gender: Mixed • Day/boarding: Day pupils

SEN provision

Detail:

Experience of:

Mild: ASP; AUT; ADD; ADHD; EBD; DYSC; DYSL; DYSP; HI;

Moderate: MLD;

Others: SPD; EAL; Sp&LD;

Summary: Latchmere Junior School is a community school, and we aim to educate any child who lives in our community, whatever their barriers to learning, as long as it does not hinder the education of the majority.

What we say about the school - the full Good Schools Guide review

Head: Since 2003, Mrs Valerie Al-Jawad MA (forties), previously deputy head and has taught at the school for 17 years. SEN specialist. Married with two grown-up daughters. Clearly loves the school and is enormously proud of it, without in any way resting on her laurels.

Entrance: From infant school on same site. Three classes per year. Since maximum class sizes were introduced for Key Stage 1, school has decided to keep classes at 30 pupils, if possible.

Exit: About 50 per cent of children to Grey Court School in Ham, the nearest state secondary school, with others to various Kingston state secondary schools. Sizeable number (up to 20) accepted each year at the highly selective Tiffin grammar schools. Handful to local independent day schools (mostly Kingston Grammar and Surbiton High).

Remarks: Latchmere and Fern Hill (qv) are the shining stars in North Kingston and beyond. Both achieve excellent results and have ferociously loyal parents, who will not hear a word said against their particular school. Two things make Latchmere stand out from other primary schools: exceptionally wide-ranging curriculum and emphasis on social skills in a broad sense.

Breadth of learning, according to the head, is what enables the school to achieve highly in the SATS tests: well above national average. Specialist teachers for art, music, social skills and French; more able linguists offered either German or Spanish. French taught from year 3; annual trips to European schools ensure a much higher standard of linguistic ability and awareness than amongst most primary schoolchildren. However, 'Let's not pretend they become great linguists,' says one dad. Parents generally are impressed by the professionalism and teamwork shown by the staff – several male teachers – and they feel that on the whole they can talk to the class teacher about individual problems. One parent described how the brighter children are given extra challenges: head gives examples of science days, citizenship conferences, maths master classes at Tiffin Girls' and Science at Greycourt.

Currently, about 50 children with special needs. These needs range from dyslexia, dyspraxia, autistic spectrum disorder to global delay. Eleven teaching assistants, including two 'higher level', who help children, together with the SEN teacher. Ten children with EAL have special provision two sessions per week.

Specialist art teacher and art room produce outstanding work, of a standard normally expected from pupils several years older. Numerous opportunities for music: through class teaching from the specialist teacher and instrumental tuition from peripatetic teachers. The school boasts two choirs and an orchestra.

Sport is strength, overseen by one of the few advanced skills teachers for PE. Heated indoor swimming pool (shared with the infants) in use from spring to autumn, large grass playing fields across the road, in addition to own playground space for hard courts. Regularly wins sporting competitions in the borough-many cups proudly displayed in the hallway. Sports day is a major event – every child's achievements earning points towards the team. More than 25 after school clubs, also plenty of after school sports which are heavily over-subscribed. Indoor sports hall planned, to be shared with the community.

Social skills programme very evident in the school: friendship bench in the playground 'it must feel good for a child feeling upset at playtime to have somewhere to go and someone to talk to,' one parent remarked – and pupil-written rules in the classrooms. Positive discipline promoted by pupils learning to take responsibility for their own actions through social skills programme. Makes a real difference, as much for the older child learning to mediate as for the child being helped. School council treated as important body – pupils want to gain a place.

No one could say that the buildings are particularly smart (but there is a programme of improvement). Outdoor play space divided into areas for different activities, both quiet and sporty, lovely signposts pointing children in the right direction: eg 'the enchanted wood' – an area of trees, paths and benches with a playhouse nestling at the end, there is also a vegetable garden, an area for ball games as well as good climbing equipment.

Unusually for the borough of Kingston, hot lunches are available – and of a surprisingly high quality. 'They actually seem to care about food here,' a father said in a surprised tone of voice. General communication with parents excellent and they are made to feel a vital part of the school. The head produces a newsletter every week, and governors' annual report written in an informative but informal style. Breakfast club, for parents with early morning commitments and a holiday club which is open to all the local schools and very well attended.

LATYMER PREP SCHOOL

36 Upper Mall, Hammersmith, London, W6 9TA

Tel: 020 8748 0303

Fax: 020 8741 4916

Email: mlp@latymerprep.org

Website: www.latymerprep.org

• Pupils: 160 girls and boys; all day • Ages: 7-11
• Religion: Non-denom • Fees: Prep £3,625
• School status: Independent • Opendays: September and November • School gender: Mixed • Day/boarding: Day pupils

SEN provision

Detail:

Now provide for in school:

Mild: ASP; ADD; ADHD; EBD; DYSL; DYSP; HI; VI; CP;

Moderate: ASP; ADD; EBD; DYSL; DYSP; HI; CP;

Severe: HI;

Others: CD; PD;

Experience of:

Mild: DYSC;

Moderate: DYSC;

Others: OCD; ODD; Epi; Eat;

Summary: The Junior School of Latymer Upper School, Latymer Prep shares its SEN provision with the senior school. A range of SEN needs are catered for, including dyslexia, dyspraxia, ADHD and Asperger's syndrome. We also have experience of dealing with chidlren with significant hearing loss and limb amputation. We have a learning support unit, as well as a school counsellor who deals with learning needs as well as broader social, emotional and familial issues.

Children are monitored throughout their time at the school. If we become concerned about a child's progress an initial assessment is conducted by the learning support unit. The school can arrange for more detailed assessments if some difficulty is indicated, though parents are expected to pay for these more-detailed assessments.

Advice is provided to teachers on how to support those with SEN, based upon the Support Unit's own evaluation as well as any additional information and analysis provided by parents and psychologists. Children with ADHD or Asperger's are provided with in-class support but we are unable to provide full, long-term in-class support.

It is worth mentioning, perhaps, that whatever a child's SEN, he or she must be of sufficient academic ability to be able to meet the demands of our curriculum. Those with SEN who would benefit from additonal time in our Entrance Assessment are allowed an additonal 25 per cent extra time, providing this request is suported by a psychologist's report.

What we say about the school - the full Good Schools Guide review

Head: Mr S P Dorrian BA (previously head of English and head of years 7 and 8 in the senior school).

Entrance: Maths, English and verbal reasoning exams at 7-plus interview.

Exit: Virtually all go on to the senior school. Very occasionally parents advised to move their child to a less academic establishment.

Remarks: Beautifully-situated building with views over the Thames from one side and lawns from the other side, plus all the senior school facilities. Has broadened the activities available since going co-ed eg circus skills as well as football at playtime. 'We have some very unsporty boys who spend all their time on stilts.' Mixed teams for all sports, dance also available – 'the boys love it'. Curriculum enriched by eg looking at famous women in history. Italian from year 3 and French in year 6. Broad curriculum benefits from not having to work towards Common Entrance.

SEN department liaise closely with the senior school; currently ten boys with statements of needs plus ten more, any pupils with suspected problems are given 'a battery of tests' to suss out their problems, school can deal with mild to moderate dyslexia et al, but if pupil has 'severe' dyslexia then parents are advised to get external help (school has neither the staff nor the time to spare). Not frightened of Asperger's – one boy currently with full-time mentor part paid for by the school and part by the parents, and can deal with moderate physical problems, CP, ADHD, profoundly deaf etc. Chaps who come armed with edpsych's reports get 25 per cent extra time in their entrance exam. Two fully trained and dedicated staff, one-to-one help, school will 'pick up and run' with pupils, but must be able to access mainstream.

LEEDS GRAMMAR SCHOOL

Alwoodley Gates, Harrogate Road, Leeds, West Yorkshire, LS17 8GS

Tel: 0113 229 1552
Fax: 0113 228 5111
Email: info@lgs.leeds.sch.uk
Website: www.leedsgrammar.com

• Pupils: 1,380 boys • Ages: 4-18 • Religion: Non-denominational • Fees: Junior school £1,683-£2,280; senior school £2,796 • School status: Independent • Opendays: October, November, January and June; sixth form January. See school website for dates • School gender: Boys • Day/boarding: Day pupils

SEN provision

Detail:
Now provide for in school:
- Mild: DYSC; DYSL; DYSP; HI; VI; CP;
- Moderate: DYSC; DYSL; DYSP; HI; CP;
- Severe: DYSC; DYSP; CP;
- Others: DEL; Epi; PD; Eat;

Experience of:
- Mild: ASP; ADD; ADHD; EBD; SpLD;
- Moderate: ASP; ADD; ADHD; SpLD;
- Severe: ASP;
- Others: SPD; EAL;

Summary: At Leeds Grammar School, we are aware that sometimes able pupils may have special learning difficulties, notably those associated with dyslexia and dyspraxia. Our policy is to welcome such pupils here. From our experience, these boys make good progress in the Leeds Grammar School environment, which is both structured and supportive.

In September 2001, we introduced a screening programme for all year 3 and year 7 pupils (as well as all new boys to the school) to identify learning difficulties. This is conducted by our specialist dyslexia teacher who is also responsible for teaching boys who have been identified. This teaching is in small groups or individually, usually on a weekly basis. Regular reports and feedback is given to parents and teachers to establish an integrated support strategy. This is part of the LGS curriculum provision and there is no extra cost to parents.

In addition, any boys who have already been identified as dyslexic before entering LGS are assessed by our specialist teacher and then offered extra support lessons where appropriate.

Please direct any queries to our learing needs coordinator, Mr Andrew Bridgewater, who will be happy to discuss related matters with you

What we say about the school - the full Good Schools Guide review

Headmaster: Since 1999, Dr Mark Bailey (early forties), read history at Durham and Cambridge. Previously Fellow in History at Caius, Cambridge, then at Corpus Christi (including some bursarial duties). Author of four books on medieval England, played rugby on the wing for England between 1984 and 1990. Wife works as freelance Human Resources consultant; young son and daughter. Unusual (no school experience) but highly successful appointment. A committed meritocrat, 'hugely ambitious for school' he says, wedded to importance of a firm academic basis for all-round education. Very visible round the place (teaches year 7 history, shadows pupils, visits lessons). Consensual leadership style – including listening seriously to pupils' views – insists on staff taking responsibility – 'HM's job is to articulate the way forward and trust others to get on with it'. Strong yet affable personality, say approving parents; he clearly relishes the challenge of his career change of direction, in a brand new school (see below).

Will be head of the merged school when the combination with Leeds Girls' High School goes ahead in July 2007.

Academic Matters: Well up the league tables; results compare favourably with similar selective grammar schools – negligible failures at A level, average 70 per cent at A/B grades, similar record at GCSE. Not a hot-house, however; any boy who passes the entrance procedure should cope, with impressive staff help. There is a real sense of academic purpose about the place and all subjects share in enviable results. Pupils noted in 1999 ISI report as 'smart, engaged and eager to learn'.

Maximum class size to GCSE is 25, with many sets at about 20; subjects almost entirely setted from year 9. Teaching mainly traditional but supported by up-to-date IT and library facilities, encouraging self-directed learning. Dual award science for all; brightest sets get beyond GCSE before year-end. All do RS to GCSE as an integral element in PSE. French, German, Latin and Greek offered. Up to five ASs per student in sixth form, boys 'encouraged' to do the lot (about 60 per cent do). Modern science block with 17 specialist labs; dedicated suites for all subjects. All boys screened for dyslexia on entry; some help given thereafter.

Staff commitment is enormous – half of them have 20+ years of experience and about a quarter have been at LGS since the 1970s. The challenge involved in a move to a completely new school seems to have invigorated those who might otherwise be fading in late career. Also a sufficient number of keen young things. One fifth women staff. Head insists on teachers 'living values they profess to teach'.

Games, Options, The Arts: Extensive windswept playing fields, with room to expand, sports hall and squash courts, swimming pool. Sport is important – strong reputation in rugby (frequent representation at county level and beyond) and cricket (this being Yorkshire, the 1st XI tend to moonlight in the tough world of league cricket). Soccer recently introduced. Many other team and individual games on offer. A lot of drama goes on – there is a studio theatre – and music has always been vigorous in this very musical city; choirs and orchestras all over the place. Plenty of opportunity beyond the curriculum for creative activities stemming from art and DT and the usual spread of clubs and societies.

Visits to the outdoor centre in splendidly wild Teesdale form part of every pupil's curriculum. Also on offer are the voluntary CCF, Scouts and the D of E Scheme.

Background and Atmosphere: In 1552 Sir William Sheafield left £14.13s. 4d. to found a school, 'for all such young scholars, youthes and children as shall come to be taught, instructed and informed'. New premises were found in 1624 and then, in 1857, increasing numbers prompted a further move to a site a mile from the city centre, with confident ecclesiastical buildings – now part of Leeds University – designed by EM Barry (brother to the then headmaster and a member of the famous architectural family). In 1997, renewed pressure of numbers and curriculum brought the courageous decision under Dr Bailey's predecessor to build a completely new school on the northern edge of Leeds. The result is a very handsome set of buildings, 'a blend of function and quality', designed by an architect who did imaginative work at the previous site. Vital historical bits from the old school are incorporated, thanks to the efforts of its extraordinary teenage historian. Few if any major schools start with an advantage like this (visitors are wafted by lift from reception to the elegant administrative area and invited to admire the campanile, piazza and porte-cochere). Purpose-building does not come cheap but expanded numbers and stringent financial control now mean that the school's future looks secure.

Clearly everyone got a shot in the arm from having to reinvent themselves on a fresh site; now settled down into a determined atmosphere which is also civilised, to a degree unusual in a large city boys' school (though of course generous and well-lit circulation space helps). The students seem genuinely proud of the place and look after it (though the sixth form centre is beginning to look a touch tatty). Rare inadequacies like art provision are being remedied. Confidence buzzes in the air and so it should.

Pastoral Care and Discipline: Traditionally form-based, with horizontal divisions into two-year sections; also all-through houses, mainly for sporting and other competitions. Chaplain offers counselling to boys of all religions. General discipline firm but understanding; key figure here is long-serving and universally admired deputy head.

Pupils and Parents: From Leeds and a wide arc to the north; significant proportions of boys of minority ethnic backgrounds reflecting the area's cultural diversity. Many professional families, especially doctors. A booming region but the school doesn't serve only the rich: bursary fund on its way to a second million pounds. Parents generally supportive and probably grateful – this is the best boys' school in the area. Old boys include Barry Cryer, Tony Harrison, Gerald Kaufman MP and Colin Montgomerie (who has given a sports-weighted bursary) and Ricky Wilson (Kaiser Chiefs).

Entrance: Mostly from local primary schools, who are pretty keen (but state secondary provision in Leeds is hardly an attraction), some from prep schools. Selection by in-house assessment from junior school, exam + interview + report at 10 to 13, interview + 5 Bs at GCSE for sixth form. Places occur at other ages from time to time. More than two applicants per place overall.

Exit: Nearly all go (predictably) to higher education: 15+ a year to Oxbridge, otherwise overwhelmingly to Ivy League northern universities (21 to Newcastle in 2001), many to medical school, also history and English. Gap years popular.

Money Matters: Up to three scholarships at 11, plus a rising number of bursaries at 11 and 16 (ongoing fundraising to increase these) to encourage bright boys from low income families.

Remarks: Excellent all-round school under strong and clear-sighted leadership, greatly enjoying its new life at Alwoodley Gates. No reason why both quiet and pushy should not prosper here, provided they are determined to join in and get the work done. There's still an element of West Riding grittiness about but the school increasingly looks more cultured and sophisticated than its competitors.

Merging with Leeds Girls' High School in July 2007 – not clear yet what the detailed implications of this are.

LEIGHTON PARK SCHOOL

Shinfield Road, Reading, Berkshire, RG2 7ED

Tel: 0118 987 9600
Fax: 01189 879 625
Email: admissions@leightonpark.reading.sch.uk
Website: www.leightonpark.reading.sch.uk

• Pupils: 450 girls and boys; 163 board • Ages: 11-18 • Religion: Quaker (all faiths welcomed) • Fees: Senior: boarding £6,950; weekly boarding £6,196; day £4,618. Junior: boarding £5,906; weekly boarding £5,267; day £3,926 • School status: Independent • Opendays: September as well as a monthly open morning and also individual meetings with head are available • School gender: Mixed • Day/boarding: Takes boarders

SEN provision

Detail:
Centre of excellence for:
Mild: DYSL;
Moderate: DYSL;
Severe: DYSL;
Now provide for in school:
Mild: DYSC; DYSP;
Moderate: DYSC; DYSP;

Summary: Leighton Park School currently offers specialist support for a number of pupils in the individual learning centre. This is provided by four well-qualified teachers, who give one-to-one help on a regular basis. Other pupils benefit from the weekly spelling group. Pupils receive support from the centre for dyslexia and similar learning difficulties, individually arranged and in close co-operation with their subject teachers. All pupils are screened on entry to the school, to determine whether additional support is appropriate. Study skills, including identifying the individual learning style, revision, organisation and mind-mapping are examples of different strategies used to help with pupils' learning.

At Leighton Park, everyone understands that pupils will have distinctive learning styles: the community fully recognises how important it is that dyslexic pupils should feel fully part of school life, with their needs openly understood and supported. Pupils often drop in to the centre for a chat, or for additional pastoral or academic support. ILC pupils regularly achieve outstandingly successful results in public examinations, and of course play a full part in the rich variety of school life outside the classroom.

SEN questionnaire details added by GSG.

What we say about the school - the full Good Schools Guide review

Head: Since 1996, Mr John Dunston MA AIL (fifties), a Churchill fellow educated at Cambridge and York universities with a degree in modern languages. The only Jewish headmaster chosen for two Quaker schools (previous headship was Sibford). Wife teaches at a local prep, two children, son is a pupil. A likeable man and diplomat manqué who accompanied the school choir on USA trip (sings baritone).

Academic Matters: For 7 consecutive years, students achieved 97 per cent or more passes at A level (99 per cent 2005). 66 per cent A/B grades at A level in 2005. Almost half the A level students take maths, and about a third physics or chemistry. Unlike the discrepancy seen in national figures, boys here perform as well as girls. Sciences taught separately as three subjects. GCSEs; 95 per cent achieved five or more A*-C, with 35 per cent at A*/A. Pupils averaged nine passes each. Religious studies, called 'beliefs and values', includes the philosophy of Quakerism. Individual learning centre (mainly for dyslexia) with highly skilled staff. New multimedia languages centre opened September 2005.

Games, Options, The Arts: An impressive list of county athletes, runners, hockey, netball and rugby players. A rugby and hockey South Africa tour made time for bush excursions and ocean safaris. Individual success at ice dance, swimming, world-class sailing. Wide choice of hobbies include ceramics, electronics, good causes, Duke of Edinburgh, photography, textiles, plus wide choice of sports and musical groups. Young Enterprise is an ambitious throng.

Choir and orchestra tour Europe regularly. A successful US tour to Philadelphia performed Fire and the Hammer – a musical written by the school's music director. 100 pupils learn a musical instrument, some to grade 8, a few to diploma. Timetabled lessons. Practice before school/lunch hour/evenings. Jazz band in finals of Music for Youth at South Bank. New music technology studio. Masses of cultural exchanges – recently with a lycée in Nantes; Barcelona, Hamburg, Athens and joint ventures with other Quaker schools. Adventure training trips recently include Ecuador (sixth form), skiing in Canada and Pembrokeshire (year 8). A level art trip to European capitals.

Background and Atmosphere: A welcome oasis of greenery, calm and gracious buildings amidst the hustle and bustle of Reading's maze of tarmac, cheek by jowl with the University of Reading in 60 acre parkland. Though not as ancient as most other Quaker schools, LP began as a public school in 1890 (though there are links with Grove House Tottenham which dates earlier) with the specific intention of educating scholars for Oxbridge. Girls were added in 1975. Boarding houses, some smart as a whistle, some a tad dowdy, but Fryer House where 11-13-year-olds live is a lively, warm environment with lots of space for recreation/prep/outdoor activities housed in a wonderful self-contained building – a three minute walk from main campus – recreational café area and skateboards/roller blades appropriately in evidence. New Dining room 'Oakview' opened October 2004, offering wide choice of high quality meals for the whole school community (breakfast, lunch and tea) plus sixth form cafe. Library to die for in the oldest building with nine separate rooms, themed artful displays prepared by a librarian who lives to make people want to go in there and read.

Pastoral Care and Discipline: Dedicated older staff inject a great deal of warmth and behind-the-scenes support. Lots of effort, so not much division between day pupils and the rest. 'Day boarders' stay for evening meal and supervised prep if required; breakfast also available if needed. All pupils participate in residential week of team building/adventure training. Anyone bringing drugs onto premises permanently excluded. Alcohol is banned.

Pupils and Parents: All major faiths represented here. 20 per cent from overseas and a sprinkle of expats but mainly from Berkshire, Oxfordshire, north Hampshire and Bucks. Only 10 per cent staff and pupils Quaker. All seem confident and vital. Dress code for senior school, uniform for years 7 and 8. No Saturday lessons so many of the boarders are weekly, hence exodus on Friday nights though much to do for those remaining. Old Leightonians: Sir David Lean, Sir Richard Rodney Bennett, Jim Broadbent, Michael Foot, Lord Caradon, Lord Frederick Seebohm (who reformed social services) and a fair clutch of MPs, Rowntrees, Cadburys, Clarks, Reckitts, Morlands and Frys.

Entrance: Tests autumn and spring for year 7-10 (though alternate dates can be set if needed); entrance tests include maths, English, non-verbal reasoning. Pupils chosen on previous report, interview and reference from current head. At sixth form about 35 enter from outside with at least five A-Cs with A*-B grades in chosen subjects.

Exit: Most go to universities (often getting firsts). Few leave at 16 for sixth form colleges.

Money Matters: Several major and minor awards. Means-tested bursaries. Friends' schools' bursaries given to those with Quaker parents. David Lean Foundation awards one annual scholarship for 100 per cent of day fees, for academic excellence.

Remarks: The feel of a busy London day school on a mini-university campus. Strong moral code and self-esteem.

LENZIE ACADEMY

Myrtle Avenue, Kirkintilloch, Lenzie, G66 4HR

Tel: 0141 776 6118

Fax: 0141 777 8121

Email: office@lenzieacademy.e-dunbarton.sch.uk

Website: www.lenzieacademy.org.uk

• Pupils: 1425 boys and girls (roughly 50/50 split); all day
• Ages: 11-18 • Religion: Non-denom • School status: State
• School gender: Mixed • Day/boarding: Day pupils

SEN provision

Detail:

Now provide for in school:
- Mild: HI;
- Moderate: HI;
- Severe: HI;

Experience of:
- Mild: ASP; ADD; ADHD; DYSL; DYSP;

Summary: Staying mum. A pity – first class inclusion and special provision for the deaf. SEN questionnaire details added by us.

What we say about the school - the full Good Schools Guide review

Rector: Since 1997, Mr Roderick (Roddy) McLelland BSc PGCE (fifties), who first came to the school as head of maths in 1985 and was previously assistant rector. He started his teaching career at Paisley Grammar, followed by five years at Williamwood High. Educated at John Neilson Institution in Paisley (now part of Paisley Grammar), studied maths at University of Strathclyde and did his PGCE at Jordanhill College of Education. Married with three children, two of whom are at uni; his daughter is still at Paisley Academy, where his wife also teaches.

A pro-active, open-door head, friendly and helpful, but very much an iron fist in a velvet glove. (Were the charming articulate pupils who had recently won the YE local final and were due to appear in Edinburgh shortly who came to borrow the trophies primed?? – but we think not, the encounter was too relaxed and natural.) He also has a splendid sense of the ridiculous. Mr McLelland runs the school with a management team of six whom we met for coffee – much talk of chocolate biscuits, each contribution examined with obvious delight, and much use of walkie talkies to keep in contact throughout the day – the bell at the wrong time was the concern during our visit – the first day of Standard Grades exams. Head keen for pupils to enter as many competitions and extra-curricular activities as possible, lots of celebrations of achievements of citizenship. A rector who believes in carrots rather than sticks, impressive. This is a school moving as one.

Academic Matters: Max class size currently 28ish, with 20 for practical classes. Five new heads of departments appointed recently: no problems with getting top class staff. Huge range of Standard Grades on offer; three sciences. Good take up of French and German, impressive variety of exchanges at junior level and two week work experience placements for older pupils in 5th and 6th years. Head hopes to add Spanish; Italian taken at Intermediate (on the wish list for Higher). Standard Grades the norm, but Intermediates available too, 18 Advanced Highers on offer, 23 Highers: subjects include tourism, food technology (looked and smelt delicious) information systems, computer studies and business management – all the usual suspects found in some, but by no means all, of the top end of the independent sector.

A magnet school: pupils from other (state) schools come to Lenzie to study Highers that are not available in their own school. Stunning computer studies results at all levels, geography is also particularly strong ('progressive' says the rector), interactive whiteboards much used. Good use too, of the eight computer suites, for teaching as well as IT. Psychology is taught by distance learning – the SCHOLAR programme, provided by Heriot Watt University. Maths results strong across the board, school makes much use of the Glasgow Maths Association lectures and joins with Strathclyde both for maths and using their biology lab for DNA work. 'Welcome Host' customer service course.

Dedicated special needs team (this is an inclusive school) with half a dozen profoundly deaf children happily integrated, some of them with special interpreters who sit in class with them. (The East Dunbartonshire Council Sensory Service was relocated here some four years ago.) 120 pupils do not have English as their first language and extra help is available. Homework club at lunchtime and supported study classes post school, 200 pupils regularly stay on – when pupils can access the ICT suites. Smashing library, with roll of shame for sixth formers who have overstayed their allotted book time; library has computers too, and pupils have a say in what books are stocked. Altogether a superb set-up.

Games, Options, The Arts: New sports hall built four years ago, not quite as big as anticipated – a top floor was on the original plan – but financial constraints meant that this stunning building is perhaps not as useful as anticipated. Sports facilities are 'slightly limited' but good links with local sports clubs; rugby, football, volleyball (enthusiastic coach on staff) plus hockey, slightly damp looking athletics track in grounds, cross-country and regular trips abroad with a fund to help those who couldn't otherwise afford it. Basketball, golf, dance, sailing – they win races even though the school has no boat.

Jolly art room, but no great airy windowed space to paint in, though good and interesting work. 'Strong art and design' says the rector, with pupils entering local competitions: ceramics as well as flat art. Good computer interaction, CAD available and nice line in CDT. Drama extra-curricular, and post school the school competes successfully in national competitions, but music highly integrated with huge department on top of the new wing, good representation in the West of Scotland youth orchestra, lots of little bands and excellent and exciting concerts, the Christmas concert particularly popular. Good jazz, keen public speaking, superb YE – since pre Jamie Oliver they have had a healthy food tuck shop (bottled water and nutrigrain bars); head hopes that he can persuade East Dunbartonshire to remove the current e-number dispensing machines during the summer (it will). Clubs post school and at lunchtime for everything, chess popular plus maths, debating and sport, fashion shows. Staff stay on unpaid. Tremendous charity input, £10,000 a year for Children in Need (wow!) plus Comic Relief, and the Tsunami appeal. Keen on World Challenge: Australia, Ecuador, Costa Rica, loads of fund-raising and good for self-sufficiency.

Background and Atmosphere: Founded in 1886 as Lenzie Academy, it was originally a private school started by Donald McQuarrie, based in what is now the Primary school on the main street, and moved to the current site nearby in 1960s. Surrounded by mixed housing, Victorian villas abut a large housing estate, and games pitches. Good wide corridors in all but the latest wing, where a one way system has been installed. Based round a slightly tatty quad, needs a face lift, with a tiny dining room which might suit fifty pupils on a good day. Uniform de rigueur, but some slightly surprising hair styles amongst the male of the species: pony tails and strawberry hair to name but two we spotted. Effective school council – year groups meet with staff and raise matters of concern (hence the padlocked lockers for each student), vibrant interactive house competitions, regular school assemblies, but not perhaps as much religious input as there might be (of any kind). New building includes provision for the disabled.

Pastoral Care and Discipline: Strong and effective PSE, this is a school with zero tolerance for bullying and abusive behaviour. A number of exclusions, but pupils know where they stand. Permanent exclusions are rare, though the occasional parent prefers to remove their offspring rather than have them excluded – perhaps one every two or three years. Sixth year pupils act as mentors for younger ones, helping with reading and dealing with minor bullying issues – they receive training from Childline.

Pupils and Parents: Loads of professionals. Decent middle class ethos prevails, mass from Glasgow, unis and local hospitals with a fair number of ethnic minorities whose mothers are nurses and fathers training for the ministry. In Mirror speak this is leafy Lenzie; school has four dedicated primary schools, but currently takes pupils from over 140 primaries and regularly has over 550 placement requests. Pupils come from nearby Torrance, Bishopbriggs, East Dunbartonshire, North Lanarkshire (the train station is handy). Fearsome parents association.

Entrance: Either automatic from dedicated primaries or by placement requests. School has strong links with local primaries; SEN staff and guidance staff spend time at the primaries during the summer terms. Every pupil coming to the school receives a letter of introduction from a current first year pupil telling them what it is like. Incoming pupils spend a two day induction period in the school following a specimen timetable.

Exit: Some leave post Standard Grades, some, but not a lot, arrive. Sixth form visit the Glasgow careers forum, 65 per cent or so to universities, more to FE colleges, and a regular trickle of three or four to Oxbridge, there is a local seminar for senior students.

Remarks: Smashing school, academically and socially strong, but buildings could do with a serious Laurence Llewellyn Bowen makeover.

Lord Williams's School

Oxford Road, Thame, Oxfordshire, OX9 2AQ

Tel: 01844 210 510

Fax: 01844 261 382

Email: Headteacher.4580@lordwilliams.oxon.sch.uk

Website: www.lordwilliams.oxon.sch.uk

• Pupils: 2,190 boys and girls; all day • Ages: 11-18

• Religion: Non-denom • School status: State

• School gender: Mixed • Day/boarding: Day pupils

SEN provision

Detail:

Now provide for in school:

Mild: ASP; AUT; ADD; ADHD; EBD; DYSC; DYSL; DYSP; HI; VI; CP;

Moderate: ASP; AUT; ADD; ADHD; EBD; MLD; DYSC; DYSL; DYSP; HI; VI; CP;

Severe: AUT; ADD; ADHD; EBD; DYSL; CP;

Others: CD; ODD; GEN; PMLD; EAL; Sp&LD; DEL; Epi; PD; Oth; Eat;

Experience of:

Mild: DS;

Moderate: DS;

Severe: VI;

Others: OCD;

Summary: Provision for Brittle Bone disease. Provision on school trips/activities for medical conditions requiring stomach feed tubes and respiration aids.

What we say about the school - the full Good Schools Guide review

Head: Acting head since Sept 2005, Mr David Wybron MA (forties). Previously head of lower school, and deputy head of Lord Williams's overall, he joined school in 1991 as head of humanities faculty. History graduate from Swansea University who taught in Cambridgeshire and Great Missenden, Bucks, before settling in Thame. Still teaches GCSE history to one class a week. A softly-spoken Welshman whose drive and determination should not be under-estimated. 'I am passionate about this place,' he assures us. Has already drawn up a two to three year plan of improvements with better GCSE results a top priority. Wife a secondary school teacher, one child at school in Aylesbury, the other at university. Took over from Michael Spencer, head since 2000.

Academic Matters: Still one of top state schools in Oxfordshire. A level results seen as major success in 2005 with 99 per cent pass rate, 74 per cent A-C grades. GCSE results might seem less impressive; 64 per cent gained five or more A*-C grades with 94 per cent exam passes overall – but still far exceeding national and county averages. OK, but could be better, says head. Focus now very much on improving those grades though and broadening choices, including vocational subjects. Head says, 'I'm looking at the core agenda for all students and looking to see how we can be sure our students get the right package and develop the right skills.' As children of all abilities entered for exams, results are pretty sound and school commended by Ofsted for adding value, 'well above the national average'. Girls beat the boys in most subjects (as per national trend) but boys come out on top in core areas of English, maths and science. Huge curriculum choice at every level. Special needs very well catered for Resource unit for 20 children with autism on site, also plenty of classroom and extra help for others with dyslexia and other learning problems. Well-stocked libraries in both lower and upper schools, regularly updated. ICT taught as subject in its own right to all from year 7, also as learning support for later studies. 10 purpose-built computer networked suites boast latest technology and are in constant demand. Loads of classroom assistants as well as subject specialists mean large classes of 30-odd are kept under control.

Games, Options, The Arts: Sports college status, also awarded an Artsmark Gold award for its creative arts provision. Both areas of school impressive, highly productive and successful. But head keen to point out, 'we are not just a sports school, we haven't slanted things so that it's just about sport.' Happy with the health, leadership, fitness and community agendas. Shared use of Thame sports centre (right next door to school), acres of playing fields and plans for all-weather pitch. Regularly produce county (sometimes national) players and winning teams. NVQ football course launched in 2005 for sixth formers. Art studios well used and well resourced. Excellent examples of work on head's study walls. Good displays at lower school. Good music uptake. Individual lessons as well as compulsory class music for all early on. Traditional orchestras now complemented by assortment of bands. Drama, dance and theatre studies all popular time-table and exam options. Impressive results too.

Background and Atmosphere: A true comprehensive. Known affectionately as Lord Bill's, it's a big school – much bigger than average secondary with 2,000+ pupils – but split over two sites about two miles apart. School founded by Lord Williams of Thame in 1575. Current set-up dates from 1971 when Lord Williams's Grammar and Wenman Secondary merged. Both sites on leafy edge of market town, well spread out, and despite high numbers on school register, there's room to breathe. Buildings mixed in age and mostly functional, parts much in need of TLC, but well laid out and absolutely buzzing. 'It's an ideas place. There's a sparkiness here about teaching and learning.' Students allowed voice in decision making process. 'Sometimes people are afraid of the student voice,' says head. 'But we harness it.' Recently played major role in choosing new caterers. (Plumped for healthy option rather than one offering fatty fry-ups and burgers.) Canteen style lunches, good selection of fresh salads, some vending machines still with the usual contents. School sites very open and security has recently been stepped up. CCTV installed at cost of £38,000 at lower school, all staff and visitors to upper school must wear ID and anyone not wearing a badge will be challenged by staff and students alike. Maintains close ties with local primaries through well-established system of networking. Much effort made to ease the transition to 'big' school through team-building activities.

Pastoral Care and Discipline: Small tutor groups, communications and family workers, plus close links with parents all provide solid student support. Nurture groups set up for students who are particularly vulnerable. Children shown how to deal with own problems too, as well as being encouraged to seek help. Few serious misdemeanours but guilty parties swiftly dealt with. Sliding scale of exclusion periods for offenders. No instant dismissal for drugs, but police will automatically be involved. Head readily admits bullying exists, but is not tolerated. All unacceptable behaviour dealt with initially in the same way – with a range of sanctions used – detentions, internal isolations and fixed term external exclusions.

Pupils and Parents: Confident, sometimes out-spoken, but articulate and secure. Hard workers will achieve and the less academically able are being increasingly catered for. Students seen on our visit appeared focused and involved in their lessons. Their relationship with staff seemed generally relaxed and informal. A socially mixed catchment area obviously results in a wide social mix at school. Some from professional backgrounds, plenty of rural and an increasing number who qualify for free school meals. Parents range from the supportive to the demanding, rather than the apathetic.

Entrance: From Oxfordshire state primaries in Thame and surrounding villages like Chinnor and Tetsworth, but also a number of Buckinghamshire schools (like Brill and Long Crendon) due to school's proximity to county border. Over-subscribed by about two to one. Head describes Lord Williams's as 'truly inclusive'.

Exit: Up to 70 per cent stay on to sixth form, most of those leaving after year 11 go onto college courses or into employment. Majority go to university or college after A levels, annually two or three to Oxbridge. No single area of expertise evident – courses and jobs right across the board.

Money Matters: Extra funding given through sports college status has been well spent and clever bit of land sale (a small triangle of unused playing field) is paying for the new all-weather pitch.

Remarks: A perennially popular school which maintains a good local reputation through its ability to do well by its students. Seen by some as a safety net for Bucks grammar school failures but hard-grafters won't be disappointed. In many respects worthy of first choice status, certainly not second best.

LYMM HIGH VOLUNTARY CONTROLLED SCHOOL

Oughtrington Lane, Lymm, Cheshire, WA13 0RB

Tel: 01925 755 458

Fax: 01925 758 439

Email: sch_lymm@warrington.gov.uk

Website: www.lymmhigh.co.uk

• Pupils: 1,960 boys and girls, all day • Ages: 11-19

• Religion: Non-denom • Fees: Free • School status: State

• Opendays: sixth form open evening November

• School gender: Mixed • Day/boarding: Day pupils

SEN provision

Detail:

Now provide for in school:

Mild: ASP; ADD; ADHD; EBD; DYSC; DYSL; DYSP; SpLD; HI; VI;

Moderate: ASP; ADD; ADHD; EBD; MLD; DYSL; DYSP; HI; VI;

Severe: ASP; ADHD; EBD; DYSL; CP;

Others: SPD; CD; OCD; ODD; TIC; EAL; Sp&LD; DEL; Epi; PD; Eat;

Experience of:

Mild: CP;

Moderate: CP;

Summary: Teaching assistants support pupils who have most significant need. Some support is provided by the Local Education Authority and some is provided by the school.

There are withdrawal groups for literacy and small groups for basic skills and SPLD input. These groups are taught using a multi-sensory approach. There are also homework and keyboard (typing) clubs. Some students have word processors.

Some pupils have support for self-esteem and behaviour modification. Students' needs are carefully screened and a range of access arrangements are provided for examinations in line with the criteria set by the examination boards.

What we say about the school - the full Good Schools Guide review

Headteacher: Since 1998, Roger A Lounds (fifties). Married with two grown children. Down to earth, enthusiastic, deemed 'very approachable' by parents. Dismisses his letters BA MSc MA DMS (Ed) DipCEdG CertEd as not making any difference to Roger Lounds the person. Passionately believes in non-selective co-education 'because society is mixed; if you can create a school that mirrors society, youngsters find it easier to cope as they grow up.' Came from challenging headships at Brumby Comprehensive in Scunthorpe and Vermuyden School, Goole.

Academic Matters: Lymm High School ranks in top 30 non-selective state schools for results. 93 per cent plus 5+ A*-Cs at GCSE. Specialist language college since 1996 – five language assistants, in separate block of eight classrooms with state of the art technology, offering German, Spanish, French, Russian, Italian, Japanese and Mandarin – 80 language online learning packages available. Staff from LHS teach and support language learning in partner primary schools; this is regarded as exemplar practice by CILT. Languages being worked into vocational corners of the curriculum – take-up improving from a low base. Many students take intermediate and advanced vocational GNVQs/Btec each year, most passing at the higher level. Hospitality and catering course, with the opportunity for study/work experience in France, and sports vocational course with work experience in Spain. New courses in art/design, fashion, health science, travel and tourism, construction, design and performing arts.

Setting in two ability 'populations' is standard throughout school in most subjects and parents like the way pupils readily move up and down sets depending on performance. Good provision for dyslexia and dyspraxia in designated block; currently 200 special needs pupils. School works closely with parents of SEN children from years 5 and 6 before transition to secondary school. Huge developments in SEN provision over past six years from single SENCo to learning development team of 25 staff working to evaluate and improve support. Extra literary sessions at 8.15am before school, lunchtime typing/homework club popular for those who need extra help and those escaping hurly burly of playground. Wheelchair-friendly sixth form, lift and automated doors. Timetabling for ground floor access if necessary lower down school. Advanced skills teacher identifies and encourages gifted and talented pupils through 'gifted scholarship programme' for over 200 pupils in all subjects including sport, using mentoring, advanced public exams, university work in addition to A levels, summer schools, outside lecturers and trainers and the National Academy for Gifted and Talented Youth in Warwick. Parents describe this area of school as 'really on the ball' and versatile with the possibility of a child having, for example, extra help for dyslexia while on the honours programme for art or sport.

LHS has links with schools in South Africa and is supporting developments at Quashana High School in a black township near East London. This school is also supported by one of Lymm's partners, Glen High in Pretoria.

Developments in teaching and learning styles are changing 'a dependency culture where pupils come to rely on teachers instead of taking responsibility for their own learning. The best teachers in any school put learning first and regard teaching as just a way to access learning.'

Games, Options, The Arts: Sport is a key strength; 'best thing about the school,' say many pupils. Head believes, 'to be the best you have to bring in the best' so employs teachers who are county coaches for hockey, has appointed an England U16 squad coach for soccer and there are strong club-school links for rugby. Vastly improved fixture lists against some of the best independent schools in the north west. Rash of county players in hockey, netball, rugby, cricket, football, tennis, athletics, cross-country – including two female county players – and under 18 male and female water polo nationals. Pupils frequently selected for England U18 Rugby Union. Rowing established at junior and senior levels. Won the gold medal at U15 in the National Schools Championship and two silver medals in the National Championships. The 22 metre pool, gym and sport hall double as local community leisure centre. Full size all-weather pitch, and recent land purchases mean the sports fields stretch out in several directions with additional pitches. Lymm HS now leads a School Sports

Development partnership involving 50 schools in Warrington and Cheshire. Chosen to be the location for the All England Netball Association North West 'Centre of Excellence' and home for the professional side 'Northern Thunder'.

Half a dozen dinghies are over-wintering in one of the quads – the school has 14 GPs, Mirrors, Lasers and Toppers and sails every weekend from April to October at local Budworth Reservoir and Tatton Mere. Summer sailing courses held at Roscolyn on Anglesey where the school has an outdoor residential centre in 38 acres – Ty'n-y-Felin is a 1600s farmhouse with new dormitory wing where all first years bond in form groups and which is busy all summer with camps. Long list of clubs and societies, several bands (one has cut CD), mainly meeting in lunch hour. D of E, Young Enterprise, Whole School Enterprise Challenge. Lots of trips to exotic locations and international sports tours(Australia 2004, South Africa 2007).

Music now a strong element of the school. All students in year 7 have musical tuition in strings and brass free of charge. Voice and oboe are also free. Music is also taught by LHS staff in partner primary schools.

Background and Atmosphere: Lymm High School, Lymm Grammar until 20+ years ago, serves a wide area of rural England. Set on a hillside with far reaching views over the Cheshire plain, all the outlooks are green. Easy access to the motorway network makes Lymm an ultra-leafy suburb – recently acclaimed the most expensive place to live in the North West with average house price over £200,000. Not quite as neat as a private school, nevertheless well-presented, with work, projects, trips and very impressive ceramics on display everywhere. Prefects on entrance doors at breaks and lunch – a nice touch and welcoming. Staff and pupils friendly and communicative. A busy place with leisure and language centres and on-site uniform shop open almost every day.

Grey and navy blue uniform described as 'comfortable' by pupils who accept ties, even in sixth form. Logoed sportswear also compulsory. School has own caterers though the dining hall looks small, 'lunchtime is not dignified,' admitted head,'we need to get a lot of children through in a short time'. School has a healthy eating policy with chips ('they're good,' say pupils) only available on one day each week. Day starts early at 8.20am.

Notable past pupils include Ruth Lea, head of the Institute of Directors and business commentator; Maurice Flanagan CBE, group managing director of Emirate Airlines; Catherine Bruton, author; Neil Fairbrother, cricketer; Richard Eggington, rower.

Pastoral Care and Discipline: Parental concerns that size of school is daunting for first years – addressed by established Five Halls system, so each child belongs to smaller unit. Two forms from each year in each of five halls – Arley, Dunham, Moreton, Tatton and Walton, each with own tie. 'It gives me more chance to say 'well done' to more children,' says head. The Halls are the backbone of the school and afford many more students the chance to succeed.

Active mentoring and pupil peer scheme through the Hall system – pastoral care seems to fall to form tutors in Hall teams. No-nonsense approach to discipline; head doesn't hesitate to temporarily exclude for serious misdemeanours and permanently exclude for assault and drugs but describes school as 'pretty clean' for its size. 'You can count the scallywags on one hand; they're great kids but we demand and expect high standards.'

Pupils and Parents: White, rural Cheshire, quintessentially middle class. Ethnic minority faces and faiths almost non-existent. Christian with a small 'c' – no church connections. Parents say they're 'bowled over' by the school and describe it as 'the cream of secondary schools for miles'.

Entrance: Non-selective. Place virtually certain for children from one of nine feeder partnership primaries. Heavily over-subscribed locally so entrance difficult from out of area – for 11+ rejects from neighbouring Trafford for example, but some with grammar school places choose Lymm High School in preference.

Exit: A good handful to Oxbridge. About 90 per cent go on to higher education, most to university.

Remarks: A forward looking, happening place; full of life and more opportunities than you would expect even from a large secondary school. Good results with a lot of fun to be had along the way.

MALSIS SCHOOL

Cross Hills, North Yorkshire, BD20 8DT

Tel: 01535 633 027
Fax: 01535 630 571
Email: admin@malsis.com
Website: www.malsis.com

• Pupils: 90 boys, 40 girls. 40 board, the rest day. Plus pre-prep with 55 pupils • Ages: 7-13, pre-prep 3-7 • Religion: Inter-denom: C of E and RC • Fees: Boarding £4,700, day £3,600; Garden House pre-prep £1,920 • School status: Independent • Opendays: Termly • School gender: Mixed • Day/boarding: Takes boarders

SEN provision

Detail:
Centre of excellence for:
- Mild: DYSL;
- Moderate: DYSL;
- Severe: DYSL;

Now provide for in school:
- Mild: ASP; AUT; ADD; ADHD; EBD; DYSC; DYSP; CP;
- Moderate: MLD; DYSC; DYSP;
- Others: SPD;

Summary: At Malsis, we treat every pupil as an individual and recognise that each of us has varying strengths and weaknesses, abilities and difficulties.

When we identify a pupil who has significantly greater difficulty in learning than the majority of children of a similar age, we respond to their specific needs by offering Learning Support.

This may take the form of additional one-to-one tuition with specialist staff on a withdrawal basis, or more general 'in-class' support with extra help in timetabled lessons. All pupils with special needs have an Individual Education Programme (IEP) which offers agreed targets, timescales and resources to help children achieve progress. All teaching staff are aware of each child's IEP, so that their needs may be met in all school settings.

We carefully and regularly monitor and review children's progress, and work in partnership with parents at all stages to build confidence and a strong sense of self-esteem.

What we say about the school - the full Good Schools Guide review

Head: Since 2004, Mr Christopher Lush MA. History at Cambridge. Married to Ingrid, two children both at Malsis. Formerly a housemaster at St Edward's Oxford, having joined the teaching staff at St Edward's in 1995 to run the history department. Before that he was an assistant housemaster at Cranleigh. A keen cricketer and hockey player, captained Eastbourne College at both sports and represented Sussex at junior level. Earlier in his career he taught at St Andrew's Prep School in Eastbourne. A caring and compassionate head – a parent who suggested that, as head was referee for a rugby match, Malsis had an advantage, received a chorus of, 'Oh no he's far too fair'.

One of the teachers (a very good one) felt some of head's changes, eg greater frequency of reports, parents' consultations etc put more work on staff but were benefiting all. Parents agree: 'the frequent ability grades as opposed to just effort are making my son raise his game – and I find the comments useful.' Lots of happy children, but not all changes welcomed by all; some staff (and a couple of pupils) voted with their feet and followed the previous head.

Entrance: Spend at least one day in school and do tests in maths and English. No longer the Yorkshire mafia, now come from Cheshire, Lancashire to Somerset and the west of Glasgow. Trickle of Services families.

Exit: The usual suspects: Oundle, Glenalmond, Shrewsbury, Giggleswick, one or two to Sedbergh, Uppingham, Eton (steady one or two), Rugby and Ampleforth. Plus Radley and Stowe. Regular stream of scholarships to all over, including music, sport and art.

Remarks: School founded in 1920 by a teacher from Giggleswick in a glorious over-the-top Victorian mansion with incredible ceilings re-painted and gilded and shining bright, set in 40 acres of games pitches and fields. Worth every inch the £500,000 that it cost for a total facelift, which extended into the many additions. Old style spiral bound prospectus comes with a series of jolly pics of children having fun and getting dirty, check out the very good website too, even has really useful recommended reading lists for children of all ages.

Busy little cheerful faces in striped shirts trot purposefully round jolly classrooms, stand up when you go into the room, hold the door open, and say Sir. Refreshing. Marvellous John Piper War Memorial Windows in the Chapel, plus the flags which used to hang on the Cenotaph in London. Chapel converts into hall theatre. School holds services on Saturday, rather than Sunday, so Sundays are 'free for activities'. Chess incredibly popular, giant-sized sets all over the place, including the library, very child-orientated. Huge range of country-type activities as well as the trad prep school type things, essential (school) equipment includes mountain bikes (Insurance cover OK if parents sign a form), fly-tying, hill-walking, canoeing, camping – including camp cooking. Swimming pool, shooting range, cross-country, nine hole golf course – remember this is not a country club. This is a busy boarding school. Day pupils have to be in school by 8.30am and stay till 6.15pm – though most stay later for clubs (over 50 of them) – they can in any case stay for supper if they want, there is no evening prep. 'Most' 10/13-year-olds do board, and one or two younger ones.

Strong academically, head sees all good work. French from 7 (regular trips to France), nativity play in French. Latin from 8 and Greek club from 10 – and surprisingly popular. Regular scholarships to top schools. Small classes, average 12, with dedicated staff.

Excellent learning support; 20 pupils currently mostly dyslexia /dyspraxia but range of others considered if they think they can help and child will cope. IEPs for those with needs, one-to-one help, regular additional reading (often with parent volunteers), small group work and setting (including holding back the weakest or advancing the brightest a year so they get to spend extra time on scholarship work for common entrance). SEN not seen as a barrier, possible to be getting extra support and work in scholarship classes. All staff informed and involved with SEN. Needs across curriculum recognised: lots of different sports and opportunities for all to represent the school, DT club provides extra time and one-to-one opportunities for those needing additional help, extra English, calligraphy and finding something child is good at, all feature. Children respond positively to those who have additional needs: great applause when tie, usually awarded for completing gruelling three peaks walk in one go, awarded to pupil with physical difficulties who managed a peak a year over three years.

Whizzy CDT, video editing, digital cameras, vibrant art room, masses of music, loads of visits to local hot spots: Manchester, Bradford, Halifax, Leeds all have orchestras and theatres. Civilised dining room with table napkins. Famous Old Boys include Simon Beaufoy who wrote The Full Monty, Martin Taylor ex of Barclays Bank and Lord Robinson (of rentals?).

MALVERN COLLEGE

College Road, Malvern, Worcestershire, WR14 3DF

Tel: 01684 581 500

Fax: 01684 581 615

Email: enquiry@malcol.org

Website: www.malcol.org

• Pupils: 355 boys and 213 girls; 449 board, 119 day. Plus own prep and pre-prep schools – 188 boys and girls • Ages: 13-18, prep and pre-prep 2-13 • Religion: C of E but ecumenical • School status: Independent • Opendays: Early in the Autumn term and May day • School gender: Mixed • Day/boarding: Takes boarders

SEN provision

Detail:

Centre of excellence for:

Mild: DYSL;

Others: EAL;

Now provide for in school:

Mild: ASP; ADD; DYSC; DYSP; HI;

Moderate: DYSL;

Experience of:

Mild: ADHD;

Others: Epi;

Summary: Malvern College has a learning support department with seven part-time, qualified, and experienced members of staff. We offer one-to-one support with literacy, numeracy and study skills to pupils with a predominantly mild specific learning difficulty. The department screens pupils for specific difficulties on entry and offers to design an individual programme to meet an individual's needs through one-to-one tuition for an additional charge. A period of diagnostic teaching follows and may result in a referral to a visiting educational psychologist for a full assessment. A pupil may receive a regular lesson once a week, attend a short block of lessons or, in the Sixth form, attend as and when required. The department writes an annual

Individual Educational Plan for each pupil that is made available to all teaching staff and is reviewed with parents at parents days. The department is continually seeking to develop links with the teaching staff and offers internal training/advice. Where appropriate, arrangements are made for special access arrangements in public exams, such as additional time, rest breaks and word processing.

The facilities are excellent and a warm, positive attitude is fostered. We offer a 'drop in facility' for pupils for private study with access to the school networked computer system, a printer and additional resources to help a pupil fully access the curriculum in their preferred learning style. We currently have three computers and are able to access a pupil's work and offer help with drafting and presentation.

What we say about the school - the full Good Schools Guide review

Head: Since 1997, Mr Hugh Carson MA PGCE (late fifties), educated Tonbridge (head boy), joined the army and discovered, whilst at Sandhurst, that he loved teaching. Came to Malvern via the Royal Tank Regiment followed by London and Reading, where he read history, history of economics and politics – which he still teaches. Came to Malvern via Epsom College, where he became housemaster, and Denstone College – a Woodard school – where he was headmaster.

Urbane and charming but serious minded too, with an underlying sense of purpose and a certain reserve; pupils hold him in high regard. He has definitely made his mark on the school. His wife, Penny, is a JP and 'freelance historian'. Both great dog lovers, his black and white spaniel is never far from his heels.

Retiring July 2006. New head is to be Mr David Dowdles, currently headmaster of Warminster School.

Academic Matters: Number of recent staff changes in heads of departments and further down the school. Malvern is one of the highest profile schools to teach the IB – with great success: about 50 per cent of sixth form pupils take this option – though, having said that, the A level results are also very good. This is not an overtly academic school but achieves good results, with a fair number of As and Bs at GCSE and A level and AS level. Placed 19th in the Times league tables of top 800 schools. Max class size 23, streamed and setted, no obvious star subject, though both maths and English strong. Economics strong in sixth form. Separate or dual award science (science labs look pretty tatty) plus impressive success in modern languages – do not be deceived; there are a number of native speakers in the school. EFL on offer to top up wobbly English for non-native speakers but good basic English essential before joining the school – and many foreigners go to the prep school at 11 before transferring to the senior school. Loads of trips abroad, German exchanges and French work experience.

Apart from the IB, the school has also pioneered the Nuffield Science course, and the Diploma of Achievement, a skills-based course that includes life skills as well as learning, healthy eating and fitness for life. The key skills qualification counts as bonus in the UCAS total. Networked Apple Macs in banks throughout the school, as well as the library, the IT dept and the houses.

Excellent dyslexia pick-up under Mrs Jackie Thomas, who runs a unit for pupils with learning difficulties at South Lodge with four part-time assistants; no facilities to deal with serious problems but lots of good advice and help. Mrs Thomas can pull up pupil's work in progress to iron out hiccups.

Games, Options, The Arts: Main games football and rugby, lots of tours abroad – but boys complain they keep being beaten by schools who do two terms of rugby rather than a mixture of football and hockey. Rackets, fives, large games hall, refurbished swimming pool in divine Victorian exterior. Adventure training at cottage in Brecon Beacons, all go there for a week. Serious popular and successful clay pigeon shooting team. Masses of music in converted Victorian monastery with monks' cells as practice rooms; former Catholic church is now a concert hall with sixth form centre in the crypt. Charming little theatre in former gym. All weather playing surface recently laid down.

Fabulous new IT block – all the normal disciplines (though dust extractor pipes have thick layer of sawdust on the inner surface which Health and Safety has required to be addressed) plus home economics and textiles – for both sexes. IT block cunningly linked to existing art department, huge exciting variety of work on show and proper (ie grown-up post-school-age) art foundation course started in September 2001 under the charismatic head of art, Mr Tim Newsholme, which leads to a Btec diploma. Strong CCF, but also extensive community service and D of E.

Background and Atmosphere: Collection of impressive Victoriana perched on sloping site beneath the Malvern Hills (imagine immaculate terracing dotted with playing fields and Betjemanesque limestone piles). Main railway line traverses the grounds. Founded in 1865, the school grew rapidly and there are now ten houses scattered throughout the brightly lit grounds – no house apparently more desirable than any other. The separate chapel built in 1899 replaces the earlier one, which has now become an imaginative double deck library. In 1992 (falling numbers, Lloyds etc) the school amalgamated with nearby Ellerslie Girls' School and Hillstone prep school – which moved into the original Ellerslie site (just up the road).

Unusually, Malvern still has in-house feeding, with around fifty pupils in each. This is both a noisy and a cosy experience – and the houseparents feel much more hands-on. Younger pupils sleep in dorms with separate studies, and graduate to study bedrooms (some said to be too small for modern Health and Safety standards, but they looked perfectly OK to us). Day pupils are either in boarding houses and stay till around 9pm or in day houses where they chose to do prep in school or at home – all day pupils can do B&B whenever parents require it. School operates on a three-week cycle, with every third weekend out from Friday lunch, masses of activities on Sundays and head is particularly proud that he usually has 'at least 400 pupils' on site during the weekend.Trousers and jackets or blazers till sixth form when boys wear 'their own suits'; dark jackets and serviceable dark striped skirts for girls who move into rather natty trouser suits at sixth form.

Pastoral Care and Discipline: Good house and tutor system; pupils allocated tutor in lower school and choose personal tutor post-GCSE. Headmaster brooks no nonsense on sin: out for drugs, out for sex, drinking is only allowed for sixth form but smoking not allowed. Persistent offenders will be required to leave the school – so there you have it. Hard, too, on petty crime.

Pupils and Parents: middle class, professional (princes to paupers) but not a posh school. 15 per cent discount for Services families, a fair number of foreigners – 'about 20 per cent climb on an aeroplane at the end of term,' says the head, that includes expats. Fair number of Germans, often for the sixth form for IB only. Not an overly sophisticated school.

Entrance: Registration and CE or separate test for state school entrants. 20 per cent from own prep school, lots from other preps (only a trickle now from Beaudesert); CE essential for these but waived for state school entrants. Sixth form entry six GCSEs at A to C for AS/A2 subjects, about seventy join the sixth form each year, mainly for IB.

Exit: 97 per cent to university – up to twenty to Oxbridge (nineteen last year) some to the States, some to Europe (the IB again), plus art college, the Services etc.

Money Matters: Demise of Assisted Places hit hard but numbers rising again and school now has own funds in place and can offer both bursarial help and scholarships. Will pick up any financial shortfall 'up to the next public exam', but parents must be upfront with the problem. Huge appeal both for bursary dosh and funds for new language labs – head proud of the fact that the school 'has no overdraft'.

Remarks: Trad co-ed rural public school with a surprising number of aces up its sleeve.

THE MANCHESTER GRAMMAR SCHOOL

Old Hall Lane, Rusholme, Manchester, Lancashire, M13 0XT

Tel: 0161 224 7201
Fax: 01612 572 446
Email: general@mgs.org
Website: www.mgs.org

• Pupils: 1,440 boys; all day • Ages: 11-18 • Religion: C of E links, but basically non-denom • Fees: £2,413 plus lunch • School status: Independent • Opendays: Early October • School gender: Boys • Day/boarding: Day pupils

SEN provision

Detail:

Now provide for in school:

Mild: ASP; ADD; ADHD; EBD; DYSC; DYSL; DYSP; SpLD; HI; VI;

Others: TIC;

Summary: The Manchester Grammar School admits pupils solely on the basis of their academic ability as assessed by performance in our entrance examination. Amongst those pupils are a number each year with specific learning difficulties both diagnosed and undiagnosed. Parents of candidates with a diagnosis are strongly encouraged to declare it prior to admission so that requirements and provision can be discussed and fully understood. Conditions routinely accommodated include autism spectrum disorders such as Asperger's; dyslexia, dyspraxia and related conditions; Tourette's syndrome and related conditions; ADD and ADHD; visual and hearing impairment; mobility restriction.

Pupils with specific learning difficulties are accommodated in normal classes subject to reasonable adjustment and supported outside the classroom by year group tutors, form tutors and the school medical services, all under the guidance of the co-ordinator of learning support. Although in normal circumstances classroom support is not provided via specialist support workers, in exceptional circumstances the school does work to make this facility available.

As an institution we are philosophically predisposed to do all we can to make a Manchester Grammar School education accessible to all pupils who can benefit from it.

What we say about the school - the full Good Schools Guide review

High Master: Since 2004, Dr Christopher Ray, educated at Rochdale Grammar School and University College London, followed by postgraduate study at Churchill College Cambridge and Balliol College Oxford. Taught at Marlborough, Framlingham, director of studies at King's College School Wimbledon. From 2001, headmaster of The John Lyon School, Harrow, who were rather surprised to see him go. Married. Has also worked at The Bank of England and for Oxford University Press, and has taught in universities (Oxford, Singapore and Oregon, USA).

Academic Matters: Outstanding academic power house, one of the best in the country. Predictably brilliant results – 85 per cent A*/A at GCSE 87 per cent A/B at A level. Quite apart from exam and league table success, school has striking academic ethos. Love of learning comes out of the boys' pores. High academic standards are valued for their own sake. Staff a mixture of old and enthusiastic and young and enthusiastic. Inevitably, the odd dud. Most are very committed, dedicated to the true aims of their profession. People want to teach at MGS and are trusted to get on with the job. Handing initiative and responsibility over is a feature of the school; a 14-year-old said, 'they help, but really it's up to us'. Increasing number of women appointees but not for political correctness, simply 'the best person for the job'.

Class sizes now reduced at lower end of school to maximum 25/26, thinning down to 22/23 in middle school, 10/12 at A level. Most take (and pass) 9-11 subjects at GCSE. Own lower school general science course to even out differences in pre-11 teaching, then all take separate sciences at GCSE. Latin optional after two years. Greek, Spanish, Russian, German, Italian. Boys 'banded' for maths, thereafter classes defined by subject grouping. RE compulsory up to 5th year. Learning support team quietly picks up fallers by the wayside, dyslexics, et al in fourth and fifth years. Membership of this 'at risk' group more a cachet than a stigma, claims head of middle school.

The academic successes of the past – long list of high-flyers in every conceivable field – does not seem to overwhelm boys; they feel cherished for what they can bring to the school, not required to live up to an impossibly high standard. The wealth of talent is mirrored by the resources for the enquiring mind. Both libraries are fantastic. The range of periodicals covering arts, physical and social sciences, current events, sport etc, tells its own tale – academic excellence fed by the intellectual ferment in the outside world. Excellent careers room and bookshop. Major new development in DT.

New pattern of post-16 curriculum is four ASs plus four A2s but very wide-ranging general studies in sixth form has been retained, with philosophy course compulsory in lower sixth; school no longer feels it can dictate a particular faith to its pupils, but believes that 'any young person leaving school at 18 without either a moral code or a structured pattern of thought relating to morality and ethics is both at risk and has not been educated'.

Homework expected to take from one hour a night (first form) to 16 self-directed hours per week in sixth. Five As at GCSE means automatic passage to sixth. If this looks unlikely, boys and parents given plenty of warning.

Games, Options, The Arts: The range of non-academic and extra-curricular activities is mind-boggling (pity about cookery – future spouses and partners may lament this omission?). Huge amount of energy invested in what goes on outside the classroom, both for its own sake and also, equally importantly, to encourage and engender self-esteem; especially popular, all-muck-in-together camps and treks and compulsory first/second year drama. Non-academic achievement valued highly. Regular visits to Edinburgh Festival. Unique full-length play-writing award, the Robert Bolt Memorial Prize, open to any pupil and judged by Royal Exchange Theatre (£500 for winner). Fantastic new sports hall, named after old boy Mike Atherton. New tennis courts (from anonymous donor). No great pressure to play games but school still licks most of the opposition; recently became first northern school to win Rosslyn Park Sevens. Music much prized. Regular visits to school by BBC Philharmonic; James MacMillan composer-in-residence in 2000; Biennial concert at St John's Smith Square.

Outstanding facilities for ceramics and fine arts and an approach by which art history, theory and practice dovetail naturally. Staffing in these two subjects greatly increased in recent years. Absence of tension between arty and sporty fraternities; each perfectly confident of their own worth.

Background and Atmosphere: Founded in 1515 by Hugh Oldham, Bishop of Exeter, a year before he founded Corpus Christi College, Oxford with which MGS has links, to educate able boys regardless of their parents' means, to go on to university and the professions, and open what the founder called the 'yate of knowledge'. Moved to present purpose-built 28-acre site in 1931, though facilities enormously extended since then. Now the biggest private senior school in the country. The founding ideals hold steady, fuelled by high master's and staff's convictions. School determined to continue to offer education to boys from less privileged backgrounds. Prides itself on being 'colour blind', ie not differentiating on grounds of race. Atmosphere very positive, vibrant, full of life, supportive, ambitious in the sense of purposeful – school sets, and rises to, challenges.

Cheerful, polite boys. Most of all, a pervading, almost tangible, love of learning, and sense of happiness, pride in achievements of all kinds.

Dining room noisy but efficient. 'Butty Bar' for older boys enamoured of fast food. Sixth formers wear school tie and tailored jackets, otherwise blue blazers. On first arriving at MGS, boys – many from small, local schools – generally feel overwhelmed by its size, despite pastoral measures to prevent this. But once they find their feet (and their classrooms), they seem never to look back.

Pastoral Care and Discipline: The caring ethos of the school, hardly touched on in its prospectus, is nonetheless real and alive. In such a big school, good pastoral care is a priority. There is a striking general standard of decency towards, and respect for, each other, unobtrusively underpinned by discipline. School goes to great lengths to catch problems early and to make available lots of different routes for boys having difficulties. Various schemes – friend (for new boys), peer support system, form tutor (key role) are backed up by less formal network, such as school nurses, who are trained in counselling. Non-teaching staff contribute to pastoral care. One teacher described as 'fairly flabbergasting' the rapport between staff and pupils. Occasionally, problems or injustices slip through the net, inevitably.

Carefully worked out and rigorously implemented drugs policy – possession means suspension, usually followed by readmission, on condition the boy concerned submits to random tests thereafter. Discipline not hampered by pointless pettiness, and occasionally rules more honoured in the breach than in the observance, eg no running in the corridors unless it's to get to the front of the lunch queue, in which case stampedes are perfectly in order; it's all visitors can do not to join in, just for the fun of it. High Master has last word on choice of captain (head boy).

Pupils and Parents: Wide range of backgrounds, social, religious, racial. One pupil commented that anyone would enjoy the school, provided they were willing to 'get involved'. And loners? Yes, so long as they 'get involved ... as loners'. Very wide catchment area. School delays start until 9:05am but even so it's a long day for some boys – dropped off early, picked up late, or facing long bus journeys both ways. Communication with parents is good on the whole – tutors encouraged to phone parents if they feel there is a problem. Otherwise contact fairly minimal, restricted to parents' evenings and reports. Parents' Society arranges events and network, including optional scheme to pair up 'old' parents with new, to aid settling-in process.

Dozens and dozens of distinguished Old Boys, including rows of FRSs, not least Sir Michael Atiyah. Also Mike Atherton, Michael Wood, the Crawley brothers, actors Ben Kingsley and Robert Powell, Robert Bolt, Steven Pimlott, and National Theatre head Nicolas Hytner, writer Alan Garner; John Ogdon, LSE boss Sir Howard Davies, Thomas de Quincey, plus several members of the Sieff family and Simon Marks. One we came across this year was Steve Robinson who runs a language school on the south western frontiers of Brazil – 'I owe an awful lot indeed to MGS. Apart from an excellent array of curricular and extra-curricular activities, the highly competitive environment exacts the very best from you and makes you into an active person who goes out there and does things. I have fond memories of my time there and I wouldn't be out here in central Brazil, running a language school if it hadn't helped broaden my horizons and expectations in life. My background in classics has been fundamental in helping me redesign the teaching of English to Brazilians and I hope to be able to publish my ideas in the near future. I think it will always be with a certain sense of pride that I recollect my time there and recognise the value of the balanced education I received.'

Entrance: Not easy. Main entry is at 11, where 550/600 boys vie for 200/210 places. Entrance by exam only. No interview (is there a risk of a bright lad missing out because of an off-day in the exam room?). 50 per cent of intake from state primaries. School draws from around 80 preps/primaries.

Exit: All but a few to degree courses, mostly trad tough subjects at older universities. Law, medicine, languages, natural sciences, history/politics popular, also accountancy. 60 or so to Oxbridge.

Money Matters: High master has clear priorities: 'money goes on bursaries and teachers' – salaries first, buildings second'. There was a large number of assisted places and their phasing out has threatened the very purpose and ethos on which the school was founded. However, massive amount of energy, determination and goodwill has been channelled into Foundation Bursary Appeal (Patron is The Prince of Wales, signalling his strong support for provision of free places at school for deprived, inner-city children). More than £10 million raised since 1998. Rigorous procedures mean that money goes to deserving cases only. School trips are often to exotic locations and can prove expensive. According to the school, dedicated fund-raising and funding for needy pupils prevent such trips from being divisive. Parents in the middle income bands might wish for a few cheaper options.

Remarks: Impressive, five star academic day school, well deserving its reputation for excellence. Its enlightened founding principles, and the vigour with which the school still carries them forward, make it exemplary among independent schools. Such is the level of intellectual challenge, as well as non-academic and extra-curricular activities, some boys must have little, if any, time or energy left over for that trifling detail, the outside world. Manchester parents with no boys, eat your hearts out.

MANOR HOUSE SCHOOL

Manor House Lane, Little Bookham, Leatherhead, Surrey, KT23 4EN

Tel: 01372 458 538
Fax: 01372 450 514
Email: admin@manorhouse.surrey.sch.uk
Website: www.manorhouse.surrey.sch.uk

• Pupils: 370 girls, all day • Ages: 11-16 • Religion: Christian non-denom • Fees: Prep/junior £1,805-£2,725; senior £3,395 • School status: Independent • Opendays: Late October, late March and late May • School gender: Girls • Day/boarding: Day pupils

SEN provision

Detail:

Now provide for in school:
- Mild: ASP; DYSC; DYSL; DYSP;
- Moderate: DYSL; VI;
- Others: EAL; Sp&LD; DEL; Epi; PD;

Experience of:
- Mild: ADD; ADHD; EBD; VI; CP;
- Moderate: MLD;
- Others: OCD; FRX; Eat;

Summary: Manor House has 63 girls who are entered on the SEN register (G&T 15; disabled 3; 45 leaning difficulties). Each child's progress is monitored and assessed by observation and by screening procedures in order to identify children with special needs to make possible their full inclusion or to ensure that they are sufficiently challenged. Support is provided within the class at first, but pupils can also be withdrawn for specialist help individually or in small groups once or twice a week for periods of 35 minutes taught by a qualified SEN tutor. Our aim is that all pupils, including one girl with Asperger's syndrome and three with physical disabilities, develop coping strategies so that they achieve their full potential.

What we say about the school - the full Good Schools Guide review

Head: Since 2000, Mrs Alison Morris BSc (fifties). Joined school in 1982 and has worked her way up the school ranks from maths teacher to deputy head and then head – she describes herself as 'a real Manor House girl.' Has two grown-up children, was educated at Sutton High and read maths and economics at University of Kent. Very smartly dressed, very business-like, yet a very friendly, approachable head who truly loves the school. One parent commented that 'she does her job well with the girls.' She knows them all by name – no mean feat for a head. Another parent summed her up by saying that 'she is very in tune with what people are trying to achieve with their girls in a realistic way.' Her warmth when dealing with parental problems – divorce etc – is much praised. Happily admits that 16 is the right age for the girls to move on 'as they need a couple of years to get in touch with the real world before university life or whatever they choose to do.'

Academic Matters: Caters for girls of all abilities from the very bright souls who do not want the pressure of the big name academic schools, to those for whom academia is not the be-all and end-all of school life. Excellent GCSE results from such a mixed bunch, with the academic girls scooping up not just bucketfuls of As and A*s, but also academic scholarships from schools such as Cheltenham Ladies, Cranleigh, and City of London Freemen's. For those wishing to pursue other avenues, there is encouragement and support and a wide range of vocational GCSEs including PE, home economics, art, music, drama and childcare. Popular optional GCSE subjects include geography (very impressive GCSE geography results), drama, and religious studies. The girls are set for maths, science and French, but not for English. The school prides itself on the introduction of Spanish – alongside French and German – a good variety of languages for such a small school. Latin is also on offer to most.

Fifteen of the current teachers have been with the school for more than ten years and many are liked and respected by the girls. They are complemented by the fresh blood of younger teachers (a few more would not go amiss). Seeing the teachers is easy, according to a mother of two girls in the school. 'You can happily walk in and will always be welcomed.' Another said, 'they are much more approachable than in other schools.' Classrooms are large and bright as are the corridors – displaying artwork by the girls.

All girls are screened for SEN and, according to the head, never turned down solely on those grounds. Currently 15 are receiving extra help. There are three part-time qualified SEN teachers and a full-time study skills support teacher for senior girls. 'Terribly supportive, fabulous' is a widely felt attitude by parents for the SEN provision. The girls are also encouraged to use computers to help them with their work if need be. Computers are gently being introduced throughout the school – with two computer rooms and a fully networked system – the school is getting there, slowly but surely, and plans are afoot for the introduction of interactive whiteboards in all the classrooms.

Games, Options, The Arts: Sports facilities on site. School praised by parents for putting out not just A teams, but regular B and the occasional C team – problem being a lack of opposition with many other schools not interested in anything other than fielding one team of top players. Games' teaching is generally very strong (though sometimes appears stretched, particularly in the busy summer months) and the school regularly gathers in sports scholarships when the sporty souls leave at 16. Music, art and drama are impressive. In line with the school ethos, everyone has an opportunity to take part, even if it is only in the back row of the chorus. Lots of music ensembles including choirs, orchestras, brass and string groups – but the teaching of individual musical instruments by outside peripatetic teachers leaves room for improvement. Average choice of after school clubs including jazz dancing and tap as well as ballet, fitness, skiing and calligraphy. D of E also popular.

Background and Atmosphere: Founded in 1920, but moved to its present site in 1937. The main building is a beautiful Queen Anne house surrounded by 17 acres of land. Allocated play areas keep the little ones happy, while idyllic grounds with flower beds and benches are at the older ones' disposal. Two small libraries – however, it does not seem to faze the girls. 'We always find what we're looking for,' was a 14 year-old's comment. School offers an 'early-birds' free of charge facility from 8am and an after-school chargeable (and not cheap) late club till 6pm. Car parking and pick ups (as with most schools) seem on the difficult side but 'we manage like clockwork,' said a satisfied parent. Administration/communications with parents is not the school's strongest point. School food also leaves something to be desired – although it is said by the girls to be improving. Cosiness a strong point – a tangibly friendly atmosphere, a pleasure to visit.

Pastoral Care and Discipline: 'To Love is To Live' is the motto of the school – a motto which seems to fit well. The size of the school means all the girls know each other. Senior girls actively help out in the junior school and spend time with the younger girls. The girls seem to feel confident approaching teachers and the head with any worries or concerns.

A peaceful community. Drugs, bullying, smoking and drinking not evident to parents. The head commented, 'you always get the odd teenage girl who thinks she knows much more than you do; in those cases, you have to set boundaries as well as win their trust'. Rewards, sanctions and rules are clearly defined within the school as well as in the girls' homework diaries! There is plenty of discipline. Girls happy and calm – break-time not as chaotic as it can be.

Pupils and Parents: A mix of parents; the children of city executives to those who come in from the state sector on well-earned scholarships, although it is fair to say most are not short of money. Many parents choose Manor House to avoid the competitiveness of the 'Surrey Schools mafia' and the academic powerhouses. Girls are friendly, polite, smartly dressed – with hair (supposed to be and mostly) its natural colour, no outrageous skirt lengths nor the ubiquitous shirts hanging out. School is very successful charity fundraiser – both the girls and the parents. Bus service available to pick up from surrounding areas (but only in the mornings) and free shuttle bus to Effingham station. Old Girls include Susan Howatch (author), Elinor Goodman (political editor Channel 4), Sarah de Carvalho (founder of the charity, Happy Children) and Rose Gray (co-owner of The River Café).

Entrance: Many enter via the junior school, but spaces are available at 11 – entrance exams in English, maths, verbal reasoning plus small group interviews. Exams not a huge hurdle, but the school is becoming more popular (about 60 girls compete for 38 places). Scholarships and bursaries available. There are often occasional places at odd times, so worth a try at most ages: girls would spend the day with peer group and take tests in maths and English.

Exit: All girls leave at 16 – leavers go everywhere from the highly academic schools to art college or drama school. List varies from year to year but usually includes: Howard of Effingham, St John's Leatherhead, Godalming College, Cranleigh, Reed's Cobham, Charterhouse and City of London Freemen's.

Money Matters: Girls from the state system can compete for The Mason Scholarship – up to 50 per cent of the fees. Other academic scholarships plus art, drama, music and sports awards.

Remarks: A small, friendly school which offers a traditional and caring environment for girls of all academic abilities. Not for the rebel or rule breaker – she would stick out like a sore thumb.

Mark College

Mark, Highbridge, Somerset, TA9 4NP

Tel: 01278 641 632

Fax: 01278 641 426

Email: post@markcollege.somerset.sch.uk

Website: www.markcollege.org.uk

• Pupils: 80 boys • Ages: 11-16 • Religion: Non-denom
• Fees: Day £4,430, weekly boarding £6,283; full £6,378
• School status: Independent • School gender: Boys
• Day/boarding: Takes boarders

SEN provision

Detail:

Centre of excellence for:
- Mild: DYSC; DYSL;
- Moderate: DYSC; DYSL;
- Severe: DYSC; DYSL;

Now provide for in school:
- Mild: DYSP;
- Moderate: DYSP;

Experience of:
- Mild: ASP; ADD; ADHD; EBD; SpLD; CP;
- Moderate: ADD; SpLD;
- Severe: DYSP; SpLD;
- Others: TIC; EAL; Sp&LD; DEL; Epi; PD;

Summary: Specialist centre for dyslexia and dyscalculia.

What we say about the school - the full Good Schools Guide review

Principal and Proprietor: Since 1986, Dr S J Chinn BSc PhD PGCE DipEd AMBDA (fifties). Read chemistry at

Leeds, then a PhD in applied physics. Head of three schools specialising in dyslexia before founding Mark. Lectures worldwide on dyslexia and maths. A spare, energetic man, a long distance runner, full of smiles and interest. Married with three children. Retired June 2005 – sold the college to Priory Education.

Since 1999, Mrs J Kay BEd (early forties). Joined Mark College in 1990 and became assistant head in 1994, headteacher in 2005.

Academic Matters: Takes boys of 'average and above average ability' with severe dyslexia, and gets them (by and large) good GCSEs. Achieves the national average in English (from an average reading age at entry of 7 years), well above in maths and humanities. Offers the full National Curriculum – no sheltering the boys from the need to shape up for the world outside. Doesn't, on the whole, believe that dyslexics can be cured but majors on coping strategies – all teaching materials and methods have been adapted for dyslexics; much use of voice recognition computers that speak back to the boys – highlight a word and you hear it.

Staff interesting and highly qualified – Dr Chinn says that all he needs to do is advertise 'class size 8' and the best come running. Boys treat staff as friends but call them 'Sir.' Chosen as a Beacon School by the DfES for excellence with dyslexics – a thoroughly deserved accolade.

Games, Options, The Arts: Sports hall, tennis courts, playing fields. Very good rugby (winners in ISA sevens 2002) and athletics (gold and other medals in ISA national championships) – typical dyslexic sports, says Dr Chinn, as no dual tasking is involved. All encouraged to do bronze D of E, some do silver. A good range of activities generally but the weekends are not packed. General studies course centres on dealing with the world after school.

Background and Atmosphere: A Georgian house with new and old outbuildings, within easy range of the M5 (junction 22). College named after the village – a quiet place with several shops, where news of misbehaviour by the boys would quickly get back to the school; half a mile up the road and the school would have been called Splot College. Boarding houses in age groups, two to a room and then one. Facilities generally not plush but everything thought through for dyslexics – eg clothes on open shelves not hidden in drawers. With the prospectus (small and grey) you get a CD-ROM containing a virtual tour of the college – another example of their excellent provision for dyslexics. Food leaves substantial room for improvement (new caterers appointed, says Dr Chinn).

Pastoral Care and Discipline: No concessions made to dyslexics' difficulties – organisation, memory, etc – boys have to learn to survive outside the school by outside standards – but difficulties are well understood and much help is given to help boys improve. A lot of boys arrive at the school with attitude problems – many have been bullied (and so may want to bully), many have had their self-confidence shaken – and close attention is paid to clearing these up. Boys agree that after the first year all is well. Boys stand up when you enter a classroom, neat and alert, smartly dressed and with regulation haircuts.

Pupils and Parents: Parents range from high society and no problem paying the fees to ordinary mortals on LEA grants. Schools aims to make its pupils confident, articulate and at ease with relationships and indeed they are a very pleasant and open lot. 'They don't fail interviews,' says Dr Chinn.

Entrance: At 11, 12 or 13. Must have been diagnosed as dyslexic, with average intelligence or above, have no 'primary behavioural or emotional problems' – ie those not resulting from dyslexia and peoples' reaction to it – and must want to learn. Apply up to two years in advance.

Exit: To schools that can offer continued support – the school keeps a list of recommended ones.

Remarks: As good as you get for those with severe dyslexia. We don't yet know what changed will follow the sale to Priory.

Marshfields School

Eastern Close, Dogsthorpe, Peterborough, Cambridgeshire, PE1 4PP

Tel: 01733 568 058
Fax: 01733 553 855
Email: aab067@peterborough.gov.uk
Website: www.marshfields.co.uk

• Pupils: 160 boys and girls, all day • Ages: 10-19
• Religion: Non-denom • School status: State
• School gender: Mixed • Day/boarding: Day pupils

SEN provision

Detail:

Centre of excellence for:
- Mild: EBD;
- Moderate: EBD; MLD;
- Others: CD;

Now provide for in school:
- Mild: ASP; AUT; ADD; ADHD; DS; DYSC; DYSL; DYSP; HI; VI; CP;
- Moderate: ASP; AUT; ADD; ADHD; DS; DYSC; DYSL; DYSP; HI; VI; CP;
- Severe: ADD; ADHD; EBD; HI; VI;
- Others: SPD; ODD; TIC; FRX; Sp&LD; DEL; Epi; PD; Eat;

Experience of:
- Mild: SpLD;
- Moderate: SpLD;
- Severe: ASP; AUT; DS; DYSC; DYSL; DYSP; SpLD; CP;
- Others: AUT(other); OCD; GEN; EAL; MSI; Oth;

Summary: Marshfields is a predominantly secondary, day school for students with moderate learning needs and global delay. Students are aged between 10 and 19 years. Students also have additional difficulties associated with their personal, social and emotional development and may have other challenges arising out of sensory or physical needs. The school has its own dedicated post-16 provision for up to 50 students. This includes a federation arrangement with Peterborough Regional College.

Marshfields is also a Specialist Technology College, providing significant learning opportunities to its family of schools, the local community and the wider region. The school has won a number of prestigious awards; most recently, it was included in Ofsted's honours list of the schools that had two or more outstanding inspections.

What we say about the school - the full Good Schools Guide review

Head: At time of writing the school is between heads, the excellent Mr Spurgeon having been exalted to be something stratospheric in Ofsted. The achievement of Marshfields clearly owes much to him and his predecessor but, he asserts, it's the quality and commitment of the staff who make this school exceptional, he couldn't have done it on its own. Observation of the school at work bears this out. 'We're a school,' they say, 'we abide by the usual criteria and we're fully inclusive. Whoever comes is fully included.' Thus do they turn the familiar criticism of special schools on its head. Marshfields isn't a last resort, it's a first resort. They rebut any gibes about segregation by showing how the school gets its students out into the community as often as possible: 'We test their learning by putting them in real life situations.' The community, at the heart of which everyone here wants the school to be, comes to Marshfields for evening courses in IT. The school maintains sprightly partnerships with local businesses, community groups and mainstream schools. Marshfields is notably gregarious, a very good mixer. Together, the staff have navigated the school into the upper reaches of acclamation, to which this guide is pleased to add its own hearty cheer.

Academic Matters: This is a specialist technology college, one of just 12 special schools in the UK to have achieved such status, and it's something the students feel good about. It has won a tranche of other awards, too. The cash injection has done no harm – 'we had here a head who was skilled in the arts of sourcing funding'. The curriculum is national, boys do as well as girls (yes, they do), and everything achieved is accredited – community work notches up Millennium Volunteers points. The focus is on employability, on equipping these children with the fullest possible portfolio of measured achievements inside the classroom and out. It is highly structured, exceedingly purposeful and rigorous. Expectations are set far higher than you'd think they could be, and they're not restricted to academic work. Best behaviour is insisted on kindly but inflexibly, uniform is worn properly, parents are called upon to get involved. It's all part of the package and it's all very concrete. These children know exactly where they stand, and it makes them feel safe. No detail is too small, eyes miss nothing. Interestingly, it's the school phobics here who are the last to let a fall of snow stop them coming to school. They claim the spirit of the school is 'joyful, positive and creative', and, do you know, they're right. Ofsted gives it top marks fulsomely across the board.

If there's any aspect of this school that is not outstanding it doesn't stand out. You quickly lose all sense that you're in a special school. Educational thinking is rooted in reality – the way the world actually is for these children. The head readily agrees that Marshfields operates diametrically differently from a Steiner school, which isn't to pit one against the other, simply to define the distinction. Class sizes have risen to around 14 (up from 10) given the high number of successful tribunal appeals. No one's nuts about this, but they're coping. Parents say the school really does meet needs and cater for all sorts, and you see this in the classroom where highly planned lessons and conspicuously nice teachers teach to each and all with masses of AppleMac laptops to abet them. Design technology thrives, as does food technology – both of them subjects which lead to jobs.

With the jobs market in mind, personal development is reckoned as important as academic attainment. Here, rigorous kindness goes hand in hand with realistic expectations. They say that 'the pupils are honest enough to recognise that this is the place for them,' that they learn to nurture pragmatic aspirations and develop compensatory personal qualities which employers will want. Work experience is a serious business, and the success of students in finding work is testimony to fine preparation and guidance. They learn life skills, they learn to make choices – 'we choose nothing for them' – and a notable ingredient is the annual residential trip for each child, irrespective of means.

Post-16 is selective, open to all in the area, so you have to apply like anyone else. Anything from one to three-year courses. Slightly set apart, enviable facilities, and don't the students know it.

Games, Options, The Arts: Lots of good art – 'many of these children are visual learners'. Lots of drama and music, some with mainstream schools. Masses of sport, some football at Peterborough United. After-school youth club.

Background and Atmosphere: Set in the northern outskirts of Peterborough in the midst of acres of suburban mediocrity. A nightmare to find – so be sure to factor in getting-lost time before leaving home. Buildings are bright light and airy, spick and span and wholly unreminiscent of a special school.

Pastoral Care and Discipline: No student admitted unless parents sign up to behaviour policy. House system. Discipline not so much overt as persistently insistent. Staff know these children very well.

Pupils and Parents: From a 25-mile radius, most from Peterborough. Racial mix reflects local reality. A high number from disadvantaged families; some children are in care. The school is for very obvious reasons a victim of its own success and crammed to the gunwales. Because the students are bused in, parents hold their own coffee mornings, and there's a League of Friends which raises money, avidly supported, a parent tells us, by even the least well off. It's a measure of gratitude. This school is 'a life-saver'.

Entrance: Statemented children. Two thirds moderate learning difficulties with additional significant challenges, especially in emotional development; some social, emotional and behavioural difficulties; a few severe learning diffs. Most join in September, but they admit throughout the year. Some come post-16.

Exit: Most leave post-16 for training or work, a matter of great pride. The school also, unusually, supports around 25 students at a local FE college.

Remarks: You are aware of cheerfulness, purpose and extraordinarily good behaviour of the most natural kind. The rigid frame of expectations makes for a notably calm, sunny social climate. But let's now hand the microphone to Baroness Mary Warnock. It was on this very spot where, in June 2005, she, er, remodelled her ideas about the role of special schools. Here she is in Their Lordships' House: 'It is one of the best and most successful schools that I have ever visited.' Bullseye, Mary.

MARY HARE GRAMMAR SCHOOL

Arlington Manor, Snelsmore Common, Newbury, Berkshire, RG14 3BQ

Tel: 01635 244 200
Fax: 01635 244 200
Email: mhgsoxbr@rmplc.co.uk
Website: www.maryhare.org.uk

• Pupils: 165 boys and girls • Ages: 11-19 • Religion: None
• Fees: Full board £21840 pa; day £18620 pa: there are 4 terms each year, so quoted termly fees seem wonderfully low!
• School status: State • School gender: Mixed
• Day/boarding: Takes boarders

SEN provision

Detail:
Centre of excellence for:
- Mild: HI;
- Moderate: HI;
- Severe: HI;
- Others: Sp&LD;

Now provide for in school:
- Mild: VI; CP;
- Moderate: VI; CP;

Experience of:
- Mild: ASP; ADD; DYSP;
- Moderate: ASP; EBD;

Summary: Mary Hare is a special non-maintained school specialising in the education of severely and profoundly hearing-impaired young people aged 5-19. The school uses an auditory/oral approach to communication, believing that this is the best method of achieving proficiency in the comprehension and use of spoken and written English. Great reliance is placed on using to the full the small amounts of remaining hearing that each student possesses, through the best available amplification systems, used in appropriate acoustic environments. Only this approach – the continuing development of listening and lip-reading skills and a teaching/learning medium of verbal language – gives that degree of access to the modern curriculum needed to realise the potential that most of our students possess; only this approach provides students such as ours with the educational, vocational and social opportunities not only to develop their talents to the full, but to contribute significantly and positively to the society in which they will choose to spend their adult life.

Although primarily specialising in hearing impairment the school does have experience of other special needs in students that are not only hearing impaired. This includes students with visual impairment and physical disabilities and some mildly on the autistic spectrum.

What we say about the school - the full Good Schools Guide review

Head: Chief Executive of Mary Hare, national charity for the education of deaf children, is Dr Ivan Tucker OBE BSc Dip Aud PhD. Strong oralist: promotes deaf children speaking. Sees technology as key. Works tirelessly not just for Mary Hare but for the national and international deaf community too. Has spent a lot of time in underprivileged countries running exchange and outreach programmes, helping the less privileged benefit from the technology, teaching and training skills that Mary Hare provides. An inspiration to all.

Principal: Since 2004, Mr D A J (Tony) Shaw BTech MEd(Aud) NPQH. Was deputy head and head of audiology at St John's Catholic School for the Deaf, Boston Spa before being appointed as vice principal at Mary Hare in 1992. Married to Ruth, an artist and designer. They have two children: the oldest recently graduated from Cambridge University, the youngest is studying A levels. Thinks he's incredibly fortunate to have a family who understand how much the job means to him; a job he genuinely believes is the best in the world.

Worked as an industrial physicist before moving across to teach deaf children. Says he was lucky – his passion for physics coincided with an exciting time in the development of technology for the deaf. Was able to harness technology in a way not previously available. Believes deafness isn't an impermeable barrier and that providing ways to ensure deaf children achieve despite their deafness is an enthralling prospect and one that Mary Hare achieves through the professionalism of the entire team. Says it's a very humbling experience to see children realise their potential and to work in a school where the partnership with parents is so strong. He worked for a long time on appeals, fighting for children to have the right to attend the school. His zeal and dedication aren't lost on parents who say he's boundlessly enthusiastic, wonderfully positive, lives on site, loves his job. Gets emotionally involved; incredibly committed.

Academic Matters: Average class size of ten, though many smaller groups in evidence. All follow National Curriculum, taking full range of GCSEs. A levels, AVCEs and key skills available in sixth form. Usual subjects on offer plus A level performance studies, photography, product design, textiles and psychology. AVCE options include business, ICT, leisure and recreation and the ever popular media studies (have own studio), also offer vocational courses in IT, care, sport and recreation to those students who want a taste of the real world of work. A few students follow a pre-advanced level curriculum in year 12. Over 80 per cent of GCSEs graded A* to C. Has terrifically high value added, almost off the scale. English speaking board exams (ESB) compulsory in the first year, optional thereinafter, say exams help develop speech and confidence.

Facilities are very good, thanks in part to massive fundraising by the school. Classrooms are spacious with desks arranged in shape of an arc so all can see the teacher at all times. Buildings acoustically treated. There's a fully resourced library with learning resource centre attached, well-equipped science labs and art and technology, housed in a super converted stable block with many inspiring works in evidence. Interactive whiteboards increasingly in use, plenty of computers etc. Modern, light dining room: tasty food, lots of choice. Good sized assembly hall with cameras and screens throughout; no last minute off-the-cuff assemblies here, they're prepared in advance with lots of visual aids and subtext appearing on the many screens. Latest development (well underway) is a new performing arts, conference and education centre to house the music department and music therapy unit as well as bring in revenue to the school.

Glowing Ofsted report with vast majority of categories rated outstanding and nothing less than good. Communication is auditory/oral. Signing isn't used in lessons but many pupils can sign and choose to do so socially. School says the educational achievements of pupils following the auditory oral approach far outstrip those of pupils following either total or bilingual approaches with added social and vocational benefits of being able to use English and communicate with the hearing community.

Parents believe the key to Mary Hare's success is allowing deaf children to learn without having to struggle to understand. They work hard to remove the barriers to learning. The training of teachers, technology, classroom set up etc all means children can get on with learning, without struggling to hear. 'It's hard enough to get through GCSE without battling with the environment. However good technology gets, it's still difficult for kids if the acoustic environment and general noise levels cannot be readily controlled.' Here everything is said in more than one way and in carefully controlled conditions. This is a school that's always trying to improve, to give pupils the best possible chance. Said one parent: 'my daughter was exhausted in mainstream just trying to understand what was being said without understanding concepts. If she worked with an LSA she'd miss chunks of what was being said. She couldn't be involved in spontaneous class discussion. Those barriers are removed here. She can get on with learning. Her mainstream school was lovely but she'd often be isolated because hearing people frequently find it too much trouble to communicate with the deaf.' And school is inclusive: for many children this is the first time they have not just been accepted by their peers but chosen. Another parent added: 'In school, these children mix only with other children who are deaf – and, paradoxically, it teaches them how to deal with hearing children and the hearing world. It is hard for parents facing this choice to believe that immersing a deaf child with other deaf children can really be the best way of preparing them for life. But it is hard to over-emphasise the success, and the high and rapid dividends, of this strategy.

At Mary Hare the children discover that they are not the odd-child-out and that they have things they want to say to other children – who want to listen to them. It gives them a courage to forge their own personalities and the insight to deal with other people. It is a process mediated by an intensive contribution from dedicated and experienced staff.

School joined forces with Starkey Laboratories to open a commercial laboratory specialising in manufacturing children's ear moulds; any problems with hearing aids can be dealt with quickly. A variety of hearing devices are used including the technologically advanced group hearing aid designed by the school. On arrival at the school, children have their hearing tested then audiologists build unique headphones for them, for use in the classroom. These plug into a computer, which recognises them. Through the headphones they can hear the teacher's voice and all their peers too; this differs to a mainstream setting where the teacher wears a microphone, so pupils can hear the teacher but can't hear peers answering questions. Cochlear implants have a box to plug into, rather than headphones. A great device, especially for teachers who control the system and can turn off the children's microphones if they don't want them to speak (every teacher and parent should have one!) Assessments open to any one in the UK, including adults.

A specialist assessment centre is available to all families in the UK. Go to family room first to chat through what's going to happen, have EP onsite, observation room, audiology and hearing aid dispensary. There are five graduate audiologists and two full-time speech and language therapists who work hard to develop listening skills, improve voice pitch, rhythm, fluency and intonation, assist with speech sounds which cause difficulty, help students develop communication tactics, extend vocabulary and develop subject-specific language. Hearing difficulties mean language acquisition tends to be way behind, will miss words that others take for granted. Say it's vital for pupils to listen to each other and to be heard.

Games, Options, The Arts: Good, well kept sports facilities: gym, own full size pool (housed in what looks like a giant greenhouse and would benefit from a cosmetic makeover or more), all weather floodlit playing area, tennis and netball courts, soccer pitches etc. Lots on offer including hockey, squash, horse riding, trampolining and golf. Plenty of fixtures against other schools, with many athletes competing at county level. Some represent the Great Britain Deaf Sports Association, notably in swimming, soccer, tennis and athletics. Not surprising then that we witnessed a boisterous game of basketball during the lunch hour with the master seriously outclassed by his energetic charges. Fantastic artwork on show, lots of sculpture, photography etc. Not a school that says no, all talents encouraged and nurtured genuinely does all it can to enable the students. Music is an important part of the curriculum with several pupils playing to grade 7 or 8. The school's annual Christmas Show is something of an event. One parent said: 'these children are deaf but they do dialogue by deaf children; and dancing by deaf children; they have a deaf orchestra; and deaf soloists, both instrumental and voice. They declaim. They act. They entertain. They dance, in troupes and as soloists. They stage challenging musicals: Grease, Chicago, the Wizard of Oz, West Side Story. Children with extreme difficulty in the basic components of speech face down an audience of 200, find they can do it, and that they enjoy doing it.' One who knows the school well told us: 'Performances of relish, style and aplomb are forthcoming from, very probably, the same children who before Mary Hare, were awkward, diffident; and not only reluctant in the extreme to take the social spotlight but quite incapable of doing so.' Latest offering is own talent competition, the Y factor, won by a band called the Deafness. Not that all are tuneful; we heard a chord clashing version of London Calling: though in fairness it was a first run through!

Background and Atmosphere: Set in lovely surroundings of 140 acres of prime Berkshire countryside, the school is named after the educationalist Mary Hare who, towards the end of the 19th Century, had a vision that deaf children were capable of realising the full potential of their intellect and had no need of shelter from the hearing society. Moved to current spacious site in 1948.

Pastoral Care and Discipline: Specialist care staff work with boarding pupils. Each boarding house has a head of house responsible to the deputy principal with waking care staff on duty throughout the night. All year 7 are housed together, with year 8-11 girls living in the Manor and the boys in Mansell House. Facilities are good, rooms bright and airy with usual common rooms, kitchens etc. Girls recently held a room decorating competition with the many, very glamorous, results still in evidence (watch out changing rooms). Super modern sixth form centre with mainly individual study bedrooms each with en-suite bathroom shared between a pair of rooms. Feels more like a university hall of residence than a boarding house. Try to get balance of promoting independence but offering level of care parents' want. Lots of trust placed on pupils but any that step out of line will suffer the consequences. Day, weekly and termly boarding options available. Plenty of clubs occupy pupils after school, ranging from scouts to snorkelling, cycling proficiency to chess and Duke of Edinburgh for the over 14s, have own youth club too. No Saturday school but range of activities at weekends including ice-skating, cinema, ten-pin bowling etc. A careers education and guidance programme plus work with Connexions help pupils prepare for life after Mary Hare.

Pupils and Parents: From all over the UK including Northern Ireland. Sixth formers, friendly, savvy group, wear own clothes: stylish, fashionable. Younger pupils smartly turned out in blazers et al. Friendships are a strength of the school. For some pupils this is the first chance they've had not to be different, to be with others who have similar difficulties. Holidays can be problematic – often life before Mary Hare was a lonely, isolated experience and holidays may mean a return to that. Parents and pupils we spoke to enthuse about the school, see it as a godsend and find it difficult to fault. Say there's a great tolerance of challenge and assertiveness, skills seen as essential in building confidence and self-worth to make way in the hearing world. Parents believe the segregation and accompanying specialist help prepares the children for the hearing world. And the preciousness of deaf culture doesn't exist here. Pupils recently had bracelets made, chose 'deaf not dumb', which sums up the Mary Hare pupil.

Entrance: School exists to meet the needs of severely and profoundly hearing impaired children. All attend assessment day. School is selective, taking those with above average potential. Majority join in year 7; though odd ones admitted at other times, these tend to be more difficult cases who've failed in mainstream and come with associated low self-esteem or behavioural difficulties. All are statemented, though will take privately funded students. Many go to tribunal, majority win, often with support from the school.

Exit: Majority stay into the sixth form and take A levels. Then vast majority to range of universities, including Oxford, Edinburgh College of Art, Bristol, Goldsmiths, Wolverhampton, some to art college etc.

Remarks: A fantastic, innovative school doing a wonderful and unique job for all those in its care. Releases youngsters from their deafness, turns out happy-high achieving children, gets results.

MARY HARE PRIMARY SCHOOL

Mill Hall, Pigeons Farm Road, Thatcham, Newbury, RG19 8XA

Tel: 01635 573 800
Fax: 01635 524 999
Email: primary@maryhare.org.uk
Website: www.maryhare.org.uk

• Pupils: 45 girls and boys • Ages: 5-12 • Religion: None
• Fees: £6,530 day; £9140 boarding
• School status: Independent • School gender: Mixed
• Day/boarding: Takes boarders

SEN provision

Summary: Mary Hare Primary caters for children with a severe or profound hearing loss. We teach children through talking using a natural aural approach, which means we make maximum use of their residual hearing. We are not selective on academic ability. We take children whom we feel are capable of developing spoken language to communicate successfully in the hearing world. We find this out by inviting the prospective pupil for a week's assessment placement. Deafness is our speciality, but we also welcome children with mild additional SEN needs.

What we say about the school - the full Good Schools Guide review

Head: Mrs Karen Smith MA PGCE TOD. A reassuringly calm demeanour. Caring, compassionate, understands the needs of pupils and parents alike.

Entrance: As for senior school but non-selective. Tends to take children with a wider range of needs than those at the senior school in part because many deaf children will cope in the primary school environment but find the academic demands of senior school too tricky.

Exit: Some to Mary Hare others to other special schools, odd one to mainstream.

Remarks: Housed in what was a former American Air Force Officers' mess. The school has lost none of its grand past with the panelled dining room, fabulous fireplace in the assembly hall, galleried landing and splendid grounds still hinting of yesteryear. The extensive grounds now house a cycle track marked out as a road with crossing points, stopping areas, children's activity playground etc. Have dedicated art room, gym and small library. Busy, cheerful pupils work in near typical primary classrooms packed full of stimulating displays.

All follow the National Curriculum adapted if necessary. Music, PE, technology and PSHE feature for all, with French for older ones. Have an auditory-oral philosophy and focus very much on language development, writing and speaking; signing isn't used. Have two one-to-one speech therapy sessions plus a weekly group session, with speech reinforced throughout their learning. Tend to come at age 8 or 9 when start to fail in mainstream. Small classes, maximum eight pupils with plenty of classroom assistants to help out and support. Technology a necessary feature, use group hearing aids for class lessons.

One of only two oral schools in the country so not surprising that pupils from all over Britain, with some exceptionally, boarding from age 5. Not an easy option: yet parents who do, say 'the memories are painful but they don't regret it.' Care taken very seriously, with each bedroom the responsibility of a key worker who assumes responsibility for all aspects of the child's welfare, not just daily routine but extending to planning individual programmes, attending Annual Reviews and of course regular contact with parents. Encourage communication, have minions, a fax machine and phones, which children can use any evening to talk to parents.

There's a fabulous indoor children's play area with café, village shop, washing machines, ovens for imaginative play used by younger boarders, and the most amazing bedrooms. Every child not only sleeps in a themed room but also on a themed bed, made for the school by a talented carpenter from Sussex, the attention to detail incredible. There's a castle room, circus with lions cage, jungle room, ocean room, Mississippi Belle with steamboat; a train room complete with carriages and engines for beds plus left luggage drawers etc. This really is the stuff of fantasy and fairytales; the biggest dilemma is for Goldilocks to choose which to sleep in. It doesn't stop there; a mural of characters adorns the corridors and closer inspection shows the characters have the faces of teachers and pupils.

Pupils work and play hard to meet the school's expectations. Parent's say, the school opens educational doorways, develops happy, confident youngsters in a lovely, caring, nurturing environment. 'I sent my child away to school but got my son back.'

Mayville High School

35-37 St Simon's Road, Southsea, Hampshire, PO5 2PE

Tel: 023 9273 4847
Fax: 023 9229 3649
Email: mayvillehighschool@talk21.com
Website: www.mayvillehighschool.com

• Pupils: 440; 205 boys, 235 girls, all day, of which nursery, 6 months-4: 42 girls and 37 boys; pre-prep, 4-7: 42 girls and 6 boys; junior school, 7-11: 58 boys, 55 girls; senior school, 11-16: 80 boys, 97 girls • Ages: 6 months to 16
• Religion: C of E, all creeds welcome
• Fees: Pre-prep £900; junior £1,675; senior £2,170
• School status: Independent
• Opendays: Tours daily, taster days by appointment
• School gender: Mixed • Day/boarding: Day pupils

SEN provision

Detail:

Centre of excellence for:
  Mild: DYSL;
  Moderate: DYSL;
Experience of:
  Mild: ASP; AUT; ADD; ADHD; DYSC; DYSP; HI; VI;
  Moderate: DYSP;
  Severe: DYSL;
  Others: SPD; Sp&LD; Eat;

Summary: The dyslexia unit was established in 1992 to provide specialist support to pupils across the age range 4-16.

Most pupils are assessed prior to school entry, in addition to this, small classes and a whole school awareness of dyslexia enable staff to quickly identify and refer pupils who may be experiencing difficulties so that they can be supported in the most effective way. All members of staff are trained to utilise the principles of Accelerated Learning, visual, auditory and kinesthetic (VAK) model and Multiple Intelligence profiling to assist pupils, especially those with dyslexia, in the most effective way.

Each pupil is regarded as a unique individual, with a unique pattern of strengths and unique ways of being clever and successful. The focus is on positive feedback, building self-esteem and confidence – maintaining high expectations while providing a 'safety net'.

Support can be delivered in a variety of ways from classroom support via an effective team of learning support assistants, to work in small groups, to individual specialist tuition with a dyslexia tutor, to support on one of our own programmes, for example Target Reading or Target Maths.

IEPs are devised from education psychology reports and in-house assessments. They are used to focus and inform teaching and to monitor the attainment of targets set. They are frequently referred to, discussed with other staff, parents and wherever appropriate, with the pupils themselves.

The structure and content of the support lesson depends on pupil age and individual needs. Each lesson is based on targets from the IEP and developed via several linked tasks with reinforcement delivered via multi-sensory games and computer programmes. Many of the games are tailor made for individual pupils and make learning so enjoyable that pupils sometimes get quite upset if they have done so well that they no longer need to attend the Unit!

What we say about the school - the full Good Schools Guide review

Head: Since 1994, Mrs Linda Owens, BEd. Has overseen what in recent years has been rapid evolution from genteel girls' school to mainstream co-ed (100 per cent when boys enter year 11 in 2006) catering for a number of particular needs locally. She and her fellow strategists have read market forces incredibly intelligently, their acumen abetted by their strong sense of what education should be about, namely, putting children in touch with the best ways of making the most of themselves. An indefatigably hard worker and a disciplinarian in a kindly old-fashioned sense – the pupils shoot to their feet and full-throatedly incant 'Good mor-orning Mrs Ow-wens' when she enters a classroom – you also see the littlest girls rushing up to hug her. Catchphrase 'everyone here is a star in some way', her words meaning what they say – this is what the school is predicated on. Teaches drama and oversees the school's monster musicals. Loves what performance does to a child's sense of itself.

Academic Matters: The spectrum is broad. They do particularly well by dyslexics and those who need the emotional nurturing of a small, caring school. It's all about focus on individual needs, of course, and it's this that's made them locally famous – 'Others say they do it, we have to do it.' Class teaching is trad, structured, careful with – we saw it happen – the clever being stretched while the rest work at their own level, and no sense of anyone looking down – or up. These children rate each other according to personal attributes, not marks, and that's instilled by the teachers. Parents say 'they lay down the building blocks of learning one by one and don't move on until everything is consolidated, no matter how much reiteration is necessary. It's very systematic.' It's also segregated. Boys, they reckon, develop differently from girls so they teach them maths, science and English separately, the boys for shorter periods according to male attention span, and bring them together for modern languages, history, geography, art, drama and sport. This is increasingly popular with members of ethnic minorities, the separate sex education in particular. One father praised the way his daughter can wear the hijab with pride, attend festivals and is encouraged to tell the other pupils at assemblies all about her faith – 'They accommodate individuality at no cost to the community.'

A number of children here are victims of the coercive, target obsessed National Curriculum – they fell behind, gave up on themselves and became the prey of all manner of emotional fallout. Refugees from other independents here, too. Mayville turns them around by, first, 'understanding the problem,' say parents, then making them feel secure, reacquainting them with success and giving them 'an amazing sense of belonging'. Discipline is strict in terms of expectations, never heavy-handed. Teachers here understand learning styles; they're up-to-date, not a bit faddish, and unusually well-qualified. Relationships are warm, often giggly. Say parents, 'they know them and they like them'. But it's 'not cushy'. The school believes that 'hitting barriers gives them the strength to overcome and learn. It sets them up for life. Our job is to keep them going though this period.'

The dyslexia unit is justly lauded by inspectors (CReSTeD DU) who know what's what, and by parents who see the difference. Highly qualified teachers do all the right polysyllabic things – multi-sensory, kinaesthetic – and they do it expertly, but this isn't the half of it. Remediation has to be much more than a mechanical process because every dyslexic is different. Kindness matters most, and it is the emotional intelligence of those who work here that generates their best work. It's all about how children feel about themselves, and one thing they certainly don't feel is sorry. This is a victim-free zone. Lots of one-to-one – 'expensive but worth it'. In addition to GCSEs, some pupils are entered for dyslexic-friendly BTecs. Some parents say they'd like to see more vocational subjects – and wish the school wouldn't worry so much about b league tables. Well, it wouldn't if they didn't.

Mayville is not a school for the marginalised. There are conventionally bright children here, too, they benefit in all the ways the rest do, they resist the urge to go off to Portsmouth Grammar at 11 and they pick up fine GCSE results. The school is currently developing a programme to stretch them even further.

Games, Options, The Arts: Sport four times a week squeezed in after lunch, fixtures with schools of similar size and they play in local leagues. Drama is big because 'it's a whole life skill'. Public speaking big, too, and they win Rotary Youth Speaks comps. Art good. Music doesn't stretch to orchestras but they do super choirs, a jazz group and rock bands. All learn recorder, then a brass instrument and violin for a term each. Fab after school clubs and supervised prep: they are open, would you believe it, from 8 till 6, 50 weeks a year.

Pastoral Care and Discipline: Strict uniform code – smart blazer – and strict behaviour code underscore the sense of security the school instils. Justly famed for its standards of care. One mum says 'I wish I could be a fly on the wall to find out exactly how they do it.' Teachers 'very approachable. Any problems, they pick up the phone or write a note.' Expectations of parents are rigorous: 'They let you know early, and they expect your backing.' Children notably pleasing in their manners and demeanour and shiningly proud of their school.

Pupils and Parents: Local. Some move to be near the school, some make quite long daily journeys. Down to earth, unsnobby. Active PTA.

Entrance: No academic hurdle. Interview. They recruit for balance, so where SENs are concerned they do turn away 'the one too many'. Dyslexia's the big thing, but they also consider dyspraxia, ADHD and mild ASD. No emotional and behavioural disorders – 'There's only so much we can do'.

Exit: Havant College v popular. Local sixth form colleges and independent sixth forms.

Money Matters: Fees decidedly competitive, and after-school care a real bargain. Academic and creative arts scholarships worth 50 per cent of fees. Some means-tested bursaries up to 80 per cent.

Remarks: Very much its own place. Very inclusive. Operating out of four town houses a stone's throw apart, they cheerfully concede 'we don't look good' yet modifications are apt and they nurture development plans. The point is this: the school's a raging little success story.

MERCHANT TAYLORS' SCHOOL

Sandy Lodge, Northwood, Middlesex, HA6 2HT

Tel: 01923 820 644
Fax: 01923 835 110
Email: info@mtsn.org.uk
Website: www.mtsn.org.uk

• Pupils: 815 boys, all day • Ages: 11-18 • Religion: Multi-faith
• Fees: £11,260 pa • School status: Independent
• Opendays: May and September • School gender: Boys
• Day/boarding: Day pupils

SEN provision

Detail:
Now provide for in school:
Mild: ASP; ADD; DYSL; DYSP; SpLD;

Summary: At Merchant Taylors' all boys are screened on entry to the school. Any needs diagnosed are discussed with parents and, wherever possible, the necessary support is provided. The school has a Learning Skills Co-ordinator who supports individual children and, more importantly, provides training and guidance for teaching staff to enable them best to integrate each pupil into the classroom environment. Achievement of pupils who have extra needs is at least as good as other pupils in the school. Extra opportunities are also provided for the gifted and talented.

What we say about the school - the full Good Schools Guide review

Headmaster: Mr Stephen Wright MA (forties) took over in 2004 from the long-serving and widely respected Jon Gabbitas. Educated at King's School, Macclesfield, and Queen's College, Cambridge. Former deputy head at

The Judd School, followed by six years as head of Borden Grammar School, north Kent. Married to Penny, a nurse, they have three children, one son at Merchant Taylors'. Very keen on sport – volleyball half blue at Cambridge – and continues to teach history and general studies. Enthusiastic gardener and opera buff.

Academic Matters: As is the case with many heads of schools near the top of the league tables, the head says he's not a great fan and then details just how good the exam results are. In this case, exceptional. Nearly 90 per cent A or B at A level, 86 per cent A and A* at GCSE. Used to demand six Bs for sixth form entry now at least three As required in the mix. 'They're looking to match schools like St Paul's,' said one parent.

Teaching a major strength of the school – with added value in every subject. Predominantly male staff oversee classes of 20 up to GCSE, 10 at AS and A level. All boys take 9 or 10 GCSEs – about 50 per cent do maths and/or French a year early. Four academic subjects at AS; most take three As. Everyone also takes AS general studies in years 12 and 13.

Wide range of subjects on offer throughout – over 20 in the sixth form. Science taught as three subjects – more able sit all three at GCSE, less do the double award. Chemistry one of most popular A levels (along with mathematics and economics). Very strong modern languages department in superbly equipped, purpose-built centre. Two thirds take two modern languages to GCSE, 50 per cent at least one at AS. All boys study French in years 7 and 8 (though this is under consideration) and begin German, Italian, Spanish or Ancient Greek in year 9. French, German, Spanish offered at AS and A, plus Italian, Japanese and Mandarin as part of the general studies programme. Latin now being phased out. English offered as three different A Levels (Eng lang, Eng lit, and Eng lang and lit).Extensive written reports three times a year, identifying strengths and weaknesses. Grades and comments sent to parents each half term, plus a full parents' evening once a year with teachers, tutors and headmaster. Study skills built into the curriculum. Once a year each boy writes his own report in considerable detail and discusses it privately with his tutor. Bright, modern library – 'a jewel' waxes the Independent Schools Inspectorate – with over 18,000 books, periodicals, tapes and CDs.

Games, Options, The Arts: Games taken seriously in this outstandingly well-equipped school. Fabulous on-site pitches, large sports hall, cricket nets, heated indoor pool, floodlit all-weather hockey pitch, lake for sailing and windsurfing, grass and hard tennis courts, squash and fives court, fencing salle, huge, level, playing field for athletics, etc. School teams in rugby, hockey, cricket – as many as four a year – and PE includes basketball, athletics, swimming and tennis. Soccer, badminton, croquet, cross-country, golf and shooting too.

Art a growing strength with a dynamic head of department – 'great man' say parents and boys – determined to add to the growing trickle leaving for top art schools. Light, spacious and well-equipped four-year-old art block with well-used display space. Gallery trips and lectures, exhibitions in school and beyond, residential courses include a week painting at St Ives. Excellent design and technology department. Self-contained music school arranged around an octagonal 150-seat recital hall seating. Annual concert at the Merchant Taylor's Hall in the City, plus a medley of orchestras, band and choirs. Active drama department with numerous large and small scale productions. Strong link with 'sister school' St Helen's Northwood, a mile away, for drama, music and other activities.

Impressive range of extra-curricular options. Over 50 clubs – everything from Scrabble to Outward Bound – including a Young Enterprise Business Company to form rival businesses and a school bank run by senior boys as a branch of Barclay's. Large cadet force – army, navy and air force – with purpose-built HG, assault course and shooting range.

Background and Atmosphere: Founded in the City of London in 1561 by the Worshipful Company of Merchant Taylors and Linen Armourers, it was then the largest school in the country. In 1933 moved to current impressive green-belt site, which remains one of the outstanding features of the school. Core of buildings still date from that period, with a dominant Deco angularity complemented by municipally neat grounds. Playing fields surround the school in an impressive sea of green. Funding clearly not an issue with recent additions including a new library and information centre, new computer centre, new politics and economics centre and a new entrance hall and sixth form. No lack of direction here – administration and management evidently clear and precise. Despite its high academic standing, the non-academic side is given equal weight, and the school sees its objective as equipping boys for the world beyond their schools days – 'a broad and balanced education that prepares pupils for life,' says the head. Old boys include Sir Edmund Spenser, Clive of India, Titus Oates, the artist Samuel Palmer and the founding editor of The Times; and, more recently, Lord Coggan, Archbishop of Canterbury and the sculptor Lynn Chadwick (whose work graces one of the many manicured lawns).

Pastoral Care and Discipline: Eight day houses and a very strong tutor system for individual guidance. Each boy is allocated a tutor on his arrival, whom he sees once a week throughout his time at the school and who monitors his progress – academic, sporting and extra-curricular – and reports regularly to parents.

Two school assemblies a week, plus one house assembly. Religious leaders from different faiths invited to address the whole school. Christian services held in the chapel. Plus a Muslim prayer room, a Jewish society, a Christian discussion group and an Asian Cultural Society. All faiths work happily together with tolerance and consideration. Probably not, however, a school for the very observant Jew, since a significant number of activities take place on Friday evenings and weekends.

School rules kept as simple as possible. Boys encouraged to show kindness, common sense and respect in their day-to-day behaviour – and good manners here are clearly not restricted to high days and holy days with evident courtesy displayed in boys' dealings with each other. Boys take considerable responsibility at registration, lunchtimes and assembly, and also run the Duke of Edinburgh Award, the Asian Culture Club and house-based teams and activities.

Series of lessons and courses on health and diet, sexual behaviour and risks of alcohol and substance abuse. Qualified school counsellor, with whom boys may book appointments and talk in confidence.

Pupils and Parents: Pupils reflect the affluent, suburban, middle class area in which the school sits – Asian, Jewish, and commuter-belt Wasps. 'Children of the Thatcher Revolution,' remarked one parent, 'with a competitive spirit to match.' Primarily local intake and points along the Metropolitan Line – Moor Park Station within walking distance. Coaches from Beaconsfield, Ealing, Harrow, Mill Hill, Radlett, Stanmore.

Entrance: 11+ entrance (about 50 per cent from the state sector) by January exam in English, maths and verbal reasoning. Boys who do well are asked to return for interview. 13+ entry – need to be registered a year in advance, with interviews in autumn preceding entry. School's own exam in all CE subjects with the scholarship exam running at the same time. Scholarship candidates invited back for further interviews. A small number of sixth form places by examination in March. Candidates must register by January 31st and will be tested in the subjects they wish to study, followed by interviews.

Exit: About 15 to Oxbridge in last two years, and another 10 to medical schools, as well as a broad range of academic subjects at Russell League universities. University and careers advice clearly a strength. Each sixth former is assigned to a senior head of department who acts as his university adviser. Careers guidance from year seven, with a careers test and a careers conference offered later. Work experience – some of which can be done abroad – is highly developed, including a companies links scheme which helps boys find work in major companies in varying sector of business and industry.

Money Matters: No separate scholarship exam but roughly a quarter receive some financial help. At least five scholarships at 11 (maximum 30 per cent of fees), 11 scholarships at 13 (up to 30 per cent of fees), one sixth form scholarship (15 per cent of fees) and one exhibition. Four internal scholarships and exhibitions in the upper and lower sixth for up to 5 per cent of fees. Music scholarships at 11, 13, 16 include one for 25 per cent of fees, one for 15, and two exhibitions of up to 10 per cent, as well as free instrumental or singing tuition. Three Assisted Places up to 100 per cent of the fees.

Remarks: A tightly-run, high-achieving academic school in beautiful surroundings preparing well-rounded and courteous boys for good universities and good jobs. New head yet to make his mark.

MERCHISTON CASTLE SCHOOL

294 Colinton Road, Edinburgh, EH13 0PU

Tel: 0131 312 2200

Fax: 0131 441 6060

Email: Admissions@merchiston.co.uk

Website: www.merchiston.co.uk

• Pupils: 430 boys (70 per cent board, 30 per cent day) • Ages: 8-18 • Religion: Non-denom • Fees: Day: £3,175-4,950; boarding £4,660-£6,925 • School status: Independent • Opendays: Information mornings (ie a morning in the life of the school): March, May, October • School gender: Boys • Day/boarding: Takes boarders

SEN provision

Detail:

Now provide for in school:

- Mild: DYSL;
- Moderate: MLD; DYSL;
- Others: EAL;

Experience of:

- Mild: ASP; ADD; ADHD; EBD; DYSC; DYSP; SpLD; HI; VI; CP;
- Moderate: ASP; ADD; ADHD; DYSP; HI;
- Severe: DYSL; HI;
- Others: CD; OCD; SLD; Epi; Eat;

Summary: Merchiston has a learning support department which gives intensive one-to-one and two-to-one tuition, particularly in the junior school. Prospective pupils go through an in depth assessment so that we can ascertain whether Merchiston would be a suitable school for them. This ensures that we know precisely the level of each pupil. The support thereafter is ongoing and adapted to that pupil's needs. Essentially, we are a mainstream school which can offer to help bright pupils requiring specific learning support, but who can independently access the curriculum in the Senior School up to and including GCSE and AS/A2 Level.

What we say about the school - the full Good Schools Guide review

Headmaster: Since 1998, Mr Andrew Hunter BA PGCE (forties), educated at Aldenham and Manchester University where he read combined studies: English, theology and biblical studies. Came to Merchiston after eight years at Bradfield, where he ended as housemaster of Army House and, before that, eight years at Worksop, housemaster of Pelham House. Trails of glory on games fields, ex-county hockey, squash and tennis player. Head admits to 'ditching his MBA' which he promised us he would complete when we first met him seven years ago. Occasionally teaches A level classes and presentation skills. An expat, he was brought up on a Kenyan coffee farm, and started school at Kenton College, Nairobi. Married to the glamorous Barbara who teaches art and design. The Hunters have three children, one son at Merchiston, one son at a special school and a daughter at St George's. Keen on the arts, theatre, wine tasting etc. He goes from strength to strength – spot of tinkering with the syllabus, mass trawling all over the UK, Europe, and the world on behalf of school, plus a dabble into building. The next great project is the sixth form house opening in September 2007, and a six million quid fundraiser is on the starting blocks (some cash already in hand following the sale of strategically placed geriatric staff houses, which will, of course have to be replaced as well). Excellent Hunter-inspired forty-five page Information Booklet that is undoubtedly the best guide to any school we have ever seen, plus a really comprehensive leaflet on exam results including a rather complicated value-added section – other schools please note.

Academic Matters: School continues to ply the mainly English system, though some may move from AS to Highers over two years. All boys must do two separate sciences at GCSE, and goodly whack go on to study science at A level. Maths, Eng and science results OK, better than the humanities, which, in many cases had a lesser take-up. The labs have all been refurbished – interesting design, repeated throughout the school, a mixture of trad tables and octagonal plinths, but not an interactive whiteboard in sight. Whiteboards at Merchiston, non-reactive and well used (torn in some places) seemed curiously old-fashioned: staff seemed pleased enough with their overhead projectors. Not that much use of computers as teaching tools either (though all must take their European Driving Licence), some pupils have their own laptops and there is a good IT suite plus more computers in the magical double-decker Spawforth library, but prep is not necessarily done online. Good showing in out-of-school activities, physics challenge, chemistry Olympiads and the like.

School now offers full junior school facilities, and littlies can start at eight. Good take-up but not that many boarders, tiny classes, max 12, but in reality smaller than this. Snazzy new Pringle Centre provides a teaching block for eight – ten-year-olds, we were treated to a treatise on tropical fish by the youngest year group, and whilst there were computers in every classroom, there was no dedicated IT area for the youngest. No dedicated dyslexia unit either, but a learning support available and all pupils screened on entry. Pupils must score 100 in IQ assessments in order to follow main curriculum and do the standard 8/9 GCSEs. Certain amount of learning support included within the fees, but extra charge if extra help needed, both for this and for EFL, but see below.

School has CReSTeD B status, though Mrs Carol Watson, head of support for learning, was fairly non-committal about the fact. No pupil taken who can't 'access mainstream education'. She heads a team of roughly four part-timers, though one of these is a four-days-a-week part-timer and she 'often comes in on her day off Friday' (and is basically in charge of the junior house). All pupils are assessed on entry on a whole year group basis for their reading riting and rithmetic, though some boys arrive already diagnosed. Support is specially geared for each pupil, all have individually tailored profiles. Timetabled support varies from year to year, with small groups for foreign languages and Latin, as much to get boys up to speed as for actual diagnosable problems. In-class support too, plus 'concentrated units' for spelling, reading and individual subjects. Maths on the whole catered for by the maths department, whilst the SEN specialists can and do provide support lower down the school, complex problems need more info and background than she feels the SEN dept can give. Lower school miss few lessons, with help available after or before class and in the evenings (boarding school), though pupils may miss Latin, French (some don't do it all) and Spanish or design technology and thereby do one GCSE less. Support for the gifted too. Mrs Watson (who is attached to a boarding house) appears to be a one man 24 hour referral unit, boys can and do come at all times. All the dys-stream catered for, plus two or three currently with 'mild Asperger's' diagnosed in-school; ADHD not a problem, physical handicap not 'a real problem': classes are re-located if access complicated; profoundly deaf boy recently went through the school with a (free) monitor paid for by West Lothian authority. Wow. Can and will scribe in exams and pupils get extra time both in school and public exams. Really quite a large number of boys 'in the system': 'looks like a lot between 80 and a 100'. Laptops not provided by the school, but masses in the special needs dept, all on the school network, and parents often buy their own. Extracurricular (ie not timetabled) classes cost extra.

Games, Options, The Arts: Rugby popular, cricket, athletics, curling back in favour, skiing, sailing etc, ditto all macho field games, well-used sports hall, and very well used swimming pool, weights room replaced by fitness centre. Golf encouraged. Wide variety of activities and successes in many areas. Popular CCF, grannie bashing and work in special schools a viable alternative, rifle range built in to school wall. Masses of trips all over the place in every discipline. Fantastic pipe band, sounding good during our visit, with some of the smallest pipers looking like embryo masons lugging their oblong bagpipe cases with grave determination. Strong choral tradition, including close harmony group, and huge number of orchestras and bands. Super art department, with terrific paintings both in the department and displayed all over the school, apparently not much take-up post school, only one to St Martins last year. Surprising, this is a strong department. History of art only within the A level curriculum, no ceramics; new printing press in the offing. DT uses Cad Cam, and good juxtaposition with computer suite and music hall – open till late.

Background and Atmosphere: Founded in 1833 by scientist Charles Chalmers, school moved from Merchiston Castle (now owned by Napier University) to the rather gaunt purpose-built Colinton House in 1930 (ruins of Colinton Castle in grounds). Set in 100 acres of park-like playing fields, with stunning views to the North. Pringle House, for junior boarders (aged eight to 12 or 13) recently much extended and a bit rabbit warreny, enclosed in its own private (secret) garden, own houseparents. Boys can climb the tree as far as the white mark, and generally allowed to be their own age without being pressurised 'to join the grown ups'. Book inspired day room, plus obligatory telly and rather complicated game of Diplomacy up on the wall. School in good heart, well used, nothing flash here but no signs of real distress either – some minor blemishes in the chipboard desks and cabin-beds. Huge amount of cash recently spent on revamping loos and individual showers.

Boys work in their dorm areas and day boys have desks in the same area. Wicked posters. First year sixth formers are billeted to each house for the year to act as monitors and have pretty snazzy kitchens to make their tasks less onerous. Cooking the flavour of the month, both in Pringle and, certainly, in Chalmers West: stunning pupil inspired kitchens. Pringle boys are running a self-financing cook-in. Older boys are encouraged to deviate from pizza and Pepsi. 'Steaks would be good,' said our guide and housemaster. Sick bay with visiting sports physiotherapists, own ultra-sound machine and a delightful bubblegum pink isolation room (which would put any self-respecting boy off thoughts of malingering). Dining hall surprisingly small, with new servery and buffet service. Food good, soup, meat and veg, acres of white bread and rice pud when we visited, impressive salad bar for a boys' school too. Boys praise the new arrangement – 'the food is still good at the end of term' – when the budget is low.

First floor Memorial Hall doubles as a chapel (service inter-denominational) and dance hall and boasts Cameron tartan cushions on removable pews, and an impressive tartan stair carpet up to the entrance. Girls are regularly corralled in from (primarily) St George's but also Kilgraston and St Margaret's for reel parties, with lots of practice before the real thing. Merchiston boys are regularly voted the best dancing partners in Scotland. Visiting girls 'not a problem' – they come and go at weekends and can join the boys in the sixth form bar. Various departments already plotting what they will do with the about-to-become redundant areas which will be freed up when the sixth form centre finally materialises; we heard three possible uses within the same number of hours. Vast number of trips and options for boarders, day pupils can join if space available.

Pastoral Care and Discipline: Good rapport between pupils and staff. The horizontal house system is said to have made bullying practically 'non-existent', and 'anyway physical bullying has been superseded by text bullying from mobile phones' (banned until senior school). Head will and has asked pupils to leave. Believes in tough love, though a couple of prefects to whom we spoke obviously hadn't heard the phrase before. Mr Hunter is keen on parent/pupil/school partnership; will take in boys who have been dissed elsewhere: both boy and parent will sign a contract and the boy will be subject to very stringent and regular drugs testing routine. NB urine testing now regarded as useless ('any fool can purchase antidotes from the Internet,' said the head) pupils are tested by hair (think Napoleon). Expect to be drugs tested if either caught or suspected of dealing, or dabbling, followed by (but nothing in black and white) temporary, or permanent exclusion. Ordinary misdemeanours (alcohol, smoking etc) are treated on their own demerits. No longer cool to smoke. Discipline seminars. Jolly school policies booklet, re-printed every year, of which head is justifiably proud, lists all the dos and don'ts of the place. Purchase of fags or booze on or off the campus and dealings with betting shops are no-go areas. Betting is a new one to the GSG but perhaps other schools aren't as clear-cut in their expectations.

Pupils and Parents: 'A down-to-earth school, rooted in values' (says the head). The only all-boys boarding school in Scotland. Strong middle class ethos, good values, no change here. Record number of pupils in the school. 14 per cent from abroad, of whom about five per cent are expats. Real foreigners come from all over, Japan, Hong Kong and Mainland China as well as the States, plus a number from Europe usually for the sixth form. Germany popular at present. No quick short stay fix, pupils must stay the full year. Head keen not to lose the boarding ethos, and littlies at Pringle are encouraged to flexi-board. Day officially ends at 4.10 pm, but pupils can stay till after tea (and presumably supper) if they want to. Must be the cheapest baby sitting service in the country. Senior boys can flexi-board too, often without charge if they are about official business – 'debates, plays and the like' – but £25 a night if for 'parental convenience'. Housemasters spend their 'ill-gotten' gains on boy treats: microwaves, new cookers. Boys open, friendly and well-mannered.

Entrance: At 8 and 10, also 11, 12 and 13, and 16 always via exams; 55 per cent pass mark at CE, boys come from prep schools all over Scotland and the north of England. Entry to sixth form automatic from inside school, others need a satisfactory report from previous school.

Exit: Refer again to the useful little booklet for details of the favoured unis – almost 80 per cent to England (Durham, Bristol, London etc, eight per cent to

Oxbridge), rest stay in Scotland (Edinburgh, Glasgow, Aberdeen). Science, engineering, economics, management/business and languages/classics/English the favoured subjects. Pupils go on to be fully paid up members of the Edinburgh mafia – law lords etc.

Money Matters: Myriads of scholarships and bursaries for almost everything but the school is working towards means-tested awards. Sibling discounts with Kilgraston, Casterton and Queen Margaret's York.

Remarks: No change. Still the top boys' school in Scotland, which extraordinary position has been achieved by defection to co-education by the rest – and it is on the way up anyway. Quite. Charismatic head, boys are encouraged to 'try their hardest, make the most of their talents and look after each other'. 'No thoughts of going co-ed,' say head, staff and boys – the latter positively shuddered at the idea.

MILL HILL COUNTY HIGH SCHOOL

Worcester Crescent, Mill Hill, London, NW7 4LL

Tel: 0844 477 2424

Fax: 020 8959 6514

Email: wynneh@mhchs.org.uk

Website: www.mhchs.org.uk

• Pupils: 1,656; roughly 55 per cent boys and 45 per cent girls, all day • Ages: 11-19 • Religion: Non-denom
• School status: State • School gender: Mixed
• Day/boarding: Day pupils

SEN provision

Detail:

Now provide for in school:

Mild: ASP; ADD; ADHD; EBD; DYSL; DYSP;

Moderate: ASP; ADD; ADHD; DYSL; DYSP;

Summary: The school has an Inclusive Learning Team which supports students with a whole range of special educational needs. The majority of additional support is offered via in-class support with limited provision outside the classroom. The school's philosophy is to provide an appropriate and inclusive learning environment in the classroom, reducing the necessity for specialist provision outside the classroom. As an Inclusion Team we address a wide range of needs covering learning, emotional and behavioural difficulties. However we do not offer a specific specialist provision. The inclusive learning department is situated upstairs in a quiet part of the school providing two large classrooms which have computers linked to the school curriculum network. The department is open from 8.00am to 4.30pm.

SEN questionnaire details added by us.

What we say about the school - the full Good Schools Guide review

Head: Since 2004, Geoffrey Thompson MA (Cantab) MBA (Ed) MIMgt. Mr Thompson came from headship of the Duchess's Community High School in Alnick. Degree subject was music. He previously taught in Bromley and was a deputy head in Norfolk. He is a performing musician, mountaineer, married with three children.

Academic Matters: Heavily over-subscribed, with high expectations and achievements. Selects 10 per cent on 'technological aptitude'. In 2005, 89 per cent of GCSE pupils got five or more A*-C grades. At A level, English, maths and the sciences are all popular. 68 per cent of A level grades were A or B in 2005, with 24 students getting at least three grades As. Strong, as one would expect, at science and maths, but very good results also for RS and English literature GCSE. Vocational options are ICT and leisure and tourism GNVQ. Other popular options are law, psychology and sociology and vocational courses including media studies and ICT. Pupils are grouped by ability for most academic subjects right from the start. Express groups of students can take one or two GCSEs in year 10, then do a one-year course in law or geography, or an AS in critical thinking.

The Inclusive Learning Team works with students with a wide range of special educational needs – mostly within mainstream lessons. Two blind students have recently joined the school. 'My son, who has dyslexia, has had plenty of support,' said a parent. 'They're helping him to achieve to his capabilities.'

Games, Options, The Arts: Perhaps surprisingly for a technology college, performing arts are important here – 10 per cent of places are given to talented musicians and 5 per cent to dancers. Everyone does combined dance and drama lessons for the first three years and can take either or both as GCSE and A level courses. 'The drama department is wonderful,' said a student. 'I love it to pieces.' There's a drama festival every autumn, often including plays written by the head of drama, and a school musical production in the spring, involving actors, dancers and musicians. 'The quality is amazing,' said a parent. There are 32 music and choral groups and six dance clubs. Art used to be the poor relation, but has improved considerably over recent years.

The school overlooks playing fields and netball courts and has a gym and sports hall. There's plenty of sport going on in PE lessons, clubs, house and school teams, alongside other activities such as Duke of Edinburgh, field trips, ski trips, language exchanges and summer camps. 'There's so much to get involved in,' said a pupil, though a parent commented that it takes organisation – 'getting a place in clubs and on trips can be competitive, so you have to be on top of what the activities are and be first in line to sign up.'

Background and Atmosphere: Its 21-acre site on the edge of the green belt should be spacious but the school is so popular that the site is almost too small for pupil numbers. It is also, incidentally, a tricky place to get to, with no tube station for miles, though buses do stop around a quarter of a mile away, and the LEA is planning to extend the existing public bus routes. The technology college status has brought extra funds for major refurbishment and building projects over the last decade, including new science and art rooms, a business and ICT centre and a media studies centre. Another round of building work has provided English, music, dance/drama rooms and a new library. This is a large school and by no means cosy, but it doesn't seem that children get lost in the crowds. 'They expect a lot but they will also put their arms around the children,' said a parent. 'Whenever we've had problems they've always solved them.'

Pastoral Care and Discipline: The school prospectus states that it is 'highly traditional in its approach to student behaviour and attitudes'. 'Their discipline is very tough and their expectations are high too,' said a parent. Sixth formers provide peer mentoring and also help with literacy in year 7. A pupil commented that her brother, who has learning difficulties, has received lots of help with friendship problems. There's a system of merit awards for service to the school and for academic achievement. Zero tolerance of selling drugs on the premises.

Pupils and Parents: The presence of the school puts a premium on house prices in the surrounding estates, with plenty of parents measuring the distance to the front gate before they buy. With a large proportion of the places going to technology and performing arts buffs and to siblings, the catchment area stretches as far as Borehamwood. So there's a good mix, ethnic and otherwise, of locals from leafy Mill Hill and families from further afield. OBs: Angus Fraser, Middlesex cricketer, and Robert Elms, journalist and broadcaster.

Entrance: Highly competitive, with over 1,300 applicants for 240 places. Looked-after children, then siblings, get first preference (siblings usually take around half the places); then the 24 with the highest scores in technological aptitude tests. There are also 24 music places, awarded after aural tests, and generally to those at around grade 4 or above, and 12 dance places. Children of staff are offered places next, and at least 10 places to those who live closest, which in practice means rather less than a mile away. Around 70 per cent go through to the sixth form; places are offered to all those who 'have previously displayed a positive attitude to study and a determination to succeed'. Entry requirements at this stage for outsiders are five Bs, including As in the subjects chosen for A level, or five Cs for vocational courses, and there are around five outside applicants for every place.

Exit: Nearly all sixth form leavers go on to university, and 7 got Oxbridge places in 2005. Law, business studies and medicine are all popular courses.

Money Matters: Not short of funds, through its technology college status and other initiatives. Plenty raised by parents.

Remarks: Successful, tightly-run state school with high standards and rigorous teaching. Strong at performing arts and sport as well as technology. 'It's a fantastic school,' said a parent. 'They expect a lot of the children and they give them the support to achieve it.'

Millfield Preparatory School

Edgarley Hall, Glastonbury, Somerset, BA6 8LD

Tel: 01458 832446

Fax: 01458 833 679

Email: admissions@millfieldprep.com

Website: www.millfieldprep.com

• Pupils: 500 boys and girls; boarding and day • Ages: 2-13
• Religion: Inter-denominational • Fees: Available on application
• School status: Independent • Opendays: May and October
• School gender: Mixed • Day/boarding: Takes boarders

SEN provision

Detail:

Now provide for in school:

Mild: AUT; DYSC; DYSL; DYSP; SpLD; HI; VI; CP;
Moderate: DYSC; DYSL; DYSP; SpLD;
Others: Sp&LD;

Experience of:

Mild: ADD; ADHD;
Moderate: ADD; ADHD;
Others: SPD;

Summary: The school has a centre to support pupils with literacy difficulties including dyslexia and other difficulties as listed. It is staffed by specialists working closely with the school staff.

What we say about the school - the full Good Schools Guide review

Head: Since 2001, Mr Kevin Cheney BA, PGCE (fifties). Educated at St George's College, Weybridge did geography at Exeter University and began his teaching career in the Royal Army Educational Corps (where he was promoted to Captain). He first joined Millfield in 1980 with his wife, Hilary, a qualified teacher, where he ran a house for five years; became head of Trinity School, Teignmouth for six years, and head of Cranmore School in 1992. Hilary provides very visible hands-on support at the school; four sons, three post-A levels, youngest at Millfield. Mr Cheney, a sporty, former county hurdler and high jumper is kind, enthusiastic and fiercely proud of his pupils. He was visibly tired and looking forward to half term during our visit, though when we left, there were parents 'who had done the tour' waiting for him and he was keen 'to get ready to go to Hong Kong tomorrow'.

Entrance: Variety of ways in. Many come via interview and report from previous head, from prep schools finishing at 11, pre-preps, overseas and local primaries. Others sit school exam in January for September entry. Can be flexible – Millfield prep will always make the effort to take pupils and has been a sanctuary for pupils unhappy or failing to thrive elsewhere. 'IQ not the only arbiter, need to see the child, not just a collection of data'. Can and will take when space available.

Exit: Vast majority go to Millfield. Transfer not automatic, with good behaviour and a satisfactory academic standard necessities. A small number move elsewhere, almost always to other independent schools.

Remarks: Extensive site spread round a bend in the road outside Glastonbury, facing the school golf course and a boarding house at the foot of the famous Tor across the road (better view if you move a tree or two). Quite difficult to find Reception, the sign posts are in just the wrong place and having started in the wrong place it is quite difficult to find reception itself. An external car park services the stunning games complex and a certain amount of titivation is being done to the two buildings nearest the road, whilst in the main house, serious chunks are being hauled down, and scaffolding obscures much of the playground. Appearance of school functional rather than beautiful, with limited attempts to co-ordinate or blend in new and less new with the Gothic Victorian pile at its heart where the head is based, and quite a lot of stuff (as in mantle pieces and the like) looks as though it has come from the Abbey itself. The previous owners used to own both. Lots of unusual touches, though – a huge outdoor chess set has moved from outside the girls' houses at the senior school (where we last saw them) to just in front of the main building, and the multi-coloured climbing wall on the outside of one building gives it the personality much of the architecture lacks, a Scandinavian style science block is on the stocks. Architecturally the place needs a Bowen Jones make-over, an enormous (three storey – why? – in the country?) cruciform classroom block was deeply muddling to this (experienced) editor, but the children seemed quite content, scurrying around like worker bees under the queen's command – well, it was end of school day and it was daylight and there were golf clubs everywhere and we do mean everywhere. Golf is the current passion.

Two new boarding houses opened in September 2003 and a pre-preparatory department, catering for pupils aged 2-7, is now based on campus in the former kitchen garden – stunning specially made Story Chair and super cosy library. Children coming into the pre-prep are automatically assessed, one-to-one groups and up to three specialist lessons a week for those who need help. The LDC is a centre of excellence, currently with more than 180 pupils in this deceptively small building, with ten tutors, five part-time and strong liaison throughout. This the school which all other prep schools recommend when they can't cope (and here this editor speaks from experience – though in the end her son did not go here).

The language development centre is second to none. And I quote from their Map of Special Needs Provision: 'Pupils from pre-prep are assigned to a class in the Preparatory School taking into account their need for extra support/access to LDC'. Study skills important. Pupils come with a range of problems from ADHD to 'mild cerebral palsy'. Pupils in the pre-prep transfer here with a 'record of phonic skills using Jolly Phonics and Sound Discovery resources as well as the pre-prep yellow files containing IEPs and records of parent discussions'. This also goes for children arriving at the school, whose edpsyched reports and problems are taken into consideration. Detailed assessments are 'carried out in the main body of the school', with ensuing discussions between the department and the heads of year groups regarding individual pupils. If their reading or spelling is more than a year behind their chronological age this is flagged 'but data is not the only aspect taken into account when determining a pupil's current needs'. It can vary from day-to-day. Each pupil on the SEN register has a Pupil Diagnostic Profile, which includes Lucid Rapid, Lucid Lass Junior, Lass Secondary, Diagnostic Reading Assessments, Spelling Tests (Young's Parents), Phonological Assessment Battery (PhAB), Aspects of The Institute of Neuro-Phylogical Psychology Assessment, Aspects of the Aston Index and they are considering a trial of the InCAS (Interactive Computerised Assessment System of the University of Durham. Brain Gym popular. The head of LDC, who is a CReSteD examiner, is also qualified in Neuro-Developmental Delay with the Institute of Neuro-Physiological Psychology: if the programme is thought beneficial for a pupil and after a positive assessment (co-ordination, balance, visual development, laterality and spatial awareness) then a 'five-ten minute a day programme using no special equipment and replicating movements from the first year of life is then implemented which gives the brain a 'second chance' to develop the reflexes needed to provide a firm foundation for learning'. This programme usually lasts about a year. (NB the much vaunted DDAT Dore programme – said by many to have a very good PR set-up – whilst based on repetitive exercise, does not replicate the first year of life – as we understand it, prescribed excercises are based on cerebellum inactivity and tested via electrodes during an assessment session). Over 120 pupils of all ages are currently attending the LDC on a regular basis, plus some 50 pupils getting additional help, with 15 on a one-to-one basis, and four doing speech and language and occupational therapy. There is also an LDC Link Tutor for those who do not qualify for total LDC immersion; these pupils may be assessed and info put on the staff Internet for follow-up. Good tie-up with houseparents when children may need extra help. All areas of life here based on efforts to find an aptitude, build self-esteem and develop the potential of every child. Special programme (Potential Academic Curriculum Excellence or PACE) undertaken by super-bright. Help at both ends of the spectrum included in fees.

Pupils follow broad curriculum with setting for maths and languages in all but first year with French taught from the first term and Spanish and Latin added by the age of 10. Plenty of exciting trips out to bolster learning, from nearby basketworks and Hinckley Point power station to London galleries and France. Class sizes small, normal maximum 16. Each child watched over by group tutor, responsible for welfare and progress, and first port of call for anxious parents. Reports are termly, with grades for effort as well as attainment. Scholarships for chess as well as academic, music, sporting and art.

Set in acres of manicured greenery, with a bubble over the tennis court in winter (some houses have their own – as opposed to the school's one). Sport as important as expected, a second sports hall was opened in 2005, an equestrian centre with two maneges (school's preferred word is arena) was built at the same time, a nine-hole golf course just for Millfield prep, a fine 25-metre pool (ditto) and all sorts of courts, pitches and fields to cater for every conceivable sport and activity. Underpinning the school's ethos, finding talent in whatever area and inspiring confidence in its wake, the games' list includes Airfix modelling and touch-typing, as well as sports from pop lacrosse and indoor go-karting to squad training for swimming, rugby and soccer. Music is particularly well-supported, with a wide range of instruments, 350 individual lessons, 29 music ensembles and 18 annual concerts. Facilities include 28 music rooms and a light and airy recital hall (currently under wraps), but junior baroque chamber orchestra plus the expected choirs et al. Art of all kinds very popular, from printmaking to ceramics via ICT, with critical discussion an integral part of its teaching.

Pupils are chatty, bubbly, confident and clearly have a fun time – head very keen that they – not he – do all the talking for the school. He does say that the school makes great efforts to preserve pupils' childhood for as long as possible and there is a welcome air of separation between the school and the town beyond. Boarding houses are particularly cosy, with great efforts made to create homes from home, with bright colours, football team duvet covers and jazzy pinboards a feature of the bedrooms. Welcoming, cheerful school with pupils treasured – whatever their special talent, be it rugby or brass-rubbing. Wonderful facilities in every sphere. Genuinely turning out well-rounded individuals and a centre of excellence for those with serious problems. Couldn't do better.

MILLFIELD SCHOOL

Butleigh Road, Street, Somerset, BA16 0YD

Tel: 01458 442 291

Fax: 01458 447 276

Email: admissions@millfieldschool.com

Website: www.millfieldschool.com

• Pupils: 1,260 boys and girls (about 75 per cent board, the rest day) • Ages: 13-18 • Religion: Inter-denominational • Fees: Available on application • School status: Independent • Opendays: May and October • School gender: Mixed • Day/boarding: Takes boarders

SEN provision

Detail:

Experience of:

Mild: ASP; ADD; ADHD; EBD; DYSC; DYSL; DYSP; SpLD; HI; VI;

Moderate: DYSL; HI; VI;

Severe: DYSL; HI;

Others: SPD; Sp&LD; Epi; Eat;

Summary: Language development unit (LDU) (English and study support for pupils with specific learning difficulties).

The language development unit has been well established for many years and has a key role within the school. Its purpose is to meet the additional needs of pupils within Millfield Senior School. It functions as an independent department with cross-curricular and pastoral links but it also works closely with the English department, teaching English Language and Literature to GCSE and providing learning support for sets of pupils in the 3rd, 4th and 5th year with specific learning difficulties or dyslexia. Its aims are to encourage and work with pupils in the development of independent learning and literacy skills, self-confidence and self-esteem as they work towards the achievement of successful GCSE and A level grades. It maintains close links with Millfield Prep School in order to facilitate a smooth transition for pupils moving across at 13+.

The LDU maintains high expectations of the pupils working within the department and are rarely disappointed by the positive and determined response they achieve as a result. The quality of relationships with pupils is regarded as a vital component in building confidence, rapport and mutual understanding as is the pace and style of teaching, taking into account different learning styles and abilities. LDU teachers maintain and share an interest in current research, training, techniques and resources in a constant effort to maximise opportunities and success for pupils and in their support and advice for fellow members of staff. Addressing issues such as motivation, organisation, work habits and self-responsibility are also regarded as important keys to building success.

At sixth form level, the LDU continues to support pupils through individual/small group tutorials, helping in the development of effective study skills, including exam and revision techniques. All students are encouraged to take responsibility for their own learning whilst having a support structure to assist them as or when necessary. Pupils/students at all stages have ready access to a dedicated networked computer workshop with specialised software to develop literacy and study skills as well as having the opportunity to engage in research or to word-process written assignments. The department is open during lunch and break times with a teacher on hand to assist pupils who need help on a drop-in basis or who simply want a quiet place to work or to complete prep. This facility is well used by pupils of all ages.

Support for pupils extends to making arrangements for exams including special arrangements for those that require them and providing advice and information for academic and pastoral staff concerning pupils with additional needs. Pupils value the contact and support they experience within the LDU during their life at Millfield and feel at ease within its supportive and encouraging culture.

What we say about the school - the full Good Schools Guide review

Head: Since 1998, Mr Peter Johnson MA CertEd (fifties). Educated at Bec (as in Tooting) Grammar (at the same time as Tory hopeful, David Davis) read geography at Oxford on army scholarship, rugby and judo blue. Retired and distinguished captain in Parachute Brigade – remains ultra-smart with tell-tale gleaming shoes; he has a deliciously confidential manner and his eyes positively sparkle when discussing successful or future projects. Fifteen years at Radley followed by seven years as head of Wrekin. Absolutely fits the Millfield bill – passionate about sport, opportunities and winkling out talent in equal measure. Has direct personal experience of inspiring confidence and providing support, as he and wife Chrissie have two sons, one a keen sportsman, one in a wheelchair (spina bifida), both high achievers making dad proud by following him into teaching. In firm control of the whole vast Millfield operation, rather like a compassionate MD, backed up by a welter of committed senior staff. New heads of physics, chemistry, drama, maths, music – 'a superb chap who enjoys rugby and now there are more boys in the choir' – plus new head of languages and history. (School can house 38 staff, the rest must rent or buy roundabout). Good young 'feisty' common room. Says 'you need a passion' to do well at Millfield.

Academic Matters: You name it, they do it, or very nearly. Huge range at GCSE, from dance to design by way of classical Greek and, of course, physical education. More than 40 A levels as well as AVCE courses in leisure and recreation and Btec in art and design. Languages, a movable feast depending on the origins of the intake, more popular here than in many schools, with French particularly strong, although with 50 nationalities represented it is not surprising. Academic Society for the brightest and the best.Staff constantly irritated by some parents' perception that Millfield's truly comprehensive, all-ability intake makes it a school solely for the nice but dim. Individual results attest that brilliance is enhanced as much as struggle is aided, and overall grades' and points' tallies have steadily increased over the last six years. School results highlight 100 top scores rather than dwell on the huge spread of results that reflect the ability range. Well-stocked library but still not open very late and only on the occasional Sunday. Head points out that Millfield's long-established and much admired language development unit supports children with IQs of 140, whose abilities are not always mirrored by their performance, as well as dyslexics, dyspraxics and the odd statemented child with severe difficulties. Mild Asperger's, autism, ADHD – some come with statements of needs and ed psychs' reports, others are identified during their school career. 'Jolly nearly' wheelchair friendly (and of course head is ultra-aware of this problem), 'but can certainly cope, enough classrooms on the ground floor'; one child at the school is deaf, hearing aid rather than monitor.Currently some 400 children get some support, for those with lesser difficulties this may be only once a week when they are taught in groups, but there is an entire English class in each year (of a greater or smaller size, ca depend) who are taught English in the SEN dept which is on the top of the academic floor, with proper classrooms as well as individual teaching units. Strong emphasis on spelling as well as on personal attention, each challenged pupil has an individual pupil profile which is constantly updated, unit is open before school, during break and at lunchtime with a drop-in centre (well used during our visit) plus some mainstream guidance for those in the main school. No shame in visiting the unit. Sixth formers meet with the unit at the start of the year, can do preps here (some concentrate better in an organised environment).Five full-time staff and two part-timers, all qualified teachers and either dyslexia qualified or with loads of experience. Strategies and help for the bright bored too, 'one-to-one', must commit to come. Some non-English speakers receive EAL teaching from specialist staffing in the Millfield English Language School (MELS), either graduating to core subjects or preparing for university interviews. Millfield may seem dauntingly large, yet classes are pocket-sized (maximum 15, usually much smaller) and the pupil:staff ratio a long-standing constant 1:7.5. Boys do just as well as girls, bucking the national trend. Staff usually stay for the long haul.

Games, Options, The Arts: 'Outstanding' barely covers the range, quality and availability of the fantastic sporting facilities for which Millfield is justly famous, 25/30 pupils compete internationally each year. Olympic-sized swimming pool, freshly upgraded sports halls, equestrian centre with indoor and outdoor arenas with fabulous accommodation for the pupils' own horses, recently increased in size: there is a waiting list for horses, polo very popular and played at Millfield Prep (£295 per term plus livery of £115 per week per pony). Pupils can take their BHSAI, as well as competing against the outside world. Purpose-built fencing salle, nine-hole golf course with indoor tuition centre (and golf clubs everywhere), indoor tennis centre (plus lots of all-weather courts), plus running track, water-based astro hockey pitches (you scoosh it with water at half time and it remains super smooth) and acres of playing fields. To further aid the quest for physical excellence, there is a well-staffed physiotherapy department and weights rooms. Predictably, Millfield teams trounce all comers as a matter of course – two pupils competed in the Commonwealth Games and one pre-teen swimmer narrowly missed the qualifying time. As head says, 'I could cover my walls just with pictures of famous Millfield sports men and women' (the admissions stairway is covered anyway, with winners from all walks of life). Two PE lessons a week the norm, including dance or orienteering for the less overtly muscled. Trips to everywhere in most disciplines.

Fantastic fine arts centre teaches everything from photography to painting, with regular artists in residence, but closed on Sundays so budding painters will have to do it elsewhere. Regular exhibitions – fab new space – from visiting artists, to staff and pupils. Outsiders invited in. Impressive new home economics dept under Leith's aegis popular with all, and massively increased design technology department positively humming (BTech as well as GCSEs on offer). New concert hall and music school under construction during our visit (Peter's Palace) should increase musical awareness in the school although huge numbers have individual music lessons and there are tripettes all over the place. The string quartet and piano trio were among the finalists at the Nat Chamber Music Competition held at St John's, Smith Square recently. Interest in academic music tends to tail off at A level. Drama well-supported, with pupils having the 500-seat Meyer Theatre at their disposal, as well as a professional-standard TV and recording studio.

Background and Atmosphere: Always a pleasure to come here – the immaculate campus is dotted with sculpture, some by artists in residence (and pupils watch them grow) and some specially commissioned, courtesy of the Millfield Sculpture Commission. Founded in 1935 by Jack Meyer with seven Indian pupils, of whom six were princes, and swiftly adopted the Robin Hood principle – squeezing money from the exceedingly rich to subsidise the needy, talented poor. From day one, in a large, rented Somerset house, he set about promoting individual ability, in whatever sphere. Millfield feels less like a school than an old-style university campus, with buildings in all directions in a mish-mash of styles, rubbing shoulders in a relaxed, appealing way rather than clashing. The new on-site boarding houses are particularly impressive, smashing kitchens with Sky and huge common rooms, almost all upper and lower sixth have individual cabins. The old boarding houses, mainly ageing manors around Street and Glastonbury, have almost all been sold off, three only remain, pupils are bused in and out. Six hundred acres of ground and school is still adding to its portfolio. Millfield is proud of having been built up from nothing and owing nothing. Used to paying its way – school hosts range of Easter revision courses and summer English language courses as well as conferences. A large dining hall, notable for its finer than average fare, sits at the heart of the campus and is given a universal thumbs up by pupils, even the vegetarians. One wall consists entirely of Olympic contenders as well as others decorated with heads of school and more ordinary mortals. Fantastic glass fronted sixth form bar, which serves real food (as indeed all school bars will have to do post November Ist). And incredible new glass cricket pavilion, the glass walls etched in cricket balls (this silly editor thought they were coffee beans until put right). Clubs for almost everything, chess highly popular.

Pastoral Care and Discipline: Seems to have eased off the throttle of 'one strike and you're out' methods of old, no doubt helped by now having a larger number of boarding pupils on campus and in clear sight. Head judges any case of bullying, drug-taking or drinking on its individual merits, although on-site drug dealing would inevitably earn a one-way ticket home, 'one sniff' and off with his head, 'unless there is a good reason why not'. Posh parents; no reason to keep the blighters. Random drug testing for individual pupils by agreement with the parents. Head acknowledges bullying cases, particularly at boarding school, can be complex – needs of the victim a priority, though. All pupils are in houses. Houseparents are usually the first port of call with problems – caring, family-orientated people making boarders feel at home (the cleaning staff important too, and we trotted off with the tutor for admissions to take in a farewell party to a lady what did for 32 years, thereby meeting a rash of houseparents, the head's wife and a raft of the cleaning squad). School keeps going throughout the term with activities for those who live abroad (though guardians etc pick up during half term and exeats). Long-standing, and successful, 'no private assignations' rule – couples would need houseparents' permission to meet. School counsellor available, as is school doctor or chaplain. Definite sense of separation from more worldly atmosphere of nearby Glastonbury – a relief. Chaplaincy centre a haven for exam-stressed pupils, plus other counsellors in the place, dedicated prayer room for Muslims. Strong community service locally.

Pupils and Parents: Sensible, mature pupils from a wide range of backgrounds, from the dyslexic sent by a local authority in north Wales to a Middle Eastern prince wallowing in cash. Girls notably smart and stylish after revision of uniform to prescribe tailored suits but tidiness very important here for boys too (though shirt tails still a problem), ties for every achievement, and the head girl has rather a natty gold brooch, senior prefects the same but in silver. Expected to work hard and play hard – not for those who duck out of being part of a team. Day pupils mostly local, boarders from anywhere and everywhere, with around 16 per cent from overseas. Increasing numbers (24 per cent) from London and the Home Counties, 'we seem to have been discovered by the trad parents and not just the first time buyers'. The list of alumni, famous and notorious, is endless, with Duncan Goodhew, John Sargeant, Tony Blackburn, James Hewitt, Ben Hollioake and Sophie Dahl just the tip of a very eclectic iceberg.

Entrance: Interview and previous head's report the usual route in, with CE used to determine set for core subjects. Millfield has anything up to 80 feeder schools but by far the largest day number come from its own prep school (see separate entry). Many more arrive than leave in the sixth form.

Exit: Most go to universities here and all over the world (America a big favourite), eight last year to Oxbridge, quite a number to sports courses at uni, Bristol is popular, also accounts, business management and law.

Money Matters: A large number of scholarships at all levels for all-rounders, sportsmen, academics, musicians and artists, dedicated scholarships for those coming in at sixth form. All are individually assessed (vestiges of the Robin Hood principle linger), nearly 50 per cent get some form of bursary, with higher special bursaries and for local hardship cases. Reassuringly expensive for the affluent – in top ten for big-budget full fees. School setting up a foundation to be able to offer more help to more.

Remarks: Impressive, good-looking school with a genuinely all-inclusive urge to seek and find the best in everyone. Strong in every area and a great confidence builder, particularly for those who have struggled elsewhere. Not for those content to hide in a corner.

MILTON ABBEY SCHOOL

Blandford Forum, Dorset, DT11 0BZ

Tel: 01258 880 484

Fax: 01258 881 194 or 01258 881 250

Email: info@miltonabbey.co.uk

Website: www.miltonabbey.co.uk

• Pupils: 220 boys (21 day boys, the rest board); 9 girls in the sixth form • Ages: 13-18 • Religion: C of E • Fees: £7,490 boarding; £5,620 day • School status: Independent • Opendays: November, February, May • School gender: Boys • Day/boarding: Takes boarders

SEN provision

Detail:

Centre of excellence for:

Mild: DYSL; DYSP;

Moderate: DYSL; DYSP;

Severe: DYSC; DYSL;

Now provide for in school:
- Mild: DYSC; SpLD; HI;
- Moderate: DYSC;
- Others: EAL;

Experience of:
- Mild: ASP; AUT; ADD; ADHD; EBD; CP;
- Moderate: ADD; ADHD; MLD;
- Others: SPD; OCD; Sp&LD; DEL; Epi; PD; Eat;

Summary: Milton Abbey has a well-resourced learning support department, staffed by fully-qualified teachers. Learning support assistants support some mainstream lessons. Pupils come at mutually agreed times. The majority of support is for pupils with dyslexia, but a range of other conditions can be supported.

What we say about the school - the full Good Schools Guide review

Headmaster: Since 1995, Mr W J (Jonathon) Hughes-D'Aeth (pronounced Daith) BA (fifty), educated at Haileybury and Liverpool, where he read geography which he still teaches throughout the school – doesn't teach as much as he would like, enjoys it a lot – 'good fun, but other bits fun as well'. Twelve year contract now abandoned ('indefinitely'), he is really enjoying 'being here in a 'little school' – not really a proper school, so enjoying real education'. No thoughts of moving anywhere. Bubbling, he has grown (perhaps a trifle literally) with the job and, when he showed us out to our car (parked somewhat perilously in front of the rugby pitches), he was instantly surrounded by chaps in diverse garb clamouring for attention. We kept an eye out of the rear window and, no, he didn't actually kick a rugby ball – but he might well have done. Obviously very popular. Previously a housemaster at Rugby, he still helps out with the CCF. Married, with four children spread all over the place – The Old Malthouse, Hanford, Haileybury and Charterhouse.

Charming, gassy, enthusiastic, keen that Milton Abbey should not be known as a special dyslexic school – 'boys are loved and treated as individuals'; the basic idea is to boost their self-confidence. Talks in metaphors (and not very good puns), 'Jaguar engines with lawn mower gearboxes'. Aims to boost self-confidence – 'how to deal with imperfections, that's what education is all about'. If a boy wants to bring back his gun dog for training, fine; the pigs, fine (Fatima and Felicity are being fattened up for summer barbies – when we last visited it was Babe who was bacon, and Bertie and Basil for barbecuing); a couple of Suffolk rams, fine; though no more than two and a half dogs (currently two beagles ex Marlborough). Captains of ferrets, captains of pigs, captains of sheep et al, if it makes a chap happy, then why not? 'If it's legal, honest, decent and doesn't scare the horses' he will try anything. 'A happy boy is a confident boy, and they are much more ready to learn'. The head believes in 'preparing chaps for life', reckons that they don't grow up 'until they are 26', loads of energy, and 'don't worry too much'. Enormously flexible, he says of pupils here that he immediately 'perceived them to be gentle men' (as in gentle/caring). But he still can't get the hang of having girlies too and still refers to his pupils as men.

Academic Matters: Huge range of ability, IQs between 80 and 156; very frustrated bright boys and the rest. A key school for helping boys with learning difficulties, dyslexics are integrated with the rest (lots of remedial help where needed and instant tutorials on anything at any time). School is anxious not to be known as a 'specialist school' and all pupils must be able to access mainstream education. That having been said, thirty per cent of the pupils come with an educational psychologist's report, a summary of which stays in the staff room and tutors and staff have instant access. Three dedicated SEN teachers plus three classroom assistants and more to come, 'dual teaching is the way forward'. Some pupils withdrawn, a core group – usually from French – five lessons a week, either one-to-one or in small groups but it varies according to need. Extra time in exams, scribing, amanuensis, laptops – 'exams really exciting time' with invigilators for every pupil with an amanuensis or a scribe – each in separate rooms. School now CReSTeD (ie indefinite learning support paid for by Services et al). No DORE or trendy exercise gismos, 'scaffolding rather than tricks'. GCSEs taken ad nauseam, no shame in failure here. 'We learn through failure,' says the head. AS levels often taken over two years and, though the A level results are perhaps not as convincing as they might be, many get A*s in their practicals, which subsequently lead to job offers after school. Spanish a popular option, and of course German speakers do German. A D or E at A level is often way beyond anything that might have been predicted. Modules as far as possible in everything. Smallish classes, max 20, 16 the norm. 'No problem' in getting staff, 'though sometimes the choice is restricted', much emphasis on staff training. Academic tutors do study skills and monitor progress; teaching staff set aside two periods each week for official tutorials or help with problems. IT popular and computers everywhere, most boys have them for private study, and laptops both in class and exam. Business studies linked to economics dept, 'excellent take-up in BTechs: countryside management popular (and two boys recently organised the delivery of 140 pheasants with 40 boys up at crack of dawn to welcome them to their release pen, the game farm was so impressed that they delivered 40 partridge for free the following day and boys organised a shoot the Saturday before our visit with nearby fathers bringing guns in on the day (no they did not shoot 180 birds). BTechs also in sports and exercise management and hospitality management, with the school currently offering a popular chalet cooking course in Shaftesbury and looking to organise its own cooking course in the kitchens which are about to undergo a serious facelift, ditto the food (wood-burning ovens, making own bread and cutting down on the Es – which 'lengthens the attention span'). BTechs = two A levels and are a 'fantastic good qualification'.

Games, Options, The Arts: Compulsory activities on Tuesday and Thursday afternoons, huge choice: art, very active theatre, boat maintenance, clay-pigeon shooting (popular), fencing, model making etc. Art and design re-vamped with the addition of good, practising (commercial-eyed) artists and 'excellent' photography. Natural history still strong with moth traps shining through the summer months. Boys do regular head counts of birds. Ferrets (captain of etc). CDT (under theatre) popular, as well as CCF. School has strong links with Royal Armoured Corps at Bovington as well as the Royal Navy and masses of D of E (oodles of golds). Indoor heated swimming pool popular, games hall has sexy under floor heating – a bonus in winter; new astroturf. Peter Allis inspired golf course (his son was here) and very enthusiastic sailing (lots of prizes) plus success in off-shore yacht masters certificates and days skipper courses. County participants in athletics.

Background and Atmosphere: Friendly, caring, prefects are called pilots and a 'big brother' atmosphere is encouraged, particularly where new and vulnerable pupils are concerned. Weirdos are not picked on and almost all recent Old Boys report that they 'loved it' at the school, though – as ever – the occasional chap slips through the net. Approving noises from prep school heads.

Magical listed grade 1 building, with fabulous plasterwork (begun by Sir William Chambers and taken over by James Wyatt), set in fold of valleys and Dorset hills. Abbot's Hall and King's Room breathtaking. School does weddings 'in the holidays', used for the occasional film and telly set; the Sallie Army have a couple of summer schools a year. Rather jolly prospectus with masses of brightly coloured inserts. School owns the fabric and grounds, diocese of Salisbury owns the Abbey – which is gorgeous – a peculiar arrangement, the diocese bought it when the place was up for sale in the thirties, to prevent it falling into 'the hands of a faith-healing group'. Locals occasionally worship here too and school uses it daily. Each year group takes chapel and even the most dyslexic read a lesson or say a prayer. School founded in mid 1950s. Modern blocks cleverly hidden, stable block converted into light classrooms plus art, music etc. Stunning theatre, with efficient CDT below (very cunning), all classrooms/sports hall/theatre quite close to hand.Houses, now with carpets, being revamped (£46,000 last year, £60,000 this), all in main building, each with its own territory.

All housemasters (one of whom is a woman, Jane Emerson) are married, family atmosphere pervades – boys know each other well, graduating from dormitory/common rooms (ie with working spaces round the beds – and much less cramped than previously) to single study bedrooms, still untidy and refreshingly scruffy. Lots of new paint everywhere, some surprisingly bright (and some currently looking a trifle worn), head aiming to bring the school 'somewhere towards the 20th century', and is going for 'the faded country house look', 'buildings and the whole environment are so important'. School not as bulging as when we first visited and could hold one or two more, but no wish to grow.

Boys are kept busy in this isolated school. Lovat trousers and jerseys, suits on Sundays, ditto for girls, who are expected to be joined by another dozen or so September 2006. Certain amount of to-ing and fro-ing still with local girls' schools – St Mary's, Godolphin, St Anthony's, and stunning new basement sixth form centre ('the best night club in Dorset'). Two fixed exeats, plus half term, but enormously flexible. Saturdays off for hunting (still), polo 'they would lose the same time if they had to go to an away match' (but no horses in school – stables converted you see, good links with local riding school). NB this is the only school where reception has Hurlingham and Country Life to read and a glossy on sporting achievements rather than recent skool mags and prospectuses.

Pastoral Care and Discipline: Housemasters, who are normally also academic tutors, plus assistant house tutors. School is small enough to pick up any worrying vibes via the bush telegraph and head usually knows within hours if drugs have been brought back. 'Boys don't like drugs because it forms cliques which are unpopular in a small school'. Rehabilitation and random drugs testing on suspicion (and boys apparently like to be able to say, when offered drugs during the exeats, 'no thanks, I am tested at school' – even if they aren't). Not automatically out for drugs but out for dealing or going OTT. Booze a permanent problem, with parents tending to slip a chap the odd six pack in the hopes that a beer here or there will keep them off drugs, and the introduction of girls will compound the problem, ditto the recent government diktat that schools can only have a bar if food is served, hence the introduction of school feasts – a massive Saturday night blow-out followed by gassing to staff 'over a beer or two'. 'Constructive restrictions' for smoking in building, plus rustication – 'if we made smoking compulsory, and Latin illegal then all the boys would sneak off to the woods to read Virgil and throw the fags in the fire'.

Pupils and Parents: Gents, plus a handful of first-time buyers, more so than previously, and from further away. A handful of real foreigners, slightly more expats, and an increasing number of Services children. Pupils are courteous, relaxed and friendly and 'really miss it when they leave'. 'Boys here have three great loves in their lives – their Ma, their Pa and the head'. Geographically widespread. Monthly rendezvous for old boys at the Duke of Wellington pub, Eaton Terrace. Presumably girls will turn up there too.

Entrance: Via CE, very flexible though, 'it's not really the school for children who need the bright lights and the Kings Road'. (Staff too, have to come for a twenty-four hour interview rather than a short sharp committee quizzing.) Boys come from all over, over 100 feeders, including all the top preps, plus state system. Girls currently from Cranleigh, Westonbirt, St Mary's Shaftesbury and the maintained sector. Entry post-GCSE if they have the right qualifications – currently five Cs or even Ds at GCSE is 'good enough'. 'But we have to be very frank and honest and say if a child is not up to it'.

Exit: Around 90 per cent to some form of further education, with 50 per cent to degree courses. (The chap who went to Peterhouse, Cambridge, at 14, graduated in 2001.) An 'increasing number positively choose not to go to uni' preferring instead to get a positive life experience: two years before the mast, a year in an African game park, coaching sport in a shanty town in India' and then hitting the jobs market. But still Cirencester, Newcastle, Bristol WE, Bournemouth, Oxford Brookes, Manchester Metropolitan all popular, as are colleges of higher education like Cheltenham and Gloucester. Boys given career briefing from the moment they arrive, and tend to opt for careers where 'they have to sell themselves' – very entrepreneurial. Practical subjects such as business studies, the record industry, and hotel and catering are popular. Some leakage (to sixth form colleges everywhere) this year post-GCSE, 'chaps tend to get restless' said our guide.

Money Matters: Some scholarships including academic, music, art, drama, sailing. Will carry pupils through exam year in cases of hardship.

Remarks: Boys' boarding school which resolutely continues to give good experienced professional help to those with learning difficulties, now with an increasing number of girls in the sixth form (a third of whom have learning difficulties). A great confidence-building place which runs on kindness and encouragement. Don't take our word for it, read Dr Rae's Letters to Parents (Harper Collins). 'What is more, the self-confidence gained by the school's pupils is not the shallow 'effortless superiority' of the traditional public schoolboy but the self-belief that comes from fighting back and proving the pessimists wrong.'

THE MOAT SCHOOL

Bishops Avenue, Fulham, London, SW6 6ED

Tel: 020 7610 9018

Fax: 020 7610 9098

Email: office@moatschool.org.uk

Website: www.moatschool.org.uk

• Pupils: 70 boys, 20 girls • Ages: 11-18

• Fees: £6,690 per term • School status: Independent

• School gender: Mixed • Day/boarding: Day pupils

SEN provision

Detail:

Centre of excellence for:
- Mild: DYSC; DYSL; DYSP;
- Moderate: DYSC; DYSL; DYSP;
- Severe: DYSC; DYSL; DYSP;

Now provide for in school:
- Mild: ADD; ADHD; SpLD; CP;
- Moderate: ADD; SpLD; CP;
- Severe: SpLD;
- Others: Epi;

Experience of:
- Mild: ASP;
- Moderate: ASP; ADHD;
- Others: Sp&LD;

Summary: The Moat is a specialist co-educational day secondary school for the education of SpLD learners. Groups are small – no more than ten in a class – Learning support assistants are linked to full class groups to provide support with literacy, numeracy and organisation. The school makes extensive use of information technology to support learning – all pupils are taught to touch-type and supplied with a fully featured, wireless-enabled laptop to use in lessons and at home. The school has the services of speech and language therapists, an art therapist, an educational psychologist and an occupational therapist. Where necessary one-to-one support is provided for literacy and numeracy. The vast majority of Staff have a specialist qualification in the teaching of SpLD learners as well as their degree in their subject specialism and their teaching qualification. All the LSAs are presently undergoing training with the Dyslexia Institute.

The approach of The Moat is to have the structure and aspirations of a mainstream school whilst using the approach of a specialist school. Everything is structured to support the learning and success of the SpLD pupil. Great emphasis is placed on the development of self-confidence and language skills. There is an extensive extra-curricular enrichment programme to help support this.

What we say about the school - the full Good Schools Guide review

Head: Since the school's founding in 1998, Mr Robert Carlysle MBA BA AKC PGCE MCoIP (mid forties). Married to Teresa, one teenage daughter. A committed Christian. Team inspector for ISI, previously deputy head of Wentworth College. Taught history until recently, is the learning support assistant for business studies – 'not as indulgent as teaching history but a great experience, I'm picking up new ideas all the time.' Focus is firmly on teaching and learning – everything else comes second – wants pupils to define themselves by what they can do. Likes to get involved. 'Sometimes we wish he'd do less, can be a lot to live up to, sees himself as captain of the ship,' say staff. Pupils say he bonds with them and parents really like him too.

Academic Matters: Max ten to a class, three or four typical for GCSE. 'We teach as they learn so we learn and adapt.' Average value-added is a commendable two grades to GCSE and a quick scan of GCSE results shows exponential dividends in the past three years: A* to C pass rate has risen from 29 per cent to a very commendable 65 per cent with over half the pupils gaining the benchmark 5 or more A*-C passes (though no A* grades yet). Art, design technology, science and business studies popular and successful at GCSE – English and maths have poorest showing. No modern foreign languages or classics otherwise all usual suspects on offer. Extra time and laptops in exams the norm.

Occupational therapist visits once a week but input extends beyond that – working with staff, parents and child to ensure delivery of a full and integrated programme. On-site speech and language therapists work with pupils on a one-to-one or in small groups. Weakest have two periods of speech and language to support GCSE. Aware that their pupils have to work much harder to succeed and that moving from their comfort zone can cause stress – 'we have to ensure pupils cope, there'll be few concessions in the world of work, we have to ensure they're at ease with dyslexia and dyspraxia and must put their hands on the controls of their life. If you're in a car and hit a hill you slow down but you don't stop ...'

You'd be hard pushed to find a staff more in tune with specific learning difficulties – all are offered continuous training and development: 'The head accepts that once we're highly trained we'll probably move on but we're all encouraged and supported – teaching and non-teaching staff – we get on great, have a lot of fun and mix socially too.' Creates lots of in-house, tailor-made resources, shares good practice. Definitely a happening place for staff – 12 are currently studying for the

Dyslexia Institute postgraduate certificate in dyslexia and literacy accredited by York University. School is keen to provide outreach support, be inclusive and share expertise with others – about to launch first conference on how to get SpLD learners to write narrative (requires sequencing – not easy for the SpLD learner). Won the Key Stage 3 stage of the TES 'newspaper in a day' (a national competition open to all schools) competition in 2004 and has been highly commended on previous occasions.

Games, Options, The Arts: Lots of music and performing arts. Careers advice provided by Connexions. Art a-plenty, supported by trips to London galleries and exhibitions (art teacher is author of books specifically for SpLD learners). Plenty of extra-curricular clubs including rowing (school on boat race route), filmmaking, wargaming, and yoga. All play sport – new head of PE inspired and enthusiastic – 'he's ex-army so we really benefit from his skills and experiences – he's even managing to get us more fixtures,' said pupils.

Prejudice abounds – not here but in the locality – 'we're a special school so some local mainstream schools are reluctant to organise fixtures against us' – outrageous! Maybe it's the fear of losing to a small special school that's hard to stomach? Bright, intelligent, articulate and often gifted youngsters – you'd be hard pushed to notice anything different about them if you met them in the street except perhaps a confidence about who they are.

Background and Atmosphere: School is part of the Constable Educational Trust, a charity. The first five pupils and seven staff crossed the threshold in 1998. School has grown and is at capacity in most years. 'We're out of step with fashion – a specialist school in the age of inclusion but we see inclusion as an entitlement to mainstream education not a compulsion'. In a residential part of Fulham but overlooking parkland, externally the school is a 1930s carbuncle – metal windows, dreary red-brick – one half given over to a state primary – the other The Moat. Step inside and the tired exterior is belied by the deceptively spacious, all mod-cons interior – 'we even had a colour specialist assigned to ensure colour matched purpose' – it works! The full National Curriculum is offered with facilities to match – well-resourced science labs, food tech, DT, art studio, music technology room, IT suite, all pupils use laptops – wireless technology throughout, super gathering room used for assemblies, lunches (packed-lunch only), drama, some games. There isn't a separate gym but there is a playground and football/basketball/netball pitch, plus tennis courts across the road and access to local sports facilities so deficiencies well catered for. 'Driving force is the knowledge that failure isn't an option – the outside world has kicked these children – there's a great financial sacrifice and emotional cost involved – we're morally obliged to succeed.'

Pastoral Care and Discipline: Breaking school rules not tolerated: two pupils expelled in the lifetime of the school – 'if they really can't follow our code we won't accommodate... it's disappointing when they're not as responsible as they might be. Pupils want to come here, the school has high aspirations for them and shame hurts; we try to addict child to success.' A small school with high staffing ratio so pupils get a lot of teacher time and – the flip side – get away with very little. A member of staff has developed a comprehensive reporting and recording system – at the touch of a button 'Teachers Pet' churns out the good and bad on any pupil: learning, test scores, targets, homework, merits, absence, so it's difficult to conjure up excuses. All staff and pupils have access to school intranet and e-mail support so no excuse for not doing homework. Usual merits, detentions, report card system for misdemeanours. Pupils are divided into two competitive houses: Bishop and Palace. Seniors nominated and trained as prefects and alerted to responsibilities under child protection. Daily gathering taken by pupils on Fridays seen as an opportunity to present ideas and to celebrate.

Pupils and Parents: A mixed bag in part because those statemented (40 per cent) receive funding from LEA; the rest are partly or wholly privately funded – sometimes involving great financial sacrifice even hardship. Professional parents tend to be from arts and media – several dyslexics among parents. All share a strong sense of relief even those making huge sacrifices. It's fine to be smart here, no one personality typifies a Moat pupil. We met quiet ones, the forthright, funny, sporty, academic, creative, dramatic (think 'Moatenders' said more than a couple) but they rub along well together sharing a tremendous team-spirit and great respect for the individual. Lots of famous patrons – no famous old boys/girls yet but one of the original pupils has gained a place at Cambridge so we're guessing it won't be too long...

Entrance: School caters for high performing child with dyslexia, dyspraxia and a few with language issues such as expressive language difficulties or problems with auditory processing – maximum 20 a year. Entry via detailed assessment including reports from previous school, ed psych, SaLT, OT reports and copy of current statement where applicable. Procedure praised: 'it was really thorough, they picked up on our child's strengths and interests and were happy to accept him but LEA wouldn't support a place for our son, said insufficient OT provision, we were really disappointed.' No sixth form, but extended age range allows for entry outside of chronological year group. All interviewed and tested, then spend an 'acquaint day' at the school. From a variety of schools including Fairleigh House, the Dominie, Blossom House.

Exit: Early days but majority of leavers to date to mainstream sixth forms, few to employment.

Money Matters: Not a rich school – all capital funding raised charitably – currently fundraising to improve school playground and outdoor facilities. 'We'd love to have a sixth form but we need £200,000 just to underwrite the costs, so it's probably not going to happen yet. It's a shame, there is a clear demand but we just don't have the cash.'

Remarks: Something special. Not for wilting wallflowers wanting to be cosseted and comforted but a hard-working haven for bright, determined dyslexics and dyspraxics who know what they want from life and will achieve when given a chance.

MOON HALL SCHOOL

Feldemore, Pasturewood Road, Holmbury St Mary, Dorking, Surrey, RH5 6LQ

Tel: 01306 731 464

Fax: 01306 731 504

Email: enquiries@moonhallschool.co.uk

Website: www.moonhall.surrey.sch.uk

• Pupils: Full-time pupils: 50 (33 boys 17girls) age 7-11. Part-time pupils: 53 age 11-13 based in Belmont Prep. 24 board (at Belmont) • Ages: 7-13 • Religion: Inter-denom • Fees: Day £3,085-£4,650; Boarding £4,395-£5,960 • School status: Independent • Opendays: See website. Parental tours are arranged on Tuesday mornings of each week • School gender: Mixed • Day/boarding: Takes boarders

---

SEN provision

Detail:

Centre of excellence for:
- Mild: DYSC; DYSL; DYSP;
- Moderate: DYSL; DYSP;
- Severe: DYSL;

Experience of:
- Mild: ADD; ADHD; HI;
- Moderate: DYSC;
- Severe: DYSC;
- Others: Sp&LD;

Summary: Moon Hall is a school catering exclusively for dyslexic children. We focus on literacy and numeracy whilst providing all usual subjects across the curriculum.

Each of our teachers holds a specialist diploma in teaching children with specific learning difficulties as well as a Phono-Graphix qualification.

Children may be with us full-time for three or four years or may come to us part-time in groups of six or seven. Those who are based in Belmont Preparatory School (whose site we share) may receive one-to-one tuition as well as group touch-typing classes.

What we say about the school - the full Good Schools Guide review

Head: Since 1993, Mrs Jill Lovett (fifties) Teaching Cert, Hornsby Dip in SpLD. Traditional in her views. Joined as first full-time member of staff in 1989, deputy head in 1991. Educated in Kent – Technical High School then to St Osyth's College (Cambridge Institute). Main subjects English and RS. Taught English in selection of local Surrey prep schools giving mainly specialist dyslexic help. Married to lawyer with one son and two daughters. One daughter teaches in mainstream education.

Entrance: Pupils must be of average ability (Verbal IQ 100 approx) or above with report from an educational psychologist indicating dyslexia. Prospective pupils carefully vetted during half day assessment. For additional fee, assessments include physiotherapy/occupational therapy/speech and language needs. School does not accept children with emotional or behavioural problems (eg ADHD or Asperger's). Unable to help those with severe speech and language or dyspraxic difficulties. Currently no pupils have statements of special educational needs. Places in demand, waiting lists for most years. Some latecomers (years 5 and 6) enter 'Omega' class – created for those who require intensive help.

Exit: Pupils usually move across to Belmont Preparatory School after year 5 (on same site. See separate entry), apart from a very few Delta pupils who may leave the site after year 6 or 7. Overall aim for all is to move to mainstream at 13 with minimal support – eg Seaford, Box Hill, Shiplake, Bloxham, Gordonstoun, Milton Abbey and Stowe. A few require more specialist schools eg Mark College and More House.

Remarks: Specialist school for youngsters with moderate dyslexia. Most will have fallen behind at other schools. Full National Curriculum aiming for competence in basic language and maths. Specialist morning tuition in very small groups (maximum 7 pupils) for English literacy and numeracy in one hour lessons. Complete class (14 pupils) re-forms in afternoon for remainder of curriculum. English course uses 'Phono-Graphix' method for reading – first in UK to adopt this throughout the school – encouraging results especially with Delta pupils (see below for definition of Delta). All teaching staff trained in special needs and have undergone specific training in Phono-Graphix. All pupils taught touch-typing from year 3 with above average OCR examination results in word processing. Excellent ICT with laptops being introduced in class. Key stage 2 results highly creditable but maths lower than English and science. No written French, oral occasionally offered. PE, music, DT taught by specialist staff in Belmont. Games likewise – Moon Hall School pupils may join Belmont teams. Meals also at Belmont. Art and DT displayed throughout the school. Individual music lessons available but not encouraged where this may conflict with core subjects. Comprehensive library including facility for parents to borrow material. Two members of staff supervise boarders' prep, one of whom hears reading. Each pupil has Personal Tutor. If required, speech and language help from visiting therapist available. Also visiting OT. Full-time therapy assistant follows recommendations of external specialists (eg optometrist and occupational therapist).

This is a CReSTeD category SP School. Founded in 1985 by Mrs Berry Baker in her home, Moon Hall, at Ewhurst, for her son. After increase in size, it relocated to Belmont School site in 1989 when the current, purpose-built building was erected. Mrs Baker became Chair of the Governors in 1998. A well staffed, well resourced school with dedicated teaching. Mrs Lovett's leadership enables all to give of their best. Lively, bright eyed, polite pupils who achieve well considering their lack of literacy on arrival.

MOOR PARK SCHOOL

Moor Park, Richards Castle, Ludlow, Shropshire, SY8 4DZ

Tel: 01584 876 061

Fax: 01584 877 311

Email: head@moorpark.org.uk

Website: www.moorpark.org.uk

• Pupils: 250 boys and girls (55/45); 70 boarding beds: full-time boarding, weekly boarding and flexi boarding, plus weekend tasters • Ages: 2 1/2-13 • Religion: RC but inter-denom • Fees: Pre-Prep £1,365-£1,710; Prep £2,535-£3,360; boarding £3,770-£4,590 • School status: Independent • Opendays: 'Every day is an open day' • School gender: Mixed • Day/boarding: Takes boarders

SEN provision

Detail:

Now provide for in school:

Mild: DYSC; DYSL; DYSP;

Moderate: DYSL; DYSP;

Others: EAL;

Experience of:

Mild: ASP; AUT; ADD; ADHD; EBD; HI; VI; CP;

Moderate: ADD; DYSC;

Severe: DYSL;

Others: OCD; Epi; PD; Oth; Eat;

Summary: Excellent learning support department, with one full-time member of staff and several part-time specialists. Teaching normally on a one-to-one basis but also some paired group work. Support may be given for gifted children, dyslexia, dyspraxia, extra help with literacy/reading, numeracy, study skills, ESL. The school is proud of its attention to the individual and the learning support department embodies this.

What we say about the school - the full Good Schools Guide review

Head: Since 2002, Mr Mike Piercy BA (forties) who had been working 'with' the school since 2001, and takes over after a turbulent time, including a couple of interregna and a new governing body. Mr Piercy, who was educated at Gresham's, read English at Leicester, worked his way up the prep school ladder via West Downs, Bishops Stortford (which he hated), Great Ballard where he was head of English and boarding, Forres Sandle Manor where he was director of studies and deputy head and finally head of Dunhurst before he came here. A bubbly, experienced head: he came clattering down the uncarpeted stairs with the energy of a 12-year-old and we bounced round the school enthusing and chatting interspersed with quite long pauses to watch a (not very needle) rugby game against a neighbouring school.

Moor Park won, most of their scrum wearing head protectors, which must have terrified the opposition (school has a reputation for 'the best teas ever'). Loads of staff changes during the debacle, not a lot recently. Working on restoring confidence, and thrilled by 'super supportive staff'. Some new staff appointed with his blessing during his 'consultative' first year (ie when he was working out his notice). Mr Piercy would like more staff houses in the grounds.

Entrance: Can take at any time if space available. At any age. All children screened at four for learning support, incoming pupils come for a day 'to see what it is all about' and are given 'standardised test'. If school concerned about learning problems they work on a suck and see policy and can give extra support where needed. One or two Asperger's children in school. The odd 'real' foreigner, ditto Services, quite a lot of grannie-ed children, plus refugees from London whose parents have bought houses locally (Gloucestershire is full).

Exit: Not many recently to Ampleforth, but Downside, Cheltenham Ladies' Coll (scholarship last year) St Mary's Ascot (recent scholarship) Winchester (scholarship). Lots to Shrewsbury, Malvern, Uppingham, Oakham (who are getting sniffier about IQs) Rugby et al. A few girls leave at 11+, most stay to 13. Several art and academic scholarships a year. Over 60 per cent won awards last year: academic, art, sport, music, all-round.

Remarks: Founded in 1964. Enormously happy little local school offering everything from baby care upwards. Taken as read, immaculate baby, nursery care till 6 pm, then add jolly pre-prep with computers and early exposure to languages and then add proper prep school with full boarding if you want it, weekly boarding, and flexi boarding (though the latter is filling up rapidly). The demand is so high for boarding that they are converting another dorm, and unless you book Thursdays and Fridays early you may not get flexi and have to go all the way. Buses for day pupils up to a radius of 45 minutes, ie Hereford and Kidderminster.

This is a gem of a school and the new head is rapidly stepping into the shoes of the much loved head but one who was ousted by a demented (to put it kindly) board of governors and was a legend in the prep school world. Trillions of options, real science at 7 (and some in the pre-prep) Latin at 10, Greek for scholars (and loads of those); max class size 18, but usually 14. Children setted at 9 in maths, but hardly notice it. Computers everywhere and subject taught.

Music department a bit shabby and head's wish list includes new music centre and new CDT centre: Henderson Hall looks functional, but sad compared to the rest of the school, much used by locals, with an out of this world grand piano just sitting there. Sports hall, and swimming pool, boarders can swim quite late in the evening. Magical art department would do credit to a senior school, entertaining ceramics and carved breeze block sculptures on show. Head of art's influence all over the shop: boys' dorms a bit severe still, but their bathrooms need to go in a glossy, ditto the girls' dorms and their bathrooms. Jaws for the boys, OTT pretty for the girls.

Fantastic regular essentially boarding weekends in school where all can do a taster sport; or, like the weekend after we visited, proper live telly production with parents invited to watch the finished product in the dining room. Pupils are already devising sets. Great pressure on parents from children having so much fun they don't want to go home (and some of those who board live less than a mile away). Last year's art weekend produced the most amazing peacocks from recycled materials which decorate the cricket pavilion, watched overall by a weird collection of totem poles.

All singing and dancing on the scholastic front, plus new classrooms (member of governors is senior builder and supplies the kits at cost with in-house management so not that expensive), more to come. All children tested on entry. Head of learning support, AMBDA qualified does all the testing, if a child is below the 'base line', they might be referred to an ed psych. There is an occasional (very rare) child who may not be 'up to the school', 'can't be everything for everyone' said the head, but 'in reality very few are turned away'. Border line children are invited for a trial day and skool tests (usually unsuspected) find out 'as much data as possible'. A fifth of the school 'have some kind of support' be it for dyslexia et al, organisational skills, mild Asperger's or just plain gifted. One mildly Aspergeral pupil whom we met during our visit recently got a scholarship to Stonyhurst. One full-time and one part-time teacher, pupils either withdrawn from class or taught in pairs or tiny groups, no in class teaching. A couple of children on the SEN spectrum don't do French, and they 'might have a child who doesn't do Latin'.

Good child play area, woods (all checked by arborists for falling branches) and children allowed to go only so far – three girls who recently went further are now temporarily banned from the woods. Tough. Ginormous bonfire in place for November 5th. Stunning Queen Anne house with various add-ons, stunning Robert Adamesque chapel in the ballroom, and terrific entrance hall with leather covered walls. V elegant, even if used for 'Blot on the landscape'.

More House School (Farnham)

Moons Hill, Frensham, Farnham, Surrey, GU10 3AP

Tel: 01252 792 303

Fax: 01252 797 601

Email: schooloffice@morehouseschool.co.uk

Website: www.morehouseschool.com

• Pupils: 200 boys, 75 board • Ages: 9-18 • Religion: RC foundation but all welcome • Fees: Day £3,135-£3,660; weekly boarding £5,280-£5,520; full boarding £5,680-£6,075 • School status: Independent • School gender: Boys • Day/boarding: Takes boarders

SEN provision

Detail:

Centre of excellence for:

- Mild: DYSL; DYSP;
- Moderate: DYSL; DYSP;
- Severe: DYSL;
- Others: Sp&LD;

Now provide for in school:

- Mild: ASP; ADD; ADHD; DYSC;
- Moderate: DYSC;
- Others: SPD;

Summary: Remediation across the curriculum, individually planned. Language processing improved by five SaLT. OT available. All staff attend specialised training to give common approach. Although often a hidden remedial component to classwork, the aim is to give all boys a normal, happy experience of school.

What we say about the school - the full Good Schools Guide review

Headmaster: Since 1993, Mr Barry Huggett (fifties), experienced scientific research and the City before moving into education. Previous job director of studies at a large prep school. Currently teaches 'maths and some RE'. Married to Gerry, a physiotherapist, who now works in the school office as admissions registrar as well as being headmaster's wife. Two children, their daughter is headmistress of a large primary school and their son is a doctor. Mr Huggett is available day and night for pupils, parents and staff.

Academic Matters: This is a specialist school, with a very supporting, caring ethos. The staff works very hard to bring out the best in every boy, all of whom will be of average intelligence but have a specific learning difficulty. Every boy has an individual education plan (IEP) with targets monitored weekly and a full 'review' each year. The school has an enviable reputation for anything creative, art and design, sculpture; 3D studies and drama are all very good – and good exam results too. Music technology introduced as a GCSE option in 2003. Pick 'n' mix GCSEs depending which boards/subjects suit best. Computers everywhere and used in GCSEs if necessary. GCSE results improving each year with many boys who had not expected to take the exams on enrolment gaining good passes. Because of their specific learning difficulties, some subjects cause the boys much difficulty but, in summer 2003, the number of boys approaching the magic 5Cs and above was close to the national average. All pupils go through a course in 'life skills', which leads to a certificate of achievement and helps boys with interview techniques, financial matters, CVs, body language and other interpersonal skills. A CReSTeD category SP school. Sixth form a new development; offers creative subjects, technology, maths and business studies. In 2004/5, English, history, theatre studies will be addded as will a new sixth form block with academic and residential areas which the students themselves have helped to design.

Games, Options, The Arts: Rugby, football, cricket, athletics and swimming plus others. Adventure training, Duke of Edinburgh, ceramics, CDT, music. There are also several school pets around including a couple of pot-bellied pigs, goats, geese, and ducks.

Background and Atmosphere: Close to Farnham, woody and spacious grounds. New buildings for IT, art and sports. Small dorms, senior single and double dorms, live-in qualified care staff. At a recent Founder's day the head boy's speech included the following, 'I remember my first day here very well. For once in my life I wasn't called names, wasn't being teased in class and wasn't desperately wishing that I was somewhere else. I had found a place where everyone seemed to understand, and was willing to help. At any time of the day or night, there was always someone there who cared about me and, in my book, that makes this place special.'

Pastoral Care and Discipline: Boys demonstrate genuine and great care for each other backed up by staff. Only one case of drug taking in many years that anyone can remember.

Pupils and Parents: Broad spectrum of society, many living locally, all of whom are uncomfortable or failing to achieve at other schools and who may have specific learning difficulties. Lots of weekly boarders with a strong cadre of full-time boarders (who have organised activity at weekends); several expats, FCO and Services families.

Entrance: Parents send any reports that there may be on a boy and talk to Gerry Huggett on the phone. They are invited for an interview, without their son, and assuming all goes well, the boy is then invited for an assessment day. If it is a boarding place this also involves an overnight stay. The boys are very welcoming and Mr Huggett says that 'everyone enjoys their assessment'; during which an up-to-date reading age, maths age and spelling age are obtained. But the main purpose is to see how the child fits in to the school environment and to make sure his total needs can be met at the school.

Exit: Up until 1999, most boys left at 16 and went into further education, predominantly with a vocational bias, especially in art and design. However, in 2004, over half of year 11 stayed on and joined the sixth form.

Money Matters: Very strong learning support throughout the curriculum but extra specialist help is available at a reasonable cost. School will try to help whenever with financial crisis/difficulty. Good value for money, no hidden extras.

Remarks: Super confidence-building in caring environment.

MORRISON'S ACADEMY

Ferntower Road, Crieff, Perthshire, PH7 3AN

Tel: 01764 653 885

Fax: 01764 655 411

Email: principal@morrisonsacademy.org

Website: www.morrisonsacademy.org

• Pupils: 171 boys, 146 girls, 28 boarders including weekly
• Ages: 3-18 • Religion: Inter-denom
• Fees: Day £850-£2,573; full boarding £5,956-£6,274; weekly boarding £4,586-£4,904 • School status: Independent
• Opendays: October and February • School gender: Mixed
• Day/boarding: Takes boarders

SEN provision

Detail:

Now provide for in school:
- Mild: DYSL; DYSP; SpLD;
- Moderate: DYSL;
- Others: EAL; DEL; Epi;

Experience of:
- Mild: ASP; ADD; EBD; HI;
- Moderate: ASP;
- Others: Eat;

Summary: The school caters for those pupils whose needs can, on the whole, be met in the mainstream classroom with their peers. At the present time we are meeting the needs of pupils with specific learning difficulties (mild/moderate dyslexia, mild dyspraxia, dysgraphia) as well as pupils with mild emotional and behavioural difficulties. A small proportion of our pupils have difficulties which respond to measures that may include individual or small group work with an additional support needs teacher. However, the vast majority will be taught in mainstream classes differentiated to suit individual need.

What we say about the school - the full Good Schools Guide review

Rector and Principal: From 2004, Mr Simon Pengelley BA PGCE (forties) who was educated at Repton, read history at Bristol and did his PGCE in London. Started his teaching career at Abingdon before moving to Strathallan where he was head of history and comes from Rossall; he spent twelve years there, ending as director of studies and deputy head. He and his wife Louise love Scotland and have 'loads of friends in the area'. So that's all right then. Has two sons, one at uni and one still at Rossall. He joins the school after an interregnum, fronted by the depute, who has returned to the common room 'and is enormously supportive'. Outgoing, enthusiastic and bubbly. When we asked about the last head but one's plan to return the ceiling of the Memorial Hall to its original height, we both rushed off to have a look; it is back to its former Victorian glory, with stained glass shining in the Perth sunshine and portraits of those who died in the First World War strategically placed round the balcony.

Academic Matters: School follows Scottish curriculum: good take up for Advanced Highers. The traditional bias towards science is slightly fading in favour of arts-based courses. Masses of computers on site and many staff have to taken their European Computer Driving Licence as have the pupils (the head of the computer department often builds his own). 17 Highers, with photography for media a recent addition at sixth form only, plus Intermediate 2 more or less across the board. Sciences perform consistently well, also maths; English Highers impressive last year, also accountancy. Goodish art and design, not really much language take up, humanities OK. Ditto geography and history. No obvious terminal cases; human biology popular at Higher level and results indicate that it is obviously either better taught or more interesting to the candidates. Can cope with special needs and programmes much used: dyslexia, dyspraxia and mild Asperger's not a problem.

Games, Options, The Arts: Masses of pitches at Dallerie, a ten-minute walk from the main buildings, and school plays all the standard games. Good rugby. Strong pipe band and very popular – with Chinese students forming a part (plus locals of course) but it does make interesting photographs. Band plays at Murrayfield rugby internationals as part of massed bands. CCF on curriculum, D of E strong, almost all get bronze, lots of silver and gold. Enthusiastic art dept in inspired converted attics but still no CAD. Music and drama strong with a stunning girls' chamber choir which plays regularly to local acclaim. 45 extra-curricular activities in total.

Background and Atmosphere: Built in 1859, this Scottish baronial-styled building with its crow stepped gables was described at the time: 'Its healthful locality and commanding view of extensive and beautifully romantic scenery cannot be surpassed, if at all equalled, by any such public building in Scotland.' The gift of Thomas Mor(r)ison, who lived in the neighbouring village of Muthill and made his fortune as a master builder in Edinburgh. He instructed his trustees to erect an institution carrying his name 'to promote the interests of mankind, having a particular regard to the education of youth and the diffusion of useful knowledge'.

Always independent, at one stage the school did have grant-aided pupils but this finished in the late 1970s. Boarding numbers declined in the 1990s but have stabilised at two houses. Some of the current boarders are Scots but many come from overseas, and add an exotic flavour to what is a fairly pedestrian environment – almost all religious festivals are celebrated. Fabulous buildings revamped following the sale of underused outlying houses. The swimming pool, the nomenclature BATHS carved in (whitewashed) stone above the entrance, is still in daily use. The original school building is fantastic with large open corridors and a terrific hall which doubles for daily assemblies and socials. A somewhat convoluted reconstruction of the former girls' school has made a jolly music room, with excellent practice rooms carved from the earlier loo block. Recording studios on the wish list. A magnificent newer build for maths and jolly attic transformation into a vast art complex.

Pastoral Care and Discipline: Excellent pastoral care and guardianship for boarders and the same applies across the school. Head quite tough on sin (early days yet) though pupils on the whole 'quite docile': 'tobacco could get you suspended and Chinese pupils do like smoking' and often arrive addicted. No booting out for fags, regular boozing could ultimately result in expulsion and use of drugs means that 'you should expect to be expelled'. Not really a street-wise school.

Pupils and Parents: Day pupils from all over the middle belt, Falkirk, Stirling, Dunblane, Comrie, Perth,

Auchterarder are bused to school. (No trains since Beeching). Masses of boarders from abroad – agencies and regularly dominie-type visits, head expects 'to show his face in the Far East shortly' and is keen to target the highland professionals, 'estate factors, solicitors, accountants and their like.'

Entrance: Children can and do arrive at any time, during the term and at the start of any term – particularly for boarding from abroad, if space available. The school operates an open presentation policy – 'we don't prevent pupils from taking exams in order to improve our statistics.' Interview and testing for nursery and junior school and more or less automatic entrance into senior school from the junior school. Some join the senior school at 11 from the state sector or from local prep schools such as Ardvrec or Craigclowan. Interview and examination. Sixth form entrants are assessed on their potential, taking into account their grades at Standard level or GCSE.

Exit: Three or four off to (usually) Scottish independent schools at either 11 or 13. Otherwise a dribble occasionally to Oxbridge, one to Cambridge last year, though four to London, Imperial and Kings. Regular mini stream usually to engineering or allied science at Imperial London, or Manchester, Newcastle, Leeds. Most stay in Scotland with law, computing, business and sciences prevailing, though sports science and sports medicine in the ribbons. Plus ca change.

Money Matters: Discounts for siblings, one or two means tested bursaries, scholarships for the final year.

Remarks: A good proud school which does well by its pupils.

THE NEW SCHOOL

Butterstone, Dunkeld, Perthshire, PH8 0HJ

Tel: 01350 724 216

Fax: 01350 724 283

Email: info@thenewschool.co.uk

Website: www.thenewschool.co.uk

• Pupils: 44 boys and girls, most of whom weekly board • Ages: 12-18 • Religion: Non-denom • Fees: Weekly boarding £9,310; day £7,581 • School status: Independent • School gender: Mixed • Day/boarding: Takes boarders

SEN provision

Detail:

Centre of excellence for:

Mild: ASP; AUT; ADD; ADHD; EBD; DYSC; DYSL; DYSP; SpLD; CP;

Moderate: ASP; AUT; ADD; DYSP;

Others: DEL;

Experience of:

Mild: HI; VI;

Moderate: EBD; DYSC; SpLD; CP;

Severe: ASP; DYSC; DYSL; DYSP; SpLD;

Others: AUT(other); CD; OCD; FRX; GEN; EAL; Sp&LD; Epi; PD; Oth; Eat;

Summary: The New School which opened in 1992 was founded by Baroness Linklater of Butterstone for the benefit of educationally fragile children, and is a mixed school providing for Monday to Friday boarding pupils, and for day pupils, with a total capacity for 45 children, aged 12 to 18, all of whom have displayed inability to develop their potential in the traditional mainstream schooling system. The school provides a uniquely supportive environment for children who have difficulties associated with neurological and developmental disorders such as autism, dyspraxia and dysphasia.

We aim to help children to realise their potential by building up confidence and self-esteem, emphasising strengths rather than allowing difficulties to become barriers to learning, and allowing them to be challenged in as normal an environment and community as possible.

Small classes, dedicated staff and a strong sense of purpose have led to an enviable ethos and unique position in the field of Scottish education.

In this small environment, using individualised educational programmes, the school enables children to move on into further education, and ultimately to be part of their community and be able to pursue happy and independent lives. The school provides an oasis of care and support where potential is unlocked and the children have the opportunity to develop educationally, socially and emotionally.

There is no substitute for a visit to the school where you will see young people at ease with themselves and their surroundings.

What we say about the school - the full Good Schools Guide review

Head: From 2006, Mr Andrew Wilson BA (Hons) CertEd NPQH (forties) who was educated at Giggleswick, read English and politics at de Montford university. He previously taught here for five years (1994-1999) and was houseparent for two. Previously deputy head at The Philip Green Memorial School in Dorset, having worked as SEN specialist at the High School of Dundee. Prior to his earlier stint at The New School he taught EFL and led a somewhat peripatetic life. Married, with a five-year-old son at the local Rudolf Steiner nursery in Dorset, his wife and son will join him in Perthshire at the end of his first academic year. A gentle soul, with flowing locks and conquistador moustache and beard, Mr Wilson says 'this is my dream job, absolutely delighted, couldn't identify a job which inspires me so much'. The governors seem equally keen.

Entrance: See below.

Exit: See below.

Remarks: Deep in the Perthshire countryside, with fantastic views in all directions, this is an inspiring school, which follows – as far as possible – a normal school curriculum but with specialist teachers, who are hard to find. With 14 ('very fortunate, they are all excellent and committed') staff, plus numerous visiting specialist teachers – speech therapists and the like – each child has a special tutor and no class is larger than eight. The pupils have a variety of problems, ranging from school refusers through the autistic spectrum plus dyspraxia, dyslexia and mild neurophysiological and social problems. Mild physical problems OK but the building is not wheelchair friendly. Children arrive here with 'a sense of failure and low self-esteem, often lack initiative and are in a downward spiral of under-achieving'. The normal school programme – often carried out to a background of music (and music is important here with pupils both composing and making their own CDs) – includes computing (campus is networked), ICT, science, home economics, a YTC enterprise centre, and fabulous (really fabulous) art and ceramics, as well as the three Rs.

French for all but no Spanish. CDT is important. Pupils sit proper exams. Good and serious games, a well-used swimming pool and an equally well-used sports hall – the ping pong table had collapsed at the time of our visit. The tennis is floodlit for evening activities. Dance and exercise popular; but fox and hounds and incredibly complicated dens are as much part of the school curriculum as maths. Days are long, children need care and loving after lessons end and indoor activities – table football and chess are popular – as well as almost any other activity. 'If a child wants to go fishing, fine'; 'if they want to go to the safari park, visit the osprey nest or climb a mountain, then we will try and organise it'. Anything and everything goes, under the strictest of supervision, and the children give concerts and plays locally and visit old folks homes. Children are encouraged to do as much for themselves as they can, and treat the staff with ease and charm – 'Mr Colley this is a teacher-free zone, you can only come in when we ask you'. Here they learn to respect both themselves and their peers, making friends – for many this is the first time in their lives.

Not as many posters round the walls as you might expect to find in a regular establishment, but pupils appear to work better in a stress-free and uncluttered zone, though how this theory equates with the amazing purple and lurid pink dormitory is anybody's guess – but it was decorated by parents in consultation with the young. Younger pupils sleep in the main building and older ones are carefully supervised in the Lodge. No fizzy drinks, e-numbers are carefully monitored, the head was doshing out naturally flavoured water when we were there. A few just come for a term or so until they are settled, but most stay the course, ending up either at Perth College or Elmwood in Cupar, Fife, where they learn horticulture and the like. A small number have made it to university.

The school gets many enquiries – it is expensive. Perth and Kinross and Dumfries and Galloway LEAs have no problem sending children here, but sometimes Mr Colley 'battles quite hard' to get appropriate funding. Eighty per cent of all children here have statements of needs. Eighty per cent funded by LEAs. The weekly boarding pattern is difficult for some and makes it impossible for pupils from further afield and the school is considering an alternative strategy – it may even clone itself further south. Founded by Baroness Linklater in 1992 in what used to be her family home, The New School has expanded and developed enormously since our first visit and runs under care commission regulations (which means the staff can cuddle). The local minister visits every fortnight or so. Exceptional. The answer to many parents' prayers. To quote one pupil 'I have some sunshine in my life'.

Newlands Manor School

Sutton Place, Seaford, East Sussex, BN25 3PL

Tel: 01323 890 309
Fax: 01323 898 420
Email: newlands1@msn.com
Website: www.newlands-school.com

• Pupils: Total 420; ages 8-13 220 pupils; ages 13-18 200 pupils • Ages: 8 to 18 • Religion: Non-Denominational
• Fees: Senior school - day fees £3,625 , boarding £5,950
• School status: Independent • School gender: Mixed
• Day/boarding: Takes boarders

SEN provision

Detail:

Centre of excellence for:
  Mild: DYSC; DYSL;
  Others: EAL;
Now provide for in school:
  Mild: DYSP;
  Moderate: DYSC; DYSL;
Experience of:
  Mild: ASP; ADD; ADHD; SpLD; HI; VI;
  Moderate: DYSP;

Summary: Newlands is a mainstream school with an excellent reputation for maximising the potential of any individual who has difficulty with literacy and numeracy. A nationally renown learning support centre, approved by CReSTeD, offers one-to-one tuition enabling pupils to restore their confidence so that they can become independent learners. By early identification of the pupils' individual learning styles, their educational programmes are tailored to their needs. Newlands thus offers continuity of learning support, in a positive and happy environment, as the pupils progress through the three sections of the school – the Pre-Prep, the Prep and the Manor.

What we say about the school - the full Good Schools Guide review

Head: Since 1998 Mr Oliver Price, BEd (Loughborough University). Oversaw the amalgamation of the three schools (pre-prep, prep and senior), now Newlands School. Big adjustments were necessary, difficult times experienced but now transformed into a more settled and positive school. Known as Buster, he's a charming, approachable, cuddly 'teddy bear' type described by parents as an honest, caring, no frills type. Married to Patricia Snowdon (in charge of the hugely successful Theatre Arts programme), they have two children in the school, one in prep and a daughter in the sixth form. Says school has developed a niche market and a national reputation for offering a broad spectrum of pupils with varying needs – a specialised and fulfilling education, whilst in the context of a mainstream school. His vision for the school is to maximise the potential of each individual, to drive on strengths and build on weaknesses, to produce decent rounded human beings so that he sees a school of smiling children.

Academic Matters: Operates as a mainstream school with small classes, where the individual is valued more than league table position. For the record, the results at GCSE and A level are slightly above the national average. In 2004, 56 per cent were graded A*/C improving in 2005 to 73 per cent. Almost all pass A level with 30 per cent A or B grades in 2005. However results alone don't give a true picture of the achievements of the school and pupils. 'There are some staggeringly bright pupils,' says the head but many results reflect the excellent teaching within the SEN department. Some children arrive after 'failing' at other schools with well below appropriate reading age yet achieve nine GCSEs and get A levels with A grades. Maths, dance, physics, art, Spanish, business studies and English literature all popular, with law and psychology newer additions to A levels. Setted from year 5 in English, maths, science and modern languages; will look at ability not obstacles. For example, one very intellectually competent pupil with data recording problems was placed in the top set. Whole school screened in reading and spelling at the beginning of Autumn term with writing speed cannily assessed (changing from a blue pen to a red pen after twenty minutes). Special exam requirements extra time, use of scribe or a transcriber, utilised as required. One dyslexic boy, whose computer skills were poor, whose writing deteriorated when under pressure, was allowed a transcriber and achieved A* in English literature and language. Of the present three Oxbridge candidates, two are dyslexics. Most parents are happy with the prep school but within the mainstream Manor School there have been murmurs of discontent. The recent inspection report revealed some unsatisfactory teaching, lack of in-service teacher training, uninviting library and inadequate boys' boarding. However, the head assures us that all the above are being addressed, particularly with the purchase of the new building.

A third of the school receives extra learning support through the Gannon Centre (warrants a separate prospectus due to its profile and specialisation). Established by a retired headmaster, Tom Gannon, who taught English and noticed that many pupils could easily accommodate facts and be discerning with them but found recording difficult. Predominantly for dyslexics but also with experience of dyspraxia, mild Asperger's and mild attention difficulties, the centre specialises in literacy and numeracy needs, often using a multi-sensory approach: 'feel it, touch it, see it'. Originally for pupils of average to above average ability, the core still fit that profile though all abilities are catered for; will take any child they think they can help. Children are withdrawn for one-to-one tuition from a mutually agreed lesson (charged as extra). 'Withdrawing them into groups almost always does not work – they do not like to admit in front of their peers that they do not understand something.' Withdrawal begins as early as pre-prep, with complete continuity through the school if required. School not suitable for those needing to be withdrawn for more than five lessons a week. Often the SEN staff stay with one pupil through their entire school life, encouraging independent learning and developing firm relationships that are the springboards for remarkable successes from previously deemed hopeless cases. Staff are all specialists, familiar with accurate diagnosis of a child's need. No SaLT or physiotherapist but pull in specialists if needed. Communication and, feedback to the Gannon Centre, plus liaison between prep and senior school is well-established.This, together with the appreciation of different learning styles by all teachers, contributes to centre's success. Parents and pupils say there is absolutely no stigma attached to a child being withdrawn to the Gannon Centre. Everywhere there is a relaxed friendly atmosphere with a supportive network; self-esteem problems vanish shortly after arrival. Many happy faces in evidence. One child decided on Newlands because 'the sun always comes out when I come here'. Many parents felt the confidence and self-assurance their children developed was a direct result of the non-pressurised, supportive environment. School also has a new international study centre offering TEFL courses in large light new classrooms.

Games, Options, The Arts: Approximately one third of the school involves itself in dance, jazz, drama and singing. Indeed the school attracts dancers of the highest calibre and currently one boy is Samba in the Lion King at the Lyceum Theatre. There is excellent specialist teaching on offer with examinations at many levels and great facilities. Three large dance studios and a good proportion of SEN pupils involved. 'The art is also highly thought of' one pupil remarked, 'it's absolutely my most favourite place to be in the whole school. Staff are open to many creative outlets, animation, photography, etc. – pupils feel inspired. The music department is small with few ensembles- but plenty of individual practice rooms. Sport has a solid reputation with good facilities including a sizable swimming pool and sports hall. The emphasis is on fun and variety. Certain activities would be encouraged for those finding competitive team games difficult, eg gym, orienteering, riding, golf. Coastal location means plenty of sailing on offer. New head of sport, changed the curriculum to ensure that years 4-5 have more co-ordinated activities, attention to flexibilities, etc.

Background and Atmosphere: Set in 21 acres, a stone's throw from the sea, the pleasant Edwardian red-brick building proves an attractive setting but some areas weary and in need of a makeover. There's nothing very glitzy, no wall to wall carpeting but there's a happy buzz amongst the children and varied and delicious food. A good proportion of boarders are Asian or African, while many are from Services families. A multi-racial group that mixes well.

Pastoral Care and Discipline: Children know they will be listened to and are valued, have good rapport with staff so little in the way of behavioural problems. Support flexes so children with attention difficulties will be given time out to help them refocus if necessary. Staff so au fait with pupils that problems are spotted quickly and nipped in the bud. The level of pastoral care is deemed a strength by parents and inspectors. A new school has been bought nearby that is large, light and will house the boys boarding and later some of the girls. Recent inspection critical of existing boys boarding facilities and associated activities; certainly the accommodation is now good but check out what is on offer at weekends etc. – other than the usual trip to the local town.

Entrance: School is not selective. SEN pupils often come to the school with educational psychologists' reports but all are tested so literacy and numeracy needs are detected. 'If we feel they have potential, we will take them but we never set a hurdle too high, too soon'.

Exit: Some to Further Education Colleges, art school or performing arts courses. Many to universities particularly helpful with SEN needs, eg Newcastle, St Mary's Exeter, Southampton or Wolverhampton.

Money Matters: Small bursary available if a child would clearly benefit but lacks the extra funds. Slight reduction for Services children.

Remarks: The prospectus picture of a girl in her white and red chorister robe running to kick a football is a fitting image of this school, reflecting an underlying spirit, learning to express itself. A mainstream school that boosts the confidence of pupils. An inclusive school for all abilities, with emphasis is on the well-rounded individual.

Nonsuch High School for Girls

Ewell Road, Cheam, Sutton, Surrey, SM3 8AB

Tel: 020 8394 1308

Fax: 020 8393 2307

Email: admissions@nonsuch.sutton.sch.uk

Website: www.nonsuchhigh.co.uk

• Pupils: 1,220 girls, all day • Ages: 11-18 • Religion: Non-denom • School status: State • Opendays: September (yr 7) and November (sixth form) • School gender: Girls • Day/boarding: Day pupils

SEN provision

Detail:

Now provide for in school:

Mild: EBD; DYSL;

Moderate: EBD; DYSL;

Severe: EBD;

Others: SPD; EAL; DEL; Epi; PD; Eat;

Experience of:

Mild: DYSP;

Summary: Miss R Isom – special educational needs co-ordinator.

A pro-forma is sent out to teachers and parents of prospective pupils in year 6 requesting information relating to SEN. This practice ensures effective continuity of provision as well as yielding valuable knowledge about potential difficulties or pastoral issues.

The progress of girls with known special educational needs is reviewed termly, generally in November, February and June. Some girls may warrant closer monitoring and therefore have a monthly review. All departments, in addition to year teams, have a mandatory agenda item of 'Pupils Causing Concern' so that both academic and pastoral needs are monitored regularly.

Initial testing for dyslexia is provided in school. Initiatives are developed for supporting individual pupils and arrangements made for any further testing so that applications for special consideration can be made for public examinations. The school liaises closely with the educational psychologist who provides valuable professional advice on those girls with special needs.

As a result of the successful piloting of a scheme to develop Social Skills, run jointly by the Educational Psychology Service and school's SENCo, the year 7 PSE programme now includes these sessions.

Regular discussion takes place with staff concerned throughout the school and particularly through the school's well-established pastoral system. Most importantly, communication is maintained with parents so that strategies for monitoring pupils with special needs are clearly understood by both home and school.

All students diagnosed as having an SEN have individual education plans that are subject to termly review. Parents are invited to attend review meetings and each student is withdrawn from a single period to enable the appropriate attention to be given to the review process. After review, a new IEP is drafted with appropriate targets. A Guide for Students and Parents of girls with dyslexia is available. Those girls requiring extra enrichment for dyslexia benefit from a lunchtime session.

Alterations have been made to the school buildings to make them more accessible to students and other visitors with physical disabillities. A lift has been installed and toilets have been adapted. The school is large, housed in six buildings, three of which are detached from the rest. Both the new and old parts of the school have three floors and there are a number of staircases and steps to negotiate.

Support for students whose first language is not English is provided through tutoring after school. This is a developing area providing language support for a defined group of pupils.

What we say about the school - the full Good Schools Guide review

Head: Since 1995, Mrs Genefer Espejo BA (mid-fifties). Previously head at a girls' comprehensive in Reading. English, despite her exotic sounding name (courtesy of her Colombian husband). Theatre, art, travelling and shopping among her interests, also a keen supporter of Southampton football club! Looks younger than her years and comes across as a woman entirely at ease with herself and her school – very pleasant manner. 'She definitely has a presence and you are in no doubt about who runs this place,' said a parent – though, as in most large state schools, the vast majority of parents have little or no face-to-face contact with her.

Academic Matters: Impressive, as you would expect from one of the top selective schools in the country. Science facilities are good – but results not so sparkling. Nice to see astronomy available as a GCSE option (school has its own observatory). At A level, English, psychology, sciences, geography and maths are among the favourite options. 'It's almost as if they don't want to be labelled as a girls' school, they are always emphasising the more traditionally masculine subjects,' said one parent. Lots of homework but parents say it is 'manageable'. 'My daughter works very hard and is definitely stretched here. In year 8 she was looking at GCSE papers,' says a mother. Definitely not a school for slackers. 'We actually chose this school because we thought it would be less pressured than Tiffin Girls but we were wrong – it is quite pushy,' says another mother. Little call for special needs support here, but SENCo assists those dyslexic pupils who are able to pass the entry test and some physical disabilities are catered for. Approximately 20 EAL students but no beginners.

Games, Options, The Arts: Sports facilities are excellent and well used, thanks in large part to an innovative deal with a David Lloyd sports club. Nonsuch was the first state school to go into such a partnership – the school leases land to the club and in return can use its facilities – including exclusive use of the swimming pool in the mornings and the tennis courts in the afternoon. Additionally as part of the deal, David Lloyd provided the school with a dedicated sports hall, a floodlit all-weather hockey pitch and a new music centre. All the usual main sports on offer and pupils compete at national and county level in several including netball, football and hockey. Tennis is popular and the school provides the ball girls for the Stella Artois tournament at Queens.

Very good reputation for music (old girls include 'cool' singer Katie Melua and harpist Lucy Wakeford) with many choirs, orchestras, and ensembles. Some 350 girls take extra-curricular music lessons and aim for grade 8 by the time they leave. Budding dancers and actresses might struggle to express themselves – some parents feel these subjects are the poor relations. 'They have spent all the money on maths and science facilities – the drama department is a temporary hut and was like that for the entire seven years I was there,' says one former pupil. (Head says work on a new drama studio will begin soon and that uptake and results for drama at both GCSE and A level are high despite the 'very modest physical means'.) Clubs and societies from cheerleading to philosophy. CCF and DofE.

Background and Atmosphere: Lovely setting on the edge of the 22 acre Nonsuch Park. Plenty of outdoor space, mix of buildings – admin and some classrooms are in the charmless original building, which has been extended in different directions with newer, fresher facilities and a few separate blocks. Workman-like rather than flashy. There was an untidy pile of clutter in the lobby when we visited at short notice. This is a school so confident of its strengths that it doesn't have to try too hard to impress. Girls are lively – even noisy. Strong house system.

Pastoral Care and Discipline: Usual system of tutors and heads of year in place, and working well. Issues dealt with rapidly – nothing festers. Discipline is strict. No major discipline problems – 'I tolerate absolutely no nonsense and treat everyone exactly the same,' says the head. Parents feel their daughters clearly know and understand the boundaries. No tolerance of smoking anywhere while in school uniform – including travel time – prefects patrol the huge school site.

Pupils and Parents: A refreshingly multicultural bunch (30 languages). Pupils proud to be here, and generally smart – school uniform kilts are difficult to shorten. Parents are mainly professional, ambitious for their daughters, and supportive of the school. Communications with parents are good – lots of up-to-date information on the website, 75 per cent of parents opts to receive and send all communication by e-mail.

Entrance: Hugely over-subscribed – in 2004 there were 830 applications (from some 50 primary schools) for 180 places. Applicants must list Nonsuch as a preferred school on the foundation grammar school application form to sit the test – two parts (maths and verbal reasoning), no interview. Places are allocated to those who pass, according to the usual criteria of siblings and proximity – families move into the area to be as near to the school doorstep as possible. However the top 50 highest scores get a place regardless of where they live. In practice the school maintains a local intake, with 95 per cent of the pupils living within 5 km of the school. 10-20 external students join the school in the sixth form.

Exit: Over 80 per cent of the girls stay on for the sixth form – of the rest some join colleges (probably in search of a mixed environment) and a few go to the private sector. At 18 most go on to university – 10 or so to Oxbridge, lots to the redbricks and a handful each year to leading medical and dental schools.

Remarks: A super school for the disciplined and hard-working, not for the rebel, slacker or drama/dance diva.

NORTH BERWICK HIGH SCHOOL

Grange Road, North Berwick, East Lothian, EH39 4QS

Tel: 01620 894 661

Fax: 01620 895 495

Email: northberwick.hs@eastlothian.gov.uk

Website: www.northberwick.e-lothian.sch.uk

• Pupils: 925 boys and girls, all day • Ages: 11-18

• Religion: Non-denom • School status: State

• School gender: Mixed • Day/boarding: Day pupils

SEN provision

Detail:

Now provide for in school:

Mild: ASP; AUT; ADD; ADHD; EBD; DYSL; DYSP; HI; VI; CP;

Moderate: MLD; HI; VI;

Severe: HI;

Others: EAL; DEL; Epi; PD;

Experience of:

Mild: DYSC; SpLD;

Moderate: ASP; AUT; ADD; ADHD; EBD; DYSL; DYSP; CP;

Severe: DYSL; CP;

Others: SPD; OCD; ODD; PMLD; MSI; Sp&LD; Eat;

Summary: North Berwick High School aims to be an inclusive one, one which meets the needs of all its children. We offer a range of services to support our most vulnerable pupils. We have two Support Bases, one aimed at pupils with pronounced Additional Support Needs and the other aimed at supporting pupils in their work in a variety of ways.

We offer support in a variety of ways: in-class support from Support Staff (both teachers and auxiliary staff); small-group tutorial work; paired reading with senior students; extra support in class from senior students; ongoing development of the curriculum in all departments.

What we say about the school - the full Good Schools Guide review

Head: Since 1999 (previous head, George Smuga, having been seconded to East Lothian Education Department), Mr Colin Sutherland BSc (forties), who comes from the West (as they say in Scotland). He started his teaching career at Garnock Academy, Kilbirnie in Ayrshire, before spending 11 years at Castlehead School in Paisley. Previously depute at Port Glasgow High School, before that assistant head at Greenock. Educated at Paisley Grammar, 'when it was still selective'. He read maths and geology at Glasgow University plus PGCE and 'masses of courses'. He would love to teach more but still does 'the odd bit, supply teaching mainly' but no set classes as such. Mr Sutherland runs the school with three depute heads, who are responsible for the school's three houses, plus a whole host of add-ons. There is also a recently-appointed school business manager.

A charming man, thoughtful and very aware of children's needs, he has a lovely sense of humour and 'just loves it here'. An enthusiastic cyclist and walker, he has not yet taken up the North Berwick vice of golf though is otherwise much involved in the community (he lives at nearby Port Seton, safely out of the catchment area).

Academic Matters: School follows Scottish system. Standard Grades followed by Highers and Advanced Highers the following year. The school picks up children from five associated primaries, the huge (over 700) Law Primary, which is adjacent and shares many of the school facilities including the fabulous local sports centre, and the much smaller local primaries of Aberlady, Athelstaneford, Dirleton and Gullane. Pupils in primary 7 visit the school before their actual arrival here and follow part of the big school timetable. There are however six parallel classes at S1 and S2, with pupils being setted for maths in S1 and S2; French is also setted in S2. Thereafter, the school runs six parallel classes, taking into account option choice, when specialist subject teaching kicks in – 'deliberately made broad to ensure that pupils' needs and interests are met within the national framework'. 'Max class size 25 (head says 'could be up to 30, but the school strives to ensure that classes contain no more than 25/26'). 18/20 for practical matters.

School consistently turns in better results than any other in East Lothian and recently ranked 37th overall in Scotland for Standard Grades and 17th for Highers. In Standard Grades biology, chemistry, English, French, geography, history and, to a lesser degree, physics, were outstanding. French writing and German less so, maths had a bad year. Pupils can take Spanish up to Intermediate level in S5/6 – usually the latter.

At Intermediate 2 (which many schools are using instead of Standard Grades) chemistry, English and maths are very strong and this trend continues at Higher level, with excellent showings across the board in English and the sciences, as well as geography, history and modern studies. Pupils take an amalgam of exams, often topping up with another batch of Highers rather than opting for Advanced Highers. Little problem with getting staff – well it's North Berwick isn't it? Head is autonomous in being able to choose his own staff ('scheme of delegation').

Good remedial back-up, children with Records of Needs not a problem, nor are those with ADHD. Double teaching in class. Laptop computers where required, plus extra time in exams and for those with learning needs, 'which cannot be tackled in the classroom'. There are 'workshops on basic processes, individual educational programmes and individual tutorials'. Reading Recovery programme, as well as educational psychologists, outreach teachers et al. Support for learning for the most able as well as for those with learning difficulties. This school has a number of profoundly deaf pupils, for whom there is an excellent programme. Blind and partially sighted pupils and wheel chairs all easily absorbed. Laudable.

In session 2003-2004, an integrated Pupil Support Faculty was established, including a Pupil Support Base in which the most vulnerable pupils have a 'sanctuary.' This was extended further in session 2004-2005 with the addition of a Base for pupils with additional support needs.

Outstanding report from HM Inspectorate of Education in January 2002.

Games, Options, The Arts: The school has an enviable collection of games pitches with the local sports centre and swimming pool next door – they have priority over local users. New astroturf. Two gyms in school, plus dance studio plus mirrors of course. Strong rugby and school recently toured Canada with great success, they all wore the kilt and the piper came too. Two current sixth formers in national squad. Plus basketball, hockey (huge fixture list for girls), badminton, netball club, sailing, swimming and local authority development officers on hand for coaching. D of E popular – head would like us to add 'VERY', with half a dozen pupils every year going to Holyrood for their Gold Award'. Trillions of clubs for everything.

Music outstanding, though no pipe band of their own, pupils (of both sexes) play with the town band. Bands, orchestras and choirs in every discipline: wind, jazz, brass, piano. Senior and junior choirs, the school sings carols outside the church for charity at Christmas, and plays at The Lodge. The school provided the brass band for the opening of the local Sea Bird Centre. Musicians have been known to come back to school and join in the school orchestra – often with no warning at all. Scottish country dancing popular, as are the regular ceilidhs, much to the amazement of the bunch of Kosovan refugees who were billeted in the town recently – 'they loved it'- (and came with extra resources).

Recording studio, huge assembly hall used for school drama, very good, and by the locals – for partying as well as plays. Deaf loop in operation. Keyboards, guitars, large number of practice rooms. Whizzy art department, absolutely fabulous, with excellent ceramics and tranches of young going on to art schools all over the country. Amazing cut glass. Fabulous screen printing (though the sewing-up was less impressive).

Artwork all over the school. Huge art library and dark room. CAD and computer links to art department, impressive DT, though mainly in wood. Home economics but not much take up. Impressive computer suites (one hundred new computers in 2004) set out like an office and due to be expanded shortly; computers and tellies in every classroom.

School is twinned, as is the town, with Kerteminde in Denmark; children do exchanges and four-weekly study visits are a regular feature. This is a growth activity.

Background and Atmosphere: The school was founded in 1893 with thirteen pupils. Originally North Berwick boasted two schools: the Parish School (which started in 1661) and the Burgh School; these amalgamated in 1868 and joined forces with the High School in 1931. The current buildings date back to 1940 and very impressive they are too. The temporary classrooms which had provided schooling for the extra post-war pupils were replaced during the 1990s and a further extension under the PPP initiative began in April 2003. This was scheduled to be complete by March 2005, and, at time of writing (autumn 2005) is at last nearly so. However, as reported in the Daily Express (so it must be true) the contractors went bust, having removed (and presumably chucked out) the specialist cabinets needed to store A1 paper and all the rest. Staff had to hunt for substitute desks at local (upmarket) scrap merchant and pupils came back to find not only a leaky roof but also fifties- style desks some of which were more suited to kindergarten than a senior school. Balfour Beatty are now in control but red faces and ruined artwork abound. Or so we hear.

Light and airy, the school must have some of the best views in Britain, with the Law to the south and views over the North Berwick coastline and the Bass Rock to the north. The school has strong links with the recently opened Sea Bird Centre, which is used for regular study, as well as providing summer and weekend jobs for impoverished pupils. A grade one bonus.

This is a community school at its best. Loads of town participation, a squad recently cleaned up the East Beach, and local countryside a haven for hands-on teaching. Masses of inter-school/town involvement, and the Community Council has recently 'donated a prize for community service which is awarded annually'. Huge library, divided into little seminar areas, as well as crannies for private study. The tidiest school we have ever visited, only two bags in evidence, the rest neatly tucked into lockers. Having patted the back, one has to say that there was quite a lot of detritus and candy bar wrappers lying around, despite the enormous (labelled) litter bins everywhere.

School operates with a three house system, a focus for pastoral care as well as discipline and games. Sibling led. Each of the three depute and heads fronts one of them. And house boards vie for imaginative notices.

Children wear their school uniform with pride; move currently afoot to introduce fleece jackets, all wear white shirts, with black and red ties and sweat shirts. Pupils not encouraged to leave the school at lunchtime but no dining rooms as such, cafeteria-style food available, and can bring packed lunch or eat in the sports centre. Head boy or girl chosen via ballot of staff and sixth form – 'not a beauty contest', said the head, the top four are then interviewed before selection. A pretty onerous task, they have to do the Burns night supper at the local Marine Hotel, which brushes up their public speaking skills. Two prize givings – the head boy and girl are principal speakers at the prize giving for S1/2/3 at the trad time in June, and then return for the senior prize giving in mid September which is followed by soft drinks, wine for the adults and nibbles in the library. Very popular.

The school closes at lunchtime on Fridays for 'staff training' which may not be over-convenient for working parents. School bus for all outlying districts. Masses of trips, for everything, all over.

Pastoral Care and Discipline: Good PSE programme in place; strong anti-bullying programme in place 'secrecy is the worst enemy'. No obvious problems with booze, fags or drugs in school, but North Berwick itself had some recent horrendous publicity with children being found paralytic on the beaches during the weekend and underage drinking is certainly a problem locally. The local community health boys take this seriously and are very 'proactive'. School is much involved in this and 'ever vigilant in educating youth'. Slight glitch last autumn when pupils were 'temporarily excluded from school for smoking cannabis at lunchtime'. Regular smoking patrol.

School uses three chaplains, two Church of Scotland and one Episcopalian, who tackle moral issues. 'An honest school', no history of theft, and most classrooms are left unlocked.

Pupils and Parents: Mostly a middle class bunch but a diverse intake, everyone from baby bankers to impoverished shepherds. Incredibly supportive, usually over 95 per cent turn up for parents' evenings, and a very strong PTA. Good at fund-raising. Minuscule number of ethnic minorities. Parent-led school board, parents, staff and a couple of members of the local community.

Entrance: Automatic from local primaries and if children of school age move into the area. At any time.

Exit: Two departure dates a year, one at Christmas, the other at the conventional end of school year. Around 80 per cent stay on for sixth year; some leave to go into 'further education', some work, 50 per cent to university, quite a mix: 'medics, law, business admin, economics, English, maths, education etc. Primarily to Scottish universities but a regular and quite impressive trickle to Oxbridge annually.

Money Matters: No child disadvantaged, good back-up from the local LEA, as well as parent-inspired foundation.

Remarks: A stunning and successful local school. Couldn't do better anywhere.

North Cestrian Grammar School

Dunham Road, Altrincham, Cheshire, WA14 4AJ

Tel: 0161 928 1856

Fax: 01619 298 657

Email: office@ncgs.co.uk

Website: www.ncgs.co.uk

• Pupils: 290 boys • Ages: 11 – 18 • Religion: Non-denom
• Fees: £2,090 • School status: Independent
• School gender: Boys • Day/boarding: Day pupils

SEN provision

Detail:

Centre of excellence for:

Mild: DYSL;

Moderate: DYSL;

Now provide for in school:

Mild: ASP; AUT; ADD; ADHD; EBD; DYSC; DYSP; SpLD; HI; VI; CP;

Moderate: ASP; AUT; ADD; ADHD; EBD; MLD; DYSC; DYSP; HI; VI; CP;

Severe: DYSL;

Others: SPD; CD; EAL; DEL; Epi;

Summary: The school has a well-established reputation for helping late developers, adding value and helping children achieve at least in line with, and often above, expectation. This reputation extends to those with various forms of special educational needs who are enocouraged to believe in themselves and helped to devlop through good pastoral care and positive teaching within a supportive learning environment. The school espouses grammar school principles and does not believe in treating those with special needs in a manner which is fundamentally different from their fellow pupils, but we do our very best to manage the curriculum and school day in such a way as to help each child thrive. The main teaching team is composed of expert classroom practititioners within their own subject, and criteria for entry include the assumption that a child will be able to cope and thrive within mainstream education. Those with special needs will be carefully monitored and allowances made in line with the particular challenge they may have to face. This is particularly helpful during examinations when additonal time can be granted to those who need it.

With two expert (self-employed) dyslexia tutors in school each week, provision is made for specialist tuition on a one-to-one basis. Individual timetables are re-arranged to accommodate such sessions within free time or standard lessons. Finance for these sessions falls outside standard fee arrangements and tuition charges are payable directly to the relevant tutor. Both dyslexia tutors are qualified to carry out formal assessment.

The school has a considerable number of pupils with dyslexia assessments and also welcomes applications from those with other forms of special needs. The structure of the curriculum and the nature of the school's mission means that such special needs are generally of mild to moderate severity, but the school is willing to look at each child as an individual and will happliy accept other conditions where we genuinely believe we can help to strengthen a child's academic performance whilst maintaining happiness and self-belief.

What we say about the school - the full Good Schools Guide review

Head: Since 1996 David Vanstone MA history, Cambridge, then PCGE and Sabbatical Union Post from Goldsmiths' College, London. Youthful early fifties. Came from six years as deputy head at Stafford Grammar. Chair of ISA, ISI Inspector. Passionate about what small schools can offer pupils in developing individual potential, speaking of 'the ethos behind the mission'. Jocular with pupils but commands friendly respect. Boys like him but say, 'he does like making speeches and the sound of his own voice'. Parents appreciate his pastoral care – 'once your son is under his wing he's really one of his boys, he looks after them like his own sons'.

Academic Matters: Founded in 1951 as a grammar school for boys who hadn't passed the 11+ and who might therefore be disadvantaged. 'People see us as a non-academic school,' says head, 'but many who have passed the 11+ actively chose our small, personal environment where they're known individually and looked after.' Justly proud of reputation for 'value-added', nurturing unfulfilled potential and enabling dyslexic boys to thrive. Two classes of 25, streamed from year 8. 14 GCSEs and 14 A level courses on offer. 73 per cent GCSEs A-C. Most boys exceed expectations, delighting parents and themselves, and many go on to university. All encouraged to develop in extra-curricular ways too. 25 per cent SEN, mostly dyslexia. Parents describe extra dyslexia tuition as, 'very available, timetabled, sympathetic, open-minded, an extra cost but marvellous'. Some boys have restricted curriculum to succeed in 6 GCSEs rather than struggling in 9, 'so they learn they can cope, to boost their confidence and self-esteem.' Boys seem willing to give up breaks to finish work. Trafford Connexions careers service and parents praise school's help in decision-making during upper years. Sixth form classes average 7 pupils.

Games, Options, The Arts: Large sports hall, gym and four tennis courts on site. 20-acre playing fields rented from National Trust with modern pavilion and changing rooms, five minutes walk through leafy suburbs, downhill there, uphill back, 'miserable in the rain after two hours football,' say boys. Very strong tradition of DofE, accounting for over half local borough's gold and silver awards. The only local school with in-house training to gold. 'Though we're a small school we try and provide everything you'd find in a bigger school,' says head. Strong emphasis on outdoor pursuits during weekends, evenings and holidays including rock climbing, snow boarding, golf, white water rafting. Well-equipped music and art rooms, private tuition on seven instruments, impressive ceramics on display round school. Recent trips include skiing in New England and theatre workshops in New York, plus less expensive outward bound nearer home.

Background and Atmosphere: Stately home aura with portico entrance, pink front door to grand carpeted entrance hall with wallpaper. Large front room of 1850s mansion was home to original 1951 intake of 39 boys, now head's study. Brand new hall seats all by former stable block housing technology. Former hall now home to library with work stations. Outdoor area at break seems cramped. Unstuffy, bustling but relaxed atmosphere prevails. 'The best thing about the school is the co-operation and understanding between boys and staff,' says head, 'they get the best out of each other.' Parents say there's a lot of fun here; teachers join drama productions, one even flick-flacks across the stage. Lunches pre-paid, compulsory. Head firmly believes, 'boys need to be fed' and while there are healthy options, defends provision of stodge, 'better than them being hungry all afternoon and I abhor Ruth Kelly's abominable attacks on vending machines. This school is full of thin boys and we educate them to make choices.' Inevitably most choose stodge but do seem to stay thin.

Pastoral Care and Discipline: On very busy A56 but boys keep to footbridge and nearby pelican crossing. Otherwise very secure with gated grounds sandwiched between Loreto prep and girls' senior schools. Caretaker and wife live on site. Classes and hall routinely locked when not in use. Boys stand for staff and the word 'sir' is on the tip of every tongue, though pupil-staff relationships friendly. Head says, 'I know every boy, not just their names but their family and whether they need me to shout at them or not'. Four houses, Grenfell, Hillary, Livingstone and Scott. Strong pastoral care, going to great lengths through year heads and form tutors, older prefects mentor lower forms. Parental contact is good, termly reports and homework diary has scope for communicating home. Parents describe school as 'very approachable' with lots of awards for effort as well as achievement but say that the influx of boys who're not thriving elsewhere before GCSE courses begin can be disrupting for existing settled boys and class groups.' Head says, 'we rarely fail a pupil and, if we do, they generally end up outside mainstream education'.

Pupils and Parents: Largely white middle class. 10 per cent Jewish, 10 per cent Muslim with strong link to local faith communities. Two thirds from nearby, others travel out from Manchester or in from far flung parts of Cheshire. Diverse but harmonious community embracing those needing extra tuition or nurturing as well as the eccentric and recalcitrant. Co-ed sixth form since September 2005 when five girls joined as response to parental requests. 'They'll flood in once word spreads,' says head. No plans to include girls from 11. Notable OBs include ice skater Nicky Slater, floating weatherman Fred Talbot, Kevin Godley – 10cc rock star, and James Goulding – Chief Executive of Deutsche Asset Management Europe, Just Pidcock – Olympic hockey medallist, Kevin Godley – 10cc rock star, Gary Davies – Radio One DJ.

Entrance: Relatively un-daunting exam looking for GCSE A-C potential, so not all pass. Papers in English, maths and reasoning in autumn term. Entry to co-ed sixth form based on anticipated GCSEs and interview with head. Some exchange of pupils at sixth form, some boys leaving for a bigger school for better transition to university, others coming here for more individual attention.

Exit: Many to university, some high flying courses.

Money Matters: Means-tested bursaries available, 'we would like to issue more,' says head who also offers some academic scholarships based on entrance exam merit.

Remarks: Justly deserved reputation for realising potential, especially in boys who, for whatever reason, have not passed 11+ and for dyslexics who can pass entrance exam. Many local boys sit exam as safety net, some 11+ passers also choose NGCS for its size and ethos of individual attention. Parents say, 'it's a brilliant school for the right boy, I can't speak highly enough of it for our son.'

NORTH HILL HOUSE

North Parade, Fromefield, Frome, Somerset, BA11 2HB

Tel: 01373 466 222

Fax: 01373 475 175

Email: andyc@nhh4as.co.uk

Website: www.nhh4as.co.uk

• Pupils: 40 boys. 12 day, 28 board • Ages: 7-18

• Religion: Non-denom • School status: Independent

• School gender: Boys • Day/boarding: Takes boarders

SEN provision

Summary: No comment taken to the point of secrecy. As if The Priory was something out of The Da Vinci Code. SEN details added by us.

What we say about the school - the full Good Schools Guide review

Principal: Since 2003, Mr Andy Cobley BEd MEd (forties) who, having worked closely with his predecessor who founded North Hill House in September 1999, took over when it became part of the Priory Group. With a background in both special and mainstream education, Mr Cobley declines elaborating further about himself, stressing that 'it's the team that matters and the approach to education ... not the personality or background of the head.' He strikes us as an energetic, focused professional who takes pride in what his staff have achieved in a short period.

Academic Matters: The school's curriculum is broad and balanced, based on the National Curriculum, but with an eclectic view of current teaching styles and philosophies. The aim is as much to develop the social and communication skills which young men with Asperger's will require to integrate effectively in society as to provide an appropriate range of educational opportunity.

All pupils are allocated a personal tutor whom they meet as regularly as necessary to sort out any difficulties or needs. Younger pupils are taught mainly in their home-base classroom in groups no larger than eight whilst older boys move between specialist areas. One-to-one teaching is used wherever necessary. The school has developed quickly from its first, positive, Ofsted inspection in May 2001. Approval has recently been granted for post-16 education.

Older boys choose from a wide range of subjects and courses with extensive use of ICT throughout the school – one computer per pupil. Success at GCSE has improved from 63 per cent of candidates obtaining A-C grades in 2003 to 74 per cent in 2004, when NHH achieved fourth position nationally for value-added tables in SEN schools. That many of the boys are of high ability was evidenced by examples seen of their written English, photography and D&T work. Science for the 21st century, which covers issues such as cloning and GM crops, is taught alongside single science for some. Food technology is taught in a state-of-the-art area which would do Jamie Oliver proud and the subject involves buying the ingredients locally out of lesson time, thereby providing realistic independence training. There are also specialist ICT, D&T and design facilities. The nature of the pupils' uneven academic development and the need for individual timetabling has already seen some as young as fourteen taking A level modules. Lessons use a variety of strategies to maintain the interest of pupils; 'smart' targets are monitored and reviewed each term and the gaining of 'excellence awards' in different subjects helps build self-esteem. Teaching staff are highly qualified with many of them engaged in further training. When we visited, the versatility of staff was obvious – one was engaged in willow work, making oddly shaped frames with pupils outside for a variety of uses; another was playing football with boys during break on an outside pitch and a few minutes later leading a discussion in an RE class about helping the less fortunate in the community.

Games, Options, The Arts: Pupils are taken to nearby Frome College for swimming and other sports as well as having the much-loved 'footie' pitch in the centre of the school around which boys have designed and placed their own mini advertising hoardings à la Stamford Bridge. There is talk of a youth club on site in collaboration with the outside community; visits are made to the cinema. There have been school visits to France. Some pupils receive individual music tuition and electric guitars are popular. Christmas show involves staff and pupils, but otherwise drama is taught within the English curriculum. Multi-functional conference room serves as the venue for daily assemblies which all staff get to lead.

Background and Atmosphere: North Hill House has moved across the road from its original buildings into larger, purpose-designed accommodation set in pleasant grounds not far from the centre of the busy market town of Frome. The immediate feel is more akin to a private clinic than a school, with an obviously high level of security both inside and outside which takes some getting used to. There is a high ratio (currently more than 2:1) of care and teaching staff to boys, but this leads to an upbeat, happy atmosphere. The individual bedrooms are en-suite and the residential accommodation is split up into attractive, small, family units including a lounge with a variety of audio-visual and other recreational facilities which boys have to learn to share. Meals are cooked on site, cater for different dietary needs and are served cafeteria style but shared by staff and boys at family tables in light and airy surroundings. 'A lot of effort goes into creating a structured and predictable environment,' explained the principal.

Pupils and Parents: Boys with Asperger's syndrome, who may be diagnosed as ASD, PDD, autistic or 'Asperger's syndrome traits', come from all over the UK as well as from Somerset and neighbouring areas. They have a poor social understanding and are often vulnerable. All UK pupils are funded by LEAs. We saw evidence of obvious trust on the part of parents in the staff as they came to leave their sons at the school. One 'closed' weekend per half-term gives residential staff a breather and boarders a chance to taste home cooking.

Entrance: Only for statemented pupils. The majority join between 7 and 13. Admissions procedure is in four stages: first, a copy of detailed files on student to assess needs; secondly, a visit by the parents to meet the principal to discuss specific needs; thirdly, a visit by student and parents to meet teaching staff informally and view the school; finally, an assessment visit to ascertain educational, communication and social needs. When a boy is accepted he is initially placed for three months followed by a meeting to review the placement. Some may be admitted for short periods only.

Exit: In 2004, all but one continued into FE within the Priory group. From 2005, boys will be able to remain at NHH until aged 18. Some return to mainstream education, some may go to part-time or full-time employment and a few have proceeded to university.

Remarks: Here is a very specialist school providing a remarkably high level of educational, social and caring support to enormously challenged boys. The dedication of the staff and the level of provision in every department is enviable. Parents of those fortunate enough to be admitted are understandably supportive and appreciative.

Notting Hill Preparatory School

95 Lancaster Road, London, W11 1QQ

Tel: 020 7221 0727

Fax: 020 7221 0332

Email: admin@nottinghillprep.com

Website: www.nottinghillprep.com

• Pupils: 70 boys and girls at present, full capacity will be 260, all day • Ages: 5-13 • Religion: Non-denom • Fees: £3,450 • School status: Independent • School gender: Mixed • Day/boarding: Day pupils

SEN provision

Detail:

Now provide for in school:

Mild: DYSC; DYSL; DYSP; SpLD;

Severe: VI;

Others: EAL; MSI; Sp&LD; DEL;

Experience of:

Mild: ADD; EBD;

Summary: Notting Hill Prep School has a well established learning support centre that strives to be a centre of excellence. The department is very well resourced and employs a full-time special needs co-ordinator. The learning centre programmes cater largely for the needs of pupils with mild learning difficulties eg dyslexia, dyspraxia and those children experiencing some speech and language difficulties.

The whole school is very well resourced in terms of IT equipment and the learning centre utilises a wide range of SpLD specific programmes, alongside assessment batteries, visual search and cognitive attainment programmes.

All pupils preparing for external examinations are able to partake in Thinking Skills and Study Skills programmes that are taught in the learning centre. Similarly, Gifted and Able pupils are able to access a wide range of software designed to stimulate, engage and challenge children. Perhaps the key to the success of the learning centre is that there is no stigma involved in using the facilities, as such a wide range and number of children throughout the school enjoy access to the facilities offered there.

What we say about the school - the full Good Schools Guide review

Head: Since September 2003, Mrs Jane Cameron BEd (early fifties) who ran the Acorn Nursery in Lansdowne Crescent for 25 years. She had long nourished the idea of taking pupils in Notting Hill (though not exclusively) up to CE. Married, with three grown-up children, Jane Cameron is approachable, realistic and respected by parents and pupils alike. She is also persistent and fun. Deputy head, David Gee BEd, was previously director of studies at Hazelwood School in Surrey.

Entrance: Already over-subscribed for tinies – waiting lists to 2010. School more or less filling up from the bottom with Jane Cameron running a twice-yearly ballot for reception and year 1; (anxious to avoid fathers with sleepless post-labour eyes racing in asking 'am I in time?') Siblings' entrance is automatic if places available. Mrs C is still principal of the Acorn – many pupils coming on but not automatic. Applicants now come from a range of nursery schools. Advertising has been word of mouth. Assessment prior to entry for seven-year-olds plus English, maths and a chat with the head. The school aiming to balance boy/girl ratio. Currently some places for older children.

Exit: To date pupils have opted for the London day schools. Parental meetings with headmistress and staff are offered well in advance of final registration dates for senior schools. Jane Cameron and David Gee are updating their knowledge of both the boarding sector and London senior schools.

Remarks: School grew from local demand – with the impetus coming from experienced teachers and local parents – partnership between parents and teachers is particularly strong. Parent profile mimics that of the Acorn – mostly creative, fashionable and successful. NHP is housed in a former school building (just south of the Westway, corner of Lancaster Road and Ladbroke Grove), purpose-built in 1902, but recently used by Camden Charities and now totally revamped with a playground at the front where parents gather and chat. The bleached-blond deputy head stands in his blazer and tie at the security gate to the playground at the beginning of each day. Parents either walk with their children, each wearing a blue rucksack marked with the pink NHP logo, across the busy intersection, or pile 'em out of four by fours.

School opens at 8.20am and pupils can stay till 4pm for free, followed by clubs till 5pm. The school is a warren of large bright rooms but no kitchen on site – organic hot scoff provided by outside caterer in the Youth Centre en face, children can bring their own packed lunch. School gym plus Youth Centre playground (nowhere near as intimidating during the day as it is at night) plus Perkes Field, Westway Sports Centre, Avondale Park and Kensington Leisure Centre available for gym and games though parents of particularly sporty children are worried about the lack of dedicated sports facilities. General sports programme from reception, team games and climbing from year 3 as well as after-school clubs for keen ones.

Dynamic head of music plays the clarinet for the school with his band, The Burning Bush, and then at the Royal Festival Hall – composes a new school song with the children every term. Art and drama from reception, regular plays and performances in assembly give the children performance confidence and weekly certificates and points are awarded to individuals in each house. These merit marks are popular and not restricted to academic skills – witness a little girl knocking on the head's door to make sure that her points were being registered! School divided into four houses (named after local roads). Heads of houses foster a 'buddy' support system. Worry box as well as the anti-bullying policy and procedure, the former has not been put into practice yet.

School follows RML (Ruth Miskin Literacy which is magical – and we mean magical) – based on 44 phonological sounds and graphemes (or Fred and Graeme sounds) – 'my turn, your turn' policy, partner work and small groups. Phenomenal. Class teachers in lower school for literacy and numeracy; max class size 20, no streaming but maths setted from nine. Specialists for those in middle and upper school; science lab now on course, Latin for all at ten, and Greek on offer. Tiny classes at the top end, so really all at scholarship level. School follows nat curriculum. Computers from reception, terrific emphasis on problem-solving and reasoning and study skills. Exam technique taught early and regular exams to practise on, ditto practice CEs, good contact between head and senior schools, though fairly steep learning curve for Mrs Cameron. Regular detailed reports home. Homework important and strong parental links – parents and children feel comfortable about 'dropping in on the head unannounced'.

Extensive 'multi-sensory' remedial help on hand from dedicated SENCo. SENCo fronts a 'three-pronged approach' one-to-one, small groups, dual teaching in class plus strategies for teaching staff in particular subjects for particular pupils. Friendly jazzy room in the attics (big enuff to hold small groups) skool can cope with the mild wild (or moderate ADHD) and the dys-strata. (The school prefers 'Specific learning difficulties'). One-to-one support costs extra. Not brill for the physically handicapped but OK if 'they can accommodate their needs'. No wheelchair access above ground level. A statemented pupil in the school part-time has a personal mentor who works across borough boundaries. Other LEAs please mark, note and act accordingly. Support, too, for pupils who 'transfer from a different education system'. No EFL.

Non-denom but major Christian and other festivals celebrated, carol service in local church. School uses all that London has to offer, oodles of visits, Nat Hist, Maritime, Museums, V & A, plus residential field trips for older pupils to Calshot activity centre in Hampshire but no lang trips abroad or exchanges as yet. School bedding down nicely, 'feels like a village school' in the centre of Notting Hill. Active parents committee and popular fairs, concerts and fundraising initiatives. Expansion in the air. The unproven record for older children does not seem to deter prospective parents, instead there is a confidence that Mrs Cameron's years of success in shaping confident, happy, creative nursery children will be extended to the older age group and, so far, it is not misplaced.

NOTTINGHAM HIGH SCHOOL

Waverley Mount, Nottingham, Nottinghamshire, NG7 4ED

Tel: 0115 978 6056

Fax: 0115 924 9716

Email: info@notthigh.rmplc.co.uk

Website: www.nottinghamhigh.co.uk

• Pupils: 847 boys, all day • Ages: 11-18 • Fees: Senior: £2,798. Junior: £2,271 • School status: Independent • Opendays: Mid November • School gender: Boys • Day/boarding: Day pupils

SEN provision

Detail:

Now provide for in school:

- Mild: DYSL; DYSP;
- Moderate: DYSC; DYSL; DYSP;
- Severe: DYSL;
- Others: Epi;

Experience of:

- Mild: ASP; AUT; ADD; ADHD; HI;
- Moderate: ASP; HI;
- Others: OCD; TIC;

Summary: The SEN department has progressed greatly in the last two years and now has three members of staff: one full-time SENCo, one part-time learning support teacher and one other teacher developing a programme of support for dyspraxics within the school. This is a new and exciting development. Our aim is to enable our pupils with learning difficulties to achieve their full potential whatever that might be. Boys needing support are withdrawn on a rota basis depending on need. This can be short-term or throughout their time at the school.

Support sessions may take the form of specific specialist dyslexic teaching or revision and study skills to support access to the curriculum. The department has a high profile within the school with an open-door policy for any boy who needs support.

What we say about the school - the full Good Schools Guide review

Head: Since 1995, Mr Chris Parker CBE BA FRSA (fifties), educated at Windsor Grammar School read geography at Bristol University and studied for his PGCE at St Catharine's College, Cambridge. Previously head of Batley Grammar School. Married to Maggie who donated the Margaret Parker cup for individual verse speaking and takes a cookery club for year 8 boys; two grown up sons. Speaks with genuine pride about his boys, knows most individually and they're comfortable with him. Says, 'boys refuel you – when you're tired, you pick up energy from them and qualities – they give so generously.' Some boys say head is out of school a lot (head agrees – chairs lots of committees and works on various projects – including assisted places and independent/state school partnerships).They add that discipline is tight and they know what won't be tolerated – but think head runs school very well and say staff he's brought in have upped the ante.

Retiring at Easter 2007.

Academic Matters: This is not a swot-house, boys don't need to be force-fed facts and figures; they are capable of independent thought and enquiry, encouraged to challenge accepted doctrine and discover the joys of serious thought and intellectual discussion. Boys say 'school has a reputation of taxing, challenging work but you find you can do it and teachers will help if you have difficulties'. All pass – 70 per cent of GCSE entries graded A/A* and commendable 80-ish per cent of A levels graded A/B. Enter lots of academic competitions – maths challenge, maths Olympiad (highest scorers), Engineer for Britain (winner most innovative award), physics and biology Olympiads (gold medal winners), to name but a few. Super well-kept facilities (save the odd bag strewn on the floor), school has many generous benefactors and it shows. Wireless networked throughout, interactive technology, super library with own laptops, DVDs, periodicals, new arts centre, well-equipped labs, DT centre etc.

Class size varies from 16 to 26 reducing to fewer than 10 in the sixth form. Lots of fizzy teaching – use technology and skills to make lessons come alive: practical demonstrations and the concrete even extend to A level mechanics – believe it's important to appreciate practical applications. Older pupils expected to research, plan, and take model lessons – it enhances understanding, makes them think. Pupils clearly appreciate dedication of staff who willingly give up free time to help boys both academically and with extra-curricular activities (45 staff assist with games alone.)

Head, a keen champion of special needs, brought in enthusiastic and very capable head of learning support who has done much rapidly to transform attitudes – lots of inset and training on learning styles, kinaesthetic learning etc. Not only have old-school staff embraced provision but children are gaining confidence to self-refer. School identifies 70 children as being in need of additional help or support, majority are dyslexics but there are a handful of dyspraxics and smattering of Asperger's, ADD, ADHD. Head fighting off those staff keen to offer extra help and support. No additional charge for those requiring one-to-one though outside help such as occupational therapy will incur a fee. They stress that the main thing is pupils requiring additional support are able to achieve. Say to pupils, 'this is you, this is your profile, you can give up, or go for it.' They go for it – SEN input reaping rewards.

Games, Options, The Arts: School motto: Together Everyone Achieves More (TEAM) summarises the spirit of the school. All are encouraged to do far more than pursue academic interests and virtually all do. Games and music are the mainstay but not the only offerings. Chess plays a large part in school life and the school boasts national champions and international representation across several age groups. Very good facilities – large sports hall, climbing wall, full size swimming pool and excellent multi-gym puts many leisure centres to shame – there's even a TV to take your mind off going the extra mile. The school's first-rate sports pitches are located a short bus-ride away and are used for school matches as well as area and national trials and training; astro-turf and additional tennis courts on the wish list. Sport is an important part of the boys' education – don't gloat over victories, happy to accept defeat. Rugby (couple of international players) and swimming particularly successful (lots of cups) but sports such as orienteering (national champions) get a look-in too. Trying to encourage and develop sport for all, especially for those where enthusiasm exceeds talent or who have difficulties such as dyspraxia. Music is active, alive and practical, numbers opting for GCSE shooting up, lots of bands (big band medal winners in Boosey and Hawkes competition), choirs, performing opportunities and now latest computer equipment adding a new dimension to music technology. Trips and tours aplenty.

Background and Atmosphere: Founded in 1513 by Dame Agnes Mellers (with help of Sir Thomas Lovell) after the death of her husband, Richard, partly in his memory but also as an act of atonement for his several wrongdoings against the people of Nottingham with the foundation deed sealed by King Henry VIII in the November. Moved to its present pleasant site in 1868. A long programme of building and development results in today's facilities. Immediate area not the most salubrious – a police raid was taking place opposite the school on the day of our visit and ladies of the night are known to pound the nearby streets (school say police efforts reducing the problem) but, apart from odd incident of graffiti, school appears to escape the downfall of its near neighbours.

Pastoral Care and Discipline: Plenty of graduated awards for good work, helping out etc. Celebrate, enjoy and respect success at any level – not just rugger buggers – mutual respect, family feel. Head or deputy sees those with 10 or more distinctions. All belong to a form and a tutor group. Forms have a horizontal structure but crux is the carefully thought-out vertically operated tutor-system – tutor even phones parents to invite them to the introductory parents' evening – get to know families as well as boys. No detentions for year 7 but one boy reported that 'detention runs from year 8 to year 11' which we thought a bit excessive! Tutor often the one batting for a boy when chips are down. Students encouraged to seek help, support or advice from any of the school nurse, tutor, form teacher, head of year, form prefect, school counsellor or other person they trust – school medical service open daily. Compulsory testing for suspected drug misuse. Bullying of all kinds dealt with promptly, boys encouraged to report all, however trivial, and certainly the many children we spoke to agreed bullying wasn't a problem, saying they felt the tutor system, where they got to know boys from all years, really helped.

Sixth formers are expected to act as role models for those younger than themselves. Usual opportunities for leadership, and for personal and social development offered through CCF, Duke of Edinburgh, young enterprise, business leadership scheme or as prefects. In addition, the organisation of house teams and events relies solely on the initiative of sixth formers and this is serious stuff – everything from four part choirs to producing, directing and co-ordinating up to 50 youngsters at a time in the uniquely inventive and dramatic verse-speaking competitions. Dire threats issued to those who might think about skiving a rehearsal or two. Plenty of joint activities with Nottingham Girls' High School: politics society, arts society, drama club and explorer scout unit as well as a couple of balls and an annual major dramatic production.

Pupils and Parents: A genuinely mixed bag – offspring of millionaires to those in care. From a wide geographical area: Nottingham, Bakewell, Loughborough, Leicestershire. 50 per cent from own junior school, 15 per cent from other independent schools, rest from state primaries. Twenty per cent identify their ethnic mix as other than white but fewer than 4 per cent have English as an additional language. Boys smartly dressed in blazers distinguished by house ties, suits in the sixth form (tufty tie for those who gain a minimum 10 grade A GCSEs), say they feel privileged to have a first-rate education and fantastic opportunities. These are genuinely grounded, rounded individuals with bags of personality and myriads of interests, not a swot in sight – we doubt arrogance, even a mild dose, would be tolerated by anyone. Many have a string of successes to their bow – grade 8 instrumentalists, national representation in the sporting, academic, and musical world but they don't let on – they present as great lads, able to hold their own in conversation and debate but with a wicked sense of humour and lovely ability to poke fun at themselves – what more could you ask? A sample of famous old Nottinghamians include Edward Balls, Jesse Boot, Kenneth Clarke, Geoff Hoon, Robert MacFarlane (author) and Andrew Turner (Olympic hurdler).

Entrance: Majority at 11 a few at 16. Occasional places available at other ages. Tests for all in English, maths and verbal reasoning, plus short interview for non-junior boys. Details about the exam are sent out in January prior to September entry. Advise all to visit school on open day in November. Entry to sixth form is by interview and achievement at GCSE, sixth form open evening held early October. Don't admit boys they feel wouldn't be happy.

Exit: Small number (between 5 and 10) leave after GCSEs. Large numbers to Oxbridge, 11 to Cambridge alone in 2004, most of rest to wide range of Russell group of universities studying for traditional gold standard degrees. Birmingham, Leeds, Manchester, Newcastle popular.

Money Matters: Generous means-tested bursaries (up to 100 per cent of fees) available at head's discretion. Believes any boy who is able should be given all the assistance necessary to attend the school. Ogden bursaries and HSBC provide 50 per cent which school must match plus additional help (if needed) via a one-off grant to offset start-up costs such as school uniform. School financially secure enough that no boy will be turned away because of a lack of funds.

Remarks: A very good school, hard to fault. Media studies types should look elsewhere though media types would do very well. Only for the seriously bright with personality and plethora of pursuits and passions.

Nunnykirk Centre for Dyslexia

Netherwitton, Morpeth, Northumberland, NE61 4PB

Tel: 01670 772 685

Fax: 01670 772 434

Email: secretary@nunnykirk.co.uk

Website: www.nunnykirk.co.uk

• Pupils: 43 of whom 20 are weekly boarders. 37 boys, 6 girls
• Ages: 9-18 • Religion: Non-denom
• School status: Independent • School gender: Mixed
• Day/boarding: Takes boarders

SEN provision

Detail:

Centre of excellence for:

Mild: DYSC; DYSL; DYSP;
Moderate: DYSC; DYSL; DYSP;
Severe: DYSC; DYSL; DYSP;
Others: DEL;

Summary: Nunnykirk specialises in pupils of average or above average ability who have specific learning difficulties. Our holistic approach ensures a curriculum specifically developed for dyslexic pupils where they can build self-esteem and confidence in a calm and supportive environment. The wide variety of subjects, hobbies, activities and games ensures that every pupil develops their potential. In addition the attention to detail in routines, diet and exercise contributes to pupils becoming mature, well-mannered, confident young people aware of community and world issues and able to move into our sixth form or on to college, where they start the next phase of their education.

What we say about the school - the full Good Schools Guide review

Head: Since 1997, Simon Dalby-Ball BSc CertEd NCA (fifties). Began life as a teacher, then diverged for a while into farm management. Has been at Nunnykirk for 18 years. Exhibits all the characteristics of the best sort of stockman – kind, non-aggressive, empathetic, conscientious, gentle – and these are, of course, eminently transferable attributes, especially to a school like this. He's a very nice man indeed whose educational philosophy is informed by seeing for himself what works. Dyslexia is the dubious beneficiary of new wonder cures daily, but Mr Dalby-Ball is not one to binge on fads – though the school's gluten-free diet, it has to be said, does have its dissers. He is alert for anything that makes a difference but he also knows that children who thrive are busy children – 'it's all down to hard work' – and is flattered that they are so knackered come Friday afternoon. Teaches rural studies. Wife Gill teaches here, too.

Academic Matters: This is a CreSTeD SP school specialising in dyslexia and all the associated info-processing quirks which huddle under that umbrella term. Ofsted were uncharacteristically charmed by what they saw but couldn't put their finger on how they did it. Cast aside all objective criteria, stop ticking boxes and switch to subjective mode – a good school is an affair of the heart. It's the individual focus, the being known and liked, that enables these children to achieve so far beyond expectation, above and beyond the application of any modish methodology. Teachers go to great lengths to find what works for each child and they keep them at it. One mum says, 'they don't make it easy just because they have difficulties.' Plenty of brilliant rapport, so good to see, heaps of praise and richly deserved mutual admiration. Tiny classes, most 4-5, max 8. Brain gym. One-to-one as necessary. Results put this school in the top 5 per cent of the value added tables. Says it all. Sixth form operational since Sept 2005.

National Curriculum, all go for GCSEs, most tackle 5-8, and there are entry levels for those who need longer. English and maths, good IT, and options spanning history and geog through photography to rural science. No modern languages – 'they can do them later if they want'. More vocational subjects coming soon. Big hands-on element in all things. Science lab completely brilliant – far from brilliantly resourced, you think, then the head points to the French window at the end of the room and says, 'It's all out there, you see...' And in your mind's eye you see them clutching nets and jars, heading for the river, theory and practice happily married.

Studies of pigs show that, though they like toys and nice buildings, they'd much rather have a good relationship with humans. Children are no different. You don't at any stage feel urgently impelled to write home about the glittering equipment in this school, nor its plushness, but the teachers are just what you'd want for a child dismayed and dented by early experiences and, dare we say it, over-demanding parents. The head picks teachers for their personal and professional attributes, then trains them on the job. It's a tiny staff, they all do lots, they are encouraged to develop their own approaches, and they all run hobbies – 'this is no place for anyone wanting to work 9-4'. Informal and shirt-sleeves-y. They are never substituted by supply teachers – continuity is all. Stability and routine are the foundations of this notably calm, notably busy school.

Games, Options, The Arts: The extra-curricular programme is an essential element of the rescue remedy, not only because achievements in other areas cross-fertilise performance in the classroom, but because parts of the academic curriculum are embedded in, especially, the rural studies programme.

Much of what they do is vigorous. Sport, given the numbers, is not competitive at school level, but they play the customary ball games and athletics. There's swimming and the use of the sports hall in Morpeth, and sailing (RYA quals) at Amble. Playing fields, all-weather surface. Annual endurance race for all, summer sports day with barbie.

Plenty of art, well done. Music brave if not symphonic. Lots of plays. D of E, of course, and scouts. Karting, mountain biking, canoeing. Bird watching. Cross-stitching, egg painting. All tastes catered for. Rural studies is the big thing – looking after the pigs, sheep, hens, ducks, geese and turkeys. They do it for real. While we were there, Maggie the sow was waiting sadly to be sent on, the arrival of 6 ewes and a tup eagerly expected. Fruit and veg home grown in the walled garden – 'we eat what we produce.' Fencing, rotavating, shed making. Brilliant therapy for the children, all this, developing a sense of responsibility, following instructions (English), measuring out the right amounts (maths). The older ones teach the younger and exert stern expectations punctuality-wise.

Background and Atmosphere: Nunnykirk was founded in 1977 for children not at home in the hurly-burly of bigger schools. Everything presently happens in the Greek revival John Dobson manor house surrounded by uncounted miles of Northumbrian loveliness. In 2006 a brand new building will arise alongside, the happy upshot of years of planning entreaties, at which time the school will lose much of its nostalgic appeal to those who cherish memories of schooldays in the 60s. It will become full boarding, too.

Pastoral Care and Discipline: Well looked after children greet visitors with unfussed naturalness. These do. No reservations, not even of any kind, on that score. Standards are high, important for those rougher diamonds when they first arrive. Manners are excellent, discipline not an issue, and they all know exactly where the line is. Smoking? Not a blind eye in the house. It's a big deal, parents instantly informed. Drugs? Out.

Weekly boarders, boys only at present, come from as far south as Birmingham and as far north as Edinburgh. No more than two to a room in the warren upstairs. It may look well worn, but boys don't mind this a bit. It's fun. Supervision levels are high, older boys guide the younger, and there's a warm welcome – 'it's a big event when someone new comes'. So much goes on in the evening there's no time for telly and it's not missed. Day pupils who can, stay on for these activities.

Food is good, the children reckon. High praise. They're not bonkers, all of them, parents either, about the gluten-free diet, and some pounce on the toaster when they get home. Additives are out, sugar rare, fish oils in, fruit abounds. The head is certain this makes a difference, makes them calmer and more focused. A written record is kept of what each child eats. Healthy living tuck shop.

There's a student council. Efforts are made to mix with the local community despite location – excellent work experience for years 10 and 11 with local businesses. Trips to the cinema and theatre. And they raise money for an even remoter school in Gambia, and mend their water pump, send them things, swap photos.

Pupils and Parents: Pupils a mixed bunch, socio-economically, spanning the 55 per cent funded by their LEA to the scions of stately homes. More girls needed. Because this is the only school of its type between Oxford and John O'Groats there's a big geographic mix, and it's why they offer weekly boarding. For many parents this is not at all what they wanted, so the school goes to great lengths to allay fears and, thereafter, keep in touch – parents united in grateful applause. Day children from 45-min radius. Big expectations made of parents – 'if work is sent home we expect it to be done – and we expect parents to help'. It's all about partnership, which means 'parents have got to make an effort, too'. There's a training day for parents where you can find out what they do, how they do it, how you can help. If your child thrives remarkably, they won't hang on – but many opt to stay nevertheless; they reckon they'll do even better. Informative website.

Entrance: Careful selection process. All the usual reports, but the (long) interview's the thing. Boys and girls here are refugees from mainstream schools with, most of them, anything from an antipathy to a horror of being educated plus a history of being teased or bullied. Repairs to damaged self-esteem are all part of the package but no entrenched EBDs of any sort, they're outside their specialism – 'if we feel we can't help there's no point'. IQs reckoned from 95 up. Formal acceptance after a trial half term when, if a child has settled, an IEP is drawn up.

Exit: Careful advice precedes post-16 decision-making, finding the right course at the right college. It's a huge leap, obviously, reliant on the self-belief they've acquired. They go on to the full rainbow – degree courses to clock making. Decided bias in favour of hands on, fresh air careers.

Money Matters: Some bursaries for private feepayers. For parents seeking to persuade their LEA to apply the statement, the news is that it's getting harder.

Remarks: Delightful and deserving. Restores children to a full sense of themselves and allows them to blossom at their own pace. Do they feel hived off? No. It's great to be where you're not the only one, where you can sometimes get top marks. This is a school you can easily fall in love with.

OAKHAM SCHOOL

Chapel Close, Oakham, Rutland, LE15 6DT

Tel: 01572 758758

Fax: 01572 758595

Email: admissions@oakham.rutland.sch.uk

Website: www.oakham.rutland.sch.uk

• Pupils: 545 boys, 530 girls; 50 per cent board, 50 per cent day • Ages: 10-18 • Religion: C of E • Fees: Jerwoods - day £3,880; day boarding £4,970; boarding £6,110. Upper/middle school - day £4,270; day boarding £5,740; boarding £7,140 • School status: Independent • Opendays: See website • School gender: Mixed • Day/boarding: Takes boarders

SEN provision

Summary: Parents are obliged to inform the school at the initial enquiry stage if their child has any learning difficulties. Early submission of any relevant paperwork will enable consideration to be given to the likely needs of the child.

The school might be able to offer learning support to students who have a specific learning difficulty. If however, it is clear that a prospective candidate requires a higher level of support than can be provided, then it is important that this is discussed openly.

Learning support may be offered to students in the form of group support in lieu of a second language in forms 1, 2 and 3 (years 7, 8 and 9) or by in-class support. This is included in the school fees. Students on the learning support register, requiring a higher level of support, may be taught in pairs or as individuals. This attracts a charge, which is added to the school bill termly.

Students in forms 4 (year 10) and above, who are on the learning support register, may be offered individual support for which there is a charge added to the bill termly.

There may be a need for some students with specific difficulties to request special concessions in external examinations. If this is the case, the school will require an educational psychologist's assessment, which specifies what is recommended. The assessment should be arranged in the summer after form 3 (year 9) and the paperwork submitted to school, so that any recommendations are in place at the start of the GCSE courses. The school examinations officer can then process this information and allow the student to practise whatever concession is permitted in the trial exams in the winter term of form 5. If this assessment recommends extra time only, then it will suffice until the student leaves school.

Anything other than a time concession requires an update of the assessment to be carried out after GCSE and in preparation for Upper School courses.

What we say about the school - the full Good Schools Guide review

Headmaster: Since 2002, Dr Joseph Spence BA PhD (mid forties. A powerhouse with immense charm. From 1992-2002, Dr Spence was Master in College at Eton ie had charge of the scholars – one of the top academic jobs in independent education. A history and politics graduate, Dr Spence is a polymath who also writes and directs plays, plays sport 'quite well', is knowledgeable about and interested in just about everything and is an acknowledged specialist (several books) on Anglo-Irish history and culture. Thus the ideal head of a school in which, traditionally, 'the total curriculum' was the byword. He has quickly got to grips with the school and, while revelling in the excellence of the sporting, musical and other activities he inherited, emphasises 'the primacy of the classroom' and now sees work 'at the heart of the total curriculum'. While at Eton he had to work to get the scholars involved with extra-curricular life, here it has been something of the other way round. However, it's working and they seem to like it! 'Delighted' and 'honest' are frequently used words in the vocabulary of this energetic, direct, highly capable and warmly welcoming head. Pupils who spot him in the Oakham streets wave affectionately. 'You must meet Oakhamians', he enthuses. 'They're having fun and I'm having more fun than all of them.' Married to a lawyer, with a son and daughter at Oakham.

Academic Matters: One of the lowest pupil:teacher ratio we have encountered at just over 7:1 though obviously this varies, depending on year and subject. Average A level class size is 10. It's been all change since 2001 when the IB became an option in the sixth. After a dip in take-up, interest is picking up and the head, wholly committed to it on academic principles, sees A level candidates becoming, eventually, a minority. Good choice of A level and IB subjects with a general spread of take-up. GCSE subjects include very popular art and design, D&T and drama. Not a league table driven school, nonetheless, results have leaped since head's advent to 74 per cent A/B at A level in 2005. Especially good: art, English, French, further maths, history, physics, RS and several minority subjects. IB results in 2005 100 per cent – average worldwide rate is 80 per cent. GCSEs 98 per cent pass rate. History imaginatively presented – wonderfully realistic WW1 trench in head of department's room plus very lively work on display. Sane policy on ICT – 'it must serve us not master us'. Internet points in every room but school does not provide the laptops. Good computerised language labs. SEN supported by 'two brilliant teachers' and school moving away from withdrawing to more in-class support. Physical disabilities copeable with onsite but some buildings separated by roads.

Games, Options, The Arts: Interesting to discover what you couldn't do here. 'Sport here is massive' asserted pupil. In addition to the standard sports, a further 30 are offered – cycling, rowing, sailing, shooting, sub aqua, fencing among them. Superb onsite pitches used by county cricket teams – 'it's better than Lords', claimed modestly proud student – two astroturfs, 25 meter pool, fitness centre and 1972 sports hall with weights room and squash courts. Achievements include victory for 1st XV rugby team in Daily Mail U18 national schools rugby cup in 2002 and 2003. Eight England schoolboy rugby internationals since 2000. Past pupils represent country in women's cricket and hockey. Duke of Edinburgh Awards scheme very big here: first school to achieve 1000 D of E golds (in 2001). CCF also strong and we witnessed inspection of massed troops by imposing RSM on our visit.

Music almost as strong. Former head of music J L Dussek 1922-83 commemorated on a plaque – presumably a descendant of Jan Ladislav Dussek? 40 per cent learn instruments, events large and small include concerts at St John's Smith Square, Southwell, Ely. Music tour to South Africa in 2003 leading to links with township schools with whom school shares charitable projects. Orchestras, bands of all kinds. Three CDs recorded by 2004. Excellent Queen Elizabeth Theatre – like a small professional theatre complete with foyer and bar and displays of ambitious, professional-looking productions. House plays and other shows abound and everyone enthusiastically involved. Both music and drama productions feature at the Edinburgh fringe. Art and design impressive, especially textiles and jewellery to art college standards – highly imaginative and creative work – very popular. Younger pupils encouraged to work alongside older students. Few boy takers at higher levels thus far. Witty work in ceramics and pottery. Superb D and T work – covetable steel and wooden hammocks on display. You want to roll up your sleeves and get in there.

Background and Atmosphere: Founded in 1584, there are still a few reminders of the school's long history in its location in the centre of this prosperous market county town, snug in the truly rolling Rutland hills. The oldest, main parts of the school have the feel of a small Cambridge college – quiet quads, old stone buildings round lawns and immaculate flower beds – civilised, donnish, conducive to study and thought. New status accorded to scholars enshrined in College House – special sanctuary with quiet study areas for those applying to Oxbridge and other high level university courses – at the heart of this carefully laid-out campus. Much is owed to pioneering head, John Buchanan, whose tenure from 1958-77 oversaw move to full independence and co-education as well as landscaped garden feel of the whole site. Present head relishes day/boarding mix and the centrality of school to town, 'we're not a capsule-like school in Oakham town that has nothing to do with it'. No weekly boarding offered here, 'this is a full boarding school for its 550 boarders,' says head and day pupils often appear to join in activities on Sundays. Day boarding, ie two or more stays during the week, a popular option. Atmosphere is civilised, collaborative, appreciative. Boarding is seen as a desirable privilege, 'I wish I'd been a boarder all the way through,' sighed one wistful sixth form recruit.

Subjects taught in, mostly, attractive 2-4 storey, purpose-built blocks, continuing the quadrangular theme, giving feel of small-scale 1960s university campus – but better designed than most. School shop where, according to a cheery sixth former, 'you can buy everything and stick it on the bill. Mum always ends up paying for her birthday card'. Superb Smallbone library – up to public library standards – spacious, well-stocked, computerised – a rare resource. Campus studded with entertaining metal sculptures (watch out for the crocodile!) by visiting Kenyan sculptor. Most boarding houses abut playing fields – peaceful and, again, reminiscent of collegiate Cambridge. All are attractive, well-maintained – large vases of flowers in entrance halls. Trips of all kinds, everywhere and excellent programme of visiting speakers, artists etc. Plans include Jerwood Sphere project – a hoped-for concert hall to serve school plus East Midlands to professional standards together with new teaching accommodation. Also wonderfully enlightened bi-partite 20:20 project – a woodland scheme to inculcate entrepreneurism, teamwork and leadership – as well as an African solar power project to provide for a whole village. Mind-broadening stuff.

Pastoral Care and Discipline: Pupils express confidence in carefully structured pastoral system – not just a written policy but one which actually does what it is designed to do. A few drugs-related incidents since Dr Spence's arrival but he relies on a policy of testing pupils if worrying reports reach him and collaboration with home. 'I'm a comfortable convert to the right to give someone a second chance – so long as they understand the policy ... I feel we've got a pretty clean campus.' A rather more honest and realistic approach than many. Super boarding houses and, unusually, all house staff also on teaching staff. Programme of room refurbishment continues and new accommodation is being built for 7th form girls and style moving from youth hostel functionality to home-like comfort. All year 13s to have own study bedroom. Lots of common rooms and meeting areas. Huge choice of excellent food in civilised dining rooms – allergy warnings on walls.

Pupils and Parents: Boys and girls, day and boarding equally mixed. Boarders mostly from 1-3 hours drive though a few from Fife to Hampshire. 85 foreign nationals from 30+ countries – numbers of Germans – direct train to Stansted helps here. 70 expat children. Day and boarding pupils from 50+ preps and juniors but largest number from Jerwoods – onsite junior school. Recent OOs include media personalities Julia Carling and Charlotte Uhlenbroek; theatre folk Katie Mitchell, Greg Hicks and Matthew MacFadyen, and international sports stars Lewis Moody, Lucy Pearson and Crista Cullen. First OO fellow of All Souls, Philip Woolfe, elected in 2003.

Entrance: Exams at 11+ (maths, English and VR), 13+ or CE (55 per cent expected though rare exceptions made for those who 'have something to offer even if they don't quite make it'. Siblings looked upon kindly. Commitment matters as does sufficient ability, 'I'm interested in people who are going to be with us from 11 or 13 until 18. I don't want to be a culler at 16,' asserts head. At 16+, minimum of 7 good GCSEs (4 As and three Bs).

Exit: All but a few to higher education and a vast range of places and courses. 2005 saw 13 Oxbridge offers and large numbers to Leeds, Newcastle, Nottingham, Durham and handfuls to Bristol, Loughborough, UCL. Business management, history, economics popular but everything else from African studies to sports science.

Money Matters: Remarkably (reasonably, says school) well-endowed. Generous spread of scholarships, exhibitions, bursaries at 11, 13 and 16 for general ability and specific talents, including sports, drama, A&D, D&T, music and chess. A new bursaries policy seeks to offer funding where most needed.

Remarks: A privileged – but unpretentious and non-spoiling start in life for the lucky. All-rounders who also like work will get the best out of it but most will love every minute here. The place somehow summed up in the fact that a new rugby coach has started a Chaucer-reading prize.

OAKWOOD HIGH SCHOOL

Chatsworth Road, Ellesmere Park, Eccles, Lancashire, M30 9DY

Tel: 0161 921 2140

Fax: 0161 921 2155

Email: oakwood.specialhighschool@salford.gov.uk

• Pupils: 163; 115 boys, 48 girls all statemented for special needs • Ages: 11-16 • Religion: non-denominational • School status: State • School gender: Mixed • Day/boarding: Day pupils

SEN provision

Detail:

Centre of excellence for:

Mild: ASP; AUT; ADD; ADHD; EBD; DS; DYSC; DYSL; DYSP;

Moderate: ASP; AUT; ADD; ADHD; EBD; DS; MLD; DYSC; DYSL; DYSP;

Severe: DYSC; DYSL; DYSP;

Others: SPD; AUT(other); FRX;

What we say about the school - the full Good Schools Guide review

Head: Since 1991, Janis Triska BEd Hons, Med, RSA Key Skills, Cert in Special Education. Previously head of Broughton Park Special School. Committed, dedicated, ambitious for children and liked by staff. Believes all children can excel, 'we provide a learning environment that enables parents and children to believe they can achieve and do well in life.' Talks of school's purpose being to serve the children, parents and community and has developed holistic approach through Oakwood Youth Club extending school's care into evenings, weekends and holidays with separate staff paid for by lottery grants. Ideas shaped by visit to a Copenhagen School with a large after-school staff and by son attending MGS, 'I wanted to transfer that culture into the state sector and I'm passionate about special needs children having the right opportunities in life.' Ofsted (2005) praised her 'excellent vision and exceptional leadership', which is 'followed and emulated by the whole staff'.

Academic Matters: Numerous awards and specialist college status in arts and technology. 2005 Ofsted report peppered with 'excellent, outstanding and exceptionally good'. Some seventy per cent gain one or more A-G GCSEs compared to fewer than thirty per cent in similar schools, making Oakwood High a top performer in its field. Particularly strong in art, design and technology as befits specialist status. Entry level certificates and ASDAN also taken and almost all children leave with a qualification. Entry level work displayed alongside GCSE work, all are celebrated with pride. Three classes each year, average size 12 with teacher, assistant (two in year 7) and some one-to-one assistants. Large learning resource room has 14 flat screen computers and library area and is haven for quieter children at lunch and breaks. Twenty computers in air conditioned ICT room and wireless network enables laptop use everywhere. Interactive whiteboards in all classrooms. All pupils learn 'sign along' sign language. All study food tech. Vocational department includes building trade skills and painting and decorating room, both used by other local schools. Dance and music room divided by moveable screen and full of children having great fun. Enthusiastic countdown in French before races in PE and science teacher uses songs for learning. Textile course has pupils making garments, giving fashion shows for a photo shoot. Art room has dark room and kiln. Pupils assessed in every subject half termly and targets are set individually.

Games, Options, The Arts: Sportsmark gold award with sports leadership courses offered. School took part in disabled section of Manchester Youth Games and lots of boys are part of Manchester United's disabled group. Ten-year-old Oakwood Youth Club, with high take-up including mainstream siblings, offers residential adventure and water sports trips, D of E, rugby, indoor bowls, swimming as well as arts and social activities and holiday projects.

Background and Atmosphere: Confident, smiling faces everywhere, great rapport between all. Brand new (2005) buildings with blue, green, yellow and orange corridors around garden with sculptures in quad and green views of playing fields or golf course on every side. Site shared with Chatsworth High School (also SEN), connected only by Primary Care Trust corridor with physios, speech therapists, nurse, hydrotherapy. 'The schools are completely separate,' says head. Entrance boasts impressive steel and bronze sculpture, 'Sinew', created in lottery grant project for children and professional artist to celebrate new school. Fabulous, colourful displays of work and photos on every wall including one recording health and beauty weekend for girls, 'to promote self-image, esteem and personal hygiene'.

School runs from 8.30am-3pm. Restaurant has three sittings, self-service with tables for four and electronic photographic swipe card described by children as 'the best thing about the school'. Fish and chip day on Fridays but Oakwood High also boasts Healthy School Award. Ambitious plans to use restaurant as café for parents waiting for clinics and midweek pensioners' specials. Year 10 is making curtains and tablecloths and serving will form part of an NVQ in catering and hospitality.

Pastoral Care and Discipline: Strong ethos of mutual care and children rise to high expectations of behaviour. Ofsted praised pupils' attitudes and helpfulness to each other. Enthusiastic cues outside classrooms before lessons. 'It's a telling school,' head says proudly, 'there are no secrets here'. School council gives pupils a voice. Detentions in break and lunch for misbehaviour, 'but we try to be more positive than negative,' say staff. Rewards scheme including citizenship award for good deeds with weekly winner's picture on wall in year 7. Uniforms of blue shirts, tucked in, logoed blue sweatshirts and blazers. Two counsellors available to children or parents two days a week.

Pupils and Parents: All children statemented for at least moderate learning difficulties. Some have physical disabilities including visual and hearing impairments and some have behavioural problems although these aren't immediately evident. Almost all white reflecting Salford population. Many from socio-economic deprived areas, over fifty per cent eligible for free school meals. Nine children in care. Parents offered workshops and support groups but uptake is low. However, parents made very positive comments to Ofsted. Head looks on parents as 'partners' and encourages feedback, 'I look on criticism as positive because we can then change to improve our service'.

Entrance: Statemented children from Salford, a few from other LEAs. Waiting list for every year. Extra care given to transition both in and out of school with year 7 based in three rooms off their own colourful, central space. Incoming year 6s make four visits and each has individual care plan so school can prepare for their arrival.

Exit: Majority to Eccles College next door for two or three years where overlap of staff gives continuity. Transition adviser supervises pro-active follow up of all leavers for a year. This aspect of school deemed a model of good practice by the government and is subject of a research paper from Pennsylvania State University.

Remarks: Very happy school encouraging the very best from its pupils. Fingers crossed and browbeat the LEA for a place.

THE OLD MALTHOUSE SCHOOL

Langton Matravers, Swanage, Dorset, BH19 3HB

Tel: 01929 422 302

Fax: 01929 422 154

Email: office@oldmalthouseschool.co.uk

Website: www.oldmalthouseschool.co.uk

• Pupils: 105; 75 boys and girls in prep school; 30 board, 45 day; 30 in pre-prep • Ages: 3-13 • Religion: C of E • Fees: Boarders £4,535; day £1,305 to £3,435 • School status: Independent • School gender: Mixed • Day/boarding: Takes boarders

SEN provision

Detail:

Experience of:

Mild: ASP; ADD; ADHD; DYSC; DYSL; DYSP; SpLD;
Moderate: DYSC; DYSL;
Others: SPD; EAL;

Summary: Extra support in both English and mathematics is available and undertaken by specialist teachers. Children are withdrawn for either one-to-one support or in small groups. Multi-sensory techniques are used wherever possible. Assessment is by LASS – computer assessment from year 1 to year 8.

What we say about the school - the full Good Schools Guide review

Head: Since 2004, Mr Richard Keeble, educated Douai and Durham (BEd English). Marinaded in good prep schools – Clifton, Farleigh and the Dragon. Ex-Hampshire cricketer. Very games-ey. Teaches English. A man with an open stance who watches the ball onto the bat and plays it straight. Dissection reveals deepdown kindness and downbeat candour. No spin. Not one to rush about with rescue remedies, despite general parlousness. He is doing more than meets the eye, yet will safeguard the spirit of this place at all costs. Parents like that – and they like him. They like his wife, Ruth, too – 'a brilliant asset, such a lovely person.' Two daughters, one at Bryanston, the other at OMH, as the Old Malthouse's aficionados style it.

Entrance: Come one, come all – so long as you pass the entry test designed to deflect deep-seated SENs. The parental mix is eclectic, no doubt about it, inclining to wellie rather than Gucci – OMH has always been a school of choice for the lost manor houses of Dorset. Minibus from Dorchester, Wool, Wareham and Swanage. Plans afoot to ship children in from Poole on the clinkety-clankety Sandbanks ferry. Perhaps the blissfullest way of getting to school this side of heaven.

Exit: There's a nostalgic link with Winchester. Nowadays, anywhere – any of the top trad schools, Wessex ones in particular, of course – Bryanston, Sherborne, Milton Abbey.

Remarks: Here's a school which snootily dropped anchor in a changing market – and almost went down, taking with it some of the best teachers and the nicest children you'll find anywhere. It's a chilling reminder of the vital importance of good governors and OMH's have now got their act together. They've shed a few, renounced nostalgia and drafted in some movers and shakers. High time. All praise to the exceptional bursar, whose wizardry with figures has seen it through – she gives you max value for fees. Can we recommend it in the year in which pupil numbers in the main school have fallen to just 66? Yes we can. Maximum kindness has been re-installed. There's a strong hand on the tiller. Numbers are rising for the first time in years. We see a sprightly bow-wave.

OMH really is a charming little school. It's the first thing you feel. Look about you. The children have an organic, free-range, look about them. The sun shines and the wind blows freshly up from the sea. You sense, not enervated routine, but open-eyed energy. Here's a school whose clothing list in the 1940s required children to pack an axe, the better to chop sticks for camps. Tree climbing has been pruned in forced deference to nanny laws, but knees still grip bark and conkers still conquer. These children retain their axe-memory.

Small school means small scale, so expect nothing grand about OMH. It's terrifically houseproud, though. There's the old house, dining room, library and excellent IT downstairs, dorms atop. It's a lovely old house. Stand in the dining room, full or empty. Feel the vibe. Then you'll understand the place. It doubles as a chapel for assemblies – they pop a cross in the food hatch. Outside, there's a cluster of wooden hut classrooms. There's the playroom, indestructible, re-varnished every holiday, resounding to the pounding of rollerblades and the hoots of jolly romping. There's a very decent sports-hall-cum-theatre with swanky classrooms on the end of it. And then there are the sports fields (all-weather pitch) and the open air pool and the tennis courts. And in the distance the sea and in the distant distance the Isle of Wight.

Two dedicated staff, one (the SENCo) is an English whizzo, plus fully trained maths special needs teacher. All children assessed on entry, roughly five per cent of children need some form of help, 'always one-to-one or small groups', no dual teaching. Small enough school to deal with most problems as they arise.

Small schools are an affair of the heart. What they lack in pediments they make up for in personality. That's the point of them. OMH teachers are as delectably characterful as teachers from way back, and you'd be forgiven for remarking on traits of mild eccentricity. But they're quality. They cut the mustard in the classroom – they bring out the best in the best and they bring on the rest. Their results stand by them. And they do so much. Take Annie Campbell. She's a collectable artist. She teaches it. She plays in the orchestra and conducts the carol service, baton in one hand, fainted chorister in the other, unfazed. There's more where she came from. Old fashioned enthusiasts. They are the school and without them OMH would be nowhere of note, so make sure you meet them. They are the reason the children are so unaffectedly courteous, easy in the company of adults. Learning support rises to three one-to-one rotated lessons a week in English, maths and study skills. All but SENs learn Latin from year 5.

In a little pond, all fishes are big. Small schools can attend to, accommodate and animate individuality. OMH is back on track here. It is freshly co-ed and the girls already look as if they've been there forever. It has modernised its boarding policy to incorporate all the flexi-options from weekly through dinner-party to last minute. The boarding tradition is strong and the head is a boarding man. Vitally needed improvements in quality of kindly care have been carried through, together with an overhaul of the diet. Day pupils are just as welcome in the new market-friendly climate. They can come for breakfast at 7.30, stay for prep, for supper and for the many evening activities – which include carving the local stone – until 8.00pm. Saturday morning school endures forever. Sport is valiantly contested and properly coached. Strong cross-country tradition. Sailing at Swanage.

OMH is a school which inspires passionate loyalty but its reputation locally has suffered in recent years from badmouthing by some disgruntled parents. Since the new regime was installed there has been nothing to complain of – indeed, everything to praise. The observable difference, in words of a parent, is that 'the teachers are all smiles again – the gloom has lifted.' Here once more – welcome back! – is a super little school where pupils flourish in their own space.

THE OLD RECTORY SCHOOL

Brettenham, Ipswich, Suffolk, IP7 7QR

Tel: 01449 736 404

Fax: 01449 737 881

Email: oldrectoryschool@aol.com

Website: www.theoldrectoryschool.com

• Pupils: 37 boys, of whom 29 board; 8 girls, of whom 5 board • Ages: 7-13 • Religion: Inter-denom • Fees: Day £4,835, boarding £6,495 • School status: Independent • School gender: Mixed • Day/boarding: Takes boarders

SEN provision

Detail:

Centre of excellence for:

Mild: DYSC; DYSL; DYSP;

Moderate: DYSC; DYSL; DYSP;

Severe: DYSC; DYSL; DYSP;

Experience of:

Mild: EBD;

Others: Sp&LD; Eat;

Summary: The Old Rectory is a specialist school for dyslexic and dyspraxic children aged 7 to 13. Pupils remain with us for one or two years, receiving an intensive programme of support which allows them to return to mainstream education at the end of this time. Key elements of the school's success are:

- Small group teaching – staff ratio of 1:6. All teachers have Diplomas in specific learning difficulties.
- Each child has a daily tutorial period with their English teacher, following a multi-sensory programme for SpLD children.
- Support for organisational difficulties – in and out of the classroom.
- Emphasis on raising self-esteem and confidence of pupils.
- Secure, comfortable family environment with excellent boarding facilities.
- Wide range of activities including School Fire Brigade.
- Emphasis on literacy and numeracy skills alongside lessons in accordance with National Curriculum.
- Additional lessons include touch-typing, thinking study skills, listening skills, handwriting, reading programme, reading development, word attack. Strong art, music and drama departments. County location with ample space for sport.

What we say about the school - the full Good Schools Guide review

Head: Since 1999, Miss Ann Furlong MA CertEd SpNeedsEdDip SpLD (forties) who first came to the school in January 1981 with the founder, Dr Martin Phillips. Educated at the Catholic Bonus Pasteur School in Bromley, she got her Cert Ed at Gloucester College of Further Education, followed by an MA (in special needs education) at the Open University and further qualifications at Chelmsford Hall, Eastbourne. She previously taught at Slinden College in Sussex, followed by a spell at Chelmsford Hall, then Slinden again, plus Bruern Abbey and five years as head of remedial teaching at King's College, Cambridge and back to The Old Rectory as head designate for a couple of terms. Quite.

Incredibly well-qualified in a number of disciplines, Miss Furlong is a quiet, thoughtful and engaging character, rather self-effacing, and perhaps not as full of exuberance as many of the heads whom we have met. Knows the children and their problems well and takes regular classes.

Retiring due to ill health.

Entrance: See below.

Exit: See below.

Remarks: This is indeed an old rectory, next to the church which is used for daily assemblies and set in five acres of deep Suffolk. The fabric of the school was bought from Mr and Mrs Phillips by Michael Murphy (whose role appears to be that of interested benefactor) in 1999.

Boarding girls live in the Coach House, recently modernised and extended. Boys live in the main house, in immaculate tidiness (can this really be so!). Lessons are either taken in a large hall subdivided into four classrooms with folding screens (The Arches which was opened by Lord Archer) or in Portakabins outside. Lots of English, maths and other trad subjects are taught in small classes (max size eight), according to ability rather than age. The school follows a modified National Curriculum, with German rather than French. Dedicated IT room, with children taught touch-typing early, but no laptops; two handwriting lessons a week match the two keyboarding lessons.

Music and drama important. Games on site, and masses of extra-curricular activity, including karate, target shooting and fire crew – the school has five fire engines which specially selected pupils can help 'crew', usually putting out controlled fires only. All the extra-curricular activities are chosen to improve motor skills.

The usual age for children coming to the school is 10 or 11, often only for a year or two; they then return either to normal mainstream schools or to schools offering continued specialist help.This is a school for the dyslexic, the dyspraxic, those with dyscalculia and the occasional fragile child. The school does not take any child with behaviour problems, nor any child on Ritalin, though there are several on efalax oil, and several wear coloured spectacles – deep pink, mauve, dark blue, which are often promoted as remedial aids.

Some children are statemented, with a few of them receiving funding from their local LEA – others are going through the process of accessing funding via a tribunal. Many of the children do not come from a boarding school background and their parents 'may have sold their house or gone without holidays' to send them here.

Female staff are invariably called Miss, and the few men Sir. No real problems in getting staff, but the head feels that it is important to have more than just the very popular groundsman as the token male role model and takes time to find men with the right qualifications – and if staff do not come with suitable dyslexia training they train at the Hornsby Centre. Occupational and speech therapists on hand.

Entrance is by an educational psychologist's report (and there is a twice yearly visit by the ed psych to all children). Plus points for good behaviour, and once a fortnight all those with the best grades for effort have a party in the jacuzzi and sauna chalet; bad points for negative behaviour, really disruptive children can be sanctioned, involving loss of privilege, and occasionally suspended or expelled.

This is a helpful little school, which sends children with special needs back into mainstream education. Worth considering.

ORWELL PARK SCHOOL

Nacton, Ipswich, Suffolk, IP10 0ER

Tel: 01473 659 225

Fax: 01473 659 822

Email: headmaster@orwellpark.co.uk

Website: www.orwellpark.co.uk

• Pupils: 163 boys, 59 girls; 75 full boarders, 81 flexible boarders; junior school 48 boys, 34 girls • Ages: Main school 7-13, Junior school 3-7 • Religion: Inter-denom • Fees: Weekly boarding £4,915-£5,465; day £1,505-£4,260 • School status: Independent • School gender: Mixed • Day/boarding: Takes boarders

SEN provision

Detail:

Now provide for in school:

Mild: ASP; ADD; ADHD; EBD; DYSC; DYSL; DYSP; HI; VI;

Moderate: ASP; ADD; ADHD; EBD; DYSC; DYSL; DYSP;

Others: SPD; EAL; Sp&LD; Epi;

Summary: The learning support department at Orwell Park runs throughout the school. We support children across all ages and abilities. We carry out an 'In-House' assessment prior to recommending individual programmes for each child on the learning support register and work closely with children, staff and parents. Children may need to be withdrawn from lessons with one of our team (including a maths specialist) or may find that in-class support offers enough help for their specific learning difficulties. We run Study Skills groups and Revision sessions prior to exams for years 7 and 8. We also have Early Morning Spelling groups, Paired Reading groups and children may follow a Typing course, where it is felt beneficial. We work closely with all outside agencies such as SaLTs, Physios, Ed. Psychs etc.

What we say about the school - the full Good Schools Guide review

Head: Since 1994, Mr Andrew Auster BA DipEd Hon FLCM FRSA (early fifties), previously head of The Downs School, Colwall and before that director of music at

King's School, Gloucester, and then Shrewsbury. Also once head of music for five years at Portslade Community College (a large comprehensive). Keen rugby player (played for English Universities, Durham, Cambridge and Gloucester RFC), accomplished musician. Wife, Liz, greatly involved in school. Three children, two of whom were pupils. Very relaxed and smiles a lot but at the same time gives the impression of being thoroughly in control. Very keen to inculcate strong moral values.

Entrance: By registration and standard assessment tests.

Exit: Impossible to list all the schools nowadays; in fact girls and boys go on to nearly all the major public schools. 2002 saw the highest number of awards and scholarships in the school's history – 19.

Remarks: A lovely place. Glorious setting, the main building is gorgeous late Georgian with Victorian additions and the facilities superb. The place has a warm, happy feel to it but still manages to look business-like and elegant. Visitors and parents can tour the 110 acres in the school's very own working fire engine. Pupils are mainly drawn from East Anglia and many have strong London connections. A nice mixture of politeness, informality and willingness to chat in both boys and girls; they are buzzing with keenness and amazingly tidy. Emphasis on academic standards is strong, with frequent internal assessments, but the head likes to think that the pupils are done slowly in the Aga rather than microwaved and this is certainly borne out by the relaxed atmosphere in the classrooms. Streaming throughout the main school, particularly in the final CE year. Plenty of quiet time – eg every day begins with a twenty-minute reading slot. Maximum class size in the main school is 16, average 12; in the junior school numbers range from 12-16.

Terrifically busy special needs department with SENCo overseeing a team of five or six. Strong support for those with dyslexia, dyspraxia, dyscalculia, mild Asperger's, ADHD but nothing too serious; must be able to access mainstream. Children with known problems before they come to the school are assessed to see if they can cope and problems for those in school are dealt with as they arise: spelling, handwriting, paired reading, maths and prep support. Study skills for couple of years during run-up to CE. One-to-one, one to two, small groups, dual teaching in class. Around seventy children get some form of help; one lesson each week is free; subsequent lessons cost extra. Outside agencies co-opted if necessary, OTs, SaLT and physios. At recent speech day head girl remarked on how well the school had helped her overcome her dyslexia, develop her confidence, developed her self-esteem and helped her make significant strides.

Plenty of adults around – each class in the junior school has a qualified teacher and an assistant – and there are six gap-year student helpers, including some from eastern Europe – the school has links here through an HMC scheme. Some exciting exchanges and events have come out of this, such as a year's stay by a young Russian concert pianist.

The spirit of competition is far from dead. Children encouraged to take part in verse, public speaking and solo singing competitions and so on and the list of school, regional and national sporting events that boys' and girls' teams compete in (and win) is endless. The head's musical bent is reflected in a breathtaking variety of activities, involving lots of the children, from concerts in St John's, Smith Square, to musicals and celebrity recitals. A concert or lecture every week, with pupils either participating or just attending. Two thirds of the pupils play an instrument, many to grade 5 and above; plenty of orchestras, bands and choirs. Forty music practice rooms in the basement, now equipped with good pianos. Unsurprisingly with all this activity, quite a few music scholarships to public schools every year. Children are kept very busy with a wide variety of activities, from sailing (the school has 10 toppers) to theatre trips, via ten-pin bowling and some very worthy charity fund-raising. The school has its own observatory (manned by a local astronomy group) with a 10-inch refractor telescope and radio station. A very flexible boarding system enables children to choose freely what they want to do. Library and IT room are open at all times and there are no silence rules. Dormitories are airy and bright. Junior school has formal family meals, main school has a cafeteria system.The junior school has expanded hugely lately, largely thanks to an enthusiastic head. They have to manage for the time being in Portakabins but these are beautifully got up, colourful and comfortable. The next major school project is the construction of a full size astroturf pitch.

Our Lady of Victories RC Primary School

Clareville Street, London, SW7 5AQ

Tel: 020 7373 4491
Fax: 020 7244 0591
Email: madeline.brading@olov.rbkc.sch.uk
Website: www.ourladyvictories.kensington-chelsea.sch.uk

• Pupils: 210, roughly 50/50 boys/girls; nursery 30
• Ages: 3-11 • Religion: RC • School status: State
• School gender: Mixed • Day/boarding: Day pupils

SEN provision

Detail:

Now provide for in school:
 Mild: DS;
 Moderate: DS;
Experience of:
 Mild: AUT; DYSL;
 Moderate: AUT; MLD; DYSL; HI;
 Others: GEN; EAL;

Summary: We have a SENCo who has been in post for five years. She works with all the outside agencies to include the educational psychology service, school nurse, speech and language provision. We have a teacher who supports the more able children. They both work alongside classroom teachers in a supportive role. We have five children with statements of special need. Two of these children have individual teacher support as part of their statement. We have SEN support which is small group withdrawal or the SEN teacher working alonside the class teacher. We also have gifted and talented support in maths and english but not other subjects. We have a child with dyslexia but are having difficulties finding a teacher to support him. We do not have the facilities to cope with children with behaviour difficulties.

What we say about the school - the full Good Schools Guide review

Head: Since 1995, Mrs Madeline Brading BEd MA (mid fifties). Born in north Wales and educated in Liverpool. She has made many improvements to school life and premises during her ten years at the school. Her MA in Staff Development is evident in the school and in the way she has involved both staff and parents in the school's development. A wizard with her budget – she has managed to make sure her pupils are provided with much more than the average state school offers.

Entrance: From practising Catholic families living in the parishes of Our Lady of Victories, Our Lady of Mount Carmel and Saint Simon Stock, which cover some parts of Earl's Court and Kensington. Attending the nursery does not guarantee you a place at 4. Unsurprisingly, the school is always over-subscribed, although there are occasional vacancies in the older age groups, so if interested, keep telephoning.

Exit: Mainly to the popular and more selective state schools; boys to The London Oratory and Cardinal Vaughan, girls to Lady Margaret and The Sacred Heart; a small percentage going into the independent sector. Scholarships have been won to James Allen, City of London and Tiffin Boys and Girls.

Remarks: One of Kensington and Chelsea's best performing primaries since the start of the league tables; awarded 'School of the Year' for 2000 by The Evening Standard, typically gets almost all to level 4 in the SATs – most to level 5 – impressive considering they have pupils speaking 18 different languages. Very high standards are expected in all areas of the curriculum and behaviour.

SEN support, five fully statemented children. Extension programme for bright pupils. Lessons well planned and delivered by enthusiastic dedicated staff (mostly long staying) who share a good range of specialist subjects between them. Class sizes are 30 max. Parents come in and help with reading and art, and are provided with training. A dip in 2003/4 due to the retirement of the excellent year 6 teacher.

Follows the National Curriculum with lots of added value but what really sets O L of V apart is that French and music are taught to all classes and Latin from 8 years. Interesting and well-stocked children's library, a huge improvement on some fee-paying schools. Very well-equipped music room, all pupils taught music theory and children learn to play the recorder and percussion. Last year the children played at Chelsea Festival with Piers Adams. Also a choir. The school also has an art room, a science room (a rarity in state primaries), computers in all classrooms and a computer suite. The head takes year 6 to Cannes on school journey each year. The music department now has key boards and runs an after school keyboard club because some of the children are so keen.

In 2004 the choir took part in the Chelsea music festival working with Harvey Brusk the composer.

After-school clubs include ballet, chess, art, Italian and Portuguese. Good sport, with a large gym, a plus as the playground is small. Cricket coach from Middlesex Colts, football coach from Queens Park Rangers. In the summer, Battersea Park for athletics, all classes swim. Children appear happy and well occupied.

Discipline is strict, very zero tolerance attitude. We imagine Mrs Brading to be quite alarming when riled! That said, the school really wants to see its pupils doing well and offers them new challenges and opportunities, not just the bare minimum. An active home-school-parish partnership is encouraged, school chaplain visits, daily prayers and school/family masses. Very Catholic maroon and grey uniform. One parent commented, 'ever since my children started here, I have felt so fortunate knowing that they will be well looked after and get a good start to their education with no corners cut. It really is an excellent school.'

THE PARK SCHOOL

Onslow Crescent, Woking, Surrey, GU22 7AT

Tel: 01483 772 057

Fax: 01483 740 976

Email: head@thepark.surrey.sch.uk

• Pupils: 85 boys, 20 girls • Ages: 11-16 • School status: State • School gender: Mixed • Day/boarding: Day pupils

SEN provision

Detail:

Now provide for in school:

Mild: AUT; EBD; DYSP; SpLD;

Moderate: AUT; ADD; ADHD; EBD; DS; DYSP; SpLD;

Severe: ASP; ADD; ADHD; DYSP; SpLD;

Others: SPD; FRX;

Experience of:

Mild: VI;

Moderate: DYSC; VI;

Severe: EBD; DYSC;

Others: OCD; Epi; PD;

Summary: The Park School is situated in Woking and maintained by Surrey LEA. It is one of seven schools in Surrey catering for pupils with Learning Difficulties and has an additional 'Language Specialism'. Six places per year group are funded for pupils with a language impairment. Staffing includes the equivalent of three full-time speech and language therapists. The school focuses on training in this area and can be described as having a Language Enriched Curriculum.

Along with the other LD schools in Surrey, The Park is moving towards being secondary age only by 2007. Numbers will remain at 100 on roll. There are 20 pupils per year group taught in classes of ten. Teachers all have teaching assistant support. Additional teaching assistants are non-class based enabling pupils to be provided with a rich diet of social development opportunities. The school has a thriving newspaper that involves pupils in reporting, photographing and interviewing. Disco dancing and gardening are other favourite sessions across the week with a full range of club opportunities keeping youngsters busy during the daily break times.

In 2004 the Investors in People assessment described the school: 'There is a relaxed but hardworking and professional feel to the school, with a strong sense of purpose in ensuring that pupils are given the opportunity to develop their potential in a safe and caring environment.'

An emphasis on staff training and development produces a confident and skilled staff who all individually contribute to achieving the aims and objectives of the organisation.

The school's accommodation is currently being upgraded. Internal adaptations to classrooms, changing rooms and offices will be finished by September 2005 and a new Science/DT classroom block is due to be completed in the autumn term.

The Park is a member of the Woking School's Federation and the Special School's Consortium providing strong community links. Opportunities are also given for pupils to access mainstream facilities or curriculum. Outreach training is provided for other schools from The Park.

What we say about the school - the full Good Schools Guide review

Head: Since 1998 Karen Eastwood BEd MA (early fifties), seconded from her post as deputy head of

Walton Leigh (an SLD school) when previous head retired through ill health. Came for six months, loved it, loved the children and thankfully, say parents, stayed. Credits success to teamwork and wanted us to mention the leadership group: 'structure is unusual, no deputy but three assistant heads and an admin officer who make up my dream team.' A good listener, a reassuringly calm demeanour, unassuming, fantastic with the children and fiercely proud of the school. Says: 'some of the children have so much potential but are damaged sometimes from their educational history, family background, child protection issues or a generally poor deal. You think you can make a difference and want to give them a wonderful time at school.'

Academic Matters: Usual facilities including DT, art and science rooms all reasonable but many soon to be upgraded including library which will become an information and resource area used for individual and small group teaching during lesson time. Average class size of ten with at least one teaching assistant per class. A very quiet and well-ordered school; pupils we saw were involved with and challenged by their work and readily explained the tasks. Work was differentiated and pupils seem very accepting of this way of working, no one was showing off or felt bullied. Such was the industrious atmosphere you'd be forgiven for thinking you were in a good prep school not a state special, no wonder parents who visit want their children to come here.

Science results are significantly better than English and maths; school say that's because the practical approach of science suits their learners. On our visit the language curriculum was being overhauled: 'we want to make the subject more practical and visual for some of our learners – 'it's about looking at different ways for different learners, we're already seeing not just results but increasingly confident children. Change involves risk but it's a calculated risk and one we're ready to take. What we have is good but it can be better and we want the best.'

We asked several of the children if they enjoyed their work; 'no' was the unanimous response but they were readily betrayed by their body language, smiles and easy relationship with the head whom they clearly cherish. Seconds later they were telling of all the good things about the school...

Games, Options, The Arts: Good provision for sports including a heated outdoor swimming pool, decent grounds with hard court and playing fields. All the usual sports offered including athletics, tennis and the ever-popular horse-riding. Play competitively against other schools and take part in events such as the Surrey youth games and Hickstead (dressage winner). Music co-ordinator Jane Brown, assisted by Simon May (composer – Howard's Way, Eastenders themes) who works at the school a couple of days a week, promotes music and drama both in school and for events such as the Guildford Cathedral special school events. Plenty of trips and visits support learning and develop social skills.

Afternoons are spent on the less academic aspects of school life. Pupil favourites: gardening clubs, disco-dancing and school newspaper groups run alongside the main curriculum: 'we experimented this year but we're building in properly next year. It's been a great success: so much hands-on experience, children enjoy themselves, relate to each other and we never have to call out a senior member of staff. Our children need the practical and vocational.'

Fabulous school garden sectioned into mini allotments – you'd be forgiven for thinking they were trying to rival Chelsea – well when did you last see runner beans in a hanging basket? That's part of the beauty: experimentation and the children get lots of help, it isn't just about planting; there's lots of practical science going on too – roots and shoots, food, water, climatic conditions and care. What's more they must be doing something right, they recently won the hanging basket category at Woking in Bloom.

Background and Atmosphere: Housed in what was a girls grammar, the school was founded in the 1960s and will become secondary only from Sept 07. Hoping for approved new building to start in July 05 which will provide additional offices, more classrooms, new science lab, DT room and free up space throughout school to create small work areas – an increasing necessity as needs of children are becoming more complex.

Pastoral Care and Discipline: There's an effective behaviour management strategy in which it's fine for children to take time out rather than allow a situation to escalate. The system is simple and graduated: reminder, warning, time out. Work on positive but importantly child can go back into a classroom with a clean slate. A senior member of staff is always available should staff need help with a serious or tricky situation or to remove a pupil from the setting. If a child misses a lesson they're expected to work with the original teacher on a 'think-sheet' where the child considers his actions. Parents are notified via a TS sticker in the child's planner and phoned whenever there's a need or worry. Staff say strategy has changed pupils: they're more positive and display less challenging behaviour, this means teaching and learning improves and so hopefully the virtuous circle continues. Offer vocational social development opportunities and run classes to work on socially acceptable conversation and behaviour. Parents say reward system of grading child every lesson makes children want to achieve.

Connexions and Woking College provide careers information and advice. Leavers have their own common room for break times where they can make drinks, have lunch, watch videos listen to music etc. Time taken to ensure all elements in place for when they leave – we met one overjoyed boy who'd taken the train to college that morning in preparation for next year – 'these things really matter.'

Pupils and Parents: A mixed bag from across Surrey: very well heeled to children of travellers. Smart uniform (blazer et al) worn with pride (school council recently asked for and got a school badge). Parents move into the area to qualify for a place. Friends of the Park organise social events including brilliant 'stars in their eyes' with set designed by a parent – not just about fundraising, get to meet other parents. Parents say get plenty of reports and opportunities to discuss any concerns. Pupils a great bunch, many with endless enthusiasm, well harnessed here but potentially overwhelming and misjudged elsewhere?

Entrance: Apply to a panel in November prior to selection for year 7 in the following September. Twenty places per year group, all statemented. Caters for pupils with learning difficulties (LD) and specific language and communication needs (SpLCN) including some on the autistic continuum. May have associated difficulties: ADD, ADHD. Approximately ten per cent have EAL requirements. Children should be significantly behind for their age, ie below level two of the National Curriculum by year 7. It's not just about how far behind they are there's usually a social communication difficulty too. Need to consider if they'll manage the school canteen, getting changed for PE etc. There used to be a separate language unit but this has gone. Those children who are offered language places (six per year) are fully integrated into the school, they get their additional therapy but everyone works together, all have an enriched curriculum as majority have a language difficulty, if they're not offered a language place they get an LD place. Language places go to those with therapy needs over and above the therapy provided. Much of the therapy is integrated in to the classroom setting and continues throughout the day and across the curriculum rather than a half-hour session here and there, though this does happen too if it's felt beneficial. Therapists (SaLT and OT) plan with teachers look at needs, key words, vocabulary and work on refining one aspect at a time.

Exit: Odd one returns to mainstream but school can't be seen as a catch-up; gap tends to widen as children get older so don't want to offer false hope. Majority to FE colleges, Guildford and Brooklands popular. Couple into employment sometimes as a result of successful work experience places.

Remarks: For those with the jury out on the inclusion debate this school looks and feels like a mainstream school, children follow the National Curriculum adapted as necessary and work in smaller groups not dissimilar to the lower sets in mainstream. They mix with their peers and with children from other years they have specialist teachers, move around the school independently wait outside classrooms before the 55 minute lessons begin, practice 'good sitting' and 'good listening' and work jolly hard. It's true they have a varied curriculum diet that includes gardening, but remember the days when rural studies and horticulture were acceptable components of the school curriculum? These children feel included because they can participate in all elements of school life not just the academic, PE, the arts but socially and emotionally too. The more able or those with a talent spend as much time as possible or desirable working in mainstream schools, the least able, especially those with more complex communication difficulties attend other special schools for some of the time if it's felt beneficial. Parents say feeling of mainstream in a specialist environment is an overwhelming selling point.

An inclusive school, an exclusive atmosphere going from strength to strength, offering a ray of sunshine in a sometimes cloudy world.

Parrs Wood High School

Wilmslow Road, East Didsbury, Manchester, M20 5PG

Tel: 0161 445 8786

Fax: 0161 445 5974

Email: pwtc@parrswood.manchester.sch.uk

Website: www.parrswood.manchester.sch.uk

• Pupils: 2,000 boys and girls; all day • Ages: 11-18

• Religion: None • School status: State

• Opendays: Late October/early November

• School gender: Mixed • Day/boarding: Day pupils

SEN provision

Detail:

Now provide for in school:

Mild: ASP; AUT; ADD; ADHD; EBD; DYSC; DYSL; DYSP; HI; VI; CP;

Moderate: ASP; ADD; ADHD; EBD; MLD; DYSC; DYSL; DYSP; HI; VI;

Severe: ASP; DYSL; HI;

Others: SPD; OCD; ODD; TIC; EAL; Sp&LD; DEL; Eat;

Experience of:

Mild: SpLD;

Moderate: AUT; CP;

Severe: ADD; ADHD; DYSP;

Others: CD; Epi;

Summary: Our SEN staff comprise a faculty within the school, with a wide range of experience across the support and teaching staff within the faculty. The support our students receive combines in-class support and one-to-one sessions with a key member of the team. We have an intervention programme aimed at raising the attainment of those students identified as working at level 3 or below in year 6 of primary school – this intervention begins during the summer term before the students arrive at Parrs Wood for year 7.

Since Sept 2004 we have also had specialist provision for hearing impaired students at the school, with the students following a mixed curriculum – supported in mainstream lessons and spending part of the school day working as a group with specialist staff in their own base within school.

What we say about the school - the full Good Schools Guide review

Head: Since 2005, partnership heads Ms Rachel Jones and Mr David Ashley, both in their forties. Ms Jones was deputy head and fixed term sole head here. She came from English teaching background with extensive experience in large, multi-cultural comprehensives in London and Manchester, and still teaches occasionally. Mr Ashley was head of Hathershaw Technology College in Oldham, where he was praised in the national press for 'driving the ICT agenda in education'. He has a design and technology teaching background.

Academic Matters: One of the first UK schools in 2004 with dual specialist status, for technology and the performing arts. Ofsted in 2001 said, 'compared with schools in the same free school meals category, results are well above average, placing them amongst the top five per cent in the country.' Of note is the school's attitude to ICT with over 1,000 computers on site, trolleys of laptops for use in lessons and a staff of five technicians. Each pupil has own electronic filing cabinet. Students can borrow a PC if they do not have one at home – access through the school's system with its many safeguards. 'We're attacking the social disadvantage,' said previous head. 100 per cent of year 9 students take ICT GNVQ (equal to 2 GCSEs at grade A-C), with extra ICT training available during lunchbreak and after school.

The school has programmes for the gifted and talented, with extra sessions after school, as well as a learning support department of 17 staff working with 198 children of designated special needs. At GCSE, 60 per cent achieves five A-C grades. Wide GCSE curriculum including PE and dance, sociology, drama, business studies and Urdu. 32 A level subjects offered here and, in 2004, 100 per cent pass rate in 90 of subjects taken. The school sets targets for each pupil from day one and offers early starts and Saturday morning sessions to those not achieving their potential. There are 118 full-time teaching staff, with a young profile (40 in post for less than five years, only 28 for 15 years or more.) Additional staff (admin, technicians and other assistants) number 120. Some subjects are streamed, some taught in mixed ability groups.Department of Education Leading Edge School working with local secondary schools to support raising standards. Future Vision award for innovation in ICT and North West regional Focus school for the Specialist Schools and Academies Trust's ICT register offering consultancy and support for other secondary schools across the region, UK and abroad.

Games, Options, The Arts: The extensive school playing fields, with airy views of trees and sky despite proximity to Manchester, can be subject to flooding from the Mersey in heavy rain, but the school also boasts an astroturf area which survives occasional submersion, as well as indoor sports halls and a fully kitted gym. There are teams for every sport imaginable and a commendable list of high placements in local and regional competitions. Community Sports Leaders Award has run for many years.

Pupils and parents say the best thing about the school is the wide range of extra-curricular activities, 'there are so many things on after school it's hard to decide what to do'. D of E, drama, music and dance productions, student governors' body, public speaking (recent area finalists in Rotary competition) and clubs for chess, maths, design technology, science, art and music, oh...and homework club nightly. Over 10 per cent of students take advantage of the wide range of instrumental lessons on offer for £15 a term or just £40 a year, including steel pans, balalaika and Indian music. 'There are loads of different bands, choirs and orchestras,' say pupils, 'and at lunchtime you can hear them practising.' Seventy per cent of the instruments are loaned from the Manchester Music Service but demand for lessons does exceed availability. Standards are high; a string quartet reached recent finals in the Music for Youth festival.

Background and Atmosphere: Today's Parrs Wood Technical College, occupied since April 2000, bears no resemblance to the former crumbling Parrs Wood High School thanks to swapping valuable school land for new premises. The new buildings are tucked away behind the huge entertainment complex that made them possible. A multiscreen cinema, bowling, health club and pizza joints now shield the school from the A34, one of Manchester's main arteries, running south from the city. The result is a quiet, leafy, ultra-modern campus where state-of-the-art, low maintenance buildings in honey-coloured brick with red painted upper floors and wave-form rooflines are softened by one elegant refurbished building which houses the music department. The new buildings are within a steel frame so internal walls can easily be altered if future teaching needs dictate. The downside of the deal is the loss of land; one of the very few criticisms on recent reports is the lack of space to expand the sixth form and for pupils to play in wet weather. Aristotle's maxim, 'we are what we repeatedly do. Excellence, then, is not an act but a habit,' is inscribed large above the entrance to the school from the main foyer where a reception office and security desk give the feel of a large new office block.

Acres of blue carpet lead to wide corridors, flanked with hundreds of lockers painted in the same jade green as the school uniform; no piles of bags and coats here. Each subject has its own coloured corridor and professionally made poster-sized sign that includes montage pictures of the students involved in relevant activities, 'look, here's me,' they delight to point out. 'We do every sort of charity fund-raising,' said head. Jade polo and sweatshirts, black in year 11, over black trousers (for girls too) or skirts are the order of the day. The atmosphere isn't refined but there's no rough air or graffiti. New dance studios; hearing impaired unit integrated into the school.

Pastoral Care and Discipline: Parents say some children are unnerved by the enormity of the school but there is a pass to a safe room with board games, reading and peer counsellors. Students belong to and wear the badge of one of four houses, Griffin, Orion, Pegasus and Phoenix, which compete for points in quizzes, sports, charity fund-raising and attendance and which 'develops a sense of belonging, togetherness, unity and community.' The school states its ethos as 'celebration and reward' and uses a system of slips for behaviour; bronze, silver and gold for good conduct and effort. Blue slips for bad behaviour counteract the good slips and students speak enthusiastically about prizes they can earn, 'you can swap slips straight away for cinema tickets or you can save them for a really good prize at the end of the year, you can even earn a CD player, and the house with the most points gets to go on a brilliant trip, like Alton Towers.' Parents say, 'the school's really encouraging, always drawing out the best and making children feel good about themselves.'

No permanent exclusions for many years. 'We work really hard to achieve that,' said last head, who also maintained tough line on drugs, and parents report that any minor bullying incidents are handled well. Presumably a tradition to be continued under new regime. Granted a Healthy School Award in 2002 for all areas of the personal education programmes.

Pupils and Parents: Thirty-five per cent pupils non-white and thirty per cent entitled to free school meals reflecting the diversity of catchment area which includes seriously disadvantaged areas and prosperous suburbs favoured by Manchester's academic and media communities. Parrs Wood has the widest and most balanced distribution of ability of any school in Manchester.

Entrance: LEA driven, hugely over-subscribed with over 600 applications for three hundred places each year, and waiting lists for every year, even the final ones.

Exit: More than 80 per cent carries on to post-16 education. After A levels 75 per cent goes on to degree courses, and some 10 per cent to other further education courses. A handful to Oxbridge yearly.

Remarks: Parents feel, 'it's fantastic, I can't praise them highly enough.' True comprehensive education at its very best for those lucky enough to secure a place.

PETER SYMONDS COLLEGE

Owens Road, Winchester, Hampshire, SO22 6RX

Tel: 01962 852 764

Fax: 01962 849 372

Email: psc@psc.ac.uk

Website: www.psc.ac.uk

• Pupils: 2,500 boys and girls; most day, 100 board • Ages: 16-18 • Religion: Non-denom but with strong links to C of E • Fees: Boarding (average) £7,000 • School status: State • Opendays: Three open evenings in November and one in February • School gender: Mixed • Day/boarding: Takes boarders

---

SEN provision

Detail:

Now provide for in school:

Mild: ASP; AUT; ADD; ADHD; EBD; DYSC; DYSL; DYSP; SpLD; HI; VI; CP;

Moderate: ADD; DYSC; DYSL; DYSP; SpLD; HI; VI; CP;

Severe: ADD; DYSC; DYSL; DYSP; SpLD; HI; VI; CP;

Others: OCD; EAL; Sp&LD; Epi; PD;

Experience of:

Mild: DS;

Moderate: ASP; EBD; DS; MLD;

Others: SPD; Eat;

Summary: The college has an experienced and well-qualified learning support department. Specialisms include dyslexia, dyspraxia, ADD, English as a second language, support for visual and hearing impairment and Asperger's. There are three co-ordinators: co-ordinator for learning difficulties, co-ordinator for physical disabilities and Inclusive learning co-ordinator. On our Adult Education Site there is an adult learning support co-ordinator. Experienced learning support assistants support both in and outside the classroom ensuring that the needs of the students are met. The services of other professionals are brought in as required.

What we say about the school - the full Good Schools Guide review

Principal: Since 1993, Mr Neil Hopkins BSc MEd (early fifties), read maths at University of East Anglia. Taught maths in a comprehensive, then Eccles Sixth Form College. Previously acting principal at Rutland Sixth Form College. Married (wife lectures in further education) with three children, all of who have been through Peter Symonds. His role is essentially general manager – five faculty heads are more in touch with the pupils themselves and he 'only knows the very good and very bad by name'. Approachable and dynamic, he is very results-orientated and has overseen a period of great expansion and building at the College. Peter Symonds is now the biggest A level centre in the country.

Academic Matters: Academically well up amongst the top 10 (out of 100) sixth form colleges. Overall A level pass rate approaching 99 per cent with over half of A levels graded A or B. AS results are equally impressive for a non-selective school. Principal keen to point out that results can be compared directly with Winchester College's when you select only the top performing 500 pupils. 'Value-added' scores were not available but are used to encourage pupils and teachers alike. Wonderful, wide selection of courses on offer – pupils can choose from 35 A level subjects. Lots of non-traditional subjects available such as performing arts (dance, theatre and music – 'outstanding' course according to the Inspectors' report), film studies and sport and PE as well as classical civilisation (but no Greek or Latin) and economics (now largely overtaken by business studies in most schools but very popular here). Some courses are 'victims of their own success' and pupils have reported that they could not study their first choices. Candidates now have to audition for performing arts and pupils cannot opt for 2 art subjects together (such as art and photography).

Numbers are huge – there are 21 sets for biology for example. No streaming though. Some unevenness in teaching is addressed by close results' monitoring and regular classroom observation. All pupils report that they have excellent and inspiring teachers, though some are reportedly less than stellar. Computers are much in evidence throughout the college and banks of them are available and used in the library.

Around 12 students a year are selected for the Hampshire Specialist Music Course on which they study two instruments to a post Grade 8 standard as well as studying for music plus two or three further A levels.

Less academic students (about 100 of the total) can pursue vocational courses – foundation and intermediate level GNVQs and/or VCEs (vocational A levels) in such subjects as health and social care or business and finance – 'much more useful than re-sitting GCSEs and struggling with A levels'. Just four GCSEs are on offer, for retakes. Academically, the pupils are watched very closely and attendance is monitored electronically by lesson. Each pupil has a tutor (who is not necessarily teaching him or her) and regular tutorial sessions to monitor progress and prepare for university entrance. Falling attendance and not handing in assignments triggers action and a letter to parents. Predicted grade summaries are sent home three times a year but parents are only encouraged to parent-teacher meetings if there is a problem. Pupils report that there is all the help they need if they ask for it – but they have to ask for it. This is not an environment for those who need spoon-feeding and pushing along.Strong learning support system in place – those with learning difficulties are actively sought out and helped in the specialist department. Some 15 per cent of pupils benefit from some form of help including essay planning and self-organisation. Corridor to learning support centre lined with pictures of successful and famous dyslexics. Similarly, those aiming for Oxbridge or competitive courses such as medicine, vet science, physiotherapy have additional guidance and interview practice. Ofsted report of 2005 rated Peter Symonds College as 'outstanding'.

Games, Options, The Arts: Pupils must choose a minimum of one activity from a long list (50+) ranging from Amnesty International to windsurfing. Progress is monitored by personal tutors and used in reference writing for university entrance. A fifth of the courses are accredited, such as the Community Sports Leader Award and the Duke of Edinburgh award. Sports are very competitive because of the large size of the school – those who were used to being in a team cannot automatically expect to be selected to play for the College. Fundraising and local community work is greatly encouraged. Drama is strong because of the performing arts course. The college orchestra, jazz band and choir all perform to a high standard.

Background and Atmosphere: Peter Symonds originally founded Christes Hospitall (no relation to Horsham school) in the sixteenth century to look after aged brethren, assist two divinity students and educate four poor boys. Sale of land during the expansion of the railways at the end of the nineteenth century allowed a boys' grammar school to be built on the current site, becoming a sixth form college in the early seventies. College buildings located on top of a grassy hill overlooking the suburbs of Winchester and train station. Town centre and lure of coffee bars and shopping just a mile away. Original late Victorian building now completely converted into enormous and comprehensive learning and resources centre (library plus) and is surrounded by marvellous, dedicated buildings purpose-built in the last ten years. Everything being used to full capacity.

Pupils socialise in giant departure lounge style common room and outside in pubs and coffee houses. Large canteen provides cheap and plentiful food. No uniform (but all pupils tidy and purposeful, with backpacks and mobile phones). Teachers are called by their first names. Friendly, casual atmosphere. This is really a half way house between school and university.

Boarding is provided in 2 houses, both mixed single en-suite rooms to sharing with three others. Quiet study time for 2 hours each evening and curfew at 10.30. 'Very happy atmosphere' report boarders.

Pastoral Care and Discipline: Discipline minimal. Although there is a zero tolerance policy on drugs and alcohol on site, there are 2 designated (outside) smoking areas. Principal has expelled occasional miscreant for possession of cannabis. 'Litter is our biggest headache'. This sudden freedom can go to their heads but surprisingly few (3 per cent) drop out. No prefect system but elected student union handles social and philanthropic matters and is the student voice on college committees. Personal tutor system greatly appreciated by students to help them with progress and direction. Full-time counsellor available for personal matters. Very little parking for students.

Pupils and Parents: Intake is 40 per cent from the three main Winchester state schools plus Perins Community School in Alresford, 15 per cent from independent day and boarding schools and the rest from far and wide – Reading, Salisbury and Isle of Wight included. Principal says you can't tell what sort of school the students came from after the first few weeks and students confirm this. Student social profile directly reflects Winchester skew towards ambitious middle classes – one teacher remarked that there is 'nothing as formidable as a Winchester mother protecting her young'.

Entrance: Deadline for application – mid-March for starting in September. Non-selective – requirement for A level courses is a minimal five grade Cs at GSCE level, which should include maths and English. Some courses are over-subscribed and an unofficial geographical selection exists for these – priority is given to the Winchester state schools. Less academically able children are encouraged to pursue vocational courses. For the Hampshire Specialist Music Course candidates have to audition on two instruments, one of which should be at grade 7/8 standard. For boarding, priority is given to Falkland Islanders, Services children and those on the Specialist Music Course. Apply early for the few remaining places.

Exit: 85 per cent to universities of all descriptions, with a steady 45 to 50 to Oxbridge.

Money Matters: Students must pay for their own books, meals and transport. Hardship funds are available, at the school's discretion.

Remarks: A huge, friendly, highly successful sixth form college which falls neatly between school and university in approach. The self-motivated can take advantage of the myriad of A level courses and resources on offer.

PHILIP GREEN MEMORIAL SCHOOL

Boveridge House, Cranborne, Wimborne, Dorset, BH21 5RU

Tel: 01725 517 218

Fax: 01725 517 968

Email: pgmschool@hotmail.com

Website: www.pgmschool.net

• Pupils: 40 boys and girls (accommodation for 44 boarders): 24 boys board, 13 girls board; plus 2 day boys and one day girl
• Ages: 11-19 boarding, 9-19 day • Religion: Ecumenical
• Fees: Full boarding £8,204; day £3,397
• School status: Independent • School gender: Mixed
• Day/boarding: Takes boarders

SEN provision

Detail:

Experience of:

Mild: ASP; AUT; ADD; ADHD; EBD; DS; DYSP; HI; VI; CP;

Moderate: ASP; AUT; ADD; ADHD; EBD; DS; MLD; DYSP;

Severe: DS; DYSP;

Others: SPD; AUT(other); OCD; ODD; FRX; GEN; SLD; Sp&LD; DEL; Epi; Eat;

Summary: Philip Green Memorial School caters for students with moderate to severe learning difficulties and speech and language problems. It provides a fully differentiated curriculum linked to both the National Curriculum and a lifeskills curriculum. We cater for a wide range of genetic disorders such as Down's syndrome, Prader-Willi syndrome, Smith Magenis syndrome and Williams syndrome amongst others.

What we say about the school - the full Good Schools Guide review

Head: Since 1998, Mrs Lesley Walter MSc, CertRCSLT, PGCE, NPQH (fifties) who runs the school with a magic wand round a rod of steel (and known as the queen witch when she is cross). Educated at Tudor Grange Grammar School, Solihull, she did her speech therapy in Birmingham, her PGCE at Oxford Brookes and her Masters at City Uni, London. She is also a qualified child protection officer and head. Head-hunted from her previous school in Oxford where she was deputy, she moved her family lock stock and parents to Dorset and hasn't stopped since. Originally called Boveridge House, the school was started in 1971 by Miss Peggie Harper who believed it was possible to educate children with learning and behaviour problems but numbers had shrunk to 17 and the school was threatened with closure for multiple reasons. Enter a female dynamo who, by dint of charming, cajoling, and downright working the system, now fronts this independent residential special school for students with moderate to severe learning difficulities and speech and language disorders – and jolly successful it is too. She should be cloned.

Entrance: Children come from all over the place, from Inverness to the south of England. The school caters for a wide variety of disabilities – not just speech and language, but Down's syndrome, Asperger's, ADHD, Smith-Magenis syndrome and Prader Willi syndrome ('loads of syndromes here'). Most have a statement of educational needs and prospective pupils come for an initial visit; if that works well then they have a 'taster visit' – usually from lunch on Thursday till teatime on Saturday. The offer of a place at the school is dependent on whether the school thinks that the prospective pupil will fit in to this gregarious family and whether the staff and the existing pupils like them, 'mustn't make waves'. The pupils themselves are an important part of the acceptance procedure. 'If the face fits.'

Exit: To colleges and places of tertiary education all over the place. Mencap special needs colleges, plus agriculture or 'supported houses' with students following normal educational places plus apprenticeships. The school works quite hard to find suitable placements.

Money Matters: Most pupils are funded by their LEAs though some are joint LEA/parental efforts and there are a couple from abroad who pay the full whack.

Remarks: Glorious Georgian (1776) house with fab plasterwork and real Delft (unused) fireplaces (in upstairs bedrooms) surrounded by terrific Gertrude Jekyll-Thomas Mawson garden. Stable block undergoing continuous conversion, with new classrooms emerging almost on an annual basis. 38 acres in all, school lets out adjacent fields to local farmers, filled with over-wintering polo ponies when we visited. Main house stands up well to the children and much used and loved. Proper library, the quiet room in the house, divine ball room, used for assemblies and parties – Christmas ball about to happen post our visit, and lots of secret planning going on. Dining room with small tables supervised by a member of staff and real table napkins and rings. Whizzo bedrooms/dorms: timetables above most beds with notes from home plus glorious views; a buzzer on the door between boys' and girls' quarters alerts staff to hormonal wanderings – and these do happen. Currently two of the young, he with Asperger's, she with Down's, who have been an item for the past two years, plan to marry in Salisbury Cathedral when they leave in two years' time. Mrs Walter is expected to be bridesmaid, complete with long frilly pink dress, and their respective parents 'all get on'. But don't be fooled, the children operate within quite narrow parameters, all children have peer mentors, a designated key worker and each of the care staff has three children in their 'key family'. All are colour coded, those under 16 wear bottle green sweat shirts, older children navy blue, the care team wear navy and red (and all wear the brightest of red jackets when taking the children off the premises) teaching staff maroon and the gardeners, cleaners and cooks wear pale blue and navy.

This is a proper community, and involved in the larger locale. All the staff are important here, with children helping in the garden and with the cleaning though cooking is confined to food technology where results last year were absolutely stunning at entry certificate level (not surprising considering the state of the art kitchen provided by The Wooden Spoon – the England, Scotland, Ireland, Wales rugby charity). Mrs W has persuaded The Wooden Spoon to ante up for another classroom conversion, currently under way. The end goal is for pupils to achieve their entry qualification certificate; last year there were also successes in English, childcare and ICT plus a creditable number of GCSEs in English, maths and science, and last year five went on to further education, seven the year before – a steady trickle.

Proper computer room. No foreign languages on the curriculum, but parents can pay for individual lessons, ditto keyboard (£7.50 and £10 per half hour). Arts and crafts in the basement, locked (keys important) fire door, plus chill out areas. The huge rumpus room boasts a not yet finished mural on this term's theme: the Victorians – slavishly studied in class, with visits to Osbourne House on the Isle of Wight, trips to museums, by playing Victorian football (complete with tasselled caps). Two common rooms, well-used, and divided by age – for those over and under 16. All carefully supervised – there are never fewer than three staff on duty down here at any one time and safety and security are paramount. No side lights anywhere ('they would throw them at each other') and the local plasterers who were repairing a damaged ceiling in an upstairs classroom screwed the door shut at night to prevent youngsters doing a spot of 'tool release', however there are darts in the senior common room ('we move the cushions before we play'), and pupils do archery with real bows and arrows. They also go ten pin bowling, to the local RDA at Wilton, to the beach in Bournemouth, the cinema, theatre and ABROAD. Every two years those who are 'up to it' take off for a week's jollity, this year it was Holland and a couple of years back Paris. Real life skills stuff – in a foreign country. The school operates on the premise that 'there is no such word as can't' and whilst pupils follow as far as possible the full National Curriculum, they also follow a parallel life skills curriculum and lessons and topics flow seamlessly into post school activities with emphasis on independent living skills and how to manage money/banking, shopping, travel and social and personal relationships.

Lots of cuddles and giggles, the children were sassy, friendly and happy. And the parents we met equally happy; it was Friday pick-up time, but not all pupils were going home (though they have to some of the time, the school only operates for 38 weeks a year). Good to see children looking so smart (pig tails the thing for the girls and done by the care workers – one of the chaps is apparently the most adept) and having such (noisy) fun.

PLYMOUTH COLLEGE

Ford Park, Plymouth, Devon, PL4 6RN

Tel: 01752 203 300

Fax: 01752 203 246

Email: mail@plymouthcollege.com

Website: www.plymouthcollege.com

• Pupils: 280 girls, 360 boys. 105 boarders, the rest day
• Ages: 11-18 • Religion: C of E • Fees: Pre-prep: £1,779, Years 1-2: £1,867, Years 3-6 £2,000
• School status: Independent • Opendays: September
• School gender: Mixed • Day/boarding: Takes boarders

SEN provision

Detail:
Now provide for in school:
Mild: DYSC; DYSL; DYSP;
Moderate: MLD;
Experience of:
Mild: ASP; ADD; HI;
Moderate: DYSL; HI;
Others: OCD; Epi;

Summary: The school welcomes a pupil who has specific learning problems so long as, with help and support, the pupil can make sound progress through the school. The support depends on the nature of the difficulty but may be individual lessons or small group tutorials. Teachers will be informed as to how they can best help a pupil and parents are kept informed of progress and what is being achieved.

Where appropriate extra time is given in exams and word processors are used. Care is taken to bear in mind any difficulties with entrance examinations.

What we say about the school - the full Good Schools Guide review

Head: Since 1990, Alan Morsley BSc ARCS CMath FIMA FRSA (sixties). Maths graduate from Imperial College, London. Began career as maths teacher at Essex comprehensive. Also worked as house master and head of maths before becoming the head of a Yorkshire independent. Married with three grown-up children. Has a passion for the history of art. Also enjoys music and cricket. Concentrates on the management demands of the schools.

Retiring in July 2006, to be replaced byDr Simon Wormleighton who has been head of Grenville College in Devon for the past three years.

Academic Matters: Strong academically. At 95 per cent, the A* to C pass rate at GCSE is the school's best ever, with A*/A grades up around 45 per cent. 60 per cent A/B at A level. Very strong economics, physics and engineering students, winning top competitions. Upper sixth students provided two of the four teams in the 2005 national final of the business CIMA Management Challenge Competition – school were runners-up in 2004. Strong sciences and business studies generally. French compulsory from year 7. Students can choose Latin, German or Classical Civilisations in year 8.

Pushes strong linguists towards Latin – also useful for medics, lawyers and English experts. Small classes: two to seven pupils is common at AS and A level; the average is about 15 lower down the school.Hot learning support system with some 80 students including some very bright who have a mild specific educational need including three Asperger's. Will take dyslexics with reasonable IQ (this is a school for those who are capable of achieving a minimum of eight GCSEs) but not so geared up for ADHDs or those with general learning problems. Any stragglers will be advised to drop a subject and will receive extra help to concentrate on the main ones. 'It really helps your child be the best they can be.'

Games, Options, The Arts: Ample on-site sporting facilities. Excellent sporting reputation. Outstanding rugby teams with Devon Cup champions in each year group. Shares on-site swimming pool with Plymouth Leander club that sees pupils swim for Great Britain. Girls' team beat other independent schools in 2005 to become HMC Schools Champions for the third year running. County successes in netball, hockey, athletics, cricket and tennis. Plenty of practice, specialist teaching and performance rooms for music including a recording studio and performance hall with professional audio and lighting equipment. Discussion groups of a director, producer, editor, DJ announcer and publicity officer develop varied performing skills. Drama is not as strong here, although it is 'up and coming'. Separate art house houses fantastic artwork with extremely broad styles. Visiting lecturers from poets to sportsmen.

Background and Atmosphere: Acquired girl's preparatory school in 1995 and the nearby St Dunstan's Independent in 2004. 'It works very well with the Prep being on a separate site. I don't think four and 18-year-olds should be on the same site,' said the head. Founded in 1877, the site is a vast maze of large buildings with a myriad of corridors and doors creating an extremely quiet school. Must be somewhat daunting for newcomers. The students seem to have masses of space – a table or even a row each although the head is determined to reduce the number of pupils to 600. Not an elite or tough city school. Adopts a more gentle, seemingly laid-back air, perhaps quietly confident. However, in class the students are extremely attentive and studious – a dream for any committed teacher.

Pastoral Care and Discipline: No behaviour problems in evidence here. 'Very helpful' resident married housemaster and housemistress and a member of the sixth form team support boarders on a one-to-one basis or in small groups. Boys are accommodated in three houses on one side of the housemaster's home, with girls in the three houses on the other side. Lots to do for weekenders, from surfing to skating.

Pupils and Parents: Overall well-presented and polite individuals. Sixth form senior prefects adorned with graduate-style gowns when accompanying visitors or on special days. Varied social and professional backgrounds. Many from the local area whose parents work at Plymouth's Derriford Hospital. Some 10 per cent foreign nationals, including 50 from Hong Kong resulting from the St Dunstan's merger; some German, South Korean and African.

Entrance: Only mildly selective, so enormous range of ability on entry, following satisfactory performance in entrance exam. Typically lower ability than neighbouring grammars on entry but GCSE and A level results compete. Six passes including maths and English are required at GCSE, including a minimum of three B grades, to enter the sixth form. Some 70 per cent enter from Prep. Intake likely to be reduced, particularly fewer foreign nationals.

Exit: Half head for traditional universities but many are increasingly staying local. Aspiring doctors, surgeons etc look to the new Peninsular Medical Training School in Plymouth, others to Plymouth University for subjects like maritime studies.

Money Matters: Some scholarships and the odd bursary.

Remarks: A huge school with ample space, excellent teaching and many opportunities to excel.

PLYMSTOCK SCHOOL

Church Road, Plymstock, Plymouth, Devon, PL9 9AZ

Tel: 01752 402 679
Fax: 01752 484 018
Email: info@plymstockschool.org.uk
Website: www.plymstockschool.org.uk

• Pupils: 1575 boys and girls, all day • Ages: 11-18
• School status: State • School gender: Mixed
• Day/boarding: Day pupils

SEN provision

Detail:

Centre of excellence for:

Mild: ASP; AUT; ADD; ADHD; EBD; DYSL; DYSP; SpLD; HI; VI;
Moderate: ASP; AUT; ADD; ADHD; EBD; MLD; DYSL; DYSP; SpLD; HI; VI;
Severe: DYSL;
Others: SPD; AUT(other); OCD; TIC; EAL; Sp&LD; DEL; Epi; PD;

Experience of:

Mild: DYSC; CP;
Moderate: DYSC; CP;
Severe: ASP; AUT; ADD; ADHD; EBD; DYSP; CP;
Others: CD; ODD; Eat;

Summary: Plymstock School has two special needs provisions: an enhanced specialist provision for pupils with Autistic Spectrum Disorder, and a large thriving learning support department meeting the needs of students with a range of additional needs.

What we say about the school - the full Good Schools Guide review

Head: Since 2002, Dr Sean Sweeney (PhD MA BMus MIMgt (late forties). Honours graduate from University of Wales. Previous managerial posts included vice principal of Stoke Dameral Community College, Plymouth, and headteacher of Ridgeway School, Plympton. A studious looking man, passionate about sport and music. As a musician, he has recorded for radio and television and has made a CD of choral and keyboard music. At Plymstock, he has taught music and general studies and played piano for school productions. Dr Sweeney has high expectations of himself and others. He likes to keep his fingers on the educational pulse – part of editorial board for international teacher development journal, external examiner, chairperson of South West Educational Leadership. His energy and enthusiasm finds him in the thick of it – active in the classroom and local community, holding officer posts on the Community Council, Civic Society, Academic Council and Plym Adult Education Governors. Parents believe his enthusiasm rubs off on his pupils. Lives in Tavistock with his wife and three children.

Academic Matters: Top (75 per cent A* to C) at GCSE for Devon. 25 A level courses, besides good GNVQ, NVQ, RSA opportunities via a training consortium. Lots of awards.

Games, Options, The Arts: Excellent reputation for county, national and international sporting achievements – hence has Specialist Sports College status. Students clinched 2003 Junior World Championship title in Mirror Dinghy class. Enviably large, outdoor floodlit sporting area with flat grass track and netball/tennis courts. Parents believe separating boys' and girls' groups for PE works. The less academic will not fade here and budding acting professionals still have a chance with drama and performing arts A level. Growing percentage of students do PE, dance and sport studies. The art adorning the corridors shouts high quality. Parents impressed with varied range of musical and dramatic performances from Shakespeare to Rock and Roll. Work experience in Germany popular for A level German students – a big confidence booster.

Background and Atmosphere: Attractive school with garden courtyards. Teachers and parents work well together. Quiet and hard-working atmosphere of which it is proud. Recent investment of £5m has replaced temporary classrooms with well-facilitated dance and drama, modern languages, mathematics, pottery and sport areas. Science, technology and humanities refurbished. Plymstock keeps up with leading edge ICT development – electronic whiteboards in every department, digital music recording.

Pastoral Care and Discipline: Parents don't seem to be the worrying type as Plymstock has a reputation for finding and supporting everyone's talent. Enhanced Specialist Provision co-ordinator for communication difficulties and intensive numeracy and literacy programme for SEN in years 7 and 8. Good extension studies for gifted/talented students through faster moving classes, earlier entry into subjects, supportive services include reading and homework club. Bullying or behavioural problems are dealt with quickly. It's 'cool to be clever at Plymstock' so ridiculing swats is out. 'Unreserved support' for any necessary punishment is expected from parents. Wheelchair friendly.

Pupils and Parents: Mixed social backgrounds, although Plymstock is more affluent than many parts of Plymouth. Parents are 'proud' to send their children to Plymstock: 'It really encourages individuals to celebrate their talents'. Students believe they achieve because the teaching is good. Olympic swimmer and gold medalist Sharon Davies came here before winning a scholarship to Kelly College.

Entrance: Pupils from eight feeder schools: Oreston, Elburton, Hooe, Dunstone, Pomphlett, Goosewell, Downham, Wembury – belonging to The Plymstock (Plymouth) Area Academic Council. This family of schools communicates well. One per cent choose Plymouth grammar schools instead.

Exit: Approximately 65 per cent of year 11 students progress to Plymstock's sixth form, others head for the local College of Further Education, the College of Art and Design, employment based training and other schools. Plymstock regularly sends students to top universities, including Oxford and Cambridge.

Remarks: Highly successful and good all-round comprehensive in a pleasant suburb of Plymouth.

PORT REGIS PREPARATORY SCHOOL

Motcombe Park, Shaftesbury, Dorset, SP7 9QA

Tel: 01747 852 566

Fax: 01747 854 684

Email: office@portregis.com

Website: www.portregis.com

• Pupils: Pupils: 350 boys and girls (57 per cent boys), 265 board, 80 day • Ages: 7-13. Plus pre-prep (around 50 boys and girls ages 3-7) and nursery with 20 children

• Religion: C of E • Fees: Day £4,795; boarding £6,155

• School status: Independent • School gender: Mixed

• Day/boarding: Takes boarders

SEN provision

Detail:

Now provide for in school:

Mild: ASP; ADD; ADHD; EBD; DYSC; DYSL; DYSP; SpLD; CP;

Moderate: DYSL;

Others: EAL; Sp&LD; Eat;

Experience of:

Mild: AUT; HI;

Moderate: ASP; MLD; DYSC; DYSP;

Others: SPD; Epi;

Summary: The term 'special needs' should not be confused with 'low ability'. Experience shows that learning difficulties can provide challenges for the brightest of children. Identification and appropriate support for such needs should take place as early as possible during a child's time at Port Regis to avoid any loss of self-confidence and to ensure that the full potential of every child is reached.

Port Regis has a well-resourced specialist department of eight experienced and qualified teachers trained to teach children with dyslexia and other special needs. We are more than able to meet the requirements of all children with mild to moderate learning difficulties who can be catered for within the normal school curriculum and who do not require a specialist school. We also have specialist staff who can provide extra tuition in mathematics, Science, French and other modern languages.

What we say about the school - the full Good Schools Guide review

Head: Since 1994, Mr Peter Dix MA BA (Natal University) (fifties) who went into the stock exchange when he left Cambridge (Jesus, classics), then decided he would rather have less dosh and more fun, so went to teach at King's, Canterbury – for sixteen years. It is always an interesting transition to move from a senior school – albeit a senior housemastership – to a prep school and, in this case it has worked superbly. His wife, Liz, BA in fashion and textiles, which she teaches at the school, is very much part of the double act. Amused and amazed that we should previously have referred to him as 'a sensitive soul hiding behind a bland exterior' – Mr Dix would have preferred to have been called anything but 'bland'. Keenly aware that people are the most important aspect of school, he strongly believes in teamwork. Hot on emphasising the positive, heaps enthusiastic praise and encouragement on children. Teaches Latin five or six periods a week and would love to teach Greek, 'but the head of classics won't let me'. Two grown-up children.

Reckons he has been 'here long enough to feel the school is ours now' and 'that it is my staff'. When he reckons that staff are underperforming, he suggests they teach something else within the school. 'Getting staff motivated is the real key; if they are happy then they inspire the children'. He has – to date – resisted all approaches from the head-hunting fraternity. Hosts the new prep school heads (IAPS) conference every two years and is pretty well forming up to be the headmaster to whom all the other heads pay heed. Usual credo about wanting children to have really good self-esteem, confidence and self-worth. Keen on pushing the academic side but not at the expense of all-rounders.

Entrance: The comments about academia above notwithstanding, the school maintains it is not 'academically selective'. Name down early, school three times over-subscribed; interview and reports from previous school where appropriate (as much for the parents as for the child). Can come at any time if space available. Can meet the requirements of those with mild to moderate learning difficulties (dyslexia, dyspraxia, dyscalculia, ADHD and Asperger's) who can be catered for within the normal school curriculum and who do not require a specialist school. All new parents are asked to fill in an educational history questionnaire and to supply relevant background information including specialist reports. Stress this isn't part of the selection process merely ensures school does its best for each child.

Exit: Bryanston, Marlborough still the flavour of the month, plus Canford, both Sherbornes (boys' school whizzing up the popularity ladder) plus a whole raft of others – head says that pupils have gone to over 70 different schools during his tenure. Impressive and regular collection of scholarships in every discipline, art, sport, music and academic.

Remarks: Not quite sure where to start here. This is undoubtedly the best-equipped school we have seen in our time with the guide (all ten editions of it); with the exception of the prospectus which is word-light, glossy picture heavy. That aside, the school has had a peripatetic career; founded in London by Dr Praetorius in 1881, then via Folkestone, Broadstairs (where there was an arch commemorating the landing of Charles II in 1683 – hence Port Regis, gateway of the king) Bryanston, Hertfordshire, and back to Wessex, arriving at Motcombe Park in 1947. Slightly younger than the school, the house itself dates from 1894, Victoriana at its most exuberant, with oak panelling and a charming galleried hall – looks like a wasted space, but is much used by all. Pretty hideous really, it was built (all eighty rooms of it) for Baron Stalbridge, younger brother of the first Duke of Westminster.

Fabulous library and grand reception rooms, the fabric is in fantastic condition, as indeed are the 150 acres of grounds, groomed and immaculate: it could be a film set. The adjoining new dining hall is sumptuous, staff (green chairs for staff) and children still sit together; table napkins and 'seriously good food'; fruit available at all times, meals are a civilised experience.

The porch of the main building is filled, rather charmingly, with roller blades; pupils spend their free time merrily roller-blading on the carriage-drive in front of the house (recent traffic management scheme prevents anyone driving straight through). Younger children live in dorms on either side of the main stairway, boys to the right, girls to the left, with older pupils living in imaginatively designed cabin-type dorms, each cabin with a bed, a sink (as the young call them) and clothes and study space. The cabins can be divided but school prefers them not to be. Flexi-boarding on offer at weekends when there is often extra space – no set exeats (there is no space during the week except for the occasional 'taster' sleepover).

Parents a mixed bunch, army, expats plus foreigners, lots from Wessex and a fair number from further east; quantity of first-time buyers. All singing and dancing on the academic front – French from the pre-prep and Latin early, Greek for the top stream, plus German, Spanish, Italian, Mandarin and Hebrew options in the evening – Spanish is a mainstream alternative to French for weaker brethren. (Indeed loads of options in the evening.) Central library recently upgraded and 'book shop' every week so 'children can order what they want and put it down on the bill' – with parents' consent. (What are libraries for? we ask ourselves.) Remedial help on hand for the weaker souls but not too weak, you understand, getting much more academic. EFL for foreigners but not many of them. Computers all over the shop – very modern, flat screen jobs; and timetabled touch-typing. Impressive CDT, art (terrific) and science block which is better equipped than many senior schools we have visited. Children start with techno-lego and move on via electronics to drawing in perspective (they really ought to do their GCSEs in CDT at Port Regis). CAD/CAM, etc, They also have e-mail access for all.

Well-resourced educational support unit (ESU) staffed by eight experienced and qualified teachers trained in dyslexia and other special needs. Additionally, specialist staff provide extra tuition in mathematics, science, French and other modern languages, as well as EAL if needed. All pupils are assessed and any significant discrepancies between tests, or evidence of poor performance, will be investigated further. Likewise any child whom teachers, tutors or parents are concerned about will be given more detailed assessment. School happy to provide names of educational psychologists (EPs) on request; EP recommendations passed on to teachers and tuition arranged. Each pupil has own individual programme, devised in consultation with the head of the ESU and tutor; extra tuition can be requested without formal assessment. Some tuition takes place in small groups, typically of two to four children: curriculum flexes so those with more severe learning difficulties do basic skills instead of French (charged as extra). Extra lessons in certain subjects will be discussed with parents of any pupil who lacks either confidence or educational background or has difficulty with the curriculum.

Music is important here, with all 8-year-olds learning the recorder and 9-year-olds the violin. 344 individual music lessons a week, more than half learn the piano. Serious orchestras and choirs, all taking good advantage of the new music school built the edge of the (tiny) lake with a recital room overlooking the water. Boys can fish in the lake (mainly carp) with permission. Drama for every child every week, with a full-time drama coach. Wind in the Willows the latest offering – the National version, of course.

The facilities are outstanding: shooting range, nine hole golf course (locals can be members and can also use all the other facilities – at no charge for the local school); so are the various gyms – one huge sports hall, and one dedicated gym, used as the National Centre for Junior Gymnastics. Plus 25-metre swimming pool, astroturfs, squash courts, judo and karate hall plus 12 specialist coaches – natty in maroon polo shirts. Masses of county championships. Pets welcome and there is a lot of extra help from parents who run cookery classes and the like (checking up on the choccie content of the school larder before making brownies that afternoon when we visited).

This is school founded on 'core Christian values', they worship at the local church, pastoral care outstanding, 'bullying is any word or act which repeatedly or deliberately sets out to hurt another' and 'breeds on boredom and disaffection and an overtly authoritarian atmosphere'. No chance of that here.

Prior Park College

Ralph Allen Drive, Combe Down, Bath, BA2 5AH

Tel: 01225 831 000

Fax: 01225 835 753

Email: admissions@priorpark.co.uk

Website: www.priorpark.co.uk

• Pupils: 300 boys, 248 girls (74 boys board, 226 day boys; 43 girls board; 205 day girls) boarding year 9 upwards • Ages: 11-18 • Religion: RC • Fees: Boarding £6,356. Day: 13+ £3,525; 11+ £3,164 • School status: Independent • Opendays: October and March • School gender: Mixed • Day/boarding: Takes boarders

SEN provision

Detail:

Centre of excellence for:

Mild: DYSL;

Summary: Prior Park College provides very limited support for up to four children (for entry into Year 7 and a further four in Year 9) with very mild dyslexia. We accept up to 10 registrations for pupils who are seeking a place on our Learning Development Programme. Currently we are unable to accept any further registrations until 2008.

What we say about the school - the full Good Schools Guide review

Head: Since 1996, Dr Giles Mercer MA DPhil (mid fifties). Went to Austin Friars School, Carlisle then read history at Churchill, Cambridge, then on to St John's, Oxford. Started career as head of history at Charterhouse before brief spell as assistant principal, MoD. Subsequently director of studies at Sherborne, then 11 years as headmaster of Stonyhurst before coming to Prior Park. Married to Caroline with one son. Likes travel, art and music. A committed Catholic with a realistically broad approach. Compassionate, articulate and approachable. Keen to emphasise positive praise whenever possible and to foster a family atmosphere in the school. Seen as an involved, effective head by parents and pupils. Cares deeply about kindness between pupils and in leading his staff from the front. Believes in maintaining a boarding ethos and structure despite vast majority of day pupils at PPC. Parents amazed at how 'he really knows pupils as individuals.'

Academic Matters: Results impressive given the broad band of ability. English and history are strongly-led departments with outstanding results at both A level and GCSE. Music, design and technology and theatre studies are impressive whilst maths results are also good with more candidates. Fewer pupils opt for physics, chemistry or modern languages at A level but there is plenty to lure them elsewhere such as music technology, sport studies and theology which all do well by their followers. Most pupils take ten subjects at GCSE with particularly good results in sciences where pupils generally have a choice between separate or dual award entry. Almost all pupils take two foreign languages in year 9 and at least one to GCSE. There is setting in all subjects by year 9 apart from English except in small subjects where there is only one set. Class sizes do not exceed 23 and are generally much smaller in GCSE sets and beyond. An excellent and over-subscribed Language Development Programme (LDP) accepts four pupils into year 7 each year and addresses mild dyslexia and dyspraxia (Asperger's syndrome also accommodated). EFL available.

Games, Options, The Arts: Fields strong teams in all ages in the major sports (rugby, hockey, netball, tennis, cricket and rounders) with good use made of its indoor heated swimming pool, gymnasium and fitness centre. Games timetabled and do not squeeze out other activities. The nearby 'Monument' playing fields were acquired from the National Trust in a swap for the landscaped grounds to which the school still has access and the astroturf is adjacent to the school buildings. Use is made of superb athletics facilities at Bath University. Hilly surroundings well-suited to x-country including an idiosyncratic annual school relay event which engenders great excitement. Army and navy sections of the CCF, D of E with expeditions in the south-west and to Europe. Facilities, coaching and choice, particularly in the upper years, ensure that sports people are more than satisfied, with some playing at county level. The less athletic can find enjoyment and recognition too.

Exceptional diversity and quality in music, drama and dance with a majority of pupils involved in one or more activities. Julian Slade Theatre hosts wide range of musical and dramatic productions; well-equipped and brilliantly managed music department oversees five choirs, orchestra, chamber strings, quartets, piano trios, jazz band, wind band and rock bands. Magnificent new classical organ was installed in the college chapel in 1996 and the chapel choir has toured extensively in Europe. Pupils have won places at all the major music colleges and several pupils are currently members of leading national youth orchestras. Boys as well as girls take dance within theatre studies and high octane performances are much appreciated. Performing arts generate a tremendous buzz. Despite a reputedly strong art department there could be more evidence of visual arts around the school.

Background and Atmosphere: Founded in 1830 and run by the Christian Brothers until 1981, Prior Park is now the largest independent, co-educational, Catholic day and boarding school in the UK. Only 20 per cent of all pupils are boarders, but the proportion increases to about one third from year 9. And with 40 per cent practising Catholics, PPC does not feel like yet another largely day school with token boarders or nominal religious affiliation. It is also unmistakably co-educational with fairly even numbers of boys and girls throughout. The magnificent Georgian architecture with a view from the 'mansion' over the grounds (much of which are now National Trust property including the famous Palladian Bridge) and Bath stretching out beyond is unsurpassed. The mansion has been painstakingly renovated and completely refurbished since the 1991 fire destroyed much of the interior. The College Chapel accommodates the whole school for weekly assemblies and mass, held roughly once each half term, plus particular feast days. Boarders have to attend mass on Sunday mornings and theology is compulsory throughout. The well established PSE programme also reflects Catholic thinking and the resident school chaplain plays a central role.

ICT has a new centre and is networked throughout including in the well-resourced and study-friendly library. Day pupils have a nominal workspace in their rather crowded house accommodation where daily prep is supervised between 4.45 and 5.45pm. Junior pupils are split into small vertical groups which counters the risk of year eights dominating. Roche and Allen are relatively civilised boarding houses for boys on the upper floors of the mansion whilst girls are accommodated in enviable surroundings in St Mary's house which occupies the nearby 'Priory'. Some day pupils opt to be in boarding houses because they prefer the ethos and flexi-boarding is popular. Most of the residential staff are Catholic as opposed to 40 per cent as a whole.

Pastoral Care and Discipline: The reward system is central to the head's philosophy and breeds a positive approach to work and behaviour. There is little evidence of a punishment culture. Pupils are generally well turned-out without being ostentatious. The deputy head is respected for being 'firm but fair' and remarkably there have been no expulsions in recent years. There is a strong counter-bullying policy. There is a good mix of 'old guard' and new staff with an average age in the common room around forty-one. All sixth formers are expected to involve themselves in running the school. Food gets a thumbs up, esp the baked spuds.

Pupils and Parents: Most come from within an hour's drive. Six daily mini-bus and coach routes transport day pupils from a 30 mile+ radius including a 7:15am start from junction 16 on the M4 which makes one wonder why those pupils don't board? Boarders generally come from further afield including a fairly traditional mix from overseas. Relatively few foreign nationals most of whom are Catholics from the Far East. Former pupils and current parents are very supportive with a range of fund-raising and social events and pages on the school website. Famous old boys include Cardinal Cormac Murphy-O'Connor, archbishop of Westminster, the impresario Sir Cameron Mackintosh, international rugby player Damian Cronin and television presenter Hugh Scully.

Entrance: Registration at least eighteen months before entrance is recommended. January entrance tests for either two or three form entry at 11+ with entrants coming from local 3-11 or 7-11 preps and about 20 per cent from state primaries. Lists close at least a year in advance for LDP applicants. About 40 pupils join at 13 with about half of them from the junior school at Cricklade, Wiltshire. November interviews for entrants into lower sixth who need a satisfactory reference and a minimum of 6 A*-C grades at GCSE with higher grades in chosen AS subjects.

Exit: Almost all to universities with Cardiff and Liverpool the most popular choices in recent years. Nine per cent to Oxbridge. Many take a gap year. A few leave after year 11.

Money Matters: Not a school for the super-rich – no five star frills. Range of scholarships and bursaries with good academic scholars typically gaining 30 per cent off fees. Services bursaries. Currently around 150 award holders. Some continuity scholarships from junior school. Generous discounts for siblings. Bus services charged monthly and quite pricey. Music tuition fees excellent value for money.

Remarks: A school which has transformed itself over the past twenty years and where most pupils will feel happy and busy. A strong Christian rather than heavily Catholic feel to the place. 'Non-Catholics are made to feel welcome and involved,' said a recent leaver. Talents can blossom here without fear of censure from peers. The only school in Bath to run along boarding school lines, even for day pupils.

QUEEN ELIZABETH GRAMMAR SCHOOL (WAKEFIELD)

154 Northgate, Wakefield, West Yorkshire, WF1 3QX

Tel: 01924 373 943

Fax: 01924 231 603

Email: admissions@qegsss.org.uk

Website: www.wgsf.org.uk

• Pupils: 720 boys • Ages: 11-18 • Religion: Inter-denom • Fees: £2,632 • School status: Independent • Opendays: Early October • School gender: Boys • Day/boarding: Day pupils

---

SEN provision

Detail:

Now provide for in school:

Mild: DYSL; DYSP;

Experience of:

Mild: ASP;

Summary: The learning support department at Queen Elizabeth's Grammar School provides continuous support for pupils at both the junior school and senior school. The SENCo is a qualified teacher of dyslexia. The department is expanding and with effect from

September 2005 there will be two members of the team. Provision includes work on: study skill/organisation, revision skills, a multisensory literacy programme, reading courses, diagnostic testing and exam concession reporting. It is a thriving department; main aims are to raise self-esteem and give the pupils the skills and strategies needed to take control of their own learning.

What we say about the school - the full Good Schools Guide review

Head: Since 2001, Mr Michael Gibbons BA AKC PGCE (forties), educated at the City of Leicester Grammar and read a double whammy history and theology at Kings, London before becoming an accountant in the City for a couple of years. Then back to do a PGCE and variously taught at Ardingly before becoming housemaster at Rugby, thereafter second master at Whitgift. An incredibly fast talker, ideas and enthusiasm come pouring out. Delightful turn of phrase – 'Gentlemen, can we please be gentlemen,' seemed to do the trick quite nicely. (The miscreants concerned shut up with alacrity.) Teaches some RS. Slightly anxious about HMI inspection, imminent at time of writing (can't see why). Married, with a son in the school and a daughter in the senior school. 'Really like it here, it is easy to be biased but I am enjoying it'. Made a 'positive choice' to come here and very much wants to 'lift the school and genuinely serve this community, with a really great school in south-west Yorkshire, doing all the things that (senior) schools should do'. Wants to strengthen the academic and help children from all backgrounds to realise their potential and aim for excellence. Numbers rising again after the Assisted Places blip.

Academic Matters: New appointment of assistant head (pastoral). 'Reasonably healthy turnover, and good mix of youth and experience in the common room'. School now operates a ten-day revolving timetable, with six fifty-minute lessons a day. Strong across the board with commendable results and, whilst still bursting with mathematicians, biology popular. English and humanities are equally good. French and German on offer to all, plus Spanish, business French and Latin. Business studies and some languages studied with the Girls' High across the road, and there is much to-ing and fro-ing across the cobbled lane. Exam results for GCSE in 2004 were good – 29 per cent A*; 69 per cent A*/A and 93 per cent B. Five parallel classes each year, max at bottom of the school 22/23 per class. Work clinics for all at lunchtime. No setting (though given the desired academic thrust, this may not be too far away?)

Computers throughout, and 'loads' of interactive whiteboards. Good remedial help on hand for mild dyslexia and the like, can 'cope' with mild Asperger's. Children are automatically screened and additional help can be organised, usually at lunchtime, laptops allowed. Fantastic double-decker library, with false floor through which the brill Victorian roof is clearly visible, the new build will return the library to an archive area and, though they would dearly love to remove the false floor, it looks as if it could be quite expensive. New build, due late 2005, includes a 240 seat theatre, learning resources centre, library, sixth form centre and English department.

Games, Options, The Arts: Art continues to blossom, both curricular and extra-curricular, still a good and popular A level subject, plus all the add-ons – terrific art department in the top of the school with masses of light. Screen printing, photography, etchings. Outstanding music, the brass section wins prizes, over 300 individual players, swing band (played in front of the Queen during her Jubilee) and junior swing bands (hired out for local weddings and things, the dosh earned funds trips abroad). Concerts often held in Wakefield Cathedral, where the junior boys provide choristers, joined by girls from the High School (BBC said second only to St Paul's). Music is often a joint activity as, indeed, is drama – Kiss Me Kate and The Mikado recent productions. School has 'use of' over 27 acres of playing fields, the senior boys play 'up the road' (which is also used by the nearby Police Academy as a helicopter landing pad – great excitement). Pavilion opened in 2000 as well as the new sports hall with special 'resilient' flooring, which is used by local rugby team and came on stream in 1999, state-of-the-art facility, and hired out to locals. Training pool for junior school only, seniors use the pool in town. This is a games school, oodles of Internationalist old boys in the field of rugby – including Mike Tindall, and masses of trips to South Africa, South America, Australia and hockey to Canada, cricket team to the West Indies. Plus cultural tours. Bridge and chess clubs well attended and 300 regularly take D of E.

Background and Atmosphere: QEGS (pronounced kwegs) for short. School founded by Royal Charter in 1591 and moved to present site in 1854. From 1944-76 it was a direct grant school and reverted to fee-paying in 1976. Marvellous Victorian Gothic façade hides a multitude of extensions and make-overs, some very imaginative and some less so. Junior school also on site, and they play games on the grass in front of the school.

Pastoral Care and Discipline: All boys carry record book at all times (homework diary) which incorporates the school rules and can be inspected by staff at any time and must be signed by parents at preordained levels. If a boy misbehaves in public, the line is to remove the record book which is then sent back to school, and the owner will be reprimanded. Ladder of sanctions, Friday afternoon staff detention for minor sin, Saturday morning (real bore, no school otherwise apart from games) detentions for more serious matters and an essay, 'set according to pupil's requirements'. Good bullying policy. Keen to educate, school holds strong beliefs and expectations. Advanced pastoral system in place, tutor first point of enquiry, followed by referral to head of year. 'No problems this year' with drugs, but automatic expulsion. Smoking equals detention, three detentions equals suspension. Suspensions and exclusions for bullying, vandalism and aggressive behaviour. Tough, but it works. NB school will also 'kick out' underperforming pupils.

Pupils and Parents: Wonderfully close to the motorways and bus and rail stations; a timetable comes with the prospectus; wide catchment area. QEGS is the 'only' acceptable alternative to the state system for miles around and progressively getting more middle class as the middle classes prefer to keep their little darlings at home. Good strong work ethic. Parents and pupils must make a 'positive choice' to come here. Fair assortment from ethnic minorities. Good breeding ground for bishops, Lincoln and York; plus John Scott, director of music at St Paul's and a tranche of internationalists.

Entrance: Not automatic from junior school, transfer is based on academic record and satisfactory results – 'may toss out if not up to it' – but less than 5 per cent each year (two or three). Those from the junior school make up 60 per cent of the first year intake, the rest coming either at 11 or 13 – most come at 11. Pre-test CE, plus interview, and then on basic CE results. Oversubscribed, last year 110 applicants applied for 47 places (the answer of course is to start at the junior school). Pupils come from local preps – though most of these now seem to go up to 16; plus state primaries. Baseline qualifications for entry at sixth form are 6 GCSEs (but most come with 7 or 8) with at least two As in subjects to be taken at AS/A level. Essentially school is looking for an 'aggressively' academic pupil, though whole lifestyle will be looked at, no 'bias to sport, music or drama'. Boys can and do move into the school at other times, subject to academic OK and space available, 'penny numbers' says the head.

Exit: Some post-GCSE occasional dropouts, one or two to art foundation courses, ditto to employment, a handful to Oxbridge, the odd one to re-takes or improved offers but the majority to degree courses all over Britain – Sheffield, Durham, Newcastle, Leeds and London the favoured destinations. Medicine and law popular.

Money Matters: Was hit hard by the end of Assisted Places. Part of the Ogden Trust (which supports 32 former state high or grammar schools with bursaries for 'talented children through independent secondary education regardless of parental ability to pay'). Bursaries of up to 100 per cent plus travel, uniform and school trips. Children must be in the state sector, high scoring at Key Stage 2, with parental income of less than £30,000 per annum. State 'education maintenance allowance', available nationally to keep pupils in sixth form, school will top up if necessary. Sprinkling of other scholarships and bursaries (which are awarded post exam and reviewed annually each year, so – no work = no sub) plus music and sixth form schols. Bursaries for choristers in junior school, paid 50/50 by school and Cathedral, but only whilst boy is in the choir. Ogden Trust sixth form science scholarships available (worth up to 100 per cent of fees) each year for a student wishing to study maths/science at A level.

Remarks: No change. The best boys' city day school in this area. Serious, unpretentious former grammar school. Results up, intake up, and very tough. Could one need more?

QUEEN MARY'S SCHOOL

Baldersby Park, Topcliffe, Thirsk, North Yorkshire, YO7 3BZ

Tel: 01845 575 000

Fax: 01845 575 001

Email: admin@queenmarys.org

Website: www.queenmarys.org

• Pupils: 215 girls; 55 boarders, mostly weekly, a dozen or so stay at weekends, plus flexi-boarding • Ages: 3-16
• Religion: C of E (Woodard school) • Fees: Reception £1,620. Pre-prep £1,950. Senior prep day from £2,990; boarding from £4,380. Senior school day £3,630; boarding £5,040
• School status: Independent • Opendays: October and April
• School gender: Girls • Day/boarding: Takes boarders

SEN provision

Detail:

Now provide for in school:
- Mild: ASP; ADD; DYSL; DYSP; HI;
- Moderate: ASP; DYSL; DYSP; HI;
- Severe: DYSL;
- Others: SPD; FRX; Epi; Eat;

Experience of:
- Mild: ADHD; EBD; DYSC; CP;
- Moderate: ADD; MLD; DYSC;
- Others: OCD; ODD; EAL; Sp&LD;

Summary: Queen Mary's is a friendly, family school and the SEN department sees itself as the hub of that environment. Any girl can visit us at any time during her school life here for whatever difficulty for as long – or short a time as it takes to set her back on the rails. The most common difficulties are dyslexia, dyspraxia and Asperger's. The department has a literacy specialist, a numeracy specialist and an early years specialist and between us we cover most problems. We also run workshops for the whole school on study skills and revision techniques.

What we say about the school - the full Good Schools Guide review

Headmaster: Since 2003, Mr Robert McKenzie Johnston MA (Cantab) (fifties), known as Mr MJ (as in emjay). Previously joint head with his wife Kate at Hanford, he was educated at Rugby, read economics at Cambridge, and taught at Shrivenham. No PGCE, grandfather's rights. In a former life he was Lt Col in the Queen's Royal Lancers, though he no longer uses the title and can't believe how lucky he is to be at Queen Mary's. The MJs live in the house, and his wife Kate, an occupational therapist, is now an assistant in the nursery: 'such fun, a perpetual three-year-old birthday party'.

Ebullient, sensitive and very on the ball, the MJs arrived at the school after a period of great turmoil; the previous heads (who did wonders re-decorating the inside of the main house)had left after a fraught proposed amalgamation with Cundall Manor, and the school had been under the guiding hand of previous much-loved heads, long since retired, Peter and Felicity Belward, for a couple of terms. Mr MJ arrived to 'a school full of tension, worry, with no development plan', 'full of lovely dedicated staff', some of whom had been in situ since the school's previous incarnation in Duncombe Park. Certain number of staff changes; the head of English, who left to teach A levels, has been replaced, and there is a new whizzy head of art. Mr MJ teaches maths to the C stream (who all therefore passed maths GCSE last year – a first for the school). The MJs' daughters come and go, living in the school when they are at home. With so few full-time boarders, the MJs treat the weekending girls as an extended family, with 'jolly trips all over the place'. As they work every weekend they take Wednesdays off and go hunting locally. Not a PC head then! Twiggy is a much loved lurcher, often amongst the children.

Academic Matters: No A level stream. This is a very mixed ability school and all take English, maths and the sciences, most (nearly all) French as well; French starts early. French e-mail exchange with school set up by previous French assistante. 'It is good because you can practise your grammar. It makes it a lot easier in exams!' seems to be the general opinion of the pupils. Excellent showing across the board at GCSE, with a pleasing number of As and A*s. Classics on offer at 11, but not that much take-up further up the school until recently, new classics-teaching chaplain has turned the tide and a couple of girls are now learning Greek as well. German results consistently good and the humanities well represented.

Streaming and setting, tiny classes. New timetable. Good and sensitive dyslexia help, with great celebration when the most dyslexic pupil in the school got her five Cs last year. Buzzy library with sagbags. Classrooms in the main building and converted outhouses, plus stunning new build for tinies. Science department boasts a greenhouse and freshwater pond for hands-on experience. A goodly supply of computers throughout, plus dedicated IT rooms, many of the girls also have their own laptops; Internet OK, but girls not allowed to used hotmail (chatrooms). Senior girls do coursework online. Tinies have computers too, and good basic three Rs in the lower school. Thirty-five staff on hand plus 12 part-timers. School never closes and girls can be found wandering around in the Easter holidays having been 'doing extra workshops' with the staff, who never seem to take holidays either.

Games, Options, The Arts: Long time head of music can't quite understand why the school does not 'revolve round music' and the place hums with junior and senior choirs and natty concerts and concertettes open to the general public as well as for inmates; impressive for a school of this size. Chapel choristers wear much coveted green sweat shirts and give regular performances both home and away. Stunning art in the attics under new head including creative textiles and ceramics, sewing machines in the DT room. Home grown art all over the place. Drama good and popular, everything about this school spells fun. Cooking timetabled, the smell of frying onions pervading the steps to the art room (instant hunger pangs and we had just had lunch).

Trad sports, with lacrosse, athletics and tennis teams all doing well. Superb equestrian facilities, children can and do bring their own ponies and ride daily (Mr MJ has started the children riding before breakfast in the summer months), outdoor manege of Olympian size, as well as rides across the local landowner's fields, Mr MJ in constant negotiation with his neighbours to increase riders' scope, cross-country course on site. Tadcaster polo club is nearby and looks like becoming the next horsy activity. Terrific little swimming pool (though the surrounding wood panelling needs help – new estate manager should help with maintenance) and tiny adjacent fenced in area for littlies. Climbing frames. Superb selection of expeditions for all, plus D of E. Canoeing on the adjacent River Swale popular in the junior school.

Background and Atmosphere: Baldersby Park is a grand Palladian mansion (Colen Campbell 1721, Jacobethanised following a fire in 1902) and was converted into residential flats in a previous existence so the girls have a rash of good sized dorms with private bathrooms. Posh. Splendid library in the former ballroom presided over by a rather dreary portrait of Nell Gwynn (why?). Glorious main hall used for daily service, with the girls sitting on the carpet, Mr MJ sitting in front of the stairs, the choir ranged behind him in serried ranks. School uniform evolves over the years with girls graduating from beige jerseys to green jerseys and royal hunting Stewart tartan kilts, slight pressure currently to change the uniform but neither the MJs nor the girls can see the point.

Staff and pupils bring their pets to school and girls are happy with the relaxed atmosphere – like an extended family – all ages mix – with a mass of sisterly teasing. Prefects lock up at night, though they may come and get Mr MJ if it is dark and they have to check the stables. Charming new-smelling chapel, resident chaplain, Mr MJ is keen that religion should be 'part of the school routine' but not rammed down the throat. The early assumption of seniority (at 16 rather than 18) gives girls confidence and maturity. All pupils have to play some part in keeping the school neat, clean and tidy. Really helpful and supportive gang of governors.

Pastoral Care and Discipline: Like home. No petty rules, and others which are bendable but there is an underlying sense of organisation. 'Suspension,' says Mr MJ, 'is a sign of failure on the part of the school and not the pupil'. Parents' requests granted when reasonable. Not a sophisticated place, no obvious sin.

Pupils and Parents: Local as opposed to county school, combination of first time buyers, local farmers, landowners and professionals and has long since shed the image of the school that looks after the daughters of local nobs. Relaxed 7.30 drop off time for working parents. Quite a lot of army families, Catterick is just up the road, some of whom pop their daughters in the school 'whilst they are based in Yorkshire' and are so pleased with the place that they leave their darlings there when they are posted elsewhere. Quite a lot of flexi-boarding, with some full-time boarders living closer than some of the day girls, ditto the flexi-boarders. ('Girls come to escape.') If girls regularly stay three nights a week they get their own permanent space rather than living in truckle beds, no charge for extra meals, only for bed. Boarding mainly from 11, and day girls often opt to stay at least on a weekly basis. Parents and pupils can use school facilities in the holidays. No real overseas presence, one or two expats. Parents run a website and are delighted to answer any queries.

Entrance: At any time, middle of term if needed. At all ages. Testette but only those with special needs beyond the school's capability are liable to be turned away.

Exit: At all ages. Some take common entrance at 11, some at 12 and some at 13. Girls have previously mainly gone to Queen Margaret's Eskrick, with one or two to Tudor Hall, Heathfield or co-eds, Uppingham, Millfield, Rugby. None appear to be leaving at this stage in 2006. Senior girls go on to do A levels at Ampleforth, St Aidan's, Ripon Grammar, Oundle, Queen Margaret's Eskrick, Uppingham etc. etc. Good collection of scholarships, music predominates, plus academic and sports.

Money Matters: Not a rich school and not endowed but scholarships for academics, music, art and sport plus bursaries for clergy daughters, sisters and Services discount.

Remarks: Useful, popular, small, girls' – predominantly weekly – boarding school without a sixth form. A home from home and a good education too. Needs one or two more bums on seats but, under the inspired guidance of (we think) one of the best headmasters around, this shouldn't prove too much of a problem.

QUEEN'S COLLEGE

Trull Road, Taunton, Somerset, TA1 4QS

Tel: 01823 272 559
Fax: 01823 338 430
Email: contact@queenscollege.org.uk
Website: www.queenscollege.org.uk

• Pupils: 710 boys and girls (160 boarders, 550 day)
• Ages: 11-18 • Religion: Methodist foundation
• Fees: Junior day £1,377-£3,342 boarding £2,629-£4,929. Senior: £3,792 day; £5,724 boarding
• School status: Independent • Opendays: A whole college open day in October and 2 further days for junior school
• School gender: Mixed • Day/boarding: Takes boarders

SEN provision

Detail:
Now provide for in school:

Mild: ASP; ADD; ADHD; DYSC; DYSL; DYSP;

Summary: We have been helping young people with dyslexia for over 28 years. Our pupils have access to the whole curriculum and are encouraged to aim as high as their academic abilities permit. Our dyslexic pupils generally do very well indeed in public examinations, many gaining an impressive number of A grades at GCSE, AS and A2 before progressing to university.

Our specialist staff, who are highly experienced and comprehensively trained, work in a well-equipped and centrally-located suite of rooms.

We are a dyslexia-friendly school and all staff receive regular in-service training to keep them up-to-date on specific learning difficulties and with useful classroom strategies which they can implement to help pupils who have difficulties.

Teaching is based on the widely accepted multi-sensory approach but we believe that there isn't one magic method that suits everyone so approaches and techniques are chosen which will be appropriate for the individual. Each pupil works at his or her own pace and for each individual the ultimate goal will be different. Pupils generally have one individual lesson each week and support continues for as long as the need exists. There is an additional charge for this support.

What we say about the school - the full Good Schools Guide review

Head: Since 2001, Mr Christopher J Alcock BSc FRSG (mid forties). Geography and anthropology graduate of Durham University, 1981. After PGCE, taught geography at Stamford School where he was boarding housemaster and rugby coach. Became deputy head of King Edward's School, Witley, in 1997. Relaxed, self-assured and pragmatic nature seems to be rubbing off on pupils. He takes an 'omni-present' approach – tries to watch every match, debate, concert performance, play, sporting fixture. Married with two sons at the school, one in senior and one in junior.

Academic Matters: 'Everyone has the chance to fulfil their potential here', said the head girl. Good raw GCSE and A level results – even better on value-added. Passionate about accelerated and individual learning – evidently working. Broadly follows National Curriculum. Huge investment in high-speed IT network linking 150 computers, mainly grouped in one of three dedicated suites including for science but many positioned in individual classrooms. It makes parents, pupils and staff proud – 'enviably this improves resourcing to enhance pupils' work'. Interactive whiteboards are also seen as an asset. Excellent teaching quality in modern languages, resulting in good marks, compensates for the bare and uninspiring classrooms, with little to show for resources.

Multi-sensory approach used to teach dyslexics, often on a one-to-one basis, although methods and techniques are adapted to suit the individual; good exam performance as a result. Supportive of SEN children generally; pupils withdrawn from classes rather than taught in class. Allowed the space to be what they are: dyspraxics thrive in individual sports like diving; ADHD pupils are allowed to 'fiddle quietly' with Blu-tac under the table. Pupils can (and do) come up to the SEN department at any time for support, advice and TLC. Informs/enlightens all colleagues about SEN difficulties through special booklet and guidance notes and through INSET. Liaises with tutors and house parents to make sure SEN children are happy and well cared for. Each pupil gets an individually designed programme to suit his/her unique needs. Expect as much from their SEN pupils as they do from the rest. Currently has former SEN pupils studying medicine, dentistry, marine biology, chemistry etc.

Games, Options, The Arts: Leadership, teamwork, confidence and self-esteem encouraged through broad, cross-curricular programme of music, drama, art, sport, Duke of Edinburgh Award and outdoor pursuits. 'You don't need to worry if your child isn't sporty as they'll soon find a sport to suit,' comments a parent. 30 acres of enviably flat playing fields, quaint benches and trees line the sides. Impressive, high-tech gym for sixth formers and staff.

A suitably noisy art room allows students to express their ideas and creativity freely. D of E is popular among pupils and staff alike – in year 10 every pupil is expected to be involved at bronze level, for older groups it is optional. Community service and charitable work comes about both under the formal D o E umbrella and via various activities specific to the school. Staff willingly give up their time to run activities as diverse as rock-climbing and computer training. 'There's something to suit every whim,' said a parent.

Background and Atmosphere: Relaxed, peaceful and friendly atmosphere. Somehow has a hint of mainstream openness about it. Sixth formers looking like they're allowed to be teenagers – chilling in the corridor, a cool kiss or hug here and there, chatting and milling in the students room. However, on entering the well-resourced, well-used media-friendly library, students knuckle-down to work. School motto 'nonscholae sed vitae discimus' ie 'We learn not for school but for life' – is followed today as it was when the school was founded in 1843. Elegant 19th century buildings combined with state-of-the-art science labs. Average class size: 17. Committed and happy teaching staff of high calibre, some who have written internationally recognised textbooks on their subjects.

Pastoral Care and Discipline: 'The pastoral care is fabulous,' say parents. 'Never heard of any bullying'. 'If you treat others the way you wish to be treated yourself then you can't go far wrong,' says head. Parents feel the house system is 'broad and challenging' but 'friendly and family-orientated'. It was the 'family feel-good factor that struck me when I visited Queens.'

Pupils and Parents: From various social backgrounds. 50 per cent of borders are Services children, the rest from all over the country and beyond.

Entrance: Broad intake. Pupils at 11, 12 or 13 sit school's own entry papers in English, maths and verbal reasoning or Common Entrance. Sixth form entry is dependent on good GCSE results and, for newcomers, a sound school report.

Exit: 65 per cent leave with all As and/or Bs. Most secure places with the Russell group of universities. Medicine, veterinary science, law and arts are popular. Dyslexics to a notably wide range of subjects: art, biology, chemistry, dentistry, electronic engineering, environmental sciences, geography, history, international business, medicine, PPE (politics, philosophy and economics) and law.

Money Matters: Awards up to eight academic scholarships a year, worth up to 50 per cent of fees. A music scholarship was won by girl in Kuala Lumpur after she auditioned via video link. Up to three boarding scholarships for seniors. Sibling discounts. A couple of boarding bursaries care for juniors whose parents fall on hard times.

Remarks: An interestingly confident school with effective teaching strategies.

Queen's Gate School

133 Queen's Gate, Kensington, London, SW7 5LE

Tel: 020 7589 3587

Fax: 020 7584 7691

Email: registrar@queensgate.org.uk

Website: www.queensgate.org.uk

• Pupils: 270 girls; all day • Ages: 11-18 • Religion: Non-denom
• Fees: Junior £2,900-£3,050 Senior: £3,625
• School status: Independent • Opendays: October
• School gender: Girls • Day/boarding: Day pupils

SEN provision

Detail:
Now provide for in school:
Mild: DYSC; DYSL; DYSP; SpLD;

Summary: SEN details added by us. Quite good for dyslexia etc, in our view

What we say about the school - the full Good Schools Guide review

Principal: Since 2006, Mrs Rosalynd Kamaryc, previously head (for ten years) of Wykeham House School in Fareham. Took over on the retirement of Mrs Angela Holyoak, the most elegant head we have interviewed and a terrific head all round.

Academic Matters: Small classes, max 20, vaguely streamed, half-termly tests, girls move up and down. Pupil:staff ratio of 7:1 which is impressive – 'good staff fairly thin on the ground' – not, you understand at Queen's Gate, where 'contracts for new staff are half a term's notice on either side during the first half term, thereafter a term's notice.' Following an earlier 'incident', all short-listed staff 'are required to teach while observed by the head of department and the principal or the head'.

Stunning male head of science (fair number of teaching chaps in evidence) who teaches chemistry, is justifiably proud of his pupils' 100 per cent As success at A level. Dedicated labs in the basement and three separate sciences taught from 11. However, sciences still the pretty poor relation, with tranches taking classical civilisation, history of art, art, theatre studies and Eng lit. Lots of desktop publishing and study skills masquerade as English. History popular, and at uni level. Languages stronger at GCSE level than at A. French, German, Italian and Spanish offered, all taught by native speakers with masses of hands-on and trips abroad. Latin for all for the first two years, and a certain take-up at GCSE. Maths (regular Monday maths clinic) and geography making a good showing. An interesting collection of specialisms: sociology, graphic communication/products and information studies. Mrs H disputes our comment that, 'this is not a place you would choose for a straight up and down academic', pointing to a string of recent successes – As across the board and honours degrees thereafter (engineering and maths would you believe), but this is a school for girls of mixed ability and they do jolly well.

Tellies, videos and computers in most classrooms, serious computer suites (cool new machines), all learn word processing, and do touch-typing in the junior school. Dyslexia provision, dyscalculia, dysphasia, you name it, two individual lessons a week. EFL as required. Not keen on behavioural problems – 'though', said Mrs Holyoak, 'there is usually a reason for it and school can often work through it.'

Games, Options, The Arts: Good sized gym, marked out for fencing in the mews of the middle house, and an impressive string of wins on the games field. Girls are bused to Battersea for tennis, rounders, hockey and basketball, and to the Kensington Sports Centre to swim and use their sports hall. Fantastic roof conversion for art suite, with fabric design, screen printing, CAD-CAM and a clever new vinyl cutting machine, lots of real hands-on stuff. Good strong work on show, much of it research based. Use made of local museums, art galleries and theatres.

Drama vibrant – the latest production was As You Like It, performed at Imperial College, the girls do everything – play every part and design the sets. Regular end of term house plays in impressive new hall (converted across two of the houses, much fund-raising, runs into the Internet library). Most take the LAMDA exams in acting and the speaking of verse and prose. Terrific music, chamber orchestra, individual lessons and popular singing; girls join the W11 choir and take part in West End musicals, much visiting the West End for opera and musicals too. Clubs for almost everything at lunchtime, girls must go to two a week, the range is huge, everything from debating, yoga, jewellery making and cookery (microwave). Hot on charity, with regular fund-raising events, and particularly keen on cancer research – sponsored readathons, spellathons.

Background and Atmosphere: Founded in 1891, the school is based in three large Victorian mansions in South Ken. The head points out that 'we've more space than you might imagine' but former broom cupboards in erstwhile mansions of this size provide useful dark rooms/tutorial rooms and offices. Immaculate, the place has recently been rewired to allow for computer/Internet access throughout. The school spreads into the mews behind and all but one of the rooms have at least two fire exits – some of them about five feet high. New pupils should probably be issued with a map, compass and bits of chalk for orienteering practice in their first few weeks.

Two libraries, not snazzy enough says the last inspection report, well-used careers library. Lots of the old features still remain, imposing marble fireplaces, ornate cornices and fire doors make curious companions. Sixth form common rooms dotted all over, ditto fifth form – much talk of tidying them up for our visit. They were – very. Walls filled with photographs, children's work and noticeboards, and a sense of calm prevails, girls remarkably well behaved, stand up when the principal enters, but sadly, they no longer curtsey or wear white gloves (haven't for years). No official uniform: T-shirts, skirts and jerseys, no facial or body piercing. Food excellent, vegetarian option, older girls may bring packed lunches which they eat in their classrooms, otherwise the whole school eats in two sessions in either the white or the black (definitely the grander) dining room. Coffee bar in the basement.

Pastoral Care and Discipline: Two of the sixth form girls are attached to each of the younger forms as 'sisters' – 'often easier to confide in than a member of staff, after all,' said our informant, 'they leave'. Mrs Holyoak is passionate about discipline, 'won't tolerate drugs', but equally won't deliver 'blanket' punishments, each case is treated individually, and wouldn't comment on 'any disciplinary subjects in school'. Not many rules. Three roll calls daily, in the morning, after lunch and before they go home, 'we are in loco parentis'. Tutor system for all (they meet twice a term). Good PSHE system in place, outside counsellor, health adviser, vigilant for anorexia.

Pupils and Parents: We would stick with our previous comment, 'pretty upper class' – 'wide range of parent' says the principal; fair enough, from a range of ethnic backgrounds, though principally of Sloane extraction. A good number of foreigners, encouraged by the principal as long as their English is up to it, 'this is London and we're a cosmopolitan city' – useful network for later gap and other travel too. Girls are fiercely loyal, delightfully mannered and very pretty. OGs: Redgraves, Sieffs, Guinnesses, Amanda de Souza, Jane Martineau, Nigella Lawson, Lucinda Lambton, Camilla Parker Bowles and Tracey Boyd, Aurelia Cecil and Suzanna Constantine. The new head of MI5, Eliza Manningham Buller, used to be on the staff.

Entrance: From junior school – three quarters of junior girls come on to the senior school – and a huge variety of other schools, confirm entry for the January exams the November before you want to come. Above all priority given to sisters and OGs' children. New arrivals throughout the year, but preferably in September, though pupils who have left and have then been unhappy at their new school often re-join again mid-term. School holds three open days a year for potential parents and it is not unusual to have 800 parents attend. Girls take London day schools' exam for entry at 11, assessment and test for entry at other times. For sixth form entry five A*-C grades with at least A in subjects to be studied at A level and B in AS subjects. Usually over-subscribed, but, because of the volatile nature of London, places do occur all over.

Exit: Tiny dribble to Oxbridge, strong medical faction at the moment, most take a gap year, otherwise to unis all over, Durham popular, some to art school. Small leakage after GCSE to other London day schools, co-ed boarding, or local sixth form colleges, either because they want a change, or a larger variety of A levels.

Money Matters: Two internal scholarships for sixth form entry.

Remarks: Plus ça change. Charming popular school, with a mixed intake, which does jolly well by its girls. Touch of the Miss Jean Brodies.

Reigate Grammar School

Reigate Road, Reigate, Surrey, RH2 0QS

Tel: 01737 222 231

Fax: 01737 224 201

Email: info@reigategrammar.org

Website: www.reigategrammar.org

• Pupils: 535 boys, 325 girls; all day • Ages: 11-18
• Religion: Non-denom • Fees: £3,303
• School status: Independent • Opendays: Main open day in October, open afternoons every month during term time
• School gender: Mixed • Day/boarding: Day pupils

SEN provision

Detail:

Experience of:

Mild: ASP; ADD; ADHD; EBD; DYSC; DYSL; DYSP;
Moderate: MLD; DYSL;
Others: Epi; Eat;

Summary: Reigate Grammar School is open to applications from any prospective pupil with a physical and/or mental impairment. The school's policy is to apply the same admissions criteria to all pupils and potential pupils regardless of any disability of which it is aware, and not to put any disabled pupil or potential pupil at a disadvantage compared to any pupil who is not disadvantaged because of a disability. All applications will be judged fairly and the school will consider any reasonable adjustments that may need to be made to cater for the child's disability.

When applying for a place, parents are asked to write to the Headmaster setting out the nature and extent of any disability, and whether or not they wish the school to take any disability into account during the admissions process.

The school currently engages two part-time learning support tutors, who are available to work with pupils on a one-to-one basis. This service is designed to assist those pupils with mild learning difficulties such as dyslexia or dyspraxia. However, the tutors' time is limited and this service is not suitable for pupils who need more help than one session each week can provide.

What we say about the school - the full Good Schools Guide review

Head: Since 2001, Mr David Thomas MA (forties), educated at Magdalen College School, Oxford where he was a chorister and later an organ scholar at Queens College Oxford. Followed a musical teaching career and was previously deputy head at Trinity, Croydon. Married to Andrea, an historian, who also teaches part-time at the school, they live in a beautiful house adjacent to the school. 'One of the main attractions of the job,' he jokes. Very business-like but friendly and easy to talk to, he enthuses about his school, 'I'm a big fan of co-ed and I love the atmosphere of this place'. Mr Thomas is very visible around the school and the children respect that – 'he comes to loads of sports matches,' said a pupil. 'A top man,' said one parent. 'The kids really like him and he's turned the place around,' said another.

Academic Matters: Strong. 75 per cent A/B grades at A level, GCSE results equally good with 60 per cent A*/A grades. Head believes the school is about more than just academic work. Generally good standards of teaching and super IT facilities with networked classrooms and interactive whiteboards. The aim is for all pupils to leave with IT qualification from the Microsoft Academy – very useful in the real world. Mr Thomas is a big fan of IT and it shows throughout the school – electronic registration is very efficient and the staff even have their own IT trainer. Well-stocked library stays open after school for homework and private study.

About 40 students with a range of needs receive help from two part-time SEN teaching staff. School is happy to discuss whether it can provide the right support for those who need it. But it would take careful consideration as to whether a SEN pupil would be happy here, as there is quite an academic pace. Those who receive extra tuition do so at extra cost to parents.

Games, Options, The Arts: Sports teaching is exceptional. Stunning 32 acre sports complex at Hartswood (about two miles from the school), complete with astro pitches, cricket field, athletics track, golf course and pavilion. All pupils are bused there to spend at least one afternoon a week taking part in a variety of sports. Netball, hockey and rounders for the girls, rugby, cricket, hockey for the boys. School is renowned for its prowess on the rugby pitch and proudly claims to field up to 18 teams on match days. Most matches are played on Saturdays, the school is mega competitive and always up there at inter school sporting competitions – the high numbers who take part are expected to show a huge level of commitment. Surprisingly little complaint from the less sporty souls, as swimming, tennis and visits to the local leisure centre for badminton and squash are also on offer. Heated outdoor pool on the site only used in the summer.

Music, art and drama receive a lot of praise from parents. Art building has an impressive range of facilities, students' work is frequently exhibited within the school and often achieves some of the best exam results. Music teaching is excellent; good facilities, opportunities for all to join in. The head continues to teach some A level music classes. 'It's my haven in the week,' he says 'and it's a good reminder of the staff workload.' Super drama department led by 'an inspirational teacher' according to parents, puts on several productions each year. Lots of individual drama successes including two students who have won places at the National Youth Theatre. Numerous after school activities including all the usual; CCF is well supported as is DofE.

Background and Atmosphere: Founded as a boys' school in 1675 and became a grammar school in the nineteenth century. Girls in the sixth form from 1976 when it became independent and fully co-ed from 1993. Located minutes from Reigate town centre, school is housed in 'hotch potch' of buildings – some very old and in need of replacement but many newer and very attractive. Outside space is at a premium. Quite a walk from class to class and to different buildings. Our pupil tour guides were none too keen on the footpath by the cemetery in the winter! 'The food is good,' say pupils and staff alike. Lots of choice. All meals served in a light airy building: 'the best place in the whole school,' said one pupil. Bit of a crackdown on uniform recently but generally not overly strict – 'life's about more than uniform,' says the head. On the whole pupils look smart – a few need reminding to tuck their shirts in and Mr Thomas does so quite regularly. More relaxed for sixth formers but still within guidelines – quite unusual but popular especially with parents.

Pastoral Care and Discipline: Head only gets involved in really serious issues and readily involves parents. Sixth formers apply each year to become mentors to the younger ones through their first years at the school. 'My mentor's lovely,' said one pupil 'she even bought me a Christmas present!' 'It's a very good idea,' commented one parent, 'although I'm not sure they get involved in serious problems – it seems to be more about going bowling and having fun.' New pupils are invited to an admissions evening in June when they are formally welcomed to the school by Mr Thomas in full cap and gown. 'Parents love it,' commented staff, and 'it's an excellent photo opportunity,' said one proud father. Comprehensive parents' handbook of school life and each term parents are invited to a parents' forum to discuss issues such as bulimia, exam stress, drugs etc. Pupils discuss the issues during the day and parents are invited in the evening. Parents find these very informative and useful – but several comment that they would like more time to discuss their child's progress on an individual basis.Discipline fairly relaxed, pupils are given space to 'get it right' and are encouraged to feel they can talk to teachers about any problems they have. Clear alcohol, drinking and smoking policy – the head and staff have dealt with occasional breaches swiftly. Very little evidence of bullying – in fact quite the opposite – but staff don't pretend it doesn't happen.

Pupils and Parents: A very unpretentious place – parents say it is just like the state grammar schools they used to attend. Pupils are a likeable bunch – confident but not full of themselves and very honest. Pupils mainly from the affluent Reigate and Redhill area and the surrounding Surrey towns. Parents from a wide variety of backgrounds: professionals, former pupils, but also plenty of first time buyers. Mega cool rating for its former pupils with many notable Old Reigatians: Norman Cook (aka DJ Fat Boy Slim) and BAFTA winning writer and comedian David Walliams are the most famous as far as pupils are concerned. Many old pupils return to the school to talk about their careers and experiences – a recent visit from David Walliams and his 'Little Britain' co star Matt Lucas was very popular with pupils and staff alike!

Entrance: Selective but not excessively so, although two applicants for every place in 2005. Majority enter at 11+, small number at 13. The school sets its own entrance exam in verbal reasoning (from 2006 this will be computerised with sample questions on the school's website), English and maths. Interview is given equal importance as is the report from previous school. The school places emphasis on academic achievement but wants to give more children an opportunity to apply, so a new test has been designed in consultation with several local state primary schools who gave it the thumbs up. Approximately 50 per cent of the pupils come from state schools, particularly Reigate Priory Junior. The rest from local preps including St Mary's Prep, which is now amalgamated with Reigate, although admission is by no means automatic. Other regular feeders include Mickelfield, The Hawthorns and New Lodge School.

Exit: About 15 per cent leave after GCSE, usually to attend the large local sixth form college. Of those who stay, around 98 per cent go on to traditional universities eg Durham, Edinburgh, York and Exeter; 5-10 students each year to Oxbridge.

Money Matters: Scholarships have a fixed value of £1,000 pa, but parents can apply for a means tested additional fee reduction up to 90 per cent. In addition, the school operates its own Assisted Places Scheme for gifted children whose parents cannot afford the fees; again this is means-tested.

Remarks: A good all round school with a strong head. Not at all posh.

Repton School

Repton, Derby, Derbyshire, DE65 6FH

Tel: 01283 559 220

Fax: 01283 559 223

Email: headmaster@repton.org.uk

Website: www.repton.org.uk

• Pupils: 595 total – 345 boys, 250 girls; 457 board, 138 day. Plus prep school 'Foremarke Hall' • Ages: 13-18 • Religion: C of E (other faiths welcome) • Fees: Boarders £7,060 day £5,240 • School status: Independent • Opendays: September • School gender: Mixed • Day/boarding: Takes boarders

SEN provision

Detail:

Now provide for in school:

Mild: DYSL;

Experience of:

Mild: DYSC; DYSP; HI;

Moderate: MLD; HI;

Severe: HI;

Others: Epi; Eat;

Summary: At Repton, we place a high value on our learning support both in terms of those with mild learning difficulties and the gifted and talented. Under the guidance of our Director of Learning Support, pupils are tested on entry and those pupils with mild learning difficulties are assisted with supplementary tuition in literacy and/or numeracy in the first year of the curriculum and then to GCSE. However, it is a vital part of our philosphy with regard to learning support that it continues throughout a pupil's time at Repton, until the Sixth form if necessary. Information on pupils' learning support requirement is shared across the curriculum.

What we say about the school - the full Good Schools Guide review

Head: Since 2003, Robert Holroyd MA (mid-forties). Educated at Birkenhead and Christ Church, Oxford. First in modern languages. Still takes French and Spanish at Repton twice a week as 'floating' teacher, stepping in where timetabled tutors allow. Previously head of department and housemaster at Radley College. Wife Penny also a teacher but now fully involved in life of school community. 'We function very much as a team,' he says. Devoted to Repton and all it stands for. Delights in having raised its profile since his appointment. 'I inherited a terrific ship and we have tried to maintain the core values of the school,' he says. 'But you won't catch us standing still.' Fervent believer in co-education. Good cricketer at Oxford, still enjoys choral music and drama. Big plans for the future. Has two daughters at Repton and its prep.

Academic Matters: Strives to extract the best from its broad intake – and frequently succeeds. Sound but unexceptional past exam results well and truly put in the shade by more recent year-on-year improvements. Latest available figures (2005) show 98 per cent overall pass rate at GCSE, 67 per cent of them A* and A. In fact every pupil got at least five A*-C grades with eight among the top marks nationwide. Top A level grades also up 4 per cent. Of the overall pass rate of virtually 100 per cent, just under a half were As, with nine students gaining four or more top grades. Lots of As taken a year early too. Most subjects set according to ability. Traditional teaching methods with all teachers living on site or in village – key to the success, says head, of the all-round boarding experience.

Good blend of ancient (library in Old Priory building) and modern (all pupils have free Internet access and own e-mail address). School's first ever full-time librarian actually in process of dragging library into 21st century after school inspectors twice highlighted it as weakness. 'I was surprised at the state the library was in when I got here,' head told school magazine, the Reptonian. Cataloguing and re-stocking now well underway, also refurnishing and carpeting planned 'to make it a more welcoming place where students will want to spend some time to read or study'. Plans include installing ICT and DVD technology in adjoining room to bring old and new learning tools together. Should be ready 2007. Computers currently located in other areas and pupils encouraged to bring own laptops for use in boarding house studies. Wide choice of subjects on offer with business studies, PE, theatre studies and IT more recent additions.

Appointment of new academic 'tsar' has seen more outside involvement in school curriculum with top business names invited to lecture students. Has also introduced electronic reporting on pupils' progress. Parents get usual end of term reports as well as mid-term updates on effort and achievement. Learning support for dyslexics. Two hours plus extra tuition a week can be given in most serious cases, though might be at the expense of French classes. Information and strategies passed to subject teachers to ensure support continues in class. Good teaching environment, new classrooms with state-of-the-art interactive whiteboards under construction, staffed by dedicated team. Students report tutors will 'go the extra mile'. Head can't speak highly enough of them! Those we saw appeared to have boundless enthusiasm and energy to spare. Prep 7-9pm each evening for both boarders and day pupils – only youngest supervised, rest work independently in house studies.

Games, Options, The Arts: Sport now in league of its own. At time of visit school celebrating huge national success. Girls' 1st XI hockey champions (U-18s) and boys victors in U-18s tennis. Repton has long been outstanding tennis school, recommended to parents by the LTA. Played all year round on outside and indoor courts. Now equally strong in hockey, much thanks to vast sports hall and similarly vast astroturf pitches. Cricket is no slouch either with county and test cricketers regularly produced. And whereas most independent boys' schools still favour rugby as the major winter sport, Repton remains among the handful to stay faithful to football – again with considerable success. (Girls also play football here, sadly with less success to date.) Large indoor pool (also used by locals). Popular extras include D of E, while CCF is compulsory for all for some time. Three half days (Tuesdays, Thursdays and Saturdays) leave time for matches and non-curricular activities. Drama thriving at all age levels. Great competition between houses. Two theatres; a small hall and a more traditional school hall waiting for a facelift. Music also flourishing, with regular choral performances and trips abroad, orchestra and variety of bands from string ensembles to rock. Best bands even get chance to record. Immensely impressive art studios. Work on show was of extremely high standard and shown prominently all round school as well as at some local businesses. (Money made from hiring out pieces goes into pot to fund foreign trips for art students.) From fine art to sculpture to wall hangings – so big, bold and brilliant. Also plenty of scope for budding photographers and architects. Old squash courts due soon for transformation into new textiles school. Where will it all end?

Background and Atmosphere: Found on the banks of the River Trent, it's absorbed into village of Repton rather than dominating it. Boarding houses can be found up leafy lanes, art department tucked down a side street, sports centre and games fields alongside another. Pavements regularly populated by throngs of well turned-out boys and girls making their way from one part of school to another. With a busy B road running through the middle, Repton was never going to be a sleepy idyll, but the school lends a certain vitality. Founded under the will of Sir John Port who died in 1557, school is fast approaching its 450th anniversary. A Bloody Mary Foundation, with a long and interesting history dating back to the medieval monastery, the peaceful heart of which still exists (minus the cloisters). Chapel a key part of weekly routine with evensong and Sunday services. Head says, 'all faiths come along to chapel and they love it. If someone from another faith wants to be excused they can be but no one has asked me yet.' School once boys only, fully co-ed since 1991. Boy/girl ratio roughly 60/40. Correspondingly there are six boys' boarding houses to four girls'. House system still very strong – all pupils return to houses for both lunch and tea. All food cooked in-house and given big thumbs up by regular diners. Small two- to four-bed dorms, sixth formers have own study bedrooms. All-age mixing in communal areas but separate common rooms for juniors and seniors 'just to give us our own space'. Emphasis on homely with mistress/master in charge seen as 'house parent'. As one girl told us, 'it's so nice to be able to take a break from whatever's been happening during the day and be with the family in your house. It's very special.'

Pastoral Care and Discipline: House system again all important. All new arrivals (whatever age) given a 'buddy' (existing Reptonian) to show them the ropes. Pupils encouraged to turn to more senior students, house parents or matron with problems. Plenty of 'motherly' input in both boys' and girls' houses. Miscreants dealt with severely though. Zero tolerance of drugs, demonstrated recently with five expulsions. 'My first and hopefully my last,' says head. Smoking and drinking both yellow card offences. Bullying (yes, there is obviously some but we are never complacent, insists head) is handled more sensitively with all parties getting involved. Parents encouraged to get involved in school activities at every level and contact with staff can be as often or infrequent as they want. Three exeats by arrangement. Some local pupils allowed to nip home on Sundays – after chapel. Good relationship between teachers and students seems based on mutual respect.

Pupils and Parents: Overall a very down-to-earth bunch. Pretentions go un-nurtured. Hard work is rewarded and with 97 per cent getting the 5+ C grades at GCSE needed to gain entry to the sixth form, is, more often than not, delivered. Uniform is compulsory – black suits and ties for the boys, grey plaid skirt and blazer for girls who can accessorise with their own choice of one-colour V-neck jumper 'for that bit of individuality'. Pupils are polite, easy-going, confident. Past OBs and OGs include author Roald Dahl, columnist and TV presenter Jeremy Clarkson and Lady Carole Blackshaw, Lady Mayoress of London. No one particular type of parent here. Some good northern hard-graft, others from the Cheshire corridor and a good smattering of professionals as well as plenty from overseas.

Entrance: Largely from own prep (sited nearby and co-ed since early 1970s). Rest from growing array of other prep schools. Head says recent good exam results making Repton first choice further afield. Common entrance pass mark required around 50 per cent but can be flexible. Takes those with special needs who can cope with the curriculum. Majority are dyslexic but can cater for others, including dyspraxics and those with severe hearing impairment. Considers needs on individual merit. As well as five Cs at GCSE, potential sixth formers also need at least Bs in chosen A level subjects. But again, rule not written in tablets of stone and other strengths will be considered.

Exit: On average, 11 students to Oxbridge, bulk of rest to northern universities, but business, drama and art all have their followers at various destinations.

Money Matters: Scholarships a-plenty. Worth up to 50 per cent of fees. Offered as academic awards, also art, drama, music and sport. Also exhibitions of around 10 per cent of fees. Open to pupils at 11, 13 and sixth form. We are assured that school's five year development plan (including new classrooms, new science centre, reworking of library, large theatre and music school and new textile school) will not mean big hike in school fees.

Remarks: No bargain but value for money. So much on offer, such an all-round experience. Repton is impossible to pigeon hole. Why would anyone want to send their child here? 'We have a strong emphasis on the whole person,' says the head. 'It's standards without snobbery. They come out of Repton proud of their schooldays but able to look out beyond the school.' A feel-good school filled with real youngsters happy to be themselves.

Riddlesworth Hall Preparatory School

Diss, Norfolk, IP22 2TA

Tel: 01953 681 246

Fax: 01953 688 124

Email: enquiries@riddlesworthhall.com

Website: www.riddlesworthhall.com

• Pupils: Nursery, prep/pre-prep – largely girls, but boys now progressing from the nursery and pre-prep; boarding from 7yrs (half of over-7s board) • Ages: main school 4-13; nursery 2-4 • Religion: C of E • Fees: Day, £1,950-£2,835 Boarding £4,620-£4,935 • School status: Independent • Opendays: Autumn and spring terms • School gender: Mixed • Day/boarding: Takes boarders

SEN provision

Detail:

Centre of excellence for:

Mild: DYSC; DYSL; DYSP; SpLD;

Moderate: DYSC; DYSL; DYSP; SpLD;

Severe: DYSC; DYSL; DYSP; SpLD;

Now provide for in school:
Mild: ASP; AUT; ADD; ADHD; EBD;
Moderate: ASP; ADD; ADHD; MLD;
Others: EAL; DEL;
Experience of:
Mild: CP;
Moderate: CP;
Others: FRX; Epi;

Summary: The specialist learning centre at Riddlesworth was created in 2004 to enable children with specific learning difficulties to receive the help they need within a Preparatory School environment. This is an arrangement unique to East Anglia and to only one other Prep School in this country. It is recognised and registered by CReSTeD – the council for the registration of schools teaching dyslexic pupils.

The centre operates within the heart of the school so that children can come to one-to-one or small group lessons during the day. For those children needing more intensive regular help we also offer parallel class groups. These children receive all their English and maths teaching within the centre, returning to the main school for all other areas of learning. The centre uses a variety of approaches to tailor individual programmes to meet the needs of every child. Phono-Graphix and the Lindamood Bell 'Seeing Stars' and 'Visualising and Verbalising' are very powerful systems which help children with specific learning difficulties, dyslexia etc. The result is great success in returning children back into the mainstream with little or sometimes no support. We work very closely with parents so that very specific needs are met together as a partnership. Consultations with parents are held on a regular basis and parents are updated as to the progress of the children. We are successful because we nurture each child. Ensuring that children are emotionally happy and ready to learn is paramount at Riddlesworth.

All outside agencies such as speech therapists, language therapy, educational psychologist etc. are available and visit the centre on a regular basis. The curriculum is based on the National Curriculum and Common Entrance Curriculum. Extra subjects such as study skills, organisational skills, memory strategies, form an important part of the Specialist Learning Centre curriculum. At Riddlesworth Specialist Learning Centre we use Phono-Graphix to promote reading and spelling. Research has shown that Phono-Graphix is a powerful and effective tool for dyslexic children. The programme can be delivered much more quickly than traditional methods and removes the worry that spelling patterns are never-ending. Our aim is to have children reading in the shortest possible time. Without doubt the use of Phono-Graphix has achieved accelerated reading improvement with all our pupils across the age range. Mrs Campbell, Head of the Specialist Learning Centre, has been involved in much of the original research when Phono-Graphix was first introduced into the United Kingdom and has had eight years experience in teaching the programme.

Maths teaching is done through various methods including the 'On Cloud Nine' maths programme devised by Linda-mood Bell. Children can be given support in one-to-one lessons, small groups or within larger classes with targeted help. The aim of the Specialist Learning Centre is to provide an excellent education, enabling children to master basic language and mathematical skills so that they can achieve their potential in mainstream classes. We strive to nurture each child, restoring confidence and developing positive attitudes to learning. This is done in a caring and warm family atmosphere. The children are given the skills and tools to overcome their difficulties and build self-esteem. The school is 'dyslexia friendly' where every teacher in the Specialist Learning Centre and main school understand and are sympathetic to, the challenges faced by children with specific learning difficulties.

Ratios of staff to pupils in the Specialist Learning Centre is no more than 1:6. All staff are qualified and experienced teachers holding Phono-Graphix and Linda-Mood Bell diplomas and diplomas in the assessment and teaching of children with specific learning difficulties and in the education of children with special needs. There are excellent links with the prep school and there are regular meetings with all school teaching staff, ensuring that everyone is kept fully informed of progress.

What we say about the school - the full Good Schools Guide review

Head: Since 2000, Mr Colin Campbell BA (fifties), educated at King George V School and read philosophy at Sussex. Previously deputy head of Belmont School in Surrey where he helped build up decimated school numbers from 90 to 200 pupils. Kind, warm, dedicated and pleasantly dreamy. Enjoys mountaineering and sailing and is introducing outdoor pursuits like scuba diving, sailing and mountain biking to the school. Wonderfully energetic wife, Julia, is head of early years department and also takes charge of special needs. She is full of fun and drive, clearly an equal partner in the Riddlesworth enterprise. Two daughters – one at St Andrew's University, the other at nearby Culford School.

Entrance: By assessment and interview. Most come from East Anglia but a school bus brings girls up from London each Sunday evening and returns them on Friday night (also daily buses to Diss and Bury). Academic scholarships for boys up to age 8 and girls up to 12 (maximum of 50 per cent of fees) and small music and art scholarships.

Exit: Most at 13, some at 11, to a wide range of jolly nice schools. Over the last three years, girls have gone on to Benenden, Gresham's, Millfield, Oundle, St George's Ascot, Badminton, Heathfield, St Mary's Wantage, Culford, Gordonstoun and Tudor Hall, to name a few. Regular schools too.

Remarks: Riddlesworth Hall made headlines in 2000 when, owing to falling numbers, the Allied Schools decided to close it. White knights, Colonel Keith Boulter (owner and head of the co-ed prep Barnardiston Hall, Haverhill) and the Reverend David Blackledge, rode in at the final hour, but not before many more parents had yanked their kids out. The new head is rebuilding the school from the bottom up (reception class is full, and numbers generally are rising strongly). He is also improving special needs provision, running more short courses for foreign youngsters (he hopes these will be reciprocal), increasing parent involvement and admitting more boys into nursery and pre-prep. An International Study Centre is being developed in the former nursery – now relocated to the main school.

Main school is housed in beautiful Georgian-style listed stately home, set in rolling lawns deep in farming country. Facilities are good for a school this size – luxuriously warm indoor swimming pool, three tennis courts, an adventure playground, hutches for pupils' pets – 'Pets' Corner' – and a wonderful feel of fresh air and open skies. Rosy cheeked, unspoilt girls walk arm in arm, and 13-year-olds still happily play with their guinea pigs. Inside, besides classrooms and pretty dormitories, lurks a good library, a decent science lab, Harry Potteresque stairways leading to mysterious rooms and passages, lots of music practice rooms, a small games room with pool table and a spectacular common room (newly revamped with glorious stuffed sofas so it looks like what it is – the sitting room of a great country house). School grub dished up in quaintly old-fashioned basement dining room (though parents speak of international days when ethnic cuisine emerges from those institutional kitchens). Academically, the school is very, very sound, shattering a decades-old reputation as a school for nice but thick country lasses. The small class sizes, dedicated teachers and individual attention have produced superb exam results (four scholarships won by recent leavers). Girls who might just drift along at other schools become high-flyers here.

Lots of games – these are competitive girls and, despite the low numbers, go on winning. Nor have low numbers hurt the range of extra-curricular options: dance, speech and drama, swimming, gym, tennis, martial arts, archery, riding four times a week and a highly successful equestrian team – pupils stable their own ponies at school – singing and tuition in a range of musical instruments are all available. 'Nearly every' girl is learning a musical instrument, says the head. The school offers brilliant flexibility – any eccentricity or interest can be accommodated and day children can stay from pre-breakfast to 8.30pm or even overnight. The school's 'family feel', individual attention and full weekend programme for boarders (including 'boarders' Friday night outings') would also suit expat families (there are special scholarships for military and diplomatic offspring). 'All the day pupils are dying to be boarders,' said one local mother.

Ages 4-7 housed in pretty former stable block opening onto own playground next to main building. Reading is brilliantly taught using the Phono-Graphix method. Everyone can read by the end of reception year (this is a school where it is common to find 3-year-olds reading).

The school is heading in a promising direction and is well worth a look. Five years from now we can foresee it being a happy, co-ed, multinational school for 2-11-year-olds. One of our favourite Riddlesworth Hall rules is, 'Be happy and cheerful'. The children seem to have no trouble following it.

RNIB New College, Worcester

Whittington Road, Worcester, Worcestershire, WR5 2JX

Tel: 01905 763 933

Fax: 01905 763 277

Email: kcampbell@rnibncw.ac.uk

Website: www.rnibncw.ac.uk

• Pupils: 75 girls and boys. 2 day, 73 board • Ages: 11-19
• Religion: Non-denom • School status: State
• School gender: Mixed • Day/boarding: Takes boarders

SEN provision

Summary: The College caters for students with a visual impairment, who are able to acess the National Curriculum at levels 2-7 at Key Stage 3 and Entry level and GCSE courses at Key Stage 4. In the Sixth form most students are studying for a wide range of AS/A2 subjects, with many going on to Higher Education. We also though offer a very flexible curriculum which could include GCSEs, ASDAN and numeracy and literacy courses. All students have mobility training, independent living skills training and ICT support as appropriate. The college also offers a very wide range of extra-curricular activites, including music, sport and drama.

The college is able to support students who have additional needs, including hearing impairment, physical disability, Asperger's syndrome, autistic spectrum disorders and social and communication needs.

What we say about the school - the full Good Schools Guide review

Principal: Acting principal, since 2004, Ms Mardy Smith MA PGCE NPQH QTVI (early fifties). Read education at Warwick and has been steering New College through transition to full independence from RNIB management. Competent and approachable; mother of five children with three grandchildren and a secondary headteacher husband. She has overseen a protracted period of restructuring that has coincided with the college achieving considerable national recognition as a centre of excellence for special education. Permanent principal expected to be appointed by September 2006.

Academic Matters: One of 12 special education institutions designated as 'trailblazers' by the DfES. Excellent results, typically well above national averages. DfES and ALIS value added indicators exceptionally strong. Curriculum is broad and balanced, giving blind and partially sighted pupils access to the National Curriculum without disapplication. Aim is to prepare pupils for three or four A levels and then higher education wherever possible. Full range of subjects at Key Stages 3 and 4 with pupils taking ten GCSE subjects typically. At least 20 subjects offered at A level including options rarely offered to blind and partially sighted students such as physics, chemistry, biology, geography, theatre studies, art and music. Small group of learning support assistants support students with additional difficulties, eg Asperger's.

Staff are recruited for teaching ability and subject knowledge, and then train after a year in post to attain qualified teacher for visually impaired (QTVI) status through a course at Birmingham University. High expectations of pupils; innovative and imaginative teaching methods. Talking apparatus, specialist software such as Jaws and Supernova which combine screen magnification, audio and Braille applications. LaTex can script advanced mathematical formulae. Course material in both visual and tactile forms. Field trips and foreign exchange visits eg with sister schools in Germany and France. Supervised prep in years 7 and 8 but from year 9 pupils are given responsibility to organise their own study time with support if required.

Games, Options, The Arts: Gym, multi-gym and indoor, heated 25 metre swimming pool. Outside there's a grass pitch and running track plus astroturf, multi-sensory maze and dry ski slope. Boathouse on the River Severn with canoeing and rowing. Impressive outdoor pursuits programme to develop decision-making and teamwork. Unusually wide range of extra-curricular activities includes everything you would expect for sighted pupils eg windsurfing, golf and chess. Summer camp for year 7 and 8 pupils in Malvern includes pony trekking and sailing. Pupils compete in acoustic shooting, including Holland open event, and international blind cricket, football and goalball matches.

Drama and art studios, music rooms and an impressive resources centre which can combine with the chapel to provide a flexible performance space cum auditorium. Majority of students participate in annual college play and three-quarters have instrumental or singing lessons and take part in a range of ensembles and concerts.

Resources department works to provide teaching aids and to transcribe print into large print or Braille. Mobility department helps pupils negotiate first the site then eg city shopping centre and independent travel on public transport. Our sixth form guide coped remarkably well even in areas of the college he rarely visited. Work experience in years 11 and 12 includes placements in businesses, schools, hospitals, theatres etc. College career staff provide intensive programme from 14+.

Background and Atmosphere: Long-serving staff have succeeded in creating a surprisingly 'normal' atmosphere considering the challenges faced by pupils. Currently undersubscribed largely as a result of recent LEA inclusion policies, but Mardy Smith feels that 'tide has turned' and that government now recognises that blind and visually impaired children will become more included in society as a result of the kind of targeted support the College is able to give. The children and older students have emotional and other needs which the college is able to address in a way which is not possible elsewhere. Residential and care staff work to create home-like atmosphere in the small boarding units and teach pupils to become independent. Student support team leader co-ordinates extra support for other disabilities such as Asperger's or additional physical difficulties. Counsellor who responds to a self-referral system by pupils 'with the normal range of adolescent problems'; educational psychologist and medical social worker at weekly doctor's surgery as well as 24 hour nursing facility.

Popular coffee bar is an out of lessons haunt run by pupils and includes an air hockey table. Younger pupils share rooms and enjoy the company but sixth formers have single bedrooms though not en-suite yet. Structured programme of independent living skills enables many to look after themselves better by the time they leave than their sighted counterparts. There is support between pupils and well-equipped areas for relaxation; pleasant central dining area with self-catering facilities in boarding houses for sixth formers who also purchase their own food. 'Discipline looks after itself' said one member of staff.

Semi-rural site with an open outlook to the Malvern Hills. Good architecture.

Pupils and Parents: Gentle, intelligent young people who are supportive of each other, and rise to the immense challenges they face with determination. They have fun too. Supportive parents and former pupils.

Entrance: Preliminary visits are arranged by a liaison teacher. After applying, pupils stay for two days and on completion of college's multi-disciplinary assessment a report will be sent to parents and other interested parties. Provisional offers are made on basis of ability to cope with full National Curriculum and according to individual need; most pupils are funded by their LEA but some sixth form students are funded by the LSC.

Exit: All students move to a wide range of courses in higher or further education, sometimes after a gap year, with many going on to higher degrees and professional training.

Remarks: Expert and dedicated staff; incredibly positive atmosphere and great camaraderie between pupils. A very special school.

The Roche School

11 Frogmore, Wandsworth, London, SW18 1HW

Tel: 020 8877 0823

Fax: 020 8875 1156

Email: office@therocheschool.co.uk

Website: www.therocheschool.co.uk

• Pupils: 205 boys and girls, all day • Ages: 3-11 • Fees: Ages 4-6 £2,560. Ages 7-10 £2,830 • School status: Independent • Opendays: November, January, February, March • School gender: Mixed • Day/boarding: Day pupils

SEN provision

Detail:

Now provide for in school:

Mild: ASP; ADD; ADHD; DS; DYSC; DYSL; DYSP; HI;

Moderate: DYSL; DYSP;

Others: EAL; Sp&LD; PD;

Experience of:

Mild: AUT;

Moderate: ASP; ADD; ADHD; DYSC;

Others: SPD;

Summary: As a non-selective school there will be a range of abilities in every class. A few of these children will have SEN. Support ranges from group to individual support as appropriate.

What we say about the school - the full Good Schools Guide review

Principal: Since 1988 Dr James Roche BSc PhD (sixties). Educated at St Paul's, read physics at Bristol and has a PhD in general relativity from Manchester. Taught for 2 years in a London state school then spent 19 years teaching A level physics at Collingham College, Kensington, where his wife Carmen taught languages. She founded the school in 1988. He teaches maths, history and RE. They have two daughters. We caught him on a bad day recovering from flu and looking quite grey (think Jon Pertwee as Dr Who) but he was a joy to chat to. Very bright, has a quote for everything. Apparently Bernard Levin said, 'institutions are best if you don't have quite enough room to run them.' So it's a compact school, but it isn't overcrowded. Handwrites everything even the children's homework indeed (thanks spy) – when he was absent from a lesson a bright pupil (dyspraxic but a maths whiz kid) insisted on setting homework in the doc's style, handwritten and complete with hints and tips! Parents say, 'he can appear to be completely off the wall (think mad professor) but he's wonderful with the children and the children adore him though he's not so at ease with parents. Children not parents are his priority, which is great.'

Entrance: Majority join in the September of their nursery or reception year but handful of occasional places crops up so always worth checking. Visit on an open morning or request an individual tour. All new entrants spend a familiarisation afternoon in school. For some reason, parents get the idea this is a special needs school – it's not, but, on the other hand, if your child has a difficulty they'll be helped. To set the record straight they have a mixed-ability intake – lots of very bright children (couple of scholars – one boy was offered four scholarships last year) some with SEN lots without. Can cater for dyslexia, dyspraxia, Asperger's, Down's syndrome, speech and language difficulties, ASD, ADD and those with EFL needs as long as they have the ability to catch up with their year group (also recognise that many children with SEN will be academically very able). Smallish site, so can only have odd one or two who require constant learning support assistance. Have flexibility, too, so if it's better for a child to be out of their chronological age group that's what they'll do. Lift (in pipeline) will improve wheelchair access. Look at the child, their profile, strengths and difficulties but it's not the place for those needing a totally different programme. Wants children who'll fit in, be integrated and included.

Exit: Some to boarding schools, majority to London day schools. At 8+ to The Harrodian, Putney High and Northcote. At 11+ to St Paul's, Lady Margaret's, Dulwich, The Hall, Ibstock Place, Wimbledon High, JAGS, Royal Russell, Kings, Bedales etc.

Remarks: Average class size of 16 ensures plenty of individual attention. Very recently praised by Ofsted, no weaknesses, couple of minor considerations. All take SATs – good results – above national norms. Most take 8+ or 11+ for next schools too so get lots of exam practice to lessen the stress. Specialist teachers for French, gym, art and music. Sets for maths and English from year 1 or year 2 to allow slower children to get a secure understanding and the high fliers to soar.

A parent of a child with dyslexia said she couldn't praise the school enough; they bend over backwards to help. If your child needs it they can have as much SEN help as necessary (though you'll be charged extra for one-to-one, and there may come a time when a specialist school is suggested if no real progress). The gifted and talented needing extension work will also be given some one-to-one help. IEPs disseminated to all staff and reviewed regularly. Team to help with dyslexia, dyspraxia and speech and language problems (have therapist). Run social skills and friendships groups if need arises. Strong belief that children with SEN enrich the school, teaching others to be kind, considerate and thoughtful.

Lessons are lively affairs that hold the children's interests – then again work's much more fun when you understand it. Have a good sprinkling of investigative and practical work with trips and visits supplementing the diet. Say it's really important to ensure children do as well here as they would anywhere.

Lots happening outside the classroom, parents wax lyrical about the amazing productions, 'my nine-year-old was in 'As You Like It'. I was cynical but she learned her lines, understood it and it's given her a taste for Shakespeare – I felt so proud.' We caught the final throes of a West Side Story rehearsal not going quite as well as hoped. Productions are very inclusive – everyone gets to perform and share the limelight. Music's popular too – lots learn instruments or sing, all have a couple of music lessons a week and there's a choir and band. We had the privilege of being shown round by the head boy and head girl – took their duties very seriously, even showing us the paper store – and fine though the facilities are we were more impressed by the children. They've a keen awareness of others, a confidence to discuss strengths and weaknesses, they're lively, interested and, try as we might to find at least one child who couldn't explain their work, we failed.

Good sized (for inner London) playground – which children would like grassed (nice idea but with the British weather probably best left), dedicated art room (impressive artwork everywhere), well-stocked library, ICT suite, science lab with apparently (according to kids) brilliant interactive white-board, good sized hall for PE, assemblies, productions, lunches. All do sport and, although school wouldn't suit aspirant athletes or potential polo players, for vast bulk of youngsters who're content with archetypal primary school sport it's just fine – usual on offer with fixtures against other schools, after school clubs (most attend at least one extra-curricular club per week) etc.

Not posh, or much patronised by the posh. Not the smartest place either (odd holey jumper and shirts hanging out brought back happy memories for this editor.) Children can be children here and they still get into all the top schools. What's more they're well-mannered and polite without a whiff of arrogance or priggishness. All children, from the non-academic through to the very brightest, are kept happy and there's a genuine belief that everyone has strengths. Older children look after younger. Mixed age tables at lunchtime (packed lunch only; no chocolate, nuts or fizzy drinks) and all of the 11+ class have a role or responsibility. Not a school where staff hide away – they're chatty and helpful just like the children.

ROEDEAN SCHOOL

Roedean Way, Brighton, East Sussex, BN2 5RQ

Tel: 01273 603 181

Fax: 01273 676 722

Email: admissions@roedean.co.uk

Website: www.roedean.co.uk

• Pupils: 387 girls, all board except for 53 • Ages: 11-18 • Religion: C of E, but all faiths are welcome • Fees: Day £4,130; boarding £7,400. Plus extra fee for those who join as international sixth formers • School status: Independent • Opendays: October and May. School recommends personal visits by appointment • School gender: Girls • Day/boarding: Takes boarders

SEN provision

Detail:

Now provide for in school:

Mild: ASP; ADD; ADHD; EBD; DYSC; DYSL; DYSP; HI; VI;

Moderate: DYSC; DYSL; DYSP;

Others: SPD; OCD; EAL; MSI; Sp&LD; Epi;

Summary: Our learning support/language skills unit was set up five years ago and has a specialist staff that covers EAL teaching, specific learning difficulties and special educational needs. We have a depth of experience in working with multi-lingual dyslexia and high ability students with specific learning difficulties. The EAL and special needs work is closely co-ordinated

What we say about the school - the full Good Schools Guide review

Head: Since 2003, Mrs Carolyn Shaw BA (English) London, PGCE Liverpool (mid fifties). Late of St Mary's, Calne where she was head for 7 years, prior to which she taught English at Cheltenham Ladies' and other schools including one in Bermuda. Lots of experience in the GSA and on various high level education committees and busily involved in the promotion of girls' education in general, this is a very active and pro-active head with a clear vision of what she wants her school to be. A seemingly inspired appointment, Mrs Shaw has the energy, dedication and leadership qualities needed to re-create this, formerly celebrated, school, as a powerhouse in the world of girls' education today. And she's nice too. Likes quoting local taxi drivers who she sees as useful sources of vox pop on the (excellent) local reputation of her charges. If the public perception of Roedean has not kept pace with its character today, Mrs Shaw is the person to change all that and, while loving the school's multi-national make-up, is already doing much to show local families that Roedean could be their local school. 'She's made it brighter, sharper, fresher,' said a parent. Above all, she's an enthusiast, enthusing wildly about the enthusiasm of her girls and her staff. It's infectious.

Academic Matters: A rare 26 A level subjects on offer – rare, that is, for a school as small as this. Subjects include German and Latin which the school is determined to support despite few current takers. Maths taken a by a huge proportion – 50 out of 81 candidates – 39 of whom got grade A in 2005. Other popular subjects include chemistry (26 takers), biology (21) and economics (22). Large proportion of As in all sciences and maths and no question that these subjects predominate in general – partly, though not entirely, through the influence of the substantial far eastern cohort. 80 per cent got A/B at A level in 2005. At GCSE, 60 per cent of the candidates obtained an A or an A*. German less popular than Spanish but resolutely supported by school and results in all languages would suggest that some girls might be missing a trick by not taking them further. EAL taken by many although a good level of English is a prerequisite for all candidates for places here – around 100 have one-to-one language/learning support which includes good support for a wide range of mild SENs. Group lessons to prepare for the IELTS exam. School's location and sloping site make wheelchair access virtually impossible though a range of other physical disabilities eg mild visual or hearing impairments catered for. Good careers room and good library with first-rate full-time staff.

Games, Options, The Arts: Around 30 sports available here including riding at Ditchling riding school where own ponies can be stabled and very active polo club, popular with girls from all types of backgrounds. Multi-purpose sports hall and additional fitness suite for older girls, inviting indoor pool and plenty of outdoor space – fields rolling seawards and robust attitude to go with it – 'we don't stop because it's raining a bit,' we were told. Girls return from matches envying the astroturfs on offer elsewhere and school currently managing doughtily without, though head says, 'in due course there will probably be one' and they do borrow a couple at nearby sports centre. Everyone takes dance for the first two years and many thereafter. Successes in many sports including, most recently, U16 netball. Lovely new adventure playground for younger girls (money raised by parents) and a great attraction to visiting prospective pupils. Arts flourish though in rooms of varying sizes and much work in many media delights the eye – super textiles, ceramics and very lively DT – all witness to clever and inspirational teaching – as are excellent results. Music is strong in good size class teaching room and many smaller spaces. Music tech 'there if you want to' but, as yet, not many do. Concerts in the wonderfully atmospheric Edwardo-Romanesque chapel or the hall or theatre – an exceptional asset with wholly flexible staging, allowing for theatre-in-the-round or an orchestra pit and seating 320. House plays, one senior and two junior productions a year. All looks professional, well-supported and enjoyed with no hint of flashiness. D of E, Young Enterprise and masses of highly enjoyable and very effective charity work. In late 2004, a 'bath race' – carrying a housemistress in a bath all the way from the school into the centre of Brighton – raised £1,200 for Water Aid.

Background and Atmosphere: You drive away from Brighton heading east, the huge marina clinking below between you and the open sea and there, in front, bolted to the hillside and above the cliffs, you see a vast, grey, pebble-dash, twin turreted and red-roofed pile and, if you don't know, wonder what on earth it could be. This is Roedean of unique and, now outmoded, reputation – with as stern an aspect as could have been wished by any Victorian schoolmarm – facing the sea and seemingly outfacing any presumptuous invader. But, the sign says 'Welcome' and welcomed you feel in this relaxed, orderly, spacious and warm – in all senses – school and any notion of being in an uninviting spot rapidly recedes.

Having begun at the end of the 19th century as a school with ten pupils and two mistresses, ten minutes walk away in Lewes Crescent, the school rapidly expanded and the present building, designed in 1898 by the former Wembley stadium architect – hence the trademark twin turrets – bears witness to the confidence, solidity and durability its redoubtable founders felt about girls' education. The building has a medieval baronial feel with huge high windows, vast tiled fireplaces and many pretty massive rooms. One feels the place could take twice the number of pupils and be far from crowded. Corridors and many other areas being cheerily redecorated when we visited – a bright primrose yellow giving a fresh, warm feel and school eagerly anticipating the arrival of smart new blue carpets. Clearly it's a nightmare to keep up and the battering of the elements visible not just outside, as patches of bubbly damp on many walls, but the place is warm, attractively and not skimpily furnished and it feels like home. A few atmospheric rather Gothic corridors and staircases and a lovely cloister area on the way to the chapel – for quiet and repose. Girls in 'French navy' uniforms seem relaxed and friendly and keen to give of their best.

Pastoral Care and Discipline: 'I don't see discipline as a problem,' says head. No drugs or similarly serious incidents in her time but 'there would be no alternative to exclusion' if anyone is caught with an illegal substance. Head sees 'respect for others as what we value here – respect of girls for girls, for different nationalities and cultures. The youngest pupil, the newest cleaner and I all merit respect from everyone – we are all equally worthy.' Integration of overseas pupils far more successful here than in many comparable schools – far less struggle in getting everyone to join in after the first few weeks. Head uncompromising about her community – 'to talk loudly in a language others can't understand is rude and can be hurtful. Everyone agrees with this and, by and large, they all speak English.'

Strong pastoral system and all staff on the alert for a long face or other signs of unhappiness or disturbance. All girls have open and wholly confidential (except in cases of actual danger) access to a counsellor. Active peer-listening scheme. Pride taken in caring for each other and family atmosphere. 'My daughter finds it a very nurturing environment,' said one parent, 'and she's very happy there'. All female teachers are called 'Madam' and head maintains it is said 'with real affection, not prissiness' – certainly borne out by what we saw. Boarding accommodation undergoing rolling programme and best upper school rooms now quite large and with en-suite bathrooms. Younger girls share in rooms of four (one of six) but all have space and all rooms are quite cosy. Some newer rooms have blu-tac embargos which seems a little sad. All sixth formers in Keswick House in single rooms with proper sized beds, good kitchen and common room. Nice touches like hot choc and coffee on tap all day. Food, in general, excellent complete with dietary warnings/info where necessary and special needs catered for. Special help given on occasions like Ramadan fasting. New wing with excellent conference room used for outside speakers, careers talks, house meeting etc. Sixth form girls do their own laundry – good practice! Other houses linked by 'bunnyruns' so you don't have to go outside from one to the other. Good support for overseas boarders includes escorted service to/from Victoria and taxis to airports. Some belongings can stay at school over hols. Excellent onsite shop sells everything including uniform. Everyone has e-mail and access to the Internet. Help for day pupils includes a bus which takes girls away from school late into the evening, after the extra-curricular activities no one wants to miss.

Pupils and Parents: From 30+ countries and every continent. Lots of Chinese, but also Thai, Russian, Korean and Europeans of all sorts. Also more than half indigenous or expat Brits, most from the south of England and school busy recruiting in this area. Clientele not the stiff upper class and diplomatic types of yesteryear but everyone and it's hard to imagine a girl who would not feel welcome here. Lots of famous ORs include Baroness Chalker, Verity Lambert, Sally Oppenheimer, Tanya Streeter, Honeysuckle Weeks, Rebecca Hall, Philipa Tattersall.

Entrance: No main feeder schools. Entry at 11, 12 or 13 is via Common Entrance, scholarship or the school's own entrance exam. All entrants are required to visit the school for interview and may spend a couple of days at the school prior to joining. Candidates should be registered as early as possible in the academic year prior to their entry in school to ensure the availability of a place.

Exit: Very few leave before 16 and then, a few, for co-ed. Some – as elsewhere – return, gratefully, after a few weeks outside. 2004 leavers went in large numbers to the LSE and to Imperial College, also to UCL, Bristol, Nottingham and Durham universities and to a long list of others. Courses in everything from cosmetic science to veterinary medicine, German to law.

Money Matters: Lots of scholarships – academic, music, sport, art or performing art – competed for at 11, 12 and 13 by exam and audition – worth up to 40 per cent fees. Sixth form schols also by exam in A level subjects and a general paper.

Remarks: Early in 2005, the new triumvirate – head/bursar/chair of governors – undertook a major overhaul of staffing and resources. The hard look at management and structure was long overdue and resulted in a more efficient system better suited to the school's needs now though some staff were lost on the way. Pupil numbers are at least holding up and in some years – notably the sixth form – over subscribed, as one would hope for a school with such a healthy spirit and so much to offer. The tough approach, though sensible, will have scared a few but the head is relaxed – 'confidence is strengthening', she says. We would be surprised if the school doesn't spur on more strongly from now on.

Head asserts, 'we're a cracking good school and I need to get parents in to see – they're overwhelmed when they come.' Previous emphasis on filling top end means you may have missed the boat there but spaces still available at the lower end and well worth getting your 11 or 13-year-old in before the word gets out.

ROKEBY SCHOOL

George Road, Kingston-upon-Thames, Surrey, KT2 7PB

Tel: 020 8942 2247

Fax: 020 8942 5707

Email: hmsec@rokeby.org.uk

Website: www.rokebyschool.net

• Pupils: 370 boys, all day • Ages: 4-13 • Religion: Non-denom • Fees: £1,660; £2,386 in years 5-8 • School status: Independent • School gender: Boys • Day/boarding: Day pupils

SEN provision

Detail:

Now provide for in school:

Mild: DYSC; DYSL; DYSP; SpLD;

Moderate: MLD; DYSC; DYSL; DYSP; SpLD;

Severe: DYSC; DYSL; DYSP;

Summary: We offer learning support to boys with difficulties accessing the curriculum, dyslexic boys, dyspraxic and boys with difficulties in maths and English. As well as study skills help. At present a learning support teacher takes 19 boys from years 3 to 8 in the Senior School. There is to be an additional part-time LS teacher from January. The junior school also offers learning support, with its own LS teacher

What we say about the school - the full Good Schools Guide review

Head: Since 1999, Mr Michael Seigel MA (early fifties), educated at St Paul's and New College, Oxford, where he read classics. Married with two teenage children, lives in Kingston by the river – 'within walking distance but I don't often do it,' he says. Author of four Latin textbooks, he teaches Latin, PHSE and also about Ancient Greece to the new intake of 7-year-olds. Cherishes hopes of one day having time to write a novel but nowadays could be mistaken for a City gent with a Guards background – tall, moustache, upright bearing and very much in control of the whole operation. He describes himself as 'sensitive to the needs of others' – some parents feel, however, that he is not averse to ruffling a few parental feathers. Departure of the previous head still regretted by some, feeling that it coincided with a certain loss of tradition but others say that Mr Seigel is dragging the school into the 21st century with success. Whichever way – he is a chap who evokes a plethora of differing comments.

Entrance: For entry at age 4 into pre-prep (known as Junior Rokeby), register ASAP from birth for a non-refundable fee of £25. Waiting list maintained on a 'first come, first served' basis, taking into account the month of birth. In the January before the year of entry (ie 20 months prior to entry date), first 100 boys are invited to an informal assessment – structured play session which has 'a formal element' – it may appear a bit harsh on such little mites (perhaps a taste of what is to come) but their parents queue up for the privilege. Subsequently, 44 boys offered places and the rest go onto another waiting list.

For entry at age 7, again put names down early – 48 places available, entrance exam – maths, English, reading and comprehension – in November, for entry the following September. No automatic transfer from Junior Rokeby, those unlikely to pass the exam are given prior warning. External candidates pay £200 (refunded if a place not awarded, but not if awarded and not taken up), set against subsequent fees. Boys come from a wide variety of pre-prep and state schools but particularly Wimbledon Common Prep and Putney Park. All parents have to dig deep into their wallets to make a £500 interest-free loan to the school, payable for each child, and refunded when the boy leaves. Three generous scholarships per year for boys aged 7/8, competed for by a separate exam in November and worth 45 per cent of fees – can be topped up in case of need. Based on academic ability but with one for potential in each of music, sport or art.

Exit: At 13, to all the top-notch schools, the main exodus to King's College School, Wimbledon, followed by St Paul's, Charterhouse, Epsom, Eton, Harrow and many others of first and upper second league. Occasionally to Tiffin's (state grammar in Kingston) and head relaxed about such boys exiting at 11.

Impressive record of academic, music and art scholarships to the favoured senior schools: recently scholarships to, amongst others, St Paul's and Wellington, an exhibition and a music scholarship to King's College and an art scholarship to St John's, Leatherhead.

Remarks: A school for seriously Surrey parents with seriously hard-working sons wanting seriously splendid academic results – and no messing. Founded in 1877, school is in a very leafy part of town off Kingston Hill and on the very swanky private residential Coombe Estate. Mainly housed in a large Victorian house which, like its neighbour, Holy Cross Preparatory School, was the home of author John Galsworthy (the Galsworthys owned several houses in the area). Site is largely built upon, there is little open space not occupied by tennis courts or an astroturf pitch, although the junior school does have its own adventure playground. Open space at the front is crammed with staff cars and is a little weedy (literally) – some judicious gardening instead of detention for errant boys would not go amiss.

Some of the classrooms in the original house are a bit on the cramped side, but the modern additions are airy and spacious, particularly the art room and the well-equipped labs. Computer suite has 24 machines and smartboard and the art department has a nice touch of a pottery room.

Academically, a school for the robust – weaklings and worriers will not enjoy it. A great deal is demanded and, if he can cope, your son will flourish and probably obtain a coveted place at one of the prestigious senior schools to which most of the pupils gravitate. If he is not up to it, he (or rather, you) will receive adequate, if unwelcome, warning that your time is up and you should move on to academic pastures new.

Average class size 16. Two parallel classes in each year until year 5, when boys are setted separately for maths and English, and then again in year 6 for French and Latin. Major change takes place in year 7, classes divided into two CE classes and what the head prefers to term a 'potential scholarship' class. All take Latin between years 5 and 8 and all in the scholarship class do Greek in their final year, with some being examined in it.

No pupils have EAL requirements but a few have mild to considerable dyslexia or dyspraxia. Parental comments that SEN provision is admirable – one mother said, 'they have done very well for my [dyslexic] son, who is a good all-rounder, managing well academically.' Another praises the school for 'picking up my son's problem very quickly'. However, such good SEN screening means some boys do not necessarily make it into senior Rokeby, which apparently has caused some parental concern.

Rokeby does nothing half-heartedly – be it academics or sport. On site, they have the all-weather pitch, which is mainly for junior Rokeby for football, rugby, rounders, cricket, short tennis and athletics in the summer. No space for senior field sports on site (land has been sold off in the past), and senior Rokeby boys are bused to Wimbledon Wanderers' Football Club grounds near the Robin Hood roundabout for football in the autumn and rugby in the winter. School is in negotiation, as we write, for the purchase of its own grounds in Worcester Park, but busing will still be necessary. No swimming pool – years 3 and 4 swim in Kingston. Head tells us that teams are not selected solely on merit – increasingly boys get the opportunity to play for the school at some stage in their career. However, as with virtually every boys' prep we see, sport is a bone of parental contention – some parents complain pupils not in the top teams can get more junior teachers and gap year students, however keen the boys may be; also a feeling that more encouragement could be given to less able but still sporty boys.

Parents speak very highly of the music tuition, describing the music teacher as 'fantastic.' All learn the violin in small groups as part of the music curriculum (hire of instrument is extra). Almost 50 per cent go on to take individual music lessons. Choir open to all. Annual Christmas music and drama production.

School has a purposeful atmosphere – you feel it is a veritable seat of learning. Uniform not especially smartly worn, but that's boys for you. Famous former pupils include actor Richard Briers and Labour historian and biographer, Professor Ben Pimlott.

Transport provision is good and very popular with parents, serving Sheen/Putney Heath areas and around Wimbledon. Shared school runs also comes into their own here (many siblings attend Holy Cross next door which eases the ferrying around). Parking near the school is problematical and has been a source of contention with local, highly articulate residents, resulting in detailed instructions issued to parents to avoid potentially inflammatory situations.

Junior Rokeby has own (teaching) head, who is responsible to Mr Seigel. Lots going on and boisterous boys – 22 maximum in class. Separate assembly hall and gym and general impression of metaphorical self-containment from main school (although share certain facilities eg canteen). Own playground in addition to adventure playground.

Rokeby is a school where parents either love the regime or moan about it (and perhaps take off to more gentle pastures) – hence the mixed reports we receive about the school. However, it cannot be denied that Rokeby comes up with the goods – excellent academic results from splendid all-rounders.

ROSSALL SCHOOL

Broadway, Fleetwood, Lancashire, FY7 8JW

Tel: 01253 774 201

Fax: 01253 774 282

Email: enquiries@rossallcorporation.co.uk

Website: www.rossallschool.org.uk

• Pupils: 407: 250 boarding, 250 day; about 40:60 girls:boys. Plus 78 in the International Study Centre • Ages: 11-18 • Religion: C of E • Fees: £2,455-£6,860 (Senior); boarding £3,005-£7,565 (IB); ISC £5,307 (below 13)-£7,570 (above 13) • School status: Independent • Opendays: October, January and April • School gender: Mixed • Day/boarding: Takes boarders

SEN provision

Detail:

Now provide for in school:

Mild: ASP; AUT; ADD; ADHD; DYSC; DYSL; DYSP;
Moderate: ADD; ADHD; MLD; DYSC; DYSL; DYSP;
Severe: DYSL;
Others: SPD;

Experience of:

Mild: HI;
Others: Epi; Eat;

Summary: Whilst there is no statutory requirement for independent schools, Rossall, following good educational practice, will as far as practicable respond to the guidelines laid down by the Code of Practice.

Provision for pupils with SEN is a matter for the school as a whole: in addition to the SEN co-ordinator, the principal, houseparents, tutors and subject teachers within senior school, the head of the junior school and head of the nursery and infant school, all have important responsiblities.

Rossall beleives in close co-operation between all those concerned including parents and outside agencies to esablish a multidisciplinary approach to the resolution of issues.

Rossall aims to educate pupils with SEN, wherever possible, alongside their peers within the normal curriculum of mainstream after giving due consideration to the appropriate wishes of the parents and to ensuring that individual pupil needs are met, so that pupils can reach their full potential and enhance their self-esteem.

What we say about the school - the full Good Schools Guide review

Headmaster of Rossall Schools: Since 2001, Mr Tim Wilbur BA PGCE (mid forties). Read history at Kent. Taught at Millfield until 1998 (housemaster), then deputy head of Sutton Valence until he came here. A serious hockey player. Married, with three children all at Rossall and all playing hockey. A modest, approachable man and a good listener. Walks about the school a lot, talks to pupils, takes school teams.

Academic Matters: Hard work insisted upon. Acceptable results overall at GCSE (86 per cent A*-C, excellent science and maths) and A level given unselective nature of intake. School by no means complacent and always looking to improve. IB taken seriously and enthusiastically by staff and pupils; one third of year do it, excellent 100 per cent per cent pass in 2005.

International Study Centre (ISC) in existence for ten years; for overseas students, mainly from Hong Kong and SE Asia, but rising numbers from Germany and Eastern Europe (parents disenchanted with domestic system and looking for secure pastoral care). Intensive English language courses lead to International GCSE or a transfer to main school (about 25 a year). As much academic integration as the organisation can cope with (eg science staff teach in both areas), and more hoped for. ISC numbers have doubled in recent years.

Special needs support taken seriously, though difficult cases have to go elsewhere. Senior SENCo doubles as housemistress and has one fully trained teacher who oversees English and maths classes during first two years in senior school. Good links too with the junior school. Currently 45 pupils turn up at the ILU (individual learning unit) twice a week for an hour long session, either one-to-one or one to three. Chiefly of the dys-strata, plus occasional mild Asperger's, ADHD or semantic pragmatic disorder (can't say a sentence the right way round). Some deaf, but not profoundly so, no mentors in living memory, the occasional statemented child. Campus not brill for wheelchairs – though they have had them. £300 per term extra for two weekly sessions: cheap. Clone the SENCo.

Games, Options, The Arts: The usual games, and famous for Rossall ('Ross') hockey, played on the beach, tides permitting, and very popular; invented in 1860s, with esoteric rules. CDT and art strong. Good music – choirs and orchestras, and professional subscription concerts, in the Sir Thomas Beecham (Old Boy) Music Schools. Performing arts building planned. Keen CCF (all three arms) includes girls; leads to Btec in year 11. School has its own outward bound award; Lake District and Yorkshire Dales used.

Background and Atmosphere: Founded in 1844 on the windswept north Fylde coast, an easy tram ride from Blackpool. Confident looking and mellow redbrick buildings open up into Oxford-type quad with a handsome chapel to one side. Healthy sea air, pretty brisk in winter, with views of the Lake District. A full programme of refurbishment of the boarding houses commenced summer 2004. Day pupils have their own houses, with studies, common rooms and changing rooms, where they can stay until 8.30 pm. Sixth form centre and bar popular with boarders and day pupils. Religious observance not obtrusive; thrice-weekly compulsory chapel 'a chance for quietness and reflection', says head. Hymn practice for all.

The ISC obviously looms pretty large – a quarter of the school, exceeded in size only by Sherborne international school. Students mix socially, eg in sports teams. Some are clearly well off, judging by the Mini-Coopers in the car park. Their parents have presumably opted for the benefits of the English system (and access to higher education), plus the security of life in west Lancashire. A full programme of events, activities and field trips runs each weekend.

Pastoral Care and Discipline: Strong anti-bullying ethos and not a druggy school. Blackpool a temptation, but head says whole-school vigilance pays off. Foreign pupils 'often set our boys and girls very fine examples'.

Pupils and Parents: Now mainly a local school, with (apart from ISC) a somewhat parochial feel. Parents are farmers and business people. A growing number of Services children. Over 50 per cent first time buyers. Chirpy, courteous students, happy to be at Rossall. (Very) Old Boys include Leslie Charteris (creator of 'The Saint'), Patrick Campbell, David Brown of Aston Martin fame, Paul Herbert and Sir Thomas Beecham.

Entrance: Entry 'flexible', and generally not a problem. All pupils assessed for dyslexia on entrance.

Exit: 95 per cent go to a wide range of universities, mainly in the north; some to Oxbridge. Gap years are popular.

Money Matters: Half a dozen or so half fee academic awards, plus one full academic and one full allrounder scholarship.

Remarks: Very successful international study centre. Trad British day/boarding side seems to be finding the competion tough, to judge by the numbers.

THE ROYAL BLIND SCHOOL

Craigmillar Park, Edinburgh, EH16 5NA

Tel: 0131 667 1100

Fax: 0131 662 9700

Email: office@royalblindschool.org.uk

Website: www.royalblindschool.org.uk

• Pupils: 130 boys and girls, boarding and day (45 pupils are based at Craigmillar Park, and the rest at the Multi-Disability Visual Impairment Centre at Canaan Lane) • Ages: 3-18 • Religion: Non-denom • Fees: Day £5,193-£5763; boarding (4 nights) £9,817-£10,450. MDVI £10,133 (day); £16,593 (boarding). Non-Scottish boarders pay about £6,000 per term on top. B&B £125+ per night. Respite: £550 per weekend; MDVI: £1,750 per weekend and £3,500 per week • School status: State • School gender: Mixed • Day/boarding: Takes boarders

SEN provision

Summary: Local authority funds visually impaired pupils.

What we say about the school - the full Good Schools Guide review

Principal: Since 2004, Mr Anthony (Tony) MacQuarrie BPhil MEd DASE CertEd (fifties). Educated in South Uist in the Western Isles, Gaelic is his first language. After reading history and English at Liverpool he taught history and English for a couple of years in mainstream before going into special education, teaching children with behavioural difficulties (the old approved school) before becoming senior teacher in charge of careers at a mixed special school for children with emotional and behaviour problems. Then took a gap year in the Western Isles with Nature Conservancy (the good life called). But he was head hunted.

Deputy head of Rochdale residential school, head of St Vincent's in Bristol for the partially sighted, where he was head hunted for a second time: to become principal of the Royal Blind. Principal of The Royal Blind School is a high profile fairly hot political potato, and Mr MacQuarrie presides over two campuses: Craigmillar Park, and the Canaan Lane Campus for MDVI pupils in Edinburgh's Morningside. A complex if rewarding job, Mr MacQuarrie is getting his head round the finer issues of the Scottish syllabus as well as dealing with paper overload from the Scottish Executive, and managing some 340 permanent staff. His wife teaches at Donaldson's School for the Deaf in Edinburgh; two grown up sons.

Academic Matters: As far as possible all pupils have regular schooling, though as most 'just' blind children are in mainstream schooling many of the students at Craigmillar come with statements or records of needs, and need full SEN back-up. Tiny tiny classes, six max and often individual, the school has a full range of specialist staff and carers, all of whom are fully trained SVA level three with an HNC in care. Senior staff are qualified social workers, and there is a rolling programme of staff training as per the Care Commission.

Scottish curriculum in all it's variety: Standard Grades (eg maths, geography, French and German), Highers and Advanced Highers as well as SQA units, clusters and courses including access and Scottish Group Awards. Pupils are assisted by every possible facility: 'vocalists', sloping desks, extra large print, Braille, Braille computers, Supernova, including laptops, which will also print normal text. Internet access from all classrooms, and extensive use of audio tapes. Pupils at Canaan Lane are wheelchair bound in the main (and some are permanently fed via a gastric tube, even in class). Some integration with the neighbouring St Peter's Primary School.

Lessons on dress sense and independent learning skills, and other forms of communication like Moon and Signing and tactile body language. Pupils are also taught not to use wild gestures: hand flinging and eye-rubbing (inappropriate behaviour).

Games, Options, The Arts: Fantastic range of facilities at Craigmillar Park, two swimming pools, one dedicated to hydrotherapy, and an excellent playground: swings and climbing frames. Two gyms: one multi-gym, and a proper 'gymnasium' which has lines painted to help ball-throwers; five children were rolling balls along them (no mean feat) when we visited. Massive extra-curricular programme with tremendous input from the local education department: skiing, hiking, handicapped driving (wow), local youth club, scouts, OTC, D of E (hot on this) bowling, judo and archery plus riding for the disabled where pupils compete internationally and do extremely well in the dressage. Stunning athletics, seven nat champs amongst FPs with four runners-up and two new records. This is not a dozy environment. Huge international involvement: the Comenius project. The soft playroom is well used and popular.

Terrific music, again tiny classes, but an awful lot of noise; enthusiastic musicians were composing electronically as well as playing. Music therapy important, as is drama. Art and design in conjunction with occupational therapy. Weekly visits to the local community, and specific visits to places of interest near and far, the Scottish Parliament, Loch Ness (though they are more likely to be sailing there). Pupils learn to shop a couple of streets away. Mobility training is important: no dogs, pupils learn to walk with the long cane, feeling their way along the pavements nearby, usually with a guide, and during our visit to Craigmillar Park there were a number gingerly feeling their way round the grounds which has dedicated pavements and hills and obstacles like gratings and bushes in the wrong place (if you follow). The mobility training extends to using buses and trains and road safety. Two hydrotherapy pools at Canaan Lane, plus music, music therapy and PE.

Background and Atmosphere: The Craigmillar Campus is based in a magnificent Victorian edifice built by Charles Leadbetter in 1874 and described by Colin McWilliam as having 'a startling south front with three rubbly sash-windowed storeys and a mansard' apparently 'an ornamental effect (was) to be aimed at without incurring much expense'. There are mutterings from those on high that Craigmillar Park should be replaced (it could never be demolished, listed and all that) by a purpose-built structure, but Mr MacQuarrie maintains that life is not purpose-built and it is better for pupils to learn to negotiate the real world, with wiggly staircases and odd corners. Craigmillar Park has lifts, and is splendidly wheelchair friendly. Huge light airy classrooms. Small dormitories, or individual rooms. All the rooms have soft toys by the door to help recognition. Impressively spacious grounds, which include

The Gatehouse Café, 'a co-operative work experience' based in the Lodge House and a sensory garden which the children look after themselves (with a little bit of help from the pros). Looking after the garden counts towards the SNQ in managing environmental resources. Glorious dining room, with fantastic views from the first floor. Make-up lessons for girls. School operates 38 weeks a year, and Mr MacQuarrie says he could fill two or three residential areas every weekend and is looking to develop 'extended residential services' – respite care and the like, and hopes to be able to buy a couple of flats nearby to act as halfway houses on the way to independent living. Canaan Lane, which is purpose-built, has six residential houses, a nursery and an early years play group.

Pastoral Care and Discipline: PSE is 'central to what we do'. Not a lot of naughtiness amongst the pupils; some problems with bullying – 'but not as much as in mainstream'. Each pupil has a named 'keyworker' for individual support who liaises with their teachers, carers, parents and social workers. Heady conference stuff. Child Protection Officer. Fantastic amount of back up, Parent counselling service, founded in 1978.

Pupils and Parents: Eclectic.

Entrance: Most of the pupils come on referral with an ed psych's report: it is a parent's right to demand specialist education for their child, but often they have a hard fight on their hands, starting with tribunals and then working up. Mr MacQuarrie would like to be able to offer short courses on living with blindness and mobility orientation for all who lose their sight as, not only children, with info on what aids and financial assistance are available. Some children, who lose their sight through illness will indeed spend a short time here coming to terms with their disability, but the LEA 'has an all or nothing' approach, and it is infinitely cheaper in mainstream.

Exit: Some to university, some to tertiary colleges – Oatridge Agricultural College in West Lothian popular, some to employment – sheltered or otherwise and some to other residential care homes.

Remarks: Challenging, successful, a beacon.

THE ROYAL HIGH SCHOOL (EDINBURGH)

East Barnton Avenue, Edinburgh, EH4 6JP

Tel: 01313 362 261

Fax: 01313 128 592

Email: admin@royalhigh.edin.sch.uk

Website: www.royalhigh.edin.sch.uk

• Pupils: 1,160; 585 boys and 575 girls, all day • Ages: 11-18
• Religion: Non-denom • School status: State
• School gender: Mixed • Day/boarding: Day pupils

SEN provision

Detail:

Now provide for in school:

Mild: ASP; ADD; ADHD; EBD; DYSC; DYSL; DYSP; HI; VI; CP;
Moderate: ADD; ADHD; EBD; DYSC; DYSL; DYSP; HI;
Severe: ADD; ADHD; EBD; DYSC; DYSL; DYSP;
Others: SPD; OCD; ODD; TIC; EAL; Sp&LD; DEL; Epi; PD; Oth; Eat;

Summary: We aim to give pupils the opportunity to achieve their potential by working together with pupils, teachers and parents within national guidelines to develop a curriculum which is flexible and accessible to all pupils. We seek to liaise with all agencies and with parents and staff to ensure an appropriate support strategy for pupils.

What we say about the school - the full Good Schools Guide review

Rector: Since 1998, Mr George M R Smuga MA DipEd (fifties) who was previously head of North Berwick High School, with a brief interregnum when he was seconded to East Lothian Education Department where he was manager of quality assurance. Educated at Kirkcaldy High School, he read politics and modern history at Edinburgh University, followed by Moray House. He had thought of a career in journalism; wrote text books, but enjoyed teaching. After Portobello High, where he built up his department as principal teacher of modern studies, he became assistant headteacher, before moving to Beeslack School in Penicuik, where he was depute rector. A man of parts then. Thoughtful, concerned and sensitive. He has two grown-up children.

Enjoys the school, enjoys the challenge and has become an expert on building control and such-like since his arrival here.

Academic Matters: Max class size 30, going down to 20 for practical subjects and much less in higher years. Certain number of new staff appointed. Maths, English and modern languages set in S1/S2, other subjects set in S3 where necessary. Strong on social subjects; modern studies popular. In 2003 sixth year student awarded the Beazley Prize from the Royal Historical Society for performance in Advanced Higher History exam. Good showing in the National Enterprising Maths competition and maths results outstanding. English impressive, CDT very strong; fair showing in the field of science; excellent human biology as well as biology department. The Nuffield Science Bursary was awarded in 2001 to one of the pupils 'to carry out an investigation into flamingo behaviour at Edinburgh zoo'. Languages trail slightly. History popular with over-subscribed library lunchtime club (library lunchtime clubs generally over-subscribed anyway). Clubs for almost everything, often curriculum related: maths, chess etc.

Computers everywhere, six suites, plus 'computers in a box' – a mobile trolley armed with 20 laptops which motors round each classroom in turn. Good support for learning; one-to-one, plus support teaching, as well as curricular support for the staff; advice on how to differentiate work sheets and the like. Sixth form help with 'paired reading for younger members. Prefects also 'befriend' younger pupils – either for specific subjects or just general back-up. Number of statemented pupils ('record of needs' as it is known in Scotland). Recognised fast track for primary pupils, who may combine studies in both places. French and German, plus optional Spanish, with Urdu on the side. Masses of trips abroad in every discipline. Year tutor stays with that class for their time at school. Classrooms and facilities used by adults and locals out of hours – this is a community school in all but name.

Games, Options, The Arts: House system (nations) in place, but mainly for games. Mass of rugby/football pitches; the school does well on the games front with masses of individual and team activities; athletics, badminton, cross-country, fencing and curling. Rugby and football for both boys and girls; plus basketball. Ski trip to the States in 2003. As ever, problems with those who think it cool not to play the game (any game). Swimming pool much used and FPs (who have a rather posh sports pavilion on campus) use all the sporting facilities (car parking a bit tight).

Music strong. Long-established pairing arrangement with Munich and Italy where school orchestras perform in each other's home towns in alternate years; outstandingly popular concert, choral and orchestra, which used to be in the Usher Hall. Jazz, woodwind, but no pipe band. Mass of choices. The Keith Thompson 'KT', singers are much in demand and contribute a sizeable amount to the Sir Malcolm Sargent Fund for Children at Christmas each year. Drama on the up, strong links with the Edinburgh Festival fringe. Art soldiering on in the current circumstances – life in a portacabin is not necessarily conducive to productivity.

Background and Atmosphere: Unique history: dates from 1128, the school 'provided education for 60 boys'; the site most people associate with the school is on Calton Hill, a site much loved by the telly news cameras. (Think overnight vigils, think home rule for Scotland). Girls admitted in 1974. Established on the current site in 1968, the school buildings have been recently completely refurbished under a PFI scheme completed August 2003 with half the school refurbished and the other half in new build. One constant however, is the memorial door, out of which each graduating student steps, to be greeted on the other side by the president of the former pupils club. The huge marble door is a memorial to those who died in the first world war and the west-facing stained-glass windows to FPs who fell in the second. 'Significant prize-giving'. Highly vaunted end of school leavers dance, often held in Edinburgh City Chambers, strong charity commitment.

Uniform worn by all, with a variety of sports and club ties. 'Bonding' week during the first year, when the whole class plus class teachers take off during November/December.

Pastoral Care and Discipline: Regular assemblies, good, strong PSE programme, school has to follow City of Edinburgh 'guidelines', so difficult to exclude, but will do so in the case of drugs, bullying, physical or otherwise, and abuse. Strong prefectorial presence. Very few 'refusers'. 'Civilised guidance strategies in place,' says the head. Regular school assemblies.

Pupils and Parents: Strong PTA and School Board organisation, basically 'affluent middle class, but a very wide intake – with a whole range of social and ethnic backgrounds', the catchment area covers Davidsons Mains, Clermiston, Blackhall and Cramond. The school is capped at a 200 pupil intake and there is always a waiting list.

Entrance: Automatic but see above. Some join the school from other state schools post standard grades, otherwise, 'penny numbers' arrive on a re-location basis.

Exit: In 2002, 91 per cent of all pupils stayed for fifth year (ie Highers) and 75 per cent stayed for sixth year. Trickle to Oxbridge, masses to the Scottish universities or tertiary education. FPs include Sir Walter Scott, Alexander Graham Bell, Lord Cockburn, Ronnie Corbett, Sarah Boyack (MSP) and the principal of St Andrew's University.

Money Matters: Current building has been revamped under the aegis of the PPP. Regular PTA fund-raising including discos and jumble sales, tranche of endowments (including Mary, Queen of Scots) provide tiny scholarships for pupils who have done well of the school; not a lot, 'just a nice wee extra'.

Remarks: This is a high school in the old fashioned sense – strong discipline and work code, good results, masses of extra-curricular activities – which also doubles as a local centre with adult learning classes and much use of the sports facilities. You can't get much better for nowt.

Royal High School, Bath GDST

Lansdown Road, Bath, BA1 5SZ

Tel: 01225 313 877

Fax: 01225 420 338

Email: d.sheppard@bat.gdst.net

Website: www.gdst.net/royalhighbath

• Pupils: 600 girls (approx 500 day, 100 boarding)

• Ages: 11-18 • Religion: Non-denom

• Fees: Seniors: boarding £4,814, day £2,455. Juniors: £1,779

• School status: Independent • Opendays: Usually a Saturday in early November and a Thursday in late April

• School gender: Girls • Day/boarding: Takes boarders

SEN provision

Detail:

Now provide for in school:

Mild: ADD; ADHD; EBD; DYSL; DYSP; HI; VI;

Moderate: MLD; DYSL;

Others: EAL; Eat;

Experience of:

Mild: ASP;

Moderate: DYSP; HI; VI;

Others: OCD; TIC;

Summary: As a selective independent school we tend to primarily provide support for students who have English as a second language and for those who demonstrate dyslexic tendendencies. As such, we have in-house peripatetic specialists available if students opt to have support lessons. These sessions (either on an individual or small group basis) tend to be timetabled outside of lesson times to cause minimum disruption to the students academic day.

What we say about the school - the full Good Schools Guide review

Head: Since 2000, Mr James Graham-Brown (fifties), previously head of Truro High School (also all girls), educated at Sevenoaks, University of Kent, University of Bristol. Popular with staff and parents. Totally committed to single-sex education (as is the head of the junior department), he is the first man to head a GDST school.

In his fifties, but seems much younger, fit (ex-professional cricketer), dapper even. Carefully spoken but with conviction, having strong opinions on education and educating girls, and sure to make his mark on the school. Teaches English to all year groups, including junior school, and PE to sixth form. Passionate about literature and theatre. Married with two teenage daughters.

Academic Matters: There was some worry about academic achievement when the two schools (Bath Royal and the High School) merged in 1998. However, both GCSE and A level results have remained consistently good (overall pass rates of over 95 per cent) across the board. With the merger of the two schools, there has been a number of staff changes and new appointments, with the result that the number of male teachers has increased – generally felt to be a good thing in a single-sex school. Sciences are strong and popular at A level, with biology in particular having consistently good results. Resources for science are impressive, with separate facilities for sixth form, and flexibility at GCSE with both double science and separate subjects. Excellent language teaching reflected in the results, and a good choice too – French, German, Spanish, Greek, Latin, Italian, Chinese. Languages not just reflecting overseas pupils – the school has a long-standing exchange programme with China and its own member of staff teaching Mandarin. Good provision for special needs, in particular dyslexia and EFL. Senior SENCo Mrs Teasdale who is also head of food technology has 60 girls on her special needs register. This is not the school for a seriously challenged girl. The Royal Bath is 'a highly academic school' and the girls 'pretty much cope extremely well'. One-to-one or small groups, £12 an hour, no lessons missed, either before, after school or during lunch.

Games, Options, The Arts: Girls are encouraged to be themselves and 'aim for excellence' in whatever field appeals. Drama is very strong, and the Memorial Hall is well kitted out for performances, of which there seems to be a continuous programme. Everyone does PE, lots of outdoor sports. Well-equipped sports hall with dance studio. Sporting achievements reflect the diversity on offer – diving, showjumping, rowing. About a third of pupils take individual music lessons, there are choirs, orchestras and a swing band. 'We don't shout about the music but it is of very high quality'. Although art is valued within the school and there are interesting, and often large, pieces of work displayed, it is only compulsory up to year 9; not many go on to art school. Technology gets more timetable time and includes information technology, design technology, and food technology (very popular). There is a programme of activities on Saturdays, and outings on Sundays, which are open to all.

Background and Atmosphere: Impressive but somehow austere Gothic architecture in the main school, not welcoming but doesn't seem to bother the girls. Huge overwhelming internal spaces and corridors seem to suppress rather than magnify noise, and the school feels cool and calm. Plenty of space, and the many common rooms encourage mixing and 'the opening up of friendships'. Lovely boarding facilities, on two sites according to age, girls sharing rooms of generous size between two or three. Sleepover facility and provision for friends to stay for tea, or to do homework, is an added bonus for working parents. Boarding is popular and usually over-subscribed. No house system for boarders – prefer vertical pastoral structure for boarders 'to promote a sense of one community', all very friendly. Four day houses, with fine names – Austen, Du Pre, Wollstonecraft and Brontë – for the whole school for competition purposes. No boys, and really very little contact with boys – 'the problem is a lack of single-sex boys' schools in the area'. Links with Beechen Cliff for drama and involvement with Kingswood for Model United Nations, also joint debating with King Edward's School. But some parents (and many girls) are disappointed that there is not more opportunity for mixing.

Pastoral Care and Discipline: Manners and courtesies are taught and expected, with a very strong emphasis on self-discipline and self-sufficiency. Smart dress code, the uniform with tweedy skirt, often worn quite short, perpetuates the 'Angela Brazil' image that the school has, in reality, moved away from. Sixth formers wear suits. Jewellery and pierced ears are discouraged and therefore decidedly low-key or absent.

Pupils and Parents: In the main, girls come from professional families where both parents work, living in the city of Bath or surrounding villages; could do with its own school bus – and parents are beginning to lobby on this front. Wide social mix; girls are confident, polite, sure of themselves and instilled with 'can do' ethos. Small numbers from overseas, the school has a policy of only two from any one country in each year group in order to encourage integration and English language learning.

Entrance: As selective as possible, by school's own exam at 11, with just under 50 per cent coming up through junior department. It is also possible to enter at years 8, 9,10 subject to passing exams in English and maths, but there are no formal dates for these. Entry to sixth form is dependent on a minimum of six GCSEs with top grades for subjects to be taken at A level.

Exit: Some leave after GCSE to join co-educational schools, majority go on to sixth form and then higher education with the overwhelming majority getting places at their first choice university.

Money Matters: The GDST has its own means-tested bursary scheme, maximum value is the full day fee. There are also a number of Trust Entrance Scholarships awarded on merit for a few year 7 entrants, these offer reduced fees (up to 50 per cent) for duration of school career. Services discount.

Remarks: A good, solid, GDST school. Not too flashy, emphasis on providing good value, all-round education with an emphasis on the academic side but no hothousing. Parents feel that the school offers good value for money – 'you might get a bit more elsewhere, but you'd be asked to pay for it'.

Rudolf Steiner School

Hood Manor, Dartington, Totnes, Devon, TQ9 6AB

Tel: 01803 762 528

Fax: 01803 762 528

Email: enquiries@steiner-south-devon.org

Website: www.steiner-south-devon.org

• Pupils: 285; 140 boys, 145 girls • Ages: 3-16

• Religion: Christian foundation • Fees: £810-£1,150

• School status: Independent • School gender: Mixed

• Day/boarding: Day pupils

SEN provision

Detail:

Now provide for in school:

Mild: DYSL; DYSP;

Moderate: MLD; DYSL;

Severe: DYSL;

Experience of:

Mild: ASP; ADD; ADHD; EBD; DYSC; HI; VI;

Moderate: ASP; EBD; DYSP;

Others: SPD; OCD; EAL; Sp&LD; Epi;

Summary: Each class is able to accept some children with specific learning difficulties. Extra help for these children is available from the dedicated learning support department.

Children with special needs will be assessed with regard to (i) their own needs (ii) the resources available in the learning support department to meet those needs and (iii) the make-up and balance of the class they are approaching. This assessment will take place before a place in the class can be offered.

Children with a statement of special educational needs can sometimes be accepted, provided local authority provision is in place to support the statement.

What we say about the school - the full Good Schools Guide review

Head: None. Non-hierarchal system; a 'college of teachers'. 'It has its ups and downs,' say parents; the principle is that sharing leadership lends itself to more diplomatic, well-rounded and better thought-out policies despite lengthier deliberation. Point of contact for parents is education manager and parent facilitator Gillian Mills, late thirties. She joined the school in 2002, following a career in local government and off-shore banking/trust fund administration. Has two children at the school; interests include gardening, walking, sailing and furthering her knowledge of Steiner Waldorf education.

Academic Matters: GCSEs not rated highly (only entered for four GCSE exams) with results in them around the national average. The Steiner curriculum focuses on the 'evolution of consciousness' eg progressing from fairy tales to farming, moving on to local, European and world-wide geography. Lots of cross-curricular links. In the upper school, ages 14-16, specialist teachers bring foreign languages, music, sports and crafts into the classroom. School trips are described as 'inspirational', 'social', 'fun' by pupils and parents. They are integrated into the curriculum theme and organised for every year including a trip to Germany to study history of art and work on a surveying project involving camping on-site. Teaching quality/commitment is high. Only one class per year and only one teacher per class, therefore teachers are like second parents – first point of call if problems arise.

Games, Options, The Arts: Pictures decorate the walls created with natural plant pigment using a 'wet on wet' Steiner technique. Everyone plays a musical instrument. Piano, violin, cello, flute, clarinet, guitar, saxophone, trumpet, trombone, horn, accordion and recorder lessons. Some parents like the way music and the arts are 'given as much preference as academic subjects'. No competitive sports (although basketball is played internally). Football forbidden except for class 9 and 10 students between 12.45 and 1.30pm on the Turnip Field on Wednesdays. Parents believe this prevents it monopolising all other sports. Football enthusiasts can join out-of-school clubs. Instead, pupils enjoy rock climbing, canoeing, swimming and Bothma gymnastics – reminiscent of Tai Chi. Duke of Edinburgh often available.

Background and Atmosphere: The South Devon Rudolf Steiner School was initially founded by parents as a small kindergarten in 1979 before settling at Hood Manor where it continues to expand. Outline planning permission to extend the upper school to cater for 16-18-year-olds has been granted, alongside a new tract of kindergarten buildings and a sports hall that would greatly improve the facilities. Appeal under way. Younger pupils confidently approach teachers. Youngsters' imagination and creativity abound, in the classroom and out. Teachers have transformed part of the attractive wooded grounds into a play area with rope-bridge and tree house. A neatly-wrapped parcel of leaves and berries will be presented to you on ordering from the children's pretend playground café. Wheat (ground and used for bread baked and eaten by the pupils) flowers, fruit and vegetables are harvested from the pupils' biodynamic garden and sold at the mid-week sale. The wild strawberries are a tasty treat for those who find them first. Parental involvement is central to school's life and well-being – mums and dads expected to clean/decorate classroom, make curtains, maintain grounds, help with class events such as camping trips, plays or transport. A grind for some parents, but they accept it's all part of the contract.

Pastoral Care and Discipline: Not an extended hippy community as some may perceive. Equally they don't put pupils into blazers and 'address people as 'sir' to create discipline'. Strict on rules. Immediate suspension if pupils found smoking at school, expulsion for third offence. Possession of drugs or alcohol can lead to immediate expulsion. No sign of graffiti. No mention of bullying or aggressiveness. Parents refer to 'strong positive relationships' between peer groups. Some parents/pupils like the continuity that they have with one teacher throughout lower and upper school (additional specialist teachers introduced in upper school). Parents say 'It's the care and consideration that teachers give to individual pupils that stands out'. Emphasis on developing the physical, emotional and spiritual side in unison.

Pupils and Parents: 'Wholesome-looking' children. Real clarity of expression on faces perhaps due to rich educational experiences. One parent said, 'I think the pupils are encouraged to ask questions to discover what there is to be discovered!' Taught to help one another. Socially delightful. 10 per cent from abroad but with English residency. Estate agents aware parents move to Dartington to be near school. Very few working class families. Lots of 'cultural creatives', former company owners, bank managers, lawyers, who have moved to Devon for its beauty and tranquillity. Many special needs. Caters well for dyslexics but serious cases may leave to benefit from LEA-funded specialist support.

Entrance: Entrance to Upper School (Class 8) is not automatic. Meetings with parents to assess 'commitment'.

Exit: At age 11 average of three pupils leave for Exeter or Kevics College, Totnes. Some to Atlantic College at 16, or Cornwall – a centre of excellence for English and dramatic art. Students mostly move on to local colleges at 16, and seem to do well there.

Money Matters: Lots of bursary places available, applicants judged on individual merit. Christmas market at nearby Totnes Civic Centre is a big fund-raiser and hugely supported by parents.

Remarks: Child-focused with a caring and homely environment.

Rugby School

Lawrence Sheriff Street, Rugby, Warwickshire, CV22 5EH

Tel: 01788 556 216
Fax: 01788 556 277
Email: registry@rugbyschool.net
Website: www.rugbyschool.net

• Pupils: 805 in total: 370 boys boarding, 75 day; 295 girls boarding 65 day • Ages: 11-18 (day pupils only at 11 and 12) • Religion: C of E • Fees: Day £6,900-13,800 pa; boarding £21,750 pa • School status: Independent • School gender: Mixed • Day/boarding: Takes boarders

SEN provision

Detail:
Now provide for in school:
Mild: DYSL; DYSP; HI; VI;
Moderate: DYSL;
Others: EAL;
Experience of:
Mild: ASP; ADD; ADHD; EBD; DYSC;
Moderate: DYSP; HI;
Others: DEL; Epi; PD; Eat;

Summary: Rugby is committed to the full development of the talents of its pupils, regarding learning disabilities more as challenges than obstacles. Provision is made on a one-to-one basis for those requiring it, and a qualified and experienced department is on hand to respond flexibly to a variety of special educational needs.

What we say about the school - the full Good Schools Guide review

Head: Since 2001, Mr Patrick Derham BA PGCE (forties), who started life on the naval training ship Arethusa, a 19th century wooden frigate, now in cold storage. Training on the Arethusa was abandoned quite suddenly, and he found himself at Pangbourne, from whence he read history at Pembroke College, Cambridge. His early teaching career was at Radley, where he became housemaster, before joining Solihull School as headmaster in 1996. He still teaches an A level set, 'vital to do it', and 'nice to teach an exam group'. He also delights in the fact that he is sitting in Thomas Arnold's study, complete with a contemporary portrait. He is potty about the Victorian period, so it is even more apt that boys (and now girls) still come and go through the staircase in the corner, through which boys could slide without having to run the gauntlet of the school secretary – as they did in the days of Tom Brown's Schooldays (and indeed as this editor did, on the way to her car). Said staircase recently starred in TV programme with Stephen Fry impersonating Thomas Arnold.

'This is not a highly selective single-sex boarding school but a broad church where everyone is encouraged to achieve their full potential.' Has had two of his own children in the school (one remains), which has worked well, 'a tribute to the school'. Not a lot of tinkering with the staff and he is first to acknowledge the change in ethos engineered by previous head Michael Mavor, who transformed a backward and bullying school into its superb present. Head conscious of modern realities – 'you're walking a political tightrope. It's important for the school to remain true to its traditions and values but we can't rest on our laurels and we have to move forward.'

Academic Matters: Has come shooting up the FT league tables, with a very strong showing in mathematics, physics, chemistry and economics at A level (and these of course may yet be improved). Recent English results phenomenal, also politics, art, classic and photography but not too many geographers, despite the extraordinary geog room. Business studies and economics popular, as is biology, interestingly computing is an A level rather than the European Driving Licence. All pupils now have their own laptops or computers and a stiff little plea is enclosed with the school bumf requesting that pupils have school issue, which makes servicing them that much easier. Many classrooms now have Prometheus whiteboards.

Wide range of languages on offer: French, German, Spanish, Russian plus Japanese, Chinese, Arabic and Italian – all getting As, might well be native speakers. Trip to St Petersburg for Russian speakers last Easter. Other trips include Paris, Vienna, Ecuador. New state of the art lang labs, with computers and software in every language. Japanese and Italian are also offered as non-examinable options. Three separate sciences at GCSE for all but the bottom set; all are streamed and setted in every subject. Class sizes max 24 and down. Labs undergoing serious rearrangement, certain amount of new build, with an interesting window in the biology lab, angled to get more sunlight; the complex must be hideous to work in. However, phase 6 of new build now complete. Transformation in the common room, much younger staff and quite a high proportion of women. Dyslexia provision on tap, OK dyspraxia ('tremendous team, getting better and better') and EFL programme in situ. Enrichment programme for academic scholars. Loads of extra-curricular clubs.

Games, Options, The Arts: 'Huge investment' recently in sports facilities but school still boasts the only listed gym in the world and it is still in use (looks like a church). Town uses their astroturfs, tennis courts and cricket wickets as well as pool – on the main campus. Rugby, cricket, tennis, hockey and athletics all stunning. Polo on the ascendancy. PE A level quite popular. Swimming pool available to all from 7am, early bird swimming.

Art flourishing and spectacular and photography dept much improved – 'outstanding' says school. Professional stuff this, locals use the studio, and 16 pupils took the subject at A level last year. GCSE drama and theatre studies offered at A level and an utterly stunning all singing and dancing Macready theatre. Oodles of productions, including a Latin play – 'magic'. Modern langs 'culture evening', recent productions include West Side Story, The Crucible, Snow White. Fantastic media studio with all the gear for pupils to practise making tapes, videos and cut their own CDs. Magical music, with masses of orchestras, bands and huge concert hall and, vibrant throughout the year, music at A level. Orchestras, choirs, ensembles – everything you would expect from a school of this size and importance. Keen voluntary CCF, loads of community service and other charity input.

Background and Atmosphere: Founded in 1567 but metamorphosed as a Victorian 'railway' school in the 19th century. Home of the famous Dr Arnold of Tom Brown's Schooldays. Head anxious to dispel the Tom Brown image. 'It has gone', he says. Imposing buildings, very much in the middle of the town, heavy traffic on one side of the campus. The glorious Victorian library has had a face lift, which, for some reason, has included covering the old stone staircase in blue nylon carpet. Why? Feels rather like north Oxford, with school houses scattered all over the place. Sixth form centre, a house in its own right, has a bar and those over 18 and house prefects allowed out into Rugby on Sat nights. Three-weekly weekends off, school buzzes at weekends – buzzes all the time really, everyone seems to be involved in half a dozen things at once.

School went fully co-ed in 1993. Now has seven houses for girls and eight for boys, which will bring the number of boarding houses to an astonishing fifteen by 2005, and increasing the boy/girl ratio to 55/45. All pupils eat in their own houses, one of the last large public schools to do this, head 'wouldn't dream of changing this' (hurrah!) – despite the fact it costs a bomb to get all the kitchens up to scratch. 'Social' eating in each others' houses by invitation. Girls' houses very civilised, particularly the sixth form one, Stanley (the food is reasonable here too). Boys' houses have been less ritzy, but a huge amount of dosh has been put into upgrading them. Refurbishing programme rather like the Forth Bridge in place. Two day houses.

Girls' uniform elegant long skirts, now redesigned so that it is possible to run in them, they swan round the place looking elegant with tweed jackets. Wish list includes new mod langs area, senior common room, and to finish the science development programme – which seemed pretty far through when we visited. School has its own language: co = roll call; levee = school prefects.

Pastoral Care and Discipline: Well, first of all forget the fagging of Tom Brown's Schooldays. Very strong pastoral care and PSHE in place and each pupil is issued with a book of Guidelines for Life at Rugby School, which details everything, from bedtime to fast food carry-outs (delivery before 9.00pm and never on Friday or Saturday). Stringent anti-bullying policy, stealing is unacceptable, final warnings and being sent home are the normal sanctions. Strict guidelines about where the sixth formers can eat and drink and how much, in place. No fags at any time. Crescent Centre = bar. Boozing in school hours has a variety of sanctions, four sins and you're out. Counselling for smokers. Using drugs does not necessarily equal out, though out if dealing, otherwise random testing may be required (and if positive, out).

Pupils and Parents: The girls' ('and boys', prompts school) co-educational school of choice. So girls from all over and not many first-time buyers here. Otherwise from the Midlands, sprinkling from overseas, Scotland regard it as 'just down the road', the north of England and London. Wide social range but school is not 'snobby' and not impressed by social credentials. 12 per cent are sons or daughters of ORs, who usually regard the place with nostalgia. ORs Rupert Brooke (who has a girls' house named after him), Bishop Hugh Montefiore,

Ian (Lord) Laing, Robert Hardy, A N Wilson and Anthony Horowitz as well as Tom King, Salman Rushdie, Lewis Carroll, Harry Flashman and Tom Brown.

Entrance: Oversubscribed, interview with school the lent term of the year before entrance – ie four terms before CE. Takes from a huge range of prep schools. Front runner is The Dragon but recent years have had a stunning 80 feeder schools. Approximately 10 per cent from overseas, either ethnic or expats. Sixth form entry equals a day-long programme of exams and interviews and six GCSEs including Bs in A level subjects – very competitive. School comments that an IQ below 110 would be struggling. Choice of house may be deferred until nearer the time of entry and, in any case, head tries to avoid clique houses.

Exit: Careers dept 'extraordinarily good'; all go on to further education (the Services are an option), with a stunning 15 per cent of leavers going to Oxbridge last year. Edinburgh and London popular, also the perennial chestnuts, Newcastle and Bristol. Not a lot going into art or music schools.

Money Matters: Huge numbers of scholarships and bursaries, and major schols for those living within ten miles of the school. Over 20 per cent on some sort of a bursary. The original foundation was for 'local boys' to be educated. Will keep any child to the next level in times of hardship. School owns property in London, including Great Ormond Street. Newly launched Arnold Foundation offers up to 100 per cent scholarships to boarders otherwise unable to afford fees. Scholarships now up to only 10 per cent but augmentable up to 100 per cent in case of need.

Remarks: Famous public school going from strength to strength. Has undergone huge changes in the last few years and is now one of the most popular, and deservedly so, number one choice among all the co-ed boarding schools. The co-ed school of choice at sixth form level and many are turned away. Friendly, hard-working and fun.

THE RUSSELL PRIMARY SCHOOL

Petersham Road, Petersham, Richmond, Surrey, TW10 7AH

Tel: 020 8940 1446

Fax: 020 8332 0985

Email: info@russell.richmond.sch.uk

Website: www.russell.richmond.sch.uk

• Pupils: 240; 120 boys and 120 girls in main school plus 52 in nursery; all day • Ages: 3-11 • Religion: Non-denom • School status: State • School gender: Mixed • Day/boarding: Day pupils

SEN provision

Detail:

Experience of:

Mild: ASP; ADD; ADHD; DYSL; DYSP;

Summary: In mainstream at The Russell School we provide an inclusive environment for children with SEN. Our SENCo co-ordinates provision for these children. In addition we have a special unit for Key Stage 1 children who have moderate to severe learning difficulties. This caters for up to eight children. There is a high adult/child ratio.

SEN questionnaire details added by us.

What we say about the school - the full Good Schools Guide review

Head: Since 2005, Mr Darren Harrison who worked in the London borough of Richmond for the previous 11 years. He comes from Cumbria but now lives locally with his wife. His interests include travelling, sport and mathematics.

Entrance: Over-subscribed every year: 34 places and 50 plus applicants. Nursery place does not guarantee place in reception class. Siblings of existing pupils have priority and then children who live closest to school. Medical and social circumstances may be taken into account. A few vacancies at seven when some transfer next door to The German School.

Exit: Two thirds to state secondary Grey Court in Richmond. Others to independent schools such as Christ's Hospital in Horsham, Hampton, Reed's (Cobham), state grammars Tiffin and Tiffin Girls' in Kingston and also to Waldegrave (Twickenham).

Remarks: Vibrant primary school with great package of family friendly, wrap-around care, providing the best of state education for those fortunate enough to obtain a place. SATS results show school compares equally with national percentages at Key Stage 1 and significantly better than national average at Key Stage 2.

School named after Lord John Russell (twice Prime Minister from 1846) who has links with Petersham. Built in 1950s (buildings a bit dated) and blessed with three acres of grounds, including two natural ponds full of frogs and newts, an outdoor summer 'classroom' consisting of an area bounded by young trees and an orchard with apples, plums and damsons, all avidly consumed when they crop by the children. Badgers and foxes on site, a 'tame-ish' woodpecker and boxes for nesting birds and bats.

Swanky location, but head says that pupils nevertheless represent the entire social range, their homes varying from those of millionaires to social housing and from a variety of national backgrounds, some with English as an additional language. One mother commented that when her family arrived from Italy, the children were given great support with learning English and were correcting their mother in no time at all! Site rather open and security might be a bit of a worry, apart from nursery playground, which is fenced and secured.

DfES recognition of 'a successful school' means funding has been granted for an additional infant teacher and a building extension, resulting in infant class size below government maximum of 30, with flexible system for teaching groups of between 17 and 25. However, junior class size is 34. Additional facilities include a multi-sensory room which is be available to all children, containing tactile objects, aural and visual experiences with fibre optics and bubbles and the like. An art room is presently being developed. ' The school is very forward thinking and constantly looking for ways to improve,' says one enthusiastic parent. Inspiring work, quotations and maxims exhibited everywhere. Pupils are encouraged to drink water from their bottles throughout the day and to eat a piece of fruit from home during circle time (for those unaware of the idiosyncrasies of the state system, circle time is when the children sit with teacher (in a circle!) and discuss issues such as 'what makes me happy?', 'what is a friend?'; the children take it in turn to speak if they want to and they can speak without interruption). Delightful practice of classes being renamed every year after, eg birds (Robin, Owl), eco-systems (Swamp, Rainforest), wild flowers or artists; each class preparing a presentation on its name at start of year.

Parents receive a curriculum information sheet for every half term, advising of the topic for period, eg 'What do we do with our rubbish?' or 'The Victorians'; it sets out what the class will be doing in each subject, when and what homework will be given out, what visits are to be made, when weekly tests will take place and how parents can help. A great idea which other primaries – state and independent – would do well to take on board.

Computers placed in clusters all over rather than in a dedicated suite, which head feels better reflects current office practice and thinking. All children have Internet access and there is one computer between five, improving on the government target of one computer between ten. The school is currently working with Microsoft on developing the skills of their teachers and improving their IT capability. They will then be used by the local authority as a key school for the training of teachers.

Super pre- and after-hours provision for children from the age of 6 months and 11 years (including meals) – nominal charges and reduction for siblings. Russell Rays is a community facility offering childcare from 7.30am until 6.00pm. The Club can even collect children from nearby schools. Also operates during school holidays. Two residential school trips every year: year 5 to Cranleigh, near Guildford and year 6 to the Isle of Wight. Infant swimming at neighbouring German School and junior swimming at Richmond. School continues to be hive of activity at lunchtimes and after school, with plethora of clubs for football (Brentford Football Club helps), cricket (MCC helps), rugby (Middlesex Rugby Club helps), tennis, netball and others ranging from choir to computers to pottery, some with small charge for materials, but no child excluded from any school activity if parents unable to contribute. Popular and well-supported evening talent shows where the children perform – acting, dancing, singing, telling jokes etc.

Exceptional unit for up to eight children of infant age with moderate to severe SEN. Dedicated learning support teacher, together with nursery nurse and special needs assistants. Has own supervised playground but some pupils can play in main playground at lunchtime and be supervised there by one of the lunchtime assistants. Regular integration sessions with mainstream classes, with full support by special assistant. Assessments take place through year. SEN pupils swim at Strathmore School and ride at a centre in Vauxhall. Clubs also open to SEN children.

One of first schools in the country to establish practice of producing self-evaluation report for staff, and head frequently asked to lecture about it – 'the idea is not to wait for someone to tell you how or why to improve.' Another of the head's innovations that has received great acclaim within the profession is ' The Gold Book', a workbook provided for each child which will contain all that child's work done in one week every term. Work is then marked and sent home for parents to see. Useful basis for parents' evening discussions (every term), as well as a keepsake for each term. Polite, well-behaved and motivated children confirmed by Ofsted report of 2000: 'The Russell is a popular school with a good reputation for advancing its pupils' academic, social and personal development.'

Nursery and reception class provision regarded locally as outstanding. Nursery takes 52 children, 26 in each of two sessions. Overseen generally by reception class teacher. Morning attenders can stay on to play for the afternoon and then, for those who want it, there is the Russell Rays Club for nominal charge.

ST AIDAN'S CHURCH OF ENGLAND HIGH SCHOOL

Oatlands Drive, Harrogate, North Yorkshire, HG2 8JR

Tel: 01423 885 814

Fax: 01423 884 327

Email: admin@st-aidans.n-yorks.sch.uk

Website: www.st-aidans.n-yorks.sch.uk

• Pupils: 1,217 boys and girls; plus 604 in the joint sixth form • Ages: 11-18 • Religion: C of E but welcomes children from all Christian traditions; allocates 5 places per year for children from other faiths 'where the circumstances are clearly exceptional' • School status: State • School gender: Mixed • Day/boarding: Day pupils

SEN provision

Detail:

Centre of excellence for:

Mild: HI;

Moderate: HI;

Severe: HI;

Now provide for in school:

Mild: DYSC; DYSL; DYSP; VI; CP;

Moderate: MLD; DYSC; DYSL; DYSP; VI; CP;

Severe: DYSC; DYSL; DYSP; VI;

Others: EAL; MSI; DEL; Epi; Eat;

Experience of:

Mild: ASP; AUT; ADD; ADHD; DS;

Moderate: ASP; AUT; ADD; ADHD; DS;

Severe: AUT;

Others: SPD; AUT(other); OCD; GEN; PMLD; SLD; Sp&LD;

Summary: St Aidan's has an outstanding reputation in the local area for care and concern for the less able and others with special educational needs. The school has a Down's syndrome child, a number with acute hearing problems and several with Asperger's at differing levels. There are 38 children in the school with a statement of special educational need.

What we say about the school - the full Good Schools Guide review

Head: Since 1989, Mr D Richards MA BD FRSA (mid fifties). Previously deputy head at Bishop Stopford C of E School, Kettering. Educated at Queen Elizabeth Grammar School, Wakefield. Read modern languages at Manchester University. Spent early part of career teaching in south Yorkshire state schools, before embarking on a degree in theology at King's, London. A teaching head with a highly visible profile around the school, often pops into lessons. A true Yorkshire man with a lovely Michael Parkinson lilt and shared passion for cricket. Has a genuinely Christian outlook on life and treats everyone with respect and kindness. Believes his early days teaching in south Yorkshire help him keep his feet firmly on the ground. He is well aware of the privileges afforded to the school and its pupils. Very highly thought of by all within and beyond the school, loyal and supportive staff, plenty of goodwill. Aims to produce pupils who are happy, tolerant, compassionate and rounded individuals. Member of QCA Advisory Committee to Tomlinson 14-19 group.

Academic Matters: Excellent value-added. Year on year, improvement in results at all levels. In 2005, 95 per cent gained five A*-Cs at GCSE with over 46 per cent A*/A considerably above the previous year. This is a proper comprehensive school, entering all children for exams, including those with special needs who are integrated into the main school (very good provision here). Head said one of his proudest moments was a pupil with Down's syndrome receiving rapturous applause at the presentation evening for gaining two GCSEs. Setting in some subjects from year 7 increasing to all academic subjects by year 10. Excellent range of A level courses; 99 per cent pass rate (52 per cent graded A/B), asssociated sixth form entered 414 A2 students – by far the largest school entry at that level. School gained specialist status in science in March 2003. Most subjects have fine accommodation adorned with first class displays of pupils' work and relevant information. The technology rooms are modern, bright and brimming with up-to-date equipment but growth of school means some lessons have to be carried out in inappropriate areas. Computers and modern technology throughout including a new £1 million data-handling suite opened in September 2004. Students regularly compete successfully in YORTEK and Young Engineers For Britain Competitions. Sixth formers have own study centres and facilities with a magnificent new library extension due to open in the spring of 2006.

Lively, innovative teaching, a variety of methods and styles, excellent use of modern technology. Pupils encouraged to think for themselves, to question and to investigate. Most classes 30 but lower ability and some options taught in smaller classes.

Games, Options, The Arts: One sports hall and one purpose-built fitness centre, well-maintained grounds. Lots of sport – strength in cricket, football and netball with many teams competing at national level. Superb new synthetic grass surface added in September 2004. Vibrant art department, with splendid displays, consistently secures excellent results at GCSE. Very good drama – one major and many minor productions performed each year, also touring theatre group puts on plays and workshops in the wider community. Eleven ensembles play under the guidance of the music department ably directed by Mark Pallant. Concert band in National Schools Prom in Royal Albert Hall in 2001; chamber choir achieved same accolade in 2003. Swing band also won National Festival event in 2004 and so become third St Aidan's ensemble in 4 years to play in Schools' Prom at Royal Albert Hall, an unrivalled achievement. Own recording studio. Good range of outdoor pursuits, several older students achieve D of E gold.

Background and Atmosphere: Founded in 1969 in the renowned spa town of Harrogate close to the famous Stray. Originally a secondary modern school, it has grown steadily to accommodate ever-increasing numbers. Latest additions include a new dining room, modern languages and maths block and beautiful Constance Green Chapel Hall (named after a Harrogate philanthropist and benefactor), renowned for its acoustics and regularly used by the wider community. Award-winning careers library staffed by full-time careers officer.

You have to come from a committed Christian background to get here but there's no feeling of religion being rammed down your throat – just a genuinely caring Christian ethos where everyone is valued. The assembly we attended had prayers and story but otherwise just messages and information. A resounding hymn would have been nice but, we are told, new from September 2004 is Christian rock band, Aidan's Flame, which has revolutionised assembly music. Uniform doesn't have a blazer. Vast majority of girls now wear trousers.

Not easy to find a real downside to the school – and this editor tried awfully hard – stopped the fat boy (but he wasn't being bullied – at least not until we arrived...), went into classes (spent longer than intended as they were interactive, dynamic, fun...), got two of the more streetwise boys (of my choosing) to show me round – kept saying how good the football was and how they weren't very good at maths but the maths teacher was great and made lessons fun and interesting! (They then tried to hijack me and take me to meet the chap!) Spoke to locals, parents (of academic, average and SEN children), staff – and still had nothing untoward to report.

Pastoral Care and Discipline: Pastoral system swings into action as soon as pupils are allocated a place. Lots of meetings and visits for parents and pupils prior to arrival, trips and weekends away help year 7 bond as a group and settle into their surroundings. Staff very much put the children first and treat them as individuals. All children in years 7 to 10 must remain in school at lunchtime. School employs its own award-winning chef and excellent health-conscious food has attracted national attention (featured in Times and on BBC). Large proportion take part in extra-curricular activities organised by staff with some parental involvement.

Harrogate is prime drug territory – an affluent area situated close to Leeds and Bradford. School very aware

– knows what goes on – effective policy of support – police involved where necessary (not usually minor first offence ie possession – though any intent to deal would involve immediate police contact). Strictly a no smoking school (staff and pupils). Any child excluded (figures are very low) can expect to receive help and support funded by the school in addition to that from the authority. Emphasis is very much on rewarding good behaviour and parental contact is usually instantaneous following any indiscretion by child – pupils very much aware of this.

Pupils and Parents: In a very middle class area – so social mix is not comprehensive – though there is the odd council house even in Harrogate. There are no pretensions here – Yorkshire folk are far too canny – and can spot a bargain – St Aidan's is certainly that – a state school that matches many independents. If you can't get in here then it's probably Ashville College, Harrogate Ladies, Leeds Grammar etc (ie parents will fork out if they have to). Parents are extremely supportive of the school (no wonder, after the efforts to secure a place). Plenty of fund-raising (though more goes to charities than to school). School raised a huge £33,000 for worthy causes in 2004-2005. Pupils are polite, articulate and considerate, demonstrating respect both for others and their environment.

Entrance: At 11. 66 per cent from town area, 34 per cent from wider area (diocese of Ripon). School very over-subscribed, lots of calls from people asking if purchasing a house in the catchment area will guarantee a place (absolutely not). Admission procedure is clearly laid down and locals know what needs to be done to get children in – 'start praying at conception, often and publicly', said one parent – and in reality it's much worse than that.

See website for full details but, in summary: approximately 150 places go to pupils living within the Harrogate catchment area and a further 76 to those outside. If more than 226 applications are received (and they always are), points are allocated as follows: where the family's main residence is within the geographical boundaries of the Archdeaconry of Richmond (9 points); frequency of attendance of the child at services, including Sunday school or Youth Fellowship in any branch of a Christian Church affiliated to Churches Together in England (weekly, fortnightly, monthly, occasionally and for how long this has been the case) (0-9 points); frequency of attendance of the parent(s) ditto (0-9 points); an older sibling in the school at the time of application (9 points); a parent or guardian working in the school (9 points); the child attends organisations working for the Church, or for the community or supports the Church in other ways, eg choristers, servers and readers (0-9 points); the voluntary service given by the child's parent or guardian to their church or to the community eg PCC membership; working for charitable organisations (0-9 points). Places allocated by the total number of points scored. Heaven's gates slammed firmly shut in the face of unbelievers; strong bias towards the middle classes in some of these criteria.

Exit: 96 per cent remain in full-time education at 16. Sixth formers – 86 per cent to higher education predominantly to northern universities, steady flow to Oxbridge, 9 per cent into employment, 5 per cent gap year.

Remarks: A top-flight state school, does well by its children regardless of ability or disposition. Only for Christians and a very few others.

St Albans School

Abbey Gateway, St Albans, Hertfordshire, AL3 4HB

Tel: 01727 855 521

Fax: 01727 843 447

Email: hm@st-albans.herts.sch.uk

Website: www.st-albans.herts.sch.uk

• Pupils: 780, all boys except for 38 girls in the sixth form • Ages: 11-19 • Religion: Multi-faith • School status: Independent • Opendays: Several throughout the year. Contact school • School gender: Boys • Day/boarding: Day pupils

SEN provision

Detail:

Experience of:

Mild: ASP; AUT; ADD; ADHD; DYSL; DYSP; HI; VI;

Others: OCD; TIC; Epi;

Summary: All our pupils are capable of coping with a rigorous academic education carried on at a rapid pace. A pupil with serious dyslexia or dyspraxia would struggle to cope. However, we recognise that even the ablest can experience specific difficulties that could prevent them achieving their fullest potential and could therefore benefit from some learning support. To this end, all new entrants are screened for previously undetected dyslexia and monitoring continues throughout a pupil's career. Where a problem is suspected, a diagnostic assessment is offered, following which an assessment by an independent educational psychologist may be recommended. Sometimes, an able pupil will have developed coping strategies which obscure a problem that comes to light only in later years as the demands of the work become more complex and staff are trained to spot such emergent difficulties. Various levels of support are available, including one-to-one tuition with a specialist teacher who is freelance but spends all her time at the school.

What we say about the school - the full Good Schools Guide review

Headmaster: Since 1993, Mr Andrew Grant MA PGCE FRSA, early fifties, a Cambridge English graduate. Active on HMC committees, Mr Grant is the perfect example of what a difference can be made to a school by a professional head with a sustained long-term commitment. He has overseen an impressive revival in his school and shows no signs of flagging. Relaxed, energetic, chatty and with appropriate toughness when required, he is good company and visibly 'hands-on'. Mr Grant communicates a buzz which permeates the place as a whole. 'I feel very personally identified with this place', he says, enjoys life 'outside the magic circle of the M25' and says of St Albans, 'it's a great place to be.' Mind you, he also modestly describes it as, 'a small cathedral city on the outskirts of our school playing fields' – but with justification! (see below). His own two boys have been pupils – one as head boy by popular choice and this, too, says a lot for the popularity and democracy of his regime. A good, solid head running a solidly strong school, now getting some of the acclaim it deserves.

Academic Matters: Everyone does GCSEs in core subjects plus three options chosen from a pretty standard range. In 2004, 100 per cent of pupils got A*-C in at least five subjects and most of those got A*-B. Top performers were art, maths, music, RS, science and the minority languages but results in all the other major subjects not far behind. History, geography, drama and business studies the most popular options. A levels, in a total of 20 subjects offered, similarly strong. Big numbers in maths and strong showings in all sciences, economics and English. Results good across the board and in The Independent's 2004 list of the country's top 50 schools, based on A level results.

As is so often the case in boys' schools (which this is, until a small number of girls move into the sixth) languages are less popular. However, a lapse in take-up in 2004 isn't typical and the school is keen to support langs, both ancient and modern. So numbers in all modern langs are again up throughout the school and Latin and Greek are picking up too. Staff changes are enlivening interest in German, so sadly threatened elsewhere. French, German and Latin are on an equal footing in year 7; pupils choose any 2 to continue into year 8. Ancient history popular and results at A/S level were the best nationwide in 2004. Big recent investments in IT – school now well-equipped with PC suites here and there and inter-active whiteboards – used effectively and enthusiastically by those staff who like them and eschewed by others who don't – a sensible policy.

Unobtrusive but efficient SEN provision with those who 'appear to need it' informally assessed by SENCo; edpsychs pulled in if necessary, pupils are assessed termly. 25 currently get some form of help (none with a statement of needs), usually one-to-one, rarely withdrawn from lessons and if they are, then they are rotated on a six weekly cycle so that no boy misses too much of the same subject. Extra help at lunchtime, post school popular. OK on dyslexia and dyspraxia, plus the occasional ADHD and those who find exams threatening. This is old fashioned proper back up, good for confidence and building self-esteem: no tricks, just patient ground work. Costs £25 per child per hour, 'works well for the school, works well for me' says the SENCo who works four full days a week and is chocabloc. School not really good for wheelchairs.

Games, Options, The Arts: In 2003, after a nine-year planning battle and two public enquiries, school finally opened 'Woollams' – 'the best school playing fields in the country'. School sold a 12-acre plot plus planning permission inside the purlieus of the city of St Albans and bought a 400-acre farm two miles down the road with the proceeds. Letting the rest, they then proceeded to level 75 acres to make 19 winter pitches for football and rugby, an all-weather hockey pitch, 7 cricket squares and 2 blocks of tennis/netball courts. Two elegant and impressive pavilions, one 'boyproof' and the other belonging to the energetic Old Albanians.

A 15-minute bus ride from the school but well worth it and pupils become gooey-eyed when they talk about it – as does the long-serving head groundsman and who can blame him? Twenty sporting activities are on offer here including all the major games but you can also try sailing, squash, badminton, aerobics, golf, cross- country athletics and table tennis. Regular tours worldwide.

The facilities are matched by the achievements. National and international honours, including, recently, three athletics internationals, an U16 England rugby cap, a Cambridge blue in hockey, two in cricket. 'Too numerous to mention' are school's representatives in county teams in many sports. In the 2005 English Schools AA national cross-country championships, half the county senior team came from St Albans. You get the picture. Younger, less sporty pupils feel that 'there's not so much to do for us' on the extra-curricular side but this apparently picks up as you move through the school in the shape of more, less physically demanding, clubs etc.

In case you think it's all sports, drama is strong and benefits from recently acquired house across the road from main school into which have been built teaching spaces and a good studio with top-class technics – a real boost for the subject. There is a large, well-equipped school hall which acts as a theatre for major productions as well as – how nice – a small outdoor theatre. School publishes 'The Albanian' – one of the most intelligent school mags we have seen. John Mole has been resident poet here for yonks – again a sensible and novel idea. Music is also strong – though music tech isn't big here – and lots of ensembles flourish. Annually, a huge tour taking many groups of all sizes goes to eg Barcelona, Paris – New York on the agenda in 2005. Annually also an oratorio concert, jointly with St Albans High, takes place in the cathedral. The school choir, which sings at school services twice weekly in the cathedral, is 60 plus strong and professional in approach and sound. We were treated to a Scarlatti motet – a privileged start to a morning for the whole school as well as for those who sing. School does not provide the choir for the cathedral – that is made up of boys and men (there is a girls' choir too) from all over the area but five pupils here are also in the cathedral choir – a double and challenging commitment but those we met who make it were articulately proud of the their involvement.

DT in first-rate new robotic suite, CDT is impressive and creative. Dof E is popular and begins with the silver award. CCF also strong. School owns Pen Arthur, a 'rugged' farmhouse in rural Wales and everyone goes there for a variety of activities and field work – a rare and well-used resource.

Background and Atmosphere: School founded in 948 making it one of the country's oldest. It is next to the cathedral and has inherited many of the foundation's buildings and some extraordinary rooms and nooks. It is not, however, the cathedral school and relations with the great building and its foundation are, says head, 'cordial, loose and ideal, with all the advantages of being thought a cathedral school and none of the disadvantages'. We know what you mean. We visited lessons in the old dungeon building and the library (well-stocked) is housed in a super ancient hall with gothic windows and yard-thick walls. Busts and memorials to the school's venerable history abound and sit comfortably with all the accoutrements of a thoroughly modern educational environment. Other buildings nestle amid beautifully kept gardens and school is reached by many via a walk over the cathedral green. A privileged setting. Strong involvement with the local community including excellent work on local conservation projects and links with local maintained schools.

Boarding went in the 1950s, the direct grant in the 1970s – 80 per cent had been on free places – and girls arrived in the sixth in 1991. Of the 40 or so new pupils into the sixth, most are girls but this still means that, proportionately, their numbers are small. The attitude of the school to them is healthy and we did not detect any of the cattle market mentality observable elsewhere. The girls, many from STAGS the local state girls' school, clearly love it and, despite – or because of? – their small numbers, thrive. A third of the staff are women. Perhaps this, together with the few girls and the sensible, unmacho attitude of the staff, makes for the relaxed, cheery and comradely atmosphere we observed throughout.

Pastoral Care and Discipline: Carefully structured tutorial system, prefects and a, now full-time, school nurse make for effective pastoral care. 'Anyone who brings drugs on site is too stupid to be here so they have to go,' says head, refreshingly. Random testing used 'on good grounds' and in co-ordination with home. Head has expelled for drugs and would again but no incidents for two years. School feels orderly but not oppressively so. A sense of self-discipline prevails. Food 'very good', enthuse pupils.

Pupils and Parents: Many come in on good network of school buses. 70+ per cent from local Herts area and about half of those from St Albans itself. The rest, including a good number of Jewish pupils, from north London, mostly from Enfield. Parents mostly professional/business/commercial and a large proportion new to independent education. A smaller number from other ethnic minorities or families where the first lang is not English. Very strong Old Albanians many of whom send their sons here and, later, their daughters. Many siblings so a strong family/community feel. Notable former pupils go back to the year dot but recent ones include Sir Tim Rice, archaeologist Lord Renfrew, film producer Mike Newell, General Sir Richard Lawson and Prof Stephen Hawking – himself.

Entrance: At 11 years old, 260 apply for 72 places. Tests in English, maths and VR and interviews all on the same day. Average IQ of 128 of those who make it. At 13, 90 applicants for up to 48 places. Tests as above plus three interviews and entry dependent on CE results. Around 50 applicants for 20+ places at 16 – predictions of A*-C at GCSE with As in A level subjects. Increasingly school the first choice and can afford to be choosy.

Exit: A very impressive list of subjects and destinations. All good solid stuff eg large numbers in 2003 to read maths at Warwick et al, equally large numbers in 2004 to read philosophy, economics or history at places such as Bath, Leicester, London. A sprinkling of Oxbridges in a spread of disciplines – all testament to a broad and serious education.

Money Matters: Variable numbers of schols worth 10-50 per cent of fees awarded on the basis of performance in the entrance tests at 11 and by separate exam at 13 and 16. Also means-tested bursaries up to 100 per cent of fees. Special bursaries for instrumental tuition from 11 and art.

Remarks: Justifiably in the Indie's top fifty on more grounds than the merely academic, unjustifiably omitted from this Guide until now, this is a correction we are happy to make. If the glitzy north London heavy-weights or the big boys in the shires are not your thing, quietly relocate to a spot on the St Albans bus route – and then gloat over your friends.

St Aloysius' College

45 Hill Street, Garnethill, Glasgow, G3 6RJ

Tel: 01413 323 190

Fax: 01413 530 426

Email: mail@staloysius.org

Website: www.staloysius.org

• Pupils: 945 boys and girls in senior school, all day; roughly 50/50 boys/girls • Ages: 11-18 • Religion: RC • Fees: £2,140-£2,313 • School status: Independent • School gender: Mixed • Day/boarding: Day pupils

SEN provision

Detail:

Now provide for in school:

Mild: DYSC; DYSL; DYSP;

Moderate: MLD; DYSL; DYSP;

Others: PMLD; Epi; Eat;

Experience of:

Mild: ASP; ADD; ADHD; VI;

Moderate: ASP; ADD; ADHD; EBD;

Severe: DYSL;

Others: TIC;

Summary: Eight members of staff are involved in the specific delivery of Learning Support. They are directed by two specialist staff, one in the senior school and one in the junior school. Learning support is based primarily in the classroom, the department striving first and foremost to work with the classroom teachers in an advisory capacity in order to provide maximum support to pupils with difficulties. As far as possible the emphasis is on enabling all pupils to follow the mainstream curriculum of the school. Other strategies are adopted as required.

What we say about the school - the full Good Schools Guide review

Head: Since 2004, Mr John Stoer BA PGCE (forties) who was educated at Dowie School, read theology at Bristol and originally went down the accountancy road, but rapidly changed to teaching, taking his PGCE at London University. A committed Catholic, he is the first lay head at St Aloysius and has always taught in the Catholic sector; starting at St Thomas More School in Chelsea, followed by being head of RE at St Philip Howard School off the East India Dock Road, thence Gunnersbury Catholic School in London where he was director of sixth form, followed by deputy head of The Campion School in Hornchurch. He comes to St Aloysius after ten years St Joseph's College in Staffordshire where he was also the first lay head. ('Steadily moving north'). A thoughtful man, entertaining and interesting, with a puckish sense of humour, Mr Stoer applied for St Aloysius because of its links with the Jesuit tradition which he first encountered at The Campion School (though it was, by then, out of Jesuit control). A theologian and a born teacher, he couldn't resist giving this editor a quick history lesson on Jesuit education via his (heavily marked in turquoise) copy of Ratio Studiorum, the Jesuit handbook, first published in 1586.

Mr Stoer arrived with a wealth of experience, a confidence to change and a subtle way of persuasion. The school, which had previously eschewed standard grades is now opting for the stronger Intermediate II (in the Scottish system) with music and religious studies taken as GCSEs (the latter is the only exam board with a Roman Catholic syllabus). Highers and advanced highers in S5 and S6. 'Real change doesn't happen quickly, you need to change hearts and minds'. No mass staff evacuations which might be expected to follow such radical surgery: just two or three who were of an age to retire. Mr Stoer and his wife, who have two children in the school, live in the West End of Glasgow.

Academic Matters: Year sizes of 156, S1 = mixed ability, but expect some setting further up the school into classes of around 22; pupils can move up and down. School moved to five one-hour lessons daily from September 2005, with ten minutes added on to the working day – five in the morning and five at the end. Curriculum in a state of flux currently, no standard grades at all, with pupils expected to aim for five highers in S5 and at least two advanced highers in S6. Recent results show that twice as many pupils took higher Latin than Italian, with French and Spanish the only other languages on offer. French, Spanish and the sciences the strongest kids on the block. English and maths perhaps a tad sad; we might expect more than 57 per cent getting A in these subjects and, frankly, nine failures in maths is too many, ditto seven in Geography. Music produced an astounding 10 out of 11 getting As at Higher grade. IT computing et al less than brilliant performers but new computing block should produce miracles 'ere long. Some of the classes are tiny – six in Latin five in drama; Spanish and media studies at A level, the latter outstandingly popular in S6. No recent take-up in Greek.

The school has heads of faculties rather than departments and it could be that some radical pruning may become necessary before too long. Impressive new computer suites used for straight IT and class learning with open access (staff not so keen on this as new Clavius building is vast and needs quite a lot of patrolling and there is no staff room in Clavius, though admittedly that was part of the original design). Dramatic chemistry labs with interesting clusters of really quite high tables round six dedicated work areas with gas and water access. Well-used library. School keen (very keen) on homework for all ages and has a dedicated learning website which children can access from home or wherever and carries lesson notes and homework assignments, homework club for all plus after school club for extra help – no stigma about popping in at any time. Huge strides in the SEN department, Mr Stoer was having a planning meeting with the head of SEN during our visit (and so of course we asked to stay). Number of pilot schemes afoot: laptops (and growing), mentoring (which is proving highly successful with four mentors now on staff) scribing, reading (team readers practise); this is a school aware of SEN disabilities and which is taking serious steps to facilitate learning. Asperger's, ADHD, dyslexia, dyspraxia, OK for the visually impaired ('we work with guidance from the eye hospital' – which includes using coloured lenses and overlays. NB apart from the dedicated Old Rectory, this is the first time this editor has come across coloured lenses being treated with anything other than lip service). Learning support either for the individual or small groups of pupils. The two new-builds have lifts, with Braille on the lift buttons, but the slope is such in the primary school that it would be impossible without hefty carriers to get a wheelchair into the classroom currently used for music.

Games, Options, The Arts: For an inner-city school there is a surprising amount of playground space (this includes car parking for important visitors – like this editor – otherwise it is hideous round here), and young were fooling around on the all-weather surface in a serious Glasgow rain at break time during our visit. Games are important in the Jesuit culture – 'sport helps pupils learn to accept both success and failure graciously' – and team games for all (at least once a week). The dedicated playing fields are down the M8 towards Stepps (our guides hadn't a clue where – they just 'slept on the bus'). Old-fashioned gym on site and impressive looking weights room. Quite good representation in rugby and regular winners of the Scottish Schools' Cup plus local and national caps in rugby, hockey and athletics. Annual rugby tour to Ireland and the occasional trip abroad. More for skiing than for rugby. Girls' games important too. Full-time co-ordinator of outdoor education and D of E just appointed, so expect masses more expos – kayaking, climbing, sailing, all good hearty stuff. The whole senior school decamps for a week's brisk outdoor education between S1 and S4, and post the public exams there are more jaunts and tripettes: walking the West Highland way, film making, trips to London and the like.

Glorious, light, sunny art department in the top of the elegantly stained-glass Mount building, nice line in flat painting, one or two jolly sculptures and some terrific fabric design plus a wizard Roman helmet made out of ring pulls from cans (our guide had been photographed in it and made sure we had seen quite how cunningly it had been made).

Music important with a vast range of instruments on offer and compulsory weekly lessons up to S2. Vibrant school orchestra, terrific and popular choir. This is a school where music really matters. Strong drama throughout the school, we were kicked out of a junior rehearsal with alacrity. Enthusiastic inter-house music as well as sport. Keen debaters; mass of clubs, chess, debating and film making popular, ditto D of E, and YE. Regular school links with other schools 'especially Jesuit ones' for exchanges and the like give pupils a 'broader outlook on life'.

Background and Atmosphere: School founded in 1859 to educate the Catholic community in the west of Scotland and is run still very much on the Jesuit principles that God is in all things, that human excellence and service to others and the 'fullest possible development of all the God-given talents of each individual' is paramount. St Aloysius College St A (St Aloysius Gonzaga 1568-91) was the patron of young people and the school is part of a network of over two thousand Jesuit seats of learning 'educating over two million students in sixty five countries', and one of the principle missions of Jesuit teaching is education. The school is based on not quite the apex of Hill Street, opposite the convent and next to the splendid Victoria Baroque Jesuit church, which the school uses for whole school mass and regular assemblies (about three times a week) – very much in the centre of Glasgow, just off the M8; brilliant for public transport and well-nigh impossible for car-bound visiting editors to find. The Hanson and Mount buildings are redbrick, serious Victoriana and have well withstood the test of time, however the two newer buildings, one housing the junior school, and the Clavius building which is home to the IT and scientific world, are already showing their age. The junior school is lovely, full of jolly hanging pics and tiny chairs in groups of six. It is fully self-contained but adjacent (and too many steps). The Clavius building, however glam it is, causes problems: the staff think it is too big to patrol, the pupils think it is 'pretty weird' to have form mass in the atrium surrounded by blocks of lockers, and the bright blue paint on the doors and cupboards is already chipping off (it has been repainted once); passages and stairs are horrendously narrow. Both new-builds are prize winners with Clavius top of the pops but neither look particularly clever next to the Rennie MacIntosh Glasgow School of Art, which is apparently just what the planners wanted.

Charming tiny little chapel in the main building, voluntary mass for all at 8.30 every morning – well-attended by parents pupils and staff and 'over by the time school starts'. Crowded during lent and the run up to exams. Crucifixes in every classroom, two Jesuits still on staff.

Pastoral Care and Discipline: New chaplain appointed. Jesuit principles pervade: formation in all things important including theology, philosophy, a commitment to ecumenism, and the resistance of atheism, materialism and consumerism, with an emphasis on 'service to others even as a lawyer or a doctor' (think UCAS forms). In the real world this means strong anti-bullying dogma in place and sin and wickedness treated with the contempt they deserve. Expect to be dismissed for trading in drugs at school, otherwise subjected to the expected scale of punishments – 'we would gradually raise the ante, but make sure that support programmes were in place to try and solve all problems in a positive way'. Sex education officially taught via RE 'and lousy', says a parent. Junior school operates discipline Stars and Stripes cards. Strong house system (based on the Jesuit saints: Campion, Loyola, Ogilvie and Xavier). Heads of houses double as guidance teachers and are responsible for 'the academic, pastoral, co-curricular and disciplinary' side of school life. Siblings in the same house as far as poss.

Pupils and Parents: Predominantly middle class core, almost exclusively RC, which, in the west of Scotland, historically means predominantly Scots, Irish and Italians, plus a tiny ethnic minority. Strongly supportive of the school, pupils come (in the main) from the wealth of suburbs that surround the city. Tranches of FPs who seem to accept that the school is progressively changing to lay staff. Fair number of first time buyers. 'Wide diversity'.

Entrance: School claims 'to admit pupils in the top half of the general population. 75 per cent of our pupils come from the top quarter of the population' – we are talking academically here. Priority given to practising Catholics and those who 'share the aims and values of Jesuit education'. More or less automatic from the junior school. Active sibling policy. Assessment, tests but previous school reports, school reference (and preferably one from the parish priest) are all taken into account. If pupils transfer from another independent school, St Aloysius checks that there are no outstanding fees as well as getting a reference.

Exit: Fair number leave post Highers with uni entry in the bag – a bare 70 per cent stay on. (Mr Stoer was surprised by this, but it is the nature of the Scottish uni entrance system and high time it was changed.) Some 95 plus per cent go on to tertiary education, the school provides a regular (tiny) trickle to the priesthood (some 15/20 pupils are serving in the local diocese) slightly larger trickle to Oxbridge. Deep reluctance to strike out from familiar territory, fair number seem to end up at Glasgow and Strathclyde unis, but they are getting 'progressively more adventurous'.

Money Matters: The school receives no state funding – not even apparently for classroom assistants for those with a record of needs which is odd. The original Jesuit concept was that their role was to educate free and the school has a certain amount of funding available. Parents are asked whether they need bursarial help at the time of application, almost automatic for families on income support, plus family discounts, but no named or dedicated bursaries. School does what it can to help. Will also try and help out if family hits financial crisis but with the usual strictures, parents must be up-front about the extent of their problems.

Remarks: A traditional and unusual school which has served the local community well – dedicated to providing 'improvement in living and learning to the greater glory of God and for the common good' (St Ignatius Loyola 1491-1556). St Aloysius has adapted well to the twenty-first century; it will be interesting to watch the developments in the exam department. So much better to get some exam practice at 16 rather than go straight to highers as previously.

St Anselm's School

Bakewell, Derbyshire, DE45 1DP

Tel: 01629 812 734

Fax: 01629 814 742

Email: headmaster@anselms.co.uk

Website: www.sanselms.co.uk

• Pupils: 195, including one-third girls. About two thirds board. 50 in pre-prep and 25 in nursery • Ages: 7-13, pre-prep 3-7 • Religion: C of E • Fees: Day: pre-prep £2160; £3,340-£4200. Boarding: £4,930 • School status: Independent • Opendays: Richard Foster believes every day is an Open Day - prospective parents are encouraged to visit on a normal working day • School gender: Mixed • Day/boarding: Takes boarders

---

SEN provision

Detail:

Now provide for in school:
- Mild: DYSC; DYSL; DYSP;
- Moderate: DYSC; DYSL;

Experience of:
- Mild: ASP; ADD; ADHD; EBD; HI; VI;
- Moderate: MLD;
- Others: SPD; EAL; Sp&LD; PD;

Summary: St Anselm's is a mainstream school and as such we welcome pupils with a broad cross-section of ability. Gifted children are stretched and those with specific learning difficulties have access to dedicated one-to-one specialist teaching. All children are fully integrated into every aspect of life at the school.

What we say about the school - the full Good Schools Guide review

Head: Since 1994, Mr Richard Foster (mid forties), energetic, friendly and very focused. Came to the school after a lifetime within the independent sector. Educated in a Kenyan prep school, Clifton College and then a BEd in history and PE at St Luke's in Exeter. Since then taught back in Kenya – including 9 years as head of Pembroke House School, 'a very English prep school'. Married to Rachel, also a qualified teacher, who helps in the pre-prep and in headmaster's wife role throughout the school. Their youngest child has just left the school, to follow the other two to Oundle. The head has no plans to leave the school and is on an open contract.

Entrance: No exam, children admitted at all ages providing there is space.

Exit: Recent scholarships include all three major academic scholarships to Oundle in 2003, when leavers gained 20 awards to schools such as Uppingham, Repton, Westonbirt, Oakham. Others in previous five years to Eton, Roedean, Rugby, Malvern, Stowe, Ampleforth, Shrewsbury, Oundle, Downe House and Moreton Hall. Non-scholarships go to a wide range of schools around the country.

Remarks: Tucked away on the edge of the attractive town of Bakewell, St Anselm's modest location belies its achievements. Superbly resourced, with a team of dedicated and enthusiastic staff, pupils appear beamingly happy. Prides itself on stretching each pupil to the limit of their potential. Visitors and staff are greeted politely as they pass and pupils show great courtesy at all times. 'I'm a bit of a stickler for manners,' says Foster.

Academically aims high, despite having no entrance exam. Around 30 pupils in each year – two classes in the transition year and three classes in the others. Setting from the age of 9 onwards (8 for maths).

Dedicated learning support team with one full-time and three peripatetic staff; about 1 in 10 take advantage of it. Follows the National Curriculum but with extras – we saw a very vigorous English lesson with 9-year-olds acting one of Shakespeare's bloodiest scenes. 'Sir, please, Sir, Can I be Hamlet next time?' Fabulous, exuberant classics master seen coaching small boy in Latin. Much emphasis on finding 'what makes the child buzz, then we can develop and nurture it.' Lots of schemes where effort is rewarded – certificates, prizes, house points, visit to Mr Foster to be congratulated after a particularly good piece of work. Parents get a grade slip every two-and-a-half weeks, to keep them abreast.

Keen on sport (four times a week), but 'we are mindful of children who are musical or artistic.' Two thirds play an instrument and all eight-year-olds p... the violin. New building – as ever – and lots of extras.

Homely boarding houses scattered about the site. Boys' dorms suitably boyish in decor, girls' are pretty and pink. New pupils have a guide in the same year and a senior mentor from the top year. One large dining-room for everyone (good).

Superb staff; blissful, confident children fizzing with energy and enthusiasm.

St Bede's School

The Dicker, Upper Dicker, Hailsham, East Sussex, BN27 3QH

Tel: 01323 843 252

Fax: 01323 442 628

Email: school.office@stbedesschool.org

Website: www.stbedesschool.org

• Pupils: 485 boys, 315 girls. About half board • Ages: 12-19 • Religion: Inter-denomination • Fees: Day £4,055; boarding £6,595 • School status: Independent • Opendays: May, September • School gender: Mixed • Day/boarding: Takes boarders

---

SEN provision

Summary: All who have contact with the department describe it as outstanding. The SENCo, Mrs Linda Gillham, in post for ten years, is very committed, efficient and with over 25 per cent of the school on the SEN register – she is also very busy. The majority of pupils with SEN are dyslexic with a wide range of abilities. Qualified staff with varying specialities give a broad service, eg all SEN teachers also teach in the main stream to GCSE. A strong inclusion policy gives pupils plenty of support and GCSEs are taken only when the pupils are ready and the choice of programme is made according to their strengths. The SEN staff are fully supported by the Headmaster and School with good communication apparent so that all departments are aware and act upon individuals needs.

What we say about the school - the full Good Schools Guide review

Head: Since 2002, Mr Stephen Cole (fiftyish) formerly head of St Paul's Collegiate in Hamilton, New Zealand. Took over from Mr Roger Perrin, who was here from the beginning (1978). Energetic and passionate about sport, remains loyal to the original philosophy of not selecting on academic grounds.

Academic Matters: Non-selective at entry but produces a good proportion of A/B grades at A level. A teacher/pupil ratio of 1 to 7 allows for lots of individual support – and the academically able have the Curriculum Enhancement Programme to keep them on the fast track. Students are not expected to take subjects where they have no natural aptitude, except English and maths. One pupil, who was floundering at a nearby, more pressurised, school and recently joined St Bede's and is now thriving (there are numerous such cases) said, 'here I am allowed to make mistakes – the pressure is off'. Another exceptionally able boy was not performing at a traditional school. Offered full academic scholarships at two top league schools, he chose St Bede's as the only school that would be flexible enough to accommodate his request to fast track some subjects so he could concentrate on a range of further subjects. Teachers take the view that for some pupils an E grade is a marvellous achievement. English, modern languages and art and media studies are particularly strong.

Games, Options, The Arts: Absolutely extraordinary choice – it's difficult to imagine anyone being bored here. All students take part in a club activities programme that runs every afternoon. Students must do one energetic activity each week but can get away with, for example, table tennis. At the moment, there are more than 140 activities on offer, with a daily choice of over 40. Clubs for everything, from car restoration to art appreciation. Facilities for the arts include a graphics design room, art studios and a photographic area and dark room. Music is a strength of the school, with nearly half the school involved in the musical programme. Numerous concerts, workshops and choirs performing every term at different levels. Parents are very welcome to attend. 'Everyone is allowed to do their own thing and is accepted for what they are but this is not an easy option and the students work hard.' Drama is doing very well and there is a new drama studio under construction which will open in January 2006. Lots of productions, musicals etc with a thriving weekly club for drama scholars. Own riding stables with a recently enlarged menage and excellent local riding. National success in tennis and swimming.

Background and Atmosphere: Leafy bit of East Sussex – many have long school runs or journeys on the school minibuses. Newly built extensions visible everywhere and on the 'to do list'. School runs the village shop and post office and helps look after the village church. An English School with a strong cosmopolitan element, staff and pupils are drawn from all the continents of the world. A happy, buzzy and diverse bunch – diversity breeds a tolerance and understanding that is perhaps the school's greatest strength.

Pastoral Care and Discipline: Parents much appreciate St Bede's' tolerant atmosphere and its caring pupil/teacher relationships. No major discipline problems reported – 'if people feel the school supports them, they're more likely to be kind to each other,' says the head. Students are told that the worst thing they can do is to make others unhappy. Strict drugs policy and anyone caught using or possessing drugs is out, and those suspected of drug use are tested. Choice of a multi-religious school meeting or an organised church service.

Pupils and Parents: About 20 per cent from overseas – 30 different countries. Most British pupils are from schools in Sussex, Surrey and Kent, with most day pupils coming from prep schools and community colleges in Sussex.

Entrance: Non-selective. Most children enter at 13 after an interview with the head, following references from the student's current school or through Common Entrance, scholarship or entrance test, although some enter in the sixth form. It is unusual for any pupil who has been interviewed and received a satisfactory report from his or her present school to be refused admission. Considerably over-subscribed, so pupils are admitted on a first come, first served basis.

Exit: Most go to university in this country, with a good number to Oxbridge. Many return to overseas universities. A sizeable number follow relatively unconventional careers, especially in art and design, theatre and dance.

Money Matters: Healthy – plenty of new builds and expansions demonstrates this. Numerous scholarships and bursaries for academic work, art, music, sport, dance and drama.

Remarks: Not a typical public school – not for tidy, traditional or tweedy types. Good for self-disciplined children who want the freedom to pursue their own interests.

St Bees School

St Bees, Cumbria, CA27 0DS

Tel: 01946 828 000

Fax: 01946 823 657

Email: mailbox@st-bees-school.co.uk

Website: www.st-bees-school.org

• Pupils: 190 boys, 120 girls. 125 board (40 weekly), the rest day • Ages: 11-18 • Religion: C of E • Fees: Day £3,107-£4,013; weekly boarding £3,985-£5,713; full boarding £4,856-£6,696 • School status: Independent • Opendays: October and May Day bank holiday • School gender: Mixed • Day/boarding: Takes boarders

SEN provision

Detail:

Now provide for in school:

Mild: DYSC; DYSL; DYSP; SpLD; HI; VI;

Moderate: DYSC; DYSL; DYSP; SpLD; HI; VI;

Others: EAL;

Experience of:

Mild: ASP; ADD; ADHD; EBD; CP;

Others: DEL; Epi; PD; Eat;

Summary: The St Bees School learning support unit is run by specialist staff catering for specific learning difficulties.

What we say about the school - the full Good Schools Guide review

Head: Since 2000, Mr Philip Capes, previously deputy head of Warminster School; engineering degree from Exeter, married to a primary school teacher, three children, one of whom attends St Bees. Safe, experienced pair of hands; an approachable head, clear about school's future. Many new staff since he arrived; planned retirement scheme for some long-servers.

Academic Matters: Broad range, from special learning unit to top scores at A level. Not a hothouse and doesn't claim to be. Much satisfaction over Ds and Es turned into Cs and above. 'Everyone is stretched,' says one satisfied parent, whose two sons' indifferent junior school achievements were turned into three As at A level – attributed to confidence instilled by being treated as an individual. Usual small school constraints on A level choices, but Latin, Greek and further maths available. GCSE – over 40 per cent at A and A*. IT, French and Spanish taught in innovative Management Centre (see below). Year 10 do some OU foundation courses. Very committed staff, who insist on hard work and high standards.

Games, Options, The Arts: Games fields everywhere in stunning 150-acre site. Rugby strong (tough fixture list), girls' sport also good. Large sports hall, squash and fives courts. Much PE teaching mixed. 60-acre 9-hole golf course on headland, shared with locals. Proximity to unspoiled part of Lake District has led to development of distinctive and successful tradition of outdoor activities. CCF for all aged 13-15. Artwork in evidence everywhere, drama lively, music very good; refurbished music school opened 2000 – many instrumental groups, choir sings in chapel and village priory, tours abroad with chamber orchestra every other year.

Background and Atmosphere: Founded as a grammar school in 1583; original schoolroom now a dining hall with past pupils' names carved on wall panels. Handsome Victorian additions in local sandstone spread over fine site 'between the sea and the sheep', and well integrated with St Bees village, where pupils wander freely. Girls admitted since 1976, so a proper co-educational school. Girls' houses in attractive terrace on the far side of useful local railway (footbridge), senior boys in two houses, one in the same building as the head. All new staff do boarding house duties. International Centre offers specialist EFL plus general courses for one year for up to 18 overseas students aged 11-16 – doubtless a useful boost to numbers. Many now from mainland China. Some join St Bees after basic course, some return home. All international pupils integrated into existing boarding houses.

Management Centre, opened in 1992, is an unusual and successful joint venture – used commercially as a conference centre in the week, by the school in evenings and at weekends.

There's a general air about the school of unhurried but purposeful activity. Working day ends for all pupils at 5.45pm – 'a boarding school with day pupils'. Various efforts to overcome inescapable sense of isolation, eg trips abroad, visits to Stratford, lecture programme, Oxbridge taster visit. Leavers' ball (with parents) a high point of social calendar.

Pastoral Care and Discipline: Housemaster/housemistress plus tutorial system. Staff: 22 male, 17 female. Claim that in a small 'family' school no one slips through the net seems reasonable, eg kitchen staff notice if someone isn't eating properly. 'Centralised matrons', husband-and-wife GP team, counsellor on call. Not much real naughtiness in this quiet backwater; pupils seem content with traditional discipline, reputedly tightened up by head since 2000. Drug supplying or sex mean the sack.

Pupils and Parents: Many local, though an increasing number from the north east (parents seeking a secure environment?); foreign nationals more in evidence further up the school. Extensive private bus system ferries day pupils to and fro, boarders picked up at nearest airports. Pupils refreshingly old-fashioned, perhaps a touch unsophisticated – neatly dressed in formal uniform, frank and unaffected in manner. Many bright boys and girls attracted to St Bees, says head, because of greater chance of representing school in multifarious activities.

Parents very supportive (some allow their names to be used in prospectus for potential parents to telephone – what a good idea); Cumbrian farmers and professionals, local industrialists (Sellafield – still – a huge employer). Very efficient marketing department; its boss goes on frequent recruiting trips abroad.

Entrance: Not very competitive – though International Centre students have to show realistic level of competence. Two-form entry, mainly from state schools, topped up at 13 and 16. Possibility of extension downwards into prep and nursery departments.

Exit: Nearly all to higher education (very little fall-out after GCSE); a sprinkling to Oxbridge, mainly to a wide range of old and new universities. 2004 leavers' list shows good cover of engineering, law, medicine; straight arts under-represented.

Money Matters: Bursaries for children of clergy, Services and former pupils, and a few for deserving cases. Up to 50 per cent academic and music scholarships; art and sports awards post-16.

Remarks: Good local school, strong reputation, not averse to change; palpable atmosphere of security in beautiful surroundings. Endless care taken over individuals.

ST CHRISTOPHER SCHOOL

Barrington Road, Letchworth, Hertfordshire, SG6 3JZ

Tel: 01462 679 301

Fax: 01462 481 578

Email: admissions@stchris.co.uk

Website: www.stchris.co.uk

• Pupils: 370 boys and girls, including 67 boarders
• Ages: 11-19 • Religion: Non-denom
• Fees: Junior school £2,415-£3,000; senior school £3,855-£6,775 • School status: Independent
• School gender: Mixed • Day/boarding: Takes boarders

SEN provision

Detail:

Experience of:

Mild: ASP; ADD; ADHD; EBD; DYSC; DYSL; DYSP; SpLD; HI; VI; CP;

Moderate: ASP; ADD; ADHD; MLD; DYSC; DYSL; DYSP; SpLD; CP;

Severe: EBD;

Others: SPD; OCD; TIC; EAL; Sp&LD; DEL; Epi; Eat;

Summary: Our strengths lie in supporting pupils with dyslexia, and dyspraxia, though not severe. Occasionally we incorporate successfully a few pupils with Asperger's syndrome.

What we say about the school - the full Good Schools Guide review

Head: Since 2004, Mr Donald Wilkinson MA MLitt (early fifties). Educated at the Royal Grammar School, Lancaster and Keble College, Oxford, where he got a history first. Previously at Manchester Grammar, Oakham and Newcastle-under-Lyme, then appointed head of Cheadle Hume in 1990. His second headship was Jerudong International School in Brunei. Married with four children; interests include sport and running ('depressingly slowly'). He feels that the traditional St Chris virtues of informality and tolerance need a strong academic underpinning. 'It has always considered itself set apart from the rest of the world but must recognise that there are important functions that the world expects it to fulfil. Good results and idealism are not mutually exclusive.'

Academic Matters: St Chris prides itself on taking children of wide-ranging abilities from 'average' upwards. Its results are very commendable, with over 98 per cent of pupils getting 5+ A*-C grades at GCSE in 2005, with 34 per cent A*/A grades. More than half of A levels were graded A or B. Art and psychology are two of the most popular A level subjects, from a list that includes photography, business studies and government and politics. Classes are small, averaging 18, with many A level classes in single figures. Pupils get a wide choice at GCSE, as only five subjects – two English, double science and maths – are compulsory. Other options include three modern languages, PE and IT. 'A broad education is vital to an individual's development but it is also vital that they are stimulated academically. I am very keen for the academic side to be as strong as it can be.'

Excellent support for individual needs from a specialist, highly-trained team. The school copes well with dyslexia and dyspraxia. A 'second to none' in-house counselling service is available. A handful of pupils have Asperger's. 'But we are certainly not a specialist unit,' says the head of Individual Needs. 'Other schools can cope better.' Some have one-to-one tuition (at extra cost), others are helped by a learning support assistant. Mainstream staff are given information and training on different needs. 'We have a strong individual needs department and we hope to make it stronger,' says the head. 'The true aim of learning support is to help with difficulties with a view to the child eventually managing on their own.'

Games, Options, The Arts: Not, traditionally, a school that excels at team sports. It is known rather for its magnificent climbing wall, its skateboard park and the outdoor pursuits club, which goes off for weekends surfing, climbing, potholing, white-water rafting. However, competitive sports are increasingly important; netballers are off to Spain and basketball is particularly popular. Standards in team sports like soccer and rugby are improving. 'Because we are so small, everyone has got a better chance of being part of a team.' Extensive playing fields, sports hall, new indoor swimming pool and the Letchworth Tennis Club is handily situated next door. At the end of the summer term the school decamps to a range of destinations from the Cotswolds to Saas Fee.

Art, including pottery, ceramics and photography, is strong at all levels, with plenty of spectacular work on display. DT is also important, with much emphasis on craftsmanship.

Plenty of performance opportunities, from major school musicals to orchestral concerts to recycled fashion shows. Great praise for the drama – 'the teacher took care to get to know all the children before he cast the play' – and the after-school music club. 'It's all about sharing and enjoying the experience of playing in a group.'

Lower sixth formers have the opportunity to spend time in Rajastan and/or Kosovo, visiting schools and development projects with which the school has had considerable involvement over the years.

Background and Atmosphere: Set up in 1915 under Theosophist principles, which include a wide age and ability range and co-education. Excellent, vegetarian meals; many Quaker influences, with pauses for silent reflection in meetings and assemblies. Self-government is central to the school ethos, and the head is in the process of reviewing the workings of the school council, which meets every two weeks. 'We need to find ways of ensuring that the council has an effective part to play. It should involve pupils in how the school operates, including what goes on in lessons. As a teacher, I like to ask pupils occasionally what works and what doesn't work.'

The 35-acre site accommodates a harmonious blend of old and new buildings, including the award-winning junior school extension, with its glazed roof and low energy use, and the new senior school IT and English building, built of wood and glass with a grass roof. The school has a very active environment committee and has won the Eco-Schools green flag award for energy monitoring.

Pastoral Care and Discipline: Liberal, caring, nurturing ethos, with no uniform and staff and pupils on first name terms. 'There's an air of tolerance here,' said a parent. 'They don't stamp on you for being eccentric.' Some parents are concerned that the greater emphasis on academic achievement may come at the expense of the liberal ethos. 'It is very important to look after children as individuals,' says the head, 'but not by allowing them to do as they please. We work for the child's best interests, but do not allow them to fulfil themselves at the expense of their work or behaviour.'

Drugs and alcohol are 'occasional problems that are dealt with as appropriate'.

No prefects: sixth formers are elected to take charge of aspects of school life such as games, the environment and social events. The boarding system has been reviewed and will continue on largely weekly boarding lines.

Pupils and Parents: A liberal lot, who have found an alternative to more hot-house, authoritarian establishments, and tend to be fiercely protective of the school ethos. The school runs a daily bus service from north London; most other pupils live nearby or along the rail route which runs from Kings Cross to Cambridge. After school, a steady stream of pupils make their way the mile or so to the station.

Entrance: Most junior school pupils move on automatically, 'unless we feel in the light of experience that the child wouldn't benefit from the senior school. We try to keep parents fully aware and school and family will make the decision together.' Outsiders come in for half a day, take part in assessments which include cognitive ability tests and extended writing, and have an interview. Parents can chat with senior staff at the same time. 'We take children whom we think will do well. We try to assess their underlying ability and to build up a rounded view.' Students coming into the sixth form need at least five grade Bs at GCSE.

Exit: A few leave after GCSEs for sixth form colleges, schools closer to home or those with greater vocational opportunities. Nearly all sixth form leavers go on to higher education – including two or three a year to Oxbridge – to do courses that range from Astrophysics at Exeter to, wonderfully, Surf Science and Technology at Plymouth.

Money Matters: A few bursaries are available for families who fall into financial difficulty, but not a hugely endowed school.

Remarks: Liberal, creative school with strong spiritual underpinning and environmental values. The new head is set on greater academic rigour; parents are happy with this while still wishing to preserve the liberal outlook.

St Christopher's School

32 Belsize Lane, Hampstead, London, NW3 5AE

Tel: 020 7435 1521

Fax: 020 7431 6694

Email: admissions@st-christophers.hampstead.sch.uk

Website: www.st-christophers.hampstead.sch.uk

• Pupils: around 235 girls; all day • Ages: 4-11 • Religion: Non-denom • Fees: £3,193, inclusive of lunch and non-residential trips • School status: Independent • School gender: Girls • Day/boarding: Day pupils

SEN provision

Detail:

Now provide for in school:

Mild: ADHD; EBD; DYSC; DYSL; DYSP; HI; VI;

Moderate: ADD; MLD; DYSC; DYSL; DYSP;

Others: CD; OCD; EAL; Sp&LD; Epi;

Experience of:

Mild: ADD;

Severe: DYSL;

Summary: Equivalent of four days support for children with mild learning or co-ordination difficulties.

What we say about the school - the full Good Schools Guide review

Headmistress: From 2003, Mrs Susan (Susie) West BA Hons PGCE MA Educational Management (fifties). Educated at Howell's, University of Newcastle, Oxford (PGCE) and OU. Began teaching career at Oakham School with 11 to 18-year-olds and to say she has had a wide range of jobs since would be an understatement. Highlights include head of St Bede's, Eastbourne pre-prep, head of English at a school in Kuala Lumpur, housemistress at Sherborne School for Girls, year 4 teacher at Sussex House, plus a few spells in business. Most recently was deputy head at Kensington Prep. Divorced with grown son, daughter in university. A breath of fresh air in the intimidating world of London preps – down to earth, straight- talking, no hint of snobbery. Always puts the girls first, occasionally exasperating some mums. Cycles to school every day from Pimlico.

Entrance: Unique, we think, and hinges entirely on the fact that the school possesses 13 classrooms rather than 14. With two classes per year group, this leaves only one room (capacity 18 girls) for reception. Now read carefully: girls born in September to February enter reception at four-and-a-half and spend seven years at the school. Those with March to August birthdays stay at nursery an extra year and start in year 1 at 5+, spending six years at the school. Name down at birth – 'we have had calls from the maternity ward'. The school closes the register at 200 names (for 38 slots) but tries to make allowances for people who have suddenly moved to the area. All places awarded on the results of assessments (of potential, not accomplishment) and play. Looking for bright berries, but also a mixture of personalities – 'some leaders, some quieter girls, the odd eccentric.' Sisters accepted automatically unless they are screamingly unsuited to the place. Vacancies arise from time to time, mainly at the end of year two. Over a third of pupils live within walking distance. Rest mainly from, Highgate, St John's Wood, Maida Vale and Islington.

Exit: Lots to South Hampstead High and Francis Holland. A few to St Paul's, Haberdashers' Aske's, City of London, Channing, North London Collegiate. Handful to boarding schools: Queenswood, Wycombe Abbey, Downe House, Badminton. Sometimes one to Henrietta Barnett.

Remarks: High-achieving, girls' prep in large, airy Victorian dwelling in leafy back road. Dates back, in a convoluted way, to 1883, but was established in its current form in 1950 by the writer Rosemary Manning. Strong family feel, sheltered, cosy, but not twee. Stairs central to proceedings, with throngs of confident little girls making their way up and down, oblivious to headmistress and teachers battling through the crowd. New uniform 100 per cent cotton – 'good for the skin but hell to launder,' said a mum. When we visited, girls were dressed in a mixture of summer and winter wear, shorts and tracksuit trousers, dresses and tunics, shoes and trainers – somehow all gelling into an attractive and comfy uniform. No specific school rules, just the word 'respect'. 'The school has a feeling of controlled but bubbling energy,' said a mother.

Years 4-6 tucked into horrific concrete classroom block out back (plans afoot for a rebuild) – lovely inside though, with super rooms for DT, science, art etc. Library and computer building designed in Scandinavian style with light wood and big windows. Unusually broad range of subjects on offer. French and Spanish both taught, plus Mandarin club, and head dreams of 'putting Latin back' in the programme. Chess part of the curriculum years 2-6. Reading taught mainly through Jolly Phonics, with other methods as back-up. No scholarship class and no setting, with exception of one investigative maths lesson per week in years 4-6. Practice tests every Friday at the beginning of year 6 help to insure that girls shine in senior school entrance exams. Homework burden can get a bit intense as girls progress up the school. Parents gush about special needs help (with no stigma attached) for the few girls – mostly younger siblings – who need support. 'They've done everything they can to help my daughter,' said one grateful parent. Another, whose daughter was attending a special programme for her disability out of school, was impressed that her form teacher had volunteered to attend a course to help her continue the programme in class. Similarly, school takes pains to integrate loners and to thwart cliquishness.

In keeping with the tradition started by Miss Manning, the school excels in music. Over 50 per cent of girls learn at least one instrument at school (plus loads outside). Four music competitions each year (wind, strings, piano and ensemble) plus senior, junior and chamber choirs, two orchestras, and – our favourite – junior and senior piano clubs to take the isolation out of learning that lonely instrument. Recently held joint concert with nearby boys' prep, The Hall, and keen to do more in this vein. High quality artwork displayed throughout school and art history taught as a separate subject in its own room. Less emphasis on PE. Cramped site allows netball, short tennis, rounders. Also some unihoc, tag rugby, cricket, pop lacrosse etc. Gymnastics in school hall which doubles as canteen. Tarmacked playground heavily used, plus small play area out back – somehow sufficient. Huge range of school trips to theatre and museums, taking advantage of London on the doorstep. Interesting parents – media, City, entertainment – with strong opinions. Extremely useful eg in helping to organise themed special studies days in the summer term with visiting speakers. Multi-cultural, though not particularly multi-ethnic. No beef, pork, ham, bacon, shellfish or nuts on menu – we suspect you're out of luck if you don't like chicken. Assembly every Monday, hymns sung, but tone is non-denominational – many children out of school on Jewish holidays.

Not traditional, not high-tech (one interactive whiteboard for 240 girls, though more to come), not woolly. But a well-thought-out and jolly nice school.

ST DAVID'S COLLEGE, LLANDUDNO

Llandudno, Conwy, LL30 1RD

Tel: 01492 875 974

Fax: 01492 870 383

Email: headmaster@stdavidscollege.co.uk

Website: www.stdavidscollege.co.uk

• Pupils: 265, 200 boys, 65 girls (170 board) • Ages: 11-18 • Religion: Non-denom • Fees: Boarding £5,260-£5,465; day £3,420 £3,553. Dyslexic pupils boarding £5,914-£6,177; day £4,032-£4,199 • School status: Independent • School gender: Mixed • Day/boarding: Takes boarders

SEN provision

Detail:

Centre of excellence for:

Mild: DYSC; DYSL; DYSP; SpLD;
Moderate: DYSC; DYSL; DYSP; SpLD;
Severe: DYSC; DYSL; DYSP; SpLD;
Others: EAL;

Experience of:

Mild: ASP; ADD; HI;
Others: SPD; DEL; Epi;

Summary: We take great pride in our whole school approach to dyslexia and related difficulties. Our emphasis is on using appropriate teaching strategies with small classes, supported by an extensive sporting and extra-curricular programme. The whole ethos is geared to raising the self-esteem of our pupils, so important if their talents are to be uncovered and nurtured.

What we say about the school - the full Good Schools Guide review

Head: Since 1991 Mr William Seymour MA (mid fifties). Educated at Aldenham (head boy) and read natural sciences at Christ's College, Cambridge. Arrived almost by chance at St David's in 1969, liked it, and stayed on, becoming director of studies, housemaster and then head. His wife, Shirley, is a huge support on the pastoral side. One of his two children attended St David's and his daughter has returned as wife to one of the living-in housemasters. A thoughtful, sympathetic man, wise to the ways of the young, and, he says, 'still much stimulated by the environment'. Committed to providing opportunities for young people for whom success, for one reason or another, has proved elusive. Nearing the end of his span – retiring July 2006, but he has established a strong team.

The new head will be Mr Christopher Condrup, currently a housemaster at Churcher's College.

Academic Matters: St David's cannot be judged in any conventional academic sense. It makes no bones about being a school for dyslexics and is rightly proud of both its sense of purpose and achievement in this field. Two thirds of the school have specific learning difficulties and receive special help. In any straight league table comparison it would languish at the lower end but, in what the children achieve against their own capacity for learning and academic success, it would tell a very different tale. Even so, there is a good range of A level options (16 including philosophy, sports science and performing arts) and a respectable showing of As and Bs. In this, and the solid 98 per cent pass rate at all grades, can be found some astonishing personal success stories.

The school has pioneered a multisensory teaching policy for dyslexic pupils, evolving a whole school approach, with much cross-referencing between mainstream and individual lessons. There is an outstanding level of specialist help, given individually or in small groups, in the superbly equipped Cadogan Centre. Surprisingly though, no central library worthy of the name and year group libraries seemed only adequate. Very strong on business studies and powerful performers in the Young Enterprise field. IT provision is excellent, as one would expect in a school like this, and it is used both intensively and extensively. CAD is a speciality, and City and Guilds qualifications are on offer. DT much enhanced by the brand-new centre opened in October 2002. Pupil/teacher ratio 6 to 1.

Games, Options, The Arts: The school aims to 'develop the whole person, promoting self-belief and confidence and meeting the needs and aspirations of each pupil'. So, the emphasis is very much on challenge, teamwork and developing physical and mental robustness and a huge range of activities is on offer. Regard is paid to conventional team games and all children take part and with fair success, but it is up in the hills of Snowdonia, the Alps, the Arctic Circle or Kilimanjaro that St David's comes into its own. There is a powerful team of outdoor activity instructors and the school is full of enthusiastic scuba-divers, kayakers, climbers, trekkers, ocean sailors, kite-buggy riders, 4x4 offroaders, skiers, fell-runners, mountain bikers etc both losing themselves and finding themselves in their own particular activity. Some even go on to represent Wales. D of E an important element. Art is very strong, and half the children learn a musical instrument. Photography is another popular speciality. Drama provision being developed with new investment in theatre equipment.

Background and Atmosphere: Founded in 1965 by John Mayor, who saw dyslexic children in the public school system sinking without trace. He acquired a fine late medieval mansion with 30 odd acres on the edge of the Snowdonia National Park in the outskirts of Llandudno in a wonderful situation and St David's was born. The heart of the school is its dark oak-panelled reception rooms, hung with fine portraits of long-departed Mostyns, but it has spread into every conceivable outbuilding and, while some of the further additions have not exactly added to the aesthetic appeal, they are very fully and inventively used (hobbies rooms, multi-gym, squash court). It has a delightful unselfconsciousness and no one, staff or children, seemed aware of tarmac walk areas that looked as if they have been the subject of a not unsuccessful carpet bomb attack, or its dingy corridors. There is however a programme of improvement, with appealing new boarding blocks for both girls and boys already up and running, in which it might be hoped that a general spruce-up one day be included. The effect, though, is friendly and all-embracing, with a good bustle about it, and a warm family atmosphere, and a feeling of care for each other. Very positive Christian ethos.

Pastoral Care and Discipline: The great benefit of a small school, says the head, is that it is difficult to get forgotten. Each pupil is supported by a veritable web of housemasters, tutors and team leaders and no area of life is overlooked. The staff profile leans towards youth, enthusiasm and energy, though there are enough grizzled veterans of the chalkface to give a good balance. Hot on bullying and drugs, though neither is a serious problem.

Pupils and Parents: The pupils are not particularly polished or sophisticated but they are confident, articulate and friendly and enormously proud of their school and what it has helped them to achieve. Dyslexia is no respecter of social or geographical barriers and the children come from every possible walk of life and every part of the country and abroad. At least 30 are statemented by different local authorities and, for others, the fees are a struggle, while at the other end of the scale, the Earl Cadogan was so delighted with what St David's did for his son that he became a school governor and the family showed their appreciation by supporting at least three major building projects which bear the family name. Quite a strong local element too, who choose the school for its good all-round education.

Entrance: Largely at 11. No formal test. Interview and school reports. At the discretion of head, who will take them if he feels children can benefit from what the school has to offer, and the school is sufficiently able to cope with such difficulties as they have. Fills school on a first come, first served basis. Some vacancies at 16.

Exit: Some to vocational courses at 16. Mainly to university, where the large majority will study the more technical subjects.

Money Matters: Excellent value, given marvellous staff/pupil ratio. Non-dyslexics pay on a slightly lower scale.

Remarks: Has no academic pretensions and would not wish to be thought of as smart. Its greatest resource is its people. What they do for children with educational difficulties and, in particular dyslexia, is just marvellous. They are given not just a high level of educational support but the wherewithal, through a huge range of sporting and creative activities, to achieve success and self-esteem and the confidence to take life's difficulties in their stride.

St Dominic's Sixth Form College

Mount Park Avenue, Harrow-on-the-Hill, Middlesex, HA1 3HX

Tel: 020 8422 8084

Fax: 020 8422 3759

Email: stdoms@stdoms.ac.uk

Website: www.stdoms.ac.uk

• Pupils: 805; just over half are girls • Ages: 16-19
• Religion: RC but other faiths accepted • School status: State
• Opendays: Contact college • School gender: Mixed
• Day/boarding: Day pupils

SEN provision

Detail:

Now provide for in school:

Mild: ASP; ADD; ADHD; EBD; DYSC; DYSL; DYSP; VI; CP;

Moderate: ASP; EBD; MLD; DYSC; DYSL; DYSP; VI; CP;

Severe: EBD; DYSL; VI; CP;

Others: EAL; Epi;

Experience of:

Mild: HI;

Moderate: ADD; ADHD; HI;

Severe: DYSC; DYSP;

Others: Eat;

Summary: The learning support department at St Dominic's Sixth Form College actively liases with parents, students, feeder schools and local SEN agencies to ensure that the support provided for those with SEN requirements is specific to their individual requirements.

During enrolment all new students are screened for learning difficulties via computerised and written assessments. This information is then used to support the students with the most effective method available. Types of support range from full-time Personal Assistants for those with severe physical difficulties, classroom assistants and one-to-one support sessions.

What we say about the school - the full Good Schools Guide review

Principal: Since 2004, Mr Patrick Harty BSc PGCE MA(Ed) NPQH, early forties, a scientist and engineer, open, relaxed and positive. Previously taught at three schools, then a first deputy headship at Parmiter's School in Watford, a second at Nicholas Breakspear RC School followed by his first headship at Marlborough School – both in St Albans. Mr Harty spent between two and four years in all his previous posts but is clearly in no hurry to move from St Dominic's about which he is infectiously enthusiastic and has plans! Faith is the common denominator here – 'our faith base is just as important as our academic performance', he stresses, and these two factors come up again and again. 'The fundamental mission for the college is to provide education for the Roman Catholics of Harrow – in a multi-faith community ... one of the reasons for our success is that we provide an academic atmosphere.' The job has its challenges and its frustrations but the rewards are palpable too and Mr Harty has the energy and the humour to take it all on. He is impressively and vigorously supported by his vice principal, Mr Mark Nicholls – they were colleagues in St Albans – and clearly enjoy working as a mutually supportive team.

Academic Matters: Teaching is good here. Staff are efficient and pupils warmly praise their dedication and care. Expert help is given to prospective pupils about their subject choices and to existing pupils about their future courses and destinations. A very good range of courses and subjects offered – A levels include art history, business studies, classical civilisation, further maths, human biology, four modern languages, PE and Latin – in addition to all the ones you'd expect. Results are impressive. More than 82 per cent A-C pass rate in 2005. 55 students got three or more A grades, with 18 getting four and two getting five. Biggest cohorts by far in biology, chemistry and psychology – results impressive in all three. Large numbers also taking the other sciences, maths, Eng lit and business studies and average 75-85 per cent A-C in most. AVCEs taken in business studies, ICT and travel and tourism with, again, respectable results or better. GNVQs taken in business – results more mixed but some stars. Few takers for modern languages but results pretty good and outstanding in Italian – all langs taught by native speakers.

SEN is good here and individuals' physical as well as educational needs can be met. Almost everywhere is accessible by wheelchair. Everyone is assessed on enrolment and individual learning programmes are constructed where necessary. A 'Skills for Life' manager, ie a SENCo with add-ons, organises support in class or one-to-one. Little EAL required. Average class size of 16 with max 22.

Games, Options, The Arts: Very little on site – simply there is no space. School borrows facilities from Harrow School down the road but for A level PE only. Games not compulsory but football and a few other sports are options in the Wednesday 'activities' slot. One tarmac playground on which football is played. New block to be opened in September 2006 will free more space for art and DT rooms and facilities – much needed. Art and design and DT taken by small but significant numbers with creditable results. Music is currently taught at a partner school but will move back on site from September 2005 and into the new block the following year. One small trapezoid drama studio – theatre studies taken by 19 students in 2004 with mixed bag of results but this is not a such a high profile subject here. Space is at such a high premium that the school's few larger rooms cannot be spared for large productions.

Work experience, trips, lectures, opera visits, talks, the Duke of Edinburgh Award scheme, conferences – there is plenty going on, though some students feel that more could be done and that peers elsewhere are offered more on the extra-curricular side. Space, again, is a factor. However, the Comenius project sponsored a trip to Malta, a politics group went to Florida, history of art to Rome and the college has good links with schools in Italy. You wouldn't come here on account of the extra-curricular but there are more opportunities here than immediately meet the eye.

Background and Atmosphere: It's like a mini mini university campus – with the stress on mini. A cluster of buildings of different ages and styles sits on a leafy bit of Harrow-on-the-Hill, surrounded by some of the priciest bits of residential north-west London. Private schools are all around – John Lyon, Orley Farm and, of course, the local Big Brother. It's quiet, attractive, enhanced by the super chapel – a 1920s bit of retro Arts and Crafts – but none of the buildings are unappealing and the site has been developed with sensitivity, since giving up being a convent school in 1979. The new four storey block is taking up outdoor space the college can ill afford to lose but needs must when you are over-subscribed 3 to 1 and teaching and IT rooms are essentials. It took 7 years to get planning permission so no one should expect the college's enviable reputation to lead to a rush of new-build to meet demand.

We visited on a sunny spring day so students were gathering everywhere, especially on the few grassy patches. On wintry days there are few places to go and the canteen, in which lunchtime sittings are, of necessity, staggered, is small and unappealing. The food is criticised – 'too expensive and horrible', we were told and certainly there was a preponderance of pasta and pies. Sales, however, are very high so it can't be all bad. There is a salad bar but a two-slice white bread sandwich was £1.20, a jacket potato with tuna mayo £1.50. There is no common room – nor plans for one – and this lack of social space is the students' main complaint. However, there are plans to extend the social space of the canteen and provide an outdoor sheltered area. Off-site there is nowhere much to go either so everything is conducive to work – and these are, in the main, highly motivated students. The atmosphere is harmonious and co-operative and discipline – mostly in the firm-but-fair hands of Mr Nicholls – is enforced, much as you'd expect at any well-run school. There may not be anywhere much to go in non-lesson time but he will make sure you go there. One such resort is the excellent, well-stocked and workful library, another is the ICT room and, by September 2006, the new building will greatly increase workspace. Considering the number of people packed in here it was surprisingly orderly and tidy – we have seen far more mess in far more august and spacious establishments.

Everyone in this very ethnically mixed college looked happily integrated and 'there is no racism here' though we did hear regrets from a few that the ethnic groups didn't mix as much as in students' previous schools. The principal was mystified at this and, certainly, the visual evidence didn't support it. Staff and students seemed on good – first name, in fact – terms and there is a feeling of mutual respect.

Pastoral Care and Discipline: The faith base of the college is crucial and homogenising although no more than 50 per cent of students are Roman Catholic. What counts is faith: 'I will expect the young person to talk about their faith at interview,' says the principal. There is a chaplain and a weekly, voluntary, mass. Everyone has two lessons weekly of Religious and Moral

Education. The staff monitors attendance very carefully and there is an electronic registration system at each lesson that picks up unauthorised absence very quickly but absenteeism isn't a problem here. Students realise how prized places are and don't want to jeopardise theirs. Tutors monitor all aspects of a student's life and progress. Many staff stay for 10 plus years – stability counts. Student council and a peer listening system. Progress grades are issued half-termly. Zero tolerance of violence and drugs.

Pupils and Parents: There are 7 boys to 9 girls because more girls meet the academic entrance requirements. Of the 50 per cent who are non-RC, 25 per cent are Hindu, 16 per cent Muslim and the rest a mix of everything else. Most live locally in Harrow but they come from more than 50 schools in five other boroughs as well as from Berks and Bucks. A commitment to religious faith is the common denominator as well as, increasingly among the non-Catholics, academic ability.

Entrance: The vast majority come from the Salvatorian College and Sacred Heart on unconditional offers. The rest must meet various criteria based on verifiable religious commitment and academic predictions. Criteria vary depending on courses applied for but, for example, for a full A level course in four subjects seven GCSE passes are required plus at least Bs in the A level subjects. All are interviewed.

Exit: Local ie the various London University colleges and Brunel predominate here but there's a good crop of other redbricks etc notably Manchester, Southampton, Leicester and so on. Lots of law, business and medical courses but there are fine arts students and teaching students – they go everywhere to do everything. It's a very impressive list and notably lacking silly courses at exploitative institutions. Students from here clearly mean to have proper careers.

Money Matters: Free if you're under 19. Excellent and enlightened system of bursaries for students and staff to fund specific projects and trips.

Remarks: Measured against its peers on academic achievement, St Doms outscores virtually all the local competition. If the serious work/faith combination does it for you and outweighs the space and facilities other places offer, get onto your priest/imam/rabbi pronto and get those grades.

St Dunstan's College

Stanstead Road, Catford, London, SE6 4TY

Tel: 020 8516 7200

Fax: 020 8516 7300

Email: jdavies@sdmail.org.uk

Website: www.stdunstans.org.uk

• Pupils: 480 boys and 340 girls, all day • Ages: 11-18
• Religion: Anglican foundation • School status: Independent
• School gender: Mixed • Day/boarding: Day pupils

SEN provision

Detail:
Now provide for in school:
Mild: ADD; ADHD; DYSC; DYSL; DYSP;
Moderate: DYSL;
Experience of:
Mild: HI;
Others: EAL; Epi;

Summary: The College wants to welcome any pupil that meets its required entrance standards.

The learning support department works on a one-to-one or small group basis with pupils. All pupils who have an identified learning need will be offered support, usually on a weekly basis. Pupils are taught in a structured, cumulative and multi-sensory way that builds on existing knowledge and provides revision and reinforcement of new learning. Strategies to support independent learning are taught and pupils are encouraged to discover their own most effective ways of learning.

There is a full-time head of learning support who screens all children on entry to the school. Pupils at St Dunstan's College whose learning needs require a heightened awareness amongst teaching staff are put on School Action and are issued with an individual education plan (IEP). Some pupils at St Dunstan's College do use laptops. This provision is co-ordinated by the head of learning support.

The college is able to offer specialist support for those pupils with dyslexia.

What we say about the school - the full Good Schools Guide review

Head: Since 2005, Ms Jane Davies BSc. She joined the College in 2000 as deputy head having been head of maths at Trinity School in Croydon.

Academic Matters: At A level 66 per cent of grades A or B, at GCSE 44 per cent A or A*. Class sizes small, 20 max in prep, pre-prep and lower senior school, smaller thereafter. Youngish staff, average 35 years, one third female. Pupils are setted for maths in years 7-9 and in all subjects for GCSE. Lessons are well structured, homework is taken seriously and there is a feeling of serious intent and work to be done around the busy and sometimes crowded school corridors. Staff training taken seriously. Achieving well especially given the competition from selective schools on its doorstep, which take the highest flyers. Very few children have special educational needs.

Games, Options, The Arts: Sport is important, although if you're not a rugger bugger you'll still fit in and get along OK. Less sporty pupils head for the popular after-school clubs – pets to chess. National U13 fives champions and school judo champions. Enthusiastic games staff include specialists such as Neil Taylor, a former county and England cricket player. One third of the school learns a musical instrument and there is plenty of activity, with two school orchestras, concerts at Southwark cathedral, six choirs, and regular overseas visits. Drama strong, with 15 in-house productions each year, an electronic workshop for learning the art of theatre production. Corridors are adorned with pupils' art – run of the mill stuff. Duke of Edinburgh Award Scheme: second nationwide for number of awards; CCF strong.

Background and Atmosphere: Originally built as a boys' school in 1888, went co-educational over ten years ago. The old building, fondly described by some as Hogwartesque, is dark and imposing, though there's some OK new build. Busy inner-city site next to a road junction is not enviable, nor is tangling with the South Circular a joyful way to spend your mornings, nor is the immediate area notably salubrious. Parents and the coaches drive inside the gates to drop the children off.

Pastoral Care and Discipline: Pastoral care is excellent, 'cannot be faulted' according to parents, a real strength of the school with a lot of effort and manpower invested in it. 'St Dunstan's picked up instantly on a special educational need for my child, which had not been noticed in two other independent prep schools. They were extremely supportive and my child was not singled out in any way.' There are heads of year, heads of section, a prefect system and mentor if needed.

Discipline is firm and the school take a harder line than the rest of society on misdemeanours. Straight out for drugs. Bullying not tolerated – it (but one hopes not the bully) is stamped on as soon as it appears.

Pupils and Parents: Parents are professional but in no way snooty – would consider Alleyn's to be stuffy, Dulwich College to be overwhelming; school suits a more laid-back, happy-go-lucky child. 30 per cent of pupils are from ethnic minorities, which reflects the immediate neighbourhood; all pupils speak English. Children come from all over south east London; coaches daily from Blackheath, New Cross, Clapham, Streatham, Farnborough and Bromley. After-school club until 5pm.

Entrance: With improving results it's become easier to recruit staff and the school is becoming more academically selective. Oversubscribed – half from the prep school and most of the rest from other independents. Exam preparation available on Saturday mornings in the autumn term.

Exit: Most pupils go to their first choice of university, one third of those are to the top tier universities to read medicine and other academic subjects. A couple to Oxbridge.

Money Matters: Competitively priced for a London day school. Around 10 pupils per year get some help with fees – to be eligible household income must be under £25,000.

Remarks: Busy, bustling feel. A useful option.

St Elizabeth's Catholic Primary School

Queen's Road, Richmond, Surrey, TW10 6HN

Tel: 020 8940 3015
Fax: 020 8332 0986
Email: info@st-elizabeths.richmond.sch.uk
Website: www.st-elizabeths.richmond.sch.uk

• Pupils: 215 boys and girls (plus 28 boys and girls in nursery), all day • Ages: 4-11, nursery 3 • Religion: Catholic • School status: State • School gender: Mixed • Day/boarding: Day pupils

SEN provision

Detail:
Now provide for in school:
- Mild: ASP; ADD; ADHD; EBD; DYSC; DYSL; DYSP; VI; CP;
- Moderate: ADD; ADHD; EBD; MLD; DYSC; DYSL; DYSP;
- Severe: DYSL;
- Others: SPD; EAL; Sp&LD; Epi; PD; Oth;

Experience of:
- Mild: AUT; DS; SpLD; HI;
- Moderate: ASP; AUT; SpLD; HI; VI;
- Severe: ASP; ADD; ADHD; EBD; DYSC; DYSP; SpLD;
- Others: CD; OCD; PMLD; SLD;

Summary: St Elizabeth's School takes particular care and concern for the children with special needs. Each child's needs are evaluated and special provision is put in place according to their needs. We cater for a wide variety of special needs which at the moment includes, dyslexia, dyspraxia, ADHD, hemiplegia, cerebal palsy, speech and language difficulties, epilepsy, semantic pragmatic difficulties, mild visual impairment and moderate learning difficulties. We are open to receiving children with an kind of special need. When children enter the school the parents may approach the headteacher or the SENCo if their child has special needs and they are concerned about their provision. Similarly the school will approach parents if they are concerned about their child. In discussion with the SENCo, class teacher and parents special needs children will have an individual education plan written for them which will be regularly monitored and reviewed. The children will receive support from one of our SEN assistants or teacher who receive ongoing training in the teaching of special needs.

St Elizabeth's School has wheelchair access and full provision for children with physical difficulties. Children with physical difficulties are able to participate in a full curriculum including going on three school journeys whilst in the junior school.

We encourage parents to have regular contact with their child's class teacher and to work alongside learning support assistants, so that a good home/school relationship is fostered.

At St Elizabeth's School we ensure that all children feel included and this is a particular area of strength. All of our children feel happy and safe at school and enjoy learning, whatever their difficulty.

What we say about the school - the full Good Schools Guide review

Head: Since 1988, Ms Christine Brett MEd (in English) BEd (in English) DipMathsEd (describes herself as 'over 21'). Educated at The Ursuline Convent, St Mary's University College (formerly part of University of London and now part of University of Surrey), where she is now a governor and King's College, London. Lives locally in Barnes and taught previously at the Catholic primaries of St Augustine's in Hammersmith and St Mary Magdalen in Mortlake; then deputy head of St Mary's, Clapham. Interests include the theatre, art, foreign travel (providing no aeroplanes involved!), reading and swimming. Likeable and sweet-natured in a way rarely encountered in the 21st century, but 'enormously efficient', according to one mother, and very on the ball educationally. Only the seventh head in the history of the school since its foundation in 1840. Teaches the strongest mathematicians once a week. Parents speak highly of her, particularly her fierce loyalty to the school, her commitment to the Catholic faith and her achievements in promoting the family atmosphere of the school. One mother said, 'she gives lots of encouragement and praise and everyone is made to feel good about something.' Another commented that she cares for each and every pupil as though her own child, but is held in some awe by the pupils.

Entrance: Oversubscribed (72 applicants for 30 places), which means that the intake is effectively 100 per cent Catholic. Realistically, don't even think about applying unless your child is baptised and in a regular or occasionally practising Catholic family within Richmond, Kew, Ham or East Sheen. Regular attenders get priority over the occasional ones. Priority is then given to those living nearest the school and to siblings of present pupils. Extent of practising Catholicism must be certified by the priest: result is large and enthusiastic attendance at local Sunday services. NB head very opposed to parents withdrawing children from school at seven to take up places in prep schools and will require an undertaking in this respect – 'if that's what parents want, they should choose it at 4.' Feels strongly that children need continuity and stability rather than a parking place for three years.

Exit: To up to 20 schools, including the state Catholic schools of Gumley House Convent, Wimbledon College, The Ursuline Convent, Sacred Heart, Cardinal Vaughan and the London Oratory; to local Richmond schools such as Waldegrave Girls, to Kingston schools Tiffin and Richard Challoner and to independent schools such as Lady Eleanor Holles, Surbiton High School, Hampton and Latymer Upper School. One mother said that 'pupils intended for independent schools tend to go to local tutors during the year before entrance exams.'

Remarks: Hugely popular state school, well regarded and chosen by many parents who could easily afford the private sector. Good SATs results – for 11-year-olds they are 'well above average' in English and science and even more so for maths when compared with schools of similar socio-economic intake. School built on present site in 1969 to unusual and appealing design incorporating semi-open-plan layout. The building floods with light – hexagonal rooms open out to the grounds and partially glazed ceilings result in conservatory-like environment – very 'Homes & Gardens' and rather appropriate in midst of local ritzy housing. Surrounded by reassuring, impressive security – locked gates during school day with entry phone access both to the site and at main entrance. Head believes that building style also leads to greater openness, willingness to share and consideration for others. Certainly we detected a noticeably caring atmosphere and the pupils are polite, well behaved and neatly attired in traditional uniform. Older children are assigned to look after younger ones who have hurt themselves. Assemblies or prayers are held each day for each class and parents are welcome to assembly on Wednesdays. Religious education report (required by Ofsted in respect of denominational education) in 2001 is extremely complimentary. Family-friendly policy continued with the 'Cam-kids' after-school care scheme run jointly with two other schools – children up to age 11 collected and walked from school to nearby Cambrian Centre until 6pm if required.

Currently, one computer to 10 children but a new ICT suite has just been built enabling 30 children at a time to be taught ICT skills. Notable annual arts week when specialists are brought in for clay modelling, tie-dying etc. Recent additions have been a super library, a light and airy group room, the ICT suite, an SEN room and an environmental room, which has French windows to the pond.

Parents include the whole spectrum of society as the catchment area is so wide. 45 children – mostly of white European heritage – have English as an additional language, and 32 have SEN (SEN co-ordinator four days per week). School premises are adapted for physical disability, with access ramps and special loo facilities. One third of the 14 staff has been here for more than five years.

Football, netball, swimming and athletics are all compulsory; school recently very successful locally at swimming and reports that parental worries about inadequate sports now less audible. Unfortunately, there is no playing field, only hard-surface provision which is basically the junior playground, with benching. However, school uses the outdoor facilities of a secondary school two minutes walk away. Infant play area is artificial grass most attractively landscaped and equipped.

About 60 learn a musical instrument. There are extra-curricular clubs but some parents would like to see more. Interesting extras include a Latin club run after school by an Oxford classicist mum, another runs a chess club and the Italian embassy provides a teacher to teach Italian for one day a week (timetabled) to ages 7-10. School keen on charitable activities – supports MacMillan Cancer Care and Catholic Children's Society, among others. Nativity play presented at The Royal Star and Garter Home, and carol singing at Richmond railway station. Very active and supportive PTA which raises impressive amount of funds every year. Parental involvement in school high and encouraged. Head says school receives 'huge support', from the governors – because of the needs of the Catholic community governors tend to stay on for longer than the period of their child's education at the school.

Nursery is separate unit on site in premises due for upgrade. Fee-paying, although in effect most children over three and a half are funded by government scheme. Same admissions criteria as the school. Some children stay all day and some are part-time – aims to be family-friendly and flexible.

Ofsted report of 2000 says: 'The very first thing that strikes a visitor to St Elizabeth's ... is how eager the pupils are to learn and how committed the staff are to achieving the highest possible standards.' As they join the queue for a place, parents obviously agree.

ST GEORGE'S SCHOOL (ASCOT)

Wells Lane, Ascot, Berkshire, SL5 7DZ

Tel: 01344 629 900
Fax: 01344 629 901
Email: office@stgeorges-ascot.org.uk
Website: www.stgeorges-ascot.org.uk

• Pupils: 290 girls; 140 board, 150 day • Ages: 11-18
• Religion: C of E • Fees: Day £4,600; boarding £7,200
• School status: Independent • Opendays: Any Tuesday or Friday by appointment • School gender: Girls
• Day/boarding: Takes boarders

SEN provision

Detail:
Experience of:

Mild: ADD; DYSC; DYSL; DYSP; VI; CP;
Moderate: MLD; DYSL; DYSP;
Others: EAL; Epi; Eat;

Summary: Some learning support leassons are given by the specialists from the Helen Arkell Dyslexia Centre.

What we say about the school - the full Good Schools Guide review

Head: Since 2005 Mrs Caroline Jordan MA PGCE (early forties). Mrs Jordan succeeded the highly respected and much-loved Mrs Joanna Grant-Peterkin. Educated at St Helen's and St Katharine's, she then went onto St Edmund Hall, Oxford to read Earth Sciences. After a period of running her own business, she then took her PGCE at Manchester University before taking her first teaching job at Wycombe Abbey. Ten years later she left there for St George's, having taught both physics and chemistry. She gained boarding experience as a housemistress and latterly joined senior management as head of sixth form and deputy senior housemistress. Married with one son.

Academic Matters: A level results excellent, 88 per cent A/B, and 2004 GCSE results were commendably good with trails of As and A* and no failures. Average take-home was AAB in 2005. All girls take science at GCSE, double for most, but single for some weaker brethren, rather than three separate sciences. Maths 'surprisingly good,' said the last head, 'and popular' – but not as popular as English, biology, history of art and theatre studies. 24 subjects offered at A level.

Foreign nationals can and do take their own languages to exam level, which has a dramatic effect on results! French on particularly fine form, with German and Spanish on offer, Russian, Japanese and Chinese also taken. No apparent Greek take-up, nor business studies and the like. Lots of IT. Inter/intra-netted computers everywhere and available at all times (though an ominous notice on the door announces 'that if more evidence of food is found in the computer room then it will be locked at the weekend'). Personal laptops can be connected to the system. Key-boarding skills are important here and girls get CLAIT and RSA qualifications. E-mail and voicemail for all.

EFL and good dyslexia/dyspraxia cover plus study skills for all, from the Helen Arkell Centre which operates from 'a new facility' ie a portacabin in the grounds.

Games, Options, The Arts: Art, textile and design strong as ever. Super fashion, make your own pattern/ball gown, and rather natty corsets on show in the entrance to the art block. Fabulous music, joined-up concerts with Eton (popular), lots of own CDs, masses of instruments – and lessons can be arranged for any instrument. Drama and public speaking popular with regular awards for the former, LAMDA exams. Photography popular, own dark room.

30-acre campus, new multi-purpose building opened in 2002. Very versatile: the hall can be used as a lecture theatre, auditorium, dance floor and for exams. Funds from the sale of Queen's Hill paid for the stunning sports hall, with enviable dance and weight training area (indoor swimming pool is next on the agenda). Games important here, especially lacrosse and tennis.

Background and Atmosphere: Founded in 1877 as a boys' prep school and converted to girls at the turn of the century. This is rhodie-land. Mega rebuild following sale of Queen's Hill, with purpose-built dorms, and interlocking classrooms – incredibly narrow claustrophobic staircases and passages everywhere – single file only. Guides said careers advice and university suggestions tiptop.

There is a certain amount of B&B (currently £25 per night) and flexi-boarding on offer. Day boarders often move to becoming real boarders further up the school. Boarders move from dorms of six to dorms of one or two (always called dorms even if it's only one). Common rooms, pay phones (mobiles OK but only in dorms) and kitchens for each year group. Sixth formers can take driving lessons and entertain boys in the common room (dinner parties still popular) and go out one night a week. Increased privileges come with age, no uniform in sixth – though our guides were wearing very smart black suits (skirt or trousers a choix), plus trips to Windsor (Eton next door) etc. Cookery club popular and sixth formers often cook their own supper.

No timetabled lessons on Saturdays, but all girls start with an hour's prep, juniors then do games, riding, drama lessons and, with the exception of four closed weekends a term, can go out from lunchtime on Saturday till Sunday evening. Complaints that there was 'not enough to do' at weekends were refuted by our guides who said there was masses to do, lots of activities organised by the girl-led school council. 'Changing rooms' a popular activity, when girls redecorate and paint their common rooms – which are then opened to great fanfare.

Pastoral Care and Discipline: Good pastoral care via house and prefectorial system; day girls are assigned to boarding houses where they have work stations – surprisingly cocooned off from each other with gloomy grey screens. Shadows for first year pupils, form deputies and year tutors for all, girls choose a personal tutor at sixth form, plus a director of studies. School operates school code, enforced on the seven deadly sins – 'girls are in big trouble' if they get involved with drugs, sex (boys in bedrooms), booze, fags, bullying, going out without permission, or theft. 'Straight out' for drugs; fags = chores, fine and gating; booze ditto and contract, strong bullying policy and 'quick follow-up'.

Pupils and Parents: From the south, rather than London but masses from further afield, around eight or nine per cent foreigners. 'No visible impact' yet from the Yorks' decision to send their daughter here. Some first time buyers.

Entrance: 'Lots of different schools', basically the toffs' prep schools: Cowarth Park, Upton House, Windsor, Maltman's, Garden House, Lady Eden's, Thomas's etc plus local primary schools. CE at 11 and 13, pass mark 50/55 per cent plus previous head's report. Plus interview. Sixth form entry, standard six GCSEs at C and above for all. B or above recommended for A level subjects; A essential for maths and science at A level plus talk to heads of departments for external pupils.

Exit: A few do leave after GCSE, going to Wellington, Stowe, Bradfield or sixth form colleges, otherwise 98 per cent to tertiary education. Small tranche to Oxbridge.

Money Matters: Academic and music scholarships on offer at 11 or 16; art and textiles, drama and sport scholarships at 16, which can be further means-tested, plus bursarial help (means tested annually) for those already in the school.

Remarks: School increasingly popular locally (ie day boarders), good for the less academic, with impressive results. Still a bit Sloane.

St George's School (Edinburgh)

Garscube Terrace, Edinburgh, EH12 6BG

Tel: 0131 311 8000

Fax: 0131 311 8120

Email: head@st-georges.edin.sch.uk

Website: www.st-georges.edin.sch.uk

• Pupils: 995 girls; 945 day, 50 board. Nursery 72 including 8 boys • Ages: 2-18 • Religion: Non-denom • Fees: £1,830-£2,120 in primary; £2,335 £2,925 senior school. Boarding £2,875 extra • School status: Independent • Opendays: October and visits are welcomed throughout the year

• School gender: Girls • Day/boarding: Takes boarders

SEN provision

Detail:

Now provide for in school:

Mild: ASP; ADD; ADHD; DYSC; DYSL; DYSP; HI; VI;

Moderate: MLD; DYSC; DYSL; DYSP;

Others: OCD; EAL; Epi; PD; Eat;

Experience of:

- Mild: EBD;
- Moderate: SpLD;
- Severe: SpLD;
- Others: Sp&LD;

Summary: Provision for additional support needs at St George's School for Girls is overseen by the Support for Learning Group, which encompasses learning support, ESOL, student welfare and development, medical and especial talents. The Support for Learning Group is a whole school resource which works with students from 3 years old to university entrance upon the basis of their individual difficulties and requirements.

The learning support department works with all areas of Support for Learning, but has a particular regard to individuals with special educational needs. The ESOL department works closely with students who have English as their second language and the Especial Talents Co-ordinator oversees provision of a suitable progamme for students identified as gifted.

Identification of additional support needs is undertaken through the school's screening programme, combined with parental/student referral and contact with the teaching staff. Provision for students with identified needs, ranging from specific learning difficulties to ESOL, is undertaken through individual tutition, small group work and co-operative teaching in whole class situations. A drop in service is also provided for students who do not require the provision outlined above, but who at times may require assistance with a specific area of work.

The learning support department has experience of working with a range of specific learning difficulties, behavioural disorders, learning difficulties and difficulties on the autistic spectrum continuum.

What we say about the school - the full Good Schools Guide review

Head: Since 1994, Dr Judith McClure CBE, MA, DPhil, FRSA, FSA (fifties). A Scot educated at Newlands Grammar School, Middlesbrough (was briefly a nun – at 18), studied law, then read history at Oxford where she got a first and lectured at Liverpool and Oxford. She came to St George's after a stint at St Helen and St Katherine, followed by an assistant headship at Kingswood and was previously head of the now merged Royal School, Bath. Married to 'portable' historian husband, Dr Roger Collins, who specialises in medieval Spain. No children.

Fast talking, super, enthusiastic head – she leapt up and down during our interview getting us yet more policy statements and exam results – larger than life and incredibly elegant – a long black dress, with shocking pink jacket and matching pashmina when we visited. 'She loves it here, loves Scotland, loves Edinburgh' and loves running St George's; she is also much involved both with the Scottish education policy makers and with the local universities. 'So much is happening, so fast, such fun.' Pretty OTT, and not necessarily every parent's cup of tea – think Miss Jean Brodie, think Edinburgh. A great exponent of single sex schools, she runs the best in Scotland and puts pupils, parents and staff in that order. 'No problems getting staff' and those who are there change jobs every so often which eliminates the boredom factor, though whether Dr McClure is reaching that particular plateau is open to debate. A five-star head, St George's is lucky to have her.

Academic Matters: School no longer narrowly academic, the courses are much broader, with girls taking units of Intermediate I and II, as well as following the English or the Scottish system as appropriate. A choice might therefore be Standard Grades, followed by a unit or two of Intermediate in lower sixth (Intermediate studies incorporate a much wider range of options than the regular exams) as well as Highers, followed by further Highers or Advanced Highers. Again extra Intermediates can be added in the upper sixth (geddit?). Equally, girls can opt for the English system after Standard Grades and switch between Highers and Advanced Highers, and ASs and A2s. It is very much horses for courses and a timetabling challenge. Oodles of As and Credit 1s in both disciplines, and 'lots of flexibility' in course selection. School employs VLE – Virtual Learning Environment – to allow students to access course work, collect work or refer to notes provided by staff online.

Pupils help with scientific research with the universities, share seminars with staff and undergraduates and take part in an impressive outreach programme which encompasses both the academic and the appreciation of the wider world. No particular bias – English, maths, languages, the sciences and the humanities are outstanding. The new, very popular, Chinese centre has girls studying Mandarin – results only now coming through – but otherwise French, German, Spanish and Russian (school is twinned with Pushkin's town, as well as schools in Moscow and St Petersburg). Good general studies and careers advice.

School is split into three distinct departments – junior, which encompasses the nursery, lower (where Dr McClure has her office) and upper. Good learning support throughout, four specialist teachers in all. Small ESOL department to help with non-nationals.

NB league tables are meaningless in this school, given that two systems are followed.

Games, Options, The Arts: Fabulous Centenary sports hall with imaginative viewing area over hall and squash courts; much used lacrosse pitches (recently upgraded) plus a floodlit all-weather pitch, all trad games played with a vengeance. Magical Robertson music centre houses untold numbers of choirs, ensembles, three orchestras, over 600 musicians. Vibrant art department, with fantastic sea sculptures (sadly the lobster didn't sing), conventional art – and some pretty rum portraits, we hope they don't really look like that – as well as pottery, textiles et al. Drama and theatre good. D of E popular, as is CCF with Merchiston (well, it would be, wouldn't it?); sixth formers join forces with brother school Edinburgh Academy and Merchiston Castle School for sport, art, music etc. Zillions of after school clubs that offer everything from keyboarding to extra IT.

Background and Atmosphere: Founded in 1888, St George's is Edinburgh's foremost school for girls and sister to Edinburgh Academy – shared holidays, sibling discounts, that sort of thing. Purpose-built 1912 complex, much altered and expanded, is still home to the school. Long corridors with classrooms but also fab recent add-ons. Lower school now in converted earlier boarding house; primary school much expanded and previously dreary classrooms totally refurbished late 2005. Stunning new dining hall (exit bridge known as Bridget) with entertainment area below has released valuable space for extra libraries and study areas. Parents can (and do) use the new dining centre as a coffee shop. Recently opened a sixth form reading room. Totally refurbished library.

Pupils have a purposeful air, mufti in sixth form. Boarders occupy a couple of converted Edwardian mansions with a purpose-built bungalow for sixth formers, singles and twins, all very jolly, lots of extra activities.

Pastoral Care and Discipline: Head has made no real expulsions, though several miscreants have been given very heavy hints that they 'move elsewhere' (two in seven years). 'No need to break out, this is a liberal environment.' The boarding housemistress tells tales of boys trying to sneak in and gaspers handing her their lighters and their Lucky Strikes when they have been rumbled – but that's only a few occasions in eleven years and none recent. 'No sniff of drugs'. Good PSE, positive behaviour policy which incorporates the best of human rights legislation.

Pupils and Parents: Boarders from the Highlands and Islands and from the borders; some from 'abroad', links and exchanges with Germantown Friends School in Philadelphia. Otherwise, good straight Scots parents, some with Charlotte Ranger background, incomers and some first time buyers. Unashamedly elitist, lots of parent/pupil forums – on every subject under the sun; The Friends of St George's for social events.

Entrance: Selective and seriously so. Via nursery and elsewhere at four-and-a-half. Otherwise, exam, school report and interview. Entry to sixth form is more or less automatic for home-grown pupils; external pupils need five A/1-C/3 passes at GCSE/Standard grade.

Exit: Usual (but rare) trickle down south at 8 and 13, a few leave after GCSE/Standard grade to go co-ed; otherwise gap, degrees, and higher education of all sorts – Scottish law popular, as are the sciences and medicine. Around 50 per cent opt for Scottish universities, Aberdeen, St Andrew's plus Edinburgh and Glasgow.

Money Matters: Bursary scheme now replaces assisted places; 'mustn't let the really bright down'. Sibling discounts which walk hand in hand with brothers at Edinburgh Academy.

Remarks: The top girls' school in Scotland, particularly in the academic field; much more liberal than previously and offering a broad sweep of academia – the main building still looks archaic but this is not a school to judge by its exterior.

St Gregory's Catholic College

Combe Hay Lane, Odd Down, Bath, BA2 8PA

Tel: 01225 832 873

Fax: 01225 835 848

Email: stgregorys_sec@bathnes.gov.uk

Website: www.st-gregorys.bathnes.sch.uk

• Pupils: 811 girls and boys, all day • Ages: 11-16
• Religion: Catholic • School status: State
• Opendays: First Thursday in October to see the school in action; last Thursday evening in September
• School gender: Mixed • Day/boarding: Day pupils

SEN provision

Detail:
Now provide for in school:
- Mild: DYSP; HI; VI; CP;
- Moderate: DYSP; HI; CP;
- Others: Sp&LD; DEL; Epi;

Experience of:
- Mild: ASP; ADD; ADHD; EBD; DYSC; DYSL;
- Moderate: ADD; EBD; MLD; DYSC; DYSL;
- Others: EAL;

Summary: It is recognised that all pupils have needs which are special to them; the curriculum provided is broad, balanced, relevant, differentiated, challenging and stimulating thus raising the standards achieved by all.

Pupils who are particularly talented or gifted are identified early and staff are encouraged to match how and what they teach to the needs of the pupil. Using National Curriculum SATs, NFER CATS and other sources of information received including from the junior schools the special needs co-ordinator identifies those who may need extra help. The nature of their needs is assessed and direction is given on how best to meet these needs. Support, resources and in school training are made available to staff in order to ensure that all pupils are given equal access to the curriculum. Text books, materials and other resources are carefully selected to be suitable and stimulating by all Curriculum leaders.

Pupils are taught in mixed ability groups for some subjects and setted for particular subjects. Consideration is made for those with special educational needs; the numbers of pupils in some classes will reflect their need for more individual guidance. Additional in-class support will be available in some lessons.

The special needs co-ordinator Mrs Miles works closely with all faculties to ensure that pupils receive the attention they require.

For all National Curriculum subjects the syllabus on offer is common for pupils, regardless of ability. The pace of work, sophistication of skills taught and the level of the content covered will reflect the pace at which the pupils can work. Teachers' expectations remain extremely high; pupils are encouraged to set for themselves realistic goals and to make every effort to achieve these as they mature and become more independent.

What we say about the school - the full Good Schools Guide review

Head: Since 2004, Raymond Friel MA(Hons) NPQH (early forties). First class degree in English from Glasgow University in 1987; PGCE from University of Wales, Aberystwyth. As head of English introduced A level English to new sixth form at St Augustine's, Trowbridge after 'good start' to career at St Charles Sixth Form College, London. Two-and-a-half years as head of St Joseph's, Salisbury which he took from 'challenging circumstances' to receiving a 'good' Ofsted rating. Then 'too good to miss' opportunity arose at St Gregory's. Thoughtful and caring head who follows long-serving predecessor. Good listener and fits St Gregory's academic and Catholic profile. 'Has handled changes with sensitivity,' say parents. Married to Janet Anne, an artist and teacher, with three sons at local Catholic primary school. Interests include sport, literature and performing arts. Former co-editor of Southfields literary review and a regular contributor to London Review of Books.

Academic Matters: Outstanding results in core subjects, especially English (with GCSE results in both language and literature more than 20 per cent above national average). Religion compulsory to GCSE. A modern foreign language compulsory for nearly all; we were particularly impressed by quality of teaching and range of languages offered. Most other subjects also strong and drama, music and dance more than justify the college's specialist performing arts status. Children streamed academically and setted in maths from the beginning of their second term in year 7. At Key Stage

4, pupils follow courses in one of three 'pathways' stretching the most able, providing qualifications alongside appropriate experience for small vocational group and giving 'mainstream' pupils a sensible compromise in terms of breadth and workload. No sense of 'second class' or disaffected pupils. Class sizes vary according to subject and ability.

All year 7 children are screened on entry. 6 statemented children and 29 with IEPs. Early morning reading programme and a lunch club for vulnerable pupils. Close liaison with range of outside agencies. SENCo works with staff to support pupils with SpLD and other special needs largely within normal timetable; learning support assistants work alongside mainstream teachers. High ranking (recently ninth in the country) for value-added at Key Stage 4 attributed in part to success of support programmes. Head of RE also runs small behaviour and attendance unit with experienced support assistant.

Games, Options, The Arts: Active sports department organises range of after school fixtures across the major games. Pupils spoilt for choice when it comes to performing arts. 220 pupils receiving instrumental tuition in school and another 100 outside. Annual tour for musicians of all kinds and many play in county bands. Parents 'really grateful' for trips abroad organised by staff. New music technology offers twilight tuition to AS level for those who can manage extra workload, likewise after-school dance and language options. Strong drama with school productions involving dance and music too. New, purpose-built dance/drama studio opened in 2003 in addition to main stage in school hall. When we visited, one of two professional dancers in residence was inspiring a creative class of uninhibited year 7 pupils. Annual Artsweek in July has performances every day and draws up to 500 Key Stage 3 pupils; stunning choice of workshops with local artists and performers volunteering their time. Artists, writers and poets, theatre visits and cross-cultural exchanges add to the heady creative mix here. Children prove resourceful in getting themselves home and many stay after school.

Background and Atmosphere: Motto: In Christo floremus (In Christ we flourish) expresses the Christian core of the school. Every day begins with corporate worship plus extra masses through year and voluntary mass in school's small chapel which also provides a sanctuary where some pupils have left touching prayer dedications in an open book. Each year group can experience a retreat and there are all kinds of good works for charity. Non-Catholics 'don't feel left out' confirm parents.

School located on attractive 12-acre site on 'socially mixed' southern edge of Bath; extensive playing fields, new astroturf for hockey and soccer plus hard tennis courts and gym. Good facilities for graphics, design and technology. Modern 12 classroom block for mathematics, geography and modern languages in spacious, purpose-built accommodation. Well-resourced and airy library; interactive whiteboards, overhead projection and plenty of computers around without being techno crazy. Pleasant bistro area for year 11 lunches with healthy food options and smart card payment system. School day begins at 8.55am and ends at 3.35pm with many getting back to far-flung homes by bus ahead of those crossing congested Bath. Strong PTFA runs fund-raising events through year.

Pastoral Care and Discipline: Deputy head (former LEA adviser and Ofsted inspector) pioneered 'peer counselling' here; truancy almost unknown with attendance monitored closely. 'Name and praise' assembly and rewards system plus clear sanctions where necessary. House system under review.

Pupils and Parents: 88 per cent Catholic; very active PTFA. Parents receive six progress reports plus full written report at end of year. Homework set by all and journals for parents to see and sign. Quite a few refugees from private sector and many staff have children here. Strong sense of community; pupils appear relaxed, confident and tolerant of each other. Those who showed us around were articulate and sensitive. Moral values and full of good works for disabled, homeless etc. Smart, green uniform has replaced dreary brown predecessor still worn by older year groups. College Senate has representatives from across years and has influenced uniform and catering changes including introduction of popular breakfast club.

Entrance: Oversubscribed. Prides itself on transition arrangements into year 7; children come from 200 square mile catchment area and complicated preference system for Catholics operates. Pupils mainly from six linked primary schools (St Benedict's, Midsomer Norton; St John's, Bath, SS Joseph and Teresa, Wells; St Mary's, Bath, St Mary's, Chippenham and St Patrick's, Corsham) plus siblings. Apply through Bath and North East Somerset LEA for admission into year 7, but apply direct to school if moving into the area.

Exit: Around 65 per cent to St Brendan's and other sixth forms; 25 per cent to further education; 10 per cent to training and employment. A few to Oxbridge via St Brendan's or other colleges.

Remarks: Much sought-after and dynamic 11-16 Catholic comprehensive which combines creativity with academic success.

ST JAMES'S CATHOLIC PRIMARY SCHOOL

260 Stanley Road, Twickenham, Middlesex, TW2 5NP

Tel: 020 8898 4670

Fax: 020 8893 3038

Email: info@st-james.richmond.sch.uk

Website: www.st-james.richmond.sch.uk

• Pupils: 280 boys and 270 girls (including 50 in the nursery), all day • Ages: 3-11 • Religion: RC only • School status: State • School gender: Mixed • Day/boarding: Day pupils

SEN provision

Detail:

Centre of excellence for:
- Mild: AUT;
- Moderate: AUT;
- Severe: AUT;

Summary: No comment. Shy? No need to be – has good provision, especially for autism. SEN details added by us.

What we say about the school - the full Good Schools Guide review

Head: Since 2000, Mrs Veronica Heffernan, BD MA (late forties). Married (to another headteacher) with two grown-up children. Previously head for 7 years at St Mary's, Chiswick. Neat and petite, she comes across as calm and very capable – completely on top of her brief of running this expanding school, while still managing to fit in some regular teaching and Friday choir practice. 'She is fantastic – and very approachable,' says one mother. 'I think the children are in awe of her and eager to please, but in a positive way.' She knows most children by name and regularly paces corridors, classrooms and playground. 'Visionary,' says another parent. 'She has fantastic ideas and is very friendly and happy.' She is strict and takes no nonsense from the children or their parents. 'I have heard her say that she won't entertain playground gossip, but if there is a genuine issue over anything you can get to see her quickly and she is very very fair,' said another mother. 'She goes by the book and I have nothing but praise for her.'

Entrance: At 3 to nursery, and 4 to the main school. Non-selective academically, children must be baptised Catholics and then admission is based on proximity to the school. Serving four parishes in Twickenham and Hampton, the school changed to 3-form entry to cope with over-subscription in 2002. But the school is still over-subscribed – 2004 saw 110 applications for 52 nursery places and 150 applications for the 90 reception places. Getting into the nursery does not guarantee a reception place but, in practice, most do go on to the main school as criteria are similar. If you want a place get to church and move nearby.

Exit: Popular choices are Hampton and The London Oratory for boys and Gumley House for girls. Recent scholarships to Kingston Grammar and also to St George's, Weybridge (for music) and St David's, Ashford (for PE).

Remarks: Brand new, state of the art accommodation, a gift for local Catholic families. Its very strong Catholic ethos and excellent academic results make it a popular choice around these parts. The school's expansion into a new building on the same site has been welcomed by parents. 'The whole place seems to have been rejuvenated,' says one happy parent. The building is attractive and the school staff worked with the architect to get things right. A good example of being 'built for the purpose' is the ICT suite – where all the computer workstations face front for whole class teaching, rather than the more usual arrangement where they face the wall. Interactive whiteboards are in every classroom – including the nursery. The front of the school is one storey, rising to two storeys at the back (with a lift as well as stairs). Nursery children enjoy an additional outside classroom. Sunny yellow decoration gives a warm, almost Mediterranean feel to the place (indeed Italian is taught from year 3, and to any interested parents after school, as part of an initiative with the Italian embassy). Great use of space outside as well, with covered ways to provide some shelter, tables for lunch in good weather, and a huge climbing frame.

St James's has been up and running since the 1960s, gradually expanding from a single entry schoo to the current 3-form entry, but retaining its good local reputation throughout. 'We heard fantastic reports of it and moved nearby to be sure of a place,' said one parent. 'We feel it has given our children a really good foundation and that they will get into a good secondary school after this.' Certainly there is a purposeful buzz about the place. Classrooms have a bright and industrious air and the children – all very smart and wearing proper ties – seem engaged in what they are doing.

Expect your child to work hard. There is a structured approach to teaching and a lot of homework (for a state school). 'I was shocked at the amount of homework – 1½ to 2 hours three nights a week when my daughter was in year 4,' said one mother. Mainly literacy and numeracy, there are spellings to learn and reading 'without fail'. The head agrees with the parents we spoke to: she says, 'It's a big commitment which means a lot of parental involvement, especially with the younger children. We expect high standards of academic excellence and behaviour here.'

But it's not all work. 'They play hard too,' said another parent. 'My kids have lots of fun and are very happy.' And don't be discouraged if your child is not an academic high-flier. Parents of children whose talents lay elsewhere seem just as pleased. 'I feel my daughter, who is not so academic, has fared very well here,' says one mother. 'She is young in her year, but got lots of extra help and has gained tremendous confidence. She is good at art and I feel this has been encouraged. The teachers seem to nourish talent, wherever it lies.' There is an SEN co-ordinator and support teacher – and facilities have been enhanced by the move to the new building, which has more quiet rooms for group and individual work and assessment. St James's also houses The George Tancred Centre for autistic children. 10 places are available here and are open to non-Catholic children. Fantastic facilities include partitioned work areas so the children can control their immediate environment and a 'time-out' room filled with soft play equipment. The playground is separated from, but adjacent to, that of the main school and a regulated number of children from the main school are allowed to go in and play with the George Tancred children at break time – and compete to do so.

Plenty of praise for a delightful and stable staff – a mix of ages, but not gender, with just one male classroom assistant. School is very good at netball (Middlesex and Surrey champions) and chess, but does not really excel in other sporting pursuits. 'There is plenty of sport played and we take part in lots of things – but we don't actually win much,' one parent reports. Musical abilities are nicely encouraged – with a dedicated teacher and practice room and annual presentations of a music cup and another for 'Most Promising' musician.

Located in a cul de sac, opposite another school, access by car in the morning is not the best. Helping to overcome this, the school is heavily involved in a 'green transport policy', running several 'walking buses' and encouraging children to ride bikes and scooters to school, where 'parking' is provided. A very Catholic school – prayers are said three times a day in classrooms and whole school gathers for mass on holy days.

St John's Beaumont School

Old Windsor, Windsor, Berkshire, SL4 2JN

Tel: 01784 432 428

Fax: 01784 494 048

Email: admissions@stjohnsbeaumont.co.uk

Website: www.stjohnsbeaumont.org.uk

• Pupils: 325 boys; 60 board, 265 day • Ages: 4-13

• Religion: RC (owned by Jesuits) • Fees: Day: pre-prep £1,999, prep £2,586-£3,682. Boarding: weekly £4,860, full £5,762

• School status: Independent • School gender: Boys

• Day/boarding: Takes boarders

SEN provision

Detail:

Now provide for in school:

Mild: DYSL; DYSP;

Moderate: DYSL;

Others: EAL;

Experience of:

Mild: ASP; ADD; EBD; DYSC; HI;

Moderate: MLD;

Others: DEL; Epi;

Summary: The school has its own SEN unit, the Campion Unit, which assesses the needs of pupils in the school and assists them as appropriate. The school can help pupils with mild dyslexia or dyspraxia.

Differentiation is a necessary part of the teachers' work in the school, which is designed to help pupils with a difficulty or those who are particularly gifted. Academically gifted children are also placed in a small class for years 7 and 8.

What we say about the school - the full Good Schools Guide review

Head: Interregnum. The remarkable, stylish and long-serving head, Mr Dermot St John Gogarty, died in a car crash in November 2005. His passionate advocacy of the Jesuit principles of service and justice, his distaste for humbug and his insistence on the importance of old-fashioned virtues like trust and honesty, show throughout the school.

Entrance: First-come-first-served, rigorously adhered to – though some turned down after educational psychologist's report, 'if we can't help them'; long waiting list. Most enter at age 4 but places are kept open for another small intake at year 3.

Exit: Eton, Ampleforth, Stonyhurst, Hampton, Harrow, Wellington, Winchester, The Oratory, Bradfield, Milton Abbey, ie the whole range, but skewed towards the more demanding senior schools.

Remarks: Fine 1888 buildings on a hilltop, by the architect of Westminster Cathedral. Lovely Gothic chapel, brand new music and drama block (there is a strong musical tradition), cheerful new junior classrooms. Everywhere inside is bright and wholesome (cleaners on constant duty), including dorms and loos. Extensive rolling grounds, bordering on Windsor Great Park, including 'one of the finest cricket squares to be found in an English prep school' and acres of woodland – one resident priest is fascinated by forestry. Following shortcomings in IT provision and library accessibility noted in recent ISI report the school has erected a purpose-built IT centre for learning and two new libraries. Usual broad curriculum, including Latin and Spanish options from year 5 and Greek for some. Streaming operates from year 5; boys and parents seem happy about this. There is a strong academic drive about the school, without the less gifted being neglected; high standards for all. A very structured, hard-working place. Class size averages 14; EAL help available, and the Campion Unit has teachers in all fields of SEN requirements.

It's a pretty sporty place – games every day and typical RC emphasis on rugby (recent tour of South Africa); swimming also very good. Pupils are kept busy right through the day; school ends for all at 6+ pm. All staff expected to offer at least one extra-curricular activity – aeromodelling to origami and cooking. The sixty full boarders have full weekend programmes, including cultural visits and relaxation time. They sleep in long, old-fashioned dorms, divided into sacrosanct cubicles; plenty of resident staff. Staff are a healthy mixture of young and long-serving and clearly relish the school's success and sense of purpose. When you sidle into a classroom they will march over and shake you by the hand, without apparently losing disciplinary hold or pedagogic flow.

Most pupils come from London and the south east; some from as far as Mexico, Korea, Japan. About 25 per cent are non-Catholic – head boy in 2004/05 was a Muslim – all denominations 'positively welcomed'. Non-Christians are invited to share as far as they feel comfortable in the school's religious life; this seemingly difficult balancing trick is managed with some ease. Parents are issued with an amazingly detailed handbook which covers everything from a mission statement to what 7-year-olds are doing at 4.05pm on Thursday. Some financial help available for deserving cases.

A famously prescriptive school, expects high standards of discipline. Successful, with a strong sense of community. 'Glammy Berkshire – turn up in the Rolls,' advises one parent. Pupils are confident, at ease with themselves and with others – much respect both ways between boys and staff; ambitious and socially alert. Everyone seems to enjoy being there.

ST JOHN'S COLLEGE SCHOOL

Grange Road, Cambridge, Cambridgeshire, CB3 9AB

Tel: 01223 353 532

Fax: 01223 355 846

Email: admissions@sjcs.co.uk

Website: www.sjcs.co.uk

• Pupils: around 250 boys, 200 girls. 50 boy and girl boarders, 400 day • Ages: 4-13 • Religion: C of E • Fees: Day £2,345-£3,180; boarding £5,023. Choristers £1,674

• School status: Independent • School gender: Mixed

• Day/boarding: Takes boarders

SEN provision

Detail:

Now provide for in school:

Mild: ASP; ADD; ADHD; EBD; DYSC; DYSL; DYSP; HI; VI; CP;

Moderate: DYSC; DYSL; DYSP; HI; CP;

Severe: HI; CP;

Others: SPD; CD; OCD; ODD; GEN; EAL; Sp&LD; DEL; Epi; PD; Eat;

Experience of:

Mild: AUT;

Summary: 'Each child is special: each child has needs: each child has special needs. These are truths as old as time, carried in the heart of any parent and any good teacher' (K L Jones, Head).

As set out in the school's Ethos and Aims, we aim 'to meet the individual needs, foster the aptitudes and nurture the growth of each child.' In this sense, the school's Individual Needs provision is part of a wider commitment to helping any child to discover his or her ability. The provisions of SENDA aside, we do not view learning difficulties as disabling but rather as obstacles to fulfilling potential which, with appropriate support, can in many cases be overcome.

This difference of emphasis has significant consequences. It is by no means the case that learning difficulties are experienced only by the less able. Indeed, the problems encountered by the most gifted children can require considerable specialist attention. St John's is therefore committed to meeting the needs of children who have an identified learning difficulty, whatever their innate ability. It is worthy of note, in this respect, that many children who gain academic awards to their senior schools have, at some point, been given Individual Needs support.

While the Individual Needs department's Procedure for Referral and Organisation of Provision (PROP) follows the approach recommended by the DfES Special Educational Needs Code of Practice 2001, the school far exceeds any statutory obligations in its approach to identifying and meeting a child's needs.

St John's has several specialist staff, trained and qualified to assess, recognise and deal with learning problems throughout the age and ability range. We do not have a separate Individual Needs 'unit' because the close relationship and constant communication between individual needs and mainstream teachers (many wear both hats) is an essential factor in the early identification and the continuing management of any difficulty. As a consequence, 'internal' assessment of children is commonplace when a difficulty has been observed and has been discussed with parents.

In a similar vein, the 'threshold' of intervention is much lower than in most schools. The vast majority of children in receipt of support will have very mild or mild specific learning difficulties. For many of these, the provision will be relatively short-term, addressing a particular concern at a particular time. For others, support may be needed throughout their time at the school and beyond.

The level of awareness of all staff is very high. There is an 'Action Plan' for every child in the school which is constantly updated and formally reviewed and attention to the individual child is a part of the culture. For children with learning difficulties, through specific training and through involvement in framing each child's individual education plan (IEP), the mainstream teachers are made fully aware of any child's difficulties and can therefore plan their teaching accordingly. In this respect, all children benefit greatly from the teachers' awareness of different learning styles, irrespective of whether they have a learning difficulty.

The level of communication with home is, likewise, very high. Parents are informed of any concern, give their permission for any assessment, discuss the outcomes of such aim is to prepare youngassessment in detail with the staff concerned and are fully involved thereafter in the creation and regular updating of a child's IEP. They meet formally and informally with a child's Individual Needs teacher to discuss progress and agree action.

The school is able to refer children to a wide range of outside agencies (educational psychologists, speech therapists, occupational therapists, optometrists, etc) all of whom work in close co-operation with the Individual Needs department. Any such referral is discussed with parents before it goes ahead and the outcome of any assessment is communicated to all mainstream teaching staff.

The effect of a learning difficulty on a child's self-esteem is of paramount concern. While the identification of a difficulty is naturally a cause for concern to parents, it is almost always a source of comfort to the child. To know that there is a difficulty and that you will be helped to overcome it is a reassuring process and, while children's self-esteem is very closely monitored and carefully nurtured by the department and by the staff as a whole, being given Individual Needs support is felt as positive by the vast majority of children concerned. It is a matter of pride, in this respect, that our children will talk openly and without embarrassment to prospective parents about their difficulties.

The range of Individual Needs teaching, as outlined below, is wide and will vary according to a child's needs.

Mainstream Support

The school offers a range of specialist support within its mainstream provision, at no additional cost to parents:

- At Byron House, we offer small group Enrichment English and mathematics support and Motor Skills Groups.
- At Senior House, Enrichment classes in English and maths continue in the 3rd form. Whilst Enrichment English continues into the 4th form, Maths Enrichment ceases with the introduction of smaller mainstream classes, grouped by ability.
- Spelling and Listening Skills clubs are offered to 3rd and 4th form children.
- Curriculum support is available to those who do not study Latin in forms 4-6.
- Touch-typing clubs exist to develop the keyboard skills of any child for whom the use of a laptop may prove beneficial.
- The school has a library of laptops for those children who will benefit from their use in the classroom. In due course, some children will move on to home-owned laptops. Provision for the use of laptops in examinations is negotiated by the school, as appropriate, with a child's future school.

Individual Needs

In addition to the above, the school generally provides, at no additional cost:

- up to two Individual Needs lessons in the Pre-Prep
- one Individual Needs lesson in forms 1-2.
- Any provision over and above this amount is charged at the rate declared in the school's annually updated fees list.

In the case of children for whom the need for support is established prior to entry to the school, while Mainstream Support is offered without additional cost, admission is subject to parental agreement to bear Individual Needs costs.

EAL

The school may admit children for whom English is an Additional Language (EAL) if it deems them able, with appropriate support, to benefit in due course from the mainstream curriculum. Until such a time, individual tuition in English is provided by a specialist teacher in place of mainstream lessons as appropriate. It is a condition of admission that the cost of such tuition should be borne by the parents.

Timetabling of Individual Needs Lessons

The individual needs of each child are taken into account when timetabling lessons. Lessons take place before school, during part of lunchtime or in specified timetable slots which cause the least disruption to mainstream teaching.

Assessment

Detailed assessment of children by the school's Individual Needs department is provided at the school's expense. Where the school proposes a referral for assessment by an educational psychologist, the school may also undertake to bear a share of the cost of the assessment. Many senior schools request an educational psychologist's assessment before granting additional time and/or the use of a laptop for exams. The school arranges this as appropriate.

Where an Individual Needs assessment by the school's staff or by an outside agency is deemed necessary prior to the offer of a place, parents of potential new entrants should expect to bear the cost of such assessment. The cost may vary according to the needs of a child but will be communicated to parents when their approval is sought for such a referral.

What we say about the school - the full Good Schools Guide review

Head: Since 1990, Mr Kevin Jones (mid forties) MA, plus unfinished thesis on how best to acquire knowledge and preserve creativity. Educated Woolverstone Hall (state boarding) and Caius, Cambridge. Previous post – deputy head in the school and before that head of drama and English at the Yehudi Menuhin School. Married with one son formerly in the school and one in the senior department. A thinker, good with children. Nice sense of humour. Comments, a propos parental observation that the school is a high pressure zone, that this is not so, he thinks, and that 'the most precious thing we can give to our children is their childhood'.

Entrance: Getting in is Cambridge prep Valhalla. Name down embryo on. No testing at 3 -'ridiculous' – but test at 7. Yearly scholarships for up to five boy choristers a year. Means-tested scholarships and bursaries at 11 for outstanding academic, music, artistic or all-round ability.

Exit: Every year gets clutch of scholarships to strong music schools – Eton, Tonbridge, Uppingham, Winchester. Gets even more academic scholarships, not to mention art, IT, DT and sports awards (about 50 per cent of leavers gain an award). Sends up to one third of boys to The Perse School in Cambridge, also to Oakham, Westminster, Rugby, Radley, Oundle, King's Canterbury etc, and one or two to East Anglian schools. A very few girls leave at 11 usually for The Perse Girls' and St Mary's Cambridge, the rest generally opt for co-educational boarding at 13.

Remarks: Wonderful prep school in a dreamy city – well worth bustling about to get in. Feels like a honeycomb of schools – kindergarten department in separate house, 'so it feels like home'; 5 to 8-year-olds are in a wing of the smart tailor-made Byron House, which provides not only classrooms but smart hall/gym, drama studio, DT, computer room, music department etc for tinies. Older pupils in a house down the road; boarders live above the shop with their own private recently refurbished and upgraded quarters – part of the £2.5 million building development (you name it, they've got it, from indoor swimming pool to junior library and new music school with individual practice rooms, song school and concert room). Adjacent property acquired and recently redeveloped provides gardens, an arts facility and a lecture theatre; space released in old buildings used to expand ICT etc.

Claims to have (and we would not dispute it) best computer facilities of any prep school – whole school networked in 1998; two computer labs and two networks of PCs for the 4 to 9-year-olds plus laptops. More importantly, the school has the staff to go with them – all teachers and classroom assistants are trained in IT in-house to the skill level achieved by leaving pupils ie very high. Recognised as the National Expert Centre for all prep schools for DT and IT. Head's aim is to 'meet individual needs of each child, so the most (and least) able children get what they need' and, with that in mind, he has come up with a number of developments – study skills (teaching children the skills of individual learning) now an integral part of the curriculum; advanced tutorial system, with one member of staff responsible for 'knowing all there is to know' about no more than ten children and their families; reporting system that allows parents to be 'fully involved' in their children's education. Also 'individual needs department' – qualified specialists backed by educational psychologist on staff. Approximately 20 per cent of pupils at any one time receive help with a 'learning difficulty'. Head hopes that a parent's comment that, 'the school's fine if you can cope but no fun for the strugglers', no longer applies – places immense emphasis on children's happiness, the need for fun and laughter and training teachers (wish more did this).

Jolly red uniform. High calibre of teachers who draw all that is best and most original from pupils. Class size never more than 20 and these are subdivided in senior years to make classes of 12-18. Terms now fit in with other schools and not university terms as hitherto. Most helpful, flexible school day/week includes weekly boarding, 'day' boarding (ie until 8.15pm) and 'staying on' (until 5.15pm) – a miracle for working parents. No longer Saturday morning school but sports coaching and optional activities. Although this is not a 'professional' games school, it has lots of sporting options with good coaching including real tennis and rowing (has produced national real tennis champions). Also the usual sports – rugby, hockey (for the girls) etc and head points out the school has produced county players in these sports plus netball, cricket, raquets, athletics and swimming.

Says a past parent, 'there seems to be some sort of magic that infuses everyone with confidence, happiness and generosity. In this atmosphere academic work prospers effortlessly and discipline appears to take care of itself while the children are so good to each other it brings a lump to your throat. In fact, at any school event it's difficult to know who is having more fun – the children, staff or parents. The head, Kevin Jones, is absolutely inspirational and has a staff of delightful characters who are adored almost without exception by the children. I must confess I'm a bit baffled by the whole thing – how can a school be this wonderful when so many others are tense, inhibited and uninspiring?' Quite.

St John's School

Epsom Road, Leatherhead, Surrey, KT22 8SP

Tel: 01372 373 000

Fax: 01372 386 606

Email: secretary@stjohns.surrey.sch.uk

Website: www.stjohnsleatherhead.co.uk

• Pupils: 417 boys plus 60 girls in sixth form • Ages: 13-18
• Religion: C of E but other denominations accepted
• Fees: Day £5,050; boarding £6,950
• School status: Independent • Opendays: October and June
• School gender: Boys • Day/boarding: Takes boarders

SEN provision

Detail:

Centre of excellence for:
- Mild: DYSL;
- Moderate: DYSL;

Now provide for in school:
- Mild: ADD; ADHD; DYSC; DYSP;
- Moderate: DYSP;
- Others: OCD; EAL;

Experience of:
- Mild: EBD; SpLD; HI; VI;
- Moderate: ADD; ADHD; DYSC; HI; VI;
- Severe: HI; VI;
- Others: Epi; Eat;

Summary: St John's is a school which welcomes students with specific learning difficulties and has been recognised locally as a centre of excellence in this respect for many years. Most students are expected to remain at the school for the full five years and many gain impressive results at A Level.

The SENCo manages the school's Special Needs Register, copies of which are given to all members of staff and updated termly. Tuition, tailored to individual needs, is available on an individual withdrawal basis, usually outside normal lesson times. Students with SpLD are usually identified before entry, but all year 9 pupils are given a series of screening tests. If this process identifies any unexpected difficulties, parents will be contacted by the head of learning support and monitoring, further assessment and individual support might be recommended. Basic skills are monitored throughtout the first three years and any student who appears to require extra help with English, maths or study habits will be referred to learning support by members of staff or parents. Support may continue into the sixth form, where the focus will be on Study Skills, including time management, note-taking and essay writing techniques. Lessons for the sixth form generally take place during a private study period. In practice, these levels of support are available to any pupil in the school, whether they have a specific learning difficulty or not. In addition, there is a programme of Study Skills, delivered throughout the school, by the Head of Learning Support.

What we say about the school - the full Good Schools Guide review

Head: Since 2004, Mr Nicholas J R Haddock MBE MA FRGS. He was educated at St Edward's School and St Edmund Hall, Oxford, where he read geography and played hockey for the University. After leaving Oxford, he was commissioned as an officer in the Royal Green Jackets, where he attained the rank of major. Married with four children. In 1998, he was awarded the MBE for work involved in planning military operations worldwide and was selected for promotion to Lieutenant Colonel but left to pursue a career in teaching.

Academic Matters: Not an academic hothouse; more of an all-round ethos catering for a broader intake of pupils. Examination results have risen sharply over the years – the percentage of GCSE top grades (A* to B) is 84 per cent. Four AS levels taken in lower sixth and usually three A2s after that. At A level, the percentage of A and B grades now stands at 76 per cent and at A2 it is 65 per cent.

The most able academic high-flyers in the area in the past have tended to gravitate towards more prominent day schools such as King's College School, Wimbledon and the Royal Grammar School, Guildford. Equally, St John's competes for potential boarders with Epsom College, Charterhouse, Winchester, Eton, Tonbridge and Lancing. One prospective parent summed up the school as, 'a good all-round school suitable for those not academic enough to get into King's,' however the head responds that a significant percentage of his pupils would be able to meet King's' academic rigour! He does accept that it remains a major challenge for St John's to become the first choice senior school for the most academically able. To this end, the school has introduced 'The Scholars' Initiative' which is designed to stretch and challenge these sought-after able pupils from day one onwards. The aim is to widen the general cultural perspective of members of a selected group by addressing matters of current affairs and political, scientific and cultural issues. Others can ask to join the group.

Up to GCSE average class size is 17, the 80 pupils in each year being divided into sets, the more able in larger sets and the less able in smaller. Average size of sixth form class is 10. Youngish (39) average age of staff. Provision for dyslexics is 'super', according to one parent, 'a great confidence booster.'

Games, Options, The Arts: About one third of pupils learn an instrument, several of them are at grade 8 standard. Tuition largely scheduled so as not to clash with academic lessons. Orchestra, wind band, two jazz bands, chapel choir, madrigal and choral societies, string quartets and more. In 2001, its 150th year, school put on a concert at St John's, Smith Square, Westminster, in presence of its patron, HRH the Duchess of Gloucester. First school allowed to perform Shakespeare in public at Globe Theatre, Southwark, in same year. New three million pound performing arts centre was officially opened in May 2003 with an auditorium, a music school and a Sixth form Social Centre. Good opportunities for sport – including conventional pitches and large astroturf pitch for hockey, football, rugby and tennis. Girls play netball and hockey. PE available at both GCSE and A level.

One mother praised the summer post-GCSE programme in particular, 'the boys had trips to France, driving theory lessons and such-like, when all my friends' children at other schools were being chucked out after the exams – a bit galling when their parents had paid for the whole term and after the children had had study leave at home as well!' Another mother with a daughter due to start at the school was a fan of lessons on Saturday morning, 'great for keeping 16-year-old girls from hanging around Guildford on Saturday mornings.'

Background and Atmosphere: Founded in 1851 in St John's Wood to educate the sons of Anglican clergy; moved to existing site in 1872. Set in the middle of a residential area in prosperous commuter town of Leatherhead. Red-brick buildings and quad, with modern chapel, which is light and airy with tiered seating, unlike a lot of older ones.

Girls (in sixth form only) from 1989 – ' brilliant integration,' says head but no plans to go fully co-ed. Girls' boarding house converted and extended from Victorian house situated just across the road from main school site. Bit of a rabbit warren but cosy and the girls like it and draw up their own rotas for minor domestic chores – not just left to domestic staff – mothers will probably approve. Two or three lower sixth girl boarders share rooms with own room in upper sixth. Another girls' house for boarders and day girls opened in September 2004. All boys' houses have day boys and three take boarders as well. Boarders initially share rather cramped dormitories for up to six, which by no stretch of the imagination could be called luxurious. 'Boarding facilities not up to much,' said a prospective parent who was put off the school by the sleeping arrangements. However, many a boy (if not their parents) may welcome the camaraderie of dorm life and, as usual, accommodation improves with age of pupil – sharing between two to five in fifth form, between two in lower sixth; own room in upper sixth.

School very proud of its computer facilities and aims to be one of the most computer literate schools in the country. Sixth form boarders have school computer provided in their houses, all linked to the school network. Splendidly equipped modern language lab. Library converted from former chapel and has good stock of 12,000 books, together with suitable videos and CDs for loan, daily broadsheet papers and periodicals, including foreign language journals. CCF compulsory for first 18 months but 50 per cent of school tend to stay on after that. Duke of Edinburgh Awards also popular with 100 or so members and 13 gold awards in 2002/03. Great inter-house rivalry.

Many day pupils make their way by train – five minutes walk from station and public bus routes from Epsom and Guildford pass the door. School minibus service from Woking under consideration.

Pastoral Care and Discipline: Head points to school's 'caring Christian ethos.' A fourth former agreed, saying that he 'likes the way that everyone looks out for each other right from the start.' Assemblies held daily in Chapel with themes being introduced by the head, chaplain, staff and pupils. Once a month pupils attend a compulsory act of worship on Sundays. No specific provision for those of faiths other than C of E.

Tutors meet all their pupils in small groups for ten minutes at start of every day and for 30 minutes on

Friday. Each year group in each house has its own tutor, with two tutors per year group for the girls. Pupils have different tutor every year as they progress through the school – means lack of continuity – but advantage is that tutor becomes very experienced with the foibles of that particular age group. Tutor meets parents of pupils within four weeks of start of academic year. Sixth formers are involved in a range of voluntary service activities including work with disabled adults and football coaching with autistic children.

Pupils neat and tidy in their navy blue blazers; sixth formers also have a uniform regime – a suit of their choice – and prospectus refreshingly says that some of the girls' uniform can be purchased from M&S. Smoking dealt with by graded system of punishment and fine. Drugs cases dealt with on an individual basis and the rules apply to offences either on or off school premises. Student Council with representatives appointed for each house and for each year group – the elected Chair liaises with head. Parents agree that pastoral provision is good.

Pupils and Parents: Unspoilt youngsters, mostly from middle class families and without a trace of arrogance in sight. Boys come from large selection of local Surrey preps and girls mainly from local independent schools. Virtually all live within 20 miles, even boarders. About 50 per cent first-time buyers, with very few expats and around 30 from overseas. Now 14 Foundationers (children of Anglican clergy, see Money Matters), probably because clergy prefer these days to educate their children in their local communities. Notable OJs include architect Lord (Richard) Rogers, archaeologist Sir Leonard Woolley, novelist Sir Anthony Hope (wrote 'The Prisoner of Zenda'), Bishop Leonard Wilson (a former Bishop of Birmingham) and Sir Paul Bryan (a Cabinet minister in Harold MacMillan's government).

Entrance: Boys enter at 13 via CE (pass mark 55 per cent) or Common Scholarship exams. The few coming from the state sector sit an internal test. Both girls and boys can enter at 16 via school's entry interview and their GCSE results, which should include at least 6 passes at A-C with a minimum of four Bs, and with B for their chosen AS level subjects.

Exit: Very few leave after GCSE, those who do invariably go to sixth form colleges. Vast majority to university – favoured ones include Oxbridge, Durham, Southampton, West of England, Bristol, Birmingham, Loughborough, Exeter and Kings College, London. About 30 per cent choose a science-based subject, the same percentage plump for humanities, then around 25 per cent a business-orientated course, the rest opting for art.

Money Matters: 170 pupils receiving some sort of fee assistance at present. Awards at 13 for academic, all-rounder/sports, music and art scholarships, ranging in value from 25 to 50 per cent of fees. Similar awards at 16. Fees for children of Anglican clergy (Foundationers) are based on total family income. School is able to offer up to 67 per cent remission of fees for Foundationers. In some cases, fee remission could be higher.

Remarks: Solid, all-round, school with good pastoral care and well sought after but lacking the glitz of its more illustrious competitors. However, a big plus – the super pupils, un-snooty and unaffected while still displaying confidence.

St John's School

Broadway, Sidmouth, Devon, EX10 8RG

Tel: 01395 513 984

Fax: 01395 514 539

Email: nrp@stjohndevon.demon.co.uk

Website: www.st-johns.devon.sch.uk

• Pupils: 220 girls and boys (including 47 in Early Birds nursery)
• Ages: 2-13 • Religion: RC/Anglican
• Fees: Day £1,460-£2,225; boarding £3,585-£4,069
• School status: Independent • Opendays: Every day
• School gender: Mixed • Day/boarding: Takes boarders

SEN provision

Detail:

Centre of excellence for:

Mild: DYSC; DYSL; DYSP;

Moderate: DYSL; DYSP;

Others: EAL;

Summary: St John's school supports pupils with special learning needs. The learning support unit is registered with CReSTeD as having effective support for dyslexic pupils. There are two highly qualified teachers (BDA) who are available for one-to-one or group teaching as well as in class support. All members of staff are familiar with the needs of the children who receive support and the sensitive support and guidance given to these pupils results in their gaining confidence and succeeding in their studies. We are pleased to note the successes of our past special needs pupils at senior school and university level.

What we say about the school - the full Good Schools Guide review

Head: Since 2005, Mrs Tessa Smith BA (Hons) PGCE DipM ACIM.

Entrance: About 60 per cent migrate from nursery. Non-selective although early registration is prudent. Reduction in fees for concurrent siblings. Children invited to spend familiarisation day prior to starting. Foreign intake usually 12 per cent. Day pupils come from 25-mile radius. Parents are typical middle class professionals. Colourful and well-stocked Early Birds nursery has six-month waiting list for 12 places.

Exit: Popular destinations are King's College, Taunton and Exeter School. Others are Blundell's, Maynards, St Margaret's, Stover or Colyton Grammar School.

Remarks: Attractive former convent with stained glass windows. Stands on hill, bordered by countryside and stunning sea view. Excellent facilities. General administration may seem muddled (school prefers 'relaxed') but parents excuse this as part and parcel of the homey atmosphere.

Main course of study is based on the Common Entrance syllabus. National Curriculum SATS at Key Stage 1 and 2 also taken. Children from year 5 are setted by ability in all subjects. Maths is a particular strength with a good number of pupils gaining gold medals in the UK maths challenge each year. Able pupils are given extension work in the 'Endeavourers' group to extend and broaden their thinking skills in preparation for scholarship work.

Major field games played – rugby, football, hockey, cricket (boys) and hockey, netball and rounders (girls). Other games or sports include athletics (eight children at National Championships 2004), swimming, tennis, basketball, cross-country running and badminton. Cricket team champions of Devon and the Western Counties (4th in National Championships 2003). Indoor sports centre encourages children to participate in a wide range of sports.

Discipline centres on rewards for good work and behaviour with the headmaster awarding special 'tokens' for work deemed to be excellent. Children thrive in the atmosphere of stressing the positive with children keen to gain stars (points) for their house. Successes are celebrated in the weekly assembly and the children thrive in the positive atmosphere that promotes positive behaviour of every kind. Prefects are assigned to each form so that the youngest children are encouraged to behave well by the older children whom they learn to respect and have confidence in.

Good pastoral care; peaceful, family environment. Boarders well cared for in fun and colourful dorms painted by the last head and family. Homesickness rapidly resolved. Day parents supportive of boarding community – frequently have boarders staying weekends; ferry them to and from birthday parties etc. After usual settling in period, children may forget to phone home! Children in general confident, self-assured and gregarious individuals.

Linked to school in St Petersburg, its pupils visit St John's to improve their English. Average 14 pupils per class. Two full-time SEN tutors and another who teaches English as a second language for foreign pupils. Careful timetabling to ensure dyslexics receive one-to-one tuition. Some pupils arrive here unable to communicate in English but that soon changes; a pupil who speaks their mother tongue is appointed as their special guardian.

Every classroom and dormitory has computers; all pupils have own e-mail address (Internet is free 8am to 6pm five days a week). Mrs Smith takes over a happy school and we await developments!

St Margaret's School for Girls

17 Albyn Place, Aberdeen, AB10 1RU

Tel: 01224 584 466

Fax: 01224 585 600

Email: info@st-margaret.aberdeen.sch.uk

Website: www.st-margaret.aberdeen.sch.uk

• Pupils: 385 girls, all day • Ages: 3-18 • Religion: Non-denom
• Fees: Juniors from £1,381 to £2,189; Seniors £2,409
• School status: Independent • School gender: Girls
• Day/boarding: Day pupils

SEN provision

Detail:

Now provide for in school:

Mild: ASP; ADD; DYSC; DYSL; CP;

Others: Sp&LD; Epi; Eat;

Experience of:

Mild: EBD; SpLD; VI;

Moderate: ASP; DYSC; DYSL; SpLD; VI;

Severe: ASP;

Others: SPD; PD;

Summary: The school told us:

St Margaret's is fortunate in being able to offer continued assistance for girls from junior classes right through to Senior school level.

Services include: Identifying specific learning difficulties using recognised diagnostic assessments; consulting with staff and parents on the nature of different learning difficulties and liaising with outside agencies where appropriate: advising on strategies both in class and at home to help overcome problems; devising and delivering individual programmes of support for pupils; advising on accelerated learning strategies for more able pupils; advising on examination provision available for pupils with noted learning difficulties and supporting study skills.

What we say about the school - the full Good Schools Guide review

Head: Since 2001, Mrs Lynn McKay BA PGCE ACCEG (fifties), who has a stunning list of schools behind her: previously head of Parsons Mead at Ashstead in Surrey, and before that deputy head of sixth form of Guildford High. Educated in Wales, she went to Ardwyn Grammar School in Aberystwyth, followed by Swansea uni where she read French (which she still teaches). Keen on Spanish, youth work and the 'extra-curricular side of school life'. She also sings and is a member of the local church choir.

Don't get the wrong impression: Mrs McKay is a modern re-invention, zinging, swinging, and totally on the top of everything. She took over a school which had 'been through a difficult year': the school is on course again. Mrs McKay's incredibly elegant office overlooks the playground and she is much entertained by the fact that when pupils want to plan something 'really wicked' they sometimes squat on the stairs immediately below her window, not realising that she can hear everything they say.

Academic Matters: Academically strong across the board, though not really such a formidable selection of subjects: Business management and information studies (one candidate only) stand out among all the usual suspects. Italian and philosophy in the pipeline, and ethics has been introduced as a non-exam subject next year. French and German, plus Latin on the langs side – all can be taken to Advanced Higher level, but hardly any classicists – though all get top grades. Tranches of excellent results in maths, English, mod langs and sciences. Head keen that girls should have the advantage of 'learning independently' and enjoy their lessons. Three new ICT suites, all intranetted, travelling trolley of laptops motors round the school.

Strong support for learning throughout the school with help for the most gifted as well as the underperformer, dyslexia, dyspraxia, ADHD and mild Asperger's all catered for, both individual and group teaching, plus support in class if needed. Each department keeps detailed notes of problems that might be 'just around the corner'. Impressive paired reading initiative where girls in senior school 'trained in specific reading techniques' work with younger pupils in their free time – apart from fostering community spirit, senior readers also get brownie points through 'certification from the Institute of Management'. The learning support team also provides EAL (TEFL-trained helpers in the nursery): Aberdeen is, after all, the oil capital of the North and has a huge through-put of non-English speakers.

Games, Options, The Arts: Stunning netball team who were Scottish champs last year. School keen on promoting team games, but loads of individual activities too: swimming important, athletics, tennis, rounders etc. Mrs McKay keen for school to have an 'ungirly' image, so food technology only up to second year (though it reappears again as preparation for living in sixth). Dramatic fabric design in art, girls make bags with their products, sewing club post school. Art and soldering 'fantastic', and juniors had art on display at Crathes castle last year. Art, music and PE can all be taken to Advanced Higher level, good music and PE results, art the least impressive, drama seems to have fallen by the wayside as an exam subject, can it really be relegated to a couple of club slots a week? Music vibrant, school uses the Kodaly method and boasts a collection of orchestras, string, chamber, jazz plus outstanding 'travelling' choir with regular trips to the States, Europe and St Paul's Cathedral. Impressive collection of FPs in the national youth orchestra. St Margaret's schools worldwide band together for choir tours, heads' chit-chat. 'Gives the school a global dimension'. Collection of clubs, but not a vast collection and some of them might be seen to be part of the school curriculum: tennis, French, dance but also debating and chess. Strong D of E proponents, regular golds. YE (finalists in 2005) and masses of charity input, strong international pupil base and good global awareness. Comprehensive careers department with every girl spending a day at BP.

Background and Atmosphere: Founded in 1846, St Margaret's is the only all girls school in the North of Scotland. Based in a hotch potch conversion of Victorian Merchant's houses (and Albyn Place and the adjacent Queens Road in Aberdeen are home to some six or seven various schools – not all of them clearly labelled, this editor happily tried to go to the (state) school next door.) The deep gardens at the back have been neatly filled in with massive new builds, and recently refurbished art studio, resources centre and dining area. Charming well-equipped library. Pupils chose lunch from a menu provided by a local restaurant, and are served by volunteer parents in a jolly nice but pretty cramped bistro style room in the basement adjacent to the recently revamped and very posh loos. Girls eat by class, own sandwiches OK. School is wheel chair friendly, lifts. Early drop off from 8am, with special provision in the nursery for tots to stay up till 5.30pm, though it costs extra if after school's official closing time. Holiday activities club run during the Easter, summer and October holidays. Nursery staff – and the nursery is called daffodil, wear charming yellow tops and green track suit bottoms. Good second-hand shop (well this is Aberdeen).

Pastoral Care and Discipline: Strong moral back ground, with joint PSE and RME syllabus. Some 15 Moslems in the school, headscarves and longer skirts OK, and pupils made to feel inclusive with Ramadan respected and a special prayer room set aside. Ecumenical assemblies. All join in the Easter service and Christmas concert and the whole school troops off to the Cathedral for St Margaret's day when the smallest have to be restrained from trying to find St Margaret's shield on the roof and falling over in the process. Girls have form teachers, with a dedicated head of guidance for each year, and can go 'to anyone if in difficulties'. Strong anti-bullying programme. Detention now apparently against human rights (not a lot of other schools seem to know this) and recalcitrant pupils get 'an extra learning opportunity to brush up their skills'. Sometimes this takes place after school ...

Pupils and Parents: Large number of first time buyers, large number of non-Brits, strong parent association. And very strong FP links, we met several coming back to help during their gap year, or just to say how they were getting on. Charming. Polite and well-mannered. Tessa Jowell was an old girl. Girls come from all the surrounding areas, as well as the city itself.

Entrance: Test for all, mini test for tinies where they play in groups and are surreptitiously assessed by experts. Siblings not usually turned away.

Exit: Regular trickle to Oxbridge, one last year, but most to Scottish universities studying an astonishing variety of subjects.

Money Matters: Couple of academic and music scholarships, means-tested from September 2005. Will keep a child to next public exam if parents have problems but with the usual caveat about parents being upfront and realistic.

Remarks: Jolly nice old fashioned school with proper values and the best of modern teaching methods. Some of the fabric is a bit sad ('although recent inspectors said it was very good') and the well-used lawn in the tiny play area is a disgrace (thanks to the recently laid new gas pipe). But if single sex education is what you want, St Margaret's is a school which does its girls exceeding well.

St Mary's Catholic School

Windhill, Bishop's Stortford, Hertfordshire, CM23 2NQ

Tel: 01279 654 901

Fax: 01279 653 889

Email: info@stmarys.net

Website: www.stmarys.net

• Pupils: 899 boys and girls, all day • Ages: 11-18
• Religion: RC • School status: State • Opendays: Early October
• School gender: Mixed • Day/boarding: Day pupils

SEN provision

Detail:
Experience of:
Mild: ASP; DYSL; DYSP; SpLD; VI;
Moderate: VI;
Others: EAL; DEL; Epi; PD;

Summary: The SEN provision at St Mary's is high quality: SEN staff are well-qualified, dedicated and experienced. SEN provision was highly praised in the recent Ofsted report. However, this high quality provision is limited in scope due to the fact that most applicants to the school are very able in academic terms.

What we say about the school - the full Good Schools Guide review

Head: Since 2001, Mr Anthony Sharpe BA MMus NPQH (late thirties). Took over from Mr Paul Jackson who had a good reputation. Has ambitious plans for the school, 'I'm not here to just oversee everything staying as it is,' he says. Educated at Cardinal Langley High School in Greater Manchester and University of Liverpool, where he studied music and divinity. Taught music and RE in Liverpool before taking up post of deputy head at Loreto RC Girls School in St Albans. Music is a passion – his liturgical compositions have been published and broadcast. Married with three young children.

Academic Matters: Pupils are taught in mixed ability groups in year 7, apart from setting in maths. In years 8 and 9 they are setted for further subjects. IT teaching has been integrated into other subjects but the head is keen to prioritise it and it is now taught as a separate subject. GCSE results are good – 70 per cent achieved five grade Cs or above in 2001 – and A level results tend to be some of the best in the area. There doesn't appear to be any major gender gap in the results. All sixth formers study a general studies programme that includes both religious education and sport. Pupils with learning difficulties are well supported and there are currently ten pupils with SEN statements. Twenty of the 50-odd teachers have been at the school for ten years or more. Average age of teaching staff is 43.

Games, Options, The Arts: Plenty of trips to theatres, exhibitions and places of interest and opportunities for travel abroad. Wide-ranging extra-curricular activities include D of E. High numbers of pupils participate in extra-curricular sports, particularly boys. Regular music and drama performances involving large numbers of pupils. Specialist Arts status, awarded in September 2003, will build further on the reputation of the school in this area. Pupils are encouraged to help in the community through the Saint Vincent-de-Paul Society.

Background and Atmosphere: Established by an order of nuns in 1896 as a girls' convent but co-ed since 1976. Situated near the centre of Bishop's Stortford on a large and pleasant site. Near to bus routes but about a 15-minute walk from the rail station. A mixture of old and new buildings. Some of the older ones are a bit scruffy and there is a big current building programme and plans for refurbishment. Recently built sixth form centre with plenty of space for both study and relaxation. Current sports facilities are adequate but plans for a first class new sports centre. Unobjectionable uniform for years 7-11; no uniform for sixth formers although they are expected to dress smartly.

Pastoral Care and Discipline: Very strong Catholic ethos. There are regular lunchtime Masses and residential retreats. Pupils report a very supportive atmosphere and find it easy to confide in teaching staff who they believe will deal swiftly and effectively with any problems, whether they are related to school – including bullying – or at home. Discipline is firm, but fair. 'We have a reputation for being strict but overall this is a happy school. We have no major discipline problems and pupils are very aware that if they cross the line, there will be sanctions,' says the head. One pupil has been excluded in the past two years. Ofsted rated leadership and management as very good and noted the very good relationships between staff and pupils, saying that staff are excellent role models.

Pupils and Parents: Predominantly Catholic families. In the past, non-Catholic pupils have fitted in well but increasing pressure for places from Catholics has meant that fewer non-Catholics have been admitted to the school over recent years. St Mary's serves the Lea Valley Deanery, which stretches from Bishop's Stortford to Hoddesdon, Cheshunt and Waltham Cross and many pupils travel significant distances across Hertfordshire and Essex. Unlike some local schools, St Mary's does not practise backdoor selection so has, the head stresses, a truly comprehensive intake. The area served is fairly affluent so pupils tend to have relatively few social problems. Very enthusiastic support and fundraising from parents through the PTA.

Entrance: Has recently expanded to five form entry. Heavily over-subscribed. First priority goes to Catholic children with a brother or sister in the school. Next in line are Catholic applicants with no sibling connection. Places are awarded according to where applicants live, with 40 per cent going to children in Bishop's Stortford and Sawbridgeworth, 40 per cent going to children in other parts of the Lea Valley Deanery and 20 per cent to those living in another five surrounding Essex parishes. Next come any other Catholic applicants who don't fit the above criteria. Criterion four offers places to those with a non-Catholic sibling in the school. Effectively, apart from rare cases, the only non-Catholics who will now be gaining a place are those who have an older sibling already at the school. Contact the school for full admissions information.

Entrance to sixth form is dependent on GCSE grades but 'some students come to us without the necessary grades if we think they can cope,' says the head. 'Equally, if students are not able to sustain the level, we ensure that they leave that course and take up alternative provision.'

Exit: A few pupils leave after GCSEs to move to other sixth forms in the area, a few go straight to work. The vast majority of those leaving the sixth form go on to further education. One or two a year head for Oxbridge but the head hopes to see this figure increase with the introduction of a new year 12 extension studies programme.

Remarks: You can more or less forget about applying to this school at the moment unless your child has been baptised in a Catholic church, although places may possibly be available again to non-Catholics following expansion to five form entry. For Catholic parents who are keen to have their children educated in their faith in a happy and academically successful environment, St Mary's should be ideal.

St Mary's College, Part of the Wrestwood Trust

Wrestwood Road, Bexhill-on-Sea, TN40 2LU

Tel: 01424 730 740

Fax: 01424 733 575

Email: adm@st-marys.bexhill.sch.uk

Website: www.st-marys.bexhill.sch.uk

• Pupils: 40 boys, 17 girls • Ages: 16-19 • Fees: Day: £11,326; Boarding: £14,000-£15,103. Additional weekends: £174.30. Fees are normally paid by LEAs • School status: State • School gender: Mixed • Day/boarding: Takes boarders

SEN provision

Summary: See St Mary's School entry.

What we say about the school - the full Good Schools Guide review

Head: Since its foundation in 1999, Mr Nigel Willis. Background in FE especially horticulture, which he's introduced to college. 'All do horticulture even selling some produce, it's very therapeutic, a great interest of mine and can open up employment opportunities.' Has a really good team, excellent working relationship with staff.

Entrance: All are assessed – four days for non-school, two days for school. Preference isn't given to St Mary's pupils. If college believe they can meet the students' needs and are best placed to do so, they will offer a place. The student must then obtain funding before a place is confirmed – first-come-first-served – once living house is full, that's it. Majority are funded by LEA – college isn't cheap – but among other things it offers a real chance of meaningful employment – excellent value compared to a possible life on benefits with resultant lack of self-esteem etc.

Exit: Post-19 transition is overseen by the community resources co-ordinator. Some go to residential colleges – Derwin (Shropshire), Ruskin Hill (Glouc), Linkage (Lincs), Hereward (Coventry), some return home and attend local FE colleges, usually those with an SEN department and employment links; others move on to supported living funded through social services usually close to a local college or employment.

Remarks: Founded in 1999 on land neighbouring the school grounds, the college occupies two low-level buildings, shares school dining hall and sports facilities but is otherwise largely autonomous. Set up to cater for the sizeable chunk of children proving difficult to place on leaving St Mary's.

College has five houses three on site – The Stables, Margate and Jalna for the most dependent and two mixed houses in Bexhill for those working towards greater independence. Accommodation is well presented, all rooms are en-suite and students have own cooking and laundry areas plus usual sitting and communal rooms. In the town houses pupils cook breakfast and supper and must shop, cook and budget for these meals. Living in town enables students to access and integrate into the local community, develop key living skills and exercise a degree of autonomy and independence.

Like the school, college has teachers, therapists and facilitators who monitor and provide for the students needs. Teaching groups are small and well supported. All students have an ILP/action plan reviewed periodically.

Aim is to prepare young people for the change from school to adult life. School is very structured adhering carefully to routines which college gradually breaks down – changing everything from course tutors, study rooms, living houses, house co-ordinators, uniform (there isn't one), travel etc. Initially some find it difficult, others adapt well and respond admirably to being treated as young adults doing more of what they want to do. Most are appreciative of independent living and say life at college is good fun.

There are two levels of course: programme 1 for students who need high level support and who are day or weekly boarders and programme 2, all fortnightly boarders, for students demonstrating greater independence and relatively higher academic achievement. A full 3-year programme is offered to guide students into the world of work.

All students have an individual timetable geared around their interests – if that's in mechanics a programme will be designed and developed around that. They continue with ASDAN, taking the adult life skills certificate, study key skills: numeracy and literacy, spend one day a week at the local FE college and wherever possible, one day a week on work experience. Other study options include GNVQ (foundation) hospitality and catering, and leisure and tourism, some do both. Business studies is also popular with many taking part in Young Enterprise – recently a successful car-wash enterprise was outdone by a pop group who professionally recorded and released a record about being SEN and being bullied. The song, 'Enough is enough' was picked up and aired by Southern Counties Radio and Meridian TV – students fronted the whole thing from making record to burning CD, and won the prize for best marketing campaign for local young enterprise.

A key aim is to make students employable. Some employers eg Hilton and Tesco are very enlightened and work closely with the college and students. Hilton not only provides carefully structured work experience placements but also funded the designer kitchen in one of the student houses. Some students so impressive they've been offered work, permanent and holidays. Activities afternoon a week, all students are encouraged to continue with sport (all do swimming). Activities include relaxation therapy and art and design. At 17 college will facilitate driving lessons, encourage a healthy attitude to drink (take to pub), openly discusses sex, relationships and what's appropriate, talk about politics and voting including postal votes. All have own bank account and participate in the independent budget scheme (like the independent travel scheme – which continues from school to college). Terrific, improving all the time. Lots of innovative ideas. Buy your ticket early, keep your fingers crossed.

St Mary's School (Bexhill-on-Sea)

Wrestwood Road, Bexhill-on-Sea, East Sussex, TN40 2LU

Tel: 01424 730 740

Fax: 01424 733 575

Email: adm@st-marys.bexhill.sch.uk

Website: www.st-marys.bexhill.sch.uk

• Pupils: 49 boys 20 girls. 90 per cent board • Ages: 7-16 • Religion: Christian • Fees: School: Day: £8,071; Boarding: £12,705-£13,808. Additional weekends: £174.30. College: Day: £11,326; Boarding: £14,000-£15,103. Additional weekends: £174.30. Fees are normally paid by LEAs • School status: Independent • School gender: Mixed • Day/boarding: Takes boarders

SEN provision

Detail:
Now provide for in school:
Mild: AUT;
Moderate: AUT;
Others: AUT(other); Sp&LD; DEL; Oth;
Experience of:
Mild: ASP;
Moderate: ASP;
Severe: ASP;

Summary: St Mary's is a registered charity. It is a Children's Trust dedicated to educating and caring for young people between 7 and 19 years of age, all of whom have complex needs. The trust has a school (7-16), a college (16-19) and is also involved in outreach work and assessments.

All our young people are within the moderate learning difficulties (MLD) range and have particular needs in regard to Speech/Language difficulties, autism, physical disabilities and complex medical conditions, all of which are met by an experienced education, therapy, care and nursing staff.

St Mary's is a DfES approved non-maintained special school.

What we say about the school - the full Good Schools Guide review

Principal/Chief Executive: Since 1991 Mr David Cassar MA FRSA FCMI CCYW CEd (fifties) previously principal of a boarding special school in Hertfordshire. Has the titles Principal/Chief Executive. A fascinating background: spent seven years in civil engineering and architecture before becoming a youth and community worker then decided to train as a teacher to get to pupils on the inside. Worked with abused children – also studied business – not a 'Jack of all trades' but a master of many. Was appointed to the school in freefall amid rumours he was there to close it down. A man of considerable vision he immediately arrested decline – called in favours from everywhere, secured charitable status by changing from an education to a children's trust, raised capital, haggled with banks and project managed the whole thing – now thriving, cutting-edge stuff. Proud that something new has been added every year – classroom block is latest work. Nobody's fool – a demanding, exacting taskmaster – an entrepreneur with a heart – undoubtedly a supplier of silk stockings to sell in wartime – drives a hard bargain, has a degree in charm and dry sense of humour. Jokes he's done it all for the money – but all agree his real motivation is undisputedly the children – staff say he's fantastic with the kids.

The Head of School (7-16) Mrs Jo Whiteman CEd BEd NPQH first joined St Mary's on a part-time basis in 1985. Appointed head in 2003, she has witnessed the vicissitudes of fortune and seen great changes over the years. Her calm demeanour, pride in and love for the children reflect her dedication and quiet determination.

Academic Matters: Every child has some form of language and communication difficulty often accompanied by other SEN including autistic spectrum disorders, physical disabilities, delicate/medical conditions or multi-sensory impairment (MSI). School has own audiology department and signing is used throughout not just for the hearing impaired but to assist those who find visual communication easier than oral. Class sizes average 8 to 10 per teacher with substantial integrated therapy as required.

The experienced teachers, speech and language, art, physio and occupational therapists, counselling psychologist, sign language tutor and care and nursing staff work collaboratively to deliver the 'waking curriculum' ensuring educational needs are balanced with therapeutic needs, life skills and ability to interact with others – good value-added across the board. Pupils follow the National Curriculum, adapted as necessary – no foreign languages at any stage, no humanities at Key Stage 4. Every pupil has an individual learning programme (ILP). Any child able enough will follow entry level or GCSE courses otherwise ASDAN forms the main curriculum vehicle when exam courses are not appropriate. There is a dedicated IT suite and IT is widely used throughout the school. Community integration is a key feature, all year 11 pupils undertake work experience and are involved with carefully selected and closely monitored community groups and activities.

Games, Options, The Arts: All take part in sport. Lots on offer including football, unihock, basketball, boccia (a game in which the athletes kick, throw or roll pliable balls down a ramp and which can be played in wheelchairs), stool ball, new age curling, riding, yoga, outdoor and adventurous activities, badminton, and tennis. School has super swimming pool with disabled access and well-equipped gym where we watched a group of children with autism perform a well co-ordinated music and movement piece they'd choreographed; we also witnessed two triumphant football teams receive hearty applause in the school assembly. Music and drama are a big part of school life as well as choir, guitar, keyboard, brass and woodwind all children are invited to take part in the annual school production written by the head of music. Other activities offered include photography (lovely montages adorn the corridors), painting/sculpture (super art therapy room), cookery in the state of the art food technology room, horticulture, Duke of Edinburgh Award, brownies, scouts plus a host of specialised activities for individuals and groups including back care and termly cultural days.

Background and Atmosphere: Founded in 1922, moved to current semi-rural location on the outskirts of Bexhill in 1946. Principal arrived in 1991 to a school with fewer than 60 children, 17 were leaving and there wasn't one referral. School has expanded rapidly over past 12 years: lots of purpose-built, light, airy facilities including assembly hall/chapel, library, sensory room, fully equipped and adapted science lab, adventure playground etc. There's terrific team spirit – everyone works together, learns from their mistakes and builds on the positive.

Pastoral Care and Discipline: Social care is at least as important as education. Care curriculum has lots of input from therapists who work in boarding houses as well as the classroom, nursing and care staff and social worker. Independence is encouraged in all aspects of life – lots of innovative and very visual ideas – pictorial 'keep safe' scheme enables pupils to express concerns about bullying, unwanted touching etc. Highly sought after Independent Travel Scheme is a real winner – pupils earn coloured cards red, amber or green. Red means a child can move within the school unsupported, the coveted green that they can access public transport and travel independently. Many never progress beyond red but each step represents a huge leap. Every aspect of life is closely monitored and frequently reviewed, personal targets were evidenced everywhere – in one boarding house targets were placed on a dart board – the closer to the bull's eye the nearer the child is to meeting their target.

There are five living areas chronologically based – youngest live in main school, some single bedrooms but up to four children may share. Accommodation has a comfortable homely feel – carpeted and well decorated with cheery curtains and pupils encouraged to personalise their living space. There is a carefully planned programme of activities which extends to theatre trips, farm visits etc. Pupils have built in friendship groups – essential, as some are not sure how to make friends – boys and girls are actively encouraged to mix and socialise through activities such as supper swap. Mobile phones are seen as an excellent way to keep in touch. Children run the school shop and school council; all belong to one of three houses with the incoming house captain interviewed and selected by the outgoing one.

Signed assemblies with hymn, pupil interaction and prayer, are held daily. Friday assembly is celebration day. Pupils eat together in the light, modern dining room, good food, lots of choice and of course special diets, cutlery, adapted seats etc. Lunch is a social occasion – we were very well looked after by the friendly, endearing pupils who told us lots about the school, the head, lessons, targets, keep safe, augmentative communication (their words not ours) – one even read the menu for us and explained the benefits of healthy eating – joined us in the salad queue but in the end couldn't resist the pull of the brunch grill – the smell of bacon...

Pupils and Parents: From throughout the country and abroad. All pupils have a communication disorder and many have complex and often unique conditions and syndromes but not behavioural difficulties. School values the partnership with parents and recognises some have struggled for a long time to get this level of care or feel guilty about entrusting the care of their child to others. Parents are encouraged to be involved and to work collaboratively with the school and can phone any time. There's a pupil–parent support group (PPSG) and a 'new parents' group as well as provision of classes such as signing. An annual reunion is held every year in May for old boys and girls and their parents.

Entrance: Referrals are made through local education departments or private referrals. Pupils are statemented for speech, language and occupational therapy and will need greater provision than LEA can offer. Entry is via detailed formal assessments and interview. A school transition advocate will help support parents through SEN tribunals and liaise with legal professionals if required.

Exit: At 16 majority seek places at St Mary's College. Otherwise mostly to FE colleges or specialist residential colleges.

Remarks: A very good school with fantastic, highly structured, integrated support at all levels – worth every penny for those lucky enough to get one of the few available places.

St Mary's School (Cambridge)

Bateman Street, Cambridge, Cambridgeshire, CB2 1LY

Tel: 01223 353 253

Fax: 01223 357 451

Email: enquiries@stmaryscambridge.co.uk

Website: www.stmaryscambridge.co.uk

• Pupils: 490 girls, 50 boarders including full-time, weekly and flexi, rest day • Ages: 11-18 • Religion: RC but all faiths welcome • Fees: Day £2,990; weekly boarding £5,290; full boarding £5,990 • School status: Independent • Opendays: October and May • School gender: Girls • Day/boarding: Takes boarders

SEN provision

Detail:

Centre of excellence for:
  Mild: EBD;
Now provide for in school:
  Mild: ADD; ADHD; DYSC; DYSL; DYSP; HI; VI; CP;
  Moderate: DYSC; CP;
  Others: SPD; OCD; EAL; MSI; DEL; Eat;
Experience of:
  Mild: ASP;
  Others: GEN; PD;

Summary: We offer in-house assessment of any pupil who enters the school with an existing educational psychologist's report or whose performance in school raises cause for concern. Pupils who have been identified as requiring extra assistance in literacy, numeracy or other study skills are offered help according to their needs. Some have private lessons in or outside lesson times with a peripatetic dyslexia specialist; others are offered tuition in small groups by members of St Mary's staff. In some cases, pupils may follow a reduced timetable in order to meet their needs.

What we say about the school - the full Good Schools Guide review

Head: Since 2001, Mrs Jayne Triffitt MA PGCE (forties), educated at Truro High School, read chemistry at St Hilda's, Oxford, where she also did her PGCE. Having benefited from a direct grant scholarship when she was at school, followed by a full grant at Oxford, Mrs Triffitt 'always wanted to put something back into education'; bright, pragmatic, with a twinkle in her eye and a memory like a computer, she has all the easy charm of someone who is not accustomed to not getting her own way. Married to the head of history at The Leys (but she got her job first), they have two young children, a son at King's College School and a daughter at St Catherine's, the main feeder school for St Mary's.

Came to the school after a period of some turmoil – five heads (two acting) in six years. A practising Catholic (and a convert) she was previously head of sixth form at one of the sister schools, St Mary's Ascot; before that, she taught for 17 years in the state system, ending with a ten year stint at La Sainte Union girls' comprehensive school where she was head of science. Mrs Triffitt arrived in Cambridge to find a much more rudderless ship than she had anticipated, 'it was incredibly challenging...the school had really good academic standards, the teachers were excellent, the pastoral care was good' but the school was falling in numbers. It wasn't 'selling itself', it was also losing money. Not surprising really, the external walls were decorated with graffiti and some parts of the inside hadn't been 'touched for thirty years'. Now, decorated in uplifting tones of cheerful yellow, cream, jonquil – except for one very nasty (inherited) bubble gum pink passage – with clean white woodwork everywhere; the school looks fresh and inviting.

With fewer than thirty boarders when she arrived, Mrs Triffitt has invested heavily in a whizzy marketing director, assistant and registrar and does a fair amount of trawling herself. A smart young bursar with an IT background (what do former army officers do now, we wonder?) and an academic housemistress in the boarding house are among the latest appointments. Plus new assistant head from an international school in Brazil. Over 60 staff, with a regular 10/15 per cent turnover. No problem appointing high calibre staff (head keen to make the right appointments and will re-advertise rather than taking a 'might-do') but cost of housing in Cambridge is high for those with families.

Academic Matters: Huge recent investment in IT, with over 250 computers around the school; dedicated computer in sixth form IT centre for girls to edit video footage – multi-split screen and high tech mikes. Recent ISI inspection high-lighted lack of teacher-skills in this direction – one suspects the young may be rather more with it than their mentors. Breezy attractive library, but possibly not enough novels or newspapers in evidence throughout the school. Efficient labs, bright and sunny on the whole, and school has a history of doing well in the biology and chemistry Olympiads; strong A level results too in the sciences, ditto GCSE. Individual or dual award.

Stunning results across the board. Actually results overall pretty outstanding, especially when you consider this is a 'fairly' unselective school. Italian about to be phased out, 'just French, German and Spanish'. Latin on hand, and the odd girl does Greek. Theology for all to GCSE, we sat in on a lesson, brilliant. Classical civilisation, drama, textiles, art and design all make a good showing. Statistics quite popular, also art and design plus psychology or RE at A level. Range of subjects at A level includes theatre studies, textiles, critical thinking, economics and business studies. Max class size 22, but most are way below, certain amount of streaming throughout, but not in science, girls can and do move up and down. Regular collection of time-tabled drop-in surgeries for girls with problems – in any subject – and much used.

The school also runs an International Study Centre. This offers a year's concentrated course in English for girls going to secondary school in the UK (and some will end up at St Mary's, but by no means all) as well as EFL, and lang labs for their own students and summer courses. Ages from 11-17. The site (which is plumb opposite the main school buildings) also accommodates an overspill from St Catherine's, the main feeder school to St Mary's. Girls from abroad at the international study centre are either found accommodation with host families nearby, or, if space available, in the main school itself.

All pupils assessed on entry for reading, spelling and maths, unit 'logs and monitors' problems at the beginning and may pick up one or two during their time at school. Dr Goddard head of SEN, plus two full team co-ordinators and specialists, plus peripatetics for one-to-one, and double teaching in class. Edpsych consulted if required. Only 'about ten' see specialists, some help available outside school, and some help with study skills, plus individual departments help out on an 'informal basis'. Norm is one lesson a week, though 'up to three' is possible. School reckons it is 'dyslexia friendly' but not Crested 'and not likely to move into that area' though there is a 'dedicated teaching space with full rescources'. Individual classes in lunchtime and post school. One girl in school diagnosed ADHD with one or two further suspicions. Will not let any pupil needing help 'slip through the net'. Good EFL provision too.

Games, Options, The Arts: An inner-city school, games pitches some distance away, pupils are bused, various hirings from The Leys, swimming pool and the like, one or two courts on site, and really quite an adequate play area. Own (smallish first floor!) gym. School plays matches on Wednesdays, and does 'jolly well' in hockey, netball with one or two county players and good match successes. Currently under 16 county netball champions. Tennis and gymnastics impressive, taster rugby sessions available in the sixth form. Regular tours abroad, hockey in Holland popular. Popular too are water sports holidays in France. Outstanding D of E, the best we have ever (and we mean ever) come across – 38 participating in gold in sixth form. Mega mega WOW factor. For any school this would be impressive, for an inner-city girls' school, this is incredible. Incredible performance too in Young Enterprise, where school regularly tops all others in the district. Can't do better than that.

Music was the weak link, new staff and getting stronger by the term. Serious investment. Bigger variety of instruments on offer, and take up encouraging, with 'lots more' extra-curricular. Three choirs (and trips abroad) two orchestras, jazz band etc. Drama 'fine', with dedicated drama room, and a couple of main school productions a year. School piloting a new Arts Council sponsored Arts Award scheme for young people which includes journalism, dance, digital film work, music and drama. Art rooms a trifle cramped but good work nonetheless, entertaining ceramics. Textiles allied to art, with huge bright classroom filled with sewing machines (brill), adaptable tailor's dummies leer out from the most unlikely corners all over the school.

The sixth form society runs their own esoteric activity programme from kayaking to wine-tasting. Varied programme of visiting speakers and debates. School hot on charity, raised £14,000 last year, and do an annual and popular Lourdes pilgrimage (the Catholic nobs' unofficial marriage market).

Background and Atmosphere: Former convent, moved out of nun-control in 1989, built round one side of the Botanic Gardens. Stunning sixth form centre in a separate building where girls, who wear their own clothes, have dedicated study areas and classrooms. Main school has a diverse collection of '60s, '70s and '90s add-ons to a primarily early Victorian structure.

Architecture at its worst in almost every case. Dorms cosy, well-used, with teddies and boy inspired posters, single rooms for those post GCSE and some for those in their GCSE year, but a map would come in handy for visiting GSG editors and suchlike. Rising popularity has meant that you have to be quite quick off the mark to book boarding before the school has filled all available beds with an influx from abroad (not more than 11 per cent in total, though it may feel more). Dedicated flexi-boarding space available. Local boarders are enthusiastic and rate the place highly – 'hilarious in the evening ... quite a lot of freedom and regular trips to Cambridge'. Junior common room full of dress-up clothes, painting kits as well as games and the inevitable telly and DVDs – the former two are a first for us. Excellent. Dining room (stools folding into tables set-up) part of brilliant halls (A+B) arrangement, noisy, busy, with good buffet, hot, veggie and cold and the food, according to our informant is 'super, all hand-made'. So there you are. Constant anorexia watch but no current concerns.

Pastoral Care and Discipline: Strong Catholic ethos. Very strong form tutor team backed up by 'six experienced heads of year'; girls get 'loads of individual attention from subject teachers' and their 'progress is noted on a personal basis'. Every girl knows that someone is watching out for her and is encouraged 'to share her problems with any member of staff with whom she is comfortable'. Happy self-confident girls. Recent report picked up a certain laxness in sixth form registration and sixth formers now have to register twice a day. Smoking, boozing, drugging – expect suspensions at the very least, head has permanently excluded two girls.

Pupils and Parents: Broad day pupil base, some very local, some commute by car, but over 100 come by train (station five minutes away). School vies with The Perse and The Leys locally. Mixture of first time buyers, dons' children, medics and lawyers plus a few (Catholic) toffs and the like from East Anglia. Good selection of weekend activities.

Entrance: Quite a number at 11, usually the entire output from St Catherine's next door, plus those who are coming at the state sector break, more at 12 and 13 plus a small influx post GCSE. Own exam throughout but not 'necessarily an easy ride'.

Exit: Fair number of locals leave after GCSE to Hills Road (qv) and a few others may go to co-ed boarding schools or merely elsewhere. That having been said, the sixth form centre appeared full of utterly happy and poised young ladies busily getting on with life. Most to unis, with impressive numbers to Oxbridge and equally impressive course selection.

Money Matters: School now financially OK. A Mary Ward school, with two Mary Ward bursaries (up to 95 per cent) at 11, one at 13 and at sixth form; these are reviewed annually; as well as academic scholarships, and music scholarships. Will 'try and help' with pupils whose families fall upon hard times, usually to the next public exam. Always worth a try.

Remarks: School on a roll. Not the sleepy neglected place it used to be.

ST MARY'S SCHOOL (MELROSE)

Abbey Park, Melrose, TD6 9LN

Tel: 01896 822 517

Fax: 01896 823 550

Email: enquiries@stmarys.newnet.co.uk

Website: www.stmarysmelrose.org.uk

• Pupils: 130 boys and girls in main school (40/60), 40 in nursery (kindergarten); 25 boarders max
• Ages: main school 4-13; nursery 2.5-4 • Religion: Non-denom
• Fees: Weekly boarding £3,990; day 3-8 £3,400; reception - upper transition £2,450; lower and upper kindergarten £20 per morning, £30. per day • School status: Independent
• Opendays: In the summer term • School gender: Mixed
• Day/boarding: Takes boarders

SEN provision

Detail:
Now provide for in school:
Mild: ADD; ADHD; EBD;
Moderate: MLD; DYSC; DYSL; DYSP;

Summary: At St Mary's, children initially screened when joining school to identify any particular learning needs. If necessary, support is provided through a 35 minute one-to-one lesson twice a week. These lessons are individually tailored to the particular needs of each pupil.

Our additional support for learning department is staffed by two experienced and appropriately qualified teachers.

What we say about the school - the full Good Schools Guide review

Head: Since 1998, Mr John Brett MA CertMusEd, MCollP GCLCM (forties) who was educated at King's Bruton but did his A levels at Yeovil College ('fantastic music A level'). Studied music at Leeds and London and trails more letters after his name than most. He came from Thomas's (Battersea) where he was head of music, and before that taught at King's Hall in Somerset. An urbane, enterprising head, he oozes confidence (and well he might) and happily chatted up children and staff on our way round. After his appointment he discovered a school firmly entrenched in the trad-boys-prep school mind-set with a newly-built, barely-used, boys' dormitory (hungry builder governor) and rooms shut up all over the place. With sixty children and 'only three in the top year group', St Mary's was a school with a problem and Mr Brett happily admits that 'the first two or three years were a rocky ride'.

His first move was 'to stop the rot', literally. Fundraising helped too, and the school is financially sound. Armed with a strong nucleus of experienced teachers (now supplemented by younger models – more professional, with loads of specialist teachers) he went out and created a new market. 'Lots of input, lots of goodwill' 'Fantastic new board of governors, senior management and structure in place', and lives on the site with his wife Clare, who teaches drama, and their two small children. Mr Brett himself, despite all his musical trail of glory, actually teaches global citizenship to the top three year groups. 'But,' he says, 'children are always popping in (to his book-lined study) to see me so that I can hear them read'.

Entrance: All things to all men. The only independent school in the borders, children come from within a 20/30 mile radius, can come mid-term at any time if space available, otherwise automatically up from kindergarten. The odd state child has been known simply to come for an 'eighteen-month blast' before going back into the maintained sector again. And some come at 11 to do CE.

Exit: 'Most but not all' stay on until they go to their senior school which may be at 11, 12, or 13, depending whether they are going to continue in the independent vein in which case it is Glenalmond, Fettes, Merchiston, Loretto, St Georges in Edinburgh as well as Longridge Towers in Berwick, Queen Margaret's York or dive back into the state sector and Earlston High School.

Money Matters: Scale of sibling reductions.

Remarks: Jolly useful little school, incredibly flexible, with flexi, weekly and day pupils; one or two toffs, but mostly farmers and local professionals who stay to the bitter end, plus 'masses of' first time buyers. Tiny classes, max 18 but usually much less, only one stream but scholars will be 'hived off' and setted at 10 if necessary. Latin and Greek from eight, 'fantastically popular teacher'. Languages from five, taster term of German, French, Spanish then specialise in French for Common Entrance. Science taught separately for the last four years, and pupils move round the staff. 'Excellent' dyslexia department, and good support for the very bright as well. Withdrawn help and staff will go into class as well – 'pretty flexible' (might be the school motto). Keen on handwriting.

Art mistress comes three times a week, and obviously pretty busy if the amount of art on display is anything to go by. Drama strong and timetabled, the school has links with local theatrical costumiers. Good music, rehearsals and lessons in functional school hall, whilst pre-prep have own gym, with Noah and his ark drawn by the young, main school has to use the hall. Somewhat surprising cloistered classroom corridor and incredible conversions and add-ons (or subtractions) on the classroom side, very rabbit warreny. Charming little Foyle library, with computers all over the place and dedicated resource centre for every age group.

Day children can stay from 7.30am (and breakfast in school) right through to 7.30pm, by which time they will have done their prep and had supper. Kindergarten can stay till 4pm, tinies wear delightful green and white check tabliers, and girls evolve from tartan gym slips to kilts. Jolly dorms upstairs, all brightly painted with splendid (unironed) stripy duvet covers. Dining room with proper menu (beware the 'sandwitch') and over-high benches for littlies to sit at the table. Brown bread only, and lots of sugar-free puds, and mainly organic as far as possible. Robert the chef comes complete with starched chef's hat and sparkling white uniform. Cor. He also makes rather natty millionaire's shortbread for the head's guests – not sugar-free at all.

Squads and teams triumph all over the place. Swimming off-site in Gala(shiels) and main games pitches just across some National Trust land. Smashing little school.

ST MARY'S SCHOOL (SHAFTESBURY)

Donhead St. Mary, Shaftesbury, Dorset, SP7 9LP

Tel: 01747 852 416

Fax: 01747 851 557

Email: registrar@st-marys-shaftesbury.co.uk

Website: www.st-marys-shaftesbury.co.uk

• Pupils: 320 girls; 205 board, rest day • Ages: 9-18

• Religion: RC • Fees: Junior boarders £6,065, day £4,140. Senior boarders £6,390, day £4,350

• School status: Independent

• School gender: Girls • Day/boarding: Takes boarders

SEN provision

Detail:

Now provide for in school:

Mild: DYSC; DYSL; DYSP;

Experience of:

Mild: ADD; ADHD;

Others: EAL; Epi; PD; Eat;

Summary: St Mary's is able to cater for pupils of at least average intelligence with mild difficulties of a dyslexic or dyspraxic nature, or mild ADD/ADHD disorders, who can access an academic curriculum. A maximum of two x 35 minute individual lessons per week are taught by specialist support staff at an additional charge. There is currently no provision for in-class support. Extra maths tuition is offered at an additional charge for pupils requiring support in the run-up to GCSE examinations, but is also available for younger pupils with weak numeracy skills.

What we say about the school - the full Good Schools Guide review

Head: Since 2003, Mrs Margaret McSwiggan MA (early fifties), who was educated at St Rita's in Brisbane and started her career teaching home economics in the state sector. She becomes the second lay head at St Mary's and was previously first lay head at Notre Dame School in Cobham, and before that at King Edward's Witley. Asked why she came to St Mary's, she simply says 'I missed boarding'. Got her MA in educational management from University of Surrey (whilst at Cobham). Married, with a daughter (at St Mary's). Loves skiing and walking and spends any spare time in Alps. Believes strongly in encouraging each girl to achieve her potential, not only academically, but also through playing a part in the life of the school. Since her arrival she has 'got rid of those awful velvet curtains', revamped the staffroom, and spent an awful lot of money on the sporting side. (Parents and pupils agree that this was money well spent – though one father grumbled that he had thought they were getting an art department and not a wretched indoor swimming pool – fear not, the art school cometh next – complete with planning permission). Her husband is big in IT. Head is also keen on IT and has revamped the IT, wireless in the boarding houses and points all over the main school. Pupils are encouraged to bring their own laptops. ECDL for all. Keen that pupils should 'achieve their potential' through IT and not in spite of it. New heads of staff include director of sport plus heads of ICT services, RE, geography and history (the latter's predecessor is now housemistress) and Mrs McS is appointing 'high calibre academics as house mistresses', and is thrilled to have a chaplain under retirement age. 'All jolly fun' said the head, who is enjoying her time at the helm here. IB in tandem currently under investigation.

Academic Matters: Results are excellent for mixed intake. Almost half the girls do A level English; RS, French and art/history of art popular too; maths and the sciences have 'smaller numbers' – ie minimal take-up. Separate sciences for all at GCSE and rather whizzy science labs with just the whiff of Dr Strangelove about them, GCSE results impressive, and an astrophysician in the making (so why so few at A level). New head of geog in place and numbers of girls taking AS and A levels on the up. Impressive classics master. One or two esoteric languages: exams usually taken by native speakers, otherwise Spanish, German and French. Trained staff stretch the most able ('through our gifted and talented programme'). 'Girls being pushed more and harder these days'. Good calibre of staff and increasing numbers of them. 'We won't give in over little things' – homework must not be late, poor work is not accepted. All screened on entry, five part-time and one full-time co-ordinator in the SEN department; good links with preps (and pre-preps come to that), and can cope with mild dyslexia etc; no ADHD or Asperger's. SEN lessons usually take the place of a language. Good provision for physical disability – has accommodated muscular dystrophy and cerebral palsy.

Games, Options, The Arts: Strong on netball, tennis and hockey, astroturf, new pool, oodles of dosh lately spent on the sports side, polo popular, but new art department not too far down the wings, planning permission and expect it in a couple of years. Old art rooms burgeoning, and with textiles (sewing machines natch – after all Mrs Mc S started her teaching career in home economics). Stunning music dept, with practice rooms and concert hall. Jazz, rock, orchestras, choirs, trips abroad. Envy making. Keen drama, LAMDA. Strong on extra-curricular activities – self-defence, modern dance, masses of clubs for just about everything and stunning cooking facilities. Duke of Edinburgh Award taken to Gold level. Retreats, pilgrimage to Lourdes (that well-known smart European marriage bureau) etc.

Background and Atmosphere: Sister school to St Mary's Ascot (the choicest of the three) and St Mary's Cambridge (the most street-wise), founded by IBVM (now CJ) in 1945. Charming converted late Victorian house with hotch potch of architectural miss matches: classrooms scattered all over the shop with a shabby wooden shack (sponge bags in the windows) home for the smallest – 'due for demolition shortly – in next stage of development – linked with art school project'. Fifty-five (ominously previous reports said sixty two) acres of rolling grounds, wonderful views and – for the boarders – rather a sense of 'being out in the sticks'. Shaftesbury three miles away does not swing; and trips to Bath and Salisbury at weekends will hardly set the world alight.

All must spend two compulsory weekends in school each term. Girls allowed cars in the sixth form, offsets the isolation a bit. Weekend activities considerably boosted in the last two years. Recent building includes new junior school, infirmary and library. Strong community happy-family feel. Boarders graduate from larger bedrooms (never dorms) to individual bedrooms (think nun's cells – head says 'individual bedrooms are actually quite spacious compared with other schools ' – yeah?) all with concealed 'sinks'. Refectory and fantastic new pastry chef 'so close to the hearts of so many'; long flowing kilts for all, curious when worn with short white (head sez 'beige' but we actually saw quite a number of white) socks, and full length for the sixth form.

Pastoral Care and Discipline: Shock horror: Mrs McSwiggan suspected drugs had been brought back to the school and called the police who arrived with every dog they could lay their hands on (search and rescue as well as drugs) and searched the school, having corralled the sixth form. Nothing found. Pupils duly impressed and neighbouring heads enchanted at the idea. 'but St Mary's...'. Fierce anti-smoking policy – fine and letter; suspended; expelled.

All newcomers (even the head) have a mentor for the first term, and welcome cards (decorating the altar during our visit) abound. Pastoral care improved and improving with increased numbers of staff per house; pupils meet with their tutor each morning. Spiritual life important, two thirds pupils Catholic, two thirds board; school chaplain takes mass in Spanish once a week. Quite a number of C of E girls, Anglican priest comes once a week and 'occasionally' celebrates eucharist in the chapel.

Pupils and Parents: Wide variety, including some from overseas (but not more than 10 per cent non-nationals) – 22 currently: Mexico, Spain, Germany, Hong Kong. Unspoilt, jolly nice, articulate, uninhibited girls – and relatively unsophisticated. One or two refugees from the hurly burly of London. Day girls go home at 6 pm. Parents largely enthusiastic about their choice, though recent personnel changes seem to have led to an increase in first time buyers. Parents wanting to use the school as a conventional prep school are scuppered as there is no provision or preparation for CE (head says 'This is not relevant because we are not a prep school, we just have two small junior classes'.

Entrance: At nine, 11, 13 and into sixth form. Tranches of scholarships in all disciplines, music, art and sport as well as academic with the option of bursarial top-up. Numbers currently steady, minimal testing for those who come into the junior school to go up to senior school.

Exit: Tiniest trickle to trad girls or co-ed senior schools, stronger trickle post GCSE to sixth form elsewhere. Of those who remain almost all to university, occasional Oxbridge candidate (head sez: 'special Oxbridge preparation classes. Each year we have at least two or three Oxbridge offers often 'post A level, so they do not appear in our statistics', loads to various art courses: foundation or history of art plus medics and chemical engineers, astrophysics.

Money Matters: Not a rich school but does its housekeeping well. Bursar an acknowledged genius.

Remarks: Jolly nice girls' Catholic boarding school, from the same stable as St Mary's Ascot, but with less social cachet, unpretentious and good at bringing out the best. Parents and pupils pleased with the increase of sport, but there are equally those who would prefer slightly sharper academic facilities. School has come a long way from the days when locals used to ride to school and leave their mounts in the stables during the day.

St Mary's School, Wantage

24-28 Newbury Street, Wantage, Oxfordshire, OX12 8BZ

Tel: 01235 773 800
Fax: 01235 760 467
Email: admissions@stmarys.oxon.sch.uk
Website: www.stmarys.oxon.sch.uk

• Pupils: 200 girls, 90+ per cent boarding • Ages: 11-19
• Religion: High Anglican • Fees: Boarding £7,330; day £4,900
• School status: Independent • School gender: Girls
• Day/boarding: Takes boarders

SEN provision

Detail:
Centre of excellence for:
  Mild: DYSC; DYSL; DYSP;
  Moderate: DYSC; DYSL; DYSP;
  Severe: DYSC; DYSL; DYSP;
  Others: EAL;
Now provide for in school:
  Mild: ASP; ADD; ADHD; EBD; VI;
  Others: SPD; DEL;
Experience of:
  Mild: HI;
  Others: Epi; Eat;

Summary: St Mary's has a unique system of academic support provided by AES (Academic Enrichment and Support), which works with every girl in the school, from the gifted to those with a specific difficulty. The well-qualified Head of Faculty is supported by a part-time member of staff and by a team of visiting teachers, all of whom are qualified and experienced in literacy and numeracy support. The visiting teachers give individual lessons, tailored to the particular needs of any girl, as required.

However, the permanent staff, as part of the school's general provision, teach all the girls in small groups, giving age-appropriate guidance on study skills, revision methods etc. They also run a prep club and provide a 'drop-in' centre for advice and guidance, and extension clubs for the gifted. The Head of Faculty organises and monitors all the provision in AES and briefs teaching staff regularly on the particular needs of individuals, also receiving feedback from teachers.

The aim of AES is to underpin the entire academic provision for each girl, according to her needs, providing everything from regular intervention where necessary to confidence-boosting sessions on an occasional basis. It is pivotal to the very high added-value that St Mary's gives to all girls or all abilities.

What we say about the school - the full Good Schools Guide review

Head: Since 1994, Mrs Susan Sowden BSc PGCE (forties), educated at Clarendon House Grammar School in Kent and read geography at King's College, London. Previously deputy head at Headington School, where she had two daughters; also has one son. Divorced and recently remarried. Also has a theological qualification, AKC, and an advanced diploma in educational management. Super lady, extremely popular with staff, pupils and parents, energetic and jolly with it. Operates totally open-door policy. 'She knows us all!' say girls appreciatively. Teaches geography.

Academic Matters: Head is determined to maintain present first-come, first-served policy which does not require demanding academic selectiveness at entry. However, recent results and her successful regime mean that there is a growing pressure on places. Excellent teacher/pupil ratio 1:6. Art is superb and much the most popular A level subject. Many go on to higher education in this and related subjects. Otherwise a good spread through all subjects and with very small A level classes. 25 A level subjects on offer. Enlightened policy of RS (compulsory) GCSE taken in year 10, followed by a year 11 course in ethics and philosophy. GCSEs at least respectable across the board; 43 per cent A*/A grades in 2005. Excellent support for EFL, EAL and SEN. 'Value added' is especially good here, girls achieving results in GCSEs and A levels beyond expectations. School is first to have complete wireless laptop computer system, virtually doing away with need for designated IT rooms – a liberating innovation especially on a site spread over several buildings. Library provision improved under new librarian over last two years.

Games, Options, The Arts: Sport, especially 'lax', is good here, remarkably so for so small a school. Huge sports hall and good sixth form gym. A horsy school – large-scale regular riding, as befits its geography and its tradition. Girls appreciate school's policy of trying to help everyone find things they are good at – will find teachers of obscure instruments if there is a demand etc. Super new music block linked to newer drama block creating many opportunities as well as increasing links with locality as residents invited for events. Art is extraordinary in the variety available – ceramics (wonderful), painting, drawing, textiles (professional), printing, pottery (done by everyone in first three years), metalwork, photography, sculpture, stone-carving, casting etc etc – and in the execution. Justifiably, the school is full of the stuff. A splendid cookery room used for years 7-10, a 'survival cookery' course, as well as a Leith Cert of Food and Wine course and other sixth form options. Resident artist, musician, dramatist and sports person an enlightened extra.

Background and Atmosphere: Gradually and naturally shedding its previous image as being for thick, rich horsy types, but not its well-earned reputation for exuberance and self-reliance. It is an immensely civilised place, set in a jumble of attractive Victorian red-brick and later buildings on a corner of the pleasant Oxfordshire town of Wantage – the town centre being only minutes walk away. Girls stress school's friendliness and there is an almost palpable gentleness in the air. A High Anglican Foundation and still centred on the splendid Anglo-Catholic chapel in the Gothic heart of the main building, the school's ethos is now a relaxed Christian one where all faiths are welcome and religion is not forced on anyone though 'chapel' is compulsory. Community service is strong, there are close ties with local old people's homes and school supports children in Africa via pen-letters as well as cash. Long-term refurbishment plans in progress, having begun with labs and needed in other areas, though 90 per cent board and boarding regarded as superb. Girls clearly happy with it and food is also excellent. Totally new school buildings on an expanded single site on the other side of the town centre due to open in late 2007.

Pastoral Care and Discipline: 'We give them responsibility for themselves and teach them how to use it', says head. 'We aren't wishy-washy.' There is a policy of 'restorative justice' actively practised in matters great and small. Few disciplinary problems and girls given much freedom to visit town, have weekends away etc. Sixth form has pool table, Sky TV and bar in JCR. 'Day boarders', ie day girls who spend some nights at school, fully integrated and welcomed. No official weekly boarding. Many staff live on site and school has good relaxed atmosphere. Good sixth form block.

Pupils and Parents: From range of local, London and national preps. Up to 15 per cent from up to 20 other nationalities make for a stimulating mix. Natural constituency 'Countryside Alliance' but increasingly business families send daughters here – a broader spectrum in all respects. Interesting bunch of OGs include ten per cent of the baronesses in the House of Lords (there by merit not inheritance, a truly extraordinary record), Dame Ruth Railton, Mrs Ian Duncan Smith, polar explorer Victoria Riches, Lady Helen Windsor and the first Who Wants to be a Millionairess, Judith Keppel. Old Girls (SMOGS) and current parents very supportive of school.

Entrance: Via school's own assessment procedure and Common Entrance at 11 plus interviews and current head's report. Few places at 12 and several more at 13. Overseas candidates assessed via current school's report and piece of written English. School does not admit to years 10 or 12 without fluent English.

Exit: To a good range of university and college courses. Excellent art results naturally produce good crop of entries to art schools.

Money Matters: Scholarships at 11 and 13. Various sixth form scholarships – academic, musical and one for an all-round contribution. All well-endowed and worth investigating.

Bursaries available particularly for daughters of clergy, St Mary's OGs and from Services families.

Remarks: School site and buildings in process of being totally replaced by a new build but ethos will remain the same – a rare mix of work, fun and caring for each other and the wider community. A lovely school, especially so if the arts are your thing and you want a happy atmosphere in a small school nestled in the Oxfordshire countryside.

The St Marylebone C of E School

64 Marylebone High Street, London, W1U 5BA

Tel: 020 7935 4704

Fax: 020 7935 4005

Email: stmaryleboneschool@yahoo.co.uk

Website: www.stmaryleboneschool.com

• Pupils: 821 • Ages: 11-18 • Religion: C of E

• School status: State • School gender: Girls

• Day/boarding: Day pupils

SEN provision

Detail:

Now provide for in school:
- Mild: AUT; ADD;
- Moderate: ADHD;
- Severe: ADHD;

Experience of:
- Mild: ADHD; DYSC; DYSL; DYSP; SpLD; HI; VI; CP;
- Moderate: ADD; DYSC; DYSL; DYSP; HI; VI;
- Severe: DYSL; DYSP; HI;
- Others: OCD; EAL; Epi; PD; Eat;

Summary: The St Marylebone School is committed to providing an inclusive education for all of its students with support provided by the SEN, EAL and Inclusion departments.

Students are assessed upon entry and we aim to ensure that all students' needs are identified and catered for as appropriate. SEN staff play a key role in providing support to SEN students during their transition to secondary school.

It is the school's aim that the majority of students will be supported within mainstream lessons. This approach focuses on teachers working in partnership with subject specialists in order to shape inclusive environments that cater both to individual need, as well as for diversity of need in the classroom.

The SEN department provides additional support outside of the curriculum through activities such as homework club and lunchtime clubs.

What we say about the school - the full Good Schools Guide review

Head: Since 1993, Mrs Elizabeth Phillips (fifties), previously at Feltham School in Hounslow. Spent 16 years abroad in places ranging from Hong Kong to Zambia; ran a language school in Rome. Neat, smart, married, with one daughter and two sons who were all educated privately but she is passionately committed to the state sector, 'I want to fight for those who have no one else to fight for them'. A historian, and 'a brilliant, inspiring teacher,' said a parent. 'She is very focused and has turned the school around,' said another.

Academic Matters: Hailed in 2000 as the most improved school in England – over the previous four years the proportion of girls achieving five good grades at GCSE shot up from 39 per cent to 89 per cent – it's now 94 per cent. Most subjects achieving 90 per cent+ A*-C grades. A level options have expanded dramatically and now include media studies, ICT, politics, RE, psychology and economics. Key Stage 3 SATs results are well above average. It is a genuinely comprehensive school, taking 25 per cent from the top ability band, 50 per cent from the middle and 25 per cent from the bottom band. 'The results are staggering considering the intake,' says the head. She puts the results down to setting pupils in all academic subjects from year 7, and to excellent teaching – 'inadequate teaching is not accepted'. 'In a good percentage of lessons learning was outstanding,' said the last Ofsted report, which talked of 'an environment for teaching and learning based on mutual respect and high expectations of all'.

The school invests highly in teachers to get a staff:student ratio of around 1:17. Although tutor groups are 33, each has two form tutors. The four tutor groups in each year divide into five ability groups and the lower sets are particularly small. 'We are here to see that all the children achieve. It is really important not to let some pupils become an underclass.' 'The teachers are very good at spotting need and doing something about it,' said a parent, 'and they get astounding results from girls who don't speak English at home.' There is an effective special needs department and a language and learning department to help those with difficulties. There is a gifted and talented programme that builds extra opportunity for able pupils with mentoring from a GT co-ordinator. In years 9 and 10 there are special programmes in history, English, maths and science for gifted and talented children, plus after-school enrichment classes. All take ICT and RS GCSEs in year 10. All the staff are specialists (it is the only state school in Westminster with a full complement of qualified mathematicians and scientists). Many girls do vocational subjects, 'it is a real preparation for the world of work and the universities are very happy to have students from the AVCE courses'.

The school runs a homework club, 'many of our girls have nowhere quiet to work. But the most deprived have to get home to look after the younger kids.' The sixth form is a haven for some boys (with their own football team, dance group and rock band) 'who had a terrible time at macho boys' schools. And accepting these boys in a girls' school has a beneficial effect on their results.'

Games, Options, The Arts: St Marylebone is a specialist Performing Arts College, 'though we're not a Fame school – the arts are for enrichment' – which awards 12 places a year to talented music, dance and drama students. All year 7 pupils get free music lessons, the head would like to expand this but lacks money and space, and all Key Stage three students have three hours a week of music, dance, drama and expressive art as well. There are two orchestras – one of which recently played concerts in Venice and Barcelona – plus salsa bands, string quartets, percussion and African drumming bands. There are major concerts three times a year, plus plays and pageants. 'I like that fact that the events involve everyone but the standards are very high,' said a parent. The school has extensive music technology equipment.

Spectacular artwork is displayed all around the school including a wide range of textiles, 'this is where you see the effects of the multi-ethnic nature of the school, and we display a whole class's work, not just the best.' The school has its own printing press that can print copies of artwork. Sport suffers from lack of space but this is being rectified (see atmosphere section). 'The girls are very competitive,' says the head. A parent comments, 'there's always something going on, like weights or dancing or keep-fit. The sports teachers are brilliant'. The school uses the sports pitches in Regents Park, All Souls gym for dance and the Seymour Baths for swimming and hopes to get access to the old Pineapple Dance Studios.

The central London location enables many cultural outings and trips in the UK and abroad include outward bound, skiing and exchanges with French and German schools. Much of this, though not skiing, is subsidised for the needy by charitable funds. 'I want to give my pupils all the music, the theatre, the trips abroad that private schoolchildren take for granted,' says the head. A group of 22 sixth formers, 'many of them inner-city pupils from high-rise estates', are off to Zambia on a World Challenge trip in 2007, building on successful trips to Vietnam and India in the past.

Background and Atmosphere: Wonderfully situated in an oasis of quiet off a paved courtyard at the top of Marylebone High Street with the Conran shop almost opposite and Regents Park across the road, albeit the six-lane Marylebone Road. Desperately tight for space. 'I've expanded into every space I can possibly think of,' says the head. The video editing room was once a coal-hole and a music practice room was once the cleaners' cupboard.

The school has recently shoe-horned three classrooms into one high-ceilinged Victorian room and many of the upper classrooms have marvellously shaped windows and ceilings. The rooms are mostly light and airy, in a colour scheme of green and white to match the school uniform. The staff room is painted tasteful blues and purples, redecorated through business sponsorship – 'I'd never have spent the money on it myself', says the head. 'We use everything we can for the children.' Newly refurbished science labs, plus new professional recording studio and two dance and drama studios. Assemblies are held in the wonderful Regency church next door. A major building programme has been approved by the DfES to create a large subterranean sports hall and a purpose-built performing arts centre with dance and drama studios, music teaching rooms, music practice rooms and art studios. This will be completed by October 2006.

Pastoral Care and Discipline: There is a peer mentoring system to help children who are having trouble settling in, making friends or coping with homework. 'The children will say there's no bullying,' says the head. 'Year 10 counsellors are there if they need someone to talk to. All the drama we do gives them confidence to speak out. They learn the ability to stand up and talk in front of the school.'

Drugs have not been a problem, 'we're really harsh about that and we do lots of preventative work. We're vigilant and strict. I expect there is smoking, especially amongst the sixth-formers, but they don't do it in the toilets or on the school premises.' In general, the school has a no-exclusion policy, 'we never write a child off.' The school has a quiet and orderly feel, with silent concentration in most of the lessons. 'Pupils' behaviour both in lessons and around the school is exemplary,' said Ofsted. 'We're nit-pickingly strict – people need to know the rules. The staff can teach here, because they're not spending their time keeping order,' says the head, who feels,'you can't take the spiritual dimension out of all this. It's not fashionable to talk about faith but I think the nation is yearning for spiritual belief.' 'There is a strong caring and achieving philosophy,' said a parent. Another said, 'it's not over-pressurised – they just help them as much as they can.'

Pupils and Parents: Mixed socially and culturally, including many races and religions. 'We have working class children, immigrants, refugees – someone needs to bother about them,' says the head. Very popular with middle class parents, some of whom undergo miraculous religious conversions a year or two before applying. Very active PTA does successful fundraising for the new building project.

Entrance: Hugely over-subscribed, with 1,027 applicants for 120 places in 2005. Apart from 12 performing arts places, religious faith is a prerequisite. Within the academic banding, about 55 per cent of places are reserved for C of E, while the others go to girls of any other faith – including Muslims, Jews, Buddhists and Zoroastrians. Girls from two linked Westminster primary schools get preference along with all Westminster Church primaries; coming from any other church primary school helps, with distance as a tie-break.

Exit: The school has a wide catchment area and because local boroughs don't pay for transport after 16, some girls leave then to go to local schools. Some high-flyers get scholarships to private schools, 'though value-added data shows that they would do better here – the boys who come in do particularly well,' says the head. All go on to higher education (about one a year to Oxbridge – parents tend to be wary of it from a social point of view) or to blue-chip training companies, apart from a few Muslim girls destined for early marriage.

Money Matters: As well as being a specialist performing arts college, St Marylebone is a beacon school and receives Excellence in Cities money for supporting gifted and talented students. All this brings in extra cash. However, one parent commented how sad it was that bidding for extra money from various sources takes up a lot of the head's time and she agrees, 'fund-raising is my nightmare – it's what I do. It's cost me five years of my life.' The result, however, is a school that is well-staffed and well-equipped, if not to lavish private school standards.

Remarks: Hugely successful and popular small girls' comprehensive in wonderful West End setting. Caring and dedicated staff, determined that girls of all abilities should succeed. A parent whose two older children went through the private sector commented, 'it's simply a brilliant school'.

St Paul's Catholic Primary School, Thames Ditton

Hampton Court Way, Thames Ditton, Surrey, KT7 0LP

Tel: 020 8398 6791

Fax: 020 8398 4275

Email: info@stpauls-thamesditton.surrey.sch.uk

• Pupils: 140 girls and 150 boys , all day • Ages: 4-11 • Religion: RC • School status: State • Opendays: June and October • School gender: Mixed • Day/boarding: Day pupils

SEN provision

Summary: No comment – in a huff with us – but good general provision, in our view. Ofsted report worth a read.

What we say about the school - the full Good Schools Guide review

Head: Since 1990, Mrs Fionnuala Johnson, BEd (late forties), married with two children, the younger one is at the school. Garners huge respect from parents, who regard her as the architect of the school's (and their children's) success. Descriptions of her vary along the spectrum from 'strong impressive leader', through 'powerful personality' to 'formidable' (we'll vouch for that) – but most also mention her caring side. 'The children adore her – tempered by due reverence,' said one mother. 'I've seen children run across the playground to hug her,' said another.

Has plenty to say about the school – of which she is fiercely proud – and is full of plans and ideas for the future. She knows all the children by name – and promises to keep this up even when the school has doubled in size. As it is, parents wonder at her grasp of all the smallest details of their lives and the praise continues – 'She's fantastic – the school is as good as it is because of her. She talks to the children quietly and they all listen – she never needs to raise her voice. They want to please her – and if ever they are in trouble and sent to see her they are not frightened, but sorry they have incurred her disapproval.'

Entrance: Heavy over-subscription has allowed funding for expansion from single to two-form entry. From 2002, the school has accepted 60 children/year (instead of 30) and the pressure has eased up a little –

but Catholic families whose children have been baptised (and you need the certificates to prove it) still take 99 per cent of the places. The school serves the parishes of Cobham, Esher and Thames Ditton, a mostly white middle class lot. It is non-selective academically – regular church attendance will get you a long way.

Exit: Where to go next is the most vexing question for parents. In 2004, the 30 year 6 pupils headed in all directions – to 14 different secondary schools. 'I just wish this school had a secondary equivalent,' sighed one mother, echoing the view of many. St Paul's pupils are guaranteed entry to the RC Salesian School in Chertsey, but few choose it. Among the more popular choices of secondary school are Wimbledon College, Ursuline High, Tiffin School and Tiffin Girls School in Kingston.

Remarks: An academically strong school with a solid Catholic ethos. Set back from a busy dual carriageway, in functional rather than beautiful accommodation, purpose-built in the mid-1960s. There is plenty of space, including a large playground and a grass playing field. The smart new block built to provide the necessary seven extra classrooms does make the older classrooms look a little tired, but good art displays line the walls and lift the spirits. A well-resourced school, with a shiny IT suite and three well-stocked libraries. All classrooms are spacious and light; and each is named after a saint – reflecting the importance of Catholic teaching at the school.

The Catholic Church schools' 'Search for Excellence' theme is seen as key here – both in the spiritual and academic development of the children. Academic standards are high. At Key Stage 2, 93 per cent gained level 4 and above in English, and 100 per cent in maths and science – there were more level 5s than 4s in all three subject areas. Many parents tell us that this is a school for academic girls rather than non-academic boys. Even parents who are not quite so dogmatic believe the environment is more suited to the academically inclined. 'It is not a hot-house, but there is just a general expectation of achievement,' said one mother. Mrs Johnson disagrees strongly – so does Ofsted, who also single out the SEN teaching for praise. The number with SEN is below the national average, but those with SEN do as well as their peers. There is an SEN teacher with two assistants on hand and the school also brings in outside specialists.

High praise from parents for an able and effective teaching staff. 'Every time we change classes we say we wish we could have that teacher again – and then the next one is just another delight,' said a mother who has had had children at the school for many years. 'Discipline is strong, the children know their boundaries and understand them,' said another. There is plenty of praise and reward, with a system of highly-prized stickers and certificates, not just for academic work but also for helpfulness, cheerfulness and so on. Prayers are said at the end of each day, and children attend mass regularly. The religious teaching really kicks in at year 3 as the children are preparing for Holy Communion.

All the parents we spoke to agree their children are happy at the school which they describe time and time again as 'very caring'. Pupils are respectful and polite – and also extremely smart – with even the reception children wearing neat ties. 'The fact they can get a four-year-old to tie a tie says a lot about this school,' enthused one mother. Mixed feelings abound over sports provision with some parents feeling it is not a particular strength, especially among the boys – though the school does well in the borough in netball and cross-country.

A real sense of community, which staff and parents are keen to maintain as the school expands. Some parents have expressed concerns that the strong sense of community they have enjoyed may be eroded as the school grows. However, the niggles are few and far between, and overall the positive comments far outweigh the negatives. It is still a first choice for parents seeking a good education for their child in a distinctively Catholic environment.

St Peter's Eaton Square C of E Primary School

Lower Belgrave Street, London, SW1W 0NL

Tel: 020 7641 4230

Fax: 020 7641 4235

Email: office.st-peters-eaton-square.westminster@lgfl.net

• Pupils: 266 primary and 50 nursery (intake 10 per term to the nursery and 40 per year to the reception class). All day
• Ages: 3-11 • Religion: C of E • School status: State
• Opendays: February • School gender: Mixed
• Day/boarding: Day pupils

SEN provision

Detail:

Experience of:

Mild: ASP; ADD; ADHD; EBD; DS; DYSC; DYSL; DYSP; HI; VI; CP;

Moderate: ADD; ADHD; EBD; DS; MLD; DYSC; DYSL; DYSP;

Severe: EBD; DYSL;

Others: CD; ODD; EAL; MSI; Sp&LD;

Summary: St Peter's is an inclusive school and supports pupils with a wide range of disabilities but it is not in effect a special school. It provides for pupils with physical, emotional and learning difficulties as well as Gifted and Talented pupils. There is a part-time special educational needs co-ordinator and one additional part-time teacher with SEN as a specialism. Pupils are taught principally within mixed ability classes appropriate to their age group.

What we say about the school - the full Good Schools Guide review

Head: Since 1992, Mr John Wright BEd MBA (in School Leadership) (fifties). Previous career in state system in London Borough of Merton and in Beaconsfield. Keen on music, especially opera, gardening, also travel planning. Fantastically thorough and efficient and makes a real point of knowing his pupils, his staff and the parents well. Keen on 'the corporate ethos' and has a real talent for 'getting us to work as a team,' said one teacher, not to mention encouraging parents to help. Comments dryly that the school's overall intake 'helps provide an environment well-matched to the society our young people will enter when they leave school'.

Entrance: Register in the academic year before the date of entry (part of the pan-London system). Two points of entry (September and January) for reception children. Nursery moves to two points of entry from the start of the 2006/7 school year. Visit school. Priority given to children whose parents attend St Peter's Church; those who attend church regularly; children with siblings in the school; children whose parents attended the school; children baptised as Anglicans etc etc. Always over-subscribed at early levels, and there is no automatic transfer (but some priority) from nursery to reception classes. Offers are made in the May preceding the year of entry.

Exit: To local state schools, particularly Greycoat Hospital, St Marylebone, Lady Margaret, Pimlico, London Nautical etc. Thirty per cent to private schools – Christ's Hospital, JAGS, City of London, Godolphin and Latymer, Clapham Hill and Streatham High etc.

Remarks: Super central London primary school which got a deservedly glowing Ofsted report. Good social mix – 'everything from duchesses to dustmen and politicians', in the words of the previous head; 'a very broad spectrum of socioeconomic backgrounds', comments the present head. Loyal parents and PTA (good fund-raisers, these), exceptionally committed and dedicated professional staff. Terrific swimming school (all except nursery and reception use nearby Queen Mother's Sports Centre pool every week). Local district swimming competitions abandoned as other schools do not commit to similar regular swimming programmes through the year. Good music and getting better all the time. Keen computers – and new computer centre opened 2000 and IT timetabled. Competent special needs provision, according to parents; school by turns forthcoming and clam-like about what's on offer. All classrooms equipped with interactive whiteboards.

Maximum class size 30 (several classes less than this). Setting for maths in junior classes. French and Mandarin now an 'option' – with parent-organised club after school on Tuesdays and Fridays, staffed by members of the Les Petites Marionettes – a start. Food reported to have improved (was ghastly). Maintenance of school supported by London Diocesan Board. Every inch of the school is used, with cunning timetabling and doubling up of rooms for various purposes. Jolly shouts from the playground (playtimes are staggered – a clever move), with a regular supply of 'midday supervisors' overseeing fair play. Library recently refurbished by active and enthusiastic parents.

School first mentioned in survey carried out by the National Society for Promoting Religious Education in 1864-7, sited in Eccleston Place. Moved to present building in 1872 on a site given by the Marquess of Westminster. Assumed its present form in 1949. Visited by HM Queen in 1972 (centenary year) and by HM Queen Mum in 1995. Strong links with St Peter's Church, and the clergy pop in and out (Church very high Anglican – so high, in fact, that a passing arsonist mistook it for Roman Catholic and burned it down not so long ago). Lots of parental involvement.

Super nursery opened in 1992 in the crypt of the Church, now on site. Morning or afternoon sessions, with groups of 25. New nursery teacher who is well respected by the parents and has made an early, very positive mark, a nursery nurse and two helpers. Has an indoor/outdoor area for structured play and opportunities for development of gross motor skills. Drawback of the main school is that it is very cramped for space (though NB, many local private schools are even more cramped) and playground can be horrifically noisy and bursting at seams at break time. Children are not 'hot-housed' - but with two-thirds of pupils reaching level 5 in year 6 they are well well ahead of national expectations.

Late 2003, school wrote to parents appealing for funds and blaming the government for financial difficulties (including a £14,000 deficit. Balance in credit during the 2003/4 school year without the need for parental donations). School requested £15 per child or £25 per family. 'In Westminster, St Peter's is consistently top in achievement but bottom in funding,' head wrote. Here is a school whose parents could, for the most part, well afford to help.

SAINT RONAN'S SCHOOL

Water Lane, Hawkhurst, Kent, TN18 5DJ

Tel: 01580 752 271
Fax: 01580 754 882
Email: info@saintronans.co.uk
Website: www.saintronans.co.uk

• Pupils: 280 boys and girls. Mainly day with flexi boarding • Ages: Nursery 2½ to reception age; pre-prep to rising 7; prep school from 7 to 13 • Religion: C of E • Fees: Nursery £314 per day of the week; pre-prep £1,995; prep £3,485. Boarding £21.50 per night • School status: Independent • Opendays: Two per term • School gender: Mixed • Day/boarding: Takes boarders

SEN provision

Detail:
Now provide for in school:
Mild: ADD; EBD; DYSC; DYSL; DYSP;
Moderate: DYSC; DYSL; DYSP;
Experience of:
Mild: ADHD;
Moderate: ADD; EBD; MLD;
Severe: DYSP;

Summary: Saint Ronan's is justly proud of its academic record. We believe that we should, and do, cater for the educational needs and aspirations of the brightest children; but we believe also that those who have any academic problems and weaknesses should be enabled to deal with the challenges of the mainstream academic programme.

To the latter end, we have a team of three specialist SEN teachers, who asses any children who are encountering difficulties within their class and, if necessary, refer them to an educational psychologist for a formal diagnosis of any specific learning difficulty.

Dyslexia, dyspraxia, ADD, ADHD, and dyscalculia are well catered for. The school SENCo liaises with parents on a regular basis and, if it is felt necessary, and in agreement with the parents, individual tuition can be arranged with one of the specialist SEN teachers.

All Pre-prep classes have their own learning support assistant, to assist with those children who are less able and group work is carried out on a weekly basis, under the supervision of the SENCo for such children.

What we say about the school - the full Good Schools Guide review

Head: Since 2003, Mr William Trelawny-Vernon (early forties). Exeter university, briefly a fund manger in the City before moving to Stowe to teach biology. Formerly 7 years as housemaster of Chatham House, Stowe. Married to Emma who teaches divinity, four young children. Very enthusiastic and energetic – has managed to bring the school into the 21st century without losing its old fashioned charm.

Entrance: By interview. No exam; children need to be of a fairly good standard but nonetheless cover a wide ability range. Pre-prep in the capable hands of Joceline Mawdsley since 2003.

Exit: About two thirds of pupils go on to public schools, of which Tonbridge, King's Canterbury, Benenden and Eton are currently the most popular. Harrow, Sevenoaks, Eastbourne and Stowe also in evidence. One or two major scholarships most years. One third go on to local grammar schools, principally Cranbrook.

Remarks: Spiritually a home from home, a relaxed and informal school where teachers are approachable and mud is unremarkable. Saint Ronan's is a quirky and unusual school with a happy and busy feel to it. Aims to develop each individual rather than impose a style, bringing out self-confidence, academically as well as socially, and independence. Academic achievement valued – it is cool to be clever for boys as well as girls. Maximum class size is 18 and average 12-14. Latin as a major subject from early on, Greek an option for the academic children in the last two years. Children streamed within their year group according to ability. Very able children can be accelerated to the year above their age group, reaching the top of the school a year early to prepare for scholarship entry to senior schools.

No longer offers full boarding but flexi-boarding is a popular option and most children ask to do this at some stage. As a result there is no longer a Sunday chapel service but visiting speakers are often invited to the Friday evensong. The chapel, which features every leaver's name and destination enrolled on boards, is used every morning for 10 minutes. The school day is a long one as the older children (9+) do not finish school until 6.30pm, but all prep is done at school and it does mean that there is plenty of time for play and fun during the day.

Sport is a major feature of the school day; games are played every afternoon, and the appointment of two sports' specialists has raised the already good standard. Major sports for the boys are football, hockey and cricket – rugby too now – and the girls play netball, hockey, rounders and tennis. There is a strong tradition of cross-country running – marvellous practice running round all those acres. Minor sports include shooting, golf (on the school's own small course), judo, gymnastics and archery. The children also seem to find time for modelling and craft as well as tending their gardens.

The school was founded in 1883 in Worthing and moved in 1946 to this rambling Victorian mansion built by an OXO magnate in 247 acres – it has its own 100 acre wood, lakes and a pinetum. There is a splendid one-time ball room (with sprung floor and painted ceiling) known as The Great Space – used as a theatre, indoor football pitch, gymnasium etc – and much loved. The children spend a lot of time outside and a favourite pastime is damming a stream called the Gulch – Wellington boots and old tracksuits essential. A school where children can be children for longer.

The stable block has recently been converted and now houses a fine science lab, an ICT department with new plasma screens, music and art departments and a well-equipped kitchen – cooking is a popular option for both boys and girls. Staff and children eat together in the new dining room where an eye can be kept on table manners.

Lots of music in the school – over two thirds learn a musical instrument, several ensembles, lunchtime concerts throughout the term. Drama part of the curriculum, two major productions a year as well as more informal reviews and mini plays and an art and music festival in the summer term.

Parents very involved in the life of the school – many help with reading for the younger children and others have formed a group to teach them Scottish dancing and there is a thriving Friends of St Ronan's parents' group who organise summer balls, parents' quizzes, Burns Night parties etc. Old Boys include artist Piers de Laszlo and cartoonist Sir Osbert Lancaster, whose Latin master used to tear up his sketches and demand prep instead. Also Charles Saumarez-Smith, Director of the National Gallery.

SANDROYD SCHOOL

Rushmore, Tollard Royal, Salisbury, Wiltshire, SP5 5QD

Tel: 01725 516 264

Fax: 01725 516 441

Email: office@sandroyd.com

Website: www.sandroyd.org

• Pupils: 158: 13 girls, 145 boys (88 full boarding, including 3 girls). Pre-prep: 22 girls and boys • Ages: 4-13 • Religion: C of E • Fees: Year 4 and above: boarding £5,450 day; day £4,550 (until 6.30pm). Year 3: boarding £4,400; day £3,350 • School status: Independent • Opendays: October • School gender: Mixed • Day/boarding: Takes boarders

SEN provision

Detail:

Now provide for in school:

Mild: ADD; ADHD; EBD; DYSC; DYSL; DYSP; VI;

Moderate: MLD; DYSC; DYSL; DYSP;

Others: SPD; OCD; Epi; Eat;

Experience of:

Mild: ASP; AUT; SpLD; HI;

Moderate: ADD;
Others: TIC; EAL; Sp&LD; DEL; PD;

Summary: Sandroyd has a learning support unit staffed by three fully qualified teachers, who have further training in dealing with children with special needs. If it is felt that a child requires a degree of individual assistance with their academic studies, we have the expertise and facilities to help them.

33 children currently receive some help. Parents may discuss the support at any time. External support services, such as an educational psychologist, speech therapist and paediatricians are consulted for further specialist support when needed.

Individual lessons last 40 minutes and take place at a convenient time for the students. Mainstream staff are kept informed of any specific difficulties. On average children receive two lessons a week but this varies depending on individual circumstances. We pride ourselves on the improvements and successes achieved by our students.

What we say about the school - the full Good Schools Guide review

Head: Since 2003, Martin Harris BSc (Hons) PGCE (fortyish). Educated at The Skinners School and read geography at Loughborough University. Began teaching at Sevenoaks Prep but has spent most of career at Ashdown House in East Sussex eventually rising to deputy head and then acting head. Keen sportsman, plays cricket, golf and tennis. Married to Catherine (a chartered physiotherapist) who plays a pastoral role in the school. Two young sons, the eldest now in the school's pre-prep. Has overseen big changes since arriving: the opening of The Walled Garden pre-prep, the introduction of girls in the main school, the debut of football(!).

Entrance: Not selective but all children are assessed and then interviewed by the head. Pupils can start at The Walled Garden from 4, at the main school generally at 7 or 8, but pupils start at all ages. Some enter at age 10 or 11, specifically for the boarding. Flexi-boarding available, but all pupils must properly board in the last two years. 70 per cent come from Wiltshire and Dorset, a few from London – a top drawer lot, with the school roll a festival of double-barrelled surnames. 16 boys from overseas, half British expats, half foreign, some of the latter receiving extra English tuition. Minibuses from Gillingham, Blandford, and now Salisbury.

Exit: Virtually all leave at 13, very occasionally one at 11 – girls now entering the school intend to stay all the way through. Sherborne the favourite destination by far but quite a few to Radley and Bryanston and several to Eton and Marlborough. Otherwise all over, far and wide. Strangely few to Canford and Dauntsey's. A couple to good state schools most years.

Remarks: A happy school, bursting with all the extras. Founded in 1888 by the Revd L H Wellesley Wesley as a 'small coaching establishment' in his own home, for 'sons of friends who were due to go to Eton'. The school was evacuated here during the war and later bought the Pitt-Rivers' family house plus paddocks, playing fields and houses for many of the staff. Still a relatively formal and traditional prep in its second year of co-education. School currently owns 55 acres within the 400 acre Rushmore estate, next door to the Rushmore Golf Course (pupils and staff play for free). The park teems with wild life and the school was undergoing something of a pheasant infestation when we visited. Slightly isolated feel, a bit of a world unto itself. The main building has elegance in its bones but a tired feeling within. Grand wood-panelled hall, with classrooms off it. Has been much added to – all very practical but not inspirational. Entire school – classrooms, dormitories, swimming pool, chapel etc under one roof, connected by a warren of corridors. Handy, as the wind can rip through the grounds as we discovered. Children terribly polite – say 'Sir', and stand up as soon as you appear. Dress code rather than uniform on school days: any check shirt, no tie, any brown shoes, green or blue cords – looks great. Girls wear a blue kilt or navy cords, blue blouse, Sandroyd sweatshirt and black shoes. Smarter wear for chapel and outings.

Still strong on traditional teaching: French from seven, Latin from nine, Greek for those who want it, plus a non-timetabled Spanish/German option. Head was keen on sharpening up the academic side when he arrived and he has been rewarded with a clutch of good awards to senior schools in recent years. Max class size 16 but average is 12 (and many are smaller). 30 children receive extra lessons – mainly for dyslexia and extra maths. Up to four sessions a week, if needed, with times varying so pupils miss different lessons or activities. Low tech IT – no interactive whiteboards, old computers – but sufficient. Four gap students, fill in here and there, read with the younger children every day.

Parents given lots of feedback: termly reports, weekly assessments for effort, twice termly assessments for achievement. Exams every term in the top two years to iron out exam technique and quell any nerves.

Big on sport, especially rugger – the school reached the National Prep School 7s final at Rosslyn Park in 2004 and won the Wiltshire U13 Rugby Cup and there is an annual rugby tour. Every boy represents the school in a rugby match and there are four IVs at the top of the school. Cricket also very strong. Girls have recently begun to play hockey against other schools – there are almost enough of them to make a team – and some have played in boys' teams. Sport every day, though some peel off to attend special lessons – roughly half the pupils do tennis coaching as an extra; many learn squash with pro who visits three times a week. Still offers pistol shooting. A quarter of the school ride – on school's own horses, or you can bring your own. School contines to host an annual National Tetrathlon with 160 children competing. Glass-like cricket pitch, three quarter size astroturf, rifle range, pets area (with few lodgers), indoor pool (18-and-a-half metres!), gym 'held together by Sellotape but well-loved'. Adventure playground for use by the youngest.

On Saturdays and Wednesday afternoons, less gamesy older children may seek refuge in the DT room, which is also open on winter evenings. Pupils make their own tuck boxes and decorate them in the holidays. The school still has general knowledge quizzes, with notable national success. Lots of activities on offer, and this is a key facet of the school. Something for everyone, from the nerdy (magic tricks, electronics, Russian) to the sporty (clay pigeon shooting, golf, fencing). God important and children attend the lovely chapel four days a week. Lively music, especially the choir, and the orchestra is 'improving'. 108 pupils learn an instrument – two of them bagpipe. 'We'll teach anything,' says the head. Violin tuition given by a house parent who used to play in The Royal Philharmonic Orchestra (and in a backing band for Elton John!). Busy art in big, airy room, with outstanding ceramics. Drama offered through class lessons and a drama club. The school has drawn up plans for a theatre, which would be a super addition, and has purchased equipment for a film-making club. Cookery in a dedicated room, organised by the mums.

Brilliant boarding with good care throughout. 7-9 boys in dorms in younger years – perfectly pleasant. Smaller dormitories of 3-4 boys in top year, and prep at this age is done in dorm – unusual for a prep school. Common room with telly, play station, table football – a stepping stone to public school. No mobile phones, except for overseas boys who keep them in the office. Good food served family style in bright and airy dining room. Fruit available all day. Snacks galore. Top year can make toast and cocoa. Exeats every third weekend. Two Sundays a term pupils must stay in school but school enthusiastically woos them to stay more – and most do. Regular Sunday outings on horseback or cycling. Swallows and Amazons camping weekend for year 4. School does all the boys' laundry, even for the day boys (it was at this point that we were sold on the place). OBs include the Lords Avon, Carrington, Snowdon, Wilberforce, Gladwyn, Sainsbury plus Archbishop Ramsay of Canterbury, Ian Gow, Max Aitken, Sir Terence Rattigan, Sir Anthony Eden, Sir Ranulph Fiennes.

The Walled Garden pre-prep opened in 2004. Still less than half full but numbers growing. Beautiful curving design, light bright and cheery – all built to child size including mini whiteboards and beautiful loos. The children play and learn confidently in their bright purple sweatshirts – very focused. Spacious outdoor play area and these littlies use the main school's swimming pool and computers. One third of them have older siblings in the school. Their day finishes at 3:30pm but many stay for a late club until 5:15 where they can take part in activities like football or pony club.

Seaford College

Lavington Park, Petworth, West Sussex, GU28 0NB

Tel: 01798 867 392

Fax: 01798 867 606

Email: seaford@clara.co.uk

Website: www.seaford.org

• Pupils: 439; 120 boarders (85 boys, 35 girls), 319 day (216 boys, 103 girls) • Ages: 10-18 • Religion: C of E • Fees: Day £4,180, juniors £3,350. Boarding £6,370, juniors £4,920 • School status: Independent • Opendays: Two a term • School gender: Mixed • Day/boarding: Takes boarders

SEN provision

Summary: Pupils are accepted on the basis of an interview with the Headmaster and assessement by the Head of Learning Support. A report from an educational psychologist is useful, and may be used in conjunction with our own assessment when making decisions on places.

On arrival, all new pupils are given screening tests to check for any difficulities or signs of dyslexia. The Head of Learning Support re-assesses each pupil who has difficulites, and designs a programme for their needs. This programme will be different for every child and may require extra tuition, usually one-to-one, but sometimes in pairs, on a once or twice a week basis. Individual reports are written on each child and copied to all teaching staff.

What we say about the school - the full Good Schools Guide review

Head: Since 1997, Mr Toby Mullins BA (economics) MBA (forties), came from a retail background, previously deputy head of Churcher's, Petersfield. A committed head, working hard to build up the school's reputation, also an inspector for ISI/HMC. Voluble, tells you like it is, emphasises regularly at school speech days that 'this Seaford is no longer the dumping ground for staff and pupils that it used to be', but some pupils with troubled histories still. Parents also regularly reminded not to moan alone but to call him on his direct line if they have any problems at all – 'we're all big boys now, let's get to the heart of the problem'. Pupils reckon they can go to him at any time, not frightened of him. Married with 2 young children, both at the school, wife active in the school.

Academic Matters: Traditional, catering for a wide range of pupil. Results improving steadily, the sixth form growing each year, pupils achieving well according to their abilities. 90 per cent plus five A* to C grades at GCSE, a fair share of As for English. Humanities and history are strong departments with brilliant staff who are popular with the pupils; lots of living history and travel included. IT is all high tech, the whole school campus has a wireless network – broadband access to the Internet from anywhere.

Children's progress is monitored carefully and study skills are taught. Learning support team regularly update themselves on new ways of assisting pupils – about one third of children have a SpLD such as dyslexia or dyscalculia (but not dyspraxia) – such pupils need to provide an educational psychologist's report, otherwise will be assessed on entry. Those who need to can work on a laptop. EFL support available but the school only has a handful of overseas pupils. Staff are predominately young and long-staying. Parents comment 'staff are approachable and work very hard here to get results with all pupils whatever their difficulties, which is no mean feat'.

Games, Options, The Arts: Sports play a very important role in school life, vast playing fields and courts of every description, all pupils participate in sporting activities every afternoon. International water based hockey pitch (makes balls go faster and players get wet as balls splosh down), only 2 schools in the country have this facility; all UK teams use the pitch for practising on, so excellent links with professional sportsmen. Regular winners of the West Sussex Cups for hockey and rugby for the under 14s. Lake for fly fishing, golf course, Multigym and clay pigeon shooting. Indoor swimming pool is next on the new building plan. Golf course not up to par.

High-profile music, no more free instrumental tuition for new pupils, but there are various orchestras and jazz band. Renowned choir in high demand to perform both here and abroad – they have made numerous CDs and are given air-time on Classic FM. Drama is equally strong, every term offers good quality dramatic and musical events with theatre studies being popular at GCSE and A level. Pupils also do LAMDA awards. The art and CDT department are well resourced – five full-time members of staff, pupils produce some excellent results. The school invites professional artists to visit and four different art A level courses are on offer.

Background and Atmosphere: Founded in 1884 and moved to Lavington Park (not surprisingly, known as Lavy Park) in 1946, pretty Georgian house set in wonderful grounds with great views of the South Downs in all directions; charming Sussex flint stone cottages for staff, ghastly collection of add-ons for teaching – changes afoot. Planning has been granted for a brand new maths and science block, scheduled for completion in January 2005. Walking round the campus feels like being in a small village, peaceful with sound of children cheering at matches in the distance. Some children find the size of grounds a little overwhelming at first – 'you definitely need an umbrella as departments are miles from each other', commented one younger pupil. Girls live in main house, boys in a cluster well past their sell-by date though redeemed by fab common rooms, sag bags, DVD, telly – Playstation 2; 'better than at home' we were told. Dorms for younger boys, sixth form have study bedrooms. Brand new boys' boarding house should be ready by September 2005.

Pastoral Care and Discipline: Tutor system, pupils say they feel well supported and there is always a housemaster/housemistress available for them to talk to. Chapel in the grounds. School has a good standard of behaviour and good manners, and consideration for others is expected. Sin – very much three strikes and you're out. Bullying – letters home, warning of suspension next time around. Out for serial wickedness. Drugs usually equals out.

Pupils and Parents: Mainly professional middle class families, on the whole affluent rather than grand, but some polo-set girls (Cowdray just up the road). Overseas pupils predominately in the sixth form. Old Boys include the De Haan brothers.

Entrance: From a variety of local preps and state primaries within a 30-mile radius; popular with Haslemere and Chichester parents. Small number of 10-year-olds, mostly at 11 or 13 by Common Entrance or school's own exam and a report from their current school.

Exit: 70 per cent stay on to do A level courses, 90 per cent then go onto university or art school, many to Central St Martin's. Leavers at 16 tend to go to local colleges for A level.

Money Matters: Annual scholarships worth £500 for art, design and technology, music both choral and instrumental, sports and academic, and sixth form.

Remarks: Definitely a good choice of school for a sporty child – facilities and training some of the best on the market; the same can be said of the art departments. Parents comment, 'its ethos lies in confidence building and developing people; whatever their strengths, staff at Seaford will help them be realised'. Kids seem happy, results speak for themselves, good for dyslexia etc.

SHEEN MOUNT PRIMARY SCHOOL

West Temple, Sheen, London, SW14 7RT

Tel: 020 8876 8394

Fax: 020 8878 6568

Email: info@sheenmount.richmond.sch.uk

Website: www.sheenmount.richmond.sch.uk

• Pupils: 450 (roughly equal numbers of boys and girls), all day • Ages: 4-11 • Religion: Non-denom • School status: State • School gender: Mixed • Day/boarding: Day pupils

SEN provision

Detail:

Now provide for in school:

Mild: ASP; AUT; ADD; EBD; DYSC; DYSL; DYSP; CP;
Moderate: AUT; ADD; EBD; DYSL; DYSP;
Severe: AUT; DYSL; DYSP;
Others: SPD; EAL; Sp&LD; Epi; PD; Eat;

Experience of:

Mild: ADHD; HI;
Moderate: CP;
Others: AUT(other); OCD; PMLD; SLD; MSI;

Summary: Our well-staffed and experienced SEN Team provides advice and resources to class teachers and parents. When further intervention is required, well-researched programmes are delivered either by a qualified SEN Teacher or a TA closely monitored by the SEN Team. Advice from external agencies is regularly sought and acted upon. We adhere firmly to the principles of early intervention and inclusion.

What we say about the school - the full Good Schools Guide review

Head: Since 1999, Mrs Elaine England (early fifties), has thirty years teaching experience, and was previously head at Stanley Infant School in Teddington. Not an obviously touchy-feely 'my door is always open' type of head, but very much a strong leader. Parents describe her as 'efficient', 'well-respected', 'dynamic', 'a good motivator' and 'very involved.' She thinks long-term and is currently planning major building works for the next ten years.

Entrance: Over-subscribed every year. Priority to very special needs then siblings. After that, it's location, location, location – not just the road you live in but the house number in that road can determine whether your child gets a place. 90 per cent of the children have been to one of the many local nurseries – too numerous to list. Unlike other local state primaries, places only rarely become available higher up the school – hardly anyone leaves Sheen Mount at 7 to go to the local prep schools, it's more likely to happen the other way round.

Exit: Mention any local independent school and someone from Sheen Mount has gone there and we're talking top academic schools: St Paul's, Lady Eleanor Holles, Putney High, Kingston Grammar, Latymer Upper, Godolphin, Hampton as well as St Catherine's, Surbiton or Halliford. Obviously lots of private tutoring goes on for the entrance exams but Mrs E feels it is unnecessary – 'we get them to the required level anyway,' but not all parents are quite that confident. Head does not try to advise parents on the choice of independent school – she admits that she doesn't know enough about them. She concentrates instead on the local state schools: Christ's, Waldegrave and Shene. Christ's is the most popular, with Waldegrave hard to get a place in from this side of the borough. With such a choice of exit schools, there is never more than a handful of pupils going on to each.

Remarks: The best primary school in the area according to parents in the know, and we are not going to argue. If you have the money, it is worth moving to be on its middle class doorstep – many see it as a real alternative to the local preps.

A sea of scooters greets you at the school gates – somehow symbolic of children who want to be at school – and as quickly as possible. Everywhere you see groups of eager, self-confident, happy children who enjoying their learning and teachers enjoying their teaching. Reception is regarded as particularly strong – described by mothers as 'a really secure and happy start', 'gets children well-socialised', though children don't all start full-time together – 'a bit divisive' say some.

'A vibrant and lively education,' say one mum, who sums up the feeling of many; parents agree that the curriculum is well-taught with lots of visits to help bring subjects to life, but some mutter that SATS results ought to be higher given the intake. Class sizes are typical of state primary schools – average about 30. Despite the high cost of local housing, staff turnover is low and there are four male teachers including a male deputy head. Parents are very welcome in school, they take an interest in what their children are learning and buy appropriate books or visit museums. At least one child was taken to Egypt because she was studying the Egyptians.

The school prides itself on the help given to children with special needs – there is a small dedicated special needs room and the SENCo is highly experienced with children with specific learning difficulties. Some parental grumbles that more minor problems in children's learning are ignored.

Music, drama and the arts are strengths – two music rooms, with mountains of individual instruments piled up on the floor reflecting the range of individual music lessons and the myriad musical groups practising each lunchtime. In the summer term there's a musical drama production and an art show, and last year the choir sang at the Royal Albert Hall.

Children introduced to a wide range of sports, rather than concentrating on winning in a few. Sports facilities are nothing special. Loads of extra-curricular activities – produces mini chess champions, as well as budding Jamie Olivers through its cookery club. 'I wouldn't eat the school lunches though,' one little girl said ruefully. 'They are inedible,' confirmed a very unfussy mother, 'its lucky children don't have to rely on them.'

Buildings pretty standard for a primary school – fairly scruffy but with loads of artwork on display. A nice computer suite is well-used and Key Stage 2 classrooms all have interactive whiteboards. All sorts of use made of the spacious grounds – reading circles, weather stations, nature trails to name but a few. The hall is being rebuilt to double it in size which should make a real difference to its usefulness for the school and the community. Parents have raised £125,000 towards the hall and more money will come to equip it! The summer fete alone raised a phenomenal £18,000. Leafy and suburban catchment, predominately middle class parents with a smattering of film stars and media types. Some of the school's success is due to these highly committed, well-off, parents – they undoubtedly know how to give generously, but some less affluent souls aren't so happy at being regularly asked for money – 'they say it will only cost me the same as a daily cappuccino – well I can only afford a cup of instant!'

SHEILING SCHOOL

Horton Road, Ashley, Ringwood, Hampshire, BH24 2EB

Tel: 01425 477 488

Fax: 01425 479 536

Email: enquiries@sheilingschool.co.uk

Website: www.sheilingschool.co.uk

• Pupils: 45, of whom 25 in the junior school (18 boys, 4 girls, 19 residential and 3 day) and 20 in the senior school (12 boys, 7 girls residential, 1 boy day) • Ages: 6-16 junior school, 16-19 senior school • Religion: Non-denom, Christian ethos • Fees: Boarding: £17,000-£22,000 according to need. Day fees: £10,000-12,000 • School status: Independent • School gender: Mixed • Day/boarding: Takes boarders

SEN provision

Detail:
Now provide for in school:

Mild: ASP; AUT; ADD; EBD; DS; DYSP; SpLD; HI; VI; CP;

Moderate: ASP; AUT; ADD; DS; MLD; DYSP; SpLD; CP;

Severe: ASP; AUT; DS; DYSP; SpLD;

Others: OCD; FRX; SLD; Sp&LD; Epi;

Summary: The Sheiling School was founded in 1951 and is a Camphill Rudolf Steiner School offering an adapted Waldorf Curriculum together with individual therapies. The school caters for up to 50 children and students aged between 6-19 years who have severe and moderate learning diffulties, including Down's syndrome, autism, Fragile X, Williams syndrome, Micrcephaly and others. Mainly residential (38 weeks) and we also offer weekly boarding and day places. The school aims to fill the gap where local and national special school facilities are not appropriate, and to provide a total environment in which children can be helped to reach their ful potential. The children and students live in extended family households with houseparents and co-workers (carers). Currently, places are purchased by 26 funding authorities throughout England and Wales.

What we say about the school - the full Good Schools Guide review

Management group: You guessed it – there's no one person in charge. Camphill communities don't have hierarchies. There's a management group, four strong, advised by delegated working groups. It's a business model that works – forthright personalities moving forward, the catalyst their shared ideal. Pooled experience is enriched by input from some impressive school council members.

Academic Matters: Therapies mix of the conventional and the anthroposophical: speech and language, physio, music, art, play, rhythmical massage, curative eurythmy, specific curative movement exercises, and colour light.

On the academic front, the Steiner influence is pervasive. Your first impression may well be the architecture, which abhors straight lines; the swoopy roofs are instantly eyecatching. Then you are arrested by the serenity of the place. The accumulation of impressions and the evidence of activity only reinforce this. It's remarkable and marvellous. Everything that happens here is touched by a particular species of calm beauty. This is the therapeutic environment and it is founded in a mode of community living predicated on the belief that the more each person gives, and the less each demands in return, the more their needs are satisfied. Everyone – not just pupils – plays their part according to their abilities and it is by these means that the school engenders independence. It's not about conformity, it's about the celebration of uniqueness, making it a colourful mosaic of character and activity, the sum greater than the parts. Here's a point of radical difference. One mum – she looked at 22 schools before discovering this one – told of how her son's challenging behaviour had been exacerbated by peremptory rules and expectations until he came here where his tantrums were absorbed and diverted, and calm entered in. It is a truly holistic approach in that the daily round is devised to nourish self-worth and personal development through work, play and coming together to enjoy meals – very important – and festivals, whether birthdays or religious and seasonal festivals. Although the ethos is based in Christian values, all religions are enthusiastically embraced.

The curriculum is based on Waldorf. For the junior school, mornings start with singing, poetry and discussion, then move on to history, geography and science. Next, pupils work one-to-one on reading, writing and maths. Afternoons are given to practical and artistic subjects – games, handcrafts, painting, gardening, eurythmy. It's all tailored and goal conscious. The senior school follows much the same programme with the addition of pre-vocational work and the development of a particular practical skill – gardening, pottery, woodwork, baking, for example. Life skills are addressed by travelling and shopping in the local community. Every week a party goes over to Bryanston to do sporty things with their students. Parents speak highly of the quality of teaching and the academic programme – 'Sheiling is part of the modern world of education'.

At the end of their first term, parents get a report which, almost all of them say, sums up their child in a way no other report has ever got near.

Background and Atmosphere: The school is a member of the Steiner-inspired anthroposophical Camphill Movement founded in Scotland in 1941 by Dr Karl König (see www.camphill.org.uk). The core belief is that, beneath any disability or emotional disturbance, a person's inner being lies undamaged. On this pinewoody 50-acre site just outside Ringwood are, also, the Lantern Community and a Waldorf school for children. At the Sheiling, the philanthropic, ascetic ideal – community, equality, no remuneration, needs met according to circumstances – is giving way to a regulatory requirement to professionalise, and there are increasing numbers of paid staff – an incongruity. To renounce materialism in order to live the life, then find the world, Ofsted and CSCI banging on your door demanding documentation with menaces is hard – and it sometimes shows. Recruitment now offers a choice of working for pay or working for love, and the community is presently assimilating the knock-ons of this new order. They call it 'living in the 21st century and keeping the best of the past'.

The hard-headed business view is that change is fuelling the dynamic and only good will come of it – all serve the inviolable ethos. Inspectors describe the school as 'unconventional' and worry that so many carers (excellent carers) don't yet have an NVQ Level 3 in caring. In response, the school is pluckily laying audit trails and piling up paperwork in pursuit of best practice. The inspectors are quizzically struck by the school's eschewal of TV and computer games – yet note that the children are terrifically busy and happy. There's an insight for you. Best practice but not as we know it. Read the Commission for Social Care Inspection (CSCI) report through the link on the school's website. It will give you a very reliable gut feeling about the place.

Up to 30 young (and not so young) volunteers – they call them co-workers – come from all over the world for a year to be care and classroom assistants in exchange for bed, board and pocket money. A few stay for ever. Give the place a young, cosmopolitan feel.

Pastoral Care and Discipline: Six boarding houses scattered about this roomy campus for between 5 and 12 children, each run by houseparents. There's one new house and very nice it is too. The others are, shall we say, a tad tatty, but in the nicest, best cared-for way. Money isn't something this community has a lot of. Rooms are homey, and children decorate them in ways which won't un-calm them. Staffing levels are extremely high – there's always heaps of human interaction going on. Meals are a highlight. Food is organic (of course), cooked on an Aga – every house has one – served on proper china. There are flowers on the table, and napkin rings. Unlike any other school you have ever seen, food is devoured with appetite, unhurriedly, with a certain formality. Meals are joyous highlights of the day, and may be followed by singing. Bedtime is for storytelling, reflection and, often, more singing.

Relationships with staff are touchingly close and trusting, consistent with the 'curative' philosophy. In this context, students develop self-awareness and build social skills. Some feel the school operates too much in a world of its own – that they ought to get out more – to which the school answers that they keep them in until they are ready, that's the whole point. As they get older, they do go out more. Parents like things the way they are. They all speak of 'one big family' and remark that the self-esteem their children develop endures. Former pupils concur.

Entrance: Children with severe learning difficulties and some moderate – autism, ADHD, epilepsy, challenging behaviour – must be able to fit in with existing pupils, some of whom are delicate. No major physical disabilities – the site is unsuitable. All statemented, referred and funded by LEA or social services. Private places available. This is an independent school and a relatively expensive placement so, if your child is offered a place, getting the statement applied is likely to take from 3 to 12 months' unflinching campaigning. The application process goes like this: 1) Have an informal look. 2) Interview with child, all reports having been sent previously. School's medical officer will be there.

3) School will offer a trial and assessment place – one full term – if it reckons it can meet care needs. Parents: start the fight for funding. School may ask for a child overnight or for a week to give them more time to decide. May offer a place on the waiting list. 4) Review at end of assessment term, when fee is set.

Exit: Almost all stay till they're 19 then seek FE College placements, usually within the Camphill family of communities – 40 of them UK-wide. Some may then move on to the Lantern or to nearby Sturts Farm; most graduate to an adult care environment.

Remarks: An extraordinary lay-by off the me-me highway of the 21st century from which you cannot hear the traffic thunder past, where good and admirable people are undeniably doing something very special. Those of a mechanical or chemical persuasion may presuppose it to be a tad cranky. You will eat your prejudices. One mum says, 'I still don't know how they do it,' but do it they do. If you go to check it out, be sure to amble down to the Lantern, where there's a very good café and shop.

Shiplake College

Shiplake Court, Shiplake, Henley-on-Thames, Oxfordshire, RG9 4BW

Tel: 0118 940 2455
Fax: 0118 9405 204
Email: registrar@shiplake.org.uk
Website: www.shiplake.org.uk

• Pupils: 306 pupils, mostly boys (16 girls in sixth form). 220 boarders • Ages: 13-18 • Religion: C of E • Fees: Day £4,445 Boarding £6,590 • School status: Independent
• Opendays: Normally October with sixth form taster day in January. See college website for more details
• School gender: Boys • Day/boarding: Takes boarders

SEN provision

Detail:
Now provide for in school:
Mild: DYSL; DYSP;

Summary: Every academic year a number of places are allocated to pupils with mild learning difficulties. Shiplake has a reputation for providing whole-school support for pupils with mild dyslexia. A new system is now in place whereby pupils requiring additional help are provided with necessary support by the learning support department. These sessions take place in addition to the main timetable.

What we say about the school - the full Good Schools Guide review

Head: Since 2004, Mr Gregg Davies. Fresh from Fettes College, Edinburgh, where he was briefly deputy head before stepping up to lead a complete transformation of Fettes prep school. Joined Fettes in 1989 as schoolmaster and games coach. Has been described to us as 'charismatic and deeply caring' and known for his 'energy, enthusiasm, total commitment and easy charm'. Top class international rugby referee and fine singer.

Academic Matters: Good value-added results. Unfussed by league table ratings – allows pupils to sit exams when they are ready, early or late. One of the first schools to accommodate pupils with specific learning difficulties, 24 mild dyslexics admitted to learning support department each year, pupils drop French to allow for specific tuition. Shiplake seems to have recognised that they had coasted along on their old reputation. Response has included appointment of head of pupil development, 16 subject teachers trained in specific learning difficulties to complement the head of learning support, three new part-time specialist teachers and additional support offered off time-table. Despite all this, reports still reach us of pupils falling through the net and not getting the learning support that parents expect them to receive.

Good overall pupil/teacher ratio – 45 full-time to 306 pupils at last count. Healthy turnover of staff after five to ten years on average. Accommodation provided for about half eases crippling cost of living in Henley area (and helps hang onto them for longer). Classrooms in newer buildings light, airy and well furnished. Good language facilities – French said to be a particular favourite, German replaced by Spanish. Maths and sciences relatively weak (in numbers, not teaching, insists head). An upper sixth boy taking chemistry, physics and biology is a rarity. A boy explained, 'Shiplake is more creative'. Currently a choice of 16 subjects at A level, theatre studies new this year. Girls slowly increasing in numbers, boarding girls from September 2006. State-of-the-art accommodation in new £2 million upper sixth house and broadening range of activities are helping.

Games, Options, The Arts: Well-earned reputation for fine sports – boys put much emphasis on it, U19 Rugby County Cup winners last season. Real strength lies in rowing (see below). Frequent race winners at National Schools Regatta at Nottingham and boys winning gold medals for GB team. Sixth form girls successful competitors in their own right. Extra-curricular rowing club for less competitive aquatic activities. Mixed fortunes at rugby (understandably struggle against much bigger schools but regularly thrash those of similar size. Large, rarely empty sports hall (squash, badminton etc), 25 metre outdoor pool very much for leisure rather than competitive use. Hockey, tennis and cricket all good – derive particular pleasure in taking on rivals Pangbourne. Foreign tours – eg rowing in Switzerland, cricket in Barbados. Plenty of travel opportunities too through CCF (no longer compulsory but still 100 strong), D of E and educational trips to likes of Kenya, Strasbourg and Brecon Beacons. Astronomy, cookery, film club and debating are all broadening the options. Pupils have to choose something extra to do. Head says, 'I don't mind if boys get bored at weekends – I just won't have them getting bored alone, so boarders staying at weekends should have lots to do.'

Art traditionally strong and current artists certainly upholding that. Fabulous work on show around the school and immensely popular A level choice. Music more for fun than a serious career option for most. 'We have a terrifically good jazz band and we hold some great rock concerts,' says head. Part of 19th century water tower sound-proofed for music practice (namely drums, keyboards and electric guitar). Drama productions in own theatre, also an open air show (often riverside) in summer. Good links with local girls' schools. Regular dances with Queen Anne's (Caversham), lots of parties with Wycombe Abbey and 'we flirt with schools in the Ascot area. They like us because our boys are well behaved,' adds head.

Background and Atmosphere: By public school standards, still relatively new. Founded in 1959 by first head, Alec Everett, as school for 120 boys. Opened up sixth form to girls forty years later in response to demand from families for female siblings to attend same school as brothers. Managed to achieve that 'without too many difficulties', girls boarding from 2006. Head insists mixed sixth form works – boys readily agree. Main building is elegant red-brick mansion which has converted well to school use. Wood panelled Great Hall doubles as dining room and assembly hall (also occasional overspill concert hall), four-bed dorms and study bedrooms above, some with balconies. Breathtaking views over tennis courts and glorious grounds to river. Despite long school days (prep till 9) and wealth of activities, a sense of calm pervades. More recent class blocks and boarding houses blend almost seamlessly with old, also barn and stables converted to theatre, careers room and more classrooms. Large site but all within easy reach. Separate upper sixth centre (College House) providing university-type accommodation. New bursar and new catering manageress investing in dramatic food improvements.

Pastoral Care and Discipline: Very supportive, they all look after each other. Head gives example, 'when a known weak reader is reading in chapel, you could hear a pin drop.' Chaplain delightful, 'genuinely Christian', matrons good at handling teenage problems and will help finding lost socks and laundry (always a problem with children who are dyslexic). Shiplake famed for its caring approach to education and this extends to all school life. Anyone found upsetting equilibrium is given marching orders. Particularly important in small school. 'Very concerned' about bullying and deals with it 'as well as anyone, providing support for all parties involved'. Boys excluded in past for this and drugs offences (sinful Henley nearby). 'I'm certainly not loath to expel,' says head, and parents would vouch for that; does not seem to be as helpful as other schools in finding a new school for the sinner. Allowed back for exams but only on daily basis (no boarding). No drink problem (licensed bar on premises).

Chapel at least once a week for assembly, also on Sunday for those still in school, central to Shiplake. House system organised according to pupils' day or boarding status – ie there's one day house, one weekly, one full boarding and two hybrid.

Pupils and Parents: More middle class professional types than there used to be. Still favoured in Surrey and SW postcode area of London, 'we get more recommendations from SW dinners than anywhere else', head jokes. Around 10 per cent overseas (Russia, Europe, Thailand, Hong Kong and Korea) and some Services. Also strong expat support. Boys appear comfortable and content. Exude confidence, not arrogance. Very polite, relaxed in appearance and keen to help. 'Chaps who leave us will have a confidence about them and a set of values from being constantly talked to about how one should conduct oneself in society,' says head. Some say that boys can lack a sense of destiny and ambition. Famous OBs, Olympic (gold medal) rower Ben Hunt-Davis, Nick Jones founder of Soho House/Babington House.

Entrance: Around 40 feeder schools, no favourites. At 13, interview with head, prep school report and CE (in order of priority). Looking for character, boys who will make the most of Shiplake, rather than outstanding academic excellence. Around 10 taken annually from state schools. Must sit school's own papers in English, maths and IQ. Early assessment for learning problems (contact school around 18 months before entry). External entry at sixth form dependent on interview; at least five C grades preferred. 'We expect people to work and turn people down if I feel they wouldn't benefit or contribute to Shiplake.' Few arrivals at sixth form – reportedly quite hard for some newcomers to fit in.

Exit: Oxford Brookes and Bristol UWE perennial favourites; also Bristol, Exeter, Leeds and Reading. Business studies and art foundation courses both popular choices in recent years as are sport and leisure. Vast bulk of leavers do degrees, diplomas, HNDs etc. Clutch of gap students.

Money Matters: Lack of charge for extras (like rowing and books) make fees pretty reasonable. Scholarships up to third of fees in music, art and sport.

Remarks: Small (fundamentally single sex) school with close-knit family approach. Boys here may not be destined for Oxbridge but charm, good manners and respect for others as well as themselves will get them far. Fills niche as demand for this kind of supportive education steps up in line with increasing academic pressure on pupils in league-chasing establishments. Parents equally supportive and fiercely defensive of Shiplake. 'The school's really brought the best out in our son,' said one. 'It's never let him down.'

SHREWSBURY SCHOOL

The Schools, Shrewsbury, Shropshire, SY3 7BA

Tel: 01743 280 552

Fax: 01743 351 009

Email: enquiry@shrewsbury.org.uk

Website: www.shrewsbury.org.uk

• Pupils: 695 boys; 565 boarding, 130 day • Ages: 13-18
• Religion: C of E • Fees: Boarding £7,180; day £5,045
• School status: Independent • Opendays: None
• School gender: Boys • Day/boarding: Takes boarders

SEN provision

Detail:

Experience of:

Mild: DYSC; DYSL; DYSP;

Others: EAL;

Summary: Although Shrewsbury is not a specialist school for boys with special educational needs, it is pleased to offer learning support to boys for whom such support is likely to be of real benefit.

All boys who enter Shrewsbury must have performed satisfactorily in our entrance tests. As a guide, we expect boys taking Common Entrance to achieve an average score of not less than 55 per cent across the subjects.

Shrewsbury's learning support department consists of six members of staff with specialist qualifications. Each works at the school to a weekly part-time timetable under the responsibility of the head of department. The work of the department is primarily geared to helping boys whose academic progress is informed by dyslexia or a specific learning difficulty (usually associated with dyslexia).

Tuition, one hour per week, is offered outside the teaching timetable and takes place in one of the four specialist rooms occupied by the learning support department.

What we say about the school - the full Good Schools Guide review

Head: Since 2001, Mr Jeremy Goulding MA (early fifties). Previously head of Haberdashers' Aske's (from 1996), and before that Prior Park, Bath. Went to school in Nottinghamshire, then Magdalen College, Oxford, where he started to read classics, then switched to philosophy and theology. Keen sportsman and accomplished cellist. Taught at Abingdon and Shrewsbury. Married to Isobel, also a philosophy and theology graduate; four children. Very able and experienced, calm and reassuring, with a twinkle in the eye. Inclusive management style – he heads a very strong staff team – but not afraid of decisions. Delighted to be back at Shrewsbury. Took over from charismatic Mr Ted Maidment, who did the school a lot of good.

Academic Matters: Very sound across the board, does very well for average as well as scholarly. English and maths remain popular at A level; all three sciences and geography healthy. School team recently represented UK in recent successful International Young Physicists Tournament. Many other successes in physics and maths Olympiads. Art spectacular, backed up by trips to everywhere including Italy and USA (with history department); classics and second and third languages well supported, also RS and business studies. Wonderful Jacobean library. AS pattern is four subjects, turning into three at A2. Boys can cope with this in the boarding school day; staff are becoming more familiar with the new exam. They give off an air of confidence about this kind of thing and certainly aren't bullied by the currently faddish assessment culture.

Learning support available for mild dyslexia, dyspraxia et al; OK for the mild wild (ADHD, Asperger's). If pupils arrive at school with an edpsych's report then they get free remedial help for the first term, thereafter it costs. Keen on boosting morale, and helping youngsters to 'work through' dyslexia (it happens). 15/20 per cent of school has some form of help, one-to-one and regular drop-in clinics. No big deal. Moderate OK for handicapped, new house wheelchair friendly, but still stairs. 'The odd disabled child not a problem,' can cope with visually and hearing impaired, with assistants if necessary. SENCo plus six fully trained staff plus one dedicated EFL teacher.

Games, Options, The Arts: Famous for rowing (marvellous facilities on the Severn, representation at national level), and strong on cricket and most games. Soccer is main winter game; cross-country club – 'The Hunt' – claims to be oldest in the world. Just about any sport can be played somewhere on the 100-acre plus site. Music very vigorous, now housed in state-of-the-art new Maidment Building; professional string quartet in residence. Drama strong – home-grown musicals transfer every other year to the Edinburgh Fringe. Lots of theatre trips – Birmingham (1 hour) and Manchester (1½ hours) theatres within day-trip reach. Wonderful Jacobean library. Many visiting speakers; despite idyllic setting, the school does not feel isolated. There are two management conferences a year, and each year one young graduate from Harvard and one from Bordeaux University come on a teaching fellowship. The annual Salopian Review, written by pupils, is a mature and stimulating production. Well-known for outward-boundish activities – camping, fell walking, leadership, based on school's farmhouse near Betws-y-Coed; and serious community work centred on Shrewsbury House youth club in Liverpool.

Background and Atmosphere: Founded in 1552 and, at one time, reckoned to be the biggest school in England; revived at the end of the 18th century, moved in 1882 to present position, across river from town. Beautiful, spacious campus, vistas everywhere, boys seen scudding about all over the place. Grounds superbly kept. Classrooms upgraded recently, now starting on boarding houses again (emphasis on quiet space for individual learning). Day boys have their own houses with studies. Houses in general very strong, excite tremendous loyalty. All staff engaged in personal tutoring one way and another, very committed; 'a 24 hours-a-day community,' says Mr Goulding, where mutual responsibility is clearly understood. 'They learn how to tolerate adults,' remarked one teacher. Staff and pupils do appear to treat each other in an enviably grown-up way.

All meals are now cafeteria-style, doubtless to the regret of some, but the food is good and the noise level acceptable. Sunday chapel plus sectional assemblies. Several school buildings available for outside use, concerts, lectures, summer activities; headmaster is keen not to be seen as 'the posh school on the hill'; in fact relations with local schools are generally good. Some drama and music with Moreton Hall, Shrewsbury Girls' High and Shrewsbury Sixth Form College.

New outpost in Thailand, Shrewsbury International School, on the Chao Phraya riverfront in Bangkok, opened September 2003 with a roll of 670, ages 3-18; cost £29 million. Follows 'same curriculum as its English original' with masses of exchanges of staff and pupils. Two reps from Shrewsbury sit on Thai school board. Headmaster Stephen Holroyd – former deputy head at Shrewsbury.

Pastoral Care and Discipline: Excellent house system picks up most personal problems, backed up by sanatorium and counselling service if needed. Boys choose their own tutors for the last two years. Good relations with parents. Headmaster takes firm line on drugs – expulsion in clear-cut cases and it doesn't matter whether the offence took place in or out of school. Little if any bad behaviour reported in town.

Pupils and Parents: Remarkably poised and civil young men as a rule; a recently appointed master was asked (genuinely) if he was enjoying his new job. Perhaps not as edgily sophisticated as in some urban schools, but none the worse for that. Parents come from a vast catchment area – many from West Midlands and Marches, also Yorks, Lancs, London, East Anglia and Scotland. Lots of sons of Old Salopians – loyalty a strong point. Pretty Middle England, really. Interesting list of former pupils includes Sir Philip Sidney, Sir Martin Rees (Astronomer Royal), Charles Darwin, Michael Heseltine, Richard Ingrams, Willie Rushton, Paul Foot, John Peel (ask to see the 1552-2002 'scrapbook').

Entrance: By CE, but the lists are pretty full, and early registration is recommended (before age 10). Many boys from top prep schools for miles around, especially Abberley and Prestfelde, also Malsis, Bramcote, Lichfield Cathedral School, Locker's Park, Aysgarth, Yarlet, Moor Park, Packwood Haugh and Kingsland Grange and increasingly from the home counties. Sixth form entry via school's entrance exam plus specified GCSE grades. No open days, all done six days a week by interviews with characterful registrar (ex-English master).

Exit: Almost all to university, a good number to Oxbridge.

Money Matters: Seventeen academic, four music scholarships at age 13, two at sixth form. Fourteen boys supported by Shrewsbury Foundation, and 200 on bursary support from the school.

Remarks: Remains one of the strongest boarding schools in the country, about which we hear virtually nothing but good; 'a school wholly at ease with itself,' says one experienced observer. Has a good blend of tradition and forward-looking attitudes, conscious of the temptation to complacency and works hard to avoid it. Leavers are confident and mature. A connoisseur's choice, and well worth slogging up/down the motorway to get to it. NB Girls from September 2007, new boarding house, sixth form only, both boarding and day; no more than a hundred, though that could be a few years hence.

SIBFORD SCHOOL

Sibford Ferris, Banbury, Oxfordshire, OX15 5QL

Tel: 01295 781 200

Fax: 01295 781 204

Email: info@sibford.oxon.sch.uk

Website: www.sibford.oxon.sch.uk

• Pupils: 391 boys and girls; 75 board, the rest day • Ages: 4-18 • Religion: Quaker • Fees: Day £1,879-£2,986; weekly boarding £4,033-£5,403; full boarding £5,688-£5,802 • School status: Independent • Opendays: Twice a term • School gender: Mixed • Day/boarding: Takes boarders

SEN provision

Detail:

Now provide for in school:

Mild: ASP; DYSL; DYSP;

Moderate: ASP; DYSL; DYSP;

Others: EAL; DEL; Oth;

Summary: No response – a pity, as this school has a particular talent for doing well by eg the delicate, the bullied and school refusers. SEN details added by us.

What we say about the school - the full Good Schools Guide review

Head: Since 2004, Mr Michael Goodwin (late forties), married with four children, and fluent in Spanish, who came from Sheringham High School and sixth form centre in Norfolk where he was head for five years. Says he felt drawn to Sibford as soon as he saw job advertised. Has big plans for school, starting with asking parents about school's strengths, their perceptions of it, changes that could be made. 'I felt the school was very special and the interview process comfirmed that for me. There is a wonderful atmosphere and ethos to the place.'

Academic Matters: Sibford is a 'gentle nurturing school' and follows the National Curriculum – with enhancements – 'more suited to our pupils' needs and talents'. There is a strong and well-known SEN department, though not more than a third of the children need remedial help, 'though sometimes, because we are good at catching dyslexia, we recognise it when it wasn't previously diagnosed and the numbers go up a bit'. However, A, AS, levels, GCSEs, GNVQs and Certificates of Achievement are regarded as equally important. The 30 per cent in the remedial stream include those with dyslexia, dyspraxia, the odd Asperger's, as well as fragile children plus refusers and those who have been bullied elsewhere – 'we are so thrilled when they break the rules'. A maximum of five pupils in each year are admitted to the learning support department and the tiny well-stocked specialist rooms only have six-sided tables. Pupils follow the mainstream curriculum, being withdrawn on a regular basis from French.

Laptops important and pupils encouraged to have one, but computers throughout, though in banks rather than dotted around – 'the staff said it was a distraction'. Internet/intranet/networked. School is trialing voice recognition software. The academic side is on the up, though university results won't set the world alight, 'it is more important to raise their self-esteem'. Having said that, this is a school where the children do hold their heads up high, look you in the eye and say hello. The normal GCSE syllabus includes English lang, possibly English lit or media studies, maths and double science plus a whole raft of options including business studies, DT, IT, music, art, textiles, drama et al. School keen to 'identify talents' and encourage self-esteem, 'GCSE results day absolute magic. Pupils who might previously have thought themselves worthless, can then judge themselves on the same basis as others.' Results surprisingly good 'by their own lights'. 'Any child who does the course can take the exam – if they want to and personally feel up to it'. Sibford is not really a high-flying school. Countryside and environment, for which the school is famous, can be taken in conjunction with single science. Numerous A level courses on offer at sixth form and can be mixed and matched with vocational qualifications. Large English as an Additional Language department, particularly well subscribed at sixth form level; pupils take EAL exams and work in tiny classes of eight.

Games, Options, The Arts: All the normal trad games are played in regular matches against other schools plus (very special this) dyspraxic children practising balancing on their tummies on fat skate boards and zooming around the gym like turtles, with dyspraxia specialists on hand, for fine motor control. Large sports hall, squash courts, proper playing fields and recently-opened swimming pool.

The arts are 'confidence building, and underpin the Quaker ethos – all have a right to be seen and be heard'. Drama, art and music are of first importance and during our trip round we found no fewer than five different groups rehearsing some form of theatrical entertainment. Art is taught in conjunction with textiles, design and technology (wood cutting is good for measurements), and music is everywhere. The aim is for children to find self-expression and give them 'wings with which to fly'.

Background and Atmosphere: School originally founded in 1842 and the charming motley collection of Cotswold stone buildings 'on the hill' were put up in the thirties. The school itself is fairly pedestrian – passages with add-ons, some spanking new boarding houses (boarding numbers down and extra houses have already been sold), staff houses look like impoverished farm workers' dwellings, contrast with Orchard Close and super duper new art and music blocks – very state of the art. Fabulous 98-acre grounds.

Masses of flowers and plants everywhere – as you might expect – and it appeared as though the Triffids were on the march, as tractor after tractor came trundling down with ever more impressive collections of greenery.

Pastoral Care and Discipline: Very strong Quaker ethos, but having said that, head locked her door when we left to go on our tour. Self-discipline and treating others with respect emphasised – 'you only abuse once', which means great freedom but, if bullying does occur, authority 'comes down like a ton of bricks'. 'Two strikes and suspension, three strikes and you're out'. Fatigues (not Quaker PC) for smoking, one warning for drugs and booze then suspension; immediate out for trading or providing. Head has only had to expel twice in three years – this is not a very streetwise place. Tutors, but every child has someone in whom they can confide.

Pupils and Parents: A mixed bunch, from those who come daily and use the school like any other, to those – often quite grand – whose children come for the special needs department. A small tranche from overseas, both for the English language department and for the special needs facility.

Entrance: Fairly relaxed at Orchard Close, though children needing help have an educational psychologist's report and an IQ test. Pupils are generally accepted if the school has the necessary staffing and provision in place to deal with specific problems and they will do their own assessment if necessary.

Exit: 'Pupils usually go to the courses they want to.' Strong emphasis on performing arts and art foundations courses, music, business and language courses or straight into employment. Majority of Orchard Close pupils go through to the senior school but some still opt for Cokethorpe, Bloxham or other local schools.

Money Matters: LEAs' contribution appreciated, otherwise not a rich school but host of scholarships at all ages, including special Orchard Close and dyslexia scholarships.

Remarks: This is a school highly thought of by parents with children needing special help either because of learning difficulties or because they find 'ordinary schools' daunting and over their heads. Friendly, fun and could be just the ticket.

SIDCOT SCHOOL

Oakridge Lane, Winscombe, BS25 1PD

Tel: 01934 843 102

Fax: 01934 844 181

Email: admissions@sidcot.org.uk

Website: www.sidcot.org.uk

• Pupils: 350 boys and girls; 146 boarders • Ages: 11-18 • Religion: Quaker • Fees: Day £1,250-£3,330; weekly boarding £5,350; full boarding £4,850-£7,200 • School status: Independent • Opendays: First Friday in October and first Bank Holiday in May. Scholarship and test day last Saturday in January • School gender: Mixed • Day/boarding: Takes boarders

SEN provision

Detail:

Now provide for in school:

Mild: ASP; ADD; ADHD; EBD; DYSC; DYSL; DYSP; HI; VI;

Moderate: MLD; DYSL;

Others: EAL; Sp&LD; DEL; Epi; Eat;

Experience of:

Mild: AUT;

Moderate: ADD; ADHD; DYSC; DYSP; HI; VI;

Others: SPD; CD; OCD; TIC;

Summary: We are a mainstream school with a learning support department and have CReSTeD registration (dyslexia). One to one tuition is available for literacy and maths, additionally we can offer support for maths in a classroom setting with an LSA. In additon we can offer provision for mild Asperger's, dyscalculia, dyspraxia, speech and language difficulties.

What we say about the school - the full Good Schools Guide review

Head: Since 2001, Mr John Walmsley BSc PGCE (fifties), educated Leeds and Lancaster universities, is a veteran traveller who taught at Mexico City International School before becoming head of IT at Simon Langton Girls' School Canterbury and deputy head at Sidcot in 1998. Married to Barbara, a stonemason and teacher, has James 14, Dominic 12, William 7 and Cissy 4. An engaging man with razor-sharp perception, was chosen against high calibre candidates while holding post of acting head. Seems like the one-school-head sort; teaches Octopush, scuba dives, enjoys cooking, cinema, music. Although not a Quaker, his father was one and he is currently an Attender (one who attends Quaker meetings). 'I want our students to engage with the world, to forge links across international boundaries and religious divides,' he says.

Academic Matters: A rare breed of school; excellent exam results within a holistic education. Ratio of staff to pupils is 1:15 and drops to 1:7 in sixth form. 65 per cent A/B grades at A level but some students take exams a year early and so don't show. In the last five years five students have been amongst the top five in the country for maths and music. 25 A level subjects. Bucks the national trends with boys doing as well as girls at GCSE – says it's because they don't have peer group pressure problems.

Highly successful English as a Foreign Language centre recently integrated into school campus, teaches intensive English language/business English/IT to up to 25 students at GCSE while maths, science, games and arts subjects are taught within shared classes amongst rest of school. Latin taught from 12 onwards.

This isn't a special needs school but they don't shy away from pupils with SEN. Dyslexics well catered for with provision monitored by CReSTeD. Lots of successes too: recent head boy and head girl got straight A grade A levels, one had dyslexia other didn't, yet the one with dyslexia had been written off by a previous school as someone who'd never achieve academically. Say it's not unusual for dyslexics to get top grades though not all do. Recognise for some, lower grade passes represent great achievement and massive success.

Games, Options, The Arts: Perfect place for a child and horse who will not be parted. Own stables on site. Though all students are encouraged to participate in wide variety of sports, compulsion does not fit with Quaker ethos. Competitive teams for rugby, football, cricket, hockey, basketball, rounders, netball, athletics on 20 acres of playing field, three short tennis courts and lush heated swimming pool. Recently Kate Reed was middle distance England runner. Vibrant table-tennis tournaments, Octopush, canoeing, fencing, riding, dry-slope skiing, golf, competitive squash, skateboard ramp and 60 activity clubs offer everything from chess, Judo, photography. Hot on public speaking, Environmental Action Group and United Nations Club.

Music school built in 1957 has lunchtime concerts for parents and locals to air the two choirs, a jazz group and the school band 'Crumpet'. One in three play instruments and 20 per cent of students learn instruments to diploma. Several go on to music colleges. Around three a year to Royal Academy. Innovative textiles department

Background and Atmosphere: It is unusual to find a school of this calibre of which so little is known. Facilities are good and current population scant because of last head being Bob-the-Builder variety, extending buildings rather than numbers. Library and luxurious sports centre donated by OB from the Cullis family. State of the art canteen. Impeccably kept gardens amid 150 acres of Cheddar countryside, buildings purpose-built over three centuries provide spacious labs/classrooms. Five un-ritzy houses on campus. Resident staff are often couples with own children so family atmosphere prevails. Does well from its inheritance – 'we sold a field for £2 million last year,' comments head.

Founded in 1699 when Quakers in the west of England set up schools to educate their children in liberal, intellectual, tolerant ideology. Equality of sexes and critical enquiry valued from year dot. Though only 15 per cent of school are now Quakers, ditto staff, emphasis on nurturing the individual and exploring potential are key to their ethos. Morning meeting based on silent worship begins each day though pupils can and do address the meetings. Strong community feel with lots happening at weekends. No Saturday school. Quaker schools celebrate and respect differences so the 10 per cent with SEN issues have high self-esteem, know they can achieve, are valued and have many fine examples of others with similar difficulties leading the way.

'Sidcot pioneered the teaching of sciences by allowing students to partake in lab experiments,' says a chirpy physics head. Visual impact of the place not lost on pupils. Art students designed a circular stained glass window for dome of new library; younger ones worked with interior designer for an eye-popping common room in indigo/saffron yellow. 'It's a very pleasant place to work; people come and stay,' say staff, 11 of whom have stayed more than a decade.

Pastoral Care and Discipline: 'College of Teachers' confers on important decisions. Teachers live by example so that 'nothing should humiliate any pupil or their religious belief'. This is obvious in relationships between pupils and staff. 20 upper sixth prefects called 'office holders' organise social events and seniors involved in running their own houses. Current head boy from Saudi, previous head boys from Russia and Thailand. Bad behaviour dealt with by Quaker gentleness rather than by stamping on it.

No alcohol served on premises though Quaker ethos does not forbid it. Not druggy. Much care taken over transition from junior, and new pupils given pupil mentor to break them in gently. Guardians arranged for foreign pupils. School choir includes staff and parents too. Barbecue parties each Friday evening at the swimming pool.

Head and staff switched on to the needs of all individuals. Recognise a child with a prestigious talent may not be straight down the line, won't fit in neatly or think as majority do but will make own way with help, support and guidance. Recognise some aspects of SpLDs are an advantage; help a child think outside the box, won't write children off, use role models where they can including parents. Say parents who chose it for three very different types of offspring – 'it is unusual to find a school which takes itself seriously academically to be this kind and caring, particularly amongst the Bristol 'hot-house' schools'.

Pupils and Parents: Not a flash school despite some well-heeled customers. Popular with media/arts folk. 25 nationalities making up 20 per cent of the pupils. A school bus and flexi boarding attracts 75 per cent locals from Glastonbury, Yeovil, Frome, Bristol. Pupils in uniform of blue and white striped shirts and grey skirts/trousers seem happy and confident. Old Scholars: Sir George Trevelyan, Robert Shackleton, George Palmer

(Huntley and Palmer) historian Edmund Ashby, Justin Webb and some of younger Dimbleby clan, Zoe Wanamaker, Tim Bevan, Deborah Warner (RSC director), one of the Baroness Millers.Each Easter old scholars gather for a week's pow-wow when pupils put on concerts/theatricals/art exhibitions. The snappy and professional newsletter, Sidcot Matters, that keeps track of recent OS successes and school news, can put to shame many a school magazine.

Entrance: Automatic entry from junior school. Entrance test at 9 and 13 can be taken at applicant's present school. Common Entrance as possible alternative to school's own entrance exam in February. A taster day and night can be arranged. Entrance to sixth form needs 6 GCSEs though the school reserves the right to be flexible. Students of EAL can enter any time of year. A genuinely mixed ability school, handful of students has a range of needs: exceptionally bright, gifted and talented, dyslexia, dyspraxia, dyscalculia, Asperger's, ADD, ADHD and physical difficulties (improved wheelchair access on cards). Looks at every single child, takes those who'll benefit from school and give a bit back, though severe SEN cases may be better placed in specialist schools; only has room for occasional child requiring a learning support assistant.

Exit: Geared up to finding right course at right institution, however talented a student. Recently helped a very bright dyslexic student who wanted to study medicine find a course with a practical bias (a great comfort to those of us who'd rather be opened up by a surgeon with a steady hand and good eye than one who's a whiz at spelling!) 70 per cent to select universities: LSE, Imperial, Exeter, Manchester, Leeds etc. 4 per cent to Royal Academy of Music and music colleges. 20 per cent to art foundation/art colleges, a couple to Oxbridge.

Money Matters: Eight academic scholarships at years 6 and 8 worth up to 25 per cent of fees. Exceptional candidates may get awards younger. At sixth form 10 major scholarships for pupils inside or outside the school planning on three A levels. Music and arts scholarships at any age for outstanding youngsters on basis of portfolio/sculpture. Six other Quaker schools in UK contribute to a fund, which distributes up to 80 per cent bursaries to Quaker families.

Remarks: An international boarding environment in a safe and secure community where every teacher can know the name of each pupil. Ideal for a bright child who might shrivel up in a pressured environment or one who needs creativity unlocking.

SLINDON COLLEGE

Slindon, Arundel, West Sussex, BN18 0RH

Tel: 01243 814 320

Fax: 01243 814 702

Email: registrar@slindoncollege.fsnet.co.uk

Website: www.slindoncollege.co.uk

• Pupils: 87, all boys, most board • Ages: 10-16

• Religion: Non-denom • School status: Independent

• Opendays: Contact school • School gender: Boys

• Day/boarding: Takes boarders

SEN provision

Detail:

Centre of excellence for:

Mild: ASP; ADD; ADHD; DYSC; DYSL; DYSP;

Moderate: ADD; ADHD; DYSC; DYSL; DYSP;

Severe: DYSL;

Others: SPD; EAL;

Experience of:

Mild: EBD;

Moderate: MLD;

Others: OCD; ODD; TIC; Sp&LD; Epi;

Summary: A centre of excellence for moderate but complex specific learning difficulties including AD(H)D, dyslexia, dyspraxia, Asperger's syndrome (mild) and others that may overlap. It is also a haven for less able or vulnerable pupils who will not thrive in large classes. It has a warm and friendly atmosphere. The school adopts a holistic approach to learning support. Small classes with experienced teachers and a large team of classroom assistants are further supported by ICT, a dyslexia unit, dietry measures, Bowen therapy and medication.

Special needs planning is present at every level. Individual education planning goes beyond the classroom and is truly unique. Every pupil is fully included, enabled, valued and encouraged.

What we say about the school - the full Good Schools Guide review

Headmaster: Since 1999, Mr Ian Graham MA BEd Cert Ed, mid-fifties. Formerly a teacher of history and PE with 25 years service at Rugby School under his belt, Mr Graham had lots of experience at housemastering and heading numerous depts including General Studies and Activities before taking up his headship at Slindon – different, eh? Perhaps not so different for a teacher clearly committed to giving the best to and getting the best out of each individual. This challenge and the attractions of the college's stunning site and buildings convinced him, and his tenure so far has overseen the development of a school with a clear focus and direction. At Rugby, he tended to take on the boys with problems or who were struggling and he has a natural touch, together with the required toughness when appropriate. Now with a staff who see things the same way – 'we know what we are about, we know what we are doing and we get on with it.' He is realistic and honest – 'it doesn't always work. I do have to move people on. It's unethical to take people's fees if a boy really doesn't want to learn.' However, it clearly does work for the vast majority who stay. 'I know every boy in the school and I know what makes him tick', says the head. Of a current leaver he says, 'he'll be a success in life and that's what we want.'

Academic Matters: 'Not a special but a specialist school', says the literature. 'It specialises in helping pupils whose needs have not been met in larger schools despite extra support because of insufficient individual tailoring.' The key to this approach seems to lie in school's 'holistic' approach and in its constant stressing of the need to create and bolster self-esteem in everyone. Helpful are the small classes – none bigger than 12, the use of individual learning plans and a highly flexible, undogmatic approach. Some boys might even be encouraged to repeat a year so that the basic skills are reinforced, allowing for a more confident step into year 10. Some make such good progress that, by year 10, they no longer need individual support and are wholly reintegrated into class.

Slindon children may well be dyslexic, dyspraxic, have mild Asperger's syndrome or mild autism, ADD, ADHD or Semantic Pragmatic Disorder or be school refusers, but often specific labels won't do and the history is one of simply not thriving educationally in the mainstream world. Hence, a special school isn't called for and a rigid approach is inappropriate. Asperger's children, for example, aren't treated to 'serious behavioural modification – we're creating the right atmosphere and then tweaking things'. SEN education at Slindon is highly sophisticated but confident enough to allow the staff to pick and choose which bits of which approach will best assist each individual. In this, the learning support department and its impressively committed head – himself a successful dyslexic – are central, together with the extensive use of trained learning support assistants in years 5-9, to strengthen the work of the specialist classroom teachers. There is an emphasis on the basic skills, primarily reading, and a range of techniques is used to help each pupil achieve in the best way for him. 'We're wrapping our education around the individual pupils,' says head. Lessons are an hour long – sensibly allowing for the disorganised to get organised and the careful conclusions to work that some such students need. Even breaks are supervised by SEN-trained staff.

Everyone does double or single science at GCSE. Everyone does ICT and takes either a GCSE or the CLAIT exam. Food technology is popular and all years 6-9 do cookery. School has a little observatory – no light pollution here – and GCSE astronomy is a recent innovation for the more able students – such a good idea. In that, as in other areas, school making good use of its assets. There is a small farm, to be expanded and developed in late 2005, allowing for animal husbandry – school lovingly cares for ducks, geese, hens, a goat and four sheep – as well as crop growing. Super Victorian conservatory already used for growing fruit and veg – students will be able to take a GNVQ in environmental studies. Those boys for whom a hefty clutch of GCSE subjects is not on are allowed to drop some and are assigned to grounds/maintenance staff and learn electrics, plumbing, painting and decorating, mowing and so on – useful for many who move on to college vocational courses – and good for self-esteem.

Not everyone here has a specific learning difficulty. In particular, the younger brothers of existing pupils, who themselves would have no problems in mainstream education, often choose to come. In addition, there are those few able but socially less robust individuals for whom Slindon is a safe and comfortable learning space. So – a wide range of results at GCSE. Some here gain grades from C-G and this represents a notable achievement. Others may gain mostly Cs and the odd A or B. PE and Food Tech score well. Art and photography sometimes get A*/A. Efforts clearly made to involve the practical in the theoretic to encourage interest in everyone. We watched a bunch of boys with small circuit boards, soldering irons, mini loudspeakers and batteries making tiny electric organs. School built two racing cars for the annual Greenpower event at Goodwood and won The Spirit of Greenpower award in 2004. This and other activities encourage both individual skills and team-building.

Games, Options, The Arts: Huge, super fields on which football and rugby are played, a floodlit court, purpose-built squash courts, archery, golf, tai kwondo, basketball, tennis, mountain biking, cross-country etc with an outdoor heated pool – open from Easter to late October, along with the Duke of Edinburgh Award Scheme – no shortage of things to do even though there is, as yet, no sports hall. Some worthy achievements here – especially in cross-country.

Lots of extra-curricular opportunities, mostly of the outdoor type but also chess, stagecraft and various musical activities. Music is popular, especially the recording studios where boys can record and then cut their performances into CDs or mini-disks. Lots of guitars and drumming here. Many learn individually with peripatetics; there is a jazz band, choir and other impromptu bands. Music is taken at GCSE. Appealingly messy art room full of primary colours, mobiles, ceramics and purposeful work. School's principle is to display everything everyone does and there is plenty of space to cover. New skateboard ramp in the gardens possibly the most popular innovation yet.

Background and Atmosphere: The site and buildings are owned by the National Trust. The house itself is Tudor Sussex flint and is an imposing grey three-storey pile on top of a superb site overlooking the south Sussex landscape – fields and woods, down, on a clear day, to the sea and the Isle of Wight. Most rooms, including dorms, look out over this deliciousness but it is probably never taken for granted – just too special. Up here you hear nothing but birdsong and a distant mechanical saw. School will celebrate its sixtieth anniversary in 2006. It's not all in perfect nick but it's impressively well-kept for a school of such a size and in such high-maintenance accommodation. Boarding is good – a choice of a 2/3 or a 5/6 bedder for juniors and 2/3 for senior boys except for the top year who have single study bedrooms of good sizes. Good common rooms and bathroom facilities. Belongings not, for the most part, kept in rooms – to help boys learn about organisation – but stored in loft rooms to which access is allowed twice daily or by pleading with matron at other times. Welcoming surgery with san next door and ensuite bathroom – not too scary if you're ill away from home. General atmosphere is very relaxed and friendly – no one could feel threatened here.

Pastoral Care and Discipline: Clear pastoral system – academic staff being also tutors with pastoral responsibilities but a strong sense of general caring for each other pervades. Resident housemaster and mistress and matron supported by evening tutors oversee the boarding side. Rewards and sanctions system maintained by the head who manages it all by much walking around and being visible. Erratic behaviour, so often part of the frustrations attendant on SENs, is accepted and treated with compassionate firmness but head will exclude a pupil if misbehaviour becomes a problem to others. Credits and prizes abound and head keeps a drawer full of chocolate bars as rewards – so much nicer than a sticky star! Food mostly cooked on site by much-loved resident cook who will even make sandwiches on demand if main menu – which looks good – doesn't appeal. Many boys on regular medication regime – Ritalin is common and seen as a very effective tool – so no one bats a proverbial. Summer term sees as much going on outside as possible including lessons, once-weekly each bbq and picnic.

Pupils and Parents: Boarders from everywhere in the UK; some few from Hong Kong – only English allowed to be spoken during the school day – and one or two from elsewhere. Day boys from as far south as the sea and within 15 miles or so around. Social mix but very few supported by LEAs so a self-limiting cohort. Small but busy PTA making a big contribution both in fund-raising and in actual physical work. Every Friday is a tea-party to which all staff go and all parents are invited – an excellent chance for a quick word about Edward's homework/chilblains/lost bat without a palaver.

Entrance: By interview with head, current school report plus ed psych's if any and assessment by head of learning support. Taster days – and nights for prospective boarders – are popular and useful. No actual tests – refreshingly enlightened.

Exit: Mostly to local colleges for vocational courses or for A levels. 'By the time they get to post-GCSE, they need to be exposed to all the things we've been protecting them from,' we were told – sensible enough.

Money Matters: Some bursaries.

Remarks: School beginning to take from year 5 from September 2005 – a good idea and they could start even younger as, by the age of 8, most problems are apparent and parents at their wits end. Slindon is a happy answer to the sort of boy for whom mainstream – whatever the in-class/out-of-class support – simply isn't right. Slindon parents exhale relief, gratitude and hope and the boys come here and no longer feel different, dim or excluded.

SLOUGH GRAMMAR SCHOOL

Lascelles Road, Slough, Berkshire, SL3 7PR

Tel: 01753 522 892

Fax: 01753 538 618

Email: office@sloughgrammar.berks.sch.uk

Website: www.sloughgrammar.berks.sch.uk

• Pupils: 1110; mixed, all day • Religion: Non-denom

• School status: State • Opendays: November

• School gender: Mixed • Day/boarding: Day pupils

SEN provision

Detail:

Now provide for in school:

- Mild: ASP; ADD; EBD; DYSL; DYSP; HI; VI; CP;
- Moderate: ASP; HI; VI; CP;
- Severe: ASP; VI;
- Others: EAL; Sp&LD; DEL; Epi; PD;

Experience of:

- Mild: ADHD;
- Moderate: ADD; DYSL;
- Severe: HI;
- Others: CD; Eat;

Summary: As a mainstream mixed selective grammar school our range of pupils with special educational needs is limited by their need to pass the entrance examinations.

In Slough we have gained a reputation for promoting inclusion for all pupils with SEN and have a proven track record of managing the needs of these young people with measurable success. We have a number of pupils with a range of physical disabilities, some of whom are wheelchair users. We will soon have a special toilet and shower facility and a physio room to ensure that we can fully meet the needs of these pupils. We also have a number of pupils with sensory impairment, some of whom are statemented. This includes both Visual Impairment and Hearing Impairment. We also have some pupils on the autistic spectrum, including a couple with Asperger's, who have varying degrees of support in the classroom. We have pupils with specific learning difficulty and their needs are met with individual support and a multi-sensory approach to teaching.

Special arrangements for examinations are made for pupils with SEN, where their needs indicate this to be appropriate.

We have a few pupils with behavioural problems who receive support as required to enable them to access the curriculum and manage their own behaviour. We are fortunate to have access to a wide variety of professionals working as specialists in the fields mentioned above. They provide invaluable support and advice for students, their families and the school staff.

What we say about the school - the full Good Schools Guide review

Head: Since 1988, Mrs Margaret Lenton BA FRSA (fifties), a historian. Previously Mrs Lenton worked in a bank and in a solicitor's office after which she became a teacher and taught in Derbyshire, Haringey and Southend, latterly as deputy head at Westcliff High School for Girls. In her long tenure as head, Mrs Lenton has appointed most of the current staff and has transformed the place into one of the best mixed grammars in the country. The Ofsted annual report for 2003/4 included SGS in its highly prestigious list of most successful schools. Mrs Lenton is highly experienced, thoughtful, quietly assertive and a firm believer in order and being tough when appropriate. 'Once you have order you can do anything,' she claims and the quiet and purposeful air of her school bears her out. She stickles over uniform – 'button!' she says as she spots an undone collar and the hole is quickly buttoned up. An eyebrow scarcely needs to be raised over a coat illegally worn inside school – it is off almost before she notices. She is regarded with respect but not fear. 'I take risks,' she says and can cite examples of sticking her neck out for her pupils or her school and getting results. This seems to be appreciated and understood by pupils and parents alike.

Not afraid to buck trends and question established tenets, Mrs Lenton learns from experience and then turns that learning into highly effective teaching practice.

Boys and girls, for example, are taught separately in some subjects for the first three years – and achieve more as a result. 'We have driven up the performance of girls doing physics ... boys prefer fact to fiction – we choose girl-friendly and boy-friendly books eg Treasure Island and Jane Eyre.' They have separate drama lessons – 'young men will not perform in front of girls.' The 2004 Ofsted inspection report, one of the most lyrical we have read, noted that there is 'very little difference between pupils of different ethnicity or sex' in terms of their achievement and praises the 'inspirational leadership' of the head. 'The danger is,' she says, 'of being in a comfort zone. I hope I'm not.' She could be – many would be – but this one clearly isn't. 'My aim in life is to create genuine, independent learners and we're not there yet.'

Academic Matters: In addition to a full National Curriculum programme, school offers a vast range of other options and opportunities. Food technology is popular – 'everyone learns how to make a samosa', as are textiles and languages – modern and ancient – both Latin and Greek are taught here. 15+ other languages also available as extra-curricular options though, perhaps surprisingly, the majority of pupils in the school – those whose families originate from the Asian sub-continent – mainly choose to study the languages and the music of their culture outside school. The sixth form offers both A levels and, since 2003, the International Baccalaureate. 'It's a really good course, it helps you to think creatively and it offers opportunities to those who don't want to specialise', asserts head. School also offers AVCEs in travel and tourism and in business studies – useful qualifications and results are a spread across the grades. School works to a fortnightly timetable facilitating a more-or-less free choice from the huge range of options.

Results in core subjects show a spread, mostly across the A/C grades, with a good sprinkling of A*s, notably in English lit and maths. Very few grades below B in the sciences. In the optional subjects, RS is very popular and the results are exemplary. Food and nutrition also does well – for both sexes. 15 A levels are offered and results seem pretty evenly spread, some subjects being vastly more popular, eg biology, chemistry and psychology, than others. Languages and RS have tiny groups at this level. First IB results expected in 2005 and eagerly awaited. This side of academic life here – as elsewhere – is sure to grow.

Overall, results are more than respectable and indicate a serious and successful approach to learning and preparation for professional life. The plan is that, by 2006, every child will have his or her own Individual Learning Plan – ie a programme and plan of work tailored to their own abilities and aptitudes. This is a dream elsewhere – here it is close to being realised. SEN not a big deal here – few with SpLD – and a SENCo and teaching assistants give, mostly, in-class help. Physical disability catered for though there is no lift but visually and hearing-impaired students are supported as are wheelchair users and few autistic spectrum pupils. Extra support and masterclasses for those identified as gifted and talented.

Smallish library with helpful full-time librarian who works closely with the academic departments. Limited but well-chosen books and extensive fiction section – again well-chosen and well-used, as is the library as a whole. Library also houses UCAS handbooks though there is a good careers library and staff elsewhere. IT is impressive – 'the equivalent of 13 computer rooms' – and the school is 'wireless' so that anyone can access anything anywhere. A system of wall-mounted screens in the corridors keeps everyone in touch with school information. A spanking new website up and running in March 2005 enables pupils and parents to access masses of information from home.

Games, Options, The Arts: Wednesday afternoon is spent on diverse 'activities' such as 'Out and About in historical Slough', digital photography, music composition, bell ringing, health and beauty, first aid, football refereeing, cycle proficiency and sports and languages galore – this is serious 'enrichment'. The 17 sports on offer include all the usuals plus badminton, 'new age kurling', and cricket at which the school is more-or-less unbeaten. School has a good, large, on-site field, several courts for tennis and netball and buses pupils to the Thames Valley Athletics Centre in Eton. Buses also go to the nearby municipal pool, the Montem Sports Centre.

Instrumental music is not huge here but there is a choir and an orchestra and five rock bands. 'They can learn jazz or rock but they have to learn it properly – the rules of composition and so on', says head. Drama also is not high profile but major productions happen in large school hall. Art is strong and painting, drawing, sculpture, cartoon animation, ceramics and textiles all produce lively and attractive results. Super aboriginal work on 'self-identity' on display when we visited. Good woodwork and DT. Artists and writers come and give masterclasses. Provision for all these subjects was described as 'good' in the recent Ofsted. In all these areas, though, as with staff and office accommodation, school suffers from a lack of space. The abilities and enthusiasm are there – more space and facilities could make a huge difference. Projects with local companies eg GSK, provide training and experience in problem-solving and the world of work. Young Enterprise students were taking orders for Valentine's Day roses when we visited. They'd been up at Nine Elms at 4.00am to get them!

Lots of trips all over the place – in and out of the country – many linguistic but also scientific and geographic as well as cross-cultural. School has links with another in China and one in Norway. School participates in the British Council's Comenius project to encourage such links.

Background and Atmosphere: The main, two-storey, long building is a classic 1930s design, brick, unbeautiful but practical. Pupils do not admire it nor its add-ons but it is well-maintained and kept in good order. In a quiet, prosperous residential road, lined with well-spaced detached houses – hardly the Slough of unfair repute. Two minutes from the M25 intersection with the M4 and just off the A4 but it feels safe, suburban and very respectable.

We saw far less litter inside the school and roundabout and fewer heaps of back-packs than in most comparable schools. Orderliness is the theme and it is palpable in every class you pass and in the disciplined and purposeful movement of pupils around the place. Some, inevitably, find the regime too rigid but most appreciate it and feel what it does for them. We met two prospective sixth formers hoping to be offered places partly because 'there's no racist fighting here' – unlike at their existing schools.

School institutions are democratic and important. Houses – Herschel, Hampden, Brunel etc, count in the school structure and cultural life as does the exemplary school council which, as in another place, has committees for such concerns as health and safety, learning and teaching, bullying, the school environment and so on. These committees research questions of importance to the school community, report back and their findings and recommendations are implemented. This is impressive democracy and is also part of the school's citizenship programme.

Sixth form centre in converted squash court. Lunch here would not delight health campaigners – a high proportion of pizzas, pies, sandwiches and crisps and a very small salad bar. The least impressive thing we saw on our visit.

One of school's major successes is in the happy co-existence of students from such diverse backgrounds. Head is clear – 'we celebrate the cultural diversity of the school, which is huge, but these are British children'. Many children are bi-lingual and you hear odd snatches of other languages as you move around but head says her parents want the children 'to absorb other languages'. She is keen to unite them in a common British heritage and 2005 sees everyone making trips to Portsmouth to learn about Nelson in the bi-centenary of his death at Trafalgar. 'I said they could have their money back if they didn't enjoy it and no one's asked for it yet.' School has British Council's International School Award status and is now also accredited as an Initial Teacher Training provider – high level stuff.

A high-flying institution with an atmosphere of high standards and aspirations. School elects 'honorary fellows' – people with no direct connection but who help in different capacities eg in careers advice or support. Ex-head of Eton – across the river – Sir Eric Anderson, came to give the prizes and, when you wait in the school's entrance foyer, a large screen shows the occasion, with staff in gowns all sitting on the platform. Screen apart, this could be a scene from fifty years ago.

Pastoral Care and Discipline: Pupils rise when a teacher enters the room. Lessons are orderly, disciplined, quiet. Pupils move along the corridors in a civilised manner and treat each other and staff with respect and courtesy. Everyone wears uniform. Zero tolerance of drug-taking and stealing but only two exclusions in recent years – for drugs. For stealing – 'I will call the police,' says head but 'we're a pretty honest community'.

Pupils and Parents: Pupils come from Slough but some from Ealing, Chiswick, Twickenham and Harrow and some from as far away as Paddington and Reading. Considerable ethnic mix but the majority is of Indian and Pakistani origin and the rest mostly white Brits. Once you're there it becomes an irrelevance. Most people's first language is English, Punjabi a not-close second. Sikhs, Muslims and Christians in more-or-less equal numbers. Very supportive parents. 90+ per cent turn up to parents' evenings and many support school in diverse ways eg work experience. Former pupils include novelist

Susan Cooper, Lord William Bradshaw, transport expert, ophthalmologist Prof Anthony Moore, Olympic swimmer Philip Hubble, Andrew Watts, opera singer.

Entrance: Via Slough 11+ NFER exam. Highly competitive – it's about five children trying for each place at 11 and about three for each sixth form place. School can afford to be highly selective – 'we're educating people who are going to be the bedrock of the community,' says head, citing the numbers of lawyers and doctors produced during her time there. The 2004 intake came from 67 primaries. For entry into year 12 students will need 5+ GCSEs at C+ for vocational subjects and 6+ good GCSEs at, at least, B in their A level subjects.

Exit: Most to study scientific or business courses. London, Brunel, City, Westminster or other local universities. Some to everywhere from Stirling to Southampton to read everything from languages to aerospace engineering, from history to drama. A few to Oxbridge.

Remarks: Impressive at all levels. Head's aim is 'to be better than we are'.

STANBRIDGE EARLS SCHOOL

Stanbridge Lane, Romsey, Hampshire, S051 0ZS

Tel: 01794 529 400

Fax: 01794 511 201

Email: admin@stanbridgeearls.co.uk

Website: www.stanbridgeearls.co.uk

• Pupils: 165 of whom 135 are boarders. 135 boys,30 girls

• Ages: 10-19 • Religion: Inter-denom

• School status: Independent • School gender: Mixed

• Day/boarding: Takes boarders

SEN provision

Detail:

Centre of excellence for:

Mild: DYSC; DYSL; DYSP; SpLD;
Moderate: DYSC; DYSL; DYSP; SpLD;
Severe: DYSC; DYSL; DYSP; SpLD;
Others: EAL; Sp&LD;

Now provide for in school:

Mild: ASP;
Moderate: ASP;
Others: SPD;

Experience of:

Mild: ADD; ADHD; EBD;
Moderate: MLD;
Others: ODD; TIC; Epi; Eat;

Summary: Stanbridge Earls School has 26 specialist staff who teach pupils one-to-one in addition to those who teach main curriculum subjects. Some of this teaching is small group work eg social and communication skills group work with Asperger's children. These specialists are fully qualified in their own areas within literacy Skills, maths skills, speech and communications skills, occupational therapy or English as a Second Language. All are based on the school campus which enables us to have a very flexible approach, particularly with those children who have complex learning difficulties. A large number of empathetic staff also enables Stanbridge Earls to be very supportive of those children who could not survive in a large school environment or who find the prospect of attending school at all too daunting. For further information see our website at www.stanbridgeearls.co.uk.

What we say about the school - the full Good Schools Guide review

Head: Since 2005, Mr Geoff Link MEd CertEd (fifties). Deputy head since 1997, his elevation has been universally acclaimed. Began his career at King's Wimbledon then wandered into Grenville College and discovered, wholly by happy mistake, the joy of working with children with SENs – 'it's so much more rewarding teaching children who have been written off.' Big, warm and obviously very nice. Emits gratifying rumbles of thunder in defence of his pupils – there's passion here, no doubt about it. Believes undimmably in 'the value of every child', sees the importance of equipping these boys and girls with social skills essential to self-reliance. Rejoices as much for the winners of best exam grades as for winners of the most meagre where they represent superhuman achievement. They've just had their best exam results for a long time but he despairs incandescently of league tables. Pupils say he made a big and immediate difference to the feel of the place, especially by taking an inflexible line with those whose behaviour mocks kindness. He's fair, they say, and the school is safer, happier, 'more relaxed' for it. Ex-England under-23 rugby player, thereafter Rosslyn Park. Two grown-up children. Enjoys walking and all things French.

Academic Matters: This is a CReSTeD category DU school, and whilst a mainstream curriculum is (more or less) followed and children take A levels, Stanbridge Earls has long had a good reputation for catering for specific learning difficulties. Learning support is offered to 160 out of 200 pupils in varying degrees, from supporting the 'fragile' pupil to help for many specific learning difficulties, including dyslexia, Asperger's, dyspraxia, dyscalculia, dysphasia and dysgraphia. Mrs Edwina Cole runs the remedial department with a large dedicated staff. Tiny classes, staff/pupil ratio of 1:6, max class size 12, but mostly eight or nine. Remedial classes are either for children withdrawn from class on a one-to-one basis, or for small groups; many subjects are also taught with a support teacher in class. An occupational and two speech therapists are on call and their time greatly over-subscribed; this is a school which treats the whole child. Impressive.

Seventy-eight pupils currently statemented, of whom 50 are paid for by their LEAs (often after Tribunal). GCSEs, A levels, NVQs, Certificates of Achievement are the norm though most take the exam at modular level. English lit, English lang, maths and science are the core curriculum subjects for GCSE. Ahead of time they have chosen to omit the obligatory foreign language – often a nightmare for the SpLD pupil. Courses are tailored to the child's interest and ability. They gladly embrace behaviour problems that derive from an SEN – from the low self-esteem which results from all that early years drubbing – but they draw the line at problems that display obduracy – there are vulnerable souls here who need space to grow. Stanbridge pupils exhibit all the jolly loquacity you expect from, especially, dyslexics and, they say, 'they develop quickly, behaviourally and emotionally, because they're so grateful and relieved to be here.' We saw this for ourselves – we were shown around by a boy declared unteachable and disruptive two years ago by his previous school. As sensitive and personable a fellow as you'd ever meet, he's just bagged a quiverful of A*s in his GCSEs.

Accelerated learning centre with an all female staff of 20 – 15 literacy specialists, 2 speech and language, 2 English as a second language and one occupational therapist (for dyspraxics). A busy, happy hub of a place, where to stand and chat is to be thoroughly in the way. There's a separate department, 7 strong, for numeracy skills – the only one of its kind. For lots of these pupils, here is where it happens. They like it. Most have regular one-to-one, and you can swap tutors on the rare occasions you don't get on with each other.

Tiny classes, most eight or nine, many fewer. Entry Level Certificates, GCSEs, A levels, NVQs and other vocational, creative and practical subjects – see their website. English, maths and science are the core curriculum subjects for GCSE. Courses are tailored to the child's interest and ability. The accent is on studying conventional academic subjects. Prep supervised in small groups and all assignments published so no one can 'forget'.

Pupils rave about the teachers. Many of these children are victims of that inability of mainstream schools to work with any but conventionally intelligent children, and endured misery before coming here. They say they are never, ever, treated dismissively or with impatience – quite the reverse, 'they simply can't do enough for you'. Observable also, and vital to the efficacy of the regenerative elixir, pupils are notably supportive of each other. Teachers irrigate them with praise. One pupil said 'I'm sure they've got one of those psychologist's reports in my file somewhere, and they may even refer to it sometimes, but the point is they know me as an individual and treat me as I am.' SENs here are addressed not clinically but holistically – emotionally, intellectually, physically and socially. You've got to say, it works. Teachers picked for quality of heart – 'they've got to give, give, give.' Very low turnover. 'If they still love it after a year, they stay forever.'

Performance table results dismal. This is because many take their exams a year late and are not counted because they are too old. In the year they were expected to take them they are counted as having got no exam passes – a real double whammy. Similar nonsense applies to A levels but not so detrimentally because fewer pupils. DfES value added score is skewed by this statistical mischiefmaking. (Should improve in the 2005 tables due to change of basis.) School say the Univ Durham MidYIS value-added scoring system shows Stanbridge is in the top 25 per cent.

Games, Options, The Arts: Usual collection of games on offer; excellent and well-used swimming pool, sports hall, plus riding, judo, archery etc. Forty different activities on offer after class – pupils must opt for five, of which three must be of a physical nature. D of E, leadership training, no CCF.

Home economics popular and fabric design. Drama strong, music good – on Tuesdays all the staff listen to any child who wants to perform anything, even if it's only a one-finger exercise on the piano. One of the ponds is well stocked for fishing, and a tributary to the River Test runs through the grounds. Art very strong and popular, CDT well supported; lots of successful entrants in all subjects at national competition level.

Background and Atmosphere: Founded in 1953 by refugees from the London world of creative arts as an 'alternative to the conventional public school'. Became renowned for its early recognition of specific learning difficulties. Charming, much altered sixteenth century manor house set in 50 acres of delightful parkland, with streams and ponds and mature trees. The campus has a spacious feel, the low rooflines abetting this. Just as well because, though the old is giving way to the creditable new, a lot of these buildings have a less than semi-permanent look to them. The pupils loyally say it's because the school spends its money on people not architecture, and they proudly showed us the WW2 theatre – ENSA would have been at home – and said, very fondly, 'This place sums the school up' – which, in many ways, it most agreeably does. This is not a rich school, but it is adequately resourced. The welcoming and helpful telephone receptionist deserves a beacon award in her own right.

Pastoral Care and Discipline: You move up a house year by year. They describe it as 'multi-layered', meaning you have a housemaster/mistress, plus the couple who are in charge of your living quarters. So easy are relationships here between staff and pupils that it's straightforward to find someone to talk to. They like to talk to the 'gappies' – the gap year students, too. Pupils call teachers 'Sir' and 'Miss.' Normal school rules apply: smoking = fines, drinking = breathalyser, counselling and gating as a last resort. Drugs testing, random after first offence. Pregnancy only ever among married staff. The atmosphere is very mainstream – prefects, etc. Blazers from year 9 on, own suit and tie for sixth formers.

Brilliant regime for years 7 and 8. They inhabit an anxiety-free zone of their own. Minimal organisational expectations of their short-term memories, so they only have to get themselves to class – everything they need is waiting for them. They go into meals first, in front, even, of the prefects. Once their self-esteem has begun to grow they are ready to embark on a gradient of responsibilities as they move up the school. Sixth formers notably self-reliant.

Most board and it works. They don't get out much, even the oldest, and they don't complain, and you wonder if they are learning enough about the beastliness of the world. It's a fine line the school must tread between putting them back together and pitching them out too soon. Around half the school in at weekends. Sixth form bar where staff drink, too – hugely approved of by the students. Food decidedly good.

Pupils and Parents: Growing number from abroad where SENs are apparently more believed in than acted on – small handfuls from France, Germany, Middle East, Far East, Africa, India. Predominantly English, countrywide catchment, with an equal number from state and independent schools. Guy 'Two Smoking Barrels' Ritchie was here.

Entrance: The interview's the thing. Ed psych report, of course, but they reckon the scores are often skewed by disinclination or despair – 'if we judged by the Wechsler scores we'd never let our best in.' They reckon IQs span 90-150. Main intake at year 7 with more in year 9 and then if places become available. Significant increase in year 10s kicked out of schools cravenly fearing for their league table places.

Exit: Around 40 per cent post-GCSE to sixth form colleges, though this number is falling because more than ever are staying on. Post-sixth form they go on to 'the conventional range of options'. They remind you – 'a SpLD simply occludes a conventional intelligence.'

Money Matters: 30 per cent of pupils funded by their LEAs (often after siege warfare and tribunal). Some bursaries and scholarships available.

Remarks: A parent sums it up nicely , 'if you'd told me when my son was nine that he'd get these GSCE results, I wouldn't have believed you.' To its long track record of expertise, Stanbridge brings a quality of rigorous kindness, and it's this that makes all the difference.

Stewart's Melville College

Queensferry Road, Edinburgh, EH4 3EZ

Tel: 0131 311 1000
Fax: 0131 311 1099
Email: principal@esmgc.com
Website: www.esms.edin.sch.uk

• Pupils: (SMC) 715 boys (almost all day) (MES) 705 girls (almost all day) • Ages: 11-18 • Religion: Non-denom • Fees: Day £2,643; boarding £5,015 • School status: Independent • Opendays: Late September • School gender: Boys • Day/boarding: Takes boarders

SEN provision

Detail:

Now provide for in school:
- Mild: DYSL;
- Moderate: DYSL;
- Others: EAL;

Experience of:
- Mild: ASP; ADD; ADHD; DYSC; DYSP; HI; VI; CP;
- Severe: DYSL;
- Others: OCD; Sp&LD; DEL;

Summary: We offer Support for Learning, both in class and in small extracted groups. In the first year some pupils are given the option to do one modern language instead of two, allowing support to be delivered instead.

What we say about the school - the full Good Schools Guide review

Principal: Since 2000, Mr David Gray BA PGCE (forties), who was educated at Fettes, read English and modern Greek at Bristol, where he did his PGCE. Taught English in a Bristol comprehensive before moving to Greece to run a language school, after which he became head of English at Leeds Grammar. Mr Gray comes to this vast conglomerate from Pocklington School in east Yorkshire, where he was head for eight years. Brought up in Inverness, he is proud of his Scottish roots and is 'keen to give something back to Scotland, having been away for almost a quarter of a century' – (his father is the wonderful, long-standing, former Conservative MP, now Lord Gray of Contin). Married, he has twin daughters and a younger son. He and his wife live on campus and she is actively 'attempting to make the place like a large family', including entertaining members of staff for dinner (an activity which has not apparently met with universal acclaim). Mr Gray himself spends part of the week in each school. We visited him at his base in Mary Erskine, where there is a strict policy of no coke vending machines; this editor was amused therefore, to see an empty crumpled coke can on the principal's desk when we arrived.

Very much a hands-on head, the principal reckons to keep sane by swimming and jogging at 7am each morning, and is a familiar sight as he cycles between the two campuses. He also 'works the room' quite beautifully, 'we all think we know him well and that he knows our children almost as well as we do,' said one father (a gift no doubt inherited from his politician father?). Keen on promoting self-confidence in his pupils, he sees himself as an 'educator'; 'no man is an island'; interdependence is important here. Mr Gray also admitted that, in a better world, he would prefer 'his pupils not to party during term time' – some hope – and maintains that 'only eleven children have been expelled for drugs offences in Scotland during the past academic year' – it is, apparently all a 'press hype'. (Head says 'we have a Personal and Social Education policy which is important in encouraging well-informed young people to make wise judgements'.)

Pupils slightly dismissive about the new regime, 'he has tightened up on our shoes and our clothes but not a lot else'. All staff wear the school badge – post Dunblane – and yet again, this editor was charmingly challenged by a pupil.

Mr Gray runs the twin senior schools with two deputy heads, and the head of the co-ed junior school, Bryan Lewis, who is also vice-principal. Mrs Lesley Douglas took over as deputy head of The Mary Erskine School in August 2002; she was previously assistant rector at The High School of Glasgow and her predecessor, Mrs Norma Rolls, moves to front up the massive new five-year ICT development programme as co-ordinator and director.

Academic Matters: Boys and girls educated together at junior school, separately from age 12-17, then combine again for the last year at school. 'Not a highly selective school', however described by an educationalist as a 'grade one academic machine'. Classes of up to 25 (20 for practical classes) setted, groups subdivided to extend the most able. School has embraced the new

Advanced Higher in depth – greater analysis, independent study, projects and dissertation and recent results show a pleasing number of As and Bs across the board in both schools. 'The Mary Erskine results are outstanding' said the principal, 'particularly on the languages front'. French, German and Spanish on offer to Higher Grade but Spanish is not available at Advanced Higher. Latin and Greek on offer, if demand high enough.

From August 2002, Standard Grades phased out in favour of Intermediate 2 (which is based primarily on unit assessments, as are Highers) except in the modern languages and maths departments. Stirring stuff this. Very good links (still) with the Merchant Company who do masses of business breakfasts and links with professional firms around Edinburgh. New IT multiplex in the pipeline, to be fronted up by Mrs Rolls. Biology dept strong links with the horticultural dept of the world famous Edinburgh Botanic Gardens. Impressive careers structure across both schools and excellent library facilities. Pupils can sign in for private study and technology is taken at GCSE level rather than following the Scottish norm.

Schools combine for sixth form, most extras, and pastoral structure – ie you might find one girl doing science at Stewart's Melville and seven boys doing RE at Mary Erskine's. With such a large sixth form, the variety of course permutations is almost limitless, though, as our informant muttered, 'the amount of free time you can wangle by saying you are taking the bus up the road is equally limitless'. Outstanding back-up for those with learning difficulties, school has its own educational psychologist; 'some on Ritalin'; 'will never abandon anyone'.

Games, Options, The Arts: Girls still better at shooting than boys and both sexes join the voluntary CCF (trillions of girls, over 400 members in all) – and at a recent camp in Scotland, produced more candidates than the rest of the schools put together. Super new floodlit astroturf. Twenty-seven rugby teams; swimming pool (at Stewart's Melville) with dramatic sixth form slump-out room adjacent, new gym (at MES), cricket pavilion (MES again). FPs and current pupils share sporting facilities at MES; mutterings about needing more – but one of the play areas at SMC is about to be developed into a new performing arts centre. Extra games pitches at Inverleith. Needle matches in almost all disciplines; with FPs representing both county and country across the board. Stunning swimming pool adjacent to dining room complex with sixth form centre above for better viewing the SMC pitches.

Incredibly strong drama (regular performances at the Edinburgh Festival and throughout the year – Sir Cameron Mackintosh much in evidence). 600 pupils were involved in Noye's Fludde – (super video) and, more recently, 80 pupils from the junior school took part in Joseph and the ATD at the Edinburgh Festival theatre. Masses of orchestras in every discipline. Pupils can learn to fly, ski (Hillend and the real thing: the Alps, Canada); brilliant debating team (regularly the Scottish Debating Champions, European Youth Parliament finalists) and SMC has represented Great Britain abroad all over the shop. Masses of clubs, for all, lunchtime and post school. Popular. Good home economics. Arts spectacular. Dramatic art room atop MES (with adjoining pottery and greenhouse), and art displayed all over.

Background and Atmosphere: Stewart's Melville campus is based round the magnificent David Rhind-designed Daniel Stewart's Hospital which opened in 1885 and merged with Melville College in 1972. Fabulous Victorian Gothic with a cluster of moderately successful modern additions, surrounded by ever-decreasing games pitches and car parks. Huge and impressive school hall. The old chapel is now a library complete with organ and stained-glass windows. Stewart's Melville is also home to the senior department of the junior school – see separate entry.

Mary Erskine was founded in 1694 (originally the Merchant Maiden Hospital) moved to Ravelston House in 1966, changing its name to The Mary Erskine School, and amalgamated with the boys' school in 1978. (Girls wear charming Mary Erskine tartan skirts, with matching Alice bands.) MES clusters in decidedly 1960s architecture – with, now, quite a lot of more modern extensions, round the charming (1791) Ravelston House: swimming pool, tennis courts, games pitches, astroturf etc. The last much used by FPs. The nursery department and the youngest classes of the junior school are also based here – see separate entry.

Two boarding houses, Dean Park House and Erskine House, furnished like large family houses and based on the edge of the Stewart's Melville campus. Tremendous family feel, boarders are encouraged to invite friends home, caring house parents. No more than 50 boarding places. Lockers for all woefully inadequate in both schools, and piles of bags everywhere. The tarmac outside both schools is hideously covered in blobs of discarded chewing gum, particularly in front of the sixth form centre at Stewart's Melville. School disputes this.

Regular buses from East and West Lothian and Fife service both schools, which operate as one, under the auspices of Erskine Stewart's Melville Governing Council. Each school, however, is fiercely proud of its individual heritage.

Pastoral Care and Discipline: Both schools have a tutorial system for the first year, followed by house system in Upper Schools which is common to both. Good links with parents. Brief is that 'all children have a right to be happy here'. Excellent anti-bullying policy, keen on 'children not slipping through the net'. Sophisticated PSE programme right up the school, including study skills. Buddy system for those coming up from junior schools. Automatic expulsion for those bringing in illicit substances – 'those on the periphery of the same incident will not necessarily be excluded but can come back in as long as they agree to random testing'. This is a policy that the principal has applied in the past, and no one has yet tested positive. Though 'each case is judged on its merits'. Fags 'unacceptable and pupils suspended'. Booze 'not an issue in school'.

Pupils and Parents: Edinburgh hotch-potch of New Town and suburbs, with many first-time buyers and lots up from England. Siblings and FPs' children. Less elitist and perhaps less dusty than some Edinburgh schools. Children living far out can spend the night when doing evening activities. Pupils 'relaxed and happy, friendly and responsible' to quote school inspector. Parent teacher group ('the red socks brigade') slightly better organised into a Friends of the School group, fund-raising, ceilidhs, 'good cash cow'.

Entrance: At 11,12, 13 or sixth form – otherwise 'by default'. Automatic from junior school. Entrance assessments held in January but can be arranged at any time. Waiting lists for some stages but just go on trying. Entrance to upper school is by interview, plus school report plus GCSEs/Standard grades (five credit passes for fifth form entry.) Numbers up, 'the number sitting our entrance exam has increased by 100 per cent in three years,' says the deputy head of Stewart's Melville. Whilst Mary Erskine's is 'buoyant, absolutely full'.

Exit: Some leakage after Standard Grades, 12 left after Highers last year, most sixth year (95 per cent) go on to university (few gap years, though growing in popularity), most opt for Scottish unis (30 per cent go south). SATS (the requirement for American Colleges) not a problem. Art college, music/drama are popular alternatives.

Money Matters: Scholarships/bursaries available, some linked to the Merchant Company, others sibling directed. 'No child will be left wanting in a (financial) crisis.'

Remarks: An outstanding school, happily focused.

STONAR SCHOOL

Cottles Park, Atworth, Melksham, Wiltshire, SN12 8NT

Tel: 01225 701 740

Fax: 01225 790 830

Email: k.ibbott@stonarschool.com

Website: www.stonarschool.com

• Pupils: 400 girls; 200 board, 200 day • Ages: 2-18 • Religion: Christian, non-denom • Fees: Senior boarding £5,550, junior boarding £4,750; day £1,600-£3,125 • School status: Independent • Opendays: November • School gender: Girls • Day/boarding: Takes boarders

---

SEN provision

Detail:

Centre of excellence for:
- Mild: DYSL;
- Moderate: DYSL;

Now provide for in school:
- Mild: ADD; DYSC; DYSP; VI;
- Moderate: MLD;
- Severe: VI;
- Others: OCD; EAL; Epi; Eat;

Experience of:
- Mild: ASP; ADHD; EBD; HI;
- Moderate: DYSP; HI; VI;
- Severe: DYSL;
- Others: Sp&LD;

What we say about the school - the full Good Schools Guide review

Head: From 2006, Mrs Shirley Shayler MA BSc(Hons). Formerly deputy head of Taunton School. She follows Mrs Claire Osborne, head since 2002, who left to become head of Rockport School in Ireland.

Academic Matters: Biology, psychology, English strong overall, also history and geography as well as geology; mod langs popular, with Chinese, Japanese as well as the trad French, German and Spanish; maths strong, as are physics and chemistry at A level. New head of drama from September 2004. Stonar is very proud to count Romola Garai as an ex-pupil. Theatre studies results pathetic at A level but unsurprisingly stronger are art, music, photography, home economics and PE. Much better showing across the board at GCSE. Trad teaching, staff mainly female, but with several senior chaps. Encouragement freely given. No problems with dyslexia, SEN teachers for both one-to-one and withdrawn from class.

Games, Options, The Arts: Super stabling for over 60 horses – 'better than the dorms' according to a mother – good sized covered indoor riding school and a mini Badminton cross-country course. Local pony clubs rent the facilities for camps etc. Famous for holding British Inter-schools One Day Event each year – and, not surprisingly, Stonar girls do extremely well in this. Currently about 150 riders in the school. Top-level riders do BHSAI (horsy qualification). Sports are taken seriously, one or two stars currently in the school, several county hockey and netball players. Fitness centre, sports hall, swimming pool, astroturf. Lively art and music does well – more play instruments than ride. Dead keen drama, with lots of productions. Imaginative on outings and trips – going as far as New Zealand, South Africa, Canada, USA.

Background and Atmosphere: Elegant Strawberry Hill Gothic house (once the home of the Fuller family), at odds with a motley collection of modern outbuildings; prep school on site (most girls move on to the senior school); separate sixth form house. Good new sixth form study centre. No five star accommodation here but comfortable enough. All dorms have been recently refurbished. Dining hall where each girl must wipe her place clean. Lots of computers – games no longer allowed on them. Girls can help with tinies in the nursery but no official qualification (Norland Nanny College just down the road). New science laboratories in November 2003. Brand new nursery opened in 2002. Parental grouses reach us that there is not enough emphasis on reading – disputed by school. Not overly tidy – relaxed, gentle, cosy. Horse boxes fill the drive at start and end of term.

Pastoral Care and Discipline: Not a problem. Lively school council consisting of girls of all ages and staff. All staff are watchful, a key part of school policy. Non-teaching house staff, 'so they are fresh at the end of the day'.

Pupils and Parents: Mutually supportive friendly girls at ease with themselves and their teachers. Around 30 children from overseas, Europeans and Far Easterners. Londoners, locals and Home Counties' girls. 180 boarders. New green and white tartan uniform popular with girls.

Entrance: Girls have to sit the entrance examinations held in January. Limited spaces for girls with special needs.

Exit: About 80 per cent go on to take degrees – London, Nottingham, lesser lights. Several follow equine careers, some to art college.

Money Matters: Scholarships at 11, 13 and 16, including for music, art, drama, sport and riding. Services bursaries available.

Remarks: Just the place to send your pony-mad daughter, where she will emerge pleasantly confident and probably with some decent exam results too. Needs now to settle down under the new head after an interregnum and a head who did not work out.

STONYHURST COLLEGE

Stonyhurst, Clitheroe, Lancashire, BB7 9PZ

Tel: 01254 827 073

Fax: 01254 827 135

Email: admissions@stonyhurst.ac.uk

Website: www.stonyhurst.ac.uk

• Pupils: 438: 305 boys, 113 girls; 281 full boarders
• Ages: 13-18 • Religion: RC but enquiries welcome from other Christian denominations • Fees: Boarding £7,101; weekly boarding £6,075; day £4,152
• School status: Independent • Opendays: Early November
• School gender: Mixed • Day/boarding: Takes boarders

SEN provision

Detail:

Centre of excellence for:

Mild: DYSL; DYSP;
Moderate: DYSL; DYSP;
Severe: DYSL;
Others: EAL;

Now provide for in school:

Mild: ASP; ADD; ADHD; EBD; DYSC; SpLD; HI; VI; CP;

Moderate: ASP; ADD; ADHD; MLD; DYSC; SpLD; HI; VI;

Severe: DYSP;

Others: DEL; Epi; PD; Eat;

Experience of:

Mild: AUT;

Summary: We have about 65 pupils here at Stonyhurst who have SEN. The majority have mainly various degrees of dyslexia. A few are dyspraxic, a couple have Asperger's and most of them cope very well in normal classes and take a range of GCSE subjects. They are 'setted' in some areas, not in others, and the sets are relatively small; some have as few as five pupils. 'Curriculum support' is delivered through small groups of pupils who usually drop one or more subjects and have lessons with the SENCo instead. If their English is weak, then they are put in her set for that subject too. They all take English Language and Literature GCSE and most of them gain B or C grades. If they are particularly intelligent and can cope in higher sets then they are encouraged to do so and they are just monitored by the SENCo. We have some in-class support but only from our Gap Students. We have no 'statemented' pupils at the present time as all our pupils are assessed privately.

What we say about the school - the full Good Schools Guide review

Head: Adrian Aylward MA (mid forties), appointed as the second lay headmaster in 1996. Educated at Worth and Oxford, where he read literae humaniores. Spent ten years in the City and industry becoming MD of a plc before entering education. His passion is philosophy and theology, the latter he teaches when he can. He is articulate, engaging and open minded, describing himself as a family man but admits to enjoying fishing when three young children permit. His wife joins in school life and 'recruits in local supermarkets!' He seeks to strengthen the clear vision of education set by the Jesuits and sees the school as a community but highly values the individual.

Departing in July 2006.

Academic Matters: Broad curriculum including astronomy (up to GCSE if demand) – own observatory for this. Average class size 17, 10 in the sixth form. Some setting. RE compulsory to GCSE, thereafter theology. Pupils are assigned a personal tutor whom they meet twice weekly to discuss progress. Broad ability intake and thus not the academic powerhouse of city day schools but a genuine wish for each pupil to fulfil their potential. Head did not publish results for league tables – 'it undermines the value of the individual'. Average results over a three-year period show 42 per cent A* and A at GCSE, 59 per cent A and B grades at A level. Maths consistently popular at A level achieving good results. 10 per cent of pupils have special needs and receive extra help – majority of these are dyslexic. Plenty of computers around linked up to the school's intranet and all pupils have their own e-mail address. Pupils do 'a quick GCSE in IT' at 13 years. Terminals in sixth form study bedrooms.

Games, Options, The Arts: A 'sport for all' policy. Compulsory sport throughout the school achieving notable success in rugby, golf, hockey and netball. Super indoor swimming pool and new all-weather pitch, the latter used by athletes training during the 2002 Commonwealth Games. School is divided vertically into four 'lines' for sporting competitions. Music is highly valued. Free instrumental tuition on an orchestral instrument is available to all pupils and maintained if satisfactory progress is made. Three pupils were recently selected for the Halle youth orchestra. The school is the proud owner of a Steinway, Bosendorfer and Bechstein and other facilities include a keyboard lab and practice rooms looking like mini greenhouses. Good DT department with plenty of scope for those artistically inclined. Outdoor pursuits in abundance – fishing, canoeing, sailing, fell walking, clay pigeon shooting etc. Further afield pupils participate in world challenge trips, this year to Peru, pilgrimages to Lourdes, D of E expeditions, to name but a few. In the second year the cadet corps is compulsory.

Background and Atmosphere: Founded by the Jesuits at St Omer in what is now northern France for English families forced to pursue a Catholic education abroad. After a succession of moves the school was given refuge at its present site in the Catholic part of Lancashire by Thomas Weld, who later donated the property to the school. The magnificent buildings are set in a 2,000-acre estate, most of which is farmed. 'I arrive each morning and cannot believe that this is my school,' comments one pupil. Each year group is termed a 'playroom' with its own common room and boarding facilities, cared for by a married couple. The girls have separate accommodation and are looked after by a housemistress. Recent developments include a magnificently refurbished and equipped library and study centre in the heart of the school and years 9 and 10 boys' dormitories have been transformed. Other parts of the school are truly splendid; huge staircases, wood panelling, polished stone, works of art, brimming with history and tradition. Some formerly hidden treasures are now exhibited in a millennium display for all to enjoy. Shared boarding accommodation (4-5 per room), lower down the school, makes way for smart study bedrooms for the sixth formers. This is essentially a full-time boarding school, 'no mass exodus at weekends' but exeats are readily approved according to pupils. Sunday afternoon appreciated by some as their only free time to do as they please, as much of the weekend is consumed by prep, excursions and church. Religion is taken seriously but is not oppressive. Now co-ed and feels as if it has always been so. Girls' have improved communication at all levels,' says head, as well as 'making the school a more cheerful place'.

Pastoral Care and Discipline: A Family Handbook sets out clear expectations of conduct and behaviour. Cases of bullying are dealt with by playroom staff and general policing by the pupil-run playroom committees. A few suspensions in the past for drug offences but 'not a drugs school'. Discipline not a major problem. The Jesuit school chaplain is singled out for special praise by pupils. Being a former pupil, but widely travelled in the interim, he is highly valued for his pastoral care and general availability.

Pupils and Parents: 'Broad mix,' comments head. More socially mixed than equivalent schools – being in Catholic Lancashire. Catholics make up 70 per cent of the total. Southern parents cite one reason for their choice being the school's lack of consumerism and the social competitiveness of some southern schools. Rich mix of accents – regional and international (25 per cent pupils are non-Brits). International links are highly valued and there has 'never been a problem with racism,' comments head. Confident, articulate and mature pupils praise the community feel of the school, which is enhanced by the playroom system. 'Looking at the whole picture,' comments one pupil, 'the school works extremely well.' Day pupils are encouraged to stay after school for studies and activities – a facility valued by parents – and may feel left out if they choose not to do so. Head disagrees, pointing out that the head boy was a day pupil for four years. Alumni include twelve martyrs, seven VCs, also Arthur Conan Doyle, Charles Laughton, General Walters, Paul Johnson, Peter Moorhouse, Bishop Hollis, Bishop Hines, Charles Sturridge, Hugh Woolridge, Jonathon Plowright, Bill Cash MP, Bruce Kent, Mark Thompson, Lords Chitnis and Talbot, Kyran Bracken and Robert Brinkley.

Entrance: From own prep (St Mary's Hall), St John's Beaumont and a variety of other schools, both here and abroad. Broad ability intake – 'for some, 6 GCSEs will be an achievement,' comments head. Academic entrance exam but other factors taken into account, particularly family connections with the school. Six GCSE passes, plus interview, for entry into sixth form. Those unable to attend for interview eg overseas pupils, write a 500 word essay explaining why they wish to come to Stonyhurst.

Exit: All over. London popular. Numbers vary to Oxbridge, but average 10 per cent over recent years. 2004 saw 10 per cent enter medical school. Art foundation, management and business courses currently look popular. Plenty of international links and scope for travel through the Jesuit community with many students taking a gap year.

Money Matters: A variety of scholarships; academic, music and art and design to a maximum of 50 per cent of fees. Some bursaries are available up to 50 per cent of fees for those in need.

Remarks: Distinguished Jesuit boarding school, steeped in history and set in beautiful surroundings, now comfortably co-ed and at capacity. A genuine concern for the individual pervades.

STOWE SCHOOL

Stowe, Buckingham, Buckinghamshire, MK18 5EH

Tel: 01280 818 323/ 818 205
Fax: 01280 818 181
Email: admissions@stowe.co.uk
Website: www.stowe.co.uk

• Pupils: 615; co-ed from 2005: 23 girls starting in the Lower School, 98 girls in sixth form. 65 day pupils, rest full-time boarders • Ages: 13-18 • Religion: C of E • Fees: Day £5,665; boarding £7,660 • School status: Independent • Opendays: Minimum 2 per term, see website. Individual visits welcomed • School gender: Mixed • Day/boarding: Takes boarders

SEN provision

Detail:
Now provide for in school:
 Mild: DYSL;
 Moderate: MLD; DYSL;
 Severe: DYSL;
 Others: EAL;
Experience of:
 Mild: ADD; ADHD; DYSC; DYSP; HI; VI;
 Moderate: ADD; DYSP;
 Severe: DYSP;
 Others: TIC; Sp&LD; Epi; Eat;

Summary: The Skills Development Centre at Stowe exists primarily to give help and support to pupils with different learning abilities, in order to help them fulfil their academic potential. Our aim is that those who have special needs should both be understood and supported, while at the same time taught to cope with and overcome their difficulties. Special help is provided within the department and close liaison maintained with the teaching staff as a whole, since all pupils are expected to remain integrated in the mainstream curriculum.

What we say about the school - the full Good Schools Guide review

Head: Since 2003, Dr Anthony Wallersteiner MA PhD (early forties), the youngest head since the legendary J F Roxburgh. Educated at King's School, Canterbury, history scholar at Trinity, Cambridge, he read history and theory of art at Kent. Dr Wallersteiner comes to Stowe from Tonbridge where he had been a housemaster, head of history and ran Oxbridge entrance; taught at St Paul's and Sherborne before that. An academic, 'unashamedly academic' he says, with a focus on raising academic standards. Stowe has finally got the head it so richly deserves, 'I want to put back the academic core, it has been missing for a while'. 'Some staff could set tougher targets' he comments, 'we need to stretch the more able'.

An open door head, Dr Wallersteiner has a cupboard full of birthday presents for pupils, hosts the head's essay society and teaches VisEd (aka visual education: an instant architectural gallop round the house and grounds) to third formers 'as much to teach myself as to get to know the boys', and history to GCSE pupils. Loves teaching, 'I don't want to develop a bunker mentality' and has promptly (with the full support of the governors) turned the previous head's building programme upside down, concentrating on art, music, drama and sports facilities.

The main building itself has been shaken (not stirred) and made to work for its living. The original library 'in the heart of the school' previously used for rather grand meetings and debates has become very much a focal point, full of desks, plasma screens and computers, the middle doors flung open, and humming with young. 'More than twice as many books taken out as this time last year' said the librarian, 'and particularly busy during the evenings and at lunchtime'. Stowe is going fully co-ed, with the first intake of junior girls in 2005. The two third formers who joined in 2004, trialling the place, were pleased as punch with the experience. Dr Wallersteiner is married to Valerie, and they have three children, two girls and a boy, currently 'up the road' at Winchester House.

Academic Matters: 'We will continue to draw out pupils from a broad academic spectrum' said Dr Wallersteiner as he raised the CE pass mark to 50 per cent. Wide range of academic abilities, streaming in all disciplines. A level and GCSE results well below what they should be – this, as we said above, is the focus of Dr Wallersteiner's attention. Four langs on offer: French, German, Spanish and Italian. Geography, design tech and production design, economics and fine art results stand tall among the weeds.

Sciences are relatively unpopular and unsuccessful – particularly strange as we sat through the note-taking session of a chemistry class, with reactive whiteboards (fascinating, you change the programme by dragging your finger along the screen) and 'fools' chemistry programmes' replicating the various experiments performed in class, online in every house, there should be no reason for uninspiring marks. The teaching tools are in place: whiteboards, smartboards, you name it – this is a school geared up to help pupils learn, regular drop in clinics between 5.30 and 6, with 'different teachers on different days' in most subjects where pupils can (officially) get one-to-one tuition. 'Trouble is', said one pupil 'the staff in charge either make you feel a bit stupid, or the ones you really want to talk to are doing something more important'.

Maths, sciences and English assignments are 'usually OK' online, though some staff 'do want hard copy'. School has wired up (neatly encased in square plastic tubing in the posh bits of the house) all over the main school and in the houses, and has a popular laptop purchase scheme. European (computer) driving licence for all, including staff (Latest results: Complete ECDL passes (7 modules): 8 passes by students – 2 passes by staff) Now piloting a new BCS (British Computer Society) course with a 4th form group. Three-week orders (assessments/progress reports etc). Artist in Residence and regular visiting speakers and seminars on a range of subjects.

The skills development centre gives help to pupils with mild to moderate learning difficulties and/or specific needs. All pupils remain integrated in the mainstream curriculum. However, while the specialist teachers in the centre are qualified and able to help with mild to moderate dyslexic and dyspraxic difficulties, they are not able to deal with severe learning difficulties and their associated behavioural and social problems.

Games, Options, The Arts: Art, sports science, and various design technology disciplines all did well at A level with almost half the A level art candidates getting A, and stunning work on the stairs of the art room, but gosh why have four separate classes teaching four different ages the same boring drawing technique at the same time? Some ultra enthusiastic staff, and artists in residence, 3D, ceramics, colour exploration and etching with copper sulphate all on offer. Schemes of co-operation with Alexander Talbot Rice to turn the proposed new art block into an art academy are in the pipeline, and Stoics past and present staged a fundraising art exhibition at Christies in 2004. Head has visions of a Yehudi Menuhin template for the new art centre, turning the school into a centre of excellence with classical training as well as modern forms of painting, drawing, sculpture, graphic arts, etc.

Drama and music poor relations in comparison, though this is improving. School says 'Congreve performances are regarded as training ground for RADA, The Guildhall or the Old Vic.'

Sport is important at Stowe, all the trad games as you might expect, rugby and cricket particularly strong with three U18 England cricket players. Girls proud of their hockey prowess. Plus fives (court due for re-vamp), athletics (track due for a re-vamp), polo popular, ditto rowing; one of the few schools to boast its own pack of beagles, about 30 pupils follow each week and much of the husbandry is done by pupils. The beagles are being kept, following the hunting ban, and are being re-trained for drag-hunting. Terrific number of options, fly fishing, martial arts and clay pigeon shooting, but sewing machines, creative textiles and dress design for all.

Thriving evangelical Christian union, D of E, pupils complain 'there are almost too many options available' music rooms, art studios are all open at weekends, and 'if we want to encourage a new activity all we have to do is persuade a member of staff'.

Background and Atmosphere: School founded in 1923. Stowe, home of the Dukes of Buckingham and Chandos, has been described as 'one of the most majestic English houses of the eighteenth century' and has recently undergone (and is still undergoing) a very serious restoration.

Mind boggling millions from Heritage Lottery funding, the fabric of the buildings are now owned by the Stowe House Preservation Trust, the 750 acres of Capability Brown designed grounds and gardens having been long given to The National Trust. During our first visit it was umbrellas in the dining room and buckets in the attic, now the place is let for weddings and bar mitzvahs and open to the public in the holidays. It was also used (as were the pupils) in the last James Bond movie. Slightly strange red carpets adorn the portrait strewn entrance hall, family pics abound, and the head's study, aka the gothic library, is a gem.

Vanbrugh, James Gibbs, William Kent and Robert Adams all had a hand in the main building and would be turning in their collective graves at some of the sixties classroom blocks. Two houses in main block much more convenient and romantic, but not quite so user-friendly, certain amount of work-space reorganisation so that boys no longer have to share cross-year common rooms. Boarding being gradually refurbished. All eat in main house, two dining rooms in action, architectural gems, pupils say 'lunch and breakfast OK salad bars and jacket potatoes, but supper pretty boring'.

Pastoral Care and Discipline: PSHE with tutors, head has clamped down quite hard on discipline and school is no longer the choice for kids bombed out of other schools, though there's a fair amount of wickedness still. Out for drugs (Augean stables syndrome not-withstanding) and out for 'continuous smoking', boozing or bullying. Prefects say they are the first line of defence on the bullying front 'but really there isn't that much around'. But housemasters/mistresses, matrons and tutors are all on call. Petty punishments are a thing of the past and are replaced by those designed to the fit the offence: litter patrol, working in the grounds, etc. Out also if pupils 'are not trying and continuously getting into trouble' but not out, say their peers 'if they are trying and making an effort'. Around 60 day boys and girls, but full boarding encouraged no flexi- or weekly on offer.

Pupils and Parents: An eclectic mix, some quite grand with other children at Eton or Winchester, and some first time buyers who occasionally appear a trifle surprised by their choice. The young gel well, 'absolutely friends for life', work together, play together, shoot together. Traditionally a school that fed the army stream, now in the maverick production game. New uniform: blue tweed blazers with gold lining, with grey trousers for the boys and short grey skirts for the girls (or visa versa if they appeal to the Equal Opportunities Commission). Dark suits of the girls' own choice (trouser or skirt) in the sixth form. Around 10 per cent from real abroad and about the same expats, a fair number from Scotland, ditto London. Exeat weekends occur mid-term. There is a strict alcohol policy, and housemasters have been issued with breathalysers – so we'll see no more Stoics paralytic in the Kings Road? Fiercely loyal old boys include Richard Branson, George Melly, Sir Peregrine Worsthorne, Lord Sainsbury and a clutch of guitarists/rock musicians/property developers. Amongst those who are no longer with us Sir Leonard Cheshire, David Niven.

Entrance: Common Entrance now 50 per cent, own exam for those from the state sector or ill-prepared and from abroad. Still seen as an excellent bet if you fail to make the grade for Eton. Places competitive for girls, though the odd place still available at odd moments. Waiting lists looming. The Dragon, Papplewick, Haileybury, Cheam all send representatives. Standard A/Bs for both girls and boys joining at sixth form level.

Exit: Occasional creature to Oxbridge (4 last year, but still too few in the head's view); otherwise around 97 per cent to uni: Edinburgh, Newcastle, Bristol and Durham all well represented, plus the odd Cirencester candidate, a number to gap year and then decide.

Money Matters: Expensive, but by no means heading the queue. Two main appeals currently: The Stowe House Preservation Trust, which is more or less up to scratch and The Stowe School Foundation which will be funding the new music school complex and increasing the scholarship and bursarial fund which is currently trailing at nearly a million quid a year. Huge numbers of bursaries, scholarships in almost every discipline, art, music, sport, academia, plus a Stowe/Harvard foundation.

Remarks: As we said last time: back in fashion once more, it's a complete winner for turning out confident young things with enough self-belief to reach great heights. With the added advantage of an academic leader who has tackled the boozing druggy culture that was prevalent head on and makes no bones about his aim for excellence in all things. We look forward to reporting slightly sharper exam success, though hopefully without loosing any of the inherent charm.

Stowford College

95 Brighton Road, Sutton, Surrey, SM2 5SJ

Tel: 020 8661 9444

Fax: 020 8661 6136

Email: stowfordsch@btinternet.com

Website: www.stowford.com

• Pupils: 100 boys and girls, all day • Ages: 6-16

• Religion: Christian non-denom

• Fees: Prep/junior £2,175-£2,255; Senior £2,265-£2,595

• School status: Independent • Opendays: November, January, February, April and May • School gender: Mixed

• Day/boarding: Day pupils

SEN provision

Detail:

Centre of excellence for:

Mild: DYSL;

Moderate: DYSL;
Others: EAL;
Now provide for in school:
Mild: DYSC; DYSP;
Others: DEL;
Experience of:
Mild: ASP;

Summary: The Senior school aims to integrate dyslexic students in a mainstream classroom where this would be beneficial to their progress. The junior department provides an intensive multi-sensory programme delivered in a small class environment.

A structured dyslexia programme is available thoughout the school using multi-sensory methods co-ordinated by the school's Director who is a trained dyslexia teacher.

Dyslexic pupils are taught English and (maths up to Year 9) with a trained dyslexia teacher in a class setting. Individual maths tutoring is also available for dyslexic pupils.

In addition a team of qualified dyslexia tutors offer individual teaching support to senior pupils on request to improve specific areas of weakness such as spelling. Students who request a tutor are withdrawn from class for 35 minute lessons and usually have 1-2 lessons per week.

What we say about the school - the full Good Schools Guide review

Head: Since 1995, Mr Richard Shakespeare (fifties), principal of Stowford as well as history and business studies teacher together with his wife, Janet, as the proprietor and teacher of specific learning difficulties. Mr S started out as deputy for Mr Hennessey (the school's founder) and went on to purchase the school with his wife in 1995. A charming, friendly man – always with a smile on his face. 'You can always hear his voice down the corridors' comments a pupil, 'we all really like him'. Mrs S is the first point of contact for first-time parents. She is also welcoming, and friendly. The couple aim to instil a family feeling into the school, something parents feel has been successfully achieved. 'They understand what a parent of a child with learning difficulties goes through,' said one parent.

Academic Matters: Although the school does not just take pupils with special needs, almost all in the junior department and half of the senior pupils have SEN provision. Accredited by CReSTeD, and thoroughly inspected by them every three years. Children are taught according to their ability: those in years 3 and 4 are combined into one class, years 5 and 6 are in two classes divided according to their need for SEN provision. Senior classes are larger, ranging from 22 in year 9 to 13 in year 10.

A multi-sensory dyslexia programme is offered throughout the school; dyspraxia exercise programmes are on hand for those who need them as well as 'brain gym' and mind stimulation lessons. As pupils move on to the senior section they are offered subjects such as thinking skills, personal development and computer skills. To the dismay of some pupils, though, design and technology is not offered beyond year 9. Most classrooms are equipped with computers and there's a somewhat outdated IT suite. Art room, science labs and classrooms are buzzing – pupils have happy smiley faces! 'No one is an odd one out here. They are all in the same boat and don't feel they are a black sheep' commented a satisfied parent.

GCSE results are rising year by year. All get five or more grades A*-G; 30 per cent plus get their five A*-C grades (though of those 75 per cent are girls). Subjects vary from art to English language and literature, languages (German and French offered from the junior section onwards), drama, history and many more.

Games, Options, The Arts: Facilities at the school need some updating. Hockey, rugby, table tennis, athletics, swimming etc. Playground not very spacious, but five nearby football pitches and a junior playing field are at the school's disposal, plus on-site tennis and badminton courts. Impressive plays: several merit awards at ISA drama competitions. Walls are covered with colourful and expressive art.

Background and Atmosphere: Founded in 1975, the main school house is set in two acres of mature, landscaped gardens together with a playground, lawns and woodlands. Parking a little difficult, which is to be expected in a 'town' school. Mr S is very proud of the family atmosphere that engulfs the school. A quiet, orderly and calm environment seems to encourage every pupil to be him/herself and feel part of a large family. Clubs on offer include drama, music and art; after school care available.

Pastoral Care and Discipline: Pastoral care is a priority in both junior and senior sections. 'Because most children at Stowford have SEN, you rarely hear of bullying or bad behaviour' according to a parent. A house system operates in the school and encouragement to pupils is never short. As well as parent 'surgery' – teacher/parent evenings – an open door policy is adopted by Mr S where he welcomes those with any queries or worries. Teachers are also very approachable either by appointment or at pick-up in the afternoons.

Pupils and Parents: Culturally and ethnically varied and diverse. Backgrounds vary from Korean to Asian and African – At least 9 children do not speak English as a first language. Mostly local children, although some travel from various London Boroughs to the school to make the most of the SEN help that is on offer. Over 50 per cent of pupils are either dyslexic or have dyspraxia, Some are school-phobic and a few suffer from mild autism or Tourette's syndrome.

Entrance: From the age of 6 via interview with the principal and Mrs S. Preferably during school hours so that parents and prospective students can see other pupils at work. A place is offered following the interview and reports from previous schools.

Exit: Mainly to further education colleges, although 10 per cent straight to employment. Around 80 per cent of those leaving go on to gain A levels. Almost 70 per cent go on to university at 18 or 19.

Money Matters: Fees are higher for younger students because extra tuition and support is needed. A small number of bursaries and scholarships.

Remarks: A specialised school, but welcomes all. A friendly, warm and comforting atmosphere that suits many children with SEN. Promotes self-confidence. A happy, sympathetic and gentle place to be.

Strathallan School

Forgandenny, Perth, Perthshire, PH2 9EG

Tel: 01738 812 546

Fax: 01738 812 549

Email: admissions@strathallan.co.uk

Website: www.strathallan.co.uk

• Pupils: 260 boys, 195 girls; all board except for 130
• Ages: 10-18 • Religion: Non-denom • Fees: Day: junior £2,882; senior £4,396. Boarding: junior £4,629; senior £6,504
• School status: Independent • School gender: Mixed
• Day/boarding: Takes boarders

SEN provision

Detail:

Experience of:

Mild: ASP; ADD; ADHD; DYSC; DYSL; DYSP; HI; VI; CP;

Moderate: MLD; DYSL;

Others: OCD; EAL; Sp&LD; Eat;

Summary: In the Inspection of standards and quality undertaken by Her Majesty's Inspectorate of Education published in June 2004 the provision of support for learning was described as good overall with many significant strengths. Strong features of support for learning included the following:

- Systematic identification of pupils with specific learning difficulties and sensitive support for individual pupils;
- Well-planned arrangements for pupils requiring special assistance with examinations;
- Informative advice to teachers on the learning needs of pupils requiring support;
- An appropriate range of programmes for pupils for whom English was an additional language;
- Effective use of the expertise of external specialists such as educational psychologists; and
- After school 'clinics' run by a number of subject departments.

The priority is to provide long-term support for individuals and groups of pupils and to respond positively to the needs of pupils referred from individual departments. Teachers have been provided with briefings on issues such as dyslexia and the focus in the last year has been on helping departments adapt approaches and materials to pupils' different needs.

The department consists of two full-time members of staff with the help of three other teachers. One of the full-time members of staff specialises in the provision for pupils in the Junior House, Riley (ages 10-13), and she works closely with the head of department whose focus is in the senior part of the school. All pupils have screening tests on entry and extensive use is made of the arrangements available under both the English and the Scottish examination systems.

What we say about the school - the full Good Schools Guide review

Head: Since 2000, Mr Bruce Thompson MA (forties) educated at Newcastle High, thence New College where he read literae humaniores (classics to the rest of us) and comes to Strathallan via Cheltenham College, where he was head of classics, and Dollar Academy – he wanted to 'try the Scottish system'. 'Loves Scotland, and loves Strathallan', as does his wife, Fabienne (French, teaches at a local prep school, worked in travel and tourism, expert skier – coaches it). The Thompsons have two young daughters and are delighted to find a young staff with similar-aged children. Head teaches classics and coaches rugby; the pupils enjoy finding him practising weights alongside them. He has a reputation for calling into houses unannounced for the odd chat with a pupil on their own ground and has lots of informal brain-storming sessions in the evenings. ('Great fun, got to kick 'em out'.) He 'needs pupil stimulation' and finds himself creating oppportunities to meet more pupils on an informal basis.

Academic Matters: Not tremendously academic (school says 'strong academic record') – but you can reach the heights from here. 2005 A level results include over 80 per cent A-B in art, business studies, Eng lit, Chinese, classical civilisation, further maths, Spanish and German. School plays the system, both Scottish and A levels. 60/70 per cent take A levels, the rest do Highers (over two years). School tries to please parents but the choice between A level and Highers is always a contentious one. All pupils do double award science at GCSE. No subject much stronger than others and exam grades are generally good across the board. DT continues to be excellent. Sophisticated computer design equipment, and pupils work here in spare time. Intranet access all over. Four separate computer rooms and computers everywhere. School has always had a reputation for picking up weaker brethren and has a smallish but effective learning support system which had a smashing HMI report in June 2004, with talk of 'systematic identification', 'sensitive support', 'informative advice'. All pupils screened on entry with psycheds brought in where necessary. One-to-one, small groups, plus after school clinics in various disciplines. Two full-time trained staff, plus three others, and a dedicated full-timer for 10-13-year-olds in Riley who has strong links with the senior school. Extra time for exams. Three week assessment orders for all – ie reports (these are becoming more commonplace).

Games, Options, The Arts: Fantastic new state-of-the-art art school over three floors with marvellous light and inspired work. Art/history combined field trips to Venice etc graphics camera and screen printing. Good music (Copeman Hart manual organ) including keen traditional Scottish music group. Popular pipe band. Lots of drama and small theatre, a clever conversion of a former dining hall, the insides cleverly scooped out (theatre doubles as an examination hall). Swimming pool curiously juxtaposed to the theatre. Swimming team developing under new coach. Sport taken seriously (hideous pale green astroturf), rugby, cricket, own golf course, skiing, CCF (boys and girls, voluntary), flying, sailing. Masses of charity work.

Background and Atmosphere: School was founded in 1913, based in 18th century country house with masses of additions, set in 150 acres. Two fantastic double-deck libraries, one with the (obviously commissioned) carpet reflecting the plaster work in the ceiling. Nice chapel, hideous dining room. Main classrooms 150 yards away beside the old stable building which has been converted into a splendidly cosy junior house, Riley. Riley now boasts a most amazing atrium plus library and music practice rooms etc. Classroom blocks undergoing programme of refurbishment, with latest improvements including three new state-of-the-art chemistry labs. Houses new and newish, boys and girls have own study bedrooms, lots of kitchens, and common room area on each floor. Much general to-ing and fro-ing, but co-ed works very well here; girls' houses out of bounds to boys on Sunday mornings so that girls 'can laze around in their dressing gowns if they want'. School facilities much used by groups during holiday period. Staff live on site in school houses, lots of young and good family feel.

Pastoral Care and Discipline: House parents live on site with two staff on duty in each house every night. Tutors often using the time available for informal chats. Mr Thompson 'aware that things happen' and talks of rustication and drugs testing 'in case of suspicion'. Punishment system for misdemeanours of 'fatigues' – jobs around the buildings and grounds – 'no shortage of them'!

Pupils and Parents: A few from the eastern bloc via the HMC placement scheme, plus Hong Kong, Germany etc. A third in all live overseas, mostly expats. School is popular with Scots (regional accents of all kinds) well-placed, an hour from both Edinburgh and Glasgow, plus a small contingent from south of the border. FPs Dominic Diamond (computer games whizzo), Colin Montgomerie (golfer), Sir Jack Shaw (Bank of Scotland), John Gray (former chairman of the Hong Kong and Shanghai Bank). Not a toffs' school, despite brief showing in the fashion stakes when David Pighills took the school co-ed.

Entrance: At 10 or 11 for the junior house (interview and test) then automatic entry, otherwise by CE – more than one attempt OK. Not a high hurdle, but popular. Later entry if space available.

Exit: More than 95 per cent to a wide range of universities (Aberdeen popular). Usually 'a few' to Oxbridge.

Money Matters: School financially strong. Junior scholarships, open scholarships and sixth form scholarship plus academic, allrounder, sport, music and art scholarships. Parents can also apply to the Ochil Trust for means-tested help with fees.

Remarks: David Pighills (the last head but one who was all that was wonderful for Strathallan) is back as chairman of the governors and, with a dynamic new head, school should be on the up again.

The Study Preparatory School

Wilberforce House, Camp Road, Wimbledon Common, London, SW19 4UN

Tel: 020 8947 6969

Fax: 020 8944 5975

Email: wilberforce@thestudyprep.co.uk

Website: www.thestudyprep.co.uk

• Pupils: 320 girls, all day • Ages: 4-11 • Religion: Non-denom • Fees: £2,795 • School status: Independent • Opendays: November and March • School gender: Girls • Day/boarding: Day pupils

SEN provision

Detail:

Now provide for in school:

Mild: ADHD; DYSC; DYSL; DYSP; SpLD;

Moderate: DYSL;

Experience of:

Mild: ADD; HI;

Moderate: ADD; ADHD; DYSC; DYSP;

Others: EAL; Epi;

Summary: The Study is non-selective at age 4 and aims to cater for those girls with specific learning difficulties such as mild to moderate dyslexia, dyspraxia and ADHD. There are flexible support groups in some years and one-to-one private tuition for those who need it. Support staffing consists of a learning support co-ordinator, four private tutors, a part-time support teacher and several teaching assistants.

What we say about the school - the full Good Schools Guide review

Headmistress: Since 2003, Ms Joyce Nicol MA Cert Ed (late forties). Took over from the popular Lindsay Bond; formerly head at Wilmslow Prep, Cheshire and Longacre School, Surrey. Parents say she is organised, unflappable and always ready to listen. Joanna Gay is deputy head, she and Mrs Nicol alternate their time between sites.

Entrance: Non-selective entry at 4+ by ballot; priority given to siblings. Thereafter girls have an informal assessment and interview for occasional places. Girls mainly local, Wimbledon and the surrounding areas of Roehampton, Kingston, Barnes and Putney.

Exit: Regularly get both music and academic scholarships at 11+. Majority go to day schools: Wimbledon, Putney and Surbiton High Schools, Lady Eleanor Holles, Kingston Grammar, Notre Dame. Some to boarding schools Woldingham, Godolphin, St Mary's Calne, odd one to the state sector.

Remarks: Lively prep school founded in 1893 by a governess, now on two sites bordering Wimbledon Common. Pre-prep girls at Wilberforce House in large purpose-built ex local authority premises, surrounded by well maintained gardens and play areas. Year 4 upwards on the original site, Spencer House, which was acquired in 1903 and has a small playground.

Both buildings have been redecorated and modernised recently. Classes are mixed ability although there is some setting for maths and English; a committed band of staff. Girls are taught to enjoy learning; certainly not a hothouse say parents, but all the girls are 'encouraged to reach their potential'. Produces confident, friendly and well adjusted girls, without pressure. Mrs Nicol is strong on staff development too. Science lab particularly well designed and the teaching is very high standard. A learning support team assists girls with specific difficulties and EFL.

A good choice of clubs, with sports being very popular; girls have been selected for SW London athletic squads and swimming teams. No sports field: makes use of the many public sports facilities in the area. Drama and public speaking also thriving – many do LAMDA exams. The head says she likes to encourage girls to try out different activities before thinking of specialising. The jewel in the crown is undoubtedly music; four choirs, an orchestra, and smaller strings groups that provide music for assemblies. The school also boasts a parent and pupil choir whose most recent performance was Mozart's Requiem. A new enthusiastic director of music appointed this term. There is always a waiting list for individual instrumental tuition, so put your name down early.

SUNNYDOWN SCHOOL

Portley House, 152 Whyteleafe Road, Caterham, Surrey, CR3 5ED

Tel: 01883 342 281

Fax: 01883 341 342

Email: head@sunnydown.surrey.sch.uk

• Pupils: 72 boys; 29 weekly boarders • Ages: 11 to 16

• Religion: non-denom • School status: State

• School gender: Boys • Day/boarding: Takes boarders

SEN provision

Detail:

Now provide for in school:

- Mild: ASP; ADD; ADHD; DYSC; DYSL; DYSP; VI;
- Moderate: ASP; DYSC; DYSP;
- Severe: ASP; DYSC;
- Others: SPD; Sp&LD; PD;

Experience of:

- Mild: AUT; HI;
- Moderate: ADD; ADHD;
- Severe: ADD; DYSP;
- Others: AUT(other);

Summary: Sunnydown School is a community special school for boys aged 11 to 16. All pupils have statements of special educational needs that identify specific learning difficulties and/or difficulties on the autistic spectrum. Pupils are taught in groups of 10 or less and follow the National Curriculum in a modified manner, to make it more accessible to the pupils. The school has an ethos of good relationships between pupils, staff and parents which Ofsted regard as outstanding.

What we say about the school - the full Good Schools Guide review

Head: Since 1982, Mr Moore Armstrong (fifties, just become a grandfather): his wife Jill also teaches history at the school – 'I did not appoint her!' Smiley, caring and respected – fierce when necessary, obviously loves coming to work. 'I could be accused of failing in ambition in not moving to another job but this is a very interesting place...' Not complacent, yet shows endless delight in boys' achievements.

Academic Matters: All the boys have Autistic Spectrum Disorder, Asperger's syndrome or very severe dyslexia and arrive at the school streetwise – albeit with behavioural and communication difficulties – but with their only academic experience one of failure (eg 11 years old with a reading age of 5). Immediate assessments of reading, comprehension and spelling set challenging targets for each boy, which are achieved and rewarded with the focus and encouragement of form teachers and learning support staff. About eight boys and two adults in each class; outgoing yet disciplined behaviour with laughter, practical examples of subjects and peer evaluation holding the kids' attention. Mainstream curriculum from year 7, good range of GCSEs; mainly focused on work related skills. Entry Level Certificates mean everyone leaves with a qualification. Effective and well-used IT room, ditto library. An excellent working environment where fear of failure does not exist; 'If they don't make it here, they won't make it anywhere.'

Games, Options, The Arts: Games and outdoor activities recognised as immensely important for 11 to 16-year-old boys. Lunch break lasts an unfashionable 80 minutes, giving everyone time to let off steam before more lessons – the basketball court is very popular, the London Towers professional team come and coach 24 boys each week. Swimming takes place in the pool at the neighbouring mainstream state school – and snowball fights between the two when the weather is right! Astroturf area enables all weather football. Sunnydown competes with the 70 other members of Surrey Special Schools Sports Association – trophies displayed in the school hall. Duke of Edinburgh Award Scheme, Ocean Youth Trust South, Army, Sea Cadets, St John's Ambulance – the biggest problem is not enough days for all the available options... many of the activities stem from pupils' suggestion books. Music is part of the curriculum but there is also an opera workshop each week. Art is of a mainstream standard – pupils recently took part in a national sculpture competition and were ranked by the V&A as one of the top ten schools in the county.

Background and Atmosphere: Friendly atmosphere as soon as you enter and are given a bright visitor's badge – each individual's needs are known without looking them up in a file. Boarders love it here – not just because of the range of evening activities – rooms are clean, bright and there are obviously no problems with stealing, since I saw mobile phones lying around and a dorm's safe box wide open. Zero tolerance to bullying means that everything is reported – including complaints such as 'So and so is not talking to me' – if that is seen as bullying then communication has to be pretty important here! The care staff is dedicated and perceptive, 6½ in total; one of the two men is an ex-pupil. Couple of whole school assemblies each week; no group religion outside RE syllabus. Two dogs (pets of care staff) and a part-time cat (belonging to head's daughter). Form tutor and care staff are the first points of contact for concerned parents yet head operates (truly) open door policy. Written report at Christmas and in July, three parents' meetings a term and pupils' statements are reviewed every year.

Pupils and Parents: From all over Surrey (weekly board available for those with long commute) and families have moved into the county to attend.

Entrance: Surrey LEA SEN panel meets each November and examines statements – the youngest with the most severe SEN come to Sunnydown. School does not really want to dilute effective size but may stretch to 80 pupils with extra facilities in the future. Open mornings for parents alone.

Exit: 95 per cent stay in education, mostly to local colleges for vocational GNVQs.

Money Matters: State financed, parents and friends contribute to extra fund-raising; a few eyebrows were raised at letter proposing a collection for Guinness (the name of the often sick – now deceased – school cat)!

Remarks: A remarkable school with a family feel, effective and inspiring for the visitor and obviously for the pupils too – old boys return to visit, normally around lunchtime... Sunnydown builds boys' self-esteem fast; one applied for a job as a apprentice at a hairdressers' and ended up cutting hair on national TV.

SURBITON PREPARATORY SCHOOL

3 Avenue Elmers, Surbiton, Surrey, KT6 4SP

Tel: 020 8390 6640

Fax: 020 8255 3049

Email: surbiton.prep@church-schools.com

Website: www.surbitonhigh.com

• Pupils: 138 boys, all day • Ages: 4-11 • Religion: Christian ethos but all denominations accepted • Fees: £1,929 (reception, years 1-2); £2,628 (years 3-6) • School status: Independent • Opendays: November • School gender: Boys • Day/boarding: Day pupils

SEN provision

Detail:

Now provide for in school:

Mild: DYSL;

Moderate: DYSL;

Others: DEL;

Experience of:

Mild: ASP; ADD; ADHD; DYSC; DYSP;

Moderate: MLD; DYSP;

Others: SPD; Epi; Eat;

Summary: A baseline assessment is undertaken when the boys join the school in reception. This is followed by an end of Reception assessment. Children are also screened in year 1 and year 2 for dyslexic type problems. If a child is causing concern at any other point, then individual assessments are also carried out. When necessary, a child might also be referred to an educational psychologist. If learning support is given to a pupil, as a result of assessments, then this is usually in the form of weekly one-to-one lessons or sometimes small group lessons.

The school ethos is one of embracing a pupil's individuality, helping him to grow in self-confidence and self-worth. Those pupils with specific learning difficulties are no exception and are supported in a caring and practical way.

What we say about the school - the full Good Schools Guide review

Head: Stephen Pryce MA BA CertEd FRSA (early fifties), with more than 30 years experience and grown-up children of his own. Roundly praised by parents. 'He is the reason I chose the school,' said one, echoed by others. 'He is absolutely wonderful, knows all the boys by name and character, very firm but very kind.' Operates an open door policy and once a week invites six pupils to 'take tea' with him (actually squash and doughnuts). 'He runs a very happy ship,' said one father.

Entrance: At 4: informal assessment in January for 20 reception places. At other times subject to availability. No need to register at birth – easier to get into than the girls' school.

Exit: With no in-house repository at 11, school achieves a very creditable set of places/scholarships at local independent schools including Hampton, Kingston Grammar, Reed's and St George's College.

Remarks: Good academically but with limited space particularly outdoors. Surbiton Prep is the junior boys' school of Surbiton High School and shares many of its facilities including dining rooms and gym (100 metres down the road, so the boys get plenty of short walks each day) and sports fields (impressive, though a three mile bus journey away). The Prep building has been a school since 1862 (it became part of Surbiton High in 1987) and, while this gives the place a certain homely charm, the downside is that physical surroundings are not great and space is at a premium. 'Reception classroom is small and hot and the toilets need doing,' said one parent. Several others voiced concerns about the playground – 'too small – no space for the boys to have a good run about,' said one. 'Not enough equipment,' said another.

Does not follow the National Curriculum to the letter (boys additionally take French from reception),- but pupils sit SATs at Key Stages 1 and 2. In 2005 at Key Stage 1, 100 per cent reached level 2 (the national target) and more than half reached level 3 – 45 per cent in English, 89 per cent in maths. At Key Stage 2, 100 per cent of pupils reached the national target level 4 in English and science, and 96 per cent did in maths. Again many bettered this: level 5s by 59 per cent of the boys in English, 81 per cent in maths and 68 per cent science. All classrooms have electronic whiteboards. Lots of opportunities for arty children – regular drama productions and a good range of music tuition available as an extra. Plenty of after-school clubs.

Pastoral care and discipline generally considered good. 'It's a very close community where the boys all know each other and the teachers all know them,' said a mother of two boys at the school. 'It's a safe and supportive environment where the children feel secure.' Any issues over behaviour problems are considered well-handled – with the occasional miracle turnaround of a difficult child. Relaxed atmosphere, boys are polite and well turned out. Parents mostly English professional couples – both working, with a sprinkling from overseas. Strong parent association with plenty going on – more social than fund-raising. 'Friendly, not snooty,' said one.

Generally a feel that the prep is a bit of a poor relation of the main school, but 'there's a happy atmosphere and they turn out a good product,' said a father – 'makes you wonder what they could do if the facilities were slightly better.'

Swiss Cottage School

Avenue Road, London, NW8 6HX

Tel: 020 7681 8080

Fax: 020 7681 8082

Email: admin@swisscottageschool.com

Website: www.swisscottage.camden.sch.uk

• Pupils: 140: 60 girls 80 boys • Ages: 2 to 16 • School status: State • School gender: Mixed • Day/boarding: Day pupils

SEN provision

Detail:

Now provide for in school:

Mild: ASP; AUT; ADD; ADHD; EBD; DS; DYSC; DYSL; DYSP; HI; VI; CP;

Moderate: ADD; ADHD; EBD; DS; DYSC; DYSL; DYSP; HI; CP;

Severe: DS; DYSP; CP;

Others: GEN; SLD; Sp&LD; DEL; Epi; PD; Eat;

Summary: All children will have learning difficulties within the moderate range as their core need (as identified by an educational psychologist) and one or more of the following as their secondary need/s:

- Physical difficulties, which can be managed within the existing level of resourcing in each department.
- Social communication difficulties, secondary to their learning difficulties.
- Moderate sensory impairment.
- Speech and language difficulties, over and above their global learning difficulties, and which will respond to the existing level of support available in the department.
- Medical problems, which can be managed within the existing resource levels.
- Emotional and behavioural problems, secondary to their other difficulties.

What we say about the school - the full Good Schools Guide review

Head: Since amalgamation in 1995 Ms Kay Bedford BEd MA (psychology) Dip Mal Ed. Previously head of a delicate school in London. Educated, trained and spent early part of career in Australia before moving to England to work in an EBD school. Always in demand – 'trouble is, the more you're out there, the more you're asked to do.' An inspirational leader, winner of a national leadership award and rated excellent by Ofsted. Unbelievably busy, she currently spends two days per week as a consultant leader in secondary schools (part of the London Challenge); is a facilitator on the mentoring-coaching course; facilitator to consultancy team at the London Leadership Centre; an ambassador for Investors In People and was actively involved with the DfES developing leading edge CPD practices, many drawing on those at Swiss Cottage. Staff say, 'we are devoted, stimulated and all share in success, her door is always open, she is the boss but she is also like another colleague – very organised, incredibly busy – but always has time for people.' Head says, 'being happy and making a difference is what's important to me'. Gets lots of offers to do other things but says she would 'miss the daily challenge, the children, parents and staff – they're all great – it's exciting.'

Academic Matters: Class size averages eight in primary, 12 in secondary with lots of teaching assistants (TAs) considerably reducing this. Has best Key Stage 3/4 value added in Camden. Pupils follow National Curriculum with lots of additions including extended literacy, life skills, music and PE. Take SATs if appropriate. At Key Stage 4 most follow the Certificate of Achievement (Level 1 to 3 on National Curriculum); many follow ASDAN youth award scheme with focus on key skills. Use 'working towards independence' for those not at level 1, some do Graded Assessment Profile in English (GAPE) – 'we don't want to fail our young people by putting them on an inappropriate route.' Good facilities including sensory room, soft play area, hydrotherapy pool, plus rooms for physio, speech therapy and music in primary department, snazzy life-skills base for all, with seniors benefiting from specialist science, art, DT, French and ICT rooms. PSHE very important – bullying awareness week turned into six weeks – important to empower children to say 'I don't like that.' Well-equipped, not just interactive white-boards and ICT but resources ranging from programmes such as mind-mapping through to cash for shopping trips (part of life-skills). Innovation and creativity very much to the fore throughout, though the head modestly claims, 'most of it isn't rocket science' – whatever it is, it works.

Learning is very individualised, based on clusters of needs with TAs delivering differentiated pre-prepared programmes so children can be finely grouped. Use lots of strategies including TEACCH and Makaton signing. Literacy seen as key, have a literacy adviser who works with staff to develop competencies, targets, reading recovery etc. Have adapted assessment of national literacy strategy, took a lot of work but upshot – everybody wants it so they're going to publish it and get some cash into bargain. Use photography and video evidence to capture learning and work hard to develop 'awe and wonder' – 'the Tsunami, death of the Pope, all have an impact on our children – we have to ensure it makes sense.' Pupils say, 'you learn a lot of things because the teachers teach you in a way you'll understand and they don't rush you.' Makaton signed assembly begins with rousing rendition of cheery school song, 'When we are together' and celebrates success – noisy, enthusiastic, brilliant!

Games, Options, The Arts: Plenty of PE (use own facilities plus local sports centre) enter and often win sporting competitions, lots of dance – funky and fun – there's even an early morning aerobics session to help children loosen and limber up plus after school clubs and holiday play schemes, additionally the newly built adventure playground for Key Stage 2 and well-equipped playgrounds for younger years mean lots of imaginative and sensory play – our favourite was the wibbly-wobbly bridge with a bell that rings as you run across it! Playtime essential for letting off steam and socialising – 'the TA helped me find people to play with and things to do at playtime, I have lots of friends and we all support each other.' Music and music therapy play an important part, school has recorded its own CD (new one in the pipeline). Art teacher genuinely enthused by quality of pupils art, a fabulous 3D guitar and associated storyboard caught our attention as did the wall hangings, textiles, fabric designs etc. When a pupil in a wheelchair panicked about using the sewing machine, the adage 'many hands make light work' turned to 'many feet make machine work' as assistance was given with operating the foot pedals.

Background and Atmosphere: Established in 1995 the result of an unpopular amalgamation of two schools, it rapidly claimed its place as one of the top schools in the country. Undoubtedly a demanding and challenging place to work, the head doesn't suffer fools – instead she's likely to work with them and turn them into shining examples of best practice! Lots of ambitious goals and targets set and met. School's received a string of awards including two school achievement awards, a place in Ofsted's Hall of Fame and champion investors in people status. Needless to say there's no problem recruiting and retaining quality staff. Not a swish cottage, would benefit from a much requested rebuild; that said, accommodation is well-maintained, adapted and frequently adjusted to meet the needs of an ever changing student population. All say school is so successful because relationships between everyone are first rate and driven by the staff relationship guidelines (highly recommended).

Pastoral Care and Discipline: Based on lots of rewards mostly centred around pupil interest and on premise that children aren't deliberately naughty – 'you never know why a child is having a bad day so you do your best for them and find strategies to help.' Push children to achieve but add 'if an activity is demanding we work on it as long as we can, then we give them something easier and less stressful.'

Believe strongly in their duty of care and use a multi-agency approach, liaising with therapists, social workers, parents etc as necessary. Create lots of opportunities for children to contribute to school, to feel proud and respect each other. Pupils told us, 'the teachers help me when I get angry and I've done brilliantly.' All have a child-speak mission statement – they know why they are at SC and what it's about. Senior children consider learning behaviours – what have adults done to help learning and what did children do. In near future, head plans to take older children out on lesson observations with her – will have checklist (and kudos by being with head) and will feed back to class thus extending dialogue. Currently working on children showing visitors around and talking about the school (our guides did a great job). Careers advice was provided by full-time Connexions adviser (relocated so replacement sought) – used as model of best practice by Ofsted – 'that's what we'd expect at Swiss Cottage,' adds head. Lunch is an important time for children to practice their social skills – youngest work towards serving selves or each other, oldest have achieved this.

Work hard on induction and transition from nursery through to the busy Year 11 programme – a day a week at college, a mentoring programme, plus lots of outings. Additionally all seniors make a speech before they leave reflecting on their time at the school, progress, best memories, expected exam results, what they're moving on to and importantly how they feel about it ('so moving – everyone cries') – those with little language are supported not only by videos and photos but also by their peers, all act as role models for the younger children and ambassadors for the school.

Pupils and Parents: From Camden and surrounding boroughs. Majority are white British, Bengali and Somali. Social and ethnic mix with 55 per cent in receipt of free school meals and 52 per cent having EAL requirements. All are fully statemented. Parents very supportive of school and school offers lots of support to the parents (and siblings) – informally whenever it's needed and formally through courses, the weekly parent advice and support group, social evenings, review meetings etc. Parents say school is fantastic – can't do enough to help – 'staff even give up a day of their holidays to run a social for parents.' One pupil told us, 'my mum's pleased I'm at Swiss Cottage, she's really proud of me.' Clearly a school with nothing to hide – we were invited to browse through comment forms from past eight years but didn't actually feel the need...

Entrance: School caters for students with moderate global learning difficulties and in addition students may have speech and language needs, physical needs – medical, gross or fine motor, emotional and or behavioural needs as a result of any or all of the aforementioned. In addition, the assessment nursery can cater for severe/profound learning difficulties and children with sensory impairment (these children will move to an appropriate school at age 5). Parents are encouraged to attend a pre-visit but a place will only be offered if the child's needs fit the admissions criteria and a place is available – no waiting lists – places seldom arise. Very much a first choice school – massively over-subscribed.

Exit: At 16 majority to local FE colleges, a couple to other schools. All would like to see school accommodate pupils beyond 16 but no space to do so in current buildings.

Money Matters: Lots of fundraising by Home School Association plus local generous benefactors helps develop and maintain resources.

Remarks: In the words of a visitor, 'the more you dig the more seams of gold you uncover.' This is what Dick Whittington failed to find; an inspirational centre of excellence – among the best we've reviewed.

Talbot Heath School

Rothesay Road, Bournemouth, Dorset, BH4 9NJ

Tel: 01202 761 881

Fax: 01202 768 155

Email: admissions@talbotheath.org

Website: www.talbotheath.org

• Pupils: 393 girls. Mainly day, but 28 girls board, weekly and full, from age 11 • Ages: 3-18 • Religion: C of E • Fees: Day: kindergarten £920, reception £1,330, junior £1,500-£2,365; senior £2900. Full boarding £1,930 on top. Weekly boarding £1,800 on top • School status: Independent • Opendays: October • School gender: Girls • Day/boarding: Takes boarders

SEN provision

Detail:

Now provide for in school:

Mild: DYSL;

Others: EAL;

Summary: As well as meeting the needs of Gifted and Talented pupils, we aim to identify and assess a child's special educational needs as early as possible, so that the individual can be helped to overcome difficulties and attain her full potential. Where possible, this is done before entry to the school. Once identified, appropriate support strategies are implemented to enable the pupil to integrate fully into the school.

Children requiring additional support will have a weekly lesson with the SENCo, either in a small group or individually, according to need. These lessons can be used to boost weaknessess in reading/comprehension/grammar/spelling/written and speaking skills/study skills and revision techniques.

The EAL teacher tutors girls individually after school in the boarding house. Progress of all children on the SEN register is monitored termly by means of a meeting with the SENCo and a representative from each faculty. Parents and pupils are kept informed of progress.

What we say about the school - the full Good Schools Guide review

Headmistress: Since 1991, Mrs Christine Dipple BA M ès Lettres PGCE (late-forties). Educated at Barnard Castle Grammar School, read French and Italian at Leeds University, followed by a master's degree in France, then PGCE at Oxford. Taught at Millfield, Sherborne School for Girls and St Swithun's (head of modern languages at last two). Married with grown-up stepdaughter. Approachable, energetic, no-nonsense head with clear ideas of standards she expects from girls. Enjoys choral singing, gardening and travel. Took over from Miss Austin-Smith, who was here from 1976.

Academic Matters: Traditional teaching and solid results. ISI report in 2001 said GCSE and A level results 'very good in relation to pupils' abilities'. 60 per cent A/B at A level and A*/A at GCSE. Offers good range of subjects, with maths and science very popular – all take dual award GCSE science and a number go on to study medicine and veterinary science at university. Most girls take nine subjects at GCSE, four at AS level and three or four at A2. Setting by ability for French and maths term after 11-year-olds start – 'we give them time to get settled,' says head – and for science at GCSE level. Majority learn two languages and there are exchange trips galore to France, Germany and Spain.

Lots of computers – each subject area has access to IT, every girl has e-mail address and there are three computer rooms for use by all. Textiles and cookery on offer in the newly equipped technology centre. Many long-serving staff – average age of teachers in senior school is 46 – and 66 per cent have been at school for more than 10 years. Head says girls are very motivated and expect staff to deliver. Higher number of male staff than in the past – deputy head is male – but men still few and far between. Class sizes range from 20 at lower end of school to 15 at GCSE stage. School has EAL teacher and caters for those with dyslexia, dyspraxia and ADHD.

Games, Options, The Arts: Sport is compulsory for all, though number of timetabled sessions decreases as girls progress through school. Particularly strong in netball, tennis, swimming and athletics – with several county champions over the years. Heated outdoor swimming pool used from May till October for lessons and lunchtime clubs. Large sports hall offers everything from aerobics and dance to fencing and trampolining. Own all-weather playing fields, netball and tennis courts.

Art impressive – with wide range of work on display, from self-portraits to stunning black and white still-life photographs. Flourishing music department – cellist Natalie Clein (former Young Musician of the Year) is an old girl as is Kate Royal, winner of the 2004 Kathleen Ferrier Award. 250 girls have instrumental lessons in school and loads of choirs, ensembles and orchestras to join – including the jazz-based Double O'Sax group which has reached the Music for Youth National Festival three times running in recent years. Excellent drama. Between ages of 11 and 14 every form has to produce a play for the annual drama festival. There is a major drama production every autumn and some go on to take theatre studies at AS and A level. Modern drama studio with state of the art sound system and computerised lighting desk.

Background and Atmosphere: Founded as Bournemouth High School in 1886. First head was Mary Broad who believed girls should have same opportunities in education as boys and shocked locals by teaching her pupils cricket and gymnastics. School moved to picturesque 24-acre purpose-built site in Talbot Woods in 1935, when it became known as Talbot Heath – school birthday is still celebrated every May. Senior school is built round two quads and has been vastly added to over the years. Girls encouraged to use grounds – walks in pinewoods, building dens etc – yet kept secure.

School prides itself on helping girls settle into routine when first join. Sparky unofficial handbook written by 11-year-olds advises new girls to 'be ready with a clear 'yes' at registration – unless you are absent!' and not to 'PANIC – unless absolutely necessary!' Tiny number of boarders lives at St Mary's boarding house, a short walk from main school building. Boarding house fairly traditional in appearance, with dormitories for younger girls and cubicles for older ones, but boarders are allowed to keep their own hamsters ('no rats,' says head firmly) and there are skateboards propped up all over the place. (See recent CSCI report on school website). Girls wear simple uniform of navy blazer, skirt, blouse and tie – vast improvement on old-fashioned grey felt hats once worn. Sixth form girls are given more freedom – no uniform (but have to look smart – no flip-flops or pierced tummy buttons on show), more free periods and sixth form common room. After-school and lunchtime clubs entirely voluntary (computers through to hand-bells) – though a puzzled sixth former told us she couldn't imagine any girl going through school without joining something. Once a year each form chooses its own charity and holds a fund-raising week. Many take part in Duke of Edinburgh award scheme and Young Enterprise. Local employers have praised Talbot Heath girls on work experience post-GCSE for being reliable, competent, able to shoulder responsibility and work as a team.

Pastoral Care and Discipline: Apart from noisy corridors, head says girls generally behave well. No girl has been suspended in recent years but head would not hesitate to do so for smoking, drinking or drugs offences in school or for persistent bullying. School has system of sanctions – order marks, detentions etc – for unsatisfactory work or behaviour. Parents always informed. Each form has two form leaders, voted for by peers each term, and there are two head girls, two deputies and a raft of prefects. In senior school, full assembly held four days a week, led by head, staff, outside speakers and girls themselves.

Pupils and Parents: Girls come from enormous catchment area – some cycle in from close by while other travel from as far afield as Beaulieu to the east and Weymouth and Portland to the west (good train service). Wide range of backgrounds, including first-time buyers of private education. Large proportion of boarders come from overseas, particularly Service families. Very friendly, purposeful, well-mannered girls, proud of their school. Confident and outgoing – but not as alarmingly sophisticated as you find in some schools. School is not snobby – very down-to-earth. Notable old girls include Dame Shirley Williams, Caroline Gledhill (first woman to receive Young Engineer of the year award) and Frances Ashcroft (first woman to receive Fellow of Royal Society award). Natalie Clein and Kate Royal (see above).

Entrance: Senior school holds entrance exam in January for the following September. Most Talbot Heath juniors progress through to senior school but all must pass exam. At 11 girls sit papers in English, maths and verbal reasoning and at 12, 13 and 14 there is a French exam too. Not too horrific a hurdle. Some girls join from state schools, others from preps like Hordle Walhampton, Castle Court, Dumpton and Durlston Court. Entry at sixth form requires a minimum of five A-C grades at GCSE and at least Bs in subjects to be studied at A level.

Exit: Three-quarters of girls stay on for sixth form – those who don't tend to leave for local FE colleges to do subjects not on offer here. Virtually all sixth form go to university – Exeter, Birmingham, Surrey, Bath currently popular choices. 10 per cent of upper sixth to Oxbridge each year.

Money Matters: Offers a wide variety of scholarships (academic, all-rounder, performing arts, music and sport) and bursaries. There are also discounts for children of parents serving in the Services and clergy.

Remarks: A happy, successful school that has moved with the times while firmly maintaining its own unique character and traditions. Suits able girls who want to work hard and get involved.

THE THOMAS HARDYE SCHOOL

Queen's Avenue, Dorchester, Dorset, DT1 2ET

Tel: 01305 266064

Fax: 01305 250510

Email: admin@thomas-hardye.dorset.sch.uk

Website: www.thomas-hardye.dorset.sch.uk

• Pupils: 2002 boys and girls, all day • Ages: 13-18

• Religion: Non-denom • School status: State

• School gender: Mixed • Day/boarding: Day pupils

SEN provision

Detail:

Centre of excellence for:

Mild: CP;

Moderate: CP;

Now provide for in school:
- Mild: HI; VI;
- Moderate: HI;
- Severe: HI;
- Others: Sp&LD;

Experience of:
- Mild: ASP; AUT; ADD; ADHD; EBD; DYSC; DYSL; DYSP;
- Moderate: ASP; AUT; ADD; ADHD; MLD; DYSC; DYSL; DYSP;
- Severe: ADHD;

Summary: The school uses the title Education Extra for its special needs provision, believing this does not label the relevant students. The SENCo and Flexible Learning Co-ordinator (also with SENCo experience) work with two other full-time teachers and a number of teaching assistants. The school has a number of young people with physical disabilities. It also has a learning support teacher and unit for students with speech and language difficulties. Students are not withdrawn from class unless this is linked to a requirement of a statement. Students work with teaching assistants and their peers in the classroom. Our students in Education Extra achieve exceptional results and many of them enter the sixth form.

What we say about the school - the full Good Schools Guide review

Head: Since 1988, Dr Iain Melvin BA PhD OBE (2005) (fifties). Educated at St Francis Grammar School, Hartlepool and read English at the University of Nottingham. Deputy head of the Royal Latin School in Buckinghamshire before taking the reins here. Married, no children. In no doubt about the excellence of his school. When asked how it differed from comprehensives in similar Dorset towns, he beamed, 'our results are much better!' Although he teaches some A level English, Dr Melvin is more a master chef, pulling everything together, than a hands-on head with his fingers in the batter. The school absorbs both his working day and much of his free time ('there are 2002 pupils here – I don't have any outside interests'). Admits that at a school of this size it is impossible to know all the pupils' names, but 'I can guarantee they all know me!' With 218 members of staff, just keeping abreast of all the teachers' names must be a trial. Masterful at weaving together a complex range of pupils, programmes and – especially – funding into a thriving and vibrant web. Inexhaustible supply of ideas – aiming to offer the IB programme as an alternative to A levels from September 2006. Not getting any younger, but as one parent of a sixth former said dismissively, 'oh, there have been rumours of him retiring for years.' Not going anywhere for now.

Academic Matters: There are some smart cookies here. In 2005, one boy gained 13 A*s in his GCSEs and several others were close behind. Nine pupils scored one of the top five marks in their GCSE subjects in the whole of the UK (two in maths). Maths particularly strong and, far and away, the most popular A level subject here. Head points out that there are more pupils doing A level maths here than in all the schools in the rest of the county combined. Science popular but results a little disappointing for a school that became a science college in 2002. Ofsted report so over the top with gushing praise that it makes embarrassing reading. Has been given every award going: Charter Mark, Schools Curriculum Award, Investor in People, Arts Mark Gold, Leading Edge School, Education Extra Award, School Achievement Awards ... you get the picture.

Being so large allows the school to provide some unusual subjects, including Latin and dance at GCSE, and sociology, dance, electronics, food technology, travel and tourism and accounting at A level. Also offers the CACHE diploma in nursery nursing. On top of all this, Hardye's is a teaching training school, working in partnership with Exeter and other universities. IT a sore point for some pupils: though well-equipped with swarms of new boxes, monitors, interactive whiteboards etc, pupils speak of perpetual printer problems down on the shop floor – while the head's printer purrs like a dream ... Some 180 pupils take advantage of SEN provision here, ranging from moderate learning difficulties (the majority) to a handful of pupils in wheelchairs. The school has a physiotherapy room, a unit for the hearing impaired, two large SEN rooms and several specialist SEN staff. And for pupils who just need a boost, there are after-school homework help sessions – well attended 'and no stigma attached,' said a pupil. A few parents of kids with minor problems (eg poor handwriting, organisational issues) felt the school could do more.

Games, Options, The Arts: Super sports facilities – floodlit Astro, sports hall with climbing wall, fitness suite, verdant playing fields, plus use of the facilities at the Dorchester Rugby Club and neighbouring leisure centre (two swimming pools). Rugby keenly played, along with football (boys and girls), cross-country, netball, athletics, traditional cricket and swimming. Vast numbers of pupils to choose from means the school's 'won' column contentedly exceeds its 'lost'. A good range of minor sports eg water polo and kayaking, plus outward bound activities. Drama, music, art and dance are all buzzing. Music department stands out, with recording studio and music tech room. Music tours, two orchestras, school music festival, lots of rock bands, annual joint concert with Imperial College, steel band, chapel choir – 'you name a cathedral, they've sung in it!' says the head. Drama in own theatre, RSC visits every second year. Small museum area displays some excellent artwork. THTV, the school's in-house television channel, shows pupil-produced programmes on a plasma-screen TV in the heart of the school, know as the Spine. Lots of charity do-gooding and recycling.

Background and Atmosphere: Thomas Hardye founded the first free school in Dorchester in 1569 (the school has nothing to do with Dorset novelist Thomas Hardy who confusingly attended school in Dorchester in the 1850s, in case you are wondering). Doubled in size in 1992 when amalgamated with local girls' school. Is now enormous, heaving, multi-layered campus. Feels more like a small university than a comprehensive – owing partly to the absence of 11 and 12 year-olds, a key element of Hardye's uniqueness. Sixth form immense. 'We think it is the largest of any comprehensive in the country,' says the head, which gives you some idea. Just in case any other school is plotting to eclipse them, Hardye's is in the process of expanding its sixth form further still, until they will be the ... SUPREME ... MASTERS ... OF ... THE ... UNIVERSE. A gigantic sixth form means better funding which 'percolates down through the rest of the school'. It also allows them to offer their good range of A level courses.

School's swish office and reception area immediately radiates a school that has its act together. Lots of new building including £2.7 million English and modern languages block with central glassed-in atrium housing 50 computers (2004). Beauteous sixth form centre, with own mini-canteen, well appreciated by the students. Class sizes pushing the boundaries in the sixth form (AS pupils we spoke to griped about tutor groups of over 30 kids) but kept smallish in the lower school.

Pastoral Care and Discipline: The few local parents who do not choose the school mainly cite pastoral matters (will my child be lost in the vastness? will he suffer peer pressure?). But parents who have taken the plunge are almost all happy here. The head points out that, by breaking the school down by year group, they have created five manageable-sized groups of children. Pupils coming into year 9 keep the same tutor for three years – helps enormously. Appearance a constant source of skirmishes, with the pupils' guerrilla tactics usually overpowering the administration. Girls' skirts worn short with, in some cases, stilettos. Barber shop visits have not greatly troubled the boys. However, the school has outflanked the pupils in the battle of the neckwear, introducing clip-on ties for new pupils in 2005. One set of Dorchester parents explained their decision to send their daughter to an independent school thus, 'she could get a perfectly good education at Hardye's. We are essentially paying £16,000 a year to make sure she wears a kilt below the knee.'

Behaviour otherwise OK, if informal. No uniform in sixth form. Out if caught in possession of drugs but head says he is 'a realist' and there have been no permanent exclusions in the past six years. Area where sixth form pupils store their bags is guarded by CCTV (a good idea). Library well used and quiet – a sea of heads earnestly down. Bullying low on list of concerns – 'it's uncool to fight here,' said a pupil.

Pupils and Parents: School is the pinnacle of Dorchester's Schools Partnership, a cohesive 4-19 educational pyramid. Hardye's has traditionally been able to count on this mainly homogeneous, middle income, non-urban catchment to provide reasonably wholesome kids with a good work ethic. Sadly, some negative aspects of youth culture are reaching even here, and Hardye pupils are not quite the bushy-tailed, fresh-faced youngsters they were when Dr Melvin first came to the school. Negligible sprinkling of ethnic diversity – most with English as their home language.

Entrance: 450 pupils at 13+ mainly from Dorchester's three middle schools. Some fifty pupils come from outside the area, from as far away as Sherborne and Blandford. Handful from local prep, Sunninghill, settle in just fine. Number seeking entry roughly matches places available. All candidates for entry to the sixth form are interviewed, including the school's own pupils. 120 new pupils enter at that stage, a few from Poole and Bournemouth's grammars, attracted here by wide range of A levels, less authoritarian sixth form and lure of the opposite sex.

Exit: At least 80 per cent to higher education. 20 per cent leave after GCSEs, most of these to further education elsewhere. Head says that none are pushed out, but that the less able tend to leave, some looking for more vocational courses. UCAS a Herculean labour here, with Dr Melvin reading every single application. Half a dozen pupils to Oxbridge most years – sometimes more.

Remarks: Bulging metropolis, humming purposefully under efficient head. Exactly what educationalists had in mind when comprehensives were first invented, and going from strength to strength.

THOMAS TELFORD SCHOOL

Old Park, Telford, Shropshire, TF3 4NW

Tel: 01952 200 000

Fax: 01952 293 294

Email: admissions@ttsonline.net

Website: www.ttsonline.net

• Pupils: 1,175 boys and girls, all day • Ages: 11-18
• Religion: Non-denom • School status: State
• Opendays: In March 18 months before proposed entry
• School gender: Mixed • Day/boarding: Day pupils

SEN provision

Summary: Thomas Telford School operates a whole School approach to special educational provision. This means that all staff are responsible for meeting special educational needs and have a responsibility for all students. Our objectives are to provide a curriculum which enables all students to realise their full learning potential. We target resources specifically for exceptionally able students and those with learning and physical difficulties and provide a whole School approach to learning support so that meeting special educational needs is an integral part of curriculum planning, delivery and assessment. We identify individual needs and provide appropriate support and utilise Information Technology fully so that students can take more control over their learning.

The extra help and learning support that is provided may take a variety of forms. For example, a specially designed learning programme; assistance from an extra teacher, technician, parent or helper in the classroom; being taught individually or in small groups; using technological equipment, eg electronic spelling aids, radio microphones and software for specific skill training as well as full wheelchair access.

Avoidance of labelling and non-segregation is fundamental to good practice. Each student is offered their curriculum entitlement, including the National Curriculum, within the context of the teaching area alongside their peers and subject teachers. Each student is given the opportunity to develop from their own starting point and progress at an appropriately challenging pace. Additionally, specialist teaching and resources are provided for students who require Learning Support.

The school employs a full-time Registered General Nurse.

No details given of SEN provision offered.

What we say about the school - the full Good Schools Guide review

Head: Since 1991, Sir Kevin Satchwell BA (early fifties). OU education degree plus a diploma in educational management. Taught PE, ran his department in two schools, then deputy head in Kirkby and head of Moseley Park in Wolverhampton, before being appointed as TTS's founding head, with the brief 'to raise educational standards in Telford and Wolverhampton'. This he has unequivocally done, hence the superhead gong. The school is very much his creation, and he's proud of it, as he is of fighting his way out of his limited background to current fame. Likes media attention and the range of visitors it brings (many turned away), but keeps closely in touch with pupils (is part of the personal tutor team, holds regular working lunches with students of all ages, runs a football team – on the day of the GSG visit was seen after school boarding a minibus with them for an away match).

A quiet, modestly confident man, down-to-earth and direct in manner. Married, with two children. Sometimes sounds like the head of a successful trad independent grammar school – which indeed the school resembles in many ways. Prides himself on innovative approach to running a school, eg day divided into 2 x 3-hour periods – a long day, especially if pupils stay for a third session (up to 5.40) for sports and activities – but no one seems to complain. Also flat management structure for staff: nine deputy/departmental heads have responsibility for the curriculum and for appointing their own teachers; Sir

Kevin claims that this releases cash for everyone else (teachers have a lightish teaching load and get overtime for extra duties).

Academic Matters: Very important (the head's first sentence in the prospectus), and very successful. The claim to be 'England's top comprehensive school' gives rise to lively and intermittent argument about how they do it – and how the exam statistics are worked out – but there is no doubt that drive towards achievement and celebration of success are hot-wired into the place. Some A level students recently wrote to the press in answer to a disparaging criticism of the school (see below): 'Our school and students are competitive and we make no apologies for that. We do not accept mediocrity, and why should we?'

Pass rates at both levels are high and rising (vocational qualifications included in the calculation); science, maths and technology A level are strong (as one might expect), also English literature, history and business studies. Languages feature pretty well at GCSE though few take them in the last two years. Still, this is a wide-ability school, and clearly something in the air makes the pupils work hard and want to do well. 'Students should feel good about being successful.' Sir Kevin would say it's all to do with an ethos of high standards, secure surroundings, staff commitment and strong parental involvement; now where have we heard all that before? Bags of encouragement and reinforcement underpins all this.

The school pioneered the use of IT early in the 1990s, and is still at the leading edge in the production of educational software – so much so that it sells its curriculum and allied material to schools nationally as part of an outreach programme, which brings in a handy £2m a year. The whole curriculum is planned in July for the following year; the claim is that it can be accessed in school or from home at any time. Quite what 'curriculum' means here is not clear – it sounds as if teachers are expendable – perhaps 'schemes of work'; but in context it has to be a bright idea, handing initiative to pupils to learn and releasing teachers from some drudgery. 'It may sound mechanistic', says the head, 'but it's very productive'.

Average class size is 24 below the sixth; groups range from 4 to 23 in years 12 and 13. 44 pupils on the SEN roll, nine of them statemented.

Games, Options, The Arts: Enormous range of games played (Sportsmark Gold with Distinction awarded), much student representation at every level up to national: football (boys have link-up with Wolves, one girl played for England), cricket, hockey, athletics, swimming, etc. etc. Inter-house competitions taken seriously; excellent facilities, including floodlit pitches. Over a hundred pupils currently involved in D of E at all levels. Performing arts are strong, especially dance and music.

Background and Atmosphere: Founded in 1991 with attractive purpose-built campus; the use of space underpins the head's philosophy. As a CTC, the school is sponsored, notably by the Mercers' Company and the Tarmac Group, who have plenty of influence on the governing board. This means the head has great freedom of action – and no anxieties because no fees to garner.

Plenty of open spaces, including open areas where two or three classes are taught simultaneously; an interesting reversion to the old schoolroom idea, which appears to work well, and certainly suits the 3-hour periods. Generally there is an impression of quiet and purposeful study, with elements of both focus and relaxation. Everywhere is carpeted, and noise levels are impressively low (no bells). Reception area could belong to a corporate HQ, with (silent) TV screens giving the latest in news and sport, and a monitor for visitors to access the school's very professional website – and indeed much of the building looks like a modern open-plan office. Neatly uniformed boys and girls (they even have TTS lab coats).

Parents encouraged to become involved in the school's life, through an advisory council and through constant monitoring of their children's progress: they get a report every three-and-a-half weeks, and are invited to comment on eg whether they are satisfied with their child's work. Much contact with personal tutors, who are encouraged to draw the diffident into the educational process; they even visit housebound parents on their own initiative. The very hard-working can be rewarded by becoming Parent of the Year.

Pastoral Care and Discipline: Vertical tutor-group system (like St Paul's London – another Mercer's school), two to three from each year in one 'family'; meets every day for 20 minutes. 'Students can see the headmaster at any time to discuss issues of concern.' Zero tolerance over bullying and use of harmful substances, inside or outside school. Uniform rules strictly enforced.

Pupils and Parents: From Wolverhampton (nine coaches ferry pupils to and fro), or from Telford town.

Obviously a wide span of social backgrounds – some families on income support and some middle class parents who, elsewhere, might have avoided comprehensives but can sniff out a successful middle class school. Ideologically-driven observers like Roy Hattersley have sought to explain academic success by accusing the school of a socially skewed selection policy, a charge vigorously countered by Sir Kevin, who points out that all CTCs have to pick in fixed proportions from the standard distribution of ability bands. The argument will doubtless continue.

Entrance: Entrants at 11+ come from a defined catchment area; no preference for siblings. Selection is 'from the full ability range ... in accordance with the criteria embodied in the funding agreement between the school and the Education Secretary', which is different from LEA schools. Within each of the nine ability bands 'places will be allocated as far as practicable over the full range of ability. The headmaster will select students ... and in exercising his professional judgement will take into account the range of ability admitted, geographical dispersal of intake, and competence in science, technology and maths.' So the head has some freedom within broad parameters. (Note carefully: applications have to be in by 30 September for the next September.) Our translation of this for eager parents would be – underlying ability is no barrier or advantage but do interest your child in something technological or mathematical. There will be geographical patches where the chances of success are higher because the level of applications is lower. This is one of the few good schools where moving to a cheaper house will give an advantage? Enthusiasm for the school, a real interest in education, and an obvious willingness to get stuck in should be on display at visits/interviews; this applies to your child too.

There may be a few places after GCSE.

Exit: Increasingly to higher education, mainly in and around the midlands – 80 per cent in 2004, with 7 per cent taking a gap year, the rest to employment or training. About a third of leavers to older universities – four to Oxford. Numbers staying on to the sixth are steadily increasing (now over 90 per cent). The school claims a low drop-out rate at university (two per cent).

Remarks: A remarkable school, proof (for some) of what a comprehensive – albeit a special one – can achieve under strong and visionary leadership. Whatever you think about the overtly competitive drive towards academic success, you can't be unaffected by the pupils' all-round confidence, and their pleasure in belonging to an institution which stimulates them in the classroom and appreciates them for what they can offer outside it; not new values by any means, but all the better for being asserted here. If you're moving to this part of the west midlands, get your form in in good time.

TIFFIN SCHOOL

Queen Elizabeth Road, Kingston Upon Thames, Surrey, KT2 6RL

Tel: 020 8546 4638
Fax: 020 8546 6365
Email: office@tiffin.kingston.sch.uk
Website: www.tiffin.kingston.sch.uk

• Pupils: 1,045 boys, all day • Ages: 11-18
• Religion: Broadly C of E, all faiths admitted
• School status: State • Opendays: Early October
• School gender: Boys • Day/boarding: Day pupils

SEN provision

Detail:
Now provide for in school:
Mild: ASP; ADD; ADHD; DYSL; DYSP;
Moderate: ASP;
Others: Epi;
Experience of:
Mild: HI;

Summary: The school currently has three statemented students, one with muscular dystrophy and two with Asperger's syndrome. These students are supported by a team of four part-time LSAs. In addition we have one support teacher who concentrates on literacy. The latter supports students with dyslexia and dyspraxia within her 1½ days per week.

What we say about the school - the full Good Schools Guide review

Head: Since 2004, Mr Sean Heslop MA Hons PGCE (mid-thirties). Read English at Queen's College, Cambridge, where he played football and cricket for the college. After early career in IT poetry publishing joined Queen Elizabeth's, Barnet, 1994 to 1997, thence to St Olave's Grammar School as head of English.

In 2000 to Ravens Wood School, Bromley, as deputy head. Clearly very committed to, influential and experienced in, pioneering work in the state sector on all fronts.

Academic Matters: Unashamedly academic, pre-applicants are warned – 'don't sit the tests if you are not up to academic rigour.' However school is also prepared to challenge existing styles of learning and teaching; the opening of the new Dempsey building in 2004 has given the school an opportunity to put innovation into practice. Another open day mantra predicts two hours homework per night – if that doesn't thrill, look elsewhere. In practice, whilst there is plenty of it, homework loads rarely match up to such daunting warnings. Results are solid – almost all pass GCSE at A*-C (65 per cent at A*/A) and 75 per cent get A/B at A level. Predictably, the quintessentially male subjects, maths and the sciences, far and away the most popular at A level. However the school's specialism is the performing arts, based upon its excellence in music, drama and dance. Broader span of success at GCSE with English language and literature eliciting some good grades.

Average class size is 30 in line with other state schools. At A and AS levels less popular subjects generate smaller classes whilst favourites strain at the seams (maths being a case in point). Any child who passes IQ-based entry exams sees automatic acceptance, therefore, broad range of special needs catered for, from Asperger's syndrome to severe physical impairment and usual range of dyslexia/dyspraxia. All benefit from free specialist support within curriculum.

Games, Options, The Arts: Detached sports hall on site, built under the auspices of Sport for All and used by the local community evenings and weekends. A great modern facility with space for 6 badminton courts and full disabled access. Outdoor sports are exiled to own playing fields, Grist's at Hinchley Wood (half an hour by public transport, sometimes coach). Timetabled sport one afternoon a week and plenty of extra-curricular ventures at lunchtime and after classes. School performs well in local independent/state leagues, particularly in rugby, cricket and rowing. Own boathouse is short walk away down at the Thames. Genuine attempts to give boys extra-curricular space to shine beyond the relentless exam machine. Strong house system with sporting and other competitions.

Music department offers individual instrumental tuition (payable termly) with acoustic practice areas; 30 per cent of boys play an instrument across several bands and orchestras. The choir has covetable links with the Royal Opera House. Modern facilities and renowned drama. Have achieved performing arts college status (brings with it D of E grant). School takes its productions to the Edinburgh Festival and on tour internationally. Art and design technology workshops are functional and up-to-date, as are IT suites.

Background and Atmosphere: Inescapably urban location, at the heart of Kingston's notorious one way traffic system. High redbrick walls largely hide it from the outside world and form a fair security/sound barrier. Inside the perimeter, grounds offer a surprising amount of outdoor space; slightly unkempt five-a-side football pitch, several tarmac quads, plus sixth form/staff-only lawns and gardens. Main school block built in 1929 is attractive and creeper laden, set just behind a smallish, heavily listed early nineteenth century school house – Elmfield – currently housing the sixth form common rooms, library and careers suite. Listed buildings, no matter what gravitas and history they lend, are, one senses, the bane of schools choked by LEA budgets. The oodles of funds that it would take to restore Elmfield to any former glory and make its interior space usable and appealing are clearly not forthcoming. Two modern extensions are sympathetic. The Dempsey building, opened in June 2004, links an existing extension to the body of the school and provides lecture theatre, new library and other teaching spaces. Overall, classrooms and facilities are of a good standard, décor is sometimes tired, but there is no sense of neglect. At the bell, well-kitted-out boys fill the corridors with chatter; relationships seem convivial. Canteen housed in worryingly ugly Nissen-hut style accommodation on the edge of the site. The school introduced a 'healthy eating regime' in September 2004 so no chips! It was well patronised at break-time on the day of visit. Options of school or packed lunch – 'food is OK.'

Pastoral Care and Discipline: New head is strict on uniform, behaviour and consistency across the school. Rules are rules, boys kept in line with well-oiled detention (ultimately suspension) system and homework clinics for those whose main misdemeanour is not keeping up. Some find it quite starchy. Conducive working atmosphere is defended at all costs. Good anti-bullying policy and pupils attest to feeling safe and supported. Prefects, form tutors and year heads keep an eye on pastoral problems. Cross three lanes of slow-moving traffic next to the school and you will reach Kaleidoscope needle exchange project with its clients jostling (and worse) on the pavements outside. Perhaps serves as a warning to their impressionable young neighbours as no major infringements of the banned substances policy have recently come to light.

School has a distinctly male vibe though 33 per cent of teaching staff are female. Plenty of social opportunities with the opposite sex, however. Pupils are much in demand for drama and other accompanying roles at local girls' schools, not least Tiffin Girls' (a mile up the road in cosier Kingston suburbs).

Pupils and Parents: Fairly solidly middle class group. Some would almost certainly have opted for the private sector if the Tiffin pass mark had not been attained and about thirty acceptees a year go that way regardless. A percentage of pupils come from low income families and school has forged social links with disadvantaged high-rise estates less than a mile away. Half of the pupils come from primary schools in Kingston borough and, despite being open to all-comers, Tiffin is well regarded as a local asset. Forty per cent of the intake is non-C of E, plenty of respect for other religions and cultures institutionally and at playground level.

Entrance: Highly selective. Catchment stretches wide across south London and Surrey – places are over-subscribed seven to one. At 11: two half-day tests, verbal and non-verbal reasoning in November of year before entry. Results are 'age-weighted'- August birthdays not disadvantaged. Top 140 are offered places (possibly a few more or if any positions are tied). The rest are put on a waiting list in order of score. Places offered up until September in the year of entry. After this doors are shut to newcomers until sixth form. Leavers are not sufficient over five years to deplete the year group/affect funding. Minimum requirements for incumbents to progress to sixth form (GCSE Grade B or above in given subject and four other passes) mean that, in principle, there could be forced departures. In practice, all measure up. Nonetheless, between 16 and 17 approximately twenty leave of their own accord to other institutions. Empty places, plus fifty new vacancies, are filled by application and a competitive set of GCSE results. Incomers settle well and often progress to be prefects after just a year in school.

Exit: Majority to higher education. Oxford is most attended university with 16 boys gaining places (4 to Cambridge). Nottingham, Warwick and various University of London colleges are also popular.

Money Matters: State funded, free for all. Manages well on limited budgets and is hot on the trail of any opportunities for extra government cash. Newsletters witness constant appeals to parents. Fundraising activities are rife, weekend car-boot sales have become something of an institution in the area. School shop retailing a dizzying range of varying ties and blazers which are used to differentiate houses, lower school, upper school and upper sixth, must turn in a fair profit. Well-supported alumni association also lends financial muscle.

Remarks: Selective state school with excellent local and national reputation. Takes academic high flyers and gets the job done with them in a humane and no nonsense way. Oddballs at primary school, who seemed too nerdy for words, will at least find like-minds here and, at best, end up folk-heroes. The super-sensitive may be happier with the smaller classes and refined atmosphere of the private sector – if they are bright enough for here, they may get a scholarship there.

TONBRIDGE GRAMMAR SCHOOL

Deakin Leas, Tonbridge, Kent, TN9 2JR

Tel: 01732 365 125

Fax: 01732 359 417

Email: office@tgs.kent.sch.uk

Website: www.tgs.kent.sch.uk

• Pupils: 1,083, mostly girls; includes about 40 boys in the sixth form; all day • Ages: 11-18 • Religion: Non-denom • School status: State • Opendays: October or tours once a month (telephone for details) • School gender: Girls • Day/boarding: Day pupils

SEN provision

Detail:

Now provide for in school:

Mild: DYSL;

Severe: DYSL;

Experience of:

Mild: ASP; ADD; ADHD;

Moderate: EBD;
Others: OCD; Epi; PD; Eat;

Summary: Our school works in close partnership with parents in dealing with children with special educational needs. This also means that outside agencies may be involved and we feel that early recognition and good communication between all parties is essential. We have a dyslexia specialist who will assess our students and provide tuition as necessary. We provide a range of laptops with good, instructive software for their use. Similarly we employ a counsellor who will give support as required. We believe that intervention with appropriate support and resources leads to improved learning, self-esteem and ultimately greater personal success.

What we say about the school - the full Good Schools Guide review

Head: Since 2005, Mrs Rosemary Joyce BA (Hons) MA, previously deputy head of Nonsuch High School for Girls in Cheam, Sutton. First degree from University of Stirling, PGCE and second degree from University of London Institute of Education. Areas of educational specialism – Religious Studies and history. Previous schools include Clarendon School Trowbridge, Aylesbury High School, Millais School Horsham.

Academic Matters: Much praise from Ofsted 2002. The school is consistently at the top of league tables. Excellent A level results in 2005 and GCSE results in 2004 and a good range of languages including Italian, Latin and Spanish – an exceptional department praised by all, with work experience done in Spain, France and Germany. English – 82 per cent A/A*. Maths teaching excellent, accelerated maths group takes GCSE in year 10. A lot take drama, 93 per cent A/A*, described as 'transformed and uplifted ' by the students – the statistics speak for themselves. Their trump card is the flexible curriculum that allows them to spread their GCSEs and take some early, giving more time for other studies, minimising exam pressure and allowing time for just the learning experience of eg drama for fun. The school is piloting AS levels in year 10 for some students. Girls learn how to be independent and manage their work load early. School now also offers the International Baccalaureate as an alternative pathway for students not wanting to follow the traditional A level route.

Staff profile is a healthy mix of young NQTs and experienced staff; calibre is top notch and kept on their toes with very effective monitoring of stats internally and externally. Any shortcomings quickly surface and mentors always on hand. Setting in maths begins in year 8 and some setting in modern languages. Generally, however, there is no streaming or fixing of labels, as this doesn't tally with the culture of being respectful of others' different and diverse strengths. Very good science, holds science careers conventions, speakers ranging from chemical engineer to a patent agent. ICT integrated into every subject. Pays attention to learning difficulties and the particularly gifted – personalised programme for those who need it including running its own summer school and Saturday enrichment sessions. 'This is certainly not a hot-house for pressurised academic success,' comments a deputy head.

Games, Options, The Arts: Corridors are decked with students' work in a nice higgledy-piggledy way, showing a full range of pupils' abilities. There are increasing amounts of work presented digitally. Technology is rated highly by the girls, teachers give 110 per cent of their time – some contemporary and dazzling garb hanging on models contrasting with a traditional but stylish green/blue tartan uniform.

Artsmark Gold re-awarded in 2004 for outstanding provision in art, dance, drama and music. Music technology studio and spectacular graphics software. Plenty going on, presently 300 students learn a full range of musical instruments, two rock bands, three choirs, two orchestras etc etc. Plenty of students involved in county and national youth orchestras as well as choirs and bands. School seeking final permission to exchange brownfield land at one end of the site for a new three-story teaching block with adjoining sports hall, drama studio and dance studio plus refurbishment of all the facilities for art and music.

Usual games are on offer and the school is well represented at county and national level (particularly at netball and hockey). Sportsmark re-awarded in 2004. One pupil managed to swim for England and still maintain a successful A level programme. There are plenty of playing fields (easily waterlogged and slushy in the winter and wide craters appear in the summer), hard and grass tennis courts, an outdoor pool and limited indoor facilities. Good partnerships with local schools under the School Sports Co-ordinator programme. Duke of Edinburgh popular at all levels. Developing programme of outreach for students through the school's specialist and leading edge status. Developing programme of international links with schools in Washington DC, Singapore and Sri Lanka. School supports the World Challenge expedition to Peru 2006.

Background and Atmosphere: Main building early 20th century, redbrick, very C grade and the only thing about this school that is. Corridors recently refurbished and the canteen very antiquated. School has expanded by scattering a hotchpotch of classrooms (a little barrack-like) on the hill; there is a newer science and technology block and 'we're thinking big on facilities' says the deputy head. The age of the current buildings does not deter the pupils' natural enthusiasm and pride in their school – they're all too productive to notice wear and tear.

Introduction of boys has proved good news, particularly in debate, 'some of these girls are as ambitious as the chaps, this is a good stepping stone for their later working environment'.The large common room is a very friendly place. Sixth form students play a major role in the running of the school and in contributing to the culture – responsibilities include publicity, environment, one2one, charity work etc.

Pastoral Care and Discipline: Parents really impressed with the confidence and level of maturity the girls achieve. Sixth form students have initiated a peer mentoring, one2one system whereby each student takes responsibility for a topic, eg anorexia; they receive counselling advice and provide confidential support for junior girls. Discipline is hardly an issue as girls are motivated. 'Perhaps one downside of being so selective is that pupils can feel they fail if they achieve a B grade. We work very hard with their self-worth and perception,' says the deputy head.

Pupils and Parents: Students come from over 70 schools, both maintained and private, mainly the surrounding areas of Tonbridge, Sevenoaks, Tunbridge Wells, some from Surrey and East Sussex. Majority are very middle class, supportive of the school, friendly and no pretensions. Small numbers from other European countries, middle east, America, Australia – attracted to the school because of its reputation and approach to language teaching. All but 15 have English as their first language. Good Old Girl network – Baroness Sharpe, Hayley Allen (Olympic diver), Rebecca Stephens (Everest mountaineer), Felicity Aston (polar explorer), Sophia Macdougall (novelist).

Entrance: 140 places via the Kent selection procedure (11+ exam), which is overseen by Kent. Usually over-subscribed. A minimum of 35 'governor places' are reserved for able pupils from outside the area but the same criteria apply as for Kent selection. Entry to sixth form 'where ability is appropriate'. The school welcomes students with special needs. Admissions latest information is available in the prospectus and on the school website.

Exit: Diverse choices – mainly to Higher Education through university, studying anything from the traditional, eg classics, medicine, law, psychology through to film and French, chemistry and forensic science, politics, early childhood studies, textiles and fashion, sports science etc. Increasing numbers to Oxbridge, including choral scholarships. Good tradition of specialist art, music and drama college places.

Money Matters: State-funded. Music bursaries available and awards in sixth form. Some academic bursary-scholarships in the sixth form. The school also co-ordinates a fund, administered exclusively by the head-teacher, to assist in cases of financial hardship.

Remarks: The façade may not be (yet) refined and polished oak but the students are top brass and so is the education.

Tower House Preparatory School

188 Sheen Lane, London, SW14 8LF

Tel: 020 8876 3323

Fax: 020 8876 3321

Email: head@towerhouse.richmond.sch.uk

• Pupils: 175 boys, all day • Ages: 4-13 • Religion: non-denom

• Fees: junior school £2,770, senior school £2,845

• School status: Independent • School gender: Boys

• Day/boarding: Day pupils

SEN provision

Detail:

Now provide for in school:

Mild: ASP; AUT; DYSC; DYSL; DYSP;

Moderate: ASP; ADD; MLD; DYSC; DYSL; DYSP;

Severe: ADHD; DYSL; VI;

Others: PD;

Experience of:

Mild: EBD; HI;

Moderate: EBD;
Others: SPD; EAL;

Summary: At Tower House we have a SENCo who monitors boys requiring learning support. Boys are withdrawn mainly from English for their English support lessons. Boys receive support lessons before school or during timetabled slots. Support lessons are taught one-to-one, or in small groups according to the boys needs. The SENCo liaises closely with staff, parents and relevant outside agencies.

What we say about the school - the full Good Schools Guide review

Head: Since 2002, Mrs Jackie Compton-Howlett (fiftyish). Initially a professional musician at Royal Academy of Music, thereafter trained and taught deaf and partially hearing children. Was previously head of Wimbledon High Junior School. Studying for doctorate in educational leadership – so brings lots of new ideas including encouraging children to 'be responsible for their own learning' and attaches great value to their views. Talks enthusiastically – 'we need everyone to turn their hands to everything, matches, and plays ... nobody escapes!' Some parents are still getting used to her new style of management. Business-like, she admits she is 'not a standing in the playground all day' type of head but adds, 'I am always here and can and do see people at the drop of a hat all day long.'

Entrance: From lots of different nursery schools mainly within couple of miles radius. Early (before 1st birthday) registration to guarantee place at 4+. Late applicants held on waiting list, many get in this way, 'people do move around here'. A few places can become available at 8+ and often taken by those from Falcons, Putney Park and Orchard House. Non-selective entry at 4. Short assessment in maths, English and non-verbal reasoning for those joining later.

Exit: Academically wide-ranging, reflecting intake. St Paul's, King's College, Epsom College, Ibstock, Hampton, Kingston Grammar, Harrodian, Latymer Upper popular among day schools with a few to board further afield at Marlborough and Charterhouse. 2004 academic scholarships to St Paul's and Bradfield with four other music and art scholarships to King's, Latymer, Emmanuel, Harrow. Discussions about destination schools begin 'earlier and earlier out of necessity with more schools pre-testing at 11,' says head, 'we now start the process in year 4'. Lots of support and advice given by a head who is trying to build contacts with heads and housemasters for the next stage.

Remarks: Small, gentle, essentially traditional (though perhaps becoming more progressive with new head) all-round prep school which has always had a cosy environment and strong sense of purpose.

Split academically and physically into junior and senior schools linked by shared, rather bijou, playground. Pressure on playground space is clearly an issue for nearly two hundred boys but they appear to make the most of it. Small area with climbing frames available for littlies and older boys encouraged to play 'gently', no bats/batons allowed. Junior school houses boys to year 3 where every inch is maximised to give bright, quirkily-shaped classrooms each adorned with two state-of-the-art computers. Boys are taught in classes of about 18 by a class teacher and assistant. Great importance attached to 3Rs and school is noted particularly for innovative ideas to get them all reading, eg paired reading schemes with senior boys very popular. Senior school housed in similarly attractive, late-Victorian building. Again, space is at a premium but there is what the head describes as, 'a lovely science lab', an extensive and much-used library, amazingly large, well-equipped new ICT suite, light airy loft-style art room. Except for these sessions, boys remain in their own classrooms for lessons, specialist teachers coming to them.

Academically, school does well for broad spectrum of needs. Strong science and maths (setting from year 3), streaming in year 8 where class splits into two groups, top CE/scholarship and other CE candidates. In-house exams held every year. In year 4 Richmond Skills and year 5 CAT tests – a thorough assessment of where children are at and what can be expected of them. Incentive scheme for both work and behaviour by system of house plus and minus points, 'life's a mirror' type chat with head v productive for ironing out any concerns. Learning support for dyslexia, dyspraxia, Asperger's and ADHD from experienced SEN specialist four days a week. No extra cost.

Lack of on-site sports facilities, so boys bused to fabulous Bank of England Sports Ground in Roehampton to play a range of sports that would impress many a bigger school – football, hockey, rugby, cricket, tennis, athletics and swimming (for ages 5-10 years). Arrival of new head has put more focus on music with 60 per cent now learning an instrument up to grade 6, although no practice sessions are timetabled. Two active choirs and orchestra practise weekly after school.

School day is longer for seniors and goes on to include after school clubs – these vary according to current pupil and staff interests and can include fencing, squash, 5-a-side football, drama, and chess. Child-care provision after school; the school is keen to be working-parent friendly. Lots of charity fundraisings, many driven by the boys – the head is particularly keen on responsibility coming with privilege and community awareness.

TreeHouse School

Woodside Avenue, Muswell Hill, London, N10 3JA

Tel: 020 8815 5424

Fax: 020 8815 5420

Email: info@treehouse.org.uk

Website: www.treehouse.org.uk

• Fees: £56,073 primary; £68,250 secondary. No extras. All LEA funded • School status: Independent • Opendays: Monthly • School gender: Mixed • Day/boarding: Day pupils

SEN provision

Summary: TreeHouse is an independent special school for children with autism. We deliver highly individualised personalised learning for our pupils using the principles of Applied Behaviour Analysis. We are based in Muswell Hill, North London and have excellent links for integration with local mainstream schools. All our pupils are funded by their home LEAs. Many of our children have multiple diagnoses but all will have a primary diagnosis of autism.

What we say about the school - the full Good Schools Guide review

Head: Since 2004, Ms Gill Bierschenk Cert Ed, previously head of St Aidan's VC Primary School in Haringey. Glamorous and elegant with a compassionate, sensitive demeanour, she exudes warmth and calm. Was encouraged to apply for the job over a coffee in Starbucks, following a head-hunting process, once conventional attempts at recruitment proved unsuccessful, then subjected to hours of gruelling interviews, psychometric testing etc. Seduced by the challenge of the school and the limitless boundaries – 'TreeHouse has done everything through learning how to do it; developed own model for the UK.' Incredibly knowledgeable, loves opening doors for children and their families, transforming expectations – 'we've had a sports day, overnight trip to a scout camp, it's great to push the boundaries. There's so much more we can do. This is an exciting place to work; we unite the best of educational practice with the rigour and intensity of scientific principles.'

Academic Matters: Grouped according to age, huge variety of ability. Curriculum loosely based on primary foundation but with heavy focus on communication, behaviour strategies and for new children, learning to learn skills. One member of staff told us proudly, 'we had a child visit in summer, he was like a whirlwind, darting about the place. He loved being outside and wouldn't go anywhere else. We had to coax him down from the climbing frame, yet today he walked to class, sat on a chair...' Curriculum covers all areas of the National Curriculum but each child has his or her own highly individualised programme and targets. The focus may be sitting at the table, eye contact, answering core instructions – depends very much on the individual. All will participate in group work but all have individual targets within that; requires large numbers of staff. Five pupils to a class, but work on a one-to-one staffing ratio with a unique staffing structure of programme specialists (tend to be bright young graduates with psychology degrees) extensively trained by TreeHouse, supported by a class leader (usually experienced programme specialists) and a programme supervisor (normally a former class leader who's a Board Certified Associate Behaviour Analyst [BCABA] and a qualified teacher). Programme consultants and two deputies complete the team.

Only 25 per cent have some expressive language, more have good receptive language so use PECs, Makaton etc. ABA is used extensively and underpins the very founding principles of the school. Traditionally, in the UK, ABA was delivered via home programmes; here, staff with training in ABA and background of working very specifically with children with autism work alongside those with a general education background. The ABA team translate targets into individual programmes. Decide what will be taught and how; down to fine detail such as what prompts to use (and how to fade); what types of reinforcement to use etc. Qualified teachers develop the curriculum in broader sense; decide scheme of work, lesson plans etc. There's great synergy between the education and the ABA teams. 'When we get it right it's really exciting but it does lead to hairy conversations from time to time.' Say – 'it's easy to make assumptions about a child; prompt them to a response when they could be independent; easy to teach a skill, but in the absence of being able to practise and reinforce they lose it again, so we have to plan systematically, opportunities for generalisation and 'maintenance' of skills, in order to sustain them. Our children don't neatly learn – they may be accomplished in some areas but have fundamental difficulties in others. Learning has to be carefully defined in very minute steps. If we're not absolutely specific about what they've achieved we may presume a particular prerequisite skill has been learned when in fact it hasn't.' Do assess against P levels but say they're way too broad to define the small but significant steps in a child's progress and aren't broken down in a sufficiently precise way – 'exposure to', 'experienced', what do these mean? Need to be certain how a child is progressing so know when to move on or change the programme so minutiae of the child, their progress, behaviours etc are painstakingly targeted, recorded and monitored on palm PC attached to each child; this is effectively their clipboard. Have devised own, continually evolving, programme. 'Can't be too prescriptive, there's a temptation to go through stages 1-10 and tick – much more of a challenge to be spontaneous and respond.'

Lots of smiling faces, eye contact and communication very much in evidence. We witnessed a heartwarming, parent–child interaction, using a mix of Makaton and language. A calm, industrious atmosphere pervaded but Gill was quick to point out life isn't always so – 'we work very hard to give the children the security they need; that can mean two or three members of staff working with one child, especially when they first come to us. Some children can be incredibly challenging. There may be outbursts but we have a dedicated staff. There's a real possibility that on occasions they may be scratched, bitten, thumped, knocked to floor; you have to be a certain sort of person to come back the next day, love that child, want to work, feel confident and not frightened to work. The staff are special, they love the children unconditionally. The rewards are high too – when a child achieves a new skill, or makes a breakthrough, it's immensely satisfying.'

We didn't see any pupil who wasn't actively engaged. Some were working individually with helpers, others in small groups – all the time being encouraged to learn, push the boundaries, try something new. Programmes are carefully designed to build a child's confidence. One child was on an eating programme, painstakingly delivered from getting the child to look at the food, touch it, place it on their tongue, and hopefully eventually, eat it. Eating can be a tricky process for children with autism, who may be averse to all but a very restrictive range of foods. Fundamental to ABA is the appropriate use of positive reinforcement. This may include using favourite foods as a reward – 'when a child does something right, it's important to reward with things they enjoy – it helps them make the connection. ABA has to be constantly reinforced. Once a child achieves a target we have an overt maintenance programme.'

Background and Atmosphere: Founded by five sets of parents in 1997, all still very much involved. Not quite a happy accident, but more than a degree of chance brought them together. All were interested in ABA but couldn't find anywhere offering it. Had high but realistic expectations for their children; it wasn't enough that they were occupied, babysat. 'We knew what we wanted, realised we could facilitate it, but recognised it wasn't something we ourselves could deliver on a day-to-day basis, so we brought in the experts.' Their clear vision and outright determination remains a beacon in the sometimes insular world of autism. The school opened when special schools were closing at a galloping rate. TreeHouse was named on the statements of the first pupils because the local authority, at the time, didn't have any autism-specific provision, and so couldn't offer a comparable alternative. Undoubtedly it has been a struggle to establish a new special school and the quest for appropriate premises has been a real challenge.

School has had more moves than a gipsy caravan, but stability beckons; this latest site will be the last. Currently housed in externally uninspiring green Portakabins, demonstrating that the best presents aren't always the ones in the glitzy wrapping. Unwrap and a smart, inspirational setting emerges. Facilities are super and plentiful for the time being. Classrooms are bright, modern, airy with quality displays; there's a good-sized hall, laundry room, bathroom, cookery room; even a mock-up dental practice in the offing. Outside there's a fabulous outdoor play area with flying fox, trampoline, playhouse, climbing wall etc. School will grow to 80 pupils in the next few years and move to a new building on the same site (planning permission and funding permitted – appeal underway). The first pupils, now in year 8, will continue at TreeHouse until they're 19. Then what? It will come as no surprise to know they're already working on this in terms of planning and delivering a curriculum that will address relationships, sex education, PSHE, and ultimately vocational education, work placements...

TreeHouse isn't just a school, it's a charity with three objectives: to run a flagship school, offer national training and accreditation for those working in field of autism and to keep autism high on the agenda, including the political agenda. To this end they recently merged with PACE, a campaigning charity that has always enjoyed an intimate relationship with TreeHouse – 'it made sense to marry.' In addition to several other schools that TreeHouse has helped establish on the mainland, they have recently worked with a parent group and the local Education and Library Board (equivalent to LEAs) to set up a new ABA units attached to a special school in N Ireland. National outreach work is something they'd like to do more of. 'There is a lot of expertise here, 72 per cent of schools are dissatisfied with the extent of their teachers' training in autism.' 'It's easy to see why spreading the word and sharing the practice is vital; there's often a willingness but insufficient expertise, that's where we have a role.'

Pastoral Care and Discipline: Have certificates for success – perhaps for allowing an apple to be touched to tongue or asking for the toilet. 'The children don't always understand but it means everything to parents and siblings; that's really important.' Parents are a priority. 'A major part of our role is working with them.' They offer training, stress that the work the school does must be reinforced, generalised and consistently applied at home too. Parents are enormously supportive of school, and the school of parents. Communication between the two is excellent: daily home–school book; weekly reports detailing progress in key areas of the curriculum; plus clinics where a parent will either work with their child, running through programmes, or observe teacher, class leader, therapist or other professional working with the child. All are videoed. A copy is given to the parent to watch at home; where separated (and separation is common), this allows the other parent to see development and ongoing assessment. Firmly believe training for parents and social occasions are a major part of their work.

TreeHouse recognise that the struggle starts with having to get a diagnosis. Parents may have to fight for a diagnosis of autism. Next, in order to access the provision needed, they battle for a statement that accurately reflects their child's needs and specifies the provision needed. Parents get exhausted and find it difficult to get proper support, entitlement, care packages, respite. 'They may be entitled to free travel but form filling, doctors letters, all are very wearing, so they miss out. We help if we can.' Work closely with outside agencies such as social services, health etc. Have good relations with local primary schools and reciprocal visits. Choosing appropriate sessions to visit mainstream schools is paramount. 'We have to plan and rehearse going in. It's essential to think of the motivation behind why the child is attending, what we're hoping to achieve and which sessions will facilitate that. We have to understand, be respectful of the schools and the pressure they're under. It's not easy for them. People think children benefit from inclusion in mainstream because they're getting the chance to communicate and socialise with other typically developing children, but this isn't necessarily the case.' Social motivation isn't hard wired in the brain of all children with autism; some will always get more satisfaction from human beings than others. School believes children do benefit from visits; they offer a chance to generalise their skills. Head says she'd love to unpick what is meant by a peer group for the children – 'one of our pupils who has language was in a mainstream setting but he wasn't in a peer group, wasn't actually accessing the curriculum, and staff didn't have the training or opportunity to undo his learning or the stages and steps his learning needed. It was breaking down. He still spends some time at his old school but most is with us.' Accessing the wider community is important, children need to get used to being with people who aren't their classmates, mustn't cocoon. Go on outings to pizza parlours, museums; have trips to local shops or similar.

Pupils and Parents: From 12 LEAs in London. 'People think we're a school for rich kids. We're not. There's a real social and ethnic mix. Some of our children have very little, not even space to run around at home.' Entry is by LEA statement; this involves persuading the local authority to fund the place.

Entrance: All have an autistic spectrum disorder, some with associated difficulties such as sensory impairment or other complex conditions affecting communication. Where co morbidity exists, autism is the priority in terms of knowing how to adapt the curriculum and teaching style. Suggest interested parents attend one of the monthly visitor afternoons. If parents feel the school would be suitable for their child, they are requested to complete an application form, giving as much information as possible. The child is assessed by the Applied Behaviour Analysis (ABA) team in the child's environment: nursery, home, wherever. If they feel they can meet the needs of the child a place will be offered. Only 20 per cent get a place; funding is the sticking point. Says that, for some parents, a bereavement /grieving process can happen following diagnosis, only to be followed by a genuine struggle to find appropriate education. 'They've had to fight, fight, then reality hits: this is a lifelong condition with no medical cure, so the only way to support a child with autism is through very specific education.' We start a programme of intervention, often beginning at home. Reactions from parents vary, from those who just want to pass responsibility to the school and have to be re-engaged, through to others who can become almost obsessive, trying everything – every diet and whim – how can they pass something up that might just work? Parents are pivotal, they know their children inside out, strengths and deficits; we need to know what they feel to be the most important next steps. School works with parents to develop an IEP and discuss long-term goals. Examine the medium term then detail the next year.

Exit: Occasionally to mainstream. Rest still working their way through the school.

Money Matters: Not a rich school. Extensive fundraising underway to support TreeHouse.

Remarks: The government stresses every child matters; at TreeHouse they really do. An incredible school; a fabulous organisation; run by highly trained professionals who not only succeed in doing a terrific job for the youngsters in their care but are seeking to bottle the success for others to share.

TRELOAR COLLEGE

London Road, Holyourne, Alton, GU34 4EN

Tel: 01420 547 400

Fax: 01420 542 708

Email: admissions@treloar.org.uk

Website: www.treloar.org.uk

• Pupils: 180, all post-16. Boys 110, girls 70. Boarders 160, day students 20 • Ages: post-16 • Fees: Residential: £7,000-£22,000 according to need. Day £4,000-£15,000 • School status: Independent • School gender: Mixed • Day/boarding: Takes boarders

SEN provision

Detail:

Centre of excellence for:
- Mild: CP;
- Moderate: CP;
- Severe: CP;
- Others: PD;

Now provide for in school:
- Mild: DYSC; DYSL; DYSP; SpLD; VI;
- Moderate: MLD; DYSC; DYSL; DYSP; SpLD; VI;
- Severe: DYSC; DYSL; DYSP;
- Others: DEL; Epi;

Experience of:
- Mild: ASP; AUT; ADD; EBD; HI;
- Moderate: HI;
- Others: OCD; TIC; GEN; EAL; Sp&LD;

Summary: Treloar College is a national specialist college for young people age 16-25 who have physical disabilities. Many also have a degree of learning difficulty or a sensory or communication impairment. The college's curriculum extends from pre-entry level through entry level, vocational Further education awards to GCE AS and A2s. Equal emphasis is given to developing independence and self-advocacy, in preparation for adult life. The college has a health centre and therapy departments, and can support students with life-limiting disabilities such as muscular dystrophy and ataxias.

What we say about the school - the full Good Schools Guide review

Head: Since 1995, Dr Graham Jowett. Yorkshireman. Educ Roundhay Boys' School, Bristol University then

University Coll, London, where he PhD-ed in biochemistry. After some scholarly tinkering with sick plants, his social conscience hi-jacked him. From hands-on mental health worker he rose to be hands-off FE department manager where his only contact with students was to sack them. Not him, no way, he's implacably compassionate. Finding Treloar, he says, 'has made sense of my career' and you begin to see why when others blow his trumpet. He's a big achiever. He's warm but enigmatically so – making the case for guides like this. Private, they say. Complex. Perhaps an alter ego is the unchained Martin Johnson poster on his wall. Has raised the college to Beacon status – the first specialist college in the country – making it demonstrably one of the two best. Those who roll out best practice are usually joined-up jargon wonks with undeveloped hearts. Not so Dr J. His rare trick is to do stats and people with equal brilliance. So it is that he wept when Ofsted came in with their rave review and – 'only someone as nerdy as me would do this' – counted all the 'outstandings' and 'very goods' in the report (118).

Has pioneered, in the teeth of every sort of objection, an initiative to enable students to form intimate relationships. They like him a lot. When dealing with a rare case of bullying, a student told us, it was the dismay he registered that sorted the matter. It's probably emotional wisdom that underpins his imperturbability. That and a sense of humour with a twist of Zen. He's a force for change, works incredibly hard, yet staff have only good words for him. Passionate – 'so passionate you don't see it' – about equality of opportunity, but also about getting students real and ready for the real world, so it's zero tolerance for not engaging or showing up late. Probably never happier than when working in the halls of residence in the evening alongside care staff. Easily accessed by anyone through his famously open door. His wife is a pro vice-chancellor. Two sons and a daughter. Weakness for morris dancing.

Academic Matters: Impressively resourced, impressively peopled. Gorgeous LRC. First names all round. Skills for life and independent living skills for all. Academic, vocational, entry and pre-entry courses – standard FE fare – and some A levels on campus. Most do three years but some, with more potential than predicted, will stay longer. Those with bags waltz through As in two, then scoot off to law school. Criticism from former students that they were not got ready for the real world has been taken on board and there's strong focus on what happens next – 'we are a transit camp to the future' – so there's lots of rigour and that species of Treloar attitude that makes you smile – a soft-eyed lad who had just converted to red rudeboy hair. Around 30 students do A levels and IB at nearby Alton College – one of the best-achieving FE colls in the UK. There's a 20-year partnership behind this and integration is seamless. It shows in the architecture, too. The Alton principal is intensely proud of the relationship and gladly goes along with the Treloar students' demandingness. When a prospective parliamentary candidate said how nice it was to see them mixing with normal people, young Ted marched into the principal's office and demanded to have him arraigned. He was recalled, and duly recanted. The students have a base in the canteen and Treloar staff on hand – 'the less we see the better'. There's shared transport and, for those who like to trundle, your battery will get you there and back with oomph still over to take you down to the pub later. Don't these students fall between two stools, living on one campus, studying in another? It seems not. 'We get the best of both worlds,' they say with one voice. Always always the push towards independence, so big focus on careers and HE planning.

Background and Atmosphere: Spacious campus. Decidedly adult atmosphere pervades – markedly different from the school. Four halls of residence with shared or single rooms plus care team. Busy, lots on at weekends, plenty of quality sport on offer. This is a place where, says Dr Jowett, 'students enjoy an emotional break from the pressures of adolescence – especially those who are fed up with being the centre of attention.' Parents are often taken aback by the rigours, which are judiciously applied, manifest as matter-of-factness and inspire gutsiness. Equal opps means something when it cuts both ways – we met one student on the office skills course about to move on to a job and into an adapted flat with his girlfriend; and we heard of another discovered the night before akimbo in his wheelchair, the worse for a drop of vodka. Road skills assessment before you're let loose in your wheelchair. Everyone has to be back by 10 – later 'so long as we know where they are'. Disability living allowance imparts independence, so there's clubbing in Alton, a crowd round the beauty counter at Boots and cabs delivering pizzas. You can feel the dynamic – 'They're in and out of love – and ditches.' Alton may not be hostile enough to be the real world, but it's not a bad rehearsal. And there's nothing careless about the care standards; they match the expectations. Self-contained flats enable final year students to rehearse living alone.

Pupils and Parents: Treloar School accounts for approx a third of the intake, the rest come from mainstream or other specialist schools and opt for Treloar because they want the complete package – ed, social, sport, being my own person in my own space.

Entrance: Disabilities as per school. Admission as per school – same four steps – except visiting days are Tuesdays.

Exit: Some to higher education, others to work if poss. Some to sheltered accomm, some go home. Some set up their own business, others work in the family firm. It's a broad spread, basically best next possible outcome.

Money Matters: Almost all students funded by the Learning and Skills Council (LSC). A smattering privately funded, either overseas students or winners of a legal claim.

Remarks: Happening and humane. Students leave full of attitude and purpose, ready to go places if that's realistic, schooled in how to make it realistically happen for, as one of them observed, 'Disability is everyday life.'

TRELOAR SCHOOL

Upper Froyle, Alton, Hampshire, GU34 4LA

Tel: 01420 526 400

Fax: 01420 526 426

Email: admissions@treloar.org.uk

Website: www.treloar.org.uk

• Pupils: 80 boys, 60 girls 110 board • Ages: 5-16 • Religion: Non-denom, but there's a notably ecumenical C of E chaplain • Fees: Boarding: £9,000-£23,000 according to need. Day £7,000-£15, 000 • School status: Independent • School gender: Mixed • Day/boarding: Takes boarders

SEN provision

Detail:

Centre of excellence for:

Mild: CP;

Moderate: MLD; CP;

Severe: CP;

Others: GEN; DEL; PD;

Now provide for in school:

Mild: VI;

Moderate: HI; VI;

Others: Sp&LD; Epi;

Experience of:

Mild: ASP; DS; DYSL; DYSP;

Summary: Treloar School provides first class education, therapy, care and independence training for young people with physical disabilities from all over the UK. We have places for 140 students; 110 boarders. Students may have a sensory or communication impairment or a learning disability as well as being physically disabled. Academically our range is very broad – we offer the full National Curriculum and GCSEs, ASDAN and modular programmes at Key Stage 4.

The majority of our students are wheelchair users. Physiotherapists, occupational therapists, speech and langauge therapists, teaching, care and nursing staff all work together to ensure each child achieves the best they can – in all aspects of life.

Developing independence of thought and action is at the heart of what we do. We work to enable young people and equip them for the life they want. Our medical centre is staffed 24 hours a day and handles routine in-patient requirements, post-operative care and medical care and support for young people with life-limiting conditions such as ducheene muscular dystrophy.

What we say about the school - the full Good Schools Guide review

Head: Since 1989, Neil Clark MA PGCE (early fifties). Schooled in Cumbria, finished at Oxford (history, football Blue). Served 15 years before the masts of mainstream maintained schools, then happened upon Treloar. Saw instantly that this was the one for him. Dry, wry, kind, engagingly rumpled. Doesn't do eminence – utilitarian office, bog standard biscuits, wall festooned with timetables and lists pinned up by their ears. Held in highly affectionate regard by parents – 'he's a non-panicker' – and by the children, to whom he relates with touching naturalness. A man of deeds: he helped set up a residential special school in Kampala and keeps in touch with it. His intriguing assertion 'This is a mainstream environment with specialist facilities and staff' makes sense when you've seen how they do things here – but you've got to see first. There's a Treloar attitude, and an estimable attitude it is, too. It is a tribute to the ethos he has helped to create that he agrees: 'Yes, feistiness is built in, here.' What does that mean? Read on.

Academic Matters: Holistic means holistic, here. Teachers are appointed to teach children. Each child is set goals agreed with his or her multi-disciplinary care team comprising medical, physio, speech and language, OT, teachers and care staff. In the words of a parent, 'All the fine details of multiple needs are dealt with together' which takes some doing in an environment where differing care needs make every child pronouncedly different. What is really extraordinary, though, is the quality of the teamworking: there are almost twice as many staff as children. So many specialisms, all those interfaces – it's a recipe for every known species of friction. You get, after all, enough bitchery among staff in a non-disabled school. There's none of that here. It is a tribute to everyone's focus on each child and a tribute, too, to the quality of their humanity. Teachers are, in the words of a former pupil, 'pushy...They used to say that if you want a job, you have to fight for the right to get it.'

The process isn't remorseless, though, it's respectful. And happy, very happy. For children in years 7-9 there are FLAME classes, Treloar's adapted conductive education programme. Everyone has a go at the National Curriculum. A range of courses from year 10 on gives every child, whatever their level, plenty to get their teeth into and accreditation at the end of it – entry level certificates, ASDAN, GCSE. Time lost to care – physio, etc – is kept to a minimum because it all happens on site (the specialists come to you), often actually in the classroom. There is huge emphasis on participation in every class. A teacher showed us a drawer full of adapted saws in design technology: 'I want each of them to feel the blade rip the wood'. No one sits out a science practical. Everyone makes music. This is because skilled and ingenious rehabilitation engineers select and customise equipment of all sorts for each child, then tweak it as necessary.

Games, Options, The Arts: Impressive sporting facilities generate impressive sporting achievements, and that means nothing less that a steady supply of GB paralympic athletes and England boccia players. Some 40 per cent of the students are national or regional stars. Everyone is urged to have a go and plenty do GCSE PE where the school's penchant for pioneering has earned it praise for the way it has rendered the syllabus accessible to disabled students. Thus we see club thrower Therese Hunt devise her training schedule for her GCSE coursework – and now she is throwing it further than the world record mark. There's a swimming pool, gym, superb staff and, in recognition of them, a Sportsmark Gold award.

Performance and self-expression are reckoned essential to personal development, and these students do things most mainstream colleges would reckon, in paralysed apology, impossible. That's the spirit, you see: fragile but fierce. Lots of music, masses of song and dance and drama, heaps of art, all superbly resourced. Cad Cam in design technology. Performance opportunities for all, not only here at school but also locally and in London. Photography, video, animation. Whatever they do here, they do it as well and as plentifully (and as joyously) as you'll find anywhere.

Background and Atmosphere: Founded in 1908 by the Lord Mayor of London, Sir William Purdie Treloar, to care for boys crippled by non-pulmonary TB. They've dropped all but his surname from the school's title because it made them look deceptively posh. The charitable trust he established accounts for the superb facilities and brings in just short of £2 million a year to the school and the college, so the educational package isn't just excellent value for money, it's subsidised, too. Industrious fundraising and strong relationships with City livery companies keep the school in the forefront, together with the quality and astuteness of the governing body. Setting: full Hampshire rural.

In less than an hour we had lost all sense that we were touring a special school. It took longer to pin down exactly why. It has something to do with things like the un-solemn sign in the entrance hall, which warns: Beware fast-moving wheelchairs. But here's the nub of it: the students' feelings of self-worth banish all awareness of their disabilities. Sure, the buildings and facilities are as good as it gets, and these things matter, which is why the school tirelessly improves them: getting about and coping when you get there are important. Hardware matters; software matters most – people – and the robust humanity of this place is what impresses deeply. We live in an age of meretricious rhetoric, meaningless at the point of utterance. But when we tried to count the empty words in the Treloar mission statement, we never got past zero. So read it. They do it. The focus is on equipping every child with as much self-reliance as possible, where self-reliance is the ability to make choices starting with the littlest, like being able to feed yourself, to the big ones: expressing your talents, getting to be what you want to be. Here is a school awash with wholeheartedness. The children, impressively busy, capture your mind with their animated, opinion-filled conversation and their respect for, and kindness to, each other. There is humour of course. Lots of that. Not all of it reverent, praise be.

Pastoral Care and Discipline: If you are considering opting for boarding, remember that living away from home for 38 weeks of the year has its downside, and you will need to weigh it: when your child comes home for the holidays social ties may have got rusty. All the more important to reassure yourself that homesickness is eased. It will be for your child – it's you who'll need to be self-supporting. The upside is that, for day children too, this may be the first time ever that they have had a social life, living among friends. Five boarding houses, each run by a care manager. Junior houses with shared rooms and Pike and Burnham Houses for the eldest, where many have single rooms. Comfy and well-equipped. Rooms display all the efflorescence of adolescence – teen bling, rock posters n stuff. As normal as normal. Changing rooms, of course. No, no, they're charging rooms – for wheelchairs! We recommend the food – and note that it has attracted a Healthy Heartbeat award. Emotional nourishment is all around, a product of the person-centeredness of everyone in every care team. As one physio has it, 'Physiotherapy is emotional support, too.' Because care needs are so insistent, though, it can sometimes take a while before you can get an adult to yourself. Emotions run high, sometimes. Children lose friends every term. Specialist psychotherapy and counselling are on hand, and an educational psychologist. Normality extends to children getting it wrong, and, when good old bad behaviour breaks the surface, normal remedies apply: talk (as much as it takes) plus, sometimes, sanctions like not going out on a jaunt, or doing a spot of community service.

Plenty to do throughout the week. Some weekly boarding. Lots of sport at the weekends and, for those who stay, a chance to get out and go shopping or take in a movie – but you have to wait (grrr) till the minibuses have brought back the gamesy types first. Big emphasis on coping skills of all sorts from cooking to getting out and about in the community. Annual holiday week in Cornwall for year 10s was the big talking point when we toured, a focus of excitement. The highly nurtured self-image of the children is rooted in their awareness of what they have learnt to do for themselves. Their responsibilities to themselves and others confer rights. Self-advocacy is the Treloar term for having opinions and representing them effectively and accountably, so there's a student council which holds the management team to account, and democratic elections for head boy and head girl. All this empowerment in early youth – it works brilliantly for shy children, too – is probably what led the Evening Standard to describe former pupil, now sit-down stand-up comedian Lawrence Clark, as 'a seasoned member of the disability movement's militant tendency'. Feisty, yes; bolshy, never.

Pupils and Parents: For children, their days at Treloar's are going to be a voyage of discovery. For parents, too. Good news, then, that this school likes parents (an awful lot only say they do). They like them dropping in, they actually really do: 'There are no hidden secrets,' says one, 'I just clip on my badge at reception and go in.' Ring when you want – no problem. There's a Parents' Association which meets to talk about matters of shared concern. It also raises money to embellish living spaces. There's a parent governor whose job it is to keep the deliberations of the governing body pupil centred. Once a term you can meet your child's carers and discuss progress and, of course, once a year you will play a major part in your child's annual review. Here's the health warning, though: you've got to keep up. Because this is, truly, a child-centred school, you won't get deference if you don't. 'Sometimes,' they say, 'we end up challenging a parent because a student's needs or aspirations have changed. Often they have become more independent or able, and a parent struggles to let go of an obligation.'

Entrance: Forty disabilities are currently represented, 70 per cent cerebral palsy. Something over 10 per cent have life-limiting conditions, 30 per cent are non-speakers and 80 per cent use wheelchairs or mobility aids. Palliative care for students with degenerative conditions. Wide geographical, socio-economic and ethnic range. Children join at all ages as parents discover the desirability of a specialist over a mainstream environment, or at the prompting of health professionals. There's an element of respite care here, of course, and everyone's a winner because there may well be a remission from school bullies, too. Who gets in? Those for whom the school reckons it can make a difference. Broadly, it's yes to physical and/or sensory impairment, no to profound learning difficulties, most autism, very challenging or violent behaviour, and some disinhibition as a result of acquired brain injury. Every child must be able to follow speech. IQ range 70 – 140.

Admissions process is four steps: 1) Ring Helen Burton (number above) and have an exploratory chat; 2) make an appointment to visit (Wednesdays, year round); 3) fill out the application form; 4) come for interview and multi-disciplinary assessment (education, care, therapy, medical, psychological). This is also when they work out how much it's going to cost. Then comes the really hard bit. Almost all children are funded by their LEA, topped up sometimes by social services and local NHS Trust. This is an expensive placement, so be prepared to fight the good fight in Churchillian mode (beaches, landing grounds, streets, the lot) to get the Statement applied – it'll take anything from 3-months to a year. They'll give you expertly targeted guidance. Excellent fact-packed prospectus, twin-tracked, half of each page for children, the other half for parents and carers. Good website.

Exit: The majority go on to Treloar College (ages 16-25) – just up the road. Mostly residential, just a few day students, and you've got to be able to get around on your own. Here there's a spectrum of academic opportunities: skills for life, independent living skills; pre-entry and entry level courses in practical subjects; some A, AS and NVQs on site plus the full range at nearby Alton College. Those who don't move up go on to another specialist college or return home and go mainstream. The buck doesn't stop when schooldays end. Oh no. The point of it all is to help students discover what they can and can't do, and what they dream of doing, so the Trust tracks former students to check the aptness of its courses and, more impressive still, works to keep them moving forwards if they get stuck. The goal always is independence (independence, independence), and they've just started up a typically impressive pioneering outreach programme – it's being piloted in Lewisham and north-west Surrey – to help any disabled person untangle a social, housing or employment snag. It's early days and it's not a magic wand. You know that, don't you? Post-19 may not be easy, especially post-Treloar.

Illustrious alumni shed light on this place. They include Julie Fernandez (she of The Office) and Ash Atallah (he who produced it). There's actor Sophie Partridge ('fierce, fragile' – Guardian), mouth and foot painter Tom Yendell, lawyer Michael Cassidy and Paralympics medal-winning swimmer Danielle Watts, holder of four world records.

Remarks: If non-disabled, you come away from this school counting not your blessings but theirs. For a parent or carer of a child with disabilities, it reconfigures expectations. Does anyone do it better?

TUDOR HALL SCHOOL

Wykham Park, Banbury, Oxfordshire, OX16 9UR

Tel: 01295 263 434

Fax: 01295 253 264

Email: abrauer@tudorhallschool.com

Website: www.tudorhall.oxon.sch.uk

• Pupils: 275 girls; 220 boarding, 55 day • Ages: 11-18

• Religion: Anglican, but makes provision for RCs

• Fees: Boarding £6,515; day £4,200

• School status: Independent • Opendays: Spring and summer

• School gender: Girls • Day/boarding: Takes boarders

SEN provision

Detail:

Now provide for in school:

Mild: ADD; EBD; DYSC; DYSL; DYSP; SpLD; CP;

Others: GEN; DEL; Oth; Eat;

Experience of:

Mild: ASP; ADHD; DS; HI; VI;

Moderate: DYSC; DYSL; DYSP;

Others: OCD; Sp&LD; Epi; PD;

Summary: We are able to provide a full, enriching and balanced curriculum to girls with a variety of mild learning difficulties, physical difficulties and medical conditions. We also provide enrichment for the gifted and talented. We are working towards accreditation by the British Dyslexia Association for Dyslexia Friendly Schools status. All of the staff in the learning support team have specialist qualifications and experience. We would be pleased to discuss any specific needs your daughter may have.

What we say about the school - the full Good Schools Guide review

Head: Since 2004, Miss Wendy Griffiths BSc PGCE (forties). Educated at Queen Elizabeth Grammar School,

Carmarthen, followed by University of Wales, where she read zoology. Taught at Tormead School (member of senior management team and head of sixth form), then became director of studies at St Catherine's, Bramley. Married to history teacher and has young daughter – they live in newly-built house in grounds. A powerhouse of energy who leads from the front. Approachable, dynamic and brimming with ideas. Still teaches biology several times a week and says, 'I love teaching – there's nothing quite like it.' Knows every girl by name and takes huge delight in their achievements, great and small.

Academic Matters: Once known as school for toffs' daughters without academic aspirations but this is certainly not the case now. Academic matters taken very, very seriously and school aims 'to get the best out of every girl.' Achieves good results and comes out well in value added data. 60 per cent plus of GCSE grades A*/A, with girls taking average of 10 subjects. Choice of 20 subjects at A level, with English by far the most popular, followed by French, art and history. 70-ish per cent of A2 and AS grades A/B.

Setting by ability for maths, science and French from first year. Majority of girls learn two languages and there are regular exchange trips to France and Germany. About one third of pupils take separate sciences at GCSE, with rest opting for dual award. Gifted and talented co-ordinator recently appointed to stretch most able girls. School has number of pupils with mild dyslexia and/or learning difficulties – they are taken out of prep periods for one-to-one help at cost of £38 per hour. 155 computers dotted throughout school; most subject areas have access to IT, every girl has e-mail address and there are light, airy computer rooms. Library equipped with 7,000 books and £3,000 a year is spent on new books – Philippa Gregory and Mark Haddon most-borrowed authors. Long-serving and supportive staff who light up with enthusiasm for school. Average age of teachers is 41 and 30 per cent have been at school for more than 10 years. Maximum class size is 24 but, in practice, groups are far smaller.

Games, Options, The Arts: Games are very important part of school life. All girls play sport (including sixth form), exuding fresh-faced enthusiasm and energy in their tartan games skirts and cheery red socks. Professional games staff who teach hockey, lacrosse, netball, rounders, athletics etc. Tennis very popular, played in the old walled garden, covered tennis court or summer-only Astro courts. Two squash courts, large sports hall (complete with basketball court, exercise bikes, weights etc), gym and swimming pool (recently covered with bubble roof for swimming in autumn term). Lots of matches at weekends – though nearest comparable games school almost an hour away.

Music school buzzes with activity. Around 75 girls have instrumental lessons in school and there are concerts galore throughout the year, featuring choirs, orchestras, even a samba band. Dynamic art department, with lots of activities at weekends – candle making, photography, jewellery design etc. Art, textiles, design technology and history of art v popular at A level. Riding, judo, cookery, ballet, tap, word processing. Strong debating and public speaking tradition, with girls taking part in mock United Nations. Lots of community service, including concerts for local OAPs and charity fund-raising. Each year girls form a Young Enterprise company with the help of local businesses. A couple of years ago enterprising pupils set up a knicker company – the most popular product was a pair of knickers emblazoned with 'Good girls go to heaven, bad girls go to Tudor Hall!' Work experience is compulsory for every pupil and there's a World Challenge expedition every two years – recent destinations have included Madagascar, Peru and Tanzania.

Background and Atmosphere: One of the oldest girls' schools in the country, founded in 1850 by the Reverend and Mrs John Todd. Has moved several times but headmistress Nesta Inglis bought stunning Wykham Park at end of World War 2 and school has been there ever since. Main building an imposing country house in honey-coloured stone set in 48 acres of rolling parkland, with maze of inter-connecting buildings added on. Each year group lives in separate bit of school, with lucky 11-year-olds ensconced in cosy Todd House, complete with jolly dorms (plastered with pictures of family and sporting heroes like Jonny Wilkinson), swings and garden where they get their own patch to look after. New girls are assigned 'keepers' from year above to help them settle in and as they move up through school they earn much-prized 'privileges.' These range from 13-year-olds who are deemed to be 'well-behaved and responsible' being allowed to go shopping on Saturday afternoons to 15-year-olds getting the chance to wear home clothes all the time.

Impressive sixth form block – lots of light, space and no uniform. Upper sixth boarders can go home every weekend if wish. Mobile phones are banned for girls in the first two years and after that there are strict rules – depending on age. Younger girls wear slightly old-fashioned bottle green cord skirts and striped blouses. The uniform was under review at the time of our visit but lots of girls said they were quite fond of it! Good, wholesome food served in bustling dining room. Lots of weekend activities and visits to Stratford-upon-Avon, Oxford, Horse of the Year Show etc. Once a year the whole school departs en masse for the day to celebrate the school's birthday – Alton Towers a popular venue. A proper 'full' boarding school – with two organised exeats each term.

Pastoral Care and Discipline: Tudor Hall's forte. Firm, clear rules and no major problems re drugs, booze etc. 'You can never be complacent,' says head, 'but they are just not big issues here.' School's motto is Habeo ut Dem – I have that I may give. School puts strong emphasis on courtesy and holds manners meetings twice a term, where each girl is awarded marks for conduct, kindness, helpfulness etc. Grade A denotes 'an outstanding member of the community' whereas grade E is 'unacceptable behaviour.'

Staff in regular e-mail contact with parents and there are meetings each year to discuss girls' progress. Each house has housemistress and assistant housemistress who take charge of pastoral care. Girls can also talk to their form tutor, the school's 'larger than life' chaplain and a newly-appointed counsellor who comes in several hours a week. Revamped house system, with mixed-age houses – they attend chapel and social events together. Head girl is chosen from lower sixth and changes every term.

Pupils and Parents: Very smiley, purposeful, well-mannered girls, proud of their school and not as frighteningly sophisticated as peers elsewhere. Ex-head girl on point of taking A levels wistful at prospect of leaving – 'it's such a way of life here,' she says. Everywhere you go girls confidently leap to open doors and answer questions. Girls come from all over the UK, many from rural areas. Very few overseas pupils. Notable old girls include Serpentine Gallery director Julia Peyton-Jones, writer Sacha Bonsor and sculptress Candida Bond.

Entrance: Register early. Entry at 11, 12 and 13. Selection process includes school report, common entrance and interview with the head, who looks for 'that special spark.' Occasional vacancy in sixth form – minimum of five GCSEs, with grades A*-B in subjects to be studied at A level.

Exit: Average of three leave post-GCSE, usually for co-ed schools. After A level most go to university – Newcastle, St Andrews, Edinburgh and Exeter current favourites.

Money Matters: Academic, music, art, drama and sport scholarships, but not for huge amounts, plus bursaries. Not a particularly rich school but manages an impressive building programme out of income.

Remarks: A wholesome, happy, successful boarding school that has moved with the times while still hanging on to its much-loved customs and traditions. Large enough to offer good range of subjects and activities but small enough for everyone to know each other. Girls make lifelong friends and school really feels like one big happy family – evidenced by the fact that so many Old Tudorians choose to send their daughters here.

TWYFORD CHURCH OF ENGLAND HIGH SCHOOL

Twyford Crescent, Acton, London, W3 9PP

Tel: 020 8752 0141

Fax: 020 8993 7627

Email: admin@twyford.ealing.sch.uk

• Pupils: 1,247, boys:girls 160:133 • Ages: 11-18

• Religion: C of E • School status: State • Opendays: October

• School gender: Mixed • Day/boarding: Day pupils

SEN provision

Detail:

Centre of excellence for:

Mild: DYSC; DYSL; CP;

Moderate: DYSL; CP;

Severe: DYSL;

Now provide for in school:

Mild: ASP; AUT; ADD; ADHD; EBD; DYSP; HI; VI;

Moderate: ASP; EBD; DYSC; DYSP; HI; VI;

Severe: ASP; DYSC; DYSP;

Summary: The school has expertise in dealing with students with dyslexia or specific learning difficulties. It has also successfully worked with students on the autistic spectrum and those with physical difficulties.

What we say about the school - the full Good Schools Guide review

Head: Since 2002, Ms Alice Hudson MA (fortyish) educated at Slough Girls' High and Leighton Park, then St Hilda's, Oxford, where she read English. Previously deputy head at Brentside HS, also in Ealing, and prior to that taught at Central Foundation Boys', Islington and Maria Fidelis, Euston. Joined Twyford in 2000, first as deputy then as acting head. Married, three young children. This was a failing school, financially, and seriously underperforming academically and socially, when Ms Hudson arrived and one needs to visit the school to believe the extraordinary turnaround she has achieved in her, so far, brief tenure. It is a unique experience for this particular, hardened, Guide editor to see so much change in every aspect of a school's life, effected with such irresistible enthusiasm, focused and intelligent rethinking, authority, conviction and energy – all articulated in an entirely disarming and infectious manner. Very much faith-inspired vision of what the school should – and could – be.

Our meeting was delayed and then punctuated by fallout from an incident before school – pupils set upon by a child from another school – and Ms Hudson was hot on the case to identify the culprit and ensure via a meeting between perpetrator and victims that it wouldn't be repeated. 'She gets involved ... you see her about ... she makes people take a pride in themselves'. Somehow she manages to teach nine periods weekly. Her idea of a 'career break' was to have three children in four years and to do a simultaneous MA in education policy. Hm! 'Profoundly', is a key word in her vocabulary. Staff pay tribute – 'she is an absolutely delightful person to work for'. Lucky school.

Academic Matters: Hugely improved results in this, academically, non-selective school. Three Bs average at A level; maths results exceptional. Choices include economics, music tech, photography (very successful), psychology, sociology. Biggest improvement in sixth form – head's especial baby – 'it's a reliable place for your high-achieving child ... we chase them much more in the sixth form', but the less academic well supported too.

ICT (we saw loads of computers) a developing area though head refreshingly cheery when asked about interactive whiteboards – 'almost nothing.' Head sees wisdom in routeing the less academic to the practical which 'can be studied alongside A level', so double AVCE in ICT popular along with other more vocational subjects. 12 per cent have SLD or SEN (65 have statements) and are well-supported, either by regular staff or from outside. 'They will be valued and survive here,' says head, 'and parents are very well supported – we have very good home-school links.' 280 pupils have EAL – first languages in this very ethnically mixed area Gujurati, Punjabi, Arabic and Urdu – but no one needs additional help in English. Proactive on modern languages – 'we identify potential linguists in year 7, accelerate them in French and, in year 8, give them a choice of German and Spanish.' RE always a feature of school life and supported by two conferences each year, often with outside speakers on moral or spiritual topics. Curriculum taught on an alternating two-week cycle which some find confusing at first but they get used to it.

Games, Options, The Arts: Remarkable playing fields, well-concealed along this urban high street site. Netball especially strong here but hockey, tennis, football, cricket, basketball too. Dance and athletics popular. Rugby coached by pros from London Wasps. Consistent successes in many sporting areas and representation in borough and regional levels. Thriving art, drama popular and lively though restricted to one well-used studio. Good and well-used music and music tech facilities, especially now with new block and state-of the-art audio-visual recording studio. Good work placement programme. Pupils enthuse about the number and quality of trips and expeditions – everywhere from St Petersburg to the New Forest for every activity imaginable – photography to water skiing. Lots of charity work.

Background and Atmosphere: School tucked behind rare bit of green along the Uxbridge Road. Main building, Grade IIA listed 'The Elms', an elegant, early Georgian house, built 1735, now well-preserved and sensibly painted in blues, houses the admin and offices side of things. A diverse mixture of less distinguished and pretty scruffy later blocks, A, B, unaccountably then D and M, house rest of school – not too much room for growth and development.

Black uniform with white shirts creates somewhat sombre impression but most pupils look tidy (head strides around, unaverse to pointing out, amicably, 'shirt!' to any wearer of stray shirt tails) and overall impression of a good-humoured, confident, mix of the boisterous and the purposeful. No uniform for the sixth. Huge ethnic diversity – 52 per cent from non-white British backgrounds, of whom the largest number from

Afro-Caribbean families; Asians make up next biggest group. Christian principles in practice evident in staff's approach to all aspects of this richly diverse community. While Anglicanism predominates, all churches and faiths are celebrated and explored here and everyone feels part of the school.

Two minutes' daily silent reflection before lessons - 'everyone is quiet', said a sixth former. 'Faith has a big profile here', says head, 'we place a high premium on formal acts of worship.' Everyone attends a termly Communion service and there is a weekly voluntary one. Assemblies are inclusive but have an unashamed Christian bias. 'The key to inter-faith issues,' believes head, 'is to be clear about what one's standpoint is.' She talks of the validity of each individual's own 'faith journey'. 'Spiritual matters are neither embarrassing nor taboo here' – a big claim but it feels legitimate. Pupils, though seldom deferential, respect teachers here – there is a good working relationship between staff and pupils at all levels. 'They stretch you as far as you can go – but not beyond what you can do,' reflected one sixth former.

Pastoral Care and Discipline: Well established system of form tutors – first resource though pupils able to talk to which member of staff they choose. Heads of year back up the tutors and pupils have regular meeting with tutors to check on targets, progress, happiness. Chaplaincy team also available. Interaction between ages encouraged – actively by sixth form mentoring to younger pupils and system of form reps. School Council much appreciated – 'it has a lot of power over changes and we can meet the governors,' we were told. Few serious problems – most pupils feeling that offending in school time and on school property 'not worth it' and seemingly a bit immature, though usual crop of minor misdemeanours.

Pupils and Parents: As above, huge ethnic mix, Christianity being the unifying principle though 30 places reserved each year for those from 'other world faiths' and Christianity itself taking in Russian/Serbian/ Eastern Orthodox along with other denominations. Pupils come from wide geographic area – Brent, Hounslow, all over Ealing and further into town. Most, though, from Christchurch junior school, half a mile away and nearly 50 other primaries. More boys than girls though this not generally perceptible. Princes and paupers here – all social strata represented and cheerfully interrelate.

Entrance: Hugely over-subscribed and getting ever more so. 2003 saw 600 applicants for 190 places and school already stretches its capacity. Complex pecking order based on family's attendance at and commitment to church, along with home's distance from school. Worth checking this out in detail before losing your heart to the place. No one is fooled by rapid conversion when your child is in year six – though it is still – widely and unsuccessfully – tried. 30 places for pupils from other world faiths where the family is committed to the idea and principles in practice of 'faith'. Sixth less stringent – though they must 'have sympathy with the aims of the school' as well as 6 GCSEs at C or above and A/B in A level subjects.

Exit: Vast and creditable range of courses and universities – two to Cambridge in 2003 and everywhere else from Exeter to Newcastle. Pupils encouraged to aim high and have aspirations while remaining realistic and practical.

Remarks: This isn't a smart school and its priorities in the last two years have been to get straight the finances, the staffing, the ethos – this has been triumphantly achieved in startlingly little time but a lot remains for this dynamic regime to accomplish.

THE UNICORN SCHOOL

Whitefield, 18 Park Crescent, Eynsham, Abingdon, Oxfordshire, OX14 1DD

Tel: 01235 530 222

Fax: 01235 530222

Email: unicorndyslexia@hotmail.com

Website: www.unicorndyslexia.co.uk

• Pupils: 40 (38 boys and 2 girls), all day • Ages: 6-12

• Fees: £3,840 • School status: Independent

• School gender: Mixed • Day/boarding: Day pupils

SEN provision

Detail:

Centre of excellence for:

Mild: DYSC; DYSL; DYSP;

Moderate: DYSC; DYSL; DYSP;

Severe: DYSC; DYSL; DYSP;

Experience of:

Mild: ASP; ADD; ADHD; EBD; HI; VI;

Moderate: ADD; ADHD; VI;

Others: SPD; FRX; DEL; PD; Eat;

Summary: The aim and philosophy of the Unicorn School is to provide specialist education for dyslexic children, from both the independent and mainstream sectors, and to teach strategies and skills to enable them to return to mainstream education as soon as possible. Pupils are taught by specialist teachers in small classes of eight to ten, with a daily half-hour of individual tuition. Educational and emotional needs are met on an individual basis as well as through a friendly atmosphere and community spirit. Parents are supported throughout the time they are associated with the school and helped to find supportive schools for their children to move on to.

What we say about the school - the full Good Schools Guide review

Head: Since 2004, Mrs Jackie Vaux MA (Oxon), BSc Psychology (forties). Joined Unicorn in 1998 as special needs co-ordinator from state sector. Modern languages graduate St Catherine's, Oxford, husband an Oxford medical tutor, four children aged 14 to 24. Very open and enthusiastic with energy to spare and to share. Hugely supportive of highly dedicated staff and derives immense pleasure from pupils' progress. (During our visit, one boy read out a poem he'd written, prompting this response from the head – 'you have no idea what a great personal achievement that was. It's wonderful.') Big plans for the future, which have governors' full support, include some expansion as have now reached capacity on current site. But head quick to point out, 'we would not change the nature of the school. We're like a family.'

Entrance: All pupils must have report from educational psychologist identifying moderate to severe dyslexia as primary need. Pupils may also have secondary needs such as dyspraxia, dyscalculia, speech and language or physical disabilities. But dyslexia is a must. Some referred from primary or prep schools, most contact though initiated by anxious parents who see their children under-achieving and floundering in schools without the specialist skills or facilities. Entry on first-come-first-served basis. Demand for places very high in year 5 when learning difficulties normally identified with waiting list usually for years 4, 5 and 6.

Exit: Pupils expected to stay between one and three years. School's stated aim is 'to try to give all the appropriate help needed to address literacy and numeracy difficulties as quickly as possible so that he/she can return to mainstream education'. Places sought at known supportive schools and parents given plenty of help and advice in finding the right one for them. Popular choices include Pangbourne College (near Reading), St Bartholomew's (near Witney), Cokethorpe (Witney).

Remarks: A small but vital school which does wonders with its children. Founded in 1991 with just five pupils, demand has forced it to grow quickly and keep moving to larger premises. It now leases a charming old boarding house from neighbouring Abingdon School in a lovely quiet area of the town beside a public park. The classrooms aren't huge, but there's no need as there are never more than 10 youngsters in them at any one time and they're well fitted out with computers in all, plus an IT suite with interactive whiteboard. Also small one-to-one tuition rooms. Lessons in numeracy and literacy held in mornings when children at their most receptive, also every child given at least 30 minutes individual teaching a day. Rest of timetable is along National Curriculum lines – including humanities, science, DT, drama, French and ICT – but tailored to specific needs. Touch-typing taught from day one. All classes very hands-on and children encouraged to develop their strengths as much as strengthen their weaknesses. SATs are taken but marked internally. Also extra exam time allowed where necessary. Teaching staff of 15, all specialists so appropriate help can be given. Children given free rein to express themselves but within disciplined and well-structured environment. Head recognises self-esteem likely to be very low and sense of failure high when new pupils arrive, so much effort spent on rebuilding confidence first and foremost. 'Children are never put in a position where they could fail here,' says head. Four sports periods a week – football, hockey, touch rugby, sailing and swimming. After-school clubs include art, shooting, table tennis and badminton. Lawns and hard play areas around the Unicorn for children to use at break. PE hall and larger sports field thanks to Abingdon School. Unicorn's long-term aim to be Centre of Excellence for Dyslexia. Saturday morning pilot project currently running for parents whose children need significant help with literacy or maths but can't afford private tuition. Staffed by volunteer specialists and already proving great success. Also for those parents who are able to pay, school will send specialist teachers into other schools to help on one-to-one basis in cases of mild dyslexia as part of Outreach programme. On money matters, Unicorn now building up capital to fund annual bursary. High teacher:pupil ratio ensures high standards of pastoral care. Children know where to turn for help and recently completed questionnaire as part of anti-bullying campaign. Vulnerable areas swiftly identified and corrected. Very supportive network of parents. Those questioned could not praise school highly enough. Said one, 'I don't know what we'd have done without it. It's been a life-saver.'

UPPINGHAM COMMUNITY COLLEGE

London Road, Uppingham, Oakham, Rutland, LE15 9TJ

Tel: 01572 823 631

Fax: 01572 821 193

Email: principal@ucc.rutland.sch.uk

Website: www.ucc.rutland.sch.uk

• Pupils: 852 boys and girls, roughly split 50:50; all day
• Ages: 11-16 • Religion: Non-denom • School status: State
• School gender: Mixed • Day/boarding: Day pupils

SEN provision

Detail:

Experience of:

Mild: ASP; AUT; ADD; EBD; DYSC; DYSL; DYSP; SpLD; HI; VI; CP;

Moderate: ASP; AUT; ADD; EBD; MLD; DYSC; DYSL; DYSP; SpLD; HI;

Severe: SpLD;

Others: EAL; DEL; Epi; PD; Eat;

Summary: The College has an excellent Additional Needs (Curriculum Support) department led by a very experienced SEN co-ordinator. The provision received particular praise in the most recent Ofsted inspection. A new Additional Needs Learning Room has just been equipped with Successmaker software to promote individual learning for children with special needs. A team of experienced teaching assistants work with students through classroom support and withdrawal.

What we say about the school - the full Good Schools Guide review

Principal: Since 2000, Mr Malcolm England MA PGCE (mid-forties), educated at the Royal Grammar School, Worcester and Worcester College, Oxford. A linguist, he succeeded the highly respected Peter Macdonald-Pearce, working closely with him prior to taking up post. Previously head of Testbourne Community School, Hampshire. One of first group to take National Professional Qualification for Headship (1998). Married, with three children. Friendly and approachable. Knows large proportion of pupils by first names.

Academic Matters: School has had specialist technology college since 1995. Most recent Ofsted report (February 2001) describes it as 'a very successful school with many significant strengths and no major weaknesses.' Particularly strong in ICT, maths, science and design technology but prides itself on being just as good in the arts. Was one of the first schools in the country to be awarded the Artsmark for excellence in the provision of arts education and has now achieved Artsmark Gold status. Full network of bang-up-to-date computers, with one computer to every four pupils. Most take ICT at GCSE and the college is currently a pilot school for the new Diploma in Digital Applications course. Good GCSE results in general (65 per cent achieved at least five grades A*-C at GCSE in 2005). Healthy mix of experienced staff – many have been here for more than ten years – and newly qualified teachers. The average class size is 28. Mixed ability classes on entry but by year 8 there is setting in maths and languages (French and German). Homework ranges from 30 minutes a night for the youngest to two-and-a-half hours for GCSE students. Parents are asked to sign their child's homework diary each week. Cheerful 'Additional Needs' room offers help to 160, often one-to-one. Can also cater for pupils needing English 'as an additional language' though there aren't many.

Games, Options, The Arts: School rightfully proud of its 'session six' courses – 40 different activities, from sport, music and dance through to chess, pottery, sign language, film making and fashion design. All students must take at least one session six course each term and some take more. Good on sport – including football, rugby, hockey, cricket, tennis, fitness, gym and dance. Large sports hall, fitness centre and extensive playing fields on school site. College also holds Sportsmark award for strengths in PE. All pupils have two games lessons every week and 25 per cent take PE at GCSE. Very popular sporting exchange link with school in Haacht, Belgium, has been going for 30 years. The college has secured most of the funding for a proposed new full-size artificial playing surface which is likely to be built in early 2006. Music strong though only 150 pupils play a musical instrument and there are lots of orchestras, choirs and bands to join. Fantastic drama studio, with specialised lighting, where assemblies are held too.

Background and Atmosphere: Set on edge of historic town of Uppingham, overlooking rolling countryside. Self-contained site is key attraction for parents. Has been a school on this site since 1920. Original red-brick school building has been vastly added-to and is now a maze of inter-connecting buildings – visitors need a map to make sense of it! More building work – to add three classrooms and extra changing facilities – taking place when we visited. Pupils enthusiastic, friendly and forthcoming. A chirpy year 8 was manning the reception desk – principal says it encourages pride in the school and everyone gets a go. College council with reps from each year group offers forum for airing ideas and suggestions on how to improve school. A recent complaint about the dreariness of the girls' cloakroom led to a group of year 11s being allowed to come in before term to redecorate in zingy greens and yellows! Principal holds 'success assembly' every half term to celebrate students' achievements both in and out of school – not simply a eulogy to the brightest students. The school also acts as a lead school for the international EC Comenius project and has links with schools in Italy, Poland and Germany.

Pastoral Care and Discipline: College logo is 'caring and challenging.' Students can talk to head of year or their form tutor, who remains with them as they progress through the school. College has structured approach of reports and detentions. Bullying is rare and swiftly dealt with in line with a charter developed by students and staff and endorsed by governors. College also has strong links with local community. There is an on-site nursery – where some year 10s choose to do work experience – an adult learning centre and an Extended Schools Centre.

Pupils and Parents: Students come from predominantly rural catchment area – around 300 from town of Uppingham itself. Increasing number from outlying areas of Oakham and Corby. Plain navy/black uniform worn, with older students getting chance to choose a different coloured sweatshirt to the rest of the school. Former pupils include Sally Reddin, shot put gold medallist at the 2000 Paralympics, and businessman John Browett, chief executive of Tesco.com.

Entrance: Comprehensive intake. Regularly over-subscribed. Priority given to pupils from seven designated primary schools in Rutland and Leicestershire and those with siblings already at the school. Parents very impressed with induction arrangements for new pupils.

Exit: Most students (around 85 per cent) continue into further education at 16. The majority go on to local sixth form colleges or FE colleges, a few to independent schools.

Remarks: A popular and thriving community school with dedicated staff and motivated students.

WALDEGRAVE SCHOOL

Fifth Cross Road, Twickenham, Middlesex, TW2 5LH

Tel: 020 8894 3244

Fax: 020 8893 3670

Email: info@waldegrave.richmond.sch.uk

Website: www.waldegrave.richmond.sch.uk

• Pupils: 1,040 girls, all day • Ages: 11-16

• Religion: Non-denom • School status: State

• School gender: Girls • Day/boarding: Day pupils

SEN provision

Detail:

Centre of excellence for:

Mild: ASP; EBD; DS; DYSC; DYSL; DYSP; HI; CP;

Moderate: DS; MLD; DYSC; DYSL; HI;

Severe: DS; DYSL;

Others: EAL; Epi;

Now provide for in school:

Mild: AUT; ADD; ADHD; SpLD; VI;

Moderate: ASP; EBD; DYSP; SpLD; VI;

Others: CD; OCD; FRX; DEL; PD; Eat;

Summary: At Waldegrave we believe pupils with special educational needs should be offered full access to a broad, balanced and relevant education, including appropriate access to the National Curriculum.

All teachers in the school share the responsibility for identifying and responding to the special educational needs of all pupils. All teachers are teachers of pupils with special educational needs.

A variety of methods is employed to meet the wide range of pupils needs: modification of materials, provision of individualised structured programmes, and the use of a range of teaching methods as well as differing degrees of support. Use is made of the learning resources centre and flexible learning methods.

What we say about the school - the full Good Schools Guide review

Head: Since 1992, Mrs Heather Flint BSocSc (Soc Admin) PGCE MA (fifties), educated at Birmingham and London universities. Has taught since 1973 in London comprehensive schools, with a break 1987-1992 when she was an adviser on educational issues to ministers in the Employment Department. Married with grown-up stepchildren. Very welcoming to visitors, bubbling with enthusiasm to show people around the school but with a slightly hurried air as she marches at top speed down the corridors. However, she gives the impression that she would make time for any girl or parent who needed her – she is very approachable. Parents describe her as 'highly respected' and 'very organised' or 'a bit formidable'.

Departing in 2006. Successor will be Mrs Philippa Nunn, currently head of Holt School in Wokingham. Married with two children.

Academic Matters: Academically, the strongest state school in the borough of Richmond – 80 per cent got 5+ GCSE A*-C grades in 2005. Most students sit nine GCSEs. In 2005, a third of GCSE grades were A*/A. One student got one of the top five marks in the country in English literature. The school feels that it, 'succeeds in setting high standards for its wide range of pupils through interesting, varied and appropriate teaching and the setting of individual challenging targets'. Curriculum adequate but not very wide – only French and German as modern foreign languages, no Latin, and currently only dual award science. Plenty of DT, and PE and IT are both taken at GCSE. For the majority, there are quite enough subjects on offer – 'my child could not cope with three foreign languages and Latin,' said a parent. A very bright pupil might not agree.

School now a specialist science school – hoping to offer single sciences to some and increase the number of girls who go on to science A levels – at present very low. Waldegrave has Beacon status and is a Leading Edge school – brings in extra money but, even so, you feel there is simply not enough for the needs of such a diverse school population. Priority recently given to ICT (all the computers, old and new, were in use on our visit) but probably what can't be afforded is more staff to increase the breadth of the curriculum and extra-curricular activities and to provide stimulus for the girls for whom an A* at GCSE is a piece of cake.

Pupils are put in sets for maths in year 7 and for science and foreign languages in year 8. Further setting as they move up the school but not for English – school feels it best taught in mixed ability groups. Targeted help for EFL (currently about 10 per cent of pupils) and for any type of special needs through an individual learning department described as 'very strong' by one parent.

Lots of voluntary extra lessons at various times throughout the day to help those who need it (apparently well-attended) – may be part of the reason for the good academic record but it could be to the detriment of extra-curricular activities. For example, all lunchtime clubs currently are extra classes for curriculum subjects, except rehearsals for the school play. After school there is orchestra, choir, drama, IT and sport but also a homework club. School day ends at 3.15pm – you wonder what the girls do for the rest of the day if they have finished their homework by 4.00. Some parental grouses on homework – 'there is an element who do not complete the work assigned...work is not always marked and returned or only very late.' School disputes both vigorously.

Games, Options, The Arts: Opportunities for sport are limited – only one small sports hall and team sports do not apparently appeal to many, eg the twice weekly after school hockey practice is for all age groups at once; only one PE lesson a week for years 7 and 9 (two for year 8). Despite this, school has achieved a Sportsmark award – the situation in other state schools is a lot worse. New dance studio soon to be built and off-site activity courses are made available from time to time. Art is a strength – school has an Artsmark silver award – and more than 50 per cent take it at GCSE. Music department described as 'lacking' by a musical family but Richmond Music Trust (a borough organisation) helps here.

Background and Atmosphere: Buildings fairly scruffy and the newer block is workmanlike rather than smart – however, lots of excellent artwork on the walls to cheer things up. Indoor space is at a premium – school is so full – but some of the outdoor space is under-used and under-maintained; the large athletics pitch doesn't show many signs of regular use. Sensible, workmanlike uniform worn by all, with skirts worn far too short by some (very common in other girls-only schools in the area too).

The only single sex state school in the borough of Richmond – more opportunities for the predominantly female staff to fill leading roles within the school and become good role models for the girls, says the head. She also feels it removes any concerns about girls not feeling 'cool' in front of boys if seen to be working, especially at more 'male' subjects like science. 'All my child's teachers are very enthusiastic and motivating and set her very high targets,' said a parent, 'but sometimes her achievements are not recognised as she does not collect her merit awards.' Perhaps too uncool to do so?

Pastoral Care and Discipline: Tutor groups (classes) keep the same form tutor right through their school career. 'I see this as a positive thing,' said a parent, who felt that his child benefited from the close relationship. Another, though, said that the tutor still did not seem to know her child after a year. Behaviour generally good – usual noise and chatter at the end of class as pupils proceed one way – lack of space – down the corridors but attentive and interested pupils in class. Opportunities to take on responsibility, eg a system of peer mediation – a group of specially trained girls available to talk through disagreements between pupils – designed to cut down on bullying. Every girl at some point takes a turn to man reception for a day and charitable activities a regular feature.

Pupils and Parents: Misses out on some of the brightest girls as the most 'pushy' parents who can't afford private school will attempt to move heaven and earth to get a place at the local grammar. School ethnically mixed and pupils and parents are also a social mix. Local 'posh' private school girls complain of bad language, taunts and smoking on the bus but are they such angels themselves, we wonder?

Entrance: From 50 local primary schools in the boroughs of Richmond and neighbouring Hounslow. Preference for SEN, girls in care, siblings (widely defined), then for girls who have expressed a preference for single sex education. A complicated and changeable system of 'quadrants' decides who get a place, based on distance (by public road or footpath) from the school. The school isn't even the central point of the four quadrants and, although the quadrant areas have not changed since 2000, the chance of success is dependent on how many people have applied from each quadrant. Hence the pattern of successful applications varies from year to year. Understanding the system should be enough to guarantee anyone a place at the school – alas, it is not. Heavily over-subscribed, a handful of girls is awarded a place each year on appeal (10 in 2004) – thus school is always over-crowded. 'The staff has to get used to it', says Mrs Flint, 'only 26 in a class would be ideal.' Most tutor groups have 28.

Exit: Currently no Richmond state schools have a sixth form, so most girls go on to the Richmond sixth form college.

Remarks: Happy atmosphere and professional feel. A girl with drive and independence could do very well here but extras like high level sport or further academic subjects would have to come from outside school.

Wellesley House School

Broadstairs, Kent, CT10 2DG

Tel: 01843 862 991

Fax: 01843 602 068

Email: office@wellesleyhouse.org

Website: www.wellesleyhouse.org

• Pupils: 80 boys, 45 girls; 80 per cent boarding • Ages: 7-13
• Religion: C of E • School status: Independent
• School gender: Mixed • Day/boarding: Takes boarders

SEN provision

Detail:

Now provide for in school:

Mild: ASP; AUT; DYSC; DYSL; DYSP; HI;

Moderate: MLD; DYSP; HI;

Severe: HI;

Others: AUT(other); EAL;

Experience of:

Mild: ADD; ADHD; EBD;

Others: CD; OCD; Sp&LD; Epi; PD; Eat;

Summary: We have a fully qualified SENCo who is a full-time member of staff. We have a specialist SENCo room fully equipped with the latest computer technology for special needs. The school operates a SEN policy which enables liaison between teaching staff and SEN staff.

SEN teaching takes place during the normal school day. Children are withdrawn from lessons or games for up to two half-hour periods a week. We can cope with most mild forms of SEN conditions under the SEN description. For a full account of our policy contact the school. We will be only too willing to discuss special needs with you.

What we say about the school - the full Good Schools Guide review

Head: Since 1990, Mr Richard Steel BSc, previously head of York House Day Preparatory School. He has three children, one son at King's Canterbury, one daughter at university and one actress daughter. Conventional, very kind man, gives impression of keeping his cards close to chest. Enjoys his role 'as setting the tone for the school', thinks of himself as a people person keeping regular contact with the staff, pupils, parents. He teaches RE to top two years and runs the school on Christian principles hoping that some will subconsciously rub off on the children. 'This is an impressionable age – we are aware that we are establishing their future life skills now.' Strongly supported by a vivacious, attractive, fit wife, Judith (swims daily and runs up main stairs in a blink) – contrasting qualities of husband and wife prove a good double act for the school.

Retiring in July 2007.

Entrance: By interview, broad range of abilities accepted. Will take special needs provided they need no more than 2 half-hour lessons per week (approx 20 such pupils now). An assessment is given to pupils entering at age 10 and over.

Exit: Majority to King's Canterbury, Eton, Benenden, Tonbridge, Harrow, Marlborough and Stowe. Handful of scholarships over the last few years but intake is broad and, as they mainly exit to major league schools, these are competitive and coveted places. 3rd Scholarship to Eton in 2003. 2004 scholarships to Radley, Benenden and Tonbridge. Exhibition to King's Canterbury (academic); to Harrow (music); chemistry Prize in CE to Rugby; geography prize in CE to Benenden. Music scholarship to Eton in 2005.

Remarks: An attractive red-brick building a short leap from the sea situated away from the city hubbub – a rambling building that houses both classrooms and boys' dorms. Mix of old with the new. A predominantly traditional boarding school, family feel pervades, also respect, order, sound principles rooted into the brickwork. Head is keen to promote new style boarding ie interactive and family centred – being blessed with unformidable, very experienced, pleasant matrons and plenty of domestic staff. 'Children are meticulously cared for and boarding is thoroughly planned,' says the head and the pastoral side is a real strength of the school, agreed by parents and inspectors alike.

Dorms are fastidiously clean and tidy – perfectly pressed clothes on the end of the new pine beds, towels and flannels hanging just so – all in light airy rooms. Junior boys sleep, work, eat and play in the junior house. Junior house girls sleep at The Orchard girls' house. Senior dorms upstairs (10-13 years) varying from 5 to 10 in a room. A Captain sleeps in each senior dorm as a responsible vigilante. Judith overseas all health/domestic matters – even holding hands for hospital visits. 'We are conscious of children growing up before their time in boarding life – we guard against that'. All girls board at Orchard House which is situated across the playing fields through an orchard of apple trees, hence the dorms named Blenheim, Russet etc. and run by geography master, Mr Nichol, and his Spanish wife – 'essential they can be feminine and have girlie time,' said a petite and efficient Mrs Nichol. There is constant communication with parents and a sound anti-bullying policy. Food is 'not great' say the pupils, vegetarian option.

2001 inspection must have come as a shock and has led to widespread improvements. Some good news – geography, English and history recognised as good (Townsend Warner winner 1998), Latin and games commended – testimony to this is that eight pupils have read classics in Oxbridge over the last five years and three old boys recently took the classics master out to dinner to thank him for sparking their interest in the subject. Good languages department offering German, Greek and Spanish has developed good links with English-speaking institute in Madrid. We witnessed an especially good English lesson where the deputy head interacted and elicited profound insights from a text, often bursting into dramatic characterisations. Pastoral and social responsibilities also highly regarded.

On the down side (and it is most encouraging to see ISI becoming more critical and objective) the inspectors reported unevenly balanced curriculum, inadequate monitoring of child and staff performance and a 'significant proportion' of below-par teaching, particularly in music and French and at Key Stage 2. This unnerved some parents and staff and served as a wake-up call to bring a refreshing breeze of modernity to the curriculum. Much has now been done to bring the curriculum up to speed. Recent reported visit from an Inspector was very complimentary about teaching and progress. New director of studies, appointed in 2004, monitoring and developing the curriculum. Inset training is also being addressed (very important when there is not much turnover of staff to keep them up-to-date with new methods in education).

Good, large and comfortable library; ICT room well-equipped and plans include networking all departments. Children's art not much in evidence on our visit but head assured us now that corridors always full of it. Art is two lessons a week with drama and design technology timetabled on a rotational basis. Music picking up and results are good. Children are streamed further up the school and because the school is small, it can tailor to individual needs. A real 'fast tracker' will progress up the school unhindered by constraints of curriculum.

Sport is very strong – enviable record as long as your arm of past and present achievements, frequently winning national and county events in hockey, rounders and cricket (only school to have produced two captains of England – Mann and Cowdrey). National winners of JET cricket 2003. Does exceptionally well in golf – greatly benefiting from their own beautiful putting green, also being neighbours with Royal St George's with first rate professionals. School has a well-equipped sports hall, sunny, heated indoor swimming pool, tennis courts, squash courts and a shooting range tucked snugly off a corner of well-manicured playing fields (.22 rifle team regularly achieve success). National winners of JET Rounders U13 competition in 2005.

Culturally, plenty going on – annual dramatic productions, general knowledge team reaching semi-finals recently at national IAPS level, chess, regular debates and fashion shows for the girls. 2002 contributed a school float for the Lord Mayor's parade – he himself an Old Boy. Children given choice with some aspects of uniform but formal wear should conform to any sports jacket, trousers, schools tie and shorts.

A classy school that is steeped in tradition and, considering boarding schools are a dying breed, surviving well (if a little below capacity); little drop-out, and, for the most part, happy parents. The school has responded robustly to 'resting on laurels' and 'lacking fizz factor'. A great deal has been achieved since the ISI report in 2001.

Westbourne House School

Shopwyke, Chichester, West Sussex, PO20 2BH

Tel: 01243 782 739

Fax: 01243 770 757

Email: whouseoffice@rmplc.co.uk

Website: www.westbournehouse.org

• Pupils: 365 (200 boys, 165 girls); 50 boys and 25 girls board • Ages: 3-7 pre-prep; 7-13 prep • Religion: C of E • Fees: Full board £4,290; day £1,800 in the pre-prep rising to £3,450 • School status: Independent • Opendays: None. The headmaster wants to see you • School gender: Mixed • Day/boarding: Takes boarders

SEN provision

Detail:
Now provide for in school:
Mild: ASP; ADD; DYSL; DYSP;

Summary: All our children enter the school having completed an assessment showing that they are able to cope with mainstream school. However, if children are flagged up as having a specific need or a need is picked up at a later date, these children will receive extra support from our excellent SEN team. SEN questionnaire details added by us.

What we say about the school - the full Good Schools Guide review

Headmaster: Since 2003, Mr Brendan Law (late thirties). Born and educated in South Africa where he taught at their first-ever multiracial school. Came by way of Sweden to Bedford School 1995, where he was meteorically made senior housemaster. Sports mad – coaches the lot. Dyed in the wool boarder. The great Colin Sharman, head for 28 years and father of today's school, says feelingly and with understatement, 'we were very lucky to get him.' Brendan (he's a first name man) is clearly an effective force and affectingly anxious to head a kind, happy, achieving school. Early changes spooked some teachers but the force is with him. Parents like him exceedingly and say his door really is always open. His wife, Linda, is seen by parents as a 'huge asset'. She does a bundle of liaison and co-ordination things – she's the school mum. Two children, one of each, both at the school. Golden retriever, just as there ought to be.

Entrance: Most from a 15-mile radius. Unfiltered for nursery and pre-prep, assessment for entry to year 3. Because this is a local school the mesh is not fine, but big SENs are urged to think again. Best get in early – roughly 36 go on from the pre-prep to be joined by 18 or so brand new year 3s. Very few chinks higher up. Scholarship: 50 per cent for music. Sundry bursaries for those who fall on hard times and 5 per cent off for brothers and sisters. Racial mix reflects the local community: almost none – but there is a charming smattering of Germans from nearby Rolls Royce. Website a touch stuffy but fully informative.

Exit: Almost all stay to year 8, then fly to the full rainbow of independent seniors of which the most flavoursome are Marlborough, Canford, Sherborne, Charterhouse, Eton, Winchester, Radley, Harrow, Wellington, Cranleigh, Portsmouth Grammar, Bryanston, Bedales, Lancing, Benenden, St Swithun's, St Mary's Ascot, Downe House. Scholarship hit rate an arrestingly high 35 per cent of all leavers (39 per cent in 2004). Eminent outgoers include R4's Marcus Brigstocke (funny) and Nick Clarke (news); and Monarch of the Glen, Alastair McKenzie.

Remarks: Here's a school which has responded nimbly to a changing market with no sense of reactive incoherence. Until 1990 it was all boys, all boarding. Now it serves a prosperous local community which prefers day early on with some weekly boarding in the last two years as a rehearsal for a boarding senior. Saturday morning school survives impregnable. Parents say the school has done the transition from the old to the now brilliantly.

Blessed with a high acre:pupil ratio, this is a spacious place with a campus-y feel and all the playing fields you can count. In the midst is the late Georgian (1840) house and, liberally disposed, the usual school buildings, some characterful, some not. They've spent well over £2 million in the last five years – including good science labs, IT, dining, classrooms and theatre – and are inordinately and justly proud that the lion's share of that came from prudently husbanded fee income. Indoor swimming pool, sports hall, separate music and art.

Academically the range is wide. Those scholarships tell it all for top-notch teaching, but parents say strugglers are well supported too because all are lauded for what they're good at: 'the teachers really care'. The accent in all things is on making children feel good about themselves. There are extension lessons for the bright and reinforcement lessons for the not-so. Emergent special needs are swiftly spotted and fixed by the superb SEN department where the emphasis is on not creating dependence: 'Our job,' says Lynda Butt, a school hero, 'is to make ourselves redundant.' Children come only if they choose and include a sprinkling of prospective scholars. She does what SENCos do best – get the other teachers talking to each other. All do SATS and results feed internal monitoring systems. Talking about the right senior school starts in year 2.

Art and ceramics flourish luxuriantly and joyously in an inspirational environment where colour blazes and craft skills are taught to the accompaniment of the romping of the imagination. Music is eye-blinkingly good. An unusual number play at grades 6-8, and 80 per cent of the children learn an instrument. Every year, fantastic scholarships and super concerts, but the rigour can be chilling. We are promised that more fun is afoot, and a broader range. Vital.

Sport is played with full fervour and results to match. Observable at every level is a high level of coaching. Whatever they teach you here they teach you to do it well. Matches well supported by parents, with lots of bonding and dogs on the many touchlines. Picnics in the grounds after Saturday lessons all year round.

Boarding is the tradition and it lives on, most popularly in years 7 and 8. No sloppy sleepover stuff, and 'although we are always open for business over weekends' almost all go home. Most sleep in the main house with some boys in outhouses, looked after by houseparents. It's not much to look at, not as fluffy as some – but the pastoral care is in place and misses little. A key feature, now copied elsewhere, is their system of Friends, trained year 8 counsellors – impressively successful and testimony to strong seriousness. Lots to do after school, it's on the up, and the point is this – the children love it.

Here is a school which does more than it says on the tin. We have never met so many parents who never thought to look elsewhere. The boys and girls are chummy, charming and bright-eyed. In an environment of humanity and hard work parents get what they want: happy, confident children who do the best they can.

Westlands School and Technology College

Westlands Lane, Torquay, Devon, TQ1 3PE

Tel: 01803 400 660

Fax: 01803 408 897

Email: cabarr@westlands.torbay.sch.uk

Website: www.westlandstc.com

• Pupils: 1,400 boys and girls • Ages: 11-18

• Religion: Non-denom • School status: State

• School gender: Mixed • Day/boarding: Day pupils

SEN provision

Detail:

Centre of excellence for:

- Mild: DYSL; HI;
- Moderate: DYSL; HI;
- Severe: DYSL; HI;

Now provide for in school:

- Mild: ADD; EBD; DYSP;
- Moderate: ADD; EBD; MLD; DYSP;
- Severe: EBD;
- Others: TIC; PMLD; SLD;

Experience of:

- Mild: DS; DYSC;
- Moderate: DYSC;
- Severe: DYSC;
- Others: MSI; Sp&LD; PD;

Summary: Considerable efforts are made to support the needs of the individual child. The school has an SEN department which supports students in lessons as well as withdrawing them for precision teaching. Specialist accommodation is provided to support the working of the department, and support is given across the complete range of academic subjects. All students are involved in a mentoring programme which seeks to support their individual needs and developments. There are specialist mentors and external agencies available to students. The school encourages the involvement of parents in this process.

What we say about the school - the full Good Schools Guide review

Head: Since 1995, Mr Michael TH Stewart TD BEd AdvDipEdMan FIMgt FRSA (fifties). A Sussex University graduate. MPhil from East Anglia University; Open University advanced management diploma. Taught in various comprehensives. Positions include head of ICT and maths departments; deputy head and education officer for a spell. Quietly confident, competent and successful. Aims to turn out all-rounders who leave to become 'responsible well-adjusted citizens with a caring attitude to others.' Former member of TA for 27 years. Married with two children; one achieved a first class honours degree after being educated at Westlands.

Academic Matters: Lots of opportunities to develop individual talents. Depending on performance, pupils can migrate between two grammar-stream sets and six non-selective ones. Varied abilities however, are reflected in overall results. Top-stream pupils and parents believe the more relaxed atmosphere leads to higher grades – 'it's a less pressurised environment than some grammar schools where bulimia and anorexia can prevail'. Popular A level choices are English, maths, art, history and geography. Other courses include NVQ business studies, GNVQs, Btec public services course. Mr Stewart equally proud of university undergraduates leaving with two Es or four As at A level. 'The school places enormous emphasis on the individual, ensuring their education and well-being are closely monitored.'

Dedicated partially-hearing unit with well-qualified staff provides extra tuition where needed. Otherwise, partially-hearing students wear hearing aids and are fully integrated into lessons. 'Teachers really seem to care above and beyond their call of duty,' say parents, and some have voluntarily learnt to sign to improve communication.

Games, Options, The Arts: Facilities to boast of – impressive soundproof media/recording studio, five ICT rooms, two drama practice rooms, dance studio, eight music rooms. Multi-purpose, sports and drama production halls. Large, well-stocked and organised library, ample computers. Uses neighbouring public swimming pool and tennis courts. Extensive sporting and extra-curricular opportunities including DJ skills, first aid, various music clubs, astronomy, aerobics, girls' football, dance. County successes in chess, rugby (Harlequins), athletics. Cricket is definite strength, lots of cup wins. Outstanding success in D of E and Ten Tors. Up and coming orchestra – first UK tour in 2003. Family-to-family exchange arrangement with French school proving popular.

Background and Atmosphere: The school doors open early and shut late. There is always something happening so pupils can and do enjoy school life to the full – important to the pupils and achieved by most. Perhaps not the world's calmest sea but a place replicating a real and normal community, where politeness is usual, and the high standards of bright and exceptionally able students entwine with the talents of slower developers. 'Pupils are proud of their new school and generally care about it,' say parents.

A technology college since September 2002, it began in 1973 with the amalgamation of two high schools. One of four bilateral schools in country. Completed rebuild in 2001, a 'breath of fresh air' say its hardworking and dedicated teachers. Hi-tech security system, with cameras in corridors and classrooms, helps to eradicate any disruptive behaviour that can creep in on occasion (extreme mixes in social backgrounds here). Everyone is screened before entering through electronic doors. Students encouraged to see themselves as part of community by taking school band to elderly people's homes, organising charity fund-raising events, helping in special schools (sixth formers).

Pastoral Care and Discipline: School's teaching ethos includes social training, although tireless efforts are not always rewarded. 'I hated my old school; everyone is friendlier at Westlands and I now enjoy going. The staff and pupils treat you as an individual and with respect.' Westlands' excellent pastoral care has resulted in Investors in People, Healthy School, Investors in Careers and School Achievement awards. In-house education welfare officer helps abate truancy. Few expulsions in current head's reign. An air of leniency and forgiveness for one-off misdemeanours. No smoking on-site for teachers and students alike. 'The dedicated parent telephone line is extremely useful', say parents, 'you can always speak with someone if necessary.'

Pupils and Parents: Two nationally designated 'deprivation wards' situated within Westlands' catchment area means pupils come from both ends of social scale – they mix happily.

Entrance: Foundation school since 2003, therefore responsible for own admissions via common admissions process. Students achieving high enough 11+ scores awarded one of 60 selective (grammar) places; usually from Torbay. 150 comprehensive places filled by students from St Marychurch, Babbacombe and Ellacombe areas of Torquay. Pupils living outside Westlands' catchment area still eligible and parental preference is acceded to wherever possible.

Exit: 10 per cent of sixth form enters from outside. 80 per cent of year 11 continue at Westlands with its 26 available courses, 12 per cent go to South Devon College, others to armed forces, public services or work placements. Up to 80 per cent to university – mainly at Plymouth, Exeter, Swansea, Bristol, Southampton. Popular choices: media, biology, business management, communication.

Remarks: Enormous scope and opportunity. Pupils feel accepted here no matter what their social background.

WESTONBIRT SCHOOL

Westonbirt, Tetbury, Gloucestershire, GL8 8QG

Tel: 01666 880 333

Fax: 01666 880 364

Email: office@westonbirt.gloucs.sch.uk

Website: www.westonbirt.gloucs.sch.uk

• Pupils: 230 girls; 140 board, 90 day • Ages: 11-18 • Religion: C of E • Fees: Day £4,580; boarding £6,635-£6,860 • School status: Independent • Opendays: Early October (Open Morning) and first Bank Holiday in May (Open Day) • School gender: Girls • Day/boarding: Takes boarders

---

SEN provision

Detail:

Centre of excellence for:

Mild: DYSC; DYSL; DYSP;

Moderate: DYSC; DYSL; DYSP;

Severe: DYSL;

Now provide for in school:

Mild: ASP; ADD; SpLD;

Moderate: MLD; SpLD;

Others: EAL;

Summary: The aim of the department is to provide full support and confidence building for all girls with learning difficulties in order to gain full access to the curriculum.

The girls are taught on a one-to-one basis by three fully qualified SpLD/dyslexia teachers, alongside a team of three specialist teachers in maths, English and Science. In addition Computer assisted Learning software (Successmaker and Dragon Dictate), is frequently used for independent learning to address specific difficulties in spelling, comprehension, writing and mathematical skills. The learning support department arranges assessments and examination concessions as necessary.

What we say about the school - the full Good Schools Guide review

Head: Since 1999, Mrs Mary Henderson MA PGCE (late forties). Educated at Berkhamsted as a day girl then read French at St Andrews and played lacrosse for Scotland. PGCE from Durham before teaching modern languages at Cheltenham Ladies' where she became a housemistress; spent four years at co-ed Warminster School before joining Westonbirt in 1996 as head of modern languages. No doubt that single sex education benefits girls. Married to retired senior lecturer from Bath University with whom she sings in local choirs and tours Europe. No children. In seventh heaven here enjoying 'sport, music and beautiful things'. Girls like and respect her as 'traditional without being old fashioned.' Genuine and candid manner; really caring – 'knows what makes girls tick' but prepared to get tough if necessary. Encourages girls to be 'keen' like her. Praises staff; touched by girls who say 'thank you.'

Academic Matters: Makes top 5 per cent in government 'value added' tables; 70-ish per cent A and B grades at A level; cheap comments about academic level should be ignored. More girls opting for science and unusually flexible timetable allows odd subject combinations. Successful art department, English popular too. Good results by smaller numbers in a range of other subjects. History buoyant; theatre studies popular but yet to achieve top grades. Latin still survives to GCSE and sometimes has takers at A level; similarly classical civilisation. RE compulsory through school but few takers for short course GCSE; many girls achieve marketable European Driving Licence qualification in ICT. Innovative Young Enterprise companies. Prep compulsory after supper for an hour and no upper limit for sixth formers who like study slots during day. One parent said school had 'transformed' his daughter and given her academic interest for first time – most parents thrilled at outcome. Cuddly EFL department accepts overseas girls without strong English and is successful at range of qualifications including IELTS for university entrance. Strong learning support includes two full and three part-timers working with a fifth of girls plus self-help access: mainly SpLD but a few dyspraxia and dyscalculia. Separate programme for talented and gifted.

Games, Options, The Arts: Sporty school: fabulous new sports centre including 25m indoor swimming pool, fitness room etc opened September 2005; lacrosse 'superb' and boasts American coach at present; regularly reach top eight nationally; girls have 'whale of a time' on triennial tour to USA; all play up to year 9 plus 50 older girls; similar numbers for tennis with year round coaching available; netball, rounders, squash and trampolining plus own nine hole golf course; hockey historically low key but gaining ground. Elite athlete runs PE and games; swimming, basketball and volleyball getting boost with futuristically designed pool and sports hall. School teams participate in local and national equestrian events – good links with nearby Beaufort polo club results in three teams; school sponsors annual Mini Horse Trials at local pony club; girls ride at local stables but no bringing Dobbin to school.

Handy connection with Leith's helped Westonbirt get in at start of prestigious five term cookery course still offered to only ten schools in UK; hadn't yet covered wine when we visited but at least girls knew that a white would go best with their tuna mousse.

Over half school learning musical instruments. 22 rehearsal rooms in outgrown music department; informal concerts in elegant Camellia House; two pipe organs to accompany élite chapel choir; jazz band and school orchestra perform less frequently. Drama centred around capacious Orangery theatre, dynamic drama department impacts strongly on timetable and extra-curricular activities. Three major productions annually; successes in local Bath festival and in speech and drama awards. We watched year 9 girls perform sensitively with masks under bubbly, imaginative direction.

Computer network points for sixth formers in study bedrooms. Vast, interconnecting art studios lend themselves to large scale work whilst DT is surprisingly well resourced; seriously impressive furniture being built here alongside feats of small scale engineering. One recent leaver joined formula one racing team having built go-kart at school. Accredited careers department paying far more than lip service with key skills day. Work experience. Sound HE advice for girls – last two head girls getting army university scholarships. Malmesbury bookseller runs browseworthy bookshop. Good library for sixth but state rooms probably rather too daunting for younger readers; budget provides for new and interesting material but Jilly Cooper still popular.

Background and Atmosphere: Magnificent neo-Renaissance pile built for ludicrously wealthy Holford family (who also founded nearby arboretum at Westonbirt) at height of Victorian age. Apparently, Stanley Kubrick had eye on front entrance at one stage but change of mind denied girls sight of Tom Cruise on their doorstep. Fortunately imbued with excellent taste, Robert Holford spared no expense here and since 1928 school has been worthy custodian of the grade 1 listed building and ornamental gardens plus 250 acres of parkland. Some dorms exquisite with plum billet in Lady Holford's boudoir; individual dressing tables as well as wardrobes. Girls' lasting memories tend to be of delightful gardens rather than of marble columns, frescoes, glass ceilings and vast state rooms. De rigueur moans about being 'in middle of nowhere' don't need taking too seriously.

Friendly atmosphere with good balance of female and male staff – much more down to earth than you'd expect. Day girls can 'sleep over' once a week for free and some buy extra nights to be with friends. Delightful guiding traditions survive eg vespers sung whilst stood around edge of Great Hall.

Classrooms huddle around former carriage and stabling courtyard making 35 minute lesson changes quicker than in most places. Discrete sixth form house above with two, well-appointed social areas is popular with older girls who customise their study bedrooms, do own laundry, eat and make snacks in ambiguously named 'piggery' plus smaller 'piglet' for coffee. Viewed from Italian garden, former gym is an eyesore waiting to be rebuilt more in keeping with environs. School food not an issue – own chef does good job. Some socialising with other schools. Popular shopping trips to Bath and Cheltenham. Senior girls can have own car at school. Own choice of dress in sixth and sensible workaday cream blouse, maroon sweater and tartan skirt for remainder. Low church tradition – not dogmatic and lots of Christian giving to charities.

Pastoral Care and Discipline: Parents praise house staff for giving quality time to girls and having 'mature approach.' Counsellor comes regularly to lend confidential support; star of a chaplain whom 'girls really trust;' qualified nursing staff in sanatorium around clock. Fines for smoking offences (some girls are bound to get caught); glass of wine permitted to sixth formers for special occasions but never spirits; tough on drugs. Night-time high jinks avoided by alarmed doors and ex-policeman patrolling grounds with Alsatian. Overall, parents like measured approach to discipline which gets girls 'on side.'

Pupils and Parents: No riffraff but many parents having to make sacrifices. Appeal to sporty, creative and willing workers. Sociable, hearty girls; resilient yet sensitive, who look neat, happy and healthy; sit by houses at lunch with staff so no hiding eating disorders; boarders do twenty minutes' housework before breakfast. Draws from further afield in UK than many competitors and not overrun with international students; absence of bitchiness; different age groups and nationalities mix surprisingly well. Famous old girls include socialites Lady Emily Compton, Lady Sybilla and Lady Natasha Rufus-Isaacs as well as Georgia Byng, children's author.

Entrance: Common entrance at 11 and 13; own exam for those outside CE system and for sixth formers outside of GCSE system (otherwise 5+ GCSEs at A*-C are needed). Main feeders Beaudesert Park, Rose Hill, St Margaret's, Calne etc; London preps such as Thomas's and Garden House; provincial preps – Leaden Hall, Godstowe and increasingly from north including Scotland. Own prep and local primaries provide some day girls. Educational psychologist's report required if special needs but only turned away if really unable to cope. 25 per cent overseas – many from Europe. All nationalities fit in remarkably well.

Exit: A few to co-ed boarding schools or day colleges after GCSE. Virtually all sixth form leavers to higher education. Possibly one or two to Oxbridge annually but generally going for wide range of courses at mixture of trad and new universities.

Money Matters: Scholarships and exhibitions offered at 11, 13 and 16 include academic, art, drama sport and music. 5 per cent sibling reductions; more for services, diplomatic and clergy daughters. Extras range from learning support to ballet.

Remarks: Turns out self-confident and accomplished young women. Few boarding schools (if any) can match setting; modern, unshockable head. Lovely atmosphere for treasured daughters.

William Ellis School

Highgate Road, London, NW5 1RN

Tel: 020 7267 9346

Fax: 020 7284 1274

Email: tanton@williamellis.camden.sch.uk

Website: www.williamellis.camden.sch.uk

• Pupils: 870 boys, all day • Ages: 11-18

• Religion: Non-denom • School status: State

• School gender: Boys • Day/boarding: Day pupils

SEN provision

Detail:

Now provide for in school:

Mild: ASP; AUT; ADD; ADHD; EBD; DYSL; DYSP;

Moderate: ASP; ADD; ADHD; EBD; MLD; DYSL; DYSP;

Severe: ASP;

Others: EAL;

Experience of:

Mild: DYSC; HI; VI; CP;

Moderate: DYSC; HI; VI; CP;

Severe: DYSC;

Others: Sp&LD;

Summary: William Ellis School has a diverse and varied population of students including some 23 per cent of its population exhibiting special educational needs. The school currently has some 50 Statemented pupils on roll and some 150 pupils on the SEN register with a wide range of additional learning, sensory or emotional needs.

William Ellis has a successful history of educating boys with Asperger's syndrome and is interested in developing this as a future strength. Other future changes will see the SEN deptartment combine with the behavioural support department to increase the effectiveness of its provision to all pupils.

William Ellis School fully supports Inclusion and is committed to policies that foster equal opportunities and equality of treatment for all its pupils.

What we say about the school - the full Good Schools Guide review

Head: Since 2002, Mr Richard Tanton BA (forties), previously head of Westminster City School. A trainee teacher at William Ellis in the early 1980s, and has since taught at Highbury Grove, Gladesmore and Archbishop Tenison's. Married to Sue, also a teacher, has three children and lives in Potters Bar. A passionate cricket, football and rugby fan, and has run the London marathon six times. A good leader, who has already strengthened some of the weaker areas of the school. 'He has lots of energy,' said a parent. 'And I was impressed that he has no truck with the culture of it not being cool to work. He encourages the boys to excel.'

Academic Matters: National average in value-added and absolute terms (ie quite good for the borough). A large percentage of its lower ability pupils achieved good Key Stage 3 SATs levels in 2003. The improvement is not so marked at GCSE, though around half the pupils get at least five A*-C grades – a very creditable result, given the student profile, and above the national average for boys (shows up well in value-added for this stage). Few boys leave the school without qualifications.

Sixth form is the 'La Swap' consortium – value-added not special here, but OK. The La Swap system can result in large classes with a wide range of ability, but it gives students a good choice of subjects, ranging from Health and Social Care GNVQ to Critical Thinking AS level and law A level, and results are at or above the national average.

Maths is a particular strength; 'The top set always does GCSE in year 10 and always does well.' Good English results, too. A specialist language college, but although there are several languages on offer, and a good take-up rate, the results are among the schools' weakest. They are, however, improving, with a stable set of teaching staff in place. Pupils here, unlike those at non-specialist schools, all try two languages and are not allowed to give up both at 14, but may be directed to vocational rather than academic courses. Talented linguists can take one language GCSE in year 10 and another in year 11, and the La Swap consortium offers a good range of languages, including Mandarin, to A level. There is also a range of vocational subjects on offer, and the head is keen to increase these options lower down the school. 'We value the vocational as well as the academic, and some boys will want to do both pathways, ending up with a good mixed portfolio of GCSEs and vocational qualifications. When boys are on a pathway where they know they can succeed they will work harder.'

Mixed ability teaching in year 7, in classes of 25, with setting from year 8 for languages and year 9 for maths and science. 'Setting too early could have a deleterious effect, as SATs results from primary schools can be misleading, so we like to let them settle. But we have some very bright boys who could cope with a fast pace from the start.' 'At the beginning of year 8 we felt our son was very bored,' said a parent. 'But we talked to his form teacher, who was very responsive.'

The Gifted and Talented programme includes summer courses for able year 6s about to join the school, a performance programme for musicians, and extension clubs in maths, sciences and languages. Talented mathematicians can be put up for university summer schools, maths days at colleges and enter Global Maths Challenges. The school devises an alternative curriculum of individual, intensive support programmes for boys who are struggling academically. 'The younger boys, in particular, can misbehave if they don't have the academic skills to cope with the curriculum. We like to work on that intensively early on.' A recent Ofsted report commented: 'The school does identify and support ... disadvantaged students well'.

Classes keep the same form teacher throughout. There are twice-yearly academic review days where boys, parents and teachers talk about assessments and set targets. 'They are a very dedicated bunch of teachers who have a good grip on each child and what to expect of him,' said a parent. 'I've always had a good sense of their ambitions for my son, and they've always been high.' Other parents comment that while staff expectations vary, 'there are a lot of young, committed male teachers who are very good role models for the boys.'

Games, Options, The Arts: A sporty school, with the usual range of clubs and fixtures and an enviable location on the edge of Hampstead Heath. The new sports hall, on the site of the old gymnasium, includes full-size basketball and badminton courts. The school uses the running track and sports pitches on the Heath, but its own outdoor space is limited to some small tarmac five-a side pitches. The head is negotiating, however, for the use of a sports field directly behind the school, owned by the Corporation of London and at present used purely for exercising police dogs.

Good, well-equipped, very lively music department. Joint orchestra with Parliament Hill girls' school next door, plus jazz and rock bands and singing groups. 'The music tends towards the popular rather than the classical, but it's very buzzy and a lot of fun for the boys,' said a parent. 'I was terribly impressed by the Christmas concert,' said another. The recent highly-praised production of Five Guys Named Mo, in conjunction with the Roundhouse, is one of several in the pipeline. 'There were 35 boys up there singing and dancing and absolutely loving it,' said a parent.

Year 7s visit the school's converted water mill in Surrey for an outdoor pursuits week. It is also the site of biology and geography field studies and extension weekends. Ski trips and plenty of language trips abroad, plus annual study trips to Russia, Spain and China.

Background and Atmosphere: Founded in 1862 in Gospel Oak by businessman William Ellis, who wanted children to be taught 'useful' subjects like science instead of rote learning, the school moved to its present site on the edge of Hampstead Heath in 1937. Recent building work – funded, astonishingly, by £4.5m from the DfES – has produced a new science and technology building plus arts and media studies rooms and sports hall. 'It's very much a community school,' said a parent. 'It's small and very local and the teachers know the boys very well.'

Pastoral Care and Discipline: 'It's quite a tough school,' said a parent. 'But it's a very happy one – the boys really enjoy being there and they feel safe.' Ofsted commented that pastoral support is a major strength of the school. On-call teachers are on hand to deal with disruptions in the class-rooms and there are CCTVs to keep an eye out for trouble-makers elsewhere. 'We do our best to get as much information as possible about the boys from their primary schools,' says the head. 'We ask what strategies worked and didn't work, so we're equipped to deal with them when they start here.' Not much bullying, by all accounts, and the school deals with it well.

The school celebrates effort and achievement with termly presentation assemblies and a prize evening in the summer term. Boys are rewarded with treats such as trips to see Lord of the Rings on its opening day or activity afternoons. 'They have an incentive to work hard and behave well,' commented a parent approvingly.

Pupils and Parents: Pupils come from a staggering 76 countries, including Afghanistan, Zimbabwe, Venezuela, Ecuador, Sierra Leone, Mauritius, Slovakia, Somalia and Kosovo. Mainly from families of neighbouring manual workers, with a few from the liberal middle classes, including some well-known political and legal families. OBs include rock guitarist Mark Bedford, journalist David Aaronovitch, England cricketer Freddie Titmus and scientist David Deitch.

Entrance: Around 550 applicants for 123 places. Admission criteria: (i) a brother in the school (ii) musical ability – there are 12 music places, chosen without audition (iii) a family connection (iv) location – in practice, within about half a mile. Takes eight statemented children a year.

Exit: About 75 per cent stay on to do A levels or vocational courses at La Swap. Of these, about 75 per cent move on to further or higher education, to do a huge range of courses at a huge range of old and new universities, including three or four a year to Oxbridge.

Money Matters: Has done well out of the DfES for building funds, and is voluntary aided by the William Ellis and Birkbeck Schools Trust, but otherwise is as hard up as most other state schools.

Remarks: Small north London comprehensive with a community feel, and bright, dedicated staff who do their best to tailor-make the work for each boy. Committed to rewarding effort and achievement and, despite the best efforts of some disruptive elements, creating a culture that values hard work, enterprise and success.

WIMBLEDON CHASE PRIMARY SCHOOL

Merton Hall Road, London, SW19 3QB

Tel: 020 8542 1413

Fax: 020 8542 1668

Email: senior.admin@wimbledonchase.merton.sch.uk

Website: www.wimbledonchase.merton.sch.uk

• Pupils: 500 boys and girls (including 105 in the nursery), all day • Ages: 3-11 • Religion: Non-denom • School status: State • School gender: Mixed • Day/boarding: Day pupils

---

SEN provision

Detail:

Now provide for in school:

Mild: HI;

Others: SLD; EAL; Sp&LD; Epi;

Experience of:

Mild: ASP; AUT; ADD; ADHD; EBD; DS; DYSC; DYSL; DYSP;

Moderate: ASP; AUT; ADD; ADHD; EBD; DS; DYSC; DYSL; DYSP; SpLD; HI;

Severe: EBD;

Others: SPD; AUT(other); CD; PD; Eat;

Summary: At Wimbledon Chase we have a special needs base for up to 10 pupils with additional learning needs. The base was named by the children as the Station (because they are on a learning journey). The children attend the Base in the mornings, where they receive their literacy and numeracy lessons from a special needs teacher and three learning support assistants. They also receive regular speech and language therapy and occupational therapy. For all other lessons, they return to their normal classes with their learning support assistants.

We pride ourselves on being a fully inclusive school. All children have equal access to the wider curriculum as well as participating in school trips, theatre workshops and sports activities.In September 06, the Special Needs Base will change to accommodate 14 children with speech, language and communication disorders.

What we say about the school - the full Good Schools Guide review

Head: Since 2001, Mrs Sue Tomes BEd (fifties), has been at the school for 30 years, moving up the ranks from head of French, senior mistress and then deputy head for 15 years. Married, a self-confessed workaholic and perfectionist, she freely admits that the school plays a major part in her life. Her lovely, large office is very homely, but when she can be prised away from work, she enjoys reading, music, travelling and collecting antiques. Mrs T also tries to maintain her links with France and is keen to support the teaching of primary modern foreign languages across the borough. A modest and unassuming woman, she is popular with pupils (knows all their names) and parents. 'She is pretty amazing,' sums up one mother. Generally seen as v. approachable and open to suggestion and famed for her huge attention to detail. 'We have to sit on her a bit sometimes or she would be ordering the jammy dodgers for the school fair,' jokes one of her many fans.

Entrance: At 3+ to nursery, and 4+ to the main school. Non-selective academically. Applicants must list the school as their first preference, with special needs taking priority, followed by the usual sibling, then proximity criteria. Families need to move close to the school to be sure of a place.

Exit: A regular trickle to selective grammars: both of the Tiffin schools, Sutton Grammar and Nonsuch, while majority move locally to Ricards Lodge, Rutlish Secondary and Raynes Park Secondary School.

Remarks: A school with a heartbeat – lively and likeable; we didn't find anyone with a bad word to say about this happy place. In fact, quite the opposite: 'My children absolutely love going to school,' says one mother. 'It's an amazing place – the opportunities it offers and the way the kids are catered for, are as near to a private school as I could get without opening a cheque book.'

At first sight it's a bit like visiting a senior school with very small pupils. Despite its location near the centre of Wimbledon, the school enjoys the size, site and facilities rarely found at primary level. Buildings date back to 1924 (when they were home to the local senior girls school) consequently there is lots of wood-panelling (slightly Harry Potterish feel to some of it), but more importantly, lots of dedicated space. In 2001, and overseen by Mrs T, the school began its conversion from middle to a primary school with its first intake of reception children and the addition of a big bright nursery. 'Its transition seemed daunting at the time, but we're out the other side and it's great,' said one mother.

Academically all is more than sound -all well above national averages at the relevant Key Stages. What makes this school really stand above other primaries is the sheer range and variety of experiences over and above the National Curriculum. The philosophy is to give children a chance to try things and to make learning fun. So there are lots of themed days and weeks (everything from maths to black history) – the highlight of which is the well-planned 'Enrichment Week' where the afternoon timetable is suspended entirely in favour of workshops on all sorts from boxing to jewellery making. 'We want to find and foster talents wherever they may lie,' says Mrs T. Talent is also nurtured through the inspiring extra-curricular activities after school and at lunchtimes – most of them free. Simple but easily lost skills like skipping, knitting and story telling are promoted via clubs, alongside the more usual sports, dancing (including tap), drama and French.(The children learn French from reception including a residential stay in France for year 5). Lots of days out and trips. Pupils and parents are hugely appreciative of the range and quality of what's on offer.

A very inclusive place (lots of Koreans, Tamil speakers make up the second largest section) – 73 pupils speak 23 different languages. With the mix of languages comes a mix of abilities – but the school does well by them all. Every EAL pupil, except a few SEN children, attained at least a level 4 in their SATS. Similarly, provision for SEN is of high quality. There is a dedicated SENCo, early identification of special needs (including a gifted and talented register) and lots of additional support and catch up programmes. Additionally, the school has a unit for children with additional learning needs (ALN), currently aimed at moderate needs, but by 2006 this is changing to cater for children with language and communication disorders. It will offer 14 places – with top priority for entrance to the school. Currently the ALN children learn in the unit in the morning (their own adapted curriculum, mostly maths and English) and join their class in the main school for the afternoon session, with support staff. There are also facilities for physically disabled children such as ramps and purpose-built toilets. Head feels this mix is good for all the children. Certainly the place is buzzing: from the front hall, packed with trophies, certificates and photographs extolling the achievements of pupils and staff, to the back door leading to beautiful grounds (well used – especially for sports and science); there's lots going on.

A happy school – it's not silent or regimented, but still has a slightly traditional feel and pupils quite smartly dressed. There is a 'positive behaviour management system' – largely stickers and crystals (full jar of gems equals golden time). All the teachers use – and encourage the children to use – 'language of choice', as in 'Is this (behaviour) a good choice? What are the consequences if I do this?' Parents encouraged to use the idea at home. The school also has a worry box, peer mediators, strong school council, buddy bus stop in the playground – all geared for children to sort out any problems. A boon for working parent is the wrap-around care on offer (breakfast and after-school) – another benefit of having the space. Even the half-day nursery children can be accommodated for the rest of the day. Hugely supportive parents are keen to help in the classroom and by raising impressive sums of money. The school returns the favour by providing a dedicated parents' room in school where helpers have somewhere to keep their things and (most importantly) get tea and biscuits!

WIMBLEDON HIGH SCHOOL

Mansel Road, London, SW19 4AB

Tel: 020 8971 0900
Fax: 020 8971 0901
Email: info@wim.gdst.net
Website: www.gdst.net/wimbledon

• Pupils: 567 girls, all day • Ages: 11-18 • Religion: Non-denom
• Fees: Junior £2,383; senior £3,063
• School status: Independent • Opendays: October
• School gender: Girls • Day/boarding: Day pupils

SEN provision

Detail:
Now provide for in school:
Mild: DYSC; DYSL; DYSP; SpLD; HI;
Moderate: MLD; DYSL; DYSP;
Severe: DYSL;
Others: EAL; Epi; Eat;
Experience of:
Mild: ADD; ADHD; EBD;

Summary: We aim to support every student to become a successful independent learner with high self-esteem. We identify and support students with particular educational needs and support them in benefiting from the academic education provided. For those identified as having specific needs we aim to provide specialist support and to help all teachers devise classroom strategies to support their learning. Study skills and time management workshops are provided for individual year groups. All students are screened for specific learning difficulties during their time in the junior school and in year 7. New entrants to the senior school in years 8-13 are also routinely screened.

We are committed to developing a close relationship with the parents, informing them about, and involving them in, all decisions. If a specific learning difficulty is identified, we hope that parents will agree to pay for support tuition and an educational psychologist's assessment if required. An Individual Educational Plan with specific targets is drawn up and the student's progress monitored closely.

There are students at Wimbledon High School with dyslexia, dyspraxia and dsycalculia. We aim to offer careful and sensitive management so that teaching and learning can proceed in a positive fashion. Both junior and senior departments have learning support co-ordinators and Able and Gifted Co-ordinators. Visiting learning support teachers come into the junior school. The senior school offers advice and links for students with English as an Additional Language.

What we say about the school - the full Good Schools Guide review

Head: Since 2001, Mrs Pamela Wilkes BEd (fifties), did her BEd at Hull University in history and theology. Previous schools include Malvern Girls' and Sutton Coldfield Girls' Grammar, where she was deputy head for 14 years. Came mid academic year after her predecessor, Dr Clough, 'left to pursue her interests as an educationalist and to take on the challenge of running a school that had been put into special measures.' She readily admits it was a difficult time to take over but she now feels well ensconced (as parents would agree). Friendly, open and positive, parents describe her as 'caring and traditional, very concerned with nurturing a caring and respectful environment.' A no-nonsense head who is expected to change the school slowly and subtly. Keen for every girl to fulfil her potential academically and socially – wants the girls to make a difference when they go out into society and to be socially aware. Her aim is to 'remove barriers so that they can all fly.' Runs an 'at home' every fortnight for any parent to drop in without an appointment – nice idea.

Academic Matters: Academic but does cater for wider range of abilities than some other girls' senior schools in the surrounding areas. Continues to turn out good results; 100 per cent GCSE entrants achieving A*-C, over 80 per cent A* or A in English and maths. Girls entering year 10 are expected to study 10 or 11 GCSEs. Offers GCSE in PE since appointing new staff and one of few schools with GCSE option of food technology. Three separate sciences are available at GCSE as well as double award. Languages include French, Spanish, and German plus Latin (30 per cent uptake) and Greek. one-to-one interviews for GCSE selection to encourage breadth and balance.

School requires at least 7 grade Bs at GCSE level to study for A levels (although some departments prefer A grades or above in the subjects chosen at A levels). The head adds, 'over the last few years, all girls have surpassed the entry requirements so none have been asked to leave.' A level results overall very good – particular aptitude for maths and geography. Good provision for special needs with appointment of dedicated part-time member of staff. Class sizes are not small – about 28 up to GCSE (with smaller groups for GCSE and above). 13 full-time male members of staff (12 in the senior school and 1 in the junior school).

Games, Options, The Arts: Nursery Road playing fields (10 minutes walk from school) providing hard and astroturf surfaces for netball, tennis, athletics and hockey with picturesque changing pavilion (original building used by the All England Tennis Club before it moved to Wimbledon Park Road). Several girls play for Surrey squads in tennis and netball. 25-metre swimming pool and fully equipped sports hall at school site. New sports club for year 10 upwards to include less traditional sports like karate. Excellent art department – arty girls make their way subsequently to Wimbledon Art School to do an art foundation year. IT well funded, keeping apace with technological developments. Thriving drama department with productions in modern and classical languages, some with the boys from King's College School. Numerous instrumental groups and choirs. Community service greatly encouraged and Duke of Edinburgh Awards. Fair selection of after-school clubs, particularly in sport, eg martial arts and trampolining.

Background and Atmosphere: Victorian redbrick buildings front Wimbledon Hill with tube and BR stations less than 10 minutes' walk away. Although quite cramped for space, new buildings are light and airy, trees have been planted and there is grass to sit on and chat. Steady programme of refurbishment. A new technology building opened summer 2005 and new performing arts centre due March 2006. Relaxed atmosphere, girls seem happy, polite and friendly. Strictly non-denominational. Assemblies run as a showcase of achievement.

Pastoral Care and Discipline: A high priority pastoral system ensures even greater care from tutors and year heads – some indications of stressing-out and bullying in the past with luck will be a thing of the past. Headmistress frequently shadows a pupil (randomly selected) for a day. Great idea – how many other heads would have the guts to do likewise? A house system has recently been implemented. Older girls already tutor younger. School rules are established through a referral system, which leads to a detention system – performing a helpful task. Three detentions and parents are involved. Pupils rarely asked to leave; head believes all behaviour is causal and can therefore be dealt with.

Pupils and Parents: Big mix of parents, multi-cultural and multi-ethnic, but definite emphasis on professional (lawyers/accountants), company directors and academics. Thriving parents' association. Girls wear smart low-key predominantly navy uniform until mock GCSEs completed – then own clothes. Sixth formers mostly jeans and smart casual clothes – not scruffy and few designer labels.

Entrance: Selective at 11: tests involve English, maths and non-verbal reasoning plus interview. Looking for independent thinkers and girls with opinions. About 35 per cent intake from own junior school – remainder from local state primaries such as Bishop Gilpin and Hollymount First School and private schools including The Study and Kensington Prep (GDST primary). For sixth form entry, external applicants sit entrance assessments including data analysis, maths, English and a narrow-gauge IQ test in verbal and non-verbal reasoning. All applicants are interviewed. Places are usually conditional on candidates achieving A grades in their preferred A level subjects and at least C grades in all other subjects.

Exit: Most girls stay on for sixth form, handful leaves for boarding school (usually family tradition) or to other sixth forms (particularly if they have been at the school since their junior days). University choice tends to be quite selective: 10 or 12 usually go to Oxbridge, other universities include Durham, Edinburgh, Exeter, with Warwick becoming more popular, and London universities (particularly for medicine). Gap year very popular.

Money Matters: Some bursaries available per year plus scholarships at 11 and 16, also music scholarship at 11 and sixth form science scholarship from OG's endowment.

Remarks: Academic school with good results, not too pushy, although not a school for the daydreamer or non-motivated. Head looks set to keep the flag flying. Strengths of the school drawn from the atmosphere and friendships.

Winchester College

College Street, Winchester, Hampshire, SO23 9NA

Tel: 01962 621 100

Fax: 01962 621 106

Email: information@wincoll.ac.uk

Website: winchestercollege.co.uk

• Pupils: 690 boys; 675 boarding, 15 day • Ages: 13-18

• Religion: C of E • Fees: Boarding £7,833; day £7,442

• School status: Independent • Opendays: June

• School gender: Boys • Day/boarding: Takes boarders

SEN provision

Detail:

Now provide for in school:

Mild: ASP; AUT; ADD; ADHD; EBD; DYSL; DYSP;

Others: EAL;

Experience of:

Mild: DYSC; HI; VI;

Others: SPD; OCD; DEL; Epi;

Summary: Winchester College currently has 127 boys who are entered on the SEN register. Pupils are assessed in the first term in order to identify any particular learning needs. Appropriate support is then provided. Those boys who are known to have specific learning needs are placed in one of two specialist classes, one lesson per day, where particular emphasis is placed on study skills. In addition, one-to-one support is provided once a week for forty minutes by an SEN tutor, usually a ten lesson course, tailored to the particular needs of the pupil. We currently have three Asperger's boys in the school and there is a small number of candidates with attention deficit disorders. Specialist help is also provided for EFL pupils.

Winchester College is a 'dyslexia friendly' school where the needs of those with special learning requirements are both accepted and understood. Many of our SEN pupils have been extraordinarily successful during their school careers, both academically and outside the taught curriculum.

What we say about the school - the full Good Schools Guide review

Headman: Since 2005, Dr Ralph (pronounced Rafe) Townsend, early fifties. Previously head of Oundle since 1999 and before that head of Sydney Grammar School, Australia and head of English at Eton. Dr Townsend is a high-flier – he has already been a head for sixteen years. A good and popular headmaster at Oundle, maintains close contact with the sixth form and staff. Some parents find him remote and anonymous, others outward going, friendly and very optimistic about the future of the school; headmagisterial colleagues seem to have a high regard for him and rate him as likely to be able to sort out Winchester's underlying difficulties. The Daily Telegraph's educational guru, John Clare talked of his 'low-key manner and consensual management style' as well as his determination. Tough – but with the housemasters having seen off his predecessor Dr Tate, amid extraordinary scenes of staff infighting, he will need to be.

Academic Matters: Outstanding academic education coupled with excellent teaching. GCSE performance statistics distorted by Winchester's use of IGCSEs, and by some boys bypassing GCSE altogether. GCSE taken on the wing at different moments, cleverest miss out GCSEs in some subjects; AS fitted in here and there, many early A levels, boys go on to take fourth or even fifth or sixth. Endless shadow of exams might daunt lesser mortals but most seem to cope well enough. Aim is less pot-hunting than breadth of learning, though the school regularly features near the top of the league. Japanese and Mandarin popular; Italian and Arabic are also now part of modern languages department. Enormous numbers take A level maths. Small but successful Greek sets; popular and excellent science.

Unique and enviable feature is 'div': unexamined general studies, one period a day with the same master ('don'), starting with broadly based European history in any aspect the teacher chooses and moving on in the sixth form to pretty well anything intellectual. Boys encouraged to take charge of discussion, can be any topic from political philosophy to reproductive and genetic ethics. Successive heads keen to promote this area, partly to counter minority utilitarian culture – bright and committed pupils make this possible. IT (criticised by recent inspection) has been completely revamped thanks to £1m legacy. Much of school networked, geography set up as beacon department; all dons have laptops, boys sometimes e-mail essays to staff. Library provision pretty lavish, excellent collections both old and new.

Several staff members trained in special needs; and the school is unique in having a full-time SENCo, as well as full and part-time assistants. All boys are assessed on entry; 135 boys currently get some form of help ranging from mild to moderate dyslexia, dyspraxia etc to fairly serious Asperger's. Ed psychs called in if necessary. Probably 6-8 chaps with ADHD on Ritalin or whatever, some pupils have nonspecific or classified problems – often with short-term memory or concentration. All sorts of tricks: eating sweets (sugar) or chewing gum can help focus. Quite often remedial team can have more problems with parents, persuading them that it is not an intellectual issue. Lessons cost £23 per hour and college is considering a bursary purely for the bright dyslexic, though will underwrite extra cost for those who find the extra charge challenging. EFL teaching on tap (some overseas boys need help). School continues to teach national and international examination systems: IGCSEs in English, mathematics and separate sciences; International A level in English.

Games, Options, The Arts: After the first year individuals are allowed to do their own thing and there is a huge number of options. Main games are soccer, cricket and the college's home-grown and robust variety of football – keen inter-house rivalry. Hugely successful cricket and tennis season in summer 2005. Glorious grounds with one of the most beautiful cricket fields in the country, stretching down to the River Itchen, where the school's famous fishing club still flourishes. Basketball good and the school is often national cross-country champion. Long-established sports centre in use for 85 hours a week, by outsiders as well as boys. No large all-weather surface – forbidden by city planners.

Large light art department with a remarkable collection of watercolours (Cotmans, Rowlandsons etc). Music is quite outstanding; college has maintained founder's 14th century provision of sixteen quiristers selected from all over the country and trained by director of chapel music to sing in chapel.Three of the last five winners of the BBC Young Chorister of the Year have come from the school. Superb results at A level, and the most successful school in England at Oxbridge choral/organ awards. 700 lessons are provided each week by a staff of more than 50 specialist teachers; there are nearly 70 music scholars. £4m music school opened in 2004. Magnificent 1960 concert hall, with panelling by a pupil of Grinling Gibbons (taken from elsewhere in the school). And so on. Drama is strong too, with more than 20 productions per year – many of them directed by boys in the school. Boys are expected to make choices and stick with them. Community service is encouraged (and the college is the third largest employer in Winchester). Charge of exclusiveness countered by boys eg manning night shelter, clearing litter in cathedral grounds. Playing fields are let to Southampton FC youth team.

Background and Atmosphere: Centre of school still the 14th century quad built by William of Wykeham, bishop of Winchester and chancellor to Richard II. Other buildings bolted on at regular intervals, giving a glorious but slightly rabbit-warrenish feeling to the place, where every stone has a history. Chapel has christening robe of Henry VII's son Arthur and some original stained glass. Wonderful grounds – on one side the town, on the other the cathedral close; long acres of playing fields stretching lushly down to water meadows. Architectural gems everywhere, including a 17th century sick house, beside which a contemporary herb garden has been planted. Everywhere, a feast for the eyes and the soul. Several buildings still used for their original purpose.

Boarding houses (mostly rambling red brick) dotted round the town in narrow streets (hard to park). Meals still eaten in houses – one of the last schools to retain this civilised (excellent for pastoral care) custom. Genuine family atmosphere fostered by hard-working housemasters. New post of assistant housemaster recently introduced to ease the burden. New system of personal tutors for years 9-11. Large house has been converted as annexe for nine last-year students.

Academic and intellectual pursuits are what the boys rate highest. In general, 'a sixth form college from age 13'; much free time and responsibility for sorting yourself out. Inevitably a few can't hack it. Scholars live in separate 14th century house – 'College', where – they claim – they are worked extremely hard; a kind of academic praetorian guard.

Housemasters are traditionally very strong – admission to Winchester is by house. Recent heads have aimed to foster an all-school sense; hence new termly cathedral service and some tidying up of disciplinary procedures – part of 'drawing more threads into the middle'. Headmaster now sees all parents as part of the application process.

Pastoral Care and Discipline: Routine discipline is house based; most parents will get to know their son's housemaster very well over five years – though things are changing and they will find themselves talking to the headmaster as well. Pastoral matters taken very seriously, as you would expect. First and second-year boys sleep in small dorms and work in 'toys' (small cubicles = more Winchester private language); older boys have reasonable studies. Winchester City is a druggy place and there are predictable strayings into pubs and clubs on Saturday nights. Housemasters accustomed to dealing independently with everyday misdemeanours. The school has tightened up on drugs. Alcohol considered more pernicious. Little truck with counsellors but expert help is always to hand. Staff expected to deal with most problems.

Pupils and Parents: Bright to brilliant, many from intellectual (upper) middle class; also contingent of clever Hong Kong Chinese and other foreign nationals. Pupils confident, charming, frank, critical, unorthodox. 'You have to be able to laugh at yourself to survive here,' said one sixth former. Irony and self-deprecation the keynote. Winchester is so good in many ways that there can be a tendency to self-absorption too; products of other schools still say that Wykehamists are out of touch with the real world. Enormous roll of distinguished Old Boys, including Willie Whitelaw, Hugh Gaitskell, Richard Crossman, Geoffrey Howe, Jeremy Morse, George Younger, Tim Brooke-Taylor, the Nawab of Pataudi, Peter Jay, Sir Humphrey Appleby. Pianists Ian Fountain and Nic Hodges and actors Hugh Dancy and Charlie Edwards are recent old boys. Another famous OB is Buffy the Vampire Slayer creator, Joss Whedon – American, but spent three years at Winchester. As he said in an interview, 'most of the things that I've done that have been truly creative have been extra-curricular. However, stories that I've written have gotten me recommendations, which was nice. At Winchester, they tried to squash a lot of things. Certainly everything I wore or said bothered them but, at the same time, I studied classic literature and drama with some of the greatest teachers out there. You couldn't help but become more creative.'

Entrance: Full to bursting. Register after boy's eighth birthday. Interview at 11, with IQ test for selection to take school's own entrance exam at 13. Pupils drawn from 170 prep schools – most popular are Pilgrims' School (on doorstep, quiristers educated there), Horris Hill, Twyford. Efforts made to encourage state school boys. Sixth form entry via exam in prospective A levels plus interview.

Exit: Very few escape university; nearly sixty gained places at Oxbridge in 2006.

Money Matters: Seventy scholars 'in-College' and about six exhibitioners a year, plus a bursary or two for Hampshire state school boys, plus a very large number of music exhibitions and two sixth form exhibitions. Hardship cases considered on merits. School working hard to widen access.

Remarks: Among the best, and possibly the sharpest of the public boarding schools in the country, wedded to traditional broad liberal education. Enormous intellectual and financial muscle. Leavers are far more rounded than ten years ago and school is making strong efforts to put familiar charge of ivory-towerishness behind it; certainly little evidence these days of the embryo coldly rational, top civil servant of received myth. For example, the school has produced more than its fair share of actors, musicians and academics in recent years.

Winchester House School

44 High Street, Brackley, Northamptonshire, NN13 7AZ

Tel: 01280 702 483

Fax: 01280 706 400

Email: office@winchester-house.org

Website: www.winchester-house.org

• Pupils: 368 boys and girls; 80 boarders (55 of whom are weekly) • Ages: 7-13, plus pre-prep 3-7 • Religion: C of E • Fees: Day: pre-prep £1,765-£2,225; prep £3,060-£3,825. Weekly and full boarding: £4,050-£5,065 • School status: Independent • Opendays: One each in Michaelmas, Lent and Summer terms • School gender: Mixed • Day/boarding: Takes boarders

SEN provision

Detail:

Experience of:

Mild: DYSC; DYSL; DYSP; HI; VI;

Moderate: MLD; DYSL; DYSP;

Others: Sp&LD;

Summary: We provide a broad, inclusive curriculum with all teaching staff recognising the full potential of each child. Support is provided through a variety of methods including extensive in-class support across the classroom range, small group work and individual withdrawal sessions. The school is fortunate in having an occupational therapist on site, a visiting speech and language therapist, and an educational psychologist who visits the school on a termly basis. Several learning support teachers also teach various aspects of the curriculum eg maths, history, classics.

On entry to the school, in addition to a screening process, parents are requested to inform the school of any previous assessments. There are strong home–school links with regular meetings and workshops for parents.

What we say about the school - the full Good Schools Guide review

Head: Since 2003, Mr Mark Seymour BA CertEd (fiftyish), an historian and previously head of Cargilfield (qv) from 2000 and senior housemaster at Haileybury. Keen cricketer. His wife Andrea has an honours degree in literature and media and has been involved in school PR. Three school-age children. Interests include playing the drums, power-boating.

Entrance: Preferably in September but now completely full with waiting lists in most year groups. Quite the reverse problem to only a couple of years ago and blamed on new head. Day pupils move up via hugely popular pre-prep (Tel: 01280 703 070), others come for an informal test. Most boarders come from within 50 mile radius.

Exit: Mostly to schools within a 60-mile radius – Rugby, St Edwards, Oundle, Uppingham, Stowe, Bloxham, etc. Girls to Tudor Hall, Downe House, Malvern Girls', Wycombe Abbey etc. Has had a good collection of awards over the years. In 2005, of the 27 pupils, a third got schols.

Remarks: Traditional co-ed prep school, now with occasional, weekly and full boarding, based in a converted Victorian hunting lodge. The school was founded in 1876, and moved to its present site in Brackley in 1923. Very much a local school, and popular as such. Keen games, athletics meetings here a great favourite. Thriving well-run pre-prep and nursery over the road, with the playing fields, sports hall and tennis courts. Library block and IT centre attached to the main building.

Sound teaching on all fronts, including Greek for the brightest, strong classics and maths for scholars. Some remedial help for dyslexia – co-ordinator is director of studies (but also trained in special needs). Maximum class size twenty, average around fifteen. New head has introduced various initiatives including, All-A-Board and Learn to Lead (leadership programme for all in upper school.

WINDLESHAM HOUSE SCHOOL

Washington, Pulborough, West Sussex, RH20 4AY

Tel: 01903 874 700
Fax: 01903 874 702
Email: office@windlesham.com
Website: www.windlesham.com

• Pupils: 160 boys, 105 girls; all board except for staff's children; Plus pre-prep with 35 boys and girls (who can spend one year in the main school as day children but must board from 9) • Ages: 8-13, pre-prep 4-7 • Religion: C of E • Fees: Little Windlesham Reception and year 1: £1,940, years 2/3: £2,250; Main prep school: 'determined at the time of entry' • School status: Independent • Opendays: October and/or March for Little Windlesham; older children and parents by appointment at any time • School gender: Mixed • Day/boarding: Takes boarders

---

SEN provision

Detail:
Now provide for in school:
- Mild: DYSC; DYSL; DYSP;
- Moderate: DYSL; HI;
- Others: EAL; Sp&LD;

Experience of:
- Mild: ADD; ADHD;
- Moderate: MLD;
- Others: Epi;

Summary: At Windlesham we cater for a broad range of abilities including the very talented and academically able children and those who may need learning support. Our curriculum is designed to meet the requirements of the Independent Schools Examination Board with their Common Entrance exams taken at 13+. We do have a number of children with special needs and aim to provide them with appropriate help, but these children must be of above average ability or they are likely to find the broad curriculum too demanding and not appropriate to their needs.

We assess the children briefly before they join the school (normally when they have an overnight stay) and we hope that any existing special needs will have been discussed with us by the child's parents. Once we have had access to any existing reports (eg from previous schools or from educational psychologists) we can arrange a programme to suit their needs. We have a team of specialist teachers, under the Head of Learning Support, who give a mixture of individual or small group lessons to the children. The number of lessons will vary according to need and to our resources. We offer support with reading, spelling, written language skills, handwriting, word-processing, touch-typing, maths, visual perceptual training and speech and language therapy. We make a charge for these lessons, and details are available on request.

Other children, after an initial settling in period, may be identified by subject teachers as having some areas of difficulty and this leads to discussion with the learning support department. In October, we give all children NFER Verbal and Non-Verbal Reasoning tests, maths, Reading and Spelling tests and these will help identify any areas of concern. After observation and discussion with the child's teachers we may give a child diagnostic tests to ascertain where the problem lies. We will inform parents at this stage and discuss the support that may be needed. It is possible to arrange a full, in-depth assessment by a visiting educational psychologist who will make recommendations for the child's educational programme and we do have the services of a speech and language therapist and occupational therapist when required.

All children have a right to a broad and balanced education and we aim to provide the necessary support for each child. This is in line with the government's Code of Practice for the teaching of children with special needs, which emphasises that the needs of the children are paramount. In order to do so, many of the children requiring learning support do not study Latin, as this is an optional subject at Common Entrance. We use this time for support lessons. Learning support lessons can also take place in the lunch hour, outside lesson time and, in a few cases, during other lessons in non-examined subjects.

What we say about the school - the full Good Schools Guide review

Head: Since 1996, Mr Philip Lough (pronounced Lock) MA PGCE (fifties), married to Mrs Christine Lough MA PGCE (fifty) who is assistant head. Both are linguists; Mr Lough was educated at Sherborne, followed by Trinity College, Oxford and Mrs Lough went to Madras College in St Andrews, followed by Aberdeen University. This is very much a joint appointment ('But – he's the boss'). The Loughs, who have three grown up children, met and married whilst doing their respective PGCEs at Durham. Both of them teach French – he to the scholars at the top end plus RE, and she to the tinies as well as preparing older children for their next step. 'Drugs, drink, relationships (including sex) and how to deal with peer pressure.' 'Learn to say no, consider the consequences'. PSHE is ongoing throughout the school and Mrs Lough masterminds the programme in conjunction with tutors 'so that children go on to their senior schools confident in their own abilities'. She also supervises the anti-bullying initiative. We had a very jolly tour round the school with Mrs Lough greeting each child by name and showing genuine interest in their various activities. The Loughs do a birthday box for pupils and ten mates, either in their flat or in the garden if the weather is OK – no balloons though, just a cake and fizz (the non-alcoholic kind). Mr Lough was previously housemaster at Marlborough and spent seventeen years there 'in various capacities', including a two year exchange with Melbourne Grammar. Before that he taught at Chafyn Grove. Thoughtful and fun, they are obviously enjoying their time at Windlesham and glowing reports come in from happy parents of children who find themselves 'watching telly and eating crisps' in the Loughs' flat to overcome a temporary blip of homesickness.

Smashing new (if made of somewhat garishly coloured paper) handbook for all pupils (no pics though) full of handy hints, school policies, individual timetables and pages for attainments and staff comments – highly praised by the inspection team (who must be colour blind).

The Loughs started The Rolling Heads, where the heads of Brambletye, Cheam, Summerfields, Beaudesert and St Andrews Eastbourne meet twice a year with their wives to discuss the vicissitudes of prep-school headmastering and how to cope with the latest government initiatives as well as sharing their better schemes and wheezes. The directors of studies, as well as heads of departments and senior management, now also have barn-storming sessions. After nine years, Mr Lough has got the situation here pretty well sussed but still complains about the problems of getting staff, 'it's not always easy but all you need is one good applicant', though at the moment they 'have a brilliant crew', many of them young and zinging (the classics master – think policemen – was organising a basketball match during our visit and speaks Mandarin into the bargain) and the school has recently appointed a whizzo new head of DT who has transformed the outward bound type activities. Splendid staff accommodation on site with 33 'units' – everything from bachelor flats to 'proper' houses but nothing 'too grand' makes staff appointments easier.

Off to head The Hall School in July 2006.

Entrance: Via registration, interview at ages eight to 10, and testing at 11. Loads from London and the south east, about a third local, and 'around 90' from overseas, mainly expats, 30 Foreign Office children, fewer than before, but still (2005) more than any other school, plus 20 Services and a collection of 15 or so non-nationals. Quite a gang of French and Spanish children coming for a term or a year or so, all by word of mouth, the Domecq family 'are a strong influence', EFL on hand. Three term entry but mainly in September, though half term or even in between if space available. Wide ability range. All prospective pupils spend a day and a night in school, attending lessons et al, to see how it works out.

Exit: To a huge range of schools, 70 per cent to co-ed and almost all to boarding schools, occasional dribble back to state sector. Good record of scholarships, nine last year with four pure academic (Downe House, Marlborough, Benenden and Sevenoaks) but only one boy. Most frequent destinations as before: Marlborough, Harrow, Stowe, Bryanston, Eton, Millfield, King's Canterbury, Sevenoaks, St Edwards, Cranleigh, Rugby. Also to Winchester (none last year), Wellington, Charterhouse, Canford etc as well as locally to Brighton, Eastbourne and Bedales.

Remarks: Broad intake, so pupils setted for English, maths, French and science; most classes 15/16, max 20. Extensive learning support based in the snazzily decorated attic but the school is not good for physical handicap, though 'one of our best rugby players' is profoundly deaf. Stunning ISI report in May 2005: 'Pupils with a wide range of needs are very well catered for. Boys and girls make good and, at times, very good progress'. Pupils both withdrawn from class (usually Latin) for individual or small groups and French taught by inspired re-working of the syllabus (Mrs L says she has learnt much about teaching French from the SEN support staff). Six jolly bright dedicated rooms in the attics, with computers accessing the school network, pupils often have their own laptops. 35 per cent of pupils on some form of support, either for the brightest or the less able, usually on the dys-strata plus the odd ADHD child – but only those with organisational dysfunction rather than behavioural problems. Not a good school for those with an IQ of less than 100, though there are the odd siblings; unit is staffed by two full-time and five part-time teachers, one of whom is a maths specialist. Currently there are two children in the school who have their own teaching assistants. Language therapy (helpful for EFL too) and experienced counsellor on hand (the latter also visits other schools and brings a wider brief to the school). Weekly staff conferences to discuss various strategies and pupil profiles. In all cases parents pay, though there may be help available from their local authorities and an individual mentor may be partially supported by the school when they also help out in class.

All pupils must board, Little Windlesham pupils after their first year (ie aged 9+). Six houses, with boys resident in one building and girls in another; bright jolly dorms, with each girl having their own bedside light (wow!) Both boys and girls have a special 'chill out' common room, where they can have supervised quiet time. Tutorial system as well as houseparents, counsellor in the school. School prides itself on its pastoral care, which is much praised by the official reports. Pastoral board in the staff room where comments, both good and bad, are logged for all to see. Lots of project work, good links with Europe, all pupils learn Spanish for two years, German is an option as an 'activity'. Latin at ten for the brighter pupils, who follow a three year course. Greek another option. New IT system in place which links up all staff houses, plus computers all over the shop, as well as a mass of interactive whiteboards. Own laptops too, 'for children recommended to have one either by us or an Ed Psych'. Impressive art and design, school likes to have a regular presence in London, with exhibitions, concerts and the like every two years. Fantastic array of options, wizard glass fusing (really professional stuff) plus pottery, film making, kayaking, pistol shooting, as well as clays, plus karate, judo, chess coaching and extra tennis and riding (these latter cost extra and equestrians, who can ride up to five times a week could bankrupt their parents at a cost of £20 or so a lesson – but the stables are just a stones throw away and the schools hosts a horse show each May). Some of the most fantastic textiles, and screen painting (the batik is to die for), impressive new kitchens and cookery particularly popular with the boys – perhaps it is the sugar craft? Windlesham has the most stunning music we have ever come across, with outstanding musical director producing and recording works of his own compilation. Last time we said that 'time listening in the cupboard was well worth while' and yes, we had a session in the cupboard again – some superb choral work, plus music for the school's latest offering of Honk deftly re-worked by the head of drama to include some eighty children with two casts. This music/drama combination is terrific, bags of enthusiasm, the place positively buzzes. Huge number of individual lessons (600 or so) any instrument can be learnt, including the pipes, the mandolin and the Jew's harp. Outstanding sport, rugby team had just come back from Scotland and the girls' hockey had spent the same weekend in the Isle of Wight, and recently three boys linked up with a Saudi Arabian school for an Arctic adventure.

Science labs recently revamped and masses of TLC expended on the buildings which no longer look a little neglected, swimming pool windows now replaced with ball-proof (jolly expensive) glass and the whole place gleaming like a new pin, new security doors being fitted, though funds are not yet in hand to start the major new build which has been in the pipeline (planning permission received) to attach a dining hall, kitchen, indoor sports hall and extra-curricular centre to the Malden Theatre. The trad dining room has a new child-height servery, with jolly plastic plates and a huge range of salads and Jamie Oliver type dishes. Masses of fruit, and a trendy machine for doshing out baked potatoes.

The main house is a splendid and distinguished old redbrick Queen Anne house on the Downs near the south coast. Last time we visited the school was installing a new sewage plant and water main; and the 60 acres of grounds, with games pitches, tennis courts, a nine-hole golf course and child-inspired woods for making dens are back to their manicured splendour, and now boast a (tiny) observatory courtesy of the Worthng Astronomical society. A small patch of garden is dedicated for pupils' plots, usually taken up by those whose parents live abroad, and who still write regularly to the (now retired) school gardener for years after they have left enquiring about their veggie plots. Loughs keen on home comforts, a fire burns in the hall from mid October till Easter. Regular bus from Putney on Sunday evenings, all pupils must stay in school for two fixed weekends but with so many from real abroad there is no general exodus and children of the same age are grouped together and taken on jollies elsewhere. School founded (elsewhere at the request of Dr Arnold of Rugby) in 1837 by the Malden family who owned and ran it until a few years ago when it became a charitable foundation, The Malden Trust. Charles Malden retired in 1994 and died several years ago, his daughter is still a governor. Efficient, caring country school – less obviously green wellie than some (good showing of pheasants in the policies though) – with purposeful children beavering away at all levels. Windlesham is a happy school, with children getting the kind of care and attention you would expect from a much smaller establishment.

The Windsor Boys' School

1 Maidenhead Road, Windsor, Berkshire, SL4 5EH

Tel: 01753 716 060
Fax: 01753 833 186
Email: windsorboys@rbwm.org
Website: www.twbs.org.uk

• Pupils: 967 boys • Ages: 13-18 • Religion: non-denom
• School status: State • Opendays: contact school for details
• School gender: Boys • Day/boarding: Day pupils

SEN provision

Detail:

Now provide for in school:

Mild: ASP; AUT; ADD; ADHD; EBD; DYSC; DYSL; DYSP; SpLD; HI; VI;

Moderate: ASP; ADD; ADHD; EBD; MLD; DYSC; DYSL; DYSP; SpLD; HI; VI;

Severe: ADD; ADHD; DYSL; DYSP; HI;

Others: AUT(other); OCD; ODD; EAL; Sp&LD; Epi; PD;

Experience of:

Mild: CP;

Severe: EBD; DYSC; SpLD; VI;

Others: CD; SLD; DEL; Eat;

Summary: It is the aim of the school to enable pupils to achieve the highest standards possible. This will be achieved within the context of a broad and balanced curriculum that embraces the National Curriculum. In the case of pupils having a learning or behavioural difficulty which is significantly greater than the majority of pupils his age, or having a disability which either prevents or hinders him from making use of the educational facility, the school's intention is to make specific provision for that pupil. The support and involvement of parents is integral to the education of all pupils, particularly those with special needs.

In the case of more able pupils the school's intention is to provide extension and enrichment to the curriculum so that they can reach their full potential.

What we say about the school - the full Good Schools Guide review

Headmaster: Since 1997, Mr Jeffrey Dawkins BA Hons (in Semitic langs) MA MEd, early fifties. Instantly likeable, open, straightforward and friendly, this is clearly a popular and effective head and, seemingly, a round peg in the appropriate hole. Despite thirty years on the wrong side of the border, a vigorous Welsh tang lingers in the speech of Mr Dawkins who has held two previous headships – in Hungerford and in Reading. While at The Prospect school in Reading he oversaw the change to grant maintained status and to specialist technology college status. He remains a prime mover in the specialist schools movement and deeply committed to it. He has a practical and hands-on approach (his hands were, in fact, mostly on the copious litter we met on our tour around his demesne. He is famous for collecting it himself, seemingly regarding it as a normal part of the job). A sense of mutual respect between him, the other staff and the boys was tangible and informed the healthy working atmosphere we felt as we went round. He challenged the odd uniform infringer and minor renegade but in a good-humoured way and was received similarly. Mr Dawkins has a justifiable pride in his school, its achievements and in his pupils, 'they're good boys in the main', and shrugs his shoulders at the neglect of general maintenance over which he has only little control. He has managed, nonetheless, an impressive amount of fund-raising and much of the new-build and renovation has come about through his efforts. A sensible, feet-on-ground head with drive and imagination – just about anyone's cup of tea.

Academic Matters: In 2002, 60 per cent of pupils gained five or more grades A*-C at GCSE. This was before the school became a Specialist School in the Arts. The last four years has seen this rise to, in 2005, 72 per cent. Similarly, at Advanced level, 78 per cent of all grades were at A, B or C; 53 per cent of grades were A/B – not bad for a full comprehensive in an area where the many well-regarded local grammars – to say nothing of one or two well-known independent boys' schools nearby – cream off the cream. Over 100 students gained their first choice place at university. School now in the top 10 percentile of all schools and colleges in the country. This is now the school of choice for many and not just on account of its famous sporting prowess.

A level subjects are a trad mix plus psychology, sports studies, theatre studies, DT. New computer-controlled, digital language centre with satellite/video links – this is high-level stuff – allows individual and distance learning but French is the only modern language to survive to A level here and few takers. ICT now better-resourced than hitherto and used intelligibly and appropriately. GCSE subjects include PE, electronics and graphics. GNVQ intermediates in IT taken in year 12 and advanced in year 13 with impressive results. When asked about performing arts college status, head says it enables them to 'use performance, music and dance to stimulate achievement across whole school'. SENCo and team of twenty, either onsite or at local 'Achievement centre', where first-rate, creative work in learning support takes place. School being adapted for the less physically able. In general, Ofsted reports well above average results in comparison with similar schools. Parents report good teaching across the curriculum. This is a school where, if you work, you can reach the heights, but there are opportunities for everyone.

Games, Options, The Arts: Famous for sport, above all, rowing. School has a boat house on the nearby Thames and, by 2003, its under 18s had won the coveted Fawley Cup at Henley five times in the previous nine years. Pictures of boats and crews everywhere and a stack of upturned boats in the car park. Similarly impressive rugby teams tour internationally – South Africa and Canada in 2004. Financial help for those who need it. Athletics and cricket also strong and everything else you'd expect played hard here too. As well as rowing. School has 1994 sports pavilion, extensive onsite fields including a large astroturf pitch. Plays cricket against the MCC! School has a Sportsmark and head feels that sport is, overall, school's strongest suit. Especially rowing.

When not rowing, boys remember that theirs is a specialist arts college and has gained an Artsmark gold award. Drama is famously good and ambitious. Lord of the Flies and Berkoff's Agamemnon among recent productions – some with girls from Windsor Girls' School. Excellent drama studio. New performing arts, exhibition hall and sixth form block in 2004. Imaginative cross-curricular work eg a languages and drama collaboration praised by Ofsted 2003. Music is formidable – every kind of instrumental tuition and bands including a full orchestra, jazz band, close harmony singers and a 'junk band' – instruments made out of old plastic bottles etc. Good recording studio. Annual themed arts week each summer provides opportunities for experimentation of all kinds and visits from celebrity writers and musicians. Art is imaginative and varied, despite somewhat shabby – though light and spacious – art room and boys actually learn to draw here. Lovely, lively and thoughtful work here and around the school – critical Ofsted report clearly bonkers. New completely refurbished and re-equipped art rooms with state-of-the-art ICT facilities will make computer art a new and exciting challenge here from autumn 2004. School has excellent 'artists in residence' scheme and benefits from charismatic and inspiring onsite sculptor in addition to dedicated regular staff. Lots of local, national and international trips – sporting, artistic, linguistic, cultural. Lots of extra-curricular options – Young Enterprise, public speaking, debating, clubs for riding, philosophy, chess etc – and then there's always rowing.

Background and Atmosphere: Main, almost handsome, redbrick building dates from school's foundation as a boys' grammar in 1908. Later blocks of various vintages and degrees of attractiveness at rear make for a somewhat cluttered and amorphous site but no building more than two storeys so a human-scale, unthreatening, almost domestic ambiance overall. Subjects taught in all redbrick faculty blocks. School became a comprehensive in 1977. Chronic lack of investment makes for a general interior shabbiness – oh for some floors without chewing gum blots! – and exterior neglect but no more here than in comparable schools elsewhere and made up for by ubiquitous worthwhile displays of work and evidence of achievement. Head is wistful, 'I'd like a laptop, projector and an electronic whiteboard in every room,' he muses. 'I'd like two million to refurbish the whole lot,' and you want to give it to him.

Inescapable distant roar of the motorway at the end of the road punctuated by traffic in and out of Heathrow a couple of miles away, nonetheless, the school feels peaceful and purposeful. Surrounded by genteel if not affluent Victorian sprawl on the way to Maidenhead, it's easy to ignore the vast regal edifice down the road if you choose to do so. Litter is a feature here but school is used by the local community until late most nights and all weekend so it's a lost battle though still gamely joined by head. House system important in all school activities. About a third of teachers are women.

Pastoral Care and Discipline: Head believes in permanent exclusion for anyone who brings drugs into school in most circumstances – not the fashionable view perhaps but the conviction of a clearly humane man. 'Traditional' is a word he uses and mostly as a term of approbation. Assemblies 'with me in my gown' are used to celebrate school successes but 'if you talk during assembly in our hall you're in detention for an hour.' Would sound familiar to – and go down well with – many parents. Atmosphere is relaxed and civilised – boys look you in the face and smile at their teachers.

Pupils and Parents: Boys come from all over Windsor, Slough and surrounds. Intake is strictly according to catchment area so applying from further afield is a waste of time. Socio-economic backgrounds greatly varied as demographics would suggest. Despite several good local grammars, this is increasingly the school of choice for the less-than-loaded parents of the less-than-brilliant prep school leavers – and there are a lot of prep schools in Berkshire. Parents put a lot into this school – it has a true sense of community and a pride in being what it is – not glitzy, not flash nor trendy. About a fifth of boys from a variety of minority ethnic heritages, predominantly Indian and Pakistani. Very few need substantial EAL help. Pupils mostly from four local middle schools and various preps.

Entrance: Via local authority registration and application. See note above about catchment areas. This school is now seriously over-subscribed. From 2006, 10 per cent of students selected by aptitude in the performing arts.

Exit: After GCSEs school loses 10 per cent to other educational establishments and 20 per cent to employment or training. The rest stay on for sixth form studies. A further 10 per cent of those will leave for employment after one year in the sixth. Of those who complete the sixth, around 90 per cent go on to higher or further education – Oxbridge to vocational courses of all kinds. A good record.

Remarks: 'Success' is a word you read a lot as you go round the school. 'Achievement' is a word the head uses frequently and there is, throughout, a sense of realistic aspiration. Parents put a lot into this school – it has a true sense of community and a pride in being what it is – not glitzy, not flash nor trendy. Quietly, carefully and with dedication this school is, in the head's words, 'building on our traditional strength with an eye to the future' and achieving impressively across the board. And on the river.

Witherslack Hall School

Witherslack, Grange-over-Sands, Cumbria, LA11 6SD

Tel: 015395 52397

Fax: 015395 52419

Email: schooloffice@witherslackhalladmin.co.uk

Website: www.witherslackhallschool.co.uk

• Pupils: 72 boys, all board • Ages: 11-19

• School status: Independent • School gender: Boys

• Day/boarding: Takes boarders

SEN provision

Detail:

Centre of excellence for:

Mild: ASP; AUT; EBD;

Moderate: ASP; AUT; EBD;

Severe: ASP; EBD;

Now provide for in school:

Mild: ADD; ADHD; DYSL; DYSP; HI; VI;

Moderate: ADD; ADHD; MLD; DYSL; HI;

Severe: ADD; ADHD;

Others: SPD; CD; OCD; ODD; Sp&LD;

Experience of:

Mild: DYSC;

Moderate: DYSC;

Others: TIC; Epi; Eat;

Summary: Witherslack Hall School caters for boys exhibiting social, emotional and behavioural difficulties. The school provides a safe, secure and caring environment for boys with: specific learning difficulties, oppositional defiant disorders, autisic spectrum disorders, attachment disorders, conduct disorders, ADHD, pathological demand avoidance disorders, anxiety and depression.

The school employs nearly 100 trained staff including a full-time educational psychologist and a CAHMS worker. In addition to the National Curriculum the deliver an extensive vocational programme including construction, rural studies, motor vehicle engineering and catering to name but a few. We also have 38 qualified care staff to manage over 25 risk-assessed recreational activities. The school has a hugely successful record of sporting achievements.

Two detached cottages are provided for post-16 provision, where each young person completes a personalised leavers' programme which incorporates all aspects of helping to live life independently. These young men will also attend local colleges with support staff.

What we say about the school - the full Good Schools Guide review

Head: Since 1998, Mr Michael Barrow BEd PGCE (in educational management) (forties). Began his teaching life as a PE and maths teacher in a mainstream school, gravitated to the children reckoned difficult, and has been standing shoulder to shoulder ever since. Energetic, robust, full of heart. The old ways of addressing the behaviour of boys like these – the exertion of stern, unbending imperatives – have given way to methods based in affection, admiration and praise, to which he subscribes wholeheartedly. Passionate about kindness and building on children's strengths, but he's no pushover, no way, nor is he an airy-fairy ideas man, he's a pragmatist: 'I work from good, solid theory,' he says, and he takes what works, what makes children feel good about themselves, will send them on their way at ease with themselves and others. Has maintained links with the mainstream, enabling him to 'pluck the best of what's going on out there' and evolve the distinctive, eclectic 'Witherslack Way'. Board member of NAES – the EBD schools association – so he's up to the minute. He's a busy networker, too. Married, two children.

Academic Matters: The accent is on putting these boys back on track, so it's all about getting focused, catching up, in an environment with a mainstream feel so they can slip back in again. National Curriculum, 14 GCSEs on offer, core subjects as you'd expect plus citizenship, single award science, mod languages at Key Stage 3. Entry levels and certs of achievement as appropriate. IQ range is approx 65-130. Lots of seriously attractive vocational options include splendid motor vehicle engineering, construction in wood n brick, and top catering, into which they are seeking to incorporate the entire core curriculum. Rural studies very hands on in the walled garden – horticulture, hens to feed. Everything here is impressively, fully resourced.

Teachers are all subject specialists. Max class size eight with up to four support assistants and key workers in there too, as many of them as necessary to keep boys on task and give help where an SpLD is hampering. Success measurable: exam results put these boys in the top 5 per cent of the government's value-added table. To see them at it is not to be aware that they have 'some of the most complex needs in the country'; the atmosphere is calm, busy, cheery. If ever it all gets too much a boy will be scooped up, taken out, urged to talk through what blew the fuse, treated kindly and, yes, suffer the sanction, but even at the bottom of a downer they talk only about the way up. Back in the classroom, meanwhile, learning must, must go on. Special literacy and numeracy support for those who need it, plus speech and language specialist.

Most leave at 16 but some whose needs will be best served stay on to do vocational courses – brickwork, catering – plus key skills both on campus and at Lancaster and Morecambe FE College. Some year 11 pupils and the post-16s live in cottages in the grounds where, under supervision, they learn to live independently.

It's a long school day, six lessons, just an hour for lunch, from 9 o'clock till 3.40 – and you come back if you haven't finished. All the while, boys are amassing points. Their scoreboards start ticking the moment they get up, they get praised for anything, everything praiseworthy – the staff are always looking to dish out points in lessons, at meals, in activities, for effort and behaviour. The most you can get at once is 3, the fewest 0 and they're added up every day at teatime. Anything less than 35 restricts your choice of evening activities and – they are pragmatic in all things, here – the amount of pocket money you get at the end of the week. It's a very clever blend of incentive with self-esteem building.

Staff, all 95 of them, are trained in emotionally intelligent methods and encouraged to build relationships with these children, some of whom urgently need positive adult role models. Absolutely no shouting ever, or angry confrontation, but unacceptable behaviour is challenged calmly and unshakably until the desired outcome is agreed on. Bags of calm kind talk based in common sense. Stability and routine make for an environment in which children observably relax and settle. They know exactly where they stand.

Games, Options, The Arts: Loads of sport, football a speciality, they were still at it at 8 o'clock the night we visited down on the floodlit hard play pitch, oblivious to the rain. All the team sports you would expect, they even have an angling team. Matches against other special schools. Fabulously resourced outdoor ed programme and, come the weekend, they're off into the hills or out in canoes on Coniston. Some good art evident, and drama and music – it's all there for them if they want it. Provision in all things is seriously impressive here.

Background and Atmosphere: One of seven schools in the expanding, privately owned Witherslack Group, all for children with special needs. Occupies Lord Derby's former hunting lodge, 1874 Tudorbethan, high up in the hills yet close to civilisation as we know it. Wild, romantic location whose beauty is not lost on the children themselves.

Pastoral Care and Discipline: The emotional health of these children is central to everything they do, so it's paramount. The ethos of the school is founded in resilience theory, summarised as: 'building on children's strengths, looking for the beauty in a person and enhancing that beauty.' Expectations made of these boys are unrelenting and good fun. Standards are extremely high. When we were there the theme of the week was 'look and listen' and plenty of laughter accompanied kind, firm insistence on eyes meeting. The day is structured, the programme busy and fatiguing, but chill out time at the end of the day (all lights out by 10) allows for telly watching and playstation games. These boys live in physical conditions that a top independent school would envy, and they look after it. Carpets, paint furniture all top notch, comfy as can be. Care staff sit with the boys and join in. Very happy, relaxed atmosphere. School supplies all uniform and toiletries, which makes for a level social playing field. Always around 25 in at weekends, and plenty to do. It's a no smoking campus, and, such are vigilance levels, there are no loopholes. All damage is paid for.

They're by no means confined to barracks, these boys. The school nurtures its community relationships – with the youth club, for example, or taking cakes they've made to old folk – and locals speak warmly of them.

Emotional and behavioural support come from the entire community, from each child's key worker in particular – 45-min weekly sessions. Frequent liaison with home, they work closely with parents, who appreciatively agree: 'They always phone to find out how the weekend went'. There is specialist support from a full-time educational psychologist and a halftime CAMHS (mental health) worker.

Pupils and Parents: A school of choice for LEAs far and wide right down to home counties. Not the sort of ethnic mix you might expect but, they shrug, 'we can only take those whom the LEAs refer'. Social range not wide, either. Parents praise 'very open communication'. Annual review of SSEN is the big stocktaking session. For parents, it can be a wrench to see their son go off to a residential school – 'We were torn apart when he had to leave home' – but the pain is short lived, they soon settle. Exemplary handbooks for new pupils and parents including curriculum booklet which tells parents what they can do to help.

Entrance: All referred by their LEA because mainstream couldn't or wouldn't cope. Would they take fee-paying pupils? 'Yes.' All manner of emotional educational and social behaviour problems here – 'there are more clinical classifications than ever' – spanning Asperger's and other ASDs through ADHD with, often, an accompanying SpLD. No criminal behaviour – no twoccers, no drugs, 'nothing likely to endanger the community. These boys know they're not reaching their potential, they know there's something wrong, they genuinely want to do something about it.' Informal, exploratory initial enquiry, then formal interview, home visit by key worker and decision to admit if the school feels it can meet the child's needs.

Exit: Back to the mainstream for post-16 courses. Some direct to work.

Remarks: Kind and commonsensical. Parents reach for all the superlatives – 'amazing people, nothing fazes them' – and tell academic and behavioural transformation stories.

Wolverhampton Grammar School

Compton Road, Wolverhampton, West Midlands, WV3 9RB

Tel: 01902 421 326

Fax: 01902 421 819

Email: wgs@wgs.org.uk

Website: www.wgs.org.uk

• Pupils: 405 boys and 285 girls, all day • Ages: 11-18 • Religion: Non-denom • Fees: £2,764 • School status: Independent • School gender: Mixed • Day/boarding: Day pupils

SEN provision

Detail:

Experience of:

Mild: HI;

Moderate: DYSP; HI;

Summary: The Opportunities through Assisted Learning (OPAL) Programme, for specific learning difficulties, is a unique unit within the school that integrates able dynamic students into an academically selective co-education school. Applicants for the OPAL Programme can be assessed by interview rather than entrance exam. The OPAL Programme provides tuition and support within the unit for 3½hrs per week. The students do not study Latin, French or German; however they have the option of Italian as a MFL. WGS is a dyslexia friendly school. GCSE and A Level OPAL results are excellent. 2003-05 GCSE – 100 per cent (5 or more at grade A-C). A2 2005 – 82 per cent at grade A/B. Entrance is at 10+, 11+ and occasionally 13+.

What we say about the school - the full Good Schools Guide review

Head: Since 1990, Dr Bernard Trafford (forties), married to Katherine, two daughters now both at University. Educated at Downside and St Edmund Hall Oxford, and secured an external doctorate in education from the University of Birmingham in 1996 whilst serving as head. Dr Trafford has spent most of his career here, except for a short spell at the Royal Grammar School in High Wycombe. Arrived in 1981 as head of music, then head of sixth form and finally head. This is a very unusual, perhaps unique, curriculum vitae within the independent school world. He has a fine voice, and continues to take an active part in the musical life of the school; (noted for organising a choir at HMC conferences.) A musician head is remarkably enough; to have achieved such rapid promotion within the same school is virtually unheard of. This says much of Dr Trafford's ability. Dr Trafford's particular educational interests are centred on the issues of inclusion and accountability in schools, where he is an acknowledged authority.

A very civilised and courteous man with, as one might expect, a relaxed approachable style. Yet that should not in any way lead you to underrate his steely purpose and real determination. Dr Trafford is someone who leads from the front and continues to immerse himself fully in the life of the school. He understands fully what the school should achieve and has led Wolverhampton through stormy waters with the advent of co-education and the ending of Assisted Places. He believes in offering his pupils a breadth of education and is determined that Wolverhampton Grammar should be a beacon of liberal, tolerant and civilised values. One of the largest new development projects in many years is the creative arts centre, which wholly expresses his educational vision.

Academic Matters: Wolverhampton Grammar School survives and indeed thrives in a very competitive market. Wolverhampton itself is blessed with at least two over-subscribed comprehensive schools as well as the very selective Wolverhampton Girls' High School as a serious academic rival. The close proximity of the King Edward's schools in Birmingham must also be taken into account. The Grammar School has solid if not spectacular results across the whole curriculum; its results at both GCSE and A level have improved steadily over the years with A level A/B grades at over 70 per cent. Given the fact that the school is not especially selective these figures are extremely impressive and place it amongst the best performing schools in the region. Art is especially strong. Not an academic hothouse. Something of a pack leader in the provision of appropriate help for bright dyslexic children: the head takes a personal interest in the OPAL programme which is specially designed for their needs.

Games, Options, The Arts: There are attractive games fields (including astroturf) hard by the main school complex as well as a newish sports hall and squash courts as well some rather underused fives courts. The school is a big player in the local and very competitive games scene. Football, netball and cricket special strengths. School offers a wide range of out-of-school activities; these include drama and debating as well as the more sporting alternatives. Outdoor education (trekking, climbing, expeditions etc) is a huge growth area at present. (23 senior students climbed Mt Kilimanjaro summer 2005). Music is an important component – several instrumental and choral groups – more than one might expect. A third of the pupils have instrumental lessons: this is a proportion that the head is endeavouring to increase.

Background and Atmosphere: School founded by the Merchant Taylors' Company in 1512. Moved to its present imposing building in the smarter suburbs of Wolverhampton in 1875. The campus still reflects the social and academic aspirations of its Victorian benefactors: the front of the school would not disgrace a university college or grand public school with all the gloss of neo-gothic antiquity by which no 19th century burgers could fail to be impressed. The atmosphere is both relaxed and purposeful. This has been aided by the development of attractive communal areas where pupils can 'chill out' during lunchtime and after school. Most of the newer building developments are attractive and the school seems to have avoided the municipal brutalism than has been inflicted on so many similar institutions. Despite the elite resonances of the site the whole atmosphere is unpretentious.

Pastoral Care and Discipline: Inclusion, involvement and empowerment are the school's watchwords in dealing with pupils' needs. Pupils are involved and listened to and nowhere is this better illustrated than in a powerful school council which is genuinely consulted on a whole range of issues. The system seems to work seamlessly and the atmosphere of openness and mutual respect that it engenders is evident throughout the school. This approach to pastoral care is genuinely innovative and clearly marks out Wolverhampton from the pack. We were especially impressed by the friendly confidence of the pupils.

Pupils and Parents: The intake is a fair cross-section of wealthier citizens of the Wolverhampton area, with pupils travelling up to 20 miles to attend. Around 30 per cent of the school is from ethnic minorities; the largest single group by far being from the Asian subcontinent. The ending of Assisted Places has narrowed the social base of the parent body – something that concerns the head and a generous scholarship fund goes some way to address. Not a 'posh' school: social pretensions are not something valued, or even tolerated. Modest fee levels appeal to less well-off parents and the school also attracts those who want something special for their children and have rejected many of the Birmingham and Wolverhampton academic and social hothouse alternatives.

Entrance: Mostly from local primary schools with a smattering from prep-schools. The school has its own entrance examination at 11 and 13, and has recently opened the 'Big Six'. This is a year 6 group of 10 to 11-year-olds where parents can choose to enter their children early into a genuinely caring academic atmosphere, without having to subject them to all the nonsense of Key Stage 2 testing. It makes much of its experimental 'learning to learn' curriculum, and has proved very popular. A cynic might suggest that this is a clever marketing ploy to grab the cream of local primary school pupils a year early – certainly it is not universally popular with local primary heads. However, it does show the kind of innovative thinking one would expect from a school led by Dr Trafford.

Exit: The vast majority go to university. One in fifteen to Oxbridge. The rest to a wide range of institutions, the largest number to the University of Birmingham. Around 10 per cent read medicine or pharmacy. Few choose 'Mickey Mouse' universities and fewer still 'Minnie Mouse' courses.

Money Matters: The school was badly hit by the ending of Assisted Places (numbers have dropped by 100 since the peak in the mid nineties.) The present size of the school seems more appropriate for the space and available facilities. Fees are competitive and there are some scholarships and bursaries for brighter and needier pupils. Money has been wisely spent on many fine facilities, but there are few of the whizzier additions that one might find in the more expensive and grander alternatives.

Remarks: A fine school with an exceptional and innovative head. Good results but also a balanced and happy environment; especially good for bright dyslexics where the Opal programme is at the top of its class.

Woodcote House School

Windlesham, Surrey, GU20 6PF

Tel: 01276 472 115

Fax: 01276 472 890

Email: info@woodcotehouseschool.co.uk

Website: www.woodcotehouseschool.co.uk

• Pupils: 105 boys, most board • Ages: 8-13
• Religion: Inter-denom • Fees: Day £3,275; boarding £4,575
• School status: Independent • School gender: Boys
• Day/boarding: Takes boarders

SEN provision

Detail:

Centre of excellence for:
- Mild: DYSL; DYSP;
- Others: EAL;

Now provide for in school:
- Mild: ASP; ADD; ADHD; EBD; DYSC; SpLD;
- Moderate: ASP; ADD; ADHD; MLD; DYSC; DYSL; DYSP; SpLD;
- Others: SPD;

Experience of:
- Mild: HI;
- Others: Sp&LD; Eat;

Summary: Woodcote has a fully qualified and very experienced special needs teacher who can deal with a variety of problems. She comes in four days per week and at present takes about 15 per cent of boys for anything between one and four sessions per week, sometimes on their own, sometimes in small groups. She is very much considered part of the full-time staff, and briefs the mainstream teachers at weekly staff meetings as to the best way to help individuals in their lessons. She is in regular contact with all the parents of boys she teaches, either in person or by telephone, and liaises closely with the educational psychologist the school recommends if formal reports are required.

In addition, boys who do not study Latin (about 25 per cent of the school) are given one extra session per week in each of maths, English and Science. In one or two cases boys are also excused French and can have individual SEN lessons arranged.

What we say about the school - the full Good Schools Guide review

Head: Since 1989, Mr Nick Paterson BA (fiftyish), educated at Westminster and Exeter University. Called 'Mr Nick' by one and all. Mr Nick's grandfather bought the school in 1931 when it was going 'but only just'. It is now a private limited company. Super wife, with older children, and they have one son at university. Mr Nick comments (in answer to our question) that his biggest challenge is continuing to instil a code of good manners, fair play and unselfishness in the face of a deteriorating situation nationally.

Entrance: Send for what is still one of the smallest prospectuses in the country (though Ludgrove and Sunningdale come close), small 'because it is vital they (the parents) come and see us with the boy and really we must get on pretty well'. Always prepared to talk to parents right up to the last moment. Takes new boys in at the beginning of all three terms.

Exit: Biggest numbers to Sherborne, Radley, Bradfield, Harrow, Shiplake, Charterhouse, Wellington, plus a dozen others.

Remarks: Super little school where each boy is carefully cocooned so that the shock of leaving 'nursery environment' will not be too much. Main problem might be the shock of leaving Woodcote for their public school. 'Generous' exeats every third week (Friday-Monday), and Mrs Nick will always make arrangements for 'abroad' boys with other families. Lots of other activities/outings on in-school weekends when parents are welcome to join in but not take out. Minuscule but extremely informative, yearly magazine which kicked off last year on the very first page: 'Food. Always the most interesting part of any small boy's day'. Keen chess, bridge, fishing, calligraphy and nice old-fashioned boy things, such as making model aeroplanes, and less old-fashioned things such as 'Warhammer' (the head is appalled at the cost). Set in its own thirty acres, which includes some attractive woods, the main building is Regency and elegant but delightfully worn at the edges, with additional modestly built classroom blocks round the back and charming little chapel across the lawn, made of corrugated iron (painted black) and wooden inside. ('Buildings like hen houses,' said one visiting parent disappointedly.) Barbour and/or Husky part of the uniform, corduroy trousers and a rather dreary brown sweater or school sweatshirt; school now runs its own clothes shop and several changes have recently been made to the uniform.

Lots of golf played on site and cricket, squash (uses courts up the road), rugger and shooting. Several parents join large ski party in early January. Head concentrates on placing boys in the school of their parents' choice rather than on getting scholarships – though they got seven in 2005. Small and very competent remedial unit – recommended by special needs organisations for dyslexia and dyspraxia. Fully-qualified teacher who works in a small unit – some 15 per cent of the boys receive help – also experienced EFL teacher.

One or two gems among the staff including the super dynamic head of science, and the archetypal schoolmaster, Colin Holman, who has been here for yonks and lives in the lodge and, amongst other things, looks after the grounds lovingly. Development programme means school now has science lab, computer centre, art and music block. Music strong – head and brilliant young head of music co-write musicals. Eighty per cent learn at least one instrument. Choir tours to Holland. New changing rooms (not before time, some might say), also astroturf hockey pitch/tennis courts and telescopic swimming pool enclosure. About one-third are sons of soldiers or expats, one-third London or local and a third from 'far afield'. One or two Thais (long-standing tie with Thailand), a few 'Europeans' (mainly Spanish). One of a dying breed – the family-owned school – and, unlike some, by and large it works. Continuing good reports.

WOODSIDE PARK INTERNATIONAL SCHOOL

Upper School, Main Office, 6 Friern Barnet Lane, London, N11 3LX

Tel: 020 8920 0600
Fax: 020 8368 3220
Email: admissions@wpis.org
Website: www.wpis.org

• Pupils: 470 boys and girls • Ages: 2-7 kindergarten and junior (4-7); 7-11 junior; 11-16 senior; 16-18 IB Diploma Centre • Religion: Non-denom • Fees: Kindergarten up to £2,100, Lower School up to £3,200, Upper School £3,550, IB £5,100. Plus lunch. Quest and EAL up to £2,400 (for 5 sessions per week) • School status: Independent • Opendays: Open day once a term; private tour upon appointment • School gender: Mixed • Day/boarding: Day pupils

SEN provision

Detail:
Now provide for in school:
Mild: DYSL;
Moderate: DYSL;
Experience of:
Mild: ASP; AUT; ADD; DYSC; DYSP;
Moderate: ASP; AUT;

Summary: We are a small mainstream school with specialist provision for the teaching of dyslexic pupils, usually by withdrawal from lessons, on a carefully arranged timetable.

What we say about the school - the full Good Schools Guide review

Head: Since 2005, Mr David Rose as head of school, former head of The British School of Houston. After working overseas for over 20 years he and his wife Vivienne are enjoying being back in UK and close to their two daughters.

Academic Matters: Two form entry, max class size 20 and often much smaller. Most of the teaching is based on 'the defining question, with pupils becoming adept at problem-solving, rather than learning by rote.' School has moved forward to true international status and follows the IB discipline. Pupils at the senior department are using the MYP – Middle Years Programme; with the IB Diploma Centre on stream, and the junior department currently waiting for accreditation of the IBO to teach their primary years programme, Woodside will be one of only two schools in the country to undertake the complete IB syllabus. For the moment run on trad lines, with pupils taking nine or ten GCSEs in a vast array of subjects. Results to hand show a scattering of A*s and As, more or less across the board. Design and technology fairly dismal – perhaps the Hall is a road too far?

French, German, Spanish, Italian, Chinese and Turkish on offer as well as the more trad subjects, as you might expect with a quantity of native speakers. Combined sciences. Strong homework ethos. 'No real problem' with staff, but the pay is not that of Inner London and recent appointments have included an Italian (maths) as well as teachers from Singapore, India and an American via Sweden. Computers all over, everywhere, but no timetabled keyboarding.

School has specialist teachers for learning support so dyslexia 'not a problem'; usually one-to-one but various disciplines are employed, including Quest. 'The aim of the Quest programme is to teach students with different learning styles to function successfully and independently in an academically challenging mainstream setting.' One statemented child in school. 'Those with ADD can be considered', but school not keen for those with recognised ADHD. The previous head of special needs at St Christopher's has been appointed as consultant. That has to be a real coup.

The EAL (either English as Alternative or Additional depending, apparently, on the day of the week) offers non-fluent English speakers extra help, in English traditions and culture as well as ABC. Again, often one-to-one. These two add-ons cost extra: cost of Quest programme up to £2,400 for five sessions per week. Cost of EAL 'add-ons' up to £1,750 for five sessions per week.

Games, Options, The Arts: Games field ten minutes' coach ride away; all the usual suspects, gym in the Hall (not vast by modern standards) and much use of local swimming and other facilities. 'Masses of joining in'.

Interesting art but, when facilities improve, this will too. Not much child-inspired art in evidence around the place. Masses of trips to museums and art galleries in London and further afield. Drama on the up. No music at all until three years ago but gradually making itself heard. Class music for all and plenty of individual tuition. Again, masses of visits to concerts and plays in London. Big blitz in 2003 for the creative arts. Clubs for almost everything, with just as many for the younger pupils as those in the senior school – choirs, handwriting, Scrabble, RE and guitar either at lunchtime or after school.

Background and Atmosphere: This is the complicated bit. School operates on four sites. The senior department was originally Friern Barnet Grammar School and still looks and feels like a grammar school – pretty scruffy, with bags in corners and older classrooms running irritatingly off each other. Woodside Park pre-prep, the kindergarten and nursery based in the rather jolly, somewhat expanded Holmewood site. The IB Diploma centre was formed in 1995 and has just moved into the new Jubilee Hall development. (Got it so far?) Senior, junior departments, and the Jubilee Hall/IB Diploma Centre are all surrounded by uniform bright blue railings; the gates are locked. The sites are really quite far apart but a school bus 'does the loop'.

The school only joined the international circuit in 2000; and the original concept (and funding) came from Dr Steven Spahn – he is on the school board and rang the director during our interview. Dr Spahn, who is American, has been involved with IB for yonks, and founded the original international school of London (no connection with the current IS of L). WPIS is sister school of The Dwight School in New York.

Children in baby school smart in bright blue track suits; pre-prep wear trad school grey trousers for boys, tunics for girls, with pretty patterned dresses for summer – blazers for all, caps for the boys, and felt hats or boaters for girls. Sadly this charming image falls off as you progress up the school, the junior dept look much as you would expect, while the senior pupils are very teenagey and the current fashion appears to be girls wearing their ties some five inches long with skirts barely longer.

IB Diploma centre is a new creation, only six years old, and whilst all singing and dancing is available here, the tradition of leaving at 16 (from the old Grammar School) dies hard, and it was sadly empty when we visited (exam leave). Centre follows recognised IB syllabus including theory of knowledge, creativity, action, service, plus the extended essay and six other subjects. French, German, Italian, Chinese and Spanish on offer, and all must do some form of science. Quest and EAL as one might expect. Laptops for all. All but one of the previous pupils have gone to university and the exception was that of choice. Staff commute between the sites, plus some part-time specialist language teachers. Informal rather grown-up atmosphere, pupils wear mufti/with a dress code.

Slight feeling of 'being out on a limb with so few pupils, and perhaps not enough interaction with the rest of the school – 'more music, drama and art would be a bonus'. Foundation year (at the centre) to get incomers up to speed. Pupils are composed of roughly 50 per cent from the senior department, and 50 per cent incomers. 'They bond well and tend to do things as a group out of school hours'. A bonus for those (most at present) from abroad on contracted 'homestay' arrangements, who are under the aegis of the pastoral director and can be met at the airport etc.

Pastoral Care and Discipline: Excellent; school follows the IB philosophy of value, system and peace, this is tolerance 'put in place'. Bullying firmly sat on, with girls having their own common room – well, they are still the smaller number. No apparent problem with drugs, or fags or booze and the gate of the senior dept (on the busy main road) was being guarded when we arrived at lunchbreak. One recent expulsion for general mischievousness. Fair amount of obvious dossing around after lessons when we visited.

Pupils and Parents: Mostly from a very small catchment area, school organises buses but, that being said, truly international, with 30/35 per cent expats. A preponderance of Japanese but also Indian, Greek, Iranians, Israelis – whatever. Senior dept slightly less international because of its grammar school roots and perceived bias but all this is changing as the school's own babies come through the system. Parents a middle class professional business bunch, quite a lot of first time buyers. International with a small i.

Entrance: 60 per cent come up from the junior dept, otherwise from state or independent local schools. Quite a lot of 'to-ing and fro-ing' with other local independent schools. Entrance by interview and previous school reports. Children arriving from overseas can come immediately if there is space available, or indeed any child moving into the area.

Exit: Some traditionally leave to go to other nearby independents, either straight from junior dept, or at 13; to Haberdashers', City of London, Henrietta Barnett etc.

Otherwise at 16 for the IB Diploma centre or to other schools or colleges of further education.

Money Matters: Scholarships fixed percentage of the fees, competitive exam at 11; plus bursaries on appeal. School runs 'a tight ship'; late payers are regularly reminded and will, if necessary, be taken to court.

Remarks: This is a school on the cusp; as the previous head freely admitted, 'there is a fair way to go' but his successor is looking to make it 'the best international school in London'. Time will tell.

WOOLGROVE SCHOOL

Pryor Way, Letchworth, Hertfordshire, SG6 2PT

Tel: 01462 622 422
Fax: 01462 622 022
Email: admin.woolgrove@thegrid.org.uk
Website: www.woolgrove.org.uk

• Pupils: 110: 82 boys and 28 girls, all day • Ages: 5-11
• Religion: non-denom • School status: State
• School gender: Mixed • Day/boarding: Day pupils

SEN provision

Detail:

Centre of excellence for:
- Mild: AUT; DYSL;
- Moderate: AUT; MLD;

Now provide for in school:
- Mild: ADD; ADHD; EBD; DS; DYSP; SpLD; HI; VI; CP;
- Moderate: ADD; ADHD; DS; DYSL; HI; VI;
- Severe: ADD; ADHD; DS;
- Others: SPD; AUT(other); OCD; FRX; GEN; EAL; Sp&LD; DEL; Epi; Eat;

Experience of:
- Mild: ASP; DYSC;
- Moderate: ASP; DYSC; DYSP; SpLD; CP;
- Severe: AUT; HI; VI;
- Others: MSI;

Summary: All pupils at Woolgrove have a moderate learning difficulty. Some have attention disorders, some have autism and some have a variety of other syndromes. We follow the National Curriculum at a level appropriate to pupils' needs. Our best resource is our staff who are experienced, well-qualified and have a committment to supporting the learning of all pupils. The majority of our staff carry out outreach work which not only supports mainstream schools, but also allows our staff to maintain strong links with mainstream education.

What we say about the school - the full Good Schools Guide review

Head: Since 2003, Mrs Bridget Walton (married, three grown up children), previously research teacher on workforce remodelling Woolgrove for a year. Quietly spoken and efficient, very confident in her team and the structured and safe environment for learning that her school provides. Has a strong vision to extend the school day as part of inclusion provision and to broaden Woolgrove's excellent speech and language facilities.

Academic Matters: A centre of excellence. Purpose-built autism base for 10 children (staff:children 1:2) consisting of three quiet rooms, a sensory room and an observation room to help parents and staff with initial 6 week assessment and thrice yearly target setting. Integration with main classes at Woolgrove is the aim, with the help of an Individual Integration Plan.

Main body of school: average class size ten pupils with teacher and at least one full-time teaching assistant (TA) or nursery nurse. English and maths are taught as separate subjects and every child has access to a computer in the classroom and in the computer suite – older ones have access to the Internet. Science, technology, history, geography are tackled partly through a topic approach. French for year 5 and 6 pupils. Part-time speech therapists (three days/week), music therapist (one day/week), art therapist (one day/week), occupational therapist (one day/week) – all work closely with teaching staff and parents.

A third of the pupils in the whole school have autism, therefore threefold communication throughout; speaking, visual clues and signing. This enhances communication and cuts down frustration. Visual timetables are present in every classroom and as the children move up the school the classrooms appear more and more like mainstream ones. Older children get used to moving environment and interruptions while surrounded by familiar teachers and assistants. Individual planning, with long, medium and short-term goals, is important, since classes do not go up necessarily as an entity – Woolgrove uses and applies the P level assessments. TAs play a large part in this and feel their role and personal development is valued, 'perhaps they should be called Teaching Partners instead of assistants'. Four TAs are doing a foundation degree with study time scheduled out of school (absences are covered by a core of regular supply teachers) each week – so they are not selected for their qualifications alone (60 applicants for a recent job). Support for most needy pupils is plentiful, but developing independence is vital, so a hand might be held on the way into assembly, but child will usually be deposited to sit with rest of class.

Every child is given a chance to excel at something – library monitors learn the Dewey system and to colour code – and behaviour in the multi-faith assemblies illustrates this with cheery, bouncy yet well-behaved children applauding the class and individual awards.

Renowned Outreach service supports pupils in mainstream schools and those who have moved on from Woolgrove through sharing expertise. INSET courses and a resource centre in school enhance this service.

Games, Options, The Arts: The school day begins with a 15 minute workout since many of the children have been bused in for at least half an hour from home or respite care. Each class has two lessons a week for gym/dance/athletics and pupils go to North Herts Leisure Centre for swimming lessons. Break times are also opportunities to learn to play in groups, new playground equipment and training in playground buddy behaviour is very successful. School owns seven acres of woodland that is being developed as a conservation area for use by local schools, with wellies and equipment available in a mobile.

Music is timetabled as well as playing a part in daily assemblies. Words and visuals help recognition of instruments and even composers in recorded music, and live piano encourages pupils' singing. Art enters the curriculum through topics eg gingerbread man competitions, a class animal assembly and also individual therapy sessions.

Membership of the School Council is gained by volunteers and peer nomination. Their input has made the boys' toilets more 'boyie' and the girls ones 'girlie' and had an influence on the variety of clubs on offer, eg line dancing, top trumps, table football, chess, computer, eco committee. Local trips in two school minibuses to go horse riding are popular and pupils are offered a place on a five day residential Adventure holiday before they leave. The main obstacle to after school clubs is space and funding – extra transport is needed to bus pupils home afterwards.

Pastoral Care and Discipline: The staff is dedicated, aware and highly organised, supported by a School Medical Officer and a School Nurse. Most are female but there are two male teachers (one awarded primary science teacher of the year recently), one male TA and a male caretaker. Children very caring and aware – liable to surround and comfort 'weeping' person even when only acting out bullying scene... Atmosphere at school is calm but busy – everyone seems to have a purpose and children are confident and curious; one piped up, 'good morning. You sound different.'

Pupils and Parents: A thriving parents' group meets regularly for coffee and family very much involved in pupils' target setting, via home/school book and face-to-face time with teachers. All parents and staff belong to Friends of Woolgrove – committee is elected at AGM but all members welcome at monthly meeting – provides opportunities for socialising and fundraising.

Entrance: Decision by LA (Children's, Schools and Families) for Hertfordshire pupils. Entry at beginning of term in which children are five, or any stage up to the beginning of year six if there are places available. Every pupil has a statement of SEN.

Exit: One or two pupils per year reintegrate back into mainstream schooling throughout school – notably one boy after only a year in the autism base! Between one and three in each year six class return to their local mainstream secondary school. After discussion with educational psychologist and parents, many move on to the Valley School in Stevenage, the secondary Moderate Learning Difficulty School.

Money Matters: State funded, with charges for ingredients in subjects such as cooking and school trips. Fundraising for enhancement of curriculum via Friends of Woolgrove. County funding for speech and language and occupational therapy, delegated school funding for art and music therapy.

Remarks: In the past two years alone Woolgrove has notched up an Active Gold Sports Award, a Healthy Schools Award, an Arts Council Gold Award, a National Mentoring Ward and an Inclusion Quality Mark. Runs an autism conference every two year which attracts parents, teachers and health service professionals countywide. A fabulous school, inspiring from the moment you pass the fish tank at the front door. Inclusive in ethos and reality and keen to spread good practice throughout Hertfordshire and beyond.

WYCLIFFE COLLEGE

Bath Road, Stonehouse, Gloucestershire, GL10 2JQ

Tel: 01453 822 432

Fax: 01453 827 634

Email: senior@wycliffe.co.uk

Website: www.wycliffe.co.uk

• Pupils: 430, two-thirds boys, one-third girls; two-thirds boarding • Ages: 13-19 • Religion: Inter-denominational • Fees: Senior school: day: £4,065-£4,465; boarding: £6,515-£7,025 (£7,925 including ESOL); prep school: day: from £1,535 in the nursery to £3,140 (years 6,7 and 8); boarding £3,620 -£4,545 • School status: Independent • Opendays: Early October and mid February • School gender: Mixed • Day/boarding: Takes boarders

SEN provision

Detail:
Centre of excellence for:
- Mild: DYSL; DYSP;
- Moderate: DYSL;
- Severe: DYSL;
- Others: EAL;

Experience of:
- Mild: ASP; ADD; ADHD;
- Moderate: DYSP;
- Others: TIC; Epi; Oth; Eat;

Summary: Wycliffe College is a CReSTeD acredited school (catgory DU), with a highly regarded learning support department, delivering specialist support to dyslexic and dyspraxic students on an individual or small group basis. The learning support department is located at the heart of the College's Advanced Learning Centre, with a suite of four rooms for individual and group tuition. The department is well resourced, with a wide range of teaching materials and textbooks, as well as networked ICT facilities and specialist software.

SEN at Wycliffe is very much a whole school issue. Our experience shows that students with dyslexia can and will achieve, if taught according to their learning preferences and strengths. The learning support department aims to enable students to develop their skills to a secure level in order to emerge as confident, independent learners with a high sense of self-worth.

To ensure this, we have set in place clear procedures to identify students with SpLDs – including dyslexia – at the earliest possible stage in their education, and to distribute detailed information and advice which informs all teaching of these pupils. Whilst some students need additional learning support within the department, others achieve with differentiation within the classroom. Close and continuous monitoring ensures that their needs are met.

Staff are very aware of the needs of dyslexic pupils and are responsive to SEN advice. Staff consult the SEN department very frequently, to ensure the students' needs are met. Good use is made of SEN information in the planning of the curriculum, which has been adapted specifically to meet the needs of SEN pupils, for example in science, English and modern languages. Departmental schemes of work all include a differentiation policy.

Although our main provision is for students with mild to moderate dyslexia and mild dyspraxia, we have supported children with mild Asperger's sydrome and one partially paralysed student. We have also provided for students with mild tic syndromes and epilepsy. Our SEN admission policy is to consider the needs of each child on an individual basis, and following this, determine whether the College can meet that child's needs, without prejudice to the needs of others.

For more details of Wycliffe's provision for dyslexic and dyspraxic pupils, please visit the CReSTeD website.

What we say about the school - the full Good Schools Guide review

Head: Since 2005, Mrs Margie Burnet Ward MA (Hons), replacing Dr Tony Collins, who left unexpectedly. Mrs Burnet Ward had been second master for three years.

Academic Matters: Standards going up judging by last few years' results. Broad intake (not massively selective) but exam success still steadily rising with 100 per cent passes at A level for first time ever in 2002 and again with 60 per cent A/B grades in 2003, 2004 and 2005. No slackers at GCSEs either. Not quite a clean sweep with recent A*-Cs ranging from a low of 85 per cent to a high of almost 92. Great emphasis placed on value-added results (school in top 10 per cent in its field). Overall GCSE grades nearly half a grade better than predicted – maths, English and art better still. Traditionally strong in sciences, impressive labs block. Outstanding DT facilities, computers on equal footing with work benches, lathes etc. Pupils produce everything from prize-winning cello to beds and chairs. ICT the lifeblood of education here. Around £600,000 spent on it in last three years – now 250 computers around school, 60 staff laptops, 30 whiteboards, whole campus networked, and more to come. The new advanced learning centre in main school building which houses the latest interactive whiteboard technology as well as provide home for maths, English, media studies, history and special needs opened in 2004, together with the state-of-the-art library which is a multi-media resource centre.

Eighty pupils currently get some form of remedial help – including one pupil with a statement of needs (and part funded by his local LEA). Two full-time and one part-time fully qualified teachers; mainly dyslexia, dyspraxia etc, not really into ADHD. Lessons vary from one-to-one, one-to-three (max and usually for help with organisational skills), and from once a week to once a fortnight or just whenever needed. 'Tearaway' success: £30 for 50 mins. As far as poss lessons held in free time, but occasionally pupils withdrawn from lessons (usually mod lang). Pupils automatically assessed on entry into pre-prep, ditto prep; school CReSTeD and much praised by them, equally by ISI. Senior SENCo will visit potential pupils who might give 'cause for concern' and have not done as well as expected in CE in their own prep schools.

Pupils profiled 'in terms of their preferred learning style.' Life skills programme for all pupils (like PSHE with knobs on) aims to develop skills like teamworking, problem-solving, creative IT, self and social awareness and 'learning how to learn.' 'There's more to education than leaving school with a set of exam certificates'. Immense interest from abroad (see Pupils and Parents). Two English language preparation courses specifically targeted at overseas students – foundation course for 14 to 16-year-olds and development year (DY) for new pre-sixth formers – both designed to get foreign pupils up to speed for English exam system. Mrs Burnet Ward explains, 'the whole point of the courses is that they are tailor-made to the needs of the individual pupils. Flexibility is very important. Those pupils will only sit GCSEs and A levels when they are ready for them, not because they're the right age.' Means some pupils stay on beyond 19. Saturday morning school for years 9, 10 and 11 only. The sixth form can have tutorials, extra lessons, use the library but must take part in games commitments in the afternoon. Masterclasses for gifted pupils.

Games, Options, The Arts: A force to be reckoned with in certain sports. Big in sculling, rowing and, more recently, basketball; very big in squash, both national and international status. Pupils currently use pool at nearby prep school. Playing fields slope gently down to A419 (road to Stroud), include all-weather cricket crease. Floodlit astroturf hockey pitch and battery of well-used squash courts. Rugby making a comeback, cricket undeniably good (seven county players), and girls' hockey another success story. Plenty of extra activities on offer, with the emphasis on active. As well as the usual D of E and CCF, there's strong scouting tradition here. Focus very much on such 'character building' experiences such as caving, climbing and canoeing. Good debaters too. Freedom of thought and speech encouraged. Drama and theatre arts popular exam choices as well as club. Wycliffe Youth Theatre has featured twice at Edinburgh Fringe. Vibrant music department and 35 per cent of pupils learn instruments. Orchestras and choirs (one with 70 pupils) aplenty, very high standard in exams and performances. Director of music described as 'an absolute star'. House music competitions a highlight of school year – 'everything stops for a week and a half beforehand,' admits Mrs Burnet Ward. 'It's a wonderful opportunity for the kids to show their creative talents.' Same goes for inter-house drama contest. Pupils' artwork on show in the new atrium space in the new School House learning area and around the school.

Background and Atmosphere: Founded by vegetarian G W Sibly in 1882 who chose Stonehouse because of its rail connections. Soon grew in size, developed strong links with scouting and 'almost an obsession' with vegetarianism – a link not entirely severed (see Money Matters). Set in 60 acres, the original listed building (housing head, admin and the advanced learning centre) has now been joined by newer additions, varied in design and age but not looking totally out of place. Intended for boys only, its single sex-status remained until the 1970s when girls arrived in the sixth form and the following decade they were welcomed throughout the school. Like many independents, took a bad hit in the 1990s recession but has made full recovery with pupil numbers now full to capacity and with a waiting list in some year groups. School council, initiated by head, gives pupils big say in running of school life – from what they wear to what they eat. Pupils had say in design of new day house and sixth form uniform. 'It teaches them they have a voice and can make a difference but it also teaches them that sometimes change can take a long time.'

True spirit of 'can-do' which always seems to have been a heart of school. Back in the 1950s, staff and pupils built and furnished their own chapel (using wood from Isle of Wight pier!). Daily assemblies held here with alternative assemblies offered to non-Christians. Fabulous new dining hall doubles as conference centre. Food, provided by outside caterers, certainly looked and smelled good. Sunday brunch unmissable, say pupils. Even so, it's a subject that invariably crops up at school council meetings – known as PM's question time. New flexi boarding house for day pupils with their own building for prep, changing for games and overnight boarding when it suits them. Sixth form boarding house second to none – boys' section boasts own sauna and jacuzzi. All rooms en-suite. Conditions for other boarders less impressive but lots of focus on personal privacy as well as communal areas. School motto: Bold and Loyal.

Pastoral Care and Discipline: House system for day pupils and boarders, each one led by housemaster/mistress with support from matron, assistant house staff and all-important team of tutors, not to mention responsible sixth formers or prefects. It's a wide but well-woven net which shouldn't let too much slip through. School rules kept to a minimum. Nine straight-forward Don'ts, with one big Do – You must obey the law. No automatic expulsions (except drug-dealing for personal financial gain) – all punishments at head's discretion. 'Taking risks is part of growing up. Kids must be allowed to make mistakes.' Fines (and then suspension for second offence) for smoking. No drugs (pupils can be randomly tested). Well-publicised anti-bullying policy. Pupils not aware of any particular problems. 'We all get on well together,'... 'we look out for each other.'

Pupils and Parents: A well-heeled bunch without a doubt. But nice with it. No artificial airs and graces – simply friendly, polite and polished – and totally unaffected. Professional backgrounds. Very supportive parents who volunteer or get roped in to help in a variety of projects as and when their skills are required. High percentage of overseas pupils – around 35 per cent – from 27 countries, including former Soviet Union, mainland China, Hong Kong and Japan as well as Europe. Also fair number of Services and children of old boys. Famous OBs include TV doctor Mark Porter, horse trainer Mark Pitman, Dome designer Derek Tuke Hastings and Sir Michael Graydon, lately Chief of the Air Staff. Famous OGs? 'There will be.'

Entrance: Bulk of year 9 entry from own prep school but increasingly from other local and further afield prep schools. Pupils there sit scholarships and Wycliffe exam, not Common Entrance. Allows school to sort them into the right sets at senior school. External candidates at 13 will sit either CE, scholarship papers or tailor-made exam. Will accept 50 per cent pass, less in cases where other strengths show. Much hangs on interview and school reports. Entry to sixth form – at least five GCSEs grade C or above.

Exit: Over 93 per cent go on to higher education. One or two Oxbridge, others far and wide (many overseas pupils continue studies in home countries). Nottingham, Birmingham, Cardiff and Bournemouth perennially popular. Lots of business and computing type courses. Large number opt for gap year. Regularly lose about 10 post-GCSE to vocational courses and sixth form colleges.

Money Matters: Scholarships available at 13 and 16 for academic excellence, art, music, DT, ICT, drama and sport. Maximum value up to 50 per cent. Some bursaries funded by Wycliffe Endowment Trust and generous Old Wycliffians. Throwback to past is existence of vegetarian scholarships (quirky but not worth much). Candidates need to write good essay on merits of being vegetarian, apparently.

Remarks: Looks good, feels good and past and present pupils seem in no doubt whatsoever that it's done them good. May not be one of the country's academic high-flyers but really puts body and soul into preparing kids for the after-school life. Somehow manages to be a modern thinker without losing any of its traditional values. High international profile might not suit all but definitely worth a long, hard look.

Questionnaire responses: What the schools told us

This section covers schools that we have not visited, but where the school's own description of their provision points up particular facilities or strengths. 'What the school told us about their SEN provision' is based on the schools' answers to our detailed questionnaire. We haven't verified this information. Like the full write-ups, it comes in two sections, 'Summary' and 'Detail', and uses the same abbreviated terms.

We asked schools to indicate for each condition how experienced they were in dealing with it: whether they had had experience of children with this condition, whether they currently provided for such children in the school or whether they regarded themselves as a centre of excellence. To see the full range of answers, and to search our schools database using them, log on to www.goodschoolsguide.co.uk/?SEN. In this book we have listed the answers in abbreviated form:

Autistic spectrum disorders

ASP — Asperger's syndrome

AUT — autism

SPD — semantic pragmatic disorder

AUT(other) — other autistic: any autistic spectrum disorder that the school does not wish to put into one of the above categories

Behavioural difficulties

ADD — attention deficit disorder

ADHD — attention deficit hyperactivity disorders

CD — conduct disorders: behaviour that violates social rules and the rights of others

EBD — emotional and behavioural difficulties

OCD — obsessive compulsive disorders

ODD — oppositional defiant disorders

TIC — Tourette's syndrome and other tic disorders

Genetic and related disorders

DS — Down's syndrome

FRX — fragile X

GEN — other genetic: indicates a special provision or expertise not listed above. A description should be included in the summary of SEN provision

Learning difficulties

MLD — moderate learning difficulties

PMLD — profound and multiple learning difficulties

SLD — severe learning difficulties

Specific learning difficulties

DYSC — dyscalculia

DYSL — dyslexia

DYSP — dyspraxia

EAL — English as an additional language: facilities for non-native speakers with little or very poor English

SpLD — other specific learning difficulties: covers an increasing number of SENs not otherwise specified, such as dysgraphia, dysphasia etc

Sensory impairment

HI — hearing impairment

MSI — multi-sensory impairment: combination of visual and hearing difficulties possibly with additional disabilities

Sp&LD — speech and language difficulties

VI — visual impairment

Medical and related needs

CP — cerebral palsy

DEL — 'delicate' children: a catch-all for conditions which require the school to take particular care with a child, although there are no learning difficulties as such. Haemophilia is an example, as might be leukaemia, cystic fibrosis or allergies

Epi	epilepsy
Eat	eating disorders: anorexia etc
PD	physical difficulties: may be specific or cover a wide range of physical disabilities
Oth	other: indicates specialist provision that does not fall within any of the descriptions above. Should be outlined in the summary

Other types of facility or support

BSU	behaviour support unit
Gifted	special provision for exceptionally gifted children
GWA	good wheelchair access. Access could be good even if the school is in a Victorian building on three floors with no lift, as long as the school is prepared to make major adjustments (eg moving a science lab) to accommodate a wheelchair user
LSU	learning support unit
POS	provides outreach support
ROS	receives outreach support
SLC	specialist language centre

ABBEY HILL SCHOOL AND PERFORMING ARTS COLLEGE

Greasley Road, Bucknall, Stoke-on-Trent, Staffordshire, ST2 8LG

Tel: 01782 234 727
Fax: 01782 234 729
Email: abbeyhill@sgfl.org.uk
Website: www.abbeyhill.stoke.sch.uk

• Pupils: 210 Mixed; Day Pupils • Age: 2 to 18
• Religion: Non-denominational • School status: State

SEN provision

Detail:
Centre of excellence for:
Mild: AUT;
Moderate: ASP; AUT; MLD;
Severe: ASP; AUT;
Others: SPD; AUT(other)
Now provide for in school:
Mild: DS; HI; VI; CP;
Moderate: DS;
Others: Sp&LD; Epi
Experience of:
Mild: ADD; ADHD; EBD; DYSC; DYSL; DYSP;
Moderate: ADD; ADHD; EBD; DYSC; DYSL; DYSP;
Severe: ADD; ADHD; EBD; DYSC; DYSL;
Others: CD; OCD; ODD; TIC; SLD; EAL; DEL; PD

Summary: School caters for students with moderate global learning difficulties but specialising in autism/ASD. Students usually have associated needs such as speech and language needs, minor sensory or physical needs, emotional and or behavioural needs. In addition the assessment nursery and reception classes can cater for children with a wider range of needs (these children may move to an appropriate school between the ages of 5 and 7).

ABBEY HILL SCHOOL TECHNOLOGY COLLEGE

Ketton Road, Hardwick Estate, Stockton-on-Tees, TS19 8BU

Tel: 01642 677 113
Fax: 01642 679 198
Email: abbeyhill@stockton.gov.uk
Website: www.abbeyhill.stockton.sch.uk

• Pupils: 233 Mixed; Day Pupils • Age: 11 to 19
• Religion: Non-denominational • School status: State

SEN provision

Detail:
Centre of excellence for:
Mild: ASP; AUT; ADD; ADHD; EBD; DS; DYSL; DYSP;
Moderate: ASP; AUT; ADD; ADHD; EBD; DS; MLD; DYSL; DYSP;
Severe: ASP; AUT; DS; DYSL; DYSP;
Others: AUT(other); CD; FRX; GEN; PMLD; SLD; MSI; Sp&LD; Epi
Now provide for in school:
Mild: DYSC; HI; VI;
Moderate: DYSC; HI; VI;
Severe: ADD; ADHD; EBD; DYSC;
Others: SPD; ODD; EAL

Summary: Abbey Hill provides for students aged 11 to 19 who have a broad range of learning difficulties. It currently operates on two sites although a purpose built facility for post-16 students will open in January 2006. The school population contains young people with profound and multiple handicap, developmentally young, severe and moderate learning difficulties. Additionally some students come from local secondary schools during a period of anxiety in their lives.

The school operates five major curriculum models which are constructed around the National Curriculum and which also retain those features of a special school which are distinctive. Attainment levels on entry are determined by Key Stage 2 SATs, NC levels and PIVATS.

We are recognised as a centre of excellence in our provision for students with autistic spectrum disorder. In November 2004 we were awarded the much coveted National Autistic Society accreditation to add to our existing Specialist School and Leading Edge School status.

In summary, we believe that we are able to provide an education which meets the needs of all of our students in a modern, well designed setting. Our motto 'Excellence is our Standard' has been endorsed by our Ofsted inspection report of October 2005 which described Abbey Hill as 'a good school with many outstanding features'.

The Abbey School

Menin Way, Farnham, Surrey, GU9 8DY

Tel: 01252 725 059
Fax: 01252 737 300
Email: info@abbey.surrey.sch.uk
Website: www.abbey.surrey.sch.uk

• Pupils: 85 Mixed; Day Pupils • Age: 8 to 16 • Religion: Non-denominational • School status: State

SEN provision

Detail:
Now provide for in school:
Mild: ASP; AUT; SpLD; HI; VI; CP;
Moderate: ASP; AUT;
Others: Epi
Experience of:
Mild: DS; DYSL;
Others: TIC

Summary: The school accepts pupils who meet the Surrey CC criteria for entry to an LD school. The school also caters for pupils on the autistic spectrum with learning difficulties; this group makes up 20 per cent of those on roll.

Abbot's Hill School

Bunkers Lane, Hemel Hempstead, Hertfordshire, HP3 8RP

Tel: 01442 240 333
Fax: 01442 269 981
Email: klewis@abbotshill.herts.sch.uk
Website: www.abbotshill.herts.sch.uk

• Pupils: 445 Girls; Day Pupils • Age: 2 to 17 • Religion: Not Applicable • School status: Independent

SEN provision

Detail:
Experience of:
Mild: ASP; ADD; ADHD; EBD; DYSC; DYSL; DYSP; HI; VI; CP;
Moderate: ASP; DYSL; DYSP; HI;
Severe: DYSL; HI;
Others: SPD; CD; OCD; Sp&LD; Epi; PD; Eat

Summary: Girls with mild specific learning difficulties and average and above intelligence are very successful at Abbot's Hill with its caring, sympathetic and nurturing environment. Small classes and skilled teachers ensure that girls thrive, as strengths are recognised and coping strategies are put into place.

Abingdon House School

4-6 Abingdon Road, London, W8 6AF

Tel: 0845 2300 426
Fax: 020 7361 0751
Email: ahs@abingdonhouseschool.co.uk
Website: www.abingdonhouseschool.co.uk

• Mixed; Day Pupils • Age: 9 • Religion: Not Applicable • School status: Independent

SEN provision

Detail:
Now provide for in school:
Mild: ASP; ADD; ADHD; EBD; DYSC; DYSL; DYSP; SpLD;
Moderate: ASP; ADD; ADHD; DYSC; DYSL; DYSP; SpLD;
Severe: DYSC; DYSL; DYSP; SpLD;
Others: Sp&LD
Experience of:
Mild: AUT;
Severe: ASP;
Others: SPD

Summary: Abingdon House School opened in January 2005 as a major new initiative in education providing a unique education for children in need of educational support.

Our class teachers are highly trained, have specialist qualifications and are effective. Our on-site multi-disciplinary team provides valuable speech and language therapy, occupational therapy and physiotherapy. Specialist literacy, maths and visual perceptual training along with music therapy are provided. We have a close association with Lyn Fry Associates for educational psychology support. Each child has a termly individual education plan with SMART targets. This is reviewed at the end of term.

Our environment is based on understanding your child's individual needs, nurturing your child's academic and social development and caring for your child's wellbeing.

Abingdon House understands the importance of discipline and boundaries. The school fosters a sense of pride and belonging that encourages your child to progress and achieve at school.

ACRES HILL PRIMARY SCHOOL

Mather Road, Sheffield, South Yorkshire, S9 4GQ

Tel: 01142 441 512
Fax: 01142 441 577
Email: enquiries@acreshill.sheffield.sch.uk
• Pupils: 240 Mixed; Day Pupils • Age: 3 to 11
• Religion: Non-denominational • School status: State

SEN provision

Detail:
Now provide for in school:
Mild: ASP; AUT; ADD; ADHD; EBD; DYSC; DYSL; DYSP; HI; VI;
Moderate: EBD; MLD; DYSL;
Severe: HI; VI;
Others: PMLD; SLD; EAL; MSI; Sp&LD; DEL; PD

Summary: Acres Hill is committed to inclusive education and this has been commented on by the inspectors in our recent successful Ofsted inspection. We have a lift between our two floors and are used to accommodating wheelchair pupils. We have staff trained in gross motor skills support and regularly run support groups for this need. Our reputation locally of good SEN support has meant that children have been deliberately transferred to our school. We have close working relations with Norfolk Special School inclusion support team. We hold termly review meetings where parents, class teachers and SENCo get together to look at progress, sort out provision for the following term and set targets.

AD ASTRA FIRST SCHOOL

Sherborn Crescent, Canford Heath, Poole, Dorset, BH17 8AP

Tel: 01202 602 113
Fax: 01202 693 330
Email: adastraschool@poole.gov.uk
• Pupils: 387 Mixed; Day Pupils • Age: 4 to 8
• Religion: Non-denominational • School status: State

SEN provision

Detail:
Now provide for in school:
Mild: ASP; ADD; ADHD; EBD; DS; DYSC; DYSL; DYSP; HI; CP;
Moderate: ASP; ADD; EBD; MLD; HI;
Others: EAL; Sp&LD
Experience of:
Mild: AUT;
Moderate: ADHD;
Others: Epi

Summary: At Ad Astra School we believe in creating a secure, accepting, collaborating and stimulating community. We seek to develop inclusive values. Our principles regarding inclusion guide our decisions about our school policies and our daily practices.

We strive to set suitable learning challenges for all our pupils and respond to pupils' diverse learning needs. We try to overcome potential barriers to learning.

We value all our pupils, acknowledge differences and disabilities and try to create a culture of respect and appreciation of everyone.

Akeley Wood School

Akeley Wood, Buckingham, Buckinghamshire, MK18 5AE

Tel: 01280 814 110
Fax: 01280 822 945
Email: enquiries@akeleywoodschool.co.uk
Website: www.akeleywoodschool.co.uk

• Pupils: 900 Mixed; Day Pupils • Age: 11 to 18 • Religion: Not Applicable • School status: Independent

SEN provision

Detail:
Now provide for in school:
Mild: ASP
Experience of:
Mild: AUT; ADD; ADHD; EBD; DYSC; DYSL; DYSP; VI;
Moderate: DYSL; DYSP;
Others: EAL; Epi; PD; Eat

Summary: The special educational needs provision is centred on a sound and caring environment in which every child is encouraged to achieve their very best. Early assessment ensures that the need for support can be quickly established. This takes the form of extra dyslexia tuition for younger children and Study Support through GCSE and A level years by highly qualified, dedicated specialist teachers.

Study Support

Study Support plays a central role in the standard of academic achievement in the school and can provide a secure base, where pupils can receive guidance and support to enable them to function to the best of their ability in the classroom and in public examinations.

Tutorial Programme

For children with more severe dyslexic-type difficulties and those requiring a greater level of support, we provide a specialist Tutorial Programme. These classes run parallel to and are an integral part of each year group, catering for a maximum of ten pupils. Whilst still following the general curriculum, the Tutorial Programme is able to offer specialist teaching in a structured, caring environment. A more multi-sensory approach to learning is provided in order to meet individual needs and to maximise pupils' potential.

Albert Bradbeer Infant and Nursery Community School

Turves Green, Northfield, Birmingham, West Midlands, B31 4RD

Tel: 0121 475 4291
Fax: 0121 477 8242
Email: enquiry@albertbi.bham.sch.uk

• Pupils: 180 Mixed; Day Pupils • Age: 2 to 7
• Religion: Non-denominational • School status: State

SEN provision

Detail:
Now provide for in school:
Mild: ASP; AUT; ADD; ADHD; EBD; DS; DYSL; DYSP; CP;
Moderate: AUT; MLD;
Others: SPD; TIC; EAL
Experience of:
Mild: HI;
Others: Sp&LD; Epi

Summary: We cater in the main for children with moderate learning difficulties but we have experience with teaching children on the autistic spectrum. We have close links to a special school where all the children are autistic. All our staff have attended training on autism. The children from this special school spend time with us (varying on staff and finance) thus being able to experience a mainstream setting. Parents/Carers are welcome to come into school at any time to discuss problems with the SENCo, who is non-class based. The SENCo meets with educational psychologists twice a term; referrals to other agencies are made when necessary. Copies of our SEN policy are available on request.

ALDERWASLEY HALL SCHOOL

Alderwasley, Belper, Derbyshire, DE56 2SR

Tel: 01629 822 586
Fax: 01629 826 661
Email: info@alderwasleyhall.com
Website: www.alderwasleyhall.com

• Pupils: 122 Mixed; Takes boarders • Age: 5 to 19
• School status: Independent

SEN provision

Detail:

Centre of excellence for:
Mild: ASP; AUT; DYSC; DYSL; DYSP;
Moderate: ASP; AUT; DYSC; DYSL; DYSP;
Severe: ASP; AUT; DYSC; DYSL; DYSP;
Others: SPD; AUT(other); OCD; TIC; Sp&LD
Now provide for in school:
Mild: ADD; ADHD; HI; VI; CP;
Moderate: ADD; ADHD;
Severe: ADD; ADHD;
Others: FRX; Epi; Eat
Experience of:
Mild: EBD;
Moderate: EBD; MLD; HI; VI; CP;
Severe: EBD;
Others: CD; ODD; MSI

Summary: The children and young people at Alderwasley Hall School have difficulties with speech, language and communication. A large percentage of students are on the Autistic Spectrum including Asperger's and a small number have associated behavioural difficulties. The school offers small classes, a high ratio of Speech and Language Therapists to students and has Occupational Therapy provision. The school offers 38 week placements to boarding and day students.

ALFRISTON SCHOOL

Penn Road, Knotty Green, Beaconsfield, Buckinghamshire, HP9 2TS

Tel: 01494 673 740
Fax: 01494 670 177
Email: office@alfriston.bucks.sch.uk

• Pupils: 120 Girls; Takes boarders • Age: 11 to 18
• Religion: Non-denominational • School status: State

SEN provision

Summary: Alfriston is a special school for girls aged between 11 and 18. The majority of pupils meet the admissions criterion of moderate learning difficultes. Most have additional emotional, social, physical or sensory impairments. There is a weekly residential provision.

ALICE STEVENS SCHOOL

Ashington Grove, Coventry, West Midlands, CV3 4DE

Tel: 024 7630 3776
Fax: 024 7630 6173
Email: admin@alicestevens.coventry.sch.uk
Website: www.alicestevens.coventry.sch.uk

• Pupils: 163 Mixed; Day Pupils • Age: 11 to 19
• Religion: Non-denominational • School status: State

SEN provision

Detail:

Now provide for in school:
Mild: ASP; AUT; ADD; ADHD; EBD; DS; DYSC; DYSL; DYSP; HI; VI;
Moderate: ASP; AUT; ADD; ADHD; EBD; DS; MLD; DYSC; DYSL; DYSP; HI; VI;
Severe: ASP; ADD; ADHD; EBD; DYSC; DYSL;
Others: CD; OCD; SLD; EAL; Sp&LD; DEL; Epi; PD; Eat
Experience of:
Mild: CP;
Moderate: CP;
Severe: DYSP; HI; VI; CP;
Others: SPD; ODD; TIC; FRX; GEN

Summary: School caters for students with moderate learning difficulties and associated complex needs, including ASD, ADHD, dyslexia, Speech and Language difficulties, and emotional/behavioural difficulties.

ALL SAINTS' CHURCH OF ENGLAND SCHOOL, WEYMOUTH

Sunnyside Road, Wyke Regis, Weymouth, Dorset, DT4 9BJ

Tel: 01305 783391
Fax: 01305 785 291
Email: office@allsaints.dorset.sch.uk
Website: www.allsaints.dorset.sch.uk
• Pupils: 933 Mixed; Day Pupils • Age: 11 to 16
• Religion: Church of England • School status: State

SEN provision

Detail:
Centre of excellence for:
Mild: DYSC; DYSL; DYSP; HI; VI;
Moderate: DYSL; DYSP;
Severe: DYSL
Now provide for in school:
Mild: ASP; ADD; ADHD; EBD; CP;
Moderate: ASP; ADD; ADHD; EBD; MLD; DYSC; HI; VI;
Severe: DYSP;
Others: OCD; TIC; DEL
Experience of:
Mild: AUT;
Moderate: AUT; CP;
Severe: ASP; ADD; EBD; DYSC;
Others: CD; ODD; FRX; PMLD; SLD; EAL; Epi; PD; Eat

Summary: The learning support department in the school is set up to provide support for pupils with a wide range of difficulties; from literacy, physical, ADHD, ASD spectum, through to emotional needs, etc. The department works with pupils from years 7 to 11. Support is provided by teaching assistants in many mainstream lessons, by small group withdrawal for basic literacy, numeracy or social skills and by one-to-one support as required. The department works closely with the teachers within the school.

The school has a dyslexia base. This is run as an integral part of the school and its pupils are fully inclusive. All pupils within the school follow the full National Curriculum.

ALPHINGTON COMBINED SCHOOL

Wheatsheaf Way, Alphington, Exeter, Devon, EX2 8RQ

Tel: 01392 254 291
Fax: 01392 421 296
Email: admin@alphington.devon.sch.uk
Website: www.alphington.devon.sch.uk
• Pupils: 394 Mixed; Day Pupils • Age: 5 to 12
• Religion: Non-denominational • School status: State

SEN provision

Detail:
Now provide for in school:
Mild: ASP; AUT; ADD; ADHD; EBD; DYSC; DYSL; DYSP; HI; VI;
Moderate: ASP; AUT; ADHD; DYSC; DYSL;
Severe: ASP; AUT; EBD;
Others: SPD; EAL; DEL; Epi; PD

Summary: Alphington Combined School is an inclusive school and we aim to provide a broad and balanced curriculum for all children whatever their educational and social needs. Our headteacher listens to teachers who express concerns about the levels of provision (human resources) that children with special educational needs need in school and, wherever possible, provides support from the school budget for these children. We believe in early intervention as a simple philosophy. To provide for and support children as early as possible seems to be the best and most sensible thing to do.

We have a number of children, particularly in the Foundation Stage, who have speech, language and communication difficulties. Whilst we do not have a unit for children requiring extra help, we work closely with Bull Meadow Speech and Language Therapists to plan and help deliver regular speech and language sessions.

As a school we have very good relationships with

external agencies such as the CIDs Team (Communication and Interaction Difficulties), the Speech and Language Therapists, the Visual Impairment sevice, the Educational Psychologist service, the Pre-School advisory service, Honeylands, the English as an Additional Language service, the Behavioural Team, Social Services and the School Nurse.

Our experience is wide in the special needs area, and we are very aware of the more complex special needs of children coming into our mainstream school at this time.

We aim for entitlement in education for all.

ANNANHILL PRIMARY SCHOOL

Grange Terrace, Kilmarnock, East Ayrshire, KA1 2JR

Tel: 01563 532 962

Fax: 01563 574 863

Email: ian.roxburgh@east-ayrshire.gov.uk

• Pupils: 421 Mixed; Day Pupils • Age: 5 to 11

• Religion: Non-denominational • School status: State

SEN provision

Detail:

Experience of:

- Mild: ASP; ADD; ADHD; EBD; DYSL; DYSP; VI; CP;
- Moderate: MLD; VI; CP;
- Others: EAL; Sp&LD; Epi; PD

Summary: We are a mainstream school with no particular specialisms. However we are able, with the support of the LA and other agencies, to cater for a range of SEN needs.

ARNHEM WHARF PRIMARY SCHOOL

1 Arnhem Place, Westferry Road, London, E14 3RP

Tel: 020 7515 4310

Fax: 020 7538 4344

Email: admin@arnhemwharf.towerhamlets.sch.uk

• Pupils: 402 Mixed; Day Pupils • Age: 3 to 11

• Religion: Non-denominational • School status: State

SEN provision

Detail:

Centre of excellence for:

- Mild: CP;
- Moderate: CP;
- Others: EAL; PD

Now provide for in school:

- Mild: ASP; ADD; ADHD; EBD; DYSC; DYSL; HI;
- Moderate: EBD; DS; MLD; DYSL;
- Others: SPD; PMLD; DEL

Summary: Arnhem Wharf is an inclusive school that can provide for children with a variety of special needs both physical and learning. The building has a lift, ramps, disabled toilets and a changing/shower room. We are committed to inclusive education and believe that every child has the right to reach their full potential. We have a committed support staff who carry out programmes under the guidance of speech therapists and physiotherapists.

Children who need extra support academically have the opportunity to work individually and in small groups on intervention programmes. We have a reading recovery teacher who works with individual children. We have strong links with Education Business Partnership and have reading and maths partners who come and work in the dinnertimes with children giving them extra support and encouragement.

Arrow Vale Community High School - A Specialist Sports College

Green Sward Lane, Matchborough West, Redditch, Worcestershire, B98 0EN

Tel: 01527 526 800
Fax: 01527 514 255
Email: office@arrowvale.worcs.sch.uk
Website: www.arrowvalehigh.worcs.sch.uk

• Pupils: 964 Mixed; Day Pupils • Age: 13 to 18
• Religion: Non-denominational • School status: State

SEN provision

Detail:
Now provide for in school:
Mild: ASP; AUT; ADD; ADHD; EBD; DYSC; DYSL; DYSP; SpLD; HI; VI; CP;
Moderate: ADD; ADHD; MLD; DYSC; DYSL; DYSP; HI; VI; CP;
Severe: CP;
Others: OCD; ODD; TIC; Sp&LD; PD; Eat

Summary: The school aims to support all pupils to achieve their full potential. It has a dynamic team of teaching assistants who work in the class and on a one-to-one basis where needed. Pupils with physical disabilites are fully intergrated into the life of the school and we have invested in a mini bus with wheelchair lift to further aid this. We also have hoists available to toilet pupils who are unable to weight bear. We have rooms that are specifically dedicated to supporting pupils who experience learning and behavioural difficulties and which also give us the opportunity to develop very flexible curricula for pupils who experience difficulties with any aspect of their school life.

Artigarvan Primary School

31 Berryhill Road, Artigarvan, Strabane, Co Tyrone, BT82 0HN

Tel: 02871 883 684
Fax: 02871 884 086
Email: info@artigarvanps.strabane.ni.sch.uk

• Pupils: 164 Mixed; Day Pupils • Age: 4 to 11
• School status: State

SEN provision

Detail:
Now provide for in school:
Mild: ASP; AUT; ADD; EBD; DYSC; DYSL; DYSP; VI; CP;
Moderate: ASP; AUT; MLD; DYSC; DYSL; DYSP; VI; CP;
Severe: CP
Experience of:
Mild: ADHD;
Moderate: ADD; EBD;
Severe: DYSC; DYSL; DYSP;
Others: CD; TIC; DEL; Epi

Summary: Artigarvan Primary School supports SEN pupils according to the Northern Ireland Code of Practice and within a carefully differentiated learning and teaching environment. Our learning support teacher works in each of the classrooms and also has the facility to withdraw individual pupils or small groups for short sessions of intensive support. We also have a number of SEN classroom assistants. The school is adapted to suit pupils with physical difficulties. To this end we strive to promote inclusion and accessibility with regard to the physical dimensions, the curricular dimensions and the social dimensions of school, all within a caring environment.

Aston Clinton School

Twitchell Lane, Aston Clinton, Aylesbury, Buckinghamshire, HP22 5JJ

Tel: 01296 630 276
Fax: 01296 632 413
Email: office@astonclinton.bucks.sch.uk
Website: www.astonclinton.bucks.sch.uk

• Pupils: 265 Mixed; Day Pupils • Age: 4 to 11
• Religion: Non-denominational • School status: State

SEN provision

Detail:
Centre of excellence for:
- Mild: SpLD;
- Moderate: SpLD;
- Others: SPD; Sp&LD

Experience of:
- Mild: CP;
- Others: PD

Summary: Ten place integrated department for children with a Statement of Special Educational Need which has 'language impairment' as the main need. The children need to be able to work in a mainstream class, and receive additional support from the Teacher and Speech and Language Therapist as well as classroom assistants.

Avigdor Hirsch Torah Temimah Primary School

Parkside, Dollis Hill, London, NW2 6RT

Tel: 02084 504 377
Fax: 02088 306 202
Email: admin@torahtemimah.brent.sch.uk

• Pupils: 188 Boys; Day Pupils • Age: 3 to 11
• Religion: Jewish • School status: State

SEN provision

Detail:
Now provide for in school:
- Mild: ASP; AUT; ADD; ADHD; EBD; DYSL; DYSP;
- Moderate: AUT; ADD; EBD; MLD; DYSL;
- Severe: EBD;
- Others: EAL; Epi

Experience of:
- Mild: DYSC; HI; VI;
- Moderate: ASP; ADHD; DYSC; DYSP; HI;
- Severe: ADD;
- Others: Sp&LD

Summary: Avigdor Hirsch Torah Temimah Primary School recognises every child's right to a broad and balanced curriculum. Each child is a valued member of our school community and we aim to enable all children to reach their full potential regardless of their ability or disability and to provide them with a caring and supportive environment. All children should be given the opportunity to become confident in themselves and be able to enjoy successfully participating in class and school activities. We aim to integrate children with special needs into mainstream classes and to identify and provide for the natural differing abilities and needs of each child.

Children with special educational needs may require the delivery of the curriculum to be differentiated according to their individual need.
We aim to support children who have:
- A significantly greater difficulty in learning than children of the same age
- A disability which hinders the child from making use of the educational facilities generally provided in the school that can be catered for within the means of our school
- A behaviour problem that is a affecting the learning process of the child, or hindering the progress of other children
- Emotional problems

In addition we will also support children who have a strength in any subject that requires a differentiated curriculum in order to stretch the child, thus enabling them to reach their full potential.

Avishayes Community Primary School

Avishayes Road, Fairway Road, Chard, Somerset, TA20 1NS

Tel: 01460 63 050
Fax: 01460 66 532
Email: office@avishayes.somerset.sch.uk
Website: www.eclipse.co.uk/avishayes
• Pupils: 300 Mixed; Day Pupils • Age: 3 to 11
• Religion: Non-denominational • School status: State

SEN provision

Detail:
Now provide for in school:
Mild: ASP; AUT; ADD; ADHD; EBD; DS; DYSC; DYSL; DYSP; HI; VI; CP;
Moderate: ADD; ADHD; EBD; MLD; DYSL; DYSP;
Others: SPD; CD; Sp&LD; Epi; PD

Summary: We are a school with considerable experience of providing for children with a wide range of special educational needs. Until four years ago, there was a unit attached to the school to which children with complex special needs in the immediate area could go, instead of having to travel more than 10 miles to a Special School in one of the bigger towns. As a result of this enhanced provision – which has now ceased as the LEA has devolved funds so that children can be included in schools even more local to themselves – we still retain many of the experienced teaching and non-teaching staff in the school. Amongst our many resources, we have excellent disabled facilities, such as lifts, adjustable beds (one with a shower) and tables, as well as fully trained staff in moving and handling. All our teaching assistants are trained to at least NVQ2 in supporting pupils within the classroom and all staff keep their expertise up-to-date by attending courses and INSET training. We have regular input and advice from a Speech and Language Therapist who helps us devise programmes for our many children with communication difficulties and from the Physiotherapist and Occupational Therapist together with the input provided by the LEA Support Services.

Babington House School

Grange Drive, Elstead Lane, Chislehurst, Kent, BR7 5ES

Tel: 020 8467 5537
Fax: 020 8295 1175
Email: enquiries@babingtonhouse.com
Website: www.babingtonhouse.com
• Pupils: 234 Girls; Day Pupils • Age: 3 to 16
• School status: Independent

SEN provision

Detail:
Now provide for in school:
Mild: DYSL; DYSP; HI;
Moderate: DYSL; DYSP; HI
Experience of:
Mild: DYSC;
Others: EAL; Sp&LD

Summary: Babington House School offers support to pupils who, although are able to work in a mainstream, mixed-ability environment, require extra help with a variety of issues. The special educational needs accepted by the school are decided on a case by case basis. Extra provision is paid for by parents or, in the case of a statemented pupil, the authority, and the amount of help is at the discretion of the school.

Bablake School

Coundon Road, Bablake, Coventry, West Midlands, CV1 4AU

Tel: 02476 271 200
Fax: 02476 271 292
Email: hmsec@bablake.rmplc.co.uk
Website: atschool.eduweb.co.uk/bablake/
• Pupils: 898 Mixed; Day Pupils • Age: 11 to 19
• School status: Independent

SEN provision

Detail:
Experience of:
Mild: DYSL;
Moderate: DYSL

Summary: The Learning Support department has its own room and contains space for individual and small group work to take place. It is well resourced with books, teaching aids and a number of computers. Three staff are responsible for monitoring the progress of pupils who experience mild or moderate dyslexia: they are Mrs C Friebe (Head of Department), Mrs K Basker and Mr D Parkins. All have some training and good experience of working with pupils with dyslexia. All pupils are screened on entry to Bablake to identify who might have dyslexia and the school works closely with parents and the Dyslexia Institute to give the best possible support and guidance for each individual.

BALNACRAIG SCHOOL

Fairmount Terrace, Perth, PH2 7AR

Tel: 01738 636 456
Fax: 01738 441 863
Email: admin.balnacraigschool@btinternet.com
• Pupils: 21 Mixed; Takes boarders • Age: 12 to 16
• Religion: Non-denominational • School status: Independent

SEN provision

Summary: An independent special school for pupils with emotional, social or behavioural difficulties (ESBD). There may be associated problems including specific learning difficulties, autistic spectrum disorders, school phobia or school refusers and those who have been excluded from education elsewhere. Some pupils have records of need. Can provide residential care for up to 52 weeks a year if required.

BANCHORY ACADEMY AND COMMUNITY EDUCATION CENTRE

Schoolhill, Banchory, Kincardineshire, AB31 5TQ

Tel: 01330 825 966
Fax: 01330 825 323
Email: banchory.aca@aberdeenshire.gov.uk
Website: www.banchoryacademy.co.uk
• Pupils: 957 Mixed; Day Pupils • Age: 11 to 18
• Religion: Non-denominational • School status: State

SEN provision

Detail:
Now provide for in school:
Mild: ADD; ADHD; EBD; DYSC; DYSL; DYSP; HI; VI;
Moderate: ADD; ADHD; EBD; MLD; DYSC; DYSL; DYSP; HI; VI;
Severe: DYSC; DYSL; DYSP;
Others: EAL; DEL; Epi; PD; Eat
Experience of:
Mild: ASP; AUT;
Moderate: ASP; AUT;
Severe: ASP;
Others: Sp&LD

Summary: There is no separate SEN base in Banchory Academy. Support for pupils with Additional Support Needs is provided through the Support for Learners team. There are a number of staff in the SfL team who have extensive experience in supporting children's learning. Provision is intended to meet the needs of all pupils, regardless of their academic ability.

Banham Marshalls College

Mill Road, Banham, Norwich, Norfolk, NR16 2HU

Tel: 01953 888 656
Fax: 01953 887 021
• Pupils: 32 Mixed; Takes boarders • Age: 7 to 16
• School status: Independent

SEN provision

Detail:
Now provide for in school:
Mild: AUT;
Moderate: AUT;
Severe: AUT;
Others: SPD; AUT(other)

Summary: Eagle House School (Norfolk) is a member of Eagle House Group which also operates a day school for children (4-19) with Austic Spectrum Disorders (ASDs) in south London. Eagle House School (Norfolk) offers residential provision on a 38-week and 52-week basis for young people (4-19) who have ASDs and moderate/severe learning difficulties. Respite is also offered. Staff are qualified and experienced in the education and care of young people with ASDs.

The school has its own clinic which includes highly qualified professionals who are experienced in working with young people with ASDs, including speech and language therapy, educational and clinical psychology, and occupational therapy.

Banister Infant School

Banister Gardens, Westrow Road, Southampton, Hampshire, SO15 2LX

Tel: 02380 393 313
Fax: 02380 393 001
Email: info@banister.southampton.sch.uk
Website: www.banister.southampton.sch.uk
• Pupils: 116 Mixed; Day Pupils • Age: 4 to 7
• Religion: Non-denominational • School status: State

SEN provision

Detail:
Now provide for in school:
Mild: CP;
Moderate: MLD;
Others: EAL; Sp&LD
Experience of:
Mild: ASP; AUT; ADD; EBD; DYSL; DYSP; HI;
Moderate: EBD; HI

Summary: Banister values the abilities and achievement of all its pupils. We believe that all children have a right to a broad and balanced curriculum which addresses their individual needs and endeavours to provide the best learning conditions for each pupil. Banister has a whole school policy for special educational needs which describes the values we hold and the provision we make so that no child should be disadvantaged. Parental involvement is sought and encouraged at all times. The class teacher and SENCo will work with parents and keep them informed about provision and progress. If necessary, advice may also be sought from other agencies such as educational psychologists and speech and language therapists.

Barking Abbey Comprehensive School and Sports College

Sandringham Road, Barking, Essex, IG11 9AG

Tel: 020 8270 4100
Fax: 020 8270 4090
Email: office@babbey.bardaglea.org.uk
Website: www.babbey.bardaglea.org.uk
• Pupils: 1660 Mixed; Day Pupils • Age: 11 to 18
• Religion: Non-denominational • School status: State

SEN provision

Detail:
Now provide for in school:
Mild: DYSC; DYSL; DYSP; HI; VI;
Moderate: MLD;
Others: EAL; Sp&LD; Epi; PD; Eat

Experience of:
Mild: ASP; AUT; ADD; ADHD; EBD;
Others: OCD; ODD; TIC

Summary: Barking Abbey School maintains a register of any pupil presenting with special educational needs. This allows the school to monitor the support and progress of the identified pupils.

Small classes have been set up, at Key Stage 3, in English, Maths, History, RE and Geography to allow for the curriculum to be made accessible and literacy skills to be developed. In-class support is provided, by a team of nine support assistants, in many science and technology areas so that pupils can make the best progress possible.

Socially SEN students are well supported by the mentoring team and the learning support units. If pupils require anger management or lack self-esteem they can join a social skills class that runs once a week throughout the year.

Reviews are held at least twice a year for those pupils named on the register. These would involve pupils, parents, mentors and any outside agency that might be involved. At the reviews the targets from the pupil's individual education plan will be looked at and new targets set.

BATTLEDOWN CHILDREN'S CENTRE

Harp Hill, Battledown, Cheltenham, Gloucestershire, GL52 6PZ

Tel: 01242 525 472
Fax: 01242 257 557
Email: admin@battledown.gloucs.sch.uk
Website: www.battledown.gloucs.sch.uk
• Mixed; Day Pupils • Age: 2 to 7
• Religion: Non-denominational • School status: State

SEN provision

Detail:
Now provide for in school:
Mild: AUT; ADD; ADHD; EBD; DS; CP;
Moderate: AUT; ADD; ADHD; EBD; DS; MLD; CP;
Severe: AUT; ADD; ADHD; EBD; DS;
Others: SPD; AUT(other); FRX; GEN; PMLD; SLD; Sp&LD; Epi; PD
Experience of:
Mild: ASP; HI; VI;
Moderate: ASP; HI; VI;
Severe: ASP; HI; VI; CP;
Others: CD; OCD; DEL

Summary: Battledown Children's Centre is a specialist Early Years Centre providing multidisciplinary assessment.

THE BEACON INFANT & NURSERY SCHOOL, BODMIN

38 Robartes Road, Bodmin, Cornwall, PL31 1JQ

Tel: 01208 72773
Fax: 01208 72773
Email: secretary@the-beacon-bod.cornwall.sch.uk
Website: www.the-beacon-bod.cornwall.sch.uk
• Mixed; Day Pupils • Age: 3 to 8
• Religion: Non-denominational • School status: State

SEN provision

Detail:
Now provide for in school:
Mild: ASP; AUT; ADD; ADHD; EBD; CP;
Moderate: ASP; AUT; ADD; ADHD; EBD; MLD; VI; CP;
Severe: ASP; AUT; ADD;
Others: SPD; Sp&LD; Epi
Experience of:
Mild: DS; DYSP; HI; VI;
Moderate: DS; DYSP; HI;
Severe: ADHD; EBD; VI;
Others: CD; FRX; SLD

Summary: We have a Child Development Centre (CDC) attached to our school. It caters for preschoolchildren, from age 3 to 5.

Children are referred to the Centre by professionals. We have multi-disciplinary assessments of the child's special edcuational needs. A Speech Therapist works in the Centre. Because of the support of the CDC our school has excellent provison for children with a range of difficulties. We provide for pupils with ASD, ADHD, severe developmental delay, CP, and rare medical disorders and syndromes such as Albinism, Turner's Syndrome,

Rubinstein Taybi Syndrome, rare epileptic conditions, and metabolic disorders such as Carntinine Defficiency, sensory impairment, hearing impaired and blind (Leber's Amaurosis).

BEAL HIGH SCHOOL

Woodford Bridge Road, Ilford, Essex, IG4 5LP

Tel: 020 8551 9378
Fax: 020 8551 9249
Email: admin.beal@redbridge.gov.uk
• Pupils: 1574 Mixed; Day Pupils • Age: 11 to 18
• Religion: Non-denominational • School status: State

SEN provision

Detail:
Centre of excellence for:
Mild: ADD; ADHD; EBD;
Moderate: ADD; ADHD; EBD; MLD;
Severe: ADHD; EBD;
Others: SLD; Epi
Now provide for in school:
Mild: ASP; AUT; DYSL; DYSP;
Moderate: ASP; AUT; DYSL; DYSP;
Severe: ASP; DS;
Others: Sp&LD
Experience of:
Mild: DYSC; HI; VI;
Others: SPD

Summary: The school's SEN provision caters for pupils with a variety of needs. A range of strategies are deployed in order to meet the individual needs of these pupils. By supporting them in their inclusion in all aspects of school life, the school helps them to become independent learners, working towards their full potential.

This provision includes support in the classroom, a National Literacy programme in year 7, social skills groups, a Linkworker system, use of support agencies, staff INSET, a SUBCO system, a SEN list, pupil IEPs, Key Stage 3 Language Support lessons, Key Stage 4 Supported Studies and Key Stage 4 Homework club.

BEATRICE TATE SCHOOL

St Jude's Road, London, E2 9RW

Tel: 020 7739 6249
Fax: 020 7613 1507
Email: head@beatricetate.towerhamlets.sch.uk
• Pupils: 65 Mixed; Day Pupils • Age: 11 to 19
• Religion: Non-denominational • School status: State

SEN provision

Detail:
Now provide for in school:
Mild: DS; HI; VI; CP;
Moderate: DS; HI; VI; CP;
Severe: DS; HI; VI; CP;
Others: PMLD; SLD; MSI; Epi; PD; Eat
Experience of:
Mild: AUT;
Moderate: AUT;
Severe: AUT

Summary: Beatrice Tate Special School is a school for secondary age pupils with severe learning difficulties, sensory impairment and physical disability.

THE BEAUCHAMP COLLEGE

Ridge Way, Oadby, Leicester, Leicestershire, LE2 5TP

Tel: 01162 729 100
Fax: 01162 715 454
Email: info@beauchamp.org.uk
Website: www.beauchamp.leics.sch.uk
• Pupils: 1957 Mixed; Day Pupils • Age: 14 to 18
• Religion: Non-denominational • School status: State

SEN provision

Detail:
Now provide for in school:
Mild: ADD; ADHD; EBD; DYSC; DYSL; DYSP; HI; VI; CP;
Moderate: ADHD; EBD; MLD; DYSC; DYSL; DYSP; HI; VI; CP;

Severe: DYSL; HI;
Others: EAL; MSI; Sp&LD; Epi; PD; Eat
Experience of:
Mild: ASP;
Severe: VI

Summary: The Beauchamp College prides itself on its inclusive nature. All students, regardless of their SEN, are fully integrated into all aspects of College. The support provided is sensitive to the age and ability of the student and allows full access to the curriculum and extra-curricular activities. Through this support we encourage the students to take more responsibility for their learning and to develop into young adults who are ready for the world of work or further education.

All students are given literacy tests on entering the College and those requiring extra support are identified and monitored closely. Parents are encouraged to take an active role in support of their child through regular communication with the College.

Beaumont Hill School

Glebe Road, Darlington, County Durham, DL1 3EB

Tel: 01325 254 000
Fax: 01325 254 222
Email: admin@beaumonthill.darlington.sch.uk
Website: www.beaumonthill.darlington.sch.uk
• Pupils: 225 Mixed; Day Pupils • Age: 2 to 19
• Religion: Non-denominational • School status: State

SEN provision

Detail:
Centre of excellence for:
Mild: ADHD; EBD; DS;
Moderate: AUT; ADHD; EBD; DS; MLD; SpLD;
Severe: AUT; ADD; ADHD; EBD; DS; SpLD;
Others: SPD; PMLD; SLD; MSI; Epi
Now provide for in school:
Mild: ASP; AUT; CP;
Moderate: ASP; ADD; CP;
Severe: ASP; CP;
Others: CD; ODD; DEL
Experience of:
Mild: HI; VI;
Moderate: HI; VI;
Severe: VI;
Others: TIC; FRX; EAL; PD; Eat

Summary: Beaumont Hill School and Technology College is a large generic special school catering for the full age range and the full range of need. There are specific areas of the school designed to meet the very special needs of our children such as a centre for pupils with Social Emotional and Behavioural Difficulties, autistic provision and provision for pupils with Profound and Multiple Learning Difficulties. Staff are trained to a high standard and the school provides an Outreach service for the LEA. All students access a relevant, age appropriate curriculum that equips them for future placements.

Bebington High Sports College

Higher Bebington Road, Bebington, Wirral, Merseyside, CH63 2PS

Tel: 01516 454 154
Fax: 01516 438 065
Email: schooloffice@bebingtonhigh.wirral.sch.uk
Website: www.bebingtonhigh-wirral.ik.org
• Pupils: 1080 Mixed; Day Pupils • Age: 11 to 18
• Religion: Non-denominational • School status: State

SEN provision

Detail:
Now provide for in school:
Mild: ASP; ADD; ADHD; EBD; DYSC; DYSL; DYSP; HI; VI; CP;
Moderate: ASP; ADD; ADHD; EBD; MLD; DYSL; DYSP; HI; VI; CP;
Severe: ADD; ADHD; EBD; DYSL; DYSP;
Others: EAL; Sp&LD
Experience of:
Mild: AUT;
Moderate: AUT; DYSC;
Severe: ASP; AUT;
Others: CD; OCD; ODD; TIC; FRX; SLD; DEL; Epi; Eat

Summary: We believe that our first responsibility is to meet the needs of all our students and their parents by providing an outstanding professional service. We provide a quality education for all students through the effective and stimulating delivery of the curriculum. We expect consistently high standards from staff and students in all areas of the school – academic, personal appearance, relationships and discipline matters.

Opportunities are provided for every individual to develop his/her maximum potential.

- We celebrate success and achievement at every opportunity.
- We strive to provide a caring and challenging environment.
- We are committed to forging an ever-stronger partnership with parents and the community.
- We have adopted a policy of continuous improvement in every aspect of the school's work and life.

Beech Hill Primary School

Linhope Road, West Denton, Newcastle upon Tyne, Tyne and Wear, NE5 2LW

Tel: 01912 678 113
Fax: 01912 641 240
Email: admin@beechhill.newcastle.sch.uk
Website: www.beechhill.newcastle.sch.uk

• Pupils: 274 Mixed; Day Pupils • Age: 3 to 11
• Religion: Non-denominational • School status: State

SEN provision

Detail:

Now provide for in school:
  Mild: DYSL; HI; CP;
  Moderate: ADD; MLD; DYSL; DYSP; VI; CP;
  Severe: EBD;
  Others: SPD; ODD; PMLD; SLD; EAL; MSI; Sp&LD; Epi; PD; Eat

Experience of:
  Mild: ASP; ADD; ADHD; DYSP;
  Moderate: ADHD; EBD

Summary: Semantic/pragmatic disorder – Language Gap programme to support abstract and concrete concepts. Speaking and Listening Programme of work from SENTASS. ADD and ADHA – classroom management policy, BIP room and human resources. Emotional-Behaviour policy (Special time in BIP room/reward system) and human resources. Moderate/severe Learning – Jolly Phonics, Progression in Phonics activities, Janie Tapster books, Animated Alphabet, ALS software programme, Breakthrough to literacy folders, B-square extra literacy and numeracy programme and extra human resource helping to support differentiated work.

Visual and hearing impaired support for SENTASS and 'B-square, Thinking Skills' programme.

Profound Multi learning – SENTASS support, Animated Alphabet, Star Spell and many other software programmes including Number and Word Shark. Individual Physical Programmes from Occupational Therapists and speech programmes from The Speech and Language Team in Newcastle.

Dyspraxia – 'Write from start' programme, Visual perception support and an exercise programme from SENTASS to support motor-co-ordination. Classroom environment support.Dyslexia – 'Phame' programme and additional human support. Beat Dyslexia books 1-4. Environment awareness support – classroom managment. Brain gym and access to water in every session.

Beech Tree School

Meadow Lane, Bamber Bridge, Preston, Lancashire, PR5 8LN

Tel: 01772 323 131
Fax: 01772 322 187
Email: beechtreeschool@easynet.co.uk
Website: www.scope.org.uk/education/schools/beechtree/

• Pupils: 14 Mixed; Takes boarders • Age: 7 to 19
• School status: Independent

SEN provision

Detail:

Now provide for in school:
  Mild: AUT; ADD; ADHD;
  Moderate: AUT; ADD; ADHD;
  Severe: AUT; ADD; ADHD; EBD;
  Others: AUT(other); PMLD; SLD

Summary: Beech Tree School provides 52-week care with on site education for children with severe and complex needs compounded by challenging behaviour.

Beechwood Lower School

Beechwood, Queen's Road, St. Peter Port, Guernsey, GY1 1PU

Tel: 01481 722123
Fax: 01481 715503
Email: Secretary@Beechwood-gsy.net

• Boys; Day Pupils • Age: 7 to 11
• Religion: Non-denominational • School status: Independent

SEN provision

Detail:
Experience of:
Mild: ASP; ADD; ADHD; EBD; DYSC; DYSL; DYSP; HI; VI;
Moderate: DYSC; DYSL; DYSP;
Severe: DYSL; DYSP;
Others: OCD; Sp&LD

Summary: Beechwood has a thriving dyslexia and learning support centre which operates throughout the school. Children are taught individually or in pairs on a withdrawal basis by fully qualified staff. The centre also plays a larger role within the wider school community.

Bell Lane Combined School

Bell Lane, Little Chalfont, Amersham, Buckinghamshire, HP6 6PF

Tel: 01494 764 521
Fax: 01494 764 903
Email: office@bell-lane.bucks.sch.uk

• Pupils: 129 Mixed; Day Pupils • Age: 3 to 11
• Religion: Non-denominational • School status: State

SEN provision

Detail:
Centre of excellence for:
Mild: DYSP;
Moderate: DYSP;
Others: Sp&LD
Now provide for in school:
Mild: ADD; ADHD; EBD; DS; DYSC; DYSL; CP;
Moderate: ADD; ADHD; EBD; DS; MLD; DYSC; DYSL; CP;
Others: SPD; CD; PMLD; Epi
Experience of:
Mild: ASP; AUT;
Moderate: ASP; AUT;
Others: FRX; GEN

Summary: Bell Lane School is a mainstream primary school that caters for children from 3 to 11 years of age. Approximately 25 per cent of the children hold a Statement of Special Educational Need and thus we have small classes and a high ratio of adults to children. We have a specialist department for children with Speech and Language Disorders and this is staffed by experienced professionals who are able to disseminate their wide range of knowledge and expertise throughout the school. The school employs their own Speech and Language Therapist and their own Occupational Therapist to ensure that children receive the regular programmes of therapy that will meet their needs. The school has won an award from the local authority for its success at including children with a wide range of needs. All children, regardless of their level of difficulty, are totally included in all their class activities and spend the bulk of their time in their mainstream classroom with their peers. They have full access to the Foundation or National Curriculum, as appropriate, and this will be differentiated as necessary to meet their individual needs. Good links with parents are high on the agenda of the school to do the best by the children, and the staff are welcoming and happy to meet prospective and existing parents by appointment. Bell Lane is a happy and welcoming school whose ethos is to make sure every child has high self esteem, feels valued, and is able to fulfil their potential both academically and socially.

Belmont House Special School

17 Racecourse Road, Londonderry, BT48 7RE

Tel: 02871 351 266
Fax: 02871 351 125
Email: info@belhs.londonderry.ni.sch.uk
Website: www.belmonthouse.ik.org/
• Pupils: 208 Mixed; Day Pupils • Age: 3 to 17
• Religion: Jewish • School status: State

SEN provision

Detail:
Centre of excellence for:
Mild: EBD;
Moderate: EBD; MLD;
Severe: EBD;
Others: CD; Sp&LD
Now provide for in school:
Mild: AUT; ADD; ADHD; DS; DYSC; DYSL; DYSP; VI; CP;
Moderate: AUT; ADD; ADHD; DS; DYSC; DYSL; DYSP; VI; CP;
Severe: ADD; ADHD; DYSC; DYSL; DYSP;
Others: SPD; OCD; ODD; FRX; DEL; Epi
Experience of:
Mild: HI;
Severe: AUT;
Others: SLD; Eat

Summary: Belmont House is set in its own grounds 100 metres from the main road on the outskirts of the city. Although surrounded by housing the school campus still preserves a rural atmosphere by being buffered from the outside world by large fields on three sides.

The Campus is made up of Learning Centres catering for a wide range of special needs including Moderate Learning Difficulties, Language Disorders and Emotional and Behaviour Difficulties.

Visit our website http://www.belmonthouse.ik.org to find out more details about each centre and the special needs provision on the campus.

We hope you find our site informative, useful and an insight into life on Belmont Campus. We are a school with traditional roots and a modern outlook. We aim to promote a positive, happy, secure environment where children of all abilities feel valued and stimulated.

Belstead School

Sprites Lane, Belstead, Ipswich, Suffolk, IP8 3ND

Tel: 01473 556 200
Fax: 01473 556 209
Email: headbelstead.kgk@e2bn.net
Website: www.belstead.suffolk.sch.uk
• Pupils: 75 Mixed; Day Pupils • Age: 11 to 19
• Religion: Non-denominational • School status: State

SEN provision

Detail:
Experience of:
Mild: ADD; ADHD; EBD; SpLD;
Moderate: ADD; ADHD; EBD; SpLD;
Severe: ADD; ADHD; SpLD;
Others: ODD

Summary: School caters for students with severe learning difficulties and in addition students may have speech and language needs, physical needs, medical, gross or fine motor or behavioural needs as a result of any or all the aforementioned.

Bennerley Fields School

Stratford Street, Cotmanhay, Ilkeston, Derbyshire, DE7 8QZ

Tel: 0115 932 6374
Fax: 0115 932 6374
Email: info@bennerleyfields.derbyshire.sch.uk
• Pupils: 75 Mixed; Day Pupils • Age: 2 to 16
• Religion: Non-denominational • School status: State

SEN provision

Detail:
Now provide for in school:
Mild: ASP; AUT; ADD; ADHD; EBD; SpLD; HI; VI;
Moderate: ASP; AUT; ADD; ADHD; EBD; MLD; SpLD; HI; VI;
Severe: ASP; AUT; ADD; ADHD; SpLD;
Others: AUT(other); SLD; MSI; Sp&LD

Summary: Bennerley Fields School provides day education for pupils between 2 and 16 years old. The school is divided into three departments: the diagnostic and assessment nursery, the junior and senior school. Pupils assessed in the nursery subsequently attend a variety of schools at the age of five years.

We cater for pupils with moderate and severe learning difficulties including Autism, speech and language difficulties, visual and/or hearing impairment and BESD. Assessment of a wide range of complex needs takes place in the nursery, particularly language and communication.

The school provides the full National Curriculum including the Foundation Stage and has recently received a School Achievement Award for standards achieved. The school has the Basic Skills Quality Mark award which acknowledges the good core curriculum. The Derbyshire Anti-Bullying Commitment award confirmed the school's good practice, which Ofsted praised. Senior pupils work towards externally accredited schemes, achieving very good results; the school is one of a few special schools nationally to be Careermark accredited. Pupils leave the school at the end of Key Stage 4 and go on to a range of further education or work related opportunities. The school prioritises the five key themes in Every Child Matters; furthering these also in initiatives such as Health Promoting Schools and the schools award scheme. The school received a very successful Ofsted in 2000. Bennerley Fields is an Investor in People.

The Bennett House School

332 Eaves Lane, 7 Park Street, Chorley, Lancashire, PR6 0DX

Tel: 01257 267 393

Fax: 01257 262 838

• Mixed; Day Pupils • Age: 2 to 7

• School status: Independent

SEN provision

Summary: We have an SEN co-ordinator on staff who liases with our LEA Area SENCo/speech therapist and educational psychologist. We provide small class groups enabling individual attention in a calm atmosphere with experienced class teachers who are able to foster close home-school links.

Beverley School

Beverley Road, Saltersgill, Middlesbrough, TS4 3LQ

Tel: 01642 277 444

Fax: 01642 277 453

Email: beverleyschool@middlesbrough.gov.uk

• Pupils: 80 Mixed; Day Pupils • Age: 3 to 19

• Religion: Non-denominational • School status: State

SEN provision

Detail:

Centre of excellence for:

Mild: ASP; AUT;

Moderate: ASP; AUT;

Severe: ASP; AUT;

Others: AUT(other)

Experience of:

Mild: ADD; ADHD;

Moderate: ADD; ADHD;

Severe: ADD; ADHD;

Others: PMLD

Summary: The children and young people at Beverley school require a very structured approach to learning and they benefit from a high staffing ratio (generally a teacher and two assistants to seven or eight pupils). Our approach is autism-specific, and designed to maintain a friendly, calm and purposeful atmosphere. Staff know pupils well, and respect their individual needs. The organisation of the school, our teaching styles and our excellent staff/pupil relationships, all minimise the stress on our pupils. This helps them to make the most of their communication and interaction skills, and to benefit fully from the educational opportunities on offer.

Historically, Beverley School was established as a School for the Deaf. Provision for children with autism was added in the 1980s and the balance of the population then steadily changed. The school has moved through a phased reorganisation, and provision for Deaf pupils has transferred to mainstream settings. Beverley is now uniquely placed as the only 100 per cent autism-specialist school and service in the Tees Valley area.

Throughout the reorganisation period, there have been many opportunities to build on the school's strengths. In partnership with Middlesbrough LEA, we are ensuring that Beverley is recognised as a regional centre of excellence for the education of children with autism. We have succeeded in recruiting and training an excellent staff team, a programme of extensive building refurbishment work has been completed, and many specialist facilities have been added.

Beverley School also provides training and advice to other schools with pupils on the autistic spectrum. This aspect of our work continues to grow, and we are building a network of contacts to support a range of genuinely inclusive options appropriate to the needs of individual pupils.

Bicester Community College

Queen's Avenue, Bicester, Oxfordshire, OX26 2NS

Tel: 01869 243 331
Fax: 01869 246 396
Email: headteacher.4030@bicester-cc.oxon.sch.uk
Website: www.bicester-cc.oxon.sch.uk
• Pupils: 1261 Mixed; Day Pupils • Age: 11 to 18
• Religion: Non-denominational • School status: State

SEN provision

Detail:

Now provide for in school:
- Mild: ASP; AUT; ADD; ADHD; EBD; DS; DYSC; DYSL; DYSP; HI; VI;
- Moderate: ASP; MLD; DYSL; DYSP;
- Others: EAL; Sp&LD

Experience of:
- Mild: CP;
- Moderate: EBD; HI;
- Others: CD; OCD; TIC; Epi; PD; Eat

Summary: The College's Achievement Centre provides support for a wide range of SEN.

Students with special educational needs are very well supported and make good progress in reaching their individual targets, and in improving reading and spelling. They achieve well in most subjects and many do well in examinations.

Teaching on the work-related programme is very good, both in basic skills lessons within school and in off-site vocational courses. Students are motivated by the practical work and learn very well because they have very good relationships with staff and good personal guidance. Teachers, vocational tutors and support staff know the students well and work very well as a team (Ofsted 2004).

Birtenshaw Hall (Children's Charitable Trust)

Darwen Road, Bromley Cross, Bolton, Lancashire, BL7 9AB

Tel: 01204 304 230
Fax: 01204 597 995
Email: enquiries@birtenshawhall.bolton.sch.uk
Website: www.birtenshawhall.bolton.sch.uk
• Pupils: 19 Mixed; Takes boarders • Age: 3 to 19
• School status: State

SEN provision

Summary: Birtenshaw Hall is a small, non-maintained day/residential school and Registered Children's Home for children and young people with severe and complex or profound and multiple learning difficulties in conjunction with either physical disablities, autistic spectrum disorder or severe medical conditions. The staff are greatly experienced in working with children and young people with degenerative and exceptional conditions, including life-threatening and life-limiting illnesses. Birtenshaw Hall is a very special place – a place where dedicated staff work in partnership with parents to provide a quality education in a caring, supportive environment.

Bishop Hedley Catholic High School

Gwaunfarren Road, Penydarren, Merthyr Tydfil, CF47 9AN

Tel: 01685 721747
Fax: 01685 385 292
Email: office@bishophedleyhigh.merthyr.sch.uk
Website: www.bishophedleyhigh.merthyr.sch.uk
• Pupils: 602 Mixed; Day Pupils • Age: 11 to 19
• Religion: Roman Catholic • School status: State

SEN provision

Detail:
Centre of excellence for:
Mild: DYSC; DYSL; DYSP;
Moderate: DYSC; DYSL;
Severe: DYSL
Now provide for in school:
Mild: ASP; AUT; ADD; ADHD; EBD; HI;
Moderate: ASP; AUT; ADD; ADHD; EBD; MLD; HI;
Severe: HI;
Others: EAL; Epi; Eat
Experience of:
Mild: DS; VI; CP;
Moderate: DYSP;
Severe: ASP; ADD; ADHD; EBD; DYSC;
Others: SPD; AUT(other); CD; OCD; ODD; TIC; Sp&LD; DEL

Summary: The school operates a whole school policy to enable pupils with a wide range of difficulties to be able to achieve their full potential and are recognised as valuable members of our school community. Every member of staff is committed to being teachers of pupils with a wide range of difficulties. We are acknowledged by our LEA to have an excellent and successful Dyslexia and Behavioural record.

BISHOP'S HATFIELD GIRLS' SCHOOL

Woods Avenue, Hatfield, Hertfordshire, AL10 8NL

Tel: 01707 275 331
Fax: 01707 270 244
Email: admin.bishophatfield@thegrid.org.uk
Website: www.bishophatfield.herts.sch.uk
• Pupils: 718 Girls; Day Pupils • Age: 11 to 18
• Religion: Non-denominational • School status: State

SEN provision

Detail:
Now provide for in school:
Mild: ADD; ADHD; EBD; DS; DYSC; DYSL; DYSP; HI; VI;
Moderate: EBD; DS; MLD; DYSL; HI;
Others: EAL; Epi

Summary: The Learning Support Faculty provides in-class support across the curriculum for pupils with special educational needs. It also provides small group and individual literacy support for pupils who need it.

Some pupils at Key Stage are taking a reduced number of GCSEs in order to receive small group curriculum and literacy support to enable them to achieve a better standard in their GCSEs.

Small group and individual support for pupils with emotional and/or behavioural difficulties is currently under development.

THE BISHOPS' BLUE COAT CHURCH OF ENGLAND HIGH SCHOOL

Vaughans Lane, Great Boughton, Chester, Cheshire, CH3 5XF

Tel: 01244 313 806
Fax: 01244 353 055
Email: school@bishopsbluecoat.cheshire.sch.uk
Website: www.bishopsbluecoat.cheshire.sch.uk
• Pupils: 1025 Mixed; Day Pupils • Age: 11 to 18
• Religion: Church of England • School status: State

SEN provision

Detail:
Now provide for in school:
Mild: ASP; ADD; EBD; DYSL; DYSP; SpLD; HI; VI; CP;
Moderate: ASP; ADD; MLD; DYSL; DYSP; SpLD; HI; VI;
Others: Sp&LD; DEL; Epi; PD; Oth

Summary: The school is Voluntary Aided and pupils with Additional Needs benefit from its Christian Ethos.

The school caters for a wide range of pupils including those with medical needs, Asperger's syndrome, Dyslexia, Dyspraxia and ADHD.

Pupils who need extra help are taught literacy skills in a small group of about 10 during English lessons. Paired reading, Paired Maths and SuccessMaker clubs run during registration times. The school has a team of 10 Classroom assistants and 3 teachers. We are currently developing a Pupil Support Centre to help pupils to remain engaged with school life, to support pupils with SEN and to provide a base for pupils who find unstructured times at school difficult (break or lunchtime). The SENCo has AMBDA status and withdraws individuals or small groups for extra literacy tuition during the school day. Good communication is maintained with external agencies and staff work closely with a variety of specialists to ensure that pupils achieve their potential in school. Mainstream staff are kept informed of the needs of pupils and their IEP targets.

Blatchington Mill School and Sixth Form College

Nevill Avenue, Hove, East Sussex, BN3 7BW

Tel: 01273 736 244
Fax: 01273 739 615
Email: admin@blatchingtonmill.brighton-hove.sch.uk
Website: www.blatchingtonmill.brighton-hove.sch.uk
• Pupils: 1668 Mixed; Day Pupils • Age: 11 to 18
• Religion: Non-denominational • School status: State

SEN provision

Detail:
Now provide for in school:
Mild: ASP; AUT; DS; DYSL; HI; CP;
Moderate: ASP; AUT; DS; DYSL; HI; CP;
Severe: DS; DYSL;
Others: CD
Experience of:
Mild: ADD; ADHD; EBD; DYSC; DYSP; VI;
Moderate: ADD; ADHD; EBD; MLD; DYSC; DYSP; VI;
Severe: ASP; AUT; DYSC; DYSP; HI; VI; CP;
Others: OCD; GEN; PMLD; SLD; DEL; Epi; Eat

Summary: The Student Support Centre at BMS offers an opportunity for all pupils to achieve to their full potential. At present there are six teachers and nineteen teaching assistants (full and part-time) who work with pupils (and the teachers of...) who have SEN. The main thrust of the SSC is supporting pupils in mainstream lessons. However, there is the flexibility to cope with pupils individual needs through small group or one-to-one work. We have the experience and knowledge of working with the diverse nature of SEN, as well as excellent working relationships with outside agencies within the local authority – Autistic Spectrum Disorder, Speech and Language, Specific Learning Difficulties, Sensory and Physical needs. We liaise regularly with parents and are always available to discuss any concerns (given appropriate notice!)

The Blue Coat C of E School

Egerton Street, Oldham, Lancashire, OL1 3SQ

Tel: 01616 241 484
Fax: 01616 284 997
Email: secretary@blue-coat.oldham.sch.uk
• Pupils: 1311 Mixed; Day Pupils • Age: 11 to 18 • Religion: Church of England • School status: State

SEN provision

Detail:
Now provide for in school:
Mild: ASP; ADD; ADHD; EBD; DYSL; DYSP; HI; VI;
Moderate: ASP; ADD; ADHD; EBD; MLD; DYSL; DYSP; HI; VI;
Severe: ASP; DYSL; HI;
Others: Sp&LD; Epi

Summary: We offer support across the curriculum for pupils with SEN. We have pupils who have MLD, Spld, EBD, hearing and visual impairment, autistic spectrum and communication difficulties. Teaching assistants provide in-class support, small group work and deliver COPE at Key Stage 4. There is a SENCo who implements the requirements of the code of practice as well as teaching and tutoring these students. There are training courses delivered to all staff concerning many aspects of SEN. We have three mentors who provide support for a wide range of children in difficulty or G&T. All agencies are employed in as many ways as possible to harness the best resources and support we can possibly give.

BOUNDSTONE COMMUNITY COLLEGE

Upper Boundstone Lane, Lancing, West Sussex, BN15 9QZ

Tel: 01903 755 894
Fax: 01903 755 848
Email: admin@boundstone.w-sussex.sch.uk
Website: www.boundstone.w-sussex.sch.uk
• Pupils: 1144 Mixed; Day Pupils • Age: 12 to 18
• Religion: Non-denominational • School status: State

SEN provision

Detail:
Experience of:
Mild: ASP; AUT; ADD; ADHD; EBD; DYSC; DYSL; DYSP; HI; VI;
Moderate: ASP; AUT; ADD; ADHD; EBD; MLD; DYSC; DYSL; DYSP; HI; VI;
Severe: EBD; DYSL; HI; VI;
Others: CD; TIC; EAL; Sp&LD

Summary: We offer 3 main areas of support:-

- Cognition and learning, including literacy/numeracy, physical, sensory, speech and language through in-class and withdrawal.
- EBD – 'Bridge' a nurture unit and in-class support.
- AEN – Curriculum catch-up and an LSU.

BOURNE GRAMMAR SCHOOL

South Road, Bourne, Lincolnshire, PE10 9JE

Tel: 01778 422 288
Fax: 01778 394 872
Email: enquiries@bourne-grammar.lincs.sch.uk
Website: www.bourne-grammar.lincs.sch.uk
• Pupils: 943 Mixed; Day Pupils • Age: 11 to 18
• Religion: Christian • School status: State

SEN provision

Detail:
Experience of:
Mild: ASP; ADD; ADHD; EBD; DYSC; DYSL; DYSP; HI; VI;
Others: Eat

Summary: The school has one SENCo and no learning support assistants. Any students who have special needs are seen by the SENCo on a regular basis and all teaching staff are informed about these students with copies of their IEPs if applicable.

BOVINGTON MIDDLE SCHOOL

Cologne Road, Bovington Camp, Wareham, Dorset, BH20 6NU

Tel: 01929 462 495
Fax: 01929 405 161
Email: office@BovingtonMid.dorset.sch.uk
Website: www.bovingtonmid.dorset.sch.uk
• Pupils: 308 Mixed; Day Pupils • Age: 9 to 13
• Religion: Non-denominational • School status: State

SEN provision

Detail:
Now provide for in school:
Mild: ASP; ADD; ADHD; EBD;
Moderate: ASP; ADD; ADHD; EBD
Experience of:
Mild: AUT; DYSC; DYSL; DYSP; HI;
Moderate: MLD; DYSL; DYSP;
Severe: ASP; ADD; EBD;
Others: CD; OCD; ODD; EAL; Epi; PD

Summary: We endeavour to include all pupils regardless of their abilities or difficulties. We have had experience including pupils with ADHD, ADD, Asperger's, Dyslexia and a wide range of learning difficulties. We pride ourselves on our team work and the relationships we build as a school with all the pupils that we support. Our teaching assistants are very well qualified in supporting pupils in the classroom and we ensure that the curriculum is differentiated to suit individual needs. We have very good links with external agencies who offer support and advice to teaching and non-teaching staff when we need it. The SEN department prides itself on its sense of humour and are prepared to try anything once! Our last Ofsted report stated that the SEN department was a strength of the school, providing very good support for SEN pupils.

Bowsland Green Primary School

Ellicks Close, Bradley Stoke, Bristol, BS32 0ES

Tel: 01454 866 766
Fax: 01454 866 765
Email: BowslandGreenPrimary.School@southglos.gov.uk
Website: www.bowslandgreen.ik.org

• Pupils: 289 Mixed; Day Pupils • Age: 4 to 11
• Religion: Non-denominational • School status: State

SEN provision

Detail:
Now provide for in school:
Mild: ASP; AUT; ADD; ADHD; EBD; DYSC; VI; CP;
Moderate: ASP; AUT; ADHD; EBD; MLD; DYSC; DYSL; DYSP;
Severe: ASP; AUT; ADHD; EBD;
Others: SLD; EAL; Sp&LD; Epi; PD

Summary: Bowsland Green Primary aims to enable pupils with special educational needs to have access to a broad and balanced curriculum encompassing the development of the whole child, whilst acknowledging parental and child involvement. We pride ourselves on our fully inclusive policy and are renowned for our excellent understanding and provision for children with special needs. We treat all parents as partners in the decision making process throughout their child's education.

Brackenfield School

128 Duchy Road, Harrogate, North Yorkshire, HG1 2HE

Tel: 01423 508 558
Fax: 01423 524 841
Email: admin@brackenfield.n-yorks.sch.uk
Website: www.brackenfieldschool.co.uk

• Pupils: 161 Mixed; Day Pupils • Age: 2 to 11
• School status: Independent

SEN provision

Detail:
Experience of:
Mild: DYSC; DYSL; DYSP;
Moderate: MLD; DYSC; DYSL; DYSP;
Others: Eat

Summary: Pupils requiring extra support are taught either in small groups or individually by our Learning Support teacher. This support takes place either in class or in a dedicated room. We also have a teacher from the Dyslexia Institute who visits the school for two mornings weekly to work with individual pupils or groups of two, as appropriate.

Bradstow School

34 Dumpton Park Drive, Broadstairs, Kent, CT10 1BY

Tel: 01843 862 123
Fax: 01843 866 648
Email: info@bradstow.wandsworth.sch.uk

• Pupils: 50 Mixed; Takes boarders • Age: 6 to 19
• Religion: Non-denominational • School status: State

SEN provision

Summary: Bradstow School caters for students who are severely disabled with autism and many have challenging behaviour and severe learning difficulties. In 2002, the DfES recognised the school as a Regional Resource for children with Autistic Spectrum Disorders and challenging behaviour.

The school has developed radical approaches to the education, support and management of pupils with challenging behaviour and ASD, that involve ensuring the environment for learning presented to the child is non-threatening and accessible to them at their own level. This approach has been recognised by Ofsted (July 05) as being highly successful, and they report that 'Pupils make remarkable progress in the way they overcome communication and social difficulties and so become able to learn.' They go on to say that 'There are many instances of remarkable change for pupils and students whose severely challenging behaviour meant that other special schools could not accommodate them.' This progress was reinforced by the parents who are reported to be ... 'very pleased with the school and feel very strongly that their children have been able to succeed and learn to communicate and be more sociable than ever before.'

BRAINTREE COLLEGE

Church Lane, Braintree, Essex, CM7 5SN

Tel: 01376 321 711
Fax: 01376 340 799
Email: enquiries@braintree.ac.uk
Website: www.braintree.ac.uk

• Pupils: 1072 Mixed; Day Pupils • Age: 16 to 99
• Religion: Non-denominational • School status: State

SEN provision

Detail:
Experience of:
Mild: ASP; AUT; ADD; ADHD; EBD; DS; DYSC; DYSL; DYSP; HI; VI; CP;
Moderate: ASP; AUT; ADD; ADHD; EBD; DS; MLD; DYSC; DYSL; DYSP; HI; VI; CP;
Severe: ASP; AUT; ADD; ADHD; EBD; DS; DYSC; DYSL; HI; VI; CP;
Others: CD; OCD; TIC; FRX; PMLD; SLD; EAL; MSI; Epi; PD

Summary: Our Learning Support department can arrange for:

- Study skills assisting students to plan and organise work
- Provision of a note taking service
- Assisting students with mobility
- Assisting students in the work place when on work experience
- Mentoring
- Supply and adaptation of equipment
- Specialist software
- Educational psychologist assessment
- Exam dispensation, scribes, reader etc
- Assessment of a specific learning difficulty eg dyslexia
- Specialist workshop dyslexia tuition
- Communicators for the deaf/hearing impaired
- Specialist tuition for the deaf
- Physiotherapy support
- Support for students with sight impairment
- In-class support with a learning support assistant
- Personal care assistants
- Scribe
- Dedicated technician for supply, maintenance and training in the use of specialist equipment/software
- Initial assessments.

BRAITHWAITE SPECIAL SCHOOL

Braithwaite Road, Keighley, West Yorkshire, BD22 6PR

Tel: 01535 603 041
Fax: 01535 691 227
Email: office@braithwaite.ngfl.ac.uk

• Pupils: 112 Mixed; Day Pupils • Age: 2 to 19
• Religion: Non-denominational • School status: State

SEN provision

Detail:
Now provide for in school:
Mild: VI; CP;
Moderate: MLD; HI;
Severe: ASP; AUT; ADD; DS;
Others: AUT(other); PMLD; SLD; EAL; Sp&LD; Epi
Experience of:
Mild: HI;
Severe: ADHD; EBD;
Others: SPD; OCD; FRX; Eat

Summary: Braithwaite School caters for pupils, aged 2 to 19 years, with a wide range of learning difficulties and associated behavioural difficulties.

Brampton Ellis C of E Junior School

Brampton Road, West Melton, Wath-on-Dearne, Rotherham, South Yorkshire, S63 6BB

Tel: 01709 760 104
Fax: 01709 875 884
Email: brampton-ellis-cofe.junior@rotherham.gov.uk

• Pupils: 244 Mixed; Day Pupils • Age: 7 to 11
• Religion: Church of England • School status: State

SEN provision

Detail:
Now provide for in school:
Mild: ASP; AUT; ADD; ADHD; EBD; DYSC; DYSL; DYSP; SpLD;
Moderate: ASP; EBD; MLD; DYSC; DYSL; DYSP;
Severe: EBD;
Others: Sp&LD; Epi; Eat

Summary: Brampton Ellis C of E Junior School fully supports the principle that children with special educational needs require the greatest possible access to a broad and balanced curriculum as determined by the National Curriculum. Children are given support as far as possible to achieve this.

We also aim to develop independence within the classroom environment. We run a variety of different programmes to meet children's specific needs and develop their potential.

The Bramptons Primary School

Harlestone Road, Chapel Brampton, Northampton, Northamptonshire, NN6 8AW

Tel: 01604 842 078
Email: head@thebramptons.northants-ecl.gov.uk

• Pupils: 70 Mixed; Day Pupils • Age: 4 to 11
• Religion: Non-denominational • School status: State

SEN provision

Detail:
Experience of:
Mild: ADD; ADHD; EBD; DYSL;
Moderate: ADD; ADHD; EBD; DYSL;
Others: EAL; Sp&LD; Oth

Summary: We provide a variety of SEN facilities for children in our school. We identify needs as early as possible and use both in-class and out of class support for the children. This support may be given by the teacher or a teaching assistant. All provision is reviewed on a regular basis and parents are kept continually informed of their child's progress and any changes to their programmes of work. We believe that by working with children with special needs from an early age we can improve their achievements and develop their attainment more quickly. We consider both under achieving children and gifted and talented children.

Brantridge School

Staplefield Place, Staplefield, Haywards Heath, West Sussex, RH17 6EQ

Tel: 01444 400 228
Fax: 01444 401 083
Email: headteacher@brantridge.greenwich.sch.uk

• Pupils: 36 Boys; Takes boarders • Age: 6 to 13
• Religion: Non-denominational • School status: Independent

SEN provision

Detail:
Now provide for in school:
Mild: ASP; AUT; ADD; ADHD; EBD; DYSC; DYSL; DYSP; SpLD; HI; VI;
Moderate: ASP; AUT; ADD; ADHD; EBD; MLD; DYSL
Severe: ADD; ADHD; EBD;
Others: SPD; AUT(other); ODD; FRX; GEN; Sp&LD; DEL; Epi

Summary: Brantridge School specialises in helping children with Behavioural, Emotional and Social Difficulties (BESD). This includes many with Social Communication difficulties. We have a reputation for taking 'hard to place' children, who don't fit easily into any of the usual categories, and helping them to reintegrate into day special or mainstream schools wherever possible. On average, 50 per cent of our leavers successfully return to mainstream.

We offer a combination of good behaviour management strategies linked to a range of therapeutic approaches.

We welcome visits from parents, LEA officers and other professionals.

BRECKENBROUGH SCHOOL

Sand Hutton, Thirsk, North Yorkshire, YO7 4EN

Tel: 01845 587 238

Fax: 01845 587 385

• Pupils: 34 Boys; Takes boarders • Age: 9 to 17

• Religion: Quaker • School status: State

SEN provision

Detail:

Now provide for in school:

Mild: ASP; AUT; ADD; ADHD; EBD; DYSC; DYSL; DYSP;

Moderate: ASP; ADD; ADHD; EBD;

Severe: ADD; ADHD; EBD;

Others: Epi

Summary: Breckenbrough School is a residential boarding school, for forty pupils aged between 9 and 17 who exhibit emotional and behavioural difficulties and high academic potential. All of our pupils have repeatedly struggled with the structure and ethos of mainstream education where their eccentricities and needs have never been adequately met. Our pupils have in effect learning differences that deserve the opportunity to be developed. We have developed expertise and success with boys diagnosed with Asperger's, ADHD, ADD and Dyslexia in recent years. The ethos reflects the philosophy of the Society of Friends. Central to the ethos is the belief in the innate good of everyone. We give our pupils the time and space to be themselves in a clear, non-confrontational, flexible structure. Where there are problems we encourage honesty in addressing them in order to move forward.

BRECON HIGH SCHOOL

Penlan, Brecon, Powys, LD3 9SR

Tel: 01874 622 361

Fax: 01874 624 855

Email: office@brecon-hs.powys.sch.uk

Website: www.brecon-hs.powys.sch.uk

• Pupils: 897 Mixed; Day Pupils • Age: 11 to 18

• Religion: Non-denominational • School status: State

SEN provision

Detail:

Now provide for in school:

Mild: ASP; AUT; DS; DYSL; DYSP; HI; VI; CP;

Moderate: ASP; AUT; DS; MLD; DYSL; DYSP; HI; VI; CP;

Severe: ASP; DYSL;

Others: EAL; DEL

Experience of:

Mild: ADD; ADHD; EBD;

Moderate: ADD; ADHD; EBD;

Severe: EBD; DYSP; HI;

Others: SPD; OCD; ODD; FRX; Sp&LD; PD; Eat

Summary: Brecon High School is a mainstream comprehensive school. The school hosts a resource base for pupils with ASD in the south of Powys. In each year group there is a mainstream support class for pupils with a range of learning needs. It has a maximum number of 15 pupils and has LSA support allocated to it. The school has a full-time Dyslexia specialist who works with pupils on a withdrawal basis. The school has recently upgraded its buildings with the installation of four lifts to improve access for disabled persons. The school also has a learning support class for pupils with moderate learning difficulties. The school has a number of LSAs who work with individual pupils and groups within mainstream lessons or if withdrawn to the learning support base.

BRIDGE OF DON ACADEMY

Braehead Way, Bridge of Don, Aberdeen, AB22 8RR

Tel: 01224 707 583
Fax: 01224 706 910
Email: accboda@rmplc.co.uk
Website: www.bridgeofdon.aberdeen.sch.uk

• Pupils: 679 Mixed; Day Pupils • Age: 11 to 18
• Religion: Non-denominational • School status: State

SEN provision

Detail:
Now provide for in school:
Mild: ASP; ADD; EBD; DYSC; DYSL; DYSP; SpLD; HI; VI;
Moderate: ASP; EBD; MLD; DYSC; DYSL; DYSP; SpLD; HI; VI;
Severe: DYSC; DYSL; SpLD;
Others: SLD; Sp&LD; Epi; PD

Summary: Our SEN base operates an inclusive practice. Our pupils attend mainstream setting for most subjects and come to the base to work on various needs/skills/homework or follow Access 2 units. The pupils are usually supported when in their mainstream classes.

The base is opened to pupils at break and lunchtime to provide a place of safety.

THE BRIDGE SCHOOL

The Brookside Building, Brookside, Telford, Shropshire, TF3 1LB

Tel: 01952 417 010
Fax: 01952 417 022

• Pupils: 142 Mixed; Day Pupils • Age: 2 to 19
• Religion: Non-denominational • School status: State

SEN provision

Summary: The Bridge provides for pupils with severe or profound learning disabilities. A large number are diagnosed with ASD. Many pupils have complex medical needs and/or additional sensory impairments. The school runs inclusive classes and we have no units.

THE BRIDGE SCHOOL

290 Reservoir Road, Erdington, Birmingham, West Midlands, B23 6DE

Tel: 0121 464 8265
Fax: 0121 464 7619
Email: enquiry@bridgesp.bham.sch.uk

• Pupils: 29 Mixed; Day Pupils • Age: 2 to 11
• Religion: Non-denominational • School status: State

SEN provision

Detail:
Now provide for in school:
Mild: DS; HI; VI; CP;
Moderate: DS; SpLD; HI; VI; CP;
Severe: EBD; DS; SpLD; HI; VI; CP;
Others: AUT(other); FRX; GEN; PMLD; SLD; EAL; MSI; Sp&LD; DEL; Epi; PD

Summary: The Bridge is a small special school which caters for the needs of 35 pupils with Severe, Profound and Multiple Learning Difficulties. Some pupils display Challenging Behaviours and others are on the Autistic Disorder Spectrum.

BRIDLINGTON SCHOOL SPORTS COLLEGE

Bessingby Road, East Riding of Yorkshire, Bridlington, YO16 4QU

Tel: 01262 672 593
Fax: 01262 607 388
Email: office@bridlingtonschool.eril.net

• Pupils: 1141 Mixed; Day Pupils • Age: 11 to 18
• School status: State

SEN provision

Detail:
Now provide for in school:
Mild: ASP; AUT; ADD; ADHD; EBD; DS; DYSC; DYSL; DYSP; HI; VI; CP;
Moderate: ASP; AUT; ADHD; EBD; DS; MLD; DYSL;

HI; VI; CP;
Severe: DS; CP;
Others: PMLD; Sp&LD; Epi; PD

Summary: The school has a strong team of committed, knowledgeable and experienced teaching staff, well supported by a qualified teaching assistant team. Together we will offer students with SEN the best possible chance to experience, and gain skills from, the full National Curriculum and leave school with the skills necessary to move into adult life, confident in their own abilities.

THE BRIER SCHOOL

Bromley Lane, Kingswinford, West Midlands, DY6 8QN

Tel: 01384 816000
Fax: 01384 816001
Email: vgrainger@brier.dudley.gov.uk

• Pupils: 135 Mixed; Day Pupils • Age: 4 to 16
• Religion: Non-denominational • School status: State

SEN provision

Detail:
Centre of excellence for:
Mild: AUT;
Moderate: AUT; MLD;
Others: Sp&LD
Now provide for in school:
Mild: ASP; ADD; ADHD; EBD; DS; DYSC; DYSL; DYSP; HI; VI;
Moderate: ASP; ADD; ADHD; EBD; DS; DYSC; DYSL; DYSP; HI; VI;
Severe: ASP; VI;
Others: CD; OCD; FRX; GEN; EAL; DEL; Epi; PD; Eat
Experience of:
Mild: SpLD; CP;
Moderate: CP;
Severe: AUT; DYSC; DYSL; DYSP;
Others: SPD; ODD; TIC

Summary: The Brier School is an all age mixed special school that aims to serve children with moderate learning difficulties or complex communication difficulties. The school is the largest special school in Dudley LEA and the flagship for SEN provision in the authority. It is located on Campus 21, a site that also houses a mainstream primary school and a mainstream secondary. As the proximity of two mainstream schools is a key factor in the culture of the school, integration into mainstream education is an option, where appropriate, open to all pupils. Such integration is arranged on an individual basis and following careful negotiation with all parties, including the child. The building itself was completed in February 2004 and thus offers state-of-the-art provision.

BROADMEAD JUNIOR SCHOOL

366 Sydenham Road, Croydon, Surrey, CR0 2EA

Tel: 020 8689 5473
Fax: 020 8665 1461
Email: admin@broadmead-jun.croydon.sch.uk

• Pupils: 297 Mixed; Day Pupils • Age: 7 to 11
• Religion: Non-denominational • School status: State

SEN provision

Detail:
Now provide for in school:
Mild: ASP; AUT; ADD; ADHD; EBD; DYSL; DYSP; SpLD; HI; VI;
Moderate: ASP; ADD; ADHD; EBD; MLD; DYSL; DYSP;
Others: EAL; Sp&LD; DEL; PD
Experience of:
Mild: DS; DYSC;
Others: FRX

Summary: Every child has individual needs and brings different experiences, talents, interests and strengths to our school. Our intention at Broadmead is to maintain an inclusive environment in which every child has access to the whole curriculum and to cultivate in all our pupils a confidence and a desire to strive towards achieving their full potential.

We aim to ensure equality of opportunity/entitlement and access for all children including those with special educational needs and to provide maximum stability and continuity for those pupils.

Brook Primary School

George Street, Wordsley, Stourbridge, West Midlands, DY8 5YN

Tel: 01384 818 835
Fax: 01384 818 836
Email: info@brook.dudley.gov.uk
Website: www.brook.dudley.gov.uk/

• Pupils: 244 Mixed; Day Pupils • Age: 5 to 11
• Religion: Non-denominational • School status: State

SEN provision

Detail:
Now provide for in school:
Mild: DS;
Moderate: DS;
Others: Sp&LD
Experience of:
Mild: ADD; ADHD; EBD; DYSC; DYSL; DYSP; SpLD; HI; VI; CP;
Moderate: ADD; ADHD; EBD; MLD; DYSC; DYSL; SpLD; CP;
Others: EAL; Epi

Summary: The school's Deputy Head is currently our special needs co-ordinator. There is a teaching assistant who withdraws children for one-to-one support on a weekly basis, if there are School Action Plus on the special needs register. Pupils with special needs have support in small groups within the classroom as a regular feature of lessons. Children with special needs statements have a dedicated worker for the hours prescribed on their statement. The school is currently building a care room and small group teaching space for children with SEN. There are ramps enabling access to parts of the building, but a single step remains from the corridor to each classroom.

Brooklands School

27 Wray Park Road, Reigate, Surrey, RH2 0DF

Tel: 01737 249 941
Fax: 01737 242 017

• Pupils: 82 Mixed; Day Pupils • Age: 11
• Religion: Non-denominational • School status: State

SEN provision

Detail:
Now provide for in school:
Mild: ASP; AUT;
Moderate: ASP; AUT;
Severe: ASP; AUT;
Others: SPD; AUT(other); PMLD; SLD

Summary: School has an assessment nursery and caters for children with severe learning difficulties (SLD), profound and multiple learning difficulties (PMLD), and autistic spectrum disorder with associated learning difficulties.

Broomfield, The South Leeds SILC

Broom Place, Leeds, West Yorkshire, LS10 3JP

Tel: 01132 771 603
Fax: 01132 771 622
Email: broomfieldschool@hotmail.com
Website: www.broomfield.leeds.sch.uk

• Pupils: 109 Mixed; Day Pupils • Age: 2 to 19
• Religion: Non-denominational • School status: State

SEN provision

Detail:
Now provide for in school:
Mild: ASP; AUT; ADD; DS; HI; VI; CP;
Moderate: ASP; AUT; DS; HI; VI; CP;
Severe: ASP; AUT; DS; VI; CP;
Others: AUT(other); FRX; EAL; MSI; Sp&LD; Epi; PD;

Summary: Broomfield is a Specialist Inclusive Learning Centre (a SILC). We operate partnerships with mainstream schools, provide outreach support to mainstream schools and advise and support in Early Years Centres. Currently 20 per cent of our pupils, all of whom have a statement of special needs, attend local primary and secondary schools, but are taught and supported by Broomfield staff. This number is planned to rise over time to 50 per cent.

Brownhills High School

Brownhills Road, Tunstall, Stoke-on-Trent, Staffordshire, ST6 4LD

Tel: 01782 233 888
Fax: 01782 834 637
Email: brownhills@sgfl.org.uk
Website: www.brownhills.stoke.sch.uk

• Pupils: 736 Mixed; Day Pupils • Age: 11 to 16
• Religion: Non-denominational • School status: State

SEN provision

Detail:
Now provide for in school:
Mild: ADD; ADHD; EBD; DYSC; DYSL; DYSP; HI; VI; CP;
Moderate: ADD; ADHD; EBD; MLD; DYSC; DYSL; DYSP; HI; VI; CP;
Severe: DYSL; DYSP;
Others: TIC; GEN; EAL; Sp&LD; DEL; Epi; PD
Experience of:
Mild: ASP; AUT;
Severe: EBD;
Others: SPD; CD; ODD

Summary: Brownhills is the wheelchair access school for the north of the city, we have lifts, ramps and high visability strips. We have a designated SEN area, with 4 computers and access to a range of ICT support programmes. Currently the school employs seven full-time Learning Support Practioners and one part-time LSP. We operate a combination of in-class support and intervention withdrawal. Our LSPs have a range of specialisms including; SPLD support, working with the physically disabled, circle time and precision teaching. As a school we work closely with a range of external agencies this includes running a monthly drop-in session in conjunction with Parent Partnership. We also have access to a family support worker, who is based in school three days a week.

Brushwood Junior School

Brushwood Road, Chesham, Buckinghamshire, HP5 3DW

Tel: 01494 786 023
Fax: 01494 793 114
Email: office@brushwood-jun.bucks.sch.uk
Website: www.brushwoodjunior.ik.org

• Pupils: 160 Mixed; Day Pupils • Age: 7 to 11
• Religion: Non-denominational • School status: State

SEN provision

Detail:
Now provide for in school:
Mild: ASP; EBD; DYSC; DYSL; DYSP; HI; VI;
Moderate: MLD; DYSC; DYSL;
Others: EAL; Sp&LD; Epi; PD
Experience of:
Mild: AUT; ADD; ADHD; DS; CP;
Moderate: ASP; EBD; DYSP; HI;
Severe: DYSC; DYSL

Summary: Brushwood's aims are:

- To creat an environment that meets the SEN of each child.
- To ensure that SEN of children are identified, assessed and provided for.
- To make clear the expectations of all partners in the process.
- To enable all children to have full access to all elements of the school curriculum.
- Finally, and most importantly to ensure that our children have a voice in this process. Empowering them in developing and growing.

Bryn Offa C of E Primary School

Rockwell Lane, Pant, Oswestry, Shropshire, SY10 9QR

Tel: 01691 830 621
Fax: 01691 839 232
Email: admin@brynoffa.shropshire.sch.uk
• Pupils: 134 Mixed; Day Pupils • Age: 5 to 11
• Religion: Church of England • School status: State

SEN provision

Detail:
Now provide for in school:
Mild: AUT; ADD; ADHD; EBD; DYSP;
Moderate: AUT; ADHD; EBD; MLD;
Severe: EBD;
Others: Sp&LD; DEL
Experience of:
Mild: DYSL;
Moderate: ADD; DYSL;
Others: SPD; CD; OCD; EAL; Epi

Summary: We have a strong tradition of supporting pupils with SEN and a belief that they can achieve to their full potential too. We have a very supportive ethos between staff, staff and children and between pupils, which helps all children to feel safe and secure and to learn well.

Bryn Primary School

Gelli Road, Bryn, Llanelli, Carmarthenshire, SA14 9TT

Tel: 01554 776 064
Fax: 01554 776064
Email: staff.bryn@ysgolccc.org.uk
Website: www.ysgolccc.org.uk/bryn/
• Pupils: 201 Mixed; Day Pupils • Age: 4 to 11
• Religion: Christian • School status: State

SEN provision

Detail:
Now provide for in school:
Mild: ASP; AUT; EBD; DYSP;
Moderate: EBD; MLD; DYSP;
Severe: DS;
Others: CD
Experience of:
Mild: ADD; ADHD; DYSL; HI;
Moderate: ADD; ADHD;
Severe: AUT; ADD; ADHD;
Others: SPD; ODD; TIC; PMLD; SLD; EAL; Sp&LD; Epi; PD

Summary: The school is willing to try and cater for children with a range of difficulties both physical and behavioural. We pride ourselves in being willing and able to accept pupils with new challenges. Our LEA's SEN department has always shown itself to be supportive of the school's efforts by providing specialist equipment for the individual child's needs. We firmly believe that we, both children and staff, can learn as much about life from children with difficulties as they can from being in mainstream school.

Brynmill Primary School

Trafalgar Place, Brynmill, Swansea, SA2 0BU

Tel: 01792 463 019
Fax: 01792 459 110
Email: Brynmill.Primary@swansea.gov.uk
• Pupils: 381 Mixed; Day Pupils • Age: 3 to 11
• School status: State

SEN provision

Detail:
Centre of excellence for:
Mild: DYSL; DYSP;
Moderate: MLD; DYSL; DYSP;
Severe: DYSL;
Others: EAL
Now provide for in school:
Mild: ASP; AUT; ADD; ADHD; EBD; DYSC;

Moderate: ASP; AUT; ADD; ADHD; EBD; DYSC;
Severe: ADHD; EBD;
Others: SPD; Sp&LD; DEL; Epi

Experience of:
Mild: HI; VI;
Moderate: HI; VI

Summary: The school employs a full-time Support Teacher, who is also the SENCo. The Support Teacher holds a Diploma in Continuing Professional Development for work done in the areas of Dyslexia and Speech and Language. She also holds AMBDA status. The school is 'Dyslexia friendly'. The school has been a pilot school, delivering a multi-agency DCD programme, devised by the County. This is currently delivered to two Key Stage 2 groups and will be extended to Key Stage 1 after Easter 2005. Having attended conferences on ADHD and Autism, we can cater for children exhibiting these difficulties. There is one pupil who has a Statement of SEN for 'Moyamoya'. She has LSA support.

Buckingham Primary School

Foscot Way, Buckingham, Buckinghamshire, MK18 1TT

Tel: 01280 812 864
Fax: 01280 812 806
Email: office@bps.bucks.sch.uk
Website: www.buckinghamprimary.co.uk

• Pupils: 570 Mixed; Day Pupils • Age: 3 to 11
• Religion: Non-denominational • School status: State

SEN provision

Detail:

Experience of:
Mild: ASP; AUT; ADD; ADHD; EBD; DS; DYSC; DYSL; DYSP; CP;
Moderate: MLD; HI; VI; CP;
Others: EAL; Sp&LD; DEL; Epi; PD; Eat

Summary: Buckingham Primary is a fully inclusive school which caters for a broad range of children with special needs. Our buildings are adapted for wheelchair users and we have disabled toilet and changing facilities in the three key areas of the site.

Bude Infant School

Broadclose Hill, Bude, Cornwall, EX23 8EA

Tel: 01288 353 798
Fax: 01288 353 798
Email: secretary@bude-inf.cornwall.sch.uk
Website: www.bude-inf.cornwall.sch.uk

• Mixed; Day Pupils • Age: 5 to 8
• Religion: Non-denominational • School status: State

SEN provision

Detail:

Now provide for in school:
Mild: ASP; AUT; ADD; ADHD; EBD; DS; DYSC; DYSL; DYSP; SpLD; HI; VI;
Moderate: ASP; AUT; ADD; ADHD; EBD; DS; DYSC; DYSL; DYSP; SpLD; HI; VI;
Severe: ADD; ADHD; EBD; DYSC; DYSL; DYSP; SpLD; HI; VI;
Others: AUT(other); CD; OCD; TIC; PMLD; SLD; EAL; MSI; Sp&LD

Summary: Bude Infant School has around 200 children on roll each year. During our last Ofsted inspection it was noted that the provision for special educational needs was a strength of the school. Bude Infant School appointed a new SENCo in September 2004 who has undertaken courses to build upon and strengthen knowledge and understanding of this area. Each teacher is thoroughly aware of the school's stand on SEN through such documentation as the school's SEN and Gifted and Talented policies. It is the classroom practitioners responsiblity to identify those whom they feel have special educational needs of any type. This is achieved through classroom observation and on going assessment.

Parental involvement is sought from the start. Parents are involved in all decisions regarding the provision for their child and copies of all the relevant paperwork is sent home. There is an open door policy in the school and parents are welcome to come in to discuss any issues they have or to raise any questions. Individual education plan targets are set by the child's class teacher and are reviewed termly but can be altered at any time if need be.

Bude Infant School is unique in so much as we have a dedicated special needs teaching assistant. In her role she may take individuals or groups of children out of class for intensive work or preparation. This is undertaken in a new SEN dedicated classroom. She can also be used within the classroom setting, depending on what the teacher deems suitable. We also have teaching assistants in the classrooms who can help the teacher address the needs of all children. Bude Infant school has a warm and friendly atmosphere and all children are valued and we have high expectations of all. Each child on the school's Record of Need is reviewed termly and their progress discussed with all the involved parties. We have had experiences of a wide range of special educational needs which has helped us to build on our good practice. There is constant communication between all members of staff regarding SEN. The school's main theory regarding SEN is that early identification is a must.

Burhill Community Infant School

Pleasant Place, Hersham, Walton-on-Thames, Surrey, KT12 4HR

Tel: 01932 225 836
Fax: 01932 240 397
Email: head@burhill.surrey.sch.uk
Website: www.burhill.surrey.sch.uk

• Pupils: 270 Mixed; Day Pupils • Age: 2 to 7
• Religion: Non-denominational • School status: State

SEN provision

Detail:

Now provide for in school:

Mild: AUT; ADD; ADHD; EBD; DYSC; DYSL; DYSP; SpLD; HI; VI;
Moderate: EBD; MLD; DYSC; DYSL; DYSP; SpLD; CP;
Severe: DYSC; DYSL; DYSP; SpLD;
Others: GEN; EAL; MSI; Sp&LD; DEL; Epi; PD

Experience of:

Mild: ASP; DS; CP;
Moderate: ASP; AUT; ADD; ADHD; HI; VI;
Severe: AUT; ADD; ADHD; EBD; HI;
Others: SPD; AUT(other); FRX

Summary: At Burhill School we are committed to offering an inclusive curriculum to ensure the best possible progress of all our pupils whatever their needs or abilities.

The school is committed to early identification of special educational need and adopts a graduated response to meeting special educational need in line with the Code of Practice 2002.

Burstow Primary School

Wheelers Lane, Smallfield, Horley, Surrey, RH6 9PT

Tel: 01342 842 010
Fax: 01342 842 935
Email: info@burstow.surrey.sch.uk

• Pupils: 377 Mixed; Day Pupils • Age: 4 to 11
• Religion: Non-denominational • School status: State

SEN provision

Detail:

Now provide for in school:

Mild: AUT; ADD; ADHD; EBD; VI; CP;
Moderate: ADD; ADHD; EBD; MLD;
Severe: ADD; ADHD;
Others: Sp&LD

Experience of:

Mild: ASP; DS; DYSC; DYSL; DYSP; SpLD; HI;
Moderate: AUT; DYSC; DYSL; HI;
Severe: EBD;
Others: SPD; CD; OCD; ODD; SLD; EAL; DEL; PD; Oth; Eat

Summary: Burstow School has a history of providing access and support to all children regardless of their disability. We can draw on a wide pool of expertise from outside agencies. We have close contacts with the Pupil Referral Unit and have children attending on a part-time basis.

We have several children with Attention Deficit Disorder, Attention Deficit/Hyperactivity Disorder and some experience with Oppositional Defiant Disorder. In all cases we attempt to integrate the children into the classroom, providing support over and above the allocated amount. We also include many Traveller children.

living in the area or passing through and have the support of the Traveller Education Service for these children.

CALDER HOUSE SCHOOL

Thickwood Lane, Colerne, Chippenham, Wiltshire, SN14 8BN

Tel: 01225 742 329
Fax: 01225 742 329
Email: headmistress@calderhouseschool.co.uk
Website: www.calderhouseschool.sagenet.co.uk

• Pupils: 50 Mixed; Day Pupils • Age: 5 to 12
• School status: Independent

SEN provision

Detail:
Centre of excellence for:
Mild: DYSL; DYSP;
Moderate: DYSL; DYSP;
Severe: DYSL;
Others: DEL
Now provide for in school:
Mild: ASP; ADD; ADHD; EBD; DYSC; SpLD; HI; VI;
Moderate: ADD; ADHD; DYSC; SpLD;
Severe: DYSC; DYSP;
Others: SPD; EAL; Sp&LD
Experience of:
Mild: CP;
Others: Epi; PD

Summary: Calder House School provides a whole school learning environment for pupils who in mainstream education have been unable to achieve their full potential. Every child has an individual learning programme tailored to deliver the support required, but has access to the full National Curriculum so that they will have 'missed' nothing when they return to mainstream education. Our team of specialist teachers is augmented by our speach and language therapist and consultant occupational therapist. We have a maximum class size of eight and a staff pupil ratio of 1:4 or better. Pupils are timetabled for their one-to-one individual suport sessions so that class teaching is not missed. Our literacy and numeracy lessons are arranged so that pupils work with children at a similar level and this is kept under constant review. Above all we are a happy school, where children are encouraged to value themselves and trust their teachers. Our fees are all inclusive. Our pupils are usually ready to return to mainstream within three years of joining us: and they keep in touch to tell us of their successes.

CALTHORPE SCHOOL SPORTS COLLEGE

Darwin Street, Highgate, Birmingham, West Midlands, B12 0TJ

Tel: 0121 773 4637
Fax: 0121 773 0708
Email: enquiry@calthorpe.bham.sch.uk
Website: www.calthorpe.bham.sch.uk

• Pupils: 270 Mixed; Day Pupils • Age: 2 to 19
• Religion: Non-denominational • School status: State

SEN provision

Detail:
Experience of:
Mild: ADHD; DYSC; DYSL; DYSP; HI; VI; CP;
Moderate: ADD; ADHD; DS; DYSC; DYSL; DYSP; HI; VI; CP;
Severe: ADD; ADHD; DS; DYSC; DYSL; DYSP; HI; VI; CP;
Others: SPD; TIC; FRX; PMLD; SLD; EAL; MSI; Sp&LD; DEL; Epi; Eat

Summary: We are a specialist sports college. School caters for pupils with severe/profound, complex needs, autism and sensory difficulties. Our well qualified and experienced team have the capacity to support the needs of students utilising the exceptional facilites at the school. Satellite provision is provided in mainstream secondary and colleges of FE.

Cambridge Centre for Sixth-form Studies

1 Salisbury Villas, Station Road, Cambridge, Cambridgeshire, CB1 2JF

Tel: 01223 716 890
Fax: 01223 517 530
Email: enquiries@ccss.co.uk
Website: www.ccss.co.uk

• Pupils: 169 Mixed; Takes boarders • Age: 20
• School status: Independent

SEN provision

Detail:
Now provide for in school:
Mild: ASP; ADD; ADHD; EBD; DYSC; DYSL; DYSP; HI; VI;
Moderate: ADD; DYSC; DYSL; DYSP; HI

Summary: We specialise in years 11,12,13. Therefore we expect the students we take to have backgrounds and capabilities which offer reasonable prospects of success in GCSE, AS, A2 exams. However, our small class size (maximum 8), the one-to-one element in all our sixth-from teaching and a pastoral system based on individual rather than form-group work, enable us to give a lot of support to students with difficulties. We can't however help in cases where behaviour or impairment is such that the student's needs make it significantly less feasible to provide good education to each member of a teaching group.

Camphill Rudolf Steiner Schools

Central Office, Murtle House, Bieldside, Aberdeen, AB15 9EP

Tel: 01224 867 935
Fax: 01224 868 420
Email: office@crss.org.uk
Website: www.camphillschools.org.uk

• Pupils: 88 Mixed; Takes boarders • Age: 3 to 19
• Religion: Non-denominational • School status: Independent

SEN provision

Summary: The Camphill-Rudolf Steiner-School is an independent voluntary school situated on three estates beside the River Dee on the outskirts of Aberdeen. The school offers residential places for full term or weekly boarders as well as day places for local pupils. The school year covers 40 weeks over 4 terms.

Camphill offers an inclusive, comprehensive holistic education programme known as 'Curative Education' for 88 pupils with complex special needs ranging from deprivation to autism from the age of 3 to 19 years. For pupils aged 16-19 years there is an Extended Schooling Programme which offers a more individualised programme geared towards graduation and preparation for the future. Cairnlee House offers further training for 12 young adults from 16-25 years. Pupils are generally funded by their local authority.

All pupils whether day or residential, belong to a life-sharing House Community which is made up of groups of one to two pupils cared for by a co-worker who guides the pupils in his/her personal care and a number of co-workers who also live in the house. In School, classes are generally grouped according to age, using the Waldorf Curriculum based on guidelines formulated by Rudolf Steiner, which encompass the Scottish 5-14 Guidelines.

In addition individual therapies are given to meet the specific needs of the pupils. Older pupils participate in a variety of craft workshops.

As part of its commitment to training, the school offers co-workers a Foundation Year and, to successful applicants, a chance to participate in the four-year BA Programme in Curative Education run in partnership with Aberdeen University.

The School is accredited with the National Autistic Society and registered with the Scottish Care Commission.

CARDIFF HIGH SCHOOL

Llandennis Road, Roath Park, Cyncoed, Cardiff, CF23 6WG

Tel: 029 2075 7741
Fax: 029 2068 0850
Email: D.Macho@cardiff.gov.uk
Website: www.cardiffhigh.cardiff.sch.uk

• Pupils: 1403 Mixed; Day Pupils • Age: 11 to 18
• Religion: Non-denominational • School status: State

SEN provision

Detail:
Experience of:
Mild: ASP; ADD; ADHD; EBD; DYSC; DYSL; DYSP; HI; VI; CP;
Moderate: ASP; ADD; ADHD; EBD; MLD; DYSC; DYSL; DYSP; HI; CP;
Severe: DYSL;
Others: FRX; EAL; Sp&LD; Epi

Summary: SEN provision at Cardiff High School is in line with the SEN Code of Practice and the LEA Guidance Criteria. Pupils receive a staged approach to help meet their needs which includes a Literacy Intervention programme, paired learning with year 12 students and extra literacy and numeracy sessions. A key element of the provision involves Learning Support Assistants who are able to offer in-class support for a variety of lessons in years 7 and 8. The learning support department prides itself on its open-door policy for pupils and teaching staff. There is also close liaison with parents and pastoral staff. The Learning Support area is available for any pupil at lunchtime with homework and computer clubs. After school sessions are available. Option subjects are offered in years 9, 10 and 11 and these are very popular. At present there are 88 pupils following the Learning Skills option in year 9 and 65 in Learning Support in Key Stage 4. The Cardiff LEA Specific Learning Difficulties Resource Base for 12 statemented dyslexic pupils is housed in Cardiff High School. More information on this provision is available from Cardiff LEA or the school.

CARNBOOTH SCHOOL

Carnbooth House, Carmunnock, Glasgow, G76 9EG

Tel: 01416 442 773
Fax: 01416 443 136
Email: carnbooth@sen.glasgow.sch.uk

• Pupils: 13 Mixed; Day Pupils • Age: 2 to 18
• Religion: Non-denominational • School status: State

SEN provision

Detail:
Experience of:
Mild: HI; VI; CP;
Moderate: AUT; HI; VI;
Severe: EBD; HI; VI;
Others: CD; OCD; GEN; PMLD; SLD; MSI; Sp&LD; Epi; PD; Eat

Summary: Carnbooth School was established in 1985 to offer day and residential facilities for children with dual sensory impairment in varying degrees and who have been assessed as requiring special education.

The present roll is 13, some of whom are day pupils and some residential according to their individual educational needs. We aim to be flexible in our support of every child and young person. For example, a split placement may best meet the needs of the individual pupil, with part of the week in Carnbooth and part in another educational establishment.

Parents should note that the working capacity of the school may vary dependent upon the number of pupils at each stage and the way in which classes are organised.

Carnbooth School is in a magnificent two storey villa within its own grounds, situated in the city of Glasgow just west of Carmunnock village.

Resident children each have their own room and the school has a comprehensive range of educational and leisure facilities including activity rooms, gymnasium, sound perception room, ultra-violet/dark room, dining/kitchen areas.

There is a facility within the school for parents to stay overnight if necessary.

The school has a non-denominational status. Within the school we aim to foster an atmosphere of love, trust and mutual respect.

Carrongrange School

Carrongrange Avenue, Larbert, Stenhousemuir, FK5 3BH

Tel: 01324 555 266
Fax: 01324 503 555
Email: carrongrangeschool@falkirk.gov.uk
Website: www.falkirk.gov.uk

• Pupils: 152 Mixed; Day Pupils • Age: 5 to 18
• Religion: Non-denominational • School status: State

SEN provision

Detail:
Now provide for in school:
- Mild: AUT; DS;
- Moderate: AUT; DS; MLD;
- Severe: AUT; DS;
- Others: FRX; PMLD; SLD

Experience of:
- Mild: ASP; ADD; ADHD; EBD; DYSC; DYSL; DYSP; HI; VI; CP;
- Moderate: ASP; ADD; ADHD; EBD; DYSC; DYSL; DYSP; HI; VI; CP;
- Severe: ASP; ADD; ADHD; EBD; DYSC; DYSL; DYSP; HI; VI; CP;
- Others: SPD; AUT(other); CD; OCD; ODD; TIC; EAL; MSI; Sp&LD; DEL; Epi

Summary: Carrongrange School is a non-denominational special school, which offers provision to pupils with moderate to severe learning difficulties. The school presently has a roll of 150 pupils aged from 10-18 years. The primary department currently has 13 pupils on the roll, the secondary 137. The school aims to provide a high quality service where the individual needs of every pupil are met through an appropriate curriculum. Here the pupils have the opportunity to work in first-class surroundings with well equipped classrooms, library and sport facilities and we continue to develop state-of-the-art facilities in computer technology.

Carter Community Sports College

Blandford Close, Hamworthy, Poole, Dorset, BH15 4BQ

Tel: 01202 676 789
Fax: 01202 670 822
Email: cartercommunitycollege@poole.gov.uk
Website: www.carter.poole.sch.uk

• Pupils: 441 Mixed; Day Pupils • Age: 12 to 16
• Religion: Non-denominational • School status: State

SEN provision

Summary: Carter Community Sports College is committed to providing equal opportunities for all students to access a broad and balanced curriculum.

Support is provided in all areas of the curriculum through small teaching groups, teaching assistants and individual tuition. Work is differentiated to enable all students to access the curriculum and to achieve their academic potential. Close links are maintained with educational support agencies and the 'Code of Practice' guides our decision making in all matters relating to educational needs.

Strategies for addressing the needs of our students are agreed in either individual education plans or Pastoral Support Plans. These plans usually involve a number of professional bodies and the support of parents is paramount to their success. We recognise the views, experiences and knowledge of parents are vital when addressing special educational needs and close contact between home and the school is encouraged.

The school employs a specialist teacher, who withdraws pupils from lessons to provide intensive support with literacy.

For further information on special needs provision, contact Miss J Caldwell, special educational needs co-ordinator.

THE CASTLE SCHOOL

Love Lane, Donnington, Newbury, Berkshire, RG14 2JG

Tel: 0163 542 976
Fax: 01635 551 725
Email: Office.castle@westberks.org
Website: www.castle.westberks.org

• Pupils: 140 Mixed; Day Pupils • Age: 2 to 19
• Religion: Non-denominational • School status: State

SEN provision

Detail:
Now provide for in school:
Mild: ASP; AUT; ADD; ADHD; DS; VI; CP;
Moderate: ASP; AUT; ADD; ADHD; DS; CP;
Severe: ASP; AUT; DS; CP;
Others: SPD; AUT(other); FRX; PMLD; SLD; MSI; Sp&LD; Epi; PD; Eat
Experience of:
Mild: EBD; DYSL; DYSP; SpLD; HI;
Moderate: EBD; MLD; DYSL; DYSP; SpLD; HI; VI;
Severe: ADHD;
Others: CD; OCD; ODD; TIC; DEL

Summary: The Castle School is a West Berkshire Education Authority Special School. It is a mixed day school which takes pupils, between the ages of 2 and 19, who have a wide range of educational needs. Our Nursery class is co-located to Victoria Park Nursery, spending time at The Castle School two afternoons per week to use the specialist facilities.

The Castle School is resourced by the Local Education Authority to provide education for 15 pupils with ASD who need a higher staffing ratio and a more intensive programme than others. At the present time there are 21 pupils who have a diagnosis of Autistic Spectrum Disorder recorded on their statement of special educational needs and 13 pupils are in the 'Resourced classes'.

CASTLE VIEW SCHOOL

Cartwright Road, Hylton Castle, Sunderland, Tyne and Wear, SR5 3DX

Tel: 01915 535 533
Fax: 01915 535 537
Email: castle.view@schools.sunderland.gov.uk
Website: www.pftp.org.uk/castleviews/

• Pupils: 937 Mixed; Day Pupils • Age: 11 to 16
• Religion: Non-denominational • School status: State

SEN provision

Detail:
Now provide for in school:
Mild: ASP; AUT; ADD; ADHD; EBD; DYSC; DYSL; DYSP; HI; VI; CP;
Moderate: EBD; MLD; HI; VI; CP;
Severe: HI;
Others: SPD; DEL; Epi; Eat
Experience of:
Mild: DS;
Moderate: ASP; AUT; ADD; ADHD; DS; DYSC; DYSL; DYSP;
Others: AUT(other); OCD; ODD; TIC; PMLD; EAL; Sp&LD; PD

Summary: Castle View School has a large number of students who are currently on the SEN register – around 28 per cent of its students on roll. Many students experience difficulty with literacy and numeracy skills which makes it difficult for them to access the curriculum.

In-class support is allocated to students to assist with their reading and comprehension skills. Students are sometimes withdrawn to work in small groups on the work being covered within the class to help consolidate the concepts being covered. Students are then returned to the class to build upon their subject knowledge and develop their skills.

Those students who experience severe literacy skills are taught for several periods a week in a small group situation where intensive help is given with phonic and word building skills. Particular focus is given to develop confidence and raise self esteem and confidence with these students. Corrective Reading is taught to non-readers and those with exceptionally weak literacy skills. A morning reading club is also available for less able readers where year 10 pupils act as mentors and encourage reading skills.

The learning support department offers a wide range of help and support to all students within the school. Support staff have developed excellent working relationships with students of all ages and offer help and advice to students throughout their school career. Staff within the department offer a wide range of lunchtime activities to encourage student participation and development of confidence and self esteem.

Castledon School

Bromfords Drive, Wickford, Essex, SS12 0PW

Tel: 01268 761 252

Fax: 01268 571 861

Email: admin@castledon.essex.sch.uk

Website: www.castledon.essex.sch.uk

• Pupils: 92 Mixed; Day Pupils • Age: 5 to 16

• Religion: Non-denominational • School status: State

SEN provision

Detail:

Now provide for in school:

Mild: ASP; AUT; ADD; ADHD; EBD; DS; DYSL; DYSP;

Moderate: ASP; AUT; ADD; ADHD; EBD; DS; MLD; DYSL; DYSP;

Severe: ASP; AUT; ADD; ADHD; DS;

Others: AUT(other); CD; OCD; ODD; TIC; Sp&LD; Epi;

Experience of:

Mild: DYSC; CP;

Moderate: DYSC;

Severe: DYSC;

Others: FRX; SLD

Summary: An outreach school catering for pupils with moderate learning difficulties, with a number of pupils educated part-time in mainstream.

The Causeway School

Larkspur Drive, Eastbourne, East Sussex, BN23 8EJ

Tel: 01323 465 700

Fax: 01323 740 097

Email: office@causeway.e-sussex.sch.uk

Website: www.causeway.e-sussex.sch.uk

• Pupils: 837 Mixed; Day Pupils • Age: 11 to 16

• Religion: Non-denominational • School status: State

SEN provision

Detail:

Now provide for in school:

Mild: ASP; AUT; ADD; ADHD; EBD; DS; DYSC; DYSL; DYSP; SpLD; VI; CP;

Moderate: ASP; ADD; ADHD; EBD; DS; MLD; DYSC; DYSL; DYSP; VI; CP;

Severe: DYSL; CP;

Others: SPD; CD; OCD; ODD; TIC; Sp&LD; Epi; Eat;

Summary: The Causeway School is co-located with Hazel Court Special School. It first opened its door to students in September 2000. It has modern facilities and shares its canteen, library and school hall with the students from Hazel Court. The co-location has brought benefits for students in both schools, with students having the opportunities to share their learning and take part in joint creative projects, including a week in Spain in year seven. Spanish is the modern foreign language taught at the school. The school operates an inclusive policy and aims to meet the individual needs of all its students. In September 2005 the school adopted a 'pathways' curriculum which provides extra support for students working below or towards recommended National Curriculum levels. It enables a more varied curriculum for selected students at Key Stage 4 that includes Work Experience and Increased Flexibility Courses at the local Further Education colleges, whilst still studying at school to achieve GCSEs in core subjects. The school has an inclusion unit that provides support for both learning and behavioural difficulties. SEN support at the school is delivered through a differentiated curriculum, in-class support, one-to-one and group withdrawal from lessons to attend specific programmes and mentoring. Students with Statements are supported in lessons by teaching assistants, ranging from full-time support to specifical targeted support depending on need.

CEDAR HALL SCHOOL

Hart Road, Thundersley, Benfleet, Essex, SS7 3UQ

Tel: 01268 774 723
Fax: 01268 776 604
Email: admin@cedarhall.essex.sch.uk
Website: www.cedarhall.essex.sch.uk

• Pupils: 124 Mixed; Day Pupils • Age: 4 to 16
• Religion: Non-denominational • School status: State

SEN provision

Detail:
Now provide for in school:
Mild: ASP; AUT; ADD; DS; DYSC; DYSL; DYSP; CP;
Moderate: ASP; AUT; ADD; DS; MLD; DYSC; DYSL; DYSP;
Severe: DYSL;
Others: FRX; Sp&LD
Experience of:
Mild: EBD; HI;
Moderate: ADHD; EBD; SpLD; HI;
Severe: ADD; DS; DYSC; SpLD;
Others: OCD; ODD; TIC; EAL; DEL; Epi

Summary: Cedar Hall School is an Essex LEA school which provides education for pupils aged between 5 and 16 who primarily experience global moderate learning difficulties but who may experience speech, language, emotional, behavioural, or autistic spectrum secondary disabilities.

CEDAR HOUSE SCHOOL

Kendal Road, Kirkby Lonsdale, Carnforth, Lancs, LA6 2HW

Tel: 01524 271 181
Fax: 01524 271 910
Email: schooloffice@cedarhouseadmin.co.uk
Website: www.cedarhouseschool.co.uk

• Pupils: 68 Mixed; Takes boarders • Age: 7 to 16
• School status: Independent

SEN provision

Detail:
Centre of excellence for:
Mild: EBD;
Moderate: EBD; MLD;
Severe: EBD;
Others: CD; ODD
Now provide for in school:
Mild: ASP; AUT; ADD; ADHD; DYSC; DYSL; DYSP; SpLD; HI; CP;
Moderate: ASP; ADD; ADHD; DYSC; DYSL; DYSP; SpLD;
Severe: ADD; ADHD; SpLD;
Others: SPD; OCD; TIC; Sp&LD; Epi
Experience of:
Mild: VI;
Moderate: AUT;
Severe: ASP; DYSP;
Others: AUT(other); SLD; DEL; PD; Eat

Summary: Cedar House School is an independent residential special school for pupils with social, emotional and behavioural difficulties. The school caters for both boys and girls and also admits day pupils from the local area. The school has excellent facilities to meet both the social and educational needs of children.

The ethos of the school supports the provision of a safe, secure and caring environment within which personal growth and development is promoted.

The school provides access to the National Curriculum and a range of examinations are offered at GCSE and Entry Level alongside alternative external accreditation.

The school is regularly inspected by client LEAs, CSCI, Ofsted and by our parent company; Witherslack Group of Schools, and has a successful record of inspection in all areas.

Chailey Heritage School

Haywards Heath Road, North Chailey, Lewes, East Sussex, BN8 4EF

Tel: 01825 724 444
Fax: 01825 723 773
• Pupils: 94 Mixed; Takes boarders • Age: 3 to 19
• School status: State

SEN provision

Summary: The ability to express ourselves, even to give a simple 'yes'or 'no' is something we all take for granted. At Chailey Heritage School, children whose active minds would otherwise be trapped by physical disability are enabled to communicate even though they can't talk, and to get around using specially adapted wheelchairs thanks to its committed team of technicians.

Chailey Heritage School caters for up to 100 of the most seriously disabled children in the country. It provides a stimulating and enjoyable learning environment for children with complex physical disabilities who, with the help of a dedicated team of teachers, care staff, support staff and volunteers, are able to reach their potential and enjoy an enhanced quality of life.

The school is unique in that it provides the whole package. Education, nursing and medical care on site from a team of top paediatricians, therapists and nurses from the South Downs Health Trust, working within the school. This partnership allows the school to develop and implement tailored learning programmes for each child, who range in age from 2 years to 19.

It also provides respite for parents in the form of a 'sleep-over' where the children can stay overnight with other children of their own age. Most of these youngsters require 24 hour care and help with just about all aspects of every-day life, so parents can't ask family or friends to step in when they need a break.

The school in Chailey, near Lewes, was founded in 1903 by Dame Grace Kimmins, a pioneer of education for children suffering from rickets, TB and even malnutrition.

Today the disabilities and associated learning difficulties are much more complex; few of the pupils can talk or walk and most have minimal use of arms and hands. Whilst the majority of children suffer from cerebral palsy, some of these youngsters have been involved in road traffic and other tragic accidents.

The school, which is nationally recognised and non-maintained, is also at the forefront of dual-placement in education which enables some pupils to attend part-time at their local school.

Challney High School for Girls

Stoneygate Road, Luton, Bedfordshire, LU4 9TJ

Tel: 01582 571 427
Fax: 01582 490 133
Email: challney.high.girls.admin@luton.gov.uk
Website: www.challneygirls.luton.sch.uk
• Pupils: 901 Girls; Day Pupils • Age: 11 to 16
• Religion: Non-denominational • School status: State

SEN provision

Detail:
Now provide for in school:
  Mild: EBD; DYSL; HI;
  Moderate: EBD; MLD; HI; VI;
  Severe: EBD;
  Others: OCD; SLD; Epi; PD
Experience of:
  Mild: DS

Summary: Support for pupils with additional or different needs is provided by the support team which includes learning, language and behaviour support and is strategically managed by the pupil support manager who is an assistant headteacher. Within the support team, learning support is co-ordinated by the learning support co-ordinator. The learning support department consists of two part-time (0.5) teachers and eight teaching assistants. The behaviour support department is co-ordinated by the behaviour support co-ordinator who works with two full-time teaching assistants. For the most part, support for pupils with special educational needs, both learning and behaviour, takes place within mainstream lessons, although both departments benefit from their own dedicated classroom for withdrawal purposes where specialist programmes can be delivered. The school is committed to the employment of higher level teaching assistants.

Charleton Church of England Primary School

West Charleton, Kingsbridge, Devon, TQ7 2AL

Tel: 01548 531 275
Fax: 01548 531 275
Email: admin@charleton-primary.devon.sch.uk
Website: www.charleton-primary.devon.sch.uk

• Pupils: 48 Mixed; Day Pupils • Age: 4 to 11
• Religion: Church of England • School status: State

SEN provision

Detail:
Centre of excellence for:
  Mild: AUT;
  Moderate: AUT
Now provide for in school:
  Mild: ASP; EBD; DYSC; DYSL; DYSP; VI;
  Moderate: ASP; EBD; DYSC; DYSL; DYSP; HI;
  Severe: AUT; DYSL; DYSP;
  Others: Sp&LD
Experience of:
  Mild: HI;
  Others: SPD; AUT(other); CD; Epi; Eat

Summary: A small supportive rural school with expertise amongst the learning support assistants in Autistic Spectrum disorders, dyspraxia, communication difficulites etc. The school prides itself on its work in building positive relationships for all children and uses such approaches as 'circle of friends', nurture groups etc. Headteacher has a background in assessment and language unit work.

Chatham Grammar School for Boys

Holcombe, Maidstone Road, Chatham, Kent, ME4 6JB

Tel: 01634 830 083
Fax: 01634 826 230
Email: info@cgsb.co.uk
Website: www.cgsb.medway.sch.uk

• Pupils: 992 Boys; Day Pupils • Age: 11 to 18
• Religion: Non-denominational • School status: State

SEN provision

Detail:
Now provide for in school:
  Mild: ASP; ADD; ADHD; EBD; DYSC; DYSL; DYSP;
  Moderate: ASP; ADD; ADHD;
  Others: SPD; TIC; EAL; Epi

Summary: Depending on the individual needs of a student, we are able to offer limited in-class support, or one-to-one outside the classroom, if timetabling allows. We currently work with a variety of needs across the whole school from years 7 to 13, including Asperger's syndrome, Visual Impairment, ADHD, Semantic pragmatic language disorder, Dyslexia, Dyspraxia and Tourette's syndrome. We have a small SEN team who are committed to the care of our students and work hard to develop a good working relationship with them, sharing and celebrating their successes.

Chatham Grammar School for Girls

Rainham Road, Chatham, Kent, ME5 7EH

Tel: 01634 851 262
Fax: 01634 571 928
Email: office@chathamgirlsgrammar.medway.sch.uk
Website: www.chathamgirlsgrammar.medway.sch.uk

• Pupils: 958 Girls; Day Pupils • Age: 11 to 18
• Religion: Non-denominational • School status: State

SEN provision

Detail:
Now provide for in school:
Mild: ASP; EBD; DYSL; DYSP;
Moderate: EBD;
Others: SPD; EAL; Epi; PD; Eat
Experience of:
Mild: DYSC;
Moderate: DYSL

Summary: Currently the school is providing SEN provision for individuals who experience a wide variety of barriers to learning. These barriers include: mild Asperger's syndrome; Semantic pragmatic disorders; mild Dyslexia and Dyspraxia; mild and moderate Emotional and Behavioural difficulties; English not being the students' first language; and medical related needs, for example Spinal Muscular Atrophy, Eating disorders and Epilepsy.

In addition, the school has very good provisions for physically disabled individuals. There is a lift in each building which has more than one floor and wheelchair access into every building on the school site. Furthermore, the school has provisions in place for 'gifted and talented' students.

At present we do not have provisions for individuals who experience moderate to severe ADD; ADHD; or moderate to severe learning difficulties; sensory impairments (i.e. severe hearing or visual impairments); or for children whose medical needs are related to Cerebral Palsy.

The SENCo at the school oversees the SEN provisions. The school also employs three Learning Support Assistants and has staff trained in first aid.

Chelfham Mill School

Chelfham, Barnstaple, Devon, EX32 7LA

Tel: 01271 850 448
Fax: 01271 850 235
Email: enquiries@chelfhammillschool.co.uk

• Pupils: 48 Boys; Takes boarders • Age: 6 to 13
• School status: Independent

SEN provision

Detail:
Now provide for in school:
Mild: ASP; AUT; ADD; ADHD; EBD; DYSL; DYSP; VI;
Moderate: ASP; AUT; ADD; ADHD; EBD; MLD; DYSL; DYSP;
Severe: ADD; ADHD; EBD; DYSL;
Others: CD; OCD; ODD; TIC; Sp&LD; Epi
Experience of:
Mild: DYSC; HI;
Moderate: DYSC; HI; VI;
Severe: DYSP;
Others: SPD; FRX; GEN; PD; Eat

Summary: Chelfham Mill opened in 1966 as a residential school, with some day places for boys aged 7 to 13+. The Mill, still a school but also a registered Children's Home, is open 52 weeks of the year although some boys only attend in term time. Chelfham has always been special, educating and providing a holistic approach to childcare and a range of therapeutic options.

Chelmsford College

Moulsham Street, Chelmsford, Essex, CM2 0JQ

Tel: 01245 265 611
Fax: 01245 266 908
Email: information@chelmsford-college.ac.uk
Website: www.chelmsford-college.ac.uk

• Pupils: 1631 Mixed; Day Pupils • Age: 16 to 99
• Religion: Non-denominational • School status: State

SEN provision

Detail:

Now provide for in school:

Mild: ASP; AUT; ADD; ADHD; EBD; DS; DYSC; DYSL; DYSP; SpLD; HI; VI; CP;

Moderate: ASP; AUT; ADD; ADHD; EBD; DS; MLD; DYSC; DYSL; DYSP; SpLD; HI; VI; CP;

Severe: DS; DYSL;

Others: SPD; AUT(other); CD; FRX; SLD; EAL; Sp&LD; Epi; PD

Summary: Discrete provision for young people with learning difficulties and disabilities in the college is provided in three full-time courses.

Starting Out

This course covers a range of activities covering independence skills, social education and practical skills. It is a course designed for young people who have moderate or severe learning difficulties. Learners take part in a range of activities to suit their individual needs. They work at their own pace and have the assistance of dedicated learning support staff in the class and at break times. Students record their achievements by collecting a portfolio of their work which is accredited through ASDAN.

The Bridge Course

This course is designed for young people with mild to moderate learning difficulties and is offered at Entry Level. The learners study a range of subjects to help them develop their personal skills. This includes preparation for work and independent living skills. Learners may attend a work experience placement as part of their studies. The course offers young people the opportunity to improve their essential skills in the areas of literacy, numeracy and IT. Learners are assessed through Edexcel Skills for Life or Edexcel Skills for Working Life. They also take the national tests in literacy and numeracy. Learning support is offered in every class according to student need.

Foundation for Work

This course is designed for young people with mild to moderate learning difficulties. The course offers young people the opportunity to improve their essential skills in the areas of literacy, numeracy and IT. Learners will study a range of subjects designed to help them prepare for the world of work. It is expected that learners will undertake a work experience placement as part of their studies. Learners' work will be accredited through C&G Entry Level Certificate in Preparing for Employment (3797). They will also take national tests in literacy and numeracy. Learning support is offered in every class according to student need. By providing a wide range of learning support the college can offer opportunites for young people with special educational needs within its mainstream provision. Please contact us for further advice and guidance on any specific issue.

CHERRY TREE PRIMARY SCHOOL AND NURSERY

Church Road, Basildon, Essex, SS16 4AG

Tel: 01268 523 017

Fax: 01268 534 784

Email: admin@cherrytree-pri.essex.sch.uk

• Pupils: 362 Mixed; Day Pupils • Age: 3 to 11

• Religion: Non-denominational • School status: State

SEN provision

Detail:

Now provide for in school:

Mild: AUT; ADD; ADHD; EBD; DYSC; DYSL; DYSP; HI; VI;

Moderate: AUT; ADD; ADHD; EBD; MLD; DYSC; DYSL; DYSP;

Severe: ADD; ADHD; EBD; DYSL; DYSP;

Others: Sp&LD; PD

Experience of:

Mild: ASP;

Moderate: HI; VI;

Severe: DYSC;

Others: CD; OCD; TIC; PMLD; SLD; EAL; Epi

Summary: We have a high number of pupils in our school with SEN, who have a wide range of needs. As such we have a lot of staff dedicated to supporting the needs of SEN pupils. We try, as much as possible, to support a pupil's needs within the classroom and through the curriculum. We work closely with a wide range of outside agencies to ensure that we are providing our children with appropriate support. We receive good support from the educational psychology service and work with them to identify barriers to children's learning, which we then strive to overcome.

We believe in early identification and have a school system for teachers to identify concerns which we can then address before a child would need to go on the special needs register. We have a number of staff in school who work on boosting these children, so that they can make good educational progress. Staff in our nursery and reception classes also liaise with health professionals who identify children with difficulties before they enter into school, therefore allowing us to gain extra support for these children from appropriate agencies.

Chessington Community College

Garrison Lane, Chessington, Surrey, KT9 2JS

Tel: 020 8974 1156
Fax: 020 8974 2603
Email: ccc@rbksch.org
Website: www.cc.kingston.sch.uk

• Pupils: 720 Mixed; Day Pupils • Age: 11 to 18
• Religion: Non-denominational • School status: State

SEN provision

Detail:
Now provide for in school:
Mild: ASP; DYSL;
Moderate: ASP; MLD; DYSL;
Severe: DYSL;
Others: SPD; EAL; Sp&LD
Experience of:
Mild: ADD; ADHD; EBD; DYSC; DYSP; HI; VI;
Moderate: ADD; ADHD; EBD; DYSC; DYSP;
Severe: ADD; ADHD; EBD; DYSC; DYSP;
Others: CD; TIC; PD

Summary: The college has a comprehensive intake but with a high proportion of students with low attainment in reading and writing skills. The large number of students with statements allows for a more extensive than usual amount of in-class support in the core and foundation subjects. There is an effective reading programme for those whose reading does not allow them to access a secondary curriculum. There is small group teaching for spelling, handwriting, basic numeracy, behaviour management, speech and language difficulties and social skills.

Chipping Norton School

Burford Road, Chipping Norton, Oxfordshire, OX7 5DY

Tel: 01608 642 007
Fax: 01608 644 530
Email: Headteacher.4010@chipping-norton.oxon.sch.uk

• Pupils: 1103 Mixed; Day Pupils • Age: 11 to 18
• Religion: Non-denominational • School status: State

SEN provision

Detail:
Centre of excellence for:
Mild: DYSL;
Moderate: MLD; DYSL
Now provide for in school:
Mild: ASP; AUT; ADD; ADHD; EBD; DYSC; DYSP; HI; CP;
Moderate: ASP; EBD; DYSC; DYSP; HI

Summary: At Chipping Norton School we strive to ensure that every pupil fulfils his or her potential both through examinations and as rounded individuals with the social skills and confidence to succeed in further education and the world of work. We have in recent years successfully included pupils with Hearing Impairment, Dyslexia, Dyspraxia, Asperger's, Emotional and Behavioral Difficulties, Physical difficulties and Moderate Learning Difficulties. Implicit in our success has been our effective partnership with outside agencies, with local special schools and most importantly with parents. We offer an appropriately differentiated curriculum to our SEN pupils in Key Stage 3 and a work related option in Key Stage 4 along with work experience and college placements to suit individual needs.

Chiswick Community School

Burlington Lane, Chiswick, London, W4 3UN

Tel: 020 8747 0031
Fax: 020 8747 6620
Email: enquiries@chiswick.hounslow.sch.uk
Website: www.chiswick.hounslow.sch.uk

• Pupils: 1253 Mixed; Day Pupils • Age: 11 to 18
• Religion: Non-denominational • School status: State

SEN provision

Detail:
Now provide for in school:
Mild: ASP; AUT; ADD; ADHD; EBD; DYSL; DYSP; CP;
Moderate: DYSL;
Others: ODD; EAL; Sp&LD; DEL; Epi; Eat
Experience of:
Mild: DYSC; HI

Summary: Chiswick School has a vibrant SEN faculty whose team works hard to address the vast range of needs presented by students. We feel strongly that every child has a right to experience success and to be valued: raising self esteem is paramount. Pupils with SEN, be it emotional, behavioural, learning or social difficulties, receive good guidance and support from the SEN faculty, Learning Mentors, Behaviour and Education Support Teams (BEST) and Behaviour Improvement Programme (BIP) teams, EAL staff and the learning support unit. Our aim is to support students whose difficulties impact upon their learning and impede progress. Pupils with learning difficulties are quickly assessed (by school staff or outside agencies) and supported in their learning. The needs of all these pupils are well known to all teachers via the SEN student booklet, keyworkers, the SEN register and liaison between support staff and other teachers. The Social Inclusion Panel is effective in deciding appropriate provision for each child and for including parents in the process. Parents are very much included in decision making where extra support needs to be provided. We feel that the learning culture for our students is good. We are committed to inclusion and want all students to feel valued. We run social skills, anger management, study skills and listening skills groups, among others, to help students enjoy a well rounded school experience. Most of our students have a positive attitude to learning and they seem to value the extra support provided. They have a desire to learn and achieve; this is illustrated by the number of students who come to the SEN homework club after school. Our faculty is stable and well-managed. The team has a genuine desire to help students and knows pupils' needs well. Staff take care to share their findings with other subject teachers to help maximise students' learning and planning is efficient. We have a friendly, dedicated team of teachers well-respected by the borough: for us, every child matters.

Christ Church Church of England High School

Millbank Road, Kingsnorth, Ashford, Kent, TN23 3HG

Tel: 01233 623 465
Fax: 01233 636 861
Email: headteacher@christ-church-ashford.kent.sch.uk

• Pupils: 1015 Mixed; Day Pupils • Age: 11 to 16
• Religion: Church of England • School status: State

SEN provision

Detail:
Centre of excellence for:
Mild: HI; CP;
Moderate: HI; CP;
Severe: HI; CP;
Others: DEL; Epi
Now provide for in school:
Mild: ASP; AUT; ADD; ADHD; EBD; DS; DYSC; DYSL; DYSP; VI;
Moderate: ASP; EBD; MLD; DYSC; DYSL; DYSP; VI;
Others: SPD; PMLD; EAL; Sp&LD; PD; Eat

Summary: Christ Church is a fully inclusive school. We are a school that has a designated unit for physically disabled pupils and one for hearing impaired pupils. The objective of the SEN department is to ensure that all pupils with special educational needs have access to a broad, balanced and relevant curriculum. These pupils may require additional resources and differentiation to ensure progress within the classroom. They are given every opportunity to be intergrated as fully as possible, both socially and educationally. Outside of the classroom they are also able to involve themselves to whatever extent they feel able to do so.

Currently we have Golden Curriculum groups in year 7, 8 and 9. These groups are for children who need additional support and 'nurturing' as most have multiple and complex special educational needs. Golden Curriculum groups are smaller in size than other teaching groups, they have highly differentiated schemes of work and teaching staff who are specifically trained in SEN.

Most SEN pupils cope well in the other teaching sets with differentiated work and support from teaching staff. All SEN pupils are monitored closely and have their work planned with their special educational needs in mind.

Christian Brothers' Grammar School

Kevlin Road, Omagh, Co Tyrone, BT78 1LD

Tel: 02882 243 567

Fax: 02882 240 656

Email: info@cbs.omagh.ni.sch.uk

• Pupils: 969 Boys; Day Pupils • Age: 11 to 18

• School status: State

SEN provision

Detail:

Now provide for in school:

Mild: EBD; DYSC; DYSL; DYSP; SpLD; HI; VI;

Moderate: HI; VI;

Severe: HI;

Others: Sp&LD

Summary: The key feature of our SEN provision is its flexibility. We feel we respond to the various needs of students by offering a range of flexible provision such as: classroom assistance, one-to-one withdrawal, small group withdrawal and a range of clubs and initiatives in key areas such as reading, spelling and handwriting. This ensures we can offer the best possible practical assistance in any student's particular area of strength or weakness.We make use of a range of baseline data such as Cognitive Abilities Testing to compile a profile of each student, carrying out further diagnostic testing and the type of provision mentioned above as the need arises.

Churchill Community College

Churchill Street, High Howdon, Wallsend, Tyne and Wear, NE28 7TN

Tel: 01912 007 260

Fax: 01912 007 264

Email: churchill.college@northtyneside.gov.uk

• Pupils: 1081 Mixed; Day Pupils • Age: 11 to 18

• Religion: Non-denominational • School status: State

SEN provision

Detail:

Now provide for in school:

Mild: ASP; ADD; ADHD; EBD; DYSC; DYSL; DYSP; HI; VI; CP;

Moderate: ADD; ADHD; EBD; DYSL; DYSP; SpLD; HI; VI; CP;

Severe: EBD; DYSL; CP;

Others: ODD; SLD; EAL; Sp&LD; DEL; Epi; PD; Eat

Experience of:

Mild: AUT;

Severe: ADD; ADHD;

Others: SPD; OCD; PMLD

Summary: Churchill College is committed to equality of opportunity and provides access to the National Curriculum for all students. We identify, through appropriate assessment, those students with special educational needs. We ensure that provision is effective in meeting these needs thus allowing the students to experience success and to feel that they are valued. We plan, organise and implement an appropiately modified curriculum where necessary. Those students, who are placed at School Action Plus, have detailed Pastoral Support Plans which are shared with all staff. All students with statements have individual education plans which are reviewed termly. Our recent Ofsted inspection acknowledged the ownership of SEN by everyone and that the majority of students had their needs met within the classroom. We were praised for our intervention programmes and the calibre of our teaching within the

SEN department. In addition our student support centre was rated as excellent in its provision for very difficult, disaffected and challenging students.

Cirencester Kingshill School

Kingshill Lane, Cirencester, Gloucestershire, GL7 1HS

Tel: 01285 651 511
Fax: 01285 885 652
Email: office@cirencesterkingshill.gloucs.sch.uk
Website: www.cirencesterkingshill.gloucs.sch.uk

• Pupils: 817 Mixed; Day Pupils • Age: 11 to 16
• Religion: Non-denominational • School status: State

SEN provision

Detail:
Now provide for in school:
Mild: ASP; AUT; ADD; ADHD; EBD; DYSC; DYSL; DYSP; SpLD; HI; CP;
Moderate: ASP; AUT; ADD; ADHD; EBD; MLD; DYSC; DYSL; DYSP; SpLD; HI; CP;
Severe: ASP; DYSL; DYSP; SpLD; HI; CP;
Others: SPD; GEN; PMLD; EAL; Sp&LD; DEL; Epi; PD; Eat

Summary: An intervention programme is available for Key Stage 3 pupils in English and maths. Reading and spelling groups are run. The Learning Support Department is open lunchtime so that any pupil can get help with skilled-based work and homework. There is also an after school homework club. All pupils receive targets which pupils and tutors agree.

We offer different types of support including general class support, support for statement pupils, literacy skill workshops, basic skill groups, key skill groups and study groups.

The Clare School

South Park Avenue, Norwich, Norfolk, NR4 7AU

Tel: 01603 454 199
Fax: 01603 451 317
Email: office@clare.norfolk.sch.uk

• Pupils: 94 Mixed; Day Pupils • Age: 3 to 19
• Religion: Non-denominational • School status: State

SEN provision

Detail:
Centre of excellence for:
Mild: HI; VI;
Moderate: HI; VI;
Severe: HI; VI;
Others: MSI; Sp&LD
Now provide for in school:
Mild: CP;
Moderate: MLD; CP;
Severe: CP;
Others: PMLD; SLD; DEL; Epi; PD; Eat

Summary: The Clare School is a mixed, day community special school for pupils, from 3 to 19 years of age, with special educational needs usually associated with physical disabilities and /or sensory impairment. Many of the pupils also have complex medical needs and learning difficulties associated with their physical or sensory disabilities. The school is located on the ring road to the south of the city and set in very pleasant grounds alongside a first and middle school.

Claremont School

Henleaze Park, Henleaze, Bristol, BS9 4LR

Tel: 0117 9247 527
Fax: 0117 9426 942
Email: claremont_sp@bristol-city.gov.uk
Website: www.claremont.bristol.sch.uk
• Pupils: 53 Mixed; Day Pupils • Age: 2 to 11
• Religion: Non-denominational • School status: State

SEN provision

Detail:
Centre of excellence for:
Mild: CP;
Moderate: CP;
Severe: CP;
Others: PMLD; MSI

Summary: Claremont School caters for children aged between 2 and 11 years old who have physical impairments and associated difficulties in learning. There are two strands within the school: one for children with Physical Impairments (PI) and one for children with Profound and Multiple Learning Difficulties (PMLD). Excellent resources and well developed expertise in working with PI and PMLD children ensure efficient and effective practice. In February 2005 Ofsted judged the school as 'Outstanding' and it had no Key Issues for improvement.

We also run an effective Outreach Service, which not only supports the transfer of children from Claremont to their local mainstream school, but also supports inclusive activities at the attached mainstream schools.

Clarendon House Grammar School

Clarendon Gardens, Ramsgate, Kent, CT11 9BB

Tel: 01843 591 074
Fax: 01843 851 824
Email: admin@clarendonhouse.kent.sch.uk
Website: www.clarendonhouse.kent.sch.uk
• Pupils: 799 Girls; Day Pupils • Age: 11 to 18
• Religion: Non-denominational • School status: State

SEN provision

Detail:
Now provide for in school:
Mild: EBD; HI;
Moderate: EBD; HI
Experience of:
Mild: ASP; AUT; DYSC; DYSL; DYSP; VI;
Moderate: MLD;
Severe: EBD;
Others: AUT(other); OCD; ODD; EAL; Epi; PD; Eat

Summary: Pupils who have specific learning needs are identified and supported through extra help in the classroom, or occasionally by withdrawal. Pupils with physical disabilities have access where needed to specialist equipment and extra support.

Cleveland College of Art and Design

Green Lane, Linthorpe, Middlesbrough, TS5 7RJ

Tel: 01642 288 000
Fax: 01642 288828
Email: student.recruitment@ccad.ac.uk
Website: www.ccad.ac.uk
• Pupils: 491 Mixed; Day Pupils • Age: 16 to 99
• Religion: Non-denominational • School status: State

SEN provision

Detail:
Now provide for in school:
- Mild: ADD; ADHD; EBD; DYSC; DYSL; DYSP; HI;
- Moderate: EBD; MLD; DYSC; DYSL; HI;
- Severe: DYSL; HI;
- Others: Sp&LD; Epi; Eat

Experience of:
- Mild: VI; CP;
- Moderate: DYSP

Summary: CCAD tries to offer appropriate support to learners with specific learning difficulties/disabilities wherever possible to enable success on a main course of study. One to one support is available from specialist lecturers to support individual student need. There are also classroom assistants to provide in class support where appropriate. The College aims to assess need prior to, or at entry either through disclosure of medical condition/learning difficulty/physical disability by the student, via interview and enrolment procedures and via screening such as Quickscan.

CLIFFDALE PRIMARY SCHOOL

Battenburg Avenue, North End, Portsmouth, Hampshire, PO2 0SN

Tel: 023 9266 2601
Fax: 023 9266 0506
Email: admin@cliffdale.portmouth.sch.uk
Website: www.cliffdale.portsmouth.sch.uk
• Pupils: 102 Mixed; Day Pupils • Age: 4 to 11
• Religion: Non-denominational • School status: State

SEN provision

Detail:
Experience of:
- Mild: EBD;
- Moderate: EBD;
- Severe: EBD

Summary: School caters for pupils with severe learning difficulties (SLD), moderate learning difficulties (MLD), autistic spectrum disorders (ASD), physical disabilities, speech and language needs and social, emotional and behavioural difficulties (SEBD) as a result of learning difficulties.

CLIPPENS SCHOOL

Brediland Road, Linwood, PA3 3RX

Tel: 01505 325 333
Fax: 01505 336 097
Email: clippens@appleomnline.net
Website: www.clippens.renfrewshire.sch.uk
• Pupils: 46 Mixed; Day Pupils • Age: 5 to 19
• Religion: Non-denominational • School status: State

SEN provision

Detail:
Centre of excellence for:
- Mild: HI; VI; CP;
- Moderate: AUT; HI; VI; CP;
- Severe: AUT; DS; HI; VI; CP;
- Others: AUT(other); FRX; PMLD; SLD; MSI; PD

Summary: Clippens is a happy school where the welfare of pupils, parents, and staff is valued. It is a special school for pupils with high level additional support needs. The school has a roll of 61 pupils who have a wide range of barriers to learning including autism, and motor and sensory impairments. The school has four departments: primary, secondary, post-16, and also accommodates the Lismore Unit which is a provision for pupils who have autism and challenging behaviour.

The school is viewed as a dynamic centre of excellence where there are high expectations for all. In addition to a school-based curriculum, much learning happens out of school with developing projects such as PE in the Community and a well established mainstream link programme. The school works hard to achieve an inclusive ethos in many different ways and this can be seen in the way broad range of ways that the school supports learning.

Cockshut Hill Technology College

Cockshut Hill, Yardley, Birmingham, West Midlands, B26 2HX

Tel: 0121 464 2122
Fax: 0121 464 2354
Email: enquiry@cockshut.bham.sch.uk
Website: www.atschool.eduweb.co.uk/cockshut

• Pupils: 1600 Mixed; Day Pupils • Age: 11 to 18
• Religion: Non-denominational • School status: State

SEN provision

Detail:
Now provide for in school:
Mild: ASP; AUT; ADD; ADHD; EBD; DYSC; DYSL; DYSP; HI; VI; CP;
Moderate: ASP; AUT; ADHD; MLD; DYSL; DYSP

Summary: The school is particularly effective in meeting the needs of pupils with learning difficulties. Many of the pupils who enter the school with extremely low reading ages leave as confident young people with qualifications. It was noted in the last Ofsted report that 'students with special educational needs make good progress when they receive specialist teaching.'

The SEN teachers, along with a team of experienced and qualified teaching assistants, build a highly supportive environment. The department has recently received considerable input from the Special Support Services concerning autism and fulfilling the needs of pupils' social training. The school is endeavouring to build expertise in this field. We also have considerable experience in supporting students with moderate dyslexia and dyspraxia.

Collegiate High School Sports College

Blackpool Old Road, Blackpool, Lancashire, FY3 7LS

Tel: 01253 300 460
Fax: 01253 395 700
Email: admin@collegiate.blackpool.sch.uk

• Pupils: 1403 Mixed; Day Pupils • Age: 11 to 16
• Religion: Non-denominational • School status: State

SEN provision

Detail:
Now provide for in school:
Mild: ASP; ADD; ADHD; EBD; DYSC; DYSL; DYSP; HI; VI; CP;
Moderate: ADD; ADHD; EBD; MLD; DYSL; DYSP; HI; VI; CP;
Severe: EBD; DYSL;
Others: Sp&LD; Epi; PD; Eat

Summary: SEN provision is a graduated response throughout the school, providing learning and behaviour support for pupils on the school's register of learning needs.

We have a staff of highly trained and experienced teachers working within the department giving both in class support and extra support lessons. We also have a highly experienced team of teaching assistants who work closely with all pupils across the different levels of need. Core lessons of English, maths and science are given priority for support and the special needs staff work closely with the class teachers to ensure our pupils are successful in their learning. Pupils are identified firstly by their Primary records and secondly they are screened for literacy levels when they arrive in Collegiate High School, to ensure we identify all those pupils with learning needs right at the start of their high school career. The department caters for all learning needs including physical diabilities, dyslexia and Asperger's syndrome.

THE COMMONWEAL SCHOOL

The Mall, Old Town, Swindon, Wiltshire, SN1 4JE

Tel: 01793 612 727
Fax: 01793 513 437
Email: head@commonweal.co.uk

• Pupils: 1112 Mixed; Day Pupils • Age: 11 to 16
• Religion: Non-denominational • School status: State

SEN provision

Detail:
Now provide for in school:
- Mild: CP;
- Moderate: MLD; CP;
- Others: PD

Experience of:
- Mild: ASP; ADD; EBD; DYSC; DYSL; DYSP; HI;
- Moderate: EBD; DYSC; DYSL; HI;
- Others: TIC; GEN; EAL; Sp&LD; DEL; Epi

Summary: Commonweal responds to a wide range of special needs. It has a specialist resource provision for students with specific learning difficulties, a specialist resource provision for students with physical disabilities, mainstream support for students with general learning difficulties, as well as providing a place this year for the first totally blind student in secondary education in Swindon LEA.

CONYERS SCHOOL

Green Lane, Yarm, TS15 9ET

Tel: 01642 783 253
Fax: 01642 783 834
Email: conyers.school@stockton.gov.uk
Website: www.conyers.Stockton.sch.uk

• Pupils: 1391 Mixed; Day Pupils • Age: 11 to 18
• Religion: Non-denominational • School status: State

SEN provision

Detail:
Experience of:
- Mild: ASP; AUT; ADD; ADHD; EBD; DYSC; DYSL; DYSP; HI; VI;
- Moderate: ASP; AUT; ADD; ADHD; EBD; MLD; DYSL; DYSP; HI;
- Others: CD; TIC; EAL; Sp&LD; Epi; PD; Eat

Summary: A number of students may experience temporary learning difficulties throughout their school career, whilst some will have ongoing special needs. At Conyers we are commited to retaining all students in mainstream classes under the supervision of subject teachers. Close collaboration between subject staff and the SEN co-ordinator ensures appropriate provision, sometimes with additional in class support from a teaching assistant.

Mr Lawton is the team leader for the school's Learning Support centre,which ensures close liaison with primary schools to provide smooth transition for students already identified as having a special need. Students may also be referred for assessment to LS teachers at any time during their time at the school. The team maintains the register of students with SEN and co-ordinates the regular up-dating of this and all other related assessments/records. Extensive liaison with outside agencies including local authority medical and social services is another important aspect of the support given to students by the team.

The school's SEN policy is fully compliant with the legal requirements of The Special Educational Needs and Discrimination Act of 2002. The governing body is pleased to confirm the success of the SEN policy for the year 2004/05, and will review SEN provision routinely this year. If you have any further queries or would like to see a copy of the full policy, please contact the school.

The Coopers' Company and Coborn School

St Mary's Lane, Upminster, Essex, RM14 3HS

Tel: 01708 250 500
Fax: 01708 226 109
Email: info@cooperscoborn.org.uk
Website: www.cooperscoborn.org.uk

• Pupils: 1264 Mixed; Day Pupils • Age: 11 to 18
• Religion: Christian • School status: State

SEN provision

Detail:
Now provide for in school:
Mild: HI; VI;
Moderate: HI
Experience of:
Mild: ASP; AUT; ADD; EBD; DYSC; DYSL; DYSP; CP;
Moderate: EBD; DYSL; DYSP;
Severe: EBD;
Others: DEL; Epi; PD; Eat

Summary: The Coopers' Company and Coborn School has relatively few students with special educational needs, however, students with specific learning difficulties are well catered for within the requirements of the SEN Code of Practice. Some in-class support can be provided if appropriate, and individual education plans support the progress of students with learning difficulties. The students are closely monitored by the SENCo and other pastoral staff. We currently employ two Learning Support Assistants who provide in class support and we offer an after school support club to ensure that homework is recorded properly and to give SEN students the chance to make a start on homework. We do not currently have an in-school referral unit. All students are expected to undertake the full curriculum at Coopers Coborn, with differentiation and support from staff to support inclusion.

The Cornelius Vermuyden School and Arts College

Dinant Avenue, Canvey Island, Essex, SS8 9QS

Tel: 01268 685 011
Fax: 01268 510 290
Email: admin@corver.rmplc.co.uk
Website: www.corver.ik.org

• Pupils: 908 Mixed; Day Pupils • Age: 11 to 16
• Religion: Non-denominational • School status: State

SEN provision

Detail:
Now provide for in school:
Mild: ASP; AUT; ADD; ADHD; EBD; DS; DYSL; DYSP; VI;
Moderate: ASP; AUT; ADD; ADHD; EBD; DS; MLD; DYSL; DYSP; HI; VI; CP;
Severe: ASP; ADD; ADHD; EBD; DS; DYSL; DYSP; VI;
Others: SPD; CD; ODD; TIC; PMLD; SLD; EAL; Epi
Experience of:
Mild: CP;
Moderate: SpLD;
Severe: SpLD; CP;
Others: AUT(other); OCD; DEL; PD

Summary: The school has a strong learning support department that helps pupils with specific difficulties including learning, physical, emotional and behavioural to have access to the National Curriculum and to achieve success. The school embraces the stepped approach outlined in the Code of Practice; some pupils are statemented and others are on School Action or Action Plus. Emphasis is on suppport in the classroom and there are opportunities for pupils to take part in group and one-to-one work. The SENCo, School Action Manager and Learning Mentor help pupils with their organisation, learning and emotional well-being; the Pupil Support Centre provides intense support for pupils who are out of the mainstream for a specific period of time; and individual personalised programmes of study including timetable adjustments, Successmaker, Smart Thinking and additional literacy ensure there is a variety of approaches so every child has opportunities to achieve their potential. The department works with pupils, staff, outside agencies and parents to ensure all pupils have the opportunity to participate in all school and extra curricular activities.

Corseford Residential School

Howwood Road, Milliken Park, Kilbarchan, Renfrewshire, PA10 2NT

Tel: 01505 702 141
Fax: 01505 702 445
Email: capability@capability-scotland.org.uk
Website: www.capability-scotland.org.uk

• Pupils: 60 Mixed; Day Pupils • Age: 3 to 18
• Religion: Non-denominational • School status: State

SEN provision

Summary: The school caters for children with significant physical difficulties and provides integrated programmes and individualised education therapies, health and personal care/support.

The Court School

Station Road, Llanishen, Cardiff, CF14 5UX

Tel: 029 2075 2713
Fax: 029 2076 3895
Email: schooladmin@thecourtsp.cardiff.sch.uk

• Pupils: 35 Mixed; Day Pupils • Age: 4 to 11
• School status: State

SEN provision

Detail:
Now provide for in school:
Mild: ADD; ADHD; EBD;
Moderate: ADD; ADHD; EBD; MLD;
Severe: ADD; ADHD; EBD;
Others: CD; ODD
Experience of:
Mild: ASP; AUT; DYSC; DYSL; DYSP;
Moderate: DYSC; DYSL; DYSP;
Others: OCD; TIC; Sp&LD; Epi

Summary: The Court School caters for primary aged pupils with severe social, emotional and behavioural difficulties. All have statements of SEN. Many have associated learning difficulties and a significant percentage are medicated for ADHD.

Craigavon Senior High School

Portadown Campus, 26-34 Lurgan Road, Portadown, Craigavon, Co Armagh, BT63 5HJ

Tel: 02838 352 222
Fax: 02838 352 200
Email: info@craigavonsenhigh.portadown.ni.sch.uk

• Pupils: 590 Mixed; Day Pupils • Age: 14 to 16
• School status: State

SEN provision

Detail:
Experience of:
Mild: ASP; AUT; ADD; ADHD; EBD; DYSC; DYSL; DYSP; SpLD; HI; VI;
Moderate: ASP; ADD; ADHD; EBD; MLD; DYSC; DYSL; DYSP; VI;
Severe: ASP; ADD; ADHD; EBD; DYSC; DYSL; DYSP;
Others: CD; OCD; ODD; TIC; PMLD; SLD; Sp&LD; DEL; Epi; PD; Eat

Summary: At Craigavon Senior High School we endeavour to meet the needs of all low ability students. We currently cater for students with low literacy and numeracy skills, medical problems such as ADHD, ADD, Asperger's syndrome and other specific medical problems. We provide a classroom assistant for those students who have a statement and have been approved by the SELB, whilst we offer additional support in all subjects by offering extra classes after school.

Cranford House School Trust Limited

Moulsford, Wallingford, Oxfordshire, OX10 9HT

Tel: 01491 651 218
Fax: 01491 652 557
Email: office@cranfordhouse.oxon.sch.uk
Website: www.cranfordhouse.oxon.sch.uk

• Pupils: 325 Mixed; Day Pupils • Age: 5 to 16
• Religion: CofE/Christian • School status: Independent

SEN provision

Detail:

Centre of excellence for:
 Mild: DYSC; DYSL;
 Moderate: DYSC; DYSL
Now provide for in school:
 Mild: HI; VI; CP;
 Moderate: VI;
 Others: EAL; Sp&LD
Experience of:
 Mild: ADD; ADHD; EBD; DYSP;
 Others: DEL; Epi; PD; Eat

Summary: The learning support department at Cranford House believes that every child has the potential to succeed. Those children who are not succeeding to their full potential within the classroom are recognised at an early age and given individual help and support with literacy, numeracy and organisational skills or with support for specific classroom assignments. In this way, as the child progresses, success is achieved at that child's individual level. Self-esteem is raised and self-confidence increased.

The Learning Support Register informs all staff of the specific difficulties of every child who is on the register. The individual education plan, which is given to all staff involved with the child, outlines the teaching objectives and strategies for implementing those subjects and is discussed at least twice a year at review meetings.

Pupils who receive learning support are offered an individual structured multi-sensory programme, which builds on the child's strengths while developing strategies to help compensate for areas of weakness. Pupils are encouraged to discuss their problems and by means of an individual education plan, communication between staff, parents and the learning support department is close, ensuring that all parties concerned carry out the programme.

By the very nature of the one-to-one relationship shared between a pupil with special educational needs and the learning support teacher, a caring and sympathetic attitude is shown at all times. Lessons are aimed at encouraging independent learning and self-confidence.

Crescent School

Bawnmore Road, Bilton, Rugby, Warwickshire, CV22 7QH

Tel: 01788 521 595
Fax: 01788 816 185
Email: admin@crescentschool.co.uk
Website: www.crescentschool.co.uk

• Pupils: 182 Mixed; Day Pupils • Age: 3 to 11
• School status: Independent

SEN provision

Detail:

Experience of:
 Mild: ASP; AUT; ADD; ADHD; EBD; DYSC; DYSL; DYSP; SpLD; HI;
 Moderate: MLD;
 Others: Sp&LD

Summary: Children with mild learning difficulties receive additional support and individual work within the classroom. Children with a more specific learning difficulty are withdrawn from a lesson for a short while several times a week for individual or paired work aimed at helping them cope in the classroom. None of our children have severe learning difficulties.

Croftlands Infant School

Oakwood Drive, Ulverston, Cumbria, LA12 9JU

Tel: 01229 894 181
Fax: 01229 894 182
Email: headteacher@croftlandsinf.cumbria.sch.uk

• Pupils: 183 Mixed; Day Pupils • Age: 3 to 7
• Religion: Non-denominational • School status: State

SEN provision

Detail:
Now provide for in school:
Mild: ASP; ADD; EBD; HI; VI;
Moderate: ASP; EBD; MLD; CP;
Others: PMLD; EAL; Sp&LD
Experience of:
Mild: AUT; ADHD; DS; DYSC; DYSL; DYSP; SpLD;
Moderate: AUT; ADD; ADHD; DYSC; HI;
Severe: VI;
Others: DEL; Oth

Summary: We currently have 40 children in school identified on our register of special educational needs. Of these, five children have statements. We cater for a range of learning needs. We have a small number of children with physical disabilities. There is a disabled toilet and changing area in the building. The building has wheelchair access throughout. Some modifications have been made to meet the needs of a child with a visual impairment. We have children in school with diabetes.

Crofton High School

High Street, Crofton, Wakefield, West Yorkshire, WF4 1NF

Tel: 01924 303 940
Fax: 01924 303 937
Email: headteacher@croftonhigh.wakefield.sch.uk
Website: www.croftonhigh.wakefield.sch.uk

• Pupils: 1145 Mixed; Day Pupils • Age: 11 to 16
• Religion: Non-denominational • School status: State

SEN provision

Detail:
Centre of excellence for:
Mild: VI;
Moderate: VI;
Severe: VI
Now provide for in school:
Mild: ADD; ADHD; EBD;
Moderate: ADD; ADHD; EBD; MLD;
Others: CD; OCD
Experience of:
Mild: DYSC; DYSL; DYSP; HI;
Moderate: DYSC; DYSL; DYSP; HI;
Severe: ADD; ADHD; EBD;
Others: Epi; PD; Eat

Summary: The school has a strong commitment to inclusion. Our SEN co-ordinator is supported by some teacher time and 6 ESAs. In the main, pupils with SEN are taught in normal classes but there is some extraction for basic skill development in Key Stage 3. The school is currently developing its strategies to address the needs of those pupils covered by the Disability Discrimination Act.

In addition the school is the LEA Centre for those with Visual Impairment. Provision is staffed with 2 teachers and 10 ESAs. In the main pupils with Visual Impairment follow the normal school curriculum which is amended as necessary to meet need.

Cromwell High School

Yew Tree Lane, Reddish, Dukinfield, Cheshire, SK16 5BJ

Tel: 01613 389 730
Fax: 01613 389 731
Email: admin@cromwell.tameside.sch.uk
Website:
www.tameside.gov.uk/edugen/new/direct/website/7005.htm

• Pupils: 61 Mixed; Day Pupils • Age: 11 to 16
• Religion: Non-denominational • School status: State

SEN provision

Summary: As a special school everything we do is focused on special educational needs. Care needs, health needs, communication needs, the need to develop key skills for life, the need for different ways to access the curriculum are all central to our purpose. We value each pupil as a complex human being with a complex identity. They may be disabled but they are so much more than that and we value their entitlement to access and be included in the widest world possible. Above all we value their entitlement to achieve success in their own terms and the celebration of personal success is central to our special educational needs policy. We offer accreditation appropriate for all pupils from the major national awarding bodies; OCR, AQA, ASDAN etc. A pupil's education is not simply about what happens in school and we are committed to a partnership with parents to support their child's achievement in whatever way is possible. We are developing ourselves as an extended school and have a vibrant, and continually expanding, extra-curricular provision.

We cater for pupils experiencing severe or profound difficulties in their learning and pupils with complex difficulties in their learning. Staff are trained in the TEACCH and PECS approaches to supporting pupils who need a very structured environment and visual communication system including pupils with Autistic Spectrum Disorder (ASD) and associated learning difficulties. In addition to their learning difficulties we cater for pupils with physical disabilities and requiring full personal care. Some pupils have experienced challenging behaviour in addition to learning difficulties. The school is a centre of excellence for addressing these needs; eliminating or minimising such incidents, and provides Team Teach behaviour management training to many other schools, colleges and social care environments in the local authority area.

Crosshill Special School

Shadsworth Road, Blackburn, Lancashire, BB1 2HR

Tel: 01254 667 713

Fax: 01254 664 449

Email: crosshill@blackburn.gov.uk

• Pupils: 94 Mixed; Day Pupils • Age: 5 to 16

• Religion: Non-denominational • School status: State

SEN provision

Detail:

Now provide for in school:

Mild: ASP; AUT; ADD; ADHD; EBD; DS; DYSC; DYSL; DYSP; SpLD; HI; VI; CP;

Moderate: ASP; AUT; ADD; ADHD; EBD; DS; MLD; DYSC; DYSL; DYSP; SpLD; HI; VI; CP;

Others: SPD; CD; EAL; Sp&LD; Epi; PD

Summary: Crosshill School caters for children aged 11-16 with complex learning difficulties. Many of the children have behaviour difficulties, as well as children on the autistic spectrum and with ADHD. A small number of pupils also have other disabilities including physical, visual and hearing.

Croyland Primary School

Croyland Road, Wellingborough, Northamptonshire, NN8 2AX

Tel: 01933 224 169

Fax: 01933 275831

Email: head@croyland-pri.northants-ecl.gov.uk

• Pupils: 320 Mixed; Day Pupils • Age: 5 to 11

• Religion: Non-denominational • School status: State

SEN provision

Detail:

Now provide for in school:

Mild: ASP; AUT; ADD; ADHD; EBD; DYSL; DYSP; HI; VI; CP;

Moderate: ASP; AUT; ADD; ADHD; EBD; MLD; DYSL; DYSP; CP;

Severe: EBD;

Others: AUT(other); EAL; Sp&LD

Experience of:

Mild: DS; SpLD;

Moderate: DS; HI; VI;

Severe: ADD; ADHD; DYSL; DYSP; HI; CP;

Others: OCD; PMLD; SLD; DEL; Epi; PD; Eat

Summary: We have a DSP for 10 children with speech and language difficulties. Currently we have a large percentage of children on the SEN register (56 per cent) with a wide range of varying needs. The school staff are extremely well trained and deal with these children in a positive and supportive manner. Our last Ofsted inspection (Jan 2004) stated that we were highly inclusive.

CUDDINGTON CROFT PRIMARY SCHOOL

West Drive, Cheam, Sutton, Surrey, SM2 7NA

Tel: 020 8642 4325
Fax: 020 8642 9808
Email: admin@cuddington-croft.surrey.sch.uk
Website: www.cuddington-croft.surrey.sch.uk
• Pupils: 483 Mixed; Day Pupils • Age: 3 to 11
• Religion: Non-denominational • School status: State

SEN provision

Detail:
Now provide for in school:
Mild: DYSL;
Moderate: DYSL;
Others: EAL
Experience of:
Mild: ASP; AUT; ADD; EBD; DYSC; HI; CP;
Moderate: EBD; DYSC;
Others: Sp&LD; DEL; Epi; PD

Summary: Special educational provision means educational provision which is additional to, or otherwise different from, the educational provision made generally for children of the same age. The kind of provision available at Cuddington Croft is most often to help to acquire literacy skills and to develop language. Sometimes support is provided to develop numeracy skills. Provision is also made for children with a physical disability and children with emotional and behaviour difficulties who will be involved in pastoral and/or disciplinary procedures with rewards and sanctions.

When a child is identified with special educational needs the school will inform the parents and with their agreement initiate support to help the child. Provision will be matched to the child's needs. The school offers a variety of provision in line with the Code of Practice.

CULFORD PREPARATORY SCHOOL

Culford, Bury St Edmunds, Suffolk, IP28 6TX

Tel: 01284 729 348
Fax: 01284 728 183
Email: admissions@culford.co.uk
Website: www.culford.co.uk
• Pupils: Mixed; Takes boarders • Age: 8 to 13
• Religion: Methodist • School status: Independent

SEN provision

Detail:
Now provide for in school:
Mild: DYSC; DYSL; DYSP; SpLD; HI

Summary: We are an independent selective school that has a very clear academic emphasis. We aim to meet individual needs within a mainstream setting through the delivery of a differentiated curriculum. We have pupils with SEN. Mild dyslexia, mild dyspraxia and mild dyscalculia are the most common difficulties. We do not have a dedicated SEN unit but we do have fully qualified specialist staff who provide learning support lessons on a withdrawal basis.

CULTS PRIMARY SCHOOL

Earlswells Road, Cults, Aberdeen, AB15 9RG

Tel: 01224 869 221
Fax: 01224 869 372
Email: enquiries@cultsprimary.aberdeen.sch.uk
Website: www.cultsprimary.aberdeen.sch.uk
• Pupils: 571 Mixed; Day Pupils • Age: 3 to 11
• Religion: Non-denominational • School status: State

SEN provision

Detail:
Now provide for in school:
Mild: ASP; AUT; ADD; ADHD; EBD; DS; DYSL; DYSP; SpLD; VI; CP;
Moderate: AUT; ADD; EBD; DS; MLD; DYSL; SpLD;

HI; VI; CP;
Others: SPD; AUT(other); EAL; MSI; Sp&LD; Epi; Eat

Summary: Cults Primary School is a large, open plan community education school. The building comprises of three teaching units with seven classes in each, from primary 1 to 7 around central resources with a nursery unit and SEN unit which is in a central position to the school. The unit was opened in 1998 as a two teacher unit for 13 children from primary 1 to 7 who have a wide range of physical needs as well as moderate learning difficulties. The children all have Records of Needs and the SEN provision follows the guidelines for admission procedures and inclusion set by the Aberdeen City Education Department and Scottish Office. The teachers who work from the unit are trained primary teachers one with a Certificate in SEN and one teacher with an SEN Diploma and a Diploma in Autism. In addition to teaching children with mild/moderate difficulties, the staff have developed expertise in autism, Down's syndrome, cerebral palsy, hearing and visual impairments and are well supported by specialists who work collaborately with each other, school staff and parents in a team approach to the individual child's needs. The children are well included into mainstream, work is differentiated through an individualised educational programme as appropriate and children are included into mainstream and supported one-to-one or within a small class group in the unit as appropriate to their needs. A two-way flow of children between class and the SEN unit is encouraged and the school encourages a buddy system where children choose to buddy a child with special needs at playtime under the supervision of the child's auxiliary where the child has designated one-to-one support. The sensory room adds a wider dimension to the curriculum to support the children's needs and we are gradually making the whole school environment more accessible to all eg within the school playground we have created pathways for wheelchair access and are incorporating inclusive play equipment. We have the best interests of all the children at heart and are ready to meet the requirements of the Additional Support for Learning Act where all children's needs should be met through a fully inclusive environment.

Cutteslowe Primary School

Wren Road, Oxford, Oxfordshire, OX2 7SX

Tel: 01865 558 944
Fax: 01865 559 755
Email: Headteacher.2522@cutteslowe.oxon.sch.uk
Website: www.cutteslowe.oxon.sch.uk

• Pupils: 238 Mixed; Day Pupils • Age: 3 to 11
• Religion: Non-denominational • School status: State

SEN provision

Detail:
Now provide for in school:
Mild: ASP; ADD; ADHD; EBD; DYSC; DYSL; DYSP; HI;
Moderate: ASP; ADD; EBD; MLD; HI;
Severe: AUT; DS; HI; VI; CP;
Others: PMLD; SLD; EAL; MSI; Sp&LD; DEL
Experience of:
Mild: AUT; DS;
Moderate: AUT; ADHD; DS; DYSC; DYSL; DYSP; CP;
Severe: ASP; ADD; ADHD; EBD; DYSC; DYSL;
Others: Epi

Summary: Cutteslowe school places a strong emphasis on inclusion. Children with special educational needs are supported by teaching assistants who work closely with teaching staff to differentiate the curriculum appropriately for pupils. There is a non-teaching SENCo who liaises closely with staff and external agencies to ensure appropriate provision. We currently provide for children with autistic spectrum disorder, Down's syndrome, cerebral palsy, visual and hearing impairment and moderate learning difficulties and behavioural difficulties.

Children with SEN may be taught in small groups or one-to-one, supported by a teaching assistant in the classroom or outside it. They have individual education plans which are reviewed termly with parents and staff in order to closely monitor progress of these pupils.

Danestone Primary School

Fairview Brae, Danestone, Aberdeen, AB22 8ZN

Tel: 01224 825 062
Fax: 01224 707 796
Email: enquiries@danestone.aberdeen.sch.uk
Website: www.danestone.aberdeen.sch.uk

• Pupils: 302 Mixed; Day Pupils • Age: 3 to 11
• Religion: Non-denominational • School status: State

SEN provision

Detail:
Experience of:
  Mild: ASP; AUT; ADD; ADHD; EBD; DS; DYSC; DYSL; DYSP; HI; VI;
  Moderate: EBD; DS; DYSC; DYSL; DYSP; HI;
  Severe: HI;
  Others: MSI; Sp&LD; PD

Summary: We happily integrate where at all possible any child with a particular need into our mainstream classes. We are particularly suited to children with physical disabilities as we are a new and modern school built totally on one level. We have two SEN auxiliaries who work with a number of children throughout the school.

Danum School Technology College

Armthorpe Road, Doncaster, South Yorkshire, DN2 5QD

Tel: 01302 831385
Fax: 01302 300109
Email: danum@danum.doncaster.sch.uk
Website: www.danum.doncaster.sch.uk

• Pupils: 1980 Mixed; Day Pupils • Age: 11 to 18
• Religion: Non-denominational • School status: State

SEN provision

Detail:
Now provide for in school:
  Mild: ASP; AUT; ADD; ADHD; EBD; DS; DYSC; DYSL; DYSP; HI; VI; CP;
  Moderate: ASP; AUT; ADD; ADHD; EBD; DS; MLD; DYSL; DYSP; HI; VI; CP;
  Severe: DYSL; HI; CP;
  Others: CD; FRX; EAL; MSI; Sp&LD; DEL; Epi; PD; Eat

Summary: Danum is a large mixed split-site comprehensive: we have a special school for pupils with profound difficulties between our two sites. We were built with lifts, disabled toilets, and before the inclusion agenda, Doncaster LEA transported all PD pupils to us. For these reasons, we have a vast experience of all sorts of physical, behavioural and learning disabilities, and a large army of fantastic LSAs, trained in eg: moving and handling, who specialise in different aspects of SEN, eg: behaviour, VI, HI, autism, etc. Pupils at Danum are accustomed to difference and diversity: we strive to ensure our ethos encourages all pupils to work together, to support each other, to understand each other's differences. SEN is important to all staff, teaching and support. We believe that we are a very caring department, determined to treat all pupils as individuals: we are a school that is willing and able to adjust the school's systems and structures so that pupils can access our curriculum, reach their full potential, academically but also extra-curricular. Through dialogue with parents, pupils, internal support, and external support agencies, we are willing to work hard, together, to include everyone. We value the close links we have built up with the local support eg: hearing and visual impairment services, behaviour support, autistic spectrum support. All pupils are included on trips, visits, extracurricular activities, and we are working hard to be an accessible and an inclusive school. We are particularly proud of our disabled athletics team which always sends qualifiers to the national finals in Blackpool. We are also proud of our success with pupils who join us with low literacy levels: four qualified teaching staff work hard with small withdrawal groups to raise reading, comprehension and spelling ages, so pupils can access the mainstream curriculum asap. Success is when they don't need us anymore!

THE DARLEY CENTRE

School Road, Ashby, Scunthorpe, DN16 2TD

Tel: 01724 843 684
Fax: 01724 281 704

• Mixed; Day Pupils • Age: 5 to 16
• Religion: Non-denominational • School status: State

SEN provision

Detail:
Now provide for in school:
Mild: ADD; ADHD; EBD; DYSC; DYSL; DYSP;
Moderate: ADD; ADHD; EBD; MLD; DYSC; DYSL; DYSP;
Others: CD; OCD; ODD
Experience of:
Mild: HI;
Severe: DYSL;
Others: TIC; DEL; Epi

Summary: The Darley Centre supports the secondary schools of North Lincolnshire with Key Stage 3 pupils who have social, emotional and/or behavioural difficulties. Pupils remain on their school role, attend The Darley Centre for an agreed period of time, up to two terms, followed by re-integration into full-time permanent educational provision. Pupils are referred via an LEA Admissions Panel of local secondary headteachers and LEA officers. Pupils approved for placement follow a pre-placement planning procedure to ensure all individual needs will be addressed. A regular individual education (IEP) review process ensures that pupil's progress is recorded, monitored and shared with all relevant parties. An individually matched curriculum aims to provide each pupil with mainstream school coping strategies for successful re-integration wherever possible. The five outcomes from Every Child Matters – Be Healthy, Stay Safe, Enjoy and Achieve, Make a Positive Contribution and Achieve Economic Well Being remain at the heart of the curriculum.

We also aim to improve the provision we offer through a process of continual self assessment, evaluating the quality of:-

- teaching
- curriculum and other activities
- leadership and management
- achievements and standards
- personal development and well-being
- the care, guidance and support for learners
- overall effectiveness.

DARTFORD GRAMMAR SCHOOL FOR GIRLS

Shepherds Lane, Dartford, Kent, DA1 2NT

Tel: 01322 223 123
Fax: 01322 294 786
Email: school@dartfordgrammargirls.kent.sch.uk
Website: www.dartfordgrammargirls.kent.sch.uk

• Pupils: 1027 Girls; Day Pupils • Age: 11 to 18
• Religion: Non-denominational • School status: State

SEN provision

Detail:
Experience of:
Mild: ADD; EBD; DYSC; DYSL; DYSP; VI;
Moderate: DYSL; DYSP; VI;
Severe: VI;
Others: EAL; Epi; Eat

Summary: We aim to consider each student as an individual and, where special provision is required to:

- provide a suitable curriculum for each student
- track the progress of such students through school
- ensure progression through all key stages and beyond for such students
- enable such students to form social and working relationships.

A copy of the full policy can be obtained from the school office on request. The school also organises a range of activities and courses to support talented students.

DAVENTRY WILLIAM PARKER SCHOOL

Ashby Road, Daventry, Northamptonshire, NN11 5QE

Tel: 01327 705 816

Fax: 01327 300 156

Email: head@dwps.northants-ecl.gov.uk

Website: www.geocities.co./dwpschool

• Pupils: 1199 Mixed; Day Pupils • Age: 11 to 16

• Religion: Non-denominational • School status: State

SEN provision

Detail:

Now provide for in school:

Mild: ASP; AUT; ADD; ADHD; EBD; DYSC; DYSL; DYSP; SpLD; HI; VI; CP;

Moderate: ASP; AUT; ADD; ADHD; EBD; MLD; DYSC; DYSL; DYSP; SpLD; HI;

Severe: ASP; ADD; ADHD; EBD;

Others: SPD; AUT(other); CD; OCD; ODD; TIC; GEN; EAL; Sp&LD; Epi; PD; Eat

Experience of:

Mild: DS;

Moderate: CP;

Severe: DYSP; HI;

Others: DEL; Oth

Summary: Provision according to individual needs of students at SA, SA+ and with statements of SEN. In class, one-to-one and small group teaching with TAs and SEN teachers – across the curriculum, years 7-11.

THE DEANERY CHURCH OF ENGLAND VOLUNTARY AIDED PRIMARY SCHOOL

Fox Hollies Road, Walmley, Sutton Coldfield, West Midlands, B76 2RD

Tel: 0121 351 6441

Fax: 0121 313 0320

Email: enquiry@deanery.bham.sch.uk

• Pupils: 449 Mixed; Day Pupils • Age: 3 to 11

• Religion: Church of England • School status: State

SEN provision

Detail:

Now provide for in school:

Mild: AUT; ADHD; EBD; DYSC; DYSL; DYSP; HI; VI;

Moderate: MLD;

Others: AUT(other); PMLD; EAL; Sp&LD; Epi

Summary: SEN provision takes many forms at Deanery. Following the authority's audit, teacher observation and parental concerns a child will be assessed. A baseline is established to ascertain the child's needs in reading, writing, speaking and listening and mathematics. Provision:

- Precision Teaching – Reading and Mathematics
- Direct Teaching – Reading
- Reading Groups – Targetting children, scoring 2/3 on the reading strand.
- Speaking and Listening – Targetting children scoring 2/3 on the sp and list. strand
- Neuro-physiological group – Children who have poor co-ordination/concentration

DEERNESS VALLEY COMPREHENSIVE SCHOOL

Bracken Court, Ushaw Moor, Durham, County Durham, DH7 7NG

Tel: 0191 373 0336
Fax: 0191 373 0710
Email: deerness.valley@durhamlea.org.uk
Website: www.deernessvalley.durham.sch.uk

• Pupils: 596 Mixed; Day Pupils • Age: 11 to 16
• Religion: Non-denominational • School status: State

SEN provision

Detail:
Centre of excellence for:
- Mild: EBD;
- Moderate: EBD; MLD;
- Severe: EBD;
- Others: DEL

Now provide for in school:
- Mild: ASP; AUT; ADD; ADHD; DYSC; DYSL; DYSP; SpLD; HI; VI;
- Moderate: ASP; AUT; ADD; ADHD; DYSC; DYSL; DYSP; SpLD; HI; VI;
- Severe: ASP; AUT; ADD; ADHD; DYSL; DYSP; SpLD; HI; VI;
- Others: SPD; CD; ODD; FRX; GEN; PMLD; SLD; Sp&LD; Epi; PD; Eat;

Summary: Deerness Valley School is fully committed to the Inclusion Agenda and those students with special educational needs. Its approach to SEN is one which encompasses the full range of need, from learning and behaviour needs to medical, physical, social and emotional needs. Every student is unique and individual and deserves to be treated with respect and with care for these needs. Deerness Valley School has strong links with external agencies to ensure that students' needs are met and has its own purpose-built Social Inclusion Centre from which multi-agency liaison is managed.

DERBY MOOR COMMUNITY SPORTS COLLEGE

Moorway Lane, Littleover, Derby, Derbyshire, DE23 2FS

Tel: 01332 766 280
Fax: 01332 270 178
Email: info@derbymoor.derby.sch.uk
Website: www.derbymoor.derby.sch.uk

• Pupils: 1340 Mixed; Day Pupils • Age: 11 to 18
• Religion: Non-denominational • School status: State

SEN provision

Detail:
Now provide for in school:
- Mild: ASP; AUT; ADD; ADHD; EBD; DYSC; DYSL; DYSP; HI; VI; CP;
- Moderate: ASP; AUT; ADD; ADHD; EBD; MLD; DYSL; DYSP; HI; VI; CP;
- Others: SPD; CD; OCD; ODD; EAL; Sp&LD; Epi; PD; Eat

Summary: DMCSC is an inclusive comprehensive school of 1400 11-16 students striving to give all children with learning and behaviour difficulties the best opportunity to develop their abilities.
- Pupils with SEN are mainly taught in mainstream classes whenever possible.
- There are approximately 250 pupils on the SEN list and 38 pupils with statements.
- There are four Learning and Language Support Teachers and the equivalent of 13 teaching assistants support these pupils in the classroom.
- Pupils in years 7 and 8 with identified literacy needs are withdrawn for additional small group work.
- Older pupils with longer term specific literacy or behavioural needs are withdrawn for additional individual support.
- Teaching assistants work in the Learning Support Base at lunchtime to help with homework or GCSE coursework.
- Teaching assistants and support teachers work in the Achievement Centre with students who have behavioural, attendance or emotional difficulties.
- Appropriate Access Arrangements are put in place for external exams such as SATs and GCSEs.

- 97.9 per cent of pupils gained 5 or more grade A*-G GCSEs and 98.7 per cent gained one or more grade A*-G GCSEs.
- The school maintains close links with outside support agencies and the LEA who are continuing to make alterations to the buildings and site to maximise access.

DERRIAGHY PRIMARY SCHOOL

14 Milltown Park, Lisburn, Co Antrim, BT28 3TU

Tel: 02890 301 012
Fax: 02890 308 334
Email: gtopping@derriaghyps.lisburn.ni.sch.uk
Website: www.derriaghyps.ik.uk
• Pupils: 125 Mixed; Day Pupils • Age: 5 to 11
• School status: State

SEN provision

Detail:
Now provide for in school:
Mild: ASP; AUT; ADD; ADHD; EBD;
Moderate: EBD; MLD; DYSP;
Others: Sp&LD
Experience of:
Mild: DYSC; DYSL;
Moderate: ASP; AUT; ADD; ADHD;
Severe: EBD;
Others: AUT(other); ODD; TIC; DEL; PD; Eat

Summary: We are a small primary school with a high percentage of children who require additional support across a range of special needs. The staff are committed and able to provide that support through a range of strategies and strengths.

DODMIRE JUNIOR SCHOOL

Rydal Road, Darlington, County Durham, DL1 4BH

Tel: 01325 380 784
Fax: 01325 240 577
Email: admin@dodmirejun.darlington.sch.uk
Website: www.dltn.site-edit.net/2652
• Pupils: 303 Mixed; Day Pupils • Age: 7 to 11
• Religion: Non-denominational • School status: State

SEN provision

Detail:
Now provide for in school:
Mild: ASP; EBD; DYSC; DYSL; DYSP; HI;
Moderate: EBD; MLD; DYSL; CP;
Severe: ADHD;
Others: SPD; EAL; Sp&LD; DEL; Epi; Eat
Experience of:
Mild: AUT; VI; CP;
Moderate: ASP; DYSP; HI;
Severe: ASP;
Others: ODD;

Summary: At Dodmire Juniors all staff believe that every child is special. We have a team of five full-time support assistants with a part-time team leader, offering a high level of support to those who need it at any given time. Most of our support staff and teachers have worked with children who have autistic spectrum disorders, ADHD, language difficulties, behavioural difficulties, children with specific physical and medical needs and those with general learning difficulties. We feel it is important to have close links with parents and the appropriate professional bodies and the wider community to aid the child's progress. All children are welcomed at Dodmire regardless of ethnicity, religion, ability, physical needs or background. The strengths of each child are promoted and celebrated whilst their weaknesses are well supported.

Don Valley High School

Jossey Lane, Scawthorpe, Doncaster, South Yorkshire, DN5 9DD

Tel: 01302 781528
Fax: 01302 786252
Email: office@donvalley.co.uk
Website: www.donvalley.co.uk

• Pupils: 1524 Mixed; Day Pupils • Age: 11 to 18
• Religion: Non-denominational • School status: State

SEN provision

Detail:
Now provide for in school:
Mild: ASP; ADD; DS; DYSC; DYSL; HI; VI; CP;
Moderate: ASP; MLD; DYSL; HI; VI;
Severe: ASP; DYSL;
Others: EAL; Sp&LD
Experience of:
Mild: AUT; ADHD; EBD; DYSP;
Moderate: AUT; ADD; ADHD; EBD; DS; DYSC;
Others: SPD; AUT(other); Epi

Summary: Don Valley School and Performing Arts College has a successful and caring special needs department. Children with Special Needs have a personalised individual curriculum and we involve parents to help with the education of their children. We take a holistic approach to our students and teach them in a happy encouraging environment. We especially cater for Asperger's syndrome.

Dorin Park School

Wealstone Lane, Upton, Chester, Cheshire, CH2 1HD

Tel: 01244 381 951
Fax: 01244 390 422

• Pupils: 70 Mixed; Day Pupils • Age: 19
• Religion: Non-denominational • School status: State

SEN provision

Detail:
Now provide for in school:
Mild: CP;
Moderate: CP;
Others: PD

Summary: Dorin Park School is a school for physically disabled pupils. We have speech therapists, occupational therapists, physiotherapists, and a hydrotherapy pool all on site.

Doucecroft School

163 High Street, Kelvedon, Colchester, Essex, CO5 9JA

Tel: 01376 570 060
Fax: 01376 570 060
Email: admin@easdoucecroft.u-net.com

• Pupils: 33 Mixed; Takes boarders • Age: 2 to 19
• School status: Independent

SEN provision

Detail:
Centre of excellence for:
Mild: AUT;
Moderate: AUT;
Severe: AUT;
Others: AUT(other)
Experience of:
Mild: HI; VI;
Moderate: ADHD; DYSP;
Others: SPD; OCD; ODD; FRX

Summary: Doucecroft provides day and weekly boarding places for pupils with autistic spectrum disorders. The National Curriculum is adapted to meet the individual needs of pupils with ASD, providing an increased emphasis on communication and physical education. Pupils are taught in small classes with a high level of adult support. Doucecroft caters for pupils with a wide range of ability and levels of autism.

DOWDALES SCHOOL

Dalton-in-Furness, Cumbria, LA15 8AH

Tel: 01229 89 7911

Fax: 01229 89 7913

Email: office@dowdales.cumbria.sch.uk

• Pupils: 975 Mixed; Day Pupils • Age: 11 to 16

• Religion: Non-denominational • School status: State

SEN provision

Detail:

Now provide for in school:

Mild: ASP; ADD; ADHD; EBD; DS; DYSC; DYSL; DYSP; HI; VI; CP;

Moderate: ASP; AUT; ADD; ADHD; EBD; DS; MLD; DYSC; DYSL; DYSP; HI; VI; CP;

Severe: DYSC; DYSL; DYSP;

Others: SPD; AUT(other); CD; OCD; ODD; TIC; EAL; Sp&LD; Epi; PD; Eat

Experience of:

Mild: AUT

Summary: The SEN department at Dowdales works as a team mainly supporting the SEN pupils by in-class support but withdrawing them as necessary for specialist teaching in dyslexia, dyscalculia and social skills. In the recent Ofsted inspection the work of the department was described as 'exemplary'.

THE DUCHESS'S COMMUNITY HIGH SCHOOL

Howling Lane, Alnwick, Northumberland, NE66 1DH

Tel: 01665 602 166

Fax: 01665 510 602

Email: admin@duchesss.northumberland.sch.uk

Website: www.duchesss.digitalbrain.com

• Pupils: 1105 Mixed; Day Pupils • Age: 13 to 18

• Religion: Non-denominational • School status: State

SEN provision

Detail:

Now provide for in school:

Mild: ASP; AUT; ADD; ADHD; EBD; DYSC; DYSL; DYSP; HI;

Moderate: ASP; ADD; EBD; DS; MLD; DYSL;

Others: PD

Experience of:

Mild: VI; CP;

Moderate: ADHD; DYSP; CP;

Others: SPD; TIC; Sp&LD

Summary: Students with special educational needs are particularly welcome in our school. A team of specialist teachers and support assistants provides additional help to students with a variety of needs. We support in class and also withdraw students for additional help. In addition to a 'Support' option in years 10 and 11, we offer vocational subjects which are accessible to all our students. Among our current students are those with learning, behavioural, physical, emotional and medical needs.

We liaise closely with our feeder middle schools and external agencies and have a thriving 'Student Support' team within school. This has evolved through our role as an extended school and we are able to involve a variety of professionals to support our work with young people in school.

THE DUCHY SCHOOL BRADNINCH

Bowley Meadow, Townlands, Blank, Bradninch, Devon, EX5 4RF

Tel: 01392 881 482

Fax: 01392 881482

Email: admin@duchy.devon.sch.uk

Website: www.duchy.devon.sch.uk

• Pupils: 201 Mixed; Day Pupils • Age: 4 to 11

• Religion: Non-denominational • School status: State

SEN provision

Detail:

Experience of:

Mild: ASP; AUT; ADD; ADHD; EBD; DS; DYSC; DYSL;

DYSP; HI; VI; CP;
Moderate: ASP; EBD; DS; MLD; DYSC; DYSL; DYSP; HI;
Severe: EBD;
Others: ODD; PMLD; SLD; EAL; Sp&LD; Eat

Summary: We are an inclusive school and as such strive to accomodate all children with special needs. We have a very supportive and clear policy for special needs children which requires the family and school to engage in a comprehensive dialogue at induction. Individual education programmes are developed for each child and are reviewed twice a year. Children can move between classes for literacy and numeracy according to their needs. Additional support can be given on a small group or one-to-one basis in the afternoons. We have an experienced team of support workers who work both in and out of the classroom. The LEA also supports the school through the Educational Psychology Service, the Communication and Interaction Disorder Team and Specialist Advisory Teacher Service (eg for visual and audio conditions.)

Dunmurry High School

River Road, Dunmurry, Belfast, BT17 9DS

Tel: 02890 622 828
Fax: 02890 620 913
Email: info@dunmurry.belfast.ni.sch.uk
• Pupils: 302 Mixed; Day Pupils • Age: 16 • School status: State

SEN provision

Detail:
Now provide for in school:
Mild: ASP; AUT; ADD; EBD; DYSC; DYSL; DYSP; SpLD;
Moderate: ASP; AUT; ADD; ADHD; EBD; MLD; DYSC; DYSL; DYSP;
Others: SPD; AUT(other); CD; Epi

Summary: We have put together a special needs package which supports our students throughout their secondary school experience. In year 8 we create a nurture group of no more than 12 children with special needs. They are taught seven subjects by their form teacher so that their experience almost mirrors that of primary school. As they move to years 9 and 10 they are still taught as a group but again by fewer staff. In years 11 and 12 they are our work related learning group taking five or six GCSEs and qualifications in work related learning. They do one day a week work experience and also participate in our XL club working on personal and social development. We also have a special needs teacher who supports students whose special needs do not require the nurture group placement. We have specially equipped rooms and have recently introduced a read well scheme. Sharing of good practice ensures that strategies used by specialist teachers can be used in mainstream classes.

Durham Gilesgate Sports College and Sixth Form Centre

Bradford Crescent, Gilesgate, Durham, County Durham, DH1 1HN

Tel: 0191 384 2217
Fax: 0191 386 3454
Email: dgsc@dgsc.org.uk
Website: www.dgsc.org.uk
• Pupils: 1169 Mixed; Day Pupils • Age: 11 to 18
• Religion: Non-denominational • School status: State

SEN provision

Detail:
Now provide for in school:
Mild: ADD; ADHD; EBD; DYSC; DYSL; DYSP; HI;
Moderate: ADHD; EBD; MLD; DYSC; DYSL;
Others: EAL; Sp&LD; Epi
Experience of:
Mild: AUT; SpLD;
Moderate: ADD; DYSP; HI;
Severe: EBD; VI;
Others: SPD; ODD; TIC; Eat

Summary: Gilesgate provides a safe and caring environment for all students. The SEN team are commited to raising achievement and self esteem for those students with additional needs. Excellent resources are available including invaluable access to specialised IT software. SEN staff have a wide range of expertise and life skills which enhances the level of support available for a wide range of learning and emotional needs of many children.

The Earl Of Dysart Primary School, Grantham

Dysart Road, Grantham, Lincolnshire, NG31 7LP

Tel: 01476 562 091

Fax: 01476 562 091

Email: enquiries@earldysart.lincs.sch.uk

• Pupils: 261 Mixed; Day Pupils • Age: 4 to 11

• Religion: Non-denominational • School status: State

SEN provision

Detail:

Now provide for in school:

Mild: AUT; DYSL; HI; VI;

Moderate: AUT; MLD; VI;

Others: PMLD; EAL; Sp&LD; PD

Experience of:

Mild: ASP; ADD; ADHD; EBD;

Moderate: ADD; ADHD; EBD;

Severe: EBD;

Others: AUT(other); CD; ODD

Summary: At the Earl of Dysart school we have a strong supportive team of Learning Support Assistants who are experienced and equipped to deal with a range of learning needs. We have a full-time learning mentor in school to support children with special needs, particularly emotional and behavioural needs. We have strong links with both the Learning Support Services and the Emotional and Behavioural Support Services. The school SENCo is currently studying for a qualification in autism.

East Norfolk Sixth Form College

Church Lane, Gorleston, Great Yarmouth, Norfolk, NR31 7BQ

Tel: 01493 662 234

Fax: 01493 441 405

Email: enquiries@enorf.ac.uk

Website: www.enorf.ac.uk

• Pupils: 1100 Mixed; Day Pupils • Age: 16 to 99

• Religion: Non-denominational • School status: State

SEN provision

Summary: The College offers full support for all students who attain the entry criteria. Students are asked about special educational or physical needs at their advisory interview prior to their start at college. All students have a personal tutor who makes arrangements for the student to access any additional support they may need while at college. The personal tutor also teaches the students so there is ample opportunity for student and tutor to talk. Extra support is available in the Skills Improvement Centre for literacy, numeracy and IT and all subjects hold weekly clinics. Counselling is available on four days of the week and the college has a health visitor and welfare officer. The examinations officer liaises with the examination boards for students with special examination requirements. The college has disabled access to most of its accommodation and provides specialist toilet facilities.

Eastcombe Primary School

Dr Crouch's Road, Eastcombe, Stroud, Gloucestershire, GL6 7EA

Tel: 01452 770 227
Fax: 01452 770 942
Email: admin@eastcombe.gloucs.sch.uk
Website: www.eastcombeprimaryschool.ik.org

• Pupils: 82 Mixed; Day Pupils • Age: 5 to 11
• Religion: Non-denominational • School status: State

SEN provision

Detail:
Now provide for in school:
Mild: EBD; DYSL;
Moderate: EBD; MLD; DYSL
Experience of:
Mild: AUT;
Moderate: AUT

Summary: Pupils are taught in mixed age classes and work is differentiated appropriately. Good use is made of learning support workers who work with individuals or small groups of pupils under the direction of the class teacher. The special needs co-ordinator works with the class teachers in drawing up and implementing individual education programmes. The headteacher has recent experience of teaching pupils with autism in a mainstream school. One class teacher has recently attended training on managing difficult behaviour in the classroom.

Eastfield Primary School and Nursery

St Alban's Close, Eastfield, Northampton, Northamptonshire, NN3 2RJ

Tel: 01604 405 042
Fax: 01604 411 509
Email: head@eastfield.northants-ecl.gov.uk
Website:
www.rmplc.co.uk/eduweb/sites/eastfieldlower/index.html

• Pupils: 218 Mixed; Day Pupils • Age: 3 to 11
• Religion: Non-denominational • School status: State

SEN provision

Detail:
Now provide for in school:
Mild: ASP; AUT; ADD; ADHD; EBD; DYSL; SpLD;
Moderate: AUT; ADD; EBD; MLD; DYSL; SpLD; CP;
Severe: EBD; CP;
Others: AUT(other); PMLD; SLD; EAL; Sp&LD; Epi; Eat
Experience of:
Mild: DYSP; VI;
Moderate: ASP; DYSP;
Others: SPD

Summary: One third of the children in our school receive one-to-one or small group support from the SENCo and her team of 14 support assistants. The ratio of available adult to child help is high for an ordinary Primary school. We have had a spectrum of special needs disabilities over the years and the team are very experienced and have many skills. Staff are continuously updating qualifications and learning new skills. All our children take part in the full curriculum and extra activities. It is a happy caring environment where children enjoy their studies and value their time with adults. Children, who start in our Nursery make significant progress in school.

EASTWICK INFANT SCHOOL

Eastwick Drive, Great Bookham, Surrey, KT23 3PP

Tel: 01372 453 672
Fax: 01372 451 236
Email: info@eastwick-infant.surrey.sch.uk
Website: www.eastwick-infant.surrey.sch.uk

• Pupils: 247 Mixed; Day Pupils • Age: 4 to 7
• Religion: Non-denominational • School status: State

SEN provision

Detail:
Now provide for in school:
Mild: ADD; ADHD; DS; DYSC; DYSL; DYSP; SpLD; HI; VI; CP;
Moderate: DS; MLD; DYSP; VI; CP;
Others: SPD; Sp&LD; Epi
Experience of:
Mild: ASP; AUT; EBD;
Moderate: ASP; AUT

Summary: The school has a 22 place special needs support unit, which caters for children with a range of needs. At present the majority of the children are on the autistic spectrum. The teachers and support staff take part in regular training to help in their teaching of autistic children. There is a wide range of support for all children including visual timetables, multi-sensory teaching and the use of Makaton.

The children have access to physiotherapy; occupational therapy once a week if they need it. We also have speech and language therapy sessions at least once a week or more if needed.

EASTWOOD GRANGE SCHOOL

Eastwood Grange, Milken Lane, Ashover, Chesterfield, Derbyshire, S45 0BA

Tel: 01246 590 255
Fax: 01246 590 215
Email: info@eastwoodgrange.com
Website: www.eastwoodgrange.com

• Pupils: 26 Boys; Takes boarders • Age: 11 to 16
• School status: Independent

SEN provision

Detail:
Now provide for in school:
Mild: ADD; ADHD; EBD;
Moderate: ADD; ADHD; EBD; MLD;
Severe: EBD;
Others: CD; ODD

Summary: Eastwood Grange is both a Children's Home and a Residential School for boys aged 11-16+ years with social, emotional and behavioural difficulties. We provide a warm, welcoming, relaxed, yet structured environment, which encourages young people to develop social, educational and practical skills and enjoy an active, fulfilling life in beautiful surroundings.

ECTON PRIMARY SCHOOL

West Street, Ecton, Northampton, Northamptonshire, NN6 0QF

Tel: 01604 409 213
Fax: 01604 409 213
Email: head@ecton-pri.northants-ecl.gov.uk

• Pupils: 62 Mixed; Day Pupils • Age: 4 to 11
• Religion: Non-denominational • School status: State

SEN provision

Detail:
Now provide for in school:
Mild: EBD; DYSC; DYSL;

Moderate: EBD; MLD; DYSL; CP;
Others: PMLD; Sp&LD
Experience of:
Mild: ASP; ADD; ADHD;
Moderate: ADD; ADHD; DYSP;
Others: Epi

Summary: The ethos of our school is centered around each child achieving their potential and enjoying their time in school. All children are special and our policies are inclusive for all children regardless of their needs and abilities. We recognise the talents of each individual child and plan to nurture their abilities and develop confidence and self esteem.

EDENHURST PREP SCHOOL

Westlands Avenue, Newcastle, Staffordshire, ST5 2PU

Tel: 01782 619 348
Fax: 01782 662 402
Email: mail@edenhurst.co.uk
Website: www.edenhurst.co.uk
• Pupils: 242 Mixed; Day Pupils • Age: 3 to 12
• School status: Independent

SEN provision

Detail:
Now provide for in school:
Mild: DYSC; DYSL; DYSP; SpLD; HI; VI;
Moderate: MLD; DYSC; DYSL; DYSP; SpLD;
Severe: DYSL;
Others: EAL; Epi
Experience of:
Mild: ADD; ADHD; EBD

Summary: A teacher from the Dyslexia Institute gives tuition to around 30 pupils during the week. From September 2006, this function will be taken over by a fully trained member of staff who will also be on hand to help other children with less specific special needs. It is thought that the school will admit more pupils with dyslexia.

ELDENE PRIMARY SCHOOL

Colingsmead, Eldene, Swindon, Wiltshire, SN3 3TQ

Tel: 01793 525 908
Fax: 01793 487 245
Email: admin@eldene-jun.swindon.sch.uk
• Pupils: 412 Mixed; Day Pupils • Age: 4 to 11
• Religion: Non-denominational • School status: State

SEN provision

Detail:
Now provide for in school:
Mild: AUT; ADHD; EBD; DYSL; DYSP; HI; VI;
Moderate: AUT; ADHD; EBD; MLD; DYSL; DYSP; CP;
Severe: AUT; ADD; ADHD;
Others: SPD; EAL; MSI; DEL; Epi; PD
Experience of:
Mild: ASP;
Moderate: ASP; HI;
Severe: ASP;
Others: OCD; TIC

Summary: Eldene Primary is a large mainstream school with experience of meeting the needs of a wide range of ability levels and needs. We also have a Special Resourced Provision for children with complex learning difficulties – a class of eight pupils who have access to mainstream lessons and activities as and when appropriate. Entry to the SRP is dictated by the LEA and all these children have the support of statements of special educational needs. We also have some children in the mainstream who have the support of a statement, plus children who have additional funding from the LEA to enable access to the curriculum.

ELMTREE SCHOOL

Elmtree Hill, Chesham, Buckinghamshire, HP5 2PA

Tel: 01494 771 474
Fax: 01494 785 254
Email: office@elmtree.bucks.sch.uk
Website: www.elmtree.bucks.sch.uk

• Pupils: 229 Mixed; Day Pupils • Age: 4 to 7
• Religion: Non-denominational • School status: State

SEN provision

Detail:
Now provide for in school:
Mild: ASP; ADHD; DYSL; DYSP
Experience of:
Mild: EBD; DS; HI; CP;
Others: Epi

Summary: Elmtree School has a specialist Language Department attached, for children with statements of special educational needs for language disorders. This excellent provision is inclusive; supporting children in their mainstream classes and helping them acquire the skills to access the curriculum. In addition the teacher in charge of the department, our speech and language therapist and the trained teaching assistants withdraw children for specialist teaching sessions. The school makes provision for a range of other special needs and has strategies in place to extend the learning of more able children, so that all our children work to achieve their potential.

ENFIELD (NEW WALTHAM) PRIMARY SCHOOL

Enfield Avenue, New Waltham, Grimsby, DN36 4RB

Tel: 01472 321 434
Fax: 01472 321 434
Email: office@ep.tlfe.org
Website: www.enfieldprimary.co.uk

• Pupils: 140 Mixed; Day Pupils • Age: 4 to 11
• Religion: Non-denominational • School status: State

SEN provision

Detail:
Now provide for in school:
Mild: ASP; AUT; DYSC; DYSL; DYSP;
Moderate: ASP; AUT; HI; CP;
Others: EAL
Experience of:
Mild: ADD; ADHD; EBD; DS;
Others: Epi

ENFIELD GRAMMAR SCHOOL

Market Place, Enfield, Middlesex, EN2 6LN

Tel: 020 8363 1095
Fax: 020 8342 1805
Email: enfgrammar@aol.com
Website: www.enfieldgrammar.com

• Pupils: 1130 Boys; Day Pupils • Age: 11 to 18
• School status: State

SEN provision

Detail:
Now provide for in school:
Mild: ASP; ADD; ADHD; EBD; DYSC; DYSL; DYSP; SpLD; HI; VI;
Moderate: EBD; MLD; DYSC; DYSL; DYSP; HI; VI;
Severe: DYSL;
Others: EAL; Sp&LD; DEL; Epi; Eat

Summary: The SEN team is made up of two tutors, two higher level teaching assistants, seven teaching assistants, a dyslexia specialist and inclusion manager and the SEN co-ordinator. Members of the team are attached to those departments in which they have expertise, for example, the teaching assistant with expertise in geography will be attached to the geography department.

Much support is provided through the teaching of smaller groups. Within these groups members of the SEN team target those pupils with particular learning difficulties. In addition each site has a student support centre enabling support, on an individual or small group basis, to be provided, eg withdrawal literacy groups.

Older pupils also provide support, either as reading buddies and peer mentors or through the homework club.

Pupil progress is regularly reported to parents.

EPINAY SCHOOL

Clervaux Terrace, Jarrow, Tyne and Wear, NE32 5UP

Tel: 0191 489 8949

Fax: 0191 483 7417

Email: hharrison@southtyneside.northerngrid.org

• Pupils: 108 Mixed; Day Pupils • Age: 4 to 16

• Religion: Non-denominational • School status: State

SEN provision

Detail:

Experience of:

Mild: DYSC; DYSL; DYSP; SpLD;

Moderate: EBD; DYSC; DYSL; DYSP; SpLD;

Severe: EBD; DYSC; DYSL; DYSP; SpLD;

Others: CD; OCD; Sp&LD

Summary: Epinay Business and Enterprise School caters for pupils with moderate global learning difficulties and in addition pupils may have speech and language needs, specific learning difficulties, emotional, health (ie mental health not medical) and behavioural needs.

EUROPEAN SCHOOL OF KARLSRUHE

Albert Schweitzer Strasse 1, D-76139 Karlsruhe 1, Germany

Tel: 00 49721680 0901

Fax: 00 49721680 0950

Email: vnsh@eursc.org

• Pupils: 1200 Mixed; Day Pupils • Age: 3 to 18

• School status: State

SEN provision

Summary: Learning support is offered on the recommendation of the class teacher to children of all age groups in the Kindergarten and the primary school. Learning support is provided in the subjects of the class curriculum in order to alleviate learning difficulties through short-term, targeted assistance. This support is delivered during normal teaching time in the classroom, or if necessary, also on a one-to-one basis, whilst ensuring that no teaching time is lost in the relevant subject area. The children receiving learning support receive an individual learning plan, which identifies their strengths and weaknesses, as well as a programme for overcoming their difficulties. After approximately six months, the progress of the individual student is discussed with parents, class teacher and deputy headteacher, and future objectives agreed.

In years 3, 4 and 5 in the primary school, children who are having problems with the foreign language can have extra tuition in the language on Wednesday afternoons – outside of normal teaching hours. On the recommendation of either the language teacher or the class teacher, in agreement with the parents, a specific programme of extra tuition can be organised for a six-month period.

FAIRMEAD SCHOOL

Mudford Road, Yeovil, Somerset, BA21 4NZ

Tel: 01935 421 295

Fax: 01935 410 552

Email: office@fairmead.somerset.sch.uk

Website: www.fairmead.ik.org

• Pupils: 79 Mixed; Day Pupils • Age: 4 to 16

• Religion: Non-denominational • School status: State

SEN provision

Summary: Fairmead Community Special School supports statemented pupils aged 5-16 with complex needs around learning, autism, behaviour, emotional and social needs, and language and communication. Increasingly our work supports pupils with SEN in partnership with health and social services.

Farney Close School

Bolney Court, Bolney, Haywards Heath, West Sussex, RH17 5RD

Tel: 01444 881 811
Fax: 01444 881 957
Email: head@farneyclose.co.uk

• Pupils: 56 Mixed; Takes boarders • Age: 11 to 17
• School status: Independent

SEN provision

Detail:

Now provide for in school:
Mild: EBD; DYSL; SpLD;
Moderate: EBD; DYSL; SpLD;
Severe: EBD; SpLD

Summary: An independent school with charitable status. Caters for children with social emotional and behavioural difficulties (SEBD) and some specific learning difficulties including dyslexia.

Farr High School & Farr Primary School

Bettyhill, by Thurso, KW14 7SS

Tel: 01641 521 217
Fax: 01641 521 203
Email: farr.high@highland.gov.uk

• Pupils: Mixed; Day Pupils • Age: 3 to 18
• Religion: Non-denominational • School status: State

SEN provision

Detail:

Now provide for in school:
Mild: ASP; EBD; DYSL; DYSP; VI;
Moderate: MLD; DYSL; CP;
Others: SPD; PMLD; Sp&LD; Eat
Experience of:
Mild: AUT;
Others: PD

Summary: The school accommodates pupils in nursery, primary and secondary. We have a small learning support base for secondary pupils when small groups or one-to-one tuition is required. All school pupils are entitled to support for learning.

We are very much an inclusive school and we strive to meet individual pupil needs. Pupils belong to the class for their year group and follow a mainstream timetable as far as possible.

Although other agencies are far away we do seek out advice and support where necessary.

Fell House School

Appletree Treatment Centre Ltd, Natland, Kendal, Cumbria, LA9 7QS

Tel: 01539 535 926
Fax: 01539 534 847

• Mixed; Day Pupils • Age: 1 to 10
• School status: Independent

SEN provision

Detail:

Centre of excellence for:
Mild: ADD; ADHD; EBD; DYSC; DYSL; DYSP; SpLD; HI; VI;
Moderate: ADD; ADHD; EBD; DYSC; DYSL; DYSP; SpLD;
Severe: ADD; ADHD; EBD; DYSC; DYSL; DYSP; SpLD;
Others: CD; OCD; ODD

Summary: Fell House helps children with emotional and behavioural difficulties and associated learning difficulties overcome their problems and re-integrate by the age of 13 years.

Felpham Community College

Felpham Way, Felpham, Bognor Regis, West Sussex, PO22 8EL

Tel: 01243 826 511
Fax: 01243 841 021
Email: fcc@felpham.org.uk
Website: www.felpham.w-sussex.sch.uk

• Pupils: 1328 Mixed; Day Pupils • Age: 11 to 18
• Religion: Non-denominational • School status: State

SEN provision

Detail:
Now provide for in school:
Mild: ASP; ADD; ADHD; EBD; DYSC; DYSL; DYSP; HI; VI;
Moderate: ASP; ADD; ADHD; EBD; MLD; DYSL; DYSP; HI;
Severe: DYSL; HI;
Others: EAL; Sp&LD; Epi
Experience of:
Mild: CP;
Moderate: DYSC; VI; CP;
Severe: VI; CP;
Others: SPD; OCD; PMLD; SLD; DEL; Eat

Summary:

- In the individual learning support department at Felpham Community College we aim to help raise all student's achievements and standards throughout the college.
- To improve the learning and teaching experience for all SEN students.
- To promote strategies to help SEN students to become independent learners.
- To communicate to all staff information and support necessary to ensure access to the National Curriculum for all students but particularly those with SEN. To ensure all students are given the opportunities to reach their full potential.

Filsham Valley School

Edinburgh Road, St Leonards-on-Sea, East Sussex, TN38 8DA

Tel: 01424 448 740
Fax: 01424 722 354
Email: office@filshamvalley.e-sussex.sch.uk
Website: www.filshamvalley.e-sussex.sch.uk

• Pupils: 963 Mixed; Day Pupils • Age: 11 to 18
• Religion: Non-denominational • School status: State

SEN provision

Detail:
Centre of excellence for:
Mild: EBD; CP;
Moderate: CP;
Others: Sp&LD
Now provide for in school:
Mild: ASP; AUT; ADD; ADHD; DYSL; DYSP; HI; VI;
Moderate: EBD; DYSL;
Severe: CP;
Others: SPD; AUT(other); CD; OCD; ODD; EAL
Experience of:
Mild: DS; DYSC; SpLD;
Moderate: ASP; AUT; ADD; ADHD; MLD; DYSP; HI; VI;
Severe: ASP; AUT; ADD; ADHD; EBD; DYSL; DYSP;
Others: TIC; MSI; DEL; Epi

Summary: Filsham Valley School has a special facility for pupils with sensory and physical needs. Provision within the special facility includes: speech and language therapy, physiotherapy, hydrotherapy, swimming, a visual impairment unit and a medical room. Pupils have access to literacy and numeracy teaching, the Youth Awards Scheme, social skills lessons and a nurture group facility.

Filton Hill Primary School

Blenheim Drive, Filton, Bristol, BS34 7AX

Tel: 01454 866 559
Fax: 01454 866 560
Email: FiltonHillPrimary.School@southglos.gov.uk
Website: www.filtonhill.ik.org

• Pupils: 207 Mixed; Day Pupils • Age: 5 to 11
• Religion: Non-denominational • School status: State

SEN provision

Detail:
Experience of:
Mild: ASP; ADD; ADHD; EBD; DYSL; DYSP;
Moderate: ASP; MLD

Summary: We have an excellent SEN department. It is led by an experienced and well qualified SENCo and she is joined by a strong team of teaching and learning support assistants. The children are assessed and then supported according to their individual needs.

Finham Park School

Green Lane, Coventry, West Midlands, CV3 6EA

Tel: 024 7641 8135
Fax: 024 7684 0803
Email: headteacher@finhampark.co.uk
Website: www.finhampark.co.uk

• Pupils: 1520 Mixed; Day Pupils • Age: 11 to 18
• Religion: Non-denominational • School status: State

SEN provision

Detail:
Now provide for in school:
Mild: ASP; AUT; ADD; ADHD; EBD; DYSL; DYSP; HI; VI;
Moderate: ASP; EBD; MLD; DYSL; DYSP; HI; VI;
Severe: DYSL;
Others: EAL; Sp&LD; Epi; PD; Eat

Experience of:
Mild: DYSC;
Moderate: AUT; ADD; ADHD; DYSC;
Severe: ASP; EBD; VI;
Others: SPD; CD; OCD; ODD; TIC; MSI

Summary: At Finham Park, students with special educational needs are taught largely in mainstream classes and are encouraged to participate fully in the whole-school curriculum. Additional support, however, is provided through the supportive studies department, and this can take various forms. Some students are supported in mainstream classes by our team of teaching assistants, whose main role is to help students access the curriculum and to encourage and assist them with their work and behaviour. In addition to this, small group and individual support lessons are set up for those students who who have high levels of specific learning needs, such as low level literacy skills. The school works closely with external support agencies to provide specialist support for conditions such as autistic spectrum disorder or sensory impairment, and this can take the form of both direct intervention with students, as well as training and advice for the staff. The school follows the guidelines set out in the Code of Practice, whereby all students with special educational needs are recorded in our SEN register which is used to communicate individual student's needs to teachers and is up-dated on a termly basis. Students' progress is monitored closely and communicated regularly to parents and carers. The school has a policy of SEN which is available to parents on request.

Forest Oak School

Lanchester Way, Castle Bromwich, Birmingham, West Midlands, B36 9LF

Tel: 01217 483 411
Fax: 01217 497 534
Email: office@forest-oak.solihull.sch.uk

• Pupils: 94 Mixed; Day Pupils • Age: 4 to 16
• Religion: Non-denominational • School status: State

SEN provision

Detail:
Now provide for in school:
Mild: ASP; AUT; ADD; ADHD; EBD;
Moderate: ASP; AUT;
Others: SPD; Epi
Experience of:
Mild: DYSC; DYSL; DYSP; HI; VI; CP;
Moderate: ADD; ADHD; EBD; DYSC; DYSL; DYSP;
Severe: ASP; AUT; ADD; ADHD; EBD;
Others: CD; Sp&LD

Summary: All of the pupils at Forest Oak have moderate learning difficulties and have statements of educational need. The difficulties cover a broad range. Pupils have access to the statutory curriculum, differentiated according to their needs. Each class has a learning support assistant. In order to support pupils with communication difficulties, staff receive training in the use of Makaton signing and the Widget symbol system.

In addition to moderate learning difficulties, Forest Oak caters for pupils with autistic spectrum disorder, ADD and ADHD, and has experience of dealing with emotional social behavioural disorders, visual and hearing impairments and physical disabilities. Staff work in conjunction with outside agencies to provide the best possible support for pupils. A speech and language therapist is attached to the school.

Pupils are assessed on an ongoing basis. Optional SATs testing is used to assess at the end of Key Stages. Pupils in Key Stage 4 are prepared for accreditation in English, maths, science and life skills. In addition, they have a choice of performing or expressive arts.

Fosse Way School

Longfellow Road, Radstock, Bath, BA3 3AL

Tel: 01761 412 198
Fax: 01761 411 751
Email: fosseway_spe@bathnes.gov.uk

• Pupils: 109 Mixed; Takes boarders • Age: 3 to 19
• Religion: Non-denominational • School status: State

SEN provision

Detail:
Now provide for in school:
Mild: ASP; AUT; ADD; ADHD; DS; DYSL; DYSP; SpLD; HI; VI; CP;
Moderate: ASP; AUT; ADD; ADHD; DS; MLD; DYSL; DYSP; SpLD; HI; VI; CP;
Severe: ASP; AUT; DS; DYSL; DYSP; SpLD; HI; CP;
Others: AUT(other); OCD; ODD; TIC; FRX; GEN; PMLD; SLD; MSI; Sp&LD; DEL; Epi; PD; Eat
Experience of:
Mild: DYSC;
Moderate: DYSC;
Severe: DYSC; VI;
Others: SPD; Oth

Summary: Fosse Way is a school for children and young people with severe and complex learning difficulties, including autistic spectrum disorders, aged 3-19 years old. There is also a weekly boarding facility for up to 14 pupils requiring 24-hour structured and consistent learning environment.

Fosse Way has a specialist technology college status.

We are a comparatively small school of about 110 pupils. The staff and governors aim to provide our young people with an education that is broadly based and tailored to meet individual needs. We create a caring, happy and positive atmosphere in which a child may fulfil his/her potential and grow in self-confidence and respect for the people and environment around them.

We believe strongly in working with local schools and the wider community, supporting students with special needs by offering expertise, training and resources.

FOXWOOD SCHOOL

Seabrook Road, Hythe, Kent, CT21 5QJ

Tel: 01303 261 155

Fax: 01303 262 355

• Pupils: 100 Mixed; Takes boarders • Age: 2 to 19

• Religion: Non-denominational • School status: State

SEN provision

Detail:

Now provide for in school:

Mild: AUT; EBD;

Moderate: AUT; EBD;

Severe: AUT; EBD;

Others: AUT(other); PMLD; SLD

Summary: Foxwood School offers flexibility and individually tailored education for pupils and students. All pupils at Foxwood School will have a statement of special educational needs issued by and maintained by their local education authority. The statement will outline each pupil or student's individual special educational needs and the educational and non-educational provision required to meet those needs. The statement will also name Foxwood School as the appropriate placement to provide for the child's additional educational needs. All pupils at Foxwood School have a range of needs including severe learning difficulties, challenging behaviour, profound and multiple learning difficulties and autism.

The school's admission policy clearly outlines the procedure and guidance for successful applications. Pupils generally come from Kent and day pupils from within easy travel distance. Support for transport is arranged through the local education authority. Where appropriate, pupils are taught to travel independently.

During the admissions procedure, parents will be asked to agree and sign the Home School Agreement (two way contract) which outlines acceptable behaviours and procedures, both at school and at home.

For day pupils/students

When a child has been assessed as in need of special educational provision, parents and pupils are invited to visit the school to view the facilities and see the school in action. The aim is to make the visit as relaxed and informal as possible, whilst at the same time being informative and supportive.

Residential Referrals

On referral by the local educational authority, the Headteacher and Head of Care would normally visit pupils at their day school and meet the parents at home. If admission is indicated and agreed the child will be discussed with a class teacher and key worker from Foxwood School, who will also visit the pupil's/student's school and meet with parents. In discussion with all parties concerned the process of admission will be determined.

The process of admission may vary. For some, an induction period will be planned to gradually acclimatise pupils to their new school and the specific arrangements for them. For others, their induction may be planned to include part-time attendance increasing to full-time. In all cases, admissions are carefully and jointly planned with parents to match specific pupil/student needs.

FULHAM CROSS SCHOOL

Munster Road, London, SW6 6BP

Tel: 020 7381 0861

Fax: 020 7386 5979

Email: fulham_cross_sch@btconnect.com

• Pupils: 598 Girls; Day Pupils • Age: 11 to 16

• Religion: Non-denominational • School status: State

SEN provision

Detail:

Now provide for in school:

Mild: EBD; HI; CP;

Moderate: EBD; MLD; HI;

Severe: EBD;

Others: EAL

Experience of:

Mild: ADD; DYSL; DYSP; VI;

Moderate: ADD; DYSL;

Others: Sp&LD; DEL; Epi; Eat

Summary: Students at Fulham Cross School are well supported by the SEN and learning support departments. A dedicated team of teaching assistants work in classrooms with students. In addition target groups of students have opportunities to work in the SEN department, within a small group with one of the two full-time SEN teachers.

At Key Stage 4 the support offered to students is flexible, encouraging them to become even more independent in their learning. Key Stage 4 support groups offer additional help with meeting coursework deadlines as well as reinforcing basic literacy and numeracy skills.

Students are set clear and achievable targets. At school, Action Tutors liaise with students in order to agree reasonable targets. These can be monitored on a daily basis as part of the pastoral care system.

The students at Fulham Cross value the support offered to them and are eager to make use of it.

Garnock Academy

School Road, Kilbirnie, KA25 7AX

Tel: 01505 682 685
Fax: 01505 684 876
Email: contactus@garnock.n-ayrshire.sch.uk
Website: www.garnockacademy.org
• Pupils: 1191 Unknown; Day Pupils • Age: 11 to 18
• Religion: Non-denominational • School status: State

SEN provision

Summary: The primary aim of Garnock Academy is that every pupil receives an appropriate education which is both challenging and attainable. In that respect pupil support is integral to all teaching and learning and is the responsibility of all those involved: the LEA, school staff, education support services, appropriate external agencies, parents and the pupil. The fact that a pupil is referred to the pupil support department simply means that at a particular time they are experiencing a difficulty which requires additional support.

We have the facility to cater for a wide range of educational needs, supporting effective teaching and learning across the curriculum. The pupil support department will aim to meet those needs through a variety of different strategies namely:

- Differentiation of the curriculum, resources and teaching strategies
- Consultancy support/staff development for other members of staff
- Cooperative or team teaching
- Tutorial support, either within the classroom, one-to-one or small group
- one-to-one counselling behaviour management programmes
- Flexibile/alternative curriculum plannning
- ASDAN target setting and monitoring of pupil progress through the use of IEPs where appropriate
- Involvement of appropriate external agencies
- On-going communication with parents.

Garratt Park School

Waldron Road, Earlsfield, Wandsworth, London, SW18 3TB

Tel: 020 8946 5769
Fax: 020 8947 5605
• Pupils: 145 Mixed; Day Pupils • Age: 11 to 18
• Religion: Non-denominational • School status: State

SEN provision

Detail:
Centre of excellence for:
Mild: AUT;
Moderate: AUT; MLD
Now provide for in school:
Mild: ASP; ADD; ADHD; EBD; DS; DYSC; DYSL; DYSP; HI; VI; CP;
Moderate: ASP; ADD; ADHD; DYSL; DYSP; HI;
Severe: ASP; DYSL;
Others: SPD; AUT(other); OCD; FRX; EAL; Sp&LD; DEL; Epi; PD; Eat
Experience of:
Mild: SpLD;
Moderate: EBD; DS; DYSC; SpLD;
Others: TIC

Summary: Garratt Park School is a special school for students with a wide range of special educational needs. The school is located in the Inner London Borough of Wandsworth and takes students from all over the Borough, as well as neighbouring boroughs.

Garratt Park School currently caters for 145 students from a wide range of economic and social backgrounds. Our current students all have statements of special educational needs that name mild/moderate learning difficulties as the major need. Examples of the types of special educational needs and additional needs that are experienced by our current students include language and communication difficulties and autistic spectrum disorder (ASD).

Garratt Park School aims to enable young people to achieve their fullest potential through a broad and balanced curriculum. All members of the school have the right to experience success within a caring community, which recognises their efforts and celebrates their achievements. Garratt Park School aims to enable its students to foster a caring, respectful attitude to others; become independent and socially competent adults; earn their living, gain job satisfaction, enjoy their learning and be eager to continue learning; take pride in themselves; develop self-confidence, an ability to communicate and acquire the skills necessary in life; be able to play a positive role in today's society and achieve their fullest potential.

The school has a base for students who have autistic spectrum disorders (ASD). In addition to this, there are a number of students with ASD within the main school. Students attached to the base are integrated into the main school for some aspects of the curriculum, as well as social integration. The school's year 12/13 curriculum reflects the recommendations of the Learning Skills Council and has well-established links with the local further education college and employers. These opportunities for students reflect our understanding of personalised learning and our commitment to promoting it.

GAY ELMS PRIMARY SCHOOL

Withywood Road, Withywood, Bristol, BS13 9AX

Tel: 0117 9030 311

Fax: 0117 9030 310

Email: gay_elms_p@bristol-city.gov.uk

Website: www.gayelmsprimary.freeserve.co.uk

• Pupils: 228 Mixed; Day Pupils • Age: 3 to 11

• Religion: Non-denominational • School status: State

SEN provision

Detail:

Now provide for in school:

Mild: ASP; AUT; ADD; ADHD; EBD; DYSC; DYSL; DYSP; HI; VI; CP;

Moderate: ASP; AUT; ADD; ADHD; EBD; MLD; DYSC; DYSL; HI; VI; CP;

Severe: ASP; AUT; ADD; ADHD; EBD; DYSC; DYSL; VI;

Others: SPD; AUT(other); EAL; MSI; Sp&LD; DEL; Epi; PD

Experience of:

Mild: SpLD;

Moderate: DYSP; SpLD;

Severe: DYSP; CP

Summary: We are a primary school which has a high proportion of local children who have special educational needs, some of whom have statements, others are provided for by the school's own resources. In the mainstream school we have a wheelchair accessible toilet, ramps, and some classrooms have widened doorways to allow greater access. We are currently having a lift installed to allow access to our upstairs corridor. The school is part of an Education Action Zone, which allows for access to greater local resources. We are part of a BLIP project for improving behaviour and attendance for children in school. The school is also part of a local speech and language therapy project. The school has an attached resource base for 27 children with an autistic spectrum disorder. All of these children have statements and admission to the resource base is through the LEA, which also manages the waiting list. Many of these pupils travel from all over Bristol to attend. In the resource base we have a specialist ASD environment, small classes of six or seven pupils and staff who are all trained and experienced in working with children who have an ASD. Pupils from the Resource Base have inclusion with their mainstream peers as appropriate.

Gayhurst School

Bull Lane, Gerrards Cross, Buckinghamshire, SL9 8RJ

Tel: 01753 882 690
Fax: 01753 887 451
Email: csnelling@gayhurst.bucks.sch.uk
Website: www.gayhurst.bucks.sch.uk

• Pupils: Boys; Day Pupils • Age: 3 to 14
• School status: Independent

SEN provision

Detail:
Now provide for in school:
Mild: ADD; ADHD; DYSC; DYSL; DYSP;
Moderate: DYSC; DYSL; DYSP;
Severe: DYSL
Experience of:
Mild: ASP; SpLD; HI;
Moderate: ADD; ADHD; SpLD; HI;
Others: SPD; EAL; Sp&LD; Epi; Eat

Summary: We provide learning support, on an individual basis, for children assessed as having specific learning difficulties, including neurodevelopmental delay, in both the junior and senior departments.

George Dixon International School and Sixth Form Centre

City Road, Edgbaston, Birmingham, West Midlands, B17 8LF

Tel: 0121 434 4488
Fax: 0121 434 3721
Email: enquiry@georgedixon.bham.sch.uk

• Pupils: 1016 Mixed; Day Pupils • Age: 11 to 18
• Religion: Non-denominational • School status: State

SEN provision

Detail:
Now provide for in school:
Mild: AUT; ADD; EBD; DYSC; DYSL; DYSP; SpLD; HI; VI;
Moderate: ADD; EBD; MLD; DYSL; HI; VI;
Others: CD; ODD; Sp&LD; Epi
Experience of:
Mild: ASP; DS; CP;
Moderate: DYSC; DYSP; SpLD;
Severe: SpLD;
Others: PMLD; SLD; DEL; Eat

Summary: At George Dixon International School we have a 'whole-school' approach to the education of students with special educational needs. All teachers share responsibility for the identification, assessment and provision appropriate to meeting individual student needs within their own curriculum area. The work of the student support department interconnects and underpins the practice of other departments. Students with special educational needs have access to all National Curriculum subjects. Students are taught in mainstream teaching groups, and are placed in groups as part of the whole school setting process. In-class learning support is provided where possible. The student support manager has prime responsibility for promoting awareness of the needs of students with special educational needs, and for encouraging and supporting the development of appropriate opportunities and resources throughout all aspects of school life. We offer extra support through: registration classes, lunchtime reading classes, after school classes, mentoring and one-to-one support in the student support base. Outside agencies work in partnership with student support and pastoral teams to support learning, behaviour and to monitor progress of individual students when required.

George Eliot Community School

Raveloe Drive, Caldwell, Nuneaton, Warwickshire, CV11 4QP

Tel: 02476 744 000
Fax: 02476 741 530
Email: admin@4156.wgfl.net

• Pupils: 805 Mixed; Day Pupils • Age: 11 to 16
• Religion: Presbyterian • School status: State

SEN provision

Detail:

Centre of excellence for:
- Mild: EBD; DYSL;
- Moderate: EBD; MLD; DYSL;
- Severe: EBD;
- Others: CD; OCD; TIC; SLD; EAL; Sp&LD

Now provide for in school:
- Mild: ASP; AUT; ADD; ADHD; DYSC; DYSP; HI; VI; CP;
- Moderate: ASP; AUT; ADD; ADHD; DYSC; DYSP; HI; CP;
- Severe: ADD; ADHD; DYSC; DYSL; DYSP;
- Others: SPD; ODD; DEL; Epi; PD

Experience of:
- Mild: DS; SpLD;
- Moderate: DS; SpLD;
- Severe: DS; SpLD;
- Others: FRX; GEN; PMLD

Summary: The learning support department staff are accessible to parents, carers and outside agencies at any time. Each child is an individual and therefore has individual needs. The learning support department have weekly one hour INSETs. These could be from a member of the department, outside agencies or other school members. INSETs have included dyslexia, dyspraxia, autistic spectrum discorder, ADHD, ethnic minority, asylum seekers, behaviour management, anger management, speech and language and social skills to enhance teaching assistants' skills. Currently we have three teaching assistants following courses on the autistic spectrum disorder, speech and language and dyslexia. New members of the department are trained and strategies taught to make sure students reach their full potential. Meetings with various subject's teams are ongoing. As a school we are committed to all students who have learning or behavioural difficulties to provide the best possible education we can.

George Hastwell School

Moor Tarn Lane, Walney Island, Barrow-in-Furness, Cumbria, LA14 3LW

Tel: 01229 475 253

Fax: 01229 471 418

• Pupils: 89 Mixed; Day Pupils • Age: 2 to 19

• Religion: Non-denominational • School status: State

SEN provision

Summary: George Hastwell is a community special school for pupils with statements of severe or profound and multiple learning difficulties. In addition, some pupils may also have hearing or visual impairments, autistic spectrum disorder, emotional/behavioural problems and cerebral palsy. The aim of the school is to provide a broad, balanced and relevant curriculum, taking into account the needs of each individual pupil. The National Curriculum is followed with, where necessary, adaptations to allow maximum participation in classroom activities. The school aims to promote the personal development of all pupils as a preparation for future life. They should acquire, as far as possible, the ability to tolerate and respect other people, as well as an appropriate balance of knowledge, understanding and skills, in an environment which promotes the enjoyment of learning.

Glebe Primary School

Sussex Road, Ickenham, Uxbridge, Middlesex, UB10 8PH

Tel: 01895 671 951
Fax: 01895 674 143
Email: glebe@hillingdongrid.org
Website: www.glebe.hillingdon.sch.uk

• Pupils: 306 Mixed; Day Pupils • Age: 3 to 11
• Religion: Non-denominational • School status: State

SEN provision

Detail:
Centre of excellence for:
Mild: HI;
Moderate: HI;
Severe: HI

Summary: We have a specialist resourced provision for hearing impaired children. We can take up to nine children who are statemented. The children are part of mainstream classes but benefit from the support of appropriately qualified and experienced staff. Individual programmes of work are drawn up for each child to reflect their diverse needs. The children also receive regular speech and language therapy. Our last Ofsted inspection in January 2003 recognised the good quality of our provision.

Glebelands School

Parsonage Road, Cranleigh, Surrey, GU6 7AN

Tel: 01483 542 400
Fax: 01483 542 401
Email: headteacher@glebelands.surrey.sch.uk
Website: www.glebelands.surrey.sch.uk

• Pupils: 898 Mixed; Day Pupils • Age: 11 to 16
• Religion: Non-denominational • School status: State

SEN provision

Detail:
Now provide for in school:
Mild: ASP; AUT; ADD; ADHD; EBD; DYSC; DYSL; DYSP; SpLD; HI; VI; CP;
Moderate: ASP; AUT; MLD; DYSC; DYSL; DYSP; SpLD; HI; CP;
Severe: DYSL;
Others: SPD; CD; OCD; ODD; TIC; EAL; Sp&LD; Epi; PD; Eat

Summary: The learning support department reinforces the school's policy of supporting and developing the child as an individual to reach his or her potential. The school believes in the entitlement of all pupils to the whole curriculum including the National Curriculum.

Pupils are supported by being withdrawn to work with specialist LS staff on Tracks Literacy, Numeracy, SuccessMaker, general literacy, language or social skills programmes. Pupils can receive support in class or by being withdrawn.

Pupils are tested termly and tuition reviewed and adapted to meet the changing needs of the pupils.

Communication with parents is welcomed.

Glen Hills Primary School

Featherby Drive, Glen Parva, Leicestershire, LE2 9NY

Tel: 01162 782 535
Fax: 01162 788 208
Email: office@glen-hills.leics.sch.uk
Website: www.glenhills.ik.org

• Pupils: 383 Mixed; Day Pupils • Age: 4 to 10
• Religion: Non-denominational • School status: State

SEN provision

Detail:
Now provide for in school:
Mild: ASP; AUT; ADD; ADHD; EBD; DYSC; DYSL; DYSP; SpLD; HI; VI; CP;
Moderate: ASP; AUT; ADD; ADHD; EBD; MLD; DYSC; DYSL; DYSP; HI; VI;
Severe: ADHD; EBD; DYSC; DYSL;
Others: ODD; PMLD; EAL; Sp&LD; Epi; PD; Oth
Experience of:
Mild: DS;
Moderate: DS; SpLD; CP;
Severe: ASP; AUT; ADD; DS; DYSP; SpLD; HI; VI; CP;

Others: SPD; AUT(other); CD; OCD; TIC; FRX; SLD; MSI; DEL; Eat

Summary: Glen Hills has long held a good reputation locally for supporting SEN pupils. A high proportion of pupils on our special needs register are from outside our catchment area. Parents apply for places specifically to get a high level of support for their children. This opinion is endorsed by our County Advice and Inspection Team and by Ofsted. (Difficulties which are not mentioned, but of which we have experience/ expertise, are Perthes syndrome, Cystic Fibrosis, Haemophilia, Epilepsy, MRSA, Juvenile Arthritis, Head injuries causing brain trauma, Leukaemia, Cancer.)

THE GORDON SCHOOLS

Castle Street, Huntly, Aberdeenshire, AB54 4SE

Tel: 01466 792 181
Fax: 01466 794 715
Email: gordonschools.aberdeenshire.sch.uk
Website: atschool.eduweb.co.uk/gordonschools.ac
• Pupils: 890 Mixed; Day Pupils • Age: 18
• Religion: Non-denominational • School status: State

SEN provision

Summary: There is a curriculum support unit integrated for pupils who have special needs. The integrated curriculum support unit caters for pupils with profound needs, in addition to facilities for support for learners and provision for pupils with social and emotional needs. There are approximately 12 pupils in the GSU.

GOSFORD HILL SCHOOL

Oxford Road, Kidlington, Oxfordshire, OX5 2NT

Tel: 01865 374 971
Fax: 01865 841 029
Email: Headteacher.4060@gosford-hill.oxon.sch.uk
Website: www.gosford-hill.oxon.sch.uk/
• Pupils: 1183 Mixed; Day Pupils • Age: 11 to 18
• Religion: Non-denominational • School status: State

SEN provision

Detail:

Now provide for in school:
- Mild: ADD; ADHD; EBD; DS; DYSL; DYSP; HI; VI;
- Moderate: ADD; ADHD; EBD; DYSL; DYSP; HI; VI;
- Severe: DYSL; HI;
- Others: EAL; PD; Oth

Experience of:
- Mild: ASP; DYSC;
- Moderate: ASP; DS;
- Severe: ADD; ADHD; EBD;
- Others: SPD; ODD; GEN; Sp&LD; Eat

Summary: Gosford Hill has a range of SEN provision operating from a well equipped base which has three work areas and a suite of computers. There is a large (16+) team of teaching assistants led by an experienced SENCo. Support is offered according to need and may take the form of withdrawal for one-to-one or group work, or in-class help. Students for whom English is not their first language are offered targetted support. The school opened a learning support unit in September 2003 which has a full-time teacher manager and designated teaching assistants. An induction course is offered to 'vulnerable' year 6 students in the summer term before transfer to Gosford Hill.

GRANGE SCHOOL

77 Dickenson Road, Rusholme, Manchester, Lancashire, M14 5AZ

Tel: 01612 484 841
Fax: 01612 486 715
Email: admin@grange.manchester.sch.uk
• Pupils: 56 Mixed; Day Pupils • Age: 4 to 19
• Religion: Non-denominational • School status: State

SEN provision

Detail:

Now provide for in school:
- Mild: AUT;
- Moderate: AUT; EBD; MLD;
- Severe: ASP; AUT; EBD;
- Others: AUT(other); SLD

Summary: Grange school caters for pupils with a diagnosis of autistic spectrum disorder leading to moderate to severe learning difficulties and in some cases challenging behaviours.

Grangefield School & Technology College

Oxbridge Avenue, Stockton-on-Tees, TS18 4LE

Tel: 01642 353 637
Fax: 01642 612 217
Email: grangefield@stockton.gov.uk
Website: www.grangefield.stockton.sch.uk
• Pupils: 1327 Mixed; Day Pupils • Age: 11 to 16
• Religion: Non-denominational • School status: State

SEN provision

Detail:
Now provide for in school:
Mild: ASP; ADHD; EBD; DYSC; DYSL; DYSP; HI; VI; CP;
Moderate: ADHD; EBD; MLD; DYSL;
Severe: EBD; DYSL;
Others: CD; OCD; ODD; TIC; FRX; EAL; Epi; PD; Eat
Experience of:
Mild: ADD;
Moderate: ASP;
Others: Sp&LD

Summary: SEN is a whole school issue. The SEN team comprises SENCo, assistant SENCo and nine LSATs. Each subject area has an allocated LSTA, although all will work as required. The Learning Zone is an area where pupils may receive individual and small group support. Pupils may be supported in-class, by withdawal or by individual programmes. In Key Stage 4 there is the opportunity to follow more vocational courses which may be individually tailored.

The Grantham Ambergate School

Dysart Road, Grantham, Lincolnshire, NG31 7LP

Tel: 01476 564 957
Fax: 01476 573 870
Email: amy.hodson@ambergate.lincs.sch.uk
• Pupils: 75 Mixed; Day Pupils • Age: 5 to 16
• Religion: Non-denominational • School status: State

SEN provision

Detail:
Now provide for in school:
Mild: ADD; ADHD; EBD;
Moderate: ADD; ADHD; EBD; MLD;
Severe: ADD; ADHD; EBD;
Others: Sp&LD; PD

Summary: School caters for students with moderate global learning difficulties and in addition students may have speech and language needs, physical needs – medical fine or gross motor, emotional and or behavioural needs as a result of any or all the aforementioned.

Grayrigg C of E School

Grayrigg, Kendal, Cumbria, LA8 9BU

Tel: 01539 824 676
Fax: 01539 824 676
Email: admin@grayrigg.cumbria.sch.uk
• Pupils: 46 Mixed; Day Pupils • Age: 4 to 11
• Religion: Church of England • School status: State

SEN provision

Detail:
Now provide for in school:
Mild: DS;
Moderate: DS
Experience of:
Mild: DYSC; DYSL; DYSP;
Moderate: DYSL;
Others: Sp&LD; DEL; Oth

Summary: Each of our two classes (one infant, one junior) has a qualified teacher working as an LSA each morning. The junior teacher and LSA both have a strong SEN background, having worked in inner-city schools with a variety of problems. The junior LSA has completed both the Reading Intervention and Maths Recovery programmes. We have a variety of computer programmes (Wordshark, Numbershark, Bubble Reef, Fuzzbuzz, to name but a few) which we can use to reinforce individual or small group work. Junior children are withdrawn from class individually, or in small groups to follow tailored programmes.

GREAT BALLARD SCHOOL

Eartham, Chichester, West Sussex, PO18 0LR

Tel: 01243 814 236
Fax: 01243 814 586
Email: gbschool@breathemail.net
Website: www.darch.co.uk
• Pupils: 102 Mixed; Takes boarders • Age: 2 to 13
• School status: Independent

SEN provision

Detail:
Now provide for in school:
- Mild: ASP; AUT; ADD; ADHD; EBD; DYSC; DYSL; DYSP;
- Moderate: MLD; DYSL; DYSP;
- Others: SPD; Sp&LD

Summary: Our school has an established learning support department that supports about 40 children on a one-to-one basis and also works with parents and outside agencies to support these children and any others within the school who have need. We cater for children from nursery through to year 8 (2-13+ years). The majority of the students on our LS register have dyslexic difficulties, or difficulties that come under that umbrella. All children are seen as individuals who make up part of a large family which is the school.

GREAT BARR PRIMARY SCHOOL

Aldridge Road, Great Barr, Birmingham, West Midlands, B44 8NT

Tel: 0121 464 2251
Fax: 0121 464 9714
Email: enquiry@grtbarr.bham.sch.uk
Website: www.grtbarr.bham.sch.uk
• Pupils: 409 Mixed; Day Pupils • Age: 5 to 11
• Religion: Non-denominational • School status: State

SEN provision

Detail:
Centre of excellence for:
- Mild: CP;
- Moderate: CP;
- Severe: CP;
- Others: DEL; Epi; PD

Now provide for in school:
- Mild: DS; DYSP; HI; VI;
- Moderate: DS; DYSP; HI; VI

Experience of:
- Mild: ASP; AUT; ADD; ADHD; EBD; DYSC; DYSL;
- Severe: DYSP; HI; VI;
- Others: MSI; Sp&LD; Eat

Summary: Great Barr Primary is a mainstream school with a facility for children with physical disabilities. Many of the children also have associated sensory difficulties. The children are all included into the mainstream classes with support. We offer additional physiotherapy, conductive education, outside agency support and opportunities to take part in disability sport as well as working alongside their peers accessing the National Curriculum.

Great Yarmouth College

Southtown, Great Yarmouth, Norfolk, NR31 0ED

Tel: 01493 655 261
Fax: 01493 653 423
Email: info@gyc.ac.uk
Website: www.gyc.ac.uk

• Pupils: 1327 Mixed; Day Pupils • Age: 16 to 99
• Religion: Non-denominational • School status: State

SEN provision

Detail:

Centre of excellence for:

Mild: ASP; AUT; ADD; ADHD; EBD; DS; DYSC; DYSL; DYSP; HI; VI; CP;
Moderate: ASP; AUT; ADD; ADHD; EBD; DS; MLD; DYSC; DYSL; DYSP; SpLD; HI; VI; CP;
Severe: ADD; EBD; DS; DYSC; DYSL; SpLD; HI; VI; CP;
Others: AUT(other); CD; OCD; ODD; FRX; PMLD; SLD; EAL; MSI; Epi; PD; Eat

Summary: GYC is a centre of excellence for SEN students 16+ years providing programmes for SLDD/PMLD/MLDD. Care is taken to ensure the correct support is in place to enhance the individual needs of each student in one-to-one or small group situations to ensure that inclusion and equal opportunities are in place to provide teaching and learning experiencies of the highest quality.

Greenacre School

Keresforth Hill Road, Barnsley, South Yorkshire, S70 6RG

Tel: 01226 287 165
Fax: 01226 295 328

• Pupils: 158 Mixed; Day Pupils • Age: 3 to 19
• Religion: Non-denominational • School status: State

SEN provision

Summary: All pupils at Greenacre have a statement of special educational needs. Their specific needs identified in their statements are met through individual education plans (IEPs), plans that include physical needs plans, personal care plans, medical care plans and behaviour modification plans as appropriate. The school recognises that all pupils are entitled to follow and benefit from the National Curriculum. Staff plan appropriate curriculum opportunities that provide exciting and stimulating learning experiences at the appropriate level for all pupils.

Greenacre School is well resourced with specialist equipment, including computers, electronic aids and interactive technology. There are specialist areas including a nursing station, hydrotherapy pool, light and sound rooms, soft play room, ICT suite, as well as food technology and design and technology rooms. A specialist music room and drama studio complete a very exciting range of facilities. There is also a room designated for parents' use.

There is a school house on Victoria Road that is used as a life skills training base for older students. The school also has access to a specially resourced house on Myrtle Street. This facility is completely accessible to all wheelchair users and provides a further invaluable life-skills teaching base.

Greenfields School

Victoria Road East, Hebburn, Tyne and Wear, NE31 1YQ

Tel: 0191 489 7480
Fax: 0191 483 7390
Email: mconway@southtyneside.northerngrid.org
Website: atschool.eduweb.co.uk/greenfields

• Pupils: 47 Mixed; Day Pupils • Age: 2 to 19
• Religion: Non-denominational • School status: State

SEN provision

Detail:

Now provide for in school:

Mild: DS; HI; VI; CP;
Moderate: AUT; DS; HI; VI; CP;
Severe: AUT; DS; CP;
Others: GEN; PMLD; SLD; MSI; Epi

Summary: Greenfields School is a day school for children and young people who experience severe/complex learning difficulties aged 2-19 years of age. We are located in South Tyneside on the Hebburn/Jarrow border. Whilst some of our pupils with most complex difficulties are based within a discrete class many and varied inclusion opportunites have been created to enable them to share learning opportunites with their Key Stage peers. Greenfields School was awarded the Healthy School Standard Award in 2002 and there is now a very strong focus on encouraging pupils/students to engage in regular activity through the wide range of clubs we offer.

GREENFIELDS SCHOOL

Goldwell Farmhouse, Tenterden Road, Biddenden, Ashford, Kent, TN27 8BS

Tel: 01580 292 523
Fax: 01580 292 354
Email: greenfieldsschool@btopenworld.com
Website: www.peperharow.org.uk
• Pupils: 15 Mixed; Day Pupils • Age: 5 to 10
• Religion: Non-denominational • School status: Independent

SEN provision

Detail:
Now provide for in school:
Mild: EBD;
Moderate: EBD;
Severe: EBD
Experience of:
Mild: ADD

Summary: Greenfields School is an independent primary school for children aged 5-11 with emotional, social and behavioural difficulties. Greenfields is part of the Goldwell Children's Home and the Peper Harow Foundation, the children's charity offering therapeutic residential, educational and outreach services to children and young people aged 5-18 with complex emotional and behavioural needs. Greenfields School has capacity for a maximum of 15 pupils – some living at Goldwell, others living locally – who are taught in small groups by well qualified staff. Greenfields School follows the National Curriculum to Key Stage 2 within a structured school week and has received an excellent Ofsted report. The Admissions Panel assesses each application.

Greenfields School creates and maintains a safe and secure environment where children are encouraged through positive reinforcement to always try their best. Pupils are stimulated and challenged within their individual capabilities and benefit from clear instruction and well-planned activities designed to meet their needs, including a structured PHSE programme. Each child has an Independent Education Plan and Behaviour Management Plan and is expected to work with staff to write, review and set new targets on a termly basis.

Every child at Greenfields is special and the school's aim is to ensure that each pupil has access to a broad and balanced curriculum in an environment that is safe, happy and stimulating, giving the child confidence and improving his/her self esteem. Greenfields makes sure that no child is disadvantaged in any area of the curriculum and has the opportunity of entering mainstream education if this is appropriate. Greenfields' positive approach encourages pupils to treat adults and children with respect and courtesy and to remember that school is primarily a place of learning.

GREENHOLME SCHOOL

392 Derby Road, Nottingham, Nottinghamshire, NG7 2DX

Tel: 01159 787 329
Fax: 01159 781 160
Email: enquiries@greenholmeschool.co.uk
Website: www.greenholmeschool.co.uk
• Pupils: 200 Mixed; Day Pupils • Age: 3 to 11
• School status: Independent

SEN provision

Detail:
Now provide for in school:
Mild: ASP; ADD; DYSC; DYSL; DYSP;
Moderate: EBD; MLD; DYSL;
Severe: DYSL;
Others: EAL
Experience of:
Mild: AUT; HI; VI; CP;
Moderate: VI

Summary: Staff are very aware of the importance of meeting the needs of all children. Our full-time staff includes an individual needs co-ordinator (SENCo), who is available to discuss, with parents, appropriate individual education programmes. Recently a new unit has been set up offering specialised tuition by a qualified dyslexia teacher to help those of our pupils with individual needs. A specialist teacher (TEFL) also provides structured language programmes, for the occasional pupil who may not have English as their first language.

Greenways School

Beechwood Road, Liverpool, Merseyside, L19 0LD

Tel: 01514 271 175
Fax: 01514 275 343
• Mixed; Day Pupils • Age: 3 to 8
• Religion: Non-denominational • School status: State

SEN provision

Detail:
Now provide for in school:
- Mild: ASP; AUT; ADD; ADHD; EBD; DYSC; DYSL; DYSP; VI; CP;
- Moderate: ASP; AUT; ADD; ADHD; EBD; MLD; DYSC; DYSL; DYSP; SpLD;
- Severe: ASP; AUT; ADD; ADHD; EBD; DYSC; DYSL; DYSP; SpLD;
- Others: SPD; AUT(other); CD; OCD; ODD; TIC; FRX; GEN; SLD; EAL; Sp&LD; DEL; Epi; Eat

Experience of:
- Mild: DS; HI;
- Moderate: HI; VI; CP;
- Others: MSI; PD

Summary: Greenways is an Assessment School for children aged between 3 and 7 years. Children are referred via the Liverpool Children's Services Pre-school Panel. Greenways caters for children with complex learning difficulties, ASD, SLD, MLD, emotional or mental health needs and behavioural difficulties. We provide assessment within the Foundation and National Curriculum areas. Our aim is that every child will be the best they can. We have the services of speech and language therapists, psychologist and community paediatrition plus access to a wide variety of support services. Children move on from Greenways to an appropriate placement when their assessment is complete.

Grendon Church of England Primary School

Main Road, Grendon, Northampton, Northamptonshire, NN7 1JW

Tel: 01933 663 208
Email: head@grendon.northants-ecl.gov.uk
• Pupils: 81 Mixed; Day Pupils • Age: 4 to 11
• Religion: Church of England • School status: State

SEN provision

Detail:
Now provide for in school:
- Mild: ASP; DYSC;
- Moderate: MLD;
- Others: DEL

Experience of:
- Mild: ADD; ADHD; EBD; DYSL; DYSP; SpLD;
- Others: EAL; Sp&LD; PD

Summary: Grendon Church Of England Primary is a small friendly school. We have a strong inclusive policy, recognising and valuing all our pupils. The school governors are always looking to improve the accessibility of the school to all pupils and members of the wider community. Recently we have built permanent wheelchair access ramps and separate disabled toilet facilities.

Grenville College

Belvoir Road, Bideford, Devon, EX39 3JP

Tel: 01237 472 212
Fax: 01237 477 020
Email: info@grenville.devon.sch.uk
Website: www.grenville.devon.sch.uk
• Pupils: 413 Mixed; Takes boarders • Age: 2 to 19
• School status: Independent

SEN provision

Detail:
Centre of excellence for:
Mild: DYSL; DYSP;
Moderate: DYSL; DYSP;
Severe: DYSL

Summary: Grenville College maintains a policy of having 30 per cent of the school register assessed as being dyslexic – that is, between 90 and 100 students out of 320. We provide considerable support for our dyslexic pupils partly through the Dyslexia Department and partly through the whole school policies towards the teaching of dyslexic pupils which ensure a dyslexia-friendly school. Grenville also provides numerous and varied opportunities for our dyslexic pupils to enhance their self-confidence and self-esteem.

GREY COURT SCHOOL

Ham Street, Ham, Richmond, Surrey, TW10 7HN

Tel: 020 8948 1173
Fax: 020 8332 2428
Email: info@greycourt.richmond.sch.uk
Website: www.greycourt.richmond.sch.uk
• Pupils: 993 Mixed; Day Pupils • Age: 11 to 16
• Religion: Non-denominational • School status: State

SEN provision

Detail:
Now provide for in school:
Mild: ASP; AUT; ADD; ADHD; EBD; DYSC; DYSL; DYSP; SpLD;
Moderate: ASP; ADD; EBD; MLD; DYSC; DYSL; DYSP;
Others: SPD; EAL; Sp&LD; Epi
Experience of:
Mild: DS; HI; VI;
Moderate: AUT; ADHD;
Severe: ASP; DYSL;
Others: ODD; Eat

Summary: The special educational needs department at Grey Court includes a team of: one SENCo, one full-time and one part-time SEN teacher, three full-time TAs and four part-time TAs. The team has specialist knowledge in autism, ADHD, dyslexia and behaviour management. SEN pupils in years 7,8 and 9 follow a fully inclusive education where they may either receive support in the classroom by TAs, or when required, work individually/ in small groups with SEN teachers. Pupils identified as needing higher levels of teacher input benefit from the smaller class size and TA support in many subjects. English classes are carefully selected using mixed ability groupings to enable peer mentoring. This has been found to encourage the less able pupil and enables the more self-conscious students to take an active part in speaking and listening assignments. This has been shown as very effective and is mirrored in our excellent English GCSE results. In years 10 and 11, Grey Court offers pathways which enable pupils to achieve vocational educational qualifications along side core subject GCSEs. The programme of extended work experience has been particularly successfully in raising pupils' self esteem whilst preparing them for the work place. Grey Court strives to ensure that each child maximises their potential by the development of close communication and supportive working relationships between pupils, parents and staff.

THE GROVE SPECIAL SCHOOL

Grove Gardens, Tweedmouth, Berwick-upon-Tweed, Northumberland, TD15 2EN

Tel: 01289 306 390
Fax: 01289 306 994
Email: admin@thegrove.northumberland.sch.uk
Website: www.thegrove.northumberland.sch.uk
• Pupils: 30 Mixed; Day Pupils • Age: 3 to 19
• Religion: Non-denominational • School status: State

SEN provision

Detail:
Experience of:
Mild: ADD; ADHD; EBD;
Moderate: ADD; ADHD; EBD;
Severe: ADD; ADHD; EBD;
Others: SPD; CD

Summary: The Grove School provides placements for children/students who have complex learning needs which covers a broad spectrum of difficulties although primarily placements are for pupils with a severe, global, cognitive, disability. In addition pupils may have speech and language, physical-medical, gross or fine motor, emotional and/or behavioural needs. A small number of our children/students have profound and multiple learning difficulties and we have developed specialist hydrotherapy and sensory facilities to support their individual needs.

GUILSBOROUGH SCHOOL

West Haddon Road, Guilsborough, Northampton, Northamptonshire, NN6 8QE

Tel: 01604 740 641

Fax: 01604 749 104

Email: head@guilsborough-sch.northants-ecl.gov.uk

Website: www.guilsborough.northants.sch.uk

• Pupils: 1350 Mixed; Day Pupils • Age: 11 to 18

• Religion: Non-denominational • School status: State

SEN provision

Detail:

Centre of excellence for:

Mild: ASP; AUT; ADD; ADHD; EBD; DYSC; DYSL; DYSP; SpLD; HI;

Moderate: ASP; EBD; MLD;

Others: PD

Now provide for in school:

Mild: DS; VI;

Moderate: AUT; ADD; ADHD; DYSC; DYSL; DYSP; SpLD; HI;

Others: SPD; AUT(other); CD; Sp&LD; Epi; Eat

Summary: The philosophy of the department is for inclusion to provide support across the whole curriculum for any student who has special eduational needs, either on a long term or temporary basis. We aim to support students within the classroom where/when possible. Some small group or individual withdrawal is offered to those students for whom an additional teaching programme is preferable. Each member of the Learning Support Team is fully trained according to DfES standards for teaching assistants; additionally, individual members have further specialisms in supporting students on the autistic spectrum; with Down's syndrome; with brain damage; with dyslexia, dyspraxia and ADHD; with speech and language difficulties and in manual handling techniques for physically disabled students. Several members of the team have counselling skills and regularly see students with emotional difficulties. There are links with designated agencies for hearing impaired and visually impaired students, for looked after children, the Traveller Education Service and the English as an Additional Language Service.

GURU NANAK SIKH VOLUNTARY AIDED SECONDARY SCHOOL

Springfield Road, Hayes, Middlesex, UB4 0LT

Tel: 020 8573 6085

Fax: 020 8561 6772

Email: gurusec@hillingdongrid.org

• Pupils: 425 Mixed; Day Pupils • Age: 11 to 18

• Religion: Sikh • School status: State

SEN provision

Detail:

Experience of:

Mild: ASP; ADD; ADHD; EBD; DYSC; DYSL; HI; VI;

Moderate: DYSL

Summary: We strive to be an inclusive school. This means that we aim to provide equal opportunities for all our students regardless of their age, gender, ethnicity, disability, attainment or background. We pay particular attention to the provision made for students and the progress made by each student. The school aims to provide all our students with a broad, balanced, relevant and differentiated curriculum. We aim to provide the necessary support to those who are experiencing learning difficulties, or whose educational development is hampered by physical, sensory, emotional or linguistic problems. It is also an expectation that pupils of exceptional ability should be challenged so that they make progress appropriate to their ability.

Assessing and Screening

Early identification of learning difficulties is a priority.

We liaise with our feeder primary schools to identify students who may experience difficulties on transfer. Visits are made to primary schools to discuss concerns with teachers, parents and students so as to ensure continuity of provision.

All new pupils are tested as part of the induction procedure to give a norm-referenced baseline of ability, in addition to achievement in literacy and numeracy. Standardised scores from Cognitive Abilities (CATs) Tests, reading ages and spelling ages are calculated and handwriting skills are assessed.

A 'Staged' model, in line with the SEN Code of Practice, has been developed. Children with SEN are placed at one of four levels on the SEN register (Monitoring, School Action, School Action Plus, Statement).

Appropriate records are kept and any child placed at School Action or above has an individual education plan; this clearly identifies special needs and SEN provision.

All subject teachers are provided with an 'Inclusion List' that identifies SEN students as well as highlighting other concerns.

The Inclusion Manager meets each half term with our educational psychologist to discuss concerns and to plan our provision. We liaise closely with the LEA advisory teachers to ensure that students receive appropriate provision.

Most students identified as requiring support will be supported through a differentiated curriculum.

Those students who have a Statement of Educational Need have additional provision as identified in their statement.

We currently have two full-time SEN Learning Support Assistants who support across the school. They and the teaching staff are encouraged to attend relevant SEN training.

The school is committed to including parents in all aspects of their child's education. Parents are kept informed of progress by regular contact through homework diary, school reports, and review meetings. They are encouraged to participate fully in the IEP/Annual Reviews and in their child's educational programme.

An annual report is presented to the school's Senior Management Team. A presentation is made to the governing body each year and termly reports are also submitted to governors.

HALL CROSS SCHOOL

Thorne Road, Doncaster, South Yorkshire, DN1 2HY

Tel: 01302 320626

Fax: 01302 322190

Email: hxadmin@hallcross.doncaster.sch.uk

• Pupils: 2104 Mixed; Day Pupils • Age: 11 to 18

• Religion: Non-denominational • School status: State

SEN provision

Detail:

Now provide for in school:

Mild: DYSL; DYSP;

Moderate: DYSL;

Severe: DYSL;

Others: EAL

Experience of:

Mild: ASP; ADD; ADHD; EBD; DYSC; HI;

Moderate: ASP; ADHD; EBD; MLD; DYSC;

Severe: ASP; DYSP;

Others: SPD; Sp&LD; Epi; Eat

Summary: Hall Cross School is a two site school. The Lower School is for Key Stage 3 students. The Upper School is for Key Stage 4 students and sixth formers. The SEN provision is different on each site.

Lower School

Standard courses we offer students on our register:-

SuccessMaker – up to two lessons per week on reading, spelling and maths. The students follow an individually tailored learning programme

Corrective Reading – one lesson a week to all students with a reading age less than 9 years. This is a structured reading scheme delivered in small groups and teaches decoding, encoding, word attack skills and basic comprehension and punctuation.

Specialist Courses

Specialist teaching for students with a statement for dyslexia. This may be available to students who do not have a statement but who we assess as having dyslexia.

Also at upper school

Toe by Toe – a highly structured reading scheme delivered on a one-to-one basis by our highly trained teaching assistants for 15 minutes three times a week. Also at upper school.

Typequick – a programme to teach keyboard skills to students with dyspraxia or students who have poor handwriting. Usually takes place three times a week during registration.

Mastering Memory – delivered by trained teaching assistants who work with students who have been identified as having problems with their visual or auditory memory. This is usually delivered twice a week for about half a term during registration.

Word Wasp – a highly structured spelling programme delivered by dyslexia specialist teachers to students who can read but have severe problems with spelling. The students have up to two 15 minute sessions per week when the specialist teacher can fit them in. Available at upper school also.

Voice Activated software – training is available to any student who finds writing difficult but who has plenty of ideas and may be underachieving. Available at upper school also.

DDAT – certain students are involved on this innovative, experimental programme. The programme is designed for students with dyslexia or dyspraxia and involves the students working twice daily with teaching assistants to do tailored exercises aimed at developing their cerebellum. The exercises are undertaken before school in the morning and during lesson 6 in the afternoon. The students involved will need to be allowed out of lesson 6 for approximately 15 minutes. Available at upper school also.

In-class support – all bottom-set English classes receive one lesson per week support from SENCo who works with the English teacher on a structured reading scheme.

Additional withdrawal maths – support for less able pupils.

Teaching assistants support statemented students in some of their English, maths and science lessons.

Upper School

Destinations – similar to SuccessMaker. Students in the lower sets at maths and English work with a teacher and a specialist teaching assistant on basic English and numeracy tasks. Classes receive one lesson per week support from SENCo.

Maths support by Key Stage 4 co-ordinator in class.

Behaviour counselling with Key Stage 4 co-ordinator.

In class support in English, maths and science with our expert teaching assistants who have specialised in specific subjects and they support our students with special reference to coursework.

In-class support – all bottom set English classes.

What the SEN Dept can assess:-

Reading age – there is a regular screening programme for all students on SEN list.

Spelling age – this is assessed along with the reading age at specified times.

Dyslexic screening – we can assess any student you feel may have a specific learning difficulty.

Vision screening

Visual perceptual difficulties – some students are sensitive to certain colours that cause them to have difficulties in reading and writing .

Learning style – we can assess the preferred learning style of students.

In year 9 all students are screened to see if they qualifiy for access arrangements in public examinations.

Hall Road Primary School

Hall Road, Hull, HU6 8PP

Tel: 01482 441 151

Fax: 01482 492 483

Email: admin@hallroad.hull.sch.uk

• Pupils: 349 Mixed; Day Pupils • Age: 3 to 11

• Religion: Non-denominational • School status: State

SEN provision

Detail:

Centre of excellence for:

Mild: EBD;

Moderate: EBD; MLD

Now provide for in school:

Mild: ASP; AUT; ADD; ADHD; DYSC; DYSL; DYSP; HI; VI; CP;

Moderate: ASP; AUT; ADD; ADHD; DYSC; DYSL; DYSP; HI; VI;

Severe: EBD; DYSC; DYSL;

Others: CD; PMLD; EAL; MSI; Sp&LD

Summary: We have good systems in place and excellent support from quality teaching assistants. Resources are regularly reviewed to ensure correct provision. We have outstanding links and excellent support from a number of outside agencies who work both from within school and as outreach teams.

HALLMOOR SCHOOL

Hallmoor Road, Kitts Green, Birmingham, West Midlands, B33 9QY

Tel: 0121 783 3972
Fax: 0121 783 3481
Email: enquiry@hallmoor.bham.sch.uk
Website: www.hallmoor.bham.sch.uk

• Pupils: 234 Mixed; Day Pupils • Age: 4 to 19
• Religion: Non-denominational • School status: State

SEN provision

Detail:
Now provide for in school:
Mild: ASP; AUT; ADD; ADHD; EBD; DS; DYSP; VI; CP;
Moderate: ASP; AUT; ADD; ADHD; DS; DYSP; CP;
Severe: ASP;
Others: SPD; TIC; FRX; GEN; SLD; EAL; Sp&LD; Epi; Eat
Experience of:
Mild: HI;
Moderate: EBD; HI; VI;
Severe: DYSP;
Others: AUT(other); OCD; ODD; PD

Summary: Hallmoor School educates and cares for children between the ages of 4 and 19. The school is divided into three very distinct departments depending on the age of the child. Our children have a range of abilities and needs, and are supported in their learning by small group teaching and individual learning programmes. All of the children need support with their learning and we have some capacity to support children with specific needs such as autism, speech and language difficulties, dyspraxia, and mild physical or medical difficulties. Excellent staff provide good support, to assist children with mild emotional and behavioural difficulties, enabling them to achieve. As pupils become students they progress to Work Related Learning activities and gain a range of external accreditation. The school achieved a School Achievement Award for improvement in 2000/2001 and has gained Investors In People status twice. More recently we have been awarded 'Basic Skills Quality Marks' for the third time, a 'Leading Aspect Award' for 'Positive Behaviour Management for Vulnerable Children and Young People' and A Birmingham School Award for 'Continuing Professional Development'.

HAMSTEAD HALL SCHOOL

Craythorne Avenue, Handsworth Wood, Birmingham, West Midlands, B20 1HL

Tel: 0121 358 5991
Fax: 0121 358 6707
Email: enquiry@hamhall.bham.sch.uk
Website: www.hamsteadhall.com

• Pupils: 1107 Mixed; Day Pupils • Age: 11 to 18
• Religion: Non-denominational • School status: State

SEN provision

Detail:
Now provide for in school:
Mild: EBD;
Moderate: EBD; MLD
Experience of:
Mild: ASP; AUT; DYSC; DYSL; DYSP; HI;
Others: EAL; Sp&LD; Epi

Summary: We are an 11-18 school with a special needs resource base which has 40 places for students. These places are allocated by SENAS. The base is a support base and all students are fully integrated into the whole school with suitable support. Students mainly have MLD, but from 2006 two places per year group will be allocated to students with speech and language difficulties. Ofsted in 2003 commented that our strengths were our inclusivity, excellent pastoral support and quality of provision. We were awarded a 1 for inclusion and a 2 overall.

HANDSWORTH WOOD GIRLS' SCHOOL

Church Lane, Handsworth, Birmingham, West Midlands, B20 2HL

Tel: 0121 554 8122
Fax: 0121 551 6805
Email: enquiry@hworthwg.bham.sch.uk
Website: www.hwgs.org.uk

• Pupils: 683 Girls; Day Pupils • Age: 11 to 18
• Religion: Non-denominational • School status: State

SEN provision

Detail:
Centre of excellence for:
Mild: HI; VI;
Moderate: MLD; HI; VI;
Severe: HI;
Others: SLD; EAL
Now provide for in school:
Mild: ASP; AUT; ADD; ADHD; EBD; DYSC; DYSL;
Moderate: ASP; AUT; ADD; ADHD; EBD; DYSL;
Severe: ASP; AUT; ADD; ADHD; EBD;
Others: SPD; AUT(other); CD; OCD; ODD; TIC; PMLD; PD

Summary: At Handsworth Wood Girls' School and the Sixth Form Centre there is a whole school approach to raising achievement of EAL/EM/SEN pupils. There is a well established system in place for:

1. Effective assessment of each and every pupil on a regular basis and dissemination of all data to all staff responsible for teaching and supporting the student.
2. Allocation of appropiate resources to support identified pupils.
3. CPD to all staff to maintain their effectiveness.
4. Establishment of strong links with parents/carers to support learning and celebration of success.

HARBOUR SCHOOL

Elms Vale Road, Dover, Kent, CT17 9PS

Tel: 01304 201 964
Fax: 01304 225 000

• Pupils: 125 Mixed; Day Pupils • Age: 5 to 16
• Religion: Non-denominational • School status: State

SEN provision

Detail:
Centre of excellence for:
Mild: ADD; ADHD; EBD; DYSL; DYSP;
Moderate: ADD; ADHD; EBD; MLD; DYSL; DYSP;
Severe: ADD; ADHD; EBD;
Others: OCD; ODD; Sp&LD
Now provide for in school:
Mild: ASP; AUT; DS; SpLD; HI; VI;
Moderate: ASP; AUT; DS; SpLD; HI; VI;
Severe: DYSL; DYSP; SpLD;
Others: TIC; Epi; PD
Experience of:
Mild: CP;
Moderate: CP;
Severe: ASP; AUT; DS

Summary: Harbour School is a mixed, day special school for children who have a combination of behaviour and learning needs. Pupils have a wide-range of learning, behaviour, social and emotional needs and some also experience difficulty with speech and language development. Many pupils have also experienced repeated failure in their previous schools and as a result have low self-esteem and often a negative attitude towards school and learning.

HARFORD MANOR, NORWICH

43 Ipswich Road, Norwich, Norfolk, NR2 2LN

Tel: 01603 451 809
Fax: 01603 453 508
Email: head@harfordmanor.norfolk.sch.uk
Website: www.harfordmanor.norfolk.sch.uk

• Pupils: 76 Mixed; Day Pupils • Age: 3 to 19
• Religion: Non-denominational • School status: State

SEN provision

Summary: The school caters for 76 students with severe and complex needs, many have autism. The local authority maintains three autistic resource bases at the school. A recent Ofsted inspection (Nov 2004) described the school as very effective.

HARLANDS PRIMARY SCHOOL

Penland Road, Haywards Heath, West Sussex, RH16 1PJ

Tel: 01444 450 782
Fax: 01444 415 352
Email: office@harlands.w-sussex.sch.uk
Website: www.harlands.w-sussex.sch.uk

• Pupils: 430 Mixed; Day Pupils • Age: 4 to 11
• Religion: Non-denominational • School status: State

SEN provision

Detail:
Now provide for in school:
Mild: ASP; AUT; ADD; ADHD; EBD; DS; DYSL; DYSP; HI;
Moderate: ASP; AUT; EBD; DYSL;
Severe: ASP;
Others: EAL; Sp&LD; PD
Experience of:
Mild: SpLD; VI;
Moderate: ADD; ADHD; MLD; VI;
Severe: VI;
Others: Epi

Summary: Harlands provides SEN support in line with the SEN Code of Practice.There is a school policy outlining the triggers for school action and extensive use is made of outside agencies.

HARMENY EDUCATION TRUST

Mansfield Road, Balerno, Midlothian, EH14 7JY

Tel: 0131 449 3938
Fax: 0131 449 7121
Email: admin@harmeny.org.uk
Website: www.harmeny.org.uk

• Pupils: 30 Mixed; Takes boarders • Age: 6 to 13
• Religion: Non-denominational • School status: Independent

SEN provision

Detail:
Centre of excellence for:
Mild: EBD;
Moderate: EBD;
Severe: EBD;
Others: ODD
Now provide for in school:
Mild: ADD; ADHD;
Moderate: ADD; ADHD;
Severe: ADD; ADHD;
Others: CD; OCD; TIC
Experience of:
Mild: ASP; AUT; DYSL; DYSP;
Moderate: MLD; DYSL;
Others: Sp&LD

Summary: Harmeny provides all year round care and education for primary age children with significant social, emotional and behavioural difficulties.

Hamond's High School

Brandon Road, Swaffham, Norfolk, PE37 7DZ

Tel: 01760 721 480
Fax: 01760 721 269
Email: office@harfordmanor.norfolk.sch.uk

• Pupils: 718 Mixed; Day Pupils • Age: 12 to 18
• Religion: Non-denominational • School status: State

SEN provision

Detail:
Now provide for in school:
Mild: ASP; AUT; ADD; ADHD; EBD; DYSC; DYSL; DYSP; SpLD; HI; VI; CP;
Moderate: ASP; AUT; ADD; ADHD; EBD; MLD; DYSC; DYSL; DYSP; SpLD; HI; VI; CP;
Severe: HI;
Others: AUT(other); EAL; Sp&LD

Summary: Hamond's is a mainstream High School catering for students between the ages of 12 and 18. A nurturing school, Hamond's has an excellent reputation for the work which we do and the support which we give our students.

The school has a Progress Centre where it is possible for us to give intensive teaching and learning time to students, either one-to-one or in small groups, as deemed appropriate and necessary.

The school also has an Improvement Centre where we work with young people whose learning behaviours need support and modification.

Hamond's is a school where inclusion is always top of the agenda and provision is made to support those in minority groups such as EAL, G&T, health and medical needs, or indeed any student who might be at risk of underachieving.

Haslingden High School

Broadway, Haslingden, Rossendale, Lancashire, BB4 4EY

Tel: 01706 215 726
Fax: 01706 219 861
Email: head@haslingden-high.lancsngfl.ac.uk

• Pupils: 1480 Mixed; Day Pupils • Age: 11 to 18
• Religion: Non-denominational • School status: State

SEN provision

Detail:
Now provide for in school:
Mild: ASP; AUT; ADD; ADHD; EBD; DYSC; DYSL; DYSP; HI; VI;
Moderate: ASP; AUT; ADD; ADHD; EBD; MLD; DYSL; DYSP; HI; VI; CP;
Severe: ASP; EBD; DYSL;
Others: SPD; EAL; Sp&LD; PD
Experience of:
Mild: DS; CP;
Moderate: DYSC;
Severe: DYSC; DYSP; HI; VI; CP;
Others: OCD; Epi; Eat

Summary: Haslingden High School's Learning Support Faculty is staffed by four full-time specialist teachers and 15 teaching assistants. This makes us one of the largest faculties in school. The work of the faculty is extremely varied and covers SEN, behaviour support and support of students from ethnic minorities. Haslingden High School is one of the largest secondary schools in Lancashire and with a truly comprehensive intake it caters for students whose needs are representative of the population at large. We therefore routinely support those with specific and moderate learning difficulties, hearing or visual impairment, speech and communication problems, behaviour or emotional difficulties, those on the autistic spectrum and many more. In recent years we have admitted several students with physical disabilites and the school has invested heavily in adapting the building to improve accessibility for this group. All teaching assistants undergo training in Moving and Handling to enhance our work with PD students. The success of the Learning Support Faculty stems from its inclusive principles and the flexibility and commitment of its highly motivated staff.

Hawthorn Community Primary School

Hawthorn Road, Kettering, Northamptonshire, NN15 7HT

Tel: 01536 512 204
Fax: 01536 512 468
Email: head@hawthorn.northants-ecl.gov.uk

• Pupils: 316 Mixed; Day Pupils • Age: 4 to 11
• Religion: Non-denominational • School status: State

SEN provision

Detail:
Experience of:
Mild: ASP; AUT; ADD; ADHD; EBD; DS; DYSL; DYSP; VI; CP;
Moderate: ASP; ADD; EBD; DS; MLD; DYSL; DYSP; VI;
Severe: HI; VI;
Others: FRX; EAL; Sp&LD; Epi; PD

Summary: Mainstream school with no specialist provision but recent successful experience of integration programme with neighbouring special school. SEN currently catered for include profound deafness, epilepsy, physical disability (brittle bone and spina-bifida, autism (mild) and moderate learning difficulties. The school has a philosophy for inclusion.

Basingstoke School Plus

Pack Lane, Basingstoke, Hampshire, RG22 5TH

Tel: 01256 336 601
Fax: 01256 330 010

• Pupils: 120 Mixed; Day Pupils • Age: 10 to 16
• Religion: Non-denominational • School status: State

SEN provision

Summary: Special needs, respite and excluded pupils. Caters for pupils with behavioural, emotional and social difficulties, together with pupils who have been, or are at risk of being, excluded.

Haycliffe School

Haycliffe Lane, Little Horton, Bradford, West Yorkshire, BD5 9ET

Tel: 01274 576 123
Fax: 01274 770 555
Email: office@haycliffe.bradford.sch.uk

• Pupils: 156 Mixed; Day Pupils • Age: 11 to 19
• Religion: Non-denominational • School status: State

SEN provision

Detail:
Now provide for in school:
Mild: AUT; EBD; DS; HI; VI;
Moderate: ASP; AUT; EBD; DS; MLD; HI;
Severe: AUT;
Others: SLD; Sp&LD; Epi

Summary: The school provides education for pupils with learning difficulties between the ages of 11 and 19 across a wide range of need, including moderate and severe difficulties. It excels in the provision of the arts and physical education, having arts mark gold and sports mark gold awards.

The Hayesbrook School

Brook Street, Tonbridge, Kent, TN9 2PH

Tel: 01732 500 600
Fax: 01732 500 556
Email: secretary@hayesbrook.kent.sch.uk
Website: www.hayesbrook.kent.sch.uk

• Pupils: 855 Boys; Day Pupils • Age: 11 to 18
• Religion: Non-denominational • School status: State

SEN provision

Detail:
Now provide for in school:
Mild: ASP; AUT; ADD; ADHD; EBD; DS; DYSC; DYSL; DYSP; HI; VI; CP;
Moderate: ASP; AUT; ADD; ADHD; EBD; DS; MLD; DYSC; DYSL; DYSP; CP;
Severe: DYSL;
Others: TIC; Sp&LD; DEL; Epi

Summary: The Hayesbrook School is a highly inclusive school that is dedicated to supporting the needs of all its students. The Inclusion Manager co-ordinates all the activities in school to maximise the effectiveness of this support. All year 7 students are screened on entry and any additional needs they may have, be it medical, learning, behavioural, social are identified. The response to these needs is a whole school one. All staff in school are responsible for providing the best environment for learning.

The staff are supported by a highly skilled learning support department and the Pastoral Team. Most of our students' needs are met in the classroom situation. More intensive work is carried out with those students who have complex difficulties, in small groups, or very occasionally on an individual basis.

Headlands School and Community Science College

Sewerby Road, East Riding of Yorkshire, Bridlington, YO16 6UR

Tel: 01262 676 198
Fax: 01262 607 907
Email: headlands.secondary@eastriding.gov.uk
Website: www.headlands.eril.net

• Pupils: 1429 Mixed; Day Pupils • Age: 11 to 18
• Religion: Non-denominational • School status: State

SEN provision

Detail:
Now provide for in school:
Mild: ASP; AUT; ADHD; EBD; DYSC; DYSL; DYSP; HI; VI; CP;
Moderate: ASP; AUT; ADHD; EBD; MLD; DYSL; HI; CP;
Severe: EBD;
Others: SPD; SLD; Sp&LD; Epi; PD
Experience of:
Mild: ADD;
Moderate: ADD; DYSP;
Severe: DYSL; DYSP;
Others: ODD; TIC; EAL; DEL; Eat

Summary: The learning support department comprises (at time of writing) two specialist teachers, fourteen learning tutors, a behaviour support manager and a behaviour support outreach worker. Support is provided for children with learning difficulties as a result of intellectual, physical, sensory, emotional and/or behavioural difficulties. This support takes many forms, including: in-class work with a learning tutor; withdrawal work to address specific difficulties eg spelling, numeracy; individual work on subjects; part-time attendance and individualised teaching; group work on specific areas, both academic and social/emotional group withdrawal for focused behavioural needs.

The aim is to provide a flexible package of support, with parents consulted to discuss individual needs and work together to ensure appropriate learning opportunities for each child.

Heathfield Primary School

The Broadway, Darlington, County Durham, DL1 1EJ

Tel: 01325 252 144

Fax: 01325 252 010

Email: admin@heathfield.darlington.sch.uk

Website: www.heathfield.dltn.net

• Pupils: 410 Mixed; Day Pupils • Age: 4 to 11

• Religion: Non-denominational • School status: State

SEN provision

Detail:

Now provide for in school:

Mild: EBD; DYSL; DYSP; HI;

Moderate: AUT; EBD; MLD; DYSL; DYSP; HI;

Severe: ADHD; EBD; DYSL; DYSP; HI;

Others: SPD; SLD; EAL; Sp&LD; DEL; Epi; PD

Experience of:

Mild: ASP; ADD; ADHD; DS; DYSC; VI; CP;

Moderate: ASP; ADD; ADHD; DS; CP;

Severe: DS;

Others: TIC

Summary: Heathfield is a fully inclusive school which provides:-

- High levels of support (13 TAs at present) allowing higher staff/pupil ratios than normal
- High levels of experience, gained over 15 years of inclusive practice, dealing with the inclusion of complex learning difficulties/fine and gross motor skills/speech and language, and emotional difficulties
- Full access with ramped approaches for all external entrances and widened doors to playgrounds etc
- Three sets of assisted toilets to allow access in all parts of the school
- Ongoing links with Beaumont Hill Special School for sharing expertise and advice
- Well developed assessment and pupil tracking
- High levels of achievement throughout the school
- A vibrant ethos of 'I Can..', which applies to all in the school
- The highest added value in the LEA 2003-4
- Inclusive provision 3-11 with the opening of new Foundation Stage in Autumn 2005 and the provision of 'wrap-around care', small group work and constant high levels of support.
- The development of gross and fine motor skills to deal with language difficulties.
- Finely tuned programs of study to support personalized learning.
- Provision for the talented and gifted children through small group support and dedicated teacher.

Heathside School

Heath Road, Ipswich, Suffolk, IP4 5SN

Tel: 01473 725 508

Fax: 01473 724 419

• Pupils: 73 Mixed; Day Pupils • Age: 3 to 11

• Religion: Non-denominational • School status: State

SEN provision

Summary: Heathside is a local authority primary school and nursery for children with severe, profound and complex learning difficulties. The special educational needs of our pupils include a wide range of communication, physical, profound and multiple learning difficulties.

As a school we work closely with colleagues from many other disciplines. Whilst recognising our different roles and responsibilities, we strongly believe that a well co-ordinated multi-professional approach provides the best level of support to meet the special educational needs of our pupils. A team philosophy is a strength of the school. This supportive network includes all the adults working with the pupils on a daily basis. The common purpose for everyone is the same – to provide the highest quality of education for all pupils. Our Charter, 'Children First', expresses our commitment to educate pupils in a challenging yet caring and sensitive way, respecting their rights as children. 'Children First' is our starting point in everything we do.

Where we feel there is a need we aim to develop specialist provision for particular groups of children. Like many other schools we have seen an increase in the number of children with autism attending the school. To better meet their needs we have introduced the TEACCH and PECS approaches across the school and have worked closely with parents and carers to ensure the success of these approaches.

Henry Hinde (Community) Infant School

Grenville Close, Bilton, Rugby, Warwickshire, CV22 7JQ

Tel: 01788 814 848
Fax: 01788 814 948
Email: admin@2424.wgfl.net

• Pupils: 60 Mixed; Day Pupils • Age: 4 to 7
• Religion: Non-denominational • School status: State

SEN provision

Detail:
Now provide for in school:
Mild: ADD; ADHD; EBD;
Moderate: ADD; ADHD; EBD; MLD;
Severe: EBD;
Others: SPD; ODD; EAL; PD
Experience of:
Mild: ASP; AUT; DYSL; DYSP; HI; VI; CP;
Moderate: ASP; AUT; DYSL; HI; CP;
Severe: ADD; ADHD;
Others: CD; OCD; TIC; Sp&LD; DEL; Epi; Eat

Summary: We endeavour to address all issues of special needs, whether it be children with learning or behavioural difficulties, the child with short term emotional problems, speech and language or physical difficulties. Parents' views are greatly respected and we encourage their involvement in all aspects of their child's education. We are especially committed to early intervention and identify children with special needs as early as possible so that action can be taken to ensure they make progress towards reaching their personal potential.

'There is good provision for pupils with special educational needs. These pupils achieve well because they are helped well by the teachers and teaching assistants.' Ofsted Report September 2003

Hensall Community Primary School

Church Lane, Hensall, Goole, Yorkshire, DN14 0QQ

Tel: 01977 661 340
Fax: 01977 661 967
Email: admin@hensall.n-yorks.sch.uk
Website: www.hensall.n-yorks.sch.uk

• Pupils: 111 Mixed; Day Pupils • Age: 4 to 11
• Religion: Non-denominational • School status: State

SEN provision

Detail:
Experience of:
Mild: DYSL;
Moderate: MLD

Summary: The aim of Hensall School is to provide all children with the opportunity to reach their full potential. All children have equal access to all areas of the curriculum and their contributions are of equal value. There is a whole school approach to the identification, assessment, provision and review of children with SEN. The school works in partnership with parents to enable them to contribute to the education of their children.

Pupils with SEN are mostly taught by their class teacher. There may be some sessions where they work individually or in small groups with a teaching assistant, to address their specific targets. Where possible these sessions are timetabled to focus on the same curriculum area as being covered by the rest of the class.

Through planning and teaching all staff endeavour to provide all children with suitable learning challenges, meet the pupils' diverse needs, minimise barriers to learning.

Hensall School uses a graduated response to the early identification, assessment and provision of SEN, which is line with the Code of Practice.

HERITAGE HOUSE SCHOOL

Cameron Road, Chesham, Buckinghamshire, HP5 3BP

Tel: 01494 771 445
Fax: 01494 775 892

• Pupils: 77 Mixed; Day Pupils • Age: 2 to 19
• Religion: Non-denominational • School status: State

SEN provision

Summary: Heritage House School is an all-age day community special school currently catering for pupils with severe learning difficulties and profound and multiple learning diffiiculties. In addition, we have a very successful TEACCH unit which caters for pupils on the autistic spectrum who have significant learning difficulties.

HERONSBRIDGE SCHOOL

Ewenny Road, Bridgend, CF31 3HT

Tel: 01656 653 974
Fax: 01656 766 270
Email: headteacher.heronsbridge@bridgend.gov.uk

• Pupils: 184 Mixed; Takes boarders • Age: 3 to 19 • School status: State

SEN provision

Summary: Admissions are controlled by the LEA. School caters for children with profound and multiple learning difficulties (PMLD), severe learning difficulties (SLD) and autisitic spectrum disorders (ASD). Currently six pupils weekly board.

HESKETH FLETCHER C OF E HIGH SCHOOL, ATHERTON

Hamilton Street, Atherton, Manchester, Lancashire, M46 0AY

Tel: 01942 882 425
Fax: 01942 887 310
Email: enquiries@admin.heskethfletcher.wigan.sch.uk

• Pupils: 999 Mixed; Day Pupils • Age: 11 to 16 • Religion: Church of England • School status: State

SEN provision

Detail:

Centre of excellence for:
- Mild: DYSL; SpLD;
- Moderate: MLD; DYSL; SpLD

Now provide for in school:
- Mild: ADD; ADHD; EBD; DS; DYSC; DYSP; HI; VI;
- Moderate: ADD; ADHD; EBD; DYSC; DYSP; HI; VI;
- Severe: DYSL; SpLD;
- Others: EAL; PD

Experience of:
- Mild: ASP; AUT; CP;
- Moderate: ASP; DS; CP;
- Severe: ADD; ADHD; DYSC; DYSP; HI; VI;
- Others: ODD; PMLD; SLD; Sp&LD; DEL; Epi

Summary: Special needs provision is centred on the learning support unit. The unit operates as a base for largely in class support, with only a small number of children catered for in the unit itself. The SEN staff consists of one SENCo and two assistant SENCos, with dedicated administrative support. The team is highly trained in the provision of the Sounds Write literacy programme. Children with social emotional and behavioural difficulties are catered for and the team works with a range of outside agencies to meet children's needs. Support staff from the team also deliver areas of the Key Stage 3 strategy. Literacy catch up programmes are delivered in the autumn term.

Hessle High School

Tranby House, Heads Lane, East Riding of Yorkshire, Hessle, HU13 0JQ

Tel: 01482 648 604
Fax: 01482 643 207
Email: hesslehigh@eastriding.gov.uk
Website: www.hesslehigh.ik.org
• Pupils: 1415 Mixed; Day Pupils • Age: 11 to 18
• Religion: Non-denominational • School status: State

SEN provision

Detail:
Now provide for in school:
Mild: ASP; DYSL; DYSP; HI; VI; CP;
Moderate: MLD; VI
Experience of:
Mild: AUT; ADD; ADHD; EBD; DYSC; SpLD;
Moderate: ASP; DYSL; DYSP; HI;
Severe: DYSL;
Others: DEL; Epi; Eat

Summary: At present Hessle High caters mainly for students with mild learning difficulties. We have three full-time teachers and 14 teaching assistants working between the two sites, Heads Lane and Boothferry Road.The majority of students are integrated and so are taught in their mainstream group. We have limited withdrawal of students from lessons and this tends to be for students with a statement of need. The aim of withdrawal and in-class support is to encourage students to become independent, both in their school life and their home life. There is access to the ground floor on both school sites for the disabled in a wheelchair, via ramps, and there is disabled access to the storey above, at the Boothferry Road site, via a lift. Both sites have a disabled toilet, ramps and hand rails. With the changes in the National Curriculum we have disapplied some of our year 10 and 11 students from French and some science lessons. This has freed up time to allow a more vocationally based timetable. Students complete a day a week at a local training provider and follow five GCSE courses. They also follow the ASDAN Award Scheme which promotes the use of key skills.

Hexham Priory School

Dene Park, Hexham, Northumberland, NE46 1HN

Tel: 01434 605 021
Fax: 01434 609 022
Email: Admin@hexham.northumberland.sch.uk
Website: www.hexham.northumberland.sch.uk
• Pupils: 40 Mixed; Day Pupils • Age: 3 to 19
• Religion: Non-denominational • School status: State

SEN provision

Detail:
Experience of:
Mild: ASP; AUT; HI; VI;
Moderate: ASP; AUT; HI; VI;
Severe: ASP; AUT;
Others: SPD; AUT(other); Sp&LD; PD

Summary: The school meets the needs of pupils with severe learning difficulties aged from 3 to 19 years. Several pupils also have a secondary disability. This may be a sensory or physical impairment or an autistic spectrum disorder. The school enjoys excellent links with a number of local mainstream schools. Seventeen pupils are dual registered: that is, they spend part of the week at our special school and part of their week at their local mainstream school.

Higham Lane School

Shanklin Drive, Nuneaton, Warwickshire, CV10 0BJ

Tel: 02476 388 123
Fax: 02476 370 550
Email: highamlane@aol.com
Website: www.higham.warwickshire.sch.uk
• Pupils: 1234 Mixed; Day Pupils • Age: 11 to 16
• Religion: Non-denominational • School status: State

SEN provision

Detail:
Now provide for in school:
Mild: ASP; AUT; ADD; ADHD; EBD; DYSC; DYSL; DYSP; SpLD; HI; VI; CP;

Moderate: ASP; AUT; ADD; EBD; MLD; DYSC; DYSL; SpLD; HI; VI; CP;
Severe: DYSL; DYSP; SpLD; CP;
Others: OCD; PMLD; SLD; EAL; Sp&LD; Epi; PD

Summary: Higham Lane has a specialist provision for students with physical difficulties. We have an experienced and well qualified SEN team who work with students with dyslexia, speech and language difficulties, physical difficulties, emotional and behavioural difficulties, autism, hearing difficulties, problems with literacy and numeracy. We support students in the classroom and we also have withdrawal groups for specialist programmes. We work with the local colleges to offer a wider range of courses for students at Key Stage 4 and we have just received an Inclusion Quality Mark for our work.

HIGHBURY SCHOOL

Lower Edge Road, Rastrick, Brighouse, West Yorkshire, HD6 3LD

Tel: 01484 716 319
Fax: 01484 721 893
Email: admin@highbury.calderdale.sch.uk

• Pupils: 40 Mixed; Day Pupils • Age: 2 to 11
• Religion: Non-denominational • School status: State

SEN provision

Detail:
Now provide for in school:
Mild: ASP; AUT; ADD; ADHD; DS; HI; VI; CP;
Moderate: ASP; AUT; ADD; ADHD; DS; SpLD; HI; VI; CP;
Severe: ASP; AUT; ADD; ADHD; DS; SpLD; HI; VI; CP;

Others: AUT(other); FRX; GEN; PMLD; SLD; MSI; Sp&LD; DEL; Epi; PD; Eat

Summary: Highbury is a community primary special school providing for children from 2 to 11 years who have a range of special educational needs, some of which are complex, and whose needs cannot be fully met in mainstream schools.

HIGHER SIDE COMMUNITY COMPREHENSIVE SCHOOL

Cumber Lane, Whiston, Prescot, Merseyside, L35 2XG

Tel: 01514 265 715
Fax: 01514 306 644
Email: higherside.de@knowsley.gov.uk
Website: www.higherside.knowsley.sch.uk

• Pupils: 757 Mixed; Day Pupils • Age: 11 to 16
• Religion: Non-denominational • School status: State

SEN provision

Detail:
Now provide for in school:
Mild: EBD; DYSL; DYSP; CP;
Moderate: MLD; DYSL;
Others: OCD; EAL; Epi
Experience of:
Mild: ASP; ADD; ADHD; DS; DYSC; HI; VI;
Moderate: ASP; EBD; DS; DYSC; DYSP;
Severe: DYSL;
Others: ODD; Sp&LD; Eat

Summary: Higherside School is committed to the support of all students to ensure that all have the best opportunity to achieve their potential. The school aims to be as flexible as possible in order to overcome barriers to learning and makes a genuine effort to listen to the views and opinions of students and parents.

Higherside staff are experienced in teaching students across the full ability range including those with moderate learning difficulties and specific literacy difficulties (dyslexia). All students are supported wherever possible in order to access the full curriculum.

Highfield Special School

Downham Road, Ely, Cambridgeshire, CB6 1BD

Tel: 01353 662 085

Fax: 01353 662 096

Email: office@Highfield.cambs-schools.net

• Pupils: 91 Mixed; Day Pupils • Age: 2 to 19

• Religion: Non-denominational • School status: State

SEN provision

Summary: Highfield School provides a secure learning environment for pupils with special educational needs. We provide excellent education and pastoral care to enable pupils to develop socially and academically.

Highfields Community Primary School

Highfield Road, Kettering, Northamptonshire, NN15 6HY

Tel: 01536 514 622

Fax: 01536 512 993

Email: head@highfields-pri.northants-ecl.gov.uk

• Pupils: 131 Mixed; Day Pupils • Age: 4 to 11

• Religion: Non-denominational • School status: State

SEN provision

Detail:

Now provide for in school:

Mild: DYSP;

Moderate: MLD; DYSP

Experience of:

Mild: ASP; EBD;

Moderate: EBD

Summary: SEN indicators begin in year 4. Children, who need specific or general support, will be put onto an individual education plan with clear targets which are set and reviewed on a termly basis. Teaching strategies and materials to be used are clearly identified. Any specialist arrangements will be recorded. Learning support assistant support for each classroom is considered based on the needs of the individuals in each classroom. A VAK approach to learning is used to support their needs. Teachers work in unison, with the special educational needs co-ordinator, to help support the child's needs and in setting new targets. When a child is not succeeding with the strategies used in school, the special educational needs co-ordinator then refers the concerns to Children and Families. Expert advice is sought from different departments, observations or assessments are carried out, and recommendations lead the new targets to be set on the individual education plans.

Children receive support on a one-to-one basis or within small groups, within differentiated lessons in the classroom mainly, but provision for some children does require withdrawal from the classroom, within small groups/on a one-to-one basis through the support of a learning support assistant. The overall aim is to provide for children's needs within the classroom. When children no longer require specific support within an Individual Educational Plan, they are taken off the register. Referrals for statements are made when persistent non-achievement of targets is evident, when the strategies and arrangements advised by outside agencies are not having an effect and when lack of progress is so significant and the child is unable to follow the programmes of work set.

Highshore School

Bellenden Road, Peckham, London, SE15 5BB

Tel: 020 7639 7211

Fax: 020 7252 9024

Email: jcheeseman@highshore.southwark.sch.uk

Website: www.highshore.southwark.sch.uk

• Pupils: 128 Mixed; Day Pupils • Age: 11 to 16

• Religion: Non-denominational • School status: State

SEN provision

Detail:

Now provide for in school:

Mild: ADHD; EBD; DS; DYSC; DYSL; DYSP; SpLD; HI; VI; CP;

Moderate: ADD; ADHD; DS; MLD; DYSC; DYSL; DYSP; SpLD; VI; CP;

Severe: DYSL; DYSP; SpLD;
Others: SPD; OCD; FRX; GEN; EAL; DEL; Epi; Eat
Experience of:
Mild: ASP; AUT; ADD;
Moderate: ASP; AUT; EBD; HI;
Severe: ASP; ADD; ADHD; DS; DYSC;
Others: AUT(other); CD; ODD; TIC; SLD; PD

Summary: Highshore is a successful mixed special needs secondary school in Peckham, South East London. Formerly a school for children with moderate learning difficulties it now caters for students with a range of difficulties with particular focus on speech and language disorders, moderate to severe learning difficulties.

HILL HOUSE SCHOOL

Rope Hill, Boldre, Lymington, Hampshire, SO41 8NE

Tel: 01590 672 147
Fax: 01590 670 535
Email: jwright@hesleygroup.co.uk
Website: www.hesleygroup.co.uk

• Pupils: 22 Mixed; Takes boarders • Age: 11 to 19
• School status: Independent

SEN provision

Detail:
Now provide for in school:
Mild: CP;
Moderate: ADD; MLD;
Severe: ADD; HI; VI;
Others: SLD; Eat

Summary: Hill House School provides for children who require 52 week provision as a result of autistic spectrum disorders and associated learning difficulties and challenging behaviour. Students are functioning broadly at the SLD/MLD range of ability.

HILLINGDON MANOR SCHOOL

Moorcroft Complex, Harlington Road, Hillingdon, Uxbridge, Middlesex, UB8 3HD

Tel: 01895 813 679
Fax: 01895 813 679
Email: hillingdonmanor@hotmail.com

• Pupils: 51 Mixed; Day Pupils • Age: 3 to 19
• School status: Independent

SEN provision

Detail:
Now provide for in school:
Mild: ASP; AUT;
Moderate: ASP;
Severe: ASP;
Others: AUT(other)

Summary: Hillingdon Manor School is an independent specialist school for children with higher functioning autism and Asperger's syndrome. It accepts pupils from the age of 3.5 years to 19 years.

The ethos of the school is based in psychological theory and neurological research. The school aims to work holistically. It does this by working with the child's family and through providing a low anxiety learning environment. This is facilitated through a genuine no blame culture where 'what works' is promoted. In addition clear rules and boundaries, consequences and personal responsibility and teamwork are built into the structure of everyday experience.

The approaches used are designed to ensure that children's emotional needs are met and that children and families are provided with structure, consistency, clarity and calmness. Training and home support is provided for parents.

Parents are required to agree to sign a contract to work with the school.

The environment gives pupils constant opportunities to win awards and achieve at exam level. Pupils have access to GCSE, ASDAN and Duke of Edinburgh Award. They also have work experience and where appropriate access to mainstream settings. Pupils are set up to succeed at all that is offered them.

The school aims to reduce the limiting effects ASD places on individuals and their families. It aims to minimise disability and maximise ability.

Hillingdon Manor School has two sites. The Lower and Middle School has children from 3.5 to 13 years and the Upper School takes children from 13 to 19 years.

Lower and Middle School is sited at Moorcroft Complex, Harlington Road, Hillingdon Middx. UB8 3HD. Tel; 01895 813679.

Upper School is sited at Stables Courtyard, Church Road, Hayes, Middx.

Telephone 020 8673 7419 E-mail; hillingdon-manor@hotmail.com

Principal; Angela Austin. B. Ed. Hons. Adv. Dip. London. HG Dip.

Headteacher; Sean Pavitt. B. Ed Hons. Adv Dip. Birmingham.

Hillside School

Foredown Road, Portslade, Brighton, East Sussex, BN41 2FU

Tel: 01273 416 979

Fax: 01273 417 512

Email: office@hillside.brighton-hove.sch.uk

Website: www.hillside.brighton-hove.sch.uk

• Pupils: 78 Mixed; Day Pupils • Age: 3 to 19

• Religion: Non-denominational • School status: State

SEN provision

Detail:

Now provide for in school:

- Mild: AUT; VI; CP;
- Moderate: AUT; MLD; VI; CP;
- Severe: DS; VI; CP;
- Others: FRX; GEN; PMLD; SLD; EAL; MSI; Sp&LD; Epi

Summary: Hillside School caters for children with a wide range of abilities between the ages of 4 and 16, all of whom have learning difficulties. We cater for pupils with profound and multiple learning difficulties, and severe learning difficulties.

Hinchliffe Mill Junior and Infant School

Waterside Lane, Holmbridge, Holmfirth, West Yorkshire, HD9 2PF

Tel: 01484 222 476

Fax: 01484 222 476

Email: office.hinchliffemill@kirklees-schools.org.uk

Website: www.hinchliffemillschool.org.uk/

• Pupils: 95 Mixed; Day Pupils • Age: 5 to 11

• Religion: Non-denominational • School status: State

SEN provision

Detail:

Now provide for in school:

- Mild: DYSC; DYSL; DYSP;
- Moderate: MLD; DYSC; DYSL; DYSP;
- Others: EAL

Experience of:

- Mild: ASP; ADD; ADHD; EBD;
- Moderate: ADD; ADHD; EBD;
- Severe: EBD;
- Others: ODD

Summary: The school has an SEN co-ordinator and an up-to-date policy. Individual needs are catered for by in-class support and in withdrawal groups with a qualified Special Needs assistant. We also have a trained Behaviour Support Worker in school.

Holly Bank School

Roe Head, Far Common Road, Mirfield, West Yorkshire, WF14 0DQ

Tel: 01924 490 833

Fax: 01924 491 464

Email: admin@hollybanktrust.com

Website: www.hollybanktrust.com

• Pupils: 37 Mixed; Takes boarders • Age: 5 to 19

• School status: State

SEN provision

Detail:

Centre of excellence for:

- Mild: CP;
- Moderate: CP;
- Severe: CP;
- Others: PMLD; SLD; MSI; Sp&LD; Epi; PD; Oth

Now provide for in school:

- Mild: VI;
- Moderate: MLD; VI;
- Severe: SpLD; VI;
- Others: GEN; DEL; Eat

Experience of:

- Mild: HI;
- Moderate: HI;
- Severe: HI

Summary: Holly Bank School is registered with the DfES for 38 weeks, as well as being registered as a Children's Home by the NCSC for 52 weeks. We offer a broad and balanced curriculum which is both sensory and developmental and incorporates the National Curriculum. Work in our post-16 department is based on realistic essential skills which equip young people for their lives in the community. Where appropriate courses are accredited through 'ALL'. We have regular links with other schools, colleges and community groups.

There is an interdisciplinary approach which includes speech and language therapy, physiotherapy, OT, nursing, education, IT and care. All students have their own indivdiual programme. Staffing levels are high, full police checks are carried out and great emphasis is placed on training and development.

We are in a beautiful semi-rural location with nearby access to the M1 and M62. Our first-class facilites also include overnight accommodation for parents. We provide a homely enviornment within a safe and secure setting. There are opportunities for our leavers to move on to supported independence housing within the Trust.

HOLMFIRTH HIGH SCHOOL

Heys Road, Thongsbridge, Holmfirth, West Yorkshire, HD9 7SE

Tel: 01484 691 460

Fax: 01484 691 469

Email: office.holmfirth@kirklees-schools.org.uk

Website: www.holmfirthhighschool.com

• Pupils: 1240 Mixed; Day Pupils • Age: 11 to 16

• Religion: Non-denominational • School status: State

SEN provision

Detail:

Now provide for in school:

- Mild: ASP; AUT; ADD; ADHD; EBD; DS; DYSC; DYSL; DYSP; SpLD; HI; VI; CP;
- Moderate: ASP; AUT; ADD; ADHD; EBD; DS; MLD; DYSC; DYSL; DYSP; SpLD; HI; VI; CP;
- Severe: ASP; AUT; ADD; ADHD; EBD; DS; DYSC; DYSL; DYSP; SpLD; HI; VI;
- Others: SPD; AUT(other); CD; OCD; SLD; EAL; MSI; Sp&LD; DEL; Epi; PD; Oth; Eat

Summary: The SEN department at this school is a thriving one. It is made up of 15 members of staff who bring with them a range of expertise and experience. For the most part educational teaching assistants (ETAs) are linked to subject departments within school. This enables them to play an important role in the department and to support students effectively within a classroom situation. There are of course occasions when it is more appropriate for an individual student to work closely with no more than one or two ETAs, so we retain the flexibility to enable this to happen. We offer a range of programmes for students with SEN, these include:

- multi-sensory literacy programmes run by a teacher for students with specific learning difficulties
- in-class support
- morning registration literacy programmes
- reading support lessons (during lesson times)
- paired reading (Key Stage 3 students reading to Key Stage 4 students during morning registration)
- a movement programme incorporating Brain Gym activities
- early morning homework support in the library each morning from 8 o'clock

- lunchtime Zig Zag club which offers help with school/homework or where students may go to play games/chat
- social skills club (particularly for students on the autistic spectrum)
- lunchtime escorts
- an alternative curriculum for students at Key Stage 4
- KRONOS and Spectrum, in school counselling/support/health provisions run by school based staff and external agencies such as school nurse, youth workers, Connexions

As a department we are also responsible for access arrangements in examinations.

The provision for students with SEN is an important whole school responsibility, we endeavour to offer a high quality service for young people and their parents/carers.

Holmwood House School

Chitts Hill, Lexden, Colchester, Essex, CO3 9ST

Tel: 01206 574 305

Fax: 01206 768 269

Email: hst@holmwood.essex.sch.uk

Website: www.holmwood.essex.sch.uk

• Pupils: 397 Mixed; Takes boarders • Age: 4 to 13

• School status: Independent

SEN provision

Detail:

Centre of excellence for:

Mild: DYSC; DYSL;

Moderate: DYSC; DYSL

Now provide for in school:

Mild: DYSP;

Moderate: DYSP

Experience of:

Mild: SpLD; HI; CP;

Others: EAL; Sp&LD; Epi; PD

Summary: We have a specialist dyslexia unit comprising three full-time teachers and three part-timers. The children can be withdrawn from class for individual lessons and the staff also provide in-class support where necessary. Other members of the teaching staff have qualifications for teaching dyslexic children and the school, in general, offers full support.

Horsington Church of England Primary School

Horsington, Templecombe, Somerset, BA8 0BW

Tel: 01963 370 358

Fax: 01963 370 117

Email: office@horsington.somerset.sch.uk

• Pupils: 99 Mixed; Day Pupils • Age: 4 to 11

• Religion: Church of England • School status: State

SEN provision

Detail:

Now provide for in school:

Mild: ADD; EBD; DYSL; DYSP; HI;

Moderate: MLD; DYSL; DYSP;

Others: EAL; Sp&LD; PD

Experience of:

Mild: ASP; AUT; DYSC;

Moderate: ASP; AUT; EBD; DYSC

Summary: Many children occasionally need extra help with some aspect of learning. At these times extra support will be offered by our special needs co-ordinator, class teachers and learning support assistants. Children who need this help are supported by extra, small group or individual support with work specifically designed for their particular needs. For the majority of time this support is offered within the classroom, but for some activities children may be withdrawn to another working space. Sometimes the school will seek additional help and advice from external services in consultation with parents. The school has pioneered a project for successful transfer of children with special educational needs to secondary provision and this is now as a model for such provision. The school has also worked successfully in partnership with the local special school.

Hove Park School and Sixth Form Centre

Nevill Road, Hangleton Way, Hove, East Sussex, BN3 8AA

Tel: 01273 295 000
Fax: 01273 295 009
Email: admin@hovepark.brighton-hove.sch.uk
Website: www.hovepark.brighton-hove.sch.uk

• Pupils: 1717 Mixed; Day Pupils • Age: 11 to 18
• Religion: Non-denominational • School status: State

SEN provision

Detail:
Centre of excellence for:
Mild: DYSL;
Moderate: DYSL;
Severe: DYSL
Now provide for in school:
Mild: ASP; AUT; ADD; ADHD; EBD; DYSC; DYSP; HI; VI; CP;
Moderate: ASP; ADD; ADHD; EBD; MLD; DYSC; DYSP; HI; VI;
Severe: ASP; VI;
Others: OCD; ODD; TIC; EAL; Sp&LD; DEL; Epi; Eat

Summary: The school maintains an SEN record. All pupils are supported in line with the Code of Practice issued by the DFES. The school has students with a variety of SEN eg SpLD, autism, speech and language difficulties, EBSD, VI, HI, MLD, medical, physical etc. Students are supported in a variety of ways, eg in-class, small group and individual withdrawal. The school is working towards implementing the 'Every Child Matters' policy and promotes inclusion.

Hugh Christie Technology College

Norwich Avenue, Tonbridge, Kent, TN10 4QL

Tel: 01732 353 544
Fax: 01732 367 833
Email: chris@hughchristie.kent.sch.uk
Website: www.hughchristie.kent.sch.uk

• Pupils: 1147 Mixed; Day Pupils • Age: 11 to 18
• Religion: Non-denominational • School status: State

SEN provision

Detail:
Now provide for in school:
Mild: ASP; AUT; ADD; ADHD; EBD; DS; DYSC; DYSL; DYSP; HI; VI; CP;
Moderate: ASP; ADD; ADHD; EBD; DS; MLD; DYSC; DYSL; DYSP; HI;
Others: SPD; TIC; EAL; Sp&LD; Epi; PD

Summary: Hugh Christie Technology College learning support department aims to provide additional support to all students from year 7 to 13 where necessary. Support is given in particular to those students who have a statement of special educational needs or diagnosed with specific difficulties i.e dyslexia, ADHD, autistic spectrum disorder (ASD), specific learning difficulties etc.

All students are screened on entry to the college using Cognitive Ability Tests plus reading and spelling test. Further assessments can be carried out should the need arise for example access arrangements for public examinations.

The students are supported by a very small team of Specialist Teachers and Learning Support Assistants (LSAs). Support is grouped and takes place either in the classroom or in the learning support department.

The department is supported by many outside agencies who can be called upon for advice i.e psychology service, attendance and behaviour service, local cluster group, social services, EWO, LEA etc.

We work closely with parents at all times and the student is always of paramount importance; we wish to make them feel valued, safe and happy.

HUMPHRY DAVY SCHOOL

Coombe Road, Penzance, Cornwall, TR18 2TG

Tel: 01736 363 559
Fax: 01736 331 042
Email: enquiries@humphry-davy.cornwall.sch.uk
Website: www.humphry-davy.cornwall.sch.uk

• Pupils: 767 Mixed; Day Pupils • Age: 11 to 16
• Religion: Non-denominational • School status: State

SEN provision

Detail:
Now provide for in school:
Mild: ASP; ADD; ADHD; EBD; DYSC; DYSP; HI; VI;
Moderate: ASP; EBD; MLD; DYSC; DYSL; DYSP; HI; VI;
Severe: DYSL; DYSP;
Others: EAL; Sp&LD; Epi; Eat
Experience of:
Mild: AUT; DS;
Others: SPD; CD; OCD; ODD; TIC

Summary: We encourage all pupils with SEN to fulfil their potential here at school. We encourage students to play to their strengths and to develop their talents. We provide in-class support with qualified TAs to assist pupils. We also extract pupils with literacy difficulties for work on our ARROW and WORDSHARK programmes. We have Maths Intervention classes to help those who find maths challenging. We run numerous programmes to help children manage their anger and to develop social skills. Children who benefit from the use of a laptop are provided with an Alphasmart machine for use in key lessons.

In September 2005 we are opening our state-of-the-art ilearn centre which will cater for those who need an individual learning programme specially developed to meet their individual needs.

HUNTERS HILL TECHNOLOGY COLLEGE

Spirehouse Lane, Blackwell, Bromsgrove, Worcestershire, B60 1QD

Tel: 0121 445 1320
Fax: 0121 445 2496
Email: enquiry@hunthill.bham.sch.uk
Website: www.huntershill.org.uk

• Pupils: 69 Mixed; Takes boarders • Age: 11 to 16
• Religion: Non-denominational • School status: State

SEN provision

Detail:
Now provide for in school:
Mild: EBD;
Moderate: EBD; MLD;
Severe: EBD

Summary: The young people who attend Hunters Hill have been identified as having moderate learning, emotional and behavioural difficulties with a wide variety of needs which, it is felt, are best met in an environment which is structured, calm and sympathetic to individuals who are insecure, lacking in confidence and have hitherto experienced failure in mainstream, day schools.

THE IFIELD SCHOOL

Cedar Avenue, Gravesend, Kent, DA12 5JT

Tel: 01474 365 485
Fax: 01474 569 744

• Pupils: 170 Mixed; Day Pupils • Age: 4 to 16
• Religion: Non-denominational • School status: State

SEN provision

Summary: Ifield School is a district special school catering for 138 pupils with special educational needs and is fully equipped to support the National Curriculum from year 1 to year 11. The school has been re-designated as the district special school for the Gravesham cluster to take pupils with more profound, severe and complex learning, communication and interaction difficulties from September 2004. The school aims to provide an attractive, welcoming and stimulating environment that can develop pupils through the effective and appropriate delivery of the National Curriculum. The school seeks to develop in all a respect for the individual and an appreciation of quality. The school understands that every child has natural talents and abilities that can stand outside of their general underlying ability and seeks to support these. The staff see that the successful re-integration of pupils, when appropriate, is of the utmost importance. Staff endeavour to create, within classes, a well organised, conducive and ordered environment. The school aims to provide a happy and cheerful ethos that enables children to develop their confidence through success and praise.

ILFRACOMBE CHURCH OF ENGLAND JUNIOR SCHOOL

Princess Avenue, Ilfracombe, Devon, EX34 9LW

Tel: 01271 863 463

Fax: 01271 863 997

Email: admin@ilfracombe-jun.devon.sch.uk

Website: www.ilfracombe-jun.devon.sch.uk

• Pupils: 537 Mixed; Day Pupils • Age: 7 to 11

• Religion: Church of England • School status: State

SEN provision

Detail:

Now provide for in school:

Mild: AUT; EBD; DYSL; HI; VI;

Moderate: ASP; AUT; EBD; MLD; HI; VI;

Severe: AUT; EBD;

Others: EAL; Sp&LD; Epi

Experience of:

Mild: ASP; ADD; ADHD; DYSC; DYSP;

Moderate: ADD; ADHD; DS; DYSC; DYSL; DYSP;

Severe: ADD; ADHD; DYSL; VI;

Others: SPD; AUT(other); OCD; ODD; TIC; Eat

Summary: At Ilfracombe C of E Junior School, we aim to provide a broad and balanced, personalised education that will develop the best in every child and enable them to grow into confident, independent young people.

We are fully committed to the principle of inclusion, and have a number of children attending this school with a range of SEN. Every child in the school has a personal target book which enables class teachers to work closely with the children in setting achievable realistic targets to raise their attainment and self esteem. Parents are actively encouraged to be involved with their child's learning and their views are highly valued.

We employ a large number of experienced support staff who work closely with class teachers and the school's special educational needs co-ordinator, to provide effective in-class support for any children experiencing difficulties with their learning.

INGLEBY ARNCLIFFE CHURCH OF ENGLAND VOLUNTARY AIDED PRIMARY SCHOOL

Ingleby Arncliffe, Northallerton, North Yorkshire, DL6 3NA

Tel: 01609 882 432

Email: admin@inglebyarncliffe.n-yorks.sch.uk

Website: www.inglebyarncliffe.n-yorks.sch.uk

• Pupils: 58 Mixed; Day Pupils • Age: 4 to 11

• Religion: Church of England • School status: State

SEN provision

Detail:

Experience of:

Mild: AUT; EBD; DYSL; SpLD; HI; VI;

Moderate: ASP; HI; VI;

Others: Sp&LD

Summary: Our provision for SEN has always been commented on as being 'good' as we have catered for a wide range of needs including children on the autistic spectrum, hearing impaired and physical disability.

INTERNATIONAL COMMUNITY SCHOOL

4 York Terrace East, Regents Park, London, NW1 4PT

Tel: 020 7935 1206
Fax: 020 7935 7915
Email: admissions@ics.uk.net
Website: www.ics.uk.net

• Pupils: 240 Mixed; Day Pupils • Age: 3 to 19
• Religion: Non-denominational • School status: Independent

SEN provision

Detail:
Now provide for in school:
Mild: ASP; AUT; ADD; ADHD; EBD; DS; DYSC; DYSL; DYSP;
Moderate: ASP; MLD; DYSL; DYSP;
Others: SPD; TIC; Sp&LD
Experience of:
Mild: HI

Summary: The school admits children from the UK and international settings into its mainstream environment. About 17 per cent of the students benefit from the student support programme that designs individual education plans (IEPs) for children with Special Education Needs. Our educational psychologist leads a team of therapists and learning support assistants who provide in-school therapy and support to students who so require. This unique model of delivery involves all teachers and staff working with each child, so that all including the parent is on the same page. The school believes passionately in integrating students with special needs and strives to be a leader in London in both provision and teacher training. A Life Skills College is being established by the school, for students aged 16-25. This will launch in the New Year, 2006.

ITCHEN COLLEGE

Middle Road, Bitterne, Southampton, Hampshire, SO19 7TB

Tel: 023 8043 5636
Fax: 023 8042 1911
Email: info@itchen.ac.uk
Website: www.itchen.ac.uk

• Pupils: 1250 Mixed; Day Pupils • Age: 16 to 99
• Religion: Non-denominational • School status: State

SEN provision

Detail:
Experience of:
Mild: ASP; AUT; ADD; ADHD; EBD; DYSC; DYSL; DYSP; SpLD; HI; VI; CP;
Moderate: ASP; ADD; ADHD; MLD; DYSC; DYSL; DYSP; SpLD; HI; VI;
Severe: DYSL; DYSP; HI; VI;
Others: OCD; TIC; EAL; Sp&LD; Epi; Eat

Summary: Itchen College's SEN provision is tailored to each individual learner – we do not run separate courses. The data shown below shows the kinds of special needs which we can deal with or have experience of. If we show that we can deal with a need, suitable provision is available.

All students are screened on admission to ensure that relevant support is available to all our students.

THE JOHN FIELDING COMMUNITY SPECIAL SCHOOL

Ashlawn Drive, Boston, Lincolnshire, PE21 9PX

Tel: 01205 363 395
Fax: 01205 357 696
Email: enquiries@john-fielding.lincs.sch.uk

• Pupils: 45 Mixed; Day Pupils • Age: 2 to 19
• Religion: Non-denominational • School status: State

SEN provision

Detail:
Experience of:
Mild: AUT; ADD; ADHD; DS; HI; VI; CP;
Moderate: AUT; DS; VI; CP;
Severe: AUT; DS; CP;
Others: PMLD; SLD; DEL; Epi; PD; Eat

Summary: We are a small school for pupils with severe learning difficulties, some of whom have sensory impairments, speech and language needs, multi-sensory, physical needs – medical gross or fine motor, are on the autistic spectrum or use wheelchairs.

KEHELLAND VILLAGE SCHOOL

Kehelland, Camborne, Cornwall, TR14 0DA

Tel: 01209 713 928
Fax: 01209 713 928
Email: secretary@kehelland.cornwall.sch.uk
Website: www.kehelland.cornwall.sch.uk
• Pupils: 63 Mixed; Day Pupils • Age: 4 to 11
• Religion: Non-denominational • School status: State

SEN provision

Detail:
Now provide for in school:
Mild: ASP; ADD; ADHD; EBD; DYSL; DYSP; HI;
Moderate: ADD; MLD; DYSL; DYSP;
Others: OCD; TIC; Sp&LD; Eat
Experience of:
Mild: DS; DYSC; VI;
Moderate: ASP; ADHD; EBD;
Others: ODD

Summary: Our school is fully inclusive. All children have equal rights. Our curriculum is designed to motivate and engage all children. We have a peer mentoring system and our children are supported with strategies which will help them learn – readiness, resilience, resourcefulness, remembering and reflection. Our children are organised into mixed aged groups (reception to year 6) for registration, personal, social, health education, emotional development and citizenship as well as all the foundation subjects, eg art, science, design and technology. The curriculum is environmentally based and linked to our guardianship of Godrevy Beach (National Trust). Our learning activities are led through team teaching and are linked to skills ladders. We encourage fun and creativity through a negotiated curriculum. Our topic based work leads the skills developed in literacy and this in turn has led to a rise in standards for all children. Currently we are developing children's thinking skills through open ended questions which allows all children to succeed. Our children are becoming confident learners. Our small school means that we know each individual child really well.

KELLS LANE PRIMARY SCHOOL

Kells Lane, Low Fell, Gateshead, Tyne and Wear, NE9 5HX

Tel: 01914 878 226
Fax: 01914 200 509
• Pupils: 404 Mixed; Day Pupils • Age: 4 to 11
• Religion: Non-denominational • School status: State

SEN provision

Detail:
Centre of excellence for:
Mild: DYSL;
Moderate: DYSL;
Severe: DYSL
Now provide for in school:
Mild: ASP; ADD; EBD; DYSC; DYSP; VI;
Moderate: ASP; EBD; MLD; DYSC; DYSP;
Others: EAL; Sp&LD; Epi; PD
Experience of:
Mild: ADHD;
Moderate: ADD; ADHD; VI;
Severe: ASP; ADD; ADHD; EBD; DYSP;
Others: SPD

Summary: Kells Lane is a mainstream school which caters for a wide range of pupils with special educational needs. A recent Ofsted inspection praised all members of staff for their inclusive practices. Staff are skilled in preparing and delivering lessons which include the most and least able pupils. Children at school action and school action plus receive individual or small group support from a learning support teacher.

Kells Lane is a dyslexia friendly school with a mainstream support base catering for statemented pupils from across Gateshead. Staff in the base hold specialised qualifications in teaching dyslexic pupils. Children receive literacy and numeracy lessons in the base during the morning and join their mainsteam classes for curriculum areas during the afternoon.

KENNET SCHOOL

Stoney Lane, Thatcham, Berkshire, RG19 4LL

Tel: 01635 862 121

Fax: 01635 871 814

Email: Office.kennet@westberks.org

Website: www.kennetschool.net

• Pupils: 1667 Mixed; Day Pupils • Age: 11 to 18

• Religion: Non-denominational • School status: State

SEN provision

Detail:

Now provide for in school:

Mild: ADD; ADHD; EBD; DYSL; HI;

Moderate: ADD; ADHD; EBD; MLD; DYSL;

Others: PMLD; SLD; PD

Experience of:

Mild: DYSC; DYSP; VI; CP;

Moderate: DYSC; DYSP;

Severe: ADD; ADHD; EBD; DYSC; DYSL; DYSP;

Others: CD; Sp&LD; DEL; Epi; Eat

Summary: It is widely acknowledged that 20 per cent of pupils need extra help at some stage in their school careers. At Kennet, we have long been clear that attention to the needs of the individual is vital. New pupils arriving in school are carefully screened to ensure that their needs are identified and met. For the majority of children, this means careful negotiation with primary schools and discussions before the child ever arrives at Kennet. We have a well-trained and enthusiastic special needs department, which ensures that the provision for children in difficulty is appropriate. This may manifest itself in work in mainstream classrooms or in small groups withdrawn, though the latter is very rare. We are careful to invest significantly in staffing in the early years of secondary education, to ensure that pupils have appropriate assistance as far as possible in classrooms, alongside their peers. We have the benefit of joint working with others from West Berkshire Education Authority, including an educational psychologist. The particular needs of pupils are communicated to staff, pupils and parents, by the use of individual education plans. These plans and statements are reviewed regularly and the reviews involve all key parties. At parents' evenings, and at other times of the year, a member of the special needs department is always available should parents require further advice.

Able, gifted and talented pupils are also often considered to have 'special needs'. We have invested a great deal of time and effort in identifying our more able pupils in recent years and in providing opportunities and support for their needs. We are delighted that some 80 pupils have already been affiliated by the Government to the National Academy for Gifted and Talented Youth. We will continue to offer masterclasses and other opportunities, including summer and Easter schools, for pupils across the whole spectrum of ability.

KENTON BAR PRIMARY SCHOOL

Ryal Walk, Newcastle upon Tyne, Tyne and Wear, NE3 3YF

Tel: 01912 860 536

Fax: 01912 862 287

Email: admin@kentonbar.newcastle.sch.uk

Website: www.newcastle-schools.org.uk/kentonbar

• Pupils: 289 Mixed; Day Pupils • Age: 3 to 11

• Religion: Non-denominational • School status: State

SEN provision

Detail:

Now provide for in school:

Mild: ASP; AUT;

Moderate: MLD;

Others: Sp&LD

Experience of:

Mild: ADHD; EBD; DS; DYSC; DYSL; DYSP; HI;

Moderate: DS;

Others: EAL

Summary: The latest Ofsted report describes the school as a 'very caring community' with a 'very strong commitment to inclusion' which gives good support for pupils with special educational needs. We also have an additionally resourced centre catering for children with autistic spectrum disorders.

KEW COLLEGE

24-26 Cumberland Road, Kew Gardens, Richmond, Surrey, TW9 3HQ

Tel: 020 8940 2039
Fax: 020 8332 9945
Email: enquiries@kewcollege.com
Website: www.kewcollege.com

• Pupils: 260 Mixed; Day Pupils • Age: 3 to 11
• Religion: Non-denominational • School status: Independent

SEN provision

Detail:
Now provide for in school:
- Mild: DYSC; DYSL; DYSP; VI;
- Others: EAL

Experience of:
- Mild: ADD; ADHD; EBD; SpLD;
- Moderate: MLD;
- Others: SPD; Sp&LD; Epi

Summary: Our qualified SENCo assesses any child referred by the class teacher and will then advise the teachers how best to help the child using multi-sensory strategies and prepare the individual education plan. The IEPs are in place to help the child achieve their full potential and strengthen their confidence.

KEYHAM LODGE SCHOOL

Keyham Lane, Leicester, Leicestershire, LE5 1FG

Tel: 01162 416 852
Fax: 01162 416 199
Email: cbruce@keyhamlodge.leicester.sch.uk

• Pupils: 46 Boys; Day Pupils • Age: 11 to 16
• Religion: Non-denominational • School status: State

SEN provision

Detail:
Centre of excellence for:
- Mild: EBD;
- Moderate: EBD

Experience of:
- Mild: ASP; ADD; ADHD; DYSC; DYSL; DYSP; HI;
- Moderate: ADD; ADHD; MLD; DYSC; DYSL; DYSP;
- Severe: ADD; ADHD; EBD;
- Others: CD; ODD; TIC; EAL; Sp&LD; Epi

Summary: Keyham Lodge caters for boys aged 11-16 with behavioural emotional and social difficulties. We also cater well for pupils who have additional needs related to generalised and specific learning difficulties and speech and language difficulties

KILSYTH ACADEMY

Balmalloch, Kilsyth, G65 9NF

Tel: 01236 822 244
Fax: 01236 824 974
Email: ht@kilsythacademy.n-lanark.sch.uk

• Pupils: 827 Mixed; Day Pupils • Age: 11 to 18
• Religion: Non-denominational • School status: State

SEN provision

Detail:
Now provide for in school:
- Mild: AUT; ADD; EBD; DYSC; DYSL; DYSP; VI;
- Moderate: ASP; MLD; DYSL;
- Others: SPD; PMLD; Epi; PD; Eat

Experience of:
- Mild: ASP; HI; CP;
- Moderate: DYSC; DYSP; HI; VI;
- Severe: ASP; DS; DYSC; DYSL; DYSP;
- Others: OCD; Sp&LD

Summary: We have general provision for pupils from our catchment area and strive to give them the best possible academic and social education in an inclusive way.

The building will be fully DDA compliant by late 2006 although there are limits to our provision up until that time.

We also have a unit (KALSP) for up to six young people from North Lanarkshire who would have difficulties coping with mainstream education because of identified SE needs.

Kilwinning Academy

Dalry Road, Kilwinning, KA13 7HD

Tel: 01294 551 316
Fax: 01294 552 980
Email: contactus@kilwinning.n-ayrshire.sch.uk
Website: www.kilwinningacademy.ssnet.co.uk
• Pupils: 1000 Mixed; Day Pupils • Age: 11 to 18
• Religion: Non-denominational • School status: State

SEN provision

Detail:
Now provide for in school:
Mild: CP;
Moderate: MLD; CP;
Others: EAL; PD
Experience of:
Mild: ASP; EBD; DYSC; DYSL; DYSP; HI; VI;
Moderate: ASP; ADHD; EBD; DYSL; DYSP; HI; VI;
Severe: DYSL

Summary: We have, in the recent past, had pupils with disabilities requiring the use of wheelchairs in Kilwinning Academy. The building has been modified for wheelchair use eg lift to upper floors, evac chairs, special equipment and modifications in Technical, Home Economics and Music. More importantly we have staff who are experienced and comfortable in working with pupils with physical disabilities. We have a good working relationship with the outside agencies who also work with these pupils. In addition over the years we have learned a great deal about the social and emotional needs of these pupils and so we are confident that systems could be put in place early in order to support pupils. We believe that we have a caring and supportive staff who will do everything they can to meet the needs, academically and socially, of individual pupils whatever their special need. There is a college of Further Education near to the school and Kilwinning Academy has developed very good links especially with the department dealing with inclusive education.

King Alfred's Community and Sports College

Portway, Wantage, Oxfordshire, OX12 9BY

Tel: 01235 225 700
Fax: 01235 225 779
Email: Headteacher.4142@kingalfreds.oxon.sch.uk
Website: www.kingalfreds.oxon.sch.uk
• Pupils: 1827 Mixed; Day Pupils • Age: 11 to 18
• Religion: Non-denominational • School status: State

SEN provision

Detail:
Centre of excellence for:
Mild: ASP; DS;
Moderate: ASP;
Severe: ASP
Now provide for in school:
Mild: AUT; ADD; ADHD; EBD; DYSL; DYSP; SpLD; HI;
Moderate: AUT; ADD; ADHD; EBD; DS; MLD; DYSL; DYSP; HI;
Severe: AUT; ADD; ADHD; EBD; DS; DYSL; DYSP; HI;

Others: SPD; AUT(other); Epi; PD
Experience of:
Mild: DYSC; VI;
Moderate: DYSC;
Severe: DYSC;
Others: EAL

Summary: King Alfred's provides support for students with SEN in all lessons – mainly via a suitably differentiated curriculum but in some instances with the additional support from teaching assistants. We are an inclusive establishment and work hard to enable all students to achieve their potential. As a training school staff are encouraged to take part in a variety of courses aimed at helping them to develop their teaching skills with regards to SEN, teaching and learning approaches, e-learning etc.

King Edward VI Grammar School, Chelmsford

Broomfield Road, Chelmsford, Essex, CM1 3SX

Tel: 01245 353 510
Fax: 01245 344 741
Email: office@kegs.org.uk
Website: www.kegs.org.uk

• Pupils: 835 Boys; Day Pupils • Age: 11 to 18
• School status: State

SEN provision

Detail:
Experience of:
Mild: ASP; ADD; ADHD; EBD; DYSL; DYSP; VI;
Others: EAL; Epi; PD; Eat

Summary: Although we are a highly academic, selective grammar school we do cater for a variety of special educational needs. We do not have a large number of students requiring extra assistance and so we do not have teaching assistants, specialist knowledge or a specialist unit. We do offer individual help for students with specific needs however and have had some experience of students with Asperger's syndrome, ADHD, ADD, visual impairments, mild speech impediments (stammering), mild dyspraxia and mild dyslexia. We have a strong pastoral system and work closely with both students and parents to overcome difficulties experienced, meeting their needs on a one-to-one basis in consultation with outside agencies. We also offer assistance with social skills, anger management and general counselling sessions where required, either in-house (we have a trained counsellor on the staff) or again using outside agencies. We do not claim to be experts in any of these areas but can hopefully provide support and encouragement.

King Edward VII and Queen Mary School

Clifton Drive South, Lytham St Annes, Lancashire, FY8 1DT

Tel: 01253 784 100
Fax: 01253 731 623
Email: principal@keqms.co.uk
Website: www.keqms.co.uk

• Pupils: 733 Mixed; Day Pupils • Age: 2 to 18
• School status: Independent

SEN provision

Detail:
Now provide for in school:
Mild: ADD; ADHD; EBD; DYSC; DYSL; DYSP; SpLD; HI; VI;
Moderate: ADD; ADHD; EBD; MLD; DYSC; DYSL; DYSP; SpLD;
Severe: DYSL; SpLD;
Others: EAL; Sp&LD; Epi; Eat

Summary: At King Edward VII & Queen Mary School the special educational needs of our pupils are met through the work of the learning support department and the individual subject/class teachers.We believe that all our students have skills, talents and abilities and as a school we have a responsibility to develop them to the full. Students with SEN are supported as necessary to help them achieve full access to the whole school curriculum. On entry into year 7 we firstly rely on information from feeder schools and parents for identifying students with SEN. The year group is screened within the first half term and any causes for concern are then further assessed. Any student, regardless of age, can, at any time, be assessed by the Head of Learning Support if there is cause for concern from teachers and/or parents. A variety of assessments are carried out to determine the type of support required.Once assessed a student, if deemed necessary, will follow one of two possible options: receive small group learning support for 2 – 2.5 hours per week with a specialist teacher or attend a weekly lunchtime study skills clinic, again run by a specialist teacher. All year 7 and 8 students receive in-class support in English lessons. Each student withdrawn for learning support has an individual education plan which is reviewed on a six-monthly basis. Those students who come to us with a statement of educational needs will continue to have their statement reviewed annually for as long as is deemed necessary. The special educational needs of our pupils include dyslexia, dyspraxia, dyscalculia, ADHD, and speech and language difficulties. We believe it to be of vital importance to work closely with students, teachers and parents when assessing a student's educational needs and when formulating a suitable individual education plan. We work hard together to ensure that every student has the best possible chance of success. J. Klenk, Head of Learning Support.

King Edward's School

Witley, Wormley, Godalming, Surrey, GU8 5SG

Tel: 01428 682 572
Fax: 01428 685 260
Email: hmsec@kesw.surrey.sch.uk
Website: www.kesw.surrey.sch.uk

• Pupils: 465 Mixed; Takes boarders • Age: 10 to 19
• School status: Independent

SEN provision

Detail:
Now provide for in school:
Mild: ASP; AUT; ADD; ADHD; EBD; DYSC; DYSL; DYSP; HI; VI;
Moderate: ASP; AUT; ADD; ADHD; EBD; MLD; DYSL; HI; VI;
Others: MSI; DEL; PD; Eat

Summary: The school caters for those with a special need for boarding, promoting both cultural and intellectual development in our pupils, together with the achievement of the best academic qualifications within each pupil's capabilities. To this end the school seeks to identify and to provide support for the particular or special needs of its pupils by:

- screening new pupils regularly in order to identify those with particular needs
- employing trained learning support teachers who are able to provide individual or small group support for pupils with particular needs
- keeping a regularly updated register of pupils who receive such help so that those who teach them are informed of their needs
- co-operating with specialist advisory teachers and allowing them access to classrooms in company with the pupil
- being flexible over the provision of co-curricular sport and activities, as well as the curriculum itself, in order to accommodate individual pupil's needs.

King James's School

St Helen's Gate, Almondbury, Huddersfield, West Yorkshire, HD4 6SG

Tel: 01484 223 930
Fax: 01484 223 934
Email: office.kingjames@kirklees-schools.org.uk

• Pupils: 780 Mixed; Day Pupils • Age: 11 to 16
• Religion: Non-denominational • School status: State

SEN provision

Detail:
Now provide for in school:
Mild: ADD; DYSC; DYSL; VI;
Moderate: MLD; DYSL;
Severe: DYSL
Experience of:
Mild: ASP; ADHD; EBD;
Moderate: ADD; ADHD; DYSC;
Severe: ADD; ADHD;
Others: Epi

Summary: King James's is a relatively small school and we aim to support our students in any way they feel they need. When pupils come to us in year 7 they take tests in a number of areas which allows us to identify anyone who may have particular difficulties. Pupils will then be given provision to match their needs. Currently we have a dyslexia specialist teacher as well as the SENCo and a small but caring and lovely team of classroom assistants.

As well as helping students overcome difficulties in literacy we also work with small groups of year 7 pupils with their maths skills. Any student who feels they need some help with homework or classwork is always welcome to come along for support and we are more than happy to talk to parents about ways in which we can support their child in school. We aim to provide a caring and supportive atmosphere, a place for children to feel safe and know they can find someone to help them whatever their difficulty.

KING'S NORTON BOYS' SCHOOL

Northfield Road, Birmingham, West Midlands, B30 1DY

Tel: 0121 628 0010

Fax: 0121 628 0080

Email: enquiry@kingsnortonboys.bham.sch.uk

Website: www.kingsnortonboys.bham.sch.uk

• Pupils: 743 Boys; Day Pupils • Age: 11 to 18

• Religion: Non-denominational • School status: State

SEN provision

Detail:

Now provide for in school:

Mild: ASP; AUT; ADD; ADHD; EBD; DYSC; DYSL; DYSP;

Moderate: MLD; DYSL;

Severe: HI;

Others: SPD; Sp&LD

Experience of:

Mild: VI;

Others: EAL

Summary: At King's Norton Boys' School, the learning support department (LSD) is responsible for dealing with boys who at any time during their school career are identified as having special educational needs. This might be related to their learning, or could be due to social, emotional or physical difficulties. If any boy is identified as having such additional needs, then they will be provided with appropriate support in school.

The LSD is run by the special educational needs co-ordinator (SENCo), with the support of a team of teaching assistants. The department operates the 'SEN Code of Practice', which outlines how a school should support pupils with special educational needs. Once a boy has been identified as requiring additional support, then he will be placed on the school database. This will ensure that his specific needs are met through an individual education plan (IEP). This plan is drawn up after consultation with subject teachers and an assessment and diagnosis of the nature of the difficulty. A pivotal part of this process is the involvement of parents; parents will be advised if it is proposed to place a boy on the SEN database, and will also be invited to take part in regular reviews of progress.

The process of support begins as soon as the boys enter year 7. The teaching assistants work closely with both the year 7 form tutors and with the lower band groups, to ensure that boys who might be struggling receive support within the classroom. Assessments in English and mathematics help us to establish which boys will need additional help. This support continues throughout years 8 and 9. In years 10 and 11 boys will receive more individualised support, depending on their GCSE choices. In addition, boys may be withdrawn to receive extra support, either on a one-to-one basis, or in small groups.

There are some occasions where the support that the school is able to offer is not sufficient. In these instances the school is able to call upon the expertise of colleagues within educational psychology, pupil and school support services, educational welfare and behaviour support. If necessary, a request will be made to the LEA for a boy to be assessed for a statement of special educational needs. If this is the case, then parents will be involved throughout the process.

KINGSFIELD SCHOOL

Brook Road, Warmley, Bristol, BS15 4JT

Tel: 01454 866 538

Fax: 01454 866 541

Email: KingsfieldSecondary.School@southglos.gov.uk

Website: www.kingsfield.s-gloucs.sch.uk

• Pupils: 1225 Mixed; Day Pupils • Age: 11 to 18

• Religion: Non-denominational • School status: State

SEN provision

Detail:

Now provide for in school:

Mild: AUT; ADD; ADHD; EBD; DYSC; DYSL; DYSP; SpLD; HI; VI; CP;

Moderate: AUT; ADD; EBD; DYSC; DYSL; DYSP; SpLD; HI;

Severe: DYSL; SpLD; HI;

Others: TIC; GEN; EAL; Sp&LD; Epi; PD

Summary: The school's special needs department consists of the SEN co-ordinator, a learning support teacher, and 8 teaching assistants. Schools meals supervisors may also have defined responsibilities for specified students during unstructured times. Each faculty has its own teaching assistant, who is deployed to meet special educational needs within that curriculum area, whilst being ultimately responsible to the co-ordinator of special needs.

The department has developed considerable experience in dealing with a wide range of special needs, from specific learning difficulties to multiple disability. As well as intervening directly to help students, the department gives direction and advice to staff through its pioneering use of learning support profiles. These are maintained and updated on the school's computer network and lie at the heart of planning, intervention and monitoring. In cases where the school has no previous experience of dealing with a particular special educational need it enlists help within the local education authority's inclusion support service. Regular visits of the psychology service and behaviour support team help identified students make a smooth transition from secondary transfer across their years of secondary schooling. The Connexions service, similarly, is involved in ensuring that statemented students have the necessary support in their transition to adult life.

Learning support can take many forms. Apart from everyday modification and differentiation of the curriculum, support may take the form of teaching assistance within the classroom, or structured skills – acquisition programmes, usually taught within small groups. The department is directly involved in the implementation of the Key Stage 3 Intervention Strategy which seeks to raise the level of attainment of identified students through the school's 'Flying Start' and 'Skills Booster' programmes. At Key Stage 4 the curriculum is adapted to give students with special needs a wide range of accredited courses, some with a strong vocational element.

Kingsfield prides itself upon its inclusive character, and seeks to ensure progression in learning by establishing high expectations for all students, and setting suitable learning challenges for them to achieve. The school sees parents as partners in education and this is particularly the case where students have a special educational need. The school draws upon parental knowledge and expertise in relation to their child and seeks to develop a sensitive and constructive relationship which helps students fulfil potential. Similarly, young people with special needs have a unique knowledge of their own circumstances and needs, and the school seeks their views and active involvement in planning for their education.

KINGSLEY COLLEGE

Woodrow Drive, Redditch, Worcestershire, B98 7UH

Tel: 01527 523 088

Fax: 01527 514 245

Email: kingsley@kingsley.worcs.sch.uk

• Pupils: 997 Mixed; Day Pupils • Age: 13 to 18

• Religion: Non-denominational • School status: State

SEN provision

Detail:

Now provide for in school:

Mild: ASP; AUT; ADD; ADHD; EBD; DYSC; DYSL; DYSP; HI; VI; CP;

Moderate: ASP; AUT; ADD; ADHD; EBD; MLD; DYSC; DYSL; DYSP; HI; VI;

Severe: ASP; ADD; ADHD; DYSL;

Others: SPD; CD; Sp&LD; DEL; Epi

Experience of:

Mild: DS; SpLD;

Moderate: DS;

Others: OCD; EAL; PD; Eat

Summary: SEN at Kingsley College caters for students with a wide variety of needs. The department is based in the learning support area of school which is self contained. In the building we cater for students with MLD and a learning support unit for students who are experiencing difficulty in mainstream school. These students can come from all years with any problem be it behaviour, learning etc. Elsewhere there is a base for students who have an autistic spectrum condition.

Each area is managed by staff with specialist expertise. All SEN staff liaise with the SENCo, curriculum staff, pastoral heads and senior management so that the students get a consistent and positive approach.

KINGSPARK SCHOOL

Gillburn Road, Dundee, DD3 0AB

Tel: 01382 432 803
Fax: 01382 432 820
Email: kingspark@dundeecity.gov.uk

• Pupils: 120 Mixed; Day Pupils • Age: 4 to 18
• Religion: Non-denominational • School status: State

SEN provision

Detail:
Experience of:
Mild: ADD; ADHD; DYSP; CP;
Moderate: AUT; ADD; ADHD; EBD; MLD; DYSP; VI;
Severe: ADD; EBD; HI; VI;
Others: GEN; EAL; MSI; Epi; PD; Eat

Summary: Kingspark School was purpose-built in the late 1970s and is, therefore, situated in a modern, well-designed building with many excellent facilities including a library, soft play room, sensory awareness room, large assembly/games hall, gymnasium, swimming pool and therapy pool, and well-equipped rooms for practical and aesthetic subjects. Together with well-heated, light and airy classrooms, these provide a very bright and pleasant working environment for pupils and staff. The school has a very open aspect, and a large grass area surrounds the building, providing attractive gardens and play areas.

Kingspark has approximately 120 pupils, aged between 5 and 18 years. All of the pupils have learning difficulties and many have additional physical disabilities or medical problems. Their educational needs can best be met, at present, in a special school like Kingspark. Almost all of the children have a 'Record of Needs' statement.

The main catchment area for the school is the City of Dundee, but pupils also attend from Angus and from Perth.

THE KINGSWAY SCHOOL

Foxland Road, Cheadle, Cheshire, SK8 4QX

Tel: 01614 287 706
Fax: 01614 914 335
Email: headteacher@kingsway.stockport.sch.uk

• Pupils: 1585 Mixed; Day Pupils • Age: 11 to 16
• Religion: Non-denominational • School status: State

SEN provision

Detail:
Now provide for in school:
Mild: ASP; AUT; ADD; ADHD; EBD; DS; DYSC; DYSL; DYSP; HI; VI; CP;
Moderate: ASP; AUT; ADD; ADHD; EBD; DS; MLD; DYSC; DYSL; DYSP; HI; VI; CP;
Severe: DYSC; DYSL;
Others: SPD; AUT(other); TIC; SLD; EAL; Sp&LD; Epi; PD

Summary: The Kingsway School is a large, split-site 11-16 comprehensive school with 1500+ students. Approximately 300 students are on the school's SEN register with a wide range of special needs, including general learning difficulties, specific learning difficulties, emotional and behavioural difficulties, speech and language difficulties, physical and sensory impairments, medical conditions and autistic spectrum disorders. We are additionally resourced for three students per year group with severe learning difficulties. The school has a policy of full inclusion, with all students attending mainstream lessons and participating in all aspects of school life, with the necessary adult support. There is a learning support base for students to use at breaktimes and for occasional withdrawn sessions, but it is not a learning support unit.

Kingswode Hoe School

Sussex Road, Colchester, Essex, CO3 3QJ

Tel: 01206 576 408
Fax: 01206 571 477
Email: admin@kingswodehoe.essex.sch.uk
• Pupils: 90 Mixed; Day Pupils • Age: 5 to 16
• Religion: Non-denominational • School status: State

SEN provision

Detail:
Centre of excellence for:
Mild: ASP; DS;
Moderate: ASP; DS; MLD;
Others: Sp&LD
Now provide for in school:
Mild: AUT; ADD; ADHD; EBD; DYSC; DYSL; DYSP; CP;
Moderate: ADD; ADHD; DYSC; DYSL;
Others: FRX; GEN; DEL; Epi; Eat
Experience of:
Mild: HI; VI;
Severe: DYSC; DYSL;
Others: SPD; CD; OCD; ODD; TIC; EAL

Summary: Kingswode Hoe School is an all aged mixed school for pupils with moderate learning difficulties. All pupils have a statement of SEN and are admitted to the school by Essex LEA. We offer a broad and balanced curriculum which includes the National Curriculum. In addition we focus on speech, language and communication through the Social Use of Language Programme (SULP) and on social skills with particular emphasis on raising self esteem. The school runs a 'buddy' system and a School Council for pupils. In Key Stage 4, we offer a range of accreditation including GCSE (maths), Entry Level and ASDAN, as well as work experience (three sessions in year 11) and college link courses in year 10 and year 11. We work closely with the Connexions service to ensure a smooth transition post-16. We are currently developing Outreach provision, allowing us to work with mainstream primary and secondary schools to support SEN pupils and to allow our pupils to have some mainstream experience. We are experienced with a range of pupils including those with Asperger's syndrome, Down's syndrome, Fragile X, Kleinfelter's, ADHD, ADD, ODD, speech and language difficulties, dyspraxia, dyslexia, dyscalculia and emotional difficulties.

Kingswood Prep. School

College Road, Lansdown, Bath, BA1 5SD

Tel: 01225 310 468
Fax: 01225 464 434
Email: schooloffice1@kingswoodschool.org.uk
Website: www.kingswood.bath.sch.uk
• Pupils: Mixed; Takes boarders • Age: 3 to 11
• Religion: Methodist • School status: Independent

SEN provision

Detail:
Now provide for in school:
Mild: DYSL;
Others: EAL
Experience of:
Mild: ASP; ADD; ADHD; DYSC; DYSP;
Others: DEL; Epi; Eat

Summary: Kingswood Prep School has a limited level of support beyond classroom differentiation, in the form of a dylexia-trained teacher who withdraws pupils individually or in small groups once or twice per week. Needs are assessed prior to registration and where necessary an individual educational programme (IEP) is written and needs addressed. Charges are made in addition to normal school fees for this service.

Knightsfield School

Knightsfield, Welwyn Garden City, Hertfordshire, AL8 7LW

Tel: 01707 376 874
Fax: 01707 321 738
Email: admin.knightsfield@thegrid.org.uk
Website: www.knightsfield.herts.sch.uk
• Pupils: 30 Mixed; Takes boarders • Age: 10 to 18
• Religion: Non-denominational • School status: State

SEN provision

Detail:
Centre of excellence for:
Mild: HI;
Moderate: HI;
Severe: HI

Summary: Built within the grounds of a mainstream secondary school, Knightsfield School offers the best of both worlds, small group teaching within a purpose built school for hearing impaired children together with inclusive educational and social opportunities in the adjacent mainstream school. We specialise in teaching pupils, who despite their hearing loss, which is usually severe to profound, are making progress in developing their language skills through the auditory-oral mode.

The school works in partnership with the neighbouring comprehensive school and the Welwyn Garden City 14 to 19 Consortium. There are opportunities for supported integration, in the mainstream link school, on a part-time basis, in a variety of subjects. Pupils can attend on a full-time basis and receive help and support from Knightsfield School staff. This unique partnership enables the school to respond flexibly and effectively to meet the needs of all our pupils.

Purpose built in 1997 for hearing impaired pupils, the school is acoustically treated throughout. The furniture and equipment are state-of-the-art and a new science lab was built in 2003 which is within the mainstream link school's Science block. The school is fully networked with a pupil computer ratio of one-to-one, access to the Internet and a huge range of hardware and software to support learning. In the residential area each pupil has his or her own comfortable study bedroom with wash basin and facilities to do homework in the evenings. The light and airy leisure rooms provide pupils with comfortable areas to relax and socialise. The 'Knight Club' offers a range of evening activities to residential and day pupils.

All teachers are qualified teachers of the deaf. New teachers are required to gain this qualification within three years of becoming members of staff. There is a speech and language therapist, support from the county audiologist, visits from a specialist careers adviser and a comprehensive work experience programme. Support from other outside professionals such as educational psychologist, occupational therapist etc can be arranged.

Our goal is to provide the best possible secondary education for deaf children. We encourage our pupils to develop their speaking and listening skills through consistent use of an auditory-oral approach. Our aim is to give each of our pupils a high quality, personalised educational experience that equips them for a full and fulfilling role in society.

KNOLLMEAD PRIMARY SCHOOL

Knollmead, Tolworth, Surbiton, Surrey, KT5 9QP

Tel: 020 8337 3778
Fax: 020 8337 4650
Email: KMP@rbksch.org
Website: www.knollmead.kingston.sch.uk/
• Pupils: 256 Mixed; Day Pupils • Age: 3 to 11
• Religion: Non-denominational • School status: State

SEN provision

Detail:
Centre of excellence for:
Mild: HI;
Moderate: HI;
Severe: HI

Summary: Knollmead has a dedicated resource for hearing impaired pupils. The resource, called the Sunshine Room, provides specialist teaching and speech and language therapy in a mainstream setting. We promote a total communication approach to ensure that individual children's needs are met.

La Salle Boys' School (Junior)

Glen Road, Belfast, BT11 8BQ

Tel: 02890 508 839

Fax: 02890 508 840

Email: info@lasalleboys.belfast.ni.sch.uk

• Pupils: 1200 Boys; Day Pupils • Age: 11 to 18

• Religion: Roman Catholic • School status: State

SEN provision

Detail:

Now provide for in school:

Mild: ASP; AUT; ADD; ADHD; EBD; DYSC; DYSL; DYSP; HI; VI; CP;

Moderate: ASP; AUT; ADD; ADHD; EBD; MLD; DYSC; DYSL; DYSP; VI; CP;

Others: EAL; Sp&LD; DEL; Epi; Eat

Experience of:

Mild: SpLD;

Moderate: SpLD; HI;

Others: CD; PD; Oth

Summary:

1. In-class support for statemented pupils. Asperger's/austic syndrome, ADHD, learning lifficulties, physical disability.
2. Literacy Support Unit.

a) To support pupils with dyslexic tendencies and pupils with learning difficulties.

b) To develop support materials for use in the linguistic phonics programme and reading/writing programmes.

c) To train support assistants in all aspects of this work.

3. Behaviour Support Unit.

On-site provision to facilitate interventions where pupils' behaviour interrupts classroom teaching with the aim to reintegrate the pupil back into the mainstream classroom as soon as possible.

Lakeside Junior & Infant School

Ontario Way, Lakeside, Cyncoed, Cardiff, CF23 6HB

Tel: 029 2076 7050

Fax: 029 2076 7051

Email: schooladmin@lakesideprm.cardiff.sch.uk

• Pupils: 534 Mixed; Day Pupils • Age: 4 to 11

• Religion: Non-denominational • School status: State

SEN provision

Detail:

Now provide for in school:

Mild: HI;

Moderate: MLD; HI;

Others: EAL

Experience of:

Mild: ASP; AUT; ADD; ADHD; EBD; DYSC; DYSL; DYSP; VI;

Moderate: ASP; ADD; EBD; DYSL; DYSP;

Others: TIC; Sp&LD

Summary: The special needs team (SENCo, SEN support teacher, SEN support assistants and headteacher) has oversight of all pupils in the school. Teachers and support staff work closely with parents to identify any pupil with any special education need, relating to learning or medical needs. Pupils are supported in class and often withdrawn for specific teaching and identified learning objectives. The SEN team works closely with the LEA's pupil support service staff who offer a wide variety of specialist advice and support. Parents are involved in their child's education throughout the year and frequent opportunities are provided for staff and parents to meet together informally or on a more formal review basis.

LAMBS LANE PRIMARY SCHOOL

Back Lane, Spencer's Wood, Reading, Berkshire, RG7 1JB

Tel: 0118 988 3820
Fax: 0118 988 7448
Email: admin@lambslane.wokingham.sch.uk
• Pupils: 198 Mixed; Day Pupils • Age: 4 to 11
• Religion: Non-denominational • School status: State

SEN provision

Summary: Lambs Lane Primary School is a mainstream school catering for children from 5 to 11 years of age. We have a resource for physically disabled children which at the moment provides for up to ten children. We are a single form entry school and all of our resource children are based within the appropriate year group. Children from the resource work with their class mates for the majority of the time although there are opportunities for children to receive physiotherapy, occupational therapy and speech and language provision in line with the requirements of their statements. We have a teacher-in-charge of the resource who is in close liaison with class teachers and class teaching assistants and if appropriate can initiate interventions for literacy or maths. Careful consideration is also given to the resources made available to children so that they can fully access the curriculum. A full-time welfare assistant sees to the medical needs of the children. In line with our inclusion policy we also have children with other disabilities including Asperger's syndrome, autism, dyslexia and speech and language disorders.

THE LANCASTER SCHOOL

Knighton Lane East, Leicester, Leicestershire, LE2 6FU

Tel: 01162 703 176
Fax: 01162 448 513
Email: admin@lancaster.leicester.sch.uk
Website: www.lancaster.leicester.sch.uk
• Pupils: 1190 Boys; Day Pupils • Age: 11 to 16
• Religion: Non-denominational • School status: State

SEN provision

Detail:
Now provide for in school:
Mild: ADD; ADHD; EBD; DYSC; DYSL; DYSP; SpLD; HI; VI; CP;
Moderate: MLD; DYSC; DYSL; DYSP; SpLD; HI; VI; CP;
Severe: DYSL;
Others: OCD; TIC; EAL; Sp&LD; DEL
Experience of:
Mild: ASP; AUT

Summary: The aims of The Lancaster School special educational needs policy are based on the aims stated in the LEA policy for SEN and guided by the SEN Code of Practice. We aim to work to ensure high levels of achievement, effective learning, progress and development for all pupils regardless of any special educational need. We make every effort to achieve maximum inclusion of pupils with SEN commensurate with meeting pupils' individual needs. All staff are teachers of special educational needs and are aware of their responsibilities towards pupils with SEN and try to exhibit and elicit a positive and sensitive attitude.

LAUNCESTON COLLEGE

Dunheved Road, Launceston, Cornwall, PL15 9JN

Tel: 01566 772 468
Fax: 01566 777 371
Email: secretary@launceston-college.cornwall.sch.uk
Website: www.launceston-college.cornwall.sch.uk
• Pupils: 1337 Mixed; Takes boarders • Age: 11 to 18
• Religion: Non-denominational • School status: State

SEN provision

Detail:
Now provide for in school:
Mild: ASP; EBD; DYSC; DYSL; DYSP; HI; VI;
Moderate: ASP; AUT; ADD; ADHD; EBD; DS; MLD; DYSL; DYSP; HI; VI; CP;
Severe: ASP; HI;
Others: CD; OCD; ODD; TIC; SLD; EAL; Sp&LD; DEL; Epi; PD

Summary: Launceston College's SEN department consists of a team of four SEN teachers, 30+ LSAs in a suite of four rooms. All pupils are tested on arrival for a reading and spelling age and, if deemed necessary, are extracted from mainstream classes for English and maths to join the SN group of 15-20 pupils. Additional individual sessions (SLD) are offered for spelling, grammar and organisational skills. Reading is taught from scratch on the Beacon Reading Program for those pupils who have a reading age of under eight years. There are 55 statements on the SEN register, plus 94 children at school Action Plus stage. There are 13 children in the Castle Area Resource Base whose needs are more specialised and who are looked after by a team of four teachers and three LSAs.

Laverock School

19 Bluehouse Lane, Oxted, Surrey, RH8 0AA

Tel: 01883 714 171
Fax: 01883 722 206
Email: office@laverock.fsnet.co.uk
Website: www.laverockschool.co.uk
• Pupils: 146 Girls; Day Pupils • Age: 3 to 11
• School status: Independent

SEN provision

Detail:
Experience of:
  Mild: ADD; ADHD; DS; HI; CP;
  Others: EAL; Epi

Summary: Laverock School is a mainstream school. The girls are of varying academic abilities and we try to ensure that each fulfils her potential by running a differentiated programme. The high achievers are extended and the slower learners receive support. Our SENCo works with the class teachers, one girl has an LSA and there is a fully trained dyslexia specialist.

Lea C of E Primary School

Lea, Ross-on-Wye, Herefordshire, HR9 7JY

Tel: 01989 750 296
Fax: 01989 750 892
Email: admin@lea-primary.hereford.sch.uk
Website: www.lea-primary.hereford.sch.uk
• Pupils: 72 Mixed; Day Pupils • Age: 5 to 11
• Religion: Church of England • School status: State

SEN provision

Detail:
Now provide for in school:
  Mild: AUT; ADD; ADHD; EBD; DYSL; HI;
  Moderate: AUT; ADD; ADHD; EBD; MLD; DYSL;
  Severe: EBD;
  Others: PMLD
Experience of:
  Mild: ASP; DS; DYSC; DYSP; VI;
  Moderate: DS; DYSC; DYSP; HI;
  Severe: DYSL;
  Others: CD; SLD; MSI; Sp&LD; Epi

Summary: At Lea C E Primary School we work hard together to make the school fully inclusive. We do not have a specialism in any particular special needs area, but we work hard at making school life and the curriculum, accessible to all pupils attending Lea. We work closely with our colleagues at the Education Centre in Hereford, calling on their expertise when necessary to support us in meeting the needs of all our pupils. In our recent Ofsted inspection we were commended on our inclusive approach.

LEOMINSTER JUNIOR SCHOOL

George Street, Leominster, Herefordshire, HR6 8JZ

Tel: 01568 612 555
Fax: 01668 610 066
Email: ljsoffice@ljs.hereford.sch.uk

• Pupils: 376 Mixed; Day Pupils • Age: 7 to 11
• Religion: Non-denominational • School status: State

SEN provision

Detail:
Now provide for in school:
Mild: ASP; AUT; EBD; DYSL; DYSP; HI; VI;
Moderate: ASP; AUT; ADD; EBD; MLD; DYSL; HI; VI;
Severe: DYSL; HI;
Others: TIC; EAL; Sp&LD; Epi
Experience of:
Mild: ADD; ADHD; CP;
Moderate: ADHD; DYSP;
Severe: ASP; ADD; ADHD; EBD;
Others: SPD; AUT(other); CD; OCD; PD

Summary: Provision for pupils with SEN has been described as a strength of the school by Ofsted. All pupils are integrated into mainstream classes with support. We have an experienced learning support teacher who works with sets for literacy/numeracy and gives extra individual/group support for pupils in the afternoons. Our SEN co-ordinator joined us in January 2005. She works half at this school and half at the local infant school ensuring a smooth transition for pupils. She oversees SEN provision, liaises with teachers on developing individual education plans and accesses additional funding and support from various agencies in Herefordshire. The school has close links with Herefordshire Learning Support Services, Herefordshire Psychology Services, Physical And Sensory Support Services, Medical and Behaviour Support Services among others. There is also access to Riding for the Disabled Association facilities, Xelerate enrichment activities and links with local outreach centres for pupils with behaviour difficulties. All pupils have the opportunity to join in out of school activities, with a wide range of clubs and outings. Children from the local special school are included in a range of activities, and allow access to their facilities if needed by individuals (eg yoga, trampolining). All staff are committed to inclusion of pupils with SEN and partnership with parents. The school ran an SEC until July 05, and the experienced support staff are now involved with supporting in mainstream classes.

THE LINDSAY SCHOOL

Forster Green Hospital, 110 Saintfield Road, Belfast, Antrim, BT8 6HD

Tel: 029 9094 4419
Fax: 028 9079 9683
Email: info@lindsayspec.belfast.ni.sch.uk

• Pupils: 24 Mixed; Day Pupils • Age: 4 to 15
• Religion: Integrated (Northern Ireland cross-community)
• School status: State

SEN provision

Summary: The Lindsay School provides education for the pupils who attend the regional Child and Family Centre. The pupils have a wide range of mental health difficulties, eg ADHD, anorexia, ASD, school refusal, self-harm, psychosis etc.

LITTLE ACORNS SCHOOL

London Beach Farm, Ashford Road, St Michaels, Tenterden, Kent, TN30 6SR

Tel: 01233 850 422
Fax: 01233 850 422

• Boys; Takes boarders • Age: 1 to 11
• School status: Independent

SEN provision

Detail:
Centre of excellence for:
Mild: ADD; ADHD; EBD;
Moderate: ADD; ADHD; EBD;
Severe: ADD; ADHD; EBD;
Others: CD; OCD; ODD

Now provide for in school:
Mild: SpLD; HI;
Moderate: MLD; HI;
Severe: HI;
Others: TIC; SLD; Sp&LD; Eat

Summary: Little Acorns is a small residential therapeutic unit offering places for up to seven children with emotional, behavioural and social difficulties. The placement provides on-site education with full access to the National Curriculum. Psychotherapy is available to all pupils. All staff are highly qualified in their respective fields.

THE LITTLEHAMPTON COMMUNITY SCHOOL

Hill Road, Littlehampton, West Sussex, BN17 6DQ

Tel: 01903 711 120
Fax: 01903 730 117
Email: enquiries@littlehampton.w-sussex.sch.uk
Website: www.littlehampton.w-sussex.sch.uk
• Pupils: 2022 Mixed; Day Pupils • Age: 11 to 18
• Religion: Non-denominational • School status: State

SEN provision

Detail:
Now provide for in school:
Mild: ASP; AUT; ADD; ADHD; EBD; DYSC; DYSL; DYSP; HI; VI;
Moderate: ASP; ADD; ADHD; MLD; DYSC; DYSL; DYSP;
Severe: DYSL;
Others: SPD; EAL; Sp&LD
Experience of:
Mild: SpLD; CP;
Moderate: AUT; HI; VI;
Severe: ADD;
Others: TIC; DEL; Epi; PD; Eat

Summary: Students who are likely to experience difficulties are identified during a liaison process with primary schools prior to transfer. All students are assessed on entry to the school. This information is used to devise support programmes for students who then receive individual work plans tailored to their specific needs. Individual education plans which set targets are regularly reviewed and are sent to parents. Fully trained Learning Support Assistants work alongside students in their regular classes. Students may also work in small groups or individually with a specialised SEN teacher. Dyslexia assessments are undertaken if appropriate. An out of hours homework club is run to provide additional help. Students with emotional and behavioural difficulties are closely monitored and supported in a Behaviour Support Unit and follow programmes which reflect the latest thinking in behaviour management. Off-site courses to improve team building and social skills are arranged on a regular basis.

LOCHINVER HOUSE SCHOOL

Heath Road, Little Heath, Potters Bar, Hertfordshire, EN6 1LW

Tel: 01707 653 064
Fax: 01707 653 064
Email: registrar@lochinverhouse.herts.sch.uk
Website: www.lochinverhouse.herts.sch.uk
• Pupils: Boys; Day Pupils • Age: 3 to 13
• School status: Independent

SEN provision

Summary: Lochinver House School has a learning support unit that provides assistance to boys that require extra support in the school. This unit works closely with all members of staff to provide the necessary support required. The SENCo can provide screening/ assessment to assist with any difficulty the child might have. The learning support unit works closely with parents and outside agencies should this be necessary.

Long Ditton St Mary's C of E Aided Junior School

Sugden Road, Long Ditton, Thames Ditton, Surrey, KT7 0AD

Tel: 020 8398 1070
Fax: 020 8398 3720
Website: www.longdittonstmarys.ik.org

• Pupils: 159 Mixed; Day Pupils • Age: 7 to 11
• Religion: Church of England • School status: State

SEN provision

Summary: We have six classes and seven teaching assistants. One TA is full-time and six are part-time. The SENCo is a full-time teacher so Class Teachers (CT) are responsible for their own children on the Code of Practice. Children are identified for academic help from examination of the tracking records of achievement kept for every individual. Other problems may be flagged up by parents, class teachers, the infant school or helpers. Children are assessed using the Surrey guidelines (FR13). Tests used are NFER Nelson reading, comprehension, maths 7-11, NARA, Vernon's spellings, PIPS and QCA end of year tests. We also bring in outside agencies (after consultation with the multi-professional team) for further assessment and advice and liaise with them regarding the writing of IEPs.

Children may be targeted for help in particular areas, eg maths, in which case they will get most or all of their help there. All children on SA+ will get their allotted two hours (or equivalent) with a TA, some may get extra. We have no specialist teachers so TAs will liaise with the CTs on work programmes and work either individually with the children or in small groups, in or out of the classroom.

Longbenton Community College

Hailsham Avenue, Longbenton, Newcastle upon Tyne, Tyne and Wear, NE12 8ER

Tel: 01912 007 423
Fax: 01912 007 850
Email: LongbentonCommunity.College@northtyneside.gov.uk
Website: www.longbenton.com/bugleweb/index.htm

• Pupils: 885 Mixed; Day Pupils • Age: 11 to 18
• Religion: Non-denominational • School status: State

SEN provision

Detail:

Now provide for in school:

Mild: ASP; ADHD; EBD; DYSC; DYSL; DYSP; HI; VI; CP;

Moderate: ASP; ADHD; EBD; MLD; DYSC; DYSL; DYSP; HI; VI; CP;

Severe: DYSL;

Others: SPD; TIC; MSI; Sp&LD; Epi

Experience of:

Mild: ADD;

Moderate: ADD;

Others: EAL; Eat

Summary: There is a strong learning support department within the college; it consists of four SEN teachers, including the learning support co-ordinator and the behaviour co-ordinator, in addition to two full-time SSAs and two part-time SSAs.

Support provided for students varies from one-to-one individual support, to small group literacy and numeracy support, alongside general in-class support. Learning support staff have received training in dyslexia, speech and language difficulties, behaviour management and working with students with sensory impairments. In addition to on-site support, the college shares a BIP-funded off-site unit for EBSD students to access as appropriate.

Longborough Church of England Primary School

Longborough, Moreton-in-Marsh, Gloucestershire, GL56 0QD

Tel: 01451 830 097

Fax: 01451 830097

Email: admin@longborough.gloucs.sch.uk

Website: www.longboroughpri2.uk.org

• Pupils: 25 Mixed; Day Pupils • Age: 4 to 11

• Religion: Church of England • School status: State

SEN provision

Detail:

Now provide for in school:

Mild: ADD; EBD; DYSC; DYSL; HI;

Moderate: ASP; MLD;

Others: PD; Eat

Experience of:

Mild: ASP; AUT; ADHD; DS;

Moderate: ADD; ADHD; EBD; DS; DYSC; DYSL;

Severe: ASP; ADD; EBD; DYSL;

Others: CD; OCD; FRX; PMLD; EAL; Sp&LD

Summary: Our classes are very small and well staffed. In addition we have a very experienced special needs co-ordinator (David Boardman) who visits the school three times a week to work with individuals and small groups of children. We have had experience of children with a wide range of disabilities/learning problems/ attention problems. Our provision is not just for children at the lower end of the special needs spectrum. Since every child is taught as an individual we are also aware of the needs of the above average pupils and arrange additional sessions for those who are Gifted and Talented.

Lord Wandsworth College

Long Sutton, Hook, Hampshire, RG29 1TB

Tel: 01256 862 201

Fax: 01256 860363

Email: info@lordwandsworth.org

Website: www.lordwandsworth.org

• Pupils: 518 Mixed; Takes boarders • Age: 11 to 18

• Religion: Non-denominational • School status: Independent

SEN provision

Detail:

Now provide for in school:

Mild: DYSC; DYSL; DYSP;

Others: EAL

Experience of:

Mild: ASP; ADD; ADHD; EBD; SpLD; HI; VI;

Moderate: ASP; ADD; ADHD; MLD; DYSC; DYSL; DYSP; SpLD;

Others: Epi; PD; Eat

Summary: The school is sympathetic to pupils with specific learning difficulties and there is a small special needs department that provides support for a range of learning difficulties. The department aims to help students to become effective learners, while ensuring that awareness of special needs is regularly reviewed so that teachers can meet students' needs across the curriculum. Students are initially identified through prep/primary liaison, screening tests and referrals by subject teachers and concerns expressed by parents. Following further investigation a programme of support is put into action ranging from differentiation within the classroom, to small group-work and one-to-one tuition with a specialist teacher. Progress is monitored and review sessions organised with pupils, staff and parents where appropriate. For further information you are welcome to contact the special needs co-ordinator on 01256 860257.

LOSSIEMOUTH HIGH SCHOOL

Coulardbank Road, Lossiemouth, Moray, IV31 6JU

Tel: 01343 812 047
Fax: 01343 814 343
Email: admin.lossiehigh@moray-edunet.gov.uk

• Pupils: Mixed; Day Pupils • Age: 11 to 18
• Religion: Non-denominational • School status: State

SEN provision

Detail:
Experience of:

Mild: ASP; AUT; ADD; ADHD; EBD; DS; DYSC; DYSL; DYSP; HI; VI; CP;
Moderate: ASP; AUT; ADD; ADHD; EBD; DS; MLD; DYSL; DYSP; HI; VI; CP;
Severe: ASP; AUT; ADD; ADHD; EBD; DS; DYSL;
Others: SPD; AUT(other); CD; OCD; FRX; PMLD; SLD; Epi

Summary: Support for learning staff In Lossiemouth High school support pupils and staff in mainstream classes and teach small groups and /or individual pupils in the support for learning base where that is appropriate. Staff in the support for learning department have a wide teaching experience in various areas of pupil support. One teacher has a background in working with emotionally disturbed young people, another comes from a special school background and has taught pupils with Down's syndrome and autistic spectrum disorders. Work is to commence in January 2006 to build a new provision which will enable Lossiemouth High School to support young people with more significant difficulties. This facility will include toilet and shower areas as well as enhanced learning and teaching areas. Wheelchair access is also part of this project. Staff in other departments in Lossiemouth High School work in collaboration with support for learning staff to support pupils and to ensure that they achieve their full potential.

THE LOYNE SCHOOL

Sefton Drive, Lancaster, Lancashire, LA1 2PZ

Tel: 01524 64543
Fax: 01524 845 118
Email: dephead@loyne.lancsngfl.ac.uk

• Pupils: 58 Mixed; Day Pupils • Age: 2 to 19
• Religion: Non-denominational • School status: State

SEN provision

Summary: The Loyne School caters for pupils aged 2-19 with a range of learning difficulties. Pupils are grouped in small classes by age and there are high staffing ratios. For pupils on the autistic continuum particular attention is paid to their learning needs with emphasis placed on visual timetables, TEACCH style teaching and assistance with social skills. Pupils with more profound learning difficulties benefit from a sensory curriculum. Particular attention is paid to communication and this is a key focus in all our work. All pupils have a regular opportunity for inclusive learning with their peer groups from mainstream settings. The school is accessible for pupils with physical difficulties. In 2004 we were identified in HMCI report as an outstanding school, following our recent Ofsted inspection.

LUMEN CHRISTI COLLEGE

Bishop Street, Londonderry, BT48 6UJ

Tel: 02871 362 595
Fax: 02871 372 544
Email: info@lumenchristi.derry.ni.sch.uk
Website: www.lumenchristicollege.uk

• Pupils: 840 Mixed; Day Pupils • Age: 11 to 18
• Religion: Roman Catholic • School status: State

SEN provision

Detail:
Experience of:

Mild: AUT; DYSL; DYSP; HI; VI;
Moderate: MLD; HI; VI;
Severe: VI;
Others: EAL; PD

Summary: Lumen Christi College has a special educational needs teacher and assistant teacher who offer tutorial help to those students identified on the special needs register or underachieving in academic performance at Key Stage 3 and 4. Students receive additional provision by withdrawal from class or in after-school sessions. The SENCo works closely with the school's educational psychologist to identify and provide Individual Educational Plans for students as required. Sixth form students peer tutor junior pupils and provide additional help through homework clubs.

Lutterworth Grammar School and Community College

Bitteswell Road, Lutterworth, Leicestershire, LE17 4EW

Tel: 01455 554 101
Fax: 01455 553 725
Email: principal@lgscc.leics.sch.uk
Website: www.lgscc.leics.sch.uk
• Pupils: 2000 Mixed; Day Pupils • Age: 14 to 19
• Religion: Church of England • School status: State

SEN provision

Detail:
Now provide for in school:
Mild: AUT; ADD; ADHD; EBD; DYSC; DYSL; DYSP; HI; VI; CP;
Moderate: EBD; MLD; DYSL; DYSP; HI; VI;
Others: CD; EAL

Summary: LGS has an excellent reputation for its achievement and progress with students who have special needs. We recently have opened (in conjunction with Lutterworth Rotary) an Enterprise Centre for teaching vocational skills to students, as well as individually designed programmes for all our special needs young people.

Our most recent PANDA data evidences the fact that our SEN students make considerably higher progress than expected and compared with all schools nationally.

Macmillan College

PO Box 8, Stockton Road, Middlesbrough, TS5 4YU

Tel: 01642 800 800
Fax: 01642 353 000
Email: office@macmillan-ctc.org.uk
Website: www.macmillan-ctc.org.uk
• Pupils: 1441 Mixed; Day Pupils • Age: 11 to 19
• School status: State

SEN provision

Detail:
Now provide for in school:
Mild: ASP; AUT; ADD; ADHD; EBD;
Moderate: ASP; AUT; ADD; ADHD;
Severe: ADD; ADHD

Summary: At Macmillan College we value all of our students, making a firm commitment to inclusive education. We strongly believe that all children have an equal right to a good education that enables them to develop and allows them to reach their full potential.

We have a commitment to high achievement and we strive to provide all of our children with a quality of education appropriate to their individual needs.

Mander Portman Woodward

3-4 Brookside, Cambridge, Cambridgeshire, CB2 1JE

Tel: 01223 350 158
Fax: 01223 366 429
Email: enquiries@cambridge.mpw.co.uk
Website: www.mpw.co.uk/cambridge
• Pupils: 88 Mixed; Day Pupils • Age: 14 to 19
• School status: Independent

SEN provision

Detail:
Now provide for in school:
Mild: DYSL; DYSP;
Others: EAL

Summary: The objectives of ESOL teaching at MPW are to help:

- those of our students who are non-native speakers of English to understand and express their content knowledge of core subjects as competently as a native speaker. They should have a knowledge of English equivalent to 5.5 (IELTS) before starting at MPW.
- those same students to obtain a Band 7 in the IELTS (International English Language Testing System) Academic exam in order to meet the English Language entry requirements demanded by universities in the UK or overseas.

Students with a mild learning difficulty will be welcomed and supported as long as they can cope with the academic demands of their chosen courses.

MANOR OAK PRIMARY SCHOOL

Sweeps Lane, St Mary Cray, Blacksmiths Lane, Orpington, Kent, BR5 3PE

Tel: 01689 828 099
Fax: 01689 825 443
Email: admin@manoroak.bromley.sch.uk

• Pupils: 133 Mixed; Day Pupils • Age: 3 to 11
• Religion: Non-denominational • School status: State

SEN provision

Detail:
Now provide for in school:
Mild: EBD;
Moderate: EBD
Experience of:
Mild: DS; DYSL; CP;
Moderate: DS; MLD;
Others: EAL

Summary: Seven place Key Stage 1 Nurture Group for pupils throughout the borough. This is a short term placement (two terms+) for children with social, emotional and/or behavioural difficulties. The aim is to work with children and then reintegrate them back to their feeder school.

MANOR SCHOOL

Chamberlayne Road, Kensal Rise, London, NW10 3NT

Tel: 020 8968 3160
Fax: 020 8968 3075
Email: admin.manor.brent@lgfl.net
Website: www.manor.brent.sch.uk

• Pupils: 119 Mixed; Day Pupils • Age: 4 to 11
• Religion: Non-denominational • School status: State

SEN provision

Summary: Manor School caters for primary age children with a variety of severe and complex learning difficulties, including autism.

We are able to provide small teaching groups from 6 to 10 pupils with a staffing ratio of at least two adults to every class. We employ our own speech and language therapists and a part-time occupational therapist. We place pupils in classes according to chronological and developmental age as well as individual needs.

MANOR SCHOOL AND SPORTS COLLEGE

Mountbatten Way, Raunds, Wellingborough, Northamptonshire, NN9 6PA

Tel: 01933 623 921
Fax: 01933 460 818
Email: head@manor.northants-ecl.gov.uk
Website: www.manorschool.northants.sch.uk

• Pupils: 789 Mixed; Day Pupils • Age: 11 to 19
• Religion: Non-denominational • School status: State

SEN provision

Detail:
Now provide for in school:
Mild: ASP; AUT; ADD; ADHD; EBD; DYSC; DYSL; DYSP; HI; CP;
Moderate: ASP; AUT; ADD; ADHD; EBD; MLD; DYSC; DYSL; DYSP; HI; CP;
Severe: ASP; EBD; CP;
Others: TIC; GEN; DEL; Epi

Summary: The school promotes full integration of all pupils into the mainstream setting. The school sees its responsibility to identify and meet individual need and to provide a caring environment. The school wishes to maintain students in accordance with the Government policy of inclusion and has many initiatives in place. Currently 3.5 per cent of the school population has a statement of special educational need.

The school has recognised expertise with physical difficulties and aims to integrate such pupils into a mainstream curriculum. The school will work with parents and individual pupils to maintain pupils in the mainstream setting unless a joint decision is made that the special needs of the individual dictate alternative provision.

Responsibility for the well-being of students with special education needs is shared between the subject teachers, the form tutors, the inclusive education team, the governing body and the parents. Parental partnership is vital for students with special education needs. The school is committed to developing a partnership with parents because the school believes that children with special educational needs have the right to work successfully alongside their peers. The school is committed to welcome pupils with learning difficulities and physical and sensory impairments. By working together we can reinforce the students positive self-image and improve learning and behaviour skills.

Haberdashers' Redcap School

32 Broomy Hill, Hereford, Herefordshire, HR4 0LH

Tel: 01432 273 594

Email: enquiries@haberdashersredcap.org

Website: www.haberdashersredcap.org

• Pupils: 78 Girls; Day Pupils • Age: 3 to 11

• Religion: Church of England • School status: Independent

SEN provision

Detail:

Experience of:

Mild: ASP; ADD; EBD; DYSL; DYSP;

Moderate: MLD; DYSL; DYSP;

Others: SPD; Sp&LD

Summary: Our pupils are supported individually in small classes, which ensures early identification of any specific learning difficulty. Children with special educational needs are usually identified and helped by the class teacher in the normal classroom environment with the support of our special education needs co-ordinator who will help to develop an individual education plan using the most up to date resources including ICT. This ensures that pupils gain confidence in any areas of difficulty under our caring and supportive staff.

Staff, parents and SENCo work together to support the child and regular reviews, which include input from the child, ensure that everyone is informed and pupils benefit tremendously from this provision. If further support is needed we may ask to refer children to outside agencies who can offer us more specialised support and advice.

We at Haberdashers' Redcap are proud of our pupils' talents and see each one as gifted. However, gifted pupils also need support in channelling their energies appropriately to ensure their potential is maximised and recognised in our community.

Market Drayton Infant and Nursery School

Longslow Road, Market Drayton, Shropshire, TF9 3BA

Tel: 01630 652 909

Fax: 01630 656 185

Email: admin@marketdrayton-inf.shropshire.sch.uk

• Pupils: 203 Mixed; Day Pupils • Age: 2 to 7

• Religion: Non-denominational • School status: State

SEN provision

Detail:

Now provide for in school:

Mild: ASP; AUT; ADD; ADHD; DYSL; DYSP; VI;

Moderate: ASP; AUT; ADD; ADHD; MLD; DYSL; DYSP; VI;

Severe: AUT; VI;

Others: SPD; AUT(other); GEN; Sp&LD; Epi; PD

Experience of:

Mild: EBD; DS; HI;

Moderate: EBD; DS; HI

Summary: We have a playgroup on site which we have taken over under 'extended schools'. This has enabled us to work with the Early Years SENCo in providing early intervention for children with SEN from the age of 2.5 years. We work with different agencies and provide inclusive education throughout up to the age of seven. We look at the child's individual needs and put into place strategies that enable us to cater for groups and individuals. We use a range of assessment tools to get a rounded picture of each child and use reports from other agencies to the full. We have a large effective team of staff who follow the Foundation Stage and Key Stage 1 policy on inclusion. We have supported and taught children with autism, Asperger's syndrome, gross and fine motor delay, hearing impairment, visual impairment, Down's syndrome, profound speech delay and children with a range of medical problems, eg Di George syndrome. We specialise in teaching and supporting children with speech delay.

MARLBOROUGH SCHOOL

Marlborough Park Avenue, Sidcup, Kent, DA15 9DP

Tel: 020 8300 6896
Fax: 020 8309 5612
Email: head.marlborough.bexley@lgfl.net
Website: www.marlborough.bexley.sch.uk

• Pupils: 75 Mixed; Day Pupils • Age: 11 to 19
• Religion: Non-denominational • School status: State

SEN provision

Detail:
Experience of:
- Mild: HI; VI; CP;
- Moderate: HI; VI; CP;
- Severe: ADD; HI; VI; CP;
- Others: ODD; FRX; GEN; Sp&LD

Summary: Marlborough School is for students who have severe, profound and complex learning difficulties. The majority of our students live within the London Borough of Bexley. It is a mixed gender school. We cater for a range of needs including medical and behavioural. 25 per cent of our students have autism and 15 per cent profound and multiple learning difficulties. Our curriculum is subject based taught by subject teachers and we also have some specialist rooms and areas, these being science, art, food technology, library, sensory room, music room and sensory garden. In Key Stage 3 the curriculum emphasis is on developing basic skills, in Key Stage 4 on practical application and in Post-16 using those skills off site. We work closely with the multi-agency team. We have a good ethos and high expectations for our students. The school caters for students who have medical, physical social and behavioural needs.

MARY ELLIOT SCHOOL

Brewer Street, Walsall, West Midlands, WS2 8BA

Tel: 01922 720 706
Fax: 01922 612 298
Email: postbox@mary-elliot.walsall.sch.uk
Website: www.mary-elliot.walsall.sch.uk/

• Pupils: 48 Mixed; Day Pupils • Age: 13 to 19
• Religion: Non-denominational • School status: State

SEN provision

Summary: Mary Elliot School is a day community school for pupils aged 14-19 with severe or profound multiple and complex learning difficulties. Our aim is to provide access to a broad balanced pupil-centred curriculum which is relevant to the needs of every pupil and which prepares them for their future life by developing the skills and abilities essential to independent adult living, acknowledging for many, the sheltered nature this may imply. We encourage the development of self-confidence, self-respect, responsibility and self-reliance, together with an awareness of and sensitivity to the needs of others. We promote a caring and stimulating environment that gives positive encouragement to all, and recognises and values the contributions of all its members.

MASCALLS SCHOOL

Maidstone Road, Paddock Wood, Tonbridge, Kent, TN12 6LT

Tel: 01892 835 366
Fax: 01892 835 648
Email: enquiries@mascalls.kent.sch.uk
Website: www.mascalls.kent.sch.uk

• Pupils: 1400 Mixed; Day Pupils • Age: 11 to 18
• Religion: Non-denominational • School status: State

SEN provision

Detail:
Now provide for in school:
Mild: ASP; EBD; DYSC; DYSL; DYSP; CP;
Moderate: ASP; EBD; MLD; DYSL; DYSP;
Others: SPD; Sp&LD
Experience of:
Mild: AUT; ADD; ADHD; HI; VI;
Moderate: ADD; ADHD; DYSC; HI; CP;
Severe: EBD;
Others: Eat

Summary: Pupils with additional educational needs are taught within mainstream classes. There is some teaching assistant support, particularly in the lower ability groups. The staff have experience of supporting pupils with a range of special needs. A call to the SENCo would be recommended so that the provision can be discussed prior to an application being made for a pupil to join the school.

MATTHEW BOULTON COLLEGE OF FURTHER AND HIGHER EDUCATION

Sherlock Street, Birmingham, West Midlands, B5 7DB

Tel: 0121 446 4545
Fax: 0121 446 4324
Email: ask@matthew-boulton.ac.uk
Website: www.matthew-boulton.ac.uk

• Pupils: 1317 Mixed; Day Pupils • Age: 16 to 99
• Religion: Non-denominational • School status: State

SEN provision

Detail:
Experience of:
Mild: ASP; AUT; ADD; EBD; DYSC; DYSP; HI; VI;
Moderate: EBD; MLD; HI; VI;
Severe: DYSL; HI; VI;
Others: Sp&LD; DEL; Epi; PD; Eat;

THE MATTHEW HOLLAND SCHOOL

Chapel Road, Selston, Nottingham, Nottinghamshire, NG16 6BW

Tel: 01773 810 321
Fax: 01773 510 262
Email: communication@matthewholland.notts.sch.uk
Website: www.matthewholland.notts.sch.uk

• Pupils: 867 Mixed; Day Pupils • Age: 11 to 18
• Religion: Non-denominational • School status: State

SEN provision

Detail:
Now provide for in school:
Mild: ASP; ADD; ADHD; EBD; DYSC; DYSL; HI; VI; CP;
Moderate: ASP; AUT; ADD; ADHD; EBD; DS; MLD; DYSC; DYSL; VI; CP;
Severe: DYSL; VI;
Others: SPD; ODD; GEN; SLD; EAL; Sp&LD
Experience of:
Mild: AUT; DYSP;
Moderate: DYSP;
Severe: ASP; EBD; DYSC;
Others: CD; PD

Summary: Matthew Holland School is fully inclusive and provides good support for pupils with special needs (Ofsted May 2004). We believe that all pupils should be supported in appropriate ways to enable them to have access to a broad, balanced curriculum. This may be through withdrawal for some lessons with support outside the classroom, or through support within the main curriculum. We have an excellent learning support unit where a variety of activities take place. Within the learning support unit, there is small group teaching for pupils in years 7-9, one-to-one coaching for pupils with specific individual needs, behaviour modification programs, work on social skills and speech and language. A range of extra curricular activities take place designed to motivate pupils and raise self-esteem. In years 8 and 9, we have some alternative curriculum in small groups. This takes place within the learning support unit. The ASDAN Life skills course is run in years 10 and 11 and there is a group of students who take part in the Schools' Link programme at West Notts College. There is a strong emphasis on supporting students to gain effective literacy skills through additional work on reading, support and specific teaching for dyslexic students and opportunities to work within small groups for some English tasks. Care is taken to ensure the curriculum is tailored to the needs of our learners and this is constantly reviewed. Support is given to some pupils at lunch and break times. This may include access to games, support for homework or just a quiet space.

McKinney Primary School Dundrod

3 Leathemstown Road, Dundrod, Co Antrim, BT29 4HX

Tel: 02890 825 375

Email: nthompson@mckinneyps.crumlin.ni.sch.uk

• Pupils: 150 Mixed; Day Pupils • Age: 5 to 11

• Religion: Non-denominational • School status: State

SEN provision

Detail:

Now provide for in school:

Mild: ASP; AUT; DYSL; DYSP; SpLD; HI; VI;

Moderate: EBD; MLD; DYSL; DYSP; HI;

Severe: AUT; DYSL; DYSP;

Others: Sp&LD; Epi

Summary: At McKinney Primary School, Dundrod we make every possible effort to provide for children's individual needs. We always take into account the child's rights and we give strong consideration to allowing a child some time to develop when he/she comes to nursery before making major decisions. We are often praised by educational psychologists from the two ELBs which serve our school for the work we do with children who have special needs.

The Meadows Primary School

Bristol Road South, Birmingham, West Midlands, B31 2SW

Tel: 0121 475 3203

Fax: 0121 478 2242

Email: enquiry@meadows.bham.sch.uk

Website: www.meadows.bham.sch.uk

• Pupils: 436 Mixed; Day Pupils • Age: 5 to 11

• Religion: Non-denominational • School status: State

SEN provision

Detail:

Now provide for in school:

Mild: AUT; ADD;

Moderate: AUT; ADD;

Severe: ASP

Summary: The school has an established reputation for the quality and consistency of its special needs provision, for mainstream and Language Unit children. A full-time mainstream special needs co-ordinator organises and monitors support for children on entry and regular assessment ensures that intervention is timely and consistent with a child's needs.

The Language Unit accommodates 26 children with statements of special need aged between 5 and 11. The children are grouped into three classes, taught by teachers with specific qualifications and expertise and supported within mainstream classes when integrating with mainstream pupils. We operate a system of 'exchange integration' where mainstream children are taught in the unit classes for certain lessons by unit staff. This arrangement benefits mainstream children for whom smaller teaching groups and more individual attention is appropriate. There are regular, on-site, qualified speech therapists, seconded to the school from the local Health Authority, who work with Unit children and some mainstream pupils during the each school day.

The Meadows School

Dudley Road East, Tividale, Oldbury, West Midlands, B69 3BU

Tel: 01215 697 080
Fax: 01215 697 081
Email: headteacher@themeadows.sandwell.sch.uk

• Pupils: 145 Mixed; Day Pupils • Age: 11 to 19
• School status: State

SEN provision

Detail:
Now provide for in school:
- Mild: AUT; ADD; ADHD; EBD; DS; HI; VI; CP;
- Moderate: AUT; ADD; ADHD; EBD; DS; MLD; HI; VI; CP;
- Severe: ASP; AUT; ADD; ADHD; EBD; DS; HI; VI; CP;
- Others: SPD; AUT(other); CD; OCD; ODD; TIC; FRX; PMLD; SLD; Sp&LD; DEL; Epi; PD; Eat

Experience of:
- Mild: ASP;
- Moderate: ASP;
- Others: MSI

Summary: The Meadows School is a secondary school for students with complex and profound learning disabilities aged 11-19 years. The school was purpose built in 2003 with state-of-the-art equipment and facilities. We have a number of awards recognising areas where the school is regarded as excellent. We have the Healthy Schools gold award, we have the NAACE mark for ICT, we have extended schools established status (we were the first special school to achieve extended school status in the country) and we have the arts mark bronze award. The Meadows School has achieved Sandwell LEA'S charter mark for inclusion. Currently we are working towards achieving Specialist Sports status to give our students all the benefits that it will bring.

Meath School

Brox Road, Ottershaw, Chertsey, Surrey, KT16 0LF

Tel: 01932 872 302
Fax: 01932 875 180

• Pupils: Mixed; Takes boarders • Age: 5 to 12
• School status: State

SEN provision

Detail:
Centre of excellence for:
- Mild: DYSP;
- Moderate: DYSP;
- Severe: DYSP;
- Others: Sp&LD

Now provide for in school:
- Mild: ASP; DYSL; HI;
- Moderate: ASP; MLD; DYSL; HI;
- Severe: DYSL; HI;
- Others: SPD; Epi

Experience of:
- Mild: AUT; ADD; ADHD; EBD; DYSC; VI;
- Moderate: AUT; ADD; ADHD; DYSC;
- Severe: DYSC;
- Others: ODD; TIC

Summary: Meath provides a multi-professional, integrated and collaborative approach to the teaching, therapy and care of children aged 5-11 years, whose primary difficulty is speech, language and communication. Children with additional or associated difficulties including learning difficulties, attention control and motor difficulties, mild visual or hearing impairments, or social interaction problems may also benefit from the provision. Ofsted inspectors commented that 'The highly skilled and collaborative multidisciplinary team of staff, generates a very strong learning culture in which pupils thrive and delivers outstanding care, support and guidance, which results in pupils feeling secure and helps them to achieve well'.

The school offers specialist practice and programmes (eg signing, Cued Articulation, Alternative, Augmentative Communication, visual supports) to enable full access to differentiated National Curriculum teaching. Each class (average 10 children) has a teacher, a full-time speech and language therapist and at least one learning support assistant. An occupational therapist supports individual children, class activities and school-wide motor skills groups and runs sensory integration sessions. A Lowenfeld play therapist works with some children individually.

MEDINA HIGH SCHOOL

Mountbatten Centre, Fairlee Road, Newport, Isle of Wight, PO30 3DX

Tel: 01983 526 523
Fax: 01983 528 791
Email: info@medina.iow.sch.uk
Website: www.medina.iow.sch.uk

• Pupils: 1062 Mixed; Day Pupils • Age: 13 to 18
• Religion: Non-denominational • School status: State

SEN provision

Detail:
Now provide for in school:
Mild: ADD; ADHD; EBD; DYSC; DYSL; DYSP; HI; VI;
Moderate: MLD; DYSL;
Others: SPD; ODD; TIC; EAL
Experience of:
Mild: ASP; AUT; CP;
Moderate: ADD; ADHD; EBD; DYSP; HI; VI; CP;
Others: OCD; DEL

Summary: Educational provision is achieved through full integration into the mainstream school. Sensitive and creative adaptation of the curriculum may be required in order to match what is taught and how it is taught to the childrens' aptitudes and abilities. This can be done by adopting appropriate teaching methods and resources which are sensitive to the expected pace of learning. Withdrawal from lessons is kept to a minimum. Each faculty area has an LSA assigned to work within that specialist subject to support statemented children. We also utilise a bungalow which has been turned into a learning centre for children who find High School difficult to access. Here a balance between practical skills and raising literacy is achieved through students engaging in projects such as gardening, cooking, carpentry, photography and community work. We strive to work towards nationally recognised qualifications such as ASDAN. Students participate in organising sailing activities, fishing trips and visits to help raise their self esteem and leadership skills. Each year we try to offer our 'special' students a residential trip to an outdoor activities centre.

MEREWAY COMMUNITY COLLEGE

Mereway, Northampton, Northamptonshire, NN4 8BU

Tel: 01604 763 616
Fax: 01604 765 036
Email: head@mcc.northants.sch.uk
Website: www.mcc.northants.sch.uk

• Pupils: 1332 Mixed; Day Pupils • Age: 11 to 18
• Religion: Non-denominational • School status: State

SEN provision

Detail:
Now provide for in school:
Mild: AUT; ADD; ADHD; EBD; DYSL; DYSP; SpLD; HI; VI; CP;
Moderate: ASP; AUT; ADD; ADHD; EBD; DS; MLD; DYSL; SpLD; HI; VI; CP;
Severe: ADD; ADHD; EBD; DYSL; HI; VI; CP;
Others: SPD; CD; OCD; ODD; TIC; GEN; EAL; Sp&LD; DEL; Epi; Eat
Experience of:
Mild: ASP; DS; DYSC;
Moderate: DYSC; DYSP;
Severe: ASP; AUT; DS; DYSC; DYSP;
Others: AUT(other); FRX

Summary: We have a large Education Support Department with two teachers, one associate teacher and 28 teaching assistants. We currently have approximately 270 students on the special needs register and cater for 40 students with widely varying statements of special educational need. Their primary needs include autism, cerebal palsy, hearing impairment, mild and moderate learning difficulties, specific learning difficulties and behavioural, social and emotional difficulties. We have a growing population of students across all year groups who have English as an Additional Language, with many languages being spoken by both students and staff.

Mexborough School

Maple Road, Mexborough, South Yorkshire, S64 9SD

Tel: 01709 585858
Fax: 01709 578080
Email: admin@mexborough.doncaster.sch.uk
• Pupils: 1142 Mixed; Day Pupils • Age: 11 to 18
• Religion: Non-denominational • School status: State

SEN provision

Detail:
Now provide for in school:
Mild: ASP; AUT; ADD; ADHD; EBD; DYSC; DYSL; DYSP; HI; VI; CP;
Moderate: ASP; AUT; ADD; ADHD; EBD; MLD; DYSC; DYSL; DYSP; HI; VI;
Others: SPD; AUT(other); TIC; FRX; DEL; Epi; Eat

Summary: Mexborough School operates an inclusive policy and educates pupils with a wide range of abilities and special educational needs.

The school has around 25 staff dedicated to providing learning support and mentoring for pupils who experience barriers to learning. These are further supported by a strong pastoral team to help pupils at all stages of secondary education.

Numeracy and literacy lessons are provided by qualified specialist teachers for special educational needs pupils in small group classes and experienced learning support assistants provide in class support for pupils with a range of learning difficulties including autism, dyslexia, discalculia, dyspraxia and moderate learning difficulties. Support is also available for pupils with physical difficulties including hearing and visual impairment.

Additional specific support is provided for individual pupils via IT based systems designed to provide personalised target setting and monitoring. Laptops are available for pupils with writing difficulties and early morning handwriting and reading classes are offered.

A homework club with extensive resources and staff support for pupils experiencing difficulties with completing or organising their homework is available after school four days per week.

A safe haven with activities is provided at lunchtimes and break-times for pupils who may experience stress in the general playground environment.

Mentors experienced in counselling pupils with emotional difficulties are available and there are strong links with external agencies to provide specialist help or resources.

Middleton School

Walnut Tree Walk, Ware, Hertfordshire, SG12 9PD

Tel: 01920 485 152
Fax: 01920 486 738
Email: admin.middleton@thegrid.org.uk
Website: www.middleton.herts.sch.uk
• Pupils: 80 Mixed; Day Pupils • Age: 4 to 11
• Religion: Non-denominational • School status: State

SEN provision

Summary: Middleton School is located in the town of Ware and pupils come from the whole of East Hertfordshire, most of them travelling to school by bus or taxi. We have had two Ofsted inspections in recent years and on both occasions the school received the highest praise with no key issues to address, the learning environment described as exceptional.

The school caters for children with moderate learning difficulties in the age range 4 to 11. There are places for approximately 92 children including provision for 12 children with autism. Although all the children have some learning difficulties it is expected that they will all make good progress and eventually leave school able to read and write and lead a perfectly normal life. They will be taught the full range of National Curriculum subjects but in smaller groups and at a pace more suited to their needs.

MIDHURST GRAMMAR SCHOOL

North Street, Midhurst, West Sussex, GU29 9DT

Tel: 01730 812 451
Fax: 01730 813 524
Email: office@midhurst-grammar.w-sussex.sch.uk
Website: www.midhurst-grammar.w-sussex.sch.uk

• Pupils: 856 Mixed; Day Pupils • Age: 13 to 18
• Religion: Church of England • School status: State

SEN provision

Detail:

Now provide for in school:
Mild: DYSC; DYSL; DYSP; VI; CP;
Moderate: MLD; DYSC; DYSL; DYSP; VI;
Severe: DYSL;
Others: Sp&LD; PD

Experience of:
Mild: ASP; AUT; ADD; ADHD; EBD; HI;
Moderate: ADD; ADHD; EBD; HI;
Others: CD; OCD; ODD; TIC; EAL; DEL; Epi; Eat

Summary: Midhurst Grammar School is a mainstream school serving all of the students within its catchment area. It has an inclusive policy and welcomes all students. The SENCo manages a team of two SEN teachers and seven teaching assistants. We provide for a range of special educational needs including students with specific learning difficulties, emotional, behavioural and social needs, sensory impairment and more general learning difficulties. The provision is worked out to suit the individual needs of each student but might include in-class support from a teaching assistant, small group learning support with an SEN teacher, speech and language support from a teacher or the senior teaching assistant. Although we have experience of working with students with autistic spectrum disorder (Asperger's syndrome) these cases have been mild to moderate. We do not have a special needs unit, students follow the National Curriculum in mainstream classes, with support to differentiate the curriculum as appropriate. We support a number of students with medical conditions. Two of the teaching assistants are trained to provide physiotherapy for students with Cystic Fibrosis; support staff and teachers are trained to deal with epileptic seizures.

MINEHEAD FIRST SCHOOL

Townsend Road, Minehead, Somerset, TA24 5RG

Tel: 01643 702 938
Fax: 01643 704 125
Email: office@mineheadfirst.somerset.sch.uk
Website: www.mineheadfirst.ik.org

• Pupils: 339 Mixed; Day Pupils • Age: 4 to 9
• Religion: Non-denominational • School status: State

SEN provision

Detail:

Now provide for in school:
Mild: DYSC; DYSL; DYSP; SpLD; HI; VI; CP;
Moderate: DYSC; DYSL; DYSP; SpLD;
Severe: DYSC; DYSL; DYSP;
Others: EAL; Epi; Eat

Experience of:
Mild: ASP; AUT; ADD; ADHD; EBD;
Moderate: ASP; AUT; ADD; ADHD; EBD; MLD; HI;
Severe: ADD; SpLD;
Others: SPD; AUT(other); GEN; PMLD; SLD; MSI; Sp&LD

Summary: Minehead First School is proud to host a specialist SEN resource base for up to 12 pupils. The resource base takes pupils from across West Somerset who have complex special needs. Entry to the RB is via the complex panel. We are committed to inclusion although we believe that inclusion is not a location. All children in the RB have specialist teaching in a small group with a high level of adult support and access to a mainstream class for activities that they are able to cope with. We have a disabled bathroom (including a shower) and a variety of outside equipment including two disabled tricycles. There is a teacher in charge of the RB and a dedicated team of assistants.

Monifieth High School

Panmurefield Road, Monifieth, DD5 4QT

Tel: 01382 534 466
Fax: 01382 532 987
Email: monifiethhigh@monifiethhigh.angus.sch.uk
Website: www.monifieth-high.org.uk

• Pupils: 1073 Mixed; Day Pupils • Age: 11 to 18
• Religion: Non-denominational • School status: State

SEN provision

Detail:
Now provide for in school:
  Mild: ASP; ADD; ADHD; EBD; DYSL; DYSP; HI;
  Moderate: ASP; ADD; EBD; MLD; DYSL; DYSP; HI; VI;
  Others: OCD; GEN; PMLD; Sp&LD; PD; Eat
Experience of:
  Mild: DYSC;
  Moderate: ADHD; DS; SpLD;
  Severe: ADD; EBD; DYSL; VI;
  Others: TIC; Epi

Summary: The main objective of the Support for Learning and Inclusion Department is to help pupils of all abilities to achieve their best across the curriculum. Inclusion is a top priority and this is made possible through consultation and collaboration with colleagues in subject departments. Co-operative teaching and development of curricular materials to meet the needs of pupils ensures successful integration into mainstream classes for the vast majority of pupils. Where more severe difficulties make only partial integration possible, the pupils spend more time in the SFLI department for 'one-to-one' or small group teaching with the construction of individualised learning plans. However, integration for various activities within the wider school community is arranged wherever this is possible. A 'Paired Reading' scheme is available to those with moderate reading difficulties while more specific language difficulties are addressed through specialised reading schemes and Alternative Assessment Arrangements for all assessments including national examinations. We also provide 'special services' in a new resource base to meet the social and emotional needs of pupils who, for example, may be returning to school after a protracted absence or who, for a variety of reasons, may feel the need for a 'secure' environment either short or long term. The Support for Learning Department places a high value on the significant contribution that can be made by parents and is committed to establishing a close working relationship between the department and home.

Moor End Technology College

Dryclough Road, Crosland Moor, Huddersfield, West Yorkshire, HD4 5JA

Tel: 01484 222 230
Fax: 01484 222 233
Email: office.moorend@kirklees-schools.org.uk
Website: www.moorendtc.digitalbrain.com/moorendtc/web/secondaryportal/

• Pupils: 791 Mixed; Day Pupils • Age: 11 to 16
• Religion: Non-denominational • School status: State

SEN provision

Detail:
Centre of excellence for:
  Mild: VI;
  Moderate: VI;
  Severe: VI
Experience of:
  Mild: AUT; DYSC; DYSL; DYSP; HI;
  Moderate: MLD;
  Others: EAL

Summary: Moor End has a team of well-qualified and experienced special needs and language development staff. The team works closely with subject teachers to ensure the right level of support is given to all children with special needs, including those requiring specialist provision for dyslexia.

In addition Moor End hosts the Kirklees resourced provision for pupils with a visual impairment. These pupils come from all over Kirklees and are provided with resources in various formats, equipment, support and specialist teaching to enable them to access the mainstream secondary school curriculum alongside their sighted peers.

Moor Nook Community Primary School

Mitton Drive, Preston, Lancashire, PR2 6EN

Tel: 01772 796 009

Fax: 01772 655 427

• Pupils: 218 Mixed; Day Pupils • Age: 3 to 11

• Religion: Non-denominational • School status: State

SEN provision

Detail:

Now provide for in school:

Mild: ASP; AUT; ADD; ADHD; EBD; DYSC; DYSL; DYSP; HI; VI;

Moderate: ASP; EBD; MLD; DYSL; DYSP;

Severe: EBD;

Others: CD; FRX; Sp&LD; Epi; PD

Summary: The proportion of the school's pupils identified as having special educational needs is much higher than the national average, as is the proportion of pupils with statements of special educational needs. The range of special educational needs includes moderate learning difficulties, emotional and behavioural difficulties, speech and communication difficulties, autism, dyslexia and dyspraxia. Pupils with special educational needs make very good progess in the Foundation Stage and good progress from years 1-6. The school has a very positive environment for learning, fully includes its pupils in all its activities and has a very strong commitment to improvement.

Moorcroft School

Bramble Close, Hillingdon, Uxbridge, Middlesex, UB8 3BF

Tel: 01895 437 799

Fax: 01895 438 123

Email: moorcroft@hillingdongrid.org

Website: www.moorcroft.hillingdon.sch.uk

• Pupils: 65 Mixed; Day Pupils • Age: 11 to 19

• Religion: Non-denominational • School status: State

SEN provision

Detail:

Now provide for in school:

Mild: AUT; ADD; ADHD; EBD; DS; HI; VI; CP;

Moderate: AUT; ADD; ADHD; EBD; DS; HI; VI; CP;

Severe: AUT; ADD; ADHD; EBD; DS; HI; VI; CP;

Others: TIC; FRX; GEN; PMLD; SLD; EAL; MSI; Sp&LD; DEL; Epi; PD; Oth; Eat

Summary: Moorcroft provides for secondary aged pupils with severe, profound and complex needs. This includes pupils with autistic spectrum disorders, sensory (hearing and vision) impairments and physical disabilities. We are positive about inclusion and pupils are based in age-based classes including all abilities but teaching arrangements include ability based lessons for core subjects. Moorcroft was recognised by Ofsted as one of the country's 'particularly successful schools' following our 2002 inspection. Moorcroft has an excellent modern building with very good facilities which support our provision for pupils with a range of different needs.

Moseley Primary School

Moseley Avenue, Coundon, Coventry, West Midlands, CV6 1AB

Tel: 024 7659 3572

Fax: 024 7660 1853

Email: headteacher@moseley.coventry.sch.uk

• Pupils: 388 Mixed; Day Pupils • Age: 3 to 11

• Religion: Non-denominational • School status: State

SEN provision

Detail:

Experience of:

Mild: ASP; AUT; ADD; ADHD; EBD; DYSC; DYSL; DYSP; SpLD; HI; VI;

Moderate: ASP; AUT; ADD; ADHD; EBD; MLD; DYSL; DYSP;

Severe: EBD; DYSL; VI;

Others: EAL; Sp&LD; Epi

MOTHERWELL COLLEGE

Dalzell Drive, Motherwell, ML1 2DD

Tel: 01698459451
Fax: 01698 232 527
Email: ikinghorn@motherwell.co.uk
Website: www.motherwell.ac.uk

• Pupils: 1800 Mixed; Takes boarders • Age: 16 to 99
• School status: Independent

SEN provision

Detail:
Centre of excellence for:
Mild: DS;
Moderate: DS; MLD;
Severe: DS
Now provide for in school:
Mild: ASP; AUT; ADD; ADHD; DYSC; DYSL; DYSP; HI; VI; CP;
Moderate: ASP; AUT; ADD; ADHD; DYSC; DYSL; DYSP; HI; VI; CP;
Severe: ASP; AUT; ADD; ADHD; DYSC; DYSL; DYSP; HI; VI; CP;
Others: SPD; AUT(other); PMLD; SLD; EAL; MSI; Epi
Experience of:
Mild: EBD;
Moderate: EBD;
Severe: EBD;
Others: OCD; TIC; FRX; Sp&LD

Summary: Motherwell College provides for students with a wide range of additional support needs. Student services provide educational support for students participating in our extensive range of vocational programmes. Following a pre-course assessment support requirments are assessed and agreed. Where personal care is identified it may require funding from Social Work services. If a student is unable to participate in our mainstream vocational programmes, we offer a personal curriculum to meet the needs of the individual. This programme will involve participation in relevant and accessible elements of college provision. A personal learning and support plan will monitor progress and guide programme development for the individual. The college has a residence which is fully accessible. Students who have personal care needs and are resident will need to appoint a care manager to agree a care plan and fund that service.

MOWBRAY SCHOOL

Masham Road, Bedale, North Yorkshire, DL8 2SD

Tel: 01677 422 446
Fax: 01677 426 056
Email: admin@mowbray.n-yorks.sch.uk
Website: www.mowbray.n-yorks.sch.uk

• Pupils: 142 Mixed; Day Pupils • Age: 3 to 16
• Religion: Non-denominational • School status: State

SEN provision

Detail:
Centre of excellence for:
Mild: AUT;
Moderate: AUT; MLD;
Severe: AUT;
Others: Sp&LD
Now provide for in school:
Mild: ASP; ADD; ADHD; EBD; DS; DYSL; DYSP; HI; VI; CP;
Moderate: ASP; ADD; ADHD; EBD; DS; DYSL; DYSP; HI; VI; CP;
Severe: ASP; ADD; ADHD; EBD; DYSL;
Others: SPD; SLD; Epi; PD

Summary: Like many special schools Mowbray is changing to meeting the needs of very complex pupils. Currently we are seeing a rise in admissions of ASD pupils and in particular children with Asperger's. In order to accommodate such children we work in partnership with local mainstream schools, which allows pupils to access a variety of GCSE courses at those schools, with specialist staffing support. We have created a specialist ASD resource for very complex primary aged pupils, run by staff with high expertise in this area. Currently 25 per cent of our pupils are ASD.

We are also seeing a rise in pupils with emotional difficulties. This affects their educational attainment, not necessarily their cognitive abilities. Their needs are enhanced through individual learning programmes, college courses and work placements. Partnerships with the speech and language resource educates 30 primary aged pupils and approximately 75 per cent of these pupils succesfully return to mainstream education by secondary transfer. The school is in a beautiful part of the world and is very well resourced and equipped to a very high standard. Parents are most welcome to contact the headteacher, who will be happy to discuss our provision with you and show you around our school. Jonathan Tearle M.Ed, B.Ed(HONS) Headteacher.

Mullion School

Meaver Road, Mullion, Helston, Cornwall, TR12 7EB

Tel: 01326 240 098
Fax: 01326 241 382
Email: enquiries@mullion-comp.cornwall.sch.uk

• Pupils: 595 Mixed; Day Pupils • Age: 11 to 16
• Religion: Non-denominational • School status: State

SEN provision

Detail:
Now provide for in school:
Mild: ASP; AUT; ADD; ADHD; EBD; DYSC; DYSL; DYSP; SpLD; HI; VI; CP;
Moderate: ASP; AUT; ADD; ADHD; EBD; DYSC; DYSL; DYSP; SpLD; HI;
Severe: ADD; ADHD; EBD; DYSC; DYSL; DYSP; SpLD; HI;
Others: SPD; CD; EAL; Sp&LD; Epi; PD; Eat

Summary: Mullion School overcomes barriers to learning by:

- setting appropriately challenging work.
- supporting pupils with numeracy, literacy and communication problems.
- planning for pupils' full participation in all activities.
- marking positively, for content and understanding.
- helping pupils to manage their behaviour and to take part in learning effectively and safely.
- helping individuals to manage their emotions and to take part in learning.
- when appropriate, taking the targets set by the SENCo and outside agencies into account when setting subject specific targets.

Nailsea School

Mizzymead Road, Nailsea, Bristol, BS48 2HN

Tel: 01275 852 251
Fax: 01275 854 512
Email: nailsch@nailsea.n-somerset.sch.uk
Website: www.nailsea.n-somerset.sch.uk

• Pupils: 1397 Mixed; Day Pupils • Age: 11 to 18
• Religion: Non-denominational • School status: State

SEN provision

Detail:
Now provide for in school:
Mild: ASP; AUT; ADD; ADHD; EBD; DYSC; DYSL; DYSP; SpLD; HI; VI; CP;
Moderate: ASP; AUT; ADD; ADHD; EBD; MLD; DYSC; DYSL; DYSP; SpLD; CP;
Severe: ASP; ADD; ADHD; EBD; DYSC; DYSL; DYSP; SpLD;
Others: SPD; AUT(other); CD; OCD; ODD; EAL; Sp&LD; DEL; Epi; PD; Eat

Summary: At Nailsea School students are identified as having special educational needs through information supplied by our primary partner schools, data from CATS tests on entry to school and open referral by teacher, student or parent. Once identified students are supported in-class by a team of eight teaching assistants and through withdrawal work in tutorials. Tutorials are taken by one of our team of five teachers. Students are mostly in pairs or some receive individual support. These are high quality and focused on the students specific needs. IEPs are issued to all staff to inform them of their specific difficulties. Tutorials are weekly and SEN students are taught in class with their peers for the remainder of the week. At Key Stage 4 students follow the ASDAN programme of study and there is a link course with Weston College to provide a more appropriate curriculum. We also offer a centre called the Small School to support students with emotional and behavioural difficulties and provide social skills work and counselling support for students in temporary crisis. The emphasis at Nailsea is very much on individual needs being met.

Netley Court School

Victoria Road, Netley Abbey, Southampton, Hampshire, SO31 5DR

Tel: 02380 453 259
Fax: 02380 455 438
Email: info@netleycourt.southampton.sch.uk
• Pupils: 35 Mixed; Day Pupils • Age: 4 to 11
• Religion: Non-denominational • School status: State

SEN provision

Detail:
Centre of excellence for:
Mild: AUT; ADD;
Moderate: AUT; ADD;
Severe: AUT
Now provide for in school:
Mild: ADHD; EBD;
Moderate: ADHD; MLD;
Severe: ADD;
Others: SPD; AUT(other); FRX; GEN; Sp&LD
Experience of:
Mild: DS; HI;
Moderate: EBD; HI;
Others: SLD

Summary: We pride ourselves on the quality of education we provide for our pupils and the ongoing opportunities we create to encourage and increase their independence.

The school is currently part of a major re-organisation of the special schools in Southampton. During the academic year 2006/2007 our current site will close and we will move to a newly adapted building. At the same time, the local school for pupils with severe learning difficulties, Ridgeway House, will close and the primary aged pupils and staff will join our school. Detailed planning at all levels is now underway to ensure that the schools work together in joint ventures.

To be a successful school, enabling pupils to make good progress and grow as individuals, it is vital to work collaboratively with parents. We value our close links with parents and look forward to working in partnership with you and providing a rewarding and challenging education for your child.

We are committed to providing a range of exciting learning opportunities relevant to every child's needs in an environment in which every child is respected and valued.

New Fosseway Lower School

Throgmorton Road, Knowle West, Bristol, BS4 1BX

Tel: 0117 3773250
Fax: 0117 3773251
Email: new_fosseway_sp@bristol-city.gov.uk
• Pupils: 77 Mixed; Day Pupils • Age: 6 to 19
• Religion: Non-denominational • School status: State

SEN provision

Detail:
Now provide for in school:
Mild: AUT; ADHD; EBD; HI; VI; CP;
Moderate: AUT; ADD; ADHD; HI; VI; CP;
Severe: AUT; ADD; ADHD; DS; SpLD; HI; VI; CP;
Others: AUT(other); CD; FRX; GEN; PMLD; SLD; MSI; Sp&LD; Epi; PD
Experience of:
Mild: ADD;
Others: ODD; TIC; EAL

Summary: This school has pupils with severe or profound and multiple learning difficulties. Some pupils have additional physical or sensory disabilities. A few also have emotional and behavioural difficulties. An increasing number have severe autistic spectrum disorder.

THE NEW SCHOOL AT WEST HEATH

Ashgrove Road, Sevenoaks, Kent, TN13 1SR

Tel: 01732 456 734
Fax: 01732 456 734
Email: principal@westheath.kent.sch.uk
Website: www.westheath.kent.sch.uk

• Pupils: 110 Mixed; Takes boarders • Age: 11 to 16
• School status: Independent

SEN provision

Detail:
Now provide for in school:
Mild: ASP; AUT; ADD; DYSL; DYSP; SpLD;
Moderate: ASP; AUT; ADD; ADHD; MLD; DYSL; DYSP; SpLD;
Severe: ASP; ADD; ADHD; EBD;
Others: AUT(other); CD; OCD; ODD; TIC; Sp&LD; DEL; Eat

Summary: Our school is an independent specialist school for day and residential youngsters aged 11-18 whose mainstream schooling has broken down. It is set in 32 acres of parkland on the edge of the historic town of Sevenoaks and accommodates students from all over the country. There are no more than 8 pupils in our classes and a team of teacher assistants and care staff complement the specialist teachers. Our children come here as a result of the trauma of abuse, horrendous bullying, bereavement or illness. Our one Aim – to rebuild damaged lives – is achieved by our specialised approach to education. We believe:

- 'In our youngsters until they can believe in themselves
- Happy people make good learners
- Change is possible, success is mandatory
- Qualifications are a good armour in life
- Shadows of the past must not be allowed to shade the future.

NEWSOME HIGH SCHOOL AND SPORTS COLLEGE

Castle Avenue, Newsome, Huddersfield, West Yorkshire, HD4 6JN

Tel: 01484 226 570
Fax: 01484 226 572
Email: office.newsome@kirklees-schools.org.uk
Website: www.newsomehigh.kirklees.sch.uk/

• Pupils: 877 Mixed; Day Pupils • Age: 11 to 16
• Religion: Non-denominational • School status: State

SEN provision

Detail:
Now provide for in school:
Mild: ASP; ADD; ADHD; EBD; DYSL; DYSP; HI; CP;
Moderate: ADD; ADHD; MLD; DYSL; DYSP; HI; CP;
Severe: DYSL; DYSP; HI; CP;
Others: SPD; EAL; DEL; Epi; PD
Experience of:
Mild: DYSC; VI;
Moderate: ASP; EBD; DYSC;
Severe: ASP; EBD;
Others: Sp&LD; Eat

Summary: Newsome has two resourced provisions within the mainstream school. We have the Kirklees Resourced Provision for pupils with hearing impairments and also the resourced provision for pupils with physical disabilities. All these pupils are fully included within the school. Hearing impaired pupils are taught alongside their peers, benefiting from teachers of the deaf and educational communicators. They also have some 'base time' to allow them to consolidate learning from other subjects. Newsome also caters for other pupils with SEN. In total we have approximately 70 statemented pupils. At the recent Ofsted inspection (Jan 2005), the overall provision for all pupils with SEN was rated as very good. All pupils are taught in mainstream classes for the majority of lessons with work being differentiated to meet their needs. We have a large team of commited, experienced support assistants who assist pupils in lesson and also extra- curricular activities.

NICOLSON INSTITUTE SCHOOL

Stornoway, Isle of Lewis, HS1 2PZ

Tel: 01851 702 275
Fax: 01851 702 645
Email: nicolson-institute@cne-siar.gov.uk
Website: www.thenicolsoninstitute.org

• Pupils: 1080 Mixed; Day Pupils • Age: 11 to 18
• Religion: Non-denominational • School status: State

SEN provision

Detail:
Experience of:
Mild: ASP; AUT; ADD; ADHD; EBD; DS; DYSC; DYSL; DYSP; HI; VI; CP;
Moderate: ASP; AUT; ADD; ADHD; EBD; DS; MLD; DYSC; DYSL; DYSP; HI; VI; CP;
Severe: ADD; ADHD; EBD; DS; DYSC; DYSL; HI; VI; CP;
Others: SPD; AUT(other); GEN; SLD; EAL; MSI; Sp&LD; Epi; PD; Eat

Summary: The Nicolson Institute has had a special class for over twenty years. Currently it has a special class of eight pupils who have moderate to severe learning difficulties. Each pupil has an individualised educational plan which takes into account their learning and social needs. The pupils in the special class have access to all subject areas in the school, taught by subject teachers, and enjoy additional special programmes. These special programmes include social and life skills, therapies, residential stays and environmental studies. Our aim is to ensure full entitlement and access to pupils with SENs to high quality education so that they can reach their full potential.

NORDEN HIGH SCHOOL & SPORTS COLLEGE

Stourton Street, Rishton, Blackburn, Lancashire, BB1 4ED

Tel: 01254 885 378
Fax: 01254 884 372

• Pupils: 658 Mixed; Day Pupils • Age: 11 to 16
• Religion: Non-denominational • School status: State

SEN provision

Detail:
Now provide for in school:
Mild: ASP; AUT; ADD; ADHD; EBD; DYSC; DYSL; DYSP; HI; VI;
Moderate: ASP; AUT; ADD; ADHD; EBD; MLD; DYSC; DYSL; DYSP; HI; VI;
Severe: DYSL; DYSP; VI;
Others: CD; OCD; ODD; FRX; PMLD; SLD; EAL; MSI; Sp&LD; DEL; Epi; PD
Experience of:
Mild: CP;
Moderate: CP;
Severe: ASP; ADD; ADHD; EBD; DYSC; HI; CP;
Others: AUT(other); TIC; Eat

Summary: Norden High School and Sports College has a dedicated team of staff supporting students with special educational needs. Eleven full-time teaching assistants and the head of learning support aim to ensure all students can achieve their maximum potential within and beyond school.

THE NORTH HALIFAX GRAMMAR SCHOOL

Moorbottom Road, Illingworth, Halifax, West Yorkshire, HX2 9SU

Tel: 01422 244 625
Fax: 01422 245 237
Email: mail@nhgs.co.uk
Website: www.nhgs.co.uk

• Pupils: 1052 Mixed; Day Pupils • Age: 11 to 18
• School status: State

SEN provision

Detail:
Now provide for in school:
- Mild: ASP; DYSL;
- Moderate: ASP; DYSL; VI;
- Severe: VI

Summary: Ofsted Inspection Report (Jan 2005) – 'There is very good provision for students with special educational needs. Teachers receive training in strategies to use in support of specific needs. In lessons teachers are fully aware of students' special needs and provide very good support'.

'Curricular provision for students who have special educational needs is very good. They follow the same curriculum as all other students and are fully included in all aspects of school life'.

Children whose special learning or behavioural needs have already been identified prior to entry into the school will receive the appropriate support and help required. Staff are informed of the particular needs of students and the implementation of strategies is monitored. The development and progress of all students is monitored and if special needs are identified then action is initiated either within the school or by using outside agencies or both. The school systems are consitent with the special educational needs Code of Practice and the school is committed to an inclusive curriculum for all students on roll. The School Guidance Counsellor is responsible for monitoring and supporting students with special needs. Parents are involved in discussions about the most appropriate strategies to support students that have special needs. The Governors' Pupils Standing Committee monitors the provision for special educational needs in the school.

NORTHFIELD ACADEMY

Granitehill Place, Aberdeen, AB16 7AU

Tel: 01224 699 715
Fax: 01224 685 239
Email: enquiries@accnorth.aberdeen.sch.uk
Website: www.northfield.aberdeen.sch.uk/

• Pupils: 1035 Mixed; Day Pupils • Age: 11 to 18
• Religion: Non-denominational • School status: State

SEN provision

Detail:
Now provide for in school:
- Mild: ADD; ADHD; EBD; DYSL; DYSP; SpLD; HI; VI;
- Moderate: ADD; ADHD; EBD; DYSL; DYSP;
- Others: CD; DEL

Experience of:
- Mild: ASP; DYSC; CP;
- Moderate: ASP; DYSC; SpLD; HI; VI;
- Severe: ADHD; EBD; DYSL; DYSP; SpLD;
- Others: OCD; ODD; TIC; PMLD; Epi

Summary: Northfield Academy is a six year comprehensive school on the North side of the City of Aberdeen in Scotland. It has a large support for learning department and houses a special needs base and a pupil support centre. The pupil support centre deals mainly with SEBD difficulties. Aberdeen City is committed to a policy of inclusion and a presumption of mainstream education. The school's timetable and working practices reflect this. The school also has a school based police officer, an educational social worker, a school counsellor and a youth worker.

NORTHWOOD COLLEGE

Maxwell Road, Northwood, Middlesex, HA6 2YE

Tel: 01923 825 446
Fax: 01923 836 526
Email: school@northwoodcollege.co.uk
Website: www.northwoodcollege.co.uk

• Pupils: 772 Girls; Day Pupils • Age: 3 to 19
• School status: Independent

SEN provision

Detail:
Now provide for in school:
- Mild: DYSC; DYSL; DYSP; HI; VI;
- Moderate: MLD; DYSL; HI;
- Severe: HI;
- Others: Epi

Summary: In the Junior school at Northwood College, two part-time staff are employed to offer support to individual girls and to small groups, notably to girls who may be dyslexic. In the senior school, girls have access to a special needs teacher. They have one-to-one lessons. This support is available to girls with learning difficulties such as dyslexia and dyspraxia. There is an extra charge for this.

NOTTON HOUSE SCHOOL

28 Notton, Lacock, Chippenham, Wiltshire, SN15 2NF

Tel: 01249 730 407
Fax: 01249 730 007
Email: notton_house_sp@bristol-city.gov.uk
• Pupils: 55 Boys; Takes boarders • Age: 9 to 16
• Religion: Non-denominational • School status: State

SEN provision

Detail:
Centre of excellence for:
Mild: EBD;
Moderate: EBD;
Severe: EBD
Now provide for in school:
Mild: ASP; ADD; ADHD;
Moderate: ASP; ADD; ADHD;
Severe: ADD; ADHD;
Others: CD; OCD; ODD; TIC
Experience of:
Mild: AUT; DYSL; DYSP;
Moderate: DYSL; DYSP;
Severe: ASP

Summary: Notton House School specialises in the care and education of boys aged between 9 and 16. In the main our pupils are of average or above academic potential and have special educational needs characterised by emotional and complex social and behavioural difficulties.

OAK LODGE PRIMARY SCHOOL

Chamberlain Crescent, West Wickham, Kent, BR4 0LJ

Tel: 020 8777 5697
Fax: 020 8776 2596
Email: admin@oaklodge.bromley.sch.uk
Website: www.oaklodge.bromley.sch.uk
• Pupils: 670 Mixed; Day Pupils • Age: 5 to 11
• Religion: Non-denominational • School status: State

SEN provision

Detail:
Now provide for in school:
Mild: ADHD; EBD; DYSC; DYSL; DYSP; HI;
Moderate: ADHD; EBD; MLD; DYSC; DYSL; DYSP;
Severe: CP;
Others: PMLD; SLD; EAL; Sp&LD; DEL
Experience of:
Mild: ASP; AUT; ADD; VI; CP;
Moderate: ASP; AUT; ADD; HI; VI; CP;
Severe: DYSC; DYSL; DYSP; HI; VI;
Others: CD; ODD; Epi; PD; Eat

Summary: Oak Lodge Primary School admits pupils irrespective of their gender, race, disability or special educational need. Children with special needs are entitled to the best kind of teaching in a positive and enriching environment with appropriate high quality resources to foster confidence and feelings of self-worth. Moreover, the content should complement, support and extend the schemes of work being delivered in the classroom. Whether the children are supported in the class or withdrawn in small groups, their learning context is carefully considered and appropriate adjustments made to help them access a broad and balanced curriculum.

OAK LODGE SCHOOL

101 Nightingale Lane, Balham, London, SW12 8NA

Tel: 020 8673 3453
Fax: 020 8673 9397
Website: www.oaklodge.wandsworth.sch.uk
• Pupils: 92 Mixed; Takes boarders • Age: 11 to 19
• Religion: Non-denominational • School status: State

SEN provision

Detail:
Now provide for in school:
Mild: SpLD;
Moderate: SpLD; HI;
Severe: HI;
Others: EAL; Sp&LD

Summary: Oak Lodge caters for severely/profoundly deaf pupils of secondary age who need British Sign Language (BSL) or Sign Supported English (SSE) to access the curriculum and everyday communication. Pupils may have additional needs including mild/moderate learning difficulties, social/emotional problems in addition to their deafness. We have developed a specialist programme to enable pupils new to this country, or new to education to succeed.

OAKES PARK SCHOOL

Hemsworth Road, Norton, Sheffield, South Yorkshire, S8 8LN

Tel: 01142 556 754
Fax: 01142 554 533
• Pupils: 52 Mixed; Day Pupils • Age: 2 to 19
• Religion: Non-denominational • School status: State

SEN provision

Summary: School caters for pupils with physical disabilities/medical difficulties and associated learning, sensory or communication difficulties. Our nursery forms the Sheffield School for Parents in Partnership with The Ryegate Centre, offering motor learning based on conductive education.

THE OAKS PRIMARY SCHOOL

Bells Lane, Druids Heath, Birmingham, West Midlands, B14 5RY

Tel: 0121 464 6272
Fax: 0121 464 6298
Email: enquiry@theoaks.bham.sch.uk
Website: www.theoaks.bham.sch.uk
• Pupils: 211 Mixed; Day Pupils • Age: 3 to 11
• Religion: Non-denominational • School status: State

SEN provision

Detail:
Now provide for in school:
Mild: ASP; AUT; ADD; ADHD; EBD; DYSP; HI; VI; CP;
Moderate: AUT; ADD; ADHD; EBD; MLD; DYSL; DYSP; HI; VI;
Severe: HI;
Others: CD; Sp&LD

Summary: The Oaks is a two storey mainstream primary school which serves an area of predominantly rented housing and very low cultural diversity. We have a higher than average number of pupils with SEN and pupils with statements for learning, autistic spectrum, sight impairment and minor physical disability. The school has toilet facilities in both Key Stage 1 and Key Stage 2 for people with mobility challenges and a recent addition is a lift to increase access around the ground floor of the school, which is on three levels. Presently years 5 and 6 are upstairs in the junior end of the school and at the moment there is no access for a wheelchair to go upstairs to those rooms or to the full computer suite, although we do have an additional smaller suite networked to the main one in the infant department. We have an experienced SENCo and a super team of well qualified teacher assistants who are familiar with working with IBPs and IEPs. We are supported by an excellent range of outside agencies who recognise the very good work we do.

Oakway Infant School

Off Oakway, Wellingborough, Northamptonshire, NN8 4SD

Tel: 01933 678 714
Fax: 01933 678 716
Email: head@oakway-inf.northants-ecl.gov.uk

• Pupils: 207 Mixed; Day Pupils • Age: 4 to 7
• Religion: Non-denominational • School status: State

SEN provision

Detail:
Now provide for in school:
Mild: ASP; AUT; ADD; ADHD; EBD; DYSC; DYSL; DYSP; HI; VI;
Moderate: ASP; AUT; ADD; ADHD; EBD; MLD; DYSC; DYSL; DYSP; HI; VI;
Severe: EBD; DYSP;
Others: EAL; MSI; Sp&LD; Epi
Experience of:
Mild: DS; SpLD;
Moderate: DS; SpLD;
Severe: ASP; ADD; ADHD; DYSC; DYSL; SpLD; HI; VI;
Others: CD; OCD; ODD; TIC; PMLD; SLD

Summary: The school offers support for children with a wide range of learning disabilities. Staff are well qualified to follow strategies that will improve a child's capacity to learn through different approaches taking into consideration the child's own style of learning. Children with behaviour difficulties enjoy the firm boundaries set by staff and the Positive Behaviour Policy encourages them to reach targets through a simple reward system. Again staff are encouraged to attend courses and improve their own approaches. The school believes no child is willfully naughty.

Offerton High School

The Fairway, Offerton, Stockport, Cheshire, SK2 5DS

Tel: 01614 839 336
Fax: 01614 199 160
Email: headteacher@offertonhigh.stockport.sch.uk
Website: www.offertonhigh.stockport.sch.uk

• Pupils: 1116 Mixed; Day Pupils • Age: 11 to 16
• Religion: Non-denominational • School status: State

SEN provision

Detail:
Now provide for in school:
Mild: ADD; ADHD; EBD; DYSC; DYSL; DYSP;
Moderate: MLD; DYSL;
Severe: DYSL;
Others: ODD; TIC; Epi; Eat
Experience of:
Mild: ASP; AUT; HI; VI; CP;
Moderate: ADD; ADHD; EBD; DYSC; DYSP; CP;
Others: OCD; Sp&LD; DEL

Summary: The Student Support Centre comprises of the Learning Support Team and the Behaviour Support Team. Learning Support caters for both moderate and specific learning difficulties and has a resourced base for MLD students. Behaviour Support caters for pupils with emotional, social and behavioural difficulties via The Oaklands LSU and Restart for pupils at risk of exclusion.

Old Stratford Primary School

Willow Grove, Old Stratford, Milton Keynes, MK19 6AZ

Tel: 01908 267 700
Fax: 01908 564 394
Email: head@oldstratford.northants-ecl.gov.uk

• Pupils: 204 Mixed; Day Pupils • Age: 4 to 11
• Religion: Non-denominational • School status: State

SEN provision

Detail:
Now provide for in school:
Mild: DYSC; DYSL; DYSP; SpLD;
Moderate: MLD; DYSC; DYSL; DYSP; SpLD;
Others: Sp&LD
Experience of:
Mild: ASP; ADD; ADHD; EBD;
Moderate: ASP; ADD; ADHD; EBD;
Others: SPD; Epi

Summary: The school has a well established process for identifying children with special needs as well as gifted and talented children. The SENCo is very experienced and receives ongoing training and updates. Each class within the school has a full-time teaching assistant who assists in the writing, planning and delivering the IEPs. The school believes in total inclusion, with all children being taught in their year groups. Specialised instruction when necessary is provided on a one-to-one basis in a comfortable, child-friendly activity room. The staff are confident to assist children with a range of mild to moderate educational and behavioural difficulties. The modern, well equipped school is situated on a level site, with ramped access for any pupils or staff with limited mobility.

OMAGH COUNTY PRIMARY SCHOOL

Campsie Road, Omagh, Co Tyrone, BT79 0AJ

Tel: 02882 242 642
Fax: 02882 251 835
Email: info@omaghcounty.omagh.ni.sch.uk
• Pupils: 415 Mixed; Day Pupils • Age: 4 to 11
• School status: State

SEN provision

Detail:
Centre of excellence for:
Mild: DYSL;
Moderate: MLD; DYSL;
Severe: DYSL
Now provide for in school:
Mild: ASP; ADHD; DYSP; VI;
Moderate: AUT; ADD; EBD;
Severe: AUT; ADD; EBD;
Others: CD; TIC; EAL; Eat

Summary: Each teacher provides a full programme of differentiated work for all the children in the class whatever their ability. Where pupils are identified as being in need of learning support they are allocated individual education plans which may be delivered by the class teacher, or in more needy cases by one of our dedicated learning support teachers.

In addition to our in-house support, the school has access to the services of our local authorities peripatetic learning service which provides for the needs of those children displaying moderate learning difficulties and more specific conditions such as dyslexia.

The school prides itself on how it meets the needs of all children in its care and currently provides for a range of conditions such as Asperger's, autism and Tourette's syndrome.

ORWELL HIGH SCHOOL

Maidstone Road, Felixstowe, Suffolk, IP11 9EF

Tel: 01394 282 628
Fax: 01394 278 831
• Pupils: 925 Mixed; Day Pupils • Age: 11 to 18
• Religion: Non-denominational • School status: State

SEN provision

Detail:
Now provide for in school:
Mild: ASP; AUT; ADD; ADHD; EBD; DYSC; DYSL; DYSP; VI;
Moderate: ASP; AUT; ADD; ADHD; EBD; MLD; DYSC; DYSL; DYSP;
Others: SPD; AUT(other); CD; OCD; ODD; TIC; Sp&LD; DEL; PD
Experience of:
Mild: HI; CP;
Others: Epi; Eat

Summary: At Orwell High School we aim to value and listen to every pupil to enable them to discover their potential and help them to achieve it. We believe every child matters and every child's needs are special.

Our SEN Team consists of specialist literacy and numeracy teachers and all of our statemented students receive the individual and small group teaching they need. We have a dedicated team of learning support assistants who work closely with SEN pupils in and out of the classroom. In addition we run a number of clubs to support these pupils and their parents – for example a lunchtime and a homework club. Our pupils needs vary, from some needing basic academic support and others needing considerable academic and social support. We work with pupils on the autistic spectrum, pupils with specific learning difficulties (dyslexia), dyspraxic pupils and those with moderate learning difficulties.

OSWALDTWISTLE BROADFIELD SCHOOL

Fielding Lane, Oswaldtwistle, Accrington, Lancashire, BB5 3BE

Tel: 01254 381 782

Fax: 01254 396 805

• Pupils: 121 Mixed; Day Pupils • Age: 4 to 16

• Religion: Non-denominational • School status: State

SEN provision

Detail:

Centre of excellence for:

Mild: AUT;

Moderate: AUT;

Severe: AUT

Now provide for in school:

Mild: ADD; ADHD; DS;

Moderate: ADD; ADHD; DS; MLD;

Severe: ADD; ADHD; DS;

Others: SPD; AUT(other); OCD; FRX; SLD; Sp&LD; Epi

OTTERHAM COMMUNITY PRIMARY SCHOOL

Marshgate, Camelford, Cornwall, PL32 9YW

Tel: 01840 261 344

Fax: 01840 261 344

Email: secretary@otterham.cornwall.sch.uk

Website: www.otterham.cornwall.sch.uk

• Pupils: 82 Mixed; Day Pupils • Age: 5 to 11

• Religion: Non-denominational • School status: State

SEN provision

Detail:

Now provide for in school:

Mild: AUT; EBD; DYSL; HI;

Moderate: DYSL; VI;

Others: SPD; SLD; Sp&LD

Experience of:

Mild: ASP; ADD

Summary: Otterham School is fully inclusive, so all children are included in mainstream classes with access to the National Curriculum in all subjects. Children with special educational needs are assessed and receive appropriate support according to their needs. The school adopts the County's recommended staged approach, from initial concern at School Action, involvement of outside agencies at School Action Plus through to full statements of need. The children at School Action Plus, and with statements are supported by teaching assistants for some or all lessons, depending on their needs. The school has reasonable wheelchair access at present, and this will be improved when the new school buildings are completed. The staff, both teaching and non-teaching, are aware of the children's special needs. Several INSET training days have been devoted to areas of special need including speech and language difficulties, communication and autistic spectrum disorder and Dyspraxia. We hope to make all children feel welcome and provide them with the opportunity to develop to their full potential.

Our Lady's Convent School

Burton Street, Loughborough, Leicestershire, LE11 2DT

Tel: 01509 263 901
Fax: 01509 236 193
Email: office@olcs.leics.sch.uk
Website: www.olcs.leics.sch.uk
• Pupils: 498 Girls; Day Pupils • Age: 3 to 18
• School status: Independent

SEN provision

Detail:
Now provide for in school:
Mild: DYSL; DYSP; VI;
Moderate: DYSL; DYSP;
Severe: DYSL;
Others: Epi
Experience of:
Mild: ASP; ADD; DYSC; HI; CP;
Moderate: HI; VI;
Severe: DYSP;
Others: SPD; EAL; Eat

Summary: We provide support for dyslexics between the ages of 5-18. Having an on site dyslexia tutor saves our pupils having to attend sessions out of school hours. Sessions are sympathetically organised so that pupils are not disadvantaged in curriculum subjects they may be good at. All the sessions in the senior department coincide with English teaching. We have teaching assistants who may assist within the classroom or who may offer out of class support. Our teaching assistants are highly qualified which is a definite strength. Our pupils are generally of average or above average intelligence and staff endeavour to allow them to fulfil their potential. Our expertise includes dyspraxics and visually impaired.

Palatine School

Palatine Road, Worthing, West Sussex, BN12 6JP

Tel: 01903 242 835
Fax: 01903 700 264
Email: office@palatine.w.sussex.sch.uk
Website: www.palatine.w-sussex.sch.uk
• Pupils: 157 Mixed; Day Pupils • Age: 11
• Religion: Non-denominational • School status: State

SEN provision

Summary: Palatine School caters for pupils with moderate learning difficulties. In addition to this some pupils have speech and language difficulties, fine/gross motor difficulties and medical conditions as well.

The school has two separate classes for pupils with Autistic Spectrum Disorder, ages 4-11. At secondary age these pupils are included into the Palatine main school secondary department.

Palfrey Junior School

Milton Street, Walsall, West Midlands, WS1 4LA

Tel: 01922 721 092
Fax: 01922 721 092
Email: postbox@palfrey-j.walsall.sch.uk
Website: www.palfrey-j.walsall.sch.uk/
• Pupils: 317 Mixed; Day Pupils • Age: 7 to 11
• Religion: Non-denominational • School status: State

SEN provision

Detail:
Now provide for in school:
Mild: ASP; AUT; ADD; ADHD; EBD; DYSC; DYSL; DYSP; HI; VI;
Moderate: AUT; ADD; ADHD; EBD; MLD; HI; VI;
Severe: VI;
Others: CD; GEN; EAL; Sp&LD; Epi; PD
Experience of:
Mild: SpLD;
Moderate: ASP;
Others: SPD; OCD; ODD; TIC; DEL

Summary: Palfrey Junior School is fully inclusive of children with a wide range of special educational needs and/or English as an Additional Language. We have expertise in working with hearing and visually impaired children, physical disabilities, ADHD, and those with learning difficulties. We have had children with dysgraphia, neurofibromatosis and agensis of the corpus callosum.

We take pride in offering all our children equal access to a rich curriculum, regardless of ability. At Palfrey we also offer pastoral care from a committed and caring staff. We believe that school should be a happy and rewarding experience for all.

PARK HIGH SPECIALIST SPORTS COLLEGE

Park Road South, Prenton, Merseyside, CH43 4UY

Tel: 0151 652 1574
Fax: 0151 653 6760
Email: schooloffice@parkhigh.wirral.sch.uk

• Pupils: 1150 Mixed; Day Pupils • Age: 11 to 16
• Religion: Non-denominational • School status: State

SEN provision

Detail:
Now provide for in school:
Mild: EBD; DYSL; DYSP; CP;
Moderate: ASP; AUT; ADD; EBD; MLD; DYSC; DYSL; VI;
Severe: EBD; DYSL; HI;
Others: EAL; Sp&LD; DEL; Epi; PD

Summary: We deliver to a number of students exhibiting a range of additional needs. A specialist Curriculum Support Team is deployed to work along side individuals and cohorts of students who are identified as requiring intervention and it is school policy to allocate teaching assistants to faculties so that students can benefit from support in many curriculum areas. Our work with ADHD students is held up as a model of good practice by our LEA and we have recently been successful with a DfES bid to pilot a project on Emotional Literacy. We have developed a comprehensive and thorough training programme for staff so that they feel confident in dealing with the demands of the Code of Practice. We maximise every opportunity to raise awareness of inclusive practices in the local community and liaise with external agencies to secure appropriate provision. Our Faculty mission statement 'It's not about how good you are, it's about how good you want to be' underpins our positive approach to inclusion and a belief that we can really make a difference to young people's futures.

PARKHALL PRIMARY SCHOOL

Seacash Walk, Antrim, BT41 1AZ

Tel: 02894 462 983
Email: info@parkhallps.antrim.ni.sch.uk

• Pupils: 443 Mixed; Day Pupils • Age: 5 to 11
• School status: State

SEN provision

Detail:
Now provide for in school:
Mild: ADD; ADHD; EBD; DYSL; DYSP; SpLD; HI; VI;
Moderate: ADD; ADHD; EBD; MLD; DYSL; DYSP; SpLD; HI;
Severe: ADD; DYSL; HI;
Others: EAL; Sp&LD; Epi
Experience of:
Mild: DYSC;
Moderate: DYSC

Summary: Parkhall Primary School is firmly committed to helping all pupils attain their fullest potential in terms of academic achievement. To this end the school operates a wide range of approaches to address the special educational needs that may arise during a child's academic career. Where a child is identified with special needs, an individual learning programme is drawn up by the class teacher and the special needs teacher. This programme may involve individual or group withdrawal to the SEN teacher or in-class support. The staff keep up to date with latest research for example, the special needs teacher has been trained in Primary Movement and is piloting this programme in Parkhall Primary School as an example of ELB Dissemination of Good Practice. There is good liaison with external professionals such as speech and language and occupational therapists to ensure that individual educational programmes are tailored to the best interests of the child.

Parsons Down Infant and Nursery School

Paynesdown Road, Thatcham, Berkshire, RG19 3TE

Tel: 01635 862 475
Fax: 01635 874 558
Email: Office.pdi@westberks.org
Website: www.parsonsdowninfant.org

• Pupils: 185 Mixed; Day Pupils • Age: 4 to 8
• Religion: Non-denominational • School status: State

SEN provision

Detail:
Now provide for in school:
Mild: ASP; AUT; ADD; ADHD; EBD; HI;
Moderate: ASP; ADD; MLD; HI;
Severe: ASP;
Others: EAL; Sp&LD
Experience of:
Mild: DYSC; DYSL; DYSP; VI; CP;
Moderate: DYSC; DYSL; DYSP; VI; CP;
Severe: VI

Summary: We are an inclusive school. We have strategies in place to support children with various special needs. We have good liaison with outside agencies and a good reputation in the community for our special needs provision. All staff involved with a child who has needs is given appropriate training. We have a comprehensive system of IEPs.

Penrice Community College

Charlestown Road, St Austell, Cornwall, PL25 3NR

Tel: 01726 72163
Fax: 01726 64901
Email: enquiries@penrice.cornwall.sch.uk
Website: atschool.eduweb.co.uk/penrice

• Pupils: 1359 Mixed; Day Pupils • Age: 11 to 16
• Religion: Non-denominational • School status: State

SEN provision

Detail:
Now provide for in school:
Mild: ASP; AUT; ADD; ADHD; EBD; DYSC; DYSL; DYSP; HI; VI;
Moderate: ASP; AUT; ADD; ADHD; EBD; DS; MLD; DYSC; DYSL; DYSP; HI; VI;
Severe: AUT; EBD; DYSL;
Others: CD; OCD; ODD; TIC; PMLD; SLD; EAL; Sp&LD; Epi; PD; Eat

Summary: Penrice Community College is a comprehensive secondary school with specialist language college status. There are approximately 1300 plus students presently on campus, of which 203 are on the college record of need. Of these, 35 are in receipt of a statement, with 69 designated at School Action Plus. The college strongly reflects the local authority's policy of inclusion, the majority of support is carried out within the class-room by a highly motivated team of teaching assistants responsible to the SENCo. In addition, each faculty has an attached TA whose primary responsibility is to support those students at School Action Plus within each subject area. Withdrawal lessons for individual students also take place to promote literacy, numeracy and study skills for many students. Ofsted, January 2004, commented on the strong leadership within the Individual Needs faculty, also praising the well motivated team of teaching assistants, as well as the strong commitment shown towards inclusion.The overall provision for children with special needs was described as very good. The Individual Needs faculty is based within its own suite, and also offers behavioural support in a discrete unit.

Penybryn School

Glasbury Road, Morriston, Swansea, SA6 7PA

Tel: 01792 799 064
Fax: 01792 781 311
Email: Pen-y-Bryn.School@swansea.gov.uk

• Pupils: 108 Mixed; Day Pupils • Age: 11 to 19
• School status: State

SEN provision

Detail:
Centre of excellence for:
Mild: AUT; ADD; ADHD; EBD; DS; DYSC; DYSL; DYSP; SpLD; HI; VI; CP;
Moderate: AUT; ADD; ADHD; EBD; DS; MLD; DYSC; DYSL; DYSP; SpLD; HI; VI; CP;
Severe: AUT; ADD; ADHD; EBD; DS; DYSC; DYSL; DYSP; SpLD; HI; VI; CP;
Others: SPD; AUT(other); CD; OCD; PMLD; SLD; MSI; Sp&LD; DEL; Epi; PD; Oth
Experience of:
Mild: ASP;
Moderate: ASP;
Others: ODD; FRX; GEN; EAL; Eat

Summary: Pen-y-Bryn is a senior day special school for pupils with moderate to severe learning disabilities aged 11 to 19. Many of the pupils have additional physical, sensory and associated behavioural difficulties. The school on its present site has been open for more than 25 years in a district called Clase, near the town of Morriston. On the campus is an all age residential autistic unit called Maytree, which is part of Pen-y-Bryn School and provides a residential regional resource for South Wales.

Peterhouse School

Preston New Road, Churchtown, Southport, Merseyside, PR9 8PA

Tel: 01704 506 682
Fax: 01704 506 683

• Pupils: 48 Mixed; Takes boarders • Age: 5 to 19
• School status: State

SEN provision

Detail:
Now provide for in school:
Mild: ASP; AUT;
Moderate: ASP; AUT;
Severe: ASP; AUT;
Others: AUT(other)

Summary: Peterhouse School provides education and care for 48 young people with autistic spectrum disorders. We provide placements on a day or residential basis. Residential placements may be weekly, termly or 52 week, and we also provide respite provision.

Phil Edwards Centre PRU

17 Sylvan Road, South Norwood, London, SE19 2RU

Tel: 020 8771 5603
Fax: 020 8771 5650
Email: office@philedwards.croydon.sch.uk
Website: www.philedwards.croydon.sch.uk

• Pupils: 48 Mixed; Day Pupils • Age: 11 to 16
• Religion: Non-denominational • School status: State

SEN provision

Detail:
Centre of excellence for:
Mild: EBD;
Moderate: EBD;
Severe: EBD;
Others: CD; ODD

Now provide for in school:
Mild: ADD; ADHD; DYSC; DYSL;
Moderate: ADD; ADHD; DYSC; DYSL;
Severe: ADD; ADHD; DYSC; DYSL
Experience of:
Mild: SpLD;
Moderate: MLD; SpLD;
Severe: VI;
Others: OCD; Eat

Summary: The Phil Edwards PRU caters for a wide range of permanently excluded pupils at Key Stage 3 and Key Stage 4 as well as some on a preventative 'Respite' placement. Although we are on the mainstream continuum we find ourselves working with increasing numbers of pupils with varying levels of SEN. We offer programmes of GCSE courses for students with emotional and behavioural issues at Key Stage 4. We also offer intervention and access to statutory assessment for pupils with moderate learning difficulties and behavioural difficulties.For pupils with specific learning difficulties we offer one-to-one 'Units of Sound' support (approved by the BDA). We conduct annual reviews for all the pupils with statements for whom we are responsible and work with the LEA, the educational psychology service and other relevant agencies. We are not intended to be a long term provision and wherever possible we seek to reintegrate excluded pupils into mainstream placements or if more appropriate into special education via the statutory assessment process. We have a full-time re-inclusion mentor who supports the students in their moves towards mainstream or special placements. The students who complete their education at the PRU until the end of Key Stage 4, have been very successful in progressing into Further Education, vocational or AS Level courses.

PHILPOTS MANOR SCHOOL

West Hoathly, East Grinstead, West Sussex, RH19 4PR

Tel: 01342 810 268
Fax: 01342 811 363
• Pupils: 55 Mixed; Takes boarders • Age: 7 to 19
• Religion: Non-denominational • School status: Independent

SEN provision

Detail:
Now provide for in school:
Mild: ADD; ADHD; EBD; SpLD;
Moderate: ASP; AUT; ADD; ADHD; EBD; MLD; SpLD;
Severe: EBD;
Others: AUT(other)

Summary: Based on the principles of Rudolph Steiner the school admits children with a broad range of emotional and behavioural difficulties. These may stem from social deprivation, a developmental disorder or an autistic spectrum disorder. The academic ability of the children or post-16 training course students range from average to moderate learning difficulties.

All children have a statement.

PHOENIX SCHOOL

49 Bow Road, London, E3 2AD

Tel: 020 8980 4740
Fax: 020 8980 6342
Email: head@phoenix.towerhamlets.sch.uk
Website: www.phoenix.towerhamlets.sch.uk
• Pupils: 120 Mixed; Day Pupils • Age: 2 to 16
• Religion: Non-denominational • School status: State

SEN provision

Detail:
Centre of excellence for:
Mild: AUT;
Moderate: AUT;
Others: AUT(other)

Summary: Phoenix is a school for pupils with a wide range of special educational needs, aged between 2 and 16 years. In September 2001 the designation of the school was changed to admit pupils with language and communication difficulties and severe learning difficulties, including those on the autistic spectrum.

The school occupies a pleasant site set back from the Bow Road in its own grounds. The area is well served by public transport and has easy access to underground stations on the District and Central lines. Bow Church station for the Docklands Light Railway is close by and buses stop almost outside the school gates. The school website is designed for parents, pupils and teachers. It will also be useful for headteachers, inspectors, administrators, educational psychologists, careers officers and social workers who may be considering placing children at Phoenix.

As a special school Phoenix offers a unique service to the children of Tower Hamlets. It is a caring, well ordered school which encourages mutual respect between staff and pupils. We believe it is important for pupils to achieve their full potential and to build upon their achievements.

The school is committed to involving parents in regular consultation and building upon a real partnership between home and school.

We expect children who come to Phoenix......

- to take advantage of the opportunities offered and reach their full potential
- to develop high standards of tolerance, care and respect for others.

We offer:

- A rich and stimulating curriculum, which is individually tailored reflecting the best of current practice.
- The National Curriculum to all our pupils.
- An environment, which supports the pupils' learning.
- The opportunity to all pupils for a successful transition from school to adult life through community and employment based activities.

Phoenix School has a bright future. It is a developing and growing school with a professional staff working alongside a multi-disciplinary team from education, health and social services. There are many new and exciting developments taking place at Phoenix, building upon well-established practices.

The changing roll and curriculum requirements have enabled us to press for new accommodation for class and specialist teaching areas, which have been supported by Tower Hamlets LEA and the DfES. The school has improved many of its facilities and will be continuing to develop its full potential.

Phoenix is committed to meeting the special needs of the children in Tower Hamlets. It is is a resource for the children and parents of Tower Hamlets which will continue to go from strength to strength. We plan to provide the very best environment for pupils at Phoenix at all times.

Plymouth Hospital School

Floor 12, Derriford Hospital, Plymouth, Devon, PL6 8DH

Tel: 01752 792 476

Fax: 01752 792 476

Email: hospital.school@plymouth.gov.uk

Website: www.plymouthhospital.plymouth.sch.uk

• Pupils: 52 Mixed; Day Pupils • Age: 3 to 16

• Religion: Non-denominational • School status: State

SEN provision

Summary: School caters for students who are out of mainstream education for medical reasons both physical and mental. There are a total of 52 funded places, all for medical reasons.

Polruan Community Primary School

St Saviour's Hill, Polruan, Fowey, Cornwall, PL23 1PS

Tel: 01726 870 402

Fax: 01726 870 161

Email: secretary@polruan.cornwall.sch.uk

Website: www.polruan.cornwall.sch.uk

• Pupils: 47 Mixed; Day Pupils • Age: 4 to 11

• Religion: Non-denominational • School status: State

SEN provision

Detail:

Experience of:

Mild: AUT; DYSC; DYSL;

Moderate: DYSL;

Others: Sp&LD

Summary: At Polruan, we welcome diversity and are able to support children with a range of educational and emotional needs, both within our two classes and through additional tuition and support. We believe that all children benefit from a wide, varied curriculum. Both classes have trained teaching assistants, we have recently upgraded our ICT provision to support ICT throughout the curriculum and for all children. Ours is a dyslexia friendly school and we are constantly seeking to improve the education, care and guidance that we give to the children in our care.

Pontville School

Black Moss Lane, Ormskirk, Lancashire, L39 4TW

Tel: 01695 578 734
Fax: 01695 579 224
Email: office@pontville.co.uk
Website: www.pontville.co.uk

• Pupils: 54 Mixed; Takes boarders • Age: 11 to 19
• School status: Independent

SEN provision

Detail:
Now provide for in school:
  Mild: ASP; AUT; ADD; DYSC; DYSL; DYSP;
  Moderate: ASP; AUT; MLD; DYSC; DYSL; DYSP;
  Severe: ASP; DYSC; DYSL; DYSP;
  Others: SPD; AUT(other); Sp&LD
Experience of:
  Mild: DS;
  Others: FRX; Epi

Summary: Pontville School provides a highly specialised and quality educational service for pupils with social communication difficulties, including: ASD, Asperger's syndrome, speech and language difficulties etc. Day and 38 week residential provision is available, with 52 week provision available via Witherslack Care children's home. The school offers a comprehensive package of accreditation opportunities including: GCSE, NVQ, Entry Level Awards, ASDAN and Unit certification. The curriculum includes access to the National Curriculum with modifications to ensure the delivery and acquisition of communication skills. The school has its own speech and language therapy department to offer individual and group therapy. Pontville is part of the well established and recognised Witherslack Group of Schools.

Portchester School

Harewood Avenue, Bournemouth, Dorset, BH7 6NZ

Tel: 01202 309 841
Fax: 01202 399 615
Email: portchester@bournemouth.gov.uk

• Pupils: 956 Boys; Day Pupils • Age: 11 to 16
• Religion: Non-denominational • School status: State

SEN provision

Detail:
Now provide for in school:
  Mild: ADD; ADHD; EBD; DYSL; DYSP;
  Moderate: ADD; ADHD; EBD; MLD; DYSL; DYSP;
  Severe: ADD; ADHD; DYSL;
  Others: PMLD; EAL; Sp&LD
Experience of:
  Mild: ASP; DYSC; HI; VI; CP;
  Moderate: ASP; DYSC; HI; VI; CP;
  Severe: ASP; EBD; CP;
  Others: SPD; AUT(other); CD; OCD; ODD; TIC; SLD; DEL; Epi; Eat

Summary: While some boys will have their needs identified before they join the school, our SEN department has assessment procedures in place to ensure the quick and effective support of all pupils who may require some assistance.

Students throughout Key Stage 3 (years 7, 8 and 9) and Key Stage 4 (years 10 and 11) may need extra support in the classroom and for this we have a strong team of teaching assistants who can support your child throughout their education, both in the classroom and in our SEN department.

At Portchester we view SEN as a whole school issue and work closely with the LEA to ensure the best advice and support is given at all times. Any specific assessment advice is passed to the relevant class tutor to enable them to use this information to enhance their teaching of individual pupils.

The school has a fast developing learning support centre and teachers with responsibilities for SEN provision. It also boasts a behavioural unit where specific support can be given to those pupils who find it difficult to cope within a mainstream setting. Much support is offered in this area including, anger management and 'problem solving skills'.

The school follows the SEN Code of Practice. In the initial SEN stages, all support is provided by our own teachers and support staff. However, if a student has a written statement of special educational needs, the school will work in tandem with the local education authority's specialist staff to ensure all the relevant provision requirement is met.

The school works together with the parents when assessing provision for a student with special needs and this partnership continues when issues or concerns arise. We also ensure this partnership extends to the contact with parents and the LEA for those pupils who have a statement for special educational needs or behaviour.

The school's SEN Policy is available from the school by written request.

If you do wish to speak to anyone regarding SEN, please feel free to phone the school; we are always happy to help and support you with all your enquiries.

English as an Additional Language

Portchester has very strong links with the LEA's 'English as an Additional Language' team (EAL) and is able to support pupils with this need.

Safeguarding School

Everyone involved in Portchester School, including staff, parents, students, community workforce and volunteers, share an objective to help keep children and young people safe by contributing to:

- Providing a safe environment for everyone to enable children and young people to achieve their full potential.
- Identifying children and young people who are suffering or likely to suffer significant harm, and taking appropriate action with the aim of making sure they are kept safe both at home and at school.

POTTERSPURY LODGE SCHOOL

Potterspury Lodge, Towcester, Northamptonshire, NN12 7LL

Tel: 01908 542 912

Fax: 01908 543 399

• Pupils: 48 Boys; Takes boarders • Age: 8 to 16

• School status: Independent

SEN provision

Detail:

Now provide for in school:

Mild: ASP; AUT; ADD; ADHD; EBD; DYSC; DYSL; DYSP;

Moderate: ASP; ADD; ADHD; EBD; MLD; DYSC; DYSL; DYSP;

Severe: EBD;

Others: OCD; ODD; TIC; Sp&LD

Experience of:

Mild: CP;

Moderate: AUT;

Severe: ASP; ADD; ADHD; DYSC; DYSL;

Others: CD; FRX; DEL; Epi; PD; Eat

Summary: Potterspury Lodge is an independent charitable trust and a company, Limited by Guarantee, approved by the DfES for boys aged 8 to 16 years who have a variety of emotional, social and behavioural difficulties and associated learning difficulties. For some time we have also provided for a significant number of students with Asperger's syndrome and currently a high proportion of our students have autistic spectrum disorders. We are actively working towards seeking accreditation with the National Autistic Society. At present we offer weekly boarding and day provision.

POWNALL HALL SCHOOL

Carrwood Road, Wilmslow, Cheshire, SK9 5DW

Tel: 01625 523 141

Fax: 01625 525 209

Email: headmaster@pownallhall.cheshire.sch.uk

Website: www.pownallhall.cheshire.sch.uk

• Pupils: 200 Mixed; Day Pupils • Age: 2 to 11

• Religion: Christian Inter-denominational

• School status: Independent

SEN provision

Detail:

Now provide for in school:

Mild: DYSC; DYSL; DYSP;

Moderate: MLD; DYSL; DYSP

Experience of:

Mild: ASP; ADD; ADHD; EBD; VI;

Others: GEN; Sp&LD; DEL

Summary: Provision for learning support is very good and it was highlighted as a strength of the school in a recent ISC inspection report. This provision is worked sensitively to support the ethos of academic excellence which is the main strength of the school. Children's progress is carefully monitored throughout the school and close liaison is maintained between form teachers and the SENCo regarding any difficulties that may have arisen. Further assessment can take place in school by the qualified SENCo or by an educational psychologist who is invited in from outside school.

There is close communication with parents and meetings are held to devise targets for IEPs. In class, support is provided in many lessons and one-to-one support is available four days a week in a bright and welcoming department. The pupils currently in the school do not present a wide spectrum of difficulties. Most difficulties seen are related to dyslexia, dyscalculia and dyspraxia. There are no children with severe learning or behavioural difficulties and all the children are expected to achieve well in mainstream classes and usually make sufficient progress to learn effectively without specialist support in the long term.

A policy for the provision of the extension of children's learning, ie for gifted and talented children, has been devised and is now in place. In the same way these children will have an IEP and targets provided for extension activities to develop their gifts and talents.

We have experience of paediatric arthritis and muscular dystrophy in mild cases where the child has been able to continue with mainstream learning.

In this way learning support can be provided at both ends of the learning spectrum.

Prestfelde School

London Road, Shrewsbury, Shropshire, SY2 6NZ

Tel: 01743 356 500

Fax: 01743 241 434

Email: office@prestfelde.net

Website: www.prestfelde.net

• Mixed; Takes boarders • Age: 3 to 14

• School status: Independent

SEN provision

Detail:

Now provide for in school:

Mild: DYSC; DYSL; DYSP; HI;

Moderate: DYSC; DYSL; DYSP;

Severe: DYSC; DYSL;

Others: DEL

Experience of:

Mild: ASP; AUT; ADD; ADHD; VI;

Moderate: ASP; MLD; HI;

Severe: DYSP; HI;

Others: SPD; EAL; Sp&LD; Epi

Summary: Prestfelde is a non-selective school with a whole school policy aimed at meeting the needs of individual pupils. The staff in the main school are aware and knowledgable about a variety of specific difficulties, such as dyslexia and dyspraxia. We have a strong learning support department, which was described as 'a major strength of the school' in a recent inspection. We specialise in specific learning difficulties (dyslexia). We have a Learning Support Centre in which we teach children individually or in small groups. It is staffed by one full-time tutor, who acts as co-ordinator, and three part-time tutors, all of whom have a diploma or certificate in SpLD teaching. We also have a CLANSA-qualified support assistant, who offers in-class support for individual children as required. We can offer a wide range of support, from basic and maths, to help with preparation for Common Entrance exams in almost any subject. We think that reading is of paramount importance and our policy is to pick up early on poor readers and put in some effective help, in co-operation with the child's form teacher. We encourage the involvement of parents. Our aim is that most children should leave the school with the necessary skills and strategies to be independent and effective learners.

PRIESTLANDS SCHOOL

North Street, Pennington, Lymington, Hampshire, SO41 8FZ

Tel: 01590 677 033
Fax: 01590 670 398
Email: info@priestlands.hants.sch.uk
Website: www.priestlands.hants.sch.uk

• Pupils: 1159 Mixed; Day Pupils • Age: 11 to 16
• Religion: Non-denominational • School status: State

SEN provision

Summary: We aim to support all students experiencing difficulties so that everyone can make the greatest possible progress in their learning. This is offered in many ways:

- In-class support with an extra adult in the classroom to help students;
- Withdrawal lessons for some students to give them extra help;
- Advice to teachers from our team of specialists to help produce teaching materials;
- Enrichment sessions providing extra help outside normal lesson times for those students who choose to come along.

Specific skills work might include personal organisation, or more advanced study skills such as speed reading, mind mapping or revision techniques. Help can be requested by the students themselves, by parents or by staff.

The support programme is managed by the special needs co-ordinator who is always pleased to discuss with parents any problems their children may be experiencing.

PRINCE ALBERT JUNIOR AND INFANT SCHOOL

Albert Road, Aston, Birmingham, West Midlands, B6 5NH

Tel: 0121 327 0594
Fax: 0121 328 2911
Email: enquiry@princealbert.bham.sch.uk
Website: www.princealbert.bham.sch.uk

• Pupils: 727 Mixed; Day Pupils • Age: 3 to 11
• Religion: Non-denominational • School status: State

SEN provision

Detail:
Now provide for in school:
Mild: ASP; AUT; ADD; EBD; DYSL; HI; VI;
Moderate: ASP; AUT; ADD; EBD; MLD; HI;
Severe: HI;
Others: PMLD; EAL; Sp&LD; DEL; Epi; PD; Oth
Experience of:
Mild: ADHD;
Moderate: ADHD

Summary: We provide opportunities for small group and individual work for children with SEN through class teachers, learning support assistants, learning mentors and specialist SEN teachers. We also have a wide range of support from outside agencies for our SEN children.

We currently provide for children with a wide range of needs including autistic spectrum disorders, behavioural problems, speech, language, hearing and sight problems, medical issues and general learning difficulties.

PRINCE WILLIAM SCHOOL

Herne Road, Oundle, Peterborough, Cambridgeshire, PE8 4BS

Tel: 01832 272 881
Fax: 01832 274 932
Email: head@princewilliam.northants-ecl.gov.uk
Website: www.pwschool.northants.sch.uk

• Pupils: 1121 Mixed; Day Pupils • Age: 13 to 18
• Religion: Non-denominational • School status: State

SEN provision

Detail:

Now provide for in school:

Mild: ASP; ADD; ADHD; EBD; DYSC; DYSL; DYSP; HI; VI; CP;

Moderate: ASP; ADD; ADHD; EBD; MLD; DYSL; DYSP; HI; VI; CP;

Severe: EBD; DYSL;

Others: CD; TIC; GEN; Epi; PD; Eat

Experience of:

Mild: AUT;

Moderate: AUT; DYSC;

Severe: CP;

Others: Sp&LD

Summary: We are an area comprehensive school. We aim to meet the learning needs of all our students providing they can access our curriculum with suitable support and/or differentiation. We have the LAIR – Learning Access Inclusion Resource. This excellent facility is well used delivering specialist support and part of the differentiated curriculum. We are inclusive and are open between 8-00 and 4-30 Monday – Thursday and until 4 on Friday. We also have the BEST (Behaviour Emotional Support Team) suite of three rooms. We work together as a student support team to ensure that all our students achieve to their very best regardless of their barrier to learning. We offer social opportunities at breaks and lunchtime and a homework club after school We are committed to increasing the skills of all teachers thus ensuring full access to the curriculum. To this end we offer twilight training sessions twice a term.

PRIOR PARK PREPARATORY SCHOOL

Calcutt Street, Cricklade, Swindon, Wiltshire, SN6 6BB

Tel: 01793 750 275

Fax: 01793 750 910

Email: officepriorparkprep@priorpark.co.uk

Website: www.priorparkschools.co.uk

• Pupils: 182 Mixed; Takes boarders • Age: 7 to 13

• Religion: CofE/RC • School status: Independent

SEN provision

Detail:

Now provide for in school:

Mild: DYSC; DYSL; DYSP;

Moderate: DYSC;

Others: EAL

Summary: Prior Park Prep is a CreSTeD school and the learning support department within the school aims to ensure that the children with mild to moderate dyslexia and dyspraxia reach their full social and educational potential by setting individual learning programmes and frequently monitoring their needs and changing situations.

PRIORY SCHOOL

Bolters Lane, Banstead, Surrey, SM7 2AJ

Tel: 01737 366 920

Fax: 01737 366 921

• Pupils: Boys; Day Pupils • Age: 3 to 13

• School status: Independent

SEN provision

Detail:

Now provide for in school:

Mild: ADD

Experience of:

Mild: DYSL; DYSP; SpLD

Summary: Two SEN departments one in the early years and one in the preparatory section. Boys causing concern are first monitored and then if needed are put on a school action IEP. In the Prep school we have a learning support teacher who is avaliable to come into the class and assist where needed. All needs are planned for within the timetabled lessons. If necessary the boy will be removed from the class and taught on a one-to-one basis but we do try and keep them within the mainstream of the lesson.

The Queen Elizabeth's High School, Gainsborough

Morton Terrace, Gainsborough, Lincolnshire, DN21 2ST

Tel: 01427 612 354
Fax: 01427 612 856
Email: office@qehs.lincs.sch.uk
Website: www.qehs.lincs.sch.uk

• Pupils: 1169 Mixed; Day Pupils • Age: 11 to 18
• Religion: Non-denominational • School status: State

SEN provision

Detail:
Experience of:
Mild: ASP; DYSL; DYSP; HI; VI;
Others: CD; OCD; Epi; Eat

Summary: Although this is a grammar school several of our students need the help of the learning support department at different times of their schooling. All these students are supported and counselled by staff with the help of the County Council's educational psychologists and specialist advisers as appropriate. We have one student with a statement of special educational needs.

All in-coming students are monitored by speaking to staff in their primary schools, reading all the transfer documentation, collating Key Stage 2 results and reviewing the results of their Richmond assessments. Richmond assessments and CATs testing takes place in the first week of the autumn term in year 7. Students who we feel would benefit from extra help with spelling, reading comprehension, mathematics or handwriting are given support at lunchtimes either by a mentor or by a member of staff. As a result of the introduction of the Key Stage 3 National Strategy, if any student were to enter the school having not achieved a level 4 or above in English and maths, they would be expected to attend extra lunchtime sessions to help them catch up.

During year 7 some students are gradually identified as being gifted. Identification is by means of primary recommendation, exam results and staff referral. This small number of students are given the chance to join the group which aims to meet four times a year for an afternoon or morning of enrichment activities.

Queen Elizabeth's School

Blandford Road, Pamphill, Wimborne, Dorset, BH21 4DT

Tel: 01202 885 233
Fax: 01202 840 703
Email: office@qe.dorset.sch.uk
Website: www.qe.dorset.sch.uk

• Pupils: 1470 Mixed; Day Pupils • Age: 19
• Religion: Church of England • School status: State

SEN provision

Detail:
Now provide for in school:
Mild: ASP; AUT; ADD; ADHD; EBD; DS; DYSC; DYSL; DYSP; SpLD; HI; VI; CP;
Moderate: ASP; ADD; DS; DYSL; DYSP;
Others: TIC; Epi; PD; Eat

Summary: Queen Elizabeth's School is a wholly inclusive school commmitted to providing a high quality individualised learning experience for every student. SEN support will therefore meet a variety of needs in a variety of ways, including in class support (the most common type of support), small group teaching in literacy and numeracy, one-to-one teaching, the use of specialised external support, and group work through our teenage drop-in centre on such issues as social skills and self-esteem.

Rainham Mark Grammar School

Pump Lane, Rainham, Gillingham, Kent, ME8 7AJ

Tel: 01634 364 151
Fax: 01634 260 209
Email: office@rainhammark.medway.sch.uk
Website: www.rainhammark.medway.sch.uk

• Pupils: 1189 Mixed; Day Pupils • Age: 11 to 18
• Religion: Non-denominational • School status: State

SEN provision

Detail:
Now provide for in school:
Mild: ASP; AUT; ADD; ADHD; EBD; DYSC; DYSL; DYSP; SpLD; HI; VI;
Moderate: ASP; AUT; ADD; ADHD; EBD; MLD; DYSL; DYSP; SpLD; HI;
Others: SPD; TIC; DEL; Epi; PD

Summary: Rainham Mark Grammar School takes great pride in the fact that it provides an excellent education for all of its pupils, irresepective of their educational needs. At various points in their education, some students are identified as having special educational needs. This could relate to some physical, medical or behavioural problem that will affect their education. The Special Eduational Needs team together with the staff at Rainham Mark work hard to ensure that the needs of all children, at all times are met. Working in close partnership with parents and other relevant agencies, every attempt is made to make certain that appropriate provision is made for pupils with special educational needs.

Ramsden Infant School

Thwaite Street, Barrow in Furness, Cumbria, LA14 1AN

Tel: 01229 89 4626
Fax: 01229 89 4627
Email: admin@ramsden.cumbria.sch.uk
• Pupils: 130 Mixed; Day Pupils • Age: 3 to 7
• Religion: Non-denominational • School status: State

SEN provision

Detail:
Now provide for in school:
Mild: ASP; AUT; ADD; ADHD; EBD; DYSL; DYSP; SpLD; HI; VI; CP;
Moderate: ASP; AUT; ADD; ADHD; EBD; MLD; DYSL; DYSP; SpLD; HI; VI;
Severe: ADD; ADHD; EBD;
Others: SPD; AUT(other); CD; OCD; ODD; TIC; SLD; MSI; Sp&LD

Summary: Ramsden strives to be an inclusive school. We appreciate that some of our children do not just have special educational needs but also social and emotional needs and we adapt our curriculum, opportunities and experiences to accommodate this. We also have a number of highly experienced teaching assistants who are able to work with children with differing specific needs. We keep track of latest research concerning specific needs and update our knowledge and understanding, acquiring appropriate resources where possible. We are always available to discuss concerns with parents and carers and have been able to support them with difficulties at home as well as school.

Ravenscliffe High School

Skircoat Green, Halifax, West Yorkshire, HX3 0RZ

Tel: 01422 358 621
Fax: 01422 329 621
Email: admin@ravenscliffe.calderdale.sch.uk
• Pupils: 115 Mixed; Day Pupils • Age: 11 to 19
• Religion: Non-denominational • School status: State

SEN provision

Detail:
Centre of excellence for:
Mild: EBD; DS; DYSL; HI; VI;
Moderate: EBD; DS; MLD; HI; VI; CP;
Severe: AUT; EBD; DS; HI; VI; CP;
Others: PMLD; SLD; MSI; Epi; PD
Now provide for in school:
Mild: ASP; ADD; ADHD; DYSP; SpLD;
Moderate: ASP; AUT; ADD; ADHD; DYSL; DYSP; SpLD;
Severe: ASP; ADD; ADHD; DYSL; DYSP; SpLD;
Others: SPD; AUT(other); CD; OCD; ODD; TIC; FRX; EAL; Sp&LD; DEL
Experience of:
Mild: AUT; CP;
Others: Eat

Summary: Ravenscliffe High School aims to provide a high quality educational provision for all its pupils. All our decisions are made with a view to meeting the individual needs of our students. We prioritise independent living skills, independent travel skills and vocational skills for our students as they progress through the school. We expect to work closely with parents and carers to ensure our students progress. Our priority is to send out students at 19 years of age who have developed independent skills at an appropriate level for their need, who will have a chance to make a meaningful contribution to society and utilise the skills they have developed whilst at the school.

Ravenscourt Park Preparatory School

16 Ravenscourt Avenue, Ravenscourt Park, London, W6 0SL

Tel: 020 8846 9153

Fax: 020 8846 9413

Website: www.rpps.co.uk

• Pupils: 259 Mixed; Day Pupils • Age: 4 to 11

• School status: Independent

SEN provision

Detail:

Now provide for in school:

Mild: DYSC; DYSL; DYSP; SpLD; CP;

Moderate: DYSC; DYSL; DYSP; SpLD

Experience of:

Mild: ASP; ADD; ADHD; EBD; DS; HI; VI;

Moderate: ADD; EBD; VI; CP;

Severe: DYSC; DYSL; DYSP; SpLD;

Others: SPD; PMLD

Summary: RPPS aims and values

- To identify at the earliest opportunity all children who need special consideration to support their physical, sensory, emotional, communication or cognitive development.
- To ensure that these children are given appropriate support to meet their needs with minimal disruption to access.
- To ensure that these children are fully included in all activities in order to promote the highest level of achievement.
- To involve parents, pupils and external agencies in developing a partnership of support at all stages.

Rawlins Community College

Loughborough Road, Quorn, Loughborough, Leicestershire, LE12 8DY

Tel: 01509 622 800

Fax: 01509 416 668

Email: enquiries@rawlinscollege.org.uk

Website: www.rawlinscollege.org.uk

• Pupils: 1346 Mixed; Day Pupils • Age: 14 to 18

• Religion: Church of England • School status: State

SEN provision

Detail:

Now provide for in school:

Mild: ASP; AUT; ADD; ADHD; EBD; DS; DYSC; DYSL; DYSP; SpLD; HI; VI; CP;

Moderate: ASP; AUT; ADD; ADHD; EBD; DS; MLD; DYSC; DYSL; DYSP; SpLD; HI; VI; CP;

Severe: ASP; AUT; ADD; ADHD; EBD; DS; DYSC; DYSL; DYSP; SpLD; HI; VI;

Others: SPD; AUT(other); CD; OCD; ODD; TIC; FRX; GEN; SLD; EAL; MSI; Sp&LD; DEL; Epi; PD; Oth; Eat;

Summary: Rawlins supports students with a variety of special educational needs across years 10, 11, 12, 13 and 14. Students are supported in mainstream classes with some students choosing a modified timetable which offers a vocational option. Some students are also offered an option which focuses on improving literacy skills. Students are encouraged to develop independence skills and take part in a wide range of college activities, including outdoor education.

The learning support department is the largest department in the college and aims to support staff and students to achieve their full potential and also to support students in moving on to further education or the workplace. The learning support department assesses students for access arrangements for GCSE, GNVQ and A Level examinations and liaises with a large number of professional agencies.

Stride is a unique full-time, three year, post-16 course for students who have moderate learning difficulties and are supported by a statement of special educational needs. The course offers a secure base from which the students can access the challenges of appropriate inclusion. Students all have an Individual Educational Programme with a curriculum specifically designed for their needs. Within the base they are taught in small groups. The curriculum includes academic skills, ASDAN life skills and independence skills and those for whom it is appropriate can access key skills programmes, GNVQs and GCSEs. Stride has two full-time teaching staff, an HLTA, and three support staff with the addition of mainstream staff teaching in their areas of expertise.

Learners with learning difficulties and disabilities post-19: Since the early 1980s, the college has offered discrete courses for learners 19+ as part of its Adult and Community Learning Programme. At the present time, courses range from full-time transition courses for a full range of learners with severe learning disabilities through to those with complex health needs. It also offers part-time courses in a variety of curriculum areas which are negotiated in a person-centred manner as required by the Valuing People white paper.

THE RED MAIDS' SCHOOL

Westbury Road, Westbury-on-Trym, Bristol, BS9 3AW

Tel: 0117 962 2641
Fax: 0117 962 1687
Email: admin@redmaids.bristol.sch.uk
Website: www.redmaids.bristol.sch.uk
• Pupils: 500 Girls; Day Pupils • Age: 7 to 19
• Religion: Non-denominational • School status: Independent

SEN provision

Detail:
Now provide for in school:
Mild: VI
Experience of:
Mild: DYSL;
Others: EAL; Eat

Summary: Girls with SEN are monitored throughout the year and reviewed in June - Support lessons can be organised as a private arrangement with a qualified teacher, these take place on a rotation basis. All staff are informed of a girl's needs. Extra time in examinations allowed throughout the school subject to appropriate documentation.

REDGATE SCHOOL

Somersall Street, Mansfield, Nottinghamshire, NG19 6EL

Tel: 01623 455 944
Fax: 01623 455 778
Email: head@redgate.notts.sch.uk
• Pupils: 30 Mixed; Day Pupils • Age: 3 to 11
• Religion: Non-denominational • School status: State

SEN provision

Detail:
Now provide for in school:
Mild: ASP; AUT; ADD; ADHD; DS; DYSL; DYSP; SpLD; HI; VI; CP;
Moderate: ASP; AUT; EBD; DS; MLD; DYSL; DYSP; SpLD; HI; VI; CP;
Severe: ASP; AUT; DYSL; DYSP; SpLD;
Others: SPD; AUT(other); OCD; ODD; TIC; FRX; GEN; SLD; Sp&LD; DEL; Epi; PD; Oth; Eat

Summary: Redgate School caters for children with wide ranging and complex educational needs. All children fall into the categories of mild, moderate or severe learning difficulties. Children at the school may also have autism, speech and language delay/disorders, Down's syndrome, emotional and behavioural needs, physical and medical needs, etc.

THE REDWAY SCHOOL

Farmborough, Netherfield, Milton Keynes, Buckinghamshire, MK6 4HG

Tel: 01908 200 000
Fax: 01908 206 420
Email: The_Redway@milton-keynes.gov.uk
• Pupils: 107 Mixed; Day Pupils • Age: 2 to 19
• Religion: Non-denominational • School status: State

SEN provision

Detail:
Experience of:
Mild: AUT; HI; VI; CP;
Moderate: HI; VI; CP;

Ribblesdale High School Technology College

Queen's Road, Clitheroe, Lancashire, BB7 1EJ

Tel: 01200 422 563
Fax: 01200 442 506
Email: enquiries@ribblesdale.org
Website: www.ribblesdale.org

• Pupils: 1278 Mixed; Day Pupils • Age: 11 to 16
• Religion: Non-denominational • School status: State

SEN provision

Detail:
Now provide for in school:
Mild: ASP; AUT; ADD; ADHD; EBD; DYSC; DYSL; DYSP; SpLD; HI; VI; CP;
Moderate: ASP; AUT; ADD; ADHD; EBD; MLD; DYSC; DYSL; DYSP; SpLD; HI; VI;
Severe: DYSC; DYSL;
Others: SPD; OCD; ODD; TIC; SLD; EAL; Sp&LD; Epi;

Summary: The department has three specialist teachers who can offer one-to-one teaching for pupils statemented or at School Action Plus with dyslexia, dyspraxia, dyscalculia, general learning difficulties and hearing impairment. We have ten teaching assistants who support pupils with learning difficulties in the classroom. The SENCo provides small group teaching for pupils at School Action who are below a reading age of ten and a spelling age of nine in our screening tests. We use the Macmillan Group reading test and the Vernon spelling test to ascertain the reading and spelling ages of all our year 7 pupils. This screening process often highlights difficulties which have not been apparent in the primary setting. We have four learning mentors whose role is to ensure a smooth transition for all year 7 pupils. The SEN department offers a nurturing environment for those vulnerable pupils who find the transition from a small primary school to a large secondary school overwhelming.

Ridge Meadow Primary School

Churchill Avenue, Chatham, Kent, ME5 0LA

Tel: 01634 861 227
Fax: 01634 862 577
Email: office@ridgemeadow.medway.sch.uk
Website: www.ridgemeadow.medway.sch.uk

• Pupils: 245 Mixed; Day Pupils • Age: 3 to 11
• Religion: Non-denominational • School status: State

SEN provision

Detail:
Now provide for in school:
Mild: ASP; ADD; ADHD; EBD; DYSC; DYSL; DYSP; HI; VI;
Moderate: ADD; ADHD; EBD; DYSL; DYSP;
Others: SPD; OCD; EAL; Sp&LD; Epi
Experience of:
Mild: AUT;
Moderate: ASP; MLD; DYSC; HI;
Severe: ADD; ADHD; DYSL; DYSP;
Others: Eat

Summary: Ridge Meadow Primary School and Nursery has a full-time SENCo whose role is to monitor the progress of pupils throughout their time at Ridge Meadow. Where additional needs for support are identified these are provided through a range of means:

1. Additional teacher support;

2. Additional support with a teaching assistant in a small group setting;

3. Booster groups based on literacy and numeracy programmes;

4. Withdrawal specialist support from the SENCo or learning support service;

We strive to recognise needs early and support children to achieve their full potential.

Ridgeway School

Moorland Road, Plympton, Devon, PL7 2RS

Tel: 01752 338 373
Fax: 01752 331 559
Email: ridgeway.school@plymouth.gov.uk
Website: www.ridgeway.plymouth.sch.uk

• Pupils: 1219 Mixed; Day Pupils • Age: 11 to 18
• Religion: Non-denominational • School status: State

SEN provision

Detail:
Now provide for in school:
Mild: ASP; AUT; ADD; ADHD; EBD; DS; DYSC; DYSL; DYSP; CP;
Moderate: ASP; AUT; ADD; ADHD; EBD; DS; MLD; DYSC; DYSL; DYSP; CP;
Severe: EBD; DYSL; DYSP;
Others: DEL; Epi; Eat

Summary: The learning support department has a literacy programme for Key Stage 3 students to improve their skills. It also has a transition group of ten students who are taught by one teacher for 50 per cent of their timetable until the spring half term in year 7.

The department supports student learning throughout the school via a number of excellent teaching assistants and a superb departmental administrator.

Ripplevale School

Chapel Lane, Ripple, Deal, Kent, CT14 8JG

Tel: 01304 373 866
Fax: 01304 381 011

• Pupils: 26 Boys; Takes boarders • Age: 9 to 16
• School status: Independent

SEN provision

Detail:
Now provide for in school:
Mild: ADD; ADHD; DYSC; DYSP; HI;
Moderate: ADD; ADHD; EBD; MLD; DYSC; DYSL; DYSP;
Severe: ADD; EBD;
Others: CD; ODD; Epi; PD; Eat
Experience of:
Mild: ASP; AUT; VI; CP;
Others: OCD; TIC; Sp&LD; DEL

Summary: Ripplevale School believes in an individual approach. The structured school day focuses on the needs of each individual through the delivery of the whole school curriculum, including a range of sporting activities and off site educational visits. Teachers and care staff work closely together to prepare Individual Educational and Care Plans designed to help each pupil overcome his difficulties while offering him the same opportunities as his peers in mainstream school.

Our caring and dedicated staff team includes qualified teachers, teaching assistants, qualified and experienced residential social workers, an educational social worker, ancillary and administrive staff. All play a significant role in the education and development of each pupil and we all work to create a warm, informal, friendly atmosphere within which the boys feel secure and confident.

Small class sizes and high staff/pupil ratios ensure each pupil receives the individual attention and support they need to experience success and start to enjoy learning. We provide the opportunity for all boys to sit a choice of subjects at GCSE level and many go onto further education.

Careers preparation is a priority at Ripplevale School. Careers lessons are timetabled and a careers adviser visits the school regularly. Work experience and visits to local industries are arranged. Our Connexions scheme ensures continuity and on-going support for school-leavers within each pupil's home area.

Risedale Community College

Hipswell, Catterick Garrison, North Yorkshire, DL9 4BD

Tel: 01748 833 501
Fax: 01748 836 149
Email: admin@risedale.n-yorks.sch.uk
Website: www.risedale.n-yorks.sch.uk

• Pupils: 581 Mixed; Day Pupils • Age: 11 to 16
• Religion: Non-denominational • School status: State

SEN provision

Detail:
Now provide for in school:
Mild: ASP; ADD; ADHD; EBD; DYSL; DYSP; HI; VI; CP;
Moderate: ASP; EBD; MLD; DYSL; HI; VI; CP;
Severe: DYSL;
Others: EAL; Sp&LD; DEL; Epi
Experience of:
Mild: AUT;
Moderate: ADHD;
Severe: EBD;
Others: SPD; CD; ODD; PD

Summary: The first aim of the learning support department at RCC is to ensure that the individual needs of all students are met. This is done by:
- liaising with other schools, PPSS and parents to ensure a successful transfer to RCC
- early identification of students with learning difficulties to assess problems and make provision for their needs
- reviewing progress of students regularly using clear systems for recording needs and for planning to meet these needs through the use of effective IEPs
- effective management of the special needs register

The second aim is to ensure that the students' self-esteem is preserved and enhanced. This is done by:
- use of appropriate language in the classrooms
- use of positive recognition for students' efforts
- celebrating success.

The third aim is to ensure that learning is enjoyable, accessible and demanding. This is done by:
- using a variety of teaching methods appropriate to students' needs
- working with departments in supporting students (and staff) to meet individual needs
- ensuring that alternative methods of recording information are made available
- employing teaching assistants, advanced teaching assistants or teachers, where resources allow, for supporting students in and out of the classroom
- differentiating lessons.

The fourth aim is to ensure that parents are included in the education of their children. This is done by:
- sending IEPs to parents
- inviting parents to reviews
- governors reporting on SEN to parents once a year

All staff at the college take on the shared responsibility of meeting the special educational needs of all students.

RNIB Sunshine House School

33 Dene Road, Northwood, Middlesex, HA6 2DD

Tel: 01923 822 538
Fax: 01923 826 227
Email: shsadmin@rnib.org.uk
Website: www.rnib.org.uk

• Pupils: 56 Mixed; Takes boarders • Age: 2 to 11
• School status: Independent

SEN provision

Detail:
Centre of excellence for:
Mild: VI;
Moderate: VI;
Severe: VI

Summary: We are a non-maintained primary special school for children with multiple disabilities and a visual impairment (MDVI). We are open weekdays, term-time only.

Our on-site residential provision is open during weekdays, term-time only. We meet all the requirements of the National Care Standards for residential special schools.

We deliver high quality teaching, providing a broad, balanced and differentiated curriculum (including the

National Curriculum and religious education) to meet the needs of the pupils. We deliver the additional curriculum needed by children with a visual impairment and provide therapies through our multi-professional staff team.

The Robert Ogden School

Clayton Lane, Thurnscoe, Rotherham, South Yorkshire, S63 0BG

Tel: 01709 874 443
Fax: 01709 870 710
Email: robert.ogden@nas.org.uk

• Pupils: 140 Mixed; Takes boarders • Age: 7 to 19
• School status: Independent

SEN provision

Detail:
Centre of excellence for:
Mild: AUT;
Moderate: ASP; AUT;
Severe: ASP; AUT;
Others: AUT(other)

Summary: In both the school and residential homes we have a wealth of experience in autistic spectrum disorders, and this is further strengthened by the breadth of knowledge held across the range of services provided by The National Autistic Society. All staff access a high standard of in-house training, following a programme of continuing professional development.

We aim to provide a stable, structured and nurturing environment in which young people with autism can achieve their full potential.

All pupils have access to a broad, balanced and relevant curriculum, including the National Curriculum where appropriate. In particular the school is able to provide: skilled and experienced teaching and care staff; psychology and speech and language therapy staff; high staffing ratios; homely and nurturing residential environment; individual education packages based on the NAS SPELL framework.

Roman Road Primary School

Roman Road, London, E6 3SQ

Tel: 020 7476 1602
Fax: 020 7511 1836
Email: admin.romanroad@pop3.newham.gov.uk

• Pupils: 240 Mixed; Day Pupils • Age: 3 to 11
• Religion: Non-denominational • School status: State

SEN provision

Detail:
Now provide for in school:
Mild: DS; DYSL; DYSP; HI;
Moderate: DYSP;
Others: PMLD; EAL; Sp&LD
Experience of:
Mild: AUT; ADD; EBD;
Moderate: EBD; MLD; HI;
Severe: ADD

Summary: In Newham all mainstream schools provide an inclusive education. Our school delivers a differentiated curriculum to suit the needs of all our children within the classroom. The only exception to this is small group teaching of the LEA's Wave 3 strategy which is a dedicated phonics skills programme, and which occurs during the Literacy Hour. Children who have identified speech and language difficulties receive small group activities delivered by teaching assistants trained by a therapist. Similarly children with identified physiotherapy needs work on an agreed programme delivered by a teaching assistant. As a very small school we are unable to provide for any additional small group work.

THE ROMSEY SCHOOL

Greatbridge Road, Romsey, Hampshire, SO51 8ZB

Tel: 01794 512 334
Fax: 01794 511 497
Email: head@romsey.hants.sch.uk
Website: www.romsey.hants.sch.uk

• Pupils: 1075 Mixed; Day Pupils • Age: 11 to 16
• Religion: Non-denominational • School status: State

SEN provision

Detail:

Experience of:

Mild: ASP; AUT; DYSL; SpLD; VI; CP;
Moderate: ASP; AUT; DYSL; SpLD; VI;
Severe: ASP;
Others: SPD; Sp&LD

Summary: Romsey Community School is a fully inclusive mainstream comprehensive for ages 11-16. learning support department classified as 'very good' in recent Ofsted inspection. Specialist Autistic Resource classified as 'excellent' in recent Ofsted report. Admission to the resource is controlled by the LEA. The learning support co-ordinator offers flexible support to all pupils with realistic levels of academic expectation. Standards of support are high.

ROSSETT SCHOOL

Green Lane, Harrogate, North Yorkshire, HG2 9JP

Tel: 01423 564 444
Fax: 01423 502 301
Email: admin@rossett.n-yorks.sch.uk
Website: www.rossett.n-yorks.sch.uk

• Pupils: 1310 Mixed; Day Pupils • Age: 11 to 18
• Religion: Non-denominational • School status: State

SEN provision

Detail:

Now provide for in school:

Mild: ASP; AUT; ADD; ADHD; EBD; DYSC; DYSL; DYSP; HI; VI;
Moderate: ASP; AUT; ADD; ADHD; EBD; MLD; DYSC; DYSL; DYSP; HI; VI;
Severe: ASP; AUT; ADD; ADHD; EBD; DYSC; DYSL; DYSP; VI;
Others: SPD; AUT(other); CD; OCD; ODD; TIC; EAL; Sp&LD; Epi; Eat

Summary: Rossett has adopted a whole school approach to special needs in which all children are valued and treated as individuals. Staff are fully briefed on the problems children may have which could be barriers to their learning and support strategies are put in place and regularly monitored. Parents are closely involved and play a vital part in the review process. The inclusion unit supports students who have emotional difficulties and those who require individual learning programmes. As a result, students on the autistic spectrum and those with related problems have been able to achieve success and fulfil their potential.

The school has an excellent team of 18 teaching assistants who help to develop children's self-confidence and support their day to day learning.

THE ROUND OAK SCHOOL AND SUPPORT SERVICE

Pound Lane, Lillington, Leamington Spa, Warwickshire, CV32 7RT

Tel: 01926 335 566
Fax: 01926 886 163
Email: admin@7030.wgfl.net

• Pupils: 85 Mixed; Day Pupils • Age: 4 to 16
• Religion: Non-denominational • School status: State

SEN provision

Detail:

Now provide for in school:

Mild: ASP; AUT; ADD; ADHD; EBD; DYSC; DYSL; DYSP; HI;
Moderate: ASP; AUT; ADD; ADHD; EBD; MLD; DYSC; DYSL; DYSP; HI;
Severe: ASP; AUT; ADD; ADHD;
Others: SPD; TIC; SLD; Sp&LD; Epi

Experience of:

Mild: DS; CP;

Moderate: DS; CP;
Severe: DS;
Others: DEL

Summary: Round Oak School caters for the needs of pupils in the Central Area of Warwickshire. All our pupils have statements for learning difficulties, and some may have additional physical, sensory or speech and language needs. We have many children with a diagnosis of autistic spectrum disorder, as well as those with ADHD and other emotional and behavioural difficulties.

Our support service works in a variety of mainstream schools, supporting children with learning and behaviour needs in their mainstream classrooms. We also make the educational provision for two adolescent units attached to a hospital in Coleshill.

THE ROWAN SCHOOL

4 Durvale Court, Furniss Avenue, Sheffield, South Yorkshire, S17 3PT

Tel: 01142 350 479
Fax: 01142 350 478
• Pupils: 61 Mixed; Day Pupils • Age: 4 to 11
• Religion: Non-denominational • School status: State

SEN provision

Detail:
Now provide for in school:
Mild: AUT; ADD; ADHD; EBD;
Moderate: ASP; AUT; ADD; ADHD; EBD;
Severe: ASP; AUT;
Others: SPD; ODD; Sp&LD
Experience of:
Mild: ASP

Summary: All children admitted to The Rowan School have a statement of special educational needs related to severe or complex communication difficulties. Currently our children are organised into eight class groups. Each class is staffed by a minimum of a teacher and a teaching and learning assistant. Additional staffing is allocated according to needs. Our curriculum is based on the six areas of learning in the Foundation Stage and on the National Curriculum with a clear emphasis on speech and language and social interaction. Children have individual timetables to meet individual needs and teaching approaches are multi-sensory to meet variety in learning styles. The Rowan School has a multi-professional approach with staff and visiting colleagues working closely together to enable each other to meet children's needs in the best ways.

ROWDEFORD SCHOOL

Rowde, Devizes, Wiltshire, SN10 2QQ

Tel: 01380 850 309
Fax: 01380 859 708
Email: admin@rowdeford.wilts.sch.uk
• Pupils: 114 Mixed; Takes boarders • Age: 11 to 16
• Religion: Non-denominational • School status: State

SEN provision

Detail:
Now provide for in school:
Mild: ASP; AUT; ADD; ADHD; EBD; DS; DYSC; DYSL; DYSP; HI; VI; CP;
Moderate: ASP; ADD; ADHD; EBD; DS; MLD; DYSC; DYSL; DYSP;
Others: SPD; OCD; ODD; TIC; FRX; SLD; Sp&LD; DEL; Epi; Eat

THE ROYAL LIBERTY SCHOOL

Upper Brentwood Road, Romford, Essex, RM2 6HJ

Tel: 01708 730 141
Fax: 01708 723 950
• Pupils: 559 Boys; Day Pupils • Age: 11 to 16
• Religion: Non-denominational • School status: State

SEN provision

Summary: The SEN department is a well-developed and dynamic team, consisiting of the SENCo and eight teaching assistants. The staff are always friendly and welcoming to all students. The SEN department offers support to all students as Key Stage 3 and Key Stage 4, this can be through revision classes, support with coursework, or the extra curricular clubs that are available during and after school clubs. These are:

- The Reading Club, which helps students to improve their reading skills, interact with others and generally improve their socialisation skills.
- The Lunchtime Club, which provides students with a base to play games, complete homework, improve upon their IT skills and their communication skills.
- The Homework Club, provides overall support for all students in all subjects who need a quiet place to work.

The department is extremely proud of the relationship that it has with parents and the students of the school. Students value the support they receive which takes in to account emotional, behavioural and social development. Students feel safe and confident. This relationship is reciprocated by the staff's willingness to support students on school and college trips.

ROYAL MASONIC SCHOOL FOR GIRLS

Rickmansworth Park, Chorleywood Road, Rickmansworth, Hertfordshire, WD3 4HF

Tel: 01923 773 168
Fax: 01923 896 729
Email: enquiries@royalmasonic.herts.sch.uk
Website: www.royalmasonic.herts.sch.uk

• Pupils: 783 Girls; Takes boarders • Age: 4 to 18
• School status: Independent

SEN provision

Detail:
Now provide for in school:
Mild: DYSC; DYSL; DYSP;
Moderate: DYSL; DYSP;
Severe: DYSL;
Others: EAL
Experience of:
Mild: ASP; ADD; ADHD; EBD; HI; VI;
Moderate: DYSC;
Others: OCD; Sp&LD; Epi; Eat

Summary: At RMS we recognise that at some stage in their academic careers all pupils will require specific help of some kind. We endeavour to monitor the pupils throughout and offer a number of services to support their learning. Individual subject teachers, form staff and special needs staff liase closely to address this area.

During the first term of year 7 we undertake a literacy-screening programme that assesses spelling, comprehension and word recognition. This indicates whether extra support is required and pupils may be asked to attend the Spelling or Reading Skills or, if specific help is necessary, one-to-one support sessions can be arranged with our special needs teacher. The school offers a programme of specialised help for those who experience dyslexia or other specific learning difficulties and parents are welcome to contact the SENCo if they have concerns in this or any other area.

Gifted pupils benefit from a wide range of national competitions and participation in FORUM, a special programme for gifted children, in addition to differentiation within the daily curriculum. Specialist support can also be provided for pupils with English as an Additional Language.

ROYAL SCHOOL FOR THE DEAF AND COMMUNICATION DISORDERS

Stanley Road, Cheadle Hulme, Cheadle, Cheshire, SK8 6RQ

Tel: 0161 610 0100
Fax: 0161 610 0101
Email: info@rsdmanchester.org
Website: www.rsdmanchester.org

• Pupils: 75 Mixed; Takes boarders • Age: 5 to 21
• School status: State

SEN provision

Detail:
Now provide for in school:
Mild: ASP; AUT; ADD; ADHD; DS; DYSP; HI; VI; CP;
Moderate: AUT; ADD; ADHD; DS; DYSP; HI; VI; CP;
Severe: AUT; DS; HI; VI; CP;
Others: PMLD; SLD; MSI; Sp&LD; DEL; Epi; PD
Experience of:
Mild: EBD; DYSL;
Moderate: EBD; MLD; DYSL;

Severe: EBD;
Others: CD; OCD; FRX; GEN; Eat

Summary: The Royal School for the Deaf and Communication Disorders (RSDCD) is a mixed day and residential co-educational, non-maintained special school with a college department. RSDCD caters for those students who have severe and complex learning difficulties, combined with significant communication difficulties, which include very limited or no oral language. RSDCD is currently divided into three departments which have different curriculum and communication emphases: deaf/severe learning difficulties support, autism support, multi sensory support. The delivery of the school and extended curriculum is supported by a multi disciplinary team: educational psychologist, SaLTs. OT, physiotherapists, audiologist, medical staff, link worker, musician in residence. RSDCD have very good recent Ofsted/Ofsted ALI/CSCI inspection reports and the post-16 department has been commended 'outstanding' in 2005 HMCI report.

ROYDON PRIMARY SCHOOL

Epping Road, Roydon, Harlow, Essex, CM19 5HN

Tel: 01279 793 152
Fax: 01279 792 009
Email: admin@roydon.essex.sch.uk
Website: www.roydon.essex.sch.uk
• Pupils: 216 Mixed; Day Pupils • Age: 4 to 11
• Religion: Non-denominational • School status: State

SEN provision

Detail:
Experience of:
Mild: DYSL; DYSP; VI; CP;
Moderate: CP;
Others: EAL

Summary: Children are encouraged to take an active part in writing and monitoring their individual education plans. They work closely with teachers and learning support assistants to achieve the targets that have been set for them. We involve parents in reviewing children's progress through regular meetings. We are trying to make our site more accessible to wheelchair users, but there are still parts of the old Victorian building which prohibit access to wheelchairs.

ROYDS HALL HIGH SCHOOL

Luck Lane, Paddock, Huddersfield, West Yorkshire, HD3 4HA

Tel: 01484 463 366
Fax: 01484 222 223
Email: office.roydshall@kirklees-schools.org.uk
• Pupils: 824 Mixed; Day Pupils • Age: 11 to 16
• Religion: Non-denominational • School status: State

SEN provision

Detail:
Now provide for in school:
Mild: ADD; ADHD; EBD; DYSC; DYSL; DYSP; HI; VI;
Moderate: ASP; ADD; ADHD; EBD; MLD; DYSC; DYSL; DYSP; HI; VI; CP;
Severe: AUT; ADD; ADHD; EBD; DYSC; DYSL;
Others: CD; ODD; TIC; EAL; DEL; Epi; Eat
Experience of:
Mild: ASP; AUT; CP;
Moderate: AUT;
Severe: ASP; HI;
Others: AUT(other); OCD; SLD

Summary: We have a highly trained team of staff who support our students in lessons. We match staff expertise to the needs of the individual student, eg ASD, dyspraxia, VI, literacy difficulties. We have a specialist resourced provision for students with a severe, specific language impairment. These students are supported by a specialist team, including a speech and language therapist, trained educational teaching assistants, and a qualified teacher of specific language impairment. We have a specialist dyslexia teacher who works with small groups of students. The provision for students is reviewed by the Additional Needs Team, which comprises the deputy headteacher, and the leaders of Key Stage 3 and Key Stage 4. This makes special educational needs a whole school issue.

Rudheath Community High School

Shipbrook Road, Rudheath, Northwich, Cheshire, CW9 7DT

Tel: 01606 42 515
Fax: 01606 46 053
Email: centraloffice@rudheathhs.cheshire.sch.uk
Website: www.rudheathhs.co.uk

• Pupils: 815 Mixed; Day Pupils • Age: 11 to 16
• Religion: Non-denominational • School status: State

SEN provision

Detail:
Now provide for in school:
Mild: ASP; AUT; ADD; ADHD; EBD; DYSL; SpLD; CP;
Moderate: ASP; AUT; ADD; ADHD; MLD; DYSL; SpLD;
Severe: EBD; DYSL;
Others: EAL; Epi; PD
Experience of:
Mild: DS; DYSC; DYSP; HI; VI;
Moderate: DS; DYSC; DYSP;
Severe: DYSP;
Others: Sp&LD

Summary: Rudheath High School has a large (60 places) unit for pupils with moderate learning difficulties.

This unit is a county resource and we draw pupils from a wide geographical area not just from our school catchment area. We pride ourselves on our inclusive education policy and philosophy and all the pupils in the special unit spend the majority of their timetabled time with their mainstream peers, with additional support where necessary. All the pupils in the unit are registered in a mixed ability mainstream form.

Rudyard Kipling Primary School

Chalkland Rise, Woodingdean, Brighton, East Sussex, BN2 6RH

Tel: 01273 303 328
Fax: 01273 304 597
Email: admin@kipling.brighton-hove.sch.uk
Website: www.kipling.brighton-hove.sch.uk

• Pupils: 391 Mixed; Day Pupils • Age: 3 to 11
• Religion: Non-denominational • School status: State

SEN provision

Detail:
Now provide for in school:
Mild: ASP; AUT; ADD; ADHD; EBD; DYSC; DYSL; DYSP; SpLD; HI;
Moderate: ASP; AUT; ADD; ADHD; EBD; DYSC; DYSL; DYSP; HI;
Severe: AUT; ADD; ADHD; EBD; DYSC; DYSL; DYSP;
Others: SPD; EAL; Sp&LD; PD

Summary: Rudyard Kipling is a mainstream primary school and currently supports children with a range of special educational need. We support children at the stages of school action and school action plus and those who have a statement of special educational need. Our current support includes that for children with literacy and numeracy difficulties, speech and language difficulties, milder sensory need, fine and gross motor difficulties, children with an autistic spectrum disorder including Asperger's, children on the dyslexic spectrum and those with a social, emotional and behavioural difficulty. We have recently become wheelchair accessible to children in Key Stage 2 (seven years and upwards). Class teachers from nursery to year 6 work closely with the special educational needs co-ordinator and parents in identifying and supporting special educational need. We aim to promote parent partnership in individual education plan target setting and offering consistency of support at home and at school. We work closely with a speech and language therapist and a speech and language support teacher. We liaise with Brighton and Hove's learning support service supporting children with more significant literacy difficulties. We also regularly liaise with an occupational therapist and physiotherapist, the autistic spectrum disorder support service, children and adolescent mental health service, school nurse and GPs. An educational psychologist supports our assessment and support for pupils where appropriate. Rudyard Kipling also houses a special facility accomodating eight pupils with a statement for autistic spectrum disorder and related difficulties. This facility has a separate team comprising of a Faciltiy co-ordinator and learning support assistants working with the children in the facility rooms and supporting their integration into mainstream school life and mainstream classes, with levels of integration varied according to need.

Ruskington Chestnut Street C of E Primary School

Chestnut Street, Ruskington, Sleaford, Lincolnshire, NG34 9DL

Tel: 01526 832 424

Fax: 01526 834 574

Email: enquiries@chestnut-street.lincs.sch.uk

• Pupils: 411 Mixed; Day Pupils • Age: 4 to 11

• Religion: Church of England • School status: State

SEN provision

Detail:

Now provide for in school:

Mild: ASP; AUT; ADD; ADHD; EBD; DYSC; DYSL; DYSP; HI; VI;

Moderate: ASP; ADD; EBD; MLD; CP;

Others: SLD; Sp&LD; Epi; PD

Experience of:

Mild: CP;

Moderate: ADHD; HI;

Severe: HI;

Others: SPD; TIC

Summary: Chestnut Street CE primary school has a very good reputation for supporting children with special needs. We have experience in supporting a wide range of needs, having at present 13 children with statements for a wide range of issues, and this is testimony to the number of parents with children with statements who positively choose this school for their children. Our last two Ofsted reports singled out SEN provision as 'excellent' and 'very good', and our SENCo is very experienced and has excellent contact with all agencies supporting SEN in Lincolnshire. We are a fully inclusive school and have entered into partnership with a special school in order to provide a child with significant needs an opportunity to be in mainstream education for part of the week. We are also very fortunate to have an excellent team of teaching assistants with expertise in supporting children with SEN. Our SENCo is recognised by the LEA for her very good practice and has been consulted on many aspects of SEN provision.

Sackville School

Tonbridge Road, Hildenborough, Tonbridge, Kent, TN11 9HN

Tel: 01732 838 888

Fax: 01732 834 999

Email: office@sackvilleschool.co.uk

Website: www.sackvilleschool.co.uk

• Pupils: 185 Mixed; Day Pupils • Age: 11 to 18

• School status: Independent

SEN provision

Detail:

Experience of:

Mild: ASP; ADD; ADHD; EBD; DYSC; DYSL; DYSP; HI;

Moderate: ASP; MLD; DYSC; DYSL; DYSP; HI;

Severe: DYSL;

Others: SPD; EAL; Sp&LD; PD

Summary: In the Lower school, we tend to concentrate on basic numeracy, literacy and spelling skills if these are weak. This is with a view to enabling the student to study more independently. However, all lessons are carefully planned to suit the needs of the individual. Once we feel that reading and spelling skills are being mastered, we tend to focus on study skills which incorporate learning strategies, information retrieval, revision and exam techniques. We value each pupil as an individual and appreciate that they all have different needs and problems. We are totally committed to trying to achieve the very best for each student in our care.

ST ANDREW'S CEVA PRIMARY SCHOOL

Ecton Brook Road, Ecton Brook, Northampton, Northamptonshire, NN3 5EA

Tel: 01604 406 486

Email: head@StAndrews-pri.northants-ecl.gov.uk

Website: www.standrews.northants.sch.uk

• Pupils: 186 Mixed; Day Pupils • Age: 11

• Religion: Church of England • School status: State

SEN provision

Detail:

Now provide for in school:

Mild: ASP; AUT;

Moderate: ASP; AUT; EBD; MLD; HI; CP;

Severe: ADD; ADHD;

Others: OCD

Summary: Our school welcomes pupils with special educational needs. Each child is taught inclusively, within mixed-ability classes, and has a range of additional one-to-one help according to need. As much as possible of this help is given within the class, rather than through withdrawal. We have very experienced SEN assistants who have worked with a range of different children over the years. We have particular experience with children who are profoundly deaf, although currently there are none on roll.

ST ANDREW'S C OF E PRIMARY SCHOOL

Park Lane, Shifnal, Shropshire, TF11 9HD

Tel: 01952 460 226

Fax: 01952 463 703

Email: admin@st-andrews-shifnal.shropshire.sch.uk

• Pupils: 293 Mixed; Day Pupils • Age: 5 to 11

• Religion: Church of England • School status: State

SEN provision

Detail:

Now provide for in school:

Mild: ASP; ADD; ADHD; EBD; DS;

Moderate: ASP; ADD; ADHD; DS; MLD;

Severe: ADD; ADHD

Experience of:

Mild: AUT; DYSP; CP;

Moderate: AUT; EBD; DYSP;

Others: SPD; Epi

Summary: Children of all abilities are taught within the school. The school aims to promote inclusion as an integral part of all pastoral care and curriculum delivery. An ongoing training programme is in place to ensure that all children are assessed at the earliest possible age and, where necessary, appropriate action taken to provide postive intervention programmes. All staff and teaching assistants work together to provide mutually beneficial information leading to children being placed on individual and group programmes where necessary. The school works alongside the learning support advisory team, educational psychologists and behaviour support at all times. Multi-agency links are made whenever necessary. The school currently caters for small munbers of children who have Down's syndrome, Asperger's syndrome, ADHD, dyspraxia and autism. The headteacher has recently returned from a two term secondment as acting headteacher at a neighbouring special school.

ST ANDREW'S SCHOOL

Lower Common, East Runton, Cromer, Norfolk, NR27 9PG

Tel: 01263 511 727
Fax: 01263 511 727

• Mixed; Day Pupils • Age: 7 to 12 • School status: Independent

SEN provision

Detail:
Centre of excellence for:
 Mild: ASP; AUT; ADD;
 Moderate: ASP; AUT
Now provide for in school:
 Mild: ADHD; DYSC; DYSL; DYSP; CP;
 Moderate: ADD; ADHD; MLD; DYSC; DYSL; DYSP;
 Severe: DYSC; DYSL; DYSP;
 Others: SPD; OCD; ODD; TIC; EAL; Sp&LD

Summary: We provide a happy, secure environment in which our pupils are valued as individuals and helped to grow academically, emotionally and socially. We provide individual work programmes for each pupil in the TEACCH system. We also provide physical therapy to improve motor co-ordination, language therapy to improve language skills and special social skills and life skills programmes.

ST ANNE'S ROMAN CATHOLIC HIGH SCHOOL, STOCKPORT

Glenfield Road, Heaton Chapel, Stockport, Cheshire, SK4 2QP

Tel: 01614 328 162
Fax: 01614 431 105
Email: headteacher@st-annes.stockport.sch.uk
Website: www.st-annes.stockport.sch.uk

• Pupils: 770 Mixed; Day Pupils • Age: 11 to 16
• Religion: Roman Catholic • School status: State

SEN provision

Detail:
Experience of:
 Mild: ASP; ADD; ADHD; DYSL; DYSP; HI; VI;
 Moderate: ASP; ADD; ADHD; EBD; DYSL; DYSP; HI; VI;
 Severe: VI;
 Others: SPD; CD; ODD; TIC; Sp&LD

Summary: The SEN department is small but effective. The SENCo teaches small groups for literacy and specific learning difficulties. We have an SEN maths teacher who has a third of her timetable in SEN and two thirds in mainstream maths. We have one classroom assistant working with pupils at stage School Action and School Action Plus. The other three classroom assistants currently working in the school work with statemented pupils.

We have one full-time teacher from the learning support service who teaches pupils with statements or at stage School Action Plus. Pupils are withdrawn from lessons to access this teaching. Teaching may be on an individual basis or in very small groups. This level of withdrawal teaching is, we believe, our great strength.

ST ANNE'S ROMAN CATHOLIC VOLUNTARY AIDED PRIMARY SCHOOL

Hylton Road, Pennywell, Sunderland, Tyne and Wear, SR4 9AA

Tel: 01915 536 860
Fax: 01915 536 862
Email: st.annes.primary@schools.sunderland.gov.uk

• Pupils: 204 Mixed; Day Pupils • Age: 5 to 11
• Religion: Roman Catholic • School status: State

SEN provision

Detail:
Now provide for in school:
 Mild: ASP; AUT; EBD; DYSL; CP;
 Moderate: EBD; MLD
Experience of:
 Mild: ADD; ADHD;

Moderate: ASP; AUT;
Others: Sp&LD

Summary: All pupils are catered for at their individual levels throughout the school, for academic, emotional and behavioural reasons. All children have individual targets to achieve and are given additional support whenever required. Some children work in small groups with an additional adult to ensure progress. Targets are sent home so parents are aware of what their child is aiming for. Parental support has proved beneficial in the past and we strive to maintain the link between school and home. Assessment is a crucial part of identifying the individual needs of the child. The children are regularly assessed throughout the year by commercially produced tests and by teacher assessments which we find is vitally important to the children's progress.

St Asaph - Esgob Morgan Junior School

Ffordd Siarl, Ashley Court, St Asaph, Denbighshire, LL17 0PT

Tel: 01745 583 690
Fax: 01745 583 690
Email: esgob.morgan@denbighshire.gov.uk
• Pupils: 135 Mixed; Day Pupils • Age: 7 to 11
• School status: State

SEN provision

Detail:
Now provide for in school:
Mild: DYSL; DYSP;
Moderate: MLD; DYSL; DYSP;
Others: EAL
Experience of:
Mild: DYSC; SpLD;
Moderate: DYSC; SpLD;
Severe: DYSC; DYSL; DYSP; SpLD;
Others: PMLD; SLD; Sp&LD

Summary: The aim of the school is to develop each individual to his/her fullest potential. Education provision is available to encompass those pupils with learning difficulties. Extra support for such children is offered once a week by a specialist teacher. Pupils are either withdrawn or given extra support in class. There is specialist one-to-one support, weekly, for pupils with a statement. Children's ability levels are recognised as being in line with the new Code of Practice. Accordingly, individual work programmes are set up to meet the needs of each child. All parents are notified if their child is on a specific stage and requires extra support. Regular monitoring of pupils with learning difficulties is carried out at the end of each term, and meetings are arranged with parents to discuss progress.

St Aubyns School

76 High Street, Rottingdean, Brighton, East Sussex, BN2 7JN

Tel: 01273 302 170
Fax: 01273 309314
Email: office@staubyns-school.org.uk
Website: www.staubynsschoolbrighton.co.uk
• Pupils: 200 Mixed; Takes boarders • Age: 4 to 13
• Religion: Church of England • School status: Independent

SEN provision

Detail:
Now provide for in school:
Mild: DYSC; DYSL; DYSP;
Moderate: DYSL; DYSP;
Severe: DYSL;
Others: EAL
Experience of:
Mild: ADD; ADHD; EBD; VI;
Moderate: EBD; DYSC;
Severe: DYSP;
Others: ODD; Sp&LD; PD

Summary: Special needs provision here comes as part of the Learning Plus programme, which assesses, monitors and provides for individual needs throughout the school. We offer in-class support in key areas, as well as individual tuition to develop the strengths and abilities with which children can succeed. We are experienced in helping those with specific learning difficulties such as dyslexia, dyspraxia or dyscalculia, offering customised tuition based on multi-sensory techniques. We also support children for whom English is an additional language as well as those who might, for whatever reason, need a short-term boost to their learning. Progress is very carefully monitored, with all staff playing an active role in ensuring that differentiated teaching – for all levels on the ability spectrum – is effective in meeting different learning needs.

Our aim is to provide confident, happy and successful learning for all pupils here, and we pride ourselves on the level to which individual needs are both recognised and supported.

St Augustine's Catholic Primary School

Hollis Lane, off Beehive Hill, Kenilworth, Warwickshire, CV8 2JY

Tel: 01926 852 943
Fax: 01926 857 073
Email: admin@3541.wgfl.net
• Pupils: 223 Mixed; Day Pupils • Age: 4 to 11
• Religion: Roman Catholic • School status: State

SEN provision

Summary: Our fundamental belief is that all children are special and have individual needs. Our aim is to meet those needs so that each child can develop their potential as a whole person, emotionally, spiritually, socially, physically and intellectually. We plan to develop a love of learning and to maximise self-esteem by providing a secure, stimulating learning environment and an appropriate programme of learning for each child. Constant monitoring by the staff team and close co-operation with parents and support services help us in this.

We call on the services of LABSS, DISCS, SALY and Ed Psych Dept, where necessary and children are supported in school, in the classroom, in small groups and occasionally one-to-one, by our teachers and TAs using a wide range of resources. We investigate new initiatives and endeavour to use them if appropriate for our children. For example we have introduced a daily exercise programme for children with co-ordination difficulties and speech and language groups to encourage good communication skills.

Over recent years we have successfully worked with several children with Asperger's syndrome and ADHD as well as general learning difficulties. We also have facilities and staff willing to support children with physical disabilities.

All children in school are encouraged to take part in sport and extra curricular activities.

St Augustine's C of E Primary School

Vicarage Lane, Scaynes Hill, Haywards Heath, West Sussex, RH17 7PB

Tel: 01444 831 371
Fax: 01444 831 078
Email: office@st-augustines.w-sussex.sch.uk
Website: www.st-augustines.w-sussex.sch.uk
• Pupils: 85 Mixed; Day Pupils • Age: 4 to 11
• Religion: Church of England • School status: State

SEN provision

Detail:
Now provide for in school:
- Mild: AUT; ADD; DYSC; SpLD;
- Moderate: MLD; SpLD;
- Severe: SpLD;
- Others: PMLD; SLD

Experience of:
- Mild: ASP

Summary: Our aim is to provide the best education we can for all children. Obviously some children will need more support than others; some will need support for a short time in specific areas, others will need more intensive and/or long term support for a variety for academic, pastoral and physical needs. We try to identify children who need support early in their time with us. Support may range from differentiated work in class to additional support in class to specific work outside of the class room. We use published schemes like the Early Literacy Strategy, Further Literacy Strategy, Springboard Maths programmes as well as less formalised, child specific support. We review all children's progress half termly and write IEPs twice a year. Parents are invited into school twice a year to discuss their child's IEP with the headteacher who is our SENCo. We are an inclusive school that strives to provide the best educational experience for all the children in our care.

St Bede's Catholic College

Long Cross, Lawrence Weston, Bristol, BS11 0SU

Tel: 0117 377 2200
Fax: 0117 377 2201
Email: st_bedes_s@bristol-city.gov.uk
Website: www.stbedescatholicschool.org.uk

• Pupils: 846 Mixed; Day Pupils • Age: 11 to 16
• Religion: Roman Catholic • School status: State

SEN provision

Detail:
Experience of:
Mild: ASP; AUT; ADD; ADHD; EBD; DYSC; DYSL; HI; CP;
Moderate: MLD

Summary: St Bede's is an 11-16 comprehensive college with students across the full ability range. We have had many successes with students who came to us with special needs. However, we would always wish to know details of the child's needs before we would claim to be able to provide for them. We have excellent links with Kingsweston Special School and have joint provision arrangements for some youngsters.

St Bernadette's Catholic Primary School

Narrow Lane, Brownhills, Walsall, West Midlands, WS8 6HX

Tel: 01543 452 921
Fax: 01543 452 921
Email: postbox@stbernadette.walsall.sch.uk
Website: www.stbernadette.walsall.sch.uk/

• Pupils: 192 Mixed; Day Pupils • Age: 3 to 11
• Religion: Roman Catholic • School status: State

SEN provision

Detail:
Now provide for in school:
Mild: ASP; ADD; ADHD; DYSC; DYSL;
Moderate: ASP; MLD; DYSC; DYSL;
Severe: DYSL;
Others: SPD; EAL
Experience of:
Mild: AUT; EBD; DYSP; CP;
Moderate: EBD; DYSP; CP;
Severe: ASP;
Others: AUT(other); CD; OCD; Epi; PD

Summary: We are a mainstream Catholic primary school who strive to include pupils with identified special needs into all areas of our curriculum. We currently have children with dyslexia, ASD and minor physical difficulties in our school. These are supported through differentiation of the curriculum and by support from learning support assistants. We have a disabled toilet and an entrance through which we have wheelchair access.

St Bernard's Catholic High School

Rating Lane, Barrow-in-Furness, Cumbria, LA13 9LE

Tel: 01229 89 4620
Fax: 01229 89 4622
Email: admin@st-bernards.cumbria.sch.uk
Website: www.st-bernards.cumbria.sch.uk

• Pupils: 847 Mixed; Day Pupils • Age: 11 to 16
• Religion: Roman Catholic • School status: State

SEN provision

Detail:
Now provide for in school:
Mild: ASP; AUT; ADD; ADHD; EBD; DYSC; DYSL; DYSP; HI;
Moderate: ASP; AUT; ADD; ADHD; EBD; MLD; DYSL; DYSP; HI;
Severe: ASP; ADD; ADHD; EBD; DYSL;
Others: SLD; Sp&LD; DEL; Epi; Eat

Experience of:
Mild: VI; CP;
Moderate: DYSC; VI;
Severe: DYSC; HI;
Others: SPD; OCD; ODD; TIC

Summary: At St Bernard's we try to meet pupils' individual needs. If you have a child with special needs and are considering St Bernard's, please make an appointment to visit the learning support department and speak to the SENCo about the type of provision that could be arranged.

St David's Roman Catholic Technology College

St Davids Way, Acklam, Middlesbrough, TS5 7EY

Tel: 01642 298 100
Fax: 01642 298 101
Email: stdavidsrcschool@middlesbrough.gov.uk
Website: www.stdavidrc.com

• Pupils: 955 Mixed; Day Pupils • Age: 11 to 16
• Religion: Roman Catholic • School status: State

SEN provision

Detail:
Centre of excellence for:
Mild: DYSL;
Moderate: MLD; DYSL
Now provide for in school:
Mild: ASP; AUT; ADD; ADHD; HI;
Others: SPD; EAL; Sp&LD; DEL
Experience of:
Mild: EBD; DS; DYSC; DYSP; SpLD; VI;
Moderate: ADD; ADHD; EBD; DYSC; DYSP; SpLD; HI;
Others: OCD; GEN; MSI; Epi; Eat

Summary: At St David's we believe that every child is important and try to provide as much help and support as we possibly can. We offer a variety of support depending upon the child's needs and try to work alongside parents to help and support their children. We have a growing department with all teaching assistants having regular training to develop and learn new skills. This is important to help pupils with a variety of needs. Pupils registered as having special educational needs receive in-class support and additional input through PLUS+ (pupil learning support service) and additional agencies such as learning and behaviour support, learning mentors.

In PLUS+ pupils can benefit from reading, spelling and comprehension workshops in year 7, 8 and 9 if necessary. We also hold pupil/ parent workshops for parents of year 7 pupils. This is to involve parents and show how we help and support the children. In years 10 and 11 we offer study and revision workshops to help pupils plan for examinations.

We offer individual appointments for children with more complex needs and refer to a number of agencies and professionals such as speech and language, English as an Additional Language, educational psychologist and complementary education.

St David's School

23/25 Woodcote Valley Road, Purley, Surrey, CR8 3AL

Tel: 020 8660 0723
Fax: 020 8645 0426
Email: office@stdavidsschool.co.uk
Website: www.stdavidsschool.co.uk

• Pupils: 165 Mixed; Day Pupils • Age: 3 to 11
• Religion: Church of England • School status: Independent

SEN provision

Detail:
Now provide for in school:
Mild: ASP; DYSL; DYSP;
Moderate: DYSL; DYSP
Experience of:
Mild: AUT; ADD; ADHD; EBD; DYSC; VI;
Moderate: ASP; DYSC; VI;
Severe: DYSL; DYSP; VI;
Others: CD; EAL; Sp&LD

Summary: As a non-selective school the children usually join us at the age of three and our educational provision therefore embraces children's needs across the spectrum. Specialist tutors are available for dyslexic and dyspraxic children. Should more specific disabilities be evident then appropriate support would be requested from outside sources and provision made within the restrictions of the building, practical facilities and the effects on the welfare and education of the other children.

St Edmund of Canterbury Catholic High School

Lordens Road, Liverpool, Merseyside, L14 8UD

Tel: 0151 489 3944/5911
Fax: 0151 4898 3058
Email: stedmund.canterbury.de@knowsley.gov.uk

• Pupils: 705 Mixed; Day Pupils • Age: 11 to 16
• Religion: Roman Catholic • School status: State

SEN provision

Detail:
Now provide for in school:
Mild: ASP; AUT; ADD; ADHD; EBD; DYSC; DYSL; DYSP; HI; VI; CP;
Moderate: ASP; ADD; ADHD; EBD; MLD; DYSC; DYSL; DYSP; HI;
Others: CD; OCD; ODD; GEN; EAL; Sp&LD; DEL; Epi; Eat

Summary: St Edmund of Canterbury High School has an extremely strong and effective SEN department which is managed by Miss C Smith who is responsible for co-ordinating provision at Key Stage 3 and 4. We support the Knowsley LEA SEN policy with its inclusive aim of promoting the presence, participation, and achievement of students with special educational needs and/or disabilities. We have clear policies for inclusion, equal opportunities and behaviour.

The department consists of, one SENCo, one assistant headteacher (line manager), one SEN consultant, one behaviour improvement manager (AHT), 3 part-time specialist support staff to assist students with learning difficulties, two first-aiders, one inclusion manager, three learning mentors, two student support workers and 14 teaching assistants. All of our staff are given advice regarding students' individual difficulties and methods in helping them to overcome their problems.

We have excellent links with outside agencies, including, Child and Adult Mental Health, Behaviour and Education Support Team, Outreach workers, Youth Offending Team, Social Services, National Health Service, Local Primary Schools, and Child Guidance. We also believe that parental involvment is the most important partnership that we could build.

Our objectives are;

- to help each student to learn, appreciate and value his/her own strengths.
- to help each child develop their full potential.
- to provide a broad and balanced curriculum, suitably differentiated to meet individual need.
- to ensure that each student feels equally valued within the school community and that positive achievements are recognised and rewarded.
- to do all that we can to make sure that each child leaves school with the core skills (such as literacy, numeracy and social independence) which she/he will need in adult life.
- that our focus be on early intervention and identification.

St Edmund's Church of England Girls' School and Sports College

Church Road, Laverstock, Salisbury, Wiltshire, SP1 1RD

Tel: 01722 328 565
Fax: 01722 421 391
Email: admin@stedmunds.rmplc.co.uk
Website: www.st-edmundsgirls.wilts.sch.uk

• Pupils: 789 Girls; Day Pupils • Age: 11 to 16
• Religion: Church of England • School status: State

SEN provision

Detail:
Now provide for in school:
Mild: ADD; ADHD; EBD; DYSL; HI; VI;
Moderate: ADD; EBD; MLD; DYSL; HI;
Severe: EBD; DYSL;
Others: ODD; TIC; EAL; Sp&LD; Epi; PD; Eat
Experience of:
Mild: ASP; AUT; DYSC; DYSP;
Moderate: ASP; ADHD; DYSC; DYSP; VI;

Severe: DYSC; DYSP;
Others: OCD; DEL

Summary: We are an inclusive school and strive to ensure that all students feel that they are supported in reaching their full potential.

We are a named SpLD unit with places for six statemented students, two members of staff are currently undertaking courses in SpLD. We also have a students' support area which is open to all. Some SpLD students are withdrawn from a small number of classes for specific support and guidance regarding literacy. In Key Stage 3 some students are disapplied from one MFL in order to work on basic literacy and numeracy skills and in Key Stage 4 some students take learning support as an option. These groups have been set up in order to ensure the students receive the support they need without having to catch up on work missed when withdrawn from an occasional lessons.

Most of our support is carried out in the classroom with subject specialist teaching assistants. Teaching assistants sometimes withdraw small groups of students from the class to work on the subject/topic being studied in a different way with a higher adult:student ratio. Teaching assistants and teachers work closely together.

There are opportunities for students to access support with homework and to attend small group sessions in order to improve skills such as fine and gross motor, social skills, sequencing and planning etc.

St Gregory's Catholic Comprehensive School

Reynolds Lane, Tunbridge Wells, Kent, TN4 9XL

Tel: 01892 527 444
Fax: 01892 546 621
Email: office@sgschool.org.uk
Website: www.sgschool.org.uk
• Pupils: 981 Mixed; Day Pupils • Age: 11 to 18
• Religion: Roman Catholic • School status: State

SEN provision

Detail:
Now provide for in school:
Mild: ASP; AUT; EBD; DYSC; DYSL; DYSP; HI;
Moderate: ASP; AUT; EBD; DYSC; DYSL; DYSP; HI;
Severe: HI;
Others: SPD
Experience of:
Mild: ADD; ADHD; DS; CP;
Moderate: ADD; ADHD; DS; MLD; VI; CP;
Others: TIC; Sp&LD; Epi

Summary: St Gregory's is pleased to host the West Kent Hearing Impaired Resource, in partnership with Kent Local Education Authority. A full-time teacher of the deaf and teaching assistants support students in and out of lessons. This provision is part of our highly-acclaimed AEN provision, which comprises SEN, G&T, Ethnic Minorities, EAL and Traveller provision, an Inclusion Unit and oversight of Equal Opportunities. Janet Cooke, AEN co-ordinator, leads a dedicated team of professionals who support and extend students' learning in and beyond the normal learning environment. The school's investment in IT, as a specialist school in maths and computing, has enabled access to computers around the school, to help individual students with their learning.

St Hild's Church of England Voluntary Aided School

King Oswy Drive, West View, Hartlepool, TS24 9PB

Tel: 01429 273 041
Fax: 01429 232 235
• Pupils: 859 Mixed; Day Pupils • Age: 11 to 16
• School status: State

SEN provision

Detail:
Centre of excellence for:
Mild: ADD; ADHD; EBD;
Moderate: MLD
Now provide for in school:
Mild: ASP;
Moderate: ASP
Experience of:
Mild: AUT; DYSC; DYSL; DYSP; SpLD; HI; VI;
Moderate: ADD; ADHD; EBD; DYSC; DYSL; DYSP; SpLD; HI; VI;

Severe: ADD; ADHD; DYSC; DYSL; DYSP; SpLD;
Others: CD; OCD; ODD; TIC; EAL; Sp&LD; DEL; Epi; PD; Eat

Summary: A suite of rooms is dedicated to SEN, the St Christopher Centre. We are an inclusive school and try to cater for pupils with SEN in an individual way. We are proud of the achievements of our SEN pupils (all six of our statemented pupils achieved at least two GCSEs in 2005). We have 100 per cent disabled access and one of our teaching assistants is a wheelchair user. We deliver a Key Stage 2/3 transfer programme which enables pupils with learning difficulties to access mainstream secondary education in a structured and supportive way.

St Ives School

Three Gates Lane, Haslemere, Surrey, GU27 2ES

Tel: 01428 643 734
Fax: 01428 644 788
Email: admin@stiveshaslemere.com
Website: www.stiveshaslemere.com
• Pupils: 140 Girls; Day Pupils • Age: 3 to 11
• School status: Independent

SEN provision

Detail:

Now provide for in school:
Mild: DYSC; DYSL;
Moderate: MLD; DYSC; DYSL;
Others: Sp&LD; Eat
Experience of:
Mild: DYSP;
Moderate: DYSP

Summary: Children requiring any degree of learning support at St Ives school are treated sensitively, sympathetically and with respect. Girls with mild to moderate learning difficulties are given strategies and study skills and there is opportunity for formal and informal assessments. Advice and recommendations from educational psychologist reports are acknowledged and communicated to all relevant staff through the child's individual education plan. Extra support is provided for any girl whenever it is felt necessary whilst she is at St Ives and this will continue for as long as it is required. Learning support is tailored to suit the individual need. The child may receive one-to-one withdrawn support, support within a small group either in or out of the class whichever is felt most appropriate and beneficial. We have a successful home/school link and treat teaching and learning as a partnership by informing parents on progress through meetings, written reports and sharing IEP reviews. The school's experienced and well informed SENCo has attended many courses on dyslexia and dyscalculia and works with every class at least once a week and therefore sees all pupils working in situ and can thus verify and observe any child giving cause for concern. The school also offers sessions of Brain Gym. Help and advice is offered to students and parents regarding the selection of senior schools. We have a good partnership with learning support staff at local senior schools which allows us to provide them with necessary information. We pride ourselves at St Ives at being aware of the Code of Practice for SEN and follow a policy which will entitle all girls to access a balanced and wide curriculum with confidence.

St James' School

22 Bargate, Grimsby, DN34 4SY

Tel: 01472 503 260
Fax: 01472 503 275
Email: enquiries@saintjamesschool.co.uk
Website: www.saintjamesschool.freeserve.co.uk
• Pupils: 221 Mixed; Takes boarders • Age: 2 to 18
• School status: Independent

SEN provision

Detail:

Now provide for in school:
Mild: ASP; ADD; DYSC; DYSL; DYSP;
Moderate: ASP; ADD; MLD; DYSC; DYSL;
Severe: DYSL;
Others: EAL; DEL; Epi

Summary: The following is a brief message from Mrs Bernice Smith, special educational needs co-ordinator (SENCo), describing the provision for special needs students at St James' School.

The main learning support unit is in The Old Rectory

– a part of St James' School – in a large classroom with very pleasant views. A further room has recently been refurbished in the Preparatory Department. Staff are experienced and sympathetic tutors working with students from years 1 to 11.

Parents may request learning support lessons prior to entry to the school; a class teacher who feels a child shows cause for concern may also seek such support.

Initially students visit the unit for a screening test (for language skills disorders or dyscalculia); parents are then informed of the findings. As a result of this a further test at the Dyslexia Institute may be recommended. The student could then begin a programme of learning support. (At present the fee for this is £12.50 for 30 minutes).

An individual education programme (IEP) is then written for the student setting realistic targets. A fresh multisensory approach is used to help the student overcome any learning differences. Strategies for self help are taught; strengths and weaknesses are carefully monitored and reports are issued to parents twice a year.

A formal review is held once a year when parents, class/subject tutors, the student and any appropriate outside agencies are invited to attend. Progress is discussed with the student and new targets are set.

Parents are also invited to visit the learning support unit on any day after 3:15pm to meet the SENCo and discuss any concerns they may have. Liason between home and school is particularly important for those students who suffer from such problems as dyslexia, dyspraxia, Asperger's disorder and attention deficit syndrome; building confidence and raising self esteem is a vital part of each child's programme.

There is also a close liason with the headteacher, departmental heads and other members of St. James' staff – all of whom receive copies of IEPs with useful classroom strategies to ensure the best possible support for the students.

St John the Baptist Catholic Comprehensive School, Woking

Elmbridge Lane, Kingfield, Woking, Surrey, GU22 9AL

Tel: 01483 729 343

Fax: 01483 727 578

Email: info@sjb.surrey.sch.uk

Website: www.sjb.surrey.sch.uk

• Pupils: 1039 Mixed; Day Pupils • Age: 11 to 18

• Religion: Roman Catholic • School status: State

SEN provision

Detail:

Now provide for in school:

Mild: ASP; AUT; ADD; ADHD; DYSC; DYSL; DYSP; HI; CP;

Moderate: ASP; ADD; EBD; MLD; DYSC; DYSL; SpLD; HI;

Severe: DYSL;

Others: SPD; CD; TIC; EAL; Sp&LD; Epi; Eat

Experience of:

Mild: DS; VI;

Moderate: ADHD; DS; DYSP;

Severe: DYSC; HI;

Others: OCD; ODD

Summary: All our students are special and all are expected to achieve their best. Students that have SEN are offered support in various ways depending on individual needs. Some are supported in class, or withdrawn from MFL for small group work. All our students take GCSEs, some undertake the ASDAN vocational qualification to a bronze or silver level. The school has an excellent pastoral system reinforced by a strong Catholic ethos.

St John's Catholic School for the Deaf (Boston Spa)

Church Street, Boston Spa, Wetherby, West Yorkshire, LS23 6DF

Tel: 01937 842 144
Fax: 01937 541 471
• Pupils: 99 Mixed; Takes boarders • Age: 3 to 19
• School status: State

SEN provision

Detail:
Now provide for in school:
Mild: ADD;
Moderate: DYSP; CP;
Severe: DYSP;
Others: Epi
Experience of:
Mild: AUT;
Moderate: AUT; MLD; DYSL

Summary: St John's is a residential and day school for pupils aged from 3 to 19 years of age. As an oral school, great emphasis is placed on developing spoken language. Our multi-disciplinary team comprises qualified teachers of the deaf, five speech and language therapists, audiologist and residential care staff. Pupils are taught in small class groups in acoustically treated classrooms using a group hearing system which has been digitally programmed to their particular hearing loss. The school has Beacon School status.

St Joseph's in the Park

The Park, Hertingfordbury, Hertford, Hertfordshire, SG14 2LX

Tel: 01992 581 378
Fax: 01992 505 202
Email: admin@stjosephsinthepark.co.uk
Website: www.stjosephsinthepark.co.uk
• Pupils: 180 Mixed; Day Pupils • Age: 2 to 11
• School status: Independent

SEN provision

Detail:
Centre of excellence for:
Mild: DYSC; DYSL; DYSP; SpLD;
Moderate: DYSL;
Severe: DYSL
Experience of:
Mild: ADD; ADHD

Summary: We aim to meet the needs of children at either end of the special educational needs spectrum. We withdraw individuals and small groups of children for both extension work and for consolidation and over learning.

Our Woodlands class accommodates up to 12 Key Stage 2 children who are dyslexic or have other specific learning difficulties. These children are taught, with a ratio of one trained member of staff to four children, every morning for English and maths. They are fully integrated into the main school for all other subjects.

St Joseph's School

Amlets Lane, Cranleigh, Surrey, GU6 7DH

Tel: 01483 272 449
Fax: 01483 276 003
Email: office@st-josephscranleigh.surrey.sch.uk
• Pupils: 69 Mixed; Takes boarders • Age: 7 to 19
• Religion: Roman Catholic • School status: State

SEN provision

Detail:
Now provide for in school:
Mild: AUT; DS; DYSP;
Moderate: AUT; DS; MLD; DYSP;
Severe: ASP; AUT; DS; DYSP;
Others: AUT(other); FRX; GEN; SLD; Sp&LD
Experience of:
Mild: ADHD;
Moderate: ADHD;
Severe: ADHD;
Others: SPD; Epi

Summary: School caters for students with MLD/SLD and those on the autistic spectrum. It also specialises in the development of learners with communication difficulties. Some learners have additional medical needs such as controlled epilepsy, asthma and allergies.

Conditions include: ADHD, ASD, Fragile X, Downs, Williams, dyspraxia.

ST KATHARINE'S CHURCH OF ENGLAND PRIMARY SCHOOL

Bridgwater Rd, Lulsgate, Felton, Bristol, BS40 9UU

Tel: 01275 472 762
Fax: 01275 472 762
Email: stkatharines.pri@n-somerset.gov.uk

• Pupils: 83 Mixed; Day Pupils • Age: 4 to 11
• Religion: Church of England • School status: State

SEN provision

Detail:
Experience of:
- Mild: AUT; ADD; EBD; DYSC; DYSL; DYSP; CP;
- Moderate: AUT; ADD; EBD; MLD; DYSL; DYSP;
- Severe: AUT; EBD; DYSL; DYSP;
- Others: CD; OCD; ODD; TIC; Sp&LD; Eat

Summary: St Katharine's C of E Primary School is a small rural primary school, which at present is sited in old Victorian buildings. A new school is being planned in the village of Felton, to open in 2006. Until that time the premises are not suitable for physically disabled people. The site is split level and the steps are stone and quite steep. The SEN policy contains a strong inclusive philosophy but we are constrained by the physical elements of the site. The school has created a special room for pupils to use with our SEN teaching assistant. 'The Den' is a very special classroom that is valued by staff, pupils and parents. It enables us to provide support for pupils both individually and in small groups. The teaching assistant is highly qualified and respected by all members of the school community. All staff work together to identify pupils with special needs as early as possible to ensure support is put in place. The Governor for SEN meets regularly with staff to maintain an overview of the quality of the provision.

SAINT LAWRENCE CHURCH OF ENGLAND PRIMARY SCHOOL

Amery Hill, Alton, Hampshire, GU34 2BY

Tel: 01420 84 400
Fax: 01420 82 148
Email: adminoffice@st-lawrence.hants.sch.uk
Website: www.schools.hants.org.uk/st-lawrence-primary/

• Pupils: 180 Mixed; Day Pupils • Age: 4 to 11
• Religion: Church of England • School status: State

SEN provision

Detail:
Now provide for in school:
- Mild: ASP; ADD; ADHD; EBD; DYSL; DYSP; HI;
- Moderate: ASP; ADD; ADHD; EBD; MLD; DYSL; HI;
- Severe: ADD; ADHD; EBD;
- Others: SPD; CD; ODD; EAL; Sp&LD

Experience of:
- Mild: DS;
- Moderate: DS;
- Others: GEN

Summary: Our school aims clearly identify our firm commitment to the inclusion of all children to our school: 'As a Church school, we will work together to develop qualities of spirit, feeling, imagination, a sense of beauty and an appreciation of human achievements and endeavour. We will encourage respect for religious and moral values and help pupils to acquire a reasoned set of attitudes, values and beliefs. Our school will increasingly take a central and visible part in the community particularly for our inclusive practice which will become an example for others to follow'. Our headteacher is Chair of Heading for Inclusion whose aim is to ensure that school leaders share good practice and expertise in this area. Our SENCo has an excellent past record in including children with a wide range of special needs ranging from Asperger's to neurofibromatosis.

ST LAWRENCE COLLEGE

College Road, Ramsgate, Kent, CT11 7AE

Tel: 01843 572931
Fax: 01843 572917
Email: ah@slcuk.com
Website: www.slcuk.com

• Pupils: 433 Mixed; Takes boarders • Age: 3 to 18
• Religion: CofE/Christian • School status: Independent

SEN provision

Detail:
Now provide for in school:
Mild: ASP; ADD; ADHD; DYSC; DYSL; DYSP;
Others: EAL
Experience of:
Mild: EBD; HI; VI;
Moderate: MLD; DYSL

Summary: SEN provision is given by a dedicated unit that has close links with all subject departments. Children with SEN attend support lessons in the unit, which is located in the main teaching block, at times and frequencies that meet their individual needs. All teaching staff have full details of the children with SEN, together with strategies that help with each individual in the classroom situation. The main aim is to maximise the learning potential of each individual so that they achieve the highest academic standards of which they are capable.

ST MARY'S CATHOLIC PRIMARY SCHOOL, MARNHULL

Old Mill Lane, Marnhull, Sturminster Newton, Dorset, DT10 1JX

Tel: 01258 820 417
Fax: 01258 820 417
Email: office@stmarymarnhull.dorset.sch.uk
Website: www.stmarymarnhull.dorset.sch.uk

• Pupils: 150 Mixed; Day Pupils • Age: 4 to 11
• Religion: Roman Catholic • School status: State

SEN provision

Detail:
Now provide for in school:
Mild: ASP; AUT; ADD; DYSL; DYSP;
Moderate: ASP; AUT; ADD; MLD; DYSL; DYSP;
Severe: DYSL;
Others: Sp&LD
Experience of:
Mild: EBD; DYSC;
Moderate: DYSC; CP;
Severe: ASP;
Others: EAL; Epi; PD; Eat

Summary: St Mary's has the advantage of being a fairly small school with class sizes less than 30. Children identified with an additional learning requirement are given extra support through group occupational therapy sessions, individual speech and language therapy and individual specialist dyslexia tutoring. For those who do not require such a specialist level of support, small groups are tutored outside the classroom for both numeracy and literacy.

ST MARY'S ISLAND CHURCH OF ENGLAND (AIDED) PRIMARY SCHOOL

Island Way West, St Mary's Island, Chatham, Kent, ME4 3ST

Tel: 01634 891 050
Fax: 01634 890 981
Email: office@st-marys-island.medway.sch.uk
Website: www.st-marys-island.medway.sch.uk

• Pupils: 293 Mixed; Day Pupils • Age: 4 to 11
• Religion: Church of England • School status: State

SEN provision

Summary: At St Mary's Island School we aim to meet the needs of all children especially those who experience difficulties in learning. We have a dedicated staff of teachers and teaching assistants who plan and work together inclusively. Children who experience difficulties in learning are assessed and supported within the classroom by teachers and teaching assistants. Parents are kept informed at all stages. Should extra help be needed, outside agencies such as educational psychologist, learning support service, speech and language therapist, health professionals etc can be contacted and brought into school. The school also offers Social Use of Language programme (SULP) for both infants and juniors. Speech and language programmes are implemented during the school day for children who need this intervention. Early additional and further literacy support groups (ELS, ALS and FLS) Springboard mathematics groups and extra phonic groups are also in place for children who experience difficulties.

St Mary's School

Packhorse Road, Gerrards Cross, Buckinghamshire, SL9 8JQ

Tel: 01753 883 370
Fax: 01753 890 966
Email: headmistress@stmarys-gx.org
Website: www.stmarys-gx.org

• Pupils: 298 Girls; Day Pupils • Age: 3 to 18
• School status: Independent

SEN provision

Detail:
Now provide for in school:
- Mild: DYSC; DYSL; DYSP; VI;
- Moderate: MLD; DYSL; HI; VI; CP

Experience of:
- Mild: EBD;
- Others: CD; EAL; Epi

Summary: St Mary's aims to support girls with special educational needs to achieve their potential, and to boost their confidence and self esteem. A learning support teacher offers guidance to girls who have sought help themselves, or have been recommended for such help by parents, teachers or educational psychologists. This teacher acts as a channel for communication between these parties, as well as providing specific help. It may take the form of class support, or individual or group sessions covering spelling or a wide range of study skills including organisation skills, time management, question analysis and planning an answer, effective reading and notetaking advice, revision and examination techniques, and counselling.

St Mary's School

5 Pottergate, Lincoln, Lincolnshire, LN2 1PH

Tel: 01522 524 622
Fax: 01522 543 637
Email: office@st-marys-prep.lincs.sch.uk
Website: www.stmarysprep.co.uk

• Pupils: 230 Mixed; Day Pupils • Age: 2 to 11
• School status: Independent

SEN provision

Summary: St Mary's Prep School offers individual help to children with special educational needs through direct one-to-one teaching from the SEN co-ordinator. Further to this children placed on the SEN register have specific programmes of work which are set out in the IEPs and which are delivered through group/class sessions. Parents receive termly IEPs and children are also encouraged to write their own IEPs. A cycle of reviews is well established when parents are invited to discuss their child's progress. St Mary's accommodates a range of specific learning difficulties; dyspraxia, dyslexia, cerebral palsy and hearing impairments.

The St Michael Steiner School

5 Merton Road, Wandsworth, London, SW18 5ST

Tel: 020 8870 0500
Email: stmichaelsteiner@dsl.pipex.com
Website: www.stmichaelsteiner.wandsworth.sch.uk

• Mixed; Day Pupils • Age: 3 to 12 • School status: Independent

SEN provision

Detail:
Now provide for in school:
- Mild: DYSC; DYSL; DYSP;
- Moderate: MLD; DYSC; DYSL; DYSP;
- Severe: DYSC; DYSL

Experience of:
- Mild: AUT; ADD; ADHD; EBD;
- Moderate: EBD;
- Others: TIC; SLD; EAL; Sp&LD

Summary: The basis of Steiner Waldorf education is observation of the child. By bringing subjects to children at the right time and by using methods which are appropriate for them at each stage of development, many common difficulties which are experienced by children can be avoided. In this sense, although we are not a special school, our whole approach is curative. However, some children still have specific difficulties, especially if they have joined the school later. We aim to meet these children's needs with a wide range of strategies including music, drama, painting, Eurythmy Therapy (a special kind of movement), speech, singing, sewing, knitting, form drawing and games. Much of this work is undertaken in the whole class as part of the regular curriculum (Please refer to our website for more information about the structure of our curriculum) but we have limited resources to offer one-to-one sessions for a few children as well. We also use more conventional strategies to help with literacy and numeracy where appropriate, but always take a holistic approach. We have a school doctor who prescribes therapies and suggests ways of working with children (Please refer to our website for information about Anthroposophical medicine). Although we have children with statements of special needs in the school, funds have only ever been granted to the school in the case of one child. Apart from contributions from parents, we have no other source of income for special needs and so we cannot provide for as many children as we would like.

ST NICHOLAS SCHOOL

Malmesbury Road, Chippenham, Wiltshire, SN15 1QF

Tel: 01249 650 435

Fax: 01249 447 033

Email: admin@st-nicholas.wilts.sch.uk

• Pupils: 67 Mixed; Day Pupils • Age: 2 to 19

• Religion: Non-denominational • School status: State

SEN provision

Detail:

Now provide for in school:

- Mild: HI; VI; CP;
- Moderate: HI; VI; CP;
- Severe: HI; VI; CP;
- Others: DEL; Epi; PD

Summary: St Nicholas is a provision for pupils in all phases of education who have a severe learning disability. This can include pupils who have ASD or a profound and multiple disability, as well as those who have a physical or sensory impairment.

In addition to their severe learning disability, pupils may have any other kind of special need – eg dyscalculia, dyslexia, EBD. Some pupils also have medical needs which affect their school day, eg epilepsy, gastrostomy.

ST PATRICK'S GRAMMAR SCHOOL

Saul Street, Downpatrick, Co Down, BT30 6NJ

Tel: 02844 619 722

Fax: 02844 619 930

Email: info@stpatricks.downpatrick.ni.sch.uk

Website: www.spgs.org.uk

• Pupils: 720 Boys; Day Pupils • Age: 11 to 19

• Religion: Roman Catholic • School status: State

SEN provision

Detail:

Now provide for in school:

- Mild: ASP; AUT; ADD; ADHD; DYSL; DYSP; VI;
- Moderate: ASP; AUT; DYSL;
- Others: PD

Experience of:

- Mild: HI;
- Moderate: ADD; ADHD; DYSP;
- Severe: DYSL;
- Others: OCD; Epi; Eat

Summary: St Patrick's has developed its SEN provision over the past five years. Under the direction of Mr R McConville (VP – Pastoral Care) and Mrs A McCann (SENCo) we have integrated children with special needs into our highly academic environment. Working with other agencies such as the SEELB, health agencies and social services we have tried to ensure that all needs are met and with the support of general and classroom assistants individual education plans are tailored to meet pupils' needs.

ST PAUL'S C OF E JUNIOR SCHOOL

Hawcoat Lane, Barrow-in-Furness, Cumbria, LA14 4HF

Tel: 01229 894 664
Fax: 01229 894 665
Email: admin@st-pauls.cumbria.sch.uk
• Pupils: 140 Mixed; Day Pupils • Age: 7 to 11
• Religion: Church of England • School status: State

SEN provision

Detail:
Now provide for in school:
Mild: ASP; DYSC; DYSL;
Moderate: ASP; ADHD; MLD; DYSL;
Others: SPD
Experience of:
Mild: AUT; HI; VI; CP;
Moderate: VI;
Severe: VI;
Others: SLD; EAL; Sp&LD; Epi; Eat

Summary: We are a small, friendly school and our aim is to enable every child to achieve their full potential. To do this we use a variety of methods and we are always interested in finding out about new ideas. At present we are running a project with the Dore Achievement Centre which involves children with specific learning difficulties taking part in twice daily exercise sessions. We provide for children with a range of autistic spectrum disorders, ADHD and specific learning difficulties within a mainstream setting. We have experience of working with both blind and partially sighted pupils. Our staff have undergone staff training to enable them to work effectively with all our pupils.

ST PETER'S CHURCH OF ENGLAND PRIMARY SCHOOL

Hallett's Way, Portishead, Bristol, BS20 6BT

Tel: 01275 843 142
Fax: 01275 845 684
Email: stpeter's.pri@n-somerset.gov.uk
• Pupils: 358 Mixed; Day Pupils • Age: 4 to 11
• Religion: Church of England • School status: State

SEN provision

Detail:
Now provide for in school:
Mild: ASP; AUT; ADD; ADHD; EBD; DYSC; DYSL; DYSP; HI; VI;
Moderate: ASP; AUT; ADD; ADHD; EBD; MLD;
Others: EAL; Sp&LD; PD
Experience of:
Mild: DS;
Moderate: DS

Summary: St Peter's School is inclusive. The building is on one level with no steps and has facilities for disabled users. Children with a variety of needs are on the roll of the school and they are included in all activities with appropriate support as required. Adult disabilities and needs are also catered for whether for staff or for visitors to the school.

St Peter's Roman Catholic Comprehensive School, South Bank

Normanby Road, South Bank, Middlesbrough, TS6 6SP

Tel: 01642 453 462

Fax: 01642 455 010

• Pupils: 453 Mixed; Day Pupils • Age: 11 to 16

• Religion: Roman Catholic • School status: State

SEN provision

Detail:

Now provide for in school:
- Mild: EBD; DYSL;
- Moderate: MLD; DYSL;
- Severe: HI

Experience of:
- Mild: ADD; ADHD; DYSP; HI; CP;
- Moderate: EBD; HI;
- Severe: DYSL;
- Others: CD; OCD; EAL; Epi; PD

Summary: There is a suite of four small rooms for SEN use. We aim to provide individualised learning for all our SEN students, whilst supporting them in full mainstream classes where possible. As part of the facility, we also operate a behaviour modification scheme in the school for students who need it. We provide reading and literacy help for all students who are attaining well below their chronological age. We have individual and small group withdrawal teaching for some students. We offer a flexible and we believe creative approach to individual's needs.

St Roch's Secondary School

40 Royston Road, Glasgow, G21 2NF

Tel: 01415 820 270

Fax: 01415 820 271

Email: headteacher@st-rochs-sec.glasgow.sch.uk

• Pupils: 723 Mixed; Day Pupils • Age: 11 to 18

• Religion: Roman Catholic • School status: State

SEN provision

Detail:

Centre of excellence for:
- Mild: HI;
- Moderate: HI;
- Severe: HI

Now provide for in school:
- Mild: EBD; DYSL; CP;
- Moderate: EBD; MLD; DYSL; CP;
- Severe: EBD; DYSL;
- Others: PD

Experience of:
- Mild: ADD; DYSC; DYSP; VI;
- Moderate: ADD; DYSP

Summary: St Roch's Secondary has a roll of approximately 800 pupils aged 11-18. There is a specialist hearing impaired unit within the school as well as specialist support for the 120+ children of asylum seekers who attend our school. Provision for the mainstream pupils is provided by a support for learning department which incorporates behaviour support as well. Many strategies are employed to support learning and behaviour needs both within and outwith the classroom. There is also a pastoral care team which looks after the welfare and many other aspects of our pupils' lives.

St Rose's High School

Beechmount Ave, Belfast, BT12 7NA

Tel: 02890 240 937
Fax: 02890 310 357
Email: info@stroses.belfast.ni.sch.uk
Website: www.stroses.belfast.ni.sch.uk

• Pupils: 575 Girls; Day Pupils • Age: 11 to 18
• Religion: Roman Catholic • School status: State

SEN provision

Detail:

Centre of excellence for:
- Mild: ADD; ADHD; EBD; HI; VI;
- Moderate: HI; VI;
- Severe: HI; VI;
- Others: EAL; MSI; Sp&LD

Now provide for in school:
- Mild: DYSL; DYSP;
- Moderate: ADD; ADHD; EBD; MLD; DYSP;
- Others: DEL; Epi; PD; Oth; Eat

Experience of:
- Mild: DYSC;
- Moderate: DYSL;
- Severe: DYSL;
- Others: OCD; FRX

Summary: St Rose's has a very strong special needs department, which offers excellent provision meeting the needs of all children in line with Code of Practice and SENDO legislation. Over the years we have gained an excellent reputation for getting the most from our SEN pupils. We have an excellent record for adding value to our pupils. We are proud to report that all our SEN students leave school with GCSE or vocational equivalent and in many cases A1 and A2 or vocational passes post-16. We have a hearing impaired unit attached.

St Stephen's Community Primary School

Roydon Road, St Stephen's, Launceston, Cornwall, PL15 8HL

Tel: 01566 772 170
Fax: 01566 773 872
Email: secretary@st-stephens-laun.cornwall.sch.uk
Website: www.st-stephens-laun.cornwall.sch.uk

• Pupils: 196 Mixed; Day Pupils • Age: 4 to 11
• Religion: Non-denominational • School status: State

SEN provision

Summary: The school has an Area Special Unit attached which takes up to 10 children from the surrounding area who have profound, complex or severe learning difficulties, some with associated additional sensory defects. It has a highly experienced teacher who leads a large team of ancillaries. It is highly praised by Ofsted and is recognised as a centre of excellence. There is a very high staff/pupil ratio reflecting the level of pupil need. The children are integrated into the mainstream school on a planned basis for some lessons or social experience, and mainstream children integrate in to the Area Special Unit as well. Within the class the children follow an individualised curriculum based around Equals and P levels and Portage and they attend from around age 4-11 years. The class has a large, well equipped sensory room and a therapy room extension. Some children go to a hydrotherapy pool, others swim with the mainstream and some go riding. In addition they have trips out and links to the local community. We have support from visiting professionals including occupational therapists, physiotherapists and speech therapists to name a few. Some children use switches to access toys and the computers. PECS communication books are encouraged for non-speaking children. Makaton sign language is also used and taught throughout the school.

In addition there are children in our mainstream with milder disabilities across the range of special needs supported with IEPs under the direction of the SENCo.

St Thomas More Roman Catholic High School Aided

Lynn Road, North Shields, Tyne and Wear, NE29 8LF

Tel: 01912 006 333

Fax: 01912 006 336

Email: StThomasMore.High@northtyneside.gov.uk

• Pupils: 1465 Mixed; Day Pupils • Age: 11 to 18

• Religion: Roman Catholic • School status: State

SEN provision

Detail:

Now provide for in school:

Mild: ADD; ADHD; EBD; DYSC; DYSL; HI;

Others: PD

Experience of:

Mild: ASP; DYSP; VI;

Moderate: MLD; HI; VI;

Others: EAL; Sp&LD; Epi

Summary: SEN provision supports the aim of the school to give each individual the opportunity to develop their full potential which entails ensuring that pupils who exhibit special needs on entry, or during their time at school, recieve appropriate support and assistance. The school strives to be inclusive in its policies and practices. Pupil progress is monitored carefully and there is a strong emphasis on developing literacy skills. Most support takes place in the mainstream classroom setting, with some withdrawal teaching for individual pupils where needed.

Samuel Pepys School

Cromwell Road, St Neots, Cambridgeshire, PE19 2EZ

Tel: 01480 375 012

Fax: 01480 375014

Email: office@samuelpepys.cambs.sch.uk

• Pupils: 93 Mixed; Day Pupils • Age: 2 to 19

• Religion: Non-denominational • School status: State

SEN provision

Detail:

Now provide for in school:

Mild: DS; CP;

Moderate: DS; MLD; CP;

Severe: AUT; DS; CP;

Others: SPD; AUT(other); FRX; PMLD; SLD; Epi; Eat

Experience of:

Mild: ADD; ADHD;

Moderate: ADD; ADHD;

Severe: ADD; ADHD;

Others: OCD; TIC

Summary: Our aims are to:

- Promote personal, social and independence skills at all levels
- Develop communication skills
- Ensure all students realise their academic potential
- Prepare students for a life after school in which they can participate fully with a strong sense of personal identity.

The majority of our pupils have severe learning difficulties. This means that we help them to achieve progress along the P Scales towards Level 1 of the National Curriculum. Improving communication and social skills is a priority and our pupils have regular access to a range of professionals to meet a variety of needs. Many of our children and young people have complex or profound and multiple learning difficulties. Often these pupils are largely dependent on adults for communication, self-care and mobility. Some may have a range of learning difficulties including the need to use augmentative and alternative communication systems.

Sandall Wood School

Leger Way, Doncaster, South Yorkshire, DN2 6HQ

Tel: 01302 322044

Fax: 01302 739927

Email: head@sandallwood.doncaster.sch.uk

• Pupils: 59 Mixed; Day Pupils • Age: 2 to 19

• Religion: Non-denominational • School status: State

SEN provision

Summary: We cater for pupils with severe physical difficulties and associated medical conditions. Increasingly the school is admitting pupils with complex, profound and multiple learning difficulties. The school has a number of pupils using alternative communication devices and operates an outreach service to pupils with a disability in mainstream schools in the area.

Sandside Lodge School

Sandside Road, Ulverston, Cumbria, LA12 9EF

Tel: 01229 894 180

Fax: 01229 894 180

• Pupils: 73 Mixed; Day Pupils • Age: 2 to 19

• Religion: Non-denominational • School status: State

SEN provision

Detail:

Now provide for in school:

Mild: CP;

Moderate: DS; CP;

Severe: DS; CP;

Others: FRX; PMLD; SLD; Epi

Summary: Sandside Lodge School caters for students with severe and complex learning difficulties. Additionally, some may have physical disabilities and approximately a third are on the autistic spectrum.

Sarah Bonnell School

Deanery Road, London, E15 4LP

Tel: 020 8534 6791

Fax: 020 8555 3793

Email: admin.sarahbonnell@pop3.newham.gov.uk

Website: www.sarahbonnell.newham.sch.uk

• Pupils: 1178 Girls; Day Pupils • Age: 11 to 16

• Religion: Non-denominational • School status: State

SEN provision

Detail:

Now provide for in school:

Mild: DYSC; DYSL; DYSP; SpLD; HI; VI; CP;

Moderate: DYSC; DYSL; DYSP; SpLD; HI; VI;

Severe: DYSC; DYSL; DYSP; SpLD; HI; VI;

Others: SPD; EAL; MSI; Sp&LD; Epi; Eat

Experience of:

Mild: ASP; AUT;

Moderate: ASP; AUT; MLD

Summary: Sarah Bonnell provides for SEN, EMA and EAL by way of the curriculum access team. This comprises of TAs and LSTs that are trained and experienced in SEN and EAL. Each member of the curriculum access staff is assigned to a designated caseload of students for whom they become their keyworker. The team assists students in accessing the school and the curriculum. This is done by way of in-class support, working with departments and group work. Some of the group work that takes place is speech and language, dyslexia programmes, Ruth Miskin Literacy2 and more. The curriculum access team also ensures that there are entry level courses in mainstream subjects for less able students and students with SEN. The team also provides access arrangements for SEN children so that they can participate fully in the exams.The curriculum access team aims to make school accessible to all students and is always working on new ways by which to do this.

Scout Road Primary School

Scout Road, Mytholmyroyd, Hebden Bridge, West Yorkshire, HX7 5JR

Tel: 01422 883 327

Fax: 01422 881 203

• Pupils: 104 Mixed; Day Pupils • Age: 4 to 11

• Religion: Non-denominational • School status: State

SEN provision

Detail:

Now provide for in school:

Mild: ASP; AUT; EBD; DS; DYSC; DYSL; DYSP; HI; VI;

Moderate: AUT; DS

Experience of:

Mild: ADD; ADHD;

Moderate: DYSL; DYSP; HI

Summary: It is the policy of Scout Road School to actively involve all in the education of children with special educational needs. The children have the opportunity to develop their full potential with the help and support of their class teacher, the special needs co-ordinator and specialist support where appropriate. The school aims to provide for all the needs of the child whilst encouraging inclusion in class and school activities.

We aim to work in full partnership with parents and the child to create the very best for all concerned.

Shenley Primary School

London Road, Shenley, Radlett, Hertfordshire, WD7 9DX

Tel: 01923 855 864

Fax: 01923 855 864

Email: admin.shenley@thegrid.org.uk

Website: www.shenley.herts.sch.uk

• Pupils: 325 Mixed; Day Pupils • Age: 3 to 11

• Religion: Non-denominational • School status: State

SEN provision

Detail:

Now provide for in school:

- Mild: EBD; DYSC; DYSL; DYSP; CP;
- Moderate: MLD; CP;
- Others: EAL; Sp&LD; PD

Experience of:

- Mild: ASP; AUT; ADD; ADHD;
- Moderate: ASP; EBD;
- Others: Epi

Summary: Shenley is an inclusive school. Equality of opportunity is a reality for our children. We take account of pupils' varied life experiences and needs. We offer a broad, balanced and differentiated curriculum which aims for all children to achieve their full potential.

Shenley primary school is committed to providing an environment that allows children with disabilities full access to all areas of learning. The school has specialist advice and support from Hertfordshire County services. We also value the knowledge, views and first hand experience parents have regarding their children. We seek to work in partnership with parents and the wider community.

Shepton Mallet Community Infants School

Waterloo Road, Shepton Mallet, Somerset, BA4 5HE

Tel: 01749 342 322

Fax: 01749 346 060

Email: office@sheptonmallet.somerset.sch.uk

• Pupils: 203 Mixed; Day Pupils • Age: 4 to 7

• Religion: Non-denominational • School status: State

SEN provision

Detail:

Centre of excellence for:

- Mild: ASP;
- Moderate: ASP;
- Others: EAL; Sp&LD

Now provide for in school:

- Mild: EBD; DYSC; DYSL; VI;
- Moderate: EBD; MLD; DYSC; DYSL;
- Severe: EBD;
- Others: ODD

Experience of:

- Mild: AUT; ADD; ADHD; DYSP; HI;
- Moderate: AUT; ADD; ADHD; DYSP;
- Others: SPD; TIC; Epi; PD; Eat

Summary: Shepton Mallet Infant School is an inclusive school which welcomes all children. We provide a happy, nurturing environment in which all children's achievements are valued and celebrated. The needs of children who may be experiencing learning, social or emotional difficulties are given a particular priority. These children receive a high level of support from a very experienced team. The SENCo (special educational needs co-ordinator) ensures that the school receives advice from the appropriate agencies, such as the Specific Literacy (dyslexia) team, or the speech and language therapist.

The SENCo works closely with the senior speech and language therapist to set programmes and targets for children with speech and language difficulties. These are carried out by trained teaching assistants and are regularly monitored and reviewed.

We have built an expertise within the school in successfully including children with Asperger's syndrome, and in supporting children with emotional difficulties.

We have been praised for our work with children for whom English is an additional language. We have set up English Language teaching groups in addition to successful strategies within each class with the support of the SENCo.

In addition to specialist provision such as Forest School Sessions, Nurture Club, Language Groups, Provision for Children with Asperger's, English as a second language, the school offers a wide range of enrichment activities.

Sherwin Knight Community Infant School

Cedar Road, Strood, Kent, ME2 2JP

Tel: 01634 338 260

Fax: 01634 296 697

Email: office@sherwinknight-inf.medway.sch.uk

Website: www.sherwinknight-inf.medway.sch.uk

• Pupils: 260 Mixed; Day Pupils • Age: 7

• Religion: Non-denominational • School status: State

SEN provision

Detail:

Now provide for in school:

Mild: ASP;

Moderate: MLD

Experience of:

Mild: AUT; ADD; ADHD; EBD; DYSL; DYSP; VI;

Moderate: ASP; AUT; ADD; ADHD; EBD;

Severe: ASP; AUT; ADD; ADHD; EBD;

Others: AUT(other); EAL; Sp&LD; Epi

Summary: We at Sherwin Knight Community Infant School are a school staff intent on finding solutions rather than focusing on problems. We believe that each pupil has individual and unique needs. However, some pupils require more support than others. If these pupils are to achieve their full potential, we must recognise this and plan accordingly. We acknowledge that a significant proportion of pupils will have special educational needs at some time in their school career. Many of these pupils may require help throughout their time in school, whilst others may need a little extra support for a short period to help overcome more temporary needs. Sherwin Knight Community Infant School aims to provide all pupils with strategies for dealing with their needs in a supportive environment, and to give them meaningful access to the curriculum. In particular, we aim:

- In our Learning and Teaching Policy we focus on the practice in the school and in particular how our system of education responds to diversity.
- to enable every pupil to experience success
- to promote individual confidence and a positive attitude
- to ensure that all pupils, whatever their special educational needs, receive appropriate educational provision through a broad and balanced curriculum that is relevant and differentiated, and that demonstrates coherence and progression in learning
- to give pupils with SEN equal opportunities to take part in all aspects of the school's provision.
- to identify, assess, record, and regularly review pupils' progress and needs
- to involve parents/carers/children in planning and supporting at all stages of their development
- to work collaboratively with parents, other professionals and support services including the educational psychology service
- to ensure that the responsibility held by all staff and governors for SEN is implemented and maintained.

All pupils should be involved in making decisions where possible right from the start of their education. The ways in which pupils are encouraged to participate should reflect the pupil's evolving maturity. Participation in education is a process that will necessitate all pupils being given the opportunity to make choices and to understand that their views matter. Confident young pupils, who know that their opinions will be valued and who can practice making choices, will be more secure and effective pupils during the school years.

Sir Charles Parsons School

Westbourne Avenue, Newcastle upon Tyne, Tyne and Wear, NE6 4ED

Tel: 01912 630 261
Fax: 01912 638 897
Email: admin@sircharlesparson.newcastle.sch.uk
Website: www.newcastle-schools.org.uk/sircharlesparsons/index.htm

• Pupils: 135 Mixed; Day Pupils • Age: 11 to 19
• Religion: Non-denominational • School status: State

SEN provision

Detail:
Centre of excellence for:
Mild: DS; CP;
Moderate: DS; CP;
Severe: DS; CP;
Others: PMLD; SLD
Now provide for in school:
Mild: ASP; DYSP; HI; VI;
Moderate: ASP; DYSP;
Severe: ASP; DYSP;
Others: FRX; MSI; Sp&LD; Epi; PD
Experience of:
Mild: AUT; ADD;
Moderate: AUT;
Severe: AUT;
Others: SPD; OCD; TIC; EAL

Summary: Sir Charles Parsons School provides places for students aged 11-19 with severe and profound and multiple learning difficulties. Students often have associated speech and language disorders and for that reason the school provides a total communication environment where augmentative forms of communication including signing and symbols are in routine use. Many students have a physical impairment, often resulting from cerebral palsy, and many have hearing and sight impairment. The school will take possession of a new £1.5 million therapy pool in the spring of 2006 and the rest of its premises will be re-built during the next three or four years.

Sir Joseph Williamson's Mathematical School

Maidstone Road, Rochester, Kent, ME1 3EL

Tel: 01634 844 008
Fax: 01634 818 303
Email: office@sirjosephwilliamson.medway.sch.uk
Website: www.sirjosephwilliamson.medway.sch.uk

• Pupils: 1056 Boys; Day Pupils • Age: 11 to 18
• School status: State

SEN provision

Detail:
Now provide for in school:
Mild: ASP; AUT; ADD; EBD; DYSC; DYSL; DYSP; HI; VI; CP;
Moderate: ASP; HI; VI; CP;
Severe: CP;
Others: SPD; Epi; PD

Summary: We provide support for pupils with physical disabililties, having excellent wheelchair access and experienced learning assistants who provide classroom support where needed, physiotherapy, etc. We also have experience of Asperger's syndrome and dyslexia and staff are provided with advice on how to support students and have all received training on autism. We belong to the Medway Dyslexia Association who provide training for staff and offer pupil/parent support.

We are the first grammar school in the Medway area to receive an 'Inclusion Mark' and inspectors noted that we offered among other things:

- High level of challenge for all pupils with appropriate support to ensure self esteem and achievement.
- Powerful sense of respect in all relationships between staff and students and between students.
- Excellent support, as a designated school, for physically disabled students who are fully included in all aspects of school life.

THE SKINNERS' SCHOOL

St John's Road, Tunbridge Wells, Kent, TN4 9PG

Tel: 01892 520 732

Fax: 01892 549 356

Email: pcdbraggins@skinners-school.org.uk

Website: www.skinners-school.co.uk

• Pupils: 737 Boys; Day Pupils • Age: 11 to 18

• School status: State

SEN provision

Detail:

Now provide for in school:

Mild: ASP; ADD; ADHD; DYSC; DYSL; DYSP;

Moderate: ASP; DYSL; DYSP

Experience of:

Mild: AUT; SpLD; HI; VI;

Moderate: HI; VI;

Others: AUT(other); TIC; EAL; PD

Summary: We are a selective boys school. We have 774 boys including 206 in the sixth form, of whom 150 boys are identified as having special educational needs, a figure we feel is higher than usual for a selective school.

The most common support is with literacy including handwriting. Typically pupils identified with SEN have mild dyslexia or dyspraxia. Pupils are assessed as necessary, not just for additional help, but to ensure they receive extra time in public examinations. A few boys have additional, on site support from the Dyslexia Institute. Some use laptops.

In recent years we have observed an increasing frequency of boys with ASD, most notably Asperger's. As a school we have had to learn appropriate teaching strategies to support these children. We will disapply elements of the National Curriculum, if appropriate, to meet the needs of the individual.

Pupils with behavioural challenges such as ADD and ADHD (Ritalin not a problem), may participate in a pastoral support programme, which includes anger management. We have experience of pupils with Tourette's and with physical difficulties. We have supported a boy who was profoundly deaf and one who was visually impaired but the hilly, Victorian site, is not ideally suited to wheelchairs. However – school has wheelchair bound parents and we will always endeavour to work out a suitable route or system to ensure they have necessary access to the site and to staff.

The school tries to be inclusive and welcoming to those able boys who have learning disabilities. We cater well for those with milder needs but may struggle to meet the needs of those with more challenging difficulties. It is important for all concerned that the needs of all our pupils, and the individual are considered. Staff have a very positive and welcoming attitude to SEN and the school has invested in training in SEN for staff. We recognise the very valuable contribution children with SEN can make to school life.

SOUTHBOROUGH SCHOOL

Hook Road, Surbiton, Surrey, KT6 5AS

Tel: 020 8391 4324

Fax: 020 8391 0177

Email: SBB@rbksch.org

Website: www.southborough.kingston.sch.uk

• Pupils: 778 Boys; Day Pupils • Age: 11 to 18

• Religion: Non-denominational • School status: State

SEN provision

Detail:

Now provide for in school:

Mild: ASP; ADD; ADHD; EBD; DYSC; DYSL; DYSP; SpLD; HI; VI; CP;

Moderate: ASP; ADD; ADHD; EBD; MLD; DYSC; DYSL; DYSP; SpLD; HI; VI; CP;

Severe: ASP; ADD; DYSC; DYSL; DYSP; SpLD;

Others: SPD; AUT(other); TIC; MSI; Sp&LD; DEL; Epi; PD; Eat

Experience of:

Mild: AUT;

Severe: ADHD; EBD;

Others: OCD

Summary: Southborough High School aims to provide an inclusive environment for all. The SEN department is well equipped and caters for students with SEN. As described by our last Ofsted inspection the provision of students with SEN is good. EAL provision is considered excellent. We have a team of very experienced staff to provide the correct support to students with SEN. The

SEN department has developed new initiatives to keep up with the growing demand of SEN and inclusion in mainstream schools.

SOUTHFIELDS COMMUNITY COLLEGE

333 Merton Road, Wandsworth, London, SW18 5JU

Tel: 020 8875 2600
Fax: 020 8874 9949
Email: info@southfields.wandsworth.sch.uk
Website: www.southfields.wandsworth.sch.uk

• Pupils: 1310 Mixed; Day Pupils • Age: 11 to 18
• Religion: Non-denominational • School status: State

SEN provision

Detail:
Centre of excellence for:
Mild: ADD; ADHD; EBD; DYSC; DYSL; DYSP; HI;
Moderate: ADD; ADHD; EBD; MLD; DYSC; DYSL; DYSP; HI;
Severe: DYSL; HI;
Others: EAL
Now provide for in school:
Mild: ASP; CP;
Others: TIC; Sp&LD
Experience of:
Mild: AUT; SpLD; VI;
Moderate: ASP; SpLD; CP;
Severe: DYSC; DYSP; SpLD;
Others: SPD; CD; OCD; ODD; SLD; Epi

Summary: Southfields Community College has been described by HMI inspectors as one of the best examples of educational inclusion they have seen (Nov. 2004). Our aim is to provide all students with the skills they need to access the curriculum and then to attain as fully as possible within the curriculum. We specialise in early literacy, SpLD (dyslexia, dyspraxia, dyscalculia); speech, language and social skills, hearing impaired support (Wandsworth HIU), English as an Additional Language and gifted and talented.Our ethos is one of inclusion and to achieve this we look carefully at the process of teaching and learning and adapt the curriculum, the delivery style and, wherever possible, the environment to suit the needs of the learner. We also acknowledge and support students in dealing with external difficulties that affect their ability to engage with the curriculum.

SOUTHLANDS SCHOOL

Beach Road, Tynemouth, North Shields, Tyne and Wear, NE30 2QR

Tel: 01912 006 348
Fax: 01912 005 674
Email: Southlands.school@northtyneside.gov.uk

• Pupils: 112 Mixed; Day Pupils • Age: 11 to 16
• Religion: Non-denominational • School status: State

SEN provision

Detail:
Now provide for in school:
Mild: ADD; ADHD; EBD;
Moderate: ADD; ADHD; EBD; DS;
Severe: ADHD;
Others: SPD; CD; OCD; ODD; TIC; Sp&LD; Epi
Experience of:
Mild: ASP; AUT; DS; DYSC; DYSL; DYSP; HI; VI;
Moderate: ASP; AUT; DYSC; DYSL; DYSP; HI;
Severe: ASP;
Others: FRX; EAL; Eat

Summary: Southlands School makes provision for young people with moderate learning difficulties and other complexities of need. It has specialist provision for a small number who have additional social, emotional and behavioural difficulties and provides supported access to local mainstream schools' GCSE curriculum for students with subject strengths. The school offers the full National Curriculum at Key Stages 3 and 4 in addition to a comprehensive work-related curriculum in a wide range of areas. These are accessed jointly by similar ability students from four local mainstream high schools as part of an inclusive programme to meet wider student needs.

SPALDING HIGH SCHOOL

Stonegate, Spalding, Lincolnshire, PE11 2PJ

Tel: 01775 722 110
Fax: 01775 762 531
Email: enquiries@spaldinghigh.lincs.sch.uk
Website: www.spaldinghigh.lincs.sch.uk

• Pupils: 952 Girls; Day Pupils • Age: 11 to 18
• Religion: Non-denominational • School status: State

EN provision

etail:
xperience of:
Mild: ADD; ADHD; EBD; DYSL; DYSP; SpLD; HI;
Moderate: ADD; EBD; DYSL; VI;
Severe: VI;
Others: OCD; EAL; Epi; PD; Eat

ummary: Spalding High School takes its special edu-ational needs provision very seriously; we are commit-d to enabling all pupils to flourish in our purposeful, sciplined and successful atmosphere. As a selective ammar school, academic achievement is of the most importance, and we shall do all we can to ncourage every pupil to fulfil his/her true potential.

SPENNYMOOR COMPREHENSIVE SCHOOL

Whitworth Lane, Spennymoor, Durham, DL16 7LN

Tel: 01388 815 634
Fax: 01388 824 840
Email: office@spennymoorschool.com
Website: www.spennymoorschool.com

• Pupils: 692 Mixed; Day Pupils • Age: 11 to 18
• Religion: Non-denominational • School status: State

EN provision

etail:
ow provide for in school:
Mild: ASP; ADD; ADHD; EBD; HI; VI;
Moderate: ASP; ADD; ADHD; EBD; MLD; HI; CP;
Others: CD; Epi; PD; Eat
Experience of:
Mild: DYSC; DYSL; DYSP;
Moderate: DYSL; DYSP;
Others: OCD; ODD; TIC; EAL; Sp&LD

Summary: The student support department, led by the SENCo, is made up of six LSAs, one youth mentor and an inclusion unit manager. The LEA's learning support services have regular involvement in school.

The school supports a variety of SEN, including some youngsters with physical disabilities; a lift is due to be installed at half-term (October 2005).

The student support team works across the whole school, supporting students in-class and in small groups, when additional help is needed. The use of 'Success-maker' – an integrated learning program which develops students' literacy and numeracy skills – is widely used in years 7 and 8.

The team has a wealth of experience, with support staff coming from a variety of backgrounds. A counselling service is available, as well as alternative curriculum packages for selected students in years 10 and 11.

The inclusion unit is central to the school and exists to support students whose behaviour may, on occasions, be more challenging.

SPRINGFIELD SCHOOL

Cawthorne Close, Southdene, Kirkby, Liverpool, Merseyside, L32 3XQ

Tel: 01515 491 425
Fax: 01515 468 995
Email: springfield.de@knowsley.gov.uk
Website: www.springfield-school.org.uk

• Pupils: 85 Mixed; Day Pupils • Age: 2 to 19
• Religion: Non-denominational • School status: State

SEN provision

Detail:
Experience of:
Mild: HI; VI;
Moderate: EBD; HI; VI;
Severe: EBD;
Others: MSI; Sp&LD; PD

Summary: Springfield School meets the needs of children and young people with physical disabilities and complex needs aged between 2 and 19. The majority of pupils, in addition to their physical needs, demonstrate learning difficulties which are moderate to very severe in nature. A significant number of pupils also exhibit sensory problems associated with auditory and visual difficulties.

Springwater School

High Street, Starbeck, Harrogate, North Yorkshire, HG2 7LW

Tel: 01423 883 214
Fax: 01423 881 465
Email: admin@springwater.n-yorks.sch.uk
Website: www.springwater.n-yorks.sch.uk

• Pupils: 40 Mixed; Day Pupils • Age: 2 to 19
• Religion: Non-denominational • School status: State

SEN provision

Detail:
Centre of excellence for:
Mild: CP;
Moderate: CP;
Severe: CP;
Others: PMLD; SLD; MSI; Epi

Summary: Springwater School provides a specialist environment and curriculum for pupils experiencing a wide range of severe learning difficulties. Additional needs may include physical, sensory and medical needs. There is a specific provision within the Primary Department for pupils with ASD. Specialist provision includes: hydrotherapy pool; sensory woodland walk; soft play room and rebound therapy. Nursing and therapy services are available on site.

Sticklepath Community School

Woodville Estate, Barnstaple, Devon, EX31 2HH

Tel: 01271 342 455
Fax: 01271 324 649
Email: admin@sticklepath-primary.devon.sch.uk
Website: www.sticklepath-primary.devon.sch.uk

• Pupils: 310 Mixed; Day Pupils • Age: 5 to 11
• Religion: Non-denominational • School status: State

SEN provision

Detail:
Now provide for in school:
Mild: ASP; AUT; ADD; ADHD; EBD; DS; DYSC; DYSL DYSP; SpLD; HI;
Moderate: ASP; AUT; ADD; ADHD; EBD; DS; MLD DYSC; DYSL; DYSP; SpLD;
Severe: ADD; ADHD; EBD; DYSL; DYSP;
Others: AUT(other); CD; TIC; GEN; EAL; Sp&LD
Experience of:
Mild: VI;
Moderate: HI; VI;
Severe: HI; VI;
Others: OCD; ODD; PMLD; SLD; MSI

Summary: We are a fully inclusive school with a high experienced special needs co-ordinator who is also fully trained Reading Recovery teacher. We believ wholeheartedly in the benefits of inclusion in all but tiny minority of cases and enjoy the enrichment that ou SEN children bring to the school. A fully equipped toil for the disabled is currently being installed although w do still have a few classrooms in huts without full dis abled access until our new building is completed. Th main building and grounds will be fully accessible c completion of the project.

Stockport College of Further and Higher Education

Wellington Road South, Stockport, Cheshire, SK1 3UQ

Tel: 0161 958 3100
Fax: 0161 480 6636
Email: admissions@stockport.ac.uk
Website: www.stockport.ac.uk
• Pupils: 1000 Mixed; Day Pupils • Age: 16 to 99
• Religion: Non-denominational • School status: State

SEN provision

Detail:
Experience of:
Mild: ASP; AUT; ADD; ADHD; EBD; DS; DYSC; DYSL; DYSP; SpLD; HI; VI; CP;
Moderate: ASP; AUT; ADD; ADHD; EBD; DS; MLD; DYSC; DYSL; DYSP; SpLD; HI; VI; CP;
Severe: ASP; DYSL; DYSP; SpLD; HI; VI;
Others: SPD; OCD; TIC; PMLD; EAL; MSI; Epi; PD; Eat

Summary: Integrated across college with support, for students with disabilities and specific learning differences. In addition to this, semi discrete skills for life vocationally based programmes for learners with below level 1 skills for life needs.

Swanage First School

Mount Scar, Swanage, Dorset, BH19 2EY

Tel: 01929 422 424
Fax: 01929 426 652
Email: office@swanagefirst.dorset.sch.uk
Website: www.swanagefirst.dorset.sch.uk
• Pupils: 210 Mixed; Day Pupils • Age: 2 to 9
• Religion: Non-denominational • School status: State

SEN provision

Detail:
Now provide for in school:
Mild: ASP; ADD; ADHD; EBD; DYSC; DYSL; DYSP; HI; VI;
Moderate: ASP; ADD; EBD; MLD; DYSL; HI;
Others: PMLD; SLD; Sp&LD; Epi
Experience of:
Mild: DS;
Moderate: ADHD; DS;
Severe: ASP; ADD; ADHD; EBD; DS

Summary: The school can cater for the wide range of special educational needs you would find in a mainstream school. Dorset does have a range of special schools that meet the specialist needs of children. Children in our school receive support from our teachers, we have a large number of teaching assistants and have access to the SEN support service who come into school weekly to provide specialist teaching.

Thomas Wolsey School

642 Old Norwich Road, Ipswich, Suffolk, IP1 6LU

Tel: 01473 467 600
Fax: 01473 462 525
• Pupils: 74 Mixed; Day Pupils • Age: 3 to 19
• Religion: Non-denominational • School status: State

SEN provision

Summary: Thomas Wolsey School is the County Community Special School for pupils who have complex physical and sensory impairment. The pupils have a wide range of educational abilities and benefit from small group teaching and a multi-professional staff team. We specialise in communication, technology access, multi-sensory curriculum, creative arts and inclusive PE. We have an Outreach Service to support inclusion of pupils with complex needs in mainstream schools.

Thomlinson Junior School

The Goose Market, High Street, Wigton, Cumbria, CA7 9PG

Tel: 016873 42432
Fax: 016973 45761
Email: thom.juniorschool@wigton.org.uk
• Pupils: 264 Mixed; Day Pupils • Age: 7 to 11
• Religion: Non-denominational • School status: State

SEN provision

Detail:
Now provide for in school:
Mild: ASP; AUT; DS; DYSP; SpLD; HI; CP;
Moderate: ASP; AUT; DS; MLD; DYSP; SpLD; HI;
Severe: SpLD;
Others: SPD; AUT(other); PMLD; SLD; MSI; PD

Summary: The school accommodates a Strategic Facility for special educational needs. This accommodates those children who have severe learning difficulties and specific special needs that can not be accommodated in their own neighbourhood school, but are not such that their needs can only be met by a special school. Admission is controlled by the Cumbria Education Service SEN Department. Depending on their individual needs, children accommodated within the Strategic Facility may be wholly or partly educated within it, or may be mainly within a mainstream class.

Thorns Community College

Stockwell Avenue, Brierley Hill, West Midlands, DY5 2NU

Tel: 01384 816 225
Fax: 01384 816 226
Email: dmountney@thorns-s.dudley.gov.uk
Website: www.thorns-s.dudley.gov.uk
• Pupils: 1360 Mixed; Day Pupils • Age: 11 to 16
• Religion: Non-denominational • School status: State

SEN provision

Detail:
Centre of excellence for:
Mild: CP;
Moderate: CP;
Severe: CP
Now provide for in school:
Mild: ASP; AUT; ADD; ADHD; EBD; DYSC; DYSL; DYSP; HI; VI;
Moderate: ASP; AUT; ADD; ADHD; EBD; MLD; DYSC; DYSL; DYSP; HI; VI;
Severe: AUT; ADD; ADHD; EBD; HI;
Others: OCD; ODD; TIC; EAL; MSI; Sp&LD; Epi

Summary: Thorns Community College provides for all students regardles of ability. We have a team of 29 learning support practitioners who support via one-to-one withdrawal and small group withdrawal but the majority of support is 'in class'. Learning support practitioners specialise in two areas, learning difficulties and physical difficulties.(Thorns is recognised by the LEA as excellent in the provision for students with physical difficulties). We also have a behaviour manager who works with students with behavioural dificulties. Thorns has a counsellor on site for four days per week and we have five learning mentors. We have links with the ASD team in the LEA and all staff have received initial training in ASD disorders whilst learning support staff who work with specific students have received further specialist training. We are committed to providing the best education possible for all local children and we admit students from across the borough with mobility difficulties.

Tile Hill Wood School and Language College

Nutbrook Avenue, Coventry, West Midlands, CV4 9PW

Tel: 024 7642 6200
Fax: 024 7642 6246
Email: enquiries@thw.coventry.sch.uk
Website: www.thw.coventry.sch.uk
• Pupils: 1370 Girls; Day Pupils • Age: 11 to 18
• Religion: Non-denominational • School status: State

SEN provision

Detail:
Centre of excellence for:
Mild: AUT; EBD; DYSL; SpLD;
Moderate: AUT; EBD; MLD; DYSL; SpLD;
Severe: DYSL; SpLD;
Others: OCD
Now provide for in school:
Mild: ASP; ADD; ADHD; DYSC; DYSP; HI; VI; CP;
Moderate: ASP; ADD; ADHD; DYSC; DYSP; HI; VI; CP;
Severe: EBD; DYSC; DYSP; HI; VI;
Others: SPD; AUT(other); CD; PMLD; MSI; Sp&LD; DEL; Epi; PD; Eat
Experience of:
Mild: DS;
Moderate: DS;
Severe: ASP; AUT; ADD; ADHD; CP;
Others: ODD; TIC; FRX; SLD

Summary: At Tile Hill Wood School and Language College we have a specialist department called 'Student Support'. The core purpose of this department is to provide and co-ordinate the support for all students in the school, whatever their need may be. There is a team of teachers, education assistants, language support assistants and learning mentors. They work both within the base as well as with students and teachers in the classroom setting. Students' needs are identified intially through our links with our feeder primary schools. Once a student arrives in our school they are assessed and their progress monitored closely. We recognise that some students find transition to a new school difficult. We aim to support these students through our Emotional Literacy and Social Skills programmes. Our recent Ofsted inspection praised the high quality of provision and noted especially that staff worked well together in supporting our students. We are able to offer specialist support for students who have specific learning dificulties, as well as specialist teacher assessments for dyslexia as well as a range of other difficulties.

TIVERTON SCHOOL

Rowington Close, Coundon, Coventry, West Midlands, CV6 1PS

Tel: 024 7659 4954
Fax: 024 7659 1575
• Pupils: 41 Mixed; Day Pupils • Age: 3 to 11
• Religion: Non-denominational • School status: State

SEN provision

Summary: Tiverton School provides for primary aged children with severe learning difficulties. We cater for a very wide range of needs within this definition including children with profound and multiple learning difficulties and children with autistic spectrum disorders. The school is staffed by a very experienced and well qualified range of teachers and classroom support staff.

TRINITY CATHOLIC SCHOOL

Beechdale Road, Aspley, Nottingham, Nottinghamshire, NG8 3EZ

Tel: 01159 296 251
Fax: 01159 426 560
Email: office@trinity.biblio.net
Website: www.trinity.biblio.net
• Pupils: 970 Mixed; Day Pupils • Age: 11 to 18
• Religion: Roman Catholic • School status: State

SEN provision

Detail:
Now provide for in school:
Mild: ASP; AUT; EBD; DYSC; DYSL; DYSP; HI;
Moderate: ASP; AUT; EBD; MLD; DYSC; DYSL; DYSP; HI;
Severe: DYSC;
Others: SLD; EAL; PD
Experience of:
Mild: ADD;
Moderate: ADD;
Severe: DYSL; DYSP;
Others: PMLD

Summary: At Trinity the SEN department has just acquired an SEN base, which children with learning difficulties can access. This room is also where parents can come to see the pupil and SENCo for meetings. Trinity has just opened an English club for its new Polish pupils. This is held every dinner and the children come of their own accord and are taught extra English. EMAG also come twice weekly here to teach. This year we have just gained two autistic children and had a solution circle workshop for them, with over 20 staff present.

We are also increasing our staff numbers to four learning support assistants. We also have a paired reading session every week for children (years 7 and 8) with literacy difficulties.

TRINITY SCHOOL

Buckeridge Road, Teignmouth, Devon, TQ14 8LY

Tel: 01626 774 138
Fax: 01626 771 541
Email: mail@trinityschool.co.uk
Website: www.trinityschool.co.uk

• Pupils: 521 Mixed; Takes boarders • Age: 2 to 19
• School status: Independent

SEN provision

Detail:
Experience of:
Mild: ASP; ADD; ADHD; EBD; DYSC; DYSL; DYSP; SpLD; HI; VI; CP;
Moderate: ASP; MLD; DYSC; DYSL; DYSP; SpLD;
Others: SPD; EAL; Sp&LD; DEL; Epi; Eat

Summary: We aim to identify a pupil's special need as soon as possible. We use the results of base-line tests, tests of self-esteem and an ongoing process of monitoring progress by subject and form teachers, to identify the possibility of a learning difficulty. If a learning difficulty is suspected we will arrange for further, more specific, testing, by an educational psychologist with the agreement of parents. The result of these tests, along with recommendations, will be circulated to subject teachers, identifying the learning style of the pupil. Extra specialist tuition will be arranged and provided by qualified staff in specialist education. We regard the pupils' self-esteem to be of vital importance to their learning and recognise that each pupil, whatever their difficulty, is an individual.

TUNBRIDGE WELLS GRAMMAR SCHOOL FOR BOYS

St John's Road, Tunbridge Wells, Kent, TN4 9XB

Tel: 01892 529 551
Fax: 01892 536 833
Email: thegrammarschool@twgsboys.kent.sch.uk
Website: www.twgsboys.kent.sch.uk

• Pupils: 1210 Boys; Day Pupils • Age: 11 to 18
• Religion: Non-denominational • School status: State

SEN provision

Detail:
Experience of:
Mild: ASP; ADD; ADHD; DYSL;
Moderate: ASP; DYSL;
Severe: DYSL;
Others: TIC

Summary: The Boys Grammar School has a limited provision for SEN within the school. On entry to the school, boys will be screened using cognitive ability tests and monitored by the staff of the school. Concerns over pupils' literacy skills will be raised with the SENCo who will carry out testing to ascertain the severity of the difficulty. Where pupils have organisational difficulties which affect their work a short course in study skills will be offered in a small group. For those students whose literacy skills are poor a course in spelling, punctuation and grammar will be provided during year 7. Students with very poor handwriting will be offered a touch typing course delivered by a specialist teacher in a group. All students placed on the school register as having difficulties will be reviewed 1/2 yearly to make sure adequate progress is being maintained following any intervention.

For those pupils who have severe dyslexia affecting their academic progress, one-to-one weekly lessons will be offered on a termly basis. However, it must be emphasised that the school has a limited amount of support time to do this so only the severest difficulties will normally be addressed.

Where students are likely to perform poorly on tests and exams, because of their difficulties, examination dispensation will be pursued, with assessments being carried out by a qualified specialist within the school.

Very few pupils receive support in the upper part of the school, but where students have persistent difficulties support may be available in terms of study and organisation sessions at a lunch time or out of lessons through negotiation with members of staff.

The school currently has one statemented pupil with Asperger's syndrome who is fully integrated into the school with support from a learning support assistant. Teaching staff are gradually becoming more familiar with this type of difficulty.

Two Trees Community High School

Two Trees Lane, Denton, Manchester, Lancashire, M34 7QL

Tel: 01613 362 719

Fax: 01613 374 337

Email: admin@twotrees.tameside.sch.uk

• Pupils: 775 Mixed; Day Pupils • Age: 11 to 16

• Religion: Non-denominational • School status: State

SEN provision

Detail:

Now provide for in school:

Mild: ASP; ADD; EBD; DYSC; DYSL; DYSP; HI; CP;

Moderate: ASP; EBD; MLD; DYSC; DYSL; DYSP; HI;

Severe: DYSL;

Others: EAL; Sp&LD

Experience of:

Mild: AUT;

Severe: EBD;

Others: SPD

Summary: We have a learning support department, staffed by eight learning support assistants, one specialist teacher and the SENCo. The pupils at Two Trees are supported in a variety of ways, from in-class support, to withdrawal sessions for small groups and also one-to-one sessions. All support is logged on individual education plans and, like the IEP targets, is reviewed and if necessary modified regularly. Learning support assistants work in the classroom, to support pupils as they access the same work as their peers, but appropriately differentiated by either the LSA or the class teacher, to match individual ability. Our learning support room is fully equipped with eight computers and we constantly assess the use of and update the software we use with our pupils. This software is matched carefully to the needs outlined on individual pupils IEPs. The pupils on our school SEN register have special needs ranging from dyslexia, dyspraxia, Asperger's syndrome to moderate learning difficulties. There are approximately 25 with a statement of special need.

Tytherington High School

Manchester Road, Macclesfield, Cheshire, SK10 2EE

Tel: 01625 610 220

Fax: 01625 610 925

Email: info@tytheringtonhs.cheshire.sch.uk

Website: www.tytheringtonhs.cheshire.sch.uk

• Pupils: 1216 Mixed; Day Pupils • Age: 11 to 18

• Religion: Non-denominational • School status: State

SEN provision

Detail:

Now provide for in school:

Mild: ASP; AUT; ADD; ADHD; EBD; DS; DYSC; DYSL; DYSP; SpLD; HI; VI;

Moderate: ASP; ADD; ADHD; EBD; DS; MLD; DYSL; DYSP; SpLD; HI; VI;

Severe: DYSL;

Others: AUT(other); CD; OCD; ODD; TIC; GEN; EAL; Sp&LD; DEL; Epi; Oth; Eat

Summary: At Tytherington, we have an excellent reputation for providing a fully inclusive education for students that have barriers to learning. The school provides both in-class and withdrawn support for pupils that have learning, behavioural and medical difficulties. These include SpLD, MLD, ESBD, ASD, DAMP, ACC and Down's syndrome. For some students, there is the option of a more supportive ethos by working within the learning support base, especially if the student returns to school on a temporary or part-time basis. The department has extensive experience of working with students that have more diverse needs too. Medical difficulties have included diabetes, visual and hearing impairment, cystic fibrosis and Crohn's disease. We are currently working towards the Inclusion Quality Mark and the Dyslexia Schools Initiative.

VALE RESOURCE BASE

c/o Northumberland Pk Community School, Trulock Road, Tottenham, London, N17 0PG

Tel: 020 8801 6111
Fax: 020 8801 1140
Email: ValeSpecial.School@haringey.gov.uk
• Pupils: 78 Mixed; Day Pupils • Age: 2 to 19
• Religion: Non-denominational • School status: State

SEN provision

Summary: Vale caters for students with physical disabilities and associated special educational needs. Many pupils have complex medical needs with sensory impairments. Due to the school's dispersed nature with resource bases within mainstream schools, the Vale is able to offer the best practice of a special school with a continuum of inclusion opportunities with our mainstream partners.

VALLEY COMPREHENSIVE SCHOOL

Baulk Lane, Worksop, Nottinghamshire, S81 7DG

Tel: 01909 475 121
Fax: 01909 530 359
Email: admin@valley.notts.sch.uk
Website: www.valley.notts.sch.uk
• Pupils: 1574 Mixed; Day Pupils • Age: 11 to 18
• Religion: Non-denominational • School status: State

SEN provision

Detail:
Now provide for in school:
Mild: ASP; AUT; ADD; ADHD; EBD; DS; DYSC; DYSL; DYSP; HI; VI; CP;
Moderate: ASP; AUT; ADD; ADHD; EBD; DS; MLD; DYSC; DYSL; DYSP; HI; VI; CP;
Severe: ASP; AUT; ADD; ADHD; EBD; DYSC; DYSL; DYSP; VI; CP;
Others: SPD; PMLD; PD; Eat

Summary: Valley School Learning Support Department
Philosophy of Department

Learning support is about removing the barriers to learning. This includes the development of basic skills, social skills, ensuring that students have access to the curriculum both academically and physically and can experience success.

It is about improving student's self-esteem, overcoming disaffection and behaviour difficulties. It also includes supporting students at times of emotional crises.

The learning support team identifies and assesses students as early as possible so teaching staff can be informed and intervention strategies put in place. Withdrawal for basic skills development needs to take place. However it is important that students are taught as much as possible with their peers in mainstream classes. The aim of in-class support is to work with teachers to help students access the curriculum and meet the objectives of the lesson.

Students are encouraged to become more independent. The relationship between the teaching assistant and teacher is very important. Effective practice is when there is shared commitment to making activities and tasks successful for all students.

Learning support staff get to know the 'whole' student. They acquire an understanding of students' difficulties and provide the security they need. Students are able to talk through their concerns and problems. Learning support staff work with students and parents to develop strategies and achieve targets.

Vandyke Upper School and Community College

Vandyke Road, Leighton Buzzard, Bedfordshire, LU7 3DY

Tel: 01525 636 700
Fax: 01525 636 701
Email: office@vandyke.beds.sch.uk

• Pupils: 1033 Mixed; Day Pupils • Age: 13 to 18
• Religion: Non-denominational • School status: State

SEN provision

Detail:
Now provide for in school:
Mild: ASP; ADD; ADHD; EBD; DYSL; DYSP; HI; VI; CP;
Moderate: ASP; ADD; ADHD; EBD; MLD; DYSL; HI; VI; CP;
Severe: ASP; DYSL; CP;
Others: EAL; Epi; PD

Summary: At Vandyke School 'Everyone Matters' including all of our students with special educational needs. As a community school, we cater for students with a wide variety of special needs and we pride ourselves on the flexibility of our provision. The npecial needs team keep staff informed about the needs of individual students and offer support both in and out of the ordinary classroom. We are supported by specialist teams from the LEA. Inclusion is important to us.

The Vines School

43 Forthbridge Road, Battersea, London, SW11 5NX

Tel: 020 7228 0602
Fax: 020 7978 7954
Email: sao@vines.wandsworth.sch.uk
Website: www.thevinesschool

• Pupils: 68 Mixed; Day Pupils • Age: 4 to 11
• Religion: Non-denominational • School status: State

SEN provision

Detail:
Now provide for in school:
Mild: ASP; AUT; ADD; ADHD; DS; DYSC; DYSL; DYSP; SpLD; HI; VI; CP;
Moderate: AUT; ADD; ADHD; DS; MLD; DYSC; DYSL; DYSP; SpLD; HI; VI; CP;
Severe: AUT; ADD; ADHD; DS; DYSP; VI;
Others: SPD; OCD; ODD; TIC; FRX; GEN; SLD; EAL; MSI; Sp&LD; DEL; Epi; PD; Eat

Summary: School caters for students with moderate global learning difficulties and in addition students may have speech and language needs, physical needs – medical, gross or fine motor, emotional and or behavioural needs as a result of any of the aforementioned.

Waddington All Saints Primary School

Mere Road, Waddington, Lincoln, Lincolnshire, LN5 9NX

Tel: 01522 820 099
Fax: 01522 820 101
Email: admin@all-saints.lincs.sch.uk

• Pupils: 451 Mixed; Day Pupils • Age: 4 to 11
• Religion: Non-denominational • School status: State

SEN provision

Detail:
Now provide for in school:
Mild: ASP; AUT; ADD; ADHD; EBD; DS; DYSC; DYSL; DYSP; HI;
Moderate: ASP; AUT; ADD; EBD; MLD; HI;
Severe: HI;
Others: AUT(other); ODD; GEN; Sp&LD

Summary: The school provides an inclusive education tailoring learning to the personalised needs of the children. Lessons have opportunities for challenge for the able as well as modification and support for those who need it. Additional adults working in school provide high quality support in class and outside it and there are specific teaching assistants for 'catch-up' programmes and booster classes. The school's SEN department is managed by an SEN manager with SEN administrator. Senior staff offer expertise in a range of special need learning and experienced teaching assistants offer daily or weekly additional support. The school has recently been commended for its strong and effective pastoral policy which provides the ethos for all pupils to achieve their best in a supportive and 'can do' culture.

WALTON PROGRESSIVE SCHOOL

Progressive Lifestyles Education Service, Rice Lane, Liverpool, Merseyside, L9 1NR

Tel: 0151 525 4004
Fax: 0151 521 5804
Email: ruthwps@btconnect.com
• Pupils: 36 Mixed; Day Pupils • Age: 8 to 19
• School status: Independent

SEN provision

Detail:
Now provide for in school:
- Mild: ASP; AUT;
- Moderate: ASP; AUT; EBD;
- Severe: ASP; AUT; EBD;
- Others: CD; PMLD; SLD

Experience of:
- Mild: ADD; ADHD; EBD;
- Moderate: ADD; ADHD;
- Severe: ADD; ADHD

Summary: A Mixed 8-19 independent day school. A wide range of difficulties are catered for including those with complex behaviour support needs, ASD, SLD, PMLD and BESD. Individual programmes and support for all children, including augmented communication, TEACCH and behaviour strategies. National curriculum is followed and adapted where appropriate. ASDAN, AQA, GCSE and essential skills are offered. There is a committed, qualified and highly experienced staff. Ofsted say:'A very good school.' The staff say: 'A happy school'

WANSTEAD HIGH SCHOOL

Redbridge Lane West, Wanstead, London, E11 2JZ

Tel: 020 8989 2791
Fax: 020 8530 8879
Email: admin.wansteadhigh@redbridge.gov.uk
Website: www.wanstead.redbridge.sch.uk
• Pupils: 1469 Mixed; Day Pupils • Age: 11 to 18
• Religion: Non-denominational • School status: State

SEN provision

Detail:
Now provide for in school:
- Mild: DYSC; DYSL; DYSP;
- Moderate: MLD; DYSL; DYSP;
- Severe: DS; DYSL; HI;
- Others: EAL; Sp&LD; Epi

Experience of:
- Mild: ASP; ADD; ADHD; EBD; HI; VI; CP;
- Moderate: ASP; ADD; ADHD; EBD; DS; DYSC; HI;
- Others: SPD

Summary: The school aims to be as inclusive as possible and caters for a range of SEN including specific learning difficulties, emotional, behavioural and social difficulties, language and communication difficulties, attention deficit disorder and general learning difficulties. We also have experience of providing for students with Down's syndrome and those with hearing impairment.

We make good use of outside specialists, for example teachers of students with language and comunication difficulties, EBSD, and hearing impairment. Our in-house specialist provision is for students with dyslexia.

WASHINGTON SCHOOL

Spout Lane, Washington, Tyne and Wear, NE37 2AA

Tel: 01912 193 845
Fax: 01912 193 848
Email: washington.school@schools.sunderland.gov.uk
• Pupils: 1026 Mixed; Day Pupils • Age: 11 to 16
• Religion: Non-denominational • School status: State

SEN provision

Detail:
Now provide for in school:
Mild: ADD; ADHD; EBD; DYSP; HI; CP;
Moderate: EBD; DYSC; DYSL;
Others: CD; TIC; EAL; Sp&LD; Epi
Experience of:
Mild: ASP; AUT;
Others: SPD; OCD; ODD; SLD; MSI

Summary: At Washington School we have a variety of ways of meeting children's special educational needs.

For those with moderate learning difficulties (MLD), we offer Curriculum Access Provision, currently staffed by four specialist SEN teachers and nine support assistants. This provision covers English and maths from year 7 up to year 11 for those children who need it, in addition to other subjects where it is felt that children are unable to integrate with mainstream classes. In Key Stage 4, children follow public exam courses to gain them the best possible qualifications, appropriate to their strengths and needs. Wherever possible, CAP children have lessons in mainstream classes with appropriate support.

We also offer in-class support to children who don't need CAP specialist teaching.

Our teaching staff are all fully qualified and as well as teaching in CAP, teach mainstream children in a variety of subjects. Our support staff have specialisms in dyslexia, speech and language difficulties and autistic spectrum disorders and we run regular extra classes and lunchtime activities for basic skills.

WATERSIDE SCHOOL

Tipner Lane, Tipner, Portsmouth, Hampshire, PO2 8RA

Tel: 023 9266 5664
Fax: 023 9265 3333
Email: t.stokes@watersideschool.co.uk
Website: www.watersideschool.co.uk

• Pupils: 70+ Mixed; Takes boarders • Age: 11 to 16
• Religion: Non-denominational • School status: State

SEN provision

Detail:
Centre of excellence for:
Mild: EBD;
Moderate: EBD;
Severe: EBD
Now provide for in school:
Mild: ASP; AUT; ADD; ADHD;
Moderate: ASP; AUT; ADD; ADHD;
Severe: ADD; ADHD;
Others: SPD; AUT(other); CD; ODD; TIC
Experience of:
Mild: DYSL; DYSP;
Moderate: DYSL; SpLD;
Severe: DYSL;
Others: Sp&LD; Epi

Summary: The school comprises four sections: the main site, which provides for around 48 secondary aged boys (and occasionally girls) with social, emotional and behavioural difficulties as well as associated learning difficulties. The unit, which is a brand new, purpose-built, self-contained annexe of the main site offers 16-18 places for more vulnerable pupils who tend to present with ASD, speech and language problems and a variety of other syndromes which make the size and activity of the main site an unsuitable environment for them. The hostel provides Monday-Friday residential places for up to 10 pupils from both sites, who benefit from a 24-hour social curriculum with qualified residential social workers. At Key Stage 4 there is a distinct Work Related Curriculum provision where pupils follow a vocational route to GCSEs and other forms of accreditation through a combination of individual tutorials, college courses, home study and work experience placements.

WAVERLEY SCHOOL

Hob Moor Road, Small Heath, Birmingham, West Midlands, B10 9BT

Tel: 0121 464 1780
Fax: 0121 464 7478
Email: enquiry@waverley.bham.sch.uk

• Pupils: 638 Mixed; Day Pupils • Age: 11 to 16
• Religion: Non-denominational • School status: State

SEN provision

Detail:

Now provide for in school:
Mild: AUT; ADD; ADHD; EBD; HI; VI;
Moderate: ADD; EBD; MLD;
Others: EAL

Experience of:
Mild: DYSL; DYSP;
Moderate: ADHD; DYSL;
Severe: ADD; EBD;
Others: TIC; Sp&LD; Epi; Eat

Summary: At Waverley School we ensure all students who are on the register are supported as well as possible. This is done in a variety of ways; teaching assistants help in all faculties, so a child who needs help in technology has that help, just as he would in English and maths. Teaching assistants also work with form teachers, so that if there is time in the form the children can be helped with their reading. SEN children are offered extra lessons after school to help with their reading as well; they are also offered opportunities to take part in the Summer School in the summer holiday. Students are given packs of extra work if they wish to use it in the holiday. When the children first arrive at the school the teaching assistants work very closely with the SEN children, particularly children who are statemented; the childen are encouraged to come to the TA office where they can come if they are finding it difficult to adjust to the new school. So, SEN children are given lots of help and support both academically and socially. At the beginning of the year we try to give the SEN children colour-coded timetables to help them find their way around the school. We ensure all the staff know who are the SEN children so that they can be as supportive as possible. The greatest strength of Waverley School is its caring and supportive environment; and this is very clear within the SEN team.

WAYLAND COMMUNITY HIGH SCHOOL

Merton Road, Watton, Norfolk, IP25 6BA

Tel: 01953 881 514
Fax: 01953 885 677
Email: office@wayland.norfolk.sch.uk

• Pupils: 697 Mixed; Day Pupils • Age: 11 to 16
• Religion: Non-denominational • School status: State

SEN provision

Detail:

Centre of excellence for:
Mild: DYSL;
Moderate: DYSL;
Severe: DYSL

Now provide for in school:
Mild: ASP; ADD; ADHD; EBD; DYSC; DYSP; HI; VI; CP;
Moderate: ASP; ADD; ADHD; EBD; VI; CP;
Others: EAL; PD

Experience of:
Mild: AUT;
Moderate: MLD; DYSP; HI;
Severe: EBD; DYSP;
Others: SPD; Sp&LD; DEL; Epi; Eat

Summary: The SEN department at Wayland Community High School is a large one currently employing a SENCo and 15 learning support assistants. The LSAs are a mixture of full and part-time staff. LSAs are deployed in a number of ways: some are employed specifically for individual pupils; some are for general support; one is employed specifically for pupils with specific learning difficulties; one is employed for a new initiative – the Gold Curriculum group – with others in the team also supporting this group; one is employed part of the time for Boys' Achievement support. The SENCo, Mrs Tyler holds the OCR Certificate for Specific Learning Difficulties and also the additional modules to enable her to assess pupils for exam dispensation. The schoo has provision, called an Additionally Resourced Facility (ARF) for pupils with specific learning difficulties (dyslexia). The provision is for six pupils at any given time, places being awarded via Pupil Access and Support Services. These pupils benefit from additonal teaching from the SENCo of up to three hours per week as well as a high level of in-class support. There are a number of pupils in school who are Asperger's, with a varying range of needs. The school is experienced in including these children. The Gold Curriculum group is essentially a nurture group for weak or vulnerable pupils who find it difficult to make the transition from primary school and who therefore may dip in achievement in year 8. The numbers of teachers they meet in a week are limited: pupils attend some subjects such as Maths, Science, PE and Music but the rest of their lessons are cross-curricular in their tutor room. The SENCo manages the group but it is taught by their form tutor with high in-class support. The SEN Department also manages the SuccessMaker IT program which addresses weaknesses in literacy and numeracy.

THE WEALD SCHOOL

Upper Station Road, Billingshurst, West Sussex, RH14 9RY

Tel: 01403 787 200
Fax: 01403 787 202
Email: office@theweald.org.uk
Website: www.weald.w-sussex.sch.uk

• Pupils: 1410 Mixed; Day Pupils • Age: 11 to 18
• Religion: Non-denominational • School status: State

SEN provision

Detail:
Now provide for in school:
Mild: DYSL; VI; CP;
Moderate: DYSL;
Severe: DYSL;
Others: EAL; Sp&LD; Epi
Experience of:
Mild: ASP; AUT; ADD; ADHD; EBD; DS; DYSC; DYSP; HI;
Moderate: ADHD; DS; MLD;
Others: OCD; ODD; TIC

Summary: The Weald Curriculum Support department is situated in a large, airy room on the first floor. Pupils use this room for a range of reasons: they may be having one-to-two literacy lessons with our specialist literacy tutor, or sessions on our SuccessMaker computer programme. Other groups that run are the Spelling Mastery small group course and the Reading Recovery programme, which is also a small group exercise. We also cater for pupils who are temporarily disabled because of broken limbs, recovering from long-term illness, although access to the first floor can be very difficult if a leg is in full plaster. Other pupils using our Curriculum Support facility, will be on shortened timetables. Thus some pupils in Key Stage 4 may be taking a reduced number of GCSEs. Pupils in Key Stage 3 may have been allowed to drop a second foreign language. We also provide a safe haven in this room for any pupil deemed by the Year Head to be in need of comforting.

WEDNESFIELD HIGH SCHOOL

Lichfield Road, Wednesfield, Wolverhampton, West Midlands, WV11 3ES

Tel: 01902 558 222
Fax: 01902 558 200
Email: wednesfieldhighschool@wolverhampton.gov.uk

• Pupils: 1264 Mixed; Day Pupils • Age: 11 to 18
• Religion: Non-denominational • School status: State

SEN provision

Detail:
Now provide for in school:
Mild: ADD; ADHD; EBD; DYSC; DYSL; DYSP; HI; VI; CP;
Moderate: ADD; ADHD; EBD; MLD; DYSL; DYSP; HI;
Others: AUT(other); CD; TIC; EAL; Sp&LD; Epi; Eat
Experience of:
Mild: ASP; AUT; DS;
Moderate: ASP; VI;
Others: PD

Summary: The Governors, headteacher and Staff of Wednesfield High School make it their SEN priority objective to meet the needs of all students. This entails a detailed assessment and identification of need upon entry which, in turn, informs the planning that underpins the level and content of the work the students undertake. The assessment also triggers, where necessary, the involvement of support agencies from outside school.

The student is consulted at every stage of the SEN process and his/her wishes are considered to be extremely important as is the help and support of parents/carers. The school has an ongoing dialogue with parents of students who have a statement of SEN.

The special needs co-ordinator (SENCo) takes responsibility for the day to day operation of SEN provision. He is assisted by a team that includes an SEN teacher, teaching assistants and mentors. Other support is provided on a regular basis by the LEA's learning support team as well as other agencies from time to time. The school has been awarded the Basic Skills Agency Charter Mark for the third time. The SENCo has been working with SEN youngsters for over 25 years.

WELLINGTON SCHOOL

Wellington Road, Timperley, Altrincham, Cheshire, WA15 7RH

Tel: 01619 284 157

Fax: 01619 279 147

Email: admin@wellington.trafford.sch.uk

Website: www.wellington.trafford.sch.uk

• Pupils: 1235 Mixed; Day Pupils • Age: 11 to 18

• Religion: Non-denominational • School status: State

SEN provision

Detail:

Now provide for in school:

Mild: ASP; ADD; ADHD; EBD; DYSC; DYSL; DYSP; SpLD; HI; VI; CP;

Moderate: ASP; ADD; ADHD; MLD; DYSC; DYSL; DYSP; SpLD; HI; VI; CP;

Severe: SpLD;

Others: SPD; TIC; EAL; MSI; Sp&LD; DEL; Epi; Eat

Experience of:

Mild: AUT;

Moderate: EBD;

Others: AUT(other); CD; OCD; PMLD; PD

Summary: Support for Learning at Wellington School

At the heart of Wellington School operates a cycle of planning, teaching and assessment, which takes into account the wide range of abilities, aptitudes and interests of all our pupils. Many students have a form of special need at some point in their school careers. These needs may be met by extra help with reading, writing, numeracy, or by special support for sensory, communication, physical, emotional or behavioural difficulties.

At Wellington School we have a special educational needs co-ordinator and a team of classroom assistants who aim to provide specialised help to both pupils and subject teachers.

How is learning support offered?

Learning support for the least able takes the form of work in small groups, concentrating especially on the basics of numeracy and literacy. Certain pupils may be withdrawn from some mainstream lessons for a time, to help them with a general or specific difficulty by providing additional help.

A partnership with parents

The pupils themselves are fully involved in all stages of decision making, the setting of goals and targets, assessment, and the review of their progress. However, we recognise that parents also play a vital part in a child's education, and that learning does not just take place in school. Therefore we encourage parents to offer their own special support with homework and with practising skills and exercises. Parents can often provide essential highlights and information about the difficulties their child may be experiencing and we are dedicated to building an effective relationship based on good communication and shared responsibility.

Partnerships with others

We share responsibility for the provision of learning support with the Local Educational Authority. Wellington School has regular access to the services of an educational psychologist who comes into school to help monitor progress, provide assessment, offer advice, and who supports the school, the parents and the pupils.

Wellington School is acknowledged as a caring, secure environment, with a very strong pastoral system, and with a committed and dedicated staff. We also have access to the services of outside agencies including the Authority's Learning Support Service, Sensory Impairment Support Service, Special Support Service, Behaviour Support Service and medical help through the School Nurse.

WEST BUCKLAND SCHOOL

West Buckland, Barnstaple, Devon, EX32 0SX

Tel: 01598 760 281
Fax: 01598 760 546
Email: headmaster@westbuckland.devon.sch.uk
Website: www.westbuckland.devon.sch.uk

• Pupils: 690 Mixed; Takes boarders • Age: 2 to 18
• School status: Independent

SEN provision

Summary: West Buckland is an inclusive school where we are willing to consider any student whom we believe we can help. Every year group has a number of pupils who have moderate learning difficulties such as dyslexia, dyspraxia and specific learning difficulties. Our learning support team (one teacher and two classroom assistants) have special needs qualifications and have these support arrangements for work in the support base and alongside subject specialists:

Age 3-18:

Meetings with staff and parents, observations across the curriculum, standardised assessments and involvement with appropriate specialists (such as educational psychologists).

Years 3-7:

In class support plus short periods of basic skills/study skills work in response to individual needs.

Year 8 and 9:

Also have timetabled learning support in groups of up to eight instead of doing a second modern foreign language.

Year 10 and 11:

Up to eight students per year may opt for learning support lessons in place of a GCSE subject. Those with the most severe needs may have the option not to take a modern language. In-class support where most needed.

Year 12 and 13:

Appointments, as necessary.

All pupils benefit from the use of IT – and many use their own laptops in class and to complete prep. The support base is usually open from 8.30am to the end of the school day at 5.00pm. Any student may seek help outside lesson times. There is also support available for Boarders' Prep four evenings a week.

We pride ourselves on having good communication with parents so we can work together to help our youngsters at school and at home. Progress is regularly reviewed and on the basis of specialist advice we seek exam dispensations (such as extra time, supervised rest breaks, use of IT) for students doing formal exams (11+, SATs, 13+, GCSE, AS and A2).

WEST KIRBY RESIDENTIAL SCHOOL

Meols Drive, West Kirby, Wirral, Merseyside, CH48 5DH

Tel: 0151 632 3201
Fax: 0151 632 0621

• Pupils: 100 Mixed; Takes boarders • Age: 5 to 16
• School status: State

SEN provision

Detail:

Experience of:

Mild: EBD;
Moderate: EBD;
Severe: ADD; ADHD; EBD;
Others: AUT(other); CD; OCD; ODD; TIC; PMLD; PD; Oth

Summary: Pupils have complex special needs and are recognised by their Local Authority as having social, medical, emotional and behavioural problems. Medical conditions include Asperger's syndrome. An initial six week assessment is carried out for all new pupils. The school offers high quality accommodation in school and covers all curriculum areas. Therapy services include a behaviour support team, speech and language, physiotherapy and an educational psychologist. The school is ideally situated for outdoor pursuits and cultural experiences, its main aim being to provide a stable, caring and stimulating environment within which pupils can come to terms with their difficulties and reach their full potential. Approximately one third of the pupils attend on a weekly boarding basis or make regular overnight stays.

West Mains School

Logie Park, East Kilbride, G74 4BU

Tel: 01355 249 938
Fax: 01355 225 814
Email: office@westmains.s-lanark.sch.uk

• Pupils: 26 Mixed; Day Pupils • Age: 5 to 8
• Religion: Non-denominational • School status: State

SEN provision

Summary: West Mains School caters for P1-P3 children who have additional support needs arising from significant speech and or language difficulties. Programmes are prepared jointly by teachers and speech and language therapists. Children attend for between one and three years and are then phased into their local mainstream school.

Westfield Technology College

Littlemoor Road, Preston, Weymouth, Dorset, DT3 6AA

Tel: 01305 833 518
Fax: 01305 835 414
Email: office@westfield.dorset.sch.uk
Website: www.westfield.dorset.sch.uk

• Pupils: 172 Mixed; Day Pupils • Age: 19
• Religion: Non-denominational • School status: State

SEN provision

Detail:
Experience of:
Mild: SpLD; HI; VI;
Moderate: SpLD; HI; VI;
Severe: SpLD; HI; VI;
Others: SPD; MSI; Sp&LD

Summary: We provide for the individual needs of children aged 3-19 with moderate learning difficulties and complex learning difficulties. Many of our pupils have a combination of sensory and learning difficulties. We also have a specialist autism base for 30 pupils.

The Westgate School

Cheriton Road, Winchester, Hampshire, SO22 5AZ

Tel: 01962 854 757
Fax: 01962 840 080
Email: contact@westgate.hants.sch.uk
Website: www.westgate.hants.sch.uk

• Pupils: 1071 Mixed; Takes boarders • Age: 11 to 16
• Religion: Non-denominational • School status: State

SEN provision

Detail:
Now provide for in school:
Mild: ASP; EBD; DS; DYSC; DYSL; DYSP; VI;
Moderate: ASP; EBD; DS; MLD; DYSC; DYSL; DYSP; VI;
Severe: EBD; DYSL; HI;
Others: GEN; PMLD; SLD; EAL; Sp&LD; DEL; PD
Experience of:
Mild: AUT; ADD; ADHD; SpLD; HI; CP;
Moderate: AUT; ADD; ADHD; SpLD; HI;
Severe: ASP; ADD; ADHD; DYSC; DYSP; SpLD; VI;
Others: SPD; AUT(other); CD; OCD; ODD; FRX; MSI; Epi; Oth; Eat

Summary: The Westgate School recognises that all pupils may have special educational needs at some stage in their school career and that it is the responsibility of all staff to ensure that these pupils have access to a broad, balanced and relevant curriculum, irrespective of ability, disability, cognitive development, cultural/ethnic or other perceived differences.

The learning support department is responsible for ensuring that these pupils' needs are identified and met so that they are able to meet their potential and develop their self-esteem.

WESTON COLLEGE

Knightstone Road, Weston-super-Mare, BS23 2AL

Tel: 01934 411 411
Fax: 01934 411 410
Email: lrc@weston.ac.uk
Website: www.weston.ac.uk

• Pupils: 1551 Mixed; Day Pupils • Age: 16 to 99
• Religion: Non-denominational • School status: State

SEN provision

Summary: The centre has a special educational needs co-ordinator (SENCo) who is aware of and operates the statutory planning and review procedure for students with a statement of special educational needs. The SENCo is also responsible for planning and reviewing the individual educational plans/personal education plans of all students who are deemed to be at School Action Plus on the Code of Practice.

Our students are young people whose needs have not been met, or cannot currently be met, within the setting of a mainstream school. Each individual is highly likely to display a range of emotional and behavioural difficulties and many have become profoundly disaffected and disengaged from the formal learning process. Some may have literacy difficulties

WESTOVER GREEN COMMUNITY SCHOOL

Westover Green, Bridgwater, Somerset, TA6 7HB

Tel: 01278 422 943
Fax: 01278 446 003
Email: office@westovergreen.somerset.sch.uk
Website: www.westovergreen.somerset.sch.uk/

• Pupils: 340 Mixed; Day Pupils • Age: 4 to 11
• Religion: Non-denominational • School status: State

SEN provision

Detail:
Now provide for in school:
Mild: ASP; ADD;
Moderate: AUT;
Others: SPD
Experience of:
Mild: DS; VI;
Moderate: EBD; MLD; DYSC; DYSL; CP;
Severe: ADD; EBD;
Others: GEN; PMLD; EAL; Sp&LD; PD

Summary: LSA support in all classes. STC in all classes. Lunchtime provision. Language Resource Base onsite - catering for complex language needs. Physio suite Good ICT provision with interactive whiteboards in nine classrooms Catering for three pupils in wheelchairs – access and differentiation.

WESTWOOD COLLEGE

The Green, Welling, Kent, DA16 2PE

Tel: 020 8304 4916
Fax: 020 8298 7121
Email: westwoodcollege@hotmail.com

• Pupils: 737 Mixed; Day Pupils • Age: 11 to 16
• Religion: Non-denominational • School status: State

SEN provision

Detail:
Now provide for in school:
Mild: DYSC; DYSL; DYSP;
Moderate: MLD; DYSL;
Severe: DYSL;
Others: EAL; Epi
Experience of:
Mild: ASP; AUT; ADD; ADHD; EBD; HI; VI;
Moderate: ADD; EBD

Summary: At Westwood College, we aim to promote the learning of all students. We provide a caring, supportive department and we encourage all students to reach their own individual potential. We work in partnership with parents and will always keep parents updated about any support we provide. The teaching assistants in the department are highly skilled individuals, who are experts at working with students of all levels of ability. Our department works very closely with mainstream staff, to ensure that a comprehensive system of support is available within the classroom. Staff are kept up to date with any special needs information which ensures a whole college response to special needs.

Westwood School

6 Hartsbourne Road, Bushey Heath, Bushey, Hertfordshire, WD23 1JH

Tel: 020 8950 1138

Email: westwood.school@virgin.net

• Mixed; Day Pupils • Age: 4 to 7 • School status: Independent

SEN provision

Detail:

Experience of:

Mild: ASP; ADD; EBD; DYSC; DYSL; DYSP; HI;
Moderate: ASP; ADD; MLD; DYSC; DYSL; DYSP; HI;
Severe: DYSP; HI;
Others: SPD; OCD; Sp&LD; Epi

Summary: As Westwood is a small caring school whose intake begins at 4+, we are equipped to identify problems which emerge as a child begins formal education. Mild forms of difficulty are supported within school. The parents of those children requiring more specialised support are guided towards finding appropriate placements.

White Rock Primary School

Davies Avenue, Paignton, Devon, TQ4 7AW

Tel: 01803 843 175

Fax: 01803 846 017

Email: admin@white-rock-primary.torbay.sch.uk

Website: www.whiterockprimary.homestead.com

• Pupils: 429 Mixed; Day Pupils • Age: 5 to 11

• Religion: Non-denominational • School status: State

SEN provision

Detail:

Now provide for in school:

Mild: ASP; AUT; ADD; ADHD; EBD; DYSC; DYSL; DYSP; HI; VI;
Moderate: ADD; ADHD; EBD; MLD; DYSC; DYSL; DYSP; HI;
Severe: EBD; DYSL;
Others: EAL; Sp&LD; DEL; Epi; PD; Eat

Summary: *Every Child is Special.*

This is the core of our belief at White Rock School. We work as a whole staff team (this includes all admin. staff, MTA's, the caretaker and any other staff employed by the school) to support and encourage the children in our care to develop skills, to grow in confidence and to try their best at all times. We offer various SEN training opportunities, many of which are open to all staff who wish to attend. Our school team is very dedicated and hard working, always striving to meet the need of any child, whatever that need might be.

We aim to deliver the curriculum in the most creative way that we can devise, giving all children equal opportunity, as is their entitlement, and the chance to succeed.

We have easy disabled access around the school site and have recently opened a purpose built medical room to cater for any physical need. We are proud of the progress through our school made by a boy with muscular dystrophy and also that of a child with moderate hearing difficulties. We have a hearing loop in the school hall and have trained staff to enable the use of radio transmitter hearing aids.

We have many excellent external agency links and can access support from a large range of sources to support a variety of needs – be they medical, emotional, behavioural, learning (across the spectrum) or anything else.

We pride ourselves on having a warm, exciting and busy, creative, fully inclusive, environment for ALL our children to grow and flourish in.

Whitehall School

117 High Street, Somersham, Cambridgeshire, PE28 3EH

Tel: 01487 840 966

Fax: 01487 840 966

Email: office@whitehallschool.com

Website: www.whitehallschool.com

• Pupils: 90 Mixed; Day Pupils • Age: 3 to 11

• School status: Independent

SEN provision

Detail:
Experience of:
Mild: DYSL;
Moderate: MLD; DYSL;
Severe: DYSL;
Others: EAL; Sp&LD

Summary: Whitehall School is non-selective but does informally assess children with known special needs when they visit the school to ensure we can best cater for their needs. We employ a learning support teacher for three mornings a week, who works one-to-one, where appropriate. We also have small class sizes (average 12-15) which enable us to provide more individualised teaching where necessary.

Willenhall School Sports College

Furzebank Way, Willenhall, West Midlands, WV12 4BD

Tel: 01902 368 221
Fax: 01902 634 253
Email: postbox@willenhall.walsall.sch.uk
Website: www.willenhall.walsall.sch.uk
• Pupils: 1561 Mixed; Day Pupils • Age: 11 to 18
• Religion: Non-denominational • School status: State

SEN provision

Detail:
Now provide for in school:
Mild: ASP; AUT; ADD; ADHD; EBD; DYSL; DYSP; HI; VI;
Moderate: ASP; AUT; ADD; ADHD; EBD; MLD; DYSL; DYSP; HI; VI;
Severe: DYSL; HI; VI;
Others: SPD; ODD; TIC; EAL; Sp&LD; Epi; PD; Eat
Experience of:
Mild: DYSC; CP;
Moderate: DYSC; CP;
Severe: EBD;
Others: CD; OCD

Summary: Willenhall School Sports College has a sound reputation in the care of SEN pupils. We take care of a wide variety of SEN pupils. We have experience in a variety of medical issues, such as ASD, epilepsy, asthma, Tourette's syndrome, ADHD and dyspraxia. We have developed some expertise in dealing with the needs of dyslexic pupils. We have had whole school training in ASD, and are now quite experienced in looking after the needs of children with Asperger's syndrome. We have good access for disabled pupils. The school has a lift, disabled toilet facilities, a toilet management room (ie changing table, fixed hoist, sluice, etc). We work closely with parents, physiotherapists, occupational therapists and Walsall's senior paediatric consultant. (He holds clinics regularly at school.)

William Henry Smith School

Boothroyd, Brighouse, West Yorkshire, HD6 3JW

Tel: 01484 710 123
Fax: 01484 721 658
• Pupils: 58 Boys; Takes boarders • Age: 8 to 16
• School status: State

SEN provision

Detail:
Centre of excellence for:
Mild: EBD;
Moderate: EBD;
Severe: EBD
Now provide for in school:
Mild: ADD; ADHD; DYSC; DYSL; DYSP; SpLD;
Moderate: ADD; ADHD; DYSC; DYSL; DYSP;
Severe: ADD; ADHD; DYSC; DYSL; DYSP
Experience of:
Mild: ASP; AUT; HI;
Moderate: MLD; SpLD;
Severe: SpLD;
Others: SPD; CD; OCD; ODD; TIC; Sp&LD; Epi; Eat

Summary: We are a renowned and highly effective non-maintained residential special school catering for boys with severe social, emotional and behavioural difficulties.

A caring, stable and stimulating environment combined with a high ratio of skilled and dedicated staff enables each young person at the school to have the opportunity to develop their full academic and social potential.

WILLOW DENE SCHOOL

Swingate Lane, London, SE18 2JD

Tel: 020 8854 9841
Fax: 020 8854 9846
Email: headteacher.willowdene.greenwich@lgfl.net
Website: www.willowdene.greenwich.sch.uk

• Pupils: 159 Mixed; Day Pupils • Age: 2 to 11
• Religion: Non-denominational • School status: State

SEN provision

Detail:
Now provide for in school:
Mild: CP;
Moderate: AUT; ADD; ADHD; MLD; HI; VI; CP;
Severe: AUT; ADD; ADHD; DS; HI; VI; CP;
Others: SPD; AUT(other); CD; OCD; ODD; FRX; GEN; PMLD; SLD; MSI; DEL; Epi; PD

Summary: Willow Dene is a large primary special school established in July 2001 following the closure/amalgamation of five separate special schools. The school aims to provide high quality education for children aged between 2 and 11 years with a wide range of learning disabilities – moderate, severe, profound and multiple learning disabilities, complex medical needs, physical disabilities and children on the autistic spectrum.

In addition to the direct provision for children, including close multi-professional working with health professionals (SaLT; physiotherapy, OT, music therapy, school nursing service etc), the school has four Outreach services – Visual Impairment Service, ASD Outreach Service, the Specific Learning Difficulties Service and the SENCo Project who work to support children with moderate to severe learning difficulties in mainstream schools. All of the outreach projects have close working links with the school as well as supporting children with learning difficulties in mainstream schools and providing training for teachers, support staff and parents.

The school had a very successful Ofsted inspection in March 2003.

WILSON STUART SCHOOL

Perry Common Road, Erdington, Birmingham, West Midlands, B23 7AT

Tel: 0121 373 4475
Fax: 0121 373 9842
Email: enquiry@wilsonst.bham.sch.uk
Website: www.wilsonst.bham.sch.uk

• Pupils: 135 Mixed; Day Pupils • Age: 2 to 19
• Religion: Non-denominational • School status: State

SEN provision

Summary: Wilson Stuart School and Sports College is an all age school catering for children with physical disabilities from 2-19.

Our aims

- To empower pupils to take their place in a modern society with as much independence, confidence, self-esteem and self awareness as possible, irrespective of any disability, gender, cultural or linguistic differences.
- To provide a safe, welcoming and effective learning environment for pupils and staff, where everybody respects the abilities, values and beliefs of others.
- To provide a broad, balanced and flexible curriculum based upon the National Curriculum, responding to pupils' individual needs and actively seeking the best possible inclusive education for each child.
- To encourage and develop a partnership between the school, our parents, other professionals, and the wider community.
- To support the development of an inclusive society by acting as a resource, and by promoting an understanding of the needs and capabilities of individuals with disabilities.
- To support the achievement of these aims by fostering the career and personal development of all staff through ongoing training, drawing on resources available at national and local level.

WIMBLEDON COLLEGE

Edge Hill, London, SW19 4NS

Tel: 020 8946 2533

Fax: 020 8947 6513

Email: enquiries@wimbledoncollege.org.uk

Website: www.wimbledoncollege.org.uk

• Pupils: 1463 Boys; Day Pupils • Age: 11 to 18

• Religion: Roman Catholic • School status: State

SEN provision

Detail:

Now provide for in school:

Mild: ASP; AUT; ADD; ADHD; EBD; DYSC; DYSL; DYSP; HI; VI; CP;

Moderate: ASP; ADD; EBD; MLD; DYSC; DYSL; DYSP; HI; VI;

Severe: DYSL; DYSP; HI; VI;

Others: SPD; EAL; DEL; Epi

Experience of:

Mild: DS;

Moderate: ADHD; DS;

Others: CD; ODD; FRX

Summary: The bulk of our provision involves in-class support, although some boys are also withdrawn both individually and in small groups, especially for assistance with maths and literacy. Sixth formers are assisted on a mentoring basis. We have access for wheelchairs, and many members of staff have been trained in providing for boys with autistic spectrum conditions and those with hearing or visual impairment.

WIMBORNE LEARNING CENTRE

School Lane, Wimborne, Dorset, BH21 1HQ

Tel: 01202 886 947

Fax: 01202 886 947

Email: b.smith@dorsetcc.gov.uk

Website: www.wimborne-lc.dorset.sch.uk

• Mixed; Day Pupils • Age: 11 to 16

• Religion: Non-denominational • School status: State

SEN provision

Summary: All our pupils are referred from mainstream schools for medical or behavioural reasons or have been permanently excluded from a mainstream school.

WINGFIELD COMPREHENSIVE SCHOOL

Wingfield Road, Rotherham, South Yorkshire, S61 4AU

Tel: 01709 513 002

Fax: 01709 511 196

Email: Wingfield.comprehensive@rotherham.gov.uk

• Pupils: 748 Mixed; Day Pupils • Age: 11 to 16

• Religion: Non-denominational • School status: State

SEN provision

Detail:

Now provide for in school:

Mild: ASP; AUT; ADD; ADHD; EBD; DYSC; DYSL; DYSP; SpLD; HI;

Moderate: ASP; AUT; ADD; ADHD; EBD; MLD; DYSC; DYSL; DYSP; SpLD; HI;

Severe: DYSL; DYSP;

Others: SPD; CD; OCD; TIC; EAL; Epi; Eat

Summary: Wingfield Comprehensive School supports the inclusion philosophy by providing for a range of students' special educational and additional needs. As well as withdrawal support for students with a variety of learning and behaviour difficulties, careful focusing of in-class support, extensive mentoring and the opportunity to access re-engagement and vocational activities, the department actively seeks the support of external agencies in order to ensure barriers to learning are overcome.

Wirral Grammar School for Girls

Heath Road, Bebington, Wirral, Merseyside, CH63 3AF

Tel: 0151 644 8282
Fax: 0151 643 1332
Email: info@wirralgrammar-girls.wirral.sch.uk
Website: www.wirralgrammar-girls.wirral.sch.uk

• Pupils: 1052 Girls; Day Pupils • Age: 11 to 18
• Religion: Non-denominational • School status: State

SEN provision

Detail:
Centre of excellence for:
- Mild: VI;
- Moderate: VI;
- Severe: VI

Now provide for in school:
- Mild: AUT; ADD; ADHD; EBD; HI; CP;
- Moderate: HI; CP;
- Severe: HI; CP;
- Others: DEL; Epi; PD

Summary: We have excellent provision for the visually impaired as we are the designated school in our area for female pupils who have passed the 11+ examination. We have good access for pupils in wheelchairs having lifts and platform lifts to all areas of the school. In our most recent Ofsted report, our overall evaluation stated, 'Procedures for identifying and making provision for gifted and talented pupils and the few with special educational needs, are exemplary.' Because of our status as a grammar school, we have no pupils with learning difficulties and only a very few pupils with mild specific learning difficulties.

Withernsea High School and Technology College

Hull Road, Withernsea, HU19 2EQ

Tel: 01964 613 133
Fax: 01964 614 560
Website: www.whs.eril.net

• Pupils: 1069 Mixed; Day Pupils • Age: 11 to 18
• Religion: Non-denominational • School status: State

SEN provision

Detail:
Now provide for in school:
- Mild: DYSP;
- Moderate: MLD; DYSL; HI; VI;
- Severe: ADD; ADHD; EBD;
- Others: CD; EAL; DEL; Epi

Summary: The school provides support for students with a wide range of special educational needs. This support takes the form of individual and/or small group teaching especially for literacy skills, speech therapy, dyslexia teaching, speech and language therapy and many other forms of learning difficulty. We have a Student Support Centre for students who present with a variety of challenging behaviours and we have some experience of helping students with severe physical handicaps. However, it must be said that the school is on two levels with no lift facility and stairs every few metres. This makes wheelchair access to classrooms impossible without an appropriate stair ascender and trained staff to operate it.

WODENSBOROUGH COMMUNITY TECHNOLOGY COLLEGE

Hydes Road, Wednesbury, West Midlands, WS10 0DR

Tel: 01215 564 951
Fax: 01215 560 134
Email: wodensborough@yahoo.co.uk

• Pupils: 1188 Mixed; Day Pupils • Age: 11 to 18
• Religion: Non-denominational • School status: State

SEN provision

Detail:
Now provide for in school:
Mild: ASP

Summary: Wodensborough is an inclusive school. We hold the Sandwell Quality mark for inclusion – Advanced status. Wodensborough has an Enhanced learning provision for specific learning difficulties, a Focused provision for deaf and hearing impaired students and is working to hold a Focussed provision for autistic spectrum disorders. These are integral to the school and form only a part of the inclusive community at Wodensborough.

WOODCHESTER ENDOWED CHURCH OF ENGLAND AIDED PRIMARY SCHOOL

Church Road, North Woodchester, Stroud, Gloucestershire, GL5 5PD

Tel: 01453 872 476
Fax: 01453 873 062
Email: admin@woodchester.gloucs.sch.uk

• Pupils: 156 Mixed; Day Pupils • Age: 5 to 11
• Religion: Church of England • School status: State

SEN provision

Detail:
Now provide for in school:
Mild: ASP; AUT; ADD; EBD;
Moderate: AUT; ADD; MLD
Experience of:
Mild: ADHD; DYSC; DYSL; DYSP; HI; VI;
Moderate: ASP; ADHD;
Others: EAL; Sp&LD; Eat

Summary: The school has a full Disability Accessibility Plan. This school is always quiet and well-ordered, and the acoustics being of good quality would not provide untoward difficulties for partially hearing children on amplification aids. The school has good signage throughout and clear procedures are in place for movement around the school. As a school we are very willing to accept children who have special needs and requirements, feeling that this is the best way to integrate such children into society and also providing our own children with important contact with those who have different needs. The main school classrooms are entirely on one level with very wide entrances that would easily facilitate wheelchairs and any other special equipment. However, the temporary classes and ICT suite are reached by stairs, but help is always available. We have the services of three learning support workers who enhance our capacity to enhance the learning of children with a variety of special needs. These assistants are extremely well-skilled in a range of different SEN areas.

Woodfield School

Glenwood Avenue, Kingsbury, London, NW9 7LY

Tel: 020 8205 1977
Fax: 020 8205 5877
Email: admin@woodfield.brent.sch.uk
Website: www.woodfield.brent.sch.uk

• Pupils: 112 Mixed; Day Pupils • Age: 18
• Religion: Non-denominational • School status: State

SEN provision

Detail:
Now provide for in school:
Mild: AUT;
Moderate: AUT; MLD;
Severe: AUT;
Others: AUT(other); Sp&LD

Summary: Woodfield School has 120 places for children aged from 11 to 18 who have moderate learning difficulties. Of these 120 places, 12 places are available for pupils with additional and complex speech and language needs and seven places for pupils on the autistic spectrum. Woodfield School is committed to providing a secure, enjoyable and stimulating learning environment which will enable pupils to realise their potential as individuals in society.

Woodlands School

Bodmin Road, Whitleigh, Plymouth, Devon, PL5 4DZ

Tel: 01752 300 101
Fax: 01752 300 102
Email: woodlands.school@plymouth.gov.uk

• Pupils: 67 Mixed; Takes boarders • Age: 2 to 17
• Religion: Non-denominational • School status: State

SEN provision

Summary: Woodlands School accommodates up to 72 physically disabled children between the ages of 2 and 16 years. Many of the pupils have additional difficulties that may also affect their learning. Teaching is based on the National Curriculum and pupils have both group and individual learning programmes. Key Stage 4 pupils follow nationally accredited courses where appropriate and a wide range of extra curricular activities are offered. Facilities include spacious classrooms, some of which are subject related, wide corridors, light sensory rooms, hydrotherapy, rebound, soft play and ball pool, every classroom has interactive whiteboards and there are sufficient computers for all pupils. The school residence offers weekly boarding and nightly respite in one and two bedded rooms for pupils at Woodlands School and those with a mobility or medical need attending Downham and Milford schools. The residence is open all year round. Emphasis is always placed on pupils becoming independent learners and there is a strong tradition of inclusion. Many pupils experience mainstream school opportunities for part of each week, normally supported by a classroom assistant from Woodlands. Some pupils transfer to their mainstream school fulltime. In addition to the teachers, nursery nurses, teaching assistants, and nurses, the Health Authority provides physiotherapy, speech and language therapy and occupational therapy where appropriate

The Wordsley School

Brierley Hill Road, Wordsley, Stourbridge, West Midlands, DY8 5SP

Tel: 01384 816 015
Fax: 01384 816 016
Email: mlambert@buckpool.dudley.gov.uk
Website: www.buckpool.dudley.gov.uk/

• Pupils: 642 Mixed; Day Pupils • Age: 11 to 16
• Religion: Non-denominational • School status: State

SEN provision

Detail:
Now provide for in school:
Mild: DYSC; DYSL; DYSP; HI;
Moderate: MLD; DYSC; DYSL; DYSP;
Others: ODD; TIC; EAL
Experience of:
Mild: ADD; ADHD; EBD; DS; VI; CP;
Moderate: ADD; ADHD; EBD; DS; HI; VI; CP;
Severe: DS; DYSC; DYSL; DYSP;
Others: CD; MSI; Sp&LD; DEL; Epi; PD; Eat

Summary: Philosophy and definition

All pupils at The Wordsley School have entitlement of support for their learning needs enabling them to develop skills, knowledge and understanding to full potential and maximum personal benefit.

We define special educational needs in terms of a staged level of difficulty a child has compared with the majority of children of the same age and the provision and resources available at each stage.

WORKSOP COLLEGE

Enquiry Office, Sparken Hill, Worksop, Nottinghamshire, S80 3AP

Tel: 01909 537 100

Fax: 01909 537 102

Email: headmaster@worksopcollege.notts.sch.uk

Website: www.worksopcollege.notts.sch.uk/

• Pupils: 401 Mixed; Takes boarders • Age: 13 to 19

• School status: Independent

SEN provision

Detail:

Now provide for in school:

Mild: DYSL; HI; CP;

Moderate: DYSL;

Others: EAL; Epi

Experience of:

Mild: ASP; ADD; ADHD; DYSC; DYSP; SpLD;

Severe: DYSL;

Others: Eat

Summary: The majority of pupils at Worksop who have special educational needs are mild to moderately dyslexic although a few have slightly more severe difficulties. All are able to cope in a normal classroom situation, although some in-class support is provided by specialist teachers. Some pupils receive additional support on a withdrawal basis, mainly one-to-one, according to need. A small percentage of pupils follow a slightly reduced curriculum in years 10 and 11. In core subjects, children are taught in sets according to their ability, which allows for a slower pace of learning for less academic pupils and enables the most able to be stretched. There are a number of overseas pupils who follow the normal curriculum, although French is usually replaced by lessons in English as an Additional Language. These lessons are taught by an experienced and qualified member of staff.

The school has a Health Care Centre staffed by qualified nurses.

YEWDALE SCHOOL

Yewdale Road, Carlisle, Cumbria, CA2 7SD

Tel: 01228 60 7557

Fax: 01228 60 7558

Email: admin@yewdale.cumbria.sch.uk

• Pupils: 213 Mixed; Day Pupils • Age: 4 to 11

• Religion: Non-denominational • School status: State

SEN provision

Detail:

Now provide for in school:

Mild: ASP; AUT; ADD; ADHD; EBD; DYSC; DYSL; DYSP; SpLD; HI; VI; CP;

Moderate: ASP; AUT; ADD; ADHD; EBD; MLD; DYSC; DYSL; DYSP; SpLD; CP;

Severe: ASP; DYSC; DYSL; DYSP; SpLD; CP;

Others: SPD; SLD; MSI; Sp&LD; DEL; Epi; PD

Summary: Yewdale School is a strategic facility for children with MLD and specific physical and medical needs and complex difficulties. We also cater successfully for children with behavioural problems. Children are fully integrated into the mainstream class situation and supported by trained staff skilled at working with children who need a carefully differentiated curriculum. We work closely with children and their parents to ensure they are well informed and involved in their child's education.

Ysgol Glanymôr School

Heol Elfed, Burry Port, Carmarthenshire, SA16 0AL

Tel: 01554 832 507
Fax: 01554 832 424
Email: glanymor@satproj.org.uk

• Pupils: 717 Unknown; Day Pupils • Age: 11 to 16
• School status: State

SEN provision

Detail:
Now provide for in school:
- Mild: ASP; AUT; ADD; ADHD; EBD; DYSC; DYSL; DYSP; HI; VI;
- Moderate: ASP; AUT; ADD; ADHD; EBD; MLD; DYSC; DYSL; DYSP; VI;
- Severe: ADD; EBD; DYSL; VI;
- Others: AUT(other); PMLD; EAL; Sp&LD; Epi

Experience of:
- Mild: DS; SpLD; CP;
- Moderate: DS; SpLD; HI; CP;
- Severe: ASP; AUT; ADHD; DS; DYSC; DYSP; SpLD; HI;
- Others: SPD; CD; ODD; SLD; MSI; Eat

Summary: At Glan-y-Mor School, we see every child as an individual. In this way, we can get to know a child's potential and provide for his/her individual needs whether underachieving or gifted and talented.

Our aim is to include all pupils within the life of the school. We achieve this by providing a holistic approach to all aspects of a child's learning. In the January 2004 Estyn report, inspectors noted that:

'The arrangements made to identify pupils who need support are thorough with very good links with primary schools leading to early identification in year 7'.

A team of specialist experienced teachers, highly trained staff and school counsellor provide academic, social, emotional and behavioural support to pupils. Support is provided in mainstream classes, dedicated teaching rooms and, if needed, during unstructured periods.

In our last inspection, the findings were:

'The provision for pupils with SEN is good and the school's response to the requirements of the Code of Practice is very good ... All pupils with SEN leave school with appropriate accreditation.'

Ysgol Uwchradd Tregaron

Tregaron, Ceredigion, SY25 6HG

Tel: 01974 298 231
Fax: 01974 298 515
Email: admin.tregaron@ceredigion.gov.uk

• Pupils: 358 Mixed; Day Pupils • Age: 11 to 18
• Religion: Non-denominational • School status: State

SEN provision

Detail:
Centre of excellence for:
- Mild: DS; DYSL; VI;
- Moderate: DS; MLD; DYSL;
- Others: EAL

Now provide for in school:
- Mild: ASP; ADD; ADHD; EBD; DYSP; HI;
- Moderate: ASP; ADD; ADHD; EBD; DYSP;
- Severe: DYSL;
- Others: SLD; Sp&LD; Epi; PD

Experience of:
- Mild: CP;
- Moderate: CP;
- Severe: EBD

Summary: The school favours a 'Whole School Policy' for pupils with SEN which provides two things:-

1. A quality of education for ALL pupils.

2. An equality of educational opportunity for ALL pupils.

Equality can be summarised as:-

a) The right to be educated with one's peers.

b) The right of education to adjust to meet individual needs.

c) The right to have one's contribution regarded on an equal basis with others. Curriculum development in a Whole School Policy takes the form of developing a curriculum which minimises the learning difficulties of its pupils.

YSGOL Y PLAS

Llanelian, Bae Colwyn, Conwy, LL29 8YY

Tel: 01492 680 601
Email: pennaeth@yplas.conwy.sch.uk
• Pupils: 64 Mixed; Day Pupils • Age: 3 to 11
• Religion: Christian • School status: State

SEN provision

Detail:
Experience of:
Mild: ASP; AUT; EBD; DYSC; DYSL; DYSP; SpLD; HI; VI; CP;
Moderate: ASP; EBD; MLD; DYSL; DYSP; HI; CP;
Severe: DYSL;
Others: OCD; EAL; DEL; Epi

Summary: We try to find teaching methods that suit the ability of every child in the school. Being a small rural school, we do feel that we are able to achieve this. We aim to secure a balanced curriculum for all children and hope that with support we can enable all children to participate in the life and work of the school to the best of their abilities, whatever their needs. The school has a policy, which ensures the early identification of a child that has difficulty and the school aims to work closely with parents to secure an effective partnership to support the child.

Chapter 6

Help for your child in the classroom

Under the Disability Discrimination Act, appropriate help must be provided by schools and colleges so that children with special needs are on a 'level playing field' with their peers. Someone with dyspraxia who writes very slowly may qualify for extra time in exams, get help with typing tuition and be permitted to use a laptop in class. Some strategies are simple and don't cost anything; for example, having a 'buddy' for a dyspraxic child who is new to the school and gets lost easily will help the child settle in. Others are complex bureaucratic processes that it may seem daunting to tackle but which can open doors to invaluable extra support.

Chapter 3 has lots of useful information on the various SEN personnel who can provide assistance in and out of the classroom, and you'll also find in this chapter information on assessments such as P levels and the ASDAN awards, which measure and celebrate achievement in different ways.

You should hope for a quiet confidence from your school about fulfilling your child's needs, but if staff appear horrified by them or flippant in their attitude to dealing with it then it's time to reconsider what is best for your child.

School Action and School Action Plus

A graduated approach to help and intervention is the norm. If your child needs extra or different help, such as teaching in a different way, getting extra help either individually or in a small group, use of specialist equipment etc, the school may recommend your child is placed on School Action or School Action Plus. School Action Plus involves outside agencies, perhaps the educational psychologist or health professionals (see Chapter 3 for information on professionals who may be involved with your child). Naturally the school has a duty to let parents know about this extra support, and school and parents should seek to work together to give the child the best possible chance of success. If your child makes good progress School Action may be discontinued.

Early Years Action and Early Years Action Plus work in much the same way for preschool children.

Individual education plans (IEPs)

A buzz word of the day, just what is an IEP and what will it mean for a child and their parents if an IEP is suggested?

Individual education plans are used in many schools, and some preschools, for children who are having greater difficulty than most in following the curriculum. An IEP pinpoints areas where a child with learning needs, behavioural problems or disabilities is experiencing difficulties. It contains targets designed to help children who require extra support. It is only used where a child needs something extra or different from others in the class. Wherever possible, the child and parents or carers should be involved in discussions and review of an IEP.

Not all schools use IEPs; some plan and record separately for each child as a matter of routine. Regardless of the system used, a successful IEP (or equivalent) should be an easy-to-understand, simple-to-use working document that is carefully monitored and regularly reviewed to best help the child. All staff who work with the child, including therapists and support staff, should be helping them attain specified goals and raise overall achievement.

Who has an IEP?

It isn't necessary for a pupil to have a statement of SEN, or even to be on School Action or School Action Plus, to have an IEP and, likewise, not all children on these programmes have IEPs. Some schools are introducing a form of IEP for all their pupils, others have group IEPs.

However, where a pupil has a statement, the setting of short-term targets and the strategies employed should be linked to the overall objectives and provision set out in the statement.

What does an IEP say?

An IEP will usually contain no more than three or four key, individual, short-term targets for the child to focus on (typically these only take up one side of A4). These may relate to aspects of the curriculum (literacy, numeracy etc), or focus on behaviour or social skills. The IEP should specify what should be taught, how it should be taught and how often, and will be based on individual need. Often targets will be set to cover not only a variety of objectives but different situations too, including working with and without support, in and out of class.

Targets should be SMART, that is: specific, measurable, achievable, relevant and time-related.

Usually an IEP will include the teaching objective (what the teacher hopes the child will learn) broken into small manageable chunks linked to a child's abilities and difficulties, enabling teacher, parent and child to see improvement. For example, the class objective may be to learn the two-times tables, but for the individual child this may be simplified to being able (and, crucially, understanding) to count on in twos, to ten.

Targets may be related to activities outside the lesson, perhaps to sit quietly at the dinner table or to play with friends, not to get angry when the lunchtime football team loses a match etc.

Targets should be clearly focused. 'To improve handwriting' is too general for most children, for example, so it may be better to break the task into more manageable chunks, perhaps first adapting to an adjusted pencil grip, or developing 'good sitting', then moving on from there.

Help to achieve targets

Any additional provision needed to meet targets, including the use of special activities or equipment, or parental involvement – perhaps how they can help with homework or support any agreed reward structure – should be identified. The IEP should outline who will help where and how – in the classroom, in a small group or in a one-to-one setting, for instance.

In some schools, where pupils have communication difficulties, schools use a target board so that pupils can visualise where they are. A particularly nice idea is a target 'dart board', showing how the closer to the bull's eye, the closer to the target being achieved. The board can be coded to show different children's progress towards their targets (or a child's progress with their individual targets).

The pupil should understand what they have to do, to successfully meet targets. The IEP should contain information on activities that will help the pupil achieve their targets as well as intervention strategies and any rewards or incentives for meeting targets. IEPs should be parent friendly, carefully monitored and regularly reviewed.

Reviewing an IEP

The IEP should be reviewed at least twice a year, more often if needs be – the review could take place every half-term or every three weeks if required. The school should involve you in the process, asking you and your child's views on progress.

When targets are met, new targets will be added. If targets are not met it will be necessary to examine why not, perhaps breaking the task down further or in some instances choosing alternative targets.

When reviewing IEPs consideration should be given to progress made, how effective the IEP has been, anything that has had a bearing on the child's progress (perhaps the child has been ill or unsettled), up-to-date information relevant to the child, and the views of the parent and the child. After considering progress, the targets to be achieved by the next review should be set by staff, with the involvement of the parents and child if possible. Of course, if targets have been achieved and help is no longer needed, a new IEP may be deemed unnecessary.

Statutory assessments and statement of special educational needs

If a school cannot meet all the child's needs from its resources it may be necessary to apply for a statement of SEN. In a few cases a statement may be applied for immediately (or even before a child starts school).

Although we still hear of parents who shun the idea, or are fearful that 'being statemented' is somehow a black mark that singles out their child as different, a statement for a child that needs it is a very positive step as it opens up doors and coffers that may otherwise remain resolutely shut.

Getting the right statement you need for your child is seldom a walk in the park. The legal side of all this is explained in Chapter 9 by David Ruebain, one of this country's leading lawyers in the field of education and disability and special needs. However, as a helpful guide to some of the practicalities of what's involved, here are some of the most frequently asked questions on the assessment and statementing process.

What is a statement of special educational needs?

A statement of special educational needs is a detailed document written by the local education authority (LEA) that describes all of a child's additional educational needs, and the special help and support a child should be given.

What is a statutory assessment?

A statutory assessment is a detailed investigation to find out a child's special educational needs, and what special help a child requires.

Why are some children assessed?

If the LEA decides that all the special help a child needs cannot be provided from within the school or preschool's resources, they will seek to issue a statement of SEN.

When will the need for statutory assessment be considered?

A statutory assessment, carried out by the LEA, may be recommended when a child has severe or complex difficulties or hasn't made enough progress through Early Years Action Plus or School Action Plus.

I would like my child to have a statutory assessment. Can I ask the LEA to do this at any time?

Yes, as long as an assessment hasn't already been made in the six months prior to the request and (the tricky bit) the LEA considers an assessment (or further assessment) is necessary.

Can anyone other than parents request an assessment?

Yes, schools and early education providers can also ask for an assessment. Again, the LEA must agree that an assessment is necessary, and with moves afoot to reduce the number of statements issued getting the LEA to agree could become an uphill struggle.

What should parents and schools do to persuade an LEA to agree to an assessment?

Present your case as clearly as possible: gather evidence and keep detailed records, and if appropriate use checklists to illustrate your case. Talk to the people who know your child well (teachers, health specialists etc). Ask for their input and support. Pass to the LEA the names of those people you feel should be contacted to give useful information about your child's needs.

Where can I find out what details should be included?

Obtain an up-to-date copy of the SEN Code of Practice (from the LEA or the DfES) as this details the evidence the LEA has to consider – it's always helpful to know how the other side prepares their case. You may also find it useful to have a parental supporter (see Chapter 8) to help you make decisions; they will advise you in a different way from those who work with your child, and will have experience of the process and understand your concerns and anxieties.

Who will the LEA ask for information and how are parents involved in the assessment process?

As part of the assessment process, the LEA will ask for information from the parent (or carer), the child's school or preschool, a doctor, an educational psychologist and anyone else involved with the child. Parents have the right to attend any interview, medical or other test during the statutory assessment but it's not always in the child's best interests for a parent to be present, so if in doubt, speak with the people assessing your child before deciding. After the LEA has collected all the advice and comments, a decision will be made whether to write a proposed statement or a note in lieu for the child.

Can I appeal if my request for a statutory assessment is refused?

Yes, you may appeal to the Special Educational Needs & Disability Tribunal (SENDIST) provided there hasn't been an assessment within the last six months.

Are there time limits in drawing up a statement?

Yes, see the table below.

Time frame	Action
Within 6 weeks	LEA must say if an assessment is to be made.
Within 16 weeks	If an LEA decides to assess a child for a statement, a proposed or draft statement must be given to parents. This should take no more than ten weeks, unless there is a valid reason such as a need to obtain extensive medical reports.
By week 18	A draft statement or notice in lieu should be issued.
Within 26 weeks	Once a draft statement has been agreed the statement should be finalised and issued.

How much detail should a statement contain?

Statements are individual and unique to each child but every statement should clearly state *in detail* the provision necessary to meet the child's needs. The LEA should determine what actions and provision are appropriate for the individual on a case-by-case basis. Where a child may be educated will be considered and although there will be cases where there needs to be flexibility to meet the child's changing special educational needs, requirements should normally be quantified in terms of hours of provision, staffing arrangements etc. Beware: some LEAs have been accused of omitting provision details from statements because of the cost to the authority, so you might have to push hard to get what your child needs.

What will a proposed statement look like?

A proposed statement will be in six parts:

Part 1	States general factual information: names, address, child's date of birth etc.
Part 2	Sets out all of a child's special educational needs.
Part 3	This is in three subsections: ■ Objectives: identifies the long-term aims of the provision to meet a child's needs. ■ Educational provision: this sets out what is required to meet the needs identified in Part 2. ■ Monitoring: this states the arrangements for reviewing targets, objectives and progress. The LEA must arrange provision set out in this section.
Part 4	Names the school a child will attend (this will be left blank in the proposed statement – see 'Identifying schools' below).
Part 5	Details any non-educational needs.
Part 6	Explains how a child will get help to meet any non-educational needs. The LEA does not have a duty to arrange provision set out here and nor does anyone else.

Am I allowed to comment on my child's proposed statement?

Yes, once you have the draft of the proposed statement you can comment on the statement and indicate anything you disagree with. The LEA must take notice of these comments. Importantly, this is the point at which you can name the school you want your child to attend (see below).

Can parents name a school for their child to attend?

Yes, you have the right to express a preference for maintained school where you wish your child to be educated, and this should be named on the draft of the proposed statement. So make sure you do your homewor on suitable schools for your child prior to this stage (se Chapter 5). It's essential to check out suitable schoo and provision in advance of the draft statement being issued so that you can make a reasoned case as to why you want your child to attend a particular school.

Does the final statement name the school?

Yes, the final statement will name the school a child will attend. Copies of the statement will be sent to you, your child's school and all other involved professionals.

What if I am unhappy with the final statement?

If you are unhappy with the final statement you can appeal to a special needs tribunal or go to mediation (see Chapters 8 and 9).

What if the LEA decides a child does not need a statement after all?

If the LEA decides the school can provide the help required without resorting to the expense and bureaucracy of a statement, a 'notice in lieu' may be issued. This means the information gleaned from the statementing process is shared with parents and a child's school, hopefully to plan future support for a child but without the backing of a formal statement. Parents have the right of appeal if a notice in lieu is issued instead of a statement.

Can the Secretary of State intervene if I am unhappy with a decision?

No, the Secretary of State cannot intervene on behalf of the parents in such cases.

Identifying schools for children with statements

Are there arrangements for expressing a preference for a particular school?

Yes, and the LEA must explain the arrangements for this as well as indicating their duty to comply with that preference. Seek out this advice during the early stages – don't wait until you receive the proposed statement.

Must my child be educated in a mainstream school?

Pupils with statements must be educated in a mainstream school unless that is incompatible with the wishes of their parents or the provision of efficient education for other children.

Can I ask for my child to be educated at an independent school?

Yes, if a parent makes representations for an independent school, and the LEA agrees this is the most appropriate school, the LEA may place the child in the school provided the school has been approved by the Secretary of State (under section 347 of the Education Act 1996) to educate children with SEN. If the school has not been approved, the LEA must seek consent from the Secretary of State (under section 347(5)(b) of the 1996 Act). Research independent schools – if you believe they will offer your child more than state schools – and be prepared to make a case.

Must the school named by parents in their child's statement be in their own LEA?

No. The LEA has to name a parent's preferred school unless either: the school is unsuitable to the child's age, ability or aptitude or to their special educational needs; or the attendance of the child at the school would be incompatible with the provision of efficient education for the children with whom they would be educated, or the efficient use of resources.

Can a school refuse to take a child with a statement if it is full?

No, the governing bodies of a maintained school named on a statement can't refuse to take a child because the school is full. However, LEAs should check out the situation before naming a school on the statement. This is especially important where infant classes are affected: statutory legislation limits class size for 5–7-year-olds (except in certain exceptional circumstances). The governing body of a school will still be under a duty to admit, although they could complain to the Secretary of State that the LEA had acted unreasonably and/or failed in a statutory duty in naming the school if it is already full (their problem, not yours).

Will the LEA provide transport for pupils with SEN?

LEAs must provide free home–school transport for any child with or without SEN where they consider that this is necessary to enable a child to attend school. Where a child attends a school other than the one the LEA considers to be the nearest suitable, the LEA does not have to provide transport but they have discretion to pay all or any part of the reasonable expenses incurred – so they can enter into special arrangements with parents.

Reviewing statements

How frequently is a statement reviewed?

LEAs must review a statement at least once every 12 months but have the right to review a statement at any time during the year.

Who is involved with the review?

Parents, the school, the LEA, therapists, the educational psychologist and any other professionals involved with the child should comment on progress made and how effective and appropriate the statement is.

Will the provision be changed at the annual review?

It can be. If the child's needs have changed, provision may change.

What format does the review take?

The annual review is in four parts: gathering information, the annual review meeting, the headteacher's report of the annual review meeting to the LEA, and the LEA's review of the statement.

What is the purpose of the meeting?

The meeting will consider whether the statement is still appropriate, examine any changes needed to the statement and decide if it should be continued or is no longer needed. Everyone involved will discuss the written views and progress made towards reaching the targets set for the year. New goals will be agreed for the coming year.

What happens before the meeting?

The child's headteacher is responsible for getting written advice from those involved and for inviting them to the review meeting. Before the meeting the school should ask parents for their views on the child's progress over the last year. Keeping a notebook or diary is a useful way of remembering key issues or concerns. Parents, a representative of the LEA and a relevant teacher must be invited to the review; other people, including the child, can attend. At least two weeks before the meeting, the school will send copies of the information received to all those invited to the review.

How should I prepare for the review meeting?

■ Think about the overall progress (or lack of progress) your child has made since the last review or statement. If you have kept a log or diary, go through it picking out important, relevant information.

■ Look at things your child finds particularly difficult or trying. If something concerns you, however trivial it may seem, mention it.

■ Look at what your child is good at and what they respond positively to as well as any areas of concern or regression.

■ Identify any changes at home or at school that might have had an impact on progress or behaviour.

■ Highlight any areas where you think your child needs more help than at present.

■ Read all the reports issued, note anything you do not understand or want clarifying and make a note of anything you want to say or ask at the meeting.

What happens at the meeting?

Everyone should be introduced and time given to read any extra reports not seen before the meeting (ask for this if it isn't offered). It's useful to take brief notes of what is said so you can check back afterwards. It may help to take a friend, relative or parental supporter.

What happens after the review meeting?

Within ten working days of the meeting, the headteacher will send a report to the LEA (and a copy to parents) detailing any agreed changes. The LEA will then decide whether to leave the statement unchanged, to amend it, to end the statement or to start a new statutory assessment, and will inform parents and the school of the decision (with reasons) in writing. Within 15 days of hearing from the LEA, parents can request a meeting to discuss any changes they may wish to make. Parental views are important and the LEA should always consider these before making any changes.

Why is the annual review in year 9 different?

In year 9 (when a child is aged 13/14) a transition plan will be drawn up to help a child prepare for the move from school to adult life. This review must include a Connexions Service representative (see Chapter 7). The Transition Plan will be reviewed each year as part of the annual review until a child leaves school.

Can parents appeal against an amended statement?

Yes, and the LEA should inform parents of the right to appeal to the SEN & Disability Tribunal (SENDIST) at the time of issuing the amended statement. You have two months from the date the letter is issued by the LEA to register your appeal. For more on appeals procedures and the Tribunal, see Chapter 9.

The National Curriculum and P levels

The National Curriculum is the framework used by all state schools in England and outlines not only what children should be taught but at what stage they should achieve particular objectives or milestones in their learning. Schools should monitor children's progress through the National Curriculum.

By the end of Key Stage 1 (age 7), the average child is expected to achieve National Curriculum level 2; this rises to level 4 at the end of Key Stage 2 (age 11) and level 5 or 6 by the end of Key Stage 3 (age 13 or 14). There are eight levels but only the most able pupils will achieve level 8, with an additional exceptional performance category for those gifted and talented children who rarely achieve beyond this. State schools enter children for national testing at the end of each of the four Key Stages (the fourth being GCSE, at which point the National Curriculum no longer applies).

It is recognised that children work at different levels according to age and ability and that for a few children even the lowest levels will be difficult to achieve. At the lower end, and in exceptional cases, schools can choose to disapply weaker students from some elements of the National Curriculum.

The P scales

Some children with special needs will be working below level 1 of the National Curriculum. They are assessed according to P scales. Pupils aged 5–16 who are working at or towards P levels are likely to need significant help and prompting with tasks and activities. P scales exist for all National Curriculum subjects, including the non-core curriculum subjects, personal, social and health education (PSHE) and religious education (RE). There are eight levels of performance, with each describing some of the important knowledge, skills and understanding that pupils may gain from the programmes of study of the National Curriculum.

Children do not undergo any formal assessment or testing and, unlike the National Curriculum, the awarding of a P level is left to the judgement of staff. It's expected that teachers will use their knowledge of the child, consider the contexts in which learning takes place and gather evidence from a variety of sources to support their decisions and to make a 'best-fit judgement' based on everyday activity and continual monitoring and assessment.

So what are P levels? The following, from *Towards the National Curriculum in Maths*, published by the DfES (2001), helps illustrate P levels:

At level 1 a pupil will: 'Encounter activities and experiences. May be passive or resistant. May show simple reflex responses. Any participation is fully prompted.' Illustrated by the example: 'Tolerate or show pleasure in hair brushing and hand massage as adult uses words like "more".'

At level 3 a pupil will: 'Begin to communicate intentionally. Seek attention through eye contact, gesture or action. Request events or activities. Participate in shared activities with less support. Sustain concentration for short periods. Explore materials in increasingly complex ways. Observe the results of their own actions with interest. Remember learned responses over more extended periods.' Illustrated by the example: 'Show some awareness of taking turns in a game or event. Offer items to people in turn.'

At level 4, subject-related attainment is introduced, eg 'Show an interest in number activities and counting', with the given example: 'Experience numbers as names – bus routes, house numbers.' By level 8 this will have graduated to: 'Begin to use number names beyond ten – number of players in a team, houses in a street or count the number of pupils in the class or group.'

Unlike the National Curriculum there is no expectation that a child will achieve a particular P scale by a given age or work through the P scales at a predetermined rate. However, attainment of a level by a particular age may help identify likely rate of progress through the P scales. The subject-related attainments of P4 to P8 are designed with transition to the National Curriculum in mind.

ASDAN: recognising, rewarding and celebrating achievement

Most schools we've visited follow the National Curriculum, albeit modified and adapted to meet the needs of the individual. Newspapers bombard us with league tables and reports of GCSE and A level exams and there's been increasing press coverage of alternative vocational awards such as NVQ. But what's on offer for those learners who achieve great personal goals and targets but find it difficult to access mainstream qualifications? How are their efforts and achievements recognised and rewarded?

Heather Fry, Head of Awards: Preparatory and Entry Level at ASDAN

ASDAN (Award Scheme Development and Accreditation Network), an awarding body approved by the Qualifications and Curriculum Authority (QCA), specialises in producing curriculum resources that promote the development of personal, social, citizenship and independence skills, and skills for working life. The awards meet the needs of learners across the ability spectrum, including those who may have difficulty following more traditional routes and qualifications.

ASDAN's special needs provision

Transition Challenge

This programme has been developed for students at Key Stage 4 (14–16 years), but can be used beyond if appropriate to the needs of the learner. Transition Challenge provides a framework of activities for developing and accrediting independent living, and personal skills, through areas of activity relating to the statutory programmes of study for Key Stage 4 National Curriculum subjects, complemented by activities contributing to the development of skills needed in adult living.

An exciting development for the Transition Challenge award is the ASDAN education partnership project with the RDA (Riding for the Disabled Association incorporating Carriage Driving). The project involves learners who take part in RDA activities as part of their school curriculum. The many varied experiences and achievements of the rider when engaged in activities at the RDA centre can be recorded as part of the Transition Challenge award. This will culminate in the rider/carriage driver receiving a dedicated ASDAN/RDA Transition Challenge award certificate, in recognition and celebration of their achievements.

Towards Independence

This programme has been developed for the adult learner (16+). The programme contains a series of modules that build into a profile of achievement. Modules include: meal preparation, self-advocacy, getting ready to go out, going to college, animal care and multi-sensory experiences. The last module is particularly suited to learners with profound and multiple learning difficulties. Towards Independence offers formal recognition for small steps in achievement towards a larger goal.

Workright

This has been developed for young people aged 14+ and adults. The aim of the programme is to develop a range of basic transferable employability skills.

Common features to all three programmes are:

- Use of levels of support: This allows differentiation of achievement between learners and provides a mechanism to record the progress of the individual. The levels of support range from No Help (NH) for those learners who can do tasks independently, to Sensory Experience (SE) appropriate for those who are engaging in an activity through the use of one or more of their senses.
- Skills recognition: key skills, basic skills and other important life skills.
- Formative student records: a portfolio of evidence which can re-engage the learner with their achievements.
- Summative records: tutor completion of an activity record book.

Certificate in Life Skills

Learners achieving any of these awards with little support (or learners looking for something more challenging) can progress onto the ASDAN Certificate in Life Skills, an entry-level qualification.

This is made up of six units: community, citizenship, home management, ICT, personal care and preparation for working life. To achieve an entry-level qualification the learner must complete any four of the six units. Unitised certification is also available, for bite-sized achievement. Progression is recognised through the three levels of the qualification in requiring the learner to demonstrate their ability to maintain skills learnt as well as recognising lateral and incremental achievements.

The qualification awarded at entry 3 facilitates progression towards qualifications at level 1, for example of ASDAN's Certificate in Personal Effectiveness (CoPE).

Entry-level qualifications are formally recognised in the National Qualifications Framework (NQF) and sit below foundation-level qualifications. Foundation-level qualifications relate to learners achieving GCSEs at grades D-G, an NVQ level 1 or a GNVQ at foundation level. Learners not able to achieve foundation-level qualifications should be working towards an entry-level qualification, to provide formal recognition of their achievements. However, it must be recognised that learners with severe and more complex learning difficulties will be working outside of the NQF, on awards such as the ASDAN Transition Challenge and Towards Independence.

How does ASDAN work?

ASDAN's operating principles are 'plan', 'do' and 'review'. The review process is paramount in identifying the next learning challenge/target. This might be progression, or involve practising and maintaining the skills/knowledge learned.

We often describe ASDAN as 'a walk-in wardrobe'. Inside the wardrobe are many 'hangers', each hanger displaying a different ASDAN award or qualification. Colleagues in schools, colleges and other providers, in consultation with ASDAN's advisory team, select a hanger or hangers appropriate to the needs of the learner. All awards and qualifications are activity based, enabling learners to develop and learn new skills in real-life contexts. The development of functional literacy and numeracy skills are implicit in all ASDAN activity.

This style of learning is very significant for learners who find it difficult to engage in formal structured literacy and numeracy sessions. It is much more exciting for a learner to engage in an activity which provides motivation and stimulation. For example, 'plan and make a journey' can readily develop both numeracy and literacy skills, in a real and relevant context.

ASDAN is practitioner-led, and awards and qualifications are written in consultation with teachers/lecturers who are at the 'chalk face' (perhaps more appropriately described as at the interactive board face!).

Contact details

ASDAN.
Web: www.asdan.org.uk
E-mail: info@asdan.org.uk
Tel: 0117 941 1126. Fax: 0117 935 1112.
Address: Wainbrook House, Hudds Vale Road,
St. George, Bristol BS5 7HY

There are currently over 5,000 centres in the UK using a range of ASDAN's curriculum resources. Increasingly ASDAN resources are being used across the globe: New Zealand, Australia, India, Kuwait and countries within Europe.

Key 4 Learning

Key 4 Learning is an organisation that provides training and consultancy on dyslexia and other hidden disabilities in schools and colleges. In its experience, students with cognitive processing differences (ie whose thinking or reasoning processes differ from the 'norm') often have low self-esteem because of under-achievement. The 'whole-school approach' promoted by Key 4 Learning, together with practical adjustments for supporting these students, will help them achieve their full potential. The consultants, who are experienced trainers, provide whole- or half-day sessions on a variety of subjects. The approach adopted is interactive, with strong use of case studies and other examples of good practice. The central aim is to strengthen the capacity of teachers and schools in supporting that significant group of students who need special forms of teaching in mainstream classrooms.

A *Toolkit for Atypical Learners* was developed by Key 4 Learning in co-operation with Manchester Grammar School. It has been successfully used in schools all over the UK and is an interactive resource enabling a whole-school approach to dyslexia, dyspraxia, attention difficulties and Asperger's syndrome in education. The toolkit explains the characteristics of hidden learning differences and provides interactive checklists as a first step to identification. Information is presented in a user-friendly format about the nature of these conditions, the impact they may have on learning and provides practical advice on how to bridge particular difficulties through strategies and adjustments for pupils to improve performance. The toolkit provides easy access through an intranet resource on CD and is supported by a loose-leaf folder.

Contact details

Key 4 Learning.
Web: www.key4learning.com
E-mail: office@key4learning.com
Tel: 01285 720964.
Address: The Old Village Stores, Chedworth, Cheltenham, Gloucestershire GL54 4AA

Extra exam support

The Joint Council for Qualifications (JCQ) has a Special Requirements committee that draws up regulations regarding access arrangements and special consideration guidance relating to candidates who are eligible for adjustments in examinations. So if, for instance, a blind child needs someone to read out the questions or a dyslexic child needs extra time in an exam, these arrangements must be approved and arranged beforehand.

Examination officers, special educational needs co-ordinators (SENCos) and subject teachers all have vital parts to play communicating the needs of individual candidates, and relating these to special arrangements for modular sessions, coursework and terminal examinations. A special arrangement is unlikely to be permitted if a child has not had such help in class on an ongoing basis. Remember that although the school decides which children require special arrangements it is the examination boards who consider each request and make a final decision. Applications for either access arrangements or special consideration must come from the examination centre entering a candidate – awarding bodies do not accept applications directly from parents. Talk to the school SENCo or contact the examination officer in the examination centre.

Deadlines are extremely important. Don't assume you can just claim extra time because 'everyone knows Tom's dyslexic'. There is much advice in the regulations and guidance booklet and on the JCQ website about when and how to apply for access arrangements or special consideration. Examination centres have a responsibility to assess need and provide access arrangements, so each awarding body invites examination centres to contact them at the earliest possibility to discuss appropriate access arrangements for individual candidates.

Applications for either access arrangements or special consideration must come from the examination centre entering a candidate – awarding bodies do not accept applications directly from parents. Talk to the school SENCo or contact the examination officer in the examination centre.

Not all arrangements requested will be accepted, because candidates will only be eligible for a particular arrangement if they have a substantial impairment; and are taking an examination where that arrangement will not interfere with the assessment itself. Examples are given in the regulations and guidance to illustrate how this might apply. However, SKILL point out that while an amanuensis, laptop etc may be provided, some students have difficulties in getting their needs met in examinations and have no redress at present. One such case involved a student with severe dyslexia and dyspraxia who used voice-activation software to complete assignments because she found writing and typing very difficult. However, the exam board wouldn't allow voice-activation software, and offered the use of an amanuensis instead. This wasn't a normal method of working for the girl and didn't provide the reasonable adjustment required.

In September 2007, amendments to the Disability Discrimination Act (DDA) will come into force for general qualifications, including GCSE and GCE examinations. Awarding bodies will be required not to vary the terms under which a qualification is issued. There will be no requirement to waive competence standards and candidates will gain credit only for what they know and can do independently.

It is important that the regulations and guidance are not taken out of context, so it is always advisable to refer to the text itself. The regulations and guidance are continually reviewed in the light of changes in legislation which affect examinations, and in the light of comments received. They are amended only once a year, and published annually in September. Make sure that you are being guided by the most up-to-date regulations.

Further information and help

Joint Council for Qualifications (JCQ).
Web: www.jcq.org.uk
Tel: 020 7638 4125. Fax: 020 7374 4343.
Address: Veritas House, 125 Finsbury Pavement,
London EC2A 1NQ

The Regulations and Guidance are available as hard copy or on the JCQ website at www.jcq.org.uk/access_arrangements.

In order to reduce the paperwork submitted by examination centres, a new computerised system is being developed by awarding bodies working with the National Assessment Agency (NAA). It currently accommodates all centre-delegated arrangements, and can be accessed via any awarding-body website.

Part 3

SOURCES OF HELP AND ADVICE

Chapter 7

What next? Help on leaving school

Once young people reach the age of 16, they can choose to stay in full-time education at their current school (if it has a sixth form), or move to a sixth-form college or a college of further education (FE). Alternatively they can find a job with training, or do a work-based learning course. What they choose to do will depend on their chosen career path, and their interests, skills and abilities.

There are lots of different routes into education, training and employment and there is no right or wrong way to go about it. On top of choosing what course they are interested in and organising appropriate support for their needs, there are many issues that young people and their parents or carers will need to work through.

If your child has a statement of special educational needs you will be invited to a transition review during your child's year 9. A representative from Connexions (see below) will also be invited, as will your child's social worker if they have one. This starts the transition process which involves having a review every year to look at the plan for the future and assess how the young person's needs may have changed.

There will be opportunities to discuss options with advisers, teachers and parents, and make visits to potential educational institutions before making a final decision. Wherever the young person chooses to continue their education or training, a full report explaining their support needs to the new institution will ensure as smooth a transition as possible.

Rights and responsibilities

Students with disabilities have a legal right not to be discriminated against at college or university, or in the work place. In September 2002, the Disability Discrimination Act (DDA) Part 4: Education came into force. Under the law, educational institutions are required to make 'reasonable' adjustments for disabled students. The law covers not only the provision of courses, but also admissions and 'student services' such as catering, counselling services and field trips.

The Disability Rights Commission works towards a society where all disabled people can participate fully as equal citizens. They can inform you about your rights under the DDA as a disabled person. Several organisations, such as RADAR and Skill, also offer advice.

The world of work

The success of individuals with specific learning difficulties in the world of work is very variable. Often, this bears little relation to actual ability, but is dependent on the environment they work in.

People whose brains process information differently have a great deal to offer the corporate world, if that world understands how to accept it. It is not surprising that a significant number of entrepreneurs are dyslexic or have other 'hidden' disabilities that made aspects of learning at school difficult. Going their own way in the business world meant they could work in the way that was best for them, and allow their particular strengths and abilities full rein. Several organisations now deliberately look to recruit people with different cognitive profiles. Innovation and different ways of approaching tasks often come easily to those who don't fit the average profile, and new ideas often are essential to business success. There are organisations (see below) that assist both employer and employee in gaining the most benefit from this approach.

Who can help?

Thinking about life after school may seem daunting, but there are many professionals and voluntary organisations that can help you.

Connexions

Connexions is the government's support service for all young people aged 13-19 in England. It offers support through personal advisers, who can provide not only careers advice but advice on health, housing, relationships, money, travel, disability and legal rights. They can also be a gateway to more specialist support, for example on drug abuse, sexual health and homelessness. Connexions personal advisers work in schools, colleges, community centres and on an outreach basis.

Just one example of a pathway into work is Janine's story.

Janine's dream had always been to work with the 'big cats', but she felt it was impossible because of her learning disabilities and mild cerebral palsy. Her Connexions service thought otherwise. Janine was helped to get a Saturday job in a local pet shop – looking after small rodents, not large lions! Her literacy and numeracy skills improved because she needed to identify and weigh out the animals' food.

Janine's school encouraged volunteering and Janine became a volunteer at a local animal rescue centre. She also started helping with a local Riding for Disabled People scheme.

Janine has abandoned the idea of big cats in favour of smaller ones; now she is on a work-based learning scheme at the Children's Zoo while she studies part time for a health and safety certificate at her local FE college. She is currently helping the staff to develop an access plan to improve access for disabled children and young people throughout the zoo.

Skill: National Bureau for Students with Disabilities

Skill is an independent national charity that promotes opportunities for disabled people in post-16 education and work-based learning throughout the UK. Skill helps disabled people across the UK make the most of their learning and employment opportunities. It operates an information and advice service, runs conferences, produces publications, conducts research projects, informs and influences key decision makers, and works with its members.

Skill's information service answers enquiries from people with any kind of disability, including mental health difficulties, physical and sensory disabilities, learning difficulties and specific learning difficulties such as dyslexia. It receives a wide range of enquiries covering topics on further and higher education, training and getting into work. Common enquiries about higher education are about funding and other support that is available for disabled students at university and college.

Skill can also help disabled students and their parents and carers to understand their rights under the Disability Discrimination Act – information booklets are available on its website or hard copies can be ordered direct.

Skill's booklet *Organisations Offering Advice and Services to Disabled People* lists voluntary organisations that may be able to provide you with specialist advice about your child's transition and other related issues. Its *Into ...* series of careers guides includes information on the routes into particular careers, profiles of disabled people who have successfully begun a career in the area, and listings of sources of further information. Titles include *Into Law, Into Architecture, Into Science and Engineering, Into Volunteering, Into Work Experience, Into Nursing and Midwifery* and *Into Art.* Check Skill's website or call its information service for further details.

As a member of Skill (the website has information on how you can join) you will be kept up to date with all the latest news and research on the issues facing disabled students. Your voice will also be added to those of others seeking to improve opportunities for disabled people in post-16 education, training and employment. Young learners with disabilities aged 13-19 can get involved with Skill by emailing jo@skill.org.uk to find out more about the exciting new Young Learners' Information Project.

Other sources

With thanks to DyslexiaWorks and Jo Todd of Key 4 Learning.

A number of organisations provide training, consultancy and resources to promote understanding of difficulties such as dyslexia, dyspraxia, attention difficulties, autistic spectrum disorders and other 'hidden' disabilities. By increasing awareness of these differences within education and employment, individuals have the opportunity to unlock their true potential.

DyslexiaWorks, for example, can offer screening, advice and guidance and, where necessary, arrange full assessments and specialist tuition for students across the board, from GCSE/A levels (it also runs training sessions in schools) to graduate and postgraduate level. It has specialists in vocational careers advice and can help find out about government funding for this transition period between school and work or higher education. It works with universities and colleges best equipped to deliver a wide range of support services which – to quote the organisation, 'can make the difference between "just getting through" and achieving a qualification which will act as a springboard to a subsequent career'.

Key 4 Learning, which works in education and the workplace, both in the UK and overseas, has produced screening tools for FE colleges and interactive toolkits for organisations and schools to promote understanding and development of the performance of employees and students who learn differently. The organisation also provides support materials and training sessions for employers, schools, colleges, universities, trade unions and individuals. Key 4 Learning's *Hidden Disabilities Toolkit* (companion to the *Toolkit for Atypical Learners* used in schools – see Chapter 6) is an interactive tool for developing skills and knowledge for both the employer and the employee, promoting the skills of all the team members.

Jo Todd, who established Key 4 Learning ten years ago, says:

> Disability legislation places a duty on employers to support their employees who have disabilities, but compliance with legislation is a secondary outcome – the first is improvement in business performance. We work with individuals to create disclosure documents that give employers a more personalised view of their strengths and appropriate adjustments that will maximise performance. This document is useful for transition from school to higher and further education as well as to employment.

Experience has shown these companies that a 'whole-organisation approach' is important if managing different abilities is to be effective and is to utilise the many gifts of different thinkers. The elements include better understanding of hidden disabilities through:

- staff awareness training
- individual identification, assessment and disclosure
- individual development through mentoring
- liaison with line managers and when appropriate internal peer groups
- reasonable adjustment and accommodation in work practice
- change in human resource policies.

The world of further and higher education

The step from school to college or university can be a huge leap if you have dyslexia, dyspraxia, autistic spectrum disorders, ADD/ADHD or other difficulties. FE colleges are often a preferred study option for post-16 students – many school leavers go on to an FE college to study a practical and skills-based subject, leading to a work-based qualification, but some study academic subjects, including AS and A levels. Success at A level can mean that the next step you consider is likely to be university.

Colleges of further education

With thanks to Dr Enid Alston, Malcolm Starr and Skill for additional information

FE colleges attract a variety of learners: those who want or need to study, either for careers or because of changes in their circumstances; those who wish to pursue a hobby or fill their time by learning something new; and adults who are looking for a change in career or who want to return to study after a break.

Qualifications undertaken vary from access or entry-level courses, to GNVQs, A levels and beyond. These are validated by accredited, examining bodies such as OCR (Oxford and Cambridge RSA) and EdExcel. Vocational courses tend to have a lot of practical content and prepare students for specific employment such as fashion, leisure, agriculture, hairdressing or building. The practical and vocational nature of many courses means work experience may play a significant part in the course.

So, FE can offer a great chance for a fresh start: the opportunity to meet new people, learn in a different environment and take courses and qualifications not available at school. However, many FE colleges have had a bad press in recent years – in 2001/2 almost one in five of all colleges inspected were judged to be inadequate. This is improving, but many FE colleges have undoubtedly suffered from a lack of funding and resources.

Colleges have amalgamated over the years and may have sites spread across a town or city. It may be wise to check out where your course would take place, how much travelling is involved, how easy it is to get to the college and the hours of study (some classes may take place during twilight hours or in the evening). The majority of FE courses are state funded, but always check funding and qualifying arrangements before committing to a course. Students in the 16–19 age group can be helped by incentives from the government such as the education maintenance allowance (EMA) and additional learner support (ALS).

If you are interested in continuing your education at an FE college, speak to your personal adviser (PA) from Connexions or Careers Scotland, who will be able to provide you with more information on suitable courses and entry requirements. Alternatively, contact your local college who will send you a prospectus and offer information and advice, including any details of forthcoming open days. Remember, inclusion of SEN students into all courses is an equal opportunities issue.

Other 16+ colleges

If the type of education or support you need is not available at your local FE college, it may be possible for you to go to a specialist or residential college. Information on these is given in the COPE Directory: Compendium of post-16 education and training in residential establishments for young people with special needs. Your local careers/Connexions service should have a copy and they should be able to help you find the best option.

The Association of National Specialist Colleges (NATSPEC) supports specialist independent colleges that provide further education and training to meet the inclusive learning needs of students with learning difficulties and/or disabilities. It also offers advice and guidance to individual learners, their families and supporters who are considering a placement at a specialist college.

The association's website offers a natty interactive college finder. This helps students locate colleges with expertise in working with particular difficulties. Still in development, we think it will be an ever-useful tool to help learners with special needs find courses. We trialled the system by first requesting a college that has expertise in helping learners with autism. This brought up an extensive list of further requirements. By checking two of the many boxes, 'opportunities to improve communication skills such as the use of Makaton, Bliss, symbols or objects of reference' and 'opportunities to learn in small steps', seven colleges were identified as meeting these requirements. However, such a tool is no replacement for personal help and advice, from those who know you and your needs well.

Information on specialist colleges and courses can also be obtained by contacting relevant charities such as the RNIB, BDA, RNID, NAS, Down's Sydrome Association, Mencap etc. Contact details can be found in Part 4.

Funding

Government funding for a place at a specialist college isn't usually available if your needs can be met at a local 'sector' college or school. However, the Learning and Skills Council (England and Wales) has a duty to fund a specialist place for a student under the age of 19 whose needs cannot be met in a 'sector' college or school. It also has the power to fund a specialist place for a student between the ages of 19 and 25 whose needs cannot be met elsewhere.

Remember, although the majority of colleges and college courses are funded by the Learning and Skills Council, some are not, so always check funding and placement arrangements for courses with each college.

In Scotland, FE colleges receive funding from the Scottish Further Education Funding Council (SFEFC) which must have regard for the needs of disabled students. College management boards have a duty to ensure adequate local provisions are made.

In Northern Ireland, colleges manage their own budgets, but are expected to present development plans to the Department for Employment and Learning (DEL). Colleges are required to identify strengths and weaknesses in current provisions for disabled students and to make proposals for improvements. An additional support fund (ASF) is available to meet the additional needs of individual students.

Note that:

■ In England, Wales and Northern Ireland you are able to get free education up to the age of 19.

■ In Scotland, you are able to get free education up to the age of 18.

In certain circumstances, such as receiving a means-tested state benefit, students aged 19 or over are eligible for a fee waiver (ie will not have to pay tuition fees).

Disability support

Colleges in England and Wales receive money to pay for additional support needed by disabled students. So disabled students can generally expect their disability-related needs to be met by the institution (similar systems exist in Scotland and Northern Ireland). Examples of this kind of support are additional teaching for dyslexic students, an interpreter for deaf students, materials in alternative formats, and specialist computer software. If you request specific equipment, such as a personal computer, you may be supplied with one for use at the college but you won't be able to take it home. In this situation, you may wish to apply to a charitable trust for funding for specialist equipment.

If you have a disability and are thinking of studying at a college of further education, do contact Skill, who will be able to advise on many practical aspects including financial help, assistance with transport etc.

Moving on to university

With thanks to Jo Todd of Key 4 Learning

By obtaining the grades necessary for university entry, you have shown that you have the intellectual capacity for the study required, but the transition to higher education imposes many other demands. Although school may have been a struggle in some ways, the environment was probably quite cosy, structured and protected when compared with the freer, unstructured and sometimes lonely first few weeks of university. Ensure you get all the help you can from teachers, support workers and careers staff in checking out course requirements and university facilities, and in obtaining the level of support you will need at university so that you can start your time there with confidence.

The support given for students with dyslexia, for example, is usually excellent in terms of IT, essay planning etc, but you can encounter problems at university that may not always be at the forefront of the disability support unit's agenda – difficulties with organisation, memory, concentration and time management are just as much saboteurs as reading and writing difficulties. Whilst at school, you may have had reminders from your parents (or houseparents if you're boarding), teachers, friends or siblings regarding dates of exams or deadlines for coursework. At university you are suddenly responsible for yourself. This means managing a budget, remembering to get assignments in on time, finding out about the Disabled Students' Allowance, remembering your house keys and where you are supposed to be and when – all this on top of the distractions of Freshers' Week!

This is an exciting time, so it is better to be well prepared before starting out. Below is an excerpt from 'Moving On', part of Key 4 Learning's *Toolkit for Atypical Students* (see page 135), which includes a number of helpful points, from notes on completing the UCAS form to practical preparations and settling in.

1. Choosing your course

■ Course requirements

■ Assessment regulations

■ Course entry

2. Completing the UCAS form

■ Remember to tick the appropriate disability box

■ Prepare your statement mentioning the positive aspects of your specific learning difficulty and how you have learned to overcome any problems

3. Support for your course

When you are sure that you have chosen the course which will allow you to demonstrate your true ability, consider the type of support you may require:

■ IT support

■ non-medical personal help, eg. note taker, proof-reader, dyslexia tutor

Compile a learning profile with your guidance teacher/learning support teacher/personal tutor before you leave school. You should include information about:

- specific examination arrangements required, eg extra time or instructions on coloured paper
- reasonable adjustments to teaching, eg plan of a lecture in advance or permission to record lectures
- reasonable adjustments to coursework, eg extra time for completion or oral feedback as well as written feedback

4. Preparation for starting

During Freshers' Week you will have many things other than academic issues on your mind! It is a good idea to spend some time before you leave home on organisation of stationery and equipment you will require when you begin your studies.

- different coloured folders and paper for each course
- evidence of your specific learning difficulties, eg an educational psychologist's report or a letter from your medical practitioner. The university will need this to register you as a disabled student so that you can have all the support to which you are entitled
- secure folder for official documents you may need, such as passport and bank details
- folder in which to keep important information, such as details about Disabled Students' Allowance, Access Centre report, address and contact name for LEA.

5. On arrival at university

- confirm your course with your academic tutor and/or department
- arrange an early time to meet your tutor to discuss your learning profile
- contact the Disability Support Unit
- visit the library or attend introductory sessions
- go to the Student Job Centre if you need to earn extra pocket money
- find out about the local laundrette or the student laundry room in halls
- make provision for mislaying keys or swipe cards – either have an extra set cut or know where to get help with access, day and night
- programme your PDA or mobile phone with your timetable and display a large copy on the wall of your room.

	Checklist	Tick
1	Have I ticked the UCAS disability box?	☐
2	In my UCAS statement have I mentioned how I overcome my difficulties and play to my strengths?	☐
3	Do I have up-to-date evidence of my specific learning difficulty, for example, an educational/clinical psychologist's report or a letter from a medical practitioner?	☐
4	Have I applied to my Local Education Authority (LEA) for funding?	☐
5	Have I applied for Disabled Students' Allowance (DSA)?	☐
6	Have I been in contact with my prospective university support staff?	☐
7	Do I have my National Insurance number?	☐
8	Do I have my passport or other photographic ID?	☐
9	Do I have my bank details?	☐
10	Have I thought about how I will organise my academic work?	☐
11	Who will I ask about library support?	☐
12	Who will I ask about arranging a 'Buddy' in my subject?	☐
13	Have I remembered to bring my learning profile?	☐
14	Have I written a list of questions to ask my tutor at the first meeting?	☐

Some students benefit from taking a gap year – they broaden their horizons and mature a little more – before moving on to further studies. Students with cognitive processing differences may need a greater amount of constructive help in planning their year out in order to gain the most benefit. A gap year is not for all students, though, with or without special educational needs. Some find that, by taking a year off, they lose the continuity of learning and may have been better off going straight to university.

Jo Todd's training ground was working in special education for 20 years, her last role being in a dyslexic unit in a large comprehensive school. Her main area of interest is developmental difference and its effect on learning, with particular reference to gifted or exceptional thinkers. Jo has received national awards for her work in raising awareness and understanding of hidden disabilities and has presented papers at conferences throughout the world. She was part of the DfES Adult Basic Skills dyslexia advisory group, participates in work for the British Dyslexia Association and the Dyspraxia Foundation, and is a trustee of the DANDA (Developmental Adult Neuro-Diversity Association).

Further information and help

See also Part 4: Useful contacts

Connexions

Web: www.connexions-direct.com, www.nacp.co.uk
Tel: 0114 281 3418. Fax: 0114 281 3419.
Address: Watsons Chambers, 5–15 Market Place, Castle Square, Sheffield S1 2GH

The link to www.nacp.co.uk/partnership-search.htm has details of Connexions' 47 local partnerships – the partnerships cover the same geographical areas as the Learning and Skills Councils. The service is managed and monitored by local management committees, which usually cover the same areas as local authorities (www.lsc.gov.uk/National/default.htm).

Skill

Web: www.skill.org.uk
Email: info@skill.org.uk
Tel: 020 7657 2337. Information service (11.30am–1.30pm Tues and 1.30–3.30pm Thurs):
Tel (voice): 0800 328 5050 (text) 0800 068 2422.
Fax: 0207 450 0650.
Address: Chapter House, 18-20 Crucifix Lane, London SE1 3JW

The website has information on all Skill's services and you can download free information booklets. To find out more about Skill membership on their site, go to About, then Membership.

Other sources

Basic Skills Agency.
Web: www.basic-skills.co.uk
Tel: 020 7405 4017. Freephone: 0800 700 987 for help, advice and information on suitable courses.
Fax: 020 7440 6626.
Email: enquiries@basic-skills.co.uk
Address: Commonwealth House, 1-19 New Oxford Street, London WC1A 1NU

DfES – Aimhigher. Website offers help and advice on going to university with sections for youngsters post-GCSE, parents and those returning to education.
Web: www.aimhigher.ac.uk/dontstop/home
Tel (free): 0800 587 8500. Textphone 0800 280 024

Disability Rights Commission.
Quasi-independent of government. Tells you what your rights are, and may help you enforce them.
Web: www.drc-gb.org
E-mail: enquiry@drc-gb.org
Tel: 0845 7622 633. Textphone: 0845 7622 644.
Fax: 0845 7778 878.
Address: DCR Helpline, Freepost MID 02164, Stratford-upon-Avon CV37 9BR

DyslexiaWorks.
Web: www.dyslexiaworks.co.uk
E-mail info@dysxlexiaworks.co.uk
Tel: 01491 636245.
Address: 3 Manor Courtyard, Hughenden Avenue, High Wycombe, Buckinghamshire HP13 5RE

Key 4 Learning.
Has worked in an advisory capacity for several government working parties; in fact its first toolkit was produced for use by the staff of the Cabinet Office and is now used across the Civil Service.
Web: www.key4learning.com
E-mail: office@key4learning.com
Tel: 01285 720964.
Address: The Old Village Stores, Chedworth, Cheltenham, Gloucestershire GL54 4AA

Learning and Skills Council (LSC).
Web: www.lsc.gov.uk
E-mail: info@lsc.gov.uk
Tel: 0845 019 4170 or (general enquiries) 0870 900 6800. Fax: 024 7649 3600.
Address: Cheylesmore House, Quinton Road, Coventry CV1 2WT

NATSPEC (Association of National Specialist Colleges). Its *Directory* lists many colleges in England and Wales (and one in Northern Ireland) that specialise in post-school education for people with special needs.
Web: www.natspec.org.uk
E-mail (Kevin O'Brien, Chief Executive): kevin.obrien43@ntlworld.com
Tel: 01509 554357.
Address: 39 Sanders Rd, Quorn, Loughborough, Leicestershire LE12 8JN

RADAR (Royal Association for Disability and Rehabilitation).
The principal organisation for (and of) the physically disabled.
Web: www.radar.org.uk
E-mail: radar@radar.org.uk
Tel: 020 7250 3222. Fax: 020 7250 0212.
Minicom: 0207 250 4119.
Address: 12 City Forum, 250 City Road, London EC1V 8AF

See also the following publications:

COPE Directory of Post-16 Education/Training in Residential Establishments. Published by Lifetime Careers Publishing.
Web: www.lifetime-publishing.co.uk
E-mail: sales@lifetime-publishing.co.uk
Tel. 01225 716023. Fax: 01225 716025.
Address: 7 Ascot Court, White Horse Business Park, Trowbridge, Wiltshire BA14 0XA

Arrangements for Placements at Specialist Colleges: learners with learning difficulties and/or disabilities for 2003/04 (Circular 02/14). Published by the Learning and Skills Council (see above).

Chapter 8

Sources of help and support

In Part 4 we have compiled a comprehensive list of sources of information, help and practical advice ranging from all-embracing websites to some tiny specialist support groups for rare conditions. Here, a few organisations describe in more detail how they work and the sort of help they provide. In each case (excepting the DfES) the information is kindly provided by the organisation concerned.

The Advisory Centre for Education (ACE)

ACE is an independent registered charity, which offers information about state education in England and Wales for parents of school-age children. This is a service which, although hardly advertised, is overwhelmingly used and much regarded for its independence, its confidentiality and the quality of its advice.

Telephone advice lines are the cornerstones of ACE, and their frequent engaged tone (but do keep trying – you will get through!) demonstrates parents' need for help and information. About half of ACE's advice calls are related to special educational needs. Parents of children with learning difficulties will know that the law in this area is complex, but an important principle of the Code of Practice for SEN is that parents should play a full part in supporting their children. ACE helps parents understand the system, offers advice on the next step to take and explains how parents can contribute to planning their children's education and appealing against decisions they feel are wrong.

As well as telephone advice, we give free advice via our website. This provides answers to frequently asked questions, a jargon buster and parents' forum as well as details of our publications and membership of ACE.

Our bestselling title is the *ACE Special Education Handbook*, which explains in parent-friendly language what parents should expect from schools and local education authorities when their child has a statement. It also provides information on key court decisions, on disability discrimination and on a range of subjects such as transport, examinations and school records. The *Handbook* costs £17.99 and can be ordered by phone or via our website. Our free advice booklets provide step-by-step advice for parents whose children have special educational needs. *Getting Extra Help*, *Asking for a Statutory Assessment*, *Getting the Statement Right* and *Understanding Annual Reviews* focus on key issues for parents and help them have their say at critical points in their children's schooling. Download them from our website or call our advice line for a copy.

ACE's exclusion helpline runs five afternoons a week, to support parents whose children have been excluded from school. Some three-quarters of these are children with SEN. The advice line was set up in response to the rising tide of permanent exclusions. ACE's expert advisers can explain how to appeal against an exclusion, how to get more support in school and how to find a new school place.

As well as special educational needs and exclusions, ACE's advice encompasses a very wide range of topics including truancy, bullying, school phobia, and school admissions.

Contact details

Advisory Centre for Education (ACE).
Web: www.ace-ed.org.uk
E-mail: enquiries@ace.dialnet.com
Freephone advice line (2pm-5pm Mon-Fri): 0808 800 5793. Freephone exclusion helpline: 0808 8000 327.
Fax: 020 7354 9069.
Address: 1 Aberdeen Studios, 22 Highbury Grove, London N5 2DQ

For a free exclusion pack, leave your contact details on 020 7704 9822.

Contact a Family

Contact a Family provides support, advice and information to families with disabled children across the UK. We take a 'one-stop shop' approach to answering enquiries from families because we recognise that their lives are often very complex and they have a range of information and support needs.

Typically, parents contact us soon after finding out that their child has a disability. The need for straightforward medical information is often the first thing that we can help with. We have information on thousands of medical conditions that affect children, including many very rare disorders. We also try to link parents up with a national support group, so that they can talk to other families who have been affected by the same condition. These groups are often small and run from the home of another family. They are a real lifeline for families, though, and a fantastic source of information on coping with a particular condition. Other parents can also tell a family how their own child coped with, for example, going to a mainstream school, or why they decided to choose a residential special school. Talking to others can help families to make up their own minds as to which course of action to take.

In the case of a very rare disorder where there is no support group we can try to link the parent one to one with another parent in the UK or abroad via our helpline or our family-linking website. If a parent wants to start a support group, we can offer development support and advice every step of the way.

The family is likely to face a range of practical problems as the child grows up. Our helpline has a large range of free factsheets covering most issues that face families with disabled children and answering common questions on rights, such as: Do I have a right to return to work part time after maternity leave? How am I going to pay the rent on a lower wage? Contact a Family would carry out a full benefits and tax credits check and advise about employment rights. Parents might also want to know about childcare for a disabled child and help from social services to adapt the family home.

We consistently find that many parents remain unaware for many years that they can claim Disability Living Allowance for their child, regardless of their own income and savings. This benefit is assessed purely on the level of care that the child needs or on the difficulty that they have getting around. Many parents are also unaware that if their child uses a wheelchair indoors they automatically qualify for money off their council tax – again, regardless of income or savings. Small concessions like this can make life much easier for families. Another example of this is the Blue Badge, which permits you to use disabled parking bays close to shops. Many families don't find out for a long time that this is not restricted to disabled adults but is also available for some children with mobility problems.

Families may also like some information specifically for the baby's father or grandparents, and this could be included in the free information pack we send within a couple of days of a parent's call. As the child grows older, we can provide information on topics such as SEN, which questions to ask when choosing a new school, coping with puberty and the transition to adulthood. This is a very complicated time, where young people need to make decisions about, say, going to college, but also about particular issues such as whether to claim Incapacity Benefit in their own right. This can affect the family's overall income and it's a time when Contact a Family often needs to advise who should claim benefits, by doing a 'better off' calculation, looking at all the options.

We also have lists of grant-making charities which can help with things like buying a washing machine or the cost of a family holiday.

We have offices in many parts of the UK which can give detailed local information. They also produce regular newsletters for local families and some run outings, workshops and social events for families.

Many professionals, including teachers, use the medical information we hold on rare conditions to help them prepare for a particular child's arrival in their classroom. This is especially the case where a condition can cause challenges in certain school situations – such as the eating problems associated with Prader-Willi syndrome, or the difficulties with co-ordination skills such as throwing and catching a ball experienced by many children with Williams syndrome.

Understanding that some challenging behaviour is linked to a medical condition is also very important for teaching staff. Individuals with Lesch-Nyhan syndrome, for example, almost always develop severe self-mutilation, including knuckle gnawing and lip biting. This compulsive behaviour is a major cause of ill health and personal distress for the individuals concerned and their families, yet remains extremely resistant to psychological and medical treatments. If teaching staff are unaware of the link between a behaviour pattern and the condition itself, they could mistake it, for example, for abuse. Contact a Family's authoritative medical information, all approved by leading medical experts, can be very helpful in such situations.

The service is free and confidential and we are registered with the Community Legal Service to provide advice at general-help level. Interpreters in over 100 community languages can be accessed through Language Line, and basic immigration advice is also available. Our website also has lots of useful information, including factsheets for families and a directory covering hundreds of rare conditions and syndromes.

Contact details

Contact a Family.
Web: www.cafamily.org.uk
Family-linking website: www.makingcontact.org
E-mail: info@cafamily.org.uk
helpline@cafamily.org.uk
Tel: 020 7608 8700. Freephone helpline (10am-4pm Mon-Fri): 0808 808 3555. Textphone (freephone): 0808 808 3556. Minicom: 020 7608 8702.
Fax: 020 7608 8701.
Address: 204–211 City Road, London EC1V 1JN

Independent Panel for Special Education Advice (IPSEA)

IPSEA is a volunteer-based organisation, whose aims are:

■ to help ensure that children with special educational needs receive the special educational provision to which they are legally entitled

■ to help ensure that the views of parents/carers and children are taken fully into account when children's needs are assessed and decisions are made about special education provision and school placement

■ to target information about our services to low-income families so that we support parents/carers who may be less confident and/or less able to fight for their children's legal entitlement to special educational provision.

IPSEA can provide help and support for parents of children with SEN in the following ways:

■ providing free independent advice

■ providing free advice on appealing to the SEN & Disability Tribunal (SENDIST; see Chapter 9), including representation when needed

■ providing free second professional opinions

■ arranging home visits for parents who need face-to-face support and/or assistance at meetings with headteachers or LEA officers.

IPSEA may be able to help if, for example:

■ you are not happy with the way the school is meeting your child's SEN

■ you want the LEA to assess your child, but they refuse

■ the LEA refuse to issue a statement after assessing your child

■ you want to appeal against a statement when it is first made or when it is amended

■ the LEA will not put the school you prefer on the statement

■ you are unhappy with the amount of help your child is being given.

Many of the volunteers who provide telephone advice and support at tribunals are themselves parents of children with special educational needs who have been helped by IPSEA in the past. Volunteers providing a second professional opinion service are trained and experienced professionals working in special education, as educational psychologists, speech therapists, teachers, etc.

Contact details

IPSEA (Independent Panel for Special Educational Advice).
Web: www.ipsea.org.uk
E-mail (for information only, not advice):
ipsea.info@intamail.com
General enquiries: 01394 380 518.

Advice line (freephone): 0800 018 4016 (10am–4pm and 7pm–9pm Mon–Thurs, 10am–1pm and 7pm–9pm Fri. During school holidays times are reduced. Please ring for availability.) Tribunal appeals only: 01394 384711. Address: IPSEA, 6 Carlow Mews, Woodbridge, Suffolk IP12 1EA

Independent Special Education Advice (ISEA) (Scotland)

Established in 1998 as a charity, ISEA is managed by parents who have a child or young person with additional support needs (formerly special educational needs). We provide free independent advice, information, practical support, advocacy and representation services across Scotland to parents/carers on their and their child's rights in law to secure the resources and provision to meet their child's education potential. Our organisation is unique in Scotland; we receive no statutory funding and are totally reliant on donations and grants.

The additional support needs legislation applies when 'a child or young person is, or is likely to be, unable without the provision of additional support to benefit from school education provided or to be provided for the child or young person'. Therefore many more children, not just those with a disability, can access this new legislation and so can also access any of our services. Examples of additional support needs include: social and emotional difficulties, English as a second language, young carers, gifted children or where home life is disrupted by homelessness or parental alcohol or drug misuse.

We currently run two projects in relation to the Additional Support for Learning (Scotland) Act 2004, which was implemented on 14 November 2005.

The DECIDE project, funded for three years by Comic Relief, has been established to enable and empower parents to Debate, Express, Consult, Influence, Discuss and Examine the new legislation. This offers a parent's telephone helpline, web page, factsheet and parents' debate room. We provide a rolling programme of training/consultation days as well as one-to-one surgeries for parents in each of the 32 local authority areas throughout Scotland. Through these processes we will be able to gather the collective views and aspirations of parents and be a watchdog on how the new legislation impacts at grass roots level, which will then enable us to present our findings to the Scottish Parliament, and ensure the collective voices of parents are heard in the campaign for improved rights to securing an education that will enable children to reach their potential.

Our Scotland's Advocacy for Education project (fondly known as SAFE) is funded for three years by the Big Lottery Fund to provide practical support to parents who are in disagreement with their local authority's decision regarding the provision and/or services to meet their child's additional support needs. The service is provided through a telephone helpline, individual case work, and providing representation and advocacy for families who are appealing against their local authority's decision via one of the many routes open to parents and young people through the 1980 and 2004 education legislation.

Contact details

ISEA (Independent Special Education Advice) (Scotland).
Website being updated at the time of writing.
Web www.isea.org.uk
E-mail: isea@whsmithnet.co.uk
Tel: 0131 454 0096. Helpline: 0131 454 0082.
Fax: 0131 454 0096.
Address: 164 High Street, Dalkeith, Midlothian EH22 1AY

DECIDE.
E-mail: plofficer@isea.org.uk
Tel/Fax: 0131 454 0096

SAFE.
E-mail: advocacy@isea.org.uk
Tel/Fax: 0131 454 0144

Parent partnership services

Under the terms of the 1996 Education Act, a local authority must arrange for the parent of any child with special educational needs in their local area to be provided with advice and information about matters relating to those needs. Parent partnership services (PPS) are the statutory services established to meet this requirement.

Parent partnership services support parents of children with SEN by offering information, advice and support. Most are based within the LEA, a few in the voluntary sector. They work with individual parents, families or carers to outline options, rights, roles and responsibilities within the SEN processes. All should provide informaion and publicity; training and support; networking and collaboration opportunities; and help to inform and influence local policy and practice. Any information, guidance and support offered should be accurate and impartial (even though they usually work within the LEA).

An independent parental supporter should be offered to any parent who would like one. They can be from the parent partnership service, a voluntary organisation, another parent or a friend. A supporter is someone who isn't involved in any decision-making processes but who can help parents to understand SEN procedures and encourage them to participate. Help may be practical: form filling; letter writing; finding information; accompanying to meetings or on school visits; or making contact with others who can help. Parental supporters will explain what is happening at the various stages and listen to any worries or concerns and help to express these.

Contact details

National Parent Partnership Network.
Web: www.parentpartnership.org.uk
Tel: 020 7843 6000.
Address: c/o Council for Disabled Children, 8 Wakeley Street, London EC1V

The Red Balloon Learner Centre Group

The first Red Balloon Learner Centre was established by Carrie Hibbert in her house in Cambridge in 1996, with a fundamental aim of helping young people who have been so badly bullied they are unable to attend school. Red Balloon offers a safe bullying-free environment, sets clear boundaries for behaviour and provides a full-time academic, pastoral and therapeutic educational programme.

Students who refuse to go to school because they have been bullied often miss out on their education. They are so fearful that the bullying behaviour will continue, that it could get worse and even result in their ending up in hospital or even being killed, that they remain hidden at home. They are frightened to go out or to answer the door, and for many their bedroom becomes both a sanctuary and a prison.

These were once 'ordinary' children who were happy to go to school, who usually made the change from primary to secondary with no apparent trauma. Yet through no fault of their own, unless having red hair, being tall for their age or overweight, being keen to do their homework, or standing out as different in some way is a fault, they are denied a satisfactory education. Surely youngsters who want to learn and succeed in education but who are bullied and teased beyond endurance deserve better?

There seems to be little or no provision for children who have been traumatised by bullying behaviour. These housebound children are denied a full-time education because they are unwilling to go to the local pupil referral units, which often cater for students who have been excluded and who are angry and disillusioned with education. The students we deal with are usually quiet and withdrawn, dogged by feelings of worthlessness and suffering from depression. The tuition they receive at home provides the basics of maths and English but no opportunity for social interaction with peers. Badly bullied students need something better if they are to recover sufficiently to play an active part in their community as young adults.

For many of our children suicide was an option with which they toyed, finding it impossible to imagine a safe place where they could learn and recover. Half of the children who come to Red Balloon have seriously thought about or attempted to take their own lives. It became clear to us that whatever we set up needed to be different from mainstream – small, safe, structured, offering a comprehensive learner-directed education together with a range of therapeutic opportunities for recovery and healing.

In the nine years we have been running, the centre has changed and developed. We offer a range of academic subjects, taking students through to GCSE if appropriate. Thirty per cent of the school time is spent in what mainstream schools commonly call 'personal and social education'. The 14 hours a week that we devote to 'emotional intelligence' comprise ethics, circle time, girl-only and boy-only group sessions (to discuss sensitive issues pertinent to the sexes), drama, art therapy, and organised social times before school and at break and lunch times. At no time are children left to play on their own, there is no staffroom, washrooms are shared and lunch is a community affair with fresh healthy food including salads, home-made bread, baked potatoes, fruit juice and fruit.

The centre takes only 12 secondary-age children, who come from both the private and the state sector. If they are from county schools the LEA pays the fees; if they are from private schools the parents pay. On a couple of occasions we have been able to offer bursaries. The length of time children are with us depends on their age and on how damaged they are. Rule of thumb says the younger the child is when they arrive the shorter the period of time they need to recover.

There are three conditions under which a child can attend. The first is that they want to come. The placement will not work if the child only attends because they are cajoled or threatened because their parent decides Red Balloon is the place for them. The second condition is that the child must want to learn and make academic progress. The Red Balloon was set up to provide a safe learning environment, not a soft option from mainstream, not a place for watching TV and playing on the computer. In fact, the children here work extremely hard. Most of the lessons are one to one, ensuring high levels of concentration and focus. The third condition is that the child must agree to behave considerately and respectfully towards the other students, the staff and the property at all times. These three conditions have stood us in good stead: throughout our nine years we have had no graffiti or wanton damage.

Once the students have regained their confidence and are back on an academic footing we prepare them to return to mainstream school, enter further education or employment.

Carrie Hibbert, Director of Red Balloon, says:

> When I look back at the young people who have been at Red Balloon and re-read the messages that I have received from parents, grandparents and the children themselves, I know that this is a resource which is needed throughout the country. (We estimate that about one child in a thousand would benefit from being at a Red Balloon at some time during their secondary school life.) I know that we have prevented some children from again attempting suicide. I know that some young people have 'found' themselves just by being given a safe and secure learning environment in which to recover.
>
> It is because this initiative has been so successful, as measured by the recovery of over 75 young people, that we are now expanding to provide Red Balloons in three more areas: North-west London, Colchester and Norwich. The fact that Barnardo's is working in partnership with us in the eastern counties speaks volumes about our work, credibility, success and future.

Contact details

The Red Balloon Learner Centre.
Director: Carrie Herbert. Co-ordinator: Ruth Loshak.
Web: www.redballoonlearner.cambs.sch.uk
E-mail: redballoon@redballoonlearner.org.uk
Tel: 01223 357714.
Address: 57 Warkworth Terrace, Cambridge CB1 1EE

SEN mediation

With additional information kindly provided by the London SEN Disagreement Resolution Service (LDRS

The Special Educational Needs and Disability Act 2001 placed a legal duty on LEAs to make independent arrangements available for the resolution of disagreements between parents or carers of children with SEN and schools and/or LEAs. This is usually offered through independent, regional mediation services.

Each region provides a confidential service which aims via mediation, to settle disputes that arise between parents of children with SEN on the one hand and LEAs or schools on the other, about the educational needs of children and how best to meet them.

Mediation is an informal process in which an independent and neutral mediator helps those involved in disputes to negotiate solutions that are acceptable to all parties. Mediation focuses on the needs of the child or young person and aims to find solutions as quickly as possible in a bid to ensure that disruption to education is kept to a minimum.

Referrals for mediation can be made by an LEA, school, parent or parent partnership service. Mediation can take place at any stage, including situations where there is no right to appeal (perhaps because a child is on School Action or School Action Plus). However, mediation works best if referrals are made as soon after a disagreement has arisen as possible. The service is voluntary and free to parents, and mediation will only take place if all sides are happy to participate. It is essential that people pa ticipate with a real desire to resolve the disagreement and a willingness to negotiate even if they cannot see a way forward prior to mediation.

Parents needn't go to mediation alone: they can bring a friend, parental supporter or similar should they wish. Any agreement reached through mediation is put in writing and signed by all parties, with each receiving a copy. This will indicate the decisions made, what is to happen, who is responsible and when.

Taking part in mediation does not prejudice any rights to appeal to the SEN & Disability Tribunal (SENDIST). In excess of 80 per cent of disputes referred to LDRS reach agreement following mediation. If you think mediation may provide the way forward, do contact your nearest provider to discuss further.

Regional SEN mediation providers

BGWS North West Regional SEN Disagreement Resolution Service

Steve Griffiths, Practice Manager

Region: Northwest Merseyside: Blackburn with Darwen; Blackpool; Bolton; Bury; Cumbria; Lancashire; Manchester; Oldham; Rochdale; Salford; Stockport; Warrington; Wigan

Web: www.bgws.org.uk
E-mail: Gayle.drs@btconnect.com
Tel: 01772 204494. Fax: 01772 204501.
Address: 15 Moor Park Avenue, Preston, Lancashire PR1 6AS

ConSENsus

Rosalind Redelsperger, Sub-Regional Co-ordinator. Admin: Diana Banks

Region: Essex, Bedfordshire, Hertfordshire, Norfolk, Suffolk

E-mail: rosalind.redelsperger@mencap.org.uk
diana.banks@mencap.org.uk
Tel: 01284 748320. Fax: 01284 723676.
Address: Mencap Regional Office, Davies House, 4 Hillside Business Park, Bury St Edmunds, Suffolk IP32 7AR

East Midlands SEN Service

Zanne Findlay, Service Manager. Admin: Teena Bates

Region: Derby City, Derbyshire, Leicester City, Leicestershire, Lincolnshire, Northampton, Northamptonshire, Nottingham City, Nottinghamshire, Rutland

Web: www.appliedmediation.co.uk
E-mail: zanne@appliedmediation.co.uk
Tel: 0800 085 3974.
Address: PO Box 45335, London SE14 5YR

FANE – Facilitating Agreement in the North East

Sue Wilson, Service Co-ordinator. Admin: Victoria Lewis

Region: North East Region: Darlington, Durham, Gateshead, Hartlepool, Middlesbrough, Newcastle, Northumberland, North Tyneside, Redcar & Cleveland, South Tyneside, Stockton, Sunderland

Web: www.fane-partnership.org.uk
E-mail: sue.wilson2@darlington.gov.uk
Tel: 01325 254548. Fax: 01325 254548.
Address: Harewood House, 14 Harewood Hill, Darlington, Co.Durham, DL3 7HY

Global Mediation Ltd

Adam Gersch, Director

Region: Bracknell Forest, Brighton & Hove, Buckinghamshire, East Sussex, Hampshire, Isle of Wight, Kent, Medway, Milton Keynes, Oxfordshire, Portsmouth, Reading, Slough, Southampton, Surrey, West Berkshire, West Sussex, Windsor & Maidenhead, Wokingham

Web: www.globalmediation.co.uk
E-mail: info@globalmediation.co.uk
Tel: 0800 064 4488. Fax: 0208 441 4101.
Address: Global Mediation Limited, 1 Oakwood Parade, London, N14 4HY

London SEN Disagreement Resolution Service

Annette Colleary, Service Manager. Admin: Kirsty Dennis

Region: London: Barking & Dagenham, Barnet, Bexley, Brent, Bromley, Camden, Corporation of London, Croydon, Enfield, Greenwich, Hackney, Hammersmith & Fulham, Haringey, Harrow, Hillingdon, Hounslow, Islington, Kensington & Chelsea, Kingston upon Thames, Lambeth, Lewisham, Merton, Newham, Redbridge, Richmond upon Thames, Southwalk, Sutton, Tower Hamlets, Waltham Forest, Wandsworth, Westminster

Web: www.londonsenmediation.org.uk
E-mail: annettec@kids-online.org.uk
kirstyd@kids-online.org.uk
Tel (freephone): 0800 389 0695. Fax: 020 7243 8512.
Address: 240 Lancaster Road, London W11 4AH

Midlands SEN Mediation

Susanna Diegel, Regional Co-ordinator.
Admin: Jenny Hinks

Region: West Midlands: Birmingham, Coventry, Dudley, Herefordshire, Sandwell, Shropshire, Solihull, Staffordshire, Stoke-on-Trent, Telford & Wrekin, Walsall, Warwickshire, Wolverhampton, Worcestershire

Web: www.midlandssenmediation.com
E-mail: admin@midlandssenmediation.com
jenny@midlandssenmediation.com
Tel: 01952 275038. Fax: 01952 520092.
Address: 48 Walker Street, Wellington, Telford TF1 1BA

Peninsula Mediation Service

Jill Holloway, Co-ordinator.
Admin: Sue Fowles or Lindsay Halford

Region: Cornwall, Devon, Plymouth, Torbay, Isles of Scilly

Web: www.peninsulamediation.co.uk
E-mail: devmed@postmaster.co.uk
info@peninsulamediation.co.uk
mediation@mediationdorset.freeserve.co.uk (admin)
Tel: 01363 777242. Fax: 01363 777734.
Address: The Red House, St Lawrence Green, Crediton, EX17 3LN

Yorkshire & Humberside SEN Mediation

Susanna Diegel, Regional Co-ordinator.
Admin: Jenny Hinks

Region: Yorkshire & Humberside: Barnsley, Bradford, Calderdale, Doncaster, East Ridings, Kingston upon Hull, Leeds, North East Lincolnshire, North Lincolnshire, North Yorkshire, Rotherham, Sheffield, Wakefield, York

Web: www.yhsenmediation.com
E-mail: admin@midlandssenmediation.com
enquiries@yhsen-mediation.com
jenny@midlandssenmediation.com
Tel (freephone): 0800 953 0662. Fax: 01952 271648.
Address: PO Box 232, Telford TF1 1ZW

Wessex Mediation

Colin Gould and Lindsey Halford, Co-ordinators

Region: Bath and North East Somerset, Bournemouth, Bristol, Dorset, Gloucestershire, North Somerset, Somerset, Poole, South Gloucestershire, Swindon, Wiltshire

Web: www.wessexmediation.com
E-mail: info@wessexmediation.co.uk
Tel: 01823 336465. Fax: 01823 352210
Address: Victoria House, Victoria St, Taunton, Somerset TA1 3FA

YoungMinds

YoungMinds is a national charity dedicated to improving and promoting the mental health of all babies, children and young people. It exists to meet the needs of parents and carers worried about the mental health of a particular child or young person – to hear their concerns and help them find a way forward. It provides comprehensive information on a range of mental health issues that affect children and young people such as depression, eating problems, self-harming, bullying and attention deficit hyperactivity disorder (ADHD).

YoungMinds believes that as parents, what we want for our children is that they live full and creative lives, be able to cope with difficult situations and make the most of their abilities. In other words, we want them to have good mental health. By this we mean having the strength and capacity to grow and develop with confidence and enjoyment, the capacity to learn from experience and to overcome difficulty and adversity. We are not talking about wanting our children to be little saints or models of perfection but children who are able to enjoy school and life and manage the ups and downs.

If you would like to know more about YoungMinds resources and our Parents Information Service, please visit www.youngminds.org.uk/whatwedo.

Contact details

YoungMinds.
Web: www.youngminds.org.uk
E-mail: enquiries@youngminds.org.uk
Tel: 020 7336 8445. Fax: 020 7336 8446.
Address: 48–50 St John Street, London EC1M 4DG

Parents Information Service.
Web: www.youngminds.org.uk/pis
Tel (freephone): 0800 018 2138 (10am-1pm Mon and Fri, 1pm-4pm Tues-Thurs, 6pm-8pm Wed)

In addition to charities and independent organisations, don't forget the government's own extensive resources, in particular the ...

Department for Education and Skills (DfES)

The DfES has more facets than a diamond (but may at times appear not to have the same clarity or sparkle). The best way of approaching it is on the web.

Choose first the facet labelled 'parents' (at the time of writing the link is obscure, towards the middle of the main page, between 'early years' and 'ICT industry'). This takes you to a page tastefully highlighted with pastel shades of grape juice and biscuit. Choose Special Needs in the left-hand menu. Contents are cheerfully helpful, if not that substantial, but those who need to know more will find lots of links to the DfES's professional facet (where the grape juice and biscuit are joined by raspberry and vomit) and to related government SEN websites. Here you can find cartloads of free documentation such as codes of practice etc. Also, when the government is in listening mode on SEN (not at the moment), this is where you can make your views known in response to consultations, green papers etc.

The search facility is worth a try too: much improved, with searches such as 'SEN' or 'inclusion' taking you straight to useful documents. Don't push it too far, though: the best that a search for 'Fragile X' can do is: 'a 108 page handbook on sand dunes, their ecosystems, environment and wildlife'.

Contact details

Web: www.dfes.gov.uk/sen
E-mail: info@dfes.gsi.gov.uk
Tel: 0870 000 2288. (Those who feel disinclined to pay the DfES for the privilege may prefer 020 7925 5000.) In our experience it often requires plenty of time and patience to get a useful answer by phone.
Fax: 01928 794 248.
Address: Sanctuary Buildings, Great Smith Street, London SW1P 3BT

Chapter 9

Special needs and the law

The Education Act (England) places a duty on parents of children of compulsory school age to ensure their child receives efficient full-time education suitable to the child's age, ability and aptitude and to any special needs the child may have either by regular attendance at school or otherwise. This is certainly a duty many parents take very seriously, even going to appeals and tribunals to ensure their child receives their entitlement. Fighting your corner can be a stressful process, but one which eventually had a positive outcome for one contributor, who describes not just the appeals process but the raw emotion involved too.

Education law is a complex business and one that's easy to misquote or misunderstand, especially now that devolved governments mean each country of the UK has its own educational legislation. So we asked leading figures in England and Scotland to explain the law. One message coming through loud and clear from all parties is always seek expert help. It doesn't have to be costly: some organisations such as IPSEA, ISEA and ACE offer help for free. If using a solicitor make sure it's someone who specialises in education law. See Chapter 8 and 'Useful contacts' in Part 4 for full details.

The support of the law

David Ruebain, education and disability lawyer (England)

Before April 1983 (when the Education Act 1981 came into force), children at school were, in effect, either considered as 'normal' or labelled with one of approximately 11 categories of disability or learning difficulty. Some of those categories had some relation to a medical or quasi-medical condition (for example 'physically handicapped' or 'blind') whilst others were somewhat curious (for example 'delicate') and some were, frankly, offensive (note, in particular, the categories of 'backward', 'maladjusted' and even 'educationally subnormal – severe').

The 1981 Act, at least in principle, sought to fundamentally transform the landscape for disabled children with a new, 'child-centred' approach designed to ensure that each child who had additional or different educational needs arising from a disability or learning difficulty had those needs individually considered and met. It introduced a process of assessment resulting in a legal document called a statement of special educational needs (known throughout educational circles as 'a statement'). In addition, the 1981 Act introduced the view that it was desirable to educate disabled and non-disabled children together wherever possible. Thus the concept of 'integration' was recognised for the first time in law, although many local education authorities (LEAs) had encouraged this approach for a number of years.

Although the 1981 Act has been repealed and replaced on a number of occasions, the key legal framework of assessments and statements and the desirability of 'inclusion' (as 'integration' evolved to become) remains in place; albeit in a much more comprehensive form. Today, the law governing provision for children with special educational needs (SEN) in England and Wales is contained primarily in Part 4 of the Education Act 1996 (itself amended by subsequent legislation; most importantly by Part 1 of the Special Educational Needs and Disability Act 2001) and in numerous regulations made by the 1996 Act. (For a timetable of relevant legislation see Part 4.)

Definitions

The 1996 Act defines SEN as arising where a child has 'a learning difficulty' which calls for special educational provision (SEP). A learning difficulty is itself defined as arising if a child:

- has a significantly greater difficulty in learning than the majority of children of the same age; or
- has a disability which prevents or hinders him/her from making use of educational facilities of a kind gen-

erally provided for children of the same age in schools within the area of the LEA; or

- is under the age of five years and is, or would be, if SEP was not made, likely to fall within the above categories when over that age.

SEP is, in turn, defined as provision which is additional to, or different from, that available in ordinary, local schools for children of that age. However, a child does not have SEN simply because they are of high ability or 'gifted' (although for some such children, there may be attendant problems arising from, perhaps, frustration or other emotional difficulties which themselves result in SEN) or solely because a child's first language is not English.

The 1996 Act gives responsibility to children with SEN up to the age of 16 or 19 (providing they remain at school).

The Code of Practice

The 1996 Act provides for the publication of a key document – the Code of Practice on Special Educational Needs – to which LEAs, schools and indeed all those involved with children with SEN must have regard. The current version was published on 1 January 2002.

Informing the Code are the fundamental principles that children with SEN should have their needs met, ordinarily in a mainstream school (or early years settings), and that the curriculum offered should be broad, balanced and relevant. Furthermore it recognises that parents play a vital role in supporting their child's education and that the views of the child should be sought and taken into account.

Critical success factors include requirements that:

- agencies, schools and LEAs work together to ensure early identification of SEN, and best practice
- professionals and parents work in partnership
- there is co-operation between agencies
- resources are managed and deployed to ensure a child's needs are met
- provision is regularly monitored and reviewed with assessments made in accordance with the prescribed time limits
- statements are clear, detailed and reviewed yearly.

The Code outlines the responsibilities of LEAs including the requirements for them to identify, assess and provide for children with SEN and to secure training, advice and support for staff providing SEN.

All maintained-sector schools, including city academies, city technology colleges, pupil referral units and early years settings that receive government funding must have a written SEN policy. There is no requirement for the majority of schools in the independent sector to have one, though many do.

The Code discusses SEN and SEP in detail and, crucially, makes a distinction between those children with SEN who require a statement and those who don't. The Code explains that some children with SEN may require LEAs to arrange the additional or different educational provision (the SEP) whilst for other children with SEN (in fact, the vast majority) their needs can be met simply by the school making its own arrangements, without the LEA needing to intervene. Such children will be classified as being at School Action or School Action Plus (or, for the very young, at Early Years or Early Years Plus. However, again, those children with more severe disabilities or learning difficulties may require, and be entitled to, a statement of SEN.

Statements

The law relating to statements is complex. Statements are unusual in law in that, if properly drafted, they provide for the most comprehensive rights for disabled people in any area of social welfare law. This is because, in short, statements should be drafted by reference to a child's needs and not directly by reference to resources, and the necessary provision to meet those needs should be set out in the statement.

You may find it helpful to look, too, at Chapter 6, which has answers to some frequently asked questions about the statementing process.

Assessments

The process of obtaining a statement through a statutory assessment may be commenced by an LEA of its own volition, or following a request from the child's parents or school.

An assessment involves the LEA obtaining reports from a number of individuals, including the parents themselves, the child in question, an LEA educational psychologist, the school or early years provision, the local health and social services authorities and others.

At the conclusion of the assessment the LEA will consider whether or not the evidence gathered indicates that the child requires a statement (in other words, whether the child's needs are such as to *require* the LEA to arrange the additional or different provision – the SEP).

If so, the LEA will produce a draft statement for consideration by the parents. The LEA will invite comment on the contents of the statement, including which school the parents consider appropriate for the child. The LEA will then consider the representations, including which school the parents have requested, and will issue a final statement. It is at this point that the statement comes into force.

Time limits for assessments

The assessment process – from first consideration by the LEA to production of a final statement – should not exceed six months in total (although there are exceptions which permit that period to be exceeded in certain limited circumstances). Within this six-month period, the following specific time limits apply:

- 6 weeks to consider whether to conduct a statutory assessment
- 10 weeks to undertake the assessment
- 2 weeks to produce a draft statement of SEN
- 8 weeks to finalise the statement.

Contents of a statement

The contents of statements are prescribed in law as follows:

Part 1: This must contain basic details about the child, including the name, date of birth, address, religion, home language and telephone number, together with the names and contact details of the child's parents. This part will also list the advice and evidence which the LEA has obtained in the assessment and which has been considered in drafting the statement.

Part 2: This should contain details of all of the child's SEN.

Part 3: This should describe all of the SEP required to meet the needs identified in Part 2. Part 3 is often defined as being an analogous to a 'prescription' to meet the 'diagnosis' of needs which has been set out in Part 2. The law requires that, usually, the provision should be particularised and detailed to a high degree, so that everyone involved in the child's education is clear as to exactly what must be arranged for them. (For example, it is not usually lawful for statements to have phrases such as 'regular speech and language therapy' since 'regular' is unclear and vague, and could mean weekly, monthly, yearly etc). Part 3 is itself subdivided into three subsections, dealing with objectives, educational provision and monitoring.

Part 4: This part should describe the school (or, exceptionally, a type of school or other provision) the child will attend.

Parts 5 and 6: These parts deal respectively with non-educational needs and non-educational provision. They are, therefore analogous to Parts 2 and 3. However, whereas the SEP set out in Part 3 *must* be 'arranged' (in other words, secured) by the LEA, the non-educational provision set out in Part 6 need not be.

Educational provision and non-educational provision

As a result of the above framework, there is a fair amount of law as to what should be in Part 3 of a statement (and therefore must be arranged by an LEA) and is covered by Part 6 of a statement (and therefore needn't be arranged by a LEA) – in other words what is, and what is not, educational. Various court cases have established that:

- Most teaching and related provision is educational (Part 3).
- Most speech and language therapy that a child requires is educational (Part 3).
- Some (but not all) occupational therapy and physiotherapy may be educational (depending on the circumstances) (and, if so, Part 3).
- Nursing support or other medical provision is unlikely to be educational (Part 6).
- Transport is unlikely to be educational (although a child may still be entitled to it under another part of the Education Act 1996) (Part 6).

■ Shelter, warmth, nourishment and clothing is unlikely to be educational (Part 6).

Choice of school

The law relating to which school should be named in Part 4 of a statement (and therefore which school the child should attend) is complicated, with sections 9, 316 and 316A of, and Schedule 27 to, the Education Act 1996 all applying.

Where a parent seeks a maintained school

If a parent requests that a maintained school (in other words, a state school, whether it be mainstream or special) be named in the statement, the LEA *must* accede to that request unless one of the following three conditions apply:

■ The school cannot meet the child's needs.

■ Other children would be adversely affected by the presence of the child at the school.

■ It would be an inefficient use of the LEA's resources for the child to attend the school.

Where a parent seeks an independent or non-maintained special school

If a parent wants an independent or non-maintained school (in other words, not a state school), the LEA must agree to this providing that it does not conflict with the duty on the LEA to have regard to the efficient use of resources. In practice, this usually means that it will only agree an independent or non-maintained special school if local maintained schools cannot meet the child's SEN.

Where a parent seeks a mainstream school

Quite apart from state/independent consideration, if a parent wants a mainstream school (in other words, an ordinary school or a school which is not a special school) named, then in addition to the above provisions, separate parts of the 1996 Act provide that the LEA must agree to this (although not necessarily the specific school that the parent has asked for). This is unless the presence of the child at a mainstream school would be incompatible with the provision of efficient education for other children *and* there is nothing that the school or LEA can do to overcome that difficulty.

If the parent is happy with what is set out in a statement (particularly with the description of SEN in Part 2, the SEP set out in Part 3 and the school or other placement named in Part 4) nothing further need happen and the LEA must arrange the SEP and the school named in the statement must admit the child.

However, if the parent does not agree with any decision of the LEA regarding the assessment and statementing process, they may have a right of appeal to the Special Educational Needs & Disability Tribunal.

Appeals to the Special Educational Needs & Disability Tribunal (SENDIST)

The tribunal was set up in 1994 to deal with appeals against decisions by LEAs concerning children with SEN. It will consider appeals on a number of grounds, including decisions by LEAs:

■ not to conduct statutory assessments

■ not to undertake statutory reassessments

■ not to make statements following statutory assessments or reassessments

■ with regard to the contents of Parts 2, 3 or 4 of a statement

■ to refuse to amend a statement to name a different maintained school

■ to cease to maintain statements.

You cannot lodge an appeal with the tribunal against any of the following:

■ how the LEA administers the help set out in the statement

■ the way in which the school meets your child's needs

■ the length of time the LEA took to carry out the assessment or the way in which it carried out the assessment

■ non-educational needs (Part 5 of the statement), or Part 6: how the LEA intends to meet those needs. (Although an LEA may arrange the provision laid out in Part 6, neither it nor anyone else has a duty to arrange it.)

However, there may be other steps that a parent can take to remedy other disputes, such as non-provision of SEP or significant delay in carrying out assessments. These include use of a complaints procedure (for the governing body, the local education authority or to the

Secretary of State), complaint to the Local Government Ombudsman or, occasionally, legal proceedings.

Appeals cannot be brought if a statement was received by a parent more than two months ago. However, if a statement is at least a year old a parent may ask for an amendment to name a different maintained school, and if the LEA refuses this the parent may bring an appeal to the tribunal. But this right of appeal does not apply for a parent who is seeking a non-maintained or independent school.

Preparing your appeal

Any appeal to the tribunal must be lodged within two months of the date that the parents receive the decision against which they are appealing.

You must give reasons why you wish to appeal. These may include:

- seeking more help or different help from that described in the statement
- showing that your child is not making satisfactory progress at a particular school and why another school may be better equipped to meet their needs
- disagreement with either the school or type of school named in Part 4 of the statement: you will need to either describe the type of school, or provide details of the school you wish your child to attend, and why.

If you do name a school you must inform the school that you are asking for it to be named on your child's statement (if it is an independent school you may need to seek approval from the Secretary of State).

It may sometimes be necessary to obtain evidence from an independent expert, such as an educational psychologist or speech and language therapist. This may be so particularly where you are seeking to show that LEA provision is unsuitable or inappropriate for your child, or that your child needs some kind of specialist provision or placement. Do think carefully about what sort of expert would properly deal with what is likely to be in dispute before a tribunal, before spending money!

The procedure provides for parents to put forward documentary evidence and to attend a hearing, which will be before a panel of three individuals consisting of a legally qualified chair and two other members who will have expertise in SEN.

The appeal process takes about four months from the date when your appeal is registered. If your appeal can be dealt with, you have 30 working days to make a case statement and provide evidence. You can add anything you feel is important but haven't mentioned previously at the hearing, so make a list. You should receive written confirmation of the date, time and place of the hearing at least ten days prior to the hearing. It takes about two weeks for appeals decisions to be issued (sometimes longer in complicated cases).

Tribunal decisions are binding on both parties (the LEA and the parents) and there is no automatic right of a further appeal. However, either party can request a review of a decision if it is considered that a key mistake has been made and, exceptionally, either party can appeal a tribunal decision to the High Court and beyond if it is considered that the tribunal has made an error of law.

On page 167, a mother describes her own – eventually successful – experience of going to SENDIST.

The tribunal provides very helpful guidance and information on appeals but it cannot advise you on whether to appeal or not. You can seek help and advice on this from parent partnerships, voluntary organisations such as IPSEA or ACE (see Chapter 8), independent parental supporters, or solicitors who specialise in SEN. Do bear in mind that education law is a specialist area and most solicitors will not have knowledge or experience of it. Most education lawyers who represent children and families are members of the Education Law Association or the Education Law Practitioners Association and will also have contracts with the Legal Services Commission (LSC), so that details may be found on the LSC's website: www.legalservices.gov.uk

Reviews and reassessments

Once a statement of SEN has been made, it must be reviewed at least once a year (although a review will not necessarily lead to any changes to the statement). If a child with a statement is due to transfer to a different phase of education (for example from primary education to secondary education), their statement must be amended by 15 February preceding the September transfer (to give parents time to conclude any appeal to the tribunal before the actual transfer, should they wish). In addition, a child with a statement may be reassessed at any time a reassessment is felt necessary.

LEAs are only responsible for children up to the age of 16, or up to the age of 19 so long as they remain on the roll of a school. For young people otherwise, responsibility lies primarily with their college or with the Learning and Skills Council (see Chapter 7).

The Disability Discrimination Act (DDA)

Since September 2002, the Disability Discrimination Act 1995 has been extended (by the Special Educational Needs and Disability Act 2001) to cover discrimination faced by disabled students in schools and colleges. The provisions apply to all schools, including independent schools and special schools.

First, the definition of disability in the DDA (in other words, which students are covered) is not the same as the definition for SEN. In particular, the DDA covers only those who have 'a physical or mental impairment which has a substantial and long term adverse effect on their ability to carry out normal day to day activities'. This definition is considered in detail in guidance produced by the Disability Rights Commission. The DDA also covers those with:

- severe disfigurements
- impairments which are controlled or corrected by the use of medication, prostheses, and aid or otherwise
- progressive symptomatic conditions
- a history of impairment
- cancer, HIV or multiple sclerosis at the point of diagnosis.

However, the DDA does not cover addiction to or dependence on nicotine, tobacco or other non-prescribed drugs or substances; hay fever; or certain mental illnesses which have anti-social consequences. Accordingly, it might be possible for a student to have special educational needs but not be disabled for the purposes of the DDA, and vice versa (although the majority of disabled students will also have special educational needs).

A student who is disabled is protected from discrimination in two ways. Firstly, they are entitled not to be treated less favourably than a non-disabled student for a reason relating to their disability without justification. Secondly, they are entitled to have reasonable adjustments made with respect to admission arrangements or in the provision of education and associated services, to prevent them being placed at a substantial disadvantage, unless the refusal to make those adjustments is 'justified'. Such adjustments may be to policies, practices, or procedures of a school but generally will not include adjusting premises (such as putting in ramps, lifts etc), nor will they usually include providing additional staff or equipment. (Although these kinds of adjustments are covered in other parts of the DDA, they are expressly excluded from the schools part of the DDA since it is generally intended that additional staff or equipment should be obtained through the SEN route and, at present, it would be too onerous on schools to have an obligation to undertake rebuilding.)

Discrimination is, however, permitted (in other words, lawful) if it is:

- in respect of a permitted form of selection, or
- where it is for reasons which are both material to the circumstances of the particular case, and substantial.

Guidance on this is available in a Code of Practice published by the Disability Rights Commission for schools.

All schools must now publish an accessibility plan and, in addition, LEAs must publish accessibility strategies. These strategies and plans are designed to show how the school or LEA will:

- increase the extent to which disabled pupils can participate in the school curriculum
- improve the physical environment of schools for the purposes of increasing the extent to which disabled pupils are able to take advantage of education and associated services
- improve the delivery to disabled pupils, within a reasonable time and in ways which are determined after taking account of their disabilities and any preferences expressed by them or their parents/carers, of information which is provided in writing to pupils who are not disabled.

If a disabled student has been discriminated against, the parent may complain to either SENDIST or, exceptionally, to an independent appeal panel. Most discrimination claims will be brought to a tribunal but if the complaint relates to the permanent exclusion of a disabled child from a maintained school, or the refusal to admit a disabled child without a statement to a maintained school, then the complaint must be brought before an independent appeal panel. If you're thinking of appealing, organisations such as IPSEA and ACE (see Part 4, Useful contacts) or your LEA can offer help and advice, and explain the sequence of procedures.

The procedures for complaining to a tribunal or independent appeal panel are similar to those for appealing in respect of SEN matters or admissions and exclusions generally. However, in the case of discrimination in schools only (as opposed to colleges or employment or service provision) compensation may not be ordered. Instead, tribunals and independent appeal panels may order a variety of remedies (assuming that they uphold the complaint of discrimination), including re-admission or admission to a school, an apology, staff training etc).

David Ruebain, who is recognised as one of England's top education and disability lawyers, heads a department of education and disability law with Levenes Solicitors. He undertakes consultation work with public, private and voluntary organisations and has a sympathetic understanding of their needs. His numerous credits include Chair of the Law Society's Mental Health and Disability Committee, member of the National Autistic Society's panel of specialist education law solicitors, member of the Disability Rights Commission panel of specialist disability discrimination solicitors, and honorary legal adviser to IPSEA. His publications include: co-author of The DDA Toolkit *(Levenes Solicitors), now in its 10th edition; and co-author of* Taking Action: A Guide for Parents of Children with Special Educational Needs *(Questions Publishing, 2000). He was winner of RADAR's 2002 People of the Year Award for Achievement in the Furtherance of Human Rights of Disabled People in the UK. In 2003 he was shortlisted for the Law Society's Gazette Centenary Award for Lifetime Achievement – Human Rights.*

Further information and help

See also Part 4: Useful contacts.

Disability Rights Commission.
Web: www.drc-gb.org
E-mail: enquiry@drc-gb.org
Tel: 0845 7622 633. Textphone: 0845 7622 644.
Fax: 0845 7778 878.
Address: DCR Helpline, Freepost MID 02164, Stratford-upon-Avon CV37 9BR

Legal Services Commission.
Web: www.legalservices.gov.uk
Tel: 020 7759 0000
Address (head office): 85 Gray's Inn Road, London WC1X 8TX

Special Educational Needs & Disability Tribunal (SENDIST).
Web: www.sendist.gov.uk
E-mail: tribunalqueries@sent.gsi.gov.uk
Tel: 020 7925 5750. Fax: 020 7925 6786.
Address: 7th floor, Windsor House, 50 Victoria Street. London SW1H 0NW

Scotland's new Education Act

On 14 November 2005 new legislation, the Additional Support for Learning (Scotland) Act 2004, replaced the sections of the Education (Scotland) Act 1980, as amended, covering children and young people with SEN.

It has taken nearly 25 years for some bright spark to realise that the 1980 Act needed to be significantly changed! That change should have been to give parents and children more rights in law and not, as was put forward, that 'the legislation was too bureaucratic and the term "Special Educational Needs" was not politically correct'. We would certainly agree that the old system was bureaucratic but, there again, we believe it was intended so to be. Parents needed to become Philadelphia lawyers (or a legal anorak) to work it out, especially if you were going to challenge your LEA. This would, of course, explain the lack of precedence being set in the Scottish law courts, unlike the rest of the UK.

Independent Special Education Advice (ISEA) (Scotland) has been at the forefront of this new legislation's passage through the Scottish Parliament. It has advocated on behalf of Scottish parents by giving both written and oral evidence, and has campaigned with various parties in order to seek in-depth debates and amendments to be put forward which would enhance and secure parents' and children's rights in law. Here ISEA gives an insight into what some of the changes in legislation mean.

From SEN to ASN

Under the 1980 Act, children and young people had SEN if they had a learning difficulty. The Education (Additional Support for Learning) (Scotland) Act 2004 introduces the new term 'additional support needs' (ASN) as a description of those who, for whatever reason, require additional support, long or short term, in order to help them make the most of their school education. Therefore the criteria have been broadened from children with a learning disability to a much wider group which includes children who are being bullied, have English as a second language, are young carers, are in care, have emotional or social difficulties, are living with parents who are abusing substances or who have mental health problems etc. But because a child falls into one of the above categories, this does not mean that additional support will be required. Whereas previously there were approximately 35,000 children in Scotland identified as having SEN, we reckon there could be as many as 100,000 children who will come under the new legislation.

Education authorities' duties to children in their area

Whereas before LEAs had a duty towards every child in their area, the new legislation only places a duty on an LEA for children who are educated in the public sector. You may be cheering at this point if you educate your child at home, but beware – your LEA can still intervene under the parent's duty to provide adequate education.

If you are in dispute with your LEA about the resources and/or provision being provided, and have withdrawn your child from school, and don't de-register them, the LEA will still have a duty. However, the Act does give a power to an LEA to help a child who has, or may have, ASN being educated at home or in an independent school at their parents' preference, but for whose school education the LEA is not responsible.

Assessments and examinations

Parents can now request their LEA to carry out an assessment and/or examination, and this can be medical and/or psychological. However, they must put it in writing, stating their preference and outlining the reasons for their request. The LEA must honour the request unless it considers it unreasonable. If this happens, the LEA must give its reason for refusing. (If requesting an assessment and/or examination, we would encourage parents to request, at the same time, whether their child requires a Co-ordinated Support Plan – see below.)

Co-ordinated Support Plan (CSP)

Prior to the ASL(Scotland) Act 2004, there were approximately 17,500 children identified as having significant and enduring SEN that required the opening and maintaining of a Record of Needs (a legal document). Under the new system, it has been estimated that 50 per cent of these children will lose the rights safeguarded under the Recording system.

The new legislation introduced a Co-ordinated Support Plan (CSP). Parents will have to write to their LEA and ask if their child requires a CSP. Criteria for a CSP are:

1. The education authority is responsible for the school education of the child.

2. The child's additional support needs are complex or have multiple factors.

3. The child's additional support needs are likely to continue for more than one year.

4. The child's needs require significant additional support to be provided by: (a) the education authority in exercise of any of their other functions as well in the exercise of their functions relating to education; or (b) one or more appropriate agencies.

In our opinion, the criteria for a CSP have been set very high and we suspect parents will, indeed, need to wear that anorak to interpret points 2 and 4 in the criteria section.

We expect over the next couple of years that parents may have to challenge the definition of 'complex' or 'multiple factors' and the word 'significant'. We did try, unsuccessfully, to have the definition of these three words clarified in the Scottish Parliament. However, clarification was gained on the issue surrounding the word 'require' in point 4. To the question 'Did the child have to actually be in receipt of the additional support or just require it, even if it was unavailable?', the Minister's response was that 'the child *would require* the additional support'. So, parents, keep this one in mind for later use.

If you are one of the lucky ones and the LEA agrees to open a CSP, the major change here will be that they will have to *specify* the additional support to be provided. No more vague statements with the dreaded words 'as appropriate', 'as necessary' or 'as required'. The statements have to provide a clear idea about what is being provided – such as 'two hours per week for one term', 'weekly therapy within a small group for six weeks' etc.

The CSP will also contain the factor or factors giving rise to the ASN, educational objectives, details of who will provide the support, the name of the school, the details of the person nominated to co-ordinate the plan, and a contact person within the LEA.

The LEA will be kept to strict time limits if a parent is requesting an assessment/examination and/or CSP. It will have no longer than four weeks from when the request, which must be recorded, is received. In the case of CSP, the LEA has 16 weeks within which to produce a completed CSP. The timescale starts from the date the LEA informs the child's parents of its proposal to establish whether a CSP is required. This means that, from the parental request to completion, it should take no more than 20 weeks. However, if the LEA cannot meet the 16 weeks timescale because of a reason expressed in the Code of Practice, it can extend the time limit, but only by another eight weeks.

The CSP has to be formally reviewed at least every 12 months. The content of the CSP can be appealed, and if the LEA refuses to open a CSP you also have the right to appeal.

Disagreements and appeals

The new Act introduces:

- Mediation – which every LEA must make available to parents and young people free of charge
- Dispute Resolution – allowing for a formal review of an individual case by an independent third party
- Additional Support Needs Tribunal.

The Additional Support Needs Tribunal will hear on:

- whether to prepare or not to prepare a CSP
- whether or not to continue a CSP
- timescales for a CSP
- non-compliance with a request for a CSP
- information contained in the CSP
- failure to review a CSP within the timescales
- request for a review by the parent or young person
- refusal of a placing request in certain circumstances.

Other routes of appeal are still in play, such as Section 70 complaints, disability discrimination, local authority appeal committees (who will still deal with exclusion appeals and 'placing request' appeals where the child does not have a CSP), Judicial Review, Ombudsman, and the Sheriff Court.

It is imperative that parents are aware of their rights in order that they access the appropriate system. With so many around, it may be possible that they can access more than one.

Placing requests

If a child has ASN, parents are now entitled to make a placing request for the child to attend an independent or a grant-aided school for children with ASN. If the LEA refuses, you can appeal (see above).

Transition

Where a child with ASN is moving from one stage of schooling to another (such as from primary to secondary), the LEA is required to seek and take account of relevant advice and information from other agencies no less than 12 months before the child is to have a change in school education. This means that the LEA will need to begin preparing for the change earlier than the 12 months before any change takes place. (The Act suggests the timescale for the transition from preschool to primary may only be six months, but you should seek clarification on this.)

Where the LEA takes advice or information from other agencies and individuals, it is also required to seek and take account of the views of the child and/or the child's parent. Remember the wording 'take account' – this does *not* mean they have to give any weight to what is received by them.

Deemed decision

Because LEAs are now governed by strict timescales, parents and young people can use the 'deemed decision' clause if the LEA does not comply within the timescales set for CSPs and placing requests. For example, if a placing request is made, the LEA has two months in which to give its written answer. If it does not respond within this two-month period it can be taken as a deemed refusal to comply with that request and an appeal can be made through the appropriate system.

The facts above are only a small indication of the changes brought about by the new legislation. We would recommend that each parent seek *independent* advice and information on their child's case – unless they are, of course, Philadelphia lawyers or anoraks.

Although we are sure that the intention to change the legislation was honourable, the gremlins crept in and we are unequivocal in our view that this new legislation is even more bureaucratic and confusing than the last one. Time will tell.

Further information and help

ISEA (Independent Special Education Advice) (Scotland).
Website being updated at the time of writing.
Web www.isea.org.uk
E-mail: isea@whsmithnet.co.uk
Tel: 0131 454 0096. Helpline: 0131 454 0082.
Fax: 0131 454 0096
Address: 164 High Street, Dalkeith, Midlothian EH22 1AY

ISEA (Scotland) has provided free, independent advice, information and practical support to parents throughout Scotland over the last six years, specifically on their and their children's legal rights under the 1980 Act. Its purpose has been to enable and empower parents to secure resources and provision so that their children reach their full potential in accordance with the Standard in Schools Act 2000. Although not all of its points were taken on board, and some were just out-voted at committee, the ones which were accepted and the amendments which were made will go some way in ensuring children are enabled to reach their potential.

Some of the practical ways in which ISEA can help parents in Scotland, including two new projects it has established, are described in Chapter 8.

Going through the tribunal experience

Here a mother describes her son's difficult experiences at school, her struggles with the system, and how her appeal to SENDIST was eventually successful.

Tom is now nearly 21 and is just finishing his gap year before starting his Foundation degree in sports conditioning and coaching. He has spent his gap year working in the French and Swiss Alps for a holiday company. He has to wait at tables, clean bedrooms, help in the kitchen, act as ski guide and anything else that requires doing. His manager told me when we went out to visit that the guests all think Tom is terrific, hardworking, an excellent team player and a mean skier! She also said that he will often diffuse tense or difficult situations that may have arisen between other members of staff or with guests with his sense of humour. My partner and I were recently married, and much to our delight Tom asked if he could make a speech at the wedding. He spoke very confidently, without notes, and had all the guests in stitches!

Tom is the youngest of my three children, all of whom are dyslexic. Tom did not speak until the age of 4. He was later than his peers in learning to walk, swim, ride a bike etc. When he started school, we realised straight away that his dyslexic difference was far greater than his brother or sister's. He attended speech therapy lessons and had extra help at school. Tom attended private school until the age of 9, when family circumstances dictated that he moved to a state primary school.

Tom had been used to small classes and one-to-one help on a regular basis. Once he moved to the state primary it took me over a year to get him statemented, and when this eventually came through Tom was entitled to half an hour per day additional help. Although this was of some help, it was nowhere near enough. However, he found primary school a fairly cosy environment and his teachers were kind and helpful. The one thing that he did find upsetting was that he was never allowed to play in the football team. Tom's coordination was immature and he found it hard to concentrate for any length of time. There were only three boys in his academic year yet Tom was not chosen for the football team and it used to break my heart to see him standing on the sidelines, desperate to join in.

Things became much worse when Tom moved to secondary school. He had always had a problem with bed-wetting and this increased. He also started to have frequent nightmares. Tom used to get lost going from classroom to classroom. He would lose his timetable and even when he had it he found it difficult to read. He was put in the bottom sets for every subject and despite the fact that he enjoyed and had some success at maths, the teacher said that he would muddle his numbers and could not copy from the board and therefore had to stay in the bottom set.

He was kept in at playtime to catch up as he struggled to copy from the board. This exacerbated the problem as he needed to run around and let off some energy during breaks. Instead there was simply no let-up. He was told off for not completing his homework diary, but as he struggled to read and write, even when he did write things down, we could not decipher what he was supposed to do when he came home in the evenings. His self-esteem was at rock bottom and he could hardly lift his chin from his chest.

His one-to-one teacher was a lovely lady, but Tom started to rely on her totally and did not make any progress at all. His teachers complained about him 'switching off'. They suggested that Tom might be having petit-mal attacks so he was tested for epilepsy on two occasions, the second time after a whole night's sleep deprivation. The tests came back negative. He was 'switching off' simply because a lot of the time he was on overload.

I ensured a fairly strict routine and listened to Tom reading every night, helping him with his homework so that he did not get into too much trouble at school. Tom also attended the Gloucestershire Dyslexia Association's Saturday one-to-one workshops. He enjoyed out-of-school activities, such as cubs, mini rugby and even speech and drama classes. These helped enormously, but school life was grim for him.

A very good friend gave us lots of support as a family and also gave Tom individual tuition both during and after school. We all felt that Tom's needs were simply not being met at school. After two years in the comprehensive, he was not only going backwards, but was getting in with the wrong lot and starting to get into trouble at school.

In March 1998 Tom had an assessment carried out by an educational psychologist. It stated that Tom had a cognitive profile indicating a severe degree of dyslexia. At the age of 13 Tom had a reading and spelling age of 7. His learning difficulties were just not being provided for at his school.

In June I went to see a solicitor in Bristol who specialised in educational tribunals. He said Tom's statement lacked the clarity or specificity which is required by law and that, despite the best efforts of the school, Tom had not achieved any measurable progress. He also said that it was obvious that a much more specialist regime was required for Tom, using approved teaching methods for the dyslexic child with teachers who are experienced and qualified in working with pupils with cognitive processing differences. The solicitor talked me through the process, warning me that it would not be an easy ride and that we would not necessarily win.

We had to gather together as much evidence and information as we could to prove that the LEA had been neglectful in their provision for Tom. This included letters from tutors, doctors, and any other professional who had helped him. I am not a naturally pushy parent and I found it very difficult to go into school and complain about how Tom was being treated. I cannot bear confrontation and neither can Tom so between us it was a wonder that we did not just put up with things and carry on letting the situation get slowly worse! However, I think that the fact that I was a single parent made me realise that if I did not stand up for my son, no one would. So I gritted my teeth and wrote to professionals, from the doctor and the educational psychologist to the solicitor to ask for help and advice. I started to do this in the summer of Tom's year 12 at school.

That summer we decided in desperation to look at a specialist school for Tom. It was a huge decision – he had very little self-confidence and so I feared he would not survive at boarding school. However, having looked at a few schools we were so impressed by the pupils, the teachers, the size of the classes and the whole-school approach to learning difficulties that these schools offered that we decided there really was no choice. He had to move or he would simply sink where he was. My parents were very kind and said that they would pay for Tom until we had his statement sorted out.

In September 1998 Tom started at a specialist school in Somerset. He was very nervous about starting at his new school. He had not been away from home very often and was still wetting the bed on a regular basis. He did not ring home for almost two weeks; I was worried sick. When he did phone he sounded like a different boy. He said 'Mum – it's great here. Nobody shouts at me when I ask for a spelling. Do you know, there are boys and girls here who are worse than me – can you imagine?!'

When he came home at half term I hardly recognised him. His chin had lifted off his chest and he was smiling. He was actually enjoying school. The bed wetting had stopped almost immediately. His new teachers had found that he was quite good at football and he occasionally played in the team. He talked animatedly about geography and science – he was starting to enjoy learning! His proudest moment was when he was put into the top maths set. Tom's skill at sport started to improve and he became a regular in the rugby and football teams as well as enjoying success at cross-country running and tennis. He was being taught in a completely different environment and everything seemed so much more positive. He was given small responsibilities such as looking after younger pupils or, later on, becoming a dorm head or a prefect. All these things helped enormously to give him self-respect and this in turn led to him wanting to learn in lessons.

When I sought reassessment of Tom's needs this was refused by the LEA, so I appealed to the tribunal. The appeal was lodged in August 1998, shortly before Tom started at the new school. It came up for hearing in January 1999 then was withdrawn by agreement on the basis that the LEA would conduct a full review. This review took place in April 1999 and I asked for amendments to Tom's statement, including the naming of his new school in Part 4.

The LEA issued its final statement in August 1999 naming the comprehensive in Part 4. I immediately appealed. During this time, Tom was seen by both the LEA's educational psychologist and an NHS Trust learning disabilities consultant psychiatrist. The results of both findings were used in evidence at the tribunal.

Before the tribunal hearing my solicitor and the LEA met and agreed as much of Tom's statement as they could apart from the subject of the placement.

On the day of the tribunal I felt very nervous, but my solicitor and friend who had come to support me were extremely positive. Tom's new headmaster was also there, as was the educational psychologist who carried out the first assessment on Tom. On the LEA side were their assistant education officer and educational psychologist and the special educational needs co-ordinator from the comprehensive school. I did not say anything during the morning but left matters to the professionals. However, at lunchtime my solicitor said that I should add anything I felt would be of help. I explained to the tribunal the complete difference in Tom since he had changed schools, especially how he could now look up with confidence. I was careful not to become emotional or tearful.

The tribunal heard that the comprehensive had not put in place cross-school strategies to address the severity of Tom's learning difficulties and to enable him to move on. Following this the LEA proposed that Tom's individual support should be increased to 6 hours 25 minutes per week, but did not say how that support should be provided or by whom. The tribunal then discussed the relative cost of placement at the two schools and found that there was not much in it by the time the extra support would have been put in place.

Two weeks later we heard the results of the tribunal and we received the amended statement at the end of January 2000, listing Tom's new school in 'Part 4, Placement Arrangements'. I was overjoyed and did allow myself some tears!

I know I could not have done it alone – the support of a specialist solicitor is paramount and I was lucky enough to have legal aid. Enormous gratitude goes to my very good friend who supported Tom and me throughout, and also huge thanks to the educational psychologist who first assessed Tom and who gave vital evidence at tribunal, and to Tom's headmaster from the specialist school who gave up so much of his time and helped Tom so much.

Tom left his new school with five GCSEs at grade C or above. He moved on to St David's College in North Wales for the sixth form, where he gained a C in sports science A level and an E in biology AS level. However, in my mind his most important result was a grade C in English language GCSE on his seventh attempt! He coached his own five-a-side football team of younger boys, took part in the paired reading scheme, was a striker in the school football team, a school prefect and was generally thought of as very worthwhile.

We all know that there is no 'magic cure' for dyslexia and Tom will always have problems, but thanks to the help of so many friends, relatives, teachers and a brilliant solicitor, Tom got the help he needed. Help that has probably changed his life forever.

My tips for taking your local education authority to tribunal are:

■ Keep records of everything – letters and reports from teachers, doctors, psychologists, friends, solicitors, headmasters.

■ Write things down in your diary such as appointments to do with your child, visits to the school, phone calls to the school. Keep all diaries for a few years. It is amazing how often you will need to check back on what happened when!

■ Don't allow the case to take over your life. Keep up the normal routine for your children and try to be positive.

■ Try to make time for activities outside school so that even if your child is hating school, he can at least have some fun!

■ At the hearings and the tribunal wear smart but normal clothes and don't get too emotional if you can help it. Just be yourself as far as you can.

■ Have a good friend (preferably with experience of tribunals!) to lean on. They will help you to keep things in perspective and help you to laugh.

Parent power prevails

Peter Woodroffe, senior solicitor and parent

'Johnny must go!' declared the head. 'Yessir', responded the father meekly. That was in the old days. Now, the father says 'Why?'

Acting for 16 years as solicitor and secretary to the court of governors of the Mill Hill School Foundation (an independent school with over 1,000 pupils) has given me an insight into how governors and heads think. As a parent and in my professional capacity, I encounter a wide variety of parental attitudes.

Parents need to be advised as to whether they have a genuine complaint or not. I do not regard it as my function to encourage disaffected parents to take a stand against the school – if they do not have a legitimate complaint, then they need to be told so firmly. The vast majority of schools act fairly and provide good pastoral care; it is only occasionally that things go wrong. In those circumstances, it is my task to negotiate a fair settlement with the school, steering the parent away from proceedings unless that is absolutely necessary. The majority of schools take a reasonably pragmatic view towards disputes and things tend only to get out of hand where there is a gung-ho bursar or head. Unfortunately, life's rich tapestry throws up such persons from time to time.

The most frequent causes of disputes are the following.

Fees (independent schools only)

In general, parents are liable to pay one term's fees in lieu of giving a clear term's notice. The reasonableness of this requirement is well established in law, and parents should expect schools to take proceedings if they do not pay. To avoid liability, a parent must show that giving a term's notice was unreasonable because of something that the school was responsible for. Examples of this might be a failure to provide promised educational support for a dyslexic child and serious injury to a child.

Bullying

This happens in every school, but today most schools go to great lengths to stamp it out. One well-known independent school expelled three boys and suspended 15 on this ground. Sometimes bullying has serious consequences: much depends upon the ability and common sense of the staff, and if it has failed to exercise proper supervision and control there may well be a claim.

My firm has recently settled a case of bullying in a well-known girls' school. As most parents know, bullying by girls is not usually physical but more subtle, causing extreme depression on the part of the victim. We are currently dealing with a case of bullying by a group of foreign pupils. This is very unusual and may well go through the courts.

If an exchange of correspondence or the commencement of proceedings exposes negligence on the part of a school, this will often lead both to a reasonable financial settlement without the need for a court hearing and to improved procedures in the school.

Breach of contract

This applies to all schools, but the rights of state-school parents can be severely curtailed by statutory procedures, for example exclusion from school.

Disputes arising out of expulsion/exclusion are serious because they are regarded as affecting the reputation of the pupil and sometimes by analogy to the parents. The all-important question is, has the head acted fairly?

It is not generally realised that the contract does not have to specify that the head will act in a fair manner. However, this is implied in every contract of education, as are the rules of natural justice. It is also likely that the Human Rights Act applies to independent schools.

The courts will be prepared to examine all aspects of an expulsion in order to establish whether or not the head has acted fairly, which gives an aggrieved parent considerable scope. Such a parent should not, though, expect to receive much by way of damages, or even their (substantial) costs back – and should expect only rarely to see their child reinstated.

What most parents want in cases of expulsion is an appeal to the governors against the head's decision, and/or an apology from the head or chairman of governors. Obtaining an apology from most heads is like drawing teeth! They teach their charges to say sorry, but appear to be unable to do so themselves. My experience is that it is usually the unfortunate chair of governors who has to give the apology for the misdeeds of the head.

Defamation apart, the law does not normally provide a right of action for an apology. This therefore has to be negotiated. I have recently settled a case involving one of Britain's more famous girls' schools in which an apology and a contribution towards costs was eventually given by the school. It arose out of a fight occurring between two girls (and believe me, when girls have a fight, they put the boys to shame!). Although, in my view, it was a case of six of one and half a dozen of the other, one girl was expelled and one was not. However, we ascertained that the latter was the daughter of a trustee who provided substantial funds to the school!

State-school parents will have to negotiate the statutory disputes procedure before they are allowed access to the courts – but would be well advised to engage a solicitor from the start.

Negligence

This is a relatively grey area of the law, but developing. It is not unreasonable for the courts to provide schools with some protection against marginal or vindictive claims, but the court of appeal has recently accepted that a school can owe a duty of care towards pupils. Whilst there is obviously an overlap with breach of contract, negligence could include a failure to educate, to take proper account of dyslexia and other learning difficulties, to supervise and control the pupils and to provide proper pastoral care. Parents might expect to receive proper recompense for expense incurred, including the additional cost of a new school, plus modest compensation for distress in appropriate cases.

Breaches of the Race Relations Act

This does not happen often but can give rise to difficult disputes because the evidence tends to be circumstantial, though I recently settled a much-publicised case at the court door. Schools sometimes settle disputes out of court on condition that there is a gagging order (which prohibits the details being made public and can apply to the parties and their lawyers or the press or both) so as to avoid adverse publicity.

Class actions

These are relatively rare but occur when a large number of pupils or parents have been affected by the same injustice. I was recently instructed by a parent representing 70 others as a result of the governors of the school hiking the fees by 25 per cent. As it happened, the contract between parents and the school required (unusually) that the governors would only implement reasonable increases. This dispute never came to court through, I suspect, sheer weight of numbers.

Student/university disputes

Disputes mainly arise out of entry qualifications, examinations and the level of degrees, and also accusations of cheating. When you reach higher education, an important difference to be aware of is that here the student rather than the parent is the client.

Going public

Infuriated parents are sometimes anxious to tell their story to the press. This is not necessarily in their best interests – or that of their child. It is necessary to measure the possibility of diminished chances of effecting a settlement once the parent has 'blown the gaff' against the threat of damaging publicity regarding the school. Some parents are sufficiently unhappy about their situation to insist upon speaking to the press before any question can arise of their being restrained by a gagging order; sometimes a press report will ginger up a school to come to the negotiating table. It is a matter of careful judgement as to what is the right course in each situation.

Costs

If a claimant succeeds in the course of proceedings, the judge normally makes an order that the defendant shall pay the claimant's costs. There is a tariff for these and the claimant usually recovers about two-thirds of the amount of their solicitors' bill. Frequently, if there is an out-of-court settlement, the terms specify that one party's legal costs, or a proportion of them, shall be paid by the other.

Parents are not normally trigger happy and do not involve themselves in proceedings unless the school takes up the cudgels first. The best advice I can give to anybody is to take out a legal protection policy. It is not expensive and can provide £100,000 or more for legal expenses and cover against an adverse order for costs. It gives a unique and necessary degree of financial muscle, particularly since most schools themselves have such a policy!

Mediation

The cost of litigation and the fear of publicity is increasingly encouraging litigants to resort to mediation. This is an informal hearing before a qualified mediator who, after hearing the main evidence and arguments, endeavours to steer the parties towards a mutual agreement. I believe that, when educational disputes get out of hand, this may well in future be the way forward.

Finally, remember that every case is different. These general comments cannot be taken to apply to an individual situation. There is no substitute for taking professional advice!

Peter Woodroffe is the senior partner of Woodroffes of 36 Ebury Street, London SW1W 0LU, and third generation of his family in the firm. He is well known to the Good Schools Guide Advisory Service.

Part 4

USEFUL CONTACTS AND REFERENCES

Useful contacts

Rather than present you with a list pages long in alphabetical order, we have divided it into sections: 'General', for those organisations that may be helpful with any aspect of SEN; 'Specific conditions', for organisations that are principally concerned with individual SEN conditions; and 'Gifted and talented pupils', for organisations concerned with exceptionally able children. There is also a list of some selected books for further reading at the end.

General

Advice

The key sites

Advisory Centre for Education (ACE).
Charity founded in 1960. Publishes guides on such subjects as how to approach primary schooling, UK school law, how to deal with the bureaucrats on SEN, school choice and appeals, home education, bullying etc.
Web: www.ace-ed.org.uk
E-mail: enquiries@ace.dialnet.com
Freephone advice line (2pm-5pm Mon-Fri):
0808 800 5793.
Freephone exclusion helpline (2pm-5pm Mon-Fri):
0808 8000 327. Fax: 020 7354 9069.
Address: 1 Aberdeen Studios, 22 Highbury Grove,
London N5 2DQ

ASDAN (Award Scheme Development and Accreditation Network).
An educational charity promoting the personal and social development of learners through the achievement of ASDAN awards, enhancing self-esteem, aspirations and contribution to the community.
Web: www.asdan.org.uk
E-mail: info@asdan.org.uk
Tel: 0117 941 1126. Fax: 0117 935 1112.
Address: Wainbrook House, Hudds Vale Road,
St. George, Bristol BS5 7HY

Citizens Advice Bureaux (CAB).
Free independent advice on a wide range of problems.
Web: www.adviceguide.org.uk, www.nacab.org.uk
Tel (admin only): 020 7833 2181.
Address: National Association of Citizens Advice Bureaux (NACAB), Myddleton House, 115-123 Pentonville Road, London N1 9LZ

Contact a Family.
Support for the families of anyone newly diagnosed with SEN. Website carries an exhaustive 'Index of Specific Conditions and Rare Disorders', often with a detailed write-up and links to organisations and websites.
Web: www.cafamily.org.uk.
Family-linking website: www.makingcontact.org
E-mail: info@cafamily.org.uk; helpline@cafamily.org.uk
Tel: 020 7608 8700. Freephone helpline (10am-4pm Mon-Fri): 0808 808 3555.
Textphone (freephone): 0808 808 3556.
Minicom: 020 7608 8702. Fax: 020 7608 8701.
Address: 204-211 City Road, London EC1V 1JN

Enquire.
Enquire is the Scottish independent advice and information service for additional support for learning (SEN). It is managed by Children in Scotland and funded by the Scottish Executive. Advice and information offered via telephone helpline, e-mail or enquiries via the website. Provides lots of useful, free publications too.
Web: www.enquire.org.uk
E-mail: info@enquire.org.uk
Helpline: 0845 123 2303. Tel (admin): 0131 222 2425.
Textphone: 0131 222 2439. Fax: 0131 228 9852.
Address: Children in Scotland, 5 Shandwick Place, Edinburgh EH2 4RG

ENABLE Scotland.
Campaigns for people with learning disabilities.
Web: www.enable.org.uk
E-mail: enable@enable.org.uk
Telephone: 0141 226 4541. Fax: 0141 204 4398.

Address (national office): 6th Floor, 7 Buchanan Street, Glasgow G1 3HL

Foundation for Conductive Education.
Teaches people with physical disabilities such as cerebral palsy, dyspraxia, multiple sclerosis, head injury, how to overcome their movement problems.
Web: www.conductive-education.org.uk
E-mail: info@conductive-education.org.uk
Tel: 0121 449 1569. Fax: 0121 449 1611.
Address: Cannon Hill House, Russell Road, Birmingham B13 8RD

Henry Spink Foundation.
A charity that collates information on therapies and sources of help for children with severe disabilities.
Web: www.henryspink.org
E-mail: info@henryspink.org
Tel: 020 7608 8789.
Address: The Henry Spink Foundation, c/o Montgomery Swann, Scotts Sufferance Wharf, 1 Mill Street, London SE1 2DE

IPSEA (Independent Panel for Special Education Advice).
Advice on legal matters regarding children with SEN, statements etc, plus 'What parents can do about seven common problems', including model letters – 'Asking for a formal assessment', 'Asking your LEA for a reassessment of your child's special educational needs' etc.
Web: www.ipsea.org.uk
E-mail (for information only, not advice):
ipsea.info@intamail.com
General enquiries: 01394 380 518.
Advice line (freephone): 0800 018 4016 (10am-4pm and 7pm-9pm Mon-Thurs, 10am-1pm and 7pm-9pm Fri. During school holidays times are reduced. Please ring for availability.) Tribunal appeals only: 01394 384711.
Address: IPSEA, 6 Carlow Mews, Woodbridge, Suffolk IP12 1EA

ISEA (Independent Special Education Advice) (Scotland).
Scottish equivalent of IPSEA. Website being updated at the time of writing.
Web www.isea.org.uk
E-mail: isea@whsmithnet.co.uk
Tel: 0131 454 0096. Helpline: 0131 454 0082.
Fax: 0131 454 0096.
Address: 164 High Street, Dalkeith, Midlothian EH22 1AY

For ISEA Northern Ireland: Tel: 01232 705654.

NASEN (National Association for Special Educational Needs).
Aims to promote the education, training, advancement and development of all those with special and additional support needs. NASEN reaches a huge readership through its journals: *British Journal of Special Education*, *Support for Learning*, new online publication Journal of Research in Special Educational Needs and the magazine *Special!* Sponsors free annual exhibitions run in association with the *Times Educational Supplement*.
Web: www.nasen.org.uk
E-mail: welcome@nasen.org.uk
Tel: 01827 311500. Fax: 01827 313005.
Address: NASEN House, 4/5 Amber Business Village, Amber Close, Amington, Tamworth, Staffordshire B77 4RP

NATSPEC (Association of National Specialist Colleges).
Its *Directory* lists many colleges in England and Wales (and one in Northern Ireland) that specialise in post-school education for people with special needs.
Web: www.natspec.org.uk
E-mail (Kevin O'Brien, Chief Executive):
kevin.obrien43@ntlworld.com
Tel: 01509 554357.
Address: 39 Sanders Rd, Quorn, Loughborough, Leicestershire LE12 8JN

Skill. National Bureau for Students with Disabilities.
A national charity promoting opportunities for young people and adults with any kind of disability in post-16 education, work-based training and entry to employment across the UK.
Web: www.skill.org.uk.
E-mail: info@skill.org.uk
Tel: 020 7657 2337

Other advice and information sites

Bullying and other such problems at school

Anti Bullying Network.
Web: www.antibullying.net
There's to be a new anti-bullying service in Scotland in April 2006, after this Guide has gone to press. You'll be able to find a link to it here.

BBC Bullying homepage. The BBC's survival guide: extensive advice, links and information.
Web: www.bbc.co.uk/schools/bullying

Bullying Online. An increasingly impressive site.
Web: www.bullying.co.uk

Childline.
Helpline for children and young people in trouble or danger. Good advice and good links.
Web: www.childline.org.uk.
Helpline: 0800 1111 (yes it really is that short).

Kidscape.
Works to prevent bullying and child abuse.
Web: www.kidscape.org.uk
Tel: 020 7730 3300. Helpline: 08451 205 204.
Fax: 020 7730 7081.
Address: Kidscape, 2 Grosvenor Gardens, London SW1W 0DH

arentline.
Advice over the telephone on problems at school and other problems of parenting.
Web: www.parentlineplus.org.uk
Tel (general): 020 7284 5500
freephone): 0808 800 2222

Red Balloon Learner Centre.
Established in 1996 with the fundamental aim of helping young people who have been so badly bullied they are unable to attend school. Director: Carrie Herbert. Co-ordinator: Ruth Loshak.
Web: www.redballoonlearner.cambs.sch.uk
E-mail: redballoon@redballoonlearner.org.uk
Tel: 01223 357714.
Address: 57 Warkworth Terrace, Cambridge CB1 1EE

ducation outside school
ducation Otherwise. A charity that advises on the education of children at home ('otherwise than at school', in he words of the statute).
Web: www.education-otherwise.org
E-mail: enquiries@education-otherwise.org
Address: PO Box 7420, London N9 9SG

ree Range Education.
Web: www.free-range-education.org.uk, the website of he book: advice on and stories of home education ncluding one from a family with autistic children).

choolHouse.
cottish site supporting home education.
Web: www.schoolhouse.org.uk.
el: 01307 463120.
Address: Schoolhouse Home Education Association, PO Box 18044, Glenrothes, Fife KY7 9AD

See also the magazine www.choiceineducation.co.uk

Information and communications technology (ICT)
BECTA (British Educational Communications and Technology Agency).
Replaced the National Council for Educational Technology (NCET). Has lots of information sheets on using ICT in special needs and inclusive education, including information on where to find free (or nearly free) software to support the education of pupils with SEN.
Web: www.becta.org.uk
E-mail: becta@becta.org.uk
Tel: 024 7641 6994.
Fax: 024 7641 1418.
Address: Millburn Hill Road, Science Park, Coventry CV4 7JJ

Iansyst.
Provides many of the software packages useful to kids with SEN – such as coloured touch-typing courses for dyspraxics. Can supply computers VAT-free for disabled customers.
Web: www.iansyst.co.uk
Tel: 01223 420101.
Address: iansyst limited, Fen House, Fen Road, Chesterton, Cambridge CB4 1UN

Groups focused on supporting those with disability and their families
Kids.
Established for more than 30 years and currently helps nearly 5,000 disabled children and young people and their families through five regional offices.
Web: www.kids.org.uk
Email: enquiries@kids.org.uk
Tel: 020 7359 3635.
Address: Kids National Office and Fundraising Department, 6 Aztec Row, Berners Road, London N1 0PW

National Parent Partnership Network. Parent partnership services are statutory services that offer information, advice and support for parents of children and young people with special educational needs. Some in the voluntary sector, most based in their local education authority (LEA) or Children's Trust, but 'at arm's length from the LEA, that is, they are able to provide impartial advice and support to parents'. More feedback to the

GSG on how good these services are would be much appreciated.
Web: www.parentpartnership.org.uk.
Tel: 020 7843 6000.
Address: c/o Council for Disabled Children,
8 Wakley Street, London EC1V 7QE

Parents Information Service.
Run by YoungMinds (see below).
Web: www.youngminds.org.uk/pis
Tel (freephone): 0800 018 2138 (10am-1pm Mon and Fri, 1pm-4pm Tues-Thurs, 6pm-8pm Wed)

YoungMinds.
A national charity dedicated to improving and promoting the mental health of all children and young people. It exists to meet the needs of parents and carers worried about the mental health of a particular child or young person, and provides comprehensive information on a range of mental health issues.
Web: www.youngminds.org.uk
E-mail: enquiries@youngminds.org.uk
Tel: 020 7336 8445. Fax: 020 7336 8446.
Address: 48-50 St John Street, London EC1M 4DG

Visual problems related to SEN

British and Irish Orthoptic Society.
Web: www.orthoptics.org.uk
Email: bos@orthoptics.org.uk
Tel: 0207 387 7992.
Fax: 0207 387 2584.
Address: Tavistock House North, Tavistock Square, London WC1H 9HX

Cerium Visual Technologies.
Provides a list of people with the specialist MIS equipment in the UK.
Web: www.ceriumvistech.com
E-mail: CeriumUK@ceriumvistech.co.uk
Tel: 01580 765211. Fax: 01580 765573.
Address: Cerium Group Headquarters,
Cerium Technology Park, Tenterden, Kent TN30 7DE

Rainbow Readers.
Dr Nadia Northway's very useful website.
Web: www.rainbowreaders.co.uk.
E-mail: admin@rainbowreaders.co.uk
Tel: 07776 191628.

Other

Bookmark Books and Disability Issues. Aims to provide support, information and signposts for parents of children with any condition which affects their reading. The site also offers book reviews and represents a useful forum for anyone interested in books and disability issues.
Web: www.bookmark.org.uk
E-mail: info@booktrust.org.uk
Tel 020 8516 2977. Fax: 020 8516 2978.
Address: 45 East Hill, London SW18 2QZ

COPE Directory of Post-16 Education/Training in Residential Establishments.
Published by Lifetime Careers Publishing.
Web: www.lifetime-publishing.co.uk
E-mail: sales@lifetime-publishing.co.uk
Tel. 01225 716023. Fax: 01225 716025.
Address: 7 Ascot Court, White Horse Business Park, Trowbridge, Wiltshire BA14 0XA

Jessica Kingsley Publishers.
Lots of good books on SEN including: *Understanding Autistic Spectrum Disorders*, Diane Yapko; *How to Understand Autism the Easy Way*, Alex Durig; *Surviving the Special Educational Needs System*, Sandy Row; and *Parenting a Child with Asperger Syndrome*, Brenda Boyd.
Web: www.jkp.com
E-mail: post@jkp.com
Tel: 020 7833 2307. Fax: 020 7837 2917.
Address: 116 Pentonville Road, London N1 9JB

Key 4 Learning.
Provides training and consultancy on dyslexia and other hidden disabilities in schools and colleges.
Web: www.key4learning.com
E-mail: office@key4learning.com
Tel: 01285 720964.
Address: The Old Village Stores, Chedworth,
Cheltenham, Gloucestershire GL54 4AA

OAASIS (Office for Advice, Assistance, Support and Information on Special Needs).
Information on a range of disorders, including develop-mental disorders. Free factsheets.
Web: www.oaasis.co.uk
E-mail: oaasis@hesleygroup.co.uk
Tel: 09068 633201 (be warned – phone calls cost 60 per minute). Fax: 01590 622687.
Address: Brock House, Grigg Lane, Brockenhurst, Hampshire SO42 7RE

Government and official agencies

Basic Skills Agency.
Web: www.basic-skills.co.uk
Email: enquiries@basic-skills.co.uk
Tel: 020 7405 4017.
Freephone: 0800 700 987 for help, advice and information on suitable courses. Fax: 020 7440 6626.
Address: Commonwealth House, 1-19 New Oxford Street, London WC1A 1NU

Connexions.
The government's support service for all young people aged 13-19 in England.
Web: www.connexions-direct.com, www.nacp.co.uk
Tel: 0114 281 3418. Fax: 0114 281 3419.
Address: Watsons Chambers, 5-15 Market Place, Castle Square, Sheffield S1 2GH

CSCI (Commission for Social Care Inspection).
Web: www.csci.org.uk
E-mail: enquiries@csci.gsi.gov.uk
Tel (head office): 020 7979 2000.
(helpline): 0845 015 0120. Fax: 020 7979 2111.
Address: 33 Greycoat Street, London SW1P 2QF

DENI (Department of Education Northern Ireland).
Website has a clear link to SEN information from the main page.
Web: www.deni.gov.uk
E-mail: mail@deni.gov.uk
Tel: 028 9127 9279. Fax: 028 9127 9100.
Address: Rathgael House, Balloo Road, Bangor, Northern Ireland BT19 7PR

DfES – Aimhigher.
Website offers help and advice on going to university with sections for youngsters post-GCSE, parents and those returning to education.
Web: www.aimhigher.ac.uk/dontstop/home
Tel (freephone): 0800 587 8500.
Textphone 0800 280 024.

DfES SEN site.
The first stop for information on government policy and procedures in England and Wales, featuring 'Parents' Guide to SEN', 'Guide to the SEN tribunal' etc. Since the rules are in the process of changing, it's one to keep in touch with.
Web: www.dfes.gov.uk/sen/
E-mail: info@dfes.gsi.gov.uk
Tel: 0870 000 2288 or 020 7925 5000.
Fax: 01928 794 248.
Address: Sanctuary Buildings, Great Smith Street, London SW1P 3BT

Disability Rights Commission.
Quasi-independent of government. Tells you what your rights are, and may help you enforce them.
Web: www.drc-gb.org
E-mail: enquiry@drc-gb.org.
Tel: 0845 7622 633. Textphone: 0845 7622 644.
Fax: 0845 7778 878.
Address: DCR Helpline, Freepost MID 02164, Stratford-upon-Avon CV37 9BR

Early Support.
Government programme to improve the quality, consistency and co-ordination of services for young disabled children and their families. Developed by the DfES in conjunction with the Department of Health and the voluntary sector. Programme materials are available free of charge to parents and those who work directly with young children and their families, in England.
Web: www.earlysupport.org.uk
Contact either Rozi Haq – E-mail: rozi.haq@rnid.org.uk, Tel: 020 7296 8238 – or Eileen Strevens: eileen.strevens@rnid.org.uk
Tel: 020 7296 8307.
Address: Early Support team, Royal National Institute for Deaf People, 19-23 Featherstone Street, London EC1Y 8SL

Estyn.
Office of HM Chief Inspector of Education and Training in Wales.
Web: www.estyn.gov.uk.
E-mail: enquiries@estyn.gsi.gov.uk (for general enquiries) or publications@estyn.gsi.gov.uk
Tel: 029 2044 6446. Fax: 029 2044 6448.
Address: Anchor Court, Keen Road, Cardiff CF24 5JW

Health Professions Council.
The independent UK-wide regulating body for many health professions including occupational, music, speech and language, and physiotherapy. Its aim is to protect the health and well-being of people who use the services of health professionals.
Web: www.hpc-uk.org
Tel. 020 7582 0866. Fax: 020 7840 9801.

Address: Park House, 184 Kennington Park Road, London SE11 4BU

HMIE.
HM Inspectorate of Education in Scotland.
Web: www.hmie.gov.uk
E-mail: enquiries@hmie.gov.uk
Tel: 01506 600200.

ISI (Independent Schools Inspectorate).
Fully independent of government.
Web: www.isinspect.org.uk
E-mail: info@isinspect.org.uk
Tel: 020 7600 0100. Fax: 020 7776 8849.
Address: CAP House, 9-12 Long Lane, London EC1A 9HA

Learning and Skills Council (LSC).
Web: www.lsc.gov.uk
E-mail: info@lsc.gov.uk
Tel: 0845 019 4170 or
(general enquiries) 0870 900 6800.
Fax: 024 7649 3600.
Address: Cheylesmore House, Quinton Road, Coventry CV1 2WT

Legal Services Commission.
Web: www.legalservices.gov.uk
Tel: 020 7759 0000
Address (head office): 85 Gray's Inn Road, London WC1X 8TX

Ofsted (Office for Standards in Education).
See website under 'Publications by topic' to view Ofsted's Guidelines for inspection, review, analysis and good practice etc regarding special schools, or for a complete list, 'A-Z of Ofsted publications'.
Web: www.ofsted.gov.uk
E-mail: freepublications@ofsted.gov.uk
Tel. 0700 263 7833.
Address: Alexandra House, 33 Kingsway, London WC2B 6SE

Scottish Executive: Special Educational Needs Advisory Forum.
See website under 'Publications' for information on 'Records of need'.
Web: www.scotland.gov.uk
E-mail: senforum@scotland.gov.uk
Tel: 08457 741741 or 0131 556 8400.
Fax: 0131 244 7943.
Address: Pupils Support Division (SEN), Area 3A (North), Victoria Quay, Edinburgh EH6 6QQ

Special Educational Needs & Disability Tribunal (SENDIST).
Web: www.sendist.gov.uk
E-mail: tribunalqueries@sent.gsi.gov.uk
Tel: 020 7925 5750. Fax: 020 7925 6786.
Address: 7th floor, Windsor House, 50 Victoria Street, London SW1H 0NW

Welsh Assembly.
Hair-tearingly tiresome website where you can spend hours and find nothing useful. Google 'SEN Wales' to find what's there.
Web: www.wales.gov.uk
Tel: 029 2082 5111.
Address: National Assembly for Wales, Cardiff Bay, Cardiff CF99 1NA

Groups focused on interacting with government

BILD (British Institute of Learning Disabilities).
Lobbies politicians and bureaucrats, and spreads good practice.
Web: www.bild.org.uk
Tel: 01562 723010.
Address: Green Street, Kidderminster, Worcestershire DY10 1JL

Disability Alliance.
'Breaking the link between poverty and disability'.
Web: www.disabilityalliance.org
E-mail: office.da@dial.pipex.com
Tel (voice and minicom): 020 7247 8776.
Fax: 020 7247 8765.
Address: Universal House, 88-94 Wentworth Street, London E1 7SA

National Children's Bureau: Council for Disabled Children.
Provides a national forum for the discussion and development of a wide range of policy and practice issues relating to service provision and support for disabled children and young people and those with SEN.
Web: www.ncb.org.uk/cdc
Tel: 020 7843 1900. Fax: 020 7843 6313.
Address: 8 Wakley Street, London EC1V 7QE

Inclusive education

Centre for Studies on Inclusive Education.
Works to promote inclusion and abolish special schools.
Web: inclusion.uwe.ac.uk/csie/csiehome.htm
Tel: 0117 328 4007. Fax 0117 328 4005.
Address: New Redland, Frenchay Campus, Coldharbour Lane, Bristol BS16 1QU

Inclusive Education.
Website produced by Learning and Teaching Scotland. Useful section on additional support for learning (the preferred alternative phrase to 'special educational needs' in Scotland).
Web: www.ltscotland.org.uk/inclusiveeducation

Parents for Inclusion.
Useful and serious site – describes themselves as: 'Parents helping parents so their disabled children can learn, make friends and have a voice in ordinary schools and throughout life'.
Web: www.parentsforinclusion.org
E-mail: info@parentsforinclusion.org
Tel (admin): 020 7735 7735 (freephone): 0800 652 3145.
Address: Unit 2, 70 South Lambeth Road,
London SW8 1RL

See also: inclusion.ngfl.gov.uk, a website produced and regularly updated by the DfES which gives detailed advice and information on inclusion.

And for the other side of the argument:

Gloucestershire Special Schools Protection League: formed to fight against the closure of local special schools, with some good general information there too, and links to the generally local and fragmented pro-special-schools lobby.
Web: www.gsspl.org.uk
Address (Secretary): Maura Woulfe, c/o Alderman Knight School, Ashchurch Road, Tewkesbury, Gloucestershire GL20 8JJ

Mediation

BGWS North West Regional SEN Disagreement Resolution Service

Steve Griffiths, Practice Manager

Region: Northwest Merseyside: Blackburn with Darwen; Blackpool; Bolton; Bury; Cumbria; Lancashire; Manchester; Oldham; Rochdale; Salford; Stockport; Warrington; Wigan

Web: www.bgws.org.uk
E-mail: Gayle.drs@btconnect.com
Tel: 01772 204494. Fax: 01772 204501.
Address: 15 Moor Park Avenue, Preston, Lancashire PR1 6AS

ConSENsus

Rosalind Redelsperger, Sub-Regional Co-ordinator. Admin: Diana Banks

Region: Essex, Bedfordshire, Hertfordshire, Norfolk, Suffolk

E-mail: rosalind.redelsperger@mencap.org.uk
diana.banks@mencap.org.uk
Tel: 01284 748320. Fax: 01284 723676.
Address: Mencap Regional Office, Davies House, 4 Hillside Business Park, Bury St Edmunds, Suffolk IP32 7AR

East Midlands SEN Service

Zanne Findlay, Service Manager. Admin: Teena Bates

Region: Derby City, Derbyshire, Leicester City, Leicestershire, Lincolnshire, Northampton, Northamptonshire, Nottingham City, Nottinghamshire, Rutland

Web: www.applied mediation.co.uk.
E-mail: zanne@appliedmediation.co.uk
Tel: 0800 085 3974.
Address: PO Box 45335, London SE14 5YR

FANE – Facilitating Agreement in the North East

Sue Wilson, Service Co-ordinator. Admin: Victoria Lewis

Region: North East Region: Darlington, Durham, Gateshead, Hartlepool, Middlesbrough, Newcastle, Northumberland, North Tyneside, Redcar & Cleveland, South Tyneside, Stockton, Sunderland

Web: www.fane-partnership.org.uk
E-mail: sue.wilson2@darlington.gov.uk
Tel: 01325 254548. Fax: 01325 254548.
Address: Harewood House, 14 Harewood Hill, Darlington, Co.Durham, DL3 7HY

Global Mediation

Adam Gersch, Director

Region: Bracknell Forest, Brighton & Hove, Buckinghamshire, East Sussex, Hampshire, Isle of Wight, Kent, Medway, Milton Keynes, Oxfordshire, Portsmouth, Reading, Slough, Southampton, Surrey, West Berkshire, West Sussex, Windsor & Maidenhead, Wokingham

Web: www.globalmediation.co.uk
E-mail: info@globalmediation.co.uk
Tel: 0800 064 4488. Fax: 0208 441 4101.
Address: Global Mediation Limited, 1 Oakwood Parade, London, N14 4HY

London SEN Disagreement Resolution Service

Annette Colleary, Service Manager. Admin: Kirsty Dennis

Region: London: Barking & Dagenham, Barnet, Bexley, Brent, Bromley, Camden, Corporation of London, Croydon, Enfield, Greenwich, Hackney, Hammersmith & Fulham, Haringey, Harrow, Hillingdon, Hounslow, Islington, Kensington & Chelsea, Kingston upon Thames, Lambeth, Lewisham, Merton, Newham, Redbridge, Richmond upon Thames, Southwalk, Sutton, Tower Hamlets, Waltham Forest, Wandsworth, Westminster

Web: www.londonsenmediation.org.uk
E-mail: annettec@kids-online.org.uk
kirstyd@kids-online.org.uk
Tel (freephone): 0800 389 0695. Fax: 020 7243 8512.
Address: 240 Lancaster Road, London W11 4AH

Midlands SEN Mediation

Susanna Diegel, Regional Co-ordinator. Admin: Jenny Hinks

Region: West Midlands: Birmingham, Coventry, Dudley, Herefordshire, Sandwell, Shropshire, Solihull, Staffordshire, Stoke-on-Trent, Telford & Wrekin, Walsall, Warwickshire, Wolverhampton, Worcestershire

Web: www.midlandssenmediation.com
E-mail: admin@midlandssenmediation.com
jenny@midlandssenmediation.com
Tel: 01952 275038. Fax: 01952 520092.
Address: 48 Walker Street, Wellington, Telford TF1 1BA

Peninsula Mediation Service

Jill Holloway, Co-ordinator. Admin: Sue Fowles or Lindsay Halford

Region: Cornwall, Devon, Plymouth, Torbay, Isles of Scilly

Web: www.peninsulamediation.co.uk
E-mail: devmed@postmaster.co.uk
info@peninsulamediation.co.uk
(admin): mediation@mediationdorset.freeserve.co.uk
Tel: 01363 777242. Fax: 01363 777734.
Address: The Red House, St Lawrence Green, Crediton, EX17 3LN

Yorkshire & Humberside SEN Mediation

Susanna Diegel, Regional Co-ordinator. Admin: Jenny Hinks

Region: Yorkshire & Humberside: Barnsley, Bradford, Calderdale, Doncaster, East Ridings, Kingston upon Hull, Leeds, North East Lincolnshire, North Lincolnshire, North Yorkshire, Rotherham, Sheffield, Wakefield, York

Web: www.yhsenmediation.com
E-mail: admin@midlandssenmediation.com
enquiries@yhsen-mediation.com
jenny@midlandssenmediation.com
Tel (freephone): 0800 953 0662. Fax: 01952 271648.
Address: PO Box 232, Telford TF1 1ZW

Wessex Mediation

Colin Gould and Lindsey Halford, Co-ordinators

Region: Bath and North East Somerset, Bournemouth, Bristol, Dorset, Gloucestershire, North Somerset, Somerset, Poole, South Gloucestershire, Swindon, Wiltshire

Web: www.wessexmediation.com
E-mail: info@wessexmediation.co.uk
Tel: 01823 336465. Fax: 01823 352210.
Address: Victoria House, Victoria Street, Taunton, Somerset TA1 3FA

Preparing for public examinations

AQA (Assessment and Qualifications Alliance).
Web: www.aqa.org.uk
E-mail: mailbox@aqa.org.uk
Tel (Manchester): 0161 953 1180.
Tel (Guildford): 01483 506506.
Fax (Manchester): 0161 273 7572.
Fax (Guildford): 01483 300 152.

CCEA (Northern Ireland Council for the Curriculum, Examinations and Assessment).
Web: www.ccea.org.uk

E-mail: info@ccea.org.uk
Tel: 028 9026 1200. Fax: 028 9026 1234.
Address: CCEA, 29 Clarendon Road, Clarendon Dock, Belfast BT1 3BG

Edexcel.
Web: www.edexcel.org.uk
Tel: 0870 240 9800. Fax: 020 7190 5700.
Address: Edexcel Customer Service, One90 High Holborn, London WC1V 7BH

JCQ (Joint Council for Qualifications).
The key agency, determining what allowances can be made for whom.
Web: www.jcq.org.uk
Tel: 020 7638 4125.
Fax: 020 7374 4343.
Address: Veritas House, 125 Finsbury Pavement, London EC2A 1NQ

OCR (Oxford Cambridge and RSA Examinations).
Web: www.ocr.org.uk
E-mail: helpdesk@ocr.org.uk
Tel: 01223 553311. Fax: 01223 552627.
Address: 1 Hills Road, Cambridge CB1 2EU

SQA (Scottish Qualifications Authority). National body in Scotland responsible for the development, accreditation, assessment and certification of qualifications other than degrees.
Web: www.sqa.org.uk.
E-mail: customer@sqa.org.uk
Tel (Customer Contact Centre): 0845 279 1000.
Fax: 0141 242 2244.
Address: Hanover House, 24 Douglas Street, Glasgow G2 7NQ or Ironmills Road, Dalkeith, Midlothian EH22 1LE

WJEC (Welsh Joint Education Committee).
Web: www.wjec.co.uk
Tel: 029 2026 5000.
Address: 245 Western Avenue, Cardiff CF5 2YX

Solicitors specialising in special needs cases

Children's Legal Centre.
A unique, independent national charity concerned with law and policy affecting children and young people, staffed by lawyers and professionals with experience in child law. The centre is funded by grants from central government and by charitable trusts.
Web: www.childrenslegalcentre.com
E-mail: clc@essex.ac.uk
Tel: 01206 872466.
Fax: 01206 874026.
Address: University of Essex, Wivenhoe Park, Colchester, Essex CO4 3SQ

Education Law Advice Line:
Tel: 0845 456 6811

Levenes.
Specialises, among other things, in education and disability law. The department is headed by David Ruebain, recognised as one of the top education and community care lawyers.
Web: www.levenes.co.uk.
E-mail: info@levenes.co.uk.
Tel: 020 8881 7777. Fax: 020 8889 6395.
Address: Ashley House, 235-239 High Road, Wood Green, London N22 8HF

Jack Rabinowicz of Teacher Sterne Selby.
Web: www.tsslaw.co.uk
E-mail: j.rabinowicz@tsslaw.com
Tel: 020 7242 3191. Fax: 020 7242 1156.
Address: 37-41 Bedford Row, London, WC1R 4JH

Robert Love of A E Smith & Sons.
E-mail: AE.Smith.Stroud@cwcom.net
Tel: 01453 757444. Fax:01453 757586.
Address: Frome House, London Road, Stroud, Gloucestershire GL5 2AF

SEN Legal.
A small firm of solicitors specialising in SEN law. We have no feedback as yet from people who have used them.
Web: www.senlegal.co.uk
E-mail: admin@senlegal.co.uk
Tel: 01284 723952. Fax: 01284 702008.
Address: 9 Looms Lane, Bury St Edmunds, Suffolk IP33 1HE

Woodroffes.
General educational problems. Peter Woodroffe specialises, among other things, in advising parents about legal matters to do with fee-paying schools.
Web: www.woodroffes.org.uk
E-mail: rbrown_woodroffes@compuserve.com
Tel: 020 7730 0001. Fax: 020 7730 7900.
Address: Woodroffes, 36 Ebury Street, London SW1W 0LU

The educational psychologist

British Psychological Society. 34,000 psychologists are members but this is a disappointingly inward-looking site with little of use to parents – except for the 'Find a psychologist' service that lists inter alia a few hundred members who offer educational psychology services.
Web: www.bps.org.uk
E-mail: enquiry@bps.org.uk
Tel: 0116 254 9568. Fax: 0116 247 0787.
Address: St Andrews House, 48 Princess Road East, Leicester LE1 7DR

Educational-Psychologist.co.uk.
'Find a psychologist' section, listing nine educational psychologists (ie very few); you can e-mail or telephone for advice. 'SEN information' section with advice on how to spot various conditions and what to do in various situations.
Web: www.educational-psychologist.co.uk
E-mail: tim@edpsych.screaming.net
edpsych@hotmail.com

Every Child Matters.
A site giving details of the educational psychology service. It includes a brief description of what an educational psychologist does, plus contact details for various services.
Web: www.everychildmatters.gov.uk/ete/psychology

National Association of School Psychologists.
A rather inward-looking US site, with not much for parents except a long and rather undigested links list.
Web: www.nasponline.org
Tel: 00 1 301 657 0270. Fax: 00 1 301 657 0275.
Address: 4340 East West Highway, Suite 402, Bethesda, MD 20814, USA

School Psychology Resources Online (US site).
Lots of links covering things such as ADD, Tourette's, dyslexia, autism, anxiety disorders, eating disorders, gifted children.
Web: www.schoolpsychology.net
Address: Office of Psychological Services, Baltimore County Public Schools, 9600 Pulaski Park Drive, Suite 118, Baltimore, MD 21220, USA

So, frankly, not much of use: the best source of advice is generally the charities related to the SEN that concerns you.

Occupational therapists, physiotherapists and music therapists

Chartered Society of Physiotherapists.
Web: www.csp.org.uk
Tel 020 7306 6666.
Address: 14 Bedford Row, London WC1R 4ED

Association of Professional Music Therapists (APMT).
The professional body for music therapists in the UK. The APMT can help you find a music therapist near to you.
Web: www.apmt.org
E-mail: APMToffice@aol.com
Tel/Fax: 020 8440 4153.
Address: 61 Church Hill Road, East Barnet, Hertfordshire EN4 8SY

British Society for Music Therapy (BSMT).
A charity promoting the use and development of music therapy. It is a source of information about music therapy.
Web: www.bsmt.org
E-mail: info@bsmt.org
Tel: 020 8441 6226.
Address: 61 Church Hill Road, East Barnet, Hertfordshire, EN4 8SY

Health Professions Council.
The independent UK-wide regulating body for many health professions including occupational, music, speech and language, and physiotherapy. Its aim is to protect the health and well-being of people who use the services of health professionals. Website includes an online register of qualified practitioners.
Web: www.hpc-uk.org
Tel. 020 7582 0866. Fax: 020 7840 9801.
Address: Park House, 184 Kennington Park Road, London SE11 4BU

Nordoff-Robbins Music Therapy Centre.
Teaching centre and clinic which provides music therapy for children and adults and a postgraduate training course.
Web: www.nordoff-robbins.org.uk
Tel: 020 7267 4496. F ax: 020 7267 4369.
Address: 2 Lissenden Gardens, London NW5 1PP

Occupational Therapists in Independent Practice (OTIP).
A specialist section of the College of Occupational Therapists. The online Directory lists members of OTIP providing a wide range of services throughout the country.

Web: www.otip.co.uk
Tel. 0800 389 4873

OT Services.
An independent occupational therapy website offering help and advice with dyspraxia assessments, stress management, medico-legal reports, disability advice, and design in the home, garden and workplace.
Web: www.otservices.co.uk
E-mail: info@otservices.co.uk
Tel/Fax: 01795 531998. Mobile: 07903 559888.
Address: PO Box 198, Faversham, Kent ME13 7YQ

Specific conditions

Attention deficit (hyperactivity) disorder (ADD/ADHD)

ADD/ADHD Ezine. Put together by parents who have been through it all; lots of links and advice, mailing list.
Web: www.adhdezine.com.
E-mail: info@adhdezine.com

ADD/ADHD Family Support Group.
Tel: 01380 726710 (Barbara and Brian Tuffill).
Address: Mrs Gillian Mead (President), 1a The High Street, Dilton Marsh, Nr Westbury, Wiltshire BA13 4DL

ADD/ADHD Information and Online Support Group.
In-depth articles on many topics, including definition and diagnosis, educational matters (including statementing with regard to ADD/ADHD children), top tips etc. Plus extensive lists of related web links and local support groups all listed by country.
Web: www.adders.org
E-mail: support@adders.org
Tel: 0870 950 3693 or 07861 134181.
Fax: 07050 666 476.
Address: Thanet ADDers ADD/ADHD Support Group, 45 Vincent Close, Broadstairs, Kent CT10 2ND

ADD diagnosis: an NHS referral: Dr Brian Toone, Department of Psychological Medicine, Kings College Hospital.
This department diagnoses ADD, follows up, and is researching into the disorder. One area of research is the link between ADD and dyslexia.
Tel: 020 7346 3226, ext. 2586
Address: Denmark Hill, London SE5 9RS.

ADDISS (National Attention Deficit Disorder Information and Support Service).
Web: www.addiss.co.uk
E-mail: info@addiss.co.uk
Tel: 020 8906 9068
Fax: 020 8959 0727.
Address: 10 Station Road, Mill Hill, London NW7 2JU

CHADD.
A high-quality US charity.
Web: www.chadd.org
Tel: 00 1 301 306 7070.
Fax: 00 1 301 306 7090.
Address: CHADD National Office, 8181 Professional Place - Suite 150, Landover, MD 20785, USA

Grey Olltwit's Software.
Free software website.
Web: www.adders.org/freeware

Asperger's syndrome, autism, pervasive developmental disorder, semantic pragmatic disorder

Allergy Induced Autism.
A charity devoted to the underlying causes and effects of autism.
Web: www.autismmedical.com

Asperger's Disorder Home Page.
Worth seeing. Features links to international websites and to other online definitions of Asperger's.
Web: www.aspergers.com

Autism Independent UK (formerly the Society for the Autistically Handicapped).
Full of Flash and other web wizardry making it painful to the eyes, but lots of good links.
Web: www.autismuk.com
E-mail: autism@rmplc.co.uk
Tel: 01536 523274. Fax: 01536 523274.
Address: 199-205 Blandford Ave, Kettering, Northamptonshire NN16 9AT

Center for the Study of Autism.
Web: www.autism.org
Address: Center for the Study of Autism, PO Box 4538, Salem, OR 97302, USA

National Autistic Society.
A clear and helpful website with good explanations of

what Asperger's and autism are, and how they affect children. Expansive links section, to other websites/ online resources and how to contact local NAS branches and other support groups nationwide.
Web: www.nas.org.uk
E-mail: nas@nas.org.uk
Tel: 020 7833 2299. Fax: 020 7833 9666.
Helpline (10am-4pm Mon-Fri): 0845 070 4004 or 0845 070 4003 (minicom).
Address (head office): 393 City Road, London EC1V 1NG

Semantic Pragmatic Disorder Webpage.
The most concentrated source that we have found for links to articles and sites on the subject.
Web: www.geocities.com/Heartland/Trail/5136

See also:

Afasic.
A parent-led organisation founded to help children with speech and language problems, and their families; also covers autistic spectrum matters.
Web: www.afasic.org.uk
E-mail: info@afasic.org.uk
Tel (admin): 020 7490 9410. Fax: 020 7251 2834.
Address: 2nd floor, 50-52 Great Sutton Street, London EC1V 0DJ

Central auditory processing disorder (CAPD)

APDUK.
A new site for those affected by CAPD.
Web: www.apduk.org
Tel (1pm-6pm): 01656 766651
(6pm-10pm): 01442 214555.
Address: Mark Mitchell, Hon Secretary APDUK, c/o Dacorum CVS, 48 High Street, Hemel Hempstead, Hertfordshire HP1 3AF

Dolfrog.
The site's layout and design is an example of how visual spatial learners or (C)APDs think and work, in comparison to non-APDs (who may find it a bit disorientating).
Web: www.dolfrog.com
The same author has a site on 'Invisible disabilities in the UK: www.geocities.com/dolfrog

Cerebral palsy, spina bifida and hydrocephalus

Association for Spina Bifida and Hydrocephalus.
A reasonable amount of information.
Web: www.asbah.org
E-mail: info@asbah.org
Tel: 01733 555988. Fax: 01733 555985.
Address: 42 Park Road, Peterborough PE1 2UQ

Capability Scotland.
The sister organisation of Scope, also has a good site.
Web: www.capability-scotland.org.uk
E-mail: ascs@capability-scotland.org.uk
Tel: 0131 313 5510. Fax: 0131 346 1681.
Textphone: 0131 346 2529.
Address: ASCS – Advice Service Capability Scotland, 11 Ellersly Road, Edinburgh EH12 6HY

Scope.
A very good website, a great deal of information on everything related to cerebral palsy and a comprehensive links section. Local support services are listed under the 'Services' heading.
Web: www.scope.org.uk
E-mail: cphelpline@scope.org.uk
Tel: 020 7619 7100. Freephone helpline (9am-9pm Mon-Fri, 2pm-6pm Sat-Sun): 0808 800 3333.
Address: 6 Market Road, London N7 9PW

Cystic fibrosis

Cystic Fibrosis Trust.
Web: www.cftrust.org.uk
E-mail: enquiries@cftrust.org.uk
Tel: 020 8464 7211. Fax: 020 8313 0472.
Address: 11 London Road, Bromley, Kent BR1 1BY

Deafness, mild hearing loss, conductive deafness, sensori-neural deafness, multi-sensory impairment (MSI)

British Deaf Association.
Exists to ensure that deaf people using sign language have the same rights and entitlement as any other citizens.
Web: www.britishdeafassociation.org.uk
E-mail: tonyp@signcommunity.org.uk
Tel: 020 7588 3520. Textphone: 020 7588 3529.
Fax: 020 7588 3527. Videophone IP: 81.138.165.105

Address: BDA London, 69 Wilson Street, London EC2A 2BB

National Deaf Children's Society.
Provides lists of deaf-friendly schools and detailed advice on what to look for.
Web: www.ndcs.org.uk
E-mail: ndcs@ndcs.org.uk
Tel: 0207 490 8656. Fax: 020 7251 5020.
Address: 15 Dufferin Street, London EC1Y 8UR

RNID (Royal National Institute for Deaf People).
Information on education is disappointingly sparse and hard to find.
Web: www.rnid.org.uk
E-mail: information@rnid.org.uk
Tel: 020 7296 8000. Textphone: 020 7296 8001.
Fax: 020 7296 8199.
Address: 23 Featherstone Street, London EC1Y 8SL

Scottish Sensory Centre.
Promotes and supports new developments in education for children and young people with sensory impairments.
Web: www.ssc.mhie.ac.uk
Tel: 0131 651 6501. Minicom: 0131 651 6067.
Address: Moray House Institute of Education, University of Edinburgh, Holyrood Road, Edinburgh EH8 8AQ

Sense: The National Deafblind and Rubella Association.
Services and support for deafblind children and adults.
Web: www.sense.org.uk
E-mail: info@sense.org.uk
Tel: 020 7272 7774. Fax: 020 7272 6012.
Textphone: 020 7272 9648.
Address: 11-13 Clifton Terrace, Finsbury Park, London N4 3SR

Sense Scotland.
Services for deafblind people, including a counselling service for young people with Usher's syndrome; a holiday scheme; further education; and residential care.
Web: www.sensescotland.org.uk
Tel: 0141 564 2444. Minicom: 0141 564 2442.
Address: 45 Finnieston Street, 5th floor, Clydeway Centre, Finnieston, Glasgow G3 8JU

Down's syndrome

Down's Syndrome Association (DSA).
Has a number of guides for parents, covering a range of medical and educational issues. Has released its support pack online as a free PDF download.
Web: www.dsa-uk.com
E-mail: info@downs-syndrome.org.uk
Tel: 0845 230 0372. Fax: 0845 230 0373.
Address: Langdon Down Centre, 2a Langdon Park, Teddington TW11 9PS

Down's Syndrome Educational Trust (DSET).
Offers an advisory and consultancy service – website not that useful in itself unless you want to subscribe for access to the Trust's online library and archive.
Web: www.downsed.org
E-mail: enquiries@downsed.org
Tel: 023 9285 5330. Fax: 023 9285 5320.
Address: The Sarah Duffen Centre, Belmont Street, Southsea, Hampshire PO5 1NA

Down's Syndrome Information Network.
Run by the DSET.
Web: www.downsed.org
E-mail: enquiries@downsed.org
Tel: 023 9285 5330. Fax: 023 9285 5320.
Address: The Sarah Duffen Centre, Belmont Street, Southsea, Hampshire PO5 1NA

Down's Syndrome Scotland.
The Scottish cousin of the DSA.
Web: www.dsscotland.org.uk
E-mail: info@dsscotland.org.uk
Tel: 0131 313 4225. Fax: 0131 313 4285.
Address: 158/160 Balgreen Road, Edinburgh EH11 3AU

Mencap.
A campaigning charity covering Down's and other brain-damage disorders.
Web: www.mencap.org.uk
E-mail: information@mencap.org.uk
Tel: 020 7454 0454. Fax: 020 7696 5540.
Address: 123 Golden Lane, London EC1Y 0RT

Mind.
The leading mental health charity in England and Wales.
Web: www.mind.org.uk
E-mail: contact@mind.org.uk
Tel: 020 8519 2122. Information helpline: 0845 766 0163.
Fax: 020 8522 1725.
Address: 15-19 Broadway, London E15 4BQ

National Down Syndrome Society (USA).
Produces a Down's syndrome education support pack for schools.

Web: www.ndss.org
E-mail: info@ndss.org
Tel (9am-5pm East Coast USA time): 00 1 212 460 9330.
Freephone: 00 1 800 221 4602. Fax: 00 1 212 979 2873.
Address: National Down Syndrome Society, 666 Broadway, New York, NY 10012, USA

Dyslexia, dyscalculia, dysgraphia

British Association for Counselling and Psychotherapy (BACP).
Web: www.bacp.co.uk
E-mail: bacp@bacp.co.uk
Tel: 0870 443 5252.
Address: BACP House, 35-37 Albert Street, Rugby, Warwickshire CV21 2SG

British Dyslexia Association (BDA).
A helpful and well put-together site; the BDA has associations for assessing and teaching dotted around the country. Good links.
Web: www.bda-dyslexia.org.uk
Tel: 0118 935 1927. Fax: 0118 935 1927.
Address: 98 London Road, Reading RG1 5AU

CReSTeD (Council for the Registration of Schools Teaching Dyslexic Pupils).
Produces a register of schools that have been through a registration procedure, including a visit by a CReSTeD selected consultant. CReSTeD does not inspect a school for aspects not connected to dyslexia, eg many of those covered in this Guide.
Web: www.crested.org.uk
E-mail: crested@crested.org.uk
Tel/Fax: 01242 604852.
Address: Greygarth, Littleworth, Winchcombe, Cheltenham, Gloucestershire GL54 5BT

Dyslexia A2Z.
A US site with wide coverage.
Web: www.dyslexiaa2z.com
E-mail: info@swindondyslexiacentre.co.uk – and there's a website there too: www.swindondyslexiacentre.co.uk, which covers dysgraphia (not often recognised in the UK).

Dyslexia Institute.
Claims to be the only national dyslexia teaching organisation in the world. Runs centres around the UK. Information includes articles about teaching children with dyslexia.
Web: www.dyslexia-inst.org.uk
E-mail: info@dyslexia.org.uk
Tel: 01784 463851. Fax: 01784 222333.
Address: Head Offce and National Training and Resource Centre, Park House, Wick Road, Egham, Surrey TW20 0HH

Dyslexia Scotland.
Launched late 2004. President Sir Jackie Stewart. Site still under construction when we last looked. Scottish Executive pledged £100,000 for the charity to work with schools, to develop best practice on supporting dyslexic children.
Web: www.dyslexiascotland.org.uk
E-mail: info@dyslexiascotland.org.uk
Tel (general office): 01786 446650.
Helpline (lo-call rate): 08448 008484.
Fax: 01786 471235.
Address: Stirling Business Centre, Wellgreen, Stirling FK8 2DZ

Dyslexia Teaching Centre.
Web: www.dyslexia-teaching-centre.org.uk
E-mail: dyslexiateacher@tiscali.org.uk
Tel: 020 7361 4790. Address: 23 Kensington Square, London W8 5HN

DyslexiaWorks.
Web: www.dyslexiaworks.co.uk
E-mail info@dysxlexiaworks.co.uk
Tel: 01491 636245.
Address: 3 Manor Courtyard, Hughenden Avenue, High Wycombe, Buckinghamshire HP13 5RE

Helen Arkell Dyslexia Centre (of which we have had excellent reports).
Web: www.arkellcentre.org.uk
E-mail: enquiries@arkellcentre.org.uk
Tel: 01252 792400. Fax: 01252 795669.
Address: Frensham, Farnham, Surrey GU10 3BW

Hornsby International Dyslexia Centre.
Web: www.hornsby.co.uk
E-mail: info@dyslexia-inst.org.uk
Tel: 01784 222300. Fax: 01784 222333.
Address: Dyslexia Institute, Park House, Wick Road, Egham, Surrey TW20 0HH

LDOnline.
An American site with lots of information on what's what in learning disorders; covers dysgraphia.

Web: www.ldonline.org
E-mail: LDOnline@weta.com

PATOSS (Professional Association of Teachers of Students with Specific Learning Difficulties).
Information on specific learning difficulties. Lists of specialists in assessment and tutoring.
Web: www.patoss-dyslexia.org
E-mail: patoss@evesham.ac.uk
Tel: 01386 712650. Fax: 01386 712716.
Address: PO Box 10, Evesham, Worcestershire WR11 1ZW

Dyspraxia, developmental verbal dyspraxia

Dyscovery Centre.
Founded by Dr Amanda Kirby, a Welsh GP who left practice to set it up when her second son was diagnosed with dyspraxia. It offers a full range of assessment and treatment for kids and adults who may have a difficulty on the Autism spectrum. Amanda Kirby speaks at conferences on SEN all over the world and has written a number of books.
Web: www.dyscovery.co.uk
E-mail: dyscovery.centre@btinternet.com
Tel: 029 2062 8222. Fax: 029 2062 8333.
Address: 4a Church Road, Whitchurch, Cardiff F14 2DZ

Dyspraxia Foundation.
Explains the condition and its symptoms well; has a network of local groups. Includes a section about dyspraxia in secondary schools.
Web: www.dyspraxiafoundation.org.uk
E-mail: dyspraxia@dyspraxiafoundation.org.uk
Tel: (10am-1pm Mon-Fri.) 01462 454986.
Fax: 01462 455052.
Address: 8 West Alley, Hitchin, Hertfordshire SG5 1EG

Iansyst.
Provides many of the software packages useful to kids with SEN – such as coloured touch-typing courses for dyspraxics. Can supply computers VAT-free for disabled customers.
Web: www.iansyst.co.uk
Tel: 01223 420101.
Address: iansyst limited, Fen House, Fen Road, Chesterton, Cambridge CB4 1UN

Emotional and behavioural difficulties (EBD), oppositional defiant disorder (ODD), conduct disorders, obsessive compulsive disorder (OCD)

A thinly supported area of SEN.

Behaviour Change Consultancy.
A commercial concern helping parents and schools to deal with these problems.
Web: www.behaviourchange.com
E-mail: WarwickDyer@behaviourchange.com
Tel (9.30am-5.30pm Mon-Fri): 0845 430 5340 (local rate) or 020 8653 9768.
Address: Behaviour Change Consultancy, 24 Rochdale, 66 Harold Road, London SE19 3TF

OCD Action.
Formerly Obsessive Action: the national organisation for obsessive compulsive disorder (OCD), body dysmorphic disorder (BDD), compulsive skin picking (CSP) and trichotillomania – a very helpful site.
Web: www.ocdaction.org.uk
E-mail: info@ocdaction.org.uk
Help and information line: 0845 390 OCDA (6232).
Office: 0870 360 OCDA (6232). Fax: 020 7288 0828.
Address: 22-24 Highbury Grove, Suite 107, London N5 2EA

SEBDA (Social, Emotional and Behavioural Difficulties Association).
Formerly AWCEBD, Association of Workers with Children with Emotional and Behavioural Difficulties.
Web: www.sebda.org
E-mail: tcole@sebda.org
Tel (Ted Cole): 01768 210510. Address: SEBDA, Church House, 1 St Andrew's View, Penrith, Cumbria, CA11 7YF

Epilepsy

British Epilepsy Association.
Plenty of information including a useful 'Parents Guide' in the 'Epilepsy Info' section. For contacts UK and worldwide, including support organisations/charities, counselling and advice services, education etc, see 'Epilepsy Organisations' under 'BEA Services'. Web: www.epilepsy.org.uk.
E-mail: epilepsy@epilepsy.org.uk.
Tel: 0113 210 8800. Fax: 0113 391 0300.
Address: New Anstey House, Gate Way Drive, Yeadon, Leeds LS19 7XY

Epilepsy Action.
National charity founded in 1950, which offers a nationwide network of branches, publishes a quarterly newsletter and has a wide range of information available.
Web: www.epilepsy.org.uk
E-mail: helpline@epilepsy.org.uk
Tel (admin/membership): 0113 210 8800.
Helpline (9am-4.30pm Mon-Thurs, 9am-4pm Fri): 0808 800 5050.
Fax (admin/membership): 0113 242 8804.
Helpline: 0808 800 5555.
Address: New Anstey House, Gate Way Drive, Yeadon, Leeds LS19 7XY

National Society for Epilepsy (NSE).
Charity established in 1892, which provides medical and other services for adults with epilepsy. Information services include leaflets, books and videos, and a helpline that gives information and listening support.
Web: www.epilepsynse.org.uk
Tel: 01494 601400.
Helpline (10am-4pm Mon-Fri): 01494 601300.
Fax: 01494 871927.
Address: Chesham Lane, Chalfont St Peter, Buckinghamshire SL9 0RJ

Fragile X

Fragile X Society.
The Society offers support, information and advice to affected families and professionals.
Web: www.fragilex.org.uk
E-mail: info@fragilex.org.uk
Tel: 01371 875100.
Address: Rood End House, 6 Stortford Road, Great Dunmow, Essex CM6 1DA

Physical disabilities

Disability Now.
An excellent starting point for disability links generally.
Web: www.disabilitynow.org.uk
E-mail: editor@disabilitynow.org.uk
Tel: 020 7619 7323. Fax: 020 7619 7331.
Address: 6 Market Road, London N7 9PW

John Grooms.
While concentrating on adult disability, this has a schools microsite 'JustLikeUs' (www.justlikeus.org.uk) – but it's mainly aimed at their new teaching pack.
Web: www.johngrooms.org.uk
Tel: 020 7452 2000. Fax: 020 7452 2001.
Address: 50 Scrutton Street, London EC2A 4XQ

RADAR
(Royal Association for Disability and Rehabilita-tion).
The principal organisation for (and of) the physically disabled.
Web: www.radar.org.uk
E-mail: radar@radar.org.uk
Tel: 0207 250 3222. Fax: 0207 250 0212.
Minicom: 0207 250 4119.
Address: 12 City Forum, 250 City Road, London EC1V 8AF

Prader-Willi/Angelman syndrome

ASSERT.
A UK-based support group run by volunteers who have direct contact with people with Angelman syndrome.
Web: www.angelmanuk.org
Address: PO Box 13694, Musselburgh, East Lothian EH21 6XZ

Prader-Willi Syndrome Association UK (PWSA).
Web: www.pwsa.co.uk
E-mail: admin@pwsa-uk.demon.co.uk
Tel (9.30am-3.30pm Mon-Fri): 01332 365676 (office hours: 9.30am-3.30pm Mon-Fri). Answerphone at other times. Fax: 01332 360401.
Address: PWSA (UK), 125a London Road, Derby DE1 2QQ

See also:

Unique – The Rare Chromosome Disorder Support Group.
Tel: 01883 330766.
Address: PO Box 2189, Caterham, Surrey CR3 5GN

ACE Centre under 'Speech and language difficulties' below.

Rett syndrome

Rett Syndrome Association UK.
A national charity offering information, advice, practical help, friendship and support to people with Rett syndrome, their families and carers.
Web: www.rettsyndrome.org.uk
E-mail: info@rettsyndrome.org.uk
Tel (national): 0870 770 3266 (local): 020 8361 5161.
Fax (national): 0870 770 3265 (local): 020 8368 6123.
Address: 113 Friern Barnet Road, London N11 3EU

Speech and language difficulties

ACE Centre (Aiding Communication in Education).
An organisation which provides a variety of services including in-depth individual assessments, information, and specialist training for parents and professionals on the use of technology for young people with physical and communication difficulties.
Web: www.ace-centre.org.uk
E-mail: info@ace-centre.org.uk
Tel (helpline): 01865 759800. Fax: 01865 759810.
Address: 92 Windmill Road, Headington, Oxford OX3 7DR

Afasic.
A parent-led organisation founded to help children with speech and language problems, and their families.
Web: www.afasic.org.uk
E-mail: info@afasic.org.uk
Tel (admin): 020 7490 9410. Fax: 020 7251 2834.
Address: 2nd floor, 50-52 Great Sutton Street, London EC1V 0DJ

ASLTIP (Association of Speech and Language Therapists in Independent Practice).
All ASLTIP therapists are Registered Members of RCSLT and registered with the Health Professions Council.
Web: www.helpwithtalking.com
E-mail: asltip@awdry.demon.co.uk
Tel (answerphone): 0870 241 3357.
Fax: 01494 488590.
Address: WSS Coleheath Bottom, Speen, Princes Risborough, Buckinghamshire HP27 0SZ

I CAN (Invalid Children's Aid Nationwide).
National charity for children with speech and language impairments.
Web: www.ican.org.uk
Tel: 0845 225 4071.
Fax: 0845 225 4072.
Address: 4 Dyers Building, London EC1N 2QP

Makaton (Vocabulary Development Project).
The most commonly used techniques for overcoming severe communication difficulties. Combines signs, symbols and speech.
Web: www.makaton.org
E-mail: mvdp@makaton.org
Tel: 01276 61390. Fax: 01276 681368.
Address: 31 Firwood Drive,Camberley, Surrey GU15 3QD

Royal College of Speech and Language Therapists (RCSLT).
Web: www.rcslt.org
E-mail: postmaster@rcslt.org
Tel: 020 7378 1200.
Fax: 020 7403 7254.
Address: 2 White Hart Yard, London SE1 1NX

Talking Point.
Website for information about speech, language and communication difficulties in children. Talking Point is run by I CAN, working with the RCSLT and Afasic.
Web: www.talkingpoint.org.uk

Tourette's syndrome and other tic disorders

Tourette Syndrome (UK) Association.
Charity that provides support, promotes medical research, educates, informs and campaigns on behalf of all those affected by Tourette's.
Web: www.tsa.org.uk
E-mail: enquiries@tsa.org.uk.
Tel: 01892 669151.
Helpline: 0845 458 1252. Admin: 01383 629600.
Address: Tourette Syndrome (UK) Association, PO Box 26149, Dunfermline KY12 9YU

Tourette Scotland.
Provides advice and support for carers and sufferers of Tourette's.
Web: www.tourettescotland.org
E-mail: info@tourettescotland.org
Tel/Fax: 01738 622008.
Address: Tourette Scotland, Support Base, 17B Hospital Street, Perth PH2 8HN

Visual impairment/blindness

Action for Blind People.
'Our mission is to inspire change and create opportunities to enable blind and partially sighted people to have equal voice and equal choice. Every year we provide direct support for more than 20,000 people.'
Web: www.afbp.org
E-mail: info@actionforblindpeople.org.uk
Tel: 020 7635 4800.
Helpline (freephone): 0800 915 4666.
Fax: 020 7635 4900.
Address: 14-16 Verney Road, London SE16 3DZ

LOOK.
Help and support for parents and their visually impaired children.
Web: www.look-uk.org
E-mail: info@look-uk.org
Tel: 0121 428 5038.
Address: Queen Alexandra College, 49 Oak Road, Birmingham B17 9TG

National Blind Children's Society (NBCS).
Web: www.nbcs.org.uk
E-mail: enquiries@nbcs.org.uk
Tel: 01278 764764.
Address: Bradbury House, Market Street, Highbridge, Somerset TA9 3BW

Partially Sighted Society.
Web: www.partsight.org.uk
E-mail: doncaster@partsight.org.uk
Tel/Fax: 020 7371 0289.
Address: The Sight Centre, 9 Plato Place, 72/74 St Dionis Road, London SW6 4TU

RNIB (Royal National Institute for the Blind).
A good chunk on education under 'Services'.
Web: www.rnib.org.uk
E-mail: helpline@rnib.org.uk
Tel (helpline): 0845 766 9999. Fax: 020 7388 2034.
Address: 105 Judd Street, London WC1H 9NE

Vision Aid.
Practical help and advice to families. Some information on Vision Aid at www.eyeconditions.org.uk/vision.htm
E-mail: visionaid@charity.vfree.com
Tel: 01204 64265. Address: 106 Junction Road, Deane, Bolton BL3 4NE

See also Sense and Sense Scotland under 'Deafness ... multi-sensory impairment (MSI)' above.

Williams syndrome

Williams Syndrome Foundation UK.
Plenty of information, diagnosis, treatment etc, including a profile of SEN. Check the 'Guidelines' section for advice for parents, teachers, families and professionals who come into contact with Williams syndrome sufferers.
Web: www.williams-syndrome.org.uk
E-mail: John.nelson-wsfoundation@btinternet.com
Tel: 01732 365152. Fax: 01732 360178.
Address: 161 High Street, Tonbridge, Kent TN9 1BX

Gifted and talented pupils

Children classed as gifted or talented are generally considered to have additional support needs rather than special educational needs, although the jury remains out in some quarters. What is evident is that having special needs does not preclude a child from being classified as gifted, talented or able. A child may well appear on both a school's SEN and their 'gifted and talented' registers.

DfES Gifted and Talented.
Aimed at schools rather than parents and children but useful for keeping pace with government initiatives.
Web: www.standards.dfes.gov.uk/giftedandtalented
E-mail: info@dfes.gsi.gov.uk

Mensa.
For bright sparks with high IQs also has a junior section and Mensa Foundation for Gifted Children.
Web: www.mensa.org.uk
E-mail: enquiries@mensa.org.uk
Tel: 01902 772771. Fax: 01902 392500.
Address: British Mensa Limited, St John's House, St John's Square, Wolverhampton WV2 4AH

National Association for Gifted Children.
Web: www.nagcbritain.org.uk
E-mail: amazingchildren@nagcbritain.org.uk
Tel: 0870 770 3217. Fax: 0870 770 3219.
Address: Suite 14, Challenge House, Sherwood Drive, Bletchley, Milton Keynes MK3 6DP

National Academy for Gifted and Talented Youth.
Offers summer schools, masterclasses etc. to talented youngsters.
Web: www.nagty.ac.uk
E-mail: gifted@warwick.ac.uk
Tel: 024 7657 4213.
Address: University of Warwick, Coventry CV4 7AL

National Association of Able Children in Education (NACE).
UK organisation providing training and a quarterly journal and other publications for education professionals working with able pupils.
Web: www.nace.co.uk
E-mail: info@nace.co.uk
Tel: 01865 861879. Fax: 01865 861880.

Address: NACE National Office, PO Box 242, Arnolds Way, Oxford OX2 9FR

World Class Tests.
An international initiative devised by the DfES to identify and assess gifted and talented students around the world. Contains information for parents and schools as well as sample questions for talented youngsters to try. Those who succeed in tests can use test grade to apply for entrance to the National Academy for Gifted and Talented Youth's talent search.
Web: www.worldclassarena.org
E-mail: information@nfer-nelson.co.uk
Tel (helpline): 0845 602 1937

Further reading

An awful lot of reading matter out there, ranging from Mark Haddon's *The Curious Incident of the Dog in the Night-time*, an insightful but fictional piece about a child with Asperger's syndrome (or even better *The Curious Incident of Tony Blair and the WMD*, an amusing parody of the former), to the most turgid of textbooks. Much will depend on your bent and need but we include a selection of texts recommended (and in some cases written) by contributors to this guide.

General

Arrangements for Placements at Specialist Colleges: learners with learning difficulties and/or disabilities for 2003/04 (Learning and Skills Council, Circular 02/14)

Bookmark Books and Disability Issues.
Aims to provide support, information and signposts for parents of children with any condition which affects their reading. The site also offers book reviews and represents a useful forum for anyone interested in books and disability issues.
Web: www.bookmark.org.uk
E-mail: info@booktrust.org.uk
Tel 020 8516 2977. Fax: 020 8516 2978.
Address: 45 East Hill, London SW18 2QZ

Jessica Kingsley Publishers.
Lots of good books on SEN.
Web: www.jkp.com
E-mail: post@jkp.com
Tel: 020 7833 2307. Fax: 020 7837 2917.
Address: 116 Pentonville Road, London N1 9JB

Surviving the Special Educational Needs System: How to be a 'Velvet Bulldozer', Sandy Row (Jessica Kingsley Publishers, 2004)

Chapter 2: Conditions

Autistic spectrum disorder (ASD)

How to Understand Autism the Easy Way, Alexander Durig (Jessica Kingsley Publishers, 2004)

Parenting a Child with Asperger Syndrome: 200 Tips and Strategies, Brenda Boyd (Jessica Kingsley Publishers, 2003) Lots of helpful advice and strategies, all clearly presented. Invaluable for parents, useful for teachers

Understanding Autistic Spectrum Disorders: Frequently Asked Questions, Diane Yapko (Jessica Kingsley Publishers, 2003). A useful (American) reference to dip into

ADD/ADHD

Learning to Slow Down and Pay Attention: A Book for Kids about ADHD, Kathleen G. Nadeau and Ellen B. Dixon. Illustrated by Charles Beyl (Magination Press, 2004). Explains ADHD in child-friendly language. Offers lots of helpful advice to the child (and parents)

Only a Mother Could Love Him: How I Lived With and Triumphed Over ADHD, Ben Polis (Hodder & Stoughton, 2005). An invaluable, inspirational and moving insight into the life of a child with ADHD

Obsessive compulsive disorder (OCD)

Touch and Go Joe: An Adolescent's Experience of OCD, Joe Wells (Jessica Kingsley, 2006). Brand new, so we haven't read it yet, but we're told it's an upbeat, honest, amusing yet realistic look at the effect of OCD on adolescent life

Tourette's syndrome

Tictionary: A Useful Reference Guide to the World of Tourette Syndrome, Asperger's Syndrome, ADHD and Obsessive Compulsive Disorder for Parents and Professionals, Becky Ottinger (Karnac Books, 2003)

Dyslexia/Dyscalculia

See also Dyspraxia

For teachers (and parents)

Day-to-Day Dyslexia in the Classroom, Joy Pollock (RoutledgeFalmer, 2nd edn, 2004)

Dyslexia: Successful Inclusion in the Secondary School, Lindsay Peer and Gavin Reid (eds) (David Fulton Publishers, 2001)

For parents (and teachers)

How Dyslexics Learn: Grasping the Nettle, Kate Saunders and Annie White. Illustrated by Jonathan Pitts (PATOSS, 2002)

How to Detect and Manage Dyslexia: A Reference and Resource Manual, Philomena Ott (Heinemann, 1997)

For potential readers

Barrington Stoke. Publishes a range of books written by leading authors, edited and presented by the publishers to make them accessible to struggling readers. This includes printing the stories on cream paper.
Web: www.barringtonstoke.co.uk
E-mail: info@barringtonstoke.co.uk
Tel: 0131 557 2020. Fax: 0131 557 6060.
Address: Sandeman House, Trunk's Close,
55 High Street, Edinburgh EH1 1SR

For maths

Mathematics for Dyslexics: A Teaching Handbook, S J Chinn and J R Ashcroft (Whurr Publishers,1998)

The National Numeracy Strategy: Guidance to support pupils with dyslexia and dyscalculia (DfES, Circular 0512/2001)

The Trouble with Maths: A Practical Guide to Helping Learners with Numeracy Difficulties, Steve Chinn (RoutledgeFalmer 2004) (winner NASEN/*TES* Teaching and Learning Book Award 2004)

Dyspraxia

Caged in Chaos: A Dyspraxic Guide to Breaking Free, Victoria Biggs (Jessica Kingsley Publishers, 2005).
A chatty book in which teenager Victoria Biggs discusses both the primary effects of her 'learning difference' – disorganisation, clumsiness and poor short-term memory – and the secondary difficulties she and other dyspraxics encounter, including bullying, low self-esteem and loneliness. A good read for any teenager or parents who find dyspraxia impinges on their life

Developmental Dyspraxia: Identification and Intervention. A Manual for Parents and Professionals, Madeleine Portwood (David Fulton Publishers, 1999). An exhaustive description by a senior educational psychologist

Dyslexia and Dyspraxia Toolkit. A very helpful guide to dyslexia and dyspraxia in the workplace. Follow the link to 'Toolkits and guides' on the Civil Service Diversity – What Works website.
Web: www.diversity-whatworks.gov.uk
Tel: 020 7276 1586. Fax: 020 7276 1483.
Address: Diversity – What Works team, Cabinet Office, Admiralty Arch, The Mall, London SW1A 2WH

Dyspraxia: A Guide for Teachers and Parents, Kate Ripley, Bob Daines and Jenny Barrett (David Fulton Publishers, 1997)

Sensory problems

Sensory Integration and the Child, A. Jean Ayres (Western Psychological Services, 1994). Available from Rompa.
Web: www.rompa.com
E-mail: sales@rompa.com
Tel: 0800 056 2323 or 01246 211777.
Fax: 01246 221802.
Address: Goyt Side Road, Chesterfield, Derbyshire S40 2PH

The Out of Synch Child: Recognising and Coping with Sensory Integration Dysfunction, Carol Stock Kranowitz (Skylight Press, 2001)

Visual impairment

Look at It This Way: Toys and Activities for Children with Visual Impairment (Play Can Help), Roma Lear (Butterworth Heinemann, 1998)

Physical difficulties

The Ali Abbas Story: The Moving Story of One Boy's Struggle for Life, Jane Warren (HarperCollins, 2004). An upbeat but moving account of how 12-year-old Ali survived a missile strike in Baghdad, was airlifted to safety and eventually came to the UK for rehabilitation and new limbs

The SEN timetable: key acts, policies and reports

1944 The Education Act establishes that children's education should be based on their age, aptitude and ability.

1978 The Warnock Report, *Special Educational Needs*, is published. This concludes that 20 per cent of the population may have special educational needs and 2 per cent may need additional support over and above what the mainstream school could provide. A key recommendation is that specialist provision for children with SEN could protect the 2 per cent and ensure that they receive appropriate provision

1981 The Education Act begins to address the needs of children with SEN. Statements of special educational needs are introduced with an emphasis placed on integration.

1993 The Education Act (now replaced by the 1996 Act) requires the Secretary of State to issue a Code of Practice giving practical guidance to local education authorities (LEAs) and the governing bodies of all maintained schools about their responsibilities for all children with SEN, including the need to assess those requiring special educational provision.

1994 The Code of Practice on the Identification and Assessment of Special Educational Needs takes effect (now replaced by a version published in 2002). Schools, LEAs and all those involved with children with SEN are required to adhere to the Code.

1996 The Education Act states: 'a child has "special educational needs" for the purposes of this Act if he has a learning difficulty which calls for special educational provision to be made for him'.

2001 The Special Educational Needs and Disability Act strengthens the right of children with SEN to attend a mainstream school, unless their parents choose otherwise or if this is incompatible with efficient education for other children, and there are no reasonable steps which the school and LEA can take to prevent that incompatibility. It states that children with SEN should be offered full access to a broad, balanced and relevant curriculum in the Foundation Stage and later years.

2001 The Disability Discrimination Act places new duties on schools not to treat disabled pupils less favourably than others, and to make reasonable adjustments to ensure that they are not disadvantaged.

2002 The revised SEN Code of Practice is introduced, building on the 1994 code. It provides a framework for developing partnerships between parents, schools, LEAs and health and social services, and places the rights of children at the heart of the process, allowing them to be heard and to take part in the decision-making process. All schools and early years settings must have regard to the Code.

2003 The green paper *Every Child Matters* focuses support on families and carers, intervention, and support for those who work with children.

2004 The white paper *Removing Barriers to Achievement* (DfES) sets out the government's long-term strategy for SEN. It builds on the proposals for the reform of children's services set out in *Every Child Matters.*

2004 *Special Educational Needs and Disability: Towards Inclusive Schools* is published by Ofsted.

2004 *Every Child Matters: Next Steps* is published by the DfES, describing what the government is proposing to do to implement the green paper and giving an overview of the Children Bill.

Phases of education, types of school and responsible bodies

Phases of education

Age	State sector	Independent equivalent
Under 5	Early years/nursery. Includes voluntary day nurseries, preschools, playgroups, childminding networks, portage services and local authority day nurseries	Nursery
5-7 (inclusive)	Key Stage 1: Reception (R), years 1-2	Pre-prep
7/8-11	Key Stage 2: years 3-6	Prep school
11-13/14	Key Stage 3: years 7-9	Prep school (Common Entrance Examination for entry to senior school is sat at age 13)
13/14-16	Key Stage 4: years 10-11	Senior school
16-18	Sixth form/further education: years 12-13	Sixth form: lower and upper sixth

Types of school

Type	Description
City technology college	These are independent all-ability (though some may set out selection criteria), non-fee-paying schools for pupils aged 11-18. Their purpose is to offer pupils of all abilities in urban areas across England the opportunity to study successfully a curriculum geared, with the help of private sector sponsors, towards the world of work. Also encouraged to innovate in the development, management and delivery of the curriculum. May have designated specialist provision.
Community	The LEA employs the school's staff, owns the school's land and buildings and has primary responsibility for deciding the arrangements for admitting pupils. (It is the admissions authority.)
Community special	The special school equivalent of mainstream community schools but caters wholly or mainly for children with statutory statements of special educational needs.
Foundation	At foundation schools the governing body is the employer and the admissions authority. The school's land and buildings are owned either by the governing body or by a charitable foundation.

Foundation special	A special school equivalent of the mainstream foundation school catering wholly or mainly for children with statutory statements of special educational needs.
Grant-maintained	A state school that has opted out of local government control but still receives central government funding from the LEA.
Independent school approved for SEN	Any school which provides full-time education for five or more pupils of compulsory school age, which is not maintained by an LEA or a non-maintained special school. Caters wholly or mainly for children with statutory statements of special educational needs. Has been approved by the DfES for SEN provision.
LEA nursery school	Any non-special school maintained by an LEA to provide education for children who have attained the age of 2 but are under compulsory school age.
Mainstream school	A generic term used to describe any school that is not a designated special school. (Term derives from mainstream education).
Maintained school	Generic term to describe any county school, grant-maintained school, grant-maintained special school, voluntary school or maintained special school.
Non-maintained special	Independent special schools in England approved by the Secretary of State for Education and Skills run as special schools which are not maintained by the state but charge fees on a non-profit-making basis. They normally cater for children with severe and/or low-incidence special educational needs. Most non-maintained special schools are run by major charities or charitable trusts.
Other independent	Any school which provides full-time education for five or more pupils of compulsory school age, which is not maintained by an LEA or a non-maintained special school, nor a grant-maintained school, and which is registered under section 70 of the Education Act 1944. Section 189 of the Education Act 1993 sets out the conditions under which an independent school may be approved by the Secretary of State as being suitable for the admission of children with statements of SEN.
Other independent special school	Any school which provides full-time education for five or more pupils of compulsory school age, which is not maintained by an LEA or a non-maintained special school. Caters wholly or mainly for children with statutory statements of SEN.
Parent and toddler playgroup	A group of parents or carers with children under school age (most of the children are below the age of 3) that provides for both children and adults. Parents remain with the children throughout the session.
Playgroups (full and extended day care)	A group that accepts children under the age of 5, without their parents, for more than four hours in any day.
Playgroups (opportunity)	A group that is set up primarily to provide for children with disabilities or learning difficulties alongside other children. The children often start at an earlier age than in a regular playgroup and staff usually have more specialist training in this field.
Playgroups (sessional)	Offer sessional care and education for children mainly aged three to five years of age cared for with or without parents, no single session lasting more than four hours and no main meal being provided by the group. Such groups are known under a variety of names, but they are all registered as playgroups.

Playing for Success	Through Playing for Success, the DfES is establishing out-of-school-hours study-support centres within top football clubs and at other sports' clubs grounds and venues. The centres use the environment and medium of football to help motivate pupils identified by their schools, as being in need of a boost to help them get back up to speed in literacy and ICT.
Portage	Portage provides a planned approach to home-based preschool education for children with developmental delay, disabilities or any other special educational needs. It works in partnership with parents or carers to enhance a child's development. An extensive Portage network exists in the UK, overseen by the National Portage Association.
Pupil referral unit (PRU)	Any school established and maintained by an LEA which is specially organised to provide education for children who are excluded, sick or otherwise unable to attend mainstream school and is not a county or special school. PRUs shouldn't be used as long-term placements for pupils with statements of SEN.
Resourced school/ additionally resourced provision	A resourced school is a mainstream school that allows pupils with severe or complex difficulties to be fully integrated and included. Additional staff and resources are provided to meet the needs of pupils with SEN. A school may be resourced for a single SEN, such as visual impairment, hearing impairment or autistic spectrum disorders, or for a number of SEN. Resourced provision enables schools not only to be inclusive but to develop the skills, expertise, specialist equipment and curricular approaches necessary to meet pupil need. Most LEAs now have resourced provision. Check out websites for details.
Special school	A school which is specially organised to make special educational provision for pupils with SEN and is approved by the Secretary of State under section 188 of the Education Act 1993.
Special units	Some mainstream schools have special units for children with moderate learning difficulties, speech and language difficulties or hearing impairment.
Voluntary aided	The governing body is the employer and the admissions authority. The school's land and buildings (apart from playing fields which are normally vested in the LEA) will normally be owned by a charitable foundation.
Voluntary controlled	The LEA is the employer and the admissions authority. The school's land and buildings (apart from the playing fields which are normally vested in the LEA) will normally be owned by a charitable foundation.

Who's responsible for meeting the law regarding special needs and disability rights?

Type of school	Responsible body
Maintained school	Governing body
Maintained nursery school	LEA
Pupil referral unit	LEA
Independent school	Proprietor
Special school not maintained by an LEA	Proprietor

Glossary and abbreviations

A2 exams taken at the end of the second year of an A level course

AAC alternative and augmentative communication

ABA applied behaviour analysis

ACE 1. Advisory Centre for Education: independent advice centre offering free and confidential advice to parents **2.** Accelerated Christian Education: a curriculum promoting flexible educational opportunities, based on Christian principles and belief that learning should be a lifelong experience, within a biblical framework

ACE Centre Aiding Communication in Education: an organisation which provides a variety of services including in-depth individual assessments, information, and specialist training for parents and professionals on the use of technology for young people with physical and communication difficulties

ADD attention deficit disorder

ADDISS Attention Deficit Disorder Information and Support Service: provides information and resources to parents, suffers, teachers and health professionals

ADHD attention deficit hyperactivity disorder

AEN additional educational need: term used to describe any type of need a learner may experience. A child may or may not have an SEN to have additional needs. Those with AEN may include teenage mothers, children of travellers, children in care, those with EAL needs etc

AENCo additional educational needs co-ordinator: tries to ensure all children have an inclusive education

Afasic organisation for children and young adults with speech, language and communication difficulties

AFBPsS Associate Fellow of the British Psychological Society

AFF Army Families Federation: independent charitable organisation for Army families

AICE Advanced International Certificate of Education

AISS approved independent special school

A level Advanced level (General Certificate of Education): second public exam in England, Wales and Northern Ireland, usually taken at age 18

ALIS Advanced Level Information System: system of value-added measurement used by many schools to aid teachers in assessing progress made by pupils post-16. *See also* MidYIS, PIPS and YELLIS

ALL accreditation for life and living

ALS additional learner support

Amanuensis someone who sits with a special needs student to help them put their thoughts on paper

AMBDA Associate Membership of the British Dyslexia Association

Aphasia loss or impairment of the faculty of speech or of understanding of language (or both), due to cerebral disease or damage; also known as dysphasia

APP Accessibility Planning Project: joint project with the Council for Disabled Children and Special Educational Needs Joint Initiative Training (SENJIT) to develop a self-review and development tool to help local authorities and schools identify ways of further improving the quality of their access-planning to increase access to education for disabled pupils

AQA Assessment and Qualifications Alliance: one of the examining bodies for GCSE and A levels, a merger of the Associated Examining Board, City & Guilds and the Northern Examinations and Assessment Board

ARCM Associate of the Royal College of Music

AS Angelman syndrome: rare genetic disorder caused by a chromosome irregularity

AS level Advanced Subsidiary GCE level: public exam equivalent to half an A level; formerly taken as a supplement to A levels but now forming the first year of a standard A level course

ASBAH Association for Spina Bifida and Hydrocephalus

ASCS Advice Service Capability Scotland

ASD autistic spectrum disorder

ASDAN Award Scheme Development and Accreditation Network: all ASDAN programmes are recognised by the DfES

ASF additional support fund

ASL additional support for learning

ASN additional support needs: broader than SEN, including those with EFL needs, young carers, teenage mums etc

ASP Asperger's syndrome

Associated Board of the Royal Schools of Music music examining board and publisher; also provides courses for teachers

ATNR asymmetric tonic neck reflex

AUT autism

AUT(other) other autistic: any autistic spectrum disorder that does not belong to the categories ASP, AUT or SPD

AVCE Advanced Vocational Certificate of Education: system of vocational qualifications, formerly GNVQ

BA Bachelor of Arts: university first degree

BAC British Accreditation Council for independent further and higher education: inspects colleges but findings not made public

BACP British Association for Counselling and Psychotherapy

Bands different academic levels for students. Some comprehensive schools divide their intake according to bands

BAS British Ability Scales

BD Bachelor of Divinity

BDA 1. British Dyslexia Association **2.** British Deaf Association

BDD body dysmorphic disorder

Beacon Schools intended to be exemplary state secondary and primary schools identified as amongst the best performing in the country in some stated way(s), eg teaching French, training new teachers etc. They are expected to work in partnership with other schools to pass on their particular areas of expertise. Now being phased out and replaced by leading edge schools (secondary) or Primary Strategy Learning Networks (PSLNs)

BEcon Bachelor of Economics

BEd Bachelor of Education: a teaching qualification

BESD behavioural emotional and social difficulties

BEST behaviour and education support team

BIBIC British Institute for Brain Injured Children: helps children with conditions affecting their sensory, social, communication, motor or learning abilities

BILD British Institute of Learning Disabilities

BIP Behaviour Improvement Programme

BLIP Behaviour and Learning Improvement Programme

BLit Bachelor of Literature: university qualification

BSA 1. Boarding Schools Association **2.** Boarding Schools Allowance within the military environment, now renamed Continuity of Education Allowance (CEA)

BSc Bachelor of Science

BSL British Sign Language

BSU behaviour support unit

BTec vocational qualification – alternative to A level – awarded by the Business and Technology Education Council and taken post-16

Bursary contribution to school fees, usually given to those from lower-income families

CAB Citizens Advice Bureaux

CAD computer-aided design

CAE computer-aided engineering

C&G City & Guilds

CAHMS Child and Adolescent Mental Health Services

Cambridge International Examinations home of the International General Certificate of Secondary Education (IGCSE) and other international equivalents to UK exams

Cantab Cambridge (from the Latin)

CAPD central auditory processing disorder

CAT cognitive ability test

CBAC Cyd-Bwyllgor Addsyg Cymru (Welsh Joint Education Committee)

CCEA Northern Ireland Council for the Curriculum, Examinations and Assessment: serves as an exam board and as the equivalent of the QCA

CCF Combined Cadet Force: paramilitary training corps for the young (boys and girls)

CD conduct disorders: behaviour that violates social rules and the rights of others

CDT craft, design and technology

CE Common Entrance: qualifying exam taken usually at 11, 12 or 13 in the private sector for entry to independent senior schools

CertEd Certificate of Education: a teaching qualification

CES Catholic Education Service

CF cystic fibrosis

CLAIT computer literacy and information technology

CLANSA Certificate for Literacy and Numeracy Support Assistants: a qualification taken by learning support assistants

CLAPA Cleft Lip and Palate Association

C of E Church of England

C of S Church of Scotland

Combined Sciences GCSE exam covering biology, chemistry and physics: counts as one GCSE

Comprehensive school takes all pupils, regardless of their ability or aptitude. Some are fully comprehensive (no entrance exam whatsoever) and others have some selective measures

Connexions the government's advice, support and information service for 13 to 19-year-olds in England

COPE Community Opportunities for Participation in Enterprise: a social enterprise company that supports adults with disabilities to participate in productive businesses

CP cerebral palsy

CPsychol Chartered Psychologist

CPVE Certificate of Pre-Vocational Education

Crammers schools that cram knowledge into the reluctant child, especially those having to re-take A levels because of low grades; not a term that the schools use of themselves – 'independent sixth-form colleges', 'tutorial colleges' or 'independent further education' is more to their taste

CREST Creativity in Science and Technology: nationally accredited award for students who complete experimental science or technology projects

CReSTeD Council for the Registration of Schools Teaching Dyslexic Pupils: charity that assesses and certifies the quality of teaching for dyslexic pupils. CReSTeD schools are placed in one of four categories: WS (withdrawal system); DU (dyslexia unit); SC (Specialist classes); SP specialist provision

CSCI Commission for Social Care Inspection

CSF cerebrospinal fluid

CSIE Centre for Studies on Inclusive Education: independent education centre that supports inclusion and will challenge exclusion

CSP **1.** compulsive skin picking **2.** Co-ordinated Support Plan: introduced under new Scottish legislation for children with additional support needs (ASN)

CSYS Certificate of Sixth Year Studies (used occasionally in Scotland)

CTC city technology college: a quasi-independent state school

DAMP deficits in attention, motor control and perceptual abilities

DCD developmental co-ordination difficulty (also termed dyspraxia)

DECIDE debate, examine, consult, influence, discuss and examine: a project established in Scotland to enable and empower parents to DECIDE the new legislation

DDA Disability Discrimination Act

DEL 1. Department for Employment and Learning (Northern Ireland) **2.** 'delicate' children: a catch-all for conditions which require the school to take particular care with a child, although there are no learning difficulties as such. Haemophilia is an example, as might be leukaemia, cystic fibrosis or allergies

DENI Department of Education Northern Ireland

DfES Department for Education and Skills (formerly the DfEE)

DI Dyslexia Institute

Differentiation adapting curriculum content to provide accessibility to all learners

DipEd Diploma of Education: a teaching qualification

DipPsychol Diploma in Psychology

Disapplication rules on how to disapply parts of the National Curriculum for those with SEN. More information at www.dfes.gov.uk/disapply

DLA Disability Living Allowance

D of E Duke of Edinburgh Award Scheme: a combination of various different activities, including demanding physical exercise, culminating in a medal

DPhil Doctor of Philosophy

DPVE Diploma in Pre-Vocational Education

DS Down's syndrome

DSP dedicated specialist provision

DT design technology

Dual Award (Science) GCSE exam covering biology, chemistry and physics: counts as two GCSEs

DVD developmental verbal dyspraxia

DYSC dyscalculia

DYSL dyslexia

Dysphasia derangement in speech due to confusion or loss of ideas arising from affection of the brain; also known as aphasia

DYSP dyspraxia

EAL English as an additional language (for non-native speakers with little or very poor English) – the latest and politically correct acronym

Eat eating disorders: anorexia etc

EBD emotional and behavioural difficulties

ECIS European Council of Independent Schools

Edexcel examining board, formerly ULEAC (University of London Examinations and Assessment Council) and BTEC (Business and Technology Education Council)

EFA essential fatty acids

EFL English as a foreign language

EMA education maintenance allowance: means tested and paid to students who continue in full-time education post-16

EMAG Ethnic Minority Achievement Grant

ENABLE Scotland organisation for people with learning disabilities and family carers

Enquire the Scottish independent advice and information service for SEN funded by the Scottish Executive

EOTAS education other than at school: provides education and support for children of school age who aren't in mainstream or special schools because they are unwell or emotionally vulnerable, and this has medical support

EP educational psychologist

Epi epilepsy

ESA educational support assistant

ESL English as a second language

ESOL English for speakers of other languages

Estyn Office of Her Majesty's Chief Inspector of Education and Training in Wales

EWS education welfare service – role now broadened to more than just catching truants

Exeat a (usually compulsory) weekend out from boarding school

FE further education

Forces the Army, Navy or Air Force, and adjuncts thereto

Foundation school a state school owned by a foundation (generally religious) which appoints some – but not most – of the governing body

Foundation special school a special school equivalent of the mainstream foundation school catering wholly or mainly for children with statutory statements of SEN. Governing body is both employer and admissions authority

FP former pupil (Scottish expression)

FRSA Fellow of the Royal Society of Arts

FRX fragile X

Gappies foreign (usually Australian, New Zealand or South African) students in their gap year working in UK independent schools

Gap year work experience projects, expeditions etc in year between school and university. Also (when in capitals) name of organisation specialising in this

G&T gifted and talented: the term used by the DfES, Ofsted and others to refer to very able pupils, ie the top 5-10 per cent of the ability range. 'Gifted' relates to ability in academic subjects, 'talented' to ability in other subjects, eg music, drama, sport. Pupils may be described as gifted or talented in one or several subjects

GBA Governing Bodies Association

GCE General Certificate of Education

GCSE General Certificate of Secondary Education: first public exam in England, Wales and Northern Ireland, taken at age 16

GDST Girls' Day School Trust (formerly called the Girls' Public Day School Trust): a foundation of private schools

GEN other genetic: indicates a special provision or expertise other than DS or FRX

Gifted special provision for exceptionally gifted children

GLD generic learning difficulties

GNVQ General National Vocational Qualification: a system of vocational qualifications, now renamed AVCE

Grammar school A type of school which selects pupils on academic merit and provides a rigorous academic education

GSA Girls' Schools' Association: female equivalent of HMC

GWA good wheelchair access

HI hearing impairment

Highers/Higher Grade Scottish public exam, usually taken one or two years after Standard Grade

HLTA higher level teaching assistant: qualified personnel who assist teachers

HMC Headmasters' and Headmistresses' Conference: a sort of headmasters' trade union (and now one or two headmistresses), mostly for public schools, whose heads belong and are considered 'top' by those in it

HMCI Her Majesty's Chief Inspectorate

HMI Her Majesty's Inspectorate

HMIE Her Majesty's Inspectorate of Education in Scotland

HND Higher National Diploma: a well-respected vocational qualification usually taken after A levels or AVCEs

Hons honours degree

Hyperkinetic disorders the correct British term for the disorders known as ADD and ADHD, terms which originate in the USA

IAPS Incorporated Association of Preparatory Schools generally considered the 'top' ones by those in it

IB International Baccalaureate: a public exam at secondary level, increasingly recognised for entry to university in the UK

I CAN Invalid Children's Aid Nationwide: a charity for children with speech and language difficulties

ICT information and communications technology

IELTS International English Language Testing System

IEP individual education plan

IGCSE International GCSE

ILP individual learning programme

Inclusion the concept that all children with special educational needs should be educated, if at all possible, in mainstream schools

Ind independent

Independent word used by fee-paying schools to describe themselves – erroneously

Independent Schools Examination Board provides examinations for pupils transferring from junior to independent senior school at the ages of 11+, 12+ and 13+. The main examination is Common Entrance. The only source of old CE papers

INPP Institute for Neuro Physiological Psychology

INSET in-service education and training

Integration educating children with SEN together with children without SEN in mainstream schools, ensuring that *all* children (as far as possible) engage in the activities of the school together

Inter-denom inter-denominational: refers to religious affiliation, supports more than one brand of Christianity

IPSEA Independent Panel for Special Education Advice. Free services include advice on legal duties of LEAs; representation at SEN tribunals for parents; second opinion given for parents who disagree with LEA decisions and assessments

IQ intelligence quotient

ISA Independent Schools Association

ISC Independent Schools Council: inspects independent schools (but is not itself independent – owned and run by the schools)

ISCis Independent Schools Council information service (not itself independent – owned and run by the schools)

ISCO Independent Schools Careers Organisation

ISEA Independent Special Education Advice: Scottish equivalent of IPSEA

ISI Independent Schools Inspectorate

IT information technology: usually referred to as ICT in schools

JCQ Joint Council for Qualifications: replaced the JCGQ (Joint Council for General Qualifications) in January 2004)

KS Key Stage(s). The National Curriculum is divided into four key stages according to pupils' ages: KS 1 for 5 to 7-year-olds, KS 2 for 7-11, KS 3 for 11-14, KS 4 for 14-16

LA local authority

LAMDA London Academy of Music and Dramatic Art

LEA local education authority

LD learning difficulties

Learning and Teaching Scotland national body sponsored by the Scottish Executive education department to provide advice, support, resources and staff development. Aims to improve attainment and achievement for all and to provide lifelong learning

LSA learning support assistant: not usually a qualified teacher but will usually have or be working towards a nationally recognised qualification. May be assigned to an individual pupil or to a group of students or class. LSA time identified on a statement is paid for by the LEA

LSC 1. Learning and Skills Council (England and Wales) **2.** Legal Services Commission

LSP learning support practitioner

LST learning support teacher- a qualified teacher

LSU leaning support unit

MA Master of Arts: university degree

Makaton a mix of sign language (adapted from British sign language), spoken word and graphic symbols. Helps children with ASD/communication difficulties

MD muscular dystrophy

MEd Master of Education: a teaching qualification

MEMSC multi-sensory, errorless, meta-cognitive, sequential and cumulative

MidYIS Middle Years Information System: a system of value-added measurement widely used in secondary schools, involving tests for years 7, 8 and 9. *See also* ALIS, YELLIS and PIPS

Mind a mental health charity

MIS Meares-Irlen syndrome

MLD moderate learning difficulties

MLitt Master of Letters

Modification amendment or alteration of any component of the National Curriculum in order to give the child access to that area of the curriculum

MSc Master of Science: university qualification

MSI multi-sensory impairment: combination of visual and hearing difficulties possibly with additional disabilities

NAS National Autistic Society

NASEN National Association for Special Educational Needs

NASS National Association of Independent Schools and Non-Maintained Special Schools

NBCS National Blind Children's Society

NC National Curriculum

NCET National Council for Educational Technology

NCSE National Council for Special Education

NFER National Foundation for Educational Research

NLD non-verbal learning disorder/disability

NMSS non-maintained special schools: list drawn up by the DfES

NNA National Assessment Agency

NNEB Diploma in Nursery Nursing

Non-denom non-denominational (refers to religious affiliation, generally means pretty low key)

NQF National Qualifications Framework

NQT Newly Qualified Teacher

NVQ National Vocational Qualification

NVR(Q) non-verbal reasoning (quotient): a test of ability used by some selective schools

OAASIS Office for Advice, Assistance, Support and Information on Special Needs

OB old boy: ie former pupil of a school

OCD obsessive compulsive disorder

OCR Oxford Cambridge and RSA Examination: a joint venture between the RSA and the University of Cambridge Local Examinations Syndicate (UCLES) that has taken on the RSA exams, CLAIT, etc. Covers all the former Oxford and Cambridge boards including GCSE and A levels

ODD oppositional defiant disorder (also known as oppositional defiance disorder)

OED Oxford English Dictionary

Ofsted Office for Standards in Education: officially the Office of Her Majesty's Chief Inspector of Schools. Inspects schools and publishes reports on them

OG old girl (ie former pupil of a school)

ONS Office for National Statistics

OT occupational therapist

Oth other: indicates specialist provision that does not fall within other specified categories

Oxbridge Oxford and/or Cambridge universities

Oxon Oxford

PAF performance assessment framework: means of assessing how well social services and related educational establishments are doing

PANDA Performance AND Assessment report

Pastoral care care of pupils on matters not related to their work, eg personal and social ones

PAT pupil achievement tracker

PD physical difficulties: may be specific or cover a wide range of physical disabilities

PDA pathological demand avoidance syndrome: a PDD related to autism and Asperger's syndrome. The individual tends to be socially manipulative and obsessionally avoid the demands of daily life

PDD pervasive development disorder

PDD (NOS) pervasive development disorder not otherwise specified

PE physical education

PECS Picture Exchange Communication System: a visual communication system used to develop communication in children with ASD and other communication disorders

Peripatetic teacher a teacher with specific expertise who travels from school to school to give appropriate specialist advice and support to the child and the school. Also called advisory teacher or support teacher

PET Preliminary English Tests: the second-level Cambridge ESOL exam

PFI private finance initiative: off-balance-sheet funding for the government, with private firms providing finance and facilities management

PFS Playing for Success: a DfES initiative using football clubs and other sports grounds for out-of-school-hours study support. Uses sport to motivate pupils and focus on literacy, numeracy and ICT

PGCE Postgraduate Certificate of Education: a teaching qualification

PhD Doctor of Philosophy: a postgraduate degree

PHSE personal, health and social education

PIPS Performance Indicators in Primary Schools: a measure of primary value-added. PIPS tracks a number of aspects of schooling as pupils move through the primary sector. *See also* ALIS, MidYIS and YELLIS

PIVATS performance indicators for value-added target setting: a mechanism to assist target setting for pupils with SEN or those who may be underachieving

PMLD profound and multiple learning difficulties

Portage Service helps and advises families who have preschool children with special needs. Offers home visits

POS provides outreach support

PPP public private partnership: *see* PFI

PPS parent partnership service

PRSE personal, religious and social education

PRU pupil referral unit

P scales used for pupils working towards level 1 of the National Curriculum

PSD personal and social development

PS(H)E personal, social (and health) education (courses)

PT physiotherapist

PTA parent-teacher association

PWS Prader-Willi syndrome

QCA Qualifications and Curriculum Authority: government body that oversees the accreditation of qualifications in England

RAD Royal Academy of Dance

RADA Royal Academy of Dramatic Art

RADAR Royal Association for Disability and Rehabilitation

RAM 1. Royal Academy of Music **2.** random access memory (computer terminology)

RAP Reasonable Adjustments Project: a Disability Equality in Education project (jointly funded by the DfES and the Disability Rights Commission) which aims to provide schools with a resource bank of practical ideas and training materials to help them make reasonable adjustments

RC Roman Catholic

RCM Royal Academy of Music

RCSLT Royal College of Speech and Language Therapists

RDA Riding for the Disabled Association – incorporating Carriage Driving

RE religious education: learning about beliefs. *See* RI and RS

Record of Need used in Scotland: similar to a statement

RI religious instruction: learning to believe. *See* RE and RS

RNIB Royal National Institute for the Blind

RNID Royal National Institute for Deaf People

ROS receives outreach support

RS religious studies: learning about beliefs. *See* RE and RI

RSA Royal Society of Arts

RSA CLAIT (now OCR) Computer Literacy and Information Technology qualification

SAFE Scotland's Advocacy for Education project, established by ISEA

SaLT speech and language therapist

SATs Standard Attainment Tests: taken by English state (and some independent) schoolchildren at 7, 11 and 14 (end of each Key Stage)

SATS test sat by American students to get into US universities

SCD speech and communication difficulties

SCE Service Children's Education: an agency that provides education (in some overseas locations) and support to Service children and their families

Scotvec a Scottish vocational qualification

SEBD social, emotional and behavioural difficulties

SEF self-evaluation form

SELB Southern Education and Library Board (Northern Ireland)

SEN special educational needs

SENAS Special Educational Needs Assessment Service

SENCo special educational needs co-ordinator: person responsible for co-ordinating special needs provision within a school

SENDIST Special Educational Needs & Disability Tribunal: an independent tribunal for appeals by parents against unresolved LEA decisions about SEN. Also considers parents' claims of disability discrimination in schools

SENNAC Special Educational Needs National Advisory Council

SENRP SEN Regional Partnerships

SEP special educational provision

Services the Army, Navy or Air Force, and adjuncts thereto

Set a group of children of similar ability within a subject and year; children can be in the top set for one subject and the bottom for others, and may move between sets

SFEFC Scottish Further Education Funding Council

SG Standard Grades: awarded by the Scottish Qualifications Authority; taken at the end of S4 and equivalent to a GCSE (replaced O-grades)

SH Scottish Highers

SHA Secondary Heads Association

SHMIS Society of Headmasters and Headmistresses of Independent Schools

SI sensory impairment

SIP 1. school improvement plan **2.** Social Inclusion Panel/Partnership

Six-inch rule rule applied at some co-educational schools whereby boys and girls may not come closer to each other than six inches (in case they get over-excited)

Skill National Bureau for Students with Disabilities

SLC specialist language centre

SLCN speech, language and communication needs

SLD severe learning difficulties

SMART specific, measurable, achievable, realistic and time-related

SPD semantic pragmatic disorder: often associated with autistic spectrum disorder

Specialist teacher advisers provide a range of services includes supporting children with sensory or physical needs

SpLCN specific language and communication needs

SpLD specific learning difficulties: a portmanteau phrase covering dyslexia, dyspraxia etc

Sp&LD speech and language difficulties

SQA Scottish Qualifications Authority: serves as an exam board for all Scottish pre-university qualifications and as the equivalent of the QCA

SSA Scottish Society for Autism

SSAFA Soldiers, Sailors, Airmen and Families Association: a welfare body looking after serving and retired military personnel and their families

SSE sign-supported English

SSEN statement of special educational need

STA specialist teacher adviser – employed by LEAs to provide specialist advice to schools on SEN

Standard Grades the Scottish equivalent of GCSE

Streaming the practice of dividing a year group into streams of similar ability: if you are in the top stream you are in the top stream for all subjects

SUBCO subject co-ordination/co-ordinator

TA teaching assistant

TEACCH Treatment and Education of Autistic and related Communication handicapped Children: a person-centred approach to autism developed in the USA that identifies and develops a support programme based on that child's abilities, interests and needs

TEFL teaching English as a foreign language

TES *Times Educational Supplement*

TIC Tourette's syndrome and other tic disorders

TLA three-letter abbreviation

TLC tender loving care

Transition Plan a plan forming part of the annual review of a child with a statement once the child reaches 14. The plan should assist with the young person's transition to adult life

Trichotillomania compulsive urge to pull hair out, resulting in alopecia

TS Tourette's syndrome

Twoccer one who Takes a car Without the Owner's Consent

UCAS Universities and Colleges Admissions Service

V very

VAK visual auditory kinaesthetic (learning styles)

Value-added a measure of the extent to which pupils' educational experience enhances their knowledge, abilities and skills

VCC Voice for the Child in Care: a charity working and campaigning for children and young people in public care

VI visual impairment

VR(Q) verbal reasoning (quotient): a test of ability used by many selective schools

Widget Rebus Symbols a reading and communication symbol system with minimum use of text

WISC III Wechsler Intelligence Scale for Children: used by psychologists; helps identify specific learning difficulties

WJEC Welsh Joint Education Committee (CBAC in Welsh)

WORD Wechsler Objective Reading Dimensions: measures attainment in literacy and helps highlight differences between predicted and actual levels of attainment

WRAT Wide Range Achievement Test

YE Young Enterprise: a hands-on business studies course

YELLIS Year Eleven Information System: a value-added monitoring system that provides a wide range of performance indicators for students aged 14-16. *See also* ALIS, MidYIS and PIPS

MAPS

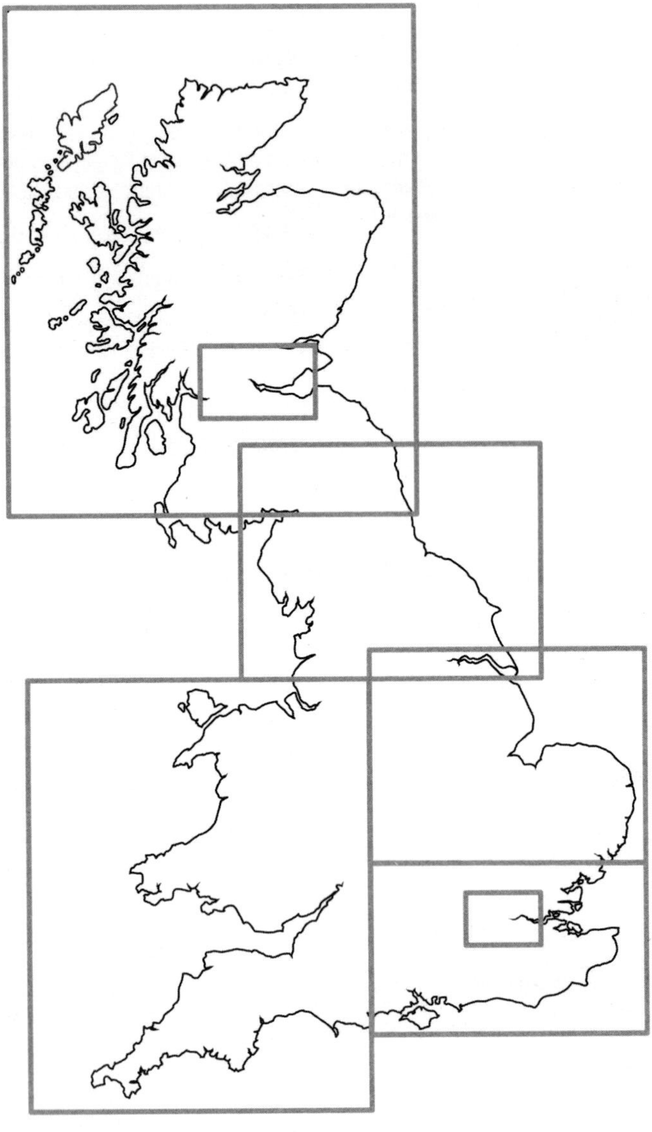

WEST MIDLANDS

1 Albert Bradbeer Infant and Nursery Community School
2 Alice Stevens School
3 Bablake School
4 Bridge School (The)
5 Brier School (The)
6 Calthorpe School Sports College
7 Cockshut Hill Technology College
8 Deanery Church of England Voluntary Aided Primary School (The)
9 Finham Park School
10 Forest Oak School
11 George Dixon International School and Sixth Form Centre
12 Great Barr Primary School
13 Hallmoor School
14 Hamstead Hall School
15 Handsworth Wood Girls' School
16 King Edward's School (Birmingham)
17 King's Norton Boys' School
18 Mary Elliot School
19 Matthew Boulton College of Further and Higher Education
20 Meadows Primary School (The)
21 Meadows School (The)
22 Moseley Primary School
23 Oaks Primary School (The)
24 Palfrey Junior School
25 Prince Albert Junior and Infant School
26 Saint Bernadette's Catholic Primary School
27 Thorns Community College
28 Tile Hill Wood School and Language College
29 Tiverton School
30 Waverley School
31 Wednesfield High School
32 Willenhall School Sports College
33 Wilson Stuart School
34 Wodensborough Community Technology College
35 Wolverhampton Grammar School
36 Wordsley School (The)

WORCESTERSHIRE

1 Abberley Hall
2 Arrow Vale Community High School - a Specialist Sports College
3 Elms School (The)
4 Hunters Hill School
5 Kingsley College
6 Malvern College
7 RNIB New College, Worcester

SOMERSET

1 Avishayes Community Primary School
2 Brymore School
3 Edington and Shapwick School
4 Fairmead School
5 Fosse Way School
6 Horsington Church of England Primary School
7 Huish Episcopi School
8 King's Bruton
9 King's Hall
10 Kingswood Prep School
11 Mark College
12 Millfield Preparatory School
13 Millfield School
14 Minehead First School
15 North Hill House
16 Prior Park College
17 Queen's College
18 Royal High School, Bath GDST
19 Saint Gregory's Catholic College
20 Shepton Mallet Community Infants School
21 Sidcot School
22 Weston College
23 Westover Green Community School

DORSET

1 Ad Astra First School
2 All Saints' Church of England School, Weymouth
3 Bovington Middle School
4 Carter Community School
5 Castle Court
6 Clayesmore Preparatory School
7 Clayesmore School
8 Gryphon School (The)
9 Knighton House School
10 Milton Abbey School
11 Old Malthouse School (The)
12 Philip Green Memorial School
13 Port Regis Preparatory School
14 Portchester School
15 Queen Elizabeth's School
16 Saint Mary's Catholic Primary School, Marnhull
17 Saint Mary's School (Shaftesbury)
18 Swanage First School
19 Talbot Heath School
20 Thomas Hardye School (The)
21 Westfield Technology College
22 Wimborne Learning Centre

BRISTOL & NORTH SOMERSET

1 Bowsland Green Primary School
2 Claremont School
3 Clifton College
4 Clifton College Preparatory School (The Pre)
5 Filton Hill Primary School
6 Gay Elms Primary School
7 Kingsfield School
8 Nailsea School
9 New Fosseway School
10 Red Maids School (The)
11 Saint Bede's Catholic College
12 Saint Katharine's Church of England Primary School
13 Saint Peter's Church of England Primary School

WALES

1 Bishop Hedley RC High School
2 Brecon High School
3 Bryn Primary School
4 Brynmill Primary School
5 Cardiff High School
6 Christ College, Brecon
7 Court School (The)
8 Heronsbridge School
9 Howell's School, Llandaff
10 Lakeside Junior and Infant School
11 Penybryn School
12 Saint Asaph - Esgob Morgan Junior School
13 Saint David's College, Llandudno
14 Ysgol Glanymôr School
15 Ysgol Uwchradd Tregaron
16 Ysgol y Plas

CHESHIRE

1 Bishops' Blue Coat Church of England High School (The)
2 Dorin Park School
3 King's School Chester
4 Pownall Hall School
5 Rudheath Community High School

MERSEYSIDE & WIRRAL

1 Bebington High Sports College
2 Greenways School
3 Higher Side Community Comprehensive School
4 Park High School
5 Peterhouse School
6 Saint Edmund of Canterbury Catholic High School
7 Springfield School
8 Walton Progressive School
9 West Kirby Residential School
10 Wirral Grammar School for Girls

GLOUCESTERSHIRE

1 Battledown Children's Centre
2 Bredon School
3 Cheltenham College Junior School
4 Cirencester Deer Park School
5 Cirencester Kingshill School
6 Commonweal School (The)
7 Dean Close School

8 Eastcombe Primary School
9 Eldene Primary School
10 Longborough Church of England Primary School
11 Prior Park Preparatory School
12 Westonbirt School
13 Woodchester Endowed Church of England Aided Primary School
14 Wycliffe College

GUERNSEY

1 Lower School

HEREFORDSHIRE

1 Lea CofE Primary School
2 Leominster Junior School
3 Margaret Allen Preparatory School (The)

WILTSHIRE

1 Appleford School
2 Calder House School
3 Notton House School
4 Rowdeford School
5 Saint Edmund's Church of England Girls' School and Sports College
6 Saint Nicholas School
7 Sandroyd School
8 Stonar School

CORNWALL

1 Altarnun Community Primary School
2 Beacon Infant and Nursery School, Bodmin (The)
3 Bude Infant School
4 Humphry Davy School
5 Kehelland Village School
6 Launceston College
7 Mullion School
8 Otterham Community Primary School
9 Penrice Community College
10 Polruan Community Primary School
11 Saint Stephen's Community Primary School

SHROPSHIRE

1 Bridge School (The)
2 Bryn Offa CofE Primary School
3 Market Drayton Infant and Nursery School
4 Moor Park School
5 Prestfelde School
6 Saint Andrew's CofE Primary School
7 Shrewsbury School
8 Thomas Telford School

GREATER MANCHESTER

1 Blue Coat CofE School (The)
2 Chethams School of Music
3 Cromwell High School
4 Grange School
5 Hesketh Fletcher CofE High School, Atherton
6 Inscape House
7 Kingsway School (The)
8 Lymm High Voluntary Controlled School
9 Manchester Grammar School (The)
10 North Cestrian Grammar School
11 Oakwood High School
12 Offerton High School
13 Parrs Wood Technology College
14 Royal Schools for The Deaf and Communication Disorders
15 Saint Anne's Roman Catholic High School, Stockport
16 Stockport College of Further and Higher Education
17 Two Trees Community High School
18 Tytherington High School
19 Wellington School

DEVON

1 Alphington Combined School
2 Blundell's School
3 Charleton Church of England Primary School
4 Chelfham Mill School
5 Dame Hannah Rogers School
6 Devonport High School for Boys
7 Duchy School Bradninch (The)
8 Grenville College
9 Ilfracombe Church of England Junior School
10 Plymouth College
11 Plymouth Hospital School
12 Plymstock School
13 Ridgeway School
14 Rudolf Steiner Junior School
15 Saint John's School
16 Sticklepath Community School
17 Trinity School
18 West Buckland School
19 Westlands School and Technology College
20 White Rock Primary School
21 Woodlands School

STAFFORDSHIRE

1 Abbey Hill School and Performing Arts College
2 Brook Primary School
3 Brownhills High School
4 Horton Lodge Community Special School

SOUTH EAST ENGLAND

BRIGTON & HOVE

1 Blatchington Mill School and Sixth Form College
2 Brighton and Hove High School
3 Brighton College
4 Brighton College Junior School Pre-preparatory
5 Brighton College Prep School
6 Hillside School
7 Hove Park School and Sixth Form Centre
8 Roedean School
9 Rudyard Kipling Primary School
10 St Aubyns School

WEST SUSSEX

1 Ardingly College
2 Bedales School
3 Bishop Luffa Church of England School, Chichester
4 Boundstone Community College
5 Brantridge School
6 Farney Close School
7 Felpham Community College
8 Great Ballard School
9 Harlands Primary School
10 Ingfield Manor School
11 Littlehampton Community School (The)
12 Midhurst Grammar School
13 Palatine School
14 Philpots Manor School
15 Saint Augustine's CofE Primary School
16 Seaford College
17 Slindon College
18 Weald School (The)
19 Westbourne House School
20 Windlesham House School

EAST SUSSEX

1 Causeway School (The)
2 Chailey Heritage School
3 Filsham Valley School
4 Frewen College
5 Glyne Gap School
6 Newlands Manor School
7 Saint Bede's School
8 Saint Mary's College Part of the Wrestwood Trust
9 Saint Mary's School Bexhill

KENT

1 Bedgebury School
2 Bradstow School
3 Chatham Grammar School for Boys
4 Chatham Grammar School for Girls
5 Christ Church Church of England High School
6 Clarendon House Grammar School
7 Cobham Hall
8 Dane Court Grammar School
9 Dartford Grammar School for Girls
10 Dover College
11 East Court School
12 Foxwood School
13 Greenfields School
14 Harbour School
15 Hayesbrook School (The)
16 Holmewood House School
17 Hugh Christie Technology College
18 Ifield School (The)
19 King's School Rochester
20 Little Acorns School
21 Mascalls School
22 New School at West Heath (The)
23 Rainham Mark Grammar School
24 Ridge Meadow Primary School
25 Ripplevale School
26 Sackville School
27 Saint Gregory's Catholic Comprehensive School
28 Saint Lawrence College
29 Saint Mary's Island Church of England (Aided) Primary School
30 Saint Ronan's School
31 Sherwin Knight Community Infant School
32 Sir Joseph Williamson's Mathematical School
33 Skinners' School (The)
34 Tonbridge Grammar School
35 Tunbridge Wells Grammar School for Boys
36 Wellesley House School

BERKSHIRE

1 Abbey School Reading (The)
2 Castle School (The)
3 Cheam School
4 Elstree School
5 Eton College
6 Hurst Lodge School
7 Kennet School
8 Lambs Lane Primary School
9 Leighton Park School
10 Mary Hare Grammar School
11 Mary Hare Primary School
12 Parsons Down Infant and Nursery School
13 Saint George's School Ascot
14 Saint John's Beaumont School
15 Shiplake College
16 Slough Grammar School
17 Windsor Boys' School (The)

HAMPSHIRE & IOW

1 Banister Infant School
2 Cliffdale Primary School
3 Farleigh School
4 Forres Sandle Manor School
5 Hawthorns School
6 Hill House School
7 Hordle Walhampton School
8 Itchen College
9 Lord Wandsworth College
10 Mayville High School
11 Medina High School
12 Netley Court School
13 Peter Symonds College
14 Priestlands School
15 Romsey School (The)
16 Saint Lawrence Church of England Primary School
17 Sheiling School

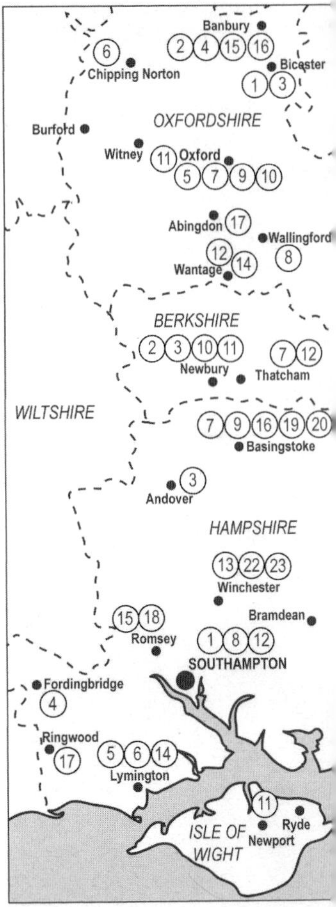

18 Stanbridge Earls School
19 Treloar College
20 Treloar School
21 Waterside School
22 Westgate School (The)
23 Winchester College

BUCKINGHAMSHIRE

1 Akeley Wood School
2 Alfriston School
3 Aston Clinton School
4 Bell Lane Combined School
5 Brushwood Junior School
6 Buckingham Primary School
7 Elmtree School
8 Gayhurst School
9 Godstowe Prep School
10 Heritage House School
11 Saint Mary's School
12 Stowe School

SURREY

1 Abbey School (The)
2 Box Hill School
3 Brooklands School
4 Burhill Community Infant School
5 Burstow Primary School
6 Caterham School
7 Coworth-Flexlands School
8 Cranleigh Preparatory School
9 Cranleigh School
10 Danes Hill School
11 Eastwick Infant School
12 Epsom College
13 Feltonfleet School
14 Freemantles School
15 Frensham Heights School
16 Glebelands School
17 King Edward's School
18 Knowl Hill School
19 Laverock School
20 Long Ditton Saint Mary's CofE Aided Junior School
21 Manor House School
22 Meath School
23 Moon Hall School
24 More House School (Farnham)
25 Park School (The)
26 Priory School
27 Reigate Grammar School
28 Saint Ives School
29 Saint John The Baptist Catholic Comprehensive School, Woking
30 Saint John's School
31 Saint Joseph's School
32 Saint Paul's Catholic Primary School, Thames Ditton
33 Sunnydown School
34 Woodcote House School

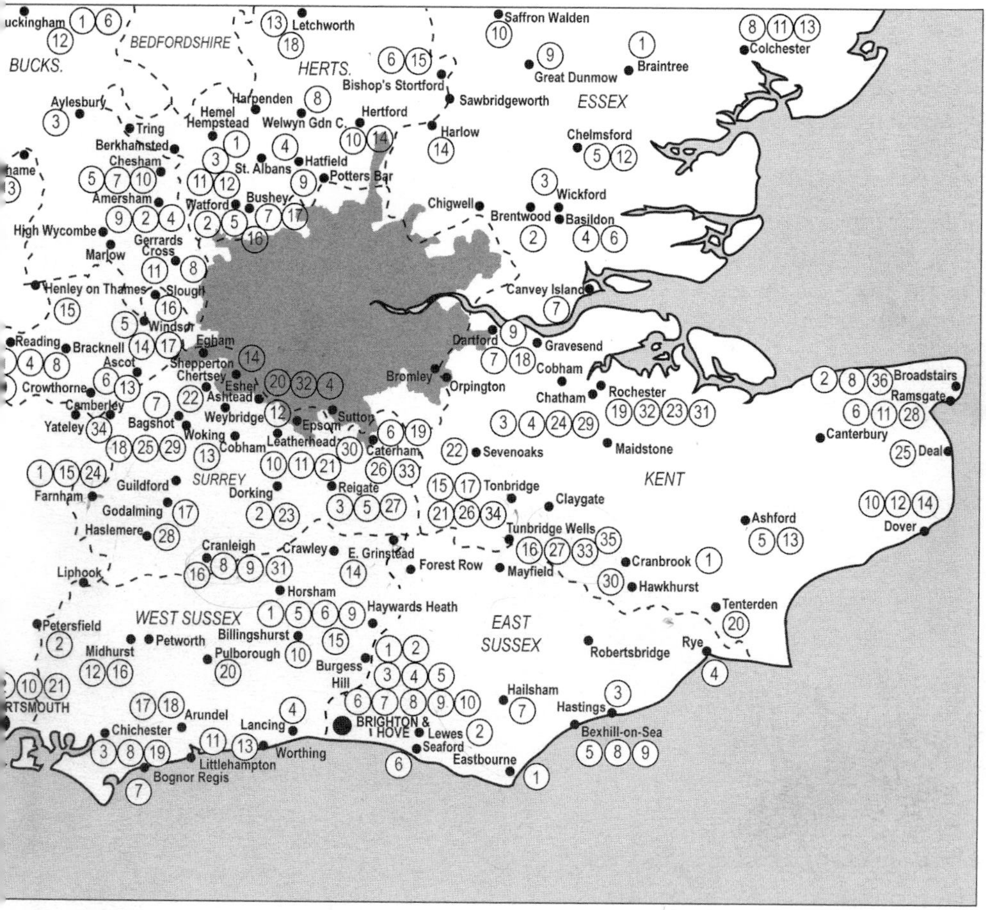

ESSEX

1 Braintree College
2 Brentwood School
3 Castledon School
4 Cedar Hall School
5 Chelmsford College
6 Cherry Tree Primary School and Nursery
7 Cornelius Vermuyden School and Arts College (The)
8 Doucecroft School
9 Felsted School
10 Friends' School
11 Holmwood House School
12 King Edward VI Grammar School, Chelmsford
13 Kingswode Hoe School
14 Roydon Primary School

OXFORDSHIRE

1 Bicester Community College
2 Bloxham School
3 Bruern Abbey School
4 Carrdus School
5 Cherwell School (The)
6 Chipping Norton School
7 Cokethorpe School
8 Cranford House School Trust Limited
9 Cutteslowe Primary School
10 d'Overbroeck's College
11 Gosford Hill School
12 King Alfred's Community and Sports College
13 Lord Williams's School
14 Saint Mary's School Wantage
15 Sibford School
16 Tudor Hall School
17 Unicorn School (The)

HERTFORDSHIRE

1 Abbot's Hill School
2 Aldenham School
3 Beechwood Park School
4 Bishop's Hatfield Girls' School
5 Edge Grove Preparatory School
6 Hertfordshire and Essex High School (The)
7 Immanuel College
8 Knightsfield School
9 Lochinver House School
10 Middleton School
11 Royal Masonic School for Girls
12 Saint Albans School
13 Saint Christopher School
14 Saint Joseph's in the Park
15 Saint Mary's Catholic School
16 Shenley Primary School
17 Westwood School
18 Woolgrove School

NORTH ENGLAND

CUMBRIA

1 Croftlands Infant School
2 Dowdales School
3 Fell House School
4 George Hastwell School
5 Grayrigg CofE School
6 Ramsden Infant School
7 Saint Bees School
8 Saint Bernard's Catholic High School
9 Saint Paul's CofE Junior School
10 Sandside Lodge School
11 Thomlinson Junior School
12 Witherslack Hall School
13 Yewdale School

STOCKTON ON TEES

1 Abbey Hill School Technology College
2 Conyers School
3 Grangefield School and Technology College

NORTHUMBERLAND

1 Duchess's Community High School (The)
2 Grove Special School (The)
3 Hexham Priory School
4 Nunnykirk Centre for Dyslexia

NORTH YORKSHIRE

1 Ashville College
2 Aysgarth School
3 Beaumont Hill School
4 Bootham School
5 Brackenfield School
6 Bramcote School, North Yorkshire
7 Breckenbrough School
8 Caedmon School
9 Dodmire Junior School
10 Easingwold School
11 Filey School
12 Giggleswick School
13 Heathfield Primary School
14 Ingleby Arncliffe Church of England Voluntary Aided Primary School
15 Mowbray School
16 Queen Mary's School
17 Risedale Community College
18 Rossett School
19 Saint Aidan's Church of England High School
20 Saint John's Catholic School for the Deaf (Boston Spa)
21 Springwater School

LANCASHIRE

1 Beech Tree School
2 Bennett House School (The)
3 Cedar House School
4 Collegiate High School Sports College
5 Crosshill Special School
6 Haslingden High School
7 King Edward VII and Queen Mary School

8 Loyne School (The)
9 Moor Nook Community Primary School
10 Norden High School and Sports College
11 Oswaldtwistle Broadfield School
12 Pontville School
13 Ribblesdale High School Technology College
14 Rossall School
15 Stonyhurst College

EAST RIDING OF YORKSHIRE

1 Beverley Grammar School
2 Birtenshaw Hall (Children's Charitable Trust)
3 Bridlington School Sports College
4 Driffield School
5 Hall Road Primary School
6 Headlands School and Community Science College
7 Hensall Community Primary School
8 Hessle High School
9 Withernsea High School and Technology College

DURHAM

1 Deerness Valley Comprehensive School
2 Durham Gilesgate Sports College and Sixth Form Centre
3 Durham High School for Girls
4 Saint Hild's Church of England Voluntary Aided School
5 Spennymoor Comprehensive School

WEST YORKSHIRE

1 Ackworth School
2 Braithwaite Special School
3 Broomfield, The South Leeds SILC
4 Crofton High School
5 Froebelian School (The)
6 Gateways School
7 Greenhead College
8 Haycliffe School
9 Highbury School
10 Hinchliffe Mill Junior and Infant School
11 Holly Bank School
12 Holmfirth High School
13 King James's School
14 Leeds Grammar School
15 Malsis School
16 Moor End Technology College
17 Newsome High School and Sports College
18 North Halifax Grammar School (The)
19 Queen Elizabeth Grammar School (Wakefield)
20 Ravenscliffe High School
21 Royds Hall High School
22 Scout Road Primary School
23 William Henry Smith School

SOUTH YORKSHIRE

1 Acres Hill Primary School
2 Birkdale School
3 Birkdale School Preparatory School
4 Brampton Ellis CofE Junior School
5 Danum School Technology College
6 Don Valley High School
7 Greenacre School
8 Hall Cross School
9 Hill House Saint Mary's
10 Mexborough School
11 Oakes Park School
12 Robert Ogden School (The)
13 Rowan School (The)
14 Sandall Wood School
15 Wingfield Comprehensive School

TYNE & WEAR

1 Beech Hill Primary School
2 Castle View School
3 Churchill Community College
4 Edenhurst Prep School
5 Epinay School
6 Greenfields School
7 Kells Lane Primary School
8 Kenton Bar Primary School
9 Longbenton Community College
10 Saint Anne's Roman Catholic Voluntary Aided Primary School
11 Saint Thomas More Roman Catholic High School Aided
12 Sir Charles Parsons School
13 Southlands School
14 Washington School

MIDDLESBROUGH

1 Beverley School
2 Cleveland College of Art and Design
3 Macmillan College
4 Saint David's Roman Catholic Technology College
5 Saint Peter's Roman Catholic Comprehensive School, South Bank

NORTHERN IRELAND

Antrim
1 Derriaghy Primary School
2 Dunmurry High School
3 La Salle Boys' School (Junior)
4 Lindsay School (The)
5 Mckinney Primary School Dundrod
6 Parkhall Primary School
7 Saint Rose's High School

Londonderry
1 Artigarvan Primary School
2 Belmont House Special School
3 Lumen Christi College

Tyrone
1 Christian Brothers' Grammar School
2 Omagh County Primary School

Down
1 Saint Patrick's Grammar School

Armagh
1 Craigavon Senior High School

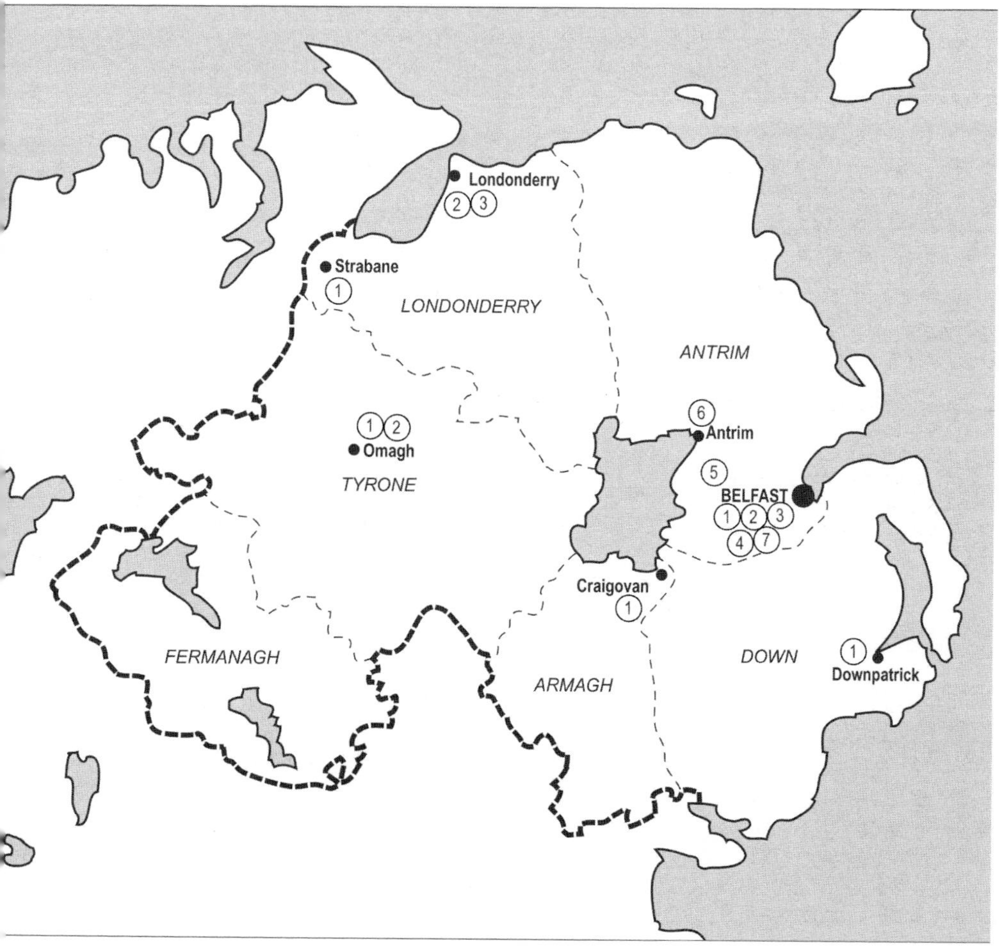

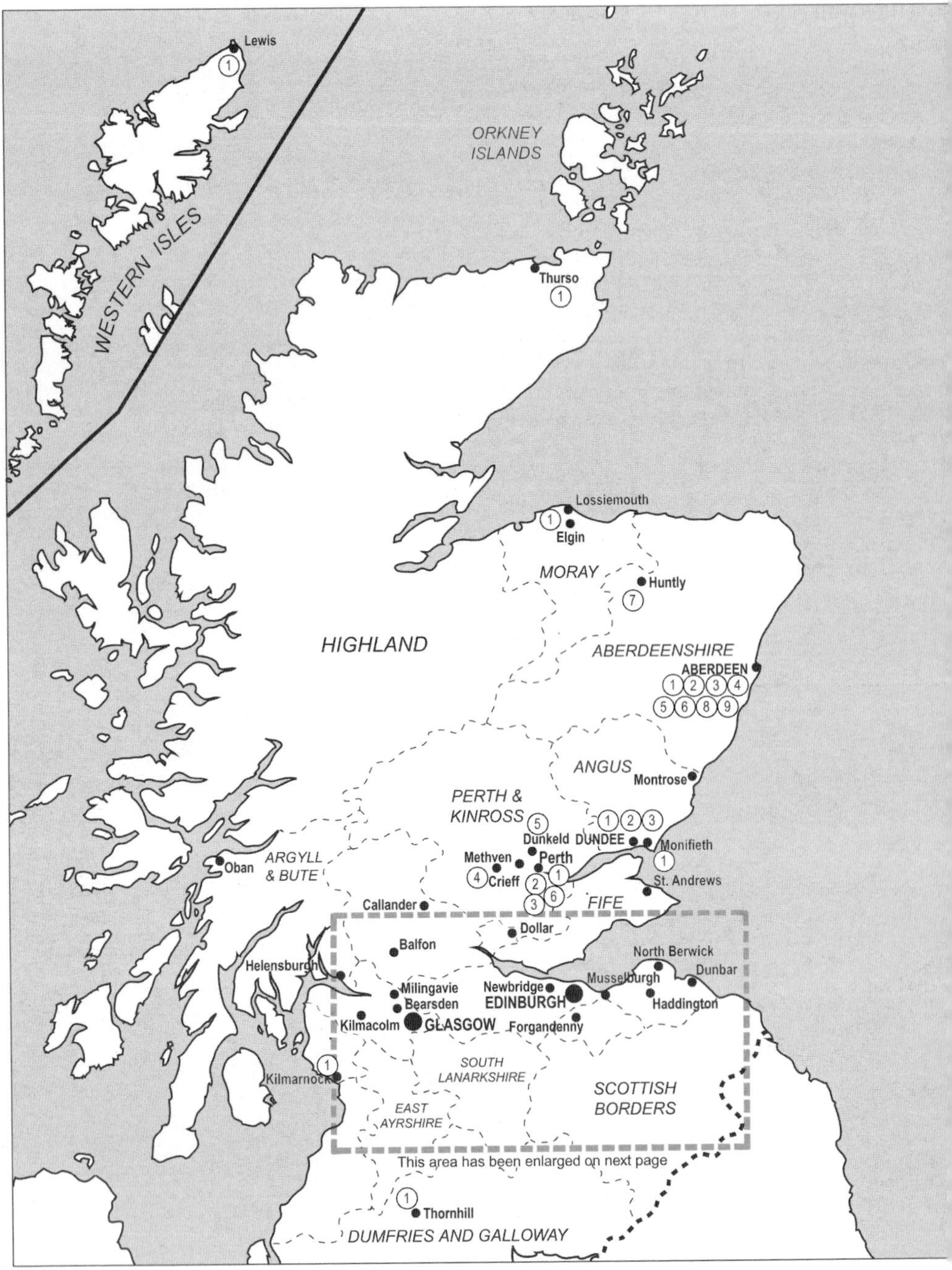
Lewis
1
ORKNEY ISLANDS
WESTERN ISLES
Thurso
1
Lossiemouth
1
Elgin
MORAY
Huntly
7
HIGHLAND
ABERDEENSHIRE
ABERDEEN
1 2 3 4
5 6 8 9
ANGUS
Montrose
PERTH & KINROSS
5
1 2 3
Dunkeld
DUNDEE
Monifieth
1
Perth
Methven
4 Crieff
2
1
3
6
St. Andrews
FIFE
Oban
ARGYLL & BUTE
Callander
Dollar
Balfon
North Berwick
Dunbar
Helensburgh
Milingavie
Bearsden
Newbridge
EDINBURGH
Musselburgh
Haddington
Kilmacolm
GLASGOW
Forgandenny
1
Kilmarnock
SOUTH LANARKSHIRE
SCOTTISH BORDERS
EAST AYRSHIRE
This area has been enlarged on next page
1
Thornhill
DUMFRIES AND GALLOWAY

SCOTLAND

DUNDEE

1 Harris Academy
2 High School of Dundee
3 Kingspark School

EDINBURGH

1 Basil Paterson Tutorial College
2 Donaldson's College
3 George Heriot's School
4 George Watson's College
5 George Watson's Primary School
6 Harmeny Education Trust
7 James Gillespie's High School
8 Merchiston Castle School
9 Royal Blind School (The)
10 Royal High School (The) (Edinburgh)
11 Saint George's School Edinburgh
12 Stewart's Melville College

CLACKMANNANSHIRE

1 Carrongrange School

GLASGOW

1 Balfron High School
2 Bearsden Academy
3 Belmont House School
4 Carnbooth School
5 Clippens School
6 Corseford Residential School
7 Craighalbert Centre (The)
8 Douglas Academy
9 High School of Glasgow Junior
10 Jordanhill School
11 Kilsyth Academy
12 Lenzie Academy
13 Motherwell College
14 Saint Aloysius' College
15 Saint Roch's Secondary School
16 West Mains School

MORAY

1 Lossiemouth High School

NORTH AYRSHIRE

1 Garnock Academy
2 Kilwinning Academy

ABERDEENSHIRE

1 Albyn School
2 Banchory Academy and Community Education Centre
3 Bridge of Don Academy
4 Camphill Rudolf Steiner Schools
5 Cults Primary School
6 Danestone Primary School
7 Gordon Schools (The)
8 Northfield Academy
9 Saint Margaret's School for Girls

EAST AYRSHIRE

1 Annanhill Primary School

EAST LOTHIAN

1 North Berwick High School

PERTH & KINROSS

1 Balnacraig School
2 Glenalmond College
3 Kilgraston School
4 Morrison's Academy
5 New School (The)
6 Strathallan School

SCOTTISH BORDERS

1 Saint Mary's School Melrose

WESTERN ISLES

1 Nicolson Institute School

HIGHLAND

1 Farr High School and Farr Primary School

ANGUS

1 Monifieth High School

DUMFRIES & GALLOWAY

1 Cademuir International School

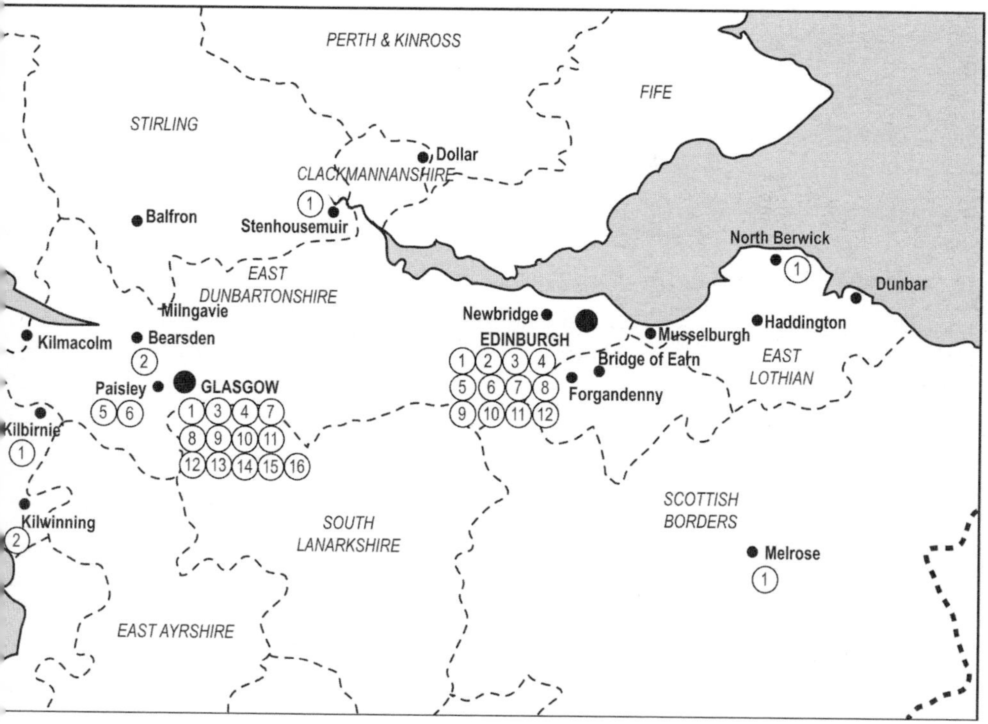

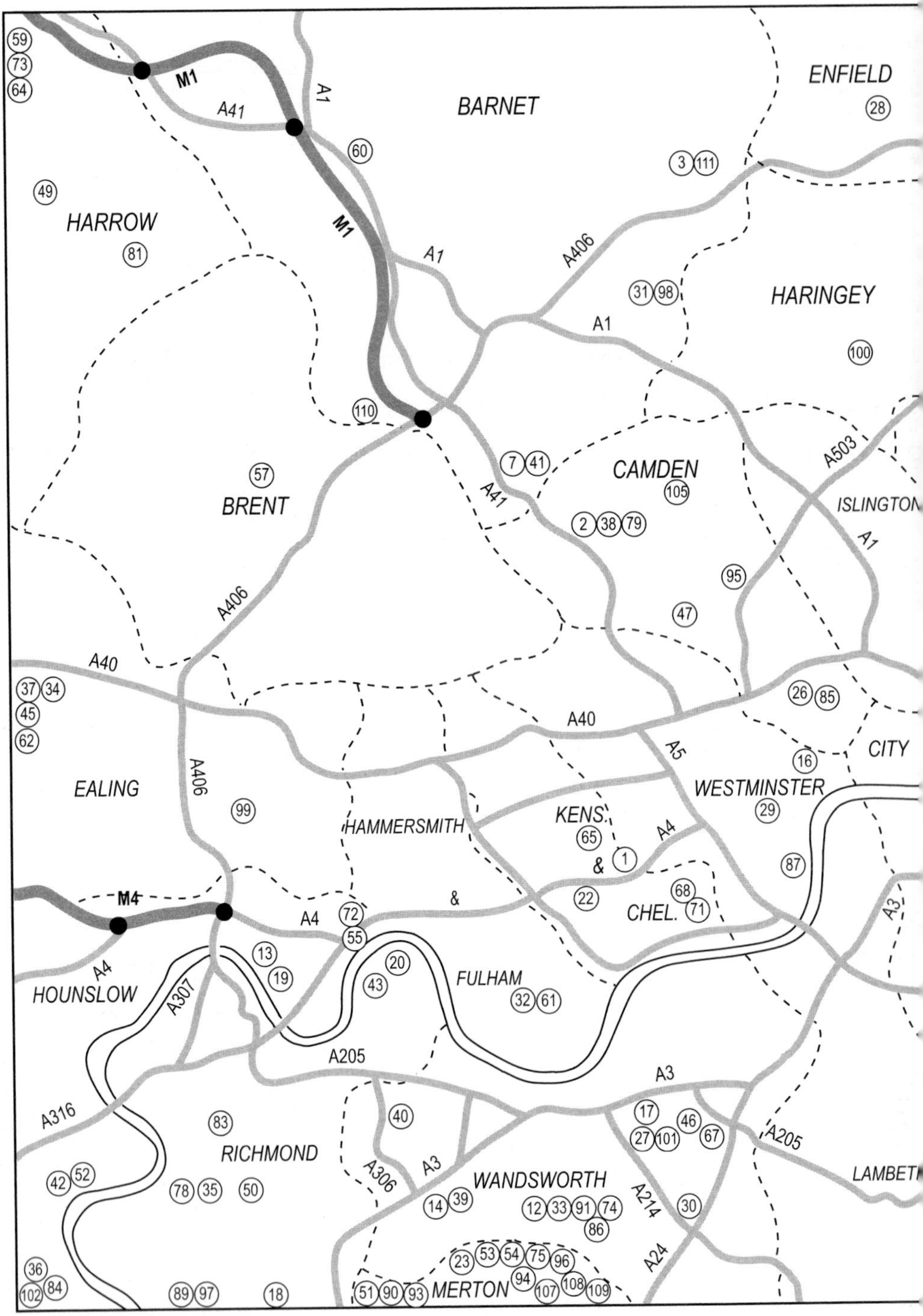
ENFIELD
BARNET
HARROW
HARINGEY
CAMDEN
BRENT
ISLINGTON
EALING
CITY
WESTMINSTER
KENS.
&
CHEL.
HAMMERSMITH
&
FULHAM
HOUNSLOW
RICHMOND
WANDSWORTH
LAMBETH
MERTON
M1
M4
A1
A41
A406
A503
A40
A5
A4
A3
A307
A316
A205
A306
A214
A24

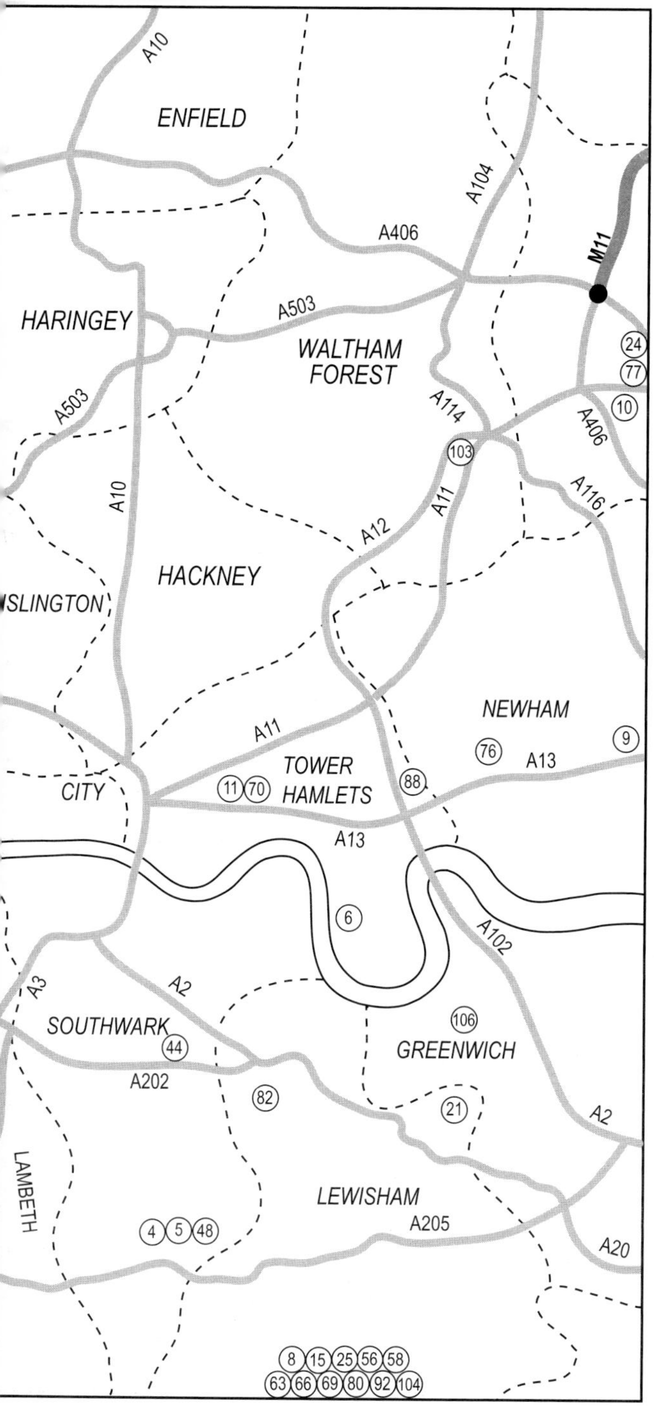

LONDON

1 Abingdon House School
2 Academy School (The)
3 Alexandra Park School
4 Alleyn's Junior School
5 Alleyn's School
6 Arnhem Wharf Primary School
7 Avigdor Hirsch Torah Temimah Primary School
8 Babington House School
9 Barking Abbey Comprehensive School and Sports College
10 Beal High School
11 Beatrice Tate School
12 Beatrix Potter Primary School
13 Belmont Primary School
14 Blossom House School
15 Broadmead Junior School
16 Cardinal Vaughan Memorial RC School (The)
17 Centre Academy
18 Chessington Community College
19 Chiswick Community School
20 Colet Court
21 Colfe's School
22 Collingham
23 Coombe Hill Infant School
24 Coopers' Company and Coborn School (The)
25 Cuddington Croft Primary School
26 Davies Laing and Dick College
27 Dominie (The)
28 Enfield Grammar School
29 Fairley House School
30 Finton House School
31 Fortismere School
32 Fulham Cross School
33 Garratt Park School
34 Glebe Primary School
35 Grey Court School
36 Gumley House RC Convent School, FCJ
37 Guru Nanak Sikh Voluntary Aided Secondary School
38 Hall School (The)
39 Hall School Wimbledon (The)
40 Hall School Wimbledon Junior School (The)
41 Hampstead School
42 Hampton School
43 Harrodian School (The)
44 Highshore School
45 Hillingdon Manor School
46 Hornsby House School
47 International Community School

48 James Allen's Preparatory School (JAPS)
49 JFS School
50 Kew College
51 Knollmead Primary School
52 Lady Eleanor Holles School (The)
53 Latchmere Infant School
54 Latchmere Junior School
55 Latymer Prep School
56 Manor Oak Primary School
57 Manor School
58 Marlborough School
59 Merchant Taylors' School
60 Mill Hill County High School
61 Moat School (The)
62 Moorcroft School
63 Nonsuch High School for Girls
64 Northwood College
65 Notting Hill Preparatory School
66 Oak Lodge Primary School
67 Oak Lodge School
68 Our Lady of Victories RC Primary School
69 Phil Edwards Centre PRU
70 Phoenix School
71 Queen's Gate School
72 Ravenscourt Park Preparatory School
73 RNIB Sunshine House School
74 Roche School (The)
75 Rokeby Senior School
76 Roman Road Primary School
77 Royal Liberty School (The)
78 Russell Primary School (The)
79 Saint Christopher's School
80 Saint David's School
81 Saint Dominic's Sixth Form College
82 Saint Dunstan's College
83 Saint Elizabeth's Catholic Primary School
84 Saint James's Catholic Primary School
85 Saint Marylebone C of E School (The)
86 Saint Michael Steiner School (The)
87 Saint Peter's Eaton Square CofE Primary School
88 Sarah Bonnell School
89 Sheen Mount Primary School
90 Southborough School
91 Southfields Community College
92 Stowford College
93 Study Preparatory School (The)
94 Surbiton Preparatory School
95 Swiss Cottage School
96 Tiffin School
97 Tower House Preparatory School
98 TreeHouse School
99 Twyford Church of England High School
100 Vale Resource Base
101 Vines School (The)
102 Waldegrave School
103 Wanstead High School
104 Westwood College
105 William Ellis School
106 Willow Dene School
107 Wimbledon Chase Primary School
108 Wimbledon College
109 Wimbledon High School
110 Woodfield School
111 Woodside Park International School

MIDLANDS & EAST ENGLAND

CAMBRIDGESHIRE

1 Cambridge Centre for Sixth Form Studies
2 Highfield Special School
3 Hills Road Sixth Form College
4 Impington Village College
5 King's College School (Cambridge)
6 Mander Portman Woodward
7 Saint John's College School
8 Saint Mary's School Cambridge
9 Samuel Pepys School

SUFFOLK

1 Barnardiston Hall Preparatory School
2 Belstead School
3 Culford Preparatory School
4 Heathside School
5 Old Rectory School (The)
6 Orwell High School
7 Orwell Park School
8 Thomas Wolsey School

NORFOLK

1 Banham Marshalls College
2 Beeston Hall School
3 Clare School (The)
4 East Norfolk Sixth Form College
5 Great Yarmouth College
6 Gresham's Preparatory School
7 Gresham's School
8 Hamond's High School
9 Harford Manor, Norwich
10 Riddlesworth Hall School
11 Saint Andrew's School
12 Wayland Community High School

LEICESTERSHIRE

1 Ash Field School
2 Beauchamp College (The)
3 Glen Hills Primary School
4 Keyham Lodge School
5 Lancaster School (The)
6 Lutterworth Grammar School and Community College
7 Our Lady's Convent School
8 Rawlins Community College

RUTLAND

1 Oakham School
2 Uppingham Community College

LINCOLNSHIRE

1 Darley Centre (The)
2 Earl Of Dysart Primary School, Grantham (The)
3 Enfield (New Waltham) Primary School
4 Grantham Ambergate School (The)
5 Queen Elizabeth's High School, Gainsborough (The)
6 Ruskington Chestnut Street CofE Primary School
7 Saint James' School
8 Saint Mary's School
9 Waddington All Saints Primary School

BEDFORDSHIRE

1 Bedford School
2 Challney High School for Girls
3 Vandyke Upper School and Community College

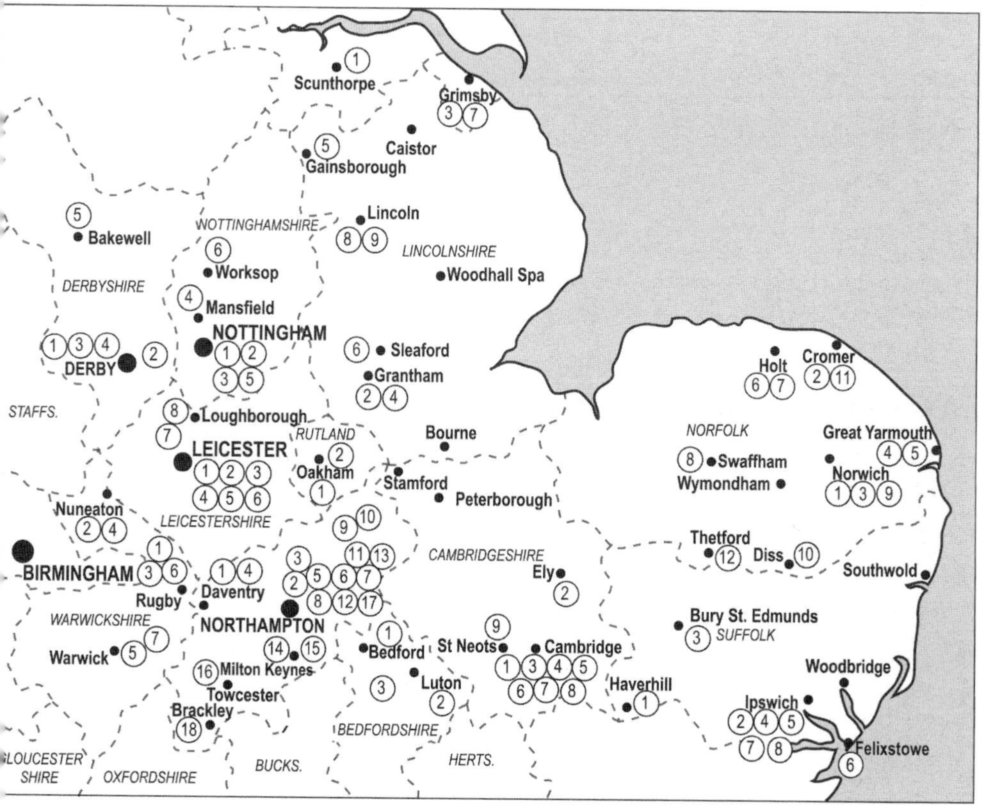

NOTTINGHAMSHIRE

1 Greenholme School
2 Matthew Holland School (The)
3 Nottingham High School
4 Redgate School
5 Trinity Catholic School
6 Valley Comprehensive School

NORTHAMPTONSHIRE

1 Ashby Fields Primary School
2 Bramptons Primary School (The)
3 Croyland Primary School
4 Daventry William Parker School
5 Eastfield Primary School
6 Ecton Primary School
7 Grendon Church of England Primary School
8 Guilsborough School
9 Hawthorn Community Primary School
10 Highfields Community Primary School
11 Manor School and Sports College
12 Mereway Community College
13 Oakway Infant School
14 Old Stratford Primary School
15 Potterspury Lodge School
16 Redway School (The)
17 St Andrews CEVA Primary School
18 Winchester House School

WARWICKSHIRE

1 Crescent School
2 George Eliot Community School
3 Henry Hinde (Community) Infant School
4 Higham Lane School
5 Round Oak School and Support Service (The)
6 Rugby School
7 Saint Augustine's Catholic Primary School

DERBYSHIRE

1 Alderwasley Hall School, Derbyshire
2 Bennerley Fields School
3 Derby Moor Community Sports College
4 Repton School
5 Saint Anselm's School

EUROPEAN SCHOOLS

Aiglon College
European School of Karlsruhe

11+ English: A Parent's Toolkit

Katherine Hamlyn

11+ English:
A Parent's Toolkit

Katherine Hamlyn

www.11PlusEnglish.com

Help your child get up to speed in English for secondary school.

Is this your child?:

*'Her class teacher just
doesn't have time to help her with the basics.'*

❍

'He just can't seem to get started with story writing.'

❍

'Her stories are lovely but she can't manage a time limit!'

❍

*'I would like him to go to a selective school, but I'm
worried that his English is not good enough.'*

❍

'She hasn't a clue about comprehensions.'

If you share any of these concerns then this is the book for you. It has been written to help parents and children work together on all aspects of English around the transition to senior schools, and specifically for children who are going to take entrance examinations for grammar schools or selective independent schools.

11+ English: a Parent's Toolkit has been distilled from Katherine Hamlyn's 25 years of experience of teaching at this level. This highly readable guide pinpoints common problems and, using child-centred techniques and games concentrating on relaxed child/parent collaboration, takes you through essential English with common sense, clarity and humour.

UNI IN THE USA

BY ALICE FISHBURN

THE UK GUIDE TO US UNIVERSITIES

WITH
ANTHONY NEMECEK
DIRECTOR OF THE EDUCATIONAL ADVISORY SERVICE OF THE US-UK FULBRIGHT COMMISSION

FOREWORD BY
STEPHEN BALDOCK
HIGH MASTER OF ST PAUL'S SCHOOL, LONDON 1992–2004

THE GOOD SCHOOLS GUIDE

UNI IN THE USA

Alice Fishburn
with Anthony Nemecek

www.UniintheUSA.com

Myths about universities in the USA abound: the cost is astronomical; you won't get in with British qualifications; the cultural chasm is unbridgeable.

Yet, in increasing numbers, British students are looking at the pleasures and possibilities that await them across the pond. And reports are favourable: once you've seen what's on offer in America, you may never look at a UCAS form again.

Choosing a university thousands of miles away is a daunting task; *Uni in the USA* is an invaluable and accurate guide to what you need to know, from formalities such as the SAT (different from SATs) and scholarships to the world of fraternities, dating etiquette and life on campus. American universities vary hugely in character, and *Uni in the USA* also provides a low-down on over two dozen of the best, from the cosy intimacy of Amherst to the high-pressure energy of Yale, via the sun-drenched sprawl of UCLA and the urban edginess of Columbia.

As a recent graduate of Harvard, British Alice Fishburn writes entertainingly and informatively from the inside on what it's like to be a Brit on American turf: the academic expectations, the social mores, the fun and frustrations.

Anthony Nemecek is director of the educational advisory service of the US–UK Fulbright Commission, the only official and independent source of information on US education in the UK. He has twenty years' experience teaching, managing and examining on both sides of the Atlantic.

There is little doubt that four years at an American college bring a fuller educational experience with greater cultural and social coherence...very few, if any, of those British pupils whom I have seen make their way to American universities have regretted their decision.'

Stephen Baldock,
former High Master of St Paul's, London

THE GOOD SCHOOLS GUIDE

The *incisive* and independent guide to the UK's best private and state schools

for ages 5-18

'One of the best aids for parents...informative and witty' – Financial Times

2006 | *11th edition*

The Good Schools Guide

As any caring parent knows, schooling is not a case of 'one size fits all' and finding the right good school for your child entails a lot of researching, worrying and trying to find satisfactory answers to questions such as:

What does a school's league table rating really mean?

Does a school's reputation rest on its academic laurels or does it turn out good all-rounders?

Will it matter that James is hopeless at sport?

Will Caroline be able to take the International Baccalaureate?

Is boarding a good idea?

Can I find help with fees?

How much does it matter that I didn't warm to the head?

The Good Schools Guide probes beyond the prospectuses to give you insider information on over 800 top schools in the UK (state and private, senior and junior, day and boarding). Its reputation for impartial critical analysis (no, schools certainly can't pay for an entry) and outspoken views has made it a consistent best-seller and, now in its eleventh edition, it offers more information than ever before. There is an update on what you can glean from inspection reports such as Ofsted and CSCI; more on boarding, especially geared to overseas readers and expats; and more advice on navigating interviews.

As an owner of *The Good Schools Guide* you are entitled to subscribe for The Good Schools Guide online – which includes everything that's in the printed version – at a substantial discount.

See www.goodschoolsguide.co.uk for details.